RETROSPECTIVE
INDEX TO
THESES
of Great Britain
and Ireland 1716~1950

RETROSPECTIVE INDEX TO THESES
of Great Britain and Ireland 1716~1950

Volume 1
SOCIAL SCIENCES AND HUMANITIES

ROGER R. BILBOUL, EDITOR

FRANCIS L. KENT, ASSOCIATE EDITOR

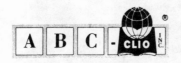

ISBN Cloth bound, volume 1: 0-903450-03-8
ISBN Cloth bound, 5 volume set: 0-903450-02-X

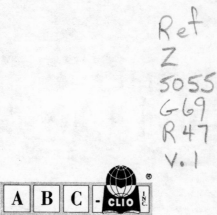

American Bibliographical Center – Clio Press, Inc.
2040 Alameda Padre Serra
Santa Barbara, California

European Bibliographical Center – Clio Press
Woodside House
Hinksey Hill
Oxford OX1 5BE, England

Computer typeset by Peter Peregrinus, Ltd.
Printed by G. A. Pindar & Son Ltd., Scarborough.

Publisher: Eric H. Boehm
Editor: Roger R. Bilboul
Associate Editor: Francis L. Kent
Editorial Board: Robert L. Collison, Head, Ealing School
                   of Librarianship
                   Kenneth W. Humphreys, Librarian, European University
                   Institute, Florence
                   Geoffrey M. Paterson, Librarian, Bedford College,
                   University of London, Editor, Aslib Index to Theses

Indexers: C. Armour
                   C.E. Bainbridge
                   J. Cummings
                   S. Marsh
                   J. Mutter
                   J. Ormston
                   J.M. Orr
                   M.D. Whalley
                   A.T. Wilcock

CONTENTS

Preface

Prior to 1950 when Aslib started its annual INDEX TO THESES there was no systematic bibliographic coverage of British theses. This work provides retrospective coverage and is, as such, an original bibliography and not a cumulation of an existing published work.

The compilation of this **Index** relied heavily on computer techniques, but we resisted the economic temptation of compiling the subject index using automatic devices such as KWIC or KWOC. Our indexers made intellectual decisions for each thesis title, assisted by a thesaurus and computer print-outs to ensure consistency and to allow users access through narrow or broad subject searches. In addition to the entry under the author index, each thesis title and its bibliographic details appear, on the average, under two subject headings. By using cross-references liberally we have managed to restrict the number of subject headings per thesis and give under broad headings such as English Literature an overall view of coverage.

The scope of our task was restricted to the compilation of this bibliography. We would have enjoyed extending this to a historical study of British theses, an area in which apparently little is known. We cannot explain, for example, why degrees based on theses took so long to be introduced in England, nor can we determine what influenced English universities to finally introduce such degrees. The foreword by Kenneth Humphreys on p.ii gives some of the data we collected and we hope that his exposé will encourage someone to undertake a study in this area.

I owe a debt of appreciation and gratitude to those many people who have assisted, encouraged and enhanced the publication of this bibliography. In particular I acknowledge the contribution of all the university librarians involved, who so readily supplied information on their theses. I appreciate Aslib's co-operation and I acknowledge the Library Association's permission to use the thesaurus developed for its **British Humanities Index**.

I cannot properly conclude this acknowledgment without expressing my thanks and appreciation to the three members of the Editorial Board, whose contribution and guidance have been most useful. The work could not have been completed without the services of Francis Kent, Associate Editor, who maintained a professional attitude in the face of countless problems. Finally, I am deeply indebted to the Publisher, Eric H. Boehm, whose encouragement and support have made this work possible. It was indeed a pleasure to work for a publisher who so well understands and has done so much for bibliographic publishing and editing. I hope this **Index** will do justice to his achievements in bibliography.

Roger R. Bilboul,
Editor.
Oxford
September 1975

i

Foreword

The aim of this publication is to provide information for scholars on the existence of theses completed for higher degrees in Great Britain and Ireland up to 1950 when Aslib began the annual publication of its lists. This first volume covers the subjects generally within the area of the social sciences and humanities and will be followed by four volumes devoted to theses in science and technology.

At a recent meeting organised by the Council of Europe a group of experts from a number of countries of Western Europe considered some of the problems posed for libraries by theses. In discussions of a report prepared by Professor Schmidt-Künsemüller, Librarian of the University of Kiel, they concluded that there were three aspects which were particularly relevant. These were bibliographical control, the availability of theses and the publication and distribution of theses. The last affects specially the librarians of universities on the continent where it is common practice for theses to be printed or multigraphed and sent to other universities on exchange. In this country on the other hand, bibliographical control and availability are outstandingly important as, unless it is later published, only one or two copies of the original thesis are deposited in a library. In fact it has not always been certain that a copy of a thesis can be found in the library of the university in which the thesis was submitted.

It is hoped that this work will offer bibliographical control of earlier theses, indicating what subjects have been treated and which universities produced certain types of theses. Researchers can check that the subject they wish to study has not already been dealt with, at least in the manner they intend to adopt. It will also provide the full bibliographic details of pre-1950 theses completed in these islands. Previously such information has been provided only by the catalogues of individual libraries except in a few cases where a university, like London, has published lists of its own theses. We have here attempted to bring all such information together in a useful form to supplement the Aslib list.

From the point of view of availability it may be generally assumed that items listed here can be obtained on inter-library loan either in the original or as a microfilm or xerox copy from the central library of the university concerned.

It may be noted that when the Aslib list was first published the Standing Conference of National and University Libraries (SCONUL) undertook in 1954 to attempt to persuade universities to agree to a standard method of dealing with theses in order to make them more easily available. A statement on the position in each university was published in Vol. II of the **Index**. By means of a coding system it was possible to know which universities would supply theses on inter-library loan, which universities could provide reprographic services and, in federal universities, where the theses were housed. SCONUL also suggested to universities that they should use forms to be signed by the authors giving permission for their theses to be available for consultation and reference.

This volume lists the titles of about 13,000 theses in the social sciences and humanities covering all universities in Great Britain and Ireland at which higher degrees were conferred before 1950. It should however be pointed out that there are a few anomalies in the listing, which arise from the methods adopted by university libraries in cataloguing or even in the preservation of their theses. It is not uncommon now for libraries to provide a separate catalogue of their theses and for universities to require that one copy of every thesis should be placed in the central university library. It was possible in the past however for these academic exercises to be considered as archival material and thus not to be deposited in the library, so that they escaped cataloguing and could also escape deposit at all. Fortunately, from the information we have collected from individual universities, such losses have not been very significant.

1. Index to Theses accepted for Higher Degrees in the universities of Great Britain and Ireland, Vol.1 1950-51, ed. by P.D. Record. London: Aslib, 1953.

It was our original intention to cover those comparatively modern theses produced as manuscript or typescript copies and dating from about 1880. In fact the first Oxford thesis recorded here is 1870 and we have also included earlier Glasgow theses from 1716, although strictly these printed theses on the continental model were not intended to come within our initial criteria. It must be stressed that this is not a work for a bibliographer of early theses [2] as it does not attempt to list the earlier printed theses whether they are full texts of theses by individuals or the broadsheets announcing the propositions to be disputed and the names of the candidates.

We received replies from all universities to which we applied for information, resulting in returns from twenty-one universities. It is of some interest to note the earliest date for a thesis in each of these universities.

Aberdeen	1883
Belfast	1910
Birmingham	1901
Bristol	1910
Cambridge	1909
Dublin, Trinity College	1921
Durham	1925
Edinburgh	1882
Glasgow	(1716)
Ireland, National University	1910
Leeds	1899
Liverpool	1889
London	1884
Manchester	1886
Nottingham	1949
Oxford	1870
Reading	1927
St. Andrews	1898
Wales	1900
Sheffield	1912

It is clear, from the figures for the humanities and for the sciences we have extrapolated from the records submitted, that only one or two universities — London and Oxford — had as many as ten theses each year before the mid-1920s. From about 1924 there were three to four times as many theses completed annually as in each of the previous years. The numbers gradually increased until the Second World War. There was then a peak period in the late 1940s. The figures for humanities theses in 1949 give some idea of the output for each university at this time and the relative importance of research.

	Science	Humanities	Total
Aberdeen	14	1	15
Belfast	28	2	30
Birmingham	65	23	65
Bristol	33	7	40
Cambridge	144	40	184
Dublin, Trinity College	15	11	26
Durham	6	8	14
Edinburgh	80	26	63

---

2. The history and development of the thesis as an educational exercise in this country has still to be written. A full bibliographical study of printed theses is also needed. The only references I could find were the articles by Cant and Johnstone: R.G. Cant 'The St. Andrews University Theses 1579 — 1747: a bibliographical introduction', Edinburgh Bibliographical Society Transactions, 2 (1938-45), 105-50, 263-72; J.F.K. Johnstone 'Notes on the academic theses of Scotland', Records of the Glasgow Bibiographical Society, 8 (1930), 81-98.

Glasgow	63	4	67
Ireland, National University	10	44	54
Leeds	71	32	103
Liverpool	56	26	82
London	392	233	625
Manchester	60	27	87
Nottingham	1	1	2
Oxford	137	100	237
Reading	8	6	14
St. Andrews	17	3	20
Sheffield	32	10	42
Wales	51	42	93

It will be evident from these figures that theses in Science Faculties were more numerous than those in the Humanities; only the National University of Ireland had a significantly larger output in the Humanities.

As I have pointed out, at both national and international level,librarians have been very concerned recently about the need for improving the bibliographic control of published material of all kinds. One important area is that of theses and the Editors hope that this publication will fill a need for researchers, bibliographers and librarians. We should like to think that it will stimulate further work on the development of thesis literature. The demand for theses has increased considerably over the past few years, indicating the greater importance given to them by scholars. This has not always been the case; in the older universities it was not considered acceptable for a scholar to be other than 'Mister'. With this attitude in mind I should like to quote from a poem on this subject by Professor A.D. Hope printed in 'Ordeal by Thesis' by Sir Keith Hancock.[3]

> The modern critics of the maggot breed
> Writhe in their carcases and seethe and feed.
> Laborious, timid, tedious at once
> Each purblind scholar and each well-trained dunce,
> From the Old World and from the New they come
> To search the rubbish heaps of Christendom!
> Is there a minor poet by others missed,
> Dull sermoneer or maudlin novelist,
> Some corpse to build a reputation on?
> A thesis swallows them and they are gone.
> Round greater tombs they mine and countermine:
> One shrieks 'Stand off, his first ten years are mine!'
> 'And mind the floreat,' Number Two replies;
> 'Well then,' shrieks Three, 'I've got him till he dies'.'
> With muck-rake zeal they ferret from the dead
> All that each genius farted, belched or said;
> Flip-flap and fly-leaves, dates and deeds and wills —
> They publish everything, from midwives' bills
> To epitaphs: whole books grow out of what
> His aunts remembered or his dad forgot.
> The scabs scratched off by genius, sought with care,
> Stuck back again, earn Doctor Budge a chair;
> And now Professor Budge, his claim made good,
> He works like dry rot through the Sacred Wood;
> Or like dead mackerel, in a night of ink
> Emits a pale gleam and a mighty stink.

3. In Postgraduate Studies in the Humanities in Australia Sydney, 1967.

Yet it must not be forgotten that not only are librarians freqently requested to obtain theses of all kinds on inter-library loan but it must be admitted, in contradiction of the spirit of the above lines, that many theses are of the greatest importance. It is to be expected that theses indeed concentrate on minutiae, but it is on painstaking research that scholarship and scholarly reputation depend. It is worth recording, for example, that Wittgenstein's **Tractatus logico-philosophicus** was a Cambridge thesis; it is duly listed in this work.

Finally, the publication would not have been possible without the very willing help we received from the librarians of all the universities of Great Britain and Ireland and we are particularly indebted to them and to their assistants for the information they supplied.

Kenneth W. Humphreys,
Birmingham,
September 1975

Introduction

Bibliographical control of British and Irish theses before 1950-51, when Aslib's annual **Index to Theses** began to be published, has hitherto been limited to a few lists covering special subjects and restricted periods. Many universities in the British Isles have not issued lists of their own theses; some have not fully catalogued or classified them. Yet theses constitute a form of academic literature which the scholar cannot ignore. By its nature a thesis is at the very least a serious piece of work carried out under scholarly direction. It usually deals with some special topic or relationship not previously treated elsewhere. It almost always contains a bibliography of source material. The **Index** of which this is the first volume is intended to record all British and Irish theses from the early eighteenth century to 1950-51, including any which may have escaped inclusion in Aslib's first volume; in its pages will be found, recorded in print for the first time, entries for the earliest intellectual efforts of many famous men and women.

Entries were reported by the universities in a number of ways. Some universities sent photocopies of catalogue cards or slips — printed, typewritten or handwritten. Some sent typed lists. Others sent printed lists, or photocopies of them. The degree of legibility and bibliographical accuracy varied considerably and the entries sent by some universities were far from consistent within themselves, in style, practice or detail. The work must therefore be looked on rather as a finding list than as a formal bibliography. No attempt has been made, and in the time available none could have been made, to achieve strict bibliographical accuracy or consistency. The vast majority of entries had perforce to be indexed by title — inspection of the originals not being practicable. Librarians were, however, most patient in helping to elucidate doubtful titles on request.

Index headings in this humanities and social sciences volume have been based on those of the **British Humanities Index**. But there are two important differences between **BHI** and the present work which have necessitated modifications and adaptations. In the first place, **BHI** is an ongoing concern, whereas our **Index** stops at 1950-51, and therefore does not include numerous topics which have arisen since then (the Arab-Israeli conflict since the establishment of the State of Israel; the European Common Market; the social implications of the computer and data bank; the establishment of new nations — Sri Lanka was still Ceylon and Zaire part of the Congo). Secondly, while **BHI** is indexing articles, we are indexing theses, which tend to be characterized by specificity of subject and by reasonably explicit titles, though to this there are exceptions which have entailed special enquiry or, all else failing, an inspired guess.

In the belief that most users of this **Index** will be looking for narrow rather than broad topics, the principle has been adopted of indexing under specific rather than general terms. Thus, a thesis on Causality or on Pragmatism will be indexed there with a cross-reference from philosophy; entries on St. Augustine will be found under Augustine of Hippo, Saint, to whom there will be cross-references from Church History; Neoplatonism; Patristics; Saints. Titles on individual persons are entered primarily under the person, with a cross-reference from the activity, aspect or topic treated. In some instances it has seemed helpful to enter the title under both the person and the activity. Full details of each title appear in both author and subject indexes. It should be possible to find a specific title under both its author and its subject as well as to gain a conspectus of what work has been done on a given topic. Personal names taking two or more forms appear as far as possible under both, or all, especially in the author index. The method adopted is to make the entry under the form reported by the university and cross-refer from the other possible form or forms. Types of name so treated include: double names such as Eynon-Smith; occasionally, married women's names such as Mary Smith née Jones (entered under both Smith, M. and Jones, M.); Irish names reported in two spellings for the same individual (O'Shuilleabháin/O'Sullivan); French, Dutch and German names with de, de la, van, von; Arabic names with al-, el-, Abdel-, etc; and, in the subject index, medieval names wherein it is not clear whether a true family name or a territorial designation is meant (such as Hue De Roteland). No consistency is claimed for the treatment of Chinese names, the form of which appears to depend largely upon the personal preference of the author of the thesis as interpreted by the university. The indexing of Welsh names follows the practice of Welsh catalogues and lists, notably the bibliography of A.E. Davies, **Traethodau ymchwil Cymraeg a Chymreig . . . . Welsh language and Welsh dissertations . . . 1887-1971**, University of Wales Press, 1973. Throughout the **Index**, the intention has been to prefer whatever may be helpful to the searcher to that which may be technically, or pedantically, correct.

It is hoped that the numerous cross-references will help to make it possible to find titles even if they are not all in the best or even in the right place. Cross-references are specifically linked to the titles that give rise to them, and certain apparent oddities necessarily result. If, for instance, there is a thesis on the theological views of a noted English literary or political figure, there will be a cross-reference to him from Theology (or appropriate related special subject), but there will be no cross-reference from English Literature or Great Britain: History unless there is also in the **Index** a thesis on his literary or political work.

Under the name of each country, if there are sufficient entries to justify subdivision, subheadings have been made for: Armed Forces; Colonies; Constitution; Economic History; Economics; Foreign Affairs; Geography; History (further subdivided by period if necessary); Parliament; Politics and Government; Social History. Entries on other subjects will be found under their names, e.g. Agriculture; Archaeology and Antiquities; Art; Church History; Education; Fiction; Food; Journalism; Land; Law; Local Government; Missions; Music; Philosophy; Poetry; Railways; Religion; Taxation; Theatre; Trade; etc. Such headings are subdivided by country if they contain sufficient titles. Thus, titles on British social history will be found under Great Britain: Social History; but titles on British journalism under Journalism: Great Britain; on British drama, under Theatre: Great Britain. Cross-references point to related headings from such general headings as Christianity; Law; Literature; Philosophy; Psychology; Religion; also to individual persons from English, French, German and other Literatures, from historical headings such as Great Britain: History, and from collective headings such as Saints. References to individuals who are prominent, or who have practised or studied, in a particular field will also be found under such headings as History, for historians; Patristics, for the Fathers of the Church; Philosophy, for philosophers; Science (and individual sciences), for the scientists; Theology, for theologians. Works on the Bible and all its parts are under Bible.

Translations are provided of titles in Irish and Welsh but not of titles in other languages. The reason for this is that while the Irish and Welsh universities may accept theses in their national languages on any subject, no university in the British Isles normally accepts a thesis in, say, French unless it deals with French history, language or literature — in which case it is unlikely to interest anyone who does not read enough French to understand the title.

Alphabetical sorting is word-by-word, and symbols have the following ordinal value - space : 0/9 A/Z (commas are ignored and hypenated words are read straight through). **Mc** is sorted as **Mac**, **St.** as **Saint** (the hyphen consequently being omitted from French names like **Saint-Just** and **Saint-Simon** so that they appear before **Sainte** and **Saints**). Roman numerals (as in names of kings, etc.) are treated as capital I's, V's, etc. and alphabetized accordingly (James, Henry; James I; James II; James, William); this is too rare an occurrence to have justified special programming or cause real inconvenience. Under each heading, titles are arranged alphabetically, **a** and **the** (but not articles in other languages) being ignored. On the other hand, **the**, when occurring as part of a subject heading, is not ignored (John Bosco, Saint; John, King of England; John of Salisbury; John, the Baptist, Saint). Subheadings of a heading normally appear in alphabetical order, but it was possible to arrange special schemes for chronological sequences (Seventeenth Century; Eighteenth Century; Nineteenth Century; where S, E, N are not in alphabetical order), and for hierarchically or logically subdivided headings such as Bible, where, after general and miscellaneous subheadings (General; Criticism and

Exegesis; Versions; Bible in Literature), Old Testament precedes New Testament and the books or groups of books are entered under each of these in canonical order. Among headings so treated are Church History; Education (where general and miscellaneous subheadings such as History, Profession, Pedagogics, etc. precede Education in individual countries, which is in turn followed by "types" of education, e.g. Adult, Higher, Physical, Secondary (itself subdivided by country), Technical, etc.); English Literature (and some other literatures); the subheading History under France, Great Britain and other countries; Jews; Missions (so as to sort History before individual mission fields); Music; Poetry, English (by period).

Each entry consists of the title, followed by its translation if it is in Irish or Welsh, the author (in the subject index), the degree and date of award, and the University.

A few small points require a word of explanation. Colleges and institutes of the University of London enjoy greater independence than those of other universities. For this reason, and because theses written by their students may still be in the institutional libraries and not in the general university library depository at Egham, the college of a London thesis is added when known. (In many instances, on the other hand, the university no longer has any ready means of ascertaining the college). Secondly, students of a number of provincial university colleges and other institutions obtained London external higher degrees before the institutions were given the right to grant their own. Theses submitted for such degrees have been reported to us by London, without specifying the external institution; these have been entered as "London, External Degree". Any thesis reported by any university is indexed, even if we know that it is not now held by the library of the university concerned. The hope always remains that a copy may at some time be found; and meanwhile the work is recorded, and the author may later have written other relevant work and, if still alive, may be traceable.

AVAILABILITY OF THESES

The following information on the availability of theses is based, with Aslib's permission, on that given in the most recent volume of the Aslib Index to Theses. The rules in force in any individual university for making theses available are subject to change; for up-to-date information the current volume should be consulted of the Aslib Index to Theses (Aslib, 3 Belgrave Square, London, SW1X 8PL).

In each instance in which it is desired to see, borrow or copy a thesis, the first approach will normally be to the library of the student's university (in London, to the University Library, Senate House; in Wales, to the National Library of Wales, Aberystwyth; in the National University of Ireland, to the Registrar, 49 Merrion Square, Dublin, for doctoral dissertations, and to the libraries of the University Colleges in Cork, Dublin and Galway, for masters' theses).

The universities with which the present Index is concerned have applied as follows the standards proposed in 1954 by the Standing Conference of National and University Libraries:

(A) At least one copy of every thesis should be deposited in the University Library: all except Wales, which deposits them in the National Library at Aberystwyth, and the National University of Ireland (masters' theses in the College libraries; doctoral dissertations with the Registrar — see preceding paragraph). But not all theses were so deposited in the past: for instance, many Oxford B. Litt. theses are not in the Bodleian and no longer survive in the library of the student's college, and in London some older theses may still be held by the libraries of constituent colleges or institutes.

(B) Subject to the author's consent, every thesis should be available for inter-library loan: all except Cambridge and the National University of Ireland. Many libraries (e.g. the Bodleian) no longer require the author's consent for the inter-library loan of theses of the period covered by the present Index.

(C)   Subject to the author's consent, every thesis should be available for copying: permission should in the first place be sought from the library concerned. Permission to copy a Cambridge thesis should be sought from the Board of Graduate Studies; permission to copy an Oxford thesis, in the first instance, from the Keeper of Western Manuscripts, Bodleian Library. Trinity College, Dublin, assumes the author's consent unless he has specifically withheld it.

(D)   Authors should signify their consent to (B) and (C) at the time of deposit. This is inapplicable to the period covered. But nearly all libraries freely allow consultation and inter-library loan of all theses more than a few years old.

The following details of the Aslib **Index to Theses**, kindly supplied by its editor, may be found helpful:

Aslib **Index to Theses**: volumes published to date:

Vol. 1,	1950 - 51;	ed.	P.D. Record	1953
Vol. 2,	1951 - 52;	ed.	P.D. Record &	
			M. Whitrow	1955
Vol. 3,	1952 - 53;	ed.	M. Whitrow	1956
Vol. 4,	1953 - 54;	ed.	M. Whitrow	1957
Vol. 5,	1954 - 55;	ed.	M. Whitrow	1958
Vol. 6,	1955 - 56;	ed.	M. Whitrow	1958
Vol. 7,	1956 - 57;	ed.	M. Whitrow	1959
Vol. 8,	1957 - 58;	ed.	M. Whitrow	1960
Vol. 9,	1958 - 59;	ed.	M. Whitrow	1961
Vol.10,	1959 - 60;	ed.	M. Whitrow	1961
Vol.11,	1960 - 61;	ed.	M. Whitrow	1962
Vol.12,	1961 - 62;	ed.	G.M. Paterson	1963
Vol.13,	1962 - 63;	ed.	G.M. Paterson	1964
Vol.14,	1963 - 64;	ed.	G.M. Paterson	1966
Vol.15,	1964 - 65;	ed.	G.M. Paterson	1967
Vol.16,	1965 - 66;	ed.	G.M. Paterson	1968
Vol.17,	1966 - 67;	ed.	G.M. Paterson	1969
Vol.18,	1967 - 68;	ed.	G.M. Paterson	1970
Vol.19,	1968 - 69;	ed.	G.M. Paterson	
			& J.E. Hardy	1971
Vol.20,	1969 - 70;	ed.	"	1973
Vol.21,	1970 - 71;	ed.	"	1973
Vol.22,	1971 - 72;	ed.	"	1974
Vol.23,	1972 - 73;	ed.	"	1975

From 1975, publication of the Aslib **Index** will no longer be tied to recording all theses accepted for higher degrees in a particular academic session. The **Index** will appear twice a year and each volume will record all theses notified to the editors by a given date. Vol. 24 is due to appear in November 1975 and will include theses accepted in 1973, 1974 and 1975.

Francis L. Kent,
Associate Editor.

Diſſertatio Philoſophica,

INAUGURALIS,

DE

Summi Numinis Exiſtentia.

QUAM

Favente Summo Numine,

Auctoritate Digniſſimi Vice-cancellarii,

JOANNIS STIRLING, V. D. M.

S. S. Th. Profeſſoris Primarii, & Academiæ Præfecti;

NEC NON

Ampliſſimi Senatus Academici Conſenſu, & celeberrimæ
Facultatis Artium Decreto,

Pro gradu Magiſterii, ſummiſque in Philoſophia & Artibus
Liberalibus, Privilegiis, & Honoribus, Rite ac
legitime conſequendis.

In Auditorio publico Academiæ Glaſguenſis,
Ad Diem *Junii* 28 Hora 10 ante Meridiem,

PROPUGNABIT

JOANNES SHERMAN *Colceſtrienſis.*

Quid enim poteſt eſſe tam apertum, tamque perſpicuum, cum Coelum
ſuſpeximus cœleſtiaque contemplati ſumus, quam *eſſe aliquod Numen*
præſtantiſſimæ mentis, quo hæc regantur? *Cic: de Nat: Deor:*

GLASGUÆ,
Ex Officina Donaldi Govan, Academiæ
Typographi, M. DCC. XVI.

Facsimile of titlepage of earliest thesis
(Glasgow, 1716)
recorded in this volume

Subject Index

Aaron
The last days of Aaron according to the Midrash *Petirat Aharon*. B. Fertleman, M.A. 1937 Manchester

Aaron ben Joseph
A comparison of the views of Aaron ben Joseph in his *Sefer Hamibhar* and his Halakic poems with the accepted views of the Karaites and Rabbanites concerning the Sabbath and other Jewish festivals. S. J. Weisz, M.A. 1942 Manchester

Aaron ha-Levi, of Barcelona
Ha-Hinukh - attributed to R. Aharon Hal-Lewi, Barcelona (13th century) - a translation and critical study. H. H. Medalie, Ph.D. 1944 Dublin, Trinity College

Abbey Theatre
The Abbey Theatre and the principal writers connected therewith. H. J. Butler, M.A. 1925 National University of Ireland

Abbeys
See Monasticism.

Abbreviations
Abbreviation by initials: a tendency in modern language studies, with special reference to the French press, 1919-1945. S. A. Champion, M.A. 1949 London, University College

Abdul-Latif, Shah
See Shah Abdul-Latif, of Bhit.

'Abdu'r-Rahīm, Mirzā
Mirza 'Abdu'r-Rahim Khan-i-Khanan: soldier, statesman and patron of letters. A. Ali, Ph.D. 1932 Cambridge

Abelard, Peter
The philosophy of Peter Abelard. R. Tatlock, M.A. 1938 Leeds

The relations between Abelard and St. Bernard. A. V. Murray, B.Litt. 1930 Oxford

Some Hellenic elements in the works of Abelard. V. G. Kirk-Duncan, B.Litt. 1941 Oxford

Abercius
1. The phraseology and style of the Pastoral Epistles. 2. The epitaph of Abercius. G. C. Richards, B.D. 1920 Oxford

Aberdare
The industrial history of the parish of Aberdare from 1800-1900. G. I. Thomas, M.A. 1943 Wales

Aberdaron
A social study of the parish of Aberdaron in the Llŷn peninsula. T. J. Hughes, M.A. 1950 Wales

Aberdeen, George Hamilton Gordon, 4th Earl of
Aberdeen and Anglo-French diplomatic relations, 1841-6. J. R. Baldwin, B.Litt. 1936 Oxford

Abi 'Aun
See 'Aun, Ibn Abi.

Ability
See also Aptitude Testing; Psychology; Intelligence Testing.

Ability and knowledge: the standpoint of the London School. F. C. Thomas, M.Sc. 1935 London, King's College

Ability, variability and improvability. E. J. G. Bradford, M.Sc. 1920 London

Ability contd.
An analysis of factors entering into geometrical ability. J. W. Withrington, M.A. 1936 London, Institute of Education

An analysis of the factors entering into mathematical ability, with special reference to children of 11 and 12. A. M. Blackwell, M.A. 1938 London, Institute of Education

The assessment of teaching ability with special reference to men students in training. J. H. Panton, M.A. 1934 London, Institute of Education

A comparative study of the mathematical ability of boys and girls in a secondary school from 12 to 14 years of age. L. Dasgupta, M.A. 1948 London, Institute of Education

A comparative study of the mathematical abilities of girls and boys in secondary schools. A. E. Cameron, M.A. 1923 London

Comparative value of certain verbal and non-verbal (primarily perceptual) tests and their relation to tests of mechanical ability. K. G. Rama Rao, Ph.D. 1933 London, University College

The development and application of statistical methods in the prediction of ability. L. Ackerson, B.Sc. 1925 Oxford

Discovering the Bluestockings, a neglected constellation of clever women. M. L. Robbie, Ph.D. 1947 Edinburgh

An enquiry into the abilities of adolescent boys in elementary schools in Bristol. G. A. Jahans, M.A. 1934 Bristol

An enquiry into the bearing of general and special abilities upon scholastic success at the beginning and end of the secondary school career. M. Ormiston, Ph.D. 1937 Leeds

A factorial analysis of ability in school physics. A. R. Berridge, M.A. 1947 London, Institute of Education

Factorial analysis of arithmetical and other abilities in junior school children. E. Appleby, Ph.D. 1939 London, Institute of Education

Factorial analysis of practical ability and its relation to other intellectual abilities and personality traits. R. M. El- Ghareib, Ph.D. 1950 Edinburgh

A factorial analysis of the abilities involved in the learning of school chemistry. G. C. Pawley, M.A. 1937 London, Institute of Education

Factors in mechanical ability in adults. D. K. Wheeler, Ph.D. 1948 London, University College

General ability and the relation between general and specific ability at different stages of school life. D. M. Turner, M.A. 1922 London

Interests of boys in relation to mental ability and environment. T. B. Kankan, M.Ed. 1936 Leeds

An investigation into mathematical abilities most closely related to logical and critical thinking. W. Bennett, M.A. 1948 London, Institute of Education

An investigation into the psychological factors of linguistic ability. P. M. M. Graham, M.A. 1942 London, Institute of Education

An investigation of mental abilities by means of non-verbal auditory material. A. Pearson, M.Ed. 1944 Leeds

Ability contd.
A new approach to the problem of individual differences, abilities and types, and their bearing on educational methods and systems. N. R. Warhadpande, B.Litt. 1949 Oxford

An objective study of the factors underlying ability in verbal expression. A. G. Scrivens, M.A. 1933 London, Institute of Education

Objective tests of the fluency factor, with special reference to its relation to ability in school subjects. W. D. Barras, M.A. 1938 London, Institute of Education

The relation between artistic ability and intelligence. E. Mewse, M.Ed. 1934 Durham

The relation between intelligence and various forms of practical ability. E. Collins, M.A. 1935 Birmingham

The relation of certain factors of imagery and immediate memory to geometrical ability. E. W. Webb, M.A. 1949 London, Institute of Education

The reliability of certain tests of practical ability. V. Prakasha, M.A. 1949 London, Institute of Education

A study in practical ability. M. McFarlane, Ph.D. 1924 London

A study of mechanical ability, with special reference to sex differences. A. A. H. el- Koussy, M.Sc. 1932 Birmingham

Tests of musical ability. H. D. Wing, M.A. 1936 London, Institute of Education

1. Tests of reasoning processes and their relation to general mental ability. 2. The mental differences between the sexes. R. C. Moore, M.A. 1915 Liverpool

The value of apprentice ability tests in Birmingham junior technical school entrance examination. T. J. Nicholas, M.A. 1942 Birmingham

Abolitionism
See Alcohol.

Aborigines
See also Primitivism.

Anthropological account of the Aborigines of western Australia together with the climate, the diseases, and the productions of the country. A. M. Robertson, M.D. 1883 Edinburgh

Economic changes in north Australian tribes. W. E. H. Stanner, Ph.D. 1938 London, School of Economics and Political Science

The family among the Australian aborigines: a sociological study. B. G. Malinowski, D.Sc. 1916 London

The position of women in Australian aboriginal society. P. M. Kaberry, Ph.D. 1938 London, School of Economics and Political Science

The relation of ritual to belief in primitive cult, with special reference to the magico-religious customs of the Australian Aborigines. E. O. James, B.Litt. 1916 Oxford

Abraham bar Hiyya
The religious philosophy of Abraham bar Hiyya, with a re-edition and translation into English of his *Hegyon Ha-nephesh*. G. B. Wigoder, D.Phil. 1947 Oxford

1

Abravanel, Isaac ben Jehudah
The blessings of Moses in post-Biblical Jewish literature: Targum versions considered and compared with the Talmud, Midrash and medieval commentators down to Abrabanel, as well as with those of Moses Mendelsohhn and Malbim. *R. H. Levy, M.A. 1945 Manchester*

A critical study of Abravanel's *Commentary on Kings. S. Kalisch, M.A. 1943 Manchester*

The influence of Alfonso Tostado on the Pentateuch commentary of Abravanel. *S. I. Gaon, Ph.D. 1943 London, Jews' College*

Absolute
Value and the philosophy of the absolute with special reference to the philosophy of Bosanquet. *J. G. F. Potter, B.Litt. 1935 Oxford*

Absolution
See Penance.

Abstraction
The concrete expression of abstract ideas in Indian philosophy, with special reference to comparison as means of evidence. *D. A. L. Stede, Ph.D. 1938 London, School of Oriental and African Studies*

A defence of abstraction. *F. K. Lennon, M.A. 1943 National University of Ireland*

The process of abstraction and concept formation. *E. F. O'Doherty, Ph.D. 1946 Cambridge*

Some experiments on the abstraction of form and colour. *O. A. Oeser, Ph.D. 1932 Cambridge*

Abū al-Ma'ālī Muhammad b. 'Ubayd Allah
The *Bayān al Adyān* by Abu'l Māil Muhammad ibn Ubayd Allāh: translation, introduction and notes. *M. A. S. Kafafi, Ph.D. 1949 London, School of Oriental and African Studies*

Abu Firas al-Hamdani
See Hamdani, Abu Firas.

Abu Tammam, Habib ibn Aus
Abu Tammam and his times. *A. Haq, D.Phil. 1925 Oxford*

Abu Tammam and his times. *A. Haq, B.Litt. 1922 Oxford*

Abu Yūsuf
An index of the traditionists quoted in *Kitāb al Kharāj* of Abū Yūsuf, together with a biography of the author. *S. A. H. Jafri, Ph.D. 1932 London, School of Oriental and African Studies*

Abulafia, Todros
An edition of: the *Sha'ar ha-Razin* of Todros Abulafia. *M. Friedlander, M.A. 1930 Manchester*

Abydos
El Arabah: explorations and excavations at Abydos, 1899-1900, including observations on modes of burial from the end of the old kingdom to the nineteenth dynasty; on the morphology of ceramic and other types; and on the dates of Egyptian employment of materials. *J. Garstang, B.Litt. 1902 Oxford*

Abyssinia
See Ethiopia.

Académie Française
La lutte romantique à l'Académie Française. *E. Jones, M.A. 1922 Birmingham*

Académie Royale des Sciences
Chemistry at the Académie Royale des Sciences from its foundation in 1666 to the middle of the eighteenth century. *J. G. Stubbs, Ph.D. 1939 London, Queen Mary College*

Accadian Language
A critical lexicon of the Accadian prayers in the rituals of expiation, with an investigation of the principles which distinguish the various series of Babylonian expiation rituals. *C. J. M. Weir, D.Phil. 1930 Oxford*

The word of God in some Accadian psalms. *E. Jones, M.A. 1949 Manchester*

Accidents
See also Liability (Law).

A contribution to the study of the human factor in the causation of accidents. *E. M. Newbold, M.Sc. 1926 London*

An historical survey of the law of inevitable accident. *R. W. Jackson, LL.D. 1936 Dublin, Trinity College*

Accountancy
Bank accounting: an examination and comparison of the accounting systems of the commercial banks in Great Britain and certain other European countries, with brief reference to the history of the matter in England. *H. C. F. Holgate, Ph.D. 1938 London, External Degree*

Accountancy contd.
Cost accounting as applied to agriculture as an aid to more productive farming. *J. S. King, Ph.D. 1928 London*

English manorial accountancy in the thirteenth and early fourteenth centuries, with special reference to the didactic treatises on the subject. *D. Oschinsky, M.A. 1942 London, School of Economics and Political Science*

An investigation into the preparation of consolidated statements for holding companies. *D. J. Bogie, Ph.D. 1948 Edinburgh*

Post-audit examination of government accounts. *P. Brennan, M.A. 1945 National University of Ireland*

Preparation of accounts from incomplete records. *J. F. Cassidy, M.Comm. 1947 National University of Ireland*

The responsibility of the public accountant to society: a comparative study of American and English practice and thought. *M. E. Murphy, Ph.D. 1940 London, School of Economics and Political Science*

A study of economic concepts of income and capital valuation, with special reference to accountancy. *G. B. Sanderson, Ph.D. 1942 London, School of Economics and Political Science*

Acculturation
See Anthropology.

Accum, Frederick
A history of food adulteration and analysis from the earliest times, to the work of Frederick Accum (1820). *F. A. Filby, Ph.D. 1933 London, University College*

Acevedo, Alonso de
La creación del mundo: a narrative poem on the cosmogony, by Alonso de Acevedo. *F. W. Pierce, M.A. 1939 Belfast*

Ackermann, Louise Victorine
Madame Louise Ackermann. *E. M. Jenkins, M.A. 1928 Leeds*

Acolastus
See Fullonius, G.

Acoustics
The acoustical and optical work of Thomas Young in relation to his contemporaries. *J. F. Robertson, M.Sc. 1938 London, University College*

The original acoustical work of Ernst Florens Friedrich Chladni and its influence on his immediate successors. *G. G. Powell, M.Sc. 1950 Wales*

Act Books
A medieval act book. *J. S. Purvis, B.D. 1943 Cambridge*

Acting
See Theatre.

Action (Philosophy)
The concept of activity. *J. Lineham, Ph.D. 1922 Bristol*

Theories of pleasure-unpleasure and its relation to action. *K. Hasegawa, Ph.D. 1926 Edinburgh*

Adam, Paul
Development of ideas in the works of Paul Adam. *K. J. Sheen, Ph.D. 1935 London, University College*

Adamantius
1. Some aspects of theology of Methodius of Olympus. 2. Some features of the theological language of the *Dialects* of Adamantius. *C. Jenkins, B.D. & D.D. 1924 Oxford*

Adams, Paul
Les romans historiques de Paul Adams (1789-1830). *M. F. Donovan, M.A. 1946 London, Birkbeck College*

Adaptation (Psychology)
An experimental investigation into adaptability to new situations. *S. R. Laycock, Ph.D. 1927 London*

A study of adaptation, with special reference to teachers. *D. M. Daldy, M.Sc. 1939 Bristol*

Addison, Joseph
Addison's literary criticism. *C. Harrison, Ph.D. 1946 Leeds*

The influence of Addison. *C. H. Porter, M.A. 1909 London*

Milton criticism from Addison to de Quincey. *K. Wood, M.A. 1950 Sheffield*

Adler, Alfred
Some psychological concepts of Alfred Adler. *E. P. Greening, M.A. 1940 Manchester*

Administrative Law
See Law, Administration of.

Adolescents
Adolescence: a study of elementary school leavers and public schoolboys of the same age. *J. L. Peterson, M.A. 1939 London, University College*

Adolescent attitudes to authority at work. *C. Tenen, M.A. 1945 Manchester*

Adolescent attitudes to authority: an investigation of the psychological factors underlying the opinions of objective authority held by young people in a particular town, and determining what they actually do when authority is exercised over them. *J. H. Price, M.A. 1943 Manchester*

The adolescent child, the newspaper reading of adolescents and adults during the War, and five other papers. *W. D. Wall, Ph.D. 1947 Birmingham*

The attitude of backward adolescents towards their school life and work. *G. A. Drummond, M.A. 1947 London, Institute of Education*

A comparative study of the interests of adolescent girls in certain urban and rural areas. *H. E. Pieris, M.A. 1949 London, Institute of Education*

A critical analysis of recent investigations into the psychology of adolescence. *D. M. Riddell, M.A. 1936 London, Institute of Education*

An enquiry into the stability of attitudes and interests of a group of adolescent girls. *M. W. Stacey, M.A. 1948 London, Institute of Education*

An enquiry into the variation of precision of movement with age during adolescence. *W. J. Sparrow, M.A. 1934 Birmingham*

An experimental study of concepts in adolescence. *R. E. Presswood, M.Ed. 1934 Leeds*

French literature and the adolescent: an inquiry into the interests of adolescents as a basis of the selection of French literature for sixth forms. *A. Lee, M.A. 1937 London, Institute of Education*

An investigation into the interests and personal attitudes of adolescents educated in schools organized according to the Dalton Plan. *R. M. Beard, M.A. 1949 London, Institute of Education*

An investigation into the out-of-school activities of a group of adolescents. *N. M. Eid, M.A. 1948 London, Institute of Education*

An investigation into the use of leaderless group discussions on topics of importance to the self and in the community with a group of adolescents. *P. J. Higginbotham, M.A. 1949 London, Institute of Education*

The leisure activities of adolescents: an investigation of the psychological functions of the various leisure activities of adolescents in a particular town, with some special references to the cinema and reading. *W. Harper, M.A. 1942 Manchester*

Psychological aspects of the change from school to work. *C. Tenen, Ph.D. 1948 Manchester*

A psychological study of the attitude of adolescents in religion and religious instruction. *J. W. Daines, Ph.D. 1949 London, External Degree*

The psychology of primary and middle adolescence in relation to religious education. *B. A. Yeaxlee, B.Litt. 1936 Oxford*

The religious and moral training of the adolescent. *W. H. Backhouse, M.Ed. 1940 Leeds*

The religious development of the adolescent. *J. B. Bradbury, M.Ed. 1947 Manchester*

Report of an enquiry into the occupations, further education and leisure interests of a number of girl wage-earners from elementary and central schools in the Manchester district, with special reference to the influence of school training on their use of leisure. *J. L. Harley, M.Ed. 1937 Manchester*

Studies in the mental imagery experienced by young adolescents during the silent reading of descriptive passages. *D. V. Coutts, Ph.D. 1947 London, Institute of Education*

Studies of employed adolescent girls in relation to their development and social background. *A. P. Jephcott, M.A. 1949 Wales*

A study of friendship among adolescents. *M. M. Shukla, M.A. 1948 London, Institute of Education*

A study of the attitude of adolescents towards school life and work. *S. B. Stacey, M.A. 1949 London, Institute of Education*

A study of the attitudes of adolescents to their own intellectual, social and spiritual development. *J. F. Forrester, Ph.D. 1946 London, Institute of Education*

A study on friendship-love in adolescence. *N. M. Iovetz-Tereshchenko, Ph.D. 1933 London, King's College*

Adoption
The theory of adoption as found in Roman law, and its development in certain countries. *T. S. Vavkoukis, B.Litt. 1909 Oxford*

Adult Education
See Education, Adult.

Adultery
La question de l'adultérie dans le théâtre français, 1750-1850. *J. H. Halloran, M.A. 1928 Leeds*

Adur, River
The agricultural geography of the Adur Basin in its regional setting. *H. C. K. Henderson, Ph.D. 1935 London, Birkbeck College*

An analysis of some of the interactions of geography and history in the Arun and Adur valleys. *A. F. A. Mutton, M.A. 1932 London, Bedford College*

Advent, Second
See Eschatology.

Advertising
Advertising, salesmanship, and the theory of value. *T. H. Silcock, D.Phil. 1936 Oxford*

The economics of advertising. *F. W. Taylor, M.Sc. 1932 London, School of Economics and Political Science*

Psychological aspects of advertising in war. *N. M. Hindmarsh, M.Sc. 1943 London, King's College*

AE
See Russell, G. W. (AE).

Aehrenthal, Alois, Count
Count Aehrenthal: a study in the foreign policy of Austria-Hungary, 1906-1912. *C. Petherick, M.A. 1936 Bristol*

Aelfric
Examination of the life and homilies of Aelfric. *C. H. Vine, B.A. 1913 Bristol*

A new edition of the Old English translation of the *Hexameron* of Basil (usually ascribed to Aelfric), with a collation of all the existing mss., and an introduction on the sources, authorship, and language of the translation. *S. J. Crawford, B.Litt. 1912 Oxford*

Aeronautics
See also Air Transport.

An experimental study of some of the psychological problems which arise in pilots who use the beam approach method of landing aircraft. *R. C. Browne, D.M. 1946 Oxford*

Field research in flying training. *C. B. Frisby, Ph.D. 1947 London, King's College and London, Birkbeck College*

The mechanical investigations of Leonardo da Vinci, with special reference to his researches on flight. *I. I. B. Hart, Ph.D. 1924 London*

The theme of flying in German literature. *M. Watson, M.A. 1939 London, Birkbeck College*

Aeschines
Aeschines as a statesman. *A. E. Palmer, M.A. 1921 Birmingham*

Aeschylus
The conception of Até from Homer to Aeschylus. *W. E. Wigley, M.A. 1940 Birmingham*

Gods and men; conceptions of a moral order in Aeschylus and Herodotus. *J. O'Mahony, M.A. 1950 National University of Ireland*

The moral and religious ideas of Aeschylus and Pindar. *E. J. King, M.A. 1937 Manchester*

The use of pictorial effect in the poetry of Aeschylus, Sophocles, and Euripides. *W. M. O. Reed, M.A. 1918 London*

The women of Sophocles and Aeschylus. *A. Hill, M.A. 1910 London*

Aesop
The fables of Aesop in the German literature of the fifteenth century, with special reference to Steinhoewel's translation. *W. Schwarz, M.A. 1939 London, University College*

Aesthetics
See also Art; Criticism; Music: Appreciation; Philosophy; Taste; and Coleridge, S. T.; Gautier, T.; Pater, W. H.; Ruskin, J.; Wordsworth, W.

Aesthetic appreciation: a comparison of two methods of training appreciation in poetry. *K. B. Leopold, M.A. 1930 London, King's College*

The aesthetic approach to theism. *T. W. Taylor, Ph.D. 1935 Cambridge*

The aesthetic doctrines of French Symbolism. *A. G. Lehmann, D.Phil. 1948 Oxford*

The aesthetic judgment. *J. Mainwaring, D.Litt. 1940 Birmingham*

Aesthetics contd.
Aesthetic of Renan. *H. W. Wardman, Ph.D. 1949 London, University College*

The analysis of some types of aesthetic judgment. *E. M. Bartlett, Ph.D. 1934 London, Bedford College*

An analysis of the function of aesthetic experience in religion. *J. G. MacGregor, D.Phil. 1945 Oxford*

An approach to a contemporary aesthetic through the 20th century visual arts. *T. Goodman, Ph.D. 1945 Dublin, Trinity College*

The confusion between moral and aesthetic ideas in Greek literary criticism and philosophy. *M. Chandler, M.A. 1933 London, Royal Holloway College*

A critical history of the main currents of modern aesthetics. *W. F. Listowel, Earl of, Ph.D. 1932 London, King's College*

A critical study of Johann Elias Schlegel's aesthetic and dramatic theory. *E. M. Wilkinson, Ph.D. 1943 London, Bedford College*

Croce and the *Einfühlung* theory on the relation of feeling to the work of art. *M. S. Meldrum, B.Litt. 1941 Oxford*

The development and significance of Oscar Wilde's theory of art and its influence upon his works. *W. M. Cubbon, M.A. 1948 Manchester*

An edition of Burke's *Sublime and Beautiful*, with notes, and an introduction dealing with the place of Burke in English aesthetics in the eighteenth century. *D. W. Jefferson, B.Litt. 1937 Oxford*

An edition of Hogarth's *Analysis of Beauty*, with an appendix of excerpts from the original manuscript drafts and a study of Hogarth's place in the aesthetic criticism of the eighteenth century. *J. T. Burke, M.A. 1935 London, King's College*

An enquiry into the use of adjectives denoting beauty in Middle High German. *R. E. Keller, M.A. 1949 Manchester*

The esthetics of Stephane Mallarmé: a study in development. *J. M. Cocking, M.A. 1939 London, King's College*

The ethical and literary appreciation: a critical analysis of Aristotle's *Poetics* in relation to current theories of aesthetics, with particular reference to the teaching of literary appreciation in schools. *S. Quan, M.A. 1945 London, King's College*

Experimental and statistical investigation of some factors influencing aesthetic judgments. *H. J. Eysenck, Ph.D. 1940 London, University College*

An experimental investigation of aesthetic judgment. *S. M. Crane, M.A. 1946 London, University College*

Experimental studies in aesthetic appreciation. *J. S. Jeffery, B.Sc. 1940 Oxford*

The feeling for natural beauty in Greek poetry. *E. Cruickshank, M.A. 1917 Wales*

The German elements in the aesthetic of the age of Wordsworth; being studies in Coleridge's aesthetic and literary theory, and its relation to contemporary German thought. *W. Howarth, Litt.D. 1928 Manchester*

The influence of German aesthetic thought on the conception of romanticism in England, 1790-1830. *T. H. Dawson, Ph.D. 1925 London*

The influence of German aesthetic philosophy on Samuel Taylor Coleridge's theory of poetry. *J. W. Sagmaster, B.Litt. 1928 Oxford*

The influence of Hobbes, Locke and Berkeley on the English and Scottish aestheticians of the eighteenth century. *J. A. C. Stevenson, Ph.D. 1949 Edinburgh*

The influence of the aesthetic point of view upon the ethics of Aristotle. *F. H. C. Brock, M.A. 1904 London*

L'esthétique de Francis Jammes. *M. H. Gray, M.A. 1949 Liverpool*

L'esthétique de Gustave Flaubert dans sa correspondence et dans ses oeuvres. *A. E. M. Nock, M.A. 1921 London*

A logical examination of non-propositional forms of thought, with special reference to aesthetics. *C. M. Fremlin, B.Litt. 1938 Oxford*

Payne Knight, Price, and the picturesque. *T. A. Heinrich, M.Litt. 1936 Cambridge*

The place of the aesthetic in education, as determined by changing social conditions, and its place in the curriculum. *A. M. B. Rosevere, M.A. 1940 Reading*

Plato and fine art. *C. C. Holly, M.A. 1942 National University of Ireland*

Aesthetics contd.
Plato's conception of beauty, and its bearing on the development of the theory of ideas. *A. C. Tunnicliffe, M.A. 1911 London*

The psychology of aesthetic experience: instinctive reaction in aesthetic experience. *H. T. Jones, B.Sc. 1924 Oxford*

Relations between aesthetic thought and painting in England in the eighteenth century. *R. Platt, M.A. 1948 Reading*

The relationship of the arts in English critical theory of the eighteenth century, with special reference to the years 1750-1780, excluding periodical essays. *K. M. Hamilton, M.A. 1940 London, University College*

Representative documents of 'aesthetic' criticism, 1866-1923, in England. *J. Byrne, M.A. 1935 Manchester*

The Rev. William Gilpin and the cult of the picturesque. *H. J. Paris, B.Litt. 1938 Oxford*

The rôle of attention in aesthetic experience. *J. B. Parry, Ph.D. 1940 London, University College*

Scholastic aesthetic. *W. J. Hyland, M.A. 1924 National University of Ireland*

A statistical study of the preference of a group of children and adults as shown by certain tests of aesthetic appreciation. *E. A. Peel, Ph.D. 1945 London, Institute of Education*

Victorian theories of literary art. *W. J. Griffiths, M.A. 1931 Wales*

Walter Pater as an exponent of aestheticism. *B. Wells, M.A. 1950 Manchester*

Afan Valley
Recent industrial changes in the Afan district (Glamorganshire), with special reference to the development of Port Talbot. *D. Davies, M.A. 1915 Wales*

Afer, Tyconius
An English translation of *Liber regularum* by Tyconius Afer. *A. R. Kent, M.A. 1943 Sheffield*

Afghanistan
The diplomatic career of Sir Claude Wade: a study of British relations with the Sikhs and Afghans, July 1823 to March 1840. *E. R. Kapadia, M.A. 1938 London, School of Oriental and African Studies*

Sultán Mahmúd of Ghazna and his times. *M. Nazim, Ph.D. 1928 Cambridge*

Africa
A comparative study of the economic development of the mandated territories in Africa. *V. R. Hadkins, M.Sc. 1940 Sheffield*

International relations on the south east coast of Africa, 1796-1856. *M. V. Jackson, Ph.D. 1938 London, King's College*

Africa, Central
The nature and development of the idea of God as held by the primitive peoples of central Africa. *V. G. Ispir, B.Sc. 1914 Oxford*

Africa, East
A comparative study of the various systems of economic development in East Africa. *C. W. Buckby, Ph.D. 1932 London, School of Economics and Political Science*

East African studies. *S. J. K. Baker, M.A. 1931 Liverpool*

The Indian problem in eastern and southern Africa. *L. James, M.A. 1940 Liverpool*

The western shores of the Indian Ocean before Vasco da Gama. *H. A. Edwards, M.A. 1930 London, Birkbeck College*

Africa, North
See also Barbary States.

Life in Vandal Africa (A.D.429-533). *J. J. Campbell, M.A. 1934 Belfast*

The life of the Christians in North Africa in the time of Tertullian. *C. B. Daly, M.A. 1938 Belfast*

The social and economic background of Christianity in North Africa down to 430, with special reference to the Donatist schism. *W. H. C. Frend, D.Phil. 1940 Oxford*

Social life in Roman Africa. *M. A. Gardiner, M.A. 1931 Belfast*

Africa, South
See South Africa.

Africa, South-West
See South-West Africa.

Africa, West
The Berlin West African Conference 1884-5. *S. E. Crowe, Ph.D. 1940 Cambridge*

Africa, West contd.
British policy in relation to Portuguese claims in West Africa, 1876 to 1884. *I. Bains, M.A. 1940 London, Bedford College*

The British West African settlements 1751-1821: a study in local administration. *E. C. Martin, Ph.D. 1924 London*

The economic revolution in British West Africa. *W. A. McPhee, Ph.D. 1925 London*

International rivalry in West Africa (1454-1559). *J. W. Blake, M.A. 1935 London, King's College*

The mapping of West Africa in the fourteenth and fifteenth centuries, as illustrative of the development of geographical ideas. *G. H. Kimble, M.A. 1931 London, King's College*

Problems of the development of French West Africa, as illustrated by Senegal and the Ivory Coast. *M. A. el M. M. Sharkawy, M.A. 1931 Liverpool*

The struggle for power on the Senegal and Gambia, 1660-1713. *T. G. Stone, M.A. 1921 London*

African Languages
See Bantu Languages; Bembe Language; Gong Languages; Mende Language; Nyanja Language; etc.

African Peoples
See Religion: Ancient and Primitive; and Amandebele; Ashanti; Azande; Bachama; Bantu; Bari; Berbers; Bete; Bushmen; Ewe; Ga; Hottentots; Ibo; Kikuyu; Kipsigi; Mende; Nupe; Umundri; Waya; Yao; Yoruba.

Agency
See also Contract (Law).
Agency in Roman and English law. *W. R. Anson, D.C.L. 1881 Oxford*

The manufacturers' agent. His economic and social significance. *J. Stephenson, D.Sc. 1922 London*

Agesilaus, King
The ancient *Lives* of Agesilaus. *P. B. Duffin, M.A. 1946 Belfast*

Aggression
See also Psychology; Sociology.
Analysis of aggression among problem children: a study of its incidence and immediate nature. *L. Jackson, B.Sc. 1942 Oxford*

Investigation into factors influencing the direction of aggressive impulses into (a) delinquency, (b) neurosis, (c) positive achievement. *L. Jackson, D.Phil. 1949 Oxford*

An investigation into the phenomena of aggressiveness. *C. P. Rawson, M.Sc. 1934 London, School of Economics and Political Science*

A psychological study of human aggressiveness. *T. P. H. McKellar, Ph.D. 1949 London, University College*

Agnosticism
A study of agnosticism and intellectual doubt in the age of Shakespeare as expressed in the literature of the period, with special reference to Marston and the Inns of Court circle. *M. G. Chamberlain, M.A. 1934 London, King's College*

Agra and Oudh, United Provinces of
, *See also Khasa, The.*
The administration of the Earl of Leicester in the United Provinces. *L. A. Hodgkinson, M.A. 1925 Liverpool*

An economic and regional geography of the United Provinces of Agra and Oudh. *S. M. T. Rizvi, Ph.D. 1937 London, External Degree*

The industrial geography of the United Provinces of Agra and Oudh. *A. M. Patel, M.A. 1948 London, University College*

An interpretation of the distribution of the population within the United Provinces of Agra and Oudh. *N. Y. Boydell, M.Sc. 1938 Leeds*

Settlements in the United Provinces of Agra and Oudh. *E. Ahmad, Ph.D. 1949 London, School of Economics and Political Science*

Agrafa
See Bible: New Testament: Apocrypha

Agricultural Co-operation
See also Co-operation.
Agricultural co-operation in the Bombay Presidency. *Y. T. Desai, M.Sc. 1930 London, School of Economics and Political Science*

Agricultural co-operation in British India. *J. Matthai, B.Litt. 1917 Oxford*

Agricultural co-operation in Sweden and its relations with the state 1929 to 1947. *R. D. Hewlett, Ph.D. 1950 Reading*

Agricultural Co-operation contd.
Agricultural co-operation in Hampshire. *H. Newman, M.Litt. 1949 Cambridge*

The consideration of alternative methods of co-operative organization in agriculture and a comparison of the results achieved by certain selected countries, viz. Great Britain, Ireland and Denmark. *R. D. Mihra, B.Litt. 1925 Oxford*

Co-operation and credit in forestry. *I. Kissin, D.Phil. 1944 Oxford*

Co-operation in agriculture and banking in British West Africa. *J. C. De Graft-Johnson, Ph.D. 1946 Edinburgh*

The Co-operative Movement in Italy, with special reference to agriculture, labour and production. *E. A. Lloyd, M.A. 1925 Wales*

The finance of co-operative organizations with special reference to methods of financing agricultural co-operatives, including state assistance. *T. T. Chang, M.Sc. 1938 Wales*

The future of agricultural co-operation in the United Provinces: an examination of co-operative experience in parts of Europe, America and India with special reference to the problems of agricultural co-operation in the United Provinces. *H. R. Chaturvedi, Ph.D. 1940 Wales*

The organization and methods of agricultural co-operation in the British Isles and the possibility of their application in the Central Provinces of India. *N. Y. Kher, Ph.D. 1949 Wales*

A study of agricultural co-operation in India based upon foreign experience. *H. L. Pasricha, Ph.D. 1931 London, School of Economics and Political Science*

A study of modern developments in agricultural co-operation in parts of Europe and North America, with reference to the problem of co-operation in India. *S. K. Kurhade, M.Sc. 1936 Wales*

Agricultural Economics
See Agriculture.

Agricultural Workers
See Agriculture.

Agriculture
See also Agricultural Co-operation; Cotton Industry; Dairy Industry; Food; Grassland; Horticulture; Land Utilization; Livestock Industry; Rice Growing Industry; Tariffs; Textiles; Woollen Industry.

Agricultural education in the Punjab. *H. S. Arora, Ph.D. 1934 London, School of Economics and Political Science*

Agricultural education in Ireland; a history. *W. S. Lawlor, M.A. 1927 National University of Ireland*

Agricultural fluctuations. *H. Belshaw, Ph.D. 1926 Cambridge*

The appraisal of agricultural productivity. *J. B. Goodson, M.A. 1939 London, Birkbeck College*

The control of agricultural prices by the State and other bodies, with special reference to British experience and the possibility of its application to post-war European agriculture. *A. Gomez Orbaneja, B.Litt. 1946 Oxford*

Cost accounting as applied to agriculture as an aid to more productive farming. *J. S. King, Ph.D. 1928 London*

An economic geography of commercialized agriculture with special reference to North America. *T. A. G. Wells, Ph.D. 1947 London, External Degree*

The economics of production on grass and arable farms. *H. J. Vaughan, B.Sc. 1924 Oxford*

Education for agriculture. *W. Mulcahy, M.A. 1946 National University of Ireland*

Farm management research technique. *R. McG. Carslaw, Ph.D. 1931 Cambridge*

The history of the development of studies in the marketing of agricultural produce and theories of marketing reforms, with some reference to the development of marketing studies in India. *A. Joshua, M.Sc. 1936 Wales*

Marketing of perishable agricultural products. *W. Mesiha, M.Com. 1930 Birmingham*

Methods in farm management analysis: an economic investigation with some illustrations and results. *W. H. Jones, M.Sc. 1933 Wales*

Methods of investigation and research in agricultural and rural economies, with special reference to economic and social studies in tropical Africa. *S. A. J. Pratt, B.Litt. 1949 Oxford*

Agriculture contd.
Methods of research on farm management. *G. Polychroniades, B.Litt. 1941 Oxford*

Monetary policy in agricultural raw material producing countries, with special reference to Egypt. *A. M. el Kaissouni, Ph.D. 1942 London, School of Economics and Political Science*

The organization of labour in tropical agriculture. *I. C. Greaves, Ph.D. 1934 London, School of Economics and Political Science*

Purposes and methods of recording and accounting as applied to agriculture, with special reference to provision and use of economic data relating to agriculture in India. *A. Singh, Ph.D. 1937 Wales*

The rationalization of agricultural production and marketing, with special reference to recent developments in central Europe. *V. Cornea, B.Litt. 1933 Oxford*

The scope and method of research in agricultural economics, with special reference to Indian agriculture. *T. G. Shirname, Ph.D. 1932 Wales*

A study of the social and economic influence of the small unit of cultivation. *E. Thomas, B.Litt. 1926 Oxford*

Systems of remuneration of labour in agriculture in relation to efficiency and performance. *W. Mackenzie, B.Litt. 1948 Oxford*

Tariffs for farmers. *D. J. Coakley, M.Comm. 1928 National University of Ireland*

Treatment of the rustic and the citizen in Elizabethan drama. *M. M. Frost, M.A. 1916 London*

Agriculture: Ancient
The agrarian programme of the democratic party. 78-59 B.C. *M. Auld, M.A. 1905 Liverpool*

The agriculture and agricultural implements of the Hebrews. *B. J. Roberts, M.A. 1936 Wales*

The agriculture of Cyrenaica in classical antiquity, with special reference to the Jewish revolt under Trajan. *E. S. Applebaum, B.Litt. 1948 Oxford*

The economic conditions of the Jews in Babylonia under the Sassanides from 200 C.E. to 500 C.E. based on Rabbinical literature: Part 1: agriculture. *J. Newman, Ph.D. 1931 London, External Degree*

The indebtedness of Vergil to Varro in the composition of the *Georgics*: a study in parallelism. *N. P. Bentley, M.A. 1929 Manchester*

Primitive agriculture. *G. P. L. Miles, Ph.D. 1942 London, School of Economics and Political Science*

Short history of ancient agriculture. *M. Gompertz, Ph.D. 1926 London*

The state of Roman agriculture in the time of the Gracchi. *C. A. I. Moore, M.A. 1914 London*

Agriculture: Australia
Developmental policy and agricultural settlement in southeastern Australia. *J. Andrews, Ph.D. 1937 Cambridge*

Agriculture: British East Africa
Conditions of agricultural and pastoral work in British East Africa. *C. W. Goffin, M.A. 1930 London, Birkbeck College*

Agriculture: Burma
The agricultural geography of the Irrawaddy delta, with special reference to rice. *K. E. Bruen, M.A. 1939 London, University College*

Agriculture: Canada
The economic geography of north-west Canada with special reference to the agricultural possibilities. *F. B. Vrooman, B.Sc. 1910 Oxford*

Agriculture: China
The position of the peasant in modern China. *W. H. Wu, Ph.D. 1939 London, School of Economics and Political Science*

Agriculture: Egypt
Changing values in Egyptian agriculture from 1800 to the present time. *G. H. Thomas, M.A. 1939 London, Birkbeck College*

Government aid to the cultivator in Egypt. *P. Hill, M.Com. 1933 Birmingham*

Post-war changes in the agricultural geography of Egypt. *H. K. Selim, M.A. 1939 Liverpool*

Agriculture: France
The influence of England on the French 'Agronomes', 1750-1789. *A. J. M. A. Bourde, Ph.D. 1949 Cambridge*

Types of agricultural villages and related systems of land utilization and division in western France and its islands. *S. Harris, M.Sc. 1930 Wales*

Agriculture: Germany

Methods of government control of agriculture in New Zealand, the United States of America, Italy, and Germany. *E. P. Weeks, D.Phil. 1940 Oxford*

Agriculture: Great Britain

An account of an investigation into the labour force employed on farms. *W. H. Senior, M.Sc. 1929 Reading*

Agrarian conditions and changes in west Wales during the sixteenth century, with special reference to monastic and chantry lands. *G. D. Owen, Ph.D. 1935 Wales*

Agrarian conditions in east Berkshire, 1560-1660. *K. A. Brewin, M.A. 1918 London*

Agrarian conditions in Herefordshire and the adjacent border during the later Middle Ages. *A. J. Roderick, Ph.D. 1938 London, School of Economics and Political Science*

Agrarian conditions in Norfolk and Suffolk during the first half of the seventeenth century. *J. Spratt, M.A. 1935 London, School of Economics and Political Science*

Agrarian conditions on the Wiltshire estates of the Duchy of Lancaster, the Lords Hungerford and the Bishopric of Winchester in the thirteenth, fourteenth and fifteenth centuries. *R. C. Payne, Ph.D. 1940 London, School of Economics and Political Science*

An agrarian survey of South Wales and the March, 1282-1415. *W. Rees, D.Sc. 1920 London*

An agricultural atlas of Scotland. *H. J. Wood, Ph.D. 1931 London, External Degree*

Agricultural change in east Cheshire, 1780-1830. *C. S. Davies, M.A. 1949 Manchester*

The agricultural geography and related distribution of population in Northumberland. *E. C. Sykes, M.A. 1931 Liverpool*

The agricultural geography of the Adur Basin in its regional setting. *H. C. K. Henderson, Ph.D. 1935 London, Birkbeck College*

Agricultural geography of southwest Lancashire. *J. F. Maguire, M.A. 1939 Liverpool*

The agricultural geography of Devon. *A. B. Shorney, M.Sc. 1943 London, External Degree*

The agricultural geography of the East Midlands-Market Harborough-Rugby area. *E. R. Payne, M.A. 1945 Wales*

Agricultural marketing in Breconshire, with special reference to different types of farming. *H. J. Meredith, M.A. 1926 Wales*

Agricultural price records: an account of the methods of recording prices and a guide to the published wholesale price records of England and Wales. *P. M. Reason, M.Sc. 1934 Reading*

The Agriculture Act, 1947. *J. F. Phillips, LL.M. 1949 Cambridge*

An analysis of the geographic factors affecting agriculture and industry in the southwest Peninsula, west of the Tamar. *S. Muckle, M.A. 1933 London, Bedford College*

An analysis of the industrial and agricultural life of south-east England. *M. B. A. Churchard, Ph.D. 1933 London, Bedford College*

The application of air photography to a study of the agricultural geography of northwest Cardiganshire. *G. M. Howe, M.Sc. 1949 Wales*

Arwystli and Cyfeilog in the sixteenth and seventeenth centuries: an agrarian and social study. *E. Evans, M.A. 1939 Wales*

Aspects of the agrarian problem in Wales in the sixteenth century. *T. Williams, M.A. 1928 Wales*

The British peasant, 1770-1820, as reflected in our literature. *B. Sampson, M.A. 1921 London*

Celtic settlement and agriculture in central Sussex. *M. Coleman, M.A. 1944 London, External Degree*

The changes in the numbers of agricultural labourers and in their wages and efficiency during the past fifty years, and the causes of these changes, with special reference to Wales. *E. Hughes, M.A. 1909 Wales*

The composition and recruitment of the agricultural labour force and their bearing on future supply. *M. A. Wilson, B.Litt. 1949 Oxford*

The control of agricultural prices by the State and other bodies, with special reference to British experience and the possibility of its application to post-war European agriculture. *A. Gomez Orbaneja, B.Litt. 1946 Oxford*

Agriculture: Great Britain contd.

The development of farm mechanization in England and Wales. *D. H. Evans, M.Sc. 1949 Nottingham*

The East Riding of Yorkshire: a study in agricultural geography. *S. E. J. Best, Ph.D. 1927 Leeds*

An economic and social survey of the parish of Badsey, Worcestershire, in which the population is engaged in an intensive form of agriculture. *E. L. Harry, M.Sc. 1931 Wales*

The economic development and organization of statutory small holdings in the south Midlands. *W. F. Darke, B.Litt. 1937 Oxford*

An economic interpretation of the agricultural statistics relating to the Bristol Advisory Province. *C. V. Dawe, Ph.D. 1935 Bristol*

An economic interpretation of the agricultural returns of the Bristol advisory province. *C. V. Dawe, Ph.D. 1932 Leeds*

The economic organization of small farms in the Northeast of Scotland. *A. A. Dawson, Ph.D. 1930 Aberdeen*

An economic study of the supply of agricultural labour in Buckinghamshire. *J. A. Mollett, M.Sc. 1949 Reading*

An economic survey of a grazing district in the Welland Valley. *J. L. Davies, M.Sc. 1927 Wales*

An economic survey of small holdings in the Vale of Evesham. *S. R. Wragg, M.A. 1937 Bristol*

An economic survey of some aspects of farming in Wales. *J. M. Jones, M.A. 1926 Wales*

An economic survey of the agriculture of Airedale and Calder Valley. *T. E. Miller, M.Sc. 1935 Leeds*

The economics of farm management in a section of Aberdeenshire. *A. D. Imper, Ph.D. 1928 Aberdeen*

The economics of poor land arable farming; based on surveys of difficult farming areas in the east Midlands. *S. M. Makings, Ph.D. 1943 London, External Degree*

The economics of Yorkshire farming: a study based on the accounts of thirty-two Yorkshire farms for the period 1928-34. *C. M. Brayshaw, M.Sc. 1937 Leeds*

English agriculture, 1760-1830. *J. Cresswell, M.Sc. 1935 London, External Degree*

English agriculture and the labourer, 1840-1885, with special reference to the depression of the 'seventies'. *N. Yates, M.A. 1930 Birmingham*

The farm worker's standard of living: a study of conditions in Shropshire in 1939. *J. B. Butler, M.Sc. 1946 London, External Degree*

The form and function of settlements in relation to types of farming in England and Wales, with an analysis of specific examples chosen from the west Midlands and elsewhere. *J. East, Ph.D. 1947 London, University College and London, External Degree*

Geographical factors influencing intensive agriculture in south west England. *W. J. Tamblin, M.Sc. 1945 London, External Degree*

The geography of Berkshire, with special reference to agriculture. *J. Stephenson, M.A. 1936 London, School of Economics and Political Science*

Gower: a regional study, with special reference to agricultural geography. *W. A. Evans, M.A. 1948 Wales*

The Hebridean crofter: a study in social geography. *G. D. New, M.A. 1925 Liverpool*

The historical geography of a part of east Sussex from 1780, with special reference to agriculture. *E. W. H. Briault, Ph.D. 1939 London, Birkbeck College*

An historical study of the agriculture of part of south-eastern Sussex from 1780. *H. B. Smith, M.A. 1940 London, Birkbeck College*

The history of English agricultural imports and exports, 1660-1713. *F. G. Carnell, B.Litt. 1945 Oxford*

The history of the agricultural geography of Great Britain since 1800. *J. McDermott, M.Sc. 1943 London, External Degree*

The influences of the improvements in agriculture during the reigns of George I and George II. *M. J. Truscott, M.A. 1914 London*

Agriculture: Great Britain contd.

An investigation of changes in population density and distribution, together with changes in agricultural practice, in Pembrokeshire during the period 1831-1931. *G. I. Lewis, M.A. 1937 Birmingham*

La politica agraria della Granbrettagna. *C. Ruini, M.Com. 1940 Birmingham*

Labour on the land since 1920. *W. H. Pedley, B.Litt. 1940 Oxford*

The land utilisation and agriculture of Somerset. *M. G. Bartlett, M.Sc. 1945 Bristol*

The migration of farmers in relation to the economic development of agriculture in Great Britain since 1880. *E. Lorrain-Smith, B.Litt. 1931 Oxford*

The Norfolk agricultural labourer, 1834-1884. *L. M. Springall, Ph.D. 1935 London, School of Economics and Political Science*

A physiological and economic study of the diets of workers in rural areas as compared with those of workers resident in urban districts. *A. B. Hill, Ph.D. 1926 London*

A portion of west Sussex: a study of agriculture and population. *E. Cook, M.A. 1939 Liverpool*

The post-war tendencies in agriculture in the county of Essex. *N. V. Scarfe, M.A. 1933 London, University College*

The practical application of wartime agricultural policy, with special reference to Highland regions. *D. R. Denman, Ph.D. 1945 London, External Degree*

The productivity of labour and standards of living in British agriculture, and a comparison with selected countries abroad. *O. J. Beilby, B.Litt. 1935 Oxford*

A regional study of the agricultural landscape of the north Exe basin. *L. R. Hawkes, M.A. 1938 London, Birkbeck College*

The revolt of the Hampshire agricultural labourers and its causes, 1812-1831. *A. M. Colson, M.A. 1937 London, King's College*

Scottish farming in the eighteenth century. *J. E. Handley, Ph.D. 1933 London, External Degree*

Some geographical aspects of the agriculture of Durham. *A. S. Gaught, Ph.D. 1939 London, External Degree*

A special enquiry into agricultural developments during the mid-eighteenth century on the estate of the Earl of Marchmont in Berwickshire. *G. S. Maxton, Ph.D. 1935 Edinburgh*

The state in relation to agriculture since 1929, with special reference to the agricultural policies of Great Britain and the United States of America. *J. T. Hsieh, B.Litt. 1938 Oxford*

A study in the use of advisory bodies by the Ministry of Agriculture and Fisheries, since 1919. *A. M. Mackintosh, B.Litt. 1949 Oxford*

A study of a rural and maritime community in the nineteenth century, with special reference to the relation between agriculture and shipping. *D. Thomas, M.A. 1928 Liverpool*

A study of profits, with special reference to the profits of farms in the East of Scotland. *E. Whittaker, Ph.D. 1932 Edinburgh*

A study of the character of the main changes in the production and distribution of agricultural produce in Cardiganshire in medieval and modern times. *G. M. Lyke, M.A. 1917 Wales*

A study of the effect of the following factors: nature of the work, lack of social intercourse, limitation of educational possibilities, migration of population and low social status upon the mental life of the modern English agricultural labourers, with special reference to Oxfordshire. *B. Barron, B.Litt. 1923 Oxford*

A survey of the agricultural geography of Mid-Craven. *K. B. Cumberland, M.A. 1938 London, External Degree*

The value of agricultural output in different regions. *O. S. Wells, M.Sc. 1937 Cambridge*

The work of women in agriculture in the late eighteenth and early nineteenth centuries, and the influence of the agrarian revolution thereon. *I. Pinchbeck, M.A. 1927 London*

Agriculture: India

Agricultural credit in India: a comparative study of arrangements for provision of agricultural credit in India and abroad. *S. M. Z. Rizvi, B.Litt. 1949 Oxford*

Agricultural development of western United Provinces. *V. N. S. Mathur, M.A. 1938 London, Birkbeck College*

Agriculture: India contd.
The agricultural geography of the Punjab. *K. S. Ahmad, Ph.D. 1939 London, University College*

The agricultural geography of Bihar. *P. Dayal, Ph.D. 1947 London, School of Economics and Political Science*

The agricultural geography of the coast plains of South India. *E. Simkins, M.A. 1927 Liverpool*

Agricultural geography of the United Provinces. *B. N. Mukerji, Ph.D. 1938 Edinburgh*

Agricultural problems and conditions in the Bombay Presidency, 1870-1914. *M. A. Tata, M.Sc. 1922 London*

Economics of agricultural marketing in India, with particular reference to oilseeds, the determination of prices, and proposals for future marketing policy. *P. Singh, B.Litt. 1949 Oxford*

Marketing of Indian agricultural produce in the United Kingdom. *M. Srinivasan, Ph.D. 1942 Wales*

Organization and finance of the marketing of the staple agricultural products in northern India. *S. A. Husain, Ph.D. 1936 London, School of Economics and Political Science*

The place and problems of rural reconstruction in the development of Indian agriculture. *V. S. Shembekar, Ph.D. 1941 Wales*

The problem of rural indebtedness in Indian economic life. *B. G. Ghate, Ph.D. 1937 London, School of Economics and Political Science*

Recent economic depression in India, with reference to agriculture and rural life. *R. K. Bhan, Ph.D. 1940 London, School of Economics and Political Science*

Rural co-operation in India. *M. M. Mahmood, B.Litt. 1922 Oxford*

Some aspects of agricultural marketing in India, with reference to developments in Western marketing systems. *R. S. Srivastava, B.Litt. 1948 Oxford*

Some factors detrimental to agriculture in the United Provinces. *G. S. Saksena, Ph.D. 1931 London, School of Economics and Political Science*

A study in rural economy of Gujarat containing suggestions for reconstruction. *J. M. Mehta, Ph.D. 1929 London*

A study of the development of agriculture in the Punjab and its economic effects. *K. S. Bajwa, Ph.D. 1928 Leeds*

Agriculture: Iraq
The agrarian question in Iraq. *U. P. Mayer, D.Phil. 1944 Oxford*

Agriculture: Ireland
Agricultural credit in Ireland. *D. J. O'Flynn, M.Econ.Sc. 1942 National University of Ireland*

Agricultural credit in Ireland. *T. J. Coyne, M.A. 1922 National University of Ireland*

Agricultural limits in the Dublin mountains. *T. F. Finch, M.Sc. 1948 Dublin, Trinity College*

Analysis of the agricultural systems of the six and the twenty-six counties. *L. P. F. Smith, M.A. 1948 National University of Ireland*

Co-operative marketing of agricultural products. *M. Murphy, M.A. 1928 National University of Ireland*

In defence of the farmer. *D. O'Sullivan, Ph.D. 1947 National University of Ireland*

Irish agriculture, 1929-1936. *T. C. Devitt, M.A. 1937 National University of Ireland*

Irish rural economics. *T. F. Duggan, M.A. 1921 National University of Ireland*

Land and peasant in Anglo-Irish literature. *E. J. Sheehy, M.A. 1932 National University of Ireland*

An outlook on agriculture and industry in post-war Eire. *M. A. O'Mahony, M.Econ.Sc. 1945 National University of Ireland*

Review of agricultural legislation in Eire, 1922-42. *D. P. Ua Buachalla, M.Econ.Sc. 1943 National University of Ireland*

Rundale and its social concomitants. *D. McCourt, M.A. 1947 Belfast*

The Rundale system in Ireland: a study of its geographical distribution and social relations. *D. McCourt, Ph.D. 1950 Belfast*

Agriculture: Italy
Methods of government control of agriculture in New Zealand, the United States of America, Italy, and Germany. *E. P. Weeks, D.Phil. 1940 Oxford*

Agriculture: Jersey
Agriculture in Jersey. *L. R. Wood, Ph.D. 1934 London, External Degree*

Agriculture: Malaysia
Malaya, with special reference to the influence of soil and climate conditions on agriculture. *A. W. King, M.A. 1936 Bristol*

Agriculture: Malta
The physical and agricultural geography of the Maltese Islands. *A. Rushton, M.Sc. 1948 London, External Degree*

Agriculture: Netherlands
The position of agriculture in the Low Countries in relation to their economic union, to their wealth and welfare, and to international organization of agriculture. *A. Verkinderen, B.Litt. 1948 Oxford*

Agriculture: New Zealand
Methods of government control of agriculture in New Zealand, the United States of America, Italy, and Germany. *E. P. Weeks, D.Phil. 1940 Oxford*

The pastoral industries of New Zealand: a study in economic geography. *R. O. Buchanan, Ph.D. 1932 London, University College*

Agriculture: Nigeria
The human geography of Nigeria in relation to physical aspects, with special reference to agriculture. *E. I. Oli, M.A. 1945 London, External Degree*

Agriculture: Pakistan
Agricultural resources of western Pakistan: a statistico-economical survey. *D. M. Qureshi, M.Sc. 1949 London, School of Economics and Political Science*

Agriculture: Rumania
The land and the peasant in Roumania. *D. Mitrany, Ph.D. 1931 London, School of Economics and Political Science*

Political aspects of the agrarian problem in Roumania, 1918-45. *H. L. Roberts, D.Phil. 1948 Oxford*

The rural revolution in Rumania and in south eastern Europe. *D. Mitrany, Ph.D. 1929 London*

Agriculture: Russia
The agricultural regions of the U.S.S.R. *W. D. Morris, M.Sc. 1946 London, King's College*

A critical survey of the Narodnik movement, 1861-1881. *A. I. S. Branfoot, Ph.D. 1926 London*

The economics of Russian farming, with particular reference to the years 1900-1916. *G. A. Pavlovsky, Ph.D. 1929 London*

The peasantry, Orthodox clergy, dissenters, and Jews, as seen by Leskov. *F. Smith, M.A. 1948 London, School of Slavonic and East European Studies*

The Russian peasant movement, 1906-1917. *L. Owen, Ph.D. 1933 London, King's College*

Soviet agriculture. *C. Penrose, M.Sc. 1946 London, School of Economics and Political Science and London, External Degree*

Agriculture: Spain
Cultivation in Spain, with some reference to trade between Spain and Great Britain. *F. F. Laidler, M.Sc. 1930 Wales*

Agriculture: Swaziland
The agricultural geography of Swaziland. *P. Scott, M.Sc. 1947 London, School of Economics and Political Science*

Agriculture: United States
Agricultural credit: being a study of recent developments in farm credit administration in the United States. *M. M. A. I. Qureshi, Ph.D. 1935 Dublin, Trinity College*

The agriculture of the semi-arid regions of the Middle West of the U.S.A. considered in relation to wheat cultivation. *J. R. Sanctuary, M.A. 1940 London, External Degree*

Methods of government control of agriculture in New Zealand, the United States of America, Italy, and Germany. *E. P. Weeks, D.Phil. 1940 Oxford*

The state in relation to agriculture since 1929, with special reference to the agricultural policies of Great Britain and the United States of America. *J. T. Hsieh, B.Litt. 1938 Oxford*

Agriculture: U.S.S.R
See Agriculture: Russia.

Aided Diarmata
Aided Diarmata Meic Fergusso Cerrbeoil (The violent death of Diarmad son of Fergus Cerrbeoil). *M. A. O'Flaherty, M.A. 1948 National University of Ireland*

Ailly, Pierre d', Cardinal
The theories of Cardinal Pierre d'Ailly concerning forms of government in Church and State with special reference to his interest in suggestions made by William of Occam. *A. E. Roberts, M.A. 1931 London, Bedford College*

Aimard, Gustave
Etude lexicographique des mots intéressants dans l'oeuvre de Gustave Aimard, étudiés dans ses romans écrits pendant les cinq années 1858-1862. *A. E. Ferguson, M.A. 1936 Leeds*

Aimeri, de Narbonne
Le caractère d'Aimeri de Narbonne d'après les chansons *Girart de Vienne, Aimeri de Narbonne, Les Enfances Guillaume, Les Narbonnais, Le Siège de Basbastre, La Prise de Cordres et de Sebille* et *La Mort Aimeri.* *A. G. R. Britten, M.A. 1936 London, Birkbeck College*

Air Transport
See also Aeronautics; Transport.

The economics of air transport. *S. J. Weiss, Ph.D. 1938 London, School of Economics and Political Science*

The international right of aerial navigation. *P. W. French, LL.D. 1915 London*

A political and economic history of the development of internal civil aviation in Great Britain, 1919-1939. *H. C. L. Leech, M.A. 1950 Manchester*

Some economic aspects of the organisation and operation of commercial air transport. *H. Birchall, Ph.D. 1936 London, External Degree*

Akbar
Faizi, Urfi, and Naziri (poets of Akbar's Court). *A. W. Khan, Ph.D. 1932 London, School of Oriental and African Studies*

Akhenaten
Akhenaten and the growth and development of monotheism in Hebrew prophecy: a comparison and a survey. *R. K. Spedding, M.A. 1932 Liverpool*

Alain-Fournier, Henri
Alain-Fournier. *M. O'Nolan, M.A. 1943 National University of Ireland*

Alary, Pierre Joseph
The political academies of France in the early eighteenth century, with special reference to the Club de l'Entresol, and to its founder the Abbé Pierre-Joseph Alary. *E. R. Briggs, Ph.D. 1932 Cambridge*

Alas, Leopoldo
Leopoldo Alas (Clarín), his work and his contemporaries. *G. J. Davies, Ph.D. 1938 Leeds*

Albanian Language
The phonology of the Indo-European elements in Albanian. *S. Mann, M.A. 1940 Bristol*

Albany, John Stewart, Duke of, Regent of Scotland
John, Duke of Albany, 1481-1536, servant of Scotland and France. *R. F. Whisker, M.A. 1939 Liverpool*

Albemarle, Isabella, Countess of
The lands of Isabella de Fortibus, Countess of Aumale: a study in thirteenth century administration. *N. Denholm-Young, B.Litt. 1929 Oxford*

Alberta
A history of the real Old Timers of Fort Edmonton (Canada) and its hinterland. *I. M. Harper, M.Litt. 1932 Cambridge*

Albertanus, of Brescia
Die Mittelhochdeutschen Uebersetzungen der Traktate des Albertanus Brixiensis. *J. K. Bostock, B.Litt. 1924 Oxford*

Albinus
See Alcuin.

Albion Schools
A survey of educational development in the borough of Ashton-under-Lyne, with special reference to Albion Schools and to the period 1840-1938. *S. D. Ashton, M.Ed. 1938 Manchester*

Albo, Joseph
A critical translation of the *Ikkarim* of Joseph Albo, with a consideration of his philosophic system and a general survey of the teaching and disputations of Jewish theologians in regard to the question of what constitutes the articles of fundamentals of the Jewish faith. *M. Bloch, M.A. 1930 Wales*

Alchemy
See also Blomefield, M.

Alchemical symbolism in Goethe's scientific and literary works. *R. D. Gray, Ph.D. 1949 Cambridge*

A conspectus of Greek alchemy. *F. S. Taylor, Ph.D. 1932 London, University College*

English alchemists before the sixteenth century. *A. Sutherland, M.Sc. 1930 London*

The experimental basis of Robert Boyle's objections to the Aristotelian and alchemical doctrines. *M. G. Odling, M.Sc. 1928 London*

Alchemy contd.
The theoretical basis and practical methods of transmutation of metals as practised by the early alchemists (before 800 A.D.). *F. S. Taylor, B.Sc. 1925 Oxford*

Alcibiades
Alcibiades. *E. E. A. Ridley, M.A. 1909 London*

Alcohol
See also Brewing Industry.

Alcohol and the nation. *G. B. Wilson, Ph.D. 1939 London, External Degree*

The law relating to the sale of intoxicating liquors in England and other countries. *R. Souttar, D.C.L. 1903 Oxford*

On the nature of dipsomania, with reference to consciousness and volition. *G. Robertson, M.D. 1894 Aberdeen*

A second study of extreme alcoholism in adults, with special reference to the Home Office inebriate reformatory data. *D. Heron, D.Sc. 1912 London*

Studies in social science: 1. The housing problem in Bristol. 2. Some social and economic effects of alcohol consumption. *H. R. Burrows, M.Com. 1932 Leeds*

Alcuin
Albinus and the history of Middle Platonism. *R. E. Witt, Ph.D. 1934 Cambridge*

Aldrich, Henry
The life and musical works of Henry Aldrich. *E. F. A. Suttle, B.Litt. 1938 Oxford*

Alemán, Mateo
The religious and philosophical background of Mateo Alemán with reference to the *Guzmán de Alfarache*. *E. Moreno, Ph.D. 1944 Cambridge*

Alembert, Jean le Rond d'
Jean d'Alembert: his activity and his thought. *R. Grimsley, D.Phil. 1948 Oxford*

Alexander, Samuel
The relation between the theory of knowledge and metaphysics in the philosophical system of Samuel Alexander. *R. I. Markus, M.A. 1948 Manchester*

Alexander, the Great
Alexander and the earthly paradise in medieval English literature. *M. M. Lascelles, B.Litt. 1927 Oxford*

The Alexander legend in medieval England. *W. Wilkinson, M.A. 1933 Leeds*

De Alexandri Magni fortuna aut virtute apud Plutarchum. *J. L. Roche, M.A. 1937 National University of Ireland*

The *Life of Alexander* in English prose (Thornton ms.). *W. Hadley, M.A. 1922 London*

Some of the continuations of the medieval French romance of *Alexander*. *E. B. Ham, D.Phil. 1927 Oxford*

Aléxandre l'Orfelin
The story of Aléxandre l'Orfelin: a critical edition. *C. E. Pickford, M.A. 1948 Manchester*

Alfieri, Vittorio
Alfieri's debt to Racine. *M. J. Oberli, B.Litt. 1937 Oxford*

Vittorio Alfieri's influence and reputation in France and England. *E. Ward, M.A. 1932 Manchester*

The work of Vittorio Alfieri considered in relation to the author's attitude to religion. *W. E. Molyneux, M.A. 1947 Manchester*

Algebra
The development of algebraic notation up to the middle of the seventeenth century. *W. Howells, M.Sc. 1930 London*

Aliens
See Nationality.

Alkali Industry
A historico-geographical survey of the alkali industry of Great Britain from 1789 to the present day. *H. Thomas, Ph.D. 1935 London, Birkbeck College*

Allegory
The attitude to allegory in poetry (1660-1715) as expressed in critical writings and as exemplified in selected allegorical poems. *P. K. Elkin, B.Litt. 1949 Oxford*

Bunyan's use of allegory in relation to the earlier English tradition. *E. B. Kenadjian, M.A. 1929 Manchester*

The methods and models of Bunyan's allegories. *R. I. Sharrock, B.Litt. 1947 Oxford*

A study of allegorical representation in *Piers Plowman*. *S. Brook, M.A. 1947 Manchester*

Allix, Pierre
Pierre Allix, life and writings. *A. H. V. de Montgomery, Ph.D. 1935 London, Birkbeck College*

Almsgiving
1. Varying treatment of the Pharisees in the Synoptic Gospels. 2. The theory of Christian almsgiving from the sub-Apostolic age to the Reformation. *C. T. Dimont, B.D. 1911 Oxford*

Alphabets
Agma: a contribution to Greek alphabetology. *L. J. D. Richardson, M.A. 1942 Wales*

The origin of the Semitic alphabet. *C. E. Goddard, Ph.D. 1927 Edinburgh*

Alps
Insolation and relief: their bearing on the human geography of Alpine regions. *A. Garnett, Ph.D. 1938 London, External Degree*

Alsace
A cultural comparison between Alsace and Lorraine, including an account of the regions round Strasbourg and Nancy. *W. H. Shepherd, M.A. 1944 Manchester*

The policies of Stanley, Granville, and Gladstone towards Luxemburg, Belgium, and Alsace-Lorraine, 1867-1871. *M. R. D. Foot, B.Litt. 1950 Oxford*

The progress of French in Alsace-Lorraine since the war. *C. M. Mole, M.A. 1925 Birmingham*

A study ot Alsace at the present time, with particular reference to its cultural history and conditions. *S. H. Paton, B.Litt. 1936 Oxford*

Altars
The Greek altar: its origins and its forms and functions down to 146 B.C. (the literary and archaeological evidence). *E. M. Hooker, M.A. 1947 London, University College and London, Birkbeck College*

1. The use of the word θυσιαστήριον and its Latin equivalent in primitive times. 2. The use of the word τράπεα and its Latin equivalent in primitive times. *G. J. Blore, B.D. 1874 Oxford*

Amandebele, The
The Amandebele tribes of southern Rhodesia: the problems of Western influence on native life and modifications of geographical and cultural values. *W. N. G. Davies, M.Sc. 1934 Wales*

Amapondo, The
Girls' initiation ceremony among the Amapondo. *J. E. S. Griffiths, Dip. Anthropology 1931 Cambridge*

Amazon, River
The Amazon Basin, with special reference to its economical development. *D. W. Shave, M.Sc. 1933 London, Birkbeck College*

Ambrose, Saint
A comparison of the styles of Gaudentius of Brescia, the *De Sacramentis* (ascribed to St. Ambrose) and the *Disdascalia Apostolorum* or *Fragmenta Veronensia*. *A. H. Birch, Ph.D. 1924 London*

1. The history of the doctrine of satisfaction from Tertullian to St. Ambrose. 2. The history of the doctrine of satisfaction from St. Augustine to St. Anselm. *G. A. Michell, B.D. & D.D. 1924 Oxford*

Studies in the vocabulary and syntax of the *Expositio Evangelii secundum Lucam* of Saint Ambrose. *A. J. B. Higgins, M.A. 1937 Wales*

Ambrose, William (Emrys)
Gweithiau llenyddol y Parch. William Ambrose, Porthmadog (Emrys) (Literary works of Rev. William Ambrose (Emrys) of Portmadoc). *M. M. Morgan, M.A. 1933 Wales*

America, Latin
See Latin America.

America, North
See North America.

America, United States of
See United States.

American Civil War
See United States: History.

American Literature
See also English Literature; and Emerson, R. W.; Hawthorne, N.; James, H.; King, H.; O'Neill, E. G.; Thoreau, H. D.; Twain, M.; Whitman, W.

English criticism of American literature during the period 1800 to 1850 as reflected in the periodicals. *J. J. Espey, B.Litt. 1938 Oxford*

American Revolution
See United States: History.

Amiel, Henri Frédéric
L'analyse d'un échec; étude sur le journal intime d'Henri-Frédéric Amiel. *E. M. Webb, M.A. 1942 Birmingham*

Amiel, Henri Frédéric contd.
The mysticism of Henri Frédéric Amiel. *H. Hunter, M.A. 1927 Leeds*

Amiens, Peace of
Dissertation on the Peace of Amiens and its rupture. *W. C. Gill, M.A. 1908 Leeds*

Amir Khusrau
The life and works of Amir Khusrau. *M. W. Mirza, Ph.D. 1930 London, School of Oriental and African Studies*

Amyln ac Amic
A comparison of the Welsh version of *Amyln ac Amic* with the French and Latin versions, with study of the grammatical forms and syntax of the Welsh version. *A. ap Gwynn, M.A. 1926 Wales*

Anabaptists
The Anabaptist movement. *R. J. Smithson, Ph.D. 1933 Glasgow*

Anaesthetics
The development of inhalation anaesthesia, with special reference to the years 1846-1900. *B. M. Duncum, D.Phil. 1945 Oxford*

Analogy
Existence and analogy. *E. L. Mascall, D.D. 1948 Oxford*

Metaphysical analogy. *J. Horgan, Ph.D. 1938 National University of Ireland*

Analysis, Mathematical
See Mathematics.

Analytic Propositions (Philosophy)
Analytic and synthetic propositions. *M. Hanlon, M.A. 1945 National University of Ireland*

Anan ben David, Book of
An inquiry into the sources of the Book of Anan, the founder of Karaism. *I. Brodie, B.Litt. 1921 Oxford*

Anatomy
See also Cuvier, G.

A critical survey of the advances made in surgery and anatomy in the *Corpus Hippocraticum* and the *De Medicina* of Celsus, with a short history of surgery and anatomy from the earliest times down to the beginning of the Christian era. *A. V. R. Don, Ch.M. 1922 Aberdeen*

Historical and other notes on the administration of the Anatomy Act. *A. MacPhail, M.D. 1923 Glasgow*

A study of anatomical eponymous nomenclature. *J. Dobson, M.Sc. 1944 Manchester*

Ancestor Cults
Ancestor worship among the southern Bantu. *D. W. T. Shropshire, B.Litt. 1927 Oxford*

Some social and religious aspects of ancestor worship in China. *D. C. Butler, Ph.D. 1929 Edinburgh*

Ancrene Riwle
The French element in the *Ancrene Riwle*. *G. C. O. Michel, M.A. 1950 Bristol*

The original language of the *Ancren Riwle*. *D. M. E. Dymes, M.A. 1922 London*

Ancrene Wisse
Grammar of the *Ancrene Wisse* (phonology and accidence). *M. B. Salu, B.Litt. 1949 Oxford*

Andhra Dynasty, The
Cultural history of the Satavahana Dynasty. *C. K. Gairola, Ph.D. 1949 London, School of Oriental and African Studies*

Andreas
Edition of the Old English poem *Andreas*. *K. R. Brooks, D.Phil. 1941 Oxford*

Andreas, Capellanus
Andreas Capellanus' *De amore*: a re-interpretation. *M. W. Dickinson, M.A. 1950 Birmingham*

Andrewes, Lancelot
The *Sermons* of Lancelot Andrewes in their relation to the growth of Anglican theology, and to the impact of doctrinal ideas upon literature in the Jacobean period. *E. J. Tinsley, B.D. 1944 Durham*

Aneirin, Book of
The Book of Aneirin. I. Williams, M.A. 1907 Wales

Angellier, Auguste
Contributions à l'étude de la poésie d'Auguste Angellier. *M. H. Galletley, M.A. 1928 Birmingham*

Angels
1. The abodes of the departed. 2. The holy angels. *F. T. Havergal, B.D. & D.D. 1888 Oxford*

Fallen angels in Jewish, Christian, and Mohammedan literature. *L. Jung, Ph.D. 1922 London*

1. The resurrection of Jesus Christ. 2. The ministry of angels as revealed in Holy Scripture. *C. C. Mills, B.D. & D.D. 1909 Oxford*

Angels contd.
1. The teaching of Holy Scripture with regard to the nature and ministry of angels. 2. The teaching of the Gospel according to St. John on the person and work of the Holy Spirit. *H. G. Lainée, B.D. 1906 Oxford*

Anglesey
The enclosure movement in Anglesey, 1788-1866. *E. J. Jones, M.A. 1924 Wales*

Anglican Church
See also Book of Common Prayer; Clapham Sect; Clergy; Episcopate; Eucharist; Methodism; and Butler, J.; Copleston, E., Bishop; Davies, R., Bishop; Gibson, E., Bishop; Juxon, W., Archbishop; Laud, W., Archbishop; Mary II, Queen; Nicholson, W., Bishop; Percy, T., Bishop; Robertson, F. W.; Rotherham, T., Archbishop; Sharp, J., Archbishop; Sherlock, T.; Smith, S.; Temple, W., Archbishop; Tenison, T., Archbishop; Tunstall, C., Bishop; Warham, W.; Watson, R., Bishop; Wesley, J.; Whitgift, J.

The Anglican Church and political parties, 1701-1737. *S. L. Chandler, M.A. 1930 Birmingham*

The Anglican tendencies in the Scottish Reformation and their bearing on the significance of the Concordat of Leith. *L. B. Taylor, B.Litt. 1932 Oxford*

The Anglican 'via media', with special reference to the ecclesiastical conditions in Lancashire during the years 1660-1689. *F. F. Rigby, M.A. 1943 Manchester*

Anglicanism: its progress until 1626. *G. E. Hart, M.A. 1922 Bristol*

Anglicanism during the Civil War and the Commonwealth. *R. Daunton-Fear, M.A. 1943 Bristol*

Archbishop Parker and the Anglican Settlement, 1558-1563. *E. M. Herne, M.A. 1928 Birmingham*

The attitude of the Church to the race problem in central South Africa during the nineteenth century, viewed in the light of New Testament principles. *S. K. Bunker, B.Litt. 1933 Oxford*

The Bishops and the poor law, 1782-1834. *W. A. Parker, M.A. 1939 Manchester*

Bossuet and the Church of England. *J. C. M. Crotty, B.Litt. 1938 Oxford*

Catholic doctine and practice in the English Church during the period 1570-1625. *R. C. Wylie, B.Litt. 1929 Oxford*

The causes of the present conflict of ideals in the Church of England. *R. D. Richardson, B.Litt. 1923 Oxford*

The Church of England and Puritanism during the primacy of Bancroft, 1604-1610. *S. B. Babbage, Ph.D. 1940 London, King's College*

The Church of England and society, 1830-1850. *C. Brackwell, M.A. 1949 Birmingham*

The Church of England and usury. *H. S. Swabey, B.D. 1949 Durham*

Church of England finances. *W. Bryn Thomas, Ph.D. 1942 London, School of Economics and Political Science*

The Church of England's contribution to popular education in England after 1833. *C. K. F. Brown, B.Litt. 1941 Oxford*

The Council of Trent and Anglican formularies. *H. E. Symonds, B.D. 1932 Oxford*

The early tractarians and the eastern Church. *P. E. O. Shaw, B.Litt. 1924 Oxford*

An enquiry into the state of public opinion from the establishment of King Henry VIII's supremacy over the Church to the close of the Lincolnshire rebellion. *W. E. Milward, M.A. 1907 Liverpool*

The evolution of the theory and doctrine of the Church of England, as exemplified by Ockham, Wyclif and Cranmer. *W. L. Moser, Ph.D. 1927 Edinburgh*

The financial basis of the established Church of England. *A. Hull, M.A. 1938 Leeds*

A history of the attempts towards reunion between the Anglican and the Eastern-Orthodox churches (especially since the sixteenth century). *W. W. Price, M.A. 1929 Birmingham*

1. Indirect proofs of the Resurrection. 2. The influence of dissent upon the Church of England. *A. E. S. Ward, B.D. & D.D. 1924 Oxford*

The influence of the Church of England and Dissent upon Methodism in the eighteenth century. *F. Hunter, M.A. 1959 Manchester*

Anglican Church contd.
1. The influence of the Continental Reformation upon the Thirty-nine Articles. *R. Milton Hay, B.D. 1924 Oxford*

The life and work of Nathaniel Woodard, with special reference to the influence of the Oxford movement on English education in the nineteenth century. *R. Perry, M.A. 1932 Bristol*

The literary influences of the Oxford Movement from 1833-1850. *T. Halliwell, M.A. 1944 Manchester*

Mary II of England and her life during the years 1689-1694: influence on politics, on the Anglican Church, and on society. *N. M. Waterson, B.Litt. 1925 Oxford*

Methodism and the Church of England in Cornwall, 1738-1838: a historical survey of Cornish Methodism, its rise, growth, and relation to the Church of England. *H. M. Brown, Ph.D. 1947 London, External Degree*

The Oxford Movement in a Manchester parish: the Miles Platting case. *H. E. Sheen, M.A. 1941 Manchester*

The parish in the seventeenth century in the North Riding. *E. Trotter, M.A. 1913 London*

The philosophical background of the Oxford Movement of the nineteenth century. *A. H. Selway, M.A. 1940 Manchester*

The relations between the Church of England and the state from 1838 to 1870. *H. K. Smith, M.A. 1946 Sheffield*

Revival of Anglicanism during the Restoration period, with special reference to the diocese of Durham. *C. H. Beaglehole, M.Litt. 1947 Durham*

Six great Anglicans. *G. W. Head, B.D. 1929 Cambridge*

Studies in the metaphysical poets of the Anglican Church in the seventeenth century. *A. J. M. Smith, Ph.D. 1931 Edinburgh*

A study of the accommodation movements between Presbytery and Episcopacy in the seventeenth century in Scotland, England and Ireland. *D. S. Hopkirk, Ph.D. 1946 Edinburgh*

A survey of attempts at religious comprehension in the Church of England in the seventeenth century, with special reference to the period from the Restoration to the Revolution. *J. W. H. Nankivell, B.Litt. 1943 Oxford*

Thomas Sherlock, Bishop of Bangor, Salisbury and London, 1728-61: his work for Church and State. *E. F. Carpenter, M.A. 1934 London, King's College*

The treatment of social and economic questions by Anglican divines during the reign of Charles II. *R. B. Schlatter, B.Litt. 1935 Oxford*

The two Oxford movements. *W. N. W. Harvey, D.D. 1947 Dublin, Trinity College*

The University of Oxford and the Church of England in the time of William Laud. *A. D. Hewlett, B.Litt. 1934 Oxford*

The various societies in the Church of England in the first half of the eighteenth century. *G. V. Portus, B.Litt. 1911 Oxford*

1. The visible Church of Christ is a congregation of faithful men, in which the pure word of God is preached, and the sacraments be duly ministered according to Christ's ordinance - Article XIX. 2. It is not lawful for the Church to ordain anything that is contrary to God's word - Article XX. *G. A. Perryn, B.D. & D.D. 1871 Oxford*

Anglo-Catholicism
See Anglican Church.

Anglo-Norman Language
The British Museum manuscript Arundel 230, with particular reference to the Psalms, and the *Livre des créatures.* *S. Bullett, M.A. 1910 London*

A comparative study of the language of the Anglo-Norman Bills of Eyre and similar documents of the Channel Isles, Gloucestershire, London and a northern area (Lancashire). *C. J. H. Topping, Ph.D. 1934 London, Birkbeck College*

Fulk-Fitz-Warin: text and a study of the language. *A. C. Wood, M.A. 1911 London*

The *Orthographia gallica*: Trinity College manuscript. *D. L. McKennan, M.A. 1935 Belfast*

The use of Anglo-Norman in private and public documents of the fourteenth and fifteenth centuries. *H. Richardson, B.Litt. 1939 Oxford*

Anglo-Norman Literature
See also Briane, G. de; Margaret, Queen of Scotland, Saint; Peckham, P. de; Pierre, d'Abernon; Trivet, N.

Anglo-Norman Literature contd.
Anglo-Norman books of courtesy and nurture. *H. R. Parsons, B.Litt. 1927 Oxford*

The Anglo-Norman *Chronicle* of Nicolas Trivet. *A. Rutherford, Ph.D. 1932 London, Birkbeck College*

Anglo-Norman didactic literature of the thirteenth century, and An Anglo-Norman life of St. Edward the Confessor. *P. Abson, Ph.D. 1921 Sheffield*

The Anglo-Norman element in Irish poetry from 1200 A.D. to 1600 A.D. *M. A. McConville, M.A. 1946 Belfast*

Anglo-Norman literature in Leinster, 1170-1570. *R. Walsh, Ph.D. 1941 National University of Ireland*

The Anglo-Norman manuscripts of the chanson de geste, *Aspremont.* *B. Proper, M.A. 1913 London*

An Anglo-Norman metrical Brut of the fourteenth century. *V. P. Underwood, Ph.D. 1937 London, University College*

The Anglo-Norman versions of the life of St. Margaret. *E. A. Francis, M.A. 1922 London*

Courtoisie in Anglo-Norman literature. *C. B. West, Ph.D. 1936 London, Birkbeck College*

An edition of the *Prose life of St. Margaret (Seinte Marherete)*, based on ms. Bodley 34 and ms. Reg. 17.A.XXVII, with a grammar and a glossary which will consider parallels in other texts of the same group. *R. A. Crook, B.Litt. 1929 Oxford*

Fulk-Fitz-Warin: text and a study of the language. *A. C. Wood, M.A. 1911 London*

Hawking literature in Anglo-Norman. *M. I. Dixon, M.Litt. 1929 Cambridge*

Jour de cendres and *Seinte confessioun*; an ed. of two Anglo-Norman poems from the ms. 312 in T.C.D. *J. W. Boyle, B.Litt. 1942 Dublin, Trinity College*

La Passiun de Seint Edmund (Gonville and Caius College ms. 435). *C. W. J. Higson, Ph.D. 1937 Cambridge*

The verbal forms in the *Mabinogion* and *Bruts.* *G. J. Williams, M.A. 1918 Wales*

The verbal forms of the *Mabinogion* and *Bruts.* *W. Griffith, M.A. 1904 Wales*

Anglo-Saxon Language
See English Language.

Anglo-Saxon Literature
See English Literature: Early and Medieval.

Animals
The animal story in German literature from the *Ecbasis Captivi* to Goethe's *Reineke Fuchs.* *L. R. Hopps, B.Litt. 1940 Oxford*

Animals in ancient Arabic poetry. *N. M. M. el-Nowaihi, Ph.D. 1942 London, School of Oriental and African Studies*

The development of the idea of the animal as a symbol of harmony in English literature. *M. Jager, Ph.D. 1932 Cambridge*

The growth of humanitarian feeling towards animals as shown in English poetry. *K. A. Fisher, M.A. 1929 Wales*

The history of tortious liability for animals. *G. L. Williams, Ph.D. 1936 Cambridge*

Leconte de Lisle: animalier. *A. S. Johnston, M.A. 1936 Belfast*

The principles of legal liability for trespass and injuries by animals. *W. N. Robson, LL.D. 1914 Leeds*

The role of incentives in animal learning. *G. C. Drew, M.A. 1948 Bristol*

Some studies in animal heat. *L. W. Chaundy, M.Sc. 1938 London, King's College*

Animism
Animism in the child's conception of the world: an experimental criticism and verification of Professor Piaget's enquiries into child animism. *R. M. Askar, M.A. 1932 Birmingham*

Animistic beliefs in Malaya. *E. M. A. A. J. Allard, D.Phil. 1941 Oxford*

Burmese animism or animism in Kengtung State, Burma. *J. H. Telford, Ph.D. 1933 Edinburgh*

Année Sociologique, L'
The sociology of religion, with special reference to the works of Professor Durkheim and other writers to *L'Année Sociologique.* *A. W. Bonsey, B.Litt. 1930 Oxford*

Anselm, Saint
Anselm and his circle: a study of the historical importance of his letters. *W. M. Mitchiner, M.A. 1945 London, Bedford College*

Anselm, Saint contd.
1. A critical study of St. Anselm's treatise *Cur deus homo?* 2. The internal evidence for the authenticity of the Gospel according to St. John. *W. R. W. Stephens, B.D. 1895 Oxford*

1. The history of the doctrine of satisfaction from Tertullian to St. Ambrose. 2. The history of the doctrine of satisfaction from St. Augustine to St. Anselm. *G. A. Michell, B.D. & D.D. 1924 Oxford*

The relation of thought to existence in Anselm's statement of the ontological argument. *A. E. Davies, M.A. 1918 London*

The theories of the atonement of Anselm and Grotius. *R. S. Franks, B.Litt. 1899 Oxford*

Anthologies
The character and use of anthologies among the Greek literary papyri, together with an edition of some unpublished papyri. *J. W. B. Barns, D.Phil. 1946 Oxford*

Anthropology
See also Aborigines; African Peoples; Celts; Indians of North America; Maori; and Ancestor Cults; Animism; Anthropometry; Burials; Death; Family; Initiation; Magic; Man; Marriage; Primitivism; Religion: Ancient and Primitive; Sacrifice; Sexual Relationships; Totemism.

The clash of race and the clash of culture. *G. L. F. Pitt-Rivers, B.Sc. 1926 Oxford*

Culture and neurosis. *R. O. R. Piddington, Ph.D. 1935 London, School of Economics and Political Science*

An enquiry into the relation between sexual opportunity and cultural condition among uncivilised peoples. *J. D. Unwin, Ph.D. 1931 Cambridge*

Monseigneur Alexandre le Roy. *W. P. O'Brien, M.A. 1949 National University of Ireland*

Primitive economics with special reference to culture contact. *M. H. Read, Ph.D. 1934 London, School of Economics and Political Science*

Psychological factors governing the education and culture of primitive peoples. *A. O'Ruairc, M.A. 1943 National University of Ireland*

The relation of repression to cultural development. *G. Whitehead, Ph.D. 1939 Edinburgh*

The relationship between food-production and social structure in simple societies. *K. E. Read, Ph.D. 1948 London, School of Economics and Political Science*

Some ancient asseverations and affirmations in the light of cultural anthropology. *W. Kirzner, M.Sc. 1934 London, School of Economics and Political Science*

State and culture, with special reference to Fichte and von Humboldt. *P. Beukes, B.Litt. 1936 Oxford*

The tools of Neanderthal man. *C. B. M. McBurney, Ph.D. 1948 Cambridge*

Anthropology: Africa
The adaptation of native custom and belief to modern conditions of civilization in South Africa. *G. R. Norton, M.A. 1939 Leeds*

Europeans and the Bantu family. *B. A. Hutchinson, Ph.D. 1945 London, External Degree*

The influence of physical conditions upon human life in the Sebou Basin. *W. Fogg, M.A. 1928 Manchester*

Observations on the extraneous influences and culture-contacts in the Tanganyika Territory in their bearing on problems of native education. *R. J. Harvey, B.Sc. 1937 Oxford*

Rank among the Swazi of the protectorate. *H. Beemer, Ph.D. 1943 London, School of Economics and Political Science*

Religion and medicine among the Ga people of the Gold Coast. *M. J. Field, Ph.D. 1936 London, University College*

The sociological importance of food with special reference to Bantu society. *A. I. Richards, Ph.D. 1930 London, School of Economics and Political Science*

The Transkeian territories: a study in acculturation. *D. D. Davies, M.A. 1948 Wales*

Anthropology: America
The social structure of Jamaica, with special reference to racial distinctions. *L. F. Henriques, D.Phil. 1948 Oxford*

Totemism among the ancient Peruvians. *J. A. Encinas, M.Sc. 1928 Cambridge*

Anthropology: Asia
A changing austric culture. *D. N. Majumbar, Ph.D. 1935 Cambridge*

Anthropology: Asia contd.
Cultural change, with special reference to the hill tribes of Burma and Assam. *E. R. Leach, Ph.D. 1947 London, School of Economics and Political Science*

Culture change in south-western India. *A. Aiyappan, Ph.D. 1937 London, School of Economics and Political Science*

Culture-contact among the Plains Gars of eastern Bengal. *J. Basu, Ph.D. 1947 London, University College*

Human sacrifice and head-hunting in Assam. *B. Gohain, M.A. 1937 London, University College*

Notes on the Reindeer Tungus of Manchuria. *E. J. Lindgren, Ph.D. 1936 Cambridge*

Observances, beliefs and customs in Sinhalese villages. *A. P. De Zoysa, Ph.D. 1928 London*

Religious cults and social structure of the Shan States of the Yunnen-Burma frontier. *J. K. Tien, Ph.D. 1948 London, School of Economics and Political Science*

Social anthropology of the Lapchas. *C. A. Stocks, B.Sc. 1927 Oxford*

Social life in Nepal. *C. J. Morris, M.Sc. 1935 Cambridge*

A study of cultural change with special reference to Turkey. *M. Turhan, Ph.D. 1949 Cambridge*

Anthropology: Great Britain
The anthropology of some coloured communities in Great Britain with comparative material on colour prejudice. *K. L. Little, Ph.D. 1945 London, School of Economics and Political Science*

The cultural contacts existing between the Bristol Channel coastlands in prehistoric times. *R. M. Prothero, M.A. 1947 Wales*

The early inhabitants of the Oxford neighbourhood, with special reference to Cassington. *C. Musgrave, B.Sc. 1939 Oxford*

Prehistoric man in the Medway Valley. *H. J. Eason, B.Sc. 1928 Oxford*

Anthropology: Oceania
An analysis of cultural change in Fiji. *W. R. Geddes, Ph.D. 1948 London, School of Economics and Political Science*

The maintenance of order in Oceania. *H. I. P. Hogbin, M.Sc. 1931 London, School of Economics and Political Science*

Modern Fiji: changes in native custom. *G. K. Roth, M.Sc. 1937 Cambridge*

The social anthropology of a western Papuan tribe (Morehead River). *F. E. Williams, B.Sc. 1934 Oxford*

Anthropology: Slavic Countries
Family organization among Slavs (as reflected in the custom of *couvade*). *J. Obrebski, Ph.D. 1934 London, School of Economics and Political Science*

Anthropometry
An anthropometric study of Welsh and English populations. *F. H. Cleaver, M.A. 1936 Wales*

An anthropometric survey of the male adolescents of the Sheffield district. *F. L. Ralphs, Ph.D. 1934 Sheffield*

Circular mentality and the pyknic body type. *M. Sahair, Ph.D. 1930 London, University College*

Estimation of stature from long bones in U. P. Indians. *B. S. Nat, M.D. 1930 Saint Andrew's*

1. A first study of the Tibetan skull. 2. A study of the Nepalese skull. *G. M. Morant, M.Sc. 1922 London*

An inquiry into the changes in the human cranium from palaeolithic times onwards, with special reference to the British Isles. *E. F. C. Tucker, B.Sc. 1927 Oxford*

Notes on artificial cranial deformation: a contribution to the study of ethnic mutilations. *E. J. Dingwall, Ph.D. 1929 London*

On the extreme individuals and the range of samples taken from a normal population. *L. H. C. Tippett, M.Sc. 1926 London*

The physical anthropology of the Gower Peninsula, studied in correlation with its settlements, archaeology, folklore and placenames. *C. H. Davies, M.A. 1927 Wales*

The physical characteristics and racial affinities of the inhabitants of the Sudan, past and present, with special reference to the human remains from Jebel Moya. *R. Mukherjea, Ph.D. 1949 Cambridge*

Anthropometry contd.
The racial history of Egypt and Nubia from predynastic to present times. *A. M. El Batrawi, Ph.D. 1940 London, University College*

A re-survey of the morphology of the nose of the different races of mankind in relation to environment. *A. Davies, M.Sc. 1931 Wales*

Southwest Wales: a study of physical anthropological characters in correlation with various distributions. *E. G. Bowen, M.A. 1926 Wales*

Studies on the primates: (1) brains of Eocene primates interpreted from endocranial casts; (2) a new interpretation of Wadjak Man; (3) a restoration of the skull and brain of the Jurassic mammal, Triconodon. *G. D. Pinkley, Ph.D. 1935 London, University College*

A study of Egyptian craniology from prehistoric to Roman times. *G. M. Morant, D.Sc. 1926 London*

A study of the English skull in medieval times, with special reference to crania in the Department of Human Anatomy, Oxford, and at Rothwell Parish Church, near Kettering, Northamptonshire. *J. Trevor, B.Sc. 1934 Oxford*

A third study of the English skull, with special reference to the Faringdon Street crania (with a subsidiary paper). *B. G. E. Hooke, M.Sc. 1927 London*

To inquire into the physical characters of the ancient inhabitants of Kish, and to compare them with those of the modern inhabitants. *D. Talbot Rice, B.Sc. 1927 Oxford*

Welsh blood groups: a contribution to the anthropology of the Welsh people. *I. M. Watkins, M.Sc. 1946 Wales*

Anthropomorphism
See God.

Antichrist
1. The Antichrist. 2. The prophet of the New Testament. *A. H. Browne, B.D. & D.D. 1905 Oxford*

Le tornoiement antecrist by Huon de Méry. *F. Davis, Ph.D. 1935 London, External Degree*

1. On Antichrist. 2. On infant baptism. *W. K. W. Chafy-Chafy, B.D. & D.D. 1891 Oxford*

Anti-Jacobin, The
The Rolliad and *The Anti-Jacobin* as literary satire. *W. H. Bryant, M.A. 1934 Wales*

Antilles
The first settlement of the maritime nations in the Spanish Antilles. *P. W. Day, M.A. 1916 London*

Antinomianism
Antinomianism in the period of English history, 1640-1660. *G. Huehns, Ph.D. 1947 London, School of Economics and Political Science*

Hanes Antinomiaeth yng Nghymru, 1650 hyd 1850 (The history of Antinomianism in Wales, 1650-1850). *R. G. Williams, M.A. 1934 Wales*

Antioch
Saladin's campaign of 1188 in northern Syria, with particular reference to the northern defences of the principality of Antioch. *J. W. Hackett, B.Litt. 1937 Oxford*

Antiquarians
See also Aubrey, J.; Bale, J.; Carew, R.; Charlett, A.; Fuller, T.; Humphreys, H., Bishop; Stukeley, W.

The literary works of Bishop Percy, with special reference to the antiquarian studies of the eighteenth century. *E. K. A. Mackenzie, Ph.D. 1943 London, Westfield College*

Anti-Semitism
See Race Relations; Jews.

Antonius, Marcus
The theme of Antony and Cleopatra in English drama. *A. May, B.Litt. 1937 Oxford*

Antwerp
A geographical study of the port of Antwerp. *J. P. Bennett, M.A. 1933 Liverpool*

Ap Rhys, Gweirydd
Gweirydd ap Rhys: ei fywyd a'i waith (Gweirydd ap Rhys: his life and his work). *E. P. Roberts, M.A. 1941 Wales*

Aphasia
A case of visual aphasia. *C. G. Davies, M.A. 1941 London, King's College*

Aphorisms
The problem of the aphorism in the writing of G. C. Lichtenberg. *J. P. Stern, Ph.D. 1950 Cambridge*

Aphraates
1. The bearing of the Rabbinical criminal code on the Jewish trial narratives of the Gospel, with a translation of the *Mishnah* and *Tosefta* of the Tractate Sanhedrin. 2. An introduction to the homilies of Aphraates. *H. Danby, B.D. 1919 Oxford*

Apocalyptic Literature
See also Revelation; and Bible: New Testament: Revelation.

Archetypes and apocalypse: a study of apocalyptic literature from the standpoint of Jungian psychology. *A. G. S. Spinks, Ph.D. 1946 London, King's College*

The influence of apocalyptic on the mind of Jesus. *W. Y. Whitehead, Ph.D. 1929 Glasgow*

The Messianic hope in the apocalyptic literature of Judaism, 200 B.C.-100 A.D. *E. Nevitt, M.A. 1930 Liverpool*

The new Hebrew Book of Enoch. *H. Olson, Ph.D. 1924 London*

The psychology of the Apocalyptists, 200 B.C.-A.D. 100. *D. S. Russell, B.Litt. 1945 Oxford*

Apocrypha
See Bible.

Apollinaire, Guillaume
The philosophy of Guillaume Apollinaire as revealed in his poetry. *P. F. Wells, M.A. 1948 Wales*

Apollinarianism
Apollinarianism. *C. E. Raven, D.D. 1923 Cambridge*

Apollinaris, Sidonius
See Sidonius Apollinaris.

Apollo
The Roman Apollo and kindred deities. *J. M. Frayn, Ph.D. 1945 Edinburgh*

Apollonius, of Perga
A discussion of the relative share of Apollonius, Hipparchus, and Ptolemy in the evolution of the theory of eccentrics and epicycles. *J. H. Wills, M.Sc. 1931 London*

Apollonius Rhodius
The influence of Apollonius Rhodius on Vergil, with special reference to the romance of *Aeneid* IV. *C. M. Worsley, M.A. 1925 Manchester*

Apologetics
See also Christianity; Theology; Origen.

Christian apologetics. *A. Richardson, D.D. 1948 Oxford*

Christianity on the offensive: a study in the task and method of Christian apologetics, with special reference to the work of Blaise Pascal and Søren Kierkegaard. *D. G. M. Patrick, Ph.D. 1943 Edinburgh*

Lucerna Fidelium le Froinsias O'Maolmhuaidh (*Lucerna Fidelium* by Froinsias O'Maolmhuaidh). *P. O'Sullivan, M.A. 1944 National University of Ireland*

Philosophy of the early Christian apologists. *D. N. Hehir, M.A. 1931 National University of Ireland*

The place of miracle in Christian apologetics in Great Britain from 1688 to the present day. *J. S. Lawton, D.Phil. 1950 Oxford*

1. Use of the Old Testament in the primitive Christian apologetic. 2. Examination of the speeches in the Acts of the Apostles with reference to this apologetic. *W. M. Pryke, B.D. 1916 Oxford*

Apostolic Succession
See Episcopate.

Appearance (Philosophy)
Bradley's treatment of 'appearance'. *M. J. A. McAra, M.A. 1926 London*

Apprenticeship
Apprenticeship at home and abroad. *P. V. Twomey, M.Comm. 1950 National University of Ireland*

Education and the apprentice. *H. A. Costigan, M.A. 1938 Liverpool*

The enforcement of a seven years' apprenticeship under the statute of artificers. *T. K. Derry, D.Phil. 1931 Oxford*

English apprenticeship and child labour: a history. *J. Dunlop, D.Sc. 1912 London*

The industrial training and education of apprentices. *R. C. Moore, M.A. 1921 Manchester*

Aptitude Testing
See also Intelligence Testing.

The construction and item analysis of aptitude tests. *E. Anstey, Ph.D. 1949 London, University College*

Aptitude Testing contd.
An endeavour to compile a test to ascertain whether a subject possesses particular capacity for science. *J. E. Hawthorne, M.Ed. 1924 Leeds*

A factorial analysis of athletic ability preparatory to the formation of a series of prognostic tests. *G. Highmore, Ph.D. 1949 London, Institute of Education*

Mechanical aptitude, its existence, nature and measurement. *J. W. Cox, D.Sc. 1928 London*

Some aspects of the measurement and maturation of mechanical aptitude in boys aged 12 to 14. *H. S. Williams, Ph.D. 1948 London, Institute of Education*

Some aspects of the measurement of technical aptitude in boys aged 12 years, with special reference to Alexander's performance scale. *B. Leff, M.A. 1949 London, Institute of Education*

Standardization of intelligence and aptitude tests in their mother tongue for secondary school children. *C. T. Philip, M.A. 1944 London, Institute of Education*

Tests of mechanical aptitude. *C. W. Shuttleworth, M.A. 1941 London, Institute of Education*

Apuleius, Lucius
An introduction and commentary to Apuleius: *Metamorphosis* XI. *J. P. J. van Rensburg, M.A. 1938 London, University College*

The religion of Apuleius. *D. J. Hill, M.A. 1940 Leeds*

Aquinas, Thomas, Saint
See Thomas Aquinas.

Arabah, El
El Arabah: explorations and excavations at Abydos, 1899-1900, including observations on modes of burial from the end of the old kingdom to the nineteenth dynasty; on the morphology of ceramic and other types; and on the dates of Egyptian employment of materials. *J. Garstang, B.Litt. 1902 Oxford*

Arabia
The Arabian East and the Far East: their commercial and cultural relations during the Graeco-Roman and the Perso-Arabian periods. *S. A. S. Hozayyen, M.A. 1933 Liverpool*

A geographical study of Saudi Arabia. *A. McK. Frodd, M.A. 1937 Liverpool*

The geography and ethnography of unknown South Arabia. *B. S. Thomas, Ph.D. 1935 Cambridge*

The influence of physical environment upon Arabian life and institutions. *S. Inayatullah, Ph.D. 1932 London, School of Oriental and African Studies*

Turkish and Egyptian rule in Arabia, 1810-1841. *A. H. M. El-Batrik, Ph.D. 1947 London, School of Oriental and African Studies*

Arabic Language
The Aden dialect of Arabic: a study of its grammatical peculiarities as compared with the classical language. *W. I. Jones, M.A. 1940 Wales*

The foreign vocabulary of the *Qurân*. *A. Jeffery, Ph.D. 1929 Edinburgh*

The grammatical characteristics of the spoken Arabic of Egypt. *I. Anis, Ph.D. 1941 London, School of Oriental and African Studies*

A list of Arabic words in the English vocabulary. *W. Taylor, M.A. 1932 Leeds*

The phonetics of the dialect of Il Karnak (upper Egypt). *T. H. O. M. Dawod, M.A. 1949 London, School of Oriental and African Studies*

1. The Rabbinic literature as an aid to the lexicography of the Hebrew bible. 2. Arabisms in Rabbinic literature. *A. Cohen, Ph.D. 1923 London*

Studies in early Arabic dialects. *C. Rabin, Ph.D. 1939 London, School of Oriental and African Studies*

The verbal piece in Egyptian Arabic: a morphological study. *A. R. M. A. Ayoub, M.A. 1949 London, School of Oriental and African Studies*

Arabic Literature
See also Abu Tammam, Habib Ibn Aus; 'Aun, Ibn Abi; Hamadhāni, Badi' al-Zamān; Hamdani, Abu Firas; Ibn Habib, Muhammad; Ibn Hāni, al-Andalusí, Muhammad; Ibn Ja'far, 'Abd Allāh b. Yahyā; Ibn Sana al-Mulk; Jahiz, Abu Uthman; Juvaini, 'Ala'al-Din 'Ata Malik b. Muhammad; Kitab al-Ikhtiyārain; Mas'uedí, Abul Hassan 'Ahi; Qartājanni, Haezím b. Muhammad; Qutayba, Ibn Muslim; Tabir al-Ruya.

Contribution of India to Arabic literature. *M. G. I. Ahmad, Ph.D. 1929 London*

Arabic Literature contd.
Ibn as-Sikkit's *Islăh al-Mantiq* according to the recensions of Al-Qālī and At-Tibrīzī. *S. A. Ahmedali, D.Phil. 1936 Oxford*

Ishmael and Hagar in the post-Biblical and Islamic literature. *H. Medalie, M.A. 1941 Manchester*

The life and social conditions of women in the primitive Islamic community as depicted in the eighth volume of Ibn Sa'd's *Tabaqat al Kubra* and the sixth volume of Ibn Hanbal's *Musnad*. *G. H. Stern, Ph.D. 1937 London, School of Oriental and African Studies*

Persian influence on Arabic court literature in the first three centuries of the Hijra. *M. H. El-Zayat, D.Phil. 1947 Oxford*

Prolegomena for a study of Arabic influences on the literature and thought of the English middle ages. *D. Metlitzky, M.A. 1938 London, University College*

Shiism and its influence on Arabic literature. *S. A. D. A. A. Khulousy, Ph.D. 1947 London, External Degree*

Some English translations of Arabic imaginative literature (1704-1838): a study of their portrayal of the Arab world, with an estimate of their influence on nineteenth century English literature. *M. A. Manzalaoui, B.Litt. 1947 Oxford*

Western influences in the Arabic literature of Egypt and Syria between 1820 and 1879. *A. N. M. A. Hasan, Ph.D. 1931 London, School of Oriental and African Studies*

Arabs and Arab Countries
See also Arabia; Egypt; Iraq; and other Arab States.

The Arabic conquest of Transoxania. *H. A. R. Gibb, M.A. 1922 London*

Causes of poverty among the rural populations of the Arab states. *P. Selwyn, B.Litt. 1947 Oxford*

Eastern influences in Chaucer with special reference to the Arabs. *E. J. S. Saigh, Ph.D. 1946 London, King's College*

Some English translations of Arabic imaginative literature (1704-1838): a study of their portrayal of the Arab world, with an estimate of their influence on nineteenth century English literature. *M. A. Manzalaoui, B.Litt. 1947 Oxford*

Aragon, Louis
Louis Aragon, a survey of his work from 1919 to 1936. *G. B. Barrett, M.A. 1936 Birmingham*

Aramaeans
The history of the Aramaeans down to the fall of Nineveh, 612 B.C. *F. Tomkinson, M.A. 1932 Wales*

Aramaic Language
See also Samaritan Language.

An Aramaic approach to the Gospels and Acts. *M. Black, D.Litt. 1944 Glasgow*

A comparison of the grammar and vocabulary of the Aramaic portions of the Old Testament with those of the Aramaic papyri and inscriptions. *H. H. Rowley, B.Litt. 1928 Oxford*

1. The language in which our Lord taught. 2. Supposed quotations from the Apostolic liturgy in the New Testament. *G. H. Gwilliam, B.D. 1890 Oxford*

1. The language used by Christ. 2. The organization of the early Christian Churches. *C. R. Perry, B.D. 1892 Oxford*

Arbitration
Anglo-American arbitration policies, 1890-1914. *O. Gollancz, Ph.D. 1940 Cambridge*

The principle of arbitration in English law treated historically. *C. E. Golding, LL.D. 1927 London*

Private law analogies in international law, with special reference to international arbitration. *H. Lauterpacht, LL.D. 1925 London*

A study of the practice and procedure of arbitration and conciliation as a voluntary principle in some British industries, with an account of state action in the field. *I. G. Sharp, Ph.D. 1940 London, School of Economics and Political Science*

Arbuckle, James
The philosophy of Francis Hutcheson and of James Arbuckle, showing the position of both in the Molesworth-Shaftesbury School and the relation of the former to the Enlightenment in Scotland. *W. R. Scott, D.Phil. 1900 Saint Andrew's*

Arcadia
The Arcadian League, 371-338 B.C. *E. A. Thompson, B.Litt. 1937 Dublin, Trinity College*

Arcanism
See Mysticism.

Archaeology and Antiquities
See also Layard, A. H., Sir; and Altars; Axes; Bronzework; Burials; Ceramics; Fountains; Jewellery; Place Names; Sculpture; Settlements; Tombs; Tools (Archaeology); Weapons.

Etude lexicographique sur le vocabulaire des textes réunis sous la lettre 'G' du *Glossaire archéologique* vol. 1, de Victor Gay. *T. Schofield, M.A. 1933 Leeds*

The prehistoric age as a subject for school study, incorporating a proposed school text-book on pre-history for children of the ages of 11 and 12. *H. E. Priestley, M.Ed. 1928 Leeds*

1. The teaching of pre-history in schools. 2. The archaeology of Somerset. *D. P. Dobson, Litt.D. 1932 Dublin, Trinity College*

The theories of an ice age. *M. Davidson, M.Sc. 1914 Belfast*

Archaeology and Antiquities: Africa
The geology, climates and cultures of the Pleistocene period in Matabeleland, southern Rhodesia. *G. Bond, Ph.D. 1949 London, External Degree*

The Stone Age archeology of Kenya Colony. *L. S. B. Leakey, Ph.D. 1931 Cambridge*

Archaeology and Antiquities: America
Archaeology of the Santa Elena Peninsula in south-west Ecuador. *G. H. S. Bushnell, Ph.D. 1947 Cambridge*

Archaeology and Antiquities: Asia
The archaeology of Gujarat (A.D. 400-1300). *H. D. Sankalia, Ph.D. 1937 London, University College*

Domestic furniture and utensils of the Han period. *J. M. F. Penny, M.A. 1941 London, Courtauld Institute of Art*

Historical conditions in patriarchal Palestine in the light of recent archaeological research. *J. Gray, Ph.D. 1949 Edinburgh*

The Mesolithic age in the Middle East. *J. Waechter, Ph.D. 1949 Cambridge*

Palestine in the seventh and sixth centuries B.C. in the light of archaeology. *E. Kendra, M.A. 1948 Leeds*

The temples of Syria of the Roman period: their dates and developments, according to the evidence of structure, decoration and inscriptions. *C. H. Heithaus, Ph.D. 1940 London, University College*

Archaeology and Antiquities: Channel Islands
The megalithic remains of the Channel Islands. *T. D. Kendrick, B.Sc. 1924 Oxford*

Archaeology and Antiquities: Egypt
See also Shabtis.

1. The Old Testament in the light of the Egyptian monuments. 2. Natural science as it affects scriptural truth. *A. E. B. Day, B.D. 1908 Oxford*

The origin of scientific excavation in Egypt and its development during the nineteenth century. *M. D. F. Cheever, M.A. 1938 London, University College*

The place of Egypt in the prehistory of the Old World, with special reference to quarternary, diluvial, climates and cultures in the Saharo-Arabian area. *S. A. Huzzayin, Ph.D. 1935 Manchester*

Archaeology and Antiquities: Europe
Indo-European influences in Hellenic civilization down to the end of the Bronze Age. *V. G. Childe, B.Litt. 1916 Oxford*

A study of the origins and distributions of some late Bronze Age industries in Western Europe. *E. E. Evans, M.A. 1931 Wales*

Archaeology and Antiquities: France
The prehistoric geography of Brittany: a study of the megalithic civilization. *D. Forde, Ph.D. 1928 London*

Archaeology and Antiquities: Great Britain
See also Roman Britain.

The archaeology of east central Wales. *H. N. Jerman, M.A. 1934 Wales*

Archaeology of the Cambridge region. *C. Fox, Ph.D. 1922 Cambridge*

The bronze and iron ages in Devon and Cornwall. *H. O'N. Hencken, M.A. 1930 Cambridge*

The distribution of early bronze age types in Scotland. *M. E. C. Mitchell, Ph.D. 1933 Edinburgh*

Archaeology and Antiquities: Great Britain contd.
The Dyfi: its people, antiquities, dialects, folklore and placenames studied in correlation to one another, with a special aim of ascertaining what degree of correlation there may be between physical anthropology, archaeology and dialect distribution. *I. C. Peate, M.A. 1924 Wales*

The excavation of the Old Parish Church of Perranzabaloe. *T. F. G. Dexter, Ph.D. 1922 Saint Andrew's*

Excavations at Bronze Age burial mounds on Stanton Moor. *J. P. Heathcote, M.A. 1930 Sheffield*

From what directions and at what times Britain was invaded by bearers of early Iron Age culture. *H. N. Savory, D.Phil. 1938 Oxford*

Hilltop camps, with special reference to those of north Cardiganshire. *R. U. Sayce, M.A. 1920 Wales*

Ideas of life and religion in pre-historic Scotland, with special reference to Mediterranean influences. *W. Edgar, Ph.D. 1934 Glasgow*

A large scale survey of groups of pre-historic earth-works in central Wales and along the Welsh Border. *I. T. Hughes, M.A. 1927 Wales*

The megalithic monuments of the coastlands of the Irish Sea and North Channel. *M. Davies, Ph.D. 1942 Manchester*

The occupation of the counties Northumberland, Durham, Cumberland, and Westmorland from the fourth to the eighth centuries, as revealed by the archaeological and historical evidence. *G. S. Keeney, B. Litt. 1935 Oxford*

The prehistoric woodlands and marshlands of England. *H. A. Wilcox, M.A. 1927 Liverpool*

1. The teaching of pre-history in schools. 2. The archaeology of Somerset. *D. P. Dobson, Litt.D. 1932 Dublin, Trinity College*

The upper palaeolithic age in the British Isles. *D. A. E. Garrod, B.Sc. 1925 Oxford*

Archaeology and Antiquities: Greece, Ancient
See Abydos; Arabah, El; Athens; Olympia; Parthenon; Sparta.

Archaeology and Antiquities: Iceland
See Landnámabók.

Archaeology and Antiquities: Ireland
The ancient stone monuments of the eastern entries into Ireland from the sea, and their British connections. *J. Garrett, M.A. 1939 Manchester*

Antiquities of E. Muskerry. *P. Hartnett, M.A. 1939 National University of Ireland*

Contributions to prehistoric archaeology, with special reference to Northern Ireland. *E. E. Evans, D.Sc. 1939 Wales*

Monumenta vetera corcagiensia, being a survey of all antiquarian remains within and around the city of Cork. *M. A. O'Leary, M.A. 1931 National University of Ireland*

Place names and antiquities of the Barony of Duhallow. *M. J. Bowman, M.A. 1934 National University of Ireland*

The place-names and antiquities of Kinalmeaky Barony, Co. Cork. *J. P. Reardon, M.A. 1930 National University of Ireland*

Prehistoric discoveries in Co. Dublin. *E. Prendergast, M.A. 1947 National University of Ireland*

Pre-historic man in Ireland. *C. P. Martin, Sc.D. 1935 Dublin, Trinity College*

Rude stone monuments of the northern portion of Co. Cork. *J. P. Conlon, M.A. 1913 National University of Ireland*

Shore dwellers of ancient Ireland. *J. M. Holland, M.A. 1912 National University of Ireland*

Some aspects of the Irish date bronze age, based on a study of the hoards of the period. *E. MacWhite, M.A. 1944 National University of Ireland*

A survey of the antiquities in the Barony of Small County, Co. Limerick. *M. J. O'Kelly, M.A. 1941 National University of Ireland*

Tráchtas ar an seana-shaoghal (An account of life long ago). *E. Ua Loinghsigh, M.A. 1936 National University of Ireland*

Archaeology and Antiquities: Malta
Excavations in Malta. *M. A. Murray, D.Litt. 1932 London, University College*

Archaeology and Antiquities: Pakistan
See Harappa.

Architecture
See also Auditoria; Houses; Staircases; Synagogues; Temples; Walls; and Chambers, W., Sir; Churriguera. J. de; Gibbs, J.; Herrera, J. de; Jones, I.; Vignola, G. B. da; Wilkins, W.; Wyatt, J.

The architectural design of streets. *R. B. Thomson, M.A. 1947 Sheffield*

Architecture and the Mediterranean climate. *M. S. Makiya, Ph.D. 1946 Cambridge*

The conservation and repair of medieval ecclesiastical buildings, with particular reference to certain selected examples. *J. R. Teggin, M.A. 1938 Manchester*

The place of architecture in a liberal education. *N. W. Goodacre, M.A. 1933 Liverpool*

The use of plastics in modern building. *P. H. Liversidge, M.A. 1950 Sheffield*

Architecture: Ancient
An account of pedimental composition from the earliest monuments to the Parthenon. *B. Tilly, M.A. 1932 London, Bedford College*

The constructional methods of ancient Hellenic architecture. *M. L. Bryer, B.litt. 1940 Oxford*

A history of Byzantine architecture with special reference to problems of origin and evolution of plan. *J. A. Hamilton, Ph.D. 1925 Edinburgh*

On the derivation and meaning of some ancient building terms. *B. O. S. Snell, M.A. 1924 London*

Private architecture in Fayyum villages of the Roman period. *S. Yeivin, M.A. 1928 London*

The problem of Greek and Egyptian influences in Ptolemaic architecture and sculpture. *I. Noshy, Ph.D. 1934 London, University College*

Ptolemaic temple architecture in Egypt: an analysis of the Greek and Egyptian elements. *T. A. Gorski, M.A. 1948 London, University College*

The relationship between classic sculpture and architecture. *G. H. Gatley, M.A. 1925 Manchester*

The theory of Roman and Renaissance vault construction, with special reference to the Pantheon, Rome, and Santa Maria della Salute, Venice. *A. G. S. Fidler, M.A. 1936 Liverpool*

Architecture: Great Britain
A catalogue of the drawings of James Gibbs in the Ashmolean Museum and their connexion with his life and work. *W. W. Crandall, B.Litt. 1933 Oxford*

Contributions to the development of English medieval architecture based largely on a first-hand study of various monuments in Oxford. *G. P. Brookfield, B.Litt. 1925 Oxford*

The development of the British railway station. *A. Arschavir, M.A. 1948 Manchester*

The distribution of traditional types of buildings on the Welsh borderland. *W. C. Chapman, M.A. 1936 Manchester*

East Anglican church architecture of the fourteenth anf fifteenth centuries, with special reference to the churches of the Stour Valley. *C. J. Ough, M.A. 1939 London, King's College*

An enquiry concerning the architectural theory and practice of Sir William Chambers, R.A. *H. M. Martienssen, Ph.D. 1949 London, Courtauld Institute of Art*

An examination of the architectural aspects of railway development in Great Britain. *B. B. Lewis, M.A. 1944 Liverpool*

An investigation into the structural and decorative characteristics of traditional domestic architecture in selected areas within the counties of Lancashire, Cheshire and Derbyshire. *W. A. Singleton, Ph.D. 1949 Manchester*

Norman domestic architecture in England. *M. E. Wood, M.A. 1934 London, University College*

The rise of neo-classic architecture in England. *L. Lawrence, M.A. 1937 London, Courtauld Institute of Art*

St. Stephen's Chapel and the architecture of the fourteenth century in London. *J. M. Hastings, Ph.D. 1947 Cambridge*

Scoto-Celtic architecture: its place among the styles. *C. Sinclair, Ph.D. 1932 Glasgow*

Architecture: Great Britain: Mackintosh, Charles Rennie
Charles Rennie Mackintosh and the secessionist movement in architecture. *A. T. Howarth, Ph.D. 1949 Glasgow*

Ark of the Covenant
1. The place of the ark in the religious thought of the early Israelites. 2. The revelation of Yahweh in tradition and history. *M. W. Myres, B.D. & D.D. 1924 Oxford*

Armagh
The fens of north Armagh. *J. M. White, Ph.D. 1932 Belfast*

Armed Forces
See also History, Military; History, Naval; and under individual countries.

Army psychiatry in and out of battle: its relationship to the soldier and to the service. *D. T. Maclay, M.D. 1947 Glasgow*

The development of military training in schools in the British Isles. *L. E. M. Savill, M.A. 1937 London, King's College*

The effect of environment on the health and efficiency of men in warships. *F. P. Ellis, M.D. 1947 Manchester*

An examination, combining the techniques of anthropology and social psychology, of the integration of western society, with special reference to the social re-adaptation of ex-prisoners of war, and the methods used to facilitate this re-adaptation. *C. T. W. Curle, B.Sc. 1947 Oxford*

Factor-analysis applied to current problems in psychology, with special reference to data obtained from H. M. forces. *E. K. C. Banks, Ph.D. 1945 London, University College*

Le militaire vu par Balzac. *B. O'Farrell, M.A. 1945 National University of Ireland*

Observations on 'neurotic' casualties in the Middle East. *I. Sutton, M.D. 1947 Manchester*

The predictive value of certain vocational tests, with special reference to personnel selection in the Army. *M. S. Stevenson, M.Sc. 1944 London, University College*

Some problems in the selection of service personnel. *E. G. Reeve, M.Sc. 1948 London, University College*

War service in a tropical country: (1) the effect of temperament; (2) as a factor in the causation of mental breakdown. *O. H. Woodcock, M.D. 1918 Manchester*

Armin, Robert
Robert Armin. *J. G. Tilney-Bassett, B.Litt. 1935 Oxford*

Arminius, Jacob
The Holy Spirit from Arminius to Wesley. *H. Watkin-Jones, D.D. 1929 Cambridge*

The influence of Arminius upon the theology of John Wesley. *A. H. S. Pask, Ph.D. 1940 Edinburgh*

Armour
See also Weapons.

The armourer and his craft. *J. F. Ffoulkes, B.Litt. 1912 Oxford*

The development of armour and costume from the fourteenth century to the seventeenth century as illustrated in the memorial brasses of Essex. *A. C. Edwards, M.A. 1937 Bristol*

The evolution of defensive armour in England, France, and Italy in the first half of the fourteenth century. *J. G. Mann, B.Litt. 1923 Oxford*

Medieval armour in Ireland, as exemplified on existing effigial monuments. *J. Hunt, M.A. 1945 National University of Ireland*

The relationship of artist and armourer in Europe during the sixteenth century, with particular reference to etching and allied techniques. *H. W. Williams, Ph.D. 1935 London, Courtauld Institute of Art*

Arnaud, François Baculard d'
The life and literary activities of Baculard d'Arnaud, with special reference to his novels. *W. M. Kerby, Ph.D. 1921 London*

Arnauld, Antoine
Antoine Arnauld and the Cartesian theory of representative ideas. *S. V. Keeling, M.A. 1926 London*

Antoine Arnauld's critique of Malebranche's philosophy as it is contained in *Des vraies et des fausses idées*. *R. V. Larmour, M.A. 1945 Belfast*

The theory of ideas in Antoine Arnauld. *E. M. Goldner, B.Litt. 1938 Oxford*

Arnim, Bettina von
Bettina von Arnim. *M. I. Malone, M.A. 1924 National University of Ireland*

Arnobius, the Elder
Arnobius' *Adversus Gentes* and the decay of paganism. *D. R. Andrews, M.A. 1934 London, Bedford College*

Arnold, Matthew
Critics of democracy: Carlyle, Arnold, Stephen (Fitzjames), Maine, Lecky. *B. E. Lippincott, Ph.D. 1931 London, School of Economics and Political Science*

The educational philosophy and influence of Matthew Arnold. *W. F. Connell, Ph.D. 1948 London, Institute of Education*

The influence of France on M. Arnold. *H. Alsop, M.A. 1914 Birmingham*

The influence of French writers on Matthew Arnold. *C. W. Wicks, M.A. 1922 Bristol*

The literary relations of Wordsworth and M. Arnold. *M. E. Green, M.A. 1927 Birmingham*

Matthew Arnold: a study of his influence on secondary school curricula. *J. E. Hollings, M.A. 1931 Birmingham*

Matthew Arnold: a study of his youth and ideas. *A. S. Cairncross, D.Litt. 1932 Glasgow*

Matthew Arnold and Germany. *J. A. Corbett, Ph.D. 1937 London, University College*

Matthew Arnold and Germany. *U. Sauerzweig, M.A. 1938 National University of Ireland*

Matthew Arnold and the literary criticism of the early nineteenth century, with special reference to Jeffrey and Hazlitt: a comparison of methods and evaluations. *J. Wilkinson, M.A. 1947 Manchester*

Matthew Arnold and Walter Pater: a study in critical attitudes. *F. Wardle, M.A. 1940 Manchester*

Matthew Arnold as a critic. *J. B. Orrick, B.Litt. 1927 Oxford*

Matthew Arnold as a critic of literature. *C. Kevin, M.A. 1930 National University of Ireland*

Matthew Arnold as a dramatic poet. *W. V. T. Coxon, M.A. 1935 Liverpool*

Matthew Arnold as a literary critic. *D. V. Marcon, M.A. 1940 London, King's College*

Matthew Arnold (the critic) as an interpreter of France. *F. J. W. Harding, B.Litt. 1948 Oxford*

Matthew Arnold's classical ideal. *M. Breathnac, M.A. 1939 National University of Ireland*

Matthew Arnold's debt to Sainte-Beuve and Renan. *O. E. Holloway, B.Litt. 1930 Oxford*

Matthew Arnold's imagery: a study in poetic method. *J. T. Green, Ph.D. 1948 Leeds*

Matthew Arnold's place in English criticism. *I. Jones, M.A. 1924 Wales*

Matthew Arnold's theory and practice of poetry. *D. G. Boys, M.A. 1923 London*

The poetry and criticism of Matthew Arnold compared. *T. Scott, M.A. 1948 Manchester*

Poetry of the Victorian age as represented by Browning and Arnold. *M. M. O'Mahony, M.A. 1942 National University of Ireland*

A study of Matthew Arnold and Ernest Renan as representative of the spirit of frustration in England and France in the nineteenth century. *J. N. Harding, M.A. 1947 Wales*

A study of Matthew Arnold's literary criticism, with special reference to the influence of Sainte-Beuve on Arnold. *O. E. Simister, M.A. 1936 Birmingham*

Arnold, of Brescia
The antecedents of the political and ecclesiastical ideas of Arnold of Brescia and his relation to the civic movement in Italy. *W. E. F. Ward, B.Litt. 1924 Oxford*

Arnold, Thomas
The religious thought and influence of Thomas Arnold of Rugby. *W. S. Baker, Ph.D. 1950 Edinburgh*

Arnulf, of Lisieux, Bishop
A critical edition of the letters of Arnulf of Lisieux. *F. Barlow, D.Phil. 1937 Oxford*

Arsenic
The history of chemical methods of detecting arsenic up to the year 1860. *J. N. T. Lintott, M.Sc. 1935 London, University College*

Art
See also Abstraction; Architecture; Aesthetics; Book Illustration; Ceramics; Colour; Enamels; Form; Iconography; Painting; Religion and Art; Sculpture.

Art in Roman life as shown in the works of Cicero. *H. G. Stokes, B.Litt. 1934 Oxford*

Art contd.
Bengal folk art. *A. Mukhopadhyay, M.A. 1941 London, School of Oriental and African Studies*

1. Body and soul. 2. Christianity and art. *P. Dearmer, B.D. & D.D. 1911 Oxford*

Buddhist art in Siam. *R. S. Le May, Ph.D. 1937 Cambridge*

A comparison of the function of imagination in the fine arts and in philosophy. *M. M. C. Chart, M.A. 1939 Reading*

External influences on west European art in the twelfth century, with special reference to Spain and the neighbouring countries. *E. F. Wellesz, B.Litt. 1948 Oxford*

The history of the Eisteddfod. *E. J. Lloyd, M.A. 1913 Wales*

The horse in Greek Art, from earliest times until the death of Alexander the Great. *M. E. Freeman, M.A. 1937 London, University College*

Illustrations of the romances in medieval English art. *R. S. Loomis, B.Litt. 1913 Oxford*

Italian art in the works of Robert Browning. *A. H. Joyce, M.A. 1904 Birmingham*

Late Celtic and Anglo-Saxon influence on continental art of the Carolingian period. *G. R. Reitlinger, B.Litt. 1923 Oxford*

The literary and artistic manifestations of neo-Platonism in the Italian Renaissance. *N. A. Robb, D.Phil. 1933 Oxford*

The origins of Byzantine art. *R. E. M. Wheeler, M.A. 1912 London*

Plato and fine art. *C. C. Holly, M.A. 1942 National University of Ireland*

Poetry and other arts in relation to life. *A. L. Stuart, Ph.D. 1944 Dublin, Trinity College*

Psychological studies of art, with special reference to pictorial art. *T. E. Dickson, Ph.D. 1937 Edinburgh*

The relationship of artist and armourer in Europe during the sixteenth century, with particular reference to etching and allied techniques. *H. W. Williams, Ph.D. 1935 London, Courtauld Institute of Art*

The relative distribution of landscape and figure art in Western Europe with some inquiry as to the causes. *H. M. Lewis, Ph.D. 1937 London, Courtauld Institute of Art*

The representation of locality in Greek art, and the ancient texts related thereto. *J. N. Schaeffer, B.Litt. 1908 Oxford*

The services of monks to art. *R. E. Swartwout, M.Litt. 1932 Cambridge*

Some barbaric elements in Carolingian art: an evaluation of Keltic, Germanic and Steppe influences in the art of the West. *H. L. Thomas, Ph.D. 1949 Edinburgh*

Studies in Greek athletic art. *K. T. Frost, B.Litt. 1907 Oxford*

Types and antitypes of the Passion in English medieval art, twelfth and thirteenth centuries. *A. C. Ritchie, Ph.D. 1935 London, Courtauld Institute of Art*

Art: Appreciation
Aos ealadhan agus oifige in Eirinn (Art students and their function in Ireland). *T. Lee, M.A. 1927 National University of Ireland*

Art and the artist in Schiller's poetry: a critical study. *W. Witte, M.A. 1943 London, External Degree*

Art judgement in school children: being an experimental study of the appreciation of pictures by secondary school boys. *K. K. Jacob, M.A. 1931 Leeds*

A comparative study of the aesthetic judgments of English and Chinese children in picture appreciation. *S. Fong, M.A. 1938 Birmingham*

The problem of illusions of reversible perspective and the effect of conation upon them. *M. I. Dunsdon, M.A. 1931 Reading*

Tests of artistic appreciation. *H. R. Maund Dewar, Ph.D. 1937 London, University College*

Art, Children's
A comparative study of drawing ability in English children by the Goodenough scale. *D. F. Tsao, M.A. 1935 London, University College*

A genetic study of the third dimension in child art, with special reference to certain aspects of phenomenal regression. *E. G. Dickinson, Ph.D. 1940 London, Institute of Education*

Art, Children's contd.
Studies of expression in children's free drawing and their response to aesthetic and other pictorial tests. *P. K. Trivedi, M.Ed. 1949 Durham*

The young child's idea of its personal environment as seen in drawings. *I. M. Farmer, M.A. 1949 Birmingham*

Arthur of Little Britain
A study of Lord Berners' translation, *Arthur of Little Britain*, with a prefatory life of the author. *S. P. Jenkins, B.Litt. 1946 Oxford*

Arthurian Legends
See also Romances.

An Anglo-Norman metrical Brut of the fourteenth century. *V. P. Underwood, Ph.D. 1937 London, University College*

The Arthurian legend. *M. J. C. Reid, Ph.D. 1937 Aberdeen*

The Arthurian legend and its revival in the nineteenth century. *C. W. Midgley, M.A. 1920 Birmingham*

The Arthurian legend in English literature down to and including Malory. *M. D. Jones, M.A. 1908 Wales*

The Arthurian legend in English literature. *R. S. Roberts, M.A. 1901 Wales*

The character of Percival in the Arthurian legend. *S. M. Powell, M.A. 1902 Wales*

Eachtra an Mhadraidh Mhaoil (The adventures of An Madradh Maol). *D. O'Laoghaire, M.A. 1942 National University of Ireland*

Early traditions concerning King Arthur's family: a study in comparative chronology. *E. E. B. Forsythe, M.A. 1938 Belfast*

An edition of *Sir Percyvell of Gales. P. Hainsworth, M.A. 1930 Leeds*

An edition of *Syre Gawene and the Carle of Carelyle. A. Kurvinen, B.Litt. 1949 Oxford*

An edition of the Middle English romance *Ywaine and Gawain. W. Lister, M.A. 1939 Manchester*

The evolution of the Merlin story in twelfth and thirteenth century French literature. *G. P. Barnes, M.A. 1950 Manchester*

An examination of Welsh versions of the *Historia regum Britanniae*, with reference to the original. *H. Lewis, M.A. 1913 Wales*

Geoffrey of Monmouth's *Chronicle* and its influence on English literature. *L. Woosnam, M.A. 1913 Wales*

La langue de *l'Atre perilleux*, poème de la Table Ronde. *B. Woledge, M.A. 1928 Leeds*

The *Lai du Cor* and its importance in the development of the chief Arthurian characters. *E. C. Southward, Ph.D. 1939 London, External Degree*

Le *Tristan* d'Eilhart d'Oberg. *A. Lofthouse, M.A. 1939 Manchester*

The legend of Gawain: its Celtic origins and its treatment in English literature. *F. W. Jones, M.A. 1911 Wales*

The Old French metrical versions of the prophecies of Merlin. *E. M. Feibusch, B.Litt. 1928 Oxford*

The presentation of King Arthur in medieval romance, with special reference to Middle English. *K. M. Sheperd, M.A. 1907 London*

Sir Gawain and the magic sword. *J. D. Jones, M.A. 1925 Wales*

The sources of book V of Malory's *Morte d'Arthur* and his treatment of them. *T. Vorontzoff, B.Litt. 1936 Oxford*

A study of some texts belonging to the Map-cycle in Italy, and especially of the *Chantari di Lancilotto*, with a short introduction on the history of the Arthurian tradition in Italy. *E. T. Griffiths, M.A. 1914 Wales*

The *avowynge of King Arthur, Sir Gawan, Sir Kaye, and Sir Bawdewyn of Bretan*: a Middle English romance from the Ireland ms. *J. A. Smith, M.A. 1938 Leeds*

Travel descriptions in Middle High German Arthurian epics. *M. O'C. Walshe, M.A. 1935 London, University College*

The Welsh version of the *Historia regum Britanniae* in Peniarth ms.44 collated with the *Red book* version, together with notes on the influence of the original on the style and construction of the Welsh, and a glossary of Welsh words whose use is illustrated by the Latin. *B. Jones, M.A. 1915 Wales*

Artificial Silk
See Rayon Industry.

Artists
See Art.

Arun, River
An analysis of some of the interactions of geography and history in the Arun and Adur valleys. *A. F. A. Mutton, M.A. 1932 London, Bedford College*

Arwystl, Huw
Gweithian barddonol Huw Arwystl (The poetical works of Huw Arwystl). *J. A. Jones, M. A. 1926 Wales*

Asaf Jah I, Mir Qamaruddin Nizamul Mulk
The life and career of Mir Qamaruddin Nizamul Mulk Asaf Jah I. *Y. Prasad, Ph.D. 1927 London*

Ascension, The
1. The condition of our Lord's body between his Resurrection and Ascension. 2. The narratives of the Ascension, critically compared and harmonized. *C. Harris, B.D. 1898 Oxford*

1. The Resurrection of Christ. 2. The Ascension of Christ. *C. H. C. Baker, B.D. 1882 Oxford*

Asceticism
The ascetical element in St. Paul. *H. F. Maxwell, B.Litt. 1934 Oxford*

Asceticism; an historical study. *J. McCann, Ph.D. 1944 Dublin, Trinity College*

1. The attitude of Christ towards the civil society of his day. 2. The Gospel and asceticism. *R. F. Rynd, B.D. 1910 Oxford*

The influence of asceticism on ideas of Christian morality from Clement and Tertullian to Siricius. *D. T. Davies, M.A. 1914 Wales*

1. Progressive revelation as illustrated in the history of Israel. 2. Asceticism and Christianity. *C. W. L. Evans, B.D. 1909 Oxford*

1. St. Mark xiv.21 and viii.38: 'Son of Man' in the Synoptic Gospels. 2. St. Mark i.11; St. Luke iii.22: 'Son of God' in the Synoptic Gospels. 3. St. Matthew xi.18-19: Our Lord's attitude towards asceticism. *F. H. Dudden, D.D. 1907 Oxford*

Ascham, Roger
Roger Ascham. *P. P. Connolly, M.A. 1949 National University of Ireland*

Ashanti, The
Customs of the Ashanti relating to birth, puberty, marriage, and death. *R. S. Rattray, B.Sc. 1925 Oxford*

The position of the chief in the modern political systems of Ashanti: a study of the influence of contemporary social changes on Ashanti political institutions. *K. A. Busia, D.Phil. 1947 Oxford*

Ashbourne
A history of Queen Elizabeth's Grammar School, Ashbourne, Derbyshire. *N. J. Frangopulo, M.Ed. 1937 Leeds*

Ashton-under-Lyne
The industrial development of Ashton-under-Lyne, 1780-1850. *F. Kenworthy, M.A. 1929 Manchester*

Asia, Central
See also Khokand, Khanate of; Seljuks.

Anglo-Russian relations from 1878-1885, with special reference to central Asia. *E. Jones, M.A. 1934 Wales*

Asian Studies
Dr. Edmund Castell, 1606-1685: studies of some aspects of eastern learning in seventeenth-century Britain. *M. Zamick, Ph.D. 1934 Saint Andrew's*

The eastern element in Lamartine. *M. J. Fisher, Ph.D. 1942 London, King's College*

Eastern influences in Chaucer with special reference to the Arabs. *E. J. S. Saigh, Ph.D. 1946 London, King's College*

The oriental elements in English poetry (1784-1859). *I. Husain, Ph.D. 1934 Edinburgh*

The Oriental tale in English prose fiction from 1740 to 1839. *E. A. Lindores, M.A. 1924 Manchester*

Orientalism in English poetry. *E. S. Broughton, M.A. 1919 London*

A study of Warburton's *The Crescent and the Cross* in relation to the literary interest in the Near East shown by English romantic writers in the eighteenth and the earlier nineteenth centuries. *M. S. Abdel-Hamid, M.A. 1948 Bristol*

True and false orientalism, with special reference to Hinduism and India, in the English poetry of the nineteenth century. *S. P. Varma, Ph.D. 1926 London*

Aspremont
See Romances.

Assam
British administration in Assam (1825-45), with special reference to the hill-tribes on the frontier. *H. Barpujari, Ph.D. 1949 London, School of Oriental and African Studies*

Cultural change, with special reference to the hill tribes of Burma and Assam. *E. R. Leach, Ph.D. 1947 London, School of Economics and Political Science*

A cultural history of Assam of the early period, c.400 A.D.-1200 A.D. *B. Barua, Ph.D. 1947 London, School of Oriental and African Studies*

East India Company's relations with Assam, 1771 to 1826. *S. K. Bhuyan, Ph.D. 1938 London, School of Oriental and African Studies*

The economic development of Assam. *N. S. Guha, M.Comm. 1937 Leeds*

The growth of local self-government in Assam, 1874-1919. *A. K. Barkakoty, Ph.D. 1949 London, School of Oriental and African Studies*

Assamese Language
Education and language problems in Assam. *S. C. Rajkhowa, M.A. 1948 London, Institute of Education*

Assize Courts
P. R. O. assize roll 505, edited with an introduction on the war-time administration of Lincolnshire, 1294-98. *W. S. Thomson, Ph.D. 1939 Edinburgh*

Association (Psychology)
The association of ideas as a psychological principle and as a principle in epistemology. *J. L. Armitage, M.A. 1913 Liverpool*

An investigation into the relation between association and intelligence. *E. P. Yule, Ph.D. 1934 Saint Andrew's*

The present status of the theory of association in the psychology of thought. *R. Coverdale, B.Litt. 1949 Oxford*

Researches in association: a psycho-physical essay. *J. O'Doherty, M.A. 1915 National University of Ireland*

Assyria
See also Nineveh; Ras Shamra-Ugarit; Sassanides; Yezidi, The.

The towns and districts of Mesopotamia in the second millenium B.C. according to the inscriptions of Tiglathpileser I. *J. J. Slotki, Ph.D. 1946 Manchester*

Astrology
Shakespeare's use of astrological terms, with an introduction on astrology and popular astrological knowledge of the period. *D. S. Collins, M.A. 1932 London, King's College*

Astronomy
See also Copernicus; Gersonides; Halley, E.; Herschel, J. F. W., Sir; Huygens, C.; Kepler, J.

Ancient Greek astronomy, with special reference to navigation and nautical astronomy. *A. W. E. Fenton, Ph.D. 1937 London, Birkbeck College*

The astronomical method of Kepler. *A. J. Taylor, Ph.D. 1932 London, University College*

The astronomical system of Copernicus. *A. Armitage, M.Sc. 1929 London*

Early history of astronomy and cosmology in India. *C. P. S. Menon, M.Sc. 1930 London*

Edmond Halley and his influence upon the progress of science in the seventeenth century. *A. C. Williams, Ph.D. 1940 London, University College*

The *Khandakhāe-dyaka* of Brahmagupta, with the commentaries of Prthūdaka for the first part, and Varuna for the second part, critically edited and translated. *B. Ghosh, D.Phil. 1940 Oxford*

The methodology of John Herschel and some of its subsequent developments. *R. MacDonald, M.Sc. 1927 London*

The origins in Greece of some physical and astral theories of the early Stoics. *M. M. Holt, M.Litt. 1938 Cambridge*

The physical and astronomical work of Christian Huygens considered in relation to that of his contemporaries. *A. E. Bell, Ph.D. 1942 London, University College*

The telescopes of Sir William Herschel. *C. T. Moss, M.Sc. 1949 London, University College*

Ate
The conception of Ate from Homer to Aeschylus. *W. E. Wigley, M.A. 1940 Birmingham*

Athanasius, Saint
For the Athanasian Creed, see Creeds.

Athanasius, Saint contd.

Athanasius' theory of redemption in the light of modern expositors. *W. L. Hall, Ph.D. 1934 Edinburgh*

The Christology of St. Athanasius. *D. Maritch, B.Litt. 1921 Oxford*

1. St. Athanasius' exposition of the divinity and Incarnation of our Lord in the anti-Arian orations. 2. St. Augustine's exposition of grace, free-will, and predestination in his anti-Pelagian treatises. *T. Hayes-Robinson, B.D. 1906 Oxford*

Atheist's Tragedy, The
The revenger's tragedy and *The atheist's tragedy*: some notes on their style and on the authorship problem. *R. A. Foakes, M.A. 1949 Birmingham*

Athelston
See Romances.

Athens
See also Cimon; Themistocles; Greece, Ancient; Parthenon.

Athenian agora. *J. P. Doherty, M.A. 1949 National University of Ireland*

Athenian foreign trade in the fifth and fourth centuries B.C. *R. J. Hopper, Ph.D. 1936 Cambridge*

The education of an Athenian. *S. C. Rowland, M.A. 1912 London*

The Four Hundred and the Thirty. *A. J. Barnett, M.A. 1901 Birmingham*

An inquiry into the purchasing power of the drachma in ancient Greece for the purpose of determining, if possible, the material conditions which prevailed in Athens during her existence as an independent state. *E. Y. Nisbet, Ph.D. 1948 Glasgow*

The political parties in Athens during the Peloponnesian War. *R. A. E. Prosser, M.A. 1926 Bristol*

Public festivals in Athenian life: the place of Attic public festivals in the lives of the people of Athens from the sixth to the fourth century B.C. *G. T. W. Hooker, M.A. 1947 London, University College and London, Birkbeck College*

Social life in Athens as depicted in Aristophanes. *M. K. Cotterill, M.A. 1907 London*

Athletics
See also Games and Sports.

A factorial analysis of athletic ability preparatory to the formation of a series of prognostic tests. *G. Highmore, Ph.D. 1949 London, Institute of Education*

Studies in Greek athletic art. *K. T. Frost, B.Litt. 1907 Oxford*

Atlases
See Maps.

Atomic Theory
The contributions to the establishment of the atomic theory made by John Dalton and his contemporaries. *J. H. White, M.Sc. 1927 London*

Atonement, The
See also Penance.

1.The doctrine of the atonement. 2. Inspiration. *L. J. G. D. Dowdall, B.D. 1881 Oxford*

1. The atonement. 2. St. Paul's doctrine of Christian ethics in relation to the Holy Spirit. *A. Robertson, B.D. & D.D. 1897 Oxford*

1. The atonement. 2. Sunday, or the Lord's day. *H. H. Merryweather, B.D. 1905 Oxford*

1. The atonement. 2. The Holy Spirit. *J. A. Smith, B.D. & D.D. 1898 Oxford*

1. The atonement. 2. The inspiration of the Scriptures. *R. W. Hiley, B.D. & D.D. 1885 Oxford*

1. The atonement. 2. The spiritual body. *C. G. H. Baskomb, B.D. 1905 Oxford*

1. The atonement. 2. The witness of the Church. *L. Ragg, B.D. 1905 Oxford*

Atonement in the light of the development of the idea of sacrifice. *E. T. H. Godwin, B.D. 1940 Leeds*

1. The Christian conception of sin. 2. The idea of atonement in the Old Testament. *L. Pullan, B.D. & D.D. 1921 Oxford*

1. The contribution of the prophets of Israel. 2. The atonement in history and life. *R. S. Cripps, B.D. 1929 Cambridge*

A critical lexicon of the Accadian prayers in the rituals of expiation, with an investigation of the principles which distinguish the various series of Babylonian expiation rituals. *C. J. M. Weir, D.Phil. 1930 Oxford*

Atonement, The contd.

The development of the doctrine of the atonement in English theology during the nineteenth century. *H. I. James, B.Litt. 1930 Oxford*

The distinctive features of the Christian doctrine of atonement as brought out by by the comparative study of religion. *P. McCall, M.A. 1947 Leeds*

The doctrine of atonement in Coleridge and Maurice. *C. W. I. Wardrop, Ph.D. 1932 Edinburgh*

1. The doctrine of sacrifice. 2. The doctrine of atonement. *A. C. Keene, B.D. 1906 Oxford*

The doctrine of the atonement and modern thought. *W. O. Phillipson, M.A. 1937 Bristol*

The doctrine of the atonement in the light of Christ's teaching and ministry. *A. MacKinnon, Ph.D. 1924 Glasgow*

1. The doctrine of the Blessed Trinity. 2. Scripture aspects of the Atonement. *B. W. Randolph, B.D. & D.D. 1901 Oxford*

1. The doctrine of the Holy Trinity. 2. The doctrine of the atonement. *R. G. Fookes, B.D. 1903 Oxford*

1. The doctrine of the Lord's Supper. 2. The doctrine of the atonement. *E. A. Glover, B.D. 1902 Oxford*

1. Doctrine of the work and office of Christ, with special reference to the atonement, during the first three centuries. 2. The relations of faith and reason in the Christian system, especially during the Apostolic and sub-Apostolic period. *F. W. Bussell, B.D. 1892 Oxford*

Exegeses of the fall: Genesis iii.1-6; the atonement: Hebrews ix.11-14; the inspiration of Holy Scripture: II Timothy iii. 15-17. *F. W. Quilter, D.D. 1872 Oxford*

The forensic theory of the atonement in its psychological aspects. *O. M. Ritchie, Ph.D. 1933 Edinburgh*

Hanes athrawiaeth yr iawn yng Nghymru yn y bedwaredd ganrif ar bymtheg (The history of the doctrine of the atonement in Wales in the nineteenth century). *J. W. Williams, M.A. 1939 Wales*

1. The Incarnation. 2. The atonement. *T. A. Purvis, B.D. & D.D. 1905 Oxford*

1. The incarnation. 2. The atonement. *M. Pryor, B.D. & D.D. 1906 Oxford*

Influence of the theory of evolution on the Christian doctrine of the atonement. *W. J. Cratchley, M.A. 1933 Bristol*

John McLeod Campbell, theologian: his theological development and trial and a new interpretation of his theory of the atonement. *E. G. Bewkes, Ph.D. 1924 Edinburgh*

1. The justice of the atonement. 2. The omnipresence of God and eschatology. *E. Lang, B.D. & D.D. 1908 Oxford*

1. The later Roman view of the Christian doctrine of the atonement. 2. The development of the penal theory of the atonement. *L. W. Grensted, B.D. 1922 Oxford*

1. The meaning, necessity, and morality of the Christian atonement. 2. The sacrament of the Lord's Supper considered as satisfying certain needs of human nature. *A. C. de Bourbel, B.D. 1896 Oxford*

1. On the atonement. 2. On infant baptism. *F. H. Woods, B.D. 1881 Oxford*

1. On the doctrine of the atonement in the Old Testament. 2. On the doctrine of the atonement in the New Testament. *H. C. Beeching, B.D. & D.D. 1911 Oxford*

Ralph Wardlaw, 1779-1853, with particular reference to his theory of the atonement and the rise of Congregationalism in Scotland. *R. D. Hyslop, Ph.D. 1947 Edinburgh*

The rational necessity of Christ's atonement. *P. Hartill, B.D. 1927 Oxford*

1. Sacrifice. 2. Atonement. *L. L. Sharper, B.D. 1874 Oxford*

1. Sin: Ἡ ἁμαρτία εστιν η ανομία. 2. The atonement: Ὁ θεὸσ αγάπη εστίν. *W.J. Oldfield, B.D. & D.D. 1907 Oxford*

A study in the doctrine of forgiveness and atonement. *D. R. Scott, Ph.D. 1923 Saint Andrew's*

The theology of James Morison, with special reference to his theories of the atonement. *C. E. Kirsch, Ph.D. 1939 Edinburgh*

The theories of the atonement of Anselm and Grotius. *R. S. Franks, B.Litt. 1899 Oxford*

Atre périleux
See Arthurian Legends.

Atreus, House of
The character and sources of the legends connected with the House of Atreus. *A. G. Way, M.A. 1935 London, King's College*

Attention
The distribution of attention. *E. N. McQueen, D.Sc. 1917 London*

Fluctuation of attention at and near the threshold. *T. C. Zok, M.A. 1938 London, University College*

Fluctuations of attention during short periods of work. *D. K. Grewal, Ph.D. 1933 London, University College*

Fluctuations of attention and the perception of meaning. *R. N. R. Wallace, M.A. 1935 London, University College*

Individual differences in fluctuation of attention. *E. R. Denton, M.A. 1943 London, University College*

Oscillation at the threshold and in mental work. *L. Chen, Ph.D. 1934 London, University College*

Oscillation of attention. *K. Sivaprakasam, Ph.D. 1934 London, University College*

Oscillation of attention: an enquiry into the effect of the degree of oscillation of ambiguous figures of varying degrees of meaning. *H. J. Hines, M.Sc. 1935 London, University College*

The pedagogical conclusion of psychological study of attention. *W. J. Messer, M.A. 1930 Reading*

A study of individual differences in the fluctuations of attention. *T. A. Purushottam, Ph.D. 1932 London, University College*

A study of the effect upon learning of a training in certain principles of attention and memorization. *L. R. Phillips, M.A. 1936 London, Institute of Education*

Attitude
Attitudes in the secondary (modern) school: an experimental investigation. *J. V. Trivett, M.A. 1949 Bristol*

An investigation of social and political attitudes. *M. Sanai, Ph.D. 1949 London, University College*

A metrical study of subject preferences in a boys' secondary school: an account of an experiment in the measurement of attitude. *C. G. Reed, M.Ed. 1939 Manchester*

Attwood, Thomas
A study of the theories of Thomas Attwood and contemporary advocates of paper money in England. *J. Sanmarti, Ph.D. 1948 London, School of Economics and Political Science*

Aubigné, Théodore Agrippa d'
D'Aubigné as a poet. *H. Knight, D.Phil. 1939 Oxford*

Aubrey, John
An edition of selected letters of John Aubrey. *E. M. Pickup, B.Litt. 1935 Oxford*

Auden, Wystan Hugh
English verse-drama from Yeats to Auden. *M. H. Brinn, M.A. 1950 Wales*

Auditoria
The auditorium. *L. Wright, M.A. 1934 Liverpool*

Auerbach, Berthold
The treatment of village life in the first four collections of Berthold Auerbach's *Schwarzwälder Dorfgeschichten*. *P. S. Pargeter, M.A. 1947 Birmingham*

Augustine of Hippo, Saint
An analysis, with commentary, of Saint Augustine of Hippo's treatises on marriage, the *De bono conjugali*, the *De adulterinis conjugiis* and the *De nuptiis et concupiscentia*. *G. G. Willis, M.A. 1939 Manchester*

Christian ethics and social institutions in the fourth century, with special reference to Augustine. *E. C. Urwin, M.A. 1920 London*

The doctrine of grace as illustrated by the experience and teaching of St. Paul, Augustine, and Luther. *R. L. Child, B.Litt. 1925 Oxford*

An examination of Mozley's treatment of the Augustinian doctrines of grace and pre-destination. *T. O. Davies, B.Litt. 1925 Oxford*

Grace and freewill in St. Paul and St. Augustine. *S. Y. Yovanovitch, B.Litt. 1920 Oxford*

1. The history of the doctrine of satisfaction from Tertullian to St. Ambrose. 2. The history of the doctrine of satisfaction from St. Augustine to St. Anselm. *G. A. Michell, B.D. & D.D 1924 Oxford*

The influence of Plotinus upon the religious philosphy of St. Augustine, with special reference to the points of difference between neoplatonism and Christianity. *W. J. Heaton, M.A. 1930 Reading*

Augustine of Hippo, Saint contd.
1. The kingdom of God. 2. The biblical and Augustinian use of the term 'grace'. *C. Knapp, B.D. 1902 Oxford*

1. On the Gospel of St. John. 2. On St. Augustine's treatise *De civitate dei. D. H. E. Keppel, B.D. 1906 Oxford*

The Platonism of Augustine's ascent to God. *S. Connolly, M.A. 1950 National University of Ireland*

Prolegomena to the *Contra academicos* of St. Augustine. *J. J. O'Meara, D.Phil. 1945 Oxford*

1. St. Athanasius' exposition of the divinity and Incarnation of our Lord in the anti-Arian orations. 2. St. Augustine's exposition of grace, free-will, and predestination in his anti-Pelagian treatises. *T. Hayes-Robinson, B.D. 1906 Oxford*

Saint Augustine's philosophy of liberal education. *T. Callaghan, Ph.D. 1942 National University of Ireland*

The vision of God in St. Augustine and Malebranche: a comparison. *D. Connell, M.A. 1947 National University of Ireland*

Augustinian Order
Ferdinando Texeda: a complete analysis of his work together with a study of his stay in England (1621? to 1631?), being a contribution to the solution of the problems connected with him. *W. McFadden, M.A. 1933 Belfast*

The history of the Augustinian canons in England before 1215, with special reference to the spread of their foundations and their relations with the secular clergy. *J. C. Dickinson, B.Litt. 1937 Oxford*

Augustus, Gaius Julius Caesar Octavius
Monumentum Ancyranum compared with other authorities for the life of Augustus. *M. H. Davies, M.A. 1912 Wales*

'Aun, Ibn Abī
A critical edition, with notes and indices, of the *Kitāb al Tashbīhāt* of Ibn Abī 'Aun. *M. A. M. Khan, Ph.D. 1939 Cambridge*

Aurangzeb, Emperor
The Court of Aurangzib as a centre of literature and learning. *R. A. Muhammadi, Ph.D. 1949 London, School of Oriental and African Studies*

Sir William Norris, Bart., and his embassy to Aurangzeb (1657-1702). *H. Das, B.Litt. 1923 Oxford*

Aurevilly, Jules Amédée Barbey d'
See Barbey d'Aurevilly, J. A.

Austen, Jane
The construction of the novel and Jane Austen. *M. J. Lavin, M.A. 1936 National University of Ireland*

The polite novel after Jane Austen. *B. C. Turner, B.Litt. 1944 Oxford*

The structure of the novel in Jane Austen, and its relationship to the work of her predecessors. *F. L. Jones, M.A. 1935 London, Queen Mary College*

Australia
See also Aborigines; Macquarie, L.

Australia and England: a study in imperial relations. *H. L. Hall, Ph.D. 1934 London, School of Economics and Political Science*

A comparison of the constitutions of the United States and Australia. *B. Jones, M.A. 1924 Wales*

Contributions to Australian geography. *J. M. Holmes, Ph.D. 1934 Glasgow*

Criminal transportation, its theory and practice, with special reference to Australia. *G. H. Fairs, M.A. 1932 Bristol*

Democratic planning in Australia, 1919-1939. *C. E. Fleming, B.Litt. 1949 Oxford*

The English activities on the north coast of Australia in the first half of the nineteenth century. *D. Howard, M.A. 1924 London*

English colonization theories, 1830-1842, with special reference to the economic and political development of the Australian colonies. *R. C. Mills, D.Sc. 1915 London*

Export demand: an attempt to measure the price and income elasticities of demand for Australian exports in 1938. *F. B. Horner, Ph.D. 1948 London, School of Economics and Political Science*

The foundation of South Australia. *R. J. Rudall, B.Litt. 1911 Oxford*

The policy of Great Britain regarding Australia, 1850-1900. *W. V. Teniswood, Ph.D. 1936 Edinburgh*

Problems of public finance in the federal states of Canada and Australia, with special reference to the scheme for India. *J. Samuel, M.Com. 1937 Leeds*

Australia contd.
The prosperity of Australia: an economic analysis. *F. C. Benham, Ph.D. 1928 London*

Some critical problems of Australian federalism. *D. N. Vohra, M.Sc. 1934 London, School of Economics and Political Science*

Some problems in the working of the Australian federation, 1927-37. *R. W. T. Cowan, B.Litt. 1939 Oxford*

State regulation of labour and industry in New South Wales. *P. A. W. Honeyman, M.A. 1922 Manchester*

The status of the federal system under the Australian constitution. *G. Greenwood, Ph.D. 1939 London, School of Economics and Political Science*

The working of federalism in Australia. *L. C. Wilcher, B.Litt. 1933 Oxford*

Austria
See also Austria-Hungary; and Beust, F. F. von, Count; Kaunitz-Rietberg, W. A. von, Prince; Metternich, C. W., Prince.

Anglo-Austrian relations during the reign of the Emperor Joseph II. *H. F. Schwarz, B.Litt. 1931 Oxford*

Austro-British relations 1863-1866, with special reference to the German question. *N. E. V. Smith, M.A. 1935 London, King's College*

The breakdown of the Anglo-Austrian Alliance, 1748-1756. *M. B. B. Cobb, M.A. 1935 London, University College*

British opinion in regard to Austria (1844 to 1867). *D. von Hirsch, Ph.D. 1946 Cambridge*

The financial reconstruction of Austria by the League of Nations, with reference to its economic consequences. *M. F. Jolliffe, M.A. 1930 Wales*

Loans and financial reconstruction in Austria. *G. R. Holden, B.Litt. 1934 Oxford*

Metternich and the English Government from the Peace of Schönbrünn. *C. S. B. Buckland, B.Litt. 1930 Oxford*

A study of the main causes for the failure of the attempt to introduce a democratic form of government in Austria after the war, with special reference to the constitution of 1920. *M. MacDonald, B.Litt. 1939 Oxford*

The survival of the Romano-Austrians. *A. F. Singer, B.Litt. 1948 Oxford*

Austria-Hungary
See also Austria; Hungary.

Count Aehrenthal: a study in the foreign policy of Austria-Hungary, 1906-1912. *C. Petherick, M.A. 1936 Bristol*

The relations between Great Britain and Austria-Hungary from the rising in Herzegovina to the Conference of Constantinople. *C. L. Wayper, Ph.D. 1950 Cambridge*

Austrian Literature
See German Literature; and references there to individual writers.

Authority
For the authority of the Bible, see Bible.

Adolescent attitudes to authority at work. *C. Tenen, M.A. 1945 Manchester*

Adolescent attitudes to authority: an investigation of the psychological factors underlying the opinions of objective authority held by young people in a particular town, and determining what they actually do when authority is exercised over them. *J. H. Price, M.A. 1943 Manchester*

Authority in Church and State, with special reference to the seventeenth century. *P. S. Belasco, Ph.D. 1928 London*

Cardinal Newman's doctrine of authority in religion. *R. S. Clements, Ph.D. 1931 Edinburgh*

The ethical basis of the State's authority. *J. Bretherton, M.A. 1937 Liverpool*

The headship of Jesus Christ as taught and vindicated by the Reformed Presbyterian Church in North America in relation to civil government. *R. M. C. Ward, Ph.D. 1939 Edinburgh*

Hindu political authority. *J. N. C. Ganguly, M.A. 1924 Birmingham*

An investigation into the development of the attitudes of children towards authority. *R. Winterbourn, Ph.D. 1941 London, Institute of Education*

John Calvin's conception of the seat of authority in religion. *R. W. McNeur, Ph. D. 1950 Edinburgh*

Authority contd.
Moral authority: an examination of external and internal authority in morals. *J. Highet, D.Phil. 1947 Oxford*

1. On the nature of authority. 2. On the essential elements of ordination. *C. H. K. Boughton, B.D. 1915 Oxford*

The origin and extent of civil authority. *J. Rickaby, B.Sc. 1901 Oxford*

The position of the chief in the modern political systems of Ashanti: a study of the influence of contemporary social changes on Ashanti political institutions. *K. A. Busia, D.Phil. 1947 Oxford*

The principle of authority in the Free Churches. *A. J. Nixon, Ph.D. 1930 London, External Degree*

Problem of authority in the continental reformers. *R. E. Davies, B.D. 1946 Cambridge*

The relations of statutory and voluntary authorities in public administration in England and Wales. *M. McKie, B.Litt. 1930 Oxford*

A study of the symbolism of political authority in Africa. *P. J. Bohannan, B.Sc. 1949 Oxford*

William of Ockham's attitude to political authority and its relation to the history of his time. *J. B. Morrall, B.Litt. 1949 Oxford*

Authorship
The profession of letters, 1780-1832: a study of the relation of author to patron, publisher, and public. *A. S. Collins, Ph.D. 1927 London*

Averroes (Ibn Rushd)
Causality in Al-Ghazali, Averroes, and Aquinas. *M. Fakhry, Ph.D. 1949 Edinburgh*

Avicenna (Ibn Sīnā
Avicenna's psychology: a critical edition, English translation, and commentary of *Kitab al-Najōt, ii.6. F. Rahman, D.Phil. 1949 Oxford*

Avogadro, Amedeo
Avogadro and Dalton: the standing in chemistry of their hypotheses. *A. N. Meldrum, D.Sc. 1904 Aberdeen*

Avon, River
See also Evesham, Vale of.

Erosion levels of the river Avon drainage basin: a comparative account of the various methods of cartographic analysis. *R. A. Yates, M.Sc. 1950 Bristol*

Axes
The domestic horse and perforated stone axes in antiquity as studied by archaeological and folklore evidence, with some suggestions as to their connections with movements of peoples. *S. J. Jones, M.A. 1928 Wales*

Ayala, Pedro Lopez de
The chronicles of Pedro the Cruel - Pedro Lopez de Ayala. *L. Taylor, Ph.D. 1931 Glasgow*

A contribution to the study of life, personality and works of Pedro Lopez de Ayala, 1332-1407. *E. W. Lloyd, Ph.D. 1930 London, King's College*

Ayrshire
Contributions to the economic geography of Ayrshire. *J. H. G. Lebon, Ph.D. 1946 London, External Degree*

Azande, The
The social organization of the Azande of the Bahr-el-Ghazal province of the Anglo-Egyptian Sudan. *E. E. Evans- Pritchard, Ph.D. 1928 London*

Babeuf, François Noël
Babouvism and the theory of proletarian dictatorship. *S. M. Cheng, Ph.D. 1934 London, School of Economics and Political Science*

Bacchylides
Epilegomena to Bacchylides. *I. Grafe, B.Litt. 1940 Oxford*

Bach, Johann Sebastian
The organ and its music from medieval times to Johann Sebastian Bach. *W. G. Allt, Mus. Doc. 1930 Edinburgh*

Bachama, The
Report of a tour to the west coast of Africa to study the education of women, 1928-29. Some notes on the Bachama tribe, Nigeria, 1928. *E. S. Fegan, Dip. Anthropology 1929 Cambridge*

Bachaumont, Louis Petit de
Etude lexicographique sur les *Mémoires secrets* (1762) par Louis Petit de Bachaumont. *R. Dunn, M.A. 1934 Leeds*

Bacon, Francis, Baron Verulam, Viscount St. Albans
Bacon's English style. *F. W. Lennon, M.A. 1936 National University of Ireland*

Bacon, Francis, Baron Verulam, Viscount St. Albans contd.
Bacon's knowledge and use of the Bible. *P. D. P. H. de E. Cole, D.Phil. 1950 Oxford*

The contribution of Francis Bacon to religious and ethical thought. *G. Wade, M.A. 1944 Leeds*

Francis Bacon and the theory and practice of formal rhetoric. *M. Walters, D.Phil. 1940 Oxford*

The literary and rhetorical background of Francis Bacon as an English man of letters. *M. Walters, M.A. 1938 London, Royal Holloway College*

The methodology of Francis Bacon. *A. Aris, M.Sc. 1926 London*

The scientific method and achievement of Aristotle and Bacon. *W. M. Dickie, Ph.D. 1925 Aberdeen*

Bacon Industry
The marketing of Canadian bacon. *A. D. B. Marshall, B.Litt. 1938 Oxford*

Bacon, Roger
Roger Bacon. *W. M. Cooper, M.A. 1910 London*

Roger Bacon. *W. H. Johnson, M.A. 1913 Birmingham*

Badsey, Worcestershire
An economic and social survey of the parish of Badsey, Worcestershire, in which the population is engaged in an intensive form of agriculture. *E. L. Harry, M.Sc. 1931 Wales*

Bage, Robert
A critical study of the novels of Robert Bage (1728-1801) and a consideration of their place in the history of the English novel. *J. H. C. Seymour, M.A. 1936 London, King's College*

The life and work of Robert Bage. *M. Greaves, B.Litt. 1938 Oxford*

Bagehot, Walter
Walter Bagehot: a study in Victorian ideas. *M. A. Nasr, Ph.D. 1949 London, School of Economics and Political Science*

Walter Bagehot: writer and critic. *T. R. Jones, M.A. 1932 Wales*

Bahaism
Studies in Bahaism. *S. N. Alter, Ph.D. 1923 Edinburgh*

Bahrein
A cemetery at Kish. A Sumerian palace. Jemdet Nasr. Bahrein and Hemamieh. Mohenjo-Daro. *E. J. H. Mackay, D.Litt. 1933 Bristol*

Bahr-el-Ghazal
The social organization of the Azande of the Bahr-el-Ghazal province of the Anglo-Egyptian Sudan. *E. E. Evans- Pritchard, Ph.D. 1928 London*

Bahrī, Qāzī Mahmūd
Qasi Mahmud Bahri: a mystic poet of the twelfth century A.H.; his times, life and work. *M. H. Syed, Ph.D. 1932 London, School of Oriental and African Studies*

Baji Rao II
Baji Rao II. *P. Gupta, Ph.D. 1936 London, School of Oriental and African Studies*

Bakery Industry
Bread making: evolution of the industry and the organisation of a modern bakery. *S. T. Rourke, M.Comm. 1927 National University of Ireland*

Balance of Payments
The balance of external payments of Nigeria during 1936. *P. A. Bower, B.Litt. 1946 Oxford*

The balance of external payments of the Gold Coast for the fiscal years 1936-37 to 1938-39. *J. Mars, M.A. 1942 Bristol*

Canada's balance of indebtedness, 1919-1933. *H. A. W. Halls, M.Sc. 1937 London, School of Economics and Political Science*

Current British payments agreements. *A. Vincent, M.Sc. 1947 London, School of Economics and Political Science*

Cyclical movements in the balance of payments. *T. C. Chang, Ph.D. 1948 Cambridge*

India's balance of international payments, 1910-11 to 1929-30. *C. A. Mehta, Ph.D. 1934 London, School of Economics and Political Science*

International cycles and Canada's balance of payments of 1921-33. *V. W. Malach, Ph.D. 1948 London, School of Economics and Political Science*

The international trade positin n of Canada, 1913-1933: an examination of the causes and characteristics of the balance of payments and the balance of trade. *W. E. Duffett, M.Sc. 1935 London, School of Economics and Political Science*

Balance of Payments contd.
The inter-relations of balances of payments and internal economic conditions, considered with special reference to selected countries in the period 1927-31. *S. D. Pollard, B.Litt. 1935 Oxford*

The relations between the English and Irish banking systems with special reference to the adjustment of the balance of payments between the countries, 1929-1939. *B. P. Menton, Ph.D. 1947 London, External Degree*

Baldwin, William
A study of the works of William Baldwin, with special reference to his connection with *The Mirror for Magistrates*. *M. Brown, M.A. 1912 London*

Bale, John
A critical study of the dramatic work of John Bale and its relation to the English dramatic tradition and contemporary developments. *W. T. Davies, B.Litt. 1936 Oxford*

John Bale, antiquary and biographer. *H. C. McCusker, M.A. 1934 London, University College*

John Bale, Protestant. *E. E. Jones, M.A. 1910 Wales*

Kynge Johan re-edited, with a study of the language of Bale in appendix. *J. H. P. Pafford, M.A. 1929 London*

Ballads
See also Carols; Hymns; Poetry; Songs.

Ballads: English, Scotch and Irish. *M. P. Fitzgerald, M.A. 1924 National University of Ireland*

A comparative study of the English, Scottish, and Hungarian popular ballad. *M. Egger, Ph.D. 1928 London*

Early Buddhist ballads and their relations to the older Upanishadic literature. *S. R. M. R. Katre, Ph.D. 1932 London, School of Oriental and African Studies*

The early history of ballad literature, with special reference to English and Scandinavian ballads. *P. H. Christophersen, Ph.D. 1943 Cambridge*

English ballads: their origin and literature. *R. R. Evans, M.A. 1911 Wales*

The historical background of the raider ballads of Liddesdale. *J. M. Couper, Ph.D. 1948 Aberdeen*

The influence of the ballad on nineteenth century poetry, with special reference to Rossetti, Morris and Swinburne. *I. M. Empson, M.A. 1933 Reading*

The light thrown by the klephtic ballads on the history of Greece in the period (1715 to 1821) before the war of Independence. *J. W. Baggally, B.Litt. 1935 Oxford*

The literary ballad in England during the romantic period. *E. Purdie, Cert.Litt. 1923 Oxford*

Old English and Hindu ballads. *G. D. Ashthana, Ph.D. 1928 London*

The origin and growth of the German ballad. *M. Lavelle, M.A. 1918 National University of Ireland*

Political ideas in Wales during the latter half of the eighteenth century as reflected in ballad literature. *A. Watkin Jones, B.Litt. 1926 Oxford*

A study of ballad collections edited in the eighteenth century. *M. E. Yockney, B.Litt. 1949 Oxford*

Survivals of the English and Scottish popular ballads in Canada: a study of the ways of tradition with verse. *M. M. Macodrum, Ph.D. 1927 Glasgow*

The works of Thomas Deloney. *F. O. Mann, B.Litt. 1912 Oxford*

Zur Entwickelungsgeschichte der Kunstballade. *M. M. Shea, M.A. 1918 National University of Ireland*

Ballet
See Dancing.

Ballistics
Ballistics in the seventeenth century. *A. R. Hall, Ph.D. 1950 Cambridge*

Ballymote, Book of
An edition of the first section of the text (Book of Ballymote, fasc. 119b-127a) with indexes and variae lectiones. *M. J. Mc Donagh, M.A. 1940 National University of Ireland*

Balzac, Honoré de
Balzac; *De amicitia*. *R. Hales, M.A. 1950 National University of Ireland*

Balzac et ses contemporains. Balzac journaliste. *A. M. Lloyd, M.A. 1935 London, King's College*

The business world in France as revealed in the works of Balzac. *L. M. Turner, M.A. 1923 Manchester*

Essai sur *Eugénie Grandet* et *Un coeur simple*. *F. V. Cass, M.A. 1920 Birmingham*

Balzac, Honoré de contd.
La bourgeoisie de province dans l'oeuvre de Balzac. *M. Wray, M.A. 1925 Manchester*

Le clergé dans l'oeuvre de Balzac. *L. Gardner, M.A. 1925 Manchester*

Le militaire vu par Balzac. *B. O'Farrell, M.A. 1945 National University of Ireland*

Le monde politique dans Balzac. *A. Clayton, M.A. 1930 Manchester*

Le rôle de la religion dans la *Comédie humaine* de Balzac. *P. A. Malt, M.A. 1937 London, King's College*

Les idées de Balzac sur la littérature. *R. van Engel, M.A. 1929 Liverpool*

Louis Lambert and the philosophy of Balzac. *H. G. J. Evans, Ph.D. 1949 London, King's College*

Néologismes dans la *Comédie humaine* de H. de Balzac, 1829-1832. *R. A. Kaye, M.A. 1923 Leeds*

Politics in the novels of Honoré de Balzac. *B. N. Parker, M.A. 1929 London*

Social questions in Balzac's novels. *F. E. Brown, Ph.D. 1934 London, King's College*

A study of Balzac's literary criticism. *H. E. Collins, Ph.D. 1937 London, Birkbeck College*

Bancroft, Richard, Archbishop
The Church of England and Puritanism during the primacy of Bancroft, 1604-1610. *S. B. Babbage, Ph.D. 1940 London, King's College*

Banim, John and Michael
The Banims; a study in Anglo-Irish literature. *M. F. Thomas, M.A. 1935 National University of Ireland*

Bank of England
The genesis of English banking, with particular reference to the private banking of the Goldsmiths, the evolution of English paper money, and the early history of the Bank of England. *R. D. Richards, Ph.D. 1928 London*

The problems of the Bank of England and the Federal Reserve System since 1927. *P. L. Hogg, M.Sc. 1935 London, School of Economics and Political Science*

Some aspects of Bank of England policy, 1780-1850. *J. K. Horsefield, M.A. 1949 Bristol*

Bank Rate
See Banks and Banking.

Bankimchandra
A critical study of the life and novels of Bankimcandra. *J. K. Dasgupta, Ph.D. 1933 London, School of Oriental and African Studies*

Bankruptcy
Conflict of laws relating to the collection of assets in bankruptcy. *W. A. L. Raeburn, LL.M. 1949 London, School of Economics and Political Science*

Criminal law as applied to bankruptcy. *H. G. Meek, LL.M. 1929 Cambridge*

The effect of the Bankruptcy and Deeds of Arrangement Act of 1913 on the law relating to bankruptcy. *A. W. Brown, LL.M. 1916 Liverpool*

The foundations of the law of bankruptcy. *R. G. Cooke, LL.M. 1924 Manchester*

The history of the English law of bankruptcy, with special reference to the origins, continental sources, and early development of the principal features of the law. *I. Treiman, D.Phil. 1927 Oxford*

Irish bankruptcy law. *P. F. Leonard, M.A. 1943 National University of Ireland*

Joint stock company failures, 1862-1914. *G. F. Todd, B.Litt. 1932 Oxford*

Banks and Banking
See also Balance of Payments; Capital; Credit; Money; Savings.

Bank accounting: an examination and comparison of the accounting systems of the commercial banks in Great Britain and certain other European countries, with brief reference to the history of the matter in England. *H. C. F. Holgate, Ph.D. 1938 London, External Degree*

Bank advances to industry. *J. G. Picton, M.Com. 1933 Birmingham*

Bankers and non-routine customers: an examination of their practical relationship. *M. H. Magrah, M.Comm. 1931 London, School of Economics and Political Science*

Dominion exchanges and central bank problems arising therefrom. *H. C. Coombs, Ph.D. 1934 London, School of Economics and Political Science*

Free banking. *V. C. Smith, Ph.D. 1935 London, School of Economics and Political Science*

Banks and Banking contd.

Functions of banks in finance of peace and war. *J. Busteed, M.Comm. 1926 National University of Ireland*

The influence of inflation and deflation on banking, based on a comparison of conditions in eastern and western Europe. *J. Kostanecki, Ph.D. 1927 London*

The international adjustment of monetary and banking systems and the proposals made since the war for the solution of the problem. *B. Samuel, M.A. 1928 Wales*

International co-operative banking (co-operative banking and co-operative banks of the world). *N. I. Barou, Ph.D. 1933 London, School of Economics and Political Science*

The law of bankers' commercial credits. *H. C. Gutteridge, LL.D. 1928 London*

A quantitative investigation of the effect of scientific lending on certain industries as viewed from the aspect of banking. *W. A. McLeish, Ph.D. 1939 Edinburgh*

Recent progress of central banking in the British Empire. *N. M. Wagle, M.Sc. 1937 London, School of Economics and Political Science*

Some recent continental commercial banking developments, with special reference to Belgium, France, Germany, Norway and Switzerland. *R. A. Crofts, M.Sc. 1938 London, External Degree*

The theory of bank rate. *C. L. Lawton, M.Sc. 1934 London, School of Economics and Political Science*

Banks and Banking: Australia
The Australian banking and credit system. *A. L. G. Mackay, M.Litt. 1931 Cambridge*

Banks and Banking: British West Africa
Co-operation in agriculture and banking in British West Africa. *J. C. De Graft-Johnson, Ph.D. 1946 Edinburgh*

Banks and Banking: Canada
A comparison of the currency and banking systems of Canada and the United States, with some reference to that of Great Britain. *C. E. Johnston, B.Litt. 1920 Oxford*

Banks and Banking: Central Europe
Currency and banking in central Europe, 1919-1938. *F. Rona, M.Sc. 1947 London, School of Economics and Political Science*

Banks and Banking: China
Cash-shop banks and their relationship to the banking system of China. *Y. H. Liang, M.A. 1936 Liverpool*

The Chinese banking with special reference to modern banks. *T. C. S. Liu, M.Com. 1931 Leeds*

The currency and banking problems of China. *S. T. Hou, Ph.D. 1935 Liverpool*

Foreign banking in China. *S. C. Feng, M.Sc. 1938 London, School of Economics and Political Science*

Joint stock banking in China. *T. L. Cho, M.Sc. 1937 London, School of Economics and Political Science*

Banks and Banking: France
Currency and banking developments in the French overseas Empire, 1939-1945. *P. L. Hogg, Ph.D. 1947 London, School of Economics and Political Science*

A study of the French banking system, with special reference to the financing of industry and to the French investment policy during the period 1815-1914. *C. Fodrio, Ph.D. 1941 London, School of Economics and Political Science*

Banks and Banking: Germany
German banking in depression and recovery, 1930-1935. *T. Prager, Ph.D. 1943 London, School of Economics and Political Science*

The German credit banks and the money market 1900-1914. *P. B. Whale, M.Com. 1924 Birmingham*

An inquiry into the nature and methods of the assistance rendered by banking to commercial enterprise in the United States of America, as compared with England and Germany particularly. *P. D. Crockett, B.Litt. 1923 Oxford*

The people's banks, with special reference to developments in Germany and Great Britain, together with a consideration of the value of its experience to India. *T. Vasudevaiya, M.A. 1936 Leeds*

The policy of the German *Reichsbank* from stabilization to the Hoover moratorium (1924-1932). *E. F. Drake, B.Litt. 1935 Oxford*

Reichsbank policy, 1923-1934. *P. T. Matthews, M. Com. 1934 Birmingham*

Banks and Banking: Great Britain
A comparison of the currency and banking systems of Canada and the United States, with some reference to that of Great Britain. *C. E. Johnston, B.Litt. 1920 Oxford*

The development of banking in the south-western counties in the nineteenth century, with particular reference to Devon and Cornwall in the period 1840-1890. *N. L. Armstrong, Ph.D. 1937 London, External Degree*

The evolution and significance of the principles of the Bank Charter Act of 1844. *J. K. Horsefield, B.A. 1937 Bristol*

Factors affecting the total flow of cheque-payments in the non-financial circulation through the clearing banks, 1919-37. *G. W. G. Browne, B.Litt. 1939 Oxford*

The genesis of English banking, with particular reference to the private banking of the Goldsmiths, the evolution of English paper money, and the early history of the Bank of England. *R. D. Richards, Ph.D. 1928 London*

The history and present position of English banks operating in foreign countries. *A. S. J. Baster, Ph.D. 1934 London, External Degree*

The history of Boyd, Benfield and Co: a study in the merchant banking in the last decade of the eighteenth century. *S. R. Cope, Ph.D. 1947 London, School of Economics and Political Science*

An inquiry into the nature and methods of the assistance rendered by banking to commercial enterprise in the United States of America, as compared with England and Germany particularly. *P. D. Crockett, B.Litt. 1923 Oxford*

The monetary and banking policy of Great Britain during and since the great depression. *M. S. Chen, M.Sc. 1939 London, School of Economics and Political Science*

The origins and early history of savings banks in Great Britain. *S. M. Proctor, M.A. 1929 Liverpool*

The people's banks, with special reference to developments in Germany and Great Britain, together with a consideration of the value of its experience to India. *T. Vasudevaiya, M.A. 1936 Leeds*

The relations between the English and Irish banking systems with special reference to the adjustment of the balance of payments between the countries, 1929-1939. *B. P. Menton, Ph.D. 1947 London, External Degree*

The rise and growth of English joint stock banking. *S. E. Thomas, Ph.D. 1934 London, External Degree*

Sir Stafford Northcote's sinking fund and the redemption of debt between 1874 and 1914. *P. C. Gordon Walker, B.Litt. 1930 Oxford*

Some aspects of Bank of England policy, 1780-1850. *J. K. Horsefield, M.A. 1949 Bristol*

Banks and Banking: Greece
Banking and monetary problems of Greece from 1931-1939. *A. Presanis, M.Sc. 1946 London, School of Economics and Political Science*

Banks and Banking: India
Banking law and practice in India. *M. L. Tannan, M.Com. 1927 Birmingham*

Banks and industrial finance in India. *R. Bagchi, Ph.D. 1937 London, University College*

Indigenous banking in India. *L. C. Jain, Ph.D. 1928 London*

Industrial banking in India. *P. P. Kallukaren, Ph.D. 1923 London*

The monetary policy of the Reserve Bank of India with special reference to the structural and institutional factors in the economy. *K. N. Raj, Ph.D. 1947 London, School of Economics and Political Science*

The people's banks, with special reference to developments in Germany and Great Britain, together with a consideration of the value of its experience to India. *T. Vasudevaiya, M.A. 1936 Leeds*

The problem of banking in India: its present situation, development, and reform. *S. M. Dhumé, Ph.D. 1922 London*

Some aspects of a central bank for India. *B. R. Shenoy, M.Sc. 1933 London, School of Economics and Political Science*

Banks and Banking: Ireland
The bank of Ireland 1783-1846. *F. G. Hall, Litt.D. 1949 Dublin, Trinity College*

Banking and currency in Ireland. *J. V. Bourke, M.Comm. 1933 National University of Ireland*

Banking systems of Ireland. *L. E. Trodden, M.A. 1926 National University of Ireland*

Banks and Banking: Ireland contd.
The relations between the English and Irish banking systems with special reference to the adjustment of the balance of payments between the countries, 1929-1939. *B. P. Menton, Ph.D. 1947 London, External Degree*

The trend of banking in Ireland since 1800. *F. G. Hall, Ph.D. 1944 Dublin, Trinity College*

Banks and Banking: Italy
1. The monastic wool trade of the thirteenth century. 2. The Italian bankers and the English Crown. *R. J. Whitwell, B.Litt. 1903 Oxford*

Banks and Banking: Turkey
Commercial banking in Turkey, with reference to the experience of certain other countries. *H. T. Ulug, M.Sc. 1946 London, School of Economics and Political Science*

Banks and Banking: United States
American banking methods. *L. M. Minty, Ph.D. 1924 London*

A comparison of the currency and banking systems of Canada and the United States, with some reference to that of Great Britain. *C. E. Johnston, B.Litt. 1920 Oxford*

The discount policy of the Federal Reserve system. *J. B. Martin, B.Litt. 1933 Oxford*

An inquiry into the nature and methods of the assistance rendered by banking to commercial enterprise in the United States of America, as compared with England and Germany particularly. *P. D. Crockett, B.Litt. 1923 Oxford*

Modern experiments in American banking reorganization. *A. M. Allen, Ph.D. 1938 London, School of Economics and Political Science*

The problems of the Bank of England and the Federal Reserve System since 1927. *P. L. Hogg, M.Sc. 1935 London, School of Economics and Political Science*

Purposes and workings of the Federal Reserve System comparatively treated. *C. W. Williams, B.Litt. 1923 Oxford*

Banks, John
A study of the dramatic works of John Banks, including a critical edition of *Vertue betray'd or, Anna Bullen: a tragedy. M. Giovannini, B.Litt. 1938 Oxford*

Bantu Languages
The comparative phonetics of the Suto-Chuana group of Bantu languages. *A. N. Tucker, Ph.D. 1929 London*

Bantu, The
Ancestor worship among the southern Bantu. *D. W. T. Shropshire, B.Litt. 1927 Oxford*

The communal idea in Bantu law. *R. P. B. Erasmus, B.Sc. 1944 Oxford*

A contribution to the study of the Bantu race (Zulus) in Natal, with reference to (1) their mode of living, racial customs and social conditions and (2) their physical and mental diseases. *A. D. Pringle, M.D. 1916 Aberdeen*

Culture contact between Bantu and European in South-East Africa as illustrated by the life of Sir Theophilus Shepstone. *D. M. Goodfellow, Ph.D. 1932 London, School of Economics and Political Science*

The effect of contact with Europeans upon a south-eastern Bantu group. *M. M. Hunter, Ph.D. 1934 Cambridge*

Europeans and the Bantu family. *B. A. Hutchinson, Ph.D. 1945 London, External Degree*

The realm of the supernatural among the south-eastern Bantu. *H. M. Gluckmann, D.Phil. 1936 Oxford*

The religious institutions and beliefs of the southern Bantu, and their bearing on the problems of the Christian missionary. *D. W. T. Shropshire, D.Phil. 1937 Oxford*

The sociological importance of food with special reference to Bantu society. *A. I. Richards, Ph.D. 1930 London, School of Economics and Political Science*

The status of women among the southern Bantu. *P. J. Bradney, B.Sc. 1950 Oxford*

Systems of land tenure among the Bantu peoples of East Africa. *J. F. M. Middleton, B.Sc. 1949 Oxford*

A translation of theological terms and ideas into the languages of evangelization, ancient and modern, particularly those of the Bantu family. *W. A. Norton, B.Litt. 1916 Oxford*

Baptism
See also Sacraments.

Baptism contd.
1.The subjects and efficacy of holy baptism. 2. Theories opposed to the fact of the Resurrection of our Lord. *T. A. Blyth, B.D. 1888 Oxford*

Argument for the resurrection. 2. Infant baptism. *S. W. B. Holbrooke, B.D. 1907 Oxford*

1. Baptism and the forgiveness of sins. 2. Absolution and the forgiveness of sins. *T. Field, B.D. & D.D. 1897 Oxford*

1. Christian baptism. 2. St. Paul's belief in the divinity of Our Lord. *H. B. Gooding, B.D. 192[Oxford*

1. Considerations on eternal punishment. 2. The baptism of infants. *E. Hermitage-Day, B.D. 1901 Oxford*

The doctrine of baptism. *E. M. Thompson, B.D. 1927 Oxford*

1. The doctrine of baptism. 2. The intermediate state. *S. Baker, B.D. 1901 Oxford*

The doctrine of baptismal regeneration in the Church of England, with special reference to the Prayer Books of 1549, 1552, and 1662. *D. G. Pratt, B.D. 1951 Oxford*

An historical examination into baptismal usage in the reformed churches of Scotland. *R. B. Hannen, Ph.D. 1948 Glasgow*

The history of Christian baptism. *C. H. Murray, B.Litt. 1927 Oxford*

A history of the controversy raised by the Reverend George Cornelius Gorham in the year 1846, and following years, in so far as it bore upon the subject of the efficacy of baptism; with a study of the pamphlets on this subject put out about this time, and an attempt to classify the doctrines of baptism expressed therein. *J. C. S. Nias, B.D. 1945 Oxford*

1. Holy baptism. 2. Holy communion. *J. Bramston, B.D. 1872 Oxford*

1. Holy baptism. 2. Redemption and the salvation consequent upon it. *G. M. Evans, B.D. 1908 Oxford*

1. Holy baptism. 2. The Resurrection and the modern mind. *A. R. H. Grant, B.D. 1920 Oxford*

1. Infant baptism. 2. The commission given to those receiving the order of Priesthood in the Church of England. *W. H. Baslow, B.D. & D.D. 1895 Oxford*

The New Testament doctrine of baptism. *W. F. Flemington, B.D. 1948 Cambridge*

1. On Antichrist. 2. On infant baptism. *W. K. W. Chafy-Chafy, B.D. & D.D. 1891 Oxford*

1. On holy baptism. 2. On episcopal government. *F. A. Walker, B.D. 1879 Oxford*

1. On the atonement. 2. On infant baptism. *F. H. Woods, B.D. 1881 Oxford*

1. On the later medieval doctrine of the Eucharistic sacrifice. 2. On the relation of confirmation to baptism according to the New Testament. *B. J. Kidd, B.D. 1898 Oxford*

1. 'One baptism for the remission of sins'. 2. 'The communion of saints'. *C. E. Jelf, B.D. & D.D. 1907 Oxford*

The Pauline notion of baptismal re-birth and the mystery religions. *J. Hackett, M.A. 1942 National University of Ireland*

The practice and doctrine of baptism in primitive Christianity. *T. C. Smith, Ph.D. 1949 Edinburgh*

1. The proper mode of holy baptism. 2. The proper subjects of holy baptism. *T. W. Lemon, B.D. & D.D. 1889 Oxford*

1. The relation of confirmation to baptism. 2. The meaning and use of the Messianic titles: 'Christ', 'Son of David', 'Son of God', 'Son of Man'. *A. Chilton, B.D. & D.D. 1906 Oxford*

1. St. Luke xxii.14-20: the institution of the Eucharist. 2. I Corinthians xv.3-8: the witness of St. Paul to the resurrection. 3. I Corinthians xv.29: baptizing for the dead. *T. H. Davies, D.D. 1910 Oxford*

1. The threefold ministry. 2. Infant baptism. *F. Moor, B.D. 1888 Oxford*

1. The *Treatise on the Apostolic tradition* of St. Hippolytus. 2. The theology of confirmation in relation to baptism. 3. The shape of the liturgy. *G. E. A. Dix, B.D. & D.D. 1949 Oxford*

1. Whether the baptism of young children is in any wise to be retained in the Church. 2. Transubstantiation overthrows the nature of a sacrament. *H. W. Yule, B.D. 1877 Oxford*

Baptists
See also McLean, A.

Baptists contd.
The Baptists and political and social conditions in Lancashire during the Industrial Revolution, 1760-1832. *C. B. Whyatt, M.A. 1948 Manchester*

The Baptists in Scotland. *J. Scott, Ph.D. 1927 Glasgow*

The educational activities of Baptists in England during the eighteenth and nineteenth centuries with particular reference to the Northwest. *J. E. Watson, M.A. 1947 Liverpool*

The relation of Baptists to Disciples (Churches) of Christ. *E. Roberts-Thomson, M.A. 1949 Bristol*

Barbados
Barbados and the Confederation Question, 1871-1885. *A. D. B. Hamilton, Ph.D. 1947 London, External Degree*

Constitutional and economic development in Barbados, 1640-1685. *V. T. Harlow, B.Litt. 1923 Oxford*

The development of executive government in Barbados and the Leeward Islands, 1660 to 1783. *F. G. Spurdle, Ph.D. 1931 London, King's College*

Barbary States
The influence of the Barbary States in international relations, with special reference to the United States. *R. K. Irons, D.Phil. 1934 Oxford*

Barbey d'Aurevilly, Jules Amédée
The Norman element in the novels of Jules Barbey d'Aurevilly. *P. A. Lewis, M.A. 1921 Wales*

Barbier, Auguste
Auguste Barbier: sa vie et son oeuvre. *J. Rowlandson, Ph.D. 1942 Đurham*

The life and work of Auguste Barbier (1805-1882). *W. W. Muirhead, M.A. 1935 London, Queen Mary College*

L'inspiration satirique d'Auguste Barbier. *E. R. Dowson, M.A. 1921 Leeds*

Barbour, John
An investigation of the rimes and phonology of Barbour's *Bruce. O. T. Williams, M.A. 1908 Wales*

Barbusse, Henri
Henri Barbusse, critique de notre temps. *V. Mallinson, M.A. 1936 Leeds*

Barclay, Alexander
The *Eclogues*, life and literary activities of Alexander Barclay. *B. M. J. White, M.A. 1926 London*

Barclay, Robert
An examination of the doctrine of the inner light in the apology of Rt. Barclay. *J. B. Russell, Ph.D. 1931 Edinburgh*

Bards
See also Celtic Languages and Literatures; Eisteddfod; Welsh Literature.

The bardic order in the fifteenth century. *T. W. L. Davies, M.A. 1910 Wales*

Bardism and romance; a study of the Welsh literary tradition. *T. G. Jones, M.A. 1915 Wales*

Dychanau ac ymrysonau'r beirdd Cymreig hyd ddiwdd yr eilfed ganrif ar bymtheg (The satires and contentions of the Welsh bards to the end of the seventeenth century). *O. Thomas, M.A. 1928 Wales*

The religious mind of the Irish bards. *J. E. Murphy, Ph.D. 1938 National University of Ireland*

The works of some fifteenth century Glamorgan bards: Ieuan Gethyn ap Ieuan ap Lleision, Rhys Brydydd, Rhisiart ap Rhys, Gwilym Tew, Llywelyn ap Hywel ap Gronwy, Lang Lewys, Llywelyn Goch y Dant, Gruffydd ap Dafydd Fychan, Ieuan Du'r Bilwg. *J. M. Williams, M.A. 1923 Wales*

Ymrysonau'r beirdd (The (poetic) contentions of the bards). *B. Rhys, M.A. 1932 Wales*

Barham, Charles Middleton, Lord
Charles Middleton, afterward Lord Barham, and naval administration, 1778-1805. *S. Riddick, M.A. 1939 Liverpool*

Bari, The
Notes on ethnography of the Bari, Uganda. *E. B. Haddon, Dip. Anthropology. 1912 Cambridge*

Barlow, William, Bishop
Some early Tudor dialogues, referred to by Sir Thomas More in his controversial works; with an account of Bishop Barlow. *A. C. Hills, M.A. 1938 London, King's College*

Barnes, Robert
The contribution of Robert Barnes to the English Reformation. *N. H. Fisher, M.A. 1950 Birmingham*

Barnes, William
William Barnes: study of the man and poet and of his work in connection with Dorset and the Dorset dialect. *J. V. Ruffell, Ph.D. 1948 London, External Degree*

Barnfield, Richard
The life and poetical works of Richard Barnfield. *E. J. N. Bramall, B.Litt. 1930 Oxford*

Baronies
See Feudalism.

Barra, Daibhí de
Amhráin is dánta Dhaibhí de Barra (Songs and poems of Daibhí de Barra). *M. R. O'Tatháin, M.A. 1932 National University of Ireland*

Barre, François Poulain de la
Feminist writers of the seventeenth century, with special reference to François Poulain de la Barre. *S. A. Richards, M.A. 1912 London*

Barrès, Maurice
Barrès en voyage: le monde extérieur dans les oeuvres de Maurice Barrès. *J. R. Taylor, M.A. 1930 Wales*

La langue et le style de Maurice Barrès. *N. E. Cledwyn, M.A. 1933 Wales*

L'appel du Rhin dans les oeuvres de Maurice Barrès avant la publication des *Bastions de l'Est*: l'influence allemande et l'évolution de sa pensée relative au problème du Rhin. *S. M. King, M.A. 1932 Leeds*

Les idées de Maurice Barrès. *E. J. Hechinger, M.A. 1946 Birmingham*

Nationalism in the works of Maurice Barrès. *R. B. Jones, M.A. 1934 Wales*

Barrow, Isaac
The sermon as persuasion in late seventeenth century France and England: a study of Bossuet, Bourdaloue, Barrow, and South. *H. Hammond, Ph.D. 1950 Cambridge*

Bartas, Guillaume de Salluste du
Du Bartas et la bible. *C. Chadwick, M.A. 1949 Liverpool*

Du Bartas in his relation to English literature, with special reference to Milton. *F. M. Mosley, M.A. 1916 London*

Barth, Karl
The controversy between Karl Barth and Emil Brunner concerning natural theology. *J. Henderson, Ph.D. 1940 Edinburgh*

The doctrine of sanctification in the theology of Karl Barth. *H. W. Tribble, Ph.D. 1937 Edinburgh*

The doctrine of the Word in relation to the Holy Scriptures as presented in the theology of Karl Barth. *J. Phillips, B.Litt. 1930 Oxford*

Karl Barth's conception of grace and its place in his theology. *H. Hirschwald, D.Phil. 1945 Oxford*

The message of Karl Barth in relation to Hinduism. *H. V. Martin, M.A. 1937 Bristol*

The relation of Karl Barth to the historic creeds and standards of the Church. *A. C. Cochrane, Ph.D. 1937 Edinburgh*

The relation of the doctrine of the Word of God to the doctrine of the *imago Dei*: a study in the theology of Karl Barth. *I. F. Morris, Ph.D. 1941 Edinburgh*

Bartholomew, Saint and Apostle
1. The Apostle Jude: is he to be identified with Jude the servant of Jesus Christ and brother of James? 2. SS. Philip, Bartholomew, Matthew, and Thomas: being an inquiry from New Testament records into the second group in the Apostolate. *A. C. Evans, B.D. 1901 Oxford*

Basel, Council of
See Roman Catholic Church.

Basil, Saint
A new edition of the Old English translation of the *Hexameron* of Basil (usually ascribed to Aelfric), with a collation of all the existing mss., and an introduction on the sources, authorship, and language of the translation. *S. J. Crawford, B.Litt. 1912 Oxford*

1. The relation of priest and prophet in the history of Israel before the exile. 2. St. Basil the Great and the monastic life. *E. F. Morison, B.D 1912 Oxford*

St. Basil's conception of Christian monasticism. *V. Pavlovitch, B.Litt. 1922 Oxford*

Basque Language
The Basque dialect of Manquina. *W. Rollo, D.Litt. 1929 Glasgow*

Benedict XIV, Pope
The contribution of Pope Benedict XIV to Church government, with special reference to the episcopate. *G. W. O. Addleshaw, B.D. 1935 Oxford*

Benedictine Order
See also Religious Orders and Societies; Cluniacs.

English Benedictines in the century preceding the dissolution, with special reference to their connexion with the universities and with learning. *W. D. Coates, B.Litt. 1931 Oxford*

Bengal
See also Saektas, The.

The administrative and judicial reforms of Lord Cornwallis in Bengal, 1786-1793, excluding the permanent settlement. *A. Aspinall, M.A. 1922 Manchester*

Bengal folk art. *A. Mukhopadhyay, M.A. 1941 London, School of Oriental and African Studies*

Culture-contact among the Plains Gars of eastern Bengal. *J. Basu, Ph.D. 1947 London, University College*

Development of social and political ideas in Bengal, 1858-84. *B. C. Bhattacharya, Ph.D. 1934 London, School of Oriental and African Studies*

An enquiry into the collections of the land revenue in Bengal, 1772-1774, from the appointment of the Committee of Circuit, May, 1772, until the introduction of the provisions of the Regulating Act, October, 1774. *R. B. Ramsbotham, B.Litt. 1924 Oxford*

Evolution of Bengal: an outline of its historical geography from the earliest times to the end of the Moslem period. . *N. N. Ghose, M.A. 1933 Liverpool*

The history of the occupation and rural administration of Bengal by the English Company from the time of Clive to the permanent settlement under Cornwallis. *W. K. Firminger, B.Litt. 1913 Oxford*

Human geography of Bengal. *A. Geddes, Ph.D. 1935 Edinburgh*

The influence of the home government on the development of the land revenue and judicial administration in the presidency of Fort William in Bengal from 1823 to 1840. *B. Mitra, M.A. 1936 London, School of Oriental and African Studies*

1. Some aspects of the economic consequences of the war for India. 2. The wealth and welfare of the Bengal Delta. *S. G. Panandikar, Ph.D. 1921 London*

Some historical aspects of the inscriptions of Bengal from the fifth to the twelfth century A.D. *B. Sen, Ph.D. 1933 London, School of Oriental and African Studies*

A study of the legal and administrative records of Dacca as illustrating the policy of Warren Hastings in East Bengal. *F. M. Sachse, B.Litt. 1934 Oxford*

The wealth and welfare of the Bengal delta. *S. G. Panandikar, D.Sc. 1926 London*

The working of the Bengal Legislative Council under the Government of India Act, 1919. . *J. G. Drummond, Ph.D. 1939 Cambridge*

Bengali Literature
See also Bankimçandra.

Changes in the status of women during the nineteenth century as reflected in Bengali literature. *J. Sen, Ph.D. 1924 London*

Benjamin b. Matisyahu, Rabbi
The *Responsa* of R. Benjamin (Ze'eb) ben Matisyahu: a contribution to the history of Jews in southern Europe at the end of the fifteenth and the beginning of the sixteenth centuries. *B. Joseph, Ph.D. 1942 London, University College*

Bennett, Enoch Arnold
A critical study of the novels of Arnold Bennett. *J. B. Simons, M.A. 1932 Wales*

The work of Arnold Bennett as a novelist. *A. E. C. Carter, M.A. 1927 Birmingham*

Bentham, Jeremy
The hedonism of Jeremy Bentham. *R. R. Bailey, Ph.D. 1938 London, University College*

The moral theory of Jeremy Bentham and William Paley. *P. Burne, M.A. 1948 London, Bedford College*

Bentinck, William Henry Cavendish, Lord
The social and administrative reforms of Lord William Bentinck. *G. Seed, Ph.D. 1949 Saint Andrew's*

Benzene
The development of the theory of substitution in the benzene nucleus, 1875-1923. *J. R. Pickering, M.Sc. 1929 London*

Beowulf
The Anglo-Saxon epic as exemplified by *Beowulf* considered in the light of the Indian epic *Rāmayana*. *I. S. Peter, Ph.D. 1930 London, King's College*

Berbers, The
Medicine among the Berbers of the Aurés. *M. W. Hilton-Simpson, B.Sc. 1921 Oxford*

Berceo, Gonzalo de
Grammar and vocabulary of the works of Gonzalo de Berceo. *M. Ephgrave, Ph.D. 1935 Leeds*

Berdyaev, Nikolai
Introduction to Berdyaev. *O. F. Clarke, B.D. 1950 Oxford*

Bergson, Henri Louis
An experimental investigation of memory of school children, with special reference to Bergson's theory. *R. K. Sur, M.Ed. 1929 Leeds*

Intuition in Bergson's philosophy. *M. Sheil, M.A. 1931 National University of Ireland*

L'influence de la philosophie de Bergson sur l'oeuvre littéraire de Marcel Proust. *E. K. McCann, M.A. 1933 Liverpool*

The method of metaphysics according to Bergson. *D. Corkery, M.A. 1937 National University of Ireland*

The philosophy of Henri Bergson. *J. McK. Stewart, D.Phil. 1911 Edinburgh*

The philosophy of M. Bergson, with special reference to his theory of knowledge. *D. J. Williams, M.A. 1916 Wales*

The philosophy of Schopenhauer in relation to pragmatism, with some reference to the history of Bergson. *M. Valiuddin, Ph.D. 1927 London*

The reality of extra-intellectual knowledge, with special reference to Bergson and pragmatism. *D. Richardson, M.A. 1917 Wales*

Rinn an bheatha: gur féidir áirdeagnufocht a bheith ann, á thagairt go speisialta do M. Bergson (The apex of life). *D. Corkery, Ph.D. 1944 National University of Ireland*

Berkeley, George, Bishop
Berkeley and Malebranche. *A. A. Luce, Litt.D. 1943 Dublin, Trinity College*

Berkeley's argument against Newtonian mathematics and its metaphysical implications. *A. E. Best, Ph.D. 1948 London, King's College*

A comparison of the philosophical system of Leibniz and Berkeley. *D. M. Sen, Ph.D. 1928 London*

A comparison of the philosophic systems of Malebranche and Berkeley. *V. S. Jha, Ph.D. 1927 London*

The conception of the self in Locke, Berkeley and Hume. *M. P. Evans, M.A. 1934 Wales*

Empiricism: a critical examination of the empirical theory of knowledge as this is expounded in certain of the works of Locke and Berkeley. *G. H. Haydock, Ph.D. 1946 Glasgow*

The ethical and social doctrines of Bishop Berkeley. *S. Azeemullah, M.A. 1924 London*

The idealism of Berkeley. *T. Crowley, M.A. 1945 National University of Ireland*

The idealism of Collier and Berkeley. *B. Thakur, Ph.D. 1937 London, University College*

The philosophical positions of Malebranche and Berkeley. *M. Ross, M.A. 1920 London*

A study of Berkeley's exposition of his new principle, from the *Commonplace book* to the second edition of the *Principles of human knowledge* (1734). *J. A. Davies, B. Litt. 1938 Oxford*

The theory of universals, with special reference to Locke, Berkeley and Hume. *O. R. Davies, M.A. 1937 Wales*

Berkenhead, John, Sir
A study of the life and works of Sir John Berkenhead. *S. P. Whitaker, M.A. 1915 London*

Berkshire
The geography of Berkshire, with special reference to agriculture. *J. Stephenson, M.A. 1936 London, School of Economics and Political Science*

Judicial proceedings under the Dictum of Kenilworth, East Berkshire. *A. L. Gregory, M.A. 1927 Manchester*

The judicial proceedings under the Dictum of Kenilworth, West Berkshire. *E. Roberts, M.A. 1927 Manchester*

The unrest in rural England in 1830, with special reference to Berkshire. *N. Gash, B.Litt. 1934 Oxford*

Berlin
Studies in the development of the Berlin salons during 1800-1820. *R. Beck, Ph.D. 1928 London*

Berlin, Conference of
The Berlin West African Conference 1884-5. *S. E. Crowe, Ph.D. 1940 Cambridge*

Berlioz, Hector
Shakespeare dans la vie et l'oeuvre de Hector Berlioz. *B. Spencer, M.A. 1936 Leeds*

Bermuda
The economic history of Bermuda in the nineteenth century. *M. R. E. Wright, M.A. 1928 Bristol*

Bernard, Charles de
La langue de Charles de Bernard. *R. Wright, M.A. 1927 Leeds*

Bernard, Jean Jacques
La 'théorie du silence' au théâtre et l'oeuvre dramatique de Jean-Jacques Bernard. *E. Marsh, M.A. 1933 Birmingham*

Bernard, Saint
The ecclesiastical relations of the reign of Stephen, with special reference to St. Bernard and the Cistercian reforming party, 1135-1154. *M. I. Megaw, M.A. 1939 Belfast*

The relations between Abelard and St. Bernard. *A. V. Murray, B.Litt. 1930 Oxford*

Bernoulli, Johann
The development of mathematical notation from Wallis to John Bernoulli. *W. Howells, Ph.D. 1933 London, External Degree*

Berthollet, Claude Louis, Comte
The controversy between Proust and Berthollet on the invariability of chemical proportions. *L. F. R. Simmonds, M.Sc. 1931 London*

Studies in the chemical work of Claude Louis Berthollet (1748-1822). *C. Ross, M.Sc. 1934 London, University College*

Bertran de Born
Word order in Old Provençal, with special reference to Flamenca and the poems of Bertran de Born. *R. J. Hilton, B.Litt. 1938 Oxford*

Bertrand de Bar-sur-Aube
Characterisation in the *Chanson de Geste* of *Girart de Vienne*, by Bertrand de Bar-sur-Aube. *K. Robinson, M.A. 1937 London, Royal Holloway College*

Bestrafte Untreue
See Minnesingers.

Bete, The
The Betes. *C. J. Pleass, Dip. Anthropology. 1928 Cambridge*

Beust, Friedrick Ferdinand von, Count
Count Beust: a study in lost causes. *J. F. Embling, M.A. 1934 Bristol*

Bevis of Hamton
Ystorya *Bown o Hamtwn*. *M. Watkin, M.A. 1913 Wales*

Beyle, Marie Henri
See Stendhal.

Bhagavad-gîtã
See Sanskrit Literature.

Bhāgavata Purāna
Some philosophical problems in the *Bhagavata Purāna*. *S. Bhattacharya, Ph.D. 1947 London, School of Oriental and African Studies*

Bhakti
See Hinduism.

Bhavabhūti
A critical edition of Bhava-bhuti's drama *Mahā-vira-caritam*. *T. Mall, B.Litt. 1914 Oxford*

Bhopal
A survey of the resources of tanning materials and the leather industry of Bhopal State, India. *G. W. Douglas, M.Sc. 1935 Leeds*

Bialik, Chaim Nachman
Jehuda Halevi and Chaim Nachman Bialik. *M. Ish-Shalom, Ph.D. 1938 London, School of Oriental and African Studies*

Bible: General
See also Apocalyptic Literature.

1.The doctrine of the atonement. 2. Inspiration. *L. J. G. D. Dowdall, B.D. 1881 Oxford*

1. The atonement. 2. The inspiration of the Scriptures. *R. W. Hiley, B.D. & D.D. 1885 Oxford*

1. The canon of Scripture. 2. The Church. *J. Chapelhow, B.D. 1876 Oxford*

1. The doctrine of immortality in the Old Testament. 2. Development of the doctrine of the fatherhood of God in the Old and New Testaments. *G. H. B. Wright, B.D. 1891 Oxford*

Bible: General contd.

Exegeses of the fall: Genesis iii.1-6; the atonement: Hebrews ix.11-14; the inspiration of Holy Scripture: II Timothy iii. 15-17. *F. W. Quilter, D.D. 1872 Oxford*

1. Genesis i, ii.1-7, iii.17-19; Psalm xix.1-3, xcv.3-7: evolution and providence. 2. St. Mark ix.48; St. John iii.36: eternal justice. 3. Genesis iii.1-10; Romans vii.18,19: will in Christian ethics. *A. J. Nilson, D.D. 1885 Oxford*

1. Genesis iv.2; Hebrews xi.4; xii.24: Abel's sacrifice. 2. St. Matthew xxvii.5-7; Romans vi.9: the Resurrection of Jesus and its effect on believers. 3. Romans viii.1-4, 14-17, 29-39: the work of the Holy Spirit. *H. T. Beebe, D.D. 1893 Oxford*

The idea of the fear of God in the Old and New Testaments. *T. J. Lander, M.A. 1938 Bristol*

The idea of witness-bearing in the Old and New Testaments. *I. G. M. Richards, M.A. 1948 Manchester*

1. Inspiration. 2. Apostolic succession of the Christian ministry. *G. Golding-Bird, B.D. & D.D. 1912 Oxford*

The land of Israel as an idea and ideal in Biblical literature. *A. Pimontel, M.A. 1937 Manchester*

1. The purpose of the Epistle to St. James. 2. The Church and Scripture. *J. J. Hannah, B.D. & D.D. 1909 Oxford*

1. The relation of the Old to the New Testament 2. The Kingdom of God. *J. C. Corlette, B.D. & D.D. 1879 Oxford*

The relation to the Old Testament of the synoptic teaching of Jesus, with some comparison of the attitude shown in the Epistles of Paul and in the Epistle to the Hebrews. *J. R. Bucher, Ph.D. 1940 Edinburgh*

1. Revelation and inspiration. 2. Christ incarnate, the reconciler and restorer of fallen man. *R. J. Wilson, B.D. & D.D. 1894 Oxford*

A study of the idea of the verbal inspiration of the Scriptures with special reference to the reformers and post-reformation thinkers of the sixteenth and seventeenth centuries. *A. A. Zaun, Ph.D. 1937 Edinburgh*

1. Verifications of Scripture from Egypt and the Holy Land. 2. The perpetual obligation of the Sabbath. *W. Allan, B.D. & D.D. 1892 Oxford*

1. The witness of the New Testament to the inspiration of the Old Testament. 2. The theology of the Epistle to the Hebrews compared with that of St. John's Gospel. *E. J. Haynes, B.D. 1900 Oxford*

Bible: Criticism and Exegesis

The biblical theology of St. Irenaeus. *J. Lawson, B.D. 1949 Cambridge*

The Antiochene exegesis of Holy Scripture up to the Council of Chalcedon. *H. E. W. Turner, B.D. 1940 Oxford*

Biblical commentators of the twelfth and thirteenth centuries, viewed as historical material, with special reference to the commentaries of Stephen Langton. *B. Smalley, Ph.D. 1929 Manchester*

Calvin's doctrine of Holy Scripture. *E. H. Pruden, Ph.D. 1931 Edinburgh*

A critical investigation into the relationship of the hermeneutical rules of the Halakah to those of the Hagadah. *D. Weisz, M.A. 1948 Manchester*

The history of the doctrine of scripture up to the Reformation. *F. J. Lambert, Ph.D. 1943 London, External Degree*

1. The influence of critical theory on the interpretation and authority of Holy Scripture. 2. Apostolic discipline as illustrated by St. Paul's epistles to the Corinthians. *H. H. Henson, B.D. 1897 Oxford*

John the Baptist and his disciples in Patristic theology: a short study in ancient Scriptural exegesis. *H. F. D. Sparks, B.D. 1937 Oxford*

1. The meaning of criticism, with special reference to the higher criticism of the Pentateuch. 2. The divine purpose in Hebrew religion. *D. C. Simpson, B.D. 1919 Oxford*

The principles of Christian hermeneutics studied in its chief varieties. *G. King, Ph.D. 1928 London*

Bible: Versions

An Aramaic approach to the Gospels and Acts. *M. Black, D.Litt. 1944 Glasgow*

The British Museum manuscript Arundel 230, with particular reference to the Psalms, and the *Livre des créatures*. *S. Bullett, M.A. 1910 London*

The Caesarean text *inter pares*. *J. E. M. Baikie, M.Litt. 1935 Cambridge*

Bible: Versions contd.

Codex Climaci rescriptus graecus. *I. A. Moir, Ph.D. 1943 Cambridge*

A commentary on the Book of Joshua, with a translation on the basis of Massoretic text and the Septuagint Version. *A. C. Anderson, Ph.D. 1943 Dublin, Trinity College*

A comparison of the grammar and vocabulary of the Aramaic portions of the Old Testament with those of the Aramaic papyri and inscriptions. *H. H. Rowley, B.Litt. 1928 Oxford*

A critical edition of the Ethiopic text of Canticles. *H. C. Gleave, B.Litt. 1948 Oxford*

A critical examination of the two main versions of the Book of Job by Bishops Morgan and Parry, with special reference to the Hebraisms in these versions, together with a new translation of the book into idiomatic Welsh. *L. E. Valentine, M.A. 1921 Wales*

A critical study of the *Peshitta* text of Psalms, books III and IV (Psalms 73-106), in relation to the Massoretic text and the Septuagint version. *E. R. Rowlands, M.A. 1939 Wales*

A critical study of the spellings of the two oldest French Psalters: 1. The Oxford, or Montebourg Psalter, 2. The Cambridge, or Canterbury Psalter. *B. L. Howarth, M.A. 1936 Manchester*

The development and sources of the Authorized Version of the English Bible. *D. Daiches, D.Phil. 1939 Oxford*

1. Doctrinal effect of the Vulgate text. 2. Original righteousness, as conceived by the Fathers, Schoolmen, and Reformers. *H. J. White, B.D. & D.D. 1918 Oxford*

An edition of the Pauline Epistles contained in ms. Parker 32, Corpus Christi College, Cambridge. *M. J. Powell, M.A. 1914 London*

An edition of the Salisbury Psalter (Salisbury ms. 150), with introduction and critical notes. *K. Sisam, B.Litt. 1915 Oxford*

An examination of the Munich and Wurtzburg fragments of the old Latin Pentateuch. *A. V. Billen, Ph.D. 1923 London*

Fragments of Gospels and pseudo-Gospels in medieval Welsh. *J. Jenkins, B.Litt. 1919 Oxford*

The Gospel according to St. Matthew: *The Clarendon Bible*, Clarendon press, 1936. *F. W. Green, B.D. 1944 Oxford*

The Greek versions of Esther. *H. J. Cook, M.A. 1948 Birmingham*

Heresies of William Tyndale: a thesis. *H. W. Callow, M.A. 1911 Liverpool*

The history and importance of the Latin versions of the Gospels in the light of modern criticism. *E. Powell, M.A. 1948 Leeds*

History of the Vulgate in England from Alcuin to Roger Bacon. *H. H. Glun, Ph.D. 1932 Cambridge*

Illustrations of the form, grammar, and language of the Epistle of St. Paul to the Romans. *M. L. Smith, B.D. & D.D. 1913 Oxford*

An index significationum to the Anglo-Saxon gloss to the Lindisfarne Gospels. *B. Hill, M.A. 1949 Birmingham*

An index verborum to the Lindisfarne Gospels. *D. E. Chadwick, M.A. 1934 Leeds*

The Latin text of the Johannine epistles, with special reference to the Spanish family. *A. W. Adams, B.D. 1950 Oxford*

The letters of Aristeas in relation to the Biblical and Apocryphal writings. *H. G. Meecham, Ph.D. 1929 Manchester*

A literary study of the Doway Bible. *L. T. Reynolds, Ph.D. 1939 National University of Ireland*

Literary study of the Doway Bible. *L. T. Reynolds, M.A. 1935 National University of Ireland*

Luther's translation of the Bible in the light of humanistic scholarship. *W. Schwarz, Ph.D. 1949 London, University College*

A Middle German Apocalypse edited from the manuscript British Museum, add. 15243. *A. T. Hatto, M.A. 1934 London, King's College*

A new edition of the Old English translation of the *Hexameron* of Basil (usually ascribed to Aelfric), with a collation of all the existing mss., and an introduction on the sources, authorship, and language of the translation. *S. J. Crawford, B.Litt. 1912 Oxford*

A new translation of the Book of Psalms from Hebrew into Amharic. *M. Gregory, B.Litt. 1936 Oxford*

Bible: Versions contd.

1. On the Septuagint. 2. On the doctrine of the Holy Trinity. *F. J. Bryant, B.D. & D.D. 1886 Oxford*

The phonology and accidence of the O.E. glosses in ms. Cotton Vespasian A1 (Vespasian Psalter). *E. V. Williams, B.Litt. 1935 Oxford*

The phonology and morphology of the Rushworth Gospels, known as Rushworth 1. *M. H. Scargill, Ph.D. 1940 Leeds*

A preparation for an edition of a critical text of selected chapters of the Syriac version of Ecclesiasticus. *W. D. McHardy, D.Phil. 1943 Oxford*

The prepositions of the New Testament, with illustrations from the papyri. *A. M. Hunter, Ph.D. 1934 Glasgow*

1. The Rabbinic literature as an aid to the lexicography of the Hebrew bible. 2. Arabisms in Rabbinic literature. *A. Cohen, Ph.D. 1923 London*

Reconstruction of the Old-Latin text or texts of the Gospels used by Saint Augustine, with a study of their character. *C. H. Milne, D.Litt. 1926 Aberdeen*

Semitisms in the New Testament in the light of later popular Greek. *R. McKinlay, Ph.D. 1927 Glasgow*

Studies in the language of the Lindisfarne Gospels. *L. Blakeley, Ph.D. 1949 Birmingham*

Studies in the morphology and syntax of the Vespasian Psalter. *R. Roberts, Ph.D. 1934 Leeds*

A study of the Middle English prose Psalter of Richard Rolle of Hampole. *D. Everett, M.A. 1920 London*

The syntax of New Testament compared with Attic Greek. *W. P. Jones, M.A. 1902 Wales*

The syntax of the New Testament compared with Attic Greek. *T. Evans, M.A. 1903 Wales*

Tatian's *Diatessaron*: introductory studies, with a portion of the Arabic version. *A. J. B. Higgins, Ph.D. 1945 Manchester*

The text of *Codex Cenannensis. G. O. Simms, Ph.D. 1950 Dublin, Trinity College*

The text of the Septuagint: its corruptions and their emendation. *W. P. M. Katz, Ph.D. 1945 Cambridge*

The three Welsh versions of the New Testament 1567, 1588, and 1620, critically compared, with special reference to the Greek original, the Latin Vulgate and the English version. *W. M. R. Davies, M.A. 1910 Wales*

The usage and influence of the Psalter in Middle and Early Modern English with special reference to the Penitential Psalms. *F. Halsey, M.A. 1933 London, King's College*

Vocalisation of the proper names in the Pentateuch according to a Syriac manuscript, Add. 12138, in the British Museum. *J. Wood, M.A. 1940 Manchester*

Bible: The Bible in Literature

Bacon's knowledge and use of the Bible. *P. D. P. H. de E. Cole, D.Phil. 1950 Oxford*

Bourdaloue and the Bible. *M. H. O'Donovan, M.A. 1926 London*

Du Bartas et la bible. *C. Chadwick, M.A. 1949 Liverpool*

The influence of the Bible in English literature of the nineteenth century. *I. M. Lloyd, M.A. 1920 Wales*

The influence of the Bible on the work of Paul Claudel. *A. M. White, Ph.D. 1932 London, Westfield College*

The influence of the Bible on English literature of the seventeenth century. *J. C. Stevenson, M.A. 1914 Birmingham*

A study of the influence of the Bible on the life and literature of Scotland in the seventeenth century. *D. Anderson, Ph.D. 1932 Glasgow*

Bible: Old Testament: General

Blood relationships of the Old Testament. *D. Jacobson, Ph.D. 1936 Cambridge*

A brief sketch of the Hebrew conception of man in the Old Testament. *D. J. Jenkins, M.A. 1937 Wales*

The conception of bliss in the Old Testament. *L. M. Jones, M.A. 1941 Wales*

Conception of reward and punishment in the Tannaitic Midrash (Mekiltah, Sifra and Sifre). *A. Melinek, Ph.D. 1944 London, Jews' College*

The conditions of labour in Israel as portrayed in the Old Testament and the Mishnah. *G. J. Roberts, M.A. 1936 Wales*

Bible: Old Testament: General contd.

1. Deuteronomy xviii.9-22: inspiration and prophecy. 2. Isaiah vi and xxi.1-10: the prophetic call, audition, and vision. I Corinthians xii-xiv: the psychology of Christian prophecy, introductory to tongues and prophecy in the Corinthian Church. *G. C. Joyce, D.D. 1909 Oxford*

1. The doctrine of immortality in the Old Testament. 2. Development of the doctrine of the fatherhood of God in the Old and New Testaments. *G. H. B. Wright, B.D. 1891 Oxford*

1. The doctrine of the future life in the Old Testament. 2. The origin of Hebrew prophecy. *J. Robertson, B.D. and D.D. 1897 Oxford*

The effect of modern criticism upon the cultural and religious values of the Old Testament. *J. E. K. Haddick, Ph.D. 1946 Dublin, Trinity College*

Ethical monotheism in Israel before Amos. *L. P. Penn, B.D. & D.D. 1924 Oxford*

Exegeses of: Deuteronomy xviii.15; Zechariah xiii.7; St.Matthew xix.17. *G. R. Price, D.D. & B.D. 1880 Oxford*

Exegeses of: I Samuel xiii.7-25 (The witch of Endor); Psalm xviii.7-17 (David's song of deliverance); Zechariah i.8,9,10; St. Matthew xvii.10, etc. (The guardianship of angels). *T. A. Blyth, D.D. 1892 Oxford*

Exegeses of: Numbers xxii; Daniel v; Acts vii. *W. D. Springett, D.D. 1888 Oxford*

Expositions of Psalms vii.4-6; Revelation xxii.1, 2; Isaiah xlix.23. *W. H. Hutton, D.D. 1919 Oxford*

1. God's purposes with regard to the Gentile world, as foreshadowed in the Old Testament. 2. Eusebius as a Christian apologist. *M. F. Argles, B.D. 1881 Oxford*

1. The heavenly doctrine of St. Mark. 2. Our Lord's use of the Old Testament. *R. H. Taylor, B.D. 1895 Oxford*

1. The history of the canon of the Old Testament, together with the Mishna and Tosephta tractate *Yadaim*. 2. The Tosephta tractate *Aboda Zara*. *R. G. Finch, Ph.D. 1931 London, External Degree*

1. Isaiah lii.13-liii.12: the servant of the Lord. 2. Genesis xv; xvii; Exodus xx and other connected passages in Deuteronomy and Jeremiah: the covenant in Israel. 3. Ezekiel xxxiii-xxxix: the new age: Israel restored. *G. A. Cooke, D.D. 1909 Oxford*

Jahweh, the God of love: a study in Old Testament theology. *R. M. Perry, Ph.D. 1937 Edinburgh*

1. The meaning of the word κύριοσ in the Septuagint and in the New Testament. 2. The prophet of Israel in his relation to God. *A. Ashton, B.D. 1909 Oxford*

1. The Old Testament: a progressive revelation of the divine character. 2. The miraculous element in the Gospels. *J. J. Turpin, B.D. 1908 Oxford*

1. The Old Testament an essential part of the revelation of God. 2. On the Epistle to the Ephesians. *W. Lock, B.D. & D.D. 1896 Oxford*

The Old Testament and the future life. *E. W. Toms, M.A. 1925 Wales*

1. The Old Testament in the light of the Egyptian monuments. 2. Natural science as it affects scriptural truth. *A. E. B. Day, B.D. 1908 Oxford*

The Old Testament morality. *G. C. Glanville, B.Litt. 1937 Oxford*

Peshat (plain exegesis) in Talmudic and Midrashic literature. *I. Frankel, Ph.D. 1949 Dublin, Trinity College*

The place of the prophet in Talmud and Midrashic literature. *S. Sperber, M.A. 1945 Manchester*

The problem of suffering in the Old Testament. *J. James, M.A. 1941 Wales*

The relations of Egypt and Syria-Palestine, with special reference to Old Testament history. *D. C. Davies, M.A. 1923 Liverpool*

The 'servant' idea in the Old Testament: its origin, its development and influence upon the Israelitish nation, with an enquiry into an alleged similar conception among other nations. *R. J. Pritchard, M.A. 1930 Wales*

The singing guilds in the Old Testament. *A. Morton, Ph.D. 1944 Saint Andrew's*

Slavery in ancient Mesopotamia and its bearing on the Old Testament. *I. Rapaport, M.A. 1939 London, King's College*

Some conceptions of Sheol: a study in Old Testament eschatology. *J. W. Swarbrick, M.A. 1922 Manchester*

Bible: Old Testament: General contd.

1. The tradition, chronology, and prophecy of the Old Testament coincident with the history of the world. 2. The infinite Creator of immortal man. *H. T. Craig, B.D. 1886 Oxford*

1. The typical significance of the history of the children of Israel. 2. The teaching of St. Paul with regard to the Holy Spirit. *W. S. Milne, B.D. 1889 Oxford*

1. The use and importance of the Old Testament in the first two centuries. 2. The first Epistle of Clement critically and dogmatically examined, with special reference to the Old Testament. *J. H. Webb, B.D. & D.D. 1907 Oxford*

1. Use of the Old Testament in the primitive Christian apologetic. 2. Examination of the speeches in the Acts of the Apostles with reference to this apologetic. *W. M. Pryke, B.D. 1916 Oxford*

1. The value of the theory of accommodation as applied to moral difficulties in the Old Testament. 2. The place of miracles among the evidences for Christianity. *P. A. Wright-Henderson, B.D. & D.D. 1903 Oxford*

Weapons and conduct of Hebrew warfare as illustrated in the Old Testament. *W. Davies, M.A. 1929 Wales*

1. The witness of the Old Testament to the immanence of God in nature and in man. 2. The theology of the Pastoral Epistle. *W. H. Fremantle, B.D. & D.D. 1895 Oxford*

Bible: Old Testament: Pentateuch

See also Creation and the Fall; Jewish Law; Judaism.

The blessings of Moses in post-Biblical Jewish literature: Targum versions considered and compared with the Talmud, Midrash and medieval commentators down to Abrabanel, as well as with those of Moses Mendelsohhn and Malbim. *R. H. Levy, M.A. 1945 Manchester*

The Book of the Covenant (Ex.xx.22-xxiii.33): a new appreciation. *J. B. Allan, Ph.D. 1926 Edinburgh*

A commentary on: Genesis i.1; ii.8; vi.17. *J. H. Shackleton Bailey, D.D. 1923 Oxford*

The conception of the covenant in the thought of Israel prior to the exile. *D. B. Gordon, Ph.D. 1938 Edinburgh*

A critical examination of recent theories of the date of Deuteronomy. *D. A. Jones, M.A. 1943 Wales*

The date, structure and authorship of the Book of Deuteronomy. *T. W. Chance, M.A. 1900 Wales*

The early Syrian Fathers on Genesis from a Syrian manuscript on the Pentateuch in the Mingana collections. *A. Levene, Ph.D. 1936 London, External Degree*

An edition of: Midrash *Haggadol* to the first five chapters of Numbers. *S. Fisch, M.A. 1933 Manchester*

Exegeses of: Genesis xii.4; xv.12; Romans iv.16,17. *F. W. Bussell, D.D. 1897 Oxford*

Exegeses of: St. John xvi.8; xvi.10; Exodus xxxiv.7. *W. R. Fremantle, B.D. & D.D. 1876 Oxford*

The exegesis of Rashi, with reference to his commentary on the Pentateuch. *H. C. R. Eltoft, M.A. 1927 Manchester*

Expositions: Exodus xxiv.9-11; St.Luke xxii.17-20; Romans v.19. *H. E. D. Blakiston, D.D. 1907 Oxford*

Expositions of: Genesis iii: the doctrine of the Fall; Ephesians iv.1-16: the unity of the Church and the functions of its ministers; I Corinthians xi.18-34. *T. H. D. Long, D.D. 1909 Oxford*

Expositions of: I Corinthians xv.29; I St. Peter iii.18-20; Genesis xlix.10. *H. Pinchin, D.D. 1899 Oxford*

Expositions of Genesis i,ii; Isaiah lii.15-liii; St. John i.1-18. *J. Barker, D.D. 1906 Oxford*

Expositions of Genesis i.1-2; Romans viii.14-16; Romans viii.22. *T. A. Branthwaite, D.D. 1907 Oxford*

Expositions of I Corinthians xv.20-58: the Resurrection; St.John iii.3-5; Genesis i: the Creation. *E. P. Lewis, D.D. 1904 Oxford*

Expositions of three selected passages from the Book of Leviticus. *E. F. Morison, D.D. 1916 Oxford*

Ezekiel and the law of holiness in Leviticus. *R. N. Edwards, M.A. 1921 Wales*

Bible: Old Testament: Pentateuch contd.

The fundamental ideas of the Holiness Code in relation to the prophetic teaching. *A. G. Fisk, Ph.D. 1930 Edinburgh*

The Halakah in Pseudojonathan on the Pentateuch (Part 1: Festivals and marriage laws). *E. Wiesenberg, Ph.D. 1952 London, Jews' College*

1. The historical and religious value of Genesis and its claim to be regarded as an inspired book. 2. Recent theories concerning the origin of life, and their probable effect upon religious thought and belief. *J. H. S. Bailey, B.D. 1913 Oxford*

The influence of Alfonso Tostado on the Pentateuch commentary of Abravanel. *S. I. Gaon, Ph.D. 1943 London, Jews' College*

The last days of Aaron according to the Midrash *Petirat Aharon*. *B. Fertleman, M.A. 1937 Manchester*

1. The meaning of criticism, with special reference to the higher criticism of the Pentateuch. 2. The divine purpose in Hebrew religion. *D. C. Simpson, B.D. 1919 Oxford*

The Midrash *Haggadol*, its authorship, its sources and its importance in Rabbinic literature. *S. Fisch, Ph.D. 1936 Manchester*

The religious institutions of the Hebrews and Jews referred to in the Hexateuch, studied in themselves and as they represent the development of religious conceptions. *R. O. Hughes, M.A. 1914 Wales*

1. The tree of the knowledge of good and evil. 2. Αἰώνιοσ: its meaning and use in the New Testament. *H. D. A. Major, B.D. 1916 Oxford*

1. The true interpretation of Genesis i. and ii.1-4. 2. The meaning of 'the generations of the heavens and the earth' in Genesis ii.4. *C. H. Waller, B.D. & D.D. 1891 Oxford*

Vocalisation of the proper names in the Pentateuch according to a Syriac manuscript, Add. 12138, in the British Museum. *J. Wood, M.A. 1940 Manchester*

Bible: Old Testament: Historical Books

The authenticity of the chronicler's account of the restoration of Israel in the light of Ezra and Nehemiah: a critical and historical study. *B. Maura, Ph.D. 1943 Edinburgh*

A critical and exegetical commentary on Mishnah tractate *Megillah*. *J. Rabbinowitz, Ph.D. 1930 Manchester*

A critical study of Abravanel's *Commentary on Kings*. *S. Kalisch, M.A. 1943 Manchester*

1. Early Christian missions in some of their relations to heathen religion. 2. The importance and function of the Book of Esther in the canon. *J. W. Williams, B.D. 1896 Oxford*

Exegeses of: Judges v.24; St. Luke i.15; Romans xvi.5. *J. Baron, B.D. & D.D. 1878 Oxford*

Expositions of: II Kings xxii: reforms of Josiah; Acts vii: the defence of Stephen; The Epistle to Philemon: St. Paul's treatment of slavery. *A. E. Joscelyne, D.D. 1898 Oxford*

Judges. *A. Earl, B.D. 1932 Cambridge*

The settlement of the Hebrews in Canaan. *M. J. C. Dinwoodie, Ph.D. 1936 Edinburgh*

Bible: Old Testament: Wisdom Books

Bohairic pericope of Wisdom and Sirach and Coptic Church Offices. *O. H. E. Burmester, Ph.D. 1933 Cambridge*

The Book of Job. *M. A. Jones, M.A. 1927 Birmingham*

1. The Christology of Clement of Alexandria. 2. The theology of the Wisdom literature. *R. B. Tollinton, B.D. 1905 Oxford*

A comparison of Hebrew and Chinese wisdom, as exemplified in the Book of Proverbs and the Analects of Confucius. *E. G. K. Hewat, Ph.D. 1934 Edinburgh*

The date and origin of Midrash psalms. *L. M. Sanker, Ph.D. 1944 London, Jews' College*

The doctrine of reward and retribution in the *Book of Proverbs*. *J. Kennedy, Ph.D. 1934 Glasgow*

1. The doctrine of the Paraclete as found in St. John xiv-xvi. 2. The preface to St. Luke's Gospel. 3. The authorship and date of Psalm cxix. *C. Knapp, D.D. 1906 Oxford*

1. The doctrine of the resurrection in the Book of Job. 2. The connection between free-will and eternal punishment. *J. T. Nance, B.D. 1881 Oxford*

1. Ecclesiastes. 2. The doctrine of the Resurrection. *T. Bramley, B.D. & D.D. 1890 Oxford*

Bible: New Testament: General contd.

Conversion: a comparison of the results formulated by recent American psychology of religion with the teaching and experience of the New Testament. *H. A. Gearhart, Ph.D. 1924 Edinburgh*

1. The date of St. Luke's Gospel and the Acts of the Apostles. 2. St. Paul's visits to Jerusalem recorded in the Acts and in the Epistle to the Galatians. *D. Walker, B.D. 1901 Oxford*

1. The doctrine of justification as set forth by St. Paul and St. James in their writings. 2. The evidence from the New Testament for the divinity of our Lord. *R. L. Langford-James, B.D. 1904 Oxford*

1. The doctrine of the Holy Trinity in the New Testament. 2. The authorship of the second Epistle of St. Peter. *S. Addleshaw, B.D. 1909 Oxford*

The doctrine of the parousia in Paul and the Synoptic Gospels. *E. Jones, B.Litt. 1924 Oxford*

The early history of the logos doctrine - the idea in Greek philosophy, with an appendix showing its relation to Hellenism, Judaism and the New Testament. *J. L. Matthews, Ph.D. 1936 London, New College*

1. The eschatology of the Gospels. 2. The authorship and destination of the Epistle to the Hebrews. *F. E. Austin, B.D. 1907 Oxford*

Exegeses of: II Corinthians iv.6-7; St. John xxi.24-25; Romans vii.7-25. *E. Moore, D.D. 1878 Oxford*

Exegeses of: John i.29-34; Philippians iv.4-9; I Timothy v.17-25. *G. C. Richards, D.D. 1924 Oxford*

Exegeses of: John iii.1-13; 14-21; I Corinthians xi.23-29. *L. St. A. Wright, D.D. 1924 Oxford*

Exegeses of: John xix.25-27; I Thessalonians ii.1-12; I Peter iii.18-20. *W. Baker, D.D. 1874 Oxford*

Exegeses of: John xx.17; Hebrews x.12-13; Romans viii.34. *A. R. H. Grant, D.D. 1924 Oxford*

Exegeses of: Judges v.24; St. Luke i.15; Romans xvi.5. *J. Baron, B.D. & D.D. 1878 Oxford*

Exegeses of: Revelation i.1-4; Romans iv.1-3; I Corinthians x.16. *F. A. Walker, D.D. 1883 Oxford*

Exegeses of: St. John vii.17; II Peter i.21; Romans iii.21-26. *F. R. Pentreath, D.D. 1878 Oxford*

Exegeses of: St.John i.4: Romans x.2; I Corinthians xv.14. *C. M. Style, D.D. 1880 Oxford*

Exegeses of: St. Matthew xiii.55; St. Matthew i.1; I Timothy ii.5. *H. D. Harper, B.D. & D.D. 1878 Oxford*

Exegeses of Acts xx.28; xvii.22-31; Ephesians iii.28. *W. K. Firminger, D.D. 1919 Oxford*

Exegeses of St. John xx.30,31; I John v.13; Acts vi.13,14. *T. W. Gilbert, D.D. 1923 Oxford*

Exegeses of St. Mark xvi.6,11; I Corinthians xv.8. *J. L. Phillips, D.D. 1920 Oxford*

Exegeses of St. Matthew xi.2-10; I Corinthians xii.31-xiii.13; Galatians iv.21-v.1. *T. H. Stokoe, D.D. 1871 Oxford*

An exposition of: Acts of the Apostles vii: Stephen's defence: Hebrews vii-ix: the heavenly priesthood of Christ: Romans viii, ix: St. Paul's doctrine of election. *R. H. Taylor, D.D. 1900 Oxford*

An exposition of: St. Luke xxiv.13-35; Acts vii.1-53 (St. Stephen's apology); the Epistle to Philemon. *B. Whitefoord, D.D. 1899 Oxford*

Expositions: Exodus xxiv.9-11; St.Luke xxii.17-20; Romans v.19. *H. E. D. Blakiston, D.D. 1907 Oxford*

Expositions of: Acts ii.42: the Christian fellowship; Acts xv.6: the ministry in the Apostolic age; St. John xvii.22: the prayer of the Lord that his Church might be one. *S. Baker, D.D. 1905 Oxford*

Expositions of: II Kings xxii: reforms of Josiah; Acts vii: the defence of Stephen; The Epistle to Philemon: St. Paul's treatment of slavery. *A. E. Joscelyne, D.D. 1898 Oxford*

Expositions of: St. Luke xii.42,43: the ministry, a stewardship; I Corinthians xii: the spiritual gifts of the Church; Romans ix.4: the Covenant or Church principle. *B. J. Kidd, D.D. 1904 Oxford*

Expositions of: St. Matthew i. and St. Luke ii; St. Luke xxiv.13-36; I Corinthians xv.29. *E. H. Day, D.D. 1905 Oxford*

Expositions of: St. Matthew iv.1-10; Acts vii.2-53; I Corinthians xiv.34,35; I Timothy ii.11-12. *H. G. Rosedale, D.D. 1901 Oxford*

Expositions of: St. Matthew v; St. Luke iv; Hebrews xi. *J. Darlington, D.D. 1904 Oxford*

Expositions of Acts xx.15-38: St. Paul's address to the elders at Miletus; Matthew iv.23: the Christ of eschatology; Hebrews i.1: The Epistle to Hebrews. *M. Jones, D.D. 1914 Oxford*

Expositions of Psalms xxxv, lxix, cix; Acts xvi.6, xviii.2-3; Romans viii.15-16. *W. J. S. Muntz, D.D. 1910 Oxford*

Expositions of Romans x-xi; Acts xviii.15-34; I Timothy iii and v. *C. Moor, D.D. 1908 Oxford*

Expositions of St. John i.1-18: the prologue; St. John xviii.33-38: within the praetorium; Ephesians i.1-14: the doctrine of grace. *H. T. Dixon, D.D. 1908 Oxford*

Expositions of St. Matthew iv.1-11: Christ's temptation; St. Luke xxii.39-44: the agony in Gethsemane; II Thessalonians ii.3-10: the second coming of Christ. *F. R. C. Bruce, D.D. 1908 Oxford*

1. The function of the prophets in Christian Church, as it may be gathered from the New Testament. 2. The Christian view of war. *J. G. Tetley, B.D. & D.D. 1901 Oxford*

The Hellenistic background of New Testament thought. *T. Harper, Ph.D. 1929 Glasgow*

How far is it true that the Christianity of the end of the second century is a departure from the teaching and ideals of the New Testament?. *R. N. Flew, B.D. 1925 Oxford*

Human personality as reflected in the psychology of the New Testament. *M. S. Pletcher, B.Litt. 1911 Oxford*

The idea of mediation as applied to Jesus Christ in the New Testament. *E. Cadvan-Jones, M.Litt. 1927 Cambridge*

The imperial policy of Claudius as reflected in the New Testament. *S. Liberty, B.D. & D.D. 1939 Oxford*

The influence of Jewish eschatology upon the New Testament. *T. E. Warner, B.Litt. 1939 Dublin, Trinity College*

1. The influence of the Apocrypha upon the language of the New Testament. 2. Paulinisms in the Epistle to the Hebrews, and their relationship to the problem of its authorship. *F. Streatfeild, B.D. 1916 Oxford*

An introduction to the literature of the New Testament. *J. Moffatt, D.Litt. 1911 Glasgow*

1. Justification by faith, as set forth in the writings of St. Paul. 2. Some New Testament evidences for the divinity of our Lord. *T. Lemmey, B.D. 1907 Oxford*

The kingdom of God in the apostolic writings. *A. M. F. Macinnes, Ph.D. 1922 Edinburgh*

1. The language in which our Lord taught. 2. Supposed quotations from the Apostolic liturgy in the New Testament. *G. H. Gwilliam, B.D. 1890 Oxford*

The laying on of hands in the New Testament and in Christian usage. *C. H. Scott, B.D. 1924 Oxford*

1. The meaning of the word κύριοσ in the Septuagint and in the New Testament. 2. The prophet of Israel in his relation to God. *A. Ashton, B.D. 1909 Oxford*

The miracles of healing in the New Testament in the light of modern psychological and psychotherapeutical research. *E. R. Micklem, B.Litt. 1921 Oxford*

The New Testament conception of δόξα. *C. B. Caird, D.Phil. 1944 Oxford*

The New Testament doctrine of perfection. *E. H. Williamson, Ph.D. 1935 Dublin, Trinity College*

New Testament eschatology in its bearing upon ethics. *E. H. Williamson, B.Litt. 1939 Dublin, Trinity College*

The New Testament idea of the Church: an historical study, with particular reference to its Hebrew and Jewish background. *M. H. Sykes, Ph.D. 1948 Manchester*

1. The New Testament teaching on the Second Advent considered in the light of subsequent history. 2. The relation of natural science to theology. *P. H. Lester, B.D. 1908 Oxford*

1. The place of the prophet in the New Testament. 2. The doctrine of the New Testament as to the moral aspect of war. *R. T. Talbot, B.D. & D.D. 1906 Oxford*

Bible: New Testament: General contd.

The priesthood of Christ, of Christians, and of the Christian ministry. 2. Public worship in the Christian Church, as described in or inferred from the New Testament. *W. D. Springett, B.D. 1880 Oxford*

1. The purpose of the Incarnation. 2. The kingdom of Christ in the New Testament. *C. L. Quibell, B.D. 1910 Oxford*

1. St. Luke xxii.14-20: the institution of the Eucharist. 2. I Corinthians xv.3-8: the witness of St. Paul to the resurrection. 3. I Corinthians xv.29: baptizing for the dead. *T. H. Davies, D.D. 1910 Oxford*

1. St. Paul's thorn in the flesh. 2. A critical examination of the use of φιλεῖν and αγαπαν in the New Testament with special reference to the exegesis of St. John xxi.15-17. *J. M. Lister, B.D. & D.D. 1899 Oxford*

The second advent: the origin of the New Testament doctrine. *T. F. Glasson, D.D. 1945 London, Richmond College*

The servant of the Lord: the influence of the Old Testament conception on the literature of the New Testament (with special reference to Isaiah lii.13-liii.12). *B. H. Sims, B.Litt. 1943 Oxford*

The source and implication of the New Testament quotations in the *Apologies* of Justin Martyr. *J. Pritchard, M.A. 1905 Wales*

Stephen: a study of his religious outlook and of its affinities in pre-Christian Jewish thought and in the New Testament. *R. Gardner, Ph.D. 1934 Saint Andrew's*

A study of the conception of life in the synoptic teaching of Jesus, and its development in the Pauline and Johannine writings. *B. S. Rude, Ph.D. 1938 Edinburgh*

A study of the New Testament sources for the life of Jesus. *E. D. Johnston, Ph.D. 1950 Manchester*

A systematic account of the ethical teaching of the New Testament. *L. H. Marshall, Ph.D. 1948 London, External Degree*

1. The theology of Justin Martyr. 2. Justin Martyr and the New Testament canon. *A. W. F. Blunt, B.D. 1918 Oxford*

The theory of the kenosis as based upon the New Testament. *J. A. Ford, Ph.D. 1928 Edinburgh*

1. The tree of the knowledge of good and evil. 2. Αἰώνιοσ: its meaning and use in the New Testament. *H. D. A. Major, B.D. 1916 Oxford*

1. The witness of the New Testament to the inspiration of the Old Testament. 2. The theology of the Epistle to the Hebrews compared with that of St. John's Gospel. *E. J. Haynes, B.D. 1900 Oxford*

1. The word σωμα in the New Testament. 2. The teaching of St. Paul's prayers. *A. J. Galpin, B.D. & D.D. 1910 Oxford*

Bible: New Testament: Gospels
See also Miracles; Parables.

The authority of Jesus and its foundation: an examination of the Gospels and the Book of Acts. *B. L. Woolf, Ph.D. 1926 Edinburgh*

1. The authorship of the Epistle to the Hebrews. 2. The authorship of the fourth Gospel as proved from internal evidence. *R. H. Morris, B.D. & D.D. 1884 Oxford*

The authorship of the Johannine literature. *J. C. West, B.D. 1926 Oxford*

1. The bearing of the Rabbinical criminal code on the Jewish trial narratives of the Gospels, with a translation of the *Mishnah* and *Tosefta* of the Tractate Sanhedrin. 2. An introduction to the homilies of Aphraates. *H. Danby, B.D. 1919 Oxford*

1. The Catholic Epistles in relation to the Gospels. 2. Some thoughts on Christian evidences and recent criticism. *R. J. Knowling, B.D. & D.D. 1896 Oxford*

1. Certain Jewish modes of thought and teaching: their influence on the form in which truth is presented in the Gospels. 2. How far and in what sense is it possible to maintain such a distinction as that implied in the phase 'essential doctrine'?. *A. E. Hillard, B.D. & D.D. 1907 Oxford*

1. The character and composition of the fourth Gospel. 2. The origin and authorship of the fourth Gospel. *R. G. Parsons, B.D. & D.D. 1924 Oxford*

1. The Christian's expectations of a palingenesis mundi finds valuable support from reason and science. 2. St.Luke xvi.9. *A. Malan, B.D. 1877 Oxford*

Bible: New Testament: Gospels contd.

1. On the divinity of Christ, as shown by his possession of the incommunicable attributes of God. 2. Internal evidence of the Johannine authorship of the fourth Gospel. *J. L. D. Smith-Dampier, B.D. 1905 Oxford*

1. On the Gospel of St. John. 2. On St. Augustine's treatise *De civitate dei*. *D. H. E. Keppel, B.D. 1906 Oxford*

1. On the import of the controversy respecting the historical character of the Gospels. 2. On the present state of the controversy. *H. Wace, B.D. 1882 Oxford*

1. The origin and characteristics of St. Mark's Gospel, and its relation to the other Synoptic Gospels. 2. The authorship, date, sources, and historical credibility of the Acts of the Apostles. *A. E. Rubie, B.D. & D.D. 1904 Oxford*

The origins of the Gospel according to St. Matthew. *G. D. Kilpatrick, B.D. 1944 Oxford*

1. Passages from the Gospels of St. Matthew and St. Mark in which Jesus enjoins 'silence'. 2. Examination of passages in which is recorded the impression made by Jesus on various classes of those who first listened to him. *A. A. David, B.D. & D.D. 1910 Oxford*

1. The political consciousness of the Marcan gospel. 2. The origins of Alexandrian Christianity. 3. The historical element in some ancient religions. *S. G. F. Brandon, D.D. 1943 Leeds*

Prayer and the four Gospels. *D. R. C. Morris, B.D. 1947 Oxford*

1. The primitive Church and its organization. 2. The kingdom of heaven in the Gospel of St. Matthew. *P. A. Micklem, B.D. & D.D. 1924 Oxford*

The problem of Mark: the sources, composition and historical value of St. Mark's Gospel. *E. L. Allen, Ph.D. 1923 London*

1. The problem of St. John's Gospel. 2. Personal immortality. *W. H. Rigg, B.D. & D.D. 1921 Oxford*

1. The providential preparation for the Church of Christ. 2. The revelation of the Church in the Gospels. *D. Stone, B.D. & D.D. 1909 Oxford*

1. The relation of the Church to the Gospels. 2. The external evidences for the Gospels in the second century. *G. F. Lovell, B.D. 1876 Oxford*

The relation of the Wisdom literature to the fourth Gospel. *H. E. Wylie, Ph.D. 1931 Edinburgh*

The relevance of the ethical teaching of Jesus to the conditions of this world order: an examination of the Sermon on the Mount. *W. R. F. Browning, B.D. 1948 Oxford*

The Resurrection in the New Testament. *H. R. Haworth, B.D. 1939 Leeds*

The Resurrection narratives. *T. J. Thorburn, D.D. 1911 Cambridge*

1. Romans iii.21-26: the doctrine of the atonement in St. Paul. 2. Romans iii.24-25; I Timothy ii.6: propitiation, redemption, reconciliation, ransom, justification. 3. Luke xvi.1-13: parable of the unrighteous steward. *F. S. G. Warman, D.D. 1911 Oxford*

St. John's Gospel vi.28-65, and the first Epistle of St. John, chapters i and iv. *W. M. Sinclair, D.D. 1892 Oxford*

1. St. Mark iv.26-29: the secret growth of the seed of the kingdom. 2. Revelation iv.4-11: the vision of the four-and-twenty elders, and the four living beings. 3. Revelation xx.1-8: the prophecy of the millennial reign. *H. E. Nolloth, B.D. 1894 Oxford*

1. St. Mark xiv.21 and viii.38: 'Son of Man' in the Synoptic Gospels. 2. St. Mark i.11; St. Luke iii.22: 'Son of God' in the Synoptic Gospels. 3. St. Matthew xi.18-19: Our Lord's attitude towards asceticism. *F. H. Dudden, D.D. 1907 Oxford*

the Semitic background of the Synoptics. *F. Bussby, B.D. 1947 Durham*

1. The Sermon on the Mount in light of today. 2. The Christian argument from the study of ethnology. *E. S. Chalk, B.D. 1921 Oxford*

1. The sources of St. Luke's Gospel. 2. St. Luke vi.20-49. 3. St. Luke xxi.1-xxii.20. *L. Ragg, D.D. 1923 Oxford*

The structure of the Gospel according to St. Mark approached from the standpoint of Formgeschichte, with a special consideration of (a) Mark ii.1.-iii.6 and (b) Mark xi.15-xii.40. *J. M. Morrison, B.Litt. 1934 Oxford*

A study of the person of Jesus Christ in the Synoptic Gospels. *L. Dezsö, Ph.D. 1930 Aberdeen*

Bible: New Testament: Gospels contd.

1. The teaching of Holy Scripture with regard to the nature and ministry of angels. 2. The teaching of the Gospel according to St. John on the person and work of the Holy Spirit. *H. G. Lainée, B.D. 1906 Oxford*

1. The teaching of the New Testament as to the divinity of our Lord and Saviour Jesus Christ. 2. The internal evidence as to the Johannine authorship of the fourth Gospel. *W. Slater, B.D. 1889 Oxford*

1. The testimony of St. Paul with regard to the resurrection of our Lord compared with that of the four Evangelists. 2. A study of the sterner side of the character of our Lord as evidenced in the narratives of the Evangelists. *A. W. Upcott, B.D. & D.D. 1906 Oxford*

To what extent do the discourses ascribed to Christ in the fourth Gospel preserve His own words?. *H. L. Jewett Williams, B.Litt. 1912 Oxford*

The transcendence of Jesus Christ: a study of the unique features of his person and work, with special reference to the fourth Gospel. *F. Cawley, Ph.D. 1934 Edinburgh*

The transition from the Synoptic to the Johannine version of the life and teaching of Jesus. *E. H. Woods, Ph.D. 1924 Edinburgh*

1. Varying treatment of the Pharisees in the Synoptic Gospels. 2. The theory of Christian almsgiving from the sub-Apostolic age to the Reformation. *C. T. Dimont, B.D. 1911 Oxford*

Bible: New Testament: Acts

The doctrine of the Holy Spirit in St. Luke and Acts. *J. B. Bernardin, B.Litt. 1925 Oxford*

1. The Acts and the Pauline Epistles. 2. The Epistle to the Romans. *C. W. Emmet, B.D. 1917 Oxford*

1. The approximate date of the Acts of the Apostles. 2. The descent into Hades. *T. H. Davies, B.D. 1905 Oxford*

The authority of Jesus and its foundation: an examination of the Gospels and the Book of Acts. *B. L. Woolf, Ph.D. 1926 Edinburgh*

A commentary on Acts xv.1-6; 6-12; 13-21. *H. Johnson, D.D. 1924 Oxford*

1. Eternal life in St. John's Gospel. 2. The leading ideas of the Acts of the Apostles. *T. W. Gilbert, B.D. 1912 Oxford*

Exegeses of: Acts xxvi.19-70; i.8; St.John xv.5. *P. W. N. Bourne, D.D. 1887 Oxford*

Exegeses of: Numbers xxii; Daniel v; Acts vii. *W. D. Springett, D.D. 1888 Oxford*

Exegeses of: St.Luke xxiv.21; Acts ii.3,4; St.John iii.5. *C. H. C. Baker, D.D. 1886 Oxford*

Expositions of: Acts ii.4: ἤρξαντο λαλεῖν ἑτέραισ γλώσσαισ; the gift of tongues; Romans iii.25: ὃν προέθετο ὁ θεὸσ ἱλαστήριον διὰ τησ πίστεωσ ἐν τω αυτου αἵματι: the meaning of ἱλαστήριον; Galatians iii.15: the legal terminology of the Epistle to the Galatians and its bearing on the question of the churches addressed by St. Paul. *D. Walker, D.D. 1904 Oxford*

Expositions of Acts i: the pre-Pentecostal Church; Acts ii-v.16: Pentecost and the first or Sadducee persecution; Acts v.17-vi. *T. S. Lea, D.D. 1910 Oxford*

The gift of the spirit in the New Testament, with special reference to Glossolalia. *M. Barnett, M.A. 1946 Manchester*

1. The interpretation of the Acts, with especial reference to Professor Ramsay's South Galatian theory. 2. Our Lord's use of π÷στισ. *H. K. Moore, B.D. & D.D. 1898 Oxford*

1. On the creed in the Acts. 2. On the appointment of rites and ceremonies in the Church. *A. L. Oldham, B.D. & D.D. 1905 Oxford*

1. On the organization of the early Church as exhibited in the Acts of the Apostles and the Pauline Epistles. 2. On the right and wrong use of the doctrine of predestination. *M. Argles, B.D. & D.D. 1891 Oxford*

1. The origin and characteristics of St. Mark's Gospel, and its relation to the other Synoptic Gospels. 2. The authorship, date, sources, and historical credibility of the Acts of the Apostles. *A. E. Rubie, B.D. & D.D. 1904 Oxford*

1. Use of the Old Testament in the primitive Christian apologetic. 2. Examination of the speeches in the Acts of the Apostles with reference to this apologetic. *W. M. Pryke, B.D. 1916 Oxford*

Bible: New Testament: Epistles

1. The Acts and the Pauline Epistles. 2. The Epistle to the Romans. *C. W. Emmet, B.D. 1917 Oxford*

1. Although the eternal power and divinity of the Creator may be learnt by reason, yet man in his present condition needs the aid of revelation to enlighten him respecting the duties of religion. 2. St. Paul is the author of the two Epistles to the Thessalonians. *J. G. Cazenove, B.D. & D.D. 1874 Oxford*

1. The authenticity of the Epistle of St. James. 2. Our Lord's brethren. *H. Maynard-Smith, B.D. & D.D. 1923 Oxford*

The authorship and authenticity of the Johannine Epistles. *S. G. Lencz, Ph.D. 1933 Aberdeen*

1. The authorship of the Epistle to the Hebrews. 2. The Christian ministry in the New Testament. *M. B. Hutchison, B.D. & D.D. 1905 Oxford*

1. The authorship of the Epistle to the Hebrews. 2. The authorship of the fourth Gospel as proved from internal evidence. *R. H. Morris, B.D. & D.D. 1884 Oxford*

1. The authorship of the Epistle to the Hebrews. 2. Galatians iii. 20. *T. W. Jex-Blake, B.D. & D.D. 1873 Oxford*

The authorship of the Johannine literature. *J. C. West, B.D. 1926 Oxford*

1. The authorship of the Pastoral Epistles. 2. The controversies dealt with in the Pastoral Epistles. *W. Leeman, B.D. & D.D. 1915 Oxford*

1. The Catholic Epistles in relation to the Gospels. 2. Some thoughts on Christian evidences and recent criticism. *R. J. Knowling, B.D. & D.D. 1896 Oxford*

1. Christ the representative man. 2. The Epistle of St. Paul the Apostle to the Ephesians. *M. J. Powell, B.D. & D.D. 1907 Oxford*

1. The Christian use of the Old Testament Apocrypha. 2. Some aspects of the value to the Church of St. Paul's first Epistle to the Corinthians. *J. E. Stocks, B.D. & D.D. 1909 Oxford*

1. The Church in the Epistle to the Ephesians. 2. The Christ of the fourth Gospel. *J. L. Phillips, B.D. 1913 Oxford*

A commentary on Philippians ii.5-11; Colossians i.13-19; Hebrews i.1-3. *T. A. Chapman, D.D. 1924 Oxford*

A commentary on Romans vi.1-4; Mark ix.44,46,48. *W. R. Cosens, B.D. & D.D. 1872 Oxford*

A commentary on St. John xvi.7; 8-11; I Corinthians xii.8-11. *T. Lemmey, D.D. 1924 Oxford*

A commentary on the Epistle to the Hebrews. *F. D. V. Narborough, B.D. 1931 Oxford*

1. The communion of saints. 2. The authorship of the Pastoral Epistles. *T. Randall, B.D. 1889 Oxford*

1. Comparison of the teaching of St. Paul and St. James as to faith and works. 2. The consideration of St. Paul's expectation as to the conversion of the Jews in Romans ix, x, xi. *S. P. Duval, B.D. and D.D. 1912 Oxford*

1. The creed of the Christian Church. 2. St. Paul's Epistles considered as a whole, with special reference to his teaching on justification. *A. Brook, B.D. 1893 Oxford*

A critical edition of Bede on the seven Catholic Epistles (or the major part thereof), based on the two early Oxford manuscripts. *C. H. M. Milne, D.Phil. 1941 Oxford*

A critical examination of the first Epistle of St. Paul to the Corinthians, with special reference to the background of the Corinthian Church. *R. F. Robbins, Ph.D. 1950 Edinburgh*

A critical investigation into the unity, date, and authorship of the 4th Gospel, and its relationship to the Johannine epistles. *W. G. Wilson, Ph.D. 1949 Dublin, Trinity College*

1. Deuteronomy xviii.9-22: inspiration and prophecy. 2. Isaiah vi and xxi.1-10: the prophetic call, audition, and vision. I Corinthians xii-xiv: the psychology of Christian prophecy, introductory to tongues and prophecy in the Corinthian Church. *G. C. Joyce, D.D. 1909 Oxford*

1. The doctrine of a future life in the Old and New Testaments 2. The authorship of the Pastoral Epistles. *N. C. W. Radcliffe, B.D. & D.D. 1909 Oxford*

1. The doctrine of the Incarnation as expounded by Wyclif. 2. Coincidences between the Epistle to St.James and the Sermon on the Mount. *E. Harris, B.D. & D.D. 1888 Oxford*

Bible: New Testament: Epistles contd.
The doctrine of the Parousia in the New Testament, with special reference to the Epistles of St. Paul. *E. L. Millen, B.D. 1939 Oxford*

1. The Epistle to the Galatians. 2. The mission of John the Baptist. *A. E. Joscelyne, B.D. 1894 Oxford*

The Epistle to the Hebrews: an enquiry into its relation to primitive tradition. *D. K. Burns, Ph.D. 1933 Edinburgh*

The epistle to the Romans. *E. E. Bradford, D.D. 1912 Oxford*

Exegeses from the Epistle to the Hebrews. *J. Ridgway, D.D. 1870 Oxford*

Exegeses of: Ephesians i.1; iv.4; iv.25. *O. J. Hogarth, D.D. 1922 Oxford*

Exegeses of: Genesis xii.4; xv.12; Romans iv.16,17. *F. W. Bussell, D.D. 1897 Oxford*

Exegeses of: I Corinthians xv.35-50; Colossians i.24; II Thessalonians i.3-10. *H. G. Cundy, D.D. 1879 Oxford*

Exegeses of: I Corinthians vii-xi; xi-xiv; xv; xvi. *H. M. Robinson, D.D. 1876 Oxford*

Exegeses of: II Corinthians iii.4-11; 12-18; Ephesians i.3-14. *G. J. Blore, D.D. 1874 Oxford*

Exegeses of: Romans iii.21-26; iv.13-25; v. 1-11. *C. McDowall, D.D. & B.D. 1882 Oxford*

Exegeses of: Romans vii.14-25; vii.28-30; ix.5. *H. Boyd, B.D. & D.D. 1879 Oxford*

Exegeses of: St.John i.18; I Corinthians xv.29; St.Matthew xviii.19. *C. E. E. Williams, D.D. 1886 Oxford*

Exegeses of I Corinthians ii.6-16; xii.7-11; II Corinthians xii.16. *G. P. Jones, D.D. 1923 Oxford*

Exegeses of I Timothy i.3; i.18; II Timothy i.13. *W. S. Tupholme, D.D. 1921 Oxford*

Exegeses of Romans iii.21-26; Romans v.1-11; I Corinthians x.23-xi.1. *G. Mackness, D.D. 1871 Oxford*

Exegeses of St. Luke viii.9-10; Romans xiv and xv.3; Hebrews x.37. *A. Povah, D.D. 1890 Oxford*

1. Exegesis of St. John iii.5 in connexion with Galatians iii.27. 2. St. Matthew xxvi.26-28 in connexion with St. Mark xiv.22-24; St. Luke xxii.19,20; I Corinthians xi.23-26, 3. Exegesis of Titus i.5. *E. S. Elwell, D.D. 1882 Oxford*

Exposition of passages from the twelfth chapter of the Epistle to the Romans: the ethical scheme of St. Paul. *C. W. L. Evans, D.D. 1914 Oxford*

Expositions of: Acts ii.4: ἤρξαντο λαλεῖν ετέραισ γλώσσαισ; the gift of tongues; Romans iii.25: ὂν προέθετο ο θεὸσ ιλαστήριον διὰ τησ πίστεωσ εν τω αυτου αἲματι: the meaning of ιλαστήριον; Galatians iii.15: the legal terminology of the Epistle to the Galatians and its bearing on the question of the churches addressed by St. Paul. *D. Walker, D.D. 1904 Oxford*

Expositions of: Genesis iii: the doctrine of the Fall; Ephesians iv.1-16: the unity of the Church and the functions of its ministers; I Corinthians xi.18-34. *T. H. D. Long, D.D. 1909 Oxford*

Expositions of: Hebrews xii.1-2; 3-17; 18-29. *J. Solloway, D.D. 1905 Oxford*

Expositions of: I Corinthians xv.1-11; 12-23; 35-58. *C. Harris, D.D. 1905 Oxford*

Expositions of: I Corinthians ix.19-22; St. Mark ix.38-40; St. Luke xx.21-26. *C. R. Perry, D.D. 1901 Oxford*

Expositions of: I Corinthians xv.29; I St. Peter iii.18-20; Genesis xlix.10. *H. Pinchin, D.D. 1899 Oxford*

Expositions of: I St. Peter i.1-ii, 10; I St. Peter ii.11-iii.22; I St. Peter iv and v. *W. R. W. Stephens, D.D. 1901 Oxford*

Expositions of: Isaiah liii; The Book of the Prophet Jonah; I Peter iii.18-20. *A. G. Pentreath, D.D. 1901 Oxford*

Expositions of: Philippians i.3-26; Philippians i.27-ii.11; Philippians iii.1-21. *C. R. D. Biggs, D.D. 1900 Oxford*

Expositions of: Romans i.17; viii.3; xi.34. *E. A. Glover, D.D. 1906 Oxford*

Expositions of: Romans viii.18-24; I Corinthians xv.29; Hebrews vi.4-6. *F. McDowall, D.D. 1897 Oxford*

Expositions of: St. John xx.30, 31: the purpose and plan of the fourth Gospel; Romans 1.17: the righteousness of God; Ephesians 1.22,23. *W. H. G. Thomas, D.D. 1906 Oxford*

Bible: New Testament: Epistles contd.
Expositions of: St. John xx.22-23: the power of absolution given to the Church; I John iii.19, 20: the Christian doctrine of conscience; Galatians ii.19-20: individual religion and the Church. *T. B. Strong, D.D. 1902 Oxford*

Expositions of: St. Matthew xii.31,32: the blasphemy against the Holy Ghost; Romans viii.19-23: the groaning creation; Galatians iii.20. *H. G. Corner, D.D. 1905 Oxford*

Expositions of Acts xx.15-38: St. Paul's address to the elders at Miletus; Matthew iv.23: the Christ of eschatology; Hebrews i.1: The Epistle to Hebrews. *M. Jones, D.D. 1914 Oxford*

Expositions of Genesis i.1-2; Romans viii.14-16; Romans viii.22. *T. A. Branthwaite, D.D. 1907 Oxford*

Expositions of I Corinthians xv.29; St. Mark xiii.26; Hebrews v.6. *F. E. Austin, D.D. 1911 Oxford*

Expositions of I Corinthians viii.4,5,6; Romans viii.7-10; Romans iii.21-25. *W. W. Longford, D.D. 1915 Oxford*

Expositions of I Corinthians xv.20-58: the Resurrection; St. John iii.3-5; Genesis i: the Creation. *E. P. Lewis, D.D. 1904 Oxford*

Expositions of I Timothy ii.8; I Peter i.10-12; II Peter i.20-21. *J. A. Evans, D.D. 1915 Oxford*

Expositions of Philippians ii.5-13; St. Luke iv.1-14; St. John viii.36-47. *E. B. Bartleet, D.D. 1915 Oxford*

Expositions of St. Matthew xxviii.1-15: I Corinthians xv.35-50; St. Luke xxiv.36-49. *F. Briggs, D.D. 1919 Oxford*

Expositions of St. Matthew v.17-48; I Corinthians xv.1-11; I Peter i.11-ii.17. *E. J. W. Houghton, D.D. & B.D. 1909 Oxford*

Expositions of the Epistle of Jude 1-8; 9-16; 17-25. *F. W. M. Woodward, D.D. 1910 Oxford*

1. The fourfold account of the resurrection of Jesus Christ in the light of the fourfold purpose of the four Gospel writers. 2. The authorship of the Epistle to the Hebrews. *E. Lane, B.D. & D.D. 1905 Oxford*

The Galatians. *M. M. Heavy, M.A. 1928 National University of Ireland*

1. General characteristics of the Epistles of the New Testament, with special illustration from the Epistle of St.James. 2.General characteristics of the Epistles of St.Paul, with special illustration from the Epistle to the Galatians. *J. F. Bright, B.D. & D.D. 1884 Oxford*

1. Grace and free will in reference to the language of Scripture and to some later theories. 2. The Epistle to the Galatians. *C. Bigg, B.D. & D.D. 1876 Oxford*

1. The gradual development of the doctrine of a future life in Holy Scripture, with special reference to the teaching of St. Paul on the resurrection-body in I Corinthians xv. 2. The Logos-Christology deduced from the writings of St. Paul. *W. O. Jenkins, B.D. & D.D. 1907 Oxford*

1. Growth of the doctrine of Jesus Christ in the Pauline Epistles. 2. The doctrine of the future life. *E. B. Bartleet, B.D. 1902 Oxford*

1. I Corinthians xv.29: baptism for the dead. 2. II Corinthians xii.7: St. Paul's thorn in the flesh. 3. I Peter iii.18-20: the spirits in prison. *J. Chapelhow, D.D. 1893 Oxford*

Illustrations of the form, grammar, and language of the Epistle of St. Paul to the Romans. *M. L. Smith, B.D. & D.D. 1913 Oxford*

1. The import and rendering of the word διαθήκη in Hebrews ix. 2. The personality and identity of St. Mary Magdalen. *H. R. C. Smith, B.D. & D.D. 1891 Oxford*

1. The influence of critical theory on the interpretation and authority of Holy Scripture. 2. Apostolic discipline as illustrated by St. Paul's epistles to the Corinthians. *H. H. Henson, B.D. 1897 Oxford*

1. The integrity of the Epistle to the Romans. 2. The argument and theology of Romans ix-xi. *A. C. Headlam, B.D. 1895 Oxford*

1. The interpretation of Psalm cx. 2. The authenticity of the Epistle of St. James. *W. S. Law, B.D. 1898 Oxford*

The language of the Pauline epistles considered in its bearing on the possible Pauline authorship of the pastoral epistles. *J. McIntyre, M.Litt. 1946 Durham*

Bible: New Testament: Epistles contd.
The Latin text of the Johannine epistles, with special reference to the Spanish family. *A. W. Adams, B.D. 1950 Oxford*

1. The Lord's Prayer: its origin, comprehensiveness, and suitability, both as a form and a model. 2. The genuineness of the pastoral epistles. *F. W. Joy, B.D. & D.D. 1895 Oxford*

1. The mediatorship of Christ as viewed from the standpoint of personality. 2. An examination of faith, with special reference to its definition in Hebrews xi. *F. G. Goddard, B.D. 1907 Oxford*

The mystical element in the Pauline Epistles. *C. McL. Currie, Ph.D. 1933 Edinburgh*

1. The Old Testament an essential part of the revelation of God. 2. On the Epistle to the Ephesians. *W. Lock, B.D. & D.D. 1896 Oxford*

1. On the Epistle to the Hebrews. 2. On the proportional reward. *W. M. Sinclair, B.D. 1888 Oxford*

1. On the organization of the early Church as exhibited in the Acts of the Apostles and the Pauline Epistles. 2. On the right and wrong use of the doctrine of predestination. *M. Argles, B.D. & D.D. 1891 Oxford*

1. The origin of the expectation of the early Advent of our Blessed Lord. 2. The relation of the Epistle to the Hebrews to St. Paul's Epistles. *H. A. Keates, B.D. 1904 Oxford*

1. The Pauline authorship of the Epistle to the Ephesians. 2. The date and authorship of the Athanasian Creed. *T. A. Branthwaite, B.D. 1903 Oxford*

Pauline ethics, with special reference to eschatology. *J. P. Lee-Woolf, B.D. 1942 Oxford*

The Pauline interpretation of history: an examination of Romans xi-xii. *E. W. Hunt, B.D. 1946 Birmingham*

1. The phraseology and style of the Pastoral Epistles. 2. The epitaph of Abercius. *G. C. Richards, B.D. 1920 Oxford*

1. The poetical structure of Isaiah xl-lv. 2. The genuineness of the second Epistle to the Thessalonians. *M. G. Glazebrook, B.D. & D.D. 1903 Oxford*

1. The priesthood of Christ in the Epistle to the Hebrews. 2. The redemption. *F. Briggs, B.D. 1910 Oxford*

The problem of the authorship of the Epistle to the Ephesians. *C. L. Mitton, Ph.D. 1949 London, External Degree*

The problem of the Pastoral Epistles, with special reference to the linguistic data. *C. S. Nye, B.D. 1934 Oxford*

1. The problem of the second Epistle of St. John. 2. The references to the Holy Spirit in the Epistle of Clement of Rome to the Corinthians. *H. J. Gibbins, B.D. 1904 Oxford*

1. Problems in the philosophy of religion raised and answered in the Book of Job. 2. St. Paul's teaching in the letters addressed to the Corinthian Church. *A. F. O'N. Williams, B.D. 1908 Oxford*

1. The purpose of the Epistle to St. James. 2. The Church and Scripture. *J. J. Hannah, B.D. & D.D. 1909 Oxford*

1. The redemption. 2. The Church in the Epistle to the Ephesians. *P. J. James, B.D. 1910 Oxford*

The relation of Jewish-Alexandrian theology, especially in Philo, to the Pauline Epistles. *W. P. Ludwig, Ph.D. 1937 Edinburgh*

The righteousness of God in the conception of St. Paul, with special reference to the Epistle to the Romans. *D. D. MacBryde, Ph.D. 1943 Edinburgh*

Romans. *R. St. John Parry, D.D. 1913 Cambridge*

1. Romans iii.21-26: the doctrine of the atonement in St. Paul. 2. Romans iii.24-25; I Timothy ii.6: propitiation, redemption, reconciliation, ransom, justification. 3. Luke xvi.1-13: parable of the unrighteous steward. *F. S. G. Warman, D.D. 1911 Oxford*

1. Romans vii.12: internal evidence of the divine origin of the law of Moses. *R. O. Davies, D.D. 1893 Oxford*

St. John's Gospel vi.28-65, and the first Epistle of St. John, chapters i and iv. *W. M. Sinclair, D.D. 1892 Oxford*

1. St. Paul and his relations to the Galatian Church. 2. Our Lord's teaching by hard sayings and parables. *C. C. Tancock, B.D. & D.D. 1899 Oxford*

Bible: New Testament: Epistles contd.
1. St. Paul's claim to be a true Apostle and the spiritual father of the Galatians (Galatians i.1,2,11,12). 2. The inadequacy of the law and its proper function and position (Galatians iii.24). 3. The attitude and responsibilities of Christians under the new law of liberty (Galatians v.i;vi.7,8). *R. B. Poole, D.D. 1886 Oxford*

St. Paul's doctrine of Christ, especially its development as revealed in his extant writings. *T. A. Lewis, B.D. 1951 Oxford*

1. Second Epistle of St. John. 2. Third Epistle of St. John. *A. R. Cole, B.D. 1874 Oxford*

1. Some general characteristics of St. Paul's Epistles, with special illustrations from the Epistle to the Galatians. 2. The intention and use of sacraments in the Christian Church. *H. D. S. Sweetapple, B.D. & D.D. 1908 Oxford*

1. A study of the first Epistle of St. Peter in its relation to the Apostle's character and history. 2. The action of divine grace through distinctive channels of human personality. *W. K. Fleming, B.D. 1909 Oxford*

1. The teaching of St. Paul on the Church in the Epistle to the Ephesians. 2. The teaching of St. Paul on the Holy Spirit. *G. P. Jones, B.D. 1908 Oxford*

The treatment of the Mosaic Law in the Epistle to the Hebrews with some comparison of the Pauline attitude. *G. G. Lloyd, Ph.D. 1946 Edinburgh*

1. The typical significance of the history of the children of Israel. 2. The teaching of St. Paul with regard to the Holy Spirit. *W. S. Milne, B.D. 1889 Oxford*

1. The use and authority of the Apocrypha. 2. The occasion and purpose of the Epistle to the Romans. *E. Bartrum, B.D. & D.D. 1885 Oxford*

The use of the Old Testament in the Epistle to the Hebrews. *R. A. Stewart, M.Litt. 1947 Cambridge*

1. 'We have an altar': Hebrews xiii.10. 2. The spiritual gifts to the Apostles: I Corinthians xii.8. *J. G. Dangar, B.D. 1877 Oxford*

1. The witness of the Old Testament to the immanence of God in nature and in man. 2. The theology of the Pastoral Epistle. *W. H. Fremantle, B.D. & D.D. 1895 Oxford*

Bible: New Testament: Revelation
1.The Apocalypse of St. John in its relation to the religion of the Empire. 2. On certain points in the Apocalypse of St. John in relation to other works in apocalyptic literature. *W. H. Hutton, B.D. 1893 Oxford*

1. The Book of Revelation. 2. The doctrine of the Church of England on the Lord's Supper compared with Scripture and the teaching of the primitive Church, and also with the teaching of the Church of Rome. *P. C. Ingroville, B.D. 1909 Oxford*

The Christology of the Apocalypse. *A. Jones, M.A. 1937 Wales*

1. The dramatic structure of the Apocalypse. 2. The mystical interpretation of the Apocalypse. *H. W. Boustead, B.D. & D.D. 1905 Oxford*

Exposition of the Book of Revelation: introduction, chapter i; ii.1-17; ii.18; iii. *E. J. Haynes, D.D. 1905 Oxford*

Expositions of Psalms vii.4-6; Revelation xxii.1, 2; Isaiah xlix.23. *W. H. Hutton, D.D. 1919 Oxford*

1. The intermediate state. 2. The date and authorship of the Apocalypse. *G. T. Jowett, B.D. & D.D. 1909 Oxford*

1. The Lord's coming and the world's end. 2. The Revelation of St. John. *W. J. L. Sheppard, B.D. & D.D. 1922 Oxford*

1. On the interpretation of the Apocalypse. 2. On the structure of the Eucharistic office. *E. C. S. Gibson, B.D. & D.D. 1895 Oxford*

1. St. Mark iv.26-29: the secret growth of the seed of the kingdom. 2. Revelation iv.4-11: the vision of the four-and-twenty elders, and the four living beings. 3. Revelation xx.1-8: the prophecy of the millennial reign. *H. E. Nolloth, D.D. 1894 Oxford*

Bible: New Testament: Apocrypha
The apocryphal Gospels. *L. St. A. Wells, B.D. 1928 Oxford*

The conception of the Resurrection, in the Apocrypha and Pseudepigrapha. *H. Anderson, Ph.D. 1950 Glasgow*

The origin and value of the Agrapha. *R. Dunkurley, Ph.D. 1927 London*

Bihar
The agricultural geography of Bihar. *P. Dayal, Ph.D. 1947 London, School of Economics and Political Science*

Industrial geography of Bihar. *S. A. Majid, Ph.D. 1949 London, School of Economics and Political Science*

Bihari Language
An edition of the unpublished Maithili ms., the *Padavali* of Govindadasa, with an analysis of its grammar and phonology. *S. Jha, Ph.D. 1934 London, School of Oriental and African Studies*

Bijāpur
The kingdom of Bijāpur. *P. M. Joshi, Ph.D. 1935 London, School of Oriental and African Studies*

Bilingualism
See also Languages: Study and Teaching.
Bilingual education in Wales, with special reference to the teaching of Welsh. *E. Evans, M.A. 1924 Wales*

The bilingual problem in Ceylon. *T. D. Jayasuriya, M.A. 1931 London, Day Training College*

The effects of bilingualism on mental development. *T. P. Lannin, Ph.D. 1946 National University of Ireland*

An experimental investigation of children's vocabularies, with special reference to the effect of bilingualism on vocabulary. *S. Wyatt, M.Ed. 1918 Manchester*

A survey of bilingualism in Wales and the Marches. *W. H. Rees, M.A. 1941 Liverpool*

Tests for the examination of the effect of bilingualism on intelligence. *W. R. Jones, M.A. 1933 Wales*

Bills of Rights
Bills of rights and federal constitutions. *K. K. Das, Ph.D. 1947 Cambridge*

Biography
See also Johnson, Samuel; Plutarch; Suetonius.
Biography in the nineteenth century as illustrated by seven biographies of English men of letters. *C. P. Hsu, B.Litt. 1947 Oxford*

An dírbheathaisnéis sa Ghaedhilg (Autobiography in Irish). *S. O'Fearchair, M.A. 1945 National University of Ireland*

English biography before 1700. *D. A. Stauffer, D.Phil. 1927 Oxford*

The materials for biography, the handling of the materials, and the techniques employed to reveal character and personality, with special reference to the work of Lockhart, Froude and Lytton Strachey, in the light of recent psychological investigation. *E. A. M. Dougary, Ph.D. 1942 Edinburgh*

Post-war biographies: their character and literary value. *D. Rees, M.A. 1934 Wales*

The pre-war biographies of Romain Rolland and their place in the ensemble of his work and of the period up to 1914. *R. A. Wilson, Ph.D. 1937 Saint Andrew's*

Some Spanish biographies of Sir Thomas More. *R. O. Jones, M.A. 1949 London, King's College*

Biology
See also Evolution; Heredity; Boussingault, J. B. J. D.; Ray, J.
The application of statistical methods to problems of biological classification. *C. R. Rao, Ph.D. 1948 Cambridge*

The biologist's approach to the mind-body problem. *J. S. Wilkie, Ph.D. 1949 London, University College*

The value and limitations of biological principles in social science. *W. Blackshaw, B.Sc. 1914 Oxford*

Biology: History
Biological research in the early days of the Royal Society. *J. L. Brewin, M.Sc. 1937 London, University College*

The contribution of J. B. J. D. Boussingault (1802-1887) to the knowledge of plant nutrition. *R. Abbott, M.Sc. 1939 London, University College*

The development of vitalistic theories in biology, especially from 1800 to 1933. *L. R. Wheeler, Ph.D. 1937 London, External Degree*

The history of the recapitulation theory. *N. F. Soyer, M.Sc. 1929 London*

Les idées biologiques de Diderot et leur influence sur son oeuvre romanesque. *S. C. De St. Mathurin, B.Litt. 1932 Oxford*

The medieval Latin versions of the Aristotelian scientific corpus, with special reference to the biological works. *S. D. Wingate, Ph.D. 1931 London, University College*

Biology: History contd.
Morphological correspondence in modern biology. *R. F. J. Withers, M.Sc. 1948 London, University College*

Biology: Study and Teaching
Biology and education. *E. J. Rutherford, M.A. 1927 Liverpool*

Biology in education. *W. A. Pritchard-Jones, M.Ed. 1935 Durham*

A comparative investigation of the influence of geography and practical biology on the understanding of the forms of reasoning involved in civics. *C. W. Atkinson, M.Ed. 1949 Leeds*

An experimental study of the biological interests of school children. *A. K. C. Ottaway, M.A. 1935 London, Institute of Education*

A record of ten years' work and experience in the teaching of biology in a senior elementary school. *F. Tyrer, M.A. 1940 Liverpool*

A study of the fundamental concepts of biology and their influence upon methods of teaching biology in schools. *F. C. Stott, M.A. 1945 London, Institute of Education*

A survey of the teaching and learning of biology. *T. L. Green, M.A. 1943 Bristol*

The value of the new-type examination for assessing attainment in biology. *F. S. Cook, M.A. 1936 London, Institute of Education*

Bion
Characteristics of the grammar and style of Bion and Moschus. *E. M. Roberts, M.A. 1908 London*

The poems attributed to Bion and Moschus. English commentary, with a new translation, introductory essays, and a complete index verborum. *J. E. Dunlop, Ph.D. 1944 London, External Degree*

Birds
Some problems connected with birds in Greek religion. *J. R. T. Pollard, B.Litt. 1947 Oxford*

Birkenhead
Birkenhead: growth and future development. *W. S. Moss, M.A. 1931 Liverpool*

The geographical development of Birkenhead. *J. E. Allison, M.A. 1939 Liverpool*

Birmingham
Birmingham: an analysis of geographical influences on the metal industries. *J. Rushton, M.Sc. 1936 London, Bedford College*

The British ports in relation to the export trade of Birmingham. *A. J. McIntosh, Ph.D. 1935 London, External Degree*

The condition of England during the revolutionary and Napoleonic periods, as illustrated by the history of Birmingham between the years 1789-1815. *D. J. Davies, M.A. 1924 Wales*

The industrial development of Birmingham and the Black Country, 1860-1914. *G. C. Allen, Ph.D. 1928 Birmingham*

Leisure as a planning problem, with special reference to the Birmingham conurbation. *R. A. Hopferwieser, M.Com. 1950 Birmingham*

The reform movement in Birmingham, 1830-1884. *H. G. Smith, Ph.D. 1930 London, External Degree*

A survey of religious life in Birmingham, 1790-1830. *C. E. B. Hubbard, M.A. 1935 Birmingham*

The Theatre Royal, Birmingham. *J. E. Cunningham, M.A. 1949 Birmingham*

Birth Rate
See Population.

Bismarck, Otto von, Prince
Bismarck and British colonial policy: the problem in South-West Africa, 1883-1885. *W. O. Aydelotte, Ph.D. 1935 Cambridge*

The social policy of Bismarck. *A. Ashley, M.A. 1912 Birmingham*

Black Death
See also Plague.

The available data for the Black Death in Wales. *W. Williams, M.A. 1920 Wales*

The Black Death, 1348-49, with special reference to cathedral registers for the mortality of the clergy. *J. Lunn, Ph.D. 1931 Cambridge*

Black Forest
Some aspects of the evolution and distribution of settlement and industries in the Black Forest region considered in relation to the geographical setting. *A. F. A. Mutton, Ph.D. 1937 London, Bedford College*

Black Mountains
The Black Mountains. A physical, agricultural and geographical survey, 1932-6. *L. S. M'Caw, M.A. 1936 Manchester*

Black Prince, The
See Edward, the Black Prince.

Black Sea
The Black Sea question during the Crimean War. *I. F. D. Morrow, Ph.D. 1927 Cambridge*

Gates of the Euxine. *L. MacCauley, M.A. 1919 National University of Ireland*

Blackmore, Richard Doddridge
A critical estimate of Richard Doddridge Blackmore's novels. *G. M. Speak, M.A. 1949 Leeds*

Blair, Hugh
Preaching in eighteenth century Scotland: a comparative study of the extant sermons of Ralph Erskine, 1685-1752; John Erskine, 1721-1803; and Hugh Blair, 1718-1800. *C. R. McCain, Ph.D. 1949 Edinburgh*

Blake, William
The lyrical poems of W. Blake. *M. H. Willetts, M.A. 1921 Birmingham*

Mystical poetry of William Blake. *P. Fullam, M.A. 1931 National University of Ireland*

Some Eastern influences on William Blake's *Prophetic Books*. *P. Nanavutty, M.Litt. 1938 Cambridge*

A study of the chief elements of mystical thought in English writers up to the time of Blake and Wordsworth. *M. Richards, M.A. 1921 Birmingham*

A study of the development of the poetry of William Blake, up to and including *The Marriage of Heaven and Hell*, with special reference to the growth of his mystical conceptions. *C. G. Williams, M.A. 1934 Wales*

The theology of William Blake. *J. G. Davis, B.D. 1946 Oxford*

William Blake and his critics. *W. L. Browne, M.A. 1944 National University of Ireland*

William Blake and the religious background of his writings. *J. P. Parry, M.A. 1947 Liverpool*

William Blake and the romantic fallacy. *A. A. Evans, M.A. 1937 Bristol*

Blasphemy
The history and scope of the offence of blasphemy cognizable by the courts Christian and the courts of common law in England. *G. D. Nokes, LL.D. 1927 London*

Blathwayt, William
The life and career of William Blathwayt, 1649-1717. *R. A. Preston, M.A. 1932 Leeds*

Blindness
For visual perception, see Perception.

Contributions to an industrial psychology of the blind. *L. G. Fuchs, M.A. 1949 London, Birkbeck College*

Contributions to the psychology of the blind: a non-verbal group test of general ability. *I. W. Langan, Ph.D. 1949 Reading*

A historical sketch of organized effort on behalf of the blind in Great Britain. *J. M. Ritchie, Ph.D. 1927 Edinburgh*

Bliss
See Joy.

Blok, Alexander Alexandrovich
The poetry of Alexander Blok. *R. Gill, Ph.D. 1938 London, External Degree*

Blomefield, Miles
Bury St. Edmund's as a literary centre, with particular reference to the activities of Miles Blomefield, b.1525, and Cox Macro, 1683-1767. *K. W. Dean, M.A. 1925 London*

Blood
The practice of blood-letting among the English from the earliest times. *B. L. Garrad, B.Litt. 1921 Oxford*

Welsh blood groups: a contribution to the anthropology of the Welsh people. *I. M. Watkins, M.Sc. 1946 Wales*

Blount, Charles, 8th Lord Mountjoy
C. Blount, 8th Lord Mountjoy. *F. M. Jones, M.A. 1946 National University of Ireland*

Bloy, Léon Marie
Le symbolisme de la pauvreté dans l'oeuvre de Léon Bloy. *E. T. Pichler, M.A. 1945 Birmingham*

Léon Bloy. *E. Beaumont, Ph.D. 1943 London, External Degree*

Bloy, Léon Marie contd.
The thought of Léon Bloy: an interpretation of the life and character of Léon Bloy, with special reference to his theology. *M. H. Williams, M.A. 1950 Wales*

Blunck, Hans Friedrich
A contribution to the study of Hans Friedrich Blunck: a study of the trilogy *Gewalt über das Feuer, Kampf der Gestirne, Streit mit den Göttern*. *A. J. Hawkes, M.A. 1933 Liverpool*

Boccaccio, Giovanni
The debt of Chaucer to Boccaccio. *G. S. Griffiths, B.Litt. 1925 Oxford*

The *Decameron* of Boccaccio, translated into French by Laurent de Premierfait, 1414. *G. S. Purkis, M.A. 1923 London*

Boccalini, Trajano
The influence of Trajano Boccalini's *Ragguagli de Parnaso* upon the English literature of the seventeenth and early eighteenth centuries. *R. Thomas, M.A. 1921 Wales*

Bodhisattva
See Buddhism.

Bodmer, Johann Jakob
J. J. Bodmer's contribution to the knowledge and appreciation of Middle High German Literature. *D. Knight, M.A. 1949 London, Bedford College*

Boehme, Jacob
The mysticism of Jacob Böhme, with special reference to his dialectic. *J. J. Stoudt, Ph.D. 1943 Edinburgh*

The reception of the works of Jacob Boehme in England in the seventeenth and eighteenth centuries. *R. E. B. Maxse, B.Litt. 1935 Oxford*

Boerhaave, Hermann
The chemical studies of Hermann Boerhaave, 1668-1738. *J. G. Knight, M.Sc. 1934 London, University College*

The life and work of Herman Boerhaave, with particular reference to his influence in chemistry. *F. W. Gibbs, Ph.D. 1949 London, University College*

Bogomilism
A history of Bogomilism in Bulgaria. *D. Obolensky, Ph.D. 1944 Cambridge*

Bohemia
See Czechoslovakia; Palacký, F.

Bohemond I, Prince of Antioch
Bohemond I of Antioch. *M. P. Brennan, M.A. 1943 Belfast*

Böhm-Bawerk, Eugen von
The influence of Böhm-Bawerk on American theories of capital and interest. *E. White, M.Sc. 1935 London, School of Economics and Political Science*

Boileau-Despréaux, Nicolas
Boileau: his influence and reputation in English literature. *M. Jenkins, M.A. 1932 Birmingham*

Pope and Boileau. *V. P. Dempsey, M.A. 1921 National University of Ireland*

Bolingbroke, Henry St. John, Viscount
Bolingbroke and Voltaire: a comparative study of their philosophical and religious ideas. *A. S. Hurn, B.Litt. 1915 Oxford*

Bolivia
The Chaco dispute: a study of pacific methods of settling international disputes. *J. W. Mallinson, M.Sc. 1939 London, School of Economics and Political Science*

Bolshevism
See Communism.

Bombay
Provincial autonomy of Bombay. *M. A. M. Patel, M.Sc. 1947 London, School of Economics and Political Science*

Bomvana, The
Ethnology of the Bomvanas. *W. A. Soga, M.D. 1894 Glasgow*

Bonaventura, Saint
The metaphysic of St. Bonaventure. *R. E. McCann, M.A. 1936 National University of Ireland*

The mystical theology of St. Bonaventura. *D. J. Dobbins, B.Litt. 1925 Oxford*

Bonet, Honoré
Linguistic study of an unedited manuscript of the *Apparition maistre Jehan de Meun* by Honoré Bonet (1398), with particular reference to the elimination of hiatus. *I. D. O. Arnold, M.A. 1927 Wales*

Bonfed, Solomon ben Reuben
Selections from Solomon ben Reuben Bonfed, translated with introduction. *A. S. Susman, M.A. 1942 Manchester*

Book Illustration
Illustrations of the romances in medieval English art. *R. S. Loomis, B.Litt. 1913 Oxford*

The use of plant-motives in marginalia of English illuminated manuscripts of the fourteenth and fifteenth centuries. *A. M. Houghton, M.A. 1942 Manchester*

Book of Aicill, The
Celtic law: with special reference to the *Senchus Mór* and the *Book of Aicill*, and a critical examination of the traces of an early Gaelic system of law in Scotland. *J. Cameron, Ph.D. 1935 Glasgow*

Book of Common Prayer
1. On the principles of worship in the Book of Common Prayer. 2. On the separate services in the Book of Common Prayer. *C. C. Mackarness, B.D. & D.D. 1914 Oxford*

A study of the linguistic features of the first Prayer Book of Edward VI (1549). *W. Straw, M.A. 1924 London*

Book Publishers and Publishing
See also Caxton, W.; Knight, C.; Minerva Press; Tonson, J.; Tottel, R.; Wolf, J.

The control of the press in England before the granting of the charter to the Stationers' Company. *W. N. Chaplin, M.A. 1935 London*

The economic aspects of book production and distribution between 1500 and 1650. *M. Plant, M.Sc. 1934 London, School of Economics and Political Science*

The English book trade: an economic history of the making and sale of books. *M. Plant, D.Sc. 1939 London, School of Economics and Political Science*

1. The English novel in France (1830-1835). 2. Index alphabétique des auteurs de romans anglais publiés en France de 1830 à 1835. *M. G. Devonshire, M.A. 1915 London*

An enquiry into the history of registration for publication in Scotland. *L. Ockrent, Ph.D. 1937 Edinburgh*

The profession of letters, 1780-1832: a study of the relation of author to patron, publisher, and public. *A. S. Collins, Ph.D. 1927 London*

The relation between author, patron, publisher, and public: 1726-1780. *A. S. Collins, M.A. 1923 London*

The Society for the Encouragement of Learning and its place in the history of publishing. *C. H. Atto, Ph.D. 1938 London, King's College*

State publishing: its methods and problems. *F. R. Cowell, Ph.D. 1938 London, External Degree*

A study of the Stationers' Register for the years 1591-1594, in relation to the social life and literature of the period. *G. B. Harrison, Ph.D. 1928 London*

A survey of the books published in English between 1603 and 1608, with a view to determining the interests of the reading public during those years. *G. J. N. Whitfield, M.A. 1935 London, King's College*

Book Reviewing
See Literature: Criticism.

Bookselling
See Book Publishers and Publishing; and Moseley, H.

Bordeaux
History of trade relations between Bordeaux and Britain in the eighteenth century, with special reference to the wine and spirit trade. *A. E. Roberts, M.A. 1926 Wales*

Bordeaux, Henry
Le mouvement régionaliste dans la littérature française moderne et l'oeuvre de Henry Bordeaux. *N. Murphy, M.A. 1926 National University of Ireland*

Borel d'Hauterive, Pétrus
Pétrus Borel: a study of his life, work and importance in French literature. *C. R. T. Saffell, Ph.D. 1941 London, External Degree*

Borgunnien, Albrecht van
Albrecht van Borgunnien's treatise on medicine and its sources. *W. L. Wardale, M.A. 1927 Liverpool*

Born, Bertran de
See Bertran de Born.

Borneo
English trade and policy in Borneo and the adjacent islands, 1667-1786. *T. C. P. Edgell, M.A. 1935 London, King's College*

Bornier, Henri de, Vicomte
Henri de Bornier: les sources de son inspiration et les influences qu'il a subies. *E. L. R. Gratz, M.A. 1912 London*

Borron, Robert de
The old French prose romance *L'estoire del Saint Graal* and its relation to Robert de Borron's poem *Le roman de l'estoire dou Graal. S. M. Scott, M.A. 1935 Manchester*

Borrow, George Henry
George Borrow. *F. E. L. E. M. Werner, M.A. 1924 Birmingham*

Borstal Institutions
Re-building character of delinquent youth: a study of the English Borstal system and of the responses of individuals to its methods of treatment. *H. E. Field, Ph.D. 1933 London, Institute of Education*

Bosanquet, Bernard
An examination of Bosanquet's doctrine of self-transcendence. *R. E. Stedman, Ph.D. 1930 Edinburgh*

The significance of the religious consciousness with special reference to Bosanquet and Ritschl. *G. H. Haydock, B.Litt. 1920 Oxford*

A study of certain doctrines found in Bosanquet's logic. *H. I. Davies, Ph.D. 1936 Cambridge*

The theory of judgment in Bradley and Bosanquet. *R. N. Kaul, B.Litt. 1928 Oxford*

The treatment of the idea of the individual in the philosophies of Bernard Bosanquet, J. M. E. McTaggart and A. N. Whitehead. *B. E. Jones, M.A. 1942 Manchester*

Value and the philosophy of the absolute with special reference to the philosophy of Bosanquet. *J. G. F. Potter, B.Litt. 1935 Oxford*

Bosley
A survey of the history of Bosley. *R. W. Lloyd-Jones, M.A. 1943 Liverpool*

Bosphorus
Gates of the Euxine. *L. MacCauley, M.A. 1919 National University of Ireland*

The history of the Bosphorus and the Dardanelles, with special reference to treaty relations: a study in international law and diplomacy. *D. B. Toye, LL.D. 1925 London*

Bossuet, Jacques Bénigne
Bossuet and mysticism. *S. D. Screech, Ph.D. 1934 London, Birkbeck College*

Bossuet and the Church of England. *J. C. M. Crotty, B.Litt. 1938 Oxford*

A critical examination of Bossuet's attitude on the question of the Gallican Church. *V. A. A. Barry, B.Litt. 1920 Oxford*

The sermon as persuasion in late seventeenth century France and England: a study of Bossuet, Bourdaloue, Barrow, and South. *H. Hammond, Ph.D. 1950 Cambridge*

Boston, Massachusetts
The House of Hancock, business in Boston, 1724 to 1775. *W. T. Baxter, Ph.D. 1946 Edinburgh*

Boston, Thomas
The life and writings of Thomas Boston of Ettrick. *W. Addison, Ph.D. 1936 Edinburgh*

Boswell, James
Boswell in the newspapers from the death of Johnson to his own death. *E. J. Willing-Denton, B.Litt. 1935 Oxford*

Botany: History
Ainmneacha aiteann i gCondae Mhuigheo (The names of furze in Co. Mayo). *P. Mc Donagh, M.A. 1948 National University of Ireland*

Contribution à l'étude de la botanologie celtique: les noms de plantes des *Four Ancient Books of Wales. P. R. Y. M. Diverres, M.A. 1915 Liverpool*

The contribution of J. B. J. D. Boussingault (1802-1887) to the knowledge of plant nutrition. *R. Abbott, M.Sc. 1939 London, University College*

The history of the study of plant response to stimuli. *M. Williams, M.Sc. 1927 London*

Outlines of the history of botany. *R. J. Harvey-Gibson, D.Sc. 1920 Aberdeen*

Peter Collinson, F.R.S., F.S.A., and his circle of friends. *N. G. B. James, B.Litt. 1923 Oxford*

Studies on the botanical researches and method of Theophrastos. *V. Sinnatamby, M.Sc. 1948 London, University College*

Botany: History contd.
The use of plant-motives in marginalia of English illuminated manuscripts of the fourteenth and fifteenth centuries. *A. M. Houghton, M.A. 1942 Manchester*

Botany: Study and Teaching
A critical study of some mechanical aids in the teaching of botany. *A. Roberts, M.A. 1933 London, Institute of Education*

The microscope in school: a consideration of the problems involved in the use of the microscope for the study of the flowering plant. *A. M. Griffiths, M.Ed. 1931 Leeds*

The teaching of botany in the history of secondary education. *A. Lennon, M.Ed. 1921 Manchester*

Bottomry
See Insurance.

Bouchardy, Joseph
Joseph Bouchardy and French melodrama. *R. V. Gardner, M.A. 1947 London, External Degree*

Boulainvilliers, Henri, Comte de
Henri de Boulainvilliers: historian and philosopher. *J. Grace, Ph.D. 1932 Cambridge*

Boulanger, Georges Ernest Jean Marie
General Boulanger. *S. S. Gee, M.A. 1938 Bristol*

Boulton and Watt
The Albion Steam Flour Mill: a chapter in the Boulton and Watt co-partnership. *O. A. Westworth, M.Com. 1930 Birmingham*

Early industrial organisation: a history of the firm of Boulton and Watt. *E. Roll, Ph.D. 1930 Birmingham*

Boulton, Matthew
The financial history of Matthew Boulton, 1759-1800. *J. E. Cule, M.Com. 1935 Birmingham*

Bourbon, Charles, Duc de
The Constable de Bourbon. *F. J. Weaver, M.A. 1906 London*

Bourdaloue, Louis
Bourdaloue and the Bible. *M. H. O'Donovan, M.A. 1926 London*

The sermon as persuasion in late seventeenth century France and England: a study of Bossuet, Bourdaloue, Barrow, and South. *H. Hammond, Ph.D. 1950 Cambridge*

Boussingault, Jean Baptiste Joseph Dieudonné
The contribution of J. B. J. D. Boussingault (1802-1887) to the knowledge of plant nutrition. *R. Abbott, M.Sc. 1939 London, University College*

Bowles, William Lisle
The Pope-Bowles controversy. *N. T. Harris, M.A. 1925 London*

William Lisle Bowles and the controversy on Pope. *W. R. Hutchison, M.A. 1946 Belfast*

Bown o Hamtwn
See Bevis of Hamton.

Boy Scouts
The psychology of the boy group with special reference to school scout troup. *D. M. Ramsden, M.Ed. 1934 Leeds*

Boyd, Benfield and Company
The history of Boyd, Benfield and Co: a study in the merchant banking in the last decade of the eighteenth century. *S. R. Cope, Ph.D. 1947 London, School of Economics and Political Science*

Boyle, Robert
The experimental basis of Robert Boyle's objections to the Aristotelian and alchemical doctrines. *M. G. Odling, M.Sc. 1928 London*

Boyle, Roger, 1st Earl of Orrery
The dramatic works of Roger Boyle, Earl of Orrery, with special reference to the rise of the heroic tragedy, including an annotated text of the unprinted *Zoroastres. F. W. Payne, M.A. 1923 London*

Bradford
Early history of the manor and parish of Bradford (W. Riding, Yorks). *K. I. Judson, M.A. 1933 London, Birkbeck College*

The growth, development and modern functions of the county borough of Bradford. *H. B. Hodgson, M.A. 1939 Leeds*

Studies in the development of the parish of Bradford, 1800-1847. *L. Flanagan, M.A. 1931 Liverpool*

Bradley, D. H.
A comparative study of the *Advaita Vēdānta* and of D. H. Bradley. *S. S. Suryanarayanan, B.Litt. 1917 Oxford*

Bradley, Francis Herbert
Bradley's treatment of 'appearance'. *M. J. A. McAra, M.A. 1926 London*

A critical exposition of Mr. Bradley's view of truth. *V. B. Evans, M.A. 1922 Wales*

A critical study of Mr. Bradley's view of truth. *V. B. Evans, B.Litt. 1923 Oxford*

An examination of Bradley's philosophy. *S. Das, Ph.D. 1929 London*

The issue between Bradley and his critics concerning the nature and reality of relations. *E. M. M. Robinson, B.Litt. 1937 Oxford*

The theory of judgment in Bradley and Bosanquet. *R. N. Kaul, B.Litt. 1928 Oxford*

The theory of judgment in the philosophies of F. H. Bradley and John Cook Wilson. *M. Ahmed, Ph.D. 1937 London, University College*

Brahmagupta
The *Khandakhae-dyaka* of Brahmagupta, with the commentaries of Prthūdaka for the first part, and Varuna for the second part, critically edited and translated. *B. Ghosh, D.Phil. 1940 Oxford*

Brahmanism
See Hinduism.

Bramwell, Byrom, Sir
The influence of Sir Byrom Bramwell on poliomyelitis. *M. B. O'Neill, M.D. 1949 Edinburgh*

Brandes, Johann Christian
Johann Christian Brandes: an examination of the plays of this dramatist contained in his *Sämtliche dramatische Schriften*, with notes on sources and translations of the plays and an account of the author's life, together with a list of his works. *J. E. Mallin, M.A. 1908 London*

Braose, William de
William de Braose. *M. Jones, M.A. 1901 Wales*

Brasenose College
See Oxford University.

Brass and Copper Industry
Geographical considerations affecting, and arising from the location and development of the copper and allied industries of the Swansea district. *S. W. Rider, M.Sc. 1923 Wales*

A geographical study of the Ndola District, northern Rhodesia, with special reference to the copper mining industry. *D. S. Cleak, M.Sc. 1938 Bristol*

The history of an eighteenth century combination in the copper-mining industry. *G. C. Allen, M.Com. 1922 Birmingham*

History of the brass and copper industries of England from Elizabethan times to the Industrial Revolution. *H. Hamilton, D.Litt. 1925 Glasgow*

The history of the growth and organization of the copper industry of Swansea and district. *W. R. John, M.A. 1912 Wales*

Wages and labour organization in the brass trades of Birmingham and district. *T. H. Kelly, Ph.D. 1930 Birmingham*

Brasses
The development of armour and costume from the fourteenth century to the seventeenth century as illustrated in the memorial brasses of Essex. *A. C. Edwards, M.A. 1937 Bristol*

English monumental brasses of the fifteenth and early sixteenth centuries with special reference (a) to the conditions of their manufacture, (b) to their characteristic forms and distribution. *M. L. Gadd, M.A. 1936 Manchester*

Bray, John Francis
A critical exposition of the social and economic ideas of John Francis Bray; and an estimate of his influence upon Karl Marx. *H. J. Carr, Ph.D. 1943 London, External Degree*

Brazil
See also Amapondo, The.

The part played by Great Britain in the separation of Brazil from Portugal, 1821-1825. *J. H. W. Liddicoat, M.A. 1927 London*

Brecon
The lordship of Brecon, 1066-1325. *W. Rees, M.A. 1914 Wales*

Breiffne Schools
The Breiffne schools and scholars. *P. O'Connell, Ph.D. 1940 National University of Ireland*

Bren, Llewelyn
See Llewelyn Bren.

Brendan, Saint
A description and classification of the mss. of the *Navigatio Sancti Brendani*. *C. E. Low, D.Phil. 1934 Oxford*

Brent, River
Historical geography of the upper Brent. *A. J. Garrett, M.A. 1935 London, King's College*

Brentano, Clemens von
The relation of music and poetry as reflected in the works of Tieck, Wackenroder and Brentano. *M. E. Atkinson, M.A. 1947 London, Bedford College*

Brescia, Arnold of
See Arnold, of Brescia.

Brethren, The
See Dunkers, The.

Breton Language
Some points of contact between Welsh and Breton. *R. W. Parry, M.A. 1912 Wales*

Breton Literature
See also Le Braz, A.; Le Goffic, C.

Le développement des idées littéraires en Bretagne sous la Restauration vu dans les pages du *Lycée Armoricain*, 1823-1831. *L. A. Zaina, M.A. 1947 Liverpool*

Breviaries
The origin of the breviary 'according to the use of the Roman Curia'. *S. J. P. Van Dijk, D.Phil. 1950 Oxford*

Brewing Industry
The organization of the brewing industry. *J. Baxter, Ph.D. 1945 London, External Degree*

Briane, Guillaume de
Une édition critique de la traduction Anglo-Normande de *La chronique de Turpin*, de Guillaume de Briane, avec introduction, notes et glossaire. *C. M. Jones, M.A. 1927 Wales*

Bridges, Robert
A study of Robert Bridges and the influence of his thought and technique on modern poetry. *H. Booth, B.Litt. 1938 Oxford*

Bridget, of Sweden, Saint
The cult of St. Bridget of Sweden in fifteenth century England. *F. R. Johnston, M.A. 1947 Manchester*

Bridgewater Canal
The financial administration of the Bridgewater Estate, 1780-1800. *E. Malley, M.A. 1929 Manchester*

Bridgewater Treatises
See Theism.

Brieux, Eugène
Eugène Brieux. *P. V. Thomas, M.A. 1912 London*

The social ideas of Eugène Brieux as expressed in his dramatic works. *E. G. Davies, M.A. 1938 Wales*

Brigantes, The
Brigantes: a study in the early history of the northern Pennines. *R. Pedley, Ph.D. 1939 Durham*

Briggs, Henry
A study of the work and methods of Henry Briggs with special reference to the theory of interpolation. *A. Waterson, Ph.D. 1941 Saint Andrew's*

Bright, John
John Bright as a critic of foreign policy. *J. E. Sanderson, M.A. 1923 Birmingham*

Brisbane
Geographical factors in the growth of Brisbane, Australia. *L. J. Jay, M.A. 1949 Birmingham*

Bristol
1. Bristol and Virginia in the seventeenth century.
2. Bristol merchants, shipwrights, etc. from the Burgess Books, 1607-1700. *N. C. P. Tyack, M.A. 1930 Bristol*

Bristol Corporation of the Poor, 1696-1834. *E. E. Butcher, M.A. 1930 Bristol*

Bristol voyages to the New World between 1576 and 1612. *E. R. Gath, M.A. 1914 Bristol*

Burgage tenure in medieval Bristol. *E. W. Veale, LL.D. 1931 London, University College*

The connection of Bristol with the African slave trade. *A. M. Richards, M.A. 1923 Bristol*

Contribution towards the study of the economic development of Bristol in the eighteenth and nineteenth centuries. *A. J. Pugsley, M.A. 1921 Bristol*

The development of transport and its effect on industries in the Bristol district. *J. Sagar, M.A. 1936 Bristol*

Bristol contd.
Early Methodism in Bristol, with special reference to J. Wesley's visits to the city, 1739-90, and their impression on the people. *W. A. Goss, M.A. 1932 Bristol*

An examination of the factors which link Bristol dock policy with the development of the tramp shipping of the port, 1840-1890. *J. R. Stevens, M.A. 1940 Bristol*

The medieval history of St. James' Bristol. *F. W. P. Hicks, M.A. 1932 Bristol*

The overseas trade of Bristol in the later Middle Ages: a study of English commerce, 1399-1485. *E. M. Carus-Wilson, M.A. 1926 London*

The parish registers of the Churches of SS. Philip and Jacob and of St. Thomas in Bristol in 1812. *D. K. Gosling, M.A. 1934 Bristol*

The parliamentary history of the City of Bristol, 1750-1790. *P. T. Underdown, M.A. 1948 Bristol*

A short history of the growth of Redcliffe. *G. Holgate, M.A. 1934 Bristol*

Bristol Channel
The cultural contacts existing between the Bristol Channel coastlands in prehistoric times. *R. M. Prothero, M.A. 1947 Wales*

Bristol Corporation of the Poor
Bristol Corporation of the Poor, 1696-1834. *E. E. Butcher, M.A. 1930 Bristol*

British and Foreign School Society
The work of the British and Foreign School Society in the training of teachers. *E. L. Hewlett, M.Ed. 1932 Manchester*

British Columbia
A consideration of geographical factors influencing the distribution of population in British Columbia. *Kenny. K. A, M.A. 1934 London, Bedford College*

British Commonwealth
See Great Britain: Colonies and Dominions.

British Guiana
The effect of the slave emancipation in British Guiana and Trinidad. *J. R. Maclean, B.Litt. 1931 Oxford*

British Honduras
See Belize.

British Museum
Antonio Panizzi, scholar and patriot. *C. Brooks, Ph.D. 1929 Manchester*

British South Africa Company
The development of Rhodesia under the British South Africa Company (1890-1914), with some indication of subsequent developments. *J. W. Fisher, M.A. 1924 Wales*

Brittany
Jean V, Duke of Brittany (1399-1442) in relation to England. *G. A. Knowlson, M.A. 1934 Liverpool*

La Bretagne, peinte par deux écrivains contemporains, A. le Braz et C. le Goffic. *H. M. Gething, M.A. 1921 Birmingham*

Louis Tiercelin and the Breton renascence. *R. Delaney, Ph.D. 1936 Leeds*

The prehistoric geography of Brittany: a study of the megalithic civilization. *D. Forde, Ph.D. 1928 London*

Brizeux, Julien Auguste
Nature as revealed in the work of Auguste Brizeux. *E. David, M.A. 1934 Wales*

Brockes, Barthold Hennrich
Barthold Hennrich Brockes' translation of James Thomson's *Seasons* and the influence of the *Seasons* on descriptive native nature poetry in Germany, with special reference to the poetry of Brockes and Christian Ewald von Kleist's poem *Der Frühling*. *G. E. W. Booy, M.A. 1940 Bristol*

Brome, Richard
The English Moor, or The Mock-marriage, by Richard Brome, edited from the manuscript in the library of Lichfield Cathedral. *A. E. R. Jenkins, B.Litt. 1941 Oxford*

Brontë, Charlotte
Charlotte Brontë. *P. P. Morris, M.A. 1945 National University of Ireland*

Brontë, Emily Jane
Emily Brontë. *B. M. Bowen, M.A. 1947 Birmingham*

Emily Brontë, with special reference to her poems. *D. J. Cooper, M.A. 1946 Leeds*

Bronze Age
See Archaeology and Antiquities.

Bronzework
The evolution of inscriptions on bronzes during the Chou period. *C.-Y. Tseng, M.A. 1937 London, Courtauld Institute of Art*

Brooke, Henry
Henry Brooke, 1703-1783. *E. M. Palser, M.A. 1907 London*

Brooks, Phillips
The religious thought of Phillips Brooks and its significance. *J. H. Grey, Ph.D. 1938 Edinburgh*

Brothers of the Christian Schools
See also John Baptist, de la Salle, Saint.

Graimeir Ghaedhilge na mBráthair (The Brothers' Irish grammar). *J. P. Egan, Ph.D. 1945 National University of Ireland*

Na Bráithre Críostamhla agus an Ghaedhilge (The Christian Brothers and the Irish language). *O'Catháin, M.A. 1945 National University of Ireland*

St. John Baptist de la Salle: the work of the Brothers of the Christian Schools, and its significance in the history of English education. *W. J. Battersby, Ph.D. 1947 London, Birkbeck College*

Brougham, Henry, 1st Baron Brougham and Vaux
The place of Lord Brougham in the history of the Whig Party. *A. Aspinall, Ph.D. 1924 Manchester*

The political career of Lord Brougham from 1805 to 1830. *N. Williams, M.A. 1913 Liverpool*

Browne, Robert
The religious element in the letters and poems of Donne, and in the works of Browne and Vaughan. *R. E. George, B.Litt. 1915 Oxford*

A thesis on Robert Browne (1550?-1633) as churchman and theologian. *D. C. Smith, Ph.D. 1936 Edinburgh*

Browne, Thomas, Sir
Sir Thomas Browne. *N. J. Sheridan, M.A. 1934 National University of Ireland*

Browne, William
The *Britannia's Pastorals* and *The Shepherd's Pipe* of William Browne. *G. Tillotson, B.Litt. 1930 Oxford*

An examination of the third book of *Britannia's Pastorals* and its attribution to William Browne of Tavistock, with a study of English fairy poetry from the time of Spenser, indicating Browne's position in its development. *I. Gourvitch, M.A. 1923 London*

Browning, Robert
Aspects of the nineteenth century quest for God as reflected in the works of Thomas Hardy, Robert Browning and Francis Thompson. *A. M. Granville, M.A. 1950 Wales*

Browning's psychology of genius as shown in *Pauline; Paracelsus; Andrea del Sarto; Cleon*. *B. G. MacCarthy, M.A. 1927 National University of Ireland*

Dramatic aspect of Browning's poetry. *J. Kelly, M.A. 1930 National University of Ireland*

Dramatic monologue of Browning. *C. Woodman, M.A. 1948 National University of Ireland*

Italian art in the works of Robert Browning. *A. H. Joyce, M.A. 1904 Birmingham*

The plays of Robert Browning in their dramatic and in their spiritual aspects. *M. A. J. McBride, M.A. 1919 London*

Poetry of the Victorian age as represented by Browning and Arnold. *M. M. O'Mahony, M.A. 1942 National University of Ireland*

Some aspects of R. Browning's philosophy of love. *J. G. Carson, M.A. 1920 Birmingham*

A study of Robert Browning's influence and reputation in the twentieth century. *A. A. Brockington, Ph.D. 1931 London, External Degree*

A study of *The ring and the book*. *M. R. Thwaites, B.Litt. 1947 Oxford*

Brownrigg, William
Chemistry in Great Britain from 1727 to 1774, with special reference to the life and scientific works of William Brownrigg, M.D., F.R.S. *J. Russell-Wood, Ph.D. 1948 London, External Degree*

Brunetière, Ferdinand
The critical system of Ferdinand Brunetière. *D. T. Davies, M.A. 1928 Wales*

Brunner, Emil
The controversy between Karl Barth and Emil Brunner concerning natural theology. *J. Henderson, Ph.D. 1940 Edinburgh*

Brut y Brenhinoedd
A comparison of the texts of the *Brut y Brenhinoedd* as found in the *Red book of Hergest* and in the Peniarth ms. 44, concluded in Llanstephan ms. 1. *O. A. Jones, M.A. 1914 Wales*

Bruts
See Anglo-Norman Literature.

Brutus, Marcus Junius
Marcus Junius Brutus: his life, times, and writings. *D. Dickson, Ph.D. 1937 Edinburgh*

Buccaneers
See Piracy.

Bucer, Martin
Martin Bucer and the English Reformation. *C. L. R. A. Hopf, D.Phil. 1943 Oxford*

Buchanan, George
The trial of George Buchanan before the Lisbon Inquisition. *J. M. Aitken, Ph.D. 1938 Edinburgh*

Büchner, Georg
The scientific materialism of Georg Büchner: a critical study. *M. U. Stang, M.A. 1942 London, External Degree*

Buchon, Jean Alexandre
Jean-Alexandre Buchon and his relations with England. *J. Hinton, M.A. 1928 London*

Buckingham, Archdeaconry
A study of the visitation books of the archdeaconry of Buckingham, 1633-6. *E. R. C. Brinkworth, B.Litt. 1948 Oxford*

Buckingham, George Villiers, 1st Duke of
Buckingham's influence on England's policy with regard to France (from October, 1623). *E. S. Goitein, M.A. 1926 London*

Buckingham, James Silk
James Silk Buckingham (1786-1855), social and political reformer. *S. T. King, M.A. 1933 London, King's College*

Buckinghamshire
Judicial proceedings under the Dictum de Kenilworth, Buckingham. *M. L. Hoyle, M.A. 1928 Manchester*

Politics and parties in the county of Buckinghamshire, 1678-1715. *C. E. S. Drew, B.Litt. 1931 Oxford*

Buddhism
See also Pali Literature.

The ' Gift of the good doctrine', containing introduction, translation and notes. *S. Tachibana, B.Litt. 1920 Oxford*

The Buddhist conception of man in relation to the Christian conception. *B. de Kretser, Ph.D. 1948 Edinburgh*

Buddhist cosmology. *W. M. McGovern, D.Phil. 1922 Oxford*

The Buddhist doctrine of insight, with special reference to the Pali text called *The path of purity*, ch. xx-xxii of *Visuddhimagga. P. M. Tin, B.Litt. 1922 Oxford*

Buddhist ideas in China on the origin of man and a translation of the *Yuen Fen Lun. T.-S. Hsü, B.Litt. 1925 Oxford*

Buddhist meditation according to the Pāli Canon of the Thera-Vāda School. *P. Vajirana, Ph.D. 1936 Cambridge*

A critical study of the *Vesaturu-da-Sanne. D. E. Hettiaratchi, Ph.D. 1948 London, External Degree*

The development of the *Bodhisattva* doctrine in Buddhist Sanskrit literature. *H. Daval, Ph.D. 1930 London, School of Oriental and African Studies*

Early history of Buddhist education in Ceylon (third century B.C. to sixteenth century A.D.). *D. D. Samaraweera, M.A. 1949 London, Institute of Education*

Early Mahayana Buddhism with special reference to the doctrine of Nagarjuna. *S. Miyamoto, D.Phil. 1927 Oxford*

Ethics of Pāli Buddhism. *S. Tachibana, D.Phil. 1922 Oxford*

The fourth noble truth: a study in Buddhist ethics. *P. L. Farkas, Ph.D. 1931 Aberdeen*

An inquiry into the socio-religious character of Chinese civilization, with special reference to those features conducive to the acceptance of Buddhism. *A. F. Wright, B.Litt. 1937 Oxford*

The position of ecclesiastics in Burmese Buddhist law. *M. H. Aung, B.Litt. 1939 Dublin, Trinity College*

Buddhism contd.
The psychology of perception in Pali Buddhism, with special reference to the theory of Bhavanga. *E. R. de S. Sarathchandra, Ph.D. 1948 London, External Degree*

The rules of discipline of Buddhist Sāmanera (novices). *S. Sumangala, B.Litt. 1920 Oxford*

1. Some heads of a Christian answer to the neo-Buddhist theosophy. 2. Some considerations, scriptural and modern, concerning sin. *T. S. Lea, B.D. 1905 Oxford*

State of Buddhism in Ceylon as revealed by the Pali commentaries of the fifth century, A.D. *K. K. D. E. W. B. Adikaram, Ph.D. 1933 London, School of Oriental and African Studies*

A translation into English of part of the *Miao fa lien hua ching. B. Kato, B.Litt. 1925 Oxford*

Buecheler, Franz
The development of the idea of personal immortality in pagan Rome, with special reference to the metrical epitaphs in Buecheler's collection. *G. E. Quinton, M.A. 1934 Bristol*

Buenos Aires
Buenos Aires and the Argentine Confederation, 1852-1861. *A. J. Walford, M.A. 1934 London, Birkbeck College*

Buganda
See Uganda.

Building Industry
An analysis of the major geographic factors affecting the production and utilization of building material in certain areas. *M. M. Cole, Ph. D. 1947 London, Bedford College*

The building trades in the Midlands in the seventeenth century. *E. F. T. Richards, M.A. 1939 Birmingham*

Incentives to work and their relation to health and efficiency with particular reference to workers in the building industry. *N. M. Davis, Ph.D. 1948 London, School of Hygiene and Tropical Medicine*

A mathematical and statistical analysis of economic phenomena connected with the building industry. *H. W. Robinson, Ph.D. 1937 London, School of Economics and Political Science*

The positions of the skilled and less skilled workman in the engineering and building trades (1914-25). *J. R. Hicks, B.Litt. 1927 Oxford*

The postwar relations of skilled and unskilled labour in the printing, building and engineering industries. *P. A. Manning, Ph.D. 1933 London, School of Economics and Political Science*

Builth
The history of the town, lordship and castle of Builth from the eleventh to the sixteenth centuries. *G. Wozencroft, M.A. 1919 Wales*

Bukhari
Al-Hadith according to al-Bukhari, with special reference to Islamic ethics. *I. H. Mougy, M.A. 1934 Manchester*

Bulgaria
A history of Bogomilism in Bulgaria. *D. Obolensky, Ph.D. 1944 Cambridge*

Bullfighting
Bullfighting in Nigeria and Portugal: a humane sport. *A. J. N. Tremearne, M.Sc. 1914 London*

Bullinger, Henry
Henry Bullinger of Zurich: his place in the Reformation with special reference to England. *T. S. Taylor, B.Litt. 1912 Oxford*

Bulmer Wapontake
Parliamentary enclosure in Bulmer Wapontake. *M. Kirk, M.A. 1948 Leeds*

Bundahesh
The Iranian recension of the Pahlavi *Bundahesh*: a philological and critical treatment of the text, with translation. *H. W. Bailey, D.Phil. 1933 Oxford*

Bunyan, John
Bunyan's use of allegory in relation to the earlier English tradition. *E. B. Kenadjian, M.A. 1929 Manchester*

The doctrine of sin in the theology of John Bunyan. *J. S. W. Irvine, Ph.D. 1930 Edinburgh*

John Bunyan: an original literary artist. *A. M. B. Rule, M.A. 1929 Birmingham*

John Bunyan as a literary artist. *N. T. Carrington, M.A. 1926 Birmingham*

The methods and models of Bunyan's allegories. *R. I. Sharrock, B.Litt. 1947 Oxford*

The pilgrim's progress of John Bunyan: sources of the allegory. *J. Foley, M.A. 1949 National University of Ireland*

Bürger, Gottfried August
Bürger's originality. *E. S. Blenkinsop, B.Litt. 1935 Oxford*

Percy's *Reliques* and the ballads of Burger. *A. Milner-Barry, M.A. 1922 Birmingham*

Burgess Books
1. Bristol and Virginia in the seventeenth century. 2. Bristol merchants, shipwrights, etc. from the Burgess Books, 1607-1700. *N. C. P. Tyack, M.A. 1930 Bristol*

Burgh, Hubert de, Earl of Kent
See De Burgh.

Burials
See also Death; Tombs.

Burial customs of the Near East with special reference to the Old Testament. *J. M. Plumley, M.Litt. 1939 Durham*

El Arabah: explorations and excavations at Abydos, 1899-1900, including observations on modes of burial from the end of the old kingdom to the nineteenth dynasty; on the morphology of ceramic and other types; and on the dates of Egyptian employment of materials. *J. Garstang, B.Litt. 1902 Oxford*

Excavations at Bronze Age burial mounds on Stanton Moor. *J. P. Heathcote, M.A. 1930 Sheffield*

The prehistoric burial chambers of England and Wales. *G. E. Daniel, Ph.D. 1938 Cambridge*

Burke, Edmund
Burke: a revaluation. *T. Concannon, M.A. 1940 National University of Ireland*

Burke and the French Revolution. *F. W. Tomlinson, M.Sc. 1928 London*

A critical review of contemporary criticism of Burke's *Reflections on the Revolution in France. A. Bonnerjee, M.Sc. 1938 London, School of Economics and Political Science*

An edition of Burke's *Sublime and Beautiful*, with notes, and an introduction dealing with the place of Burke in English aesthetics in the eighteenth century. *D. W. Jefferson, B.Litt. 1937 Oxford*

The effects of the French Revolution on English literature, with special reference to Burke. *H. W. Hampton, M.A. 1910 Birmingham*

The fortunes of rationalism in English political thought from the publication of Burke's *Reflections on the French Revolution* to the end of the nineteenth century. *G. Meara, M.A. 1933 Wales*

Legal philosophy of Edmund Burke. *J. B. Jaworczykowski, D.Phil. 1949 Oxford*

The literary aspect of Burke. *W. Barry, M.A. 1949 National University of Ireland*

The political thought of Edmund Burke. *A. B. C. Cobban, Ph.D. 1926 Cambridge*

The religious ideas of Edmund Burke. *L. D. Cowley, Ph.D. 1947 London, External Degree*

A study of the sublime, with special reference to the theory of Edmund Burke. *C. S. Ware, M.A. 1949 Wales*

Burma
Administrative beginnings in British Burma, 1826-1843. *B. J. Stewart, Ph.D. 1931 London, School of Oriental and African Studies*

Cultural change, with special reference to the hill tribes of Burma and Assam. *E. R. Leach, Ph.D. 1947 London, School of Economics and Political Science*

1. Early English intercourse with Burma, 1587-1743. 2. The Dalhousie-Phayre correspondence, 1852-1856. *D. G. E. Hall, D.Litt. 1931 London, King's College*

The history of Burma up to 1824. *G. E. Harvey, B.Litt. 1923 Oxford*

Sir Charles Crosthwaite and the consolidation of Burma. *M. S. May-Oung, B.Litt. 1930 Oxford*

Burmese Language
The development of the Burmese language in the medieval period. *M. Wun, B.Litt. 1939 Oxford*

Burmese Literature
The Burmese drama - with reference to the Elizabethan drama. *M. H. Aung, Ph.D. 1933 Dublin, Trinity College*

Konmara Pya Zat, by U Pok Ni, edited with introduction, translation and commentary. *H. Pe, Ph.D. 1944 London, School of Oriental and African Studies*

Burnell, Robert
A biographical sketch of Robert Burnell, with materials for his life. *U. W. Hughes, B.Litt. 1936 Oxford*

Burns, Robert
Burns and religion. *A. B. Jamieson, M.A. 1928 Birmingham*

Nature in the poetry of Robert Burns. *T. M. King, B.Litt. 1943 Dublin, Trinity College*

Robert Burns as the culmination of a literary tradition. *J. Kelleher, M.A. 1938 National University of Ireland*

Bury St. Edmunds
Bury St. Edmund's as a literary centre, with particular reference to the activities of Miles Blomefield, b.1525, and Cox Macro, 1683-1767. *K. W. Dean, M.A. 1925 London*

Bushe, Charles K
Life of Charles K. Bushe, Lord Chief Justice. *M. Brind, M.A. 1919 National University of Ireland*

Bushmen, The
The tribal system in South Africa: a study of the Bushmen and Hottentots. *I. Schapera, Ph.D. 1929 London*

Bushnell, Horace
The doctrine of the person and work of Christ in Horace Bushnell's theology. *D. N. MacMillan, Ph.D. 1935 Edinburgh*

Business Management
See also Industrial Management.

Business control by budget. *D. J. Garden, Ph.D. 1936 Manchester*

The cost problems and price policies of industrial enterprises: a study into the relationships between economic theory and practical business policies. *D. C. Hague, M.Com. 1949 Birmingham*

An investigation into the theoretical and practical aspects of office mechanization. *J. G. Davidson, Ph.D. 1939 Edinburgh*

New developments in costing techniques as an aid to managerial control. *A. E. M. Hegazy, Ph.D. 1950 Birmingham*

A study of business organization in the printing trade. *N. Branton, M.Com. 1937 London, External Degree*

Trends in business organisation in Great Britain since 1856, with special reference to the financial structure of companies, the mechanism of investment and the relations between the shareholder and the company. *J. B. Jeffreys, Ph.D. 1938 London, School of Economics and Political Science*

Butler, James, 2nd Duke of Ormonde
Ireland and the administration of James Butler, 2nd Duke of Ormonde, Lord Lieutenant of Ireland, 1703-1707. *G. E. I. Crosby, M.A. 1935 Liverpool*

Butler, Joseph, Bishop
Butler's contribution to ethical science. *W. B. Roberts, M.A. 1917 Liverpool*

The ethical theory of Bishop Butler. *W. P. Blevin, M.A. 1908 London*

Butler, Samuel
Samuel Butler as a satirist. *R. O. Harmshaw, M.A. 1928 Birmingham*

Buwaihid Dynasty
The early history of the Buwaihid Dynasty beginning with 320 to 356 A.H. *S. Hasan, Ph.D. 1928 London*

Byland Abbey
The Cistercian Movement in the north of England, with special reference to the early history of Byland Abbey. *P. Auty, B.Litt. 1934 Oxford*

Byrhtferth
A critical edition of the *Handboc* or *Enchiridion* of Byrhtferth. *S. J. Crawford, D.Phil. 1930 Oxford*

Byrom, John
John Byrom, F.R.S., 1691-1763: his religious thought and its relation to the movements of his time. *A. R. Hubbuck, Ph.D. 1947 Edinburgh*

The life and writings of John Byrom. *L. G. E. Barker, M.A. 1933 London, University College*

Byron, George Gordon, 6th Baron
The attitude of Wordsworth and Byron towards Napoleon. *R. Griffith, M.A. 1949 Wales*

Baironizm v poezii Lermontova (Byronism in the poetry of Lermontov). *H. Brennan, M.A. 1915 London*

Byron and Shelley considered as types of the revolutionary spirit. *J. J. Jackson, M.A. 1912 London*

Byron and the 'Postscript of the Augustans'. *M. G. Phillips, M.A. 1916 London*

Byron, the dramatist. *M. Norton, M.A. 1940 Birmingham*

Byron, George Gordon, 6th Baron contd.
The Byronic superman in England and Germany. *E. C. Hentschel, M.A. 1936 London, University College*

Byron's artistic truth. *T. Keegan, M.A. 1941 National University of Ireland*

Goethe's influence on Byron and Scott. *M. J. Roberts, M.A. 1915 Wales*

The influence of Byron on Lermontov. *S. K. Mukherjea, B.Litt. 1945 Oxford*

The influence of Byron on Russian poetry. *W. Matthews, Ph.D. 1926 London*

Lamartine et Byron. *E. M. Wright, M.A. 1938 London, King's College*

Lord Byron and Nikolaus Lenau: a comparative study. *S. Korninger, M.A. 1950 Sheffield*

The origins of Byronism in English literature. *R. Ackermann, M.A. 1924 Birmingham*

The social and literary environment of Byron's *Don Juan. N. V. L. Hill, M.A. 1946 Birmingham*

Wordsworth, Coleridge, Byron, Shelley and the French Revolution. *P. R. Griffin, M.A. 1925 National University of Ireland*

Byzantine Church
The Byzantine liturgies. *H. Holloway, M.A. 1918 Belfast*

The Norwegian rite: a study of the Byzantine liturgy. *H. Holloway, D.D. 1934 Belfast*

Byzantine Empire
Church and society in the East Roman Empire from the death of Constantine VIII to the rise of Alexius Comnenus. *J. M. Hussey, Ph.D. 1934 London, Westfield College*

Essay on the Byzantine revival, 717-1071. *E. M. Hale, M.A. 1913 Birmingham*

The Hesychast controversy, with special reference to the *Byzantina historia* of Nicephorus Gregoras and the *Historia* of John Cantacuzenus. *T. A. Hart, M.A. 1949 London, Bedford College*

The intellectual and moral standards of Anna Comnena. *G. G. Buckler, D.Phil. 1927 Oxford*

Lower Nubia in the early Byzantine period. *L. P. Kirwan, B.Litt. 1935 Oxford*

The revival of learning at Constantinople in the eleventh century, with special reference to Michael Psellos. *J. M. Hussey, B.Litt. 1932 Oxford*

Cacao
See Cocoa Industry.

Cadoc, Saint
The Latin life of St. Cadoc: a textual and lexicographical study. *H. D. Emanuel, M.A. 1950 Wales*

Caedmon
Caedmon: the first English poet. *T. W. Breen, M.A. 1951 National University of Ireland*

Caernarvonshire
The Caernarvonshire squires, 1558-1625. *E. G. Jones, M.A. 1936 Wales*

The enclosure movement in Caernarvonshire, with special reference to the Porth-yr-aur papers. *G. A. Plume, M.A. 1935 Wales*

Caerwent
Caerwent and the Roman occupation of South Wales. *V. E. N. Williams, M.A. 1924 Wales*

Caesar, Caius Julius
A study of certain aspects of word order in the prose works of Julius Caesar. *R. S. Davis, M.A. 1938 Wales*

Caiquiez, Louis Charles
The early plays of Louis-Charles Caiquiez, melodramatist (1762-1842): his literary ascendants and descendants. *F. W. M. Draper, Ph.D. 1927 London*

Cairnes, John Elliott
The economics of J. E. Cairnes. *G. H. Van Loo, M.Sc. 1938 London, University College*

J. E. Cairnes. *M. J. Sheehy, M.Econ.Sc. 1941 National University of Ireland*

Cairo Genizah
An edition of: a manuscript of the seventeenth century containing unpublished Hebrew poems by Sa'adia Longo from the *Cairo Genizah. R. A. Cole, M.A. 1948 Manchester*

Calais
The history of Calais under the deputyship of Arthur Plantagenet, Lord Lisle, 1533-1540. *J. Leese, M.A. 1929 Manchester*

Calcutta
History of the East India Company's settlement at Calcutta, 1711-1717, Vol. II. *C. R. Wilson, B.Litt. 1901 Oxford*

Calderón de la Barca, Pedro
Culteranism in the Spanish theatre of the seventeenth century, with particular reference to the works of Calderón de la Barca. *E. M. Wilson, Ph.D. 1933 Cambridge*

The religious dramas of Calderón. *R. Silva, M.A. 1939 Liverpool*

The sources of Calderon's *Principe constante. A. E. Sloman, D.Phil. 1948 Oxford*

Calhoun, John Caldwell
The political ideas of John C. Calhoun. *R. L. Humber, B.Litt. 1923 Oxford*

California
A geographical study of California. *R. Abbott, M.A. 1949 London, External Degree*

Some relationships between power and economic development, with special reference to California. *E. M. Francis, Ph.D. 1939 Cambridge*

Calvin, Jean
Calvin as a literary artist. *E. M. Farrington, M.A. 1945 Belfast*

Calvin's doctrine of Holy Scripture. *E. H. Pruden, Ph.D. 1931 Edinburgh*

Calvin's doctrine of the Lord's Supper in its relation to other sacramental types. *A. Barclay, Ph.D. 1926 Edinburgh*

The conception of the mission of the Church in early reformed theology, with special reference to Calvin's theology and practice in Geneva. *W. H. Clark, Ph.D. 1928 Edinburgh*

Determinism in Calvin. *J. H. Powell, Ph.D. 1928 Edinburgh*

The doctrine of Calvin: parts I and II. *W. G. Cazalet, B.D. & D.D. 1924 Oxford*

The doctrine of the Holy Spirit in John Calvin. *G. Walters, Ph.D. 1949 Edinburgh*

The holiness of God in John Calvin and Rudolph Otto. *W. M. Elliot, Ph.D. 1938 Edinburgh*

John Calvin's conception of the seat of authority in religion. *R. W. McNeur, Ph. D. 1950 Edinburgh*

John Calvin's doctrine of the sovereignty of God. *R. T. L. Liston, Ph.D. 1930 Edinburgh*

The relevancy of Calvin to modern issues within Protestantism. *A. H. Leitch, Ph.D. 1941 Cambridge*

Calvinism
For Calvinistic Methodism, see Methodism.

Public worship in sixteenth century Calvinism. *F. O. Reed, B.Litt. 1934 Oxford*

The relations between Calvinism and social and political thought in the United Kingdom. *R. W. Wilde, M.A. 1933 Manchester*

The rise and decline of Calvinism in England during the archiepiscopate of Whitgift. *B. M. H. Thompson, B.Litt. 1932 Oxford*

Cambodia
Indian political and cultural influence in Cambodia (Kambuja) from the sixth to the fourteenth centuries. *B. R. Chatterji, Ph.D. 1926 London*

Cambridge
The representative history of the county, town and university of Cambridge, 1689-1832. *D. Cook, Ph.D. 1935 London, University College*

Cambridge University
The representative history of the county, town and university of Cambridge, 1689-1832. *D. Cook, Ph.D. 1935 London, University College*

Some Cambridge contacts with France during Tudor and early Stuart times. *T. S. Wyatt, M.Litt. 1938 Cambridge*

Thomas Cartwright and Cambridge, 1547-71. *W. B. Whitaker, M.A. 1924 Bristol*

Cambridgeshire
Judicial investigations under the Dictum of Kenilworth, Cambridgeshire. *C. C. Bayley, M.A. 1929 Manchester*

Judicial proceedings in Cambridgeshire under the Dictum of Kenilworth. *K. H. Holden, M.A. 1929 Manchester*

Judicial proceedings under the Dictum of Kenilworth, Cambridgeshire. *S. Cohen, M.A. 1929 Manchester*

A regional study of south Cambridgeshire, with reference to relevant contiguous areas. *M. J. Buckerfield, M.A. 1946 London, Birkbeck College*

Cambridgeshire contd.
The representative history of the county, town and university of Cambridge, 1689-1832. *D. Cook, Ph.D. 1935 London, University College*

Cambry, Jacques de
La vie et l'oeuvre de Jacques de Cambry (1749-1807). *W. M. Landers, Ph.D. 1946 London, External Degree*

Camoens, Luis de
A study of the life and works of William Julius Mickle, translator of *The Lusiad* (1734-1788). *G. West, M.A. 1932 London, King's College*

Campan, Jeanne Louise Henriette
Madame Campan and her work at Ecouen. *M. G. Tillett, M.A. 1941 Reading*

Campbell, Alexander
The theology of Alexander Campbell in relation to the origin of the Disciples. *J. R. Kellems, Ph.D. 1926 Edinburgh*

Campbell, John McLeod
John McLeod Campbell, theologian: his theological development and trial and a new interpretation of his theory of the atonement. *E. G. Bewkes, Ph.D. 1924 Edinburgh*

Campbell, Thomas
The poetry of Thomas Campbell. *W. I. Sanday, B.Litt. 1943 Oxford*

Campion, Thomas
A study of Thomas Campion as critic and poet. *S. H. Atkins, M.A. 1931 London, King's College*

Thomas Campion (1567-1620): a study of his English works, with particular reference to the influence of music and classical studies on his theory and practice as a metrist. *C. M. Francis, B.Litt. 1938 Oxford*

Canaan
The Hebrew conquest of Canaan. *M. O. Paulden, M.A. 1931 Liverpool*

The settlement of the Hebrews in Canaan. *M. J. C. Dinwoodie, Ph.D. 1936 Edinburgh*

Canada
See also Alberta; Bay Islands; British Columbia; Labrador; Maritime Provinces; Newfoundland; Nova Scotia; Prince Edward Island.

Canada: Armed Forces
The development of Canadian naval bases. *A. L. Pidgeon, B.Litt. 1948 Oxford*

Canada: Constitution
See also Federalism.

The constitutional history of Canada in its earlier days; and the early trading companies of New France. *H. P. Biggar, B.Litt. 1899 Oxford*

Le pouvoir constituant au Canada depuis les origines jusqu'a nos jours. *P. E. Renaud, Ph.D. 1927 London*

Process of constitutional amendment in Canada. *P. Gérin-Lajoie, D.Phil. 1948 Oxford*

Studies in the evolution of dominion status (a) the Governor Generalship of Canada and (b) the development of Canadian nationalism. *G. Neuendorff, Ph.D. 1941 London, School of Economics and Political Science*

Canada: Economics
Canada in boom and depression, 1924 to 1935. *W. J. Hasler, M.Sc. 1936 London, School of Economics and Political Science*

Canada's balance of indebtedness, 1919-1933. *H. A. W. Halls, M.Sc. 1937 London, School of Economics and Political Science*

Canadian monetary and fiscal developments since 1929. *J. E. L. Graham, B.Litt. 1939 Oxford*

The economic history of the province of Canada, 1845-1851. *G. N. Tucker, Ph.D. 1930 Cambridge*

The economics of the settlement of the Prairie Provinces of Canada, 1900-1931. *S. Common, Ph.D. 1933 London, School of Economics and Political Science*

The international trade position of Canada, 1913-1933: an examination of the causes and characteristics of the balance of payments and the balance of trade. *W. E. Duffett, M.Sc. 1935 London, School of Economics and Political Science*

Problems of public finance in the federal states of Canada and Australia, with special reference to the scheme for India. *J. Samuel, M.Com. 1937 Leeds*

The Reciprocity Treaty of 1854: its history, its relation to British colonial and foreign policy and to the development of Canadian fiscal autonomy. *D. C. C. Masters, D.Phil. 1935 Oxford*

Canada: Foreign Affairs
Canada and the Far East. *C. J. Woodsworth, Ph.D. 1940 London, School of Economics and Political Science*

The external affairs of Canada, 1926-1934. *E. B. Rogers, M.Sc. 1935 London, School of Economics and Political Science*

Canada: Geography
The economic geography of north-west Canada with special reference to the agricultural possibilities. *F. B. Vrooman, B.Sc. 1910 Oxford*

Economic geography of North America. *W. McComish, M.Sc. 1936 London, External Degree*

The economics of the settlement of the Prairie Provinces of Canada, 1900-1931. *S. Common, Ph.D. 1933 London, School of Economics and Political Science*

Geographical factors in the development of the Maritime Provinces. *A. S. Gaught, M.A. 1932 London, King's College*

The geography and administration of northern Canada. *T. Lloyd, D.Sc. 1949 Bristol*

A regional survey of the prairie provinces of Canada. *A. W. Richards, M.A. 1924 Liverpool*

Canada: History
See also Merchant Adventurers Company.

British opinion on the federation of Canada. *J. A. Gibson, B.Litt. 1934 Oxford*

British policy and Canada, 1774-91: a study in eighteenth century mercantilism. *G. S. Graham, Ph.D. 1929 Cambridge*

British policy towards Canada, 1812-1837. *K. L. P. Martin, B.Litt. 1921 Oxford*

Canada in British politics from 1763-1783. *M. G. Reid, B.Litt. 1922 Oxford*

A comparison of the British system of colonial government in the American colonies during the half-century preceding the Revolution with that in British Canada before the rebellion of 1837. *W. J. Mulholland, B.Litt. 1920 Oxford*

Great Britain and the evolution of the western part of the international boundary of Canada. *J. O. McCabe, Ph.D. 1941 Glasgow*

The life of Sir Edmund Walker Head, Bart. *J. A. Gibson, D.Phil. 1938 Oxford*

Lord Selkirk's work in Canada. *C. B. Martin, B.Litt. 1912 Oxford*

Political unrest in the Canadian Northwest, with special reference to the first Riel Rebellion, 1869-70. *G. F. G. Stanley, B.Litt. 1932 Oxford*

Political unrest in upper Canada, 1815-1836. *A. Dunham, Ph.D. 1924 London*

The purpose and immediate operation of the Canada Act of 1791. *F. H. Soward, B.Litt. 1922 Oxford*

The second Riel Rebellion, 1870-86. *G. F. G. Stanley, D.Phil. 1935 Oxford*

Self-government in Canada and how it was achieved: the story of Lord Durham's Report. *F. Bradshaw, D.Sc. 1904 London*

The Union Bill of 1822 and the subsequent union schemes in their relation to British policy in Canada prior to 1837. *E. J. Hutchins, B.Litt. 1929 Oxford*

The work of Sir Edmund Head in British North America 1848-61. *D. G. G. Kerr, Ph.D. 1937 London, King's College*

Canada: Politics and Government
The determinants of Canadian federalism. *D. H. Gillis, Ph.D. 1948 London, School of Economics and Political Science*

The geography and administration of northern Canada. *T. Lloyd, D.Sc. 1949 Bristol*

Newfoundland, the tenth province of Canada: the case for union examined. *H. B. Mayo, D.Phil. 1948 Oxford*

Studies in the evolution of dominion status (a) the Governor Generalship of Canada and (b) the development of Canadian nationalism. *G. Neuendorff, Ph.D. 1941 London, School of Economics and Political Science*

Canada: Social History
A history of the real Old Timers of Fort Edmonton (Canada) and its hinterland. *I. M. Harper, M.Litt. 1932 Cambridge*

Canals
See also Bridgewater Canal.

Canals contd.
The ancient Egyptian canals between the Mediterranean and the Red Sea: their problems for the sciences of geology, geography, engineering and history. *W. M. Alexander, D.Sc. 1919 Glasgow*

The English canal system in its geographical and industrial relations. *R. W. G. Bryant, M.Sc. 1939 London, School of Economics and Political Science*

English coasting trade and inland navigation from 1600 to 1750. *T. S. Willan, D.Phil. 1934 Oxford*

Canfield, Benedict
Benedict Canfield (William Fitch), Capuchin: the man and his writings. *C. J. Reel, B.Litt. 1948 Oxford*

Canning, George
The domestic relations of George Canning. *J. Veitch, M.A. 1927 Liverpool*

George Canning and the Tory schism, 1809-1822. *J. Veitch, Ph.D. 1932 Liverpool*

Canon Law
See Law, Ecclesiastical.

Canonisation
See Saints.

Cantacuzenus, John
The Hesychast controversy, with special reference to the *Byzantina historia* of Nicephorus Gregoras and the *Historia* of John Cantacuzenus. *T. A. Hart, M.A. 1949 London, Bedford College*

Canterbury
Canterbury Cathedral priory: a study in monastic administration. *R. A. L. Smith, Ph.D. 1941 Cambridge*

Christ Church, Canterbury, and the *sede vacante* jurisdiction of Canterbury during the thirteenth century. *M. M. Morgan, B.Litt. 1938 Oxford*

Custodia essexae: a study of the conventual property held by the Priory of Christ Church, Canterbury, in the counties of Essex, Suffolk and Norfolk. *J. F. Nichols, Ph.D. 1930 London, King's College*

Canterbury, Province of
The minor corporations of the secular cathedrals of the province of Canterbury (excluding the Welsh sees) between the thirteenth century and 1536, with special reference to the minor canons of St. Paul's Cathedral from their origin in the twelfth century to the visitations of Bishop Gilson in 1724. *A. R. B. Fuller, M.A. 1947 London, Birkbeck College*

Cantillon, Richard
Richard Cantillon; his position in the history of economic doctrines. *J. Nagle, M.Sc. 1930 National University of Ireland*

Cape of Good Hope
Constitutional development at the Cape of Good Hope, 1795-1854. *G. von W. Eybers, M.A. 1916 London*

Capital
British capital export, 1900-1913. *J. H. A. M. Lenfant, Ph.D. 1949 London, School of Economics and Political Science*

Capital formation and the economic order: an analytical study, with special reference to the case of a poor country. . *Y. L. Wu, Ph.D. 1946 London, School of Economics and Political Science*

Capital structure and depression. *L. M. Lachmann, M.Sc. 1935 London, School of Economics and Political Science*

The concept of capital in economic theory. *R. Zafiriou, Ph.D. 1945 London, School of Economics and Political Science*

English capital theory in the light of recent developments (with special reference to Ricardo and Jevons). *S. Goldman, M.Sc. 1933 London, School of Economics and Political Science*

The export of capital. *C. K. Hobson, D.Sc. 1914 London*

Fluctuation in new capital issues on the London money market, 1899-1913. *G. L. A. Ayres, M.Sc. 1934 London, School of Economics and Political Science*

The import of capital. *R. Wilson, D.Phil. 1930 Oxford*

The influence of Böhm-Bawerk on American theories of capital and interest. *E. White, M.Sc. 1935 London, School of Economics and Political Science*

The marginal productivity of capital, with special reference to the U.S.A. *L. Tarshis, Ph.D. 1940 Cambridge*

Capital contd.
A statistical examination of how industry adapts itself to changes in the volume of output and the effects of such changes on the amounts of fixed and working capital employed. *W. A. Tweddle, Ph.D. 1938 Cambridge*

The theory of value on the capital market. *H. Makower, Ph.D. 1937 London, School of Economics and Political Science*

Capital Punishment
See Punishment.

Capitalism
See also Industrial Management.

Capitalist enterprise and social progress. *M. H. Dobb, Ph.D. 1925 London*

Capitulations
The capitulations and the mixed tribunals generally. *T. Francoudi, LL.D. 1915 London*

The legal obligations arising out of treaty relations between China and other states. *M. T. Z. Tyau, LL.D. 1916 London*

Capponi, Niccolo
The last Florentine Republic, to the fall of Niccolo Capponi. *C. Roth, B.Litt. 1923 Oxford*

Capus, Alfred
A contribution to the study of the plays of Alfred Capus. *F. L. Heath, Ph.D. 1930 London, University College*

Caravaggio, Michelangelo Amerighi
An estimate of Caravaggio and his influence on the succeeding generation in Italy. *F. Ashford, M.A. 1936 London, University College*

Cardiff
History of Port of Cardiff in relation to its hinterland with special reference to the years 1830-1914. *T. M. Hodges, M.Sc. 1946 London, External Degree*

Cardigan
History of the town and castle of Cardigan. *G. Owen, M.A. 1907 Wales*

Careers
See also Education, Vocational; Employment; Vocational Guidance.

An enquiry into the careers of these pupils who enter the secondary school after their second attempt in the admission examination. *D. M. Coombes, M.A. 1935 Birmingham*

An enquiry into the nature of the difficulties experienced by university students in choosing a career. *V. C. Chamberlain, M.A. 1950 Manchester*

Factors in occupational maladjustment: a comparative study of the careers of employed and unemployed lads in a typical London district. *S. M. Bevington, Ph.D. 1933 London, External Degree*

Occupational interests in relation to intelligence. *J. L. Stephen, M.A. 1938 London, University College*

Some investigations concerning the work of a central school in relation to the future occupations of its pupils. *A. D. Hawkins, M.Sc. 1933 Birmingham*

A study of the choice of occupation among secondary school pupils. *W. R. Hecker, M.A. 1937 London, Institute of Education*

A study of vocational wishes of a group of secondary school pupils in relation to their interests, scholastic attainments and attitudes. *B. R. Pasricha, M.A. 1949 London, Institute of Education*

A vocational investigation of some of the factors affecting the early industrial careers of elementary-school boys. *A. W. Heim, Ph.D. 1940 Cambridge*

Carew, Richard
Richard Carew. *A. K. Hamilton Jenkin, B.Litt. 1924 Oxford*

Carew, Thomas
An edition of the poetical works of Thomas Carew, with introduction and notes. *S. R. Dunlap, D.Phil. 1939 Oxford*

Carey, Henry
Henry Carey, poet, dramatist and satirist. *F. T. Wood, Ph.D. 1930 London, External Degree*

Caribbean Sea and Islands
See West Indies.

Carle, Lancelot de
The life and works of Lancelot de Carle. *L. C. Harmer, Ph.D. 1937 Cambridge*

Carleton, William
William Carleton. *E. O'Connor, M.A. 1939 National University of Ireland*

William Carleton, novelist; a study in Anglo-Irish literature. *T. O'Mahony, M.A. 1934 National University of Ireland*

Carlo Emanuele I, Duke of Savoy
The relations between James VI and I and Carlo Emanuele I, Duke of Savoy. *J. Thompson, Ph.D. 1942 Saint Andrew's*

Carlyle, Thomas
Carlyle and Emerson. *N. Cogan, M.A. 1915 National University of Ireland*

Critics of democracy: Carlyle, Arnold, Stephen (Fitzjames), Maine, Lecky. *B. E. Lippincott, Ph.D. 1931 London, School of Economics and Political Science*

The influence of German literature on English literature in the early nineteenth century, with special reference to Thomas Carlyle. *B. J. Morse, M.A. 1929 Wales*

The religious thought of Thomas Carlyle. *D. E. Roberts, Ph.D. 1948 Edinburgh*

St. Simon and Carlyle to 1835. *T. F. Thompson, M.A. 1939 Birmingham*

Studies in the thought of Thomas Carlyle. *I. M. Christie, M.A. 1947 Belfast*

The theme of 'Bildung' in *Wilhelm Meister*, and the moral and religious teaching of the early Carlyle to 1843. *G. F. Senior, M.A. 1950 Manchester*

Carmarthen
The history of the town and castle of Carmarthen to 1603. *D. M. Roberts, M.A. 1908 Wales*

Carmarthenshire
Carmarthenshire under the Tudors. *T. H. Lewis, M.A. 1919 Wales*

Carmelite Order
See also Religious Orders and Societies.

Some aspects of the English Carmelites in the first half of the fifteenth century. *M. E. Turner, M.A. 1933 Manchester*

Carmina Latina Epigraphica
Religious ideas in the *Carmina Latina Epigraphica.* *W. S. Williams, M.A. 1939 Wales*

Carnwyllion
A study of the economic development of the commote of Carnwyllion from 1500. *J. H. Morgan, M.A. 1933 Wales*

Caroline, Queen of England
Queen Caroline and literature. *M. Lindley, M.A. 1927 Liverpool*

Carols
See also Hymns; Songs.

English songs and carols of the fifteenth century: text and transcriptions of the music. *J. Copley, M.A. 1940 Leeds*

Carossa, Hans
Hans Carossa and the Goethean tradition. *P. Mecklenburg, Ph.D. 1944 National University of Ireland*

Carriage
The carrier's liability. *E. G. M. Fletcher, LL.D. 1932 London, External Degree*

The liability for safe carriage of goods in Roman-Dutch law. *T. E. Donges, LL.D. 1925 London*

Carrier, Jean Baptiste
Jean-Baptiste Carrier and the Terror in the Vendée. *E. H. Carrier, M.A. 1915 Liverpool*

Carthage
The Carthaginians as depicted in Livy, Polybius, and other ancient writers. *G. Adams, M.A. 1922 London*

Carthage, Saint
Vocabulary to lives of St. Carthage. *M. Lucy, M.A. 1915 National University of Ireland*

Cartography
See Maps.

Cartwright, John
Major John Cartwright: his place in contemporary radical movements. *A. A. Eaglestone, B.Litt. 1930 Oxford*

Cartwright, Thomas
Thomas Cartwright and Cambridge, 1547-71. *W. B. Whitaker, M.A. 1924 Bristol*

Cartwright, William
An edition of *The royall slave* by William Cartwright, with a consideration of the manuscript newly acquired by the British Museum together with a short life of Cartwright and a general survey of his dramatic works. *N. Clark, M.A. 1932 London, University College*

An edition of William Cartwright's *The ordinary.* *E. R. Gebhardt, B.Litt. 1933 Oxford*

The life and poems of William Cartwright. *R. C. Goffin, M.A. 1914 London*

Cary, Henry Francis
Henry Francis Cary, 1772-1844, translator of Dante: a study. *R. W. King, M.A. 1919 London*

Cary, John
The life and writings of John Cary. *H. T. Lane, M.A. 1932 Bristol*

Caryll, John
John Caryll, Pope's friend. *S. K. Mugaseth, B.Litt. 1936 Oxford*

Cassington
The early inhabitants of the Oxford neighbourhood, with special reference to Cassington. *C. Musgrave, B.Sc. 1939 Oxford*

Castelar y Ripoll, Emilio
The influence of Emilio Castelar on the formation and fortunes of the Spanish Republic of 1873. *J. A. Brandt, B.Litt. 1925 Oxford*

Castell, Edmund
Dr. Edmund Castell, 1606-1685: studies of some aspects of eastern learning in seventeenth-century Britain. *M. Zamick, Ph.D. 1934 Saint Andrew's*

Castile
The part of Castile in the Hundred Years' War. *A. Christelow, B.Litt. 1934 Oxford*

Castillo Solórzano, Alonso del
A critical study of the novels of D. Alonso de Castillo Solorzano. *P. N. Dunn, M.A. 1949 London, King's College*

Castle Lyons
Castle Lyons, the works-depot of the twentieth Legion at Holt, Denbighshire: a description and history of the site, with a catalogue of the pottery and other objects found, its place in the history of the Roman occupation of north Wales, together with a study of an aspect of the Romano-British pottery industry. *W. F. Grimes, M.A. 1930 Wales*

Castlereagh, Robert Stewart, 2nd Marquis of Londonderry
The act of legislative union between Great Britain and Ireland, with special reference to the political career of Castlereagh. *H. M. Hyde, M.A. 1933 Belfast*

Castlereagh and the Holy Alliance. *H. C. Hamilton, M.A. 1926 Birmingham*

The life of Viscount Castlereagh, second Marquess of Londonderry. *R. V. Holt, B.Litt. 1910 Oxford*

Casuistry
English casuistry of the seventeenth century and its relations with medieval and Jesuit casuistry. *T. Wood, M.A. 1947 Leeds*

Jeremy Taylor and seventeenth century English casuistry, with special reference to the *Ductor dubitantium.* *T. Wood, B.D. 1945 Leeds*

Catechism
See Religious Education.

Categories (Logic)
The nature and function of the categories in the philosophy of Immanuel Kant, James Ward, S. Alexander. *J. V. Bateman, Ph.D. 1933 Edinburgh*

Cathedrals
See also under the names of individual cathedrals and cathedral cities.

The cathedral system in the Church of Ireland since the disestablishment. *H. A. Boyd, B.Litt. 1950 Dublin, Trinity College*

The minor corporations of the secular cathedrals of the province of Canterbury (excluding the Welsh sees) between the thirteenth century and 1536, with special reference to the minor canons of St. Paul's Cathedral from their origin in the twelfth century to the visitations of Bishop Gilson in 1724. *A. R. B. Fuller, M.A. 1947 London, Birkbeck College*

Catherine of Alexandria, Saint
A comparative study of four Old French versions of the life of Saint Catherine of Alexandria. *W. L. Williams, M.A. 1944 Wales*

Die niederdeutsche gereimte Katharinenlegende der Brüsseler Hs.No.II.143, und ihr Verhältnis zu dem mitteldeutschen Wolfenbüttler Fragmenten: Text und Untersuchung. *W. E. Collinson, M.A. 1912 London*

Trī tonna dibhfheirge Dé agus *Beatha Chaitriona* (*The three surges of God's wrath* and *The life of Catherine*). *E. J. Edmonds, M.A. 1930 National University of Ireland*

Catholic Apostolic Church
The Catholic Apostolic church, sometimes called Irvingite: an historical study. *P. E. O. Shaw, Ph.D. 1935 Edinburgh*

Cato, Marcus Porcius, the Younger
Cato Minor. *J. O'Donovan, M.A. 1945 National University of Ireland*

Catullus
The influence of Catullus in the sixteenth century in France. *M. G. Morrison, Ph.D. 1940 Cambridge*

The limitations imposed upon Latin lyric poetry by the special nature of the Latin language, with special reference to Horace and Catullus. *F. N. Miles, M.A. 1933 Wales*

The relation of Catullus and the Augustan elegiac Latin poets to Alexandrian literature. *M. E. Fish, M.A. 1918 London*

The syntax of archaic Latin, with special reference to the usage of Catullus and Lucretius. *A. L. Thomas, M.A. 1913 Wales*

Causality
Causality. *D. McCarthy, M.A. 1940 National University of Ireland*

Causality and freedom. *J. Strain, M.A. 1920 Belfast*

Causality in Al-Ghazali, Averroes, and Aquinas. *M. Fakhry, Ph.D. 1949 Edinburgh*

Cause, value and God. *T. A. Burkill, Ph.D. 1941 Manchester*

An examination of the notion of cause in the light of recent contributions to the philosophy of nature. *R. L. Saw, Ph.D. 1927 London*

Exemplary causality in the philosophy of St. Thomas. *P. Creed, M.A. 1947 National University of Ireland*

Kant's treatment of causality. *A. C. Ewing, D.Phil. 1923 Oxford*

The relations of science to philosophy, with special reference to the conceptions of substance and causation. *J. Owen, M.A. 1908 Wales*

The religious conception of intermediary beings in relation to the idea of causation. *W. J. Beale, Ph.D. 1935 Sheffield*

The treatment of causality in the philosophy of Hume. *J. M. Weldon, M.A. 1930 National University of Ireland*

Cavour, Camille Benso di
The early life and letters of Cavour. *A. J. B. Whyte, Litt.D. 1927 Dublin, Trinity College*

Caxton, William
A biographical study of William Caxton, with special reference to his life and work in the Low Countries. *W. J. B. Crotch, M.A. 1927 London*

Critical edition of Caxton's *Fayttes of armes and of chivalrye. A. T. P. Byles, Ph.D. 1933 London, External Degree*

The *Dicts and Sayings of the philosophers. C. F. Buhler, Litt.D. 1947 Dublin, Trinity College*

Introduction and glossary to the *Book of the Ordre of Chyvalry*, translated and printed by William Caxton from a French version of the Catalan tract by Ramon Lull, entitled *Le Libre del Orde de Cavayleria*; and to Adam Loutfut's Scottish transcription, made in 1494 and contained in Harleian ms. 6149 at the British Museum. *A. T. P. Byles, M.A. 1925 London*

A study of Caxton's Ovid. *A. E. Wilmott, M.A. 1909 London*

The work and importance of W. Caxton. *G. A. Tyrrell, M.A. 1922 Birmingham*

Cazalis, Henri
See Lahor, J.

Céitinn, Seathrún
Coimheas idir stíl Chéitinn agus stíl *Desiderius* (A comparison between the style of Céitinn and the style of *Desiderius*). *S. Ní hEaluighthe, M.A. 1943 National University of Ireland*

Celsus
A comparison of the pagan apologetic of Celsus against Christianity as contained in Origen's *Contra Celsum*, and the neo-Hindu attitude to Christianity as represented in the works of Vivekananda, and an estimate of the value of Origen's reply for Christian apologetics against neo-Hinduism. *J. R. Chandran, B.Litt. 1949 Oxford*

A critical survey of the advances made in surgery and anatomy in the *Corpus Hippocraticum* and the *De Medicina* of Celsus, with a short history of surgery and anatomy from the earliest times down to the beginning of the Christian era. *A. V. R. Don, Ch.M. 1922 Aberdeen*

Celtic Church
The Celtic church in England after the synod of Whitby. *J. L. G. Meissner, M.A. 1927 Belfast*

Celtic Church contd.
Queen Margaret and the influence she exerted on the Celtic Church in Scotland. *T. R. Barnett, Ph.D. 1925 Edinburgh*

Ritual background of Celtic heroes and saints: a study of some of the survivals of pagan elements in early Celtic Christianity. *A. D. Reese, M.A. 1937 Wales*

Celtic Languages and Literatures
See also Breton; Irish; Scottish (Gaelic); Welsh.

The affinities of Italic and Celtic. *J. L. Jones, M.A. 1909 Wales*

Contribution à l'étude de la botanologie celtique: les noms de plantes des *Four Ancient Books of Wales. P. R. Y. M. Diverres, M.A. 1915 Liverpool*

A contribution to Celtic philology. *E. Mac an Fhailghigh, M.A. 1939 National University of Ireland*

The influence of Celtic literature on that of England. *J. O. M. McCaffrey, M.A. 1938 National University of Ireland*

The Nibelungen saga in Celtic literature. *M. O'Doherty, M.A. 1916 National University of Ireland*

Sgoláirí Ceiltise (Celtic scholars). *M. C. MacConformhaoile, M.A. 1936 National University of Ireland*

A study, critical, historical and linguistic, of the earliest relations between Celts and Germans. *C. S. Elston, Ph.D. 1933 London, Birkbeck College*

The verbal system in bardic poetry. *J. B. Arthurs, M.A. 1942 Belfast*

Celts
Celtic ethnology and culture. *E. J. O'Driscoll, M.A. 1928 National University of Ireland*

The eschatology of the ancient Celts. *D. O. Jones, M.A. 1927 Wales*

The psychological nature and origin of the belief in fairies in Celtic countries. *W. Y. E. Wentz, B.Sc. 1910 Oxford*

A study, critical, historical and linguistic, of the earliest relations between Celts and Germans. *C. S. Elston, Ph.D. 1933 London, Birkbeck College*

Cenannensis, Codex
See Kells, Book of.

Central Society of Education
Sir Thomas Wise and the Central Society of Education. *I. D. Harry, M.A. 1932 Wales*

Ceramics
The Attic *stamnos. B. Philippakis, D.Phil. 1950 Oxford*

Black figured skyphoi. *A. Veinoglou, M.A. 1941 Reading*

Castle Lyons, the works-depot of the twentieth Legion at Holt, Denbighshire: a description and history of the site, with a catalogue of the pottery and other objects found, its place in the history of the Roman occupation of north Wales, together with a study of an aspect of the Romano-British pottery industry. *W. F. Grimes, M.A. 1930 Wales*

Demotic ostraka from the collections at Oxford, Paris, Berlin, Vienna, and Cairo. *G. Mattha, D.Phil. 1936 Oxford*

A descriptive report on publications dealing with Greek and demotic ostraca. *G. Mattha, B.Litt. 1933 Oxford*

Early archaic red-figure vase painting during the period 530-510 B.C. *P. Pitt, M.A. 1937 Birmingham*

The economic development of the North Staffordshire potteries since 1730, with special reference to the Industrial Revolution. *J. Thomas, Ph.D. 1934 London, School of Economics and Political Science*

The economic history of the Staffordshire pottery industry. *E. S. Dane, M.A. 1929 Sheffield*

El Arabah: explorations and excavations at Abydos, 1899-1900, including observations on modes of burial from the end of the old kingdom to the nineteenth dynasty; on the morphology of ceramic and other types; and on the dates of Egyptian employment of materials. *J. Garstang, B.Litt. 1902 Oxford*

Fifty years of Greek vase-painting: Euphronios and his contemporaries. *E. Radford, M.A. 1913 London*

The human geography of the English pottery industry. *E. J. M. Haynes, B.Litt. 1925 Oxford*

An investigation of Mycenaean pottery from the Levant and of some local variations of Mycenaean pottery. *F. H. Stubbings, Ph.D. 1948 Cambridge*

Ceramics contd.
Middle Attic black-figure painting, with special reference to vases in the Manchester district. *J. M. T. Charlton, M.A. 1940 Manchester*

Minor Attic black figured vases in north-western museums. *B. Mulholland, M.A. 1950 Manchester*

The organization of the Athenian pottery industry. *D. M. Edwards, M.A. 1940 Manchester*

The pottery of the Hellenistic period to the rise of the Aretine wares. *F. N. Pryce, M.A. 1913 Wales*

Prehistoric pottery in China. *G. D. Wu, Ph.D. 1937 London, Courtauld Institute of Art*

The progress of labour organization in the pottery industry of Great Britain. *W. H. Warburton, B.Litt. 1928 Oxford*

Roman amphorae. *M. H. Callender, Ph.D. 1950 Durham*

Selected south Italian vases of the Manchester Museum. *A. Cambitoglou, M.A. 1948 Manchester*

Studies in early pottery of the Near East. *H. Frankfort, M.A. 1923 London*

Studies in South Indian pottery. *T. B. Nayar, M.A. 1931 London, University College*

Cereals Industry
See also Flour Milling Industry.

Comparative study of cereal supplies, marketing and prices in the Punjab, Great Britain, Denmark, France, U.S.A., and Canada. *M. S. Niaz, B.Litt. 1950 Oxford*

The grain trade between England and North Germany, 1815-1870. *H. G. Arnold, M.A. 1930 Manchester*

Certainty
The doctrine of assurance in the experience and thought of the eighteenth century, with special reference to John Wesley. *A. S. Yates, Ph.D. 1949 Leeds*

Philosophy of certitude. *T. J. McGrath, M.A. 1915 National University of Ireland*

Cervantes Saavedra, Miguel de
Algunas ideas religiosas y morales de Cervantes. *G. A. Johnson, M.A. 1942 National University of Ireland*

Cervantes, with special reference to *Don Quixote*, in English literature until 1781. *A. H. Mayor, B.Litt. 1926 Oxford*

The influence of Cervantes on English literature of the eighteenth century. *M. Salmons, M.A. 1929 Manchester*

Céspedes y Meneses, Gonzalo de
The life and works of Gonzalo de Céspedes y Meneses, with bibliographical notes on the Spanish novel of the seventeenth century. *J. A. Bourne, Ph.D. 1937 Cambridge*

Ceylon
See also Sinhalese, The.

Ceylon under the British occupation: its political and economic development, 1795-1833. *C. R. de Silva, Ph.D. 1932 London, King's College*

Constitutional developments in Ceylon during the period 1928-48. *S. Namasivayam, B.Phil. 1948 Oxford*

1. Dictionary of Pali Proper Names. 2. Vamsatthappakasini, or commentary on the *Mahāvamsa*. 3. The extended *Mahāvamsa. G. P. Malalasekera, D. Lit. 1938 London, External Degree*

The distribution of population and the development of settlements in Ceylon. *A. Giniġé, M.A. 1930 London, School of Economics and Political Science*

The evolution of the economic geography of early Ceylon. *P. F. Xavier, M.A. 1930 Liverpool*

A historical criticism of *Mahavamsa. G. C. Mendis, Ph.D. 1931 London, School of Oriental and African Studies*

The physiographic evolution of Ceylon. *K. Kularatnam, M.A. 1944 London, External Degree*

The state of society in Ceylon as depicted in the *Saddharma-ratnavaliya* and other Sinhalese literature of the thirteenth century. *M. B. Ariyapala, Ph.D. 1949 London, School of Oriental and African Studies*

Chaco
The Chaco dispute: a study of pacific methods of settling international disputes. *J. W. Mallinson, M.Sc. 1939 London, School of Economics and Political Science*

Chadderton, Lancashire
The social, economic and administrative development of Chadderton, 1847-1914. *E. Beech, M.A. 1949 Manchester*

Chadwick, Edwin
Edwin Chadwick and the public health movement, 1832-1854. *R. A. Lewis, Ph.D. 1949 Birmingham*

Chaga, The
The educational system of the Chaga, with special reference to 1. The light thrown by social anthropology on the origins of education. 2. The theories of the nature of education and of educational psychology. 3. The educational planning of the present day. *O. F. Raum, Ph.D. 1938 London, External Degree*

Chalmers, Thomas
The theology of Thomas Chalmers. *W. P. Huie, Ph.D. 1949 Edinburgh*

Chalukyas, The
History of the Western Chalukyas (political and administrative). *G. Raychaudhuri, Ph.D. 1948 London, School of Oriental and African Studies*

Chamberlayne, William
Some aspects of the life and literary work of William Chamberlayne of Shaftesbury, 1619-1689. *A. E. Parsons, Ph.D. 1924 London*

Chambers, William, Sir
An enquiry concerning the architectural theory and practice of Sir William Chambers, R.A. *H. M. Martienssen, Ph.D. 1949 London, Courtauld Institute of Art*

Chamisso, Adalbert von
Studien zur Entstehungsgeschichte von Chamissos *Peter Schlemihl. P. M. Herzmark, M.A. 1926 London*

Chance (Philosophy)
Aristotle's conception of chance in nature and in human life. *H. Weiss, M.Litt. 1945 Cambridge*

Contingency. *M. Lebus, M.A. 1919 London*

Channel Islands
See also Guernsey; Jersey.

The importance of the Channel Islands in British relations with the Continent during the thirteenth and fourteenth centuries: a study in historical geography. *D. T. Williams, M.A. 1927 Wales*

A study of the administration of the Channel Islands in the thirteenth and early fourteenth centuries, based mainly upon the assize rolls and other unprinted documents. *J. H. Le Patourel, D.Phil. 1934 Oxford*

Channing, William Ellery
The theological and religious teaching of William Ellery Channing. *A. D. Williams, Ph.D. 1937 Edinburgh*

Chansons de Geste
See Romances.

Chantari di Lancilotto
A study of some texts belonging to the Map-cycle in Italy, and especially of the *Chantari di Lancilotto*, with a short introduction on the history of the Arthurian tradition in Italy. *E. T. Griffiths, M.A. 1914 Wales*

Chantries
Agrarian conditions and changes in west Wales during the sixteenth century, with special reference to monastic and chantry lands. *G. D. Owen, Ph.D. 1935 Wales*

Some aspects of the chantry system in Lancashire. *M. F. Coogan, M.A. 1944 Manchester*

The suppression of chantries in England. *S. E. Hodgson, M.A. 1931 Leeds*

Chapman, George
Chapman's method of translating Homer: being studies in books I, II, and XVIII of the *Iliad*, and book V of the *Odyssey. M. M. Weale, M.A. 1920 London*

An edition of *The Shadow of Night*, by George Chapman. *M. A. Gateson, B.Litt. 1938 Oxford*

George Chapman: a critical assessment of his poetry, dramatic and non-dramatic, with particular reference to his philosophical development insofar as it influences his medium. *B. Bruckshaw, M.A. 1950 Manchester*

George Chapman: life and works (exclusive of translations); the relationship of the poems to the tragedies, 1559-1634. *M. Treadgold, M.A. 1936 London, Bedford College*

Chapman, George contd.
Stoicism and political theory in the tragedies of George Chapman. *L. F. Haddakin, M.A. 1948 London, University College*

A study of George Chapman's *Shadow of night. C. Symes, M.A. 1948 Birmingham*

Chapone, Hester
The life and works of Hester Chapone. *I. H. Robinson, B.Litt. 1936 Oxford*

Character
See also Psychology.

Ability to estimate character. *J. Wedeck, Ph.D. 1933 London, University College*

Character and intelligence: an attempt at an exact study of character. *E. Webb, D.Sc. 1914 London*

The child's environment and its influence on the development of character and the origin of the neuroses. *T. M. Hornik, B.Sc. 1943 Oxford*

Error and variability of judgment in routine work: their relation to assessments of character. *J. D. Gobat, Ph.D. 1938 London, External Degree*

Organized character. *S. Bryant, D.Sc. 1884 London*

Regeneration and the new psychology, with special reference to character changes. *A. D. Dodd, Ph.D. 1935 Edinburgh*

Character Books
Books of character of the seventeenth century. *G. P. Williams, M.A. 1906 Wales*

The seventeenth century character, with a brief sketch of its anticipations in English literature, and a bibliography of character books published in the seventeenth and eighteenth centuries. *T. B. Wheeler, M.A. 1911 Wales*

Charities
The Chatham Chest. *E. G. Mawson, M.A. 1931 Liverpool*

The development of subscription charity schools in England and Wales, from the close of the seventeenth to the close of the eighteenth century, with special reference to London and district. *H. J. Larcombe, Ph.D. 1928 London*

A history of Charity School education and a statistical survey of some measures of educational growth. *R. W. Hitchcock, Ph.D. 1938 London, King's College*

The influence of charity on education in England. *F. Mitchell, M.Ed. 1930 Manchester*

The place of charity and voluntary social service in the life of the community. *C. Braithwaite, Ph.D. 1938 London, External Degree*

The position and duties of the King's almoner, 1255-1327. *M. E. Lack, M.A. 1949 London, Royal Holloway College*

A statistical study of the growth of charity schools. *R. W. Hitchcock, M.A. 1933 London, Institute of Education*

Charles Albert, King of Sardinia
The foreign policy of Charles Albert (1848-9), with special reference to England. *J. P. H. Myres, B.Litt. 1932 Oxford*

Charles II, King of England
The administration of Scotland during the reigns of Charles II and James VII. *W. B. Gray, B.Litt. 1920 Oxford*

Charlett, Arthur
The correspondence of Arthur Charlett (Master of University College, 1692-1722) in its antiquarian and historical aspects. *S. G. Gillam, B.Litt. 1948 Oxford*

Charroi de Nîmes
See Romances.

Charters
See also Archives.

Anglo-Saxon charters. *A. J. Robertson, Ph.D. 1934 Cambridge*

A linguistic study of the Tournay charters acquired by the British Museum in 1914. *W. G. Walmsley, M.A. 1921 London*

Study of early English charters. *W. F. Binchy, M.A. 1929 National University of Ireland*

The town charters granted under the Protectorate. *B. L. K. Henderson, M.A. 1909 London*

Chartier, Alain
Alain Chartier and the political conditions of France in the year 1422. *W. P. Ellis, M.A. 1934 Liverpool*

Alain Chartier's *Quadrilogue invectif. D. Kirkland, M.A. 1935 Liverpool*

Chartists
Chartism and the Churches, with special reference to Lancashire: an account of the Churches and social reform in the Chartist period. *N. J. McLellan, Ph.D. 1947 Edinburgh*

The Chartist movement in Wales. *M. Williams, M.A. 1919 Wales*

Knowledge Chartism: a study of the influence of Chartism on nineteenth century educational development in Great Britain. *R. A. Jones, M.A. 1938 Birmingham*

The machinery of public order in England during the Chartist period, 1837-1848. *F. C. Mather, M.A. 1948 Manchester*

Social aspects of the Chartist movement. *H. J. R. Bennett, M.A. 1927 Birmingham*

Chasles, Philarète
Philarète Chasles and his connection with England. *A. G. D. Page, M.A. 1931 London, East London College*

Chateaubriand, François René de, Vicomte
Chateaubriand and Flaubert. *M. E. Clayton-Chance, M.A. 1921 Birmingham*

Châteaubriand's earliest critics in England, 1797-1822. *E. B. Hughes, Ph.D. 1939 London, Queen Mary College*

A contribution to the study of Chateaubriand's *Vie de Pance. M. Purcell, M.A. 1931 London, University College*

A contribution to the study of the sources of the *Génie du Christianisme. M. Dempsey, Ph.D. 1927 London*

An edition of: Châteaubriand, Lettre à M. de Fontanes sur la campagne romaine. *J. M. H. Gautier, M.A. 1950 Manchester*

Etude sur la correspondence de François-René de Châteaubriand, des années 1789-1823. *M. L. Harris, M.A. 1914 Birmingham*

Le mal de René. *K. M. O'Flaherty, Ph.D. 1943 National University of Ireland*

A study of the language of Chateaubriand's 'American' books, viz., *Atala, René, Les Natchez* and the *Voyage en Amérique*, with additional notes on the language of *Le dernier Abencérage. H. E. Hebb, M.A. 1926 Leeds*

Châteaubriant, Alphonse de
Le vocabulaire d'Alphonse de Châteaubriant. *R. F. Walker, M.A. 1936 Leeds*

Chatham Chest, The
The Chatham Chest. *E. G. Mawson, M.A. 1931 Liverpool*

Chatterton, Thomas
Chatterton, Thomas. *M. E. Lynam, M.A. 1946 National University of Ireland*

Chaucer, Geoffrey
The attitude of Chaucer towards chivalry, the Church and the people, compared with that of Langland, Wycliffe and Gower. *J. F. Evans, M.A. 1911 Wales*

Certain adverbial usages in Chaucer. *A. Pearce, M.A. 1928 Manchester*

Chaucer and Langland as painters of English life. *M. Donegan, M.A. 1948 National University of Ireland*

Chaucer and mediaeval romantic literature. *A. B. Southerns, M.A. 1913 National University of Ireland*

The debt of Chaucer to Boccaccio. *G. S. Griffiths, B.Litt. 1925 Oxford*

The development of literary criticism in England until 1800, as seen by the treatment of the works of Geoffrey Chaucer and Edmund Spenser. *D. M. Smith, M.A. 1923 Wales*

Dunbar's debt to Chaucer. *D. Burnicle, M.A. 1934 Birmingham*

Eastern influences in Chaucer with special reference to the Arabs. *E. J. S. Saigh, Ph.D. 1946 London, King's College*

The elements of Chaucer's narrative art. *L. E. H. Quick, M.A. 1917 Bristol*

English heroic line structure from Chaucer to Wyatt. *W. F. Pyle, Ph.D. 1933 Dublin, Trinity College*

An examination into some elements of Spenser's psychological vocabulary, with reference to that of Chaucer. *M. Topham, M.A. 1931 Manchester*

An examination of certain portions of the French element in Chaucer's vocabulary. *H. Goldstraw, M.A. 1931 Manchester*

Chaucer, Geoffrey contd.
Geoffrey Chaucer and Guillaume de Machaut. L. Febvre, M.A. 1948 National University of Ireland

The influence of Chaucer, Gower, and Lydgate on the Scottish poets in the fifteenth and early sixteenth centuries. P. W. Thomson, B.Litt. 1915 Oxford

Introduction and notes to the Reves tale. L. Blakeley, M.A. 1946 Birmingham

Prose works of Chaucer. M. O'Gorman, M.A. 1937 National University of Ireland

The relation of Chaucer to chivalry. L. M. Evans, M.A. 1911 Wales

The relation of Chaucer to chivalry. T. G. Williams, M.A. 1909 Wales

The rise of the Scottish Chaucerians. W. B. Inglis, Ph.D. 1930 Glasgow

The Scottish Chaucerians. T. P. Lamnin, M.A. 1941 National University of Ireland

A study in Chaucer: the English poet's nature lore. J. Haynes, M.A. 1917 National University of Ireland

A study of Chaucer's diction and terms for womanly beauty. S. Ganguly, Ph.D. 1940 London, University College

A study of Chaucer's narrative methods in The Book of Duchesse, The Parlement of foules, The Hous of fame, Troilus and Criseyde and The Canterbury tales. G. M. Stephens, M.A. 1933 Wales

The syntax of Chaucer's Troilus and Criseyde. D. J. Rogers, M.A. 1925 Wales

Chaundler, Thomas
Thomas Chaundler. S. F. Bridges, B.Litt. 1949 Oxford

Chauny (Aisne)
Histoire générale de la ville de Chauny (Aisne) de sa fondation au commencement de la Troisième République. R. S. Clegg, M.A. 1939 Leeds

Chauvelin, Germain Louis de
The life and ministry of Chauvelin, with particular reference to French foreign policy between 1731 and 1737. A. M. Wilson, B.Litt. 1927 Oxford

Chefoo, Convention of
See Great Britain: Foreign Affairs: China.

Chekhov, Anton Pavlovich
Anton Chehov: a critical study. W. A. Gerhardi, B.Litt. 1923 Oxford

Chemical Industry
An analytical survey of the influence of the development of chemical theory during the nineteenth century upon the evolution of chemical industry, with special reference to East London. W. A. Parks, M.Sc. 1950 London, West Ham Municipal College

The geography of the chemical industry of western Europe. H. Thomas, M.A. 1923 Wales

The growth and development of the chemical industry. L. F. Haber, Ph.D. 1949 London, External Degree

Chemistry: History
See also Alchemy; Benzene; Fermentation; Gases; Halogen; Sulphuric Acid; and Berthollet, C. L.; Boerhaave, H.; Boyle, R.; Davy, H., Sir; Garbett, S.; Lomonossov, M.; Maquer, P. J.; Rozier, J.; Stahl, G. E.; Wollaston, W. H.; etc.

An analytical survey of the influence of the development of chemical theory during the nineteenth century upon the evolution of chemical industry, with special reference to East London. W. A. Parks, M.Sc. 1950 London, West Ham Municipal College

Avogadro and Dalton: the standing in chemistry of their hypotheses. A. N. Meldrum, D.Sc. 1904 Aberdeen

Chemistry at the Académie Royale des Sciences from its foundation in 1666 to the middle of the eighteenth century. J. G. Stubbs, Ph.D. 1939 London, Queen Mary College

Chemistry at the early meetings of the Royal Society of London. D. J. Lysaght, M.Sc. 1934 London, University College

Chemistry at the Royal Society, 1687-1727. D. J. Lysaght, Ph.D. 1937 London, University College

Chemistry in Great Britain from 1727 to 1774, with special reference to the life and scientific works of William Brownrigg, M.D., F.R.S. J. Russell-Wood, Ph.D. 1948 London, External Degree

The controversy between Proust and Berthollet on the invariability of chemical proportions. L. F. R. Simmonds, M.Sc. 1931 London

Chemistry: History contd.
The development of analytical method in chemistry from 1790 to 1830. F. A. Filby, M.Sc. 1929 London

Early development of views regarding acids, alkalies, and salts, until the time of Graham. N. Taylor, M.Sc. 1930 London

The electro-chemical researches of Sir Humphrey Davy. W. C. Walker, M.Sc. 1929 London

Gay Lussac's law of gaseous volumes and the influence on chemical theory up to 1860. H. A. Filmer, M.Sc. 1928 London

The history of chemical methods of detecting arsenic up to the year 1860. J. N. T. Lintott, M.Sc. 1935 London, University College

The history of stereochemistry up to 1890. E. M. L. Brown, M.Sc. 1949 London, University College

The history of the theories of chemical affinity from Boyle to Berzelius. J. Ellowitz, M.Sc. 1927 London

The influence of chemical theory upon chemical nomenclature and symbolism from the period of Lavoisier to that of Laurent. F. J. Pearson, M.Sc. 1929 London

A review of the radical and type theories in organic chemistry from the time of Berzelius to that of Kekulé, including the development of the theory of valency. M. Davis, M.Sc. 1927 London

Rise and development of chemistry in medieval Islam. E. J. Holmyard, M.Sc. 1925 Bristol

A study of the chemistries of Lemery, Freind, Baume, and Watson, and of the development of chemical thought from 1675 to 1787. S. D. M. Waters, M.Sc. 1931 London

The work of Williamson and its relation to the type theory of Wurtz. J. Harris, M.Sc. 1926 London

1. Work on the history of chemistry in medieval Islam. 2. Work on the teaching of chemistry in this country. E. J. Holmyard, D.Litt. 1928 Bristol

Chemistry: Study and Teaching
The application of scientific method to the teaching of chemistry. H. V. Hillman, M.A. 1947 London, Institute of Education

The basic difficulties of chemistry teaching in the matriculation course with special reference to the practical work. N. F. Newbury, M.A. 1930 Liverpool

A critical analysis of didactic methods in chemistry and their effect upon the educational development of the child. B. A. Lewis, M.A. 1930 Liverpool

The educational value of chemistry with proposals for its treatment in the school curriculum. H. Milnes, M.A. 1928 Liverpool

An examination of school text books in chemistry. J. M. Pullan, M.A. 1932 London, Day Training College

A factorial analysis of the abilities involved in the learning of school chemistry. G. C. Pawley, M.A. 1937 London, Institute of Education

The importance and place of physical sciences in a liberal education, with special reference to the study of physical chemistry in a secondary school curriculum. R. R. Finney, M.A. 1928 Liverpool

The place of chemistry in a rural secondary school. A. Ferriday, M.Sc. 1930 Liverpool

The proper scope of quantitative work in science in secondary schools, with particular reference to chemistry. W. C. J. Ward, M.A. 1927 London

A statistical analysis of the performance of boys and girls in science (physics and chemistry). K. V. Chary, M.A. 1948 London, Institute of Education

A vocational study of chemistry with its applications to education. N. Greenwood, M.Ed. 1924 Leeds

1. Work on the history of chemistry in medieval Islam. 2. Work on the teaching of chemistry in this country. E. J. Holmyard, D.Litt. 1928 Bristol

Chénier, André
André Chénier: poète du dix-huitième siècle. O. M. Wilson, M.A. 1933 Belfast

L'influence d'André Chénier sur l'oeuvre de Victor Hugo jusqu'à 1840. A. B. Nimmo, M.A. 1948 Liverpool

Cherokee Indians
The religion of the Cherokee Indians. O. C. Seymour, Ph.D. 1934 Edinburgh

Chertsey, Abbey of
The Abbey of Chertsey and its manors under Abbot John de Rutherwyk, 1307-1347. E. Toms, Ph.D. 1935 London, King's College

Cheshire
Contributions to the history of the earldom and county of Chester, 1237-1399, with a study of the household of Edward the Black Prince and its relations with Cheshire. M. Sharp, Ph.D. 1925 Manchester

The earls and earldom of Chester to 1254. A. B. Targett, M.A. 1913 Wales

The economic and social history of Cheshire in the reign of the three Edwards. H. J. Hewitt, Ph.D. 1926 London

Rural settlement in East Cheshire: a study in historical geography. P. F. Kenworthy, M.A. 1949 Manchester

Chester
The historical geography of Chester. G. Conzen, M.A. 1942 Manchester

The Roman occupation of north Wales and Chester. W. E. Griffiths, M.A. 1947 Wales

Chesterfield
The growth of the borough and the distribution and density of population in the Chesterfield region since the Industrial Revolution. F. C. Couzens, Ph.D. 1941 London, External Degree

A survey of the principal economic activities of the Chesterfield district, realistically and historically treated. G. W. Cobham, M.Sc. 1942 London, External Degree

Chesterton, Gilbert Keith
The philosophy of G. K. Chesterton. M. Rocks, M.A. 1941 National University of Ireland

Chettle, Henry
The life and work of Henry Chettle (c. 1560-1607). H. Jenkins, M.A. 1933 London, University College

Chhatrapati, Shahu
The reign of Shahu Chhatrapati, 1708-1749 A.D. A. G. Powar, Ph.D. 1934 London, School of Oriental and African Studies

Chicago
The ocean port of Chicago. M. E. Wilson, M.Sc. 1926 London

Chichele, Henry, Archbishop
Constitutions of Archbishop Chichele. B. G. Carroll, M.A. 1932 Manchester

Parliament and Convocation, with special reference to the pontificate of Henry Chichele, 1413-1443. M. Oldfield, M.A. 1938 Manchester

Ch'ien Hung, Emperor of China
A translation with critical notes of a ms. in the British Museum written by the Chinese Emperor Ch'ien Hung, and entitled A treatise on the recognition of faults. J. P. Bruce, M.A. 1907 London

Child Psychology
See also Behaviour; Bilingualism; Children, Gifted; Children, Retarded; Dreams; Educational Psychology; Intelligence; Personality; Psychoanalysis; Reading.

Analysis of aggression among problem children: a study of its incidence and immediate nature. L. Jackson, B.Sc. 1942 Oxford

Children's conception of adult life. P. M. Freston, M.A. 1945 London, Birkbeck College and London, King's College

The child's environment and its influence on the development of character and the origin of the neuroses. T. M. Hornik, B.Sc. 1943 Oxford

A comparative study of drawing ability in English children by the Goodenough scale. D. F. Tsao, M.A. 1935 London, University College

A comparative study of speech development and motor co-ordination in children of twenty-four to forty months by means of specially devised tests. E. R. W. Unmack, Ph.D. 1939 London, University College

A comparative study of the mental ability of normal and subnormal children. A. Abelson, D.Sc. 1920 London

A comparative study of the mental development of European and south Indian children. M. Varughese, M.A. 1937 London, Bedford College

A comparative study of the aesthetic judgments of English and Chinese children in picture appreciation. S. Fong, M.A. 1938 Birmingham

A comparison of the mental patterns of English children with those of a comparable age in British Guiana. F. W. E. Case, M.A. 1947 London, Institute of Education

The daydreams of children: their importance for education. G. H. Green, B.Litt. 1921 Oxford

Child Psychology contd.
The effects of different conditions of temperature and ventilation on the mental output and mental fatigues of school children. *A. H. Seymour, Ph.D. 1936 London, University College*

Emotional development and the infant school: the play curriculum as an aid to emotional adjustment and growth. *A. E. Price, M.A. 1940 Leeds*

Emotional development in young children. *E. H. Hughes, Ph.D. 1934 London, Bedford College*

An enquiry into curiosity as shown in the written questions of children and adolescents. *W. A. Simson, M.A. 1946 Birmingham*

Evacuation problems: a study of difficult children in hostels. *H. T. Lyons, M.A. 1943 London, Institute of Education*

An experimental and theoretical study of humour in children. *J. M. Williams, M.A. 1945 London, University College*

An experimental investigation into cognitive development in infants of one to two years of age. *M. Loewenheim, Ph.D. 1945 London, University College*

An experimental investigation of 'fluency' (of imagination and association), in school children. *B. D. Karvé, M.Ed. 1929 Leeds*

Factors in the mental processes of school children. 1. Visual and autditory imagery. 2. On the nature of the specific mental factors. 3. Factors concerned in the school subjects. *N. Carey, D.Sc. 1916 London*

Individual differences of behaviour in early infancy, and an objective method for recording them. *M. Balint, M.Sc. 1945 Manchester*

The influence of the form of a question upon children. *C. W. Good, M.A. 1937 London, University College*

An inquiry into the perception and memory of time relations, and particularly into the development of the time concept among high school children. *J. N. W. Hanter, Ph.D. 1934 Edinburgh*

An investigation concerning the inter-relations of social and economic status, Stanford-Binet and performance I.Q., estimates of probable vocational success, the Otis Primary A Group intelligence test in a group of mentally defective children, and the free association test as a measure of intelligence. *H. M. Cohen, M.D. 1936 Liverpool*

An investigation into the development of the attitudes of children towards authority. *R. Winterbourn, Ph.D. 1941 London, Institute of Education*

The moral development of the child. *H. E. Piggott, M.A. 1903 Wales*

Moral reasoning of the child and its relation to mental age. *M. K. Ahmed, M.A. 1936 London, University College*

The primitive in the psychology of the modern child. *F. Duckworth, M.A. 1940 London*

The problem of the European child in Shanghai (China). *M. A. Hadden, M.D. 1933 Dublin, Trinity College*

Psychological and social differences between A, B and C groups in senior schools, and their relation to the differential birth rate. *A. N. V. Harris, M.A. 1942 Birmingham*

The psychological functions involved in the child's use of fantasy and fiction; and, the child's response to fictional characters and its relationship to personality traits. *G. A. Foulds, M.A. 1943 Liverpool*

The psychological grounds of preference of shapes by school children. *E. L. Griffiths, M.A. 1927 Wales*

The psychological needs of children: a critical survey with a discussion of confirmatory evidence. *S. Bhalla, M.A. 1949 London, Institute of Education*

A psychological study of ownership in children. *D. W. McElwain, Ph.D. 1937 London, University College*

A psychological study of poetry-writing by children. *G. Smith, D.Phil. 1940 Oxford*

A psychological study of the development of religious beliefs among children and young persons. *J. Bradshaw, M.Sc. 1949 London, University College*

The social development of a child from birth to 18 months. *H. H. Stern, M.A. 1947 London, King's College*

Some family factors in the development of children's behaviour patterns. *M. Ravden, Ph.D. 1947 London, External Degree*

Child Psychology contd.
Some mental changes in the growth of children and their significance for education. *P. S. Moffat, Ph.D. 1938 Edinburgh*

Some psychological characteristics of educationally retarded children. *H. Highfield, M.A. 1935 London, University College*

A study of certain aspects of the psychology of the pre-adolescent child. *F. S. Hewitt, M.A. 1945 Liverpool*

A study of children's activity with plastic material and some interpretations of play in infancy. *E. M. Hall, M.A. 1938 Birmingham*

A study of interests in relation to the needs of children. *K. P. Choudhury, M.A. 1948 London, Institute of Education*

A study of the archetypes in children's fantasies. *I. Best, M.A. 1949 Leeds*

A study of the attitude towards war of a group of secondary school-children, aged 14-15. *S. Dutt, M.A. 1949 London, Institute of Education*

Study of the causal factors and subsequent development of excessive shyness, lack of self-confidence and allied conditions among children. *G. T. Lakhani, Ph.D. 1934 Edinburgh*

A study of the factors influencing the general development of the child during the pre-school years by means of record forms. *A. H. Bowley, Ph.D. 1940 London, External Degree*

The study of the primary emotions in young children with special reference to the emotion of fear. *M. C. Moore, M.A. 1914 Liverpool*

A study of the reactions of older children to air-raid conditions in 1940-41. *M. H. Ouseley, M.A. 1948 London, Institute of Education*

Suggestibility in children. *S. H. Cracknell, M.Sc. 1922 London*

The young child's idea of its personal environment as seen in drawings. *I. M. Farmer, M.A. 1949 Birmingham*

Child Welfare
See also Adoption.

An analysis of some case records from a London child guidance clinic. *M. Bose, M.A. 1947 London, Institute of Education*

The attitude of society towards the young since the Industrial Revolution. *W. Hindshaw, M.Ed. 1920 Manchester*

Education and industrialism: a study of the way in which changes in industrial organizations have led to changes in the use of child labour, and to the growth in England of a system of education based on compulsory school attendance. *C. J. Gill, M.A. 1938 Liverpool*

The education of children engaged in industry in England, 1833-76. *A. H. Robson, Ph.D. 1930 London, King's College*

The education of children in hospital schools. *I. Nichols, M.A. 1938 Liverpool*

English apprenticeship and child labour: a history. *J. Dunlop, D.Sc. 1912 London*

Fosterage in early and medieval Ireland. *J. A. Henchy, Ph.D. 1942 National University of Ireland*

Fosterage in old Irish law. *S. O'hInnse, M.A. 1940 National University of Ireland*

An historical study of the provision made for the social (as distinct from the scholastic) welfare of children and young persons in England since 1800. *C. L. H. Cowper, M.A. 1930 London, King's College*

The influence of environment on the fen children of Holland, Lincs. *A. Hinchley, M.Ed. 1939 Durham*

An inquiry into the boy and girl welfare movement in England. *M. A. H. Quraishi, M.Ed. 1930 Leeds*

Observations of the evolution of public health law and administration with special reference to its bearing on mother and child. *M. S. S. Jones, M.D. 1925 Liverpool*

Poverty and some of its effects upon schoolchildren. *E. N. Nash, M.Ed. 1941 Durham*

Royal wardship in the reign of King John, with reference to chapters 3-6 of the Magna Carta of 1215. *M. A. Renshaw, M.A. 1947 Manchester*

Woman and child industrial labour in the Bombay Presidency. *Z. A. Ahmad, Ph.D. 1935 London, School of Economics and Political Science*

Childhood
The child and childhood in the poetry of the French Romantic period, studied particularly in the works of Lamartine, Vigny, Victor Hugo, Sainte Beuve and De Musset. *R. F. C. Davies, M.A. 1929 Wales*

The child in poetry. *M. Handley, M.A. 1906 Birmingham*

The child in the German drama, from the time of Goethe and Schiller. *M. Titterton, M.A. 1908 Birmingham*

Child portraiture in English prose. *E. R. Williams, M.A. 1912 Bristol*

Childhood in English poetry. *E. M. Hall, M.A. 1921 Wales*

Childhood in English poetry. *A. Scott, M.A. 1935 Belfast*

Children in Greek literature from the heroic to the golden age. *S. Allott, B.Litt. 1943 Dublin, Trinity College*

A comparative study of children in English and French literature 1900 to 1914. *H. C. Davis, M.A. 1934 London, East London College*

Etude de l'enfant chez quelques romanciers du 19e siècle. *G. M. Barker, M.A. 1916 Birmingham*

On child life in medieval English literature. *P. H. Whittaker, M.A. 1932 Liverpool*

A portrayal of childhood in German fiction from Keller to Carcesa. *J. M. Berneaud, Ph.D. 1950 Saint Andrew's*

Studies in the treatment of the child in English literature. *W. A. Whiting, M.A. 1921 London*

Children: Law
See also Child Welfare; Juvenile Delinquency.

Abilities and disabilities of minors in the law of South Africa and Ceylon and allied systems. *M. Donaldson, B.Litt. 1949 Oxford*

The law of negligence, with particular reference to children. *A. J. C. Hirst, LL.M. 1929 Leeds*

Royal wardship in the reign of King John, with reference to chapters 3-6 of the Magna Carta of 1215. *M. A. Renshaw, M.A. 1947 Manchester*

Children: Psychology
See Child Psychology.

Children and Religion
See Religious Education.

Children, Gifted
Retardation in children of high intelligence. *V. M. McLaren, Ph.D. 1950 Glasgow*

Children, Handicapped
A critical enquiry into the training of defective children in England. *A. R. Akhunji, M.Ed. 1932 Leeds*

The development of language expression and language appreciation in the congenitally deaf child. *F. L. Denmark, M.A. 1930 Liverpool*

The education of the crippled child in England. *N. Garry, M.A. 1933 Leeds*

A history of deaf education in Scotland, 1760-1939. *T. J. Watson, Ph.D. 1949 Edinburgh*

The incidence and causes of minor degrees of deafness in elementary school children. *A. H. Gale, D.M. 1933 Oxford*

Myopia and the education of the myopic scholar in Scotland. *A. M. MacGillivray, M.D. 1930 Saint Andrew's*

Residual capacity to hear of pupils in schools for the deaf. *A. I. Goodman, M.D. 1947 Manchester*

The scholastic attainments of children with impaired hearing. *M. D. H. Sheridan, M.A. 1945 Liverpool*

Children, Retarded
See also Educational Psychology.

The backward child in the elementary school. *B. B. Wakelam, M.A. 1942 Birmingham*

The C child, with special reference to the C child in senior schools. *C. P. Rochester, M.A. 1939 Birmingham*

A clinical survey of the applicability of intelligence tests to the study of mental deficiency in children. *T. Ferguson, M.D. 1924 Edinburgh*

A comparative study of the mental ability of normal and subnormal children. *A. Abelson, D.Sc. 1920 London*

The diagnosis and treatment of the dull and backward child. *G. F. Sleight, Ph.D. 1933 London, Day Training College*

Children, Retarded contd.
An enquiry into the physical conditions and social circumstances of mentally subnormal children attending elementary schools in the city of Lincoln. *E.J. Findlay, M.D. 1934 Glasgow*

An experimental approach to remedial reading for dull and backward junior pupils. *E. A. Taylor, M.Ed. 1942 Leeds*

An experimental research on the problem of teaching geography to backward boys in present day senior schools. *F. S. Cassidy, M.Ed. 1937 Leeds*

An investigation into the educability of children suffering from cerebral palsy, spastic paralysis. *F. E. Schonell, Ph.D. 1950 Birmingham*

An investigation into the incidence of convergence insufficiency among school children, with an examination by means of the Thematic Apperception test into the personality of some difficult or retarded children showing this condition. *D. H. Archibald, B.Sc. 1944 Oxford*

An investigation into the stability of personal relations among educationally sub-normal children living in an institution. *H. Murray, M.Sc. 1949 Sheffield*

An investigation of the causes of backwardness at the qualifying stage, with particular reference to the percentage of children scholastically retarded owing to unsuitability of curriculum. Non-scholastic tests, mechanical aptitude tests, technical information tests, and a practical test for 'backward' children. *M. M. MacTaggart, Ph.D. 1928 Edinburgh*

Perceptual ability of defective children. *A. Waite, M.A. 1938 London, King's College*

The problem of the backward child. *E. M. Costello, M.A. 1938 National University of Ireland*

Remedial reading for dull senior boys. *L. Holdsworth, M.Ed. 1939 Leeds*

Report of an investigation into the secondary school careers of children who were not selected by the head teachers of elementary schools as likely to benefit by a secondary education. *H. A. Evans, M.A. 1938 Birmingham*

Retardation in children of high intelligence. *V. M. McLaren, Ph.D. 1950 Glasgow*

Some aspects of the problem of the educable mentally defective child and its place in society. *S. J. Kay, M.A. 1935 Liverpool*

Some psychological characteristics of educationally retarded children. *H. Highfield, M.A. 1935 London, University College*

A study of sociability with special reference to backward children in a secondary modern school. *N. K. Henderson, Ph.D. 1949 London, Institute of Education*

Children's Books and Reading
Elementary schools and schoolbooks in England at the close of the eighteenth and beginning of the nineteenth centuries. *P. H. Sandall, M.A. 1929 London*

Léightheoireacht agus caitheamh-aimsire bhuachaillí an bhaile mhór (The reading and pastimes of boys in big towns). *S. Mac Cuinn, M.A. 1942 National University of Ireland*

Manners and morals of the seventeenth and eighteenth centuries as revealed in books written for the young. *I. E. Thrift, Ph.D. 1935 London, King's College*

The place of children's books in English education during the first half of the nineteenth century, with special reference to the Hofland Collection. *A. J. Leech, M.Ed. 1941 Leeds*

A study of children's books from 1700-1825. *F. V. Barry, B.Litt. 1921 Oxford*

Children's Games
See also Games and Sports; Play.

Children's games. *L. H. Yodaiken, B.Litt. 1942 Dublin, Trinity College*

Emotional development and the infant school: the play curriculum as an aid to emotional adjustment and growth. *A. E. Price, M.A. 1940 Leeds*

A study of children's activity with plastic material and some interpretations of play in infancy. *E. M. Hall, M.A. 1938 Birmingham*

Chilterns, The
An inquiry into the changing distribution of population in the Chilterns since 1821. *R. S. G. Brocklebank, Ph.D. 1937 London, University College*

China
See also Kiangsu; Peiping; Shanghai; Wuhan.

China: Constitution
The Chinese constitution. *V. Y. Chiu, Ph.D. 1921 London*

China: Economics
British loans to China from 1860 to 1913, with special reference to the period 1894-1913. *C. Chung-Sieu, Ph.D. 1940 London, School of Economics and Political Science*

Kaihsienkung: economic life in a Chinese village. *H. T. Fei, Ph.D. 1938 London, School of Economics and Political Science*

The problem of international technical assistance to China. *R. W. Weise, M.Sc. 1940 London, School of Economics and Political Science*

A survey of the position and prospects of domestic industries in north China. *M. S. Valentine, M.A. 1938 Liverpool*

The system of Chinese public finance: a comparative study. *C. Lee, Ph.D. 1935 London, School of Economics and Political Science*

China: Foreign Affairs
American diplomatic policy in China, 1928-33. *J. W. Christopher, D.Phil. 1948 Oxford*

Anglo-Chinese diplomacy, 1895-1911. *T. T. G. Mar, Ph.D. 1929 London*

Anglo-Chinese diplomatic relations. *H. C. Pei, Ph.D. 1939 London, School of Economics and Political Science*

Anglo-Chinese relations, 1834-1860. *S. D. Wooldridge, M.A. 1930 Birmingham*

Anglo-Chinese relations and the Macartney embassy (1775-1800). *E. H. Pritchard, D.Phil. 1933 Oxford*

British diplomatic relations with China, 1854-1869. *W. Davies, M.A. 1938 Wales*

China's frontier's problems. *T. C. Chen, Ph.D. 1937 London, School of Economics and Political Science*

China's political fin-de-siècle, 1900: a study in the diplomatic relations of the powers with China. *P. Joseph, Ph.D. 1926 London*

Christian missions and foreign relations in China: an historical study. *C. M. Drury, Ph.D. 1932 Edinburgh*

The legal obligations arising out of treaty relations between China and other states. *M. T. Z. Tyau, LL.D. 1916 London*

The Margary Affair and the Convention of Chefoo. *S. T. Wang, B.Litt. 1938 Oxford*

Treaty relations between China and Great Britain: a study of international law and diplomacy. *C. L. Hsia, Ph.D. 1922 Edinburgh*

The United States and Old World diplomacy, 1898 to 1914, with special reference to China. *R. G. Shiman, Ph.D. 1930 London, School of Economics and Political Science*

China: Geography
Contributions to the climatology and geomorphology of Sino-Tibet and central China. *J. B. Hanson-Lowe, Ph.D. 1949 London, External Degree*

An exercise book of the geography of China. *E. W. Sawdon, M.A. 1922 Birmingham*

A geographical study of China, with special reference to the means of transport. *C. M. Bao, Ph.D. 1940 London, School of Economics and Political Science*

China: History
See also Ch'ien Hung, Emperor of China; Wang an Shih.

China's political fin-de-siècle, 1900: a study in the diplomatic relations of the powers with China. *P. Joseph, Ph.D. 1926 London*

The Great Powers and the Far East, from the seizure of Kiao-chau to the Boxer Settlement, 1897-1901. *M. I. Grimshaw, M.A. 1929 Birmingham*

An inquiry into the socio-religious character of Chinese civilization, with special reference to those features conducive to the acceptance of Buddhism. *A. F. Wright, B.Litt. 1937 Oxford*

Liu Hsiang and the Hsin Hsü. *W. B. D. Doxford, Ph.D. 1937 London, School of Oriental and African Studies*

Some aspects of the Taiping rebellion in China, 1850-64. *J. C. Cheng, Ph.D. 1950 Cambridge*

China: Politics and Government
Modern China: a political study. *S. G. Cheng, D.Sc. 1921 London*

China: Politics and Government contd.
The theory and practice of Chinese democracy. *C. Pakey, Ph.D. 1939 London, School of Economics and Political Science*

China: Social History
All for China: an account of the life and labour of Mrs. E. H. Edwards of Taiynanfu, Shensi. *H. R. Williamson, M.A. 1922 London*

China as treated by English and French writers in the first half of the eighteenth century. *S. P. Yu, B.Litt. 1932 Oxford*

China in the English literature of the eighteenth century. *C. S. Ch'ien, B.Litt. 1937 Oxford*

An examination of certain Chinese institutions, customs, aesthetic concepts, and achievements, with a view to determining how far they could be naturalized in the practice and teaching of the Christian Church in China. *J. H. Pratt, B.Litt. 1935 Oxford*

Feudal society in ancient China. *H. L. Tai, Ph.D. 1939 London, School of Economics and Political Science*

The position of the peasant in modern China. *W. H. Wu, Ph.D. 1939 London, School of Economics and Political Science*

A study of the Chinese moral traditions and its social values. *F. C. Wei, Ph.D. 1929 London*

Chinese Language
Chinese religion: an approach through the Hakka Chinese dictionary. *E. Parry, B.D. 1940 Leeds*

The phonetics of Pekingese. *D. M. Beach, Ph.D. 1923 London*

Chinese Literature
See also Ch'ien Hung, Emperor of China; Li, Po.

Prose literature of the T'ang period as contained in the T'ang collection of reprints. *E. D. Edwards, D.Litt. 1931 London, External Degree*

Speeches of the states (The Kuo Yü): a translation with introduction and notes. *B. S. Bonsall, D.Litt. 1932 London, External Degree*

A translation into English of part of the *Miao fa lien hua ching*. *B. Kato, B.Litt. 1925 Oxford*

Chirk
The history of the lordship and castle of Chirk, 1282-1660. *M. Jones, M.A. 1920 Wales*

Chivalry
The attitude of Chaucer towards chivalry, the Church and the people, compared with that of Langland, Wycliffe and Gower. *J. F. Evans, M.A. 1911 Wales*

Critical edition of Caxton's *Fayttes of armes and of chivalrye*. *A. T. P. Byles, Ph.D. 1933 London, External Degree*

The decline of chivalry as shown in the French literature of the fifteenth century, with special reference to poetry and drama. *K. H. Francis, Ph.D. 1948 London, External Degree*

Foreign chivalry at the Court of Edward III. *F. Schenck, B.Litt. 1912 Oxford*

Introduction and glossary to the *Book of the Ordre of Chyvalry*, translated and printed by William Caxton from a French version of the Catalan tract by Ramon Lull, entitled *Le Libre del Orde de Cavayleria*; and to Adam Loutfut's Scottish transcription, made in 1494 and contained in Harleian ms. 6149 at the British Museum. *A. T. P. Byles, M.A. 1925 London*

The relation of Chaucer to chivalry. *L. M. Evans, M.A. 1911 Wales*

The relation of Chaucer to chivalry. *T. G. Williams, M.A. 1909 Wales*

The theme of honour as present in the English drama, 1485-1642, with special reference to the dramatic use of the duel. *F. R. Cooper, M.A. 1946 London, King's College*

The treatment in literature of the ideal of chivalry in the nineteenth century with reference to medieval documents. . *M. Diggle, M.Litt. 1928 Cambridge*

Chladni, Ernst Florens Friedrich
The original acoustical work of Ernst Florens Friedrich Chladni and its influence on his immediate successors. *G. G. Powell, M.Sc. 1950 Wales*

Choiseul-Amboise, Etienne François de, Duc
Choiseul's foreign policy relative to England. *M. J. McCormick, M.A. 1911 Liverpool*

Cholmley, Hugh, Sir
An edition of the memoirs of Sir Hugh Cholmley, with a contribution on his life and on the Civil War in Yorkshire. *T. H. Brooke, B.Litt. 1937 Oxford*

Chrétien de Troyes
A comparison of the use of the subjunctive in Gautier d'Arras and Chrétien de Troyes. *E. Hugh, M.A. 1919 Wales*

Christ
See Jesus Christ.

Christ Church, Oxford
See Oxford University.

Christian Councils
See Church History.

Christian Doctrine
See Christianity.

Christian Science
The philosophic and psychological implications of Christian Science. *A. H. Bambridge, B.Litt. 1930 Oxford*

Christian Union
The attempts at Presbyterian-Episcopal accommodation in Scotland and their influence on modern movements of unity. *M. J. Roberts, Ph.D. 1949 Glasgow*

1. The conception of personality in relation to the present outlook and to the Christian doctrine of God. 2. Intercommunion and Christian reunion. *E. A. Burroughs, B.D. & D.D. 1921 Oxford*

The doctrine of the unity of the Church, with special reference to the works of Khomaikov and Moehler. *S. Bolshakoff, D.Phil. 1943 Oxford*

Expositions of: Acts ii.42: the Christian fellowship; Acts xv.6: the ministry in the Apostolic age; St. John xvii.22: the prayer of the Lord that his Church might be one. *S. Baker, D.D. 1905 Oxford*

Expositions of: Genesis iii: the doctrine of the Fall; Ephesians iv.1-16: the unity of the Church and the functions of its ministers; I Corinthians xi.18-34. *T. H. D. Long, D.D. 1909 Oxford*

An historical and critical study of the Christian unity movements since the Peace of Westphalia. *G. J. Slosser, Ph.D. 1928 London*

The idea of the unity of the Church: a study of its development in the first three centuries. *W. N. Jamison, Ph.D. 1948 Edinburgh*

1. Idolatry. 2. The place of unity in the ideal of a Church. *H. A. James, B.D. 1874 Oxford*

The quest for unity. *J. Murphy, D.Litt. 1925 Glasgow*

1. The re-union of the Christian Church, viewed under some of its present aspects. 2. Man in God's image as revealed in Scripture. *J. P. Way, B.D. & D.D. 1896 Oxford*

1. The unity of the Church. 2. The person and work of God the Holy Ghost. *T. H. A. Houblon, B.D. & D.D. 1903 Oxford*

The unity of the Church and the reunion of the Churches. *N. Zernov, D.Phil. 1932 Oxford*

Christianity
See also Apologetics; Asceticism; Belief; Creation and the Fall; Creeds; Eschatology; Jesus Christ; Kingdom of God; Liturgy and Ritual; Mary, Virgin; Prophecy; Sacrifice; Saints; Salvation; Sin; Soul; Sunday.

1. Body and soul. 2. Christianity and art. *P. Dearmer, B.D. & D.D. 1911 Oxford*

1. Certain Jewish modes of thought and teaching: their influence on the form in which truth is presented in the Gospels. 2. How far and in what sense is it possible to maintain such a distinction as that implied in the phase 'essential doctrine'?. *A. E. Hillard, B.D. & D.D. 1907 Oxford*

The Christian element in Shelley's religious thought. *E. A. Buttler, M.A. 1919 Birmingham*

Christianity and modern humanism. *D. H. G. Stewart, Ph.D. 1939 Edinburgh*

1. Christianity and pantheism. 2. The heavenly priesthood of our Lord. *H. R. Cavalier, B.D. 1906 Oxford*

The dependence of St. Paul upon the pre-Pauline Christian tradition. *A. M. Hunter, D.Phil. 1939 Oxford*

Disinterestedness and its conditions: a limited comparison between the ethics of Christianity and of scientific humanism as represented in particular by the *Ethics* of Professor Nicholai Hartmann. *R. G. Norburn, M.A. 1940 Manchester*

An edition of British Museum ms. Harley 2372. *L. E. Rogers, B.Litt. 1934 Oxford*

The ethical idea of love and its central position in Christian ethics down to St. Cyprian. *Y. Davies, B.Litt. 1918 Oxford*

Christianity contd.
Evolution and the Christian doctrine of human worth: a vindication of human values from the standpoint of biology, anthropology and psychology. *R. Paton, Ph.D. 1931 Edinburgh*

Expositions of: Acts ii.4: ἤρξαντο λαλεῖν ἑτέραισ γλώσσαισ; the gift of tongues; Romans iii.25: ὃν προέθετο ὁ θεὸσ ἱλαστήριον ξιὰ τησ πίστεωσ εν τω αυτου αἵματι: the meaning of ἱλαστήριον; Galatians iii.15: the legal terminology of the Epistle to the Galatians and its bearing on the question of the churches addressed by St. Paul. *D. Walker, D.D. 1904 Oxford*

1. Illustrations of the doctrines of Christianity from natural religion. 2. The value of evidences in Christian theology. *H. R. Huckin, B.D. 1874 Oxford*

The influence of asceticism on ideas of Christian morality from Clement and Tertullian to Siricius. *D. T. Davies, M.A. 1914 Wales*

The influence of Plotinus upon the religious philosphy of St. Augustine, with special reference to the points of difference between neoplatonism and Christianity. *W. J. Heaton, M.A. 1930 Reading*

The interpretation of some aspects of Christian doctrine and practice in the light of Sigmund Freud's conceptions of the development and structure of the mind. *R. S. Lee, D.Phil. 1947 Oxford*

1. Justification by faith. 2. Christianity as a civilizing agent. *C. E. E. Williams, B.D. 1882 Oxford*

A manual of Christian evidences. *A. L. Williams, D.D. 1911 Cambridge*

Milton's treatise *On Christian doctrine* and its relation to *Paradise lost*. *W. A. Sewell, B.Litt. 1933 Oxford*

On philosophical aspects of Christian ethics. *G. F. Barbour, Ph.D. 1910 Edinburgh*

1. On the origin and affinities of the Lord's Supper and the Passover. 2. On the traces of Gentilism in Christianity. *H. E. D. Blakiston, B.D. 1901 Oxford*

1. On the persistence of Arcanism. 2. On the place of mysticism in Christianity. *H. Marriott, B.D. 1915 Oxford*

Origen's doctrine of tradition. *R. P. C. Hanson, D.D. 1950 Dublin, Trinity College*

The originality of Christianity. *J. H. Templeton, Ph.D. 1946 Dublin, Trinity College*

1. Progressive revelation as illustrated in the history of Israel. 2. Asceticism and Christianity. *C. W. L. Evans, B.D. 1909 Oxford*

1. The purpose of the Epistle to St. James. 2. The Church and Scripture. *J. J. Hannah, B.D. & D.D. 1909 Oxford*

The reciprocal influence of Roman law and Christianity. *J. W. Jones, Ph.D. 1925 London*

1. The resurrection. 2. Christianity necessary to a true view of personality. *S. Bickersteth, B.D. & D.D. 1905 Oxford*

Revolt and Christian orthodoxy in the German lyric since 1890. *O. Weinstock, M.A. 1949 Leeds*

1. Some non-Jewish sources of the Christian religion. 2. The Maccabean period as an element in the preparation for Christianity. *R. J. Campbell, B.D. & D.D. 1919 Oxford*

The source and implication of the New Testament quotations in the *Apologies* of Justin Martyr. *J. Pritchard, M.A. 1905 Wales*

Sufficiency of Christianity. *R. S. Sleigh, Ph.D. 1923 Aberdeen*

1. Utrum Christus venisset si Adam non peccasset. 2. The New Testament doctrine of the Christian character and its development. *L. Hands, B.D. 1907 Oxford*

Christianity: History
See Church History.

Christianity and Other Religions
The Bhagavadgita and the Gospel. *W. G. Mulligan, B.Litt. 1941 Dublin, Trinity College*

The Buddhist conception of man in relation to the Christian conception. *B. de Kretser, Ph.D. 1948 Edinburgh*

1. Certain Jewish modes of thought and teaching: their influence on the form in which truth is presented in the Gospels. 2. How far and in what sense is it possible to maintain such a distinction as that implied in the phase 'essential doctrine'?. *A. E. Hillard, B.D. & D.D. 1907 Oxford*

The Christian attitude to other religions. *E. C. Dewick, D.D. 1950 Cambridge*

Christianity and Other Religions contd.
A comparison between Christian theism and the religious beliefs of certain tribes in West Africa. *E. N. Jones, B.Litt. 1925 Oxford*

A comparison of ideas of salvation in Hinduism and Christianity, with special reference to the Bhakti religions. *F. W. Dillistone, B.D. 1933 Oxford*

A comparison of the pagan apologetic of Celsus against Christianity as contained in Origen's *Contra Celsum*, and the neo-Hindu attitude to Christianity as represented in the works of Vivekananda, and an estimate of the value of Origen's reply for Christian apologetics against neo-Hinduism. *J. R. Chandran, B.Litt. 1949 Oxford*

1. The development of Judaism and its influence upon Christianity. 2. Christian life in the first days of the Church. *C. Moor, B.D. 1904 Oxford*

1. Early Christian missions in some of their relations to heathen religion. 2. The importance and function of the Book of Esther in the canon. *J. W. Williams, B.D. 1896 Oxford*

An examination of certain Chinese institutions, customs, aesthetic concepts, and achievements, with a view to determining how far they could be naturalized in the practice and teaching of the Christian Church in China. *J. H. Pratt, B.Litt. 1935 Oxford*

An investigation of the methods of presentation of Christianity to the Gentiles by the early Church, and an examination of China's religious heritage with a view to similarity of approach. *F. A. Smalley, B.Litt. 1933 Oxford*

Islam in the twentieth century: the relevance of Christian theology and the relation of the Christian mission to its problems. *A. K. Cragg, D.Phil. 1950 Oxford*

The Jewish and Christian doctrine of good and evil spirits: its origin and development. *E. Langton, D.D. 1942 London, External Degree*

The message of Karl Barth in relation to Hinduism. *H. V. Martin, M.A. 1937 Bristol*

The mystery religions and the Christian sacraments. *J. E. Barlow, B.D. 1942 Leeds*

1. The position of Jesus Christ in Mohammedanism. 2. Our risen Lord's appearances in Galilee. *A. E. Richardson, B.D. 1902 Oxford*

The relation of the human soul to God in Hinduism and Christianity. *P. B. Means, B.Litt. 1923 Oxford*

Ritual background of Celtic heroes and saints: a study of some of the survivals of pagan elements in early Celtic Christianity. *A. D. Reese, M.A. 1937 Wales*

The spiritual campaign between Christians and pagans from Lactantius to Augustine. *H. Muller, B.Litt. 1945 Oxford*

A study in the relationship between the Jewish people and Jesus Christ. *J. Jocz, Ph.D. 1945 Edinburgh*

Christianity and Political and Social Questions
See also Citizenship; Ethics.

Christian attitudes to war and peace: a study of the four main types, with a foreword by W. P. Paterson. *T. S. K. Scott-Craig, Ph.D. 1938 Edinburgh*

Christian socialism: its rise and development, its economic and social results, and its relation to other working class movements. *I. Evans, M.A. 1912 Wales*

Christian sociology, 1920-1940: a review and critical estimate of the main trends of the period. *H. F. Leatherland, Ph.D. 1947 Edinburgh*

Christianity and education in the first five centuries A.D. *J. V. Patton, B.Litt. 1916 Oxford*

1. The Christian's duty to the State. 2. The lawfulness of war. *J. G. W. Tuckey, B.D. 1924 Oxford*

The evolution of the franchise in England, with special reference to the Reform Act of 1869, and to the political influence of organized Christianity. *W. G. H. Cook, M.Sc. 1922 London*

The humanitarian movement in England in the eighteenth century, with special reference to the relation between the revival in religious life and industrial change: a study in the sociology of religion. *W. J. Warner, Ph.D. 1929 London*

The influence of Christianity on social progress as illustrated by the career of Lord Shaftesbury. *J. W. Bready, Ph.D. 1927 London*

1. Israel and society: the Jewish religion's contribution towards social integration. 2. Christianity and society: our Lord's work considered sociologically. *H. Johnson, B.D. 1917 Oxford*

Christianity and Political and Social Questions contd.

The nature and significance of Christian sociology. *G. H. Gibson, M.A. 1936 Bristol*

1. The place of the prophet in the New Testament. 2. The doctrine of the New Testament as to the moral aspect of war. *R. T. Talbot, B.D. & D.D. 1906 Oxford*

The relation of theology to social theory and action in the Christian Social Movement in England from 1877 to 1914. *E. V. Newman, B.Litt. 1936 Oxford*

The relations between Calvinism and social and political thought in the United Kingdom. *R. W. Wilde, M.A. 1933 Manchester*

Robert Owen and Christian Socialism. *F. Fraser, Ph.D. 1927 Edinburgh*

The social and economic ideas in the writings of religious leaders, 1660-1688. *R. B. Schlatter, D.Phil. 1938 Oxford*

The social and religious thought of Charles Kingsley and his place in the English Christian Socialist Movement of 1848-54. *H. W. West, Ph.D. 1947 Edinburgh*

A study of Troeltsch's treatment of Christianity as a doctrine of society. *K. T. Henderson, B.Litt. 1925 Oxford*

The teaching of Christ on social questions. *D. H. Morgan, M.A. 1944 Wales*

Christine de Pisan

Glossaire des vieux mots qu'on trouve dans *Le dit de Poissy*, poème écrit en avril 1400 par Christine de Pisan. *A. M. Binas, M.A. 1926 Leeds*

Trois poèmes de Christine de Pisan: (a) *L'epistre au dieu d'amour*; (b) *Le dit de la rose*; (c) *Le débat de deux amants*. *W. J. Tiffin, M.A. 1929 Leeds*

Christology

See Jesus Christ.

Christophe, Jean

Jean-Christophe et la musique. *C. M. Bedson, M.A. 1942 Birmingham*

Christopher, Saint

St. Christopher in Old and Middle English literature and in the contemporary iconography. *W. G. Croker, M.A. 1931 Wales*

Chronique de Turpin, la

La tradition manuscrite et la phonétique des principaux textes de la version Johannis de *La Chronique de Turpin*. *R. N. Walpole, M.A. 1936 Wales*

Chronology

Clausulae and Platonic chronology. *L. Billig, M.A. 1920 London*

The sense of time and its relation to the teaching of chronology. *M. Kaye, M.A. 1933 Leeds*

Church and State

See also Church History; Anglican Church; Roman Catholic Church; Hooker, R.

1659-1660: a study in the interaction of political and religious forces in the period between the fall of Richard Cromwell and the restoration of Charles II. *J. L. Nightingale, M.Litt. 1936 Durham*

Archbishop Winchelsey: a sketch of a critical period in the relations between Church and State. *F. Barton, M.A. 1912 London*

Authority in Church and State, with special reference to the seventeenth century. *P. S. Belasco, Ph.D. 1928 London*

Bishops and the secular power in the writings of Gregory of Tours. *S. Mullins, B.Litt. 1950 Oxford*

Catholic opinion and the ecclesiastical policy of the government in France (1869-70). *J. W. Pickersgill, B.Litt. 1933 Oxford*

Church and society in the East Roman Empire from the death of Constantine VIII to the rise of Alexius Comnenus. *J. M. Hussey, Ph.D. 1934 London, Westfield College*

Church and state in early Christian Ireland. *W. Nugent, M.A. 1949 National University of Ireland*

City-state and Church. *A. A. T. Ehrhardt, Ph.D. 1944 Cambridge*

The concordats between the Holy See and England in the fourteenth and fifteenth centuries. *M. J. George, M.A. 1915 Liverpool*

The constitutional position of the Church in the Norman kingdom of Sicily, 1130-94, with special reference to the relations between papacy, monarchy, metropolitan and immediate sees. *J. M. Shaxby, B.Litt. 1933 Oxford*

The *Defensor minor* of Marsilius de Mainardini of Padua. *C. K. Brampton, B.Litt. 1922 Oxford*

Church and State contd.

An edition of Book I of Hooker's *Ecclesiastical polity* with an introductory essay dealing with the subject matter of the book and with the author's position in the history of political thought. *H. R. Charles, M.A. 1928 Wales*

Episcopal appointments and patronage in the reign of Edward II: a study in the relations of Church and State. *W. E. L. Smith, Ph.D. 1931 Edinburgh*

Parliament and Convocation, with special reference to the pontificate of Henry Chichele, 1413-1443. *M. Oldfield, M.A. 1938 Manchester*

People v. prince: some political doctrines of Mariana and the early Jesuits. *S. G. Griffin, M.A. 1931 National University of Ireland*

The politics of Hooker. *F. J. J. Shirley, Ph.D. 1931 London, External Degree*

The relation of Church and State with special reference to the growth of the idea of religious toleration in England under James I, 1603-1616. *P. Doyle, M.A. 1928 London*

Relations between Church and State in England between 1829 and 1839. *F. M. Scully, B.Litt. 1935 Oxford*

The relations between the Roman Government and Christianity down to the end of the second century. *A. M. Hollis, B.D. 1931 Oxford*

The relations of the bishops and citizens of Salisbury (New Sarum) between 1225 and 1612. *F. Street, M.A. 1915 London*

Scottish royal ecclesiastical policy, 1107-1214, with special reference to foreign influence in the spread of the monastic orders and the personnel of the episcopate in Scotland. *G. W. S. Barrow, B.Litt. 1950 Oxford*

An t-aighneas idir chill agus tuaith 'sa tseanscéaluidheacht Ghaedhilge (The conflict between church and state in Old Irish storytelling). *S. Breathnach, M.A. 1940 National University of Ireland*

Church, Doctrine of

See also Clergy; Episcopate; Prophecy; Worship. For the Communion of Saints, see Saints.

1. Acts vii.38; St. Luke vii.3; St. Matthew xvi.21: the pre-Christian doctrine of the Εκκλησία and non-political organizations. 2. St. Matthew xvi.18: Gospel teaching direct or indirect, as to the Εκκλησία. 3. Acts ii.42: the earliest Christian community. *A. C. Headlam, D.D. 1903 Oxford*

1. The atonement. 2. The spiritual body. *C. G. H. Baskomb, B.D. 1905 Oxford*

1. The atonement. 2. The witness of the Church. *L. Ragg, B.D. 1905 Oxford*

1. The biblical conception of the kingdom of heaven. 2. 'Tu es Petrus'. *B. H. B. Attlee, B.D. 1910 Oxford*

The bride of Christ; an enquiry into the nuptial element in early Christianity. *C. L. Chavasse, B.Litt. 1940 Dublin, Trinity College*

1. The canon of Scripture. 2. The Church. *J. Chapelhow, B.D. 1876 Oxford*

1. Church government. 2. The Apocrypha in relation to the Church. *H. G. Rosedale, B.D. 1897 Oxford*

1. The Church in the Epistle to the Ephesians. 2. The Christ of the fourth Gospel. *J. L. Phillips, B.D. 1913 Oxford*

1. The communion of saints. 2. The nature of the Resurrection body. *J. E. Sheppard, B.D. & D.D. 1900 Oxford*

1. The conception of the Church in Holy Scripture and the early Christian writers. 2. The conception of the Church in the writings of the Reformers. *H. Gee, B.D. & D.D. 1898 Oxford*

A critical survey of recent British work on the Church and ministry. *T. D. O. Edwards, M.A. 1940 Bristol*

The dissenting Reformed Churches of England with respect to the doctrine of the Church from 1870 to 1940, with special reference to the Congregational Churches. *J. W. Grant, D.Phil. 1948 Oxford*

The doctrine of the Church and the sacraments in Hugh of Saint Victor. *W. F. Whitman, B.Litt. 1924 Oxford*

The doctrine of the church as exemplified in the life and works of James Ussher, Archbishop of Armagh. *R. B. Knox, Ph.D. 1948 Belfast*

Church, Doctrine of contd.

The doctrine of the Church in Anglican theology, 1833-52, with particular reference to the conception of doctrinal authority. *F. A. Gain, B.Litt. 1950 Oxford*

1. The doctrine of the objective presence in the Eucharist. 2. The Church and the world. *T. B. Strong, B.D. 1899 Oxford*

The doctrines of the Church and the ministry held by the principal Anglican and Continental reformers. *W. D. F. Hughes, B.Litt. 1923 Oxford*

The elements of Hildebrand's conception of the Church. *D. Dymond, M.A. 1915 London*

1. Eternal life in relation to the Incarnation. 2. The idea of the Church in the Gospels. *W. Hobhouse, B.D. & D.D. 1918 Oxford*

Expositions of: Acts ii.42: the Christian fellowship; Acts xv.6: the ministry in the Apostolic age; St. John xvii.22: the prayer of the Lord that his Church might be one. *S. Baker, D.D. 1905 Oxford*

Expositions of: Genesis iii: the doctrine of the Fall; Ephesians iv.1-16: the unity of the Church and the functions of its ministers; I Corinthians xi.18-34. *T. H. D. Long, D.D. 1909 Oxford*

Expositions of: St. Luke xii.42,43: the ministry, a stewardship; I Corinthians xii: the spiritual gifts of the Church; Romans ix.4: the Covenant or Church principle. *B. J. Kidd, D.D. 1904 Oxford*

The idea of the Church in the New Testament and its development in the first two centuries. *G. Johnson, Ph.D. 1941 Cambridge*

1. The Incarnation in relation to our daily life. 2. The priesthood of the laity in the Church of Christ. *C. G. Browne, B.D. & D.D. 1908 Oxford*

Issues dividing western Christendom on the doctrine of the Church in the sixteenth and seventeenth centuries. *R. H. Wilmer, D.Phil. 1948 Oxford*

John Calvin's conception of the seat of authority in religion. *R. W. McNeur, Ph. D. 1950 Edinburgh*

La religion et l'église dans l'oeuvre de Stendhal. *J. Sankey, M.A. 1935 Liverpool*

Luther's doctrine of the Church in his early writings. *H. A. Preus, Ph.D. 1928 Edinburgh*

The New Testament idea of the Church: an historical study, with particular reference to its Hebrew and Jewish background. *M. H. Sykes, Ph.D. 1948 Manchester*

1. On the holy Catholic Church. 2. On the sacraments. *B. S. Tupholme, B.D. & D.D. 1888 Oxford*

One body in Christ: a study in the relationship of the Church to Christ in the teaching of the Apostle Paul. *E. Best, Ph.D. 1948 Belfast*

1. The providential preparation for the Church of Christ. 2. The revelation of the Church in the Gospels. *D. Stone, B.D. & D.D. 1909 Oxford*

1. The redemption. 2. The Church in the Epistle to the Ephesians. *P. J. James, B.D. 1910 Oxford*

1. The relation of the Church to the kingdom of God. 2. The meaning of the words of institution in I Corinthians xi.24, 25. *H. L. Goudge, B.D. & D.D. 1910 Oxford*

1. The relation of the Church to the Gospels. 2. The external evidences for the Gospels in the second century. *G. F. Lovell, B.D. 1876 Oxford*

1. The Scriptures: the rule of faith. 2. The Church. *J. E. Cox, B.D. & D.D. 1870 Oxford*

1. Some aspects of modern criticism with reference to the Book of Jonah. 2. St. Paul's doctrine of the Church. *E. C. Unmack, B.D. 1924 Oxford*

The teaching of John Hus concerning the Church. *J. H. S. Burleigh, B.Litt. 1922 Oxford*

1. The teaching of St. Paul on the Church in the Epistle to the Ephesians. 2. The teaching of St. Paul on the Holy Spirit. *G. P. Jones, B.D. 1908 Oxford*

Church History

See also Catholic Apostolic Church; Celtic Church; Nestorian Church; Orthodox Churches; Roman Catholic Church; and Christian Union; Church, Doctrine of; Church and State; Heresies; Clergy; Episcopate; Liturgy and Ritual; Missions; Monasticism; Religious Orders and Societies; Saints; Sermons.

Church History: General

The authority of oecumenical councils, in the Eastern Orthodox, the Roman Catholic, and the Anglican Churches. *N. Nickoloff, B.Litt. 1925 Oxford*

Church History: Early Church

See also Patristics; and Augustine of Hippo, Saint; Hippolytus, Saint; Isidore, of Seville, Saint; John Chrysostom, Saint; Justin, Martyr, Saint; Novatian; Paul, Saint and Apostle; Synesius, of Cyrene; Tertullian; Theodoret, Bishop of Cyros.

The attitude of the Roman Government to Christianity from Nero to Marcus Aurelius. *M. H. Evans, M.A. 1909 Wales*

The basis of Christian morals in the second and third centuries. *G. F. Thompson, M.A. 1924 Sheffield*

Christian ethics and social institutions in the fourth century, with special reference to Augustine. *E. C. Urwin, M.A. 1920 London*

Christian healing; a consideration of the place of spiritual healing in the Church of today in the light of examination of the doctrine and practice of the Ante-Nicene Church. *E. Frost, Ph.D. 1940 London, King's College*

The Christian inscriptions of North Africa: a study in the popular religion of the early (Western) Church. *I. T. Gillan, Ph.D. 1943 Edinburgh*

Christianity in Africa, A.D. 180-258. *T. A. Johnston, M.A. 1924 National University of Ireland*

Christianity in Asia, and evidences of the Church's power and influence in the province to A.D.325, in the light of Christian epigraphy. *E. Bristow, M.A. 1926 Manchester*

The Church and the councils of the early fifth century. *H. Spencer, M.A. 1915 Liverpool*

The conception of the *Civitas Christiana* in the thought of the early Church. *E. Langstadt, Ph.D. 1938 Cambridge*

1. The Council of Constantinople and the Nicene Creed. 2. The early Roman baptismal creed. *F. J. Badcock, B.D. & D.D. 1922 Oxford*

A critical examination of the first Epistle of St. Paul to the Corinthians, with special reference to the background of the Corinthian Church. *R. F. Robbins, Ph.D. 1950 Edinburgh*

1. The development of Judaism and its influence upon Christianity. 2. Christian life in the first days of the Church. *C. Moor, B.D. 1904 Oxford*

The Didache and early Christianity. *F. G. Lowe, M.A. 1932 Bristol*

1. Doctrine of the work and office of Christ, with special reference to the atonement, during the first three centuries. 2. The relations of faith and reason in the Christian system, especially during the Apostolic and sub-Apostolic period. *F. W. Bussell, B.D. 1892 Oxford*

The effect of the fall of Jerusalem in A.D. 70 on the Christian Church. *S. G. F. Brandon, B.D. 1939 Leeds*

The elements in early Christianity, down to the end of the fourth century, which helped to prepare the way for later Christian intolerance, and the relation of these elements to the early Christian conception of God as love. *L. A. Garrard, B.D. 1935 Oxford*

England and the Great Schism of the West. *C. M. Saum, M.A. 1916 Liverpool*

An examination of the central themes of St. Mark's Gospel in relation to the beliefs of the Apostolic Church. *T. A. Burkill, D.Phil. 1947 Oxford*

1. The growth ot belief in a future state. 2. The organization and worship of the early Christian Churches as exhibited in the New Testament. *C. Erskine, B.D. 1901 Oxford*

How far is it true that the Christianity of the end of the second century is a departure from the teaching and ideals of the New Testament?. *R. N. Flew, B.D. 1925 Oxford*

The influence of Roman law on the history and doctrine of the Christian church during the first three centuries. *W. Phillips, Ph.D. 1931 Edinburgh*

The intellectual and social phenomena which determined the triumph of Christianity in Italy. *J. Mathias, M.A. 1925 Wales*

The introduction of Christianity into the British Islands, illustrated by the lives of the saints. *F. N. Davis, B.Litt. 1905 Oxford*

An investigation of the methods of presentation of Christianity to the Gentiles by the early Church, and an examination of China's religious heritage with a view to similarity of approach. *F. A. Smalley, B.Litt. 1933 Oxford*

Justin Martyr and his witness to the beliefs, practice and sufferings of the Christians of his day. *M. B. Owen, M.A. 1941 Wales*

Church History: Early Church contd.

1. The language used by Christ. 2. The organization of the early Christian Churches. *C. R. Perry, B.D. 1892 Oxford*

The life of the Christians in North Africa in the time of Tertullian. *C. B. Daly, M.A. 1938 Belfast*

North Italian Christianity, A.D.350-461. *J. P. Naish, B.Litt. 1921 Oxford*

1. On the organization of the early Church as exhibited in the Acts of the Apostles and the Pauline Epistles. 2. On the right and wrong use of the doctrine of predestination. *M. Argles, B.D. & D.D. 1891 Oxford*

The persecution under Diocletian. *G. W. Richardson, M.A. 1924 London*

1. The political consciousness of the Marcan gospel. 2. The origins of Alexandrian Christianity. 3. The historical element in some ancient religions. *S. G. F. Brandon, D.D. 1943 Leeds*

1. The primitive Church and its organization. 2. The kingdom of heaven in the Gospel of St. Matthew. *P. A. Micklem, B.D. & D.D. 1924 Oxford*

1. The *Quicumque Vult.* 2. The discipline of the early Church. *R. S. P. Chesshire, B.D. & D.D. 1910 Oxford*

The relation of the Eastern Churches to Rome before the schism of Photius. *S. H. Scott, D.Phil. 1927 Oxford*

Relations of Pope Gregory the Great with the churches in the Roman Empire of the East. *W. J. Boast, M.A. 1931 Birmingham*

The religious experience of the Church of the Apostolic Age. *P. G. S. Hopwood, B.Litt. 1925 Oxford*

The religious experience of the primitive Church. *P. S. S. Hopwood, Ph.D. 1935 Glasgow*

The social and economic background of Christianity in North Africa down to 430, with special reference to the Donatist schism. *W. H. C. Frend, D.Phil. 1940 Oxford*

Some aspects of the relation between Neo-Platonism and Christianity in the later Roman Empire. *A. Weissbruth, M.A. 1937 London, University College*

Church History: Medieval

See also Crusades; and Aelfric; Anselm, Saint; Arnold, of Brescia; Bernard, Saint; Theodore, of Tarsus, Archbishop.

A critical edition of the *Quattuor determinationes patris Willelmi Wydeforde de ordine fratrum minorum contre Wycliff et Wyclyvianos in materia de religion. M. D. Dobson, B.Litt. 1932 Oxford*

The influence of economic factors in the Gregorian reform of the eleventh century. *D. B. Zema, Ph.D. 1940 Cambridge*

'The mirror of fools': a study in church history chiefly of the twelfth century. *R. Sidgwick, M.A. 1908 Birmingham*

Church History: Reformation and Counter-Reformation

See also Evangelicalism; Nonconformity; Protestantism; Puritanism; and Calvin, J.; Eccius, I.; Lambert, F.; Luther, M.; and below, under individual countries.

The conception of Church order and ministry under Luther and the early Lutheran Church considered in the light of non-Roman Christianity in Scandinavia, Germany, and the British Isles to-day. *H. H. W. Kramm, D.Phil. 1940 Oxford*

The Council of Trent and Anglican formularies. *H. E. Symonds, B.D. 1932 Oxford*

Disputatio I. Eccii et M. Lutheri, Lipsiae, Labita 1519: translation with critical introduction and notes. *A. McPherson, B.D. 1931 Edinburgh*

The influence of John Hus on Europe to the time of the Reformation, with special reference to central and eastern Europe. *J. Sedlo, Ph.D. 1943 Edinburgh*

The Jesuits and the Council of Trent. *G. Duckworth, B. Litt. 1939 Oxford*

Problem of authority in the continental reformers. *R. E. Davies, B.D. 1946 Cambridge*

The Reformation and the religion of the spirit: a critical study of the life and teaching of Hans Denck. *A. Coutts, Ph.D. 1921 Edinburgh*

Standards of Catholicism during the period of the Councils and at the Reformation. *H. K. Douglass, B.Litt. 1921 Oxford*

Church History: Canada

Settlements and churches in Nova Scotia, 1749-1776: the origin of Protestant Churches in relation to settlement, from the founding of Halifax to the American Revolution. *I. F. Mackinnon, Ph.D. 1930 Edinburgh*

Church History: Denmark

Dr. Johannes Macchabaeus (John MacAlpin): Scotland's contribution to the Reformation in Denmark. *M. A. F. Bredahl Petersen, Ph.D. 1937 Edinburgh*

Paul Eliasen and the Danish Reformation. *E. H. Dunkley, B.D. 1942 Oxford*

The Reformation in Denmark. *E. H. Dunkley, D.D. 1945 Oxford*

Church History: England

See also Anglican Church; Baptists; Congregationalism; Evangelicalism; Lollards; Methodism; Nonconformity; Puritanism; and Chichele, H., Archbishop; Hallum, R., Bishop; Kilwardby, R., Archbishop; Langton, S., Archbishop; Marprelate, M.; Neville, R., Bishop; Roger, Bishop of Worcester; Rutherwyk, J. de, Abbot; Spottiswoode, J., Archbishop.

The attitude of Chaucer towards chivalry, the Church and the people, compared with that of Langland, Wycliffe and Gower. *J. F. Evans, M.A. 1911 Wales*

The Celtic church in England after the synod of Whitby. *J. L. G. Meissner, M.A. 1927 Belfast*

The changes of the Reformation period in Durham and Northumberland. *B. N. Wilson, Ph.D. 1939 Durham*

Character and importance of the religious settlement in Tudor England. *C. A. Francis, M.A. 1936 National University of Ireland*

Chartism and the Churches, with special reference to Lancashire: an account of the Churches and social reform in the Chartist period. *N. J. McLellan, Ph.D. 1947 Edinburgh*

The Church in the reign of Edward I, with special reference to the register of Archbishop Peckham. *B. E. Brimson, M.A. 1909 Wales*

The Church in the reign of Edward I. *D. T. Price, M.A. 1907 Wales*

The Church under the Lancastrians. *P. H. Jones, M.A. 1910 Wales*

Clerical taxation and consent in the reign of Edward I. *H. S. Deighton, B.Litt. 1935 Oxford*

A comparison of the influence of Wycliffe and Luther upon the Reformation in England. *W. H. Leighton, M.A. 1927 Birmingham*

The condition of the clergy at the time of the Reformation in England. *M. K. R. Cotton, M.A. 1916 London*

The contribution of Robert Barnes to the English Reformation. *N. H. Fisher, M.A. 1950 Birmingham*

Disputes about episcopal elections in England in the reign of Henry III, with special reference to some unpublished Durham documents. *W. K. Evers, B.Litt. 1936 Oxford*

Ecclesiastical letter-books of the thirteenth century. *R. M. T. Hill, B.Litt. 1936 Oxford*

The ecclesiastical relations of the reign of Stephen, with special reference to St. Bernard and the Cistercian reforming party, 1135-1154. *M. I. Megaw, M.A. 1939 Belfast*

Edward I and the church. *F. E. Sweetinburgh, M.A. 1917 Birmingham*

The effect of the Marian and Elizabethan religious settlements upon the clergy of the City of London, 1553-64. *E. L. C. Mullins, M.A. 1948 London, University College*

The effect of the Reformation on the supply of schools in England during the sixteenth century. *F. F. Rigby, M.Ed. 1941 Manchester*

The effects of the Reformation on the social conditions of England, 1535-1570. *I. V. Harriss, M.A. 1915 Birmingham*

The enforcement of the Lateran decrees in England in the reign of Henry III. *E. M. Lang, B.Litt. 1931 Oxford*

England a papal fief: repudiation. *A. J. Williams, M.A. 1925 Liverpool*

England and the Great Schism of the West. *C. M. Saum, M.A. 1916 Liverpool*

English ecclesiastical baronies and knight service, especially in the thirteenth and fourteenth centuries. *H. M. Chew, Ph.D. 1926 London*

Church History: England contd.
The English Reformation as reflected in the life and works of Thomas Becon, 1512 to 1567. *D. S. Bailey, Ph.D. 1947 Edinburgh*

The episcopate in the reign of Henry III. *M. E. Gibbs, B.Litt. 1932 Oxford*

The evolution of radical theory after the Reformation. *A. J. Clark, M.A. 1910 London*

An examination of the views of John Wesley in relation to the Protestant Reformation. *R. G. Ashman, Ph.D. 1949 Wales*

A factual and analytical account of the religious awakening in the United Kingdom in the years 1855-65. *J. E. Orr, D.Phil. 1948 Oxford*

Frank almoign: a study of ecclesiastical tenure in England chiefly in the fourteenth and fifteenth centuries. *E. G. Kimball, B.Litt. 1927 Oxford*

Growth of sabbatarianism in England from 1558 to 1658. *W. A. Leaper, M.A. 1919 National University of Ireland*

Growth of the idea of religious toleration in England from 1689 to 1727. *A. B. Miller, Ph.D. 1939 Edinburgh*

Henry Bullinger of Zurich: his place in the Reformation with special reference to England. *T. S. Taylor, B.Litt. 1912 Oxford*

The history of the Church in the reign of Edward III. *H. M. Jones, M.A. 1914 Wales*

The humanitarian movement in England in the eighteenth century, with special reference to the relation between the revival in religious life and industrial change: a study in the sociology of religion. *W. J. Warner, Ph.D. 1929 London*

The influence of bishops and of members of cathedral bodies in the intellectual life of England, 1066 to 1216. *E. Rathbone, Ph.D. 1936 London, King's College*

1. The influence of the Continental Reformation upon the Thirty-nine Articles. *R. Milton Hay, B.D. 1924 Oxford*

Introduction and glossary to the Old English version of Bede's *Ecclesiastical history of the English people. M. R. Jeffery, M.A. 1935 Leeds*

John Byrom, F.R.S., 1691-1763: his religious thought and its relation to the movements of his time. *A. R. Hubbuck, Ph.D. 1947 Edinburgh*

The Laudian Party, 1649-1662, and its influence on the Church settlement of the Restoration. *R. S. Bosher, Ph.D. 1949 Cambridge*

The light thrown by the papal registers on papal provisions, and some ecclesiastical abuses in the English Church during the time of Pope John XXII. *A. P. Deeley, M.A. 1927 Manchester*

Martin Bucer and the English Reformation. *C. L. R. A. Hopf, D.Phil. 1943 Oxford*

Ms. Balliol 354: Richard Hill's *Commonplace Book. D. C. Browning, B.Litt. 1935 Oxford*

Oglethorpe and social and religious movements in England and Georgia. *L. F. Church, Ph.D. 1928 London*

The personnel and political activities of the English Episcopate during the reign of Edward II. *K. Edwards, M.A. 1937 London, Royal Holloway College*

The Reformation and the English universities. *W. B. Merritt, M.A. 1938 National University of Ireland*

The Reformation in the diocese of Lincoln as illustrated by the life and work of Bishop Longland (1521-47). *G. E. Wharhirst, B.Litt. 1938 Oxford*

The religious relations of England and Scotland in the early reformation period. *D. Davidson, B.Litt. 1923 Oxford*

Secular instruction and incidental information in English vernacular sermon literature of the later Middle Ages, 1150-1450. *W. Lister, M.Ed. 1945 Manchester*

Some aspects of Church life in England during the reign of Edward III. *K. L. Wood-Legh, Ph.D. 1933 Cambridge*

Some aspects of the religious history of Norfolk in the fifteenth century. *C. B. Firth, M.A. 1910 London*

A study of certain letter books in the possession of the Dean and Chapter of Durham as illustrations of the life of the Church in England in the later thirteenth century. *F. Barlow, B.Litt. 1934 Oxford*

The style and syntax of the *Historia ecclesiastica* of Bede. *R. Ottley, M.A. 1935 London, Queen Mary College*

Church History: England contd.
A survey of religious life in Birmingham, 1790-1830. *C. E. B. Hubbard, M.A. 1935 Birmingham*

Church History: Ethiopia
The religious history of the Abyssinian races. *H. J. Weld-Blundell, B.Litt. 1911 Oxford*

Church History: France
See also Arnulf, of Lisieux, Bishop; Bossuet, J. B.; Dupanloup, F. A. P.; Juvenal des Ursins, J., Archbishop; Poullain, V.; Richer, E.

Catholic opinion and the ecclesiastical policy of the government in France (1869-70). *J. W. Pickersgill, B.Litt. 1933 Oxford*

The characteristics of the early Christian Church in Wales, considered especially in relation to the Churches in Ireland and in Gaul. *E. Davies, B.Litt. 1934 Oxford*

Constitutional history of the French Church, 1438-1682. *F. Streatfeild, D.Phil. 1921 Oxford*

Francis Lambert of Avignon (1487-1530): a study in Reformation origins. *R. L. Winters, Ph.D. 1936 Edinburgh*

Church History: Germany
The development of the catechism and of the catechetical instruction of children in the church consequent upon the religious changes in Germany during the sixteenth century. *J. Clement, M.A. 1945 National University of Ireland*

Studies in the history and administration of the German Church from 1225 to 1275, with special reference to the Province of Cologne. *F. R. Lewis, D.Phil. 1936 Oxford*

Church History: Ireland
Beatha Giollasius - Giolla Iosa (1135-1174) (The life of Giollasius - disciple of Jesus (1135-1174)). *A. Ní Mhaoldhomhnaigh, M.A. 1938 National University of Ireland*

The characteristics of the early Christian Church in Wales, considered especially in relation to the Churches in Ireland and in Gaul. *E. Davies, B.Litt. 1934 Oxford*

Church reform in Ireland before 1550. *J. G. Flanagan, M.A. 1946 National University of Ireland*

Cornelius O'Mulrian, Bishop of Killaloe (1576-1617) and the Counter-Reformation. *M. MacPhillips, M.A. 1928 National University of Ireland*

The counter-reformation in Ireland under the Tudor sovereigns. *E. M. Brown, M.A. 1922 National University of Ireland*

Henry VIII and the Irish Church. *J. C. P. Proby, B.Litt. 1925 Oxford*

Jesuit Mission to Ireland. *J. Corboy, M.A. 1941 National University of Ireland*

Mary Tudor's Irish policy and the Counter-Reformation. *B. Lee, M.A. 1930 National University of Ireland*

Vocabulary to lives of St. Carthage. *M. Lucy, M.A. 1915 National University of Ireland*

Church History: Italy
The constitutional position of the Church in the Norman kingdom of Sicily, 1130-94, with special reference to the relations between papacy, monarchy, metropolitan and immediate sees. *J. M. Shaxby, B.Litt. 1933 Oxford*

The effect of the religious movement on the origin and early growth of the Milanese commune during the eleventh century. *S. M. Brown, B.Litt. 1929 Oxford*

The effect of the religious reformation on Italy between 1520 and 1550. *G. K. Brown, Ph.D. 1931 Edinburgh*

Church History: Norway
The Norwegian rite: a study of the Byzantine liturgy. *H. Holloway, D.D. 1934 Belfast*

Church History: Portugal
The treasure of São Roque: a sidelight on the Reformation. *W. Telfer, B.D. 1932 Cambridge*

Church History: Scotland
See also Church of Scotland; Episcopal Church in Scotland; Knox, J.; McAlpin, J.; Wishart, G.

The Anglican tendencies in the Scottish Reformation and their bearing on the significance of the Concordat of Leith. *L. B. Taylor, B.Litt. 1932 Oxford*

The Church in Shetland during the sixteenth and seventeenth centuries. *E. W. Wallis, Ph.D. 1940 Edinburgh*

Church order in Scotland. *W. C. Thom, Ph.D. 1924 Aberdeen*

Church History: Scotland contd.
Ecclesiastical polity and religious life in Scotland during the Commonwealth and Protectorate. *M. B. MacGregor, Ph.D. 1929 Glasgow*

An examination of the grants of land made to the Scottish Church in the twelfth and thirteenth centuries, with special reference to secular services. *T. Davidson, Ph.D. 1930 Edinburgh*

The historical setting of the Scottish covenants of the reign of Charles I. *J. W. McEwan, Ph.D. 1930 Glasgow*

The history of Church discipline in Scotland. *I. M. Clark, Ph.D. 1926 Aberdeen*

The influence of England on the Scottish Reformation. *D. Davidson, Ph.D. 1926 Edinburgh*

The later convenanting movement, with special reference to religion and ethics. *H. C. Macpherson, Ph.D. 1923 Edinburgh*

The life of James Sharp, archbishop of St. Andrews. *A. T. Miller, Ph.D. 1940 Edinburgh*

Musicians of the Scottish Reformation, with special reference to Crown policy c.1560-1650. *J. McQuaid, Ph.D. 1949 Edinburgh*

The political factor in the Scottish Reformation, national and international, with special reference to the relations between England and Scotland in the years immediately preceding the Reformation. *J. C. T. Hunter, B.Litt. 1925 Oxford*

The religious relations of England and Scotland in the early reformation period. *D. Davidson, B.Litt. 1923 Oxford*

Scottish ecclesiastical influence upon Irish Presbyterianism from the non-subscription controversy to the union of the synods. *R. Allen, M.A. 1940 Belfast*

Scottish Lollardry and its contribution to the Reformation in Scotland, with special reference to the Lollards of the West. *T. M. A. MacNab, Ph.D. 1933 Glasgow*

A study of the accommodation movements between Presbytery and Episcopacy in the seventeenth century in Scotland, England and Ireland. *D. S. Hopkirk, Ph.D. 1946 Edinburgh*

Church History: Serbia
The history of the Church of Serbia from the foundation of its independence to the fall of the patriarchate (1219-1463 A.D.). *A. Yelissiye, B.Litt. 1919 Oxford*

History of the Serbian Church under Turkish rule. *P. Yevtić, B.Litt. 1919 Oxford*

Church History: Spain
See Margarit, J., Cardinal; Ximénes, F. de C., Cardinal.

Church History: Sweden
The Counter-Reformation in Sweden. *C. J. A. Oppermann, M.A. 1922 London*

On the liturgy of the Swedish Church: a) mass offices prepared by individuals between 1535 and 1576; b) mass offices prepared by committees between 1599 and 1716. *E. Y. Esskildsen, B.D. 1917 Oxford*

Church History: Switzerland
Henry Bullinger of Zurich: his place in the Reformation with special reference to England. *T. S. Taylor, B.Litt. 1912 Oxford*

Church History: U.S.S.R.
The humiliated Christ in modern Russian thought. *N. Gorodetzky, B.Litt. 1938 Oxford*

The peasantry, Orthodox clergy, dissenters, and Jews, as seen by Leskov. *F. Smith, M.A. 1948 London, School of Slavonic and East European Studies*

Church History: Wales
See also Jones, John (Talsarn); Jones, R.

The attitude of Wales towards the Reformation. *A. Davies, M.A. 1911 Wales*

The characteristics of the early Christian Church in Wales, considered especially in relation to the Churches in Ireland and in Gaul. *E. Davies, B.Litt. 1934 Oxford*

Cysylltiad y diwygiadau crefyddol o 1730 hyd 1850 â llenyddiaeth y cyfnod (The connection of religious revivals from 1730 to 1850 with the literature of the period). *L. E. Evans, M.A. 1934 Wales*

The ecclesiastical and religious position in the diocese of Llandaff in the reign of Queen Elizabeth. *H. M. Isaacs, M.A. 1928 Wales*

The ecclesiastical history of Glamorgan during the Middle Ages up to 1188, with special reference to the period A.D. 1056-1188. *L. C. Simons, M.A. 1914 Wales*

Church History: Wales contd.
Ffwleriaeth yng Nghumru (Fullerism in Wales). *T. E. Jones, M.A. 1934 Wales*

The history of the Counter-Reformation in Wales. *T. C. Jones, B.Litt. 1924 Oxford*

A history of the origins and development of the Celtic church in Wales, between the years 450 A.D. and 630 A.D. *J. W. James, D.D. 1931 Durham*

1. A history of the Puritan Movement in Wales. 2. Religious development in Wales (1654-1662). 3. The Puritan visitation of Jesus College, Oxford, and the principalship of Dr. Michael Roberts (1648-1657). *T. Richards, D.Litt. 1924 Wales*

The Reformation in the diocese of Llandaff. *L. Thomas, B.Litt. 1926 Oxford*

The religious and social condition of Wales at the outbreak of the Glyndwr movement, with special reference to the attitude of the clergy, both regular and secular, to the movement. *J. R. Gabriel, M.A. 1906 Wales*

The social and religious history of Wales from 1350 to 1550 as reflected in the literature of the period. *C. H. Thomas, Ph.D. 1940 National University of Ireland*

The Welsh Church and Welsh politics in the war of Owen Glyndwr. *J. T. Davies, M.A. 1920 Liverpool*

The Welsh church under Edward I. *E. Thomas, M.A. 1912 Wales*

Church in Australia
The constitutional history of the Church in Australia. *R. A. Giles, B.Litt. 1929 Oxford*

Church Music
See also Carols; Hymns; Organ.

Musicians of the Scottish Reformation, with special reference to Crown policy c.1560-1650. *J. McQuaid, Ph.D. 1949 Edinburgh*

The neumes and Irish liturgical mss. *A. G. Fleischmann, M.A. 1932 National University of Ireland*

The Puritans and music, with special reference to the Commonwealth period. *W. M. Lewis, M.A. 1917 Wales*

The relations between theology and music viewed in the light of the works of theologians and the decisions of ecclesiastical authorities. *E. R. Routley, B.D. 1946 Oxford*

A review of fifteenth century church music in England, with special reference to the Pepys ms. 1236. *D. M. G. Bird, M.Litt. 1941 Cambridge*

Church of England
See Anglican Church.

Church of Ireland
See also Swift, J.; Ussher, J.

The articles of the Church of Ireland of 1615. *R. L. Wallace, Ph.D. 1949 Edinburgh*

The cathedral system in the Church of Ireland since the disestablishment. *H. A. Boyd, B.Litt. 1950 Dublin, Trinity College*

The economic results of the disestablishment of the Irish Church. *H. F. Shearman, Ph.D. 1944 Dublin, Trinity College*

Henry VIII and the Irish Church. *J. C. P. Proby, B.Litt. 1925 Oxford*

Church of Scotland
See also Darien Scheme.

The attempts at Presbyterian-Episcopal accommodation in Scotland and their influence on modern movements of unity. *M. J. Roberts, Ph.D. 1949 Glasgow*

The Darien scheme and the Church of Scotland. *J. C. Ramsay, Ph.D. 1949 Edinburgh*

The Eucharistic rite in the liturgy of the Church of Scotland. *J. M. Barkley, D.D. 1949 Dublin, Trinity College*

The General Assembly of the Church of Scotland in the year 1638: a study from contemporary documents of its origin, proceedings and importance. *N. Meldrum, Ph.D. 1924 Edinburgh*

Ministerial stipends in the Church of Scotland from 1560 to 1633. *N. V. Hope, Ph.D. 1944 Edinburgh*

Witchcraft and the Church of Scotland subsequent to the Reformation. *J. Gilmore, Ph.D. 1948 Glasgow*

Church Plate
The treasure of São Roque: a sidelight on the Reformation. *W. Telfer, B.D. 1932 Cambridge*

Treasures of the Surrey churches in the diocese of Guildford. *C. K. F. Brown, M.A. 1942 Leeds*

Church Union
See Christian Union.

Churches of Christ
See Disciples of Christ.

Churchill, Charles
Charles Churchill. *J. Lewis, M.A. 1945 Bristol*

A study of Charles Churchill. *T. B. Shepherd, M.A. 1934 London, Birkbeck College*

Churchill, Randolph Spencer, Lord
The political career of Lord Randolph Churchill. *M. Dempsey, M.A. 1949 Liverpool*

Churriguera, José de
The position of José de Churriguera in the development of Spanish Baroque architecture. *Sir J. L. Martin, Ph.D. 1936 Manchester*

Cibber, Colley
The Cibbers, father and son, as actors, dramatists and writers. *P. T. Rees, M.A. 1931 Wales*

Colley Cibber, actor-manager, dramatist and historian of the theatre. *L. M. Shaw, M.A. 1928 Liverpool*

The life of Colley Cibber. *K. Goyne, M.A. 1937 London, Courtauld Institute of Art*

Cibber, Theophilus
The Cibbers, father and son, as actors, dramatists and writers. *P. T. Rees, M.A. 1931 Wales*

Cicero
Art in Roman life as shown in the works of Cicero. *H. G. Stokes, B.Litt. 1934 Oxford*

Changes in educational ideals from Cicero and Quintilian to the Carolingian renaissance. *A. Hurworth, M.A. 1923 Leeds*

The character of Cicero as exhibited in his letters. *T. E. Davies, M.A. 1916 Wales*

Cicero and the supernatural. *M. T. Heyes, M.A. 1922 Liverpool*

Cicero as a translator. *E. M. Montgomery, M.A. 1931 London, Bedford College*

Cicero's educational theory. *G. B. Smith, M.Ed. 1934 Manchester*

Cicero's ideas on deity and universe. *W. V. Denard, B.Litt. 1948 Dublin, Trinity College*

Cicero's recall from exile. *H. G. Leaver, M.A. 1924 Manchester*

Cicero's study of Greek literature, with special reference to Cicero as a translator. *M. D. J. Adams, M.A. 1932 Wales*

Contributions to a commentary on Cicero's speech *Pro Rabirio Postumo. E. A. Joels, M.A. 1924 London*

The history of the οικείωσιο doctrine, with special reference to Cicero *De Finibus* v. *J. M. Mingay, B.Litt. 1950 Oxford*

Notes on Cicero: *In Vatinium. L. G. Pocock, M.A. 1924 London*

A palaeographical study of the manuscript of Cicero's *De Oratore* (Harl. 2736) in the British Museum. *H. L. Macdonald, M.A. 1924 London*

The philosophy of Cicero. *T. E. Cottrell, M.A. 1914 Birmingham*

The poems of Cicero. *W. W. Ewbank, Ph.D. 1932 London, External Degree*

Rome and Roman models in Cicero's philosophical and rhetorical writings. *F. H. R. Solmsen, Ph.D. 1936 Cambridge*

Cimon
Cimon and Themistocles: a comparison and a contrast. *A. W. Barth, M.A. 1907 London*

Cinema
The effect of a recruitment film on the attitude of school leavers to nursing as a career. *A. J. W. Jeffery, M.Ed. 1950 Manchester*

A measurement of the effect of group discussion on the understanding and appreciation of films. *E. B. Simpson, M.A. 1947 London, Institute of Education*

The social and emotional effects of the recreational film on adolescents of 13 and 14 years of age in the West Bromwich area. *B. Kesterton, Ph.D. 1948 Birmingham*

The theory and practice of film observation: and experimental investigation into the child's attitudes to educational and entertainment films. *A. M. Lewis, M.A. 1938 London, Institute of Education*

The value of films in the teaching of history. *F. Consitt, Ph.D. 1931 Leeds*

Cinque Ports
The growth of the organization of the Cinque Ports Confederation. *K. M. E. Murray, B.Litt. 1932 Oxford*

Cirencester
Cirencester and its region: a study in Cotteswold geography. *R. W. Brooker, M.A. 1937 Reading*

Cistercian Order
See also Religious Orders and Societies.

The Cistercian movement. *C. Brien, M.A. 1926 Birmingham*

The Cistercian Movement in the north of England, with special reference to the early history of Byland Abbey. *P. Auty, B.Litt. 1934 Oxford*

The ecclesiastical relations of the reign of Stephen, with special reference to St. Bernard and the Cistercian reforming party, 1135-1154. *M. I. Megaw, M.A. 1939 Belfast*

Cities and Towns
See Town and Country Planning.

Citizenship
See also Nationality.

The analysis and testing of civics in a school civics experiment. *M. J. Heavyside, M.Ed. 1949 Leeds*

1. The Christian's duty to the State. 2. The lawfulness of war. *J. G. W. Tuckey, B.D. 1924 Oxford*

A comparative investigation of the influence of mechanical and linguistic training on the understanding of the forms of reasoning involved in civics. *G. Edwards, M.Ed. 1949 Leeds*

A comparative investigation of the influence of geography and practical biology on the understanding of the forms of reasoning involved in civics. *C. W. Atkinson, M.Ed. 1949 Leeds*

Education for citizenship in China. *K. T. Sun, M.A. 1936 Leeds*

Education for world-citizenship: the modern doctrines of instinct, heredity, social science, and aesthetics, and their bearing on educational aim, method, organization and administration. *S. L. Dasvarma, M.A. 1922 London, University College*

History and education for citizenship in grammar schools. *W. H. Burston, M.A. 1947 Bristol*

The types of political relation established between Rome and other communities in Italy from the earliest recorded times to the close of the Republic, and their contribution to the conception of citizenship adopted by the Roman Empire during the first three centuries A.D. *A. N. Sherwin-White, D.Phil. 1937 Oxford*

Citrus Fruit Growing Industry
The citrus fruit growing industry: its geographical distribution and conditions. *S. G. Dyer, Ph.D. 1930 London, Birkbeck College*

Civil Aviation
See Air Transport.

Civil Liberties
See Freedom.

Civil Service
See also Public Administration.

The administrative staff of the Roman emperors at Rome from Augustus to Alexander Severus. *G. R. C. Davies, D.Phil. 1947 Oxford*

An administrative study of the development of civil service in India during the Company's régime. *A. K. Ghosal, Ph.D. 1940 London, School of Economics and Political Science*

Civil service discipline in modern democracies: an essay on the code of official conduct in England, U.S.A. and France. *J. K. Hsiang, M.Sc. 1938 London, School of Economics and Political Science*

A comparative study of the higher classes of administrative officials, in the British Civil Service on the one hand, and the American Federal system on the other. *D. K. Price, B.Litt. 1935 Oxford*

The development of the Indian civil service. *S. C. Parasher, M.Sc. 1947 London, School of Economics and Political Science*

An examination of the theory and practice of appointments in the reigns of Henry III and Edward I (1216-1307), and of their historical significance. *P. H. Scotney, M.A. 1927 London*

The history of the Canadian civil service. *R. M. Dawson, M.Sc. 1920 London*

The personnel organization of the British civil service: a study of structure as related to function. *S. G. King, M.Sc. 1945 London, External Degree*

Post-entry training in the civil service: a study of the positive state. *A. M. Smith, Ph.D. 1945 London, School of Economics and Political Science*

The settlement of wages in government employment. *E. C. Shepherd, B.Litt. 1923 Oxford*

Civil Service contd.
Some problems connected with the influence of the freedmen upon the civil service under Claudius. P. R. Hiscock, M.A. 1947 Reading

A study of the Civil Service of Northern Ireland. T. Kelly, M.A. 1936 Belfast

Civil War, 1642-1646
See Great Britain: History: Seventeenth Century.

Clapham Sect, The
The Clapham Sect. E. M. F. Howse, Ph.D. 1934 Edinburgh

Clare, John
John Clare: a life. J. W. Tibble, M.A. 1935 Leeds

Clare, Suffolk
A history of Clare, Suffolk, with special reference to its development as a borough during the Middle Ages, and to its importance as a centre of the woollen industry in the fifteenth to seventeenth centuries. G. A. Thornton, Ph.D. 1927 London

Clarendon, Edward Hyde, 1st Earl of
Clarendon as a historian. D. D. Richards, M.A. 1913 Wales

The value of Clarendon as a historian. N. M. Smith, M.A. 1906 Wales

Clarin
See Alas, L.

Clarke, Samuel
Samuel Clarke and his contemporaries: a revaluation of Clarke's philosophical position based upon an examination of his relations with his contemporaries. M. B. Lucas, Ph.D. 1940 London, King's College

Class (Sociology)
See Aristocracy; Labour; Middle Classes.

Classical Studies
See also Greece, Ancient; Rome; Greek and Latin Language and Literature; and Tyrwhitt, T.; Verrall, A. W.

The ancient classics: their place in modern education. P. J. Ryan, M.A. 1927 National University of Ireland

The changing values in the critical and literary outlook of the seventeenth century, as manifested in English verse translation from the Greek and Latin classics. S. Musgrove, D.Phil. 1944 Oxford

The classical element in English poetry of the nineteenth century. E. A. Williams, M.A. 1908 Wales

Classical mythology and classical subjects in the work of some of the nineteenth century poets. E. M. Lea, M.A. 1921 Birmingham

The history of the study of the classics in Wales during the sixteenth century. G. D. Roberts, B.Litt. 1923 Oxford

L'idée de l'antiquité Gréco-Latin dans Jean-Jacques Rousseau. A. Quinton, M.A. 1924 Liverpool

Matthew Arnold's classical ideal. M. Breathnac, M.A. 1939 National University of Ireland

Quaestiones hydraulicae. E. J. A. Kenny, M.Litt. 1936 Cambridge

Shakespeare's debt to classical antiquity. G. C. Hingley, M.A. 1912 Birmingham

Claudel, Paul
The imagery of Paul Claudel. D. M. Willis, M.A. 1933 Manchester

The influence of the Bible on the work of Paul Claudel. A. M. White, Ph.D. 1932 London, Westfield College

Influences dans le drame de Paul Claudel. J. C. van L. Decreus, M.A. 1945 Leeds

La Spiritualité de Claudel. D. Mulligan, M.A. 1951 National University of Ireland

Paul Claudel. S. Rickman, M.A. 1936 Birmingham

A study of the ideas of Paul Claudel, as expressed in his plays and poems. R. E. Horne, M.A. 1939 Wales

Clémanges, Nicholas Poillevilain de
The letters of Nicholas Poillevilain de Clémanges, 1363(4)-1437. F. J. Moorhead, M.A. 1936 Liverpool

The life and writings of Nicolas de Clémanges: a study in repercussions of the Schism and Conciliar Movement. M. H. Bell, M.A. 1948 London, Bedford College

Clement I, Pope, Saint
1. The problem of the second Epistle of St. John. 2. The references to the Holy Spirit in the Epistle of Clement of Rome to the Corinthians. H. J. Gibbins, B.D. 1904 Oxford

Clement I, Pope, Saint contd.
1. The use and importance of the Old Testament in the first two centuries. 2. The first Epistle of Clement critically and dogmatically examined, with special reference to the Old Testament. J. H. Webb, B.D. & D.D. 1907 Oxford

Clement, of Alexandria
1. The Christology of Clement of Alexandria. 2. The theology of the Wisdom literature. R. B. Tollinton, B.D. 1905 Oxford

The Christology of Clement of Alexandria. V. A. S. Little, D.Phil. 1938 Oxford

Studies in Clement of Alexandria. R. P. Casey, Ph.D. 1924 Cambridge

Clénard, Nicolas
See Cleynaerts, N.

Cleopatra, Queen of Egypt
Cleopatra on the English stage. O. C. de C. Ellis, M.A. 1946 Sheffield

The theme of Antony and Cleopatra in English drama. A. May, B.Litt. 1937 Oxford

Clergy
See also Episcopate; Ordination.

Astudiaeth feirniadol o'r Didache a llenyddiaeth Gristionogol arall o gynnyrch y ddwy ganrif gyntaf, a ysgrifennwyd yn yr iaith Roeg, ynghyda chyfeiriad arbennig at ddatblygiad y Weinidogaeth a'r Gwasanaethau Eglwysig (A critical study of the Didache and other Christian literature in Greek of the first and second centuries, with special reference to the development of the ministry and the church services). E. J. Lloyd, Ph.D. 1946 Wales

1. The authorship of the Epistle to the Hebrews. 2. The Christian ministry in the New Testament. M. B. Hutchison, B.D. & D.D. 1905 Oxford

The clergy of the English secular cathedrals in the fourteenth century, with special reference to the church of Salisbury. K. Edwards, Ph.D. 1940 Manchester

The clergyman, the schoolmaster and the governess in the novel of the eighteenth century. H. D. Pearson, M.A. 1920 London

The condition of the clergy at the time of the Reformation in England. M. K. R. Cotton, M.A. 1916 London

The condition of the English parish clergy from the Reformation to 1660, with special reference to the dioceses of Oxford, Gloucester, and Worcester. D. M. Barratt, D.Phil. 1949 Oxford

A critical survey of recent British work on the Church and ministry. T. D. O. Edwards, M.A. 1940 Bristol

The doctrines of the Church and the ministry held by the principal Anglican and Continental reformers. W. D. F. Hughes, B.Litt. 1923 Oxford

Education for the Christian ministry. A. Sims, M.A. 1945 Bristol

The effect of the Marian and Elizabethan religious settlements upon the clergy of the City of London, 1553-64. E. L. C. Mullins, M.A. 1948 London, University College

Expositions of: St. Luke xii.42,43: the ministry, a stewardship; I Corinthians xii: the spiritual gifts of the Church; Romans ix.4: the Covenant or Church principle. B. J. Kidd, D.D. 1904 Oxford

Grievances of the English clergy in the late thirteenth and early fourteenth centuries, with special reference to the gravamina of 1309. U. R. Q. Henriques, B.Litt. 1940 Oxford

The history of the English clergy, 1800-1900. C. K. F. Brown, D.Phil. 1949 Oxford

1. Inspiration. 2. Apostolic succession of the Christian ministry. G. Golding-Bird, B.D. & D.D. 1912 Oxford

Le clergé dans l'oeuvre de Balzac. L. Gardner, M.A. 1925 Manchester

The naval chaplain in Stuart times. W. F. Scott, D.Phil. 1935 Oxford

1. On eternal punishment. 2. On Anglican orders. E. S. Elwell, B.D. 1878 Oxford

The organisation of a college of secular priests as illustrated by the records of the College of Holy Trinity, Arundel, 1380-1544. R. B. K. Petch, M.A. 1940 London, King's College

Parish clergy in the diocese of Exeter in the century after the Black Death. G. R. Dunstan, M.A. 1939 Leeds

Clergy contd.
The parish clergy of rural Oxfordshire from the institution of Bishop John Butler (1777) to the translation of Bishop Samuel Wilberforce (1869), with particular reference to their non-ecclesiastical activities. D. McClatchey, D.Phil. 1949 Oxford

The place of the secular clergy in the society of fifteenth century England. G. Templeman, M.A. 1936 London, School of Economics and Political Science

The priesthood of Christ, of Christians, and of the Christian ministry. 2. Public worship in the Christian Church, as described in or inferred from the New Testament. W. D. Springett, B.D. 1880 Oxford

The problem of the second marriage of priests in the Orthodox Church of the East. M. Yanoshevitch, B.Litt. 1921 Oxford

1. The relation of priest and prophet in the history of Israel before the exile. 2. St. Basil the Great and the monastic life. E. F. Morison, B.D 1912 Oxford

The relations between the Mendicant Friars and the secular clergy in England during the century after the issue of the bull Super Cathedram (1300). J. L. Copeland, M.A. 1937 London, Royal Holloway College

The rôle of the parson in the literature of the eighteenth century in England and Germany. M. E. Daw, M.A. 1937 London, King's College

The sacred ministry and its relation to marriage in the Holy Eastern Orthodox Church. C. Knetes, B.Litt. 1909 Oxford

Three expositions of Holy Scripture on the earliest conception of the nature of the Christian ministry. A. E. B. Day, D.D. 1913 Oxford

1. The threefold ministry. 2. Infant baptism. F. Moor, B.D. 1888 Oxford

Cleveland, Yorkshire
See Yorkshire.

Cleynaerts (Clenardus or Clénard), Nicolas
Nicolai Clenardi epistolae. L. J. F. Welton, Ph.D. 1935 Liverpool

Clifford, Thomas, 1st Lord Clifford of Chudleigh
A biography of Thomas Clifford, first Lord Clifford of Chudleigh. J. J. S. Shaw, Ph.D. 1935 Glasgow

Climate
See also Rain.

Architecture and the Mediterranean climate. M. S. Makiya, Ph.D. 1946 Cambridge

The climate and climatic regions of Chile. H. A. Matthews, Ph.D. 1931 London, University College

Climatic aspect of the permanent settlement of the white man in the tropics: an essay in acclimatization. G. J. Cons, M.A. 1929 London

Climatic cycles and their influence upon human history. M. S. Vercoe-Rogers, M.A. 1928 London

Climatic variation in the Argentine, with special reference to problems of climatic classification. J. E. Walsh, M.Sc. 1934 London, Birkbeck College

Cold: its demands and suggestions: a study of the importance of environment in the development of Eskimo culture. D. Nusbaum, D.Phil. 1939 Oxford

Contributions to the climatology and geomorphology of Sino-Tibet and central China. J. B. Hanson-Lowe, Ph.D. 1949 London, External Degree

Early distribution and valleyward movement of population in south Britain; a relief model of Wales; climatology in correlation with geography; human geography in Britain. W. E. Whitehouse, M.A. 1916 Wales

The organization of a climatological station in a secondary school, and the introduction of this work into the geography syllabus. D. Peter, M.Ed. 1930 Manchester

The seasonal distribution (of temperature) over the British Isles. L. F. Lewis, M.Sc. 1947 Bristol

Clive, Catherine
A study of the life and times of Kitty Clive. P. J. Crean, Ph.D. 1933 London, External Degree

Clive, Robert, Baron Clive of Plassey
The history of the occupation and rural administration of Bengal by the English Company from the time of Clive to the permanent settlement under Cornwallis. W. K. Firminger, B.Litt. 1913 Oxford

Clodius Pulcher
The political activity of Clodius, particularly in relation to the triumvirs. M. D. Whitehouse, M.A. 1916 London

Cloth Industry
See Woollen Industry.

Clothing Industry
See also Costume; Footwear Industry; Hat Industry; Hosiery Industry; Tailoring Industry.

A history of the Londonderry shirt industry. *E. H. Slade, M.A. 1937 Belfast*

Location theory and the clothing industry: a study of the factors of industrial location, with particular reference to their influence on the clothing industry. *J. R. Long, Ph.D. 1949 Leeds*

World consumption of clothing wools. *F. J. C. Cronjé, Ph.D. 1939 Cambridge*

Cloud of Unknowing, The
An edition from the manuscripts of the *Cloud of Unknowing*, with an introduction, notes, and glossary. *P. Hodgson, D.Phil. 1936 Oxford*

An edition, from the manuscripts, of some of the prose pieces which have been attributed to the author of the *Cloud of unknowing* with an introduction and notes. *P. Hodgson, B.Litt. 1934 Oxford*

Clough, Arthur Hugh
Arthur Hugh Clough and his poetry. *I. P. Alexander, M.A. 1939 Birmingham*

Arthur Hugh Clough and his age. *N. J. Sheppard, M.A. 1938 National University of Ireland*

The intellectual life of A. H. Clough, with particular reference to his poetry. *G. P. Johari, B.Litt. 1949 Oxford*

Club de l'Entresol
The political academies of France in the early eighteenth century, with special reference to the Club de l'Entresol, and to its founder the Abbé Pierre-Joseph Alary. *E. R. Briggs, Ph.D. 1932 Cambridge*

Cluniacs
See also Religious Orders and Societies; Benedictine Order.

The history of the Cluniacs in England and Wales. *E. M. Fussell, M.A. 1917 Wales*

Clydach, River
The geography of the drainage areas of the Cynon and Clydach Rivers on the eve of the Industrial Revolution. *D. S. Prosser, M.Sc. 1945 Wales*

Clyde, River
The influence of geographical factors on the economic evolution of Scotland to the beginning of the eighteenth century, mainly as revealed in the development of overseas trade, especially that of the Clyde ports. *J. Walker, Ph.D. 1928 Edinburgh*

Coal Industry
The development of a safety lamp. *J. R. Morgan, M.Sc. 1927 London*

Coal Industry: Great Britain
An analysis of the industrial and agricultural life of south-east England. *M. B. A. Churchard, Ph.D. 1933 London, Bedford College*

Changes in the marketing of coal brought about by the Coal Mines Act of 1930, with special reference to Lancashire. *A. Roberts, Ph.D. 1939 Manchester*

The coal export trade of the United Kingdom, 1910-1920, with special reference to south Wales. *D. W. Lloyd, M.A. 1922 Wales*

The coal industry. *W. Prest, M.A. 1934 Leeds*

The coal industry in the seventeenth century. *A. J. Allaway, B.A. 1931 Sheffield*

The coal mining industry in Great Britain: yesterday, today and tomorrow. *F. H. Robinson, M.Sc. 1927 London*

A detailed survey of the history and development of the south Wales coal industry, c.1750 to c.1850. *L. B. Collier, Ph.D. 1941 London, External Degree*

The development of organized marketing in the British coal industry. *A. Beacham, M.A. 1937 Liverpool*

The development of south Wales anthracite coal area, with special reference to its industrial and labour organizations. *T. H. Griffiths, M.A. 1922 Wales*

An economic and historical survey of the development of the anthracite industry with special reference to the Swansea Valley. *D. G. John, M.A. 1923 Wales*

The economic aspect of coal-mining in South Yorkshire. *F. A. Gordon, M.Com. 1926 Birmingham*

Forms of organization in the British coal industry. *A. M. Neuman, Ph.D. 1933 London, School of Economics and Political Science*

The history, condition and prospects of the South Wales coalfield, considered mainly from the point of view of markets and industrial organisation. *J. O. Cheetham, M.A. 1921 Wales*

Coal Industry: Great Britain contd.
History of coal during the Industrial Revolution. *J. J. Jory, Ph.D. 1931 London, External Degree*

The history of English coal mining, 1500-1750. *A. W. R. Moller, D.Phil. 1933 Oxford*

The history of English coal-mining in the seventeenth century. *A. W. R. Moller, B.Litt. 1923 Oxford*

The history of the Barry Dock and Railways Company in relation to the development of the south Wales coalfield. *L. N. A. Davies, M.A. 1938 Wales*

A history of the trade disputes and the formation and operation of the several sliding scale agreements in the South Wales coal trade, 1870 to 1903, with special reference to the work of Sir William Thomas Lewis, 1st Baron Merthyr of Senghenydd. *B. Evans, M.A. 1944 Wales*

The history of trade unionism in the coal-mining industry of north Wales up to 1914. *E. Rogers, M.A. 1928 Wales*

Hours of work in the coal-mining industry of Great Britain since the early part of the nineteenth century, with special reference to Northumberland and Durham, and with an account of certain movements connected therewith. *N. H. Booth, B.Litt. 1930 Oxford*

Industrial and social conditions in the Wrexham coalfield (1800-1860). *D. T. Morgan, M.A. 1927 Liverpool*

The influence of recent changes in the social environment on the outlook and habits of individuals, with special reference to mining communities in south Wales. *W. H. Davies, M.A. 1933 Wales*

The influence of the coal trade on the merchant shipping and foreign trade of Great Britain during the second half of the nineteenth century. *E. Pritchard, B.Litt. 1925 Oxford*

Labour organization of miners of South Yorkshire from 1858-1914. *F. Machin, B.Litt. 1930 Oxford*

Movements of mining population in the anthracite area of south Wales. *E. J. Howells, M.Sc. 1938 Wales*

The Nottinghamshire coalfield: a geographical interpretation. *L. Dennis, M.A. 1936 London, External Degree*

A regional and economic survey of the anthracite area of Carmarthenshire. *D. T. Rosser, M.A. 1948 Wales*

Social survey of East Kent coalfield. *V. L. Hughes, Ph.D. 1934 London, School of Economics and Political Science*

Some effects of state interference in the British coal industry, with special reference to the period 1930-39. *N. Branton, Ph.D. 1944 London, External Degree*

Some psychological aspects of employment in the coal-mining industry, with special reference to the Ayrshire coalfield in Scotland. *W. D. Stewart, B.Litt. 1933 Oxford*

The south Wales anthracite industry, with special reference to changes in business organization since government decontrol in 1921, and their social effects. *D. J. Davies, M.A. 1930 Wales*

The south Wales coal trade in its international and marketing aspects, 1921-1926. *B. Thomas, M.A. 1928 Wales*

The south Wales coalfield during government control, 1914-1921. *J. Thomas, M.A. 1925 Wales*

A study of employment in coalmining and agriculture in the Wrexham area. *A. E. Hayes, M.A. 1948 Liverpool*

A study of the Daucleddau coalfield, Pembrokeshire. *G. Edwards, M.A. 1950 Birmingham*

The vend of coal, 1700-1830. *J. Symes, M.A. 1928 Leeds*

Wakefield and district as a traditional area in the Yorkshire, Derbyshire and Nottinghamshire coalfield. *E. H. Varley, M.Sc. 1935 London, Birkbeck College*

The Welsh coal trade during the Stuart period, 1603-1709. *B. M. Evans, M.A. 1928 Wales*

Coal Industry: India
Indian coal trade. *J. Guhathakurta, M.Sc. 1937 London, School of Economics and Political Science*

Coal Industry: Poland
The Polish Upper Silesian coal industry since the War. *H. L. Brooks, M.Sc. 1939 London, School of Economics and Political Science*

Coal Industry: United States
The bituminous coal industry in the United States of America. *E. Daniel, M.A. 1949 Wales*

An enquiry into the major geographical factors conditioning the production and distribution of coal and iron in the United States of America. *P. W. Bryan, Ph.D. 1924 London*

Coal Industry: U.S.S.R
The coal industry of the U.S.S.R. *D. E. J. Roberts, M.Sc. 1948 London, School of Economics and Political Science*

The coal resources of Russia. *M. Clough, M.Sc. 1931 London, School of Economics and Political Science*

Coastline
Certain aspects of coast erosion in the English Channel with special reference to the coast-defence problems of the town of Sidmouth, Devon. *W. P. Baron, M.A. 1931 London, External Degree*

Changes in the sand dune coasts of south Wales, with special reference to an investigation in the Newton-Merthyr Mawr area. *L. S. Higgins, M.A. 1932 Wales*

The coastal lands of southwest Lancashire and some of their problems. *C. Taylor, M.A. 1932 Liverpool*

Hull and the North Sea coastlands. *V. J. Gorner, M.Sc. 1948 London, External Degree*

The law of the foreshore and the right of access thereto. *W. Bennison, LL.D. 1914 London*

The movement of sand on beaches by waves and other action. *C. A. M. King, Ph.D. 1950 Cambridge*

Soil erosion in North America. *G. Winram, M.A. 1944 London, External Degree*

Studies of the Scottish shoreline. *S. Ting, Ph.D. 1937 Glasgow*

Cobbett, William
The political influence of William Cobbett, 1794-1815. *E. Knox, M.A. 1907 Liverpool*

Cobden, Richard
The Coventry silk-ribbon industry from the introduction of the use of the Dutch engine loom (c.1770) to the Cobden Commercial Treaty (1860). *H. Miles, B.Litt. 1930 Oxford*

Cocker, Edward
An account of the treatment of the fundamental operations of arithmetic, as applied to whole numbers, fractions and decimals, in the printed English Arithmetics, up to and including Cocker's *Arithmetic* (1678). *J. Jones, M.Sc. 1931 Wales*

Cocoa Industry
The production and marketing of cocoa in the western provinces of Nigeria, with some consideration of government control of marketing and prices from 1939 to 1946. *E. Bailey, M.A. 1947 Sheffield*

Some economics aspects of the cacao industry of Trinidad. *C. Y. Shepherd, Ph.D. 1937 London, External Degree*

Co-education
See also Education; Girls: Education; Women: Education.

The advantages and disadvantages of co-education. *M. E. Matthews, M.A. 1925 Birmingham*

Co-education: a statistical enquiry into the attitude of teachers towards co-education, and a comparative study of the emotional development of children trained in co-educational and other institutions. *F. E. Moreton, Ph.D. 1939 London, Institute of Education*

Co-education: an analysis of the work and principles of the mixed schools. *G. Clark, M.A. 1937 Liverpool*

Co-education, with special reference to the adolescent. *N. K. Mirz, M.A. 1931 Leeds*

The development of co-education in English secondary schools. *J. H. Bury, M.A. 1941 Reading*

Some apparent effects of co-education, suggested by a statistical investigation of examination results. *G. Tyson, M.Ed. 1930 Manchester*

The years between: an enquiry into the bases of co-education for adolescents, and some account of its practice. *A. Lloyd, M.A. 1936 Birmingham*

Coffey Family
Filidheacht mhuintir Chobhtaigh (The poetry of the Coffey family). *A. Mac Dhubhain, M.A. 1940 National University of Ireland*

Cognition
Cognition: its psychological analysis, its metaphysical conditions, and its epistemological value. *L. J. Walker, M.A. 1909 London*

Cognition contd.
An experimental investigation into cognitive development in infants of one to two years of age. *M. Loewenheim, Ph.D. 1945 London, University College*

Influences of volition in mental testing, or influences of conation on cognition. *E. H. Wild, Ph.D. 1926 London*

The objective mode of cognition: its metaphysical ground, logical sphere and the modification in its use in the passage from primitive man to the positive scientist. *O. A. Wheeler, M.A. 1911 Wales*

A study of certain aspects of *prima facie* extra-sensory cognition. *V. G. Kirk-Duncan, D.Phil. 1944 Oxford*

The subjective character of cognition and the pre-sensational development of perception. *R. B. Cattell, Ph.D. 1929 London*

Coinage
See Numismatics.

Cokain, Aston, Sir
The life and work of Sir Aston Cokain. *D. Raychaudhuri, M.A. 1933 London, University College*

Coleridge, Hartley
A biography of Hartley Coleridge. *E. L. Griggs, Ph.D. 1927 London*

Coleridge, Samuel Taylor
Aspects of the religious thought of S.T. Coleridge. *F. H. Grewe, M.A. 1947 Sheffield*

Classical and medieval inspiration in the poetry of Coleridge, Keats and Shelley. *H. A. Needham, M.A. 1921 Birmingham*

Coleridge as a religious thinker. *H. D. Frazer-Hurst, Ph.D. 1939 Dublin, Trinity College*

Coleridge on Shakespeare: an essay in correlation. *P. H. Williamson, M.A. 1948 Manchester*

Coleridge's contributions to periodical literature. *I. D. Adams, M.A. 1935 London, Bedford College*

Coleridge's dramatic criticism. *T. O'Flynn, M.A. 1946 National University of Ireland*

Coleridge's theory of communication. *B. G. Hardy, M.A. 1949 London, University College*

A critical edition of Coleridge's marginalia to Tennemann's *Geschichte der Philosophie* (1798-1817), with introduction and notes. *K. H. Coburn, B.Litt. 1932 Oxford*

A critical examination of Herder's thought, with special reference to its parallels in Coleridge. *G. A. Wells, M.A. 1949 London, University College*

The doctrine of atonement in Coleridge and Maurice. *C. W. I. Wardrop, Ph.D. 1932 Edinburgh*

An edition of the *Friend* by S. T. Coleridge. *B. E. Rooke, Ph.D. 1949 London, University College*

The German elements in the aesthetic of the age of Wordsworth; being studies in Coleridge's aesthetic and literary theory, and its relation to contemporary German thought. *W. Howarth, Litt.D. 1928 Manchester*

The influence of German aesthetic philosophy on Samuel Taylor Coleridge's theory of poetry. *J. W. Sagmaster, B.Litt. 1928 Oxford*

The mutual influence of William Wordsworth and Samuel Taylor Coleridge. *J. Bradshaw, M.A. 1914 Liverpool*

The origins and course of Coleridge's reaction against Locke and Kant. *J. Coles, M.A. 1949 Wales*

The prosodic and historical aspects of some poems by S. T. Coleridge. *P. White, M.A. 1925 Birmingham*

The religious philosophy of Samuel Taylor Coleridge. *H. E. G. Hinds, Ph.D. 1935 Edinburgh*

The romantic poetry of S. T. Coleridge. *G. A. Mackenzie, M.A. 1926 Birmingham*

Scientific terminology and analogy in Coleridge's poetic theory and practice. *R. Stein, B.Litt. 1946 Oxford*

Wordsworth, Coleridge, Byron, Shelley and the French Revolution. *P. R. Griffin, M.A. 1925 National University of Ireland*

Colette, Sidonie Gabrielle Claudine
The epithet and Colette. *E. Kirkman, M.A. 1942 Leeds*

Colleges
See Education, Higher; and under the names of individual colleges and universities.

Collier, Arthur
The idealism of Collier and Berkeley. *B. Thakur, Ph.D. 1937 London, University College*

Collingwood, Robert George
Professor Collingwood's conception of the relations between metaphysics and history, and its consequences for the theory of truth. *C. K. Grant, D.Phil. 1949 Oxford*

Collins, William Wilkie
The life and works of Wilkie Collins. *T. J. H. Haines, M.A. 1936 Wales*

Sensational elements in Dickens and Collins. *A. R. Jolly, M.A. 1943 Manchester*

Collinson, Peter
Peter Collinson, F.R.S., F.S.A., and his circle of friends. *N. G. B. James, B.Litt. 1923 Oxford*

Colman, George
The life and works of George Colman the Elder. *S. M. Lund, M.A. 1928 London*

Cologne
Studies in the history and administration of the German Church from 1225 to 1275, with special reference to the Province of Cologne. *F. R. Lewis, D.Phil. 1936 Oxford*

Colon (Kolom), Joseph, Rabbi
Life and times of Rabbi Joseph Colon (Kolom), 1420-1480. *M. H. Rabinowicz, Ph.D. 1948 London, Jews' College*

Colonization
General works only. See also the subheading Colonies under individual colonizing powers, and under the names of individual colonies.

The Berlin West African Conference 1884-5. *S. E. Crowe, Ph.D. 1940 Cambridge*

Education as a factor in colonial development, with special reference to Java. *B. A. Fletcher, M.A. 1934 Bristol*

International relations between Great Britain, Germany and the United States in the Samoan Islands. *L. M. Williams, M.A. 1938 Wales*

International rivalry in Samoa, 1845-1884. *S. R. Masterman, M.A. 1933 London, Bedford College*

International rivalry in West Africa (1454-1559). *J. W. Blake, M.A. 1935 London, King's College*

Origin and growth of the protectorate system, with special study of the system as developed in British colonial history 1800 to 1848. *W. E. Philpott, M.A. 1934 London, King's College*

The Pacific, its past and future and the policy of the great powers from the eighteenth century. *G. H. Scholefield, D.Sc. 1919 London*

The struggle for supremacy in the Pacific. *P. H. Wang, M.Sc. 1937 London, School of Economics and Political Science*

The struggles of the European powers for possession in Guiana, 1667-1713. *M. Fisher, M.A. 1926 London*

Studies in pre-Gracchan colonization. *E. T. Salmon, Ph.D. 1933 Cambridge*

Colour
History of the theories of colour vision from Young (1800) to the present time. *E. C. Millington, M.Sc. 1930 London*

Individual differences in colour memory. *P. N. Rozdon, Ph.D. 1932 Edinburgh*

On ιερóσ, ιεϱóσ, ιϱóσ; and on the colour words in Homer. *C. M. Mulvany, B.Litt. 1897 Oxford*

Psychochromaesthesia: an investigation of the nature and development of coloured thinking in childhood. *M. E. Bickersteth, Ph.D. 1923 Edinburgh*

Reactions to colour and form. *D. Lindsey, M.A. 1947 Manchester*

Some experiments on the abstraction of form and colour. *O. A. Oeser, Ph.D. 1932 Cambridge*

The specific nature of colour and form memories. *M. M. Said, M.Sc. 1929 Birmingham*

Colum, Pádraig
Padraig Colum. *C. Kinsella, M.A. 1949 National University of Ireland*

Comedy
Comedy as a literary form. See also Theatre. For individual writers, see under their names.

Anglo-Irish writers of comedies, 1690-1790. *J. Markey, M.A. 1929 National University of Ireland*

Aspects of the economic and social background of comedy in the early seventeenth century. *L. C. Knights, Ph.D. 1936 Cambridge*

Comedy and the theory of comedy in Germany from 1700-1750, with special reference to foreign influences. *B. Aikin-Sneath, Ph.D. 1935 London, University College*

Comedy contd.
Comedy in the Irish theatre; its genius. *J. Horgan, M.A. 1936 National University of Ireland*

The comedy of humours and the comedy of manners. *B. M. Leslie, M.A. 1923 Belfast*

The comedy of manner, 1700-1780. *S. M. Lund, Ph.D. 1933 London, East London College*

Comic theory and criticism from Steele to Hazlitt. *S. M. Tave, D.Phil. 1950 Oxford*

The *commedia erudita* and Elizabethan Comedy. *D. J. Gordon, Ph.D. 1941 Cambridge*

The 'country' in Restoration comedy. *J. H. Cretney, M.A. 1950 Nottingham*

English comedians in Germany in the sixteenth and seventeenth centuries. *W. I. Lucas, M.A. 1930 Bristol*

The evolution of the Spanish *comedia* from the close of the seventeenth century to the present day, with special reference to the period 1835-1898. *M. M. Couper, Ph.D. 1936 Edinburgh*

Fragments of Attic comedy. *M. Whittaker, M.Litt. 1934 Cambridge*

Galsworthy's conception of comedy. *H. Bilbrough, M.A. 1948 Manchester*

The historical evidence contained in Aristophanes and in the fragments of the Old Attic Comedy. *B. H. G. Williams, B.Litt. 1932 Oxford*

How far does Roman comedy represent Roman life and sentiment?. *J. R. Hughes, M.A. 1907 Wales*

The influence of French farce on English sixteenth century drama. *I. R. Maxwell, B.Litt. 1935 Oxford*

Influence of Jonson on Restoration comedy (1660-1700). *E. J. Potter, M.A. 1939 London, King's College*

The influence of Molière on Restoration comedy (1660-1720). *A. L. Stoddart, M.A. 1919 Birmingham*

La comédie en France entre Molière et Marivaux. *W. C. Donlon, M.A. 1937 London, King's College*

Latin influence on Tudor comedy. *A. J. Kearns, M.A. 1935 National University of Ireland*

Le pédant dans la comédie italienne du cinquecento, et sa descendance directe dans la comédie française jusqu'à Molière. *A. Gill, M.A. 1934 Manchester*

L'influence espagnole sur la comédie française du dix-septième siècle. *J. L. Milner, M.A. 1913 Liverpool*

Minor comedies in the eighteenth century. *F. A. Smith, M.A. 1929 Birmingham*

Nivelle de la Chaussée et *La comédie larmoyante*. *A. Jay, M.A. 1913 Liverpool*

The person of quality in Restoration comedy. *G. R. Kotwal, B.Litt. 1938 Oxford*

Post-Restoration comedy, 1700-25. *F. N. W. Bateson, B.Litt. 1926 Oxford*

Pride, love, and reason in the characters of the *nueva Comedia*. *H. Eames, M.Litt. 1933 Cambridge*

Realism in the Elizabethan drama, with special reference to citizen comedy. *H. I. Wilkie, Ph.D. 1923 Edinburgh*

The relation between theory and practice in Elizabethan and Jacobean comedy, 1570-1616. *N. E. Orna, M.A. 1948 London, University College*

The relation of Euripides to 'new comedy', with special reference to Menander. *M. Andrews, M.A. 1922 London*

The relation of the seventeenth century 'character' to the comedy of manners. *E. D. Ratledge, M.A. 1933 Manchester*

The slave in ancient comedy. *F. K. Beese, M.A. 1939 Wales*

The slaves of Greek comedy compared with those of Plautus and Terence. *W. G. Williams, M.A. 1911 London*

Social and political comedy in France from 1815 to 1848, and its origins. *S. L. England, Ph.D. 1932 London, East London College*

Social ideas in comedy, 1860-1920. *S. S. Smith, B.Litt. 1924 Oxford*

Society in French comedy from the death of Molière to 1715. *M. Hughes, M.A. 1925 Wales*

Some aspects of the development of seventeenth century comedy. *L. E. MacGibney, M.A. 1942 Belfast*

Comedy contd.
A study of the burlesque drama from D'Avenant to Fielding. *R. K. Kapur, B.Litt. 1934 Oxford*

Tirso de Molina and the *nueva comedia*. *J. Pomfret, M.A. 1935 Birmingham*

The transition from Jacobean to Restoration comedy, with special reference to social and theatrical factors. *M. M. Mahood, M.A. 1944 London, King's College*

Women in ancient comedy. *A. Page, M.A. 1947 Manchester*

Commerce
See Trade; Education, Commercial.

Commercial Law
The commercial law of ancient Athens to 323 B.C. *E. S. F. Ridout, Ph.D. 1935 London, University College*

History of the development of mercantile law in India, with special reference to the law of incorporated trading companies. *A. M. M. A. A. Siddinqi, LL.D. 1928 London*

An introduction to English maritime and commercial law. *F. R. Sanborn, Ph.D. 1924 Oxford*

The law of trade combinations, a study in comparative international law. *A. Neugröschel, Ph.D. 1942 London, School of Economics and Political Science*

The position of foreign merchants in England during the reign of Edward III, mainly from the legal standpoint. *A. Beardwood, B.Litt. 1924 Oxford*

Some aspects of Canadian legislation with regard to trade practices and business policy. *C. J. Gardner, M.Sc. 1940 London, School of Economics and Political Science*

Commines, Philippe de
See Commynes, P. de.

Commodities
General Works only. For particular commodities, see under their names.

The economic function of organized speculation in commodities. *A. B. Mitchell, B.Litt. 1938 Oxford*

Indian commodity market speculation. *L. N. Misra, Ph.D. 1932 London, School of Economics and Political Science*

International commodity agreements and world trade expansion. *H. Tyszynski, Ph.D. 1949 London, School of Economics and Political Science*

Restriction of the supply of staple commodities. *E. A. Stoffregen, Ph.D. 1931 London, School of Economics and Political Science*

Commons, House of
See Great Britain: Parliament.

Communications
See also Gong Languages.

The development of communications in northwest Wales. *M. O. Hernaman, M.A. 1945 London, Birkbeck College*

The development of communications in Glamorgan, with special reference to the growth of industry between 1760 and 1840. *E. Walker, M.A. 1947 Wales*

The economic geography of southern Rhodesia, with special reference to communications. *E. Fisher, M.A. 1924 Liverpool*

History of the development of the means of communication in the County of Monmouth. *M. A. Swallow, Ph.D. 1932 London, School of Economics and Political Science*

International legal and military control of cables and wireless in time of war, with special reference to the present war. *G. I. Phillips, B.Litt. 1918 Oxford*

Telecommunications: their significance as a factor in economic developments. *J. Smith, Ph.D. 1946 London, External Degree*

Transport and communication in medieval Wales. *W. H. Waters, M.A. 1923 Wales*

Communion, Holy
See Eucharist.

Communism
See also Marx, K.

Babouvism and the theory of proletarian dictatorship. *S. M. Cheng, Ph.D. 1934 London, School of Economics and Political Science*

The breakdown of post-war democracy in central Europe: analysis of authoritarian methods and possibilities of their control. *K. J. Neumann, D.Phil. 1944 Oxford*

The German Communist movement, 1918-1923. *N. B. Blumberg, D.Phil. 1950 Oxford*

Communism contd.
The philosophy of Bolshevism. *D. O'Brien, M.A. 1934 National University of Ireland*

The relation of the first international working men's association to the war of 1870 and the ensuing communard movements in Paris, Lyons, and Marseilles. *C. D. Edwards, B.Litt. 1924 Oxford*

The social and intellectual background of the 'déclassé' members of the Paris Commune of 1871. *E. Astington, M.A. 1939 Manchester*

Community
Classification of communities by means of occupations. *E. H. Selwood, Ph.D. 1932 London, Birkbeck College*

Community: a sociological study, being an attempt to set out the nature and fundamental laws of social life. *R. M. Maciver, D.Phil. 1915 Edinburgh*

The structure of community: a study in personal relationships. *G. H. Gibson, Ph.D. 1945 London, University College*

Commynes, Philippe de
The word order of subject, verb, régimes and attributes in Commines. *L. Priestley, M.A. 1948 Leeds*

Comnena, Anna
The intellectual and moral standards of Anna Comnena. *G. G. Buckler, D.Phil. 1927 Oxford*

Companies
See also Corporations.

The auditing of private limited company accounts in its relations to taxation. *E. C. Turner, M.Com. 1923 Birmingham*

A comparison between the English limited company and the French societé anonyme. *J. A. Streichenberger, B.Litt. 1932 Oxford*

Extra-territorial non-mining companies in Nigeria in peace and war. *H. Mars, B.Litt. 1945 Oxford*

The financial control of British joint stock companies. *H. M. Davies, M.Com. 1940 Birmingham*

An investigation into the preparation of consolidated statements for holding companies. *D. J. Bogie, Ph.D. 1948 Edinburgh*

Joint stock companies in Great Britain, 1890-1930. *A. Essex-Crosby, M.Com. 1937 London, School of Economics and Political Science*

Joint stock company failures, 1862-1914. *G. F. Todd, B.Litt. 1932 Oxford*

The reorganisation of company capital. *K. C. Chu, M.Com. 1939 Birmingham*

Companies, Public Utility
The load factor as a factor in fixing rates and charges for public utility undertakings. *M. F. Farrar, M.A. 1930 Leeds*

Local public utilities in relation to local government. *J. H. Warren, M.A. 1936 Liverpool*

Municipal enterprise in Germany : a study of German local utilities before and after the war. *B. M. Piplani, Ph.D. 1939 London, School of Economics and Political Science*

Personnel administration in public utility enterprises, with special reference to railways and to Chinese conditions. *C. H. Chi, M.Sc. 1938 London, School of Economics and Political Science*

Company Law
A comparative study of the rules of private international law relating to partnerships and to corporations, with special reference to the laws of France and of Egypt. *M. S. Guenena, LL.D. 1924 London*

An economic analysis of existing English legislation concerning the limited liability company. *M. E. Rix, M.Sc. 1936 London, External Degree*

Economic aspects of company law. *T. K. Liston, M.A. 1925 National University of Ireland*

History and development of company law in Great Britain and Ireland. *I. Boden, M.A. 1947 National University of Ireland*

History of the development of mercantile law in India, with special reference to the law of incorporated trading companies. *A. M. M. A. A. Siddinqi, LL.D. 1928 London*

The interpretation of company law in the light of equitable principles, with particular regard to the duties of directors and promoters. *B. A. Wortley, LL.M. 1934 Leeds*

Legal problems of limited companies in English and German law, with references to American law. *W. B. P. Horrwitz, D.Phil. 1946 Oxford*

Protection of minorities of shareholders by the law. *A. K. Chandra, LL.D. 1944 Dublin, Trinity College*

Public policy in company law. *P. J. Polyvios, B.Litt. 1944 Oxford*

Comparative Religion
See Religion.

Comte, Auguste
The influence of Auguste Comte and the rise of positivism in England up to the formation of the English Positivist Society in 1867. *W. L. Presswood, Ph.D. 1935 Sheffield*

The influence of Auguste Comte on the economics of John Stuart Mill. *A. Weinberg, Ph.D. 1949 London, External Degree*

Positivism with special reference to Auguste Comte and the Viennese circle of philosophy. *M. F. Browne, M.A. 1944 National University of Ireland*

Conall Gulban
Eachtra Chonaill Ghulban (*The adventures of Conall Gulban*). *R. A. O'Scannláin, M.A. 1941 National University of Ireland*

Conation
See Will.

Concepts
The ability to arrange concepts in order and the relation of this ability to reasoning. *J. H. Clapham, M.A. 1935 London, Institute of Education*

The concept. *J. Brough, M.A. 1911 Wales*

The development of concepts. *H. L. Fowler, Ph.D. 1928 London*

An experimental study of concepts in adolescence. *R. E. Presswood, M.Ed. 1934 Leeds*

The process of abstraction and concept formation. *E. F. O'Doherty, Ph.D. 1946 Cambridge*

Concert of Europe
See Europe: History.

Conditioning (Psychology)
The philosophy of the conditioned. *W. F. Baird-Smith, M.A. 1922 Liverpool*

Condorcet, Jean Antoine Nicolas Caritat de, Marquis
Condorcet as an educationalist. *C. E. Gittins, M.A. 1935 Wales*

The ideas of democracy in the eighteenth century as shown in the writings of Condorcet. *D. Williams, M.A. 1928 Wales*

Confidence (Psychology)
A study of confidence in a group of secondary school children. *J. A. M. Davis, M.A. 1944 London, Institute of Education*

Confirmation
See also Sacraments.

1. The grace of confirmation. 2. The Christian observance of the Lord's day. *E. J. Gough, B.D. & D.D. 1900 Oxford*

The laying on of hands in the New Testament and in Christian usage. *C. H. Scott, B.D. 1924 Oxford*

1. On the later medieval doctrine of the Eucharistic sacrifice. 2. On the relation of confirmation to baptism according to the New Testament. *B. J. Kidd, B.D. 1898 Oxford*

1. The place and work of the prophets in the Catholic Church. 2. The laying on of hands. *T. H. May, B.D. & D.D. 1924 Oxford*

1. The relation of confirmation to baptism. 2. The meaning and use of the Messianic titles: 'Christ', 'Son of David', 'Son of God', 'Son of Man'. *A. Chilton, B.D. & D.D. 1906 Oxford*

1. The theory of sacraments and the varying use of the term in theology. 2. Confirmation or laying on of hands as recorded and taught in the New Testament. *C. E. Farran, B.D. & D.D. 1910 Oxford*

1. The *Treatise on the Apostolic tradition* of St. Hippolytus. 2. The theology of confirmation in relation to baptism. 3. The shape of the liturgy. *G. E. A. Dix, B.D. & D.D. 1949 Oxford*

Conflict of Laws
See Law.

Confucianism
A comparison of Hebrew and Chinese wisdom, as exemplified in the Book of Proverbs and the Analects of Confucius. *E. G. K. Hewat, Ph.D. 1934 Edinburgh*

The social morality of Confucianism: a Christian appraisal. *A. N. MacLeod, Ph.D. 1938 Edinburgh*

A study of the *Analects* of Confucius. *W. J. Lindsay, M.A. 1925 Belfast*

Congo
British diplomacy and the Anglo-Congo Treaty of 1894. *Y. S. Wei, Ph.D. 1949 Cambridge*

Food and leisure among the African youth of Leopoldville (Belgian Congo): a study of the adaptation of African youth to urban life. *S. A. M. A. J. M. Comhaire-Sylvain, B.Litt. 1948 Oxford*

Congo contd.
The founding of the Congo Free State, with special reference to the work of Sir Henry Morton Stanley. *G. P. Jones, M.A. 1935 Wales*

Congregationalism
See also Nonconformity; and Browne, R.; Edwards, J.; Forsyth, P. T.

1603-1685: Presbyterians and Independents, their relations to the government and its effect on their relations with one anothe. *E. Ingham, M.A. 1935 Manchester*

Annibyniaeth yng Ngorllewin Morgannwg, 1646-1816 (Congregationalism in West Glamorgan, 1646-1816). *R. L. Hugh, M.A. 1945 Wales*

The dissenting Reformed Churches of England with respect to the doctrine of the Church from 1870 to 1940, with special reference to the Congregational Churches. *J. W. Grant, D.Phil. 1948 Oxford*

The Evangelical revival and Congregationalism. *F. C. Rogers, M.A. 1909 Liverpool*

The origin of the Independents in the reign of Elizabeth. *A. M. M. Wallbank, M.A. 1927 Birmingham*

The origins and early history of independency in Suffolk to 1688. *H. D. Greenwood, B.Litt. 1949 Oxford*

The origins of Congregationalism in Scotland. *G. L. S. Thompson, Ph.D. 1932 Edinburgh*

The origins of the English Independents. *D. H. Jones, M.A. 1929 Birmingham*

Ralph Wardlaw, 1779-1853, with particular reference to his theory of the atonement and the rise of Congregationalism in Scotland. *R. D. Hyslop, Ph.D. 1947 Edinburgh*

The rise and development of English separatist and separatistic congregations during the years 1553-1640. *C. Burrage, B.Litt. 1909 Oxford*

William Prynne's ideal State Church, and his views on the sectaries, Independents. *E. Stephenson, M.A. 1929 Manchester*

Congreve, William
A life of William Congreve. *D. C. Taylor, B.Litt. 1925 Oxford*

Connaught
Grace O'Malley: a 16th century heroine of the province of Connaught. *K. M. Ward, M.A. 1934 National University of Ireland*

Conrad, Joseph
Conrad the novelist. *D. J. Murphy, M.A. 1949 National University of Ireland*

The construction of Joseph Conrad's novels and stories. *G. P. Wakefield, M.A. 1950 Liverpool*

Craftsmanship in Conrad. *S. F. Moscrop, M.A. 1926 Liverpool*

Joseph Conrad. *M. J. Scott, M.A. 1926 Birmingham*

Joseph Conrad. *F. M. S. Jack, M.A. 1941 Birmingham*

Joseph Conrad: a study of his style. *T. Throssell, M.A. 1947 Liverpool*

The philosophy of Joseph Conrad. *D. K. Ellis, M.A. 1949 Wales*

Conscience
1. Conscience and moral law. 2. Cases of conscience. *K. E. Kirk, B.D. 1922 Oxford*

The doctrine of conscience in British philosophy. *E. W. Hirst, M.A. 1908 London*

The doctrine of conscience in British philosophy. *E. W. Hirst, B.Sc. 1908 Oxford*

Expositions of: St. John xx.22-23: the power of absolution given to the Church; I John iii.19, 20: the Christian doctrine of conscience; Galatians ii.19-20: individual religion and the Church. *T. B. Strong, D.D. 1902 Oxford*

1. The limits of conscience. 2. The doctrine of eternal rewards and punishments. *F. W. Quilter, B.D. 1872 Oxford*

A psychological analysis of Kant's doctrine of conscience. *A. Oates, M.A. 1931 Liverpool*

The psychology of conscience, with special reference to its relation to the Christian doctrine of man. *R. H. Beaven, M.Litt. 1939 Cambridge*

A study of the conception of conscience in the philosophy of Martin Heidegger and Karl Jaspers. *A. B. Downing, M.A. 1947 Manchester*

A study of the idea of conscience, with particular reference to the thought of Jeremy Taylor. *M. W. Eckel, B.Litt. 1950 Oxford*

Conscience contd.
The theory of conscience or moral sense, as found in some eighteenth century writers. *J. R. Beresford, M.A. 1914 Liverpool*

Consciousness
The feeling aspect of the religious consciousness. *A. Nicolson, Ph.D. 1929 Edinburgh*

The implications of immortality in the moral consciousness. *M. M. Morris, M.A. 1925 Wales*

Life and consciousness. *E. Daly, M.A. 1944 National University of Ireland*

The nature and extent of conative control of some contents of consciousness. *W. J. Messer, M.Sc. 1927 London*

The nature of consciousness in Hindu philosophy. *S. K. Saksena, Ph.D. 1939 London, School of Oriental and African Studies*

Conservatism
See also Liverpool, R. B. J., Earl of.

The attitude of the Tory Party to labour questions, 1832-46. *R. L. Hill, B.Litt. 1928 Oxford*

The evolution of the Tory party, 1783-1815. *M. M. Ashworth, M.A. 1925 Manchester*

George Canning and the Tory schism, 1809-1822. *J. Veitch, Ph.D. 1932 Liverpool*

The romantic element in English conservatism, 1789-1850. *H. W. Arndt, B.Litt. 1940 Oxford*

The Tory Party in the reign of George I. *L. W. Hanson, B.Litt. 1930 Oxford*

Toryism from 1745 to 1761. *T. E. Howard, M.A. 1939 Liverpool*

Considérant, Victor
Political and social ideas of Victor Considérant. *S. K. Shastri, M.Sc. 1936 London, School of Economics and Political Science*

Consideration (Law)
The doctrine of consideration treated historically and comparatively. *P. N. Daruvala, LL.D. 1913 London*

Conspiracy
Conspiracy as a tort and as a crime in English law, treated historically. *D. Harrison, LL.D. 1923 London*

The law relating to combinations. *A. L. Haslam, D.Phil. 1929 Oxford*

Constant de Rebecque, Henri Benjamin
Benjamin Constant as a political writer (1814-20). *F. E. Newman, B.Litt. 1931 Oxford*

Constantinople, Council of
See Church History: Early Church.

Constitutional Law
Constitutional law. *L. MacDermott, M.A. 1934 National University of Ireland*

Constitutional principles re-examined in the light of modern administrative law. *M. R. R. Davies, Ph.D. 1948 Cambridge*

Consumption (Economics)
Family budget data and price elasticities of demand. *C. E. V. Leser, M.Sc. 1941 London, School of Economics and Political Science*

Some aspects of the economics of consumption. *J. R. E. Phillips, M.A. 1938 Wales*

Theories of consumption, with reference to demand for and supply of foodstuffs in Great Britain. *E. M. Jones, M.A. 1939 Wales*

Conti, Antonio
Antonio Conti e il suo posto nella letteratura del settecento. *M. C. Cave, M.A. 1922 London*

Contingency (Philosophy)
See Chance.

Contraband
See Smuggling.

Contract (Law)
Assignment of contracts and choses in action. *J. S. Khergamvala, LL.D. 1915 London*

A comparative study of the problem of consent in the formation of contract in French and English law. *G. L. Chrétien, D.Phil. 1949 Oxford*

Critical studies upon the texts and the theory of the *beneficium cedendarum actionum* and *venditio nominis*. *K. Lipstein, Ph.D. 1937 Cambridge*

The development of the conception of the proper law of a contract in English private international law. *N. C. H. Dunbar, Ll.M. 1940 Sheffield*

The economics of loyalty contracts. *W. A. Lewis, Ph.D. 1940 London, School of Economics and Political Science*

Contract (Law) contd.
The effects of notice on contracts for the sale of land with particular reference to the registration of land charges. *R. G. Rowley, LL.D. 1948 Leeds*

The history of contract in early English equity. *W. T. Barbour, B.Litt. 1912 Oxford*

Impossiblity of performance of contract. *R. G. McElroy, Ph.D. 1934 Cambridge*

The influence of equitable ideas concerning property in the development of the law of contract as illustrated by (1) the passing of property under invalid contracts, and (2) contracts for the benefit of third persons. *A. M. Finlay, Ph.D. 1938 London, School of Economics and Political Science*

The influence of Roman law on the development of the consensual contracts in the law of Scotland. *F. S. Batchelor, Ph.D. 1938 Glasgow*

Interference with contract and unfair competition. *F. R. Batt, M.A. 1933 Wales*

The law of mistake in contract. *G. I. Joseph, B.Litt. 1936 Oxford*

The local law applicable to contracts with a foreign element. *M. Friedman, LL.M. 1940 Leeds*

The measure of damages in actions for breach of mercantile contract. *G. T. Washington, B.Litt. 1930 Oxford*

Mistake in contract. *A. B. Levy, LL.M. 1942 Bristol*

Mistake in the English law of contract. *R. J. A. David, Ph.D. 1935 Cambridge*

Mistake in the formation of contracts. *J. G. Williamson, B.Litt. 1938 Oxford*

Mistake in the law of contract. *J. T. Molony, LL.M. 1933 Cambridge*

Obligation contract in French and English law. *F. d'E. de Charmoy, LL.M. 1936 Cambridge*

Private international law of contracts on a comparative basis. *J. J. Van Schaik, D.Phil. 1949 Oxford*

Quasi-contract. *R. H. Kersley, LL.M. 1932 Cambridge*

The rights and duties of third parties. *E. B. Heap, LL.M. 1938 Leeds*

The rules of private international law determining capacity to contract. *F. T. Cheng, LL.D. 1916 London*

Some aspects of the discharge of contracts in English and Continental law. *C. Szladits, LL.M. 1949 London, School of Economics and Political Science*

Convents
See Monasticism.

Conversion
See Religious Conversion.

Conveyancing
The history and development of the conveyance on sale of land. *S. Johnson, LL.D. 1916 London*

Cooke, Henry
The influence of the Rev. Henry Cooke on the political life of Ulster. *J. Jamieson, M.A. 1950 Belfast*

Cooley, Cattle-Raid of
See Romances.

Cooper, Anthony Ashley, 1st Earl of Shaftesbury
Anthony Earl of Shaftesbury (1671-1713) and the German classical writers of the eighteenth century. *M. A. Morland, Ph.D. 1946 London, External Degree*

The ministerial career of the first Earl of Shaftesbury, 1660-73. *K. H. D. Haley, B.Litt. 1949 Oxford*

Cooper, Anthony Ashley, 3rd Earl of Shaftesbury
Shaftesbury (the author of *The Characteristics*) as a literary critic. *R. L. Brett, B.Litt. 1940 Oxford*

The third Earl of Shaftesbury and the background of English romanticism. *J. R. Brewer, M.A. 1947 London, University College*

Cooper, Anthony Ashley, 7th Earl of Shaftesbury
The 7th Earl of Shaftesbury as a social reformer. *E. M. Wightman, M.A. 1923 Birmingham*

The influence of Christianity on social progress as illustrated by the career of Lord Shaftesbury. *J. W. Bready, Ph.D. 1927 London*

Co-operation
Control and management in co-operative retail societies. *W. G. Symons, M.Com. 1936 Birmingham*

Co-operation at home and abroad: a description and analysis. *C. R. Fay, D.Sc. 1909 London*

Co-operative credit in the Punjab. *T. Singh, Ph.D. 1927 London*

Co-operation contd.
The co-operative movement in Japan. *K. Ogata, Ph.D. 1923 London*

The Co-operative Movement in Italy, with special reference to agriculture, labour and production. *E. A. Lloyd, M.A. 1925 Wales*

The cooperative organization in British India. *S. P. Sanyal, M.A. 1940 Leeds*

Economics of the Consumers' Co-Operative Movement. *J. W. Ruddock, M.Sc. 1939 London, School of Economics and Political Science*

Efficiency of capital raising, investment and financial administration in consumers' co-operative production. *H. Mars, M.Com. 1937 Birmingham*

Industrial relations in the distributive trades, with special reference to the Co-operative Movement. *J. Huddleston, M.A. 1938 Leeds*

Industrial relations in the British Co-operative Movement. *J. Tizard, B.Litt. 1949 Oxford*

Production in the consumers' co-operative movement. *G. B. Jenkin, M.Com. 1934 Birmingham*

Recent aspects of the co-operative movement in Ireland. *M. Raghaillaigh, M.A. 1929 National University of Ireland*

Copernicus
The astronomical system of Copernicus. *A. Armitage, M.Sc. 1929 London*

Copleston, Edward, Bishop
Edward Copleston, bishop of Llandaff. *W. J. Cratchley, B.Litt. 1938 Oxford*

Coppard, Alfred Edgar
A critical appreciation of the modern short story, with particular reference to Mr. A. E. Coppard. *W. John, M.A. 1936 Wales*

Coppée, François
François Coppée: a critical study of his works. *R. Allen, M.A. 1923 Wales*

Copper Industry
See Brass and Copper Industry.

Copyright
See Book Publishers and Publishing.

Corbet, John
John Corbet, 1619-1680. *A. Grime, Ph.D. 1932 Edinburgh*

Corbière, Edouard Joachim
The influence of Baudelaire, Laforgue and Corbière on the poetry of T. S. Eliot. *C. M. Shanahan, M.A. 1949 Manchester*

Corcyra
See Corfu.

Corfu
Phases of Corcyraean history. *C. C. Cremin, M.A. 1931 National University of Ireland*

Corinth
A history of Corinth from the earliest times to the death of Alexander. *J. O'Neill, M.A. 1919 National University of Ireland*

History of independent Corinth. *W. Fitzpatrick, M.A. 1915 National University of Ireland*

Cork, City
An economic history of Cork City to 1800. *W. O'Sullivan, M.A. 1936 National University of Ireland*

An economic history of the Port of Cork from 1813 to 1900. *P. J. McCarthy, M.Econ.Sc. 1949 National University of Ireland*

Monumenta vetera corcagiensia, being a survey of all antiquarian remains within and around the city of Cork. *M. A. O'Leary, M.A. 1931 National University of Ireland*

Cork, County
A regional survey of Cork County geology and geography. *C. S. O'Connell, M.A. 1942 National University of Ireland*

Rude stone monuments of the northern portion of Co. Cork. *J. P. Conlon, M.A. 1913 National University of Ireland*

Cork, Diocese
The ruined parish churches of the diocese of Cork. *M. H. J. Brunicardi, M.A. 1913 National University of Ireland*

Corneille, Pierre
Christophorus Kormart's adaptations of Pierre Corneille's *Polyeucte* and *Héraclius* and their relation to the contemporary German drama of the seventeenth century. *P. H. Powell, M.A. 1936 Wales*

Elizabethan tragedy contrasted with the classical drama of Corneille and Racine. *F. E. Jope, M.A. 1910 Birmingham*

Corneille, Pierre contd.
La jeunesse de Corneille et la formation de son génie. *G. M. N. Robinson, M.A. 1948 Birmingham*

Cornwall
An analysis of the geographic factors affecting agriculture and industry in the southwest Peninsula, west of the Tamar. *S. Muckle, M.A. 1933 London, Bedford College*

The geographical development of West Cornwall. *C. F. W. R. Gullick, B.Litt. 1934 Oxford*

The geography of Cornwall and its control over human activity. *G. H. Skinner, M.A. 1934 Bristol*

The historical geography of Cornwall. *N. J. G. Pounds, Ph.D. 1945 London, External Degree*

On the causes and course of the rebellion of 1549 in Devon and Cornwall. *W. J. Blake, M.A. 1909 London*

Population changes in Cornwall in relation to economic resources. *T. W. McGuinness, Ph.D. 1944 London, King's College*

The West Penwith Peninsula of Cornwall, considered from the point of view of archaeological evidences concerning development of settlements. *D. H. Watkins, M.A. 1930 Wales*

Cornwall, Edmund, Earl of
Edmund, Earl of Cornwall, and his place in history. *L. M. Midgley, M.A. 1930 Manchester*

Cornwall, Richard, Earl of
The early years of Richard, Earl of Cornwall. *L. W. Kelley, M.A. 1912 Liverpool*

Richard, Earl of Cornwall, King of the Romans (1257-1272). *F. R. Lewis, M.A. 1934 Wales*

Cornwallis, Charles, 1st Marquis
The administrative and judicial reforms of Lord Cornwallis in Bengal, 1786-1793, excluding the permanent settlement. *A. Aspinall, M.A. 1922 Manchester*

The history of the occupation and rural administration of Bengal by the English Company from the time of Clive to the permanent settlement under Cornwallis. *W. K. Firminger, B.Litt. 1913 Oxford*

Coroners
The antiquity and development of the office of coroner: a study in English legal history. *H. F. Galpin, D.C.L. 1896 Oxford*

Corporations
See also Companies.

The public corporation in Great Britain. *A. L. Gordon, D.Phil. 1936 Oxford*

The residence and domicil of corporations. *A. Farnsworth, Ph.D. 1938 London, External Degree*

Theory and practice of corporative economics. *K. White, B.Litt. 1937 Oxford*

Corsica
See Paoli, P. di.

Cosmology
Buddhist cosmology. *W. M. McGovern, D.Phil. 1922 Oxford*

The cosmology of Plato and the background of early Greek philosophy. *J. L. Bowers, B.Litt. 1950 Dublin, Trinity College*

Early history of astronomy and cosmology in India. *C. P. S. Menon, M.Sc. 1930 London*

La creación del mundo: a narrative poem on the cosmogony, by Alonso de Acevedo. *F. W. Pierce, M.A. 1939 Belfast*

Moral evil in relation to modern cosmological theory. *W. R. Matthews, M.A. 1912 London*

Studies in the establishment ot the heliocentric theory. *A. Armitage, Ph.D. 1947 London, University College*

Cost of Living
See Prices; Standard of Living.

Costs
Cost analysis in the gas industry. *T. Brown, M.Com. 1946 Birmingham*

Costing and prices in British industry. *C. C. Saxton, D.Phil. 1941 Oxford*

Influence of the cost of inland transport on the development of production, trade and traffic, with special reference to India. *F. P. Antia, Ph.D. 1930 London, School of Economics and Political Science*

New developments in costing techniques as an aid to managerial control. *A. E. M. Hegazy, Ph.D. 1950 Birmingham*

Retailing costs and technical progress. *H. Smith, B.Litt. 1934 Oxford*

Costume
The development of armour and costume from the fourteenth century to the seventeenth century as illustrated in the memorial brasses of Essex. *A. C. Edwards, M.A. 1937 Bristol*

Greek dress. *E. B. Abrahams, M.A. 1907 London*

Cotswolds, The
Cirencester and its region: a study in Cotteswold geography. *R. W. Brooker, M.A. 1937 Reading*

The regional geography of the Cotteswolds. *C. A. Simpson, B.Sc. 1923 Oxford*

The South Cotswolds. *F. G. Morris, M.A. 1933 Bristol*

Cottin, Sophie
Madame Cottin et le roman sentimental. *L. C. Sykes, D.Phil. 1940 Oxford*

Cotton, Charles
The life and work of Charles Cotton. *E. M. Turner, B.Litt. 1935 Oxford*

The poetry of Charles Cotton. *E. Taylor, M.A. 1937 Liverpool*

Cotton Industry
The Alexandria cotton market. *M. A. R. Hafez, M.A. 1938 Manchester*

The British cotton industry in depression. *Y. N. Hsu, Ph.D. 1941 Cambridge*

The British cotton trade with China. *C. S. Woo, M.Com. 1913 Birmingham*

Concentration and localization of the British cotton industry, 1825-1850. *A. J. Taylor, M.A. 1947 Manchester*

The contribution of water power development to the progress of the cotton-spinning industry, with particular reference to the Bolton district (period 1770-1845). *E. J. Foulkes, M.A. 1943 Wales*

Cotton finance and its relation to the currency and credit system of Egypt. *E. Hallett, Ph.D. 1946 London, External Degree*

The cotton industry in the Madras Presidency, with special reference to the domestic and factory systems. *G. Ranganayakula, B.Litt. 1926 Oxford*

Cotton production in the Nile basin outside Egypt. *M. E. A. A. Hindia, M.A. 1943 London, School of Economics and Political Science*

Cotton production, with special reference to Egypt. *A. M. Ahmed, M.Sc. 1946 London, External Degree*

The development of the cotton industry in India from the early nineteenth century. *S. Deshpande, B.Litt. 1924 Oxford*

The family economy of the workers in the cotton industry during the period of the Industrial Revolution, 1784-1833. *F. Collier, M.A. 1921 Manchester*

Geographical factors affecting the cotton industry in Lancashire as compared with India. *M. C. Saxton, M.A. 1921 Liverpool*

History of the cotton industry of India. *J. N. Varma, M.Sc. 1922 London*

The history of the cotton-mill industry in western India. *K. B. Bharucha, Ph.D. 1927 London*

Lancashire cotton famine. *W. O. Henderson, Ph.D. 1932 London, School of Economics and Political Science*

The Luddite disturbances throughout the cotton manufacturing area in 1812. *D. Halstead, M.A. 1917 Liverpool*

Manufactured Indian cotton goods in England and their influence on English economic history about 1680-1720. *P. J. Thomas, B.Litt. 1922 Oxford*

The provision for the welfare of women and young workers in the cotton industry. *R. K. K. Lee, M.A. 1949 Liverpool*

The recent extension of cotton growing. *T. D. Woo, M.Com. 1912 Birmingham*

A survey of the problems of reorganization of the cotton industry of Great Britain. *M. Grossu, Ph.D. 1941 Manchester*

Coulomb, Charles Augustin de
The physical work of C. A. de Coulomb. *G. R. Sharp, M.Sc. 1936 London, University College*

Council of Florence
See Roman Catholic Church.

Counter-Reformation
See Church History: Reformation and Counter-Reformation.

Coupar Angus Abbey
The economic administration of Coupar Angus Abbey, 1440-1560. *J. L. Morgan, Ph.D. 1929 Glasgow*

Courcy, Jean de
A contribution to the study of *Le chemin de vaillance*, a fifteenth-century allegorical poem by Jean de Courcy. *A. J. McCrae, Ph.D. 1934 London, University College*

Courier, Paul Louis
L'archaisme et les procédés littéraires chez P. L. Courier. *E. F. Cash, M.A. 1914 Birmingham*

Court of Sapience
The sources of the *Court of Sapience*; a Middle English religious and didactic poem. *C. F. Bühler, Ph.D. 1930 Dublin, Trinity College*

Courtoisie
See also Chivalry.

Anglo-Norman books of courtesy and nurture. *H. R. Parsons, B.Litt. 1927 Oxford*

Courtoisie in Anglo-Norman literature. *C. B. West, Ph.D. 1936 London, Birkbeck College*

Courtoisie in the *roman d'aventures* of the thirteenth century. *A. D. Crow, B.Litt. 1933 Oxford*

L'amitié masculine dans les romans courtois. *O. L. M. Hellman, M.A. 1945 London, Birkbeck College*

Les idées courtoises dans l'*Ipomeden* de Hue de Roteland. *K. G. Traneker, M.A. 1927 Birmingham*

Studies in the language of manners in England from the eleventh to the eighteenth centuries. *J. E. Colledge, M.A. 1935 Liverpool*

Courts of Law
See also Law; Assize Courts; Probation.

The contribution of the English courts to the development of international law. *T. Finkelstein, B.Litt. 1939 Oxford*

The court leet of Southampton and leet jurisdiction in general. *F. J. C. Hearnshaw, M.A. 1908 London*

The Court of Requests in the reign of Elizabeth. *W. B. J. Allsebrook, M.A. 1936 London, University College*

The Court of Star Chamber, 1603-41, with special reference to the period 1625-41. *H. E. I. Phillips, M.A. 1939 London, University College*

The Court of Star Chamber in the reign of Queen Elizabeth. *E. Skelton, M.A. 1931 London, University College*

The Court of Taunton in the sixteenth and seventeenth centuries. *R. G. H. Whitty, M.A. 1932 London, External Degree*

Critical edition of the Norwich Mayor's Court minute books (1630-3), with introduction describing functions of the court at that time. *W. L. Sachse, B.Litt. 1937 Oxford*

The Exchequer Chamber, being the assembly of all the judges of England for matters of law. *M. Hemmant, Ph.D. 1929 London*

An inquiry into the procedure of the Supreme Court of New South Wales. *J. A. Harney, B.Litt. 1939 Oxford*

The judiciary in relation to legislation and constitutional development during the reigns of Henry VII and Henry VIII. *J. J. MacGinley, M.A. 1915 London*

Local government in Wales, sixteenth to eighteenth centuries, as exemplified by the work of the Quarter Sessions in the County. *T. H. Lewis, Ph.D. 1941 London, External Degree*

The Middlesex magistrate, 1760 to 1820: social and economic aspects of the work of J.P.'s. *I. E. V. Forrester, M.A. 1934 London, School of Economics and Political Science*

The place of judiciary in the modern state with special reference to the English judiciary. *C. L. Chien, Ph.D. 1936 London*

Principles of justice observed by courts of justice in England. *F. E. B. Ferns, LL.M. 1956 Manchester*

Sheriffs and sheriff courts in Scotland prior to the union of the Crowns in 1603, with special reference to the Fife records at the sixteenth century. *W. C. Dickinson, Ph.D. 1924 Saint Andrew's*

The working of the Court of King's Bench in the fifteenth century. *M. Blatcher, Ph.D. 1936 London, University College*

Cousin, Victor
Victor Cousin and the Romantic Movement. *P. R. Hardy, M.A. 1932 London, King's College*

Covenanters
See Church History: Scotland.

Covenants (Law)
Recent developments in the law of restrictive covenants affecting land. *R. G. Rowley, LL.M. 1942 Leeds*

Covent Garden, The Adventures of
The reaction against the prose romance of the seventeenth century, with special reference to *The adventures of Covent Garden. A. C. Coolidge, B.Litt. 1929 Oxford*

Coventry
The City of Coventry in the Restoration period, 1660-1688. *N. Upright, M.A. 1944 Manchester*

Coventry: a study in urban geography. *G. L. Marson, M.A. 1949 Liverpool*

Coventry and the Municipal Corporations Act, 1835: an investigation of the workings of Coventry Corporation mainly between 1750 and 1835, and a critical examination of the Commissioners' Report of 1833. *S. E. Kerrison, M.A. 1939 Birmingham*

Coventry and Lichfield, Diocese of
The diocese of Coventry and Lichfield during the Reformation, with special reference to parochial life. *D. E. Lindop, B.Litt. 1937 Oxford*

Cowley, Abraham
The English writings of Abraham Cowley. *G. Walton, M.Litt. 1939 Cambridge*

Some aspects of seventeenth century learning as exhibited in the *Davideis* of Abraham Cowley. *J. F. Kermode, M.A. 1947 Liverpool*

Cowper, William
Cowper, as revealed in his letters and poems. *E. Yates, M.A. 1917 Birmingham*

The place of Cowper in eighteenth century literature. *G. W. Hastings, M.A. 1908 Wales*

William Cowper: his attitude to nature and religion. *G. A. E. Cornforth, M.A. 1929 Birmingham*

William Cowper and the eighteenth century. *C. Houlihan, M.A. 1949 National University of Ireland*

Cranborne, Dorset, Manor of
Economic changes in the manor of Cranborne (Dorset) in the sixteenth and seventeenth centuries. *E. B. Clarke, B.Litt. 1939 Oxford*

Crashaw, Richard
Francis Thompson: a study of his relation to George Herbert, Henry Vaughan and Richard Crashaw. *C. Bergin, M.A. 1948 National University of Ireland*

The religious use of symbol in Crashaw and his predecessors. *T. O. Haworth, M.A. 1950 Manchester*

Richard Crashaw. *D. Lamont, M.A. 1941 National University of Ireland*

Richard Crashaw, poet and mystic: a critical biography. *F. E. Barker, M.A. 1922 London*

A short study of Richard Crashaw: his time and his work. *C. J. Curtin, M.A. 1946 National University of Ireland*

Crassus, Marcus Licinius, Triumvir
The life and times of Marcus Licinius Crassus, Triumvir. *J. Thompson, Ph.D. 1941 Edinburgh*

Plutarch's *Life of Crassus*: with historical commentary. *A. S. Osley, Ph.D. 1942 London, External Degree*

Creation and the Fall
1. The Christian idea of sin and original sin. 2. The doctrine of the Trinity in the early Fathers. *E. J. Bicknell, B.D. & D.D. 1923 Oxford*

1. The Christian view of the natural world. 2. The unjust steward. *H. Costley-White, B.D. & D.D. 1924 Oxford*

The concept of creation in the metaphysics of St. Thomas. *J. F. Cummins, M.A. 1943 National University of Ireland*

The conception of creation considered in its bearing upon the relation of the finite individual to God. *M. E. Clarke, M.A. 1920 London*

1. Doctrinal effect of the Vulgate text. 2. Original righteousness, as conceived by the Fathers, Schoolmen, and Reformers. *H. J. White, B.D. & D.D. 1918 Oxford*

The doctrine of original sin in the light of some recent psychological and anthropological theories. *K. C. Dykes, M.A. 1943 Manchester*

The doctrine of the fall: a question of validity. *H. T. Powell, D.D. 1929 Durham*

1. The doctrine of the fall in relation to evolution. 2. The fall and the Incarnation. *G. C. Joyce, B.D. 1904 Oxford*

Exegeses of the fall: Genesis iii.1-6; the atonement: Hebrews ix.11-14; the inspiration of Holy Scripture: II Timothy iii. 15-17. *F. W. Quilter, D.D. 1872 Oxford*

Creation and the Fall contd.
Expositions of: Genesis iii: the doctrine of the Fall; Ephesians iv.1-16: the unity of the Church and the functions of its ministers; I Corinthians xi.18-34. *T. H. D. Long, D.D. 1909 Oxford*

Expositions of: St. Matthew xii.31,32: the blasphemy against the Holy Ghost; Romans viii.19-23: the groaning creation; Galatians iii.20. *H. G. Corner, D.D. 1905 Oxford*

Expositions of I Corinthians xv.20-58: the Resurrection; St. John iii.3-5; Genesis i: the Creation. *E. P. Lewis, D.D. 1904 Oxford*

1. The historical and religious value of Genesis and its claim to be regarded as an inspired book. 2. Recent theories concerning the origin of life, and their probable effect upon religious thought and belief. *J. H. S. Bailey, B.D. 1913 Oxford*

The idea of creation in Christian thought. *J. H. Templeton, B.Litt. 1943 Dublin, Trinity College*

The mind of God in creation: or a philosophic enquiry into the nature of creation. *R. L. Matchette, M.A. 1920 Belfast*

Modern theories of the fall of man and original sin. *L. Watson, M.Litt. 1949 Durham*

A new edition of the Old English translation of the *Hexameron* of Basil (usually ascribed to Aelfric), with a collation of all the existing mss., and an introduction on the sources, authorship, and language of the translation. *S. J. Crawford, B.Litt. 1912 Oxford*

1. On creation. 2. On the person of Christ. *W. Hooper, B.D. & D.D. 1887 Oxford*

1. On original sin. 2. On justification. *W. Bree, B.D. & D.D. 1893 Oxford*

1. On the anticipative or prophetic character of the several stages of the Creation. 2. The order of the hours of the day in the Gospel according to St. John is the same as that in the other Gospels. *C. Pritchard, B.D. & D.D. 1880 Oxford*

1. The tree of the knowledge of good and evil. 2. Aἰώνιος: its meaning and use in the New Testament. *H. D. A. Major, B.D. 1916 Oxford*

1. The unveiling of the Fall. 2. Re-creation: a new aspect of evolution. *C. W. Formby, B.D. & D.D. 1924 Oxford*

1. Utrum Christus venisset si Adam non peccasset. 2. The New Testament doctrine of the Christian character and its development. *L. Hands, B.D. 1907 Oxford*

Creativity
A study of the psychology of the creative processes, with particular reference to literary production. *R. Thomas, D.Sc. 1932 Wales*

Credit
The Australian banking and credit system. *A. L. G. Mackay, M.Litt. 1931 Cambridge*

Co-operative credit in the Punjab. *T. Singh, Ph.D. 1927 London*

The law relating to commercial letters of credit. The relationship between banker and seller under a confirmed credit promised to perform an existing duty. *A. G. Davis, Ph.D. 1939 London, School of Economics and Political Science*

The relative influence of money and credit on general prices. *J. Rejan, Ph.D. 1922 Edinburgh*

Creeds
See also Arianism; Trinity, The.

1. Apostolic teaching and the teaching of the creeds in relation to that of our Lord. 2. The doctrine of immortality, Jewish and Christian. *W. C. Tuting, B.D. & D.D. 1911 Oxford*

1. The Athanasian Creed consonant with the word of God. 2. The true doctrine of election involves no injustice. *F. N. Oxenham, B.D. & D.D. 1896 Oxford*

1. The Chalcedonian definition of the faith, and the inter-relation of the four great heresies on the Incarnation. 2. The historic value of the episcopate in the early Church as a witness and a guarantee. *T. H. Bindley, B.D. 1893 Oxford*

1. The communion of saints. 2. The Athanasian Creed. *A. G. Pentreath, B.D. 1897 Oxford*

1. The Council of Constantinople and the Nicene Creed. 2. The early Roman baptismal creed. *F. J. Badcock, B.D. & D.D. 1922 Oxford*

1. The creed of the Christian Church. 2. St. Paul's Epistles considered as a whole, with special reference to his teaching on justification. *A. Brook, B.D. 1893 Oxford*

1. The creeds: their origin and value. 2. The communion of saints. *H. G. Cundy, B.D. 1876 Oxford*

Creeds contd.

1. The creeds: their origin and value. 2. The intermediate state. *F. R. Pentreath, B.D. 1874 Oxford*

1. The divine fatherhood. 2. The Apostles' Creed. *K. D. Knowles, B.D. & D.D. 1924 Oxford*

1. Holy Scripture: the rule of faith. 2. 'I believe in one God'. *D. M. Owen, B.D. 1877 Oxford*

1. 'I believe in one God'. 2. 'I look for the resurrection of the dead'. *T. H. Stokoe, B.D. 1871 Oxford*

1. The Incarnation of our Lord. 2. The three creeds. *W. S. Tupholme, B.D. 1903 Oxford*

The oecumenical creeds of the ancient church: problems of their origin and development. *W. T. Williams, M.A. 1943 Wales*

1. On the creed in the Acts. 2. On the appointment of rites and ceremonies in the Church. *A. L. Oldham, B.D. & D.D. 1905 Oxford*

1. 'One baptism for the remission of sins'. 2. 'The communion of saints'. *C. E. Jelf, B.D. & D.D. 1907 Oxford*

1. The origin and development of the Apostles' Creed. 2. The real meaning of the Arian controversy. *J. M. Walker, B.D. & D.D. 1914 Oxford*

1. The Pauline authorship of the Epistle to the Ephesians. 2. The date and authorship of the Athanasian Creed. *T. A. Branthwaite, B.D. 1903 Oxford*

1. Presence of a creed in the New Testament. 2. The Resurrection, or the cardinal features of Apostolic teaching. *B. Whitefoord, B.D. 1895 Oxford*

The principle of nonsubscription to creeds and confessions of faith as exemplified in Irish Presbyterian history. *R. Allen, Ph.D. 1944 Belfast*

1. The *Quicumque Vult*. 2. The discipline of the early Church. *R. S. P. Chesshire, B.D. & D.D. 1910 Oxford*

The relation of Karl Barth to the historic creeds and standards of the Church. *A. C. Cochrane, Ph.D. 1937 Edinburgh*

1. That a brief summary of credenda was drawn up at a very early date in Apostolic times and probably by the Apostolic College, the reception of which was a condition of baptism; and that this preliminary summary was subsequently amplified and expanded by a more full statement with which the baptized were furnished for their edification and advancement in Christian knowledge. 2. A consideration of such passages in the Apostolic writings as apparently contain quotations from this primitive creed. *A. Jessopp, B.D. & D.D. 1870 Oxford*

Crewe

The social and economic development of Crewe, 1830-1880. *W. H. Chaloner, M.A. 1937 Manchester*

The social and economic development of Crewe, 1800-1923. *W. H. Chaloner, Ph.D. 1939 Manchester*

Crime and Criminals
See also Criminal Law; Juvenile Delinquency; Transportation.

Cambridgeshire and its lunatic paupers and criminals. *E. M. Hampson, M.A. 1926 Liverpool*

Certain mental disorders in relation to gross antisocial conduct. *T. Christie, M.D. 1936 Saint Andrew's*

Criminal transportation, its theory and practice, with special reference to Australia. *G. H. Fairs, M.A. 1932 Bristol*

Criminality in youth: a medico-legal study. *J. Baker, M.D. 1901 Aberdeen*

The press and crime. *R. Sinha, M.Sc. 1949 London, School of Economics and Political Science*

Crimean War, 1854-1856
The Black Sea question during the Crimean War. *I. F. D. Morrow, Ph.D. 1927 Cambridge*

The genesis of the Crimean War. *H. E. Howard, M.A. 1932 London, King's College*

Criminal Law
See also Extradition.

The abnormal subject and responsibility for crime. *M. S. S. Jones, M.D. 1926 Liverpool*

An account of the progress of penal reform in England from 1810-1930, together with some conclusions. *H. H. Ayscough, Ph.D. 1933 London, School of Economics and Political Science*

The Christian principle of redemption in its application to penal reform. *M. S. Bradley, B.Litt. 1929 Oxford*

Criminal law as applied to bankruptcy. *H. G. Meek, LL.M. 1929 Cambridge*

Criminal Law contd.
Criminal law reform during Peel's tenure of office as Home Secretary, 1822-27. *J. A. Gulland, M.A. 1930 London, University College*

Criminal responsibilities in India. *V. V. Chowdary, LL.D. 1928 London*

The criminal responsibility of lunatics: a study in comparative law. *H. Oppenheimer, LL.D. 1908 London*

Criminal responsibility in English law. *W. L. Rao, Ph.D. 1931 Sheffield*

The doctrine of culpa. *J. S. Sandars, D.C.L. 1885 Oxford*

England and the criminal legislation of Egypt, from 1882. *E. Sarofim, D.Phil. 1949 Oxford*

The English criminal and criminal ecclesiastical law of sex morality and its effect upon the organization of the family. *G. May, LL.D. 1933 London, School of Economics and Political Science*

Evidence of a prisoner's character. *A. J. Ellison, LL.M. 1928 Cambridge*

Evolutionary aspects and critical analysis of the English criminal law in its relation to mental disorder, with particular reference to crimes against the person. *K. S. Sharples, LL.M. 1950 Manchester*

The history of *mens rea* in the law of homicide. *A. W. G. Kean, M.Litt. 1939 Cambridge*

The law and practice relating to habitual criminals. *N. R. Morris, Ph.D. 1949 London, School of Economics and Political Science*

The legal attitude toward mental abnormality: a comparative analysis of the historical and modern criminal law tests of responsibility, with respect to insanity, in England, Scotland and the United States of America. *S. Polsky, Ph.D. 1950 Edinburgh*

The legal conception of criminal responsibility in view of modern theories of criminology. *C. B. Porter, Ph.D. 1924 Edinburgh*

Mens rea or imputability under the law of England. *D. A. Stroud, LL.D. 1913 London*

Monograph on the modern law relating to criminal appeals to the King in Council. *S. K. Datta Guptar, LL.M. 1931 Cambridge*

A study of the change in meaning of French criminal law terms, with special reference to colloquial and literary usage. *D. R. T. Goodwin, M.A. 1936 Manchester*

A study of the criminal law and its administration in South Africa, Southern Rhodesia and Kenya. *H. J. Simons, Ph.D. 1936 London, School of Economics and Political Science*

The writ of habeas corpus. *H. P. Letcher, LL.D. 1934 London, External Degree*

Criticism
See also Aesthetics; Art: Criticism; Literature: Criticism; Music: Criticism; Poetry: Criticism.

The authentic philosophy of W. Pater. *D. M. Hateley, M.A. 1921 Birmingham*

The criticisms of Walter Pater. *D. L. Chadwick, M.A. 1928 Birmingham*

Germany's relations to France in drama and criticism between 1870 and 1890. *T. P. Williams, M.A. 1936 Wales*

The relationship of the arts in English critical theory of the eighteenth century, with special reference to the years 1750-1780, excluding periodical essays. *K. M. Hamilton, M.A. 1940 London, University College*

Croce, Benedetto
Croce and the *Einfühlung* theory on the relation of feeling to the work of art. *M. S. Meldrum, B.Litt. 1941 Oxford*

The education theory of Benedetto Croce. *F. E. Tomkinson, M.A. 1929 Liverpool*

Crocodile, The
The Nuremberg legend of the crocodile. *L. A. Triebel, M.A. 1914 London*

Croker, John Wilson
John Wilson Croker's contributions to the *Quarterly review*, with and estimate of his work in them as a literary critic. *R. M. Campbell, B.Litt. 1937 Oxford*

Cromwell, Oliver
Cromwell and Mazarin, 1656-1658: an account of the Anglo-French alliance leading to the conquest of Dunkirk. *J. A. Williamson, M.A. 1909 London*

Cromwell in French literature of the Restoration period, 1815-1830. *E. B. Hughes, M.A. 1931 London, East London College*

Cromwell, Oliver contd.
Oliver Cromwell's view of his political mission in the light of his theological and ecclesiastical presuppositions. . *R. S. Paul, D.Phil. 1949 Oxford*

Cromwell, Ralph, Lord
Ralph, Lord Cromwell, and his household: studies in relation to household accounts in the possession of Lord de l'Isle and Dudley. *E. M. Price, M.A. 1949 London, King's College*

Cromwell, Thomas, Earl of Essex
A biography of Thomas Cromwell. *R. B. Merriman, B.Litt. 1899 Oxford*

Thomas Cromwell: aspects of his administrative work. *G. R. Elton, Ph.D. 1949 London, University College*

Crónica de Morea
The language of the *Cronica de Morea. F. W. Hodcroft, M.A. 1950 Manchester*

Cross
See Jesus Christ.

Crowds
The crowd: collective and individual aspects in Elizabethan drama, 1580-1610. *A. M. McGregor, M.A. 1927 London*

Crowland
The organization of the manor, with reference to the estates of Crowland Abbey. *F. M. Page, Ph.D. 1930 Cambridge*

Crown Lands
The Domesday of Crown Lands: a study of the Parliamentary confiscations, surveys and sales during the Commonwealth. *S. J. Madge, D.Sc. 1938 London, School of Economics and Political Science*

Crusades
See also Bohemond I, Prince of Antioch; Knights Templar, The.

The crusades of St. Louis. *M. B. Thomason, M.A. 1913 Birmingham*

The early years of Richard, Earl of Cornwall. *L. W. Kelley, M.A. 1912 Liverpool*

The economic and political preliminaries of the Crusade of Henry Despenser, Bishop of Norwich in 1383. *A. P. R. Coulborn, Ph.D. 1931 London, University College*

England and the Crusades during the reign of Henry III. *W. F. Mumford, M.A. 1924 Manchester*

The influence of the Crusades on the contemporary religious life in Scotland. *T. Low, Ph.D. 1933 Glasgow*

Military methods employed by the Latin states in Syria, 1097 to 1192. *R. C. Smail, Ph.D. 1948 Cambridge*

Projects of crusade in the fifteenth century. *G. W. Pym, M.A. 1925 Liverpool*

Saladin's campaign of 1188 in northern Syria, with particular reference to the northern defences of the principality of Antioch. *J. W. Hackett, B.Litt. 1937 Oxford*

Cuba
The mission to Spain of Pierre Soulé, 1853-5: a study in the Cuban diplomacy of the United States, with special reference to contemporary opinion. *A. A. Ettinger, D.Phil. 1930 Oxford*

Cubbon, Mark, Sir
The administration of Mysore under Sir Mark Cubbon (1834 to 1861). *K. N. V. Sastri, Ph.D. 1931 London, University College*

Cūhrā, The
The speech and customs of the Cūhrās of the Panjab. *A. M. Daula, Ph.D. 1935 London, School of Oriental and African Studies*

Culhwch ac Olwen
See Romances.

Cumberland
The geography and administration of services in the county of Cumberland. *A. F. Young, M.A. 1934 Liverpool*

The Roman occupation of west Cumberland. *A. H. N. Williams, M.A. 1927 Wales*

Cumberland, Richard
Law as basis of morality in the philosophy of Hobbes, Cumberland and Locke. *M. Balaguer, Ph.D. 1937 London, University College*

Cunningham, John
An edition of the poems of John Cunningham (1729-73). *D. P. Shepherd, B.Litt. 1941 Oxford*

Curel, François de, Vicomte
François de Curel, dramatist and philosopher. *A. K. Tucker, Ph.D. 1931 London, University College*

Curel, François de, Vicomte contd.
The ideas of François de Curel as expressed in his dramatic works. *W. James, M.A. 1931 Wales*

La psychologie et les idées dans le théâtre de François de Curel. *F. C. W. Dowson, M.A. 1929 Birmingham*

Curia
See Roman Catholic Church.

Curiosity (Psychology)
An enquiry into curiosity as shown in the written questions of children and adolescents. *W. A. Simson, M.A. 1946 Birmingham*

Curran, John Philpot
John Philpot Curran. *J. A. MacCauley, M.A. 1939 National University of Ireland*

Currency
See Money. For Coinage, see Numismatics.

Cursor Mundi
The phonology and accidence of the Cotton ms. of the *Cursor mundi* considered with especial reference to the Northumbrian dialect of Old English. *L. Fenwick, M.A. 1947 Manchester*

The syntax of *Cursor Mundi*. *D. J. Rogers, B.Litt. 1932 Oxford*

Custodia Essexae
Custodia essexae: a study of the conventual property held by the Priory of Christ Church, Canterbury, in the counties of Essex, Suffolk and Norfolk. *J. F. Nichols, Ph.D. 1930 London, King's College*

Customs and Excise
See also Staple.

British policy in relation to the origin of the Chinese Imperial Maritime Customs Service, 1850-4 inclusive. *J. K. Fairbank, B.Litt. 1931 Oxford*

The last period of the great farm of the English customs (1660-1671). *C. C. Crews, M.A. 1935 London, King's College*

Mr. Customer Smythe, customer of the Port of London, 1570-89. *L. L. S. Lowe, B.Litt. 1950 Oxford*

The organisation of the English customs system, 1696 to 1786. *B. E. Hoon, Ph.D. 1934 London, King's College*

The origin of the Chinese maritime customs. *J. K. Fairbank, D.Phil. 1936 Oxford*

The railway and customs policy of the South African states and colonies. *J. Van der Poel, Ph.D. 1929 London*

Cuvier, Georges
Work of Cuvier. *E. E. White, M.Sc. 1947 London, External Degree*

Cymmrodorion, Honourable Society of
The history of the Honourable Society of Cymmrodorion. *H. M. Jones, M.A. 1939 Wales*

Cymreigyddion y Fenni Society
Cymdeithes Cymreigyddion y Fenni a'i chynhyrchion pwsicaf gyda sylw manylach i waith Thomas Stephens, Merthyr (The Cymreigyddion y Fenni Society and its most important productions, with special reference to the work of Thomas Stephens of Merthyr). *M. Gregory, M.A. 1948 Wales*

Cynddelw Brydydd Mawr
Astudiaeth feirniadol o farddoniaeth Cynddelw Brydydd Mawr, o ran iaith a gwerth llenyddol (A critical study of the poetry of Cynddelw Brydydd Mawr, with special reference to language and literary value). *D. M. Lloyd, M.A. 1932 Wales*

Cynewulf
A critical edition of Cynewulf's *Elene*. *P. O. E. Gradon, Ph.D. 1948 London, King's College*

Cynicism
The Cynic philosophers in the second century of the Christian era. *W. Rees, M.A. 1917 Wales*

The Cynics from the first century to the fall of the Western Empire, with a special study of the problem of fate and free-will as treated by the Stoics and Cynics of the same period. *W. Rees, B.Litt. 1919 Oxford*

Cynon, River
The geography of the drainage areas of the Cynon and Clydach Rivers on the eve of the Industrial Revolution. *D. S. Prosser, M.Sc. 1945 Wales*

Cyprus
Cyprus under the Turks, 1571-1878. *H. C. Luke, B.Litt. 1919 Oxford*

Cyril of Alexandria, Saint
The theology of St. Cyril of Alexandria. *S. H. Scott, B.Litt. 1911 Oxford*

Czech Language
The structure of neologisms in Russian and Czech. *J. O. Ellis, Ph.D. 1948 London, School of Slavonic and East European Studies*

Czechoslovakia
The German-Czech national conflict in Bohemia, 1879-1893. *H. G. Skilling, Ph.D. 1940 London, School of Slavonic and East European Studies*

Monetary reconstruction in Czechoslovakia. *S. Konovaloff, B.Litt. 1927 Oxford*

The rôle of men of science in the Czech National Revival Movement, 1790-1848. *J. G. F. Druce, M.A. 1942 London, School of Slavonic and East European Studies*

Dafydd Llwyd ap Llywelyn ap Gruffudd
Gwaith Dafydd Llwyd o Fathafarn (The work of Dafydd Llwyd of Mathafarn). *W. L. Richards, M.A. 1947 Wales*

Dafydd, Meurig
Bywyd a gwaith Meurig Dafydd (Llanisien) a Llywelyn Siôn (Llangewydd) (The life and work of Meurig Dafydd (Llanisien) and Llywelyn Jones (Llangewydd)). *T. O. Phillips, M.A. 1937 Wales*

Dafydd Trefor
The poetical works of Syr Dafydd Trefor. *S. E. I. George, M.A. 1929 Wales*

Dairy Industry
An analysis of the variation in costs of milk production. *A. L. Jolly, Ph.D. 1940 London, South Eastern Agricultural College*

Certain aspects of food consumption, with special reference to milk. *H. S. Booker, M.Sc. 1938 London, School of Economics and Political Science*

Control schemes in raw materials and foodstuffs in relation to the problems of the dairy industry in New Zealand. *E. P. Haslam, B.Litt. 1938 Oxford*

The cooperative marketing of eggs. *E. C. Colbeck, M.Com. 1933 Leeds*

Dairying in the Irish agricultural economy. *J. I. Fitzpatrick, Ph.D. 1946 Dublin, Trinity College*

Desirable objectives for the milk-producing industry in Great Britain: some problems involved and their prospect of solution. *H. E. Garrett, B.Litt. 1950 Oxford*

The economic geography of the milk supply of London. *E. R. Dudlyke, M.A. 1937 London, School of Economics and Political Science*

Economic studies of the poultry industry. *J. H. Smith, M.Sc. 1937 Wales*

An economic study of dairy herd depreciation. *J. Harrison, M.Sc. 1939 Reading*

The geography of the milk supply of London down to 1921. *E. Cross, B.Litt. 1925 Oxford*

An investigation into the consumer-demand for milk in the city of Leeds. *E. R. Bransby, Ph.D. 1938 London, External Degree*

Livestock improvement in the dairy industry of England and Wales: a study of economic factors involved. *J. D. Empson, B.Litt. 1950 Oxford*

The maintenance of the winter milk supply during war-time. *K. L. Blaxter, Ph.D. 1944 Reading*

The nature of demand for dairy produce in the United Kingdom, with particular reference to New Zealand supplies. *M. M. Cooper, B.Litt. 1937 Oxford*

The organization of the egg industry, with special reference to England and Wales. *R. Coles, M.Sc. 1938 London, School of Economics and Political Science*

A problem in agricultural marketing: an investigation in Yorkshire and Sussex into the consumer-demand for milk. *E. R. Bransby, M.Sc. 1935 London, South Eastern Agricultural College*

Production and marketing of milk and milk products in United Kingdom and western Europe with special reference to co-operative methods and their application under Indian conditions. *D. S. Saraswat, Ph.D. 1949 Glasgow*

Psychological and psychophysical studies of craftsmanship in dairying. *R. Harper, Ph.D. 1949 Reading*

The recent history and the present state of the marketing of milk and dairy produce in Northern Ireland. *R. P. Cotton, M.Com.Sc. 1942 Belfast*

A regional analysis of English milk production. *H. Palca, M.Sc. 1944 London, School of Economics and Political Science*

Dairy Industry contd.
Some aspects of the history and development of dairying in Carmarthenshire. *J. Lewis, M.Sc. 1948 Wales*

A statistical and economic survey of certain aspects of the beef producing, dairying and cattle rearing industries in Great Britian between 1939 and 1945. *J. G. Marley, M.A. 1947 Manchester*

A survey of egg supplies and consumption in a Midland market town. *J. B. Butler, M.Com. 1939 Birmingham*

Dalip Singh, Maharaja
Biography of Maharaja Dalip Singh. *K. S. Thaper, B.Litt. 1934 Oxford*

Dall, Robert
The life of the Reverend Robert Dall, 1745-1828. *P. Smallpage, M.A. 1929 Liverpool*

Dalmatia
Immigration and settlement in the province of Dalmatia from the first Roman contacts to the death of Commodus. *A. J. N. Wilson, D.Phil. 1949 Oxford*

Dalrymple, David, Lord Hailes
The correspondence of Bishop Percy with Sir David Dalrymple, Lord Hailes, and George Paton of Edinburgh, with introduction and notes. *A. F. Falconer, B.Litt. 1934 Oxford*

Dalton, John
Avogadro and Dalton: the standing in chemistry of their hypotheses. *A. N. Meldrum, D.Sc. 1904 Aberdeen*

The contributions to the establishment of the atomic theory made by John Dalton and his contemporaries. *J. H. White, M.Sc. 1927 London*

Dalton Plan
See Education: Great Britain.

Damages
A discourse on the law relating to the doctrine of remoteness of damage. *G. B. Ditcher, LL.M. 1949 Sheffield*

Dancing
The art of the dance in French literature from Theophile Gautier to Paul Valéry. *D. M. Hornby-Priddin, Ph.D. 1948 London, Bedford College*

Studies in Indian dancing as depicted in painting and sculpture and the representations of the musical ragas in painting. *M. Chandra, Ph.D. 1934 London, School of Oriental and African Studies*

Danes, The
Edward the Elder and the Danes. *F. T. Wainwright, Ph.D. 1944 Reading*

Daniel, Samuel
The life and works of Samuel Daniel. *H. Sellers, B.Litt. 1916 Oxford*

Poetical works of Samuel Daniel. *J. P. Hooper, M.A. 1938 National University of Ireland*

Samuel Daniel. *G. T. Lloyd, M.A. 1931 Birmingham*

Samuel Daniel: a biographical and critical study. *C. M. Roebuck, B.Litt. 1926 Oxford*

A study in comparative literature, based on the works of S. Daniel, J. du Bellay. *W. A. Wain, M.A. 1921 Birmingham*

Danish Literature
See Grundtvig, N. F. S.; Oehlenschläger, A. G.

D'Annunzio, Gabriele
Gabriele d'Annunzio, with special reference to his sojourn to France from 1911-1915. *R. Jones, M.A. 1943 Wales*

Dante Alighieri
A comparative study of the figures of speech in early Provençal and Italian lyrical poetry, down to and including Dante's *Vita nuova* and *Rime*. *I. M. Agnew, Ph.D. 1926 Edinburgh*

Henry Francis Cary, 1772-1844, translator of Dante: a study. *R. W. King, M.A. 1919 London*

The teaching of Dante on the human intellect, with special reference to the doctrine of St. Thomas Aquinas. *F. S. Foster, Ph.D. 1947 Cambridge*

Danube, River
The Danube: its history and its economic and political development. *A. Puscariu, Ph.D. 1928 Birmingham*

Dardanelles
The history of the Bosphorus and the Dardanelles, with special reference to treaty relations: a study in international law and diplomacy. *D. B. Toye, LL.D. 1925 London*

Darfur
The history of Darfur from A.D. 1200 to 1700. *A. J. Arkell, B.Litt. 1939 Oxford*

Darien Scheme
The Darien scheme and the Church of Scotland. *J. C. Ramsay, Ph.D. 1949 Edinburgh*

Darío, Rubén
Rubén Darío. *E. P. Crowe, M.A. 1947 National University of Ireland*

Darley, George
George Darley and the Elizabethan revival in the Romantic period. *K. W. Wild, M.A. 1914 Liverpool*

The life and work of George Darley. *C. C. Abbott, Ph.D. 1926 Cambridge*

The prose work of George Darley. *G. Crozier, M.A. 1924 Liverpool*

Darwin, Erasmus
The life, times and work of Erasmus Darwin. *E. Blackwell, M.A. 1949 London, Royal Holloway College*

Date-Growing Industry
A geographical analysis of the date-palm industry of Iraq. *A. H. el Dabbagh, M.A. 1948 Birmingham*

Daudet, Alphonse
Dickens et Daudet. *F. M. Gibson, M.A. 1913 Birmingham*

La description de la nature dans les oeuvres d'Alphonse Daudet. *M. Carmichael, M.A. 1916 Liverpool*

Daunou, Pierre Claude François
Pierre Claude François Daunou (1761-1840); a literary and biographical essay. *R. H. Clark, Ph.D. 1939 London, Queen Mary College*

D'Avenant, William, Sir
Sir William d'Avenant as a transition dramatist. *M. Lansdale, M.A. 1929 Manchester*

David, Saint
The life of St. David by Giraldus Cambrensis. *T. B. Jones, M.A. 1934 Wales*

Davidson, John
The poetry of John Davidson, 1857-1909. *S. H. Best, M.A. 1931 Birmingham*

Davidson, John, of Prestonpans
John Davidson of Prestonpans, (1549?-1604). *R. M. Gillon, Ph.D. 1935 Edinburgh*

Davies, James (Iaco ab Dewi)
Bywyd a gwaith Iaco ab Dewi (The life and work of Iaco ab Dewi). *G. H. Hughes, M.A. 1939 Wales*

Davies, John
Bywyd a gwaith Dr. John Davies, Mallwyd (The life and work of Dr. John Davies, Mallwyd). *R. F. Roberts, M.A. 1950 Wales*

Davies, John, Sir
An edition of *Nosce teipsum* by Sir John Davies, with a prefatory study of his poetry. *T. J. Childs, B.Litt. 1939 Oxford*

Davies, Richard, Bishop
The life and work of Bishop Richard Davies. *G. Williams, M.A. 1947 Wales*

Davis, Walter (Gwalter Mechain)
Gwallter Mechain: ei hanes, ei waith a'i safonau beirniadol (Gwallter Mechain; his life story, his work, and his standards of criticism). *J. T. Owen, M.A. 1928 Wales*

Davy, Humphrey, Sir
A conspectus of the scientific work of Sir Humphrey Davy, Bart. *P. C. Davey, M.Sc. 1949 London, University College*

The electro-chemical researches of Sir Humphrey Davy. *W. C. Walker, M.Sc. 1929 London*

Day, John
A critical study of *The Fair maid of the exchange* and its attribution to Thomas Heywood, and the relation of the play to Markham and Machin's *Dumb knight* and the works of John Day and Thomas Dekker. *S. R. Golding, M.A. 1922 London*

Studies in John Day. *S. R. Golding, Ph.D. 1930 London, King's College*

De Burgh, Elizabeth
Household administration in the fourteenth century, with special reference to the household of Elizabeth de Burgh, Lady of Clare. *C. A. Musgrave, M.A. 1923 London*

De Burgh, Family, Earls of Ulster
The De Burgh earls of Ulster. *O. Lamont, M.A. 1947 Belfast*

De Burgh, Hubert, Earl of Kent
Hubert de Burgh. *S. H. F. Johnston, B.Litt. 1933 Oxford*

Hubert de Burgh. *C. Ellis, M.A. 1912 Wales*

De Burgh, Hubert, Earl of Kent contd.
The relations between Crown and Baronage in England between 1216 and 1232, with especial reference to the administration of Hubert de Burgh. *G. Malbon, M.A. 1940 London, External Degree*

De Hoghton, Family
A calendar of the de Hoghton deeds and papers. *J. H. Lumby, M.A. 1936 Liverpool*

De la Mare, Walter
The poetry of Mr. Walter de la Mare. *M. Dawson, M.A. 1931 Liverpool*

Prose works of Walter de la Mare. *V. M. M. O'Brien, M.A. 1949 National University of Ireland*

Walter de la Mare: a critical study. *D. Hytch, M.A. 1931 Birmingham*

De Lafléchère, John William
See Fléchère, J. W. de la.

De Quincey, Thomas
De Quincey. *S. Patton, M.A. 1943 National University of Ireland*

De Quincey's prose style. *A. E. G. Sephton, M.A. 1946 Liverpool*

Milton criticism from Addison to de Quincey. *K. Wood, M.A. 1950 Sheffield*

Deafness
See also Children, Handicapped.

A history of deaf education in Scotland, 1760-1939. *T. J. Watson, Ph.D. 1949 Edinburgh*

Dean, Forest of
The Forest of Dean in its relations with the Crown during the twelfth and thirteenth centuries. *M. L. Bazeley, M.A. 1911 London*

The historical geography of the Forest of Dean. *F. T. Baber, M.A. 1949 Wales*

The historical geography of the Forest of Dean during the seventeenth century. *J. C. Stuttard, M.Sc. 1942 Cambridge*

Death
See also Burials; Eschatology; Tombs.

The cult of the dead in North America. *E. O. James, Ph.D. 1925 London*

The development of the concept of death. *H. S. Anthony, M.A. 1939 London, University College*

Necessity for legislative reform in Scotland in regard to uncertified deaths. *J. Glaister, M.D. 1885 Glasgow*

Primitive beliefs about the dead as a preparation for the Christian doctrine of immortality. *D. McDougall, Ph.D. 1937 Edinburgh*

The recurrence of the death theme in Spanish poetry from minstrel to 20th century. *C. De Wolf, Ph.D. 1938 Dublin, Trinity College*

Some philosophical considerations about the survival of death. *C. Lewy, Ph.D. 1943 Cambridge*

Some Rabbinical beliefs and customs connected with death and mourning. *L. Mendelsohn, M.A. 1910 London*

Studies on fatality in sentimental pre-Romantic French literature, 1725-62. *B. J. Schlumberger, M.A. 1922 London*

Death Duties
See Succession.

Debt
Assignments of debts in England from the twelfth to the twentieth centuries. *S. J. Bailey, LL.M. 1930 Cambridge*

The law relating to legal remedies against debtors, treated historically and comparatively. *J. S. Carpenter, LL.D. 1918 London*

Décade philosophique, La
La *Décade philosophique* et la fin de la philosophie en France au début du dix-neuvième siècle. *R. Fargher, D.Phil. 1941 Oxford*

Dee, River
The physical and historical background of the Dee estuary. *J. A. Young, M.A. 1926 Liverpool*

Defoe, Daniel
A critical study of Defoe's *Review*, and other journals of its day, with particular emphasis on the social life of the age. *A. B. Stapleton, Ph.D. 1924 London*

Daniel De Foe, his mind and art. *S. Sen, M.Litt. 1947 Cambridge*

The novels of Daniel Defoe. *W. S. Tomkinson, B.Litt. 1925 Oxford*

The rise of journalism to Defoe. *A. M. Underhill, M.A. 1929 Birmingham*

Defoe, Daniel contd.
The verse satires of Daniel Defoe. *A. M. Wilkinson, M.A. 1949 Manchester*

Degrevant, Sir
See Romances.

Deguileville, Guillaume de
Le *pèlerinage de la vie humaine* de Guillaume de Deguileville d'après le texte du manuscrit French 2 de la John Rylands Library, Manchester. *M. Lofthouse, M.A. 1929 Manchester*

Deimier, Pierre de
Deimier. *A. B. Thomas, M.A. 1907 Wales*

Deism
C. Blount, 8th Lord Mountjoy. *F. M. Jones, M.A. 1946 National University of Ireland*

Kant's religious theory and its relation to English deism. *T. M. Greene, Ph.D. 1924 Edinburgh*

Dekker, Thomas
The collaboration of Dekker and Middleton. *M. Baird, B.Litt. 1928 Oxford*

A critical edition of the *Famous Historie of Sir Thomas Wyat*, by Thomas Dekker and John Webster. *E. M. F. Martin, M.A. 1930 London, University College*

A critical study of *The Fair maid of the exchange* and its attribution to Thomas Heywood, and the relation of the play to Markham and Machin's *Dumb knight* and the works of John Day and Thomas Dekker. *S. R. Golding, M.A. 1922 London*

Dekker and the artizan in the Elizabethan drama. *M. M. M. Mackinlay, M.A. 1949 Manchester*

Dekker as a dramatist. *H. M. Moore, M.A. 1933 National University of Ireland*

The plague pamphlets of T. Dekker, with an account of the plague in London from 1603 to 1630. *F. P. Wilson, D.Litt. 1921 Birmingham*

The prose works of Dekker. *F. P. Wilson, M.A. 1912 Birmingham*

The prose works of Thomas Dekker. *F. P. Wilson, B.Litt. 1913 Oxford*

Delaney, Thomas
The prose works of Thomas Deloney. *E. M. MacDonald, M.A. 1931 Birmingham*

Delcassé, Théophile
The diplomatic relations between England and France from 1898 to June 1905: the policy of M. Delcassé and the making of the Anglo-French *Entente. E. J. Parry, M.A. 1932 Wales*

Delescluze, Louis Charles
Le groupe Delécluze et son rôle dans le mouvement romantique. *E. P. E. Long, M.A. 1938 Liverpool*

Delhi
The administration of the sultanate of Delhi. *I. H. Qureshi, Ph.D. 1939 Cambridge*

The sultanate of Delhi, 1206 to 1290 A.D. *A. B. M. Habibullah, Ph.D. 1936 London, School of Oriental and African Studies*

Delict
Formalism and progress in the early Roman law of delict. *D. Daube, Ph.D. 1936 Cambridge*

The principles of the Roman-Dutch law of delict as illustrated in the law of Ceylon, with a special chapter on the liability of the Crown to be sued in tort in Ceylon. *L. A. Rajapakse, LL.D. 1925 London*

Delinquency
Investigation into factors influencing the direction of aggressive impulses into (a) delinquency, (b) neurosis, (c) positive achievement. *L. Jackson, D.Phil. 1949 Oxford*

Delinquency, Juvenile
See Juvenile Delinquency.

Deloney, Thomas
The growth of realism in Elizabethan fiction, with special reference to Greene, Nashe and Deloney. *E. L. G. Giles, M.A. 1937 Wales*

The works of Thomas Deloney. *F. O. Mann, B.Litt. 1912 Oxford*

Delos
The history of Delos. *W. A. Laidlow, Litt.D. 1933 Dublin, Trinity College*

Delphi
The metopes of the treasury of the Athenians at Delphi. *W. R. Agard, B.Litt. 1923 Oxford*

Demand (Economics)
Family budget data and price elasticities of demand. *C. E. V. Leser, M.Sc. 1941 London, School of Economics and Political Science*

Demand (Economics) contd.
A study in demand analysis. *D. Cochrane, Ph.D. 1949 Cambridge*

Democracy
The breakdown of post-war democracy in central Europe: analysis of authoritarian methods and possibilities of their control. *K. J. Neumann, D.Phil. 1944 Oxford*

Critics of democracy: Carlyle, Arnold, Stephen (Fitzjames), Maine, Lecky. *B. E. Lippincott, Ph.D. 1931 London, School of Economics and Political Science*

Democracy as a practical ideal. *H. W. Locke, M.A. 1922 Birmingham*

Democracy in English fiction. *D. O'Keeffe, M.A. 1941 National University of Ireland*

The democratic spirit in English poetry up to the time of the French Revolution. *G. L. Davies, M.A. 1929 Wales*

Dissent and democracy. *F. M. Scully, M.A. 1937 Bristol*

The ideas of democracy in the eighteenth century as shown in the writings of Condorcet. *D. Williams, M.A. 1928 Wales*

Inquiry into institutional safeguards on the freedom of the individual in the modern democratic state. *S. Rolbant, Ph.D. 1946 London, School of Economics and Political Science*

The modern democratic movement as reflected in the English poets. *E. Bainton, M.A. 1911 Birmingham*

The use of schools as instruments of democracy. *C. J. Buckley, M.Sc. 1948 London, School of Economics and Political Science*

Demography
See Population.

Demonology
See also Faust.

The controversy regarding Richard Dugdale, the 'Surey demoniac'. *J. E. Roberts, M.A. 1944 Manchester*

1. Demoniacal possession. 2. The intermediate state. *R. W. M. Pope, B.D. 1877 Oxford*

Demonology, magic, and witchcraft in the English drama, 1580-1642. *F. M. N. Trefethen, M.Litt. 1950 Cambridge*

Descriptions of the Devil and his works in early English literature and the development of these ideas in relation to doctrine. *A. B. Lewis, Ph.D. 1939 London, University College*

The devil in English literature from the Middle Ages to 1700. *W. M. Mountford, Ph.D. 1931 London, External Degree*

The Faust theme in English literature, with an introduction on pre-Faustus conceptions of the devil, and a complete bibliography of English Faust publications. *D. W. Oates, M.A. 1918 Wales*

The Jewish and Christian doctrine of good and evil spirits: its origin and development. *E. Langton, D.D. 1942 London, External Degree*

1. On the intermediate state. 2. On demoniacal possession. *J. Evans, B.D. & D.D. 1906 Oxford*

The Yezidis, or 'devil-worshippers' of Assyria: an investigation into their social and religious cult. *M. K. MacLeod, Ph.D. 1933 Edinburgh*

Denck, Hans
The Reformation and the religion of the spirit: a critical study of the life and teaching of Hans Denck. *A. Coutts, Ph.D. 1921 Edinburgh*

Denham, John, Sir
A critical study of the life and works of Sir John Denham. *K. M. Rowe, M.A. 1931 Reading*

Denmark
Denmark and Britain. *R. A. Atkinson, M.Com.Sc. 1933 Belfast*

Dentistry
The law relating to medical, dental, and veterinary practice. *F. Bullock, LL.D. 1928 London*

Department Stores
See Retail Trade.

Depression (Economics)
See Trade Cycles.

Depression (Psychology)
The differential diagnosis of depressive states, with an inquiry into the suicidal impulse: an investigation conducted by a method of experimental psychology. *A. Guirdham, B.Sc. 1935 Oxford*

Derby
The county borough of Derby in relation to the surrounding region. *E. C. Vollans, B.Litt. 1949 Oxford*

Derby, Henry, Earl of
Medieval travel as illustrated by the wardrobe accounts of Henry, Earl of Derby, 1390-1393. *G. Stretton, M.A. 1924 London*

Derwent, River
Density, distribution and housing of population in the middle Derwent basin. *F. C. Couzens, M.A. 1937 London, Birkbeck College*

Descartes, René
Antoine Arnauld and the Cartesian theory of representative ideas. *S. V. Keeling, M.A. 1926 London*

The cogito ergo sum: an analytic study in the metaphysics of René Descartes. *M. Versfeld, Ph.D. 1934 Glasgow*

The concept of self from Descartes to Kant, with some reference to immortality. *E. G. Braham, Ph.D. 1935 London, King's College*

The conception of teleology in modern philosophy from Descartes to Kant. *T. Evans, M.A. 1927 Wales*

A critical discussion of the sources of Spinoza, with special reference to Maimonides and Descartes. *H. L. Roth, D.Phil. 1922 Oxford*

Descartes' world, or Treatise on light. *A. Wechsler, M.Sc. 1931 London*

The development of the theory of space from Descartes to Kant. *A. W. P. Wolters, M.A. 1910 London*

The freewill problem in modern philosophy from Descartes to Kant. *J. Pitts, Ph.D. 1933 London, External Degree*

The idea of God in Descartes, Spinoza and Leibniz. *M. A. Davies, M.A. 1935 Wales*

The influence of mathematics on the philosophy of Descartes. *J. R. Andress, M.A. 1927 Manchester*

The influence of religious dogma on metaphysical speculation in the philosophy of Descartes, with special reference to the psychological aspect. *J. J. Hartland-Swann, Ph.D. 1946 London, External Degree*

The method of Descartes. *S. Galin, M.Sc. 1927 London*

The methodology of Descartes. *A. J. Taylor, M.Sc. 1927 London*

The origins of the Cartesian view of rational explanation and certain aspects of its influence on later philosophy. *R. I. Markus, Ph.D. 1950 Manchester*

The physical work of Descartes. *F. Wootton, M.Sc. 1927 London*

The problem of value in early modern philosophy, with special reference to Descartes. *D. J. McCracken, M.A. 1934 Belfast*

The problem of value in early modern philosophy: a study of Descartes, Geulincx and Spinoza. *D. J. McCracken, Ph.D. 1936 Belfast*

Studies in the Cartesian philosophy. *N. Smith, D.Phil. 1903 Saint Andrew's*

Design Argument
See Theism.

Desires (Psychology)
Some conditions affecting the growth and permanence of desires. *I. B. Saxby, D.Sc. 1918 London*

Desmaizeaux, Pierre
An agent in Anglo-French relationships: Pierre Desmaizeaux. *J. H. Broome, Ph.D. 1949 London, University College*

Peter Desmaizeaux (1673?-1745): life and works. *F. Beckwith, M.A. 1936 Leeds*

Despenser, Henry, Bishop
The economic and political preliminaries of the Crusade of Henry Despenser, Bishop of Norwich in 1383. *A. P. R. Coulborn, Ph.D. 1931 London, University College*

Determinism
See also Free Will.

Determinism in Calvin. *J. H. Powell, Ph.D. 1928 Edinburgh*

The determinism of Jonathan Edwards. *W. L. Lewis, M.A. 1949 Bristol*

Fate, determinism and free will in religion and philosophy. *J. Westbury-Jones, D.D. 1936 Oxford*

Determinism contd.
Free will and determinism. *T. Donovan, M.A. 1914 National University of Ireland*

Devil, The
See Demonology.

Devon
The development of quarter sessions government in Devon in the nineteenth century and the transition to county council government. *D. R. Tucker, M.A. 1949 London, External Degree*

The economic geography of the county of Devon: a study of the factors controlling the geographical distribution of the chief occupations. *W. P. Baron, Ph.D. 1938 London, External Degree*

A geography of Devon. *B. H. Cudmore, M.A. 1947 Bristol*

On the causes and course of the rebellion of 1549 in Devon and Cornwall. *W. J. Blake, M.A. 1909 London*

The ownership and occupation of the land in Devonshire, 1650-1800. *W. G. Hoskins, Ph.D. 1938 London, External Degree*

The trade and industry of Devonshire in the later Middle Ages. *F. A. Mace, M.A. 1925 London*

Village-patterns and distributions in East Devon. *H. M. Mortimer, M.A. 1940 London, External Degree*

Dewey, John
A critical study of Dewey's theory of moral values. *B. E. Cornelius, Ph.D. 1924 Edinburgh*

'Instrumentalism': a methodological exposition of the philosophy of John Dewey. *S. G. Sathaye, Ph.D. 1944 London, University College*

Pragmatism and education: the philosophy of John Dewey. *E. A. Weir, M.A. 1943 Manchester*

Dialects
See Language; and under individual languages.

Diaper, John William
An edition of the complete works of William Diaper. *D. Broughton, Ph.D. 1947 Leeds*

Diaries
English personal letters and private diaries of 1640-1680: a study of the general mental attitude of the period as illustrated by individual types, together with a brief examination of the colloquial language of the time. *M. T. Williamson, Ph.D. 1929 London*

Diaspora
See Jews: History.

Dicenta, Joaquín
The dramas of Joaquín Dicenta. *H. B. Hall, M.A. 1950 Liverpool*

Dickens, Charles
Charles Dickens and Charles Kingsley as social critics. *S. W. Percival, M.A. 1947 Manchester*

Charles Dickens and the eighteenth century tradition of the novel. *L. R. Burrows, M.A. 1948 Sheffield*

Charles Dickens as a regional novelist. *E. H. London, M.A. 1949 Wales*

Charles Dickens' contribution to the social novel, 1836-1850. *H. Clarke, M.A. 1947 Birmingham*

Dickens et Daudet. *F. M. Gibson, M.A. 1913 Birmingham*

An examination of the methods of Dickens and Thackeray in the characterization of women. *E. C. McGahan, M.A. 1946 Wales*

France in the life and works of Dickens. *V. C. Wood, M.A. 1949 Liverpool*

The reception of the works of Charles Dickens in Germany. *E. N. Gummer, B.Litt. 1938 Oxford*

Schools and schoolmasters in Dickens. *W. R. Swale, M.A. 1933 Birmingham*

Sensational elements in Dickens and Collins. *A. R. Jolly, M.A. 1943 Manchester*

The social ideas of Charles Dickens, and their influence upon his art as a novelist. *F. E. Stanbury, M.A. 1934 Wales*

Social reform in the novels of Charles Dickens. *H. E. Davies, M.A. 1935 Wales*

Dictionaries
See also under individual languages.

English compound nouns of the type used in personal descriptions; a supplement to the chronology of the new English dictionary. *D. D. Pilkington, M.A. 1920 London*

The place of Johnson's dictionary in the history of English lexicography. *A. W. Read, B.Litt. 1933 Oxford*

Dictionaries contd.
Pre-Johnson developments in English lexicography. *C. Donnellan, M.A. 1932 National University of Ireland*

Dicts and Sayings of the Philosophers, The
The *Dicts and Sayings of the philosophers. C. F. Buhler, Litt.D. 1947 Dublin, Trinity College*

Didascalia Apostolorum
A comparison of the styles of Gaudentius of Brescia, the *De Sacramentis* (ascribed to St. Ambrose) and the *Disdascalia Apostolorum* or *Fragmenta Veronensia. A. H. Birch, Ph.D. 1924 London*

Diderot, Denis
Diderot et la musique. *R. L. Evans, M.A. 1932 Birmingham*

Les idées biologiques de Diderot et leur influence sur son oeuvre romanesque. *S. C. De St. Mathurin, B.Litt. 1932 Oxford*

A study of Diderot's novel *La religieuse. M. K. Hancox, M.A. 1944 Birmingham*

Dierx, Léon
La poésie de Léon Dierx. *M. B. Stephens, M.A. 1929 Belfast*

Diffusion of Useful Knowledge, Society for the
The history of the Society for the Diffusion of Useful Knowledge. *T. L. Jarman, B.Litt. 1933 Oxford*

The Society for the Diffusion of Useful Knowledge, 1826-48. *M. C. Grobel, M.A. 1933 London, University College*

Digby, Kenelm, Sir
Sir Kenelm Digby: a study of his life and works, chiefly between the years 1633-1644. *P. W. Edwards, M.A. 1946 Birmingham*

Digger Movement, The
The Digger Movement in the English Revolution. *D. W. Petegorsky, Ph.D. 1940 London, School of Economics and Political Science*

Dihlavi, Amire Hasan
The life and works of Amire Hasan Dihlavi. *M. I. Borrah, Ph.D. 1931 London, School of Oriental and African Studies*

Dilthey, Wilhelm
A critical examination of Dilthey's theory of the historical and social studies only. *H. A. Hodges, D.Phil. 1932 Oxford*

Dio Cassius
The constitution of the Roman principate under Augustus in theory and practice, with a special consideration of the edicts from Cyrene and the value of the speech of Maecenas in Dio lii as evidence for the Augustan age. *M. Hammond, B.Litt. 1928 Oxford*

Diodorus Siculus
The humanism of John Skelton, with special reference to his translation of Diodorus Siculus. *H. L. R. Edwards, Ph.D. 1938 Cambridge*

Dionysius of Halicarnassus
The place of Dionysius of Halicarnassus in the development of prose-criticism. *J. F. Lockwood, Ph.D. 1936 London, University College*

Dionysius, the Areopagite
The influence of the pseudo Dionysius the Areopagite on the philosophy of St. Thomas Aquinas. *S. J. Curtis, Ph.D. 1931 London, External Degree*

Dionysius, Tyrant of Syracuse
Dionysius the second: tyrant of Syracuse. *J. Gaynor, M.A. 1947 National University of Ireland*

Diplomacy
British practice of diplomatic protection of subjects abroad. *K. H. Hwang, Ph.D. 1949 Cambridge*

The conduct of English diplomacy in the fourteenth century. *G. P. Cuttino, D.Phil. 1938 Oxford*

Economic background of the modern diplomacy of the Great Powers in the Far East since the World War. *T. K. Chow, M.Sc. 1934 London, School of Economics and Political Science*

The law of diplomatic immunity. *R. G. Jones, Ph.D. 1949 Cambridge*

The United States and Old World diplomacy, 1898 to 1914, with special reference to China. *R. G. Shiman, Ph.D. 1930 London, School of Economics and Political Science*

Diplovatatius
Study of the antecedents of the *De Claris jurisconsultis* of Diplovatatius. *H. Koeppler, D.Phil. 1936 Oxford*

Disarmament
See War and Peace.

Disciples of Christ
The biography of Barton Warren Stone, with particular reference to the origin of the Christian Church in the west, and its influence on the Disciples of Christ. *V. E. Kellems, Ph.D. 1928 Edinburgh*

History of the British Churches of Christ. *A. C. Watters, Ph.D. 1940 Edinburgh*

The original doctrines of the Disciples of Christ: a critical evaluation. *J. W. Hastings, Ph.D. 1929 Edinburgh*

The relation of Baptists to Disciples (Churches) of Christ. *E. Roberts-Thomson, M.A. 1949 Bristol*

The theology of Alexander Campbell in relation to the origin of the Disciples. *J. R. Kellems, Ph.D. 1926 Edinburgh*

Disposition
Some tests of disposition. *E. J. Weeks, M.A. 1927 London*

Disraeli, Benjamin, 1st Earl of Beaconsfield
Disraeli. *D. I. Hart, M.A. 1921 Birmingham*

Disraeli as a writer of political novels. *R. B. Ives, M.A. 1924 Birmingham*

A dissertation upon Benjamin Disraeli as a man of letters. *K. V. Cherian, M.A. 1932 Liverpool*

The political novels of Disraeli. *T. G. John, M.A. 1918 Wales*

Dissenters
See Nonconformity.

Dissenting Academies
See Education, Higher.

Distress (Law)
History of the law of distress for rent and damage feasant. *F. A. Enever, LL.D. 1929 London*

Distribution
See Economics.

Distributive Trades
See Retail Trade.

Ditchfield Grant, The
An edition of 4 Charles I. Rot. Pat. 4 Car.I. 33A-33C: The Ditchfield Grant of September 25. *E. M. Lewis, M.A. 1930 Leeds*

Divination
See also Fate; Oracles.

Divination in Greek tragedy. *F. A. Dunne, M.A. 1945 National University of Ireland*

Divination in Homer and the tragedians. *T. Fahy, M.A. 1914 National University of Ireland*

The waters of divination. *W. R. Halliday, B.Litt. 1910 Oxford*

Divorce
See Marriage.

Dobson, William
William Dobson. *B. M. Spencer, M.A. 1937 London, Courtauld Institute of Art*

Docks
See Ports and Harbours.

Dodona
See Oracles.

Domestic Servants
Domestic workers in hospitals: a field of women's employment. *M. S. Eaton, Ph.D. 1948 London, School of Economics and Political Science*

Les valets et les servantes dans la comédie de Molière. *F. C. Roe, M.A. 1920 Birmingham*

Servants and satellites: a consideration of some minor Italian social types of the eighteenth century attendant upon the giovin signore of Parini's satire *Il giorno. W. Radcliffe, M.A. 1937 Manchester*

Domicile
The law of domicile in relation to death duties. *H. G. Bell, LL.D. 1914 London*

Dominican Order
See also Religious Orders and Societies; Thomas Aquinas, Saint; Kilwardby, R., Archbishop.

The Franciscans and Dominicans in Yorkshire. *L. M. Goldthorp, M.A. 1932 Leeds*

Some secular activities of the English Dominicans during the reigns of Edward I, Edward II, and Edward III (1272-1377). *R. D. Clarke, M.A. 1930 London, University College*

Studies in thirteenth century English Dominican history. *W. A. Hinnebusch, D.Phil. 1939 Oxford*

Domitian, Emperor
The early career, accession and domestic policy of the Emperor Domitian. *R. A. Gillespie, M.A. 1937 London, Birkbeck College*

Domna, Julia
See Julia Domna.

Don Quixote
See Cervantes Saavedra, M. de.

Donatism
The social and economic background of Christianity in North Africa down to 430, with special reference to the Donatist schism. *W. H. C. Frend, D.Phil. 1940 Oxford*

Donne, John
The Donne world picture. *V. MacAlister, M.A. 1944 National University of Ireland*

The early life and poetry of John Donne. *I. A. Shapiro, M.A. 1926 Birmingham*

The mystical element in the religious poetry of the seventeenth century (1600-1660), together with an anthology of Donne's sermons illustrative of his theology and mysticism. *I. Husain, Ph.D. 1935 Edinburgh*

Platonism and mysticism in J. Donne, H. Vaughan and T. Traherne. *C. G. M. Roberts, M.A. 1913 Bristol*

The poetry of John Donne. *C. O'Leary, M.A. 1949 National University of Ireland*

The prose style of John Donne in his *Sermons. G. Lilly, M.A. 1947 Liverpool*

The prose works of John Donne. *E. M. Simpson, D.Phil. 1923 Oxford*

The prose works of John Donne. *R. P. Coffin, B.Litt. 1921 Oxford*

The prose works of John Donne. *M. N. Bailey, M.A. 1913 Birmingham*

The relationship of form and content in the work of Donne. *E. G. Lewis, M.A. 1932 Wales*

The religious element in the letters and poems of Donne, and in the works of Browne and Vaughan. *R. E. George, B.Litt. 1915 Oxford*

The sermons of Donne and Taylor. *W. E. Brooke, M.A. 1935 Birmingham*

Donne, John, the Younger
A critical edition of the poems printed by John Donne the Younger in 1660 as written by William Herbert, Earl of Pembroke, and Sir Benjamin Ruddier. *M. A. Beese, B.Litt. 1935 Oxford*

Dorset
Feudal aspect of Domesday survey of Somerset and Dorset in connexion with the Barony of Moiun (Dunster Castle) and analogous feudal estates, based upon contemporary public and local records. *M. F. Moore, Ph.D. 1930 London, King's College*

The progress of enclosures in the county of Dorset since 1700. *G. B. Endacott, B.Litt. 1938 Oxford*

William Barnes: study of the man and poet and of his work in connection with Dorset and the Dorset dialect. *J. V. Ruffell, Ph.D. 1948 London, External Degree*

Dostoevsky, Feodor Mikhailovich
The influence of the Russian novel on French thinkers and writers, with particular reference to Tolstoy and Dostoevsky. *F. W. J. Hemmings, D.Phil. 1949 Oxford*

Doughty, Charles Montagu
A critical examination of the prose and verse of C. M. Doughty. *A. Treneer, B.Litt. 1931 Oxford*

Douglas, Gawain
An edition of the prologues to Gavin Douglas's *Eneados. E. Bennett, B.Litt. 1938 Oxford*

Gawain Douglas. *J. P. Breslin, M.A. 1942 National University of Ireland*

A study of Gawayne Douglas's translation of Vergil's *Aeneid. I. M. Le Chavetois, M.A. 1909 London*

Douglas, Thomas, 5th Earl of Selkirk
Lord Selkirk's work in Canada. *C. B. Martin, B.Litt. 1912 Oxford*

Dowson, Ernest
A study of the life and writings of Ernest Dowson. *R. Cummings, M.A. 1947 Wales*

Dracontius, Blossius Aemilius
The syntax and language of Dracontius. *A. Hudson-Williams, M.Litt. 1934 Cambridge*

Drake, Francis, Sir
Sir Francis Drake: explorer. *K. M. Keegan, M.A. 1924 Birmingham*

Drama
See Theatre.

Drapery Trade
A history of the Shrewsbury Drapers' Company during the seventeenth century, with particular reference to the Welsh woollen trade. *D. J. Evans, M.A. 1950 Wales*

Dravidian Language
Indo-Aryan loan-words in Malayalam, with a study of some Dravidian loans in Sanskrit. *K. G. Varma, Ph.D. 1934 London, School of Oriental and African Studies*

Drawing
See also Art, Children's.

A catalogue of the drawings of James Gibbs in the Ashmolean Museum and their connexion with his life and work. *W. W. Crandall, B.Litt. 1933 Oxford*

The drawings by Raphael in the Ashmolean Museum, Oxford: an account of the formation of the collection and its acquisition by the University. *D. M. Sutton, B.Litt. 1944 Oxford*

Gainsborough's landscape drawings and their place in the development of English landscape drawing and painting. *M. W. Woodall, Ph.D. 1937 London, Courtauld Institute of Art*

Drayton, Michael
The life and work of Drayton with particular reference to the *Polyolbion* and its sources. *I. Gourvitch, Ph.D. 1930 London, King's College*

A variorum text of the sonnets of Michael Drayton and a critical study of the different versions. *K. M. Constable, B.Litt. 1929 Oxford*

Dreams
The day dream and the terror dream. *G. H. Green, M.A. 1926 Wales*

The daydreams of children from infancy to adolescence considered as evidence of the nature of psychological development. *G. H. Green, Ph.D. 1925 London*

The dream in primitive cultures. *J. S. Lincoln, Ph.D. 1935 London, School of Economics and Political Science*

Dream literature in the English Romantic period (1780-1830), with a consideration of some writers of the later nineteenth century. *S. Evans, M.A. 1938 Wales*

Dreams in Old Norse literature and their affinities in folklore. *G. D. Kelchner, Ph.D. 1934 Cambridge*

Tabir al-Ruya (interpretation of dreams): sources, philosophy, influence, etc. *M. Al-Hashimi, Ph.D. 1948 London, School of Oriental and African Studies*

Drehem
The tablets from Drehem. *T. Fish, Ph.D. 1928 Cambridge*

Dreyfus, Alfred
The Dreyfus affairs in the life and works of Charles Péguy. *W. T. John, Ph.D. 1948 London, King's College*

Drinking
See Alcohol.

Droste-Hülshoff, Annette Elisabeth von, Baroness
Nature in the works of Annette von Droste-Hülshoff. *L. van Z. Smit, Ph.D. 1932 London, University College*

Women writers in Germany in the beginning of the nineteenth century, with special reference to Annette von Droste-Hülshoff. *E. Matthews, M.A. 1925 Wales*

Drug Industry
Economic survey of pharmaceutical retailing. *S. M. P. McCaul, M.Econ.Sc. 1949 National University of Ireland*

Drug Traffic
The activities of the League of Nations in relation to the traffic of opium and other dangerous drugs, in particular, emphasizing the illicit traffic as a significant factor in the situation. *A. D. Hooper, M.A. 1936 Wales*

Drummond, Thomas
The administration of Thomas Drummond in Ireland (1835-40). *T. F. Kelly, M.A. 1941 National University of Ireland*

Drummond, William
Ben Jonson's conversations with William Drummond of Hawthornden. *R. F. Patterson, D.Litt. 1922 Glasgow*

Dryden, John
Criticism and appreciation of Elizabethan drama: Dryden to Swinburne. *F. C. Baxter, Ph.D. 1933 Cambridge*

Dryden: the biographies before 1900. *J. M. Osborn, B.Litt. 1937 Oxford*

Dryden, John contd.
Dryden's heroic plays. *B. J. Pendlebury, M.A. 1921 Birmingham*

Literary patronage in the time of Dryden. *J. J. E. Palmer, B.Litt. 1940 Oxford*

The political and literary background of *Absalom and Achitophel*. *H. T. Cunningham, B.Litt. 1939 Oxford*

Du Bellay, Guillaume and Martin
The *Mémoires* of Guillaume and Martin Du Bellay: a contribution to the history of French historiography in the sixteenth century. *J. D. Duncanson, M.A. 1938 London, King's College*

Dublin
History of the Dublin Chamber of Commerce, 1760-1860. *P. L. Prendeville, M.Comm. 1930 National University of Ireland*

The trade of Dublin. *D. K. Smee, Ph.D. 1929 London*

Ducis, Jean François
The adaptations of Shakespeare by Jean-François Ducis; with special reference to the influence of the classical tradition on French tragedy. *S. E. F. Macdonald, Ph.D. 1929 Edinburgh*

Ducis and De Vigny considered as interpreters of Shakespeare. *R. J. Evans, M.A. 1909 Wales*

Duclos, Henri
Henri Duclos. *H. Jefferson, Ph.D. 1942 Dublin, Trinity College*

Dudley, Edmund
Life and works of Edmund Dudley. *D. M. Brodie, Ph.D. 1935 Cambridge*

Dugdale, Richard
The controversy regarding Richard Dugdale, the 'Surey demoniac'. *J. E. Roberts, M.A. 1944 Manchester*

Duguit, Leon
Recent critiques of the doctrine of the sovereignty with special reference to the writings of Professor Leon Duguit. *W. D. Handcock, B.Litt. 1930 Oxford*

Duhallow
Place names and antiquities of the Barony of Duhallow. *M. J. Bowman, M.A. 1934 National University of Ireland*

Duhamel, Georges
A study in French of Georges Duhamel. *O. Abrioux, Ph.D. 1949 Aberdeen*

Dumas, Alexandre
Les femmes selon Dumas: une étude. *M. T. Gibson, M.A. 1915 Birmingham*

Dumas, Alexandre, the Younger
The ethical doctrine of Alexandre Dumas fils, as expressed in his plays. *T. Jones, M.A. 1941 Wales*

The social ideas of Dumas fils. *M. Gordon, M.A. 1924 Liverpool*

Dumfriesshire
The regional and economic geography of Dumfriesshire. *J. A. McIver, M.Sc. 1948 London, School of Economics and Political Science*

Dumping (Economics)
Dumping. *E. S. Mason, B.Litt. 1923 Oxford*

Dunbar, William
Dunbar's debt to Chaucer. *D. Burnicle, M.A. 1934 Birmingham*

William Dunbar and John Skelton. *J. W. Musson, M.A. 1939 Bristol*

Dundas, Henry, Viscount Melville
Henry Dundas and the government of India, 1784-1800. *D. Thornton, M.A. 1925 Liverpool*

Dunkers, The
The Dunkers: their origins, migrations, doctrines, and development. *J. T. Peters, Ph.D. 1942 Edinburgh*

Dunkirk
Cromwell and Mazarin, 1656-1658: an account of the Anglo-French alliance leading to the conquest of Dunkirk. *J. A. Williamson, M.A. 1909 London*

Dunlavin
Ancient history of Dunlavin. *P. Walsh, M.A. 1926 National University of Ireland*

Duns Scotus, John
The philosophy of John Duns Scotus. *C. R. S. Harris, Ph.D. 1924 Oxford*

The voluntarism of Duns Scotus. *T. F. McDonagh, M.A. 1923 National University of Ireland*

Dunstan, Saint
1. The life of St. Dunstan. 2. The work of St. Dunstan at Glastonbury. *J. K. Floyer, B.D. & D.D. 1922 Oxford*

Dunster
Feudal aspect of Domesday survey of Somerset and Dorset in connexion with the Barony of Moiun (Dunster Castle) and analogous feudal estates, based upon contemporary public and local records. *M. F. Moore, Ph.D. 1930 London, King's College*

Dupanloup, Félix Antoine Philibert
Mgr. Dupanloup as an educator. *P. D. Fox, M.A. 1949 National University of Ireland*

Dupin, Amandine, Baronne Dudevant
See Sand, George.

Duran, Profiat
Al t'he kaboteca (Be not like your fathers): a polemical work by Ephodi (Prophiat Duran), critically edited on the basis of manuscripts and provided with a translation. *I. Goodman, Ph.D. 1935 Glasgow*

Durham
The archaeology of Roman Durham. *K. A. Steer, Ph.D. 1938 Durham*

Civic government of Durham, 1780-1835. *M. Todd, M.A. 1924 Liverpool*

Durham Cathedral Priory
The administration and agrarian policy of the manors of Durham Cathedral Priory. *E. M. Halcrow, B.Litt. 1949 Oxford*

Durham, County
The changes of the Reformation period in Durham and Northumberland. *B. N. Wilson, Ph.D. 1939 Durham*

Durham, Diocese of
A calendar of the register of Cuthbert Tunstall, Bishop of Durham. *G. Hinde, Ph.D. 1933 London, External Degree*

Revival of Anglicanism during the Restoration period, with special reference to the diocese of Durham. *C. H. Beaglehole, M.Litt. 1947 Durham*

Durkheim, Emile
Durkheim's conception of religion. *V. T. Arsitch, B.Litt. 1922 Oxford*

Durkheim's social theory with special reference to the position of the individual in society. *J. Rowland, M.A. 1948 London, Bedford College*

The sociology of religion, with special reference to the works of Professor Durkheim and other writers to *L'Année Sociologique*. *A. W. Bonsey, B.Litt. 1930 Oxford*

Dutch Language
The influence of Middle Dutch and Middle Low German on English speech. *E. C. Llewellyn, B.Litt. 1930 Oxford*

A middle Dutch version of the *Speculum humanae salvationis*. *C. L. T. Hermus, Ph.D. 1937 London, External Degree*

Dutch Literature
See also Effen, J. van.

Justus van Effen and English influences in Dutch literature. *W. J. B. Pienaar, Ph.D. 1925 London*

The literary relations between Germany and the Netherlands in the sixteenth century. *M. Bülbring, M.A. 1939 London, University College*

Duty
The relation between the state and the individual considered in the light of its bearing on the conception of duty. *W. E. G. Sekyi, M.A. 1918 London*

Dye Industry
Studies in the history of dyeing. *C. Ross, Ph.D. 1946 London, University College*

Dyer, Edward, Sir
The life of Sir Edward Dyer, 1543-1607. *C. J. Reynolds, B.Litt. 1930 Oxford*

Dyer, John
The life and works of John Dyer. *K. W. Campbell, Cert.Litt. 1918 Oxford*

The life and writings of John Dyer (1701-1757). *A. H. Collins, M.A. 1930 London, King's College*

A study of John Dyer, in the light of new manuscript material. *E. Parker, B.Litt. 1938 Oxford*

Dyfi
The Dyfi: its people, antiquities, dialects, folklore and placenames studied in correlation to one another, with a special aim of ascertaining what degree of correlation there may be between physical anthropology, archaeology and dialect distribution. *I. C. Peate, M.A. 1924 Wales*

Easements
See Land (Law).

East India Company
See also India; Persia; Persian Gulf; Trade.

East India Company contd.
The activities of the English East India Company in Persia and the Persian Gulf, 1616-57. *W. C. Palmer, Ph.D. 1933 London, King's College*

An administrative study of the development of civil service in India during the Company's régime. *A. K. Ghosal, Ph.D. 1940 London, School of Economics and Political Science*

Commercial relations between India and England, 1600-1757. *B. Krishna, Ph.D. 1922 London*

The East India Co. crisis (1770-1773). *R. Beard, M.A. 1928 Birmingham*

East India Company's relations with Assam, 1771 to 1826. *S. K. Bhuyan, Ph.D. 1938 London, School of Oriental and African Studies*

History of the East India Company's settlement at Calcutta, 1711-1717, Vol. II. *C. R. Wilson, B.Litt. 1901 Oxford*

The history of the occupation and rural administration of Bengal by the English Company from the time of Clive to the permanent settlement under Cornwallis. *W. K. Firminger, B.Litt. 1913 Oxford*

The influence of the East India Company 'interest' on the English government, 1813-1833. *C. H. Philips, M.A. 1937 Liverpool*

The judicial administration of the East India Company in Bengal, 1765-1782. *B. B. Misra, Ph.D. 1947 London, School of Oriental and African Studies*

The organization of the English factories in the East Indies, 1600-1642. *M. W. Thomas, M.A. 1920 London*

Parliament and the affairs of the East India Company, 1765-1784. *G. F. Pecker, M.A. 1910 Liverpool*

The relations between Oudh and the East India Company from 1785 to 1801. *P. Basu, Ph.D. 1938 London, School of Oriental and African Studies*

The relations between the Board of Commissioners for the Affairs of India and the Court of Directors, 1784-1816. *P. Chandra, Ph.D. 1933 London, School of Economics and Political Science*

Revenue administration of the Sirkars under the E.I.C. down to 1802. *L. Sundaram, Ph.D. 1930 London, School of Oriental and African Studies*

Trade and war in the eastern seas, 1803-1810. *C. N. Parkinson, Ph.D. 1935 London, King's College*

East Indies
English expeditions to the Dutch East Indies during the Revolutionary and Napoleonic Wars. *S. G. Rainbow, M.A. 1933 London, East London College*

The geographical basis, character and organization of the import trade of London from the East Indies, with special reference to the twentieth century. *L. Brettle, B.Litt. 1930 Oxford*

The organization of the English factories in the East Indies, 1600-1642. *M. W. Thomas, M.A. 1920 London*

The Portuguese in India and the East Indies 1497-1548. *T. H. Jenkins, M.A. 1924 Birmingham*

East, Near
See Middle East.

Eastern Orthodox Church
See Orthodox Churches.

Eastern Question
See Middle East.

Ebbw Vale
The economic, industrial and social history of Ebbw Vale during the period 1775-1927, being a study in the origin and development of an industrial district of south Wales in all its aspects. *A. G. Jones, M.A. 1929 Wales*

Eccius, I.
Disputatio I. Eccii et M. Lutheri, Lipsiae, Labita 1519: translation with critical introduction and notes. *A. McPherson, Ph.D. 1931 Edinburgh*

Ecclesiastical Law
See Law, Ecclesiastical.

Eckhart, Johannes
The special character of Eckhart's mysticism studied with reference in particular to his German works. *S. E. Smith, B.Litt. 1946 Oxford*

Econometrics
The building of econometric models, with special reference to the investment process. *S. J. Prais, M.Com 1950 Birmingham*

Economic Geography
See Geography.

Economic History
See Economics: History.

Economics
See also Agriculture; Commodities; Co-operation; Demand; Dumping; Finance; Industry; Labour; Marketing; Ports and Harbours; Profit; Shipping; Trade; Trade Unions; Transport; Utility (Economics); Value (Economics); Wages and Salaries.

The application of certain Keynesian concepts to international trade, with special reference to the multiplier. *E. J. Mishan, M.Sc. 1948 London, School of Economics and Political Science*

Budget control: a study of fiscal policy as an instrument for regulating economic fluctuations. *K. Chang, M.A. 1947 Leeds*

Bunadas na h-economuíocta (The basis of economics). *S. MacCurtain, M.A. 1928 National University of Ireland*

The conception of surplus in theoretical economics. *A. Dasgupta, Ph.D. 1936 London, School of Economics and Political Science*

Economic nationalism. *M. Moore, M.Econ.Sc. 1943 National University of Ireland*

Economic phenomena before and after war. *S. Secerov, M.Sc. 1918 London*

The economics of reparations. *E. M. Sage, M.A. 1930 Wales*

Effects of war on national economy. *C. Morris, M.A. 1945 National University of Ireland*

The equilibrium analysis of a monetary economy. *S. P. Chambers, M.Sc. 1934 London, School of Economics and Political Science*

Essay on economic planning. *J. Tobin, M.Econ.Sc. 1938 National University of Ireland*

The ethics of economic values. *P. Byrne, M.A. 1932 National University of Ireland*

Four essays in economic inertia. *D. Kopanitsas, M.Sc. 1950 Cambridge*

Government planning: changing opinions, 1931-1947. *R. G. Steward, M.Sc. 1949 London, School of Economics and Political Science*

Industrial fluctuations in a changing economy. *G. L. S. Shackle, Ph.D. 1937 London, School of Economics and Political Science*

An luach sa chóus eacnomaidheachta fé stiúir (Value in a planned economy). *P. J. Lynch, Ph.D. 1939 National University of Ireland*

The new economics and industrial capacity. *J. D. Richards, M.Com. 1936 Birmingham*

Outline of international economic disintegration and reconstruction. *M. Sheehy, M.Econ.Sc. 1944 National University of Ireland*

The principle of official independence. *R. M. Dawson, D.Sc. 1922 London*

The problem of economic development of backward countries (with special reference to Poland). *S. F. Gawel, B.Litt. 1947 Oxford*

The psychological factor in economic theory. *B. H. Higgins, M.Sc. 1935 London, School of Economics and Political Science*

Psychological laws and economic activity. *R. T. Harry, M.A. 1924 Wales*

The psychology of economics. *T. Templeton, Ph.D. 1927 Glasgow*

The relative influence of money and credit on general prices. *J. Rejan, Ph.D. 1922 Edinburgh*

Restrictive intervention. *J. W. Burton, Ph.D. 1942 London, School of Economics and Political Science*

Studies in economic development and international trade. *I. G. Patel, Ph.D. 1950 Cambridge*

A study of certain industries in relation to increasing and diminishing returns. *G. T. Jones, Ph.D. 1929 Cambridge*

A study of the teaching of Jesus in its application to modern economic problems. *M. Charles, B.Litt. 1935 Oxford*

Theory and practice of corporative economics. *K. White, B.Litt. 1937 Oxford*

War economics of primary producing countries. *A. R. Prest, Ph.D. 1949 Cambridge*

Economics: History
See also Cairnes, J. E.; Cantillon, R.; Comte, A.; Godwin, W.; Keynes, J. M., 1st Baron; Longfield, S. M.; MacLeod, H. D.; Malthus, T. R.; Marshall, A.; Mill, J. S.; Morris, W.; Ricardo, D.; Roscher, W.; Senior, N. W.; Thornton, H.; Tucker, J.

The concept of natural law in the history of economic thought. *M. Sweeney, M.A. 1947 National University of Ireland*

Economics: History contd.
The development of the concept of surplus in economic thought from Mun to Mill. *R. L. Meek, Ph.D. 1949 Cambridge*

Economic theories of the nineteenth century which were based on a critical study of the conception of nationality. *P. Henry, M.Econ.Sc. 1941 National University of Ireland*

The growth of economic individualism in England in modern times: Part I : introductory to the end of the Middle Ages. *H. M. Robertson, M.A. 1926 Leeds*

Influence of Malthus on economic thought. *C. S. Harrington, M.A. 1915 National University of Ireland*

The inter-relations of balances of payments and internal economic conditions, considered with special reference to selected countries in the period 1927-31. *S. D. Pollard, B.Litt. 1935 Oxford*

Montesquieu: his political and economic ideas. *P. Jordan, Ph.D. 1930 London, School of Economics and Political Science*

The place of social and economic history in education. *M. V. Gregory, M.Ed. 1929 Manchester*

Primitive economics with special reference to culture contact. *M. H. Read, Ph.D. 1934 London, School of Economics and Political Science*

Economics: Study and Teaching
The case for teaching economics in schools. *K. van den Toorn, M.Ed. 1939 Leeds*

Studies in economic methodology. *S. P. du T. Viljoen, Ph.D. 1928 London*

The teaching of economics in the secondary schools of India. *M. P. Sarkar, M.Ed. 1927 Leeds*

Economics, Agricultural
See Agriculture.

Economics, Welfare
See Welfare Economics.

Edda
The Volsung episode in the *Prose Edda* (*Edda Snorra Sturlasonar*): the Volsung episode in relation to its sources. *M. Townend, M.A. 1942 Leeds*

Edgeworth, Maria
Maria Edgeworth; a study in Anglo-Irish literature. *E. M. MacCarthy, M.A. 1934 National University of Ireland*

Maria Edgeworth: her place in the history of the English novel. *E. M. F. Samson, B.Litt. 1925 Oxford*

Maria Edgeworth and the novel. *E. G. Ewens, Ph.D. 1946 Dublin, Trinity College*

Edinburgh
The Burgh of the Canongate and its court. *A. H. Anderson, Ph.D. 1949 Edinburgh*

Edinburgh Magazine
Edinburgh Magazine: 1739-1826. *D. S. M. Imrie, Ph.D. 1936 Saint Andrew's*

Edmund, Saint
La Passiun de Seint Edmund (Gonville and Caius College ms. 435). *C. W. J. Higson, Ph.D. 1937 Cambridge*

Education: General
For the study and teaching of particular subjects, see under the subject. For the education of handicapped children, see also Child Psychology; Children, Handicapped; Children, Retarded. See also Cinema; Co-education; Examinations; Girls: Education; Handicrafts; Intelligence Testing; Women: Education.

Education and employment: a study of the employments of juveniles with reference to vocational guidance and education. *B. P. Jones, M.Ed. 1927 Manchester*

Education and employment. *A. Oldroyd, M.A. 1915 Liverpool*

Education and the creation of a common culture. *W. S. Black, M.Ed. 1937 Manchester*

Education in relation to employment in a rural area and in an industrial area. *C. B. Bardsley, M.A. 1939 Liverpool*

Education in some ideal commonwealths. *L. G. Beddis, M.Ed. 1932 Manchester*

Freedom in education: a critical interpretation of some historical views. *W. J. McCallister, Ph.D. 1930 London, External Degree*

Instinct and education. *J. T. Mulley, M.Ed. 1933 Leeds*

An investigation into some aspects of the problem of transfer of training. *G. P. Meredith, M.Ed. 1926 Leeds*

Education: General contd.
The mathematical definition of education. *C. Gategno, M.A. 1948 London, Institute of Education*

Music and education. *G. H. Jones, M.A. 1932 Birmingham*

Personality and its relation to the school as an ideal society. *W. N. Chalmers, M.A. 1924 Liverpool*

The place of practical instruction in education. *A. B. Neal, M.A. 1923 Wales*

The place of social and economic history in education. *M. V. Gregory, M.Ed. 1929 Manchester*

The place of the aesthetic in education, as determined by changing social conditions, and its place in the curriculum. *A. M. B. Rosevere, M.A. 1940 Reading*

Practical education. *K. M. Yusufuddin, M.A. 1930 Leeds*

The present position of the discussion concerning formal training. *W. J. Owen, M.A. 1920 Wales*

The principle of individuality in education. *S. J. Willis, Ph.D. 1930 Dublin, Trinity College*

Problems of democratic education. *M. Kaye, Ph.D. 1928 London*

Right to educate. *J. J. Byrne, M.A. 1942 National University of Ireland*

The sea in education. *J. E. de C. Ireland, Ph.D. 1950 Dublin, Trinity College*

Social contacts of education. *J. H. Nicholson, M.A. 1923 Bristol*

Education: History
See also Arnold, M.; Arnold, T.; Ascham, R.; Campan, J. L.; Condorcet, J. A. N. C. de, Marquis; Croce, B.; Dewey, J.; Dupanloup, F. A. P.; Fénelon, F. de S. de la M.; Ford, J.; Froebel, F. W. A.; Grundtvig, N. F. S.; Hegel, G. W. F.; Herbart, J. F.; Hey, S.; Hogg, Q.; Jones, G.; Kay-Shuttleworth, J. P., Sir; Kingsley, C.; Laurie, S. S.; Luther, M.; Maintenon, F. d'A. de, Marquise; Molière, J. B. P.; Montessori, M.; Mulcaster, R.; Mundella, A. J.; Owen, R.; Pestalozzi, J. H.; Quintilian; Rabelais, F.; Rousseau, J. J.; Ruskin, J.; Spencer, H.; Stow, D.; Stuart, J.; Wyse, T., Sir.

Changes in educational ideals from Cicero and Quintilian to the Carolingian renaissance. *A. Hurworth, M.A. 1923 Leeds*

Christianity and education in the first five centuries A.D. *J. V. Patton, B.Litt. 1916 Oxford*

The contribution of certain nineteenth century scientists to the development of educational values. *L. W. Chaundy, M.A. 1950 Reading*

Different views of the nature of mental activity, more especially in connection with educational theory. *G. A. Lewis, M.A. 1908 Wales*

Education and the social novel. *J. I. B. Johnson, M.A. 1947 Bristol*

Education in the ideal states of the seventeenth century. *N. G. Cottrell, M.A. 1935 Birmingham*

Education with a tradition: an account of the educational work of the Society of the Sacred Heart, 1800-1935. *M. F. M. O'Leary, Ph.D. 1935 London, External Degree*

The educational ideas of John Locke, 1632-1704. *J. Cummings, M.A. 1932 Liverpool*

The educational ideas of the Encyclopaedists. *T. J. James, Ph.D. 1946 London, External Degree*

The educational ideas of Wolfgang Ratke. *G. H. Turnbull, M.A. 1913 Liverpool*

The educational ideas of Wordsworth. *H. E. Winn, M.A. 1925 London*

Educational principles in the practice of Don Bosco and his successors. *J. L. O'Reilly, M.A. 1948 National University of Ireland*

The educational theories of François Rabelais. *A. G. Morris, M.Ed. 1939 Manchester*

The educational theory of the English Utilitarians. *A. H. Cheshire, M.A. 1923 Liverpool*

The English Utilitarians and education. *D. Gandy, M.A. 1921 Liverpool*

An initial study of Quintilian's theory of education. *B. J. Ward, M.A. 1943 National University of Ireland*

An investigation into the extent to which a social conception of education is to be found in the works of English writers of the eighteenth and nineteenth centuries. *A. W. Parry, M.A. 1911 Wales*

J. J. Rousseau et son influence dans l'enseignement pratique, surtout en France et en Angleterre. *A. J. Walker, M.A. 1906 Birmingham*

Education: History contd.
John Sturm. *J. Harvey, Ph.D. 1926 Glasgow*

Joseph Priestley, LL.D., F.R.S., and his influence on eighteenth century education. *C. J. Rhodes, M.Ed. 1932 Manchester*

La théorie de l'éducation chez Molière. *B. L. V. Kay, M.A. 1912 Liverpool*

The making of the ratio-studiorum, 1548-1599 A.D. *A. B. Farrell, Ph.D. 1932 National University of Ireland*

Na h-Iosánaigh agus aithbheochaint an l'éighinn cuimre (The Jesuits and the Renaissance). *S. O'Catháin, Ph.D. 1941 National University of Ireland*

The place of rhetoric in education in the first century A.D. and at the present day. *M. F. Moor, B.Litt. 1922 Oxford*

The political and educational ideas and ideals of John Knox. *D. C. B. Gordon, Ph.D. 1926 Edinburgh*

Quintilian's 'orator' as the type of the educated man. *H. M. Darbyshire, M.A. 1928 Liverpool*

Quintilian's theory of education. *R. J. Griffiths, M.A. 1914 Wales*

Quintilian's theory of education. *N. O. Parry, M.A. 1919 Wales*

Rabelais the educator. *F. W. Moss, M.Ed. 1928 Leeds*

The relation of social and educational theory at the opening of the nineteenth century. *G. J. Kenwrick, M.A. 1927 London*

The Renaissance humanists and education. *W. J. Campion, Ph.D. 1940 National University of Ireland*

The revival of learning at Constantinople in the eleventh century, with special reference to Michael Psellos. *J. M. Hussey, B.Litt. 1932 Oxford*

Some aspects of seventeenth century learning as exhibited in the *Davideis* of Abraham Cowley. *J. F. Kermode, M.A. 1947 Liverpool*

A study of H. G. Wells's contributions to education. *T. G. Evans, M.A. 1931 Wales*

The study of rhetoric in England as represented in the educational writings of the sixteenth century, and a classified catalogue of educational writings published in England and of English educational works published abroad before 1640. *G. D. M. Davies, M.A. 1934 London, King's College*

The teaching of Latin by the Jesuits, with special reference to the *ratio studiorum*. *B. C. Grant, M.A. 1920 Wales*

The teaching of Latin by the Jesuits, with special reference to the *ratio studiorum*. *D. B. Jones, M.A. 1922 Wales*

The theory and aim of education; some Thomistic principles. *P. O'C. Ryan, M.A. 1929 National University of Ireland*

The theory of education in Plato's *Laws*. *H. W. Lemon, M.Ed. 1920 Manchester*

Vives and aspects of renaissance education. *K. O'Shea, M.A. 1926 National University of Ireland*

Wordsworth and education. *P. Sandbach, M.A. 1926 Liverpool*

Education: Profession
The Arab conception of the ideal teacher in Arabic pedagogical literature. *G. D. Shahla, M.A. 1938 London, Institute of Education*

The assessment of teaching ability with special reference to men students in training. *J. H. Panton, M.A. 1934 London, Institute of Education*

The clergyman, the schoolmaster and the governess in the novel of the eighteenth century. *H. D. Pearson, M.A. 1920 London*

A comparative study of the training of full-time teachers of commercial subjects in England and France 1946 to 1949. *T. A. Hempstock, M.A. 1950 Sheffield*

The development of university participation in the training of teachers in England and Wales. *M. G. Goss, M.A. 1949 London, King's College*

The dominie in English literature. *J. E. Mason, M.A. 1928 Birmingham*

An enquiry into the development of training of teachers. *A. B. Berlas, M.A. 1949 London, Institute of Education*

Education: Profession contd.
An experiment of group methods of teaching English composition with some consideration of their effects on attainment and attitude and a sociometric study of the groups involved. *J. E. Richardson, M.A. 1948 London, Institute of Education*

A functional conception of the training of post-primary school teachers, with special reference to New Zealand. *A. H. W. Harte, Ph.D. 1948 London, Institute of Education*

The history of the training of teachers for secondary schools in England (approx. 1846 to 1930). *M. G. Fitch, M.A. 1931 London, King's College*

The investigation of factors useful in predicting teaching ability with special reference to the teaching of mathematics and science. *W. A. Skinner, M.Ed. 1947 Manchester*

Le pédant dans la comédie italienne du cinquecento, et sa descendance directe dans la comédie française jusqu'à Molière. *A. Gill, M.A. 1934 Manchester*

The planning, design and equipment of residential colleges for the training of teachers. *T. O. Haunch, M.A. 1950 Sheffield*

The problem of tenure of assistant masters in secondary schools. *A. Sinclair, M.Ed. 1940 Manchester*

Problems of teacher training in Nigeria considered in connection with educational developments in British tropical Africa. *T. T. Solaru, M.A. 1948 London, Institute of Education*

The relation of certain problems to the training of teachers in the United States, Ontario, France, Scotland and Germany. *O. E. Ault, Ph.D. 1935 Edinburgh*

The relations between schoolmaster and administrator: from the point of view of the secondary school, with special reference to: the legislation and developments during recent years; a comparison of the systems of England and those of Germany and France; the relations existing between the internal (the schoolmaster) and the external (the governors and director) authority of the school. *J. T. Hewson, M.Ed. 1931 Durham*

Schools and schoolmasters in Dickens. *W. R. Swale, M.A. 1933 Birmingham*

Selection of students for training as teachers. *G. E. R. Burroughs, Ph.D. 1950 Birmingham*

The social and economic status of the elementary school teacher in England, 1833-1870. *G. W. Hughes, M.Ed. 1936 Manchester*

Some aspects of the social position of the professional teacher at various periods in the history of education. *C. Chegwidden, M.A. 1933 Wales*

A statistical study of the judgments of a group of teachers as shown by their preferences among their pupils. *D. Cockburn, M.Ed. 1949 Durham*

A study of adaptation, with special reference to teachers. *D. M. Daldy, M.Sc. 1939 Bristol*

A study of attitude towards teaching as a career. *K. M. Evans, M.A. 1946 London, King's College*

A study of the attitude of women (students, teachers and former teachers) towards teaching as a career. *J. M. Champ, M.A. 1948 London, Institute of Education*

A study of the attitudes of teachers in England towards their course of training. *T. V. Thimme Gowda, M.A. 1946 London, Institute of Education*

A study of the factor pattern of the social conscience of intending teachers. *C. H. J. Smith, M.A. 1947 London, Institute of Education*

The teacher's functions. *F. McPolin, Ph.D. 1941 National University of Ireland*

The training of a teacher. *T. J. Daly, M.A. 1914 National University of Ireland*

The training of teachers in England and Wales: a critical survey. *L. G. E. Jones, Ph.D. 1926 London*

The training of teachers in England and Wales during the nineteenth century. *R. W. Rich, Ph.D. 1934 London, External Degree*

The training of teachers in India. *S. C. Chatterji, Ph.D. 1942 Dublin, Trinity College*

The training of women teachers in British India. *S. Webb, M.A. 1930 London, King's College*

The work of the British and Foreign School Society in the training of teachers. *E. L. Hewlett, M.Ed. 1932 Manchester*

Education: Pedagogics
See also Parents and Teachers; Psychodrama.

Education: Pedagogics contd.

An approach to the study of education in the light of an evolutionary psychology. *I. H. Hoskins, M.A. 1948 London, Institute of Education*

The development of scientific pedagogy. *E. Quine, B.Sc. 1914 Liverpool*

Education as a pure science. *A. Pinsent, M.A. 1921 London*

An examination of benefits to be derived from school educational visits. *J. A. Dicker, M.A. 1940 London, Institute of Education*

An experimental investigation into some effects upon children of infant school methods based on spontaneous activity as compared with more formal methods. *D. E. M. Gardner, M.A. 1940 Leeds*

Experimental work in educational guidance in a mixed selective central school. *W. E. Davies, M.Ed. 1943 Manchester*

Extra curricular activity: its place and scope in the two senior forms of a secondary (grammar) school. *M. D. B. Folland, M.A. 1946 Birmingham*

An historical enquiry into the teaching of history in the elementary training college and public elementary school, with some consideration of both the development of the study of history and of pedagogic theory in relation to the problem of teaching history in the training college. *F. L. Bowman, M.Ed. 1919 Manchester*

Intellectual and moral claims in education:an historico-philosophical argument. *J. Bowman, M.A. 1929 National University of Ireland*

Open-air schools. *T. H. Bridson, M.Ed. 1942 Manchester*

The personal relationship in teaching. *A. W. Hollis, M.A. 1935 Birmingham*

The principle of balance in the curriculum. *R. P. H. Blore, M.A. 1921 London*

Problems of the two-teacher school. *M. F. Cronin, M.A. 1935 National University of Ireland*

The project method, illustrated from the history of India during the British period. *H. S. Bhai, M.Ed. 1935 Leeds*

Psychological theories of instinct and their influence on educational theory and practice. *B. C. Kar, M.A. 1949 London, Institute of Education*

The relationship between interest, aptitude and achievement as shown by an enquiry into curricula in four secondary modern schools. *E. M. Uprichard, Ph.D. 1947 London, Institute of Education*

Saint Augustine's philosophy of liberal education. *T. Callaghan, Ph.D. 1942 National University of Ireland*

The school curriculum in relation to life. *N. I. Parvathi, M.A. 1934 Leeds*

School journeys and visits: their place in modern education. *R. B. Grove, M.A. 1940 Leeds*

School societies: their organization as part of the curriculum. *M. Clapham, M.Ed. 1939 Leeds*

The scope and value of the open-air school. *M. E. Cliff, M.D. 1934 Manchester*

A study of interest in school subjects among secondary school pupils at different ages (a contribution to educational guidance). *C. M. Lambert, M.A. 1944 London, Institute of Education*

A study of the layout of school books in its relevant appreciation and comprehension. *A. E. Philpot, M.A. 1948 London, Institute of Education*

Teaching pupils how to study, with special reference to the study of history. *S. A. Williams, M.A. 1918 London*

The theory of punishment, with special reference to education. *G. E. Lee, M.A. 1917 London*

The use of schools as instruments of democracy. *C. J. Buckley, M.Sc. 1948 London, School of Economics and Political Science*

The Wytham scheme: an experiment in open-air education. *L. S. Smedley, M.A. 1942 Sheffield*

Education: Administration
See also Trusts.

The administration of education, 1902-1914. *L. F. W. White, Ph.D. 1934 London, School of Economics and Political Science*

Divisional executives under the Education Act, 1944. *G. W. R. Lines, M.Ed. 1948 Leeds*

Education under changing government, with special reference to Alsace since the Great War. *C. R. S. Manders, M.A. 1939 London, Institute of Education*

Education: Administration contd.

Educational administration. *K. R. Ramaswamy, M.Ed. 1929 Leeds*

The history and character of educational inspection in England. *J. Leese, Ph.D. 1934 London, King's College*

The position of Part III Authorities in the English education system. *N. B. Mortimer, Ph.D. 1946 London, External Degree*

The relations between schoolmaster and administrator: from the point of view of the secondary school, with special reference to: the legislation and developments during recent years; a comparison of the systems of England and those of Germany and France; the relations existing between the internal (the schoolmaster) and the external (the governors and director) authority of the school. *J. T. Hewson, M.Ed. 1931 Durham*

The reorganization of an independent school. *F. W. Hodgson, M.A. 1950 Birmingham*

Some aspects of educational administration, with special reference to its organization and problems in boroughs and county boroughs. *J. E. Smart, Ph.D. 1930 London, School of Economics and Political Science*

Some aspects of English educational administration. *F. G. E. Manns, M.Sc. 1936 London, School of Economics and Political Science*

The working of the principle of co-option, with special reference to education committees. *T. Chapman, M.A. 1938 Manchester*

Education: Africa

The principals and mechanisms of education among primitive peoples and the applications of these in European-controlled education of the natives in Africa. *T. J. A. Yates, Ph.D. 1933 London, School of Economics and Political Science*

Education: America: North American Indians

A monograph on the native education among the North American Indians, and its effect upon adult behaviour. *J. M. Evans, M.Ed. 1923 Manchester*

Education: Bahamas

A history of Bahamian education. *A. D. Peggs, M.Ed. 1947 Durham*

Education: British Somaliland

Education in British Somaliland. *T. R. Holland, M.A. 1949 Reading*

Education: Burma

Comparative survey of education in Burma and a few countries with a rural background, e.g., Turkey and Scandinavia. *B. Ghosh, M.A. 1947 London, Institute of Education*

A survey of the development of education in Burma. *M. Ohn, M.Ed. 1940 Leeds*

A survey of the history of education in Burma before the British conquest and after. *K. Maung, M.A. 1929 London*

Education: Ceylon

The bilingual problem in Ceylon. *T. D. Jayasuriya, M.A. 1931 London, Day Training College*

A crticial review of researches in the United Kingdom on selection for secondary education, with suggestions for their application to Ceylon. *D. G. Sugathadasa, M.A. 1948 London, Institute of Education*

Early history of Buddhist education in Ceylon (third century B.C. to sixteenth century A.D.). *D. D. Samaraweera, M.A. 1949 London, Institute of Education*

Education in Ceylon. *D. J. N. Perera, M.A. 1920 London*

Education in Ceylon since British occupation. *A. Cumaraswamy, M.A. 1932 London, King's College*

English and English education in Ceylon. *E. F. C. Ludowyk, Ph.D. 1936 Cambridge*

Some influences that changed the educational system of Ceylon between 1900 and 1945. *P. Saverimuttu, M.A. 1949 London, Institute of Education*

Education: China

Ancient and modern educational theory in China. *T. I. Ho, Ph.D. 1936 London, Institute of Education*

Education in modern China, with special reference to the influence upon it of Western civilization. *V. W. W. S. Purcell, Ph.D. 1936 Cambridge*

The treatment of Europe in Chinese school textbooks. *H. T. Wu, M.A. 1949 London, Institute of Education*

The village school and rural reconstruction in China. *C. S. Wang, M.A. 1941 London, Institute of Education*

Education: Denmark

N. F. S. Grundtvig and the Danish Folk High School Movement. *G. N. M. Davies, Ph.D. 1928 Wales*

Report on existing educational institutions in Denmark. *F. E. B. Rost, M.A. 1928 London*

Education: East Africa

The application of psychological tests to certain problems of native education in East Africa. *R. A. C. Oliver, Ph.D. 1933 Edinburgh*

Education: East Indies

The education of overseas Chinese: a comparative study of Hong Kong, Singapore and the East Indies. *T. C. Cheng, M.A. 1949 London, Institute of Education*

Education: Egypt

Education in Egypt before British control. *J. Williams, M.Ed. 1934 Durham*

An enquiry into inequalities of educational opportunities in Egypt. *H. M. Ammar, M.A. 1949 London, Institute of Education*

An examination into the present educational opportunities for Egyptian girls in Egypt. *P. Sageman, M.A. 1937 London, King's College*

French and British influences in Egyptian education. *S. I. Hammad, M.A. 1949 London, Institute of Education*

The organisation of education in Egypt, with special reference to the future of elementary (primary) education. *S. A. A. M. Shehata, M.A. 1940 London, Institute of Education*

A study of certain aspects of education in England and in Egypt. *M. H. Makhzangi, M.A. 1933 Birmingham*

Education: France
See also Port Royal; Saint-Cyr.

A comparative study in the methods employed in England and France for the grouping of children and young persons in different types of schools. *S. P. Chatterji, Ph.D. 1936 London, King's College*

Education et morale dans les écoles en France. *E. F. Freeman, M.A. 1934 Birmingham*

A study of the respective places and contributions of parent and teacher in child education, with special reference to the parent and parent-teacher organizations in France and England. *B. E. S. Sturgiss, M.A. 1937 Bristol*

Education: France: History

Condorcet as an educationalist. *C. E. Gittins, M.A. 1935 Wales*

A contribution to the history of the educational tradition inherited from Madame de Maintenon. *M. S. Smith, Ph.D. 1927 London*

The 'Ecole Unique' in France: an historical survey of the movement, an appreciation of its aims, with some reference to political and social implications, and an account of the objects hitherto achieved. *W. H. Porter, M.A. 1938 London, Courtauld Institute of Art*

Education and the French Revolution. *J. G. Worth, B.Litt. 1921 Oxford*

Education in France during the Revolutionary and Napoleonic era (1789-1815). *E. W. Bishop, M.A. 1927 London*

Education of women in the early nineteenth century: some French points of view. *L. Gavan Duffy, M.A. 1916 National University of Ireland*

Education under changing government, with special reference to Alsace since the Great War. *C. R. S. Manders, M.A. 1939 London, Institute of Education*

Educational theories of the French Revolution. *J. Duffy, M.A. 1949 National University of Ireland*

The establishment of state intermediate education in France. *W. M. Brownlie, Ph.D. 1934 Glasgow*

La comparaison des idées de Rousseau et de Fénelon sur l'education. *A. H. Ashworth, M.A. 1911 Liverpool*

La place de Rousseau dans le mouvement pédagogique en France aux dix-septième et dix-huitième siècles. *M. J. Smith, Ph.D. 1935 Edinburgh*

La renaissance de l'éducation en France, 1764-1833. *F. V. van der Byl, Ph.D. 1934 Dublin, Trinity College*

The little schools of Port Royal. *H. Clive-Barnard, B.Litt. 1911 Oxford*

L'Université impériale. *W. I. Moore, M.A. 1920 London*

Education: France: History contd.
Schools in Gaul from the defeat of the Franks by Julian to their rise under Chlodowig. *T. J. Haarhoff, B.Litt. 1918 Oxford*

Studies in the history and influence of the education of boys at Port Royal and in the older Oratorian colleges of France. *W. N. Littlejohns, M.A. 1948 London, King's College*

Education: Germany
Education development in the county of Aachen after the war, with specific reference to teachers. *J. T. Gleave, M.Ed. 1947 Durham*

The influence of the Youth Movement on German education. *G. Thomson, Ph.D. 1935 Glasgow*

The system of education in Germany since the war. *G. U. Bhatt, M.Ed. 1931 Leeds*

Education: Gold Coast
The provision and administration of education in the Gold Coast from 1765 to 1865. *F. L. Bartels, M.A. 1949 London, Institute of Education*

Education: Great Britain
See also Diffusion of Useful Knowledge, Society for the; National Society, The.

Breaks with tradition: an inquiry, with special reference to the gradual development of the industrial element in education. *B. Fitzpatrick, M.A. 1938 National University of Ireland*

Catholic continuity in English education. *M. R. O'Nealon, M.A. 1933 National University of Ireland*

Changes in the trend and distribution of our school population, and their effects on education. *R. S. Walshaw, M.Ed. 1940 Manchester*

A comparative study in the methods employed in England and France for the grouping of children and young persons in different types of schools. *S. P. Chatterji, Ph.D. 1936 London, King's College*

A comparative study of Indian and English education. *R. N. Mohanty, M.A. 1940 Leeds*

A comparison of the educational system of Athens (400-300 B.C.) with that of England at the present day. *H. V. Loseby, M.Ed. 1934 Leeds*

A critical estimate of the educational theory and practice of the Society of Friends as seen in their schools in England. *W. A. C. Stewart, Ph.D. 1947 London, Institute of Education*

The development of the study of the national language, literature and history in the educational system of Wales. *J. Hughes, M.A. 1922 Wales*

The Education Act, 1944, and its development from earlier legislation. *M. Harrison, M.A. 1945 Leeds*

Education in Caernarvonshire, considered in relation to the social and cultural background. *J. L. Morgan-Jones, B.Litt. 1938 Oxford*

Education in rural England. *W. C. Primmer, M.Ed. 1945 Manchester*

The education of the crippled child in England. *N. Garry, M.A. 1933 Leeds*

Educational experience in the present war-time army and its bearing on national problems of education. *E. F. Wilson, M.Ed. 1944 Leeds*

The foundations of Welsh education: a study of the relationship of an educational system to its social environment. *E. R. Thomas, M.A. 1943 Birmingham*

Height and weight of school children in East Sussex. *W. R. Dunstan, M.Sc. 1923 London*

The history and character of educational inspection in England. *J. Leese, Ph.D. 1934 London, King's College*

An investigation into the interests and personal attitudes of adolescents educated in schools organized according to the Dalton Plan. *R. M. Beard, M.A. 1949 London, Institute of Education*

An investigation into the social and educational aspects of pupil migration in Scotland. *H. S. Mackintosh, Ph.D. 1941 Aberdeen*

Myopia and the education of the myopic scholar in Scotland. *A. M. MacGillivray, M.D. 1930 Saint Andrew's*

The next step in education: raising the school-leaving age to fifteen years. *A. Lewis, M.Ed. 1931 Manchester*

Nonconformist academies in Wales (1662-1862). *H. P. Roberts, M.A. 1922 Liverpool*

The operation of the Education Act of 1936 in a county area. *W. F. Herbert, M.Ed. 1943 Manchester*

Education: Great Britain contd.
Problems of population and education in the new housing estates, with special reference to Norris Green. *N. Williams, M.A. 1938 Liverpool*

Salient features of Scottish education. *W. Meiklejohn, M.A. 1931 National University of Ireland*

Some aspects of feminine education in England during the seventeenth century. *F. Cameron, M.A. 1949 Liverpool*

Some aspects of needed educational reform. *M. Harrison, M.Ed. 1942 Leeds*

Some implications of post-war educational reconstruction in the Bristol area. *G. H. Sylvester, M.A. 1944 Bristol*

The state and compulsory education. *F. Murray, M.A. 1943 National University of Ireland*

A study of certain aspects of education in England and in Egypt. *M. H. Makhzangi, M.A. 1933 Birmingham*

A study of the respective places and contributions of parent and teacher in child education, with special reference to the parent and parent-teacher organizations in France and England. *B. E. S. Sturgiss, M.A. 1937 Bristol*

The supply of education in England and the growth of public provision, 1833-1921. *D. H. Coulson, M.Ed. 1939 Leeds*

West Ham, its educational problems and its educational facilities. *H. W. Brand, M.A. 1935 London, King's College*

Education: Great Britain: History
The activities of Catholics in the matter of education in England. *A. P. Braddock, M.A. 1917 London*

The administration of education, 1902-1914. *L. F. W. White, Ph.D. 1934 London, School of Economics and Political Science*

The aims and methods of the English humanist educators of the sixteenth century. *J. S. Williams, M.A. 1914 Liverpool*

1. The ancient and modern learning of England. 2. The *Battle of the Books. A. C. L. Guthkelch, M.A. 1907 London*

The attitude of the Welsh Independents towards working class movements, including public education, from 1815 to 1870. *R. I. Parry, M.A. 1931 Wales*

The Bengali Muslims and English education (1765-1835). *M. F. Rahman, M.A. 1948 London, Institute of Education*

A brief history of education in Durham County in the eighteenth century, with a special reference to elementary education. *H. W. C. Eisel, M.Ed. 1941 Durham*

The career of A. J. Mundella, with special reference to his Sheffield connections. *M. Higginbotham, M.A. 1941 Sheffield*

Church and chapel as sources and centres of education in Wales during the second half of the nineteenth century. *L. S. Jones, M.A. 1940 Liverpool*

The Church of England's contribution to popular education in England after 1833. *C. K. F. Brown, B.Litt. 1941 Oxford*

A comparison of English and Scottish education, 1870-1948. *B. Dutt, M.Ed. 1950 Leeds*

The conflict of social, political and religious ideals in English education, 1660-1714. *L. W. Cowie, M.A. 1947 London, King's College*

The contribution of Methodism to popular education, 1800-1850. *H. F. Mathews, M.A. 1946 Liverpool*

The contribution of the Evangelical revival to the philosophy and practice of education. *A. W. Morton, D.Phil. 1949 Oxford*

A critical and historical study of the relations between the State and education from 1886 to 1926. *E. Whitehead, B.Litt. 1934 Oxford*

The development and a criticism of the theory and practice of education as found in imaginative literature of the nineteenth century and after. *H. M. Hooper, M.A. 1920 London*

The development of education in Bury to 1870. *H. Hope, M.Ed. 1933 Manchester*

The development of education in the Isle of Man. *E. W. Corbett, M.Ed. 1931 Manchester*

The development of education in Barnsley in the nineteenth century, prior to direct state intervention. *H. C. Hillary, M.A. 1941 Sheffield*

Education: Great Britain: History contd.
The development of education in Nottingham during the nineteenth and the early twentieth century with special reference to the history of University College. *E. M. Becket, M.A. 1922 London*

The development of education in Sunderland during the nineteenth century. *A. C. M. Herdson, M.Ed. 1931 Durham*

The development of Parliamentary opinion in respect to education, 1832-1870. *M. K. Wilkinson, M.A. 1925 Wales*

The development of primary and post-primary education in England during the present century. *S. N. Sen, M.A. 1937 Leeds*

The development of subscription charity schools in England and Wales, from the close of the seventeenth to the close of the eighteenth century, with special reference to London and district. *H. J. Larcombe, Ph.D. 1928 London*

Early Quaker education. *D. G. B. Hubbard, M.A. 1939 London, King's College*

The Education Act of 1870: an analysis of underlying ideas and opinions, and their influence on the English educational system. *A. H. Skillicorn, M.Sc. 1927 London*

Education and industrialism: a study of the way in which changes in industrial organizations have led to changes in the use of child labour, and to the growth in England of a system of education based on compulsory school attendance. *C. J. Gill, M.A. 1938 Liverpool*

Education and the English industrial revolution. *V. C. Vaman Rao, Ph.D. 1939 Dublin, Trinity College*

Education in Aberdeenshire before 1872. *I. J. Simpson, Ph.D. 1942 Aberdeen*

Education in England in the middle ages. *A. W. Parry, D.Sc. 1919 London*

Education in the Commonwealth, 1642-60. *E. W. Bishop, Ph.D. 1942 London, King's College*

The education of children engaged in industry in England, 1833-76. *A. H. Robson, Ph.D. 1930 London, King's College*

The education of English Catholics, 1559-1800. *W. F. Hastings, M.A. 1923 London*

The education of English women in the seventeenth century. *P. W. Smith, M.A. 1921 London*

The educational activities of Baptists in England during the eighteenth and nineteenth centuries with particular reference to the Northwest. *J. E. Watson, M.A. 1947 Liverpool*

Educational aspects of the Romantic Movement in Britain. *A. R. Paterson, Ph.D. 1941 Glasgow*

Educational needs and opportunities in English villages, 1870-1902. *P. G. Byles, B.Litt. 1925 Oxford*

The educational work of Robert Owen. *A. M. Black, Ph.D. 1949 Saint Andrew's*

The effect of the Education Act of 1918 on future local educational organization. *J. W. Murray, M.A. 1923 Liverpool*

The effect of the Reformation on the supply of schools in England during the sixteenth century. *F. F. Rigby, M.Ed. 1941 Manchester*

English Catholic education from the Reformation to Catholic emancipation (1580-1829). *M. V. Sweeney, M.Ed. 1946 Leeds*

Essex schools before 1600. *H. G. Williams, M.A. 1924 London*

The ethical value of education as provided and presented by public authorities during the past thirty years (1890-1920). *R. MacDonald, M.A. 1925 Liverpool*

Four centuries of school education in the Pottery Towns and Newcastle-under-Lyme, 1548-1948. *L. Goldschmidt, M.A. 1948 Birmingham*

The Gawdys of West Harling, Norfolk: a study of education and social life in the seventeenth century. *C. D. Price, M.A. 1950 Wales*

A general survey of the School Board Movement as it affected Monmouthshire, with special reference to the town of Newport. *D. E. Davies, M.A. 1927 Wales*

The growth of the public system of education in England and Wales, 1895-1935. *G. A. N. Lowndes, B.Litt. 1937 Oxford*

Education: Great Britain: History contd.
An historical survey of education in Angus to the year 1872 from original and contemporary sources, embracing early education and the beginning of systematic education; the parish school system; burgh schools, schools of industry and the origin and establishment of infant schools. *J. C. Jessop, Ph.D. 1930 Saint Andrew's*

A history of Charity School education and a statistical survey of some measures of educational growth. *R. W. Hitchcock, Ph.D. 1938 London, King's College*

The history of church schools in Swansea during the nineteenth century to 1870. *A. L. Trott, M.A. 1941 Wales*

A history of deaf education in Scotland, 1760-1939. *T. J. Watson, Ph.D. 1949 Edinburgh*

The history of education and educational institutions in Nottinghamshire, excluding the City of Nottingham, from 1800 to 193. *E. M. Becket, Ph.D. 1936 London, External Degree*

The history of education in Warrington. *R. Charlesworth, M.Ed. 1936 Manchester*

A history of education in Bradford during the period of the Bradford School Board (1870-1904). *A. J. Evans, M.A. 1947 Leeds*

A history of education in Halifax during the nineteenth century. *J. L. Hanson, M.Ed. 1940 Leeds*

The history of education in the British army up to 1939. *T. H. Hawkins, M.Ed. 1945 Leeds*

History of education in Oldham. *P. Lord, M.Ed. 1938 Manchester*

A history of education in York, 1780-1902. *E. Benson, Ph.D. 1933 London, External Degree*

The history of education in Wales from 1870, with special reference to secondary education to 1920. *T. I. Ellis, M.A. 1930 Wales*

A history of education in the towns of Barry and Penarth together with the neighbouring parishes of Leckwith, Llandough juxta Penarth, Lavernock, Sully, St.Andrews, Wenvoe, Highlight, Perthkerry and Penmark during the period 1860-1930. *J. Thomas, M.A. 1933 Wales*

The history of education in Lichfield, as illustrating the development of education in England. *J. R. Lindley, M.A. 1942 Birmingham*

History of Hampton-upon-Thames in the sixteenth and seventeenth centuries, with special reference to educational foundations. *B. Garside, M.A. 1930 London, University College*

A history of popular education in Wakefield, 1780-1902. *C. Brown, M.Ed. 1937 Leeds*

The history of Quaker education in England, 1647-1903. *L. J. Stroud, M.Ed. 1945 Leeds*

The history of the Society for the Diffusion of Useful Knowledge. *T. L. Jarman, B.Litt. 1933 Oxford*

The influence of 1848 on education. *O. W. Sinclair, M.A. 1916 London*

The influence of bishops and of members of cathedral bodies in the intellectual life of England, 1066 to 1216. *E. Rathbone, Ph.D. 1936 London, King's College*

The influence of charity on education in England. *F. Mitchell, M.Ed. 1930 Manchester*

The influence on educational thought of (1) Ruskin (2) Wordsworth. *W. O. Delaney, M.A. 1924 Liverpool*

An investigation into public opinion and the passing of the Education Act of 1870. *R. B. Grove, M.A. 1949 London, Institute of Education*

John Wesley and education. *A. H. Body, M.Ed. 1935 Manchester*

Knowledge Chartism: a study of the influence of Chartism on nineteenth century educational development in Great Britain. *R. A. Jones, M.A. 1938 Birmingham*

Leaders of humanism in English education: Humphrey, Duke of Gloucester, William Grocyn, Thomas Linacre, Bishop Richard Foxe. *C. H. Winstanley, M.A. 1930 Liverpool*

The life and work of Nathaniel Woodard, with special reference to the influence of the Oxford movement on English education in the nineteenth century. *R. Perry, M.A. 1932 Bristol*

The life, works and letters of Hannah More, with special reference to her influence in the social and educational movements of the eighteenth and early nineteenth centuries. *W. J. E. Moul, M.A. 1933 London, King's College*

Education: Great Britain: History contd.
The mendicants and English education in the thirteenth century. *I. H. Tolley, M.A. 1924 London*

An outline of the history of education in Bradford before 1870. *H. E. Walsh, M.Ed. 1936 Leeds*

The passing of the Education Act of 1870: a study of the formation of public opinion, 1843-1870. *E. E. Rich, Ph.D. 1932 London, School of Economics and Political Science*

The place of children's books in English education during the first half of the nineteenth century, with special reference to the Hofland Collection. *A. J. Leech, M.Ed. 1941 Leeds*

The place of the Royal Institution of South Wales in the history of scientific and general education in the nineteenth century. *H. M. Davies, M.A. 1940 Wales*

The progress of education in Bristol. *H. J. Larcombe, M.A. 1924 Bristol*

The reform of the dual system in England and Wales, 1941-44. *M. A. Travis, M.A. 1949 London, King's College*

The relation between the State and the development of a system of popular education in England and Wales. *G. H. Gopsill, M.A. 1938 Birmingham*

Religious uniformity and English education in the sixteenth century. *N. Wood, Ph.D. 1928 London*

The rise and development of education in the Staffordshire Potteries. *H. Goldstraw, M.Ed. 1935 Manchester*

The rise of education in England. *J. Thomas, M.A. 1902 London*

St. Helen's, 1845 and afterwards: an illustration of educational developments. *W. A. Fawcett, M.A. 1936 Liverpool*

St. John Baptist de la Salle: the work of the Brothers of the Christian Schools, and its significance in the history of English education. *W. J. Battersby, Ph.D. 1947 London, Birkbeck College*

Scottish experiments in rural education from the eighteenth century to the present day, with special reference to rural arts and crafts. *J. Mason, Ph.D. 1931 Edinburgh*

Sir Thomas More and education. *E. M. Chesters, M.A. 1923 Liverpool*

Some aspects of Jesuit education before the suppression. *M. Kennelly, M.A. 1948 National University of Ireland*

Some schools of north Lancashire: the record of a study of the history of the oldest schools of the Hundreds of Amounderness and Lonsdale. *C. W. Hutton, M.Ed. 1924 Leeds*

Spurley Hey's contribution to the origin and development of central schools. *T. H. Williams, M.A. 1938 Sheffield*

The state and education in the 18th century. *E. F. Braley, LL.D. 1932 Dublin, Trinity College*

The State and school education, 1640-60, in England and Wales: a survey based on printed sources. *W. A. L. Vincent, B.Litt. 1944 Oxford*

State intervention in education in England under the Early Stuarts. *L. G. Young, M.A. 1938 London, King's College*

State intervention in English education as illustrated by the relations between the State and the teacher in the early half of the nineteenth century. *J. Cross, M.A. 1932 Liverpool*

A statistical study of the growth of charity schools. *R. W. Hitchcock, M.A. 1933 London, Institute of Education*

Studies in intellectual life in England from the middle of the fifteenth century till the time of Colet. *N. D. Hurnard, D.Phil. 1935 Oxford*

A study of factors that influenced action in regard to the education of the unemployed boy during the inter-war years. *E. S. Conway, M.A. 1941 Liverpool*

A study of the development towards the principles and practice of modern education as shown in the Dissenting Academies in England. *G. W. Thomas, M.A. 1949 London, Institute of Education*

A study of the history and development of the School Medical Service in Liverpool from 1908 to 1939, and an attempt to assess its consequences on the health of the Liverpool school child. *J. Riddell, M.A. 1946 Liverpool*

A survey of educational development in the borough of Ashton-under-Lyne, with special reference to Albion Schools and to the period 1840-1938. *S. D. Ashton, M.Ed. 1938 Manchester*

Education: Great Britain: History contd.
Thomas Tyrwhitt (1730-86) and his contribution to English scholarship. *T. J. A. Monaghan, D.Phil. 1947 Oxford*

Three centuries of Birmingham educational development. *A. I. Burrow, M.A. 1931 Birmingham*

Welsh schools of the fifteenth and sixteenth centuries. *L. S. Knight, M.A. 1914 Wales*

Wesleyan Methodism's contribution to national education (1739-1902). *H. Cloke, M.A. 1936 London, King's College*

The work of religious societies in English education, 1660-1870. *F. M. Osborne, M.A. 1925 London*

Education: Greece, Ancient
A comparison of the educational system of Athens (400-300 B.C.) with that of England at the present day. *H. V. Loseby, M.Ed. 1934 Leeds*

The education of an Athenian. *S. C. Rowland, M.A. 1912 London*

Greek elementary education and its critics (down to Aristotle). *A. R. Simpson, Ph.D. 1944 London, External Degree*

Ideals of education in Isocrates and Plato. *D. Gilbert, M.A. 1937 London, Westfield College*

Plato and the Greek problem in education. *M. O'Connell, M.A. 1926 National University of Ireland*

The significance of rhythm in the Platonic system of education. *M. F. R. Limrick, M.A. 1915 Liverpool*

Education: Hong Kong
The education of overseas Chinese: a comparative study of Hong Kong, Singapore and the East Indies. *T. C. Cheng, M.A. 1949 London, Institute of Education*

Education: India
Ancient Indian education: an enquiry into its origin, development, and ideals. *F. E. Keay, M.A. 1917 London*

Ancient Indian education. *M. T. Vyas, M.A. 1926 London*

The Bengali Muslims and English education (1765-1835). *M. F. Rahman, M.A. 1948 London, Institute of Education*

A comparative study of Indian and English education. *R. N. Mohanty, M.A. 1940 Leeds*

A critical study of the educational problem in Bengal, with special reference to secondary education. *B. Rahman, M.Ed. 1927 Leeds*

A critical survey of the educational development and conditions in the state of Hyderabad (Deccan) with suggestions and recommendations for further improvement. *S. M. H. Nakavi, M.Ed. 1937 Leeds*

A critical survey of the growth of primary education in the Punjab since the annexation, 1847-1947, British period. *M. Q. H. Khan, M.A. 1949 London, King's College*

The development of Anglo-Indian education and its problems. *H. R. H. Daniell, M.Ed. 1941 Leeds*

Development of education in Orissa under the British (1803-1946). *B. N. Rath, M.A. 1948 London, Institute of Education*

The development of education in H.E.H. the Nizam's dominions. *M. Ramkrishniah, M.Ed. 1946 Leeds*

The development of education in Mysore and present day needs. *K. R. K. Ananthan, M.Ed. 1937 Leeds*

Development of Muslim education in India under the British rule. *B. A. Hashmi, M.A. 1927 Leeds*

Development of the educational system in Hyderabad, Deccan. *Z. Syed, M.Ed. 1938 Leeds*

The early history of female education in India. *R. B. Mathur, Ph.D. 1947 London, School of Oriental and African Studies*

Education and language problems in Assam. *S. C. Rajkhowa, M.A. 1948 London, Institute of Education*

Education in Madras. *S. Gowrie, M.A. 1948 Bristol*

The education of the depressed classes in India. *S. A. Haque, M.Ed. 1938 Leeds*

An examination of Indian education since the year 1813, in the light of modern educational principles. *L. P. D'Souza, M.A. 1935 London, Institute of Education*

Female education in Bengal. *V. I. Alphonso, M.A. 1931 London, King's College*

Education: India contd.

The history and development of rural education in the United Provinces of Agra and Oudh, from 1840 to 1926. *S. N. Chaturvedi, M.A. 1931 London, King's College*

The history of education in Madras, with special reference to elementary education. *T. Vasudevaiya, M.Ed. 1939 Leeds*

The history of education in Orissa. *J. Harichandan, M.Ed. 1947 Leeds*

A history of education in ancient India, from the earliest times to the beginning of the Christian era: from the *Rig-Veda* to the Smritis. *M. R. Desai, M.Ed. 1935 Leeds*

A history of the education of the Shudra untouchables before and under the British rule in India, c. 2000 B.C. to 1947. *R. S. Kalota, M. Ed. 1950 Durham*

Indian education and possible lines of its advancement. *K. S. Vakil, M.Ed. 1923 Leeds*

The influence of Western education in India. *M. H. Khan, Ph.D. 1942 Dublin, Trinity College*

An intelligence and educational survey of the eleven-year-olds in the government high schools of the United Provinces of Agra and Oudh, India. *S. Lall, Ph.D. 1945 Edinburgh*

Muhammadan education in Bengal, with special reference to primary education. *A. F. M. A. Khan, M.Ed. 1940 Leeds*

New education for the new India. *D. Rout, B.Litt. 1948 Dublin, Trinity College*

The organization and control of education in Bengal. *A. R. Khan, M.Ed. 1940 Leeds*

The origin and development in Bengal of the principles involved in Sir Charles Wood's despatch on education of 19th July, 1854. *D. P. Sinha, M.A. 1939 London, School of Oriental and African Studies*

The position of English in a national system of education for Bengal. *M. P. West, D.Phil. 1927 Oxford*

Principles of educational reconstruction, with special reference to conditions in the North West Frontier Province. *K. Khan, M.Ed. 1938 Leeds*

Principles of reconstruction of a curriculum suited to the village conditions in India, with special reference to Travancore. *P. S. Abraham, M.Ed. 1944 Leeds*

The problem of education in the Bombay Presidency, with special reference to higher education. *R. V. Paruleker, M.Ed. 1924 Leeds*

The problem of education in India with special reference to school education. *T. V. Apparsundaram, M.Ed. 1924 Leeds*

Rural education in Sind. *S. J. Narsian, M.Ed. 1938 Leeds*

Rural education in the Bombay Presidency. *G. T. Mirchandani, M.Ed. 1938 Leeds*

Sind: its educational past and present. *B. K. Shaikh, M.Ed. 1938 Leeds*

State and private enterprise in education in British India. *M. A. Ali, M.Ed. 1928 Leeds*

The state in its relation to education in India. *J. M. Sen, M.Ed. 1922 Leeds*

A study of modern principles of mental hygiene, with special reference to Indian education. *S. Bhan, M.A. 1937 London, Institute of Education*

A survey and critical study of some experiments in 'national' education in India. *A. Basu, M.A. 1932 London, King's College*

Tagore at Shantinekatan, or Sir Rabindranath Tagore's educational experiment at Shantinekatan. *H. S. D. Chaturvedi, M.Ed. 1929 Leeds*

The teaching of humanities in India. *J. N. Dudeja, M.A. 1934 Leeds*

The training of teachers in India. *S. C. Chatterji, Ph.D. 1942 Dublin, Trinity College*

Women's education in India. *I. Khan, M.A. 1947 London, Institute of Education*

Education: Ireland

The board of national education in Ireland. *F. O'Connor, M.A. 1917 National University of Ireland*

The Breiffne schools and scholars. *P. O'Connell, Ph.D. 1940 National University of Ireland*

Education: Ireland contd.

1. Catholic education in Ireland, 1774-1824: illustrated from the diocesan records of Kildare and Leighlin. 2. The Confraternity of Christian Doctrine in Ireland, 1775-1835. *M. A. Brenan, Ph.D. 1934 National University of Ireland*

Catholic popular education in Ireland (1750-1870). *J. Fitzsimons, Ph.D. 1941 National University of Ireland*

Combined agricultural and literary education in Ireland, 1765-1865. *J. J. Holland, Ph.D. 1926 National University of Ireland*

Education in Ireland in the sixteenth century. *S. M. M. McCoy, Ph.D. 1936 National University of Ireland*

Education in Ireland in the penal times. *J. H. McHugh, M.A. 1941 National University of Ireland*

An enquiry into the financial implications of the educational reforms proposed by the Federal Council of Teachers in Northern Ireland. *H. R. Brown, M.Com.Sc. 1944 Belfast*

The Hedge schools of Kerry. *M. L. O'Connor, M.A. 1949 National University of Ireland*

Irish education since the union, a historical and critical study. *P. T. Walshe, Ph.D. 1928 Dublin, Trinity College*

Legal aspects of education in Ireland. *T. J. Neylon, Ph.D. 1942 National University of Ireland*

Mixed education in Ireland 1824-1884. *R. P. J. Batterberry, Ph.D. 1939 National University of Ireland*

Newman, his work in Ireland, and his educational theory and practice. *R. J. McHugh, Ph.D. 1947 National University of Ireland*

P. H. Pearse as an educationalist. *J. Treanor, M.A. 1942 National University of Ireland*

Phases of education in Galway city during the 18th and early part of the 19th century. *K. P. Hackett, M.A. 1935 National University of Ireland*

The Popular Catholic School in Ireland. *P. J. Dowling, Ph.D. 1929 London*

Sgoltacha agus sgoláiri Fairche na Gaillimhe, 1500-1731 (Schools and scholars of the diocese of Galway, 1500-1731). *P. O'Laoighidh, M.A. 1946 National University of Ireland*

Sir William Wyse, Irish pioneer in educational reform. *W. J. Bradley, Ph.D. 1945 Dublin, Trinity College*

Stair an oideachais i bhfairche Chluain-fearta, 1700-1885 (The history of education in the diocese of Clonfert, 1700-1885). *D. P. Nolan, M.A. 1941 National University of Ireland*

Survey of the history of education in Corca Laighdne (Diocese of Ross) from earliest times to 1825. *C. A. Kennedy, M.A. 1942 National University of Ireland*

Education: Islam

The Arab conception of the ideal teacher in Arabic pedagogical literature. *G. D. Shahla, M.A. 1938 London, Institute of Education*

The Bengali Muslims and English education (1765-1835). *M. F. Rahman, M.A. 1948 London, Institute of Education*

Development of Muslim education in India under the British rule. *B. A. Hashmi, M.A. 1927 Leeds*

The educational ideas of the Muslims in the middle ages. *A. H. Fahmy, M.A. 1937 Birmingham*

Muhammadan education in Bengal, with special reference to primary education. *A. F. M. A. Khan, M.Ed. 1940 Leeds*

Education: Jamaica

The education of Jamaica: its historical background and possible future developments. *R. N. Murray, M.A. 1947 London, Institute of Education*

Education: Java

Education as a factor in colonial development, with special reference to Java. *B. A. Fletcher, M.A. 1934 Bristol*

Education: Jews

Hebrew education from 1000 to 150 B.C. *J. J. Slotki, M.A. 1929 Manchester*

The history of Jewish education in Central Europe from the beginning of the seventeenth century to 1782 (the Edict of Toleration issued by Joseph II of Austria). *I. Fishman, Ph.D. 1941 London, External Degree*

Jewish education in Talmud and contemporary sources. *B. A. Collins, M.A, 1946 National University of Ireland*

Education: Jews contd.

1. The place of education in the life of the ancient Hebrews. 2. St. Paul's ideal of labour. *F. T. Ingle, B.D. 1923 Oxford*

Schools and methods of Jewish education in Palestine and Babylon up to the close of the Talmud. *H. M. Lazarus, M.A. 1913 London*

A study in ancient Hebrew education. *J. Weingreen, Ph.D. 1931 Dublin, Trinity College*

Education: Malaya

A comparative study of the intelligence and educability of Malays and Chinese in Malaya and its significance in relation to educational policy. *G. E. D. Lewis, Ph.D. 1949 London, Institute of Education*

A history of educational policy of the Straits Settlements from 1800 to 1925 (*circa*). *D. D. Chelliah, Ph.D. 1940 London, External Degree*

Education: Mauritius

Education in Mauritius, with special reference to the Royal College. *C. G. Wise, M.Ed. 1932 Manchester*

Education: Netherlands

A study of the educational system of Holland. *H. N. Lowe, M.A. 1927 Liverpool*

Education: Nigeria

Education in Nigeria. *G. Martlew, M.A. 1934 Liverpool*

Education in Nigeria: a critical study of policy and practice in the light of modern principles of education. *C. A. Ekere, M.A. 1945 London, Institute of Education*

The education of the West African peoples, with especial reference to the Yoruba tribes of southern Nigeria. *H. Dallimore, B.Litt. 1929 Oxford*

Problems of teacher training in Nigeria considered in connection with educational developments in British tropical Africa. *T. T. Solaru, M.A. 1948 London, Institute of Education*

Education: Rome

Cicero's educational theory. *G. B. Smith, M.Ed. 1934 Manchester*

The education of women under the Roman Empire. *E. Symes, M.A. 1909 London*

Roman education under the Empire. *A. O. Gwynn, B.Litt. 1919 Oxford*

Roman education under the Empire. *A. O. Gwynn, M.A. 1915 National University of Ireland*

Education: Russia

History of Russian educational policy, 1801-1917. *N. Hans, Ph.D. 1926 London*

Education: Scandinavia

Comparative survey of education in Burma and a few countries with a rural background, e.g., Turkey and Scandinavia. *B. Ghosh, M.A. 1947 London, Institute of Education*

Education: Sierra Leone

Child training in Sierra Leone: a description of education in relation to society. *L. J. B. Pratt, M.Ed. 1949 Durham*

Education: Singapore

The education of overseas Chinese: a comparative study of Hong Kong, Singapore and the East Indies. *T. C. Cheng, M.A. 1949 London, Institute of Education*

Education: South Africa

Education in the Union of South Africa. *J. H. Washington, Ph.D. 1924 London*

Natal education: its history and methods. *E. A. Pope, M.A. 1916 Liverpool*

Education: Spain

Aspects of Spanish education. *H. V. Dacombe, M.A. 1935 London, King's College*

The development of education in Spain since 1900. *J. C. Develin, D.Phil. 1935 Oxford*

Education: Sweden

Education in Sweden. *G. Reith, Ph.D. 1950 Edinburgh*

Education: Switzerland

The education system of French Protestant Switzerland (Cantons of Geneva, Vaud and Neuchâtel. *E. G. Barnard, M.A. 1931 London, King's College*

Education: Tanganyika

The educational system of the Chaga, with special reference to 1. The light thrown by social anthropology on the origins of education. 2. The theories of the nature of education and of educational psychology. 3. The educational planning of the present day. *O. F. Raum, Ph.D. 1938 London, External Degree*

Education: Tanganyika contd.
Observations on the extraneous influences and culture-contacts in the Tanganyika Territory in their bearing on problems of native education. *R. J. Harvey, B.Sc. 1937 Oxford*

Education: Turkey
Comparative survey of education in Burma and a few countries with a rural background, e.g., Turkey and Scandinavia. *B. Ghosh, M.A. 1947 London, Institute of Education*

Education: United States
American colonial colleges. *S. K. Wilson, Ph.D. 1925 Cambridge*

Education, Adult
Adult education. *D. Daly, M.A. 1924 National University of Ireland*

Adult education: a survey from the beginning of the nineteenth century. *M. A. Buntine, Ph.D. 1925 Edinburgh*

Adult education in England. *J. D. Hoy, M.A. 1931 Birmingham*

Adult education in North Staffordshire: its history and development. *H. C. Miller, M.Ed. 1928 Manchester*

Adult education in the county of Cornwall: its development and present position. *H. L. Hudson, M.A. 1946 London, King's College*

A comparative study of some forms of adult education in England, the United States, Denmark and Sweden, with special reference to rural areas, together with a scheme of adult education in Ceylon. *K. L. V. Alagiyawanna, M.A. 1948 London, Institute of Education*

Continuation and technical education in the Irish Free State. *L. S. Pearson, M.A. 1932 London, King's College*

Continuation schools, with special reference to the continuative clauses of the Education Act, 1918. *W. R. Garland, M.Sc. 1925 London*

A critical enquiry into adult education with some suggestions for its application to India. *B. Indiramma, M.Ed. 1930 Leeds*

The day continuation school in England. *K. Brooksbank, M.Ed. 1939 Manchester*

The early development of the university extension movement under the influence of James Stuart. *H. Gordon, M.A. 1941 Sheffield*

Education and the army. *S. T. R. Hancock, M.Ed. 1949 Manchester*

The educational welfare of the industrial adolescent, with special reference to day continuation schools. *H. Hanks, M.A. 1940 London, King's College*

The effect of six months' instruction in school subjects on some mental factors of adults. *W. B. Walls, M.Ed. 1945 Leeds*

Evening education in England, with special reference to London. *F. Johnson, Ph.D. 1937 London, King's College*

The history and present status of adult education in the Punjab (India). *D. I. Lal, M.A. 1948 London, Institute of Education*

The history of adult and technical education in Skipton-in-Craven, during the nineteenth century. *J. MacGregor, M.Ed. 1949 Leeds*

A history of the development of adult education in England. *J. Stott, M.A. 1930 Liverpool*

An investigation into the principles and methods of adult education. *H. Newton, M.A. 1923 London*

Irish continuation school and the adolescent. *J. Sexton, M.A. 1942 National University of Ireland*

The London compulsory day continuation schools: January, 1921-July, 1922. *L. Brooks, M.A. 1923 London*

The place of the evening institute in further education in the East Midlands. *J. T. Fielding, M.Ed. 1950 Nottingham*

Residential adult education in England. *L. Speak, M.A. 1949 Leeds*

Some comparisons between evening class attenders in the Black Country and non-attenders. *A. B. Turner, M.A. 1932 Bristol*

Spiritual values in adult education. *B. A. Yeaxlee, Ph.D. 1925 London*

The voluntary day continuation schools in London. *A. H. Surman, M.A. 1949 London, Institute of Education*

Education, Commercial
A comparative study of the training of full-time teachers of commercial subjects in England and France 1946 to 1949. *T. A. Hempstock, M.A. 1950 Sheffield*

A critical and comparative survey of modern tendencies in commercial education at home and abroad. *F. R. Montague, M.Ed. 1936 Leeds*

The development of commercial education in England, from medieval times. *H. L. Jones, M.Ed. 1927 Manchester*

The development of commercial education on Merseyside since 1900. *E. C. Colbeck, M.A. 1945 Liverpool*

Educational practice in relation to industry and commerce. *I. V. Brown, M.A. 1919 London*

A factorial analysis of skill in commercial subjects at the secondary school level. *R. Seddon, Ph.D. 1949 London, Institute of Education*

The selection and training of pupils for commerce in the senior school. *W. E. Quine, M.Ed. 1945 Leeds*

Selection for commercial courses in junior technical schools. *G. B. Hill, M.Ed. 1950 Manchester*

Training for commerce in post-primary schools. *J. H. McInnes, M.Ed. 1934 Durham*

Training for industry and commerce: present defects and future remedies. *J. L. Tomlinson, M.Com. 1937 Leeds*

Education, Elementary
Advanced instruction in the elementary school. *F. A. Norwell, M.A. 1931 Liverpool*

Certain dangers to health which result from the present system of public elementary education in Scotland. *A. Campbell, M.D. 1883 Glasgow*

The Christian churches and the formation and maintenance of a system of state-aided elementary education in England and Wale. *E. G. Broad, M.A. 1938 Bristol*

Classification of children in the elementary school. *G. S. Leonard, M.A. 1927 Birmingham*

Conditions in the elementary school system of today, which result in strain, physical and mental, upon the child. *R. A. Taylor, M.A. 1929 Manchester*

Continuity and change in education: the origins of elementary education in England at the beginning of the nineteenth century, and recent proposals for development and change. *A. Grant, M.A. 1930 Liverpool*

A contribution to the history of elementary education in Manchester, up to 1870, with special reference to national schools. *T. R. Hughes, M.Ed. 1937 Manchester*

A contribution to the history of elementary education in north Wales up to 1870, with special reference to national schools. *T. R. Hughes, M.A. 1935 Liverpool*

Co-operation between county education authorities and authorities for elementary education only, with special reference to the county council of the West Riding of Yorkshire and the Borough of Ossett. *A. Sauvain, M.Ed. 1943 Manchester*

A critical survey of the auxiliary means of selection employed in examinations in public elementary schools for free special places in secondary schools. *G. Baron, M.Ed. 1937 Leeds*

A critical survey of the growth of primary education in the Punjab since the annexation, 1847-1947, British period. *M. Q. H. Khan, M.A. 1949 London, King's College*

The dame schools of Great Britain. *J. H. Higginson, M.A. 1939 Leeds*

The development of nursery and elementary schools in Great Britain. *W. A. Singleton, M.A. 1945 Liverpool*

The development of the modern infant school. *M. Looney, M.A. 1928 National University of Ireland*

Education among some preliterate peoples. *M. Eastham, M.A. 1940 Leeds*

The education of children in hospital schools. *I. Nichols, M.A. 1938 Liverpool*

The effects of war conditions on elementary education in the Borough of Altrincham. *W. K. Warting, M.Ed. 1943 Manchester*

Education, Elementary contd.
The educational aims of pioneers in elementary Welsh education, 1730-1870. *F. Williams, M.A. 1929 Wales*

The effect of nursery training on the responses of children in the Merrill-Terman tests. *C. P. K. Amma, M.Ed. 1920 Leeds*

Elementary education among the Greeks during the sixth, fifth and fourth centuries B.C., dealing with both educational practice, theory and criticism. *W. M. Bull, M.A. 1932 London, King's College*

Elementary education in India and abroad. *G. Singh, M.Sc. 1918 London*

Elementary education in Irak in the times of the 'Abbāsids. *A. H. Al-Hillī, Ph.D. 1949 Manchester*

Elementary education in England from 1870 to 1918. *B. Mukharji, M.A. 1923 Leeds*

Elementary education in the Babylonian Talmud. *N. Morris, M.A. 1932 London, King's College*

The elementary school and national life. *F. M. Wilcox, M.A. 1930 Liverpool*

Elementary schools and schoolbooks in England at the close of the eighteenth and beginning of the nineteenth centuries. *P. H. Sandall, M.A. 1929 London*

Emotional development and the infant school: the play curriculum as an aid to emotional adjustment and growth. *A. E. Price, M.A. 1940 Leeds*

The English elementary school considered as an agent of social transformation, 1870-1918. *E. G. Pells, B.Litt. 1928 Oxford*

An enquiry into the abilities of adolescent boys in elementary schools in Bristol. *G. A. Jahans, M.A. 1934 Bristol*

The evolution of local administration in English elementary education during the period 1833-1930 with special consideration of the problems of finance, administrative areas and inspection. *G. P. McHugh, M.Ed. 1932 Durham*

The evolution of the English elementary day school up to 1902, containing a history of the Hunslet national schools. *G. G. Gamble, M.Ed. 1945 Leeds*

An experimental investigation into some effects upon children of infant school methods based on spontaneous activity as compared with more formal methods. *D. E. M. Gardner, M.A. 1940 Leeds*

Froebel's principles and their relationship to the theory and practice of infant education today. *L. Stowe, M.A. 1940 Leeds*

Greek elementary education and its critics (down to Aristotle). *A. R. Simpson, Ph.D. 1944 London, External Degree*

Hegel's theory and practice of education, and problems of girls' education in elementary schools. *M. Mackenzie, M.A. 1908 Wales*

The history and development of nursery education in Manchester and Salford. *G. M. Wood, M.Ed. 1934 Manchester*

The history and development of boys' preparatory schools in England. *F. C. Pritchard, M.A. 1938 London, King's College*

A history of elementary education in Leeds prior to 1870. *H. Fligg, M.Ed. 1938 Leeds*

A history of elementary education in the Punjab. *S. Y. Shah, M.A. 1937 Bristol*

The history of elementary school inspection, 1839-1902. *J. Leese, M.Ed. 1931 Manchester*

The imagination of the school-child and its relation to his proficiency in the different subjects of the elementary school curriculum. *T. Boyce, M.A. 1917 Liverpool*

Music in elementary education. *C. W. J. Hooper, M.A. 1942 Leeds*

The organization of elementary education in Liverpool since the passing of the Education Act of 1918, with special reference to the provision of facilities for post-primary education. *W. J. Malley, M.A. 1936 Liverpool*

The physique of elementary school children, with special reference to their mentality: a statistical study bearing on social economics. *E. G. Habakkuk, M.Sc. 1924 Wales*

The preparatory department as it exists in some public, grammar, and secondary schools, and its curriculum. *F. J. Downs, M.Ed. 1944 Leeds*

Primary education in Assam in the light of economic, social and political development in India. *G. Hussain, M.A. 1948 London, Institute of Education*

Education, Elementary contd.

Primary education in Bengal: its history and problems. *R. Husain, M.A. 1939 Leeds*

Primary education in the Central Provinces and Berar. *G. V. Bernard, M.Ed. 1939 Leeds*

The primary school in England: survey and a forecast. *H. Bryett, M.A. 1929 Liverpool*

The problems of English elementary education since 1870: the evolution of opinion and the development of the system. . *H. A. Grimshaw, M.Sc. 1918 London*

Problems of primary education in Assam. *S. Das, M.Ed. 1940 Leeds*

The purpose of the elementary school. *J. D. Allen, M.A. 1928 Liverpool*

The rural bias and the rural primary school. *P. O'Meara, M.A. 1935 National University of Ireland*

Rural education. *A. E. Luery, M.Ed. 1921 Leeds*

Rural education. *W. G. Torrance, M.A. 1930 Birmingham*

Scottish experiments in rural education from the eighteenth century to the present day, with special reference to rural arts and crafts. *J. Mason, Ph.D. 1931 Edinburgh*

A short history of elementary education in the United Provinces of Agra and Oudh (India) 1813-1935. *S. A. Qazi, M.Ed. 1937 Leeds*

Some changes brought about by wartime evacuation in the conduct of public elementary schools and in the attainments of their pupils. *J. K. Grant, M.A. 1943 Liverpool*

A statistical enquiry into the relative popularity of school subjects in the elementary schools of Worcestershire. *J. J. Shakespeare, M.A. 1934 Birmingham*

Study as an aim in primary teaching. *M. A. Conneely, M.A. 1935 National University of Ireland*

A study of elementary education in Malta and the problems affecting its development. *R. S. Thompson, M.Ed. 1943 Durham*

A study of the problem of infant education. *P. M. Vesavevala, M.Ed. 1931 Leeds*

A survey of the financial aspect of elementary education. *J. Corlett, Ph.D. 1928 London*

The teaching of history in the preparatory school. *W. H. Sankey, M.Ed. 1923 Manchester*

A thesis on re-organization in rural elementary education, based on independent observation and study, 1924-1928. *W. Webster, M.Ed. 1928 Leeds*

Value of present-day infant school training methods. *M. T. Crisham, M.A. 1935 National University of Ireland*

Education, Higher
See also under the names of individual colleges and universities.

American colonial colleges. *S. K. Wilson, Ph.D. 1925 Cambridge*

Coláistí na Bainríoghna, a mbunú 's a mbliadhanta tosaigh 1845-1856 (Queen's Colleges, their foundation and early years, 1845-1856). *V. B. Jennings, M.A. 1947 National University of Ireland*

The constitutions for the promotion of University graduates in England, 1417-1438. *J. Flitcroft, M.A. 1937 Manchester*

The curricula of the Dissenting Academies in the reign of George III. *H. J. McLachlan, M.A. 1930 Manchester*

The curriculum of the Dissenting Academies, with special reference to factors determining it, 1660-1800. *J. W. A. Smith, M.Ed. 1950 Durham*

The early development of the university extension movement under the influence of James Stuart. *H. Gordon, M.A. 1941 Sheffield*

Education in the fourteenth and fifteenth centuries, with special reference to the development of the universities of northern Europe. *G. R. Potter, Ph.D. 1927 Cambridge*

English Benedictines in the century preceding the dissolution, with special reference to their connexion with the universities and with learning. *W. D. Coates, B.Litt. 1931 Oxford*

An enquiry into the nature of the difficulties experienced by university students in choosing a career. *V. C. Chamberlain, M.A. 1950 Manchester*

Higher education: its organization, administration and finance, with special reference to the county borough of Bootle. *W. H. Otter, M.A. 1936 Liverpool*

Education, Higher contd.

Higher education in Lancashire in the nineteenth century. *E. Smith, B.Litt. 1922 Oxford*

The influence of the university on the development of its region. *R. H. Toy, Ph.D. 1950 Dublin, Trinity College*

L'enseignement supérieur et la Révolution française. *T. J. Barling, M.A. 1948 Birmingham*

The London Polytechnic movement, with special reference to Quintin Hogg. *F. Johnson, M.A. 1929 London*

Newman's work for university education in Ireland. *J. S. F. McGrath, D.Phil. 1948 Oxford*

Nonconformist academies in Wales (1662-1862). *H. P. Roberts, M.A. 1922 Liverpool*

Nonconformist academies in Wales in the eighteenth century. *W. P. Thomas, M.A. 1928 Wales*

The origins and development of the university movement in Wales, with particular reference to the period 1800-1889. *I. J. Morgan, M.A. 1929 Wales*

The problem of the higher education of girls in the Bombay Presidency. *V. A. Ajgaonkar, M.Ed. 1940 Leeds*

The Reformation and the English universities. *W. B. Merritt, M.A. 1938 National University of Ireland*

The Scottish universities, 1826-1906. *J. R. Peddie, D.Litt. 1927 Glasgow*

Scottish university studies, 1800-1850. *E. Wilson, M.Ed. 1948 Leeds*

Some Cambridge contacts with France during Tudor and early Stuart times. *T. S. Wyatt, M.Litt. 1938 Cambridge*

A study in student life in a medieval university, with particular reference to Oxford and Paris. *H. Moyns, B.Litt. 1931 Oxford*

A study of the development towards the principles and practice of modern education as shown in the Dissenting Academies in England. *G. W. Thomas, M.A. 1949 London, Institute of Education*

A survey of the German university system during the Weimar Republic. *J. W. Gray, M.A. 1936 London, King's College*

The Universities and College Estates Acts, 1858-1880. *C. L. Shadwell, D.C.L. 1898 Oxford*

Urdu as the medium of higher instruction. *S. B. Sayeed, M.Ed. 1935 Leeds*

Education, Physical
See also Children's Games; Games and Sports.

An experimental investigation into the effects of physical training on personality. *F. J. Milverton, M.Ed. 1940 Leeds*

A study of the educational values of physical tests and measurements for boys 11+ to 15+. *B. C. Thomas, M.Ed. 1945 Manchester*

A system of physical education for schoolboys in India. *S. C. Chatterji, M.Ed. 1928 Leeds*

Education, Primary
See Education, Elementary.

Education, Religious
See Religious Education.

Education, Rural
See Education, Elementary.

Education, Secondary

The analysis of teachers' estimates and pupils' performance at the stage of entry to secondary education. *D. J. Alexander, M.A. 1947 London, Institute of Education*

The attitude of grammar school pupils and their parents to education, religion and sport. *W. Glassey, M.Ed. 1943 Manchester*

A comparison of forms of public provision for secondary education in English-speaking North America with those of England and an historical interpretation of some differences that emerge. *A. B. Currie, Ph.D. 1937 London, Institute of Education*

The contribution of a secondary school to vocational adjustment. *R. M. Jones, M.Ed. 1944 Manchester*

A critical study of external examinations and of their influence on secondary education. *J. F. G. O'Meara, M.A. 1944 National University of Ireland*

A critical survey of the auxiliary means of selection employed in examinations in public elementary schools for free special places in secondary schools. *G. Baron, M.Ed. 1937 Leeds*

Education, Secondary contd.

A crtical review of researches in the United Kingdom on selection for secondary education, with suggestions for their application to Ceylon. *D. G. Sugathadasa, M.A. 1948 London, Institute of Education*

The educational needs of the senior school boy. *J. E. Nicholson, M.Ed. 1940 Manchester*

An enquiry into the bearing of general and special abilities upon scholastic success at the beginning and end of the secondary school career. *M. Ormiston, Ph.D. 1937 Leeds*

An enquiry into the predictive value of grammar school entrance examinations. *D. Rutter, M.Ed. 1949 Durham*

An experimental study of standardized tests for selecting secondary school pupils. *P. T. Verghese, M.Ed. 1938 Leeds*

A historical sketch of the curricula of secondary schools. *M. Hogan, M.A. 1944 National University of Ireland*

An investigation into the reliability of various entrance examinations for pupils about to enter secondary and central selective schools. *C. Skelton, M.A. 1938 Leeds*

An investigation into the significance of teachers' assessments of the personal attributes of their pupils for secondary school selection. *S. Nath, M.A. 1948 London, Institute of Education*

An investigation into the use of estimated factor scores in describing and comparing a group of secondary and senior school boys of 11+. *J. J. B. Dempster, M.A. 1944 London, Institute of Education*

An investigation of recent tendencies in secondary education in England and America, and their implications for the reorganization of secondary education in New Zealand. *A. L. M. Perry, Ph.D. 1938 London, Institute of Education*

An investigation, using the discussion group technique, of some of the social relationships of secondary modern school children. *D. Wilson, M.A. 1949 Liverpool*

A metrical study of subject preferences in a boys' secondary school: an account of an experiment in the measurement of attitude. *C. G. Reed, M.Ed. 1939 Manchester*

An organization for the senior school and its influence upon curricula. *S. Overington, M.A. 1942 Sheffield*

Practical estimation of pupil's progress in secondary schools. *A. C. Paterson, Ph.D. 1928 Glasgow*

The problem of tenure of assistant masters in secondary schools. *A. Sinclair, M.Ed. 1940 Manchester*

The recruitment of secondary school pupils. *F. C. Thomas, Ph.D. 1939 London, External Degree*

The relations between abilities in grammar school subjects and their bearing upon school organization. *A. G. Ellis, M.Ed. 1948 Durham*

The relationship between interest, aptitude and achievement as shown by an enquiry into curricula in four secondary modern schools. *E. M. Uprichard, Ph.D. 1947 London, Institute of Education*

Report of an investigation into the secondary school careers of children who were not selected by the head teachers of elementary schools as likely to benefit by a secondary education. *H. A. Evans, M.A. 1938 Birmingham*

The scope, curriculum and organization of the modern school. *H. Price, M.A. 1935 Liverpool*

Secondary school selection. *W. A. C. Bishop, M.Sc. 1940 Wales*

Selection for secondary education. *L. E. Kitchen, M.A. 1945 Bristol*

The selection of children for secondary education. *A. James, M.Sc. 1925 Birmingham*

Self-government in the secondary school. *F. C. Raggatt, M.Ed. 1949 Durham*

Sex problems in boys' secondary schools. *S. M. Price, M.Ed. 1940 Manchester*

The significance of long-term persistence to successful attainment in the grammar school. *A. Wetherill, M.Ed. 1946 Leeds*

Some investigations concerning the work of a central school in relation to the future occupations of its pupils. *A. D. Hawkins, M.Sc. 1933 Birmingham*

Some problems of secondary education in the light of group psychology. *T. F. Green, M.A. 1927 Sheffield*

Education, Vocational contd.
The application of vocational selection and guidance methods in a technical college. *H. Rochester, M.A. 1938 Birmingham*

A critical enquiry into the growth and development of junior instruction centres. *C. M. Craggs, M.Ed. 1936 Leeds*

The genesis of the American system of vocational education. *D. W. Humphreys, M.A. 1936 London, King's College*

The improvement of vocational education in China. *M. Chen, M.A. 1938 Leeds*

The introduction of a vocational bias into schools in North India. *S. C. Chatterji, M.A. 1939 Leeds*

The Junior Instruction Centre. *O. E. Evans, M.A. 1939 Liverpool*

Part- and full-time vocational schools in Germany. *A. Rodgers, M.Ed. 1939 Leeds*

A study of the junior instruction centre based on material from the Wrexham district. *H. K. Evans, M.A. 1937 Liverpool*

A study of the provision for vocational training in the advanced courses of girls' secondary schools, with special reference to electricity. *M. J. Gordon, M.A. 1941 London, King's College*

A survey of junior instruction centres, with special reference to Durham County. *R. Gallon, M.Ed. 1940 Manchester*

Vocational aspects of education - elementary, secondary and technical. *H. O. Hughes, M.A. 1933 Birmingham*

Vocational education in India, with special reference to the Central Provinces and Berar. *M. H. Rao, M.Ed. 1939 Leeds*

Vocational guidance and selection, with special reference to the industries and occupations of Sheffield. *V. H. Hoskins, Ph.D. 1926 Sheffield*

A vocational study of chemistry with its applications to education. *N. Greenwood, M.Ed. 1924 Leeds*

Educational Psychology
See also Ability; Adolescents; Attention; Authority; Child Psychology; Children, Retarded; Children's Games; Confidence (Psychology); Games and Sports; Imagery; Imagination; Instinct; Intelligence Testing; Learning; Perseveration; Reading; Speech.

An analysis of learning curves and of factors in economical learning. *J. M. Blackburn, Ph.D. 1934 Cambridge*

An analysis of mental patterns and their function in the process of education. *I. A. E. M. El Labban, M.A. 1938 London, Institute of Education*

An analysis of reasoning ability in school children, with a view to determining the nature and extent of any group factor involved. *J. H. Murdoch, Ph.D. 1933 London, Institute of Education*

An analysis of the attitude of children towards certain school subjects, and the measure of correlation between attitude and attainment. *D. Jordan, M.A. 1937 London, Institute of Education*

An analysis of the factors underlying the process of observation. *E. A. Peel, M.A. 1938 London, Institute of Education*

The anti-social child within the school. *V. J. Long, M.A. 1939 Bristol*

The application of the hormic theory in psychology to the theory of religious education. *R. I. Morris, Ph.D. 1945 Edinburgh*

An approach to the study of education in the light of an evolutionary psychology. *I. H. Hoskins, M.A. 1948 London, Institute of Education*

The assessment of social attitudes of school children. *C. D. Butler, M.A. 1949 London, Institute of Education*

A comparative study of theories of factor analysis and their relations to analysis of variance, with special reference to psychology and education. *M. Zakaria, M.A. 1948 London, Institute of Education*

A comparative study of the effects of auditory and other distractions on the output and accuracy in simple addition. *W. T. Watts, M.A. 1938 London, Institute of Education*

A comparative study of the effects of continuous and intermittent auditory distraction on the mental output of children. *N. F. H. Butcher, M.A. 1938 London, Institute of Education*

Educational Psychology contd.
Conditions in the elementary school system of today, which result in strain, physical and mental, upon the child. *R. A. Taylor, M.A. 1929 Manchester*

The contribution of abnormal psychology to the problems of normal education. *A. F. Watts, M.A. 1917 London*

Different views of the nature of mental activity, more especially in connection with educational theory. *G. A. Lewis, M.A. 1908 Wales*

The effect on general reasoning ability of training in functional thinking in arithmetic. *M. Williams, M.A. 1938 London, Institute of Education*

An examination of the learning process, with special reference to the Gestalt psychology. *G. C. Bathurst, Ph.D. 1939 London, Institute of Education*

An experimental study of mental processes involved in the comprehension of historical narrative. *G. W. Bassett, Ph.D. 1940 London, Institute of Education*

Experimental work in educational guidance in a mixed selective central school. *W. E. Davies, M.Ed. 1943 Manchester*

Factors in the mental processes of school children. 1. Visual and auditory imagery. 2. On the nature of the specific mental factors. 3. Factors concerned in the school subjects. *N. Carey, D.Sc. 1916 London*

Homework and leisure time activities. *N. F. Millington, M.A. 1938 Birmingham*

The individual and the group in education. *W. J. Wheeler, M.A. 1936 Birmingham*

The influence of socio-economic factors on school progress and personality development. *O. Metcalfe, M.A. 1950 Birmingham*

Instinct in man: a contribution to the psychology of education. *J. Drever, Ph.D. 1916 Edinburgh*

Instinctive aspects of education. *J. Donovan, M.A. 1935 National University of Ireland*

Interest as a factor in the transfer of training from the inculcation of mathematical principles to problems in reasoning. *D. T. Jones, M.A. 1937 London, Institute of Education*

The interests of some junior technical school boys. *D. J. Tisdell, M.A. 1942 Birmingham*

An investigation into backwardness in arithmetic in the junior school. *R. H. Adams, M.A. 1940 London, Institute of Education*

An investigation into the causes of backwardness in geography among secondary school children. *H. K. Ault, M.A. 1940 London, Institute of Education*

An investigation into the psychological factors of linguistic ability. *P. M. M. Graham, M.A. 1942 London, Institute of Education*

An investigation into the problems of forgetting of different kinds of material by school children. *G. Ahmad, M.Ed. 1937 Leeds*

An investigation of social attitudes in school children. *H. E. Crocket, Ph.D. 1940 London, University College*

An investigation of some of the factors involved in arithmetical ability in school children. *K. S. Cooke, Ph.D. 1933 London, External Degree*

A new approach to the problem of individual differences, abilities and types, and their bearing on educational methods and systems. *N. R. Warhadpande, B.Litt. 1949 Oxford*

The new psychology and education. *J. C. Das Gupta, Ph.D. 1941 Dublin, Trinity College*

The prevalence of eidetic imagery among school-children and its educational significance. *H. Teasdale, M.Ed. 1932 Leeds*

Psychological aspects of the change from school to work. *C. Tenen, Ph.D. 1948 Manchester*

Psychological factors governing the education and culture of primitive peoples. *A. O'Ruairc, M.A. 1943 National University of Ireland*

The psychology of reasoning with special reference to educational problems. *E. V. Staynor, M.A. 1932 London, Day Training College*

1. The psychology of time. 2. Modern psychology and education. *M. Sturt, Ph.D. 1932 Birmingham*

Punishment in schools. *K. D. Hopkins, M.A. 1938 Birmingham*

The relationship between interest, aptitude and achievement as shown by an enquiry into curricula in four secondary modern schools. *E. M. Uprichard, Ph.D. 1947 London, Institute of Education*

Educational Psychology contd.
The school group - its leaders and leadership. *J. Chance, M.A. 1933 Birmingham*

The scope and value of psychological testing, with special reference to the examination of scholarship candidates for further education. *H. V. Clark, M.A. 1936 Liverpool*

The significance of long-term persistence to successful attainment in the grammar school. *A. Wetherill, M.Ed. 1946 Leeds*

Some problems of secondary education in the light of group psychology. *T. F. Green, M.A. 1927 Sheffield*

A statistical study of the judgments of a group of teachers as shown by their preferences among their pupils. *D. Cockburn, M.Ed. 1949 Durham*

Studies in: estimates of intelligence and non-intelligence qualities; temperament; left-handedness; scholastic achievement; the energy concept; and the biological significance of intelligence. *D. W. R. Oates, D.Sc. 1930 Wales*

A study in vocational guidance, with special reference to the importance of interests. *A. Crowther, Ph.D. 1937 Cambridge*

A study of the attitudes of adolescents to their own intellectual, social and spiritual development. *J. F. Forrester, Ph.D. 1946 London, Institute of Education*

The teaching of the mother tongue in Great Britain and France and the educational and psychological principles underlying it. *A. Moar, Ph.D. 1940 London, Institute of Education*

The use of standardized tests in recording the mental progress of elementary school children, and the value of such records in selecting individuals for higher education. *R. Williams, M.A. 1935 Liverpool*

Edward I, King of England
Edward I as a foreign statesman. *H. Instein, B.Litt. 1933 Oxford*

Edward II, King of England
The career of Peter of Gavaston and his place in history. *A. A. Taylor, M.A. 1938 London, Royal Holloway College*

Edward III, King of England
Edward III's war finance, 1337-41: transactions in wool and credit operations. *E. B. Fryde, D.Phil. 1947 Oxford*

Foreign chivalry at the Court of Edward III. *F. Schenck, B.Litt. 1912 Oxford*

Edward, the Black Prince
Contributions to the history of the earldom and county of Chester, 1237-1399, with a study of the household of Edward the Black Prince and its relations with Cheshire. *M. Sharp, Ph.D. 1925 Manchester*

Edward, the Confessor, Saint, King of England
Anglo-Norman didactic literature of the thirteenth century, and An Anglo-Norman life of St. Edward the Confessor. *P. Abson, Ph.D. 1921 Sheffield*

A study of the life of Edward the Confessor, as contained in ms Fonds français 1416, of the Bibliothèque Nationale. *C. J. Crozier, M.A. 1937 Belfast*

Edward, the Elder, King of Wessex
Edward the Elder and the Danes. *F. T. Wainwright, Ph.D. 1944 Reading*

Edwards, E. H.
All for China: an account of the life and labour of Mrs. E. H. Edwards of Taiynanfu, Shensi. *H. R. Williamson, M.A. 1922 London*

Edwards, Jonathan
Determinism in the theological system of Jonathan Edwards. *J. N. Thomas, Ph.D. 1937 Edinburgh*

The determinism of Jonathan Edwards. *W. L. Lewis, M.A. 1949 Bristol*

The theology of Jonathan Edwards: its historical antecedents and its distinctive features. *H. S. Curr, B.Litt. 1912 Oxford*

Edwards, Lewis
Bywyd a gwaith Dr. Lewis Edwards (The life and work of Dr. Lewis Edwards). *T. L. Evans, M.A. 1948 Wales*

Edwards, Roger
Bywyd a gwaith Roger Edwards o'r Wyddgrug (The life and work of Roger Edwards of Mold). *G. T. Jones, M.A. 1933 Wales*

Effen, Justus van
Justus van Effen and English influences in Dutch literature. *W. J. B. Pienaar, Ph.D. 1925 London*

Egberht, King of Wessex
The life and times of Egberht, King of Wessex, 802 to 839. *A. J. Thorogood, M.A. 1931 Reading*

Egg Industry
See Dairy Industry.

Egypt: Economics
See also Cotton Industry.

The costs of transport and the location of industry in Great Britain and Egypt. *A. A. A. Ismail, Ph.D. 1942 Birmingham*

Economic development of Egypt since 1876. *A. R. Fikry, M.Sc. 1918 London*

Economic federation with special references from the individual conditions of Egypt, past and present. *M. F. Leheta, Ph.D. 1926 Leeds*

The financial question and the reorganization of the Egyptian administration, 1865-1885. *H. K. S. Abulleef, M.A. 1948 Bristol*

Geographical features in the future development of Egypt. *A. B. Mountjoy, M.A. 1949 Reading*

The introduction of perennial irrigation in Egypt and its effects on the rural economy and population problems of the country. *I. A. Farid, Ph.D. 1937 London, University College*

Labour question in Egypt. *M. F. Leheta, M.Com. 1923 Birmingham*

The monetary system of Egypt. *M. A. Rifaat, Ph.D. 1935 London, School of Economics and Political Science*

The post-war industrial development of Egypt. *M. T. Sokkar, M.Com. 1940 Leeds*

Production policies and their impact on problems of marketing and international trade in modern Egypt. *G. E. M. A. Said, Ph.D. 1949 Birmingham*

The public finances of modern Egypt, with special reference to the period 1876-1942. *A. M. K. El Bey, Ph.D. 1946 London, School of Economics and Political Science*

A statistical survey of the development of capital investment in Egypt since 1880. *M. M. Hamdi, Ph.D. 1943 London, School of Economics and Political Science*

The structure of modern industry in Egypt. *A. A. I. El-Gritley, Ph.D. 1947 London, School of Economics and Political Science*

A study of the national income of Egypt. *M. A. Anis, Ph.D. 1949 London, School of Economics and Political Science*

Egypt: Foreign Affairs
The European Powers and the British occupation of Egypt, 1882-1885. *M. Phillips, M.A. 1937 Wales*

Foreign relations of Egypt in the fifteenth century (1422-1517). *M. M. Ziada, Ph.D. 1930 Liverpool*

Turkish and Egyptian rule in Arabia, 1810-1841. *A. H. M. El-Batrik, Ph.D. 1947 London, School of Oriental and African Studies*

Egypt: Geography
A geographical study of the Egyptian oases. *M. M. Mousa, Ph.D. 1938 Liverpool*

Egypt: History
See also Mehemet Ali.

The beginnings of the Egyptian Question and the rise of Mehemet Ali, 1800-1812. *S. Ghorbal, M.A. 1924 London*

British policy in reference to Mehemet Ali, 1839-41. *W. G. Turner, M.A. 1928 London*

The Nationalist movement in Egypt, 1879-1882. *M. S. Ashur, M.A. 1925 Birmingham*

Palmerston's attitude towards Mehemet Ali, 1834-8, with an introduction on the development of the Near Eastern question, 1788-1834. *R. L. Baker, B.Litt. 1928 Oxford*

Some aspects of British interest in Egypt in the late eighteenth century, 1775-1798. *M. A. Anis, Ph.D. 1950 Birmingham*

Egypt: Parliament
Parliamentary institutions and political parties in Egypt, 1866-1924. *J. Landau, Ph.D. 1949 London, School of Oriental and African Studies*

Egypt: Politics and Government
The financial question and the reorganization of the Egyptian administration, 1865-1885. *H. K. S. Abulleef, M.A. 1948 Bristol*

The legal principles governing the situational status of Egypt. *M. H. Fahmy, LL.D. 1928 London*

Parliamentary institutions and political parties in Egypt, 1866-1924. *J. Landau, Ph.D. 1949 London, School of Oriental and African Studies*

Egypt: Social History
An Egyptian in Ireland. *I. Rashad, Ph.D. 1922 National University of Ireland*

The national characteristics of the modern Egyptians. *N. Kamel, M.A. 1942 London, School of Economics and Political Science*

Egypt, Ancient
The administration of the Twelfth Dynasty: a phase in the development of government in ancient Egypt. *R. M. Cox, M.A. 1935 London, University College*

The influence of ancient Egypt on Greek and Mycenaean religious cults before the Hellenistic age. *J. G. Griffiths, M.A. 1936 Liverpool*

The Keftiu-people of the Egyptian monuments. *G. A. Wainwright, B.Litt. 1914 Oxford*

1. The origin of Christian monasticism in Egypt. 2. The history of Christian monasticism in Egypt to the close of the fourth century. *W. H. MacKean, B.D. & D.D. 1919 Oxford*

The place of Egypt in the prehistory of the Old World, with special reference to quarternary, diluvial, climates and cultures in the Saharo-Arabian area. *S. A. Huzzayin, Ph.D. 1935 Manchester*

The position of women in ancient Egypt. *M. S. Palmer, M.A. 1929 Manchester*

The racial history of Egypt and Nubia from predynastic to present times. *A. M. El Batrawi, Ph.D. 1940 London, University College*

The relations of Egypt and Syria-Palestine, with special reference to Old Testament history. *D. C. Davies, M.A. 1923 Liverpool*

Eichendorff, Joseph
Eichendorff's ideas of romanticism. *K. E. Finney, M.A. 1913 Birmingham*

Eire
See Ireland.

Eisteddfod
See also Bards.

The history of the Eisteddfod. *E. J. Lloyd, M.A. 1913 Wales*

Ekkehart I
Ekkehard's *Waltharius*. *A. H. Page, M.A. 1932 London, Bedford College*

Ekkehart IV
The annotations of Ekkehart IV in the Orosius ms. St. Gall 621: a contribution to the question of the nature of ancient glosses. *J. N. C. Clark, Ph.D. 1931 Edinburgh*

Eleanor of Castile, Queen
The enquiry into complaints against the ministers of Eleanor of Castile (1291-1292), its administrative and legal significanc. *M. E. Fenwick, M.A. 1931 London, Royal Holloway College*

Elections
See also Great Britain: Parliament.

The Clare election, 1828. *H. P. Carberry, M.A. 1934 Liverpool*

Elections to the House of Commons in the reign of William III. *J. H. Plumb, Ph.D. 1936 Cambridge*

The general election of 1710. *M. E. Ransome, M.A. 1938 London, Royal Holloway College*

The general elections of 1705. *E. A. Cunnington, M.A. 1938 London, University College*

Northamptonshire county elections and electioneering (1695-1832), based mainly on the Isham and Cartwright muniments. *E. G. Forrester, B.Litt. 1939 Oxford*

The Oxfordshire election of 1754. *R. J. Robson, B.Litt. 1947 Oxford*

Electrical Engineering
Electrical engineering economics. *D. J. Bolton, M.Sc. 1928 London*

The growth and progress of the electrical manufacturing industry in Great Britain. *E. Yates, M.A. 1937 Manchester*

Electricity: History
1. The beginnings of the scientific career of Joseph Priestley. 2. The detection and estimation of electric charges in the eighteenth century. 3. Animal electricity before Galvani. *W. C. Walker, Ph.D. 1937 London, University College*

A concise history of the beginning of the ionic theory, its development from the end of the eighteenth century to the conclusion of Faraday's work. *E. M. James, M.Sc. 1926 London*

The development of mathematical theories of electricity prior to Maxwell, with special reference to the concept potential. *M. E. J. Carr, M.Sc. 1949 London, University College*

Electricity: History contd.
Experimental methods on electricity during the first quarter of the nineteenth century, with special reference to the development of Voltaic apparatus. *H. J. Cramp, M.Sc. 1937 London, King's College*

The historical development of Ohm's law and the evolution of a standard of electrical resistance. *H. J. Winter, Ph.D. 1946 London, External Degree*

The origins of dynamo-electric apparatus. *J. R. Tugwood, M.Sc. 1945 London, University College*

A survey of the theories of the conduction of electricity through solutions from 1800-1876 (Carlisle and Nicholson to Kohlrausch). *C. H. Bailey, M.Sc. 1938 London, External Degree*

Theories of light and electricity in the eighteenth century. *G. N. Spriggs, M.Sc. 1926 London*

Electricity: Study and Teaching
An experimental investigation of the benefit derived from the employment of specially designed equipment for instruction in fundamental electrical and radio theory. *M. E. Claxton, M.Ed. 1950 Durham*

A study of the provision for vocational training in the advanced courses of girls' secondary schools, with special reference to electricity. *M. J. Gordon, M.A. 1941 London, King's College*

Electricity Supply Industry
The development of the electricity supply industry in Great Britain. *S. Judek, Ph.D. 1947 Edinburgh*

Electricity Supply Board. *B. O'Brien, M.A. 1942 National University of Ireland*

A geographical study of electricity generation and distribution in the northwest region. *T. H. King, M.A. 1949 Liverpool*

The organization of electricity supply in Great Britain. *H. H. Ballin, Ph.D. 1942 London, School of Economics and Political Science*

Power resources and utilization in the United Provinces. *P. K. Dutt, M.A. 1947 London, School of Economics and Political Science*

The relations of the state to electricity undertakings in Great Britain and Germany. *D. M. French, B.Litt. 1934 Oxford*

Some relationships between power and economic development, with special reference to California. *E. M. Francis, Ph.D. 1939 Cambridge*

Elegy
See Poetry.

Elementary Education
See Education, Elementary.

Eleusinian Mysteries
See Religion: Greece, Ancient.

Elias, Brother
Brother Elias and the government of the Franciscan Order, 1217-39. *R. B. Clark, Ph.D. 1950 Cambridge*

Eliasen, Paul
Paul Eliasen and the Danish Reformation. *E. H. Dunkley, B.D. 1942 Oxford*

Eliezer bar Nathan, Rabbi
The Life and works of Rabbi Eliezer bar Nathan of Mainz. *I. H. Levine, Ph.D. 1939 London, Jews' College*

Eliot, George
The effect of George Eliot the thinker on George Eliot the novelist. *B. Y. Deakin, M.A. 1947 Manchester*

George Eliot. *F. M. Lee, M.A. 1941 Birmingham*

George Eliot as an analyst of the social life of England in the nineteenth century. *I. Azmy, M.A. 1949 Sheffield*

Rustics and rural life in the novels of George Eliot, George Meredith and Thomas Hardy. *A. M. Vévar, M.A. 1940 Wales*

Eliot, Thomas Stearns
The earlier poetic method of T. S. Eliot and its background. *G. Patterson, M.Litt. 1937 Dublin, Trinity College*

The influence of Baudelaire, Laforgue and Corbière on the poetry of T. S. Eliot. *C. M. Shanahan, M.A. 1949 Manchester*

The poetry of T. S. Eliot. *D. E. S. Maxwell, Ph.D. 1950 Dublin, Trinity College*

T. S. Eliot as poet. *D. MacDonagh, M.A. 1939 National University of Ireland*

Ellenborough, Edward Law, Earl of
Lord Ellenborough's ideas on Indian policy. *K. I. Garrett, M.A. 1935 London, Birkbeck College*

Elliott, Ebenezer
Ebenezer Elliott: a study, including an edition of his works. *E. R. Seary, Ph.D. 1932 Sheffield*

Elliott, Henry, Sir
Sir Henry Elliott, British Ambassador at Constantinople, 1867-77, with particular reference to the period 1867-74. *D. T. Rees, M.A. 1940 Wales*

Ellis, George
George Ellis, Esquire: a study. *M. Baker, M.A. 1923 London*

Ellis, William
William Ellis and his work for education. *F. W. Robinson, M.A. 1919 London*

Elmham, Thomas de
An edition of: Thome Elmham *Gesta Henrici Quinti. F. Taylor, Ph.D. 1938 Manchester*

Emblem Books
The English emblem books. *R. Freeman, Ph.D. 1941 Cambridge*

Emerson, Ralph Waldo
Carlyle and Emerson. *N. Cogan, M.A. 1915 National University of Ireland*

Emerson and the romantic revival. *F. J. Yealy, Ph.D. 1930 Cambridge*

The spiritual outlook of Ralph Waldo Emerson. *E. B. Bostock, Ph.D. 1948 Edinburgh*

Emigration and Immigration
See also Migration.

Alien immigration into and alien communities in London, 1558 to 1640. *I. Scouloudi, M.Sc. 1936 London, School of Economics and Political Science*

The anthropology of some coloured communities in Great Britain with comparative material on colour prejudice. *K. L. Little, Ph.D. 1945 London, School of Economics and Political Science*

British migration to western Australia, 1829-1850. *M. Harris, Ph.D. 1934 London, School of Economics and Political Science*

Chinese coolie emigration to countries within the British Empire. *P. C. Campbell, M.Sc. 1922 London*

A contribution to the study of emigration from north Wales to the United States of America, 1800-1850. *E. K. R. R. Roberts, M.A. 1931 Liverpool*

Education for Empire settlement: a study of juvenile migration. *A. G. Scholes, Ph.D. 1930 Edinburgh*

Emigration from the British Isles, 1815-1921. *W. A. Carrothers, Ph.D. 1921 Edinburgh*

Emigration to British North America under the early Passenger Acts, 1803-1842. *K. A. Walpole, M.A. 1929 London*

The geographical background of white settlement in the Kenya highlands. *I. J. Fielding, M.Sc. 1947 London, School of Economics and Political Science*

A history of emigration from the United Kingdom to North America, 1763-1912. *S. C. Johnson, D.Sc. 1913 London*

An investigation into the causes, extent and character of emigration from the northern parts of Ireland to colonial America, with particular reference to the activities in Ireland of promoters of American lands. *R. J. Dickson, Ph.D. 1949 Belfast*

The Irish emigration: a study in demography. *N. G. Nolan, Ph.D. 1936 National University of Ireland*

Irish immigration into Great Britain, 1798-1838. *B. M. Kerr, B.Litt. 1939 Oxford*

Italian immigration into the Argentine Republic. *M. B. Lord, M.A. 1939 Manchester*

Midland immigrations. *O. G. Pickard, M.Com. 1940 Birmingham*

Migration from the United Kingdom to North America, 1840-1850. *F. M. I. Morehouse, Ph.D. 1926 Manchester*

Migration to Australia and New Zealand: post-war experience, present position, and future possibilities. *W. D. Forsyth, B.Litt. 1939 Oxford*

New Orleans as a port of immigration. *A. A. Conway, M.A. 1949 London, University College*

The quality of immigration into eastern Australia before 1851. *R. B. Madgwick, D.Phil. 1935 Oxford*

Some anthropological aspects of Mexican immigrant settlement in Dallas, Texas. *H. D. Gunn, M.A. 1949 London, School of Economics and Political Science*

A study of emigration from Great Britain, 1802 to 1860. *N. M. G. Page, Ph.D. 1931 London, School of Economics and Political Science*

Emigration and Immigration contd.
A study of the economics of international migration, 1820-1914. *R. Rostowski, Ph.D. 1943 Edinburgh*

Emotion
Co-education: a statistical enquiry into the attitude of teachers towards co-education, and a comparative study of the emotional development of children trained in co-educational and other institutions. *F. E. Moreton, Ph.D. 1939 London, Institute of Education*

Emotional development in young children. *E. H. Hughes, Ph.D. 1934 London, Bedford College*

Emotional fluctuations in women. *M. Kerr, Ph.D. 1938 London, Bedford College*

An enquiry into the relation of language to emotion, with special reference to its influence on thought and behaviour. *M. Collins, M.A. 1921 Liverpool*

An experimental study of emotion. *M. S. Muhiyuddin, M.Ed. 1922 Leeds*

The psychology of the emotions. *J. F. Kelly, M.A. 1945 National University of Ireland*

A study of emotion by means of free association in conjunction with the psycho-galvanic reflex. *J. M. Forbes, Ph.D. 1935 London, University College*

The study of the primary emotions in young children with special reference to the emotion of fear. *M. C. Moore, M.A. 1914 Liverpool*

Empedocles
Empedocles, the poet; his style and metre. *J. Bennett, Ph.D. 1940 Dublin, Trinity College*

Empiricism
See also Berkeley, G., Bishop; Hume, D.; Locke, J.; Ward, J.

Empiricism. *C. H. Whiteley, Ph.D. 1950 Birmingham*

Empiricism: a critical examination of the empirical theory of knowledge as this is expounded in certain of the works of Locke and Berkeley. *G. H. Haydock, Ph.D. 1946 Glasgow*

Employment
See also Women in Industry.

An analysis of wage-rates in Britain in relation to employment levels since 1920. *W. H. Mason, M.Sc. 1949 London, External Degree*

The determinants of the level of employment. *J. J. J. Baudewyns, B.Phil. 1947 Oxford*

The development of industries in Eire since 1924, with special reference to (a) employment, and (b) The national income and its distribution. *D. C. Doolan, M.Econ.Sc. 1944 National University of Ireland*

The development of industries in Eire since 1924, with special reference to (a) employment, and (b) the national income and its distribution. *J. M. Colfer, M.Econ.Sc. 1944 National University of Ireland*

The development of industries in Eire since 1924, with special reference to (a) employment, (b) the national income and its distribution. *D. F. O'Farrell, M.Econ.Sc. 1944 National University of Ireland*

Employment and unemployment in the 26 counties. *J. J. Walsh, M.Econ.Sc. 1941 National University of Ireland*

The employment of juveniles and young persons (14-18) in the West Riding wool textile industry, with some reference to the effect of the raising of the school-leaving age and release for part-time further education. *J. W. Scarf, B.Phil. 1947 Oxford*

Employment trends in Saorstát Eireann. *J. P. O'Neill, M.A. 1937 National University of Ireland*

Factors in occupational maladjustment: a comparative study of the careers of employed and unemployed lads in a typical London district. *S. M. Bevington, Ph.D. 1933 London, External Degree*

The higher education and employment of women in the twentieth century. *E. Y. Angus, M.A. 1931 London, School of Economics and Political Science*

The impact of international economic fluctuations on employment and incomes in New Zealand, 1929-1939, and the nature and effects of public policy towards it, with some comparative study of Australia and Canada in the same period. *N. S. McIvor, Ph.D. 1949 London, School of Economics and Political Science*

Industrial combination and unemployment. *W. E. Salt, M.A. 1924 Sheffield*

Employment contd.
An investigation into the causes that render large numbers of boys unable to obtain employment on reaching early manhood, with special reference to the conditions of boy life and labour in Birmingham. *A. J. Freeman, B.Litt. 1914 Oxford*

The juvenile employment service. *J. M. Dawson, M.A. 1948 London, Bedford College*

Juvenile unemployment in the south Wales industrial region: an economic and statistical enquiry. *G. Meara, Ph.D. 1935 Wales*

A national employment service: Great Britain's experience. *S. Warrington, M.Sc. 1947 London, External Degree*

New Zealand's policy in international trade and its relation to employment policy. *K. A. Blakey, M.Sc. 1947 London, School of Economics and Political Science*

The problem of unemployment in Eire. *E. F. Murphy, M.Econ.Sc. 1945 National University of Ireland*

Problems of juvenile employment. *A. D. K. Owen, M.Com. 1929 Leeds*

Some aspects of employment psychology. *K. H. Edwards, M.Ed. 1932 Durham*

A study of factors that influenced action in regard to the education of the unemployed boy during the inter-war years. *E. S. Conway, M.A. 1941 Liverpool*

A study of juvenile unemployment in West Ham. *C. V. Dawe, M.Comm. 1933 Leeds*

A study of some social and industrial problems involved in modern, large-scale employment of labour in unskilled work, based on observation and investigation in a wartime filling factory. *V. C. Stone, M.A. 1945 Liverpool*

A survey of industrial trends in employment in the West Riding of Yorkshire since 1921. *J. F. Topping, M.Com. 1946 Leeds*

Unemployment and depression in Australia, 1929-32. *E. R. Walker, Ph.D. 1933 Cambridge*

Unemployment in Britain, with special reference to the period from 1909 to the present time. *W. H. Beveridge, D.Sc. 1930 London, School of Economics and Political Science*

Unemployment in British industries, 1815-1850. *A. D. Gayer, D.Phil. 1931 Oxford*

Unemployment in Germany (since the war). *K. I. Wiggs, Ph.D. 1932 London, School of Economics and Political Science*

Unemployment insurance: a study of schemes of assisted insurance. *J. G. Gibbon, D.Sc. 1911 London*

Enamels
Medieval Spanish enamels. *W. L. Hildburgh, Ph.D. 1937 London, University College*

Encina, Juan de la
Juan del Encina and the origin of the Spanish drama. *M. I. D. J. A. A. Bernard, M.A. 1931 London, King's College*

Enclosures
East Sussex landownership: the structure of rural society in an area of old enclosure, 1733-87. *D. K. Worcester, Ph.D. 1950 Cambridge*

Enclosure in Leicestershire, 1485-1607. *L. A. Parker, M.A. 1948 London, External Degree*

The enclosure movement in Anglesey, 1788-1866. *E. J. Jones, M.A. 1924 Wales*

The enclosure movement in Caernarvonshire, with special reference to the Porth-yr-aur papers. *G. A. Plume, M.A. 1935 Wales*

The Enclosure Movement in south Wales during the Tudor and early Stuart periods. *T. I. J. Jones, M.A. 1936 Wales*

The Norfolk Rising under Robert Kett, 1549. *W. H. T. Walker, M.A. 1921 Wales*

On the causes and course of the rebellion of 1549 in Devon and Cornwall. *W. J. Blake, M.A. 1909 London*

Parliamentary enclosure in Bulmer Wapontake. *M. Kirk, M.A. 1948 Leeds*

Parliamentary enclosure in Oxfordshire, 1696-1882. *W. E. Tate, B.Litt. 1947 Oxford*

Parliamentary enclosures in Lindsey, or the enclosures of the eighteenth and nineteenth centuries as they affected Lindsey. *T. H. Swales, M.A. 1936 Leeds*

The progress of enclosures in the county of Dorset since 1700. *G. B. Endacott, B.Litt. 1938 Oxford*

Enclosures contd.
The social and economic circumstances of Ket's rebellion, 1549. *R. J. Hammond, M.A. 1934 London, School of Economics and Political Science*

Encyclopaedias
The development of natural philosophy as reflected by the English and French Encyclopaedias of the eighteenth century. *L. H. Shave, Ph.D. 1941 London, University College*

The educational ideas of the Encyclopaedists. *T. J. James, Ph.D. 1946 London, External Degree*

Energy
See Power Supply.

Enfances Guillaume
A contribution to the study of the *Enfances Guillaume* in the versions contained in the mss. Royal 20D XI (British Museum, London) and français 24369 (Bibliothèque Nationale, Paris). *D. McMillan, Ph.D. 1938 London, University College*

Engineering
The history of the development of the steam engine to the year 1850, with special reference to the work of West-country engineers. *W. R. M. Caff, M.Sc. 1937 London, External Degree*

Quaestiones hydraulicae. *E. J. A. Kenny, M.Litt. 1936 Cambridge*

The scientific history of the steam engine. *W. A. Marshall, M.Sc. 1930 London*

Engineering: Study and Teaching
An analysis of the abilities, interests and qualities of personality of a representative group of engineering apprentices. *A. G. Beverstock, M.A. 1946 London, Institute of Education*

A comprehensive survey of the mathematical education of engineers. *J. D. Stewart, Ph.D. 1948 Aberdeen*

Education for the engineering industry with special reference to Wakefield and the West Riding. *G. F. Johnson, M.Ed. 1940 Leeds*

A study of aptitude for engineering drawing at the age of 13, with reference to the selection of entrants to technical schools. *B. S. Howard, M.A. 1945 London, Institute of Education*

Engineering Industry
The antecedents and beginnings of the Amalgamated Society of Engineers. *T. H. Robinson, B.Litt. 1928 Oxford*

Early industrial organisation: a history of the firm of Boulton and Watt. *E. Roll, Ph.D. 1930 Birmingham*

An economic history of shipbuilding and marine engineering. *W. S. Cormack, Ph.D. 1930 Glasgow*

The financial history of Matthew Boulton, 1759-1800. *J. E. Cule, M.Com. 1935 Birmingham*

A geographical study of the distribution of the engineering industry in England and Wales. *A. J. B. Budge, M.A. 1933 Liverpool*

A history of civil engineering. *C. J. Merdinger, D.Phil. 1949 Oxford*

An introduction to the economic development of the mechanical engineering industry, 1750-1900. *A. T. Kings, M.Sc. 1923 London*

The positions of the skilled and less skilled workman in the engineering and building trades (1914-25). *J. R. Hicks, B.Litt. 1927 Oxford*

The postwar relations of skilled and unskilled labour in the printing, building and engineering industries. *P. A. Manning, Ph.D. 1933 London, School of Economics and Political Science*

Recent changes in the structure and training of labour in the British engineering industry, and their future trends. *A. F. Nagib, Ph.D. 1945 Manchester*

England
See Great Britain.

England, Bank of
See Bank of England.

English Channel
Certain aspects of coast erosion in the English Channel with special reference to the coast-defence problems of the town of Sidmouth, Devon. *W. P. Baron, M.A. 1931 London, External Degree*

English Language
See also Ancrene Wisse; Bede, the Venerable; Book of Common Prayer; Chaucer, G.; Names, Personal; Place Names; Schwob, M.

The affiliations of Germanic. *G. C. Britton, M.A. 1949 Birmingham*

The alliterative diction of early Middle English poetry. *B. Allen, M.A. 1921 London*

English Language contd.
Anglo-Saxon charters. *A. J. Robertson, Ph.D. 1934 Cambridge*

Certain adverbial usages in Chaucer. *A. Pearce, M.A. 1928 Manchester*

The colloquial movement in English prose from 1660 to 1704. *A. Chilton, M.A. 1948 London, Queen Mary College*

A contribution to the study of nineteenth century slang. *K. Foster, M.A. 1929 London*

The ellipsis of the subject pronoun (and related phenomena) in English in the twelfth, thirteenth and fourteenth centuries. *W. F. J. Roberts, M.A. 1933 London, University College*

English colloquial idiom in the eighteenth century. *J. Platt, Ph.D. 1925 London*

English grammarians, 1450-1650: a critical survey, a study in the development of a logical system of grammar for English. *G. K. Cooke, M.A. 1938 London, Queen Mary College*

English influence on the German language: some indications. *A. Oakey, M.A. 1931 Birmingham*

English influences on the written form of the language and on the literature of Scotland, 1500-1625. *M. A. Bald, B.Litt. 1925 Oxford*

English personal letters and private diaries of 1640-1680: a study of the general mental attitude of the period as illustrated by individual types, together with a brief examination of the colloquial language of the time. *M. T. Williamson, Ph.D. 1929 London*

The expansion of the English language in Scotland. *L. W. Sharp, Ph.D. 1927 Cambridge*

Grammar of the *Ancrene Wisse* (phonology and accidence). *M. B. Salu, B.Litt. 1949 Oxford*

Historical studies in the syntax and phraseology of present-day English. *S. Bergerhoff, Ph.D. 1945 Leeds*

A history of the Scandinavian influence on the English language. *E. S. Olszewska, B.Litt. 1934 Oxford*

The influence of Middle Dutch and Middle Low German on English speech. *E. C. Llewellyn, B. Litt. 1930 Oxford*

An investigation into the history of the use of English in Ireland in medieval times, with special reference to the nature of the dialects and the influence of standard English. *J. J. Hogan, B.Litt. 1926 Oxford*

Kynge Johan re-edited, with a study of the language of Bale in appendix. *J. H. P. Pafford, M.A. 1929 London*

The language and dialect of *Sir Gawain and the Green Knight, Pearl, Patience and purity. J. P. Oakden, M.A. 1927 Manchester*

The language and style of William Salesbury. *D. Mark, M.A. 1903 Wales*

The language of the Elizabethan drama. *M. Evans, Ph.D. 1940 Cambridge*

The language of the Middle English lyric. *G. E. Morris, B.A. 1937 Sheffield*

Linguistic activity at the court of Henry VIII. *A. Le Lièvre, Ph.D. 1950 Cambridge*

The noun and pronoun of address in the seventeenth and eighteenth centuries. *P. Gurrey, Ph.D. 1926 London*

On grammatical mood in Ben Jonson's comedies. *S. Potter, M.A. 1924 London*

On ornamental words (a preliminary essay): a contribution to the study of poetic diction in English literature. *B. Groom, M.A. 1915 London*

On the pronouns in seventeenth and eighteenth century English. *A. B. Badger, M.A. 1930 London, University College*

The original language of the *Ancren Riwle. D. M. E. Dymes, M.A. 1922 London*

The origins of Old English orthography, with special reference to the representation of the spirants and w. *J. E. Blomfield, B.Litt. 1935 Oxford*

The phonology and accidence of the O.E. glosses in ms. Cotton Vespasian A1 (Vespasian Psalter). *E. V. Williams, B.Litt. 1935 Oxford*

The phonology and morphology of the Rushworth Gospels, known as Rushworth 1. *M. H. Scargill, Ph.D. 1940 Leeds*

Some aspects of expression in the poetry of the early nineteenth century. *M. L. Jackson, M.A. 1940 Belfast*

English Language contd.
Studies in the language of Robert Smith Surtees (1805-1864). *M. G. Owen, M.A. 1939 Liverpool*

Studies in the language of manners in England from the eleventh to the eighteenth centuries. *J. E. Colledge, M.A. 1935 Liverpool*

Studies in the language of Milton: parts 1-2. *E. Holmes, M.A. 1923 Liverpool*

Studies in the language and syntax of Ben Jonson. *B. I. Evans, M.A. 1922 London*

A study of the language of the metrical chronicle of Robert of Gloucester. *V. G. Salmon, M.A. 1949 London, University College*

A study of the linguistic features of the first Prayer Book of Edward VI (1549). *W. Straw, M.A. 1924 London*

A study of the themes of weak verbs in Old English and the older stages of the other Germanic languages. *A. F. Thyagaraju, M.A. 1935 London, King's College*

Style in composition. *D. Canham, M.A. 1923 National University of Ireland*

The style of the *Honourable history of Friar Bacon and Friar Bungay. N. A. Marten, M.A. 1948 Birmingham*

Syncope and apocope in Old English. *H. Peers, M.A. 1932 Leeds*

The syntax of Chaucer's *Troilus and Criseyde. D. J. Rogers, M.A. 1925 Wales*

The syntax of *Cursor Mundi. D. J. Rogers, B.Litt. 1932 Oxford*

Tennyson's diction. *D. C. Jones, M.A. 1925 Liverpool*

The use of case in Old English to express comparison. *G. W. Small, B.Litt. 1927 Oxford*

The verbal forms in the *Mabinogion* and *Bruts. G. J. Williams, M.A. 1918 Wales*

The verbal forms of the *Mabinogion* and *Bruts. W. Griffith, M.A. 1904 Wales*

English Language: Dialects
An account of the dialect of Staithes in the North Riding of Yorkshire. *M. S. Lawson, M.A. 1949 Leeds*

Dialect in Tudor drama. *H. M. Hulme, M.A. 1937 London, Courtauld Institute of Art*

The dialect of Bubwith in the East Riding of Yorkshire. *A. E. Langrick, M.A. 1949 Leeds*

The dialect of Lindsey. *J. E. Oxley, M.A. 1934 London, King's College*

The dialect of Lower Calderdale (Yorks). *J. A. Sheard, Ph.D. 1940 London, King's College*

The dialect of Radcliffe: a contribution to a survey of the regional dialects of Lancashire. *W. Barlow, M.A. 1934 Liverpool*

The dialect of the *Pricke of Conscience*, together with a collation of mss. Galba E IX and Harley 4196. *J. Lightbown, M.A. 1935 Leeds*

The dialects of the West Midlands between 1150-1450. *M. S. Serjeantson, D.Phil. 1926 Oxford*

English as spoken in Cork City. *D. J. Leahy, M.A. 1915 National University of Ireland*

A grammar of the dialect of Farmborough (North Somerset): historical and descriptive, with dialect specimens and an appendix on the Scandinavian element. *F. C. Perry, M.A. 1917 Leeds*

Grammar of the dialect of Tarbolton (Ayrshire). *T. Wright, Ph.D. 1929 Glasgow*

A history of the Kentish dialect, with special reference to agricultural terms. *B. M. H. Carr, M.A. 1947 London, King's College*

An investigation into the history of the use of English in Ireland in medieval times, with special reference to the nature of the dialects and the influence of standard English. *J. J. Hogan, B.Litt. 1926 Oxford*

The language and dialect of *Sir Gawain and the Green Knight, Pearl, Patience and purity. J. P. Oakden, M.A. 1927 Manchester*

The living dialect of Broughton-in-Furness. *M. G. Round, M.A. 1949 Leeds*

The living dialect of Byers Green. *H. Orton, B.Litt. 1924 Oxford*

The older French element in the vocabulary of the English dialects. *F. M. Williams, B.Litt. 1947 Oxford*

On the French element in the English regional dialects. *P. E. Stott, M.A. 1934 Liverpool*

English Language: Dialects contd.
The phonology and accidence of the Cotton ms. of the *Cursor mundi* considered with especial reference to the Northumbrian dialect of Old English. *L. Fenwick, M.A. 1947 Manchester*

A phonology of the old Northumbrian texts. *M. Miller, Ph.D. 1930 Leeds*

The relation of standard English to the modern dialects in their treatment of the gutturals. *H. C. K. Wyld, B.Litt. 1899 Oxford*

The Sierra Leone patois: a study of its growth and structure, with especial reference to the teaching of English in Sierra Leone. *H. A. E. Sawyerr, M.Ed. 1940 Durham*

Some phonological features of the dialect of London and of the surrounding areas in the fifteenth century. *B. A. Mackenzie, B.Litt. 1926 Oxford*

Studies in language mainly in relation to Derbyshire, Staffordshire and Shropshire from 1500 to 1700, from Church accounts. *H. M. Hulme, Ph.D. 1947 London, External Degree*

A study in the living Durham dialect: a contribution to an English linguistic atlas. *J. L. Bailes, M.A. 1948 Leeds*

A study of the dialect of the Old English homilies in the twelfth century ms. Vespasian D XIV. *F. H. T. Williams, M.A. 1945 London, King's College*

A study of the English dialects of Ireland, 1172-1800. *P. J. Irwin, Ph.D. 1935 London, Birkbeck College*

The Surrey dialect in Middle English in relation to the dialects of the adjacent counties. *D. L. Cavers, B.Litt. 1929 Oxford*

William Barnes: study of the man and poet and of his work in connection with Dorset and the Dorset dialect. *J. V. Ruffell, Ph.D. 1948 London, External Degree*

English Language: Etymology
English compound nouns of the type used in personal descriptions; a supplement to the chronology of the new English dictionary. *D. D. Pilkington, M.A. 1920 London*

The English element in Welsh. *T. H. Williams, M.A. 1911 Wales*

English loan words in literary Welsh. *R. W. Jones, M.A. 1907 Wales*

An examination into some elements of Spenser's psychological vocabulary, with reference to that of Chaucer. *M. Topham, M.A. 1931 Manchester*

An examination of certain portions of the French element in Chaucer's vocabulary. *H. Goldstraw, M.A. 1931 Manchester*

An index significationum to the Anglo-Saxon gloss to the Lindisfarne Gospels. *B. Hill, M.A. 1949 Birmingham*

The influence of chemical theory upon chemical nomenclature and symbolism from the period of Lavoisier to that of Laurent. *F. J. Pearson, M.Sc. 1929 London*

The influence of French on the development of the English vocabulary from 1600 onwards. *T. Quayle, M.A. 1913 London*

A list of Arabic words in the English vocabulary. *W. Taylor, M.A. 1932 Leeds*

The military and naval terms in the Norman and Anglo-Saxon chronicles of the twelfth century. *G. C. Johnson, Ph.D. 1949 Leeds*

The obsolescence of words: a study, based chiefly on the *New English Dictionary*, of changes in our vocabulary since circa 1650. *E. B. Dike, Ph.D. 1933 Edinburgh*

The older French element in the vocabulary of the English dialects. *F. M. Williams, B.Litt. 1947 Oxford*

On the derivation and meaning of some ancient building terms. *B. O. S. Snell, M.A. 1924 London*

On the French element in the English regional dialects. *P. E. Stott, M.A. 1934 Liverpool*

The place of Johnson's dictionary in the history of English lexicography. *A. W. Read, B.Litt. 1933 Oxford*

Sea terms in early English literature. *W. J. Redbond, M.A. 1934 London, King's College*

Some aspects of the work of the Anglo-Latin twelfth century satirists: the loan words in Gothic, with some account of the pronunciation of that language. *E. P. Bates, M.A. 1910 London*

A study of Chaucer's diction and terms for womanly beauty. *S. Ganguly, Ph.D. 1940 London, University College*

English Language: Etymology contd.
A study of the vocabulary of the English settlers in Ireland before 1600. *P. J. Irwin, M.A. 1931 London, Birkbeck College*

English Language: Phonetics
Comparative phonetics of English and Roumanian. *J. O. Stefanovici, Ph.D. 1927 London*

A comparison of the phonetic systems of English and Welsh, and the application of such comparative study in the practical teaching of English in Welsh schools. *M. Davies, M.A. 1923 Wales*

English pronunciation in the seventeenth and eighteenth centuries: and essays upon shorthand and literature. *W. Matthews, Ph.D. 1934 London, Birkbeck College*

The interpretation of diphthongal spellings in Old English, with special reference to the phonological problems presented by the fracture spellings in Cambridge University Library manuscript Ii.1.33. *C. R. Quirk, M.A. 1949 London, University College*

The intonation of American English. *E. T. Anderson, M.A. 1939 London, University College*

An investigation of the rimes and phonology of Barbour's *Bruce*. *O. T. Williams, M.A. 1908 Wales*

A phonology of the old Northumbrian texts. *M. Miller, Ph.D. 1930 Leeds*

The production of dipthongs by 'breaking' in Old English from 700 to 900. *A. Campbell, B.Litt. 1931 Oxford*

The relation of standard English to the modern dialects in their treatment of the gutturals. *H. C. K. Wyld, B.Litt. 1899 Oxford*

Some phonological features of the dialect of London and of the surrounding areas in the fifteenth century. *B. A. Mackenzie, B.Litt. 1926 Oxford*

A study of the pronunciation of English during the seventeenth and eighteenth centuries as shown by the contemporary writers of shorthand. *W. Matthews, M.A. 1931 London, Birkbeck College*

Varieties of pronunciation in sixteenth century standard English (the vowels of stressed syllables). *H. Brown, B.Litt. 1926 Oxford*

Vowel sounds in poetry, their music and tone colour. *M. M. Macdermott, Ph.D. 1941 Glasgow*

English Language: Study and Teaching
A comparison of the phonetic systems of English and Welsh, and the application of such comparative study in the practical teaching of English in Welsh schools. *M. Davies, M.A. 1923 Wales*

Composition as mental and aesthetic training. *D. E. T. Owen, M.Ed. 1919 Manchester*

Critical analysis of objective studies in the teaching of English. *D. Bagley, M.A. 1935 London, Institute of Education*

English and English education in Ceylon. *E. F. C. Ludowyk, Ph.D. 1936 Cambridge*

The English language in Ceylon. *H. A. Passé, Ph.D. 1948 London, External Degree*

An enquiry into the correlation of certain mental tests with ability in different types of English composition. *O. J. K. Cotton, M.A. 1932 Birmingham*

An examination of the postulate that there is no improvement over the session in English language in the pre-senior part-time day courses at a technical school, involving the formulation of two equivalent tests in English. *W. Bolas, M.A. 1948 Birmingham*

An experiment of group methods of teaching English composition with some consideration of their effects on attainment and attitude and a sociometric study of the groups involved. *J. E. Richardson, M.A. 1948 London, Institute of Education*

An experimental study of a new method of grammar teaching and its bearing on composition. *V. M. Brown, M.A. 1936 London, Institute of Education*

An experimental study of diagnostic tests in English. *F. E. Schonell, M.A. 1940 London, University College*

The function of English studies in educational reconstruction. *G. W. Hartley, M.A. 1945 Leeds*

The history of Old English and Old Norse studies in England from the time of Francis Junius till the end of the eighteenth century. *J. A. W. Bennett, D.Phil. 1938 Oxford*

The influence exercised by the development of English prose and literary criticism upon the teaching of the vernacular tongue and study of literature in English schools. *C. Rees, M.A. 1909 Wales*

English Language: Study and Teaching contd.
An investigation into disability in spelling. *F. J. Schonell, Ph.D. 1932 London, Day Training College*

An investigation into the influence of written corrections of the work in arithmetic and English in a senior girls' school. *D. Bloomer, M.A. 1944 Liverpool*

An investigation on methods of marking composition. *B. M. D. Cast, M.A. 1939 London, University College*

Lessing's study and knowledge of English language and literature. *P. Levy, M.A. 1935 London, University College*

The method of teaching English in Chinese middle schools. *Y. N. Chang, M.Ed. 1937 Leeds*

The method of teaching the English group of subjects in junior technical schools. *G. B. Talbot, M.A. 1939 Wales*

Observation of a method of teaching English in secondary schools. *R. V. Rosetti, M.A. 1949 London, Institute of Education*

Outlines of the history of the study of English in theory and practice (1550-1800). *M. M. Lewis, M.A. 1922 London*

The place and teaching of English in early adolescence. *W. C. Watson, M.A. 1914 Liverpool*

The position of English in a national system of education for Bengal. *M. P. West, D.Phil. 1927 Oxford*

Problems in the teaching of English. *L. G. O'Flynn, M.A. 1936 National University of Ireland*

The provision of schemes of work in the English subjects for pupils of the new age group in senior modern schools. *F. C. Willmott, M.A. 1940 Bristol*

The relation of grammar and composition to the training of appreciation. *E. P. Jewitt, M.A. 1923 London*

The relationship between imagery and the teaching of English. *J. E. Mason, M.Ed. 1928 Leeds*

The Sierra Leone patois: a study of its growth and structure, with special reference to the teaching of English in Sierra Leone. *H. A. E. Sawyerr, M.Ed. 1940 Durham*

The status of French and English in the Neutral Islands, 1635-1763. *G. M. Fletcher, M.A. 1930 London, King's College*

A study in the teaching of English composition in a girls' modern secondary school: an investigation into the relative merits of two different methods. *M. Kelsall, M.A. 1947 Liverpool*

A survey, historical and critical, of the methods and textbooks employed in the teaching of English in English schools. *R. Reynolds, M.A. 1925 Liverpool*

The teaching of English as a second language in India, with special reference to Hyderabad Deccan. *A. M. Pothan, M.Ed. 1938 Leeds*

The teaching of English in the Gaeltacht primary school. *P. Hynes, M.A. 1935 National University of Ireland*

The teaching of English in the middle and high schools in the Presidency of Bombay. *K. D. Desai, M.Ed. 1938 Leeds*

The teaching of English to Indian pupils. *I. Husain, M.Ed. 1933 Leeds*

Training in style through literary appreciation, with special reference to pupils aged ten to fifteen. *G. W. Hartley, M.Ed. 1927 Leeds*

English Literature: General and Miscellaneous
Cervantes, with special reference to *Don Quixote*, in English literature until 1781. *A. H. Mayor, B.Litt. 1926 Oxford*

The character sketch: its growth and development in English literature. *M. M. Brooks, M.A. 1914 London*

Child portraiture in English prose. *E. R. Williams, M.A. 1912 Bristol*

The development of the idea of the animal as a symbol of harmony in English literature. *M. Jager, Ph.D. 1932 Cambridge*

The devil in English literature from the Middle Ages to 1700. *W. M. Mountford, Ph.D. 1931 London, External Degree*

The dominie in English literature. *J. E. Mason, M.A. 1928 Birmingham*

English influences in Russian literature, from 1700 to 1830. *W. K. Matthews, M.A. 1923 Manchester*

English literature: the rudiments of its art and craft. *E. V. Downs, M.A. 1921 Wales*

English Literature: General and Miscellaneous contd.

An examination of certain prose rhythms as used in the works of Lyly, Browne, Milton, Lamb and Shaw. *H. G. Parfitt, M.A. 1940 Wales*

Geoffrey of Monmouth's *Chronicle* and its influence on English literature. *L. Woosnam, M.A. 1913 Wales*

The growth and development of regional literature in the West Midlands. *R. J. W. Bodenham, M.A. 1932 Birmingham*

India and the Near East in English literature. *M. D. Taseer, Ph.D. 1936 Cambridge*

India's contribution to imaginative English literature. *R. Pitman, M.A. 1920 Birmingham*

The influence of Celtic literature on that of England. *J. O. M. McCaffrey, M.A. 1938 National University of Ireland*

The influence of English literature on the German novel and drama in the period 1880-1900. *A. E. Eastlake, Ph.D. 1937 London, Birkbeck College*

The influence of English literature on Urdu literature. *S. A. Latif, Ph.D. 1924 London*

The influence of English writers on Gérard de Nerval. *J. K. Evans, M.A. 1939 Manchester*

The influence of Roman satire on English literature. *A. H. Hill, M.A. 1910 Birmingham*

Justus van Effen and English influences in Dutch literature. *W. J. B. Pienaar, Ph.D. 1925 London*

The Kingdom of God in English literature. *H. Pitts, M.A. 1920 National University of Ireland*

La dette anglaise de Victor Hugo. *L. M. J. Couturier, M.A. 1912 London*

Land and peasant in Anglo-Irish literature. *E. J. Sheehy, M.A. 1932 National University of Ireland*

Les interprétations critiques de la littérature anglaise en France pendant le Second Empire. *E. Holder, M.A. 1928 Leeds*

Literary life in England and France betwen the years 1066 and 1400. *J. Scotland, M.Litt. 1929 Cambridge*

The London coffee-houses, and their literary associations down to the death of Anne. *J. Williams, B.Litt. 1936 Oxford*

Ovid in English literature. *S. Rose, M.A. 1922 London*

The poor in English literature. *E. O'Driscoll, M.A. 1917 National University of Ireland*

The rhythm of English prose. *A. Classe, D.Litt. 1940 Glasgow*

The seven deadly sins in English literature. *D. V. Ives, M.A. 1931 London, Westfield College*

Some representative versions of the Faust-theme in English literature. *V. D. Benjamin, M.A. 1936 Manchester*

Studies in the treatment of the child in English literature. *W. A. Whiting, M.A. 1921 London*

The treatment of the supernatural in English literature from Shakespeare to Coleridge together with some consideration of the subject in its relation to the metaphysical and mystical side of literature. *G. M. H. Harcourt-Smith, M.A. 1907 London*

Wales and the Welsh in English literature from the beginning of the sixteenth to the beginning of the nineteenth century. *W. J. Hughes, M.A. 1919 Wales*

English Literature: Criticism
See also Literature: Criticism; and Addison, J.; De Quincey, T.; Taine, H. A.; Walsh, W.

Dr. Johnson's knowledge of the English writers to the year 1600 (excluding Shakespeare). *D. B. Saunders, B.Litt. 1935 Oxford*

Eighteenth century literary criticism up to Dr. Johnson, with particular reference to the criticism of Shakespeare, Milton and the metaphysical poets. *M. J. Ince, M.A. 1948 Manchester*

Emile Montégut: critic of English literature. *J. W. Skinner, Ph.D. 1926 London*

England and her writers in the works of Anatole France (1844-1924). *H. C. Ault, M.A. 1928 Birmingham*

Goethe's knowledge of English literature. *J. Boyd, B.Litt. 1923 Oxford*

Goethe's knowledge of English literature. *M. S. Woolf, M.A. 1907 Birmingham*

The indebtedness of Klopstock to English literature. *D. R. Swaine, M.A. 1919 Wales*

English Literature: Criticism contd.
John Wilson Croker's contributions to the *Quarterly review*, with and estimate of his work in them as a literary critic. *R. M. Campbell, B.Litt. 1937 Oxford*

Klopstock in England: a chapter in Anglo-German literary relations. *L. Couch, Ph.D. 1928 London*

Lessing's knowledge and criticism of English literature. *L. H. Kay, M.A. 1912 Birmingham*

Lessing's study and knowledge of English language and literature. *P. Levy, M.A. 1935 London, University College*

The literary criticism of Richard Hurd (1719-1808). *M. J. Hourd, B.Litt. 1932 Oxford*

The literary criticism of Walter Pater. *M. Gopal, B.Litt. 1933 Oxford*

Literary history in England in the eighteenth century, before Warton's *History of English poetry*. *T. A. H. Scott, B.Litt. 1939 Oxford*

A pioneer in the work of propagating a knowledge of England and English literature in France, being an investigation into the Abbé Prévost's relations with England and English literature, with special reference to his *Le pour et contre, Cleveland, Mémoires d'un homme de qualité* and *Lettres de Mentor à un jeune seigneur*. *J. C. Carpenter, M.A. 1915 Wales*

Pope's knowledge of English literature from Chaucer to Dryden. *E. G. Midgley, B.Litt. 1950 Oxford*

The rise of the Scottish Chaucerians. *W. B. Inglis, Ph.D. 1930 Glasgow*

Sainte-Beuve's critical appreciation of English literature. *E. M. Phillips, M.A. 1923 Wales*

The Scottish Chaucerians. *T. P. Lamnin, M.A. 1941 National University of Ireland*

Sir Walter Scott in Germany. *F. E. Gauntlett, M.A. 1920 London*

A study of English dramatic criticism during the period 1870-1900, with special reference to the work of Bernard Shaw, William Archer, A. B. Walkley, and H. A. Jones. *A. C. D. Walters, M.A. 1944 Wales*

English Literature: Study and Teaching
See English Language: Study and Teaching.

English Literature: Early and Medieval
See also Anglo-Norman Literature; Arthurian Legends; Chivalry; Morality Plays; Mystery Plays; Passion Plays; Romances; and Aelfric; Ancrene Riwle; Andreas; Atheist's Tragedy, The; Barbour, J.; Bede, the Venerable; Beowulf; Caedmon; Caxton, W.; Chaucer, G.; Cloud of Unknowing; Court of Sapience; Cynewulf; Genesis and Exodus; Gower, J.; Guthlac, Saint; Hali Meidenhad; Judith; Langland, W.; Longtoft, P.; Lydgate, J.; Malory, T., Sir; Mannyng, R.; Michael, of Kildare; Of Goode Maneres; Phoenix; Pricke of Conscience; Revenger's Tragedy, The; Robert of Gloucester; Rolle, R., of Hampole; Sawles Warde; Thomas, of Erceldoune; Townley Mysteries; Ullerston, R.; Vision de Saint Paul; William, of Nassyngton; Wonders of the East; Wycliffe, J.

An analysis of dramatic speech in English literature before 1550. *S. E. J. Hodge, M.A. 1947 London, Birkbeck College*

Anglo-Saxon chronicles. *J. Murphy, Ph.D. 1931 National University of Ireland*

The Battle of Maldon. *E. D. Laborde, Ph.D. 1931 London, External Degree*

A comparison between the styles of Old English and Norse historical prose. *K. M. Quinn, M.A. 1932 London, King's College*

A critical edition of the *Handboc or Enchiridion* of Byrhtferth. *S. J. Crawford, D.Phil. 1930 Oxford*

De Lanterne de Lig't, transcribed from the ms. Harleian 2324, with an introduction, notes and glossary. *L. M. Swinburn, M.A. 1914 London*

Descriptions of the Devil and his works in early English literature and the development of these ideas in relation to doctrine. *A. B. Lewis, Ph.D. 1939 London, University College*

An edition of the *Liflade ant te Passium of Seinte Juliene* (ms. Bodley 34). *S. T. R. O. D'Ardenne, B.Litt. 1933 Oxford*

An edition of the metrical life of St. Robert of Knaresborough. *J. Bazire, M.A. 1949 Leeds*

An edition of *The parlement of the thre ages*. *M. Y. Offord, B.Litt. 1948 Oxford*

English Literature: Early and Medieval contd.
English social life as displayed in the literature of the thirteenth and fourteenth centuries. *D. E. Thomas, B.Litt. 1921 Oxford*

A glossary to the Middle English poem *Genesis and Exodus*, with explanatory notes on the text. *A. Merrall, M.A. 1941 Manchester*

Heathenism and its echo in Anglo-Saxon poetry. *J. P. Gaffney, M.A. 1935 National University of Ireland*

Marcel Schwob et les écrivains anglosaxons, précédé d'un aperçu sur Marcel Schwob et la littérature anglo-saxonne. *D. M. Salmon, M.A. 1927 Leeds*

Medieval English satire. *W. E. Smith, M.A. 1914 Birmingham*

Middle English sermons from the Worcester chapter: ms. F 10, edited. *D. M. Grisdale, M.A. 1936 Leeds*

A new edition of *Handlyng synne* and *Medytacyuns*. *G. H. Naish, Ph.D. 1936 London, External Degree*

On child life in medieval English literature. *P. H. Whittaker, M.A. 1932 Liverpool*

Popular medical knowledge in fourteenth century English literature. *I. B. Jones, M.A. 1934 Liverpool*

Prolegomena for a study of Arabic influences on the literature and thought of the English middle ages. *D. Metlitzky, M.A. 1938 London, University College*

Religious teaching in early English literature before the Conquest. *L. R. Sherman, B.Litt. 1914 Oxford*

St. Christopher in Old and Middle English literature and in the contemporary iconography. *W. G. Croker, M.A. 1931 Wales*

Sea terms in early English literature. *W. J. Redbond, M.A. 1934 London, King's College*

The sources of the *Court of Sapience*; a Middle English religious and didactic poem. *C. F. Bühler, Ph.D. 1930 Dublin, Trinity College*

The spirit of Anglo-Saxon literature as reflected in later English. *J. Murphy, M.A. 1926 National University of Ireland*

Studies in the Troy story in Middle English. *B. D. Wright, Ph.D. 1924 London*

Traces of Persian influence upon English literature during the fifteenth and sixteenth centuries. *M. L. K. Suratgar, Ph.D. 1939 London, University College*

The vernacular English literature, 871-1066, as illustrative of the social history of that period. *J. Cook, M.A. 1931 Wales*

English Literature: Sixteenth Century
See also Baldwin, W.; Bale, J.; Barclay, A.; Batman, S.; Blomefield, M.; Browne, R.; Canfield, B.; Chettle, H.; Daniel, S.; Davies, J., Sir; Deloney, T.; Douglas, G.; Dunbar, W.; Dyer, E., Sir; Gascoigne, G.; Goff, T.; Googe, B.; Greene, R.; Grimald, N.; Hakluyt, R.; Harrington, J., Sir; Hawes, S.; Heywood, J.; Howard, H., Earl of Surrey; Hudson, T.; Jack Juggler; Lodge, T.; Lyly, J.; Marlowe, C.; Mirror for Magistrates; Moore, Thomas, Sir, Saint; Nashe, T.; Norton, T.; Painter (Paynter), W.; Peele, G.; Redford, J.; Rollo, Duke of Normandy; Salesbury, W.; Shakespeare, W.; Sidney, P., Sir; Skelton, J.; Southwell, R.; Spenser, E.; Stonyhurst, R.; Taverner, R.; Turberville, G.; Udall, N.; Whetstone, G.; Wyatt, T., Sir.

A century of epigrams: the influence of Latin epigram upon English epigram in the Elizabethan age, with special reference to Martial. *P. B. Corbett, M.A. 1938 Sheffield*

Elizabethan pirated dramas, with special reference to the 'bad' quartos of *Hamlet, Henry V, Romeo and Juliet*: with an appendix on the problem of *The Taming of the Shrew*. *G. I. Duthie, Ph.D. 1939 Edinburgh*

English influences on the written form of the language and on the literature of Scotland, 1500-1625. *M. A. Bald, B.Litt. 1925 Oxford*

The Englishman's conception of the Italian in the age of Shakespeare. *J. Fellheimer, M.A. 1935 London, King's College*

Folklore in Elizabethan prose literature. *P. E. Thornley, M.A. 1929 Wales*

The study of Elizabethan literature at the end of the eighteenth and the beginning of the nineteenth centuries. *A. G. Jones, B.Litt. 1923 Oxford*

English Literature: Sixteenth Century contd.
A study of the Stationers' Register for the years 1591-1594, in relation to the social life and literature of the period. *G. B. Harrison, Ph.D. 1928 London*

Traces of Persian influence upon English literature during the fifteenth and sixteenth centuries. *M. L. K. Suratgar, Ph.D. 1939 London, University College*

The treatment of nature in Elizabethan literature. *P. B. Devilly, M.A. 1936 National University of Ireland*

English Literature: Seventeenth Century
See also Pamphlets; and Andrewes, L.; Armin, W.; Bacon, F., Baron Verulam, Viscount St. Albans; Banks, J.; Beaumont, F.; Behn, A.; Berkenhead, J., Sir; Boyle, R., 1st Earl of Orrery; Brome, R.; Browne, T., Sir; Browne, W.; Bunyan, J.; Butler, S.; Campion, T.; Carew, R.; Carew, T.; Caryll, J.; Cartwright, W.; Chamberlayne, W.; Chapman, G.; Cokain, A., Sir; Cotton, C.; Cowley, A.; Crashaw, R.; Daniel, S.; D'Avenant, W., Sir; Day, J.; Dekker, T.; Denham, J., Sir; Digby, K., Sir; Donne, J.; Drayton, M.; Drummond, W.; Dryden, J.; Fairfax, E.; Fanshawe, R.; Ferrar, N.; Field, N.; Fletcher, G., the Younger; Fletcher, J.; Ford, J.; Fuller, T.; Godolphin, S., 1st Earl of; Greville, F., 1st Baron Brooke; Habington, W.; Hall, John; Hall, Joseph, Bishop; Herbert, E., 1st Baron Herbert of Cherbury; Herbert, G.; Heywood, T.; Howard, R., Sir; Howell, J.; James I, King of England, and VI of Scotland; Johnson, B.; Killigrew, T.; Kynaston, F., Sir; Lee, N.; L'Estrange, R., Sir; Machin, L.; Markham, G.; Marston, J.; Marvell, A.; Massinger, P.; May, T.; Mayne, J.; Middleton, T.; Milton, J.; Motteux, P. A.; Mountford, W.; Oldham, J.; Otway, T.; Overbury, T., Sir; Parrot, H.; Peacham, H.; Pepys, S.; Perkins, W.; Philips, K.; Prior, M.; Ralegh, W., Sir; Randolph, T.; Reynolds, H.; Rich, B.; Rowley, S.; Rowley, W.; Sedley, C., Sir; Settle, E.; Shadwell, T.; Sheffield, J., Duke of Buckingham; Shirley, J.; Southerne, T.; Stanley, T.; Stapylton, R., Sir; Sylvester, J.; Taylor, Jeremy; Taylor, John; Tourneur, C.; Traherne, T.; Vaughan, H.; Walsh, W.; Webster, J.; Wilde, G.; Wilde, R.; Wilmot, J., Earl of Rochester; Wilson, J.; Wilson, R., the Elder.

Academic writings of Irish exiles in the seventeenth century. *T. Wall, Ph.D. 1943 National University of Ireland*

Boileau: his influence and reputation in English literature. *M. Jenkins, M.A. 1932 Birmingham*

The colloquial movement in English prose from 1660 to 1704. *A. Chilton, M.A. 1948 London, Queen Mary College*

The development of letter writing in the seventeenth century with a study of its bearing on the essay and the novel. *R. M. Scrimgeour, M.A. 1928 London*

The development of scientific and philosophical prose in the seventeenth century. *H. F. Hallesy, M.A. 1949 Wales*

Earlier and later seventeenth century prose. *N. Lynch, M.A. 1930 National University of Ireland*

The effect of the advance in scientific knowledge upon seventeenth century literature. . *L. L. Ross, M.A. 1912 Birmingham*

England's literary debt to Spain, 1603-1642. *G. E. Hawk, B.Litt. 1928 Oxford*

English influences on the written form of the language and on the literature of Scotland, 1500-1625. *M. A. Bald, B.Litt. 1925 Oxford*

English literature of the Picturesque School (c. 1680 to 1780) in relation to the art of printing. *C. M. Davies, M.A. 1931 London, Westfield College*

The influence of scientific speculation on imaginative literature in the seventeenth century. *G. E. Neilson, M.A. 1923 Bristol*

The influence of the Bible on English literature of the seventeenth century. *J. C. Stevenson, M.A. 1914 Birmingham*

The influence of Trajano Boccalini's *Ragguagli de Parnaso* upon the English literature of the seventeenth and early eighteenth centuries. *R. Thomas, M.A. 1921 Wales*

The melancholy humour - a study of one aspect of English literature, circa 1590-1640. *M. P. Mcgrath, M.A. 1943 Bristol*

The natural man and the noble savage in English literature in the seventeenth and eighteenth centuries. *W. T. Foster, B.Litt. 1916 Oxford*

English Literature: Seventeenth Century contd.
The reaction against the prose romance of the seventeenth century, with special reference to *The adventures of Covent Garden. A. C. Coolidge, B.Litt. 1929 Oxford*

Reactions in literature of the relations between Scotland and England in the seventeenth and eighteenth centuries: an attempt at tracing England's literary discovery of Scotland. *J. Galloway, Ph.D. 1930 Edinburgh*

The relation between court and literature in the seventeenth century (1579-1700). *M. T. Ferrario, M.A. 1917 Birmingham*

The relation of the seventeenth century 'character' to the comedy of manners. *E. D. Ratledge, M.A. 1933 Manchester*

The rise and progress of Euphuism in English literature. *T. A. Baggs, M.A. 1912 Birmingham*

The seventeenth century character, with a brief sketch of its anticipations in English literature, and a bibliography of character books published in the seventeenth and eighteenth centuries. *T. B. Wheeler, M.A. 1911 Wales*

Seventeenth century pamphlets and the development of prose style. *J. Shaw, M.A. 1949 Leeds*

Some changes in the prose style of the seventeenth century. *A. Wanning, Ph.D. 1938 Cambridge*

A study of the development of the 'character-sketch' in the seventeenth century, with special reference to its relations with the contemporary literature. *L. G. Murphy, M.A. 1920 London*

English Literature: Eighteenth Century
See also Addison, J.; Bage, R.; Blake, W.; Boswell, J.; Brooke, H.; Burke, E.; Burns, R.; Byron, J.; Carey, H.; Chapone, H.; Churchill, C.; Cibber, C.; Colman, G.; Congreve, W.; Cowper, W.; Cunningham, J.; Darwin, E.; Defoe, D.; Dyer, J.; Ellis, G.; Falconer, W.; Farmer, R.; Fergusson, R.; Fielding, H.; Gay, J.; Goodwin, W.; Granville, G., Lord Lansdowne; Graves, R.; Gray, T.; Johnson, C.; Johnson, S.; King, W.; Lennox, C.; Lillo, G.; Luxborough, H., Baroness; Mackenzie, H.; Macpherson, J.; Macro, C.; Mickle, W. J.; Moore, E.; Moore, J.; More, H.; Murphy, A.; Parnell, T.; Percy, T., Bishop; Philips, A.; Philips, J.; Pindar, P.; Pope, A.; Prior, M.; Radcliffe, A.; Ramsay, A.; Reeve, C.; Richardson, S.; Rowe, N.; Shenstone, W.; Smart, C.; Smollett, T. G.; Sterne, L.; Swift, J.; Tatler, The; Theobald, L.; Thomson, J.; Tickell, T.; Walpole, H., 4th Earl of Orford; Warburton, W., Bishop; Ward, E.; Warton, J.; Young, E.

The British peasant, 1770-1820, as reflected in our literature. *B. Sampson, M.A. 1921 London*

China as treated by English and French writers in the first half of the eighteenth century. *S. P. Yu, B.Litt. 1932 Oxford*

China in the English literature of the eighteenth century. *C. S. Ch'ien, B.Litt. 1937 Oxford*

The eighteenth century rhetoricians. *R. Entwistle, Ph.D. 1930 London, Birkbeck College*

English literature of the Picturesque School (c. 1680 to 1780) in relation to the art of printing. *C. M. Davies, M.A. 1931 London, Westfield College*

The influence of Cervantes on English literature of the eighteenth century. *M. Salmons, M.A. 1929 Manchester*

The influence of Spenser on English literature of the early eighteenth century, 1700-1750. *J. L. Rushton, Ph.D. 1934 Sheffield*

An investigation into the extent to which a social conception of education is to be found in the works of English writers of the eighteenth and nineteenth centuries. *A. W. Parry, M.A. 1911 Wales*

L'influence littéraire de Jean Jacques Rousseau en Angleterre. *H. V. Jervis, M.A. 1913 Liverpool*

Literary groups of the first half of the eighteenth century. *A. S. S. Aiyar, Ph.D. 1935 London, King's College*

Methodism and the literature of the eighteenth century. *T. B. Shepherd, Ph.D. 1938 London, Birkbeck College*

The natural man and the noble savage in English literature in the seventeenth and eighteenth centuries. *W. T. Foster, B.Litt. 1916 Oxford*

The place of natural history in English literature, 1789-1846. *W. A. Rawnsley, M.A. 1938 London, King's College*

Queen Caroline and literature. *M. Lindley, M.A. 1927 Liverpool*

English Literature: Eighteenth Century contd.
Reactions in literature of the relations between Scotland and England in the seventeenth and eighteenth centuries: an attempt at tracing England's literary discovery of Scotland. *J. Galloway, Ph.D. 1930 Edinburgh*

The relation between author, patron, publisher, and public: 1726-1780. *A. S. Collins, M.A. 1923 London*

The rôle of the parson in the literature of the eighteenth century in England and Germany. *M. E. Daw, M.A. 1937 London, King's College*

Sentiment and sensibility in English literature of the eighteenth century. *F. Coventry, Ph.D. 1942 Cambridge*

Some aspects of the treatment of the Psalms and of the song of Solomon in English eighteenth century literature. *B. Simmons, M.A. 1937 London, King's College*

Some English translations of Arabic imaginative literature (1704-1838): a study of their portrayal of the Arab world, with an estimate of their influence on nineteenth century English literature. *M. A. Manzalaoui, B.Litt. 1947 Oxford*

Some studies in the moral climate of the mid-eighteenth century in England, as expressed in a representative selection of the prose literature of the period 1740-1786. *E. K. Laycock, M.Litt. 1946 Cambridge*

The spirit of 18th century Ireland as reflected in its literature (in the English language). *P. B. Devilly, M.A. 1937 National University of Ireland*

The study of personality in English neo-classical literature. *A. A. Stewart, Ph.D. 1933 London, King's College.*

English Literature: Nineteenth Century
See also Romanticism; and Arnold, M.; Austen, J.; Banim, J.; Banim, M.; Barnes, W.; Beckford, W.; Beddoes, T. L.; Blackmore, R. D.; Borrow, G. H.; Bowles, W. L.; Bridges, R.; Brontë, E. J.; Browning, R.; Byron, G. G., 6th Baron of Rochdale; Campbell, T.; Carleton, W.; Carlyle, T.; Clare, J.; Clough, A. H.; Coleridge, H.; Coleridge, S. T.; Collins, W. W.; Darley, G.; Davidson, J.; De Quincey, T.; Dickens, C.; Disraeli, B., 1st Earl of Beaconsfield; Doughty, C. M.; Dowson, E.; Edgeworth, M.; Eliot, G.; Elliott, E.; Ferguson, S., Sir; Fitzgerald, E.; Froude, J. A.; Galt, J.; Gaskell, E. C.; Gissing, G.; Griffin, G.; Hardy, T.; Hawker, R. S.; Hazlitt, W.; Hemans, F. D.; Hogg, J.; Hood, T.; Hopkins, G. M.; Hunt, L.; Ireland, W. H.; Jefferies, R.; Johnson, L.; Jones, H. A.; Keats, J.; Ker, W. P.; Kingsley, C.; Kingston, W. H. G.; Lamb, C.; Landor, R. E.; Landor, W. S.; Lang, A.; Le Fanu, J. S.; Lever, C. J.; Lewis, M. G.; Lockhart, J. G.; Macdonald, G.; Meredith, G.; Meynell, A.; Montagu, B.; Moore, T.; Morris, W.; Opie, A.; Pater, W. H.; Patmore, C. K. D.; Peacock, T. L.; Phillips, S.; Pinero, A. W., Sir; Reade, C.; Reynolds, F.; Robertson, T. W.; Rossetti, C. G.; Rossetti, D. G.; Ruskin, J.; Scott, W., Sir; Scott, W. B.; Shelley, P. B.; Southey, R.; Spence, T.; Stevenson, R. L.; Surtees, R. S.; Swinburne, A. C.; Taylor, H., Sir; Tennyson, A., 1st Baron; Thackeray, W. M.; Thompson, F.; Trollope, A.; Wade, T.; Warburton, B. E. G.; Wesley, C.; White, W. H.; Wilde, O. F. O'F. W.; Wilson, J. (Christopher North); Wordsworth, D.; Wordsworth, W.

Alfred de Musset et la littérature anglaise. *E. M. Pool, M.A. 1914 Liverpool*

The Byronic superman in England and Germany. *E. C. Hentschel, M.A. 1936 London, University College*

Deutschlands Einfluss auf die englisch-irische Literatur in der ersten Hälfte des 19. Jahrhunderts. *R. M. Maxwell, M.A. 1944 National University of Ireland*

The development and a criticism of the theory and practice of education as found in imaginative literature of the nineteenth century and after. *H. M. Hooper, M.A. 1920 London*

Dream literature in the English Romantic period (1780-1830), with a consideration of some writers of the later nineteenth century. *S. Evans, M.A. 1938 Wales*

The effects of the French Revolution on English literature, with special reference to Burke. *H. W. Hampton, M.A. 1910 Birmingham*

English accounts and views of Norwegian life and literature, especially in the nineteenth century. *C. J. B. Burchardt, B.Litt. 1918 Oxford*

George Darley and the Elizabethan revival in the Romantic period. *K. W. Wild, M.A. 1914 Liverpool*

English Literature: Nineteenth Century contd.
The greater women novelists of the Victorian age. *E. M. Dolan, M.A. 1945 National University of Ireland*

The influence of Emile Zola on English literature. *D. G. Lewis, M.A. 1943 Wales*

The influence of German thought in English literature of the first half of the nineteenth century. *T. W. Jenkins, M.A. 1926 Wales*

The influence of the Bible in English literature of the nineteenth century. *I. M. Lloyd, M.A. 1920 Wales*

The influence of the Italian *Risorgimento* in English literature. *M. H. Ensor, M.A. 1917 Wales*

An investigation into the extent to which a social conception of education is to be found in the works of English writers of the eighteenth and nineteenth centuries. *A. W. Parry, M.A. 1911 Wales*

Irish women writers 1800-35. *S. J. C. Harrison, Ph.D. 1947 Dublin, Trinity College*

Jean-Alexandre Buchon and his relations with England. *J. Hinton, M.A. 1928 London*

L'Angleterre et la littérature anglaise dans les *Archives littéraires de l'Europe* (1804-1808). *A. C. Cullerne, M.A. 1939 Liverpool*

The literary influences of the Oxford Movement from 1833-1850. *T. Halliwell, M.A. 1944 Manchester*

Mysticism in nineteenth century English literature. *E. H. Thomas, M.A. 1924 Wales*

The place of natural history in English literature, 1789-1846. *W. A. Rawnsley, M.A. 1938 London, King's College*

The Russian Romantics and English literature. *T. A. Wolff, M.A. 1947 London, Bedford College*

Sainte-Beuve et l'Angleterre: le critique et le poète dans leurs rapports avec certains écrivains anglais. *A. F. Powell, M.A. 1920 London*

The social aspects of the rise and decay of literary culture in Mold and Holywell, 1820-1900. *D. J. Jones, M.A. 1929 Liverpool*

Some English translations of Arabic imaginative literature (1704-1838): a study of their portrayal of the Arab world, with an estimate of their influence on nineteenth century English literature. *M. A. Manzalaoui, B.Litt. 1947 Oxford*

A study of certain aspects of nineteenth century periodical criticism (1798-1842) especially in its influence on and attitude to new literary movements. *J. Kinghorn, Ph.D. 1939 Edinburgh*

Theodor Fontane and England; a critical study in Anglo-German literary relations in the nineteenth century. *C. A. B. E. Jolles, M.A. 1947 London, Birkbeck College*

Use of the Greek myth in English literature from 1800 to 1850. *E. M. Liptrot, M.A. 1929 Manchester*

Victorian theories of literary art. *W. J. Griffiths, M.A. 1931 Wales*

English Literature: Twentieth Century
See also Realism; and Auden, W. H.; Belloc, J. H. P.; Bennett, E. A.; Chesterton, G. K.; Conrad, J.; Coppard, A. E.; De la Mare, W.; Eliot, T. S.; Forster, E. M.; Galsworthy, J.; Granville-Barker, H.; Greene, G.; Housman, A. E.; Hudson, W. H.; Huxley, A. L.; Joyce, J.; Kipling, R.; Lawrence, D. H.; Machen, A.; Mansfield, K.; Maugham, W. S.; Monkhouse, A.; Moore, G.; Muir, E.; Noyes, A.; O'Casey, S.; O'Grady, S. J.; Reid, F.; Russell, G. W. (AE); Shaw, G. B.; Sheehan, P. A.; Shiels, G.; Strachey, G. L.; Synge, J. M.; Walpole, H. S., Sir; Walter, E.; Wells, H. G.; Yeats, W. B.

A comparative study of children in English and French literature 1900 to 1914. *H. C. Davis, M.A. 1934 London, East London College*

Erotic and neurotic traits in post-Victorian English literature. *A. R. Williams, M.A. 1939 Wales*

The evidence of contemporary French memoirs, letters and periodicals with regard to the influence of English literature. *E. H. Partridge, B.Litt. 1924 Oxford*

Modern Irish literature in the English language. *J. Harbison, M.A. 1928 Belfast*

Enoch, Book of
The new Hebrew Book of Enoch. *H. Olson, Ph.D. 1924 London*

Entailment
Propositions asserting entailment relations. *S. Körner, Ph.D. 1944 Cambridge*

Entertainments
The wayside entertainer in Wales in the nineteenth century. *R. W. Jones, M.A. 1939 Liverpool*

Enthusiasm
The history of enthusiasm as a factor in the religious and social problems of the eighteenth century. *E. C. Walker, Ph.D. 1930 London, King's College*

Environment
Environment and the theories of instinct. *N. Roth, M.A. 1936 London, King's College*

The Hooghly and its region: a study of human adjustmnt to changing environments. *B. Mukherjee, Ph.D. 1948 London, School of Economics and Political Science*

The influence of physical environment upon Arabian life and institutions. *S. Inayatullah, Ph.D. 1932 London, School of Oriental and African Studies*

Interests of boys in relation to mental ability and environment. *T. B. Kankan, M.Ed. 1936 Leeds*

Mental development with special reference to school conditions and health. *J. G. Bannell, M.A. 1916 Liverpool*

The relation between the distribution of intelligence and the social environment. *P. Moshinsky, Ph.D. 1937 London, School of Economics and Political Science*

The relationship of juvenile delinquency and environment in an industrial town. *A. Royds, M.Ed. 1936 Manchester*

Epics
See also Romances; Girart, de Roussillon; Homer; Mahābhaerata; Rāmayana; Southey, R.; Troy; Vega Carpio, L. F. de; Virgil; etc.

(a) The origin and development of the heroic poem in England, with some account of its relationship to the heroic romance and the heroic play; (b) The Trojan legend in England. *A. E. Parsons, D.Litt. 1932 London, External Degree*

The Anglo-Saxon epic as exemplified by *Beowulf* considered in the light of the Indian epic *Rāmayana. I. S. Peter, Ph.D. 1930 London, King's College*

A catalogue of names of persons in the German court epics: an examination of the literary sources and dissemination together with notes on the etymologies of the more important names. *F. W. Chandler, M.A. 1936 London, Birkbeck College*

The epic in Hindi literature. *H. C. Roy, Ph.D. 1949 London, School of Oriental and African Studies*

The French biblical epic in the seventeenth century. *R. A. Sayce, D.Phil. 1949 Oxford*

Golyddan; ei fywyd a'i weithiau, gyda chyfeiriad arbennig at yr arwrgerdd Gymraeg (Golyddan; his life and his works, with special reference to the Welsh epic). *H. C. Bassett, M.A. 1935 Wales*

The Hürnen Seyfrid: a study in origins. *K. C. King, Ph.D. 1938 London, University College*

La tradition manuscrite et la phonétique des principaux textes de la version Johannis de *La Chronique de Turpin. R. N. Walpole, M.A. 1936 Wales*

A linguistic study of the Franco-Italian epics. *G. Mellor, M.A. 1950 Manchester*

Milton's heroic poetry: a comparative study with reference to Sanskrit epic. *V. R. Movva, Ph.D. 1949 Wales*

The theory of the epic in France in the eighteenth century. *O. R. Taylor, M.A. 1939 Wales*

Epicureanism
Epicureanism in Roman life and literature. *J. J. Hunter, B.Litt. 1932 Oxford*

Epicurus
Lucretius as translator of Epicurus: a study in poetical mood. *C. E. Pyke, M.A. 1939 Bristol*

Epidemics
See also Public Health.

Epidemics in schools: a statistical analysis of data of the sickness experience in eighteen public schools, collected during the years 1935 to 1939. *E. A. Cheeseman, Ph.D. 1947 London, School of Hygiene and Tropical Medicine*

Epigrams
A century of epigrams: the influence of Latin epigram upon English epigram in the Elizabethan age, with special reference to Martial. *P. B. Corbett, M.A. 1938 Sheffield*

Epilepsy
The Terman-Merrill intelligence scale in testing institutionalized epileptics. *E. A. Eattell, M.Sc. 1945 London, Birkbeck College*

Epiphanius, Saint
The writings of St. Epiphanius. *P. Ierides, B.Litt. 1926 Oxford*

Episcopal Church in Scotland
See Church History: Scotland; and Douglas, G., Bishop; Forbes, P., Bishop; Kennedy, J., Bishop; Leighton, R., Archbishop.

Episcopate
See also Church, Doctrine of; Church History.

1. The Chalcedonian definition of the faith, and the inter-relation of the four great heresies on the Incarnation. 2. The historic value of the episcopate in the early Church as a witness and a guarantee. *T. H. Bindley, B.D. 1893 Oxford*

The contribution of Pope Benedict XIV to Church government, with special reference to the episcopate. *G. W. O. Addleshaw, B.D. 1935 Oxford*

1. The divinity of the Holy Spirit. 2. Episcopal government in the early Church. *J. W. Stanbridge, B.D. 1876 Oxford*

1. The Incarnation. 2. Apostolic succession. *E. P. Lewis, B.D. 1896 Oxford*

1. On holy baptism. 2. On episcopal government. *F. A. Walker, B.D. 1879 Oxford*

1. Prophecy in the Christian Church. 2. The evolution of the episcopate. *F. H. Wales, B.D. 1897 Oxford*

Epistemology
See also Cognition; Empiricism; Idealism; Memory; Realism; and Berkeley, G., Bishop; Locke, J.; Malebranche, N.; Thomas Aquinas, Saint; Wilson, J. C.

The à priori elements in religious experience: an epistemological study. *R. Griffiths, Ph.D. 1930 Edinburgh*

Ability and knowledge: the standpoint of the London School. *F. C. Thomas, M.Sc. 1935 London, King's College*

The aim and achievement of scientific method: an epistemological essay. *T. P. Nunn, D.Sc. 1907 London*

Aspects of the problem of knowledge and truth. *L. A. Reid, M.A. 1923 Wales*

The association of ideas as a psychological principle and as a principle in epistemology. *J. L. Armitage, M.A. 1913 Liverpool*

Can a neutral monist theory of knowledge give an adequate account of memory. *N. R. Knatchbull-Hugessen, B.Litt. 1938 Oxford*

A critical examination of Hume's epistemolgy with reference to its bearing on modern problems. *C. A. M. Maund, Ph.D. 1936 London, Bedford College*

The doctrine of knowledge of John Locke and contemporary English Platonism. *A. E. Best, M.A. 1940 Manchester*

The function of scepticism in the development of knowledge. *J. M. Bhatt, Ph.D. 1934 London, University College*

The fundamental problems of neo-scholastic epistemology. *L. Proserpio, M.A. 1913 Liverpool*

Hegelian epistemology. *C. W. Wolfe, B.Litt. 1938 Dublin, Trinity College*

Indian epistemology. *J. Prasad, Ph.D. 1930 Cambridge*

Kantian and scholastic theory of knowledge. *D. J. Cannon, M.A. 1945 National University of Ireland*

Kant's distinction between constitutive and regulative principles of knowledge. *F. E. England, M.A. 1922 London*

Knowledge: pure and perceptual. *E. Sideropoulo, Ph.D. 1931 London, University College*

The philosophy of M. Bergson, with special reference to his theory of knowledge. *D. J. Williams, M.A. 1916 Wales*

The rational, the arational, and the irrational in the epistemology of theism: an essay in the philosophy of faith. *J. F. Butler, Ph.D. 1936 Manchester*

The reality of extra-intellectual knowledge, with special reference to Bergson and pragmatism. *D. Richardson, M.A. 1917 Wales*

The relation between empiricism and scepticism in Hume's theory of knowledge. *E. H. Ziegelmeyer, Ph.D. 1938 London, King's College*

The relation between the theory of knowledge and metaphysics in the philosophical system of Samuel Alexander. *R. I. Markus, M.A. 1948 Manchester*

The relation of psychology to the theory of knowledge. *A. Cuming, Cert.Sc. 1916 Oxford*

Epistemology contd.
The relation of theology to epistemology, with special reference to Hume. *R. J. Tree, M.A. 1939 Wales*

Relativity of human knowledge. *C. Maguire, M.A. 1911 National University of Ireland*

A study in the philosophy of Charles Bernard Renouvier, with special reference to his theory of knowledge. *A. H. Murray, D.Phil. 1931 Oxford*

Views concerning the epistemology of morals held by some of the British moralists of the eighteenth century, with especial reference to the anti-empiricist views of Richard Price and Thomas Reid. *D. Rafilovitch, D.Phil. 1940 Oxford*

Equity
The distinctions and anomalies arising out of the equitable doctrine of the legal estate. *R. M. P. Willoughby, LL.D. 1911 London*

The equitable doctrine of election. *R. H. R. Tee, LL.D. 1923 London*

Equity and the lapse of time. *J. Brodie, LL.M. 1936 Leeds*

Erasmus, Desiderius
Opus epistolarum Desiderii Erasmi Roterodami. *P. S. Allen, D.Litt. 1925 Oxford*

Eratosthenes, of Cyrene
Eratosthenes as a representative of Hellenistic culture. *E. A. Knight, M.A. 1930 London, King's College*

Erceldoune, Thomas of
 See Thomas of Erceldoune.

Erewash Valley, The
The economic development of the Erewash Valley: a study in economic geography. *E. Pearson, M.Sc. 1936 London, External Degree*

Erigena, John Scotus
The system of Erigena, a study in Christian thought. *R. R. Hartford, D.D. 1948 Dublin, Trinity College*

Ernst, Paul
Paul Ernst and the political mission of the poet. *W. E. Anderson, M.A. 1937 Manchester*

Erosion
Certain aspects of coast erosion in the English Channel with special reference to the coast-defence problems of the town of Sidmouth, Devon. *W. P. Baron, M.A. 1931 London, External Degree*

The denudation chronology of northeast Wales. *A. N. Harris, Ph.D. 1947 London, Birkbeck College*

Soil erosion in North America. *G. Winram, M.A. 1944 London, External Degree*

Error
The problem of error. *P. J. Halligan, M.A. 1946 National University of Ireland*

The psychology of error. *J. T. Bradley, Ph.D. 1930 London, External Degree*

Erskine, John
Preaching in eighteenth century Scotland: a comparative study of the extant sermons of Ralph Erskine, 1685-1752; John Erskine, 1721-1803; and Hugh Blair, 1718-1800. *C. R. McCain, Ph.D. 1949 Edinburgh*

Erskine, Ralph
Preaching in eighteenth century Scotland: a comparative study of the extant sermons of Ralph Erskine, 1685-1752; John Erskine, 1721-1803; and Hugh Blair, 1718-1800. *C. R. McCain, Ph.D. 1949 Edinburgh*

Erskine, Thomas
The contribution of Thomas Erskine of Linlathen and his writings to Scottish theology. *J. C. Conn, Ph.D. 1935 Saint Andrew's*

The influence, direct and indirect, of the writings of Erskine of Linlathen on religious thought in Scotland. *R. A. Reid, Ph.D. 1930 Edinburgh*

The religious thought of Thomas Erskine of Linlathen: its origin, nature and influence. *H. H. Williams, B.D. 1943 Leeds*

Eryxias
The pseudo-platonic dialogue *Eryxias*. *D. E. Eichholz, M.Litt. 1934 Cambridge*

Eschatology
 See also Death; Soul.
1. The abodes of the departed. 2. The holy angels. *F. T. Havergal, B.D. & D.D. 1888 Oxford*

1. Apostolic teaching and the teaching of the creeds in relation to that of our Lord. 2. The doctrine of immortality, Jewish and Christian. *W. C. Tuting, B.D. & D.D. 1911 Oxford*

Eschatology contd.
1. Aspects of Christ as viewed in succesive ages of the Church. 2. The doctrine of a future life. *J. Darlington, B.D. 1899 Oxford*

The belief in immortality as a religious sanction for progress. *C. M. Coltman, B.Litt. 1922 Oxford*

The Christian doctrine of immortality, in the light of anthropological evidence and philosophic principles. *G. W. Burningham, M.A. 1935 Leeds*

1. The Christian's expectations of a palingenesis mundi finds valuable support from reason and science. 2. St.Luke xvi.9. *A. Malan, B.D. 1877 Oxford*

A comparison of the teachings of Spinoza and McTaggart on immortality. *H. V. M. Jones, M.A. 1936 Wales*

The concept of self from Descartes to Kant, with some reference to immortality. *E. G. Braham, Ph.D. 1935 London, King's College*

The conception of eternal life, with special reference to the Johannine writings. *M. Popovitch, B.Litt. 1922 Oxford*

1. Considerations on eternal punishment. 2. The baptism of infants. *E. Hermitage-Day, B.D. 1901 Oxford*

The contribution of Victorian poets to the development of the idea of immortality. *L. D. Weatherhead, M.A. 1926 Manchester*

1. The creeds: their origin and value. 2. The intermediate state. *F. R. Pentreath, B.D. 1874 Oxford*

1. Demoniacal possession. 2. The intermediate state. *R. W. M. Pope, B.D. 1877 Oxford*

The development of the idea of personal immortality in pagan Rome, with special reference to the metrical epitaphs in Buecheler's collection. *G. E. Quinton, M.A. 1934 Bristol*

1. The doctrine of a future life in the Old and New Testaments 2. The authorship of the Pastoral Epistles. *N. C. W. Radcliffe, B.D. & D.D. 1909 Oxford*

1. The doctrine of baptism. 2. The intermediate state. *S. Baker, B.D. 1901 Oxford*

1. The doctrine of immortality in the Old Testament. 2. Development of the doctrine of the fatherhood of God in the Old and New Testaments. *G. H. B. Wright, B.D. 1891 Oxford*

The doctrine of reward and retribution in the *Book of Proverbs. J. Kennedy, Ph.D. 1934 Glasgow*

1. The doctrine of the future life in the Old Testament. 2. The origin of Hebrew prophecy. *J. Robertson, B.D. and D.D. 1897 Oxford*

1. The doctrine of the mediation of Christ. 2. The testimony of the Church as to the doctrine of the descent of Christ into hell. *S. J. M. Price, B.D. & D.D. 1905 Oxford*

The doctrine of the Parousia in the New Testament, with special reference to the Epistles of St. Paul. *E. L. Millen, B.D. 1939 Oxford*

The doctrine of the parousia in Paul and the Synoptic Gospels. *E. Jones, B.Litt. 1924 Oxford*

1. The doctrine of the resurrection in the Book of Job. 2. The connection between free-will and eternal punishment. *J. T. Nance, B.D. 1881 Oxford*

Early Greek thought on the life of the soul after death. *W. G. Bower, M.A. 1905 London*

An edition of *Nosce teipsum* by Sir John Davies, with a prefatory study of his poetry. *T. J. Childs, B.Litt. 1939 Oxford*

1. The eschatological beliefs of Jesus. 2. Extract teaching *in re* synoptic Gospels. *J. L. L. Fulford, B.D. & D.D. 1913 Oxford*

Eschatology and manticism in Old Norse literature. *H. R. Ellis, Ph.D. 1940 Cambridge*

Eschatology and the Christian understanding of history, with special reference to the biblical and metaphysical background. *E. C. Rust, B.D. 1947 Oxford*

The eschatology of the ancient Celts. *D. O. Jones, M.A. 1927 Wales*

The eschatology of the Book of Job. *B. Sove, B.Litt. 1931 Oxford*

1. The eschatology of the Gospels. 2. The authorship and destination of the Epistle to the Hebrews. *F. E. Austin, B.D. 1907 Oxford*

The eschatology of the Psalter: a study in the religious development of Israel as reflected in the Psalms, with special reference to the destinies of the individual and the nation. *S. Jellicoe, B.D. 1944 Durham*

Eschatology contd.
The eschatology of the third Gospel. *E. Edmonds-Smith, B.D. 1929 Oxford*

1. Eternal life in relation to the Incarnation. 2. The idea of the Church in the Gospels. *W. Hobhouse, B.D. & D.D. 1918 Oxford*

1. Eternal life in St. John's Gospel. 2. The leading ideas of the Acts of the Apostles. *T. W. Gilbert, B.D. 1912 Oxford*

Formgeschichte, eschatology, and the life of Jesus. *W. Neil, Ph.D. 1936 Glasgow*

1. The future life in light of the theory of evolution. 2. The doctrine of salvation. *C. E. Beeby, B.D. 1888 Oxford*

1. God: Creator, Redeemer, Sanctifier. 2. Gehenna. *E. H. Cross, B.D. & D.D. 1890 Oxford*

1. The gradual development of the doctrine of a future life in Holy Scripture, with special reference to the teaching of St. Paul on the resurrection-body in I Corinthians xv. 2. The Logos-Christology deduced from the writings of St. Paul. *W. O. Jenkins, B.D. & D.D. 1907 Oxford*

1. Growth of the doctrine of Jesus Christ in the Pauline Epistles. 2. The doctrine of the future life. *E. B. Bartleet, B.D. 1902 Oxford*

1. The growth of belief in a future state. 2. The organization and worship of the early Christian Churches as exhibited in the New Testament. *C. Erskine, B.D. 1901 Oxford*

1. The Hebrew doctrine of immortality in the light of other religions. 2. The Hebrew doctrine of sacrifice in the light of other religions. *G. H. Jones, B.D. & D.D. 1907 Oxford*

The implications of immortality in the moral consciousness. *M. M. Morris, M.A. 1925 Wales*

The influence of Jewish eschatology upon the New Testament. *T. E. Warner, B.Litt. 1939 Dublin, Trinity College*

The influence of ritual on primitive belief with regard to the life after death in Polynesia, Melanesia, and Indonesia. *R. L. B. Moss, B.Sc. 1922 Oxford*

1. The intermediate state. 2. The resurrection of the body. *L. Bradyll-Johnson, B.D. 1918 Oxford*

1. The intermediate state. 2. The date and authorship of the Apocalypse. *G. T. Jowett, B.D. & D.D. 1909 Oxford*

1. The intermediate state. 2. The nature of Christ's risen body. *E. N. Dew, B.D. 1890 Oxford*

Iranian influence on Jewish and Christian eschatology. *P. Hadfield, B.D. 1944 Leeds*

1. The justice of the atonement. 2. The omnipresence of God and eschatology. *E. Lang, B.D. & D.D. 1908 Oxford*

1. The limits of conscience. 2. The doctrine of eternal rewards and punishments. *F. W. Quilter, B.D. 1872 Oxford*

1. The Lord's coming and the world's end. 2. The Revelation of St. John. *W. J. L. Sheppard, B.D. & D.D. 1922 Oxford*

1. The Lord's day. 2. The intermediate state. *H. J. Wilkins, B.D. & D.D. 1906 Oxford*

The medieval conception of heaven and hell as shown by English religious and didactic literature from 1150. *H. A. C. Green, M.A. 1923 London*

Muhammad's idea of the last judgment and its sources. *J. R. Buchanan, Ph.D. 1927 Edinburgh*

New Testament eschatology in its bearing upon ethics. *E. H. Williamson, B.Litt. 1939 Dublin, Trinity College*

1. The New Testament teaching on the Second Advent considered in the light of subsequent history. 2. The relation of natural science to theology. *P. H. Lester, B.D. 1908 Oxford*

The Old Testament and the future life. *E. W. Toms, M.A. 1925 Wales*

1. On eternal punishment. 2. On Anglican orders. *E. S. Elwell, B.D. 1878 Oxford*

1. On justification by faith. 2. On Hades. *H. T. Beebe, B.D. 1889 Oxford*

1. On the doctrine of the descent of Christ into hell. 2. On the doctrine of final perseverance. *G. Arbuthnot, B.D. & D.D. 1908 Oxford*

1. On the Epistle to the Hebrews. 2. On the proportional reward. *W. M. Sinclair, B.D. 1888 Oxford*

1. On the intermediate state. 2. On demoniacal possession. *J. Evans, B.D. & D.D. 1906 Oxford*

Eschatology contd.
1. The origin of the expectation of the early Advent of our Blessed Lord. 2. The relation of the Epistle to the Hebrews to St. Paul's Epistles. *H. A. Keates, B.D. 1904 Oxford*

Pauline ethics, with special reference to eschatology. *J. P. Lee-Woolf, B.D. 1942 Oxford*

Personal immortality as a moral postulate. *H. Edwards, D.Phil. 1922 Liverpool*

Personality and immortality in modern philosophy. *E. G. Braham, M.A. 1927 Bristol*

Plato's doctrine of personal immortality. *J. E. Parry, M.A. 1918 Wales*

1. Prayer. 2. The intermediate state. *E. G. Banks, B.D. & D.D. 1890 Oxford*

1. The problem of St. John's Gospel. 2. Personal immortality. *W. H. Rigg, B.D. & D.D. 1921 Oxford*

The problem of self and immortality. *E. G. Braham, B.A. 1925 Bristol*

1. Reasonableness of the considerations which form the ground of Christian hope. 2. The moral value of the doctrine of final judgement. *C. J. Thompson, B.D. & D.D. 1893 Oxford*

Roman ideas of immortality. *M. L. Hall, M.A. 1919 Bristol*

The Romans and immortality. *N. Merritt, M.A. 1933 Birmingham*

1. The scientific aspect of biblical eschatology. 2. The parable of the unjust steward. *A. N. Malan, B.D. & D.D. 1898 Oxford*

The second advent: the origin of the New Testament doctrine. *T. F. Glasson, D.D. 1945 London, Richmond College*

Shelley's philosophic thought, with special reference to his view of immortality. *E. L. Robertson, M.Litt. 1941 Cambridge*

Some aspects of personality in British and American idealism from the time of T. H. Green, with some reference to immortality. *E. G. Braham, M.A. 1930 Liverpool*

Some conceptions of Sheol: a study in Old Testament eschatology. *J. W. Swarbrick, M.A. 1922 Manchester*

Some metaphysical implications of the judgment. *P. V. Blanshard, B.Sc. 1920 Oxford*

Some philosophical considerations about the survival of death. *C. Lewy, Ph.D. 1943 Cambridge*

1. The state of the departed. 2. The communion of Saints. *W. Baker, B.D. 1871 Oxford*

A treatise on purgatory by Tschudi. *I. A. Knowles, Ph.D. 1925 Glasgow*

Eschenbach, Wolfram von
The extent to which Wolfram von Eschenbach is indebted for his poem *Parzival* to French and other foreign sources. *M. Williams, M.A. 1907 Wales*

Eskimos, The
Cold: its demands and suggestions: a study of the importance of environment in the development of Eskimo culture. *D. Nusbaum, D.Phil. 1939 Oxford*

Espinosa, Pedro
Pedro Espinosa and his work. *A. Lumsden, M.A. 1943 Liverpool*

Essays
The origin and development of the English prose essay to the making of the *Tatler. A. M. Paynter, M.A. 1910 London*

The periodical essay from 1750 to 1760. *A. E. Darke, M.A. 1936 Liverpool*

The reflection of contemporary religious thought in the essays of the eighteenth century. *E. M. A. Barnes, M.A. 1913 Birmingham*

Essex
Custodia essexae: a study of the conventual property held by the Priory of Christ Church, Canterbury, in the counties of Essex, Suffolk and Norfolk. *J. F. Nichols, Ph.D. 1930 London, King's College*

Historical geography of southeast Essex. *R. Coles, Ph.D. 1934 London, King's College*

Judicial investigations under the Dictum of Kenilworth, Essex. *H. Roberts, M.A. 1928 Manchester*

Essex, Walter Devereux, 1st Earl of
The problem of Lord Essex in Ireland. *L. Duggan, M.A. 1926 National University of Ireland*

Estaunié, Edouard
French provincial life in the novels of Edouard Estaunié, with some reference to contemporary writers. *J. W. White, M.A. 1949 London, King's College and London, Birkbeck College*

Esthonian Language
The phonetics of Estonian (including some notice of intonation). *L. Krass, M.A. 1943 London, University College*

Estienne, Robert
The press of Robert Estienne, 1526-1550: a historical study. *A. E. Tyler, D.Phil. 1949 Oxford*

Etching
The relationship of artist and armourer in Europe during the sixteenth century, with particular reference to etching and allied techniques. *H. W. Williams, Ph.D. 1935 London, Courtauld Institute of Art*

Ethics
See also Conscience; Duty; Evil; Forgiveness; Humanism; Justice; Objectivity; Personality; Pleasure; Punishment; Self-Consciousness; Sexual Relationships; Sin; Utilitarianism; War and Peace. For references to writers on Ethics, see also Philosophy; Theology.

The abuse of rights. *F. E. J. Justice, Ph.D. 1943 National University of Ireland*

The aims and method of ethics. *L. W. Cronkhite, B.Sc. 1908 Oxford*

Cause, value and God. *T. A. Burkill, Ph.D. 1941 Manchester*

Character: an essay on natural ethics. *T. F. Walsh, M.A. 1914 National University of Ireland*

The claim of morality. *N. H. G. Robinson, D.Litt. 1948 Glasgow*

A comparative study of the recent ethical theories of idealism, pragmatism, and realism. *P. M. Hamilton, B.Litt. 1922 Oxford*

The conditions of moral responsibility. *M. Fenn, M.A. 1948 Wales*

The contribution of science teaching to moral training. *G. R. Rumsey, M.A. 1926 London*

A critical and experimental study in the development of moral ideas. *R. Miller, Ph.D. 1928 Edinburgh*

A critical examination of some current tendencies in the theory of human conduct. *I. L. G. Sutherland, Ph.D. 1924 Glasgow*

De summo bono. *J. Wright, M.A. 1761 Glasgow*

The development of moral ideas in children and adolescents. *B. M. Swainson, D.Phil. 1949 Oxford*

Disinterestedness and its conditions: a limited comparison between the ethics of Christianity and of scientific humanism as represented in particular by the *Ethics* of Professor Nicholai Hartmann. *R. G. Norburn, M.A. 1940 Manchester*

Dissertation on the relations of morality and religion. *W. J. Davies, M.A. 1946 Liverpool*

Ernest Renan: moraliste. *A. L. G. Fréchet, Ph.D. 1943 Belfast*

The ethical implications of a monadistic metaphysic. *J. K. Majumdar, Ph.D. 1923 London*

The ethical implications of modern psychology. *J. Gray, M.A. 1928 Birmingham*

The ethical limitations of some modern psychology. *W. E. Smith, M.A. 1934 Leeds*

The ethics of economic values. *P. Byrne, M.A. 1932 National University of Ireland*

Ethics of right and good. *E. F. O'Doherty, M.A. 1939 National University of Ireland*

An examination of the ultimate postulates of morality. *S. Roy, M.A. 1913 London*

The function of reason in relation to the moral idea and the part played by experience. *C. M. Thompson, M.A. 1922 London*

Habits in moral training. *J. J. Ruan, M.A. 1936 National University of Ireland*

Individual differences and moral training. *T. Leonard, M.A. 1938 National University of Ireland*

La controverse sur la moralité du théâtre après la lettre à d'Alembert de J. J. Rousseau. *M. M. Moffat, M.A. 1930 Liverpool*

The limits of obligation. *M. Krizewsky, M.A. 1923 London*

Logic and the foundations of ethics. *H. P. Reichmann, D.Phil. 1943 Oxford*

Ethics contd.
Man's sense of moral obligation: the inevitable psychological aspect of a universal ethical process by which man in his freedom deals with the necessity of self-transcendence through some accepted principle of value. *J. S. A. Worboys, Ph.D. 1936 London, External Degree*

The metaphysical basis of ethics. *D. Jones, M.A. 1904 Wales*

The metaphysical basis of moral obligation. *J. E. Turner, M.A. 1921 Liverpool*

Moral attitudes in relation to upbringing, personal adjustment and social opinion. *S. Brahmachari, Ph.D. 1938 London, University College*

Moral authority: an examination of external and internal authority in morals. *J. Highet, D.Phil. 1947 Oxford*

The moral development of the child. *H. E. Piggott, M.A. 1903 Wales*

The moral end as moral excellence. *J. B. Danquah, Ph.D. 1927 London*

The moral ideal and its bearing on theism. *G. Charlesworth, M.A. 1945 Liverpool*

The moral judgments and their theistic implications. *Y. L. Jackson, Ph.D. 1940 Edinburgh*

Moral reasoning of the child and its relation to mental age. *M. K. Ahmed, M.A. 1936 London, University College*

The nature of moral obligation. *W. Tonge, M.A. 1940 Manchester*

Phenomenology and the theory of moral values. *C. B. Kidd, Ph.D. 1935 Saint Andrew's*

A philosophical analysis of the claim of religion to be a guide to human conduct, individual and social. *J. Davies, M.A. 1940 Wales*

The place of reason in ethics. *S. E. Toulmin, Ph.D. 1949 Cambridge*

The psychological and ethical basis of the problem of peace. *H. V. Hall, M.A. 1932 Wales*

The reality of morals. *J. M. MacLoughlin, Ph.D. 1942 National University of Ireland*

Reason and morals: an enquiry into the first principles of ethics. *I. Levine, D.Litt. 1924 Glasgow*

The relation between morality and religion in primitive society. *E. A. Shattock, B.Litt. 1927 Oxford*

The religious and moral training of the adolescent. *W. H. Backhouse, M.Ed. 1940 Leeds*

The right of private judgment in matters of conduct: its growth and value. *G. K. Hawes, M.A. 1931 Manchester*

The significance for metaphysics of the presuppositions of morality. *T. T. Jones, M.A. 1929 Wales*

Some ethical implications of the new psychology. *J. E. Abraham, M.A. 1926 Belfast*

Some recent theories with regard to the metaphysical foundations of ethics. *D. J. Jones, M.A. 1912 Wales*

The source of morality in human nature. *S. S. Dhamoon, M.A. 1932 London, King's College*

Spiritual values in adult education. *B. A. Yeaxlee, Ph.D. 1925 London*

The State and the moral life. *I. N. Menon, B.Litt. 1922 Oxford*

A study of moral education. *G. Fraser, B.Sc. 1923 Oxford*

Suggestion in relation to the moral value of ideas. *I. H. W. Lawrence, M.A. 1911 London*

The theory of reality as perfect, with special reference to its bearing on ethics. *D. E. Roberts, M.A. 1916 Wales*

Ethics: Christian
1. The application of our Lord's moral teaching to modern needs. 2. The Lord's Prayer as a guide to public worship. *F. A. M. Spencer, B.D. 1923 Oxford*

1. The atonement. 2. St. Paul's doctrine of Christian ethics in relation to the Holy Spirit. *A. Robertson, B.D. & D.D. 1897 Oxford*

The basis of Christian morals in the second and third centuries. *G. F. Thompson, M.A. 1924 Sheffield*

Christian ethics and social institutions in the fourth century, with special reference to Augustine. *E. C. Urwin, M.A. 1920 London*

Christian ethics in Victorian philosophy. *D. Davies, B.Litt. 1932 Oxford*

Ethics: Christian contd.

Christian moral judgment: an enquiry into the character of Christian moral judgment as evidenced by a study of St. Paul's conception of the relation between law and gospel. *J. N. Ward, M.A. 1944 Manchester*

The ethical idea of love and its central position in Christian ethics down to St. Cyprian. *Y. Davies, B.Litt. 1918 Oxford*

Exposition of passages from the twelfth chapter of the Epistle to the Romans: the ethical scheme of St. Paul. *C. W. L. Evans, D.D. 1914 Oxford*

A historical study of the ethical atmosphere at the beginning of the Christian era. *A. N. Rose, M.A. 1912 Birmingham*

New Testament eschatology in its bearing upon ethics. *E. H. Williamson, B.Litt. 1939 Dublin, Trinity College*

The notion of *virtus moralis* in S. Thomas Aquinas and its sources. *B. B. Magrath, B.Litt. 1948 Oxford*

On philosophical aspects of Christian ethics. *G. F. Barbour, Ph.D. 1910 Edinburgh*

Pauline ethics, with special reference to eschatology. *J. P. Lee-Woolf, B.D. 1942 Oxford*

A re-examination of the apparent antithesis between the theological doctrine of grace and the ethical doctrine of the categorical imperative. *J. E. Davies, B.Litt. 1944 Oxford*

The relation of religion to morals in Christianity. *C. Mackinlay, M.Litt. 1940 Durham*

The relation of St. Paul's ethics to his doctrine of salvation. *H. W. Kerley, Ph.D. 1949 Edinburgh*

The relevance of the ethical teaching of Jesus to the conditions of this world order: an examination of the Sermon on the Mount. *W. R. F. Browning, B.D. 1948 Oxford*

1. The sacrament of the Lord's Supper. 2. The obligation of the decalogue upon Christians. *A. H. Austen-Leigh, B.D. 1872 Oxford*

A systematic account of the ethical teaching of the New Testament. *L. H. Marshall, Ph.D. 1948 London, External Degree*

The theme of 'Bildung' in *Wilhelm Meister*, and the moral and religious teaching of the early Carlyle to 1843. *G. F. Senior, M.A. 1950 Manchester*

Three religious moralists. *S. M. Vos, M.Litt. 1950 Cambridge*

Truth, unity, and goodness as aspects of being in the writings of St. Thomas Aquinas. *W. W. S. March, B.Litt. 1941 Oxford*

Ethics: Europe

Albrecht Ritschl and the problem of value. *H. B. Hendershot, Ph.D. 1933 Edinburgh*

The British moralists. *J. W. Macleod, B.Litt. 1933 Oxford*

Butler's contribution to ethical science. *W. B. Roberts, M.A. 1917 Liverpool*

The development of Kant's ethical philosophy, with especial reference to his English precursors. *A. C. Mason, M.A. 1913 London*

The development, significance, and some limitations of Hegel's ethical teaching. *W. S. Chang, D.Phil. 1923 Oxford*

English theories of moral obligation from Hobbes to Stephen. *F. J. Smith, B.Sc. 1900 Oxford*

The ethical and social doctrines of Bishop Berkeley. *S. Azeemullah, M.A. 1924 London*

The ethical doctrine of Alexandre Dumas fils, as expressed in his plays. *T. Jones, M.A. 1941 Wales*

The ethical ideas of John Locke and their antecedents. *W. G. Hilton, M.A. 1929 Manchester*

The ethical theory of Bishop Butler. *W. P. Blevin, M.A. 1908 London*

The ethical theory of Nietzsche. *H. Morris-Jones, B.Litt. 1937 Oxford*

The ethical value of education as provided and presented by public authorities during the past thirty years (1890-1920). *R. MacDonald, M.A. 1925 Liverpool*

Hume's theory of ethics: a study of the *Enquiry concerning the Principles of Morals*. *R. E. O. White, M.A. 1950 Liverpool*

Kant's view of the relation between theology and ethics. *W. M. Watt, B.Litt. 1933 Oxford*

Law as the basis of morality in the philosophy of Hobbes, Cumberland and Locke. *M. Balaguer, Ph.D. 1937 London, University College*

Ethics: Europe contd.

Lessings ethische Ansichten. *I. C. Morton, M.A. 1925 Birmingham*

Manners and morals of the seventeenth and eighteenth centuries as revealed in books written for the young. *I. E. Thrift, Ph.D. 1935 London, King's College*

Moral preoccupations in the life and work of Marcel Proust. *J. L. Moffat, Ph.D. 1948 Bristol*

The moral theory of Richard Price. *R. Thomas, Ph.D. 1928 London*

The problem of moral freedom with reference to its discussion in recent philosophy and in particular in the *Ethics* of Nicolai Hartmann. *H. D. Lewis, M.A. 1934 Wales*

The relation of morality to self-consciousness in the philosophy of T. H. Green. *L. Golomb, M.A. 1946 Sheffield*

The relations between ethics and metaphysics, with special reference to the works of Spinoza, Kant and T. H. Green. *J. P. Davies, M.A. 1922 Wales*

Schleiermacher's ethics. *A. P. Kelso, B.Sc. 1913 Oxford*

Views concerning the epistemology of morals held by some of the British moralists of the eighteenth century, with especial reference to the anti-empiricist views of Richard Price and Thomas Reid. *D. Rafilovitch, D.Phil. 1940 Oxford*

Voltaire's conception of the origin and function of morality. *J. M. Jeffreys, M.A. 1947 London, University College*

Ethics: Greek and Roman

The confusion between moral and aesthetic ideas in Greek literary criticism and philosophy. *M. Chandler, M.A. 1933 London, Royal Holloway College*

The development in religious and ethical thought as discerned in the *Iliad* and the *Odyssey*. *E. I. Jones, M.A. 1915 Wales*

Development of ethical thought of Plato and Aristotle. *K. P. Smyth, M.A. 1933 National University of Ireland*

The ethical end of Plato's theory of ideas. *F. A. Cavenagh, M.A. 1909 London*

Ethics of Plato. *J. Callaghan, M.A. 1915 National University of Ireland*

The history of the οικείωσισ doctrine, with special reference to Cicero *De Finibus* v. *J. M. Mingay, B.Litt. 1950 Oxford*

The influence of the aesthetic point of view upon the ethics of Aristotle. *F. H. C. Brock, M.A. 1904 London*

The moral and religious ideas of Aeschylus and Pindar. *E. J. King, M.A. 1937 Manchester*

The moral teaching of Euripides. *D. Marshall, M.A. 1913 Birmingham*

Obligations between man and man in Euripides. *E. A. J. Marsh, M.A. 1906 London*

Plato's theory of ethics as contained in the early dialogues. *S. S. Orr, M.A. 1942 Belfast*

Some historical examples in the Roman moralists. *H. M. Phillipson, M.A. 1929 Manchester*

The stoicism of Lucius Annaeus Seneca, with special reference to ethics. *E. A. Hopkins, M.A. 1943 London, Bedford College*

Ethics: Islam

Al-Hadith according to al-Bukhari, with special reference to Islamic ethics. *I. H. Mougy, M.A. 1934 Manchester*

Ethics: Jewish

The Old Testament morality. *G. C. Glanville, B.Litt. 1937 Oxford*

R. Jonah b. Abraham of Gerona: his life and ethical works. *A. T. Shrock, Ph.D. 1936 London, External Degree*

A study of the *Tibb-el-Nufus* (medicine of the soul) of Rabbi Joseph-bar-Jehuda (Aqnin), from the Bodleian ms. Huntingdon 518, together with a short life of the author. *A. S. Doniach, B.Litt. 1921 Oxford*

1. The value of the theory of accommodation as applied to moral difficulties in the Old Testament. 2. The place of miracles among the evidences for Christianity. *P. A. Wright-Henderson, B.D. & D.D. 1903 Oxford*

Ethics: Oriental

Chinese ethics. *E. Parry, M.A. 1943 Leeds*

Ethics of Pāli Buddhism. *S. Tachibana, D.Phil. 1922 Oxford*

Ethics: Oriental contd.

The fourth noble truth: a study in Buddhist ethics. *P. L. Farkas, Ph.D. 1931 Aberdeen*

The practical theology and ethics of Shah Waliullah of Dihli. *A. J. Halepota, D.Phil. 1949 Oxford*

A study of the Chinese moral traditions and its social values. *F. C. Wei, Ph.D. 1929 London*

A translation with critical notes of a ms. in the British Museum written by the Chinese Emperor Ch'ien Hung, and entitled *A treatise on the recognition of faults*. *J. P. Bruce, M.A. 1907 London*

Ethics: United States

A critical study of Dewey's theory of moral values. *B. E. Cornelius, Ph.D. 1924 Edinburgh*

Ethiopia

Anglo-Italian relations, 1884-5, and the Italian occupation of Massawah. *F. T. Fries, Ph.D. 1940 Cambridge*

The Geneva treatment of the Manchurian and Abyssinian crises. *M. P. Lee, Ph.D. 1946 London, School of Economics and Political Science*

The growth of British influence in Abyssinia and on the African coast of the Red Sea from 1840 to 1885. *M. M. Law, M.A. 1931 London, King's College*

Ethnology

See also Anthropology; and African Peoples; Celts; Indians of North America.

Ethnographic maps of Macedonia, 1730-1918. *H. R. Wilkinson, M.A. 1948 Liverpool*

The ethnology of China proper. *C. H. Liu, B.Sc. 1932 Oxford*

1. The Sermon on the Mount in light of today. 2. The Christian argument from the study of ethnology. *E. S. Chalk, B.D. 1921 Oxford*

Vocabulaire ethnographique d'une région des Pyrenées centrales. *W. D. Elcock, M.A. 1933 Manchester*

Etiquette

Anglo-Norman books of courtesy and nurture. *H. R. Parsons, B.Litt. 1927 Oxford*

Courtoisie in the *roman d'aventures* of the thirteenth century. *A. D. Crow, B.Litt. 1933 Oxford*

Manners and morals of the seventeenth and eighteenth centuries as revealed in books written for the young. *I. E. Thrift, Ph.D. 1935 London, King's College*

Middle class conduct books in the seventeenth century. *H. Mews, M.A. 1934 London, King's College*

Eucharist

See also Sacraments.

Anglican Eucharistic theology from 1700 to 1845. *H. J. Coulson, B.Litt. 1939 Oxford*

1. The Book of Revelation. 2. The doctrine of the Church of England on the Lord's Supper compared with Scripture and the teaching of the primitive Church, and also with the teaching of the Church of Rome. *P. C. Ingroville, B.D. 1909 Oxford*

Calvin's doctrine of the Lord's Supper in its relation to other sacramental types. *A. Barclay, Ph.D. 1926 Edinburgh*

1. The Christology of St. John of Damascus. 2. The Eucharistic doctrine of St. John of Damascus. *C. A. Brereton, B.D. 1910 Oxford*

1. The conception of personality in relation to the present outlook and to the Christian doctrine of God. 2. Intercommunion and Christian reunion. *E. A. Burroughs, B.D. & D.D. 1921 Oxford*

1. The doctrinal significance of the Lord's Supper. 2. The Gospel according to St. Luke in its literary relations to the Gospels according to the other Synoptists and to St. John. *C. R. W. Biggs, B.D. 1896 Oxford*

1. The doctrine of the Lord's Supper. 2. The doctrine of the atonement. *E. A. Glover, B.D. 1902 Oxford*

1. The doctrine of the New Testament on the Supper of the Lord. 2. The doctrine of the Church of England on the Supper of the Lord. *W. H. G. Thomas, B.D. 1901 Oxford*

1. The doctrine of the objective presence in the Eucharist. 2. The Church and the world. *T. B. Strong, B.D. 1899 Oxford*

1. The doctrine of the person of Christ in the Fathers of the first two centuries. 2. The doctrine of the Holy Eucharist in the same period. *A. N. Claye, B.D. & D.D. 1907 Oxford*

The Eucharistic rite in the liturgy of the Church of Scotland. *J. M. Barkley, D.D. 1949 Dublin, Trinity College*

Eucharist contd.
1. The Gallican liturgy. 2. Consecration and communion in the English rite. *L. St. A. Wright, B.D. 1916 Oxford*

A history of the development of the Eucharist to 150 A.D. *T. A. Littleton, B.D. 1948 Leeds*

1. Holy baptism. 2. Holy communion. *J. Bramston, B.D. 1872 Oxford*

1. The meaning, necessity, and morality of the Christian atonement. 2. The sacrament of the Lord's Supper considered as satisfying certain needs of human nature. *A. C. de Bourbel, B.D. 1896 Oxford*

Meditations on the Supper of Our Lord. *M. G. Keating, M.A. 1919 Bristol*

1. On the interpretation of the Apocalypse. 2. On the structure of the Eucharistic office. *E. C. S. Gibson, B.D. & D.D. 1895 Oxford*

1. On the later medieval doctrine of the Eucharistic sacrifice. 2. On the relation of confirmation to baptism according to the New Testament. *B. J. Kidd, B.D. 1898 Oxford*

On the liturgy of the Swedish Church: a) mass offices prepared by individuals between 1535 and 1576; b) mass offices prepared by committees between 1599 and 1716. *E. Y. Esskildsen, B.D. 1917 Oxford*

1. On the origin and affinities of the Lord's Supper and the Passover. 2. On the traces of Gentilism in Christianity. *H. E. D. Blakiston, B.D. 1901 Oxford*

The order for the administration of the Lord's Supper or Holy Communion as set forth in the prayer books of the Church of England, of the Church of Scotland, and of the Episcopal Church in the United States of America. *J. B. Langstaff, B.Litt. 1916 Oxford*

The psychology of eucharistic worship. *F. F. Thompson, Ph.D. 1938 Edinburgh*

1. The relation of the Church to the kingdom of God. 2. The meaning of the words of institution in I Corinthians xi.24, 25. *H. L. Goudge, B.D. & D.D. 1910 Oxford*

1. The sacrament of the Lord's Supper. 2. The obligation of the decalogue upon Christians. *A. H. Austen-Leigh, B.D. 1872 Oxford*

The sacrament of the Lord's Supper in early Methodism. *J. C. Bowmer, M.A. 1949 Leeds*

1. St. Luke xxii.14-20: the institution of the Eucharist. 2. I Corinthians xv.3-8: the witness of St. Paul to the resurrection. 3. I Corinthians xv.29: baptizing for the dead. *T. H. Davies, D.D. 1910 Oxford*

1. St. Paul and the mystery religions. 2. The Incarnation and the Eucharist. *H. L. James, B.D. & D.D. 1924 Oxford*

1. Studies in the Holy Eucharist. 2. Ecclesiastes. *E. H. Rudkin, B.D. 1924 Oxford*

A study of the passion narratives, with special reference to the Last Supper. *H. L. Franklin, B.Litt. 1935 Oxford*

1. Sufficiency of Holy Scripture for salvation - Article VI. 2. The sacrament of the Lord's Supper - Article XXVIII. *H. Robinson, B.D. & D.D. 1871 Oxford*

The teaching of the Eastern Church with regard to the Holy Eucharist in the sixteenth and seventeenth centuries. *H. Basdekas, B.Litt. 1914 Oxford*

This, our sacrifice. *T. F. Jalland, B.D. 1934 Oxford*

1. True and false conceptions of the Eucharist as a sacrifice. 2. The grounds of the observance of the Lord's day. *W. B. C. Wilder, B.D. 1902 Oxford*

1. Whether the baptism of young children is in any wise to be retained in the Church. 2. Transubstantiation overthrows the nature of a sacrament. *H. W. Yule, B.D. 1877 Oxford*

Eucken, Rudolf Christoph
The metaphysics of the spiritual life; the philosophy of Rudolf Eucken. *J. F. Burke, M.A. 1945 National University of Ireland*

Eulenberg, Herbert
Die Neuromantik in Drama Herbert Eulenbergs. *F. W. Schoberth, M.A. 1937 Wales*

Euphronios
Fifty years of Greek vase-painting: Euphronios and his contemporaries. *E. Radford, M.A. 1913 London*

Euphuism
See also English Literature: Seventeenth Century; Lyly, J.

Euphuism contd.
The rise and progress of Euphuism in English literature. *T. A. Baggs, M.A. 1912 Birmingham*

Euripides
Alcestis. M. E. Norris, M.A. 1910 London

The attitude of Euripides towards the popular religious thought of the day. *J. S. Davies, M.A. 1907 Wales*

A dissertation on *Medea. M. M. Gillies, Ph.D. 1924 Edinburgh*

Euripides and his relation to the religion of his time. *E. D. Evans, M.A. 1909 Wales*

The *Iphigenia in Aulis* of Euripides. *R. P. Baker, M.A. 1926 Birmingham*

The moral teaching of Euripides. *D. Marshall, M.A. 1913 Birmingham*

Obligations between man and man in Euripides. *E. A. J. Marsh, M.A. 1906 London*

A reconsideration of Verrall's criticism of Euripides. *A. C. Edwards, M.A. 1931 Birmingham*

The relation of Euripides to 'new comedy', with special reference to Menander. *M. Andrews, M.A. 1922 London*

Rhetoric in Euripides and Menander. *J. M. Aitken, B.Litt. 1936 Oxford*

Studies in the late plays of Euripides. *V. Knowles, M.A. 1938 Manchester*

Three plays of Euripides in relation to the social background of his time. *R. F. Willetts, M.A. 1938 Birmingham*

The use of pictorial effect in the poetry of Aeschylus, Sophocles, and Euripides. *W. M. O. Reed, M.A. 1918 London*

Virgil's use of Homer and Euripides in the third book of the *Aeneid. N. E. Sutton, M.A. 1948 Manchester*

Europe: Constitutions
Federalism in central and eastern Europe. *R. A. J. Schlesinger, Ph.D. 1945 London, University College*

The new constitutions of Europe: a comparative study of post-war European constitutions, with special reference to Germany, Poland, Czechoslovakia, the Kingdom of the Serbs, Croats, and Slovenes, and the Baltic States. *A. H. Morley, B.Litt. 1925 Oxford*

Europe: Economics
The European recovery programme. *J. St. Freybyia, M.Econ.Sc. 1950 National University of Ireland*

Tariffs and stability in commercial relations in the post-war period, with special regard to Central Europe. *V. Jalea, Ph.D. 1931 Birmingham*

Europe: History
See also Church History; Crusades; Holy Roman Empire; Hundred Years' War; Jews: History; Thirty Years' War.

The breakdown of post-war democracy in central Europe: analysis of authoritarian methods and possibilities of their control. *K. J. Neumann, D.Phil. 1944 Oxford*

British policy and opinion and the second Hague conference. *H. S. W. Corrigan, M.A. 1934 London, King's College*

Castlereagh and the Holy Alliance. *H. C. Hamilton, M.A. 1926 Birmingham*

The circumstances of the Treaty of Dover. *A. H. Madan, M.A. 1909 Birmingham*

The Eastern Question and European diplomacy in the period 1876-1878, with special reference to British policy. *W. A. Gauld, M.A. 1923 Liverpool*

Europe and Morocco, particularly from 1900-1911. *E. T. Glendon, M.A. 1923 Birmingham*

European alliances and ententes, 1879-85: a study of contemporary British information. *A. Ramm, M.A. 1937 London, Bedford College*

The European Concert, June 1854-July 1855. *G. B. Henderson, Ph.D. 1934 Cambridge*

The Great Powers and Tunis, 1878-1881. *M. M. Safwat, Ph.D. 1940 London, School of Economics and Political Science*

The influence of 1848 on education. *O. W. Sinclair, M.A. 1916 London*

Liverpool during the Seven Years War. *M. Buchan-Sydserff, M.A. 1934 Liverpool*

The policy of Great Britain with reference to the Continental revolutions of 1848-9. *C. F. Strong, M.A. 1921 London*

Europe: History contd.
Serbia in international politics from the insurrection of Herzegovina (1875) to the Congress of Berlin (1878). *M. D. Stojanovic, Ph.D. 1930 London, King's College*

The slave trade in European diplomacy, 1814-1818. *E. Smallpage, M.A. 1922 Liverpool*

The social and economic background of attempts at a Concert of Europe from 1804 to 1825. *H. G. A. V. Schenk, D.Phil. 1943 Oxford*

A study of the relationship between the diplomatic and commercial policies of France, Germany, Italy, Russia, and Austria-Hungary, 1871-1914. *W. Koren, B.Litt. 1934 Oxford*

Tentatives toward European union: a survey of the progress made in the last half-century in the development of selected public international organizations which tend toward unifying Europe. *G. L. Powell, B.Litt. 1949 Oxford*

The Triple Alliance and the War of Devolution. *M. O. Noël-Paton, Ph.D. 1931 London, University College*

Europe: Social History
The geographical background to community of interests among the northern European peoples. *W. R. Mead, Ph.D. 1947 London, External Degree*

The historical, economic and cultural importance of the Loess soil of Europe. *T. S. Williams, M.Sc. 1928 Wales*

The treatment of Europe in Chinese school textbooks. *H. T. Wu, M.A. 1949 London, Institute of Education*

Eusebius, of Caesarea
1. God's purposes with regard to the Gentile world, as foreshadowed in the Old Testament. 2. Eusebius as a Christian apologist. *M. F. Argles, B.D. 1881 Oxford*

Evangelicalism
See also Protestantism; Clapham Sect; Fléchère, J. W. de la; Jay, W.

The attitude of the Evangelicals to the Empire and imperial problems (1820-1850). *A. F. Madden, D.Phil. 1950 Oxford*

A comparative study of the old and new types of revivalism, with special relation to the influence of contemporary religious thought and practice. *S. T. McCloy, B.Litt. 1922 Oxford*

The contribution of the Evangelical revival to the philosophy and practice of education. *A. W. Morton, D.Phil. 1949 Oxford*

Cysylltiad y diwygiadau crefyddol o 1730 hyd 1850 â llenyddiaeth y cyfnod (The connection of religious revivals from 1730 to 1850 with the literature of the period). *L. E. Evans, M.A. 1934 Wales*

The Evangelical revival and Congregationalism. *F. C. Rogers, M.A. 1909 Liverpool*

The Evangelical revival in eighteenth century England as reflected in the life and work of William Romaine, 1714-1795. *D. G. Davis, Ph.D. 1949 Edinburgh*

The Evangelicals in Oxford, 1735-1871. *J. S. Reynolds, B.Litt. 1950 Oxford*

The political activities of the 'Saints', 1800-1833. *F. U. Woods, M.A. 1924 Manchester*

A psychological estimate of evangelical experience. *W. G. Parker, Ph.D. 1948 London, Richmond College*

The religious awakening of 1858-60 in Great Britain and Ireland. *O. Bussey, Ph.D. 1947 Edinburgh*

The rise and development of the evangelical movement in the Highlands of Scotland from 1688 to 1800. *J. MacInnes, Ph.D. 1941 Edinburgh*

Evans, Daniel Silvan
Aspects of Welsh lexicography in the nineteenth century, with special reference to the contribution of Daniel Silvan Evans. *R. E. Hughes, M.A. 1941 Liverpool*

Evans, Evan
Evan Evans (Ieuan Fardd), 1731-1788. Hanes ei fywyd a'i gysylltiadau llenyddol (Evan Evans (Ieuan Fardd), 1731-1788. The history of his life and his literary connections). *A. Lewis, M.A. 1950 Wales*

Evans, John (I. D. Ffraid)
Bywyd a gwaith John Evans (I. D. Ffraid) (Life and work of John Evans (I. D. Ffraid)). *W. L. Roberts, M.A. 1950 Wales*

Evans, Mary Ann
See Eliot, George.

Evans, Theophilus
Ffynonellau, arddull a chymeriad gwaith llenyddol Theophilus Evans (Sources, style and character of the literary work of Theophilus Evans). *D. Thomas, M.A. 1937 Wales*

Evesham, Vale of
See also Avon, River.

An economic survey of small holdings in the Vale of Evesham. *S. R. Wragg, M.A. 1937 Bristol*

A geographical study of the Vale of Evesham. *E. Hardman, M.A. 1930 Manchester*

Evidence
A comparative study of the law of evidence in the Continental and common law systems. *H. A. A. P. O. Hammelmann, D.Phil. 1947 Oxford*

The hearsay rule. *R. W. Baker, B.Litt. 1947 Oxford*

The psychology of evidence. *N. G. M. Prichard, M.Sc. 1930 London, King's College*

The rationale of the rules of evidence, being an enquiry into the basis and development of the principal rules of evidence in English law, with a few suggestions for reform. *C. S. Watson, LL.D. 1917 London*

Evil
See also Sin.

The cosmic significance of Christian redemption. *A. D. Galloway, Ph.D. 1950 Cambridge*

Evil according to St Thomas. *C. Lucey, M.A. 1930 National University of Ireland*

Evil and world order in Shakespeare's tragedies. *J. G. Hanrahan, M.A. 1947 National University of Ireland*

A history of the rise and development of the problem of evil in ancient European philosophy up to the end of the second century A.D. *B. A. G. Fuller, B.Sc. 1905 Oxford*

Moral evil in relation to modern cosmological theory. *W. R. Matthews, M.A. 1912 London*

1. On the subservience of evil to the purposes of God. 2. On the office of the Holy Spirit as the perfector of the works of God the Father. *G. H. West, B.D. & D.D. 1889 Oxford*

The paradox of evil. *F. Jolley, M.A. 1949 Liverpool*

The personification of supreme evil in Christian thought: a study of origins. *W. H. A. Learoyd, D.D. 1940 Durham*

Problem of evil in Francis Thompson's poetry. *F. X. Lobo, M.A. 1945 National University of Ireland*

The problem of evil in pre-Christian religions. *R. C. J. Wilkins, M.A. 1940 Leeds*

The problem of evil in the philosophy of Leibniz. *A. B. Lavelle, Ph.D. 1935 Sheffield*

The problem of evil in the thought of F. R. Tennant. *C. G. Werner, Ph.D. 1950 Edinburgh*

The problem of evil with special reference to the *Theodicee* of Leibniz. *H. Cunliffe-Jones, B.Litt. 1932 Oxford*

The problem of evil with special reference to Hindu philosophy. *E. Ahmad Shah, B.Litt. 1922 Oxford*

St. Thomas and the problem of evil. *T. Connellan, M.A. 1944 National University of Ireland*

The subject of evil in Greek philosophy. *E. J. Widdows, M.A. 1911 Bristol*

Theism and the problem of evil. *J. R. Jones, M.A. 1929 Wales*

Evolution
See also Teleology.

The bearing of the conception of evolution upon the problem of the inclusion of individual minds within reality as a whole. *E. E. Harris, B.Litt. 1933 Oxford*

The concept of emergent evolution. *A. Richardson, M.A. 1929 Liverpool*

1. The doctrine of the fall in relation to evolution. 2. The fall and the Incarnation. *G. C. Joyce, B.D. 1904 Oxford*

Evolution. *H. D. Griffith, Ph.D. 1946 Dublin, Trinity College*

Evolution and freedom: does evolution preclude moral freedom?. *J. Maycock, M.A. 1938 Liverpool*

Evolution and the spirit of man. *J. P. Milum, Ph.D. 1926 London*

The evolutionary hypothesis and its implications: a critical exposition and discussion with special reference to the theories of naturalistic, creative and emergent evolution. *B. L. Jones, M.A. 1934 Liverpool*

Evolution contd.
The evolutionary theory of sin. *A. J. Long, B.D. 1948 Oxford*

1. The future life in light of the theory of evolution. 2. The doctrine of salvation. *C. E. Beeby, B.D. 1888 Oxford*

1. Genesis i, ii.1-7, iii.17-19; Psalm xix.1-3, xcv.3-7: evolution and providence. 2. St. Mark ix.48; St. John iii.36: eternal justice. 3. Genesis iii.1-10; Romans vii.18,19: will in Christian ethics. *A. J. Nilson, D.D. 1885 Oxford*

The influence of paleontology on the theory of evolution. *A. V. Spratt, M.Sc. 1927 London*

Influence of the theory of evolution on the Christian doctrine of the atonement. *W. J. Cratchley, M.A. 1933 Bristol*

The place of instinct in the evolution of the mind in man and the lower animals from the biological and psychological points of view. *A. Kefalas, M.A. 1926 Liverpool*

The theories of the origin of species critically viewed. *E. Poonen, M.D. 1889 Aberdeen*

The theory of evolution in science, ethics and religion, with special reference to its teleological nature, tracing the development of the theory in question from Lamarck to our own day. *W. W. Pearson, B.Sc. 1907 Oxford*

1. The unveiling of the Fall. 2. Re-creation: a new aspect of evolution. *C. W. Formby, B.D. & D.D. 1924 Oxford*

Ewe, The
The social organization of the Ewe-speaking people: an analytical and comparative study. *B. E. Ward, M.A. 1948 London, School of Economics and Political Science*

Examinations
A comparative study of the factors entering into the boys' and girls' results in a special place examination. *W. H. King, M.A. 1945 London, Institute of Education*

A comparison of free-place and fee-paying boys in a municipal secondary school (1916-1925), together with investigations concerning the reliability of the admission examination. *E. Worthington, M.A. 1930 Birmingham*

A critical analysis of the results of a school certificate examination. *W. H. King, Ph.D. 1949 London, Institute of Education*

A critical study of external examinations and of their influence on secondary education. *J. F. G. O'Meara, M.A. 1944 National University of Ireland*

A critical survey of the auxiliary means of selection employed in examinations in public elementary schools for free special places in secondary schools. *G. Baron, M.Ed. 1937 Leeds*

An enquiry into the careers of these pupils who enter the secondary school after their second attempt in the admission examination. *D. M. Coombes, M.A. 1935 Birmingham*

An enquiry into the predictive value of grammar school entrance examinations. *D. Rutter, M.Ed. 1949 Durham*

An enquiry into the relative achievements of boys and girls at a first School Certificate examination, in the six commoner subjects of the curriculum. *R. Field, M.A. 1935 Birmingham*

Errors in French prose composition made by school children under examination conditions. *W. J. Tiffin, M.Ed. 1929 Leeds*

Examinations: their origins, development and functions. *D. J. Williams, M.A. 1946 Liverpool*

An experimental study of standardized tests for selecting secondary school pupils. *P. T. Verghese, M.Ed. 1938 Leeds*

External examinations as a factor in the development of science subjects in secondary schools. *F. F. Crossley, M.A. 1947 Liverpool*

External examinations in the schools and their probable development: a critical survey. *A. B. Clegg, M.A. 1935 London, King's College*

An illustrative study of examination marks by the methods of factor analysis and the analysis of variance. *M. K. B. Harwood, Ph.D. 1943 London, Bedford College*

An investigation into the reliability of various entrance examinations for pupils about to enter secondary and central selective schools. *C. Skelton, M.A. 1938 Leeds*

An investigation of methods of examination at the 'qualifying stage'. *D. M. McIntosh, Ph.D. 1939 Saint Andrew's*

Examinations contd.
An investigation of school mathematics, mainly with the object of discovering by scientific method whether or not it is justifiable to include arithmetic, algebra and geometry as one group for school certificate and matriculation examination. *H.W. Oldham, Ph.D. 1936 Reading*

Misfits in a secondary grammar school: a study of academic failures, 1935-1944. *H. Lowther, M.Ed. 1948 Manchester*

A multiple factor analysis of the results obtained from certain mental tests and some school examinations. *A. Aris, M.A. 1938 London, Institute of Education*

New type achievement examinations in science. *H. P. Wood, M.Ed. 1941 Manchester*

The reliability of an entrance scholarship examination as a means of predicting school certificate results. *T. E. Stubbins, M.Ed. 1937 Leeds*

The school report and record as a factor in the junior scholarship examination. *W. Healey, M.Ed. 1939 Leeds*

The scope and value of psychological testing, with special reference to the examination of scholarship candidates for further education. *H. V. Clark, M.A. 1936 Liverpool*

Secondary school selection. *W. A. C. Bishop, M.Sc. 1940 Wales*

Selection for secondary education. *L. E. Kitchen, M.A. 1945 Bristol*

The selection of children for secondary education. *A. James, M.Sc. 1925 Birmingham*

The selection of entrants to the junior technical school. *N. A. Lewis, M.Ed. 1944 Manchester*

Some apparent effects of co-education, suggested by a statistical investigation of examination results. *G. Tyson, M.Ed. 1930 Manchester*

Some aspects of the examination problem. *H. Rahman, M.A. 1936 Birmingham*

A study of the Middlesex junior technical school entrance examination: being an investigation into the methods adopted and their value for the selection of junior technical school pupils. *W. H. J. Knight, M.A. 1949 London, Institute of Education*

A study of the prognostic value of examinations set as a test for admission into Middlesex secondary schools. *R. W. Dutton, M.A. 1934 London, Institute of Education*

Technique of examining children, based on the *New Examiner* by Dr. P. B. Ballard (1923). *F. MacPolin, M.A. 1934 National University of Ireland*

A theoretical and experimental study of the nature and extent of predetermination of score-scatter by the type of test-paper used. *D. A. Walker, Ph.D. 1937 Edinburgh*

The validity and reliability of a secondary school entrance test: being the follow-up over a period of six years of the examination in a rural area. *S. F. Marshall, M.A. 1940 London, Institute of Education*

The value of the new-type examination for assessing attainment in biology. *F. S. Cook, M.A. 1936 London, Institute of Education*

Exchange Rates
See Money.

Exeter, Diocese
The fabric rolls of Exeter cathedral, 1374-1514. *D. F. Findlay, Ph.D. 1939 Leeds*

Parish clergy in the diocese of Exeter in the century after the Black Death. *G. R. Dunstan, M.A. 1939 Leeds*

Experience
Experience in relation to the real. *W. J. Downes, M.A. 1923 London*

Finite and absolute experience: a study in contrasts. *F. H. Cleobury, Ph.D. 1941 London, External Degree*

Individual experience in the philosophy of Leibniz. *A. H. Talukder, M.A. 1935 London, University College*

Exploration
See Voyages and Travels.

Extradition
Extradition of political offenders. *K. U. Szantyr, M.Litt. 1949 Cambridge*

Extraterritoriality
See also Territorial Waters.

British extraterritorial jurisdiction. *J. A. Watson, LL.D. 1927 London*

Extraterritoriality contd.
Extra-territorial non-mining companies in Nigeria in peace and war. *H. Mars, B.Litt. 1945 Oxford*

The legal obligations arising out of treaty relations between China and other states. *M. T. Z. Tyau, LL.D. 1916 London*

System of extra-territoriality in Japan, 1855-99. *F. C. Jones, M.A. 1930 Bristol*

Eye, Northamptonshire
A study of parish government: illustrated by documents from the parish chest of Eye, Northants. *R. A. Shannon, M.A. 1949 London, External Degree*

Ezuttaccan
Ezuttaccan and his age. *C. A. Menon, Ph.D. 1938 London, School of Oriental and African Studies*

Fabian Society
See also Labour Party.

Fabian doctrine and its influence in English politics. *A. M. McBriar, D.Phil. 1949 Oxford*

Fabian thought and social change in England from 1884-1914. *R. D. Howland, Ph.D. 1942 London, School of Economics and Political Science*

Fabianism as the climax of the new liberalism. *S. G. Ikoku, M.Sc. 1949 London, External Degree*

Fables
The fables of Aesop in the German literature of the fifteenth century, with special reference to Steinhoewel's translation. *W. Schwarz, M.A. 1939 London, University College*

The fables of Phaedrus: a commentary critical and exegetical, with an introduction on the poet, his style, language and prosody, the mss, and the development of the fable in classical literature. *G. A. Leary, M.A. 1947 Manchester*

La vie au foyer: usages et coutumes au moyen âge d'après la littérature populaire de l'époque, et particulièrement les fabliaux. Essai historique et linguistique. *N. Haycocks, M.A. 1929 Manchester*

A Vatican manuscript of the Greek fabulist Ignatius Diaconus. *E. J. Vaughan, M.A. 1928 London*

Factories
The career of A. J. Mundella, with special reference to his Sheffield connections. *M. Higginbotham, M.A. 1941 Sheffield*

Factory inspection in Great Britain. *T. K. Djang, Ph.D. 1940 London, School of Economics and Political Science*

Factory labour in the Punjab. *A. Mukhtar, Ph.D. 1928 London*

The factory system and the factory acts, 1802-1850. *G. Baylis, M.A. 1930 Birmingham*

The social and economic consequences of the development of the factory system in India as compared with England. *G. M. Broughton, D.Sc. 1924 London*

Fair Maid of the Exchange, The
A critical study of *The Fair maid of the exchange* and its attribution to Thomas Heywood, and the relation of the play to Markham and Machin's *Dumb knight* and the works of John Day and Thomas Dekker. *S. R. Golding, M.A. 1922 London*

Fairbairn, Andrew Martin
The theology of A. M. Fairbairn. *A. W. Loos, Ph.D. 1939 Edinburgh*

Fairfax, Edward
A text of Edward Fairfax's *Eclogues*, with an introductory essay on Fairfax's place in the history of English poetry. *C. G. Bell, B.Litt. 1939 Oxford*

Fairies
See Fairy Tales.

Fairs
Historical survey of the Somerset and Bristol fairs. *N. F. Hulbert, M.A. 1935 Bristol*

Medieval fairs in England. *J. Bennison, M.A. 1911 London*

Yorkshire fairs and markets to the end of the eighteenth century. *K. L. McCutcheon, M.Litt. 1935 Durham*

Fairy Tales
Andrew Lang as a writer of fairy tales and romances. *R. G. L. Green, B.Litt. 1944 Oxford*

An examination of the third book of *Britannia's Pastorals* and its attribution to William Browne of Tavistock, with a study of English fairy poetry from the time of Spenser, indicating Browne's position in its development. *I. Gourvitch, M.A. 1923 London*

The fairy tales and fantasies of George Macdonald. *M. M. McEldowney, B.Litt. 1934 Oxford*

Fairy Tales contd.
French fairy tales in the eighteenth century. *E. M. Buckle, Ph.D. 1927 London*

The psychological nature and origin of the belief in fairies in Celtic countries. *W. Y. E. Wentz, B.Sc. 1910 Oxford*

A study of the archetypes in children's fantasies. *I. Best, M.A. 1949 Leeds*

A study of the Middle English Breton lays, with reference to fairy lore, folk-lore and origins. *G. A. Pye, M.A. 1936 London, Birkbeck College*

Faith
See also Justification; Antinomianism.

By faith alone: an inquiry into the nature of saving faith. *H. F. L. Cocks, D.D. 1942 London, New College*

Certainty through faith: an examination of the religious philosophy of Peter Taylor Forsyth. *A. F. Simpson, Ph.D. 1949 London, External Degree*

1. Comparison of the teaching of St. Paul and St. James as to faith and works. 2. The consideration of St. Paul's expectation as to the conversion of the Jews in Romans ix, x, xi. *S. P. Duval, B.D. and D.D. 1912 Oxford*

1. The doctrine of resurrection. 2. The rational basis of faith. *J. M. Willoughby, B.D. 1902 Oxford*

1. Doctrine of the work and office of Christ, with special reference to the atonement, during the first three centuries. 2. The relations of faith and reason in the Christian system, especially during the Apostolic and sub-Apostolic period. *F. W. Bussell, B.D. 1892 Oxford*

Faith. *W. R. Inge, D.D. 1909 Cambridge*

Faith and reason in the works of Bishop Pecock. *G. F. Nuttall, B.D. 1937 Oxford*

1. Faith, the organ of religious knowledge. 2. Human free-will not inconsistent with the almighty power of God. *A. P. P. Cust, B.D. & D.D. 1880 Oxford*

1. Holy Scripture: the rule of faith. 2. 'I believe in one God'. *D. M. Owen, B.D. 1877 Oxford*

1. Holy Scripture, the sole rule of faith. 2. On the limits to be imposed upon the exercise of private judgment in the interpretation of the rule of faith. *G. Mackness, B.D. 1871 Oxford*

1. The interpretation of the Acts, with especial reference to Professor Ramsay's South Galatian theory. 2. Our Lord's use of πιστισ. *H. K. Moore, B.D. & D.D. 1898 Oxford*

1. The mediatorship of Christ as viewed from the standpoint of personality. 2. An examination of faith, with special reference to its definition in Hebrews xi. *F. G. Goddard, B.D. 1907 Oxford*

1. The nature of faith. 2. The effects of faith. *E. F. D. Hutton, B.D. & D.D. 1870 Oxford*

1. On repentance. 2. On faith. *R. O. Davies, B.D. 1889 Oxford*

1. The resurrection of Jesus Christ in its relation to the Christian faith. 2. The person and work of the Holy Spirit. *D. M. Davis, B.D. & D.D. 1909 Oxford*

1. The Sacraments. 2. Faith and works. *S. N. Tebbs, B.D. 1874 Oxford*

1. The Scriptures: the rule of faith. 2. The Church. *J. E. Cox, B.D. & D.D. 1870 Oxford*

1. The theological virtue of faith. 2. The teaching of the Apostles on the duty of receiving the faith revealed by God. *R. W. Randall, B.D. & D.D. 1892 Oxford*

The wings of faith. *H. V. Martin, Ph.D. 1947 Bristol*

Faith Healing
See Healing, Spiritual.

Faizi
Faizi, Urfi, and Naziri (poets of Akbar's Court). *A. W. Khan, Ph.D. 1932 London, School of Oriental and African Studies*

Falakī-i-Shirwānī
Falakī-i-Shirwānī: his times, life and works. *H. Hasan, Ph.D. 1929 London*

Falconer, William
The life and works of William Falconer (1732-70). *M. K. Joseph, B.Litt. 1939 Oxford*

Falkland Islands
The occupation of the Falkland Islands. *W. C. Down, Ph.D. 1927 Cambridge*

Fall, The
See Creation and the Fall.

Family
Blood relationships of the Old Testament. *D. Jacobson, Ph.D. 1936 Cambridge*

A comparative study of the family law in the Chinese and English legal systems. *C. W. Pak, Ph.D. 1940 London, King's College*

The correlation between intelligence and size of family. *H. E. G. Sutherland, Ph.D. 1930 Edinburgh*

The English criminal and criminal ecclesiastical law of sex morality and its effect upon the organization of the family. *G. May, LL.D. 1933 London, School of Economics and Political Science*

Ethical aspects of the family. *A. Smith, Ph.D. 1945 London, School of Economics and Political Science*

Europeans and the Bantu family. *B. A. Hutchinson, Ph.D. 1945 London, External Degree*

Family allowances. *R. J. O'Halloran, M.Econ.Sc. 1940 National University of Ireland*

Family allowances and the compensation fund. *H. H. R. Vibart, B.Litt. 1924 Oxford*

The family among the Australian aborigines: a sociological study. *B. G. Malinowski, D.Sc. 1916 London*

Family organization among Slavs (as reflected in the custom of *couvade*). *J. Obrebski, Ph.D. 1934 London, School of Economics and Political Science*

The functioning of a north China family. *L. K. Hsu, Ph.D. 1940 London, School of Economics and Political Science*

The influence of Christianity on the family and domestic relations in Roman law. *D. Brook, D.C.L. 1896 Oxford*

The Khasa family law in the Himalayan districts of the United Provinces, India. *L. D. Joshi, LL.D. 1927 London*

Marriage and family life among educated Africans in urban areas of the Gold Coast. *A. I. Crabtree, M.Sc. 1949 London, School of Economics and Political Science*

Variations in working-class family expenditure. *J. L. Nicholson, M.Sc. 1949 London, School of Economics and Political Science*

Fanaticism
See also Enthusiasm.

Fanaticism: a psychological analysis. *J. Djamour, M.A. 1947 London, School of Economics and Political Science*

Fanshawe, Richard, Sir
The life and works of Sir Richard Fanshawe, 1608 to 1666. *H. B. Williams, M.A. 1934 London, East London College*

Far East
See also China; Japan; Malaysia; etc.

The Arabian East and the Far East: their commercial and cultural relations during the Graeco-Roman and the Perso-Arabian periods. *S. A. S. Hozayyen, M.A. 1933 Liverpool*

Economic background of the modern diplomacy of the Great Powers in the Far East since the World War. *T. K. Chow, M.Sc. 1934 London, School of Economics and Political Science*

Etudes d'exotisme contemporain: les romanciers français et l'extrème-orient. *G. O. Rees, M.A. 1940 Wales*

The Great Powers and the Far East, from the seizure of Kiao-chau to the Boxer Settlement, 1897-1901. *M. I. Grimshaw, M.A. 1929 Birmingham*

Farm Co-operatives
See Agricultural Co-operation.

Farmer, Richard
An edition of the correspondence between Thomas Percy and Dr. Richard Farmer (B.M. Add. ms. 28222). *C. Brooks, B.Litt. 1932 Oxford*

Farming
See Agriculture.

Fascism
See also National Socialism.

The economic aspects of Fascism. *G. B. Harris, M.Com.Sc. 1932 Belfast*

Fate
See also Divination.

The conception of fate, and its development in the Latin literature of the later Republic and the early Empire. *M. M. Simpson, M.A. 1919 Liverpool*

Fiction, French contd.
Realistic tendencies in French prose fiction of the seventeenth century, with special reference to the realistic novel in the nineteenth century. *C. W. Gribble, M.A. 1923 Wales*

The *roman comique* in England. *D. M. Pope, M.A. 1906 London*

Romans de caserne à tendances naturalistes, 1887-1899. *E. Burnett, Ph.D. 1937 Leeds*

The sea novel in French literature, 1830-1870. *H. F. Collins, M.A. 1924 London*

The social novel in France, 1848-1871. *P. H. Spencer, Ph.D. 1949 Cambridge*

A study of the reception of French realistic fiction in Victorian England and of its influence upon the English novel. *W. C. D. Pacey, Ph.D. 1941 Cambridge*

The terror novel in French literature: its influence on the French novel of 1820-45. *H. W. Wood, M.A. 1922 London*

Fiction, German
Beitrag zum Studium der deutschen Kriegsromane. *A. F. Cunningham, M.A. 1932 Liverpool*

The development of modern German prose fiction since 1880. *E. J. Snee, M.A. 1910 London*

Gottfried Keller and the German Künstlerroman. *G. B. Priest, M.A. 1945 Manchester*

Handwerk und Handwerker in der deutschen erzählenden Literatur vom Ausgang des achtzehnten Jahrhunderts bis zur Gegenwart. *C. E. Robert, M.A. 1939 Liverpool*

The Industrial Revolution as reflected in the German novel. *J. L. Mowat, Ph.D. 1927 Aberdeen*

The influence of English literature on the German novel and drama in the period 1880-1900. *A. E. Eastlake, Ph.D. 1937 London, Birkbeck College*

A portrayal of childhood in German fiction from Keller to Carcesa. *J. M. Berneaud, Ph.D. 1950 Saint Andrew's*

A study of the German novel between 1850 and 1870 in its relations to French and English influences. *C. L. Shelley, M.A. 1930 Wales*

A study of the *Grosstadtroman* in modern German literature. *W. L. Morgan, M.A. 1936 Wales*

Fiction, Greek
The Greek novel. *D. M. Miller, M.A. 1912 London*

Fiction, Hungarian
Social criticism in the Hungarian novel (1620-1850). *A. Rubin, Ph.D. 1945 London, External Degree*

Fiction, Irish
An gearr-scéal sa nua-Ghaedhilg (The short story in modern Irish). *M. MacGiollacuda, M.A. 1946 National University of Ireland*

An t-aighneas idir chill agus tuaith 'sa tseanscéaluidheacht Ghaedhilge (The conflict between church and state in Old Irish storytelling). *S. Breathnach, M.A. 1940 National University of Ireland*

Fiction, Italian
Shakespeare and the Italian 'novellieri'. *M. M. Wright, Ph.D. 1950 Manchester*

Fiction, Japanese
A comparative study of some aspects of modern Japanese and English fiction. *I. R. Sato, M.Litt. 1939 Cambridge*

Fiction, Russian
The growth of the Russian psychological novel. *B. M. Hill, Ph.D. 1931 London, King's College*

Le roman russe en France à la fin du dix-neuvième siècle considéré au point de vue de l'influence exercée par Tolstoi sur Paul Margueritte et Romain Rolland. *L. Godinski, Ph.D. 1923 London*

Fiction, Scottish
The petty Scots novel. *H. M. MacKenzie, Ph.D. 1945 Edinburgh*

Fiction, Spanish
The development of the novel in Spain between 1700 and 1849 and its relation to public taste in narrative prose. *R. F. Brown, Ph.D. 1939 Liverpool*

Galdós as creator of the modern Spanish novel. *L. B. Walton, B.Litt. 1926 Oxford*

The influence of Spanish picaresque fiction on English novelists to the end of the eighteenth century. *D. T. V. Leadbeater, M.A. 1942 Wales*

The influence of the Spanish picaresque novel in the French literature of the seventeenth century, with special reference to Sorel's *Francion* (1623-33). *G. M. Willing, B.Litt. 1931 Oxford*

Fiction, Spanish contd.
The life and works of Gonzalo de Céspedes y Meneses, with bibliographical notes on the Spanish novel of the seventeenth century. *J. A. Bourne, Ph.D. 1937 Cambridge*

Regionalism in Spanish fiction from 1654 to the present day, with especial reference to Pereda. *J. Manson, Ph.D. 1938 Edinburgh*

Fiction, Urdu
A critical survey of the development of the Urdu novel and short story. *S. A. B. Suhrawardy, Ph.D. 1941 London, School of Oriental and African Studies*

Fiction, Welsh
The Welsh novel. *R. M. Jones, M.A. 1923 Wales*

Fidanza, John of
See Bonaventura, Saint.

Fiduciaries
Treatise on the law of fiduciary relationships. *E. Vinter, LL.M. 1932 Cambridge*

Field, Nathan
Specimen of an edition of Nathan Field's *A Woman is a Weathercocke* (1612) and *Amends for Ladies* (1618, 1639). *N. J. Endicott, B.Litt. 1929 Oxford*

Fielding, Henry
A critical edition of *Pasquin* and *The historical register* by Henry Fielding. *E. O. Davies, B.Litt. 1948 Oxford*

Fielding as an observer of life and a reformer of contemporary manners. *H. K. Banerji, B.Litt. 1923 Oxford*

Fielding en France. *L. M. Stead, M.A. 1914 Leeds*

Fielding's plays. *C. MacDonald, B.Litt. 1924 Oxford*

Henry Fielding and his attitude towards the law and towards legal reform. *B. M. Jones, M.A. 1932 Wales*

Henry Fielding, critic of his times. *A. C. Coolidge, Ph.D. 1937 Dublin, Trinity College*

The plays of Fielding, and their influence on the technique of the novels. *G. McDonald, M.A. 1939 Liverpool*

The social and political satire in the novel of the eighteenth century (1740-1780), with special reference to Fielding and Smollett. *W. E. Roberts, M.A. 1932 Wales*

Figures of Speech
A comparative study of the figures of speech in early Provençal and Italian lyrical poetry, down to and including Dante's *Vita nuova* and *Rime*. *I. M. Agnew, Ph.D. 1926 Edinburgh*

Verbal imagery and figures of speech in Propertius: a study of some aspects of poetic technique. *S. R. Pope, M.A. 1942 Liverpool*

Fiji
The career of Sir John Thurston, Governor of Fiji, 1888-1897. *J. Millington, M.A. 1947 London, Birkbeck College*

Filmer, Robert, Sir
The political thought of Sir Robert Filmer and his royalist contemporaries. *S. M. E. Trood, M.A. 1922 London*

Films
See Cinema.

Finance
See also Balance of Payments; Banks and Banking; Capital; Gold Standard; Interest; Investment; Money; Securities; Stocks and Shares; Taxation; Unit Trusts.

Budget control: a study of fiscal policy as an instrument for regulating economic fluctuations. *K. Chang, M.A. 1947 Leeds*

Financial integration within the British Empire. *A. S. J. Baster, M.Comm. 1930 London, School of Economics and Political Science*

Foreign exchange control. *H. Metcalf, M.Com. 1939 Leeds*

Foreign lending. *W. K. Duke, M.Sc. 1939 London, School of Economics and Political Science*

German borrowings abroad, 1924-30. *A. F. K. Schlepegrell, B.Litt. 1934 Oxford*

National and local finance: a review of the relations between the central and local authorities in England, France, Belgium, and Prussia during the nineteenth century. *J. W. Grice, D.Sc. 1911 London*

The principles of federal public finance. *D. Ivor, Ph.D. 1947 London, School of Economics and Political Science*

Finance contd.
Problems of public finance arising in federal constitutions. *M. M. Khan, M.Sc. 1936 London*

Ricardo's contributions to financial theory examined in the light of modern theory. *A. N. A. Hamid, Ph.D. 1936 Leeds*

The technique of government borrowing: a study of the methods employed by the British Treasury in its borrowing operations, 1914-39. *Y. C. Ma, Ph.D. 1942 London, School of Economics and Political Science*

Finch, Daniel, 2nd Earl of Nottingham
The administration of Daniel Finch, second Earl of Nottingham, as Secretary of State under Queen Anne, 1702-4. *W. A. Aiken, M.Litt. 1933 Cambridge*

Fingerprints
Association of fingerprints. *H. Waite, D.Sc. 1915 London*

Firmin, Thomas
Thomas Firmin, F.R.S. (1632-1697). *H. W. Stephenson, D.Phil. 1949 Oxford*

Firtéar, Pádraig
Amhráin ghrádha ó'n Mhumhain; cnuasacht a bailigheadh as láimhscríbhinní Phádruig Fhéirtéir, Coláiste na h-Oillsgoile Baile Atha Cliath (Love songs from Munster; a collection from the manuscripts of Pádraig Feirtéar in University College Dublin). *P. O'hUllacháin, M.A. 1939 National University of Ireland*

Firtéar, Piaras
Faisnéis bhreise ar Phiaras Fhirtéar (Further information on Piaras Firtéar). *M. C. Mhac an tSaoi, M.A. 1945 National University of Ireland*

Fisher, John
See John Fisher, of Rochester, Saint.

Fisheries and Fishing Industry
British policy in the North American cod fisheries with special reference to foreign competition, 1776-1819. *G. O. Rothney, Ph.D. 1939 London, King's College*

A geography of the East Anglican herring fishery. *P. C. Walton, M.A. 1948 London, King's College*

History of Irish fisheries. *M. Hourihane, M.A. 1927 National University of Ireland*

The Irish fishing industry. *J. C. U. Moloney, M.A. 1950 National University of Ireland*

The Scottish herring industry. *A. R. Murison, Ph.D. 1930 Glasgow*

The sea fisheries of Northern Ireland. *J. B. Arnold, M.Com.Sc. 1942 Belfast*

A study in the use of advisory bodies by the Ministry of Agriculture and Fisheries, since 1919. *A. M. Mackintosh, B.Litt. 1949 Oxford*

A study of the port of Fleetwood, with special reference to its position in the west coast fishing industry. *D. Peter, M.A. 1932 Manchester*

The technology and economics of fishing in relation to Hawaiian culture. *R. A. Scobie, M.A. 1949 London, School of Economics and Political Science*

Fitch, William
See Canfield, Benedict.

Fitzgerald, Edward
Fitzgerald and the Persian poets, with an edition of *Salaman and Absal*; also a literal translation in English of the original poem by the Persian poet, Jami. *S. Din, B.Litt. 1933 Oxford*

The life of Edward Fitzgerald. *A. M. Terhune, Ph.D. 1940 Cambridge*

Fitzralph, Richard
An essay introductory to the *De pauperie Salvatoris* of Richard Fitzralph, books v-vii. *H. C. Hughes, Ph.D. 1928 Manchester*

Flaccus, Valerius
See Valerius Flaccus, G.

Flamenca
Word order in Old Provençal, with special reference to Flamenca and the poems of Bertran de Born. *R. J. Hilton, B.Litt. 1938 Oxford*

Flanders
Relations between England and Flanders, 1603-1618. *N. Applegate, M.A. 1948 Leeds*

Flaubert, Gustave
Chateaubriand and Flaubert. *M. E. Clayton-Chance, M.A. 1921 Birmingham*

De l'emploi des images, métaphores et comparaisons dans *Madame Bovary*. *A. E. S. Treves, B.Litt. 1929 Oxford*

Essai et notes sur *Trois contes* de G. Flaubert. *M. Simkins, M.A. 1925 Birmingham*

Flaubert, Gustave contd.

Essai sur *Eugénie Grandet* et *Un coeur simple. F. V. Cass, M.A. 1920 Birmingham*

Etude préliminaire à une biographie de Gustave Flaubert. *L. Ditchfield, M.A. 1932 Birmingham*

Gustave Flaubert as a literary critic. *J. I. Adam, M.A. 1927 Manchester*

Le sentiment poétique chez Flaubert. *G. M. Mason, M.A. 1945 Bristol*

L'élément régional dans l'oeuvre de Flaubert. *A. Crossley, M.A. 1928 Manchester*

L'esthétique de Gustave Flaubert dans sa correspondence et dans ses oeuvres. *A. E. M. Nock, M.A. 1921 London*

Normandy in the works of Gustave Flaubert. *J. L. Verney-Boys, M.A. 1947 London, King's College*

Flavius Claudius Julianus
See Julian, the Apostate, Emperor.

Fléchère, John William de la
The evangelical revival as reflected in the life and works of John William de la Fléchère, 1729-1785. *W. C. Lockhart, Ph.D. 1936 Edinburgh*

Flecker, James Elroy
Poetry of James Elroy Flecker. *H. P. Mahon, M.A. 1942 National University of Ireland*

Fleetwood
A study of the port of Fleetwood, with special reference to its position in the west coast fishing industry. *D. Peter, M.A. 1932 Manchester*

Fletcher, Giles, the Younger
Giles Fletcher the Younger: a bibliographical and critical study. *J. Grundy, M.A. 1947 London, Bedford College*

Fletcher, John
The application of the test from imagery to certain plays in the Beaumont-Fletcher canon with a view to ascertaining the shares therein of J. Fletcher and P. Massinger. *S. R. Boltiansky, Ph.D. 1938 Manchester*

An edition of the Brogyntyn manuscript of John Fletcher's *Demetrius and Enanthe*, with an examination of its relationship to the text as printed in the first folio of 1647. *M. S. M. Cook, B.Litt. 1950 Oxford*

Female characterization in Jacobean tragedy, with special consideration of the tragedies of Heywood, Webster, Middleton, Beaumont and Fletcher. *A. E. Bufton, M.A. 1939 Wales*

Flint
Flint: the castle and town in the thirteenth and fourteenth centuries. *E. O. Parry, M.A. 1927 Wales*

Flintshire
A contribution to the early history of Flintshire, with special reference to the See of St. Asaph. *J. F. Sharpe, M.A. 1924 Liverpool*

The industrial history of Flintshire in the nineteenth century. *P. T. Williams, M.A. 1933 Liverpool*

The industrialization of Flintshire in the nineteenth century, being an examination of the changes and development in the principal industries from 1815 to 1914. *C. R. Williams, M.A. 1950 Wales*

Floovant, Chanson de
See Romances.

Flore et Blanceflor
See Romances.

Florence
The last Florentine Republic, to the fall of Niccolo Capponi. *C. Roth, B.Litt. 1923 Oxford*

The last Florentine Republic, 1527-1530. *C. Roth, D.Phil. 1925 Oxford*

The problem of Paolo Vitelli, *condottiere* in the service of Florence. *E. B. Darke, M.A. 1909 London*

Florence, Council of
See Roman Catholic Church.

Flour Milling Industry
The Albion Steam Flour Mill: a chapter in the Boulton and Watt co-partnership. *O. A. Westworth, M.Com. 1930 Birmingham*

Flying
See Aeronautics.

Fogazzaro, Antonio
Antonio Fogazzaro: *Romanziere. M. Viani, M.A. 1941 National University of Ireland*

Folk Lore
See also Arthurian Legends; Fairy Tales; Legends; Magic; Mythology; Sagas; Songs.

Folk Lore contd.
Cnuasacht béaloideasa ós na Déisibh (Folklore from the Deise). *T. O'Faoláin, M.A. 1942 National University of Ireland*

Custom and belief connected with precious stones, as shown in the Middle English verse of the fourteenth century. *P. J. Heather, Ph.D. 1931 London, External Degree*

Das Werden und Vergehen von Sitte und Brauch in Hessen und Wales. *J. M. Donaldson, Ph.D. 1939 Edinburgh*

Folklore in Elizabethan prose literature. *P. E. Thornley, M.A. 1929 Wales*

Mono-Alu folklore. *G. C. W. C. Wheeler, D.Sc. 1927 London*

Psychological factors in serial reproduction. *J. Prasad, M.Sc. 1930 Cambridge*

Seanchus ó Bhaile Mhúirne (Folklore from Ballyvourney). *S. O'Ceilleachair, M.A. 1944 National University of Ireland*

Serbian traditional folk-poetry in England, France, and Germany in the nineteenth century. *D. Subotić, B.Litt. 1927 Oxford*

A study of the Middle English Breton lays, with reference to fairy lore, folk-lore and origins. *G. A. Pye, M.A. 1936 London, Birkbeck College*

The use and value of folklore in the teaching of geography. *H. B. Hodgson, M.Ed. 1935 Leeds*

Fontane, Theodor
Fontane as a social novelist. *A. R. Robinson, Ph.D. 1950 Edinburgh*

The influence of the French novelists on Theodor Fontane, with reference to the German novel of the latter part of the nineteenth century. *K. A. Horsfield, M.A. 1933 Manchester*

The Prussian aristocracy in the social novels of Theodor Fontane. *W. C. R. Billington, M.A. 1946 Birmingham*

Theodor Fontane. *K. Hayens, D.Litt. 1921 Glasgow*

Theodor Fontane and England; a critical study in Anglo-German literary relations in the nineteenth century. *C. A. B. E. Jolles, M.A. 1947 London, Birkbeck College*

Fonts
The decoration of Norman baptismal fonts in relation to English twelfth century sculpture. *R. Marcousé, Ph.D. 1940 London, Courtauld Institute of Art*

Food
See also Agriculture; Bacon Industry; Brewing Industry; Cereals Industry; Dairy Industry; Fisheries and Fishing Industry; Fruit Industry; Meat Industry; Sugar Industry; Tea Industry; etc.

Certain aspects of food consumption, with special reference to milk. *H. S. Booker, M.Sc. 1938 London, School of Economics and Political Science*

Economic aspects of the production and distribution of branded food products. *J. L. McKindlay, M.A. 1939 Liverpool*

The effects of irrigation on movements of population, and on the food supply of the world, with special reference to America. *J. N. L. Baker, B.Litt. 1924 Oxford*

Food and leisure among the African youth of Leopoldville (Belgian Congo): a study of the adaptation of African youth to urban life. *S. A. M. A. J. M. Comhaire-Sylvain, B.Litt. 1948 Oxford*

Food price policy in the United Kingdom during the war, 1939-45. *J. L. A. Lavault, B.Phil. 1947 Oxford*

The food supply of Great Britain. *A. W. Roach, M.Sc. 1938 London, External Degree*

Government control of food prices. *G. F. Drummond, M.Sc. 1923 London*

A history of food adulteration and analysis from the earliest times, to the work of Frederick Accum (1820). *F. A. Filby, Ph.D. 1933 London, University College*

The marketing of food, fodder and livestock in the London area in the seventeenth century, with some reference to the sources of supply. *P. V. McGrath, M.A. 1947 London, Queen Mary College*

A physiological and economic study of the diets of workers in rural areas as compared with those of workers resident in urban districts. *A. B. Hill, Ph.D. 1926 London*

Food contd.
The relationship between food-production and social structure in simple societies. *K. E. Read, Ph.D. 1948 London, School of Economics and Political Science*

The sociological importance of food with special reference to Bantu society. *A. I. Richards, Ph.D. 1930 London, School of Economics and Political Science*

A study of special measures designed to improve the nutriture of certain population groups in the United Kingdom which are particularly susceptible to malnutrition. *M. E. Macbeth, B.Litt. 1947 Oxford*

A survey of egg supplies and consumption in a Midland market town. *J. B. Butler, M.Com. 1939 Birmingham*

Theories of consumption, with reference to demand for and supply of foodstuffs in Great Britain. *E. M. Jones, M.A. 1939 Wales*

Footwear Industry
Devolution in industry: an enquiry into the scale of production in the boot and shoe manufacturing industry. *L. E. Warner, M.Com. 1925 Birmingham*

A geographical study of the boot and shoe trade in England. *C. P. Sargent, M.Sc. 1932 London, University College*

A history of the boot, shoe and slipper industries in Rossendale. *P. Cronkshaw, M.A. 1945 Manchester*

Forbes, Duncan
The life and letters of Duncan Forbes of Culloden, Lord President of the Court of Session, 1685-1747. *G. Menary, D.Litt. 1937 Glasgow*

Forbes, Patrick, Bishop
The times, life and thought of Patrick Forbes, Bishop of Aberdeen, 1618-1635. *W. G. S. Snow, Ph.D. 1940 Edinburgh*

Ford, John
John Ford. *M. J. Sargeaunt, B.Litt. 1931 Oxford*

John Ford. *H. V. D. Dyson, B.Litt. 1924 Oxford*

John Ford. *A. J. Clarke, M.A. 1916 National University of Ireland*

John Ford (1801-1875): the life, work and influence of a Quaker schoolmaster. *L. J. Stroud, Ph.D. 1947 London, External Degree*

Forestry
The administration of the royal forests of England during the thirteenth century. *R. K. J. Grant, Ph.D. 1938 Wales*

The composition and distribution of woods in Northern Ireland from the sixteenth century down to the establishment of the first Ordnance Survey. *E. M. McCracken, M.Sc. 1944 Belfast*

Co-operation and credit in forestry. *I. Kissin, D.Phil. 1944 Oxford*

The disposal of woodland produce. *R. C. W. Davey, M.Sc. 1938 London*

The distribution of woodland, present and past, in the Nant Ffrancon Valley, and other parts of Caernarvonshire. *L. M. Hodgson, M.Sc. 1933 Wales*

Forestry in Ireland. *S. Morrissey, M.A. 1938 National University of Ireland*

The land utilisation reports of Sutherlandshire: with a special account of the reclamation schemes and the deer forests. *F. T. Smith, M.Sc. 1938 London, King's College*

The prehistoric woodlands and marshlands of England. *H. A. Wilcox, M.A. 1927 Liverpool*

Forgiveness
1. Baptism and the forgiveness of sins. 2. Absolution and the forgiveness of sins. *T. Field, B.D. & D.D. 1897 Oxford*

An enquiry into the psychological, ethical and religious implications underlying the concept of forgiveness. *E. H. Morris, M.A. 1930 Wales*

1. Justification. 2. The forgiveness of sins. *N. H. C. Ruddock, B.D. and D.D. 1898 Oxford*

Mental therapy and the forgiveness of sins: a clinical view of the results of sin, with psychological studies of religious leaders as approaches to the application of the work of Christ in the experience of forgiveness. *A. P. Guiles, Ph.D. 1934 Edinburgh*

The relation of the Christian doctrine and experience of forgiveness to psychological health. *D. Rose, M.A. 1948 Birmingham*

A study in the doctrine of forgiveness and atonement. *D. R. Scott, Ph.D. 1923 Saint Andrew's*

Form
See also Aesthetics.

Form contd.
The doctrine of matter and form in the early English Franciscans. *D. E. Sharp, D.Phil. 1927 Oxford*

Form and function. *C. S. Russell, D.Sc. 1921 Glasgow*

The psychological grounds of preference of shapes by school children. *E. L. Griffiths, M.A. 1927 Wales*

The psychology of shape. *H. P. Bridges, M.A. 1931 London, King's College*

Reactions to colour and form. *D. Lindsey, M.A. 1947 Manchester*

Some experiments on the abstraction of form and colour. *O. A. Oeser, Ph.D. 1932 Cambridge*

The specific nature of colour and form memories. *M. M. Said, M.Sc. 1929 Birmingham*

Forster, Edward Morgan
Action, theme and symbol in the novels of E. M. Forster. *M. Farris, M.A. 1946 Liverpool*

E. M. Forster. *J. K. Walton, B.Litt. 1944 Dublin, Trinity College*

E. M. Forster: a critical and historical estimate. *W. A. S. Keir, B.Litt. 1949 Oxford*

Forsyth, Peter Taylor
Certainty through faith: an examination of the religious philosophy of Peter Taylor Forsyth. *A. F. Simpson, Ph.D. 1949 London, External Degree*

The theology of P. T. Forsyth, 1848 to 1921. *W. L. Bradley, Ph.D. 1949 Edinburgh*

Fortibus, Isabella de
See Albemarle, I., Countess of.

Fortuna
Fortune in Elizabethan drama: an attempt to discover, chiefly from plays written between 1570 and 1620, the conception of that period concerning the person and activities of the goddess Fortuna. *R. Chapman, M.A. 1947 London, King's College*

Foster, John
John Foster, 1770-1843, and his contribution to religious thought. *S. T. Habel, Ph.D. 1945 Edinburgh*

The political career of the Right Hon. John Foster, last speaker of the Irish House of Commons. *N. D. Emerson, Ph.D. 1930 Dublin, Trinity College*

Fostering of Children
See Child Welfare.

Foucault, Léon
The scientific works of Léon Foucault. *J. A. Chaldecott, M.Sc. 1949 London, University College*

Fountains
Greek fountain buildings before 300 B.C. *B. Dunkley, M.A. 1936 London, University College*

Fourier, Joseph, Baron
Operational methods in mathematics from Leibniz to Fourier. *K. A. C. Humphreys, M.Sc. 1949 London, External Degree*

Fournier, Henri Alain-
See Alain-Fournier, H.

Fox, Henry
The political career of Henry Fox in the years 1753-1763. *T. W. Riker, B.Litt. 1908 Oxford*

Foxe, Richard, Bishop
Leaders of humanism in English education: Humphrey, Duke of Gloucester, William Grocyn, Thomas Linacre, Bishop Richard Foxe. *C. H. Winstanley, M.A. 1930 Liverpool*

France
See also Alsace; Brittany; Flanders; Gascony; Gaul; Normandy.

France: Armed Forces
The Anglo-French and Anglo-Belgian military and naval conversations from the *Entente* to the Great War. *D. C. Wadman, M.A. 1939 Wales*

France: Colonies
The French survival in North America. *W. E. Arnell, M.Sc. 1946 London, External Degree*

History of French colonial policy, 1870-1925. *S. H. Roberts, D.Sc. 1929 London*

France: Constitution
The idea of sovereignty of the people, and the constitutional legislation of the French National Assembly, 1789-1791. *E. Thompson, Ph.D. 1948 London, External Degree*

The role of the Prime Minister in France. *Y. Haikal, Ph.D. 1936 London, School of Economics and Political Science*

France: Constitution contd.
Some elements of recent constitutional and administrative tendencies in France, Germany and United States of America: an introductory study. *H. Finer, M.Sc. 1922 London*

France: Economics
See also Turgot, A. R. J., Baron de l'Aulne.

The business world in France as revealed in the works of Balzac. *L. M. Turner, M.A. 1923 Manchester*

French monetary policy 1930 to 1939. *P. J. Siebenberg, M.Com. 1946 Birmingham*

The history of free trade in France during the eighteenth and nineteenth century, with special reference to the individual thinkers. *M. M. Collinson, M.Com. 1944 Birmingham*

The problem of Anglo-French commercial rivalry in the reign of Charles II. *M. A. Priestley, B.Litt. 1949 Oxford*

A study of the French banking system, with special reference to the financing of industry and to the French investment policy during the period 1815-1914. *C. Fodrio, Ph.D. 1941 London, School of Economics and Political Science*

France: Foreign Affairs
Aberdeen and Anglo-French diplomatic relations, 1841-6. *J. R. Baldwin, B.Litt. 1936 Oxford*

Anglo-French relations, 1904-1906. *J. D. Hargreaves, M.A. 1948 Manchester*

Anglo-French relations (1871-1904), with special reference to the problem of the Franco-German rivalry. *M. H. Jones, M.A. 1938 Wales*

The Anglo-French struggle for the control of Dutch foreign policy, 1755 to 1763. *A. M. C. Le Mesurier, M.A. 1934 London, University College*

British relations with France from the establishment of the Directory to the coup d'état of Fructidor. *J. R. Bracken, B.Litt. 1939 Oxford*

Buckingham's influence on England's policy with regard to France (from October, 1623). *E. S. Goitein, M.A. 1926 London*

The character of British relations with France, 1859-1865. *M. A. Anderson, M.A. 1949 London, Bedford College*

Choiseul's foreign policy relative to England. *M. J. McCormick, M.A. 1911 Liverpool*

The connection between France and England in the reign of Louis XI. *T. J. Griffiths, M.A. 1917 Wales*

The diplomatic relations between England and France during the years 1558-1564. *M. Booth, M.A. 1934 London, University College*

The diplomatic relations between England and France from 1898 to June 1905: the policy of M. Delcassé and the making of the Anglo-French Entente. *E. J. Parry, M.A. 1932 Wales*

England and the Bourbon restoration. *D. Higgins, M.A. 1922 Liverpool*

English embassies to France in the reign of Edward I: their personnel, powers, equipment and objects. *M. C. L. Salt, M.A. 1927 London*

The establishment of the French Protectorate over Tunis: its diplomatic history from the Congress of Berlin to the formation of the Triple Alliance, July 1878 to May 1882. *T. Lewis, M.A. 1950 Wales*

The Franco-Italian rapprochement, 1898-1902. *E. R. Lewis, M.A. 1937 Wales*

Franco-Scottish relations from 1290 to 1390. *R. W. Pilgrim, B.Litt. 1936 Oxford*

The German policy of the pre-Fructidorian Directory. *S. S. Biro, D.Phil. 1923 Oxford*

Idealism and foreign policy: a study on the relations of Great Britain with Germany and France, 1860-1890. *A. A. W. Ramsay, Ph.D. 1925 Edinburgh*

The influence of the Italian Question on Anglo-French relations, 1856-60, from the Treaty of Paris to the annexation of Savoy and Nice. *H. M. Vincent, M.A. 1948 Oxford*

L'ambassade française à Londres, 1792-1793. *J. T. Stoker, M.A. 1935 Leeds*

The nature and methods of parliamentary control over foreign policy in France since the signature of the Treaty of Versailles, 28 June 1919. *J. Howard, B.Litt. 1938 Oxford*

The relations between England and France during the Great Rebellion: the Civil War. *D. A. Bigby, M.A. 1912 London*

The relations between England and France during the Aberdeen-Guizot Ministries (1841-6). *G. Wozencroft, Ph.D. 1932 London, King's College*

France: Foreign Affairs contd.
Relations between England and France, 1589-1603. *E. M. Griffiths, M.A. 1921 Birmingham*

The relations between Louis Napoleon and Great Britain from 1848 to the outbreak of the Crimean war. *F. W. Wright, M.A. 1925 Birmingham*

The relations of France and England in the reign of Richard II. *N. B. Lewis, M.A. 1922 Manchester*

The relations of the British Government with the émigrés and royalists of western France, 1793-1795. *A. King, Ph.D. 1931 London, University College*

A view of Anglo-French relations, 1389-1399. *J. Burr, M.A. 1936 Liverpool*

France: Geography
The geography of France: regional and economic. *H. R. Ormsby, D.Sc. 1932 London, School of Economics and Political Science*

France: History: General
The French invasions of England from the twelfth century to the nineteenth (1101-1860). *A. R. Rhys-Pryce, M.A. 1928 Belfast*

The isolation of France. *J. R. Lester, M.A. 1937 Birmingham*

France: History: Early and Medieval
See also Crusades; Feudalism; Hundred Years' War; Louis IX, Saint, King of France.

The English in the South of France from the accession of Henry III to the death of the Black Prince. *N. L. Frazer, M.A. 1906 London*

The Northmen in France. *A. W. Kirkaldy, B.Litt. 1902 Oxford*

France: History: Fifteenth Century
See also Orléans, C., Duc d'.

Alain Chartier and the political conditions of France in the year 1422. *W. P. Ellis, M.A. 1934 Liverpool*

Remonstrances au Roy pour la réformation du royaume, by Jean Juvenal des Ursins, with introduction and notes. *D. Kirkland, Ph.D. 1938 Liverpool*

France: History: Sixteenth Century
See also Bourbon, C., Duc de.

The French ascendancy in Scotland, 1554-1560. *G. H. C. Burley, M.A. 1929 Birmingham*

France: History: Seventeenth Century
See also Maintenon, F. d'A. de, Marquise; Mazarin, Jules, Cardinal; Sully, M. de B. de, Duc.

France: History: Eighteenth Century
See also Chauvelin, G. L. de; Saint Simon, L. de R., Duc de.

The Peace of Paris, 1763. *Z. E. Rashed, Ph.D. 1949 Liverpool*

Turgot: intendent of Limoges, 1761 to 1774. *D. Dakin, Ph.D. 1936 London, Birkbeck College*

France: History: French Revolution
See also Raynal, G. T. F.

Burke and the French Revolution. *F. W. Tomlinson, M.Sc. 1928 London*

A critical review of contemporary criticism of Burke's *Reflections on the Revolution in France. A. Bonnerjee, M.Sc. 1938 London, School of Economics and Political Science*

Dylanwad y chwyldro Ffrengig ar lenyddiaeth Cymru (The influence of the French Revolution on the literature of Wales). *J. J. Evans, M.A. 1926 Wales*

Education and the French Revolution. *J. G. Worth, B.Litt. 1921 Oxford*

The effects of the French Revolution on English literature, with special reference to Burke. *H. W. Hampton, M.A. 1910 Birmingham*

The historians of the French Revolution prior to 1823. *W. Percival, M.A. 1929 Manchester*

The influence of radical doctrine in the French Revolution on English drama in the time of Thomas Holcroft, 1776 to 1806. *W. V. Aughterson, Ph.D. 1936 London, King's College*

The influence of the French Revolution on the political and social life of Wales. *W. P. Williams, M.A. 1925 Wales*

The influence of the French Revolution on the English Romantic poets. *F. C. Moore, M.A. 1918 London*

An inquiry into the nature, extent and implications of the socialism of the French Revolution, during the period of the revolutionary government. *J. C. Searle, Ph.D. 1935 London, School of Economics and Political Science*

France: History: French Revolution contd.
Jean-Baptiste Carrier and the Terror in the Vendée. *E. H. Carrier, M.A. 1915 Liverpool*

L'enseignement supérieur et la Révolution française. *T. J. Barling, M.A. 1948 Birmingham*

Marie Antoinette and the French Revolution. *R. E. A. Jones, M.A. 1946 Wales*

Naval expeditions to Ireland at the time of the French Revolution. *P. B. Bradley, M.A. 1923 National University of Ireland*

The 'noblesse' in France in 1789: a study of opinion. *B. Thomas, M.A. 1950 Wales*

The political ideas of Saint-Just, with special reference to the work of the Committee of Public Safety. *J. P. Yang, B.Litt. 1937 Oxford*

The relations of the British Government with the émigrés and royalists of western France, 1793-1795. *A. King, Ph.D. 1931 London, University College*

The rural Third Estate in France in 1789: a study in opinion. *A. Davies, M.A. 1939 Wales*

St. Just: his place in the French Revolution. *L. P. McCarthy, B.Litt. 1927 Oxford*

Saint-Just and the French Revolution. *W. F. Molloy, M.A. 1915 National University of Ireland*

The social relations of England and France, 1763-1793, in connection with their effect on the Revolutionary era. *C. H. Lockitt, M.A. 1911 London*

Wordsworth, Coleridge, Byron, Shelley and the French Revolution. *P. R. Griffin, M.A. 1925 National University of Ireland*

France: History: Nineteenth Century
See also Boulanger, G. E. J. M.; Louis Philippe, King of France; Napoleon I Bonaparte, Emperor of France; Napoleon III, Emperor of France.

The annexation of Savoy and Nice by Napoleon III, 1860. *F. R. Scott, B.Litt. 1924 Oxford*

The attitudes of France to the South American colonies, 1822-6. *W. E. Edwards, Ph.D. 1933 Cambridge*

Catholic opinion and the ecclesiastical policy of the government in France (1869-70). *J. W. Pickersgill, B.Litt. 1933 Oxford*

The Congress policy of Napoleon III. *W. F. F. Grace, M.A. 1925 Liverpool*

Dissertation on the Peace of Amiens and its rupture. *W. C. Gill, M.A. 1908 Leeds*

Napoleon III and Russia. *A. S. Walker, M.A. 1917 Birmingham*

Napoleon III and the panic of 1859. *H. G. Fox, M.A. 1930 Birmingham*

France: History: Twentieth Century
The problems of French security, 1918-1920, with special reference to the military terms and the western frontier of Germany. *W. M. Jordan, Ph.D. 1940 London, School of Economics and Political Science*

France: Parliament
The committees (commissions) in the chambers of the French Parliament (1875 to present time) and their influence on ministerial responsibility. *R. K. Gooch, Ph.D. 1924 Oxford*

The French Senate. *J. N. Khosla, Ph.D. 1933 London, School of Economics and Political Science*

The nature and methods of parliamentary control over foreign policy in France since the signature of the Treaty of Versailles, 28 June 1919. *J. Howard, B.Litt. 1938 Oxford*

The *Parlement* of Paris under Charles VI and Charles VII. *R. Windsor, M.A. 1940 Liverpool*

Parliaments and the Peace Treaty: a comparative study of the reactions of the British and French Parliaments to the Treaty of Peace of 1919. *B. Ling, Ph.D. 1938 London, School of Economics and Political Science*

France: Politics and Government
See also Club de l'Entresol.

The influence of Wellington on the internal politics of France, 1815-18. *A. I. Jones, B.Litt. 1935 Oxford*

Le mouvement régionaliste dans la littérature française moderne et l'oeuvre de Henry Bordeaux. *N. Murphy, M.A. 1926 National University of Ireland*

Liberal political thought in France, 1815-1848. *P. W. E. Curtin, Ph.D. 1939 London, School of Economics and Political Science*

France: Politics and Government contd.
L'influence des évènements politiques jusqu'à la grande guerre (1914) sur l'oeuvre d'Anatole France. *J. M. Mark, M.A. 1939 Belfast*

France: Social History
The bourgeois in French literature of the fourteenth century. *M. G. Liddle, Ph.D. 1925 London*

Critical and historical edition of B. L. de Muralt's *Letters describing the character and customs of the English and French nations,* 1726, with an introduction and notes. *S. C. Gould, B.Litt. 1931 Oxford*

The development of *préciosité* in the seventeenth century: a literary and social study. *B. G. Treloar, D.Phil. 1948 Oxford*

The evidence of English visitors on the social and economic conditions of France, 1763-89 (May). *J. A. R. Pimlott, B.Litt. 1934 Oxford*

France in the life and works of Dickens. *V. C. Wood, M.A. 1949 Liverpool*

France in the writings of Henry James; a bibliography of the writings of Henry James. *D. Hamer, M.A. 1924 Liverpool*

French provincial life in the novels of Edouard Estaunié, with some reference to contemporary writers. *J. W. White, M.A. 1949 London, King's College and London, Birkbeck College*

The influence of France on M. Arnold. *H. Alsop, M.A. 1914 Birmingham*

La bourgeoisie de province dans l'oeuvre de Balzac. *M. Wray, M.A. 1925 Manchester*

La vie au foyer: usages et coutumes au moyen âge d'après la littérature populaire de l'époque, et particulièrement les fabliaux. Essai historique et linguistique. *N. Haycocks, M.A. 1929 Manchester*

Les valets et les servantes dans la comédie de Molière. *F. C. Roe, M.A. 1920 Birmingham*

Literary and social dandyism in England and France between 1780 and 1850. *S. C. Gould, D.Phil. 1950 Oxford*

Louis Philippe's France as seen by English women. *E. Grünwald, Ph.D. 1948 London, University College*

Matthew Arnold (the critic) as an interpreter of France. *F. J. W. Harding, B.Litt. 1948 Oxford*

The rural Third Estate in France in 1789: a study in opinion. *A. Davies, M.A. 1939 Wales*

The social and intellectual background of the 'déclassé' members of the Paris Commune of 1871. *E. Astington, M.A. 1939 Manchester*

Society in French comedy from the death of Molière to 1715. *M. Hughes, M.A. 1925 Wales*

A study of Swinburne's relations with France. *J. I. Davies, M.A. 1932 Wales*

The *Tiers Estat* in medieval French literature. *L. Reed, M.A. 1945 Wales*

The vocabulary of sport in present-day France. *J. E. Travis, M.A. 1933 Manchester*

France, Anatole
Anatole France, critique de son milieu. *W. C. Phelps, M.A. 1933 Birmingham*

England and her writers in the works of Anatole France (1844-1924). *H. C. Ault, M.A. 1928 Birmingham*

The influence of Voltaire upon Anatole France. *H. E. Whittle, Ph.D. 1939 London, External Degree*

Les dieux ont soif (de Anatole France): étude sur la documentation et la genèse du roman. *M. Living-Taylor, M.A. 1942 Manchester*

L'influence des évènements politiques jusqu'à la grande guerre (1914) sur l'oeuvre d'Anatole France. *J. M. Mark, M.A. 1939 Belfast*

The socialistic theory of Anatole France as expressed in his literary works. *J. H. Thomas, M.A. 1928 Wales*

Francis, Saint
Beatha san Phroinsias maille le brollach agus gluais (*The life of St. Francis,* with preface and commentary). *P. O'Domhnalláin, M.A. 1937 National University of Ireland*

Franciscan Order
See also Religious Orders and Societies; Francis, Saint; Elias, Brother; Odoricus, Friar; William, of Wydford.

Benedict Canfield (William Fitch), Capuchin: the man and his writings. *C. J. Reel, B.Litt. 1948 Oxford*

Brother Elias and the government of the Franciscan Order, 1217-39. *R. B. Clark, Ph.D. 1950 Cambridge*

Franciscan Order contd.
The doctrine of matter and form in the early English Franciscans. *D. E. Sharp, D.Phil. 1927 Oxford*

Duanaire bhrathar mbocht d'Ord S. Froinsias (Poems of the Franciscan Brothers). *J. A. McGrath, Ph.D. 1945 National University of Ireland*

The Franciscans and Dominicans in Yorkshire. *L. M. Goldthorp, M.A. 1932 Leeds*

The Franciscans in medieval English life (1224-1348). *V. Green, B.Litt. 1936 Oxford*

Rialacha na dtrí n-Ord S. Froinsias (The rules of the three Orders of St. Francis). *C. O'Broin, M.A. 1938 National University of Ireland*

Some political activities of the Franciscan friars in England in the thirteenth century. *I. J. Saunders, M.A. 1935 Wales*

Frank Almoign
Frank almoign: a study of ecclesiastical tenure in England chiefly in the fourteenth and fifteenth centuries. *E. G. Kimball, B.Litt. 1927 Oxford*

Frankfurt-am-Main
The influence of American ideas at Frankfurt-am-Main, 1848-9. *J. A. Hawgood, M.A. 1928 London*

Franklin, William
Governor William Franklin. *F. M. Doherty, B.Litt. 1931 Oxford*

Fraser, James
James Fraser of Brea, 1639 to 1699: his life and writings, with special reference to his theory of universal redemption and its influence on religious thought in Scotland. *D. Fraser, Ph.D. 1944 Edinburgh*

Fraticelli
The nature and extent of the heresy of the Fraticelli. *D. L. Douie, Ph.D. 1930 Manchester*

Fratres Arvales
The records of the *Fratres Arvales*. *A. Kilgour, Ph.D. 1939 Saint Andrew's*

Fraud
The statute of frauds, paragraph 4, in the light of its judicial interpretation. *J. Williams, Ph.D. 1932 Cambridge*

Free Churches
See Nonconformity.

Free Trade
See also Dumping (Economics); Tariffs.

Free trade and protection in the Netherlands, 1819-1825. *H. R. C. Wright, Ph.D. 1949 Cambridge*

The growth of free trade ideas, 1800-1830. *W. J. Rawle, M.Com. 1939 Birmingham*

The history of free trade in France during the eighteenth and nineteenth century, with special reference to the individual thinkers. *M. M. Collinson, M.Com. 1944 Birmingham*

History of the free trade movement and its effects on Irish trade and commerce. *M. J. C. Keane, M.A. 1922 National University of Ireland*

The nature and effects of protective policy in Ireland from 1922-1939. *W. J. L. Ryan, Ph.D. 1949 Dublin, Trinity College*

The origins of the tariff reform movement. *B. H. Smith, M.A. 1938 Birmingham*

Sir Robert Peel and the Free Trade movement in the first half of the nineteenth century, especially during the years 1842-1847. *W. W. Rollinson, M.A. 1930 Birmingham*

Some aspects of protection and its relation to economic development in New Zealand. *G. C. Billing, Ph.D. 1934 London, School of Economics and Political Science*

Free Will
See also Determinism; Predestination; Will.

The Cynics from the first century to the fall of the Western Empire, with a special study of the problem of fate and free-will as treated by the Stoics and Cynics of the same period. *W. Rees, B.Litt. 1919 Oxford*

The doctrine of the freedom of the will according to English empiricism and transcendental idealism. *J. L. Williams, B.Sc. 1904 Oxford*

1. The doctrine of the resurrection in the Book of Job. 2. The connection between free-will and eternal punishment. *J. T. Nance, B.D. 1881 Oxford*

Free Will contd.
1. Faith, the organ of religious knowledge. 2. Human free-will not inconsistent with the almighty power of God. *A. P. P. Cust, B.D. & D.D. 1880 Oxford*

Fate, determinism and free will in religion and philosophy. *J. Westbury-Jones, D.D. 1936 Oxford*

Free will and determinism. *T. Donovan, M.A. 1914 National University of Ireland*

Free will and predestination in early Islam. *W. M. Watt, Ph.D. 1944 Edinburgh*

Freewill and time: a consideration of the metaphysical implications in regard to the nature of time, of the ethical doctrine of freewill. *A. E. Teale, B.Litt. 1937 Oxford*

The freewill problem in modern philosophy from Descartes to Kant. *J. Pitts, Ph.D. 1933 London, External Degree*

1. Grace and free will in reference to the language of Scripture and to some later theories. 2. The Epistle to the Galatians. *C. Bigg, B.D. & D.D. 1876 Oxford*

Grace and freewill in St. Paul and St. Augustine. *S. Y. Yovanovitch, B.Litt. 1920 Oxford*

An historical review of the nature of time and its connexion with value, in so far as these bear on the problems of personal freedom and human purpose. *W. A. Merrylees, B.Litt. 1923 Oxford*

Kant's conception of the freedom of the will. *W. J. Stephens, M.A. 1905 Wales*

1. Predestination and free will. 2. The resurrection of the holy. *E. E. Bradford, B.D. 1904 Oxford*

Freedom
Causality and freedom. *J. Strain, M.A. 1920 Belfast*

Civic liberty in the 20th century. *F. Woods, M.A. 1935 National University of Ireland*

The development of Luther's conception of liberty as found in his early writings (until 1521). *W. F. Sunday, Ph.D. 1924 Edinburgh*

The development of the political ideas of Wordsworth and Shelley, with special reference to their conception of freedom. *G. O. Roberts, M.A. 1938 Wales*

The doctrines of God and freedom in the philosophy of Spinoza. *W. Madgen, M.A. 1928 Liverpool*

Evolution and freedom: does evolution preclude moral freedom?. *J. Maycock, M.A. 1938 Liverpool*

Fundamental rights. *P. P. Ryan, M.A. 1941 National University of Ireland*

Fundamental rights articles in the Irish constitution. *B. P. O'Kelly, M.A. 1946 National University of Ireland*

The idea of liberty in relation to State and non-State organizations in England. *S. Ray, Ph.D. 1922 London*

Inquiry into institutional safeguards on the freedom of the individual in the modern democratic state. *S. Rolbant, Ph.D. 1946 London, School of Economics and Political Science*

Libertas as a political idea at Rome during the late Republic and early Principate. *C. Wirszubski, Ph.D. 1947 Cambridge*

The liberty of the subject. *E. Deller, LL.D. 1916 London*

The liberty of the subject in England during the period 1803-1832. *H. P. Bridges, LL.D. 1926 London*

The meaning of freedom. *M. Moore, M.A. 1922 Birmingham*

The metaphysical implications of freedom. *R. Topping, M.A. 1937 Belfast*

The metaphysical problems involved in the nature and range of the concept of freedom and its relation to the concept of mechanism. *W. H. Jefferson, M.A. 1922 Liverpool*

Milton and civil liberty. *E. A. H. Clifford, M.A. 1941 Reading*

The origins of the petition of right. *L. Ehrlich, B.Litt. 1916 Oxford*

The principles of individual right. *W. A. Beers, LL.D. 1944 Dublin, Trinity College*

The problem of freedom. *B. K. Mallik, B.Sc. 1924 Oxford*

The problem of liberty in relation to the development of voluntary associations. *W. E. Styler, M.A. 1937 Birmingham*

Freedom contd.
The problem of moral freedom with reference to its discussion in recent philosophy and in particular in the *Ethics* of Nicolai Hartmann. *H. D. Lewis, M.A. 1934 Wales*

Researches in the history of the rights of the subject in England. *L. E. D. Horanszky de Hora, Ph.D. 1927 Aberdeen*

Freedom of the Press
Freedom of the press in Ireland 1784-1842. *B. Inglis, Ph.D. 1950 Dublin, Trinity College*

The history of freedom of speech and of the press in England since 1900. *A. F. Dawn, M.Sc. 1933 London, School of Economics and Political Science*

The struggle for the freedom of the press from Caxton to Cromwell. *W. M. Clyde, Ph.D. 1929 Saint Andrew's*

The struggle for the freedom of the press, 1819-1832. *W. H. Wickwar, M.A. 1926 London*

Freemasonry
Bearlagair na saor (Masons' jargon). *S. Toibin, M.A. 1931 National University of Ireland*

Freiligrath, Hermann Ferdinand
Ferdinand Freiligraths Verbannungsjahre in London. *G. W. Spink, Ph.D. 1931 Edinburgh*

Freind, John
A study of the chemistries of Lemery, Freind, Baume, and Watson, and of the development of chemical thought from 1675 to 1787. *S. D. M. Waters, M.Sc. 1931 London*

French Language
See also Académie Française; Bernard, C. de; Hugo, V. M.; Longuyon, J. de; Marie de France; Provençal Language and Literature.

Aspects de l'imagination et du langage dans l'oeuvre de Jean Giraudoux. *E. C. Cure, M.A. 1946 London, Birkbeck College*

A commentary on Racine's *Andromaque*: a study of vocabulary, syntax, style. *H. O'Sullivan, M.A. 1945 Manchester*

A comparative study of the development of strong perfects in French, Provençal, Spanish and Italian. *A. D. Neal, M.A. 1939 Manchester*

A comparison of the use of the subjunctive in Gautier d'Arras and Chrétien de Troyes. *E. Hugh, M.A. 1919 Wales*

Critical edition of a portion of the epic poem (of Girart de Roussillon), with study of the language of the poet and of the existing manuscripts. *W. M. Hackett, M.A. 1937 Manchester*

A critical edition of the epic poem Girart de Roussillon, with notes, complete glossary, and linguistic introduction. *W. M. Hackett, D.Phil. 1950 Oxford*

A critical study of the spellings of the two oldest French Psalters: 1. The Oxford, or Montebourg Psalter, 2. The Cambridge, or Canterbury Psalter. *B. L. Howarth, M.A. 1936 Manchester*

A critical survey of the Old French element in English surnames. *S. D. Straw, M.A. 1919 London*

A first contribution to the study of the linguistics of the unpublished thirteenth century prose-romance entitled *Le Roman de Laurin, fils de Marques le Seneschal. L. G. M. Thorpe, Ph.D. 1949 London, External Degree*

Introduction to a study of the linguistic influence of France on Spain in the Middle Ages. *D. R. Sanders, M.A. 1930 Manchester*

James Howell and his relation to France, the French language and literature. *T. J. Thomas, M.A. 1926 Wales*

La chanson de Roland : its origin and its language. *M. M. McHugh, M.A. 1920 National University of Ireland*

La langue de Paul Arène (1843-1896). *A. H. Addy, M.A. 1936 Leeds*

La langue et le style de Maurice Barrès. *N. E. Cledwyn, M.A. 1933 Wales*

La littérature et la langue françaises dans l'oeuvre et dans la vie de R. L. Stevenson. *G. Colquhoun, M.A. 1933 Liverpool*

La syntaxe des propositions adverbiales dans *Huon de Bordeaux. A. F. Church, M.A. 1934 London, Birkbeck College*

La tradition manuscrite et la phonétique des principaux textes de la version Johannis de *La Chronique de Turpin. R. N. Walpole, M.A. 1936 Wales*

The language of J. K. Huysmans. *A. C. Smith, Ph.D. 1930 London, King's College*

The linguistic ideas of Charles Nodier. *S. Daiches, B.Litt. 1940 Oxford*

French Language contd.
Linguistic study of an unedited manuscript of the *Apparition maistre Jehan de Meun* by Honoré Bonet (1398), with particular reference to the elimination of hiatus. *I. D. O. Arnold, M.A. 1927 Wales*

A linguistic study of the Franco-Italian epics. *G. Mellor, M.A. 1950 Manchester*

A linguistic study of the Tournay charters acquired by the British Museum in 1914. *W. G. Walmsley, M.A. 1921 London*

The mensuration of French verse-rhythm based upon experimental investigation of the properties of stress-accent. *J. W. Jeaffreson, M.A. 1924 London*

Noun valency in French: a study of the determination of the noun and a contribution to the study of the word-group. *J. K. Williams, M.A. 1933 Wales*

The older French element in the vocabulary of the English dialects. *F. M. Williams, B.Litt. 1947 Oxford*

On the French element in the English regional dialects. *P. E. Stott, M.A. 1934 Liverpool*

The popular element in the vocabulary and syntax of *L'Assommoir* of E. Zola, 1877. *H. Bottomley, M.A. 1931 Manchester*

The position of the adjective in modern French prose. *Mrs. J. A. Hutchinson, Ph.D. 1949 Cambridge*

A primer of French pronunciation. *S. W. Grace, M.A. 1920 London*

The progress of French in Alsace-Lorraine since the war. *C. M. Mole, M.A. 1925 Birmingham*

Psychology of the language and style of préciosité. *J. G. Morley, B.Litt. 1939 Oxford*

Remarques sur la diction poétique de l'école romane. *Z. Taylor, M.A. 1928 Manchester*

Some aspects of the French element in the Middle English lyric. *D. M. Jenkins, M.A. 1912 London*

Standard speech and dialects in sixteenth century France. *A. Halliwell, M.A. 1933 Manchester*

A study of French word-order in the sixteenth century with special reference to inversion of the subject. *R. Metcalf, M.A. 1949 Leeds*

A study of the language of Chateaubriand's 'American' books, viz., *Atala, René, Les Natchez* and the *Voyage en Amérique*, with additional notes on the language of *Le dernier Abencérage. H. E. Hebb, M.A. 1926 Leeds*

A syntactical study of the verb in modern French, with special reference to Pierre Hamp. *L. G. Evans, M.A. 1928 Manchester*

The syntax of Bernard de Ventadorn. *A. Leach, M.A. 1932 Manchester*

The syntax of *Le Charroi de Nîmes. W. Barwise, M.A. 1936 Manchester*

The syntax of Marie de France as studied in her *Lais. J. B. Davies, M.A. 1938 Wales*

The syntax of the past participle in the Middle French period, c. 1320-c. 1500. *J. Eker, M.A. 1930 Manchester*

Syntaxe du *Roman de Reinbert. B. R. Griffiths, M.A. 1947 London, University College*

The use of the subjunctive mood in the *Mémoires du Duc de Saint-Simon. F. H. Tristram, M.A. 1913 Wales*

French Language: Dialects
The comparative phonetics of French and the dialects of Caux and Bray. *J. P. A. Vinay, M.A. 1937 London, University College*

A critical examination of the *Atlas linguistique de la France* in so far as it concerns the island of Guernsey. *J. P. Collas, B.Litt. 1934 Oxford*

Le parler de Bar-le-Duc au moyen âge de'après des documents d'archives. *E. F. Harris, M.A. 1924 Birmingham*

Le parler de Toul et de ses environs d'après des documents d'archives. *E. M. Scott, M.A. 1923 London*

Le toponyme baki: étude philologique sur l'apport francique dans la Wallonie. *J. O. Potter, M.A. 1950 Birmingham*

Les mots dialectaux dans la littérature française contemporaine. *W. Padfield, M.A. 1921 Liverpool*

Sources and dialect of a French didactic poem on geography. *E. C. Halket, M.A. 1919 London*

Vocabulaire ethnographique d'une région des Pyrénées centrales. *W. D. Elcock, M.A. 1933 Manchester*

French Language: Etymology

A basic minimum French vocabulary. *E. Astington, M.Ed. 1950 Manchester*

Etude lexicographique des mots intéressants dans l'oeuvre de Gustave Aimard, étudiés dans ses romans écrits pendant les cinq années 1858-1862. *A. E. Ferguson, M.A. 1936 Leeds*

Etude lexicographique sur le vocabulaire des textes réunis sous la lettre 'G' du *Glossaire archéologique* vol. 1, de Victor Gay. *T. Schofield, M.A. 1933 Leeds*

Etude sur le vocabulaire du *Voyage en Espagne* de Théophile Gautier. *W. W. Padgett, M.A. 1924 Leeds*

Etude sur le vocabulaire de Prosper Mérimée au point de vue du néologisme. *W. Brown, M.A. 1925 Leeds*

Examen de vocabulaire des *Travailleurs de la mer*. *J. H. Hird, M.A. 1925 Leeds*

An examination of certain portions of the French element in Chaucer's vocabulary. *H. Goldstraw, M.A. 1931 Manchester*

Glossaire aux branches II et Va du *Roman du Renart*. *N. H. Burnell, M.A. 1926 Leeds*

Glossaire des vieux mots qu'on trouve dans *Le dit de Poissy*, poème écrit en avril 1400 par Christine de Pisan. *A. M. Binas, M.A. 1926 Leeds*

The historical development of heraldic terms, with especial consideration of 'armes parlantes'. *H. E. Tomlinson, M.A. 1942 Manchester*

The influence of French on the development of the English vocabulary from 1600 onwards. *T. Quayle, M.A. 1913 London*

Le vocabulaire d'Alphonse de Châteaubriant. *R. F. Walker, M.A. 1936 Leeds*

Les néologismes de *Notre Dame* de Victor Hugo. *E. Bate, M.A. 1924 Leeds*

L'évolution sémantique du mot 'raison' d'après les textes du XVIIe siècle. *R. H. Pickering, M.A. 1946 Manchester*

The military and naval terms in the Norman and Anglo-Saxon chronicles of the twelfth century. *G. C. Johnson, Ph.D. 1949 Leeds*

Néologismes dans *la Comédie humaine* de H. de Balzac, 1829-1832. *R. A. Kaye, M.A. 1923 Leeds*

The nomenclature of chips and shavings in France: · a study in linguistic geography. *M. R. Roberts, M.A. 1933 Manchester*

A study of the change in meaning of French criminal law terms, with special reference to colloquial and literary usage. *D. R. T. Goodwin, M.A. 1936 Manchester*

Une étude du vocabulaire des premières oeuvres en prose de Victor Hugo (1823-1834). *S. Wormald, M.A. 1924 Leeds*

The vocabulary of sport in present-day France. *J. E. Travis, M.A. 1933 Manchester*

French Language: Phonetics

The comparative phonetics of French and the dialects of Caux and Bray. *J. P. A. Vinay, M.A. 1937 London, University College*

The influence of orthography upon pronunciation in sixteenth and seventeenth century French. *M. Baker, M.A. 1934 Manchester*

French Language: Study and Teaching

Attempts made before the sixteenth century to improve the speaking and writing of the French language in England. *A. Owen, M.A. 1921 Wales*

A comparison of the aims, conditions and methods of teaching French to the child and the adult, with special reference to secondary schools and London senior commercial institutes. *F. L. Pascoe, M.A. 1929 London*

A contribution to the study of French as taught in England: thirteenth to fifteenth centuries. *J. Nicholson, Ph.D. 1936 London, University College*

Errors in French prose composition made by school children under examination conditions. *W. J. Tiffin, M.Ed. 1929 Leeds*

Factors conditioning achievement in French among a group of adolescents. *A. B. Raybould, M.A. 1946 Birmingham*

French in a Midland grammar school. *A. H. Griffin, M.A. 1936 Birmingham*

French literature and the adolescent: an inquiry into the interests of adolescents as a basis of the selection of French literature for sixth forms. *A. Lee, M.A. 1937 London, Institute of Education*

French Language: Study and Teaching contd.

La littérature française dans l'enseignement secondaire de garçons en France. *C. A. E. Williams, M.A. 1936 Birmingham*

Prognostic tests of aptitude in modern foreign languages, with special reference to French. *R. V. Dawson, M.Ed. 1947 Leeds*

The status of French and English in the Neutral Islands, 1635-1763. *G. M. Fletcher, M.A. 1930 London, King's College*

A study of the suitability of certain courses used in the teaching of French to first year grammar school pupils. *D. G. Burns, M.A. 1949 Birmingham*

The teaching of the mother tongue in French secondary schools for girls. *C. E. Armstrong, M.Ed. 1931 Leeds*

The teaching of the vernacular in French secondary schools: a study in methods. *B. K. Sarjent, M.A. 1940 Reading*

Texts and text-books in the teaching of French and German. *F. J. Stafford, M.Ed. 1918 Manchester*

Vocabulary tests for French. *R. J. E. Martin, M.A. 1932 London, King's College*

French Literature

This heading includes Belgian and Swiss Literature in the French language. For specific literary forms, see references under Literature. See also Académie Française; Breton Literature; Provençal Language and Literature.

French Literature: General and Miscellaneous

The influence of French literature on Spanish literature. *A. C. Darck, M.A. 1924 Liverpool*

Literary life in England and France betwen the years 1066 and 1400. *J. Scotland, M.Litt. 1929 Cambridge*

The outlaw in French literature. *P. E. Friend, M.A. 1922 London, University College*

French Literature: Criticism

Goethe's knowledge of French literature. *B. Barnes, B.Litt. 1926 Oxford*

The influence of French literary theory and practice on the work of George Gissing and George Moore. *M. P. Jones, M.A. 1936 Wales*

The influence of Nietzsche's French reading on his thought and writing. *W. D. Williams, D.Phil. 1950 Oxford*

James Howell and his relation to France, the French language and literature. *T. J. Thomas, M.A. 1926 Wales*

La littérature et la langue françaises dans l'oeuvre et dans la vie de R. L. Stevenson. *G. Colquhoun, M.A. 1933 Liverpool*

French Literature: Study and Teaching

See French Language: Study and Teaching.

French Literature: Early and Medieval

See also Anglo-Norman Literature; Arthurian Legends; Poetry, Provençal; Romances; Troubadours; and Beaujeu, Renaud de; Bertran de Born; Bonet, H.; Chartier, A.; Chrétien de Troyes; Christine de Pisan; Commynes, P. de; Courcy, J. de; Flamenca; Gautier, d'Arras; Girart, de Roussillon; Guillaume, de Lorris; Guillaume, de Machaut; Guiot, de Provins; Hue de Roteland; Longuyon, J. de; Marie, de France; Pierre, de Nesson; Roman d'Eustache le Moine; Taillevent, M.; Ventadorn, B. de; Vision de Saint Paul.

The bourgeois in French literature of the fourteenth century. *M. G. Liddle, Ph.D. 1925 London*

Claude Fauchet's knowledge of Old French literature. *S. W. Bisson, B.Litt. 1929 Oxford*

A comparison of *Piers Plowman* with some earlier and contemporary French allegories. *D. L. Owen, M.A. 1909 London*

Contribution à l'étude du *Manuel des Péchés*. *E. J. F. Arnould, Ph.D. 1936 London, External Degree*

Contribution to the study of the style in the earliest French prose romances. *S. G. Thomas, Ph.D. 1948 London, University College*

The decline of chivalry as shown in the French literature of the fifteenth century, with special reference to poetry and drama. *K. H. Francis, Ph.D. 1948 London, External Degree*

The evolution of the Merlin story in twelfth and thirteenth century French literature. *G. P. Barnes, M.A. 1950 Manchester*

La vie au foyer: usages et coutumes au moyen âge d'après la littérature populaire de l'époque, et particulièrement les fabliaux. Essai historique et linguistique. *N. Haycocks, M.A. 1929 Manchester*

French Literature: Early and Medieval contd.

Patriotism in Old French literature: eleventh to fifteenth century. *J. Williams, Ph.D. 1933 London, External Degree*

Some aspects of the cult of the Virgin Mary in medieval French literature. *N. V. Williams, M.A. 1927 Wales*

The *Tiers Estat* in medieval French literature. *L. Reed, M.A. 1945 Wales*

French Literature: Sixteenth Century

See also Bartas, G. de S. du; Bellay, J. du; Carle, L. de; Garnier, R.; Habert, F.; Lemaire, J.; Margaret, Queen of Navarre; Marot, C.; Montaigne, M. E. de; Rabelais, F.; Ronsard, P. de; Tyard, P. de.

Contribution à l'étude des écrivains scientifiques en France au seizième siècle. *R. E. Ockenden, M.A. 1935 London, King's College*

The influence of Platonism on certain French authors of the sixteenth century. *M. E. Taylor, M.Litt. 1930 Cambridge*

Ovide en France durant la première partie du seizième siècle. *G. M. M. Morisset, Ph.D. 1934 London, Birkbeck College*

Satire in French literature from 1525 to 1560, with particular reference to the sources and the technique. *C. A. Mayer, Ph.D. 1949 London, University College*

French Literature: Seventeenth Century

See also Allix, P.; Aubigné, T. A. d'; Boileau-Despréaux, N.; Bossuet, J. B.; Bourdaloue, L.; Corneille, P.; Fénelon, F. de S. de la M.; La Calprenède, G. de C. de; La Mothe le Vayer, F. de; Mairet, J.; Maucroix, F.; Molière, J. B. P.; Montchrestien, A. de; Pascal, B.; Racine, J.; Regnier, M.; Rotrou, J. de; Saint Evremond, C. M. de St. D., Seigneur de; Scarron, P.; Schelandre, J. de; Sévigné, M. de.

The artificial or 'precious' element in French literature during the period 1627-1730, from d'Urfé to Marivaux. *J. Craig, M.A. 1910 London*

The development of *préciosité* in the seventeenth century: a literary and social study. *B. G. Treloar, D.Phil. 1948 Oxford*

Feminist writers of the seventeenth century, with special reference to François Poulain de la Barre. *S. A. Richards, M.A. 1912 London*

The influence of the Spanish picaresque novel in the French literature of the seventeenth century, with special reference to Sorel's *Francion* (1623-33). *G. M. Willing, B.Litt. 1931 Oxford*

Le portrait dans la littérature en prose au dix-septième siècle. *O. G. Davies, M.A. 1938 Bristol*

L'influence de l'Angleterre dans la littérature française dans la première moitié du dix-septième siècle: esquisse de cette question. *G. Hainsworth, M.A. 1929 Leeds*

Spenser et la Pléiade. *W. L. Renwick, B.Litt. 1921 Oxford*

French Literature: Eighteenth Century

See also Arnaud, F. B. d'; Bachaumont, L. P. de; Cambry, J. de; Chenier, A.; Condorcet, J. A. N. C. de, Marquis; Daunou, P. C. F.; Desmaizeaux, P.; Diderot, D.; Ducis, J. F.; Holbach, P. H. D. d', Baron; La Chaussée, P. C. N. de; Lesage, A. R.; Lussan, M. de; Marivaux, P. C. de C. de; Mercier, L. S.; Mirabeau, H. G. R., Comte de; Montesquieu, C. de S. de, Baron; Raynal, G. T. F.; Rétif de la Bretonne, N. E.; Rousseau, J. J.; Saint Just, L. A. de; Saint Lambert, J. F. de; Saint Pierre, J. H. B. de; Volney, C. F. C. de, Comte; Voltaire, F. M. A. de.

China as treated by English and French writers in the first half of the eighteenth century. *S. P. Yu, B.Litt. 1932 Oxford*

The educational ideas of the Encyclopaedists. *T. J. James, Ph.D. 1946 London, External Degree*

The evolution of French classical tragedy in the eighteenth century to the death of Voltaire. *I. H. Williams, Ph.D. 1930 Wales*

Les parodies dramatiques des oeuvres de Voltaire. *M. J. Laird, M.A. 1912 Leeds*

Studies on fatality in sentimental pre-Romantic French literature, 1725-62. *B. J. Schlumberger, M.A. 1922 London*

The theory of the epic in France in the eighteenth century. *O. R. Taylor, M.A. 1939 Wales*

Volney et la littérature française à la fin du dix-huitième siècle. *M. D. Moorhead, M.A. 1922 Belfast*

French Literature: Nineteenth Century
See also Romanticism; and Ackermann, L.; Adam, Paul; Aimard, G.; Amiel, H. F.; Angellier, A.; Arène, P.; Balzac, H. de; Barbey d'Aurevilly, J. A.; Barbier, A.; Baudelaire, C. P.; Bernard, C. de; Borel d'Hauterive, P.; Bornier, H. de, Vicomte; Brizeux, J. A.; Brunetière, F.; Buchon, J. A.; Chasles, P.; Châteaubriand, F. R., de, Vicomte; Chénier, A.; Constant de Rebecque, H. B.; Coppée, F.; Cottin, S.; Courier, P. L.; Daudet, A.; Delescluze, L.; Dierx, L.; Dumas, A., the Younger; Flaubert, G.; Fromentin, E.; Gautier, T.; Genlis, S. F., Comtesse de; Gilkin, I.; Gobineau, J. A. de, Comte; Gourmont, R. de; Guérin, E. de; Heredia, J. M. de; Hervieu, P.; Hugo, V. M.; Huysmans, J. K.; Janin, J. G.; Jouy, V. J. E. de; Labiche, E.; Laforgue, J.; Lahor, J.; Lamartine, A. M. L. de; Lamennais, F. R. de; Las Cases, E. A. D. M. J. de, Comte; Latouche, H. J. A. T.; Le Braz, A.; Leconte de Lisle, C. M. R.; Loti, P.; Mallarmé, S.; Maupassant, G. de; Mendès, C.; Mérimée, P.; Moréas, J.; Musset, A. de; Nerval, G. de; Nodier, C.; Ozanam, A. G.; Pasquier, E. D. de, Duc; Péguy, C.; Picard, L. B.; Pixerécourt, G. de; Renan, E.; Richepin, J.; Rimbaud, A.; Rollinat, M.; Sainte-Beuve, C. A.; Samain, A.; Sand, G.; Sarcey, F.; Schwob, M.; Scribe, A. E.; Staël, A. L. G. de, Baronne; Stendhal; Sue, E.; Sully-Prudhomme, R. F. A.; Verhaeren, E.; Verlainè, P.; Veuillot, L. F.; Viennet, J. P. G.; Vigny, A. de, Comte; Wey, F.; Zola, E.

The art of the dance in French literature from Theophile Gautier to Paul Valéry. *D. M. Hornby-Priddin, Ph.D. 1948 London, Bedford College*

The Catholic revival in French literature from Huysmans to Péguy. *E. Beaumont, M.A. 1940 London, King's College*

Contemporary English opinions of the French literature of 1820-1840. *H. Yare, M.A. 1927 Liverpool*

Cromwell in French literature of the Restoration period, 1815-1830. *E. B. Hughes, M.A. 1931 London, East London College*

Dylanwadau Ffrengig ar lenyddiaeth Gymreig y bedwaredd ganrif ar bymtheg (French influences on nineteenth century Welsh literature). *E. M. Evans, M.A. 1926 Wales*

French works in contemporary British reviews (1800-1820). *E. S. Roberts, M.A. 1928 Liverpool*

Germany's relations to France in drama and criticism between 1870 and 1890. *T. P. Williams, M.A. 1936 Wales*

The influence of French literature upon German prose and dramatic literature from 1880 to 1900. *A. H. King, Ph.D. 1934 London, Birkbeck College*

The influence of Ossian on the chief French writers of the Romantic period. *D. J. Lewis, M.A. 1909 Wales*

The influence of the Russian novel on French thinkers and writers, with particular reference to Tolstoy and Dostoevsky. *F. W. J. Hemmings, D.Phil. 1949 Oxford*

La muse française et l'école romantique. *W. F. Allen, M.A. 1909 Wales*

L'influence de l'école Saint-Simonienne sur la littérature française jusqu'en 1850. *I. Sinovitch, M.A. 1922 Leeds*

Neo-Hellenism in French literature from 1850-1900. *A. D. Bryant, Ph.D. 1931 London, East London College*

French Literature: Twentieth Century
See also Alain-Fournier, H.; Aragon, L.; Barbusse, H.; Barrès, M.; Bataille, H.; Bazin, R.; Benda, J.; Bernard, J. J.; Bloy, L. M.; Bordeaux, H.; Brieux, E.; Caiquiez, L. C.; Capus, A.; Châteaubriant, A. de; Claudel, P.; Colette, S. G. C.; Curel, F. de, Vicomte, Duclos, H.; Duhamel, G.; Estaunié, E.; France, A.; Gide, A.; Giraudoux, J.; Gourmont, R. de; Guerin, C.; Guttinguer, U.; Jammes, F.; Le Cardonnel, L.; Le Goffic, C.; Le Roy, E.; Maeterlinck, M., Count; Mauriac, F.; Péguy, C.; Proust, M.; Prouvost, A.; Psichari, E.; Régnier, H. de; Renard, J.; Rivière, J.; Rolland, R.; Romains, J.; Rostand, E.; Signoret, E.; Spire, A.; Supervielle, J.; Thibaudet, A.; Valéry, P.; Vielé-Griffin, F.; Vitta, E.

A comparative study of children in English and French literature 1900 to 1914. *H. C. Davis, M.A. 1934 London, East London College*

The evidence of contemporary French memoirs, letters and periodicals with regard to the influence of English literature. *E. H. Partridge, B.Litt. 1924 Oxford*

French Literature: Twentieth Century contd.
La littérature belge de langue française entre les deux guerres. *A. W. F. Dalby, M.A. 1948 Bristol*

Le pessimisme sous l'occupation allemande, 1940-1944: un aspect de la litterature contemporaine. *K. E. Collins, M.A. 1947 Birmingham*

Les mots dialectaux dans la littérature française contemporaine. *W. Padfield, M.A. 1921 Liverpool*

Postwar tendencies in French literature. *A. J. Leventhal, Ph.D. 1933 Dublin, Trinity College*

French Revolution
See France: History: French Revolution.

Freud, Sigmund
A critical examination of Sigmund Freud's theory of personality. *N. F. Chubb, M.A. 1937 London, University College*

The interpretation of some aspects of Christian doctrine and practice in the light of Sigmund Freud's conceptions of the development and structure of the mind. *R. S. Lee, D.Phil. 1947 Oxford*

Freytag, Gustav
Social history and domestic manners as reflected in the works of Gustav Freytag and Wilhelm Raabe. *M. W. E. Jones, M.A. 1932 Wales*

Friaries
See Monasticism.

Friendly Societies
The development of the great affiliated friendly societies from their humble and often obscure origins in the eighteenth century. *W. T. Bushrod, M.A. 1924 Manchester*

Some aspects of a fall in the rate of mortality as affecting the financial position of friendly societies and sickness funds. *R. R. Brodie, Ph.D. 1932 London, External Degree*

Friends, Society of
See also Barclay, R.; Ford, J.; Jones, R. M.; Kelsall, J.; Pennington, I.

Bristol Quakerism. *R. S. Mortimer, M.A. 1946 Bristol*

A critical estimate of the educational theory and practice of the Society of Friends as seen in their schools in England. *W. A. C. Stewart, Ph.D. 1947 London, Institute of Education*

The discipline of the Society of Friends as a regular national body, with particular reference to church government based on a study of the epistles of the yearly meetings, 1669 to 1738. *W. A. Lloyd, Ph.D. 1947 Cambridge*

The doctrine of the "inner light": its European development immediately prior to the foundation of the Society of Friends, and in that Society from the time of George Fox to the present day. *H. B. Miner, Ph.D. 1936 Edinburgh*

Early Quaker education. *D. G. B. Hubbard, M.A. 1939 London, King's College*

The history of Quaker education in England, 1647-1903. *L. J. Stroud, M.Ed. 1945 Leeds*

The political and economic relations of English and American Quakers, 1750-85. *A. T. Gary, D.Phil. 1935 Oxford*

The political ideas of the Quakers of the seventeenth century. *P. S. Belasco, M.Sc. 1926 London*

Quakerism and public service, chiefly between 1832 and 1867. *E. I. J. Martineau, B.Litt. 1938 Oxford*

The rise, progress, and decline of the Quaker movement in Scotland. *G. B. Burnet, Ph.D. 1937 Glasgow*

Social conditions in Ireland in the seventeeth and eighteenth centuries, as illustrated by early Quaker records. *I. Grubb, M.A. 1916 London*

The Society of Friends in Glamorgan, 1654-1900. *M. F. Williams, M.A. 1950 Wales*

The theology of the early Friends with special reference to that of Isaac Pennington. *R. H. Ion, B.D. 1947 Oxford*

Friendship
Φιλία: an edition of Aristotle, *Nicomachean Ethics*, VIII and IX. *G. Percival, PH.D. 1938 Cambridge*

L'amitié masculine dans les romans courtois. *O. L. M. Hellman, M.A. 1945 London, Birkbeck College*

A study of friendship among adolescents. *M. M. Shukla, M.A. 1948 London, Institute of Education*

A study on friendship-love in adolescence. *N. M. Iovetz-Tereshchenko, Ph.D. 1933 London, King's College*

The treatment of friendship by Schiller and Shakespeare. *E. A. Parker, M.A. 1911 Birmingham*

Fries, Jakob Friedrich
The philosophy of J. F. Fries. *G. Ewan, Ph.D. 1921 Edinburgh*

Froebel, Friedrich Wilhelm August
Froebel's principles and their relationship to the theory and practice of infant education today. *L. Stowe, M.A. 1940 Leeds*

Fromentin, Eugène
Eugène Fromentin, his life and works. *E. Tranmer, M.A. 1921 Birmingham*

Froude, James Anthony
The materials for biography, the handling of the materials, and the techniques employed to reveal character and personality, with special reference to the work of Lockhart, Froude and Lytton Strachey, in the light of recent psychological investigation. *E. A. M. Dougary, Ph.D. 1942 Edinburgh*

Fruit Industry
The British fruit market: with special reference to South Africa. *G. P. Beyleveld, M.Sc. 1940 London, School of Economics and Political Science*

The organization of wholesale distribution in Great Britain of fruit, flowers, and vegetables of domestic and foreign origin. *W. Drake, M.Com. 1941 London, External Degree*

Some aspects of the fruit growing industry in the County of Kent. *L. Napolitan, M.Sc. 1946 London, School of Economics and Political Science*

The West Riding rhubarb industry. *F. C. Henwood, M.Com. 1934 Birmingham*

Frustration
See Will.

Fuel Industry
See also Coal Industry; Gas Industry.

Fuel policy in France and Great Britain. *M. J. J. Verroeulst, B.Phil. 1947 Oxford*

Industrial fuel problems under wartime conditions. *N. Y. Kiroff, M.Sc. 1943 Leeds*

Fulk Fitz-Warin
See Anglo-Norman Literature.

Fuller, Thomas
Thomas Fuller, D. D. *M. Flynn, M.A. 1936 National University of Ireland*

Fullerism
See Church History: Wales.

Fullonius, Gulielmus
Palsgrave's translation of *Acolastus* (by Gulielmus Fullonius). *P. L. Carver, Ph.D. 1934 Leeds*

Funerary Monuments
See Tombs.

Furniture
Domestic furniture and utensils of the Han period. *J. M. F. Penny, M.A. 1941 London, Courtauld Institute of Art*

The history of Welsh domestic art from the sixteenth century as exhibited in the native furniture, with a study of its relation to the furniture of other parts of the British Isles and the continent of Europe. *D. R. Jones, M.A. 1925 Wales*

Fynglwyd, Iorwerth
The poems of Iorwerth Fynglwyd. *D. R. Jones, M.A. 1909 Wales*

Ga, The
Religion and medicine among the Ga people of the Gold Coast. *M. J. Field, Ph.D. 1936 London, University College*

Gadesden, Joannes de, Anglicus
Rosa anglica. *W. P. Wulff, Ph.D. 1931 National University of Ireland*

Gaelic Language
See Irish Language; Scottish Language, Gaelic.

Gainsborough, Thomas
Gainsborough's landscape drawings and their place in the development of English landscape drawing and painting. *M. W. Woodall, Ph.D. 1937 London, Courtauld Institute of Art*

Galdós, Benito Pérez
See Pérez Galdós, B.

Galen, Claudius
Galen's physiology, with special reference to the vascular system. *J. Prendergast, B.Litt. 1930 Oxford*

Galicia
The Galician revival in the nineteenth and twentieth centuries, in both Castilian and Galician culture. *F. S. Reckert, M.Litt. 1949 Cambridge*

Gallicanism
Edmond Richer and the revival of Gallicanism, 1600-1630. *D. O. Soper, Ph.D. 1929 London*

Galsworthy, John
Galsworthy's conception of comedy. *H. Bilbrough, M.A. 1948 Manchester*

Galsworthy's contribution to modern drama. *S. G. Rees, M.A. 1937 Wales*

John Galsworthy: some ideas in the plays and novels, in the essays and stories. *B. A. Ruck, M.A. 1928 Birmingham*

The novel technique of John Galsworthy. *S. H. Davies, M.A. 1932 Wales*

Galt, John
The life and work of John Galt. *J. W. Aberdein, Ph.D. 1934 Aberdeen*

Galway
Old Galway: history of an English colony in Ireland. *M. J. D. O'Sullivan, D.Litt. 1943 National University of Ireland*

The siege of Galway, 1651-1652. *P. Callan, M.A. 1931 National University of Ireland*

Gambia
The Gambia. *H. R. Jarrett, M.Sc. 1947 London, External Degree*

The struggle for power on the Senegal and Gambia, 1660-1713. *T. G. Stone, M.A. 1921 London*

Games and Sports
See also Athletics; Children's Games; Leisure.

The attitude of grammar school pupils and their parents to education, religion and sport. *W. Glassey, M.Ed. 1943 Manchester*

Contributions to the study of the vocabulary of sport in contemporary German. *C. E. Adams, M.A. 1935 Liverpool*

The pscyhology of the 'organized group game' with special reference to its place in the play system and its educational value. *M. J. Reaney, D.Sc. 1916 London*

Some business aspects of association football and county cricket in England: a study of certain aspects of the organization of games dependent upon gate receipts. *L. N. Harding, M.Sc. 1941 London, School of Economics and Political Science*

Sports centres; their planning and construction. *G. J. Powis, M.A. 1948 Sheffield*

The vocabulary of sport in present-day France. *J. E. Travis, M.A. 1933 Manchester*

Garbett, Samuel
Samuel Garbett, 1717-1803, a Birmingham pioneer. *P. S. Bebbington, M.Com. 1938 Birmingham*

Gardens and Gardening
See also Horticulture.

Gardens and gardening in the Roman world. *J. Lawson, M.A. 1945 Manchester*

Garnier, Robert
Robert Garnier et quelques aspects de la poésie dramatique au seizième siècle. *D. M. Smith, M.A. 1940 Wales*

Garrick, David
The family correspondence of David Garrick. *D. Wecter, B.Litt. 1929 Oxford*

Gars, The
Culture-contact among the Plains Gars of eastern Bengal. *J. Basu, Ph.D. 1947 London, University College*

Gas Industry
Cost analysis in the gas industry. *T. Brown, M.Com. 1946 Birmingham*

The economics of the gas industry. *F. Wright, M.A. 1925 Leeds*

Factors determining the size of gas undertakings. *R. C. Harman, M.Sc. 1938 London, School of Economics and Political Science*

Gascoigne, George
An edition, with indtroduction, notes, and glossary, of George Gascoigne's *A hundreth sundrie flowres*. *C. T. Prouty, Ph.D. 1939 Cambridge*

George Gascoigne, his life and works. *G. Ambrose, B.Litt. 1926 Oxford*

Gascoigne, Thomas
The life and works of Thomas Gascoigne. *W. A. Pronger, B.Litt. 1932 Oxford*

Gascony
Some aspects of the political and administrative history of Gascony from 1303-1307. *E. C. P. Stuart, Ph.D. 1927 London*

Gases
The development of the gas laws from Boyle to Van der Waals. *W. S. James, M.Sc. 1928 London*

Gases contd.
Gay Lussac's law of gaseous volumes and the influence on chemical theory up to 1860. *H. A. Filmer, M.Sc. 1928 London*

History of the discovery of the gases of the air and of their physical and chemical properties. *M. M. Haslam, M.Sc. 1929 London*

Gaskell, Elizabeth Cleghorn
Elizabeth Cleghorn Gaskell: a study of her writings. *A. S. Whitfield, B.Litt. 1926 Oxford*

Mrs. Gaskell: life and works. *W. K. Railton, M.A. 1940 Wales*

Mrs Gaskell, with special reference to the social reform novel, 1830-1850. *J. T. Lancaster, M.Litt. 1927 Cambridge*

Gaudentius, of Brescia, Saint
A comparison of the styles of Gaudentius of Brescia, the *De Sacramentis* (ascribed to St. Ambrose) and the *Disdascalia Apostolorum* or *Fragmenta Veronensia*. *A. H. Birch, Ph.D. 1924 London*

Gaul
The organization and administration of the Tres Galliae, 49 B.C.-283 A.D. *M. P. Kerr, M.A. 1924 Manchester*

The political and social organization of Gaul under the Roman Empire. *E. J. Rowland, M.A. 1910 Wales*

The political and social organization of Gaul under the Roman Empire. *J. Hooson, M.A. 1912 Wales*

Roman civilization in the three Gauls during the first three centuries of Roman rule. *H. W. Lawton, M.A. 1923 Wales*

Romanization of the three Gauls. *J. R. Moran, M.A. 1919 National University of Ireland*

The social and economic history of Cisalpine Gaul under the early Empire to the death of Trajan. *G. E. F. Chilver, D.Phil. 1936 Oxford*

Gauss, Carl Friedrich
The work of Hansteen and Gauss on the law of magnetic force, with some account of the work of their predecessors. *J. J. Reynolds, M.Sc. 1949 London, University College*

Gautier d'Arras
A comparison of the use of the subjunctive in Gautier d'Arras and Chrétien de Troyes. *E. Hugh, M.A. 1919 Wales*

The romance of *Eracle* by Gautier d'Arras: its sources, composition, and place in contemporary literature. *C. J. Hayes, B.Litt. 1935 Oxford*

Gautier, Théophile
Étude sur le vocabulaire du *Voyage en Espagne* de Théophile Gautier. *W. W. Padgett, M.A. 1924 Leeds*

Théophile Gautier. *J. H. Tamlyn, M.A. 1921 Wales*

Théophile Gautier: critique d'art. *S. E. Higgins, M.A. 1947 Belfast*

Théophile Gautier et le dandysme. *J. M. Milner, M.A. 1939 Leeds*

Gaveston, Piers
The career of Peter of Gavaston and his place in history. *A. A. Taylor, M.A. 1938 London, Royal Holloway College*

Gawain
See Arthurian Legends.

Gawdy, Family
The Gawdys of West Harling, Norfolk: a study of education and social life in the seventeenth century. *C. D. Price, M.A. 1950 Wales*

Gay, John
The life and works of John Gay. *W. A. Pickering, M.A. 1934 Birmingham*

Gay, Victor
Etude lexicographique sur le vocabulaire des textes réunis sous la lettre 'G' du *Glossaire archéologique* vol. 1, de Victor Gay. *T. Schofield, M.A. 1933 Leeds*

Gazul, Clare
See Mérimée, P.

Gearnon, Antóin
Parrthas an Anma le Antóin Gearnon (*The Paradise of the soul* by Antóin Gearnon). *J. Faulkner, M.A. 1938 National University of Ireland*

Gellius, Aulus
A commentary on the subject matter of the *Noctes Atticae* of Aulus Gellius, Bk. I. *H. M. Hornsby, Ph.D. 1931 Dublin, Trinity College*

Genesis and Exodus (poem)
A glossary to the Middle English poem *Genesis and Exodus*, with explanatory notes on the text. *A. Merrall, M.A. 1941 Manchester*

Genlis, Stephanie Félicité, Comtesse de
Madame de Genlis, educationist. *P. J. Ward, Ph.D. 1934 Cambridge*

Gentile, Giovanni
A conception of religion deduced from the works of Giovanni Gentile. *A. A. Lion, B.Litt. 1927 Oxford*

Gentleman's Journal
The novels in *The Gentleman's Journal*. *E. E. Sandeen, B.Litt. 1933 Oxford*

Geoffrey, of Monmouth
An examination of Welsh versions of the *Historia regum Britanniae*, with reference to the original. *H. Lewis, M.A. 1913 Wales*

Geoffrey of Monmouth's *Chronicle* and its influence on English literature. *L. Woosnam, M.A. 1913 Wales*

The Welsh version of the *Historia regum Britanniae* in Peniarth ms.44 collated with the *Red book* version, together with notes on the influence of the original on the style and construction of the Welsh, and a glossary of Welsh words whose use is illustrated by the Latin. *B. Jones, M.A. 1915 Wales*

Geography
See also Climate; Coastline; Erosion; Forestry; Land Utilization; Maps; Population; Sea; Settlements; Tropics; Villages. For the geography of individual areas, see under their names.

Effects of government interference in modifying the influence of natural advantages. *D. C. T. Mekie, Ph.D. 1925 Edinburgh*

Imperial military geography. *D. H. Cole, Litt.D. 1935 Dublin, Trinity College*

Insolation and relief: their bearing on the human geography of Alpine regions. *A. Garnett, Ph.D. 1938 London, External Degree*

Geography: History
The development of mathematical geography among the Greeks. *P. M. L. Brock, M.A. 1935 London, King's College*

The development of the concept of natural regions, and its value in the furtherance of geographical thought. *E. W. Lemarchand, M.A. 1929 London*

Geographical materials in the writings of al-Mas'udi. *S. M. Ahmad, B.Litt. 1947 Oxford*

The knowledge of India possessed by Arab geographers down to the fourteenth century A.D., with special reference to southern India. *S. M. H. Nainar, Ph.D. 1938 London, School of Oriental and African Studies*

The mapping of West Africa in the fourteenth and fifteenth centuries, as illustrative of the development of geographical ideas. *G. H. Kimble, M.A. 1931 London, King's College*

Sources and dialect of a French didactic poem on geography. *E. C. Halket, M.A. 1919 London*

Studies in Tudor geography. *E. G. R. Taylor, D.Sc. 1930 London, External Degree*

A study of *pays* as units of regional treatment: a comparison of France and England. *G. Bowen, M.A. 1935 Liverpool*

Geography: Study and Teaching
See also Thevet, A.

A comparative investigation of the influence of geography and practical biology on the understanding of the forms of reasoning involved in civics. *C. W. Atkinson, M.Ed. 1949 Leeds*

The correlation of history and geography in the primary schools. *T. J. O'Meara, M.A. 1936 National University of Ireland*

An enquiry into the methods of teaching geography and sources of geography material. *A. E. Wilson, M.Ed. 1934 Leeds*

An evaluation of the position of regional and other studies in geography in the curricula envisaged for the three main streams in secondary education in England and Wales. *R. W. L. Walden, M.A. 1949 Wales*

An experimental research on the problem of teaching geography to backward boys in present day senior schools. *F. S. Cassidy, M.Ed. 1937 Leeds*

An investigation into the attitudes of boys and girls towards the content of, and the methods of, teaching geography in grammar schools. *D.B. Bartlett, M.A. 1948 London, Institute of Education*

An investigation into the causes of backwardness in geography among secondary school children. *H. K. Ault, M.A. 1940 London, Institute of Education*

Geography: Study and Teaching contd.
An investigation into the efficacy of outdoor work in improving the attainment of training college students in, and their attitude towards, the subject of geography. *J. L. Oliver, M.A. 1948 London, Institute of Education*

An investigation into the interest of children in school geography, with special reference to the development of interest in girls between the ages of 11 and 16 years. *A. M. Smyth, M.A. 1946 London, Institute of Education*

An investigation into the relationship between interest in and knowledge of school geography, by means of a series of attitude tests. *I. L. M. Long, M.A. 1949 London, Institute of Education*

An investigation of the factors involved in the geographical work of boys and girls. *C. L. Heywood, M.A. 1938 London, Institute of Education*

The organization of a climatological station in a secondary school, and the introduction of this work into the geography syllabus. *D. Peter, M.Ed. 1930 Manchester*

The place and value of human geography in Irish primary schools. *T. Mahony, M.A. 1934 National University of Ireland*

Psychological problems in the teaching of geography. *E. W. Jones, M.A. 1931 London, Day Training College*

Regional survey and its application in schools. *E. M. Pilkington, M.Ed. 1921 Manchester*

Scientific method in the teaching of geography with special reference to the teaching of geography in 'modern schools'. *J. A. Glason, M.A. 1932 Reading*

A study of the factors underlying relational thinking in school geography. *J. E. Daniel, M.A. 1936 London, Institute of Education*

The syllabus, teaching and value of geography in a rural fenland grammar school. *H. Slater, M.Ed. 1933 Manchester*

The teaching of geography in England from 1886 to 1916. *E. M. Bradley, M.Ed. 1917 Manchester*

The teaching of geography in the secondary school, with special reference to maps and map-work. *P. G. Moss, M.A. 1931 Liverpool*

The teaching of geography in primary schools: an investigation as to the psychological approach in the teaching of different aspects of geography to children of primary school age. *E. David, M.A. 1944 Birmingham*

The teaching of geography in postwar secondary education. *J. J. Branigan, M.A. 1945 Leeds*

The use and value of folklore in the teaching of geography. *H. B. Hodgson, M.Ed. 1935 Leeds*

Geography, Agricultural
See Agriculture.

Geology
The life and work of A. G. Werner, 1749-1817, and his influence on his contemporaries. *M. M. Mathews, M.Sc. 1935 London, University College*

Some aspects of the geological work of Johan Jacob Scheuchzer including a translation of his *Herbarium Deluvianum* of 1709. *B. D. Tyrrell, M.Sc. 1934 London, University College*

Geometry
The development in ancient Greece of the concept of number in arithmetic and geometry. *J. L. Stirk, M.Sc. 1947 London, University College*

A history of the introduction and development of projective methods in geometry. *A. Geary, M.Sc. 1928 London*

The nature of geometrical axioms, being an essay on the theory of geometrical knowledge. *J. S. E. T. Greenwood, M.A. 1922 London*

Geometry: Study and Teaching
An analysis of factors entering into geometrical ability. *J. W. Withrington, M.A. 1936 London, Institute of Education*

Considerations on the teaching of mathematics, especially geometry - being mainly a comparison of the 'oral' method and the method of 'learning by experience'. *L. Wilkes, M.A. 1930 Birmingham*

The geometrical concepts of children from five to eight years of age. *E. M. Williams, M.A. 1934 London, Institute of Education*

An investigation into the possibility of the development of spatial perception in children in their first year of secondary education, in preparation for their introduction to formal geometry. *V. T. Brownless, M.A. 1949 London, King's College*

Geometry: Study and Teaching contd.
Prognostic tests of school geometry. *E. W. M. Potts, M.A. 1934 London, Institute of Education*

A psychological approach to the teaching of geometry. *B. H. Bond, M.A. 1935 Birmingham*

The relation of certain factors of imagery and immediate memory to geometrical ability. *E. W. Webb, M.A. 1949 London, Institute of Education*

A supplementary school course in geometry, designed for more advanced students. *W. Garner, M.Ed. 1930 Manchester*

The teaching of geometry: historically and psychologically treated, with an experimental investigation in reference to the correlation of imagery and geometrical ability. *R. J. Fulford, M.Sc. 1923 Birmingham*

The teaching of geometry in secondary schools. *G. B. Jackson, M.Ed. 1924 Manchester*

George, Stefan
A critical analysis of the presentation of ideas connected with the figure of the hero in the works of Stefan George and his circle. *M. G. Sims, M.A. 1947 London, Birkbeck College*

The unity of thought in the early works of Stefan George. *F. E. Wölcken, Ph.D. 1937 Edinburgh*

Georgia, U.S.
Oglethorpe and social and religious movements in England and Georgia. *L. F. Church, Ph.D. 1928 London*

Gerald, of Wales
See Giraldus, Cambrensis.

Geraldine Rebellion
See Ireland: History.

Gerdil, Giacinto Sigismondo, Cardinal
Cardinal Gerdil and ontologism. *M. J. Conlon, M.A. 1924 National University of Ireland*

Germain, George, Viscount Sackville
Lord George Germain. *G. H. Gilcriest, M.A. 1914 Liverpool*

German Language
See also Kolbenheyer, E. G.

Ausdrucksverstärkung im Mittelhochdeutschen: mit besonderer Berücksichtigung der Zusammensetzungen. *S. M. Ward, M.A. 1949 Birmingham*

Contributions to the study of the influence of German loanwords in Swedish vocabulary. *C. T. Hansson, M.A. 1949 Liverpool*

Contributions to the study of the vocabulary of sport in contemporary German. *C. E. Adams, M.A. 1935 Liverpool*

A critical survey of theories relating to the origin of the Germanic and High German sound-shifts, with an introduction on the general problem of sound-change. *B. Rayburn, M.A. 1942 Manchester*

English influence on the German language: some indications. *A. Oakey, M.A. 1931 Birmingham*

An enquiry into the use of adjectives denoting beauty in Middle High German. *R. E. Keller, M.A. 1949 Manchester*

The influence of Middle Dutch and Middle Low German on English speech. *E. C. Llewellyn, B. Litt. 1930 Oxford*

The maritime vocabulary of the middle high German poem *Kudrun*. *K. Cuthbert, M.A. 1945 Belfast*

Mundart Peter Roseggers, mit einer Abhandlung über seine Leben und seine Waldheimat aus seinen längeren Romanen. *A. Rodgers, M.A. 1931 Leeds*

The origins of Yiddish in the German language. *M. H. Malits, M.A. 1942 Wales*

Phonetik und Flexionslehre der Osnabrücker Mundart. *A. E. Niblett, M.A. 1911 Birmingham*

Recent German prose usage. *W. Witte, Ph.D. 1935 Aberdeen*

The Rhenish school of German philology. *J. C. Gilbertson, M.A. 1938 Manchester*

A study, critical, historical and linguistic, of the earliest relations between Celts and Germans. *C. S. Elston, Ph.D. 1933 London, Birkbeck College*

Texts and text-books in the teaching of French and German. *F. J. Stafford, M.Ed. 1918 Manchester*

Zur Geschichte der umschreibenden Konjugation im Deutschen. *J. M. Clark, M.A. 1913 London*

German Literature
This heading includes Austrian and Swiss literature in the German language. For specific literary forms, see references under Literature.

German Literature: General and Miscellaneous
The animal story in German literature from the *Ecbasis Captivi* to Goethe's *Reineke Fuchs*. *L. R. Hopps, B.Litt. 1940 Oxford*

Christ in German epic and dramatic literature. *I. M. Southall, M.A. 1914 Birmingham*

Das dritte Reich: a study of the idea of the 'third kingdom' in German literature, with special reference to the classical and romantic periods. *A. Stansfield, M.A. 1932 Manchester*

German influence on Scott. *H. Burgis, M.A. 1916 London*

The idea of *Wandlung* in German literature. *C. Jones, M.A. 1935 London, Birkbeck College*

Prométhée dans la littérature allemande. *K. M. Ingold, M.A. 1924 Belfast*

The theme of flying in German literature. *M. Watson, M.A. 1939 London, Birkbeck College*

German Literature: Early and Medieval
See also Arthurian Legends; Minnesingers; Nibelungen; Romances; Sagas; and Eschenbach, W. von; Havich, of Cologne; Judith; Kudrun; Meier Helmbrecht.

Die niederdeutsche gereimte Katharinenlegende der Brüsseler Hs.No.II.143, und ihr Verhältnis zu dem mitteldeutschen Wolfenbüttler Fragmenten: Text und Untersuchung. *W. E. Collinson, M.A. 1912 London*

The fables of Aesop in the German literature of the fifteenth century, with special reference to Steinhoewel's translation. *W. Schwarz, M.A. 1939 London, University College*

J. J. Bodmer's contribution to the knowledge and appreciation of Middle High German Literature. *D. Knight, M.A. 1949 London, Bedford College*

Marien Himmelfahrt: ein mittelhochdeutsches Gedicht kritisch. *F. Norman, M.A. 1925 London*

The position of women as reflected in medieval German didactic literature. *E. D. Barber, M.A. 1940 Manchester*

1. The use of *exempla* in Middle High German Literature. 2. The legend of the Virgin as knight. *M. D. Howrie, Ph.D. 1922 London*

German Literature: Sixteenth Century
See also Sachs, H.

The literary relations between Germany and the Netherlands in the sixteenth century. *M. Bülbring, M.A. 1939 London, University College*

Sprachliche, literarische und kulturelle Untersuchung der *Regensburger Chronik* des Leonhard Widmann. *F. Gossman, M.A. 1940 London, King's College*

German Literature: Seventeenth Century
See Grimmelshausen, H, J. C. von; Gryphius, A.; Kolbenheyer, E. G.

German Literature: Eighteenth Century
See also Brandes, J. C.; Brockes, B. H.; Bürger, G. A.; Goethe, J. W. von; Hagedorn, F. von; Herder, J. G. von; Kleist, E. C. von; Klopstock, F. G.; Lessing, G. E.; Lichtenberg, G. C.; Novalis; Schiller, J. C. F. von; Schlegel, A. W. von; Schlegel, J. E.; Wackenroder, W. H.

Anthony Earl of Shaftesbury (1671-1713) and the German classical writers of the eighteenth century. *M. A. Morland, Ph.D. 1946 London, External Degree*

Baroque survivals in literary theory and practice of the early German enlightenment, 1700-1750. *H. K. Kettler, Ph.D. 1938 Cambridge*

The development of *Weltschmerz* in German literature from *Werther* to the beginning of the Romantic movement. *W. Rose, Ph.D. 1923 London*

The rôle of the parson in the literature of the eighteenth century in England and Germany. *M. E. Daw, M.A. 1937 London, King's College*

Types of social ideals in German literature (from Sturm-und-Drang to Romanticism). *L. W. Kahn, M.A. 1936 London, University College*

Zwei unbekannte Fassungen von Gedichten: über die *Fünfzehn Zeichen* und *Das jüngste Gericht*: Text und Untersuchungen. *L. A. Willoughby, M.A. 1903 London*

German Literature: Nineteenth Century
See also Romanticism; and Auerbach, B.; Brentano, C. von; Büchner, G.; Chamisso, A. von; Droste-Hulshoff, A. E. von, Baroness; Eichendorff, J.; Ernot, P.; Fichte, J. G.; Fontane, T.; Freiligrath, H. F.; Freytag, G.; Grillparzer, F.; Halm, F.; Hebbel, C. F.; Heine, H.; Heyse, P. J. L. von; Hoffmann, E. T. W. (Amadeus); Hölderlin, J. C. F.; Holstein, F. von, Baron; Keller, G.; Kleist, H. von; Klinger, F. M. von; Körner, K. T.;

Gibbs, James
A catalogue of the drawings of James Gibbs in the Ashmolean Museum and their connexion with his life and work. *W. W. Crandall, B.Litt. 1933 Oxford*

Gibraltar
Gibraltar as a British possession to 1783. *C. P. R. Clarke, B.Litt. 1934 Oxford*

Gibson, Edmund, Bishop
Edmund Gibson, Bishop of London (1669-1748). *N. Sykes, D.Phil. 1923 Oxford*

Gide, André
André Gide. *K. G. Brooks, M.A. 1931 Birmingham*

André Gide and the individual. *G. P. F. Jeffares, Ph.D. 1950 Dublin, Trinity College*

The individualism of André Gide: its character and origin. *D. L. Thomas, M.A. 1945 Wales*

The strain of Protestantism in the works of André Gide. *E. Perrett, M.A. 1928 Wales*

Gift of Tongues
Edward Irving and the gift of tongues: an historical and psychological study. *A. L. Drummond, Ph.D. 1930 Edinburgh*

Expositions of: Acts ii.4: ἤρξαντο λαλεῖν ετέραιϛ γλώσσαιϛ; the gift of tongues; Romans iii.25: ὸν προέθετο ο θεὸσ ιλαστήριον ξιὰ πίστεωσ εν τω αυτου αἵματι: the meaning of ιλαστήριον; Galatians iii.15: the legal terminology of the Epistle to the Galatians and its bearing on the question of the churches addressed by St. Paul. *D. Walker, D.D. 1904 Oxford*

The gift of the spirit in the New Testament, with special reference to Glossolalia. *M. Barnett, M.A. 1946 Manchester*

Gildas, Saint
A study of the syntax and vocabulary of the *De excidio Britanniae* of Gildas. *G. R. Williams, M.A. 1935 Wales*

Gilkin, Iwan
L'oeuvre d'Iwan Gilkin. *F. Polderman, M.A. 1917 Birmingham*

Gilpin, William
The Rev. William Gilpin and the cult of the picturesque. *H. J. Paris, B.Litt. 1938 Oxford*

Giraldus, Cambrensis
Giraldus Cambrensis: *De Invectionibus*, transcribed from the Vatican manuscript and edited with an historical introduction. *W. S. Davies, M.A. 1921 Wales*

The life of St. David by Giraldus Cambrensis. *T. B. Jones, M.A. 1934 Wales*

Types of social life illustrated by the writings of Gerald of Wales. *D. Humphreys, B.Litt. 1936 Oxford*

Girart, de Roussillon
A comparative study of Girart de Roussillon and the Tristan poems. *E. S. Murrell, B.Litt. 1926 Oxford*

Critical edition of a portion of the epic poem (of Girart de Roussillon), with study of the language of the poet and of the existing manuscripts. *W. M. Hackett, M.A. 1937 Manchester*

A critical edition of the epic poem Girart de Roussillon, with notes, complete glossary, and linguistic introduction. *W. M. Hackett, D.Phil. 1950 Oxford*

Giraudoux, Jean
Aspects de l'imagination et du langage dans l'oeuvre de Jean Giraudoux. *E. C. Cure, M.A. 1946 London, Birkbeck College*

Le théâtre de Jean Giraudoux. *T. E. Lawrenson, M.A. 1941 Manchester*

Le théâtre de Jean Giraudoux: sa conception, sa réalization. *C. A. J. Lejeune, M.A. 1950 Liverpool*

Girls
Les jeunes filles dans le théâtre d'Alfred de Musset. *S. Courtney, M.A. 1950 National University of Ireland*

Studies of employed adolescent girls in relation to their development and social background. *A. P. Jephcott, M.A. 1949 Wales*

Girls: Education
See also Co-education; Education; Women: Education.

An account of the education of women and girls in England in the time of the Tudors. *D. M. Meads, Ph.D. 1929 London*

A comparison of girls' junior technical schools in London and Paris. *D. A. Pannett, M.A. 1939 London, King's College*

Girls: Education contd.
The curriculum in girls' secondary schools, with special reference to England and Egypt. *Z. el-Sharani, M.A. 1939 Bristol*

The education of girls in England from 1600 to 1800. *E. M. D. Morris, M.A. 1926 London*

An examination into the present educational opportunities for Egyptian girls in Egypt. *P. Sageman, M.A. 1937 London, King's College*

Hegel's theory and practice of education, and problems of girls' education in elementary schools. *M. Mackenzie, M.A. 1908 Wales*

An investigation into the curriculum of girls' secondary schools. *N. Jones, M.A. 1927 London*

L'education des filles d'après les idées de Fénelon. *W. F. Robson, M.A. 1924 Liverpool*

Les idées de Madame de Maintenon sur l'éducation des filles, comparées à celles qui ont cours à notre époque. *L. F. Barker, M.A. 1912 Liverpool*

The problem of the higher education of girls in the Bombay Presidency. *V. A. Ajgaonkar, M.Ed. 1940 Leeds*

Some aspects of feminine education in England during the seventeenth century. *F. Cameron, M.A. 1949 Liverpool*

A study of the Abbe de Fénelon's treatise *De l'education des filles*, considered in relation to the educational ideas of his contemporaries. *A. W. Hughes, M.A. 1944 Wales*

A study of the provision for vocational training in the advanced courses of girls' secondary schools, with special reference to electricity. *M. J. Gordon, M.A. 1941 London, King's College*

A study of the training for leisure occupations offered in a senior girls' school in an industrial area, together with an industrial enquiry into the use made of this training by the girls after their entry into employment. *O. I. Morgan, M.Ed. 1942 Manchester*

The technical high school, with special reference to girls. *H. Todd, M.Ed. 1941 Leeds*

Girls, Delinquent
See Juvenile Delinquency.

Gissing, George Robert
The influence of French literary theory and practice on the work of George Gissing and George Moore. *M. P. Jones, M.A. 1936 Wales*

Gladstone, William Ewart
The influence of Parliament upon the foreign policy of the Gladstone Government, 1868-74. *S. Lambert, M.A. 1949 London, Bedford College*

The internationalism in the work and thought of William Ewart Gladstone, with reference to present-day theory and practice of internationalism. *J. D. Evans, M.A. 1938 Wales*

The theological opinions of William Ewart Gladstone. *H. S. Curr, Ph.D. 1941 Edinburgh*

Glamorgan
The development of communications in Glamorgan, with special reference to the growth of industry between 1760 and 1840. *E. Walker, M.A. 1947 Wales*

The ecclesiastical history of Glamorgan during the Middle Ages up to 1188, with special reference to the period A.D. 1056-1188. *L. C. Simons, M.A. 1914 Wales*

The history of the counties of Glamorgan and Monmouth during the Great Civil War, 1642-1648. *L. J. Thomas, M.A. 1914 Wales*

The Norman lordship of Glamorgan: its settlement and early organization to the death of Gilbert de Clare, 1314. *G. N. Jones, M.A. 1921 Wales*

Wales and the Marches in the reign of Edward II, with special reference to Glamorgan and the revolt of Llewelyn Bren. *T. A. Dyke, M.A. 1912 Wales*

Glapthorne, Henry
The plays and poems of Henry Glapthorne, with a biography and critical apparatus. *J. H. Walter, Ph.D. 1935 London, University College*

Glas, John
John Glas: a study of the origins, development and influence of the Glasite Movement. *J. T. Hornsby, Ph.D. 1936 Edinburgh*

Glass Industry
Economics and organization of the glass improvement industry in England. *E. A. Beech, M.Sc. 1940 London, External Degree*

The history of the Midland glass industry, with special reference to the flint glass section. *D. N. Sandilands, M.Com. 1927 Birmingham*

Glass, Stained and Painted
Medieval painted glass in England, 1170-1501. *P. Nelson, Ph.D. 1930 Liverpool*

Globe Theatre, The
The Globe and the Romantic tendency. *T. R. Davies, M.A. 1904 Wales*

Gloucester, Diocese of
The administration of the diocese of Gloucester, 1547-79. *F. D. Price, B.Litt. 1940 Oxford*

Gloucestershire
The economic geography of Gloucestershire. *S. L. Hockey, M.A. 1935 Bristol*

The scarplands of the Wiltshire-Gloucestershire-Somerset borders: a regional study, with particular reference to urban and rural settlement. *I. G. Youldon, M.A. 1945 London, King's College*

Gloux, Olivier
See Aimard, G.

Glyndwr, Owen
The religious and social condition of Wales at the outbreak of the Glyndwr movement, with special reference to the attitude of the clergy, both regular and secular, to the movement. *J. R. Gabriel, M.A. 1906 Wales*

The Welsh Church and Welsh politics in the war of Owen Glyndwr. *J. T. Davies, M.A. 1920 Liverpool*

Gnosticism
The conception of redemption in the gnostic theologies of the first and second centuries. *J. B. Corston, Ph.D. 1938 Edinburgh*

Diaspora Judaism and syncretism, with special reference to the question of the origins of Gnosticism. *R. McL. Wilson, Ph.D. 1946 Cambridge*

Irenaeus and Gnosticism. *A. D. Livingstone, Ph.D. 1934 Edinburgh*

Marcion and his influence. *E. C. Blackman, B.D. 1947 Cambridge*

Gobineau, Joseph Arthur de, Comte
Le Comte Arthur Joseph de Gobineau: souvenirs. *Nı Mháille, M.A. 1945 National University of Ireland*

The novels and short stories of the Conte de Gobineau. *E. Noble, Ph.D. 1931 Dublin, Trinity College*

A study of the literary works of the Comte de Gobineau. *I. M. Beveridge, M.A. 1923 London*

God
See also Holy Spirit; Jesus Christ; Kingdom of God; Logos; Trinity, The.

Akhenaten and the growth and development of monotheism in Hebrew prophecy: a comparison and a survey. *R. K. Spedding, M.A. 1932 Liverpool*

Anthropomorphism and science: a study of the development of ejective cognition in the individual and the race. *O. A. Wheeler, D.Sc. 1916 London*

The arguments for the unity of God in medieval Jewish philosophy. *B. Cherrick, M.A. 1937 Manchester*

Aspects of the idea of God in western thought. *A. J. Badcock, M.A. 1949 Liverpool*

Aspects of the nineteenth century quest for God as reflected in the works of Thomas Hardy, Robert Browning and Francis Thompson. *A. M. Granville, M.A. 1950 Wales*

Cardinal Gerdil and ontologism. *M. J. Conlon, M.A. 1924 National University of Ireland*

Cause, value and God. *T. A. Burkill, Ph.D. 1941 Manchester*

1. Christianity and pantheism. 2. The heavenly priesthood of our Lord. *H. R. Cavalier, B.D. 1906 Oxford*

Cicero's ideas on deity and universe. *W. V. Denard, B.Litt. 1948 Dublin, Trinity College*

1. A comparison of the idea of divine sonship in Pauline and Johannine theology. The origin of the title Κύριοσ as applied to our Lord in the New Testament. *P. R. Brinton, B.D. & D.D. 1922 Oxford*

The concept of monotheism in its historical manifestations. *G. Evans, M.A. 1924 Bristol*

The conception of creation considered in its bearing upon the relation of the finite individual to God. *M. E. Clarke, M.A. 1920 London*

1. The conception of personality in relation to the present outlook and to the Christian doctrine of God. 2. Intercommunion and Christian reunion. *E. A. Burroughs, B.D. & D.D. 1921 Oxford*

God contd.

The contemplation of supersensible being in Plato's writings, compared with the apprehension of God through Christ in the writings of St. Paul. *A. Bairactaris, B.Litt. 1944 Oxford*

The content of our natural knowledge of God in the philosophy of St. Thomas Aquinas. *E. Quinn, M.A. 1948 Leeds*

A critical study of John Locke's examination of Père Malebranche's opinion of seeing all things in God. *C. G. Jones, M.A. 1949 Wales*

The day of Jahweh and some relevant problems. *L. Černý, B.Litt. 1944 Oxford*

De summi numinis existentia. *J. Sherman, M.A. 1716 Glasgow*

1. The development of Hebrew monotheism. 2. The prophecies of Amos. *H. Jones, B.D. 1924 Oxford*

Difficulties in the conception of an infinite God. *W. Powell, M.A. 1910 Wales*

1. The divine fatherhood. 2. The Apostles' Creed. *K. D. Knowles, B.D. & D.D. 1924 Oxford*

'Divine personality', studied in the light of recent tendencies in philosophy and theology. *R. Adams, Ph.D. 1946 Dublin, Trinity College*

Divine power: being a historical study based on Sanskrit texts. *S. K. Das, Ph.D. 1925 London*

1. The doctrine of immortality in the Old Testament. 2. Development of the doctrine of the fatherhood of God in the Old and New Testaments. *G. H. B. Wright, B.D. 1891 Oxford*

1. The doctrine of the being and nature of God. 2. The Incarnation of our Lord. *T. A. Chapman, B.D. 1907 Oxford*

The doctrine of the Godhead in St.Gregory Nazianzen, with special reference to its Trinitarian and Christological aspects. *D. Martynowski, B.Litt. 1939 Oxford*

The doctrine of the knowledge of God. *T. H. L. Baker, B.D. 1950 Cambridge*

The doctrines of God and freedom in the philosophy of Spinoza. *W. Madgen, M.A. 1928 Liverpool*

Does man aspire naturally to the vision of God?. *P. K. Bastable, Ph.D. 1945 National University of Ireland*

The elements in early Christianity, down to the end of the fourth century, which helped to prepare the way for later Christian intolerance, and the relation of these elements to the early Christian conception of God as love. *L. A. Garrard, B.D. 1935 Oxford*

Ethical monotheism in Israel before Amos. *L. P. Penn, B.D. & D.D. 1924 Oxford*

The evolution of the idea of God. *A. M. Chirgwin, M.A. 1921 Bristol*

An examination of Hume's treatment of the problems of divine existence and providence. *R. J. Tree, B.Litt. 1941 Oxford*

Expositions of: St. John xx.30, 31: the purpose and plan of the fourth Gospel; Romans 1.17: the righteousness of God; Ephesians 1.22,23. *W. H. G. Thomas, D.D. 1906 Oxford*

The fear of God: a study of the fear of God in the Christian religion. *R. F. Miller, Ph.D. 1930 Edinburgh*

1. God: Creator, Redeemer, Sanctifier. 2. Gehenna. *E. H. Cross, B.D. & D.D. 1890 Oxford*

God and creatures in the philosophy of St. Thomas Aquinas and A. N. Whitehead. *W. A. Whitehouse, B.Litt. 1940 Oxford*

1. God and the world. 2. The cultus of the Sacred Heart in light of the hypostatic union. *W. Farrar, B.D. 1895 Oxford*

God the absolute. *T. G. Dunning, Ph.D. 1926 Glasgow*

The holiness of God in John Calvin and Rudolph Otto. *W. M. Elliot, Ph.D. 1938 Edinburgh*

1. Holy Scripture: the rule of faith. 2. 'I believe in one God'. *D. M. Owen, B.D. 1877 Oxford*

1. 'I believe in one God'. 2. 'I look for the resurrection of the dead'. *T. H. Stokoe, B.D. 1871 Oxford*

The idea of God as expounded in the works of James and Ritschl. *R. Richards, M.A. 1921 Wales*

The idea of God in Descartes, Spinoza and Leibniz. *M. A. Davies, M.A. 1935 Wales*

The idea of God in the philosophy of William James and James Ward. *S. J. Theodore, B.Litt. 1925 Oxford*

God contd.

The idea of God in the philosophy of Fichte. *J. G. Slevin, M.A. 1939 National University of Ireland*

The idea of God, with special reference to James and Ritschl. *R. Richards, B.Litt. 1921 Oxford*

The idea of the Deity in primitive thought. *E. A. Hunt, M.A. 1939 Leeds*

The idea of the fear of God in the Old and New Testaments. *T. J. Lander, M.A. 1938 Bristol*

The image of God in man: an enquiry into the doctrine of human nature. *L. J. Carter, D.D. 1943 Durham*

Immanence. *W. L. Jones, M.A. 1930 Wales*

The immanence of God in Rabbinical literature. *J. Abelson, M.A. 1909 London*

The immutability of God. *J. W. A. Howe, B.D. 1948 Durham*

The impassibility of God. *J. K. Mosley, D.D. 1926 Cambridge*

The indwelling God. *E. C. Dewick, B.D. 1938 Cambridge*

The influence of anthropomorphism upon the Christian view of God, and the world. *W. F. Phillips, B.Litt. 1911 Oxford*

1. Internal evidences of revelation in Holy Scripture. 2. The immutability of God. *C. H. Golding-Bird, B.D. 1908 Oxford*

Jahweh, the God of love: a study in Old Testament theology. *R. M. Perry, Ph.D. 1937 Edinburgh*

John Calvin's doctrine of the sovereignty of God. *R. T. L. Liston, Ph.D. 1930 Edinburgh*

1. The justice of the atonement. 2. The omnipresence of God and eschatology. *E. Lang, B.D. & D.D. 1908 Oxford*

The justification of God. *A. R. Ankers, M.A. 1943 Bristol*

Kant's conception of God in its metaphysical development, together with a translation of the *Nova Dilucidatio*. *F. E. England, Ph.D. 1928 London*

Karl Heim's conception of the approach to knowledge of God. *T. E. Hill, Ph.D. 1937 Edinburgh*

1. The leading methods of Old Testament prophecy. 2. The teaching of the prophets in regard to Jehovah's relation to Israel. *G. W. Wade, B.D. & D.D. 1901 Oxford*

Lotze's conception of divine personality. *M. Davies, M.A. 1910 London*

Man's knowledge of God as treated by St. Thomas Aquinas. *R. L. Patterson, Ph.D. 1933 London, University College*

1. The meaning of the word κύριοσ in the Septuagint and in the New Testament. 2. The prophet of Israel in his relation to God. *A. Ashton, B.D. 1909 Oxford*

Monotheistic ideas in Hebrew Wisdom literature and their influence on early Christianity. *E. C. Burleigh, M.A. 1950 Bristol*

1. The nature and being of God. 2. The doctrine of the sacraments as 'effective signs of grace'. *E. G. Burr, B.D. & D.D. 1909 Oxford*

The nature and development of the idea of God as held by the primitive peoples of central Africa. *V. G. Ispir, B.Sc. 1914 Oxford*

The nature and knowledge of God (or the Absolute) in the philosophy of Plotinus. *J. P. Murray, Ph.D. 1928 London*

1. On anthropomorphism in Scripture and doctrine. 2. On seven new homilies of Macarias. *G. L. Marriott, B.D. 1918 Oxford*

1. On the existence of God. 2. On the sufficiency of Holy Scripture for salvation. *R. Martin, B.D. & D.D. 1886 Oxford*

1. On the subservience of evil to the purposes of God. 2. On the office of the Holy Spirit as the perfector of the works of God the Father. *G. H. West, B.D. & D.D. 1889 Oxford*

The ontological argument. *R. P. Anschutz, Ph.D. 1928 Edinburgh*

The ontological proof of the existence of God in modern philosophy from Descartes to Kant. *G. H. Langley, M.A. 1909 London*

Origin of belief in one God in the Greek world. *C. R. King, M.A. 1932 London, Birkbeck College*

Pantheism in English poetry, with special reference to Wordsworth and Shelley. *J. I. Wensley, M.A. 1917 Wales*

The pantheism of Spinoza. *W. Keogh, M.A. 1930 National University of Ireland*

God contd.

Philosophical proofs of the existence of God. *J. B. Raju, B.Sc. 1914 Oxford*

1. The place of the ark in the religious thought of the early Israelites. 2. The revelation of Yahweh in tradition and history. *M. W. Myres, B.D. & D.D. 1924 Oxford*

Plato's idea of God and the soul in their mutual relations. *C. Dunsby, M.A. 1912 Birmingham*

Proofs of the being of God. *H. Roberts, M.A. 1921 Wales*

A psychological study of the origins of monotheism. *A. I. Allenby, D.Phil. 1949 Oxford*

Ramanuja's conception of the Deity. *B. Kumarappa, Ph.D. 1930 London, School of Oriental and African Studies*

The relation of the concepts of immanence and personality. *J. E. H. Thomas, M.A. 1920 Liverpool*

The relation of the human soul to God in Hinduism and Christianity. *P. B. Means, B.Litt. 1923 Oxford*

The relation of thought to existence in Anselm's statement of the ontological argument. *A. E. Davies, M.A. 1918 London*

The righteousness of God in the conception of St. Paul, with special reference to the Epistle to the Romans. *D. D. MacBryde, Ph.D. 1943 Edinburgh*

Schleiermacher's idea of God. *M. U. Conditt, Ph.D. 1923 Edinburgh*

1. The scope and method of rational theology. 2. The proof of the being of God. *H. J. Bidder, B.D. 1877 Oxford*

Sources of theory of 'Lordship and grace'. *W. Salmon, M.A. 1934 National University of Ireland*

A study in divine immanence in man. *F. H. Allen, B.D. 1944 Oxford*

The study of apprehension of deity from the psychological and epistemological point of view. *E. F. B. Moore, Ph.D. 1944 Dublin, Trinity College*

A study of some of the philosophical grounds for the rejection of the idea of God by recent humanism. *A. H. Dakin, D.Phil. 1938 Oxford*

Thou who art. *J. A. T. Robinson, Ph.D. 1946 Cambridge*

1. The tradition, chronology, and prophecy of the Old Testament coincident with the history of the world. 2. The infinite Creator of immortal man. *H. T. Craig, B.D. 1886 Oxford*

The vision of God in St. Augustine and Malebranche: a comparison. *D. Connell, M.A. 1947 National University of Ireland*

1. The witness of the Old Testament to the immanence of God in nature and in man. 2. The theology of the Pastoral Epistle. *W. H. Fremantle, B.D. & D.D. 1895 Oxford*

Godolphin, Sidney, 1st Earl of
An edition of the poems of Sidney Godolphin. *W. Dighton, B.Litt. 1927 Oxford*

Gods
See also Mythology; Religion: Ancient and Primitive; and Apollo; Até; Fortuna; Isis; Mars; etc.

Aurelius Prudentius Clemens *Contra Symmachum*, Books I-II, including introduction, translation, commentary, bibliography, together with translation of Symmachus' third *Relatio* and St. Ambrose's reply. *K. Harrison, Ph.D. 1935 Dublin, Trinity College*

Foreign deities worshipped in Israel in the period of the monarchy: their character and origin. *C. H. Phillips, M.A. 1938 Wales*

The psychological role of the mother in the origin of the religious sentiment: a psychological study of mother-goddess cults, with special reference to India. *G. D. Boaz, D.Phil. 1942 Oxford*

The relation between corn-gods and other world deities. *S. R. Burstein, M.A. 1924 Wales*

The underworld and its deities in the Ras Shamra texts. *W. F. Fleet, M.A. 1938 Manchester*

Godwin, William
The economics and political theory of William Godwin and his debt to French thinkers. *H. K. Prescot, D.Phil. 1931 Oxford*

The influence of William Godwin on Shelley. *H. P. Kingston, M.A. 1932 Birmingham*

A life of William Godwin. *F. K. Brown, D.Phil. 1925 Oxford*

The novels of William Godwin. *C. E. L. Land, M.A. 1938 Birmingham*

William Godwin: his life, work and influences. *M. K. White, M.A. 1921 Sheffield*

Godwin, William contd.
William Godwin, philosopher and man of letters. *M. R. Williams, M.A. 1923 Bristol*

Goethe, Johann Wolfgang von
Alchemical symbolism in Goethe's scientific and literary works. *R. D. Gray, Ph.D. 1949 Cambridge*

Contemporary English opinion of Goethe as a dramatic poet. *T. H. Adams, M.A. 1908 Birmingham*

The female characters in Grillparzer's drama, as contrasted with those in Goethe's and Schiller's. *A. V. Burgess, M.A. 1907 Wales*

Goethe and Hauptmann: comparative study. *W. Airston, M.A. 1914 Birmingham*

Goethe as a political thinker. *G. F. Beckh, M.A. 1918 Bristol*

Goethe's influence on Byron and Scott. *M. J. Roberts, M.A. 1915 Wales*

Goethe's knowledge of English literature. *J. Boyd, B.Litt. 1923 Oxford*

Goethe's knowledge of English literature. *M. S. Woolf, M.A. 1907 Birmingham*

Goethe's knowledge of French literature. *B. Barnes, B.Litt. 1926 Oxford*

Hans Carossa and the Goethean tradition. *P. Mecklenburg, Ph.D. 1944 National University of Ireland*

Joy and sorrow and the like in the poetic language of Klopstock, Schiller and Goethe. *A. Schwarzchild, Ph.D. 1940 Edinburgh*

Some aspects of Goethe's *Pandora*. *M. L. Goodbody, M.A. 1938 Bristol*

The theme of 'Bildung' in *Wilhelm Meister*, and the moral and religious teaching of the early Carlyle to 1843. *G. F. Senior, M.A. 1950 Manchester*

Thoman Mann's writings on Goethe (with special reference to his novel *Lotte in Weimar*. *R. W. E. Weil, B.Litt. 1950 Dublin, Trinity College*

Thomas Mann's relation to Goethe and its significance for his own development. *H. Eichner, Ph.D. 1949 London, University College*

Wilhelm Meister's Wanderjahre; a critical re-examination and re-valuation. *R. Lissau, M.A. 1941 London, University College*

Goff, Thomas
The tragedies of Thomas Goff. *K. Blythe, M.A. 1940 Sheffield*

Gold
History of the theory of international gold movements. *F. I. Shaffner, B.Litt. 1928 Oxford*

International gold movements. *H. Lal, Ph.D. 1949 London, School of Economics and Political Science*

The theory of gold supply with special reference to the problems of the Witwatersrand. *W. J. Busschau, D.Phil. 1936 Oxford*

Gold Coast
See also Ashanti, The; Ga, The.

The balance of external payments of the Gold Coast for the fiscal years 1936-37 to 1938-39. *J. Mars, M.A. 1942 Bristol*

British policy in relation to the Gold Coast, 1815-1850. *P. G. James, M.A. 1935 London, King's College*

The English establishments on the Gold Coast in the second half of the eighteenth century. *E. C. Martin, M.A. 1921 London*

The Gold Coast, a geographical study. *W. J. Dyer, M.A. 1934 Bristol*

Gold Standard
Controversies about the gold standard, 1921-1932: a critical survey of the international literature. *E. Knobloch, M.Sc. 1935 London, School of Economics and Political Science*

The effect of the breakdown of the international gold standard on India. *R. Doraiswamy, M.Sc. 1937 London, School of Economics and Political Science*

Federal Reserve gold policy, 1921-32, and the working of the gold standard. *A. Hayes, B.Litt. 1933 Oxford*

The gold standard. *C. R. Curtis, M.Sc. 1933 London, External Degree*

The gold standard in South Africa, a gold-producing country, 1920-34. *E. M. Walton, B.Litt. 1943 Oxford*

Golding, Arthur
Arthur Golding's translation of Ovid's *Metamorphoses*. *E. M. W. Hovell, M.A. 1909 London*

Goldoni, Carlo
Goldoni and Gozzi. *V. M. F. M. A. Rudnyánszky de Dezsar, B.Litt. 1941 Dublin, Trinity College*

L'oeuvre française de Carlo Goldoni. *E. R. Lloyd, M.A. 1938 Manchester*

Goldsmith, Oliver
Oliver Goldsmith as essayist and critic. *F. O. Matthiessen, B.Litt. 1925 Oxford*

Gong Languages
A comparative study of some Central African gong-languages. *J. F. Carrington, Ph.D. 1946 London, External Degree*

Góngora y Argote, Luis de
Don Luis de Góngora. *J. E. Doyle, M.A. 1929 National University of Ireland*

Gontier, de Soignies
A critical edition of the poems of Gontier de Soignies. *C. H. Royle, B.Litt. 1937 Oxford*

Gonzalo, de Berceo
See Berceo, G. de.

Googe, Barnabe
Barnabe Googe. *M. Nacnab, M.A. 1918 London*

Gordon, Charles George
The mission of General Gordon in the Sudan, 18 January, 1884-26 January 1885. *M. F. Shukry, M.A. 1937 Liverpool*

Gordon, George, Lord
The causes of Anti-Romanist fanaticism in Great Britain in the eighteenth century, with special reference to the Lord George Gordon Riots. *K. Morris, M.A. 1926 Wales*

The Gordon riots, 1780. *L. H. Thraves, M.A. 1910 Liverpool*

Gorham, George Cornelius
A history of the controversy raised by the Reverend George Cornelius Gorham in the year 1846, and following years, in so far as it bore upon the subject of the efficacy of baptism; with a study of the pamphlets on this subject put out about this time, and an attempt to classify the doctrines of baptism expressed therein. *J. C. S. Nias, B.D. 1945 Oxford*

Gospels
See Bible: New Testament.

Gothic Language
Some aspects of the work of the Anglo-Latin twelfth century satirists: the loan words in Gothic, with some account of the pronunciation of that language. *E. P. Bates, M.A. 1910 London*

Goulburn, Henry
The political career of Henry Goulburn, 1784-1856. *W. J. Stranz, M.Litt. 1950 Durham*

Gourmont, Rémy de
A contribution to the study of the ideas of Rémy de Gourmont. *J. E. White, Ph.D. 1934 London, University College*

A study of Rémy de Gourmont as a literary critic, with special reference to his connection with the Symbolist Movement in French poetry from 1885-1900. *G. Rees, M.A. 1937 Wales*

Government, Local
See Local Government.

Government, Systems of
See also Authority; Federalism; Political Theory; Sovereignty.

The idea of government during the Puritan rebellion. *W. O'Brien, M.A. 1929 Liverpool*

Popular ideas concerning government during the latter half of the seventeenth century. *S. M. E. Trood, D.Litt. 1932 London, External Degree*

A study of devolution, with special reference to the government of Northern Ireland. *P. N. S. Mansergh, D.Phil. 1936 Oxford*

The theories of Cardinal Pierre d'Ailly concerning forms of government in Church and State with special reference to his interest in suggestions made by William of Occam. *A. E. Roberts, M.A. 1931 London, Bedford College*

Theory of government in ancient India. *B. Prasad, Ph.D. 1926 London*

Govindadāsa
An edition of the unpublished Maithili ms., the *Padavali* of Govindadasa, with an analysis of its grammar and phonology. *S. Jha, Ph.D. 1934 London, School of Oriental and African Studies*

Gower
Gower: a regional study, with special reference to agricultural geography. *W. A. Evans, M.A. 1948 Wales*

Gower contd.
The physical anthropology of the Gower Peninsula, studied in correlation with its settlements, archaeology, folklore and placenames. *C. H. Davies, M.A. 1927 Wales*

A survey of the manor in seventeenth century Gower. *G. H. Eaton, M.A. 1936 Wales*

Gower, John
The attitude of Chaucer towards chivalry, the Church and the people, compared with that of Langland, Wycliffe and Gower. *J. F. Evans, M.A. 1911 Wales*

The influence of Chaucer, Gower, and Lydgate on the Scottish poets in the fifteenth and early sixteenth centuries. *P. W. Thomson, B.Litt. 1915 Oxford*

Goya y Lucientes, Francisco José de
The followers of Goya. *E. E. Harris, Ph.D. 1934 London, University College*

Gozzi, Carlo, Conte
Goldoni and Gozzi. *V. M. F. M. A. Rudnyánszky de Dezsar, B.Litt. 1941 Dublin, Trinity College*

Gracchus, Gaius Sempronius
The legislation of Caius Gracchus considered especially in relation to the Order of the Equites. *G. A. Le Chavetois, M.A. 1912 London*

Grace
The antecedents and meaning of the modern evangelical conception of grace. *H. D. Gray, Ph.D. 1935 Edinburgh*

1. Christ descended into hell. 2. After we have received the Holy Ghost, we may depart from grace given, and fall into sin, and by the grace of God we may arise again, and amend our lives. *J. W. Caldicott, B.D. & D.D. 1874 Oxford*

The doctrine of grace: historically and dogmatically considered. *E. Jauncey, D.D. 1940 Durham*

The doctrine of grace as illustrated by the experience and teaching of St. Paul, Augustine, and Luther. *R. L. Child, B.Litt. 1925 Oxford*

An examination of Mozley's treatment of the Augustinian doctrines of grace and pre-destination. *T. O. Davies, B.Litt. 1925 Oxford*

Expositions of St. John i.1-18: the prologue; St. John xviii.33-38: within the praetorium; Ephesians i.1-14: the doctrine of grace. *H. T. Dixon, D.D. 1908 Oxford*

1. Grace and free will in reference to the language of Scripture and to some later theories. 2. The Epistle to the Galatians. *C. Bigg, B.D. & D.D. 1876 Oxford*

Grace and freewill in St. Paul and St. Augustine. *S. Y. Yovanovitch, B.Litt. 1920 Oxford*

Karl Barth's conception of grace and its place in his theology. *H. Hirschwald, D.Phil. 1945 Oxford*

1. The kingdom of God. 2. The biblical and Augustinian use of the term 'grace'. *C. Knapp, B.D. 1902 Oxford*

The problem of the will considered with special reference to the English school of idealists and the relation of their conclusions briefly to the doctrine of grace. *C. R. Batten, M.A. 1927 London*

A re-examination of the apparent antithesis between the theological doctrine of grace and the ethical doctrine of the categorical imperative. *J. E. Davies, B.Litt. 1944 Oxford*

Sources of theory of 'Lordship and grace'. *W. Salmon, M.A. 1934 National University of Ireland*

1. A study of the first Epistle of St. Peter in its relation to the Apostle's character and history. 2. The action of divine grace through distinctive channels of human personality. *W. K. Fleming, B.D. 1909 Oxford*

1. The theology of Gregory the Great. 2. Gregory's doctrine of man and the means of grace. *F. H. Dudden, B.D. 1903 Oxford*

Gracián, Baltasar
Aspects of the style of the *Criticón* of Baltasar Gracián with reference to the theories of his *Agudeza y arte de ingenio*. *T. E. May, M.A. 1937 Manchester*

A contribution to the study of the influence of Baltasar Gracián (1601 to 1658), with an index to the moral ideas of the *Criticón* and to the aesthetic ideas of the *Agudeza* with a complete bibliography of Gracianism. *E. Sarmiento, Ph.D. 1931 London, King's College*

Grafton, Augustus Henry Fitzroy, 3rd Duke of
The Duke of Grafton. *G. M. Imlach, M.A. 1914 Liverpool*

Graham, James, Sir
Sir James Graham as politician and Home Secretary, 1818-46. *D. W. J. Johnson, B.Litt. 1948 Oxford*

Grail, The Holy
The old French prose romance *L'estoire del Saint Graal* and its relation to Robert de Borron's poem *Le roman de l'estoire dou Graal. S. M. Scott, M.A. 1935 Manchester*

Stair an Naoimhghréadhla; aistriúchán (A translation of *Stair an Naoimhghréadhla*). *L. O'hUigın, M.A. 1939 National University of Ireland*

Grammar
See Language.

Grammar Schools
See Education, Secondary.

Grampound
The parliamentary representation of Grampound. *R. C. D. Jasper, M.A. 1940 Leeds*

Grand Tour
See Voyages and Travels.

Granville, George, Lord Lansdowne
A critical study of George Granville, Lord Lansdowne. *F. E. Handasyde, B.Litt. 1931 Oxford*

Granville-Barker, Harley
Experiments in technique: a study of the plays of Harley Granville Barker. *E. I. Smith, M.A. 1948 Liverpool*

Grassland
The economic possibilities of the northern and eastern savannas. *A. Fairgrieve, M.A. 1924 Liverpool*

An economic survey of a grazing district in the Welland Valley. *J. L. Davies, M.Sc. 1927 Wales*

An economic survey of the management and utilization of grassland in Great Britain. *J. Pearce, Ph.D. 1950 Reading*

The economics of production on grass and arable farms. *H. J. Vaughan, B.Sc. 1924 Oxford*

The structure and development of the brush-prairie of the White Earth Indian Reservation. *J. Ewing, D.Sc. 1916 Aberdeen*

Grates
A history of the domestic grate. *J. P. H. Curnin, M.Sc. 1934 London, University College*

Graunz Jaianz, De
A critical edition of *De Graunz Jaianz. G. E. Brereton, B.Litt. 1930 Oxford*

Graves, Richard
Richard Graves (1715-1804). *R. Hook, M.A. 1935 London, King's College*

Gray, Thomas
Gray and romanticism. *D. Williams, M.A. 1907 Wales*

Great Britain
For counties, towns, etc., see under their names.

Great Britain: Armed Forces
See also Barham, C. M., Lord; Maitland, T., Sir; Saint Vincent, J. J., Earl; Wilson, R. T., Sir.

The adhesion of the Royal Navy to Parliament at the outbreak of the Civil War. *I. G. Powell, M.A. 1919 London*

The administration of the navy in the reign of Edward III. *R. M. Hedley, M.A. 1922 Manchester*

The Anglo-French and Anglo-Belgian military and naval conversations from the *Entente* to the Great War. *D. C. Wadman, M.A. 1939 Wales*

The army 1815-54 as an institution: to be considered as regards the administration, organization, composition, and its relations to the political and social conditions of the country. *M. F. Cunliffe, B.Litt. 1947 Oxford*

The battles of King Edward I. *J. R. Richards, M.A. 1914 Wales*

The British navy and the Anglo-American war of 1812-1815. *K. S. Dent, M.A. 1949 Leeds*

Colonial Admiralty jurisdiction in the seventeenth century. *H. J. Crump, Ph.D. 1930 London, King's College*

The defence of the north-west border of England against the Scots in the first half of the fourteenth century. *T. Wood, M.A. 1937 Manchester*

The development of Portsmouth as a naval base as illustrating the growth of British naval policy. *H. J. Sparks, M.A. 1911 London*

The development of the British Army, 1899 to 1914. *J. K. Dunlop, Ph.D. 1936 London, Queen Mary College*

Great Britain: Armed Forces contd.
Education and the army. *S. T. R. Hancock, M.Ed. 1949 Manchester*

Educational experience in the present war-time army and its bearing on national problems of education. *E. F. Wilson, M.Ed. 1944 Leeds*

English naval administration at the close of the seventeenth century. *K. W. Wood, M.A. 1935 Leeds*

The English Navy during the Revolution of 1688 and its condition at the commencement of the reign of William III and Mary. *E. B. Powley, B.Litt. 1925 Oxford*

The history of education in the British army up to 1939. *T. H. Hawkins, M.Ed. 1945 Leeds*

A history of the English forces employed in Ireland, 1641-1649. *H. Hazlett, M.A. 1935 Belfast*

A history of the military forces operating in Ireland, 1641-1649. *H. Hazlett, Ph.D. 1938 Belfast*

The influence of topographical conditions on the English campaigns in Wales in the twelfth and thirteenth centuries. *D. W. Rees, M.A. 1923 Wales*

Life in the British Army in relation to social conditions. *T. H. McGuffie, M.A. 1940 London, King's College*

The Lords Commissioners of the Admiralty, 1689-1714. *G. F. James, M.A. 1937 Birmingham*

Maritime activity under Henry VII. *W. E. C. Harrison, M.A. 1931 London, King's College*

Military system of Edward III. *A. E. Prince, B.Litt. 1929 Oxford*

Naval administration 1603-1628. *N. Clayton, Ph.D. 1935 Leeds*

The naval chaplain in Stuart times. *W. F. Scott, D.Phil. 1935 Oxford*

Naval construction in the reign of James I. *M. Exley, M.A. 1949 Leeds*

Naval developments under Henry VIII. *W. H. Sankey, M.A. 1926 Manchester*

The navy under the early Stuarts and its influence on English history. *C. D. Penn, M.A. 1913 London*

The organization and administration of the Elizabethan foreign military expeditions, 1585-1603. *C. G. Cruickshank, D.Phil. 1940 Oxford*

Plymouth Dock: a survey of the development of the Royal Dockyard in Hamoaze during the sailing ship era. *A. E. Stephens, Ph.D. 1940 London, Birkbeck College*

The principles of the treatment of ex-service men from the time of Elizabeth. *W. E. Passey, Dip.Soc.Sci. 1924 Liverpool*

The Select Committee of 1861 on colonial military expenditure and its antecedents. *M. G. Chappell, M.A. 1934 London, Westfield College*

Visual training in the Royal Navy during the war years: an historical and critical study. *G. Halliday, M.Ed. 1950 Manchester*

The Welsh soldier in England's armies of the thirteenth and fourteenth centuries. *T. L. Williams, M.A. 1915 Wales*

Great Britain: Colonies and Dominions
See also Africa, West; Alberta; Australia; Bechuanaland; British Columbia; Canada; Falkland Islands; Fiji; Gibraltar; Gold Coast; India; Labrador; Malta; Natal; Newfoundland; Nova Scotia; Prince Edward Island; Rhodesia; Sierra Leone; South Africa; West Indies; and Clive, R., Baron Clive of Plassey; Cornwallis, C., 1st Marquis; Goulburn, H.; Hastings, W.; Maitland, T., Sir; Norris, W., Sir; Shore, J., Sir; Smith, H. G. W., Sir; Thurston, J. B., Sir.

The attitude of the Evangelicals to the Empire and imperial problems (1820-1850). *A. F. Madden, D.Phil. 1950 Oxford*

Britain's colonies in world trade. *F. Meyer, Ph.D. 1945 London, School of Economics and Political Science*

British colonial administration, 1841-52. *W. P. Morrell, D.Phil. 1927 Oxford*

The British Commonwealth and the United Nations. *C. C. Aikman, Ph.D. 1948 London, School of Economics and Political Science*

British imperial policy in relation to Madagascar, 1810-1896. *R. E. P. Wastell, Ph.D. 1944 London, King's College*

British opinion and colonial policy, 1783-1839, in particular, the origin of the ideas of the colonial reformers. *A. J. Weir, Ph.D. 1924 Edinburgh*

Great Britain: Colonies and Dominions contd.
British opinion on the development of the commonwealth of nations, 1895-1914. *F. S. Morley, Ph.D. 1932 Edinburgh*

British policy in relation to Portuguese claims in West Africa, 1876 to 1884. *I. Bains, M.A. 1940 London, Bedford College*

Chatham's colonial policy. *K. Hotblack, D.Sc. 1917 London*

Colonial Admiralty jurisdiction in the seventeenth century. *H. J. Crump, Ph.D. 1930 London, King's College*

The contribution of Wales to the British Empire in the sixteenth and seventeenth centuries. *W. A. Bebb, M.A. 1920 Wales*

The development of ideas as to the relations which should exist between the United Kingdom and the Dominions since the grant of responsible self-government. *H. D. Hall, B.Litt. 1920 Oxford*

The distribution of functions among central government departments in the United Kingdom, with some comparison of the United States of America and British dominions. *C. N. Yang, D.Phil. 1948 Oxford*

English colonization theories, 1830-1842, with special reference to the economic and political development of the Australian colonies. *R. C. Mills, D.Sc. 1915 London*

Financial integration within the British Empire. *A. S. J. Baster, M.Comm. 1930 London, School of Economics and Political Science*

The movement towards imperial preference in Great Britain and the self-governing dominions in recent years, with special reference to some aspects of empire marketing. *I. David, M.A. 1930 Wales*

Origin and growth of the protectorate system, with special study of the system as developed in British colonial history 1800 to 1848. *W. E. Philpott, M.A. 1934 London, King's College*

The Press and the colonies. *H. F. G. Tucker, M.A. 1936 Bristol*

The Reciprocity Treaty of 1854: its history, its relation to British colonial and foreign policy and to the development of Canadian fiscal autonomy. *D. C. C. Masters, D.Phil. 1935 Oxford*

The Royal instructions to colonial governors, 1783-1854: a study in British colonial policy. *J. C. Beaglehole, Ph.D. 1929 London*

Great Britain: Constitution
The administrative work of the Lord Chancellor in the early seventeenth century. *J. S. Wilson, Ph.D. 1927 London*

The common law in the sixteenth century. *J. F. Myers, M.A. 1950 Liverpool*

A comparative study of the offices of the Prime Minister of Great Britain and the President of the United States of America: a study in comparative political institutions. *T. F. Fan, M.Sc. 1933 London, School of Economics and Political Science*

Constitutional and diplomatic aspects of the ordinances of 1311. *M. H. Mills, M.A. 1912 London*

Constitutional aspects of the ministry of Lord North. *A. B. Archer, M.A. 1910 Liverpool*

The council under Henry IV. *P. G. Harvey, B.Litt. 1932 Oxford*

The English Cabinet. *Y. Yu, Ph.D. 1937 London, School of Economics and Political Science*

English constitutional history and political ideas from the death of Oliver Cromwell to the fall of Clarendon. *H. N. Mukerjee, B.Litt. 1933 Oxford*

English monarchy fifteenth to seventeenth century. *D. McCann, M.A. 1939 National University of Ireland*

The function and influence of privy councillors in Parliament in the early seventeenth century. *D. Keane, M.A. 1930 London, University College*

The Great Council in the fifteenth century. *T. F. T. Plucknett, M.A. 1917 London*

The jurisdiction of the Privy Council under the Tudors. *E. F. White, M.A. 1918 London*

The King's Secretary and the Signet Office in the fifteenth century. *A. J. Otway-Ruthven, Ph.D. 1937 Cambridge*

The office of Secretary of State, 1681-1782. *M. A. Thomson, D.Phil. 1931 Oxford*

A preliminary study of the chronicles and instruments for a constitutional history of the years 1296-1301 in England. *H. Rothwell, Ph.D. 1930 Cambridge*

Great Britain: Constitution contd.
The presidency of the U.S.A. and the premiership of Great Britain: a comparative study of patronage. *E. G. Ashcroft, M.Sc. 1946 London, School of Economics and Political Science*

The Privy Council under the Tudors. *G. E. Taylor, M.A. 1928 Birmingham*

The Radical attitude towards the Monarchy and the House of Lords, 1868-85. *E. G. Collieu, B. Litt. 1936 Oxford*

The relations of Sir Robert Peel with the Crown, 1837-46. *J. W. Horton, B.Litt. 1950 Oxford*

Some aspects of the King's household in the reign of Henry V, 1413-1422. *E. H. de L. Fagan, M.A. 1935 London, University College*

Studies in constitutional ideas in England during the fifteenth century. *S. B. Chrimes, Ph.D. 1933 Cambridge*

A study, mainly from royal Wardrobe accounts, of the nature and organization of the King's messenger service from the reign of John to that of Edward III inclusive. *M. C. Hill, M.A. 1939 London, Royal Holloway College*

A study of social and constitutional tendencies in the early years of Edward III, as illustrated more especially by the events connected with the ministerial enquiries of 1340, and the following years. *D. Hughes, M.A. 1913 London*

The Tudor Privy Council. *D. M. Gladish, M.A. 1915 London*

Under-Secretaries of State, 1755-1775. *L. Scott, M.A. 1950 Manchester*

Great Britain: Economic History
See also Customs and Excise; South Sea Bubble; and Huskisson, W.; Stewart, J., Sir; Tucker, J.

British policy in the North American cod fisheries with special reference to foreign competition, 1776-1819. *G. O. Rothney, Ph.D. 1939 London, King's College*

Budgetary policy, rates of interest, and company profits during the recovery period, 1932-1937. *C. Nuttall, Ph.D. 1940 Birmingham*

The causes and progress of the growth of economic individualism in England in the sixteenth and at the beginning of the seventeenth century. *H. M. Robertson, Ph.D. 1930 Cambridge*

The crisis of 1825. *E. Thomas, M.Sc. 1938 London, School of Economics and Political Science*

The economic policy of the Board of Trade, 1696-1714. *R. G. Mathias, B.Litt. 1939 Oxford*

Edward III's war finance, 1337-41: transactions in wool and credit operations. *E. B. Fryde, D.Phil. 1947 Oxford*

The effects produced by economic changes upon social life in England in the fifteenth century. *A. Abram, D.Sc. 1909 London*

The evolution of industries and settlements between Merthyr Tydfil and Abergavenny from 1740 to 1840. *C. Davies, M.A. 1949 Wales*

Financial and commercial policy under the Protectorate. *M. P. Ashley, D.Phil. 1933 Oxford*

The gold and silver thread monopolies granted by James I, 1611-1621. *M. A. Abrams, Ph.D. 1930 London, School of Economics and Political Science*

Home and foreign investment in Great Britain, 1870-1913. *A. K. Cairncross, Ph.D. 1936 Cambridge*

The industrial development of the Rhondda Valleys to 1910. *E. D. Lewis, M.A. 1940 Wales*

The industrial history of London (1630-1640), with special reference to the suburbs and those areas claiming exemption from the authority of the Lord Mayor. *J. L. Archer, M.A. 1934 London, School of Economics and Political Science*

Italian financiers of the fifteenth and sixteenth centuries with special reference to Pallavicino and Spinola and their share in Elizabethan finance. *B. Hall, M.Sc. 1928 London*

Manufactured Indian cotton goods in England and their influence on English economic history about 1680-1720. *P. J. Thomas, B.Litt. 1922 Oxford*

Mr. Gladstone's fiscal and financial policy, 1841 to 1845. *F. E. Hyde, Ph.D. 1931 London, School of Economics and Political Science*

The position of London in national affairs, 1658-1661, having special regard to political and economic aspects. *M. B. Weinstock, M.A. 1934 London, School of Economics and Political Science*

Great Britain: Economic History contd.
The problem of Anglo-French commercial rivalry in the reign of Charles II. *M. A. Priestley, B.Litt. 1949 Oxford*

Great Britain: Economics: Finance
See also Balance of Payments; Bank of England; Taxation; and Attwood, T.

British war finance for 12 months, April 1, 1940-April, 1941. *J. J. Byrne, M.A. 1941 National University of Ireland*

British wartime finance. *E. E. Cotton, M.Com.Sc. 1943 Belfast*

Budget studies and the measurement of living costs and standards. *E. A. Winslow, Ph.D. 1923 London*

Budgetary policy, with special reference to the trade cycle. *R. P. N. Poduval, Ph.D. 1940 London, University College*

The burden of British public debt. *O. V. Reddi, M.Sc. 1949 London, University College*

The creation and liquidation of public debt in the United Kingdom during the eighteenth and nineteenth centuries, economically and financially regarded. *C. P. Spruill, B.Litt. 1922 Oxford*

Current British payments agreements. *A. Vincent, M.Sc. 1947 London, School of Economics and Political Science*

The exchequer in the reign of Edward III, 1327-1377: a preliminary investigation. *D. M. Broome, Ph.D. 1923 Manchester*

The financial problems of Great Britain during the war 1939-1945, with special reference to Anglo-Egyptian financial relations. *A. A. F. Haikel, M.Comm. 1948 Leeds*

Financial reconstruction in England, 1815-1822. *A. W. Acworth, B.Litt. 1925 Oxford*

The financial relations between the Crown and the City of London in the reigns of Edward I to Henry VII (excluding Parliamentary taxation). *G. J. de C. Mead, M.A. 1936 London, King's College*

The financial relationship between Great Britain and Northern Ireland 1931 to 1945. *M. C. Mathur, M.Com.Sc. 1947 Belfast*

A history of the commercial and financial relations between England and Ireland from the period of the Revolution. *A. E. Murray, D.Sc. 1903 London*

The history of the public debts of the United Kingdom from 1815 to 1939, and the economic doctrine relating thereto. *R. O. Roberts, M.A. 1942 Wales*

Jewish finance in England, 1216-1290, with special reference to royal revenue. *P. Elman, M.A. 1935 London, School of Economics and Political Science*

1. The monastic wool trade of the thirteenth century. 2. The Italian bankers and the English Crown. *R. J. Whitwell, B.Litt. 1903 Oxford*

The powers of inquisition into and control over public finance exercised by the House of Commons, more especially by its committees. *F. B. Chubb, D.Phil. 1950 Oxford*

Public borrowing, 1649-1660, with special reference to government borrowing in the City of London between 1640 and 1650. *W. P. Harper, M.Sc. 1927 London*

Sir Stafford Northcote's sinking fund and the redemption of debt between 1874 and 1914. *P. C. Gordon Walker, B.Litt. 1930 Oxford*

The technique of government borrowing: a study of the methods employed by the British Treasury in its borrowing operations, 1914-39. *Y. C. Ma, Ph.D. 1942 London, School of Economics and Political Science*

Great Britain: Economics: Industry
See also Industrial Revolution.

Costing and prices in British industry. *C. C. Saxton, D.Phil. 1941 Oxford*

The costs of transport and the location of industry in Great Britain and Egypt. *A. A. A. Ismail, Ph.D. 1942 Birmingham*

The development of industry and trade in the Middle Severn Valley. *T. W. Birch, M.Sc. 1933 London, External Degree*

The development of the Tees-side industrial area. *R. Hewitt, M.Sc. 1940 London, University College*

The economic, industrial and social history of Ebbw Vale during the period 1775-1927, being a study in the origin and development of an industrial district of south Wales in all its aspects. *A. G. Jones, M.A. 1929 Wales*

Government and industry during the Protectorate (1653-8). *G. D. Ramsay, B.Litt. 1933 Oxford*

Great Britain: Economics: Industry contd.
The industrial competitive strength of the United Kingdom compared with that of some other industrial countries, with special reference to the post-war period. *I. M. Khan, Ph.D. 1932 Leeds*

The industrial development of Ashton-under-Lyne, 1780-1850. *F. Kenworthy, M.A. 1929 Manchester*

The industrial development of the Llynfi, Ogmore and Garw valleys, with special reference to transport facilities in the are. *T. Bevan, M.A. 1928 Wales*

The industrial development of Birmingham and the Black Country, 1860-1914. *G. C. Allen, Ph.D. 1928 Birmingham*

The industrial history of the Rhymney Valley, with regard to the iron, steel and tinplate industries, coal mining, lead mining, smelting and quarrying. *J. Davies, M.Sc. 1926 Wales*

The industrialization of Flintshire in the nineteenth century, being an examination of the changes and development in the principal industries from 1815 to 1914. *C. R. Williams, M.A. 1950 Wales*

The industries of the south of Russia and the competition with England. *S. B. Meyer, M.Com. 1910 Birmingham*

The integration of industry in the United States of America and Great Britain, with special reference to financial control and the capitalization of joint-stock companies. *H. A. Marquand, M.A. 1928 Wales*

The location of Britain's newer industries in the southeast and midlands. *M. C. Daly, M.Sc. 1944 Cambridge*

The modern tendency towards industrial combination in some spheres of British industry: its forms and developments, their causes and determinant circumstances. *G. R. Carter, M.A. 1911 Wales*

Present British Government policy with regard to the control of, and the assistance to, the private sector of industry. *P. G. A. Combaux, M.Sc. 1948 London, School of Economics and Political Science*

The problem of industrial restriction: a comparative study of industrial reorganization in the British basic industries, 1929-39. *A. Beacham, Ph.D. 1942 Belfast*

Profits in British industry from 1924 to 1935: an investigation into the profits made by certain public companies in Great Britain in the years from 1924 to 1935. *R. S. Hope, D.Phil. 1949 Oxford*

Sequence of movements of indices of industrial fluctuations in Great Britain (1885-1914 and 1919-1930). *J. R. H. Shaul, M.Sc. 1934 London, School of Economics and Political Science*

A survey of British industrial history, 1914-1921. *W. A. Orton, M.Sc. 1921 London*

Great Britain: Foreign Affairs
See also Gordon, C. G.; Russell, O., Lord; Wade, C., Sir.

British foreign policy, 1850-1871. *J. C. Kite, M.A. 1916 Birmingham*

British policy and opinion and the second Hague conference. *H. S. W. Corrigan, M.A. 1934 London, King's College*

The conduct of English diplomacy in the fourteenth century. *G. P. Cuttino, D.Phil. 1938 Oxford*

The effects of the Boer War on British diplomatic relations (1899-April, 1904). *R. Hughes, M.A. 1941 Wales*

European alliances and ententes, 1879-85: a study of contemporary British information. *A. Ramm, M.A. 1937 London, Bedford College*

The foreign policy of England from the peace of Nimeguen to the death of King Charles II. *J. W. Williams, B.Litt. 1910 Oxford*

The foreign policy of Wellington, 1828-30. *A. C. F. Beales, M.A. 1927 London*

The House of Commons and foreign policy between the first and second Reform Acts. *A. C. Turner, B.Litt. 1948 Oxford*

The importance of the Channel Islands in British relations with the Continent during the thirteenth and fourteenth centuries: a study in historical geography. *D. T. Williams, M.A. 1927 Wales*

The influence of Parliament upon the foreign policy of the Gladstone Government, 1868-74. *S. Lambert, M.A. 1949 London, Bedford College*

The mercantile aspect of English foreign policy during the reign of Charles II. *D. G. E. Hall, M.A. 1917 London*

Great Britain: Foreign Affairs: Netherlands contd.
The policies of Stanley, Granville, and Gladstone towards Luxemburg, Belgium, and Alsace-Lorraine, 1867-1871. *M. R. D. Foot, B.Litt. 1950 Oxford*

Relations between England and Flanders, 1603-1618. *N. Applegate, M.A. 1948 Leeds*

Great Britain: Foreign Affairs: Persia
Anglo-Persian relations, 1856-1907. *K. C. Cleak, M.A. 1938 Bristol*

Question of international law in Anglo-Iranian diplomatic relations. *A. A. Dehkan, Ph.D. 1938 London, School of Economics and Political Science*

The relations of Britain and Persia, 1800-1815. *S. F. Shadman, Ph.D. 1939 London, School of Economics and Political Science*

Great Britain: Foreign Affairs: Poland
Great Britain and the Polish Question, 1863. *W. F. F. Grace, Ph.D. 1925 Cambridge*

Great Britain: Foreign Affairs: Portugal
The attitude of the British Government to the Portuguese revolution of 1826-1834. *P. M. Cowell, M.A. 1927 London*

Great Britain: Foreign Affairs: Roman Catholic Church
Anglo-Papal relations, 1213-1216. *S. M. Whileblood, M.A. 1948 Manchester*

The English activities of Cardinal Ottobuono, Legate of the Holy See. *A. Lewis, M.A. 1937 Manchester*

The legation of Cardinal Otto, 1237-41. *D. M. Williamson, M.A. 1947 Manchester*

Relations of the British Government and the Roman Catholic Church in Ireland 1508-1829. *G. D. Sanderson, Ph.D. 1930 Dublin, Trinity College*

Great Britain: Foreign Affairs: Russia
Anglo-Russian relations and the formation of the Anglo-Russian Agreement, 1903-1907. *A. W. Hopkins, M.A. 1937 Wales*

Anglo-Russian relations from 1878-1885, with special reference to central Asia. *E. Jones, M.A. 1934 Wales*

British conceptions of Russia and Russian policy, 1837-41. *J. H. Gleason, B.Litt. 1932 Oxford*

Economic relations between England and Russia in the sixteenth century. *M. W. Smith, M.A. 1918 Wales*

Movements for Anglo-Russian reconciliation and alliance from March 1890 to December 1903. *H. H. Page, M.A. 1933 Birmingham*

The relations between Great Britain and Russia from 1848 to 1856. *A. R. Cooke, M.A. 1920 Birmingham*

The relations between Great Britain and Russia, 1870-1899. *A. E. Jones, M.A. 1917 Birmingham*

Great Britain: Foreign Affairs: Sardinia
Anglo-Sardinian relations: January, 1859-March, 1860. *M. Whibley, M.A. 1923 London*

Great Britain: Foreign Affairs: Savoy
The relations between James VI and I and Carlo Emanuele I, Duke of Savoy. *J. Thompson, Ph.D. 1942 Saint Andrew's*

Great Britain: Foreign Affairs: Scandinavia
Denmark and Britain. *R. A. Atkinson, M.Com.Sc. 1933 Belfast*

The position of England towards the Baltic powers, i.e. Denmark and Sweden including the Hanse towns, from 1689-1697. *M. Lane, M.A. 1911 London*

A study of the relations between England and the Scandinavian countries in the seventeenth century, based upon the evidence of acquaintance in English writers with Scandinavian languages, literatures, and myths. *M. E. Seaton, M.A. 1920 London*

Great Britain: Foreign Affairs: Serbia
Diplomatic relations between England and Serbia from the return of Milos to the death of Michael, 1859-1867. *E. F. Robinson, M.A. 1925 London*

Great Britain: Foreign Affairs: South Africa
The policy of the British Government towards the South African Dutch republics, 1848-1872. *C. W. de Kiewiet, Ph.D. 1927 London*

Great Britain: Foreign Affairs: Spain
Anglo-Spanish diplomatic and commercial relations, 1731-59. *J. O. McLachlan, Ph.D. 1937 Cambridge*

British policy and the Spanish marriages, 1841-1846. *E. J. Parry, Ph.D. 1934 London, School of Economics and Political Science*

Great Britain: Foreign Affairs: Spain contd.
The relations between Great Britain and the Spanish colonies, 1808-12. *A. I. Langnas, Ph.D. 1938 London, School of Economics and Political Science*

The significance of British policy towards Spain, 1859-68. *S. Doyle, M.A. 1949 London, Bedford College*

Great Britain: Foreign Affairs: Switzerland
English foreign policy during the reign of William III: in particular the relations of England with the Swiss Protestants. *L. A. Robertson, B.Litt. 1926 Oxford*

Great Britain: Foreign Affairs: United States
Anglo-American arbitration policies, 1890-1914. *O. Gollancz, Ph.D. 1940 Cambridge*

Anglo-American relations with regard to the Panama Canal project, 1897-1903. *S. P. Kramer, M.Litt. 1938 Cambridge*

Aspects of Anglo-American relations, 1899-1906. *L. M. Gelber, B.Litt. 1933 Oxford*

The British attitude towards the American Civil War. *C. I. Payne, M.A. 1928 Birmingham*

The British navy and the Anglo-American war of 1812-1815. *K. S. Dent, M.A. 1949 Leeds*

British policy in its relation to the commerce and navigation of the United States of America from 1794 to 1807. *W. H. Elkins, D.Phil. 1936 Oxford*

British public opinion on Anglo-American relations, 1805-1812. *D. R. Currie, Ph.D. 1935 Saint Andrew's*

A history of the development of British public opinion of Anglo-American relations, 1783-1794. *D. S. Reid, Ph.D. 1934 Saint Andrew's*

The reception of the American constitution in Britain, 1787-1848. *D. H. Pattinson, M.A. 1941 Birmingham*

The relations of Great Britain and the United States of America during the Spanish-American War of 1898. *H. Holroyde, M.A. 1947 Sheffield*

The relations of Great Britain and America, especially from 1861-1866. *E. E. Baker, M.A. 1920 Birmingham*

The slave trade and Anglo-American relations, 1807-1862. *A. T. Milne, M.A. 1930 London, University College*

Great Britain: Foreign Affairs: U.S.S.R
The Soviet Question in British politics. *C. G. Bolte, B.Litt. 1949 Oxford*

Great Britain: Geography
Contributions to the knowledge of the drainage, morphology and structure of the Wessex region of southern England. *D. L. Linton, M.Sc. 1930 London, King's College*

Early distribution and valleyward movement of population in south Britain; a relief model of Wales; climatology in correlation with geography; human geography in Britain. *W. E. Whitehouse, M.A. 1916 Wales*

French travellers in England from 1820 to 1830. *E. Jones, M.A. 1925 Wales*

The geographical determination of natural regions with special reference to the Welsh border. *J. E. Richards, B.Sc. 1930 Oxford*

The geographical reasons for the growth of the population of south Staffordshire, east Warwickshire and Leicestershire from 1801-1931. *G. M. Sarson, Ph.D. 1937 London, External Degree*

The historical geography (ancient) of Northamptonshire and the southeast Midlands. *S. B. Harris, M.Sc. 1945 London, External Degree*

Great Britain: History
See also Ireland: History; London; Scotland: History; Wales: History; and under particular counties, towns, etc.

Great Britain: History: General
The French invasions of England from the twelfth century to the nineteenth (1101-1860). *A. R. Rhys-Pryce, M.A. 1928 Belfast*

Researches in medical history, being an investigation into the causes of death of the kings of England from William I to William IV. *J. Rae, M.D. 1911 Aberdeen*

Great Britain: History: Early and Medieval
See also Charters; Chivalry; Crusades; Danes, The; Feudalism; Hundred Years' War; Kenilworth, Dictum of; Mercia; Saxons, The; Wessex; and Bacon, R.; Bede, the Venerable; Braose, W. de; Burgh, H. De-, Earl of Kent; Burnell, R.; Cornwall, Edmund, Earl of; Cornwall, Richard, Earl of; Edward I, King of England; Edward II, King of England; Edward III, King of England; Edward, the Black Prince; Edward, the Confes-

Great Britain: History: Early and Medieval contd.
sor, Saint, King of England; Gaveston, P.; Henry III, King of England; John, King of England; Montfort, S. de, Earl of Leicester; Neville, R., Bishop; Pembroke, William Marshal, 1st Earl of; Rivaux, P. de.

The Anglo-Norman *Chronicle* of Nicolas Trivet. *A. Rutherford, Ph.D. 1932 London, Birkbeck College*

Anglo-Saxon chronicles. *J. Murphy, Ph.D. 1931 National University of Ireland*

Baronial reform and rebellion, 1259-1267. *E. F. Jacob, Ph.D. 1924 Oxford*

The Black Death, 1348-49, with special reference to cathedral registers for the mortality of the clergy. *J. Lunn, Ph.D. 1931 Cambridge*

A collection of the acta of John, Lord of Ireland and Count of Mortain, with a study of his household. *M. Jones, M.A. 1949 Manchester*

Edward I as a foreign statesman. *H. Instein, B.Litt. 1933 Oxford*

The English in the South of France from the accession of Henry III to the death of the Black Prince. *N. L. Frazer, M.A. 1906 London*

The enquiry into complaints against the ministers of Eleanor of Castile (1291-1292), its administrative and legal significanc. *M. E. Fenwick, M.A. 1931 London, Royal Holloway College*

The financing and organization of the household of the Queens of England during the first part of the fourteenth century. *A. M. Best, M.A. 1916 London*

The great roll of the pipe for the ninth year of the reign of King Richard the first, Michaelmas 1197 (pipe roll 43) now first typed from the original in the custody of the Master of the Rolls. *H. M. Grace, M.A. 1929 Reading*

The great roll of the pipe for the ninth year of the reign of King John, Michaelmas, 1207 (pipe roll 53). *A. M. Kirkus, M.A. 1942 Reading*

The great roll of the pipe for the seventh year of the reign of King John, Michaelmas 1205. *S. Smith, Ph.D. 1937 Reading*

Henry V as conqueror in France, and the Lancastrian experiment in Normandy. *E. Wragg, M.A. 1916 Birmingham*

The Hungerford family in the later middle ages. *J. L. Kirby, M.A. 1939 London, King's College*

The importance of Winchester as capital of England from the tenth to the twelfth century. *P. Meadows, M.A. 1911 London*

The Norman conquests in Wales up to 1100 A.D. *J. W. Wilkinson, M.A. 1901 Wales*

The organization of the English occupation in Scotland, 1296-1461. *D. W. H. Marshall, B.Litt. 1925 Oxford*

Persons and politics in the early years of Richard II, 1377-1388. *N. B. Lewis, M.A. 1928 Manchester*

The position of foreign merchants in England during the reign of Edward III, mainly from the legal standpoint. *A. Beardwood, B.Litt. 1924 Oxford*

The relations between Crown and Baronage in England between 1216 and 1232, with especial reference to the administration of Hubert de Burgh. *G. Malbon, M.A. 1940 London, External Degree*

The relations between England and Scotland during the minority of Alexander III and during the Barons' War. *W. A. Cane, M.A. 1923 Manchester*

Richard II's coup d'état of 1397. *L. B. Meyer, M.A. 1908 London*

Royal wardship in the reign of King John, with reference to chapters 3-6 of the Magna Carta of 1215. *M. A. Renshaw, M.A. 1947 Manchester*

Scutages and aids in England, particularly in the fourteenth century. *H. M. Chew, M.A. 1921 London*

The Sokemen of the southern Danelaw in the eleventh century. *B. Dodwell, M.A. 1936 London, Bedford College*

Some political activities of the Franciscan friars in England in the thirteenth century. *I. J. Saunders, M.A. 1935 Wales*

A study of Anglo-Welsh political relations, with special reference to constitutional matters, 1218-1282. *A. J. Roderick, M.A. 1935 Wales*

A study of the *Parker Chronicle* (449-597 A.D.) in the light of more recent archaeological, place name and topographical evidence. *G. J. Copley, Ph.D. 1947 London, King's College*

Great Britain: History: Early and Medieval contd.
A study of the syntax and vocabulary of the *De excidio Britanniae* of Gildas. *G. R. Williams, M.A. 1935 Wales*

Great Britain: History: Fifteenth Century
See also Bedford, John, Duke of, Regent of France; Gascoigne, T.; Worcester, John Tiptoft, Earl of.

The career of Thomas, Duke of Gloucester. *H. G. Wright, M.A. 1931 London, Birkbeck College*

An edition of: Thome Elmham *Gesta Henrici Quinti. F. Taylor, Ph.D. 1938 Manchester*

Henry VII's relations with Scotland and Ireland, 1485-98. *A. E. Horsfield, Litt.D. 1932 Dublin, Trinity College*

La captivité de Charles d'Orléans d'après les manuscrits anglais. *L. Lailavoix, M.A. 1911 London*

London and the Wars of the Roses, 1445-1461. *M. I. Peake, M.A. 1925 London*

The relations between Henry VII and Wales. *W. T. Williams, M.A. 1914 Wales*

The relations of Henry VII with Scotland and Ireland (1485-1497) illustrated from episodes in the life of Sir Henry Wyatt (c. 1460-1537). *A. E. Conway, M.A. 1926 London*

Scotland and the Wars of the Roses, 1435-85. *C. Macrae, D.Phil. 1939 Oxford*

Thomas Rotherham, Archbishop of York and Chancellor of England: his life and times. *M. F. Howard-Robinson, M.A. 1940 Sheffield*

Great Britain: History: Sixteenth Century
See also Church History: Reformation and Counter-Reformation; and Barlow, W., Bishop; Dudley, E.; Henry VIII, King of England; Kett, R.; More, Thomas, Sir, Saint; Northumberland, John Dudley, Duke of; Norton, T.; Walsingham, F., Sir; Warham, W.

Bodleian mss. relating to the later Tudors, with special reference to the currency literature of the period. *F. J. Routledge, B.Litt. 1920 Oxford*

Dissolution of monasteries in England: social and economic results. *M. J. Prendergast, M.A. 1937 National University of Ireland*

Foreign influences on Scottish politics, 1578-1582. *H. M. Wallace, M.A. 1932 London, Westfield College*

The last years of a frontier: a history of the borders during the reign of Elizabeth. *D. L. W. Tough, B.Litt. 1920 Oxford*

The Norfolk Rising under Robert Kett, 1549. *W. H. T. Walker, M.A. 1921 Wales*

On the causes and course of the rebellion of 1549 in Devon and Cornwall. *W. J. Blake, M.A. 1909 London*

The problem of the North in the early years of Queen Elizabeth's reign. *S. Charlesworth, Ph.D. 1931 Sheffield*

The social and economic circumstances of Ket's rebellion, 1549. *R. J. Hammond, M.A. 1934 London, School of Economics and Political Science*

A study of Spanish and Celtic influences on Elizabethan history. *D. J. Mathew, Litt.D. 1933 Dublin, Trinity College*

Thomas Cromwell: aspects of his administrative work. *G. R. Elton, Ph.D. 1949 London, University College*

Tudor rule in Ireland in the reigns of Henry VII and Henry VIII, with special reference to the Anglo-Irish financial administration. *D. B. Quinn, Ph.D. 1934 London, King's College*

Great Britain: History: Seventeenth Century
See also East India Company; Friends, Society of; Jacobites; Religious Tolerance; Star Chamber; and Blathwayt, W.; Clifford, T., 1st Lord Clifford of Chudleigh; Cooper, A. A., 1st Earl of Shaftesbury; Cromwell, O.; Digby, K., Sir; Hesilrige, A., Sir; Howard, W., Earl of Escrick; Hyde, L., Earl of Rochester; James I, King of England, and VI of Scotland; Laud, W., Archbishop; Lilburne, J.; Mary II, Queen of England; Morgan, T., Sir; Peters, H.; Pym, J.; Smythe, T., Sir; Sunderland, Robert Spencer, 2nd Earl; Talbot, C., Duke of Shrewsbury; Vane, H., Sir; Walwyn, W.; Williams, J., Archbishop.

The adhesion of the Royal Navy to Parliament at the outbreak of the Civil War. *I. G. Powell, M.A. 1919 London*

An analysis of the opposition to the major-generals, with special reference to Yorkshire and the North. *H. Greenleaves, B.Litt. 1927 Oxford*

Great Britain: History: Seventeenth Century contd.
The Catholics in England, 1649-60, with special reference to their political significance. *E. M. B. Cottrell, B.Litt. 1932 Oxford*

The circumstances of the Treaty of Dover. *A. H. Madan, M.A. 1909 Birmingham*

The Civil War in Somerset, 1642-1646. *C. W. Terry, M.A. 1913 London*

The Civil War in Warwickshire, 1642-6, with an introduction on the representation of Warwickshire in the Long Parliament. *P. H. Billingham, B.Litt. 1927 Oxford*

A critical study of the political activities of Andrew Marvell. *I. C. Robbins, Ph.D. 1926 London*

The Crown and municipal corporations, 1679 to 1688: an aspect of the English revolution. *W. J. Fowler, M.A. 1935 Reading*

The Digger Movement in the English Revolution. *D. W. Petegorsky, Ph.D. 1940 London, School of Economics and Political Science*

An edition of the memoirs of Sir Hugh Cholmley, with a contribution on his life and on the Civil War in Yorkshire. *T. H. Brooke, B.Litt. 1937 Oxford*

England and the Orangist Party from 1665 to 1672. *R. R. Goodison, M.A. 1934 London, University College*

The English Revolution and the doctrines of resistance and non-resistance, 1688 to 1714: a study in sovereignty. *J. C. Corson, Ph.D. 1934 Edinburgh*

The first Dutch war. *A. C. Dewar, B.Litt. 1917 Oxford*

Government and industry during the Protectorate (1653-8). *G. D. Ramsay, B.Litt. 1933 Oxford*

Great Civil War in Shrewsbury. *H. Beaumont, M.A. 1934 Sheffield*

The historical setting of the Scottish covenants of the reign of Charles I. *J. W. McEwan, Ph.D. 1930 Glasgow*

The history of the counties of Glamorgan and Monmouth during the Great Civil War, 1642-1648. *L. J. Thomas, M.A. 1914 Wales*

The Leveller Movement. *J. Fitzgibbon, M.A. 1939 National University of Ireland*

Mary II of England and her life during the years 1689-1694: influence on politics, on the Anglican Church, and on society. *N. M. Waterson, B.Litt. 1925 Oxford*

The moderate Royalists and Puritans, and the conception of sovereignty in England prior to the Civil War. *A. S. H. Hill, Ph.D. 1933 London, School of Economics and Political Science*

The Monmouth rebellion. *C. D. Curtis, M.A. 1939 Bristol*

The part played by Walwyn and Overton in the Leveller Movement. *J. E. Speak, M.A. 1949 Leeds*

Persecution and toleration in the period 1660 to 1690. *L. M. Burtt, M.A. 1922 Birmingham*

The political faith of the English nonjurors. *L. M. Hawkins, Ph.D. 1927 London*

The political significance of the career of the Earl of Tyrconnell in Irish history and its relation to the cause of James II. 1685 to 1691. *M. E. Brady, M.Litt. 1932 Cambridge*

Political theories in England during the seventeenth century, with special reference to the social contract. *E. R. Jones, M.A. 1903 Wales*

Politics and parties in the county of Buckinghamshire, 1678-1715. *C. E. S. Drew, B.Litt. 1931 Oxford*

The principal secretaries of state under the earlier Stuarts. *F. M. G. Higham, Ph.D. 1921 Manchester*

The proclamations issued by Charles I during the years 1642-6, both during his progress to Oxford and his residence there until the surrender of the city in 1646, relating especially to Oxford and neighbouring counties. *E. J. S. Parsons, B.Litt. 1935 Oxford*

Public order and popular disturbances in England, 1689-1714. *M. Beloff, B.Litt. 1937 Oxford*

Puritanism in Hampshire and the Isle of Wight from the reign of Elizabeth to the Restoration. *W. H. Mildon, Ph.D. 1934 London, External Degree*

The Republican Party in England from the Restoration to the Revolution, 1660-1688. *J. Walker, Ph.D. 1931 Manchester*

Great Britain: History: Seventeenth Century contd.
The Rye House Plot: with special reference to its place in the Exclusion Contest and its consequences till 1685. *D. J. Milne, Ph.D. 1949 London, Bedford College*

Shrewsbury, Oswestry, and the Welsh wool trade in the seventeenth century, especially in connexion with the crisis and Parliament of 1621. *T. C. Mendenhall, B.Litt. 1936 Oxford*

Social and economic policy and projects during the interregnum, 1640-1660. *M. James, Ph.D. 1927 London*

Titus Oates and the Popish plot. *R. C. F. Dolley, M.A. 1911 London*

The town charters granted under the Protectorate. *B. L. K. Henderson, M.A. 1909 London*

The Upper House during the Protectorates of Oliver and Richard Cromwell. *M. C. Hart, M.A. 1929 London*

Wales and the border counties in relation to the Popish plot. *I. M. O'Leary, M.A. 1924 Wales*

Wolverhampton and the Great Civil War, 1642-1645. *T. J. Larkin, M.A. 1928 Birmingham*

Great Britain: History: Eighteenth Century
For the American War of Independence, see United States: History. See also Bolingbroke, Henry St. J., Viscount; Burke, E.; Finch, D., 2nd Earl of Nottingham; Fox, H.; Germain, G., Viscount Sackville; Grafton, A. H. F., 3rd Duke of; Harley, R., 1st Earl of Oxford; Jenkinson, C., 1st Earl of Liverpool; Lyttleton, G., 1st Baron; Pitt, W., 1st Earl of Chatham; Russell, J., 4th Duke of Bedford; Savile, G., Sir; Shelburne, William Petty, 2nd Earl of; Shippen, W.; Wedderburn, A., 1st Earl of Rosslyn; Yorke, C.

Canada in British politics from 1763-1783. *M. G. Reid, B.Litt. 1922 Oxford*

The causes of Anti-Romanist fanaticism in Great Britain in the eighteenth century, with special reference to the Lord George Gordon Riots. *K. Morris, M.A. 1926 Wales*

The correspondence between King George III and John Robinson. *M. M. Schofield, M.A. 1937 Manchester*

The domestic policy of Robert Harley and the Tory Ministry from 1710-1714. *W. T. H. Bolton, M.A. 1930 London, Bedford College*

English expeditions to the Dutch East Indies during the Revolutionary and Napoleonic Wars. *S. G. Rainbow, M.A. 1933 London, East London College*

English policy and the execution of the treaty of Paris. *W. E. E. Mosse, Ph.D. 1950 Cambridge*

The maritime powers and the evolution of war aims of the Grand Alliance, 1701-1704. *P. J. Welch, M.A. 1940 London, University College*

The operation of the English Navigation Acts during the eighteenth century. *E. H. Rideout, M.A. 1931 Liverpool*

The Peace of Paris, 1763. *Z. E. Rashed, Ph.D. 1949 Liverpool*

The political relations of the Chatham party. *G. K. Grierson, M.A. 1907 Liverpool*

Politics and parties in the county of Buckinghamshire, 1678-1715. *C. E. S. Drew, B.Litt. 1931 Oxford*

Public order and popular disturbances in England, 1689-1714. *M. Beloff, B.Litt. 1937 Oxford*

The reform movement in England previous to the French Revolution. *R. J. McAlpine, M.A. 1907 Liverpool*

Transcription of Harcourt Papers. *M. P. Joyce, M.A. 1947 National University of Ireland*

The union of England and Scotland considered with regard to the action of English statesmen and the development of opinion in England. *P. W. Skirrow, B.Litt. 1927 Oxford*

Great Britain: History: Nineteenth Century
See also Chartists; Crimean War 1854-1856; Luddites; Orangist Party; Radicalism; Saints, The; and Bright, J.; Brougham, H., 1st Baron Brougham and Vaux; Canning, G.; Cartwright, J.; Castlereagh, Robert Stewart, 2nd Marquis of Londonderry; Churchill, R. S., Lord; Disraeli, B., 1st Earl of Beaconsfield; Gladstone, W. E.; Graham, J., Sir; Grey, C., 2nd Earl; Horton, R. J. W., Sir; Hume, J.; Liverpool, R. B. Jenkinson, 2nd Earl of; Melbourne, W. Lamb, 2nd Viscount; Palmerston, H. J. Temple, 3rd Viscount; Parkes, J.; Peel, R., Sir; Tierney, G.; Wellesley, A., 1st Duke of Wellington; Wilson, R. T., Sir.

Great Britain: History: Nineteenth Century contd.
Castlereagh and the Holy Alliance. *H. C. Hamilton, M.A. 1926 Birmingham*

The importance of the religious bodies in the political development of England between the end of the eighteenth century and the beginning of the Oxford Movement. *W. H. B. Twamley, Ph.D. 1925 Cambridge*

The machinery of public order in England during the Chartist period, 1837-1848. *F. C. Mather, M.A. 1948 Manchester*

The political economists and the politicians from Waterloo to the Reform Bill. *S. G. Checkland, M. Com. 1947 Birmingham*

The political influence of William Cobbett, 1794-1815. *E. Knox, M.A. 1907 Liverpool*

The Radical attitude towards the Monarchy and the House of Lords, 1868-85. *E. G. Collieu, B. Litt. 1936 Oxford*

The Reform Bills of 1884 and 1885. *R. C. Reed, M.A. 1949 Wales*

The reform movement in Birmingham, 1830-1884. *H. G. Smith, Ph.D. 1930 London, External Degree*

The Reform movement in Tyneside and Wearside, 1812-1832. *M. B. G. Allan, M.A. 1919 Liverpool*

The unrest in rural England in 1830, with special reference to Berkshire. *N. Gash, B.Litt. 1934 Oxford*

The work of Sir Robert Peel as Secretary of State for the Home Department, 1822-1830. *E. A. W. Kinsey, M.A. 1927 Manchester*

The standard of appreciation shown by the public during the conclusion of the Napoleonic War of the period of depression and insurgence, 1800-1830. *G. G. Urwin, M.A. 1947 London, External Degree*

Great Britain: Parliament
See also Elections.

The Addled Parliament of 1614. *T. L. Moir, Ph.D. 1950 Dublin, Trinity College*

The adhesion of the Royal Navy to Parliament at the outbreak of the Civil War. *I. G. Powell, M.A. 1919 London*

Aspects of the history of the Commons in the fourteenth century. *D. Rayner, Ph.D. 1934 Manchester*

The borough franchise in the first half of the seventeenth century. *W. A. Taffa, M.A. 1926 London*

The boroughs of north Wales: their parliamentary history from the Act of Union to the first Reform Act (1535-1832). *G. Roberts, M.A. 1929 Wales*

British labour and Parliament, 1867-1893. *W. K. Lamb, Ph.D. 1934 London, School of Economics and Political Science*

The causes of the movement for radical parliamentary reform in England, between 1763 and 1789, with special reference to the influence of the so-called Rational Protestants. *G. B. M. Whale, B.Litt. 1930 Oxford*

The comparative study of parliamentary representation in the new borough constituencies created in 1832. *S. F. Woolley, M.A. 1937 London, External Degree*

The composition, organization, and character of the House of Commons, 1640-1653. *R. N. Kershaw, B.Litt. 1923 Oxford*

The Convention Parliament, 1688-9. *A. Simpson, D.Phil. 1939 Oxford*

County representatives in the Parliaments of Edward III. *K. L. Wood-Legh, B.Litt. 1929 Oxford*

The deviations of the parliamentary system of the United Kingdom since 1911. *P. H. Siriex, B.Litt. 1934 Oxford*

The effects of the Reform Bill of 1832 on Liverpool, and the contrast provided by Manchester, 1830-1842. *W. K. Hunt, M.A. 1924 Manchester*

Elections to the House of Commons in the reign of William III. *J. H. Plumb, Ph.D. 1936 Cambridge*

An enquiry into the change in the character of the House of Commons 1832-1901. *J. A. Thomas, Ph.D. 1926 London*

The evolution of the franchise in England, with special reference to the Reform Act of 1869, and to the political influence of organized Christianity. *W. G. H. Cook, M.Sc. 1922 London*

The general election of 1710. *M. E. Ransome, M.A. 1938 London, Royal Holloway College*

The general elections of 1705. *E. A. Cunnington, M.A. 1938 London, University College*

Great Britain: Parliament contd.
The historical development of private bill procedure and standing orders in the House of Commons. *O. C. Williams, B.C.L. & D.C.L. 1946 Oxford*

The history of the fourth Parliament of William III. *J. F. H. Beddow, B.Litt. 1913 Oxford*

The House of Commons and foreign policy between the first and second Reform Acts. *A. C. Turner, B.Litt. 1948 Oxford*

The influence of Parliament upon the foreign policy of the Gladstone Government, 1868-74. *S. Lambert, M.A. 1949 London, Bedford College*

Irish parliamentary representation 1891-1910. *F. S. L. Lyons, Ph.D. 1947 Dublin, Trinity College*

Irish parliamentary representation, 1800-1830. *G. D. Sullivan, B.Litt. 1950 Dublin, Trinity College*

Joseph Parkes of Birmingham and the part which he played in radical reform movements from 1825 to 1845. *J. K. Buckley, M.A. 1924 London*

Lord John Russell and the development of relations between Parliament, Cabinet and parties, 1832-1852. *M. E. Gibbs, M.A. 1928 Manchester*

Mercantile interests in the House of Commons, 1710-13. *M. D. Cox, M.A. 1949 Manchester*

Parliament and the affairs of the East India Company, 1765-1784. *G. F. Pecker, M.A. 1910 Liverpool*

Parliament in the reign of Richard II. *M. McKisack, B.Litt. 1924 Oxford*

The parliamentary franchise in the English boroughs in the Stuart period. *E. C. Whitworth, M.A. 1926 London*

The parliamentary history of Reading between 1750 and 1850. *R. C. J. Baily, M.A. 1944 Reading*

The parliamentary history of the City of Bristol, 1750-1790. *P. T. Underdown, M.A. 1948 Bristol*

Parliamentary reform in Great Britain: a critical analysis of existing proposals, with constructive comments. *F. M. Hardie, D.Phil. 1937 Oxford*

The parliamentary representation of the county of York from the earliest Parliaments to 1601. *A. Gooder, Ph.D. 1933 Leeds*

The parliamentary representation of Grampound. *R. C. D. Jasper, M.A. 1940 Leeds*

The Parliamentary representation of Monmouthshire and the Monmouth boroughs, 1536-1832. *E. E. Havill, M.A. 1949 Wales*

The parliamentary representation of Glamorgan, 1536-1832. *L. B. John, M.A. 1934 Wales*

The parliamentary representation of Wales and Monmouthshire during the nineteenth century, but mainly until 1870. *O. Parry, M.A. 1924 Wales*

Parliamentary representation in the sixteenth century. *W. S. Dann, M.A. 1911 London*

Parliaments and the Peace Treaty: a comparative study of the reactions of the British and French Parliaments to the Treaty of Peace of 1919. *B. Ling, Ph.D. 1938 London, School of Economics and Political Science*

The Pensionary or Long Parliament of Charles II. *W. C. Abbott, B.Litt. 1897 Oxford*

The personnel of Parliament, 1571. *H. Brady, M.A. 1927 Manchester*

The personnel of Parliament, 1597. *C. M. Davey, M.A. 1927 Manchester*

The personnel of Parliament under Henry IV. *J. W. Muir, M.A. 1924 London*

The personnel of the House of Commons in 1422. *J. S. Roskell, D.Phil. 1941 Oxford*

Personnel of the Parliament of 1593. *E. E. Trafford, M.A. 1948 London, University College*

Personnel of the Parliament of 1584-85. *H. Matthews, M.A. 1948 London, University College*

Petitions in Parliament under the Lancastrians, from, or relating to, towns. *M. A. Rose, M.A. 1926 London*

The powers of inquisition into and control over public finance exercised by the House of Commons, more especially by its committees. *F. B. Chubb, D.Phil. 1950 Oxford*

The private member of Parliament, 1833-1868. *J. K. Glynn, Ph.D. 1949 London, School of Economics and Political Science*

Public opinion and Parliament since 1832. *D. C. Johnson, B.Litt. 1922 Oxford*

The Reform Bills of 1884 and 1885. *R. C. Reed, M.A. 1949 Wales*

Great Britain: Parliament contd.
The Select Committee of 1861 on colonial military expenditure and its antecedents. *M. G. Chappell, M.A. 1934 London, Westfield College*

A study of the Knights of the Shire returned to Parliament by Bedfordshire during the Middle Ages. *M. A. Fletcher, M.A. 1933 London, University College*

A study of the parliamentary burgesses during the first half of the fifteenth century, based on the returns of London, York, Norwich, Bristol and Southampton between 1413 and 1437. *J. Lawson, M.A. 1936 Manchester*

The Tory attitude towards parliamentary reform (1815-1832). *E. M. Atkins, M.A. 1931 London, King's College*

Great Britain: Parliament: Lords
The House of Lords in the reign of William III, 1688-1702. *A. S. Turberville, B.Litt. 1912 Oxford*

The House of Lords under Elizabeth. *J. E. Neale, M.A. 1915 Liverpool*

The political activity and influence of the House of Lords, 1603-1629. *D. J. Dawson, B.Litt. 1950 Oxford*

The Radical attitude towards the Monarchy and the House of Lords, 1868-85. *E. G. Collieu, B. Litt. 1936 Oxford*

The Upper House during the Protectorates of Oliver and Richard Cromwell. *M. C. Hart, M.A. 1929 London*

The Victorian House of Lords. *A. L. Sachar, Ph.D. 1923 Cambridge*

Great Britain: Politics and Government
See also Conservatism; Fabian Society; Independent Labour Party; Labour Party; Liberalism.

The administration of the Yorkist kings. *J. R. Lander, M.Litt. 1950 Cambridge*

Administrative legislation and adjudication in Great Britain and the United States. *E. R. Baltzell, D.Phil. 1923 Oxford*

The administrative relations between England and Ireland, 1660-1670. *E. M. B. Robinson, M.A. 1927 Manchester*

The Anglican Church and political parties, 1701-1737. *S. L. Chandler, M.A. 1930 Birmingham*

The conception of political party in England in the period 1740-83. *D. Thomson, Ph.D. 1938 Cambridge*

The development of parties during the ministry of Danby. *E. S. de Beer, M.A. 1923 London*

The distribution of functions among central government departments in the United Kingdom, with some comparison of the United States of America and British dominions. *C. N. Yang, D.Phil. 1948 Oxford*

The English idea of the 'social contract' theory of government in English political theory, from the Reformation to the Revolution of 1688. *J. A. Thomas, M.A. 1923 Wales*

The evolution of the administration of the Treasury in England during the years 1660-1714. *D. M. Gill, M.A. 1919 London*

An examination of the theory and practice of appointments in the reigns of Henry III and Edward I (1216-1307), and of their historical significance. *P. H. Scotney, M.A. 1927 London*

Judicial control exercised over local authorities compared with that exercised over Government departments. *M. B. Cairns, M.A. 1947 Bristol*

Lord John Russell and the development of relations between Parliament, Cabinet and parties, 1832-1852. *M. E. Gibbs, M.A. 1928 Manchester*

Political opinion in the north of England, 1780-1837. *F. B. Walker, M.A. 1913 Belfast*

The position of London in national affairs, 1658-1661, having special regard to political and economic aspects. *M. B. Weinstock, M.A. 1934 London, School of Economics and Political Science*

The relations between central and local government in England and Wales in the period 1923-1933, treated with reference both to the policy and to the public discussions. *J. Lewis, M.A. 1936 Wales*

The relations of statutory and voluntary authorities in public administration in England and Wales. *M. McKie, B.Litt. 1930 Oxford*

Great Britain: Politics and Government contd.
The respective spheres of the State and of voluntary organizations in the prevention and relief of poverty in London at the present day. *L. H. Bell, M.A. 1935 London, School of Economics and Political Science*

Great Britain: Privy Council
See Great Britain: Constitution.

Great Britain: Social History
See also Etiquette; Feudalism; Friendly Societies; Letters; Poor Law; Spas; Vagrancy; and Buckingham, J. S.; Cooper, A. A., 7th Earl of Shaftesbury; Defoe, D.; Dickens, C.; Fielding, H.; Percival, T.

Andrew Marvell and the culture of his time: a study in the relationship of his poetry to some aspects of seventeenth century society. *D. Davison, M.A. 1949 Sheffield*

Britain and Britons in the eyes of the eighteenth-century Germans. *K. H. B. Kirby, Ph.D. 1934 London, King's College*

Chaucer and Langland as painters of English life. *M. Donegan, M.A. 1948 National University of Ireland*

The Comte de Mirabeau in England. *W. R. Fryer, B.Litt. 1940 Oxford*

The condition of England during the revolutionary and Napoleonic periods, as illustrated by the history of Birmingham between the years 1789-1815. *D. J. Davies, M.A. 1924 Wales*

Contemporary life, literature and society as reflected in Ben Jonson's works. *E. C. Dunn, Ph.D. 1922 London*

Das deutsche Bild vom heutigen England nach Uebersetzungen und Schulbüchern, 1918-1932. *A. H. Johnstone, Ph.D. 1934 Edinburgh*

The development of the feminist idea in England (1789-1833). *R. J. T. Saywell, M.A. 1936 London, King's College*

The economic and social condition of England on the eve of the Industrial Revolution, with special reference to Lancashire. *L. W. Moffit, Ph.D. 1921 Edinburgh*

The effects of the Reformation on the social conditions of England, 1535-1570. *I. V. Harriss, M.A. 1915 Birmingham*

The effects produced by economic changes upon social life in England in the fifteenth century. *A. Abram, D.Sc. 1909 London*

Emigration from Taunton to N. England 1625-1645. *H. J. Wickenden, M.A. 1929 Bristol*

England and the English in the Icelandic sagas. *J. M. Keays-Young, B.Litt. 1928 Oxford*

England and the English as presented in Michelet's *History of France. D. Starke, M.A. 1922 London*

England in the Icelandic sagas. *C. E. Tyler, Ph.D. 1926 Sheffield*

English personal letters and private diaries of 1640-1680: a study of the general mental attitude of the period as illustrated by individual types, together with a brief examination of the colloquial language of the time. *M. T. Williamson, Ph.D. 1929 London*

English social life as displayed in the literature of the thirteenth and fourteenth centuries. *D. E. Thomas, B.Litt. 1921 Oxford*

The English yeomanry in the seventeenth century. *I. D. A. Abbott, B.Litt. 1928 Oxford*

The Englishman as a character in the French fiction of the eighteenth century. *P. L. Evans, M.A. 1923 Manchester*

Fabian thought and social change in England from 1884-1914. *R. D. Howland, Ph.D. 1942 London, School of Economics and Political Science*

The Franciscans in medieval English life (1224-1348). *V. Green, B.Litt. 1936 Oxford*

The Gawdys of West Harling, Norfolk: a study of education and social life in the seventeenth century. *C. D. Price, M.A. 1950 Wales*

George Eliot as an analyst of the social life of England in the nineteenth century. *I. Azmy, M.A. 1949 Sheffield*

Health, wealth, and population in the early days of the Industrial Revolution. *M. C. Buer, D.Sc. 1927 London*

Heine in England in the nineteenth century. *K. H. B. Kirby, M.A. 1927 London*

Great Britain: Social History contd.
An historical study of the provision made for the social (as distinct from the scholastic) welfare of children and young persons in England since 1800. *C. L. H. Cowper, M.A. 1930 London, King's College*

The influence of bishops and of members of cathedral bodies in the intellectual life of England, 1066 to 1216. *E. Rathbone, Ph.D. 1936 London, King's College*

L'Angleterre dans l'oeuvre de Mme. de Staël. *D. Distance, M.A. 1935 Belfast*

Literary and social dandyism in England and France between 1780 and 1850. *S. C. Gould, D.Phil. 1950 Oxford*

Manners and morals in the English novel between Richardson and Jane Austen. *E. K. Brooks, M.A. 1942 Leeds*

Manners and morals of the seventeenth and eighteenth centuries as revealed in books written for the young. *I. E. Thrift, Ph.D. 1935 London, King's College*

Mme. de Staël and England: a study of Mme. de Staël's English acquaintances, and of her reputation and influence in England. *R. A. Jones, M.A. 1928 London*

The novel of industrial town life from Mrs. Gaskell to Arnold Bennett. *J. C. Suffolk, M.A. 1939 Sheffield*

The origins of the Young England Movement. *R. V. G. Bader, B.Phil. 1950 Saint Andrew's*

The penetration of English ideas into France (1680-1720), with special reference to Pierre Bayle. *K. Natzio, B.Litt. 1929 Oxford*

A pioneer in the work of propagating a knowledge of England and English literature in France, being an investigation into the Abbé Prévost's relations with England and English literature, with special reference to his *Le pour et contre, Cleveland, Mémoires d'un homme de qualité* and *Lettres de Mentor à un jeune seigneur. J. C. Carpenter, M.A. 1915 Wales*

The place of property in English culture. *J. A. Waites, Ph.D. 1946 Manchester*

The place of the secular clergy in the society of fifteenth century England. *G. Templeman, M.A. 1936 London, School of Economics and Political Science*

Poetry and the rustic in the eighteenth century. *A. W. Florance, M.A. 1935 Bristol*

Political and social ideas in England, 1820-37. *C. H. Driver, M.A. 1926 London*

The position and duties of the King's almoner, 1255-1327. *M. E. Lack, M.A. 1949 London, Royal Holloway College*

Prosper Mérimée and England. *D. Brittain, M.A. 1926 Manchester*

Protestant nonconformity and some social and economic questions, 1660-1800. *E. D. Bebb, Ph.D. 1934 Sheffield*

Ralph, Lord Cromwell, and his household: studies in relation to household accounts in the possession of Lord de l'Isle and Dudley. *E. M. Price, M.A. 1949 London, King's College*

Religious separation and moral authority: some aspects of religious intolerance in England, 1603-1660. *I. C. Coltman, M.A. 1949 London, School of Economics and Political Science*

Robert Owen and social legislation. *E. Lloyd, M.A. 1932 Wales*

Rustics and rural life in the novels of George Eliot, George Meredith and Thomas Hardy. *A. M. Vévar, M.A. 1940 Wales*

Saint-Evremond in England. *W. M. Daniels, M.A. 1906 London*

Smollett as critic of social conditions in eighteenth century England. *W. Eastwood, M.A. 1949 Sheffield*

The social and intellectual background of the Reign of Queen Anne as reflected in the *Tatler* and *Spectator. J. M. King, M.A. 1938 London, King's College*

The social and political influence of Methodism in the Napoleonic period. *M. L. Edwards, Ph.D. 1934 London, King's College*

The social condition of England during the seventeenth century as illustrated by the Southampton documents. *F. W. Camfield, M.A. 1907 London*

Great Britain: Social History contd.
The social life of 'the town' as represented by some of the Elizabethan dramatists. *M. N. Howlett, M.A. 1912 London*

The social relations of England and France, 1763-1793, in connection with their effect on the Revolutionary era. *C. H. Lockitt, M.A. 1911 London*

The social structure of an English county town. *E. R. R. Power, Ph.D. 1937 London, School of Economics and Political Science*

The social structure of the English shires on the Welsh border between the Norman conquest and the fourteenth century. *M. U. Apps, Ph.D. 1944 Leeds*

Some aspects of social and political life in England during the nineteenth century in relation to contemporary theory. *N. M. Waterson, M.A. 1921 Birmingham*

Some aspects of street life in medieval England. *G. T. Salusbury-Jones, B.Litt. 1938 Dublin, Trinity College*

Some studies in the moral climate of the mid-eighteenth century in England, as expressed in a representative selection of the prose literature of the period 1740-1786. *E. K. Laycock, M.Litt. 1946 Cambridge*

Study of juvenile delinquency, with special reference to social influences and social control in Birmingham and district. *C. Hyde, M.A. 1933 Birmingham*

A study of social and constitutional tendencies in the early years of Edward III, as illustrated more especially by the events connected with the ministerial enquiries of 1340, and the following years. *D. Hughes, M.A. 1913 London*

A study of the influence of the Victorian home on the religious development of the child in the last three decades of the nineteenth century. *W. L. Land, B.Litt. 1948 Oxford*

A study of the Stationers' Register for the years 1591-1594, in relation to the social life and literature of the period. *G. B. Harrison, Ph.D. 1928 London*

Sunday in the eighteenth century, 1677-1837. *W. B. Whitaker, Ph.D. 1937 London, King's College*

Thackeray's attitude towards the society of his time, as revealed in his writings of 1836-1847. *A. Webster, M.A. 1948 Manchester*

The treatment of social and economic questions by Anglican divines during the reign of Charles II. *R. B. Schlatter, B.Litt. 1935 Oxford*

Types of social life illustrated by the writings of Gerald of Wales. *D. Humphreys, B.Litt. 1936 Oxford*

The vernacular English literature, 871-1066, as illustrative of the social history of that period. *J. Cook, M.A. 1931 Wales*

Great Southern Railway Company
See Railways.

Great Trek
See South Africa.

Greece
British policy towards the change of dynasty in Greece in the years 1862-3. *E. Prevelakis, B.Litt. 1949 Oxford*

The light thrown by the klephtic ballads on the history of Greece in the period (1715 to 1821) before the war of Independence. *J. W. Baggally, B.Litt. 1935 Oxford*

A study of the official and unofficial relations between Greece and Turkey from the armistice of Mudros to the present day. *E. L. B. Curtis, M.Sc. 1933 London, School of Economics and Political Science*

Greece, Ancient
See also Hellenism; Houses; Philosophy: Greece, Ancient; Religion: Greece, Ancient; Theatre: Greece, Ancient; and Arcadia; Athens; Corfu; Corinth; Delos; Macedon; Mycenae; Nicopolis; Sparta; Syracuse; Thessaly; Troy. See also Agesilaus, King; Alcibiades; Alexander, the Great; Cimon; Pericles; Themistocles.

Discipline of Greek armies. *G. D. Roberts, M.A. 1927 Wales*

The distribution of power between the federal government and the constituent states in Greek federations. *E. S. F. Ridout, M.A. 1926 London*

The Greek, the barbarian and the slave. *H. Harris, M.Litt. 1929 Cambridge*

Greece, Ancient contd.
Hellas and its background. *O. L. Jones, M.A. 1937 Birmingham*

An historical account of beekeeping in Greece and Rome during the classical period. *H. M. Fraser, Ph.D. 1930 London, External Degree*

The history and nature of the dowry among the ancient Greeks. *F. A. Collie, M.A. 1905 Wales*

The influence of Greek life and Greek culture on the writings and teachings of St. Paul. *J. Jones, M.A. 1919 Wales*

An inquiry into the purchasing power of the drachma in ancient Greece for the purpose of determining, if possible, the material conditions which prevailed in Athens during her existence as an independent state. *E. Y. Nisbet, Ph.D. 1948 Glasgow*

The life and times of Hiero II, King of Syracuse. *W. H. Davies, M.A. 1935 Wales*

Light thrown by the works of Lucian on contemporary life. *W. J. Gibb, Ph.D. 1929 London*

Origin of belief in one God in the Greek world. *C. R. King, M.A. 1932 London, Birkbeck College*

The place of oligarchy in the development of Greece. *M. L. Gordon, Cert.Litt. 1917 Oxford*

The political parties in Athens during the Peloponnesian War. *R. A. E. Prosser, M.A. 1926 Bristol*

Rome, Greece and Macedon to 196 B.C. *M. Duggan, M.A. 1934 National University of Ireland*

The size of the Persian army in the invasion of Greece 480 B.C. *F. C. F. Maurice, D.Litt. 1930 London*

A study of the conditions which led to the Athenian and Spartan tyrannies, and the effect of these tyrannies on the foreign policy of other states. *M. O. Wason, Ph.D. 1946 Glasgow*

Three plays of Euripides in relation to the social background of his time. *R. F. Willetts, M.A. 1938 Birmingham*

Trade routes between mainland Greece and the West, from the Geometric Age until the end of the sixth century B.C. *B. L. Bailey, M.A. 1935 London, Westfield College*

The Trojan as conceived by Greeks of the fifth century B.C.: a comparison between the literary and artistic records. *G. C. Cook, M.A. 1937 London, University College*

Greek Language
See also Inscriptions; Papyri. For linguistic studies of Greek versions of the Bible or parts thereof, see Bible: Versions.

Adjectives of light and colour in Greek lyric poetry. *R. A. Cole, Ph.D. 1948 Dublin, Trinity College*

Agma: a contribution to Greek alphabetology. *L. J. D. Richardson, M.A. 1942 Wales*

Aristotelian antecedents in the philosophical vocabulary of the New Testament. *R. A. Ward, M.A. 1946 London, Birkbeck College*

Aristotelian usages in the philosophical vocabulary of the New Testament. *R. A. Ward, Ph.D. 1949 London, Birkbeck College*

Characteristics of the grammar and style of Bion and Moschus. *E. M. Roberts, M.A. 1908 London*

Classical etymology as revealed in Greek and Latin literature. *J. O. Anderson, M.A. 1930 London, Bedford College*

The colloquial element in the language of Attic tragedy. *P. T. Stevens, Ph.D. 1939 Aberdeen*

The 'common' or Hellenistic Greek in the light of recent research. *H. C. Waddell, M.A. 1921 Belfast*

A grammatical and lexical study of the Greek inscriptions of Phrygia in Asia Minor. *D. E. Evans, B.Litt. 1917 Oxford*

Grammatical characteristics of Lycurgus. *M. I. Thomas, M.A. 1907 London*

Greek loan words in Latin literature down to the time of Cicero. *I. A. Jones, M.A. 1915 Wales*

Ictus lengthening in Homer. *D. Castello, M.A. 1912 London*

1. The influence of the Apocrypha upon the language of the New Testament. 2. Paulinisms in the Epistle to the Hebrews, and their relationship to the problem of its authorship. *F. Streatfeild, B.D. 1916 Oxford*

The knowledge of Greek in England in Anglo-Saxon times. *A. Anderson, B.Litt. 1922 Oxford*

On ιεροσ, ιεροσ, ιροσ; and on the colour words in Homer. *C. M. Mulvany, B.Litt. 1897 Oxford*

Greek Language contd.
On certain Greek particles. *E. R. Manley, M.A. 1921 London*

The prepositions of the New Testament, with illustrations from the papyri. *A. M. Hunter, Ph.D. 1934 Glasgow*

The problem of the Pastoral Epistles, with special reference to the linguistic data. *C. S. Nye, B.D. 1934 Oxford*

Semitisms in the New Testament in the light of later popular Greek. *R. McKinlay, Ph.D. 1927 Glasgow*

A study of the Laconian dialect. *D. E. Evans, M.A. 1913 Wales*

The syntax of New Testament compared with Attic Greek. *W. P. Jones, M.A. 1902 Wales*

The syntax of New Testament Greek in the light of recent papyrological discoveries. *S. I. Buse, M.A. 1945 Wales*

The syntax of the New Testament compared with Attic Greek. *T. Evans, M.A. 1903 Wales*

Greek Literature
See also Anthologies; Comedy; Heroes in Literature; Mythology; Papyri; Tragedy; and Aeschines; Aeschylus; Aristides; Aristophanes; Bacchylides; Bion; Empedocles; Eratosthenes, of Cyrene; Euripides; Herodotus; Homer; Ignatius, Diaconus; Leonidas, of Tarentum; Lucian; Lycurgus; Menander; Moschus; Pindar; Plato; Plutarch; Sidonius Apollinaris; Simonides; Sophocles; Thucydides; Xenophon.

Astudiaeth feirniadol o'r Didache a llenyddiaeth Gristionogol arall o gynnyrch y ddwy ganrif gyntaf, a ysgrifennwyd yn yr iaith Roeg, ynghyda chyfeiriad arbennig at ddatblygiad y Weinidogaeth a'r Gwasanaethau Eglwysig (A critical study of the Didache and other Christian literature in Greek of the first and second centuries, with special reference to the development of the ministry and the church services). *E. J. Lloyd, Ph.D. 1946 Wales*

Children in Greek literature from the heroic to the golden age. *S. Allott, B.Litt. 1943 Dublin, Trinity College*

Cicero's study of Greek literature, with special reference to Cicero as a translator. *M. D. J. Adams, M.A. 1932 Wales*

The concept of wisdom in Greek and Hebrew literature. *J. P. Dempsey, M.A. 1946 National University of Ireland*

Κτίσεωσ πόλεων: an examination of the Greek foundation legend as a literary form. *E. W. W. Cumbers, M.A. 1939 London, King's College*

Magic in Greek and Latin literature. *J. E. Lowe, M.A. 1922 London*

Medea and Jason in Greek and Roman literature. *M. Curran, M.A. 1939 Manchester*

Roman Philhellenism as a factor in the literary revival of Greek under Hadrian and Antonines. *W. A. Odell, M.A. 1920 Birmingham*

The theme of the deserted heroine in classical literature. *J. M. Williams, M.A. 1935 Wales*

The treatment of love and marriage in classical Greek literature. *M. Wilkins, M.A. 1924 London*

Wit and humour in early Greek literature. *R. H. Kidd, M.A. 1941 National University of Ireland*

Wit and humour in early Greek literature. *R. H. Kidd, B.Litt. 1941 Dublin, Trinity College*

Greek Orthodox Church
Popular religion in the Orthodox Church of modern Greece. *W. D. Nutting, B.Litt. 1925 Oxford*

Green, Thomas Hill
The moral philosophy of T. H. Green. *H. D. Lewis, B.Litt. 1935 Oxford*

The relation of morality to self-consciousness in the philosophy of T. H. Green. *L. Golomb, M.A. 1946 Sheffield*

The relations between ethics and metaphysics, with special reference to the works of Spinoza, Kant and T. H. Green. *J. P. Davies, M.A. 1922 Wales*

Greene, Robert
Elizabethan rogues and vagabonds: their life, manners and representation in contemporary literature, especially in connexion with the so-called coney-catching pamphlets of Robert Greene. *F. Aydelotte, B.Litt. 1907 Oxford*

The growth of realism in Elizabethan fiction, with special reference to Greene, Nashe and Deloney. *E. L. G. Giles, M.A. 1937 Wales*

The pamphlets of Greene. *G. Van Santvoord, B.Litt. 1917 Oxford*

Greene, Robert contd.
Robert Greene's later prose works. *W. H. Lewis, M.A. 1927 Bristol*

A study of the prose works of R. Greene. *A. V. Smith, M.A. 1927 Birmingham*

The style of the *Honourable history of Friar Bacon and Friar Bungay*. *N. A. Marten, M.A. 1948 Birmingham*

Gregoras Nicephorus
The Hesychast controversy, with special reference to the *Byzantina historia* of Nicephorus Gregoras and the *Historia* of John Cantacuzenus. *T. A. Hart, M.A. 1949 London, Bedford College*

Gregory, Bishop of Tours
Bishops and the secular power in the writings of Gregory of Tours. *S. Mullins, B.Litt. 1950 Oxford*

Gregory I, Saint, Pope, 'The Great'
The political influence of Pope Gregory the Great in Italy. *H. V. W. Lewis, M.A. 1913 Wales*

Relations of Pope Gregory the Great with the churches in the Roman Empire of the East. *W. J. Boast, M.A. 1931 Birmingham*

1. The theology of Gregory the Great. 2. Gregory's doctrine of man and the means of grace. *F. H. Dudden, B.D. 1903 Oxford*

Gregory, Isabella Augusta, Lady
The work of Lady Gregory: her contribution to the Irish dramatic and literary revival. *M. Pick, M.A. 1940 London, Bedford College*

Gregory, James
James Gregory: a survey of his work in mathematical analysis. *A. Inglis, Ph.D. 1933 Saint Andrew's*

Gregory Nazianzen, Saint
The doctrine of the Godhead in St.Gregory Nazianzen, with special reference to its Trinitarian and Christological aspects. *D. Martynowski, B.Litt. 1939 Oxford*

The teaching of salvation in the orations of St. Gregory of Nazianzus. *M. Stoyanovitch, B.Litt. 1922 Oxford*

Gregory VII, Saint, Pope
The elements of Hildebrand's conception of the Church. *D. Dymond, M.A. 1915 London*

Greville, Fulke, 1st Baron Brooke
Fulke Greville and his literary relations. *E. Wright, M.A. 1930 Manchester*

The life and work of Fulke Greville, Lord Brooke. *J. F. Macvane, B.Litt. 1935 Oxford*

The life and works of Fulk Greville: a study of his poetry and of the political and religious ideas revealed in it (1554-1628). *E. Carrick, M.A. 1936 London, Bedford College*

Grey, Charles, 2nd Earl
Earl Grey's native policy in South Africa, with special reference to Natal. *P. Lee, M.A. 1930 Sheffield*

Griffin, Gerald
Gerald Griffin; a study in Anglo-Irish literature. *M. McElligott, M.A. 1936 National University of Ireland*

Gerald Griffin. *M. McElligott, M.A. 1936 National University of Ireland*

Grillparzer, Franz
The classic, romantic and specific Spanish elements in the dramas of Grillparzer and Halm. *D. Evans, M.A. 1912 Wales*

The female characters in Grillparzer's drama, as contrasted with those in Goethe's and Schiller's. *A. V. Burgess, M.A. 1907 Wales*

Franz Grillparzer; Leben, Wirken und Werden. *M. O'Connell, M.A. 1945 National University of Ireland*

Grillparzer and England. *J. Johnstone, M.A. 1931 Birmingham*

Grillparzer and his early tragic heroines: Sappho, Medea, Hero. *D. Yates, M.A. 1925 Birmingham*

Grillparzer's Pessimismus. *M. Curran, M.A. 1919 National University of Ireland*

The sources of Grillparzer's *Ein Bruderzwist in Habsburg* (1849). *R. Beck, M.A. 1926 London*

Grimald, Nicholas
An investigation of Nicholas Grimald's association with Tottel's *Miscellany*. *H. J. Byrom, M.A. 1927 London*

Grimm, Hans
The English background to the works of Hans Grimm. *I. C. Knopf, M.A. 1939 London, University College*

Grimmelshausen, Hans Jakob Christopher von
A contribution to the study of Grimmelshausen. *B. G. Birch, M.A. 1932 Bristol*

Grocers, Company of
A study of the merchant class of London in the fifteenth century, with special reference to the Company of Grocers. *S. L. Thrupp, Ph.D. 1931 London, University College*

Grocyn, William
Leaders of humanism in English education: Humphrey, Duke of Gloucester, William Grocyn, Thomas Linacre, Bishop Richard Foxe. *C. H. Winstanley, M.A. 1930 Liverpool*

Grotius, Hugo
The development of the 'just war' conception, especially since Grotius. *G. D. Roos, B.Litt. 1936 Oxford*

The theories of the atonement of Anselm and Grotius. *R. S. Franks, B.Litt. 1899 Oxford*

Grou, Jean Nicolas
Jean Nicolas Grou, 1731-1803, the man and his work. *R. C. Pitts, Ph.D. 1947 Edinburgh*

Group Psychology
Group consciousness, with special reference to educational applications. *K. T. Sen, Ph.D. 1922 Edinburgh*

Group psychology in its bearing on homiletics. *F. H. Caldwell, Ph.D. 1934 Edinburgh*

The individual and the group in education. *W. J. Wheeler, M.A. 1936 Birmingham*

The influence of the relations between groups upon the inner life of groups, with special reference to black and white in the Southern States of the United States during the nineteenth century. *H. W. Roberts, M.A. 1934 London, School of Economics and Political Science*

An investigation into the use of leaderless group discussions on topics of importance to the self and in the community with a group of adolescents. *P. J. Higginbotham, M.A. 1949 London, Institute of Education*

The method and presuppositions of group psychology. *W. R. Dennes, D.Phil. 1923 Oxford*

The psychology of the boy group with special reference to school scout troup. *D. M. Ramsden, M.Ed. 1934 Leeds*

Some problems of secondary education in the light of group psychology. *T. F. Green, M.A. 1927 Sheffield*

Gruffudd ab Ieuan ap Llywelyn Fychan
Gweithiau Gruffudd ab Ieuan ap Llywelyn Fychan (The works of Gruffudd ab Ieuan ap Llywelyn Fychan). *J. Lloyd, M.A. 1911 Wales*

The poetical works of Gruffudd ab Ieuan ap Llywelyn Fychan. *T. Roberts, M.A. 1910 Wales*

Gruffydd Hiraethog
The works of Gruffydd Hiraethog. *W. Richards, M.A. 1925 Wales*

Grundtvig, Nikolai Frederik Severim
N. F. S. Grundtvig and the Danish Folk High School Movement. *G. N. M. Davies, Ph.D. 1928 Wales*

Grünewald, Matthias
Matthias Grünewald. *C. Mitchell, B.Litt. 1938 Oxford*

Gryphius, Andreas
Andreas Gryphius and the Elizabethan drama. *D. B. Evans, M.A. 1950 Wales*

Guarantees
Some difficulties with the English law of suretyship. *T. Raleigh, D.C.L. 1896 Oxford*

Guarini, Giovanni Battista
Guarini and the English pastoral. *S. E. Dimsey, B.Litt. 1927 Oxford*

Guérin, Charles
The poetry of Charles Guérin, with special reference to his versification. *D. Dowson, M.A. 1922 Manchester*

Guérin, Eugénie de
La sensibilité d'Eugénie de Guérin. *A. M. De. Ciniphéic, M.A. 1947 National University of Ireland*

Guernsey
A critical examination of the *Atlas linguistique de la France* in so far as it concerns the island of Guernsey. *J. P. Collas, B.Litt. 1934 Oxford*

Guernsey. *G. H. Dury, M.A. 1944 London, External Degree*

The human geography of the Island of Guernsey. *E. C. Barrington, M.A. 1934 London, Birkbeck College*

Guet, Jacques Joseph du
Life, works and literary theories of Jacques-Joseph du Guet. *R. E. Nicholls, Ph.D. 1936 London, University College*

Guiana
The Guianas. *D. R. Morgan, M.Sc. 1938 London, External Degree*

The struggles of the European powers for possession in Guiana, 1667-1713. *M. Fisher, M.A. 1926 London*

Guilbert de Pixerécourt, René Charles
See Pixerécourt, G. de.

Guilds
See also Staple.

The Bristol craft guilds during the sixteenth and seventeenth centuries. *F. H. Rogers, M.A. 1949 Bristol*

The economic organization of the medieval borough with special reference to Leicester and its guild merchants. *E. H. Smith, M.A. 1912 Wales*

England and the Teutonic *Hanse. A. Weiner, M.A. 1904 Wales*

The history of Reading in the later Middle Ages, considered with special reference to the importance of the gild merchant in medieval seignorial boroughs. *N. H. Gibbs, D.Phil. 1935 Oxford*

A history of the Shrewsbury Drapers' Company during the seventeenth century, with particular reference to the Welsh woollen trade. *D. J. Evans, M.A. 1950 Wales*

The influence and development of the industrial guilds in the larger provincial towns under James I and Charles I, with special reference to the formation of new corporations for the control of industry. *F. J. Fisher, M.A. 1931 London, School of Economics and Political Science*

National guilds as a wage system. *M. Healy, M.A. 1920 National University of Ireland*

The old English gild system. *C. W. Hodgetts, M.A. 1941 Leeds*

The Roman Collegia. *M. L. Macgregor, M.A. 1931 London, Birkbeck College*

The singing guilds in the Old Testament. *A. Morton, Ph.D. 1944 Saint Andrew's*

The social and economic conditions of the members of the *Collegia* from Constantine to Theodosius II. *W. Utley, M.A. 1925 London*

Studies in the guild drama in London, from 1515 to 1550, in the records of the Drapers' Company. *P. G. Lusher, Ph.D. 1940 London, University College*

The trade gilds of the Eastern provinces of the Roman Empire (exclusive of Egypt) during the first three centuries A.D. *E. M. Thomas, B.Litt. 1934 Oxford*

The transactions between the merchants of the Staple and the Lancastrian government, 1449-1461. *W. I. Haward, Ph.D. 1932 London, Bedford College*

Guillaume, de Briane
See Briane, G. de.

Guillaume, de Lorris
L'influence de Guillaume de Lorris sur quelques poètes français du quatorzième siècle. *E. A. Alexander, M.A. 1948 Belfast*

Guillaume, de Machaut
Geoffrey Chaucer and Guillaume de Machaut. *L. Febvre, M.A. 1948 National University of Ireland*

Guillén, Pero
The poetical works of Pero Guillén de Sevilla. *W. W. Grave, Ph.D. 1928 Cambridge*

Guiot, de Provins
The preparation of a critical edition of a thirteenth century French satirical poem *La Bible de Guiot de Provins*, with a linguistic and literary study and a glossary. *J. Orr, B.Litt. 1913 Oxford*

Guizot, François
Guizot as a historian of England. *G. N. Eeles, B.Litt. 1926 Oxford*

La collaboration de François Guizot au *Publiciste. W. A. Cummins, M.A. 1930 Liverpool*

Gujarat
The archaeology of Gujarat (A.D. 400-1300). *H. D. Sankalia, Ph.D. 1937 London, University College*

Gujarat contd.
Discussion and determination of the most adequate method to be employed in the study of the interrelation and interaction of the economic, ethical, and religious factors in the life of organized communities, as illustrated in the case of the Vaishnava communities of Gujerat. *N. A. Thoothi, D.Phil. 1925 Oxford*

A study in rural economy of Gujarat containing suggestions for reconstruction. *J. M. Mehta, Ph.D. 1929 London*

Gujarati Language
Accent in Gujarāti. *N. G. Saswadkar, M.A. 1929 London*

Selections from *Sadavasyaka vrtti* of Tarunaprabha, critically edited: a study of the Gujrati language in the fourteenth century A.D. *P. B. Pandit, Ph.D. 1949 London, School of Oriental and African Studies*

A study of the Gujarati language in the sixteenth century, with special reference to the ms. Balavabodha to Upadisamata. *T. N. Dave, Ph.D. 1931 London, School of Oriental and African Studies*

Gun Trade
History of the Birmingham gun trade. *D. W. Young, M.Com. 1936 Birmingham*

Guthlac, Saint
An edition of the Old English poem of *Saint Guthlac. B. Thompson, Ph.D. 1931 Leeds*

The structure and conditions of authorship of the Old English poem on St. Guthlac. *H. A. Jones, M.A. 1938 Manchester*

Gutiérrez, Antonio García
Two Spanish Romantics: Antonio García Gutiérrez and Juan Eugenio Hartzenbusch. *J. V. Gorner, M.A. 1929 Liverpool*

Guto'r Glyn
Gwaith Guto'r Glyn (The work of Guto'r Glyn). *J. L. Williams, M.A. 1927 Wales*

Guttinguer, Ulric
The life and works of Ulric Guttinguer: being a contribution to the history of the Romantic movement in France. *C. H. Dickson, Ph.D. 1940 London, University College*

Gwidw
A study and comparison of French and Welsh texts of the story of Gwidw. *S. A. Harwin, M.A. 1929 Wales*

Gwilym Hiraethog
See Rees, W.

Gwyliedydd
Hanes llenyddol y *Gwyliedydd* (1822-1837), gyda mynegai i'w gynnwys (The literary history of the *Gwyliedydd* (1822-1837), with an index to its contents). *L. M. Jones, M.A. 1936 Wales*

Gwynedd
The *cymwds* of Gwynedd prior to the Edwardian conquest of Wales. *G. L. Jones, M.A. 1919 Wales*

The military geography of Gwynedd in the thirteenth century. *G. R. J. Jones, M.A. 1949 Wales*

Gynecology and Obstetrics
Fashions in gynecology during the last century, with remarks thereon. *B. K. Robb, M.D. 1884 Aberdeen*

Obstetrical difficulties of a recently qualified doctor, with some observations on the teaching of obstetrics to undergraduates. *K. Watson, M.D. 1941 Dublin, Trinity College*

On the history and development of obstetrical forceps, with special reference to the application and use of Kielland forceps. *R. A. Stephen, M.D. 1933 Aberdeen*

Habeas Corpus
See Criminal Law.

Habert, François
L'inspiration antique dans *La jeunesse du Nanny de Lyesse* par François Habert. *G. M. M. Morisset, M.A. 1929 London*

Habington, William
An edition of the poetical works of William Habington with a critical introduction. *K. C. B. Allott, B.Litt. 1938 Oxford*

Habit
Habits in moral training. *J. J. Ruan, M.A. 1936 National University of Ireland*

Habitus and habit. *G. O'Hara, M.A. 1949 National University of Ireland*

A psychological enquiry into the function and importance of habit in human life. *F. A. Farley, M.A. 1934 Leeds*

Hades
See Eschatology.

Hagadah
See Judaism.

Hagar
Ishmael and Hagar in the post-Biblical and Islamic literature. *H. Medalie, M.A. 1941 Manchester*

Hagedorn, Friedrich von
The German Aufklärung as reflected in the works and character of Friedrich von Hagedorn. *M. E. Davies, M.A. 1938 Wales*

Hagiography
See Saints.

Hague, Conference of
British policy and opinion and the second Hague conference. *H. S. W. Corrigan, M.A. 1934 London, King's College*

Hair in Art
Methods of representing hair in the wall-paintings of Theban tombs. *E. J. H. Mackay, M.A. 1922 Bristol*

Hakluyt, Richard
The Principal Navigations, Voyages, Traffiques, and Discoveries of the English Nation, by Richard Hakluyt. *F. West, M.A. 1927 Liverpool*

Halakah
See Jewish Law.

Halesowen Abbey
The importance of Halesowen Abbey in the life of the English people. *A. G. Pound, M.A. 1926 Birmingham*

Halevi, Jehuda
Jehuda Halevi and Chaim Nachman Bialik. *M. Ish-Shalom, Ph.D. 1938 London, School of Oriental and African Studies*

Hāli
Hāli as poet, critic and biographer, and his influence on Urdu literature. *M. T. Husain, Ph.D. 1935 London, School of Oriental and African Studies*

Hali Meidenhad
A critical edition of *Hali Meidenhad. W. F. J. Roberts, Ph.D. 1949 London, University College*

A critical text of *Hali Meidhad,* together with a grammar and glossarial notes. *A. F. Colborn, B.Litt. 1934 Oxford*

Halifax
See also Waterhouse Charity.

The government and growth of the parish of Halifax, 1760-1848. *J. W. Houseman, M.A. 1928 Liverpool*

A history of the Waterhouse Charity, Halifax. *J. Clayton, M.A. 1943 Leeds*

Halifax, Charles Montagu, 1st Earl
Tendencies of seventeenth century thought as exhibited in the writings of Lord Halifax. *C. E. Hughes, M.A. 1932 London, Bedford College*

Hall, John
John Hall: a study of his non-political works. *P. S. Havens, B.Litt. 1928 Oxford*

The prose works of John Hall of Durham. *J. W. Pendleton, B.Litt. 1934 Oxford*

Hall, Joseph, Bishop
A critical study of the prose-works of Bishop Joseph Hall, 1574-1656. *H. Fisch, B.Litt. 1948 Oxford*

Joseph Hall (1574-1656), satirist, character writer and controversialist. *J. K. Campbell, M.A. 1937 London, Birkbeck College*

Hall, Robert
Robert Hall, 1764-1831: a study of his thought and work. *G. J. Griffin, Ph.D. 1948 Edinburgh*

Halley, Edmond
Edmond Halley and his influence upon the progress of science in the seventeenth century. *A. C. Williams, Ph.D. 1940 London, University College*

Edmond Halley and the problems of terrestrial magnetism. *A. C. Williams, M.Sc. 1937 London, University College*

Hallum, Robert, Bishop
Robert Hallum. *F. D. Hodgkiss, M.A. 1931 Manchester*

Halm, Friedrich
The classic, romantic and specific Spanish elements in the dramas of Grillparzer and Halm. *D. Evans, M.A. 1912 Wales*

Halogen
The discovery of halogen. *J. G. Stubbs, M.Sc. 1931 London*

Hamadhānī, Badī' al-Zamān
A translation, with commentary, of the *Makāmas* of Badī-al-Zamān Hamadhānī. *W. J. Prendergast, B.Litt. 1914 Oxford*

Hamburg
The cultural, commercial and political relations between the State of Hamburg and Great Britain from 1890 to 1914. *O. J. M. Jolles, M.A. 1938 Wales*

Hamdani, Abu Firas
The poetry of Abu Firas al-Hamdani. *A. A. Atik, D.Phil. 1948 Oxford*

Hamelin, Octave
The elements of representation: a critical study of the philosophy of O. Hamelin. *L. J. Beck, D.Phil. 1936 Oxford*

Hamilton, Alexander
Political theory of Alexander Hamilton. *B. M. Mayers, Ph.D. 1938 London, School of Economics and Political Science*

Hammarapi (Hammurabi), Code of
Marriage law and ceremonial in the Code of Hammarapi. *J. Paterson, Ph.D. 1929 Glasgow*

Hamp, Pierre
A syntactical study of the verb in modern French, with special reference to Pierre Hamp. *L. G. Evans, M.A. 1928 Manchester*

Hampshire
Southampton: a factor in the economic development of the Hampshire Basin. *K. C. Boswell, M.Sc. 1936 London, External Degree*

Hampton Court Conference
Hampton Court Conference. *H. F. Humbert, Ph.D. 1940 Edinburgh*

Hampton-upon-Thames
History of Hampton-upon-Thames in the sixteenth and seventeenth centuries, with special reference to educational foundations. *B. Garside, M.A. 1930 London, University College*

Hancock, House of
The House of Hancock, business in Boston, 1724 to 1775. *W. T. Baxter, Ph.D. 1946 Edinburgh*

Handicrafts
See also Woodwork.

Handicraft in education: its rise and progress in English elementary and secondary schools. *G. A. Williams, M.A. 1936 Liverpool*

Handwerk und Handwerker in der deutschen erzählenden Literatur vom Ausgang des achtzehnten Jahrhunderts bis zur Gegenwart. *C. E. Robert, M.A. 1939 Liverpool*

Handwork and science: their contribution to cultural education. *H. Cordingley, M.Ed. 1938 Leeds*

The mental and moral discipline of handicraft in schools. *P. F. Smith, M.A. 1931 Liverpool*

The pedagogics of school handiwork. *W. Lewis, M.A. 1913 Wales*

Scottish experiments in rural education from the eighteenth century to the present day, with special reference to rural arts and crafts. *J. Mason, Ph.D. 1931 Edinburgh*

Some principles involved in the teaching of handwork, with special reference to the junior school. *T. V. Walsh, M.A. 1941 Leeds*

Handlyng Synne
See William, of Waddington.

Handwriting
Local peculiarities of handwriting in documentary papyri of the Roman period. *M. E. Dicker, M.A. 1929 London*

Problems of personality development in the light of graphological analysis. *E. F. C. Kronheimer, B.Sc. 1942 Oxford*

Hanse, The
The building of the Hanseatic League from its earliest days until 1370. *L. M. Seckler, M.A. 1929 Birmingham*

England and the Teutonic *Hanse. A. Weiner, M.A. 1904 Wales*

The position of England towards the Baltic powers, i.e. Denmark and Sweden including the Hanse towns, from 1689-1697. *M. Lane, M.A. 1911 London*

Hansteen, Christoph
The work of Hansteen and Gauss on the law of magnetic force, with some account of the work of their predecessors. *J. J. Reynolds, M.Sc. 1949 London, University College*

Happiness
See Joy. For Hedonism, see Philosophy.

Harappa
Harappa in Asia. *A. H. Christie, M.A. 1950 Manchester*

The script of Mohenjodaro and Harappa, and its relation to other scripts. *G. G. R. Hunter, D.Phil. 1930 Oxford*

Harcourt Family
Transcription of Harcourt Papers. *M. P. Joyce, M.A. 1947 National University of Ireland*

Hardenberg, Friedrich von
See Novalis.

Hardware Industry
The hardware export trade. *E. A. White, M.Com. 1922 Birmingham*

Hardy, Thomas
The artistic method of Thomas Hardy, novelist. *F. E. Ward, M.A. 1921 Birmingham*

Aspects of the nineteenth century quest for God as reflected in the works of Thomas Hardy, Robert Browning and Francis Thompson. *A. M. Granville, M.A. 1950 Wales*

A critical study of the novels of Thomas Hardy. *R. Williams, M.A. 1914 Wales*

Early life and works of Thomas Hardy, 1840-1878. *H. Reed, M.A. 1936 Birmingham*

The early work of Thomas Hardy. *W. R. Rutland, 1935. 195. Oxford*

The grounds of pessimism in Thomas Hardy's view of life. *R. Moir, M.A. 1947 Manchester*

Novels of Thomas Hardy. *J. B. S. O'Kelly, M.A. 1948 National University of Ireland*

The regionalism of Thomas Hardy. *J. D. Brennan, M.A. 1948 National University of Ireland*

Samuel Johnson and Thomas Hardy, their attitudes to the problem of suffering: a comparative study. *H. H. Mountfield, M.A. 1948 Liverpool*

Study of the prosody and diction of Hardy's lyric poetry. *M. Davies, M.A. 1943 Wales*

The Dynasts by T. Hardy. *J. F. Taylor, M.A. 1925 Birmingham*

Thomas Hardy. *W. R. Rutland, D.Phil. 1937 Oxford*

Thomas Hardy: His views on life and nature. *J. H. Francis, M.A. 1913 Wales*

Thomas Hardy's analysis of human nature: a psychological study of the Wessex novels. *A. J. Horrocks, Ph.D. 1931 London, External Degree*

The tragic aspect of life, as presented by T. Hardy. *E. Parsons, M.A. 1932 Birmingham*

The use of poetry by Thomas Hardy. *T. H. Bevan, M.A. 1936 Wales*

Harington, John, Sir
Sir John Harington's translation of *Orlando Furioso. B. E. Burton, B.Litt. 1939 Oxford*

Harley, Robert, 1st Earl of Oxford
The domestic policy of Robert Harley and the Tory Ministry from 1710-1714. *W. T. H. Bolton, M.A. 1930 London, Bedford College*

The political evolution of Robert Harley, 1702-12. *K. C. Turpin, B.Litt. 1940 Oxford*

Harrington, James
Conceptions of property in England from Harrington to Marx. *W. S. Evans, Ph.D. 1942 Sheffield*

Harris, Howell
The origin and growth of the Methodist Movement in Wales in the eighteenth century, in the light of the unpublished mss. correspondence of Howell Harris at Trevecka. *M. H. Jones, Ph.D. 1929 Wales*

Hartmann, Nicolai
Disinterestedness and its conditions: a limited comparison between the ethics of Christianity and of scientific humanism as represented in particular by the *Ethics* of Professor Nicholai Hartmann. *R. G. Norburn, M.A. 1940 Manchester*

The problem of moral freedom with reference to its discussion in recent philosophy and in particular in the *Ethics* of Nicolai Hartmann. *H. D. Lewis, M.A. 1934 Wales*

Hartzenbusch, Juan Eugenio
Two Spanish Romantics: Antonio García Gutiérrez and Juan Eugenio Hartzenbusch. *J. V. Gorner, M.A. 1929 Liverpool*

Hasmonean Dynasty
See Jews: History.

Hastings, Warren
Hastings' experiment in the judicial system. *N. J. M. Yusuf, Ph.D. 1930 London, School of Economics and Political Science*

Hastings, Warren contd.
The relationship of Warren Hastings to the government of Oudh. *E. Macmillan, M.A. 1912 Liverpool*

The Residency in Oudh during the administration of Warren Hastings, 1772-85. *C. C. Bracewell, M.A. 1922 Manchester*

A study of the legal and administrative records of Dacca as illustrating the policy of Warren Hastings in East Bengal. *F. M. Sachse, B.Litt. 1934 Oxford*

Hat Industry
The development of the felt hat manufacturing industry of Lancashire and Cheshire. *H. Housley, M.A. 1929 Manchester*

The history of the straw hat and straw plaiting industries of Great Britain to 1914, with special reference to the social conditions of the workers engaged in them. *J. G. Dony, Ph.D. 1941 London, School of Economics and Political Science*

Hauptmann, Gerhart
Gerhart Hauptmann. *J. Johnston, M.A. 1914 National University of Ireland*

Goethe and Hauptmann: comparative study. *W. Airston, M.A. 1914 Birmingham*

Growth of the naturalist drama in Germany, with special reference to Gerhart Hauptmann. *B. E. Thomas, M.A. 1931 Wales*

Social sympathy and the scientific impulse in the naturalistic work of Gerhart Hauptmann. *J. Barnes, M.A. 1937 Manchester*

The weak man as 'hero' in the works of Gerhart Hauptmann. *E. R. Gross, M.A. 1947 Belfast*

Hausa Language
Hausa-English dictionary and English-Hausa vocabulary. *G. P. Bargery, D.Litt. 1937 London, School of Oriental and African Studies*

Hausa, The
The ban of the Bari. *A. J. T. Nremicarne, M.Sc. 1914 London*

Havich, of Cologne
Sankt Stephans Leben. R. J. McClean, M.A. 1930 London, School of Economics and Political Science

Hawaii
The technology and economics of fishing in relation to Hawaiian culture. *R. A. Scobie, M.A. 1949 London, School of Economics and Political Science*

Hawes, Stephen
A biographical and literary study of Stephen Hawes, with special reference to the minor poems. *G. S. Humphreys, M.A. 1928 London*

Hawker, Robert Stephen
R. S. Hawker, poet and mystic: a study of his life, character and writings. *M. F. Burrows, M.A. 1925 London*

Hawkesworth, John
John Hawkesworth: a biography and a critical study of his work in the periodicals. *H. E. Webster, M.A. 1949 London, Birkbeck College*

Hawking
Hawking literature in Anglo-Norman. *M. I. Dixon, M.Litt. 1929 Cambridge*

Hawthorne, Nathaniel
Nathaniel Hawthorne: a monograph. *H. S. White, B.Litt. 1922 Oxford*

Hazlitt, William
The bias of Hazlitt. *J. K. Thomas, M.A. 1931 Liverpool*

The function of the literary critic, with special reference to the work of Hazlitt. *W. R. Niblett, B.Litt. 1930 Oxford*

Keats and Hazlitt in their personal and literary relations. *H. M. Keyes, B.Litt. 1937 Oxford*

Matthew Arnold and the literary criticism of the early nineteenth century, with special reference to Jeffrey and Hazlitt: a comparison of methods and evaluations. *J. Wilkinson, M.A. 1947 Manchester*

William Hazlitt. *M. W. Patton, M.A. 1937 National University of Ireland*

Head, Edmund Walker, Sir
The life of Sir Edmund Walker Head, Bart. *J. A. Gibson, D.Phil. 1938 Oxford*

The work of Sir Edmund Head in British North America 1848-61. *D. G. G. Kerr, Ph.D. 1937 London, King's College*

Headington, Oxfordshire
The manor of Headington. *E. Evans, B.Litt. 1928 Oxford*

Healing, Spiritual
An attempted synthesis of Christian spiritual healing and psychotherapy. *M. Gregory, D.Phil. 1938 Oxford*

Healing, Spiritual contd.
Christian healing; a consideration of the place of spiritual healing in the Church of today in the light of examination of the doctrine and practice of the Ante-Nicene Church. *E. Frost, Ph.D. 1940 London, King's College*

Faith healing under the Roman Empire: a translation of the sacred orations of Aristides Aelius, together with an introduction. *F. W. Lockwood, M.A. 1935 London, Birkbeck College*

Healing. *G. G. Dawson, D.D. 1936 Cambridge*

Healing, pagan and Christian. *G. G. Dawson, Ph.D. 1935 London, Richmond College*

Health, Public
See Public Health.

Healy, John
A translation, with a commentary, of the sermons of Father John Healy of Dunleer. *J. F. Hicks, M.A. 1947 Belfast*

Hearing
Variations in the normal range of children's voices: variations in range of tone audition: variations in pitch discrimination. *T. Anderson, Ph.D. 1937 Edinburgh*

Heat
See also Thermometers.

Experimental investigations in the study of heat in the eighteenth century. *K. M. Hollingworth, M.Sc. 1948 London, University College*

French contributions to the science of heat in the first half of the nineteenth century. *M. A. Bentham, M.Sc. 1928 London*

Heath, Robert
An edition of Robert Heath's *Clarastella* of 1650. *R. T. Swartz, B. Litt. 1929 Oxford*

Heaven, Kingdom of
See Kingdom of God.

Hebbel, Christian Friedrich
An analysis of the short stories by Ludwig Tieck and Friedrich Hebbel, with special reference to style and structure. *H. H. J. Jensen, M.A. 1947 London, Bedford College*

C. F. Hebbel's realism in theory and practice. *G. B. Rees, Ph.D. 1926 London*

Friedrich Hebbel's theory of tragedy. *C. A. M. Sym, Ph.D. 1936 Edinburgh*

The significance of Friedrich Hebbel for the German drama of the later nineteenth century. *L. F. R. Van Raalte, M.A. 1922 London*

The sources of Hebbel's *Agnes Bernauer*. *A. Löwenstein, M.A. 1908 London*

Woman versus man: a study of the relationships and differences between the sexes as a source of tragedy in the life and chief dramas of F. Hebbel. *H. J. Pargeter, M.A. 1950 Birmingham*

Hebrew Language
See also Aramaic Language; Samaritan Language.

The Babylonian-Hebrew punctuation. *D. Mann, M.A. 1906 London*

Christian Hebraists in sixteenth-century England. *A. Schper, Ph.D. 1944 London, Courtauld Institute of Art*

A critical examination of the two main versions of the Book of Job by Bishops Morgan and Parry, with special reference to the Hebraisms in these versions, together with a new translation of the book into idiomatic Welsh. *L. E. Valentine, M.A. 1921 Wales*

The Eliu and Jahweh speeches in the Book of Job, investigated from the literary and linguistic points of view. *D. R. Rogers, M.A. 1915 Wales*

The evolution of the syntax of post-biblical Hebrew. *C. Rabin, D.Phil. 1943 Oxford*

Hebraic studies in seventeenth century England. *A. D. Hallam, M.A. 1949 Leeds*

The historical continuity of Hebrew, with special reference to its medieval and modern phases. *M. Friedlander, Ph.D. 1933 Manchester*

The participial formations of the germinate verbs. *B. Halper, M.A. 1909 London*

Studies on the Hebrew verb. *H. L. Ginsberg, Ph.D. 1930 London, External Degree*

Hebrew Literature
See also Bible: Old Testament; Cairo Geniza; Romances; and Aaron ha-Levi, of Barcelona; Abulafia, Todros; Bonfed, Solomon ben Reuben;

Hebrew Literature contd.
Sa'adia Longo. For Hagadah and Talmud, see Judaism. For Halakah, Mishnah and Tosefta, see Jewish Law. For Midrash, see Bible: Old Testament.

The concept of wisdom in Greek and Hebrew literature. *J. P. Dempsey, M.A. 1946 National University of Ireland*

The Hasmonean dynasty in Jewish literature before A.D. 70. *F. J. Glendenning, M.A. 1949 Sheffield*

Ishmael and Hagar in the post-Biblical and Islamic literature. *H. Medalie, M.A. 1941 Manchester*

Jehuda Halevi and Chaim Nachman Bialik. *M. Ish-Shalom, Ph.D. 1938 London, School of Oriental and African Studies*

The parables and similes of the Rabbis: agricultural and pastoral. *A. Feldman, Ph.D. 1925 London*

1. The Rabbinic literature as an aid to the lexicography of the Hebrew bible. 2. Arabisms in Rabbinic literature. *A. Cohen, Ph.D. 1923 London*

The social life of the Jews of N. France in the XII-XIV centuries, as reflected in the Rabbinical literature of the period. *L. I. Rabinowitz, Ph.D. 1937 London, External Degree*

The use of the Old Testament in the Epistle to the Hebrews. *R. A. Stewart, M.Litt. 1947 Cambridge*

Hebrews
See Jews.

Hebrides, The
The Hebridean crofter: a study in social geography. *G. D. New, M.A. 1925 Liverpool*

Hedge Schools
The Hedge schools of Kerry. *M. L. O'Connor, M.A. 1949 National University of Ireland*

Hedonism
See Philosophy.

Hegel, Georg Wilhelm Friedrich
The development, significance, and some limitations of Hegel's ethical teaching. *W. S. Chang, D.Phil. 1923 Oxford*

Hegel and Germany. *B. P. Kehoe, Ph.D. 1932 National University of Ireland*

Hegel and modern philosophy. *J. O. Wisdom, Ph.D. 1933 Dublin, Trinity College*

Hegelian epistemology. *C. W. Wolfe, B.Litt. 1938 Dublin, Trinity College*

Hegel's theory and practice of education, and problems of girls' education in elementary schools. *M. Mackenzie, M.A. 1908 Wales*

The influence of Hegel's philosophy upon theology in Wales from 1850 to the present day. *P. J. Jones, M.A. 1927 Wales*

Quality, quantity and relation with special reference to the philosophy of Hegel. *S. B. Jones, M.A. 1923 Wales*

The relation of the Christian revelation to history, with special reference to Ritschlian and Hegelian tendencies. *J. MacWilliam, B.Litt. 1911 Oxford*

The educational theory involved in the philosophy of Hegel. *H. M. Cameron, M.A. 1918 London*

Heidegger, Martin
A study of the conception of conscience in the philosophy of Martin Heidegger and Karl Jaspers. *A. B. Downing, M.A. 1947 Manchester*

Heim, Karl
Karl Heim's conception of the approach to knowledge of God. *T. E. Hill, Ph.D. 1937 Edinburgh*

Heine, Heinrich
Heine in England in the nineteenth century. *K. H. B. Kirby, M.A. 1927 London*

Heine's imagery, in its relation to his personality and thought. *K. Webber, D.Phil. 1943 Oxford*

Sir W. Scott and H. Heine: an enquiry into the relations between the two writers. *F. T. Smallwood, M.A. 1910 Birmingham*

Heliocentric Theory
See Cosmology.

Hell
See Eschatology.

Hellenism
See also Greece, Ancient; Greek Language; Greek Literature.

The development of Hellenism during the fifteenth and sixteenth centuries. *R. R. Bolgar, Ph.D. 1940 Cambridge*

Hellenism contd.
The early history of the logos doctrine - the idea in Greek philosophy, with an appendix showing its relation to Hellenism, Judaism and the New Testament. *J. L. Matthews, Ph.D. 1936 London, New College*

Eratosthenes as a representative of Hellenistic culture. *E. A. Knight, M.A. 1930 London, King's College*

Friedrich Hölderlin's place in the German neo-Hellenic movement. *M. Montgomery, B. Litt. 1918 Oxford*

Greek and Judaistic individualism in the Hellenistic age, in their similarity and contrast, and their relation to the concept of the Messiah. *H. D. Hilliard, M.A. 1932 Bristol*

Hellas and its background. *O. L. Jones, M.A. 1937 Birmingham*

The Hellenistic background of New Testament thought. *T. Harper, Ph.D. 1929 Glasgow*

Indo-European influences in Hellenic civilization down to the end of the Bronze Age. *V. G. Childe, B.Litt. 1916 Oxford*

An investigation of the problem of Greek influence upon the religious thought of Judaism in the Hellenistic age. *A. R. Johnson, Ph.D. 1931 Wales*

Neo-Hellenism in French literature from 1850-1900. *A. D. Bryant, Ph.D. 1931 London, East London College*

Roman Philhellenism as a factor in the literary revival of Greek under Hadrian and the Antonines. *W. A. Odell, M.A. 1920 Birmingham*

Some Hellenic elements in the works of Abelard. *V. G. Kirk-Duncan, B.Litt. 1941 Oxford*

Helston
History of Helston, 1768-91. *H. S. Toy, M.A. 1931 Bristol*

Hemans, Felicia Dorothea
Felicia Hemans: the basis of a biography by Temple Lane (pseud.). *M. I. Leslie, Ph.D. 1943 Dublin, Trinity College*

Henley
The medieval borough of Henley: 1. its history; 2. its constitution. *P. M. Briers, B.Litt. 1935 Oxford*

Henrietta, Island
The Company of Adventurers to the islands of Providence and Henrietta: its foundation and history, 1630-1634. *A. P. Newton, M.A. 1910 London*

Henry III, King of England
The personal disputes between Henry III and Simon and Eleanor de Montfort. *M. M. Wade, B.Litt. 1939 Oxford*

Henry VIII, King of England
Sir Thomas More and the divorce. *E. Edkins, M.A. 1916 Liverpool*

Heraclitus, of Ephesus
The philosophy of Heraclitus as contained in his fragments. *E. E. Dodd, M.A. 1920 Wales*

Heraldry
The historical development of heraldic terms, with especial consideration of 'armes parlantes'. *H. E. Tomlinson, M.A. 1942 Manchester*

Herbals
Llysieulyfr meddyginiaethol a briodolir i William Salesbury (A medicinal herbal attributed to William Salesbury). *E. S. Roberts, M.A. 1917 Wales*

Herbart, Jean Frédéric
A critical exegesis of the concept of freedom in the educational systems of Pestalozzi and Herbart. *J. E. Parry, B.Litt. 1928 Oxford*

Herbert, Edward, 1st Baron Herbert of Cherbury
Lord Herbert of Cherbury: a study of his personality and writings. *D. W. H. Watson, M.A. 1950 Liverpool*

Herbert, George
Francis Thompson: a study of his relation to George Herbert, Henry Vaughan and Richard Crashaw. *C. Bergin, M.A. 1948 National University of Ireland*

George Herbert and Nicholas Ferrar: a study of thought and imagery in Jacobean devotional literature. *B. Blackstone, Ph.D. 1936 Cambridge*

Nicholas Ferrar and George Herbert: their work and times. *G. L. Maber, M.A. 1947 Manchester*

Studies in the life and writings of George Herbert. *K. I. Barrett, M.A. 1934 London, King's College*

Herbert, William, 1st Earl of Pembroke
A critical edition of the poems printed by John Donne the Younger in 1660 as written by William Herbert, Earl of Pembroke, and Sir Benjamin Ruddier. *M. A. Beese, B.Litt. 1935 Oxford*

Hercules
Hercules in Greek and Roman tragedy (Euripides, Sophocles, Seneca). *L. Ball, M.A. 1937 Manchester*

Herder, Johann Gottfried von
A critical examination of Herder's thought, with special reference to its parallels in Coleridge. *G. A. Wells, M.A. 1949 London, University College*

The genesis of Herder's literary theories. *W. B. Savigny, M.A. 1939 Manchester*

Herder's contribution to the Romantic philosophy of history, with special reference to the theological implications. *G. W. Bromiley, Ph.D. 1943 Edinburgh*

Herder's relationship to German romanticism, with special reference to the theory of literary criticism. *G. Parker, D.Phil. 1939 Oxford*

Herder's treatment of his English sources in the Volkslieder. *D. F. Schumacher, M.A. 1936 London, University College*

Macpherson's *Ossian* in the works of Johann Gottfried v. Herder. *H. T. Betteridge, M.A. 1933 Birmingham*

The religious philosophy of Herder and Schleiermacher studied in relation to the influence upon them of Leibniz, Spinoza, and Kant. *M. E. Sandbach-Marshall, M.A. 1928 London*

Herder, Johnann Gottfried von
Herder's Humanitätsideal. *F. McEachran, B.Litt. 1930 Oxford*

Heredia, José Maria de
L'influence du culte de la forme sur la pensée de J. M. de Heredia. *N. Smith, M.A. 1918 Birmingham*

Heredity
The history and criticism of the theory of acquired characteristics. *M. A. Washbrook, M.Sc. 1929 London*

An investigation into the relation between intelligence and inheritance. *E. M. Lawrence, Ph.D. 1930 London, School of Economics and Political Science*

Theories of heredity in the nineteenth century. *E. J. Hatfield, M.Sc. 1928 London*

The treatment of problems of heredity before the twentieth century. *F. R. H. Hora, M.Sc. 1926 London*

Herefordshire
The historical geography of Herefordshire. *E. H. Wilkinson, Ph.D. 1945 Bristol*

The plain of Hereford: a geographical study of the evolution of local life. *E. I. England, M.A. 1935 Liverpool*

Heresies
See Antinomianism; Apollinarianism; Arianism; Bogomilism; Fraticelli; Gnosticism; Jansenism; Lollards; Monophysites; Montanism; Pelagianism; Socinianism.

Hergest, Red Book of
See Red Book of Hergest.

Hermas
The Shepherd of Hermas. H. H. Currie, D.Litt. 1921 Glasgow

Hermeneutics
See Bible: Criticism and Exegesis.

Herodotus
The attitude of Herodotus towards the gods and religion. *A. K. Morris, M.A. 1939 Wales*

A comparison of the principles and methods of Herodotus and Thucydides as historians. *T. B. Davis, M.A. 1901 Wales*

Gods and men; conceptions of a moral order in Aeschylus and Herodotus. *J. O'Mahony, M.A. 1950 National University of Ireland*

The purpose and function of the speeches in Herodotus. *L. Solmsen, M.Litt. 1938 Cambridge*

The relation between Herodotus and Sophocles. *M. Davenport, M.A. 1936 Manchester*

Heroes in Literature
See also Epics.

(a) The origin and development of the heroic poem in England, with some account of its relationship to the heroic romance and the heroic play; (b) The Trojan legend in England. *A. E. Parsons, D.Litt. 1932 London, External Degree*

The Byronic superman in England and Germany. *E. C. Hentschel, M.A. 1936 London, University College*

A comparison between the tragedies and histories of Shakespeare with special reference to the heroes. *L. Watson, M.A. 1910 Birmingham*

Heroes in Literature contd.
A critical analysis of the presentation of ideas connected with the figure of the hero in the works of Stefan George and his circle. *M. G. Sims, M.A. 1947 London, Birkbeck College*

Grillparzer and his early tragic heroines: Sappho, Medea, Hero. *D. Yates, M.A. 1925 Birmingham*

Legendary and historical figures in Hellenistic-Oriental popular literature. *M. Braun, Ph.D. 1937 Cambridge*

Ritual background of Celtic heroes and saints: a study of some of the survivals of pagan elements in early Celtic Christianity. *A. D. Reese, M.A. 1937 Wales*

The theme of the deserted heroine in classical literature. *J. M. Williams, M.A. 1935 Wales*

The weak man as 'hero' in the works of Gerhart Hauptmann. *E. R. Gross, M.A. 1947 Belfast*

Herrera, Francisco de
The paintings of Francisco de Herrera the Elder. *J. S. Thacher, Ph.D. 1936 London, Courtauld Institute of Art*

Herrera, Juan de
Juan de Herrera, 1530-97: his life, art, and influence on the architecture of the sixteenth and seventeenth centuries in Spain. *J. L. Martin, Sir, M.A. 1932 Manchester*

Herrera y Reissig, Julio
Report on the study of Julio Herrera y Reissig. *E. Colquhoun, M.A. 1944 Liverpool*

Herring Fishing Industry
See Fisheries and Fishing Industry.

Herschel, John Frederick William, Sir
The methodology of John Herschel and some of its subsequent developments. *R. MacDonald, M.Sc. 1927 London*

The telescopes of Sir William Herschel. *C. T. Moss, M.Sc. 1949 London, University College*

Hertfordshire
A survey of local government in Hertfordshire, 1700 to 1832. *H. Adams, Ph.D. 1931 London, External Degree*

Hervieu, Paul
A critical study of the drama of Paul Hervieu (1857-1915). *H. L. Williams, M.A. 1935 Wales*

Hesilrige, Arthur, Sir
The place of Sir Arthur Hesilrige in English politics, 1659-60. *G. H. Brown, B.Litt. 1948 Oxford*

Hesse, Hermann
The romantic element in the prose-works of Hermann Hesse. *M. B. Benn, M.A. 1948 London, University College*

Hesychasts
The Hesychast controversy, with special reference to the *Byzantina historia* of Nicephorus Gregoras and the *Historia* of John Cantacuzenus. *T. A. Hart, M.A. 1949 London, Bedford College*

Hexateuch
See Bible: Old Testament: Pentateuch.

Hey, Spurley
Spurley Hey's contribution to the origin and development of central schools. *T. H. Williams, M.A. 1938 Sheffield*

Heyse, Paul Johann Ludwig von
Paul Heyse's dramatic use of language in his *Novellen. E. N. V. Hedley, M.A. 1949 Belfast*

Heywood, John
Studies in the life of John Heywood and the Canon Heywood. *A. W. Reed, M.A. 1916 London*

Heywood, Thomas
A critical study of *The Fair maid of the exchange* and its attribution to Thomas Heywood, and the relation of the play to Markham and Machin's *Dumb knight* and the works of John Day and Thomas Dekker. *S. R. Golding, M.A. 1922 London*

Female characterization in Jacobean tragedy, with special consideration of the tragedies of Heywood, Webster, Middleton, Beaumont and Fletcher. *A. E. Bufton, M.A. 1939 Wales*

Hicks, George Dawes
Some aspects of theism, particularly of its treatment by three modern theistic authors: A. S. Pringle-Pattison, F. R. Tennant, G. D. Hicks. *G. T. Eddy, M.A. 1940 Birmingham*

Hiero II, King of Syracuse
Hiero II. king of Syracuse (B.C. 269-215). *B. McCarthy, M.A. 1950 National University of Ireland*

The life and times of Hiero II, King of Syracuse. *W. H. Davies, M.A. 1935 Wales*

Hieronymus, Eusebius Sophronius
See Jerome, Saint.

Higden, Ralph
A study of the language of the various texts of Trevisa's translation of Higden's *Polychronicon*. *A. C. Cawley, M.A. 1938 London, University College*

Higher Education
See Education, Higher.

Highways
See Roads.

Hilary, of Poitiers, Saint
THE Christology of St. Hilary of Poitiers. *A. J. G. Hawes, Ph.D. 1928 London*

Hildebrand, Saint
See Gregory VII, Saint, Pope.

Hill, Richard, Sir
Ms. Balliol 354: Richard Hill's *Commonplace Book*. *D. C. Browning, B.Litt. 1935 Oxford*

Hillel
The schools of Shammai and Hillel with special reference to their influence upon the development of the Jewish *Halachah*. *B. Unterman, M.A. 1937 Liverpool*

Hindi Language
A critical edition and translation of the *Padumavati* of Malik Muhammad Jayasi: a study of the Hindi (Avadhi) language in the sixteenth century. *L. Dhar, Ph.D. 1940 London, School of Oriental and African Studies*

Hindi Literature
See also Jayasi, Malik Muhammad; Tulsidās.

The epic in Hindi literature. *H. C. Roy, Ph.D. 1949 London, School of Oriental and African Studies*

Hinduism
See also Karma; Maya; Philosophy: India; Reincarnation; Salvation; Sankara; Sanskrit Literature; Soul; Vedas. For Hinduism and Christianity, see Christianity and Other Religions.

The *Bhaeratıfyanaetyasastra*, translated with introduction and notes. *I. Subramania, M.A. 1919 London*

A comparison of the pagan apologetic of Celsus against Christianity as contained in Origen's *Contra Celsum*, and the neo-Hindu attitude to Christianity as represented in the works of Vivekananda, and an estimate of the value of Origen's reply for Christian apologetics against neo-Hinduism. *J. R. Chandran, B.Litt. 1949 Oxford*

The conception of *karma* and reincarnation in Hindu religion and philosophy. *P. Yevtic, Ph.D. 1927 London*

The cult of Rudra-Siva: an historical survey. *Y. Vanshi, Ph.D. 1938 London, School of Oriental and African Studies*

Discussion and determination of the most adequate method to be employed in the study of the interrelation and interaction of the economic, ethical, and religious factors in the life of organized communities, as illustrated in the case of the Vaishnava communities of Gujerat. *N. A. Thoothi, D.Phil. 1925 Oxford*

Hindu political authority. *J. N. C. Ganguly, M.A. 1924 Birmingham*

The history and literature of the Gauīyad Vaisnavas and their relation to other medieval Vaisnavas schools. *S. Das, Ph.D. 1935 London, School of Oriental and African Studies*

The history and present state of Hinduism in Ceylon. *J. Cartman, M.A. 1950 Manchester*

History of Kanauj to the Moslem conquest. *R. S. Tripathi, Ph.D. 1929 London*

The mantras in the *Asvalāyana-Grihya sūtra*. *V. M. Apte, Ph.D. 1936 Cambridge*

The mysticism of Hindu Bhakti literature, considered especially with reference to the mysticism of the fourth gospel. *A. J. Appasamy, D.Phil. 1922 Oxford*

The nature of consciousness in Hindu philosophy. *S. K. Saksena, Ph.D. 1939 London, School of Oriental and African Studies*

The philosophy of Rāmānuja as compared with that of Camkara. *G. G. Dandoy, B.Sc. 1909 Oxford*

The place of the *Bhagavadgītā* in Indian thought. *G. Howells, B.Litt. 1906 Oxford*

The position of women in ancient India according to the *Dharmásāstras*. *S. N. Ajgaonkar, B.Litt. 1925 Oxford*

The problem of evil with special reference to Hindu philosophy. *E. Ahmad Shah, B.Litt. 1922 Oxford*

Hinduism contd.
Puranas: their composition and correlation. *K. N. Sitaram, Ph.D. 1922 London*

The religious and moral teaching of Tulsidās in his poem *Rāmcharitmanās*. *J. M. Macfie, Ph.D. 1929 Edinburgh*

The religious observances ordained for every day of the Hindu year, with special reference to customs observed in the Maratha country, together with the origin of these observances, whether traceable to legends, astronomical causes, or other sources. *M. M. Underhill, B.Litt. 1921 Oxford*

Some philosophical problems in the *Bhagavata Purāna*. *S. Bhattacharya, Ph.D. 1947 London, School of Oriental and African Studies*

True and false orientalism, with special reference to Hinduism and India, in the English poetry of the nineteenth century. *S. P. Varma, Ph.D. 1926 London*

Hindustani Language
The development of Hindustani in its early stages, especially as seen in translations and adaptations from Persian. *M. B. Malik, Ph.D. 1939 London, School of Oriental and African Studies*

Hipparchus
A discussion of the relative share of Apollonius, Hipparchus, and Ptolemy in the evolution of the theory of eccentrics and epicycles. *J. H. Wills, M.Sc. 1931 London*

Hippocrates
A critical survey of the advances made in surgery and anatomy in the *Corpus Hippocraticum* and the *De Medicina* of Celsus, with a short history of surgery and anatomy from the earliest times down to the beginning of the Christian era. *A. V. R. Don, Ch.M. 1922 Aberdeen*

Pseudo-Hippocrates philosophus. *A. L. Peck, Ph.D. 1929 Cambridge*

Hippolytus
Le thème de Phèdre et d'Hippolyte dans le théâtre français avant Racine. *W. Newton, M.A. 1938 Manchester*

Hippolytus, Saint
1. Early Christian prophecy. 2. St. Hippolytus and the Church. *A. C. Lawson, B.D. 1924 Oxford*

1. The *Treatise on the Apostolic tradition* of St. Hippolytus. 2. The theology of confirmation in relation to baptism. 3. The shape of the liturgy. *G. E. A. Dix, B.D. & D.D. 1949 Oxford*

Hispanic Languages
See also Spanish Language.

A re-examination of the problem of radical-changing verbs in the Hispanic languages with a critical account of the theories so far brought forward to explain them. *D. M. Atkinson, M.A. 1948 Sheffield*

Historia Regum Britanniae
See Geoffrey, of Monmouth.

Historians
See History, Writing of.

Historical Fiction
See Fiction.

Historical Geography
See Geography.

Historical Novels
See Fiction.

Historical Studies
See History: Study and Teaching.

History
The children of the sun: a study in the early history of civilization. *W. J. Perry, D.Sc. 1929 London*

The Christian interpretation of history as exemplified in the writings of Jacques Maritain and Reinhold Niebuhr. *W. E. Tyree, Ph.D. 1949 Edinburgh*

A comparison of the treatment of historical subjects by Aristophanes and Thucydides. *W. J. Jones, M.A. 1911 Wales*

A critical examination of Dilthey's theory of the historical and social studies only. *H. A. Hodges, D.Phil. 1932 Oxford*

Eschatology and the Christian understanding of history, with special reference to the biblical and metaphysical background. *E. C. Rust, B.D. 1947 Oxford*

Herder's contribution to the Romantic philosophy of history, with special reference to the theological implications. *G. W. Bromiley, Ph.D. 1943 Edinburgh*

The historical evidence contained in Aristophanes and in the fragments of the Old Attic Comedy. *B. H. G. Williams, B.Litt. 1932 Oxford*

History contd.
An idealist conception of history. *E. J. Widdows, Ph.D. 1922 Bristol*

The ideas of time and history in the development of thought up to the end of the eighteenth century. *W. von Leyden, D.Phil. 1944 Oxford*

Medievalism in the works of Rossetti and William Morris. *E. Hall, M.A. 1912 London*

The nature of historical explanation. *P. L. Gardiner, B.Litt. 1950 Oxford*

The problem of the plurality of forms at the University of Oxford in the thirteenth century. *D. A. P. Callus, D.Phil. 1938 Oxford*

The psychology of S. Paul. *W. N. W. Harvey, B.Litt. 1941 Dublin, Trinity College*

The relations of history and science. *R. I. Aaron, M.A. 1923 Wales*

A theological study of the relationship of time and eternity, with special reference to the modern philosophy of history. *J. Marsh, D.Phil. 1946 Oxford*

The theory of sovereignty in history. *W. D. Handcock, M.A. 1926 Bristol*

Twentieth-century criticism of the sociological theories of Karl Marx, and especially of his economic or materialistic interpretation of history. *B. J. I. Lewis, M.A. 1932 Wales*

History: Study and Teaching
An analysis of the factor patterns obtained from tests of history given to boys of different ages. *G. F. Maw, M.A. 1937 London, Institute of Education*

An attempt to consider a syllabus in world history suitable for a 'senior' school. *P. N. Wilshere, M.A. 1931 London, Day Training College*

A consideration of some of the text books on modern history used in secondary schools since 1860 illustrating the development in the theory and practice of history teaching. *W. A. Pilsbury, M.A. 1944 Reading*

The correlation of history and geography in the primary schools. *T. J. O'Meara, M.A. 1936 National University of Ireland*

A critical examination of a deductive method of teaching history in secondary schools. *W. T. Selley, M.Ed. 1939 Manchester*

The development of history teaching in schools and its application to the Indian high school. *M. A. Talib, M.Ed. 1941 Leeds*

An experimental study of mental processes involved in the comprehension of historical narrative. *G. W. Bassett, Ph.D. 1940 London, Institute of Education*

An historical enquiry into the teaching of history in the elementary training college and public elementary school, with some consideration of both the development of the study of history and of pedagogic theory in relation to the problem of teaching history in the training college. *F. L. Bowman, M.Ed. 1919 Manchester*

History and education for citizenship in grammar schools. *W. H. Burston, M.A. 1947 Bristol*

The history syllabus of the senior school, being a consideration of the principles of selection. *A. H. Blake, M.A. 1934 London, Institute of Education*

Problems in teaching of history in Irish primary schools. *D. Downey, M.A. 1934 National University of Ireland*

The subject matter of history in junior schools. *E. R. H. Nunn, M.A. 1929 London*

The teaching of history. *A. Barter, M.A. 1926 Liverpool*

The teaching of history. *E. L. Hasluck, M.A. 1919 London*

The teaching of history in the preparatory school. *W. H. Sankey, M.Ed. 1923 Manchester*

The teaching of history of boys of eleven to fifteen. *C. E. Jones, M.Ed. 1926 Leeds*

Teaching pupils how to study, with special reference to the study of history. *S. A. Williams, M.A. 1918 London*

The value of films in the teaching of history. *F. Consitt, Ph.D. 1931 Leeds*

History, Military
See also Armed Forces.

The art of war in Ancient India. *P. C. Chakravarti, Ph.D. 1938 London, School of Oriental and African Studies*

The maritime powers and the evolution of war aims of the Grand Alliance, 1701-1704. *P. J. Welch, M.A. 1940 London, University College*

History, Military contd.
The military and naval terms in the Norman and Anglo-Saxon chronicles of the twelfth century. *G. C. Johnson, Ph.D. 1949 Leeds*

Military methods employed by the Latin states in Syria, 1097 to 1192. *R. C. Smail, Ph.D. 1948 Cambridge*

Military unrest as described by Tacitus. *R. J. Philpot, M.A. 1950 Wales*

Soldiers' songs of the thirteenth and fourteenth centuries. *G. E. Morris, M.A. 1947 Sheffield*

History, Naval
See also Armed Forces.

Muslim sea power in the eastern Mediterranean from the seventh to the tenth century: studies in naval organization. *A. M. Fahmy, Ph.D. 1948 London, School of Oriental and African Studies*

The principles and policies of the Nine Power Treaty of 1922 in the light of subsequent developments. *Y. Ming, D.Phil. 1941 Oxford*

History, Writing of
See also Dio Cassius; Herodotus; Livy; Salvian; Tacitus; Thucydides; and Carlyle, T.; Clarendon, Edward Hyde, 1st Earl of; Commynes, P. de; Dalrymple, D., Lord Hailes; Du Bellay, G.; Du Bellay, M.; Ferrières, G. C. de, Comte; Gibbon, E.; Guizot, F.; Higden, R.; Mably, G. B. de; Michelet, J.; Ozanam, A. F.; Paris, M.; Tocqueville, A. C. H. C. de.

A comparison between the styles of Old English and Norse historical prose. *K. M. Quinn, M.A. 1932 London, King's College*

The development of historical writing among the Moslems in Spain. *S. Goldman, D.Phil. 1936 Oxford*

English influences on French historians during the seventeenth century. *E. A. E. Mitchell, M.Litt. 1932 Cambridge*

German historiography and the evolution of German political ideas in the nineteenth century. *J. W. Jennings, Ph.D. 1949 London, School of Economics and Political Science*

The historians of the French Revolution prior to 1823. *W. Percival, M.A. 1929 Manchester*

The Muslim historians of India, from 1205-1259. *W. H. Andalib-i-Shadani, Ph.D. 1934 London, School of Oriental and African Studies*

Ralph Thoresby and his circle, with special reference to the state of English historical scholarship in his time. *J. J. Saunders, M.A. 1936 London, External Degree*

Hittites, The
Hittite prayers of Mursili II. *O. R. Gurney, D.Phil. 1939 Oxford*

Hobbes, Thomas
The conceptions of natural law and natural right, with special reference to Hobbes, Spinoza, Locke and Rousseau. *N. S. B. Powell, M.A. 1932 Wales*

English theories of moral obligation from Hobbes to Stephen. *F. J. Smith, B.Sc. 1900 Oxford*

Law as the basis of morality in the philosophy of Hobbes, Cumberland and Locke. *M. Balaguer, Ph.D. 1937 London, University College*

The theory of sovereignty in the philosophy of Thomas Hobbes. *H. Jones, M.A. 1936 Liverpool*

Hoeffding, Harald
Examination and criticism of Hoeffding's contribution to the psychology of religious conviction. *A. W. Baillie, M.A. 1924 Manchester*

Hoffmann, Ernst Theodor Wilhelm (Amadeus)
The fantastic element in the characters of E. T. A. Hoffmann. *M. I. Brogden, B.Litt. 1947 Oxford*

Hoffmann and Nerval. *C. R. Buxton, M.A. 1950 Manchester*

The influence of the earlier romanticists on E. T. A. Hoffmann. *G. D. Millar, M.A. 1915 London*

Hofland Collection
The place of children's books in English education during the first half of the nineteenth century, with special reference to the Hofland Collection. *A. J. Leech, M.Ed. 1941 Leeds*

Hofmannsthal, Hugo von
Stoff, Stimmungen und Form der Lyrik Hugo von Hofmannsthals. *L. McGearty, M.A. 1947 National University of Ireland*

Hogarth, William
An edition of Hogarth's *Analysis of Beauty*, with an appendix of excerpts from the original manuscript drafts and a study of Hogarth's place in the aesthetic criticism of the eighteenth century. *J. T. Burke, M.A. 1935 London, King's College*

Hogg, James
James Hogg. *W. J. Merry, D.Litt. 1922 Glasgow*

James Hogg: the Ettrick Shepherd. *E. C. Batho, M.A. 1920 London*

Hogg, Quintin
The London Polytechnic movement, with special reference to Quintin Hogg. *F. Johnson, M.A. 1929 London*

Holbach, Paul Heinrich Dietrich d', Baron
The influence of the French revolutionary theorists (Voltaire, Rousseau, D'Holbach etc.) upon Shelley. *G. C. Rosser, M.A. 1939 Wales*

Some aspects of the life and thought of Baron d'Holbach. *J. Lough, Ph.D. 1938 Cambridge*

Holcroft, Thomas
The influence of radical doctrine in the French Revolution on English drama in the time of Thomas Holcroft, 1776 to 1806. *W. V. Aughterson, Ph.D. 1936 London, King's College*

Hölderlin, Johann Christian Friedrich
A comparison of Friedrich Hölderlin and John Keats in their respective backgrounds. *G. Guder, Ph.D. 1942 Edinburgh*

Friedrich Hölderlin's place in the German neo-Hellenic movement. *M. Montgomery, B. Litt. 1918 Oxford*

Hölderlin's Anschauungen vom Beruf des Dichters in Zusammenhang mit dem Stil seiner Dichtung. *L. S. Salzberger, D.Phil. 1950 Oxford*

Holinshed, Raphael
A comparison of Shakespeare's use of Holinshed and Plutarch in his English and Greek-Roman history plays. *E. A. Donnan, Ph.D. 1950 Manchester*

Holland
See Netherlands.

Holland, Lincolnshire
See Lincolnshire.

Holme
A critical edition of the twelfth century sections of Cott. ms. Galba E ii (register of the Abbey of St. Benet of Holme). *J. R. West, Ph.D. 1927 London*

Holstein, Friedrich von, Baron
Policy of Baron von Holstein. *M. P. Hornik, D.Phil. 1942 Oxford*

Holy Alliance
See Europe: History.

Holy Communion
See Eucharist.

Holy Land
See Palestine.

Holy Roman Empire
A comparison of the local administration and law courts of the Carolingian Empire with those of the West Saxon kings. *H. M. Cam, M.A. 1909 London*

The Emperor Lewis IV and the Curia from 1330 to 1347: canon law and international politics in the first half of the fourteenth century. *H. S. Offler, Ph.D. 1939 Cambridge*

The part played by the aristocracy in the later Carolingian Empire, with special reference to Germany. *J. H. Matthews, Ph.D. 1949 Cambridge*

The significance of Canossa. *L. P. Hope, Ph.D. 1931 Edinburgh*

Holy See
See Roman Catholic Church.

Holy Spirit
See also Gift of Tongues; Trinity, The.

1. The atonement. 2. St. Paul's doctrine of Christian ethics in relation to the Holy Spirit. *A. Robertson, B.D. & D.D. 1897 Oxford*

1. The atonement. 2. The Holy Spirit. *J. A. Smith, B.D. & D.D. 1898 Oxford*

The blessing of the Holy Spirit. *J. E. Fison, B.D. 1950 Oxford*

1. Christ, our righteousness. 2. The doctrine of the Holy Spirit. *J. G. Simpson, B.D. & D.D. 1909 Oxford*

1. The deity of Christ and of the Holy Spirit as revealed in the New Testament. 2. The Scriptural evidence for the Resurrection of Christ. *C. J. Casher, B.D. 1899 Oxford*

Holy Spirit contd.
1. The divinity of the Holy Spirit. 2. Episcopal government in the early Church. *J. W. Stanbridge, B.D. 1876 Oxford*

1. The divinity of the Son. 2. The personality of the Holy Ghost. *H. M. Robinson, B.D. 1876 Oxford*

1. The doctrine of God the Holy Spirit. 2. The Old Testament revelation: a divine preparation for the Incarnation. *J. Barker, B.D. 1902 Oxford*

The doctrine of the Holy Spirit in St. Luke and Acts. *J. B. Bernardin, B.Litt. 1925 Oxford*

The doctrine of the Holy Spirit in John Calvin. *G. Walters, Ph.D. 1949 Edinburgh*

1. The doctrine of the Paraclete as found in St. John xiv-xvi. 2. The preface to St. Luke's Gospel. 3. The authorship and date of Psalm cxix. *C. Knapp, D.D. 1906 Oxford*

Expositions of: St. Matthew xii.31,32: the blasphemy against the Holy Ghost; Romans viii.19-23: the groaning creation; Galatians iii.20. *H. G. Corner, D.D. 1905 Oxford*

1. Genesis iv.2; Hebrews xi.4; xii.24: Abel's sacrifice. 2. St. Matthew xxvii.5-7; Romans vi.9: the Resurrection of Jesus and its effect on believers. 3. Romans viii.1-4, 14-17, 29-39: the work of the Holy Spirit. *H. T. Beebe, D.D. 1893 Oxford*

The gift of the spirit in the New Testament, with special reference to Glossolalia. *M. Barnett, M.A. 1946 Manchester*

The Holy Spirit and the Gospel tradition. *C. K. Barrett, B.D. 1948 Cambridge*

The Holy Spirit from Arminius to Wesley. *H. Watkin-Jones, D.D. 1929 Cambridge*

The Holy Spirit in Puritan faith and experience. *G. F. Nuttall, D.D. 1944 Oxford*

The Holy Spirit in thought and experience. *T. Rees, Ph.D. 1922 London*

The Johannine doctrine of the Holy Spirit. *E. A. Betts, Ph.D. 1932 Edinburgh*

1. The nature and purpose of the Pentecostal gift. 2. The Holy Spirit in the Church. *A. C. Downer, B.D. & D.D. 1908 Oxford*

1. On the doctrine of God the Son. 2. On the doctrine of God the Holy Ghost. *H. G. Corner, B.D. 1901 Oxford*

1. On the subservience of evil to the purposes of God. 2. On the office of the Holy Spirit as the perfector of the works of God the Father. *G. H. West, B.D. & D.D. 1889 Oxford*

1. The part taken by the Holy Spirit in the salvation of man. 2. The law of Moses: a preparation for the reception of Christianity. *H. A. Spyero, B.D. 1873 Oxford*

1. The personality and divinity of the Holy Spirit. 2. Growth: a feature in the kingdom of the spirit. *W. H. Hutchings, B.D. & D.D. 1907 Oxford*

1. The problem of the second Epistle of St. John. 2. The references to the Holy Spirit in the Epistle of Clement of Rome to the Corinthians. *H. J. Gibbins, B.D. 1904 Oxford*

1. The resurrection of Jesus Christ in its relation to the Christian faith. 2. The person and work of the Holy Spirit. *D. M. Davis, B.D. & D.D. 1909 Oxford*

Revelation and the Holy Spirit. *F. W. Canfield, D.D. 1933 London, External Degree*

St. Paul's conception of the Spirit. *R. Jones, D.D. 1928 Belfast*

1. The sphere of the miraculous at different epochs of the Church and of Christian life. 2. The personality and office of the Holy Spirit. *C. H. O. Daniel, B.D. & D.D. 1904 Oxford*

1. The teaching of Holy Scripture with regard to the nature and ministry of angels. 2. The teaching of the Gospel according to St. John on the person and work of the Holy Spirit. *H. G. Lainée, B.D. 1906 Oxford*

1. The teaching of St. Paul on the Church in the Epistle to the Ephesians. 2. The teaching of St. Paul on the Holy Spirit. *G. P. Jones, B.D. 1908 Oxford*

1. The Thomistic doctrine of the sacramental form or matter. 2. The reality of the Holy Spirit's indwelling in the souls of the sanctified. *W. K. Firminger, B.D. 1905 Oxford*

1. The typical significance of the history of the children of Israel. 2. The teaching of St. Paul with regard to the Holy Spirit. *W. S. Milne, B.D. 1889 Oxford*

Holy Spirit contd.
1. The unity of the Church. 2. The person and work of God the Holy Ghost. *T. H. A. Houblon, B.D. & D.D. 1903 Oxford*

1. The witness to the divinity of our Lord. 2. Operations of the Holy Spirit in the individual soul. *C. A. H. Green, B.D. 1907 Oxford*

Holywell
The social aspects of the rise and decay of literary culture in Mold and Holywell, 1820-1900. *D. J. Jones, M.A. 1929 Liverpool*

Home Economics
The family economy of the workers in the cotton industry during the period of the Industrial Revolution, 1784-1833. *F. Collier, M.A. 1921 Manchester*

Household administration in the fourteenth century, with special reference to the household of Elizabeth de Burgh, Lady of Clare. *C. A. Musgrave, M.A. 1923 London*

Household economics: its place in the scheme of national education. *C. Houghton, M.Ed. 1918 Manchester*

Homer
The barony of Odysseus. *S. Benton, B.Litt. 1933 Oxford*

Chapman's method of translating Homer: being studies in books I, II, and XVIII of the *Iliad*, and book V of the *Odyssey. M. M. Weale, M.A. 1920 London*

The conception of Até from Homer to Aeschylus. *W. E. Wigley, M.A. 1940 Birmingham*

The development in religious and ethical thought as discerned in the *Iliad* and the *Odyssey. E. I. Jones, M.A. 1915 Wales*

Divination in Homer and the tragedians. *T. Fahy, M.A. 1914 National University of Ireland*

The history of Homeric criticism among the Greeks. *W. S. Wright, M.A. 1927 London*

Ictus lengthening in Homer. *D. Castello, M.A. 1912 London*

Introduction and notes to Pope's Homer's *Iliad. M. Macmillan, D.Litt. 1902 Birmingham*

On ιερόσ, ιερόσ, ιρόσ; and on the colour words in Homer. *C. M. Mulvany, B.Litt. 1897 Oxford*

Pope's version of the *Iliad*, considered as illustrating his theory of translation and his conception of the heroic style. *W. H. Jowsey, B.Litt. 1949 Oxford*

A study of Virgil's methods of adapting Homer, based on Macrobius's list of parallel passages. *R. F. Morgan, M.A. 1936 Wales*

The technique of the Odyssey. *J. G. Bell, M.A. 1938 Manchester*

The treatment of Odysseus in Homeric and post-Homeric Greek poetry. *W. E. Hughes, M.A. 1913 Wales*

Vergil and Homer: a study of the fifth book of Vergil's *Aeneid. W. S. Booth, M.A. 1925 Manchester*

Virgil's use of Homer and Euripides in the third book of the *Aeneid. N. E. Sutton, M.A. 1948 Manchester*

Homiletics
See Sermons.

Hong Kong
The geographical growth and development of Hong Kong, 1841-1941. *S. G. Davis, Ph.D. 1946 London, External Degree*

Honour
See Chivalry.

Hood, Thomas
The achievement of Thomas Hood as a serious poet. *E. G. Hauger, M.A. 1948 Leeds*

Thomas Hood: a critical study. *R. E. Davies, Ph.D. 1937 London, University College*

Hooghly, River
The Hooghly and its region: a study of human adjustmnt to changing environments. *B. Mukherjee, Ph.D. 1948 London, School of Economics and Political Science*

Hook, Theodore Edward
Theodore Hook: his life and works. *R. A. Jones, M.A. 1932 Wales*

Hooke, Robert
The contributions of Robert Hooke to the physical sciences. *J. R. Morgan, M.Sc. 1931 London, University College*

Hooker, Richard
An edition of Book I of Hooker's *Ecclesiastical polity* with an introductory essay dealing with the subject matter of the book and with the author's position in the history of political thought. *H. R. Charles, M.A. 1928 Wales*

The place of Hooker in the history of thought. *P. Munz, Ph.D. 1949 Cambridge*

The politics of Hooker. *F. J. J. Shirley, Ph.D. 1931 London, External Degree*

Richard Hooker. *A. P. d'Entrèves, D.Phil. 1933 Oxford*

Hop Industry
The hop industry. *H. H. Parker, Ph.D. 1933 London, External Degree*

Hope
1. Reasonableness of the considerations which form the ground of Christian hope. 2. The moral value of the doctrine of final judgement. *C. J. Thompson, B.D. & D.D. 1893 Oxford*

Hopkins, Gerard Manley
Fr. Gerard Manley Hopkins. *J. M. Hayes, M.A. 1941 National University of Ireland*

Gerard Manley Hopkins: a study of poetic idiosyncrasy in relation to poetic tradition. *W. H. Gardner, Ph.D. 1942 London, External Degree*

Gerard Manley Hopkins: poetic imagery. *D. J. Lynch, M.A. 1950 National University of Ireland*

Gerard Manley Hopkins and his poetry. *J. Stephenson, M.A. 1939 National University of Ireland*

Gerard Manley Hopkins as literary critic. *N. H. Newhouse, M.A. 1949 Liverpool*

Hopkins and Milton. *A. P. Lehane, M.A. 1949 National University of Ireland*

The poetry of Gerard Manley Hopkins. *W. Morrissey, M.A. 1937 Liverpool*

Three modern mystics: Thompson, Patmore, Hopkins. *J. M. Ryan, M.A. 1937 National University of Ireland*

Horace
The characteristics of the Augustan age reflected in Virgil and Horace. *G. Etheridge, M.A. 1911 Birmingham*

Horace: his views on life. *G. M. Norman, M.A. 1919 Birmingham*

Horace as a literary critic. *G. S. T. Lee, M.A. 1908 London*

How far did Virgil, Horace and Tacitus supply the want of a middle voice in Latin by the use of the so-called passive?. *M. Cartwright, M.A. 1906 Wales*

The limitations imposed upon Latin lyric poetry by the special nature of the Latin language, with special reference to Horace and Catullus. *F. N. Miles, M.A. 1933 Wales*

Literary and philosophical models and sources of the satirical writings of Horace. *W. E. Vine, M.A. 1905 London*

Livy and Horace on the origins of the Roman drama. *R. A. Browne, Ph.D. 1931 Cambridge*

The love of nature and rustic life in Horace, Tibullus, and Propertius. *M. J. Wrigley, M.A. 1933 Manchester*

The stoic element in Horace. *E. H. Job, M.A. 1933 Manchester*

Horne, Richard Hengist
Richard Hengist Horne: a literary biography. *A. H. Warren, B.Litt. 1939 Oxford*

Horror in Fiction
The tale of mystery and terror. *T. O. Rees, M.A. 1937 Wales*

The terror novel and Sir Walter Scott: a study in literary influence. *K. M. Lobb, Ph.D. 1939 London, External Degree*

The terror novel in French literature: its influence on the French novel of 1820-45. *H. W. Wood, M.A. 1922 London*

Horse Racing
Turf in Ireland. *R. O'Doherty, M.A. 1942 National University of Ireland*

Horses
The domestic horse and perforated stone axes in antiquity as studied by archaeological and folklore evidence, with some suggestions as to their connections with movements of peoples. *S. J. Jones, M.A. 1928 Wales*

The horse in Greek Art, from earliest times until the death of Alexander the Great. *M. E. Freeman, M.A. 1937 London, University College*

Horsham
Horsham and its functions, local and regional: past, present and future. *H. F. Pearmain, M.A. 1944 London, Birkbeck College*

Horticulture
See also Gardens and Gardening.

The development and present structure of the horticultural industry of Middlesex and the London region. *L. G. Bennett, Ph.D. 1950 Reading*

A historical and economic study of the development and organization of the market gardening industry in the Vale of Evesham. *H. J. Meredith, B.Litt. 1929 Oxford*

The horticultural industries of Worcestershire. *J. E. Blundell, M.Com. 1929 Birmingham*

The organization of wholesale distribution in Great Britain of fruit, flowers, and vegetables of domestic and foreign origin. *W. Drake, M.Com. 1941 London, External Degree*

Horton, Robert John Wilmot, Sir
Sir R. J. Wilmot Horton, Bart., politician and pamphleteer. *E. G. Johnes, M.A. 1936 Bristol*

Hosiery Industry
The British hosiery trade: its history and organization. *F. A. Wells, Ph.D. 1931 London, School of Economics and Political Science*

The policy of industrial concentration during the war, with special reference to the hosiery industry. *S. A. Taylor, Ph.D. 1949 London, School of Economics and Political Science*

The structure and organization of the British hosiery industry. *S. A. Taylor, M.Sc. 1942 London, School of Economics and Political Science*

Hospital Management
See Hospitals.

Hospitals
Domestic workers in hospitals: a field of women's employment. *M. S. Eaton, Ph.D. 1948 London, School of Economics and Political Science*

The education of children in hospital schools. *I. Nichols, M.A. 1938 Liverpool*

The hospital-school and the residential special school, with particular reference to teaching in orthopaedic hospital wards. *A. A. J. Macdiarmid, Ph.D. 1946 Glasgow*

Kitchens: a thesis on domestic and large kitchens, including those to hospitals, canteens, schools and hotels. *R. B. Wragg, M.A. 1947 Sheffield*

The organization, personnel and functions of the medieval hospital in the later Middle Ages. *M. A. Seymour, M.A. 1946 London, King's College*

The Rotunda Hospital - 1745-1945. *O'D. T. D. Browne, Litt. D. 1947 Dublin, Trinity College*

Hotels
The design and development of the commercial hotel. *H. I. Ashworth, M.A. 1930 Manchester*

Kitchens: a thesis on domestic and large kitchens, including those to hospitals, canteens, schools and hotels. *R. B. Wragg, M.A. 1947 Sheffield*

Hottentot Language
The phonetics of the Hottentot language. *D. M. Beach, D.Litt. 1932 London, University College*

Hottentots, The
The tribal system in South Africa: a study of the Bushmen and Hottentots. *I. Schapera, Ph.D. 1929 London*

House of Commons
See Great Britain: Parliament.

House of Lords
See Great Britain: Parliament.

Houses
See also Architecture; Furniture; Grates; Kitchens; Staircases; Walls.

The Greek house. *B. C. Rider, M.A. 1906 London*

The Irish house. *C. Ua Danacair, M.A. 1945 National University of Ireland*

Norman domestic architecture in England. *M. E. Wood, M.A. 1934 London, University College*

Private architecture in Fayyum villages of the Roman period. *S. Yeivin, M.A. 1928 London*

Roman villas in Britain: their nature and distribution. *M. G. A. Webster, M.A. 1920 Liverpool*

Roman villas in Britain. *J. E. A. Liversidge, M.Litt. 1949 Cambridge*

The villas of Roman Britain, and their place in the life of the province. *C. A. F. Berry, Ph.D. 1949 London, External Degree*

The Welsh house: a study in folk culture, and other papers. *I. C. Peate, D.Sc. 1941 Wales*

Houses of Parliament
See also Great Britain: Parliament.

Housing
The application of the social survey to problems of housing and town and country planning. *D. Chapman, Ph.D. 1948 London, External Degree*

The economics of housing. *J. J. Clarke, M.A. 1919 Liverpool*

The housing legislation in England, 1851-67, with special reference to London. *V. Zoond, M.A. 1932 London, King's College*

The housing movement in Ireland. *W. C. Hogan, M.Econ.Sc. 1942 National University of Ireland*

An inquiry into the housing of seasonal workers in Scotland. *E. M. McVail, M.D. 1915 Glasgow*

Labour and housing in an Indian city: a study in the economic conditions of the wage-earning classes in Bombay. *A. R. Burnett-Hurst, M.Sc. 1923 London*

The present position of the housing problem in and around London. *A. H. Hogarth, D.M. 1908 Oxford*

Problems of population and education in the new housing estates, with special reference to Norris Green. *N. Williams, M.A. 1938 Liverpool*

Studies in social science: 1. The housing problem in Bristol. 2. Some social and economic effects of alcohol consumption. *H. R. Burrows, M.Com. 1932 Leeds*

Housman, Alfred Edward
A. E. Housman. *K. O'Flaherty, M.A. 1939 National University of Ireland*

Howard, Henry, Earl of Surrey
Henry Howard, Earl of Surrey. *E. R. Casady, B.Litt. 1931 Oxford*

Howard, Robert, Sir
The dramatic work of Sir Robert Howard. *J. C. Mallison, M.A. 1923 Manchester*

Howard, William, Earl of Escrick
The political career of William, third Lord Howard of Escrick (1626?-94). *P. H. Goodman, B.Litt. 1948 Oxford*

Howe, Richard
The Howes and the American Revolution. *T. S. Anderson, D.Phil. 1930 Oxford*

Howe, William, Sir
The Howes and the American Revolution. *T. S. Anderson, D.Phil. 1930 Oxford*

Howell, James
James Howell and his relation to France, the French language and literature. *T. J. Thomas, M.A. 1926 Wales*

A study of the 'Familiar letters of James Howell. *L. M. Thomas, M.A. 1931 Wales*

Hoysala Dynasty
The dynastic history of the Hoysala kings. *J. D. M. Derrett, Ph.D. 1949 London, School of Oriental and African Studies*

Hsin Hsü
Liu Hsiang and the Hsin Hsü. *W. B. D. Doxford, Ph.D. 1937 London, School of Oriental and African Studies*

Hsün-tze
A study of the moral philosophy of Hsün-tze with special reference to the relation between knowledge and morality. *C. S. Lo, B.Litt. 1939 Oxford*

Huch, Ricarda
Ricarda Huch and E. G. Kolbenheyer as historical novelists: a contribution to the problem of the development of the historical novel in Germany. *F. R. J. Russell, M.A. 1937 London, University College*

Hudson, Thomas
Thomas Hudson (1701-1779), his life and work. *E. M. Davies, M.A. 1938 London, Courtauld Institute of Art*

Thomas Hudson's *Histoire de Judith*, edited with an introduction, notes, appendices, and glossary. *J. Craigie, Ph.D. 1940 Edinburgh*

Hudson, William Henry
The work of W. H. Hudson. *J. V. Williams, M.A. 1950 Wales*

Hue de Roteland
Les idées courtoises dans l'*Ipomeden* de Hue de Roteland. *K. G. Traneker, M.A. 1927 Birmingham*

Hügel, Friedrich von, Baron
Baron Friedrich von Hügel's place in the modernist movement. *J. C. G. Tiley, B.Litt. 1940 Oxford*

The inter-relations of nature and supernature in Von Hügel's *Philosophy of Religion*. *W. H. John, M.A. 1941 Wales*

Hugh, of Saint Victor
The doctrine of the Church and the sacraments in Hugh of Saint Victor. *W. F. Whitman, B.Litt. 1924 Oxford*

Hugo, Victor Marie
Etude sur la poésie de Victor Hugo et de Tennyson. *M. B. Henderson, M.A. 1915 Birmingham*

Examen de vocabulaire des *Travailleurs de la mer*. *J. H. Hird, M.A. 1925 Leeds*

Italy in the drama of Victor Hugo: sources and characteristics. *P. E. Crump, M.A. 1919 London*

La dette anglaise de Victor Hugo. *L. M. J. Couturier, M.A. 1912 London*

Le Romantisme du *Memorial de Sainte-Helene* et son influence sur Victor Hugo. *L. A. Rozelaar, M.A. 1924 London*

Le romantisme et le théâtre de Victor Hugo. *B. P. Thomas, M.A. 1916 Birmingham*

Les neólogismes de *Notre Dame* de Victor Hugo. *E. Bate, M.A. 1924 Leeds*

L'influence d'André Chénier sur l'oeuvre de Victor Hugo jusqu'á 1840. *A. B. Nimmo, M.A. 1948 Liverpool*

The sea in the poetry of Victor Hugo. *R. Hemingway, M.A. 1917 Liverpool*

Une étude du vocabulaire des premières oeuvres en prose de Victor Hugo (1823-1834). *S. Wormald, M.A. 1924 Leeds*

Victor Hugo and the English stage. *V. E. A. Bowley, M.A. 1927 London*

Victor Hugo comme critique de Shakespeare, avec une étude spéciale de son oeuvre intitulée *William Shakespeare*. *G. Davies, M.A. 1915 Wales*

Victor Hugo et la peine de mort. *H. Lonsdale, M.A. 1922 Leeds*

Victor Hugo et le mélodrame. *A. M. Ahearne, M.A. 1942 National University of Ireland*

Victor Hugo in the light of English criticism and opinion during the nineteenth century. *V. E. A. Bowley, Ph.D. 1944 London, Queen Mary College*

Hull
A description of the trade and shipping of Hull during the seventeenth century, and the trade organizations and kindred societies within the port. *W. J. Davies, M.A. 1937 Wales*

The history of the port of Hull to the end of the fourteenth century. *W. R. Jones, M.A. 1943 Wales*

Hull and the North Sea coastlands. *V. J. Gorner, M.Sc. 1948 London, External Degree*

Hull Grammar School
The history of the Hull Grammar School. *T. A. Laughlin, M.Ed. 1945 Leeds*

Human Rights
See Freedom.

Humanism
See also Ascham, R.; Buchanan, G.; Erasmus, D.; John, of Salisbury; Skelton, J.

The aims and methods of the English humanist educators of the sixteenth century. *J. S. Williams, M.A. 1914 Liverpool*

Christianity and modern humanism. *D. H. G. Stewart, Ph.D. 1939 Edinburgh*

Disinterestedness and its conditions: a limited comparison between the ethics of Christianity and of scientific humanism as represented in particular by the *Ethics* of Professor Nicholai Hartmann. *R. G. Norburn, M.A. 1940 Manchester*

Humanism in England during the fifteenth century up to 1485. *R. Weiss, D.Phil. 1938 Oxford*

Humanism in German secondary education: an attempt to trace its influence in the XIXth and XXth centuries. *L. P. De la Perrelle, Ph.D. 1940 London, King's College*

The humanism of John Skelton, with special reference to his translation of Diodorus Siculus. *H. L. R. Edwards, Ph.D. 1938 Cambridge*

Leaders of humanism in English education: Humphrey, Duke of Gloucester, William Grocyn, Thomas Linacre, Bishop Richard Foxe. *C. H. Winstanley, M.A. 1930 Liverpool*

Luther's translation of the Bible in the light of humanistic scholarship. *W. Schwarz, Ph.D. 1949 London, University College*

The problem of humanism. *F. R. Shields, M.A. 1906 London*

The Renaissance humanists and education. *W. J. Campion, Ph.D. 1940 National University of Ireland*

Humanism contd.
A study of some of the philosophical grounds for the rejection of the idea of God by recent humanism. *A. H. Dakin, D.Phil. 1938 Oxford*

Humanitarianism
Gospel and humanitarianism. *F. Hildebrandt, Ph.D. 1941 Cambridge*

The humanitarian movement in England in the eighteenth century, with special reference to the relation between the revival in religious life and industrial change: a study in the sociology of religion. *W. J. Warner, Ph.D. 1929 London*

Humayun
The history of Humayun from 1530-1540 A.D. *S. Banerji, Ph.D. 1925 London*

Humboldt, Karl Wilhelm von, Baron
State and culture, with special reference to Fichte and von Humboldt. *P. Beukes, B.Litt. 1936 Oxford*

Hume, David
An analysis of Hume's views on the influence of reason on conduct. *R. M. Kydd, B.Litt. 1944 Oxford*

Arguments for theism from design in nature with special reference to Hume, Paley, and Kant. *P. P. Elliott, B.Litt. 1926 Oxford*

The conception of the self in Locke, Berkeley and Hume. *M. P. Evans, M.A. 1934 Wales*

A critical examination of Hume's epistemolgy with reference to its bearing on modern problems. *C. A. M. Maund, Ph.D. 1936 London, Bedford College*

An examination of Hume's treatment of the problems of divine existence and providence. *R. J. Tree, B.Litt. 1941 Oxford*

Hume's doctrine of imagination. *S. A. Kerr, B.Litt. 1930 Oxford*

Hume's theory of ethics: a study of the *Enquiry concerning the Principles of Morals*. *R. E. O. White, M.A. 1950 Liverpool*

The influence of Hume in British theology. *J. I. Brice, Ph.D. 1948 London, Richmond College*

Philosophical atomism: a comparative study of the theories of Hume and Bertrand Russell. *D. S. Barlingay, M.A. 1927 London*

The relation between empiricism and scepticism in Hume's theory of knowledge. *E. H. Ziegelmeyer, Ph.D. 1938 London, King's College*

The relation of theology to epistemology, with special reference to Hume. *R. J. Tree, M.A. 1939 Wales*

The Scottish answer to Hume. *G. O. Kyd, B.Litt. 1932 Oxford*

The theory of universals, with special reference to Locke, Berkeley and Hume. *O. R. Davies, M.A. 1937 Wales*

The treatment of causality in the philosophy of Hume. *J. M. Weldon, M.A. 1930 National University of Ireland*

The treatment of relations by Locke and Hume. *M. R. Anand, Ph.D. 1929 London*

Hume, Joseph
Joseph Hume, M.P.: political activities, 1818-1825. *C. G. Smith, M.A. 1921 Liverpool*

Humour
Analysis of humour. *K. M. Sayons, B.Litt. 1949 Oxford*

Comic theory and criticism from Steele to Hazlitt. *S. M. Tave, D.Phil. 1950 Oxford*

An experimental and theoretical study of humour in children. *J. M. Williams, M.A. 1945 London, University College*

An experimental study of humour. *R. Ghosh, Ph.D. 1938 London, University College*

An greann i sgríbhinní na n-úghdar seo leanas: 1. Pádraig Ua Conaire. 2. An Seabhach. 3. An t-Athair Peadar Ua Laoghaire (The humour in the writings of Pádraig Ua Conaire, An Seabhach, An t-Athair Peadar Ua Laoghaire). *M. Ní Thuana, M.A. 1938 National University of Ireland*

Humour in the novels of Paul Fechter. *T. H. Storey, M.A. 1940 Belfast*

Humour, irony, and satire as employed by the young German writers. *E. Goldstücker, B.Litt. 1942 Oxford*

Sources of wit and humour in Plautus. *M. Grahy, M.A. 1930 National University of Ireland*

Wit and humour in early Greek literature. *R. H. Kidd, M.A. 1941 National University of Ireland*

Wit and humour in early Greek literature. *R. H. Kidd, B.Litt. 1941 Dublin, Trinity College*

Humphrey, Duke of Gloucester
Leaders of humanism in English education: Humphrey, Duke of Gloucester, William Grocyn, Thomas Linacre, Bishop Richard Foxe. *C. H. Winstanley, M.A. 1930 Liverpool*

Humphreys, Humphrey, Bishop
Bishop Humphrey Humphreys (1648-1712): a study of the literary and antiquarian movements in Wales in the seventeenth and early eighteenth centuries. *E. G. Wright, M.A. 1948 Liverpool*

Hundred Years' War
The part of Castile in the Hundred Years' War. *A. Christelow, B.Litt. 1934 Oxford*

The war with France in 1377. *A. F. O'D. Alexander, Ph.D. 1934 London, External Degree*

Hungary
See also Austria-Hungary.

The Rumanian claims in Hungary before the peace conference. *J. M. Cabot, B.Litt. 1924 Oxford*

Hungerford Family, The
The Hungerford family in the later middle ages. *J. L. Kirby, M.A. 1939 London, King's College*

Hunslet
The early history of Hunslet. *G. G. Gamble, M.A. 1948 Leeds*

The evolution of the English elementary day school up to 1902, containing a history of the Hunslet national schools. *G. G. Gamble, M.Ed. 1945 Leeds*

Hunt, Leigh
A descriptive and critical bibliography of Leigh Hunt's prose writings. *A. Mitchell, Ph.D. 1924 Edinburgh*

Leigh Hunt, journalist, essayist, and critic. *G. D. Stout, B.Litt. 1923 Oxford*

Huon de Bordeaux
La syntaxe des propositions adverbiales dans *Huon de Bordeaux*. *A. F. Church, M.A. 1934 London, Birkbeck College*

Hurd, Richard
The literary criticism of Richard Hurd (1719-1808). *M. J. Hourd, B.Litt. 1932 Oxford*

Hürnen Seyfrid
The Hürnen Seyfrid: a study in origins. *K. C. King, Ph.D. 1938 London, University College*

Hus, John
The influence of John Hus on Europe to the time of the Reformation, with special reference to central and eastern Europe. *J. Sedlo, Ph.D. 1943 Edinburgh*

The teaching of John Hus concerning the Church. *J. H. S. Burleigh, B.Litt. 1922 Oxford*

Huskisson, William
William Huskisson (1770-1834), imperial statesman and economist. *S. M. Hardy, Ph.D. 1943 London, Birkbeck College*

Hutcheson, Francis
The philosophy of Francis Hutcheson and of James Arbuckle, showing the position of both in the Molesworth-Shaftesbury School and the relation of the former to the Enlightenment in Scotland. *W. R. Scott, D.Phil. 1900 Saint Andrew's*

Hutchinson, Jonathan, Sir
The life and work of Sir Jonathan Hutchinson, 1828-1913, with an account of his family biography and of some aspects of nineteenth century life and thought, particularly in science and medicine. *A.E. Wales, Ph.D. 1948 Leeds*

Huxley, Aldous Leonard
Aldous Huxley's quest for truth; a study of the ideas as developed in his novels and other writings. *G. S. N. Lutsky, M.A. 1943 Birmingham*

The novels of Aldous Huxley as an expression of a philosophy of life. *D. R. Godfrey, Ph.D. 1949 Dublin, Trinity College*

The works of Aldous Huxley, with special reference to his philosophy. *I. C. H. Freeman, M.A. 1939 Wales*

Huxley, Thomas Henry
The teaching of science in England during the latter half of the nineteenth century, and Huxley's influence on its development. *W. Hall, M.A. 1931 Sheffield*

Huygens, Christian
The physical and astronomical work of Christian Huygens considered in relation to that of his contemporaries. *A. E. Bell, Ph.D. 1942 London, University College*

Huysmans, Joris Karl
The Catholic revival in French literature from Huysmans to Péguy. *E. Beaumont, M.A. 1940 London, King's College*

Huysmans, Joris Karl contd.
The language of J. K. Huysmans. *A. C. Smith, Ph.D. 1930 London, King's College*

Hyde, Laurence, Earl of Rochester
The political career of Laurence Hyde, Earl of Rochester, in its illustration of government policy, and party groupings under Charles II and James II. *M. F. Yates, Ph.D. 1935 London, Royal Holloway College*

Hydrography
See Sea.

Hymns
See also Church Music; and Luther, M.; Montgomery, J.; Newton, J.; Toplady, A. M.; Watts, I.; Wesley, C.

Assyrian prayers and hymns. *M. Sidersky, B.Litt. 1922 Oxford*

Augustus Montague Toplady, hymn-writer and theologian, with special reference to his controversy with John Wesley. *J. Maycock, Ph.D. 1946 Edinburgh*

Emynwyr gogledd Cymru hyd y flwyddyn 1800 (The hymn-writers of North Wales to 1800). *G. Tibbott, M.A. 1926 Wales*

Emynyddiaeth Cymru hyd 1740 (The hymnology of Wales up to 1740). *D. J. Thomas, M.A. 1922 Wales*

Englische Ubersetzungen von Martin Luthers geistlichen Liedern bis zum Jahre 1800. *H. Buchinger, M.A. 1939 Bristol*

The influence of the Methodist revival on Welsh hymnology, with particular reference to the hymns of William Williams of Pantycelyn. *L. Jones, B.Litt. 1922 Oxford*

Isaac Watts' work in hymnology, with special regard to its derivative and original features. *H. Escott, Ph.D. 1950 Edinburgh*

A study of the contribution of the Church in Wales to the development of Welsh hymnology, with special reference to the period A.D. 1740 to A.D. 1900. *J. H. Williams, M.A. 1940 Liverpool*

A study of the hymnology of the Methodist revival in Wales, with particular reference to the hymns of Williams, Pantycelyn. *L. Jones, M.A. 1921 Wales*

A study of the life and writings of St. John of Damascus. *B. Anagnostopoulos, B.Litt. 1950 Oxford*

Hypostatic Union
See Jesus Christ: Person and Work.

Hywel Davi
The works of Hywel Davi. *H. D. Thomas, M.A. 1913 Wales*

Hywel Dda
Hywel Dda, together with an outline of the origins, affinities, and history of the laws called after his name. *W. H. Harris, B.Litt. 1913 Oxford*

The law of obligation in the laws of Hywel Dda in the light of Roman and early English (Anglo-Saxon) law. *W. E. Daniels, LL.D. 1937 Dublin, Trinity College*

The laws of Hywel Dda. *D. Jenkins, LL.M. 1949 Cambridge*

Ibn Aqnin, Joseph b. Juda, Rabbi
A study of the *Tibb-el-Nufus* (medicine of the soul) of Rabbi Joseph-bar-Jehuda (Aqnin), from the Bodleian ms. Huntingdon 518, together with a short life of the author. *A. S. Doniach, B.Litt. 1921 Oxford*

Ibn as-Sikkīt
Ibn as-Sikkīt's *Islāh al Mantiq* according to the recensions of Al-Qālī and At-Tibrīzī. *S. A. Ahmedali, D.Phil. 1936 Oxford*

Ibn Habīb, Muhammad
An introduction to the *Kitāb al-Muhabbar* of Muhammad ibn Habīb, together with an edition of its first twenty folios, with indices and explanatory notes. *I. Lichtenstädter, D.Phil. 1937 Oxford*

Ibn Hāni', al-Andalusī, Muhammad
Diwan of Ibn Hani. *Z. Ali, D.Phil. 1925 Oxford*

Ibn Hani and his times. *Z. Ali, B.Litt. 1924 Oxford*

Ibn Ja'far, 'Abd Allāh b. Yahyā
An edition with translation of: Ibn Ja'far; chapter the eleventh of *Liqāh al Khawātir wa-jilā' al-basā'ir*. *J. L. Pollard, M.A. 1950 Manchester*

Ibn Sanā' al Mulk
Dīwān Ibn Sanā' al Mulk, with commentary and indexes. *M. A. Haq, D.Phil. 1938 Oxford*

Ibn Sīnā
See Avicenna.

Ibn Taimiya
Ibn Taimiya and his projects of reform. *S. Haque, Ph.D. 1937 London, School of Oriental and African Studies*

Ibo, The
The Ibo people. *S. R. Smith, Ph.D. 1930 Cambridge*

The Ika-Ibo people, Benin Province, S. Nigeria. *H. L. M. Butcher, Dip. Anthropology. 1931 Cambridge*

Ibsen, Henrik
The influence of Ibsen's theatre in both its range and quality on English drama. *E. Ostick, M.A. 1928 Bristol*

Modern British drama in relation to the plays of Ibsen. *V. T. Jones, M.A. 1928 Liverpool*

Ice Age
See Archaeology and Antiquities.

Iceland
Aspects of the Sturlung age, with special reference to *Sturlunga Saga*: a study in the life and literature of Iceland during the twelfth and thirteenth centuries. *R. G. Thomas, Ph.D. 1943 Wales*

Iceland, in the light of modern geography. *T. V. Sheppard, M.Sc. 1935 London, King's College*

Icelandic Language
The study of Icelandic in England in the eighteenth century. *A. M. Cambridge, M.A. 1931 London, University College*

Icelandic Literature
See also Edda; Sagas; and Jochumsson, M.; Stephensen, M.

William Morris's treatment of his Icelandic sources. *A. M. Morton, B.Litt. 1935 Oxford*

Iconography
See also Saints.

The early iconography of the Tree of Jesse. *A. Watson, Ph.D. 1935 London, External Degree*

The iconography of local saints in Tuscan painting from the thirteenth to the end of the fifteenth century. *G. Kaftal, D.Phil. 1946 Oxford*

The relationship between iconography of the Middle Ages and medieval English drama. *J. I. Jones, M.A. 1939 Wales*

Types and antitypes of the Passion in English medieval art, twelfth and thirteenth centuries. *A. C. Ritchie, Ph.D. 1935 London, Courtauld Institute of Art*

Idealism
See also Individualism; Bradley, F. H.; Green, T. H.; Lotze, R. H.

A comparative study of the recent ethical theories of idealism, pragmatism, and realism. *P. M. Hamilton, B.Litt. 1922 Oxford*

Contemporary idealists and their critics. *S. Dasgupta, Ph.D. 1922 Cambridge*

Freedom of the will according to Kant and the English Idealists. *J. L. Williams, M.A. 1902 Wales*

The idea of *Wandlung* in German literature. *C. Jones, M.A. 1935 London, Birkbeck College*

The idealism of Berkeley. *T. Crowley, M.A. 1945 National University of Ireland*

The idealism of Collier and Berkeley. *B. Thakur, Ph.D. 1937 London, University College*

The idealist theory of truth. *E. T. Evans, M.A. 1948 Wales*

The influence of Spinozism on the religious philosophy of German Idealism. *F. H. Burkhardt, B.Litt. 1935 Oxford*

La renaissance de l'idéalisme et sa réaction sur le théâtre en France, 1890-1900. *D. Knowles, M.A. 1931 Leeds*

1. Lotze's theory of reality. 2. Lotze's relation to idealism. *E. E. Thomas, D.Litt. 1922 Wales*

The pragmatic reaction to absolute idealism in English philosphy. *J. E. Gregory, M.A. 1949 Sheffield*

The problem of individuality and its implications for modern idealism. *C. D. Deshmukh, Ph.D. 1933 London, University College*

The problem of the will considered with special reference to the English school of idealists and the relation of their conclusions briefly to the doctrine of grace. *C. R. Batten, M.A. 1927 London*

A re-examination of some questions at issue between idealists and realists with regard to the subject-object relation and the nature of mind. *J. R. Jones, D.Phil. 1946 Oxford*

Idealism contd.
Some aspects of personality in British and American idealism from the time of T. H. Green, with some reference to immortality. *E. G. Braham, M.A. 1930 Liverpool*

A theory of direct realism and the relation of realism to idealism. *J. E. Turner, Ph.D. 1925 Liverpool*

The transformation of an old ideal: Aristotle-Aquinas-modern idealism. *H. W. Perkins, M.A. 1928 Bristol*

Ideas
The ethical end of Plato's theory of ideas. *F. A. Cavenagh, M.A. 1909 London*

The genesis of Plato's theory of ideas. *D. Tarrant, M.A. 1909 London*

Ideas and revelation. *P. W. Kingston, B.D. 1928 Cambridge*

The Platonic conception of the soul and its relation to the ideas. *M. M. Towne, M.A. 1928 London*

Plato's conception of beauty, and its bearing on the development of the theory of ideas. *A. C. Tunnicliffe, M.A. 1911 London*

The position of the soul and its relation to the ideas in Plato's metaphysic. *M. Hirst, M.A. 1912 London*

The recent controversy over the ideal theory of Plato. *M. E. Hirst, M.A. 1911 Birmingham*

Suggestion in relation to the moral value of ideas. *I. H. W. Lawrence, M.A. 1911 London*

The theory of ideas in Antoine Arnauld. *E. M. Goldner, B.Litt. 1938 Oxford*

Idolatry
Lollard doctrine, with special reference to the controversy over image-worship and pilgrimages. *J. Crompton, B.Litt. 1950 Oxford*

Ieuan Brydydd Hir Hynaf
The works of Tudur Penllyn and Ieuan Brydydd Hir Hynaf. *A. Jenkins, M.A. 1921 Wales*

Igboland
The divine Umundri Kings of Igboland. *M. D. W. Jeffreys, Ph.D. 1934 London, University College*

Ignatius, Diaconus
A Vatican manuscript of the Greek fabulist Ignatius Diaconus. *E. J. Vaughan, M.A. 1928 London*

Ignatius of Antioch, Saint
A study of the life and writings of St. Ignatius of Antioch, and St. Irenaeus, with special reference to their personal religion and its influence on their work and teaching. *A. P. Carleton, D.D. 1934 Oxford*

Ika-Ibo, The
See Ibo, The.

Illegitimacy (Law)
The law of illegitimacy. *W. Hooper, LL.D. 1911 London*

Illumination of Books and Manuscripts
See Book Illustration.

Illusions (Philosophy)
Error and illusion. *J. N. Chubb, D.Phil. 1937 Oxford*

Imagery
See also Figures of Speech.

The application of the test from imagery to certain plays in the Beaumont-Fletcher canon with a view to ascertaining the shares therein of J. Fletcher and P. Massinger. *S. R. Boltiansky, Ph.D. 1938 Manchester*

Christina Rossetti: the imagery in her English poetry. *D. M. Parsons, M.A. 1948 London, King's College*

De l'emploi des images, metaphores et comparaisons dans *Madame Bovary. A. E. S. Treves, B.Litt. 1929 Oxford*

An experimental contribution to the function of imagery. *E. S. Alton, Ph.D. 1932 London, University College*

An experimental investigation of auditory imagery. *M. Kerr, M.A. 1931 Manchester*

Factors in the mental processes of school children. 1. Visual and autditory imagery. 2. On the nature of the specific mental factors. 3. Factors concerned in the school subjects. *N. Carey, D.Sc. 1916 London*

Gerard Manley Hopkins: poetic imagery. *D. J. Lynch, M.A. 1950 National University of Ireland*

Heine's imagery, in its relation to his personality and thought. *K. Webber, D.Phil. 1943 Oxford*

Henry Vaughan: with a special study of his imagery. *E. Holmes, B.Litt. 1928 Oxford*

Imagery contd.
The image in the works of Marcel Proust. *H. C. R. Stockwell, Ph.D. 1942 London, King's College*

Imagery and learning. *A. M. Jenkin, M.A. 1930 London, Bedford College*

Imagery and learning: a further study. *A. M. Jenkin, Ph.D. 1933 London, Bedford College*

The imagery in the works of Fritz Reuter. *R. H. Zernick, M.A. 1947 London, Birkbeck College*

Imagery of Kalidasa and the theory of poetics. *P. De Costa, Ph.D. 1949 London, School of Oriental and African Studies*

The imagery of Paul Claudel. *D. M. Willis, M.A. 1933 Manchester*

The imagery of the metaphysical poets of the seventeenth century. *T. H. Jones, M.A. 1949 Wales*

Images and literary imagery. *D. H. Farrar, Ph.D. 1931 London, Bedford College*

The prevalence of eidetic imagery among schoolchildren and its educational significance. *H. Teasdale, M.Ed. 1932 Leeds*

The relation of certain factors of imagery and immediate memory to geometrical ability. *E. W. Webb, M.A. 1949 London, Institute of Education*

The relationship between imagery and the teaching of English. *J. E. Mason, M.Ed. 1928 Leeds*

Studies in the mental imagery experienced by young adolescents during the silent reading of descriptive passages. *D. V. Coutts, Ph.D. 1947 London, Institute of Education*

The subject matter and imagery of the poetical works of Thomas Lovell Beddoes. *G. H. Moxon, M.A. 1923 Liverpool*

The use and purpose of imagery in the tragedy of Webster, Tourneur and Middleton. *J. R. Jones, M.A. 1941 Wales*

The use of imagery in the odes of Pindar. *K. Kilburn, M.A. 1950 Liverpool*

The use of pictorial effect in the poetry of Aeschylus, Sophocles, and Euripides. *W. M. O. Reed, M.A. 1918 London*

Verbal imagery and figures of speech in Propertius: a study of some aspects of poetic technique. *S. R. Pope, M.A. 1942 Liverpool*

Webster's imagery and what it tells us. *J. A. Storey, Ph.D. 1944 Dublin, Trinity College*

Imagination
Aspects de l'imagination et du langage dans l'oeuvre de Jean Giraudoux. *E. C. Cure, M.A. 1946 London, Birkbeck College*

A comparison of the function of imagination in the fine arts and in philosophy. *M. M. C. Chart, M.A. 1939 Reading*

The daydreams of children: their importance for education. *G. H. Green, B.Litt. 1921 Oxford*

The imagination of the school-child and its relation to his proficiency in the different subjects of the elementary school curriculum. *T. Boyce, M.A. 1917 Liverpool*

The influence of scientific speculation on imaginative literature in the seventeenth century. *G. E. Neilson, M.A. 1923 Bristol*

A psychological study of the poetical imagination of Wordsworth and Shelley. *E. M. E. Haydon, M.A. 1914 London*

Quantitive and qualitative analysis of imagination. *K. Sivaprakasam, M.Sc. 1931 London, University College*

A study of imagination in children of five years. *R. F. Griffiths, M.Sc. 1931 London, University College*

Immanence
See God.

Immigration
See Emigration and Immigration.

Immortality
See Eschatology.

Immunity
The law of diplomatic immunity. *R. G. Jones, Ph.D. 1949 Cambridge*

The waiver of jurisdictional immunities. *J. M. Schmidt, Ph.D. 1941 Cambridge*

Imperialism
The conflict of nationalism and imperialism with particular reference to the Near and Middle East. *M. Awad, Ph.D. 1926 London*

Lord Shelburne and British imperialism, 1763-83. *R. A. Humphreys, Ph.D. 1933 Cambridge*

Incarnation
See also Jesus Christ; Apollinarianism. For the Kenotic theory, see Jesus Christ: Person and Work.

And the word became flesh. *A. A. Fulton, Ph.D. 1947 Dublin, Trinity College*

1. The Chalcedonian definition of the faith, and the inter-relation of the four great heresies on the Incarnation. 2. The historic value of the episcopate in the early Church as a witness and a guarantee. *T. H. Bindley, B.D. 1893 Oxford*

1. A critical study of St. Anselm's treatise *Cur deus homo*? 2. The internal evidence for the authenticity of the Gospel according to St. John. *W. R. W. Stephens, B.D. 1895 Oxford*

1. The doctrine of God the Holy Spirit. 2. The Old Testament revelation: a divine preparation for the Incarnation. *J. Barker, B.D. 1902 Oxford*

1. The doctrine of the being and nature of God. 2. The Incarnation of our Lord. *T. A. Chapman, B.D. 1907 Oxford*

1. The doctrine of the fall in relation to evolution. 2. The fall and the Incarnation. *G. C. Joyce, B.D. 1904 Oxford*

1. The doctrine of the Incarnation as expounded by Wyclif. 2. Coincidences between the Epistle to St.James and the Sermon on the Mount. *E. Harris, B.D. & D.D. 1888 Oxford*

1. Eternal life in relation to the Incarnation. 2. The idea of the Church in the Gospels. *W. Hobhouse, B.D. & D.D. 1918 Oxford*

The ideas of incarnation in the non-Christian religions, and the Christian doctrine of the incarnation. *E. C. Pallot, Ph.D. 1938 London, Richmond College*

1. The Incarnation. 2. Apostolic succession. *E. P. Lewis, B.D. 1896 Oxford*

1. The incarnation. 2. The atonement. *M. Pryor, B.D. & D.D. 1906 Oxford*

1. The Incarnation. 2. The atonement. *T. A. Purvis, B.D. & D.D. 1905 Oxford*

1. The Incarnation. 2. The Christian doctrine of sin. *H. V. S. Eck, B.D. & D.D. 1924 Oxford*

1. The Incarnation in relation to our daily life. 2. The priesthood of the laity in the Church of Christ. *C. G. Browne, B.D. & D.D. 1908 Oxford*

1. The Incarnation of our Lord. 2. The three creeds. *W. S. Tupholme, B.D. 1903 Oxford*

1. The mode of the Incarnation. 2. The indebtedness of the Pauline theology to Roman law. *W. J. S. Muntz, B.D. 1906 Oxford*

1. On the disputed verses, I John v.7,8. 2. On the Incarnation. *W. J. Ward, B.D. 1904 Oxford*

1. On the Incarnation. 2. On justification by faith. *R. W. Tattersall, B.D. 1892 Oxford*

1. Our Lord's knowledge as man. 2. St. Paul and his Gospel. *W. S. Swayne, B.D. 1918 Oxford*

1. The purpose of the Incarnation. 2. The kingdom of Christ in the New Testament. *C. L. Quibell, B.D. 1910 Oxford*

1. Revelation and inspiration. 2. Christ incarnate, the reconciler and restorer of fallen man. *R. J. Wilson, B.D. & D.D. 1894 Oxford*

1. St. Paul and the mystery religions. 2. The Incarnation and the Eucharist. *H. L. James, B.D. & D.D. 1924 Oxford*

Income, National
The development of industries in Eire since 1924, with special reference to (a) employment, and (b) the national income and its distribution. *J. M. Colfer, M.Econ.Sc. 1944 National University of Ireland*

The development of industries in Eire since 1924, with special reference to (a) employment, and (b) The national income and its distribution. *D. C. Doolan, M.Econ.Sc. 1944 National University of Ireland*

The development of industries in Eire since 1924, with special reference to (a) employment, (b) the national income and its distribution. *D. F. O'Farrell, M.Econ.Sc. 1944 National University of Ireland*

National income of Palestine. *P. J. Loftus, Ph.D. 1948 London, External Degree*

Problems in the measurement of national income and wealth. *A. D. Guerreiro, B.Litt. 1945 Oxford*

Some aspects of the inequality of incomes in modern communities. *H. Dalton, D.Sc. 1920 London*

Income, National contd.
A study of methods of national income measurements, with special reference to the problems of India. *V. K. Chopra, Ph.D. 1949 London, School of Economics and Political Science*

A study of the national income of Egypt. *M. A. Anis, Ph.D. 1949 London, School of Economics and Political Science*

Income Tax
The British income tax in the twentieth century, with special reference to public enquiries and to the legislation relating to the subject. *D. E. Evans, M.A. 1925 Wales*

The British income tax since 1900. *A. H. F. Dolley, B.Litt. 1929 Oxford*

A comparative and critical study of the income tax laws of Great Britain and the United States. *H. B. Spaulding, Ph.D. 1926 London*

A comparative study of the Roumanian and British income tax. *V. G. Vasiliu, Ph.D. 1932 London, School of Economics and Political Science*

The evolution of the Indian income tax. *J. P. Niyogi, Ph.D. 1929 London*

The incidence of income tax. *W. H. Coates, Ph.D. 1928 London*

The incidence of income taxes. *D. Black, Ph.D. 1937 Glasgow*

Income tax and its evasion: a history of post-war practice. *J. D. Radcliffe, M.Com.Sc. 1938 Belfast*

Income tax in Ireland. *C. P. MacCarthy, M.Comm. 1918 National University of Ireland*

Residence of an individual for purposes of income tax. *G. W. Bedell, LL.M. 1932 Cambridge*

Some existing anomalies in British income tax law affecting resident foreigners and non-resident British subjects. *B. A. Smith, LL.D. 1927 London*

Some special aspects of British income tax. *J. G. G. Botting, M.Sc. 1945 London, External Degree*

Independent College, Bala
Brwydr y 'Ddau Gyfansoddiad', 1877-1885 (The conflict of the 'Two Constitutions', 1877-1885). *R. G. Owen, M.A. 1941 Wales*

Bywyd a gwaith Dr. Lewis Edwards (The life and work of Dr. Lewis Edwards). *T. L. Evans, M.A. 1948 Wales*

Independent Labour Party
The Independent Labour Party. *C. T. Solberg, B.Litt. 1939 Oxford*

India
See also Agra and Oudh, United Provinces of; Assam; Bengal; Bhopal; Bihar; Bijapur; Bombay; Calcutta; Delhi; Gujarat; Kerala; Madras; Mysore; North West Frontier Province; Oudh; Punjab; Sind; Travancore.

India: Constitution
See also Civil Service.

Communal representation and Indian self-government. *I. J. Bahadoorsingh, B.Litt. 1944 Oxford*

The constitutional relations of the Marquess Wellesley with the home authorities. *B. L. Frazer, M.A. 1917 Liverpool*

A critical exposition of Indian constitutional reforms with special reference to 'dyarchy'. *S. Datta, Ph.D. 1923 London*

Discretionary powers in the Indian Government, with special reference to district administration. *B. Chand, Ph.D. 1938 London, School of Economics and Political Science*

Distribution of powers between the federal and state legislatures in the draft-constitution of India. *K. K. Rao, LL.M. 1949 London, University College and London, School of Oriental and African Studies*

Influence of European political doctrines upon the evolution of the Indian Government institutions and practice (1858-1938). *G. Prashad, Ph.D. 1942 London, School of Economics and Political Science*

Lord Macaulay and the Indian Legislative Council (1834-1838). *C. D. Dharkar, M.A. 1931 London, School of Oriental and African Studies*

The origins and development to 1892 of the Indian National Congress. *I. M. Jones, M.A. 1946 London, School of Oriental and African Studies*

The position of the Viceroy and Governor of India. *A. Rudra, Ph.D. 1938 London, School of Economics and Political Science*

The problem of federation in India, with special reference to economic relations. *J. N. Bhan, Ph.D. 1949 London, School of Economics and Political Science*

India: Constitution contd.
Relations of the Governor General and Council with the Governor and Council of Madras under the Regulation Act, 1773. *A. Dasgupta, Ph.D. 1930 London, School of Oriental and African Studies*

India: Economic History
Capital development of India, 1860-1913. *A. Krishnaswami, Ph.D. 1941 London, School of Economics and Political Science*

Consumer expenditure in India, 1931-32 to 1940-41. *R. C. Desai, Ph.D. 1948 Cambridge*

Financial history of Mysore, 1799-1831. *M. H. Gopal, Ph.D. 1930 London, School of Economics and Political Science*

An historical survey of the financial policy (with its economic and general results) of the Government of India, from 1857 to 1900. *H. S. Bhai, Ph.D. 1934 Leeds*

Indian foreign trade, 1900-1931 and its economic background. *W. B. Raghaviah, Ph.D. 1937 Edinburgh*

Indian provincial finance (1919-37), with special reference to the United Provinces. *B. R. Misra, Ph.D. 1939 London, School of Economics and Political Science*

The national income of British India, 1931-32. *V. K. R. V. Rao, Ph.D. 1937 Cambridge*

The origin and early history of public debt in India. *P. Datta, Ph.D. 1931 London, School of Economics and Political Science*

1. Some aspects of the economic consequences of the war for India. 2. The wealth and welfare of the Bengal Delta. *S. G. Panandikar, Ph.D. 1921 London*

State policy and economic development in Mysore State since 1881. *U. Abbayambal, Ph.D. 1931 London, School of Economics and Political Science*

A study of agricultural co-operation in India based upon foreign experience. *H. L. Pasricha, Ph.D. 1931 London, School of Economics and Political Science*

India: Economics
An analysis of the Indian price structure from 1861. *A. K. Ghosh, Ph.D. 1949 London, School of Economics and Political Science*

Basic Indian industries. *H. R. Soni, M.Sc. 1925 London*

Development of Indian public finance during the war, April 1939 to March 1946. *S. Misra, Ph.D. 1949 London, School of Economics and Political Science*

Development of large scale industries in India and their localisation. *N. S. Sastri, Ph.D. 1943 London, School of Economics and Political Science*

The economic development of India. *V. Anstey, D.Sc. 1930 London, School of Economics and Political Science*

The effect of the breakdown of the international gold standard on India. *R. Doraiswamy, M.Sc. 1937 London, School of Economics and Political Science*

The financial problems of Indian states under federation. *M. A. W. Khan, Ph.D. 1935 London, School of Economics and Political Science*

Indian finance, 1860-1898: from the mutiny to the stabilization of exchange. *C. N. Vakil, M.Sc. 1921 London*

Indian industry and its problems (vol. 1: factors in industrial development). *H. R. Soni, D.Sc. 1933 London, School of Economics and Political Science*

Industrial conditions in modern India. *P. P. Pillai, Ph.D. 1923 London*

Industrial finance and management in India. *N. Das, Ph.D. 1937 London, School of Economics and Political Science*

Industrial organization in India, with special reference to industrial finance and labour. *P. S. Lokanathan, D.Sc. 1934 London, School of Economics and Political Science*

Influence of the cost of inland transport on the development of production, trade and traffic, with special reference to India. *F. P. Antia, Ph.D. 1930 London, School of Economics and Political Science*

International monetary policy since 1919, with special reference to India. *D. C. Ghose, M.Sc. 1948 London, School of Economics and Political Science*

The problem of rural indebtedness in Indian economic life. *B. G. Ghate, Ph.D. 1937 London, School of Economics and Political Science*

India: Economics contd.
Problems of public finance in the federal states of Canada and Australia, with special reference to the scheme for India. *J. Samuel, M.Com. 1937 Leeds*

Provincial decentralization of imperial finance in British India. *B. R. Ambedkar, M.Sc. 1921 London*

1. Public administration in ancient India. 2. A study of Indian economics. *P. Banerjea, D.Sc. 1916 London*

War and post-war public debt of India. *D. L. Dube, Ph.D. 1930 London, School of Economics and Political Science*

India: Foreign Affairs
Economic and political relations of India with Iran and Afghanistan since 1900. *T. Basu, M.Litt. 1942 Cambridge*

The foreign policy of Lord Minto, 1807-13. *K. M. Sarkar, M.Litt. 1937 Cambridge*

Indian political and cultural influence in Cambodia (Kambuja) from the sixth to the fourteenth centuries. *B. R. Chatterji, Ph.D. 1926 London*

India: Geography
The knowledge of India possessed by Arab geographers down to the fourteenth century A.D., with special reference to southern India. *S. M. H. Nainar, Ph.D. 1938 London, School of Oriental and African Studies*

Production and international exchange of wheat, with reference to the economic geography of India, and a further reference to world wheat position. *S. K. Bedekar, M.Sc. 1936 Wales*

India: History
See also Andhra Dynasty; East India Company; Hoysala Dynasty; Lodi Dynasty; Magadha; Maharashtra; Marathi; Mithila; Mughal Empire; Paramara Dynasty; Rohilla, The; Tamils; and Clive, R., Baron Clive of Plassey; Cornwallis, C., 1st Marquis; Dalip Singh, Maharaja; Hastings, W.; Norris, W., Sir; Shore, J., Sir.

The administration of Mysore under Sir Mark Cubbon (1834 to 1861). *K. N. V. Sastri, Ph.D. 1931 London, University College*

The administration of the sultanate of Delhi. *I. H. Qureshi, Ph.D. 1939 Cambridge*

Anglo-Sikh relations (1839-49). *K. C. Khanna, Ph.D. 1932 London, School of Oriental and African Studies*

The art of war in Ancient India. *P. C. Chakravarti, Ph.D. 1938 London, School of Oriental and African Studies*

British policy on the northeast Frontier of India (1826-86). *S. Gupta, D.Phil. 1948 Oxford*

British public opinion regarding Indian policy at the time of the mutiny. *J. Holmes, M.A. 1936 London, Birkbeck College*

The Chisti and Suhrawardi movements in India to the middle of the sixteenth century. *S. N. Hasan, D.Phil. 1948 Oxford*

Court life in ancient India, A.D. 300-700. *R. V. Deshmukh, B.Litt. 1929 Oxford*

Decline of the kingdom of Magadha from c.455 A.D. to c.1000 A.D. *B. P. Sinha, Ph.D. 1948 London, School of Oriental and African Studies*

The diplomatic career of Sir Claude Wade: a study of British relations with the Sikhs and Afghans, July 1823 to March 1840. *E. R. Kapadia, M.A. 1938 London, School of Oriental and African Studies*

The downfall of Tipu Sultan, 1793-99. *S. Datta, Ph.D. 1924 London*

The dynastic history of northern India from c. 916 to 1196 A.D. *H. Ray, Ph.D. 1930 London, School of Oriental and African Studies*

The dynasties of the Gupta period. *J. C. De, M.A. 1922 London*

1. Early English intercourse with Burma, 1587-1743. 2. The Dalhousie-Phayre correspondence, 1852-1856. *D. G. E. Hall, D.Litt. 1931 London, King's College*

The foreign policy of Lord Minto, 1807-13. *K. M. Sarkar, M.Litt. 1937 Cambridge*

Henry Dundas and the government of India, 1784-1800. *D. Thornton, M.A. 1925 Liverpool*

A history of self-government in India from ancient times to 1914. *V. R. Adige, B.Litt. 1924 Oxford*

The history of the Paramāra Dynasty in Malwa, Arthuna and Chandravati (A.D. 808-1310). *D. Ganguli, Ph.D. 1931 London, School of Oriental and African Studies*

India: History contd.
History of the Western Chalukyas (political and administrative). *G. Raychaudhuri, Ph.D. 1948 London, School of Oriental and African Studies*

The influence of the home government on the development of the land revenue and judicial administration in the presidency of Fort William in Bengal from 1823 to 1840. *B. Mitra, M.A. 1936 London, School of Oriental and African Studies*

The interaction of England and India during the early years of George III. *D. Dudley, M.A. 1909 Liverpool*

Lord Ellenborough's ideas on Indian policy. *K. I. Garrett, M.A. 1935 London, Birkbeck College*

The military system of the Mahrattas: its origin and development from the time of Shivaji to the fall of the Mahratta Empire. *S. Sen, B.Litt. 1927 Oxford*

The Muslim historians of India, from 1205-1259. *W. H. Andalib-i-Shadani, Ph.D. 1934 London, School of Oriental and African Studies*

Muslim rule in Sind in the eighth, ninth and tenth centuries. *A. A. Puri, Ph.D. 1936 London, School of Oriental and African Studies*

The north west frontier of India, 1890-1908. *C. C. Davies, Ph.D. 1926 Cambridge*

The northwest frontier policy of the Mughals, 1556-1658. *M. Jahangir Khan, Ph.D. 1937 Cambridge*

The Paramara dynasty of Malwa. *S. Dasgupta, M.A. 1922 London*

Peace and war in ancient India. *W. S. Armour, B.Litt. 1921 Oxford*

Persian poetry of the kings of India. *S. Y. Hashmi, Ph.D. 1933 London, School of Oriental and African Studies*

The political and cultural history of the Panjab, including the North West Frontier Province in its earliest period. *L. Chandra, Ph.D. 1940 London, School of Oriental and African Studies*

The political history of Maharashtra from the earliest times to circa 1000 A.D. *V. R. Deoras, Ph.D. 1940 London, School of Oriental and African Studies*

The Portuguese in India and the East Indies 1497-1548. *T. H. Jenkins, M.A. 1924 Birmingham*

Proceedings in Parliament with regard to the government of India, 1763-1773. *J. C. Airey, M.A. 1911 Liverpool*

The project method, illustrated from the history of India during the British period. *H. S. Bhai, M.Ed. 1935 Leeds*

The relations between the Board of Commissioners for the Affairs of India and the Court of Directors, 1784-1816. *P. Chandra, Ph.D. 1933 London, School of Economics and Political Science*

The relations of the British Government in India with the Indian States, 1813-1823. *M. S. Mehta, Ph.D. 1928 London*

Rise and fall of the Rohilla power in Hindustan, 1707 to 1774. *A. F. M. K. Rahman, Ph.D. 1936 London, School of Oriental and African Studies*

Social and political life in the Vijayanagara Empire, A.D. 1346-1646. *B. A. Saletore, Ph.D. 1931 London, School of Oriental and African Studies*

The socio-economic organization of northern India (c.200 A.D.-c.600 A.D.). *R. Sarker, Ph.D. 1947 London, School of Oriental and African Studies*

Sovereignty in ancient Indian polity: a study in the evolution of the early Indian state. *H. Sinha, Ph.D. 1935 London, School of Oriental and African Studies*

The sultanate of Delhi, 1206 to 1290 A.D. *A. B. M. Habibullah, Ph.D. 1936 London, School of Oriental and African Studies*

India: Politics and Government
British Indian amdinistration: an historical study. *K. F. Ramaswami Aiyangar, M.Sc. 1936 London, School of Economics and Political Science*

Communal representation and Indian self-government. *I. J. Bahadoorsingh, B.Litt. 1944 Oxford*

The development of political institutions in the State of Travancore, A.D. 1885-1924. *V. M. Ittyerah, B.Litt. 1930 Oxford*

Development of the Indian administrative and financial system, 1858-1905, with special reference to the relations between the central government and the provinces. *P. J. Thomas, D.Phil. 1935 Oxford*

A history of self-government in India from ancient times to 1914. *V. R. Adige, B.Litt. 1924 Oxford*

India: Politics and Government contd.
Influence of European political doctrines upon the evolution of the Indian Government institutions and practice (1858-1938). *G. Prashad, Ph.D. 1942 London, School of Economics and Political Science*

Muslims in India: a political analysis (from 1885-1906). *R. A. Zakaria, Ph.D. 1948 London, School of Oriental and African Studies*

1. Public administration in ancient India. 2. A study of Indian economics. *P. Banerjea, D.Sc. 1916 London*

Revenue administration of the Sirkars under the E.I.C. down to 1802. *L. Sundaram, Ph.D. 1930 London, School of Oriental and African Studies*

Rise and growth of Indian liberalism. *M. A. Buch, Ph.D. 1937 London, School of Economics and Political Science*

The social and administrative reforms of Lord William Bentinck. *G. Seed, Ph.D. 1949 Saint Andrew's*

The state in ancient India (North): a study in the structure and practical working of political institutions in Northern India in ancient times. *B. Prased, D.Sc. 1928 London*

India: Social History
Cultural history of the Satavahana Dynasty. *C. K. Gairola, Ph.D. 1949 London, School of Oriental and African Studies*

Discussion and determination of the most adequate method to be employed in the study of the inter-relation and interaction of the economic, ethical, and religious factors in the life of organized communities, as illustrated in the case of the Vaishnava communities of Gujerat. *N. A. Thoothi, D.Phil. 1925 Oxford*

English social life in India in the eighteenth century. *T. G. P. Spear, Ph.D. 1932 Cambridge*

India and the Near East in English literature. *M. D. Taseer, Ph.D. 1936 Cambridge*

The influence of Islam on Indian culture. *T. Chand, D.Phil. 1922 Oxford*

Life and conditions of the people of Hindustan (1200-1550 A.D.). *K. M. Ashraf, Ph.D. 1932 London, School of Oriental and African Studies*

Mental and moral culture in India in the Middle Ages. *R. Ahmad, Ph.D. 1932 London, King's College*

Some aspects of the earliest social history of India, especially the pre-Buddhistic ages. *S. C. Sarkar, D.Phil. 1923 Oxford*

Indian Literature (in English)
See also Tagore, Rabindranath, Sir; and Poetry, English: India.

India's contribution to imaginative English literature. *R. Pitman, M.A. 1920 Birmingham*

Indian Ocean
The western shores of the Indian Ocean before Vasco da Gama. *H. A. Edwards, M.A. 1930 London, Birkbeck College*

Indian Religions
See Buddhism; Hinduism; Pancaratra; Sikhism; etc.

Indians of North America
See also Cherokee Indians; Malecites; Micmacs.

The four quarter concept in aboriginal America. *J. B. Tompkins, Ph.D. 1934 London, University College*

The indigenous tribes of British Columbia and European influence upon them. *E. L. Gillies, Ph.D. 1923 Edinburgh*

The material culture of the Bay Islands. *R. W. de F. Feachem, M.Sc. 1948 Cambridge*

A monograph on the native education among the North American Indians, and its effect upon adult behaviour. *J. M. Evans, M.Ed. 1923 Manchester*

Some aspects of the totemism of north-west America. *F. C. J. M. Barbeau, B.Sc. 1910 Oxford*

The structure and development of the brush-prairie of the White Earth Indian Reservation. *J. Ewing, D.Sc. 1916 Aberdeen*

Individualism
See also Freedom; Idealism; Primitivism.

André Gide and the individual. *G. P. F. Jeffares, Ph.D. 1950 Dublin, Trinity College*

The bearing of the conception of evolution upon the problem of the inclusion of individual minds within reality as a whole. *E. E. Harris, B.Litt. 1933 Oxford*

Individualism contd.
The conditions psychological and sociological of the development of individuality amongst peoples of rudimentary culture. *W. D. Wallis, B.Sc. 1910 Oxford*

The development and value of the conception of individuality. *K. M. Goffin, M.A. 1910 London*

Greek and Judaistic individualism in the Hellenistic age, in their similarity and contrast, and their relation to the concept of the Messiah. *H. D. Hilliard, M.A. 1932 Bristol*

Identity, individuality, personality. *J. C. Bacon, Ph.D. 1924 Bristol*

The individual and his relation to the common good. *J. A. Townson, M.A. 1934 Liverpool*

Individual experience in the philosophy of Leibniz. *A. H. Talukder, M.A. 1935 London, University College*

The individual in some recent British thought. *S. McK. Rosen, Ph.D. 1931 London, School of Economics and Political Science*

Individualism in the *Deutsche Dramen* of Carl Zuckmayer. *M. Graham, M.A. 1950 Belfast*

The individualism of André Gide: its character and origin. *D. L. Thomas, M.A. 1945 Wales*

On the consciousness of the universal and the individual. *F. A. P. Aveling, D.Sc. 1912 London*

The place of the individual in some sociological theories. *H. G. Woodford, B.A. 1924 Bristol*

Political individualism of John Locke. *G. Bull, M.Litt. 1933 Cambridge*

The principle of individuality in education. *S. J. Willis, Ph.D. 1930 Dublin, Trinity College*

The problem of individuality and its implications for modern idealism. *C. D. Deshmukh, Ph.D. 1933 London, University College*

The rise of individualism, with special reference to Locke. *R. Bermingham, M.A. 1937 National University of Ireland*

Royce's theory of the individual. *W. T. Jones, B.Litt. 1933 Oxford*

Spinoza's conception of human individuality. *M. F. Hoballah, Ph.D. 1943 London, University College*

The treatment of the idea of the individual in the philosophies of Bernard Bosanquet, J. M. E. McTaggart and A. N. Whitehead. *B. E. Jones, M.A. 1942 Manchester*

Individuation
The account of individuation in Plato's early dialogues. *E. T. Keep, M.A. 1947 Wales*

Knowledge of the particular in St. Thomas Aquinas, including a discussion of the principle of individuation. *W. G. Maclagan, Ph.D. 1928 Edinburgh*

Indo-Aryan Languages
See Indo-European Languages and Literatures.

Indo-European Culture
Indo-European influences in Hellenic civilization down to the end of the Bronze Age. *V. G. Childe, B.Litt. 1916 Oxford*

Indo-European Languages and Literatures
See also Assamese; Bihari; Dravidian; Gujarati; Hindi; Hindustani; Kanarese; Kharosthi; Malayalam; Marathi; Pali; Prakrit; Punjabi; Sanskrit; Urdu.

The gradual breakdown of inflexion in the Indo-European languages. *A. S. R. Rundle, Ph.D. 1949 London, External Degree*

Indo-Aryan loan-words in Malayalam, with a study of some Dravidian loans in Sanskrit. *K. G. Varma, Ph.D. 1934 London, School of Oriental and African Studies*

The phonology of the Indo-European elements in Albanian. *S. Mann, M.A. 1940 Bristol*

The Thraco-Illyrian language. *B. F. C. Atkinson, Ph.D. 1926 Cambridge*

Induction
See Logic.

Industrial Development
See the subheadings Economic History and Economics under individual countries.

Industrial Law
The course of public opinion and legal decision, including legislation, relating to economic combination and monopoly, mainly in Great Britain, in the period 1880-1914. *L. D. F. Peck, M.A. 1929 Wales*

Industrial Law contd.
The development of factory legislation from 1833-47: a study of legislative and administrative evolution. *M. W. Thomas, Ph.D. 1948 London, University College*

English factory legislation considered with regard to its economic effects and methods of administration. *A. Harrison, D.Sc. 1903 London*

Factory legislation and its administration, 1891-1924. *H. A. Mess, Ph.D. 1926 London*

The factory system and the factory acts, 1802-1850. *G. Baylis, M.A. 1930 Birmingham*

The Irish Labour Court. *M. C. Hamilton, M.Econ.Sc. 1949 National University of Ireland*

Post-war labour legislation in India: a comparison with Japan. *S. Sinha, Ph.D. 1932 London, School of Economics and Political Science*

Sir Robert Peel the elder, and early factory legislation. *F. E. Manning, M.A. 1932 Bristol*

State regulation of labour and industry in New South Wales. *P. A. W. Honeyman, M.A. 1922 Manchester*

Industrial Management
See also Business Management.

The decentralization of industry. *E. H. C. Rutland, Ph.D. 1934 London, School of Economics and Political Science*

Development councils: a study of state co-operation with private industry. *W. J. Prichard, M.Com. 1949 Leeds*

1. Extension of statistical theory to certain problems arising in sampling inspection in industry. 2. A critical examination of Neyman and Pearson's 'L1' test and certain alternative tests. *A. V. Sukhatme, Ph.D. 1935 London, University College*

Industrial administration. *B. J. Lynch, Ph.D. 1934 Belfast*

Industrial combination and unemployment. *W. E. Salt, M.A. 1924 Sheffield*

Industrial finance and management in India. *N. Das, Ph.D. 1937 London, School of Economics and Political Science*

The manufacturers' agent. His economic and social significance. *J. Stephenson, D.Sc. 1922 London*

The modern tendency towards industrial combination in some spheres of British industry: its forms and developments, their causes and determinant circumstances. *G. R. Carter, M.A. 1911 Wales*

The new issue market and the finance of industry. *R. F. Henderson, Ph.D. 1950 Cambridge*

Planning and production control in Soviet State industries. *G. R. Barker, M,Com. 1950 Birmingham*

A quantitative investigation of the effect of scientific lending on certain industries as viewed from the aspect of banking. *W. A. McLeish, Ph.D. 1939 Edinburgh*

The significance of the effects of changes in data, and in particular in the supply of money, upon the structure of industrial production in a modern capitalist economy. *C. J. Harman, M.Sc. 1935 London, External Degree*

Some aspects of industrial organization. *T. de la Barra, Ph.D. 1924 Glasgow*

Some organizations of industrial employers in England in the early nineteenth century. *M. Jones, M.A. 1933 Manchester*

A statistical investigation of post-war industrial trends, with particular reference to employment, mechanization and output. *C. R. Curtis, Ph.D. 1942 London, External Degree*

Industrial Psychology
See Psychology, Industrial.

Industrial Relations
See also Arbitration; Industrial Management; Labour; Trade Unions; Wages and Salaries; Work.

Experiments in the maintenance of industrial peace. *M. E. Liddall, B.A. 1923 Bristol*

The general strike during one hundred years. *A. Plummer, M.Sc. 1927 London*

Industrial relations in road transport. *T. E. A. K. Jackson, Ph.D. 1946 Manchester*

Industrial relations in the distributive trades, with special reference to the Co-operative Movement. *J. Huddleston, M.A. 1938 Leeds*

Industrial relations in the British Co-operative Movement. *J. Tizard, B.Litt. 1949 Oxford*

Industrial Relations contd.
Industrial unrest. *L. Ludford, M.Com. 1918 Birmingham*

The movements for shorter hours, 1840-75. *J. S. Hodgson, D.Phil. 1940 Oxford*

The question of personnel in a socialized industry. *T. K. Hitch, Ph.D. 1937 London, School of Economics and Political Science*

The settlement of labour disputes in Canada. *N. M. Rogers, B.Litt. 1922 Oxford*

A study of the practice and procedure of arbitration and conciliation as a voluntary principle in some British industries, with an account of state action in the field. *I. G. Sharp, Ph.D. 1940 London, School of Economics and Political Science*

Industrial Revolution
The Baptists and political and social conditions in Lancashire during the Industrial Revolution, 1760-1832. *C. B. Whyatt, M.A. 1948 Manchester*

Certain aspects of the Industrial Revolution in South Wales, 1760-1850. *A. H. John, Ph.D. 1940 Cambridge*

The economic and social condition of England on the eve of the Industrial Revolution, with special reference to Lancashire. *L. W. Moffit, Ph.D. 1921 Edinburgh*

The economic development of the North Staffordshire potteries since 1730, with special reference to the Industrial Revolution. *J. Thomas, Ph.D. 1934 London, School of Economics and Political Science*

Education and the English industrial revolution. *V. C. Vaman Rao, Ph.D. 1939 Dublin, Trinity College*

The family economy of the workers in the cotton industry during the period of the Industrial Revolution, 1784-1833. *F. Collier, M.A. 1921 Manchester*

Health, wealth, and population in the early days of the Industrial Revolution. *M. C. Buer, D.Sc. 1927 London*

The history of the Industrial Revolution in Monmouthshire. *T. E. Jones, M.A. 1929 Wales*

Industrial Revolution and the textile industries of Somerset. *H. C. Oram, M.A. 1930 Bristol*

The Industrial Revolution as reflected in the German novel. *J. L. Mowat, Ph.D. 1927 Aberdeen*

The Industrial Revolution in the textile industries of Wiltshire. *H. R. Exelby, M.A. 1928 Bristol*

Nottinghamshire in the eighteenth century: a study of the movements leading to the industrial revolutions of the nineteenth century. *J. D. Chambers, Ph.D. 1927 London*

Women workers and the Industrial Revolution, 1750-1850. *I. Pinchbeck, Ph.D. 1930 London, School of Economics and Political Science*

Industrial Training
An economic and social analysis of the effects of state-aid for industrial training and professional education, with special reference to the Swansea and Aberystwyth districts. *W. King, M.A. 1921 Wales*

Education for industry on the northeast coast. *R. Harding, M.Ed. 1934 Durham*

The industrial training and education of apprentices. *R. C. Moore, M.A. 1921 Manchester*

Industrial training, with special reference to the conditions prevailing in London. *N. B. Dearle, D.Sc. 1915 London*

Recent changes in the structure and training of labour in the British engineering industry, and their future trends. *A. F. Nagib, Ph.D. 1945 Manchester*

A report on the recent development and present position of education for industry in Belgium. *L. J. Dyer, M.A. 1939 London, King's College*

Some temperament traits in relation to industrial efficiency: a study of a group of workers by interviews, tests, assessments and records. *G. W. Goodall, Ph.D. 1938 London, School of Hygiene and Tropical Medicine*

A survey of my present situation in technical education, including its relation with industry. *A. V. Harrison, M.A. 1938 Bristol*

Industry
See also Production. For individual industries, see under their names. For industrial development in a particular country, see the subheadings Economic History and Economics under the country.

A contrast between private enterprise and nationalisation of industry. *T. J. Connolly, M.A. 1927 National University of Ireland*

The demarcation of industries. *E. R. L. Watkins, M.Com. 1931 Birmingham*

Industry contd.
Politics and industry in the state. *F. S. Milligan, M.A. 1921 Birmingham*

Some theoretical aspects of industrialization of advanced agricultural countries, illustrated from New Zealand experience. *H. W. Larsen, Ph.D. 1948 London, University College*

A statistical study in the structure of industry. *A. Shenfield, M.Com. 1939 Birmingham*

Industry, Location of
The development of communications in Glamorgan, with special reference to the growth of industry between 1760 and 1840. *E. Walker, M.A. 1947 Wales*

Development of large scale industries in India and their localisation. *N. S. Sastri, Ph.D. 1943 London, School of Economics and Political Science*

A geographical study of the localization and migration of iron and steel manufacture in the North East of England (Northumberland, Durham, and the North Riding). *L. R. Jones, Ph.D. 1925 London*

Localisation of industrial production in Eire. *M. J. Hayden, M.Econ.Sc. 1938 National University of Ireland*

Location of industrial establishments. *A. S. Emre, M.Sc. 1946 London, School of Economics and Political Science*

Location of industry. *R. J. Cuffel, B.Phil. 1947 Oxford*

Location theory and the clothing industry: a study of the factors of industrial location, with particular reference to their influence on the clothing industry. *J. R. Long, Ph.D. 1949 Leeds*

The measurement and causes of the localisation of industry, with special reference to the industries of Birmingham and distric. *A. J. Wensley, M.Com. 1936 Birmingham*

Migration in Great Britain since 1927, with special reference to the industrial population. *V. M. Lamb, B.Litt. 1939 Oxford*

The policy of industrial concentration during the war, with special reference to the hosiery industry. *S. A. Taylor, Ph.D. 1949 London, School of Economics and Political Science*

The recent industrialization of the northern and western sectors of Greater London. *D. H. Smith, Ph.D. 1933 London, Birkbeck College*

A study of the changes in the geographical distribution of industry and population in England and Wales during the twentieth century. *J. E. S. Orrin, M.A. 1932 Wales*

Infants
See Children.

Infinity
Continuity and infinity in modern mathematics and philosophy. *J. P. Duminy, B.Sc. 1923 Oxford*

Inflation
See Money.

Inheritance
See Succession.

Inheritance Tax
See Succession.

Initiation
From initiation to conversion. *H. W. Sendall, M.A. 1942 Leeds*

Girls' initiation ceremony among the Amapondo. *J. E. S. Griffiths, Dip. Anthropology 1931 Cambridge*

On initiative magic. *R. F. Fortune, Dip. Anthropology. 1912 Cambridge*

Inland Waterways
See Canals.

Innisfallen
Annála Inse Fáithleann i mBaile Atha Cliath: díoglaim annála, A.D. 250-1320, H.I.7. Coláiste na Tríonóide, Ath Cliath (*The Annals of Inisfallen* in Dublin: an analytical description, A.D. 250-1320 from Ms. H.I.7. Trinity College, Dublin). *C. O'Cuilleanáin, Ph.D. 1944 National University of Ireland*

Inns of Court
A study of agnosticism and intellectual doubt in the age of Shakespeare as expressed in the literature of the period, with special reference to Marston and the Inns of Court circle. *M. G. Chamberlain, M.A. 1934 London, King's College*

Inquisition, The
The trial of George Buchanan before the Lisbon Inquisition. *J. M. Aitken, Ph.D. 1938 Edinburgh*

Inscriptions

The Christian inscriptions of North Africa: a study in the popular religion of the early (Western) Church. *I. T. Gillan, Ph.D. 1943 Edinburgh*

Christianity in Asia, and evidences of the Church's power and influence in the province to A.D.325, in the light of Christian epigraphy. *E. Bristow, M.A. 1926 Manchester*

A grammar of the old Kanarese inscriptions, including a study of Sanskrit and Prakrit loanwords. *A. N. P. Narasimhia, Ph.D. 1933 London, School of Oriental and African Studies*

A grammatical and lexical study of the Greek inscriptions of Phrygia in Asia Minor. *D. E. Evans, B.Litt. 1917 Oxford*

1. The Old Testament in the light of the Egyptian monuments. 2. Natural science as it affects scriptural truth. *A. E. B. Day, B.D. 1908 Oxford*

The origin, significance, and history of the Stoichedon style in Greek inscriptions. *R. P. Austin, B.Litt. 1935 Oxford*

Phonology of the Sinhalese inscriptions up to the end of the tenth century A.D. *B. P. F. Wijeratne, Ph.D. 1944 London, School of Oriental and African Studies*

The preparation of a handbook of south Arabian epigraphy. *A. F. L. Beeston, D.Phil. 1937 Oxford*

The script of Mohenjodaro and Harappa, and its relation to other scripts. *G. G. R. Hunter, D.Phil. 1930 Oxford*

Some historical aspects of the inscriptions of Bengal from the fifth to the twelfth century A.D. *B. Sen, Ph.D. 1933 London, School of Oriental and African Studies*

The study of the language of the Tamil inscriptions of the seventh and eighth centuries A.D. *K. Kanapathippillai, Ph.D. 1936 London, School of Oriental and African Studies*

The Thraco-Illyrian language. *B. F. C. Atkinson, Ph.D. 1926 Cambridge*

The towns and districts of Mesopotamia in the second millenium B.C. according to the inscriptions of Tiglathpileser I. *J. J. Slotki, Ph.D. 1946 Manchester*

Inshā Allāh Khān Inshā

A critical estimate of Insha Allah Khan Insha as poet and grammarian. *S. S. B. Ahmad, Ph.D. 1949 London, School of Oriental and African Studies*

Insight

The Buddhist doctrine of insight, with special reference to the Pali text called *The path of purity*, ch. xx-xxii of *Visuddhimagga. P. M. Tin, B.Litt. 1922 Oxford*

Factors involved in problem solving, with special reference to the problem of insight. *S. C. Mumford, Ph.D. 1937 London, Bedford College*

Inspiration

Inspiration in the ancient world: examination of the beliefs current among the Ancient Greeks and Romans in regard to inspiration whether experienced in a state of ectasy or in full consciousness. *A. Grant, M.A. 1939 London, King's College*

Inspiration, Scriptural

See Bible.

Instinct

Environment and the theories of instinct. *N. Roth, M.A. 1936 London, King's College*

Instinct: its nature and place in human life. *O. C. Carmichael, B.Sc. 1917 Oxford*

Instinct and education. *J. T. Mulley, M.Ed. 1933 Leeds*

Instinct in man: a contribution to the psychology of education. *J. Drever, Ph.D. 1916 Edinburgh*

Instincts and education: an enquiry concerning the instincts in education. *P. Banerji, M.Ed. 1927 Leeds*

The place of instinct in the evolution of the mind in man and the lower animals from the biological and psychological points of view. *A. Kefalas, M.A. 1926 Liverpool*

Psychological theories of instinct and their influence on educational theory and practice. *B. C. Kar, M.A. 1949 London, Institute of Education*

Insurance

The external relations of life assurance companies (ordinary branch): an historical view. *C. T. Smith, M.Sc. 1945 London, School of Economics and Political Science*

An historical and critical analysis of British health insurance. *S. L. Bull, M.Sc. 1938 London, School of Economics and Political Science*

Insurance contd.

The origin and early history of insurance, including the contract of bottomry. *C. J. Trenerry, D.Sc. 1907 London*

Principles and practice of health insurance as applied to India. *J. Agrawala, Ph.D. 1948 Wales*

Some aspects of a fall in the rate of mortality as affecting the financial position of friendly societies and sickness funds. *R. R. Brodie, Ph.D. 1932 London, External Degree*

The theory and practice of credit insurance in international trade. *E. Shenkman, Ph.D. 1934 London, School of Economics and Political Science*

Intelligence

An analysis of current views of the nature of intelligence. *H. H. Penny, Ph.D. 1935 London, Institute of Education*

Browning's psychology of genius as shown in *Pauline; Paracelsus; Andrea del Sarto; Cleon. B. G. MacCarthy, M.A. 1927 National University of Ireland*

Character and intelligence: an attempt at an exact study of character. *E. Webb, D.Sc. 1914 London*

Class distinctions as reflected in the German novel of the nineteenth century: aristocracy: middle classes: intellectuals, 1830 to 1900. *E. Kohn-Bramstedt, Ph.D. 1936 London, School of Economics and Political Science*

A comparative study of the intelligence and educability of Malays and Chinese in Malaya and its significance in relation to educational policy. *G. E. D. Lewis, Ph.D. 1949 London, Institute of Education*

The correlation between intelligence and size of family. *H. E. G. Sutherland, Ph.D. 1930 Edinburgh*

A critical evaluation of certain scales of intelligence, with special reference to the effects of coaching and practice. *J. H. Wilson, Ph.D. 1929 London*

The history and value of the distinction between intellect and intuition. *R. I. Aaron, D.Phil. 1926 Oxford*

Intelligence, concrete and abstract: a study in differential traits. *W. P. Alexander, Ph.D. 1936 Glasgow*

An investigation into the comparative intelligence and attainments of Jewish and non-Jewish school-children. *A. G. Hughes, Ph.D. 1928 London*

An investigation into the relation between intelligence and inheritance. *E. M. Lawrence, Ph.D. 1930 London, School of Economics and Political Science*

An investigation into the relation between association and intelligence. *E. P. Yule, Ph.D. 1934 Saint Andrew's*

Language and intelligence. *C. J. Holloway, D.Phil. 1947 Oxford*

Newman and intellectual culture. *F. J. Toner, M.A. 1945 National University of Ireland*

Perseveration, perseverance, character and intelligence. *S. G. Raine, Ph.D. 1935 London, King's College*

Quickness and intelligence: an enquiry concerning the existence of a general speed factor. *E. Bernstein, Ph.D. 1922 London*

The relation between artistic ability and intelligence. *E. Mewse, M.Ed. 1934 Durham*

The relation between intelligence and various forms of practical ability. *E. Collins, M.A. 1935 Birmingham*

The relation between the distribution of intelligence and the social environment. *P. Moshinsky, Ph.D. 1937 London, School of Economics and Political Science*

The relation of intelligence to performance in school. *J. S. Gittins, M.A. 1936 London, Institute of Education*

Relation of intuition and intellect. *G. M. Khan, M.A. 1933 London, King's College*

The relationship between intelligence and speed of working. *C. G. Adams, M.A. 1925 Bristol*

Report upon an enquiry into a child's vocabulary: how far it is indicative of intelligence and influence by social status. *E. M. Johns, M.A. 1949 Reading*

A sociological analysis of some intellectual groups in American society from 1912-1930. *D. H. Schwartz, Ph.D. 1940 London, School of Economics and Political Science*

Intelligence contd.

The sociological function of intellectuals in modern society: a study of some social movements in post-war Germany. *R. J. Baker, Ph.D. 1936 London, School of Economics and Political Science*

Some aspects of the developing 'intelligence'. *J. J. Strasheim, Ph.D. 1925 London*

Some modern theories of intelligence: exposition and criticism. *P. Kelleher, M.A. 1934 National University of Ireland*

Speed and accuracy as related to intelligence and perseverance. *C. C. Howard, Ph.D. 1932 London, University College*

The speed factor in intelligent reactions. *J. D. Sutherland, Ph.D. 1931 Edinburgh*

Studies in: estimates of intelligence and non-intelligence qualities; temperament; left-handedness; scholastic achievement; the energy concept; and the biological significance of intelligence. *D. W. R. Oates, D.Sc. 1930 Wales*

A study of the general knowledge of London school children in relation to intelligence. *D. M. Inman, Ph.D. 1936 London, Institute of Education*

A study of the intelligence of Anglo-Chinese children. *P. Hu, M.Sc. 1936 London, University College*

The teaching of Dante on the human intellect, with special reference to the doctrine of St. Thomas Aquinas. *F. S. Foster, Ph.D. 1947 Cambridge*

The theory of active and passive intellect from Aristotle to Aquinas. *S. J. Curtis, M.A. 1922 London*

Intelligence Testing

See also Aptitude Testing.

The analysis of a pictorial test of intelligence. *A. G. Joselin, M.A. 1947 London, Institute of Education*

An analysis of the factors entering into results of tests based upon the logical principles of mathematics. *J. W. Jenkins, Ph.D. 1939 London, Institute of Education*

The application of factor analysis to the study of the individual items of a non-verbal test. *R. Edwards, M.Ed. 1950 Manchester*

An application of mental tests to university students. *H. D. J. White, Ph.D. 1926 London*

The application of the Binet-Simon scale to normal English children. *R. C. Moore, M.Sc. 1919 Liverpool*

An attempt to trace the course of the development of some mental capacities by the application of mental tests to children from five to fifteen years of age. *F. M. E. Bickersteth, Cert.Sc. 1916 Oxford*

A clinical survey of the applicability of intelligence tests to the study of mental deficiency in children. *T. Ferguson, M.D. 1924 Edinburgh*

A comparison of verbal (oral) and pictorial tests of intelligence. *C. M. Davey, Ph.D. 1924 London*

The construction and validation of a group test of intelligence for English children of 13 years of age upwards. *D. Ray, M.A. 1948 London, Institute of Education*

The construction and validation of a test of mental ability. *M. E. Calvert, M.A. 1946 London, Institute of Education*

The construction of mental tests. *C. S. Slocombe, Ph.D. 1925 London*

The construction, standardization and validation of an orally presented group test of intelligence for children between the ages of 8 and 11. *J. Cornwell, M.A. 1950 Birmingham*

A contribution to the standardization of the Terman-Merrill intelligence test. *J. M. Gibbs, M.A. 1939 London, University College*

A contribution towards the standardization of the new revised Stanford Binet test of intelligence (Terman and Merrill) for use with English children aged four to six years. *N. Glucksohn, M.A. 1939 London, University College*

A critical inquiry into the practical value of mental tests in secondary schools. *A. Brier, M.Ed. 1924 Leeds*

The diagnostic significance of the Terman-Merrill scale. *M. E. Highfield, M.A. 1945 London, University College and London, Institute of Education*

The effect of coaching and practice on intelligence tests. *S. R. Johri, M.Ed. 1937 Leeds*

The effect of nursery training on the responses of children in the Merrill-Terman tests. *C. P. K. Amma, M.Ed. 1920 Leeds*

Effect of practice in intelligence tests. *K. J. Dave, M.A. 1938 London, University College*

Intelligence Testing contd.

The effect of six months' instruction in school subjects on some mental factors of adults. *W. B. Walls, M.Ed. 1945 Leeds*

An enquiry into the correlation of motor ability with 'g'. *W. E. Phipps, M.A. 1939 Birmingham*

An enquiry into the correlation of certain mental tests with ability in different types of English composition. *O. J. K. Cotton, M.A. 1932 Birmingham*

An experimental investigation into the distribution of intelligence in different schools by means of non-verbal tests. *D. G. Sumithra, M.Ed. 1933 Leeds*

An experimental investigation into the comparative validity of some non-verbal tests of intelligence. *F. Islam, M.A. 1934 Leeds*

An experimental study of school children with regard to some racial mental differences. *C. Rangachar, M.Ed. 1930 Leeds*

A factorial analysis of mental tests. *Z. Swanson, Ph.D. 1950 Edinburgh*

Factorial analysis of practical ability and its relation to other intellectual abilities and personality traits. *R. M. El- Ghareib, Ph.D. 1950 Edinburgh*

A factorial study of picture tests for young children, with special reference to the appearance of a space factor among boys. *M. A. Mellone, Ph.D. 1944 Edinburgh*

Influences of volition in mental testing, or influences of conation on cognition. *E. H. Wild, Ph.D. 1926 London*

An intelligence and educational survey of the eleven-year-olds in the government high schools of the United Provinces of Agra and Oudh, India. *S. Lall, Ph.D. 1945 Edinburgh*

The intelligence of a representative group of Scottish children. *A. M. Macmeeken, Ph.D. 1939 Edinburgh*

Intelligence tests and their uses in the secondary school. *A. J. Phillips, M.Ed. 1926 Manchester*

An investigation concerning the inter-relations of social and economic status, Stanford-Binet and performance I.Q., estimates of probable vocational success, the Otis Primary A Group intelligence test in a group of mentally defective children, and the free association test as a measure of intelligence. *H. M. Cohen, M.D. 1936 Liverpool*

An investigation in the use of informal objective tests in physics in the lower forms of a secondary school. *H. J. Davies, M.Sc. 1942 Wales*

An investigation into the mental abilities of the children of Trinidad. *B. J. Bedell, Ph.D. 1950 Edinburgh*

An investigation into the relationship between memory and intelligence. *J. G. Ingham, Ph.D. 1949 London, Institute of Psychiatry*

An investigation into the use of non-verbal tests of intelligence in India. *T. C. Vicary, M.A. 1938 London, Institute of Education*

An investigation into the use of estimated factor scores in describing and comparing a group of secondary and senior school boys of 11+. *J. J. B. Dempster, M.A. 1944 London, Institute of Education*

An investigation of the causes of backwardness at the qualifying stage, with particular reference to the percentage of children scholastically retarded owing to unsuitability of curriculum. Non-scholastic tests, mechanical aptitude tests, technical information tests, and a practical test for 'backward' children. *M. M. MacTaggart, Ph.D. 1928 Edinburgh*

Investigation of the dependence of tests of attainment in school subjects on 'g', 'f' and 'p' factors. *M. Robins, M.A. 1939 London, King's College*

The measurement of mental ability and school achievement. *J. Sullivan, M.A. 1926 National University of Ireland*

Measuring intelligence of Indian children. *V. V. Kamat, Ph.D. 1939 Edinburgh*

Mental tests and their relation to the central factor. *W. Stephenson, Ph.D. 1930 London, University College*

A multiple factor analysis of the results obtained from certain mental tests and some school examinations. *A. Aris, M.A. 1938 London, Institute of Education*

A new application of the theory of neogenesis to the problem of mental testing. *M. Fortes, Ph.D. 1930 London, University College*

Intelligence Testing contd.

Non-linguistic tests of mental ability. *F. J. Graw, Ph.D. 1926 London*

Objective tests of the fluency factor, with special reference to its relation to ability in school subjects. *W. D. Barras, M.A. 1938 London, Institute of Education*

On the standardization of group tests of intelligence, and the interpretation of their results. *F. C. Thomas, M.A. 1930 London, Day Training College*

On the upper limit of the growth of intelligence as determined by mental testing. *E. R. Collie, Ph.D. 1925 Edinburgh*

The performances of related individuals in tests mainly educative and mainly reproductive mental tests used in genetic studies. *J. C. Raven, M.Sc. 1936 London, King's College*

Practical estimation of pupil's progress in secondary schools. *A. C. Paterson, Ph.D. 1928 Glasgow*

Prognostic tests of ability in modern languages. *S. R. Mills, M.A. 1941 London, Courtauld Institute of Art*

The qualitative analysis of intelligence tests. *H. S. Perera, M.A. 1922 London*

The relative significance of various types of mental tests for education prognosis. *W. S. Flack, Ph.D. 1929 London*

The reliability of certain tests of practical ability. *V. Prakasha, M.A. 1949 London, Institute of Education*

The reliability of group tests as tests of intelligence. *W. H. Stockdale, M.Ed. 1924 Manchester*

The reliability of mental tests. *G. A. Ferguson, Ph.D. 1940 Edinburgh*

The scope and value of psychological testing, with special reference to the examination of scholarship candidates for further education. *H. V. Clark, M.A. 1936 Liverpool*

Some factors of effectiveness in mental ('intelligence') tests. *S. A. Hamid, M.A. 1923 London*

Some mental determinants of scholastic achievement. *A. C. D. Gowda, M.Ed. 1932 Leeds*

Standardization of intelligence and aptitude tests in their mother tongue for secondary school children. *C. T. Philip, M.A. 1944 London, Institute of Education*

A study of the inconstancy of intelligence in relation to the problems of selection for secondary education at eleven plus. *J. C. Daniels, M.Ed. 1948 Durham*

A study of the methods for the validation of test items. *M. F. Khan, M.A. 1948 London, Institute of Education*

A survey, historical and critical, of intelligence tests. *J. H. Wilson, M.Ed. 1923 Leeds*

The Terman-Merrill intelligence scale in testing institutionalized epileptics. *E. A. Eattell, M.Sc. 1945 London, Birkbeck College*

Tests for the examination of the effect of bilingualism on intelligence. *W. R. Jones, M.A. 1933 Wales*

The use of standardized tests in recording the mental progress of elementary school children, and the value of such records in selecting individuals for higher education. *R. Williams, M.A. 1935 Liverpool*

The value of intelligence tests in the selection of candidates for entrance to secondary schools. *H. D. Amos, M.A. 1930 Wales*

Interest

The influence of Böhm-Bawerk on American theories of capital and interest. *E. White, M.Sc. 1935 London, School of Economics and Political Science*

Risk, interest rates, and security prices. *W. Blair, B.Litt. 1938 Oxford*

The social function of interest. *E. J. Hegarty, M.A. 1949 National University of Ireland*

A statistical study of the economic forces affecting the rate of interest with special reference to recent developments. *J. F. L. Bray, Ph.D. 1935 London, School of Economics and Political Science*

The theory of interest and the concept of social justice. *T. F. Divine, Ph.D. 1938 London, School of Economics and Political Science*

Usury and the principles of the Muhammadan law. *M. S. Ali Khan, D.Phil. 1928 Oxford*

Wicksell's theory of interest and influence. *S. Adler, M.Sc. 1932 London, School of Economics and Political Science*

Intermediate State
See Eschatology.

International Court of Justice
The Hague arbitrations: a history, 1899-1922. *R. W. Anderson, B.Litt. 1923 Oxford*

International Finance
See Finance.

International Labour Organization
Antecedents of the International Labour Organization. *J. W. Follows, B.Litt. 1932 Oxford*

Canada in the International Labour Organisation. *T. Le M. Carter, M.Sc. 1939 London, School of Economics and Political Science*

The International Labour Office (League of Nations): certain aspects of international administration raised in connection with the early development of the International Labour Organization. *E. B. Behrens, Ph.D. 1924 London*

International Labour Organization as an object lesson in international functional co-operation. *P. M. Michaels, M.Sc. 1949 London, School of Economics and Political Science*

The International Labour Organization as an international legislator. *D. Garantch, Ph.D. 1940 London, School of Economics and Political Science*

1. Labour's Magna Carta. 2. The international labour organizations of the League of Nations. *A. Chisholm, D.Litt. 1922 Glasgow*

International Law
See Law, International.

International Politics
See Politics, International.

International Trade
See Trade, International.

Interviewing
How we judge our fellows: an investigation into the value of an interview as a means of estimating general intelligence. *E. H. Magson, D.Sc. 1925 London*

The psychological interview (a survey of methods and practical results in cases of educational and occupational difficulty). *H. I. Champernowne, Ph.D. 1940 London, School of Hygiene and Tropical Medicine*

Intuition
An examination of the meaning and use of the term intuition. *L. J. Belton, M.A. 1946 Sheffield*

The history and value of the distinction between intellect and intuition. *R. I. Aaron, D.Phil. 1926 Oxford*

Intuition and discursive understanding. *H. Bulcock, M.A. 1919 Liverpool*

Intuition in Bergson's philosophy. *M. Sheil, M.A. 1931 National University of Ireland*

Relation of intuition and intellect. *G. M. Khan, M.A. 1933 London, King's College*

Inventions
See Patent Law.

Investment
See also Securities; Stocks and Shares; Unit Trusts.

The building of econometric models, with special reference to the investment process. *S. J. Prais, M.Com 1950 Birmingham*

Divergence between the marginal private and marginal social net product in foreign investments. *M. Gryziecka, M.Sc. 1949 London, School of Economics and Political Science*

Home and foreign investment in Great Britain, 1870-1913. *A. K. Cairncross, Ph.D. 1936 Cambridge*

Liquidity-preference: a study of investment. *A. J. Brown, D.Phil. 1939 Oxford*

State control of investment. *K. K. F. Zawadzki, M.Sc. 1949 London, School of Economics and Political Science*

Ionian Islands
British occupation of the Ionian Islands, 1815-64. *S. F. Markham, B.Litt. 1926 Oxford*

The Ionian Islands under the administration of Sir Thomas Maitland, 1816-1824. *B. R. Pearn, M.A. 1924 London*

Ipswich
A study of the function of Ipswich as a centre in East Anglia, and its development as a port since 1805. *A. J. Starr, M.Sc. 1939 London, Birkbeck College*

Wolsey's colleges at Oxford and Ipswich. *F. Bate, M.A. 1905 Liverpool*

Iran
See Persia.

Iraq
See also Buwaihid Dynasty; Mesopotamia; Basra; Mosul.

British interests in the Tigris-Euphrates Valley, 1856-88. *W. Bamforth, M.A. 1948 London, Bedford College*

The geographical aspects of the Mosul Question. *M. Awad, M.A. 1926 Liverpool*

Government and administration of Iraq: a study in political development. *P. W. Ireland, Ph.D. 1936 London, School of Economics and Political Science*

The rebirth of a nation: the kingdom of Irak. *M. S. Hassan, M.A. 1928 London*

Ireland
See also Celts; Connaught; Galway; Northern Ireland.

Ireland: Constitution
The constitution and government of the Irish Free State. *P. N. S. Mansergh, B.Litt. 1933 Oxford*

The council in Ireland, 1399-1452. *M. C. Griffith, B.Litt. 1935 Oxford*

Fundamental rights articles in the Irish constitution. *B. P. O'Kelly, M.A. 1946 National University of Ireland*

The powers of government in the constitution of Ireland. *G. A. Lee, M.A. 1941 National University of Ireland*

The Senate in the Irish constitution. *C. Gavan-Duffy, M.A. 1947 National University of Ireland*

Ireland: Economics
Aspects of Irish industrialisation. *M. J. MacCormac, M.A. 1948 National University of Ireland*

The development of industries in Eire since 1924, with special reference to (a) employment, and (b) The national income and its distribution. *D. C. Doolan, M.Econ.Sc. 1944 National University of Ireland*

The development of industries in Eire since 1924, with special reference to (a) employment, and (b) the national income and its distribution. *J. M. Colfer, M.Econ.Sc. 1944 National University of Ireland*

Dissertation on the economy of Eire since the emergency began. *H. A. Moynihan, M.Econ.Sc. 1944 National University of Ireland*

Economic aspects of the problem of industrial power in Ireland. *F. A. Murphy, M.Econ.Sc. 1950 National University of Ireland*

Economic effects of the Great War 1914-18 on Ireland. *F. McDermott, M.A. 1940 National University of Ireland*

An economic history of Ireland. *D. A. Chart, Litt.D. 1922 Dublin, Trinity College*

The economic results of the disestablishment of the Irish Church. *H. F. Shearman, Ph.D. 1944 Dublin, Trinity College*

The economic, social, and administrative problem of the congested districts of Ireland. *A. F. Blair, M.Comm. 1930 National University of Ireland*

Effects of recent social legislation in Ireland on industry. *J. A. O'Brien, M.Comm. 1942 National University of Ireland*

Extension of governmental activity in the economic sphere in the Irish Free State from 1922-1935. *B. M. Byrne, M.A. 1935 National University of Ireland*

The financial administration of Ireland to 1817. *T. J. Kiernan, Ph.D. 1930 London, School of Economics and Political Science*

The financing of industry in Ireland, excluding the six counties of N.I. *T. M. O'Sullivan, M.Econ.Sci. 1947 National University of Ireland*

A history of the commercial and financial relations between England and Ireland from the period of the Revolution. *A. E. Murray, D.Sc. 1903 London*

History of the Dublin Chamber of Commerce, 1760-1860. *P. L. Prendeville, M.Comm. 1930 National University of Ireland*

Industrial revival in Eire. *C. A. Pyne, M.Econ.Sc. 1938 National University of Ireland*

Localisation of industrial production in Eire. *M. J. Hayden, M.Econ.Sc. 1938 National University of Ireland*

An outlook on agriculture and industry in post-war Eire. *M. A. O'Mahony, M.Econ.Sc. 1945 National University of Ireland*

Self-sufficiency in the Irish Free State. *D. J. Doran, M.A. 1936 National University of Ireland*

Ireland: Economics contd.
The State and industry in Ireland. *J. A. Leahy, M.Econ.Sc. 1948 National University of Ireland*

A survey of taxation and government expenditure in the Irish Free State, 1922-1936. *S. Kepple, M.A. 1938 National University of Ireland*

Ireland: Foreign Affairs
The Irish in Scotland, 1798-1845. *J. E. Handley, M.A. 1941 National University of Ireland*

Relations, historical and literary, between Ireland and Scandinavia from the ninth century to the thirteenth. *J. I. Young, Ph.D. 1930 Cambridge*

The relations of the disaffected Irish with Spain during the reign of Elizabeth Tudor. *T. Huston, M.A. 1937 Belfast*

Scoto-Irish intercourse in the latter part of the sixteenth century. *H. F. Kelleher, M.A. 1931 National University of Ireland*

Ireland: Geography
A geographical study of the Eire-Northern Ireland boundary. *J. G. Thomas, M.A. 1949 Wales*

Ireland: History
See also Monasticism; and Curran, J. P.; Foster, J.; O'Connell, D.; O'Neill, H., 2nd Earl of Tyrone; Pearse, P. H.; Perrot, J., Sir; Tyrconnell, Richard Talbot, 1st Earl of.

The act of legislative union between Great Britain and Ireland, with special reference to the political career of Castlereagh. *H. M. Hyde, M.A. 1933 Belfast*

The administration of Thomas Drummond in Ireland (1835-40). *T. F. Kelly, M.A. 1941 National University of Ireland*

Annála Inse Fáithleann i mBaile Atha Cliath: díoglaim annála, A.D. 250-1320, H.I.7. Coláiste na Tríonóide, Ath Cliath (*The Annals of Inisfallen* in Dublin: an analytical description, A.D. 250-1320 from Ms. H.I.7. Trinity College, Dublin). *C. O'Cuilleanáin, Ph.D. 1944 National University of Ireland*

An Bhoromha as *Leabhar mor Leacáin*, 295 ro a 24-310 ro a 12 (The Boru tribute, from the *Book of Lecan*, 295r 24-310r 12). *G. O'hArgain, M.A. 1950 National University of Ireland*

A critical edition with introduction and commentary of Spenser's *A view of the present state of Ireland. M. T. Perks, B.Litt. 1924 Oxford*

Earl of Tyrone's rebellion. *R. Singleton, M.A. 1915 Liverpool*

The earlier history of the Home Rule movement. *D. Freeling, M.A. 1927 Birmingham*

Early Corca Laidhe history. *F. O'Driscoll, M.A. 1943 National University of Ireland*

Early Ireland: an essay in historical geography. *W. Fitzgerald, M.A. 1925 Liverpool*

Freedom of the press in Ireland 1784-1842. *B. Inglis, Ph.D. 1950 Dublin, Trinity College*

Gearaltaigh Deasmhumhan i bfilidheacht na Gaedhilge (1350-1800) (The Desmond Geraldines in Irish poetry (1350-1800)). *P. D. O'Cillin, M.A. 1945 National University of Ireland*

Geinealaigh Earann (Irish genealogies). *R. O'h-Allmháin, M.A. 1942 National University of Ireland*

Henry VII's relations with Scotland and Ireland, 1485-98. *A. E. Horsfield, Litt.D. 1932 Dublin, Trinity College*

A history of the English forces employed in Ireland, 1641-1649. *H. Hazlett, M.A. 1935 Belfast*

A history of the military forces operating in Ireland, 1641-1649. *H. Hazlett, Ph.D. 1938 Belfast*

History of Tir Conaill in the 16th century. *J. O'Donnell, M.A. 1946 National University of Ireland*

Idircheartú ar stair na hEireann (An interpretation of Irish history). *P. O'Briáin, M.A. 1939 National University of Ireland*

Ireland and the administration of James Butler, 2nd Duke of Ormonde, Lord Lieutenant of Ireland, 1703-1707. *G. E. I. Crosby, M.A. 1935 Liverpool*

Irish Catholics and Legislative Union, 1800. *T. A. Burke, M.A. 1943 National University of Ireland*

The Leix-Offaly Plantation. *B. L. Rowan, M.A. 1940 National University of Ireland*

The Londonderry plantation, with special reference to the resulting relations between the Crown and the city, 1609-41. *T. W. D. Moody, Ph.D. 1934 London, University College*

Ireland: History contd.
The more immediate effects of the American revolution on Ireland (1775-1785). *T. M. O'Connor, M.A. 1938 Belfast*

Naval expeditions to Ireland at the time of the French Revolution. *P. B. Bradley, M.A. 1923 National University of Ireland*

The part played by Kinsale in history from Elizabeth to Cromwell. *T. E. McAdoo, M.A. 1914 National University of Ireland*

The plantation of Ulster. *S. G. Kennedy, M.A. 1925 National University of Ireland*

The political and social teachings of the Young Irelanders, 1842-1848. *G. R. Clarke, M.A. 1936 Belfast*

The problem of Lord Essex in Ireland. *L. Duggan, M.A. 1926 National University of Ireland*

Relations of the British Government and the Roman Catholic Church in Ireland 1508-1829. *G. D. Sanderson, Ph.D. 1930 Dublin, Trinity College*

The Saxon element in early Irish history. *A. M. Scarre, M.A. 1908 Liverpool*

Service of Scottish mercenary forces in Ireland. *G. A. Hayes-McCoy, M.A. 1932 National University of Ireland*

The service of the Scottish mercenary forces in Ireland, from 1565 to 1603, with an account of the mercenary system in Ireland and of its effect on Scottish history. *G. A. Hayes-McCoy, Ph.D. 1934 Edinburgh*

The siege of Galway, 1651-1652. *P. Callan, M.A. 1931 National University of Ireland*

Some aspects of the Geraldine rebellion. *M. McCarthy, M.A. 1926 National University of Ireland*

Studies of Ireland under Strafford. *W. H. A. O'Grady, Litt.D. 1922 Dublin, Trinity College*

Tudor rule in Ireland in the reigns of Henry VII and Henry VIII, with special reference to the Anglo-Irish financial administration. *D. B. Quinn, Ph.D. 1934 London, King's College*

Uí Fidgente, a kingdom of the Eoganachta. *F. Barrett, M.A. 1942 National University of Ireland*

Zoilomastix of Don Philip O'Sullivan Beare. *T. J. O'Connell, M.A. 1941 National University of Ireland*

Ireland: Parliament
The Clare election, 1828. *H. P. Carberry, M.A. 1934 Liverpool*

Irish Parliament of Queen Anne. *F. L. O'Leary, M.A. 1944 National University of Ireland*

The medieval Irish Parliament. *H. Scott, M.A. 1914 London*

The political career of the Right Hon. John Foster, last speaker of the Irish House of Commons. *N. D. Emerson, Ph.D. 1930 Dublin, Trinity College*

Ireland: Politics and Government
The administrative relations between England and Ireland, 1660-1670. *E. M. B. Robinson, M.A. 1927 Manchester*

Central and local administration in Ireland under George II. *J. L. McCracken, Ph.D. 1948 Belfast*

The civil administration of Ireland, 1801-1846. *S. M. Houghton, M.A. 1924 Manchester*

The economic, social, and administrative problem of the congested districts of Ireland. *A. F. Blair, M.Comm. 1930 National University of Ireland*

Príomh-Rialtas agus rialtas áitiúil (Central and local government). *E. O'Cathdin, M.Econ.Sc. 1929 National University of Ireland*

Ireland: Social History
The congested districts of Ireland. *I. Hynes, M.Econ.Sc. 1944 National University of Ireland*

The economic, social, and administrative problem of the congested districts of Ireland. *A. F. Blair, M.Comm. 1930 National University of Ireland*

An Egyptian in Ireland. *I. Rashad, Ph.D. 1922 National University of Ireland*

Everyday life in Ireland in the second half of the seventeenth century. *E. MacLysaght, M.A. 1937 National University of Ireland*

Meon agus tréithe na ndaoine sa nua-sgéalaidheacht (The mind and characteristics of the ordinary people in modern literature). *M. O'Mordha, M.A. 1946 National University of Ireland*

Social and political ideas in Ireland in the 18th century. *R. B. McDowell, Ph.D. 1938 Dublin, Trinity College*

Ireland: Social History contd.
Social conditions in Ireland in the seventeeth and eighteenth centuries, as illustrated by early Quaker records. *I. Grubb, M.A. 1916 London*

The spirit of 18th century Ireland as reflected in its literature (in the English language). *P. B. Devilly, M.A. 1937 National University of Ireland*

The treatment of national character in the novels of Charles Lever. *M. Lancaster, M.A. 1935 Liverpool*

The undertakers in Ireland and their relations with the Lords Lieutenant, 1724-1771. *J. L. McCracken, M.A. 1942 Belfast*

Ireland, Northern
See Northern Ireland.

Ireland, William Henry
W. H. Ireland: his life and works. *D. A. P. Saunders, M.A. 1936 Wales*

Irenaeus, Saint
The biblical theology of St. Irenaeus. *J. Lawson, B.D. 1949 Cambridge*

Irenaeus and Gnosticism. *A. D. Livingstone, Ph.D. 1934 Edinburgh*

Irenaeus and the fourth gospel: the value of his testimony. *J. McP. Fleck, Ph.D. 1925 Edinburgh*

Irenaeus of Lugdunum. *F. R. M. Hitchcock, Litt.D. 1949 Dublin, Trinity College*

1. The life and teaching of Irenaeus. 2. Irenaean fragments. *F. G. Lowe, Ph.D. 1938 Bristol*

A study of the life and writings of St. Ignatius of Antioch, and St. Irenaeus, with special reference to their personal religion and its influence on their work and teaching. *A. P. Carleton, D.D. 1934 Oxford*

Irish Free State
See Ireland.

Irish Language
Ainmneacha aiteann i gCondae Mhuigheo (The names of furze in Co. Mayo). *P. Mc Donagh, M.A. 1948 National University of Ireland*

Aithbheochaint na Gaedhilge (The Irish language revival). *S. Barruadh, M.A. 1928 National University of Ireland*

Bearlagair na saor (Masons' jargon). *S. Toibin, M.A. 1931 National University of Ireland*

Canamhain chois fhairrge (Dialects of the sea side). *T. MacD. De Bhaldraithe, Ph.D. 1942 National University of Ireland*

Canamhaint oirthuaiscirt Mhuigheo (The dialects of south-east Mayo). *J. Burke, M.A. 1941 National University of Ireland*

Canamhainti an Chláir (Dialects of Co. Clare). *G. Clune, Ph.D. 1936 National University of Ireland*

Canamhaintí Gaedhilge (Irish dialects). *M. Flatley, M.A. 1933 National University of Ireland*

Coim mheas na gcanamhan (A comparison of dialects). *P. O'Kelly, M.A. 1944 National University of Ireland*

Comhainmneacha, samhail-ainmneacha agus diúltadha Gaedhilge (Irish synonyms, homonyms and negatives). *P. G. O'Raghallaigh, M.A. 1947 National University of Ireland*

Córus bhriathardha *Chatréim Cellaig* as an Leabhar Breac (The verbal system of *Catréim Cellaig* in the Leabhar Breac). *T. P. O'Coincheanainn, M.A. 1945 National University of Ireland*

Foras focal an Athar Peadar O'Laoghaire (The vocabulary of Father Peter O'Leary). *M. J. D. Normoyle, Ph.D. 1942 National University of Ireland*

Forus feasa ar ghraiméir lobháin (An outline of the Louvain grammar). *J. Egan, M.A. 1938 National University of Ireland*

Gaedhilgeóirí Chorcaighe i dTosach ré na haithbheodhchana (Cork scholars of the Irish language at the beginning of the revival). *E. I. Ni Choindealbháin, M.A. 1941 National University of Ireland*

Gaelic catechisms in Ireland. *J. J. Corkery, M.A. 1944 National University of Ireland*

Graiméar ar an ainm san *Oileánach* le Tomás O'Criomhtháin (The grammar of the noun as used in *An tOileánach* by Tomás O'Criomhtháin). *D. O'Conchubháir, M.A. 1944 National University of Ireland*

Graimeir Ghaedhilge na mBráthair (The Brothers' Irish grammar). *J. P. Egan, Ph.D. 1945 National University of Ireland*

Irish Language contd.
Iarmbéarladha na Gaedhilge agus a dtionchur ar an ainm (Irish particles and their influence on the noun). *D. F. O'Murchadha, M.A. 1941 National University of Ireland*

Inter-relations of Ireland and Wales as evidenced by the tradition, languages and literatures of both countries. *C. O'Rahilly, M.A. 1919 Wales*

The language and literature of Dublin - a survey 1172-1942. *J. L. Clarke, M.A. 1938 National University of Ireland*

The letter R (Hessen's Irish lexicon). *J. Kavanagh, Ph.D. 1940 National University of Ireland*

Meath na teangan (The decline of the language). *E. Ni Shúilliobháin, M.A. 1930 National University of Ireland*

Múineadh litridheachta na Gaedhilge 'sa nGaedhealtacht (The teaching of Irish literature in the Irish-speaking area). *T. Mac A'ghoill, M.A. 1934 National University of Ireland*

Na Bráithre Críostamhla agus an Ghaedhilge (The Christian Brothers and the Irish language). *O'Catháin, M.A. 1945 National University of Ireland*

Nasalization in Irish. *P. O'Donnell, M.A. 1915 National University of Ireland*

Relative construction in Middle Irish; a study of some morphological and syntactical changes in the expression of the relative. *B. O'Cuiv, M.A. 1940 National University of Ireland*

Sgotha cainte na Gaedhilge (Irish idioms). *P. N. Dineen, M.A. 1942 National University of Ireland*

Some studies in the development from Middle to Modern Irish based on the Annals of Ulster. *S. O'Catháin, M.A. 1929 National University of Ireland*

Somplaí de Ghaedhilge Bheanntraí (Examples of Bantry Irish). *S. O'Brian, M.A. 1929 National University of Ireland*

Taighde ar dheilbh-eolas na meán-Gaeilge (An investigation of the morphology of Middle Irish). *B. MacGiolla Choilleadh, M.A. 1943 National University of Ireland*

Taighde ar dheilbheolus an 13-14 céad. Corus briathardha *Beatha Fheichin Thobhair* (A study of 13th and 14th century morphology. The verbal system of *Beatha Fheichin Thobhair*). *M. M. M. Rushe, M.A. 1948 National University of Ireland*

Taighde ar feidhm na réimíreann mbriathardha (An investigation of the function of verbal prefixes). *S. MacRéamoinn, M.A. 1943 National University of Ireland*

Taighde ar na h-iolraidh atá le fagháil i saothar an Athar Pheadair (Research on the plural forms used in the work of Father Peadar). *D. O'Mathghamhna, M.A. 1944 National University of Ireland*

Vocabulary to lives of St. Carthage. *M. Lucy, M.A. 1915 National University of Ireland*

Irish Literature
For Irish literature in the English language, see English Literature, and references there to individual writers. For the study and teaching of Irish literature, see Irish Language. See also Romances; and Aided Diarmata; Ballymote, Book of; Barra, D. de; Céitinn, S.; Conall Gulban; Firtéar, Padraig; Firtéar, Piaras; Francis, Saint (Life of); Gearnon, A.; Gregory, I. A., Lady; Innisfallen; Leabhar Gabhála; Leabhar Laighneach; Leabhar Muimhneach; MacAingil, A.; Macpherson, J.; MacPiarais, P.; Maolmodach, Saint; Ni Laeri, M. B.; O'Bruacháin, T. G.; O'Bruadair, D.; O'Ceallaigh, T.; O'Conaire, P. Og; O'Conchubhair, T.; O'Criomhtháin, T.; O'Cuirnin, P. D.; O'Donnghaile, E.; Oengus; O'Gadhra, S.; O'Grianna, S. (Máire); O'Laoghaire, D.; O'Leary, P.; O'Longáin, M. O.; O'Maolchonaire, Clan; O'Siochfhradha, P.; O'Suilleabháin, D.; Owen, the Red; Ruarcach; Sadhbh; Trumpet of Heaven.

Academic writings of Irish exiles in the seventeenth century. *T. Wall, Ph.D. 1943 National University of Ireland*

An béaloideas sa bhFiannuidheacht (The oral tradition of the Fenian Cycle). *M. Ni Bhrádaigh, M.A. 1948 National University of Ireland*

Inter-relations of Ireland and Wales as evidenced by the tradition, languages and literatures of both countries. *C. O'Rahilly, M.A. 1919 Wales*

Irish Gaelic literature (verse) in translation. *K. W. Heaslip, B.Litt. 1950 Dublin, Trinity College*

Irish women writers 1800-35. *S. J. C. Harrison, Ph.D. 1947 Dublin, Trinity College*

Irish Literature contd.
The language and literature of Dublin - a survey 1172-1942. *J. L. Clarke, M.A. 1938 National University of Ireland*

Litríocht na Gaedhilge in san gceathru asis deag (Irish Literature in the fourteenth century). *P. Quigley, M.A. 1951 National University of Ireland*

Meon agus tréithe na ndaoine sa nua-sgéalaidheacht (The mind and characteristics of the ordinary people in modern literature). *M. O'Mordha, M.A. 1946 National University of Ireland*

Múineadh litridheachtla na Gaedhilge 'sa nGaedhealtacht (The teaching of Irish literature in the Irish-speaking area). *T. Mac A'ghoill, M.A. 1934 National University of Ireland*

Nua-litríocht na Gaedhilge agus cainnt na ndaoine (Modern Irish literature and popular expression). *P. P. O'Maoldhomhnaigh, M.A. 1943 National University of Ireland*

Págántacht san Ruadhraigheacht agus san Fhiannaigheacht (Paganism in the Red Branch Cycle and the Fenian Cycle). *S. Nic Craith, M.A. 1939 National University of Ireland*

Prós na Gaeilge (Irish prose). *K. Golden, Ph.D. 1947 National University of Ireland*

Relations, historical and literary, between Ireland and Scandinavia from the ninth century to the thirteenth. *J. I. Young, Ph.D. 1930 Cambridge*

Saoghal agus saothar triair sgríobhnóirí Gaedhilge : Pádraig Mac Piarais, Micheál Breathnach agus Pádraig O'Conaire (The lives and works of three Irish writers: Pádraig Mac Piarais, Micheál Breathnach and Pádraig O'Conaire). *C. Nic Concairrge, M.A. 1941 National University of Ireland*

Seventeenth century satire in Irish, with special reference to the Páirlemént Cholinne Tomáis. *H. R. McAdoo, Ph.D. 1940 Dublin, Trinity College*

Stair litríochta na Gaedhilge: Draoithe (The history of Irish literature: druids). *M. B. O'Briáin, M.A. 1939 National University of Ireland*

Taighde i gcóir stair litridheachta na Nua Ghaedhilge ó 1882 anuas (Research on the history of modern Irish literature since 1882). *M. O'Droighneain, M.A. 1929 National University of Ireland*

Trı tonna dibhfheirge Dé agus Beatha Chaitriona (The three surges of God's wrath and The life of Catherine). *E. J. Edmonds, M.A. 1930 National University of Ireland*

Irish Society, The
The foundation and early history of the Irish Society, 1609-25. *M. E. Perrott, M.A. 1920 London*

Iron Age
See Archaeology and Antiquities.

Iron and Steel Industry
See also Engineering Industry; Gun Trade; Nail Industry; Needlemaking Industry; Pens; Tube Industry.

The British iron and steel trades since 1920. *E. Davies, M.A. 1937 Wales*

Capacity and pricing in the British iron and steel industry under the Federation. *I. Steven, B.Litt. 1940 Oxford*

The charcoal iron trade in the Midlands, 1690-1720. *B. L. C. Johnson, M.A. 1950 Birmingham*

Costs, prices, and investment in the British iron and steel industries 1924-37. *J. H. B. Tew, Ph.D. 1941 Cambridge*

The development of the iron and steel industry of North Lancashire and South Cumberland in relation to geographical factors. *G. B. Cheetham, M.Sc. 1937 Leeds*

The development of the south Wales tinplate industry, with special reference to 1919-1939. *E. E. Watkin, M.A. 1949 Wales*

The early history of the iron industry in the Dudley area, with special reference to the claims of Dudley. *W. J. Jenkins, M.A. 1929 Wales*

The economic geography of the tinplate industry in south Wales. *W. J. Lewis, M.Sc. 1943 London, External Degree*

The effects of tariffs on industries, with especial reference to the tinplate industry. *J. H. Jones, M.A. 1904 Wales*

An enquiry into the major geographical factors conditioning the production and distribution of coal and iron in the United States of America. *P. W. Bryan, Ph.D. 1924 London*

Factorial analysis and its bearing on selection and placement of workers in the Tata iron and steel factory, Jamshedpur, India: first survey. *B. Dhar, Ph.D. 1947 Edinburgh*

Iron and Steel Industry contd.
A geographical study of the localization and migration of iron and steel manufacture in the North East of England (Northumberland, Durham, and the North Riding). *L. R. Jones, Ph.D. 1925 London*

The geography of the iron industry of Northamptonshire, Rutland and South Lincolnshire. *S. H. Beaver, M.A. 1931 London, University College*

The historical geography of the Furness iron industry. *B. A. Rayner, M.A. 1924 Liverpool*

The historical geography of the Sheffield iron and steel industries. *E. V. Lane, M.A. 1923 Liverpool*

The history and development of the iron and steel welded tube trade, with particular reference to the rise and eventual decline of the trade in the town of Wednesbury, Staffordshire. *S. J. Langley, M.Com. 1948 Birmingham*

The reconstruction of the iron, steel and tinplate industries of south Wales since the war. *W. J. Walters, M.A. 1928 Wales*

Some aspects of the British iron and steel industry from 1927-35, with special reference to the tinplate and steel sheet industry. *G. Schulz, B.Litt. 1938 Oxford*

A study of industrial relations in the British tinplate industry, 1874-1939. *E. H. Jones, M.A. 1940 Wales*

The tinplate industry, 1914-23. *H. J. Thomas, M.Com. 1923 Birmingham*

Two partnerships of the Knights: a study of the Midland iron industry in the eighteenth century. *R. A. Lewis, M.A. 1949 Birmingham*

The Wealden iron industry. *M. Richards, Ph.D. 1924 London*

Irrawaddy, River
The agricultural geography of the Irrawaddy delta, with special reference to rice. *K. E. Bruen, M.A. 1939 London, University College*

Irrigation
The effects of irrigation on movements of population, and on the food supply of the world, with special reference to America. *J. N. L. Baker, B.Litt. 1924 Oxford*

The introduction of perennial irrigation in Egypt and its effects on the rural economy and population problems of the country. *I. A. Farid, Ph.D. 1937 London, University College*

Irving, Edward
Edward Irving and the gift of tongues: an historical and psychological study. *A. L. Drummond, Ph.D. 1930 Edinburgh*

An examination of the views of Edward Irving concerning the person and work of Jesus Christ. *P. E. Davies, Ph.D. 1928 Edinburgh*

Irvingites
See Catholic Apostolic Church.

Ishmael
Ishmael and Hagar in the post-Biblical and Islamic literature. *H. Medalie, M.A. 1941 Manchester*

Isidore of Seville, Saint
The sources of the *De ecclesiasticis officiis* of St. Isidore of Seville. *A. C. Lawson, D.D. 1937 Oxford*

Isis
The cult of Isis in Italy: an account of its external history. *M. S. Salem, Ph.D. 1937 Liverpool*

The cult of Isis in Italy under the Empire. *I. D. Bertram, M.A. 1934 London, Bedford College*

Islam
See also Qur'ān; Rābia al-'Adawiyya al-Qayriyya; Seljuks, The; Waliullah, Shah.

Free will and predestination in early Islam. *W. M. Watt, Ph.D. 1944 Edinburgh*

The influence of Mohammedanism on Western civilization. *C. F. Adams, M.A. 1910 London*

The influence of the western Caliphate on the medical system of Europe. *D. Campbell, B.Sc. 1923 Oxford*

Islam in the twentieth century: the relevance of Christian theology and the relation of the Christian mission to its problems. *A. K. Cragg, D.Phil. 1950 Oxford*

Moslem polemics against Jews and Judaism. *M. Perlmann, Ph.D. 1941 London, School of Oriental and African Studies*

Muhammad's idea of the last judgment and its sources. *J. R. Buchanan, Ph.D. 1927 Edinburgh*

Muhammad's prophetic office as portrayed in the Qur'ān. *J. C. Wilson, Ph.D. 1949 Edinburgh*

Palestine as a type region of the Mohammedan world. *D. C. Goodson, M.A. 1935 Reading*

Islam contd.
1. The position of Jesus Christ in Mohammedanism. 2. Our risen Lord's appearances in Galilee. *A. E. Richardson, B.D. 1902 Oxford*

Islam: History
Al-Junayd: a study of a third/ninth century mystic with an edition and annotated translation of his writings. *A. H. Abdel-Kader, Ph.D. 1948 London, School of Oriental and African Studies*

The civil war between Amin and Ma'mūn. *S. A. Hamdi, M.A. 1948 London, School of Oriental and African Studies*

The effect of geographical factors on the spread of Islam with special reference to Africa. *H. M. Gohar, M.A. 1930 Bristol*

Geographical factors conditioning the eastward spread of Islam in Asia. *S. Conway, M.A. 1926 Liverpool*

An index of the traditionists quoted in *Kitāb al Kharāj* of Abū Yūsuf, together with a biography of the author. *S. A. H. Jafri, Ph.D. 1932 London, School of Oriental and African Studies*

An inquiry into the causes of the failure of the Mu'tazilite movement. *A. Subhan, B.Litt. 1945 Oxford*

An introduction to the chronicle called *Muffaril al Kutub li Akhbar Bani Ayyub* by Jamal ad Din b. Wasi. *C. Waddy, Ph.D. 1934 London, School of Oriental and African Studies*

Muslim sea power in the eastern Mediterranean from the seventh to the tenth century: studies in naval organization. *A. M. Fahmy, Ph.D. 1948 London, School of Oriental and African Studies*

The scholasticism of Christianity and of Islam so far as they are represented by the *Summa contra gentiles* of St. Thomas Aquinas and the *Nihayatu-l-igdam fi ilmil-kalam* of Al Shahrastani. *A. Guillaume, B.D. & D.D. 1934 Oxford*

Islam: India
The influence of Islam on Indian culture. *T. Chand, D.Phil. 1922 Oxford*

Muslim rule in Sind in the eighth, ninth and tenth centuries. *A. A. Puri, Ph.D. 1936 London, School of Oriental and African Studies*

Muslims in India: a political analysis (from 1885-1906). *R. A. Zakaria, Ph.D. 1948 London, School of Oriental and African Studies*

Islam: Sects
The *Bayān al-Adyān* by Abu'l Māīl Muhammad ibn Ubayd Allāh: translation, introduction and notes. *M. A. S. Kafafi, Ph.D. 1949 London, School of Oriental and African Studies*

Doctrines and history of the Ismā'ili Da'wat in Yemen. *A. H. F. Hamdani, Ph.D. 1931 London, School of Oriental and African Studies*

Panjabi Sufi poets. *L. Rama Krishna, Ph.D. 1934 London, School of Oriental and African Studies*

Shiism and its influence on Arabic literature. *S. A. D. A. A. Khulousy, Ph.D. 1947 London, External Degree*

Some aspects of Shī'īte propaganda under the Fātimids in Egypt. *H. I. Hassan, Ph.D. 1927 London*

Studies on the history of the Qarmati and Ismaili movements from the eighth to the eleventh centuries. *B. Lewis, Ph.D. 1939 London, External Degree*

Islamic Law
See also Women, Status of.

Deviations from the Anglo-Muhammadan law with reference to the Maplahs of Malabar. *H. Ali, LL.D. 1931 London, University College*

The effect of legislative enactments and judicial pronouncements on the civil law of the Muhammadans in the United Provinces of Agra and Oudh on matters other than family relations, administration and arbitration. *M. Nasim, LL.D. 1929 London*

Limited interests in Muhammadan law. *K. Tyabji, B.Litt. 1947 Oxford*

Muslim law of marriage. *M. U. I. S. Jung, LL.D. 1926 Dublin, Trinity College*

An outline of the system of the administration of justice under the Muslims in India, based mainly upon cases decided by Muslim courts between 1206 and 1750. *M. B. Ahmad, M.Litt. 1939 Cambridge*

Usury and the principles of the Muhammadan law. *M. S. Ali Khan, D.Phil. 1928 Oxford*

Islay
Islay: a study in island geography. *D. Sutherland, Ph.D. 1929 Glasgow*

Ismail, Khedive of Egypt
The Khedive Ismail and slavery in the Sudan. *M. F. Shukry, Ph.D. 1935 Liverpool*

Ismailis
See Islam.

Isocrates
Ideals of education in Isocrates and Plato. *D. Gilbert, M.A. 1937 London, Westfield College*

Isoko, The
The Isoko clans of the Niger Delta. *J. W. Welch, Ph.D. 1937 Cambridge*

Israel
See also Canaan; Jews; Judaism; Palestine; Prophecy.

The authenticity of the chronicler's account of the restoration of Israel in the light of Ezra and Nehemiah: a critical and historical study. *B. Maura, Ph.D. 1943 Edinburgh*

The conditions of labour in Israel as portrayed in the Old Testament and the Mishnah. *G. J. Roberts, M.A. 1936 Wales*

The early traditions of Israel. *C. A. Simpson, B.D. & D.D. 1944 Oxford*

1. The evolution of the revelation of God traced through the crises in the history of Israel during the period from Moses to Elijah. 2. The evolution of the revelation of God traced through the crises in the history of Israel during the eighth century B.C. *C. C. Atkinson, B.D. & D.D. 1898 Oxford*

The influence of the religious and ethical idealism of the prophets on the cultus of old Israel. *J. Mayne, Ph.D. 1934 Edinburgh*

An investigation into the origin and growth of the conception of theocracy in Israel. *G. H. Davies, M.A. 1929 Wales*

1. Isaiah lii.13-liii.12: the servant of the Lord. 2. Genesis xv; xvii; Exodus xx and other connected passages in Deuteronomy and Israel. 3. Ezekiel xxxiii-xxxix: the new age: Israel restored. *G. A. Cooke, D.D. 1909 Oxford*

The king in Israel. *A. A. Jones, M.A. 1947 Birmingham*

The land of Israel as an idea and ideal in Biblical literature. *A. Pimontel, M.A. 1937 Manchester*

The movement towards 'scribism' in the history of Israel. *J. W. Lightley, M.A. 1912 Belfast*

The Pauline interpretation of history: an examination of Romans xi-xii. *E. W. Hunt, B.D. 1946 Birmingham*

Problems suggested by the names and traditions of the Iraelitish tribes. *H. W. Hogg, B.Litt. 1904 Oxford*

1. Progressive revelation as illustrated in the history of Israel. 2. Asceticism and Christianity. *C. W. L. Evans, B.D. 1909 Oxford*

1. The relation of priest and prophet in the history of Israel before the exile. 2. St. Basil the Great and the monastic life. *E. F. Morison, B.D 1912 Oxford*

Weapons and conduct of Hebrew warfare as illustrated in the Old Testament. *W. Davies, M.A. 1929 Wales*

Isserls, Moses, Rabbi
The works of Rabbi Moses Isserls as a source of the history of the Jews in Poland in the sixteenth century. *M. S. Lew, Ph.D. 1941 London, Jews' College*

Italian Language
See also Italic Language.

Alessandro Manzoni's writings on the Italian language: a chronological reconstruction. *E. M. B. Reynolds, Ph.D. 1948 London, University College*

A comparative study of the development of strong perfects in French, Provençal, Spanish and Italian. *A. D. Neal, M.A. 1939 Manchester*

A linguistic study of the Franco-Italian epics. *G. Mellor, M.A. 1950 Manchester*

Italian Literature
See also Alfieri, V.; Ariosto, L.; Boccaccio, G.; Boccalini, T.; Dante Alighieri; Fogazzaro, A., Giacomino, da Verona; Goldoni, C.; Gozzi, Carlo, Conte; Guarini, G. B.; Jacopone da Todi; Machiavelli, N. di B. dei; Manzoni, A.; Mazzini, G.; Parini, G.; Pascoli, G.; Politian, A.; Ricciboni, H.; Rolli, P. A.; Sannazaro, J.; Verri, P.

Antonio Conti e il suo posto nella letteratura del settecento. *M. C. Cave, M.A. 1922 London*

The dialogue in Italian in the sixteenth century. *I. M. Dron, Ph.D. 1940 Edinburgh*

The influence of Italian literature on Spenser and Sidney. *E. W. Cedervall, M.A. 1920 Wales*

Italian Literature contd.
Influence of Italian literature on Ragusan poetry in the sixteenth century. *J. Torbarina, Ph.D. 1930 London, King's College*

Italian influence on the Elizabethan lyrics, more especially in connection with madrigals connection with madrigals. *C. K. Saunders, M.A. 1909 London*

Le lettere italiane del nostro secolo. *C. Pellizzi, D.Litt. 1932 London, University College*

The literary and artistic manifestations of neo-Platonism in the Italian Renaissance. *N. A. Robb, D.Phil. 1933 Oxford*

Thomas James Mathias and his place in Anglo-Italian literary relations. *K. Speight, M.Litt. 1938 Cambridge*

Vincenzo Martinelli and his circle in London, 1748-1774. *E. H. Thorne, Ph.D. 1946 London, University College*

Italic Language
See also Italian Language.

The affinities of Italic and Celtic. *J. L. Jones, M.A. 1909 Wales*

Italy
See also Florence; Lombardy; Rome; and Arnold, of Brescia; Cavour, C. B. di; D'Annunzio, G.; Machiavelli, N. di B. dei; Medici, L. de'; Panizzi, A., Sir.

Italy: Foreign Affairs
Anglo-Italian relations, 1884-5, and the Italian occupation of Massawah. *F. T. Fries, Ph.D. 1940 Cambridge*

The Franco-Italian rapprochement, 1898-1902. *E. R. Lewis, M.A. 1937 Wales*

The geographical background of political problems associated with the Italo-Jugoslav frontier. *A. E. F. Moodie, Ph.D. 1942 London, Birkbeck College*

The influence of English diplomacy on Italy. *V. E. L. Doorly, M.A. 1912 London*

The influence of the Italian Question on Anglo-French relations, 1856-60, from the Treaty of Paris to the annexation of Savoy and Nice. *H. M. Vincent, B.Litt. 1948 Oxford*

Italy: Geography
The poems of Virgil considered in connection with the geography of Italy, including the natural features and animal and plant life. *A. H. Birch, M.A. 1912 Wales*

Travel in Italy in the first century before Christ. *A. H. Watts, M.A. 1915 London*

Italy: History
British policy in the Italian Question (1866-1871). *H. E. Priestley, Ph.D. 1931 London, Birkbeck College*

Giangaleazzo Visconti, Duke of Milan, and the unity of Italy. *D. M. Bueno de Mesquita, Ph.D. 1939 Cambridge*

The influence of the Italian *Risorgimento* in English literature. *M. H. Ensor, M.A. 1917 Wales*

The last Florentine Republic, to the fall of Niccolo Capponi. *C. Roth, B.Litt. 1923 Oxford*

The last Florentine Republic, 1527-1530. *C. Roth, D.Phil. 1925 Oxford*

Palmerston and the dawn of Italian independence, 1830-1851. *C. F. Strong, Ph.D. 1925 London*

The political influence of Pope Gregory the Great in Italy. *H. V. W. Lewis, M.A. 1913 Wales*

Swinburne and the Italian Risorgimento. *J. M. Forster, M.A. 1934 Birmingham*

Tuscany and the Italian Risorgimento, 1859-60. *F. J. Skinner, M.A. 1921 London*

Italy: Politics and Government
Pre-Fascist Italy: the rise and fall of the parliamentary régime. *M. Hentze, Ph.D. 1938 London, School of Economics and Political Science*

Italy: Social History
The Englishman's conception of the Italian in the age of Shakespeare. *J. Fellheimer, M.A. 1935 London, King's College*

The grand tour in Italy in the sixteenth, seventeenth and eighteenth centuries. *E. M. Hutton, Ph.D. 1937 Cambridge*

The intellectual and social phenomena which determined the triumph of Christianity in Italy. *J. Mathias, M.A. 1925 Wales*

Italy in the drama of Victor Hugo: sources and characteristics. *P. E. Crump, M.A. 1919 London*

La cultura nell'Italia settentrionale sec. XIII. *K. M. A. O'Byrne, M.A. 1932 National University of Ireland*

Italy: Social History contd.
The place of Italy in the life and works of Ludwig Tieck. *E. C. V. Stopp, Ph.D. 1938 Cambridge*

Servants and satellites: a consideration of some minor Italian social types of the eighteenth century attendant upon the giovin signore of Parini's satire *Il giorno. W. Radcliffe, M.A. 1937 Manchester*

Ivory Coast
See also Bete.

Problems of the development of French West Africa, as illustrated by Senegal and the Ivory Coast. *M. A. el M. M. Sharkawy, M.A. 1931 Liverpool*

Jack Juggler
Collation of a reprint of *Jack Juggler* prepared in collaboration with Dr. W. W. Greg for the Malone Society, with an essay on the development of the Tudor interlude as a dramatic form. *E. L. Smart, M.A. 1934 London, University College*

Jacob, of Serug
Three homilies against the Jews by Jacob of Serug, edited with introduction, translation and notes. *I. K. Cosgrove, Ph.D. 1931 London, External Degree*

Jacobite Rebellion, 1745
See Scotland: History.

Jacobites
The development of Jacobite ideas and policy, 1689-1746. *G. H. Jones, D.Phil. 1950 Oxford*

The Jacobites in England and Wales, 1689-1723. *A. C. Turnbull, M.A. 1949 Liverpool*

The political faith of the English nonjurors. *L. M. Hawkins, Ph.D. 1927 London*

Jacopone da Todi
Jacopone dei Benedetti da Todi: a religious poet of the thirteenth century. *W. G. Austen, B.Litt. 1925 Oxford*

Jacques, de Longuyon
See Longuyon, J. de.

Jade
The evolution of technique in Chinese jade carving. *S. H. Hansford, M.A. 1946 London, Courtauld Institute of Art*

Jahiz, Abu Uthman Amr ibn Bahr ibn Mahbub
Jahiz: his life and work. *M. Bazbur Rehman, Ph.D. 1923 Cambridge*

Jahweh
See God.

Jalālu'd-Dīnī Rūmī
See Rūmī Jalālu'd-Dīn.

Jamaica
The constitutional development of Jamaica, with special reference to the control of the revenue, 1660-1729. *A. M. Whitson, M.A. 1928 Manchester*

Constitutional experiments in Jamaica. *H. L. Da Costa, B.Litt. 1948 Oxford*

Constitutional struggles in Jamaica, 1748-1776. *J. W. Herbert, M.A. 1927 London*

The place of Sir Henry Morgan in the history of Jamaica. *M. Hunter, B.Litt. 1934 Oxford*

The social, economic and political problems of the Stuart settlement of Jamaica. *R. W. Harris, M.A. 1943 Bristol*

James, Henry
The contribution of Henry James to the development of the modern novel. *E. M. Young, M.A. 1931 Wales*

The element of symbolism in the later novels and stories of Henry James. *M. Farris, Ph.D. 1949 Liverpool*

An essay on the method of Henry James. *E. V. Barton, M.A. 1950 Reading*

France in the writings of Henry James; a bibliography of the writings of Henry James. *D. Hamer, M.A. 1924 Liverpool*

Henry James: with special reference to his longer novels. *B. W. Bromage, M.A. 1924 Birmingham*

The life and work of Henry James, with special reference to the development of his attitude to the craft of letters, and to the 'international situation'. *A. T. G. Edwards, M.A. 1931 Wales*

Major novels of Henry James. *B. Dillon, M.A. 1947 National University of Ireland*

James I, King of England, and VI of Scotland
An enquiry into the social and political state of Scotland as reflected in the *Basilicon Doron* of James I. *W. Falconer, Ph.D. 1925 Edinburgh*

The finances of James VI, 1567-1603. *R. S. Brydon, Ph.D. 1925 Edinburgh*

James I, King of England, and VI of Scotland contd.
The relation of Church and State with special reference to the growth of the idea of religious toleration in England under James I, 1603-1616. *P. Doyle, M.A. 1928 London*

The relations between James VI and I and Carlo Emanuele I, Duke of Savoy. *J. Thompson, Ph.D. 1942 Saint Andrew's*

The vernacular writings of King James VI and I. *S. R. Dunlap, B.Litt. 1937 Oxford*

James II, King of England, and VII of Scotland
The administration of Scotland during the reigns of Charles II and James VII. *W. B. Gray, B.Litt. 1920 Oxford*

James, of Compostela, Saint
See also Santiago.

The cult and pilgrimage of St. James of Compostela, Spain, and their effects on the life and thought of the people in the northwestern corner of Spain. *H. W. Howes, M.A. 1938 Wales*

The functional aspects of the legend of St. James of Compostela. *W. H. Howes, Ph.D. 1934 London, School of Economics and Political Science*

James, William
The contribution of William James to the philosophy and psychology of religion. *F. B. Gear, Ph.D. 1939 Edinburgh*

The idea of God as expounded in the works of James and Ritschl. *R. Richards, M.A. 1921 Wales*

The idea of God in the philosophy of William James and James Ward. *S. J. Theodore, B.Litt. 1925 Oxford*

The idea of God, with special reference to James and Ritschl. *R. Richards, B.Litt. 1921 Oxford*

Jammes, Francis
Francis Jammes. *J. F. Galleymore, M.A. 1942 Birmingham*

Francis Jammes. *I. Rahilly, M.A. 1940 National University of Ireland*

L'esthétique de Francis Jammes. *M. H. Gray, M.A. 1949 Liverpool*

Janin, Jules Gabriel
Jules Janin, l'homme et le critique dramatique. *H. J. G. Godin, M.A. 1938 Belfast*

Jules Janin, romancier et conteur. *H. J. G. Godin, Ph.D. 1940 Belfast*

Jansenism
See also Antoine, A.; Nicole, P.; Pascal, B.; Port-Royal.

The little schools of Port Royal. *H. Clive-Barnard, B.Litt. 1911 Oxford*

Studies in the history and influence of the education of boys at Port Royal and in the older Oratorian colleges of France. *W. N. Littlejohns, M.A. 1948 London, King's College*

Japan
British foreign policy in relation to the Russo-Japanese war. *R. W. Barnett, B.Litt. 1937 Oxford*

British foreign policy in relation to Japan, 1890 to 1902. *W. A. Silk, M.A. 1944 Wales*

The economic and political problems of Japanese colonization. *W. P. C. Trafford, M.A. 1919 Wales*

A geographical study of the expansion of Japan in relation to the Japanese population problem. *L. E. Ward, M.A. 1932 Liverpool*

The industry and trade of Japan in modern times. *S. Uyehara, M.Sc. 1926 London*

Japanese foreign policy since 1915, with special reference to the events in 1931 and 1932. *W. J. A. Harris, M.Sc. 1940 London, School of Economics and Political Science*

A study in Japanese economics. *T. H. Sanders, M.Com. 1914 Birmingham*

System of extra-territoriality in Japan, 1855-99. *F. C. Jones, M.A. 1930 Bristol*

Yoshida Shōin, forerunner of the Meiji restoration. *H. J. J. M. van Straelen, Ph.D. 1949 Cambridge*

Japanese Language
On the relationship of the Japanese language. Sketch of a history of Japanese literary studies made by Europeans. . *F. Hawley, M.A. 1933-34 Liverpool*

Japanese Literature
Heian literature, with special reference to the Uta-Monogatari. *H. Roggendorff, M.A. 1940 London, School of Oriental and African Studies*

Japanese Literature contd.
On the relationship of the Japanese language. Sketch of a history of Japanese literary studies made by Europeans. . *F. Hawley, M.A. 1933-34 Liverpool*

Jason
Medea and Jason in Greek and Roman literature. *M. Curran, M.A. 1939 Manchester*

Jaspers, Karl
A study of the conception of conscience in the philosophy of Martin Heidegger and Karl Jaspers. *A. B. Downing, M.A. 1947 Manchester*

Jay, William
Evangelicalism in England in the first half of the nineteenth century as exemplified in the life and works of William Jay, 1769-1853. *H. E. Pressly, Ph.D. 1950 Edinburgh*

Jayasi, Malik Muhammad
A critical edition and translation of the *Padumavati* of Malik Muhammad Jayasi: a study of the Hindi (Avadhi) language in the sixteenth century. *L. Dhar, Ph.D. 1940 London, School of Oriental and African Studies*

Jean l'Aumônier, Saint
La vie de saint Jean l'aumônier. *A. Hill, M.A. 1936 Sheffield*

Jean V, Duke of Brittany
Jean V, Duke of Brittany (1399-1442) in relation to England. *G. A. Knowlson, M.A. 1934 Liverpool*

Jebel Moya
The physical characteristics and racial affinities of the inhabitants of the Sudan, past and present, with special reference to the human remains from Jebel Moya. *R. Mukherjea, Ph.D. 1949 Cambridge*

Jechiel, Asher Ben, Rabbi
The life of the Jews in Spain in the times of R. Asher B. Jechiel, as furnished by his *Responsa. H. Freedman, Ph.D. 1930 London, External Degree*

Jefeth Ibn Ali, The Karaite
A commentary on the Book of Joel, by Jefeth Ibn Ali the Karaite. *S. M. Lehrman, Ph.D. 1927 London*

Jefferies, Richard
Richard Jefferies: the interpreter of nature. *M. Kear, M.A. 1925 Liverpool*

Jefferson, Thomas
The political theory of Thomas Jefferson. *O. Rockey, B.Litt. 1925 Oxford*

Jeffrey, Francis
Matthew Arnold and the literary criticism of the early nineteenth century, with special reference to Jeffrey and Hazlitt: a comparison of methods and evaluations. *J. Wilkinson, M.A. 1947 Manchester*

Jemdet Nasr
A cemetery at Kish. A Sumerian palace. Jemdet Nasr. Bahrein and Hemamieh. Mohenjo-Daro. *E. J. H. Mackay, D.Litt. 1933 Bristol*

Jenkinson, Charles, 1st Earl of Liverpool
Charles Jenkinson as Secretary at War, with special reference to the period from the general election of September 1780 to the fall of North's administration in March 1782. *O. R. Gee, B.Litt. 1949 Oxford*

The political papers of Charles Jenkinson, 1760-1765. *N. S. Jucker, M.A. 1936 Manchester*

Jerdan, William
The Literary Gazette under the editorship of William Jerdan. *K. M. Shawcross, B.Litt. 1937 Oxford*

Jerome, Saint
The letters of St. Jerome as illustrating the condition of society in the fourth century. *J. Duff, B.Litt. 1925 Oxford*

St. Jerome's Epistles. *L. Hughes, B.D. & D.D. 1923, Oxford*

St. Jerome's *Letters* and *Lives of the Hermits*, with reference to (i) art and style; (ii) social and historical significance. *E. Coleiro, Ph.D. 1949 London, King's College*

Jersey
Feudalism in Jersey. *A. F. Luce, M.A. 1924 London*

Jerusalem
The archaeology of Herod's Temple: incorporating a commentary on the tractate *Middoth. F. J. Hollis, D.D. 1931 London, King's College*

The effect of the fall of Jerusalem in A.D. 70 on the Christian Church. *S. G. F. Brandon, B.D. 1939 Leeds*

Jesse, Tree of
The early iconography of the Tree of Jesse. *A. Watson, Ph.D. 1935 London, External Degree*

Jesters
Studies in the development of the fool in the Elizabethan drama. *O. M. Busby, M.A. 1916 London*

Jesuits
See also Missions; Religious Orders and Societies; Southwell, R.

Jesuit Mission to Ireland. *J. Corboy, M.A. 1941 National University of Ireland*

The Jesuits and the Council of Trent. *G. Duckworth, B. Litt. 1939 Oxford*

John Oldham (1653-83), *Satyrs on the Jesuits*: a critical text with introduction and notes. *H. F. Brooks, B.Litt. 1934 Oxford*

The making of the ratio-studiorum, 1548-1599 A.D. *A. B. Farrell, Ph.D. 1932 National University of Ireland*

Na h-Iosánaigh agus aithbheochaint an l'éighinn cuimre (The Jesuits and the Renaissance). *S. O'Catháin, Ph.D. 1941 National University of Ireland*

People v. prince: some political doctrines of Mariana and the early Jesuits. *S. G. Griffin, M.A. 1931 National University of Ireland*

Robert Southwell. *W. F. Stead, B.Litt. 1936 Oxford*

A study of the Jesuit Mission of 1580 with particular reference to its effects on Catholicism in England. *M. E. Whelan, M.A. 1927 Liverpool*

The teaching of Latin by the Jesuits, with special reference to the *ratio studiorum. B. C. Grant, M.A. 1920 Wales*

The teaching of Latin by the Jesuits, with special reference to the *ratio studiorum. D. B. Jones, M.A. 1922 Wales*

Jesuits: History
Some aspects of Jesuit education before the suppression. *M. Kennelly, M.A. 1948 National University of Ireland*

Jesus Christ
See also Antichrist; Ascension; Atonement; Incarnation; Kingdom of God; Logos; Messiah; Miracles; Parables; Redemption; Resurrection; Trinity. For the Second Coming, see Eschatology.

Jesus Christ: Life and Teaching
1. The application of our Lord's moral teaching to modern needs. 2. The Lord's Prayer as a guide to public worship. *F. A. M. Spencer, B.D. 1923 Oxford*

1. The attitude of Christ towards the civil society of his day. 2. The Gospel and asceticism. *R. F. Rynd, B.D. 1910 Oxford*

1. The authenticity of the Epistle of St. James. 2. Our Lord's brethren. *H. Maynard-Smith, B.D. & D.D. 1923 Oxford*

1. The bearing of the Rabbinical criminal code on the Jewish trial narratives of the Gospel, with a translation of the *Mishnah* and *Tosefta* of the Tractate Sanhedrin. 2. An introduction to the homilies of Aphraates. *H. Danby, B.D. 1919 Oxford*

1. Christ descended into hell. 2. After we have received the Holy Ghost, we may depart from grace given, and fall into sin, and by the grace of God we may arise again, and amend our lives. *J. W. Caldicott, B.D. & D.D. 1874 Oxford*

The chronology of the public ministry of Jesus. *G. Ogg, D.Litt. 1936 Saint Andrew's*

1. The condition of our Lord's body between his Resurrection and Ascension. 2. The narratives of the Ascension, critically compared and harmonized. *C. Harris, B.D. 1898 Oxford*

1. The consideration of our Lord's Messianic consciousness in the light of his use of the Old Testament. 2. A critical study of the pericope in St. John vii.53-viii.11. *C. E. Blakeway, B.D. & D.D. 1910 Oxford*

A critical investigation into the philosophical, ecclesiastical and other influences on Ernest Renan's *Vie de Jésus. A. W. Mackie, Ph.D. 1931 Glasgow*

1. The deity of Christ and of the Holy Spirit as revealed in the New Testament. 2. The Scriptural evidence for the Resurrection of Christ. *C. J. Casher, B.D. 1899 Oxford*

1. The documentary evidence for the Virgin Birth. 2. The doctrine of the Virgin Birth. *G. L. Prestige, B.D. 1923 Oxford*

1. The eschatological beliefs of Jesus. 2. Extract teaching *in re* synoptic Gospels. *J. L. L. Fulford, B.D. & D.D. 1913 Oxford*

An essay introductory to the *De pauperie Salvatoris* of Richard Fitzralph, books v-vii. *H. C. Hughes, Ph.D. 1928 Manchester*

Jesus Christ: Life and Teaching contd.
1. The evidence for the resurrection of Jesus Christ. 2. The divinity of Christ argued from his claim to sinlessness. *H. F. P. Davson, B.D. 1908 Oxford*

Expositions of: St. Matthew iv.3, 4: St. Luke iv.3,4: the first temptation; St. Matthew iv.5; St. Luke iv.9: the second temptation; St. Matthew iv.8-11; St. Luke iv.5-8: the third temptation. *C. J. Casher, D.D. 1903 Oxford*

Expositions of St. Matthew iv.1-11: Christ's temptation; St. Luke xxii.39-44: the agony in Gethsemane; II Thessalonians ii.3-10: the second coming of Christ. *F. R. C. Bruce, B.D. 1908 Oxford*

Formgeschichte, eschatology, and the life of Jesus. *W. Neil, Ph.D. 1936 Glasgow*

God's love in the teaching of Jesus according to the synoptic Gospels. *A. Cairns, Ph.D. 1937 Belfast*

1. The heavenly doctrine of St. Mark. 2. Our Lord's use of the Old Testament. *R. H. Taylor, B.D. 1895 Oxford*

The historical evidence for the Virgin birth. *V. Taylor, Ph.D. 1922 London*

The influence of apocalyptic on the mind of Jesus. *W. Y. Whitehead, Ph.D. 1929 Glasgow*

The influence of environment on the form of the gospel of Jesus. *H. S. Mackenzie, Ph.D. 1925 Edinburgh*

An interpretation of the apocalyptic teaching of Jesus. *W. M. Grant, Ph.D. 1928 Aberdeen*

The inter-relation of the doctrine of the work of Christ and the person of Christ during the first five centuries of the Church. *A. H. Bonser, B.D. 1948 Leeds*

Jesus' conception of man in the Synoptic Gospels. *D. K. Allen, Ph.D. 1928 Edinburgh*

Jesus' teaching on man and modern psychological theories. *M. B. Birnie, M.A. 1947 Bristol*

1. The language in which our Lord taught. 2. Supposed quotations from the Apostolic liturgy in the New Testament. *G. H. Gwilliam, B.D. 1890 Oxford*

1. The language used by Christ. 2. The organization of the early Christian Churches. *C. R. Perry, B.D. 1892 Oxford*

1. The Lord's Prayer: its origin, comprehensiveness, and suitability, both as a form and a model. 2. The genuineness of the pastoral epistles. *F. W. Joy, B.D. & D.D. 1895 Oxford*

The *Meditations on the Passion* ascribed to Richard Rolle. *M. M. Morgan, M.A. 1947 London, Bedford College*

The moral dynamic in the synoptic teaching of Jesus. *J. Safely, Ph.D. 1928 Edinburgh*

1. The neo-Platonic tribute to the faith. 2. A study of the two records of our Lord's genealogy. *F. R. C. Bruce, B.D. 1904 Oxford*

Nicholas Love's fifteenth century translation of the *Meditationes vitae Christi*: a study, with special reference to the Passion section. *E. Jones, M.A. 1949 London, Bedford College*

1. On the historic Christ. 2. On the sacraments. *J. H. Skrine, B.D. & D.D. 1912 Oxford*

1. The parabolic teaching of our Saviour. 2. The temptation of our Saviour. *H. B. Gray, B.D. & D.D. 1892 Oxford*

1. Passages from the Gospels of St. Matthew and St. Mark in which Jesus enjoins 'silence'. 2. Examination of passages in which is recorded the impression made by Jesus on various classes of those who first listened to him. *A. A. David, B.D. & D.D. 1910 Oxford*

1. The position of Jesus Christ in Mohammedanism. 2. Our risen Lord's appearances in Galilee. *A. E. Richardson, B.D. 1902 Oxford*

1. The preaching of Christ and his Apostles. 2. In what sense and with what limitations is it true to say that correct theological belief is necessary to salvation?. *H. Temple, B.D. & D.D. 1899 Oxford*

1. The relation of the Psalms to Christ. 2. The resurrection of Jesus Christ. *J. H. Hopkinson, B.D. & D.D. 1909 Oxford*

The relation to the Old Testament of the synoptic teaching of Jesus, with some comparison of the attitude shown in the Epistles of Paul and in the Epistle to the Hebrews. *J. R. Bucher, Ph.D. 1940 Edinburgh*

The relevance of the ethical teaching of Jesus to the conditions of this world order: an examination of the Sermon on the Mount. *W. R. F. Browning, B.D. 1948 Oxford*

Jesus Christ: Life and Teaching contd.

1. The Resurrection of Christ. 2. The Virgin Birth of Christ. *R. Waterfield, B.D. & D.D. 1924 Oxford*

1. The resurrection of Jesus Christ. 2. The ministry of angels as revealed in Holy Scripture. *C. C. Mills, B.D. & D.D. 1909 Oxford*

1. The resurrection of Jesus Christ considered as a historical and dogmatic problem. 2. The outlook of Jesus upon the future. *A. E. J. Rawlinson, B.D. 1921 Oxford*

1. St. Mark xiv.21 and viii.38: 'Son of Man' in the Synoptic Gospels. 2. St. Mark i.11; St. Luke iii.22: 'Son of God' in the Synoptic Gospels. 3. St. Matthew xi.18-19: Our Lord's attitude towards asceticism. *F. H. Dudden, D.D. 1907 Oxford*

1. The Sermon on the Mount in light of today. 2. The Christian argument from the study of ethnology. *E. S. Chalk, B.D. 1921 Oxford*

1. The sinlessness of Christ. 2. The Resurrection as the main evidence for Christianity. *M. J. Barrington-Ward, B.D. & D.D. 1919 Oxford*

Smaointe beatha Chríost, i astriú gaedhilge a chuir Tomas Gruamdha O Bruacháin (fl. c.1450), ar an *Meditationes vitae Christi* (*Thoughts on the life of Christ*; an Irish translation by Tomás Gruamdha O Bruacháin (fl. c.1450) of *Meditationes vitae Christi*). *C. O'Maonaigh, M.A. 1941 National University of Ireland*

A study of the conception of life in the synoptic teaching of Jesus, and its development in the Pauline and Johannine writings. *B. S. Rude, Ph.D. 1938 Edinburgh*

A study of the New Testament sources for the life of Jesus. *E. D. Johnston, Ph.D. 1950 Manchester*

A study of the passion narratives, with special reference to the Last Supper. *H. L. Franklin, B.Litt. 1935 Oxford*

A study of the teaching of Jesus in its application to modern economic problems. *M. Charles, B.Litt. 1935 Oxford*

The substance and method of our Lord's teaching viewed in the light of modern educational and psychological thought. *D. Miletitch, B.Litt. 1922 Oxford*

A survey of the fundamental ideas in the mind of Christ as interpreted in the theological literature of Britain and America since *Ecce homo* (1865). *A. White, Ph.D. 1927 Edinburgh*

The teaching of Christ on social questions. *D. H. Morgan, M.A. 1944 Wales*

The temptations of Jesus, with special reference to the history of their interpretation. *J. B. Berry, Ph.D. 1930 Edinburgh*

1. The testimony of St. Paul with regard to the resurrection of our Lord compared with that of the four Evangelists. 2. A study of the sterner side of the character of our Lord as evidenced in the narratives of the Evangelists. *A. W. Upcott, B.D. & D.D. 1906 Oxford*

1. The times and prophecy of Amos. 2. The chronology of the life of our Lord. *J. Solloway, B.D. 1901 Oxford*

To what extent do the discourses ascribed to Christ in the fourth Gospel preserve His own words?. *H. L. Jewett Williams, B.Litt. 1912 Oxford*

The transition from the Synoptic to the Johannine version of the life and teaching of Jesus. *E. H. Woods, Ph.D. 1924 Edinburgh*

The Virgin Birth in history and faith. *D. A. Edwards, B.D. 1943 Oxford*

1. The Virgin birth of the Lord Jesus Christ. 2. The person of our Lord and the kenotic theory. *F. S. G. Warman, B.D. 1907 Oxford*

1. The witness to the divinity of our Lord. 2. Operations of the Holy Spirit in the individual soul. *C. A. H. Green, B.D. 1907 Oxford*

Jesus Christ: Person and Work

1. The approximate date of the Acts of the Apostles. 2. The descent into Hades. *T. H. Davies, B.D. 1905 Oxford*

1. Aspects of Christ as viewed in succesive ages of the Church. 2. The doctrine of a future life. *J. Darlington, B.D. 1899 Oxford*

Athrawiaeth y Drindod a pherson Crist yng Nghymru o 1860 (The doctrine of the Trinity and the Person of Christ in Wales from 1860). *C. Rogers, M.A. 1934 Wales*

Athrawiaeth y 'kenosis' mewn diwinyddiarth Gymraeg (Phil. ii, 5-8) (The doctrine of the 'kenosis' in Welsh theology (Phil. ii, 5-8)). *H. J. Parry, M.A. 1938 Wales*

Jesus Christ: Person and Work contd.

The authority of Jesus and its foundation: an examination of the Gospels and the Book of Acts. *B. L. Woolf, Ph.D. 1926 Edinburgh*

British and American Christology from 1889-1914. *J. S. Lawton, B.D. 1944 Oxford*

The Chalcedonian formula in the twentieth century: an examination of recent trends in Christology. *J. B. Saunders, B.D. 1947 Oxford*

Christ in German epic and dramatic literature. *I. M. Southall, M.A. 1914 Birmingham*

1. Christ, our righteousness. 2. The doctrine of the Holy Spirit. *J. G. Simpson, B.D. & D.D. 1909 Oxford*

1. Christ, the desire of all nations. 2. Christ, the light and the life of men. *C. Crowden, B.D. & D.D. 1884 Oxford*

1. Christ the representative man. 2. The Epistle of St. Paul the Apostle to the Ephesians. *M. J. Powell, B.D. & D.D. 1907 Oxford*

1. Christian baptism. 2. St. Paul's belief in the divinity of Our Lord. *H. B. Gooding, B.D. 1921 Oxford*

1. Christianity and pantheism. 2. The heavenly priesthood of our Lord. *H. R. Cavalier, B.D. 1906 Oxford*

The Christ-mysticism of St. Paul. *T. Caldwell, Ph.D. 1927 Saint Andrew's*

A Christological study, being a critical investigation of Christological data supplied from an examination of Gospel sources on the lines of an acceptance of the four-document hypothesis. *H. G. Hatch, Ph.D. 1928 London*

1. The Christology of Clement of Alexandria. 2. The theology of the Wisdom literature. *R. B. Tollinton, B.D. 1905 Oxford*

The Christology of St. Athanasius. *D. Maritch, B.Litt. 1921 Oxford*

The Christology of St. Hilary of Poitiers. *A. J. G. Hawes, Ph.D 1928 London*

1. The Christology of St. John of Damascus. 2. The Eucharistic doctrine of St. John of Damascus. *C. A. Brereton, B.D. 1910 Oxford*

The Christology of the Apocalypse. *A. Jones, M.A. 1937 Wales*

The Christology of the earliest gospel. *J. L. Ayre, Ph.D. 1922 Edinburgh*

The Christology of the second century apologists, with special reference to the philosophical influences. *V. A. S. Little, B.Litt. 1920 Oxford*

1. Christus condemnator. 2. The Johannine idea of life. *W. J. House, B.D. and D.D. 1924 Oxford*

1. The Church in the Epistle to the Ephesians. 2. The Christ of the fourth Gospel. *J. L. Phillips, B.D. 1913 Oxford*

1. A comparison of the idea of divine sonship in Pauline and Johannine theology. The origin of the title Κύριοσ as applied to our Lord in the New Testament. *P. R. Brinton, B.D. & D.D. 1922 Oxford*

1. The deity of Christ and of the Holy Spirit as revealed in the New Testament. 2. The Scriptural evidence for the Resurrection of Christ. *C. J. Casher, B.D. 1899 Oxford*

The divine sympathy: an essay on kenotic Christology. *S. H. Evans, B.D. 1944 Durham*

1. The divinity of the Son. 2. The personality of the Holy Ghost. *H. M. Robinson, B.D. 1876 Oxford*

1. The doctrine of justification as set forth by St. Paul and St. James in their writings. 2. The evidence from the New Testament for the divinity of our Lord. *R. L. Langford-James, B.D. 1904 Oxford*

The doctrine of the Christ in St. Mark's Gospel. *A. A. Morrison, Ph.D. 1948 Saint Andrew's*

The doctrine of the Godhead in St.Gregory Nazianzen, with special reference to its Trinitarian and Christological aspects. *D. Martynowski, B.Litt. 1939 Oxford*

1. The doctrine of the mediation of Christ. 2. The testimony of the Church as to the doctrine of the descent of Christ into hell. *S. J. M. Price, B.D. & D.D. 1905 Oxford*

The doctrine of the person and work of Christ in Horace Bushnell's theology. *D. N. MacMillan, Ph.D. 1935 Edinburgh*

1. The doctrine of the person of Christ in the Fathers of the first two centuries. 2. The doctrine of the Holy Eucharist in the same period. *A. N. Claye, B.D. & D.D. 1907 Oxford*

Jesus Christ: Person and Work contd.

1. Doctrine of the work and office of Christ, with special reference to the atonement, during the first three centuries. 2. The relations of faith and reason in the Christian system, especially during the Apostolic and sub-Apostolic period. *F. W. Bussell, B.D. 1892 Oxford*

The dogmatic implications of the hypostatic union, with special reference to St. John of Damascus. *A. C. Iliescu, D.Phil. 1939 Oxford*

1. The evidence for the resurrection of Jesus Christ. 2. The divinity of Christ argued from his claim to sinlessness. *H. F. P. Davson, B.D. 1908 Oxford*

An examination of the Chalcedonian Christology. *J. S. McArthur, B.D. 1929 Oxford*

An examination of the views of Edward Irving concerning the person and work of Jesus Christ. *P. E. Davies, Ph.D. 1928 Edinburgh*

An exposition of: Acts of the Apostles vii: Stephen's defence: Hebrews vii-ix: the heavenly priesthood of Christ: Romans viii, ix: St. Paul's doctrine of election. *R. H. Taylor, D.D. 1900 Oxford*

1. God and the world. 2. The cultus of the Sacred Heart in light of the hypostatic union. *W. Farrar, B.D. 1895 Oxford*

1. Growth of the doctrine of Jesus Christ in the Pauline Epistles. 2. The doctrine of the future life. *E. B. Bartleet, B.D. 1902 Oxford*

The headship of Jesus Christ as taught and vindicated by the Reformed Presbyterian Church in North America in relation to civil government. *R. M. C. Ward, Ph.D. 1939 Edinburgh*

The humiliated Christ in modern Russian thought. *N. Gorodetzky, B.Litt. 1938 Oxford*

1. The hypostatic union. 2. The nature of our Lord's resurrection body. *T. H. D. Long, B.D. 1904 Oxford*

The idea of mediation as applied to Jesus Christ in the New Testament. *E. Cadvan-Jones, M.Litt. 1927 Cambridge*

The inter-relation of the doctrine of the work of Christ and the person of Christ during the first five centuries of the Church. *A. H. Bonser, B.D. 1948 Leeds*

1. Israel and society: the Jewish religion's contribution towards social integration. 2. Christianity and society: our Lord's work considered sociologically. *H. Johnson, B.D. 1917 Oxford*

1. Justification by faith, as set forth in the writings of St. Paul. 2. Some New Testament evidences for the divinity of our Lord. *T. Lemmey, B.D. 1907 Oxford*

The kenotic theory in its bearing on the humanity of Our Lord. *J. G. T. Thomas, B.D. 1947 Leeds*

1. Logos Christology: its validity and value. 2. The nature of the Gospel and its place in sacramental theory. *W. W. Longford, B.D. 1911 Oxford*

The meaning of the term 'Son of God' in the Synoptic Gospels, and its antecedents. *K. A. Saunders, B.Litt. 1922 Oxford*

The meaning of the title 'Son of Man' in the Gospels. *W. H. Cadman, B.Litt. 1920 Oxford*

1. The meaning of the Transfiguration. 2. The Gospel histories in the Koran dogmatically considered. *F. W. M. Woodward, B.D. 1906 Oxford*

1. The mediatorship of Christ as viewed from the standpoint of personality. 2. An examination of faith, with special reference to its definition in Hebrews xi. *F. G. Goddard, B.D. 1907 Oxford*

Mental therapy and the forgiveness of sins: a clinical view of the results of sin, with psychological studies of religious leaders as approaches to the application of the work of Christ in the experience of forgiveness. *A. P. Guiles, Ph.D. 1934 Edinburgh*

Modern psychology and the Catholic doctrine of the person of Christ. *J. B. Noss, Ph.D. 1928 Edinburgh*

1. On creation. 2. On the person of Christ. *W. Hooper, B.D. & D.D. 1887 Oxford*

1. On the divinity of Christ, as shown by his possession of the incommunicable attributes of God. 2. Internal evidence of the Johannine authorship of the fourth Gospel. *J. L. D. Smith-Dampier, B.D. 1905 Oxford*

1. On the doctrine of God the Son. 2. On the doctrine of God the Holy Ghost. *H. G. Corner, B.D. 1901 Oxford*

1. On the doctrine of the descent of Christ into hell. 2. On the doctrine of final perseverance. *G. Arbuthnot, B.D. & D.D. 1908 Oxford*

Jesus Christ: Person and Work contd.
One body in Christ: a study in the relationship of the Church to Christ in the teaching of the Apostle Paul. *E. Best, Ph.D. 1948 Belfast*

The philosophical implications of the doctrine of the person of Christ in the definition of Chalcedon. *N. D. Davies, B.D. 1927 Oxford*

1. The priesthood of Christ in the Epistle to the Hebrews. 2. The redemption. *F. Briggs, B.D. 1910 Oxford*

The priesthood of Christ, of Christians, and of the Christian ministry. 2. Public worship in the Christian Church, as described in or inferred from the New Testament. *W. D. Springett, B.D. 1880 Oxford*

1. The prophets of the Old Testament and their influence. 2. St. Paul's conception of Christ. *H. T. Dixon, B.D. 1904 Oxford*

The psychological and philosophical implications of the kenotic Christology. *W. E. Harding, M.A. 1932 Manchester*

1. The purpose of the Incarnation. 2. The kingdom of Christ in the New Testament. *C. L. Quibell, B.D. 1910 Oxford*

The relation between the person of Christ and the principle of redemption, especially as propounded by D. F. Strauss, A. E. Biedermann and E. P. W. Troeltsch. *H. T. Kerr, Ph.D. 1936 Edinburgh*

1. The relation of confirmation to baptism. 2. The meaning and use of the Messianic titles: 'Christ', 'Son of David', 'Son of God', 'Son of Man'. *A. Chilton, B.D. & D.D. 1906 Oxford*

1. The resurrection of our Lord Jesus Christ. 2. The doctrine of the kenosis. *G. H. Oakshott, B.D. & D.D. 1909 Oxford*

1. St. Athanasius' exposition of the divinity and Incarnation of our Lord in the anti-Arian orations. 2. St. Augustine's exposition of grace, free-will, and predestination in his anti-Pelagian treatises. *T. Hayes-Robinson, B.D. 1906 Oxford*

1. St. Mark xiv.21 and viii.38: 'Son of Man' in the Synoptic Gospels. 2. St. Mark i.11; St. Luke iii.22: 'Son of God' in the Synoptic Gospels. 3. St. Matthew xi.18-19: Our Lord's attitude towards asceticism. *F. H. Dudden, D.D. 1907 Oxford*

St. Paul's doctrine of Christ, especially its development as revealed in his extant writings. *T. A. Lewis, B.D. 1951 Oxford*

1. The sinlessness of Christ. 2. The Resurrection as the main evidence for Christianity. *M. J. Barrington-Ward, B.D. & D.D. 1919 Oxford*

A study in the relationship between the Jewish people and Jesus Christ. *J. Jocz, Ph.D. 1945 Edinburgh*

A study of the person of Jesus Christ in the Synoptic Gospels. *L. Dezsö, Ph.D. 1930 Aberdeen*

1. The teaching of the New Testament as to the divinity of our Lord and Saviour Jesus Christ. 2. The internal evidence as to the Johannine authorship of the fourth Gospel. *W. Slater, B.D. 1889 Oxford*

The terms 'pleroma' and 'kenosis' in the theology of St. Paul, with special reference to the person of Jesus Christ. *J. B. Reid, Ph.D. 1949 Edinburgh*

The theory of the kenosis as based upon the New Testament. *J. A. Ford, Ph.D. 1928 Edinburgh*

The transcendence of Jesus Christ: a study of the unique features of his person and work, with special reference to the fourth Gospel. *F. Cawley, Ph.D. 1934 Edinburgh*

Two ancient Christologies. *R. V. Sellers, D.D. 1939 Cambridge*

1. The Virgin birth of the Lord Jesus Christ. 2. The person of our Lord and the kenotic theory. *F. S. G. Warman, B.D. 1907 Oxford*

Jevons, William Stanley
English capital theory in the light of recent developments (with special reference to Ricardo and Jevons). *S. Goldman, M.Sc. 1933 London, School of Economics and Political Science*

Jewellery
Ancient Indian jewellery (from the earliest times to the medieval period). *R. V. Ravi Varma, M.A. 1933 London, University College*

Custom and belief connected with precious stones, as shown in the Middle English verse of the fourteenth century. *P. J. Heather, Ph.D. 1931 London, External Degree*

The history, development and organisation of the Birmingham jewellery trade. *J. C. Roche, M.Com. 1926 Birmingham*

Jewellery contd.
Lebar lapiderachta Fionnguine Meic Maeltuile: a medieval Irish lapidary. *C. E. Keane, M.A. 1941 National University of Ireland*

Magical jewels of the Middle Ages and Renaissance, particularly in England. *J. Evans, Cert.Litt. 1920 Oxford*

Jewish Law
See also Ark of the Covenant; Bible: Old Testament; Judaism.

1. The bearing of the Rabbinical criminal code on the Jewish trial narratives of the Gospel, with a translation of the *Mishnah* and *Tosefta* of the Tractate Sanhedrin. 2. An introduction to the homilies of Aphraates. *H. Danby, B.D. 1919 Oxford*

Biblical land and property laws, with some account of their amplification in the Mishnah. *J. Vainstein, Ph.D. 1946 Glasgow*

The blessings of Moses in post-Biblical Jewish literature: Targum versions considered and compared with the Talmud, Midrash and medieval commentators down to Abrabanel, as well as with those of Moses Mendelsohhn and Malbim. *R. H. Levy, M.A. 1945 Manchester*

Conception of reward and punishment in the Tannaitic Midrash (Mekiltah, Sifra and Sifre). *A. Melinek, Ph.D. 1944 London, Jews' College*

The conditions of labour in Israel as portrayed in the Old Testament and the Mishnah. *G. J. Roberts, M.A. 1936 Wales*

A critical and exegetical commentary on Mishnah tractate *Megillah. J. Rabbinowitz, Ph.D. 1930 Manchester*

A critical comparison between *Pirke Aboth* and *Aboth de Rabbi Nathan*, with special reference to their relationship and a possible common source. *S. Margulies, M.A. 1949 Manchester*

A critical investigation into the relationship of the hermeneutical rules of the Halakah to those of the Hagadah. *D. Weisz, M.A. 1948 Manchester*

Ha-Hinukh - attributed to R. Aharon Hal-Lewi, Barcelona (13th century) - a translation and critical study. *H. H. Medalie, Ph.D. 1944 Dublin, Trinity College*

The Halakah in Pseudojonathan on the Pentateuch (Part 1: Festivals and marriage laws). *E. Wiesenberg, Ph.D. 1952 London, Jews' College*

1. The history of the canon of the Old Testament, together with the Mishna and Tosephta tractate *Yadaim*. 2. The Tosephta tractate *Aboda Zara. R. G. Finch, Ph.D. 1931 London, External Degree*

Mishnah *Horayoth*, with critical and explanatory notes. *P. R. Weis, M.A. 1942 Manchester*

Mosaicarum et Romanarum legum collatio. *M. Hyamson, LL.D. 1912 London*

The Oath of the Lord, being a critical and analytical exposition of the Halakhah of the judicial imposition of the Biblical oath of the Bailees in conjunction with a discussion of the general laws relevant to it. *W. Kirzner, M.A. 1930 London, King's College*

1. Romans vii.12: internal evidence of the divine origin of the law of Moses. *R. O. Davies, D.D. 1893 Oxford*

1. St. Paul's claim to be a true Apostle and the spiritual father of the Galatians (Galatians i.1,2,11,12). 2. The inadequacy of the law and its proper function and position (Galatians iii.24). 3. The attitude and responsibilities of Christians under the new law of liberty (Galatians v.i;vi.7,8). *R. B. Poole, D.D. 1886 Oxford*

The schools of Shammai and Hillel with special reference to their influence upon the development of the Jewish *Halachah. B. Unterman, M.A. 1937 Liverpool*

Sifra (voluntary offerings). *M. Ginsberg, Ph.D. 1934 London, King's College*

The status of the labourer in Jewish law and society in the Tannaitic period. *H. J. Heinemann, M.A. 1949 Manchester*

Tosefta *Pesachim*, translated and annotated, with a comparative study of Mishnah and Tosefta *Pesachim. S. Fundaminsky, Ph.D. 1949 London, External Degree*

Translation of *Sifre*, chapters 1-3, with introduction and notes. *M. Ginsberg, M.A. 1930 London, King's College*

The treatment of the Mosaic Law in the Epistle to the Hebrews with some comparison of the Pauline attitude. *G. G. Lloyd, Ph.D. 1946 Edinburgh*

Jews: History
See also Canaan; Hebrew Literature; Israel; Jewish Law; Judaea; Judaeo-Spanish Language; Judah; Judaism; Karaism; Prophecy; Yiddish Language; and Josephus, F.

Anti-semitism in the Greco-Roman Diaspora (323 B.C.-325 A.D.). *J. J. Graneek, M.A. 1938 Birmingham*

1. Comparison of the teaching of St. Paul and St. James as to faith and works. 2. The consideration of St. Paul's expectation as to the conversion of the Jews in Romans ix, x, xi. *S. P. Duval, B.D. and D.D. 1912 Oxford*

The Covenant in the life of Israel. *G. H. Davies, B.Litt. 1933 Oxford*

The development of the Rabbinate in central Europe during the years 1348-1648. *A. Tobias, Ph.D. 1945 London, Jews' College*

The economic conditions of the Jews in Babylonia under the Sassanides from 200 C.E. to 500 C.E. based on Rabbinical literature: Part 1: agriculture. *J. Newman, Ph.D. 1931 London, External Degree*

The eschatology of the Psalter: a study in the religious development of Israel as reflected in the Psalms, with special reference to the destinies of the individual and the nation. *S. Jellicoe, B.D. 1944 Durham*

1. The evolution of the revelation of God traced through the crises in the history of Israel during the period from Moses to Elijah. 2. The evolution of the revelation of God traced through the crises in the history of Israel during the eighth century B.C. *C. C. Atkinson, B.D. & D.D. 1898 Oxford*

The exilic age and contemporary thought. *C. F. Whitley, Ph.D. 1949 Dublin, Trinity College*

The Hasmonean dynasty in Jewish literature before A.D. 70. *F. J. Glendenning, M.A. 1949 Sheffield*

The Hebrew conquest of Canaan. *M. O. Paulden, M.A. 1931 Liverpool*

The Hebrews and the Babylonian captivity. *J. Davies, M.A. 1934 Liverpool*

The Jewish community in Rome, from its foundation until A.D. 313. *M. E. Jacombs, M.A. 1915 Birmingham*

The Jewish economic, religious and social life in medieval Europe, as illustrated by the *Responsa* of Rabbi Meir ben Baruch of Rothenburg (1215-1293). *A. Cohen, Ph.D. 1941 Wales*

The Jews in the city of Rome during the first centuries B.C. and A.D., including a study of the references to them in Greek and Latin writers. *J. H. Michael, M.A. 1913 Wales*

Le Juif au théâtre en France. *C. S. Edelstein, M.A. 1922 Leeds*

Moslem polemics against Jews and Judaism. *M. Perlmann, Ph.D. 1941 London, School of Oriental and African Studies*

The position of the Jewish community in Palestine in the first two centuries after the Exile. *G. L. Jones, M.A. 1930 Wales*

The religious element in anti-Semitism up to the time of Charlemagne in the West and Leo the Isaurian in the East. *J. W. Parkes, D.Phil. 1934 Oxford*

The *Responsa* of R. Benjamin (Ze'eb) ben Matisyahu: a contribution to the history of Jews in southern Europe at the end of the fifteenth and the beginning of the sixteenth centuries. *B. Joseph, Ph.D. 1942 London, University College*

The *Responsa* of the Babylonian Geonim as a source of Jewish history. *J. Mann, M.A. 1915 London*

The 'servant' idea in the Old Testament: its origin, its development and influence upon the Israelitish nation, with an enquiry into an alleged similar conception among other nations. *R. J. Pritchard, M.A. 1930 Wales*

The settlement of the Hebrews in Canaan. *M. J. C. Dinwoodie, Ph.D. 1936 Edinburgh*

1. Some non-Jewish sources of the Christian religion. 2. The Maccabean period as an element in the preparation for Christianity. *R. J. Campbell, B.D. & D.D. 1919 Oxford*

A special study of the language and contents of Josephus' *Jewish Antiquities*, books 11-20. *R. J. H. Shutt, Ph.D. 1936 Durham*

Stone and pillar cult among the Western Semites, with special reference to the Hebrews. *C. W. McMurray, Ph.D. 1934 Edinburgh*

The story of Judith in German and English Literature. *E. Purdie, M.A. 1916 London*

Jews: History contd.
A study in the relationship between the Jewish people and Jesus Christ. *J. Jocz, Ph.D. 1945 Edinburgh*

A study of the chapters concerning the history of the Jews in Voltaire's *Introduction à l'essai sur les moeurs et l'esprit des nations*. *E. Koutaissoff, B.Litt. 1939 Oxford*

Three homilies against the Jews by Jacob of Serug, edited with introduction, translation and notes. *I. K. Cosgrove, Ph.D. 1931 London, External Degree*

1. The typical significance of the history of the children of Israel. 2. The teaching of St. Paul with regard to the Holy Spirit. *W. S. Milne, B.D. 1889 Oxford*

Jews: France
The social life of the Jews of N. France in the XII-XIV centuries, as reflected in the Rabbinical literature of the period. *L. I. Rabinowitz, Ph.D. 1937 London, External Degree*

Jews: Germany
The social sources of National Socialist anti-Semitism. *E. G. Reichmann, Ph.D. 1945 London, School of Economics and Political Science*

Jews: Great Britain
The economic and social development of the Jews in England, 1730-1860. *J. Rumyaneck, Ph.D. 1933 London, School of Economics and Political Science*

An investigation into the comparative intelligence and attainments of Jewish and non-Jewish school-children. *A. G. Hughes, Ph.D. 1928 London*

Jewish finance in England, 1216-1290, with special reference to royal revenue. *P. Elman, M.A. 1935 London, School of Economics and Political Science*

The position and history of the Jews in England in the thirteenth century. *E. Dakin, M.A. 1912 Wales*

The relief of the Jewish disabilities in England (1829-58). *I. Shapira, M.A. 1934 London, Queen Mary College*

Jews: Lithuania
The Jewish Question in the district of Wilno in 1880-1914. *H. M. Winawer, B.Phil. 1948 Oxford*

Jews: Poland
The works of Rabbi Moses Isserls as a source of the history of the Jews in Poland in the sixteenth century. *M. S. Lew, Ph.D. 1941 London, Jews' College*

Jews: Russia
The peasantry, Orthodox clergy, dissenters, and Jews, as seen by Leskov. *F. Smith, M.A. 1948 London, School of Slavonic and East European Studies*

A study of the Musar movement. *K. Rosen, M.A. 1943 Manchester*

Jews: Spain
The life of the Jews in Spain in the times of R. Asher B. Jechiel, as furnished by his *Responsa*. *H. Freedman, Ph.D. 1930 London, External Degree*

The *Responsa* of Rabbi Solomon ben Adreth of Barcelona, 1235-1310, as a source of the history of Spain. Studies in the communal life of the Jews in Spain as reflected in the *Responsa*. *I. Epstein, Ph.D. 1923 London*

Jhang
The social life and institutions of Jhang and suggestions for their reorganization. *Y. Shah, M.Ed. 1925 Leeds*

Jiménez, Francisco de Cisneros, Cardinal
See Ximénez.

Joachim, of Fiore, Abbot
Studies in the reputation and influence of the Abbot Joachim of Fiore, chiefly in the fifteenth and sixteenth centuries. *M. E. Reeves, Ph.D. 1932 London, Westfield College*

Jochumsson, Matthias
A collected edition of the hitherto uncollected and unpublished poems of Matthías Jochumsson. *C. Jackson, M.A. 1931 Leeds*

Matthias Jochumsson: a biographical and critical study. *C. Jackson, Ph.D. 1934 Manchester*

Jofroi, de Waterford
The sermons of Jofroi de Waterford, with a critical, historical and philological study of the text. *D. Pinchbeck, Ph.D. 1936 London, Birkbeck College*

John Baptist, de la Salle, Saint
St. John Baptist de la Salle: the work of the Brothers of the Christian Schools, and its significance in the history of English education. *W. J. Battersby, Ph.D. 1947 London, Birkbeck College*

John Bosco, Saint
Educational principles in the practice of Don Bosco and his successors. *J. L. O'Reilly, M.A. 1948 National University of Ireland*

John Chrysostom, Saint
Dialogus Palladii de vita S. Ioannis Chrysostomi. *P. R. Norton, D.Phil. 1923 Oxford*

John Fisher, of Rochester, Saint
An edition of three unedited sermons by John Fisher (1459-1535), together with a bibliography of his printed works. *J. F. McMahon, B.Litt. 1949 Oxford*

John, King of England
A collection of the acta of John, Lord of Ireland and Count of Mortain, with a study of his household. *M. Jones, M.A. 1949 Manchester*

John of Damascus, Saint
1. The Christology of St. John of Damascus. 2. The Eucharistic doctrine of St. John of Damascus. *C. A. Brereton, B.D. 1910 Oxford*

The dogmatic implications of the hypostatic union, with special reference to St. John of Damascus. *A. C. Iliescu, D.Phil. 1939 Oxford*

A study of the life and writings of St. John of Damascus. *B. Anagnostopoulos, B.Litt. 1950 Oxford*

John, of Jandun
The *Defensor pacis* of Marsilio of Padua and John of Jandun: its relation to political theories developed in France during the reign of Philip IV. *M. J. Tooley, M.A. 1921 London*

John, of Lancaster, 1st Duke of Bedford
John, first Duke of Bedford: his work and policy in England, 1389-1435. *S. B. Chrimes, M.A. 1929 London*

John, of Salisbury
A critical edition of the text of the latters of John of Salisbury. *W. J. Millor, Ph.D. 1939 London, University College*

Early medieval humanism, as exemplified in the life and writings of John of Salisbury. *H. Liebschuetz, M.A. 1947 London, External Degree*

John of Salisbury: a pre-Renaissance humanist. *M. A. Valerio, M.A. 1946 National University of Ireland*

John of Salisbury and 12th century humanism. *T. Brady, M.A. 1931 National University of Ireland*

John of Trevisa
A study of the language of the various texts of Trevisa's translation of Higden's *Polychronicon*. *A. C. Cawley, M.A. 1938 London, University College*

John, Saint and Apostle
1. Christus condemnator. 2. The Johannine idea of life. *W. J. House, B.D. and D.D. 1924 Oxford*

The Johannine doctrine of the Holy Spirit. *E. A. Betts, Ph.D. 1932 Edinburgh*

The religious thought of St. John. *E. K. Lee, M.Litt. 1945 Durham*

John, the Baptist, Saint
1. The Epistle to the Galatians. 2. The mission of John the Baptist. *A. E. Joscelyne, B.D. 1894 Oxford*

John the Baptist and his disciples in Patristic theology: a short study in ancient Scriptural exegesis. *H. F. D. Sparks, B.D. 1937 Oxford*

1. The ministry of John the Baptist. 2. The sources, purpose, and arrangement of St. Luke's Gospel. *L. J. M. Bebb, B.D. 1899 Oxford*

The problem of John the Baptist. *J. H. L. Brown, Ph.D. 1940 Glasgow*

John, the Baptist, Saint, Hospital of, Dublin
Register of the hospital of S. John the Baptist without the New Gate. *W. E. St.J. Brooks, Litt.D. 1935 Dublin, Trinity College*

John, the Baptist, Saint, Hospital of, Marlborough
The history of Marlborough Grammar School, 1550-1944, with some account of the medieval Hospital of St. John Baptist, Marlborough. *A. R. Stedman, M.A. 1945 London, King's College*

Johnson, Charles
Life and works of Charles Johnson (1679-1748). *M. M. Dias, M.A. 1941 London, Birkbeck College*

Johnson, Lionel
Lionel Johnson, 1867 to 1902: a biographical and critical study. *D. H. Millar, M.A. 1947 Belfast*

Johnson, Samuel
Dr Johnson on poetic genius. *J. A. Daly, M.A. 1947 National University of Ireland*

Dr. Johnson's knowledge of the English writers to the year 1600 (excluding Shakespeare). *D. B. Saunders, B.Litt. 1935 Oxford*

The earlier literary criticism of Samuel Johnson. *P. K. Hesketh-Williams, B.Litt. 1940 Oxford*

Johnson, Samuel contd.
Johnson's knowledge of English poetry before 1650. *W. B. C. Watkins, B.Litt. 1931 Oxford*

Johnson's *Lives of the Poets*. *D. Murphy, M.A. 1936 National University of Ireland*

Johnson's prose style. *W. V. Reynolds, B.Litt. 1931 Oxford*

The place of Johnson's dictionary in the history of English lexicography. *A. W. Read, B.Litt. 1933 Oxford*

Samuel Johnson and Thomas Hardy, their attitudes to the problem of suffering: a comparative study. *H. H. Mountfield, M.A. 1948 Liverpool*

Samuel Johnson as a reviewer. *M. E. O'Brien, B.Litt. 1946 Oxford*

The sources of Dr. Johnson's *Lives of the Poets*. *B. B. Evans, B.Litt. 1930 Oxford*

Johnston, Archibald, Lord Wariston
The ecclesiastical politics of Archibald Johnston, Lord Wariston, 1611-1663. *D. Cameron, Ph.D. 1930 Edinburgh*

Jonah ben Abraham, Rabbi
R. Jonah b. Abraham of Gerona: his life and ethical works. *A. T. Shrock, Ph.D. 1936 London, External Degree*

Jones, Evan (Ieuan Gwynedd)
Ieuan Gwynedd: ei fywyd a'i waith (Ieuan Gwynedd; his life and his work). *S. J. Jones, M.A. 1931 Wales*

Jones, Griffith
The educational and literary work of Griffith Jones, Llanddowror. *T. J. Owen, M.A. 1923 Wales*

The life and work of Griffith Jones, Llanddowror, 1683-1761. *J. G. T. Thomas, M.A. 1940 Leeds*

Jones, Henry Arthur
Henry Arthur Jones and the dramatic renaissance in England. *F. M. Northend, M.A. 1940 London, Bedford College*

Jones, Inigo
The theoretical drawings of Inigo Jones: their sources and scope. *C. F. Rowe, M.A. 1947 London, Warburg Institute*

Jones, John (Gellilyfdy)
The lives and labours of John Jones and Robert Vaughan, scribes of the sixteenth and seventeenth centuries. *S. Jones, M.A. 1926 Wales*

Jones, John (Glanygors)
Traethawd beirniadol ar fywyd a gwaith John Jones, Glanygors (Critical essay on the life and work of John Jones, Glanygors). *J. H. Morgan, M.A. 1929 Wales*

Jones, John Morris, Sir
Lle John Morris Jones yn yr adfywiad llenyddol o 1886 (The place of John Morris Jones in the literary revival from 1886). *G. J. Evans, M.A. 1945 Wales*

Jones, John (Talhaiarn)
Talhaiarn. *H. J. James, M.A. 1919 Wales*

Jones, John (Talsarn)
A review and revision of the biography of John Jones, Talsarn, by Owen Thomas. *D. E. Jenkins, M.A. 1924 Liverpool*

Jones, Llywellyn
Bywyd a gwaith Meurig Dafydd (Llanisien) a Llywelyn Siôn (Llangewydd) (The life and work of Meurig Dafydd (Llanisien) and Llywelyn Jones (Llangewydd)). *T. O. Phillips, M.A. 1937 Wales*

Jones, Richard
Richard Jones o'r Wern: his life and work. *E. Jones-Roberts, M.A. 1947 Liverpool*

Jones, Robert
A critical study of the writings of Robert Jones, Rhoslan. *W. G. Williams, M.A. 1937 Liverpool*

Jones, Rufus Matthew
The religious teaching of Rufus M. Jones. *A. J. Miller, Ph.D. 1936 Edinburgh*

Jonson, Benjamin
Ben Jonson and the Latin comedy. *J. McKay, M.A. 1939 National University of Ireland*

Ben Jonson's conversations with William Drummond of Hawthornden. *R. F. Patterson, D.Litt. 1922 Glasgow*

Contemporary life, literature and society as reflected in Ben Jonson's works. *E. C. Dunn, Ph.D. 1922 London*

English masques, 1604-1640, with special reference to Ben Jonson. *R. E. Brettle, M.A. 1922 London*

Jonson, Benjamin contd.
Influence of Jonson on Restoration comedy (1660-1700). *E. J. Potter, M.A. 1939 London, King's College*

An inquiry into the extent and nature of Ben Jonson's familiar knowledge of classical Latin authors, and the reflection and influence of that knowledge on his work and character. *W. McArthur, Ph.D. 1940 Glasgow*

On grammatical mood in Ben Jonson's comedies. *S. Potter, M.A. 1924 London*

Studies in the language and syntax of Ben Jonson. *B. I. Evans, M.A. 1922 London*

Joseph bar Jehuda (Aqnin)
See Ibn Aqnin, Joseph b. Juda.

Josephus, Flavius
A special study of the language and contents of Josephus' *Jewish Antiquities*, books 11-20. *R. J. H. Shutt, Ph.D. 1936 Durham*

Joule, James Prescott
The growth of the doctrine of the conservation of energy, up to and including the work of Joule. *C. N. Lewis, M.Sc. 1937 London, External Degree*

Journalism
See also Freedom of the Press; Literature: Criticism.

An examination of the critical periodical literature of the Romantic revival. *R. W. Faint, M.A. 1925 London*

The press and crime. *R. Sinha, M.Sc. 1949 London, School of Economics and Political Science*

The press and foreign affairs. *R. W. Desmond, Ph.D. 1936 London, School of Economics and Political Science*

The press and the modern state. *D. A. Hartman, Ph.D. 1930 London, School of Economics and Political Science*

Journalism: France
See also Lycée Armoricain; Publiciste, le; Sillon; and Balzac, H. de; Boulainvilliers, H., Comte de.

Abbreviation by initials: a tendency in modern language studies, with special reference to the French press, 1919-1945. *S. A. Champion, M.A. 1949 London, University College*

The evidence of contemporary French memoirs, letters and periodicals with regard to the influence of English literature. *E. H. Partridge, B.Litt. 1924 Oxford*

The political importance of the newspaper press in the French Restoration period, 1814-30. *I. Fozzard, B.Litt. 1949 Oxford*

The press articles of Charles Nodier. *P. A. Charles, M.A. 1931 Wales*

Journalism: Great Britain
See also Edinburgh Magazine; Gentleman's Journal; Gwyliedydd; Literature Gazette; London Journal; London Magazine; Punch; Quarterly Review; Retrospective Review; Tatler; and Hawksworth, J.; Taylor, John.

Boswell in the newspapers from the death of Johnson to his own death. *E. J. Willing-Denton, B.Litt. 1935 Oxford*

Coleridge's contributions to periodical literature. *I. D. Adams, M.A. 1935 London, Bedford College*

The collection and dissemination of news during the time of Shakespeare, with particular reference to the news pamphlets, 1590-1610. *D. C. Collins, Ph.D. 1938 London, External Degree*

A critical study of Defoe's *Review*, and other journals of its day, with particular emphasis on the social life of the age. *A. B. Stapleton, Ph.D. 1924 London*

Dramatic criticism in early nineteenth century periodicals (1800-1830), and its influence on the contemporary drama. *A. C. Norenius, Ph.D. 1931 London, East London College*

The early newspaper press in Berkshire (1723 to 1855). *K. G. Burton, M.A. 1950 Reading*

English criticism of American literature during the period 1800 to 1850 as reflected in the periodicals. *J. J. Espey, B.Litt. 1938 Oxford*

The English press and the Moroccan crisis of 1911. *H. G. Riddell, M.A. 1949 Liverpool*

French works in contemporary British reviews (1800-1820). *E. S. Roberts, M.A. 1928 Liverpool*

The growth of the English periodical in the eighteenth century. *J. G. Ames, B.Litt. 1899 Oxford*

The history of the agitation against the stamp duty on newspapers, 1830-1855. *M. C. Moore, M.A. 1935 London, King's College*

Journalism: Great Britain contd.
The *London Journal*, 1719-1738. *K. L. Joshi, M.A. 1937 London, Courtauld Institute of Art*

London theatres, 1700 to 1714, as reflected in the periodical press of the time. *A. Jackson, Ph.D. 1936 London, External Degree*

The newspaper in Scotland. *R. M. W. Cowan, D.Litt. 1946 Glasgow*

Nineteenth century periodical criticism, 1800-1860. *R. G. Cox, Ph.D. 1940 Cambridge*

The part the press played: the influence of the Press upon international relationships during the years 1896-1914. *M. Lewis, M.A. 1930 Birmingham*

The periodical essay from 1750 to 1760. *A. E. Darke, M.A. 1936 Liverpool*

The presentation of the Manchurian Question in the English press 1931-1933. *K. C. Cheng, Ph.D. 1938 London, School of Economics and Political Science*

The Press and the colonies. *H. F. G. Tucker, M.A. 1936 Bristol*

A review of the criticisms of Keats and Shelley in *The Edinburgh*, *The Quarterly* and *Blackwood's*. *A. Campbell, M.A. 1929 Liverpool*

The rise and progress of the periodical press in Wales up to 1860. *C. Evans, M.A. 1926 Wales*

The rise of journalism to Defoe. *A. M. Underhill, M.A. 1929 Birmingham*

The rise of the critical review in the eighteenth century. *J. J. Champenois, B.Litt. 1913 Oxford*

Serial publication and the development of the art of the major novelists, c. 1845-1870. *Z. N. Geffen, M.Litt. 1949 Cambridge*

A study of newspapers of the Civil War, Commonwealth and Protectorate, in certain of their literary aspects. *H. S. Myers, M.A. 1921 London*

Journalism: Ireland
1. Early Irish journalism 2. The early newsheets. *T. M. Cahill, M.A. 1937 National University of Ireland*

Journalism: Italy
Pietro Verri's *Caffè* and periodical literature in Italy during the second half of the eighteenth century. *A. Del Re, M.A. 1921 London*

Journalism: Spain
A critical analysis of sixty-five periodicals published in Madrid between 1823-1854. *R. F. Brown, M.A. 1934 Liverpool*

Journalism: United States
See Locke, R. A.

Jouy, Victor Joseph Etienne de
Le rôle d'Etienne de Jouy dans la polémique romantique. *N. E. Anderson, M.A. 1937 Liverpool*

Joy
The conception of bliss in the Old Testament. *L. M. Jones, M.A. 1941 Wales*

A study of joy based on the theory found in Shand's *Foundations of character*. *D. M. Grierson, M.A. 1917 London*

Joyce, James
James Joyce and the evolution of the creative artist: a study of his life and works in relation to the age and his environment. *D. W. James, M.A. 1936 Wales*

James Joyce's use of symbolism. *G. M. Davenport, B.Litt. 1950 Oxford*

Judaea
Judaea under the procurators. *L. Robinson, M.Litt. 1927 Cambridge*

The Roman province of Judaea before 70 A.D. *D. D. Fielding, M.A. 1933 Manchester*

Judaeo-Arabic Literature
See Ibn Aqnin, Joseph b. Juda, Rabbi.

Judaeo-Spanish Language
Investigations into the Judaeo-Spanish of the Balkan Peninsula, with particular reference to Roumania and Yugoslavia. *C. M. Jopson, Ph.D. 1930 London, King's College*

Judaism
See also Ark of the Covenant; Bible: Old Testament; Israel; Jewish Law; Jews; Messiah; Passover; Prophecy; Purim; Sabbath; Sacrifice; Synagogues; and Abraham bar Hiyya; Albo, J.; Benjamin b. Matisyahu, Rabbi; Colon (Kolon), J., Rabbi; Eliezer bar Nathan, Rabbi; Ibn Aqnin, Joseph b. Juda, Rabbi; Isserls, M., Rabbi; Jechiel, Asher ben, Rabbi; Jonah b. Abraham, Rabbi; Kimchi, D., Rabbi; Maimonides, M.; Meir b. Baruch, Rabbi; Philo, of Alexandria; Solomon b. Adreth, Rabbi.

Judaism contd.
Al t'he kaboteca (Be not like your fathers): a polemical work by Ephodi (Prophiat Duran), critically edited on the basis of manuscripts and provided with a translation. *I. Goodman, Ph.D. 1935 Glasgow*

The attitude of the Talmud towards trade and commerce. *H. Erin, M.A. 1937 Manchester*

The blessings of Moses in post-Biblical Jewish literature: Targum versions considered and compared with the Talmud, Midrash and medieval commentators down to Abrabanel, as well as with those of Moses Mendelsohhn and Malbim. *R. H. Levy, M.A. 1945 Manchester*

A comparison of the views of Aaron ben Joseph in his *Sefer Hamibhar* and his Halakic poems with the accepted views of the Karaites and Rabbanites concerning the Sabbath and other Jewish festivals. *S. J. Weisz, M.A. 1942 Manchester*

A critical comparison between *Pirke Aboth* and *Aboth de Rabbi Nathan*, with special reference to their relationship and a possible common source. *S. Margulies, M.A. 1949 Manchester*

A critical investigation into the relationship of the hermeneutical rules of the Halakah to those of the Hagadah. *D. Weisz, M.A. 1948 Manchester*

A critical translation of the *Ikkarim* of Joseph Albo, with a consideration of his philosophic system and a general survey of the teaching and disputations of Jewish theologians in regard to the question of what constitutes the articles of fundamentals of the Jewish faith. *M. Bloch, M.A. 1930 Wales*

1. The development of Judaism and its influence upon Christianity. 2. Christian life in the first days of the Church. *C. Moor, B.D. 1904 Oxford*

Diaspora Judaism and syncretism, with special reference to the question of the origins of Gnosticism. *R. McL. Wilson, Ph.D. 1946 Cambridge*

The direct and indirect influences of geographical conditions upon Hebrew religion. *H. G. Sanders, M.A. 1937 Manchester*

The early history of the logos doctrine - the idea in Greek philosophy, with an appendix showing its relation to Hellenism, Judaism and the New Testament. *J. L. Matthews, Ph.D. 1936 London, New College*

Elementary education in the Babylonian Talmud. *N. Morris, M.A. 1932 London, King's College*

Hebrew and Jewish sources of the *Qûran*. *J. C. Hughes, M.A. 1909 Wales*

1. The Hebrew doctrine of immortality in the light of other religions. 2. The Hebrew doctrine of sacrifice in the light of other religions. *G. H. Jones, B.D. & D.D. 1907 Oxford*

The history and principles of the Hebrew professional scribes. *M. Lutzki, B.Litt. 1935 Oxford*

How came our faith. *W. A. L. Elmslie, D.D. 1947 Cambridge*

The influence of sanctuaries on the legislation and history of early Israel. *R. Brinker, M.A. 1944 Manchester*

An investigation into the origin and growth of the conception of theocracy in Israel. *G. H. Davies, M.A. 1929 Wales*

An investigation of the problem of Greek influence upon the religious thought of Judaism in the Hellenistic age. *A. R. Johnson, Ph.D. 1931 Wales*

1. Israel and society: the Jewish religion's contribution towards social integration. 2. Christianity and society: our Lord's work considered sociologically. *H. Johnson, B.D. 1917 Oxford*

The Jewish and Christian doctrine of good and evil spirits: its origin and development. *E. Langton, D.D. 1942 London, External Degree*

Jewish education in Talmud and contemporary sources. *B. A. Collins, M.A, 1946 National University of Ireland*

Maimonides on the Jewish creed. *J. Abelson, M.A. 1909 London*

1. The meaning of criticism, with special reference to the higher criticism of the Pentateuch. 2. The divine purpose in Hebrew religion. *D. C. Simpson, B.D. 1919 Oxford*

Moslem polemics against Jews and Judaism. *M. Perlmann, Ph.D. 1941 London, School of Oriental and African Studies*

The movement towards 'scribism' in the history of Israel. *J. W. Lightley, M.A. 1912 Belfast*

Judaism contd.
The nature, need and destiny of man in Jewish thought from the Exile to the Advent. *J. R. Roberts, M.A. 1941 Wales*

The parables and similes of the Rabbis: agricultural and pastoral. *A. Feldman, Ph.D. 1925 London*

Paul and Rabbinic Judaism. *W. D. Davies, D.D. 1948 Wales*

Peshat (plain exegesis) in Talmudic and Midrashic literature. *I. Frankel, Ph.D. 1949 Dublin, Trinity College*

The Pharisees: a critical investigation. *J. Bowman, D.Phil. 1945 Oxford*

The place of the prophet in Talmud and Midrashic literature. *S. Sperber, M.A. 1945 Manchester*

The relation of Jewish-Alexandrian theology, especially in Philo, to the Pauline Epistles. *W. P. Ludwig, Ph.D. 1937 Edinburgh*

The religious institutions of the Hebrews and Jews referred to in the Hexateuch, studied in themselves and as they represent the development of religious conceptions. *R. O. Hughes, M.A. 1914 Wales*

Some influences of Greek philosophy on Jewish thought and teaching in Apocryphal literature and Philo Judaeus. *C. W. Mann, M.A. 1934 Liverpool*

Some liturgical and ceremonial aspects of Jewish worship exhibited in the Psalter. *C. C. Keet, Ph.D. 1927 London*

Stephen: a study of his religious outlook and of its affinities in pre-Christian Jewish thought and in the New Testament. *R. Gardner, Ph.D. 1934 Saint Andrew's*

The use of musical instruments in Jewish and Assyro-Babylonian religious ceremonial compared. *L. Glickman, M.A. 1942 Manchester*

1. Varying treatment of the Pharisees in the Synoptic Gospels. 2. The theory of Christian almsgiving from the sub-Apostolic age to the Reformation. *C. T. Dimont, B.D. 1911 Oxford*

Judaism: Soul
Rabbinic ideas of the soul. *W. Hirsch, Ph.D. 1946 London, External Degree*

Jude, Saint and Apostle
1. The Apostle Jude: is he to be identified with Jude the servant of Jesus Christ and brother of James? 2. SS. Philip, Bartholomew, Matthew, and Thomas: being an inquiry from New Testament records into the second group in the Apostolate. *A. C. Evans, B.D. 1901 Oxford*

Judgment
For the Last Judgment, see Eschatology.

Ability to estimate character. *J. Wedeck, Ph.D. 1933 London, University College*

Error and variability of judgment in routine work: their relation to assessments of character. *J. D. Gobat, Ph.D. 1938 London, External Degree*

The experimental study of the mental processes involved in judgment. *B. Stevanovic, Ph.D. 1926 London*

Structure and function of judgement. *P. E. C. Fair, M.A. 1915 National University of Ireland*

The theory of judgment in Bradley and Bosanquet. *R. N. Kaul, B.Litt. 1928 Oxford*

The theory of judgment in the philosophies of F. H. Bradley and John Cook Wilson. *M. Ahmed, Ph.D. 1937 London, University College*

Judgments, Moral
See Ethics.

Judith
The story of Judith in German and English Literature. *E. Purdie, M.A. 1916 London*

Julia Domna
Julia Domna. *N. F. C. Rae, Ph.D. 1932 Saint Andrew's*

Julian of Norwich
An edition of ms. Sloane 2499 of *Sixteen Revelations of Divine love* by Julian of Norwich. *F. Reynolds, M.A. 1947 Leeds*

Julian, the Apostate, Emperor
1. On the policy of the Emperor Julian. 2. On the theology of the Emperor Julian. *E. J. Martin, B.D. 1914 Oxford*

Juliana, Saint
An edition of the *Liflade ant te Passium of Seinte Juliene* (ms. Bodley 34). *S. T. R. O. D'Ardenne, B.Litt. 1933 Oxford*

An edition of the Old English *Juliana. R. E. Woolf, B.Litt. 1949 Oxford*

Junayd
Al-Junayd: a study of a third/ninth century mystic with an edition and annotated translation of his writings. *A. H. Abdel-Kader, Ph.D. 1948 London, School of Oriental and African Studies*

Jung, Carl Gustav
Archetypes and apocalypse: a study of apocalyptic literature from the standpoint of Jungian psychology. *A. G. S. Spinks, Ph.D. 1946 London, King's College*

Jung's theory of psychological types: a critical estimate. *T. M. Davie, Ph.D. 1931 Edinburgh*

The psychology of C. G. Jung in relation to religious thought and experience. *F. Roberts, M.A. 1946 Birmingham*

Junior Instruction Centres
See Education, Vocational.

Junius, Francis
The history of Old English and Old Norse studies in England from the time of Francis Junius till the end of the eighteenth century. *J. A. W. Bennett, D.Phil. 1938 Oxford*

Juno in Arcadia
Juno in Arcadia: an edition of the anonymous masque in the British Museum ms. Egerton 1994, with introduction and notes. *R. C. Elsley, M.A. 1950 Birmingham*

Jurieu, Pierre
Pierre Jurieu: his political ideas and activities. *A. J. E. Capon, Ph.D. 1939 London, External Degree*

Jurisprudence
See Law.

Justice
The conception of justice in leading British moralists of the eighteenth and nineteenth centuries. *H. Williams, M.Litt. 1944 Cambridge*

The development of the concept of justice in English modern philosophy. *C. M. Coltman, M.A. 1912 London*

Plato's ideal of justice. *F. A. Martin, M.A. 1944 National University of Ireland*

Shakespeare and the idea of justice. *M. V. H. Parker, B.Litt. 1950 Oxford*

Justification
See also Salvation.

1. The creed of the Christian Church. 2. St. Paul's Epistles considered as a whole, with special reference to his teaching on justification. *A. Brook, B.D. 1893 Oxford*

1. The doctrine involved in Article XIII. 2. The historical account of the doctrine. *J. O. Johnston, B.D. & D.D. 1914 Oxford*

1. The doctrine of justification as set forth by St. Paul and St. James in their writings. 2. The evidence from the New Testament for the divinity of our Lord. *R. L. Langford-James, B.D. 1904 Oxford*

1. Justification. 2. The forgiveness of sins. *N. H. C. Ruddock, B.D. and D.D. 1898 Oxford*

1. Justification by faith. 2. Christianity as a civilizing agent. *C. E. E. Williams, B.D. 1882 Oxford*

1. Justification by faith, as set forth in the writings of St. Paul. 2. Some New Testament evidences for the divinity of our Lord. *T. Lemmey, B.D. 1907 Oxford*

1. On justification by faith. 2. On Hades. *H. T. Beebe, B.D. 1889 Oxford*

1. On original sin. 2. On justification. *W. Bree, B.D. & D.D. 1893 Oxford*

1. On the Incarnation. 2. On justification by faith. *R. W. Tattersall, B.D. 1892 Oxford*

1. The Resurrection of our Lord. 2. Justification. *E. C. Dermer, B.D. 1874 Oxford*

St. Paul's doctrine of justification: its origin, significance, and adequacy. *L. J. Tizard, B.Litt. 1929 Oxford*

Justin, Martyr, Saint
Justin Martyr and his witness to the beliefs, practice and sufferings of the Christians of his day. *M. B. Owen, M.A. 1941 Wales*

The source and implication of the New Testament quotations in the *Apologies* of Justin Martyr. *J. Pritchard, M.A. 1905 Wales*

The theological teaching of Justin Martyr. *D. Peshitch, B.Litt. 1921 Oxford*

1. The theology of Justin Martyr. 2. Justin Martyr and the New Testament canon. *A. W. F. Blunt, B.D. 1918 Oxford*

The theology of Justin Martyr. *E. R. Goodenough, D.Phil. 1923 Oxford*

Jute Industry
The jute industry of Dundee, 1830-1855. *O. Graham, M.A. 1928 Manchester*

Juvainī, 'Ala'al-Dīn 'Atā Malik b. Muhammad
Studies on the *Ta'rikh-i-Jahān-Gushā* of Juvayni. *J. A. Boyle, Ph.D. 1947 London, School of Oriental and African Studies*

Juvenal
The history of the Flavian period, and in particular of the reign of Domitian, especially as reflected in the works of the poets Juvenal, Martial, and Statius. *A. G. Barnes, M.A. 1936 Manchester*

Roman life and manners as depicted in Martial and Juvenal. *M. Lamb, M.A. 1920 London*

Roman society in the reign of Trajan as seen in the writings of Tacitus, Juvenal and Pliny the Younger. *M. M. Gough, M.A. 1908 Birmingham*

Juvenal des Ursins, Jean, Archbishop
Remonstrances au Roy pour la réformation du royaume, by Jean Juvenal des Ursins, with introduction and notes. *D. Kirkland, Ph.D. 1938 Liverpool*

Juvenile Delinquency
See also Borstal Institutions.

Criminality in youth: a medico-legal study. *J. Baker, M.D. 1901 Aberdeen*

Emotional factors in juvenile delinquency. *R. W. Hamilton, B.Sc. 1941 Oxford*

A juvenile court survey. *W. L. Chinn, M.A. 1933 Birmingham*

Juvenile delinquency in Egypt. *H. el Saaty, Ph.D. 1946 London, School of Economics and Political Science*

Juvenile delinquency, with special reference to the Children and Young Persons Act, 1933: a survey of the work of the Lancashire Education Authority in carrying out the duties imposed upon it by the Children and Young Persons Act, 1933. *H. Procter, M.A. 1942 Liverpool*

On the incidence, causation, and treatment of juvenile delinquency. *J. A. K. Bonnar, M.Sc. 1948 Cambridge*

Re-building character of delinquent youth: a study of the English Borstal system and of the responses of individuals to its methods of treatment. *H. E. Field, Ph.D. 1933 London, Institute of Education*

Recent trends in the delinquency of girls: a study of cases recorded by the City of Oxford Education Authority, Nov. 1933-Dec. 1946. *M. C. Grain, B.Litt. 1949 Oxford*

The relationship of juvenile delinquency and environment in an industrial town. *A. Royds, M.Ed. 1936 Manchester*

Significant factors in the growth of juvenile delinquency. *J. H. Bagot, M.A. 1939 Liverpool*

A study of conditions related to the delinquency of a group of boys in an approved school. *A. E. Adams, M.A. 1944 London, Institute of Education*

Study of juvenile delinquency, with special reference to social influences and social control in Birmingham and district. *C. Hyde, M.A. 1933 Birmingham*

Juxon, William, Archbishop
The life of Archbishop Juxon. *J. R. M. Etherington, B.Litt. 1940 Oxford*

Kabir
Kabir and the movements springing from his influence. *H. E. Smart, B.Litt. 1921 Oxford*

Kaihsienkung
Kaihsienkung: economic life in a Chinese village. *H. T. Fei, Ph.D. 1938 London, School of Economics and Political Science*

Kalidasa
Imagery of Kalidasa and the theory of poetics. *P. De Costa, Ph.D. 1949 London, School of Oriental and African Studies*

The works of Kalidasa. *S. K. Gupta, B.Litt. 1913 Oxford*

Kanarese Language
See also Inscriptions.

Kanarese influence in Old Marathi (Jñānesvari). *R. V. Jahagirdar, M.A. 1928 London*

Kanauj
History of Kanauj to the Moslem conquest. *R. S. Tripathi, Ph.D. 1929 London*

Kant, Immanuel
Arguments for theism from design in nature with special reference to Hume, Paley, and Kant. *P. P. Elliott, B.Litt. 1926 Oxford*

Kant, Immanuel contd.
The category of personality in relation to Kant's three postulates of the practical reason: freedom, immortality, God. *R. W. Thompson, M.A. 1907 London*

Commentary on Kant's *Critique of Judgment. H. W. Cassirer, Ph.D. 1938 Glasgow*

The concept of self from Descartes to Kant, with some reference to immortality. *E. G. Braham, Ph.D. 1935 London, King's College*

The conception of self-consciousness in pre-Kantian and Kantian philosophy. *A. A. Iqbal, M.A. 1924 London*

The conception of teleology, with special reference to the views of Spinoza, Leibniz, and Kant. *D. M. Jones, M.A. 1911 Wales*

The conception of teleology in modern philosophy from Descartes to Kant. *T. Evans, M.A. 1927 Wales*

A critical examination of Kant's treatment of the self. *D. Davies, M.A. 1920 Wales*

A criticism of the Kantian dualism. *T. A. Burkill, M.A. 1940 Manchester*

The development of Kant's ethical philosophy, with especial reference to his English precursors. *A. C. Mason, M.A. 1913 London*

The development of the theory of space from Descartes to Kant. *A. W. P. Wolters, M.A. 1910 London*

An examination of Kant's early writings in their relation to the critical works, with special reference to the method, the transcendental logic, and the theory of truth and error. *J. A. M. De Menasce, B.Litt. 1925 Oxford*

Freedom of the will according to Kant and the English Idealists. *J. L. Williams, M.A. 1902 Wales*

The freewill problem in modern philosophy from Descartes to Kant. *J. Pitts, Ph.D. 1933 London, External Degree*

Kantian and scholastic theory of knowledge. *D. J. Cannon, M.A. 1945 National University of Ireland*

Kant's conception of God in its metaphysical development, together with a translation of the *Nova Dilucidatio. F. E. England, Ph.D. 1928 London*

Kant's conception of the freedom of the will. *W. J. Stephens, M.A. 1905 Wales*

Kant's distinction between constitutive and regulative principles of knowledge. *F. E. England, M.A. 1922 London*

Kant's philosophy of religion: Professor Laird's notes and extract from Professor Taylor's report. *K. Dunbar, M.A. 1915 Belfast*

Kant's religious theory and its relation to English deism. *T. M. Greene, Ph.D. 1924 Edinburgh*

Kant's treatment of causality. *A. C. Ewing, D.Phil. 1923 Oxford*

Kant's view of object and objectivity. *A. W. James, M.A. 1908 London*

Kant's view of our knowledge of the self. *N. Bandyopadhyay, Ph.D. 1932 London, University College*

Kants' view of space about 1769. *C. B. Garnett, Ph.D. 1932 Edinburgh*

Kant's view of the relation between theology and ethics. *W. M. Watt, B.Litt. 1933 Oxford*

The origins and course of Coleridge's reaction against Locke and Kant. *J. Coles, M.A. 1949 Wales*

The possibility of mathematics in the philosophy of Kant. *B. A. Farrell, B.Litt. 1939 Oxford*

The problem of error in the contribution of Kant to modern idealistic logic. *A. A. Lion, D.Phil. 1930 Oxford*

Problems raised by Kant's treatment of the self. *D. Davies, Ph.D. 1923 Glasgow*

A psychological analysis of Kant's doctrine of conscience. *A. Oates, M.A. 1931 Liverpool*

The relations between ethics and metaphysics, with special reference to the works of Spinoza, Kant and T. H. Green. *J. P. Davies, M.A. 1922 Wales*

Sense-perception according to Kant. *G. M. Broughton, M.A. 1909 London*

The theory of personality in modern philosophy from Kant to Lotze. *E. A. J. Berthen, M.A. 1911 London*

Karaism
See also Jews; Judaism.

Karaism contd.
A commentary on the Book of Joel, by Jefeth Ibn Ali the Karaite. *S. M. Lehrman, Ph.D. 1927 London*

A comparison of the views of Aaron ben Joseph in his *Sefer Hamibhar* and his Halakic poems with the accepted views of the Karaites and Rabbanites concerning the Sabbath and other Jewish festivals. *S. J. Weisz, M.A. 1942 Manchester*

An inquiry into the sources of the Book of Anan, the founder of Karaism. *I. Brodie, B.Litt. 1921 Oxford*

Karma
The conception of *karma* and reincarnation in Hindu religion and philosophy. *P. Yevtic, Ph.D. 1927 London*

Kaunitz-Rietberg, Wenzel Anton von, Prince
The career of Prince Kaunitz, Austrian chancellor, 1753-1792. *M. G. Tucker, M.A. 1937 Bristol*

Kautilya
Indian civil law according to Kautilya. *Y. D. Sharma, D.Phil. 1945 Oxford*

Kay-Shuttleworth, James Phillips, Sir
The life and work of Sir James Kay-Shuttleworth. *F. Smith, Ph.D. 1923 Wales*

Keats, John
Classical and medieval inspiration in the poetry of Coleridge, Keats and Shelley. *H. A. Needham, M.A. 1921 Birmingham*

A comparison of Friedrich Hölderlin and John Keats in their respective backgrounds. *G. Guder, Ph.D. 1942 Edinburgh*

A definition of Keats' idea of poetry based on an examination of (1) his letters, (2) variants of his poems, (3) sources of his poems. *K. B. Ridley, B.Litt. 1923 Oxford*

The development of Keats's idea of poetry. *H. Simons, M.A. 1927 Wales*

The influence of Keats during the late nineteenth century. *H. King, M.A. 1923 Birmingham*

An interpretation of Keats' *Endymion. H. C. Notcutt, Ph.D. 1921 London*

Keats and criticism. *P. Purcell, M.A. 1937 National University of Ireland*

Keats and Hazlitt in their personal and literary relations. *H. M. Keyes, B.Litt. 1937 Oxford*

Keats and Spenser. *S. Iyengar, M.A. 1936 London, University College*

Keats as a critic. *P. Pye, M.A. 1917 National University of Ireland*

Keats as literary critic. *H. M. Greaves, M.A. 1918 Birmingham*

Keats' literary theories, as expressed in his letters and as exemplified in his poems. *K. Box, M.A. 1947 Manchester*

Keats' theory and practice of poetry. *M. A. Cordery, M.A. 1939 Reading*

The literary reputation of John Keats in England from 1817 to 1888. *C. C. Fei, M.A. 1937 Liverpool*

A review of the criticisms of Keats and Shelley in *The Edinburgh, The Quarterly* and *Blackwood's. A. Campbell, M.A. 1929 Liverpool*

A study of Keats's *Endymion. C. Godfrey, M.A. 1949 Liverpool*

Keftiu, The
The Keftiu-people of the Egyptian monuments. *G. A. Wainwright, B.Litt. 1914 Oxford*

Keller, Gottfried
Gottfried Keller and the German Künstlerroman. *G. B. Priest, M.A. 1945 Manchester*

Gottfried Keller's Weltanschauung. *I. McCourt, Ph.D. 1932 Edinburgh*

Gottfried Keller's *Züricher Novellen. F. G. Kinnear, Ph.D. 1922 Edinburgh*

Kellers religiöse Entwicklung. *M. Nı Shuibhne, M.A. 1942 National University of Ireland*

A study of Gottfried Keller's three last *Novellen* cycles, with special reference to his *Weltanschauung. H. Davies, M.A. 1937 Wales*

Kells, Book of
The text of *Codex Cenannensis. G. O. Simms, Ph.D. 1950 Dublin, Trinity College*

Kelly, Hugh
Hugh Kelly (1739-77). *N. Dawson, B.Litt. 1931 Oxford*

Kelsall, John
John Kelsall: a study in religious and economic history. *H. G. Jones, M.A. 1938 Wales*

Kenfig
The history of the borough of Kenfig to 1485. *J. H. Lewis, M.A. 1922 Wales*

Kenilworth
Kenilworth castle and priory. *E. N. Wells, M.A. 1923 Birmingham*

Kenilworth, Dictum of
Judicial investigations under the Dictum of Kenilworth, Cambridgeshire. *C. C. Bayley, M.A. 1929 Manchester*

Judicial investigations under the Dictum of Kenilworth, Northamptonshire. *E. H. Graham, M.A. 1930 Manchester*

Judicial investigations under the Dictum of Kenilworth, Essex. *H. Roberts, M.A. 1928 Manchester*

Judicial proceedings in Cambridgeshire under the Dictum of Kenilworth. *K. H. Holden, M.A. 1929 Manchester*

The judicial proceedings under the Dictum of Kenilworth in Sussex and Kent. *A. Buckley, M.A. 1927 Manchester*

Judicial proceedings under the Dictum de Kenilworth, Northamptonshire. *T. W. Byrne, M.A. 1932 Manchester*

Judicial proceedings under the Dictum de Kenilworth, Buckingham. *M. L. Hoyle, M.A. 1928 Manchester*

Judicial proceedings under the Dictum de Kenilworth, in Northamptonshire. *M. M. Rothwell, M.A. 1929 Manchester*

Judicial proceedings under the Dictum de Kenilworth. *M. L. Hoyle, Ph.D. 1934 Manchester*

Judicial proceedings under the Dictum of Kenilworth, Cambridgeshire. *S. Cohen, M.A. 1929 Manchester*

Judicial proceedings under the Dictum of Kenilworth, East Berkshire. *A. L. Gregory, M.A. 1927 Manchester*

The judicial proceedings under the Dictum of Kenilworth, Surrey. Revised text. *L. M. Round, M.A. 1928 Manchester*

The judicial proceedings under the Dictum of Kenilworth, West Berkshire. *E. Roberts, M.A. 1927 Manchester*

Kennedy, James, Bishop
James Kennedy, Bishop of St. Andrews. *A. I. Cameron, Ph.D. 1924 Edinburgh*

Kenosis
See Jesus Christ: Person and Work.

Kent
The judicial proceedings under the Dictum of Kenilworth in Sussex and Kent. *A. Buckley, M.A. 1927 Manchester*

Kenya
See also Kikuyu; Nairobi.

The Indian problem in Kenya. *P. L. Maini, M.Sc. 1944 London, School of Economics and Political Science*

The problems of the European community in Kenya. *A. C. Woodcock, M.A. 1949 Leeds*

Kepler, Johannes
The astronomical method of Kepler. *A. J. Taylor, Ph.D. 1932 London, University College*

Ker, William Paton
The critical writings of W. P. Ker. *L. P. Ball, M.A. 1940 Liverpool*

Kerala
Regional geography of Kerala. *G. Kuriyan, Ph.D. 1946 London, External Degree*

Kett, Robert
The Norfolk Rising under Robert Kett, 1549. *W. H. T. Walker, M.A. 1921 Wales*

On the causes and course of the rebellion of 1549 in Devon and Cornwall. *W. J. Blake, M.A. 1909 London*

The social and economic circumstances of Ket's rebellion, 1549. *R. J. Hammond, M.A. 1934 London, School of Economics and Political Science*

Ketubah
See Marriage.

Keynes, John Maynard, 1st Baron
Over-saving, or Keynes doctrine. *A. E. M. Duynstee, M.Econ.Sc. 1947 National University of Ireland*

Kharosthi Language
The development of the Kharosthi script. *C. C. Das Gupta, Ph.D. 1947 Cambridge*

Kormart, Christophorus
Christophorus Kormart's adaptations of Pierre Corneille's *Polyeucte* and *Héraclius* and their relation to the contemporary German drama of the seventeenth century. *P. H. Powell, M.A. 1936 Wales*

Körner, Karl Theodor
Quellen-Studien zu Theodor Körners *Leier und Schwert. M. Koerner, M.A. 1912 London*

Korzeniowski, Konrad Jozef Teodor
See Conrad, Joseph.

Kotzebue, August von
Kotzebue: a reconsideration of his place in European drama. *L. F. Thompson, M.A. 1926 London*

Kudrun
The maritime vocabulary of the middle high German poem *Kudrun. K. Cuthbert, M.A. 1945 Belfast*

Kynaston, Francis, Sir
The life and work of Sir Francis Kynaston. *H. G. Seccombe, B.Litt. 1933 Oxford*

La Calprenède, Gauthier de Costes de
La Calprenède, romancier. *T. J. Wilson, D.Phil. 1927 Oxford*

La Chaussée, Pierre Claude Nivelle de
Nivelle de la Chaussée et *La comédie larmoyante. A. Jay, M.A. 1913 Liverpool*

La Mettrie, Julien Offray de
La philosophie de La Mettrie. *H. V. George, M.A. 1946 Birmingham*

La Mothe le Vayer, François de
La Mothe le Vayer: contribution à l'étude du libertinage au dix-septième siècle. *F. L. Wickelgren, M.A. 1922 London*

Labé, Louise
Louise Labé. *E. D. Laracy, M.A. 1940 National University of Ireland*

Labiche, Eugène
Labiche's technique of comedy. *S. H. S. Hoyle, M.A. 1935 Manchester*

Labour
See also Employment; Industrial Law; Industrial Relations; Industrial Revolution; Labour Party.

Alfred Marshall as an economist, with special reference to wages and working class. *P. Whelan, M.Econ.Sc. 1945 National University of Ireland*

The attitude of the Tory Party to labour questions, 1832-46. *R. L. Hill, B.Litt. 1928 Oxford*

The attitude of the Welsh Independents towards working class movements, including public education, from 1815 to 1870. *R. I. Parry, M.A. 1931 Wales*

The black-coated worker in London. *F. D. Klingender, Ph.D. 1934 London, School of Economics and Political Science*

British and Continental labour policy: the political labour movement and labour legislation in Great Britain, France, and the Scandinavian countries, 1900-1922. *B. G. De Montgomery, D.Phil. 1923 Oxford*

British labour and Parliament, 1867-1893. *W. K. Lamb, Ph.D. 1934 London, School of Economics and Political Science*

Changes in the theory and public opinion concerning the status and interests of a wage-earning class in Great Britain during the period 1600-1800. *I. Jones, M.A. 1928 Wales*

The conditions of labour in Israel as portrayed in the Old Testament and the Mishnah. *G. J. Roberts, M.A. 1936 Wales*

The daily ebb and flow of labour between home and workplace in English industrial areas. *K. K. Liepmann, Ph.D. 1942 London, School of Economics and Political Science*

Dekker and the artizan in the Elizabethan drama. *M. M. M. Mackinlay, M.A. 1949 Manchester*

The economic ideas of the urban industrial working class of England during the years 1800-1850. *W. H. Warburton, M.Com. 1939 Birmingham*

An enquiry into the use of leisure amongst the working classes of Liverpool. *T. M. Middleton, M.A. 1931 Liverpool*

Human problems of organisation in industry. *B. L. S. Fontaine, M.Sc. 1939 London, University College*

An inquiry into the prospects that the children of the unskilled have of becoming skilled. *E. L. Lewis, Ph.D. 1923 Glasgow*

Labour contd.
Labour and housing in an Indian city: a study in the economic conditions of the wage-earning classes in Bombay. *A. R. Burnett-Hurst, M.Sc. 1923 London*

Labour and war: the theory of labour action to prevent war. *B. F. Braatoy, Ph.D. 1934 London, School of Economics and Political Science*

Labour in the merchant service 1850-1920. *A. McGeogh, M.Com. 1921 Birmingham*

Labour in the Third Reich. *P. J. Lynch, M.Econ.Sc. 1936 National University of Ireland*

Labour migration: a study of the mobility of labour. *A. E. C. Hare, Ph.D. 1933 London, School of Economics and Political Science*

Labour migration in England, 1800-1850. *A. Redford, Ph.D. 1922 Manchester*

Labour question in Egypt. *M. F. Leheta, M.Com. 1923 Birmingham*

Labour theory of value in classical economics. *E. L. Kennedy, M.A. 1946 National University of Ireland*

Les compagnons du tour de France par George Sand et les milieux ouvriers sociaux contemporains. *F. Hyslop, M.A. 1923 Manchester*

The lower classes in the novel from Lesage to 1789. *Z. W. Goddard, M.A. 1932 London, King's College*

The market for native labour in South Africa. *S. T. Van der Horst, Ph.D. 1939 London, School of Economics and Political Science*

Methodism and the working classes of England (1800-1850). *R. F. Wearmouth, Ph.D. 1935 London, School of Economics and Political Science*

The mobility of labour in the principal industries of Somersetshire, 1923-1933. *W. G. Morgan, M.A. 1934 Wales*

A physiological and economic study of the diets of workers in rural areas as compared with those of workers resident in urban districts. *A. B. Hill, Ph.D. 1926 London*

The positions of the skilled and less skilled workman in the engineering and building trades (1914-25). *J. R. Hicks, B.Litt. 1927 Oxford*

The postwar relations of skilled and unskilled labour in the printing, building and engineering industries. *P. A. Manning, Ph.D. 1933 London, School of Economics and Political Science*

Poverty and the wage-earning classes. *M. McSweeney, M.A. 1914 National University of Ireland*

The recreations and amusements of the industrial working class in the second quarter of the nineteenth century, with special reference to Lancashire. *K. Allan, M.A. 1947 Manchester*

The status of the labourer in Jewish law and society in the Tannaitic period. *H. J. Heinemann, M.A. 1949 Manchester*

Studies in labour supply and labour costs. *B. Thomas, Ph.D. 1932 London, School of Economics and Political Science*

Studies of labour wastage and sickness absence. *P. H. Chatterjee, Ph.D. 1941 London, University College*

Variations in working-class family expenditure. *J. L. Nicholson, M.Sc. 1949 London, School of Economics and Political Science*

Labour Law
See Industrial Law.

Labour Party
See also Fabian Society; Independent Labour Party; Socialism.

Economic and political origins of the Labour party from 1884 to 1906. *D. Good, Ph.D. 1936 London, School of Economics and Political Science*

An examination of the Labour Party during its formative years, 1900-1920. *R. T. Spooner, M.A. 1949 Birmingham*

Labour's foreign policy, 1919-24. *T. Z. Winnicki, M.Litt. 1950 Cambridge*

Labrador
The history of Newfoundland and Labrador, 1754 to 1783. *G. O. Rothney, M.A. 1934 London, King's College*

Labrunie, Gérard de
See Nerval, G. de.

Laforgue, Jules
The influence of Baudelaire, Laforgue and Corbière on the poetry of T. S. Eliot. *C. M. Shanahan, M.A. 1949 Manchester*

The literary theory of Jules Laforgue. *O. Jacobs, B.Litt. 1950 Oxford*

Lagan Valley
The economic history of the Lagan Valley, 1800-50. *E. R. R. Green, B.Litt. 1945 Dublin, Trinity College*

Lahor, Jean
La vie et l'oeuvre de Jean Lahor. *L. Hawksworth, M.A. 1939 Liverpool*

Laity
See Church, Doctrine of.

Lamarck, Jean Baptiste Pierre Antoine de Monet, Chevalier de
The theory of evolution in science, ethics and religion, with special reference to its teleological nature, tracing the development of the theory in question from Lamarck to our own day. *W. W. Pearson, B.Sc. 1907 Oxford*

Lamartine, Alphonse Marie Louis de
The eastern element in Lamartine. *M. J. Fisher, Ph.D. 1942 London, King's College*

La pensée dans la poésie de Lamartine. *R. R. McLernon, Ph.D. 1940 Belfast*

Lamartine et Byron. *E. M. Wright, M.A. 1938 London, King's College*

Les romans de Lamartine. *M. J. Fisher, M.A. 1937 London, King's College*

Sensibilité auditive de Lamartine. *D. J. Staples, M.A. 1949 London, Birkbeck College*

Lamb, Charles
Charles Lamb. *N. Wilson, M.A. 1939 National University of Ireland*

The literary criticism of C. Lamb. *N. I. Chaloner, M.A. 1916 Birmingham*

The personal element in the essays of Elia. *I. D. Druller, M.A. 1919 Birmingham*

Lambert, Franz (François Lambert of Avignon)
Francis Lambert of Avignon (1487-1530): a study in Reformation origins. *R. L. Winters, Ph.D. 1936 Edinburgh*

Lambert, Louis
Louis Lambert and the philosophy of Balzac. *H. G. J. Evans, Ph.D. 1949 London, King's College*

Lamennais, Félicité Robert de
A study of the development of Lamennais' thought. *G. M. Prys, M.A. 1923 Wales*

Lancashire
Agricultural geography of southwest Lancashire. *J. F. Maguire, M.A. 1939 Liverpool*

The Baptists and political and social conditions in Lancashire during the Industrial Revolution, 1760-1832. *C. B. Whyatt, M.A. 1948 Manchester*

Chartism and the Churches, with special reference to Lancashire: an account of the Churches and social reform in the Chartist period. *N. J. McLellan, Ph.D. 1947 Edinburgh*

The coastal lands of southwest Lancashire and some of their problems. *C. Taylor, M.A. 1932 Liverpool*

The correlation of industries in southeast Lancashire, with special reference to the potentialities of other European and eastern textile countries in world trade. *G. V. M. Davies, M.Sc. 1930 Wales*

The economic and social condition of England on the eve of the Industrial Revolution, with special reference to Lancashire. *L. W. Moffit, Ph.D. 1921 Edinburgh*

The historical geography of southwest Lancashire prior to the Industrial Revolution. *F. Walker, M.A. 1937 Liverpool*

Lancashire Elizabethan recusants. *J. S. Leatherbarrow, M.A. 1940 Manchester*

North Lancashire: its economic condition in the thirteenth and fourteenth centuries. *H. Horton, M.A. 1949 Manchester*

The practice and functions of local government as illustrated in Lancashire towns in the century before the Municipal Corporations Act (1835) with a consideration of the more immediate effects of the reform. *W. Scrivens, M.A. 1934 Liverpool*

Quo warranto proceedings for the county of Lancaster. *A. Cantle, M.A. 1935 London, King's College*

Southwest Lancashire: a study of the recent changes in industry and population. *G. Tatham, M.A. 1932 Liverpool*

Lancaster
The history of the port of Lancaster, with special reference to the years 1750-1825. *E. Thompson, M.A. 1935 Manchester*

Lancelot de Carle
See Carle, L. de.

Land (Law)
See also Conveyancing.

Acquisition of easements in English law. *S. Dean, LL.M. 1926 Liverpool*

Biblical land and property laws, with some account of their amplification in the Mishnah. *J. Vainstein, Ph.D. 1946 Glasgow*

A comparison of settlements of registered land in England and Australasia. *R. C. Connell, Ph.D. 1948 London, King's College*

The distinctions and anomalies arising out of the equitable doctrine of the legal estate. *R. M. P. Willoughby, LL.D. 1911 London*

The economic objects and results of land legislation in Ireland in the Gladstonian era. *E. R. Nuttall, M.A. 1936 Wales*

The effects of notice on contracts for the sale of land with particular reference to the registration of land charges. *R. G. Rowley, LL.D. 1948 Leeds*

An enquiry into the collections of the land revenue in Bengal, 1772-1774, from the appointment of the Committee of Circuit, May, 1772, until the introduction of the provisions of the Regulating Act, October, 1774. *R. B. Ramsbotham, B.Litt. 1924 Oxford*

The historical background of the English land law from 1535. *S. H. Brookfield, M.A. 1935 Liverpool*

The imperial land regulations as applied to Canada, 1763-1841. *N. Macdonald, Ph.D. 1932 Edinburgh*

The incidence of local rates and of taxes upon the unearned increment of land. *W. B. Cowcher, B.Litt. 1914 Oxford*

Jamaican land law. *V. B. Grant, LL.M. 1948 London, External Degree*

Nigerian land law and custom. *T. O. Elias, Ph.D. 1949 London, University College*

The operation of the provisions of the Law of Property Act, 1925, regarding undivided shares in land. *T. L. Morgan, LL.M. 1938 Wales*

Problems presented by easements to the purchaser of land. *R. L. Young, B.Litt. 1935 Oxford*

The protection of persons acquiring interests in land from limited owners. *D. C. Sealy-Jones, LL.M. 1947 London, External Degree*

Recent developments in the law of restrictive covenants affecting land. *R. G. Rowley, LL.M. 1942 Leeds*

Registration of title to land in Eire. *J. G. Lyons, M.A. 1946 National University of Ireland*

Land Tenure: Great Britain
See also Enclosures; Feudalism; Quo Warranto.

Burgage tenure in medieval Bristol. *E. W. Veale, LL.D. 1931 London, University College*

The development of leasehold tenure in South Lancashire, with special reference to the seventeenth century. *H. L. Jones, M.A. 1924 Manchester*

The Domesday of Crown Lands: a study of the Parliamentary confiscations, surveys and sales during the Commonwealth. *S. J. Madge, D.Sc. 1938 London, School of Economics and Political Science*

East Sussex landownership: the structure of rural society in an area of old enclosure, 1733-87. *D. K. Worcester, Ph.D. 1950 Cambridge*

An economic study of the ownership and tenure of agricultural land in Oxfordshire. *R. W. Gardner, Ph.D. 1950 Reading*

An examination of the grants of land made to the Scottish Church in the twelfth and thirteenth centuries, with special reference to secular services. *T. Davidson, Ph.D. 1930 Edinburgh*

The extent and value of the lands in London and Southwark occupied by the religious houses (including the prebends of St. Paul's and St. Martin's le Grand), the parish churches and churchyards, and the inns of the abbots and bishops, before the dissolution of the monasteries. *M. B. Honeybourne, M.A. 1930 London, Bedford College*

Frank almoign: a study of ecclesiastical tenure in England chiefly in the fourteenth and fifteenth centuries. *E. G. Kimball, B.Litt. 1927 Oxford*

The history of land-ownership since 1870, with special reference to conditions in Cambridgeshire. *J. J. Macgregor, B.Litt. 1938 Oxford*

History of the law of distress for rent and damage feasant. *F. A. Enever, LL.D. 1929 London*

The honor of Leicester: a study in descent and administration, with special reference to the Leicestershire fees of the honor. *L. Fox, M.A. 1938 Manchester*

Land Tenure: Great Britain contd.
Indefeasibility of registered titles: a comparative study. *M. E. Bathurst, Ph.D. 1949 Cambridge*

The machinery of manorial administration, with special reference to the lands of the Bishopric of Winchester, 1208-1454. *E. Swift, M.A. 1930 London, King's College*

Materials for the study of urban ground rent. *H. W. Singer, Ph.D. 1937 Cambridge*

The ownership and occupation of the land in Devonshire, 1650-1800. *W. G. Hoskins, Ph.D. 1938 London, External Degree*

Position of a tenant for life under a trust for sale of land. *E. H. Scammell, LL.M. 1948 London, King's College*

Property in land in south Bedforshire, with special reference to the land tax assessments, 1750-1832. *E. O. Payne, Ph.D. 1939 London, School of Economics and Political Science*

A reconsideration of some of the more important rules governing equitable apportionments between tenant for life and remainderman. *C. A. Smith, Ll.M. 1938 Sheffield*

The sequestration of estates 1643-1660. *E. Chesney, Ph.D. 1928 Sheffield*

A study of the small landowner and of the tenantry during the years 1780-1832 on the basis of the land tax assessments. *E. Davies, D.Phil. 1926 Oxford*

Tenant-right valuations. *D. R. Denman, M.Sc. 1940 London, External Degree*

The Universities and College Estates Acts, 1858-1880. *C. L. Shadwell, D.C.L. 1898 Oxford*

Land Tenure: Ireland
Irish land purchase. *P. C. Smyth, M.Comm. 1928 National University of Ireland*

Local registration of title in Saorstát Eireann. *F. J. Mangan, M.A. 1932 National University of Ireland*

The reform of Irish land tenures. *J. F. Burke, D.Sc. 1917 London*

Size of holdings, with particular reference to Irish conditions. *J. T. Godfrey, M.Econ.Sc. 1942 National University of Ireland*

The struggle for tenant-right in Ulster, 1829 to 1850. *B. A. Kennedy, M.A. 1943 Belfast*

Land Tenure: Other Countries
The evolution of modern land-settlement policy in Australasia. *J. E. F. Jenks, B.Litt. 1930 Oxford*

The influence of the home government on the development of the land revenue and judicial administration in the presidency of Fort William in Bengal from 1823 to 1840. *B. Mitra, M.A. 1936 London, School of Oriental and African Studies*

The influence of the home government on land revenue and judicial administration in the presidency of Fort William in Bengal from 1807-1822. *B. S. Baliga, Ph.D. 1934 London, School of Oriental and African Studies*

Land administration in Iraq from the Muhammadan period to present times, based on original Arabic sources and official administration reports. *A. Platts, Ph.D. 1927 London*

Land tenure in Syria and Lebanon and its economic effects, with some suggestions for reform. *P. J. Klat, B.Phil. 1948 Oxford*

The land-system in South India between c.800 A.D. and 1200 A.D. *K. M. Gupta, Ph.D. 1926 London*

Law of landlord and tenant in Malabar. *V. K. John, LL.D. 1926 London*

Problems of land tenure in modern Africa. *R. M. Peet, M.Sc. 1948 London, School of Economics and Political Science*

The rural organization of an Indian province (Bengal) dealing with land tenures, etc. *H. N. Sanyal, Ph.D. 1928 London*

Systems of land tenure among the Bantu peoples of East Africa. *J. F. M. Middleton, B.Sc. 1949 Oxford*

Land Utilization: Great Britain
The agricultural geography of Norfolk, with special reference to changes in land utilisation and human occupancy. *J. E. G. Mosby, Ph.D. 1938 London, School of Economics and Political Science*

Changes in land utilization in the Towy Valley, Carmarthenshire, since the end of the eighteenth century. *B. L. Davies, M.A. 1938 Wales*

Changes in land utilization in the southeast of Denbighshire, 1840-1938. *J. B. Jarvis, M.A. 1940 Wales*

Land Utilization: Great Britain contd.
Changes in land utilization in the Upper Severn Valley, Montgomeryshire, during the period 1750-1936. *L. S. Andrews, M.Sc. 1940 Wales*

The drainage of the Fens and its effects upon the parishes of the south divison of the Bedford level, 1600-1850. *L. M. Warren, M.A. 1927 London*

An economic survey of the management and utilization of grassland in Great Britain. *J. Pearce, Ph.D. 1950 Reading*

The economics of use and conservation of agricultural land, with particular reference to grasslands in England and Wales. *O. T. W. Price, D.Phil. 1949 Oxford*

Imperial land policy, 1783-1848. *R. G. Riddell, B.Litt. 1934 Oxford*

The land utilisation and agriculture of Somerset. *M. G. Bartlett, M.Sc. 1945 Bristol*

The land utilisation in Wiltshire, with special reference to Salisbury Plain. *A. H. Fry, M.A. 1939 London, Birkbeck College*

The land utilisation of Cheshire. *E. P. Boon, M.Sc. 1941 London, King's College*

The land utilisation of Huntingdonshire. *D. W. Fryer, M.Sc. 1942 London, School of Economics and Political Science*

The land utilisation of the London basin: a study of the existing conditions and historical changes, 1840-1935. *E. C. Willatts, Ph.D. 1937 London, External Degree*

The land utilisation reports of Sutherlandshire: with a special account of the reclamation schemes and the deer forests. *F. T. Smith, M.Sc. 1938 London, King's College*

Land utilization in Somerset. *T. A. Stuart-Menteath, B.Sc. 1937 Oxford*

Land utilization survey of Breconshire. *R. M. Whyte, M.A. 1943 Wales*

The Lothians. Reports of the Land Utilization Survey of Britain, parts 16-18. *P. Scola, M.Sc. 1944 London, School of Economics and Political Science*

Merioneth, part 33 of the *Land of Britain*: the final report of the land utilization survey. *L. A. Holliday, Ph.D. 1948 London, King's College*

The progress of land settlement in England since 1892, with an historical introduction. *G.-L. Von dem Knesebeck, B.Litt. 1935 Oxford*

A report on an investigation of land-utilization in east Yorkshire before the enclosures. *H. King, M.A. 1933 Liverpool*

A survey of the land utilization of Banffshire and Angus. *E. B. Dobson, M.A. 1947 London, King's College*

Types of land use in Caernarvonshire. *M. E. Otter, M.A. 1945 Liverpool*

The utilization of Caithness, Ross and Cromarty, Perth, Argyll and the Hebrides. *S. W. E. Vince, M.Sc. 1947 London, School of Economics and Political Science*

Land Utilization: Ireland
A geographical interpretation of the land utilization of the Belfast region. *D. A. Hill, M.A. 1948 London, External Degree*

Irish land and its problems. *J. Gannon, M.A. 1939 National University of Ireland*

Land Utilization: Other Countries
The development of land policy in Australia with special reference to New South Wales. *W. H. Wynne, Ph.D. 1926 Cambridge*

The land problems of Iraq. *S. Haider, Ph.D. 1942 London, School of Economics and Political Science*

Land reclamation in the Nile Delta: its geographical background and significance. *Z. R. G. Rashidi, M.A. 1940 Leeds*

Types of agricultural villages and related systems of land utilization and division in western France and its islands. *S. Harris, M.Sc. 1930 Wales*

Landnámabók
Landnámabók: the book of the settlement of Iceland. *C. G. Thornton, Ph.D. 1938 Cambridge*

Landor, Robert Eyres
Robert Eyres Landor. *F. G. Peace, M.A. 1931 Leeds*

Landor, Walter Savage
The attitude of W. S. Landor towards the political situations of his day. *N. R. McIntosh, M.A. 1914 Birmingham*

The English poetry of Walter Savage Landor before 1812. *R. H. Super, B.Litt. 1937 Oxford*

Landor, Walter Savage contd.
The *Hellenics* of Walter Savage Landor: an introductory study. *J. F. Arnott, B.Litt. 1938 Oxford*

Studies in the prose works of Walter Savage Landor. *A. Davenport, M.A. 1936 Liverpool*

W. S. Landor as a critic. *E. Fisher, M.A. 1914 Birmingham*

Walter Savage Landor. *M. J. W. Craig, Ph.D. 1944 Dublin, Trinity College*

Walter Savage Landor as a satirist and controversialist in the spheres of law and religion. *E. R. Hughes, M.A. 1949 Wales*

The women characters of W. S. Landor. *D. G. Cope, M.A. 1917 Birmingham*

Lang, Andrew
Andrew Lang as a writer of fairy tales and romances. *R. G. L. Green, B.Litt. 1944 Oxford*

Langbaine, Gerard, the Younger
Gerard Langbaine the Younger. *H. S. Harvey, B.Litt. 1937 Oxford*

Langland, William
The attitude of Chaucer towards chivalry, the Church and the people, compared with that of Langland, Wycliffe and Gower. *J. F. Evans, M.A. 1911 Wales*

The B-text of *Piers Plowman*, passus XVIII-XX. *G. J. Kane, Ph.D. 1946 London, University College*

Chaucer and Langland as painters of English life. *M. Donegan, M.A. 1948 National University of Ireland*

A comparison of *Piers Plowman* with some earlier and contemporary French allegories. *D. L. Owen, M.A. 1909 London*

A critical edition of Piers Plowman, context, prologue and passus i-iv. *A. G. Mitchell, Ph.D. 1939 London, University College*

A critical text of the C-text of *Piers Plowman*, passus 9 and 10. *E. L. Parish, M.A. 1933 London, University College*

The genealogy of the C. text manuscripts of *Piers Plowman. B. F. Allen, M.A. 1923 London*

Interpretation of text of *Piers Plowman. T. P. Dunning, M.A. 1936 National University of Ireland*

Piers Plowman: an interpretation of A-Text. *T. P. Dunning, Ph.D. 1938 National University of Ireland*

Piers Plowman as a work of moral theology. *G. Hjort, Ph.D. 1932 Cambridge*

A preliminary investigation of the pedigree of the B-text mss. of *Piers Plowman. E. Chick, M.A. 1914 London*

Problems connected with the three texts of *Piers the Plowman. F. A. R. Carnegie, M.A. 1923 London*

A study of allegorical representation in *Piers Plowman. S. Brook, M.A. 1947 Manchester*

Langtoft, Peter
The establishment of the original text of Peter Langtoft's chronicle, part 2, as translated by Robert Mannyng of Brunne, by a collation of the two extant mss. - Petyt ms. 511, vol. 7, in the Inner Temple Library and Lambeth ms. 131, in the Lambeth Palace Library. *W. E. Porter, M.A. 1930 Leeds*

Langton, Stephen, Archbishop
Biblical commentators of the twelfth and thirteenth centuries, viewed as historical material, with special reference to the commentaries of Stephen Langton. *B. Smalley, Ph.D. 1929 Manchester*

The *Questiones* of Stephen Langton. *A. L. Gregory, Ph.D. 1929 Manchester*

Stephen Langton as a defender of English liberty. *E. D. Parry, M.A. 1923 Wales*

A study of the archiepiscopal household of Stephen Langton and a collection of his acta. *K. Major, B.Litt. 1931 Oxford*

Language
See also Alphabets; Dictionaries; Meaning (Philosophy); Phonetics; Speech; and under individual languages or groups of languages.

The conflict between the logical and the historical standpoint in fundamental questions of grammar, with reference to Latin. *D. T. Roberts, M.A. 1907 Wales*

The development of language expression and language appreciation in the congenitally deaf child. *F. L. Denmark, M.A. 1930 Liverpool*

The development of language in children. *M. M. Lewis, Ph.D. 1935 London, External Degree*

Language contd.
An enquiry into the relation of language to emotion, with special reference to its influence on thought and behaviour. *M. Collins, M.A. 1921 Liverpool*

1. Ethical language. 2. Meaning and generality (and three other papers). *A. E. Duncan-Jones, Ph.D. 1937 Birmingham*

The history of the German controversy on the origin of language. *J. H. W. Rosteutscher, Ph.D. 1937 Cambridge*

Language and intelligence. *C. J. Holloway, D.Phil. 1947 Oxford*

Language and nature study. *D. N. Mac Donnell, M.A. 1934 National University of Ireland*

The principles of semantics. *S. Ullmann, D.Litt. 1948 Glasgow*

Report upon an enquiry into a child's vocabulary: how far it is indicative of intelligence and influence by social status. *E. M. Johns, M.A. 1949 Reading*

Subject and predicate: a contribution to the theory of grammatical analysis. *M. M. G. Sandmann, D.Litt. 1949 Glasgow*

Languages: Study and Teaching
See also Bilingualism; Cleynaerts, N.; Murray, J. A. H., Sir; Verrall, A. W.; and under individual languages.

An account of the 'direct method' in modern language teaching, its origin and development. *L. A. Baker, M.Ed. 1924 Manchester*

A critical enquiry into the teaching of modern languages in France. *S. Wormald, M.Ed. 1933 Leeds*

A critical study of Quintilian's system of language teaching. *J. Hill, M.A. 1930 Sheffield*

An experimental enquiry into the value of silent reading in the teaching of modern languages in schools. *D. St.J. C. Gurney, M.Ed. 1931 Leeds*

The influence of present day linguistic theory on the teaching of modern languages in schools. *A. A. Jacka, M.A. 1934 London, Institute of Education*

An investigation into the psychological factors of linguistic ability. *P. M. M. Graham, M.A. 1942 London, Institute of Education*

Language teaching in Kikuyu schools. *L. J. Beecher, M.A. 1937 London, Institute of Education*

Linguistic ability considered in relation to general intelligence in senior school children. *A. Morgan, M.A. 1940 Wales*

Linguistic problems and their treatment in antiquity. *W. S. Allen, Ph.D. 1948 Cambridge*

Prognostic tests of ability in modern languages. *S. R. Mills, M.A. 1941 London, Courtauld Institute of Art*

Prognostic tests of aptitude in modern foreign languages, with special reference to French. *R. V. Dawson, M.Ed. 1947 Leeds*

The reading approach in modern language teaching, with some reference to Australian needs and conditions. *P. J. Lynch, M.A. 1938 National University of Ireland*

The relation between language and thought as illustrated by the experience of teaching through a foreign medium. *C. H. Schmidt, 1922 B.Litt Oxford*

A study of abstract thinking and linguistic development with reference to the education of a child of 'average' intelligence. *I. E. Campbell, Ph.D. 1943 Reading*

The teaching of free composition in modern languages. *A. G. Morris, M.A. 1944 Liverpool*

Teaching of modern languages (with special reference to Irish) in primary schools. *F. J. O'Tierney, M.A. 1913 National University of Ireland*

The teaching of modern languages. *A. C. Purcell, M.A. 1945 National University of Ireland*

The teaching of the mother tongue in Great Britain and France and the educational and psychological principles underlying it. *A. Moar, Ph.D. 1940 London, Institute of Education*

The testing of aptitude for foreign languages. *B. F. Hobby, M.A. 1942 Birmingham*

Lansdowne, Lord
See Granville, G.

Lanterne of Light
De Lanterne of Lig't, transcribed from the ms. Harleian 2324, with an introduction, notes and glossary. *L. M. Swinburn, M.A. 1914 London*

Lapcha, The
Social anthropology of the Lapchas. *C. A. Stocks, B.Sc. 1927 Oxford*

Las Cases, Emmanuel Augustin Dieu-Donné Martin Joseph de, Comte
Le Romantisme du *Memorial de Sainte-Helene* et son influence sur Victor Hugo. *L. A. Rozelaar, M.A. 1924 London*

Last Judgment
See Eschatology.

Lateran Decrees
See Church History: Great Britain.

Latin America
See also Antilles; Argentina; Bolivia; Mexico; New Galicia; Paraguay; etc.

The activities of Spain on the Pacific Coast of South America, and her war with the 'Confederation of the Andes' (Chile, Peru, Bolivia and Ecuador), 1860-1886. *J. G. S. Ward, Ph.D. 1939 London, Birkbeck College*

The Amazon Basin, with special reference to its economical development. *D. W. Shave, M.Sc. 1933 London, Birkbeck College*

The attitudes of France to the South American colonies, 1822-6. *W. E. Edwards, Ph.D. 1933 Cambridge*

The government of the United States and Latin American independence. *J. J. Auchmuty, Ph.D. 1935 Dublin, Trinity College*

Los Alemanes en la conquista de América. *J. G. Healy, Ph.D. 1936 National University of Ireland*

Latin Language
See also Inscriptions. For linguistic studies of Latin versions of the Bible or parts thereof, see Bible: Versions.

Bede's use of cases and prepositions in his historical works. *G. Cowan, M.Litt. 1936 Cambridge*

Catalogue raisonné of the subjunctive in Plautus. *H. Thomas, D.Litt. 1909 Birmingham*

The conflict between the logical and the historical standpoint in fundamental questions of grammar, with reference to Latin. *D. T. Roberts, M.A. 1907 Wales*

The diminutive in Roman *satura. T. T. Thomas, M.A. 1946 Wales*

How far did Virgil, Horace and Tacitus supply the want of a middle voice in Latin by the use of the so-called passive?. *M. Cartwright, M.A. 1906 Wales*

An index verborum to the Lindisfarne Gospels. *D. E. Chadwick, M.A. 1934 Leeds*

The Latin life of St. Cadoc: a textual and lexicographical study. *H. D. Emanuel, M.A. 1950 Wales*

The limitations imposed upon Latin lyric poetry by the special nature of the Latin language, with special reference to Horace and Catullus. *F. N. Miles, M.A. 1933 Wales*

Livian usage with respect to sequence of tenses in *oratio obliqua. J. L. Horrocks, M.A. 1937 Liverpool*

The methods of the medieval translators of Greek philosophical works into Latin. *L. Minio-Paluello, D.Phil. 1947 Oxford*

The popular element in the language of Plautus. *J. R. Jones, M.A. 1911 Wales*

Some aspects of the work of the Anglo-Latin twelfth century satirists: the loan words in Gothic, with some account of the pronunciation of that language. *E. P. Bates, M.A. 1910 London*

Studies in the language of the Lindisfarne Gospels. *L. Blakeley, Ph.D. 1949 Birmingham*

Studies in the morphology and syntax of the Vespasian Psalter. *R. Roberts, Ph.D. 1934 Leeds*

Studies in the vocabulary and syntax of the *Expositio Evangelii secundum Lucam* of Saint Ambrose. *A. J. B. Higgins, M.A. 1937 Wales*

A study of certain aspects of word order in the prose works of Julius Caesar. *R. S. Davis, M.A. 1938 Wales*

A study of the syntax and vocabulary of the *De excidio Britanniae* of Gildas. *G. R. Williams, M.A. 1935 Wales*

The style and syntax of the *Historia ecclesiastica* of Bede. *R. Ottley, M.A. 1935 London, Queen Mary College*

The *Summa* of Petrus Helias on Priscian, *Institutiones Grammaticae*, XVII and XVIII. *J. E. Tolson, M.A. 1950 Liverpool*

The syntax and language of Dracontius. *A. Hudson-Williams, M.Litt. 1934 Cambridge*

The syntax of archaic Latin, with special reference to the usage of Catullus and Lucretius. *A. L. Thomas, M.A. 1913 Wales*

Latin Language contd.
Syntax of Terence. *J. T. Allardice, D.Litt. 1926 Saint Andrew's*

The Tacitean use of prepositions, with a few remarks on the tendency of Latin to become an analytical language. *S. P. Record, M.A. 1907 London*

Virgil glosses in Latin glossaries. *A. F. G. Dall, Ph.D. 1922 Saint Andrew's*

The writings of C. Velleius Paterculus: his style and grammar. *A. P. Martin, M.A. 1908 London*

Latin Language: Etymology
Classical etymology as revealed in Greek and Latin literature. *J. O. Anderson, M.A. 1930 London, Bedford College*

An edition of British Museum ms. Harley 2257. *P. Haworth, B.Litt. 1928 Oxford*

Greek loan words in Latin literature down to the time of Cicero. *I. A. Jones, M.A. 1915 Wales*

Latin loan words in Welsh and words that are cognate in Welsh and Latin. *J. Lloyd-Jones, B.Litt. 1908 Oxford*

Latin Language: Study and Teaching
A comparative study of two methods of approach in the teaching of Latin. *I. W. Jones, M.A. 1949 London, Institute of Education*

A historical survey of the teaching of Latin from medieval times. *N. L. Lythgoe, M.Ed. 1918 Manchester*

Latin in the secondary school. *F. S. Fothergill, M.Ed. 1937 Durham*

Method of teaching the intermediate Latin course in secondary schools. *J. J. Whelan, M.A. 1935 National University of Ireland*

The teaching of Latin by the Jesuits, with special reference to the *ratio studiorum. B. C. Grant, M.A. 1920 Wales*

The teaching of Latin by the Jesuits, with special reference to the *ratio studiorum. D. B. Jones, M.A. 1922 Wales*

The teaching of Latin in England: a critical and historical survey. *C. N. Worden, Ph.D. 1938 London, King's College*

Latin Literature
See also Afer, Tyconius; Ambrose, Saint; Apuleius; Brutus; Catullus; Cicero; Gellius, Aulus; Horace; Jerome, Saint; Juvenal; Livy; Lucan; Lucretius; Macrobius; Manilius; Martial; Ovid; Paterculus, C. Velleius; Petronius; Plautus; Pliny, the Elder; Pliny, the Younger; Pollio, G. Asinius; Propertius; Prudentius; Quintilian; Seneca; Sidonius Apollinaris; Statius; Tacitus; Terence; Tertullian; Tibullus; Valerius Flaccus, G.; Varro; Virgil.

Ce que Molière doit aux auteurs latins. *D. Bowie, M.A. 1912 Liverpool*

The conception of fate, and its development in the Latin literature of the later Republic and the early Empire. *M. M. Simpson, M.A. 1919 Liverpool*

An examination of the supernormal psychical phenomena recorded in Latin literature. *F. T. Walton, M.A. 1934 Birmingham*

Greek loan words in Latin literature down to the time of Cicero. *I. A. Jones, M.A. 1915 Wales*

An inquiry into the extent and nature of Ben Jonson's familiar knowledge of classical Latin authors, and the reflection and influence of that knowledge on his work and character. *W. McArthur, Ph.D. 1940 Glasgow*

Latin influence on Tudor comedy. *A. J. Kearns, M.A. 1935 National University of Ireland*

Magic in Greek and Latin literature. *J. E. Lowe, M.A. 1922 London*

Medea and Jason in Greek and Roman literature. *M. Curran, M.A. 1939 Manchester*

The native Italian element in early Roman religion as illustrated by Latin literature up to the end of the first century B.C. *J. J. Jones, M.A. 1919 Wales*

The pre-Hellenistic stage in the evolution of the literary art at Rome. *E. A. Hooton, B.Litt. 1913 Oxford*

Roman and imperial sentiment in the literature of the Empire: Augustus to Constantine. *R. D. McLellan, Ph.D. 1934 London, University College*

Rome and Roman models in Cicero's philosophical and rhetorical writings. *F. H. R. Solmsen, Ph.D. 1936 Cambridge*

Some historical examples in the Roman moralists. *H. M. Phillipson, M.A. 1929 Manchester*

Latin Literature contd.
The theme of the deserted heroine in classical literature. *J. M. Williams, M.A. 1935 Wales*

Latin Literature, Medieval and Later
See also Romances; and Albertanus, of Brescia; Amlyn ac Amic; Andreas Capellanus; Bede, the Venerable; Cadoc, Saint; Crashaw, R.; Fitzralph, R.; Fullonius, G.; Gaudentius, of Brescia, Saint.

Life in Spain during the fifth and sixth centuries A.D. (based chiefly on the works of contemporary Latin writers). *M. I. Thomas, Ph.D. 1934 London, External Degree*

The revival of Latin Literature in the eighth century A.D. *M. T. Rigg, M.A. 1935 London, Birkbeck College*

Latium
The local cults of ancient Latium outside Rome, with the exception of Ostia. *T. G. Thomas, M.A. 1930 Wales*

Latouche, Hyacinthe Joseph Alexandre Thabaud (Henri de)
Henri de Latouche. *M. W. Pye, Ph.D. 1928 London*

Laud, William, Archbishop
The Laudian Party, 1649-1662, and its influence on the Church settlement of the Restoration. *R. S. Bosher, Ph.D. 1949 Cambridge*

Life and work of William Laud, 1628-39, with special reference to his social and political activities. *K. L. McElroy, D.Phil. 1943 Oxford*

The University of Oxford and the Church of England in the time of William Laud. *A. D. Hewlett, B.Litt. 1934 Oxford*

Lauderdale, John Maitland, Duke of
Scotland under Lauderdale. *E. E. B. Thomson, Ph.D. 1928 Saint Andrew's*

Launching of the Mary
See Mountford, W.

Laundry and Dry-Cleaning Industry
A study in the laundry industry of the general conditions of work and management which may influence the health and well-being of laundry operatives. *H. G. Maule, Ph.D. 1949 London, School of Hygiene and Tropical Medicine*

Laurent, Auguste
The influence of chemical theory upon chemical nomenclature and symbolism from the period of Lavoisier to that of Laurent. *F. J. Pearson, M.Sc. 1929 London*

Laurie, Simon Somerville
The educational writings of Simon Somerville Laurie, M.A., LL.D., F.E.I.S., F.R.S.E., 1829-1909, first Bell Professor of the theory, history and art of education in the University of Edinburgh, 1876-1903. *H. M. Knox, Ph.D. 1949 Edinburgh*

Lavoisier, Antoine Laurent
The influence of chemical theory upon chemical nomenclature and symbolism from the period of Lavoisier to that of Laurent. *F. J. Pearson, M.Sc. 1929 London*

Law
See also Agency; Arbitration; Bankruptcy; Children: Law; Company Law; Conspiracy; Contract; Damages; Debt; Dentistry; Evidence; Fiduciaries; Immunity; Justice; Liability; Local Government; Medicine; Monopoly; Mortgage; Nuisance; Partnership; Property; Succession; Tort; Trade Unions; Transport; Treason; Trusts; Women, Status of. For Civil Liberties, see Freedom.

Comparative jurisprudence and legal reform. *E. Cohn, Ph.D. 1946 London, University College*

The doctrine of judicial precedent: its history and importance as a source of law. *T. E. Lewis, Ph.D. 1928 Cambridge*

Early law and religion: a study in the relationship between the primitive rules of law and the early ideas of magic and religion. *H. N. Wright, LL.D. 1919 London*

The end and aim of law. *J. L. Duncan, Ph.D. 1931 Edinburgh*

An examination of some modern theories of the relation of state to law, with special reference to their application to the juristic doctrine of corporate personality. *F. Hallis, D.Phil. 1927 Oxford*

An examination of the basis of the distinction between primary and secondary characterisation in conflict of laws. *R. M. Allott, LL.M. 1948 Sheffield*

The governance of the rule of law: an investigation into the relationship between the political theories, the legal system and the social background in the competitive society. *F. Neumann, Ph.D. 1936 London, School of Economics and Political Science*

Law contd.
Law and equity. *A. McAndrew, M.A. 1936 National University of Ireland*

Law as the basis of morality in the philosophy of Hobbes, Cumberland and Locke. *M. Balaguer, Ph.D. 1937 London, University College*

The philosophy of law of St. Thomas Aquinas. *F. H. Hunt, Ph.D. 1942 Cambridge*

The relation between international law and municipal law. *C. Chi-wu Chu, D.Phil. 1949 Oxford*

Some aspects of the proper law. *S. Farren, LL.M. 1947 London, University College*

The study of law: an essential element in a modern liberal education. *W. McK. O'Kane, LL.D. 1940 Belfast*

Study of the antecedents of the *De Claris jurisconsultis* of Diplovatatius. *H. Koeppler, D.Phil. 1936 Oxford*

Substance and procedure in the conflict of laws. *E. H. Ailes, D.Phil. 1929 Oxford*

Law: Bantu
The communal idea in Bantu law. *R. P. B. Erasmus, B.Sc. 1944 Oxford*

Law: Burma
The position of ecclesiastics in Burmese Buddhist law. *M. H. Aung, B.Litt. 1939 Dublin, Trinity College*

Law: Ceylon
The principles of the Roman-Dutch law of delict as illustrated in the law of Ceylon, with a special chapter on the liability of the Crown to be sued in tort in Ceylon. *L. A. Rajapakse, LL.D. 1925 London*

Law: Great Britain
The action on the case: the development of the action as reflected on the plea rolls of the sixteenth and seventeenth centuries. *A. K. Kiralfy, Ph.D. 1949 London, King's College*

An analysis of the nature, history and content of the doctrine of public policy in relation to the common law. *J. Wicks, B.Litt. 1941 Oxford*

The assignability of choses in action at common law. *D. J. C. King, LL.M. 1939 Bristol*

Celtic law: with special reference to the *Senchus Mór* and the *Book of Aicill*, and a critical examination of the traces of an early Gaelic system of law in Scotland. *J. Cameron, Ph.D. 1935 Glasgow*

The civil responsibility of lunatics. *W. G. H. Cook, LL.D. 1920 London*

The common law in the sixteenth century. *J. F. Myers, M.A. 1950 Liverpool*

The constitutional significance of delegated legislation. *J. A. G. Griffith, LL.M. 1948 London, School of Economics and Political Science*

The defence of compulsory necessity in the civil law. *A. T. Carter, D.C.L. 1893 Oxford*

The early history of *Placita coram rege. M. Tyson, Ph.D. 1927 Manchester*

Henry Fielding and his attitude towards the law and towards legal reform. *B. M. Jones, M.A. 1932 Wales*

The history and place of public policy in English private law. *C. L. Emrich, D.Phil. 1938 Oxford*

Hywel Dda, together with an outline of the origins, affinities, and history of the laws called after his name. *W. H. Harris, B.Litt. 1913 Oxford*

The influence of public opinion on the development of English law from 1880-1914. *S. D. Temkin, M.A. 1938 Liverpool*

The influence of Roman law on the development of the consensual contracts in the law of Scotland. *F. S. Batchelor, Ph.D. 1938 Glasgow*

The law of Wales and the Marches as connected with the history of English law. *H. Owen, D.C.L. 1900 Oxford*

Law reform in England since 1921. *J. J. Kenny, M.A. 1949 National University of Ireland*

The laws of Hywel Dda. *D. Jenkins, LL.M. 1949 Cambridge*

The machinery of public order in England during the Chartist period, 1837-1848. *F. C. Mather, M.A. 1948 Manchester*

The nature and scope of public policy in English law. *H. N. Tucker, D.C.L. 1946 Oxford*

On the common law of England with respect to waters, with special references to the possibility of applying it to varying natural circumstances. *W. A. B. Musgrave, D.C.L. 1890 Oxford*

Law: Great Britain contd.
The practical utility to English lawyers of the study of Roman law. *W. Masterman, D.C.L. 1881 Oxford*

Public policy in English law. *W. S. M. Knight, B.Litt. 1923 Oxford*

Public policy in English law. *J. M. Grosse, LL.M. 1948 Sheffield*

Sheriffs and sheriff courts in Scotland prior to the union of the Crowns in 1603, with special reference to the Fife records at the sixteenth century. *W. C. Dickinson, Ph.D. 1924 Saint Andrew's*

Status in the common law. *R. H. Graveson, Ph.D. 1941 London, King's College*

The use of fictions in English law. *W. Geddes, M.A. 1931 Liverpool*

Law: Greece, Ancient
Law and the community, being aspects of political experiment and the theory in the sixth and fifth centuries in Hellas. *M. H. Martin, D.Phil. 1936 Oxford*

Unwritten laws of Greece. *M. S. Moore, M.A. 1947 National University of Ireland*

Law: India
Deviations from the Anglo-Muhammadan law with reference to the Maplahs of Malabar. *H. Ali, LL.D. 1931 London, University College*

The effect of legislative enactments and judicial pronouncements on the civil law of the Muhammadans in the United Provinces of Agra and Oudh on matters other than family relations, administration and arbitration. *M. Nasim, LL.D. 1929 London*

Hastings' experiment in the judicial system. *N. J. M. Yusuf, Ph.D. 1930 London, School of Economics and Political Science*

Indian civil law according to Kautilya. *Y. D. Sharma, D.Phil. 1945 Oxford*

The influence of the home government on the development of the land revenue and judicial administration in the presidency of Fort William in Bengal from 1823 to 1840. *B. Mitra, M.A. 1936 London, School of Oriental and African Studies*

The influence of the home government on land revenue and judicial administration in the presidency of Fort William in Bengal from 1807-1822. *B. S. Baliga, Ph.D. 1934 London, School of Oriental and African Studies*

The judicial administration of the East India Company in Bengal, 1765-1782. *B. B. Misra, Ph.D. 1947 London, School of Oriental and African Studies*

The law relating to minors as applied by the British courts in India. *E. J. Trevelyan, D.C.L. 1906 Oxford*

An outline of the system of the administration of justice under the Muslims in India, based mainly upon cases decided by Muslim courts between 1206 and 1750. *M. B. Ahmad, M.Litt. 1939 Cambridge*

The Taluqdari law of Oudh, with special reference to the alienation of property *inter vivos*, and its devolution on death testate and intestate. *Q. Ahmad, LL.D. 1928 London*

Law: Ireland
History of legal procedure in Ireland since 1600. *J. Nash, M.A. 1945 National University of Ireland*

Law: Italy
The judicial system of Fascist Italy. *D. Wang, Ph.D. 1939 London, School of Economics and Political Science*

Law: Nigeria
Law and British administration in South-eastern Nigeria. *E. U. Udoma, Ph.D. 1944 Dublin, Trinity College*

Law: Oceania
The maintenance of order in Oceania. *H. I. P. Hogbin, M.Sc. 1931 London, School of Economics and Political Science*

Law, Administration of
See also Assize Courts; Coroners; Courts of Law.

The British background of the American theory of judicial review. *L. T. Chapin, Ph.D. 1938 Edinburgh*

The characteristics of administrative law. *F. J. Port, LL.D. 1927 London*

Constitutional principles re-examined in the light of modern administrative law. *M. R. R. Davies, Ph.D. 1948 Cambridge*

Departmental legislation and the problem of safeguards in England and Egypt. *S. Z. A. Asfour, Ph.D. 1949 Manchester*

Law, Administration of contd.
International administrative legislation under the Covenant of the League of Nations (with special reference to municipal application). *P. Bradley, Ph.D. 1936 London, School of Economics and Political Science*

The judicial function in the modern state. *N. Bouropoulos, Ph.D. 1949 London, School of Economics and Political Science*

Law and the executive. *B. Schwartz, Ph.D. 1948 Cambridge*

Legal aid. *R. Egerton, LL.M. 1946 Cambridge*

Law, Commercial
See Commercial Law.

Law, Constitutional
See Constitutional Law.

Law, Criminal
See Criminal Law.

Law, Ecclesiastical
See also Blasphemy.

The Emperor Lewis IV and the Curia from 1330 to 1347: canon law and international politics in the first half of the fourteenth century. *H. S. Offler, Ph.D. 1939 Cambridge*

English canonists in the later Middle Ages: a historical biographical and literary study. *K. R. N. St. J. Wykeham-George, B.Litt. 1937 Oxford*

The English criminal and criminal ecclesiastical law of sex morality and its effect upon the organization of the family. *G. May, LL.D. 1933 London, School of Economics and Political Science*

Pre-Reformation Church courts in the diocese of Canterbury. *B. L. Woodcock, B.Litt. 1950 Oxford*

A study of the controversy concerning the application of Roman canon law in England during the Middle Ages. *B. Allen, B.Litt. 1923 Oxford*

Law, Industrial
See Industrial Law.

Law, International
See also International Court of Justice. For the international law on particular subjects, see under the subject, e.g. Capitulations; Extraterritoriality; Nationality; Recognition; Rivers; Servitudes; Smuggling; Territorial Waters; Treaties; etc.

A comparative study of the rules of private international law relating to partnerships and to corporations, with special reference to the laws of France and of Egypt. *M. S. Guenena, LL.D. 1924 London*

The contribution of the English courts to the development of international law. *T. Finkelstein, B.Litt. 1939 Oxford*

The growth and development of international law in Africa. *H. S. McC. Hill, D.C.L. 1900 Oxford*

The history of the Bosphorus and the Dardanelles, with special reference to treaty relations: a study in international law and diplomacy. *D. B. Toye, LL.D. 1925 London*

The international law of territorial waters, with special reference to the coasts of Scotland. *W. M. Newlands, Ph.D. 1935 Edinburgh*

International private law in Scotland with special reference to the choice of law. *R. R. Taylor, Ph.D. 1947 Glasgow*

The international right of aerial navigation. *P. W. French, LL.D. 1915 London*

International servitudes: rights in foreign territory. *F. A. Vali, Ph.D. 1932 London, School of Economics and Political Science*

The law of trade combinations, a study in comparative international law. *A. Neugröschel, Ph.D. 1942 London, School of Economics and Political Science*

Legal aspects of international cooperation for the assistance of refugees. *S. Andracki, M.Sc. 1949 London, School of Economics and Political Science*

The legal principles governing the situational status of Egypt. *M. H. Fahmy, LL.D. 1928 London*

Municipal tribunals and international law: The development of international law by English and French courts in the nineteenth century. *D. B. McCown, Ph.D. 1938 London, School of Economics and Political Science*

The part played by the intention of the parties in determining the system of law applicable. *R. C. Graves, LL.D. 1925 London*

Private law analogies in international law, with special reference to international arbitration. *H. Lauterpacht, LL.D. 1925 London*

Public international law as relating to international rivers. *J. E. Candioglou, LL.D. 1919 London*

Law, International contd.
Public policy in private international law. *L. F. Moller, B.Litt. 1938 Oxford*

Public policy in private international law. *R. A. Samek, M.Litt. 1948 Cambridge*

Question of international law in Anglo-Iranian diplomatic relations. *A. A. Dehkan, Ph.D. 1938 London, School of Economics and Political Science*

Recognition in international law. *T. C. Chen, D.Phil. 1948 Oxford*

The refugee and international law. *E. R. Casper, LL.M. 1948 London, University College*

The relation between international law and municipal law. *C. Chi-wu Chu, D.Phil. 1949 Oxford*

The responsibility of states and the Calvo and Drago doctrines. *J. L. Aguilar de Leon, D.Phil. 1947 Oxford*

The rules of international private law relating to the transfer of movable, immovables, and choses in action. *H. E. Davies, LL.D. 1928 London*

The rules of private international law determining capacity to contract. *F. T. Cheng, LL.D. 1916 London*

Some Latin American contributions to the development of international law. *H. Arias, LL.D. 1911 London*

Law, Islamic
See Islamic Law.

Law, Jewish
See Jewish Law.

Law, Maritime
See Maritime Law.

Law, Roman
See also Roman-Dutch Law.

Attempt and participation in Roman penal law. *W. Rothenberg, M.Litt. 1941 Cambridge*

Critical studies upon the texts and the theory of the *beneficium cedendarum actionum* and *venditio nominis*. *K. Lipstein, Ph.D. 1937 Cambridge*

Formalism and progress in the early Roman law of delict. *D. Daube, Ph.D. 1936 Cambridge*

The influence of Christianity on the family and domestic relations in Roman law. *D. Brook, D.C.L. 1896 Oxford*

The influence of Roman law on the development of the consensual contracts in the law of Scotland. *F. S. Batchelor, Ph.D. 1938 Glasgow*

The influence of Roman law on the history and doctrine of the Christian church during the first three centuries. *W. Phillips, Ph.D. 1931 Edinburgh*

1. The mode of the Incarnation. 2. The indebtedness of the Pauline theology to Roman law. *W. J. S. Muntz, B.D. 1906 Oxford*

Mosaicarum et Romanarum legum collatio. *M. Hyamson, LL.D. 1912 London*

Offences against the State in Roman law and the courts which were competent to take cognizance of them. *P. M. Schisas, LL.D. 1924 London*

The practical utility to English lawyers of the study of Roman law. *W. Masterman, D.C.L. 1881 Oxford*

The reciprocal influence of Roman law and Christianity. *J. W. Jones, Ph.D. 1925 London*

The theory of adoption as found in Roman law, and its development in certain countries. *T. S. Vavkoukis, B.Litt. 1909 Oxford*

The Twelve Tables. *A. A. Prankerd, D.C.L. 1887 Oxford*

Law, Roman-Dutch
See Roman-Dutch Law.

Law, William
The relation of William Law to John Wesley and the beginnings of Methodism. *E. W. Baker, Ph.D. 1941 Edinburgh*

Lawrence, David Herbert
The literary influences on D. H. Lawrence's poems and novels. *R. K. Sinha, D.Phil. 1950 Oxford*

The novels of D. H. Lawrence: a critical study. *C. A. Wanklyn, M.A. 1950 Sheffield*

Personal relationships in the work of D. H. Lawrence. *H. B. Cardwell, M.A. 1947 Leeds*

Laws, Conflict of
See Law.

Layard, Austin Henry, Sir
The last embassy of Sir Austin Henry Layard (March, 1877-August, 1878). *B. Williams, M.A. 1939 Wales*

Le Braz, Anatole
La Bretagne, peinte par deux ecrivains contemporains, A. le Braz et C. le Goffic. *H. M. Gething, M.A. 1921 Birmingham*

Le Cardonnel, Louis
Louis de Cardonnel. *P. Aykroyd, Ph.D. 1927 Dublin, Trinity College*

Le Clerc, Jean
Leclerc et la république des lettres. *A. M. Barnes, D.Phil. 1935 Oxford*

Le Fanu, Joseph Sheridan
Sheridan Le Fanu. *M. Colbert, M.A. 1946 National University of Ireland*

Le Goffic, Charles
Charles Le Goffic: his poetry and poetic criticism. *W. S. Barnard, M.A. 1937 London, Bedford College*

La Bretagne, peinte par deux ecrivains contemporains, A. le Braz et C. le Goffic. *H. M. Gething, M.A. 1921 Birmingham*

Le Roy, Alexandre, Bishop
Monseigneur Alexandre le Roy. *W. P. O'Brien, M.A. 1949 National University of Ireland*

Le Roy, Eugène
Eugène Le Roy. *C. M. Foley, M.A. 1929 Birmingham*

Le Vayer, Francçois de la Mothe
See *La Mothe le Vayer, F. de.*

Leabhar Gabhála
Lebor Gabala (*The book of invasions*). *M. Flatley, M.A. 1934 National University of Ireland*

Leabhar Laighneach
Research on the saga-lists called *A & B* contained in, respectively, *The Book of Leinster* and ms.H.3.17 (T.C.D.) and mss.23.N.10 (R.I.A.), Rawl. B512 and Harleian 5280, together with research on the tales included therein, with special emphasis upon those which are now lost. *F. McCann, M.A. 1950 Belfast*

Sgéalta as an *Leabhar Laighneach* (Stories from the *Book of Leinster*). *O. Nı Fharrachtáin, M.A. 1941 National University of Ireland*

Sgéalta as *Leabhar Laighean* (Tales from the *Book of Leinster*). *P. O'Maolchatha, M.A. 1936 National University of Ireland*

The verbal system of the *Book of Leinster* version of the *Táin bó Cúalnge*. *M. MacDermott, M.A. 1939 National University of Ireland*

Leabhar Muimhneach
An *Leabhar Muimhneach* (*The Book of Munster*). *S. B. O'Donnchadha, M.A. 1937 National University of Ireland*

Lead Industry
Lead and silver industry in Wales, 1558-1750. *L. Jones, B.Litt. 1924 Oxford*

The lead industry in Cardiganshire. *L. Jones, M.A. 1915 Wales*

The lead mining industry of Cardiganshire, 1700-1830. *O. Beynon, M.A. 1938 Wales*

Leadership
The school group - its leaders and leadership. *J. Chance, M.A. 1933 Birmingham*

A sociological study of leadership in primitive society. *H. Powdermaker, Ph.D. 1928 London*

League of Nations
See also *International Court of Justice; International Labour Organization.*

The activities of the League of Nations in relation to the traffic of opium and other dangerous drugs, in particular, emphasizing the illicit traffic as a significant factor in the situation. *A. D. Hooper, M.A. 1936 Wales*

The attitude of the German Government towards membership of the League of Nations. *D. Jenkins, M.A. 1939 Wales*

The Council of the League of Nations: a constitutional study, with special reference to its composition. *A. B. O. Davies, M.A. 1930 Wales*

The evolution of the Assembly of the League of Nations as a parliamentary body. *N. E. Skrimshire, M.Sc. 1932 London, School of Economics and Political Science*

The financial reconstruction of Austria by the League of Nations, with reference to its economic consequences. *M. F. Jolliffe, M.A. 1930 Wales*

The Geneva treatment of the Manchurian and Abyssinian crises. *M. P. Lee, Ph.D. 1946 London, School of Economics and Political Science*

League of Nations contd.
International administrative legislation under the Covenant of the League of Nations (with special reference to municipal application). *P. Bradley, Ph.D. 1936 London, School of Economics and Political Science*

The League of Nations and national minorities. *P. Barber, M.A. 1924 Wales*

The League of Nations and the problem of a universal peace organization. *G. Schwarzenberger, Ph.D. 1936 London, School of Economics and Political Science*

League sanctions: an account of the origins and interpretations of Article XVI of the Covenant, and an attempt to estimate its significance. *A. S. Millward, M.Sc. 1934 London, School of Economics and Political Science*

The mandates system in the B and C territories. *E. Helmer, Ph.D. 1928 London*

The methods employed by the Council of the League of Nations to settle international disputes in pursuance of the terms of the Covenant. *T. P. Evans, Ph.D. 1930 London, School of Economics and Political Science*

The modifications made necessary in the doctrine of sovereignty in international law by the creation of the League of Nations. *J. Stone, LL.M. 1930 Leeds*

The origin and evolution of the Assembly of the League of Nations. *P. Samuel, M.A. 1935 Wales*

The position of small States in the League of Nations. *S. S. Jones, D.Phil. 1936 Oxford*

The Secretariat General of the League of Nations: an experiment into international administration. *F. C. Y. C. Wright, Ph.D. 1931 London, External Degree*

The United States and the League of Nations, with special reference to co-operation. *H. L. Sainer, M.Sc. 1946 London, School of Economics and Political Science*

Learning
See also *Children, Retarded; Memory.*

A critical survey of theories underlying experimental study of the effects of reward and punishment on school learning. *M. I. Shamin, M.A. 1948 London, Institute of Education*

Economy in motor learning. *M. V. Gopalaswami, Ph.D. 1923 London*

An examination of the learning process, with special reference to the Gestalt psychology. *G. C. Bathurst, Ph.D. 1939 London, Institute of Education*

The Gestalt theory of learning and some of its implications for educational theory and practice. *K. Pickett, B.Litt. 1949 Oxford*

Imagery and learning. *A. M. Jenkin, M.A. 1930 London, Bedford College*

Imagery and learning: a further study. *A. M. Jenkin, Ph.D. 1933 London, Bedford College*

The learning methods of mental defectives. *M. Stuart, M.Ed. 1944 Manchester*

The plateau: a study of periods of arrested progress in motor learning. *E. Healey, M.Ed. 1934 Leeds*

The role of incentives in animal learning. *G. C. Drew, M.A. 1948 Bristol*

A study of the effect upon learning of a training in certain principles of attention and memorization. *L. R. Phillips, M.A. 1936 London, Institute of Education*

A study of the influence of various types of incentives upon learning. *B. M. Wright, Ph.D. 1938 Edinburgh*

A study of the learning process. *A. F. Walwyn, M.A. 1921 London*

A survey of the learning process with special reference to perception, with experimental work on three forms of perception. *C. F. Exley, M.Ed. 1927 Leeds*

Time intervals in learning and memory. *J. C. Tsao, Ph.D. 1949 Cambridge*

Leather Industry
English leather glove trade. *M. K. Fudge, M.A. 1930 Bristol*

The influence of geography upon the development, distribution, and organization of the leather industry of Great Britain. *J. I. Roper, B.Litt. 1924 Oxford*

A survey of the resources of tanning materials and the leather industry of Bhopal State, India. *G. W. Douglas, M.Sc. 1935 Leeds*

Leather Industry contd.
The Walsall and Midlands leather trades; a study in their history and organisation from the earliest times to the present day. *E. Tonkinson, M.Com. 1948 Birmingham*

Lecky, William Edward Hartpole
Critics of democracy: Carlyle, Arnold, Stephen (Fitzjames), Maine, Lecky. *B. E. Lippincott, Ph.D. 1931 London, School of Economics and Political Science*

Leconte de Lisle, Charles Marie René
Leconte de Lisle: animalier. *A. S. Johnston, M.A. 1936 Belfast*

L'élément barbare chez Leconte de Lisle. *A. A. B. Fairlie, D.Phil. 1943 Oxford*

Les différentes formes d'imagination chez Leconte de Lisle. *J. Shrives, M.A. 1924 Birmingham*

Les idées de Leconte de Lisle. *W. F. H. Whitmarsh, M.A. 1925 Birmingham*

The visual impressions in the poems of Leconte de Lisle. *W. Herrmann, M.A. 1950 Bristol*

Ledwidge, Francis
Francis Ledwidge. *M. MacDermott, M.A. 1946 National University of Ireland*

Lee, Nathaniel
An edition of three tragedies by Nathaniel Lee: *Sophonisba, The Rival Queeens, Theodosius*; with bibliographical and critical introduction and notes. *E. Hodgson, M.A. 1947 Leeds*

The life and works of Nathaniel Lee. *M. Hasan, D.Phil. 1937 Oxford*

Leeward Islands
The development of executive government in Barbados and the Leeward Islands, 1660 to 1783. *F. G. Spurdle, Ph.D. 1931 London, King's College*

Legends
See also *Folk Lore; Mythology; and Argonauts; Arthurian Legends; Faust; Jason; Medea; Prometheus; Troy; etc.*

A historical survey and critique of the theories propounded concerning the Carolingian legends. *W. H. Thomas, M.A. 1929 Wales*

Κτίσεισ πόλεων: an examination of the Greek foundation legend as a literary form, *E. W. W. Cumbers, M.A. 1939 London, King's College*

Legendary and historical figures in Hellenistic-Oriental popular literature. *M. Braun, Ph.D. 1937 Cambridge*

The religious observances ordained for every day of the Hindu year, with special reference to customs observed in the Maratha country, together with the origin of these observances, whether traceable to legends, astronomical causes, or other sources. *M. M. Underhill, B.Litt. 1921 Oxford*

William Morris as an interpreter of northern legend. *E. M. Kenyon, M.A. 1928 Manchester*

Leibniz, Gottfried Wilhelm von, Baron
A comparison of the philosophical system of Leibniz and Berkeley. *D. M. Sen, Ph.D. 1928 London*

The conception of teleology, with special reference to the views of Spinoza, Leibniz, and Kant. *D. M. Jones, M.A. 1911 Wales*

Four philosophical controversies engaged in by Leibniz and certain other philosophers of the later seventeenth and early eighteenth centuries. *R. T. H. Redpath, Ph.D. 1940 Cambridge*

The idea of God in Descartes, Spinoza and Leibniz. *M. A. Davies, M.A. 1935 Wales*

Individual experience in the philosophy of Leibniz. *A. H. Talukder, M.A. 1935 London, University College*

Is the general standpoint of the *Theodicée* inconsistent with the philosophical views expressed in Leibnitz' other works?. *L. Brehaut, B.Sc. 1913 Oxford*

Operational methods in mathematics from Leibniz to Fourier. *K. A. C. Humphreys, M.Sc. 1949 London, External Degree*

The penetration of the philosophy of Leibniz in France. *W. H. Barber, D.Phil. 1950 Oxford*

The problem of evil in the philosophy of Leibniz. *A. B. Lavelle, Ph.D. 1935 Sheffield*

The problem of evil with special reference to the *Theodicee* of Leibniz. *H. Cunliffe-Jones, B.Litt. 1932 Oxford*

The problem of the relation between the ultimate ground and the individual members of the universe, as treated by Spinoza and Leibniz. *W. G. Sleight, M.A. 1907 London*

The relation between Leibniz and Lotze. *E. E. Thomas, M.A. 1910 Wales*

Leicester
The activities of the corporation of the borough of Leicester from 1688 to 1835. *R. W. Greaves, D.Phil. 1936 Oxford*

The economic organization of the medieval borough with special reference to Leicester and its guild merchants. *E. H. Smith, M.A. 1912 Wales*

Leicestershire
Aspects of the economic development of some Leicestershire estates in the fourteenth and fifteenth centuries. *R. H. Hilton, D.Phil. 1940 Oxford*

Enclosure in Leicestershire, 1485-1607. *L. A. Parker, M.A. 1948 London, External Degree*

The honor of Leicester: a study in descent and administration, with special reference to the Leicestershire fees of the honor. *L. Fox, M.A. 1938 Manchester*

Leighton, Robert, Archbishop
Archbishop Leighton: his characteristic position as theologian and ecclesiastic. *D. S. Hopkirk, B.Litt. 1926 Oxford*

Leinster
An Bhoromha as *Leabhar mor Leacáin*, 295 ro a 24-310 ro a 12 (The Boru tribute, from the *Book of Lecan*, 295r 24-310r 12). *G. O'hArgain, M.A. 1950 National University of Ireland*

Leinster, Book of
See Leabhar Laighneach.

Leisure
See also Games and Sports; Play; Recreation.

The changing meaning of leisure and the problems created. *T. H. Marshall, M.A. 1942 London, Institute of Education*

The development of organized leisure-time activities for young persons in England, with particular reference to London. *S. E. Barnes, M.A. 1947 London, Institute of Education*

Education for leisure in the elementary school. *G. H. Holroyd, M.A. 1941 Leeds*

An enquiry into the use of leisure amongst the working classes of Liverpool. *T. M. Middleton, M.A. 1931 Liverpool*

Food and leisure among the African youth of Leopoldville (Belgian Congo): a study of the adaptation of African youth to urban life. *S. A. M. A. J. M. Comhaire-Sylvain, B.Litt. 1948 Oxford*

Homework and leisure time activities. *N. F. Millington, M.A. 1938 Birmingham*

An investigation into the out-of-school activities of a group of adolescents. *N. M. Eid, M.A. 1948 London, Institute of Education*

Léightheoireacht agus caitheamh-aimsire bhuachailli an bhaile mhór (The reading and pastimes of boys in big towns). *S. Mac Cuinn, M.A. 1942 National University of Ireland*

The leisure activities of adolescents: an investigation of the psychological functions of the various leisure activities of adolescents in a particular town, with some special references to the cinema and reading. *W. Harper, M.A. 1942 Manchester*

Leisure as a planning problem, with special reference to the Birmingham conurbation. *R. A. Hopferwieser, M.Com. 1950 Birmingham*

The nature and function of adolescent leisure pursuits. *C. Rivett, M.A. 1947 Manchester*

The problem of leisure. *H. W. Durant, Ph.D. 1940 London, External Degree*

Psychological functions of leisure reading. *R. Oliver, M.A. 1949 Manchester*

The recreations and amusements of the industrial working class in the second quarter of the nineteenth century, with special reference to Lancashire. *K. Allan, M.A. 1947 Manchester*

Report of an enquiry into the occupations, further education and leisure interests of a number of girl wage-earners from elementary and central schools in the Manchester district, with special reference to the influence of school training on their use of leisure. *J. L. Harley, M.Ed. 1937 Manchester*

The social and emotional effects of the recreational film on adolescents of 13 and 14 years of age in the West Bromwich area. *B. Kesterton, Ph.D. 1948 Birmingham*

A study of leisure-time interests. *A. Pennington, M.Ed. 1950 Durham*

A study of the growth of the provision of public facilities for leisure time occupations by local authorities of Merseyside. *E. H. Roberts, M.A. 1933 Liverpool*

Leisure contd.
A study of the leisure activities of school children in a Middlesex secondary (mixed) school. *J. Struthers, M.A. 1939 London, Institute of Education*

A study of the training for leisure occupations offered in a senior girls' school in an industrial area, together with an industrial enquiry into the use made of this training by the girls after their entry into employment. *O. I. Morgan, M.Ed. 1942 Manchester*

Leith, Concordat of
See Church History: Scotland.

Leix-Offaly Plantation
See Ireland: History.

Lemaire, Jean
La plainte du Désire by Jean Lemaire: critical edition with notes. *D. Yabsley, M.A. 1929 London*

Lemery, Lewis
A study of the chemistries of Lemery, Freind, Baume, and Watson, and of the development of chemical thought from 1675 to 1787. *S. D. M. Waters, M.Sc. 1931 London*

Lenau, Nikolaus
Lord Byron and Nikolaus Lenau: a comparative study. *S. Korninger, M.A. 1950 Sheffield*

Lennox, Charlotte
Charlotte Lennox. *U. Todd-Naylor, B.Litt. 1931 Oxford*

The life and writings of Charlotte Lennox, 1720-1804. *A. M. Kynaston, M.A. 1936 London, Birkbeck College*

León, Luis de
Luis de León; vida y obras. *J. Redmond, M.A. 1933 National University of Ireland*

Leonardo da Vinci
The mechanical investigations of Leonardo da Vinci, with special reference to his researches on flight. *I. I. B. Hart, Ph.D. 1924 London*

Leonidas, of Tarentum
The poems of Leonidas of Tarentum. *A. M. Thomas, M.A. 1937 Wales*

Lermontov, Mikhail Yurevich
Baironizm v poezii Lermontova (Byronism in the poetry of Lermontov). *H. Brennan, M.A. 1915 London*

The influence of Byron on Lermontov. *S. K. Mukherjea, B.Litt. 1945 Oxford*

Leroux, Pierre
Contribution à l'étude de la pensée de Pierre Leroux. *F. D. David, M.A. 1916 London*

La genèse de la doctrine littéraire de Pierre Leroux. *M. H. Johnes, M.A. 1949 Wales*

Lesage, Alain René
The lower classes in the novel from Lesage to 1789. *Z. W. Goddard, M.A. 1932 London, King's College*

Leskov, Nikolai Semenovich
The peasantry, Orthodox clergy, dissenters, and Jews, as seen by Leskov. *F. Smith, M.A. 1948 London, School of Slavonic and East European Studies*

Lessing, Gotthold Ephraim
The art of exposition in Lessing's prose works, with special reference to the polemical writings. *F. J. Stopp, Ph.D. 1948 London, University College*

Lessings ethische Ansichten. *I. C. Morton, M.A. 1925 Birmingham*

Lessing's knowledge and criticism of English literature. *L. H. Kay, M.A. 1912 Birmingham*

Lessing's *Laokoon* and its English predecessors. *C. R. Bingham, M.A. 1938 London, University College*

Lessing's study and knowledge of English language and literature. *P. Levy, M.A. 1935 London, University College*

L'Estrange, Roger, Sir
Sir Roger L'Estrange: pamphleteer, essayist, and man of letters; with an estimation of his influence on the development of English prose. *G. Kitchin, B.Litt. 1910 Oxford*

Letters
The character of Cicero as exhibited in his letters. *T. E. Davies, M.A. 1916 Wales*

The development of letter writing in the seventeenth century with a study of its bearing on the essay and the novel. *R. M. Scrimgeour, M.A. 1928 London*

Egyptian epistolography from the eighteenth to the twenty-first dynasties. *A. M. Bakir, B.Litt. 1941 Oxford*

Letters contd.
English personal letters and private diaries of 1640-1680: a study of the general mental attitude of the period as illustrated by individual types, together with a brief examination of the colloquial language of the time. *M. T. Williamson, Ph.D. 1929 London*

The evidence of contemporary French memoirs, letters and periodicals with regard to the influence of English literature. *E. H. Partridge, B.Litt. 1924 Oxford*

The letters of Samuel Pepys and his immediate family circle. *H. T. Heath, B.Litt. 1938 Oxford*

The letter-writers of the eighteenth century. *J. J. Jory, M.A. 1912 Wales*

Lettish Language
The phonetics of the Lettish language. *G. S. Lowman, Ph.D. 1931 London, University College*

Levallois, Jules
Jules Levallois. *J. G. Hass, M.A. 1929 Birmingham*

Levant Company
British trade with Turkey and the decline of the Levant Company, 1790-1825. *I. S. Russell, M.A. 1932 Manchester*

A history of the Levant Company. *A. C. Wood, D.Phil. 1934 Oxford*

The history of the Levant Company 1603-1681: a study in commercial history. *W. Roby, M.A. 1927 Manchester*

The later history of the Levant Company, 1753-1825. *I. S. Russell, Ph.D. 1935 Manchester*

The Levant Company after 1640. *G. P. Ambrose, B.Litt. 1933 Oxford*

Leveller Movement
See Great Britian: History: Seventeenth Century.

Lever, Charles James
Charles Lever: Irish novelist. *D. A. N. Abernethy, B.Litt. 1937 Dublin, Trinity College*

Charles Lever, novelist. *M. J. Duffy, M.A. 1949 National University of Ireland*

The treatment of national character in the novels of Charles Lever. *M. Lancaster, M.A. 1935 Liverpool*

Levi b. Gershon
See Gersonides.

Lewis Glyn Cothi
The unpublished poems of Lewis Glyn Cothi as found in the Peniarth manuscripts. *E. O. James, M.A. 1911 Wales*

Lewis, Matthew Gregory
The life and letters of Matthew Gregory Lewis (1775-1818). *L. B. Marshall, M.A. 1929 London*

Lewis Morganwg
See Llywelyn ap Rhisiart.

Lewis, William Thomas, Sir
A history of the trade disputes and the formation and operation of the several sliding scale agreements in the South Wales coal trade, 1870 to 1903, with special reference to the work of Sir William Thomas Lewis, 1st Baron Merthyr of Senghenydd. *B. Evans, M.A. 1944 Wales*

Lexicography
See Dictionaries.

Li Po
A comparison of Shelley and Li Po as poets of nature. *C. Li, B.Litt. 1936 Oxford*

Liability (Law)
See also Accidents; Tort.

Legal liability of public authorities and local administrative bodies. *G. E. Robinson, LL.D. 1914 London*

Liability for dangerous things. *J. Charlesworth, LL.D. 1922 London*

Libanius
Studies in the orations of Libanius. *G. Middleton, D.Litt. 1920 Aberdeen*

Libel
The *carmen famosum* of the neoteric school. *R. J. M. Lindsay, M.A. 1950 Belfast*

Liber Regularum
An English translation of *Liber regularum* by Tyconius Afer. *A. R. Kent, M.A. 1943 Sheffield*

Liberalism
Fabianism as the climax of the new liberalism. *S. G. Ikoku, M.Sc. 1949 London, External Degree*

The Irish influence on the Liberal movement in England, 1789-1832, with special reference to the period 1815-32. *R. Cassirer, Ph.D. 1940 London, School of Economics and Political Science*

Liberalism contd.
Liberal political thought in France, 1815-1848. *P. W. E. Curtin, Ph.D. 1939 London, School of Economics and Political Science*

Liberalism in England 1880-1914. *W. G. K. Duncan, Ph.D. 1931 London, School of Economics and Political Science*

The organisation of the Whig Party during the exclusion crisis 1678 to 81. *V. H. Simms, M.A. 1934 London, University College*

Rise and growth of Indian liberalism. *M. A. Buch, Ph.D. 1937 London, School of Economics and Political Science*

The transition from Whiggism to liberalism. *D. G. Southgate, D.Phil. 1949 Oxford*

The Whig Party, 1702-1708. *E. L. Ellis, M.A. 1949 Wales*

The Whig Party, 1807-12. *M. Roberts, D.Phil. 1935 Oxford*

The Whigs and their relations with William III from 1689-1698. *A. K. Powis, M.A. 1947 London, King's College*

Liberia
The economic history of Liberia. *G. W. Brown, Ph.D. 1938 London, School of Economics and Political Science*

Liberty
See Freedom.

Libraries
See also Panizzi, A., Sir.

The circulating libraries of the eighteenth century. *H. M. Hamlyn, M.A. 1948 London, Birkbeck College*

The first century of the library of Corpus Christi College, Oxford (1517-1617). *J. R. Liddell, B.Litt. 1933 Oxford*

Les cabinets de lecture en France, 1800-1850. *M. M. Tirol, Ph.D. 1926 London*

The provision of books in the centrally-organized religious orders before 1400. *K. W. Humphreys, B.Litt. 1949 Oxford*

The public library service under English local government. *D. Sarjeant, Ph.D. 1935 London, School of Economics and Political Science*

Lichtenberg, Georg Christoph
The problem of the aphorism in the writing of G. C. Lichtenberg. *J. P. Stern, Ph.D. 1950 Cambridge*

Liddesdale
The historical background of the raider ballads of Liddesdale. *J. M. Couper, Ph.D. 1948 Aberdeen*

Light
Descartes' world, or Treatise on light. *A. Wechsler, M.Sc. 1931 London*

The history of the knowledge of the spectrum. *G. M. Catling, M.Sc. 1926 London*

A survey of the early work on the diffraction of light. *D. Pardoe, M.Sc. 1946 London, External Degree*

Theories of light and electricity in the eighteenth century. *G. N. Spriggs, M.Sc. 1926 London*

Theories of light to Fresnel. *E. D. East, M.Sc. 1926 London*

Theories of light to the time of Fresnel. *A. Johnstone, M.Sc. 1926 London*

Lighters
See Ports and Harbours.

Lilburne, John
John Lilburne and his relation to the first phase of the Leveller Movement, 1638-1649. *P. E. Gregg, Ph.D. 1939 London, School of Economics and Political Science*

The political ideas of the English Radicals, particularly in Nonconformist circles, from John Lilburne to John Wilkes. *B. H. Lewis, M.A. 1926 Wales*

Lillo, George
George Lillo, 1693-1739. *E. M. W. McKee, B.Litt. 1939 Oxford*

The life, work and influence of George Lillo. *T. C. Rogers, Ph.D. 1937 London, Queen Mary College*

Limerick
History and functions of the Limerick Chamber of Commerce. *D. O'Connor, M.Econ.Sc. 1938 National University of Ireland*

Limoges
Turgot: intendent of Limoges, 1761 to 1774. *D. Dakin, Ph.D. 1936 London, Birkbeck College*

Linacre, Thomas
Leaders of humanism in English education: Humphrey, Duke of Gloucester, William Grocyn, Thomas Linacre, Bishop Richard Foxe. *C. H. Winstanley, M.A. 1930 Liverpool*

Lincoln, Diocese
The diocese of Lincoln under Bishops Repingdon and Fleming. *M. Archer, B.Litt. 1936 Oxford*

The Reformation in the diocese of Lincoln as illustrated by the life and work of Bishop Longland (1521-47). *G. E. Wharhirst, B. Litt. 1938 Oxford*

Report on the Chapter Acts of Lincoln Cathedral, 1402-1427. *M. Archer, M.A. 1936 Liverpool*

Lincolnshire
Contributions towards the study of the historical geography of Lincolnshire. *S. H. King, Ph.D. 1945 London, King's College*

The early historical geography of Lindsey. *K. Wareham, M.A. 1919 Liverpool*

The influence of environment on the fen children of Holland, Lincs. *A. Hinchley, M.Ed. 1939 Durham*

Lincolnshire: some aspects of its geography, with special reference to the Wolds. *J. Bygott, B.Sc. 1914 Oxford*

Norman Lincolnshire. *G. H. Marshall, M.A. 1948 Leeds*

P. R. O. assize roll 505, edited with an introduction on the war-time administration of Lincolnshire, 1294-98. *W. S. Thomson, Ph.D. 1939 Edinburgh*

Parliamentary enclosures in Lindsey, or the enclosures of the eighteenth and nineteenth centuries as they affected Lindsey. *T. H. Swales, M.A. 1936 Leeds*

The social and economic condition of the Holland division of Lincolnshire from 1642 to 1660. *G. M. Hipkin, B.Litt. 1930 Oxford*

Lindisfarne Gospels
See Bible: Versions.

Lindsey
See Lincolnshire.

Linen Industry
Effects of the war on Irish linen industry. *W. J. Larmor, M.Com.Sc. 1921 Belfast*

The linen industry of Northern Ireland. *J. K. Forbes, M.Sc. 1939 London, External Degree*

Linguistics
See Language.

Linquet, Henri
Henri Linquet: his political and social theory. *A. B. Handler, M.Sc. 1934 London, School of Economics and Political Science*

Lintot, Firm
The firm of Lintot. *M. W. Barnes, M.A. 1942 London, Bedford College*

Lisbon
The treasure of São Roque: a sidelight on the Reformation. *W. Telfer, B.D. 1932 Cambridge*

Lisle, Arthur Plantagenet, Lord
The history of Calais under the deputyship of Arthur Plantagenet, Lord Lisle, 1533-1540. *J. Leese, M.A. 1929 Manchester*

Lisle, Charles Marie René Leconte de
See Leconte de Lisle, C. M. R.

List, Franz
The idea of the German 'national mission' as expressed by Fichte, List and Treitschke. *S. G. Graber, M.Sc. 1949 London, School of Economics and Political Science*

Lista y Aragón, Alberto
Alberto Lista y Aragón: a report on investigations of his life and work. *J. C. J. Metford, M.A. 1940 Liverpool*

Literary Criticism
See Literature: Criticism.

Literary Gazette
The Literary Gazette under the editorship of William Jerdan. *K. M. Shawcross, B.Litt. 1937 Oxford*

Literary Patronage
See Patronage.

Literary Societies
The literary and philanthropic societies of the eighteenth century: their services to and influence upon Welsh literature. *A. Lewis, M.A. 1921 Wales*

Literature
See also Aphorisms; Authorship; Biography; Character Books; Comedy; Creativity; Emblem Books; Epics; Epigrams; Essays; Fables; Fairy Tales; Fiction; Figures of Speech; Humour; Imagery; Journalism; Legends; Letters; Masques;

Literature contd.
Music and Literature; Mysticism; Ornament; Pamphlets; Parody; Patronage; Poetry; Religious Literature; Rhetoric; Riddles; Romanticism; Satire; Sermons; Tragedy; Translations.

The concept of the reason and of its function in seventeenth and eighteenth century philosophy and literature. *H. A. Taylor, Ph.D. 1938 London, University College*

The effect of the advance in scientific knowledge upon seventeenth century literature. . *L. L. Ross, M.A. 1912 Birmingham*

The influence of scientific speculation on imaginative literature in the seventeenth century. *G. E. Neilson, M.A. 1923 Bristol*

The literary landscapes of the eighteenth century. *E. Reynard, B.Litt. 1927 Oxford*

The present condition of historical drama in England. *T. A. Smith, M.A. 1934 Bristol*

Some elements of sentimentalism in the literature of the eighteenth century. *C. Hanson, M.A. 1948 Sheffield*

A study of the psychology of the creative processes, with particular reference to literary production. *R. Thomas, D.Sc. 1932 Wales*

The transition from epic to romance. *C. H. Southerns, M.A. 1913 National University of Ireland*

Literature: Criticism
See also Criticism; and Arnold, M.; Bridges, R.; Brunetière, F.; Cooper, A. A., 3rd Earl of Shaftesbury; Hazlitt, W.; Herder, J. G. von; Hunt, L.; Jeffrey, F.; Johnson, S.; Keats, J.; Lamb, C.; Landor, W. S.; Lessing, G. E.; Levallois, J.; Planche, G.; Richards, I. A.; Ruskin, J.; Sainte-Beuve, C. A.; Taine, H. A.; Veuillot, L. F.; Warton, J.; Warton, T.

An attempt to trace the rise of English literary criticism. *J. C. James, M.A. 1914 Wales*

Charles Le Goffic: his poetry and poetic criticism. *W. S. Barnard, M.A. 1937 London, Bedford College*

Charles Péguy as a literary critic. *A. M. B. Rosevere, Ph.D. 1938 London, King's College*

Coleridge's dramatic criticism. *T. O'Flynn, M.A. 1946 National University of Ireland*

The confusion between moral and aesthetic ideas in Greek literary criticism and philosophy. *M. Chandler, M.A. 1933 London, Royal Holloway College*

The contribution of modern psychology to literary criticism. *E. R. Bentley, B.Litt. 1939 Oxford*

A contribution to the study of Albert Thibaudet as a critic of the novel. *M. K. Leiper, Ph.D. 1939 London, University College*

A contribution to the study of Catulle Mendès as critic. *B. Gravenall, Ph.D. 1939 London, University College*

Critic liteardha ar saothar an Athar Peadar O'Laoghaire (A literary criticism of the work of Father Peadar O'Laoghaire). *M. U. O'Maolchumaidh, M.A. 1931 National University of Ireland*

The critical system of Ferdinand Brunetière. *D. T. Davies, M.A. 1928 Wales*

The critical writings of W. P. Ker. *L. P. Ball, M.A. 1940 Liverpool*

The critics of the eighteenth century, before Wordsworth and Coleridge. *A. Fisher, M.A. 1911 London*

The development of critical theories in England, 1660-1771. *E. F. Chapman, Ph.D. 1935 London, King's College*

Development of English literary criticism during the eighteenth century. *W. F. Miles, Ph.D. 1922 Cambridge*

The development of literary criticism in England until 1800, as seen by the treatment of the works of Geoffrey Chaucer and Edmund Spenser. *D. M. Smith, M.A. 1923 Wales*

English book-reviewing in the last half of the eighteenth century. *W. D. Sutcliffe, D.Phil. 1943 Oxford*

English criticism of American literature during the period 1800 to 1850 as reflected in the periodicals. *J. J. Espey, B.Litt. 1938 Oxford*

English literary criticism from Shaftesbury's *Characteristics* to Reynolds' *Discourses. W. Rees, Ph.D. 1926 London*

Literature: Criticism contd.
The ethical and literary appreciation: a critical analysis of Aristotle's *Poetics* in relation to current theories of aesthetics, with particular reference to the teaching of literary appreciation in schools. *S. Quan, M.A. 1945 London, King's College*

The evolution of English literary criticism. *W. Uncles, M.A. 1928 Belfast*

French works in contemporary British reviews (1800-1820). *E. S. Roberts, M.A. 1928 Liverpool*

Gerard Manley Hopkins as literary critic. *N. H. Newhouse, M.A. 1949 Liverpool*

Gwallter Mechain: ei hanes, ei waith a'i safonau beirniadol (Gwallter Mechain; his life story, his work, and his standards of criticism). *J. T. Owen, M.A. 1928 Wales*

The heroic couplet in the eighteenth century: a study of critical theory and poetic practice, with special emphasis on the development of style and content. *L. J. Jolley, M.A. 1938 London, University College*

Horace as a literary critic. *G. S. T. Lee, M.A. 1908 London*

Joseph Warton as a literary critic. *R. M. Baine, B.Litt. 1939 Oxford*

Keats and criticism. *P. Purcell, M.A. 1937 National University of Ireland*

Keats as a critic. *P. Pye, M.A. 1917 National University of Ireland*

Keats' literary theories, as expressed in his letters and as exemplified in his poems. *K. Box, M.A. 1947 Manchester*

Le Père Rapin, critique littéraire. *S. R. C. Long, Ph.D. 1936 London, Birkbeck College*

Les idées de Balzac sur la littérature. *R. van Engel, M.A. 1929 Liverpool*

Les interprétations critiques de la littérature anglaise en France pendant le Second Empire. *E. Holder, M.A. 1928 Leeds*

Life, works and literary theories of Jacques-Joseph du Guet. *R. E. Nicholls, Ph.D. 1936 London, University College*

Literary criticism in the age of Pope. *W. D. Parry, M.A. 1919 Wales*

Literary criticism in the plays of Aristophanes. *S. M. Hooker, M.A. 1913 London*

Literary criticism of Plautus, ancient and modern. *G. M. Francis, M.A. 1948 Wales*

Matthew Arnold as a literary critic. *D. V. Marcon, M.A. 1940 London, King's College*

Ozanam, historien et critique littéraire. *P. J. A. Aubry, Ph.D. 1932 London, Birkbeck College*

The place of Dionysius of Halicarnassus in the development of prose-criticism. *J. F. Lockwood, Ph.D. 1936 London, University College*

The place of Gaston Paris in romance studies. *D. J. A. Ross, M.A. 1936 London, University College*

The poetry and criticism of Matthew Arnold compared. *T. Scott, M.A. 1948 Manchester*

The reception of the works of Charles Dickens in Germany. *E. N. Gummer, B.Litt. 1938 Oxford*

Relationship of journalism to literature. *F. R. Leavis, Ph.D. 1924 Cambridge*

A review of the criticisms of Keats and Shelley in *The Edinburgh, The Quarterly* and *Blackwood's. A. Campbell, M.A. 1929 Liverpool*

The rise of English literary criticism. *S. H. Watkins, M.A. 1907 Wales*

The rise of the critical review in the eighteenth century. *J. J. Champenois, B.Litt. 1913 Oxford*

The *roman comique* in England. *D. M. Pope, M.A. 1906 London*

Ruskin as a literary critic. *E. M. Hewetson, M.A. 1938 London, King's College*

Samuel Johnson as a reviewer. *M. E. O'Brien, B.Litt. 1946 Oxford*

Scottish poetics and literary criticism from James VI to Francis Jeffrey. *T. S. Lawson, Ph.D. 1930 Edinburgh*

Some aspects of modern criticism. *M. Galway, M.A. 1929 Belfast*

Studies in early Tudor criticism, literary and linguistic, up to 1558. *E. J. Sweeting, M.A. 1938 London, Royal Holloway College*

A study of Balzac's literary criticism. *H. E. Collins, Ph.D. 1937 London, Birkbeck College*

Literature: Criticism contd.
A study of certain aspects of nineteenth century periodical criticism (1798-1842) especially in its influence on and attitude to new literary movements. *J. Kinghorn, Ph.D. 1939 Edinburgh*

A study of Matthew Arnold's literary criticism, with special reference to the influence of Sainte-Beuve on Arnold. *O. E. Simister, M.A. 1936 Birmingham*

A study of Rémy de Gourmont as a literary critic, with special reference to his connection with the Symbolist Movement in French poetry from 1885-1900. *G. Rees, M.A. 1937 Wales*

A study of Ste. Beuve's criticisms of English and German literatures. *J. R. Kinnes, Ph.D. 1928 Edinburgh*

A study of the development of the meaning of the word 'romance' (romantic) as used in literary criticism. *H. M. Harris, M.A. 1911 London*

A study of the literary criticism of John Gibson Lockhart, with a bibliography of his critical writings. *M. O. Hildyard, Ph.D. 1928 London*

A study of the significance and variations in meaning and usage of certain important terms of literary criticism during the period from the late seventeenth to the late eighteenth century. *D. M. Niblett, B.Litt. 1938 Oxford*

A study of Thomas Campion as critic and poet. *S. H. Atkins, M.A. 1931 London, King's College*

Tennyson and the reviewers, 1827-51: a study of the growth of Tennyson's reputation and of the influence of the critics upon his poetry. *E. F. Shannon, D.Phil. 1949 Oxford*

Trends in modern criticism, 1800-1940. *D. F. Mercer, B.Litt. 1949 Oxford*

Victor Hugo in the light of English criticism and opinion during the nineteenth century. *V. E. A. Bowley, Ph.D. 1944 London, Queen Mary College*

Literature: Study and Teaching
The ethical and literary appreciation: a critical analysis of Aristotle's *Poetics* in relation to current theories of aesthetics, with particular reference to the teaching of literary appreciation in schools. *S. Quan, M.A. 1945 London, King's College*

The influence exercised by the development of English prose and literary criticism upon the teaching of the vernacular tongue and study of literature in English schools. *C. Rees, M.A. 1909 Wales*

Literary appreciation in the elementary school. *W. Heron, M.Ed. 1923 Leeds*

A standardized test of literary appreciation. *E. D. Williams, M.A. 1937 London, University College*

Training in style through literary appreciation, with special reference to pupils aged ten to fifteen. *G. W. Hartley, M.Ed. 1927 Leeds*

Liturgy and Ritual
See also Baptism; Book of Common Prayer; Breviaries; Confirmation; Eucharist; Festivals; Marriage; Sacraments; and under individual religions and sects.

Astudiaeth feirniadol o'r Didache a llenyddiaeth Gristionogol arall o gynnyrch y ddwy ganrif gyntaf, a ysgrifennwyd yn yr iaith Roeg, ynghyda chyfeiriad arbennig at ddatblygiad y Weinidogaeth a'r Gwasanaethau Eglwysig (A critical study of the Didache and other Christian literature in Greek of the first and second centuries, with special reference to the development of the ministry and the church services). *E. J. Lloyd, Ph.D. 1946 Wales*

Bohairic pericopae of Wisdom and Sirach and Coptic Church Offices. *O. H. E. Burmester, Ph.D. 1933 Cambridge*

A comparative study of some aspects of ritual in the simpler and more developed communities. *J. F. Bulsara, Ph.D. 1930 London, School of Economics and Political Science*

1. The Gallican liturgy. 2. Consecration and communion in the English rite. *L. St. A. Wright, B.D. 1916 Oxford*

1. The growth ot belief in a future state. 2. The organization and worship of the early Christian Churches as exhibited in the New Testament. *C. Erskine, B.D. 1901 Oxford*

The heart of the Christian life or Christian worship in its history and teaching. *J. M. Barkley, Ph.D. 1946 Dublin, Trinity College*

The influence of ritual on primitive belief with regard to the life after death in Polynesia, Melanesia, and Indonesia. *R. L. B. Moss, B.Sc. 1922 Oxford*

Liturgy and Ritual contd.
1. The language in which our Lord taught. 2. Supposed quotations from the Apostolic liturgy in the New Testament. *G. H. Gwilliam, B.D. 1890 Oxford*

The non-Eucharistic services of the early Church. *C. W. Dugmore, B.D. 1940 Oxford*

1. On the creed in the Acts. 2. On the appointment of rites and ceremonies in the Church. *A. L. Oldham, B.D. & D.D. 1905 Oxford*

1. The origin of the daily service. 2. The aim and structure of the daily service. *J. Cott, B.D. & D.D. 1874 Oxford*

The place of seasonal ritual in the medieval English drama. *H. J. Hammerton, M.A. 1944 Leeds*

The place of the congregation in liturgical worship. *B. R. Beasley, M.A. 1945 Leeds*

The priesthood of Christ, of Christians, and of the Christian ministry. 2. Public worship in the Christian Church, as described in or inferred from the New Testament. *W. D. Springett, B.D. 1880 Oxford*

The psychology of Christian public worship: a study in the more practical aspects of some of the typical liturgies and worships of Western Christianity. *G. E. Osborn, Ph.D. 1935 Edinburgh*

The relation of ritual to belief in primitive cult, with special reference to the magico-religious customs of the Australian Aborigines. *E. O. James, B.Litt. 1916 Oxford*

Ritual and mythology in Australia: an historic study. *A. P. Elkin, Ph.D. 1927 London*

1. The *Treatise on the Apostolic tradition* of St. Hippolytus. 2. The theology of confirmation in relation to baptism. 3. The shape of the liturgy. *G. E. A. Dix, B.D. & D.D. 1949 Oxford*

The use of liturgical orders of service in the worship of the so-called Presbyterian Dissenters. *A. E. Peaston, B.Litt. 1936 Oxford*

The worship of the early Christian Church as reflected in the New Testament literature, and its influence on the development of doctrine. *A. B. Macdonald, Ph.D. 1932 Edinburgh*

A study of the use of the Psalms in Christian worship, as reflected in the pre-Reformation liturgies and service-books. *J. A. Lamb, Ph.D. 1946 Edinburgh*

Liu Hsiang
Liu Hsiang and the Hsin Hsü. *W. B. D. Doxford, Ph.D. 1937 London, School of Oriental and African Studies*

Liverpool
The industrial geography of Liverpool and district. *D. D. E. Rodgers, M.A. 1933 Liverpool*

Liverpool during the Seven Years War. *M. Buchan-Sydserff, M.A. 1934 Liverpool*

The making of modern Liverpool, 1760-1820. *H. A. Turner, M.A. 1939 Birmingham*

Problems of population and education in the new housing estates, with special reference to Norris Green. *N. Williams, M.A. 1938 Liverpool*

Studies in the history of Liverpool, 1756-1783. *W. M. Barrow, M.A. 1925 Liverpool*

A study of the history and development of the School Medical Service in Liverpool from 1908 to 1939, and an attempt to assess its consequences on the health of the Liverpool school child. *J. Riddell, M.A. 1946 Liverpool*

Liverpool, Robert Banks Jenkinson, 2nd Earl
The colonial policy of the Liverpool administration, with special reference to British settlement in South Africa. *I. E. Edwards, M.A. 1931 Wales*

Lord Liverpool and Liberal Toryism, 1820 to 1827. *W. R. Brock, Ph.D. 1943 Cambridge*

Lord Liverpool as prime minister. *S. Y. Mathias, M.A. 1913 Liverpool*

Livestock Industry
An analysis of the geographical conditions influencing the development of the stock industries in the Irish Free State. *D. K. Smee, M.A. 1927 London*

An economic history of live stock in Ireland since the famine. *J. O'Donovan, B.Litt. 1931 Oxford*

An economic study of cattle and sheep production, with particular reference to Welsh farm stock enterprises. *B. H. Roberts, M.Sc. 1949 Wales*

The economics of the store cattle industry, with special reference to Wales. *W. J. Thomas, M.Sc. 1946 Wales*

Livestock Industry contd.
Factors affecting the prices of livestock in Great Britain. *K. A. H. Murray, B.Litt. 1931 Oxford*

A geographical distribution of selected breeds of British cattle and sheep: a study in environmental factors. *J. O'Connor, Ph.D. 1949 London, School of Economics and Political Science*

Livestock improvement in the dairy industry of England and Wales: a study of economic factors involved. *J. D. Empson, B.Litt. 1950 Oxford*

The marketing of food, fodder and livestock in the London area in the seventeenth century, with some reference to the sources of supply. *P. V. McGrath, M.A. 1947 London, Queen Mary College*

The production and the consumption of animal foodstuffs, with special reference to the British Empire. *E. W. Shanahan, D.Sc. 1919 London*

Some aspects of livestock marketing in Great Britain and North America. *G. P. Wibberley, Ph.D. 1941 Wales*

A statistical and economic survey of certain aspects of the beef producing, dairying and cattle rearing industries in Great Britian between 1939 and 1945. *J. G. Marley, M.A. 1947 Manchester*

A study of some economic aspects of the sheep industry of Devon, with special reference to changes in the practice of sheep farming on the red loams of mid-Devon. *S. T. Morris, M.Sc. 1936 Wales*

Livy
The Carthaginians as depicted in Livy, Polybius, and other ancient writers. *G. Adams, M.A. 1922 London*

The importance of the Veronese palimpsest in the first decade of Livy. *C. M. Knight, M.A. 1910 London*

Livian usage with respect to sequence of tenses in *oratio obliqua. J. L. Horrocks, M.A. 1937 Liverpool*

Livy and Horace on the origins of the Roman drama. *R. A. Browne, Ph.D. 1931 Cambridge*

The sources and compositions of Livy, books XXXI-XLV. *A. H. McDonald, Ph.D. 1938 Cambridge*

Llandaff, Diocese
The disposal of the monastic property in the diocese of Llandaff at the time of the Reformation. *T. J. Edwards, M.A. 1928 Wales*

The ecclesiastical and religious position in the diocese of Llandaff in the reign of Queen Elizabeth. *H. M. Isaacs, M.A. 1928 Wales*

The Reformation in the diocese of Llandaff. *L. Thomas, B.Litt. 1926 Oxford*

Llawdden
Barddoniaeth Llawdden a Rhys Nanmor (The poetry of Llawdden and Rhys Nanmor). *M. G. Headley, M.A. 1938 Wales*

Llewelyn Bren
Wales and the Marches in the reign of Edward II, with special reference to Glamorgan and the revolt of Llewelyn Bren. *T. A. Dyke, M.A. 1912 Wales*

Lleyn, William
The poems of William Lleyn. *J. C. Morrice, M.A. 1902 Wales*

Llwyd, Morgan
Y dylanwadau llenyddol, crefyddol ac athronyddol ar Forgan Llwyd (Literary, religious and philosophical influences on Morgan Llwyd). *E. L. Evans, M.A. 1926 Wales*

Llywelyn ap Rhisiart (Lewys Morganwg)
Gweithiau Lewys Morganwg (The works of Lewys Morganwg). *E. J. Saunders, M.A. 1922 Wales*

Local Government
See also Education; Public Health; Taxation.

A comparison of the local administration and law courts of the Carolingian Empire with those of the West Saxon kings. *H. M. Cam, M.A. 1909 London*

Deconcentration and decentralisation in modern local government. *P. Y. Pao, Ph.D. 1937 London, School of Economics and Political Science*

Local government and central control. *H. Hall, D.C.L. 1906 Oxford*

Local public utilities in relation to local government. *J. H. Warren, M.A. 1936 Liverpool*

Local Government: Africa
Social and political aspects of the development of municipal government in Kenya, with special reference to Nairobi. *M. Parker, Ph.D. 1949 London, School of Economics and Political Science*

Local Government: Africa contd.
Urban native administration in tropical Africa, British and Belgian. *J. L. L. Comhaire, D.Phil. 1948 Oxford*

Local Government: China
Reform of Chinese city government based on European experience. *N. Liu, Ph.D. 1931 London, School of Economics and Political Science*

Local Government: France
Local government in France since 1918, with special reference to the financial and administrative relations of central and local authorities. *J. C. Develin, B.Litt. 1934 Oxford*

Local Government: Germany
Central and local government in Germany, with reference to the Weimar Constitution of 1919. *D. A. Worgan, M.A. 1932 Wales*

Local Government: Great Britain
The administration of the counties of Norfolk and Suffolk in the reign of Henry IV. *G. E. Morey, M.A. 1941 London, University College*

Administrative and clerical staffs in the local government service of England and Wales. *E. H. Martyn, M.Sc. 1922 London*

The application of the Local Government Act, 1929, to London. *B. H. Chubb, M.Sc. 1940 London, School of Economics and Political Science*

Central control and the employment of Exchequer grants in British local government. *H.-S. Lee, Ph.D. 1950 Glasgow*

Civic government of Durham, 1780-1835. *M. Todd, M.A. 1924 Liverpool*

The committee system in local government. *F. H. E. T. Rose, M.Sc. 1938 London, School of Economics and Political Science*

Coventry and the Municipal Corporations Act, 1835: an investigation of the workings of Coventry Corporation mainly between 1750 and 1835, and a critical examination of the Commissioners' Report of 1833. *S. E. Kerrison, M.A. 1939 Birmingham*

The Crown and municipal corporations, 1679 to 1688: an aspect of the English revolution. *W. J. Fowler, M.A. 1935 Reading*

Defects in local government arising from the distribution of areas, with special reference to north Wales. *H. W. Evans, LL.M. 1938 Wales*

Delegation in local government law. *J. M. Hawksworth, LL.M. 1950 Sheffield*

The development of city government in the United States and the United Kingdom, with special reference to the period since 1870. *E. S. Griffith, D.Phil. 1925 Oxford*

The development of quarter sessions government in Devon in the nineteenth century and the transition to county council government. *D. R. Tucker, M.A. 1949 London, External Degree*

The economic organization of the medieval borough with special reference to Leicester and its guild merchants. *E. H. Smith, M.A. 1912 Wales*

The English civic chronicles during the fifteenth and sixteenth centuries. *R. Flenley, B.Litt. 1910 Oxford*

English local authority expenditure, 1913-32. *J. Sykes, Ph.D. 1935 Leeds*

English local finance. *G. H. Austin, Ph.D. 1921 Sheffield*

The finance of capital expenditure by English local authorities. *W. Riley, M.A. 1931 Manchester*

The geography and administration of services in the county of Cumberland. *A. F. Young, M.A. 1934 Liverpool*

The growth and development of the municipal element in the principality of north Wales up to the close of the fourteenth century. *E. A. Lewis, M.A. 1902 Wales*

The growth of self-government in the Borough of Southampton as illustrated by its charters and letters patent. *H. W. Lidden, Ph.D. 1923 London*

A history of local government in the West Riding of Yorkshire since 1888. *H. Roberts, M.Com. 1943 Leeds*

History of the laws, usages and constitutions of the early English boroughs; the original constitution of municipal corporations; and the source of their powers of legislation and administration. *J. J. Williams, LL.D. 1928 Sheffield*

Imperial subventions towards services administered by local authorities in England and Wales. *C. G. Holden, M.Com. 1925 Birmingham*

Local Government: Great Britain contd.
Judicial control exercised over local authorities compared with that exercised over Government departments. *M. B. Cairns, M.A. 1947 Bristol*

The local administration of the sheriff in the thirteenth century. *M. A. Hennings, M.A. 1916 London*

Local authorities: internal financial control. *A. H. Marshall, Ph.D. 1937 London, External Degree*

Local finance (England and Wales). *D. Rollinson, M.Com. 1924 Birmingham*

Local government areas and the replanning of the Black Country. *J. S. Symonds, M.Com. 1948 Birmingham*

Local government, finance and functions in Wales, as affected by post-war changes. *J. C. Gray, M.A. 1941 Wales*

Local government in the principality of Wales during the sixteenth and seventeenth centuries, as illustrated mainly by the extant data relating to the county of Merioneth. *I. ap O. Edwards, M.A. 1924 Wales*

Local government in Wales, sixteenth to eighteenth centuries, as exemplified by the work of the Quarter Sessions in the County. *T. H. Lewis, Ph.D. 1941 London, External Degree*

Local government under the Tudors. *N. M. Brameld, M.A. 1916 London*

The medieval boroughs of Snowdonia. *E. A. Lewis, M.A. 1912 Wales*

The municipal borough as a health unit. *J. D. Kershaw, M.D. 1939 London, University College*

Municipal origins: an account of English private bill legislation relating to local government, 1740-1835; with a chapter on private bill procedure. *F. H. Spencer, D.Sc. 1911 London*

The office of sheriff in Scotland: its origin and early development. *C. A. Malcolm, Ph.D. 1922 Edinburgh*

Petitions in Parliament under the Lancastrians, from, or relating to, towns. *M. A. Rose, M.A. 1926 London*

The place of the parish in local government, 1600-1650. *K. L. McElroy, B.Litt. 1925 Oxford*

Powers of local authorities. *H. J. Richards, LL.M. 1930 Cambridge*

The practice and functions of local government as illustrated in Lancashire towns in the century before the Municipal Corporations Act (1835) with a consideration of the more immediate effects of the reform. *W. Scrivens, M.A. 1934 Liverpool*

Principles of governing the exercise of the powers and duties of local authorities. *J. C. Smith, LL.M. 1948 Leeds*

Problems of areas in English local government. *V. D. Lipman, D.Phil. 1947 Oxford*

Problems of English rural administration illustrated by the three parishes of St. Mary Cray, St. Paul's Cray and Orpington, Kent. *A. W. Webster, M.Sc. 1922 London*

Rating reform. *M. R. R. Davies, M.LL. 1943 Leeds*

The relations between central and local government in England and Wales in the period 1923-1933, treated with reference both to the policy and to the public discussions. *J. Lewis, M.A. 1936 Wales*

Scots burgh finances prior to 1707. *G. S. Pryde, Ph.D. 1926 Saint Andrew's*

Some aspects of the administrative control of local government in England. *S. Tarnowski, Ph.D. 1936 London, School of Economics and Political Science*

A study of English local government from a legal standpoint, with particular reference to the early development of country administration, illustrated by a comparison of the application of certain principles of local government in medieval and in modern times. *H. B. Williams, LL.D. 1925 London*

A study of local government in Wales under the Commonwealth with special reference to its relations with the central authority. *T. M. Bassett, M.A. 1941 Wales*

A study of parish government: illustrated by documents from the parish chest of Eye, Northants. *R. A. Shannon, M.A. 1949 London, External Degree*

A survey of local government in Hertfordshire, 1700 to 1832. *H. Adams, Ph.D. 1931 London, External Degree*

Local Government: India
Financing of local authorities in British India. *A. N. Banerji, Ph.D. 1941 London, School of Economics and Political Science*

The growth of local self-government in Assam, 1874-1919. *A. K. Barkakoty, Ph.D. 1949 London, School of Oriental and African Studies*

Local finance in India. *G. C. Varma, Ph.D. 1932 London, School of Economics and Political Science*

Local self-government in the Madras Presidency, 1850-1919. *K. K. Pillay, D.Phil. 1948 Oxford*

The rural organization of an Indian province (Bengal) dealing with land tenures, etc. *H. N. Sanyal, Ph.D. 1928 London*

Village government in British India. *J. Matthai, D.Sc. 1916 London*

Local Government: Ireland
Central and local administration in Ireland under George II. *J. L. McCracken, Ph.D. 1948 Belfast*

Evolution and history of local government law in Ireland. *I. K. Lynch, M.A. 1948 National University of Ireland*

Irish local government. *R. O'Hanrahan, M.A. 1927 National University of Ireland*

Local Government in Ireland. *M. V. Conlon, M.A. 1931 National University of Ireland*

Príomh-Rialtas agus rialtas áitiúil (Central and local government). *E. O'Catháin, M.Econ.Sc. 1929 National University of Ireland*

The undertakers in Ireland and their relations with the Lords Lieutenant, 1724-1771. *J. L. McCracken, M.A. 1942 Belfast*

Local Government: United States
The development of city government in the United States and the United Kingdom, with special reference to the period since 1870. *E. S. Griffith, D.Phil. 1925 Oxford*

Locke, John
The conception of the self in Locke, Berkeley and Hume. *M. P. Evans, M.A. 1934 Wales*

The conceptions of natural law and natural right, with special reference to Hobbes, Spinoza, Locke and Rousseau. *N. S. B. Powell, M.A. 1932 Wales*

A critical study of John Locke's examination of Père Malebranche's opinion of seeing all things in God. *C. G. Jones, M.A. 1949 Wales*

The doctrine of knowledge of John Locke and contemporary English Platonism. *A. E. Best, M.A. 1940 Manchester*

The educational ideas of John Locke, 1632-1704. *J. Cummings, M.A. 1932 Liverpool*

Empiricism: a critical examination of the empirical theory of knowledge as this is expounded in certain of the works of Locke and Berkeley. *G. H. Haydock, Ph.D. 1946 Glasgow*

The ethical ideas of John Locke and their antecedents. *W. G. Hilton, M.A. 1929 Manchester*

The idea of substance in Locke's philosophy. *J. H. Abraham, M.A. 1930 London, University College*

The influence of Locke on Rousseau. *E. T. Davies, M.A. 1914 Wales*

Law as the basis of morality in the philosophy of Hobbes, Cumberland and Locke. *M. Balaguer, Ph.D. 1937 London, University College*

The monetary theories of John Locke. *J. S. Raj, M.Sc. 1937 London, University College*

The origins and course of Coleridge's reaction against Locke and Kant. *J. Coles, M.A. 1949 Wales*

The origins of the political opinions of John Locke. *A. H. Maclean, Ph.D. 1948 Cambridge*

Political individualism of John Locke. *G. Bull, M.Litt. 1933 Cambridge*

The rise of individualism, with special reference to Locke. *R. Bermingham, M.A. 1937 National University of Ireland*

The theology of John Locke. *D. G. Wright, Ph.D. 1938 Edinburgh*

The theory of property in the eighteenth century: its historical antecedents with special reference to England and Locke. *W. Larkin, Ph.D. 1928 London*

The theory of universals, with special reference to Locke, Berkeley and Hume. *O. R. Davies, M.A. 1937 Wales*

The treatment of relations by Locke and Hume. *M. R. Anand, Ph.D. 1929 London*

Locke, Richard Adams
Richard Locke: a record of a strenuous life. *F. M. Ward, M.A. 1937 Bristol*

Lockhart, John Gibson
The materials for biography, the handling of the materials, and the techniques employed to reveal character and personality, with special reference to the work of Lockhart, Froude and Lytton Strachey, in the light of recent psychological investigation. *E. A. M. Dougary, Ph.D. 1942 Edinburgh*

A study of the literary criticism of John Gibson Lockhart, with a bibliography of his critical writings. *M. O. Hildyard, Ph.D. 1928 London*

Lodge, Thomas
Studies in the works of Thomas Lodge. *A. Walker, Ph.D. 1926 London*

Lodi Dynasty
The Lodi dynasty A.D. 1451 to 1526. *S. A. Shere, M.A. 1934 London, School of Oriental and African Studies*

Logic
See also Categories; Certainty; Entailment; Individuation; Intelligence; Intuition; Thinking; Truth.

The ability to arrange concepts in order and the relation of this ability to reasoning. *J. H. Clapham, M.A. 1935 London, Institute of Education*

An absolute logical criterion. *G. H. Malan, D.Phil. 1916 Glasgow*

An analysis of reasoning ability in school children, with a view to determining the nature and extent of any group factor involved. *J. H. Murdoch, Ph.D. 1933 London, Institute of Education*

A comparative investigation of the influence of mechanical and linguistic training on the understanding of the forms of reasoning involved in civics. *G. Edwards, M.Ed. 1949 Leeds*

The concept of the reason and of its function in seventeenth and eighteenth century philosophy and literature. *H. A. Taylor, Ph.D. 1938 London, University College*

Concerning propositions and their truth. *D. E. Miller, M.A. 1931 London, Bedford College*

The dualism of practical reason. *W. Owen, M.A. 1915 Wales*

The effect on general reasoning ability of training in functional thinking in arithmetic. *M. Williams, M.A. 1938 London, Institute of Education*

An examination of the deductive logic of J. S. Mill. *R. Jackson, D.Litt. 1938 Saint Andrew's*

A factorial analysis of reasoning ability. *S. E. Nakar, M.A. 1949 London, Institute of Education*

The function of reason in relation to the moral idea and the part played by experience. *C. M. Thompson, M.A. 1922 London*

Indian logic in the light of Western thought. *P. W. French, M.A. 1919 London*

Indian logic of Nyaya system. *H. N. Randle, D.Phil. 1927 Oxford*

Inductive methods: historical and critical examination. *C. K. Murphy, M.A. 1913 National University of Ireland*

Interest as a factor in the transfer of training from the inculcation of mathematical principles to problems in reasoning. *D. T. Jones, M.A. 1937 London, Institute of Education*

An investigation into mathematical abilities most closely related to logical and critical thinking. *W. Bennett, M.A. 1948 London, Institute of Education*

La doctrine de l'a priori chez Aristote. *G. Casey, M.A. 1934 National University of Ireland*

L'évolution sémantique du mot 'raison' d'après les textes du XVIIe siècle. *R. H. Pickering, M.A. 1946 Manchester*

Logic and mathematics, with special reference to Bertrand Russell. *M. Kelleher, M.A. 1942 National University of Ireland*

Logic and the foundations of ethics. *H. P. Reichmann, D.Phil. 1943 Oxford*

The logical characteristics of expression. *M. MacDonald, Ph.D. 1934 London, University College*

The logical theory of the term: a critical examination of the traditional doctrine. *A. Klein, M.A. 1910 London*

Logical types from the axiomatic point of view. *O. Helmer-Hirschberg, Ph.D. 1936 London, Bedford College*

Lotze's logic and its relations to current logical doctrine in England. *B. Edgell, M.A. 1899 Wales*

Logic contd.
Many-valued logic. *A. Rose, M.Sc. 1950 Manchester*

Modern idealistic logic and the problem of relations. *H. B. Acon, D.Phil. 1935 Oxford*

A modern introduction to logic. *L. S. Stebbing, D.Litt. 1931 London, Bedford College*

Moral reasoning of the child and its relation to mental age. *M. K. Ahmed, M.A. 1936 London, University College*

The nature of logical constructions and their bearing on metaphysical analysis. *M. E. Daniels, Ph.D. 1933 London, Bedford College*

The place of reason in ethics. *S. E. Toulmin, Ph.D. 1949 Cambridge*

The primacy of the practical reason. *D. P. Jones, M.A. 1920 Liverpool*

The problem of error in the contribution of Kant to modern idealistic logic. *A. A. Lion, D.Phil. 1930 Oxford*

The province of logic and its relation to grammar, metaphysics, and psychology with special reference to the view of Cook Wilson. *R. G. F. Robinson, B.Litt. 1927 Oxford*

Psychological meaning with special reference to logical meaning. *R. S. Birch, Ph.D. 1927 Edinburgh*

The psychological study of reasoning. *J. D. Horgan, M.A. 1923 National University of Ireland*

The psychology of reasoning, being an experimental study of the mental processes involved in reasoning. *V. K. K. Menon, M.A. 1929 London*

The psychology of reasoning with special reference to educational problems. *E. V. Staynor, M.A. 1932 London, Day Training College*

Reason and the limits of reason. *F. E. Quick, M.A. 1933 Liverpool*

Reasoning in children from 7 to 11 years of age. *K. Nahapiet, M.A. 1933 Birmingham*

The reasoning of children aged 7 years. *S. B. Gupta, M.Ed. 1932 Leeds*

A study of certain doctrines found in Bosanquet's logic. *H. I. Davies, Ph.D. 1936 Cambridge*

A study of inductive reasoning in children of about 13 years of age. *M. M. Shukla, M.A. 1948 London, Institute of Education*

A study of the possibility of improving habits of thought in school children by a training in logic. *E. F. White, M.A. 1935 London, Institute of Education*

1. Tests of reasoning processes and their relation to general mental ability. 2. The mental differences between the sexes. *R. C. Moore, M.A. 1915 Liverpool*

The theory of logical types. *L. D. Bowden, B.Litt. 1950 Oxford*

Tractatus logicophilosophicus. L. Wittgenstein, M.Litt. 1929 Cambridge

Logos
The conception of the logos in Greek philosophy from 300 B.C. to 200 A.D. *K. M. Curtis, M.A. 1913 London*

The doctrine of the Word in relation to the Holy Scriptures as presented in the theology of Karl Barth. *J. Phillips, B.Litt. 1930 Oxford*

The early history of the logos doctrine - the idea in Greek philosophy, with an appendix showing its relation to Hellenism, Judaism and the New Testament. *J. L. Matthews, Ph.D. 1936 London, New College*

The foundations of the doctrine of the Logos in the prologue to the fourth gospel. *K. Harper, M.Litt. 1947 Durham*

1. The gradual development of the doctrine of a future life in Holy Scripture, with special reference to the teaching of St. Paul on the resurrection-body in I Corinthians xv. 2. The Logos-Christology deduced from the writings of St. Paul. *W. O. Jenkins, B.D. & D.D. 1907 Oxford*

1. The Logos as the interpreter of God the Father. 2. The Book of Job critically considered with special reference to the faith and needs of the present day. *P. D. Eyre, B.D. & D.D. 1900 Oxford*

1. Logos Christology: its validity and value. 2. The nature of the Gospel and its place in sacramental theology. *W. W. Longford, B.D. 1911 Oxford*

The relation of the doctrine of the Word of God to the doctrine of the *imago Dei*: a study in the theology of Karl Barth. *I. F. Morris, Ph.D. 1941 Edinburgh*

Lollards
See also Wycliffe, J.

The detection and trial of Lollards from 1414-1428. *K. M. Keeley, M.A. 1936 Manchester*

Lollard doctrine, with special reference to the controversy over image-worship and pilgrimages. *J. Crompton, B.Litt. 1950 Oxford*

Lollardry in London on the eve of the Reformation. *E. J. Davis, M.A. 1913 London*

Scottish Lollardry and its contribution to the Reformation in Scotland, with special reference to the Lollards of the West. *T. M. A. MacNab, Ph.D. 1933 Glasgow*

Wyclif and Lollardry in England. *W. H. Leighton, M.A. 1925 Birmingham*

Lombardy
Paul the Deacon, and the *Historia Langobardorum*. *M. H. Blyton, M.A. 1935 London, Birkbeck College*

Lomonossov, Mikhail
The chemical studies of Michael Lomonossov, 1711-1765. *Y. A. Bick, M.Sc. 1949 London, University College*

London
See also Battersea; Westminster.

Alien immigration into and alien communities in London, 1558 to 1640. *I. Scouloudi, M.Sc. 1936 London, School of Economics and Political Science*

The black-coated worker in London. *F. D. Klingender, Ph.D. 1934 London, School of Economics and Political Science*

A century's extension of passenger transport facilities (1830-1930) within the present London Transport Board's area, and its relation to population spread. *M. L. Moore, Ph.D. 1948 London, Birkbeck College*

Civic factions in London and their relation to political parties, 1376-99. *R. Bird, M.A. 1922 London*

The correspondence of the City of London. *G. F. Chapple, Ph.D. 1938 London, Birkbeck College*

An edition of 4 Charles I. Rot. Pat. 4 Car.I. 33A-33C: The Ditchfield Grant of September 25. *E. M. Lewis, M.A. 1930 Leeds*

The extent and value of the lands in London and Southwark occupied by the religious houses (including the prebends of St. Paul's and St. Martin's le Grand), the parish churches and churchyards, and the inns of the abbots and bishops, before the dissolution of the monasteries. *M. B. Honeybourne, M.A. 1930 London, Bedford College*

The financial relations between the Crown and the City of London in the reigns of Edward I to Henry VII (excluding Parliamentary taxation). *G. J. de C. Mead, M.A. 1936 London, King's College*

A history of the Italian exiles in London, 1816-1848. *M. C. W. Wicks, Ph.D. 1930 Edinburgh*

The housing legislation in England, 1851-67, with special reference to London. *V. Zoond, M.A. 1932 London, King's College*

The industrial history of London (1630-1640), with special reference to the suburbs and those areas claiming exemption from the authority of the Lord Mayor. *J. L. Archer, M.A. 1934 London, School of Economics and Political Science*

The land utilisation of the London basin: a study of the existing conditions and historical changes, 1840-1935. *E. C. Willatts, Ph.D. 1937 London, External Degree*

London, 1801-51: a geographical study. *O. H. K. Spate, Ph.D. 1938 Cambridge*

London and the Wars of the Roses, 1445-1461. *M. I. Peake, M.A. 1925 London*

The London coffee-houses, and their literary associations down to the death of Anne. *J. Williams, B.Litt. 1936 Oxford*

The London lighterage trade: its history, organisation and economics. *C. L. Wheble, M.Sc. 1939 London, School of Economics and Political Science*

The minor corporations of the secular cathedrals of the province of Canterbury (excluding the Welsh sees) between the thirteenth century and 1536, with special reference to the minor canons of St. Paul's Cathedral from their origin in the twelfth century to the visitations of Bishop Gilson in 1724. *A. R. B. Fuller, M.A. 1947 London, Birkbeck College*

Mr. Customer Smythe, customer of the Port of London, 1570-89. *L. L. S. Lowe, B.Litt. 1950 Oxford*

London contd.
The northeastern expansion of London since 1770. *H. Rees, M.Sc. 1946 London, School of Economics and Political Science*

The position of London in national affairs, 1658-1661, having special regard to political and economic aspects. *M. B. Weinstock, M.A. 1934 London, School of Economics and Political Science*

The present position of the housing problem in and around London. *A. H. Hogarth, D.M. 1908 Oxford*

Public borrowing, 1649-1660, with special reference to government borrowing in the City of London between 1640 and 1650. *W. P. Harper, M.Sc. 1927 London*

The recent industrialization of the northern and western sectors of Greater London. *D. H. Smith, Ph.D. 1933 London, Birkbeck College*

St. Stephen's Chapel and the architecture of the fourteenth century in London. *J. M. Hastings, Ph.D. 1947 Cambridge*

Some effects of the slum clearance schemes of the London County Council. *A. R. Holmes, M.Sc. 1947 London, School of Economics and Political Science*

A study of the merchant class of London in the fifteenth century, with special reference to the Company of Grocers. *S. L. Thrupp, Ph.D. 1931 London, University College*

A study of the nunnery of St. Mary Clerkenwell and its property with an edition of its cartulary. *W. O. Hassall, D.Phil. 1941 Oxford*

London Magazine
The London Magazine (1820-9). *T. R. Hughes, B.Litt. 1931 Oxford*

London Missionary Society
The London Missionary Society in South Africa during the years 1798-1836. *D. K. Clinton, B.Litt. 1935 Oxford*

Principles and characteristics of missionary policy during the last fifty years, as illustrated by the history of the London Missionary Society. *N. Goodall, D.Phil. 1950 Oxford*

Londonderry
The Londonderry plantation, with special reference to the resulting relations between the Crown and the city, 1609-41. *T. W. D. Moody, Ph.D. 1934 London, University College*

Longfield, S. Mountifort
Study of the economic writings of S. Mountifort Longfield. *R. D. C. Black, Ph.D. 1943 Dublin, Trinity College*

Longland, John, Bishop
The Reformation in the diocese of Lincoln as illustrated by the life and work of Bishop Longland (1521-47). *G. E. Wharhirst, B. Litt. 1938 Oxford*

Longuyon, Jacques de
Etude sur la langue de Jacques de Longuyon. *F. T. H. Fletcher, M.A. 1923 Birmingham*

Recherches sur la syntaxe de Jacques de Longuyon dans *les voeux du paon*, manuscript w. *W. T. Faulks, M.A. 1932 Birmingham*

Vénus et sa chambre dans *Les voeux du paon* de Jacques de Longuyon. *C. O. Gooderson, M.A. 1942 Birmingham*

Löns, Hermann
A study of the life, thought and works of Hermann Löns. *H. Heyworth, M.A. 1939 Leeds*

Lonsdale
A survey of the geographical factors that have controlled the history of Lonsdale. *M. E. Butler, M.A. 1921 Liverpool*

Lope de Vega
See Vega Carpio, L. F. de.

Lopez de Villalobos, Ruy
Lopez de Villalobos: a critical study. *J. Ballantine, M.A. 1932 Belfast*

Lords, House of
See Great Britain: Parliament.

Lord's Prayer
See Jesus Christ: Life and Teaching.

Lord's Supper
See Eucharist.

Lorraine
See Alsace.

Lorris, Guillaume de
See Guillaume, de Lorris.

Los Angeles
A geographical study of the Los Angeles region of southern California. *J. Garst, Ph.D. 1931 Edinburgh*

Loti, Pierre
La vie coloniale dans le roman anglais et français: étude sur Rudyard Kipling et Pierre Loti. *C. Frebault, M.A. 1926 Birmingham*

La vocation dans les romans de P. Loti. *P. I. Ross, M.A. 1927 Birmingham*

L'art de la prose chez Pierre Loti. *A. R. Wise, M.A. 1935 Birmingham*

Quelques aspects de l'étude de Pierre Loti. *D. M. Auld, M.A. 1929 Birmingham*

The religion of Pierre Loti. *F. Taylor, M.A. 1934 Manchester*

Lotze, Rudolf Hermann
Lotze's conception of divine personality. *M. Davies, M.A. 1910 London*

Lotze's logic and its relations to current logical doctrine in England. *B. Edgell, M.A. 1899 Wales*

Lotze's metaphysical unity of things. *S. Newman, M.A. 1910 London*

1. Lotze's theory of reality. 2. Lotze's relation to idealism. *E. E. Thomas, D.Litt. 1922 Wales*

The relation between Leibniz and Lotze. *E. E. Thomas, M.A. 1910 Wales*

The theistic philosophy of Hermann Lotze. *A. K. Rule, Ph.D. 1923 Edinburgh*

The theory of personality in modern philosophy from Kant to Lotze. *E. A. J. Berthen, M.A. 1911 London*

Louis IX, Saint, King of France
The crusades of St. Louis. *M. B. Thomason, M.A. 1913 Birmingham*

St. Louis: a study of medieval kingship. *W. A. Riley, M.A. 1917 Liverpool*

Louis Philippe, King of France
Louis Philippe. *C. I. Gavin, Ph.D. 1931 Aberdeen*

Louis Philippe's France as seen by English women. *E. Grünwald, Ph.D. 1948 London, University College*

Louisiana
Napoleon Bonaparte and the sale of Louisiana to the United States. *E. W. Lyon, B.Litt. 1928 Oxford*

Love
Andreas Capellanus' *De amore*: a re-interpretation. *M. W. Dickinson, M.A. 1950 Birmingham*

The elements in early Christianity, down to the end of the fourth century, which helped to prepare the way for later Christian intolerance, and the relation of these elements to the early Christian conception of God as love. *L. A. Garrard, B.D. 1935 Oxford*

The ethical idea of love and its central position in Christian ethics down to St. Cyprian. *Y. Davies, B.Litt. 1918 Oxford*

The Platonic conception of love in the work of Pontus de Tyard. *H. O. C. Phillips, M.A. 1949 Wales*

1. St. Paul's thorn in the flesh. 2. A critical examination of the use of $\varphi\iota\lambda\epsilon\div\nu$ and $\alpha\gamma\alpha\pi\alpha\nu$ in the New Testament, with special reference to the exegesis of St. John xxi.15-17. *J. M. Lister, B.D. & D.D. 1899 Oxford*

Shakespeare's philosophy of love. *W. F. Luckman, M.A. 1929 Birmingham*

Some aspects of R. Browning's philosophy of love. *J. G. Carson, M.A. 1920 Birmingham*

Some comparisons between Welsh and Irish love poetry. *M. A. Kennedy, M.A. 1943 National University of Ireland*

A study on friendship-love in adolescence. *N. M. Iovetz-Tereshchenko, Ph.D. 1933 London, King's College*

The treatment of love and marriage in classical Greek literature. *M. Wilkins, M.A. 1924 London*

Love, Christopher
The life and letters of Christopher Love, 1618-1651. *M. H. Jones, M.A. 1932 Wales*

The life of Christopher Love and his relation to contemporary movements. *C. G. Criddle, M.A. 1933 Wales*

Love, Nicholas
Nicholas Love's fifteenth century translation of the *Meditationes vitae Christi*: a study, with special reference to the Passion section. *E. Jones, M.A. 1949 London, Bedford College*

Lucan
Comparáid idir an *Pharsalia* agus an *Cath Cathardha* (*Pharsalia* and *Cath Cathardha* compared). *S. O'Luing, M.A. 1939 National University of Ireland*

The influence of the *Metamorphoses* of Ovid on Lucan. *E. S. Edees, M.A. 1931 Manchester*

Lucan contd.
Marcus Lucanus as a representative stoic and rhetorician of the Neronian period. *E. R. Thomas, M.A. 1920 Wales*

Lucanus, Marcus Annaeus
See Lucan.

Lucaris, Cyril
Cyril Lucaris, his life and works. *G. A. Hadjiantoniou, Ph.D. 1948 Edinburgh*

Lucian
Light thrown by the works of Lucian on contemporary life. *W. J. Gibb, Ph.D. 1929 London*

Lucian as a critic and lover of art. *D. G. Roberts, M.A. 1910 London*

Lucius Septimius Severus, Roman Emperor
The Emperor Lucius Septimius Severus. *M. Platnauer, B.Litt. 1915 Oxford*

Lucretius
Lucretius as translator of Epicurus: a study in poetical mood. *C. E. Pyke, M.A. 1939 Bristol*

The philosophy of Titus Lucretius Carus: its position in the history of thought and its relation to contemporary Roman life. *H. L. O'Connor, Ph.D. 1928 London*

The syntax of archaic Latin, with special reference to the usage of Catullus and Lucretius. *A. L. Thomas, M.A. 1913 Wales*

Luddites, The
The Luddite disturbances and the machinery of order. *F. O. Darvall, Ph.D. 1933 London, External Degree*

The Luddite disturbances throughout the cotton manufacturing area in 1812. *D. Halstead, M.A. 1917 Liverpool*

Luden, Heinrich
Heinrich Luden and the origins of the Luden Nationalist movement. *W. E. Brown, M.A. 1929 Birmingham*

Ludwig, Otto
Otto Ludwig's character portrayal. *D. M. Leek, B.Litt. 1948 Oxford*

Lully, Jean Baptiste
The recitative of Lully. *H. Ludlam, M.A. 1948 Sheffield*

Lumiere (la) as Lais
See Peckham, P. de.

Lussac, Gay
Gay Lussac's law of gaseous volumes and the influence on chemical theory up to 1860. *H. A. Filmer, M.Sc. 1928 London*

Lussan, Marguérite de
Marguérite de Lussan and the historical novel in the first half of the eighteenth century. *D. A. Cuff, Ph.D. 1932 Cambridge*

Lute Music
English lute music and its writers, from the earliest records until the introduction of the 'French' lute. *R. E. Newton, B.Litt. 1938 Oxford*

Luther, Martin
A comparison of the influence of Wycliffe and Luther upon the Reformation in England. *W. H. Leighton, M.A. 1927 Birmingham*

The development of Luther's conception of liberty as found in his early writings (until 1521). *W. F. Sunday, Ph.D. 1924 Edinburgh*

Disputatio I. Eccii et M. Lutheri, Lipsiae, Labita 1519: translation with critical introduction and notes. *A. McPherson, Ph.D. 1931 Edinburgh*

The doctrine of grace as illustrated by the experience and teaching of St. Paul, Augustine, and Luther. *R. L. Child, B.Litt. 1925 Oxford*

Englische Ubersetzungen von Martin Luthers geistlichen Liedern bis zum Jahre 1800. *H. Buchinger, M.A. 1939 Bristol*

Law and gospel and their relationship in the theology of Luther. *K. R. Bridston, Ph.D. 1949 Edinburgh*

Luther's doctrine of the Church in his early writings. *H. A. Preus, Ph.D. 1928 Edinburgh*

Luther's translation of the Bible in the light of humanistic scholarship. *W. Schwarz, Ph.D. 1949 London, University College*

Martin Luther as an educator. *G. E. Bell, M.Ed. 1949 Durham*

Lutheran Church
The conception of Church order and ministry under Luther and the early Lutheran Church considered in the light of non-Roman Christianity in Scandinavia, Germany, and the British Isles to-day. *H. H. W. Kramm, D.Phil. 1940 Oxford*

Luxborough, Henrietta, Baroness
Lady Luxborough and her circle. *B. M. A. Edge, M.A. 1930 Birmingham*

Luxemburg
The Grand Duchy of Luxembourg: its human and economic geography. *K. C. Edwards, Ph.D. 1948 London, External Degree*

The Luxemburg crisis of 1867, with special reference to British policy. *G. A. Craig, B.Litt. 1938 Oxford*

The policies of Stanley, Granville, and Gladstone towards Luxemburg, Belgium, and Alsace-Lorraine, 1867-1871. *M. R. D. Foot, B.Litt. 1950 Oxford*

Lycée Armoricain
Le développement des idées littéraires en Bretagne sous la Restauration vu dans les pages du *Lycée Armoricain*, 1823-1831. *L. A. Zaina, M.A. 1947 Liverpool*

Lycurgus
Grammatical characteristics of Lycurgus. *M. I. Thomas, M.A. 1907 London*

Lydgate, John
The influence of Chaucer, Gower, and Lydgate on the Scottish poets in the fifteenth and early sixteenth centuries. *P. W. Thomson, B.Litt. 1915 Oxford*

Lying
See Truth.

Lyly, John
The relation of Shakespeare to Lyly. *E. M. King, M.A. 1908 London*

Lyons
Lyons as a market of ideas from B.C. 43-1307 A.D. *M. Berryman, M.A. 1910 London*

Lyttleton, George, 1st Baron
The life and works of George, Lord Lyttleton, 1709-1773. *A. V. Rao, Ph.D. 1929 London*

Mabinogion
Cystrawen arddodiaid ym Mhedair Cainc y Mabinogi (The syntax of prepositions in the Four Branches of the Mabinogi). *M. Rees, M.A. 1935 Wales*

Cystrawen y frawddeg yn y Pedair Cainc yn Llyfr Gwyn Rhydderch (The syntax of the sentence in the Four Branches in the White Book of Rhydderch). *G. M. Richards, M.A. 1933 Wales*

The verbal forms in the *Mabinogion* and *Bruts*. *G. J. Williams, M.A. 1918 Wales*

The verbal forms of the *Mabinogion* and *Bruts*. *W. Griffith, M.A. 1904 Wales*

Mably, Gabriel Bonnot de
Gabriel Bonnot de Mably. *E. A. Whitfield, Ph.D. 1928 London*

Mably and Montesquieu. *R. Fargher, B.Litt. 1938 Oxford*

McAdam, John Loudon
John Loudon McAdam, colossus of roads. *R. H. Spiro, Ph.D. 1950 Edinburgh*

MacAingil, Aodh
Beatha agus saothar Aodha Mhic Aingil (The life and work of Aodh Mac Aingil). *T. O'Cléirigh, M.A. 1925 National University of Ireland*

MacAlpin, John
Dr. Johannes Macchabaeus (John MacAlpin): Scotland's contribution to the Reformation in Denmark. *M. A. F. Bredahl Petersen, Ph.D. 1937 Edinburgh*

Macarias, of Egypt, Saint
1. On anthropomorphism in Scripture and doctrine.
2. On seven new homilies of Macarias. *G. L. Marriott, B.D. 1918 Oxford*

Macartney, George, 1st Earl
Anglo-Chinese relations and the Macartney embassy (1775-1800). *E. H. Pritchard, D.Phil. 1933 Oxford*

Macaulay, Thomas Babington, 1st Baron Macaulay
Lord Macaulay and the Indian Legislative Council (1834-1838). *C. D. Dharkar, M.A. 1931 London, School of Oriental and African Studies*

Maccabees, Books of the
See Bible: Old Testament: Apocrypha.

Maccabees, Dynasty
See Jews: History.

MacCurdy, John Thomson
MacCurdy's doctrine of patterns. *C. E. Rees, M.Sc. 1930 Bristol*

Macdonald, George
The fairy tales and fantasies of George Macdonald. *M. M. McEldowney, B.Litt. 1934 Oxford*

Macedon
The rival claims of Sparta and Macedon to the leadership of Greece in the late third century B.C. *E. M. Green, M.A. 1924 London*

Rome, Greece and Macedon to 196 B.C. *M. Duggan, M.A. 1934 National University of Ireland*

Macedonia
Ethnographic maps of Macedonia, 1730-1918. *H. R. Wilkinson, M.A. 1948 Liverpool*

Machabaeus, Johannes
See MacAlpin, J.

Machaut, Guillaume de
See Guillaume, de Machaut.

Machen, Arthur
The life and works of Arthur Machen, with special reference to his novels and tales. *D. P. M. Michael, M.A. 1940 Wales*

Machiavelli, Niccolo di Bernardo dei
Machiavelli. *G. D. Freyer, Ph.D. 1940 Dublin, Trinity College*

Machin, Lewis
A critical study of *The Fair maid of the exchange* and its attribution to Thomas Heywood, and the relation of the play to Markham and Machin's *Dumb knight* and the works of John Day and Thomas Dekker. *S. R. Golding, M.A. 1922 London*

Machworth, Humphrey, Sir
An examination of Sir Humphrey Machworth's industrial activities, with special reference to the Governor and Company of the Mine Adventurers of England. *S. Evans, M.A. 1950 Wales*

Mackenzie, Henry
The novels of Henry Mackenzie. *P. Bradszky, M.A. 1941 Birmingham*

A study of Henry Mackenzie. *H. M. Richmond, Ph.D. 1923 London*

McLean, Archibald
Archibald McLean, 1733-1812, Baptist pioneer in Scotland. *R. D. Mitchell, D. 1950 Edinburgh*

MacLeod, Henry Dunning
The economics of Henry Dunning MacLeod. *J. S. Pattison, Ph.D. 1940 London, School of Economics and Political Science*

Macpherson, James
The influence of Ossian on the chief French writers of the Romantic period. *D. J. Lewis, M.A. 1909 Wales*

Macpherson's *Ossian*. *L. E. Fitter, M.A. 1908 Birmingham*

Macpherson's *Ossian* and its relation to English literature from 1760 to 1850. *E. O'Connor, M.A. 1939 National University of Ireland*

Macpherson's *Ossian* in the works of Johann Gottfried v. Herder. *H. T. Betteridge, M.A. 1933 Birmingham*

MacPiarais, Pádraig
An tAthair Peadar Ua Laoghaire agus Pádraig Mac Piarais, i gcomh-mheas agus i gcodarsna (Father Peadar Ua Laoghaire and Pádraig Mac Piarais, compared and contrasted). *B. Pléamonn, M.A. 1943 National University of Ireland*

Tráchtas ar Phádraig Mac Piarais (A thesis on Pádraig Mac Piarais). *S. C. O'Morain, M.A. 1931 National University of Ireland*

Macquarie, Lachlan
A colonial autocracy: New South Wales under Governor Macquarie, 1810-1821. *M. Phillips, D.Sc. 1908 London*

Macquarie, Governor of New South Wales, 1809-1821. *B. H. Travers, B.Litt. 1949 Oxford*

Macrae, Clan
History of the clan Macrae. *A. Macrae, M.A. 1905 London*

Macro, Cox
Bury St. Edmund's as a literary centre, with particular reference to the activities of Miles Blomefield, b.1525, and Cox Macro, 1683-1767. *K. W. Dean, M.A. 1925 London*

Macrobius, Ambrosius Theodosius
A study of Virgil's methods of adapting Homer, based on Macrobius's list of parallel passages. *R. F. Morgan, M.A. 1936 Wales*

McTaggart, John McTaggart Ellis
A comparison of the teachings of Spinoza and McTaggart on immortality. *H. V. M. Jones, M.A. 1936 Wales*

The treatment of the idea of the individual in the philosophies of Bernard Bosanquet, J. M. E. McTaggart and A. N. Whitehead. *B. E. Jones, M.A. 1942 Manchester*

Madagascar
British imperial policy in relation to Madagascar, 1810-1896. *R. E. P. Wastell, Ph.D. 1944 London, King's College*

Madras
A geographical study of Madras City. *G. D. Watkins, M.Sc. 1929 London*

Local self-government in the Madras Presidency, 1850-1919. *K. K. Pillay, D.Phil. 1948 Oxford*

Relations of the Governor General and Council with the Governor and Council of Madras under the Regulation Act, 1773. *A. Dasgupta, Ph.D. 1930 London, School of Oriental and African Studies*

Some problems of urbanization in India: based on a study of Madras City. *C. W. Ranson, B.Litt 1937 Oxford*

Madrigals
See also Weelkes, T.

Italian influence on the Elizabethan lyrics, more especially in connection with madrigals connection with madrigals. *C. K. Saunders, M.A. 1909 London*

Maeterlinck, Maurice, Count
Maurice Maeterlinck: a study of the development of his drama and philosophy. *J. C. Hartley, M.A. 1950 Sheffield*

Quelques aspects de Maurice Maeterlinck. *G. I. Wanklin, M.A. 1928 Birmingham*

Magadha
Decline of the kingdom of Magadha from *c.*455 A.D. to *c.*1000 A.D. *B. P. Sinha, Ph.D. 1948 London, School of Oriental and African Studies*

Mithila and Magadha, 700 A.D.-1100 A.D. *L. Jha, Ph.D. 1948 London, School of Oriental and African Studies*

Origin and development of Māgadhī. *A. Banerji Sastri, D.Phil. 1922 Oxford*

Magic
Anglo-Saxon magic. *H. J. R. Money-Kyrle, B.Sc. 1924 Oxford*

A comparative study of magical practices among the Anglo-Saxons. *W. Bonser, Ph.D. 1927 London*

Demonology, magic, and witchcraft in the English drama, 1580-1642. *F. M. N. Trefethen, M.Litt. 1950 Cambridge*

Early law and religion: a study in the relationship between the primitive rules of law and the early ideas of magic and religion. *H. N. Wright, LL.D. 1919 London*

The language of suggestion, magic and propaganda. *A. O. Waligorski, Ph.D. 1938 London, School of Economics and Political Science*

Magic in Greek and Latin literature. *J. E. Lowe, M.A. 1922 London*

The magical element in the calendar of Numa. *A. P. Hyslop, Ph.D. 1925 Aberdeen*

Magical jewels of the Middle Ages and Renaissance, particularly in England. *J. Evans, Cert.Litt. 1920 Oxford*

Magico-religious beliefs and practices in primitive society: a sociological interpretation of their therapeutic aspects. *K. R. Stewart, Ph.D. 1948 London, School of Economics and Political Science*

On initiative magic. *R. F. Fortune, Dip. Anthropology. 1912 Cambridge*

The relation of ritual to belief in primitive cult, with special reference to the magico-religious customs of the Australian Aborigines. *E. O. James, B.Litt. 1916 Oxford*

Some aspects of the relation of primitive medicine to magic. *B. M. Broadhurst, B.Sc. 1928 Oxford*

Magna Carta
See Great Britain: History: Early and Medieval.

Magnetism
An outline of the development of ideas on magnetism from 1600-1820. *F. S. Hansford, M.Sc. 1931 London*

Magnetism, Terrestrial
Edmond Halley and the problems of terrestrial magnetism. *A. C. Williams, M.Sc. 1937 London, University College*

Experimental methods in terrestrial magnetism in the late eighteenth and early nineteenth centuries. *F. Butler, M.Sc. 1934 London, University College*

The work of Hansteen and Gauss on the law of magnetic force, with some account of the work of their predecessors. *J. J. Reynolds, M.Sc. 1949 London, University College*

Mahabharata, The
The social and legal position of women in ancient India as represented by a critical study of the epics: the *Mahabharata* and the *Ramayana*. *S. N. Ajgaonkar, D.Phil. 1927 Oxford*

Maharashtra
The political history of Maharashtra from the earliest times to circa 1000 A.D. *V. R. Deoras, Ph.D. 1940 London, School of Oriental and African Studies*

Mahavamsa
1. Dictionary of Pali Proper Names. 2. Vamsatthappakasini, or commentary on the *Mahaevamsa*. 3. The extended *Mahaevamsa*. *G. P. Malalasekera, D. Lit. 1938 London, External Degree*

A historical criticism of *Mahavamsa*. *G. C. Mendis, Ph.D. 1931 London, School of Oriental and African Studies*

Mahayana
See Philosophy: India.

Mahmūd, Sultan of Ghazna
Sultán Mahmúd of Ghazna and his times. *M. Nazim, Ph.D. 1928 Cambridge*

Mahratta, The
See Marathi, The.

Maidstone
Historical geography of Maidstone. *V. E. Morant, M.A. 1948 London, Birkbeck College*

Mailu
The natives of Mailu: preliminary results of the Robert Mond research work in British New Guinea. *S. G. Malinowski, D.Sc. 1916 London*

Maimonides, Moses
A critical discussion of the sources of Spinoza, with special reference to Maimonides and Descartes. *H. L. Roth, D.Phil. 1922 Oxford*

Maimonides on the Jewish creed. *J. Abelson, M.A. 1909 London*

The social and political ideas of Maimonides. *Z. Schwarz, M.Sc. 1926 London*

Maine, Henry James Sumner, Sir
Critics of democracy: Carlyle, Arnold, Stephen (Fitzjames), Maine, Lecky. *B. E. Lippincott, Ph.D. 1931 London, School of Economics and Political Science*

Maintenon, Françoise d'Aubigné de, Marquise
A contribution to the history of the educational tradition inherited from Madame de Maintenon. *M. S. Smith, Ph.D. 1927 London*

Les idées de Madame de Maintenon sur l'éducation des filles, comparées à celles qui ont cours à notre époque. *L. F. Barker, M.A. 1912 Liverpool*

Madame de Maintenon. *A. Crutchley, M.A. 1912 Birmingham*

Madame de Maintenon and Saint Cyr. *H. C. Barnard, M.A. 1928 London*

Máire
See O'Grianna, S.

Mairet, Jean
Jean Mairet and his tragedies. *J. C. Mahoney, B.Litt. 1932 Oxford*

Maitland, Thomas, Sir
The colonial administrations of Sir Thomas Maitland. *G. W. Dixon, B.Litt. 1938 Oxford*

The Ionian Islands under the administration of Sir Thomas Maitland, 1816-1824. *B. R. Pearn, M.A. 1924 London*

Makerfield, Lancashire
Historical geography of the Makerfield district in south Lancashire. *H. Fairhurst, M.A. 1922 Liverpool*

Malabar
Deviations from the Anglo-Muhammadan law with reference to the Maplahs of Malabar. *H. Ali, LL.D. 1931 London, University College*

Malatesta, Family
The Malatesta of Rimini. *P. J. Jones, D.Phil. 1950 Oxford*

Malaya
See Malaysia.

Malayalam Language and Literature
See also Ezuttaccan.

Indo-Aryan loan-words in Malayalam, with a study of some Dravidian loans in Sanskrit. *K. G. Varma, Ph.D. 1934 London, School of Oriental and African Studies*

Malaysia
British Malaya, 1824-1867, with an introductory sketch of its history from 1786-1824. *L. A. Mills, Ph.D. 1924 Oxford*

Malaysia contd.
A geographical study of the population problems of Malaysia. *B. M. Husain, M.A. 1942 Liverpool*

Malaya, with special reference to the influence of soil and climate conditions on agriculture. *A. W. King, M.A. 1936 Bristol*

The political geography of Malaya. *E. H. G. Dobby, Ph.D. 1945 London, Birkbeck College*

Maldon, Battle of
The Battle of Maldon. *E. D. Laborde, Ph.D. 1931 London, External Degree*

Malebranche, Nicolas
Antoine Arnauld's critique of Malebranche's philosophy as it is contained in *Des vraies et des fausses idées*. *R. V. Larmour, M.A. 1945 Belfast*

Berkeley and Malebranche. *A. A. Luce, Litt.D. 1943 Dublin, Trinity College*

A comparison of the philosophic systems of Malebranche and Berkeley. *V. S. Jha, Ph.D. 1927 London*

A critical exposition of the theory of knowledge in Malebranche. *R. W. Church, D.Phil. 1930 Oxford*

A critical study of John Locke's examination of Père Malebranche's opinion of seeing all things in God. *C. G. Jones, M.A. 1949 Wales*

The metaphysic of Malebranche. *M. Ginsberg, M.A. 1915 London*

The philosophical positions of Malebranche and Berkeley. *M. Ross, M.A. 1920 London*

The vision of God in St. Augustine and Malebranche: a comparison. *D. Connell, M.A. 1947 National University of Ireland*

Malecites
Studies in the life and culture of the Malecites and Micmacs. *W. H. Mechling, B.Litt. 1916 Oxford*

Mallarmé, Stéphane
The esthetics of Stephane Mallarmé: a study in development. *J. M. Cocking, M.A. 1939 London, King's College*

Paul Valéry and the Mallarmean heritage: a literary and psychological study. *R. S. Jones, Ph.D. 1949 London, King's College*

Malone, Edmond
The correspondence between Edmond Malone and Thomas Percy (preserved in the Bodleian in mss. 26, 27, 37 and 39). *A. Tillotson, B.Litt. 1933 Oxford*

Malone as Shakespearean commentator. *M. Hanly, M.A. 1913 National University of Ireland*

Malory, Thomas, Sir
The Arthurian legend in English literature down to and including Malory. *M. D. Jones, M.A. 1908 Wales*

The romance of *Tristan and Iseult* in Malory's *Le Morte Darthur*: a study of the sources. *E. Vinaver, B.Litt. 1922 Oxford*

The sources of book V of Malory's *Morte d'Arthur* and his treatment of them. *T. Vorontzoff, B.Litt. 1936 Oxford*

Malta
Malta as a British colony, 1824-1851. *H. I. Lee, M.A. 1949 London, Bedford College*

The physical and agricultural geography of the Maltese Islands. *A. Rushton, M.Sc. 1948 London, External Degree*

Maltese Language
The structure of Maltese: a study in mixed grammar and vocabulary. *J. Aquilina, Ph.D. 1940 London, School of Oriental and African Studies*

Malthus, Thomas Robert
Influence of Malthus on economic thought. *C. S. Harrington, M.A. 1915 National University of Ireland*

Malthus and his relation to contemporary economic writers. *W. Rees, M.A. 1927 Wales*

Man
See also Anthropology.

A brief sketch of the Hebrew conception of man in the Old Testament. *D. J. Jenkins, M.A. 1937 Wales*

The conception of creation considered in its bearing upon the relation of the finite individual to God. *M. E. Clarke, M.A. 1920 London*

A critical examination of the interpretation of man in the early writings of Karl Marx. *M. M. Davies, M.A. 1948 Wales*

Evolution and the spirit of man. *J. P. Milum, Ph.D. 1926 London*

Man contd.
Feuerbach's reconstruction of philosophy as the study of man. *R. Bach, M.A. 1948 London, Birkbeck College*

The image of God in man: an enquiry into the doctrine of human nature. *L. J. Carter, D.D. 1943 Durham*

Jesus' conception of man in the Synoptic Gospels. *D. K. Allen, Ph.D. 1928 Edinburgh*

Jesus' teaching on man and modern psychological theories. *M. B. Birnie, M.A. 1947 Bristol*

The natural man and the noble savage in English literature in the seventeenth and eighteenth centuries. *W. T. Foster, B.Litt. 1916 Oxford*

The nature, need and destiny of man in Jewish thought from the Exile to the Advent. *J. R. Roberts, M.A. 1941 Wales*

The nature of man. *H. A. Watson, D.D. 1911 Cambridge*

The nature of man in the living religions. *F. H. Hilliard, Ph.D. 1944 London, King's College*

The relation between the psychological and religious interpretations of man. *B. W. De Mel, B.Litt. 1947 Oxford*

Management
See Agriculture; Business Management; Industrial Management.

Manchukuo
The economic organization of Manchoukuo, with particular reference to specific features exemplifying the special characteristics of the modern economic system in the Far East. *E. S. Kirby, Ph.D. 1938 London, External Degree*

Manchuria
The colonization and settlement of Manchuria. *A. Gaskell, M.A. 1932 Liverpool*

The Geneva treatment of the Manchurian and Abyssinian crises. *M. P. Lee, Ph.D. 1946 London, School of Economics and Political Science*

Notes on the Reindeer Tungus of Manchuria. *E. J. Lindgren, Ph.D. 1936 Cambridge*

The presentation of the Manchurian Question in the English press 1931-1933. *K. C. Cheng, Ph.D. 1938 London, School of Economics and Political Science*

Mandates
See League of Nations.

Mangan, James Clarence
James Clarence Mangan. *L. Mangan, M.A. 1932 National University of Ireland*

Mangan als Übersetzer Schillers. *P. Reilly, M.A. 1946 National University of Ireland*

Manilius
Manilius. *C. T. H. Walker, B.Litt. 1902 Oxford*

Mann, Thomas
Die Synthese des Bürgers und des Künstlers bei Thomas Mann. *P. Reilly, Ph.D. 1949 National University of Ireland*

The reception of Thomas Mann in England and America, a critical study. *D. A. R. H. Webster, M.A. 1940 London, University College*

Recurrent themes in the works of Thomas Mann. *J. M. Lindsay, Ph.D. 1950 Aberdeen*

Thoman Mann's writings on Goethe (with special reference to his novel *Lotte in Weimar*. *R. W. E. Weil, B.Litt. 1950 Dublin, Trinity College*

Thomas Mann: a study of his work in relation to the main currents of thought in nineteenth-century Germany. *E. Heller, Ph.D. 1948 Cambridge*

Thomas Mann: the development of his social philosophy and its relation to his art. *D. N. Mitchell, M.A. 1945 Leeds*

Thomas Mann's relation to Goethe and its significance for his own development. *H. Eichner, Ph.D. 1949 London, University College*

Mannyng, Robert
The establishment of the original text of Peter Langtoft's chronicle, part 2, as translated by Robert Mannyng of Brunne, by a collation of the two extant mss. - Petyt ms. 511, vol. 7, in the Inner Temple Library and Lambeth ms. 131, in the Lambeth Palace Library. *W. E. Porter, M.A. 1930 Leeds*

Manorial Life, Manors
See Feudalism.

Manpower
See Labour.

Mansfield, Katherine
The art of Katherine Mansfield. *Y. Servais, M.A. 1937 National University of Ireland*

Manticism
See Prophecy.

Manual Dexterity
See Motor Performance.

Manuel des Péchés
See William, of Waddington.

Manuscripts
See also Book Illustration.

The annotations of Ekkehart IV in the Orosius ms. St. Gall 621: a contribution to the question of the nature of ancient glosses. *J. N. C. Clark, Ph.D. 1931 Edinburgh*

Clár na láimhscríbhinní san leabharlainn, Coláiste no hOllscoile Corcaigh (Catalogue of manuscripts in the library of University College, Cork). *M. E. O'Donoghue, Ph.D. 1943 National University of Ireland*

Codex Climaci rescriptus graecus. *I. A. Moir, Ph.D. 1943 Cambridge*

A descriptive catalogue of the mss. in the library at University College, London, with an appendix of unpublished medieval German documents. *D. K. Coveney, Ph.D. 1930 London, University College*

Eagar ar shleachta as 24 p9 (An edition of extracts from ms. 24 p9). *B. O'hUallacháin, M.A. 1941 National University of Ireland*

A palaeographical study of the manuscript of Cicero's *De Oratore* (Harl. 2736) in the British Museum. *H. L. Macdonald, M.A. 1924 London*

The rise and development of the Ketubah. *J. Statman, M.A. 1910 London*

A study of the additions and alterations in mss. Bodley 340 and 342. *N. R. Ker, B.Litt. 1933 Oxford*

Manzoni, Alessandro
Alessandro Manzoni's writings on the Italian language: a chronological reconstruction. *E. M. B. Reynolds, Ph.D. 1948 London, University College*

Manzoni. *E. Volpi, M.A. 1941 National University of Ireland*

Maolmodach, Saint
Beatha Mhaolmhodaigh naomhtha (The life of St. Maolmodach). *S. MacOireachtaigh, M.A. 1934 National University of Ireland*

Maori, The
Briton and Maori: a comparative study of the relations between the races, 1840-1848. *S. E. Greville, M.A. 1910 London*

The effect of civilization on the Maori race, with special reference to health and disease. *J. A. Courie, M.D. 1913 Glasgow*

Maps
See also Geography.

An analysis of the cartographical material in John Speed's *Theatre of the Empire of Great Britaine*. *M. B. John, M.Sc. 1945 Wales*

An analysis of the 'one-inch to the mile' ordnance survey map of Great Britain, with special reference to the methods of production and the persistence or change of conventional symbols throughout successive editions of the map. *D. E. Roberts, M.Sc. 1946 Wales*

Aspects of modern cartography. *I. J. Curnow, Ph.D. 1925 London*

Erosion levels of the river Avon drainage basin: a comparative account of the various methods of cartographic analysis. *R. A. Yates, M.Sc. 1950 Bristol*

Ethnographic maps of Macedonia, 1730-1918. *H. R. Wilkinson, M.A. 1948 Liverpool*

The history of cartographical symbols. *E. M. J. Campbell, M.A. 1946 London, Birkbeck College*

The life and writings of John Cary. *H. T. Lane, M.A. 1932 Bristol*

The mapping of West Africa in the fourteenth and fifteenth centuries, as illustrative of the development of geographical ideas. *G. H. Kimble, M.A. 1931 London, King's College*

The psychology of the use of a map. *W. C. Quayle, M.A. 1916 Liverpool*

Recent developments in the mathematical theory of mapping. *D. Grindley, M.A. 1929 Wales*

The teaching of geography in the secondary school, with special reference to maps and map-work. *P. G. Moss, M.A. 1931 Liverpool*

Maquer, P. J
The chemical studies of P. J. Maquer (1718-1784). *L. J. M. Coleby, M.Sc. 1935 London, University College*

Marathi Language
Kanarese influence in Old Marathi (Jñānesvari). *R. V. Jahagirdar, M.A. 1928 London*

Some problems in the nasalization of Marāthī. *V. N. Sardesai, M.A. 1929 London*

Marathi, The
Matheran folk songs. *M. Macmillan, D.Litt. 1903 Birmingham*

The military system of the Mahrattas: its origin and development from the time of Shivaji to the fall of the Mahratta Empire. *S. Sen, B.Litt. 1927 Oxford*

The religious observances ordained for every day of the Hindu year, with special reference to customs observed in the Maratha country, together with the origin of these observances, whether traceable to legends, astronomical causes, or other sources. *M. M. Underhill, B.Litt. 1921 Oxford*

Marchmont, Earl of
A special enquiry into agricultural developments during the mid-eighteenth century on the estate of the Earl of Marchmont in Berwickshire. *G. S. Maxton, Ph.D. 1935 Edinburgh*

Marcion
Marcion and his influence. *E. C. Blackman, B.D. 1947 Cambridge*

Margaret, Queen of Navarre
The inspiration and sources of Marguerite de Navarre. *E. M. Jones, M.A. 1929 Wales*

Margaret, Saint, Queen of Scotland
The Anglo-Norman versions of the life of St. Margaret. *E. A. Francis, M.A. 1922 London*

An edition of *Seinte Marherta*. *F. M. Mack, Ph.D. 1934 London, King's College*

An edition of the *Prose life of St. Margaret (Seinte Marherete)*, based on ms. Bodley 34 and ms. Reg. 17.A.XXVII, with a grammar and a glossary which will consider parallels in other texts of the same group. *R. A. Crook, B.Litt. 1929 Oxford*

Queen Margaret and the influence she exerted on the Celtic Church in Scotland. *T. R. Barnett, Ph.D. 1925 Edinburgh*

Welsh hagiography with special reference to Saint Margaret. *H. Hughes- Roberts, M.A. 1949 Liverpool*

Margarit, Joan, Cardinal
The life, works and ideas of Cardinal Margarit. *R. B. Tate, M.A. 1950 Belfast*

Margary Affair
The Margary Affair and the Convention of Chefoo. *S. T. Wang, B.Litt. 1938 Oxford*

Marguerite, de Navarre
See Margaret, Queen of Navarre.

Margueritte, Paul
Le roman russe en France à la fin du dix-neuvième siècle considéré au point de vue de l'influence exercée par Tolstoi sur Paul Margueritte et Romain Rolland. *L. Godinski, Ph.D. 1923 London*

Mari
The city of Mari, with special reference to the archaeological material. *B. E. Morgan, M.A. 1950 Manchester*

Mariana, Juan
People v. prince: some political doctrines of Mariana and the early Jesuits. *S. G. Griffin, M.A. 1931 National University of Ireland*

Marie Antoinette, Queen of France
Marie Antoinette and the French Revolution. *R. E. A. Jones, M.A. 1946 Wales*

Marie de France
The syntax of Marie de France as studied in her *Lais*. *J. B. Davies, M.A. 1938 Wales*

Marien Himmelfahrt
Marien Himmelfahrt: ein mittelhochdeutsches Gedicht kritisch. *F. Norman, M.A. 1925 London*

Maritain, Jacques
The Christian interpretation of history as exemplified in the writings of Jacques Maritain and Reinhold Niebuhr. *W. E. Tyree, Ph.D. 1949 Edinburgh*

Maritime Law
See also Commercial Law; Smuggling; Territorial Waters.

The doctrine of continuous voyage, 1756-1815. *O. H. Mootham, M.Sc. 1926 London*

Evolution in the law and practice of blockade. *J. S. Bridges, LL.D. 1919 London*

An introduction to English maritime and commercial law. *F. R. Sanborn, Ph.D. 1924 Oxford*

The law of maritime liens. *J. G. T. Price, LL.D. 1940 Wales*

Maritime Law contd.
The law of private property at sea in time of war. *R. J. W. Hurd, LL.D. 1915 London*

The law of the foreshore and the right of access thereto. *W. Bennison, LL.D. 1914 London*

Maritime settlements and disputes. *C. T. Sutton, M.Com. 1936 London, School of Economics and Political Science*

The origin of the sea codes. *R. F. Wright, LL.D. 1943 Dublin, Trinity College*

Prize law during the Great War. *C. J. Colombo, LL.D. 1925 London*

The recent history of the law of maritime liens. *J. G. T. Price, M.A. 1935 Wales*

Maritime Provinces, The
Geographical factors in the development of the Maritime Provinces. *A. S. Gaught, M.A. 1932 London, King's College*

Marivaux, Pierre Carlet de Chamblain de
La comédie en France entre Molière et Marivaux. *W. C. Donlon, M.A. 1937 London, King's College*

Marivaux' debt to his predecessors in the drama. *L. N. Laurier, Ph.D. 1941 London, King's College*

Market Gardening
See Horticulture.

Marketing
Co-operative marketing of agricultural products. *M. Murphy, M.A. 1928 National University of Ireland*

The economic implications of conditions in the production and marketing of primary commodities since the Great War. *C. H. Thompson, M.Com. 1939 Birmingham*

The history of the development of studies in the marketing of agricultural produce and theories of marketing reforms, with some reference to the development of marketing studies in India. *A. Joshua, M.Sc. 1936 Wales*

The marketing of Australian and New Zealand primary products. *W. M. Smith, Ph.D. 1932 London, School of Economics and Political Science*

The marketing of non-ferrous metals. *H. L. Ellis, M.Com. 1926 Birmingham*

Marketing of perishable agricultural products. *W. Mesiha, M.Com. 1930 Birmingham*

Marketing research. *D. A. Holmes, M.A. 1946 National University of Ireland*

Production policies and their impact on problems of marketing and international trade in modern Egypt. *G. E. M. A. Said, Ph.D. 1949 Birmingham*

A study of methods of investigation and research in marketing, and an assessment of their contributions to the solution of problems of producers and to the general economic efficiency of the organizations lying between producers and consumers. *M. B. Ghatge, Ph.D. 1936 Wales*

Markets
Athenian agora. *J. P. Doherty, M.A. 1949 National University of Ireland*

A comparative study of the *fora* of the Roman Empire. *I. Purchon, M.A. 1933 Wales*

Yorkshire fairs and markets to the end of the eighteenth century. *K. L. McCutcheon, M.Litt. 1935 Durham*

Markham, Gervase
A critical study of *The Fair maid of the exchange* and its attribution to Thomas Heywood, and the relation of the play to Markham and Machin's *Dumb knight* and the works of John Day and Thomas Dekker. *S. R. Golding, M.A. 1922 London*

Marlborough Grammar School
The history of Marlborough Grammar School, 1550-1944, with some account of the medieval Hospital of St. John Baptist, Marlborough. *A. R. Stedman, M.A. 1945 London, King's College*

Marlowe, Christopher
Art of Marlowe. *E. MacLaughlin, M.A. 1916 National University of Ireland*

The development of Marlowe's attitude towards aspiration. *A. Hinchliffe, M.A. 1948 Manchester*

An elucidation of the death of Christopher Marlowe, through an examination of the lives and interests of certain of his associates. *E. W. de Kalb, Ph.D. 1929 Cambridge*

Marlowe's influence on Shakespeare and *Richard III*. *J. Gately, M.A. 1912 National University of Ireland*

Marlowe's presentation of human destiny. *R. V. Johnson, M.A. 1949 Manchester*

Marot, Clément
The poetry of Clément Marot. *M. A. H. Bradbury, M.A. 1915 Belfast*

Marprelate, Martin
John Penry and the Marprelate controversy in the light of recent research. *D. D. Phillips, M.A. 1914 Wales*

Marriage
See also Adultery.

An analysis, with commentary, of Saint Augustine of Hippo's treatises on marriage, the *De bono conjugali*, the *De adulterinis conjugiis* and the *De nuptiis et concupiscentia*. *G. G. Willis, M.A. 1939 Manchester*

A comparative study of bride wealth in Africa, with special reference to kinship structure and tribal organization. *M. M. Tew, B.Sc. 1948 Oxford*

Comparison between the divorce law of the British Commonwealth, U.S.A., and certain continental systems of law, with particular regard to the execution of foreign judgments. *F. Welt, Ph.D. 1941 Edinburgh*

Customary law of Buddhist marriages in British Burma. *Maung Thein, Ph.D. 1941 London, University College*

The development of marriage in ancient India. *B. C. Paul, Ph.D. 1949 London, School of Oriental and African Studies*

The development of sacramental ideas in relation to the institution of marriage. *A. E. Smart, M.A. 1942 Leeds*

Foreign marriages and divorces: the rules of private international law relating to marriage and divorce. *W. E. Wilkinson, LL.D. 1918 London*

The Halakah in Pseudojonathan on the Pentateuch (Part 1: Festivals and marriage laws). *E. Wiesenberg, Ph.D. 1952 London, Jews' College*

The history and nature of the dowry among the ancient Greeks. *F. A. Collie, M.A. 1905 Wales*

1. The history of marriage and divorce. 2. The development of monogamy among the Jews in the Old Testament. *S. A. Leathley, B.D. & D.D. 1916 Oxford*

Marriage and family life among educated Africans in urban areas of the Gold Coast. *A. I. Crabtree, M.Sc. 1949 London, School of Economics and Political Science*

Marriage law and ceremonial in the Code of Hammarapi. *J. Paterson, Ph.D. 1929 Glasgow*

Matrimonial causes in the conflict of laws: a comparative study. *J. G. Fleming, D.Phil. 1948 Oxford*

Muslim law of marriage. *M. U. I. S. Jung, LL.D. 1926 Dublin, Trinity College*

The problem of the second marriage of priests in the Orthodox Church of the East. *M. Yanoshevitch, B.Litt. 1921 Oxford*

Regulation of marriage in the New Hebrides. *T. T. Barnard, Ph.D. 1924 Cambridge*

The rise and development of the Ketubah. *J. Statman, M.A. 1910 London*

The sacred ministry and its relation to marriage in the Holy Eastern Orthodox Church. *C. Knetes, B.Litt. 1909 Oxford*

The treatment of love and marriage in classical Greek literature. *M. Wilkins, M.A. 1924 London*

Mars
The meaning and the development of the cult of Mars at Rome. *E. H. Clement, B.Litt. 1939 Oxford*

Marsden, Samuel
Samuel Marsden: a pioneer of civilization in the South Seas. *S. M. Johnstone, M.A. 1928 Belfast*

Marshall, Arthur
Alfred Marshall as an economist, with special reference to wages and working class. *P. Whelan, M.Econ.Sc. 1945 National University of Ireland*

Marshlands
See Fens.

Marsilius, of Padua
The *Defensor minor* of Marsilius de Mainardini of Padua. *C. K. Brampton, B.Litt. 1922 Oxford*

The *Defensor pacis* of Marsilio of Padua and John of Jandun: its relation to political theories developed in France during the reign of Philip IV. *M. J. Tooley, M.A. 1921 London*

Marston, John
The dramatic art of John Marston. *D. M. R. Salter, M.A. 1920 Bristol*

John Marston. *R. E. Brettle, D.Phil. 1927 Oxford*

Marston, John contd.
A study of agnosticism and intellectual doubt in the age of Shakespeare as expressed in the literature of the period, with special reference to Marston and the Inns of Court circle. *M. G. Chamberlain, M.A. 1934 London, King's College*

A study of John Marston as a satirist, considered generally and with special reference to contemporary writers. *R. C. Davies, M.A. 1922 London*

A study of John Marston's satires, 1598-9. *R. P. Warren, B.Litt. 1930 Oxford*

Martial
A century of epigrams: the influence of Latin epigram upon English epigram in the Elizabethan age, with special reference to Martial. *P. B. Corbett, M.A. 1938 Sheffield*

The history of the Flavian period, and in particular of the reign of Domitian, especially as reflected in the works of the poets Juvenal, Martial, and Statius. *A. G. Barnes, M.A. 1936 Manchester*

Roman life and manners as depicted in Martial and Juvenal. *M. Lamb, M.A. 1920 London*

Martineau, James
The theism of James Martineau. *G. O. McCulloh, Ph.D. 1938 Edinburgh*

Martinelli, Vincenzo
Vincenzo Martinelli and his circle in London, 1748-1774. *E. H. Thorne, Ph.D. 1946 London, University College*

Martyrdom
See Saints.

Marvell, Andrew
Andrew Marvell (1621-78); an interpretation. *A. B. O'Shea, M.A. 1950 National University of Ireland*

Andrew Marvell and the culture of his time: a study in the relationship of his poetry to some aspects of seventeenth century society. *D. Davison, M.A. 1949 Sheffield*

A critical study of the political activities of Andrew Marvell. *I. C. Robbins, Ph.D. 1926 London*

Marvell and poetry. *W. H. Irwin, M.A. 1935 National University of Ireland*

Marx, Karl
See also Communism.

Conceptions of property in England from Harrington to Marx. *W. S. Evans, Ph.D. 1942 Sheffield*

A critical examination of the philosophic principles basic to Karl Marx's *Capital*. *D. C. Jones, M.A. 1946 Wales*

A critical examination of the interpretation of man in the early writings of Karl Marx. *M. M. Davies, M.A. 1948 Wales*

The evolution of Marx's social and political ideas, with special reference to the period 1840-1848. *E. Y. Wu, Ph.D. 1939 London, School of Economics and Political Science*

An examination of some problems of Marxist philosophy. *A. M. Mardiros, M.Litt. 1943 Cambridge*

Karl Marx and his system. *W. Larkin, M.A. 1916 National University of Ireland*

Pierre-Joseph Proudhon et Karl Marx. *W. Pickles, M.A. 1927 Leeds*

Some aspects of the social philosophy of Karl Marx. *J. F. Holt, B.Litt 1943 Dublin, Trinity College*

The teachings of Karl Marx: their influence on English labour organizations, 1850-1900. *H. Morgans, M.A. 1936 Wales*

Twentieth-century criticism of the sociological theories of Karl Marx, and especially of his economic or materialistic interpretation of history. *B. J. I. Lewis, M.A. 1932 Wales*

Mary II, Queen of England
Mary II of England and her life during the years 1689-1694: influence on politics, on the Anglican Church, and on society. *N. M. Waterson, B.Litt. 1925 Oxford*

Mary Magdalen, Saint
1. The import and rendering of the word διαθήκη in Hebrews ix. 2. The personality and identity of St. Mary Magdalen. *H. R. C. Smith, B.D. & D.D. 1891 Oxford*

Mary, Virgin
For the Virgin Birth, see Jesus Christ: Life and Teaching.

Aspects of the devotion to the Blessed Virgin Mary in thirteenth-century English lyric poetry. *G. T. Shepherd, M.A. 1948 London, King's College*

Mary, Virgin contd.
The Blessed Virgin Mary in Middle English verse. *M. F. McKeough, M.A, 1939 National University of Ireland*

Gwyrthyeu e wynvydedic Veir: astudiaeth gymharol ohonynt fel y'u ceir hwynt yn llawysgrifau Peniarth 14, Peniarth 5 a Llanstephan 27 (The Miracles of the Blessed Mary: a comparative study of them as they are found in the manuscripts Peniarth 14, Peniarth 5, and Llanstephan 27). *L. H. Angell, M.A. 1938 Wales*

Marian poetry in Irish, a comparative study. *J. D. Frizelle, M.A. 1949 National University of Ireland*

Marien Himmelfahrt: ein mittelhochdeutsches Gedicht kritisch. *F. Norman, M.A. 1925 London*

Some aspects of the cult of the Virgin Mary in medieval French literature. *N. V. Williams, M.A. 1927 Wales*

Une introduction aux *Miracles de Nostre Dame par personnages*. *N. Stratford, M.A. 1941 Sheffield*

1. The use of *exempla* in Middle High German Literature. 2. The legend of the Virgin as knight. *M. D. Howrie, Ph.D. 1922 London*

Maryland
Maryland and the American Revolution. *M. J. Broadbent, M.A. 1949 Sheffield*

Masques
See also Juno in Arcadia.

English masques, 1604-1640, with special reference to Ben Jonson. *R. E. Brettle, M.A. 1922 London*

A study of the seventeenth century masque. *R. Banks, M.A. 1912 Birmingham*

Mass
See Eucharist.

Massawah
Anglo-Italian relations, 1884-5, and the Italian occupation of Massawah. *F. T. Fries, Ph.D. 1940 Cambridge*

Massinger, Philip
The application of the test from imagery to certain plays in the Beaumont-Fletcher canon with a view to ascertaining the shares therein of J. Fletcher and P. Massinger. *S. R. Boltiansky, Ph.D. 1938 Manchester*

The life and writings of Philip Massinger. *A. K. McIlwraith, D.Phil. 1931 Oxford*

Philip Massinger. *M. Walsh, M.A. 1931 National University of Ireland*

Philip Massinger. *A. Cox, M.A. 1913 National University of Ireland*

Mas'ūdī, Abul Hassan 'Alī
Geographical materials in the writings of al-Mas'udi. *S. M. Ahmad, B.Litt. 1947 Oxford*

Matabeleland
The geology, climates and cultures of the Pleistocene period in Matabeleland, southern Rhodesia. *G. Bond, Ph.D. 1949 London, External Degree*

Materialism
See also Holbach, P. H. D. d', Baron; La Mettrie, J. O. de; Marx, K.

The hylomorphic concept in psychology. *P. Barry, M.A. 1942 National University of Ireland*

Some aspects of the life and thought of Baron d'Holbach. *J. Lough, Ph.D. 1938 Cambridge*

Materials, Strength of
History of ideas on the behaviour of materials under stress (from 1650 to 1850). *S. B. Hamilton, M.Sc. 1934 London, University College*

Mathematics
See also Algebra; Arithmetic; Geometry; Infinity; and Alembert, J. le R. d'; Briggs, H.; Gregory, J.

The mathematical definition of education. *C. Gattegno, M.A. 1948 London, Institute of Education*

The nature of mathematical thinking. *F. W. Mitchell, Ph.D. 1937 London, Institute of Education*

Scientific method as exemplified in qualitative analysis. *F. W. Turner, M.A. 1928 London*

The use of graphs and charts in the mining industry. *C. L. Caine, M.A. 1948 Sheffield*

Mathematics: History
The concept of continuity: its development in Greek thought before Aristotle. *A. T. Nicol, Ph.D. 1938 Cambridge*

The development of mathematical notation from Wallis to John Bernoulli. *W. Howells, Ph.D. 1933 London, External Degree*

The history of the introduction of infinitesimals. *F. W. Brown, M.Sc. 1930 London*

Mathematics: History contd.
The increasing rigour in mathematical demonstration: a historical study. *E. Rees, M.A. 1926 Wales*

The influence of mathematics on the philosophy of Descartes. *J. R. Andress, M.A. 1927 Manchester*

John Wallis, and his place in the history of science. *J. F. Scott, Ph.D. 1935 London, University College*

Logic and mathematics, with special reference to Bertrand Russell. *M. Kelleher, M.A. 1942 National University of Ireland*

The nature of mathematics. *J. W. L. Stuart, M.Sc. 1946 London, External Degree*

Operational methods in mathematics from Leibniz to Fourier. *K. A. C. Humphreys, M.Sc. 1949 London, External Degree*

The place of mathematical history in school mathematics. *R. G. Ruscoe, M.A. 1925 London*

The possibility of mathematics in the philosophy of Kant. *B. A. Farrell, B.Litt. 1939 Oxford*

A study of mathematical methods in England to the thirteenth century. *F. A. Yeldham, Ph.D. 1932 London, University College*

Unified field theories: the theories of Kaluza and Klein, Weyl, Eddington and Einstein. *J. F. Ratcliffe, M.Sc. 1934 Wales*

Mathematics: Study and Teaching
(1) Some of the textbooks used in the teaching of elementary mathematics in Scotland prior to the year 1800. (2) Development of the mathematical curriculum in the Scottish schools during the same period. *D. K. Wilson, Ph.D. 1932 Glasgow*

An analysis of the correlations between results of mathematical tests compiled according to the principles of Gestalt psychology and a teacher's estimate of mathematical ability in school children. *R. J. Otter, M.A. 1949 London, Institute of Education*

An analysis of the factors entering into results of tests based upon the logical principles of mathematics. *J. W. Jenkins, Ph.D. 1939 London, Institute of Education*

An analysis of the factors entering into mathematical ability, with special reference to children of 11 and 12. *A. M. Blackwell, M.A. 1938 London, Institute of Education*

A comparative study of the mathematical ability of boys and girls in a secondary school from 12 to 14 years of age. *L. Dasgupta, M.A. 1948 London, Institute of Education*

A comparative study of the mathematical abilities of girls and boys in secondary schools. *A. E. Cameron, M.A. 1923 London*

A comprehensive survey of the mathematical education of engineers. *J. D. Stewart, Ph.D. 1948 Aberdeen*

Considerations on the teaching of mathematics, especially geometry - being mainly a comparison of the 'oral' method and the method of 'learning by experience'. *L. Wilkes, M.A. 1930 Birmingham*

A critical account of certain experiments in the realist approach to the teaching of mathematics in post-primary schools. *H. G. Jones, M.A. 1941 Liverpool*

The doctrine of recapitulation in its application to the teaching of mathematics. *J. S. Ross, M.A. 1923 London*

An experiment in the measurement and modification of attitude towards mathematics. *A. M. Khan, M.A. 1948 London, Institute of Education*

An experimental investigation into the processes of solving arithmetical problems by children in a modern school. *J. M. Rooum, M.Ed. 1936 Leeds*

An experimental study into the backwardness of elementary schoolboys in arithmetic. *T. N. K. Rao, M.Ed. 1934 Leeds*

A factor analysis of tests of functional thinking in mathematics. *J. E. Jayasuriya, M.A. 1949 London, Institute of Education*

The factors contributing to successful mathematical attainment in boys and girls of a secondary school. *L. C. Parslow, M.A. 1942 London, Institute of Education*

The formation and modification of mental attitudes towards mathematics. *E. M. Stokes, M.Sc. 1946 Manchester*

The history of the teaching of school mathematics in England during the last fifty years. *C. F. Retter, M.A. 1936 London, Institute of Education*

Mathematics: Study and Teaching contd.
Interest as a factor in the transfer of training from the inculcation of mathematical principles to problems in reasoning. *D. T. Jones, M.A. 1937 London, Institute of Education*

An investigation into mathematical abilities most closely related to logical and critical thinking. *W. Bennett, M.A. 1948 London, Institute of Education*

An investigation into the possibility of measuring attitude towards mathematics by means of a test based on values and situations. *V. H. Bhanot, M.A. 1949 London, Institute of Education*

The investigation of factors useful in predicting teaching ability with special reference to the teaching of mathematics and science. *W. A. Skinner, M.Ed. 1947 Manchester*

An investigation of school mathematics, mainly with the object of discovering by scientific method whether or not it is justifiable to include arithmetic, algebra and geometry as one group for school certificate and matriculation examination. *H.W. Oldham, Ph.D. 1936 Reading*

Matamaitice 'sna bun-scoileannaibh (Mathematics in primary schools). *P. O'Faoláin, M.A. 1928 National University of Ireland*

Mathematical education. *W. H. Parry, M.A. 1912 National University of Ireland*

The mathematical education of the adolescent, with particular reference to the work in central and senior schools. *W. Goom, M.Ed. 1937 Manchester*

The mathematical laboratory in secondary schools. *T. H. Pickles, M.Ed. 1926 Leeds*

Mathematics and natural science in English education. *J. Macwillie, M.A. 1933 Liverpool*

Mathematics teaching in senior schools based on the suggestions of the Board of Education pamphlet no. 101. *H. Dibden, M.A. 1937 Bristol*

Mental tests as a means of classifying secondary school pupils in mathematics. *W. S. Flack, M.Sc. 1924 Birmingham*

The place and value of mathematics in secondary schools. *W. Flemming, M.A. 1949 Liverpool*

The place of mathematical history in school mathematics. *R. G. Ruscoe, M.A. 1925 London*

Practical mathematics: the approach of the post-primary pupil to the study of mathematics. *F. J. Williams, M.Ed. 1928 Manchester*

The relative values of certain individual and group methods used in practice periods in the teaching of elementary mathematics. *N. R. Hoggarth, M.A. 1938 London, Institute of Education*

Some considerations on the teaching of mathematics. *T. W. Hall, M.A. 1936 National University of Ireland*

The teaching of elementary mathematics in secondary schools. *T. C. Batten, M.A. 1934 Liverpool*

The teaching of mathematics: an enquiry into the aims and methods in schools of various types, with a view to securing a greater degree of coordination between (a) school and school, (b) school and after-school activities. *T. H. Jackson, M.Ed. 1937 Manchester*

Matheran, Bombay
Matheran folk songs. *M. Macmillan, D.Litt. 1903 Birmingham*

Mathias, Thomas James
A study of the life and work of Thomas James Mathias, 1754-1835. *W. K. Spicer, M.A. 1946 London, Birkbeck College*

Thomas James Mathias and his place in Anglo-Italian literary relations. *K. Speight, M.Litt. 1938 Cambridge*

Matter (Philosophy)
The doctrine of matter and form in the early English Franciscans. *D. E. Sharp, D.Phil. 1927 Oxford*

The notion of matter in the later philosophy of Plato. *W. A. Greatbatch, M.A. 1922 London*

Some studies in the history of ideas on the discontinuity of matter and energy. *D. R. Peck, M.Sc. 1946 London, External Degree*

Matthew, Saint and Apostle
1. The Apostle Jude: is he to be identified with Jude the servant of Jesus Christ and brother of James? 2. SS. Philip, Bartholomew, Matthew, and Thomas: being an inquiry from New Testament records into the second group in the Apostolate. *A. C. Evans, B.D. 1901 Oxford*

Maucroix, François
Maucroix. *R. W. Ladborough, Ph.D. 1935 Cambridge*

Maugham, William Somerset
The plays of W. Somerset Maugham. *G. Hughes, M.A. 1939 Wales*

Maupassant, Guy de
Etude du pessimisme de Guy de Maupassant. *B. E. Collins, M.A. 1933 Birmingham*

Guy de Maupassant's works in England. *P. W. Packer, Ph.D. 1946 London, Birkbeck College*

The influence of Guy de Maupassant on the English short story, 1800-1900. *F. T. Bullen, M.A. 1928 Liverpool*

Le Normand d'après Guy de Maupassant. *L. F. Monnaie, M.A. 1926 London*

Mauriac, François
Catholicism in the work of François Mauriac. *R. J. North, M.A. 1947 London, King's College*

Maurice, Frederick Denison
The doctrine of atonement in Coleridge and Maurice. *C. W. I. Wardrop, Ph.D. 1932 Edinburgh*

Frederick Denison Maurice. *A. C. Smith, M.A. 1950 Sheffield*

Mauritius
Education in Mauritius, with special reference to the Royal College. *C. G. Wise, M.Ed. 1932 Manchester*

The expedition to Mauritius in 1810 and the establishment of British control. *A. G. Field, M.A. 1932 London, Birkbeck College*

May, Thomas
The comedies of Thomas May. *H. B. Spencer, B.Litt. 1933 Oxford*

Maya
The doctrine of *Maya* in the system of the Vedanta. *P. D. Shastri, B.Sc. 1911 Oxford*

Mayne, Jasper
A critical edition of Jasper Mayne's *The citie match* and *The amorous warre*, with a biographical and critical introduction. *G. C. Bannerjee, B.Litt. 1936 Oxford*

Mazarin, Jules
Cromwell and Mazarin, 1656-1658: an account of the Anglo-French alliance leading to the conquest of Dunkirk. *J. A. Williamson, M.A. 1909 London*

Mazzini, Giuseppe
The significance of Mazzini's literary work. *U. Limentani, Ph.D. 1947 London, Birkbeck College*

Meaning (Philosophy)
See also Language.

Fluctuations in meaning (in binocular rivalry). *J. C. A. Corea, M.A. 1939 London, University College*

Fluctuations of attention and the perception of meaning. *R. N. R. Wallace, M.A. 1935 London, University College*

Meaning. *W. O. Stapledon, Ph.D. 1925 Liverpool*

Oscillation of attention: an enquiry into the effect of the degree of oscillation of ambiguous figures of varying degrees of meaning. *H. J. Hines, M.Sc. 1935 London, University College*

Psychological meaning with special reference to logical meaning. *R. S. Birch, Ph.D. 1927 Edinburgh*

Measurement
A critical study of the idea of dimensions. *R. P. W. Lewis, M.Sc. 1949 Wales*

The economic significance of weights and measures: a study in the progress towards uniformity. *H. Robinson, M.A. 1948 Liverpool*

The evolution of the physical units. *S. Galin, Ph.D. 1934 London, University College*

Meat Industry
International regulation in the meat trade. *R. G. Hampton, Ph.D. 1938 London, School of Economics and Political Science*

Mechanics
A discussion of the relative share of Apollonius, Hipparchus, and Ptolemy in the evolution of the theory of eccentrics and epicycles. *J. H. Wills, M.Sc. 1931 London*

The history of mechanics up to and including the work of Newton. *E. C. Henstock, Ph.D. 1938 London, External Degree*

The mechanical investigations of Leonardo da Vinci, with special reference to his researches on flight. *I. I. B. Hart, Ph.D. 1924 London*

The rise of mechanics. *E. C. Henstock, M.Sc. 1934 London, University College*

Some aspects of the measurement and maturation of mechanical aptitude in boys aged 12 to 14. *H. S. Williams, Ph.D. 1948 London, Institute of Education*

Mechanics' Institutes
The mechanics' institute movement in Lancashire and Yorkshire, 1824 to 1850, with special reference to the institutions at Manchester, Ashton-under-Lyne and Huddersfield. *M. Tylecote, Ph.D. 1930 Manchester*

Mechanism
A critical exposition of mechanism and vitalism, with special reference to their philosophical implications. *H. Williams, M.A. 1932 Wales*

The mechanical view of nature since Descartes. *J. C. Hardwick, B.Sc. 1923 Oxford*

The metaphysical problems involved in the nature and range of the concept of freedom and its relation to the concept of mechanism. *W. H. Jefferson, M.A. 1922 Liverpool*

Medea
Medea and Jason in Greek and Roman literature. *M. Curran, M.A. 1939 Manchester*

Medical Profession
See Medicine: Study and Teaching.

Medical Services
See Public Health.

Medici, Lorenzo de'
The life and character of Lorenzo de Medici, with special consideration of the conflicting views entertained by historians. *B. Thomas, M.A. 1921 Wales*

Medicine
See also Anaesthetics; Black Death; Blood; Dentistry; Epidemics; Gynecology and Obstetrics; Healing, Spiritual; Herbals; Museums; Plague; Public Health; Respiration; Rheumatic Diseases; Surgery.

Medicine: History
See also Celsus; Gadesden, J. de, Anglicus; Galen, C.; Hippocrates; Hutchinson, J., Sir; Moore, J.; Percival, T.

Albrecht van Borgunnien's treatise on medicine and its sources. *W. L. Wardale, M.A. 1927 Liverpool*

Bywyd a gwaith Dr. Owen Owen Roberts, 1793-1866 (Life and work of Dr. Owen Owen Roberts, 1793-1866). *E. H. Owen, M.A. 1939 Wales*

Bywyd a gwaith y Dr. Siôn Dafydd Rhys (The life and work of Dr. John David Rhys). *T. Parry, M.A. 1929 Wales*

Chinese medicine: a comparison with Renaissance and Stuart medicine. *E. W. Smerdon, M.D. 1913 Edinburgh*

Greek medicine in the fifth and fourth centuries B.C. *W. C. Wake, M.Sc. 1946 London, External Degree*

The influence of the western Caliphate on the medical system of Europe. *D. Campbell, B.Sc. 1923 Oxford*

Medical museums: an historical and bibliographical study. *L. W. G. Malcolm, Ph.D. 1933 Cambridge*

Medicine among the Berbers of the Aurés. *M. W. Hilton-Simpson, B.Sc. 1921 Oxford*

Origin and development of Arabian medicine. *M. Z. Siddiqi, Ph.D. 1925 Cambridge*

Popular medical knowledge in fourteenth century English literature. *I. B. Jones, M.A. 1934 Liverpool*

Pseudo-Hippocrates philosophus. *A. L. Peck, Ph.D. 1929 Cambridge*

Researches in medical history, being an investigation into the causes of death of the kings of England from William I to William IV. *J. Rae, M.D. 1911 Aberdeen*

Short historical sketches of Ayur-Vedic or Hindu system of medicine. *A. Mirza, M.D. 1900 Edinburgh*

Some aspects of primitive medicine. *J. M. Fisher, Ph.D. 1949 Cambridge*

Some aspects of the relation of primitive medicine to magic. *B. M. Broadhurst, B.Sc. 1928 Oxford*

Medicine: Law
Historical and other notes on the administration of the Anatomy Act. *A. MacPhail, M.D. 1923 Glasgow*

The law relating to medical, dental, and veterinary practice. *F. Bullock, LL.D. 1928 London*

Medicine: Study and Teaching
Medical education and the rise of the general practitioner, 1760-1860. *R. E. Franklin, Ph.D. 1950 Birmingham*

Obstetrical difficulties of a recently qualified doctor, with some observations on the teaching of obstetrics to undergraduates. *K. Watson, M.D. 1941 Dublin, Trinity College*

Medicine: Study and Teaching contd.
Preliminary medical education. *W. A. G. Laing, M.D. 1886 Glasgow*

Meditation
Buddhist meditation according to the Pāli Canon of the Thera-Vāda School. *P. Vajiranana, Ph.D. 1936 Cambridge*

Mediterranean, The
The ancient Egyptian canals between the Mediterranean and the Red Sea: their problems for the sciences of geology, geography, engineering and history. *W. M. Alexander, D.Sc. 1919 Glasgow*

Muslim sea power in the eastern Mediterranean from the seventh to the tenth century: studies in naval organization. *A. M. Fahmy, Ph.D. 1948 London, School of Oriental and African Studies*

The place of the olive in the economy of the Mediterranean region. *K. De La Mare, B.Litt. 1930 Oxford*

The trade of Southampton with the Mediterranean. *A. A. Ruddock, Ph.D. 1940 London, School of Economics and Political Science*

Medway, River
Prehistoric man in the Medway Valley. *H. J. Eason, B.Sc. 1928 Oxford*

Megillah
See Bible: Old Testament: Historical Books (Esther).

Mehemet Ali, Viceroy of Egypt
The beginnings of the Egyptian Question and the rise of Mehemet Ali, 1800-1812. *S. Ghorbal, M.A. 1924 London*

British policy in reference to Mehemet Ali, 1839-41. *W. G. Turner, M.A. 1928 London*

Palmerston's attitude towards Mehemet Ali, 1834-8, with an introduction on the development of the Near Eastern question, 1788-1834. *R. L. Baker, B.Litt. 1928 Oxford*

Meier Helmbrecht
A metrical examination of the Middle High German poem *Meier Helmbrecht*. *A. Bastow, M.A. 1935 Leeds*

Meir Baruch, Rabbi
The Jewish economic, religious and social life in medieval Europe, as illustrated by the *Responsa* of Rabbi Meir ben Baruch of Rothenburg (1215-1293). *A. Cohen, Ph.D. 1941 Wales*

Meisgyn
Astudiaeth o enwau lleoedd cwmwd Meisgyn, gyda sylw arbennig i blwyf Llantrisant (A study of the placenames of the commote of Meisgyn, with special reference to the parish of Llantrisant). *R. J. Thomas, M.A. 1933 Wales*

Meister Albertus Lere
A critical edition of *Meister Albertus Lere* with introduction and notes. *J. K. Bostock, Ph.D. 1922 London*

Mejía, Pedro
The life, works, and learning of Pedro Mejía, with a study of the sources of the *Silva de Varia Lección*. *W. D. Moore, M.A. 1934 Belfast*

Melancholy
The melancholy element in English poetry from Widsith to Chaucer. *T. R. Hughes, M.A. 1928 Wales*

The melancholy humour - a study of one aspect of English literature, circa 1590-1640. *M. P. Mcgrath, M.A. 1943 Bristol*

Melanesia
Economic aspects of culture contact in eastern Melanesia, with special reference to the influence of a monetary economy. *C. S. Belshaw, Ph.D. 1948 London, School of Economics and Political Science*

Melbourne, William Lamb, 2nd Viscount
Political life of Lord Melbourne. *N. F. Atkinson, M.A. 1919 Liverpool*

Melodrama
See Theatre.

Melvill, Henry
Henry Melvill, 1798 to 1871: a study of his theological thought and homiletical method. *R. G. Young, Ph.D. 1949 Edinburgh*

Memory
Can a neutral monist theory of knowledge give an adequate account of memory. *N. R. Knatchbull-Hugessen, B.Litt. 1938 Oxford*

The development and present status of the trace theory of memory. *B. R. Gomulicki, B.Litt. 1950 Oxford*

An examination of the manner in which prose passages are memorised by pupils between the ages of 10 and 13. *C. D. Wostenholm, M.Sc. 1936 Sheffield*

Memory contd.
An experimental investigation of memory of school children, with special reference to Bergson's theory. *R. K. Sur, M.Ed. 1929 Leeds*

Experimental study of some verbal factors in perceiving and remembering. *K. R. L. Hall, D.Phil. 1949 Oxford*

A further study of volitional frustration in respect of uncompleted tasks. *T. Walsh, Ph.D. 1942 London, King's College*

The history of a list of nonsense syllables committed to memory in 1912, being a preliminary enquiry into the process of forgetting. *R. J. Bartlett, M.Sc. 1921 London*

An investigation into the relationship between memory and intelligence. *J. G. Ingham, Ph.D. 1949 London, Institute of Psychiatry*

Memory; a psychological study. *J. Sullivan, M.A. 1915 National University of Ireland*

The most economical unit of memorizing with recitation. *S. A. Hamid, Ph.D. 1926 London*

Nature and conditions of memory progress. *H. C. Vincent, M.A. 1919 Liverpool*

On the memory of completed and uncompleted tasks: a study of volitional frustration. *T. Walsh, M.A. 1940 London, King's College*

Preference and affective influence as factors in recall. *G. H. Miles, D.Sc. 1916 London*

The psychological basis of memory. *J. O. Edwards, Ph.D. 1928 London*

The relation of certain factors of imagery and immediate memory to geometrical ability. *E. W. Webb, M.A. 1949 London, Institute of Education*

Retentivity in the special senses. *E. H. Walters, Ph.D. 1929 London*

The role of interpolated experience in remembering. *K. D. Sinha, M.Sc. 1949 Cambridge*

The role of memory in education. *L. Duggan, Ph.D. 1948 National University of Ireland*

Should children learn poems as 'wholes' or in 'parts'. *E. W. Sawdon, M.A. 1926 Birmingham*

The specific nature of colour and form memories. *M. M. Said, M.Sc. 1929 Birmingham*

A study of memory and its importance for the theory of knowledge. *E. S. Budden, D.Phil. 1935 Oxford*

A study of the effect upon learning of a training in certain principles of attention and memorization. *L. R. Phillips, M.A. 1936 London, Institute of Education*

Theories of memory. Studies in the theory of memory. *B. Edgell, D.Litt. 1924 Wales*

Time intervals in learning and memory. *J. C. Tsao, Ph.D. 1949 Cambridge*

The effects of time interval on recall. *V. N. Hall, M.A. 1935 London, King's College*

Menander
The characterization of women in Plautus and Terence and the fragments of Menander. *M. Watts, M.A. 1919 London*

The philosophy of Menander and its sources. *D. P. Maw, M.A. 1948 Manchester*

The relation of Euripides to 'new comedy', with special reference to Menander. *M. Andrews, M.A. 1922 London*

Rhetoric in Euripides and Menander. *J. M. Aitken, B.Litt. 1936 Oxford*

The traditional estimate of Menander, as affected by the discovery of the new fragments. *W. G. Waddell, M.A. 1914 London*

Mende Language
A study of the Mende language. *K. H. Crosby, Ph.D. 1939 London, External Degree*

Mende, The
An anthropological survey of the Mende people of Sierra Leone, with special reference to their social structure and material culture and their relation to the geographical environment. *A. C. Lamb, Ph.D. 1946 Leeds*

Mendès, Catulle
A contribution to the study of Catulle Mendès as critic. *B. Gravenall, Ph.D. 1939 London, University College*

Mendicant Friars
See Religious Orders and Societies.

Mendip Hills
A geographical survey of the Mendip Hills showing their effect upon human activities in the region. *M. Powell, B.Sc. 1927 Oxford*

Mens Rea
See Criminal Law.

Mental Health
See also Children, Retarded.

The abnormal subject and responsibility for crime. *M. S. S. Jones, M.D. 1926 Liverpool*

An analysis of 'p' (perseveration) tests, with special reference to schizophrenic conditions. *E. M. McDonnell, M.A. 1934 London, University College*

An attempt to assess the importance of some of the usually accepted causes of mental abnormality: a clinical and statistical study of 500 psychiatric patients. *A. R. Norton, D.M. 1947 Oxford*

Cambridgeshire and its lunatic paupers and criminals. *E. M. Hampson, M.A. 1926 Liverpool*

Certain mental disorders in relation to gross antisocial conduct. *T. Christie, M.D. 1936 Saint Andrew's*

The child's environment and its influence on the development of character and the origin of the neuroses. *T. M. Hornik, B.Sc. 1943 Oxford*

The civil responsibility of lunatics. *W. G. H. Cook, LL.D. 1920 London*

The criminal responsibility of lunatics: a study in comparative law. *H. Oppenheimer, LL.D. 1908 London*

Culture and neurosis. *R. O. R. Piddington, Ph.D. 1935 London, School of Economics and Political Science*

Evolutionary aspects and critical analysis of the English criminal law in its relation to mental disorder, with particular reference to crimes against the person. *K. S. Sharples, LL.M. 1950 Manchester*

Historical landmarks in the treatment of insanity. *A. J. MacGregor, M.D. 1892 Edinburgh*

Investigation into factors influencing the direction of aggressive impulses into (a) delinquency, (b) neurosis, (c) positive achievement. *L. Jackson, D.Phil. 1949 Oxford*

The legal attitude toward mental abnormality: a comparative analysis of the historical and modern criminal law tests of responsibility, with respect to insanity, in England, Scotland and the United States of America. *S. Polsky, Ph.D. 1950 Edinburgh*

The physique of elementary school children, with special reference to their mentality: a statistical study bearing on social economics. *E. G. Habakkuk, M.Sc. 1924 Wales*

The psychology of insanity. *B. Hart, M.D. 1912 London*

The psychology of the unconscious, with special reference to mental disorder, its cause and cure. *J. Blacow, M.A. 1936 Liverpool*

The psychosis and the psychoneuroses. *T. Beston, M.D. 1920 London*

A study of modern principles of mental hygiene, with special reference to Indian education. *S. Bhan, M.A. 1937 London, Institute of Education*

Word deafness: a psychological contribution to the study of mental defect. *L. G. Fildes, Ph.D. 1929 London*

Mercantilism
British policy and Canada, 1774-91: a study in eighteenth century mercantilism. *G. S. Graham, Ph.D. 1929 Cambridge*

The mercantile aspect of English foreign policy during the reign of Charles II. *D. G. E. Hall, M.A. 1917 London*

Mercantile interests in the House of Commons, 1710-13. *M. D. Cox, M.A. 1949 Manchester*

A study of the mercantile system: an analysis of its influence on England, Ireland and the American colonies. *C. Shortt, M.A. 1929 National University of Ireland*

Mercenaries
Service of Scottish mercenary forces in Ireland. *G. A. Hayes-McCoy, M.A. 1932 National University of Ireland*

The service of the Scottish mercenary forces in Ireland, from 1565 to 1603, with an account of the mercenary system in Ireland and of its effect on Scottish history. *G. A. Hayes-McCoy, Ph.D. 1934 Edinburgh*

Merchant Adventurers Company
The Company of Adventurers to the islands of Providence and Henrietta: its foundation and history, 1630-1634. *A. P. Newton, M.A. 1910 London*

Merchant Banks
See Banks and Banking.

Merchant Navy
See Shipping.

Merchants
See also Guilds; Mercantilism; Trade.

A study of the merchant class of London in the fifteenth century, with special reference to the Company of Grocers. *S. L. Thrupp, Ph.D. 1931 London, University College*

Mercia
Offa of Mercia in history and tradition. *A. E. Smith, M.A. 1942 Leeds*

Mercier, Louis Sébastien
Bibliographie critique des ouvrages de Louis Sébastien Mercier. *T. V. Benn, Ph.D. 1925 Leeds*

Meredith, George
George Meredith. *A. Trenur, M.A. 1922 London*

George Meredith: his aims and achievements as a novelist. *M. A. I. Seabourne, M.A. 1936 Wales*

The prose style of George Meredith. *J. Birmingham, M.A. 1927 Liverpool*

Technical theory and practice in George Meredith's novels. *S. H. Davies, Ph.D. 1935 London, King's College*

The women of George Meredith. *E. Conroy, M.A. 1912 Wales*

The works of George Meredith. *M. S. Gretton, B.Litt. 1926 Oxford*

Mérimée, Prosper
Etude sur le vocabulaire de Prosper Mérimée au point de vue du néologisme. *W. Brown, M.A. 1925 Leeds*

Le scepticisme de Prosper Mérimée. *F. B. Shaw, M.A. 1923 Birmingham*

Le théâtre de Clara Gazul. *F. W. Moss, M.A. 1924 Leeds*

Mérimée nouvelliste. *M. White, M.A. 1941 National University of Ireland*

Prosper Mérimée and England. *D. Brittain, M.A. 1926 Manchester*

Merioneth
The industrial development of Merioneth, 1750-1820, being an investigation into the economic organization and history of certain distinctive industries in the county during this period. *M. J. Jones, M.A. 1937 Wales*

Local government in the principality of Wales during the sixteenth and seventeenth centuries, as illustrated mainly by the extant data relating to the county of Merioneth. *I. ap O. Edwards, M.A. 1924 Wales*

Merlin
See Arthurian Legends.

Merrill-Terman Tests
See Intelligence Testing.

Merseyside
North Wales and Merseyside. *D. Williams, M.A. 1932 Liverpool*

Merton College
See Oxford University.

Méry, Joseph Houon de
Le tornoiement antecrist by Huon de Méry. *F. Davis, Ph.D. 1935 London, External Degree*

Mesolithic Age
See Archaeology and Antiquities.

Mesopotamia
See also Assyria; Iraq.

British interests in the Tigris-Euphrates Valley, 1856-88. *W. Bamforth, M.A. 1948 London, Bedford College*

Studies on the economic life of Mesopotamia in the tenth century. *A. A. A. K. Duri, Ph.D. 1942 London, School of Oriental and African Studies*

Messiah
See also Jesus Christ; Judaism.

1. The consideration of our Lord's Messianic consciousness in the light of his use of the Old Testament. 2. A critical study of the pericope in St. John vii.53-viii.11. *C. E. Blakeway, B.D. & D.D. 1910 Oxford*

1. The ethical and spiritual ideas of the Psalms. 2. The doctrine of the Messiah in the Psalms. *P. F. Eliot, B.D. & D.D. 1891 Oxford*

Messiah contd.
Greek and Judaistic individualism in the Hellenistic age, in their similarity and contrast, and their relation to the concept of the Messiah. *H. D. Hilliard, M.A. 1932 Bristol*

Jewish conceptions of the Messiah and the kingdom of God as reflected in certain specified texts between 150 B.C. and A.D. 100, with special reference to the political implications. *P. C. Young, B.Litt. 1940 Oxford*

The Messianic hope in the apocalyptic literature of Judaism, 200 B.C.-100 A.D. *E. Nevitt, M.A. 1930 Liverpool*

1. The relation of confirmation to baptism. 2. The meaning and use of the Messianic titles: 'Christ', 'Son of David', 'Son of God', 'Son of Man'. *A. Chilton, B.D. & D.D. 1906 Oxford*

Metal Industry
Birmingham: an analysis of geographical influences on the metal industries. *J. Rushton, M.Sc. 1936 London, Bedford College*

Cost accounts in the metal industry. *H. E. Parkes, M.Com. 1920 Birmingham*

The marketing of non-ferrous metals. *H. L. Ellis, M.Com. 1926 Birmingham*

The regional development of the metallurgical industries of south-east Carmarthenshire. *L. W. Evans, M.A. 1937 Wales*

Metalwork
See also Church Plate.

Metal-workers in early Ireland. *B. P. Rooney, M.A. 1946 National University of Ireland*

Metaphysical Poets
See Poetry, English: Seventeenth Century.

Metaphysics
See also Eschatology; Ethics; Freedom; Idealism; Ideas; Logic; Mind; Mysticism; Obligation; Realism; Soul; Value (Philosophy). For writers on Metaphysics, see Philosophy.

A commentary on Aristotle's *Metaphysics*, Book 12. *M. J. Troy, M.A. 1942 National University of Ireland*

A comparison between the metaphysics of St. Thomas Aquinas and the metaphysics of Aristotle to illustrate the relation of Scholasticism and Aristotelianism. *H. J. W. Carpenter, B.Litt. 1926 Oxford*

The concept of creation in the metaphysics of St. Thomas. *J. F. Cummins, M.A. 1943 National University of Ireland*

Creativity, process and entity in the philosophy of A. N. Whitehead. *M. Haldar, Ph.D. 1949 London, King's College*

De summi numinis existentia. *J. Sherman, M.A. 1716 Glasgow*

An enquiry into the foundations of Whitehead's metaphysic of experience. *I. Leclerc, Ph.D. 1949 London, King's College*

The ethical implications of a monadistic metaphysic. *J. K. Majumdar, Ph.D. 1923 London*

The influence of religious dogma on metaphysical speculation in the philosophy of Descartes, with special reference to the psychological aspect. *J. J. Hartland-Swann, Ph.D. 1946 London, External Degree*

The metaphysic of St. Bonaventure. *R. E. McCann, M.A. 1936 National University of Ireland*

The metaphysical basis of ethics. *D. Jones, M.A. 1904 Wales*

The metaphysical implications of freedom. *R. Topping, M.A. 1937 Belfast*

The method of metaphysics according to Bergson. *D. Corkery, M.A. 1937 National University of Ireland*

The nature of logical constructions and their bearing on metaphysical analysis. *M. E. Daniels, Ph.D. 1933 London, Bedford College*

The notion of substance in the *Metaphysics* of Aristotle. *V. Pouliot, B.Litt. 1933 Oxford*

The origin and significance of the logicoanalytic method in metaphysics. *J. W. Reeves, Ph.D. 1934 London, Bedford College*

Relation. *P. K. Bastable, M.A. 1939 National University of Ireland*

The relation between the theory of knowledge and metaphysics in the philosophical system of Samuel Alexander. *R. I. Markus, M.A. 1948 Manchester*

The relations between ethics and metaphysics, with special reference to the works of Spinoza, Kant and T. H. Green. *J. P. Davies, M.A. 1922 Wales*

Metaphysics contd.
The significance for metaphysics of the presuppositions of morality. *T. T. Jones, M.A. 1929 Wales*

Some metaphysical aspects of modern physical science. *D. O'Donoghue, M.A. 1945 National University of Ireland*

Some metaphysical implications of the judgment. *P. V. Blanshard, B.Sc. 1920 Oxford*

Subject and object: a study of some aspects of the new realism. *N. Speller, M.A. 1917 Birmingham*

The Vedanta: its place as a system of metaphysics. *N. K. Datta, Ph.D. 1921 London*

Metempsychosis
See Soul.

Methodism
See also Anglican Church; Dall, R.; Wesley, C.; Wesley, J.; Whitefield, G.; Williams, W.

The aims and practices of the English Dissenters from the end of Anne's reign to the rise of the Wesleyan Movement. *D. Coomer, M.A. 1944 Liverpool*

Bywyd a gwaith Dr. Lewis Edwards (The life and work of Dr. Lewis Edwards). *T. L. Evans, M.A. 1948 Wales*

The contribution of Methodism to popular education, 1800-1850. *H. F. Mathews, M.A. 1946 Liverpool*

Cyfraniad Methodistiaeth Galfinaidd i lenyddiaeth Gymraeg o 1811 hyd 1864 (The contribution of Calvinistic Methodism to the literature of Wales from 1811 ro 1864). *J. P. Williams, M.A. 1928 Wales*

Early Methodism in Bristol, with special reference to J. Wesley's visits to the city, 1739-90, and their impression on the people. *W. A. Goss, M.A. 1932 Bristol*

Early Methodist associations and societies in Wales. *M. Gelly, M.A. 1919 Wales*

The forms and psychology of worship in the Free Church tradition, with special reference to Methodism. *J. Bishop, M.A. 1947 Bristol*

The history of Methodism in the eighteenth century. *R. A. F. Mears, B.Litt. 1925 Oxford*

The influence of the Church of England and Dissent upon Methodism in the eighteenth century. *F. Hunter, M.A. 1959 Manchester*

The influence of the Methodist movement on social life in Wales. *E. C. Lloyd, B.Litt. 1921 Oxford*

The introduction and development of Wesleyanism in Scotland. *D. L. MacFarlane, Ph.D. 1931 Edinburgh*

John Newton and the early Methodists. *J. Laver, B.Litt. 1923 Oxford*

Methodism and the Church of England in Cornwall, 1738-1838: a historical survey of Cornish Methodism, its rise, growth, and relation to the Church of England. *H. M. Brown, Ph.D. 1947 London, External Degree*

Methodism and the English Romantic Movement. *F. C. Gill, M.A. 1936 Liverpool*

Methodism and the literature of the eighteenth century. *T. B. Shepherd, Ph.D. 1938 London, Birkbeck College*

Methodism and the working classes of England (1800-1850). *R. F. Wearmouth, Ph.D. 1935 London, School of Economics and Political Science*

Methodism from the death of Wesley, 1791, to the Wesleyan centenary, 1839. *R. F. Wearmouth, M.A. 1928 Birmingham*

The Methodist contribution to nineteenth century secondary education. *F. C. Pritchard, Ph.D. 1947 London, External Degree*

The origin and growth of the Methodist Movement in Wales in the eighteenth century, in the light of the unpublished mss. correspondence of Howell Harris at Trevecka. *M. H. Jones, Ph.D. 1929 Wales*

The origins and influence of Methodism in the north Staffordshire Potteries before 1820. *R. Moss, M.A. 1949 London, Birkbeck College*

The relation of the Methodist movement to political thought in England, 1800-1850, with special reference to Methodist records. *C. J. Christian, M.A. 1936 Manchester*

The relation of William Law to John Wesley and the beginnings of Methodism. *E. W. Baker, Ph.D. 1941 Edinburgh*

The rise and growth of Welsh Wesleyan Methodism to 1858. *A. H. Williams, M.A. 1932 Wales*

Methodism contd.
The sacrament of the Lord's Supper in early Methodism. *J. C. Bowmer, M.A. 1949 Leeds*

The social and political influence of Methodism in the Napoleonic period. *M. L. Edwards, Ph.D. 1934 London, King's College*

The social and psychological conditions of the rise and development of Methodism. *W. L. Jones, Ph.D. 1939 Liverpool*

Wesleyan Methodism's contribution to national education (1739-1902). *H. Cloke, M.A. 1936 London, King's College*

Methodius, Saint
1. Some aspects of theology of Methodius of Olympus. 2. Some features of the theological language of the *Dialects* of Adamantius. *C. Jenkins, B.D. & D.D. 1924 Oxford*

Metternich, Clemens Wenzeslaus, Prince
Metternich and the English Government from the Peace of Schönbrünn. *C. S. B. Buckland, B.Litt. 1930 Oxford*

Mexico
See also New Galicia.

British relations with Mexico, 1859-62. *R. B. Chapman, B.Litt. 1936 Oxford*

Meyer, Conrad Ferdinand
Conrad Ferdinand Meyer in his relationship to the theory of the Novelle. *A. L. Anderson, Ph.D. 1924 Edinburgh*

Meynell, Alice
Alice Meynell. *C. E. Callan, M.A. 1926 Birmingham*

Alice Meynell. *T. I. Elmes, M.A. 1949 National University of Ireland*

The works of Alice Meynell. *M. C. McLernan, M.A. 1937 Liverpool*

The works of Alice Meynell. *M. Graham, M.A. 1942 Birmingham*

Michael, of Kildare
Michael of Kildare: earliest traces of Anglo-Irish poetry. *M. Musgrave, M.A. 1912 National University of Ireland*

Michelet, Jules
England and the English as presented in Michelet's *History of France*. *D. Starke, M.A. 1922 London*

Michelstown, Ireland
The geography of Michelstown, its demesne and surrounding country, in the Barony of Condons and Clangibbon about the year 1841. *D. V. Henning, M.Sc. 1948 Dublin, Trinity College*

Mickle, William Julius
A study of the life and works of William Julius Mickle, translator of *The Lusiad* (1734-1788). *G. West, M.A. 1932 London, King's College*

Micmacs
Studies in the life and culture of the Malecites and Micmacs. *W. H. Mechling, B.Litt. 1916 Oxford*

Middle Ages
Medievalism in the works of Rossetti and William Morris. *E. Hall, M.A. 1912 London*

Some aspects of the cult of medievalism in nineteenth century poetry. *M. F. Doolan, M.A. 1936 Belfast*

Middle Classes
The bourgeois in French literature of the fourteenth century. *M. G. Liddle, Ph.D. 1925 London*

Class distinctions as reflected in the German novel of the nineteenth century: aristocracy: middle classes: intellectuals, 1830 to 1900. *E. Kohn-Bramstedt, Ph.D. 1936 London, School of Economics and Political Science*

La bourgeoisie de province dans l'oeuvre de Balzac. *M. Wray, M.A. 1925 Manchester*

The presentation of the liberal middle class in the novels and *Novellen* of Friedrich Spielhagen. *N. Roberts, M.A. 1949 Birmingham*

Middle East
See also Levant Company; Cyprus; Egypt; Palestine; Syria; Turkey.

British foreign policy in the Near East from the Congress of Berlin to the accession of Ferdinand of Coburg. *W. N. Medlicott, M.A. 1926 London*

British policy in the Middle East, 1874-80. *L. E. Frechtling, D.Phil. 1939 Oxford*

A comparative review of rainfall régimes with a marked winter maximum in areas bordering the Eastern Mediterranean. . *T. M. Whitaker, M.A. 1941 Manchester*

Middle East contd.
The conflict of nationalism and imperialism with particular reference to the Near and Middle East. *M. Awad, Ph.D. 1926 London*

Ecclesiastical opinion in England on the Eastern Question from the Treaty of Paris to the Treaty of Berlin. *S. B. R. Poole, M.A. 1934 London, King's College*

Great Britain, Russia and the Eastern Question (1832-1841). *G. H. Bolsover, Ph.D. 1933 London, King's College*

India and the Near East in English literature. *M. D. Taseer, Ph.D. 1936 Cambridge*

The Mesolithic age in the Middle East. *J. Waechter, Ph.D. 1949 Cambridge*

Palmerston's attitude towards Mehemet Ali, 1834-8, with an introduction on the development of the Near Eastern question, 1788-1834. *R. L. Baker, B.Litt. 1928 Oxford*

The policy of Lord Palmerston in the Near Eastern Question from the date of his accession to office in November, 1830, to the date of his retirement in August, 1841. *M. H. Mackenzie, B.Litt. 1928 Oxford*

A study of Warburton's *The Crescent and the Cross* in relation to the literary interest in the Near East shown by English romantic writers in the eighteenth and the earlier nineteenth centuries. *M. S. Abdel-Hamid, M.A. 1948 Bristol*

Middle English Language and Literature
See English Language; English Literature: Early and Medieval.

Middlesex
The economic administration of Middlesex from the accession of Charles II to the death of George II: studies in the records of Quarter-sessions. *E. G. Dowdell, D.Phil. 1929 Oxford*

Rural Middlesex under the Commonwealth: a study based principally upon the Parliamentary surveys of the royal estates. *S. J. Madge, M.Sc. 1922 London*

Middleton, Thomas
The collaboration of Dekker and Middleton. *M. Baird, B.Litt. 1928 Oxford*

An edition of Middleton's *Women beware women* and *A chaste maid in Cheapside*, with an introduction and notes. *M. L. E. Fisher, B.Litt. 1937 Oxford*

Female characterization in Jacobean tragedy, with special consideration of the tragedies of Heywood, Webster, Middleton, Beaumont and Fletcher. *A. E. Bufton, M.A. 1939 Wales*

Thomas Middleton. *R. C. Bald, Ph.D. 1929 Cambridge*

The use and purpose of imagery in the tragedy of Webster, Tourneur and Middleton. *J. R. Jones, M.A. 1941 Wales*

Midrash
See Bible: Old Testament.

Migration
See also Emigration and Immigration; Refugees.

The domestic horse and perforated stone axes in antiquity as studied by archaeological and folklore evidence, with some suggestions as to their connections with movements of peoples. *S. J. Jones, M.A. 1928 Wales*

Economics of migration. *J. Isaac, Ph.D. 1942 London, School of Economics and Political Science*

The effects of irrigation on movements of population, and on the food supply of the world, with special reference to America. *J. N. L. Baker, B.Litt. 1924 Oxford*

Emigration from Taunton to N. England 1625-1645. *H. J. Wickenden, M.A. 1929 Bristol*

Labour migration in England, 1800-1850. *A. Redford, Ph.D. 1922 Manchester*

Labour mobility: its measurement and causes. *H. W. Robinson, D.Phil. 1939 Oxford*

Migration in Great Britain since 1927, with special reference to the industrial population. *V. M. Lamb, B.Litt. 1939 Oxford*

A new statement of the facts regarding the movements of peoples in China, with respect to the natural features. *E. E. Gomersall, M.Sc. 1921 Wales*

Sample analyses of migration into the Oxford district. *G. H. Daniel, D.Phil. 1939 Oxford*

Milan
The effect of the religious movement on the origin and early growth of the Milanese commune during the eleventh century. *S. M. Brown, B.Litt. 1929 Oxford*

Milan contd.
The French conquest and administration of the Milanese, 1499-1572. *W. MacDougall, D.Litt. 1924 Glasgow*

Miletus
The history of Miletus down to the anabasis of Alexander. *A. G. Dunham, M.A. 1913 London*

Militarism
The development of the militant spirit among primitive peoples. *P. H. Brodie, B.Sc. 1917 Oxford*

Military History
See History, Military.

Military Service
See Armed Forces.

Military Training
See Armed Forces.

Milk
See Dairy Industry.

Mill, John Stuart
An examination of the deductive logic of J. S. Mill. *R. Jackson, D.Litt. 1938 Saint Andrew's*

The influence of Auguste Comte on the economics of John Stuart Mill. *A. Weinberg, Ph.D. 1949 London, External Degree*

The political theory of J. S. Mill. *W. L. Kendall, M.Sc. 1926 London*

Milton, John
The architectonics of *Paradise lost. J. Goode, M.A. 1921 Birmingham*

A critical study of Milton's *Samson Agonistes. W. R. Parker, B.Litt. 1934 Oxford*

Du Bartas in his relation to English literature, with special reference to Milton. *F. M. Mosley, M.A. 1916 London*

Eighteenth century literary criticism up to Dr. Johnson, with particular reference to the criticism of Shakespeare, Milton and the metaphysical poets. *M. J. Ince, M.A. 1948 Manchester*

Hopkins and Milton. *A. P. Lehane, M.A. 1949 National University of Ireland*

The influence of Milton on English poetry up to 1770. *W. J. Williams, M.A. 1907 Wales*

The influence of Milton upon the poetry of the eighteenth century. *W. Morgan, M.A. 1918 Wales*

The influence of Spenser on Milton. *J. M. Foster, M.A. 1945 London, King's College*

John Milton: the making of an epic poet. *J. Goode, D.Litt. 1929 Birmingham*

Milton - the last Elizabethan. *C. Renwick, M.A. 1947 National University of Ireland*

Milton and civil liberty. *E. A. H. Clifford, M.A. 1941 Reading*

Milton as a politician and a political thinker. *T. Henshaw, M.A. 1926 Wales*

Milton, as he reveals himself in his prose. *K. Ford, M.A. 1919 National University of Ireland*

Milton criticism from Addison to de Quincey. *K. Wood, M.A. 1950 Sheffield*

Milton's editors and commentators from Patrick Hume to Todd. *H. Oras, B.Litt. 1928 Oxford*

Milton's heroic poetry: a comparative study with reference to Sanskrit epic. *V. R. Movva, Ph.D. 1949 Wales*

Milton's reputation in France in the seventeenth century. *F. C. Sepianu, B.Litt. 1941 Oxford*

Milton's treatise *On Christian doctrine* and its relation to *Paradise lost. W. A. Sewell, B.Litt. 1933 Oxford*

Paradise lost and the seventeenth-century reader. *B. Rajan, Ph.D. 1946 Cambridge*

Studies in the background of Milton's prose. *A. E. Barker, Ph.D. 1937 London, University College*

Studies in the language of Milton: parts 1-2. *E. Holmes, M.A. 1923 Liverpool*

The study of Milton in the first half of the eighteenth century. *E. Noble, M.A. 1914 London*

A study of Milton's reputation at home and abroad between the years 1660-1714. *T. E. P. Horsfall, B.Litt. 1929 Oxford*

A study of the workings of Milton's imagination as revealed in the portrayal of the chief characters in *Paradise Lost, Paradise Regained* and *Samson Agonistes. G. M. Shapcott, M.A. 1930 London, Bedford College*

Mind
See also Mental Health; Psychiatry; Psychoanalysis; Psychology.

Mind contd.
The interpretation of some aspects of Christian doctrine and practice in the light of Sigmund Freud's conceptions of the development and structure of the mind. *R. S. Lee, D.Phil. 1947 Oxford*

Mind and the universal frame. *M. S. Fitzpatrick, M.A. 1934 National University of Ireland*

A re-examination of some questions at issue between idealists and realists with regard to the subject-object relation and the nature of mind. *J. R. Jones, D.Phil. 1946 Oxford*

Mineral Water Industry
The early history of chemical studies on mineral waters. *K. W. Ulyatt, M.Sc. 1948 London, University College*

Minerva Press, The
A study of the publications of the Minerva Press: 1790-1820. *D. Blakey, Ph.D. 1933 London, King's College*

Mines and Mining
See also under the names of individual metals, ores, etc.

Ancient mining in Spain. *A. O'Donovan, M.Litt. 1934 Cambridge*

The application of time and work study to the mining industry. *E. J. Daniell, M.Eng. 1944 Sheffield*

Changes of population in west Cornwall with the rise and decline of mining. *T. W. McGuinness, M.Sc. 1938 London, Birkbeck College*

An examination of Sir Humphrey Machworth's industrial activities, with special reference to the Governor and Company of the Mine Adventurers of England. *S. Evans, M.A. 1950 Wales*

Legislation relating to mining, XIX century, 1840-1887. *A. T. Flight, Ph.D. 1937 London, School of Economics and Political Science*

Mining in the Lake counties in the sixteenth century. *J. D. S. Paul, Ph.D. 1926 London*

Movements of mining population in the anthracite area of south Wales. *E. J. Howells, M.Sc. 1938 Wales*

The policy of the Tudors in regard to the mines in Ireland. *M. E. O'Dea, M,A. 1931 National University of Ireland*

Roman mines in Europe. *O. Davies, Litt.D. 1947 Dublin, Trinity College*

The technical education of the mine worker with special reference to the effect of the industry on the receptivity of the student. *R. L. Hay, M.Ed. 1935 Durham*

The use of graphs and charts in the mining industry. *C. L. Caine, M.A. 1948 Sheffield*

Minnesingers
See also Vogelweide, W. von der.

Bestrafte Untreue, eine allegorische mittelhochdeutsche Minnerede, herausgegeben. *J. A. Wilks, M.A. 1920 London*

The Minnesingers in relation to contemporary politics. *M. M. Green, M.A. 1909 Birmingham*

Studien über die älteren Minnesänger mit Ubersetzungsversuchen. *W. Lee, M.A. 1903 Birmingham*

Minorca
Minorca under British rule. *E. Murdie, M.A. 1932 London, King's College*

Minorities and Minority Problems
See Population.

Minors
The law relating to minors as applied by the British courts in India. *E. J. Trevelyan, D.C.L. 1906 Oxford*

Minufiya Province
Geographical study of Minufiya province: the physical character and the human response. *L. Saad, Ph.D. 1950 Reading*

Mira de Amescua, Antonio
The dramatic art of Mira de Amescua. *M. M. C. McCallum, M.A. 1936 Liverpool*

Mirabeau, Honoré Gabriel Riqueti, Comte de
The Comte de Mirabeau in England. *W. R. Fryer, B.Litt. 1940 Oxford*

Miracles
The controversy concerning miracles in England during the seventeenth and eighteenth centuries, with special reference to the period 1700-1750. *E. K. Feaver, Ph.D. 1937 Edinburgh*

An examination of the nature and function of miracle stories in the formation of the Gospel tradition. *A. Richardson, B.D. 1940 Oxford*

Miracles in history and in modern thought. *C. J. Wright, Ph.D. 1931 London, External Degree*

Miracles contd.
1. Miracles in the light of modern science. 2. The Trinitarian formula in the writings of Novatian. *W. Y. Fausset, B.D. 1914 Oxford*

The miracles of healing in the New Testament in the light of modern psychological and psychotherapeutical research. *E. R. Micklem, B.Litt. 1921 Oxford*

1. The Old Testament: a progressive revelation of the divine character. 2. The miraculous element in the Gospels. *J. J. Turpin, B.D. 1908 Oxford*

1. On the credibility of miracles. 2. The efficacy of the sacraments. *F. McDowell, B.D. 1890 Oxford*

1. On the history of the doctrine of the Holy Trinity. 2. On miracles. *L. J. T. Darwall, B.D. 1886 Oxford*

1. On the kingdom of God as depicted in the New Testament. 2. On miracles. *A. W. H. Adrian, B.D. 1892 Oxford*

The place of miracle in Christian apologetics in Great Britain from 1688 to the present day. *J. S. Lawton, D.Phil. 1950 Oxford*

1. The sacrificial worship of the Hebrews. 2. The miraculous element in the Gospels. *J. Benoy, B.D. 1891 Oxford*

1. The sphere of the miraculous at different epochs of the Church and of Christian life. 2. The personality and office of the Holy Spirit. *C. H. O. Daniel, B.D. & D.D. 1904 Oxford*

1. The value of the theory of accommodation as applied to moral difficulties in the Old Testament. 2. The place of miracles among the evidences for Christianity. *P. A. Wright-Henderson, B.D. & D.D. 1903 Oxford*

Miracles de Nostre Dame
See Romances.

Mirror for Magistrates
A study of the works of William Baldwin, with special reference to his connection with *The Mirror for Magistrates. M. Brown, M.A. 1912 London*

Mirror of Fools
'The mirror of fools': a study in church history chiefly of the twelfth century. *R. Sidgwick, M.A. 1908 Birmingham*

Mishnah
See Jewish Law.

Missions
See also Church History; London Missionary Society; Marsden, S.

Missions: History
1. Early Christian missions in some of their relations to heathen religion. 2. The importance and function of the Book of Esther in the canon. *J. W. Williams, B.D. 1896 Oxford*

1. The mission of the Twelve. 2. The teaching of the Christ on the kingdom. *E. L. Macassey, B.D. 1924 Oxford*

The missionary activity of the ancient Nestorian Church. *J. Stewart, Ph.D. 1925 Edinburgh*

Principles and characteristics of missionary policy during the last fifty years, as illustrated by the history of the London Missionary Society. *N. Goodall, D.Phil. 1950 Oxford*

Missions: Africa
The beginnings of missionary enterprise in South Africa, 1795-1812. *K. M. Reynolds, M.A. 1927 London*

The London Missionary Society in South Africa during the years 1798-1836. *D. K. Clinton, B.Litt. 1935 Oxford*

The religious institutions and beliefs of the southern Bantu, and their bearing on the problems of the Christian missionary. *D. W. T. Shropshire, D.Phil. 1937 Oxford*

A translation of theological terms and ideas into the languages of evangelization, ancient and modern, particularly those of the Bantu family. *W. A. Norton, B.Litt. 1916 Oxford*

The work of the Catholic Church in British tropical Africa: a study in co-operation. *M. Thornton, Ph.D. 1933 London, External Degree*

Missions: Central Europe
The conversion of the Slovenes. *A. L. Kuhar, Ph.D. 1950 Cambridge*

Missions: Ceylon
A study of the history of Christianity in Ceylon in the British period from 1796 to 1903, with special reference to the Protestant missions. *C. N. V. Fernando, B.Litt. 1942 Oxford*

Missions: China
All for China: an account of the life and labour of Mrs. E. H. Edwards of Taiynanfu, Shensi. *H. R. Williamson, M.A. 1922 London*

The Christian Church of the T'ang Dynasty. *J. Foster, M.A. 1938 Birmingham*

Christian missions and foreign relations in China: an historical study. *C. M. Drury, Ph.D. 1932 Edinburgh*

Missions: India
The achievements of Christian missionaries in India, 1794-1833. *K. Ingham, D.Phil. 1949 Oxford*

1. Pelagianism. 2. Recent attempts to establish undogmatic Christianity in India. *F. E. Warren, B.D. 1873 Oxford*

A study of missionary policy and methods in Bengal from 1793 to 1905. *W. B. S. Davis, Ph.D. 1942 Edinburgh*

Missions: Jamaica
Protestant missions in Jamaica, being a critical survey of mission policy from 1754 to the present day. *J. W. Kilpatrick, Ph.D. 1944 Edinburgh*

Missions: New Zealand
The influence of the evangelical spirit on a policy of trusteeship towards native races, as illustrated by the records of certain missionary societies dealing with New Zealand (1814-54). *A. F. Madden, B.Litt. 1939 Oxford*

Mitchel, John
John Mitchel. *M. C. Lynch, M.A. 1943 National University of Ireland*

Mithila
Mithila and Magadha, 700 A.D.-1100 A.D. *L. Jha, Ph.D. 1948 London, School of Oriental and African Studies*

Mitre, Bartolome
The political career of Bartolome Mitre, 1852-1891. *A. J. Walford, Ph.D. 1940 London, University College*

Mizauld, Antoine
The life and works of Antoine Mizauld. *R. E. Ockenden, Ph.D. 1941 London, External Degree*

Modernism
Baron Friedrich von Hügel's place in the modernist movement. *J. C. G. Tiley, B.Litt. 1940 Oxford*

The sources, growth, and value of English modernism. *G. V. Jones, B.Litt. 1931 Oxford*

Modus Tenendi Parliamentum
Suggestions concerning the date and authorship of the *Modus Tenendi Parliamentum. D. K. Hodnett, M.A. 1918 Bristol*

Moehler, Johann Adam
The doctrine of the unity of the Church, with special reference to the works of Khomaikov and Moehler. *S. Bolshakoff, D.Phil. 1943 Oxford*

Moh Tih
The philosophy of Moh Tih. *K. C. Chang, M.A. 1926 Liverpool*

Mohammedanism
See Islam.

Mohenjo-Daro
A cemetery at Kish. A Sumerian palace. Jemdet Nasr. Bahrein and Hemamieh. Mohenjo-Daro. *E. J. H. Mackay, D.Litt. 1933 Bristol*

The script of Mohenjodaro and Harappa, and its relation to other scripts. *G. G. R. Hunter, D.Phil. 1930 Oxford*

Mold
The social aspects of the rise and decay of literary culture in Mold and Holywell, 1820-1900. *D. J. Jones, M.A. 1929 Liverpool*

Molière, Jean Baptiste Poquelin
Ce que Molière doit aux auteurs latins. *D. Bowie, M.A. 1912 Liverpool*

The influence of Molière on Restoration comedy (1660-1720). *A. L. Stoddart, M.A. 1919 Birmingham*

La comédie en France entre Molière et Marivaux. *W. C. Donlon, M.A. 1937 London, King's College*

La psychologie de Molière. *E. M. Kennedy, M.A. 1916 National University of Ireland*

La théorie de l'éducation chez Molière. *B. L. V. Kay, M.A. 1912 Liverpool*

Les comédies-ballets de Molière. *J. V. Hughes, M.A. 1947 Liverpool*

Les valets et les servantes dans la comédie de Molière. *F. C. Roe, M.A. 1920 Birmingham*

Molière: his philosophy of religion. *C. R. M. Williams, M.A. 1922 Wales*

Molière, Jean Baptiste Poquelin contd.
Molière as a national dramatist of France. *R. Murray, M.A. 1916 National University of Ireland*

Shakespeare and Molière, with special reference to comedy. *E. C. Kimpton, M.A. 1908 London*

Molina, Tirso de
Tirso de Molina and the *nueva comedia. J. Pomfret, M.A. 1935 Birmingham*

Molinos, Miguel de
Molinos and the implications of the spirit of quietism. *R. A. Agnew, Ph.D. 1935 Edinburgh*

Monarchomachi
The Monarchomachi: a study in the political philosophy of the sixteenth century. *R. N. C. Hunt, B.Litt. 1925 Oxford*

Monarchy
See Kingship.
English monarchy fifteenth to seventeenth century. *D. McCann, M.A. 1939 National University of Ireland*

Monastic Orders
See Religious Orders and Societies.

Monasticism
See also Religious Orders and Societies; Church History; and under the names of individual abbeys, convents, monasteries, etc.

The origin, ideal and early history of monachism. *E. H. Humphreys, M.A. 1925 Bristol*

1. The origin of Christian monasticism in Egypt. 2. The history of Christian monasticism in Egypt to the close of the fourth century. *W. H. MacKean, B.D. & D.D. 1919 Oxford*

1. The relation of priest and prophet in the history of Israel before the exile. 2. St. Basil the Great and the monastic life. *E. F. Morison, B.D 1912 Oxford*

Rise and earliest development of Christian monasticism with a study of its origin. *J. R. M. Forbes, Ph.D. 1928 Edinburgh*

St. Basil's conception of Christian monasticism. *V. Pavlovitch, B.Litt. 1922 Oxford*

Monasticism: Great Britain
Agrarian conditions and changes in west Wales during the sixteenth century, with special reference to monastic and chantry lands. *G. D. Owen, Ph.D. 1935 Wales*

The disposal of the monastic property in the diocese of Llandaff at the time of the Reformation. *T. J. Edwards, M.A. 1928 Wales*

Dissolution of English monasteries: social and economic effects. *J. Magee, M.A. 1941 National University of Ireland*

Dissolution of monasteries in England: social and economic results. *M. J. Prendergast, M.A. 1937 National University of Ireland*

The dissolution of the English nunneries. *H. T. Jacka, M.A. 1917 London*

The dissolution of the monasteries in Lincolnshire. *G. A. F. Hodgett, M.A. 1947 London, External Degree*

The extent and value of the lands in London and Southwark occupied by the religious houses (including the prebends of St. Paul's and St. Martin's le Grand), the parish churches and churchyards, and the inns of the abbots and bishops, before the dissolution of the monasteries. *M. B. Honeybourne, M.A. 1930 London, Bedford College*

The greater English monasteries and their knights, 1066-1215. *J. D. Anderson, B.Litt. 1948 Oxford*

Monasticism in Cheshire. *H. J. Hewitt, M.A. 1917 Liverpool*

Relations between English monasteries and their patrons in the thirteenth century. *S. M. Chevenix Trench, B.Litt. 1950 Oxford*

Scottish monasticism: its relations with the Crown and the Church to the year 1378. *D. E. Easson, Ph.D. 1928 Saint Andrew's*

Some chapters in the history of English nunneries in the later Middle Ages. *E. E. Power, M.A. 1916 London*

Monasticism: Ireland
The decline of the native Irish monasticism from the ninth to the twelfth centuries. *R. B. Knox, M.A. 1944 Belfast*

The monastic round towers of Ireland. *C. B. Phipps, Ph.D. 1935 Dublin, Trinity College*

Survivals of Irish monastic church organisation in late medieval and early modern times. *J. G. Barry, M.A. 1949 National University of Ireland*

Money
See also Banks and Banking; Capital; Finance; Gold Standard; Numismatics.

A 100% reserve plan in relation to monetary theories of the trade cycle. *J. E. Weinrich, M.Sc. 1948 London, School of Economics and Political Science*

Commercial fluctuations and currency disturbances of the seventeenth century. *W. J. Hinton, M.A. 1915 Wales*

The control of money. *R. C. Bernhard, M.Sc. 1936 London, School of Economics and Political Science*

Dominion exchanges and central bank problems arising therefrom. *H. C. Coombs, Ph.D. 1934 London, School of Economics and Political Science*

The equilibrium analysis of a monetary economy. *S. P. Chambers, M.Sc. 1934 London, School of Economics and Political Science*

The evolution of the money market (1835-1915). *E. T. Powell, D.Sc. 1915 London*

Exchange control. *H. K. M. Heuser, Ph.D. 1938 London, School of Economics and Political Science*

Exchange control and clearing agreements in 1931-37. *V. M. Bhatt, M.Sc. 1939 London, School of Economics and Political Science*

Foreign exchange control. *H. Metcalf, M.Com. 1939 Leeds*

Inconvertible paper money in relation to the foreign exchanges and international trade. *W. H. Lyon, M.A. 1925 Liverpool*

The influence of inflation and deflation on banking, based on a comparison of conditions in eastern and western Europe. *J. Kostanecki, Ph.D. 1927 London*

The international adjustment of monetary and banking systems and the proposals made since the war for the solution of the problem. *B. Samuel, M.A. 1928 Wales*

International monetary policy since 1919, with special reference to India. *D. C. Ghose, M.Sc. 1948 London, School of Economics and Political Science*

The legal aspect of money, with special reference to comparative and private international law. *F. A. A. Mann, LL.D. 1938 London, School of Economics and Political Science*

Monetary policy and dynamic change. *H. Barger, Ph.D. 1937 London, School of Economics and Political Science*

Monetary policy in agricultural raw material producing countries, with special reference to Egypt. *A. M. el Kaissouni, Ph.D. 1942 London, School of Economics and Political Science*

The monetary theories of John Locke. *J. S. Raj, M.Sc. 1937 London, University College*

The money and foreign exchange problems, with special reference to the monetary experience of Great Britain and the course of the dollar-sterling exchange in 1919-1925. *P. George, M.Sc. 1928 Wales*

Money and monetary policy in early times. *A. R. Burns, Ph.D. 1926 London*

Post-war developments in monetary theory. *I. M. Kapur, M.Sc. 1934 London, School of Economics and Political Science*

The problems of international exchange in 1914-1920. *A. M. Lewis, M.A. 1921 Wales*

Recent monetary problems of some primary producing countries. *A. R. Conan, M.Sc. 1938 London, School of Economics and Political Science*

The relative influence of money and credit on general prices. *J. Rejan, Ph.D. 1922 Edinburgh*

Resumption of cash payments: the problems as illustrated by the experience of various countries in the nineteenth century. *E. G. Wilson, Ph.D. 1928 London*

Seasonal variations in the demand for money. *M. S. Adiseshiah, Ph.D. 1938 London, School of Economics and Political Science*

Some reversions to former standards of money. *E. L. Hargreaves, Ph.D. 1924 London*

A study of the course of forward exchange rates during the last few years. *L. C. Duncan, M.Sc. 1934 London, School of Economics and Political Science*

Systems of limitation of currency. *G. R. Elvey, B.Litt. 1926 Oxford*

Tendencies of seventeenth century thought as exhibited in the writings of Lord Halifax. *C. E. Hughes, M.A. 1932 London, Bedford College*

Money contd.
Velocity of circulation of money. *R. Arakie, M.Sc. 1934 London, School of Economics and Political Science*

Money: Canada
Canadian monetary and fiscal developments since 1929. *J. E. L. Graham, B.Litt. 1939 Oxford*

Money: Central Europe
Currency and banking in central Europe, 1919-1938. *F. Rona, M.Sc. 1947 London, School of Economics and Political Science*

Money: China
The problems of monetary reform in China. *T. T. Cheng, M.Sc. 1937 London, School of Economics and Political Science*

Money: Egypt
The monetary system of Egypt. *M. A. Rifaat, Ph.D. 1935 London, School of Economics and Political Science*

Money: Far East
The currency and banking problems of China. *S. T. Hou, Ph.D. 1935 Liverpool*

Effects of the world economic depression on Far Eastern currencies. *L. M. Nadkarni, M.Sc. 1937 London, School of Economics and Political Science*

Money: France
Currency and banking developments in the French overseas Empire, 1939-1945. *P. L. Hogg, Ph.D. 1947 London, School of Economics and Political Science*

Modern monetary theories in France. *J. G. Zighdis-Papaioannou, Ph.D. 1939 London, School of Economics and Political Science*

Money: Great Britain
An analysis of the stock and flow of money in England and Wales since 1925. *R. M. Goodwin, B.Litt. 1937 Oxford*

Bodleian mss. relating to the later Tudors, with special reference to the currency literature of the period. *F. J. Routledge, B.Litt. 1920 Oxford*

British monetary policy and practice, 1927-33. *K. Gupta, M.Sc. 1938 London, University College*

A comparative study of the English and American money markets. *S. Y. Liu, Ph.D. 1927 London*

Currency history and the currency problem, 1914-1923. *A. E. Feavearyear, M.Sc. 1923 London*

The great recoinage of 1696-99 (a particular study of the question on currency devaluation). *M. H. Li, Ph.D. 1937 London, School of Economics and Political Science*

History of the London discount market. *W. T. C. King, Ph.D. 1936 London, School of Economics and Political Science*

The monetary and banking policy of Great Britain during and since the great depression. *M. S. Chen, M.Sc. 1939 London, School of Economics and Political Science*

The monetary reform of 1821. *P. C. Kimball, B.Litt. 1930 Oxford*

A study of the theories of Thomas Attwood and contemporary advocates of paper money in England. *J. Sanmarti, Ph.D. 1948 London, School of Economics and Political Science*

Money: Greece
Banking and monetary problems of Greece from 1931-1939. *A. Presanis, M.Sc. 1946 London, School of Economics and Political Science*

Money: Greece, Ancient
An inquiry into the purchasing power of the drachma in ancient Greece for the purpose of determining, if possible, the material conditions which prevailed in Athens during her existence as an independent state. *E. Y. Nisbet, Ph.D. 1948 Glasgow*

Money: India
The monetary policy of the Reserve Bank of India with special reference to the structural and institutional factors in the economy. *K. N. Raj, Ph.D. 1947 London, School of Economics and Political Science*

The organization of the Indian money market. *M. N. Asnodkar, M.Sc. 1923 London*

The problem of the rupee. *B. R. Ambedkar, D.Sc. 1923 London*

The problem of the standards of the Indian currency. *A. Sadeque, Ph.D. 1948 London, School of Economics and Political Science*

Money: Ireland
Banking and currency in Ireland. *J. V. Bourke, M.Comm. 1933 National University of Ireland*

Investigation into the Loans Guarantee Acts of Northern Ireland. *J. Munn, M.Com.Sc. 1943 Belfast*

Money: Poland
Polish monetary policy and trade fluctuations, 1924-1939. *S. Smierzchaiski, M.Sc. 1945 London, School of Economics and Political Science*

Money: United States
A comparative study of the English and American money markets. *S. Y. Liu, Ph.D. 1927 London*

Monetary and financial experiments in the U. S. A., 1933-35. *E. C. Acheson, Ph.D. 1939 London, School of Economics and Political Science*

A study of sound and unsound currency in Massachusetts from 1690 to 1763. *A. V. Barber, B. Litt. 1929 Oxford*

Money Lending
See Usury.

Mongolia
The economic development and prospects of Inner Mongolia (Chahar, Suiyuan, and Niugria). *Y. T. Chang, M.A. 1929 Liverpool*

Studies on the Ta'rikh-i-Jahān-Gushā of Juvayni. *J. A. Boyle, Ph.D. 1947 London, School of Oriental and African Studies*

Monism
Can a neutral monist theory of knowledge give an adequate account of memory. *N. R. Knatchbull-Hugessen, B.Litt. 1938 Oxford*

The ethical implications of a monadistic metaphysic. *J. K. Majumdar, Ph.D. 1923 London*

Science and monism: an historical and critical discussion of the monistic tendencies in the natural sciences. *W. P. D. Wightman, Ph.D. 1933 London, External Degree*

Monkhouse, Allan
The dramatic work of Allan Monkhouse. *H. C. Vaughan, M.A. 1949 Wales*

Monkstown
Baile na Manach: a dhinnsheanchus agus a stair (Monkstown: its topography and history). *T. O'Criodáin, M.A. 1942 National University of Ireland*

Monmouth
The history of the counties of Glamorgan and Monmouth during the Great Civil War, 1642-1648. *L. J. Thomas, M.A. 1914 Wales*

History of the development of the means of communication in the County of Monmouth. *M. A. Swallow, Ph.D. 1932 London, School of Economics and Political Science*

Monmouth, James
The Monmouth rebellion. *C. D. Curtis, M.A. 1939 Bristol*

Mono-Alu, Islands
Mono-Alu folklore. *G. C. W. C. Wheeler, D.Sc. 1927 London*

Monogamy
See Marriage.

Monophysites
Theodoret, bishop of Cyros and follower of the Antioch school in the Monophysite controversy, A.D. 441-457. *J. Malathouras, B.Litt. 1921 Oxford*

Monopoly
The course of public opinion and legal decision, including legislation, relating to economic combination and monopoly, mainly in Great Britain, in the period 1880-1914. *L. D. F. Peck, M.A. 1929 Wales*

The gold and silver thread monopolies granted by James I, 1611-1621. *M. A. Abrams, Ph.D. 1930 London, School of Economics and Political Science*

The law relating to combinations. *A. L. Haslam, D.Phil. 1929 Oxford*

Monotheism
See God.

Montagu, Basil
Literary work and literary friendships of Basil Montagu, Q.C. *M. C. Crum, B.Litt. 1950 Oxford*

Montaigne, Michel Eyquem de
Exposé des données actuelles de la question des idées religieuses de Montaigne. *M. Hopp, M.A. 1926 London*

The fortunes of Montaigne. *A. M. Boase, Ph.D. 1930 Cambridge*

Montaigne, Michel Eyquem de contd.
The indebtedness of Shakespeare and English writers to Montaigne and his *Essays*. D. J. E. Williams, M.A. 1917 Wales

Montaigne in England in the seventeenth century, with special reference to the *Essay*. P. B. Whitt, Ph.D. 1934 London, East London College

Montanism
Phrygia and Montanism. G. S. P. Freeman, B.Litt. 1940 Oxford

A study of early Montanism and its relation to the Christian church. W. G. Murdoch, Ph.D. 1946 Birmingham

Montchrestien, Antoine de
The sources and inspiration of Montchrestien's dramatic works and his place in French tragedy. D. S. Moss, M.A. 1927 Wales

Montégut, Jean Baptiste Joseph Emile
Emile Montégut: critic of English literature. J. W. Skinner, Ph.D. 1926 London

Montesquieu, Charles de Secondat de, Baron
The influence of Montesquieu upon the American constitution. R. W. Ferguson, M.A. 1912 London

Les idées de Montesquieu sur la religion. J. D. Berbiers, M.A. 1929 Liverpool

Mably and Montesquieu. R. Fargher, B.Litt. 1938 Oxford

Montesquieu: his political and economic ideas. P. Jordan, Ph.D. 1930 London, School of Economics and Political Science

Montesquieu: his political and economic ideas. P. Jordan, Ph.D. 1930 London, External Degree

Montesquieu and English thought. F. T. H. Fletcher, D.Litt. 1935 Birmingham

Montessori, Maria
Montessori and her inspirers. R. J. Fynne, M.A. 1921 London

Montfort, Simon de, Earl of Leicester
The personal disputes between Henry III and Simon and Eleanor de Montfort. M. M. Wade, B.Litt. 1939 Oxford

Simon de Montfort and his times. D. T. Hughes, M.A. 1910 Wales

Montgomerie, Alexander
A study of Scottish vernacular poetry in the reign of James VI; with a new text of the poems of Alexander Montgomerie. G. S. C. Stevenson, B.Litt. 1911 Oxford

Montgomery
The medieval lordship of Montgomery. D. Ward, M.A. 1924 Wales

Montgomery, James
The religious thought of James Montgomery. R. T. Williamson, Ph.D. 1950 Edinburgh

Montreal
The development of the port of Montreal: a study of the modification of geographical values. S. B. Gosling, M.A. 1932 Reading

Monumentum Ancyranum
Monumentum Ancyranum compared with other authorities for the life of Augustus. M. H. Davies, M.A. 1912 Wales

Moore, Edward
Moore en France de 1757 à 1830. D. E. Moore, M.A. 1934 Liverpool

Moore, George
The art of George Moore: his theory and practice. G. L. Jones, M.A. 1936 Liverpool

The influence of French literary theory and practice on the work of George Gissing and George Moore. M. P. Jones, M.A. 1936 Wales

The novels of George Moore. H. H. Noyes, Ph.D. 1938 London, Birkbeck College

Novels of George Moore. B. P. Misra, Ph.D. 1947 Dublin, Trinity College

Moore, John
John Moore, 1729 to 1802. S. Ray, Ph.D. 1936 London, University College

Moore, Thomas
An appreciation of Thomas Moore. M. Murphy, M.A. 1928 National University of Ireland

Biographical and critical study of Thomas Moore. M. Murphy, Ph.D. 1931 National University of Ireland

The poetry of Thomas Moore. J. J. Coghlan, M.A. 1920 National University of Ireland

Satirical poems of Thomas Moore. M. O'Riordan, M.A. 1946 National University of Ireland

Moral Philosophy
See Ethics.

Morality Plays
See also Mystery Plays.

Bywyd a gwaith Twm o'r Nant a'i le yn hanes yr Anterliwt (The life and work of Twm o'r Nant and his place in the history of the 'Interlude'). G. M. Ashton, M.A. 1944 Wales

The influence of the morality play upon the regular Elizabethan drama. G. E. Hollingworth, M.A. 1915 London

Yr anterliwd Gymraeg (The Welsh interlude). G. G. Evans, M.A. 1938 Wales

Yr anterliwt Gymraeg: ei ffynonellau, ei chrefftwaithm a'i gwerth fel arwddocâd o ddiwylliant y bobl (The Welsh 'interlude'; its sources, craftsmanship, and value as an indication of the culture of the people). T. J. R. Jones, M.A. 1939 Wales

Moray Firth
The geography of the Moray Firth lowlands, with special reference to distribution of settlements, and with special attention to the tract between the rivers Ness and Spey; Inverness and Cullen. F. H. W. Green, M.Sc. 1935 London, School of Economics and Political Science

The physical geography of the Moray Firth from Golspie to Port Gordon. A. Ogilvie, B.Sc. 1915 Oxford

Moray, Robert, Sir
The biography of Sir Robert Moray, 1608-1673. A. Robertson, B.Litt. 1912 Oxford

More, Hannah
Hannah More as a blue stocking. H. H. Davis, B.Litt. 1927 Oxford

The life, works and letters of Hannah More, with special reference to her influence in the social and educational movements of the eighteenth and early nineteenth centuries. W. J. E. Moul, M.A. 1933 London, King's College

More, Paul Elmer
A study of the development of the critical thought of Paul Elmer More. J. N. Harding, Ph.D. 1949 Birmingham

More, Thomas, Sir, Saint
An examination of the *Epigrammata* of Sir Thomas More and of their importance in his life and writings. R. Lester, M.A. 1937 London, King's College

Les traductions françaises de l'*Utopie* et l'influence de Thomas Morus en France au seizième siècle. J. Boyle, M.A. 1949 Liverpool

Sir Thomas More and education. E. M. Chesters, M.A. 1923 Liverpool

Sir Thomas More and the divorce. E. Edkins, M.A. 1916 Liverpool

Sir Thomas More as a satirist in his epigrams and *Utopia*. C. A. Thompson, B.Litt. 1947 Oxford

The social life and doctrine of St. Thomas More. H. Nolan, M.A. 1942 National University of Ireland

Some early Tudor dialogues, referred to by Sir Thomas More in his controversial works; with an account of Bishop Barlow. A. C. Hills, M.A. 1938 London, King's College

Some Spanish biographies of Sir Thomas More. R. O. Jones, M.A. 1949 London, King's College

Moréas, Jean
Contemporary theories of French prosody as exemplified in the works of Jean Moréas. B. L. Edmondson, M.A. 1922 Manchester

Contribution à l'étude de Jean Moréas. N. Niklaus, Ph.D. 1934 London, University College

La vie et les poésies de Jean Moréas. N. M. Firth, M.A. 1923 Leeds

L'évolution des thèmes poétiques dans l'oeuvre de Jean Moréas. P. E. Thompson, M.A. 1950 Manchester

Morgan, Henry, Sir
The place of Sir Henry Morgan in the history of Jamaica. M. Hunter, B.Litt. 1934 Oxford

Morgan, Thomas, Sir
Sir Thomas Morgan, Bart., 1604-1679, 'soldier of fortune'. D. G. Lewis, M.A. 1930 Wales

Morgenstern, Christian
Christian Morgenstern's relations to Nietzsche. J. H. Saxton, M.A. 1936 London, University College

Morison, James
The theology of James Morison, with special reference to his theories of the atonement. C. E. Kirsch, Ph.D. 1939 Edinburgh

Mormons
The Mormon doctrine of salvation and the nineteenth century background. E. L. Clitheroe, Ph.D. 1936 Edinburgh

Morocco
British policy in relation to Morocco, 1902-6. E. W. Edwards, M.A. 1939 Wales

Economic development of Morocco under French protection. T. H. Jupp, M.A. 1935 Bristol

The English press and the Moroccan crisis of 1911. H. G. Riddell, M.A. 1949 Liverpool

Europe and Morocco, particularly from 1900-1911. E. T. Glendon, M.A. 1923 Birmingham

Morris, Edward
Bywyd a gwaith Edward Morris, Perthi Llwydion (The life and work of Edward Morris, Perthi Llwydion). G. Jones, M.A. 1941 Wales

Morris, William
The *Defence of Guenevere* and other poems by W. Morris. J. Allen, M.A. 1913 Bristol

The development of thought in the writings and work of William Morris. P. Segal, M.A. 1939 London, University College

The early and late Morris. D. I. E. Huband, M.A. 1924 Birmingham

The influence of the ballad on nineteenth century poetry, with special reference to Rossetti, Morris and Swinburne. I. M. Empson, M.A. 1933 Reading

The literary work of William Morris as an expression of his social ideas. T. Cusack, M.A. 1941 Belfast

Medievalism in the works of Rossetti and William Morris. E. Hall, M.A. 1912 London

The prose tales of William Morris. W. E. Lloyd, M.A. 1930 Liverpool

The prose works of W. Morris. F. Gibbons, M.A. 1915 Birmingham

The social and economic ideas of William Morris and their relation to those of his times. E. L. John, M.A. 1944 Wales

A study of some of the influences traceable in the poetry of William Morris. C. M. Arscott, M.A. 1917 London

A study of *The Life and death of Jason, The earthly Paradise*, and *Sigurd the Volsung*, with special reference to Morris's treatment of his sources. C. M. Arscott, Ph.D. 1928 London

A study of the mythology and legend in the creative poetry of William Morris. E. Shannon, M.A. 1938 National University of Ireland

The treatment of Old Norse literature in the works of William Morris, with particular reference to *Sigurd the Volsung*. C. M. James, M.A. 1932 Wales

William Morris. E. M. Twyman, M.A. 1924 Birmingham

William Morris as an interpreter of northern legend. E. M. Kenyon, M.A. 1928 Manchester

William Morris's treatment of his Icelandic sources. A. M. Morton, B.Litt. 1935 Oxford

The works of Morris and of Yeats in relation to early saga literature. A. D. M. Hoare, Ph.D. 1930 Cambridge

The works of William Morris in relation to the Norse sagas. A. D. M. Hoare, M.Litt. 1927 Cambridge

Mortality
See also Population.

An analysis of the influence of social conditions on different causes of infant deaths and on stillbirths and neonatal deaths in county boroughs of England and Wales during the years 1928-1938. M. A. Bauer, M.Sc. 1944 Birmingham

Infantile mortality in Egypt, with some reference to the experience of Great Britain. H. Hassanein, Ph.D. 1945 London, School of Economics and Political Science

Some aspects of a fall in the rate of mortality as affecting the financial position of friendly societies and sickness funds. R. R. Brodie, Ph.D. 1932 London, External Degree

A statistical study of the incidence of still births in England and Wales and its possible relation to social influences. I. Sutherland, D.Phil. 1948 Oxford

A study of mortality and fertility trends and of various indices related thereto. A. H. Pollard, Ph.D. 1948 London, External Degree

Morte d'Arthur, le
See Malory, Thomas, Sir.

Mortgage (Law)
The Roman and English law of mortgage. *A. W. G. Ranger, D.C.L. 1884 Oxford*

Mortimer, Family
The family of Mortimer. *B. P. Evans, Ph.D. 1934 Wales*

Morus Dwyfech
Gweithiau barddonol Morus Dwyfech (The poetic works of Morus Dwyfech). *O. Owens, M.A. 1944 Wales*

Morys, Huw (Eos Ceiriog)
Bywyd a gwaith Huw Morys (Pont y Meibon) (1622-1709). *D. Jenkins, M.A. 1948 Wales*

Mosaic Law
See Jewish Law.

Moschus
Characteristics of the grammar and style of Bion and Moschus. *E. M. Roberts, M.A. 1908 London*

The poems attributed to Bion and Moschus. English commentary, with a new translation, introductory essays, and a complete index verborum. *J. E. Dunlop, Ph.D. 1944 London, External Degree*

Moseley, Humphrey
Humphrey Moseley, bookseller. *J. C. Reed, B.Litt. 1928 Oxford*

Moslems
See Islam.

Mosul
The geographical aspects of the Mosul Question. *M. Awad, M.A. 1926 Liverpool*

Motherhood
See also Parenthood.

The psychological role of the mother in the origin of the religious sentiment: a psychological study of mother-goddess cults, with special reference to India. *G. D. Boaz, D.Phil. 1942 Oxford*

Motion
Plato's later philosophy of motion. *J. B. Skemp, Ph.D. 1937 Edinburgh*

A study of simple harmonic motion, 1450-1850. *A. E. Bell, M.Sc. 1938 London, University College*

Motor Car Industry
See also Road Transport.

Rationalisation in relation to the economic situation of the British motor industry. *S. T. Hughes, M.Com. 1950 Birmingham*

Motor Performance
The acquisition of motor habits. *V. H. Hazlitt, M.A. 1917 London*

The automatization of voluntary movements. *B. Hla, Ph.D. 1934 London, King's College*

An enquiry into the correlation of motor ability with 'g'. *W. E. Phipps, M.A. 1939 Birmingham*

An experimental study of certain forms of manual dexterity. *J. N. Langdon, Ph.D. 1933 London, External Degree*

The plateau: a study of periods of arrested progress in motor learning. *E. Healey, M.Ed. 1934 Leeds*

A study of rhythm and psychological methods of developing regularity of time and stress in movement. *S. Nurullah, M.Ed. 1927 Leeds*

Motteux, Peter Anthony
Peter Anthony Motteux: a biography with a bibliography of his works. *R. N. Cunningham, B.Litt. 1929 Oxford*

Mountfort, William
An edition of the *Launching of the Mary. J. H. Walter, M.A. 1930 London, University College*

Mozley, James Bowling
An examination of Mozley's treatment of the Augustinian doctrines of grace and pre-destination. *T. O. Davies, B.Litt. 1925 Oxford*

Mughal Empire
See also Asaf Jah I; Aurangzeb, Emperor; Humayun; Shahgahan, Emperor.

The Court of Aurangzib as a centre of literature and learning. *R. A. Muhammadi, Ph.D. 1949 London, School of Oriental and African Studies*

The Mogul diplomacy from Akbar to Aurangzeb. *A. Rahim, Ph.D. 1932 London, School of Oriental and African Studies*

The northwest frontier policy of the Mughals, 1556-1658. *M. Jahangir Khan, Ph.D. 1937 Cambridge*

The political structure of the Mughal Empire in northern India and its practical working up to the year 1657. *I. Hasan, Ph.D. 1932 London, School of Oriental and African Studies*

Mughal Empire contd.
The provincial government of the Mughals: 1556 to 1659 A.D. *P. Saran, Ph.D. 1936 London, School of Oriental and African Studies*

Muhi-ud-Dīn Ibn al-'Arabī
The mystical philosophy of Muhyid-Dín Ibnul-'Arabí. *A. E. Affifi, Ph.D. 1930 Cambridge*

Muir, Edwin
Edwin Muir and Scottish letters. *M. O'Leary, M.A. 1948 National University of Ireland*

Mulcaster, Richard
The positions and elementarie of Richard Mulcaster. *G. M. Miller, M.A. 1934 Leeds*

Richard Mulcaster and his pedagogic doctrines: a study of the realistic movement in Elizabethan education. *R. A. Mackie, Ph.D. 1933 Glasgow*

Müller, Wilhelm
Studies in the lyric poetry of Wilhelm Müller, with special reference to his relations to the Romanticists. *M. E. A. Harris, Ph.D. 1922 London*

Munda Tribes
A changing austric culture. *D. N. Majumbar, Ph.D. 1935 Cambridge*

Mundella, Anthony John
The career of A. J. Mundella, with special reference to his Sheffield connections. *M. Higginbotham, M.A. 1941 Sheffield*

Munster, Book of
See Leabhar Muimhneach.

Muralt, Béat Louis de
Critical and historical edition of B. L. de Muralt's *Letters describing the character and customs of the English and French nations*, 1726, with an introduction and notes. *S. C. Gould, B.Litt. 1931 Oxford*

Murder
The history of *mens rea* in the law of homicide. *A. W. G. Kean, M.Litt. 1939 Cambridge*

Murle, The
The political system of the Murle. *B. A. Lewis, B.Sc. 1950 Oxford*

Murphy, Arthur
A study of the life and dramatic works of Arthur Murphy. *E. Cockroft, Ph.D. 1931 London, External Degree*

Murray, James Augustus Henry, Sir
Some letters of Sir James Murray. *E. Robson, M.A. 1948 Manchester*

Murray, John, Sir
A critical edition of the Persian correspondence of Col. Sir John Murray. *I. M. Khan, M.A. 1925 London*

Musar Movement, The
A study of the Musar movement. *K. Rosen, M.A. 1943 Manchester*

Muscovy Company
The policy and activities of the Muscovy Company in the late sixteenth and early seventeenth centuries. *M. Wretts-Smith, M.Sc. 1920 London*

The Russia Company. *G. M. Posnette, M.A. 1919 Birmingham*

Museums
Medical museums: an historical and bibliographical study. *L. W. G. Malcolm, Ph.D. 1933 Cambridge*

Music: General
See also Carols; Church Music; Hymns; Lute Music; Madrigals; Opera; Organ; Pianoforte; Singing; Songs.

The basis of musical artistry. *H. S. Wilson, Ph.D. 1948 London, Trinity College*

The conflict of musical opinion in the early eighteenth century: based on a study of certain critical writings of the period. *G. S. Jackson, B.Litt. 1949 Oxford*

The expressiveness of music. *W. J. Foxell, Ph.D. 1927 London*

Music and the theory of signs. *O. H. McDonald, M.Litt. 1949 Cambridge*

Music: Ancient
The Byzantine liturgies. *H. Holloway, M.A. 1918 Belfast*

The Greek modes. *J. F. Mountford, M.A. 1917 Birmingham*

A musical history of the Arabs: from the days of idolatry to the time of the Buwaihids. *H. G. Farmer, Ph.D. 1926 Glasgow*

Studies in Greek music with special reference to the harmoniai. *J. F. Mountford, D.Litt. 1921 Birmingham*

Music: Australia
The Percy Grainger materials preserved in the Anderson papers in the National Library of Scotland. *T. Shearer, B.Litt. 1935 Oxford*

Music: France
See also Berlioz, H.; Christophe, J.; Guillaume, de Machaut; Lully, J. B.

Music: Germany
See Bach, J. S.; Hoffmann, E. T. A.

Music: Great Britain
See also Lute Music; Madrigals; and Aldrich, H.; Weelkes, T.

The Elizabethan lyric and its relations with contemporary music. *D. J. Jones, M.A. 1939 Wales*

English instrumental music from the Reformation to the Restoration, with particular reference to the first half of the seventeenth century. *R. Donington, B.Litt. 1946 Oxford*

Musicians of the Scottish Reformation, with special reference to Crown policy c.1560-1650. *J. McQuaid, Ph.D. 1949 Edinburgh*

The Puritans and music, with special reference to the Commonwealth period. *W. M. Lewis, M.A. 1917 Wales*

Some aspects of music in England in the seventeenth century. *F. M. Harrison, Ph.D. 1935 London, Royal College of Music*

Music: India
Studies in Indian dancing as depicted in painting and sculpture and the representations of the musical ragas in painting. *M. Chandra, Ph.D. 1934 London, School of Oriental and African Studies*

Music: Ireland
A short general survey of the history of Irish folk music. *A. O'Connor, M.A. 1934 National University of Ireland*

Music: Italy
See Palestrina, G. P.

Music: Appreciation
The aesthetic appreciation of music and its training. *G. F. Sims, M.A. 1938 Birmingham*

An experimental investigation of the musical response of school-children. *J. H. Higginson, M.Ed. 1935 Leeds*

An investigation into the development of musical ability of children in a selective general school, with special reference to the effects of age, intelligence and training, together with a plan for a one-year course of work in rudiments of music and musical appreciation. *E. R. E. Caffyn, M.A. 1946 Reading*

Musical ability and appreciation: an investigation into its measurement, distribution and development: a contribution to the psychology of music using a new series of standardized tests. *H. D. Wing, Ph.D. 1941 London, University College*

The problem of listening to music. *E. M. Payne, M.A. 1933 Bristol*

The psychology of music, with special reference to its appreciation, perception, and composition. *P. E. Vernon, Ph.D. 1932 Cambridge*

The psychology of musical appreciation: an analysis of the bases and nature of the experience of listening to music. *C. E. Robertson, Ph.D. 1936 Durham*

Music: Study and Teaching
The application of musical tests to the study of individual reactions to music. *J. Meiklejohn, Ph.D. 1940 Glasgow*

Aptitude tests for performance on violinda (violin-type instrument). *H. B. Priestley, M.A. 1949 London, Institute of Education*

The development of musical ability with special reference to aural technique and sight reading. *A. J. Irvine, Ph.D. 1940 Glasgow*

An enquiry into the development of a new method of class music teaching based on the principles of Gestalt psychology. *G. I. Thomas, Ph.D. 1949 London, Institute of Education*

An experimental study of musical ability in schoochildren. *H. Lowery, M.Ed. 1927 Leeds*

Ideals in school music. *J. M. Sykes, M.A. 1939 Bristol*

An investigation into the development of musical ability of children in a selective general school, with special reference to the effects of age, intelligence and training, together with a plan for a one-year course of work in rudiments of music and musical appreciation. *E. R. E. Caffyn, M.A. 1946 Reading*

Music and education. *G. H. Jones, M.A. 1932 Birmingham*

Music: Study and Teaching contd.

Music in education. *R. M. Hayes, M.A. 1947 National University of Ireland*

Music in elementary education. *C. W. J. Hooper, M.A. 1942 Leeds*

Music in general education. *J. L. O'Ferrall, M.A. 1927 National University of Ireland*

Music in primary and secondary schools with special regard to its aesthetic and disciplinary values. *J. H. Fussell, M.A. 1936 Bristol*

Music is a language and should be taught as such. *R. J. W. Hurd, Ph.D. 1929 London*

Musical ability and appreciation: an investigation into its measurement, distribution and development: a contribution to the psychology of music using a new series of standardized tests. *H. D. Wing, Ph.D. 1941 London, University College*

Musical education in Tudor times, 1485-1603. *D. G. T. Harris, M.A. 1938 Liverpool*

The perception of musical relationships by school children: an anlysis of experimental data and a discussion of practical and theoretical issues. *A. Chadwick, M.Ed. 1949 Leeds*

Percussion playing and recorder playing in schools. *E. Priestley, M.Ed. 1942 Leeds*

Psychological factors in musical education and in the musical development of the child. *J. Mainwaring, M.A. 1931 Birmingham*

Rhythm and its significance in musical education: a study of the fundamental principles of rhythm, their development in musical composition and their rôle in musical education. *E. Wilson, M.A. 1941 Leeds*

The significance of rhythm in musical education. *J. W. James, M.A. 1938 Liverpool*

Singing disability in school children. *T. Pollock, M.Ed. 1950 Durham*

A study of the development as a school subject of music from the beginning of the nineteenth century to the present time in England and Wales, with special reference to official reports. *G. I. Thomas, M.A. 1943 Wales*

Tests of musical ability. *H. D. Wing, M.A. 1936 London, Institute of Education*

Tests of musical talent. *R. M. Drake, Ph.D. 1931 London, University College*

The use of visual and auditory aids in the class teaching of music. *R. R. Dale, M.Ed. 1936 Leeds*

Variations in the normal range of children's voices: variations in range of tone audition: variations in pitch discrimination. *T. Anderson, Ph.D. 1937 Edinburgh*

Music and Literature
See also Diderot, D.

French verse in classical metres, and the music to which it was set, of the last quarter of the sixteenth century. *D. P. Walker, D.Phil. 1940 Oxford*

Music and drama have a common origin. *H. P. Thomas, Ph.D. 1939 London, Trinity College*

Music and English poetry. *K. M. Wilson, Ph.D. 1925 Cambridge*

Music and poetry in the sixteenth century. *B. Pattison, Ph.D. 1934 Cambridge*

Music as a didactic element in Renascence literature. *M. Hammond, M.A. 1912 London*

The relation of music and poetry as reflected in the works of Tieck, Wackenroder and Brentano. *M. E. Atkinson, M.A. 1947 London, Bedford College*

The relationship between English poetry and music in the seventeenth century. *E. F. Hart, M.A. 1949 London, King's College*

The use of music in the Elizabethan theatre: an enquiry into the dramatic value of the musical element in the drama of the Elizabethan period. *S. Knox, M.Litt. 1939 Durham*

The use of song in the Elizabethan drama. *M. F. Dunn, M.A. 1929 Liverpool*

Musical Instruments
See also Lute; Organ; Pianoforte.

Ancient musical instruments of Ireland. *M. J. Bowman, B.Mus. 1933 National University of Ireland*

Arabic musical instruments, from a ms. in the Farmer collection. *J. B. Hardie, Ph.D. 1946 Glasgow*

The use of musical instruments in Jewish and Assyro-Babylonian religious ceremonial compared. *L. Glickman, M.A. 1942 Manchester*

Musical Taste (Psychology)
See Music: Appreciation.

Muskerry

Antiquities of E. Muskerry. *P. Hartnett, M.A. 1939 National University of Ireland*

Barúntacht Mhúscraighe (The barony of Muskerry). *D. F. Ua Buachalla, M.A. 1942 National University of Ireland*

Stair agus seanchas Iár-Mhúscraighe, agus filíocht le S. Máistir O'Conaill agus le Tadhg O'Síothcháin, agus giotaí le fillibh (The history and lore of West Muskerry, and poetry by S. Máistir O'Conaill, Tadhg O'Síothcháin and others). *D. MacCarthaigh, M.A. 1937 National University of Ireland*

Musset, Alfred de

Alfred de Musset et la littérature anglaise. *E. M. Pool, M.A. 1914 Liverpool*

Le proverbe dramatique et Alfred de Musset. *V. A. Cullingworth, M.A. 1935 Birmingham*

Les jeunes filles dans le théâtre d'Alfred de Musset. *S. Courtney, M.A. 1950 National University of Ireland*

Mycenae
Mycenaean religion. *J. E. John, M.A. 1915 Wales*

Mycology
An outline of the history of mycology up to about 1884. *I. M. Wilson, M.Sc. 1931 London*

Myers, Leopold Hamilton
A study of L. H. Myers as a philosophical novelist. *B. Das, B.Litt. 1950 Oxford*

Myopia
Myopia and the education of the myopic scholar in Scotland. *A. M. MacGillivray, M.D. 1930 Saint Andrew's*

Mysore
The administration of Mysore under Sir Mark Cubbon (1834 to 1861). *K. N. V. Sastri, Ph.D. 1931 London, University College*

Financial history of Mysore, 1799-1831. *M. H. Gopal, Ph.D. 1930 London, School of Economics and Political Science*

Industrial development of Mysore. *R. Balakrishna, Ph.D. 1939 London, School of Economics and Political Science*

State policy and economic development in Mysore State since 1881. *U. Abbayambal, Ph.D. 1931 London, School of Economics and Political Science*

Mystery Plays
See also Morality Plays; Townley Mysteries.

Quelques personnages comiques dans les mystères français de la Passion et autres du quinzième siècle. *J. J. Milne, D.Litt. 1926 Birmingham*

Some aspects of the English scriptural drama in relation to the times. *E. C. Oakden, M.A. 1918 Birmingham*

The York, Chester and Towneley cycles: a comparison of their contents and their outstanding characteristics of treatment. *F. M. Clulow, M.A. 1933 Birmingham*

Mysticism
See also Hinduism; Quietism; Religion; Theology; and Bahrıf, Q. M.; Blake, W.; Eckhart, J.; Ferrar, N.; Hopkins, G. M.; Hugh, of Saint Victor; Joachim, of Fiore, Abbot; Jones, R. M.; Julian, of Norwich; Kabir; Muhi-ud-Dıfn Ibn al-'Arabıf; Patmore, C.; Teresa, of Avila, Saint; Thompson, F.

Al-Junayd: a study of a third/ninth century mystic with an edition and annotated translation of his writings. *A. H. Abdel-Kader, Ph.D. 1948 London, School of Oriental and African Studies*

Bossuet and mysticism. *S. D. Screech, Ph.D. 1934 London, Birkbeck College*

The Christ-mysticism of St. Paul. *T. Caldwell, Ph.D. 1927 Saint Andrew's*

Cyfriniaeth yn llenyddiaeth Gymreig (Mysticism in Welsh literature). *J. I. Williams, M.A. 1926 Wales*

The doctrine of the "inner light': its European development immediately prior to the foundation of the Society of Friends, and in that Society from the time of George Fox to the present day. *H. B. Miner, Ph.D. 1936 Edinburgh*

The English mystics of the fourteenth century. *W. B. Brash, B.Litt. 1919 Oxford*

An examination of the doctrine of the inner light in the apology of Rt. Barclay. *J. B. Russell, Ph.D. 1931 Edinburgh*

Henry Vaughan: a study in the relation of poetry and mysticism. *M. M. Bruckshaw, M.A. 1950 Manchester*

Mysticism contd.

The influence of the pseudo Dionysius the Areopagite on the philosophy of St. Thomas Aquinas. *S. J. Curtis, Ph.D. 1931 London, External Degree*

The interpretation of the Song of Solomon in the Spanish mystics. *I. I. Macdonald, Ph.D. 1930 Cambridge*

The mystical element in the Pauline Epistles. *C. McL. Currie, Ph.D. 1933 Edinburgh*

The mystical element in the religious poetry of the seventeenth century (1600-1660), together with an anthology of Donne's sermons illustrative of his theology and mysticism. *I. Husain, Ph.D. 1935 Edinburgh*

The mystical element in Walt Whitman. *J. H. Bodgener, M.A. 1932 Liverpool*

Mysticism and nature: an enquiry into the attitude of the mystics to the natural world. *J. Dalby, D.D. 1948 Oxford*

Mysticism in nineteenth century English literature. *E. H. Thomas, M.A. 1924 Wales*

Mysticism in poetry; a study of AE, W. B. Yeats and Rabindranath Tagore. *A. C. Bose, Ph.D. 1937 Dublin, Trinity College*

Mysticism in the early nineteenth century poetry in England. *H. M. Gurbaxani, Ph.D. 1928 London*

Mysticism in the poetry of Wordsworth, Shelley and Tagore. *B. Sengupta, B.Litt. 1947 Dublin, Trinity College*

Mysticism in Wordsworth. *J. Adams, M.A. 1927 Wales*

The mysticism of George Sand. *L. V. Powles, Ph.D. 1939 London, External Degree*

The mysticism of Henri Frédéric Amiel. *H. Hunter, M.A. 1927 Leeds*

The mysticism of Hindu Bhakti literature, considered especially with reference to the mysticism of the fourth gospel. *A. J. Appasamy, D.Phil. 1922 Oxford*

The mysticism of Jacob Böhme, with special reference to his dialectic. *J. J. Stoudt, Ph.D. 1943 Edinburgh*

The mysticism of the fourth Gospel. *L. B. Hazzard, Ph.D. 1927 Edinburgh*

The nature of the mystical in the poetry of Francis Thompson. *T. McClintock, M.A. 1947 Manchester*

1. On the persistence of Arcanism. 2. On the place of mysticism in Christianity. *H. Marriott, B.D. 1915 Oxford*

Philosophical issues raised by mystical experience. *J. E. Storey, M.A. 1929 Liverpool*

Platonism and mysticism in J. Donne, H. Vaughan and T. Traherne. *C. G. M. Roberts, M.A. 1913 Bristol*

R. S. Hawker, poet and mystic: a study of his life, character and writings. *M. F. Burrows, M.A. 1925 London*

The reception of the works of Jacob Boehme in England in the seventeenth and eighteenth centuries. *R. E. B. Maxse, B.Litt. 1935 Oxford*

The relation of mysticism and philosophy. *S. T. Richards, M.A. 1915 Liverpool*

Richard Crashaw, poet and mystic: a critical biography. *F. E. Barker, M.A. 1922 London*

1. St. Paul and the mystery religions. 2. The Incarnation and the Eucharist. *H. L. James, B.D. & D.D. 1924 Oxford*

Scottish mysticism in the seventeenth century, with special reference to Samuel Rutherford. *C. N. Button, Ph.D. 1927 Edinburgh*

A study of the chief elements of mystical thought in English writers up to the time of Blake and Wordsworth. *M. Richards, M.A. 1921 Birmingham*

Thesis on the philosophic character of English fourteenth century mysticism. *J. Short, Ph.D. 1929 Edinburgh*

Three modern mystics: Thompson, Patmore, Hopkins. *J. M. Ryan, M.A. 1937 National University of Ireland*

The validity of mystical knowledge. *J. W. McAlpine, Ph.D. 1931 Edinburgh*

Mythology
See also Folk Lore; Gods; Hercules; Hippolytus; Jason; Legends; Medea; Prometheus; Troy; etc.

An analysis of the mythology of Orpheus. *E. M. Dance, Ph.D. 1939 Cambridge*

Aspects of the mythology in W. B. Yeats' poetry. *P. Ure, M.A. 1944 Liverpool*

Mythology contd.
The burlesque of mythology in seventeenth century Spanish poetry. *T. W. Keeble, Ph.D. 1948 London, King's College*

The character and sources of the legends connected with the House of Atreus. *A. G. Way, M.A. 1935 London, King's College*

Classical mythology and classical subjects in the work of some of the nineteenth century poets. *E. M. Lea, M.A. 1921 Birmingham*

The cult of Isis in Italy: an account of its external history. *M. S. Salem, Ph.D. 1937 Liverpool*

Dualism in Greek and Roman mythology. *M. I. Machin, Ph.D. 1933 London, University College*

The Helen myth in Greek literature. *W. C. Reid, M.A. 1948 Belfast*

The Italian element in Vergil's mythology. *E. M. Palmer, M.A. 1929 Manchester*

Meydum and Memphis: the formula in the light of mythology. *G. A. Wainwright, B.A. 1911 Bristol*

Ritual and mythology in Australia: an historic study. *A. P. Elkin, Ph.D. 1927 London*

A study of the mythology and legend in the creative poetry of William Morris. *E. Shannon, M.A. 1938 National University of Ireland*

Thessaly in the thirteenth century B.C. and the origin of the Centaur-Lapithai myth. *N. Bachtin, Ph.D. 1934 Cambridge*

Use of the Greek myth in English literature from 1800 to 1850. *E. M. Liptrot, M.A. 1929 Manchester*

Yeats and Celtic mythology. *A. J. Barrett, M.A. 1948 National University of Ireland*

Nādir Shāh
Nādir Shāh. *L. Lockhart, Ph.D. 1935 London, School of Oriental and African Studies*

Naga, The
An investigation into the social sanctions of the Naga tribes of the Indo-Burma border. *R. Needham, B.Litt. 1950 Oxford*

Nail Industry
The hand-made nail trade of Birmingham and district. *E. I. Davies, M.Com. 1933 Birmingham*

The hand-made nail trade of Dudley and district. *K. Henn, M.Com. 1927 Birmingham*

Nairobi
Social and political aspects of the development of municipal government in Kenya, with special reference to Nairobi. *M. Parker, Ph.D. 1949 London, School of Economics and Political Science*

Nala-ki Bata
An edition with translation, grammatical study, and glossary of a text *Nala-ki bata. B. S. Pandit, Ph.D. 1933 London, School of Oriental and African Studies*

Names, Botanical
Ainmneacha aiteann i gCondae Mhuigheo (The names of furze in Co. Mayo). *P. Mc Donagh, M.A. 1948 National University of Ireland*

Contribution à l'étude de la botanologie celtique: les noms de plantes des *Four Ancient Books of Wales. P. R. Y. M. Diverres, M.A. 1915 Liverpool*

Names, Geographical
See Place Names.

Names, Personal
A catalogue of names of persons in the German court epics: an examination of the literary sources and dissemination together with notes on the etymologies of the more important names. *F. W. Chandler, M.A. 1936 London, Birkbeck College*

A critical survey of the Old French element in English surnames. *S. D. Straw, M.A. 1919 London*

1. Dictionary of Pali Proper Names. 2. Vamsatthappakasini, or commentary on the *Mahaevamsa.* 3. The extended *Mahāvamsa. G. P. Malalasekera, D. Lit. 1938 London, External Degree*

An historical investigation into the survival of Anglo-Saxon personal names into the English surname period. *W. M. Taylor, M.A. 1914 London*

A study of anatomical eponymous nomenclature. *J. Dobson, M.Sc. 1944 Manchester*

Vocalisation of the proper names in the Pentateuch according to a Syriac manuscript, Add. 12138, in the British Museum. *J. Wood, M.A. 1940 Manchester*

Names, Place
See Place Names.

Nandi, The
The political organization of the Nandi. *G. W. B. Huntingford, B.Sc. 1947 Oxford*

Nanmor, Dafydd
The poetical works of Dafydd Nanmor. *T. Roberts, M.A. 1910 Wales*

Napoleon I Bonaparte, Emperor of France
The attitude of Wordsworth and Byron towards Napoleon. *R. Griffith, M.A. 1949 Wales*

The contemporary English view of Napoleon. *F. J. MacCunn, B.Litt. 1913 Oxford*

Napoléon et sa légende à travers le roman, le conte et la nouvelle jusqu'à la fin du Second Empire. *I. M. Fothergill, M.A. 1928 Wales*

Rousseau et Napoléon. *F. G. Healey, M.A. 1949 Birmingham*

Napoleon III, Emperor of France
The annexation of Savoy and Nice by Napoleon III, 1860. *F. R. Scott, B.Litt. 1924 Oxford*

British diplomacy and the recognition of Louis Napoleon. *M. E. Clark, M.A. 1922 London, King's College*

Narodnik Movement
See Agriculture: Russia.

Nashe, Thomas
The growth of realism in Elizabethan fiction, with special reference to Greene, Nashe and Deloney. *E. L. G. Giles, M.A. 1937 Wales*

The place of Thomas Nashe in the learning of his time. *M. McLuhan, Ph.D. 1944 Cambridge*

Thomas Nashe and English fiction. *E. Costello, M.A. 1932 National University of Ireland*

Nassyngton, William of
See William, of Nassyngton.

Natal
See also Bantu, The.

The development of the white community in Natal, 1845-72. *W. P. Bromiley, Ph.D. 1937 London, King's College*

Earl Grey's native policy in South Africa, with special reference to Natal. *P. Lee, M.A. 1930 Sheffield*

National Debt
See under the subheading Economics of individual countries.

National Income
See Income, National.

National Socialism
See also Fascism.

Genesis of national socialism. *T. D. F. Williams, M.A. 1946 National University of Ireland*

An investigation into the effects of National Socialism on secondary education in Germany and some problems involved in its reconstruction. *J. W. Powell, M.Ed. 1948 Durham*

Propaganda in National Socialist Germany. *O. Friedmann, M.Sc. 1947 London, School of Economics and Political Science*

The social sources of National Socialist anti-Semitism. *E. G. Reichmann, Ph.D. 1945 London, School of Economics and Political Science*

National Society, The
The educational history of the National Society, 1811-1833. *H. J. Burgess, M.A. 1949 London, Institute of Education*

Nationalism
The conflict of nationalism and imperialism with particular reference to the Near and Middle East. *M. Awad, Ph.D. 1926 London*

Economic nationalism. *M. Moore, M.Econ.Sc. 1943 National University of Ireland*

Heinrich Luden and the origins of the Luden Nationalist movement. *W. E. Brown, M.A. 1929 Birmingham*

The idea of the German 'national mission' as expressed by Fichte, List and Treitschke. *S. G. Graber, M.Sc. 1949 London, School of Economics and Political Science*

Johann Gottlieb Fichte and the genesis of the Nationalist movement in Germany. *C. J. Child, M.A. 1934 Birmingham*

Nationalism in the works of Maurice Barrès. *R. B. Jones, M.A. 1934 Wales*

Nationalist currents in nineteenth-century socialist doctrines. *V. T. C. E. F. Egger, Ph.D. 1949 London, School of Economics and Political Science*

The principle of self-determination, with special reference to President Wilson. *T. H. Kuo, B.Litt. 1935 Oxford*

Self-determination. *Z. N. Mahmoud, Ph.D. 1947 London, King's College*

Nationality
See also Citizenship.

Cases in English courts concerning unrecognized states or governments. *P. L. Bushe-Fox, LL.M. 1935 Cambridge*

Economic theories of the nineteenth century which were based on a critical study of the conception of nationality. *P. Henry, M.Econ.Sc. 1941 National University of Ireland*

The international juridical condition, in respect of nationality, of the former inhabitants of the Ottoman Empire under the Treaty of Lausanne, in Egypt and in the mandated territories. *P. P. J. Ghali, B.Litt. 1931 Oxford*

Nationality: its meaning, developments and problems. *B. Joseph, Ph.D. 1928 London*

1. Nationality and its problems. 2. The fall of feudalism in France. *S. Herbert, M.A. 1923 Wales*

Nationality within the British Commonwealth of Nations. *E. F. W. Gey van Pittins, Ph.D. 1928 London*

Naturalization as a sub-division of private international law. *F. B. Edwards, B.Litt. 1913 Oxford*

An quis civis in duabus civitatibus esse possit?. *T. Tumbleton, D.C.L. 1886 Oxford*

The sentiment of nationality. *J. J. Cater, Ph.D. 1924 Edinburgh*

The status of aliens in Egypt since 1937, with a sketch of the historical development of their position and a comparison of the present law in Egypt with the British law as to aliens. *G. E. Barakat, B.Litt. 1950 Oxford*

Natural History
See also Hudson, W. H.

A commentary on Pliny's *Natural History*, book VII. *A. E. J. Hann, Ph.D. 1949 London, Birkbeck College*

The place of natural history in English literature, 1789-1846. *W. A. Rawnsley, M.A. 1938 London, King's College*

Pliny: *Natural History*, book 2, vol. 1 (2). *D. J. Campbell, Ph.D. 1935 Aberdeen*

Ronsard's natural history. *M. E. Alan, B.Litt. 1943 Dublin, Trinity College*

Natural Law
The concept of natural law in the history of economic thought. *M. Sweeney, M.A. 1947 National University of Ireland*

The conceptions of natural law and natural right, with special reference to Hobbes, Spinoza, Locke and Rousseau. *N. S. B. Powell, M.A. 1932 Wales*

The law of nature: the Patristic conception as contrasted with the Thomist. *J. Dalby, B.D. 1942 Oxford*

Thomistic concept of natural law in ethics. *M. B. Crowe, M.A. 1945 National University of Ireland*

Naturalization
See Nationality.

Nature
See also Chance (Philosophy).

Ailneacht na Tuaithe (The beauty of the countryside). *S. O'Buachalla, M.A. 1942 National University of Ireland*

A comparative study of the nature poetry of Ieuen Glan Geirionydd, Alun, Islwyn and Ceiriog. *W. R. Jones, M.A. 1923 Wales*

A comparison of Shelley and Li Po as poets of nature. *C. Li, B.Litt. 1936 Oxford*

The Hebrew conception of nature, especially as illustrated by the prophets. *O. H. M. Lehmann, B.Litt. 1947 Oxford*

The inter-relations of nature and supernature in Von Hügel's *Philosophy of Religion. W. H. John, M.A. 1941 Wales*

La description de la nature dans les oeuvres d'Alphonse Daudet. *M. Carmichael, M.A. 1916 Liverpool*

La philosophie du retour à la nature chez Jean-Jacques Rousseau, et applications practiques de son système. *R. F. Britton, M.A. 1949 Liverpool*

Language and nature study. *D. N. Mac Donnell, M.A. 1934 National University of Ireland*

Les soirées de Mêdan as a manifesto of naturalism. *J. J. Starck, Ph.D. 1948 London, King's College*

The love of nature and rustic life in Horace, Tibullus, and Propertius. *M. J. Wrigley, M.A. 1933 Manchester*

Nature contd.
The mechanical view of nature since Descartes. *J. C. Hardwick, B.Sc. 1923 Oxford*

Mysticism and nature: an enquiry into the attitude of the mystics to the natural world. *J. Dalby, D.D. 1948 Oxford*

Naturalism in Spanish poetry from the origins to 1900. *R. M. Macandrew, D.Litt. 1929 Aberdeen*

Nature as revealed in the work of Auguste Brizeux. *E. David, M.A. 1934 Wales*

Nature in English poetry from 1610 to 1660. *D. E. Brook, M.A. 1936 Liverpool*

Nature in the poetry of Ronsard. *H. S. Mayall, M.A. 1931 Manchester*

Nature in the poetry of Robert Burns. *T. M. King, B.Litt. 1943 Dublin, Trinity College*

Nature in the works of Annette von Droste-Hülshoff. *L. van Z. Smit, Ph.D. 1932 London, University College*

Nature observance in Anglo-Saxon poetry. *M. Madden, M.A. 1937 National University of Ireland*

Nature studies in Greek poetry. *G. Soutar, D.Litt. 1898 Saint Andrew's*

The place of nature in French classical tragedy. *E. E. MacCabe, M.A. 1920 National University of Ireland*

Richard Jefferies: the interpreter of nature. *M. Kear, M.A. 1925 Liverpool*

Social sympathy and the scientific impulse in the naturalistic work of Gerhart Hauptmann. *J. Barnes, M.A. 1937 Manchester*

A study in Chaucer: the English poet's nature lore. *J. Haynes, M.A. 1917 National University of Ireland*

Tráchtas ar nádúir-fhilíocht na Gaedhilge (A treatise on Irish nature poetry). *B. Ua Nualláin, M.A. 1934 National University of Ireland*

The treatment of nature in Elizabethan literature. *P. B. Devilly, M.A. 1936 National University of Ireland*

Tuairisgí Nádúra i Trı Truagha na Sgéalaidheachta (Accounts of nature in the *Three Sorrowful Stories*). *M. Nı Mhathghamhna, M.A. 1943 National University of Ireland*

Virgil as an observer of nature. *A. I. Craig, M.A. 1909 Birmingham*

Nau Tarz i Murassa
A comparative study of the *Nau Tarz i Murassa*, and a history of Urdu prose from the earliest times down to 1775. *S. S. Husain, Ph.D. 1933 London, School of Oriental and African Studies*

Naval History
See History, Naval.

Navigation
See also Neckam, A.

Ancient Greek astronomy, with special reference to navigation and nautical astronomy. *A. W. E. Fenton, Ph.D. 1937 London, Birkbeck College*

Naziri
Faizi, Urfi, and Naziri (poets of Akbar's Court). *A. W. Khan, Ph.D. 1932 London, School of Oriental and African Studies*

Nazism
See National Socialism.

Ndola
A geographical study of the Ndola District, northern Rhodesia, with special reference to the copper mining industry. *D. S. Cleak, M.Sc. 1938 Bristol*

Neagh, Lough
The Lough Neagh shore area: its physical evolution and human utilization. *M. Addison, M.Sc. 1945 Belfast*

Near East
See Middle East.

Neath
The historical geography of the Neath region up to the eve of the Industrial Revolution. *C. D. J. Trott, M.A. 1946 Wales*

Neckam, Alexander
Alexander Neckam. *R. W. Hunt, D.Phil. 1936 Oxford*

Needlemaking Industry
An account of the needle industry up to the beginning of the factory system. *S. H. Hardy, M.Com. 1940 Birmingham*

Needlework
Prognostic tests for the selection of students for advanced courses in needlework. *I. A. Hughes, M.A. 1935 London, Institute of Education*

Negligence (Law)
Contributory negligence. *J. L. McQuitty, LL.D. 1940 Dublin, Trinity College*

The law of negligence, with particular reference to children. *A. J. C. Hirst, LL.M. 1929 Leeds*

Neohellenism
See Hellenism.

Neoplatonism
See also Augustine of Hippo, Saint; Plotinus; Synesius of Cyrene, Bishop.

The Christology of the second century apologists, with special reference to the philosophical influences. *V. A. S. Little, B.Litt. 1920 Oxford*

The influence of neo-Platonism on the life and thought of St. Augustine. *J. Anderson, Ph.D. 1927 Glasgow*

The influence of Plotinus upon the religious philosphy of St. Augustine, with special reference to the points of difference between neoplatonism and Christianity. *W. J. Heaton, M.A. 1930 Reading*

The literary and artistic manifestations of neo-Platonism in the Italian Renaissance. *N. A. Robb, D.Phil. 1933 Oxford*

1. The neo-Platonic tribute to the faith. 2. A study of the two records of our Lord's genealogy. *F. R. C. Bruce, B.D. 1904 Oxford*

Some aspects of the relation between Neo-Platonism and Christianity in the later Roman Empire. *A. Weissbruth, M.A. 1937 London, University College*

Nepal
Outline of social life in Central Nepal. *C. J. Morris, Dip. Anthropology. 1931 Cambridge*

Nerval, Gérard de
Hoffmann and Nerval. *C. R. Buxton, M.A. 1950 Manchester*

The influence of English writers on Gérard de Nerval. *J. K. Evans, M.A. 1939 Manchester*

Nesson, Pierre
See Pierre, de Nesson.

Nestorian Church
The missionary activity of the ancient Nestorian Church. *J. Stewart, Ph.D. 1925 Edinburgh*

Nestroy, Johann
Die Gestaltungsmittel der Komoedie bei Johann Nestroy. *G. Seidmann, M.A. 1945 Belfast*

Nestroys Parodien: ihre Technik und Methode. *K. Jones, M.A. 1927 London*

Netherlands
The Anglo-French struggle for the control of Dutch foreign policy, 1755 to 1763. *A. M. C. Le Mesurier, M.A. 1934 London, University College*

The development of the Dutch political party system, 1848-1901. *H. H. Ginsburg, B.Litt. 1948 Oxford*

Diplomatic relations between Great Britain and the Dutch Republic, 1714-1721. *R. M. R. H. Hatton, Ph.D. 1947 London, University College*

The Dutch barrier, 1709-1719. *I. A. Morison, Ph.D. 1929 London*

England and the establishment of the United Kingdom of the Netherlands, 1813-1816. *G. Renier, Ph.D. 1929 London*

The first Dutch war. *A. C. Dewar, B.Litt. 1917 Oxford*

Free trade and protection in the Netherlands, 1819-1825. *H. R. C. Wright, Ph.D. 1949 Cambridge*

Neuroses
See Mental Health.

Neutrality
The doctrine of continuous voyage, 1756-1815. *O. H. Mootham, M.Sc. 1926 London*

Neville, Ralph, Bishop
Ralph Neville, Bishop of Chichester and Chancellor. *J. M. B. Fradin, B.Litt. 1942 Oxford*

New Brunswick
Distribution of population in New Brunswick and Prince Edward Island. *A. D. Jones, M.A. 1933 Liverpool*

New France
The constitutional history of Canada in its earlier days; and the early trading companies of New France. *H. P. Biggar, B.Litt. 1899 Oxford*

New Galicia
The audiencia of New Galicia in the sixteenth century: a study in Spanish colonial government. *J. H. Parry, Ph.D. 1939 Cambridge*

New Guinea
See also Mailu.

New Jersey
Governor William Franklin. *F. M. Doherty, B.Litt. 1931 Oxford*

New Orleans
New Orleans as a port of immigration. *A. A. Conway, M.A. 1949 London, University College*

New South Wales
A colonial autocracy: New South Wales under Governor Macquarie, 1810-1821. *M. Phillips, D.Sc. 1908 London*

Constitutional development in New South Wales, 1788-1856. *A. C. V. Melbourne, Ph.D. 1931 London, King's College*

The economic development of the coastal regions of Victoria and New South Wales. *H. Swift, M.A. 1939 Liverpool*

Macquarie, Governor of New South Wales, 1809-1821. *B. H. Travers, B.Litt. 1949 Oxford*

New Testament
See Bible: New Testament.

New York
The causes of the revolution in New York, 1691-1760: a study of taxation and of the effects of England's commercial restrictions, prefaced by a sketch of the colony's political history. *B. Miles, B.Litt. 1905 Oxford*

New Zealand
See also Maori, The.

An analysis of economic fluctuations in New Zealand. *C. G. F. Simkin, D.Phil. 1949 Oxford*

The colonization of New Zealand. *J. S. Marais, D.Phil. 1925 Oxford*

Depression, recovery and reconstruction in New Zealand, 1929-1937: the effects of economic depression, of economic nationalism and of changes in world economic trends upon a pastoral-producing country. *J. P. Belshaw, Ph.D. 1937 Manchester*

Early settlement in the South Island of New Zealand, with special reference to the North and East. *R. K. Wilson, M.A. 1947 London, University College*

England and New Zealand. *A. J. Harrop, Ph.D. 1926 Cambridge*

New Zealand aspirations in the Pacific in the nineteenth century. *A. Ross, Ph.D. 1950 Cambridge*

New Zealand public finance. *A. R. F. Mackay, Ph.D. 1936 London, School of Economics and Political Science*

Social reform in New Zealand. *C. M. P. Brown, M.Sc. 1938 Cambridge*

Some theoretical aspects of industrialization of advanced agricultural countries, illustrated from New Zealand experience. *H. W. Larsen, Ph.D. 1948 London, University College*

New Zealand Literature
Literature in New Zealand. *E. H. McCormick, M.Litt. 1936 Cambridge*

Newark
The historical geography of the Newark area as illustrating changes in the importance of geographical factors. *H. M. Keating, M.A. 1929 London*

Newcastle Emlyn
The early history of Newcastle Emlyn, to include a study of the data relating to the castle, town and lordship down to the Act of Union, 1536. *T. J. James, M.A. 1913 Wales*

Newcastle-upon-Tyne
The trade of Newcastle-upon-Tyne and the northeast coast, 1600-1640. *B. Hall, Ph.D. 1933 London, School of Economics and Political Science*

Newfoundland
The development of government in Newfoundland, 1638-1713. *A. M. Field, M.A. 1924 London*

The economic geography of Newfoundland. *A. F. Martin, B.Sc. 1938 Oxford*

The establishment of constitutional government in Newfoundland, 1783-1832. *A. H. McLintock, Ph.D. 1938 London, King's College*

History of Newfoundland, 1713-1763. *J. Paterson, M.A. 1931 London, King's College*

Newfoundland contd.
The history of Newfoundland and Labrador, 1754 to 1783. *G. O. Rothney, M.A. 1934 London, King's College*

Newfoundland in colonial policy, 1775-1793. *W. L. Morton, B.Litt. 1935 Oxford*

Newfoundland, the tenth province of Canada: the case for union examined. *H. B. Mayo, D.Phil. 1948 Oxford*

Newman, John Henry, Cardinal
Cardinal Newman. *H. M. Herrick, M.A. 1932 Liverpool*

Cardinal Newman's doctrine of authority in religion. *R. S. Clements, Ph.D. 1931 Edinburgh*

A critical study of Newman's *Apologia pro vita sua*. *G. Lahey, B.Litt. 1949 Oxford*

Newman and intellectual culture. *F. J. Toner, M.A. 1945 National University of Ireland*

Newman, his work in Ireland, and his educational theory and practice. *R. J. McHugh, Ph.D. 1947 National University of Ireland*

Newman's work for university education in Ireland. *J. S. F. McGrath, D.Phil. 1948 Oxford*

The religious philosophy of Newman. *J. G. Jones, Ph.D. 1934 Edinburgh*

The theology of John Newman. *W. J. Cratchley, Ph.D. 1936 Bristol*

Newport
Port developments and commerce of Newport, 1835-1935. *E. M. E. Davies, M.A. 1938 Wales*

Newspapers
See Journalism.

Newton, Isaac, Sir
Berkeley's argument against Newtonian mathematics and its metaphysical implications. *A. E. Best, Ph.D. 1948 London, King's College*

The history of mechanics up to and including the work of Newton. *E. C. Henstock, Ph.D. 1938 London, External Degree*

Newton, John
John Newton and the early Methodists. *J. Laver, B.Litt. 1923 Oxford*

Nezāmi, of Ganjeh
The life and times of Nezāmi of Ganjeh. *G. H. Daeraeb Khan, M.A. 1932 London, School of Oriental and African Studies*

Ní Laeri, Máire Buidhe
Filíocht Mháaire Bhuidhe Ní Laeri (The poems of Máire Buidhe Ní Laeri). *D. O'Donoghue, M.A. 1929 National University of Ireland*

Nibelungen
See also Hebbel, C. F.

The Nibelungen saga in Celtic literature. *M. O'Doherty, M.A. 1916 National University of Ireland*

The study and literary treatment of the *Nibelungen* legend and *Nibelungenlied* from 1752 to the present time. *N. M. Thorp, D.Phil. 1938 Oxford*

Nice
The annexation of Savoy and Nice by Napoleon III, 1860. *F. R. Scott, B.Litt. 1924 Oxford*

Nicene Creed
See Creeds.

Nicole, Pierre
The life and work of Pierre Nicole. *N. J. Abercrombie, D.Phil. 1933 Oxford*

Nicolson, William, Bishop
The political and ecclesiastical activities of William Nicolson, Bishop of Carlisle (1702-1718). *P. J. Dunn, M.A. 1931 London, King's College*

Nicopolis
Nicopolis: a study based on eastern and western sources, and an examination of the battlefield and its approaches. *A. S. Atiya, Ph.D. 1933 London, School of Oriental and African Studies*

Niebuhr, Reinhold
The Christian interpretation of history as exemplified in the writings of Jacques Maritain and Reinhold Niebuhr. *W. E. Tyree, Ph.D. 1949 Edinburgh*

Nietzsche, Friedrich Wilhelm
The attack on Christendom made by Kierkegaard and Nietzsche. *C. Bonifazi, M.A. 1950 Bristol*

Christian Morgenstern's relations to Nietzsche. *J. H. Saxton, M.A. 1936 London, University College*

The ethical theory of Nietzsche. *H. Morris-Jones, B.Litt. 1937 Oxford*

The influence of Nietzsche's French reading on his thought and writing. *W. D. Williams, D.Phil. 1950 Oxford*

Nigeria
See also Bachama; Ewe; Hausa; Ibo; Igboland; Isoko; Nupe; Umundri; Yoruba.

The human geography of Nigeria in relation to physical aspects, with special reference to agriculture. *E. I. Oli, M.A. 1945 London, External Degree*

International rivalry in the bights of Benin and Biafra, 1815-1885. *W. H. Scotter, Ph.D. 1934 London, King's College*

Law and British administration in South-eastern Nigeria. *E. U. Udoma, Ph.D. 1944 Dublin, Trinity College*

Notes on some tribes of Kabba province. *B. Kennett, Dip. Anthropology. 1931 Cambridge*

Nineveh
See also Assyria.

The history of the Aramaeans down to the fall of Nineveh, 612 B.C. *F. Tomkinson, M.A. 1932 Wales*

Nobility
See Aristocracy.

Nodier, Charles
Charles Nodier: romancier et conteur, 1780-1844. *B. Taylor, M.A. 1938 Birmingham*

The linguistic ideas of Charles Nodier. *S. Daiches, B.Litt. 1940 Oxford*

Nodier, conteur. *H. J. Barker, M.A. 1923 Liverpool*

The press articles of Charles Nodier. *P. A. Charles, M.A. 1931 Wales*

Nonconformity
See also Anabaptists; Baptists; Clapham Sect; Congregationalism; Disciples of Christ; Methodism; Missions; Presbyterianism; Protestantism; Scottish Reformed Church; and Bale, J.; Baxter, R.; Beecher, L.; Cromwell, O.; Glas, J.; Knox, J.; Powell, V.

The aims and practices of the English Dissenters from the end of Anne's reign to the rise of the Wesleyan Movement. *D. Coomer, M.A. 1944 Liverpool*

Early nonconformity in Lincolnshire. *J. Plumb, M.A. 1940 Sheffield*

The forms and psychology of worship in the Free Church tradition, with special reference to Methodism. *J. Bishop, M.A. 1947 Bristol*

History of the laws against the nonconforming churches in Ireland in the 17th and 18th centuries. *R. D. Edwards, M.A. 1931 National University of Ireland*

1. Indirect proofs of the Resurrection. 2. The influence of dissent upon the Church of England. *A. E. S. Ward, B.D. & D.D. 1924 Oxford*

Nonconformist academies in Wales (1662-1862). *H. P. Roberts, M.A. 1922 Liverpool*

Nonconformist academies in Wales in the eighteenth century. *W. P. Thomas, M.A. 1928 Wales*

The nonconformity of Richard Baxter. *I. Morgan, Ph.D. 1944 London, Richmond College*

The political importance of English Protestant nonconformity, 1673-88. *R. R. Osborn, B. Litt. 1937 Oxford*

The principle of authority in the Free Churches. *A. J. Nixon, Ph.D. 1930 London, External Degree*

Protestant nonconformity and some social and economic questions, 1660-1800. *E. D. Bebb, Ph.D. 1934 Sheffield*

A psychological study of some aspects of the religious consciousness of seventeenth century England: considered with particular reference to the psychological factors involved in the development of English 'dissent'. *A. G. S. Spinks, M.A. 1939 London, University College*

The Reverend Richard Baxter and Margaret Charlton: being an examination of *The Breviate of a Life of Margaret Charlton* by Richard Baxter (1681). *J. T. Wilkinson, M.A. 1930 Birmingham*

Some contributions to the early history of Nonconformity in Rossendale. *K. Gray, M.A. 1942 Wales*

A statistical study of the development of Nonconformity in north Wales in the nineteenth century, with special reference to the period 1850-1901. *W. A. Evans, M.A. 1928 Liverpool*

Non-Jurors
See Jacobites.

Norfolk
The administration of the counties of Norfolk and Suffolk in the reign of Henry IV. *G. E. Morey, M.A. 1941 London, University College*

Norfolk contd.
The agricultural geography of Norfolk, with special reference to changes in land utilisation and human occupancy. *J. E. G. Mosby, Ph.D. 1938 London, School of Economics and Political Science*

Contributions towards the study of the historical geography of Norfolk, with special reference to West Norfolk. *S. H. King, M.A. 1937 London, King's College*

The Norfolk Rising under Robert Kett, 1549. *W. H. T. Walker, M.A. 1921 Wales*

Some aspects of the religious history of Norfolk in the fifteenth century. *C. B. Firth, M.A. 1910 London*

Norman Antiquities
Norman Lincolnshire. *G. H. Marshall, M.A. 1948 Leeds*

Norman Conquest
See Great Britain: History: Early and Medieval.

Normandy
For the Norman Conquest, see Great Britain: History: Early and Medieval. See also Rollo, Duke of Normandy.

The family of de la Pomerai of Beri, 1066-1719, with appendix post 1720. *E. B. Powley, M.A. 1941 Liverpool*

Henry V as conqueror in France, and the Lancastrian experiment in Normandy. *E. Wragg, M.A. 1916 Birmingham*

Le Normand d'après Guy de Maupassant. *L. F. Monnaie, M.A. 1926 London*

The Norman element in the novels of Jules Barbey d'Aurevilly. *P. A. Lewis, M.A. 1921 Wales*

Normandy in the works of Gustave Flaubert. *J. L. Verney-Boys, M.A. 1947 London, King's College*

The Northmen in France. *A. W. Kirkaldy, B.Litt. 1902 Oxford*

Norms (Psychology)
The concept of norms in the theology of Ernst Troeltsch. *L. S. Eby, Ph.D. 1932 Edinburgh*

Norris, William, Sir
Sir William Norris, Bart., and his embassy to Aurangzeb (1657-1702). *H. Das, B.Litt. 1923 Oxford*

Norsemen
Norse relations with Wales. *B. G. Charles, M.A. 1932 Wales*

The Northmen in France. *A. W. Kirkaldy, B.Litt. 1902 Oxford*

The position of women in Norway in Viking times. *E. S. Eames, M.Litt. 1950 Cambridge*

North America
The French survival in North America. *W. E. Arnell, M.Sc. 1946 London, External Degree*

North, Christopher
See Wilson, John.

North, Frederick, 8th Lord North
Constitutional aspects of the ministry of Lord North. *A. B. Archer, M.A. 1910 Liverpool*

North Sea
Hull and the North Sea coastlands. *V. J. Gorner, M.Sc. 1948 London, External Degree*

Report on hydrographical investigations in the Faroe-Shetland Channel and the northern part of the North Sea during the years 1904-1905. *A. J. Robertson, D.Sc. 1906 Saint Andrew's*

North West Frontier Province, India
A general geographical account of the N. W. F. Province of India. *M. A. K. Durrani, M.A. 1939 London, School of Economics and Political Science*

The political and cultural history of the Panjab, including the North West Frontier Province in its earliest period. *L. Chandra, Ph.D. 1940 London, School of Oriental and African Studies*

Northamptonshire
The historical geography (ancient) of Northamptonshire and the southeast Midlands. *S. B. Harris, M.Sc. 1945 London, External Degree*

Judicial investigations under the Dictum of Kenilworth, Northamptonshire. *E. H. Graham, M.A. 1930 Manchester*

Judicial proceedings under the Dictum de Kenilworth, Northamptonshire. *T. W. Byrne, M.A. 1932 Manchester*

Judicial proceedings under the Dictum de Kenilworth, in Northamptonshire. *M. M. Rothwell, M.A. 1929 Manchester*

Northamptonshire contd.
Northamptonshire county elections and electioneering (1695-1832), based mainly on the Isham and Cartwright muniments. *E. G. Forrester, B.Litt. 1939 Oxford*

Northcote, Stafford, Sir
Sir Stafford Northcote's sinking fund and the redemption of debt between 1874 and 1914. *P. C. Gordon Walker, B.Litt. 1930 Oxford*

Northern Ireland
See also Cooke, H.; De Burgh, Family, Earls of Ulster.

The financial relationship between Great Britain and Northern Ireland 1931 to 1945. *M. C. Mathur, M.Com.Sc. 1947 Belfast*

A geographical study of the Eire-Northern Ireland boundary. *J. G. Thomas, M.A. 1949 Wales*

The influence of the Rev. Henry Cooke on the political life of Ulster. *J. Jamieson, M.A. 1950 Belfast*

Irish Catholics and Legislative Union, 1800. *T. A. Burke, M.A. 1943 National University of Ireland*

Northern Ireland: a study in human and economic geography. *J. W. Darbyshire, M.A. 1933 Liverpool*

The plantation of Ulster. *S. G. Kennedy, M.A. 1925 National University of Ireland*

The problem of Lord Essex in Ireland. *L. Duggan, M.A. 1926 National University of Ireland*

Rural life in Northern Ireland and other papers. *J. McF. Mogey, D.Sc. 1948 Belfast*

A study of devolution, with special reference to the government of Northern Ireland. *P. N. S. Mansergh, D.Phil. 1936 Oxford*

Northumberland
The agricultural geography and related distribution of population in Northumberland. *E. C. Sykes, M.A. 1931 Liverpool*

The changes of the Reformation period in Durham and Northumberland. *B. N. Wilson, Ph.D. 1939 Durham*

The older settlements of north Northumberland: a study in geography and history. *C. P. M. Olsen, M.A. 1947 London, University College*

Northumberland, John Dudley, Duke of
The life and times of John Dudley, Earl of Warwick and Duke of Northumberland, 1504(?)-1553. *C. Struge, Ph.D. 1927 London*

Norton, Thomas
Biographical study of T. Norton. *P. F. Chapman, M.A. 1931 Bristol*

Norway
See also Norsemen.

English accounts and views of Norwegian life and literature, especially in the nineteenth century. *C. J. B. Burchardt, B.Litt. 1918 Oxford*

Studies in human geography in the highland regions of Norway. *E. W. Milne, D.Sc. 1934 Aberdeen*

Norwegian Literature
See also Ibsen, H.

English accounts and views of Norwegian life and literature, especially in the nineteenth century. *C. J. B. Burchardt, B.Litt. 1918 Oxford*

Norwich
Critical edition of the Norwich Mayor's Court minute books (1630-3), with introduction describing functions of the court at that time. *W. L. Sachse, B.Litt. 1937 Oxford*

Finance accounts of Norwich Cathedral Priory, 1272-1377. *H. W. Saunders, D. Litt. 1927 Glasgow*

Notaries
English notaries at the Papal Curia in the fifteenth century with special reference to W. Swan. *D. Newell, Ph.D. 1934 Manchester*

The origin and early history of the office of notary, with a foreword by the Right Honourable the Viscount Dunedin. *J. C. Brown, Ph.D. 1935 Edinburgh*

Nottingham
The development of education in Nottingham during the nineteenth and the early twentieth century with special reference to the history of University College. *E. M. Becket, M.A. 1922 London*

Nottinghamshire
The factors which have influenced settlement and the movements of population within the plain of Nottingham. *H. M. Keating, Ph.D. 1933 London, External Degree*

The human and economic development of Nottingham and the associated district. *K. C. Edwards, M.A. 1931 London, External Degree*

Nottinghamshire contd.
Nottinghamshire in the eighteenth century: a study of the movements leading to the industrial revolutions of the nineteenth century. *J. D. Chambers, Ph.D. 1927 London*

Nova Scotia
British rule in Nova Scotia, 1713-1784. *W. S. MacNutt, M.A. 1932 London, King's College*

The history of Nova Scotia prior to 1763. *J. B. Brebner, B.Litt. 1925 Oxford*

Origins of self-government in Nova Scotia, 1815-1836. *J. S. Martell, Ph.D. 1935 London, King's College*

Novalis
Novalis, Friedrich von Hardenberg, in English translation. *G. A. Black, Ph.D. 1936 London, University College*

Novatian
1. Miracles in the light of modern science. 2. The Trinitarian formula in the writings of Novatian. *W. Y. Fausset, B.D. 1914 Oxford*

The theology of Novatian. *D. M. Cooper, Ph.D. 1944 London, King's College*

Novels
See Fiction.

Noyes, Alfred
Poetry of Alfred Noyes. *E. Coyle, M.A. 1933 National University of Ireland*

Nubia
Lower Nubia in the early Byzantine period. *L. P. Kirwan, B.Litt. 1935 Oxford*

The racial history of Egypt and Nubia from predynastic to present times. *A. M. El Batrawi, Ph.D. 1940 London, University College*

Nuisance
The nature and scope of civil liability in nuisance. *W. A. McRae, B.Litt. 1936 Oxford*

Nature and scope of private nuisance. *I. Cash, B.Litt. 1939 Oxford*

Number Theory
The development in ancient Greece of the concept of number in arithmetic and geometry. *J. L. Stirk, M.Sc. 1947 London, University College*

The Germanic numerals and numeral-systems. *J. McKenzie, Ph.D. 1938 Leeds*

An investigation into the development of number concepts in young children. *M. M. Smith, M.A. 1943 Leeds*

An uimhir dhéide i saothar na n-úghdar seo leanas. 1. An t-ath. P. O'Laoghaire. 2. P. O'Conaire. 3. An Seabhac (The number two as used in the works of P. O'Laoghaire, P. O'Conaire, and An Seabhac). *R. O'Domnabháin, M.A. 1942 National University of Ireland*

Uimhreacha i saothar an ath. P. O'Laoghaire (Numbers as used in the work of Father Peadar O'Laoghaire). *S. O'Riáin, M.A. 1939 National University of Ireland*

Numenius
The life and philosophy of Numenius. *B. S. Page, M.A. 1926 Birmingham*

Numidia
History of Numidia under the Roman Republic. *S. M. Gates, M.A. 1917 London*

Numismatics
The coin hoards of Roman Britain. *A. S. Robertson, M.A. 1936 London, University College*

The coinage of ancient Palestine from the second century B.C. to the fourth century of the Christian era. *A. Mallinson, B.Litt. 1924 Oxford*

The coinages of Illyria and Paeonia from the early fourth century B.C. until the establishment of Roman provinces in these countries. *J. M. F. May, B.Litt. 1937 Oxford*

Inscriptions on old English coins up to 1154. *L. Woosnam, Ph.D. 1921 Cambridge*

The place of coinage in Greek foreign trade down to the end of the fifth century B.C. *A. H. Lloyd, Ph.D. 1929 Cambridge*

Nunneries
See Monasticism.

Nupe, The
The political and religious structure of Nupe society (northern Nigeria). *S. F. Nadel, Ph.D. 1935 London, School of Economics and Political Science*

Nuremberg
Die Familiengeschichte der Köler. *H. S. M. Amburger, Ph.D. 1928 London*

The Nuremberg legend of the crocodile. *L. A. Triebel, M.A. 1914 London*

Nursery Schools
See Education, Elementary.

Nursing Profession
The effect of a recruitment film on the attitude of school leavers to nursing as a career. *A. J. W. Jeffery, M.Ed. 1950 Manchester*

Nyanja Language
The phonetics of a Nyanja speaker, with particular reference to the phonological structure of the word. *T. Hill, M.A. 1948 London, School of Oriental and African Studies*

Nyasaland
See also Waya; Yao.

The history of Nyasaland and northeastern Rhodesia, 1875-95. *A. J. Hanna, Ph.D. 1948 London, King's College*

Nyaya
See Philosophy: India.

Oases
A geographical study of the Egyptian oases. *M. M. Mousa, Ph.D. 1938 Liverpool*

Oates, Titus
Titus Oates and the Popish plot. *R. C. F. Dolley, M.A. 1911 London*

Wales and the border counties in relation to the Popish plot. *I. M. O'Leary, M.A. 1924 Wales*

Oaths
The Oath of the Lord, being a critical and analytical exposition of the Halakhah of the judicial imposition of the Biblical oath of the Bailees in conjunction with a discussion of the general laws relevant to it. *W. Kirzner, M.A. 1930 London, King's College*

Oberg, Eilhart von
Le *Tristan* d'Eilhart d'Oberg. *A. Lofthouse, M.A. 1939 Manchester*

Objectivity
Kant's view of object and objectivity. *A. W. James, M.A. 1908 London*

Obligation
The law of obligation in the laws of Hywel Dda in the light of Roman and early English (Anglo-Saxon) law. *W. E. Daniels, LL.D. 1937 Dublin, Trinity College*

O'Brien, James Bronterre
The life of James Bronterre O'Brien. *A. Plummer, B.Litt. 1928 Oxford*

O'Bruacháin, Tomás Gruamdha
Smaointe beatha Chriost, i astriú gaedhilge a chuir Tomas Gruamdha O Bruacháin (fl. c.1450), ar an *Meditationes vitae Christi* (*Thoughts on the life of Christ*; an Irish translation by Tomás Gruamdha O Bruacháin (fl. c.1450) of *Meditaciones vitae Christi*). *C. O'Maonaigh, M.A. 1941 National University of Ireland*

O'Bruadair, Daibhí
Dáibhí O'Bruadair; a bheatha agus a shaothar (Daibhí O'Bruadair: his life and work). *S. M. MagUidhir, M.A. 1937 National University of Ireland*

Observation
See Perception.

Obstetrics
See Gynecology and Obstetrics.

O'Casey, Sean
The plays of Sean O'Casey. *C. Houghton, M.A. 1942 Birmingham*

Occupations
See Careers.

Classification of communities by means of occupations. *E. H. Selwood, Ph.D. 1932 London, Birkbeck College*

O'Ceallaigh, Tomás
An t-athair Tomás O'Ceallaigh agus a shaothar, maille le réamh-rádh, nótaí agus eile (Fr. Tomás O'Ceallaigh and his work, with preface, notes etc). *T. S. O'Laoighidh, M.A. 1941 National University of Ireland*

O'Conaire, Pádraig Og
An chómhacht a bhí ag an Athair Peadar O'Laoghaire agus ag Pádraig O'Conaire (The extent of the influence of Father Peadar O'Laoghaire and Pádraig O'Conaire). *T. P. O'Laochdha, M.A. 1941 National University of Ireland*

An greann i sgríbhinní na n-úghdar seo leanas: 1. Pádraig Ua Conaire. 2. An Seabhach. 3. An t-Athair Peadar Ua Laoghaire (The humour in the writings of Pádraig Ua Conaire, An Seabhach, An t-Athair Peadar Ua Laoghaire). *M. Ní Thuana, M.A. 1938 National University of Ireland*

O'Conaire, Pádraig Og contd.
Pádraig Og O'Conaire agus Máire: saoghal agus saothar na mbeirte (Pádraig Og O'Conaire and Máire: their lives and works). *T. Plover, M.A. 1950 National University of Ireland*

An uimhir dhéide i saothar na n-úghdar seo leanas. 1. An t-ath. P. O'Laoghaire. 2. P. O'Conaire. 3. An Seabhac (The number two as used in the works of P. O'Laoghaire, P. O'Conaire, and An Seabhac). *R. O'Domnabháin, M.A. 1942 National University of Ireland*

O'Conchubhair, Bonaventura
Buaidh na Naomh-Chroiche; aistriú a rinne Bonaventura O'Conchubhair, O.F.M. ar *Triumphus Crucis* le Girolamo Savonarola (*The triumph of the Holy Cross*; a translation by Bonaventura O'Conchubhair, O.F.M. of *Triumphus Crucis* by Girolamo Savonarola). *C. O'Gioballáin, M.A. 1938 National University of Ireland*

O'Conchubhair, Tomás
Filíocht Thomáis Uí Chonchubhair (The poetry of Tomás.O'Conchubhair). *M. E. Ní Dhonnchadha, M.A. 1941 National University of Ireland*

O'Connell, Daniel
Daniel O'Connell and Catholic emancipation. *N. E. L. Guest, M.A. 1931 Birmingham*

O'Conor, Charles
Early life of C. O'Conor, 1710. *C. O'Conor, M.A. 1930 National University of Ireland*

O'Criomhtháin, Tomás
Graiméar ar an ainm san *Oileánach* le Tomás O'Criomhtháin (The grammar of the noun as used in *An tOileánach* by Tomás O'Criomhtháin). *D. O'Conchubháir, M.A. 1944 National University of Ireland*

O'Cuirnín, Pádraig Dubh
Pádraig Dubh O'Cuirnín tiugh-fhile na nGael (Pádraig Dubh O'Cuirnín, popular poet of the Irish). *J. A. McGrath, Ph.D. 1945 National University of Ireland*

Odo of Cheriton
Life and works of Odo of Cheriton. *A. C. Friend, D.Phil. 1936 Oxford*

O'Donnghaile, Eoghan
Duanta Eoghain Uí Dhonnghaile agus duanta eile ó indé (The poems of Eoghan O'Donnghaile and other poems of yesterday). *R. O'Tierney, M.A. 1937 National University of Ireland*

Odoricus, Friar
Fford y Brawt Odric, o'r Llanstephan ms. 2; ei gymharu âr gwreiddiol, gyda nodiadau gramadegol a geirfa (*The journey of Brother Odoric*, from the Llanstephan ms. 2; compared with the original and with grammatical notes and a vocabulary). *S. J. Williams, M.A. 1925 Wales*

Oehlenschläger, Adam Gottlob
A study of Oehlenschläger. *M. Roseby, M.A. 1913 London*

Oengus
Aislinge Oenguso (The vision of Oengus). *F. Shaw, M.A. 1931 National University of Ireland*

Of Goode Maneres
A booke yntytuled *Of goode maneres*. *F. E. Pearn, M.A. 1914 London*

Officers' Training Corps
See Armed Forces.

O'Gadhra, Séan
Dánta agus amhráin an fhile Séan O' Gadhra. *S. MacDomhnaill, M.A. 1936 National University of Ireland*

Oglethorpe, James Edward
Oglethorpe and social and religious movements in England and Georgia. *L. F. Church, Ph.D. 1928 London*

O'Grady, Standish James
Standish James O'Grady. *L. J. Wrenne, M.A. 1944 National University of Ireland*

O'Grianna, Séamus (Máire)
Pádraig Og O'Conaire agus Máire: saoghal agus saothar na mbeirte (Pádraig Og O'Conaire and Máire: their lives and works). *T. Plover, M.A. 1950 National University of Ireland*

Saothar Mháire (The work of Máire). *S. O'hUalla-cháin, M.A. 1939 National University of Ireland*

Oil Industry
The economic organisation of the Rumanian oilfields, with special reference to the problems of international competition. *D. G. Mateescu, Ph.D. 1929 Birmingham*

Oilseed Industry
See Fats and Oils.

O'Kelly, Seamus
Seamus O'Kelly. *A. O'Hanlon, M.A. 1946 National University of Ireland*

O'Laoghaire, Domhnall
Filíocht Dhomhnaill Uí Laoghaire 1827-1911 (The poetry of Domhnall O'Laoghaire, 1827-1911). *E. C. Ní Bhuachalla, M.A. 1941 National University of Ireland*

O'Laoghaire, Peadar
See O'Leary, P.

Old Catholic Churches
The origin and history of the Old Catholic group of churches, their doctrinal and liturgical position; and the development of their relations with other non-papal communions. *W. H. de Voil, Ph.D. 1937 Edinburgh*

Old Norse Language
The history of Old English and Old Norse studies in England from the time of Francis Junius till the end of the eighteenth century. *J. A. W. Bennett, D.Phil. 1938 Oxford*

Old Norse Literature
A comparison between the styles of Old English and Norse historical prose. *K. M. Quinn, M.A. 1932 London, King's College*

Dreams in Old Norse literature and their affinities in folklore. *G. D. Kelchner, Ph.D. 1934 Cambridge*

The treatment of Old Norse literature in the works of William Morris, with particular reference to *Sigurd the Volsung. C. M. James, M.A. 1932 Wales*

Old Saxon Language
Die altsaechsischen Nominalkomposita: ihrer Bildung und Bedeutung nach Untersucht. *C. T. Carr, M.A. 1926 Manchester*

The Old Saxon vocabulary and its relationship to the other Germanic dialects. *W. B. Lockwood, M.A. 1946 Bristol*

Old Testament
See Bible: Old Testament.

Oldham, John
The complete works of John Oldham (1653-83): edited with an introduction, biographical and critical textual apparatus, and explanatory notes: with an appendix, containing an analysed transcript of the autograph drafts of Oldham's poems in ms. Rawlinson Poet. 123. *H. F. Brooks, D.Phil. 1939 Oxford*

John Oldham (1653-83), *Satyrs on the Jesuits*: a critical text with introduction and notes. *H. F. Brooks, B.Litt. 1934 Oxford*

John Oldham, poet and satirist. *R. Brown, B.Litt. 1927 Oxford*

O'Leary, Peter
An chómhacht a bhí ag an Athair Peadar O'Laoghaire agus ag Pádraig O'Conaire (The extent of the influence of Father Peadar O'Laoghaire and Pádraig O'Conaire). *T. P. O'Laochdha, M.A. 1941 National University of Ireland*

Critic liteardha ar saothar an Athar Peadar O'Laoghaire (A literary criticism of the work of Father Peadar O'Laoghaire). *M. U. O'Maolchu-maidh, M.A. 1931 National University of Ireland*

Foras focal an Athar Peadar O'Laoghaire (The vocabulary of Father Peter O'Leary). *M. J. D. Normoyle, Ph.D. 1942 National University of Ireland*

An greann i sgríbhinní na n-úghdar seo leanas: 1. Pádraig Ua Conaire. 2. An Seabhach. 3. An t-Athair Peadar Ua Laoghaire (The humour in the writings of Pádraig Ua Conaire, An Seabhach, An t-Athair Peadar Ua Laoghaire). *M. Ní Thuana, M.A. 1938 National University of Ireland*

Séadna. *M. B. Uí Chroitigh, M.A. 1942 National University of Ireland*

Taighde ar na h-iolraidh atá le faghail i saothar an Athar Pheadair (Research on the plural forms used in the work of Father Peadar). *D. O'Mathg-hamhna, M.A. 1944 National University of Ireland*

An t-Athair Peadar agus na sean sgéalta (Father Peter (O'Leary) and his treatment of the old stories). *B. M. Ní Shionnaigh, M.A. 1942 National University of Ireland*

An tAthair Peadar Ua Laoghaire agus Pádraig Mac Piarais, i gcomh-mheas agus i gcodarsna (Father Peadar Ua Laoghaire and Pádraig Mac Piarais, compared and contrasted). *B. Pléamonn, M.A. 1943 National University of Ireland*

An uimhir dhéide i saothar na n-úghdar seo leanas. 1. An t-ath. P. O'Laoghaire. 2. P. O'Conaire. 3. An Seabhac (The number two as used in the works of P. O'Laoghaire, P. O'Conaire, and An Seabhac). *R. O'Domnabháin, M.A. 1942 National University of Ireland*

O'Leary, Peter contd.
Uimhreacha i saothar an ath. P. O'Laoghaire (Numbers as used in the work of Father Peadar O'Laoghaire). *S. O'Riáin, M.A. 1939 National University of Ireland*

Oligarchy
The place of oligarchy in the development of Greece. *M. L. Gordon, Cert.Litt. 1917 Oxford*

Olive
The place of the olive in the economy of the Mediterranean region. *K. De La Mare, B.Litt. 1930 Oxford*

O'Longáin, Micheál Og
Micheál Og O'Longáin. *T. O'Murchadha, M.A. 1940 National University of Ireland*

Olympia
The temple of Zeus at Olympia. *R. K. Hack, B.Litt. 1908 Oxford*

O'Malley, Grace
Grace O'Malley: a 16th century heroine of the province of Connaught. *K. M. Ward, M.A. 1934 National University of Ireland*

Oman
See Sharqiya.

O'Maolchonaire, Clan
Cnuasacht dán a rinne seisear de mhuinntir ua Maolchonaire (A collection of poems by six of the Ua Maolchonaire clan). *S. O'Connell, M.A. 1934 National University of Ireland*

Saothar filídheachta Thuileagna Uí Mhaolchonaire (The poetic works of Tuileagna O'Maolchonaire). *M. O'Flaherty, M.A. 1936 National University of Ireland*

O'Maolmhuaidh, Froinsias
Lucerna Fidelium le Froinsias O'Maolmhuaidh (*Lucerna Fidelium* by Froinsias O'Maolmhuaidh). *P. O'Sullivan, M.A. 1944 National University of Ireland*

O'Molloy, Francis
See O'Maolmhuaidh, F.

O'Mulrian, Cornelius, Bishop
Cornelius O'Mulrian, Bishop of Killaloe (1576-1617) and the Counter-Reformation. *M. MacPhil-lips, M.A. 1928 National University of Ireland*

O'Neill, Eugene Gladstone
Eugene O'Neill. *K. Pounder, M.A. 1947 Birmingham*

Eugene O'Neill and modern dramatic technique. *K. J. Lorimer, M.A. 1947 London, Bedford College*

O'Neill, Hugh, 2nd Earl of Tyrone
An historical study of the career of Hugh O'Neill, second earl of Tyrone, 1550c.-1616. *J. K. Graham, M.A. 1938 Belfast*

O'Neill, Turlough Luineach
Turlough Luineach O'Neill. *P. McSweeney, M.A. 1927 National University of Ireland*

Ontological Argument
See God.

Opera
Aspects of the early English opera libretto. *I. Porter, Ph.D. 1938 Leeds*

The development of dramatic opera in England. *D. M. Walmsley, Ph.D. 1928 London*

Venetian operatic stage, 1637-1700. *S. P. E. C. W. Towneley-Worsthorne, D.Phil. 1950 Oxford*

Opie, Amelia
The life and works of Mrs. Amelia Opie. *M. E. Macgregor, Ph.D. 1932 London, King's College*

Optics
The acoustical and optical work of Thomas Young in relation to his contemporaries. *J. F. Robertson, M.Sc. 1938 London, University College*

Oracles
See also Divination; Prophecy; Religion: Greece, Ancient.

The Delphic oracle: its early history influence and fall. *T. Dempsey, M.A. 1916 National University of Ireland*

The influence of oracles on human conduct in Greek tragedy. *M. Smith, M.A. 1950 Manchester*

The oracle at Dodona. *K. M. Beyon, M.A. 1928 Bristol*

Orange Free State
The Orange Free State: a study in the inter-relation of geography and history. *M. Dawson, M.A. 1926 London*

Orangist Party
England and the Orangist Party from 1665 to 1672. *R. R. Goodison, M.A. 1934 London, University College*

Oratorians
The little schools of Port Royal. *H. Clive-Barnard, B.Litt. 1911 Oxford*

The part played by the French Oratory in the secondary education of France during the years 1614-1792. *J. H. Hamnett, M.A. 1947 Birmingham*

Studies in the history and influence of the education of boys at Port Royal and in the older Oratorian colleges of France. *W. N. Littlejohns, M.A. 1948 London, King's College*

Ordination
See also Sacraments; Clergy.

The doctrine of orders in the Reformed Churches in the sixteenth and seventeenth centuries. *J. L. Ainslie, Ph.D. 1935 Edinburgh*

1. Infant baptism. 2. The commission given to those receiving the order of Priesthood in the Church of England. *W. H. Baslow, B.D. & D.D. 1895 Oxford*

1. On the nature of authority. 2. On the essential elements of ordination. *C. H. K. Boughton, B.D. 1915 Oxford*

Semikhah, ordination: its origin, function, and history in Rabbinical literature. *J. Neumann, M.A. 1945 Manchester*

Orfeo, Sir
See Romances.

Orford, Robert, Bishop
Robert of Orford and his place in the scholastic controversies at Oxford in the late thirteenth century, with an edition of his *Reprobationes* of Giles of Rome. *A. P. Vella, B.Litt. 1946 Oxford*

Organ
The organ and its music from medieval times to Johann Sebastian Bach. *W. G. Allt, Mus. Doc. 1930 Edinburgh*

Oriental Studies
See Asian Studies.

Origen
A comparison of the pagan apologetic of Celsus against Christianity as contained in Origen's *Contra Celsum*, and the neo-Hindu attitude to Christianity as represented in the works of Vivekananda, and an estimate of the value of Origen's reply for Christian apologetics against neo-Hinduism. *J. R. Chandran, B.Litt. 1949 Oxford*

The ecclesiastical and philosophical background of Origen's thought, with special reference to the work *De principiis*. *E. Evans, B.D. 1925 Oxford*

Origen's doctrine of tradition. *R. P. C. Hanson, D.D. 1950 Dublin, Trinity College*

Original Sin
See Creation and the Fall.

Orléans, Charles, Duc d'
La captivité de Charles d'Orléans d'après les manuscrits anglais. *L. Lailavoix, M.A. 1911 London*

Ormskirk
The region of Ormskirk. *F. Robinson, M.A. 1928 Liverpool*

Ornament (Literature)
A study of ornament in western Europe from 1180 to the middle of the seventeenth century. *J. Evans, D.Litt. 1930 London, University College*

Orosius
The annotations of Ekkehart IV in the Orosius ms. St. Gall 621: a contribution to the question of the nature of ancient glosses. *J. N. C. Clark, Ph.D. 1931 Edinburgh*

O'Rourke, Irish poet
See Ruarcach.

Orpheus
An analysis of the mythology of Orpheus. *E. M. Dance, Ph.D. 1939 Cambridge*

Orthodox Churches
See also Church History; and Byzantine Church; Greek Orthodox Church.

The early tractarians and the eastern Church. *P. E. O. Shaw, B.Litt. 1924 Oxford*

A history of the attempts towards reunion between the Anglican and the Eastern-Orthodox churches (especially since the sixteenth century). *W. W. Price, M.A. 1929 Birmingham*

The peasantry, Orthodox clergy, dissenters, and Jews, as seen by Leskov. *F. Smith, M.A. 1948 London, School of Slavonic and East European Studies*

Relations of Pope Gregory the Great with the churches in the Roman Empire of the East. *W. J. Boast, M.A. 1931 Birmingham*

Orthographia Gallica
The *Orthographia gallica*: Trinity College manuscript. *D. L. McKennan, M.A. 1935 Belfast*

Orvieto
Medieval Orvieto: the political history of an Italian city state, 1157-1334. *D. P. Waley, Ph.D. 1950 Cambridge*

O'Siochfhradha, P.
An greann i sgríbhinní na n-úghdar seo leanas: 1. Pádraig Ua Conaire. 2. An Seabhach. 3. An t-Athair Peadar Ua Laoghaire (The humour in the writings of Pádraig Ua Conaire, An Seabhach, An t-Athair Peadar Ua Laoghaire). *M. Ní Thuana, M.A. 1938 National University of Ireland*

Saothar an tSeahaic - staidéar agus léirmheas ar na fuirmeacha bhriathardha ann (The work of An Seabhac - a study and criticism of his verbal forms). *C. M. Ní Raghallaigh, M.A. 1943 National University of Ireland*

An uimhir dhéide i saothar na n-úghdar seo leanas. 1. An t-ath. P. O'Laoghaire. 2. P. O'Conaire. 3. An Seabhac (The number two as used in the works of P. O'Laoghaire, P. O'Conaire, and An Seabhac). *R. O'Domnabháin, M.A. 1942 National University of Ireland*

Ossian
See Macpherson, J.

Ostia
The social and economic history of Ostia. *F. H. Wilson, D.Phil. 1935 Oxford*

Ostraca
See Ceramics.

Ostrovsky, Aleksandr
The dramatic art of Ostrovsky. *I. M. Beasley, Ph.D. 1931 London, External Degree*

O'Súilleabháin, Diarmuid
Dánta Dhiarmada Uí Shúilleabháin i. MacDomhnaill Mic Fhinghín Chaoill (The poems of Diarmuid O'Súilleabháin i. Mac Domhnaill, son of Finghín Caoll). *S. Ní Loingsigh, M.A. 1934 National University of Ireland*

Oswestry
Some aspects of the history of the lordship of Oswestry to A.D. 1300. *D. C. Roberts, M.A. 1939 Wales*

Otto, Cardinal
The legation of Cardinal Otto, 1237-41. *D. M. Williamson, M.A. 1947 Manchester*

Otto, Rudolph
The holiness of God in John Calvin and Rudolph Otto. *W. M. Elliot, Ph.D. 1938 Edinburgh*

Ottobuono, de' Fieschi, Cardinal (Pope Adrian V)
The English activities of Cardinal Ottobuono, Legate of the Holy See. *A. Lewis, M.A. 1937 Manchester*

Otuel
See Romances.

Otway, Thomas
An edition of the works of Thomas Otway, with biography and commentary. *J. C. Ghosh, D.Phil. 1929 Oxford*

The life and works of Thomas Otway. *J. C. Ghosh, B.Litt. 1923 Oxford*

Otway: his indebtedness in tragedy to French drama and to the *Nouvelles de Saint-Réal*. *K. E. Ashwell, M.A. 1908 London*

A study of Thomas Otway. *P. Whyatt, B.Litt. 1915 Oxford*

Oudh
See also Agra and Oudh, United Provinces of.

The relations between Oudh and the East India Company from 1785 to 1801. *P. Basu, Ph.D. 1938 London, School of Oriental and African Studies*

The relationship of Warren Hastings to the government of Oudh. *E. Macmillan, M.A. 1912 Liverpool*

The Residency in Oudh during the administration of Warren Hastings, 1772-85. *C. C. Bracewell, M.A. 1922 Manchester*

Outlaws
The outlaw in French literature. *P. E. Friend, M.A. 1922 London, University College*

Ouville, Antoine le Metel d'
The dramatic works of Antoine le Metel, Sieur d'Ouville. *F. J. Williams, Ph.D. 1936 London, Birkbeck College*

Overbury, Thomas, Sir
An edition of the *Characters* of Sir Thomas Overbury. *W. J. Paylor, B.Litt. 1933 Oxford*

Overton, Richard
The part played by Walwyn and Overton in the Leveller Movement. *J. E. Speak, M.A. 1949 Leeds*

Ovid
Arthur Golding's translation of Ovid's *Metamorphoses*. *E. M. W. Hovell, M.A. 1909 London*

The Elizabethan Ovid: a study of the Ovidian spirit in Elizabethan poetry, 1589 to 1616. *J. Forrest, Ph.D. 1945 Edinburgh*

The influence of the *Metamorphoses* of Ovid on Lucan. *E. S. Edees, M.A. 1931 Manchester*

Octovien de Saint Gelais's translation of Ovid's *Heroides*. *K. M. A. Popham, B.Litt. 1937 Oxford*

Ovid in English literature. *S. Rose, M.A. 1922 London*

Ovide en France durant la première partie du seizième siècle. *G. M. M. Morisset, Ph.D. 1934 London, Birkbeck College*

A study of Burney ms. 311: the prose arguments to the *Metamorphoses* of Ovid. *U. D. Hunt, M.A. 1923 London*

A study of Caxton's Ovid. *A. E. Wilmott, M.A. 1909 London*

Owen, John
John Owen, D.D., Puritan preacher and ecclesiastical statesman, with particular reference to his proposals for a settlement of religion and his views on toleration. *J. C. W. Davis, M.A. 1949 Liverpool*

The life and work of the Rev. John Owen D.D., the Puritan divine, with special reference to the Socinian controversies of the seventeenth century. *R. G. Lloyd, Ph.D. 1942 Edinburgh*

Owen, Robert
The educational work of Robert Owen. *A. M. Black, Ph.D. 1949 Saint Andrew's*

Robert Owen and Christian Socialism. *F. Fraser, Ph.D. 1927 Edinburgh*

Robert Owen and social legislation. *E. Lloyd, M.A. 1932 Wales*

Owen the Red
Duanta Eoghain Ruaidh mhic an bháird (Poems of Owen the Red, son of the bard). *T. Reilly, Ph.D. 1931 National University of Ireland*

Owen, Wilfred
A comparative study of the war poetry of Siegfried Sassoon and Wilfred Owen. *M. Palmer, M.A. 1950 Manchester*

Owenson, Sydney, Lady Morgan
The life and works of Sydney Owenson, Lady Morgan. *A. H. L. Stevenson, B.Litt. 1935 Oxford*

Oxford
See also Headington.

Contributions to the development of English medieval architecture based largely on a first-hand study of various monuments in Oxford. *G. P. Brookfield, B.Litt. 1925 Oxford*

Oxford Movement
See Anglican Church.

Oxford University
The administration of the estates of Merton College in the fourteenth century. *E. C. Lowry, D.Phil. 1933 Oxford*

Brasenose College in the time of Principal Ralph Cawley (1770-7). *W. T. Coxhill, B.Litt. 1946 Oxford*

The correspondence of Arthur Charlett (Master of University College, 1692-1722) in its antiquarian and historical aspects. *S. G. Gillam, B.Litt. 1948 Oxford*

1. A history of the Puritan Movement in Wales. 2. Religious development in Wales (1654-1662). 3. The Puritan visitation of Jesus College, Oxford, and the principalship of Dr. Michael Roberts (1648-1657). *T. Richards, D.Litt. 1924 Wales*

Life and works of Dr. Wm. King of Christ Church (1663-1712). *C. J. Horne, B.Litt. 1940 Oxford*

The problem of the plurality of forms at the University of Oxford in the thirteenth century. *D. A. P. Callus, D.Phil. 1938 Oxford*

A study in student life in a medieval university, with particular reference to Oxford and Paris. *H. Moyns, B.Litt. 1931 Oxford*

A study of the University letter book (FF) 1509-1535. *K. F. Lindsay-Macdougall, B.Litt. 1950 Oxford*

The University of Oxford and the Church of England in the time of William Laud. *A. D. Hewlett, B.Litt. 1934 Oxford*

Wolsey's colleges at Oxford and Ipswich. *F. Bate, M.A. 1905 Liverpool*

Oxfordshire
The Oxfordshire election of 1754. *R. J. Robson, B.Litt. 1947 Oxford*

Papyri contd.
The language of the non-literary papyri of the first four centuries. *L. R. Palmer, Ph.D. 1933 Cambridge*

Local peculiarities of handwriting in documentary papyri of the Roman period. *M. E. Dicker, M.A. 1929 London*

The syntax of New Testament Greek in the light of recent papyrological discoveries. *S. I. Buse, M.A. 1945 Wales*

Parables
1. The Christian view of the natural world. 2. The unjust steward. *H. Costley-White, B.D. & D.D. 1924 Oxford*

The parables and similes of the Rabbis: agricultural and pastoral. *A. Feldman, Ph.D. 1925 London*

Parables of the synoptic Gospels. *B. T. D. Smith, D.D. 1937 Cambridge*

1. The parabolic teaching of our Saviour. 2. The temptation of our Saviour. *H. B. Gray, B.D. & D.D. 1892 Oxford*

1. St. Paul and his relations to the Galatian Church. 2. Our Lord's teaching by hard sayings and parables. *C. C. Tancock, B.D. & D.D. 1899 Oxford*

1. The scientific aspect of biblical eschatology. 2. The parable of the unjust steward. *A. N. Malan, B.D. & D.D. 1898 Oxford*

Paraguay
The Chaco dispute: a study of pacific methods of settling international disputes. *J. W. Mallinson, M.Sc. 1939 London, School of Economics and Political Science*

Letras Armas de la Provincia del Paraguay de los años de 1626 y 1627. *R. Offor, Ph.D. 1926 London*

Paramara Dynasty
The history of the Parămara Dynasty in Malwa, Arthuna and Chandravati (A.D. 808-1310). *D. Ganguli, Ph.D. 1931 London, School of Oriental and African Studies*

The Paramara dynasty of Malwa. *S. Dasgupta, M.A. 1922 London*

Pardo Bazan, Emilia, Condesa
La Condesa Emilia Pardo Bazan: novelista. *E. P. O'Connell, M.A. 1948 National University of Ireland*

Parenthood
See also Fertility; Motherhood.

Cultural and psychological problems in education for parenthood. *A. Heron, M.Sc. 1949 Manchester*

Parents and Teachers
The relation of parents to schools: an enquiry into the advisability and the practicability of organizing co-operation between the home and the school. *C. M. Arscott, M.Ed. 1922 Manchester*

A study of the respective places and contributions of parent and teacher in child education, with special reference to the parent and parent-teacher organizations in France and England. *B. E. S. Sturgiss, M.A. 1937 Bristol*

Parini, Giuseppe
Servants and satellites: a consideration of some minor Italian social types of the eighteenth century attendant upon the giovin signore of Parini's satire *Il giorno*. *W. Radcliffe, M.A. 1937 Manchester*

Paris, Conference of, 1919-1920
See World War I, 1914-1918.

Paris, Gaston
The place of Gaston Paris in romance studies. *D. J. A. Ross, M.A. 1936 London, University College*

Paris, Matthew
An examination of the charges brought against the friars by Matthew Paris. *W. Alty, M.A. 1911 Wales*

Paris, Treaty of
English policy and the execution of the treaty of Paris. *W. E. E. Mosse, Ph.D. 1950 Cambridge*

The Peace of Paris, 1763. *Z. E. Rashed, Ph.D. 1949 Liverpool*

Paris University
A study in student life in a medieval university, with particular reference to Oxford and Paris. *H. Moyns, B.Litt. 1931 Oxford*

Parish History
Parish registers of individual churches will be found under their names.

The origin of the parish. *M. W. Neilson, Ph.D. 1928 Aberdeen*

The parish in the seventeenth century in the North Riding. *E. Trotter, M.A. 1913 London*

The place of the parish in local government, 1600-1650. *K. L. McElroy, B.Litt. 1925 Oxford*

Parish History contd.
The Vicarage system in Western Europe in the later middle ages, c.1200-1500. *R. A. R. Hartridge, Ph.D. 1929 London*

Parker Chronicle
A study of the *Parker Chronicle* (449-597 A.D.) in the light of more recent archaeological, place name and topographical evidence. *G. J. Copley, Ph.D. 1947 London, King's College*

Parker, Matthew, Archbishop
Archbishop Parker and the Anglican Settlement, 1558-1563. *E. M. Herne, M.A. 1928 Birmingham*

Parkes, Joseph
Joseph Parkes of Birmingham and the part which he played in radical reform movements from 1825 to 1845. *J. K. Buckley, M.A. 1924 London*

The Parlement of the Thre Ages
An edition of *The parlement of the thre ages*. *M. Y. Offord, B.Litt. 1948 Oxford*

Parliamentary Government
See also under individual countries.

The evolution of the Assembly of the League of Nations as a parliamentary body. *N. E. Skrimshire, M.Sc. 1932 London, School of Economics and Political Science*

Second chambers in theory and practice. *H. B. Lees-Smith, D.Sc. 1927 London*

Some aspects of comparative parliamentary procedure. *N. M. Perera, Ph.D. 1932 London, School of Economics and Political Science*

Parnasse, The
See also Poetry, French.

The metric of the Parnassians. *D. B. Anthony, M.A. 1910 Wales*

The origins and milieux of the Parnasse. *O. T. Evans, M.A. 1932 Wales*

Parnassus Plays, The
The three *Parnassus Plays*. *J. B. Leishmann, B.Litt. 1928 Oxford*

Parnell, Thomas
Thomas Parnell: his life and works. *M. Martin, B.Litt. 1930 Oxford*

Parody
Literary parody and burlesque of the seventeenth and eighteenth centuries. *H. R. Bennett, M.A. 1914 London*

Parousia
See Eschatology.

Parrot, Henry
A critical edition, with introduction and explanatory notes, of ms. Malone 14. *H. A. Buchan, B.Litt. 1934 Oxford*

Parthenon, The
The interpretation of the pediments of the Parthenon. *L. M. Willis, M.A. 1910 London*

Parthia
Parthia and her relations with Rome from 27 B.C. to A.D. 228. *A. T. Owen, M.A. 1920 Wales*

Rome and Parthia, 70-29 B.C. *A. Sandys-Wood, B.Litt. 1949 Oxford*

Particulars (Philosophy)
Knowledge of the particular in St. Thomas Aquinas, including a discussion of the principle of individuation. *W. G. Maclagan, Ph.D. 1928 Edinburgh*

Partnership
A comparative study of the law of partnership in England and France. *F. H. Dean, LL.M. 1932 Manchester*

An examination of the law of partnership in Roman law, with special reference to points of analogy and contrast in English law. *W. P. Cobbett, D.C.L. 1887 Oxford*

Parzival
See Romances.

Pascal, Blaise
The nature of religious knowledge according to Pascal. *J. C. Mears, M.A. 1948 Wales*

The revival of Pascal in France, 1880-1923. *D. M. Eastwood, D.Phil. 1933 Oxford*

The scientific method of Pascal. *P. H. J. Lagarde, B.Litt. 1933 Oxford*

Pascoli, Giovanni
Affinities and differences between Giovanni Pascoli and English and French poets: English and French inspiration in his poetry. *E. B. Pendleton, M.A. 1947 London, Bedford College and London, Birkbeck College*

Giovanni Pascoli: a contribution to the study of his Italian poems. *G. S. Purkis, Ph.D. 1927 London*

Pasquier, Étienne Denis de, Duc
La critique littéraire d'Étienne Pasquier dans les *Recherches de la France* et les *Lettres*. *M. M. MacLean, M.A. 1941 Liverpool*

Passion Plays
See Mystery Plays.

Passioun de Saint Edmund
See Anglo-Norman Literature.

Passover
History of the Passover. *J. B. Segal, D.Phil. 1939 Oxford*

1. On the origin and affinities of the Lord's Supper and the Passover. 2. On the traces of Gentilism in Christianity. *H. E. D. Blakiston, B.D. 1901 Oxford*

Tosefta *Pesachim*, translated and annotated, with a comparative study of Mishnah and Tosefta *Pesachim*. *S. Fundaminsky, Ph.D. 1949 London, External Degree*

Patagonia
Hanes a llenyddiaeth cychwyniad a datblygiad mudiad y wladfa Gymreig ym Mhatagonia (The history and literature of the origin and development of the Welsh colony in Patagonia). *N. H. Cadfan, M.A. 1942 Wales*

Llenyddiaeth Gymraeg y Wladfa (The Welsh literature of the Colony (in Patagonia)). *R. B. Williams, M.A. 1931 Wales*

Patent Law
The doctrine of invention in its connexion with the law relating to letters patent for inventions. *T. M. Stevens, D.C.L. 1897 Oxford*

Early history of the English law relating to letters patent for inventions. *R. Champness, LL.M. 1930 Cambridge*

An historical and comparative study of patentability. *R. E. Burns, B.Litt. 1935 Oxford*

Patent rights for scientific discoveries. *C. J. Hamson, LL.M. 1935 Cambridge*

Pater, Walter Horatio
The authentic philosophy of W. Pater. *D. M. Hateley, M.A. 1921 Birmingham*

The criticisms of Walter Pater. *D. L. Chadwick, M.A. 1928 Birmingham*

The literary criticism of Walter Pater. *M. Gopal, B.Litt. 1933 Oxford*

Matthew Arnold and Walter Pater: a study in critical attitudes. *F. Wardle, M.A. 1940 Manchester*

Walter Pater as an exponent of aestheticism. *B. Wells, M.A. 1950 Manchester*

Paterculus, C. Velleius
The writings of C. Velleius Paterculus: his style and grammar. *A. P. Martin, M.A. 1908 London*

Path of Purity
See Buddhism.

Patmore, Coventry
Three modern mystics: Thompson, Patmore, Hopkins. *J. M. Ryan, M.A. 1937 National University of Ireland*

The works of Coventry Patmore. *E. T. Downing, B.Litt. 1930 Oxford*

Paton, George
The correspondence of Bishop Percy with Sir David Dalrymple, Lord Hailes, and George Paton of Edinburgh, with introduction and notes. *A. F. Falconer, B.Litt. 1934 Oxford*

Patriotism
The history of English patriotism. *E. C. W. Stratford, D.Sc. 1913 London*

Patriotism in English poetry, 1702-1832. *S. L. Przegonia-Kryński, B.Litt. 1947 Oxford*

Patriotism in Old French literature: eleventh to fifteenth century. *J. Williams, Ph.D. 1933 London, External Degree*

Patristics
See also Church History; Theology; and Ambrose, Saint; Augustine of Hippo, Saint; Clement of Alexandria; Cyril of Alexandria, Saint; Epiphanius, Saint; Gaudentius, of Brescia, Saint; Gregory I, Saint, Pope, 'The Great'; Gregory Nazianzen, Saint; Hermas; Ignatius of Antioch, Saint; Irenaeus, Saint; John, of Damascus, Saint; Justin, Martyr, Saint; Novatian; Origen; Tertullian.

Belief in beings superhuman and subhuman: an examination of the part played by this belief in the Patristic theology up to the Council of Nicaea. *H. A. Blair, B.D. 1945 Oxford*

The criticism of the Greek philosophers in the Ante-Nicene Fathers. *G. Hutchins, M.A. 1934 Bristol*

Patristics contd.
1. The doctrine of the Trinity in St. Paul's Epistles.
2. The growth of Christian dogma and of Christian belief as evidenced by the apologists of the second century. *W. A. Spooner, B.D. & D.D. 1903 Oxford*

The Greek mysteries as presented in the early Christian Fathers. *D. J. Davies, M.A. 1915 Wales*

John the Baptist and his disciples in Patristic theology: a short study in ancient Scriptural exegesis. *H. F. D. Sparks, B.D. 1937 Oxford*

The law of nature: the Patristic conception as contrasted with the Thomist. *J. Dalby, B.D. 1942 Oxford*

Patronage
An examination of the theory and practice of appointments in the reigns of Henry III and Edward I (1216-1307), and of their historical significance. *P. H. Scotney, M.A. 1927 London*

Literary patronage in the time of Dryden. *J. J. E. Palmer, B.Litt. 1940 Oxford*

The presidency of the U.S.A. and the premiership of Great Britain: a comparative study of patronage. *E. G. Ashcroft, M.Sc. 1946 London, School of Economics and Political Science*

The profession of letters, 1780-1832: a study of the relation of author to patron, publisher, and public. *A. S. Collins, Ph.D. 1927 London*

The relation between author, patron, publisher, and public: 1726-1780. *A. S. Collins, M.A. 1923 London*

The relations of English poets and patrons between 1780-1830. *H. Deeming, M.A. 1922 London*

Paul, Saint and Apostle
The ascetical element in St. Paul. *H. F. Maxwell, B.Litt. 1934 Oxford*

1. The authorship of the Epistle to the Hebrews. 2. Galatians iii. 20. *T. W. Jex-Blake, B.D. & D.D. 1873 Oxford*

Christian moral judgment: an enquiry into the character of Christian moral judgment as evidenced by a study of St. Paul's conception of the relation between law and gospel. *J. N. Ward, M.A. 1944 Manchester*

The Christ-mysticism of St. Paul. *T. Caldwell, Ph.D. 1927 Saint Andrew's*

The contemplation of supersensible being in Plato's writings, compared with the apprehension of God through Christ in the writings of St. Paul. *A. Bairactaris, B.Litt. 1944 Oxford*

1. The date of St. Luke's Gospel and the Acts of the Apostles. 2. St. Paul's visits to Jerusalem recorded in the Acts and in the Epistle to the Galatians. *D. Walker, B.D. 1901 Oxford*

The dependence of St. Paul upon the pre-Pauline Christian tradition. *A. M. Hunter, D.Phil. 1939 Oxford*

The doctrine of grace as illustrated by the experience and teaching of St. Paul, Augustine, and Luther. *R. L. Child, B.Litt. 1925 Oxford*

The doctrine of predestination in St. Paul and Stoicism. *B. Joannidis, B.Litt. 1932 Oxford*

Grace and freewill in St. Paul and St. Augustine. *S. Y. Yovanovitch, B.Litt. 1920 Oxford*

The influence of Greek life and Greek culture on the writings and teachings of St. Paul. *J. Jones, M.A. 1919 Wales*

1. Justification by faith, as set forth in the writings of St. Paul. 2. Some New Testament evidences for the divinity of our Lord. *T. Lemmey, B.D. 1907 Oxford*

1. The mode of the Incarnation. 2. The indebtedness of the Pauline theology to Roman law. *W. J. S. Muntz, B.D. 1906 Oxford*

The moral dynamic of the Christian experience according to St. Paul. *G. R. Johnson, Ph.D. 1922 Edinburgh*

One body in Christ: a study in the relationship of the Church to Christ in the teaching of the Apostle Paul. *E. Best, Ph.D. 1948 Belfast*

1. Our Lord's knowledge as man. 2. St. Paul and his Gospel. *W. S. Swayne, B.D. 1918 Oxford*

Paul and Rabbinic Judaism. *W. D. Davies, D.D. 1948 Wales*

The Pauline notion of baptismal re-birth and the mystery religions. *J. Hackett, M.A. 1942 National University of Ireland*

1. The place of education in the life of the ancient Hebrews. 2. St. Paul's ideal of labour. *F. T. Ingle, B.D. 1923 Oxford*

Paul, Saint and Apostle contd.
1. The prophets of the Old Testament and their influence. 2. St. Paul's conception of Christ. *H. T. Dixon, B.D. 1904 Oxford*

The psychology of S. Paul. *W. N. W. Harvey, B.Litt. 1941 Dublin, Trinity College*

The relation of St. Paul's ethics to his doctrine of salvation. *H. W. Kerley, Ph.D. 1949 Edinburgh*

1. St. Paul and his relations to the Galatian Church. 2. Our Lord's teaching by hard sayings and parables. *C. C. Tancock, B.D. & D.D. 1899 Oxford*

1. St. Paul and the mystery religions. 2. The Incarnation and the Eucharist. *H. L. James, B.D. & D.D. 1924 Oxford*

1. St. Paul's claim for dogmatic theology. 2. The resurrection of Jesus Christ: the keystone of the faith. *W. C. Eppstein, B.D. & D.D. 1905 Oxford*

1. St. Paul's claim to be a true Apostle and the spiritual father of the Galatians (Galatians i.1,2,11,12). 2. The inadequacy of the law and its proper function and position (Galatians iii.24). 3. The attitude and responsibilities of Christians under the new law of liberty (Galatians v.i;vi.7,8). *R. B. Poole, D.D. 1886 Oxford*

St. Paul's conception of the Spirit. *R. Jones, D.D. 1928 Belfast*

St. Paul's doctrine of justification: its origin, significance, and adequacy. *L. J. Tizard, B.Litt. 1929 Oxford*

1. St. Paul's thorn in the flesh. 2. A critical examination of the use of φιλεῖν and ἀγαπᾶν in the New Testament, with special reference to the exegesis of St. John xxi.15-17. *J. M. Lister, B.D. & D.D. 1899 Oxford*

The social implications of the teaching of St. Paul. *R. H. Jennings, Ph.D. 1938 Edinburgh*

1. Some aspects of modern criticism with reference to the Book of Jonah. 2. St. Paul's doctrine of the Church. *E. C. Unmack, B.D. 1924 Oxford*

The terms 'pleroma' and 'kenosis' in the theology of St. Paul, with special reference to the person of Jesus Christ. *J. B. Reid, Ph.D. 1949 Edinburgh*

1. The word σῶμα in the New Testament. 2. The teaching of St. Paul's prayers. *A. J. Galpin, B.D. & D.D. 1910 Oxford*

Paul (Warnefried), the Deacon
Paul the Deacon, and the *Historia Langobardorum*. *M. H. Blyton, M.A. 1935 London, Birkbeck College*

Paulinus, of Nola, Saint
Saint Paulinus of Nola. *M. Curran, Ph.D. 1944 Manchester*

Pauperism
See Poverty.

Peace
See War and Peace.

Peacham, Henry
Studies in the work of Henry Peacham. *M. C. Pitman, M.A. 1933 London, Royal Holloway College*

A study of Henry Peacham's *Minerva Britanna*. *R. G. Rhoads, B.Litt. 1927 Oxford*

Peacock, Thomas Love
1. The life and works of Thomas Love Peacock. 2. A bibliography of Thomas Love Peacock. *C. E. Jones, Ph.D. 1927 London*

The novels of T. L. Peacock. *J. H. Kerrigo, M.A. 1921 Birmingham*

Peacock and the novel of ideas. *L. Stone, M.A. 1949 National University of Ireland*

Pearse, Patrick Henry
P. H. Pearse as an educationalist. *J. Treanor, M.A. 1942 National University of Ireland*

Peasantry
See Agriculture.

Peckham, John, Archbishop
The Church in the reign of Edward I, with special reference to the register of Archbishop Peckham. *B. E. Brimson, M.A. 1909 Wales*

Peckham, Pierre de
A description of the manuscripts of *La Lumiere as Lais*, by Pierre de Peckham, an Anglo-Norman poem of the thirteenth century, and a comparison of the poem with its Latin source. *M. D. Legge, B.Litt. 1928 Oxford*

Pecock, Reginald, Bishop
Bishop Reginald Pecock. *V. H. H. Green, B.D. 1945 Cambridge*

The *Donet* by Reginald Pecock, collated with the *Poore mennis myrrour*. *E. V. Hitchcock, Ph.D. 1924 London*

Pecock, Reginald, Bishop contd.
Faith and reason in the works of Bishop Pecock. *G. F. Nuttall, B.D. 1937 Oxford*

Pedagogic Theory
See Education: Pedagogics.

Pedro I, King of Castile
The character of Don Pedro in the chronicles, romancero, and Spanish theatre up to 1700. *N. E. Gardiner, M.Litt. 1939 Cambridge*

Peel, Robert, Sir
Criminal law reform during Peel's tenure of office as Home Secretary, 1822-27. *J. A. Gulland, M.A. 1930 London, University College*

The relations of Sir Robert Peel with the Crown, 1837-46. *J. W. Horton, B.Litt. 1950 Oxford*

Sir Robert Peel and the Free Trade movement in the first half of the nineteenth century, especially during the years 1842-1847. *W. W. Rollinson, M.A. 1930 Birmingham*

Sir Robert Peel the elder, and early factory legislation. *F. E. Manning, M.A. 1932 Bristol*

The work of Sir Robert Peel as Secretary of State for the Home Department, 1822-1830. *E. A. W. Kinsey, M.A. 1927 Manchester*

Peele, George
George Peele, (1558-1596?): poet and dramatist. *J. O'Leary, M.A. 1935 National University of Ireland*

The life of George Peele, dramatist, with the text, canon and interpretation of his works. *H. M. Dowling, M.A. 1934 Wales*

The old wives' tale by G. Peele: a study of the literary and folklore aspects of the play. *G. H. Dix, M.A. 1910 London*

Peers
See Aristocracy.

Péguy, Charles
Charles Péguy as a literary critic. *A. M. B. Rosevere, Ph.D. 1938 London, King's College*

The Dreyfus affairs in the life and works of Charles Péguy. *W. T. John, Ph.D. 1948 London, King's College*

Les idées sociales de Charles Péguy. *U. Riordan, M.A. 1931 National University of Ireland*

L'évolution de la pensée de Charles Péguy. *M. A. Doherty, M.A. 1936 Birmingham*

The work of Charles Péguy. *R. M. Harrison, Ph.D. 1933 London, Westfield College*

Péguy, Charles Pierre
The Catholic revival in French literature from Huysmans to Péguy. *E. Beaumont, M.A. 1940 London, King's College*

Peiping
An historical geography of Peiping. *J. C. Hou, Ph.D. 1949 Liverpool*

Peirol, Troubadour
The poems of the Provençal troubadour Peirol. *S. C. Aston, Ph.D. 1940 Cambridge*

Pelagianism
1. Pelagianism. 2. Recent attempts to establish undogmatic Christianity in India. *F. E. Warren, B.D. 1873 Oxford*

1. St. Athanasius' exposition of the divinity and Incarnation of our Lord in the anti-Arian orations. 2. St. Augustine's exposition of grace, free-will, and predestination in his anti-Pelagian treatises. *T. Hayes-Robinson, B.D. 1906 Oxford*

Peloponnesian War
See Greece, Ancient.

Pembroke
The castle and borough of Pembroke during the Middle Ages. *H. Reese, M.A. 1927 Wales*

The history of the town and castle of Pembroke to 1603. *E. P. Jones, M.A. 1905 Wales*

Pembroke, William Marshal, 1st Earl of
William the Marshal. *M. Salmon, M.A. 1909 Wales*

Pembrokeshire
An investigation of changes in population density and distribution, together with changes in agricultural practice, in Pembrokeshire during the period 1831-1931. *G. I. Lewis, M.A. 1937 Birmingham*

Manorial organization in medieval Pembrokeshire. *G. W. Skone, M.A. 1928 Wales*

The medieval boroughs of Pembrokeshire. *P. G. Sudbury, M.A. 1947 Wales*

The reaction of English Pembrokeshire to the social and intellectual movement of modern Wales since 1689. *E. R. Griffiths, M.A. 1927 Wales*

Penal Law
See Criminal Law.

Penance
See also Atonement, The; Forgiveness.

1. Baptism and the forgiveness of sins. 2. Absolution and the forgiveness of sins. T. Field, B.D. & D.D. 1897 Oxford

The origins of private penance. R. C. Mortimer, B.D. 1938 Oxford

The theology of Novatian. D. M. Cooper, Ph.D. 1944 London, King's College

Pennines, The
Brigantes: a study in the early history of the northern Pennines. R. Pedley, Ph.D. 1939 Durham

Landforms of the western slopes of the Pennines. L. M. E. Vincent, B.Sc. 1924 Oxford

Pennington, Isaac
The theology of the early Friends with special reference to that of Isaac Pennington. R. H. Ion, B.D. 1947 Oxford

Penry, John
See Marprelate, Martin.

Pens
The Birmingham steel pen trade. F. L. Timings, M.Com. 1926 Birmingham

Pentateuch
See Bible: Old Testament.

Penwith
Notes on the early history of the Hundred of Penwith in Cornwall, with a more detailed history of the parish of Phillack with its dependent chapelry of Gwithian. J. H. Rowe, M.A. 1931 Leeds

The West Penwith Peninsula of Cornwall, considered from the point of view of archaeological evidences concerning development of settlements. D. H. Watkins, M.A. 1930 Wales

Pepys, Samuel
The letters of Samuel Pepys and his immediate family circle. H. T. Heath, B.Litt. 1938 Oxford

Perception
See also Abstraction; Colour; Sensory Perception.

An analysis of factors in certain tests of sensory recognition. M. K. B. Harwood, M.A. 1935 London, Institute of Education

An analysis of the factors underlying the process of observation. E. A. Peel, M.A. 1938 London, Institute of Education

An analysis of the visual perception of movement. H. R. De Silva, Ph.D. 1928 Cambridge

Aristotle's theory of perception. S. G. Hulyalkar, M.A. 1939 London, University College

A case of visual aphasia. C. G. Davies, M.A. 1941 London, King's College

The changes in visual acuity during the course of dark adaptation. A. J. Marshall, Ph.D. 1939 London, University College

Comparative value of certain verbal and non-verbal (primarily perceptual) tests and their relation to tests of mechanical ability. K. G. Rama Rao, Ph.D. 1933 London, University College

A critical discussion of the status of sense-data. W. S. Barlingay, Ph.D. 1930 London, University College

The effect of change of meaning on periodicity in the perception of ambiguous figures. E. H. De Alwis, M.A. 1940 London, University College

Experimental study of some verbal factors in perceiving and remembering. K. R. L. Hall, D.Phil. 1949 Oxford

Fluctuations of attention and the perception of meaning. R. N. R. Wallace, M.A. 1935 London, University College

A genetic study of the third dimension in child art, with special reference to certain aspects of phenomenal regression. E. G. Dickinson, Ph.D. 1940 London, Institute of Education

The growth of visual perception in children. W. Line, Ph.D. 1929 London

The influence of volition upon the perception (cognition) of visual items, relations and correlates. E. O. Mercer, Ph.D. 1935 London, King's College

An investigation into the possibility of the development of spatial perception in children in their first year of secondary education, in preparation for their introduction to formal geometry. V. T. Brownless, M.A. 1949 London, King's College

An investigation of the factors in tests involving the visual perception of space. A. A. H. El Koussy, Ph.D. 1934 London, University College

Perception contd.
The object of perception. H. H. Price, B.Sc. 1923 Oxford

On the after effect of seen movement. S. A. Wohlgemuth, D.Sc. 1911 London

The part played by kinaesthetic experience in perception and in thinking. W. Strzalkowski, D.Phil. 1946 Oxford

The perception of size and its connexion with the perception of space. R. B. Joynson, B.Litt. 1949 Oxford

Perceptual ability of defective children. A. Waite, M.A. 1938 London, King's College

The psychology of perception in Pali Buddhism, with special reference to the theory of Bhavanga. E. R. de S. Sarathchandra, Ph.D. 1948 London, External Degree

The range and nature of the factors in perceptual tests. G. Clarke, Ph.D. 1937 London, University College

The real and the apparent in mature sense-perception. A. O. Delo-Dosumu, M.A. 1923 London

Realist theories of perception. A. R. M. Murray, Ph.D. 1932 Cambridge

Sensation and experience: an enquiry into the data of psychology. V. Haas, M.A. 1944 Wales

Sense-perception according to Kant. G. M. Broughton, M.A. 1909 London

Some factors in visual perception. J. W. Cox, M.Sc. 1919 London

Some influences upon perception. F. M. Miller, M.A. 1937 London, King's College

Some modern theories of perception. C. A. Hogan, B.Litt. 1931 Oxford

The subjective character of cognition and the presensational development of perception. R. B. Cattell, Ph.D. 1929 London

A survey of the learning process with special reference to perception, with experimental work on three forms of perception. C. F. Exley, M.Ed. 1927 Leeds

The temporal arrangement of errors or failures in perceptual work. S. Ghosh, Ph.D. 1949 London, University College

The theory of sense-perception in the writings of Plotinus. J. P. Murray, M.A. 1924 London

The ultra-perceptive faculty. J. Hettinger, Ph.D. 1939 London, King's College

Percival
See Romances.

Percival, Thomas
Dr. Thomas Percival, a medical pioneer and social reformer, 1740-1804. R. B. Hope, M.A. 1947 Manchester

Percy, Thomas, Bishop
The correspondence between Edmond Malone and Thomas Percy (preserved in the Bodleian in mss. 26, 27, 37 and 39). A. Tillotson, B.Litt. 1933 Oxford

The correspondence of Bishop Percy with Sir David Dalrymple, Lord Hailes, and George Paton of Edinburgh, with introduction and notes. A. F. Falconer, B.Litt. 1934 Oxford

The correspondence of Bishop Percy and Thomas Warton. M. G. Robinson, B.Litt. 1935 Oxford

An edition of the correspondence between Thomas Percy and Dr. Richard Farmer (B.M. Add. ms. 28222). C. Brooks, B.Litt. 1932 Oxford

The literary correspondence (1757-1781) of Bishop Percy. P. G. Thomas, M.A. 1928 Wales

The literary works of Bishop Percy, with special reference to the antiquarian studies of the eighteenth century. E. K. A. Mackenzie, Ph.D. 1943 London, Westfield College

Percy's Reliques and its influence. M. J. Peaty, M.A. 1914 Birmingham

Percy's Reliques and the ballads of Burger. A. Milner-Barry, M.A. 1922 Birmingham

The revival of early literature in England and Scotland from Percy to Scott, 1765-1802. A. E. Jensen, Ph.D. 1933 Edinburgh

Pereda, José María de
Regionalism in Spanish fiction from 1654 to the present day, with especial reference to Pereda. J. Manson, Ph.D. 1938 Edinburgh

The setting and characters in the novels of Pereda. W. Johnson, M.A. 1936 Birmingham

Perellós, Ramón de, Visconde
The life of Ramón de Perellós, Viscount of Roda and Perellós. S. Costello, M.A. 1930 Belfast

Peretti, Felice
See Sixtus V, Pope.

Pérez de Ayala, Ramón
Pérez de Ayala, novelist. J. McDonnel, B.Litt. 1947 Oxford

Ramón Pérez de Ayala. N. J. Lamb, M.A. 1940 Liverpool

Pérez de Oliva, Fernan
El maestro Fernan Pérez de Oliva. W. C. Atkinson, M.A. 1925 Belfast

Pérez Galdós, Benito
Costumbrismo in the novels of Pérez Galdós. V. N. R. McCririck, M.A. 1949 Birmingham

Galdós as creator of the modern Spanish novel. L. B. Walton, B.Litt. 1926 Oxford

Perfection
The New Testament doctrine of perfection. E. H. Williamson, Ph.D. 1935 Dublin, Trinity College

The path to perfection, an examination and restatement of John Wesley's doctrine of Christian perfection. W. E. Sangster, Ph.D. 1942 London, Richmond College

Pericles
Plutarch's Life of Pericles. W. H. Plommer, D.Phil. 1948 Oxford

Periodicals
See Journalism.

Perkins, William
The work and significance of William Perkins. R. A. Sisson, M.Litt. 1949 Cambridge

Perranzabaloe, Cornwall
The excavation of the Old Parish Church of Perranzabaloe. T. F. G. Dexter, Ph.D. 1922 Saint Andrew's

Perrot, John, Sir
Sir John Perrot. P. C. C. Evans, M.A. 1940 Wales

Persecution, Religious
See Religious Tolerance.

Perseverance
1. On the doctrine of the descent of Christ into hell. 2. On the doctrine of final perseverance. G. Arbuthnot, B.D. & D.D. 1908 Oxford

1. That the doctrine of a future state did form part of the revelation to man in the times preceding our Lord's birth. 2. That the so-called doctrine of final perseverance can be established by sufficient evidence from Holy Scripture, and is held by the Church of England in her seventeenth Article. F. Bedwell, B.D. 1874 Oxford

Perseveration
An analysis of 'p' (perseveration) tests, with special reference to schizophrenic conditions. E. M. McDonnell, M.A. 1934 London, University College

An enquiry into some perseverative tendencies in school children. K. B. S. Gupta, M.Ed. 1928 Leeds

An experimental study of perseveration. K. H. Edwards, M.Sc. 1934 Cambridge

An experimental study of some tests of perseveration. H. Islam, M.Ed. 1940 Leeds

Perseveration. L. H. Allison, M.A. 1937 Reading

Perseveration and difficult children. W. J. Piennaar, Ph.D. 1929 London

Perseveration, perseverance, character and intelligence. S. G. Raine, Ph.D. 1935 London, King's College

Perseveration tests of temperament. R. B. Cattell, M.A. 1932 London, Day Training College

Speed and accuracy as related to intelligence and perseveration. C. C. Howard, Ph.D. 1932 London, University College

A survey of perseveration and perseverance tests. J. Darroch, Ph.D. 1936 Edinburgh

Pershore Abbey
The history of Pershore Abbey and its estates. R. A. L. Smith, M.A. 1938 London, School of Economics and Political Science

Persia
See also Buwaihid Dynasty; Seljuks.

The activities of the English East India Company in Persia and the Persian Gulf, 1616-57. W. C. Palmer, Ph.D. 1933 London, King's College

Anglo-Persian relations, 1856-1907. K. C. Cleak, M.A. 1938 Bristol

Caliphate and kingship in medieval Persia. A. H. Siddiqi, Ph.D. 1934 London, School of Oriental and African Studies

Persia contd.
The campaign of Xerxes from the Persian side. *J. A. Dodd, M.A. 1913 London*

A critical edition of the Persian correspondence of Col. Sir John Murray. *I. M. Khan, M.A. 1925 London*

A critical examination of the *Tarikh-i-Bayhaqi*. *S. M. Siddiq, Ph.D. 1930 London, School of Oriental and African Studies*

The diplomatic relations of Persia with Britain, Russia and Turkey, 1815-1830. *F. Adamiyat, Ph.D. 1949 London, School of Economics and Political Science*

Economic and political relations of India with Iran and Afghanistan since 1900. *T. Basu, M.Litt. 1942 Cambridge*

Introduction to the *Tarikh-i-Bayhaqi*. *Q. S. K. Husaini, Ph.D. 1930 London, School of Oriental and African Studies*

Nādir Shāh. *L. Lockhart, Ph.D. 1935 London, School of Oriental and African Studies*

Persian history from 820-1056 A.D. *M. Ata, Ph.D. 1932 Dublin, Trinity College*

Question of international law in Anglo-Iranian diplomatic relations. *A. A. Dehkan, Ph.D. 1938 London, School of Economics and Political Science*

The relations of Britain and Persia, 1800-1815. *S. F. Shadman, Ph.D. 1939 London, School of Economics and Political Science*

The rise of Persian independence 820-1056 A.D. *A. M. Ud-Din, Ph.D. 1935 Dublin, Trinity College*

The size of the Persian army in the invasion of Greece 480 B.C. *F. C. F. Maurice, D.Litt. 1930 London*

Persian Gulf
The activities of the English East India Company in Persia and the Persian Gulf, 1616-57. *W. C. Palmer, Ph.D. 1933 London, King's College*

Persian Language
The Iranian recension of the Pahlavi *Bundahesh*: a philological and critical treatment of the text, with translation. *H. W. Bailey, D.Phil. 1933 Oxford*

Persian Literature
See also Dihlavi; Faizi; Falakī-i-Shirwanī; Naziri; Nezāmi; Rūmī, Urfi.

Fitzgerald and the Persian poets, with an edition of *Salaman and Absal*; also a literal translation in English of the original poem by the Persian poet, Jami. *S. Din, B.Litt. 1933 Oxford*

Introduction to the *Jawámi'u'l-hikáyát wu lawámi'ur-riwáyát*. *A. H. M. Nizámu'd-Din, Ph.D. 1924 Cambridge*

The Persian *Ghazal*: its origin, development and characteristics. *F. A. Karim, B.Litt. 1932 Oxford*

Persian influence on Arabic court literature in the first three centuries of the Hijra. *M. H. El-Zayat, D.Phil. 1947 Oxford*

Traces of Persian influence upon English literature during the fifteenth and sixteenth centuries. *M. L. K. Suratgar, Ph.D. 1939 London, University College*

Personality
See also Ability; Self; Temperament (Psychology).

An analysis of the abilities, interests and qualities of personality of a representative group of engineering apprentices. *A. G. Beverstock, M.A. 1946 London, Institute of Education*

Aspects of personality: a study in the inter-correlation of certain estimates of personal qualities. *D. Howie, Ph.D. 1936 London, Institute of Education*

The category of personality in relation to Kant's three postulates of the practical reason: freedom, immortality, God. *R. W. Thompson, M.A. 1907 London*

1. The conception of personality in relation to the present outlook and to the Christian doctrine of God. 2. Intercommunion and Christian reunion. *E. A. Burroughs, B.D. & D.D. 1921 Oxford*

A critical examination of Sigmund Freud's theory of personality. *N. F. Chubb, M.A. 1937 London, University College*

The development of the individual. *C. H. Jackson, Ph.D. 1941 Dublin, Trinity College*

Disintegration of the personality in the work of Marcel Proust. *S. Jones, M.A. 1940 Wales*

An experimental investigation into the effects of physical training on personality. *F. J. Milverton, M.Ed. 1940 Leeds*

An experimental investigation into some aspects of character. *S. H. Cracknell, Ph.D. 1939 London, King's College*

Personality contd.
Explanatory concepts in the theory of personality. *F. V. Smith, Ph.D. 1948 London, Birkbeck College*

Human personality as reflected in the psychology of the New Testament. *M. S. Pletcher, B.Litt. 1911 Oxford*

The idea of personality in Greek philosophy. *D. J. O'Connor, Ph.D. 1940 London, Birkbeck College*

Identity, individuality, personality. *J. C. Bacon, Ph.D. 1924 Bristol*

The implications of perfection as capable of realization in the finite self, being a consideration of the ethical conditions of personality. *V. Dimitrieff, M.A. 1919 London*

The incorporate person. *H. K. Wang, Ph.D. 1941 London, University College*

The influence of socio-economic factors on school progress and personality development. *O. Metcalfe, M.A. 1950 Birmingham*

The influence on concepts of the personality of recent advances in physiology. *U. M. Williams, B.Litt. 1949 Oxford*

The nature of personality. *R. J. F. Trotter, M.A. 1947 Liverpool*

Personality analysis from the clinical point of view. *E. M. Westburgh, Ph.D. 1933 Edinburgh*

Personality and immortality in modern philosophy. *E. G. Braham, M.A. 1927 Bristol*

Personality and impersonality: a study in the philosophy of religion. *W. G. Mulligan, Ph.D. 1944 Dublin, Trinity College*

Personality and its relation to the school as an ideal society. *W. N. Chalmers, M.A. 1924 Liverpool*

Personality in recent philosophy. *S. C. Lazarus, Ph.D. 1924 Oxford*

The philosophy of personalism, a study in the philosophy of the human person. *J. A. Creaven, M.A. 1941 National University of Ireland*

Problems of personality development in the light of graphological analysis. *E. F. C. Kronheimer, B.Sc. 1942 Oxford*

The psychological functions involved in the child's use of fantasy and fiction; and, the child's response to fictional characters and its relationship to personality traits. *G. A. Foulds, M.A. 1943 Liverpool*

The relation of the concepts of immanence and personality. *J. E. H. Thomas, M.A. 1920 Liverpool*

Religion as an integrative principle in human personality. *R. H. King, M.Litt. 1938 Cambridge*

1. The resurrection. 2. Christianity necessary to a true view of personality. *S. Bickersteth, B.D. & D.D. 1905 Oxford*

The significance in the philosophy of religion of the integration of personality through adaptation to reality. *A. G. Stuart, B.Litt. 1932 Oxford*

Some aspects of personality in British and American idealism from the time of T. H. Green, with some reference to immortality. *E. G. Braham, M.A. 1930 Liverpool*

A study in the philosophy of personality. *H. D. Oakeley, D.Litt. 1930 London, King's College*

The study of personality in English neo-classical literature. *A. A. Stewart, Ph.D. 1933 London, King's College*

The theory of personality in modern philosophy from Kant to Lotze. *E. A. J. Berthen, M.A. 1911 London*

Personality, Corporate
An examination of some modern theories of the relation of state to law, with special reference to their application to the juristic doctrine of corporate personality. *F. Hallis, D.Phil. 1927 Oxford*

Personality Tests
A comparison of methods of assessing personality in children. *M. A. Cunningham, M.A. 1948 London, University College*

An examination of some recent developments in testing personality, and an experimental investigation on the measurement of personality in senior school-children. *H. P. Williamson, M.Sc. 1929 Birmingham*

An experiment in assessing personality. *I. Ramzy, Ph.D. 1948 London, University College*

Factors affecting the reliability of self-estimates in answering personality questionnaires. *S. M. Mohsin, Ph.D. 1948 Edinburgh*

Personality Tests contd.
An investigation into the incidence of convergence insufficiency among school children, with an examination by means of the Thematic Apperception test into the personality of some difficult or retarded children showing this condition. *D. H. Archibald, B.Sc. 1944 Oxford*

Temperamental tests: an experimental investigation into some points of character and temperament. *E. A. Allen, Ph.D. 1926 London*

Personnel Management
Personnel administration in public utility enterprises, with special reference to railways and to Chinese conditions. *C. H. Chi, M.Sc. 1938 London, School of Economics and Political Science*

Personnel in retail distribution, with special reference to the training of juvenile employees. *H. W. Clark, M.Com. 1937 Birmingham*

The predictive value of certain vocational tests, with special reference to personnel selection in the Army. *M. S. Stevenson, M.Sc. 1944 London, University College*

The question of personnel in a socialized industry. *T. K. Hitch, Ph.D. 1937 London, School of Economics and Political Science*

Some problems in the selection of service personnel. *E. G. Reeve, M.Sc. 1948 London, University College*

Pessimism
Grillparzer's Pessimismus. *M. Curran, M.A. 1919 National University of Ireland*

The grounds of pessimism in Thomas Hardy's view of life. *R. Moir, M.A. 1947 Manchester*

Le pessimisme de Voltaire entre 1759 et 1769. *K. Rockett, M.A. 1939 Manchester*

Pestalozzi, Jean Henri
A critical exegesis of the concept of freedom in the educational systems of Pestalozzi and Herbart. *J. E. Parry, B.Litt. 1928 Oxford*

Petakopadesa
The editing of the *Petakopadesa*, with critical apparatus and commentary. *A. Barua, Ph.D. 1933 London, School of Oriental and African Studies*

Peter, Saint and Apostle
1. The biblical conception of the kingdom of heaven. 2. 'Tu es Petrus'. *B. H. B. Attlee, B.D. 1910 Oxford*

1. A study of the first Epistle of St. Peter in its relation to the Apostle's character and history. 2. The action of divine grace through distinctive channels of human personality. *W. K. Fleming, B.D. 1909 Oxford*

Peter Thomas, Saint
St. Peter Thomas, 1305-1366. *S. T. Manbre, M.A. 1937 Liverpool*

Peters, Hugh
The careers and opinions of Hugh Peters and Sir Henry Vane the Younger. *J. M. Patrick, B.Litt. 1936 Oxford*

Petronius
The minor poems of Petronius, with special reference to his literary and philosopical outlook. *J. D. Marcantoni, M.A. 1938 London, Queen Mary College*

Petronius Arbiter, Gaius
The satirical element in Petronius. *E. Jenkins, M.A. 1932 Wales*

Phaedrus
The fables of Phaedrus: a commentary critical and exegetical, with an introduction on the poet, his style, language and prosody, the mss, and the development of the fable in classical literature. *G. A. Leary, M.A. 1947 Manchester*

Pharisees
See Judaism.

Pharmaceutical Industry
See Drug Industry.

Phenomenology
Phenomenology and the theory of moral values. *C. B. Kidd, Ph.D. 1935 Saint Andrew's*

Philanthropic Societies
The literary and philanthropic societies of the eighteenth century: their services to and influence upon Welsh literature. *A. Lewis, M.A. 1921 Wales*

Philhellenism
See Hellenism.

Philip, Saint and Apostle
1. The Apostle Jude: is he to be identified with Jude the servant of Jesus Christ and brother of James? 2. SS. Philip, Bartholomew, Matthew, and Thomas: being an inquiry from New Testament records into the second group in the Apostolate. *A. C. Evans, B.D. 1901 Oxford*

Philips, Ambrose
The life and works of Ambrose Philips. *M. G. T. Segar, B.Litt. 1929 Oxford*

Philips, John
The life of John Philips. *M. G. Lloyd Thomas, B.Litt. 1925 Oxford*

Philips, Katherine
The life and works of Katherine Philips. *A. Woodward, Cert.Litt. 1920 Oxford*

Philistinism
The satire of the Philistine and philistinism in German literature from Sturm und Drang to Heine. *E. G. C. McIlvenna, Ph.D. 1936 Edinburgh*

Phillips, Stephen
The dramatic work of Stephen Phillips. *G. C. Griffiths, M.A. 1934 Wales*

Philo, Judaeus
The relation of Jewish-Alexandrian theology, especially in Philo, to the Pauline Epistles. *W. P. Ludwig, Ph.D. 1937 Edinburgh*

Some influences of Greek philosophy on Jewish thought and teaching in Apocryphal literature and Philo Judaeus. *C. W. Mann, M.A. 1934 Liverpool*

The use of the Old Testament in the Epistle to the Hebrews. *R. A. Stewart, M.Litt. 1947 Cambridge*

Philology
See Language.

Philosophy
See also Absolute; Abstraction; Aesthetics; Analogy; Belief; Causality; Certainty; Chance; Cosmology; Cynicism; Determinism; Empiricism; Epistemology; Ethics; Evolution; Fate; Form; Free Will; Freedom; Geometry; History; Idealism; Ideas; Imagination; Individualism; Infinity; Justice; Logic; Logos; Mathematics; Matter; Mechanism; Metaphysics; Natural Law; Neoplatonism; Pessimism; Political Theory; Positivism; Pragmatism; Rationalism; Realism; Relations; Scepticism; Soul; Stoicism; Substance; Synthetic Propositions; Teleology; Theology; Thinking; Time; Vitalism; Will.

A comparison of Hebrew and Chinese wisdom, as exemplified in the Book of Proverbs and the Analects of Confucius. *E. G. K. Hewat, Ph.D. 1934 Edinburgh*

The mechanical view of nature since Descartes. *J. C. Hardwick, B.Sc. 1923 Oxford*

Medieval philosophy and the approach to modern thought. *W. A. Painter, Ph.D. 1929 Bristol*

The mind-body problem in the light of recent philosophical theories. *D. Richards, Ph.D. 1943 London, Birkbeck College*

Philosophical issues raised by mystical experience. *J. E. Storey, M.A. 1929 Liverpool*

Philosophy and poetry: a study of their combination and an evaluation of its success. *J. J. Hartland-Swann, B.Litt. 1949 Oxford*

Philosophy and science. *J. Feeley, M.A. 1948 National University of Ireland*

The problem of the relationship between mind and body. *S. T. Han, M.A. 1912 Liverpool*

Recent philosophy and recent social movements. *J. W. Scott, D.Phil. 1919 Glasgow*

The relation of mysticism and philosophy. *S. T. Richards, M.A. 1915 Liverpool*

The relations of science to philosophy, with special reference to the conceptions of substance and causation. *J. Owen, M.A. 1908 Wales*

The solution of concrete problems. *H. A. Pollard, M.A. 1942 Birmingham*

A study of the sublime, with special reference to the theory of Edmund Burke. *C. S. Ware, M.A. 1949 Wales*

Tractatus logicophilosophicus. *L. Wittgenstein, M.Litt. 1929 Cambridge*

Philosophy: Australia
See Alexander, S.

Philosophy: Austria
See Freud, S.; Rilke, R. M.

Philosophy: China
See Confucianism; Hsün-Tze; Moh Tih.

Philosophy: Denmark
See Hoffding, H.; Kierkegaard, S. A.

Philosophy: France
See also Décade Philosophique; Physiocrats, The; and Bayle, P.; Bergson, H. L.; Boulainvilliers, H., Comte de; Comte, A.; Cousin, V.; Descartes, R.; Hamelin, O.; La Mettrie, J. O. de; Leroux, P.; Malebranche, N.; Montesquieu, C. de S. de, Baron; Rauh, F.; Renan, E.; Renouvier, C. B.; Vauvenargues, L. de C., Marquis de; Voltaire, F. M. A. de.

A bibliography of eighteenth century English translations of certain French philosophic writers of the Age of Reason. *H. B. Evans, M.A. 1938 Birmingham*

A study in the development of French thought in the second half of the nineteenth century. *J. A. Gunn, Ph.D. 1921 Liverpool*

Philosophy: Germany
See also Boehme, J.; Dilthey, W.; Feuerbach, L. A.; Fichte, J. G.; Fries, J. F.; Hegel, G. W. F.; Herder, J. G. von; Jaspers, K.; Kant, I.; Kolbenheyer, E. G.; Leibniz, G. W. von, Baron; Lotze, R. H.; Marx, K.; Nietzsche, F. W.; Schelling, F. W. J. von; Schleiermacher, F. D. E.; Schopenhauer, A.; Tennemann, W. G.; Troeltsch, E.

The influence of German thought in English literature of the first half of the nineteenth century. *T. W. Jenkins, M.A. 1926 Wales*

Philosophy: Great Britain
See also Arbuckle, J.; Bacon, R.; Bentham, J.; Bosanquet, B.; Bradley, F. H.; Burke, E.; Clarke, S.; Collier, J.; Collingwood, R. G.; Cumberland, R.; Duns Scotus, J.; Erigena, J. S.; Felltham, O.; Green, T. H.; Hobbes, T.; Hume, D.; Hutcheson, F.; Locke, J.; McTaggart, J. McT. E.; Mill, J. S.; Price, R.; Pringle-Pattison, A. S.; Reid, T.; Russell, B. A. W., 3rd Earl; Smith, A.; Spencer, H.; Ward, J.; Whitehead, A. N.; Wilson, J. C.

Christian ethics in Victorian philosophy. *D. Davies, B.Litt. 1932 Oxford*

The crowning phase in the critical philosophy. *R. A. C. MacMillan, Ph.D. 1912 Glasgow*

The development and significance of English philosophic method. *T. M. Forsyth, D. Phil. 1908 Edinburgh*

The development of Kant's ethical philosophy, with especial reference to his English precursors. *A. C. Mason, M.A. 1913 London*

The problem of the plurality of forms at the University of Oxford in the thirteenth century. *D. A. P. Callus, D.Phil. 1938 Oxford*

The Scottish answer to Hume. *G. O. Kyd, B.Litt. 1932 Oxford*

Philosophy: Greece and Rome   *See also Apuleius, L.; Aristotle; Celsus; Cicero; Dicts and Sayings of the Philosophers; Epicurus; Eryxias; Galen, C.; Heraclitus, of Ephesus; Hippocrates; Libanius; Lucretius; Menander; Numenius; Origen; Plato; Plotinus; Pythagoras; Seneca; Synesius of Cyrene, Bishop; Theophrastus.*

The criticism of the Greek philosophers in the Ante-Nicene Fathers. *G. Hutchins, M.A. 1934 Bristol*

The development of the platonic theory of forms. *J. D. Mabbott, B.Litt. 1923 Oxford*

The Greek philosophical background of *pneuma*, in its relation to early Christian thought. *J. E. Yates, M.A. 1939 Manchester*

The influence of Plato on the philosophy of the Empire 53-180 A.D. *C. M. Chilcott, M.A. 1922 London*

The methods of the medieval translators of Greek philosophical works into Latin. *L. Minio-Paluello, D.Phil. 1947 Oxford*

Philosophical survey of Roman religion. *F. Comerford, M.A. 1946 National University of Ireland*

Some influences of Greek philosophy on Jewish thought and teaching in Apocryphal literature and Philo Judaeus. *C. W. Mann, M.A. 1934 Liverpool*

Philosophy: India   *See also Buddhism; Hinduism; Pancaratra; Saiva Siddhaenta; Saktas, The; Sankara; Sikhism.*

A comparative study of the *Advaita Vêdânta* and of D. H. Bradley. *S. S. Suryanarayanan, B.Litt. 1917 Oxford*

The conceptions of time, space, and motion in early Indian philosophy. *N. S. Junankar, D.Phil. 1937 Oxford*

The concrete expression of abstract ideas in Indian philosophy, with special reference to comparison as means of evidence. *D. A. L. Stede, Ph.D. 1938 London, School of Oriental and African Studies*

Philosophy: India contd.
A critical examination of some theories of the external world in Indian philosophy. *E. R. Sarathchandra, M.A. 1949 London, University College*

The criticisms of the Sāmkhya philosophy in the texts of other Indian systems. *N. S. Junankar, B.Litt. 1935 Oxford*

The doctrine of *Maya* in the system of the Vedanta. *P. D. Shastri, B.Sc. 1911 Oxford*

The fundamental principles of Sankara-Vedānta. *B. Raychaudhuri, Ph.D. 1922 London*

Indian logic of Nyaya system. *H. N. Randle, D.Phil. 1927 Oxford*

The nature of consciousness in Hindu philosophy. *S. K. Saksena, Ph.D. 1939 London, School of Oriental and African Studies*

The philosophy of Rāmānuja as compared with that of Camkara. *G. G. Dandoy, B.Sc. 1909 Oxford*

Ramanuja's conception of the Deity. *B. Kumarappa, Ph.D. 1930 London, School of Oriental and African Studies*

A rational justification of the main principles of Advaita-Vedanta philosophy. *A. L. Gregson, Ph.D. 1947 London, Birkbeck College*

Some aspects of Mahayana and its relation with Hinayana. *N. Datta, D.Litt. 1930 London, School of Oriental and African Studies*

The Vedanta: its place as a system of metaphysics. *N. K. Datta, Ph.D. 1921 London*

Vedanta and Spinoza: a comparative study. *M. S. Modak, Ph.D. 1928 London*

The Vedānta doctrine according to Nimbārka, with a translation of his *Bhāsya*, together with the supercommentary of Srīnivāsa. *R. Bose, D.Phil. 1937 Oxford*

Philosophy: Islam
See also Averroes; Ghazali; and references under Arabic and Persian Literature.

Ibn Taimiya and his projects of reform. *S. Haque, Ph.D. 1937 London, School of Oriental and African Studies*

Philosophy: Italy
See Gentile, G.

Philosophy: Jewish
See Judaism.

Philosophy: Netherlands
See Spinoza, B. de.

Philosophy: Russia
See Berdyaev, N.; Solovieff, V. S.

Philosophy: Switzerland
See Rousseau, J. J.

Philosophy: U.S.A
See Dewey, J.; James, W.; Royce, J.

Philosophy and Religion
See Religion and Philosophy.

Phlogiston
The history of the phlogiston theory. *J. H. White, Ph.D. 1932 London, University College*

Phoenix
A critical edition, with introduction, glossary and notes of the Old English poem *Phoenix*. *E. M. Raynes, M.A. 1948 London, Bedford College*

Phonetics
See also Language.

Articulation tests: an application of experimental phonetic methods to measuring the efficiency of communication systems. *D. B. Fry, Ph.D. 1947 London, University College*

A critical survey of theories relating to the origin of the Germanic and High German sound-shifts, with an introduction on the general problem of sound-change. *B. Rayburn, M.A. 1942 Manchester*

Photius, Schism of
See Church History: Early Church.

Photography
A short study in the early history of photography. *M. F. Bailey, M.Sc. 1946 London, University College*

Photography, Aerial
The application of air photography to a study of the agricultural geography of northwest Cardiganshire. *G. M. Howe, M.Sc. 1949 Wales*

Photosynthesis
The contributions of Priestley, Ingenhausz, Senebier and N. T. de Saussure to our knowledge of photosynthesis and respiration. *E. W. Lambert, M.Sc. 1937 London, External Degree*

Phrygia
Phrygia and Montanism. *G. S. P. Freeman, B.Litt. 1940 Oxford*

Phylip, Sion
Phylipiaid Ardudwy, with the poems of Sion Phylip in the Cardiff Free Library collection. *W. Davies, M.A. 1912 Wales*

Physical Education
See Education, Physical.

Physics
See also Atomic Theory; Electricity; Heat; Light; Magnetism; Materials, Strength of; Sound; Chladni, E. F. F.; Coulomb, C. A. de; Descartes, R.; Foucault, L.; Neckam, A.; Rowlands, H.

Physics: History
The evolution of the physical units. *S. Galin, Ph.D. 1934 London, University College*

The growth of the doctrine of the conservation of energy, up to and including the work of Joule. *C. N. Lewis, M.Sc. 1937 London, External Degree*

The history of the law of conservation of matter. *A. N. Kothare, M.Sc. 1937 London, University College*

The origins in Greece of some physical and astral theories of the early Stoics. *M. M. Holt, M.Litt. 1938 Cambridge*

The physical and astronomical work of Christian Huygens considered in relation to that of his contemporaries. *A. E. Bell, Ph.D. 1942 London, University College*

Some studies in the history of ideas on the discontinuity of matter and energy. *D. R. Peck, M.Sc. 1946 London, External Degree*

Studies in cohesion, 1650-1850. *E. C. Millington, Ph.D. 1943 London, External Degree*

Physics: Study and Teaching
Adolescent education in county boroughs and industrial districts, and the place of physics in the reorganised schools. *H. G. Wilkinson, M.Ed. 1932 Durham*

The aims of physics teaching in secondary schools. *E. Denne, M.Sc. 1946 London, External Degree*

The educational value of the study of physics from the standpoint of method. *J. E. Phillips, M.A. 1924 Wales*

A factorial analysis of ability in school physics. *A. R. Berridge, M.A. 1947 London, Institute of Education*

Individual experimental work in physics in the junior forms of grammar schools. *L. S. Joyce, M.Ed. 1949 Durham*

Physical science in the non-selective modern school. *L. J. Kay, M.A. 1929 London*

A statistical analysis of the performance of boys and girls in science (physics and chemistry). *K. V. Chary, M.A. 1948 London, Institute of Education*

The teaching of physics in secondary schools up to the standard of the school certificate examination. *T. K. Henthorne, M.A. 1933 Liverpool*

The teaching of physics to junior pupils, ages 11½ to 14½ years, with particular regard to the period 12½ to 13½ years. *B. F. Brown, M.A. 1938 Liverpool*

Physiocrats, The
The Physiocrats and Adam Smith. *W. F. Keane, M.A. 1915 National University of Ireland*

Physiology
The claim of physiology to be regarded as one of the humanities. *C. L. G. Pratt, M.A. 1936 Liverpool*

Galen's physiology, with special reference to the vascular system. *J. Prendergast, B.Litt. 1930 Oxford*

The influence on concepts of the personality of recent advances in physiology. *U. M. Williams, B.Litt. 1949 Oxford*

Piaget, Jean
Animism in the child's conception of the world: an experimental criticism and verification of Professor Piaget's enquiries into child animism. *R. M. Askar, M.A. 1932 Birmingham*

Pianoforte
The pianoforte: its history traced to the Great Industrial Exhibition of 1851. *R. E. M. Harding, Ph.D. 1931 Cambridge*

Picard, Louis Benoit
The life and work of Louis-Benoit Picard. *F. F. Brotherton, M.A. 1943 Manchester*

Pierre, d'Abernon
Le secré de secrez of Pierre d'Abernun; a critical edition. *O. A. Beckerlegge, Ph.D. 1938 Sheffield*

Pierre, de Nesson
A critical edition of the *Vigilles des mors* of Pierre de Nesson, based on the two manuscripts in the British Museum. *N. Jones, M.A. 1942 Wales*

Pierre, de Peckham
See Peckham, P. de.

Piers Plowman
See Langland, W.

Pilgrimages
The cult and pilgrimage of St. James of Compostela, Spain, and their effects on the life and thought of the people in the northwestern corner of Spain. *H. W. Howes, M.A. 1938 Wales*

Lollard doctrine, with special reference to the controversy over image-worship and pilgrimages. *J. Crompton, B.Litt. 1950 Oxford*

Pindar
The moral and religious ideas of Aeschylus and Pindar. *E. J. King, M.A. 1937 Manchester*

The use of imagery in the odes of Pindar. *K. Kilburn, M.A. 1950 Liverpool*

Pindar, Peter
Peter Pindar: satirist. *H. R. S. Coldicott, B.Litt. 1913 Oxford*

Pinero, Arthur Wing, Sir
The dramatic art of Pinero. *W. J. C. Morgan, M.A. 1933 Wales*

Pipe Rolls
The great roll of the pipe for the ninth year of the reign of King John, Michaelmas, 1207 (pipe roll 53). *A. M. Kirkus, M.A. 1942 Reading*

The great roll of the pipe for the ninth year of the reign of King Richard the first, Michaelmas 1197 (pipe roll 43) now first typed from the original in the custody of the Master of the Rolls. *H. M. Grace, M.A. 1929 Reading*

The great roll of the pipe for the seventh year of the reign of King John, Michaelmas 1205. *S. Smith, Ph.D. 1937 Reading*

Piracy
See also Morgan, T., Sir.

The buccaneers in Jamaica. *C. H. Haring, B.Litt. 1909 Oxford*

Wales and piracy: a study in Tudor administration, 1500-1640. *C. E. Hughes, M.A. 1937 Wales*

Pirke Aboth
See Jewish Law.

Pisa, Council of
See Roman Catholic Church.

Pisan, Christine de
See Christine de Pisan.

Pistoia, Synod of, 1786
See Roman Catholic Church.

Pitt, William, 1st Earl of Chatham
Chatham's colonial policy. *K. Hotblack, D.Sc. 1917 London*

Criticism of Horace Walpole's treatment of William Pitt, Earl of Chatham, 1760-1768. *G. M. Dalrymple, M.A. 1909 Liverpool*

The political relations of the Chatham party. *G. K. Grierson, M.A. 1907 Liverpool*

Pixerécourt, Guilbert de
A contribution to the study of the melodrama of Guilbert de Pixerécourt, with special reference to his treatment of his sources. *W. G. Hartog, M.A. 1908 London*

Place Names
Anglesey placenames. *G. M. Jones, M.A. 1926 Wales*

Anglesey placenames: a contribution to Welsh history and ethnography. *E. R. Jones, M.A. 1911 Wales*

Astudiaeth o enwau lleoedd cwmwd Meisgyn, gyda sylw arbennig i blwyf Llantrisant (A study of the placenames of the commote of Meisgyn, with special reference to the parish of Llantrisant). *R. J. Thomas, M.A. 1933 Wales*

Astudiaeth o enwau lleoedd (plwyfi, trefydd, pentrefydd, tref-ddegymau, mynddoedd, afonydd, cymeodd, llynnoedd) sir Drefaldwyn (A study of place names (parishes, towns and villages, townships, mountains, rivers, valleys, lakes) of Montgomeryshire). *D. M. Ellis, M.A. 1935 Wales*

The chief elements in Norfolk placenames: a contribution to the study of place nomenclature. *O. K. Schram, M.A. 1924 Wales*

Enwau lleoedd yng nghymydau Caerwedros a Mabwynion, Ceredigion (The placenames in the commotes of Cardiganshire and Mabwynion). *G. M. Griffiths, M.A. 1948 Wales*

Place Names contd.
Le toponyme baki: étude philologique sur l'apport francique dans la Wallonie. *J. O. Potter, M.A. 1950 Birmingham*

Log-Ainmneacha Barúntacht Uí Bhadhamhna agus an Bharraigh Ruaidh (The place names of the Baronies of Ibane and Barryroe). *P. O'Niatháin, M.A. 1942 National University of Ireland*

Non-Celtic placenames in Wales and Monmouthshire. *B. G. Charles, Ph.D. 1935 London, University College*

The non-Celtic placenames of the Scottish border counties. *M. G. Williamson, Ph.D. 1943 Edinburgh*

The phonology of the placenames of Shropshire. *J. P. Scott, M.A. 1924 Liverpool*

The physical anthropology of the Gower Peninsula, studied in correlation with its settlements, archaeology, folklore and placenames. *C. H. Davies, M.A. 1927 Wales*

Place names and antiquities of the Barony of Duhallow. *M. J. Bowman, M.A. 1934 National University of Ireland*

The place names of Norfolk. *O. K. Schram, Ph.D. 1927 Cambridge*

The place names of Nottinghamshire. *H. Mutschmann, M.A. 1912 Liverpool*

The place names of the county of West Lothian. *A. Macdonald, Ph.D. 1937 Edinburgh*

The place-names and antiquities of Kinalmeaky Barony, Co. Cork. *J. P. Reardon, M.A. 1930 National University of Ireland*

The place-names of Essex. *P. H. Reaney, Ph.D. 1931 London, East London College*

The place-names of Holland, south-east Lincolnshire. *L. W. H. Payling, Ph.D. 1940 London, University College*

The place-names of Kesteven. *L. W. H. Payling, M.A. 1936 Leeds*

The place-names of Lindsey (north Lincolnshire). *I. M. Bower, Ph.D. 1940 Leeds*

The placenames of Midlothian. *N. Dixon, Ph.D. 1947 Edinburgh*

The place-names of the North Riding of Yorkshire. *A. H. Smith, Ph.D. 1926 Leeds*

A study of the placenames of Merioneth. *T. H. Williams, M.A. 1931 Wales*

A study of the place-names of the pre-Conquest Kentish charters. *T. E. A. Acum, M.A. 1923 London*

Vocalisation of the proper names in the Pentateuch according to a Syriac manuscript, Add. 12138, in the British Museum. *J. Wood, M.A. 1940 Manchester*

Plague
See also Black Death.

The plague pamphlets of T. Dekker, with an account of the plague in London from 1603 to 1630. *F. P. Wilson, D.Litt. 1921 Birmingham*

Planche, Gustave
Un critique littéraire de l'époque romantique: Gustave Planche. *R. H. Clark, M.A. 1934 London, Queen Mary College*

Plastics
The use of plastics in modern building. *P. H. Liversidge, M.A. 1950 Sheffield*

Plate, River
The historical geography of the River Plate region, 1810-1900. *H. J. Savory, M.A. 1937 Manchester*

Plateaus
The form of the plateau in south Wales. *K. L. Goskar, M.Sc. 1935 Wales*

Plato
See also Neoplatonism.

7th and 8th *Epistles* and *Laws* of Plato. *P. O'Connell, M.A. 1944 National University of Ireland*

The account of individuation in Plato's early dialogues. *E. T. Keep, M.A. 1947 Wales*

Albinus and the history of Middle Platonism. *R. E. Witt, Ph.D. 1934 Cambridge*

City State and Nation State: a study of the political theory of Plato and Aristotle in relation to the modern State. *R. J. F. Chance, Ph.D. 1927 London*

Clausulae and Platonic chronology. *L. Billig, M.A. 1920 London*

The contemplation of supersensible being in Plato's writings, compared with the apprehension of God through Christ in the writings of St. Paul. *A. Bairactaris, B.Litt. 1944 Oxford*

Plato contd.

The cosmology of Plato and the background of early Greek philosophy. *J. L. Bowers, B.Litt. 1950 Dublin, Trinity College*

Development of ethical thought of Plato and Aristotle. *K. P. Smyth, M.A. 1933 National University of Ireland*

The development of the platonic theory of forms. *J. D. Mabbott, B.Litt. 1923 Oxford*

The doctrine of knowledge of John Locke and contemporary English Platonism. *A. E. Best, M.A. 1940 Manchester*

The early dialectic of Plato. *J. J. Maxwell, M.A. 1908 London*

The Eleusinian mysteries, with special reference to their influence upon Plato. *W. Edwards, M.A. 1914 Wales*

The ethical end of Plato's theory of ideas. *F. A. Cavenagh, M.A. 1909 London*

Ethics of Plato. *J. Callaghan, M.A. 1915 National University of Ireland*

An examination of the nature and significance of Plato's theory of degrees of sapheneia. *W. F. Hicken, D.Phil. 1949 Oxford*

The genesis of Plato's theory of ideas. *D. Tarrant, M.A. 1909 London*

The *Greater Alcibiades* attributed to Plato: an introduction and commentary, together with an appendix on the language and the style. *R. S. H. Bluck, Ph.D. 1949 Edinburgh*

The *Hippias major* attributed to Plato, with introductory essay and commentary. *D. Tarrant, Ph.D. 1931 London, External Degree*

Ideals of education in Isocrates and Plato. *D. Gilbert, M.A. 1937 London, Westfield College*

The influence of Plato on the philosophy of the Empire 53-180 A.D. *C. M. Chilcott, M.A. 1922 London*

The influence of Platonic philosophy on Elizabethan poetry. *A. Fretter, M.A. 1911 Birmingham*

The influence of Platonism on certain French authors of the sixteenth century. *M. E. Taylor, M.Litt. 1930 Cambridge*

The interpretation of Plato's *Timaeus*. *E. R. Benjamin, Ph.D. 1928 Edinburgh*

Moral and national aspects of platonic and modern play. *B. Healy, M.A. 1940 National University of Ireland*

The notion of matter in the later philosophy of Plato. *W. A. Greatbatch, M.A. 1922 London*

Plato and fine art. *C. C. Holly, M.A. 1942 National University of Ireland*

Plato and Pythagoreanism. *A. H. Ewen, M.A. 1923 London*

Plato and the Greek problem in education. *M. O'Connell, M.A. 1926 National University of Ireland*

Plato and the poets. *J. A. Turner, M.A. 1932 National University of Ireland*

Plato and the subconscious. *A. Little, M.A. 1923 National University of Ireland*

The Platonic conception of the soul and its relation to the ideas. *M. M. Towne, M.A. 1928 London*

Platonism and mysticism in J. Donne, H. Vaughan and T. Traherne. *C. G. M. Roberts, M.A. 1913 Bristol*

The Platonism of Augustine's ascent to God. *S. Connolly, M.A. 1950 National University of Ireland*

Plato's conception of beauty, and its bearing on the development of the theory of ideas. *A. C. Tunnicliffe, M.A. 1911 London*

Plato's doctrine of personal immortality. *J. E. Parry, M.A. 1918 Wales*

Plato's idea of God and the soul in their mutual relations. *C. Dunsby, M.A. 1912 Birmingham*

Plato's ideal of justice. *F. A. Martin, M.A. 1944 National University of Ireland*

Plato's later philosophy of motion. *J. B. Skemp, Ph.D. 1937 Edinburgh*

Plato's philosophical theism. *J. W. Griffiths, M.A. 1920 Wales*

Plato's philosophical theism. *J. W. Griffiths, M.A. 1919 London*

Plato's psychology in its bearing on the development of will. *M. H. Wood, M.A. 1905 London*

Plato's theory of ethics as contained in the early dialogues. *S. S. Orr, M.A. 1942 Belfast*

Plato contd.

The position of the soul and its relation to the ideas in Plato's metaphysic. *M. Hirst, M.A. 1912 London*

The pseudo-platonic dialogue *Eryxias*. *D. E. Eichholz, M.Litt. 1934 Cambridge*

Psychology of Plato. *J. O'Shea, M.A. 1915 National University of Ireland*

The recent controversy over the ideal theory of Plato. *M. E. Hirst, M.A. 1911 Birmingham*

The relation between the individual good and the social good, in Plato. *C. E. Faithfull, M.A. 1915 London*

The relation of θεωρία to πράξισ in Plato's *Republic* and Aristotle's *Ethics*. *F. L. Ghey, M.A. 1907 London*

Shelley and Plato: a study in literary relationship. *G. Coope, M.A. 1931 Birmingham*

Spiritualism of Plato and Aristotle. *H. F. Carroll, M.A. 1913 National University of Ireland*

A study of the relation of Plato's philosophy to theism. *C. H. Rose, M.A. 1922 Birmingham*

The theory of education in Plato's *Laws*. *H. W. Lemon, M.Ed. 1920 Manchester*

Tuairimí oideachais Phlatón. *C. O'Broin, M.A. 1939 National University of Ireland*

Plautus

Catalogue raisonné of the subjunctive in Plautus. *H. Thomas, D.Litt. 1909 Birmingham*

The characterization of women in Plautus and Terence and the fragments of Menander. *M. Watts, M.A. 1919 London*

An investigation of the development and character of the influence of Terence and Plautus on the earlier English drama, with some account of fifteenth and sixteenth century editions of their plays in England. *T. C. Rising, M.A. 1933 London, King's College*

The light thrown by Plautus on Roman social life of his time. *B. Carpenter, M.A. 1917 London*

Literary criticism of Plautus, ancient and modern. *G. M. Francis, M.A. 1948 Wales*

The popular element in the language of Plautus. *J. R. Jones, M.A. 1911 Wales*

The slaves of Greek comedy compared with those of Plautus and Terence. *W. G. Williams, M.A. 1911 London*

Sources of wit and humour in Plautus. *M. Grahy, M.A. 1930 National University of Ireland*

Play

See also Children's Games; Entertainments; Games and Sports; Leisure; Recreation.

An historical study of the provision for play and recreation in Manchester. *W. G. Jackson, M.Ed. 1940 Manchester*

Moral and national aspects of platonic and modern play. *B. Healy, M.A. 1940 National University of Ireland*

Psychological theories of play and their influence upon education theory and practice. *J. Dasgupta, M.A. 1949 London, Institute of Education*

Plays

See Theatre.

Pleasure

Pleasure as a criterion of worth. *J. Drake, M.A. 1917 London*

Theories of pleasure-unpleasure and its relation to action. *K. Hasegawa, Ph.D. 1926 Edinburgh*

Pléiade

See French Literature: Sixteenth Century.

Pliny (Gaius Plinius Secundus), the Elder

A commentary on Pliny's *Natural History*, book VII. *A. E. J. Hann, Ph.D. 1949 London, Birkbeck College*

Pliny: *Natural History*, book 2, vol. 1 (2). *D. J. Campbell, Ph.D. 1935 Aberdeen*

Pliny (Gaius Plinius Secundus), the Younger

Roman society in the reign of Trajan as seen in the writings of Tacitus, Juvenal and Pliny the Younger. *M. M. Gough, M.A. 1908 Birmingham*

Plotinus

The influence of Plotinus upon the religious philosphy of St. Augustine, with special reference to the points of difference between neoplatonism and Christianity. *W. J. Heaton, M.A. 1930 Reading*

The nature and knowledge of God (or the Absolute) in the philosophy of Plotinus. *J. P. Murray, Ph.D. 1928 London*

Plotinus contd.

Plotinus's conception of the unconscious. *D. D. Stuurman, B.Litt. 1937 Oxford*

The theology of Plotinus. *A. R. Pastor, B.Litt. 1920 Oxford*

The theory of sense-perception in the writings of Plotinus. *J. P. Murray, M.A. 1924 London*

Plunkett, Joseph Mary

The poetry of Joseph Mary Plunkett. *M. Leahy, M.A. 1949 National University of Ireland*

Plutarch

A comparison of Shakespeare's use of Holinshed and Plutarch in his English and Greek-Roman history plays. *E. A. Donnan, Ph.D. 1950 Manchester*

De Alexandri Magni fortuna aut virtute apud Plutarchum. *J. L. Roche, M.A. 1937 National University of Ireland*

Plutarch's *Life of Crassus*: with historical commentary. *A. S. Osley, Ph.D. 1942 London, External Degree*

Plutarch's *Life of Pericles*. *W. H. Plommer, D.Phil. 1948 Oxford*

Plymouth

The city port of Plymouth: an essay in geographical interpretation. *C. B. M. Sillick, Ph.D. 1938 London, Bedford College*

Plymouth Dock: a survey of the development of the Royal Dockyard in Hamoaze during the sailing ship era. *A. E. Stephens, Ph.D. 1940 London, Birkbeck College*

Plymouth Haven. *A. E. Stephens, M.Sc. 1936 London, Birkbeck College*

Pneumatics

Pneumatics in the seventeenth century. *D. Rowbottom, M.Sc. 1943 London, External Degree*

Poetry

See also Ballads; Bards; Carols; Epics; Hymns; Imagery; Romances; Songs. For references to individual poets, see under English Literature; French Literature; Latin Literature; etc. For religious poetry, see Religious Literature.

Contemporary poetic drama. *N. D. Lawlor, M.A. 1944 National University of Ireland*

Dr Johnson on poetic genius. *J. A. Daly, M.A. 1947 National University of Ireland*

From inspiration to erudition: studies in the development of the notion 'poeta doctus'. *M. J. McGann, M.A. 1950 Belfast*

The illogical element in poetry, with a study of its application by romantic and limitation by classical poets. *R. R. Graves, B.Litt. 1925 Oxford*

Imagery of Kalidasa and the theory of poetics. *P. De Costa, Ph.D. 1949 London, School of Oriental and African Studies*

The influence of German aesthetic philosophy on Samuel Taylor Coleridge's theory of poetry. *J. W. Sagmaster, B.Litt. 1928 Oxford*

Matthew Arnold's theory and practice of poetry. *D. G. Boys, M.A. 1923 London*

Organic rhythm. *J. Thompson, M.A. 1920 National University of Ireland*

Philosophy and poetry: a study of their combination and an evaluation of its success. *J. J. Hartland-Swann, B.Litt. 1949 Oxford*

Poetic diction. *A. O. Barfield, B.Litt. 1927 Oxford*

Poetry and other arts in relation to life. *A. L. Stuart, Ph.D. 1944 Dublin, Trinity College*

Politian's vernacular poems and their relation to his theory of poetry. *J. M. S. Cotton, B.Litt. 1934 Oxford*

A psychological study of poetry-writing by children. *G. Smith, D.Phil. 1940 Oxford*

The quarrel between poetry and philosophy. *M. E. Day, M.A. 1911 Birmingham*

The rise and development of the pastoral, with special reference to the English pastoral. *M. L. Bleby, M.A. 1906 Birmingham*

Romantic poets and language. *J. J. Hogan, M.A. 1923 National University of Ireland*

Some aspects of the cult of medievalism in nineteenth century poetry. *M. F. Doolan, M.A. 1936 Belfast*

Some tendencies and developments in recent poetry. *A. J. Sheldrick, M.A. 1921 Wales*

The use of poetry as a dramatic medium in the twentieth century. *M. Coldwell, M.A. 1940 Wales*

Poetry: Appreciation

Aesthetic appreciation: a comparison of two methods of training appreciation in poetry. *K. B. Leopold, M.A. 1930 London, King's College*

Aims and problems in the teaching of poetry at the secondary school stage. *K. E. Morgan, M.A. 1948 Liverpool*

Poetic appreciation: an essay in assessment. *I. L. Mumford, M.A. 1946 London, King's College*

Should children learn poems as 'wholes' or in 'parts'. *E. W. Sawdon, M.A. 1926 Birmingham*

Some aesthetic and psychological factors in the appreciation of poetry. *W. Howarth, M.Ed. 1920 Manchester*

A study of responses to poetry. *N. C. Martin, M.A. 1949 London, Institute of Education*

Poetry: Criticism

Safonau beirniadu barddoniaeth yng Nghymru yn y bedwaredd ganrif ar bymtheg (The standards of the criticism of poetry in Wales in the nineteenth century). *H. L. Williams, M.A. 1935 Wales*

Poetry, Anglo-Norman

The lyrical poems of the Harleian ms. 2253, British Museum. *J. A. Gibson, M.A. 1914 London*

Poetry, Arabic

Animals in ancient Arabic poetry. *N. M. M. el-Nowaihi, Ph.D. 1942 London, School of Oriental and African Studies*

The development of *El-Ghazal* in Arabic poetry. *A. H. K. M. Z. Kanani, Ph.D. 1948 London, School of Oriental and African Studies*

The influence of Arabic poetry on the development of Persian poetry. *U. M. K. Daudpota, Ph.D. 1927 Cambridge*

The theory and practice of 'poetic diction' in English, with reference to the same in Arabic and French. *L. H. K. Awad, M.Litt. 1941 Cambridge*

Poetry, Bengali

Realism in contemporary Bengali poetry as compared and considered with reference to realism in English poetry from the last decade of the nineteenth century. *B. Banerjee, Ph.D. 1937 London, King's College*

Poetry, Celtic

See also below, Irish.

The verbal system in bardic poetry. *J. B. Arthurs, M.A. 1942 Belfast*

Poetry, Classical

See also below, Greek; Latin.

The classical element in English poetry of the nineteenth century. *E. A. Williams, M.A. 1908 Wales*

Poetry, English: General

Childhood in English poetry. *E. M. Hall, M.A. 1921 Wales*

Childhood in English poetry. *A. Scott, M.A. 1935 Belfast*

A comparative study of English lyric poetry from a Polish point of view, illustrated by an anthology, a critical commentary, and verse translations into Polish. *J. M. Pietrkiewicz, Ph.D. 1947 London, King's College*

The democratic spirit in English poetry up to the time of the French Revolution. *G. L. Davies, M.A. 1929 Wales*

Doctrina poetarum. *H. M. Gaffney, M.A. 1939 National University of Ireland*

Doctrina poetarum: a survey of the doctrinal content of English poetry from Caedmon to Scott in the light of the *Summa theologica* of St. Thomas Aquinas. *S. J. C. Gaffney, Ph.D. 1938 National University of Ireland*

English elegy. *K. Kavanagh, M.A. 1933 National University of Ireland*

The growth of humanitarian feeling towards animals as shown in English poetry. *K. A. Fisher, M.A. 1929 Wales*

The influence of the Faust legend on English poetry. *E. H. Harris, M.A. 1912 Belfast*

Music and English poetry. *K. M. Wilson, Ph.D. 1925 Cambridge*

On certain similarities between Persian and English poetry. *G. O. H. Ansari, M.A. 1925 London*

On ornamental words (a preliminary essay): a contribution to the study of poetic diction in English literature. *B. Groom, M.A. 1915 London*

Orientalism in English poetry. *E. S. Broughton, M.A. 1919 London*

Poetry, English: General contd.

The 'prentice years of English poetry. *J. Whelan, M.A. 1926 National University of Ireland*

The revival of the sonnet. *M. L. Skentelbery, M.A. 1941 National University of Ireland*

The sea in English poetry. *J. F. O'Mahony, M.A. 1942 National University of Ireland*

Theology in English poetry. *S. J. C. Gaffney, Ph.D. 1941 National University of Ireland*

The theory and practice of 'poetic diction' in English, with reference to the same in Arabic and French. *L. H. K. Awad, M.Litt. 1941 Cambridge*

Vowel sounds in poetry, their music and tone colour. *M. M. Macdermott, Ph.D. 1941 Glasgow*

Poetry, English: Early and Medieval

The alliterative diction of early Middle English poetry. *B. Allen, M.A. 1921 London*

Aspects of the devotion to the Blessed Virgin Mary in thirteenth-century English lyric poetry. *G. T. Shepherd, M.A. 1948 London, King's College*

The Blessed Virgin Mary in Middle English verse. *M. F. McKeough, M.A, 1939 National University of Ireland*

Custom and belief connected with precious stones, as shown in the Middle English verse of the fourteenth century. *P. J. Heather, Ph.D. 1931 London, External Degree*

The diction of alliterative poetry in English in the fourteenth and fifteenth centuries. *L. F. Casson, B.Litt. 1937 Oxford*

An edition of the Old English poem *Crist* A and B, lines 1 to 866. *S. Das, Ph.D. 1936 London, University College*

The English religious lyric in the Middle Ages. *J. J. Underwood, M.A. 1937 National University of Ireland*

An enquiry into the possible existence of an alternative school of poetry in Middle English: a linguistic and metrical approach. *J. P. Oakden, Ph.D. 1929 Manchester*

Heathenism and its echo in Anglo-Saxon poetry. *J. P. Gaffney, M.A. 1935 National University of Ireland*

The language of the Middle English lyric. *G. E. Morris, B.A. 1937 Sheffield*

The medieval English lyric. *J. F. MacInerney, M.A. 1932 National University of Ireland*

The melancholy element in English poetry from Widsith to Chaucer. *T. R. Hughes, M.A. 1928 Wales*

Nature observance in Anglo-Saxon poetry. *M. Madden, M.A. 1937 National University of Ireland*

A new edition of the Middle British lyrics of ms. Harley 2253 in the British Museum. *G. L. Brook, Ph.D. 1934 Leeds*

Rhai agweddau ar ganu rhydd cynnar Cymru, g yda sylw arbennig i'w gysylltiadau â chanu Saesneg (Some aspects of the free early poetry of Wales, with special reference to its connections with English poetry). *B. Rees, M.A. 1940 Wales*

The sea in Old English poetry. *W. J. F. Davies, M.A. 1948 Wales*

Some aspects of the French element in the Middle English lyric. *D. M. Jenkins, M.A. 1912 London*

Some medieval elements in early Tudor poetry. *M. S. Lodge, M.A. 1948 Sheffield*

A study of fifteenth century English lyric verse from manuscripts and printed editions, with special attention to metrical form. *B. H. N. G. Geary, B.Litt. 1934 Oxford*

A study of the Middle English Breton lays, with reference to fairy lore, folk-lore and origins. *G. A. Pye, M.A. 1936 London, Birkbeck College*

Poetry, English: Sixteenth Century

See also Tottel, R.

The Elizabethan lyric and its relations with contemporary music. *D. J. Jones, M.A. 1939 Wales*

The historical, non-dramatic poetry of the period 1550-1642. *W. J. Price, M.A. 1914 Liverpool*

The influence of Platonic philosophy on Elizabethan poetry. *A. Fretter, M.A. 1911 Birmingham*

Italian influence on the Elizabethan lyrics, more especially in connection with madrigals connection with madrigals. *C. K. Saunders, M.A. 1909 London*

The lyrics and songs of the Elizabethan drama. *H. Morris, M.A. 1912 Wales*

Metrical theory and practice in the Elizabethan lyric. *C. M. Ing, D.Phil. 1949 Oxford*

Poetry, English: Sixteenth Century contd.

The poet and his audience: non-dramatic poetry of the sixteenth century. *J. W. Saunders, B.Litt. 1949 Oxford*

The rise and development of the pastoral, with special reference to the English pastoral. *M. L. Bleby, M.A. 1906 Birmingham*

A study of verse-satire and epigram, 1595-1603. *S. H. Atkins, Ph.D. 1937 London, External Degree*

Poetry, English: Seventeenth Century

An anthology of seventeenth century verse by poets hitherto almost unknown, with accounts of their lives and a critical survey of their work. *L. B. Marshall, Ph.D. 1932 London, University College*

A critical edition of the poems printed by John Donne the Younger in 1660 as written by William Herbert, Earl of Pembroke, and Sir Benjamin Ruddier. *M. A. Beese, B.Litt. 1935 Oxford*

The debt of English poetry in the seventeenth century to Théophile and Saint-Amant. *J. Short, B.Litt. 1941 Oxford*

Eighteenth century literary criticism up to Dr. Johnson, with particular reference to the criticism of Shakespeare, Milton and the metaphysical poets. *M. J. Ince, M.A. 1948 Manchester*

The Elizabethan Ovid: a study of the Ovidian spirit in Elizabethan poetry, 1589 to 1616. *J. Forrest, Ph.D. 1945 Edinburgh*

Evolution and character of the Elizabethan lyric. *S. K. Banerjee, Ph.D. 1931 Edinburgh*

The evolution of the Elizabethan sonnet. *J. W. Lever, M.A. 1945 Manchester*

Guarini and the English pastoral. *S. E. Dimsey, B.Litt. 1927 Oxford*

The imagery of the metaphysical poets of the seventeenth century. *T. H. Jones, M.A. 1949 Wales*

The influence of the metaphysical poets on post-war poetry. *M. Corbett, M.A. 1938 National University of Ireland*

The late eighteenth and early nineteenth century editions of the metaphysical poets, with notes on their editors and publishers: an enquiry into the revival of interest in metaphysical poetry and the influence of that revival. *R. Moore, M.A. 1932 London, King's College*

Metaphysical poetry in the seventeenth century. *M. B. Masoroon, M.A. 1933 Bristol*

The metaphysical style: its use and development. *J. E. V. Crofts, B.Litt. 1914 Oxford*

Minor English verse narrative, 1600-1651. *F. Burton, M.A. 1936 Sheffield*

Nature in English poetry from 1610 to 1660. *D. E. Brook, M.A. 1936 Liverpool*

The relationship between English poetry and music in the seventeenth century. *E. F. Hart, M.A. 1949 London, King's College*

The rise of 'metaphysical' poetry in England. *M. B. Douglas, M.A. 1913 Birmingham*

Studies in the metaphysical poets of the Anglican Church in the seventeenth century. *A. J. M. Smith, Ph.D. 1931 Edinburgh*

A study of the influence of politics on poetry during the years 1640 to 1660. *L. C. Bennett, M.A. 1924 London*

A study of the song-books and poetical miscellanies of the seventeenth century. *A. K. D. Gupta, Ph.D. 1931 Edinburgh*

Symbolism in English metaphysical poetry, with special reference to Donne, Herbert and Vaughan. *M. A. Khan, Ph.D. 1948 London, Queen Mary College*

A transcript and catalogue of Bodleian ms. Malone 16. *R. A. White, B.Litt. 1931 Oxford*

Verse satire in the reign of Charles II. *P. Cutler, M.A. 1940 London, Queen Mary College*

Poetry, English: Eighteenth Century

The development of descriptive poems in the English poetry of the eighteenth century. *R. Thomas, M.A. 1949 Wales*

Eighteenth century ideas of taste as reflected chiefly in the poetry of the period. *P. C. Das, Ph.D. 1936 Edinburgh*

Eighteenth century poetical miscellanies. *T. R. Bailey, Ph.D. 1933 London, External Degree*

The elegy in the eighteenth century. *J. Fisher, B.Litt. 1929 Oxford*

English lyric in the eighteenth century. *O. Doughty, B.Litt. 1923 Oxford*

Poetry, Hebrew
Ancient Hebrew poetry as illustrated by a ms. of the seventeenth century from the *Cairo Genizah*. *M. Wallenstein, Ph.D. 1938 Manchester*

Some unpublished Hebrew poems of the fifteenth and sixteenth centuries forming part of the Montefiore collection of manuscripts, transcribed, translated and annotated. *A. Wallenstein, M.A. 1941 Manchester*

The writing and recital of ancient Hebrew poetry. *I. W. Slotki, D.Litt. 1932 Manchester*

Poetry, Indian
Panjabi Sufi poets. *L. Rama Krishna, Ph.D. 1934 London, School of Oriental and African Studies*

Poetry, Irish
The Anglo-Norman element in Irish poetry from 1200 A.D. to 1600 A.D. *M. A. McConville, M.A. 1946 Belfast*

Cnuasacht filidheachta ó Iár-Mhúsgraighe (An anthology of poetry from West Muskerry). *C. M. Ní Bhuachalla, M.A. 1942 National University of Ireland*

Dánta as láimhscríbhinn i gColáiste Cholmáin, Mainistir Fhearmuighe (Poems from a manuscript in St. Colman's College, Fermoy). *S. O'Mathghamhna, M.A. 1939 National University of Ireland*

Dánta droch-shaoil (1800-1845) (Poems of the hard life, 1800-1845). *S. O'Tuama, M.A. 1931 National University of Ireland*

Dánta polaitíochta san Ghaoluinn, 1782-1848 (Political poems in the Gaoluinn, 1782-1848). *E. P. De Blaghd, M.A. 1946 National University of Ireland*

Díoscán de dhánta gearra (A short selection of syllabic poems). *P. Teidhirs, M.A. 1948 National University of Ireland*

Dréachtaí filíochta a cumadh do sna Grásaigh, i gCo. Cille Coinnigh, idir 1704 agus 1742 (Poetry composed for the Grace family in Co. Kilkenny between 1704 and 1742). *R. Breathnach, M.A. 1938 National University of Ireland*

Duanaire bhrathar mbocht d'Ord S. Froinsias (Poems of the Franciscan Brothers). *J. A. McGrath, Ph.D. 1945 National University of Ireland*

Duanaire do Chloinn Chárthaigh (An anthology of poems written for the McCarthy family). *N. M. Ní Cheallacháin, M.A. 1939 National University of Ireland*

Duanta Eoghain Uí Dhonnghaile agus duanta eile ó indé (The poems of Eoghan O'Donnghaile and other poems of yesterday). *R. O'Tierney, M.A. 1937 National University of Ireland*

Filí Chathair Chorcaigh 1730-80 (Cork City poets 1730-1780). *P. O'Callanáin, M.A. 1933 National University of Ireland*

Filí Mhúsgraighe agus go sonradhach filí Baile Mhuirne (The poets of Muskerry and particularly the poets of Ballyvourney). *M. Ní Chuill, M.A. 1934 National University of Ireland*

Filíocht ó láimhscríbhinn ó co. an Chláir. Filíocht Stainndis Aodha Uí Ghráda, Bhriain Uí Luanna agus Shéamais Mhic Chruitinn (Poetry from a manuscript from Co. Clare, including the poetry of Stainndis Aodh O'Gráda, Briain O'Luanna and Séamas Mac Cruitinn). *L. MacCarthaigh, M.A. 1937 National University of Ireland*

Gearaltaigh Deasmhumhan i bfilidheacht na Gaedhilge (1350-1800) (The Desmond Geraldines in Irish poetry (1350-1800)). *P. D. O'Cillín, M.A. 1945 National University of Ireland*

Geinealach Dál gCais, agus triúr filí na 18adh aoise (The Dal Cais geneology and three eighteenth-century poets). *J. O'Brien, Ph.D. 1944 National University of Ireland*

The life and work of George Darley. *C. C. Abbott, Ph.D. 1926 Cambridge*

Marian poetry in Irish, a comparative study. *J. D. Frizelle, M.A. 1949 National University of Ireland*

Nua fhilidheacht na Gaedilge (Modern Irish poetry). *M. MacConroi, M.A. 1926 National University of Ireland*

The religious mind of the Irish bards. *J. E. Murphy, Ph.D. 1938 National University of Ireland*

Some comparisons between Welsh and Irish love poetry. *M. A. Kennedy, M.A. 1943 National University of Ireland*

Poetry, Irish contd.
Stair agus seanchas Iár-Mhúscraighe, agus filíocht le S. Máistir O'Conaill agus le Tadhg O'Síothcháin, agus giotaí le fillibh (The history and lore of West Muskerry, and poetry by S. Máistir O'Conaill, Tadhg O'Síothcháin and others). *D. MacCarthaigh, M.A. 1937 National University of Ireland*

A study of the poetry of the Irish *Annals* up to the year 1,000 A.D. *O. McKernan, M.A. 1938 Belfast*

Tráchtas ar fhilidheacht na 17 aoise (A treatise on 17th century poetry). *C. Pléimeanne, M.A. 1933 National University of Ireland*

Tráchtas ar nádúir-fhilíocht na Gaedhilge (A treatise on Irish nature poetry). *B. Ua Nualláin, M.A. 1934 National University of Ireland*

Poetry, Italian
A comparative study of the figures of speech in early Provençal and Italian lyrical poetry, down to and including Dante's *Vita nuova* and *Rime*. *I. M. Agnew, Ph.D. 1926 Edinburgh*

Spirito e motivi dei poeti crepuscolari. *K. Speight, M.A. 1933 Manchester*

Poetry, Latin
The *carmen famosum* of the neoteric school. *R. J. M. Lindsay, M.A. 1950 Belfast*

The epyllion from Theocritus to Ovid. *M. M. Crump, D.Litt. 1930 London, University College*

The influence of Roman satire on English literature. *A. H. Hill, M.A. 1910 Birmingham*

The minor Latin didactic poets. *H. E. Gould, M.A. 1931 London, Birkbeck College*

The origins of Latin love-elegy. *A. A. Day, Ph.D. 1937 London, University College*

The relation of Catullus and the Augustan elegiac Latin poets to Alexandrian literature. *M. E. Fish, M.A. 1918 London*

Roman society of the Republic as revealed in the comic poets. *E. L. Gilham, M.A. 1920 London*

Shakespeare's debt to Latin poetry. *P. C. Brown, M.A. 1912 Birmingham*

Stoicism in Latin poetry (to the end of the Augustan period). *A. Cooper, M.A. 1918 Birmingham*

Studies in Livy, Lucan, and Seneca, and some additional notes on Latin poetry. *W. B. Anderson, D.Litt. 1916 Aberdeen*

Poetry, Persian
The influence of Arabic poetry on the development of Persian poetry. *U. M. K. Daudpota, Ph.D. 1927 Cambridge*

On certain similarities between Persian and English poetry. *G. O. H. Ansari, M.A. 1925 London*

Persian poetry of the kings of India. *S. Y. Hashmi, Ph.D. 1933 London, School of Oriental and African Studies*

Persian poets in India and their works. *R. Ahmad, M.A. 1926 London*

Poets and poetry of modern Iran. *M. Ishaque, Ph.D. 1940 London, School of Oriental and African Studies*

Poetry, Provençal
A comparative study of the figures of speech in early Provençal and Italian lyrical poetry, down to and including Dante's *Vita nuova* and *Rime*. *I. M. Agnew, Ph.D. 1926 Edinburgh*

Poetry, Russian
The influence of Byron on Russian poetry. *W. Matthews, Ph.D. 1926 London*

Some problems of the *Tale of the expedition of Igor*, a Russian poem of the twelfth century. *N. M. Iovetz-Tereshchenko, B.Litt. 1928 Oxford*

Poetry, Sanskrit
A study of metres in the older *Upanisads*. *P. N. Majmudar, M.A. 1930 London, School of Oriental and African Studies*

Poetry, Scottish
The influence of Chaucer, Gower, and Lydgate on the Scottish poets in the fifteenth and early sixteenth centuries. *P. W. Thomson, B.Litt. 1915 Oxford*

Scottish poetics and literary criticism from James VI to Francis Jeffrey. *T. S. Lawson, Ph.D. 1930 Edinburgh*

A study of Scottish vernacular poetry in the reign of James VI; with a new text of the poems of Alexander Montgomerie. *G. S. C. Stevenson, B.Litt. 1911 Oxford*

Poetry, Serbo-Croatian
Influence of Italian literature on Ragusan poetry in the sixteenth century. *J. Torbarina, Ph.D. 1930 London, King's College*

Poetry, Serbo-Croatian contd.
Serbian traditional folk-poetry in England, France, and Germany in the nineteenth century. *D. Subotić, B.Litt. 1927 Oxford.*

Poetry, Spanish
The burlesque of mythology in seventeenth century Spanish poetry. *T. W. Keeble, Ph.D. 1948 London, King's College*

Naturalism in Spanish poetry from the origins to 1900. *R. M. Macandrew, D.Litt. 1929 Aberdeen*

The recurrence of the death theme in Spanish poetry from minstrel to 20th century. *C. De Wolf, Ph.D. 1938 Dublin, Trinity College*

Poetry, Welsh
Accented verse: a study of the development of free metre poetry in Welsh literature until the beginning of the seventeenth century. *D. L. Jenkins, M.A. 1921 Wales*

Barddoniaeth arwrol yn y Gymraeg (Heroic poetry in Welsh). *D. H. Jenkins, M.A. 1924 Wales*

Barddoniaeth Huw Cae Llwyd, Ieuan ap Huw Cae Llwyd, Ieuan Dyfi a Gwerful Mechain. *L. Harries, M.A. 1933 Wales*

Bugeilgerddi a rhieingerddi Cymraeg y 18fed a'r 19eg ganrif (Welsh pastoral and love poems of the eighteenth and nineteenth centuries). *D. J. Jones, M.A. 1930 Wales*

A comparative study of the nature poetry of Ieuen Glan Geirionydd, Alun, Islwyn and Ceiriog. *W. R. Jones, M.A. 1923 Wales*

Contemporary lyrical poetry. *N. M. Edwards, M.A. 1925 Wales*

Datblygiad y delyneg mewn llenyddiaeth Cymreig (Development of the lyric in Welsh literature). *M. L. Huws, M.A. 1916 Wales*

Datblygiad y gelfyddyd ysgrifennu caneuon yng Nghymru yn y XIX ganrif (The development of the art of song-writing in Wales in the XIX century). *T. H. J. Rees, M.A. 1930 Wales*

Efrydiau yn nharddiad a datblygiad geirfa ac arddull beirdd Cymraeg y cynfnod 1800-1842 (Studies on the source and development of the vocabulary and style of Welsh poets of the period 1800-1842). *H. Rees, M.A. 1929 Wales*

The history of the Modern Movement in Welsh poetry. *M. Evans, M.A. 1921 Wales*

Iaith a ieithwedd y cerddi rhydd cynnar (The language and style of the early free poems). *H. M. Evans, M.A. 1937 Wales*

Poems of Bedo Brwynllys. *W. R. Watkin, M.A. 1909 Wales*

The poetical works of Bedo Aerddrem, Bedo Brwynllys and Bedo Phylip Bach. *R. Stephen, M.A. 1907 Wales*

Rhai agweddau ar ganu rhydd cynnar Cymru, g yda sylw arbennig i'w gysylltiadau â chanu Saesneg (Some aspects of the free early poetry of Wales, with special reference to its connections with English poetry). *B. Rees, M.A. 1940 Wales*

Some comparisons between Welsh and Irish love poetry. *M. A. Kennedy, M.A. 1943 National University of Ireland*

The transition in Welsh poetry between 1450 and 1600. *G. R. Jones, M.A. 1925 Wales*

The works of some fifteenth century Glamorgan bards: Ieuan Gethyn ap Ieuan ap Lleision, Rhys Brydydd, Rhisiart ap Rhys, Gwilym Tew, Llywelyn ap Hywel ap Gronwy, Lang Lewys, Llywelyn Goch y Dant, Gruffydd ap Dafydd Fychan, Ieuan Du'r Bilwg. *J. M. Williams, M.A. 1923 Wales*

Y daroganau Cymraeg hyd at amser y Tuduriaid, gan roi sylw arbennig i'r cywyddau brud (The Welsh prophecies up to the time of the Tudors, with special reference to the prophetic cywyddau). *R. W. Evans, M.A. 1935 Wales*

Ymrysonau'r beirdd (The (poetic) contentions of the bards). *B. Rhys, M.A. 1932 Wales*

Poland
Great Britain and the Polish Question, 1863. *W. F. F. Grace, Ph.D. 1925 Cambridge*

Polish-Ukrainian relations, 1919-39. *Z. Sliwowski, B.Phil. 1947 Oxford*

The problem of economic development of backward countries (with special reference to Poland). *S. F. Gawel, B.Litt. 1947 Oxford*

Police
The English police system and its applicability to rural China. *C. Chang, Ph.D. 1937 London, School of Economics and Political Science*

Police contd.
The work of Sir Robert Peel as Secretary of State for the Home Department, 1822-1830. *E. A. W. Kinsey, M.A. 1927 Manchester*

Poliomyelitis
The influence of Sir Byrom Bramwell on poliomyelitis. *M. B. O'Neill, M.D. 1949 Edinburgh*

Politian, Angelo
Politian's vernacular poems and their relation to his theory of poetry. *J. M. S. Cotton, B.Litt. 1934 Oxford*

Political Parties
See Communism; Conservatism; Independent Labour Party; Labour Party; Liberalism; Socialism; and under the subheadings History and Politics of individual countries.

Political Philosophy
See Political Theory.

Political Science
See Political Theory.

Political Theory
See also Authority; Christianity and Political and Social Questions; Communism; Democracy; Government, Systems of; Law; Radicalism; Rationalism; Religion and Politics; Socialism; Utopias.

De imperii civilis origine. *B. Webb, M.A. 1750 Glasgow*

The idea of the state and its realisation. *W. Walsh, M.A. 1936 National University of Ireland*

Influence of European political doctrines upon the evolution of the Indian Government institutions and practice (1858-1938). *G. Prashad, Ph.D. 1942 London, School of Economics and Political Science*

The Monarchomachi: a study in the political philosophy of the sixteenth century. *R. N. C. Hunt, B.Litt. 1925 Oxford*

Political theory and educational practice. *J. Hudson, M.A. 1941 Liverpool*

Politics and industry in the state. *F. S. Milligan, M.A. 1921 Birmingham*

The pragmatic revolt in politics. *W. Y. Elliott, D.Phil. 1923 Oxford*

The principles of political obligation of the modern state. *F. C. Meng, B.Litt. 1938 Oxford*

The relation between the state and the individual considered in the light of its bearing on the conception of duty. *W. E. G. Sekyi, M.A. 1918 London*

Tennyson's religious, social and political ideas in relation to his time. *L. J. Smethurst, M.A. 1948 London, King's College*

Political Theory: Ancient
City State and Nation State: a study of the political theory of Plato and Aristotle in relation to the modern State. *R. J. F. Chance, Ph.D. 1927 London*

The commentaries on the *Politics* of Aristotle in the late thirteenth and early fourteenth centuries, with reference to the thought and political life of the time. *C. J. Martin, D.Phil. 1949 Oxford*

Law and the community, being aspects of political experiment and the theory in the sixth and fifth centuries in Hellas. *M. H. Martin, D.Phil. 1936 Oxford*

Political Theory: Bohemia
The life and work of František Palacký, with special reference to his political ideas of nationality and government. *J. E. Williams, M.A. 1925 Wales*

Political Theory: France
See also Jurieu, P.; Rousseau, J. J.; Saint Simon, C. H., Comte de.

Benjamin Constant as a political writer (1814-20). *F. E. Newman, B.Litt. 1931 Oxford*

The *Defensor pacis* of Marsilio of Padua and John of Jandun: its relation to political theories developed in France during the reign of Philip IV. *M. J. Tooley, M.A. 1921 London*

George Sand as a political theorist. *A. K. Tucker, M.A. 1922 London*

Henri Linquet: his political and social theory. *A. B. Handler, M.Sc. 1934 London, School of Economics and Political Science*

Le monde politique dans Balzac. *A. Clayton, M.A. 1930 Manchester*

Les idées politiques de George Sand. *M. H. Birtwell, M.A. 1926 Manchester*

The political academies of France in the early eighteenth century, with special reference to the Club de l'Entresol, and to its founder the Abbé Pierre-Joseph Alary. *E. R. Briggs, Ph.D. 1932 Cambridge*

Political Theory: France contd.
Politics in the novels of Honoré de Balzac. *B. N. Parker, M.A. 1929 London*

Montesquieu: his political and economic ideas. *P. Jordan, Ph.D. 1930 London, School of Economics and Political Science*

Political Theory: Germany
See also Marx, K.

Adalbert Stifter's attitude towards the state. *K. H. G. Spalt, M.A. 1938 Birmingham*

German historiography and the evolution of German political ideas in the nineteenth century. *J. W. Jennings, Ph.D. 1949 London, School of Economics and Political Science*

Goethe as a political thinker. *G. F. Beckh, M.A. 1918 Bristol*

Political Theory: Great Britain
See also Bagehot, W.; Bray, J. F.; Burke, E.; Carlyle, T.; Filmer, R., Sir; Godwin, W.; Hamilton, A.; Harrington, J.; Locke, J.; Mill, J. S.; Paine, T.; Sidney, A.

Contemporary political thought in England. *L. Rockow, Ph.D. 1925 London*

Disraeli as a writer of political novels. *R. B. Ives, M.A. 1924 Birmingham*

English constitutional history and political ideas from the death of Oliver Cromwell to the fall of Clarendon. *H. N. Mukerjee, B.Litt. 1933 Oxford*

The English idea of the 'social contract' theory of government in English political theory, from the Reformation to the Revolution of 1688. *J. A. Thomas, M.A. 1923 Wales*

The impact of politics on literature in the reign of Queen Anne. *H. R. Hoggart, M.A. 1940 Leeds*

The influence of the Renaissance on the English conception of the State. *F. W. E. C. Caspari, B.Litt. 1936 Oxford*

The main tendencies in English political philosophy in the nineteenth century. *M. McKie, M.A. 1925 Wales*

Milton as a politician and a political thinker. *T. Henshaw, M.A. 1926 Wales*

Montesquieu and English thought. *F. T. H. Fletcher, D.Litt. 1935 Birmingham*

The political economists and the politicians from Waterloo to the Reform Bill. *S. G. Checkland, M. Com. 1947 Birmingham*

The political ideas and influence of John Wesley. *M. L. Edwards, M.A. 1927 Wales*

Political ideas in Wales during the latter half of the eighteenth century as reflected in ballad literature. *A. Watkin Jones, B.Litt. 1926 Oxford*

The political ideas of the Quakers in the seventeenth century. *P. S. Belasco, M.Sc. 1926 London*

The political importance of Dr. Price. *B. M. Parry, M.A. 1934 Liverpool*

Political thought in Wales, 1789-1846. *T. Evans, M.A. 1924 Wales*

The political thought of Edmund Burke. *A. B. C. Cobban, Ph.D. 1926 Cambridge*

The political thought of the English Romanticists. *C. C. Brinton, D.Phil. 1923 Oxford*

The political thought of Victorian poets. *A. K. Davis, B.Litt. 1923 Oxford*

Some aspects of social and political life in England during the nineteenth century in relation to contemporary theory. *N. M. Waterson, M.A. 1921 Birmingham*

Stoicism and political theory in the tragedies of George Chapman. *L. F. Haddakin, M.A. 1948 London, University College*

A study of the influence of politics on poetry during the years 1640 to 1660. *L. C. Bennett, M.A. 1924 London*

The transition from individualist to socialist political thinking in England. *C. C. Cheng, B.Phil. 1948 Oxford*

Uthred of Boldon: a study in fourteenth century political theory. *C. H. Thompson, Ph.D. 1936 Manchester*

Political Theory: Islamic
The development of political thought and practice in Islam, 1-232 A.H./622-847 A.D. *M. J. Ramzi, Ph.D. 1948 Glasgow*

Political Theory: Jewish
See also Spinoza, B. de.

Political Theory: Jewish contd.
The social and political ideas of Maimonides. *Z. Schwarz, M.Sc. 1926 London*

Political Theory: Spain
Political philosophy of Suarez. *C. H. Scanlan, M.A. 1939 National University of Ireland*

Political Theory: United States
The political ideas of John C. Calhoun. *R. L. Humber, B.Litt. 1923 Oxford*

Politics, International
See also League of Nations; United Nations; War and Peace.

The Eastern Question and European diplomacy in the period 1876-1878, with special reference to British policy. *W. A. Gauld, M.A. 1923 Liverpool*

The influence of the Barbary States in international relations, with special reference to the United States. *R. K. Irons, D.Phil. 1934 Oxford*

International co-operation: a study of its causes and forms. *T. Cristureanu, Ph.D. 1932 London, School of Economics and Political Science*

International relations on the south east coast of Africa, 1796-1856. *M. V. Jackson, Ph.D. 1938 London, King's College*

The internationalism in the work and thought of William Ewart Gladstone, with reference to present-day theory and practice of internationalism. *J. D. Evans, M.A. 1938 Wales*

Labour's foreign policy, 1919-24. *T. Z. Winnicki, M.Litt. 1950 Cambridge*

The part the press played: the influence of the Press upon international relationships during the years 1896-1914. *M. Lewis, M.A. 1930 Birmingham*

Public opinion in international relations. *W. W. Wade, M.Sc. 1948 London, School of Economics and Political Science*

The Saar territory as a factor in international relations, 1920-1932. *M. Lambert, Ph.D. 1936 London, School of Economics and Political Science*

Serbia in international politics from the insurrection of Herzegovina (1875) to the Congress of Berlin (1878). *M. D. Stojanovic, Ph.D. 1930 London, King's College*

The United States and Old World diplomacy, 1898 to 1914, with special reference to China. *R. G. Shiman, Ph.D. 1930 London, School of Economics and Political Science*

Pollanus, Valerandus
See Poullain, V.

Pollio, Gaius Asinius
Asinius Pollio and his part in the Roman Revolution. *J. Fogarty, M.A. 1943 National University of Ireland*

Polybius
The Carthaginians as depicted in Livy, Polybius, and other ancient writers. *G. Adams, M.A. 1922 London*

Polychronicon
See Higden, R.

Polynesia
Economic organization of Polynesian societies. *R. W. Firth, Ph.D. 1927 London*

Pomeroy, Family of
The family of de la Pomerai of Beri, 1066-1719, with appendix post 1720. *E. B. Powley, M.A. 1941 Liverpool*

Pompeii
The development of social and economic life at Pompeii. *R. C. Carrington, D.Phil. 1933 Oxford*

Poor Law
See also Poverty.

The administration of the poor laws in Ireland till 30th November, 1921, and in Northern Ireland from the 1st December, 1921, till present date. *H. Miller, M.Com.Sc. 1942 Belfast*

The assistance of the poor in Paris and in the northeastern French provinces, 1614 to 1660, with special reference to the letters of S. Vincent de Paul. *E. Archer, Ph.D. 1936 London, School of Economics and Political Science*

The Bishops and the poor law, 1782-1834. *W. A. Parker, M.A. 1939 Manchester*

The conditions and needs of the cottage homes child (poor law), together with a short history of the rise and development of the cottage homes system. *J. Edwardson, M.A. 1923 Liverpool*

Poor Law contd.
The development of the poor laws in Caernarvonshire and Anglesey, 1815-1914. *C. F. Hughes, M.A. 1945 Wales*

The English Poor Law of 1834, with special reference to its working between 1834 and 1847: a study in social pathology. *J. M. Mackinnon, M.A. 1930 London, University College*

The English Poor Laws and social conditions. *D. Marshall, Ph.D. 1926 Cambridge*

A history of the workhouse system to the end of the eighteenth century, with special reference to the period from 1722 to 1732, and the industrial aspect. *E. M. M. Zucker, M.A. 1925 Manchester*

Organisation and administration of relief during the great famine. *T. P. O'Neill, M.A. 1946 National University of Ireland*

Phases of poor law policy and administration, 1760-1834. *J. H. Howard, M.A. 1921 Liverpool*

Poor law adminstration in Glamorganshire before the Poor Law Amendment Act of 1834. *W. E. Allin, M.A. 1936 Wales*

The Poor Law of 1601, with some consideration of modern developments of the poor law problem. *G. Boone, M.A. 1917 Birmingham*

Some aspects of the history of the administration of the Poor laws in Birmingham between 1730 and 1834. *M. McNaulty, M.A. 1942 Birmingham*

The treatment of vagrancy and the relief of the poor and destitute in the Tudor period, based upon the local records of London to 1552 and Hull to 1576. *K. Anderson, Ph.D. 1933 London, Royal Holloway College*

Pope, Alexander
Alexander Pope as a satirist in prose. *D. Broughton, M.A. 1943 London, Birkbeck College*

The bases of Pope's *Essay on man*. *F. B. Thornton, B.Litt. 1937 Oxford*

Introduction and notes to Pope's Homer's *Iliad*. *M. Macmillan, D.Litt. 1902 Birmingham*

John Caryll, Pope's friend. *S. K. Mugaseth, B.Litt. 1936 Oxford*

Pope and Boileau. *V. P. Dempsey, M.A. 1921 National University of Ireland*

The Pope-Bowles controversy. *N. T. Harris, M.A. 1925 London*

Pope's knowledge of English literature from Chaucer to Dryden. *E. G. Midgley, B.Litt. 1950 Oxford*

Pope's relations with his contemporaries. *N. T. Harris, Ph.D. 1933 London, University College*

Pope's version of the *Iliad*, considered as illustrating his theory of translation and his conception of the heroic style. *W. H. Jowsey, B.Litt. 1949 Oxford*

The reputation of Alexander Pope during the early years of the nineteenth century, 1800-30. *J. D. Davies, M.A. 1940 London, Queen Mary College*

A study of Pope's satire. *C. R. Bishop, Ph.D. 1937 London, King's College*

William Lisle Bowles and the controversy on Pope. *W. R. Hutchison, M.A. 1946 Belfast*

Pope, Walter
Walter Pope: a study of his life and works. *A. B. Dugan, B.Litt. 1935 Oxford*

Popes
See Roman Catholic Church.

Popish Plot
See Great Britain: History: Seventeenth Century.

Population
See also Emigration and Immigration; Family; Fertility; Migration; Mortality; Refugees.

Density of population in Europe, including special treatment of two countries about 1801 and 1861. *J. P. Ryder, M.A. 1935 Manchester*

Fertility of marriage and population growth. *L. R. Connor, M.Sc. 1926 London*

The interpretation of age frequency data. *E. R. Clarke, M.Ed. 1933 Manchester*

The League of Nations and national minorities. *P. Barber, M.A. 1924 Wales*

Political thought and the population problem. *N. Roth, M.Sc. 1939 London, School of Economics and Political Science*

Population fluctuation studies in biotic communities. *J. R. Carpenter, B.Sc. 1938 Oxford*

Population contd.
The techniques of sampling with special reference to demographic enquiries in undeveloped countries. *P. S. You, Ph.D. 1949 London, School of Economics and Political Science*

Population: Africa, East
The settlement of Indians on the margins of the Indian Ocean. *W. R. Rayner, M.A. 1934 London, Birkbeck College*

Population: Arabia
The settlement of Indians on the margins of the Indian Ocean. *W. R. Rayner, M.A. 1934 London, Birkbeck College*

Population: Asia
The Chinese in southeastern Asia and the East Indies. *G. J. Miles, M.A. 1932 London, Birkbeck College*

Population: Australia
A contribution to the demography (including some remarks on the climate, hygienic, and other conditions) of South Australia. *T. Borthwick, M.D. 1891 Edinburgh*

Population: Burma
Some aspects of the population problem in Burma. *B. N. Kaul, Ph.D. 1930 London, School of Economics and Political Science*

Population: Canada
A consideration of geographical factors influencing the distribution of population in British Columbia. *Kenny. K. A, M.A. 1934 London, Bedford College*

Distribution of population in New Brunswick and Prince Edward Island. *A. D. Jones, M.A. 1933 Liverpool*

Population: Ceylon
A discussion of the geographical factors affecting the distribution of population in Ceylon. *C. L. H. Geary, M.A. 1929 London*

The distribution of population and the development of settlements in Ceylon. *A. Ginigé, M.A. 1930 London, School of Economics and Political Science*

The Sinhalese in Ceylon: a study in historical and social geography. *D. D. M. Gooneratne, M.A. 1930 Liverpool*

Population: China
The Chinese in southeastern Asia and the East Indies. *G. J. Miles, M.A. 1932 London, Birkbeck College*

The education of overseas Chinese: a comparative study of Hong Kong, Singapore and the East Indies. *T. C. Cheng, M.A. 1949 London, Institute of Education*

The legal status of the Chinese abroad. *T. Huang, Ph.D. 1936 London, School of Economics and Political Science*

A new statement of the facts regarding the movements of peoples in China, with respect to the natural features. *E. E. Gomersall, M.Sc. 1921 Wales*

Population: Egypt
The introduction of perennial irrigation in Egypt and its effects on the rural economy and population problems of the country. *I. A. Farid, Ph.D. 1937 London, University College*

Population: France
French refugees in England from the Restoration to the death of William III. *A. W. Nicholls, B.Litt. 1923 Oxford*

Some changes in the distribution of population in Brittany. *M. E. Orsman, M.A. 1932 Wales*

Population: Great Britain
The agricultural geography and related distribution of population in Northumberland. *E. C. Sykes, M.A. 1931 Liverpool*

An anthropometric study of Welsh and English populations. *F. H. Cleaver, M.A. 1936 Wales*

Changes in the distribution of the population since 1800. *W. R. Luke, M.A. 1939 London, External Degree*

Changes in the trend and distribution of our school population, and their effects on education. *R. S. Walshaw, M.Ed. 1940 Manchester*

Changes of population in west Cornwall with the rise and decline of mining. *T. W. McGuinness, M.Sc. 1938 London, Birkbeck College*

Cleveland and Teesside: a geographical study of population and occupational changes since 1800. *I. Bowes, M.A. 1948 London, Bedford College*

The conditions of the rural population of England and Wales, 1870-1928, in relation to migration and its effects in age and sex selection; income and standards of living; changes in social organization. *D. J. Davies, Ph.D. 1931 Wales*

Population: Great Britain contd.
Density, distribution and housing of population in the middle Derwent basin. *F. C. Couzens, M.A. 1937 London, Birkbeck College*

The distribution of rural population with particular reference to the Vale of Evesham. *S. W. Brown, B.Litt. 1925 Oxford*

Early distribution and valleyward movement of population in south Britain; a relief model of Wales; climatology in correlation with geography; human geography in Britain. *W. E. Whitehouse, M.A. 1916 Wales*

The factors which have influenced settlement and the movements of population within the plain of Nottingham. *H. M. Keating, Ph.D. 1933 London, External Degree*

French refugees in England from the Restoration to the death of William III. *A. W. Nicholls, B.Litt. 1923 Oxford*

The geographical reasons for the growth of the population of south Staffordshire, east Warwickshire and Leicestershire from 1801-1931. *G. M. Sarson, Ph.D. 1937 London, External Degree*

A geographical study of the recent distribution of population and types of settlement in mid-Wales and along the central Welsh border, with special reference to Radnorshire. *W. R. Saunders, B.Litt. 1925 Oxford*

The growth of the borough and the distribution and density of population in the Chesterfield region since the Industrial Revolution. *F. C. Couzens, Ph.D. 1941 London, External Degree*

Hanes a llenyddiaeth cychwyniad a datblygiad mudiad y wladfa Gymreig ym Mhatagonia (The history and literature of the origin and development of the Welsh colony in Patagonia). *N. H. Cadfan, M.A. 1942 Wales*

A history of the Italian exiles in London, 1816-1848. *M. C. W. Wicks, Ph.D. 1930 Edinburgh*

The influence of physical geography upon the history of settlement and distribution of population in Sussex. *W. H. Parker, B.Sc. 1939 Oxford*

An inquiry into the changing distribution of population in the Chilterns since 1821. *R. S. G. Brocklebank, Ph.D. 1937 London, University College*

An investigation into the social and educational aspects of pupil migration in Scotland. *H. S. Mackintosh, Ph.D. 1941 Aberdeen*

An investigation of changes in population density and distribution, together with changes in agricultural practice, in Pembrokeshire during the period 1831-1931. *G. I. Lewis, M.A. 1937 Birmingham*

Llenyddiaeth Gymraeg y Wladfa (The Welsh literature of the Colony (in Patagonia)). *R. B. Williams, M.A. 1931 Wales*

Movements of mining population in the anthracite area of south Wales. *E. J. Howells, M.Sc. 1938 Wales*

Population changes in Cornwall in relation to economic resources. *T. W. McGuinness, Ph.D. 1944 London, King's College*

Population in Central Wales: changes in number and distribution, 1801-1931. *J. E. C. Jenkins, M.A. 1939 London, King's College*

Population in the dales of North East England. *A. E. Smailes, M.A. 1934 London, University College*

Population migration to and from Warwickshire and Staffordshire, 1841-1901. *R. Lawton, M.A. 1950 Liverpool*

Population movements in the British Isles since 1921. *R. S. Walshaw, M.A. 1937 Liverpool*

Population movements in Scotland, 1770-1850. *D. F. Macdonald, D.Phil. 1933 Oxford*

A portion of west Sussex: a study of agriculture and population. *E. Cook, M.A. 1939 Liverpool*

Psychological and social differences between A, B and C groups in senior schools, and their relation to the differential birth rate. *A. N. V. Harris, M.A. 1942 Birmingham*

Recent and prospective population trends in Great Britain and certain other countries. *G. G. Leybourne, M.A. 1935 Liverpool*

Rural depopulation in Wales, 1881-1901. *R. Jones, M.A. 1911 Belfast*

Rural settlements and the distribution of rural population in Northamptonshire. *E. E. Field, M.Sc. 1931 London, External Degree*

Population: Great Britain contd.
A sociological and statistical study of the population of the Vale of Glamorgan during the first half of the nineteenth century. *M. I. Williams, M.A. 1939 Wales*

Some aspects of population in Bristol. *E. Grebenik, M.Sc. 1941 London, School of Economics and Political Science*

A statistical study of the rural population of Wales in the nineteenth and twentieth centuries. *W. King, Ph.D. 1929 Wales*

A study of English vital statistics, with special emphasis on marriage statistics and social or occupational class differences. *K. T. Lim, Ph.D. 1938 Liverpool*

A study of statistics of population and occupations in the countries and urban and rural districts of Wales, 1901-31. *M. A. Richards, M.Sc. 1942 Wales*

A study of the changes in the geographical distribution of industry and population in England and Wales during the twentieth century. *J. E. S. Orrin, M.A. 1932 Wales*

A study of the changes in the distribution and density of population in Worcestershire during the period 1841-1931, and of the geographical factors involved. *E. R. G. Wood, M.A. 1950 Birmingham*

Survey of the effects of the 1939-45 war and of the immigration of former city-dwellers on a Midland township. *W. M. Whiteley, M.Com. 1948 Birmingham*

Population: India
Distribution of population in the United Provinces of Agra and Oudh (India). *C. S. Sinha, M.A. 1933 London, Birkbeck College*

Distribution of population in the Tamil country. *V. S. Swaminathan, M.Sc. 1931 London, University College*

The Indian problem in eastern and southern Africa. *L. James, M.A. 1940 Liverpool*

The Indian problem in Kenya. *P. L. Maini, M.Sc. 1944 London, School of Economics and Political Science*

An interpretation of the distribution of the population within the United Provinces of Agra and Oudh. *N. Y. Boydell, M.Sc. 1938 Leeds*

The settlement of Indians on the margins of the Indian Ocean. *W. R. Rayner, M.A. 1934 London, Birkbeck College*

Some social aspects of the minority problem in India. *R. S. Bhatt, M.A. 1936 London, School of Economics and Political Science*

Population: Ireland
The congested districts of Ireland. *I. Hynes, M.Econ.Sc. 1944 National University of Ireland*

Inter-relation between geographical factors and population decline in Ireland since the famine of 1845-47. *P. M. McNamara, Ph.D. 1932 London, School of Economics and Political Science*

The population of Ireland from 1750 to 1846, and the social and economic factors associated with its increase. *K. H. Connell, Ph.D. 1948 London, External Degree*

Population: Italy
A history of the Italian exiles in London, 1816-1848. *M. C. W. Wicks, Ph.D. 1930 Edinburgh*

Population: Japan
A geographical study of the expansion of Japan in relation to the Japanese population problem. *L. E. Ward, M.A. 1932 Liverpool*

Population: Malaysia
A geographical study of the population problems of Malaysia. *B. M. Husain, M.A. 1942 Liverpool*

Population: Mexico
Some anthropological aspects of Mexican immigrant settlement in Dallas, Texas. *H. D. Gunn, M.A. 1949 London, School of Economics and Political Science*

Population: Northern Ireland
The population and settlement in Northern Ireland. *R. D. James, M.A. 1948 Wales*

Population: Norway
The Fiord peoples. *C. B. Fawcett, B.Litt. 1913 Oxford*

A population study of Aust Agder fylke (county), Norway. *K. Bartholomew, M.Sc. 1949 London, University College*

Population: South Africa
Some recent trends in the status history of the coloured people of South Africa. *C. Sofer, M.Sc. 1949 London, School of Economics and Political Science*

Poquelin, Jean Baptiste
See Molière, J. B. P.

Port Books
A calendar and analysis, with introduction, of two Elizabethan port books (E190/5/1 and E190/5/6). *F. E. Leese, B.Litt. 1950 Oxford*

Port Talbot
Recent industrial changes in the Afan district (Glamorganshire), with special reference to the development of Port Talbot. *D. Davies, M.A. 1915 Wales*

Port-Royal
See also Jansenism.

The little schools of Port Royal. *H. Clive-Barnard, B.Litt. 1911 Oxford*

Studies in the history and influence of the education of boys at Port Royal and in the older Oratorian colleges of France. *W. N. Littlejohns, M.A. 1948 London, King's College*

Ports and Harbours
See also individual ports, e.g. Belize; Bristol; Cardiff; Chicago; Cinque Ports; Fleetwood; Hull; Madras; Montreal; New York; Newcastle-upon-Tyne; Newport; Plymouth; Portsmouth; Southampton; etc.

The administration of ports. *J. H. Hannay-Thompson, Ph.D. 1938 Edinburgh*

The British ports in relation to the export trade of Birmingham. *A. J. McIntosh, Ph.D. 1935 London, External Degree*

The free port system in the British West Indies, 1766-1815. *L. F. Horsfall, Ph.D. 1939 London, King's College*

The London lighterage trade: its history, organisation and economics. *C. L. Wheble, M.Sc. 1939 London, School of Economics and Political Science*

The Pacific ports of Canada. *F. A. Arrowsmith, M.A. 1936 London, School of Economics and Political Science*

The ports of Western India: a study in the physical, economic and historical factors controlling port development. *A. N. Harris, M.A. 1932 Reading*

The present and future organization of British ports and harbours. *W. McC. Scammell, M.Com.Sc. 1947 Belfast*

Portsmouth
The development of Portsmouth as a naval base as illustrating the growth of British naval policy. *H. J. Sparks, M.A. 1911 London*

Portugal
The attitude of the British Government to the Portuguese revolution of 1826-1834. *P. M. Cowell, M.A. 1927 London*

British policy in relation to Portuguese claims in West Africa, 1876 to 1884. *I. Bains, M.A. 1940 London, Bedford College*

Geographical factors in the evolution of Portugal as a political unit. *G. R. Morris, M.A. 1936 Liverpool*

The part played by Great Britain in the separation of Brazil from Portugal, 1821-1825. *J. H. W. Liddicoat, M.A. 1927 London*

The Portuguese in India and the East Indies 1497-1548. *T. H. Jenkins, M.A. 1924 Birmingham*

Positivism
See also Comte, A.

The English Positivists. *T. Nyland, M.A. 1937 London, School of Economics and Political Science*

The influence of Auguste Comte and the rise of positivism in England up to the formation of the English Positivist Society in 1867. *W. L. Presswood, Ph.D. 1935 Sheffield*

Positivism with special reference to Auguste Comte and the Viennese circle of philosophy. *M. F. Browne, M.A. 1944 National University of Ireland*

The theories of logical positivism. *M. Black, Ph.D. 1939 London, University College*

Postal Services
The development of rates of postage. *A. D. Smith, D.Sc. 1917 London*

Postal Services contd.
Some aspects of staff organization in the Postal Service with special reference to (a) the general history and development of the movement since 1895; (b) the struggle for official recognition; (c) the efforts to secure full civil rights; and (d) the working of Whitleyism. *L. M. Smith, B.Litt. 1931 Oxford*

Pottery
See Ceramics.

Poullain, Valérand
The Liturgia sacra and Professio fidei catholicae of Valerandus. *J. Gordon, Ph.D. 1928 Edinburgh*

Poultry Industry
See Dairy Industry.

Poussin, Nicolas
The history of theories of painting in Italy and France, 1400-1700, with special reference to Poussin. *A. F. Blunt, Ph.D. 1935 Cambridge*

Poverty
See also Poor Law.

Causes of poverty among the rural populations of the Arab states. *P. Selwyn, B.Litt. 1947 Oxford*

The doctrine of poverty in its religious, social and political aspects, as illustrated by some XII-XIII century movements. *J. L. Flajszer, Ph.D. 1943 London, School of Economics and Political Science*

An essay introductory to the De pauperie Salvatoris of Richard Fitzralph, books v-vii. *H. C. Hughes, Ph.D. 1928 Manchester*

Le symbolisme de la pauvreté dans l'oeuvre de Léon Bloy. *E. T. Pichler, M.A. 1945 Birmingham*

Pauperism and vagrancy in Cambridgeshire to 1834. *E. M. Hampson, Ph.D. 1931 Cambridge*

The poor in English literature. *E. O'Driscoll, M.A. 1917 National University of Ireland*

Poverty and some of its effects upon schoolchildren. *E. N. Nash, M.Ed. 1941 Durham*

Poverty and the wage-earning classes. *M. McSweeney, M.A. 1914 National University of Ireland*

The respective spheres of the State and of voluntary organizations in the prevention and relief of poverty in London at the present day. *L. H. Bell, M.A. 1935 London, School of Economics and Political Science*

The treatment of poverty in Norfolk, from 1700 to 1859. *M. F. Prichard, Ph.D. 1950 Cambridge*

Powell, Vavasor
The life, work and thought of Vavasor Powell (1617-70). *R. T. Jones, D.Phil. 1947 Oxford*

Vavasor Powell (1617-1670): an account of his life, with special reference to religious movements in Wales in his time. *D. E. Walters, M.A. 1933 Liverpool*

Power Supply
See Electricity Supply Industry; Fuel Industry; Gas Industry; Oil Industry.

Pragmatism
A criticism of pragmatism. *T. Fu, M.A. 1917 Birmingham*

The pragmatic reaction to absolute idealism in English philosphy. *J. E. Gregory, M.A. 1949 Sheffield*

The pragmatic revolt in politics. *W. Y. Elliott, D.Phil. 1923 Oxford*

The pragmatic theory of truth, with especial regard to the question whether it implies a distinction between reality as it is known and reality as it is in itself. *S. S. S. Browne, B.Litt. 1929 Oxford*

The primacy of the practical reason. *D. P. Jones, M.A. 1920 Liverpool*

The reality of extra-intellectual knowledge, with special reference to Bergson and pragmatism. *D. Richardson, M.A. 1917 Wales*

The relations between voluntarism and pragmatism as illustrated by the development of French voluntaristic philosophy from Maine de Biran to Professor Bergson: with especial reference to the Bergsonian notion of truth and its development in the 'new philosophy'. *L. S. Stebbing, M.A. 1912 London*

Prakrit Language and Literature
A grammar of the old Kanarese inscriptions, including a study of Sanskrit and Prakrit loan-words. *A. N. P. Narasimhia, Ph.D. 1933 London, School of Oriental and African Studies*

Prayer
Assyrian prayers and hymns. *M. Sidersky, B.Litt. 1922 Oxford*

Prayer contd.
1. The Christian doctrine and some non-Christian theories of sin. 2. The nature and reaonableness of prayer. *H. T. Pinchin, B.D. 1895 Oxford*

1. The efficacy of prayer. 2. The efficacy of sacraments. *E. C. Maclure, B.D. & D.D. 1890 Oxford*

1. The Lord's day. 2. The efficacy of prayer. *E. R. Currie, B.D. & D.D. 1888 Oxford*

1. The Lord's Prayer: its origin, comprehensiveness, and suitability, both as a form and a model. 2. The genuineness of the pastoral epistles. *F. W. Joy, B.D. & D.D. 1895 Oxford*

The origin and development of prayer and its place in the life of primitive peoples. *H. H. C. Bee, M.A. 1942 Leeds*

The philosophy of prayer, developed on a psychological basis. *G. V. W. Subley, M.A. 1927 London*

The place of prophetic intercession in Old Testament religion. *G. R. Conning, Ph.D. 1934 Edinburgh*

1. Prayer. 2. The intermediate state. *E. G. Banks, B.D. & D.D. 1890 Oxford*

Prayer and its psychology. *A. J. Hodge, Ph.D. 1930 London, External Degree*

Prayer and the four Gospels. *D. R. C. Morris, B.D. 1947 Oxford*

1. The scientific objections to the utility of prayer. 2. The Book of Job and the problems arising out of it. *T. F. Royds, B.D. 1910 Oxford*

Prayer Books
See Book of Common Prayer; Breviaries.

Preaching
See Sermons.

Precious Stones
See Jewellery.

Predestination
1. The Athanasian Creed consonant with the word of God. 2. The true doctrine of election involves no injustice. *F. N. Oxenham, B.D. & D.D. 1896 Oxford*

The doctrine of predestination in St. Paul and Stoicism. *B. Joannidis, B.Litt. 1932 Oxford*

An examination of Mozley's treatment of the Augustinian doctrines of grace and pre-destination. *T. O. Davies, B.Litt. 1925 Oxford*

An exposition of: Acts of the Apostles vii: Stephen's defence: Hebrews vii-ix: the heavenly priesthood of Christ: Romans viii, ix: St. Paul's doctrine of election. *R. H. Taylor, D.D. 1900 Oxford*

Free will and predestination in early Islam. *W. M. Watt, Ph.D. 1944 Edinburgh*

1. On the organization of the early Church as exhibited in the Acts of the Apostles and the Pauline Epistles. 2. On the right and wrong use of the doctrine of predestination. *M. Argles, B.D. & D.D. 1891 Oxford*

1. Predestination and free will. 2. The resurrection of the holy. *E. E. Bradford, B.D. 1904 Oxford*

1. St. Athanasius' exposition of the divinity and Incarnation of our Lord in the anti-Arian orations. 2. St. Augustine's exposition of grace, free-will, and predestination in his anti-Pelagian treatises. *T. Hayes-Robinson, B.D. 1906 Oxford*

1. That the doctrine of a future state did form part of the revelation to man in the times preceding our Lord's birth. 2. That the so-called doctrine of final perseverance can be established by sufficient evidence from Holy Scripture, and is held by the Church of England in her seventeenth Article. *F. Bedwell, B.D. 1874 Oxford*

Prehistory
See Archaeology and Antiquities.

Prejudice
The social and cultural basis of prejudice. *S. S. McIntyre, Ph.D. 1950 Edinburgh*

Preparatory Schools
See Education, Elementary.

Pre-Raphaelite Movement, The
See also English Literature; Painting.

A bibliographical and reference guide to the life and works of Dante Gabriel Rossetti, with a study of the Pre-Raphaelite Movement. *J. B. Gregory, Ph.D. 1931 London, King's College*

Presbyterianism
See also Church of Scotland; Irving, E.; Love, C.; Rutherford, S.; Witherspoon, J.

Presbyterianism contd.
1603-1685: Presbyterians and Independents, their relations to the government and its effect on their relations with one anothe. *E. Ingham, M.A. 1935 Manchester*

The attempts at Presbyterian-Episcopal accommodation in Scotland and their influence on modern movements of unity. *M. J. Roberts, Ph.D. 1949 Glasgow*

Classical Presbyterianism in England, 1643-1660. *C. E. Surman, M.A. 1949 Manchester*

Contribution of the Scottish Church to New Brunswick Presbyterianism from its earliest beginnings until the time of the Disruption, and afterwards, 1784 to 1852. *F. E. Archibald, Ph.D. 1933 Edinburgh*

The early history of the Presbyterian church in western Canada from the earliest times to the year 1881. *J. C. Walker, Ph.D. 1928 Edinburgh*

English Presbyterian thought from 1662 to the foundation of the Unitarian Movement. *O. M. Griffiths, Ph.D. 1933 Bristol*

The General Assembly of 1610: a critical investigation. *G. C. Wadsworth, Ph.D. 1930 Edinburgh*

The General Assembly of the Kirk as the rival of the Scottish Parliament, 1560-1618. *E. E. MacQueen, Ph.D. 1927 Saint Andrew's*

The headship of Jesus Christ as taught and vindicated by the Reformed Presbyterian Church in North America in relation to civil government. *R. M. C. Ward, Ph.D. 1939 Edinburgh*

An inquiry into the origins of the Presbyterian Church polity in Scotland, as devised by the reformers of the sixteenth century. *J. G. MacGregor, Ph.D. 1923 Edinburgh*

Origin and early development of Presbyterianism in Virginia. *D. L. Beard, Ph.D. 1932 Edinburgh*

The principle of nonsubscription to creeds and confessions of faith as exemplified in Irish Presbyterian history. *R. Allen, Ph.D. 1944 Belfast*

Puritanism and its Presbyterian development in the time of Elizabeth. *A. Peel, B.Litt. 1912 Oxford*

The relations between the English and Scottish Presbyterian movements to 1604. *G. Donaldson, Ph.D. 1938 London, University College*

The relations between the Irish Presbyterians and the government from the Declaration of Indulgence (1687) to the repeal of the Test Act (1780). *J. C. Beckett, M.A. 1942 Belfast*

The Scots Confession of 1560: its sources and distinctive characteristics. *T. Muir, Ph.D. 1926 Edinburgh*

Scottish ecclesiastical influence upon Irish Presbyterianism from the non-subscription controversy to the union of the synods. *R. Allen, M.A. 1940 Belfast*

The Southern Presbyterian Church and the doctrine of the spirituality of the Church. *T. H. Spence, Ph.D. 1929 Edinburgh*

A study of the accommodation movements between Presbytery and Episcopacy in the seventeenth century in Scotland, England and Ireland. *D. S. Hopkirk, Ph.D. 1946 Edinburgh*

The use of liturgical orders of service in the worship of the so-called Presbyterian Dissenters. *A. E. Peaston, B.Litt. 1936 Oxford*

The *Westminster Confession of Faith*: being an account of the printing and preparation of its seven leading editions to which is appended a critical text with notes thereon. *S. W. Carruthers, Ph.D. 1929 Edinburgh*

Press
See Freedom of the Press; Journalism; Printing.

Preston
Preston: the interrelations of town and region. *H. B. Rodgers, M.A. 1950 Manchester*

Prévost, Antoine François, Abbé
A pioneer in the work of propagating a knowledge of England and English literature in France, being an investigation into the Abbé Prévost's relations with England and English literature, with special reference to his *Le pour et contre, Cleveland, Mémoires d'un homme de qualité* and *Lettres de Mentor à un jeune seigneur. J. C. Carpenter, M.A. 1915 Wales*

Price, Richard
The aims and work of Richard Price, 1723-1791. *B. Jenkins, M.A. 1927 Wales*

Price, Richard contd.
A dissertation comprising a critical commentary and analysis of the system of intuitional ethics expounded by R. Price. *E. S. Price, M.A. 1930 Bristol*

The ethical philosophy of Richard Price. *M. Thomas, M.A. 1921 Wales*

The moral theory of Richard Price. *R. Thomas, Ph.D. 1928 London*

The political importance of Dr. Price. *B. M. Parry, M.A. 1934 Liverpool*

The religious thought of Richard Price, 1723-1791. *B. A. Norris, Ph.D. 1950 Edinburgh*

Views concerning the epistemology of morals held by some of the British moralists of the eighteenth century, with especial reference to the anti-empiricist views of Richard Price and Thomas Reid. *D. Rafilovitch, D.Phil. 1940 Oxford*

Price, Uvedale, Sir
Payne Knight, Price, and the picturesque. *T. A. Heinrich, M.Litt. 1936 Cambridge*

Prices
Agricultural price records: an account of the methods of recording prices and a guide to the published wholesale price records of England and Wales. *P. M. Reason, M.Sc. 1934 Reading*

An analysis of the Indian price structure from 1861. *A. K. Ghosh, Ph.D. 1949 London, School of Economics and Political Science*

Aspects of resale price control, with special reference to conditions in the U.K. *A. P. Zentler, M.Sc. 1941 London, School of Economics and Political Science*

Budget studies and the measurement of living costs and standards. *E. A. Winslow, Ph.D. 1923 London*

Cost of living index figure. *D. Hutchinson, M.Econ.Sc. 1938 National University of Ireland*

The economics of control: a theory of authoritarian pricing and production. *A. Lerner, Ph.D. 1942 London, School of Economics and Political Science*

Price control in Great Britain, 1939-1946, with special reference to non-food consumers' goods. *M. Eccleshall, B.Litt. 1950 Oxford*

Price determination under monopoly and competition: a theory of structural integration. *G. Horwill, M.Com. 1948 Birmingham*

Price policy in the short period. *N. A. Morling, M.Com. 1931 Birmingham*

The relative influence of money and credit on general prices. *J. Rejan, Ph.D. 1922 Edinburgh*

Some contributions to a study of work, wages and prices in Wales in the sixteenth century. *A. B. Jones, M.A. 1933 Wales*

The theory of international price relationships: an historical survey. *C. Y. Wu, Ph.D. 1937 London, School of Economics and Political Science*

Valorization under public auspices. *J. Kipps, B.Litt. 1929 Oxford*

Pricke of Conscience
The dialect of the *Pricke of Conscience*, together with a collation of mss. Galba E IX and Harley 4196. *J. Lightbown, M.A. 1935 Leeds*

Priestley, Joseph
1. The beginnings of the scientific career of Joseph Priestley. 2. The detection and estimation of electric charges in the eighteenth century. 3. Animal electricity before Galvani. *W. C. Walker, Ph.D. 1937 London, University College*

Joseph Priestley, LL.D., F.R.S., and his influence on eighteenth century education. *C. J. Rhodes, M.Ed. 1932 Manchester*

Priests
See Clergy.

Primary Education
See Education, Elementary.

Primitivism
See also Anthropology; Religion: Ancient and Primitive; Tattooing.

The conditions psychological and sociological of the development of individuality amongst peoples of rudimentary culture. *W. D. Wallis, B.Sc. 1910 Oxford*

The development of the militant spirit among primitive peoples. *P. H. Brodie, B.Sc. 1917 Oxford*

La philosophie du retour à la nature chez Jean-Jacques Rousseau, et applications practiques de son système. *R. F. Britton, M.A. 1949 Liverpool*

Primitivism contd.
The principals and mechanisms of education among primitive peoples and the applications of these in European-controlled education of the natives in Africa. *T. J. A. Yates, Ph.D. 1933 London, School of Economics and Political Science*

Prince Edward Island
Distribution of population in New Brunswick and Prince Edward Island. *A. D. Jones, M.A. 1933 Liverpool*

The establishment of British government in Isle St. John (Prince Edward Island) 1758-1784. *H. J. Champion, M.A. 1934 London, King's College*

Pringle-Pattison, Andrew Seth
The philosophy of A. S. Pringle-Pattison. *A. H. Norman, B.Litt. 1936 Oxford*

Some aspects of theism, particularly of its treatment by three modern theistic authors: A. S. Pringle-Pattison, F. R. Tennant, G. D. Hicks. *G. T. Eddy, M.A. 1940 Birmingham*

Printing
See also Caxton, W.; Estienne, R.; Tottel, R.; Wolf, J.

The control of the press in England before the granting of the charter to the Stationers' Company. *W. N. Chaplin, M.A. 1935 London*

An economic survey of the printing industry in Bristol. *E. J. Propert, M.A. 1934 Bristol*

English literature of the Picturesque School (c. 1680 to 1780) in relation to the art of printing. *C. M. Davies, M.A. 1931 London, Westfield College*

The postwar relations of skilled and unskilled labour in the printing, building and engineering industries. *P. A. Manning, Ph.D. 1933 London, School of Economics and Political Science*

Printing in the Mascarene Islands (Ile de France and Bourbon) from 1767 to 1810. *M. M. A. Toussaint, Ph.D. 1947 London, External Degree*

Some economic aspects of printing. *A. Qaiyum, M.Com. 1939 Leeds*

A study of business organization in the printing trade. *N. Branton, M.Com. 1937 London, External Degree*

Prior, Matthew
Matthew Prior and his literary relations with France. *W. P. Barrett, Ph.D. 1932 Cambridge*

Priscian
The *Summa* of Petrus Helias on Priscian, *Institutiones Grammaticae*, XVII and XVIII. *J. E. Tolson, M.A. 1950 Liverpool*

Prisons
Evidence of a prisoner's character. *A. J. Ellison, LL.M. 1928 Cambridge*

Houses of correction in England and Wales. *W. E. Passey, M.A. 1936 Liverpool*

Humanitarian and religious elements in early English prison reform, 1773-1835. *R. S. E. Hinde, B.Phil. 1948 Oxford*

The system of gaol delivery as illustrated in the extant gaol delivery rolls of the fifteenth century. *M. E. H. J. Gollancz, M.A. 1936 London, King's College*

Probation
An analysis of the records of some 750 male probationers in the city of Coventry. *E. W. Hughes, M.A. 1942 Birmingham*

Problem-Solving (Psychology)
Factors involved in problem solving, with special reference to the problem of insight. *S. C. Mumford, Ph.D. 1937 London, Bedford College*

Proclamations, Royal
The proclamations issued by Charles I during the years 1642-6, both during his progress to Oxford and his residence there until the surrender of the city in 1646, relating especially to Oxford and neighbouring counties. *E. J. S. Parsons, B.Litt. 1935 Oxford*

Production
The economic implications of conditions in the production and marketing of primary commodities since the Great War. *C. H. Thompson, M.Com. 1939 Birmingham*

The economics of control: a theory of authoritarian pricing and production. *A. Lerner, Ph.D. 1942 London, School of Economics and Political Science*

Efficiency in production control. *N. Buchanan, Ph.D. 1937 Belfast*

Fluctuations in human output. *S. J. F. Philpott, D.Sc. 1932 London, University College*

Production contd.
The limits to the effectiveness of the system of payment by results as an incentive to production. *P. A. Manning, M.A. 1924 Manchester*

Planning and production control in Soviet State industries. *G. R. Barker, M,Com. 1950 Birmingham*

The problem of industrial restriction: a comparative study of industrial reorganization in the British basic industries, 1929-39. *A. Beacham, Ph.D. 1942 Belfast*

Production policies and their impact on problems of marketing and international trade in modern Egypt. *G. E. M. A. Said, Ph.D. 1949 Birmingham*

Recent monetary problems of some primary producing countries. *A. R. Conan, M.Sc. 1938 London, School of Economics and Political Science*

The significance of the effects of changes in data, and in particular in the supply of money, upon the structure of industrial production in a modern capitalist economy. *C. J. Harman, M.Sc. 1935 London, External Degree*

Soviet economic life and the general categories of economic analysis: comparative studies of the forms of value, distribution and production under Soviet and other systems of economic organization. *H. E. Ronimois, Ph.D. 1949 London, School of Economics and Political Science*

A statistical examination of how industry adapts itself to changes in the volume of output and the effects of such changes on the amounts of fixed and working capital employed. *W. A. Tweddle, Ph.D. 1938 Cambridge*

A study of certain industries in relation to increasing and diminishing returns. *G. T. Jones, Ph.D. 1929 Cambridge*

Wages and capitalist production. *V. G. Edelberg, Ph.D. 1935 London, School of Economics and Political Science*

Profit
The measurement of profit and the incidence of taxation. *R. W. Moon, B.Phil. 1948 Oxford*

Profits. *J. P. Beddy, D.Econ.Sc. 1941 National University of Ireland*

Profits in British industry from 1924 to 1935: an investigation into the profits made by certain public companies in Great Britain in the years from 1924 to 1935. *R. S. Hope, D.Phil. 1949 Oxford*

A study of certain industries in relation to increasing and diminishing returns. *G. T. Jones, Ph.D. 1929 Cambridge*

A study of profits, with special reference to the profits of farms in the East of Scotland. *E. Whittaker, Ph.D. 1932 Edinburgh*

The variations of real wages and profit margins in relation to the trade cycle. *S. C. Tsiang, Ph.D. 1945 London, School of Economics and Political Science*

Prometheus
Prométhée dans la littérature allemande. *K. M. Ingold, M.A. 1924 Belfast*

Promotion of Christian Knowledge, Society for the
Hanes yr S.P.C.K. yn Sir Gaerfyrddin o 1700 hyd 1750, gyda chyfeiriad arbennig at John Vaughan, Cwrt Derllys, a'i waith (The history of the S.P.C.K. in Carmarthenshire from 1700 to 1750, with special reference to John Vaughan, Cwrt Derllys, and his work). *M. Clement, M.A. 1940 Wales*

Pronunciation
See Phonetics.

Propaganda
The language of suggestion, magic and propaganda. *A. O. Waligorski, Ph.D. 1938 London, School of Economics and Political Science*

Propaganda in National Socialist Germany. *O. Friedmann, M.Sc. 1947 London, School of Economics and Political Science*

Propertius
The love of nature and rustic life in Horace, Tibullus, and Propertius. *M. J. Wrigley, M.A. 1933 Manchester*

Verbal imagery and figures of speech in Propertius: a study of some aspects of poetic technique. *S. R. Pope, M.A. 1942 Liverpool*

Property
See also Conveyancing; Distress.

Ususfructus and *dominium*. *K. Kagan, M.Litt. 1945 Cambridge*

The application in Roman-Dutch law of the principle *mobilia non habent sequelam* with special reference to the law of South Africa. *M. H. Barry, B.Litt. 1925 Oxford*

Property contd.
Biblical land and property laws, with some account of their amplification in the Mishnah. *J. Vainstein, Ph.D. 1946 Glasgow*

British incomes and property. *J. C. Stamp, D.Sc. 1916 London*

Conceptions of property in England from Harrington to Marx. *W. S. Evans, Ph.D. 1942 Sheffield*

Donatio mortis causa in Roman, English, and American law. *D. W. Logan, D.Phil. 1939 Oxford*

An enquiry into the attitudes of adults in a Lancashire urban area towards property. *J. A. Waites, M.A. 1944 Manchester*

The equitable doctrine of election. *R. H. R. Tee, LL.D. 1923 London*

Evolution of the proprietary status of woman under the common law of the Hindus with special reference to the quantum of interest in immovable property acquired by way of inheritance and partition. *B. M. Patnaik, LL.M. 1948 London, School of Economics and Political Science*

A historical study of the law relating to the assignment of choses in action. *O. R. Marshall, Ph.D. 1948 London, University College*

The influence of equitable ideas concerning property in the development of the law of contract as illustrated by (1) the passing of property under invalid contracts, and (2) contracts for the benefit of third persons. *A. M. Finlay, Ph.D. 1938 London, School of Economics and Political Science*

Jurisdiction of English courts in relation to foreign immovables. *G. B. A. Coker, LL.M. 1947 London, University College*

The law of private property at sea in time of war. *R. J. W. Hurd, LL.D. 1915 London*

The law relating to documents of title to goods. *H. G. Purchase, LL.D. 1931 London, King's College*

The modern law of real property. *G. C. Cheshire, D.C.L. 1927 Oxford*

The operation of the provisions of the Law of Property Act, 1925, regarding undivided shares in land. *T. L. Morgan, LL.M. 1938 Wales*

Ownership in relation to character. *M. E. Wakefield, M.A. 1917 London*

The place of property in English culture. *J. A. Waites, Ph.D. 1946 Manchester*

Possessory liens in English law. *L. E. Hall, LL.D. 1916 London*

The possessory remedies in Roman-Dutch law. *T. W. Price, Ph.D. 1941 Cambridge*

The primitive Roman law of property: its probable origin, its principles and their application. *J. A. Neale, D.C.L. 1886 Oxford*

Right to support of land and buildings by underground water and semi-solids. *F. B. Brook, LL.M. 1932 Cambridge*

Rights in property: a psychological study. *E. Beaglehole, Ph.D. 1931 London, School of Economics and Political Science*

The rules of international private law relating to the transfer of movable, immovables, and choses in action. *H. E. Davies, LL.D. 1928 London*

The slave's *peculium* in Rome and the protection afforded to it by Roman law before the year 180 A.D. *E. M. Thomas, M.A. 1927 Wales*

A study of the rules of private international law relating to the transfer and acquisition of rights in movable property, *inter vivos*, with the exception of bankruptcy. *W. J. Holleman, B.Litt. 1924 Oxford*

The Taluqdari law of Oudh, with special reference to the alienation of property *inter vivos*, and its devolution on death testate and intestate. *Q. Ahmad, LL.D. 1928 London*

The theory of property in the eighteenth century: its historical antecedents with special reference to England and Locke. *W. Larkin, Ph.D. 1928 London*

Prophecy
See also Bible: Old Testament : Prophets; Divination; Oracles.

Akhenaten and the growth and development of monotheism in Hebrew prophecy: a comparison and a survey. *R. K. Spedding, M.A. 1932 Liverpool*

1. Deuteronomy xviii.9-22: inspiration and prophecy. 2. Isaiah vi and xxi.1-10: the prophetic call, audition, and vision. I Corinthians xii-xiv: the psychology of Christian prophecy, introductory to tongues and prophecy in the Corinthian Church. *G. C. Joyce, D.D. 1909 Oxford*

Prophecy contd.
1. The doctrine of the future life in the Old Testament. 2. The origin of Hebrew prophecy. *J. Robertson, B.D. and D.D. 1897 Oxford*

1. The doctrine of the Holy Trinity. 2. Prophecy and the prophets of Israel. *N. Davies, B.D. 1924 Oxford*

1. Early Christian prophecy. 2. St. Hippolytus and the Church. *A. C. Lawson, B.D. 1924 Oxford*

Early vaticinatory material in Welsh, with a study of some English parallels known to Welsh writers. *M. E. Griffiths, M.A. 1927 Wales*

Eschatology and manticism in Old Norse literature. *H. R. Ellis, Ph.D. 1940 Cambridge*

1. The function of the prophets in Christian Church, as it may be gathered from the New Testament. 2. The Christian view of war. *J. G. Tetley, B.D. & D.D. 1901 Oxford*

The Hebrew conception of nature, especially as illustrated by the prophets. *O. H. M. Lehmann, B.Litt. 1947 Oxford*

Hebrew prophecy as illustrated by the vision and message of second Isaiah. *R. S. McHardy, B.Litt. 1923 Oxford*

1. The history of Old Testament prophecy. 2. The study of the Psalms. *L. Owen, B.D. 1924 Oxford*

1. The leading methods of Old Testament prophecy. 2. The teaching of the prophets in regard to Jehovah's relation to Israel. *G. W. Wade, B.D. & D.D. 1901 Oxford*

1. The meaning of the word κύριοσ in the Septuagint and in the New Testament. 2. The prophet of Israel in his relation to God. *A. Ashton, B.D. 1909 Oxford*

Muhammad's prophetic office as portrayed in the Qur'ān. *J. C. Wilson, Ph.D. 1949 Edinburgh*

1. On the anticipative or prophetic character of the several stages of the Creation. 2. The order of the hours of the day in the Gospel according to St. John is the same as that in the other Gospels. *C. Pritchard, B.D. & D.D. 1880 Oxford*

The origin and development of Old Testament prophecy, with an examination of alleged similar phenomena among non-Israelitish people. *G. Rees, M.A. 1917 Wales*

The origin of Hebrew prophecy. 2. The development of prophecy in Israel after the time of Samuel. *L. Davies, B.D. & D.D. 1919 Oxford*

1. The place and work of the prophets in the Catholic Church. 2. The laying on of hands. *T. H. May, B.D. & D.D. 1924 Oxford*

The place of prophetic intercession in Old Testament religion. *G. R. Conning, Ph.D. 1934 Edinburgh*

The place of the prophet in Talmud and Midrashic literature. *S. Sperber, M.A. 1945 Manchester*

1. The place of the prophet in the New Testament. 2. The doctrine of the New Testament as to the moral aspect of war. *R. T. Talbot, B.D. & D.D. 1906 Oxford*

1. Prophecy in the Christian Church. 2. The evolution of the episcopate. *F. H. Wales, B.D. 1897 Oxford*

1. The prophets: the characteristics of their teaching, and their influence on the religious and political life of Israel. 2. The resurrection of our Lord: its evidences and its hints as to a future life. *W. H. Powell, B.D. & D.D. 1909 Oxford*

1. The prophets of Israel up to the fall of Samaria. 2. The function of prophecy illustrated by the prophets of Judah. *J. E. Hatch, B.D. & D.D. 1915 Oxford*

The Rabbinic conception of prophecy. *H.A. Fischel, Ph.D. 1945 Edinburgh*

1. The relation of priest and prophet in the history of Israel before the exile. 2. St. Basil the Great and the monastic life. *E. F. Morison, B.D 1912 Oxford*

Study of the Hebrew prophets. *T. W. Lacey, M.A. 1931 Bristol*

Y daroganau Cymraeg hyd at amser y Tuduriaid, gan roi sylw arbennig i'r cywyddau brud (The Welsh prophecies up to the time of the Tudors, with special reference to the prophetic cywyddau). *R. W. Evans, M.A. 1935 Wales*

Propositions
See Logic.

Prostitution
Prostitution and sex promiscuity in several countries at the present time. *G. M. Hall, M.A. 1932 Liverpool*

Protection
See Free Trade; Tariffs.

Protectorates
See Colonization.

Protestantism
See also Nonconformity; and references there.

The causes of the movement for radical parliamentary reform in England, between 1763 and 1789, with special reference to the influence of the so-called Rational Protestants. *G. B. M. Whale, B.Litt. 1930 Oxford*

The conception of the mission of the Church in early reformed theology, with special reference to Calvin's theology and practice in Geneva. *W. H. Clark, Ph.D. 1928 Edinburgh*

The doctrine of orders in the Reformed Churches in the sixteenth and seventeenth centuries. *J. L. Ainslie, Ph.D. 1935 Edinburgh*

English foreign policy during the reign of William III: in particular the relations of England with the Swiss Protestants. *L. A. Robertson, B.Litt. 1926 Oxford*

The evangelical doctrine of conversion, Lutheran and Reformed. *B. Citron, Ph.D. 1946 Edinburgh*

Ferdinando Texeda: a complete analysis of his work together with a study of his stay in England (1621? to 1631?), being a contribution to the solution of the problems connected with him. *W. McFadden, M.A. 1933 Belfast*

The first and second editions (English and Latin) of the service book used by the English congregation of Marian exiles in Geneva, 1556-1559; arranged in parallel columns, and edited with introduction and notes showing the origins and usages of the rite. *W. D. Maxwell, Ph.D. 1929 Edinburgh*

The Gordon riots, 1780. *L. H. Thraves, M.A. 1910 Liverpool*

The nature and function of dogma in the symbolo-fidéisme of the Paris School. *G. P. Moscherosch, Ph.D. 1950 Edinburgh*

The origin and history of the Old Catholic group of churches, their doctrinal and liturgical position; and the development of their relations with other non-papal communions. *W. H. de Voil, Ph.D. 1937 Edinburgh*

Protestant nonconformity and some social and economic questions, 1660-1800. *E. D. Bebb, Ph.D. 1934 Sheffield*

The relevancy of Calvin to modern issues within Protestantism. *A. H. Leitch, Ph.D. 1941 Cambridge*

Settlements and churches in Nova Scotia, 1749-1776: the origin of Protestant Churches in relation to settlement, from the founding of Halifax to the American Revolution. *I. F. Mackinnon, Ph.D. 1930 Edinburgh*

The strain of Protestantism in the works of André Gide. *E. Perrett, M.A. 1928 Wales*

Studies in the making of the English Protestant tradition. *E. G. Rupp, B.D. 1946 Cambridge*

Proudhon, Pierre Joseph
Pierre-Joseph Proudhon et Karl Marx. *W. Pickles, M.A. 1927 Leeds*

Proust, Marcel
Disintegration of the personality in the work of Marcel Proust. *S. Jones, M.A. 1940 Wales*

The image in the works of Marcel Proust. *H. C. R. Stockwell, Ph.D. 1942 London, King's College*

L'influence de la philosophie de Bergson sur l'oeuvre littéraire de Marcel Proust. *E. K. McCann, M.A. 1933 Liverpool*

The metaphysical basis of the work of Marcel Proust. *S. Jones, Ph.D. 1949 Cambridge*

Moral preoccupations in the life and work of Marcel Proust. *J. L. Moffat, Ph.D. 1948 Bristol*

Proust, William
The controversy between Proust and Berthollet on the invariability of chemical proportions. *L. F. R. Simmonds, M.Sc. 1931 London*

Prouvost, Amédée
Amédée Prouvost: poète, 1877-1909. *R. F. Stockwin, M.A. 1936 Birmingham*

Provençal Language and Literature
See also Flamenca.

A comparative study of the development of strong perfects in French, Provençal, Spanish and Italian. *A. D. Neal, M.A. 1939 Manchester*

Word order in Old Provençal, with special reference to Flamenca and the poems of Bertran de Born. *R. J. Hilton, B.Litt. 1938 Oxford*

Proverbs
Certain aspects of Russian proverbs. *A. I. Guershoon, Ph.D. 1938 London, School of Slavonic and East European Studies*

Seanuiocla Chonnacht le minighthe's nótaí (Proverbs of Connaught, with the author's notes). *T. S. Melia, Ph.D. 1938 National University of Ireland*

Providence
1. Genesis i, ii.1-7, iii.17-19; Psalm xix.1-3, xcv.3-7: evolution and providence. 2. St. Mark ix.48; St. John iii.36: eternal justice. 3. Genesis iii.1-10; Romans vii.18,19: will in Christian ethics. *A. J. Nilson, D.D. 1885 Oxford*

History of the concept of providence. *A. M. Armstrong, Ph.D. 1943 Edinburgh*

Providence, Island
The Company of Adventurers to the islands of Providence and Henrietta: its foundation and history, 1630-1634. *A. P. Newton, M.A. 1910 London*

Prudentius, Aurelius Clemens
Aurelius Prudentius Clemens *Contra Symmachum*, Books I-II, including introduction, translation, commentary, bibliography, together with translation of Symmachus' third *Relatio* and St. Ambrose's reply. *K. Harrison, Ph.D. 1935 Dublin, Trinity College*

The manuscripts of Prudentius. *E. O. Winstedt, B.Litt. 1903 Oxford*

Prudentius and the problems of his age: an exposition and appreciation of the *Apotheosis* and *Hamartigenia* of Aurelius Prudentius Clemens. *W. L. Davies, M.A. 1939 Wales*

Prudentius *Psychomachia* and French allegorical poetry of the Middle Ages. *S. C. M. Treharne, M.A. 1929 Wales*

Prudentius' treatment of Roman religion. *R. E. Roberts, M.A. 1938 Wales*

Prynne, William
Caroline puritanism as exemplified in the life and work of William Prynne. *T. Fitch, Ph.D. 1949 Edinburgh*

William Prynne's ideal State Church, and his views on the sectaries, Independents. *E. Stephenson, M.A. 1929 Manchester*

Prys, Edmwnd
Edmwnd Prys: hanes ei fywyd a chasgliad o'i weithiau (Edmwnd Prys; the history of his life and a collection of his works). *J. W. Roberts, M.A. 1938 Wales*

Prys, Thomas
Barddoniaeth Tomos Prys o Blas Iolyn (The poetry of Thomas Prys of Plas Iolyn). *W. Rowlands, M.A. 1912 Wales*

Pryse, John Robert (Golyddan)
Golyddan; ei fywyd a'i weithiau, gyda chyfeiriad arbennig at yr arwrgerdd Gymraeg (Golyddan; his life and his works, with special reference to the Welsh epic). *H. C. Bassett, M.A. 1935 Wales*

Psellos, Michael
The revival of learning at Constantinople in the eleventh century, with special reference to Michael Psellos. *J. M. Hussey, B.Litt. 1932 Oxford*

Psichari, Ernest
Ernest Psichari. *C. J. Henry, M.A. 1949 National University of Ireland*

Ernest Psichari: l'homme et son oeuvre. *F. T. Devlin, M.A. 1938 National University of Ireland*

Psychiatry
See also Mental Health; Psychoanalysis.

Army psychiatry in and out of battle: its relationship to the soldier and to the service. *D. T. Maclay, M.D. 1947 Glasgow*

Aspects of prognosis in psychiatry. *D. T. Bardon, M.D. 1943 Dublin, Trinity College*

An attempt to assess the importance of some of the usually accepted causes of mental abnormality: a clinical and statistical study of 500 psychiatric patients. *A. R. Norton, D.M. 1947 Oxford*

The conception of value in psychological medicine. *C. P. Blacker, D.M. 1931 Oxford*

The study of temperament of neurotic persons by means of aspiration tests. *H. T. Himmelweit, Ph.D. 1945 London, Maudsley Hospital*

Psychical Research
An examination of the supernormal psychical phenomena recorded in Latin literature. *F. T. Walton, M.A. 1934 Birmingham*

Psychoanalysis
See also Psychiatry; Sublimation; and Freud, S.; Jung, C. G.

Psychoanalysis contd.

A psychological and statistical study of certain psychoanalytical character types. *D. S. Trouton, M.A. 1947 London, University College*

The statistical significance of certain psychoanalytical types in children. *R. Cole, M.A. 1947 London, University College*

Psychodrama

A study of psychodrama as a classroom technique. *J. M. Bridgewater, M.A. 1949 London, Institute of Education*

Psychological Tests
See also Aptitude Testing; Intelligence Testing; Perseveration; Personality Tests; Psychology, Experimental; Tachistoscope.

The application of psychological tests to certain problems of native education in East Africa. *R. A. C. Oliver, Ph.D. 1933 Edinburgh*

Comparative value of certain verbal and non-verbal (primarily perceptual) tests and their relation to tests of mechanical ability. *K. G. Rama Rao, Ph.D. 1933 London, University College*

The development and application of statistical methods in the prediction of ability. *L. Ackerson, B.Sc. 1925 Oxford*

An experimental analysis of certain performance tests. *E. J. J. Price, B.Sc. 1939 Oxford*

Overstress in endurance tests. *S. Wright, M.Sc. 1934 Belfast*

Researches in the measurement of human performance. *N. H. Mackworth, Ph.D. 1947 Cambridge*

Some effects of social and educational opportunities upon mental tests. *C. R. McRae, Ph.D. 1925 London*

A study of the factors underlying the intercorrelations of verbal, mathematical, and form perception tests. *O. R. Russell, Ph.D. 1935 Edinburgh*

A study of the Gestalten problem concerning completed and uncompleted test-items. *A. R. Pachauri, Ph.D. 1934 London, University College*

1. Tests of reasoning processes and their relation to general mental ability. 2. The mental differences between the sexes. *R. C. Moore, M.A. 1915 Liverpool*

Psychology
See also Ability; Abstraction; Adaptation; Adolescents; Aggression; Association; Attention; Attitude; Belief; Child Psychology; Conditioning; Confidence; Consciousness; Creativity; Death; Delinquency; Desires; Disposition; Dreams; Emotion; Employment; Epistemology; Error; Ethics; Experience; Fanaticism; Friendship; Group Psychology; Habit; Humour; Imagery; Imagination; Instinct; Judgment; Leadership; Logic; Love; Meaning; Memory; Mental Health; Mind; Motor Performance; Norms; Perception; Perseveration; Personality; Play; Prejudice; Problem Solving; Psychiatry; Psychoanalysis; Repression; Self; Self-Consciousness; Skill; Sleep; Stress; Subconscious, The; Sublimation; Suggestibility; Thinking; Unconscious; War and Peace; Will; Women: Psychology.

The biologist's approach to the mind-body problem. *J. S. Wilkie, Ph.D. 1949 London, University College*

Circular mentality and the pyknic body type. *M. Sahair, Ph.D. 1930 London, University College*

The contribution of modern psychology to literary criticism. *E. R. Bentley, B.Litt. 1939 Oxford*

The curve of output during a continued series of tasks varying in nature. *M. K. B. Harwood, M.Sc. 1937 London, University College*

Dextrality and sinistrality of hand and eye. *T. L. Woo, Ph.D. 1928 London*

The effects of volition and affective states upon muscular work. *R. P. R. Westgate, Ph.D. 1934 London, King's College*

The ethical implications of modern psychology. *J. Gray, M.A. 1928 Birmingham*

Experimental and statistical investigation of some factors influencing aesthetic judgments. *H. J. Eysenck, Ph.D. 1940 London, University College*

Fluctuations in meaning (in binocular rivalry). *J. C. A. Corea, M.A. 1939 London, University College*

The hylomorphic concept in psychology. *P. Barry, M.A. 1942 National University of Ireland*

Individual psychology - its nature, assumptions and limitations. *D. E. Lake, M.A. 1939 Bristol*

Influence of rest pauses on fluctuations of mental output. *F. W. Warburton, Ph.D. 1945 London, University College*

Psychology contd.

Influence of short rest pauses on fluctuations in mental output. *F. W. Warburton, M.A. 1938 London, University College*

Lessons of the war for psychological theory. *W. N. Maxwell, M.A. 1921 Belfast*

Mental development with special reference to school conditions and health. *J. G. Bannell, M.A. 1916 Liverpool*

The mind-body problem in the light of recent philosophical theories. *D. Richards, Ph.D. 1943 London, Birkbeck College*

The nature of psychological enquiries. *R. S. Peters, M.A. 1949 London, Birkbeck College*

The nervous temperament: its definition and history: its expression in industry and importance from the point of view of health and efficiency. *M. Smith, D.Sc. 1930 London, School of Hygiene and Tropical Medicine*

The psychological factor in economic theory. *B. H. Higgins, M.Sc. 1935 London, School of Economics and Political Science*

Psychological laws and economic activity. *R. T. Harry, M.A. 1924 Wales*

The psychological needs of children and their relation to behaviour. *C. Sanders, Ph.D. 1938 London, Institute of Education*

The psychological study of reasoning. *J. D. Horgan, M.A. 1923 National University of Ireland*

The psychology of aesthetic experience: instinctive reaction in aesthetic experience. *H. T. Jones, B.Sc. 1924 Oxford*

The psychology of economics. *T. Templeton, Ph.D. 1927 Glasgow*

The psychology of S. Paul. *W. N. W. Harvey, B.Litt. 1941 Dublin, Trinity College*

The psychology of shape. *H. P. Bridges, M.A. 1931 London, King's College*

Psychology of the language and style of préciosité. *J. G. Morley, B.Litt. 1939 Oxford*

The psychology of the unconscious, with special reference to mental disorder, its cause and cure. *J. Blacow, M.A. 1936 Liverpool*

Regeneration and the new psychology, with special reference to character changes. *A. D. Dodd, Ph.D. 1935 Edinburgh*

Relations and complex qualities. *S. Arulnandy, M.Sc. 1931 London, University College*

Retentivity in the special senses. *E. H. Walters, Ph.D. 1929 London*

The rôle of attention in aesthetic experience. *J. B. Parry, Ph.D. 1940 London, University College*

A statistical study of individual preferences with olfactory stimuli. *M. M. Davies, M.A. 1938 London, University College*

A statistical study of physical and mental types. *I. Cohen, Ph.D. 1940 London, University College*

Statistics and psychology. *H. G. Stead, Ph.D. 1925 London*

The status of secondary qualities in the light of contemporary research. *D. G. James, M.A. 1928 Wales*

Studies of labour wastage and sickness absence. *P. H. Chatterjee, Ph.D. 1941 London, University College*

A study of psycho-somatic correlations, with especial reference to the affective states. *W. H. Shepley, M.D. 1943 Manchester*

A study of surprise. *M. M. Desai, Ph.D. 1937 London, University College*

A study of the threshold in relation to subliminal impressions and allied phenomena. *R. P. B. Pillai, Ph.D. 1938 London, University College*

Theory and practice of psychology, and other papers. *L. W. Jones, D.Sc. 1939 Wales*

Psychology: History
See also Avicenna; MacCurdy, J. T.

An examination into some elements of Spenser's psychological vocabulary, with reference to that of Chaucer. *M. Topham, M.A. 1931 Manchester*

An examination of Bosanquet's doctrine of self-transcendence. *R. E. Stedman, Ph.D. 1930 Edinburgh*

Jesus' teaching on man and modern psychological theories. *M. B. Birnie, M.A. 1947 Bristol*

La psychologie de Molière. *E. M. Kennedy, M.A. 1916 National University of Ireland*

Psychology: History contd.

Modern psychology and the validity of Christian experience. *C. H. Valentine, Ph.D. 1926 London*

The new psychology, its origins, and development. *A. McCrea, M.A. 1924 Belfast*

Psychology of Plato. *J. O'Shea, M.A. 1915 National University of Ireland*

Studies in pre-Lockian psychology. *J. White, D.Sc. 1898 London*

Psychology, Child
See Child Psychology.

Psychology, Educational
See Educational Psychology.

Psychology, Experimental
See also Adaptation; Aptitude Testing; Intelligence Testing; Measurement; Personality Tests; Psychological Tests; Reading; Suicide.

An analytic and experimental study of relation and correlate finding. *I. Cohen, M.A. 1936 London, University College*

Curves of output produced by one individual. *F. H. Akil, Ph. D. 1949 London, University College*

The differential diagnosis of depressive states, with an inquiry into the suicidal impulse: an investigation conducted by a method of experimental psychology. *A. Guirdham, B.Sc. 1935 Oxford*

The effects of different conditions of temperature and ventilation on the mental output and mental fatigues of school children. *A. H. Seymour, Ph.D. 1936 London, University College*

An experimental investigation of aesthetic judgment. *S. M. Crane, M.A. 1946 London, University College*

An experimental investigation of certain phenomena due to oscillation in mental efficiency. *H. W. Oldham, M.A. 1931 Reading*

Factor-analysis applied to current problems in psychology, with special reference to data obtained from H. M. forces. *E. K. C. Banks, Ph.D. 1945 London, University College*

Fluency and lying: an experiment designed to study the relations between a number of tests of fluency and temperamental and intellectual traits, and also their relationship to a behaviour problem, namely, lying. *G. M. Hammond, M.A. 1946 London, Birkbeck College*

Individual differences in dark adaptation. *L. R. Phillips, Ph.D. 1939 London, University College*

Interaction of figural after-effects. *L. Weiskrantz, B.Sc. 1950 Oxford*

An investigation into temperament: its relation to intelligence, and special abilities. *F. E. MacNeill, Ph.D. 1942 Edinburgh*

Measuring fluctuation in mental work. *E. R. Denton, Ph.D. 1949 London, University College*

Periods of arrested progress in the acquisition of skill. *M. D. Smith, Ph.D. 1930 Cambridge*

Relation between intelligence quotient and curves of output (mental). *C. P. Sinha, M.Sc. 1949 London, University College*

The study of fluctuations in homogeneous mental tasks. *R. Ratha, Ph.D. 1949 London, University College*

The study of temperament of neurotic persons by means of aspiration tests. *H. T. Himmelweit, Ph.D. 1945 London, Maudsley Hospital*

A study of the Rorschach test. *A. Sen, Ph.D. 1949 London, University College*

The temporal arrangement of errors or failures in perceptual work. *S. Ghosh, Ph.D. 1949 London, University College*

Psychology, Industrial
See also Work.

Contributions to an industrial psychology of the blind. *L. G. Fuchs, M.A. 1949 London, Birkbeck College*

The main economic results of industrial psychology. *H. D. Harrison, M.Com. 1923 Birmingham*

The psychological conditions in two representative factories. *F. Orde, M.A. 1937 London, University College*

Some psychological aspects of employment in the coal-mining industry, with special reference to the Ayrshire coalfield in Scotland. *W. D. Stewart, B.Litt. 1933 Oxford*

Psychology, Occupational
See Careers.

Psychology, Religious
See also Belief; Evangelicalism; Initiation; Man; Metaphysics; Mind; Mysticism; Prayer; Religious Conversion; Religious Experience; Revelation; Theology.

A critical examination of the theory of sublimation, together with a consideration of its relevance for religion. *J. T. Davies, Ph.D. 1944 London, Richmond College*

A critical exposition of the methods and results of the American School of religious psychology: a study in the psychology of religion. *A. R. Uren, Ph.D. 1924 Edinburgh*

Examination and criticism of Hoeffding's contribution to the psychology of religious conviction. *A. W. Baillie, M.A. 1924 Manchester*

Mental therapy and the forgiveness of sins: a clinical view of the results of sin, with psychological studies of religious leaders as approaches to the application of the work of Christ in the experience of forgiveness. *A. P. Guiles, Ph.D. 1934 Edinburgh*

Problems of religious psychology in the works of the French naturalistic and psychological novelists. *P. W. Gower, M.A. 1932 London, King's College*

The psychological role of the mother in the origin of the religious sentiment: a psychological study of mother-goddess cults, with special reference to India. *G. D. Boaz, D.Phil. 1942 Oxford*

A psychological study of some aspects of the religious consciousness of seventeenth century England: considered with particular reference to the psychological factors involved in the development of English 'dissent'. *A. G. S. Spinks, M.A. 1939 London, University College*

A psychological study of the development of religious beliefs among children and young persons. *J. Bradshaw, M.Sc. 1949 London, University College*

Psychology and religious education. *D. F. Wilson, B.Litt. 1927 Oxford*

The psychology of C. G. Jung in relation to religious thought and experience. *F. Roberts, M.A. 1946 Birmingham*

The psychology of religious belief. *L. J. Belton, M.A. 1927 Birmingham*

The psychology of religious expression and its relation to religious education. *L. P. Star, Ph.D. 1942 Dublin, Trinity College*

Recent developments of psychological study upon religion. *J. C. Flower, Ph.D. 1925 Cambridge*

Recent psychological theories of the origin of religion. *J. K. Benton, Ph.D. 1934 Edinburgh*

The relationship of instinctive and rational factors in the religous attitude: a psychological inquiry. *W. M. R. Rusk, Ph.D. 1927 Edinburgh*

Religion as a factor in personal synthesis. *R. S. Lee, B.Litt. 1927 Oxford*

Religion as an integrative principle in human personality. *R. H. King, M.Litt. 1938 Cambridge*

Religious revivals in the light of modern psychological theory. *I. G. Grimshaw, Ph.D. 1933 Edinburgh*

Revelation and the unconscious. *R. S. Frayn, Ph.D. 1940 London, Richmond College*

A study of the relation between the imaginative and rational aspects of religion. *H. J. Smith, B.Litt. 1936 Oxford*

Psychoneurosis
See Mental Health.

Psychosis
See Mental Health.

Psychotherapy
An attempted synthesis of Christian spiritual healing and psychotherapy. *M. Gregory, D.Phil. 1938 Oxford*

The concept of sea in psycho-therapy. *R. W. Wilde, Ph.D. 1945 Dublin, Trinity College*

Ptolemy, Claudius
A discussion of the relative share of Apollonius, Hipparchus, and Ptolemy in the evolution of the theory of eccentrics and epicycles. *J. H. Wills, M.Sc. 1931 London*

Public Administration
See also Civil Service.

The attainment of efficiency in the state service. *E. N. Gladden, Ph.D. 1936 London, External Degree*

The relations of statutory and voluntary authorities in public administration in England and Wales. *M. McKie, B.Litt. 1930 Oxford*

Public Health
See also Epidemics.

Public Health contd.
The accommodation for the sick provided at certain public schools for boys in England. *W. Champneys, D.M. 1929 Oxford*

Certain dangers to health which result from the present system of public elementary education in Scotland. *A. Campbell, M.D. 1883 Glasgow*

Edwin Chadwick and the public health movement, 1832-1854. *R. A. Lewis, Ph.D. 1949 Birmingham*

Epidemics in schools: a statistical analysis of data of the sickness experience in eighteen public schools, collected during the years 1935 to 1939. *E. A. Cheeseman, Ph.D. 1947 London, School of Hygiene and Tropical Medicine*

Fifty years of public health and social welfare in Bath, 1896-1945. *J. F. Blackett, M.A. 1949 Bristol*

Height and weight of school children in East Sussex. *W. R. Dunstan, M.Sc. 1923 London*

A history of the public health of the borough of Reading up to 1872. *R. W. Daltry, M.A. 1933 Reading*

The municipal borough as a health unit. *J. D. Kershaw, M.D. 1939 London, University College*

Observations of the evolution of public health law and administration with special reference to its bearing on mother and child. *M. S. S. Jones, M.D. 1925 Liverpool*

The physique of elementary school children, with special reference to their mentality: a statistical study bearing on social economics. *E. G. Habakkuk, M.Sc. 1924 Wales*

The place of health education in the advancement of public health. *K. O. A. Vickery, M.D. 1947 London, St. Bartholomew's Hospital Medical College*

Public health in Leeds, 1836-1848. *D. C. Wollman, M.A. 1949 Leeds*

Some principles of health education in their historical relationships. *H. S. Davies, M.D. 1946 London, School of Hygiene and Tropical Medicine and London, King's College*

A study of the history and development of the School Medical Service in Liverpool from 1908 to 1939, and an attempt to assess its consequences on the health of the Liverpool school child. *J. Riddell, M.A. 1946 Liverpool*

Town sanitation in the sixteenth century, based on the records of a group of provincial towns. *J. H. Thomas, B.Litt. 1929 Oxford*

Public Opinion
See also Journalism.

British opinion on the development of the commonwealth of nations, 1895-1914. *F. S. Morley, Ph.D. 1932 Edinburgh*

British public opinion regarding Indian policy at the time of the mutiny. *J. Holmes, M.A. 1936 London, Birkbeck College*

The concept of public opinion and its measurement. *S. F. Rae, Ph.D. 1939 London, School of Economics and Political Science*

Das deutsche Bild vom heutigen England nach Uebersetzungen und Schulbüchern, 1918-1932. *A. H. Johnstone, Ph.D. 1934 Edinburgh*

Ecclesiastical opinion in England on the Eastern Question from the Treaty of Paris to the Treaty of Berlin. *S. B. R. Poole, M.A. 1934 London, King's College*

The Elizabethan drama as the newspaper of the age; a study of the influence of external controlling factors on the drama of the early seventeenth century as a potential medium for reflecting popular opinion on political and social questions. *L. F. Turner, M.A. 1938 London, University College*

An enquiry into the state of public opinion from the establishment of King Henry VIII's supremacy over the Church to the close of the Lincolnshire rebellion. *W. E. Milward, M.A. 1907 Liverpool*

The evolution of British public opinion with regard to Germany as reflected in the press and journals of opinion between 1895 and 1903. *R. E. Houseman, M.A. 1934 London, Birkbeck College*

The movement of opinion in England concerning America prior to the declaration of American independence. *D. G. Martin, M.A. 1911 Liverpool*

Public opinion and Parliament since 1832. *D. C. Johnson, B.Litt. 1922 Oxford*

Public opinion and the acquisition of Bechuanaland and Rhodesia, 1868-1896. *D. Trevor, Ph.D. 1936 London, School of Economics and Political Science*

Public opinion and the movement for disarmament, 1888-98. *M. Tate, B.Litt. 1935 Oxford*

Public Opinion contd.
Public opinion in international relations. *W. W. Wade, M.Sc. 1948 London, School of Economics and Political Science*

The standard of appreciation shown by the public during the conclusion of the Napoleonic War of the period of depression and insurgence, 1800-1830. *G. G. Urwin, M.A. 1947 London, External Degree*

Public Schools
See Education, Secondary.

Public Works
Municipal enterprise in Germany : a study of German local utilities before and after the war. *B. M. Piplani, Ph.D. 1939 London, School of Economics and Political Science*

Public works policy. *S. O'Hart, M.A. 1938 National University of Ireland*

Publiciste, le
La collaboration de François Guizot au *Publiciste*. *W. A. Cummins, M.A. 1930 Liverpool*

Publishing
See Book Publishers and Publishing; Journalism.

Publius Terentius Afer
See Terence.

Punch
Social satire and literary burlesque in *Punch*, 1841-1850. *A. Sutcliffe, M.A. 1937 Manchester*

Punishment
See also Criminal Law; Eschatology.

Conception of reward and punishment in the Tannaitic Midrash (Mekiltah, Sifra and Sifre). *A. Melinek, Ph.D. 1944 London, Jews' College*

A critical survey of theories underlying experimental study of the effects of reward and punishment on school learning. *M. I. Shamin, M.A. 1948 London, Institute of Education*

The ethics of punishment. *W. H. Smyth, M.A. 1920 Belfast*

The idea of punishment in moral and political theory. *H. S. Sodhi, Ph.D. 1931 London, University College*

The problem of capital punishment. *J. Oldfield, D.C.L. 1901 Oxford*

Theories of punishment. *H. A. Lloyd, M.A. 1937 Wales*

The theory of punishment, with special reference to education. *G. E. Lee, M.A. 1917 London*

Punjab
The agricultural geography of the Punjab. *K. S. Ahmad, Ph.D. 1939 London, University College*

A geographical analysis of the development of the Canal Colonies region of the Punjab. *F. J. Fowler, Ph.D. 1938 Leeds*

The Panjab as a sovereign state, 1799-1839. *G. Lall, Ph.D. 1923 London*

The political and cultural history of the Panjab, including the North West Frontier Province in its earliest period. *L. Chandra, Ph.D. 1940 London, School of Oriental and African Studies*

Punjab industries. *A. A. Sheikh, M.A. 1945 London, University College*

Reorganisation of the Punjab Government, 1847-57. *R. C. Lai, Ph.D. 1937 London, School of Oriental and African Studies*

The rise to power of Ranjit Singh. *M. S. Cheema, B.Litt. 1925 Oxford*

The social life and institutions of Jhang and suggestions for their reorganization. *Y. Shah, M.Ed. 1925 Leeds*

Some geographical factors in the history of the Punjab from 712 A.D. to 1605 A.D. with special reference to river control of settlement. *M. I. R. Khan, Ph.D. 1930 London, University College*

Punjabi Language
Phonology of Panjābī as spoken about Ludhiana. *B. D. Jain, Ph.D. 1926 London*

The speech and customs of the Cūhrās of the Panjab. *A. M. Daula, Ph.D. 1935 London, School of Oriental and African Studies*

Puranas
See Hinduism.

Purchase, Law of
See Sale, Law of.

Purgatory
See Eschatology.

Purim
A critical and exegetical commentary on Mishnah tractate *Megillah*. *J. Rabbinowitz, Ph.D. 1930 Manchester*

Puritanism
See also Cartwright, T.; Owen, J.; Prynne, W.

Caroline puritanism as exemplified in the life and work of William Prynne. *T. Fitch, Ph.D. 1949 Edinburgh*

The Church of England and Puritanism during the primacy of Bancroft, 1604-1610. *S. B. Babbage, Ph.D. 1940 London, King's College*

Early English puritanism as exemplified in the life and works of Henry Smith. *D. E. Nelson, Ph.D. 1939 Edinburgh*

1. A history of the Puritan Movement in Wales. 2. Religious development in Wales (1654-1662). 3. The Puritan visitation of Jesus College, Oxford, and the principalship of Dr. Michael Roberts (1648-1657). *T. Richards, D.Litt. 1924 Wales*

The Holy Spirit in Puritan faith and experience. *G. F. Nuttall, D.D. 1944 Oxford*

The idea of government during the Puritan rebellion. *W. O'Brien, M.A. 1929 Liverpool*

The influences of Puritanism on English life and character. *N. Popplewell, Ph.D. 1931 Edinburgh*

John Penry and the Marprelate controversy in the light of recent research. *D. D. Phillips, M.A. 1914 Wales*

The kingdom at the threshold: a study of the apocalyptic element in English puritanism in the sixteenth and seventeenth centuries. *P. B. Hawkridge, Ph.D. 1943 London, Richmond College*

The puritan classical movement of Elizabeth's reign. *E. Bibby, M.A. 1929 Manchester*

Puritanism and its Presbyterian development in the time of Elizabeth. *A. Peel, B.Litt. 1912 Oxford*

Puritanism in Hampshire and the Isle of Wight from the reign of Elizabeth to the Restoration. *W. H. Mildon, Ph.D. 1934 London, External Degree*

The Puritans and music, with special reference to the Commonwealth period. *W. M. Lewis, M.A. 1917 Wales*

The worship of the English Puritans during the sixteenth, seventeenth and early eighteenth centuries. *D. H. M. Davies, D.Phil. 1943 Oxford*

Pym, John
John Pym. *E. M. Beebee, M.A. 1915 Birmingham*

Pythagoras
Plato and Pythagoreanism. *A. H. Ewen, M.A. 1923 London*

Qartājannī, Hāzim b. Muhammad
An edition of: Al-Qártajannī's *Maqsúrah. M. M. Allam, Ph.D. 1945 Manchester*

Quakers
See Friends, Society of.

Quarterly Review
John Wilson Croker's contributions to the *Quarterly review*, with and estimate of his work in them as a literary critic. *R. M. Campbell, B.Litt. 1937 Oxford*

Queen's Colleges, Ireland
Coláistí na Bainríoghna, a mbunú 's a mbliadhanta tosaigh 1845-1856 (Queen's Colleges, their foundation and early years, 1845-1856). *V. B. Jennings, M.A. 1947 National University of Ireland*

Quietism
Molinos and the implications of the spirit of quietism. *R. A. Agnew, Ph.D. 1935 Edinburgh*

Quintilian
Changes in educational ideals from Cicero and Quintilian to the Carolingian renaissance. *A. Hurworth, M.A. 1923 Leeds*

A critical examination of the educational theory of Quintilian. *H. Leverton, M.Ed. 1939 Leeds*

A critical study of Quintilian's system of language teaching. *J. Hill, M.A. 1930 Sheffield*

An initial study of Quintilian's theory of education. *B. J. Ward, M.A. 1943 National University of Ireland*

The major declamations of Pseudo-Quintilian. *I. M. L. Colonna, M.A. 1939 London, University College*

Quintilian's 'orator' as the type of the educated man. *H. M. Darbyshire, M.A. 1928 Liverpool*

Quintilian's theory of education. *R. J. Griffiths, M.A. 1914 Wales*

Quintilian's theory of education. *N. O. Parry, M.A. 1919 Wales*

Quintus, of Smyrna
Quintus of Smyrna. *M. J. M. Wagner, M.A. 1932 London, University College*

Quiro, Juan de
La famosa toledana of Juan de Quiro. *R. Alcock, M.A. 1916 Liverpool*

Quo Warranto
Quo warranto proceedings for the county of Lancaster. *A. Cantle, M.A. 1935 London, King's College*

Qur'ān
The foreign vocabulary of the *Qurân. A. Jeffery, Ph.D. 1929 Edinburgh*

Hebrew and Jewish sources of the *Qûran. J. C. Hughes, M.A. 1909 Wales*

1. The meaning of the Transfiguration. 2. The Gospel histories in the Koran dogmatically considered. *F. W. M. Woodward, B.D. 1906 Oxford*

Muhammad's prophetic office as portrayed in the Qur'ān. *J. C. Wilson, Ph.D. 1949 Edinburgh*

Qutayba, Ibn Muslim
The life and works of Ibn Qutayba. *I. M. Husseini, Ph.D. 1934 London, External Degree*

Raabe, Wilhelm
Social history and domestic manners as reflected in the works of Gustav Freytag and Wilhelm Raabe. *M. W. E. Jones, M.A. 1932 Wales*

Rabbinic Literature
See Hebrew Literature.

Rabelais, François
The educational theories of François Rabelais. *A. G. Morris, M.Ed. 1939 Manchester*

Etude sur l'authenticité du 5e livre de Rabelais. *C. D. Jukes, M.A. 1924 Birmingham*

Rabelais the educator. *F. W. Moss, M.Ed. 1928 Leeds*

Rābia' al-'Adawiyya al-Qayriyya
The life and teachings of Rābia' al-'Adawiyya al-Qayriyya of Basra together with some account of the place of the women saints in Islam. *M. Smith, Ph.D. 1928 London*

Race Relations
See also Prejudice; Slavery.

The anthropology of some coloured communities in Great Britain with comparative material on colour prejudice. *K. L. Little, Ph.D. 1945 London, School of Economics and Political Science*

The attitude of the Church to the race problem in central South Africa during the nineteenth century, viewed in the light of New Testament principles. *S. K. Bunker, B.Litt. 1933 Oxford*

Briton and Maori: a comparative study of the relations between the races, 1840-1848. *S. E. Greville, M.A. 1910 London*

The clash of race and the clash of culture. *G. L. F. Pitt-Rivers, B.Sc. 1926 Oxford*

An experimental study of school children with regard to some racial mental differences. *C. Rangachar, M.Ed. 1930 Leeds*

The influence of the relations between groups upon the inner life of groups, with special reference to black and white in the Southern States of the United States during the nineteenth century. *H. W. Roberts, M.A. 1934 London, School of Economics and Political Science*

Native segregation in Southern Rhodesia: a study of social policy. *R. McGregor, Ph.D. 1940 London, External Degree*

The psychology of colour prejudice. *S. P. Adinarayansih, M.A. 1939 London, University College*

Race and racism in the Union of South Africa. *J. D. Hatton, M.A. 1948 National University of Ireland*

The social structure of Jamaica, with special reference to racial distinctions. *L. F. Henriques, D.Phil. 1948 Oxford*

The sociology of race relations in southeast Asia with special reference to British Malaya. *M. Freedman, M.A. 1948 London, School of Economics and Political Science*

Some recent trends in the status history of the coloured people of South Africa. *C. Sofer, M.Sc. 1949 London, School of Economics and Political Science*

Racine, Jean
Alfieri's debt to Racine. *M. J. Oberli, B.Litt. 1937 Oxford*

A commentary on Racine's *Andromaque*: a study of vocabulary, syntax, style. *H. O'Sullivan, M.A. 1945 Manchester*

Elizabethan tragedy contrasted with the classical drama of Corneille and Racine. *F. E. Jope, M.A. 1910 Birmingham*

Racine, Jean contd.
L'action dans la tragédie de Racine. *A. C. Conlin, M.A. 1949 National University of Ireland*

Le développement de la tragédie racinienne jusqu'à *Andromaque. H. T. Barnwell, M.A. 1949 Birmingham*

The religion of Jean Racine. *J. A. M. MacDonogh, B.Litt. 1939 Dublin, Trinity College*

Radcliffe, Ann
The work of Mrs. Radcliffe and its influence on later writers. *J. M. S. Tompkins, M.A. 1921 London*

Radicalism
See also Marx, K.; O'Brien, J. B.

English radicalism, 1832-1852. *S. Maccoby, Ph.D. 1934 London, School of Economics and Political Science*

The influence of radical doctrine in the French Revolution on English drama in the time of Thomas Holcroft, 1776 to 1806. *W. V. Aughterson, Ph.D. 1936 London, King's College*

Major John Cartwright: his place in contemporary radical movements. *A. A. Eaglestone, B.Litt. 1930 Oxford*

The political ideas of the English Radicals, particularly in Nonconformist circles, from John Lilburne to John Wilkes. *B. H. Lewis, M.A. 1926 Wales*

The Radical attitude towards the Monarchy and the House of Lords, 1868-85. *E. G. Collieu, B.Litt. 1936 Oxford*

Some aspects of Lancashire radicalism, 1816-21. *W. W. Kinsey, M.A. 1927 Manchester*

Radicalism (Theology)
The evolution of radical theory after the Reformation. *A. J. Clark, M.A. 1910 London*

Radio Telegraphy
See Communications.

Radishchev, Alexander Nikolaevich
Alexander Nikolaevich and his contacts with French and German thinkers. *D. M. Lang, Ph.D. 1950 Cambridge*

Radnor
The boroughs of Radnor to the Act of Union and beyond. *R. M. Morgan, M.A. 1911 Wales*

A geographical study of the recent distribution of population and types of settlement in mid-Wales and along the central Welsh border, with special reference to Radnorshire. *W. R. Saunders, B.Litt. 1925 Oxford*

Raetia
See Rhaetia.

Railways
The comparative economics of railways and roads for pioneer development abroad. *J. E. Holmstrom, Ph.D. 1932 London, School of Economics and Political Science*

The international organization of railway communications. *A. W. Rees, M.A. 1938 Wales*

Personnel administration in public utility enterprises, with special reference to railways and to Chinese conditions. *C. H. Chi, M.Sc. 1938 London, School of Economics and Political Science*

Railway organization and administration. *J. Taylor, Ph.D. 1925 Edinburgh*

Railway statistics: their history and economic significance. *A. L. Clift, M.Com. 1925 Birmingham*

The role of the state in the development of railways. *H. M. Jagtiani, M.Sc. 1923 London*

The State railways of Europe. *C. F. Roediger, B.Litt. 1909 Oxford*

Railways: Great Britain and Ireland
The construction of the London underground railways: a study of the creation of an important public utility by private enterprise. *C. A. Luzzetti, B.Litt. 1939 Oxford*

The development of legislation relating to the powers of railway companies to charge for the carriage of merchandise traffic. *D. G. Ineson, LL.D. 1923 Leeds*

The development of road transport in conjunction with railways for the conveyance of merchandise in England and Wales. *J. M. Hanna, M.Sc. 1936 London, School of Economics and Political Science*

The development of the British railway station. *A. Arschavir, M.A. 1948 Manchester*

English railways, their development and their relation to the state. *L. Cleveland-Stevens, D.Sc. 1915 London*

Railways: Great Britain and Ireland contd.
An examination of the architectural aspects of railway development in Great Britain. *B. B. Lewis, M.A. 1944 Liverpool*

Great Southern Railways Company. *J. McGartoll, M.A. 1939 National University of Ireland*

A history and survey of the road-transport operations of the British railways. *J. P. Wallace, M.A. 1947 Wales*

The history of the Barry Dock and Railways Company in relation to the development of the south Wales coalfield. *L. N. A. Davies, M.A. 1938 Wales*

History of the Eastern Counties Railway in relation to contemporary economic development. *E. Doble, Ph.D. 1939 London, School of Economics and Political Science*

The public accounts and statistical returns of English railways. *K. Y. Pao, M.Com. 1912 Birmingham*

Railways: Other Countries
Development of Indian railways, 1842-1928. *N. Sanyal, Ph.D. 1929 London*

Indian railways: rates and regulation. *N. B. Mehta, Ph.D. 1925 London*

The railway and customs policy of the South African states and colonies. *J. Van der Poel, Ph.D. 1929 London*

The railways of West Africa: a geographical and historical analysis. *R. J. Church, Ph.D. 1943 London, External Degree*

South African railway policy, with special reference to rates and the development of the primary industries. *S. H. Frankel, Ph.D. 1928 London*

Rain
A comparative review of rainfall régimes with a marked winter maximum in areas bordering the Eastern Mediterranean. . *T. M. Whitaker, M.A. 1941 Manchester*

The Rainfall régimes of the Western United States of America. *W. H. Hogg, M.Sc. 1938 London, University College*

Rainfall variability: world and continental distribution. *W. J. King, M.Sc. 1938 London, Queen Mary College*

A study of climatic correlations, with special reference to the Indian monsoon, based upon a review of conditions in abnormal seasons. *H. Hollas, M.A. 1933 Manchester*

A study of the rainfall fluctuations in China: their causes and effects. *E.-L. Liu, D.Phil. 1940 Oxford*

Ralegh, Walter, Sir
The poems of Sir Walter Ralegh. *A. M. C. Latham, B.Litt. 1927 Oxford*

Ramanuja
See Philosophy: India.

Ramayana
The Anglo-Saxon epic as exemplified by *Beowulf* considered in the light of the Indian epic *Rāmayana*. *I. S. Peter, Ph.D. 1930 London, King's College*

The social and legal position of women in ancient India as represented by a critical study of the epics: the *Mahabharata* and the *Ramayana*. *S. N. Ajgaonkar, D.Phil. 1927 Oxford*

Ramsay, Allan
Allan Ramsay and the Scottish vernacular revival (circa seventeenth and eighteenth centuries). *H. Lister, M.A. 1934 London, Birkbeck College*

Ramsay, William Mitchell, Sir
1. The interpretation of the Acts, with especial reference to Professor Ramsay's South Galatian theory. 2. Our Lord's use of π÷στισ. *H. K. Moore, B.D. & D.D. 1898 Oxford*

Randolph, Thomas
A study of Randolph's *Amyntas* and its relation to contemporary pastoral drama. *G. M. Oswin, B.Litt. 1941 Oxford*

Three plays of Thomas Randolph: *Aristippus, The Conceited pedler, The Muses looking-glasse*: with introduction, collations and notes. *Z. M. Isaacs, Ph.D. 1926 Sheffield*

Ranjit Singh
See Singh, Ranjit.

Raphael (Raffaello Sanzio)
The drawings by Raphael in the Ashmolean Museum, Oxford: an account of the formation of the collection and its acquisition by the University. *D. M. Sutton, B.Litt. 1944 Oxford*

Rapin, René
Le Père Rapin, critique littéraire. *S. R. C. Long, Ph.D. 1936 London, Birkbeck College*

Ras Shamra-Ugarit
See also Ugaritic Language.

Sacrifice at Ugarit. *D. McK. L. Urie, Ph.D. 1944 Saint Andrew's*

The underworld and its deities in the Ras Shamra texts. *W. F. Fleet, M.A. 1938 Manchester*

Rashdall, Hastings
The religious philosophy of Hastings Rashdall. *D. E. Roberts, Ph.D. 1936 Edinburgh*

Rashi, Solomon b. Isaac, Rabbi
The exegesis of Rashi, with reference to his commentary on the Pentateuch. *H. C. R. Eltoft, M.A. 1927 Manchester*

Rashi as philologist. *J. Pereira-Mendoza, M.A. 1939 Manchester*

Rates
See Local Government: Great Britain.

Rationalism
An attempt to ascertain the conditions and final import of a rational experience. *E. M. Byrne, M.A. 1940 National University of Ireland*

The conflict between rationalism and romanticism in the works of Ernest Renan. *B. L. Beynon, M.Litt. 1936 Cambridge*

The fortunes of rationalism in English political thought from the publication of Burke's *Reflections on the French Revolution* to the end of the nineteenth century. *G. Meara, M.A. 1933 Wales*

Kierkegaard's critique of rationalism. *A. T. McKinnon, Ph.D. 1950 Edinburgh*

The origins of the Cartesian view of rational explanation and certain aspects of its influence on later philosophy. *R. I. Markus, Ph.D. 1950 Manchester*

Ratke, Wolfgang
The educational ideas of Wolfgang Ratke. *G. H. Turnbull, M.A. 1913 Liverpool*

Rauh, Frédéric
La philosophie de l'expérience moral: Frédéric Rauh. *C. E. H. Marin, B.Litt. 1921 Oxford*

Ray, John
Studies in the biological work of John Ray. *D. C. Gunawardena, M.Sc. 1934 London, University College*

Raynal, Guillaume Thomas Francis
Guillaume Thomas Francis Raynal: his life, writings, political views, and his influence on the French Revolution. *M. C. Flockhart, B.Litt. 1923 Oxford*

Rayon Industry
The development and organization of the artificial silk industry in Great Britain. *E. Jones, M.A. 1940 Wales*

Reade, Charles
Charles Reade: his methods, characterizations, and place in English literature. *J. Hopkins, M.A. 1929 Wales*

Reading
See also Children, Retarded.

The adolescent child, the newspaper reading of adolescents and adults during the War, and five other papers. *W. D. Wall, Ph.D. 1947 Birmingham*

An experimental approach to remedial reading for dull and backward junior pupils. *E. A. Taylor, M.Ed. 1942 Leeds*

An experimental enquiry into the value of silent reading in the teaching of modern languages in schools. *D. St.J. C. Gurney, M.Ed. 1931 Leeds*

Eyedness and handedness in relation to certain difficulties in reading. *H. C. Dalby, Ph.D. 1933 London, Bedford College*

A factorial analysis of the reading ability in 10 year old primary school children. *J. A. Richardson, M.A. 1949 Birmingham*

Fiction and the reading public. *Q. D. Leavis, Ph.D. 1932 Cambridge*

Psychological functions of leisure reading. *R. Oliver, M.A. 1949 Manchester*

Remedial reading for dull senior boys. *L. Holdsworth, M.Ed. 1939 Leeds*

Studies in the mental imagery experienced by young adolescents during the silent reading of descriptive passages. *D. V. Coutts, Ph.D. 1947 London, Institute of Education*

A study of backwardness in reading among London elementary school children. *E. G. Hume, M.A. 1926 London*

A study of some mental processes involved in reading. *R. W. Pickford, Ph.D. 1932 Cambridge*

Reading contd.
A survey of reading ability. *C. M. Fleming, Ph.D. 1931 Glasgow*

A survey of the books published in English between 1603 and 1608, with a view to determining the interests of the reading public during those years. *G. J. N. Whitfield, M.A. 1935 London, King's College*

Reading, Berkshire
The history of Reading in the later Middle Ages, considered with special reference to the importance of the gild merchant in medieval seignorial boroughs. *N. H. Gibbs, D.Phil. 1935 Oxford*

The parliamentary history of Reading between 1750 and 1850. *R. C. J. Baily, M.A. 1944 Reading*

Realism
See also Pragmatism; and Scarron, P.; Thomas Aquinas, Saint.

The bearing of the conception of evolution upon the problem of the inclusion of individual minds within reality as a whole. *E. E. Harris, B.Litt. 1933 Oxford*

C. F. Hebbel's realism in theory and practice. *G. B. Rees, Ph.D. 1926 London*

A comparative study of the recent ethical theories of idealism, pragmatism, and realism. *P. M. Hamilton, B.Litt. 1922 Oxford*

Degrees of truth and reality. *S. E. Hooper, M.A. 1918 London*

Experience in relation to the real. *W. J. Downes, M.A. 1923 London*

The growth of realism in the fiction of the sixteenth and seventeenth centuries, with special reference to the development of the picaresque novel. *E. L. G. Giles, Ph.D. 1943 London, Birkbeck College*

1. Lotze's theory of reality. 2. Lotze's relation to idealism. *E. E. Thomas, D.Litt. 1922 Wales*

Modern developments of realism. *G. C. Field, B.Sc. 1912 Oxford*

'New realism' contrasted with 'critical realism'. *H. I. Frith, M.A. 1924 Manchester*

The pragmatic theory of truth, with especial regard to the question whether it implies a distinction between reality as it is known and reality as it is in itself. *S. S. S. Browne, B.Litt. 1929 Oxford*

Realism: an attempt to trace its origin and its development. *S. Z. Hasan, D.Phil. 1925 Oxford*

Realism in Anglo-Irish fiction, 1916-1940. *V. H. S. Mercier, Ph.D. 1945 Dublin, Trinity College*

Realism in contemporary Bengali poetry as compared and considered with reference to realism in English poetry from the last decade of the nineteenth century. *B. Banerjee, Ph.D. 1937 London, King's College*

Realism in English poetry, 1700-1783. *R. G. Ralph, M.A. 1940 London, King's College*

Realism in Irish drama. *J. B. McGuire, Ph.D. 1941 Dublin, Trinity College*

Realistic tendencies in French prose fiction of the seventeenth century, with special reference to the realistic novel in the nineteenth century. *C. W. Gribble, M.A. 1923 Wales*

Reality and spirit. *A. Allardyce, M.A. 1924 Bristol*

A re-examination of some questions at issue between idealists and realists with regard to the subject-object relation and the nature of mind. *J. R. Jones, D.Phil. 1946 Oxford*

The relation of thought to reality. *H. A. Overstreet, B.Sc. 1901 Oxford*

Russian realism and the development of the English novel, 1880-1914 - a study in literary influence. *L. D. Reedy, Ph.D. 1938 Dublin, Trinity College*

Scarron and the Realistic Movement of the seventeenth century. *E. Evans, M.A. 1937 Wales*

Subject and object: a study of some aspects of the new realism. *N. Speller, M.A. 1917 Birmingham*

A theory of direct realism and the relation of realism to idealism. *J. E. Turner, Ph.D. 1925 Liverpool*

The theory of reality as perfect, with special reference to its bearing on ethics. *D. E. Roberts, M.A. 1916 Wales*

Twentieth century realism in England and America. *T. E. Jessop, B.Litt. 1924 Oxford*

Reasoning
See Logic.

Rebecca Riots
See Wales: History.

Recall
See Memory.

Recapitulation Theory
See Biology.

Recognition
Recognition in international law. T. C. Chen, D.Phil. 1948 Oxford

Recreation
See also Games and Sports; Leisure; Play.

An historical study of the provision for play and recreation in Manchester. W. G. Jackson, M.Ed. 1940 Manchester

Play centres in England. G. S. Smith, M.Ed. 1921 Manchester

The recreations and amusements of the industrial working class in the second quarter of the nineteenth century, with special reference to Lancashire. K. Allan, M.A. 1947 Manchester

Recusants
See Roman Catholic Church: Great Britain.

Red Book of Hergest
A comparison of the texts of the *Brut y Brenhinoedd* as found in the *Red book of Hergest* and in the Peniarth ms. 44, concluded in Llanstephan ms. 1. O. A. Jones, M.A. 1914 Wales

The Welsh version of the *Historia regum Britanniae* in Peniarth ms.44 collated with the *Red book* version, together with notes on the influence of the original on the style and construction of the Welsh, and a glossary of Welsh words whose use is illustrated by the Latin. B. Jones, M.A. 1915 Wales

Red Sea
The ancient Egyptian canals between the Mediterranean and the Red Sea: their problems for the sciences of geology, geography, engineering and history. W. M. Alexander, D.Sc. 1919 Glasgow

The growth of British influence in Abyssinia and on the African coast of the Red Sea from 1840 to 1885. M. M. Law, M.A. 1931 London, King's College

The Periplus of the Erythraean Sea. J. L. Whiteley, Ph.D. 1940 London, Birkbeck College

Redemption
Athanasius' theory of redemption in the light of modern expositors. W. L. Hall, Ph.D. 1934 Edinburgh

The Christian principle of redemption in its application to penal reform. M. S. Bradley, B.Litt. 1929 Oxford

The conception of redemption in the gnostic theologies of the first and second centuries. J. B. Corston, Ph.D. 1938 Edinburgh

1. The history of the doctrine of satisfaction from Tertullian to St. Ambrose. 2. The history of the doctrine of satisfaction from St. Augustine to St. Anselm. G. A. Michell, B.D. & D.D. 1924 Oxford

1. Holy baptism. 2. Redemption and the salvation consequent upon it. G. M. Evans, B.D. 1908 Oxford

James Fraser of Brea, 1639 to 1699: his life and writings, with special reference to his theory of universal redemption and its influence on religious thought in Scotland. D. Fraser, Ph.D. 1944 Edinburgh

The place of redemptive mediation in the history of religion. A. Brown, M.A. 1938 Leeds

1. The priesthood of Christ in the Epistle to the Hebrews. 2. The redemption. F. Briggs, B.D. 1910 Oxford

1. The redemption. 2. The Church in the Epistle to the Ephesians. P. J. James, B.D. 1910 Oxford

The relation between the person of Christ and the principle of redemption, especially as propounded by D. F. Strauss, A. E. Biedermann and E. P. W. Troeltsch. H. T. Kerr, Ph.D. 1936 Edinburgh

1. Utrum Christus venisset si Adam non peccasset. 2. The New Testament doctrine of the Christian character and its development. L. Hands, B.D. 1907 Oxford

Redford, John
An edition of the play *Wyt and science* by John Redford, from British Museum additional manuscript 15233. A. Brown, M.A. 1949 London, University College

Reele, George
Early Elizabethan dramatic style with particular regard to the works of George Reele. H. C. Chang, Ph.D. 1949 Edinburgh

Rees, William (Gwilym Hiraethog)
Cyfraniad Dr. William Rees (Gwilym Hiraethog) i fywyda llên ei gyfnod (The contribution of Dr. William Rees to contemporary life and literature). T. E. Davies, M.A. 1931 Wales

Reeve, Clara
Clara Reeve. E. J. Gadsby, M.A. 1926 London

Clara Reeve: her life and works. H. H. Santmyer, B.Litt. 1927 Oxford

The novels of Clara Reeve. J. K. Reeves, B.Litt. 1932 Oxford

Reformation
See Church History: Reformation and Counter-Reformation.

Refugees
French refugees in England from the Restoration to the death of William III. A. W. Nicholls, B.Litt. 1923 Oxford

A history of the Italian exiles in London, 1816-1848. M. C. W. Wicks, Ph.D. 1930 Edinburgh

Legal aspects of international cooperation for the assistance of refugees. S. Andracki, M.Sc. 1949 London, School of Economics and Political Science

The refugee and international law. E. R. Casper, LL.M. 1948 London, University College

Regensburg
Sprachliche, literarische und kulturelle Untersuchung der *Regensburger Chronik* des Leonhard Widmann. F. Gossman, M.A. 1940 London, King's College

Régnier, Henri de
The creative imagination of Henri de Régnier. P. M. Smith, B.Litt. 1938 Oxford

Henri de Régnier: le poète. J. B. Hanson, D.Phil. 1945 Oxford

Henri de Régnier: poète symboliste. D. MacBride, M.A. 1937 Belfast

Régnier, Mathurin
The language and style ot Mathurin Régnier. H. Knight, B.Litt. 1935 Oxford

Reid, Forrest
A critical study of the writings of Forrest Reid. J. Boyd, B.Litt. 1945 Dublin, Trinity College

Reid, Thomas
Views concerning the epistemology of morals held by some of the British moralists of the eighteenth century, with especial reference to the anti-empiricist views of Richard Price and Thomas Reid. D. Rafilovitch, D.Phil. 1940 Oxford

Reincarnation
The conception of *karma* and reincarnation in Hindu religion and philosophy. P. Yevtic, Ph.D. 1927 London

Relations (Philosophy)
The issue between Bradley and his critics concerning the nature and reality of relations. E. M. M. Robinson, B.Litt. 1937 Oxford

The treatment of relations by Locke and Hume. M. R. Anand, Ph.D. 1929 London

Relativity
The implications of the theory of relativity with respect to religious thought. H. D. Anthony, Ph.D. 1925 London

Religion
See also Buddhism; Christianity; Islam; Judaism; Shintoism; etc.; and Agnosticism; Asceticism; Casuistry; Demonology; Ethics; Evil; God; Gods; Inspiration; Mysticism; Oracles; Poverty; Religious Education; Sacrifice; Science and Religion; Theology; Worship.

Algunas ideas religiosas y morales de Cervantes. G. A. Johnson, M.A. 1942 National University of Ireland

The attitude of grammar school pupils and their parents to education, religion and sport. W. Glassey, M.Ed. 1943 Manchester

Burns and religion. A. B. Jamieson, M.A. 1928 Birmingham

Coleridge as a religious thinker. H. D. Frazer-Hurst, Ph.D. 1939 Dublin, Trinity College

A comparative study of the old and new types of revivalism, with special relation to the influence of contemporary religious thought and practice. S. T. McCloy, B.Litt. 1922 Oxford

A conception of religion deduced from the works of Giovanni Gentile. A. A. Lion, B.Litt. 1927 Oxford

Durkheim's conception of religion. V. T. Arsitch, B.Litt. 1922 Oxford

Religion contd.
Exposé des données actuelles de la question des idées religieuses de Montaigne. M. Hopp, M.A. 1926 London

The influence of religious dogma on metaphysical speculation in the philosophy of Descartes, with special reference to the psychological aspect. J. J. Hartland-Swann, Ph.D. 1946 London, External Degree

The influence of Romanticism on Renan's historical treatment of religious beliefs. K. M. Barnett, M.A. 1931 London, Bedford College

Kellers religiöse Entwicklung. M. Nı Shuibhne, M.A. 1942 National University of Ireland

La religion et l'église dans l'oeuvre de Stendhal. J. Sankey, M.A. 1935 Liverpool

La religion et les hommes. M. Dior, M.A. 1943 National University of Ireland

Les idées de Montesquieu sur la religion. J. D. Berbiers, M.A. 1929 Liverpool

The religion of Jean Racine. J. A. M. MacDonogh, B.Litt. 1939 Dublin, Trinity College

The religion of Pierre Loti. F. Taylor, M.A. 1934 Manchester

The religious ideas of Renan. C. Smith, Ph.D. 1949 London, King's College

The religious philosophy of Herder and Schleiermacher studied in relation to the influence upon them of Leibniz, Spinoza, and Kant. M. E. Sandbach-Marshall, M.A. 1928 London

The sociology of religion, with special reference to the works of Professor Durkheim and other writers to *L'Année Sociologique*. A. W. Bonsey, B.Litt. 1930 Oxford

Religion: Ancient and Primitive
See also Ancestor Cults; Burials; Primitivism.

Arnobius' *Adversus Gentes* and the decay of paganism. D. R. Andrews, M.A. 1934 London, Bedford College

The cult of Isis in Italy: an account of its external history. M. S. Salem, Ph.D. 1937 Liverpool

Early law and religion: a study in the relationship between the primitive rules of law and the early ideas of magic and religion. H. N. Wright, LL.D. 1919 London

The fall of paganism. A. E. Wilson, M.A. 1914 Birmingham

The fall of paganism. E. M. C. Hunt, M.A. 1913 Birmingham

Foreign deities worshipped in Israel in the period of the monarchy: their character and origin. C. H. Phillips, M.A. 1938 Wales

Heathenism and its echo in Anglo-Saxon poetry. J. P. Gaffney, M.A. 1935 National University of Ireland

The idea of the Deity in primitive thought. E. A. Hunt, M.A. 1939 Leeds

The idea of the soul in primitive religion. J. W. Gregory, M.A. 1939 Leeds

Ideas of life and religion in pre-historic Scotland, with special reference to Mediterranean influences. W. Edgar, Ph.D. 1934 Glasgow

1. Idolatry. 2. The place of unity in the ideal of a Church. H. A. James, B.D. 1874 Oxford

The influence of ancient Egypt on Greek and Mycenaean religious cults before the Hellenistic age. J. G. Griffiths, M.A. 1936 Liverpool

Magico-religious beliefs and practices in primitive society: a sociological interpretation of their therapeutic aspects. K. R. Stewart, Ph.D. 1948 London, School of Economics and Political Science

Meydum and Memphis: the formula in the light of mythology. G. A. Wainwright, B.A. 1911 Bristol

The nature and development of the idea of God as held by the primitive peoples of central Africa. V. G. Ispir, B.Sc. 1914 Oxford

The origin and development of prayer and its place in the life of primitive peoples. H. H. C. Bee, M.A. 1942 Leeds

Págántacht san Ruadhraigheacht agus san Fhiannaigheacht (Paganism in the Red Branch Cycle and the Fenian Cycle). S. Nic Craith, M.A. 1939 National University of Ireland

1. The political consciousness of the Marcan gospel. 2. The origins of Alexandrian Christianity. 3. The historical element in some ancient religions. S. G. F. Brandon, D.D. 1943 Leeds

Religion: Ancient and Primitive contd.
The practice of Eastern cults at Rome and their influence to 200 A.D. *M. T. Skues, M.A. 1908 London*

The quarrel of Horus and Seth, from Egyptian and classical sources. *J. G. Griffiths, D.Phil. 1950 Oxford*

The relation between corn-gods and other world deities. *S. R. Burstein, M.A. 1924 Wales*

The relation between morality and religion in primitive society. *E. A. Shattock, B.Litt. 1927 Oxford*

The relation of ritual to belief in primitive cult, with special reference to the magico-religious customs of the Australian Aborigines. *E. O. James, B.Litt. 1916 Oxford*

The religion of the Cherokee Indians. *O. C. Seymour, Ph.D. 1934 Edinburgh*

The religion of the Yorubas, especially in relation to the religion of ancient Egypt. *J. O. Lucas, D.D. 1942 Durham*

Religious practices and beliefs of Uganda. *A. K. Nyabongo, B.Litt. 1936 Oxford*

Religious practices and beliefs of Uganda. *A. K. Nyabongo, D.Phil. 1939 Oxford*

The significance of 'mana' in primitive life and thought. *J. R. Course, M.A. 1940 Leeds*

Some ancient asseverations and affirmations in the light of cultural anthropology. *W. Kirzner, M.Sc. 1934 London, School of Economics and Political Science*

Some aspects of the totemism of north-west America. *F. C. J. M. Barbeau, B.Sc. 1910 Oxford*

Stone and pillar cult among the Western Semites, with special reference to the Hebrews. *C. W. McMurray, Ph.D. 1934 Edinburgh*

The use of musical instruments in Jewish and Assyro-Babylonian religious ceremonial compared. *L. Glickman, M.A. 1942 Manchester*

West African religion, illustrated from the beliefs and practices of the Yoruba, Ewe, Akan and kindred peoples. *E. G. S. Parrinder, Ph.D. 1946 London, External Degree*

The word of God in some Accadian psalms. *E. Jones, M.A. 1949 Manchester*

Yoruba paganism, or the religious beliefs of the West African negroes, particularly of the Yoruba tribes of southern Nigeria. *S. S. Farrow, Ph.D. 1924 Edinburgh*

Religion: Asia
The concept of sin in the great religions of the East. *G. C. Barber, Ph.D. 1938 London, Richmond College*

The history of Oriental cults among the Greeks. *U. E. Pulling, M.A. 1911 London*

The practice of Eastern cults at Rome and their influence to 200 A.D. *M. T. Skues, M.A. 1908 London*

Religion: China
Chinese religion: an approach through the Hakka Chinese dictionary. *E. Parry, B.D. 1940 Leeds*

An investigation of the methods of presentation of Christianity to the Gentiles by the early Church, and an examination of China's religious heritage with a view to similarity of approach. *F. A. Smalley, B.Litt. 1933 Oxford*

Religion: Ethiopia
The religious history of the Abyssinian races. *H. J. Weld-Blundell, B.Litt. 1911 Oxford*

Religion: France
Religious controversies in the sixteenth century, and their influence in France and England. *I. Georgević, B.Litt. 1919 Oxford*

Religion: Great Britain
The geographical distribution of religious denominations in Wales in its relation to racial and social factors. *J. E. Daniel, M.A. 1928 Wales*

The history of religion in Wales from 1600 to 1640. *M. D. A. Hughes, B.Litt. 1930 Oxford*

The religious awakening of 1858-60 in Great Britain and Ireland. *O. Bussey, Ph.D. 1947 Edinburgh*

Religious controversies in the sixteenth century, and their influence in France and England. *I. Georgević, B.Litt. 1919 Oxford*

Religion: Greece, Ancient
The attitude of Aristophanes towards the traditional conception of religion and religious observances in Athens. *F. G. Francis, M.A. 1921 London*

The attitude of Euripides towards the popular religious thought of the day. *J. S. Davies, M.A. 1907 Wales*

Religion: Greece, Ancient contd.
The attitude of Herodotus towards the gods and religion. *A. K. Morris, M.A. 1939 Wales*

The attitude of the Greek dramatic poets to the religious cults of their day. *C. F. B. Broadbent, M.A. 1920 London*

Cults of Rhodes. *T. F. Donnelly, M.A. 1938 National University of Ireland*

The development in religious and ethical thought as discerned in the *Iliad* and the *Odyssey*. *E. I. Jones, M.A. 1915 Wales*

The Eleusinian mysteries. *R. H. Harte, M.A. 1927 Belfast*

The Eleusinian mysteries, with special reference to their influence upon Plato. *W. Edwards, M.A. 1914 Wales*

Euripides and his relation to the religion of his time. *E. D. Evans, M.A. 1909 Wales*

The evolution of religion in Greece from the earliest times to the time of Hesiod. *A. Lemarchant, M.A. 1920 Belfast*

Gods and men; conceptions of a moral order in Aeschylus and Herodotus. *J. O'Mahony, M.A. 1950 National University of Ireland*

The Greek mysteries as presented in the early Christian Fathers. *D. J. Davies, M.A. 1915 Wales*

The history of Oriental cults among the Greeks. *U. E. Pulling, M.A. 1911 London*

The influence of ancient Egypt on Greek and Mycenaean religious cults before the Hellenistic age. *J. G. Griffiths, M.A. 1936 Liverpool*

Inspiration in the ancient world: examination of the beliefs current among the Ancient Greeks and Romans in regard to inspiration whether experienced in a state of ectasy or in full consciousness. *A. Grant, M.A. 1939 London, King's College*

The moral and religious ideas of Aeschylus and Pindar. *E. J. King, M.A. 1937 Manchester*

Mycenaean religion. *J. E. John, M.A. 1915 Wales*

Origins of Hellenistic king-worship. *C. M. O'Neill, M.A. 1927 National University of Ireland*

Some problems connected with birds in Greek religion. *J. R. T. Pollard, B.Litt. 1947 Oxford*

Religion: India
The origin and development of Indian religion as presented by Vedic literature to the end of the Sutra period. *P. S. Deshmukh, D.Phil. 1927 Oxford*

The social function of religion in a South Indian community. *M. N. Srinivas, D.Phil. 1947 Oxford*

Religion: Rome
1.The Apocalypse of St. John in its relation to the religion of the Empire. 2. On certain points in the Apocalypse of St. John in relation to other works in apocalyptic literature. *W. H. Hutton, B.D. 1893 Oxford*

The attitude of Virgil and other Augustan poets to the religion of Rome. *A. J. McIver, B.Litt. 1932 Oxford*

The cult of Isis in Italy under the Empire. *I. D. Bertram, M.A. 1934 London, Bedford College*

The development of the idea of personal immortality in pagan Rome, with special reference to the metrical epitaphs in Buecheler's collection. *G. E. Quinton, M.A. 1934 Bristol*

1. Early Spartan civilisation. 2. Influence of Dionysus cult on Roman religion. *J. J. Tierney, M.A. 1932 National University of Ireland*

The fall of paganism in the Western Roman Empire, 311-395 A.D. *A. E. Wilson, D.Litt. 1927 Birmingham*

Inspiration in the ancient world: examination of the beliefs current among the Ancient Greeks and Romans in regard to inspiration whether experienced in a state of ectasy or in full consciousness. *A. Grant, M.A. 1939 London, King's College*

The local cults of ancient Latium outside Rome, with the exception of Ostia. *T. G. Thomas, M.A. 1930 Wales*

The magical element in the calendar of Numa. *A. P. Hyslop, Ph.D. 1925 Aberdeen*

The meaning and the development of the cult of Mars at Rome. *E. H. Clement, B.Litt. 1939 Oxford*

The native Italian element in early Roman religion as illustrated by Latin literature up to the end of the first century B.C. *J. J. Jones, M.A. 1919 Wales*

Philosophical survey of Roman religion. *F. Comerford, M.A. 1946 National University of Ireland*

Religion: Rome contd.
The policy of the Roman Government towards non-Roman religions from Augustus to Trajan, with special reference to the treatment of such religions in Rome and Italy. *U. C. Fitzhardinge, B.Litt. 1940 Oxford*

The practice of Eastern cults at Rome and their influence to 200 A.D. *M. T. Skues, M.A. 1908 London*

Prudentius' treatment of Roman religion. *R. E. Roberts, M.A. 1938 Wales*

The religion of Apuleius. *D. J. Hill, M.A. 1940 Leeds*

Religion: Russia
The religious philosophy in Russia in the nineteenth century. *J. Stoyanovic, Ph.D. 1926 London*

Religion and Art
The influence of anthropomorphic art on religious belief and practice. *V. A. Demant, B.Litt. 1924 Oxford*

Religion and Philosophy
1. The Christian's expectations of a palingenesis mundi finds valuable support from reason and science. 2. St.Luke xvi.9. *A. Malan, B.D. 1877 Oxford*

Dharmnu Tattvajnan (the philosophy of religion). *W. G. Mulligan, Litt.D. 1949 Dublin, Trinity College*

F. M. Klinger's attitude to religion. *H. M. Waidson, M.A. 1938 Birmingham*

Kant's philosophy of religion: Professor Laird's notes and extract from Professor Taylor's report. *K. Dunbar, M.A. 1915 Belfast*

The metaphysical status of religion. *H. R. Trenaman, Ph.D. 1935 London, King's College*

Molière: his philosophy of religion. *C. R. M. Williams, M.A. 1922 Wales*

On the significance of inter-communication in the philosophy of religion. *J. C. Ballantyne, M.A. 1930 Liverpool*

Personality and impersonality: a study in the philosophy of religion. *W. G. Mulligan, Ph.D. 1944 Dublin, Trinity College*

The philosophy of religion. *D. M. Edwards, Ph.D. 1925 London*

1. Problems in the philosophy of religion raised and answered in the Book of Job. 2. St. Paul's teaching in the letters addressed to the Corinthian Church. *A. F. O'N. Williams, B.D. 1908 Oxford*

The religious conception of intermediary beings in relation to the idea of causation. *W. J. Beale, Ph.D. 1935 Sheffield*

The religious philosophy in Russia in the nineteenth century. *J. Stoyanovic, Ph.D. 1926 London*

The significance in the philosophy of religion of the integration of personality through adaptation to reality. *A. G. Stuart, B.Litt. 1932 Oxford*

Studies in the philosophy of religion. *G. Galloway, D.Phil. 1905 Saint Andrew's*

Religion and Politics
See also Christianity and Political and Social Questions; Church and State.

1659-1660: a study in the interaction of political and religious forces in the period between the fall of Richard Cromwell and the restoration of Charles II. *J. L. Nightingale, M.Litt. 1936 Durham*

The importance of the religious bodies in the political development of England between the end of the eighteenth century and the beginning of the Oxford Movement. *W. H. B. Twamley, Ph.D. 1925 Cambridge*

Religion and Science
See Science and Religion.

Religion, Comparative
The Buddhist conception of man in relation to the Christian conception. *B. de Kretser, Ph.D. 1948 Edinburgh*

The distinctive features of the Christian doctrine of atonement as brought out by the comparative study of religion. *P. McCall, M.A. 1947 Leeds*

The ideas of incarnation in the non-Christian religions, and the Christian doctrine of the incarnation. *E. C. Pallot, Ph.D. 1938 London, Richmond College*

The mystery religions and the Christian sacraments. *J. E. Barlow, B.D. 1942 Leeds*

Supernatural birth in historical religions. *S. E. Starrels, Ph.D. 1936 London, King's College*

Religious Conversion

The biblical doctrine of conversion. A. C. Underwood, B.Litt. 1920 Oxford

Conversion: a comparison of the results formulated by recent American psychology of religion with the teaching and experience of the New Testament. H. A. Gearhart, Ph.D. 1924 Edinburgh

The evangelical doctrine of conversion, Lutheran and Reformed. B. Citron, Ph.D. 1946 Edinburgh

From initiation to conversion. H. W. Sendall, M.A. 1942 Leeds

A psychological study of religious conversion. W. L. Jones, M.A. 1935 Reading

Regeneration and the new psychology, with special reference to character changes. A. D. Dodd, Ph.D. 1935 Edinburgh

Religious conversion in Great Britain (1700-1850): a psychological and historical enquiry. F. W. B. Bullock, M.Litt. 1934 Cambridge

A study in the phenomena of prostration arising from a conviction of sin. A. McNaughton, Ph.D. 1937 Edinburgh

The theology of Christian conversion in the light of New Testament teaching, and with special reference to the works of Søren Kierkegaard. W. Fitch, Ph.D. 1946 Glasgow

Religious Education

See also Brothers of the Christian Schools; Friends, Society of; Jesuits; Methodism; Oratorians; Roman Catholic Church and Education; Sunday Schools.

The application of the hormic theory in psychology to the theory of religious education. R. I. Morris, Ph.D. 1945 Edinburgh

Christian education in the first four centuries. L. Millar, Ph.D. 1944 Dublin, Trinity College

Church and chapel as sources and centres of education in Wales during the second half of the nineteenth century. L. S. Jones, M.A. 1940 Liverpool

Corporate religious worship as practised in a group of secondary modern schools, and its value to adolescents. E. M. Smith, M.A. 1946 Birmingham

Correlation of religion in Catholic pedagogy. M. M. Marnane, M.A. 1948 National University of Ireland

The development of the catechism and of the catechetical instruction of children in the church consequent upon the religious changes in Germany during the sixteenth century. J. Clement, M.A. 1945 National University of Ireland

Developments since 1870 in the teaching of religion in the public elementary schools of England, with special reference to senior schools. O. White, B.Litt. 1939 Oxford

An examination of some educational implications of the New Testament gospels. G. Needham, M.A. 1949 London, Institute of Education

Gaelic catechisms in Ireland. J. J. Corkery, M.A. 1944 National University of Ireland

Methods of teaching religion. J. T. McMahon, Ph.D. 1928 National University of Ireland

Moral and religious education at Athens in the fifth century B.C. T. W. Henry, M.A. 1915 Liverpool

The problem of religious education in secondary' schools. S. R. Woods, M.A. 1943 Bristol

The psychological approach to religious education. T. R. Foulger, M.A. 1930 London, Day Training College

A psychological study of the attitude of adolescents in religion and religious instruction. J. W. Daines, Ph.D. 1949 London, External Degree

Psychology and religious education. D. F. Wilson, B.Litt. 1927 Oxford

The psychology of primary and middle adolescence in relation to religious education. B. A. Yeaxlee, B.Litt. 1936 Oxford

The psychology of religious expression and its relation to religious education. L. P. Star, Ph.D. 1942 Dublin, Trinity College

The religious and moral training of the adolescent. W. H. Backhouse, M.Ed. 1940 Leeds

The religious development of the adolescent. J. B. Bradbury, M.Ed. 1947 Manchester

Religious education. F. S. Popham, Ph.D. 1933 Dublin, Trinity College

Religious education: revolution or renaissance?. F. H. K. Terry, Ph.D. 1939 National University of Ireland

Religious Education contd.

Religious instruction in secondary schools: an enquiry and some suggestions. T. A. Grocock, M.A. 1940 Birmingham

Religious teaching in secondary schools. D. S. Bellamy, M.Ed. 1932 Leeds

A statistical enquiry into the religious ideas of children, and some application in religious education. F. E. Moreton, M.A. 1931 Birmingham

A study of the influence of the Victorian home on the religious development of the child in the last three decades of the nineteenth century. W. L. Land, B.Litt. 1948 Oxford

The teaching of religious knowledge in secondary schools. K. M. Roach, M.A. 1934 Birmingham

Towards Christian education; a psychological approach. E. A. Crawford, Ph.D. 1946 Dublin, Trinity College

Religious Experience

See also Inspiration.

The à priori elements in religious experience: an epistemological study. R. Griffiths, Ph.D. 1930 Edinburgh

An analysis of the function of aesthetic experience in religion. J. G. MacGregor, D.Phil. 1945 Oxford

1. The experience of religion. 2. The religion of experience. E. M. Venables, B.D. 1924 Oxford

Modern psychology and the validity of Christian experience. C. H. Valentine, Ph.D. 1926 London

The moral dynamic of the Christian experience according to St. Paul. G. R. Johnson, Ph.D. 1922 Edinburgh

Nature of religious experience. R. H. Thoviss, Ph.D. 1923 Cambridge

The part of experience in theological knowledge. E. L. Wenger, B.D. 1947 Oxford

The place of fear as a determinant of religious thought and practice. A. C. Lamb, M.A. 1942 Sheffield

Religious experience and its objective reference. H. Roberts, Ph.D. 1927 Cambridge

The religious experience of the primitive Church. P. S. S. Hopwood, Ph.D. 1935 Glasgow

Schleiermacher's theory of the nature of religious experience. K. Edward, Ph.D. 1915 Edinburgh

The significance of the religious consciousness with special reference to Bosanquet and Ritschl. G. H. Haydock, B.Litt. 1920 Oxford

The study of apprehension of deity from the psychological and epistemological point of view. E. F. B. Moore, Ph.D. 1944 Dublin, Trinity College

Religious Literature

See also Hymns; Morality Plays; Mystery Plays; Sermons.

Astudiaeth feirniadol o'r Didache a llenyddiaeth Gristionogol arall o gynnyrch y ddwy ganrif gyntaf, a ysgrifennwyd yn yr iaith Roeg, ynghyda chyfeiriad arbennig at ddatblygiad y Weinidogaeth a'r Gwasanaethau Eglwysig (A critical study of the Didache and other Christian literature in Greek of the first and second centuries, with special reference to the development of the ministry and the church services). E. J. Lloyd, Ph.D. 1946 Wales

Devotional prose written on the Continent during the reign of Elizabeth. D. A. U. Antona-Traversi, B.Litt. 1937 Oxford

An edition of British Museum ms. Harley 2372. L. E. Rogers, B.Litt. 1934 Oxford

Ein Beitrag zum Studium der geistlichen Lyrik des siebzehnten Jahrhunderts. M. F. Richey, M.A. 1916 London

Elizabethan recusant literature, 1559-1582. A. C. Southern, Ph.D. 1946 London, University College

The English religious lyric in the Middle Ages. J. J. Underwood, M.A. 1937 National University of Ireland

George Herbert and Nicholas Ferrar: a study of thought and imagery in Jacobean devotional literature. B. Blackstone, Ph.D. 1936 Cambridge

A history of English religious poetry from 1500 to 1700. H. J. L. Robbie, Ph.D. 1928 Cambridge

An introduction to the Jesuit theatre. W. H. McCabe, Ph.D. 1929 Cambridge

Jour de cendres and Seinte confessioun; an ed. of two Anglo-Norman poems from the ms. 312 in T.C.D. J. W. Boyle, B.Litt. 1942 Dublin, Trinity College

Religious Literature contd.

The literature of the religious revival in eighteenth century England. G. M. Maddocks, M.A. 1950 Wales

The liturgical origin and the didactic purpose of the medieval drama. A. J. Hogan, Ph.D. 1928 Cambridge

The medieval conception of heaven and hell as shown by English religious and didactic literature from 1150. H. A. C. Green, M.A. 1923 London

The medieval English religious lyric. R. H. Robbins, Ph.D. 1938 Cambridge

The mystical element in the religious poetry of the seventeenth century (1600-1660), together with an anthology of Donne's sermons illustrative of his theology and mysticism. I. Husain, Ph.D. 1935 Edinburgh

The poetry of the Catholic revival. M. M. Macauliffe, M.A. 1938 National University of Ireland

The poets of the Oxford Movement. G. Phillips, M.A. 1926 Liverpool

Popular religious works of the eighteenth century: their vogue and influence. I. W. J. Machin, Ph.D. 1939 London, External Degree

Religious currents in modern German-Swiss literature. A. M. Meyer, M.A. 1923 Liverpool

Religious lyric verse in fifteenth century England. M. N. McKeough, Ph.D. 1941 National University of Ireland

The religious mind of the Irish bards. J. E. Murphy, Ph.D. 1938 National University of Ireland

Religious teaching in early English literature before the Conquest. L. R. Sherman, B.Litt. 1914 Oxford

Sacred verse and the Oxford Movement. E. M. Butterworth, M.A. 1923 Liverpool

The sources of the Court of Sapience; a Middle English religious and didactic poem. C. F. Bühler, Ph.D. 1930 Dublin, Trinity College

Three religious poets of the seventeenth century. M. MacDonald, M.A. 1933 National University of Ireland

Two old French religious poems from a ms. in the library of Trinity College, Dublin. W. H. Lyons, Ph.D. 1937 Dublin, Trinity College

Religious Orders and Societies

See also Monasticism; and under the names of individual orders and societies, e.g. Augustinian Order; Carmelite Order; Cistercian Order; Cluniacs; Dominican Order; Franciscan Order; Jesuits; Knights Templar; Oratorians.

The Celtic monastics on the Continent. R. R. Lindsay, Ph.D. 1927 Glasgow

An examination of the charges brought against the friars by Matthew Paris. W. Alty, M.A. 1911 Wales

The friars in England. E. E. Smith, M.A. 1908 Birmingham

The friars in Wales. R. C. Easterling, M.A. 1912 Wales

The mendicants and English education in the thirteenth century. I. H. Tolley, M.A. 1924 London

The provision of books in the centrally-organized religious orders before 1400. K. W. Humphreys, B.Litt. 1949 Oxford

The relations between the Mendicant Friars and the secular clergy in England during the century after the issue of the bull Super Cathedram (1300). J. L. Copeland, M.A. 1937 London, Royal Holloway College

Religious societies (ecclesiolae in ecclesia) from 1500 to 1800, excluding those of the Church of Rome. F. W. B. Bullock, Ph.D. 1938 Cambridge

Scottish royal ecclesiastical policy, 1107-1214, with special reference to foreign influence in the spread of the monastic orders and the personnel of the episcopate in Scotland. G. W. S. Barrow, B.Litt. 1950 Oxford

Some aspects of the history of the English friars in the thirteenth century. W. J. Whitehouse, M.A. 1923 Birmingham

The various societies in the Church of England in the first half of the eighteenth century. G. V. Portus, B.Litt. 1911 Oxford

The work and influence of the friars in England for the first 50 years. E. M. Davies, M.A. 1915 Birmingham

The work of religious societies in English education, 1660-1870. F. M. Osborne, M.A. 1925 London

Religious Poetry
See Religious Literature.

Religious Societies
See Religious Orders and Societies.

Religious Tolerance
See also Christian Union; Hampton Court Conference.

The Declaration of Indulgence of 1672, including an introduction tracing the development of the question of toleration from 1660 to 1672. *F. Bate, B.Litt. 1907 Oxford*

The elements in early Christianity, down to the end of the fourth century, which helped to prepare the way for later Christian intolerance, and the relation of these elements to the early Christian conception of God as love. *L. A. Garrard, B.D. 1935 Oxford*

Growth of the idea of religious toleration in England from 1689 to 1727. *A. B. Miller, Ph.D. 1939 Edinburgh*

The idea of toleration under the later Stuarts. *G. S. Plant, Ph.D. 1936 London, School of Economics and Political Science*

John Owen, D.D., Puritan preacher and ecclesiastical statesman, with particular reference to his proposals for a settlement of religion and his views on toleration. *J. C. W. Davis, M.A. 1949 Liverpool*

Persecution and toleration in the period 1660 to 1690. *L. M. Burtt, M.A. 1922 Birmingham*

The relation of Church and State with special reference to the growth of the idea of religious toleration in England under James I, 1603-1616. *P. Doyle, M.A. 1928 London*

Religious separation and moral authority: some aspects of religious intolerance in England, 1603-1660. *I. C. Coltman, M.A. 1949 London, School of Economics and Political Science*

Religious toleration in England in the years immediately following the Restoration. *E. L. Orme, M.A. 1918 Bristol*

Religious uniformity and English education in the sixteenth century. *N. Wood, Ph.D. 1928 London*

Renaissance, The
The influence of the Renaissance on the English conception of the State. *F. W. E. C. Caspari, B.Litt. 1936 Oxford*

The influence of the romantic poem of Ariosto upon the critical thought of the Renaissance. *M. M. Wright, M.A. 1947 Manchester*

Na h-Iosánaigh agus aithbheochaint an l'éighinn cuimre (The Jesuits and the Renaissance). *S. O'Catháin, Ph.D. 1941 National University of Ireland*

The Renaissance humanists and education. *W. J. Campion, Ph.D. 1940 National University of Ireland*

Renan, Ernest
Aesthetic of Renan. *H. W. Wardman, Ph.D. 1949 London, University College*

The conflict between rationalism and romanticism in the works of Ernest Renan. *B. L. Beynon, M.Litt. 1936 Cambridge*

A critical investigation into the philosophical, ecclesiastical and other influences on Ernest Renan's *Vie de Jésus*. *A. W. Mackie, Ph.D. 1931 Glasgow*

Ernest Renan: moraliste. *A. L. G. Fréchet, Ph.D. 1943 Belfast*

The influence of Romanticism on Renan's historical treatment of religious beliefs. *K. M. Barnett, M.A. 1931 London, Bedford College*

Matthew Arnold's debt to Sainte-Beuve and Renan. *O. E. Holloway, B.Litt. 1930 Oxford*

The religious ideas of Renan. *C. Smith, Ph.D. 1949 London, King's College*

A study of Matthew Arnold and Ernest Renan as representative of the spirit of frustration in England and France in the nineteenth century. *J. N. Harding, M.A. 1947 Wales*

Renard, Jules
Jules Renard, 1864-1910. *H. C. Cooksey, M.A. 1924 London*

Renaud de Montauban
See Romances.

Renouvier, Charles Bernard
A study in the philosophy of Charles Bernard Renouvier, with special reference to his theory of knowledge. *A. H. Murray, D.Phil. 1931 Oxford*

Rent
See Land Tenure.

Repentance
See also Atonement; Penance; Sin.

Moral and psychological factors in repentance. *G. A. Brown, Ph.D. 1939 Edinburgh*

1. On repentance. 2. On faith. *R. O. Davies, B.D. 1889 Oxford*

Representativeness
Antoine Arnauld and the Cartesian theory of representative ideas. *S. V. Keeling, M.A. 1926 London*

The elements of representation: a critical study of the philosophy of O. Hamelin. *L. J. Beck, D.Phil. 1936 Oxford*

Repression
Aspects of inhibition. *B. F. Clarke, B.Litt. 1948 Oxford*

The relation of repression to cultural development. *G. Whitehead, Ph.D. 1939 Edinburgh*

Respiration
The contributions of Priestley, Ingenhausz, Senebier and N. T. de Saussure to our knowledge of photosynthesis and respiration. *E. W. Lambert, M.Sc. 1937 London, External Degree*

Early contributions to our knowledge of respiration. *F. H. C. Butler, M.Sc. 1928 London*

Restoration, The
See Great Britain: History: Seventeenth Century.

Resurrection, The
See also Jesus Christ.

1. The subjects and efficacy of holy baptism. 2. Theories opposed to the fact of the Resurrection of our Lord. *T. A. Blyth, B.D. 1888 Oxford*

Argument for the resurrection. 2. Infant baptism. *S. W. B. Holbrooke, B.D. 1907 Oxford*

1. The biblical teaching as to the Resurrection. 2. The Patristic teaching as to the Resurrection. *R. L. Moore, B.D. 1924 Oxford*

Buaidh na Naomh-Chroiche; aistriú a rinne Bonaventura O'Conchubhair, O.F.M. ar *Triumphus Crucis* le Girolamo Savonarola (*The triumph of the Holy Cross*; a translation by Bonaventura O'Conchubhair, O.F.M. of *Triumphus Crucis* by Girolamo Savonarola). *C. O'Gioballáin, M.A. 1938 National University of Ireland*

1. The communion of saints. 2. The nature of the Resurrection body. *J. E. Sheppard, B.D. & D.D. 1900 Oxford*

1. The communion of saints. 2. The resurrection of the dead. *J. Aden, B.D. & D.D. 1876 Oxford*

The conception of the Resurrection, in the Apocrypha and Pseudepigrapha. *H. Anderson, Ph.D. 1950 Glasgow*

1. The deity of Christ and of the Holy Spirit as revealed in the New Testament. 2. The Scriptural evidence for the Resurrection of Christ. *C. J. Casher, B.D. 1899 Oxford*

1. The doctrine of resurrection. 2. The rational basis of faith. *J. M. Willoughby, B.D. 1902 Oxford*

1. The doctrine of the Holy Trinity. 2. The reality of the resurrection of Christ. *S. C. Morgan, B.D. & D.D. 1881 Oxford*

1. The doctrine of the resurrection in the Book of Job. 2. The connection between free-will and eternal punishment. *J. T. Nance, B.D. 1881 Oxford*

1. Ecclesiastes. 2. The doctrine of the Resurrection. *T. Bramley, B.D. & D.D. 1890 Oxford*

1. The evidence for the resurrection of Jesus Christ. 2. The divinity of Christ argued from his claim to sinlessness. *H. F. P. Davson, B.D. 1908 Oxford*

An examination of the literary and historical evidence of the Resurrection of Jesus Christ, together with an estimate of its value from the standpoint of modern thought. *W. E. Conkling, B.Litt. 1922 Oxford*

Expositions of I Corinthians xv.20-58: the Resurrection; St. John iii.3-5; Genesis i: the Creation. *E. P. Lewis, D.D. 1904 Oxford*

1. The fourfold account of the resurrection of Jesus Christ in the light of the fourfold purpose of the four Gospel writers. 2. The authorship of the Epistle to the Hebrews. *E. Lane, B.D. & D.D. 1905 Oxford*

1. Genesis iv.2; Hebrews xi.4; xii.24: Abel's sacrifice. 2. St. Matthew xxvii.5-7; Romans vi.9: the Resurrection of Jesus and its effect on believers. 3. Romans viii.1-4, 14-17, 29-39: the work of the Holy Spirit. *H. T. Beebe, D.D. 1893 Oxford*

1. The Gospel narratives of the Resurrection. 2. The sources of St. Mark's Gospel. *N. P. Williams, B.D. 1921 Oxford*

Resurrection, The contd.
1. The gradual development of the doctrine of a future life in Holy Scripture, with special reference to the teaching of St. Paul on the resurrection-body in I Corinthians xv. 2. The Logos-Christology deduced from the writings of St. Paul. *W. O. Jenkins, B.D. & D.D. 1907 Oxford*

1. Holy baptism. 2. The Resurrection and the modern mind. *A. R. H. Grant, B.D. 1920 Oxford*

1. The hypostatic union. 2. The nature of our Lord's resurrection body. *T. H. D. Long, B.D. 1904 Oxford*

1. 'I believe in one God'. 2. 'I look for the resurrection of the dead'. *T. H. Stokoe, B.D. 1871 Oxford*

1. Indirect proofs of the Resurrection. 2. The influence of dissent upon the Church of England. *A. E. S. Ward, B.D. & D.D. 1924 Oxford*

1. The intermediate state. 2. The resurrection of the body. *L. Bradyll-Johnson, B.D. 1918 Oxford*

1. The intermediate state. 2. The nature of Christ's risen body. *E. N. Dew, B.D. 1890 Oxford*

1. The position of Jesus Christ in Mohammedanism. 2. Our risen Lord's appearances in Galilee. *A. E. Richardson, B.D. 1902 Oxford*

1. Predestination and free will. 2. The resurrection of the holy. *E. E. Bradford, B.D. 1904 Oxford*

1. Presence of a creed in the New Testament. 2. The Resurrection, or the cardinal features of Apostolic teaching. *B. Whitefoord, B.D. 1895 Oxford*

1. The problem of pain as treated in the Book of Job. 2. The place of the resurrection ot our Lord in the plan of salvation. *J. A. Evans, B.D. 1907 Oxford*

1. The prophets: the characteristics of their teaching, and their influence on the religious and political life of Israel. 2. The resurrection of our Lord: its evidences and its hints as to a future life. *W. H. Powell, B.D. & D.D. 1909 Oxford*

1. The relation of the Psalms to Christ. 2. The resurrection of Jesus Christ. *J. H. Hopkinson, B.D. & D.D. 1909 Oxford*

1. The resurrection. 2. Christianity necessary to a true view of personality. *S. Bickersteth, B.D. & D.D. 1905 Oxford*

The Resurrection in the New Testament. *H. R. Haworth, B.D. 1939 Leeds*

The Resurrection narratives. *T. J. Thorburn, D.D. 1911 Cambridge*

1. The Resurrection of Christ. 2. The Ascension of Christ. *C. H. C. Baker, B.D. 1882 Oxford*

1. The Resurrection of Christ. 2. The Virgin Birth of Christ. *R. Waterfield, B.D. & D.D. 1924 Oxford*

1. The resurrection of Jesus Christ in its relation to the Christian faith. 2. The person and work of the Holy Spirit. *D. M. Davis, B.D. & D.D. 1909 Oxford*

1. The resurrection of Jesus Christ. 2. The ministry of angels as revealed in Holy Scripture. *C. C. Mills, B.D. & D.D. 1909 Oxford*

1. The resurrection of Jesus Christ considered as a historical and dogmatic problem. 2. The outlook of Jesus upon the future. *A. E. J. Rawlinson, B.D. 1921 Oxford*

1. The resurrection of our Lord Jesus Christ. 2. The doctrine of the kenosis. *G. H. Oakshott, B.D. & D.D. 1909 Oxford*

1. The Resurrection of our Lord. 2. Justification. *E. C. Dermer, B.D. 1874 Oxford*

Resurrection of the body. *J. T. Darragh, D.D. 1921 Dublin, Trinity College*

1. St. Luke xxii.14-20: the institution of the Eucharist. 2. I Corinthians xv.3-8: the witness of St. Paul to the resurrection. 3. I Corinthians xv.29: baptizing for the dead. *T. H. Davies, D.D. 1910 Oxford*

1. St. Paul's claim for dogmatic theology. 2. The resurrection of Jesus Christ: the keystone of the faith. *W. C. Eppstein, B.D. & D.D. 1905 Oxford*

1. The sinlessness of Christ. 2. The Resurrection as the main evidence for Christianity. *M. J. Barrington-Ward, B.D. & D.D. 1919 Oxford*

1. The testimony of St. Paul with regard to the resurrection of our Lord compared with that of the four Evangelists. 2. A study of the sterner side of the character of our Lord as evidenced in the narratives of the Evangelists. *A. W. Upcott, B.D. & D.D. 1906 Oxford*

Retail Trade
See also Marketing; Trade.

Retail Trade contd.
Control and management in co-operative retail societies. *W. G. Symons, M.Com. 1936 Birmingham*

Departmental stores. *J. M. Harries, M.A. 1950 Sheffield*

Industrial relations in the distributive trades, with special reference to the Co-operative Movement. *J. Huddleston, M.A. 1938 Leeds*

The organization of retail trade in the borough of Llanelly, with special reference to the retailing of foodstuffs. *W. S. Adams, M.A. 1940 Wales*

Personnel in retail distribution, with special reference to the training of juvenile employees. *H. W. Clark, M.Com. 1937 Birmingham*

Retail goodwill valuation. *G. S. Brownlow, M.Sc. 1940 London, External Degree*

Retailers' buying associations. *T. M. Davies, M.A. 1936 Wales*

Retailing costs and technical progress. *H. Smith, B.Litt. 1934 Oxford*

The social and economic effects of the development of multiple shops in the United Kingdom and the United States of America. *G. A. Jeremy, M.A. 1927 Wales*

A study of methods of investigation and research in marketing, and an assessment of their contributions to the solution of problems of producers and to the general economic efficiency of the organizations lying between producers and consumers. *M. B. Ghatge, Ph.D. 1936 Wales*

Retarded Children
See Children, Retarded.

Rétif de la Brétonne, Nicolas Edmé
Rétif de la Brétonne. *Z. W. Goddard, Ph.D. 1935 London, King's College*

Retrospective Review, The
The Retrospective Review: its origin, aims, and contributors. *C. J. Dastur, B.Litt. 1939 Oxford*

Reuter, Fritz
The imagery in the works of Fritz Reuter. *R. H. Zernick, M.A. 1947 London, Birkbeck College*

Revelation
See also Theism; and Hegel, G. W. F.; Ritschl, A. For the Book of the Revelation, see Bible: New Testament.

1. Although the eternal power and divinity of the Creator may be learnt by reason, yet man in his present condition needs the aid of revelation to enlighten him respecting the duties of religion. 2. St. Paul is the author of the two Epistles to the Thessalonians. *J. G. Cazenove, B.D. & D.D. 1874 Oxford*

1. The evolution of the revelation of God traced through the crises in the history of Israel during the period from Moses to Elijah. 2. The evolution of the revelation of God traced through the crises in the history of Israel during the eighth century B.C. *C. C. Atkinson, B.D. & D.D. 1898 Oxford*

Ideas and revelation. *P. W. Kingston, B.D. 1928 Cambridge*

1. Internal evidences of revelation in Holy Scripture. 2. The immutability of God. *C. H. Golding-Bird, B.D. 1908 Oxford*

1. The place of the ark in the religious thought of the early Israelites. 2. The revelation of Yahweh in tradition and history. *M. W. Myres, B.D. & D.D. 1924 Oxford*

1. Progressive revelation as illustrated in the history of Israel. 2. Asceticism and Christianity. *C. W. L. Evans, B.D. 1909 Oxford*

The relation of the Christian revelation to history, with special reference to Ritschlian and Hegelian tendencies. *J. MacWilliam, B.Litt. 1911 Oxford*

Revelation: an interpretation in the terms of modern conceptions of personality. *J. Pickthall, Ph.D. 1924 Edinburgh*

1. Revelation and inspiration. 2. Christ incarnate, the reconciler and restorer of fallen man. *R. J. Wilson, B.D. & D.D. 1894 Oxford*

Revelation and the Holy Spirit. *F. W. Canfield, D.D. 1933 London, External Degree*

Revelation and the unconscious. *R. S. Frayn, Ph.D. 1940 London, Richmond College*

1. That the doctrine of a future state did form part of the revelation to man in the times preceding our Lord's birth. 2. That the so-called doctrine of final perseverance can be established by sufficient evidence from Holy Scripture, and is held by the Church of England in her seventeenth Article. *F. Bedwell, B.D. 1874 Oxford*

Revenge
The use of revenge as a tragic theme in Greek tragedy, Seneca, and Elizabethan revenge plays. *J. S. Middlemas, M.A. 1949 Manchester*

Revenger's Tragedy, The
The revenger's tragedy and *The atheist's tragedy*: some notes on their style and on the authorship problem. *R. A. Foakes, M.A. 1949 Birmingham*

Revolution
General Works only. See also Communism; and under the subheadings History and Politics of individual countries.

Byron and Shelley considered as types of the revolutionary spirit. *J. J. Jackson, M.A. 1912 London*

The influence of the French revolutionary theorists (Voltaire, Rousseau, D'Holbach etc.) upon Shelley. *G. C. Rosser, M.A. 1939 Wales*

Revue Britannique
The *Revue britannique*: its origins in 1825 and its early history to 1840. *K. M. Jones, M.A. 1938 Wales*

Reynolds, Frederic
The life and works of Frederic Reynolds, dramatist, 1764-1841. *M. H. A. Collins, M.A. 1929 London*

Reynolds, Henry
Mythomystes and *The tale of Narcissus* by Henry Reynolds: edited with introduction and notes. *E. M. T. Duffy, M.A. 1948 Liverpool*

Rhaetia
A historical and cultural survey of the Roman limes of Germania Superior and Raetia. *O. P. F. Kendall, M.A. 1931 London, University College*

Rhetoric
The Aristotelian and scholastic doctrine of opposition. *H. F. Lyne, M.A. 1945 National University of Ireland*

The eighteenth century rhetoricians. *R. Entwistle, Ph.D. 1930 London, Birkbeck College*

The literary and rhetorical background of Francis Bacon as an English man of letters. *M. Walters, M.A. 1938 London, Royal Holloway College*

The place of rhetoric in education in the first century A.D. and at the present day. *M. F. Moor, B.Litt. 1922 Oxford*

Rhetoric in Euripides and Menander. *J. M. Aitken, B.Litt. 1936 Oxford*

Rhetoric in Welsh oratory and poetry, 1789-1840. *J. T. Jones, M.A. 1924 Liverpool*

The study of rhetoric in England as represented in the educational writings of the sixteenth century, and a classified catalogue of educational writings published in England and of English educational works published abroad before 1640. *G. D. M. Davies, M.A. 1934 London, King's College*

Rheumatic Diseases
A summary of recent research bearing on the relation of social factors to the incidence of rheumatic diseases in childhood, with an analysis of new data bearing on the subject. *E. O. Humphreys, M.A. 1930 Liverpool*

Rhine, River
L'appel du Rhin dans les oeuvres de Maurice Barrès avant la publication des *Bastions de l'Est*: l'influence allemande et l'évolution de sa pensée relative au problème du Rhin. *S. M. King, M.A. 1932 Leeds*

Rhodes
Cults of Rhodes. *T. F. Donnelly, M.A. 1938 National University of Ireland*

Rhodesia
See also Amandebele, The; Matabeleland; Ndola.

The achievement of self-government in Southern Rhodesia, 1898-1923. *J. D. Fage, Ph.D. 1950 Cambridge*

The development of Rhodesia under the British South Africa Company (1890-1914), with some indication of subsequent developments. *J. W. Fisher, M.A. 1924 Wales*

The economic geography of southern Rhodesia, with special reference to communications. *E. Fisher, M.A. 1924 Liverpool*

The history of Nyasaland and northeastern Rhodesia, 1875-95. *A. J. Hanna, Ph.D. 1948 London, King's College*

Native segregation in Southern Rhodesia: a study of social policy. *R. McGregor, Ph.D. 1940 London, External Degree*

Public opinion and the acquisition of Bechuanaland and Rhodesia, 1868-1896. *D. Trevor, Ph.D. 1936 London, School of Economics and Political Science*

Rhondda
The industrial development of the Rhondda Valleys to 1910. *E. D. Lewis, M.A. 1940 Wales*

Rhymney Valley
The industrial history of the Rhymney Valley, with regard to the iron, steel and tinplate industries, coal mining, lead mining, smelting and quarrying. *J. Davies, M.Sc. 1926 Wales*

Rhys, John David
Bywyd a gwaith y Dr. Siôn Dafydd Rhys (The life and work of Dr. John David Rhys). *T. Parry, M.A. 1929 Wales*

Rhys Nanmor
Barddoniaeth Llawdden a Rhys Nanmor (The poetry of Llawdden and Rhys Nanmor). *M. G. Headley, M.A. 1938 Wales*

Rhythm
See Music; Poetry; Speech.

Ricardo, David
English capital theory in the light of recent developments (with special reference to Ricardo and Jevons). *S. Goldman, M.Sc. 1933 London, School of Economics and Political Science*

Ricardo's contributions to financial theory examined in the light of modern theory. *A. N. A. Hamid, Ph.D. 1936 Leeds*

Ricci, Scipione de, Bishop
Bishop Scipio dei Ricci and the Synod of Pistoia: a critical survey. *C. A. Bolton, B.Litt. 1937 Oxford*

Riccoboni, Helena
Madame Riccoboni: her life and works; her place in the literary history of the eighteenth century. *E. A. Crosby, M.A. 1919 London*

Rice Growing Industry
The agricultural geography of the Irrawaddy delta, with special reference to rice. *K. E. Bruen, M.A. 1939 London, University College*

International production and exchange of rice, with special reference to production, market demand and consumption of rice in India and Burma. *A. Khan, Ph.D. 1939 Wales*

The marketing of padi in Siam. *C. M. B. Thomas, M.A. 1933 Bristol*

The rice economy of China. *J. C. C. Wu, Ph.D. 1948 Liverpool*

Rice growing in British Malaya. *H. S. Ong, M.A. 1936 London, External Degree*

Rich, Barnaby
A biography of Barnabe Riche. *E. M. Hinton, B.Litt. 1928 Oxford*

The life and works of Barnaby Rich. *J. Campbell, B.Litt. 1921 Oxford*

Rich, John
John Rich and the eighteenth century stage. *L. V. Paulin, M.A. 1936 London, University College*

Richard of St. Victor
The *De tribus processionibus* of Richard of Saint Victor: a critical text with introduction. *W. J. Tulloch, M.A. 1945 Liverpool*

Richards, Ivor Armstrong
The critical theories of Dr. I. A. Richards. *V. N. Dhavale, D.Phil. 1949 Oxford*

Richardson, Jonathan
The work and theories of Jonathan Richardson the Elder (1665 to 1745). *G. W. Snelgrove, Ph.D. 1936 London, Courtauld Institute of Art*

Richardson, Samuel
Richardson's conception of narrative art. *C. Y. Wu, M.A. 1949 Liverpool*

Richardson's influence on the women novelists of the eighteenth century. *U. Todd-Naylor, Ph.D. 1935 London, University College*

The value of sentiment to the characterization in the novels of Samuel Richardson. *T. H. Jones, M.A. 1946 Wales*

Richardson, William
A study of William Richardson, with special reference to his Shakespearian criticism. *M. Boulton, B.Litt. 1948 Oxford*

Richepin, Jean
The life and poetry of Jean Richepin. *S. Balin, M.A. 1937 Sheffield*

Richer, Edmund
Edmond Richer and the revival of Gallicanism, 1600-1630. *D. O. Soper, Ph.D. 1929 London*

Richmond, Yorkshire
A history of Richmond School, Yorkshire. *L. P. Wenham, M.Ed. 1947 Durham*

Roman Catholic Church
*See also Breviaries; Church History; Eucharist;
Heresies; Inquisition; Monasticism.*

Anglo-Papal relations, 1213-1216. *S. M. White-
blood, M.A. 1948 Manchester*

Catholicism in the work of François Mauriac. *R. J.
North, M.A. 1947 London, King's College*

The Emperor Lewis IV and the Curia from 1330 to
1347: canon law and international politics in the
first half of the fourteenth century. *H. S. Offler,
Ph.D. 1939 Cambridge*

English notaries at the Papal Curia in the fifteenth
century with special reference to W. Swan. *D.
Newell, Ph.D. 1934 Manchester*

The legation of Cardinal Otto, 1237-41. *D. M.
Williamson, M.A. 1947 Manchester*

The manuscript tradition of the *Practica* of the
Council of Florence. *J. Gill, Ph.D. 1949 London,
King's College*

Relations of Pope Gregory the Great with the churches in the Roman Empire of the East. *W. J. Boast,
M.A. 1931 Birmingham*

The Roman Collegia. *M. L. Macgregor, M.A. 1931
London, Birkbeck College*

Standards of Catholicism during the period of the
Councils and at the Reformation. *H. K. Douglass,
B.Litt. 1921 Oxford*

The work of the 'deputation of reform' during the
early stages of the Council of Basel. *R. L. H. Lloyd,
B.Litt. 1936 Oxford*

Roman Catholic Church: Great Britain
See also Newman, J. H.

The Catholic body in England from 1715 to 1829,
with special reference to the Catholic laity. *C. P.
Purcell, B.Litt. 1927 Oxford*

The Catholics in England, 1649-60, with special
reference to their political significance. *E. M. B.
Cottrell, B.Litt. 1932 Oxford*

The causes of Anti-Romanist fanaticism in Great
Britain in the eighteenth century, with special
reference to the Lord George Gordon Riots. *K.
Morris, M.A. 1926 Wales*

The concordats between the Holy See and England
in the fourteenth and fifteenth centuries. *M. J.
George, M.A. 1915 Liverpool*

The early history of Roman Catholic emancipation,
1760-1793. *F. E. Round, M.A. 1930 Birmingham*

Elizabethan recusant literature, 1559-1582. *A. C.
Southern, Ph.D. 1946 London, University College*

England a papal fief: repudiation. *A. J. Williams,
M.A. 1925 Liverpool*

The English Catholics, 1649-1660. *E. M. M. Hurst,
M.A. 1929 Liverpool*

Great Britain and the Roman question. *E. M.
Wiskemann, M.Litt. 1928 Cambridge*

Lancashire Elizabethan recusants. *J. S. Leatherbarrow, M.A. 1940 Manchester*

The laws against Roman Catholic recusants, illustrated from the history of the North Riding of
Yorkshire. *J. M. Price, M.A. 1922 Wales*

The light thrown by the papal registers on papal
provisions, and some ecclesiastical abuses in the
English Church during the time of Pope John XXII.
A. P. Deeley, M.A. 1927 Manchester

The movement for Catholic emancipation, 1807-
1829. *A. Quirk, M.A. 1913 Liverpool*

The revival of Roman Catholicism in South Wales
in the late eighteenth and early nineteenth centuries. *G. J. J. Lynch, M.A. 1941 Wales*

St. Peter Thomas, 1305-1366. *S. T. Manbre, M.A.
1937 Liverpool*

Some aspects of the sufferings of Catholics under
the penal laws in the reign of James I. *T. W. Lennon, M.A. 1939 Liverpool*

A study of the Jesuit Mission of 1580 with particular reference to its effects on Catholicism in
England. *M. E. Whelan, M.A. 1927 Liverpool*

Titus Oates and the Popish plot. *R. C. F. Dolley,
M.A. 1911 London*

Wales and the border counties in relation to the
Popish plot. *I. M. O'Leary, M.A. 1924 Wales*

Roman Catholic Church: Ireland
Daniel O'Connell and Catholic emancipation. *N.
E. L. Guest, M.A. 1931 Birmingham*

Roman Catholic Church: Ireland contd.
Early life of C. O'Conor, 1710. *C. O'Conor, M.A.
1930 National University of Ireland*

The history of penal laws against Irish Catholics
from 1534 to 1691 (Treaty of Limerick). *R. W.
Edwards, Ph.D. 1934 London, King's College*

Irish Catholics and Legislative Union, 1800. *T. A.
Burke, M.A. 1943 National University of Ireland*

Relations of the British Government and the
Roman Catholic Church in Ireland 1508-1829. *G.
D. Sanderson, Ph.D. 1930 Dublin, Trinity College*

Roman Catholic Church: Italy
Bishop Scipio dei Ricci and the Synod of Pistoia: a
critical survey. *C. A. Bolton, B.Litt. 1937 Oxford*

The monastery of Vivarium and its historical
importance. *M. Stanley, B.Litt. 1939 Oxford*

The political influence of Pope Gregory the Great
in Italy. *H. V. W. Lewis, M.A. 1913 Wales*

Roman Catholic Church: Sweden
Sweden and the Papacy, 822-1248. *C. J. A. Oppermann, Ph.D. 1931 London, External Degree*

Roman Catholic Church and Education
The activities of Catholics in the matter of education in England. *A. P. Braddock, M.A. 1917 London*

Catholic continuity in English education. *M. R.
O'Nealon, M.A. 1933 National University of Ireland*

1. Catholic education in Ireland, 1774-1824: illustrated from the diocesan records of Kildare and
Leighlin. 2. The Confraternity of Christian Doctrine in Ireland, 1775-1835. *M. A. Brenan, Ph.D.
1934 National University of Ireland*

Catholic popular education in Ireland (1750-
1870). *J. Fitzsimons, Ph.D. 1941 National University of Ireland*

Correlation of religion in Catholic pedagogy. *M. M.
Marnane, M.A. 1948 National University of Ireland*

The education of English Catholics, 1559-1800. *W.
F. Hastings, M.A. 1923 London*

Education with a tradition: an account of the educational work of the Society of the Sacred Heart,
1800-1935. *M. F. M. O'Leary, Ph.D. 1935 London,
External Degree*

Educational principles in the practice of Don Bosco
and his successors. *J. L. O'Reilly, M.A. 1948
National University of Ireland*

English Catholic education from the Reformation
to Catholic emancipation (1580-1829). *M. V.
Sweeney, M.Ed. 1946 Leeds*

The growth and present status of Catholic secondary education in the province of Bombay. *E. A.
Pires, M.A. 1942 London, Institute of Education*

An historical account of Catholic education in
England, with special reference to educational activities in the Salford diocese. *W. Whalley, M.Ed.
1938 Manchester*

Pioneer movements in Catholic education, Cork
City, 1750-1850. *J. J. Queenan, M.A. 1928
National University of Ireland*

The Popular Catholic School in Ireland. *P. J.
Dowling, Ph.D. 1929 London*

Some aspects of Jesuit education before the suppression. *M. Kennelly, M.A. 1948 National
University of Ireland*

Roman de Laurin
A first contribution to the study of the linguistics of
the unpublished thirteenth century prose-romance
entitled *Le Roman de Laurin, fils de Marques le
Seneschal*. *L. G. M. Thorpe, Ph.D. 1949 London,
External Degree*

Roman de Reinbert
Syntaxe du *Roman de Reinbert*. *B. R. Griffiths,
M.A. 1947 London, University College*

Roman d'Eustache Le Moine
An examination of the historical basis of the
Roman d'Eustache le Moine. *G. A. Thorn, M.A.
1949 Leeds*

Roman Empire
See Rome.

Roman Law
See Law, Roman.

Romance Languages
The development of Latin *u* and Germanic *w* in the
Romance languages. *F. Whitehead, D.Phil. 1933
Oxford*

Romances
*See also Arthurian Legends; Epics; English Lite-
rature; French Literature; German Literature;
Irish Literature; Welsh Literature.*

Romances contd.
Alexander and the earthly paradise in medieval
English literature. *M. M. Lascelles, B.Litt. 1927
Oxford*

The Anglo-Norman manuscripts of the chanson de
geste, *Aspremont*. *B. Proper, M.A. 1913 London*

Astudiaeth o chwedl *Culhwch ac Olwen* (A study
of the legend of Culhwch and Olwen). *I. L. Foster,
M.A. 1935 Wales*

Bardism and romance; a study of the Welsh literary
tradition. *T. G. Jones, M.A. 1915 Wales*

Breuddwyd Pawl a *Phurdan Padrig* (*The Dream of
St. Paul* and *The Purgatory of St. Patrick*). *J. E. C.
Williams, M.A. 1936 Wales*

Chanson de geste and prose romance in French literature of the fifteenth and early sixteenth centuries.
H. R. Conrad, Ph.D. 1937 Cambridge

Characterisation in the *Chanson de Geste* of *Girart
de Vienne*, by Bertrand de Bar-sur-Aube. *K.
Robinson, M.A. 1937 London, Royal Holloway
College*

Chwedl *Troelus a Chresyd* yn Gymraeg fel y ceir hi
yn llawysgrif Peniarth 106 (The legend of *Troilus
and Cressida* in Welsh as it is found in ms. Peniarth
106). *W. B. Davies, M.A. 1932 Wales*

A comparative study of four Old French versions of
the life of Saint Catherine of Alexandria. *W. L.
Williams, M.A. 1944 Wales*

A comparative study of Girart de Roussillon and
the Tristan poems. *E. S. Murrell, B.Litt. 1926
Oxford*

A comparative study of the French, Welsh and
Latin versions of the *Purgatoire de Saint Patrice
(Purdan Padrif)*. *I. Jenkins, M.A. 1929 Wales*

A comparison between *Owein a Luned* and *Yvain,
or Le Chevalier au Lion*. *M. Morgan, M.A. 1910
Wales*

Contribution à étude de Flore et Blanceflor. *E. G.
Chettle, M.A. 1920 Birmingham*

Contribution to the study of the style in the earliest
French prose romances. *S. G. Thomas, Ph.D. 1948
London, University College*

A contribution to the study of the *Chanson de
Geste de Simon de Pouille*. *W. Davies, M.A. 1921
London*

Courtoisie in the *roman d'aventures* of the thirteenth century. *A. D. Crow, B.Litt. 1933 Oxford*

A critical study of the episodic Tristan poems. *J. M.
Telfer, B.Litt. 1949 Oxford*

Die niederdeutsche gereimte Katharinenlegende
der Brüsseler Hs.No.II.143, und ihr Verhältnis zu
dem mitteldeutschen Wolfenbüttler Fragmenten:
Text und Untersuchung. *W. E. Collinson, M.A.
1912 London*

Dissertation sur *La chanson de Floovant*. *F. H.
Bateson, M.A. 1932 Leeds*

Eachtra Choinn Láidir Mic Bacaigh binne Gulban
(The adventures of Conn Láidir son of Bacach
binne Gulban). *M. Mac Donagh, M.A. 1939
National University of Ireland*

Eachtra Muireadhaigh Mhic Diaindheirg (*The
adventures of Muireadach son of Diaindearg*). *S.
O'hOisin, M.A. 1945 National University of Ireland*

Eachtraí buile Shuibhne ingaedhilg an lae indiu
(The adventures of Buile Suibhne, in modern
Irish). *S. O'Laoghaire, M.A. 1929 National
University of Ireland*

An edition of *Sir Amadace*. *M. N. Smith, M.A.
1934 Leeds*

An edition of that part of the prose romance of
Lancelot du lac which corresponds to Chrétien de
Troyes' *Conte de la Charrette*, with introduction and
notes. *G. Hutchings, D.Phil. 1936 Oxford*

An edition of the Middle English romance of
Athelston. *G. Taylor, M.A. 1934 Leeds*

An edition of the Middle English romance of
Athelston with literary and linguistic introduction,
notes, and a glossary. *A. M. Trounce, B.Litt. 1932
Oxford*

The extent to which Wolfram von Eschenbach is
indebted for his poem *Parzival* to French and other
foreign sources. *M. Williams, M.A. 1907 Wales*

Feudal law in the *chansons de geste*. *L. Owen, M.A.
1914 Wales*

A first contribution to the study of the linguistics of
the unpublished thirteenth century prose-romance
entitled *Le Roman de Laurin, fils de Marques le
Seneschal*. *L. G. M. Thorpe, Ph.D. 1949 London,
External Degree*

Romances contd.

Floire et Blancheflor. M. M. Pelan, Ph.D. 1937 Belfast

Floire et Blancheflor: a critical edition of the popular version. E. H. Robinson, M.A. 1935 Manchester

Glossaire aux branches II et Va du *Roman du Renart.* N. H. Burnell, M.A. 1926 Leeds

Gwyrtheyu e wynvydedic Veir: astudiaeth gymharol ohonynt fel y'u ceir hwynt yn llawysgrifau Peniarth 14, Peniarth 5 a Llanstephan 27 (The Miracles of the Blessed Mary: a comparative study of them as they are found in the manuscripts Peniarth 14, Peniarth 5, and Llanstephan 27). L. H. Angell, M.A. 1938 Wales

Hebrew-German romances and tales and their relation to the romantic literature of the Middle Ages. L. Landaw, M.A. 1911 London

Histoire poétique de Guillaume au court nez: recherches sur les chansons de geste. K. M. G. Smith, Ph.D. 1925 Leeds

Illustrations of the romances in medieval English art. R. S. Loomis, B.Litt. 1913 Oxford

Iomramh Mhaoldúin: aiste, tex, aistriu (Iomramh Mhaoldúin: introduction, text and translation). C. O'Cuilleanáin, M.A. 1932 National University of Ireland

La chanson de Floovant: étude critique et édition. F. H. Bateson, D. Litt. 1938 Leeds

La chanson de Roland : its origin and its language. M. M. McHugh, M.A. 1920 National University of Ireland

La syntaxe des propositions adverbiales dans *Huon de Bordeaux.* A. F. Church, M.A. 1934 London, Birkbeck College

La vision de Saint Paul: a comparative study in the French, Latin and Welsh literatures of the Middle Ages. T. G. Davies, M.A. 1934 Wales

Le caractère d'Aimeri de Narbonne d'après les chansons *Girart de Vienne, Aimeri de Narbonne, Les Enfances Guillaume, Les Narbonnais, Le Siège de Basbastre, La Prise de Cordres et de Sebille* et *La Mort Aimeri.* A. G. R. Britten, M.A. 1936 London, Birkbeck College

Le *Tristan* d'Eilhart d'Oberg. A. Lofthouse, M.A. 1939 Manchester

The *Life of Alexander* in English prose (Thornton ms.). W. Hadley, M.A. 1922 London

The old French prose romance *L'estoire del Saint Graal* and its relation to Robert de Borron's poem *Le roman de l'estoire dou Graal.* S. M. Scott, M.A. 1935 Manchester

Preliminary studies on the alliterative version of the *Gest hystoriale* as compared with the original Latin of Guido delle Colonne. A. M. Roberts, M.A. 1920 London

The presentation of King Arthur in medieval romance, with special reference to Middle English. K. M. Sheperd, M.A. 1907 London

The romance of *Eracle* by Gautier d'Arras: its sources, composition, and place in contemporary literature. C. J. Hayes, B.Litt. 1935 Oxford

The romance of the *Seven Sages of Rome* in the French, Latin and Welsh literatures of the Middle Ages. G. John, M.A. 1926 Wales

The romance of *Tristan and Iseult* in Malory's *Le Morte Darthur:* a study of the sources. E. Vinaver, B.Litt. 1922 Oxford

An Rudhraigheacht 'sa bheuloidis (The Red Branch Knights in the oral tradition). A. O'Ceallaigh, M.A. 1945 National University of Ireland

Sdair na Traoi do réir láimhscríbhinne A.11 (*The history of Troy* as in ms. A.11). S. M. MacGiolla Mhártain, M.A. 1945 National University of Ireland

Sir Orfeo: introduction, text, commentary, and glossary. A. J. Bliss, B.Litt. 1948 Oxford

Sir Orfeo, edited with introduction, notes, translation and glossary. C. Bullock, Ph.D. 1926 London

Some of the continuations of the medieval French romance of *Alexander.* E. B. Ham, D.Phil. 1927 Oxford

Stair an Naoimhgréadhla: aistriúchán (A translation of *Stair an Naoimhghréadhla*). L. O'hUigin, M.A. 1939 National University of Ireland

A study of a hitherto unconsidered Yvain manuscript (National Library of Wales, add. ms.444W - Yvain Williams ms.530). M. M. McRitchie, M.A. 1929 Wales

Romances contd.

A study of Lord Berners' translation, *Arthur of Little Britain,* with a prefatory life of the author. S. P. Jenkins, B.Litt. 1946 Oxford

A study of the English romance of *Sir Tristrem* in relation to its source. D. F. Aitken, B.Litt. 1927 Oxford

A study of *The Life and death of Jason, The earthly Paradise,* and *Sigurd the Volsung,* with special reference to Morris's treatment of his sources. C. M. Arscott, Ph.D. 1928 London

A study of the mss. of the *Chanson d'Aspremont* in the Bibliothèque Nationale in Paris. C. I. Wilson, Ph.D. 1923 London

A study of the supernatural in Middle English verse romances. G. L. Preedy, M.A. 1918 Bristol

Study of the version of *Titus and Vespasian* contained in the ms. British Museum additional 10289. M. E. D. Honey, M.A. 1907 London

The syntax of *Le Charroi de Nîmes.* W. Barwise, M.A. 1936 Manchester

Táin Bó Cuailnge; arna hiomlánú agus arna heagar, as iomad seanteacs, agus arna gléasadh faoi chulaith na-Gaeilge (The Cattle-raid of Cooley: its completion and edition from numerous old texts and its treatment in modern Irish). S. O'Cathasiagh, M.A. 1943 National University of Ireland

The text of the Fillingham *Otuel* with a thesis upon it (ms. additional 37492, British Museum). C. Hulme, M.A. 1922 London

The avowynge of King Arthur, Sir Gawan, Sir Kaye, and Sir Bawdewyn of Bretan: a Middle English romance from the Ireland ms. J. A. Smith, M.A. 1938 Leeds

The romance of Sir Degrevant: edited from the mss, at Lincoln and Cambridge, with introduction, notes and glossary. . L. F. Casson, Ph.D. 1942 Edinburgh

Three fifteenth century manuscripts of *Renaud de Montauban* (British Museum, Royal 16 G. ii, Royal 15 E. vi and Sloane 960). M. R. Boyd, M.A. 1905 London

Tóruidheacht ar Lorg Chriosta (Following the footsteps of Christ). B. Garry, M.A. 1945 National University of Ireland

Trn tonna dibhfheirge Dé agus Beatha Chaitriona (The three surges of God's wrath and The life of Catherine). E. J. Edmonds, M.A. 1930 National University of Ireland

Uí Chonchubhair Chonnacht sa bhfilídheacht (The O'Connors of Connaught in poetry). M. G. Mac Confhaola, M.A. 1942 National University of Ireland

Une introduction aux *Miracles de Nostre Dame par personnages.* N. Stratford, M.A. 1941 Sheffield

Ystorya Bown o Hamtwn. M. Watkin, M.A. 1913 Wales

The verbal system of the *Book of Leinster* version of the *Táin bó Cúalnge.* M. MacDermott, M.A. 1939 National University of Ireland

Roman-Dutch Law

The application in Roman-Dutch law of the principle *mobilia non habent sequelam* with special reference to the law of South Africa. M. H. Barry, B.Litt. 1925 Oxford

The liability for safe carriage of goods in Roman-Dutch law. T. E. Donges, LL.D. 1925 London

The possessory remedies in Roman-Dutch law. T. W. Price, Ph.D. 1941 Cambridge

The principles of the Roman-Dutch law of delict as illustrated in the law of Ceylon, with a special chapter on the liability of the Crown to be sued in tort in Ceylon. L. A. Rajapakse, LL.D. 1925 London

Romantic Movement
See Romanticism.

Romanticism

A comparison of the treatment of romantic motives in Sir Philip Sidney's *Arcadia* and in typical earlier and later romances. M. Moens, M.A. 1912 London

The conflict between rationalism and romanticism in the works of Ernest Renan. B. L. Beynon, M.Litt. 1936 Cambridge

Die Neuromantik in Drama Herbert Eulenbergs. F. W. Schoberth, M.A. 1937 Wales

Educational aspects of the Romantic Movement in Britain. A. R. Paterson, Ph.D. 1941 Glasgow

Eichendorff's ideas of romanticism. K. E. Finney, M.A. 1913 Birmingham

Romanticism contd.

El romanticismo en España. H. Ahern, M.A. 1929 National University of Ireland

Emerson and the romantic revival. F. J. Yealy, Ph.D. 1930 Cambridge

An examination of the critical periodical literature of the Romantic revival. R. W. Faint, M.A. 1925 London

German Romanticism. I. M. J. McBryan, M.A. 1916 National University of Ireland

The Globe and the Romantic tendency. T. R. Davies, M.A. 1904 Wales

Gray and romanticism. D. Williams, M.A. 1907 Wales

Herder's contribution to the Romantic philosophy of history, with special reference to the theological implications. G. W. Bromiley, Ph.D. 1943 Edinburgh

Herder's relationship to German romanticism, with special reference to the theory of literary criticism. G. Parker, D.Phil. 1939 Oxford

The influence of German aesthetic thought on the conception of romanticism in England, 1790-1830. T. H. Dawson, Ph.D. 1925 London

The influence of Ossian on the chief French writers of the Romantic period. D. J. Lewis, M.A. 1909 Wales

The influence of Romanticism on Renan's historical treatment of religious beliefs. K. M. Barnett, M.A. 1931 London, Bedford College

The influence of the earlier romanticists on E. T. A. Hoffmann. G. D. Millar, M.A. 1915 London

The influence of the French Revolution on the English Romantic poets. F. C. Moore, M.A. 1918 London

La lutte romantique à l'Académie Française. E. Jones, M.A. 1922 Birmingham

La muse française et l'école romantique. W. F. Allen, M.A. 1909 Wales

Le groupe Delécluze et son rôle dans le mouvement romantique. E. P. E. Long, M.A. 1938 Liverpool

Le rôle d'Etienne de Jouy dans la polémique romantique. N. E. Anderson, M.A. 1937 Liverpool

Le Romantisme. E. H. Jennings, M.A. 1909 Birmingham

The life and works of Ulric Guttinguer: being a contribution to the history of the Romantic movement in France. C. H. Dickson, Ph.D. 1940 London, University College

Methodism and the English Romantic Movement. F. C. Gill, M.A. 1936 Liverpool

The political thought of the English Romanticists. C. C. Brinton, D.Phil. 1923 Oxford

The relation of form and subject in the romantic movement of English Literature. T. E. Casson, B.Litt. 1911 Oxford

The relation of political and social ideas to the novel of the English romantic revival. A. C. Kettle, Ph.D. 1942 Cambridge

The romantic element in the prose-works of Hermann Hesse. M. B. Benn, M.A. 1948 London, University College

The romantic movement in Russia. L. Segal, M.A. 1919 Birmingham

Romantic poets and language. J. J. Hogan, M.A. 1923 National University of Ireland

Sir George Beaumont, and his contacts with English Romanticism. E. G. Mitchell, M.A. 1938 London, Queen Mary College

Socialism and romanticism in France, 1830-1848. H. J. Hunt, D.Phil. 1931 Oxford

Some elements of sentimentalism in the literature of the eighteenth century. C. Hanson, M.A. 1948 Sheffield

A study of the development of the meaning of the word 'romance' (romantic) as used in literary criticism. H. M. Harris, M.A. 1911 London

The third Earl of Shaftesbury and the background of English romanticism. J. R. Brewer, M.A. 1947 London, University College

Victor Cousin and the Romantic Movement. P. R. Hardy, M.A. 1932 London, King's College

Rome
See also Africa, North; Dalmatia; Gaul; Germania Superior; Judaea; Latium; Numidia; Palestine; Rhaetia; Roman Britain; Sardinia.

Rome contd.
The theory of Roman and Renaissance vault construction, with special reference to the Pantheon, Rome, and Santa Maria della Salute, Venice. *A. G. S. Fidler, M.A. 1936 Liverpool*

Rome: Armed Forces
The development of the Roman fleets under the Empire. *L. F. Fitzhardinge, B.Litt. 1933 Oxford*

Roman sea power. *D. Murphy, M.A. 1916 National University of Ireland*

Rome: Constitution
The constitution of the Roman principate under Augustus in theory and practice, with a special consideration of the edicts from Cyrene and the value of the speech of Maecenas in Dio lii as evidence for the Augustan age. *M. Hammond, B.Litt. 1928 Oxford*

The legislation of Caius Gracchus considered especially in relation to the Order of the Equites. *G. A. Le Chavetois, M.A. 1912 London*

Rome: History
See also Augustus, Gaius Julius Caesar Octavius, Emperor; Brutus, Marcus Junius; Cato, Marcus Porcius, the Younger; Crassus, Marcus Licinius; Gracchus, Caius Sempronius; Julia Domna; Julian, the Apostate, Emperor; Lucius Septimus Severus, Emperor; Pollio, Gaius Asinius; Scipio, Publius Cornelius; Vespasianus, Titus Flavius, Emperor.

The attitude of the Roman Government to Christianity from Nero to Marcus Aurelius. *M. H. Evans, M.A. 1909 Wales*

Cicero's recall from exile. *H. G. Leaver, M.A. 1924 Manchester*

Development of the idea of Rome up to the fall of the Western Empire. *E. F. Ryan, M.A. 1911 National University of Ireland*

The early career, accession and domestic policy of the Emperor Domitian. *R. A. Gillespie, M.A. 1937 London, Birkbeck College*

The evidence of Salvian for the causes of the fall of the Roman Empire in the West. *W. R. Davies, M.A. 1941 Wales*

A historical and cultural survey of the Roman limes of Germania Superior and Raetia. *O. P. F. Kendall, M.A. 1931 London, University College*

History of Numidia under the Roman Republic. *S. M. Gates, M.A. 1917 London*

The history of Sardinia under the Roman Republic. *E. M. Adams, M.A. 1917 London*

The history of the Flavian period, and in particular of the reign of Domitian, especially as reflected in the works of the poets Juvenal, Martial, and Statius. *A. G. Barnes, M.A. 1936 Manchester*

The imperial policy of Claudius as reflected in the New Testament. *S. Liberty, B.D. & D.D. 1939 Oxford*

Judaea under the procurators. *L. Robinson, M.Litt. 1927 Cambridge*

Libertas as a political idea at Rome during the late Republic and early Principate. *C. Wirszubski, Ph.D. 1947 Cambridge*

Palestine under Roman administration 6-66 A.D. *M. Aberbach, M.A. 1947 Leeds*

Parthia and her relations with Rome from 27 B.C. to A.D. 228. *A. T. Owen, M.A. 1920 Wales*

The philosophic and aristocratic opposition to the Flavian emperors. *R. L. James, Ph.D. 1938 London, University College*

The political activity of Clodius, particularly in relation to the triumvirs. *M. D. Whitehouse, M.A. 1916 London*

The political and social organization of Gaul under the Roman Empire. *E. J. Rowland, M.A. 1910 Wales*

The political and social organization of Gaul under the Roman Empire. *J. Hooson, M.A. 1912 Wales*

The relations between the Roman Government and Christianity down to the end of the second century. *A. M. Hollis, B.D. 1931 Oxford*

Roman civilization in the three Gauls during the first three centuries of Roman rule. *H. W. Lawton, M.A. 1923 Wales*

The Roman province of Judaea before 70 A.D. *D. D. Fielding, M.A. 1933 Manchester*

Romanization of the three Gauls. *J. R. Moran, M.A. 1919 National University of Ireland*

Rome and Parthia, 70-29 B.C. *A. Sandys-Wood, B.Litt. 1949 Oxford*

Rome: History contd.
Rome, Greece and Macedon to 196 B.C. *M. Duggan, M.A. 1934 National University of Ireland*

The social and economic history of Cisalpine Gaul under the early Empire to the death of Trajan. *G. E. F. Chilver, D.Phil. 1936 Oxford*

The source and growth of the legend of the association of Troy with the foundation of Rome. *M. E. M. Hamilton, M.A. 1932 London, Bedford College*

Studies in pre-Gracchan colonization. *E. T. Salmon, Ph.D. 1933 Cambridge*

The survival of the Romano-Austrians. *A. F. Singer, B.Litt. 1948 Oxford*

The types of political relation established between Rome and other communities in Italy from the earliest recorded times to the close of the Republic, and their contribution to the conception of citizenship adopted by the Roman Empire during the first three centuries A.D. *A. N. Sherwin-White, D.Phil. 1937 Oxford*

Virgil's treatment of Roman history. *G. A. L. Heward, M.A. 1908 Wales*

Rome: Politics and Government
The administrative staff of the Roman emperors at Rome from Augustus to Alexander Severus. *G. R. C. Davies, D.Phil. 1947 Oxford*

The composition and functions of the local councils of the cities of the province of Africa under the early Roman Empire up to Constantine. *C. V. M. Lucas, Ph.D. 1937 London, Westfield College*

Family influence in Roman politics from Hannibal's invasion to the Battle of Pydna. *J. R. Cummings, B.Litt. 1935 Oxford*

The organization and administration of the Tres Galliae, 49 B.C.-283 A.D. *M. P. Kerr, M.A. 1924 Manchester*

The political and administrative system of Sulla. *J. E. Taylor, B.Litt. 1924 Oxford*

Some problems connected with the influence of the freedmen upon the civil service under Claudius. *P. R. Hiscock, M.A. 1947 Reading*

Rome: Social History
See also Epicureanism; Guilds; Hellenism; Latin Literature; Religion: Rome; Theatre.

The chief Roman satirists and the historical value of their works, as a picture of their times. *J. E. S. Turner, M.A. 1918 Birmingham*

A comparative study of the *fora* of the Roman Empire. *I. Purchon, M.A. 1933 Wales*

The development of social and economic life at Pompeii. *R. C. Carrington, D.Phil. 1933 Oxford*

The fall of paganism in the Western Roman Empire, 311-395 A.D. *A. E. Wilson, D.Litt. 1927 Birmingham*

An historical account of beekeeping in Greece and Rome during the classical period. *H. M. Fraser, Ph.D. 1930 London, External Degree*

How far does Roman comedy represent Roman life and sentiment?. *J. R. Hughes, M.A. 1907 Wales*

The Jewish community in Rome, from its foundation until A.D. 313. *M. E. Jacombs, M.A. 1915 Birmingham*

The Jews in the city of Rome during the first centuries B.C. and A.D., including a study of the references to them in Greek and Latin writers. *J. H. Michael, M.A. 1913 Wales*

The letters of St. Jerome as illustrating the condition of society in the fourth century. *J. Duff, B.Litt. 1925 Oxford*

The light thrown by Plautus on Roman social life of his time. *B. Carpenter, M.A. 1917 London*

The non-military aspects of the Roman occupation of Wales. *B. Jones, M.A. 1935 Wales*

The policy of the Roman Government towards non-Roman religions from Augustus to Trajan, with special reference to the treatment of such religions in Rome and Italy. *U. C. Fitzhardinge, B.Litt. 1940 Oxford*

The position of women among the Romans. *A. M. Holmes, M.A. 1932 London, University College*

Roman and imperial sentiment in the literature of the Empire: Augustus to Constantine. *R. D. McLellan, Ph.D. 1934 London, University College*

Roman life and manners as depicted in Martial and Juvenal. *M. Lamb, M.A. 1920 London*

Roman society in the reign of Trajan as seen in the writings of Tacitus, Juvenal and Pliny the Younger. *M. M. Gough, M.A. 1908 Birmingham*

Rome: Social History contd.
Roman society of the Republic as revealed in the comic poets. *E. L. Gilham, M.A. 1920 London*

Rome and Roman models in Cicero's philosophical and rhetorical writings. *F. H. R. Solmsen, Ph.D. 1936 Cambridge*

Seneca the philosopher as a source for Roman private life. *J. F. Leddy, B.Litt. 1934 Oxford*

The social and economic history of Ostia. *F. H. Wilson, D.Phil. 1935 Oxford*

The social legislation of the Roman Empire from Augustus to Constantine, and the policy of its authors. *J. F. Leddy, D.Phil. 1938 Oxford*

The use of wealth by the Romans from 150 to 50 B.C. *E. Thomas, M.A. 1947 London, Birkbeck College*

Vergil's Roman campagna. *B. Tilly, Ph.D. 1940 London, External Degree*

Rome, Church of
See Roman Catholic Church.

Ronsard, Pierre de
Les trois manières de Ronsard. *M. O'Donovan, M.A. 1946 National University of Ireland*

Nature in the poetry of Ronsard. *H. S. Mayall, M.A. 1931 Manchester*

Ronsard's natural history. *M. E. Alan, B.Litt. 1943 Dublin, Trinity College*

Rosa Anglica
Rosa anglica. *W. P. Wulff, Ph.D. 1931 National University of Ireland*

Roscher, Wilhelm
Wilhelm Roscher, his life and works. *W. D. D. Brewer, M.Com. 1924 Birmingham*

Rosegger, Peter
Mundart Peter Roseggers, mit einer Abhandlung über seine Leben und seine Waldheimat aus seinen längeren Romanen. *A. Rodgers, M.A. 1931 Leeds*

Roses, Wars of the
See Great Britain: History: Fifteenth Century.

Rossendale
Studies in the economic development of Rossendale. *G. H. Tupling, Ph.D. 1925 London*

Rossetti, Christina Georgina
Christina Rossetti. *J. E. McLoughlin, M.A. 1947 National University of Ireland*

Christina Rossetti: as a lyrical poet. *A. Kamen, M.A. 1927 Wales*

Christina Rossetti: the imagery in her English poetry. *D. M. Parsons, M.A. 1948 London, King's College*

D.G. and C. Rossetti. *A. P. Crowley, M.A. 1940 National University of Ireland*

Rossetti, Dante Gabriel
A bibliographical and reference guide to the life and works of Dante Gabriel Rossetti, with a study of the Pre-Raphaelite Movement. *J. B. Gregory, Ph.D. 1931 London, King's College*

D. G. Rossetti. *C. M. Titmuss, M.A. 1924 Birmingham*

Dante Gabriel Rossetti and his influence on English poetry until the end of the nineteenth century: a study of the poetic tendencies of the period, 1870-1900. *D. C. Davies, M.A. 1924 Wales*

D.G. and C. Rossetti. *A. P. Crowley, M.A. 1940 National University of Ireland*

Gabriele Rossetti in England. *E. R. P. Vincent, D.Phil. 1933 Oxford*

The influence of the ballad on nineteenth century poetry, with special reference to Rossetti, Morris and Swinburne. *I. M. Empson, M.A. 1933 Reading*

Medievalism in the works of Rossetti and William Morris. *E. Hall, M.A. 1912 London*

The poetry of Dante Gabriel Rossetti, with special reference to style. *E. W. Blackbird, M.A. 1934 Liverpool*

Rostand, Edmond
Edmond Rostand et son oeuvre dramatique. *G. H. Holden, M.A. 1922 Birmingham*

The romantic element in Rostand, with special reference to *Cyrano de Bergerac* and *Chantecler*. *A. C. Hitchens, M.A. 1927 Manchester*

Roteland, Hue de
See Hue de Roteland.

Rotherham, Thomas, Archbishop
Thomas Rotherham, Archbishop of York and Chancellor of England: his life and times. *M. F. Howard-Robinson, M.A. 1940 Sheffield*

Rotrou, Jean de
Quelques traces de L'influence espagnole au théâtre français du 17e siècle: Lope de Vega et J. Rotrou. *F. Astley, M.A. 1928 Birmingham*

Rotrou's conception of the tragic, with reference to *Hercule Mourant* and *Venceslas. F. K. Dawson, M.A. 1950 Manchester*

Roumania
See Rumania.

Rousseau, Jean Jacques
The conceptions of natural law and natural right, with special reference to Hobbes, Spinoza, Locke and Rousseau. *N. S. B. Powell, M.A. 1932 Wales*

The doctrinaire novel, 1760-1830, with special reference to J. J. Rousseau. *D. S. Johns, M.A. 1926 Manchester*

Histoire de la publication des *Confessions* (1775-1789): contribution aux études Rousseauistes. *M. A. Mills, M.A. 1940 Leeds*

The influence of Locke on Rousseau. *E. T. Davies, M.A. 1914 Wales*

The influence of the French revolutionary theorists (Voltaire, Rousseau, D'Holbach etc.) upon Shelley. *G. C. Rosser, M.A. 1939 Wales*

J. J. Rousseau et son influence dans l'enseignement pratique, surtout en France et en Angleterre. *A. J. Walker, M.A. 1906 Birmingham*

Jean Jacques Rousseau. *W. Boyd, D.Phil. 1911 Glasgow*

La comparaison des idées de Rousseau et de Fénelon sur l'education. *A. H. Ashworth, M.A. 1911 Liverpool*

La controverse sur la moralité du théâtre après la lettre à d'Alembert de J. J. Rousseau. *M. M. Moffat, M.A. 1930 Liverpool*

La philosophie du retour à la nature chez Jean-Jacques Rousseau, et applications practiques de son système. *R. F. Britton, M.A. 1949 Liverpool*

La place de Rousseau dans le mouvement pédagogique en France aux dix-septième et dix-huitième siècles. *M. J. Smith, Ph.D. 1935 Edinburgh*

L'idée de l'antiquité Gréco-Latin dans Jean-Jacques Rousseau. *A. Quinton, M.A. 1924 Liverpool*

L'influence littéraire de Jean Jacques Rousseau en Angleterre. *H. V. Jervis, M.A. 1913 Liverpool*

Rousseau and De Tocqueville. *V. Buranelli, M.A. 1948 National University of Ireland*

Rousseau and English poetry, 1785-1824. *M. A. Cox, M.A. 1911 Birmingham*

Rousseau et Napoléon. *F. G. Healey, M.A. 1949 Birmingham*

Un manuscrit inédit de Jean-Jacques Rousseau: la première rédaction des lettres écrites de la montagne. *J. S. Spink, M.A. 1932 Leeds*

Roussillon, Girart de
See Girart, de Roussillon.

Rowe, Nicholas
A critical appreciation and survey of the works of Nicholas Rowe. *J. Fletcher, B.Litt. 1939 Oxford*

The life and work of Nicholas Rowe, 1674-1718. *A. Jackson, M.A. 1929 London*

Nicholas Rowe. *J. R. Sutherland, B.Litt. 1926 Oxford*

Rowland, Daniel
Hanes a llafur llenyddol Daniel Rowland (The life and literary work of Daniel Rowland). *D. J. O. Jones, M.A. 1937 Wales*

Rowlands, Henry
The life and works of Henry Rowlands. *W. G. Jones, M.A. 1936 Wales*

Rowley, Samuel and William
The life and works of Samuel and William Rowley, with a special examination of the evidence for the authorship of the more important doubtful plays and of plays written in collaboration. *M. E. Dickson, M.A. 1931 London, East London College*

Royal Institution of South Wales
The place of the Royal Institution of South Wales in the history of scientific and general education in the nineteenth century. *H. M. Davies, M.A. 1940 Wales*

Royal Society
Biological research in the early days of the Royal Society. *J. L. Brewin, M.Sc. 1937 London, University College*

Chemistry at the early meetings of the Royal Society of London. *D. J. Lysaght, M.Sc. 1934 London, University College*

Royal Society contd.
Chemistry at the Royal Society, 1687-1727. *D. J. Lysaght, Ph.D. 1937 London, University College*

A study of English natural theology in the seventeenth century, illustrating some results of the influence of the scientific spirit upon religious thought in England during the earlier years of the Royal Society. *E. B. Vincent, B.Litt. 1927 Oxford*

The history of the Royal Society (1667) by Thomas Sprat, bishop of Rochester, edited from the original copies and mss, together with the comments of Henry Stubbe and others; remarks on the life of the author; a list of his works; notes, appendices and bibliography. *H. W. Jones, Ph.D. 1948 Leeds*

Royce, Josiah
Critical examination of the religious position of Josiah Royce. *J. B. Toomay, Ph.D. 1934 Edinburgh*

Royce's theory of the individual. *W. T. Jones, B.Litt. 1933 Oxford*

Rozier, Jean
Chemistry in Rozier's journal, 1771-1794. *E. W. J. Neave, Ph.D. 1949 London, University College*

Ruarcach
Filídheacht na Ruarcach (The poetry of O'Rourke). *E. Hegarty, M.A. 1939 National University of Ireland*

Rubber Trade
The rubber market. *A. W. Martin, M.Com. 1911 Birmingham*

Ruddier, Benjamin, Sir
A critical edition of the poems printed by John Donne the Younger in 1660 as written by William Herbert, Earl of Pembroke, and Sir Benjamin Ruddier. *M. A. Beese, B.Litt. 1935 Oxford*

Ruiz, Juan
El Libro de buen amor of Juan Ruiz. *J. W. Barker, Ph.D. 1924 Cambridge*

Rumania
The constitution of Roumania. *G. Munteanu, Ph.D. 1935 London, School of Economics and Political Science*

The Rumanian claims in Hungary before the peace conference. *J. M. Cabot, B.Litt. 1924 Oxford*

Rumanian Language
Comparative phonetics of English and Roumanian. *J. O. Stefanovici, Ph.D. 1927 London*

Rūmī, Jalālu'd-Dīn
An edition of the *Masnavi*, by Jalalu'd-Dīn Rūmī, Vol. I - Translation; Vol. II - Commentary. *C. E. Wilson, Ph.D. 1925 London*

Fīhi mā fīhi, or the table-talk of Jalālu'ddīn Rūmī *K. A. Khan, Ph.D. 1942 Cambridge*

Rundale
Rundale and its social concomitants. *D. McCourt, M.A. 1947 Belfast*

The Rundale system in Ireland: a study of its geographical distribution and social relations. *D. McCourt, Ph.D. 1950 Belfast*

Runge, Philipp Otto
Tieck and Runge: a study in the relationship of literature and the fine arts in the German Romantic period, with special reference to Franz Sternbald. *J. B. C. Grundy, Ph.D. 1929 London*

Rural Districts
See Local Government: Great Britain.

Rural Settlements
See Settlements.

Ruskin, John
The affinity between the aesthetic and social philosophy of Ruskin and the teaching of Wordsworth. *M. E. Needham, M.A. 1931 Birmingham*

The influence on educational thought of (1) Ruskin (2) Wordsworth. *W. O. Delaney, M.A. 1924 Liverpool*

John Ruskin as a critic of literature. *A. H. R. Ball, M.A. 1921 Birmingham*

John Ruskin as a writer of prose. *A. H. R. Ball, M.A. 1924 Liverpool*

John Ruskin as social reformer. *F. U. Stribley, M.A. 1925 Birmingham*

Ruskin as a literary critic. *E. M. Hewetson, M.A. 1938 London, King's College*

Russell, Bertrand Arthur William, 3rd Earl
Logic and mathematics, with special reference to Bertrand Russell. *M. Kelleher, M.A. 1942 National University of Ireland*

Philosophical atomism: a comparative study of the theories of Hume and Bertrand Russell. *D. S. Barlingay, M.A. 1927 London*

Russell, George, William (AE)
The early years of George Russell (AE) and his connection with the theosophical movement. *W. M. Gibbon, Ph.D. 1947-48 Dublin, Trinity College*

Mysticism in poetry; a study of AE, W. B. Yeats and Rabindranath Tagore. *A. C. Bose, Ph.D. 1937 Dublin, Trinity College*

Russell, John, 1st Earl
Lord John Russell and the development of relations between Parliament, Cabinet and parties, 1832-1852. *M. E. Gibbs, M.A. 1928 Manchester*

Russell, John, 4th Duke of Bedford
The public life of John, 4th Duke of Bedford (1710-1771). *R. H. Owen, M.A. 1923 Wales*

Russell, Odo, Lord
Lord Odo Russell as British Ambassador in Berlin, 1872-1878. *W. A. Taffs, Ph.D. 1932 London, University College*

Russia
See also U.S.S.R.; Panslavism; Slavophilism; Crimean War, 1854-1856.

Anglo-Russian relations and the formation of the Anglo-Russian Agreement, 1903-1907. *A. W. Hopkins, M.A. 1937 Wales*

Anglo-Russian relations from 1878-1885, with special reference to central Asia. *E. Jones, M.A. 1934 Wales*

British conceptions of Russia and Russian policy, 1837-41. *J. H. Gleason, B.Litt. 1932 Oxford*

A critical survey of the Narodnik movement, 1861-1881. *A. I. S. Branfoot, Ph.D. 1926 London*

Development of pan-Slavist thought in Russia from Karazin to Danilevski, 1800-1870. *F. L. Fadner, Ph.D. 1949 London, School of Slavonic and East European Studies*

The economic development of Russia from 1905-1914: with special reference to trade, industry and finance. *M. S. Miller, Ph.D. 1925 London*

The growth and interrelations of political groups and parties in Russia, 1898-May 1906. *D. W. Treadgold, D.Phil. 1949 Oxford*

The industries of the south of Russia and the competition with England. *S. B. Meyer, M.Com. 1910 Birmingham*

Movements for Anglo-Russian reconciliation and alliance from March 1890 to December 1903. *H. H. Page, M.A. 1933 Birmingham*

Napoleon III and Russia. *A. S. Walker, M.A. 1917 Birmingham*

The relations between Great Britain and Russia from 1848 to 1856. *A. R. Cooke, M.A. 1920 Birmingham*

The relations between Great Britain and Russia, 1870-1899. *A. E. Jones, M.A. 1917 Birmingham*

Russia Company
See Muscovy Company.

Russian Language
The structure of neologisms in Russian and Czech. *J. O. Ellis, Ph.D. 1948 London, School of Slavonic and East European Studies*

The use of verbal prefixes in Russian. *V. M. Du Feu, M.A. 1949 London, School of Slavonic and East European Studies*

Russian Literature
See also Blok, A. A.; Chekhov, A. P.; Dostoevsky, F. M.; Lermontov, M. Y.; Leskov, N. S.; Ostrovsky, A.; Radishchev, A. N.; Tale of the Expedition of Igor; Tolstoi, L. N., Count; Tyuchev, F. I.

English influences in Russian literature, from 1700 to 1830. *W. K. Matthews, M.A. 1923 Manchester*

Russian realism and the development of the English novel, 1880-1914 - a study in literary influence. *L. D. Reedy, Ph.D. 1938 Dublin, Trinity College*

The Russian Romantics and English literature. *T. A. Wolff, M.A. 1947 London, Bedford College*

Rutherford, Mark
See White, W. H.

Rutherford, Samuel
Samuel Rutherford, propagandist and exponent of Scottish Presbyterianism: an exposition of his position and influence in the doctrine and politics of the Scottish church. *W. McM. Campbell, Ph.D. 1937 Edinburgh*

Scottish mysticism in the seventeenth century, with special reference to Samuel Rutherford. *C. N. Button, Ph.D. 1927 Edinburgh*

Rutherwyk, John de, Abbot
The Abbey of Chertsey and its manors under Abbot John de Rutherwyk, 1307-1347. *E. Toms, Ph.D. 1935 London, King's College*

Ruthwell Cross
The Dream of Rood and Ruthwell Cross. *J. R. O'Donoghue, M.A. 1929 National University of Ireland*

Rye House Plot
See Great Britain: History: Seventeenth Century.

Sa'adia Longo
An edition of: a manuscript of the seventeenth century containing unpublished Hebrew poems by Sa'adia Longo from the *Cairo Genizah*. *R. A. Cole, M.A. 1948 Manchester*

Saar, The
The Saar territory as a factor in international relations, 1920-1932. *M. Lambert, Ph.D. 1936 London, School of Economics and Political Science*

Sabbatarianism
See Sunday.

Sabbath
See also Sunday.

A comparison of the views of Aaron ben Joseph in his *Sefer Hamibhar* and his Halakic poems with the accepted views of the Karaites and Rabbanites concerning the Sabbath and other Jewish festivals. *S. J. Weisz, M.A. 1942 Manchester*

1. The Hebrew sabbath. 2. The Christian Sunday. *G. L. Porcher, B.D. 1923 Oxford*

1. The origin and religious significance of the Jewish Sabbath. 2. The history and meaning of the Christian Sunday. *H. R. Gamble, B.D. & D.D. 1919 Oxford*

1. Verifications of Scripture from Egypt and the Holy Land. 2. The perpetual obligation of the Sabbath. *W. Allan, B.D. & D.D. 1892 Oxford*

Sachs, Hans
Hans Sachs's dramatic adaptation of *Dares and Dictys*. *F. I. Wiener, M.A. 1945 Manchester*

Sacraments
See also Baptism; Confirmation; Eucharist; Marriage; Ordination; Penance.

Calvin's doctrine of the Lord's Supper in its relation to other sacramental types. *A. Barclay, Ph.D. 1926 Edinburgh*

The doctrine of the Church and the sacraments in Hugh of Saint Victor. *W. F. Whitman, B.Litt. 1924 Oxford*

1. The efficacy of prayer. 2. The efficacy of sacraments. *E. C. Maclure, B.D. & D.D. 1890 Oxford*

John Wyclif and his interpretation of the sacraments. *H. G. Harold, Ph.D. 1940 Edinburgh*

1. Logos Christology: its validity and value. 2. The nature of the Gospel and its place in sacramental theory. *W. W. Longford, B.D. 1911 Oxford*

The mystery religions and the Christian sacraments. *J. E. Barlow, B.D. 1942 Leeds*

1. The nature and being of God. 2. The doctrine of the sacraments as 'effective signs of grace'. *E. G. Burr, B.D. & D.D. 1909 Oxford*

1. On the credibility of miracles. 2. The efficacy of the sacraments. *F. McDowell, B.D. 1890 Oxford*

1. On the historic Christ. 2. On the sacraments. *J. H. Skrine, B.D. & D.D. 1912 Oxford*

1. On the holy Catholic Church. 2. On the sacraments. *B. S. Tupholme, B.D. & D.D. 1888 Oxford*

1. On the Holy Trinity. 2. On the sacraments. *A. B. O. Wilberforce, B.D. & D.D. 1897 Oxford*

The philosophical implications of the sacramental principle. *C. Lampert, D.Phil. 1943 Oxford*

1. The Sacraments. 2. Faith and works. *S. N. Tebbs, B.D. 1874 Oxford*

1. Some general characteristics of St. Paul's Epistles, with special illustrations from the Epistle to the Galatians. 2. The intention and use of sacraments in the Christian Church. *H. D. S. Sweetapple, B.D. & D.D. 1908 Oxford*

1. The theory of sacraments and the varying use of the term in theology. 2. Confirmation or laying on of hands as recorded and taught in the New Testament. *C. E. Farran, B.D. & D.D. 1910 Oxford*

1. The Thomistic doctrine of the sacramental form or matter. 2. The reality of the Holy Spirit's indwelling in the souls of the sanctified. *W. K. Firminger, B.D. 1905 Oxford*

Sacred Heart, Society of the
Education with a tradition: an account of the educational work of the Society of the Sacred Heart, 1800-1935. *M. F. M. O'Leary, Ph.D. 1935 London, External Degree*

Sacred Heart, The
1. God and the world. 2. The cultus of the Sacred Heart in light of the hypostatic union. *W. Farrar, B.D. 1895 Oxford*

Sacrifice
See also Altars.

Atonement in the light of the development of the idea of sacrifice. *E. T. H. Godwin, B.D. 1940 Leeds*

The attitude of Judaism towards the sacrificial system. *L. Ginsburg, B.Litt. 1936 Oxford*

1. The doctrine of sacrifice. 2. The doctrine of atonement. *A. C. Keene, B.D. 1906 Oxford*

1. Enquiry into the nature of sacrifice. 2. Primitive sacrifice as perfected and completed by Christianity. *S. P. T. Prideaux, B.D. 1912 Oxford*

1. The Hebrew doctrine of immortality in the light of other religions. 2. The Hebrew doctrine of sacrifice in the light of other religions. *G. H. Jones, B.D. & D.D. 1907 Oxford*

Human sacrifice and head-hunting in Assam. *B. Gohain, M.A. 1937 London, University College*

1. The meaning and history of Jewish sacrifice and sacrificial ideas. 2. The attitude to sacrifice of the critics of the Old Testament. *F. C. N. Hicks, B.D. & D.D. 1924 Oxford*

The meaning of sacrifice. *R. E. Money- Kyrle, Ph.D. 1929 London*

1. Sacrifice. 2. Atonement. *L. L. Sharper, B.D. 1874 Oxford*

Sacrifice at Ugarit. *D. McK. L. Urie, Ph.D. 1944 Saint Andrew's*

Sacrifice in the period of the Hebrew monarchy: its theory and practice. *J. G. Harris, M.A. 1950 Wales*

1. The sacrificial worship of the Hebrews. 2. The miraculous element in the Gospels. *J. Benoy, B.D. 1891 Oxford*

Semikha or the laying on of the hands of the sacrifice. *J. Herzog, M.A. 1912 London*

This, our sacrifice. *T. F. Jalland, B.D. 1934 Oxford*

Sadhbh
Toruigheacht Shaidhbhe (The pursuit of Sadhbh). *T. O'Broin, M.A. 1936 National University of Ireland*

Toruigheacht Shaidhbh inghine Eoghain Oig (*The pursuit of Sadhbh, daughter of Eoghan Og*). *R. De Barún, M.A. 1932 National University of Ireland*

Sagas
Aspects of the Sturlung age, with special reference to *Sturlunga Saga*: à study in the life and literature of Iceland during the twelfth and thirteenth centuries. *R. G. Thomas, Ph.D. 1943 Wales*

A biographical study of the western Icelandic sagas, giving a full account of the lives of the principal characters, with genealogical tables showing their descent from the first settlers. *G. A. Hight, B.Litt. 1918 Oxford*

The cultivation of saga during the Dark Ages. *C. E. Wright, Ph.D. 1936 Cambridge*

An edition of *Hrafnkelssaga Freysgotha*, with introduction, normalized text, notes and glossary. *W. Rees, M.A. 1921 Wales*

An edition of *Hrómundar saga Greipssonar*. *A. G. Hooper, M.A. 1930 Leeds*

An edition of the *Bragða Olvis* saga and rimur. *A. G. Hooper, Ph.D. 1932 Leeds*

An edition of the *Saga of Porgils and Haflioi* (from Sturlunga Saga). *U. M. Brown, B.Litt. 1949 Oxford*

An edition of *Viga Glúms Saga* from the manuscripts, with introduction and notes. *E. O. G. Turville-Petre, B.Litt. 1934 Oxford*

England and the English in the Icelandic sagas. *J. M. Keays-Young, B.Litt. 1928 Oxford*

England in the Icelandic sagas. *C. E. Tyler, Ph.D. 1926 Sheffield*

Eschatology and manticism in Old Norse literature. *H. R. Ellis, Ph.D. 1940 Cambridge*

An examination of the sources of the *Thidrikssaga*. *W. E. D. Stephens, M.A. 1937 London, University College*

Gunnlaugssaga Ormstungu: a critical edition. *L. M. Small, Ph.D. 1925 Edinburgh*

Icelandic church saga. *J. C. F. Hood, D.D. 1943 Durham*

Sagas contd.
Legal procedure and the conduct of the feud in the Icelandic sagas. *G. Jones, M.A. 1929 Wales*

A literary analysis of the *Grettissaga* showing the composite nature of the Old Norse historical saga. *E. G. Ingram, M.A. 1908 London*

A new translation of the Icelandic *Saga of Hoensa-Dorir*. *O. Smith, M.A. 1945 Bristol*

The position of women in Icelandic life and social economy as shown in the Icelandic sagas. *R. G. Thomas, M.A. 1939 Wales*

Research on the saga-lists called *A & B* contained in, respectively, *The Book of Leinster* and ms.H.3.17 (T.C.D.) and mss.23.N.10 (R.I.A.), Rawl. B512 and Harleian 5280, together with research on the tales included therein, with special emphasis upon those which are now lost. *F. McCann, M.A. 1950 Belfast*

The sea and seafaring as described in the *Islendinga Sögur*. *P. J. B. Griffiths, M.A. 1935 Wales*

Some characters of the Red Branch saga. *B. A. MacNulty, M.A. 1920 National University of Ireland*

A study of Snorri Sturlason's *Saga of Olaf Tryggvasn*. *M. C. Greening, M.A. 1931 London, Westfield College*

A topographical study of the sagas of the Vestfirðirand of their traditions. *I. L. Gordon, Ph.D. 1930 Leeds*

The Volsung episode in the *Prose Edda* (*Edda Snorra Sturlasonar*): the Volsung episode in relation to its sources. *M. Townend, M.A. 1942 Leeds*

The works of Morris and of Yeats in relation to early saga literature. *A. D. M. Hoare, Ph.D. 1930 Cambridge*

The works of William Morris in relation to the Norse sagas. *A. D. M. Hoare, M.Litt. 1927 Cambridge*

St. Alban's
The Abbey of St. Albans under John of Whethamstede. *C. E. Hodge, Ph.D. 1933 Manchester*

The history of the abbey of St. Alban's. *L. F. R. Williams, B.Litt. 1913 Oxford*

Saint Amant, Antoine Girard de
The debt of English poetry in the seventeenth century to Théophile and Saint-Amant. *J. Short, B.Litt. 1941 Oxford*

St. Asaph
A contribution to the early history of Flintshire, with special reference to the See of St. Asaph. *J. F. Sharpe, M.A. 1924 Liverpool*

St. Bertin
The Abbey of St. Bertin and its neighbourhood, 900-1350. *G. W. Coopland, D.Litt. 1914 Liverpool*

Saint Cyr
Madame de Maintenon and Saint Cyr. *H. C. Barnard, M.A. 1928 London*

St. David's, Diocese
The diocese of St. David's during the first half of the eighteenth century, including a study of the relevant data in the *Ottley Papers*. *J. V. Davies, M.A. 1936 Wales*

Saint Evremond, Charles Marguetel de St. Denis, Seigneur de
Saint Evremond in England. *J. C. Lowe, M.A. 1932 Birmingham*

Saint-Evremond in England. *W. M. Daniels, M.A. 1906 London*

Saint Gelais, Octovien de
Octovien de Saint Gelais's translation of Ovid's *Heroides*. *K. M. A. Popham, B.Litt. 1937 Oxford*

St. Helena
The history of St. Helena and the route to the Indies, 1659-1702. *W. C. Palmer, M.A. 1924 London*

St. Helens
Economic and social development in St. Helens in the latter half of the eighteenth century. *J. R. Harris, M.A. 1950 Manchester*

St. Helen's, 1845 and afterwards: an illustration of educational developments. *W. A. Fawcett, M.A. 1936 Liverpool*

Saint Just, Louis Antoine de
The political ideas of Saint-Just, with special reference to the work of the Committee of Public Safety. *J. P. Yang, B.Litt. 1937 Oxford*

St. Just: his place in the French Revolution. *L. P. McCarthy, B.Litt. 1927 Oxford*

Saint-Just and the French Revolution. *W. F. Molloy, M.A. 1915 National University of Ireland*

Saint Lambert, Jean François de
A study of Saint Lambert, the man and the poet. *R. A. C. Milligan, B.Phil. 1950 Saint Andrew's*

Saint Mary and Saint Michael, Nunnery, Stamford
The history of the Nunnery of St. Mary and St. Michael outside Stamford. *W. M. Sturman, M.A. 1944 London, Queen Mary College*

Saint Mary, Nunnery, Clerkenwell
A study of the nunnery of St. Mary Clerkenwell and its property with an edition of its cartulary. *W. O. Hassall, D.Phil. 1941 Oxford*

St. Paul's Cathedral
The minor corporations of the secular cathedrals of the province of Canterbury (excluding the Welsh sees) between the thirteenth century and 1536, with special reference to the minor canons of St. Paul's Cathedral from their origin in the twelfth century to the visitations of Bishop Gilson in 1724. *A. R. B. Fuller, M.A. 1947 London, Birkbeck College*

St. Pierre, Jacques Henri Bernardin de
Etude sur les procédés littéraires de B. de St. Pierre. *H. A. Hatfield, M.A. 1913 Birmingham*

Saint Simon, Claude Henri, Comte de
St. Simon and Carlyle to 1835. *T. F. Thompson, M.A. 1939 Birmingham*

Saint Simon, Louis de Rouvroy, Duc de
L'influence de l'école Saint-Simonienne sur la littérature française jusqu'en 1850. *I. Sinovitch, M.A. 1922 Leeds*

The use of the subjunctive mood in the *Mémoires du Duc de Saint-Simon. F. H. Tristram, M.A. 1913 Wales*

St. Vincent
An economic survey of St.Vincent. *G. Wright, M.Com. 1928 Leeds*

Saint Vincent, John Jervis, Earl
The early life and services of Sir John Jervis, Lord St. Vincent, and their influence on his later career and character. *W. F. Scott, B.Litt. 1929 Oxford*

Sainte-Beuve, Charles Augustin
Matthew Arnold's debt to Sainte-Beuve and Renan. *O. E. Holloway, B.Litt. 1930 Oxford*

Sainte-Beuve et l'Angleterre: le critique et le poète dans leurs rapports avec certains écrivains anglais. *A. F. Powell, M.A. 1920 London*

Sainte-Beuve's critical appreciation of English literature. *E. M. Phillips, M.A. 1923 Wales*

A study of Matthew Arnold's literary criticism, with special reference to the influence of Sainte-Beuve on Arnold. *O. E. Simister, M.A. 1936 Birmingham*

A study of Ste. Beuve's criticisms of English and German literatures. *J. R. Kinnes, Ph.D. 1928 Edinburgh*

Saints
See also Ambrose; Anselm; Athanasius; Augustine, of Hippo; Bartholomew; Basil; Bernard; Bonaventura; Bridget, of Sweden; Cadoc; Catherine, of Alexandria; Clement I, Pope; Cyril, of Alexandria; David; Dunstan; Edward, the Confessor, King of England; Epiphanius; Francis; Gaudentius, of Brescia; Gildas; Gregory I, Pope, 'The Great'; Gregory Nazianzen; Hilary, of Poitiers; Hippolytus; Ignatius, of Antioch; Irenaeus; Isidore, of Seville; James, of Compostella; Jean, l'Aumonier; Jerome; John, the Baptist; John, Chrysostom; John, of Damascus; John Fisher, of Rochester; Jude; Juliana; Justin, Martyr; Macarias, of Egypt; Maolmodach; Margaret, Queen of Scotland; Mary Magdalen; Mary, Virgin; Matthew; Methodius; More, Thomas; Patrick; Paul; Paulinus, of Nola; Peter; Peter Thomas; Philip; Robert, of Knaresborough; Stephen; Teresa, of Avila; Theodore, of Tarsus; Archbishop; Thomas; Thomas a Becket, Archbishop; Thomas Aquinas; Tikhon, of Voronezh. For books of the New Testament written by Saints, see Bible: New Testament. See also Iconography; Sanctification.

The Biblical use of the word μάρτυσ and the idea of martyrdom. *J. Lowe, M.A. 1939 Manchester*

Cerddi'r Saint a'u cymharu â'r bucheddau cyfatebol (The poems of the Saints and their comparison with the corresponding lives). *D. J. Jones, M.A. 1929 Wales*

1. The communion of saints. 2. The authorship of the Pastoral Epistles. *T. Randall, B.D. 1889 Oxford*

1. The communion of saints. 2. The Athanasian Creed. *A. G. Pentreath, B.D. 1897 Oxford*

Saints contd.
1. The communion of saints. 2. The nature of the Resurrection body. *J. E. Sheppard, B.D. & D.D. 1900 Oxford*

1. The communion of saints. 2. The resurrection of the dead. *J. Aden, B.D. & D.D. 1876 Oxford*

1. The creeds: their origin and value. 2. The communion of saints. *H. G. Cundy, B.D. 1876 Oxford*

Ecclesiastical authority and the canonizations of saints in the western Church. *E. W. Kemp, B.D. 1944 Oxford*

The introduction of Christianity into the British Islands, illustrated by the lives of the saints. *F. N. Davis, B.Litt. 1905 Oxford*

1. 'One baptism for the remission of sins'. 2. 'The communion of saints'. *C. E. Jelf, B.D. & D.D. 1907 Oxford*

Ritual background of Celtic heroes and saints: a study of some of the survivals of pagan elements in early Celtic Christianity. *A. D. Reese, M.A. 1937 Wales*

1. The state of the departed. 2. The communion of Saints. *W. Baker, B.D. 1871 Oxford*

Study of the lives of seven saints in the ms. Cotton Domitian XI, British Museum. *V. M. W. Marks, M.A. 1915 London*

1. The sufficiency of Holy Scripture. 2. The communion of saints. *S. Phillips, B.D. & D.D. 1889 Oxford*

Welsh hagiography with special reference to Saint Margaret. *H. Hughes- Roberts, M.A. 1949 Liverpool*

Saints, The
The political activities of the 'Saints', 1800-1833. *F. U. Woods, M.A. 1924 Manchester*

Saiva Siddhānta
Saiva Siddhānta: a religio-philosophical system of south India. *V. R. Ranganathan, B.Litt. 1923 Oxford*

Theology of the *Saivagamas*, being a survey of the doctrines of the Saiva Siddhanta and Virasaivism. *S. C. Nandimath, Ph.D. 1930 London, School of Oriental and African Studies*

Saktas, The
The Saktas of Bengal. *E. A. Payne, B.Litt. 1927 Oxford*

Saladin
Saladin's campaign of 1188 in northern Syria, with particular reference to the northern defences of the principality of Antioch. *J. W. Hackett, B.Litt. 1937 Oxford*

Sale, Law of
The law as to the transfer of title in sale of goods. *D. A. Ismail, LL.M. 1934 Leeds*

On purchasing. *A. C. Tate, M.Com. 1934 Birmingham*

The protection of a purchaser under the old law and the new. *S. E. Brown, LL.M. 1927 Leeds*

Salesbury, William
Astudiaeth o weithgarwch llenyddol William Salesbury (A study of the literary activity of William Salesbury). *W. A. Mathias, M.A. 1949 Wales*

The language and style of William Salesbury. *D. Mark, M.A. 1903 Wales*

Llysieulyfr meddyginiaethol a briodolir i William Salesbury (A medicinal herbal attributed to William Salesbury). *E. S. Roberts, M.A. 1917 Wales*

Salesmanship
Advertising, salesmanship, and the theory of value. *T. H. Silcock, D.Phil. 1936 Oxford*

Salisbury
The clergy of the English secular cathedrals in the fourteenth century, with special reference to the church of Salisbury. *K. Edwards, Ph.D. 1940 Manchester*

The relations of the bishops and citizens of Salisbury (New Sarum) between 1225 and 1612. *F. Street, M.A. 1915 London*

Salisbury, John of
See John, of Salisbury.

Salisbury Psalter
An edition of the Salisbury Psalter (Salisbury ms. 150), with introduction and critical notes. *K. Sisam, B.Litt. 1915 Oxford*

Saljūqs, The
See Seljuks, The.

Salt Industry
The Indian salt industry, trade and taxation, 1756-1932. *B. Ghosh, Ph.D. 1933 London, School of Economics and Political Science*

Salvation
See also Antinomianism; Atonement; Faith; Jesus Christ; Justification; Redemption; Repentance.

A comparison of ideas of salvation in Hinduism and Christianity, with special reference to the Bhakti religions. *F. W. Dillistone, B.D. 1933 Oxford*

The experience of salvation in the sub-Apostolic period. *G. Matthews, B.Litt. 1910 Oxford*

1. The future life in light of the theory of evolution. 2. The doctrine of salvation. *C. E. Beeby, B.D. 1888 Oxford*

1. Holy baptism. 2. Redemption and the salvation consequent upon it. *G. M. Evans, B.D. 1908 Oxford*

A middle Dutch version of the *Speculum humanae salvationis. C. L. T. Hermus, Ph.D. 1937 London, External Degree*

The Mormon doctrine of salvation and the nineteenth century background. *E. L. Clitheroe, Ph.D. 1936 Edinburgh*

1. On the existence of God. 2. On the sufficiency of Holy Scripture for salvation. *R. Martin, B.D. & D.D. 1886 Oxford*

1. The part taken by the Holy Spirit in the salvation of man. 2. The law of Moses: a preparation for the reception of Christianity. *H. A. Spyero, B.D. 1873 Oxford*

1. The preaching of Christ and his Apostles. 2. In what sense and with what limitations is it true to say that correct theological belief is necessary to salvation?. *H. Temple, B.D. & D.D. 1899 Oxford*

1. The problem of pain as treated in the Book of Job. 2. The place of the resurrection ot our Lord in the plan of salvation. *J. A. Evans, B.D. 1907 Oxford*

The relation of St. Paul's ethics to his doctrine of salvation. *H. W. Kerley, Ph.D. 1949 Edinburgh*

The soteriology of John Wesley. *P. W. Hoon, Ph.D. 1936 Edinburgh*

A study in soteriology with special reference to the ransom theory in its origin, historical setting and significance. *C. T. Chapman, Ph.D. 1946 London, King's College*

1. The sufficiency of Holy Scripture. 2. The communion of saints. *S. Phillips, B.D. & D.D. 1889 Oxford*

1. Sufficiency of Holy Scripture for salvation - Article VI. 2. The sacrament of the Lord's Supper - Article XXVIII. *H. Robinson, B.D. & D.D. 1871 Oxford*

The teaching of salvation in the orations of St. Gregory of Nazianzus. *M. Stoyanovitch, B.Litt. 1922 Oxford*

Salvian
The evidence of Salvian for the causes of the fall of the Roman Empire in the West. *W. R. Davies, M.A. 1941 Wales*

Samain, Albert
Albert Samain. *D. E. C. Hall, M.A. 1936 London, Bedford College*

Les confidences de Samain dans le *Jardin de l'Infante. W. E. Jackson, M.A. 1926 Birmingham*

Samaritan Language
Basis for a Samaritan grammar. *M. Mansoor, Ph.D. 1944 Dublin, Trinity College*

Sāmkhya
See Philosophy: India.

Samoa
International relations between Great Britain, Germany and the United States in the Samoan Islands. *L. M. Williams, M.A. 1938 Wales*

International rivalry in Samoa, 1845-1884. *S. R. Masterman, M.A. 1933 London, Bedford College*

Samuel, Edward
Edward Samuel: ei oes a'i waith (Edward Samuel; his age and his work). *J. Edwards, M.A. 1924 Wales*

Sanctification
The doctrine of sanctification in the theology of Karl Barth. *H. W. Tribble, Ph.D. 1937 Edinburgh*

Sanctuary
The influence of sanctuaries on the legislation and history of early Israel. *R. Brinker, M.A. 1944 Manchester*

Sand, George
George Sand as a political theorist. *A. K. Tucker, M.A. 1922 London*

Les compagnons du tour de France par George Sand et les milieux ouvriers sociaux contemporains. *F. Hyslop, M.A. 1923 Manchester*

Sand, George contd.
Les idées politiques de George Sand. *M. H. Birtwell, M.A. 1926 Manchester*

Les romans champêtres de George Sand. *M. B. Gibson, M.A. 1940 Belfast*

The mysticism of George Sand. *L. V. Powles, Ph.D. 1939 London, External Degree*

Sankara
The philosophic system of Sankara. *P. Johanns, B.Litt. 1921 Oxford*

Sankt Stephans Leben
See Havich, of Cologne.

Sannazaro, Jacopo
Sannazaro: a study of his Latin works. *M. T. Heyes, Ph.D. 1933 London, External Degree*

Sanskrit Language
A grammar of the old Kanarese inscriptions, including a study of Sanskrit and Prakrit loanwords. *A. N. P. Narasimhia, Ph.D. 1933 London, School of Oriental and African Studies*

Indo-Aryan loan-words in Malayalam, with a study of some Dravidian loans in Sanskrit. *K. G. Varma, Ph.D. 1934 London, School of Oriental and African Studies*

The Nirukta and the Nighantu. *L. Sarup, Ph.D. 1920 Oxford*

On the interpretation of some doubtful words in the *Atharvaveda. T. Choudhury, Ph.D. 1930 London, School of Oriental and African Studies*

A Rigvedic index: being a complete collection of Sayana's interpretations of Rigvedic words, both when those interpretations are inconsistent with one another and when they differ from the interpretations of western scholars. *C. Kunhan Raja, Ph.D. 1924 Oxford*

Studies in the word-order of Sanskrit prose. *P. Lahiri, Ph.D. 1933 London, School of Oriental and African Studies*

Sanskrit Literature
See also Bhavabhūti; Brahmagupta; Kalidasa; Rāmayana; Vedas; Vetālapañcavimśati.

The Bhagavadgita and the Gospel. *W. G. Mulligan, B.Litt. 1941 Dublin, Trinity College*

Concordance to the *Bhagavad Gita*; supplement: annotated translation of the *Bhagavad Gita. J. R. K. de Lingen, Ph.D. 1948 Edinburgh*

A critical edition of the *Atharvaprātiśakhya* with a comparative study of the *Caturādhyāyikā*, with translation and notes. *S. Kanta, D.Phil. 1937 Oxford*

A critical edition of the *Kapisthala-Katha-Samhita*, first astaka. *R. Vira, Ph.D. 1930 London, School of Oriental and African Studies*

The development of the *Bodhisattva* doctrine in Buddhist Sanskrit literature. *H. Daval, Ph.D. 1930 London, School of Oriental and African Studies*

Early Buddhist ballads and their relations to the older Upanishadic literature. *S. R. M. R. Katre, Ph.D. 1932 London, School of Oriental and African Studies*

Milton's heroic poetry: a comparative study with reference to Sanskrit epic. *V. R. Movva, Ph.D. 1949 Wales*

The place of the *Bhagavadgītā* in Indian thought. *G. Howells, B.Litt. 1906 Oxford*

Principles of the adjudgment of value in literature from Sanskrit sources. *S. Dasgupta, Ph.D. 1948 Cambridge*

Some philosophical problems in the *Bhagavata Purāna. S. Bhattacharya, Ph.D. 1947 London, School of Oriental and African Studies*

Studies in the Sanskrit drama. *V. G. Bhat, Ph.D. 1933 Cambridge*

A study of metres in the older *Upanisads. P. N. Majmudar, M.A. 1930 London, School of Oriental and African Studies*

The Vaikhānasa Dharma Praśna. *S. Sankar, M.A. 1915 London*

Santa Elena Peninsula
Archaeology of the Santa Elena Peninsula in southwest Ecuador. *G. H. S. Bushnell, Ph.D. 1947 Cambridge*

Santa Maria della Salute, Venice
The theory of Roman and Renaissance vault construction, with special reference to the Pantheon, Rome, and Santa Maria della Salute, Venice. *A. G. S. Fidler, M.A. 1936 Liverpool*

Santiago de Compostela
The cult and pilgrimage of St. James of Compostela, Spain, and their effects on the life and thought of the people in the northwestern corner of Spain. *H. W. Howes, M.A. 1938 Wales*

Santiago de Compostela, Galicia, Spain: an attempt to prove that it was a prehistoric settlement. *H. W. Howes, M.Sc. 1924 Wales*

Sarcey, Francisque
Les théories dramatiques de Francisque Sarcey. *E. M. Papenfus, Ph.D. 1926 London*

Sardinia
Anglo-Sardinian relations: January, 1859-March, 1860. *M. Whibley, M.A. 1923 London*

The foreign policy of Charles Albert (1848-9), with special reference to England. *J. P. H. Myres, B.Litt. 1932 Oxford*

The history of Sardinia under the Roman Republic. *E. M. Adams, M.A. 1917 London*

Sarmiento, Félix Rubén Garcia
See Dario, R.

Sassanides
The economic conditions of the Jews in Babylonia under the Sassanides from 200 C.E. to 500 C.E. based on Rabbinical literature: Part 1: agriculture. *J. Newman, Ph.D. 1931 London, External Degree*

Sassoon, Siegfried
A comparative study of the war poetry of Siegfried Sassoon and Wilfred Owen. *M. Palmer, M.A. 1950 Manchester*

Sastras
See Hinduism.

Satan
See Demonology.

Satire
Alexander Pope as a satirist in prose. *D. Broughton, M.A. 1943 London, Birkbeck College*

A century of English prose satire. *S. Powell, M.A. 1914 National University of Ireland*

The chief Roman satirists and the historical value of their works, as a picture of their times. *J. E. S. Turner, M.A. 1918 Birmingham*

The development of satire in prose, 1640-1660. *E. B. Carter, M.A. 1948 Manchester*

The diminutive in Roman *satura. T. T. Thomas, M.A. 1946 Wales*

Dychanau ac ymrysonau'r beirdd Cymreig hyd ddiwdd yr eilfed ganrif ar bymtheg (The satires and contentions of the Welsh bards to the end of the seventeenth century). *O. Thomas, M.A. 1928 Wales*

English political satire, 1800-1830. *J. E. Oxley, Ph.D. 1941 London, Birkbeck College*

Humour, irony, and satire as employed by the young German writers. *E. Goldstücker, B.Litt. 1942 Oxford*

The influence of Greece on Roman *satura. J. H. Jones, M.A. 1933 Wales*

The influence of Roman satire on English literature. *A. H. Hill, M.A. 1910 Birmingham*

L'inspiration satirique d'Auguste Barbier. *E. R. Dowson, M.A. 1921 Leeds*

Literary and philosophical models and sources of the satirical writings of Horace. *W. E. Vine, M.A. 1905 London*

Medieval English satire. *W. E. Smith, M.A. 1914 Birmingham*

The Nuremberg legend of the crocodile. *L. A. Triebel, M.A. 1914 London*

The origin and development of the Roman *satura. E. M. Steuart, M.A. 1914 London*

Peter Pindar: satirist. *H. R. S. Coldicott, B.Litt. 1913 Oxford*

The preparation of a critical edition of a thirteenth century French satirical poem *La Bible de Guiot de Provins*, with a linguistic and literary study and a glossary. *J. Orr, B.Litt. 1913 Oxford*

Samuel Butler as a satirist. *R. O. Harmshaw, M.A. 1928 Birmingham*

Satire in Elizabethan drama. *P. Brady, Ph.D. 1942 National University of Ireland*

Satire in English nineteenth century verse. *T. Job, M.A. 1925 Wales*

Satire contd.
Satire in French literature from 1525 to 1560, with particular reference to the sources and the technique. *C. A. Mayer, Ph.D. 1949 London, University College*

The satire of the Philistine and philistinism in German literature from Sturm und Drang to Heine. *E. G. C. McIlvenna, Ph.D. 1936 Edinburgh*

The satirical element in Petronius. *E. Jenkins, M.A. 1932 Wales*

Satirical poems of Thomas Moore. *M. O'Riordan, M.A. 1946 National University of Ireland*

Servants and satellites: a consideration of some minor Italian social types of the eighteenth century attendant upon the giovin signore of Parini's satire *Il giorno. W. Radcliffe, M.A. 1937 Manchester*

Seventeenth century satire in Irish, with special reference to the Páirlemént Cholinne Tomáis. *H. R. McAdoo, Ph.D. 1940 Dublin, Trinity College*

Sir Thomas More as a satirist in his epigrams and *Utopia. C. A. Thompson, B.Litt. 1947 Oxford*

The social and political satire in the novel of the eighteenth century (1740-1780), with special reference to Fielding and Smollett. *W. E. Roberts, M.A. 1932 Wales*

Social satire and literary burlesque in *Punch*, 1841-1850. *A. Sutcliffe, M.A. 1937 Manchester*

Some aspects of the work of the Anglo-Latin twelfth century satirists: the loan words in Gothic, with some account of the pronunciation of that language. *E. P. Bates, M.A. 1910 London*

Spenser as a satirist. *P. Brady, M.A. 1936 National University of Ireland*

A study of John Marston as a satirist, considered generally and with special reference to contemporary writers. *R. C. Davies, M.A. 1922 London*

A study of Pope's satire. *C. R. Bishop, Ph.D. 1937 London, King's College*

A study of the life and work of Thomas James Mathias, 1754-1835. *W. K. Spicer, M.A. 1946 London, Birkbeck College*

A study of the life and works of Sir John Berkenhead. *S. P. Whitaker, M.A. 1915 London*

A study of verse-satire and epigram, 1595-1603. *S. H. Atkins, Ph.D. 1937 London, External Degree*

The Rolliad and *The Anti-Jacobin* as literary satire. *W. H. Bryant, M.A. 1934 Wales*

Traethawd beirniadol ar fywyd a gwaith John Jones, Glanygors (Critical essay on the life and work of John Jones, Glanygors). *J. H. Morgan, M.A. 1929 Wales*

Verse satire in the reign of Charles II. *P. Cutler, M.A. 1940 London, Queen Mary College*

The verse satires of Daniel Defoe. *A. M. Wilkinson, M.A. 1949 Manchester*

Walter Savage Landor as a satirist and controversialist in the spheres of law and religion. *E. R. Hughes, M.A. 1949 Wales*

Saudi Arabia
See Arabia.

Saul, of Tarsus
See Paul, Saint and Apostle.

Savanna
See Grassland.

Savile, George, Sir
A biographical sketch of Sir George Savile, 1726-1784, with an appendix of his letters. *T. Lightbound, M.A. 1916 Liverpool*

Savings
Factors governing the supply of savings in Great Britain since the war. *E. A. Radice, D.Phil. 1938 Oxford*

Over-saving, or Keynes doctrine. *A. E. M. Duynstee, M.Econ.Sc. 1947 National University of Ireland*

Psychological factors in saving and spending. *G. Wagner, M.A. 1939 London, University College*

A review of savings and savings institutions. *R. G. Barry, M.Comm. 1948 National University of Ireland*

Savonarola, Girolamo
Buaidh na Naomh-Chroiche; aistriú a rinne Bonaventura O'Conchubhair, O.F.M. ar *Triumphus Crucis* le Girolamo Savonarola (*The triumph of the Holy Cross*; a translation by Bonaventura O'Conchubhair, O.F.M. of *Triumphus Crucis* by Girolamo Savonarola). *C. O'Gioballáin, M.A. 1938 National University of Ireland*

Savoy
The annexation of Savoy and Nice by Napoleon III, 1860. *F. R. Scott, B.Litt. 1924 Oxford*

The relations between James VI and I and Carlo Emanuele I, Duke of Savoy. *J. Thompson, Ph.D. 1942 Saint Andrew's*

Sawles Warde
An edition of the Middle English homily *Sawles Warde*, with notes, glossary and full critical and textual apparatus. *R. M. Wilson, M.A. 1931 Leeds*

Saxons, The
The Saxon element in early Irish history. *A. M. Scarre, M.A. 1908 Liverpool*

Scandinavia
Relations, historical and literary, between Ireland and Scandinavia from the ninth century to the thirteenth. *J. I. Young, Ph.D. 1930 Cambridge*

Scandinavian Languages and Literatures
See also Icelandic; Norwegian; Swedish.

A history of the Scandinavian influence on the English language. *E. S. Olszewska, B.Litt. 1934 Oxford*

Relations, historical and literary, between Ireland and Scandinavia from the ninth century to the thirteenth. *J. I. Young, Ph.D. 1930 Cambridge*

A study of the relations between England and the Scandinavian countries in the seventeenth century, based upon the evidence of acquaintance in English writers with Scandinavian languages, literatures, and myths. *M. E. Seaton, M.A. 1920 London*

Scarron, Paul
Paul Scarron et la littérature espagnole: les emprunts et l'influence espagnole dans son oeuvre. *M. H. Gill, M.A. 1932 Leeds*

Scarron and the Realistic Movement of the seventeenth century. *E. Evans, M.A. 1937 Wales*

Scepticism
The function of scepticism in the development of knowledge. *J. M. Bhatt, Ph.D. 1934 London, University College*

Le scepticisme de Prosper Mérimée. *F. B. Shaw, M.A. 1923 Birmingham*

Scheffel, Joseph Victor von
Die Verwertung der Quellen und Motive in Scheffels *Ekkehard* und *Hugideo*. *R. S. Eaton, M.A. 1930 Manchester*

Schelandre, Jean de
The place of Jean de Schelandre in the development of the French tragedy. *H. Smitherman, M.A. 1912 London*

Scheldt, The
Great Britain and the Scheldt, 1814-1839. *S. T. Bindoff, M.A. 1933 London, University College*

Schelling, Friedrich Wilhelm Joseph von
Schelling to Feuerbach. *J. H. Chadwick, M.A. 1910 London*

Scheuchzer, Johan Jacob
Some aspects of the geological work of Johan Jacob Scheuchzer including a translation of his *Herbarium Deluvianum* of 1709. *B. D. Tyrrell, M.Sc. 1934 London, University College*

Schiller, Johann Christoph Friedrich von
Art and the artist in Schiller's poetry: a critical study. *W. Witte, M.A. 1943 London, External Degree*

The female characters in Grillparzer's drama, as contrasted with those in Goethe's and Schiller's. *A. V. Burgess, M.A. 1907 Wales*

Joy and sorrow and the like in the poetic language of Klopstock, Schiller and Goethe. *A. Schwarzchild, Ph.D. 1940 Edinburgh*

Mangan als Übersetzer Schillers. *P. Reilly, M.A. 1946 National University of Ireland*

The treatment of friendship by Schiller and Shakespeare. *E. A. Parker, M.A. 1911 Birmingham*

Schism of Photius
See Church History: Early Church.

Schlegel, Johann Elias
A critical study of Johann Elias Schlegel's aesthetic and dramatic theory. *E. M. Wilkinson, Ph.D. 1943 London, Bedford College*

Schleiermacher, Friedrich Daniel Ernst
The religious philosophy of Herder and Schleiermacher studied in relation to the influence upon them of Leibniz, Spinoza, and Kant. *M. E. Sandbach-Marshall, M.A. 1928 London*

Schleiermacher's ethics. *A. P. Kelso, B.Sc. 1913 Oxford*

Schleiermacher's idea of God. *M. U. Conditt, Ph.D. 1923 Edinburgh*

Schleiermacher, Friedrich Daniel Ernst contd.
Schleiermacher's theory of the nature of religious experience. *K. Edward, Ph.D. 1915 Edinburgh*

Schnitzler, Artur
Arthur Schnitzler. *M. M. Cohen, M.A. 1935 Birmingham*

The work of Arthur Schnitzler. *H. S. Reiss, Ph.D. 1945 Dublin, Trinity College*

Scholasticism
See Theology.

School Medical Service
See Public Health.

Schools
See Education.

Schwob, Marcel
Marcel Schwob et les écrivains anglosaxons, précédé d'un aperçu sur Marcel Schwob et la littérature anglo-saxonne. *D. M. Salmon, M.A. 1927 Leeds*

Science
See also Alchemy; Astronomy; Biology; Botany; Chemistry; Cosmology; Heat; Heredity; Magnetism; Mycology; Phlogiston; Photography; Photosynthesis; Physics; Pneumatics; etc.

The aim and achievement of scientific method: an epistemological essay. *T. P. Nunn, D.Sc. 1907 London*

The ideal of science. *E. O'Mahony, M.A. 1919 National University of Ireland*

Philosophy and science. *J. Feeley, M.A. 1948 National University of Ireland*

The relations of science to philosophy, with special reference to the conceptions of substance and causation. *J. Owen, M.A. 1908 Wales*

Science and monism: an historical and critical discussion of the monistic tendencies in the natural sciences. *W. P. D. Wightman, Ph.D. 1933 London, External Degree*

Some metaphysical aspects of modern physical science. *D. O'Donoghue, M.A. 1945 National University of Ireland*

Science: History
See also Aristotle; Bacon, F., Baron Verulam, Viscount St. Albans; Brownrigg, W.; Descartes, R.; Draper, J. W.; Foucault, L.; Hutchinson, J., Sir; Huxley, T. H.; Mizauld, A.; Neckam, A.; Tennant, S.; Whewell, W.

Contribution à l'étude des écrivains scientifiques en France au seizième siècle. *R. E. Ockenden, M.A. 1935 London, King's College*

The contribution of certain nineteenth century scientists to the development of educational values. *L. W. Chaundy, M.A. 1950 Reading*

The development of natural philosophy as reflected by the English and French Encyclopaedias of the eighteenth century. *L. H. Shave, Ph.D. 1941 London, University College*

The development of scientific and philosophical prose in the seventeenth century. *H. F. Hallesy, M.A. 1949 Wales*

The foundation and early history of the Irish Society, 1609-25. *M. E. Perrott, M.A. 1920 London*

The historical significance of science. *A. J. Whitmarsh, M.Sc. 1941 Birmingham*

Historical survey of theories concerning the elementary nature of matter, with special reference to the four element theory and its overthrow by modern scientific work. *H. A. Reason, M.Sc. 1936 London, External Degree*

Inspiration in science: a study of the genesis of scientific ideas. *E. B. Tanner, M.Sc. 1932 Liverpool*

The medieval Latin versions of the Aristotelian scientific corpus, with special reference to the biological works. *S. D. Wingate, Ph.D. 1931 London, University College*

The relations of history and science. *R. I. Aaron, M.A. 1923 Wales*

Robert Kilwardby's *Tractatus de ortu scientiarum*. *K. F. Delany, B.Litt. 1925 Oxford*

The rôle of men of science in the Czech National Revival Movement, 1790-1848. *J. G. F. Druce, M.A. 1942 London, School of Slavonic and East European Studies*

The scientific method of Pascal. *P. H. J. Lagarde, B.Litt. 1933 Oxford*

Scientific terminology and analogy in Coleridge's poetic theory and practice. *R. Stein, B.Litt. 1946 Oxford*

Studies in natural philosophy of India. *S. P. Desai, M.Sc. 1934 London, University College*

Science: History contd.
Studies in the history of the physical sciences. *N. H. de V. Heathcote, Ph.D. 1947 London, External Degree*

Science: Study and Teaching
A comparative study of the scientific interests of adults and of boys of the same social class. *L. F. R. Simmonds, M.A. 1936 London, Institute of Education*

A comparative study of the curriculum (with special reference to science) of the secondary schools of England and the U.S.A.; and implications for the curriculum of Bombay secondary schools. *F. S. Chothia, M.A. 1948 London, Institute of Education*

A comparison of the free topic method with the experiment demonstration method of teaching science in a senior school. *D. H. T. Horne, M.A. 1942 London, Institute of Education*

The construction of a test of scientific method. *W. Sheard, M.Ed. 1950 Manchester*

The contribution of science teaching to moral training. *G. R. Rumsey, M.A. 1926 London*

The contributions of Robert Hooke to the physical sciences. *J. R. Morgan, M.Sc. 1931 London, University College*

An endeavour to compile a test to ascertain whether a subject possesses particular capacity for science. *J. E. Hawthorne, M.Ed. 1924 Leeds*

External examinations as a factor in the development of science subjects in secondary schools. *F. F. Crossley, M.A. 1947 Liverpool*

The first two years of general science work in a secondary school. *S. Law, M.Ed. 1937 Manchester*

Handwork and science: their contribution to cultural education. *H. Cordingley, M.Ed. 1938 Leeds*

An historical survey of science instruction in Liverpool. *J. A. Hall, M.A. 1930 Liverpool*

History of science teaching in England. *D. M. Turner, Ph.D. 1928 London*

The history of science teaching in English schools since 1870. *F. G. Small, M.Sc. 1926 London*

The history of the teaching of science in Scottish schools. *D. J. S. Sutherland, Ph.D. 1939 Saint Andrew's*

The importance and place of physical sciences in a liberal education, with special reference to the study of physical chemistry in a secondary school curriculum. *R. R. Finney, M.A. 1928 Liverpool*

The influence of science teaching on the development of secondary education, with particular reference to the City of Birmingham. *C. Foster, M.A. 1940 London, King's College*

The interests of boys in the junior forms of a secondary school in relation to the teaching of science. *T. T. Richards, M.Sc. 1939 Wales*

An investigation into the relative value of methods of teaching science in selective central schools. *W. N. Howard, M.Sc. 1930 Sheffield*

An investigation into the teaching of science to non-science specialists at the post-certificate stage, with special reference to the needs of these pupils in later life. *L. G. Smith, M.A. 1934 London, Institute of Education*

The investigation of factors useful in predicting teaching ability with special reference to the teaching of mathematics and science. *W. A. Skinner, M.Ed. 1947 Manchester*

An investigation of the scientific interests of girls aged 12-13 years. *D. A. Glenister, M.A. 1932 London, Day Training College*

Mathematics and natural science in English education. *J. Macwillie, M.A. 1933 Liverpool*

The modern approach in science teaching, having particular reference to courses for secondary school pupils of 11-16 years of age. *W. Atherton, M.Ed. 1939 Manchester*

Natural science as an element in a liberal education: its proper place and treatment in the curriculum of schools. *A. B. Moffat, M.A. 1934 Liverpool*

Natural science in Irish rural schools. *F. J. Magee, M.A. 1921 National University of Ireland*

New type achievement examinations in science. *H. P. Wood, M.Ed. 1941 Manchester*

The place of educational visits in the teaching of science in primary (junior) and secondary schools, and the facilities for such visits in London and other English cities. *A. G. Bastin, M.A. 1948 Bristol*

The position and teaching of science in co-educational schools. *J. Morris, M.A. 1929 Liverpool*

Science: Study and Teaching contd.
Principles of science, with application to certain problems in the teaching of physics and chemistry. *E. E. Jardine, M.A. 1916 Leeds*

The project method applied to the teaching of elementary science in Indian schools. *A. R. Mohajer, M.Ed. 1937 Leeds*

The proper scope of quantitative work in science in secondary schools, with particular reference to chemistry. *W. C. J. Ward, M.A. 1927 London*

Science and observation. *E. R. Dinsmore, M.A. 1935 London, Institute of Education*

Science and scientific method in secondary education. *J. Reilly, M.A. 1914 National University of Ireland*

Science in the secondary school: its adaptation to an appreciation of life. *C. W. Wood, M.Ed. 1933 Manchester*

Science in the senior school. *G. Nunn, M.A. 1937 Liverpool*

Science teaching in schools, with respect to the proposed reorganization of the educational system. *J. C. Murphy, M.A. 1934 Liverpool*

The scientific interests of children in relation to the teaching of science. *L. C. Comber, M.A. 1938 London, Institute of Education*

Scientific method as exemplified in qualitative analysis. *F. W. Turner, M.A. 1928 London*

Scientific method in ancient and medieval times. *E. M. Smewing, M.Sc. 1934 London, University College*

A short thesis on the origin and development of science teaching in English schools. *A. Samad, M.A. 1930 Leeds*

Some problems in the presentation of popular science. *W. E. Flood, Ph.D. 1949 Birmingham*

Some problems in the teaching of science. *A. J. White, M.A. 1926 London*

A survey and criticism of the scope of natural science teaching in girls' secondary schools with proposals for increasing its practical value. *I. Rowland, M.A. 1927 Liverpool*

A survey of science teaching in the senior school. *J. A. Lawton, M.A. 1941 Leeds*

A survey of the history of science teaching in English schools since 1870. *W. J. Parrish, M.Sc. 1926 London*

The teaching of general science in a secondary modern school for boys. *R. Ryder, M.A. 1948 Liverpool*

The teaching of science in elementary schools. *W. Staton, M.A. 1935 Liverpool*

The teaching of science in England during the latter half of the nineteenth century, and Huxley's influence on its development. *W. Hall, M.A. 1931 Sheffield*

The teaching of science in the junior school. *W. R. Fielding, M.Ed. 1932 Manchester*

The teaching of science to the Chinese. *L. G. Morgan, M.A. 1932 London, Day Training College*

The treatment of some scientific activities in the senior school. *C. Bevers, M.Ed. 1935 Leeds*

Science and Religion
1. Miracles in the light of modern science. 2. The Trinitarian formula in the writings of Novatian. *W. Y. Fausset, B.D. 1914 Oxford*

1. The New Testament teaching on the Second Advent considered in the light of subsequent history. 2. The relation of natural science to theology. *P. H. Lester, B.D. 1908 Oxford*

1. The Old Testament in the light of the Egyptian monuments. 2. Natural science as it affects scriptural truth. *A. E. B. Day, B.D. 1908 Oxford*

Prolegomena to the study of the relationship between science and religion. *A. W. Heathcote, Ph.D. 1949 London, External Degree*

Religious certainty: an enquiry into the nature and conditions of religious certainty in relation to the modern scientific attitude. *F. E. Reynolds, Ph.D. 1935 Edinburgh*

A study of English natural theology in the seventeenth century, illustrating some results of the influence of the scientific spirit upon religious thought in England during the earlier years of the Royal Society. *E. B. Vincent, B.Litt. 1927 Oxford*

Scientific Method
See Science.

Scilly Islands
The Scilly Islands during Tudor and Stuart times (approx. 1547-1700). *T. F. G. Matthews, B.Litt. 1943 Oxford*

Scipio, Publius Cornelius (Scipio Africanus)
Some neglected aspects of Scipio Africanus. *H. H. Scullard, Ph.D. 1930 London, University College*

Scotland: Armed Forces
The military forces and the public revenue of Scotland, 1660-1688. *W. B. Gray, Ph.D. 1921 Edinburgh*

The rise of a Scottish navy, 1460-1513. *F. W. Robertson, Ph.D. 1934 Edinburgh*

Scotland: Constitution
The Scottish Privy Council, 1603-1625: its composition and its work. *W. Taylor, Ph.D. 1950 Edinburgh*

Scotland: Economics
The finances of James VI, 1567-1603. *R. S. Brydon, Ph.D. 1925 Edinburgh*

The influence of geographical factors on the economic evolution of Scotland to the beginning of the eighteenth century, mainly as revealed in the development of overseas trade, especially that of the Clyde ports. *J. Walker, Ph.D. 1928 Edinburgh*

Scotland: Foreign Affairs
Franco-Scottish relations from 1290 to 1390. *R. W. Pilgrim, B.Litt. 1936 Oxford*

The French ascendancy in Scotland, 1554-1560. *G. H. C. Burley, M.A. 1929 Birmingham*

The Irish in Scotland, 1798-1845. *J. E. Handley, M.A. 1941 National University of Ireland*

The last years of a frontier: a history of the borders during the reign of Elizabeth. *D. L. W. Tough, B.Litt. 1920 Oxford*

The relations between England and Scotland during the minority of Alexander III and during the Barons' War. *W. A. Cane, M.A. 1923 Manchester*

Scoto-Irish intercourse in the latter part of the sixteenth century. *H. F. Kelleher, M.A. 1931 National University of Ireland*

Scotland: Geography
Some aspects of the early historical geography of Scotland. *H. Fairhurst, M.A. 1933 Liverpool*

Scotland: History
See also Albany, John Stewart, Duke of, Regent of Scotland; Charles II, King of England; Jacobites; James I, King of England, and VI of Scotland; James II, King of England, and VII of Scotland; Moray, R., Sir.

The administration of Scotland during the reigns of Charles II and James VII. *W. B. Gray, B.Litt. 1920 Oxford*

Foreign influences on Scottish politics, 1578-1582. *H. M. Wallace, M.A. 1932 London, Westfield College*

Henry VII's relations with Scotland and Ireland, 1485-98. *A. E. Horsfield, Litt.D. 1932 Dublin, Trinity College*

The military forces and the public revenue of Scotland, 1660-1688. *W. B. Gray, Ph.D. 1921 Edinburgh*

Musicians of the Scottish Reformation, with special reference to Crown policy c.1560-1650. *J. McQuaid, Ph.D. 1949 Edinburgh*

The organization of the English occupation in Scotland, 1296-1461. *D. W. H. Marshall, B.Litt. 1925 Oxford*

Scotland and the Wars of the Roses, 1435-85. *C. Macrae, D.Phil. 1939 Oxford*

Scotland under Lauderdale. *E. E. B. Thomson, Ph.D. 1928 Saint Andrew's*

Scottish colonial schemes prior to the Union. *G. P. Insh, D.Litt. 1922 Glasgow*

Service of the Scottish mercenary forces in Ireland. *G. A. Hayes-McCoy, M.A. 1932 National University of Ireland*

The service of the Scottish mercenary forces in Ireland, from 1565 to 1603, with an account of the mercenary system in Ireland and of its effect on Scottish history. *G. A. Hayes-McCoy, Ph.D. 1934 Edinburgh*

The sources for the history of the Highlands. *J. A. Maclean, Ph.D. 1939 Aberdeen*

Strategy and tactics in medieval Scotland. *J. D. Forbes, Ph.D. 1927 Edinburgh*

The union of England and Scotland considered with regard to the action of English statesmen and the development of opinion in England. *P. W. Skirrow, B.Litt. 1927 Oxford*

Scotland: Parliament
The General Assembly of the Kirk as the rival of the Scottish Parliament, 1560-1618. *E. E. MacQueen, Ph.D. 1927 Saint Andrew's*

Scotland: Social History
An enquiry into the social and political state of Scotland as reflected in the *Basilicon Doron* of James I. *W. Falconer, Ph.D. 1925 Edinburgh*

Scottish culture in the seventeenth century (1603-1660). *K. N. Colvile, Ph.D. 1930 Edinburgh*

Scott, Walter, Sir
German influence on Scott. *H. Burgis, M.A. 1916 London*

Goethe's influence on Byron and Scott. *M. J. Roberts, M.A. 1915 Wales*

The historical novel in Scott and his imitators. *G. N. Goodman, M.A. 1914 Birmingham*

The revival of early literature in England and Scotland from Percy to Scott, 1765-1802. *A. E. Jensen, Ph.D. 1933 Edinburgh*

Scott the interpreter, or Scott and the novel. *H. Murphy, Ph.D. 1931 Glasgow*

Scott's use of fact in the novels: a study in the relation of fact and fiction. *G. S. Morris, M.A. 1938 Wales*

Sir W. Scott and H. Heine: an enquiry into the relations between the two writers. *F. T. Smallwood, M.A. 1910 Birmingham*

Sir Walter Scott. *B. J. Doyle, M.A. 1938 National University of Ireland*

Sir Walter Scott: his influence on life and letters. *A. Smart, Ph.D. 1938 Aberdeen*

Sir Walter Scott and the drama with some account of the theatre in Edinburgh. *W. G. Dustan, Ph.D. 1933 Edinburgh*

Sir Walter Scott in Germany. *F. E. Gauntlett, M.A. 1920 London*

The terror novel and Sir Walter Scott: a study in literary influence. *K. M. Lobb, Ph.D. 1939 London, External Degree*

Walter Scott et le roman frénétique. *R. W. Hartland, D.Litt. 1927 Birmingham*

Scott, William Bell
Life and works of William Bell Scott. *J. W. Roche, M.A. 1930 London, University College*

Scottish Highlands
A social and economic history of the Higlands of Scotland from the Revolution of 1689 to the Forty-five. *H. Holdsworth, M.A. 1936 Leeds*

The sources for the history of the Highlands. *J. A. Maclean, Ph.D. 1939 Aberdeen*

Transformation of the Highlands of Scotland. *H. J. Ewart, Ph.D. 1935 Aberdeen*

Scottish Language, Gaelic
Allan Ramsay and the Scottish vernacular revival (circa seventeenth and eighteenth centuries). *H. Lister, M.A. 1934 London, Birkbeck College*

The Gaelic dialect of North Uist. *J. Macpherson, Ph.D. 1945 Edinburgh*

Gaelic dialects. *G. Henderson, B.Litt. 1899 Oxford*

The pronouns and pronominal adjectives in early Scots down to 1603. *M. Wattie, B.Litt. 1927 Oxford*

The Scots vernacular revival. *J. M. G. Alexander, M.A. 1913 London*

Studies in the language of Bellenden's *Boece*. *E. A. Sheppard, Ph.D. 1936 London, University College*

Scottish Literature
See also English Literature, and references there to individual writers.

English influences on the written form of the language and on the literature of Scotland, 1500-1625. *M. A. Bald, B.Litt. 1925 Oxford*

The French background of Middle Scots literature. *J. M. Smith, Ph.D. 1933 Edinburgh*

A study of the influence of the Bible on the life and literature of Scotland in the seventeenth century. *D. Anderson, Ph.D. 1932 Glasgow*

Scottish Reformed Church
The worship of the Scottish Reformed Church, 1550-1638. *W. McMillan, Ph.D. 1925 Edinburgh*

Scotus, John Duns
See Duns Scotus, J.

Screens, Rood
Figure paintings on rood screens in the churches of Norfolk and south Devonshire. *A. M. Baker, Ph.D. 1938 London, Courtauld Institute of Art*

Scribe, Augustine Eugène
A contribution to the study of the historical comedies of Scribe. *I. C. Thimann, Ph.D. 1934 London, University College*

Scribes
See Judaism.

Scripture
See Bible.

Sculpture
Accessory elements in Chinese Buddhist sculpture to the end of the sixth century. *J. H. Lindsay, M.A. 1938 London, Courtauld Institute of Art*

An account of pedimental composition from the earliest monuments to the Parthenon. *B. Tilly, M.A. 1932 London, Bedford College*

The chariot group of the Mausoleum. *J. B. K. Preedy, M.A. 1909 London*

The dating of early Hellenistic statues. *A. W. Lawrence, B.Litt. 1925 Oxford*

The decoration of Norman baptismal fonts in relation to English twelfth century sculpture. *R. Marcousé, Ph.D. 1940 London, Courtauld Institute of Art*

Dedalus: a study of Dorian plastic art in the seventh century B.C. *R. J. H. Jenkins, Ph.D. 1936 Cambridge*

A descriptive and bibliographical list of Irish figure sculptures of the early Christian period, with a critical assessment of their significance. *E. H. L. Sexton, B.Litt. 1940 Oxford*

Features distinctive of Buddhist sculpture in China. *W. Y. Willetts, M.A. 1946 London, Courtauld Institute of Art*

Greek sculpture and painting. *D. J. Finn, M.A. 1910 National University of Ireland*

Greek sculpture of the period between Pheidias and Praxiteles. *B. Ashmole, B.Litt. 1924 Oxford*

The interpretation of the pediments of the Parthenon. *L. M. Willis, M.A. 1910 London*

The metopes of the treasury of the Athenians at Delphi. *W. R. Agard, B.Litt. 1923 Oxford*

Middle Egyptian stelae in the British Museum to the end of the Middle Kingdom. *M. F. L. Macadam, D.Phil. 1935 Oxford*

The natural basis of sculptural forms. *R. C. Calvert, M.A. 1936 Belfast*

The Oxford school of sculptors from 1550-1800. *J. E. K. Esdaile, B.Litt. 1935 Oxford*

The problem of Greek and Egyptian influences in Ptolemaic architecture and sculpture. *I. Noshy, Ph.D. 1934 London, University College*

The relationship between classic sculpture and architecture. *G. H. Gatley, M.A. 1925 Manchester*

Sculpture in Britain, with special reference to its nature as a community art between 500 B.C. and 1900 A.D., being an analysis of the progress of community psychological states in Britain and its relation to the development of British sculpture. *R. H. Seddon, Ph.D. 1946 Reading*

A study of Anglo-Saxon stone sculpture in central and southern England. *F. Cottrill, M.A. 1931 London, University College*

Wooden figure sculpture in Ireland until the 17th century. *C. MacLeod, M.A, 1944 National University of Ireland*

Sea
See also History, Naval; Maritime Law; Shipbuilding; Shipping; Smuggling; Territorial Waters; Transport; Voyages and Travels.

Canamhain chois fhairrge (Dialects of the sea side). *T. MacD. De Bhaldraithe, Ph.D. 1942 National University of Ireland*

The concept of sea in psycho-therapy. *R. W. Wilde, Ph.D. 1945 Dublin, Trinity College*

German sea poetry. *M. F. Liddell, D.Phil. 1925 Birmingham*

Greek poetry and the sea. *J. N. Kemp, M.A. 1938 London, University College*

The maritime vocabulary of the middle high German poem *Kudrun. K. Cuthbert, M.A. 1945 Belfast*

Report on hydrographical investigations in the Faroe-Shetland Channel and the northern part of the North Sea during the years 1904-1905. *A. J. Robertson, D.Sc. 1906 Saint Andrew's*

The sea and seafaring as described in the *Islendinga Sögur. P. J. B. Griffiths, M.A. 1935 Wales*

The sea in education. *J. E. de C. Ireland, Ph.D. 1950 Dublin, Trinity College*

Sea contd.
The sea in English poetry. *J. F. O'Mahony, M.A. 1942 National University of Ireland*

The sea in French poetry from 1870 to the present day. *D. M. Vinnicombe, M.A. 1928 London*

The sea in Old English poetry. *W. J. F. Davies, M.A. 1948 Wales*

The sea in Shelley. *T. A. G. Dowling, M.A. 1946 National University of Ireland*

The sea in the poetry of Victor Hugo. *R. Hemingway, M.A. 1917 Liverpool*

The sea novel in French literature, 1830-1870. *H. F. Collins, M.A. 1924 London*

Sea terms in early English literature. *W. J. Redbond, M.A. 1934 London, King's College*

Sebou, River
The influence of physical conditions upon human life in the Sebou Basin. *W. Fogg, M.A. 1928 Manchester*

Secondary Education
See Education, Secondary.

Securities
See also Stocks and Shares.

Liens accessory of securities. *R. Pilkington, LL.M. 1928 Leeds*

The nature and effect of floating securities. *F. S. Clark, LL.D. 1922 London*

Sedley, Charles, Sir
The life and works of Sir Charles Sedley. *V. de S. Pinto, D.Phil. 1927 Oxford*

Seinte Marherta
See Margaret, Saint, Queen of Scotland.

Selby
Two obedientiary rolls of Selby Abbey. *B. Smith, M.A. 1949 Leeds*

Self
The concept of self from Descartes to Kant, with some reference to immortality. *E. G. Braham, Ph.D. 1935 London, King's College*

The conception of the self in Locke, Berkeley and Hume. *M. P. Evans, M.A. 1934 Wales*

A critical examination of Kant's treatment of the self. *D. Davies, M.A. 1920 Wales*

An enquiry into the philosophical significance and justification of self-respect. *R. V. Feldman, Ph.D. 1937 London, University College*

An examination of Bosanquet's doctrine of self-transcendence. *R. E. Stedman, Ph.D. 1930 Edinburgh*

Factors affecting the reliability of self-estimates in answering personality questionnaires. *S. M. Mohsin, Ph.D. 1948 Edinburgh*

Kant's view of our knowledge of the self. *N. Bandyopadhyay, Ph.D. 1932 London, University College*

The nature of the self: an historical survey from Descartes to James, with a constructive essay. *A. W. Massey, M.A. 1935 Liverpool*

The problem of self and immortality. *E. G. Braham, B.A. 1925 Bristol*

Problems raised by Kant's treatment of the self. *D. Davies, Ph.D. 1923 Glasgow*

Self-Consciousness
The conception of self-consciousness in pre-Kantian and Kantian philosophy. *A. A. Iqbal, M.A. 1924 London*

Recent psychological theories of self-consciousness. *J. C. Bacon, M.A. 1923 Wales*

The relation of morality to self-consciousness in the philosophy of T. H. Green. *L. Golomb, M.A. 1946 Sheffield*

Seljuks, The
Contributions to the study of Seljūq institutions. *A. K. S. Lambton, Ph.D. 1939 London, School of Oriental and African Studies*

A critical study of the sources for the history of the Saljūqs of Persia and Syria. *V. A. Hamdani, D.Phil. 1938 Oxford*

The decline of the Saljuqid Empire (1092-1117). *Sanaullah, Ph.D. 1935 London, School of Oriental and African Studies*

Semantics
See Language.

Semikhah
See Ordination (Jewish).

Semitic Languages
See also Accadian; Arabic; Aramaic; Hebrew; Samaritan.

Semitic Languages contd.
The origin of the Semitic alphabet. *C. E. Goddard, Ph.D. 1927 Edinburgh*

Rashi as philologist. *J. Pereira-Mendoza, M.A. 1939 Manchester*

Semitisms in the New Testament in the light of later popular Greek. *R. McKinlay, Ph.D. 1927 Glasgow*

Senchus Mór, The
Celtic law: with special reference to the *Senchus Mór* and the *Book of Aicill,* and a critical examination of the traces of an early Gaelic system of law in Scotland. *J. Cameron, Ph.D. 1935 Glasgow*

Seneca, Lucius Annaeus
The Elizabethan translations of Seneca's tragedies. *E. M. Spearing, M.A. 1912 London*

The Roman conception of tragedy as exemplified especially in Seneca. *R. A. Browne, M.A. 1927 Wales*

A Roman of the early Empire: Lucius Annaeus Seneca. *J. C. McQuaid, M.A, 1918 National University of Ireland*

Seneca the philosopher as a source for Roman private life. *J. F. Leddy, B.Litt. 1934 Oxford*

Seneca the younger as a critic of his age. *P. J. Lee, M.A. 1934 Manchester*

Seneca's philosophy. *E. G. Hughes, M.A. 1908 Birmingham*

The stoicism of Lucius Annaeus Seneca, with special reference to ethics. *E. A. Hopkins, M.A. 1943 London, Bedford College*

The stoicism of Seneca. *S. W. Edge, M.A. 1927 Liverpool*

The *Suasoriae* of Seneca the Elder. *W. A. Edward, D.Litt. 1924 Glasgow*

Senegal
Problems of the development of French West Africa, as illustrated by Senegal and the Ivory Coast. *M. A. el M. M. Sharkawy, M.A. 1931 Liverpool*

The struggle for power on the Senegal and Gambia, 1660-1713. *T. G. Stone, M.A. 1921 London*

Senior, Nassau William
The place of Nassau William Senior (1790 to 1864) in the development of economic thought. *M. E. Bowley, Ph.D. 1936 London, External Degree*

Sensory Perception
See Perception.

Septuagint
See Bible: Versions.

Serbia
Diplomatic relations between England and Serbia from the return of Milos to the death of Michael, 1859-1867. *E. F. Robinson, M.A. 1925 London*

The international relations of Serbia 1848-1860. *E. F. Malcolm-Smith, Ph.D. 1926 Cambridge*

Serbia in international politics from the insurrection of Herzegovina (1875) to the Congress of Berlin (1878). *M. D. Stojanovic, Ph.D. 1930 London, King's College*

Sermons
See also Aelfric; Andrewes, L.; Aphraates; Blair, H.; Donne, J.; Erskine, J.; Erskine, R.; Healy, J.; Jacob, of Serug; Jofroi, de Waterford; John Fisher, of Rochester, Saint; King, H.; Macarias, of Egypt, Saint; Melvill, H.; Sully, M. de; Taylor, Jeremy.

English preaching, 1221-1293. *J. M. Sweet, B.Litt. 1950 Oxford*

English pulpit oratory from Andrewes to Tillotson: a study of its literary aspects. *W. F. Mitchell, B.Litt. 1931 Oxford*

English pulpit oratory in its relation to literary style and thought, 1680-1850. *D. K. Somerville, Ph.D. 1943 Aberdeen*

Etude sur l'éloquence de la chaire française du 17e siècle. *A. W. Lineham, M.A. 1905 Birmingham*

Group psychology in its bearing on homiletics. *F. H. Caldwell, Ph.D. 1934 Edinburgh*

Medieval preaching in England as illustrated by the period c.1350 to 1450. *G. R. Owst, Ph.D. 1924 London*

Middle English sermons from the Worcester chapter: ms. F 10, edited. *D. M. Grisdale, M.A. 1936 Leeds*

The north English homily collection, with a study of the tales contained therein. *G. H. Gerould, B.Litt. 1901 Oxford*

Sermons contd.
Preaching in eighteenth century Scotland: a comparative study of the extant sermons of Ralph Erskine, 1685-1752; John Erskine, 1721-1803; and Hugh Blair, 1718-1800. *C. R. McCain, Ph.D. 1949 Edinburgh*

Seanmóirí na Gaeilge (Irish sermons). *M. A. O'Spolláin, M.A. 1948 National University of Ireland*

Secular instruction and incidental information in English vernacular sermon literature of the later Middle Ages, 1150-1450. *W. Lister, M.Ed. 1945 Manchester*

The sermon as persuasion in late seventeenth century France and England: a study of Bossuet, Bourdaloue, Barrow, and South. *H. Hammond, Ph.D. 1950 Cambridge*

A study of the dialect of the Old English homilies in the twelfth century ms. Vespasian D XIV. *F. H. T. Williams, M.A. 1945 London, King's College*

Servitudes
International servitudes: rights in foreign territory. *F. A. Vali, Ph.D. 1932 London, School of Economics and Political Science*

Servitudes in the law of Scotland: principles, sources and influences which have affected the law. *T. A. Ross, Ph.D. 1932 Edinburgh*

Seth, Andrew
See Pringle-Pattison, A. S.

Settle, Elkanah
Elkanah Settle: his life and works. *W. E. Gibson, M.A. 1938 Wales*

Settlements
See also Landnámabók; Population; Villages; and under the subheading Social History of individual countries; also under Land (Law); Land Tenure.

Climatic aspect of the permanent settlement of the white man in the tropics: an essay in acclimatization. *G. J. Cons, M.A. 1929 London*

The economic possibilities of land settlement. *A. W. Menzies-Kitchin, Ph.D. 1939 Cambridge*

Settlements: Great Britain
Celtic settlement and agriculture in central Sussex. *M. Coleman, M.A. 1944 London, External Degree*

The distribution and functions of urban settlements in East Anglia. *R. E. Dickinson, Ph.D. 1934 London, University College*

Distribution of settlements in the Solway Firth Plain. *J. M. Houston, B.Sc. 1946 Oxford*

The economic and social results of statutory land settlement in the south of England. *W. F. Darke, Ph.D. 1936 London, University College*

The evolution of settlement in the Teify Valley. *E. Jones, M.Sc. 1945 Wales*

The factors which have influenced settlement and the movements of population within the plain of Nottingham. *H. M. Keating, Ph.D. 1933 London, External Degree*

The form and function of settlements in relation to types of farming in England and Wales, with an analysis of specific examples chosen from the west Midlands and elsewhere. *J. East, Ph.D. 1947 London, University College and London, External Degree*

A functional classification of settlement in Breckland. *J. Carter, B.Litt. 1950 Oxford*

The geography of rural settlement in the Durham region. *H. Thorpe, M.Litt. 1937 Durham*

The geography of the Moray Firth lowlands, with special reference to distribution of settlements, and with special attention to the tract between the rivers Ness and Spey; Inverness and Cullen. *F. H. W. Green, M.Sc. 1935 London, School of Economics and Political Science*

The growth of settlement in the Swansea Valley. *J. M. Davies, M.A. 1942 Wales*

The influence of physical geography upon the history of settlement and distribution of population in Sussex. *W. H. Parker, B.Sc. 1939 Oxford*

Iron age settlements in Kintyre: Kildonan Bay. *H. Fairhurst, Ph.D. 1940 Glasgow*

The Norse settlements in northwest Yorkshire. *J. T. Day, M.A. 1939 Liverpool*

The occupation of the counties Northumberland, Durham, Cumberland, and Westmorland from the fourth to the eighth centuries, as revealed by the archaeological and historical evidence. *G. S. Keeney, B. Litt. 1935 Oxford*

Settlements: Great Britain contd.
The older settlements of north Northumberland: a study in geography and history. *C. P. M. Olsen, M.A. 1947 London, University College*

The origin of settlements in the Cheshire Plain: an essay in historical geography. *W. J. Varley, M.A. 1934 Wales*

The planning and conditions of settlement in Wales during the Dark Ages and medieval period, from first-hand knowledge obtained by means of archaeological investigations. *T. Lewis, M.Sc. 1927 Wales*

Rural settlement in East Cheshire: a study in historical geography. *P. F. Kenworthy, M.A. 1949 Manchester*

Rural settlements and the distribution of rural population in Northamptonshire. *E. E. Field, M.Sc. 1931 London, External Degree*

The scarplands of the Wiltshire-Gloucestershire-Somerset borders: a regional study, with particular reference to urban and rural settlement. *I. G. Youldon, M.A. 1945 London, King's College*

Settlement types and their distribution in northeast Yorkshire. *H. Jessop, M.Sc. 1938 Leeds*

A study of rural settlement in Somerset. *B. M. Swainson, M.A. 1932 London, External Degree*

The West Penwith Peninsula of Cornwall, considered from the point of view of archaeological evidences concerning development of settlements. *D. H. Watkins, M.A. 1930 Wales*

The Wey River Basin: a study of human settlement and economic development in the valley, with particular reference to present day conditions. *G. A. T. F. Hooper, M.A. 1935 London, Birkbeck College*

Settlements: Other Countries
The colonization and settlement of Manchuria. *A. Gaskell, M.A. 1932 Liverpool*

Developmental policy and agricultural settlement in southeastern Australia. *J. Andrews, Ph.D. 1937 Cambridge*

The distribution of population and the development of settlements in Ceylon. *A. Ginigé, M.A. 1930 London, School of Economics and Political Science*

Early settlement in the South Island of New Zealand, with special reference to the North and East. *R. K. Wilson, M.A. 1947 London, University College*

The economics of the settlement of the Prairie Provinces of Canada, 1900-1931. *S. Common, Ph.D. 1933 London, School of Economics and Political Science*

A history of the settlement of the western firths of Iceland. *F. Mosby, M.A. 1931 Leeds*

Immigration and settlement in the province of Dalmatia from the first Roman contacts to the death of Commodus. *A. J. N. Wilson, D.Phil. 1949 Oxford*

Santiago de Compostela, Galicia, Spain: an attempt to prove that it was a prehistoric settlement. *H. W. Howes, M.Sc. 1924 Wales*

The settlement of Palestine in the Bronze age and its connexion with geographical and human factors. *B. S. J. Isserlin, B.Litt. 1948 Oxford*

Settlements and churches in Nova Scotia, 1749-1776: the origin of Protestant Churches in relation to settlement, from the founding of Halifax to the American Revolution. *I. F. Mackinnon, Ph.D. 1930 Edinburgh*

Settlements in the United Provinces of Agra and Oudh. *E. Ahmad, Ph.D. 1949 London, School of Economics and Political Science*

Some geographical factors in the history of the Punjab from 712 A.D. to 1605 A.D. with special reference to river control of settlement. *M. I. R. Khan, Ph.D. 1930 London, University College*

Severn, River
The development of industry and trade in the Middle Severn Valley. *T. W. Birch, M.Sc. 1933 London, External Degree*

Sévigné, Marie de Rabutin-Chantal, Marquise de
Les lectures de Madame de Sévigné. *H. T. Lawrence, M.A. 1934 Leeds*

Sexual Relationships
See also Adultery.

A contribution to the psychology of common sexual perversions. *C. Glen, M.D. 1939 Glasgow*

The English criminal and criminal ecclesiastical law of sex morality and its effect upon the organization of the family. *G. May, LL.D. 1933 London, School of Economics and Political Science*

Sexual Relationships contd.
An enquiry into the relation between sexual opportunity and cultural condition among uncivilised peoples. *J. D. Unwin, Ph.D. 1931 Cambridge*

The nature of sex: a study of the metaphysical and moral character of sex. *N. Patrinacos, D.Phil. 1950 Oxford*

Origins of the Christian sex ethic. *D. R. Mace, Ph.D. 1942 Manchester*

Prostitution and sex promiscuity in several countries at the present time. *G. M. Hall, M.A. 1932 Liverpool*

Sex problems in boys' secondary schools. *S. M. Price, M.Ed. 1940 Manchester*

Woman versus man: a study of the relationships and differences between the sexes as a source of tragedy in the life and chief dramas of F. Hebbel. *H. J. Pargeter, M.A. 1950 Birmingham*

Shabtis
A study of shabti-figures, with special reference to the Manchester collection. *M. S. Palmer, Ph.D. 1945 Manchester*

Shadwell, Thomas
A study of Thomas Shadwell. *D. M. Walmsley, M.A. 1924 London*

Shafi'i, Muhammad ibn Idris al-
The *Risalah* of Shafi'i. *M. Eliash, B.Litt. 1919 Oxford*

Shaftesbury, Earls of
See Cooper.

Shah Abdul-Latif, of Bhit
Shah Abdul Latif of Bhit, his poetry, life and times: a study of literary, social and economic conditions in eighteenth century Sind. *H. T. Sorley, D.Litt. 1938 Aberdeen*

Shahgahan, Emperor
History of Shahgahan of Dihli. *B. P. Saksena, Ph.D. 1931 London, School of Oriental and African Studies*

The reign of the Emperor Shah Jehan. *N. L. Ahmed, B.Litt. 1927 Oxford*

Shahrastani, Al
The scholasticism of Christianity and of Islam so far as they are represented by the *Summa contra gentiles* of St. Thomas Aquinas and the *Nihayatu-l-igdam fi ilmil-kalam* of Al Shahrastani. *A. Guillaume, B.D. & D.D. 1934 Oxford*

Shakespeare, William
A comparison between the tragedies and histories of Shakespeare with special reference to the heroes. *L. Watson, M.A. 1910 Birmingham*

Dramatic creation as exemplified in Shakespeare's plays. *H. Brown, D.Litt. 1927 Glasgow*

Elizabethan pirated dramas, with special reference to the 'bad' quartos of *Hamlet, Henry V, Romeo and Juliet*: with an appendix on the problem of *The Taming of the Shrew*. *G. I. Duthie, Ph.D. 1939 Edinburgh*

Evil and world order in Shakespeare's tragedies. *J. G. Hanrahan, M.A. 1947 National University of Ireland*

The first folio. *J. C. Deary, M.A. 1916 National University of Ireland*

The genesis of Shakespeare's *Hamlet*. *A. Scotland, Ph.D. 1930 Glasgow*

Hamlet dans les oeuvres françaises depuis 1700 jusqu'à la *Préface du Cromwell*. *A. Wood, M.A. 1920 Liverpool*

The indebtedness of Shakespeare and English writers to Montaigne and his *Essays*. *D. J. E. Williams, M.A. 1917 Wales*

The influence of Shakespeare on the eighteenth century drama (1700-1780). *M. A. Pink, M.A. 1920 London*

King Lear, a study. *P. F. Donovan, M.A. 1928 National University of Ireland*

Marlowe's influence on Shakespeare and *Richard III*. *J. Gately, M.A. 1912 National University of Ireland*

Normality of Shakespeare. *T. Tuomey, M.A. 1931 National University of Ireland*

The problems arising out of Shakespeare's *Troilus and Cressida*. *A. G. Lucas, M.A. 1913 Wales*

The relation of Shakespeare to Lyly. *E. M. King, M.A. 1908 London*

Shakespeare and Molière, with special reference to comedy. *E. C. Kimpton, M.A. 1908 London*

Shakespeare and the comic spirit. *E. J. C. Large, M.A. 1923 Birmingham*

Shakespeare, William contd.
Shakespeare and the idea of justice. *M. V. H. Parker, B.Litt. 1950 Oxford*

Shakespeare and the Italian 'novellieri'. *M. M. Wright, Ph.D. 1950 Manchester*

Shakespeare and the neo-romance. *E. C. Pettet, B.Litt. 1944 Dublin, Trinity College*

Shakespeare dans la vie et l'oeuvre de Hector Berlioz. *B. Spencer, M.A. 1936 Leeds*

Shakespeare's dramatic technique in the opening scenes of his tragedies. *P. Weil-Norden, M.A. 1950 Birmingham*

Shakespeare's final vision: the *Tempest. R. T. O'Kelly, M.A. 1941 National University of Ireland*

Shakespeare's philosophy of love. *W. F. Luckman, M.A. 1929 Birmingham*

Shakespeare's prose. *M. O'Dwyer, M.A. 1930 National University of Ireland*

Shakespeare's prose. *D. L. Bligh, M.A. 1921 National University of Ireland*

Shakespeare's use of astrological terms, with an introduction on astrology and popular astrological knowledge of the period. *D. S. Collins, M.A. 1932 London, King's College*

Some aspects of Shakespeare's philosophy of life. *V. F. Honniball, M.A. 1911 Birmingham*

The winter's tale: a study. *S. L. Bethall, M.A. 1950 Wales*

The tragedy of *Julius Caesar. M. Macmillan, D.Litt. 1902 Birmingham*

The treatment of friendship by Schiller and Shakespeare. *E. A. Parker, M.A. 1911 Birmingham*

The women in Shakespeare's plays: a critical study from the dramatic and psychological points of view, and in relation to the development of Shakespeare's art. *A. M. Mackenzie, D.Litt. 1924 Aberdeen*

Shakespeare, William: Adaptations
The adaptations of Shakespeare by Jean-François Ducis; with special reference to the influence of the classical tradition on French tragedy. *S. E. F. Macdonald, Ph.D. 1929 Edinburgh*

Alfred de Vigny's translation of Othello: its place in the history of French drama. *M. E. O'Dowd, M.A. 1917 National University of Ireland*

Ducis and De Vigny considered as interpreters of Shakespeare. *R. J. Evans, M.A. 1909 Wales*

L'appréciation de Shakespeare en France: avec mention particulière des traductions et des représentations de Macbeth, 1700 à 1900. *M. Brown, M.A. 1948 Birmingham*

The *Othello* of Alfred de Vigny as compared with that of Shakespeare. *M. Whiteley, M.A. 1920 Manchester*

Shakespeare adaptations from Dryden to Garrick. *D. Corvesor, Ph.D. 1926 London*

Shakespeare, William: Criticism
Coleridge on Shakespeare: an essay in correlation. *P. H. Williamson, M.A. 1948 Manchester*

Editors of Shakespeare. *D. M. Southall, M.A. 1923 Birmingham*

Eighteenth century literary criticism up to Dr. Johnson, with particular reference to the criticism of Shakespeare, Milton and the metaphysical poets. *M. J. Ince, M.A. 1948 Manchester*

English Shakespearian criticism in the eighteenth century. *H. S. Robinson, M.Litt. 1930 Cambridge*

The French critics of Shakespeare, with a bibliography of works dealing with the history of Shakespearean study, criticism, and representation in France. *E. A. Craddock, M.A. 1914 London*

The history of the literary criticism of Shakespeare in Germany. *E. M. R. Stadler, B.Litt. 1912 Oxford*

L'appréciation de Shakespeare en France: avec mention particulière des traductions et des représentations de Macbeth, 1700 à 1900. *M. Brown, M.A. 1948 Birmingham*

Ludwig Tieck's Shakespearean criticism. *H. Moses, M.A. 1939 London, University College*

Malone as Shakespearean commentator. *M. Hanly, M.A. 1913 National University of Ireland*

Othello in Shakespeare criticism. *M. Carroll, M.A. 1946 National University of Ireland*

Shakespeare criticism in France in the nineteenth century. *F. T. Barton, B.Litt. 1919 Oxford*

Shakespeare illustration and design. *W. M. Merchant, M.A. 1950 Wales*

Shakespeare, William: Criticism contd.
A sketch of the progress of English Shakespearian study, with special reference to the nineteenth century. *M. D. Belgrave, M.A. 1908 London*

A study of William Richardson, with special reference to his Shakespearian criticism. *M. Boulton, B.Litt. 1948 Oxford*

A survey of English Shakespearean criticism, 1907-1939. *F. E. Hawdon, M.A. 1948 London, External Degree*

Victor Hugo comme critique de Shakespeare, avec une étude spéciale de son oeuvre intitulée *William Shakespeare. G. Davies, M.A. 1915 Wales*

The work of Theobald and his predecessors on the text of Shakespeare. *H. M. King, Ph.D. 1940 London, External Degree*

Shakespeare, William: Production
The acting tradition in England between 1800 and 1830, with special reference to Shakespeare's plays. *G. E. Batchelor, Ph.D. 1939 London, King's College*

The influence of the boy actor on Shakespeare's dramatic technique. *W. R. Davies, B.Litt. 1938 Oxford*

Shakespeare in Serbia. *V. Popovitch, Ph.D. 1925 London*

Shakespeare on the London stage in the days of Coleridge, Hazlitt, and Lamb. *A. B. Staniforth, B.Litt. 1933 Oxford*

Shakespeare on the modern English stage. *F. M. Warner, Ph.D. 1928 London*

Shakespeare's actors: their importance and possible influence upon Shakespeare as a playwright. *J. M. Whittington, M.A. 1948 Manchester*

Shakspeare in India: a general survey of Shakespeare's vogue in India. *S. Gupta, Ph.D. 1924 London*

A short history of Shakespearean production. *J. Huang, M.Litt. 1937 Cambridge*

Shakespeare, William: Sources
A comparison of Shakespeare's use of Holinshed and Plutarch in his English and Greek-Roman history plays. *E. A. Donnan, Ph.D. 1950 Manchester*

Shakespeare's debt to classical antiquity. *G. C. Hingley, M.A. 1912 Birmingham*

Shakespeare's debt to Latin poetry. *P. C. Brown, M.A. 1912 Birmingham*

Shakespeare's history. *M. McD. Bodkin, M.A. 1922 National University of Ireland*

The study of Shakespeare's sources from Langbaine to Malone. *H. O. E. Andersson, B.Litt. 1949 Oxford*

Shammai
The schools of Shammai and Hillel with special reference to their influence upon the development of the Jewish *Halachah. B. Unterman, M.A. 1937 Liverpool*

Shan States
Religious cults and social structure of the Shan States of the Yunnen-Burma frontier. *J. K. Tien, Ph.D. 1948 London, School of Economics and Political Science*

Shand, Alexander Faulkner
A study of joy based on the theory found in Shand's *Foundations of character. D. M. Grierson, M.A. 1917 London*

Shanghai
The International Settlement at Shanghai. *Y. Ch'en, Ph.D. 1940 London, School of Economics and Political Science*

The problem of the European child in Shanghai (China). *M. A. Hadden, M.D. 1933 Dublin, Trinity College*

Shantinekatan
Tagore at Shantinekatan, or Sir Rabindranath Tagore's educational experiment at Shantinekatan. *H. S. D. Chaturvedi, M.Ed. 1929 Leeds*

Shantung
A regional study of Shantung and its significance in the life of north China. *P. C. Tsou, M.A. 1939 Liverpool*

Shares
See Stocks and Shares.

Sharp, James, Archbishop
The life of James Sharp, archbishop of St. Andrews. *A. T. Miller, Ph.D. 1940 Edinburgh*

Sharp, John, Archbishop
Life and times of John Sharp. *A. T. Hart, B.D. 1944 Cambridge*

Sharqiya
The people of Sharqiya: their racial history, serology, physical characters, demography and conditions of life. *A. M. Ammaer, Ph.D. 1940 Manchester*

Shaw, George Bernard
Bernard Shaw in Germany: the first phase. *G. A. Davis, M.A. 1930 London, King's College*

Shaw's contribution to the theory and practice of modern English drama. *T. F. Bennett, M.A. 1929 Wales*

The social background of Shaw's early plays. *M. M. Cooper, M.A. 1947 Sheffield*

Sheehan, Patrick Augustus
The creative work of Canon Sheehan. *T. J. F. McElligott, M.A. 1942 National University of Ireland*

Sheep Farming
See Livestock Industry.

Sheffield
The career of A. J. Mundella, with special reference to his Sheffield connections. *M. Higginbotham, M.A. 1941 Sheffield*

The human geography of Sheffield and the surrounding district. *M. McInnes, B.Litt. 1923 Oxford*

Vocational guidance and selection, with special reference to the industries and occupations of Sheffield. *V. H. Hoskins, Ph.D. 1926 Sheffield*

Sheffield, John, Duke of Buckingham
An edition of the dramatic works of John Sheffield, Duke of Buckinghamshire. *B. B. Banerjee, B.Litt. 1937 Oxford*

Shelburne, William Petty, 2nd Earl of
The career of the Earl of Shelburne, 1760-1783. *E. M. Scrimiger, M.A. 1909 Liverpool*

Lord Shelburne and British imperialism, 1763-83. *R. A. Humphreys, Ph.D. 1933 Cambridge*

Shelley, Percy Bysshe
Byron and Shelley considered as types of the revolutionary spirit. *J. J. Jackson, M.A. 1912 London*

The Christian element in Shelley's religious thought. *E. A. Buttler, M.A. 1919 Birmingham*

Classical and medieval inspiration in the poetry of Coleridge, Keats and Shelley. *H. A. Needham, M.A. 1921 Birmingham*

A comparison of Shelley and Li Po as poets of nature. *C. Li, B.Litt. 1936 Oxford*

The crusade of Shelley against tyranny. *F. Whitehouse, M.A. 1922 Birmingham*

The development of the political ideas of Wordsworth and Shelley, with special reference to their conception of freedom. *G. O. Roberts, M.A. 1938 Wales*

The early development of Shelley. *W. S. Ashley, M.A. 1908 Birmingham*

The influence of the French revolutionary theorists (Voltaire, Rousseau, D'Holbach etc.) upon Shelley. *G. C. Rosser, M.A. 1939 Wales*

The influence of William Godwin on Shelley. *H. P. Kingston, M.A. 1932 Birmingham*

The life of Percy Bysshe Shelley, 1792-1818. *W. E. Peck, D.Phil. 1922 Oxford*

Mysticism in the poetry of Wordsworth, Shelley and Tagore. *B. Sengupta, B.Litt. 1947 Dublin, Trinity College*

Pantheism in English poetry, with special reference to Wordsworth and Shelley. *J. I. Wensley, M.A. 1917 Wales*

A psychological study of the poetical imagination of Wordsworth and Shelley. *E. M. E. Haydon, M.A. 1914 London*

A review of the criticisms of Keats and Shelley in *The Edinburgh, The Quarterly* and *Blackwood's. A. Campbell, M.A. 1929 Liverpool*

The sea in Shelley. *T. A. G. Dowling, M.A. 1946 National University of Ireland*

Shelley and Plato: a study in literary relationship. *G. Coope, M.A. 1931 Birmingham*

Shelley in Italy, and his use of Italian literature. *W. P. Scott, B.Litt. 1925 Oxford*

Shelley's outlook on life as revealed in his poetry. *E. M. Cox, M.A. 1916 National University of Ireland*

Shelley's philosophic thought, with special reference to his view of immortality. *E. L. Robertson, M.Litt. 1941 Cambridge*

Shelley's translations from Greek. *B. Farrington, M.A. 1917 National University of Ireland*

Shelley, Percy Bysshe contd.
Wordsworth, Coleridge, Byron, Shelley and the French Revolution. *P. R. Griffin, M.A. 1925 National University of Ireland*

Shenstone, William
1. The letters of William Shenstone. 2. William Shenstone: a chapter in eighteenth century taste. *M. Williams, D.Litt. 1939 London, External Degree*

William Shenstone: a chapter in eighteenth century taste. *M. Williams, Ph.D. 1928 London*

Shepherd of Hermas
See Hermas.

Sheppey, Isle of
The Isle of Sheppey and the Swale. *K. R. MacDonald, M.A. 1949 London, King's College*

Shepstone, Theophilus, Sir
Culture contact between Bantu and European in South-East Africa as illustrated by the life of Sir Theophilus Shepstone. *D. M. Goodfellow, Ph.D. 1932 London, School of Economics and Political Science*

Sheridan, Richard Brinsley Butler
Sheridan. *M. McGoris, M.A. 1941 National University of Ireland*

Sherlock, Thomas, Bishop
Thomas Sherlock, Bishop of Bangor, Salisbury and London, 1728-61: his work for Church and State. *E. F. Carpenter, M.A. 1934 London, King's College*

Shetland Islands
Historical geography of the Shetland Islands. *A. C. O'Dell, M.Sc. 1933 London, King's College*

Shiels, George
George Shiels as the exponent of modern Irish comedy. *J. J. Kelly, M.A. 1951 National University of Ireland*

Shi'ism
See Islam: Sects.

Shintoism
Konko-kyo: a sect of modern Shintoism. *E. M. Clark, Ph.D. 1924 Edinburgh*

A review of recent work on primitive Japanese Shinto. *G. B. Stigant, M.Sc. 1936 London, School of Economics and Political Science*

Shipbuilding
An economic history of shipbuilding and marine engineering. *W. S. Cormack, Ph.D. 1930 Glasgow*

The history of iron shipbuilding on the Queen's Island up to July, 1874. *D. Rebbeck, Ph.D. 1950 Belfast*

The shipbuilding industry on the east and south coasts of England in the fifteenth century. *M. A. S. Hickmore, M.A. 1937 London, School of Economics and Political Science*

The shipyards of Britain - a geographical and historical analysis. *D. Rebbeck, B.Litt. 1946 Dublin, Trinity College*

Shippen, William
William Shippen as an opposition leader (1714-43). *C. T. R. Buckley, B.Litt. 1930 Oxford*

Shipping
Changes in the economic structure of the British shipping industry since the Great War. *B. Bramwell, M.A. 1939 Liverpool*

The co-ordination of market forces in ocean tramp shipping, with special reference to the period 1920-1939. *H. Gripaios, M.Sc. 1949 London, School of Economics and Political Science*

A description of the trade and shipping of Hull during the seventeenth century, and the trade organizations and kindred societies within the port. *W. J. Davies, M.A. 1937 Wales*

An examination of the factors which link Bristol dock policy with the development of the tramp shipping of the port, 1840-1890. *J. R. Stevens, M.A. 1940 Bristol*

Irish maritime development. *B. Collender, M.Econ.Sc. 1946 National University of Ireland*

Irish maritime development. *M. J. Byrne, M.Econ.Sc. 1946 National University of Ireland*

Irish maritime development. *R. B. Walsh, M.Econ.Sc. 1946 National University of Ireland*

Labour in the merchant service 1850-1920. *A. McGeogh, M.Com. 1921 Birmingham*

The operation of the English Navigation Acts during the eighteenth century. *E. H. Rideout, M.A. 1931 Liverpool*

Port developments and commerce of Newport, 1835-1935. *E. M. E. Davies, M.A. 1938 Wales*

Shipping contd.
The shipmoney levies under Charles I, and their influence upon local feeling. *S. E. Foster, M.A. 1914 London*

A study of a rural and maritime community in the nineteenth century, with special reference to the relation between agriculture and shipping. *D. Thomas, M.A. 1928 Liverpool*

Shirley, James
A critical edition of James Shirley's *The court secret*. *M. S. Sundaram, B.Litt. 1934 Oxford*

A critical edition of *St. Patrick for Ireland* (1640) by James Shirley. *H. M. Macmullan, B.Litt. 1931 Oxford*

An edition of the poems of James Shirley as contained in the 1646 *Poems*, Bodl. ms. Rawl. Poet. 88 and B.M. Add. ms. 33998. *R. G. Howarth, B.Litt. 1931 Oxford*

James Shirley. *J. P. O'Donnell, M.A. 1939 National University of Ireland*

James Shirley, dramatist. *M. Breen, M.A. 1936 National University of Ireland*

Shōin, Yoshida
Yoshida Shōin, forerunner of the Meiji restoration. *H. J. J. M. van Straelen, Ph.D. 1949 Cambridge*

Shops
See Retail Trade.

Shore, John, Sir
The Governor-Generalship of Sir John Shore, 1793-8. *A. W. Mahmood, B.Litt. 1939 Oxford*

Short Stories
See Fiction.

Shorthand
English pronunciation in the seventeenth and eighteenth centuries: and essays upon shorthand and literature. *W. Matthews, Ph.D. 1934 London, Birkbeck College*

A study of the pronunciation of English during the seventeenth and eighteenth centuries as shown by the contemporary writers of shorthand. *W. Matthews, M.A. 1931 London, Birkbeck College*

Shrewsbury
Great Civil War in Shrewsbury. *H. Beaumont, M.A. 1934 Sheffield*

The medieval borough of Shrewsbury. *J. G. Speake, M.A. 1939 Wales*

Shrewsbury, historical geography and present survey. *G. J. Fuller, M.A. 1940 London, External Degree*

Shrewsbury, Charles, Duke of
See Talbot, C., Duke of Shrewsbury.

Shudra, The
A history of the education of the Shudra untouchables before and under the British rule in India, c. 2000 B.C. to 1947. *R. S. Kalota, M. Ed. 1950 Durham*

Shuibhne
See Romances.

Siam
See Thailand.

Sicily
The government of Sicily under Philip II of Spain: a study in the practice of empire. . *H. G. Königsberger, Ph.D. 1949 Cambridge*

Sidmouth, Devon
Certain aspects of coast erosion in the English Channel with special reference to the coast-defence problems of the town of Sidmouth, Devon. *W. P. Baron, M.A. 1931 London, External Degree*

Sidney, Algernon
The political ideas of Algernon Sidney. *E. T. Davies, M.A. 1940 Wales*

Sidney, Philip, Sir
A comparison of the treatment of romantic motives in Sir Philip Sidney's *Arcadia* and in typical earlier and later romances. *M. Moens, M.A. 1912 London*

The influence of Italian literature on Spenser and Sidney. *E. W. Cedervall, M.A. 1920 Wales*

The literary programme of the early *Arcadia* with special reference to poetic diction. *V. Simcock, M.A. 1950 Liverpool*

Sir P. Sidney's *Astrophel and Stella*. *A. M. Seal, M.A. 1917 Birmingham*

Sidonius Apollinaris
In Apollinaris Sidonii *Carmina quaestiones et notae exegeticae*. *W. H. Semple, M.A. 1929 Belfast*

Quaestiones exegeticae Sidonianae. *S. H. Semple, Ph.D. 1927 Cambridge*

Sidonius Apollinaris contd.
Sidonius Apollinaris and his age. *C. E. Stevens, B.Litt. 1930 Oxford*

Sierra Leone
See also Mende, The.

British policy in relation to Sierra Leone, 1808-1852. *G. R. Mellor, M.A. 1935 London, King's College*

The human geography of Sierra Leone. *R. W. Steel, B.Sc. 1939 Oxford*

The Sierra Leone patois: a study of its growth and structure, with special reference to the teaching of English in Sierra Leone. *H. A. E. Sawyerr, M.Ed. 1940 Durham*

Sifre
See Jewish Law.

Signoret, Emmanuel
Emmanuel Signoret: l'homme et l'oeuvre. *I. F. Marsden, M.A. 1927 Leeds*

Sikhavalañda
An examination of Sikhavalañda. *M. D. Ratnasuriya, Ph.D. 1931 London, External Degree*

Sikhism
See also Singh, Ranjit.

Anglo-Sikh relations (1839-49). *K. C. Khanna, Ph.D. 1932 London, School of Oriental and African Studies*

Philosophy of Sikhism. *S. S. Gyani, Ph.D. 1938 London, School of Oriental and African Studies*

Silk Industry
The Coventry silk-ribbon industry from the introduction of the use of the Dutch engine loom (c.1770) to the Cobden Commercial Treaty (1860). *H. Miles, B.Litt. 1930 Oxford*

Economic organization of the export trade of Kashmir and Indian silks, with special reference to their utilization in the British and the French markets. *R. C. Rawlley, M.Sc. 1918 London*

Economics of the silk industry: a study in industrial organization. *R. C. Rawlley, D.Sc. 1919 London*

Geographical basis of natural silk industry of West Pennines. *C. L. Mellowes, M.A. 1933 London, External Degree*

The silk industry in London, 1760-1830, with special reference to the condition of the wage-earners and the policy of the Spitalfields Acts. *W. M. Jordon, M.A. 1931 London, University College*

Sillon
Une histoire du *Sillon*. *M. B. Purcell, M.A. 1931 Birmingham*

Silver
Lead and silver industry in Wales, 1558-1750. *L. Jones, B.Litt. 1924 Oxford*

The silver market during and since the war. *R. N. Vaidya, M.Sc. 1923 London*

Simonides
Simonides of Ceos. *R. E. Ker, M.A. 1930 Belfast*

Sin
See also Atonement; Penance; Evil; Forgiveness. For Original Sin, see Creation and the Fall.

1. Baptism and the forgiveness of sins. 2. Absolution and the forgiveness of sins. *T. Field, B.D. & D.D. 1897 Oxford*

1. Christ descended into hell. 2. After we have received the Holy Ghost, we may depart from grace given, and fall into sin, and by the grace of God we may arise again, and amend our lives. *J. W. Caldicott, B.D. & D.D. 1874 Oxford*

1. The Christian conception of sin. 2. The idea of atonement in the Old Testament. *L. Pullan, B.D. & D.D. 1921 Oxford*

1. The Christian doctrine and some non-Christian theories of sin. 2. The nature and reaonableness of prayer. *H. T. Pinchin, B.D. 1895 Oxford*

1. The Christian idea of sin and original sin. 2. The doctrine of the Trinity in the early Fathers. *E. J. Bicknell, B.D. & D.D. 1923 Oxford*

The concept of sin in the great religions of the East. *G. C. Barber, Ph.D. 1938 London, Richmond College*

The doctrine of sin in the theology of John Bunyan. *J. S. W. Irvine, Ph.D. 1930 Edinburgh*

The evolutionary theory of sin. *A. J. Long, B.D. 1948 Oxford*

1. The Incarnation. 2. The Christian doctrine of sin. *H. V. S. Eck, B.D. & D.D. 1924 Oxford*

1. Man's solution of the problem of sin. 2. God's solution of the problem of sin. *A. P. Shepherd, B.D. 1924 Oxford*

Sin contd.
Mental therapy and the forgiveness of sins: a clinical view of the results of sin, with psychological studies of religious leaders as approaches to the application of the work of Christ in the experience of forgiveness. *A. P. Guiles, Ph.D. 1934 Edinburgh*

The new psychology and the Christian doctrine of sin. *C. E. Barbour, Ph.D. 1927 Edinburgh*

The origin of the sense of sin in man. *E. Silsby, M.Sc. 1921 London*

The psychological approach to the problem of sin. *E. J. Johanson, B.Litt. 1929 Oxford*

The seven deadly sins in English literature. *D. V. Ives, M.A. 1931 London, Westfield College*

1. Sin: 'H αμαρτία εστιν η ανομί α. 2. The atonement: 'Ο Θεόσ αγάπη εστίν. *W. J. Oldfield, B.D. & D.D. 1907 Oxford*

1. Some heads of a Christian answer to the neo-Buddhist theosophy. 2. Some considerations, scriptural and modern, concerning sin. *T. S. Lea, B.D. 1905 Oxford*

Stiúraitheoir an pheacaigh (The director of the sinner). *D. O'hEalnighthe, M.A. 1943 National University of Ireland*

A study in the phenomena of prostration arising from a conviction of sin. *A. McNaughton, Ph.D. 1937 Edinburgh*

Sind
The British conquest of Sind. *K. A. Chishti, M.A. 1938 London, School of Oriental and African Studies*

Muslim rule in Sind in the eighth, ninth and tenth centuries. *A. A. Puri, Ph.D. 1936 London, School of Oriental and African Studies*

Shah Abdul Latif of Bhit, his poetry, life and times: a study of literary, social and economic conditions in eighteenth century Sind. *H. T. Sorley, D.Litt. 1938 Aberdeen*

Singh, Ranjit
The rise to power of Ranjit Singh. *M. S. Cheema, B.Litt. 1925 Oxford*

Singing
See also Music.

Singing disability in school children. *T. Pollock, M.Ed. 1950 Durham*

A study of backwardness in singing among school children. *A. E. Fieldhouse, Ph.D. 1937 London, Institute of Education*

Variations in the normal range of children's voices: variations in range of tone audition: variations in pitch discrimination. *T. Anderson, Ph.D. 1937 Edinburgh*

Sinhalese Language
An historical examination of Sinhalese case-syntax from the beginning of the tenth century to the end of the thirteenth century A.D. *C. E. Godakumbura, Ph.D. 1945 London, External Degree*

Phonology of the Sinhalese inscriptions up to the end of the tenth century A.D. *B. P. F. Wijeratne, Ph.D. 1944 London, School of Oriental and African Studies*

Sinhalese Literature
The state of society in Ceylon as depicted in the *Saddharma-ratnavaliya* and other Sinhalese literature of the thirteenth century. *M. B. Ariyapala, Ph.D. 1949 London, School of Oriental and African Studies*

Sinhalese, The
The Sinhalese in Ceylon: a study in historical and social geography. *D. D. M. Gooneratne, M.A. 1930 Liverpool*

Sinu, River
A geographical description of the basin of the River Sinu, in the State of Colombia, South America, with special reference to the geographical conditions of selected areas. *A. W. Guest, B.Sc. 1930 Oxford*

Sir Degrevant
See Romances.

Sir Percyvell of Gales
See Romances.

Sir Tristrem
See Romances.

Sirkars, The
Revenue administration of the Sirkars under the E.I.C. down to 1802. *L. Sundaram, Ph.D. 1930 London, School of Oriental and African Studies*

Sivasvāmin
An edition of the *Kapphinābhyudaya* of Sivasvāmin with a discussion of the Prākrit exemplified in it. *G. Shankar, B.Litt. 1933 Oxford*

Sixtus V, Pope
The family and early life of Sixtus V. *W. T. Selley, M.A. 1934 Bristol*

Skelton, John
The humanism of John Skelton, with special reference to his translation of Diodorus Siculus. *H. L. R. Edwards, Ph.D. 1938 Cambridge*

John Skelton and the early Renaissance: a biographical and critical study. *I. A. Gordon, Ph.D. 1936 Edinburgh*

The life and works of John Skelton. *H. L. R. Edwards, M.A. 1934 Wales*

The poetical works of John Skelton, Laureate, 1460-1529. *H. Harvey, M.A. 1912 London*

William Dunbar and John Skelton. *J. W. Musson, M.A. 1939 Bristol*

Skill
The relation between the simultaneous constituents in an act of skill. *C. E. Beeby, Ph.D. 1927 Manchester*

Slate Industry
A general survey of the slate industry of Caernarvonshire and Merionethshire. *W. M. Richards, M.A. 1933 Liverpool*

A history of the slate quarryman in Caernarvonshire in the nineteenth century. *G. Ellis, M.A. 1931 Wales*

The slate industry in north Wales, with special reference to Merioneth. *E. L. Lewis, M.A. 1917 Wales*

The slate industry of north Wales: a study of the changes in economic organization from 1780 to the present day. *D. D. Pritchard, M.A. 1935 Wales*

Slavery
Abolitionist societies (1787-1838). *E. C. Toye, M.A. 1936 London, King's College*

British measures for the suppression of the slave trade from the west coast of Africa, 1807-1833. *E. I. Herrington, M.A. 1923 London*

Colonial policy and slavery in South Africa, 1806-26. *I. E. Edwards, B.Litt. 1937 Oxford*

A comparative study of the forms of slavery. *F. B. Steiner, D.Phil. 1949 Oxford*

The connection of Bristol with the African slave trade. *A. M. Richards, M.A. 1923 Bristol*

The conomic aspect of the abolition of the West Indian slave trade and slavery. *E. E. Williams, D.Phil. 1938 Oxford*

The development of abolitionism, 1807-23. *T. M. Birtwhistle, M.A. 1948 London, Birkbeck College*

The effect of the slave emancipation in British Guiana and Trinidad. *J. R. Maclean, B.Litt. 1931 Oxford*

The emancipation of the slaves in Jamaica and its results. *W. M. Cousins, Ph.D. 1928 London*

Expositions of: II Kings xxii: reforms of Josiah; Acts vii: the defence of Stephen; The Epistle to Philemon: St. Paul's treatment of slavery. *A. E. Joscelyne, D.D. 1898 Oxford*

Freedmen in the early Roman Empire. *A. M. Duff, B.Litt. 1926 Oxford*

Great Britain and the suppression of the Cuban slave trade, 1817-1865. *L. H. Cawte, M.A. 1934 London, King's College*

The Greek, the barbarian and the slave. *H. Harris, M.Litt. 1929 Cambridge*

History of slave compensation, 1833-45. *R. E. P. Wastell, M.A. 1933 London, King's College*

Ireland and U.S. slavery. *J. Maher, M.A. 1929 National University of Ireland*

The Khedive Ismail and slavery in the Sudan. *M. F. Shukry, Ph.D. 1935 Liverpool*

The slave in ancient comedy. *F. K. Beese, M.A. 1939 Wales*

The slave trade and Anglo-American relations, 1807-1862. *A. T. Milne, M.A. 1930 London, University College*

The slave trade at Mauritius, 1811-29. *M. K. Jones, B.Litt. 1936 Oxford*

The slave trade in European diplomacy, 1814-1818. *E. Smallpage, M.A. 1922 Liverpool*

Slavery and its abolition, particularly with regard to England's efforts for its extinction to the year 1846, and with especial reference to the West Indies. *W. Whalley, M.A. 1926 Manchester*

Slavery in ancient Mesopotamia and its bearing on the Old Testament. *I. Rapaport, M.A. 1939 London, King's College*

Slavery contd.
Slavery in Pharaonic Egypt. *A. M. Bakir, D.Phil. 1946 Oxford*

Slavery in the first two centuries of the Roman Empire. *R. H. Barrow, B.Litt. 1926 Oxford*

The slaves of Greek comedy compared with those of Plautus and Terence. *W. G. Williams, M.A. 1911 London*

The slave's *peculium* in Rome and the protection afforded to it by Roman law before the year 180 A.D. *E. M. Thomas, M.A. 1927 Wales*

The social and economic condition of the unfree classes in England, from the twelfth to the fourteenth century, with special reference to the eastern counties. *N. Neild, M.A. 1908 London*

Some problems connected with the influence of the freedmen upon the civil service under Claudius. *P. R. Hiscock, M.A. 1947 Reading*

Slavophilism
See also Panslavism.

Russia and the West in the teaching of the Slavophiles: a study of a romantic ideology. *N. V. Riasanovsky, D.Phil. 1949 Oxford*

Sleep (Psychology)
The nature of sleep: a critical survey of the principal theories. *A. Carr, B.Litt. 1949 Oxford*

Slum Clearance
See Town and Country Planning.

Small County, Co. Limerick
A survey of the antiquities in the Barony of Small County, Co. Limerick. *M. J. O'Kelly, M.A. 1941 National University of Ireland*

Smart, Christopher
Christopher Smart. *C. B. Abbott, B.Litt. 1927 Oxford*

Smell
A statistical study of individual preferences with olfactory stimuli. *M. M. Davies, M.A. 1938 London, University College*

Smith, Adam
The Physiocrats and Adam Smith. *W. F. Keane, M.A. 1915 National University of Ireland*

Smith, Harry George Wakelyn, Sir
Sir Harry Smith in South Africa. *E. B. Hawkins, B.Litt. 1923 Oxford*

Smith, Henry
Early English puritanism as exemplified in the life and works of Henry Smith. *D. E. Nelson, Ph.D. 1939 Edinburgh*

Smith, Sydney
Sydney Smith: his works and their significance. *J. Murphy, M.A. 1935 Liverpool*

Smith, Thomas
See Smythe, T., Sir.

Smith, William
William Smith, American loyalist, 1728-83. *M. S. Sinclair, B.Litt. 1928 Oxford*

Smollett, Tobias George
Smollett as critic of social conditions in eighteenth century England. *W. Eastwood, M.A. 1949 Sheffield*

Smollett's reputation and influence in the eighteenth century, chiefly as novelist. *W. A. G. Scott, B.Litt. 1948 Oxford*

The social and political satire in the novel of the eighteenth century (1740-1780), with special reference to Fielding and Smollett. *W. E. Roberts, M.A. 1932 Wales*

Smuggling
Jurisdiction in marginal seas over foreign smuggling vessels and subjects. *W. E. Masterson, LL.D. 1928 London*

The law of contraband. *I. I. Dollond, B.Litt. 1941 Dublin, Trinity College*

The law of contraband of war. *H. R. Pyke, LL.D. 1916 London*

The law of contraband with reference to transit to neutral ports. *T. Baty, D.C.L. 1901 Oxford*

Smyrna
A history of Smurna from the earliest times to 180 A.D. *C. J. Cadoux, M.A. 1911 London*

Smythe, Nicholas
Mr. Customer Smythe, customer of the Port of London, 1570-89. *L. L. S. Lowe, B.Litt. 1950 Oxford*

Smythe, Thomas, Sir
Thomas Smith, merchant adventurer. *S. G. Evans, M.A. 1949 Leeds*

Snowdonia
The medieval boroughs of Snowdonia. *E. A. Lewis, M.A. 1912 Wales*

Soap Industry
Some studies in the history of soap manufacture. *F. W. Gibbs, M.Sc. 1937 London, University College*

Social Credit Party
A history of the social credit movement. *E. E. McCarthy, M.A. 1947 Leeds*

Social Democratic Party
The rise and decline of the German Social Democratic Party. *N. D. Herman, M.A. 1949 Sheffield*

Social History
See Sociology.

Social Reform
See also Sociology.

Capitalist enterprise and social progress. *M. H. Dobb, Ph.D. 1925 London*

The influence of recent changes in the social environment on the outlook and habits of individuals, with special reference to mining communities in south Wales. *W. H. Davies, M.A. 1933 Wales*

John Ruskin as social reformer. *F. U. Stribley, M.A. 1925 Birmingham*

Mrs Gaskell, with special reference to the social reform novel, 1830-1850. *J. T. Lancaster, M.Litt. 1927 Cambridge*

Recent philosophy and recent social movements. *J. W. Scott, D. Phil. 1919 Glasgow*

Social reform in New Zealand. *C. M. P. Brown, M.Sc. 1938 Cambridge*

Unacknowledged motivations in some social movements. *P. C. Hopkins, Ph.D. 1927 London*

Social Security
See also Employment; Insurance; Social Services.

Social insurance, a study of the destitution caused by the early death of the wage earner. *M. Sclare, M.A. 1923 Leeds*

Social legislation and theory in Great Britain from 1906 to 1914. *T. W. Price, B.Litt. 1930 Oxford*

Social security and Ireland. *T. J. Clancy, M.Econ.Sc. 1951 National University of Ireland*

Social security in south Rhodesia. *F. T. Russell, Ph.D. 1947 London, External Degree*

Unemployment insurance: a study of schemes of assisted insurance. *J. G. Gibbon, D.Sc. 1911 London*

Social Services
See also Social Security; Welfare Economics.

Aspects of taxation and expenditure in the United Kingdom, 1890-1914, with special reference to the growth of the social services. *E. M. Bowen, M.A. 1934 Wales*

Effects of recent social legislation in Ireland on industry. *J. A. O'Brien, M.Comm. 1942 National University of Ireland*

Fifty years of public health and social welfare in Bath, 1896-1945. *J. F. Blackett, M.A. 1949 Bristol*

The relation of theology to social theory and action in the Christian Social Movement in England from 1877 to 1914. *E. V. Newman, B.Litt. 1936 Oxford*

Social service in the Irish Free State. *P. C. Byrne, M.A. 1937 National University of Ireland*

Social services in Eire. *E. Donnelly, Ph.D. 1943 Dublin, Trinity College*

Social services in Ireland. *P. M. Dunne, M.Econ.Sc. 1948 National University of Ireland*

A statistical examination of post-war developments of selected public social services on Merseyside. *H. Silcock, M.A. 1941 Liverpool*

Social Surveys
See also Housing; Town and Country Planning.

Survey of the effects of the 1939-45 war and of the immigration of former city-dwellers on a Midland township. *W. M. Whiteley, M.Com. 1948 Birmingham*

Tregaron: a sociological study of a Welsh rural community. *E. Jones, Ph.D. 1947 Wales*

Socialism
See also Fabian Society; Labour Party; National Socialism; and Considérant, V.; Owen, R.; Proudhon, P. J.

The development of English socialism from 1848 to 1884. *M. John, M.A. 1934 London, Bedford College*

Fabian thought and social change in England from 1884-1914. *R. D. Howland, Ph.D. 1942 London, School of Economics and Political Science*

Socialism contd.
An inquiry into the nature, extent and implications of the socialism of the French Revolution, during the period of the revolutionary government. *J. C. Searle, Ph.D. 1935 London, School of Economics and Political Science*

Nationalist currents in nineteenth-century socialist doctrines. *V. T. C. E. F. Egger, Ph.D. 1949 London, School of Economics and Political Science*

Socialism and romanticism in France, 1830-1848. *H. J. Hunt, D.Phil. 1931 Oxford*

The socialistic tendencies of Emile Zola as expressed in his literary works. *F. S. McCutcheon, M.A. 1929 Wales*

The socialistic theory of Anatole France as expressed in his literary works. *J. H. Thomas, M.A. 1928 Wales*

Sociétés Anonymes
See Companies.

Society of Friends
See Friends, Society of.

Society of Jesus
See Jesuits.

Socinianism
See also Godwin, W.

The life and work of the Rev. John Owen D.D., the Puritan divine, with special reference to the Socinian controversies of the seventeenth century. *R. G. Lloyd, Ph.D. 1942 Edinburgh*

The rise and spread of Socinianism in England before 1689. *H. J. McLachlan, D.Phil. 1949 Oxford*

Sociology
See also Alcohol; Christianity and Political and Social Questions; Fiction; Leisure; Population; Poverty; Race Relations; Settlements; Statistics; and Année Sociologique; Aristotle; Balzac, H. de; Dickens, C.; Durkheim, E.; Kingsley, C.; Morris, W.; Robertson, J. M.; Shaw, G. B.; Wesley, J.

The assessment of social attitudes of school children. *C. D. Butler, M.A. 1949 London, Institute of Education*

A critical examination of Dilthey's theory of the historical and social studies only. *H. A. Hodges, D.Phil. 1932 Oxford*

The ethical and social doctrines of Bishop Berkeley. *S. Azeemullah, M.A. 1924 London*

An examination, combining the techniques of anthropology and social psychology, of the integration of western society, with special reference to the social re-adaptation of ex-prisoners of war, and the methods used to facilitate this re-adaptation. *C. T. W. Curle, B.Sc. 1947 Oxford*

An examination of some recent theories of social progress. *T. B. Bottomore, M.Sc. 1949 London, School of Economics and Political Science*

Herbert Spencer's theory of social justice. *J. E. Asirvatham, Ph.D. 1925 Edinburgh*

A history of social and economic theory in Palestine down to the monarchy. *D. W. Davies, M.A. 1938 Wales*

An investigation of social attitudes in school children. *H. E. Crocket, Ph.D. 1940 London, University College*

An investigation, using the discussion group technique, of some of the social relationships of secondary modern school children. *D. Wilson, M.A. 1949 Liverpool*

Les idées sociales de Charles Péguy. *U. Riordan, M.A. 1931 National University of Ireland*

Moral attitudes in relation to upbringing, personal adjustment and social opinion. *S. Brahmachari, Ph.D. 1938 London, University College*

The place of social and economic history in education. *M. V. Gregory, M.Ed. 1929 Manchester*

The place of the individual in some sociological theories. *H. G. Woodford, B.A. 1924 Bristol*

Problems of method in the social sciences. *A. S. Nash, M.Sc. 1938 London, School of Economics and Political Science*

The relation between the individual good and the social good, in Plato. *C. E. Faithfull, M.A. 1915 London*

The relation of social and educational theory at the opening of the nineteenth century. *G. J. Kenwrick, M.A. 1927 London*

Security, authority and society; an ethnological introduction into sociology. *E. Manheim, Ph.D. 1937 London, School of Economics and Political Science*

Sociology contd.
Social criticism in the Hungarian novel (1620-1850). *A. Rubin, Ph.D. 1945 London, External Degree*

The social determination of ideologies: being a study of a Welsh mining community. *G. H. Armbruster, Ph.D. 1940 London, School of Economics and Political Science*

The social development of a child from birth to 18 months. *H. H. Stern, M.A. 1947 London, King's College*

Social factors in German-Swiss literature since 1850. *K. H. G. Spalt, Ph.D. 1940 Birmingham*

The social ideas of Dumas fils. *M. Gordon, M.A. 1924 Liverpool*

The social implications of the teaching of St. Paul. *R. H. Jennings, Ph.D. 1938 Edinburgh*

Social problems and social theories during the sixteenth century (1520-70), with special reference to the writings of More, Starkey, Crowley, Ascham, Latimer and Elyott. *R. T. Davies, M.A. 1921 Wales*

The sociology of the Yoruba. *N. A. Fadipe, Ph.D. 1940 London, School of Economics and Political Science*

The structure of community: a study in personal relationships. *G. H. Gibson, Ph.D. 1945 London, University College*

Tennyson's religious, social and political ideas in relation to his time. *L. J. Smethurst, M.A. 1948 London, King's College*

The theoretical basis of William Temple's social teaching. *R. Craig, Ph.D. 1950 Saint Andrew's*

The theory of interest and the concept of social justice. *T. F. Divine, Ph.D. 1938 London, School of Economics and Political Science*

Tragedy in France in the eighteenth century, 1700-1789: its literary and sociological value. *H. C. Ault, D.Litt. 1948 Birmingham*

The value and limitations of biological principles in social science. *W. Blackshaw, B.Sc. 1914 Oxford*

Sogdian Language
A grammar of Manichean Sogdian. *I. Gerschewitsch, Ph.D. 1943 London, School of Oriental and African Studies*

Soldiers
See Armed Forces.

Solomon b. Adreth, Rabbi
The *Responsa* of Rabbi Solomon ben Adreth of Barcelona, 1235-1310, as a source of the history of Spain. Studies in the communal life of the Jews in Spain as reflected in the *Responsa*. *I. Epstein, Ph.D. 1923 London*

Solomon b. Isaac
See Rashi, Solomon b. Isaac, Rabbi.

Solon
The work and life of Solon. *K. Freeman, M.A. 1922 Wales*

Solovieff, Vladimir Sergeevich
Vladimir Solovieff's religious philosophy. *J. Stoyanović, B.Litt. 1919 Oxford*

Somerset
See also Mendip Hills.

The Civil War in Somerset, 1642-1646. *C. W. Terry, M.A. 1913 London*

Feudal aspect of Domesday survey of Somerset and Dorset in connexion with the Barony of Moiun (Dunster Castle) and analogous feudal estates, based upon contemporary public and local records. *M. F. Moore, Ph.D. 1930 London, King's College*

The mobility of labour in the principal industries of Somersetshire, 1923-1933. *W. G. Morgan, M.A. 1934 Wales*

The scarplands of the Wiltshire-Gloucestershire-Somerset borders: a regional study, with particular reference to urban and rural settlement. *I. G. Youldon, M.A. 1945 London, King's College*

Somerset 1800-1830: an inquiry into social and economic conditions. *J. F. Lawrence, M.Litt. 1941 Durham*

1. The teaching of pre-history in schools. 2. The archaeology of Somerset. *D. P. Dobson, Litt.D. 1932 Dublin, Trinity College*

The Vale of Somerset: study of economic development and types of settlement in relation to physical character. *F. G. H. Coster, Cert.Litt. 1919 Oxford*

Songs
See also Ballads; Carols; Hymns; Madrigals.

Songs contd.
Amhráin ghrádha ó'n Mhumhain; cnuasacht a bailigheadh as láimhsgríbhinní Phádruig Fhéirtéir, Coláiste na h-Oillsgoile Baile Atha Cliath (Love songs from Munster; a collection from the manuscripts of Pádraig Feirtéar in University College Dublin). *P. O'hUllacháin, M.A. 1939 National University of Ireland*

Datblygiad y gelfyddyd ysgrifennu caneuon yng Nghymru yn y XIX ganrif (The development of the art of song-writing in Wales in the XIX century). *T. H. J. Rees, M.A. 1930 Wales*

English song in the seventeenth century. *W. A. Maynard, B.Litt. 1950 Oxford*

English songs and carols of the fifteenth century: text and transcriptions of the music. *J. Copley, M.A. 1940 Leeds*

Ethical and social features of the German people in the fifteenth and sixteenth centuries, as represented in the Volkslied of the period. *W. Rose, M.A. 1914 Birmingham*

French song in the seventeenth century: poets and musicians. *W. McArthur, M.A. 1925 London*

The lyrics and songs of the Elizabethan drama. *H. Morris, M.A. 1912 Wales*

Matheran folk songs. *M. Macmillan, D.Litt. 1903 Birmingham*

Soldiers' songs of the thirteenth and fourteenth centuries. *G. E. Morris, M.A. 1947 Sheffield*

Staidéar ar roinnt seanamhrán Gaelige (A study of a selection of old Irish songs). *C. MacMathúna, M.A. 1949 National University of Ireland*

A study of the song-books and poetical miscellanies of the seventeenth century. *A. K. D. Gupta, Ph.D. 1931 Edinburgh*

The use of lyrics in German drama. *R. Weil, B.Litt. 1950 Oxford*

The use of song in the Elizabethan drama. *M. F. Dunn, M.A. 1929 Liverpool*

Sonnets
See Poetry.

Sophocles
The Palatine manuscript of Sophocles. *G. F. Forsey, M.A. 1912 London*

The relation between Herodotus and Sophocles. *M. Davenport, M.A. 1936 Manchester*

Sophoclei chori persona tragica. *I. Errandonea, B.Litt. 1922 Oxford*

The use of pictorial effect in the poetry of Aeschylus, Sophocles, and Euripides. *W. M. O. Reed, M.A. 1918 London*

The women of Sophocles. *K. N. Toy, M.A. 1911 Birmingham*

The women of Sophocles and Aeschylus. *A. Hill, M.A. 1910 London*

Sorel, Charles
The influence of the Spanish picaresque novel in the French literature of the seventeenth century, with special reference to Sorel's *Francion* (1623-33). *G. M. Willing, B.Litt. 1931 Oxford*

Soteriology
See Salvation.

Soul

Aristotle's conception of the soul. *E. E. Spicer, M.A. 1933 London, King's College*

1. Body and soul. 2. Christianity and art. *P. Dearmer, B.D. & D.D. 1911 Oxford*

The Christian doctrine of the origin of the soul. *A. W. Argyle, B.D. 1939 Oxford*

Early Greek thought on the life of the soul after death. *W. G. Bower, M.A. 1905 London*

The Greek philosophical background of *pneuma*, in its relation to early Christian thought. *J. E. Yates, M.A. 1939 Manchester*

The idea of the soul in primitive religion. *J. W. Gregory, M.A. 1939 Leeds*

Metempsychosis in Western thought. *R. W. Shields, B.D. 1943 Leeds*

The Platonic conception of the soul and its relation to the ideas. *M. M. Towne, M.A. 1928 London*

Plato's idea of God and the soul in their mutual relations. *C. Dunsby, M.A. 1912 Birmingham*

The position of the soul and its relation to the ideas in Plato's metaphysic. *M. Hirst, M.A. 1912 London*

The relation of the human soul to God in Hinduism and Christianity. *P. B. Means, B.Litt. 1923 Oxford*

Soulé, Pierre
The mission to Spain of Pierre Soulé, 1853-5: a study in the Cuban diplomacy of the United States, with special reference to contemporary opinion. *A. A. Ettinger, D.Phil. 1930 Oxford*

Sound
The propagation of sound in air, in solids, and in liquids: the development of the subject during the period c.1615-c.1830. *S. A. Dyment, M.Sc. 1930 London*

South Africa
See also British South Africa Company; London Missionary Society; Natal; Orange Free State; Race Relations; Swaziland; Transkei; Transvaal; and Smith, H. G. W., Sir; and Bantu; Bushmen; Hottentots.

The adaptation of native custom and belief to modern conditions of civilization in South Africa. *G. R. Norton, M.A. 1939 Leeds*

British relations with the Transvaal from 1874 to 1881. *W. G. Murray, D.Phil. 1937 Oxford*

Colonial policy and slavery in South Africa, 1806-26. *I. E. Edwards, B.Litt. 1937 Oxford*

The colonial policy of the Liverpool administration, with special reference to British settlement in South Africa. *I. E. Edwards, M.A. 1931 Wales*

The development of the white community in Natal, 1845-72. *W. P. Bromiley, Ph.D. 1937 London, King's College*

Earl Grey's native policy in South Africa, with special reference to Natal. *P. Lee, M.A. 1930 Sheffield*

The effects of the Boer War on British diplomatic relations (1899-April, 1904). *R. Hughes, M.A. 1941 Wales*

The Indian problem in eastern and southern Africa. *L. James, M.A. 1940 Liverpool*

The policy of the British Government towards the South African Dutch republics, 1848-1872. *C. W. de Kiewiet, Ph.D. 1927 London*

The prelude to the Great Trek. *J. L. Holloway, D.Sc. 1917 London*

Race and racism in the Union of South Africa. *J. D. Hatton, M.A. 1948 National University of Ireland*

The unification of South Africa, 1806-1909. *J. H. Washington, M.Sc. 1921 London*

South African Literature
South African travel literature in English to the end of the seventeenth century. *N. H. MacKenzie, Ph.D. 1940 London, University College*

South America
See Latin America.

South Downs, The
A contribution to the geomorphology of the South Downs. *B. W. Sparks, M.A. 1949 London, University College*

South, Robert
Dr. Robert South. *C. M. Webster, B.D. 1951 Oxford*

Prolegomena to a study of Robert South: a bibliography of his miscellaneous works (1654-1717) with appendices. *W. M. T. Dodds, M.A. 1946 London, University College*

The sermon as persuasion in late seventeenth century France and England: a study of Bossuet, Bourdaloue, Barrow, and South. *H. Hammond, Ph.D. 1950 Cambridge*

South Sea Bubble
The political aspect of the South Sea bubble. *E. Wagstaff, M.A. 1934 London, University College*

South Sea Company
The South Sea Company and the Assiento. *L. E. M. Batcheler, M.A. 1924 London*

Southampton
The borough organization of Southampton in the sixteenth century. *C. E. Boden, M.A. 1920 London*

A geographical study of the port of Southampton. *G. H. J. Daysh, B.Litt. 1925 Oxford*

The growth of self-government in the Borough of Southampton as illustrated by its charters and letters patent. *H. W. Lidden, Ph.D. 1923 London*

Southampton: a factor in the economic development of the Hampshire Basin. *K. C. Boswell, M.Sc. 1936 London, External Degree*

The trade of Southampton with the Mediterranean. *A. A. Ruddock, Ph.D. 1940 London, School of Economics and Political Science*

Work and wealth in Southampton: an essay in civic economy. *P. Ford, Ph.D. 1933 London, External Degree*

Southerne, Thomas
Life and Works of Thomas Southerne. *C. E. J. Leech, M.A. 1932 London, East London College*

Southey, Robert
R. Southey and his poetry. *A. C. Harrison, M.A. 1920 Birmingham*

Robert Southey: a critical biography. *D. Rintoul, Ph.D. 1940 Edinburgh*

Southey, as seen in his epics. *D. D. Stuart, B.Litt. 1939 Oxford*

Southwell, Robert
Blessed Robert Southwell, S.J. *E. J. Sweetman, M.A. 1936 National University of Ireland*

An introduction to an edition of the poems of Robert Southwell. *J. H. Macdonald, B.Litt. 1930 Oxford*

Robert Southwell. *W. F. Stead, B.Litt. 1936 Oxford*

Robert Southwell. *F. Donnelly, M.A. 1929 National University of Ireland*

South-West Africa
Bismarck and British colonial policy: the problem in South-West Africa, 1883-1885. *W. O. Aydelotte, Ph.D. 1935 Cambridge*

The foreign policy of the Gladstone administration of 1880-1885, with special reference to German policy in South-west Africa. *D. E. Searle, M.A. 1933 Wales*

Sovereignty
See also Capitulations; Extraterritoriality; Kingship; Servitudes.

The acquisition of sovereignty over unappropriated territory. *M. F. Levey, LL.D. 1914 London*

The English Revolution and the doctrines of resistance and non-resistance, 1688 to 1714: a study in sovereignty. *J. C. Corson, Ph.D. 1934 Edinburgh*

The moderate Royalists and Puritans, and the conception of sovereignty in England prior to the Civil War. *A. S. H. Hill, Ph.D. 1933 London, School of Economics and Political Science*

The modifications made necessary in the doctrine of sovereignty in international law by the creation of the League of Nations. *J. Stone, LL.M. 1930 Leeds*

Recent critiques of the doctrine of the sovereignty with special reference to the writings of Professor Leon Duguit. *W. D. Handcock, B.Litt. 1930 Oxford*

Some aspects of the problem of sovereignty. *T. D. M. Rees, M.A. 1949 Wales*

Sovereignty in ancient Indian polity: a study in the evolution of the early Indian state. *H. Sinha, Ph.D. 1935 London, School of Oriental and African Studies*

The theory of sovereignty in Germany from 1811 to 1921. *R. Emerson, Ph.D. 1927 London*

The theory of sovereignty in the philosophy of Thomas Hobbes. *H. Jones, M.A. 1936 Liverpool*

The theory of sovereignty in history. *W. D. Handcock, M.A. 1926 Bristol*

Space
The development of the theory of space from Descartes to Kant. *A. W. P. Wolters, M.A. 1910 London*

An investigation of the factors in tests involving the visual perception of space. *A. A. H. El Koussy, Ph.D. 1934 London, University College*

Kants' view of space about 1769. *C. B. Garnett, Ph.D. 1932 Edinburgh*

Spain
See also Hundred Years' War; Latin America.

The activities of Spain on the Pacific Coast of South America, and her war with the 'Confederation of the Andes' (Chile, Peru, Bolivia and Ecuador), 1860-1886. *J. G. S. Ward, Ph.D. 1939 London, Birkbeck College*

Anglo-Spanish diplomatic and commercial relations, 1731-59. *J. O. McLachlan, Ph.D. 1937 Cambridge*

The attitudes of France to the South American colonies, 1822-6. *W. E. Edwards, Ph.D. 1933 Cambridge*

The audiencia of New Galicia in the sixteenth century: a study in Spanish colonial government. *J. H. Parry, Ph.D. 1939 Cambridge*

British policy and the Spanish marriages, 1841-1846. *E. J. Parry, Ph.D. 1934 London, School of Economics and Political Science*

Spain contd.
British relations with the Spanish colonies in the Caribbean 1713-1739. *L. F. Horsfall, M.A. 1935 London, King's College*

A commentary on certain aspects of the Spanish Armada drawn from contemporary sources. *J. P. R. Lyell, B.Litt. 1932 Oxford*

The cult and pilgrimage of St. James of Compostela, Spain, and their effects on the life and thought of the people in the northwestern corner of Spain. *H. W. Howes, M.A. 1938 Wales*

The first settlement of the maritime nations in the Spanish Antilles. *P. W. Day, M.A. 1916 London*

The Galician revival in the nineteenth and twentieth centuries, in both Castilian and Galician culture. *F. S. Reckert, M.Litt. 1949 Cambridge*

The government of Sicily under Philip II of Spain: a study in the practice of empire. . *H. G. Königsberger, Ph.D. 1949 Cambridge*

Life in Spain during the fifth and sixth centuries A.D. (based chiefly on the works of contemporary Latin writers). *M. I. Thomas, Ph.D. 1934 London, External Degree*

The relations between Great Britain and the Spanish colonies, 1808-12. *A. I. Langnas, Ph.D. 1938 London, School of Economics and Political Science*

The relations of the disaffected Irish with Spain during the reign of Elizabeth Tudor. *T. Huston, M.A. 1937 Belfast*

The *Responsa* of Rabbi Solomon ben Adreth of Barcelona, 1235-1310, as a source of the history of Spain. Studies in the communal life of the Jews in Spain as reflected in the *Responsa*. *I. Epstein, Ph.D. 1923 London*

The significance of British policy towards Spain, 1859-68. *S. Doyle, M.A. 1949 London, Bedford College*

Spanish economic policy and its relation to trade with England, culminating in the Treaty of 1667. *J. C. Salyer, B.Litt. 1948 Oxford*

Spanish sea power in the Mediterranean during the reign of Philip II. *C. A. H. Hartmann, B.Litt. 1922 Oxford*

Spanish Language
A comparative study of the development of strong perfects in French, Provençal, Spanish and Italian. *A. D. Neal, M.A. 1939 Manchester*

A critical edition of the British Museum manuscript of the *Dialogo de las Lenguas*, with a prefatory essay in three part. *J. H. Perry, M.A. 1920 London, School of Economics and Political Science*

Grammar and vocabulary of the works of Gonzalo de Berceo. *M. Ephgrave, Ph.D. 1935 Leeds*

The history of the study of Spanish in England from 1500 to 1808. *E. F. Vosper, B.Litt. 1926 Oxford*

Introduction to a study of the linguistic influence of France on Spain in the Middle Ages. *D. R. Sanders, M.A. 1930 Manchester*

The language of the *Cronica de Morea*. *F. W. Hodcroft, M.A. 1950 Manchester*

The teaching of Spanish to Welsh-speaking pupils. *R. M. Williams, M.A. 1939 Liverpool*

Spanish Literature
Acevedo, A. de; Alas, L.; Alemán, M.; Ayala, P. L. de; Berceo, G. de; Calderón de la Barca, P.; Cervantes Saavedra, M. de; Céspedes y Meneses, G. de; Crónica de Morea; Darıo, R.; Dicenta, J.; Encina, J. de la; Espinosa, P.; Gongora y Argote, L. de; Gracián, B.; Guillen, P.; Gutiérrez, A. G.; Hartzenbusch, J. E.; León, L. de; Lista y Aragón, A.; Mejıa, P.; Mira de Amescua, A.; Molina, T. de; Pereda, J. M. de; Pérez de Ayala, R.; Pérez de Oliva, F.; Pérez Galdós, B.; Quiro, J. de; Rojas Zorrilla, F. de; Ruiz, J.; Scarron, P.; Valdés, A. P.; Valdés, J. de; Vega, G. de la; Vega, V. de la; Vega Carpio, L. F. de.

The character of Don Pedro in the chronicles, romancero, and Spanish theatre up to 1700. *N. E. Gardiner, M.Litt. 1939 Cambridge*

El romanticismo en España. *H. Ahern, M.A. 1929 National University of Ireland*

England's literary debt to Spain, 1603-1642. *G. E. Hawk, B.Litt. 1928 Oxford*

The Galician revival in the nineteenth and twentieth centuries, in both Castilian and Galician culture. *F. S. Reckert, M.Litt. 1949 Cambridge*

The influence of French literature on Spanish literature. *A. C. Darck, M.A. 1924 Liverpool*

L'influence espagnole sur la comédie française du dix-septième siècle. *J. L. Milner, M.A. 1913 Liverpool*

Spanish Literature contd.
The return to the Golden Age in Spanish Literature. *L. A. Murray, M.A. 1924 Liverpool*

Spanish-American War, The
The relations of Great Britain and the United States of America during the Spanish-American War of 1898. *H. Holroyde, M.A. 1947 Sheffield*

Sparta
1. Early Spartan civilisation. 2. Influence of Dionysus cult on Roman religion. *J. J. Tierney, M.A. 1932 National University of Ireland*

The rival claims of Sparta and Macedon to the leadership of Greece in the late third century B.C. *E. M. Green, M.A. 1924 London*

The second Spartan Empire, 405-379 B.C. *H. W. Parke, Litt.D. 1933 Dublin, Trinity College*

Spas
The development of the spa in England and Wales. *D. K. Baron, M.A. 1938 Manchester*

Spectator, The
The social and intellectual background of the Reign of Queen Anne as reflected in the *Tatler* and *Spectator*. *J. M. King, M.A. 1938 London, King's College*

Speculum Humanae Salvationis
A middle Dutch version of the *Speculum humanae salvationis*. *C. L. T. Hermus, Ph.D. 1937 London, External Degree*

Speech
See also Children, Retarded; Stammering.

A comparative study of speech development and motor co-ordination in children of twenty-four to forty months by means of specially devised tests. *E. R. W. Unmack, Ph.D. 1939 London, University College*

The development of a child's speech: a study of the growth of vocabulary and the progress in linguistic ability during the third and fourth years. *J. Hunter, M.Ed. 1932 Manchester*

An experimental investigation of children's vocabularies, with special reference to the effect of bilingualism on vocabulary. *S. Wyatt, M.Ed. 1918 Manchester*

A historical and critical survey of the study of speech-melody, 1775 to 1923. *M. L. Barker, Ph.D. 1925 Edinburgh*

An investigation into the relative efficacy of different methods of speech instruction, including some study of factors influencing speech. *P. Royston, M.A. 1945 London, Institute of Education*

An investigation of the attitude of training college students towards the importance of good speech. *C. C. Bell, M.A. 1934 London, Institute of Education*

An objective study of the factors underlying ability in verbal expression. *A. G. Scrivens, M.A. 1933 London, Institute of Education*

Observations on the speech of a child. *E. Norman, M.A. 1931 Reading*

Report upon an enquiry into a child's vocabulary: how far it is indicative of intelligence and influence by social status. *E. M. Johns, M.A. 1949 Reading*

Some consideration of the causes of defects in the rhythm of speech. *W. Hodgkins, M.A. 1938 Manchester*

Speed, John
An analysis of the cartographical material in John Speed's *Theatre of the Empire of Great Britaine*. *M. B. John, M.Sc. 1945 Wales*

Spence, Thomas
Thomas Spence and his connections. *O. D. Rudkin, M.A. 1924 London*

Spencer, Herbert
The educational ideas of Herbert Spencer. *N. M. T. Walker, Ph.D. 1929 Glasgow*

Herbert Spencer's theory of social justice. *J. E. Asirvatham, Ph.D. 1925 Edinburgh*

Spencer in Ireland. *P. Henley, M.A. 1926 National University of Ireland*

Spenser, Edmund
An analytic study of the sources of Spenser's diction in *Shepheardes Calender*. *J. W. W. Scott, Ph.D. 1928 Saint Andrew's*

A critical edition with introduction and commentary of Spenser's *A view of the present state of Ireland*. *M. T. Perks, B.Litt. 1924 Oxford*

Criticism of Spenser in the eighteenth century. *G. A. Sambrook, M.A. 1929 Liverpool*

Spenser, Edmund contd.
The development of literary criticism in England until 1800, as seen by the treatment of the works of Geoffrey Chaucer and Edmund Spenser. *D. M. Smith, M.A. 1923 Wales*

Edmond Spenser: an essay on Renaissance poetry. *W. L. Renwick, D.Litt. 1926 Glasgow*

An examination into some elements of Spenser's psychological vocabulary, with reference to that of Chaucer. *M. Topham, M.A. 1931 Manchester*

An examination of the third book of *Britannia's Pastorals* and its attribution to William Browne of Tavistock, with a study of English fairy poetry from the time of Spenser, indicating Browne's position in its development. *I. Gourvitch, M.A. 1923 London*

The influence of Italian literature on Spenser and Sidney. *E. W. Cedervall, M.A. 1920 Wales*

The influence of Spenser on English literature of the early eighteenth century, 1700-1750. *J. L. Rushton, Ph.D. 1934 Sheffield*

The influence of Spenser on Milton. *J. M. Foster, M.A. 1945 London, King's College*

Influence of Spenser on succeeding poets. *K. J. Harney, M.A. 1919 National University of Ireland*

Keats and Spenser. *S. Iyengar, M.A. 1936 London, University College*

The old and new elements in Spenser's poetry. *M. H. Irvine, M.Litt. 1932 Cambridge*

Poetry of place in Spenser's *Faerie Queene*. *M. Nı Shúilleabháin, M.A. 1944 National University of Ireland*

The sound images in Spenser's poetry. *J. H. Jagger, M.A. 1909 London*

Spenser as a satirist. *P. Brady, M.A. 1936 National University of Ireland*

Spenser as philosopher. *P. J. McShane, M.A. 1935 Birmingham*

Spenser et la Pléiade. *W. L. Renwick, B.Litt. 1921 Oxford*

Spenser's debt to Ariosto and Tasso. *F. J. Keane, M.A. 1920 National University of Ireland*

The story of *Argalus and Parthenia*. *J. R. B. Horden, B.Litt. 1946 Oxford*

Studies in the diction of Spenser. *E. C. Ivatt, M.A. 1911 London*

A study of Spenser's *Complaints*. *B. E. C. Davis, M.A. 1915 London*

Style in Spenser. *J. H. Steel, D. Litt. 1917 Glasgow*

Spielhagen, Friedrich
The presentation of the liberal middle class in the novels and *Novellen* of Friedrich Spielhagen. *N. Roberts, M.A. 1949 Birmingham*

Spinola, Ambrogio, Marquis of Balbases
Italian financiers of the fifteenth and sixteenth centuries with special reference to Pallavicino and Spinola and their share in Elizabethan finance. *B. Hall, M.Sc. 1928 London*

Spinoza, Benedict de
A comparison of the teachings of Spinoza and McTaggart on immortality. *H. V. M. Jones, M.A. 1936 Wales*

The conception of teleology, with special reference to the views of Spinoza, Leibniz, and Kant. *D. M. Jones, M.A. 1911 Wales*

The conceptions of natural law and natural right, with special reference to Hobbes, Spinoza, Locke and Rousseau. *N. S. B. Powell, M.A. 1932 Wales*

A critical discussion of the sources of Spinoza, with special reference to Maimonides and Descartes. *H. L. Roth, D.Phil. 1922 Oxford*

The doctrines of God and freedom in the philosophy of Spinoza. *W. Madgen, M.A. 1928 Liverpool*

The idea of God in Descartes, Spinoza and Leibniz. *M. A. Davies, M.A. 1935 Wales*

The influence of Spinozism on the religious philosophy of German Idealism. *F. H. Burkhardt, B.Litt. 1935 Oxford*

The pantheism of Spinoza. *W. Keogh, M.A. 1930 National University of Ireland*

The problem of the relation between the ultimate ground and the individual members of the universe, as treated by Spinoza and Leibniz. *W. G. Sleight, M.A. 1907 London*

The relations between ethics and metaphysics, with special reference to the works of Spinoza, Kant and T. H. Green. *J. P. Davies, M.A. 1922 Wales*

Spinoza's conception of human individuality. *M. F. Hoballah, Ph.D. 1943 London, University College*

Spinoza, Benedict de contd.
Spinoza's political and ethical philosophy. *R. A. Duff, Ph.D. 1904 Glasgow*

Vedanta and Spinoza: a comparative study. *M. S. Modak, Ph.D. 1928 London*

Spire, André
André Spire. *V. G. Orgel, Ph.D. 1942 Dublin, Trinity College*

Spirituality
La Spiritualité de Claudel. *D. Mulligan, M.A. 1951 National University of Ireland*

La spiritualité de Fénelon. *J. A. Mullins, Ph.D. 1948 National University of Ireland*

The metaphysics of the spiritual life; the philosophy of Rudolf Eucken. *J. F. Burke, M.A. 1945 National University of Ireland*

1. The personality and divinity of the Holy Spirit. 2. Growth: a feature in the kingdom of the spirit. *W. H. Hutchings, B.D. & D.D. 1907 Oxford*

Reality and spirit. *A. Allardyce, M.A. 1924 Bristol*

Sports
See Games and Sports.

Spottiswoode, John, Archbishop
John Spottiswoode, Archbishop and Chancellor, as churchman, historian and theologian. *J. Perry, Ph.D. 1950 Edinburgh*

Sprat, Thomas, Bishop
The history of the Royal Society (1667) by Thomas Sprat, bishop of Rochester, edited from the original copies and mss, together with the comments of Henry Stubbe and others; remarks on the life of the author; a list of his works; notes, appendices and bibliography. *H. W. Jones, Ph.D. 1948 Leeds*

Staël, Anne Louise Germaine de, Baronne
L'Angleterre dans l'oeuvre de Mme. de Staël. *D. Distance, M.A. 1935 Belfast*

Le féminisme de Madame de Staël. *E. M. Standring, M.A. 1941 Manchester*

Madame de Staël and August Wilhelm Schlegel. *M. M. Curtis, Cert.Litt. 1917 Oxford*

Madame de Staël et les idéologues. *G. E. Gwynne, M.A. 1949 Wales*

Mme. de Staël and England: a study of Mme. de Staël's English acquaintances, and of her reputation and influence in England. *R. A. Jones, M.A. 1928 London*

Stafford, Humphrey, 1st Duke of Buckingham
Humphrey Stafford, first Duke of Buckingham: an estimate of the significance of his political activities. *H. Cole, M.A. 1945 London, King's College*

Staffordshire
Industrial geography of north Staffordshire. *A. B. Hollowood, M.Sc. 1940 London, External Degree*

Population migration to and from Warwickshire and Staffordshire, 1841-1901. *R. Lawton, M.A. 1950 Liverpool*

Stahl, Georg Ernst
Studies in the chemical work of Stahl. *L. J. M. Coleby, Ph.D. 1938 London, University College*

Staircases
The development of the British staircase. *E. F. Sekler, Ph.D. 1948 London, Warburg Institute*

Stamford
The history of the Nunnery of St. Mary and St. Michael outside Stamford. *W. M. Sturman, M.A. 1944 London, Queen Mary College*

Stammering
Spasmophemia. *M. Fahmy, Ph.D. 1949 Cambridge*

Stammering in children and a method of treatment. *R. M. M. Atkinson, M.Ed. 1922 Manchester*

A study of the numerous causes chiefly psychological, of stammering in school children. *E. B. Dickinson, M.D. 1939 Glasgow*

Stamp Duty
The history of the agitation against the stamp duty on newspapers, 1830-1855. *M. C. Moore, M.A. 1935 London, King's College*

Standard of Living
A comparative view of the cost of living, and standard of life and comfort, obtaining in a new and in an old country, as exemplified in the cases of South Africa and England. *J. M. Rees, M.A. 1911 Wales*

Family budget data and price elasticities of demand. *C. E. V. Leser, M.Sc. 1941 London, School of Economics and Political Science*

The farm worker's standard of living: a study of conditions in Shropshire in 1939. *J. B. Butler, M.Sc. 1946 London, External Degree*

The standard of life. *E. Roberts, M.Sc. 1928 London*

Standard of Living contd.
Variations in working-class family expenditure. *J. L. Nicholson, M.Sc. 1949 London, School of Economics and Political Science*

Stanley, Henry Morton, Sir
The founding of the Congo Free State, with special reference to the work of Sir Henry Morton Stanley. *G. P. Jones, M.A. 1935 Wales*

Stanley, Thomas
Thomas Stanley: a biographical and critical study, with some account of the influence of Marinism on the lyric of the later seventeenth century. *L. M. Cumming, Ph.D. 1924 Edinburgh*

Stanton Moor
Excavations at Bronze Age burial mounds on Stanton Moor. *J. P. Heathcote, M.A. 1930 Sheffield*

Staple
See also Commodities; Customs and Excise; Guilds; Woollen Industry.

The history of the staple at Westminster in the reign of Richard II. *J. S. A. Macaulay, B.Litt. 1934 Oxford*

The transactions between the merchants of the Staple and the Lancastrian government, 1449-1461. *W. I. Haward, Ph.D. 1932 London, Bedford College*

Stapylton, Robert, Sir
The Stepmother by Sir Robert Stapylton. *T. B. Smart, M.A. 1938 Sheffield*

Star Chamber
The Court of Star Chamber, 1603-41, with special reference to the period 1625-41. *H. E. I. Phillips, M.A. 1939 London, University College*

The Court of Star Chamber in the reign of Queen Elizabeth. *E. Skelton, M.A. 1931 London, University College*

Statistics
The development and application of statistical methods in the prediction of ability. *L. Ackerson, B.Sc. 1925 Oxford*

1. Extension of statistical theory to certain problems arising in sampling inspection in industry. 2. A critical comparison of Neyman and Pearson's 'L1' test and certain alternative tests. *A. V. Sukhatme, Ph.D. 1935 London, University College*

The interpretation of age frequency data. *E. R. Clarke, M.Ed. 1933 Manchester*

Statistics and psychology. *H. G. Stead, Ph.D. 1925 London*

Studies in statistics: social, political, and medical. *G. B. Longstaff, M.D. 1891 Oxford*

A study of English vital statistics, with special emphasis on marriage statistics and social or occupational class differences. *K. T. Lim, Ph.D. 1938 Liverpool*

The techniques of sampling with special reference to demographic enquiries in undeveloped countries. *P. S. You, Ph.D. 1949 London, School of Economics and Political Science*

Statius, Publius Papinius
The history of the Flavian period, and in particular of the reign of Domitian, especially as reflected in the works of the poets Juvenal, Martial, and Statius. *A. G. Barnes, M.A. 1936 Manchester*

Status
See also Women, Status of.

Status in the common law. *R. H. Graveson, Ph.D. 1941 London, King's College*

Steel Industry
See Iron and Steel Industry.

Stehr, Hermann
Hermann Stehr: sein Leben und sein Werk. *W. H. Finch, M.A. 1940 Liverpool*

Stendhal
La religion et l'église dans l'oeuvre de Stendhal. *J. Sankey, M.A. 1935 Liverpool*

Stendhal: ce qu'il a écrit et ce qu'il a lu en anglais. *J. Bryce, M.A. 1911 Birmingham*

Stendhal, dramatic theorist and playwright. *C. E. Hurren, Ph.D. 1934 London, Bedford College*

Stephen, James Fitzjames, Sir
Critics of democracy: Carlyle, Arnold, Stephen (Fitzjames), Maine, Lecky. *B. E. Lippincott, Ph.D. 1931 London, School of Economics and Political Science*

Stephen, Saint
Stephen: a study of his religious outlook and of its affinities in pre-Christian Jewish thought and in the New Testament. *R. Gardner, Ph.D. 1934 Saint Andrew's*

Stephens, James
Poetry and prose of James Stephens. *M. F. Herlihy, M.A. 1945 National University of Ireland*

Prose works of James Stephens. *W. J. Hogan, M.A. 1949 National University of Ireland*

Stephens, Thomas
Cymdeithes Cymreigyddion y Fenni a'i chynhyrchion pwsicaf gyda sylw manylach i waith Thomas Stephens, Merthyr (The Cymreigyddion y Fenni Society and its most important productions, with special reference to the work of Thomas Stephens of Merthyr). *M. Gregory, M.A. 1948 Wales*

Stephensen, Magnus
The journal (Sept. 1st-Oct. 10th, 1807) of the Icelander, Magnus Stephensen: a newly-discovered manuscript, edited with translation, notes, glossary and appendices. *S. L. Pálsson, M.A. 1947 Leeds*

Sterne, Laurence
The French sources of Sterne. *C. F. Jones, Ph.D. 1931 London, Birkbeck College*

Sterne: an autobiography extracted from his writings. *M. H. Russell, B.Litt. 1930 Oxford*

Steuart, James, Sir
Sir James Steuart. *S. Sen, Ph.D. 1947 London, School of Economics and Political Science*

Stevenson, Robert Louis
La littérature et la langue françaises dans l'oeuvre et dans la vie de R. L. Stevenson. *G. Colquhoun, M.A. 1933 Liverpool*

Stevenson's method as writer and critic. *E. C. Latimer, M.A. 1917 Liverpool*

Stifter, Adalbert
Adalbert Stifter. *P. J. Leahy, M.A. 1945 National University of Ireland*

Adalbert Stifter's attitude towards the state. *K. H. G. Spalt, M.A. 1938 Birmingham*

Stockholm
The Stockholm region: a geographical study. *R. T. Cornish, M.Sc. 1949 London, King's College*

Stockport
The economic and social development of Stockport, 1815-1836. *P. M. Giles, M.A. 1950 Manchester*

The history of Stockport Grammar School. *B. Varley, M.Ed. 1943 Manchester*

Stocks and Shares
See also Investment; Securities; Unit Trusts.

The British investor and his sources of information. *N. J. Grieser, M.Sc. 1940 London, School of Economics and Political Science*

The effects of a stock market boom upon industry and commerce with special reference to American experience, 1924-30. *B. H. Morris, B.Litt. 1933 Oxford*

The new issue market and the finance of industry. *R. F. Henderson, Ph.D. 1950 Cambridge*

The operations of underwriting and issuing houses, with particular reference to the Irish Free State. *M. M. Connor, M.Comm. 1937 National University of Ireland*

Risk, interest rates, and security prices. *W. Blair, B.Litt. 1938 Oxford*

Stock Exchange and state control. *J. J. Davy, M.A. 1924 National University of Ireland*

Transfers of shares and debentures in private international law. *W. A. F. P. Steiner, LL.M. 1948 London, School of Economics and Political Science*

Stoicism
See also Cynicism; Free Will; Lucan; Seneca.

The Cynics from the first century to the fall of the Western Empire, with a special study of the problem of fate and free-will as treated by the Stoics and Cynics of the same period. *W. Rees, B.Litt. 1919 Oxford*

The doctrine of predestination in St. Paul and Stoicism. *B. Joannidis, B.Litt. 1932 Oxford*

The influence of other philosophies on later Stoicism. *H. A. Channing, M.A. 1948 London, Royal Holloway College*

The origins in Greece of some physical and astral theories of the early Stoics. *M. M. Holt, M.Litt. 1938 Cambridge*

The stoic element in Horace. *E. H. Job, M.A. 1933 Manchester*

Stoicism and political theory in the tragedies of George Chapman. *L. F. Haddakin, M.A. 1948 London, University College*

Stoicism and Wordsworth. *I. Watson, M.A. 1911 Birmingham*

Stoicism contd.
Stoicism in Latin poetry (to the end of the Augustan period). *A. Cooper, M.A. 1918 Birmingham*

The stoicism of Seneca. *S. W. Edge, M.A. 1927 Liverpool*

Stone Age
See Archaeology and Antiquities.

Stone, Barton Warren
The biography of Barton Warren Stone, with particular reference to the origin of the Christian Church in the west, and its influence on the Disciples of Christ. *V. E. Kellems, Ph.D. 1928 Edinburgh*

Stonyhurst, Richard
Studies in the life and English works of Richard Stonyhurst (1547-1618). *N. P. Grose, M.A. 1948 London, Westfield College*

Storm, Hans Theodor Woldsen
Theodor Storm's prose style: a study in the evolution of the literary style and construction of novellen based on the original mss. *C. F. Allen, Ph.D. 1926 Edinburgh*

Stour, River
A geographical survey of the basin of the Warwickshire Stour. *J. K. B. Ingham, M.Sc. 1938 Leeds*

Stow, David
David Stow, his life and work, 1793-1864. *R. E. Houseman, M.Ed. 1938 Manchester*

Strachey, Giles Lytton
The materials for biography, the handling of the materials, and the techniques employed to reveal character and personality, with special reference to the work of Lockhart, Froude and Lytton Strachey, in the light of recent psychological investigation. *E. A. M. Dougary, Ph.D. 1942 Edinburgh*

Strafford, Thomas Wentworth, 1st Earl of
Irish trade in the time of Strafford. *H. M. Davis, M.A. 1911 London*

Studies of Ireland under Strafford. *W. H. A. O'Grady, Litt.D. 1922 Dublin, Trinity College*

Strasbourg University
John Sturm. *J. Harvey, Ph.D. 1926 Glasgow*

Strathmore
Strathmore in the eighteenth century. A study in historical geography. *A. J. Jameson, M.Sc. 1938 Manchester*

Streets
See Roads; Town and Country Planning.

Stress (Psychology)
Men under stress. *P. Delap, M.D. 1945 Dublin, Trinity College*

Overstress in endurance tests. *S. Wright, M.Sc. 1934 Belfast*

Strikes
See Industrial Relations.

Stuart, James
The early development of the university extension movement under the influence of James Stuart. *H. Gordon, M.A. 1941 Sheffield*

Stukeley, William
The life and work of Dr. William Stukeley (1687-1765). *S. Piggott, B.Litt. 1946 Oxford*

Sturlason, Snorri
See Sagas.

Sturm, John
John Sturm. *J. Harvey, Ph.D. 1926 Glasgow*

Styal, Cheshire
The social and economic history of Styal, 1750-1850. *W. C. Lazenby, M.A. 1949 Manchester*

Suárez, Francisco de
Political philosophy of Suarez. *C. H. Scanlan, M.A. 1939 National University of Ireland*

Subconscious, The
Plato and the subconscious. *A. Little, M.A. 1923 National University of Ireland*

Sublimation
A critical examination of the theory of sublimation, together with a consideration of its relevance for religion. *J. T. Davies, Ph.D. 1944 London, Richmond College*

Substance
The notion of substance in the *Metaphysics* of Aristotle. *V. Pouliot, B.Litt. 1933 Oxford*

The relations of science to philosophy, with special reference to the conceptions of substance and causation. *J. Owen, M.A. 1908 Wales*

Succession
See also Property.

Succession contd.
The administration of a deceased's estate in Muhammadan law: an historical and comparative study. *M. I. H. Zagday, Ph.D. 1945 London, University College*

The administration of and succession to estates in the Straits Settlements. *C. H. W. Payne, LL.D. 1932 London, External Degree*

Administration of foreign estates. *E. L. Burgin, LL.D. 1913 London*

De conjecturis ultimarum voluntatum. *W. P. Emerton, D.C.L. 1883 Oxford*

Death duties on entailed estates. *J. P. Cleary, LL.D. 1927 London*

The economics of inheritance in Ireland. *C. J. F. MacCarthy, M.Comm. 1949 National University of Ireland*

Encumbered Estates Act. *J. Kent, M.A. 1931 National University of Ireland*

The English law of wills treated historically and especially with suggestions for advisable reforms. *M. Salisbury, LL.D. 1911 London*

Irish death duty code. *S. J. Ronan, M.A. 1947 National University of Ireland*

The law of domicile in relation to death duties. *H. G. Bell, LL.D. 1914 London*

The legal incidence of the death duties. *K. McFarlane, LL.D. 1933 London, External Degree*

The origin and nature of the legal rights of spouses and children in the Scottish law of succession. *J. C. Gardner, Ph.D. 1927 Edinburgh*

Succession and partition in Marumakkatayam law. *K. K. Pandalai, LL.D. 1914 London*

The Taluqdari law of Oudh, with special reference to the alienation of property *inter vivos*, and its devolution on death testate and intestate. *Q. Ahmad, LL.D. 1928 London*

Theory and practice of the inheritance taxes in the American commonwealth. *G. E. Putnam, B.Litt. 1910 Oxford*

The theory of State succession, with special reference to English and Colonial law. *A. B. Keith, D.C.L. 1907 Oxford*

Turkey and state succession. *O. Eralp, Ph.D. 1939 London, External Degree*

Sudan
See also Darfur; Nubia; Azande, The.

The mission of General Gordon in the Sudan, 18 January, 1884-26 January 1885. *M. F. Shukry, M.A. 1937 Liverpool*

The social organization of the Azande of the Bahr-el-Ghazal province of the Anglo-Egyptian Sudan. *E. E. Evans-Pritchard, Ph.D. 1928 London*

The Sudan and the Mahdist Revolution of 1881-85. *M. A. Shibeika, Ph.D. 1949 London, Bedford College*

Süe, Eugène
Le roman social d'Eugène Süe. *J. Moddy, B.Litt. 1925 Oxford*

Suetonius Tranquillus, Gaius
A commentary, mainly, but not exclusively, devoted to its historical aspects, on the *Vita Divi Vespasiani* of C. Suetonius Tranquillus. *A. W. Braithwaite, B.Litt. 1926 Oxford*

Suez Canal
The history of the Suez Canal Concession, 1854-1866. *M. Kassim, M.A. 1924 London*

Suffering
The problem of suffering in the Old Testament. *J. James, M.A. 1941 Wales*

Samuel Johnson and Thomas Hardy, their attitudes to the problem of suffering: a comparative study. *H. H. Mountfield, M.A. 1948 Liverpool*

Suffering as a religious problem, with special reference to the Book of Job and the Psalter. *E. Jones, M.A. 1944 Wales*

Suffolk
The administration of the counties of Norfolk and Suffolk in the reign of Henry IV. *G. E. Morey, M.A. 1941 London, University College*

Sufism
See Islam: Sects.

Sugar Industry
British sugar taxation since the Napoleonic wars. *J. L. Mackie, Ph.D. 1939 London, School of Economics and Political Science*

The international regulation of sugar bounties. *I. G. Jones, M.A. 1940 Wales*

Sugar Industry contd.
The international sugar problem. *F. Boyer de la Giroday, B.Phil. 1947 Oxford*

A study of some influences in the development of the British beet-sugar industry. *C. Burgess, Ph.D. 1932 Cambridge*

The sugar trade: a study in economic geography. *C. J. Robertson, Ph.D. 1930 London, School of Economics and Political Science*

The sugar trade of Bristol. *I. V. Hall, M.A. 1925 Bristol*

Suggestibility
Suggestibility in children. *S. H. Cracknell, M.Sc. 1922 London*

Suicide
The differential diagnosis of depressive states, with an inquiry into the suicidal impulse: an investigation conducted by a method of experimental psychology. *A. Guirdham, B.Sc. 1935 Oxford*

Motivation of attempted suicide: an investigation of 87 cases of unsuccessful suicide, Edinburgh, 1932 to 1933. *E. T. Stoneman, Ph.D. 1933 Edinburgh*

Sulla, Lucius Cornelius
The political and administrative system of Sulla. *J. E. Taylor, B.Litt. 1924 Oxford*

Sully, Maurice de
The French version of the sermons of Maurice de Sully. *C. A. Robson, B.Litt. 1939 Oxford*

Sully, Maximilien de Béthune de, Duc
Sully: l'homme et son oeuvre d'après *Les économies royales*. *E. Westall, M.A. 1947 Liverpool*

Sully-Prudhomme, René François Armand
La pensée religieuse de Sully-Prudhomme d'après son oeuvre poétique. *M. A. Doise, M.A. 1935 London, King's College*

Sulphuric Acid
The history of the manufacture of sulphuric acid up to 1860. *A. Walker, M.Sc. 1934 London, University College*

Sumatra
Aspects of the economic geography of Sumatra. *A. J. James, M.A. 1949 Wales*

Sumerian Antiquities
See also Jemdet Nasr; Kish.

A cemetery at Kish. A Sumerian palace. Jemdet Nasr. Bahrein and Hemamieh. Mohenjo-Daro. *E. J. H. Mackay, D.Litt. 1933 Bristol*

The city of Mari, with special reference to the archaeological material. *B. E. Morgan, M.A. 1950 Manchester*

Sunday
See also Sabbath.

1. The atonement. 2. Sunday, or the Lord's day. *H. H. Merryweather, B.D. 1905 Oxford*

1. The grace of confirmation. 2. The Christian observance of the Lord's day. *E. J. Gough, B.D. & D.D. 1900 Oxford*

Growth of sabbatarianism in England from 1558 to 1658. *W. A. Leaper, M.A. 1919 National University of Ireland*

1. The Hebrew sabbath. 2. The Christian Sunday. *G. L. Porcher, B.D. 1923 Oxford*

1. The Lord's day. 2. The efficacy of prayer. *E. R. Currie, B.D. & D.D. 1888 Oxford*

1. The Lord's day. 2. The intermediate state. *H. J. Wilkins, B.D. & D.D. 1906 Oxford*

1. The origin and religious significance of the Jewish Sabbath. 2. The history and meaning of the Christian Sunday. *H. R. Gamble, B.D. & D.D. 1919 Oxford*

Sunday in the eighteenth century, 1677-1837. *W. B. Whitaker, Ph.D. 1937 London, King's College*

1. True and false conceptions of the Eucharist as a sacrifice. 2. The grounds of the observance of the Lord's day. *W. B. C. Wilder, B.D. 1902 Oxford*

Sunday Observance
See Sunday.

Sunday Schools
A comparative study of the Sunday School Movement in England and Wales. *D. M. Griffith, M.A. 1923 Wales*

The history and development of the Sunday school in England. *W. A. Christie, M.A. 1937 Liverpool*

Sunderland
The development of education in Sunderland during the nineteenth century. *A. C. M. Herdson, M.Ed. 1931 Durham*

Sunderland, Robert Spencer, 2nd Earl
The life of Robert Spencer, 2nd Earl of Sunderland, 1640-1702, with special reference to his work as secretary of state. *P. L. Norrish, M.A. 1936 Liverpool*

Supernatural, The
Belief in beings superhuman and subhuman: an examination of the part played by this belief in the Patristic theology up to the Council of Nicaea. *H. A. Blair, B.D. 1945 Oxford*

Cicero and the supernatural. *M. T. Heyes, M.A. 1922 Liverpool*

A comparative study of the supernatural element in Elizabethan drama and in modern drama. *M. Kilduff, M.A. 1937 Liverpool*

The idea of the supernatural and of the transcendent in primitive and modern theistic thought. *T. J. E. Hopkins, M.A. 1934 Liverpool*

The inter-relations of nature and supernature in Von Hügel's *Philosophy of Religion*. *W. H. John, M.A. 1941 Wales*

The realm of the supernatural among the southeastern Bantu. *H. M. Gluckmann, D.Phil. 1936 Oxford*

A study of the supernatural in Middle English verse romances. *G. L. Preedy, M.A. 1918 Bristol*

Supernatural birth in historical religions. *S. E. Starrels, Ph.D. 1936 London, King's College*

The supernatural in German drama of the early nineteenth century. *E. Bennett, M.A. 1919 Birmingham*

Supernaturalism in English poetry, 1750-1850. *M. Phillips, Ph.D. 1930 London, East London College*

The treatment of the supernatural in English literature from Shakespeare to Coleridge together with some consideration of the subject in its relation to the metaphysical and mystical side of literature. *G. M. H. Harcourt-Smith, M.A. 1907 London*

Supervielle, Jules
The function of poetry and primitive psychology in the work of Jules Supervielle. *L. Allen, M.A. 1949 Manchester*

Surgery
A critical survey of the advances made in surgery and anatomy in the *Corpus Hippocraticum* and the *De Medicina* of Celsus, with a short history of surgery and anatomy from the earliest times down to the beginning of the Christian era. *A. V. R. Don, Ch.M. 1922 Aberdeen*

The history and present position of Chinese surgery; surgical characteristics of the Chinese, and the prospects of western surgical practice in China. *J. C. Thomson, M.D. 1892 Edinburgh*

Some thirteenth century French versions of the *Chirurgia* of Roger of Salerno. *D. J. A. Ross, Ph.D. 1940 London, University College*

Surnames
See Names, Personal.

Surrey
Historical geography of Surrey about the year 1800. *P. M. Wilkins, M.Sc. 1942 London, School of Economics and Political Science*

The judicial proceedings under the Dictum of Kenilworth, Surrey. Revised text. *L. M. Round, M.A. 1928 Manchester*

Surtees, Robert Smith
Studies in the language of Robert Smith Surtees (1805-1864). *M. G. Owen, M.A. 1939 Liverpool*

Sussex
An analysis of some of the interactions of geography and history in the Arun and Adur valleys. *A. F. A. Mutton, M.A. 1932 London, Bedford College*

Celtic settlement and agriculture in central Sussex. *M. Coleman, M.A. 1944 London, External Degree*

East Sussex landownership: the structure of rural society in an area of old enclosure, 1733-87. *D. K. Worcester, Ph.D. 1950 Cambridge*

The economic geography of Sussex during the fourteenth century, with special reference to the county's relations with lands across the sea. *R. A. Pelham, M.A. 1930 Wales*

The historical geography of a part of east Sussex from 1780, with special reference to agriculture. *E. W. H. Briault, Ph.D. 1939 London, Birkbeck College*

The influence of physical geography upon the history of settlement and distribution of population in Sussex. *W. H. Parker, B.Sc. 1939 Oxford*

The judicial proceedings under the Dictum of Kenilworth in Sussex and Kent. *A. Buckley, M.A. 1927 Manchester*

Sussex contd.
Physical controls in the historical geography of the Sussex estuaries. *F. G. Morris, M.A. 1931 London, School of Economics and Political Science*

A portion of west Sussex: a study of agriculture and population. *E. Cook, M.A. 1939 Liverpool*

Sutherlandshire
The land utilisation reports of Sutherlandshire: with a special account of the reclamation schemes and the deer forests. *F. T. Smith, M.Sc. 1938 London, King's College*

Swale, River
The Isle of Sheppey and the Swale. *K. R. MacDonald, M.A. 1949 London, King's College*

Swan, William
English notaries at the Papal Curia in the fifteenth century with special reference to W. Swan. *D. Newell, Ph.D. 1934 Manchester*

Swansea
The economic development of the Swansea area. *D. J. Price, M.A. 1932 London, School of Economics and Political Science*

Swaziland
The human geography of Swaziland. *D. M. Doveton, B.Litt. 1937 Oxford*

Rank among the Swazi of the protectorate. *H. Beemer, Ph.D. 1943 London, School of Economics and Political Science*

Sweden
Parliamentary government as it exists in Sweden. *W. E. Sandelius, B.Litt. 1923 Oxford*

The Stockholm region: a geographical study. *R. T. Cornish, M.Sc. 1949 London, King's College*

Sweden and the Papacy, 822-1248. *C. J. A. Oppermann, Ph.D. 1931 London, External Degree*

Swedish Language
Contributions to the study of the influence of German loanwords in Swedish vocabulary. *C. T. Hansson, M.A. 1949 Liverpool*

Swift, Jonathan
1. The ancient and modern learning of England. 2. The *Battle of the Books*. *A. C. L. Guthkelch, M.A. 1907 London*

The homocentric attitude of Swift's writings. *M. O'Shea, M.A. 1935 National University of Ireland*

Jonathan Swift: an Augustan poet. *J. Fletcher, M.A. 1950 Manchester*

Jonathan Swift: dean and pastor. *R. W. Jackson, Litt. D. 1939 Dublin, Trinity College*

Jonathan Swift, 1696-1717: early satires and politics. *A. R. P. Shield, M.A. 1939 Birmingham*

Swift et Voltaire. *B. F. Rice, M.A. 1935 Birmingham*

Swinburne, Algernon Charles
Criticism and appreciation of Elizabethan drama: Dryden to Swinburne. *F. C. Baxter, Ph.D. 1933 Cambridge*

The influence of the ballad on nineteenth century poetry, with special reference to Rossetti, Morris and Swinburne. *I. M. Empson, M.A. 1933 Reading*

A study of Swinburne's relations with France. *J. I. Davies, M.A. 1932 Wales*

Swinburne and the Italian Risorgimento. *J. M. Forster, M.A. 1934 Birmingham*

Swinburne, *The Queen Mother* and the *Mary Stuart* trilogy: an investigation into Swinburne's sources of inspiration and into the use made of historical documents. *E. F. James, M.A. 1932 Bristol*

Swiss Literature
For Swiss Literature in the French and German languages, see French Literature; German Literature. See also under individual authors, e.g. Amiel, H. F.; Calvin, J.; Keller, G.; Meyer, C. F.

Switzerland
The policy of Switzerland in the construction of the collective peace system. *J. B. Knapp, B.Litt. 1936 Oxford*

Sylvester, Joshua
Studies in the life and works of Joshua Sylvester (1564-1618). *L. Parsons, M.A. 1948 London, Westfield College*

Symbolism
See also Totemism.

The aesthetic doctrines of French Symbolism. *A. G. Lehmann, D.Phil. 1948 Oxford*

The cult of obscurity in French symbolist poetry. *J. C. Ireson, M.A. 1949 London, External Degree*

The element of symbolism in the later novels and stories of Henry James. *M. Farris, Ph.D. 1949 Liverpool*

Symbolism contd.
Essai sur la poésie symboliste en France. *M. Hayes, M.A. 1920 National University of Ireland*

James Joyce's use of symbolism. *G. M. Davenport, B.Litt. 1950 Oxford*

Le symbolisme de la pauvreté dans l'oeuvre de Léon Bloy. *E. T. Pichler, M.A. 1945 Birmingham*

The nature and function of dogma in the symbolo-fidéisme of the Paris School. *G. P. Moscherosch, Ph.D. 1950 Edinburgh*

The part played by symbols in thinking, with special reference to belief, and cognate states. *J. L. Evans, D.Phil. 1945 Oxford*

The part played by the use of symbols in the attainment of knowledge. *W. B. Gallie, B.Litt. 1937 Oxford*

The religious use of symbol in Crashaw and his predecessors. *T. O. Haworth, M.A. 1950 Manchester*

Some essential conditions of symbolism. *E. M. M. Whetwall, Ph.D. 1927 London*

Symbolism in English metaphysical poetry, with special reference to Donne, Herbert and Vaughan. *M. A. Khan, Ph.D. 1948 London, Queen Mary College*

Synagogues
The architectural development of the synagogue. *H. Rosenau, Ph.D. 1940 London, Courtauld Institute of Art*

Synesius of Cyrene, Bishop
The letters of Synesius of Cyrene, Metropolitan Bishop of Ptolemais in the Libyan Pentapolis, tr. into English with a commentary and an introductory essay. *J. C. Stewart, Ph.D. 1923 Edinburgh*

Synesius as a representative of Greek thought and culture during the period immediately preceding its eclipse. *H. T. Tristram, B.Litt. 1925 Oxford*

Synge, John Millington
Synge and Anglo-Irish literature. *D. Corkery, M.A. 1929 National University of Ireland*

Synthetic Propositions (Philosophy)
Analytic and synthetic propositions. *M. Hanlon, M.A. 1945 National University of Ireland*

Syracuse
Dionysius the second: tyrant of Syracuse. *J. Gaynor, M.A. 1947 National University of Ireland*

Early Syracuse. *G. R. Cussen, M.A. 1921 National University of Ireland*

Hiero II. king of Syracuse (B.C. 269-215). *B. McCarthy, M.A. 1950 National University of Ireland*

The life and times of Hiero II, King of Syracuse. *W. H. Davies, M.A. 1935 Wales*

Syria
See also Antioch; Crusades; Seljuks, The.

English travellers in Syria. *E. J. S. Saigh, M.A. 1942 Leeds*

The history of the Aramaeans down to the fall of Nineveh, 612 B.C. *F. Tomkinson, M.A. 1932 Wales*

Military methods employed by the Latin states in Syria, 1097 to 1192. *R. C. Smail, Ph.D. 1948 Cambridge*

The relations of Egypt and Syria-Palestine, with special reference to Old Testament history. *D. C. Davies, M.A. 1923 Liverpool*

Syriac Language
A preparation for an edition of a critical text of selected chapters of the Syriac version of Ecclesiasticus. *W. D. McHardy, D.Phil. 1943 Oxford*

Vocalisation of the proper names in the Pentateuch according to a Syriac manuscript, Add. 12138, in the British Museum. *J. Wood, M.A. 1940 Manchester*

Tabir al-Ruya
Tabir al-Ruya (interpretation of dreams): sources, philosophy, influence, etc. *M. Al-Hashimi, Ph.D. 1948 London, School of Oriental and African Studies*

Tachistoscope
The perception of tachistoscopically exposed letters. *A. G. Caws, Ph.D. 1933 London, King's College*

Tacitus, Gaius Cornelius
How far did Virgil, Horace and Tacitus supply the want of a middle voice in Latin by the use of the so-called passive?. *M. Cartwright, M.A. 1906 Wales*

Tacitus, Gaius Cornelius contd.
Military unrest as described by Tacitus. *R. J. Philpot, M.A. 1950 Wales*

Roman society in the reign of Trajan as seen in the writings of Tacitus, Juvenal and Pliny the Younger. *M. M. Gough, M.A. 1908 Birmingham*

A study of Tacitus' motives and techniques in the writing of the *Annals. B. Walker, M.A. 1947 Manchester*

The Tacitean use of prepositions, with a few remarks on the tendency of Latin to become an analytical language. *S. P. Record, M.A. 1907 London*

Tagore, Rabindranath, Sir
Mysticism in poetry; a study of AE, W. B. Yeats and Rabindranath Tagore. *A. C. Bose, Ph.D. 1937 Dublin, Trinity College*

Mysticism in the poetry of Wordsworth, Shelley and Tagore. *B. Sengupta, B.Litt. 1947 Dublin, Trinity College*

The poetry and dramas of Rabindranath Tagore. *E. J. Thompson, Ph.D. 1924 London*

Rabindranath Tagore - poet, mystic and teacher. *R. M. le F. Burrows, B.Litt. 1947 Dublin, Trinity College*

Tagore at Shantinekatan, or Sir Rabindranath Tagore's educational experiment at Shantinekatan. *H. S. D. Chaturvedi, M.Ed. 1929 Leeds*

Taillevent, Michault
Michault Taillevent: poet of fifteenth-century Burgundy. *J. H. Watkins, M.A. 1948 Wales*

Tailoring Industry
The development of rationalization in the Leeds men's tailoring industry, with particular reference to scientific management. *E. I. H. Silman, Ph.D. 1933 Leeds*

Trends in the men's tailoring industry of Great Britain. *E. Finlay, Ph.D. 1947 London, External Degree*

Táin bó Cúalnge
See Romances.

Taine, Hippolyte Adolphe
The critical system of Hippolyte Taine. *J. H. P. Lamont, M.A. 1926 Wales*

English literature in the critical work of Taine. *P. E. Phillips, M.A. 1931 Wales*

Talbot, Charles, Duke of Shrewsbury
Shrewsbury, 1660-1718. *D. H. Somerville, D.Litt. 1933 Glasgow*

Talbot, Matthew
Aistriúcháin ar scéal beathadh Mhaitiais Talbóid ó Bhéarla an Athar Séamus O Casaide (A translation from the English of a biography of Matthew Talbot by Fr. Séamas O Casaide). *L. Breathnach, M.A. 1936 National University of Ireland*

Tale of the Expedition of Igor, The
Some problems of the *Tale of the expedition of Igor,* a Russian poem of the twelfth century. *N. M. Iovetz-Tereshchenko, B.Litt. 1928 Oxford*

Talhaiarn
See Jones, John (Talhaiarn).

Talmud
See Judaism.

Tamils
Distribution of population in the Tamil country. *V. S. Swaminathan, M.Sc. 1931 London, University College*

T'ang Dynasty
The Christian Church of the T'ang Dynasty. *J. Foster, M.A. 1938 Birmingham*

T'ang Literature
See also Chinese Literature.

Tanganyika
A study in regional division as applied to the northern part of Tanganyika Territory. *B. G. Brasington, Ph.D. 1935 London, Birkbeck College*

Tar Industry
The problems and development of cartelization in the British tar industry. *N. R. Bishop, Ph.D. 1944 London, External Degree*

Tariffs
See also Free Trade.

The effects of tariffs on industries, with especial reference to the tinplate industry. *J. H. Jones, M.A. 1904 Wales*

History of Indian tariff. *N. J. Shah, Ph.D. 1923 London*

Indian tariffs in relation to industry and taxation. *H. L. Dey, D.Sc. 1933 London, School of Economics and Political Science*

Tariffs contd.
The origins of the tariff reform movement. *B. H. Smith, M.A. 1938 Birmingham*

Preferential tariffs in the British Empire. *R. M. Campbell, Ph.D. 1929 London*

The regulation of tariffs by recent international agreements, as exemplified by the practice of Great Britain and the United States. *C. H. McKenna, B.Litt. 1938 Oxford*

Tariffs: a study in method. *T. E. G. Gregory, D.Sc. 1922 London*

Tariffs and stability in commercial relations in the post-war period, with special regard to Central Europe. *V. Jalea, Ph.D. 1931 Birmingham*

Tariffs for farmers. *D. J. Coakley, M.Comm. 1928 National University of Ireland*

Tarunaprabha
Selections from *Sadavasyaka vrtti* of Tarunaprabha, critically edited: a study of the Gujrati language in the fourteenth century A.D. *P. B. Pandit, Ph.D. 1949 London, School of Oriental and African Studies*

Tasso, Torquato
Spenser's debt to Ariosto and Tasso. *F. J. Keane, M.A. 1920 National University of Ireland*

Taste
See also Aesthetics.

Taste (Aesthetics)
Eighteenth century ideas of taste as reflected chiefly in the poetry of the period. *P. C. Das, Ph.D. 1936 Edinburgh*

1. The letters of William Shenstone. 2. William Shenstone: a chapter in eighteenth century taste. *M. Williams, D.Litt. 1939 London, External Degree*

Tatian
Tatian's *Diatessaron:* introductory studies, with a portion of the Arabic version. *A. J. B. Higgins, Ph.D. 1945 Manchester*

Tatler, The
The origin and development of the English prose essay to the making of the *Tatler. A. M. Paynter, M.A. 1910 London*

The social and intellectual background of the Reign of Queen Anne as reflected in the *Tatler* and *Spectator. J. M. King, M.A. 1938 London, King's College*

Tattooing
Tattooing and other forms of body-marking among primitive peoples. *W. D. Hambly, B.Sc. 1918 Oxford*

Taunton
The Court of Taunton in the sixteenth and seventeenth centuries. *R. G. H. Whitty, M.A. 1932 London, External Degree*

Emigration from Taunton to N. England 1625-1645. *H. J. Wickenden, M.A. 1929 Bristol*

The history of Taunton under the Tudors and Stuarts. *R. G. H. Whitty, Ph.D. 1938 London, External Degree*

Taverner, Richard
Life and writings of Richard Taverner. *J. B. W. Hughes, M.A. 1932 London, King's College*

Taxation
See also Income Tax; Land; Succession.

The causes of the revolution in New York, 1691-1760: a study of taxation and of the effects of England's commercial restrictions, prefaced by a sketch of the colony's political history. *B. Miles, B.Litt. 1905 Oxford*

Evasion in taxation. *A. V. Tranter, Ph.D. 1927 London*

The measurement of profit and the incidence of taxation. *R. W. Moon, B.Phil. 1948 Oxford*

The nature and first principle of taxation. *R. Jones, D.Sc. 1915 London*

Recent progress in the application of theories of taxation. *R. W. Green, B.Litt. 1920 Oxford*

Taxation and capital formation. *O. A. Gomez, M.Sc. 1942 London, School of Economics and Political Science*

Taxation: Egypt
The recent development of the tax system in Egypt. *A. G. Mohammed, M.Com. 1940 Leeds*

Taxation: Great Britain
Aspects of taxation and expenditure in the United Kingdom, 1890-1914, with special reference to the growth of the social services. *E. M. Bowen, M.A. 1934 Wales*

Taxation: Great Britain contd.
The auditing of private limited company accounts in its relations to taxation. *E. C. Turner, M.Com. 1923 Birmingham*

British sugar taxation since the Napoleonic wars. *J. L. Mackie, Ph.D. 1939 London, School of Economics and Political Science*

Clerical taxation and consent in the reign of Edward I. *H. S. Deighton, B.Litt. 1935 Oxford*

A comparison of the war taxation of Great Britain and the United States of America from 1914. *D. M. Sandral, B.Litt. 1922 Oxford*

The economic effects of the taxation of business reserves, with particular reference to allowances for depreciation and obsolescence. *M. E. Wharam, M.A. 1931 Birmingham*

English taxation, 1640-1799. *W. Kennedy, D.Sc. 1913 London*

Indirect taxation in the United Kingdom, 1913-14 to 1924-25. *C. O. George, Ph.D. 1934 London, External Degree*

Records of tax assessments, 1642-1651. *M. M. Colyer, M.A. 1922 London, King's College*

Redistribution of incomes through public finance in 1937. *T. Barna, Ph.D. 1943 London, School of Economics and Political Science*

War taxation. *C. P. McCarthy, M.Comm. 1918 National University of Ireland*

Taxation: India
Indian tariffs in relation to industry and taxation. *H. L. Dey, D.Sc. 1933 London, School of Economics and Political Science*

Revenue administration of the Sirkars under the E.I.C. down to 1802. *L., Sundaram, Ph.D. 1930 London, School of Oriental and African Studies*

Taxation: Ireland
The economic effect of some aspects of our current taxation system. *M. D. McGuane, M.A. 1949 National University of Ireland*

History and law of Irish local taxation. *H. A. Frazer, M.Sc. 1936 London, External Degree*

Present system of direct taxation in Eire. *J. P. McHale, M.Comm. 1947 National University of Ireland*

A survey of taxation and government expenditure in the Irish Free State, 1922-1936. *S. Kepple, M.A. 1938 National University of Ireland*

Taxation: Islam
The Muhammadan *jizyah* or capitation tax. *A. L. F. Dons, B.Litt. 1922 Oxford*

Taxation: Rome
Some 'voluntary' taxes of the Roman Empire. *E. C. Wordsworth, M.A. 1912 Birmingham*

Taxation: United States
A comparison of the war taxation of Great Britain and the United States of America from 1914. *D. M. Sandral, B.Litt. 1922 Oxford*

Taylor, Henry, Sir
Life and works of Sir Henry Taylor. *H. E. Williams, M.A. 1948 London, Queen Mary College*

Taylor, Jeremy
Jeremy Taylor: a study of his style. *E. M. Mackenzie, M.Litt. 1938 Cambridge*

Jeremy Taylor and seventeenth century English casuistry, with special reference to the *Ductor dubitantium. T. Wood, B.D. 1945 Leeds*

The life, times and writings of Jeremy Taylor. *C. J. Stranks, M.Litt. 1937 Durham*

The sermons of Donne and Taylor. *W. E. Brooke, M.A. 1935 Birmingham*

A study of the idea of conscience, with particular reference to the thought of Jeremy Taylor. *M. W. Eckel, B.Litt. 1950 Oxford*

Taylor, John
John Taylor, water poet and journalist. *M. Rushforth, M.A. 1934 London, University College*

Taylor, Tom
Tom Taylor: life and works. *C. V. Myers, M.Litt. 1933 Cambridge*

Tchekhov, Anton Pavlovich
See Chekhov, A. P.

Tea Industry
The growth and development of the Indian tea industry and trade. *S. M. Akhtar, Ph.D. 1932 London, School of Economics and Political Science*

Tea Industry contd.
The tea trade. *F. H. S. Williams, M.Sc. 1938 London, School of Economics and Political Science*

Teaching, Teachers
See Education: Profession. For the study and teaching of individual subjects, see under the subjects.

Technical Education
See Education, Technical.

Technology
From research laboratory to production line: a study in the economics of technological change. *C. S. Solo, Ph.D. 1949 London, School of Economics and Political Science*

Retailing costs and technical progress. *H. Smith, B.Litt. 1934 Oxford*

Technical theory and practice in George Meredith's novels. *S. H. Davies, Ph.D. 1935 London, King's College*

Tees, River
Cleveland and Teesside: a geographical study of population and occupational changes since 1800. *I. Bowes, M.A. 1948 London, Bedford College*

The development of the Tees-side industrial area. *R. Hewitt, M.Sc. 1940 London, University College*

A survey of the estuary of the river Tees. *B. A. Southgate, D.Sc. 1936 Aberdeen*

Telecommunications
See Communications.

Teleology
Athrawiaeth y diewedd (The doctrine of the end). *R. S. Rogers, M.A. 1934 Wales*

The conception of teleology, with special reference to the views of Spinoza, Leibniz, and Kant. *D. M. Jones, M.A. 1911 Wales*

The conception of teleology in modern philosophy from Descartes to Kant. *T. Evans, M.A. 1927 Wales*

The history of the οικεί ωσισ doctrine, with special reference to Cicero *De Finibus* v. *J. M. Mingay, B.Litt. 1950 Oxford*

The idea of teleology in the light of modern philosophy. *S. P. Whitehouse, B.Litt. 1938 Oxford*

The theory of evolution in science, ethics and religion, with special reference to its teleological nature, tracing the development of the theory in question from Lamarck to our own day. *W. W. Pearson, B.Sc. 1907 Oxford*

Telescopes
The telescopes of Sir William Herschel. *C. T. Moss, M.Sc. 1949 London, University College*

Telugu, The
The political history of the Telugu country, from *c.* A.D. 1000 to A.D. 1565. *P. Sreenivasachar, Ph.D. 1933 London, School of Oriental and African Studies*

Temperament (Psychology)
An experimental investigation of some theories of temperament types. *E. Mountford, M.A. 1938 London, King's College*

A factorial analysis of temperament factors. *C. J. Adcock, Ph.D. 1947 London, Birkbeck College*

The nature of temperament: a study of some fundamental factors. *S. Biesheuvel, Ph.D. 1933 Edinburgh*

The psychological doctrine of temperament. *C. Bloor, M.A. 1925 London*

Temple, William
The theoretical basis of William Temple's social teaching. *R. Craig, Ph.D. 1950 Saint Andrew's*

Temples
The temples of Syria of the Roman period: their dates and developments, according to the evidence of structure, decoration and inscriptions. *C. H. Heithaus, Ph.D. 1940 London, University College*

Tenancy
See Land Tenure.

Tenison, Thomas, Archbishop of Canterbury
The life and times of Thomas Tenison, 1636-1715. *E. F. Carpenter, Ph.D. 1943 London, King's College*

Tennant, Frederick Robert
The problem of evil in the thought of F. R. Tennant. *C. G. Werner, Ph.D. 1950 Edinburgh*

Some aspects of theism, particularly of its treatment by three modern theistic authors: A. S. Pringle-Pattison, F. R. Tennant, G. D. Hicks. *G. T. Eddy, M.A. 1940 Birmingham*

Tennant, Smithson
The life and work of Smithson Tennant M.D., F.R.S., 1761-1815, with an account of some aspects of eighteenth and early nineteenth century science. *A. E. Wales, M.Sc. 1940 Leeds*

Tennemann, Wilhelm Gottlieb
A critical edition of Coleridge's marginalia to Tennemann's *Geschichte der Philosophie* (1798-1817), with introduction and notes. *K. H. Coburn, B.Litt. 1932 Oxford*

Tennyson, Alfred, 1st Baron
Etude sur la poésie de Victor Hugo et de Tennyson. *M. B. Henderson, M.A. 1915 Birmingham*

The reputation of Tennyson from the date of his earliest work up to the present time. *S. C. Boorman, M.A. 1935 London, Queen Mary College*

Tennyson and the reviewers, 1827-51: a study of the growth of Tennyson's reputation and of the influence of the critics upon his poetry. *E. F. Shannon, D.Phil. 1949 Oxford*

Tennyson's diction. *D. C. Jones, M.A. 1925 Liverpool*

Tennyson's religious beliefs. *B. Colgrave, M.A. 1910 Birmingham*

Tennyson's religious, social and political ideas in relation to his time. *L. J. Smethurst, M.A. 1948 London, King's College*

Virgil and Tennyson: a parallel study. *L. S. Graham, M.A. 1917 Birmingham*

Terence (Publius Terentius Afer)
Ancient editions of Terence. *J. D. Craig, D.Litt. 1929 Saint Andrew's*

The characterization of women in Plautus and Terence and the fragments of Menander. *M. Watts, M.A. 1919 London*

An investigation of the development and character of the influence of Terence and Plautus on the earlier English drama, with some account of fifteenth and sixteenth century editions of their plays in England. *T. C. Rising, M.A. 1933 London, King's College*

The slaves of Greek comedy compared with those of Plautus and Terence. *W. G. Williams, M.A. 1911 London*

Syntax of Terence. *J. T. Allardice, D.Litt. 1926 Saint Andrew's*

Teresa, of Avila, Saint
Santa Teresa y sus obras. *B. C. Barrett, M.A. 1948 National University of Ireland*

The visions and locutions of St. Theresa. *J. Gibbs, B.Litt. 1940 Oxford*

Terman-Merrill Scale
See Intelligence Testing.

Territorial Waters
See also Extraterritoriality; Law, International.

The international law of territorial waters, with special reference to the coasts of Scotland. *W. M. Newlands, Ph.D. 1935 Edinburgh*

Tertullian, Quintus Septimus Florens
The Christianity of Tertullian, studied in its growth and historical relations. *A. Gaunt, B.Litt. 1912 Oxford*

1. The history of the doctrine of satisfaction from Tertullian to St. Ambrose. 2. The history of the doctrine of satisfaction from St. Augustine to St. Anselm. *G. A. Michell, B.D. & D.D. 1924 Oxford*

A study of the early writings of Tertullian with particular reference to the *Apologeticum*. *B. Wilson, M.A. 1948 Liverpool*

Tertullian the jurist. *W. Rankin, Ph.D. 1929 Aberdeen*

Tewkesbury
The borough of Tewkesbury, 1575-1714. *M. F. Redmond, M.A. 1950 Birmingham*

Texeda, Ferdinando
Ferdinando Texeda: a complete analysis of his work together with a study of his stay in England (1621? to 1631?), being a contribution to the solution of the problems connected with him. *W. McFadden, M.A. 1933 Belfast*

Textbooks
See Education: Pedagogics.

Textiles
See also Cotton Industry; Linen Industry; Rayon Industry; Silk Industry; Thread Industry; Woollen Industry; etc.

The cloth industry in Essex and Suffolk. *J. E. Pilgrim, M.A. 1938 London, School of Economics and Political Science*

Textiles contd.
The correlation of industries in southeast Lancashire, with special reference to the potentialities of other European and eastern textile countries in world trade. *G. V. M. Davies, M.Sc. 1930 Wales*

A geographical survey of the textile industries of the West of England. *R. P. Beckinsale, D.Phil. 1949 Oxford*

A history of Islamic textiles up to the Mongol conquest. *R. B. Serjeant, Ph.D. 1940 Cambridge*

Industrial Revolution and the textile industries of Somerset. *H. C. Oram, M.A. 1930 Bristol*

The Industrial Revolution in the textile industries of Wiltshire. *H. R. Exelby, M.A. 1928 Bristol*

The organization of the British textile finishing industry from 1920-1938. *J. W. Reidy, M.A. 1946 Manchester*

The textile industry of Australia. *O. T. Troutman, M.Com. 1939 Birmingham*

Women in the textile industries and trade of fifteenth century England. *M. K. Dale, M.A. 1928 London*

Thackeray, William Makepeace
An examination of the methods of Dickens and Thackeray in the characterization of women. *E. C. McGahan, M.A. 1946 Wales*

Some aspects of characterization in Thackeray. *R. B. Hunter, M.A. 1938 Belfast*

Thackeray's attitude towards the society of his time, as revealed in his writings of 1836-1847. *A. Webster, M.A. 1948 Manchester*

Thailand
Siamese state ceremonies: their history and function. *H. G. Q. Wales, Ph.D. 1932 London, School of Economics and Political Science*

Thames, River
Contribution to the study of the geomorphology and drainage development of the Lower Thames Basin. *B. R. Ross, Ph.D. 1932 London, External Degree*

Theatre
See also Aesthetics; Auditoria; Comedy; Literature; Masques; Morality Plays; Mystery Plays; Tragedy; and Bouchardy, J.; Chapman, G.; Cibber, C.; Clive, C.; Garrick, D.; Globe Theatre; Jonson, B.; Kelly, H.; Langbaine, G., the Younger; Moore, E.; Parnassus Plays; Shakespeare, W.: Production; Theatre Royal (Birmingham). For references to individual dramatists see under English Literature; French Literature; Greek Literature, etc.

Contemporary poetic drama. *N. D. Lawlor, M.A. 1944 National University of Ireland*

Drámaidheacht na scol (School dramatics). *C. O'Rónáin, M.A. 1938 National University of Ireland*

La controverse sur la moralité du théâtre après la lettre à d'Alembert de J. J. Rousseau. *M. M. Moffat, M.A. 1930 Liverpool*

The last days of the medieval religious stage, particularly in England. *H. C. Gardiner, Ph.D. 1941 Cambridge*

Les théories dramatiques de Francisque Sarcey. *E. M. Papenfus, Ph.D. 1926 London*

The main aspects of the post-war drama. *L. I. Lewis, M.A. 1933 Wales*

New aspects of dramatic work in secondary schools, with especial reference to the value of a model stage. *E. F. Dyer, M.Ed. 1935 Durham*

Poetic drama of the nineteenth century, from 1800 to 1830. *U. Nagchaudhuri, Ph.D. 1927 London*

A study of the manuscripts of theatrical and dramatic interest preserved in the British Museum, 1660-1720. *G. E. Batchelor, M.A. 1929 London*

Theatre: Austria
Aspects of the development of the Viennese theatre between 1866 and 1914. *H. B. Garland, Ph.D. 1935 Cambridge*

Theatre: Burma
The Burmese drama - with reference to the Elizabethan drama. *M. H. Aung, Ph.D. 1933 Dublin, Trinity College*

Theatre: France
Contribution á l'étude du théâtre en France pendant la révolution. *A. M. J. B. Souza, Ph.D. 1926 London*

English contributions to experiments in French drama in the eighteenth century. *H. A. Saer, Ph.D. 1934 London, Bedford College*

Theatre: France contd.

Etude sur la conception intuitive de l'action dramatique dans le théâtre français de 1885 à 1904. *E. H. Falk, Ph.D. 1942 Manchester*

Experiments with the unexpressed in the modern French drama. *M. Daniels, Ph.D. 1948 Edinburgh*

The French romantic drama on modern subjects. *D. O. Evans, D.Phil. 1923 Oxford*

The French theatre in the 18th century. *M. J. Flynn, M.A. 1943 National University of Ireland*

A general view of the influence of the French drama on that of England between 1660 and 1714. *S. E. Goggin, M.A. 1908 London*

Germany's relations to France in drama and criticism between 1870 and 1890. *T. P. Williams, M.A. 1936 Wales*

Joseph Bouchardy and French melodrama. *R. V. Gardner, M.A. 1947 London, External Degree*

La question de l'adultérie dans le théâtre français, 1750-1850. *J. H. Halloran, M.A. 1928 Leeds*

La renaissance de l'idéalisme et sa réaction sur le théâtre en France, 1890-1900. *D. Knowles, M.A. 1931 Leeds*

Le Juif au théâtre en France. *C. S. Edelstein, M.A. 1922 Leeds*

Le théâtre classique en France et la tradition nationale. *R. R. Stephens, M.Litt. 1935 Durham*

Le théâtre naturaliste: origin and development. *O. Wardman, Ph.D. 1930 London, External Degree*

Le thème de Phèdre et d'Hippolyte dans le théâtre français avant Racine. *W. Newton, M.A. 1938 Manchester*

L'oeuvre française de Carlo Goldoni. *E. R. Lloyd, M.A. 1938 Manchester*

Marivaux' debt to his predecessors in the drama. *L. N. Laurier, Ph.D. 1941 London, King's College*

Notes sur un choix d'oeuvres dramatiques au dix-neuvième siècle. *N. M. Bévenot, M.A. 1913 Liverpool*

Otway: his indebtedness in tragedy to French drama and to the *Nouvelles de Saint-Réal. K. E. Ashwell, M.A. 1908 London*

Quelques traces de L'influence espagnole au théâtre français du 17e siècle: Lope de Vega et J. Rotrou. *F. Astley, M.A. 1928 Birmingham*

Stendhal, dramatic theorist and playwright. *C. E. Hurren, Ph.D. 1934 London, Bedford College*

A study in the dramatic relationships of France, Spain and England in the seventeenth century. *L. du G. Peach, Ph.D. 1921 Sheffield*

Victor Hugo et le mélodrame. *A. M. Ahearne, M.A. 1942 National University of Ireland*

Woman's rights and feminism in the contemporary French theatre. *C. R. Bagley, B.Litt. 1922 Oxford*

Theatre: Germany

The child in the German drama, from the time of Goethe and Schiller. *M. Titterton, M.A. 1908 Birmingham*

Christophorus Kormart's adaptations of Pierre Corneille's *Polyeucte* and *Héraclius* and their relation to the contemporary German drama of the seventeenth century. *P. H. Powell, M.A. 1936 Wales*

Das bürgerliche Trauerspiel. *E. Power, M.A. 1927 National University of Ireland*

The evolution of the historical drama in Germany during the first half of the nineteenth century. *G. A. C. Houston, M.A. 1919 London*

Expressionist drama in modern Germany. *W. T. Owen, M.A. 1931 Wales*

The German drama under the influence of the Great War and the revolution. *H. F. Koenigsgarten, D.Phil. 1944 Oxford*

Germany's relations to France in drama and criticism between 1870 and 1890. *T. P. Williams, M.A. 1936 Wales*

Growth of the naturalist drama in Germany, with special reference to Gerhart Hauptmann. *B. E. Thomas, M.A. 1931 Wales*

The influence of English literature on the German novel and drama in the period 1880-1900. *A. E. Eastlake, Ph.D. 1937 London, Birkbeck College*

The influence of French literature upon German prose and dramatic literature from 1880 to 1900. *A. H. King, Ph.D. 1934 London, Birkbeck College*

Kotzebue: a reconsideration of his place in European drama. *L. F. Thompson, M.A. 1926 London*

Theatre: Germany contd.

Medieval themes in modern German drama since 1900. *E. R. Tigg, Ph.D. 1937 London, External Degree*

The problem of history and drama in German dramatic theory and practice in the nineteenth century. *H. M. L. Lund, M.A. 1943 London, Bedford College*

Some phases of the historical German drama since Schiller's death: the patriotic, the antique Roman and the revolutionary. *M. D. I. Lloyd, M.A. 1912 Wales*

A study of the technique of German drama from Goethe to Hebbel. *H. B. Edwards, M.A. 1936 Wales*

The supernatural in German drama of the early nineteenth century. *E. Bennett, M.A. 1919 Birmingham*

The use of lyrics in German drama. *R. Weil, B.Litt. 1950 Oxford*

Theatre: Great Britain

An account of the English stage in the last years before Garrick. *U. M. Ellis-Fermor, B.Litt. 1922 Oxford*

The acting tradition in England during the period 1730-1760. *H. C. Wiltshire, M.A. 1935 London, Queen Mary College*

The acting tradition in England between 1800 and 1830, with special reference to Shakespeare's plays. *G. E. Batchelor, Ph.D. 1939 London, King's College*

An analysis of dramatic speech in English literature before 1550. *S. E. J. Hodge, M.A. 1947 London, Birkbeck College*

Andreas Gryphius and the Elizabethan drama. *D. B. Evans, M.A. 1950 Wales*

The Cibbers, father and son, as actors, dramatists and writers. *P. T. Rees, M.A. 1931 Wales*

Cleopatra on the English stage. *O. C. de C. Ellis, M.A. 1946 Sheffield*

Collaboration between playwrights in the Elizabethan drama. *E. J. Burton, M.A. 1930 London, University College*

A comparative study of the supernatural element in Elizabethan drama and in modern drama. *M. Kilduff, M.A. 1937 Liverpool*

Contributions to the history of the English theatre and drama in Wales, 1737-1843. *C. J. L. Price, M.A. 1939 Wales*

The court stage, 1660-1702. *E. Boswell, Ph.D. 1930 London, University College*

A critical study of the dramatic work of John Bale and its relation to the English dramatic tradition and contemporary developments. *W. T. Davies, B.Litt. 1936 Oxford*

Criticism and appreciation of Elizabethan drama: Dryden to Swinburne. *F. C. Baxter, Ph.D. 1933 Cambridge*

The crowd: collective and individual aspects in Elizabethan drama, 1580-1610. *A. M. McGregor, M.A. 1927 London*

The debt of the eighteenth century novel to the drama. *P. M. Adair, M.A. 1942 Belfast*

Dekker and the artizan in the Elizabethan drama. *M. M. M. Mackinlay, M.A. 1949 Manchester*

Demonology, magic, and witchcraft in the English drama, 1580-1642. *F. M. N. Trefethen, M.Litt. 1950 Cambridge*

The development of the tragic consciousness in Elizabethan drama. *C. F. Obermeyer, Ph.D. 1928 London*

Dialect in Tudor drama. *H. M. Hulme, M.A. 1937 London, Courtauld Institute of Art*

Dramatic creation as exemplified in Shakespeare's plays. *H. Brown, D.Litt. 1927 Glasgow*

Dramatic criticism in early nineteenth century periodicals (1800-1830), and its influence on the contemporary drama. *A. C. Norenius, Ph.D. 1931 London, East London College*

Dramatic theory and the rhymed heroic play. *C. V. Deane, Ph.D. 1929 Cambridge*

The Elizabethan drama as the newspaper of the age; a study of the influence of external controlling factors on the drama of the early seventeenth century as a potential medium for reflecting popular opinion on political and social questions. *L. F. Turner, M.A. 1938 London, University College*

English drama from Robertson. *J. Herman, Ph.D. 1921 Cambridge*

Theatre: Great Britain contd.

English drama of the mid-nineteenth century. *E. R. Reynolds, Ph.D. 1934 Cambridge*

The English stage and the English scene (Elizabeth to Victoria). *G. Morris, M.A. 1950 National University of Ireland*

English verse drama: its history and its place in the twentieth century. *A. C. R. Taylor, M.Litt. 1934 Cambridge*

Expressionism in modern English drama. *L. W. A. Andrew, M.A. 1938 Bristol*

Fortune in Elizabethan drama: an attempt to discover, chiefly from plays written between 1570 and 1620, the conception of that period concerning the person and activities of the goddess Fortuna. *R. Chapman, M.A. 1947 London, King's College*

Galsworthy's contribution to modern drama. *S. G. Rees, M.A. 1937 Wales*

A general view of the influence of the French drama on that of England between 1660 and 1714. *S. E. Goggin, M.A. 1908 London*

The historical play in the age of Elizabeth. *J. C. Hipkins, M.A. 1910 Birmingham*

The history and significance of the early Elizabethan drama. *W. P. Davies, M.A. 1910 Wales*

The history and significance of the early Elizabethan drama. *T. Mathews, M.A. 1908 Wales*

The history and significance of the early Elizabethan drama. *J. M. Judd, M.A. 1914 Wales*

The history of the drama in Essex from the fifteenth century to the present time. *W. A. Mepham, Ph.D. 1937 London, Queen Mary College*

The influence of British drama on the Indian stage, with special reference to western India. *R. K. Yajnik, Ph.D. 1932 London, East London College*

Influence of Elizabethan drama on heroic tragedy. *J. D. Carey, M.A. 1929 London*

The influence of French farce on English sixteenth century drama. *I. R. Maxwell, B.Litt. 1935 Oxford*

The influence of Latin drama on Elizabethan drama. *F. Hale, M.A. 1920 Birmingham*

The influence of radical doctrine in the French Revolution on English drama in the time of Thomas Holcroft, 1776 to 1806. *W. V. Aughterson, Ph.D. 1936 London, King's College*

The influence of Shakespeare on the eighteenth century drama (1700-1780). *M. A. Pink, M.A. 1920 London*

The influence of the morality play upon the regular Elizabethan drama. *G. E. Hollingworth, M.A. 1915 London*

The influence of the stage and its appurtenances on drama. *C. P. Duncan, M.A. 1949 National University of Ireland*

An investigation of the development and character of the influence of Terence and Plautus on the earlier English drama, with some account of fifteenth and sixteenth century editions of their plays in England. *T. C. Rising, M.A. 1933 London, King's College*

Italian and English pastoral drama of the Renaissance: a comparative study. *V. M. Jeffery, M.A. 1922 London*

John Rich and the eighteenth century stage. *L. V. Paulin, M.A. 1936 London, University College*

The language of the Elizabethan drama. *M. Evans, Ph.D. 1940 Cambridge*

London theatres, 1700 to 1714, as reflected in the periodical press of the time. *A. Jackson, Ph.D. 1936 London, External Degree*

The lyrics and songs of the Elizabethan drama. *H. Morris, M.A. 1912 Wales*

Modern British drama in relation to the plays of Ibsen. *V. T. Jones, M.A. 1928 Liverpool*

Monologue, soliloquy and aside in the pre-Restoration drama. *B. L. Joseph, D.Phil. 1946 Oxford*

The place of seasonal ritual in the medieval English drama. *H. J. Hammerton, M.A. 1944 Leeds*

Private performances and amateur theatricals (excluding the academic stage) from 1580 to 1660, with an edition of one or more of the plays presented before the Earl of Westmorland, 1640-1650. *C. E. J. Leech, Ph.D. 1935 London, Queen Mary College*

Prologues and epilogues of the Restoration period, 1660-1700, considered in relation to the audience, theatrical conditions, and the dramatic productivity of the age. *S. M. Rosenfeld, M.A. 1925 London*

Theatre: Great Britain contd.
Realism in the Elizabethan drama, with special reference to citizen comedy. *H. I. Wilkie, Ph.D. 1923 Edinburgh*

Records of early drama in Scotland. *A. J. Mill, Ph.D. 1925 Saint Andrew's*

The relationship between iconography of the Middle Ages and medieval English drama. *J. I. Jones, M.A. 1939 Wales*

Romantic drama, 1780-1830, considered in the light of the theatrical history of the period. *K. C. Musafar, Ph.D. 1924 London*

Satire in Elizabethan drama. *P. Brady, Ph.D. 1942 National University of Ireland*

The significance of domestic drama in English literature, with special reference to four extant Elizabethan domestic tragedies, and with an excursus on their authorship. *H. M. Davies, M.A. 1911 Wales*

Sir Walter Scott and the drama with some account of the theatre in Edinburgh. *W. G. Dustan, Ph.D. 1933 Edinburgh*

The social life of 'the town' as represented by some of the Elizabethan dramatists. *M. N. Howlett, M.A. 1912 London*

Some aspects of the English scriptural drama in relation to the times. *E. C. Oakden, M.A. 1918 Birmingham*

Some conventions of Elizabethan drama. *A. E. Outram, D.Phil. 1939 Oxford*

Staging in England from the earliest times to 1576, with special reference to the stage directions. *G. Baldwin, M.A. 1931 Manchester*

Staging in the Restoration: with special reference to stage directions in the plays of the time. *F. W. Payne, Ph.D. 1926 London*

The staging of Elizabethan plays. *V. L. Taylor, M.A. 1911 Birmingham*

Studies in the development of the fool in the Elizabethan drama. *O. M. Busby, M.A. 1916 London*

Studies in the guild drama in London, from 1515 to 1550, in the records of the Drapers' Company. *P. G. Lusher, Ph.D. 1940 London, University College*

Studies in the theatrical companies and actors of Elizabethan times, with special reference to the period 1616-1642. *G. E. Bentley, Ph.D. 1930 London, East London College*

A study in the dramatic relationships of France, Spain and England in the seventeenth century. *L. du G. Peach, Ph.D. 1921 Sheffield*

A study of the burlesque drama from D'Avenant to Fielding. *R. K. Kapur, B.Litt. 1934 Oxford*

A study of the dramatic monologue, with special consideration of its development in the Victorian age. *M. G. Philpot, M.A. 1920 London*

The study of the pre-Shakespearian drama before Malone. *H. H. Sargeant, B.Litt. 1940 Oxford*

A study of the seventeenth century masque. *R. Banks, M.A. 1912 Birmingham*

The theme of Antony and Cleopatra in English drama. *A. May, B.Litt. 1937 Oxford*

The theme of honour as present in the English drama, 1485-1642, with special reference to the dramatic use of the duel. *F. R. Cooper, M.A. 1946 London, King's College*

Thomas Lovell Beddoes and the dramatists of the Elizabethan Age. *H. W. Donner, B.Litt. 1932 Oxford*

Treatment of the rustic and the citizen in Elizabethan drama. *M. M. Frost, M.A. 1916 London*

Victor Hugo and the English stage. *V. E. A. Bowley, M.A. 1927 London*

Victorian drama as the reflection of the age. *D. Walsh, M.A. 1942 National University of Ireland*

The Welsh character and his development in English drama, 1590-1642. *B. Pierce-Jones, M.A. 1949 Manchester*

The witch in the English drama. *M. M. C. Pollard, Cert.Litt. 1917 Oxford*

Theatre: Greece, Ancient
The historical evidence contained in Aristophanes and in the fragments of the Old Attic Comedy. *B. H. G. Williams, B.Litt. 1932 Oxford*

The structure and scenic arrangements of the Greek theatre. *G. E. Holding, M.A. 1907 Wales*

Theatre: India
The Bengali drama: its origin and development. *P. Guhathakurta, Ph.D. 1926 London*

The influence of British drama on the Indian stage, with special reference to western India. *R. K. Yajnik, Ph.D. 1932 London, East London College*

Studies in the Sanskrit drama. *V. G. Bhat, Ph.D. 1933 Cambridge*

Theatre: Ireland
The Abbey Theatre and the principal writers connected therewith. *H. J. Butler, M.A. 1925 National University of Ireland*

Comedy in the Irish theatre; its genius. *J. Horgan, M.A. 1936 National University of Ireland*

Drámaidheacht na Gaedhilge (The dramatisation of Irish). *T. Kavanagh, M.A. 1929 National University of Ireland*

The dramatic movement in Ireland. *K. E. Murphy, M.A. 1922 Birmingham*

The history of Anglo-Irish drama from the earliest period up to 1750. *P. Kavanagh, Ph.D. 1944 Dublin, Trinity College*

Realism in Irish drama. *J. B. McGuire, Ph.D. 1941 Dublin, Trinity College*

Theatre: Italy
Italian and English pastoral drama of the Renaissance: a comparative study. *V. M. Jeffery, M.A. 1922 London*

Theatre: Jesuits
An introduction to the Jesuit theatre. *W. H. McCabe, Ph.D. 1929 Cambridge*

Theatre: Rome
The influence of Latin drama on Elizabethan drama. *F. Hale, M.A. 1920 Birmingham*

An investigation of the development and character of the influence of Terence and Plautus on the earlier English drama, with some account of fifteenth and sixteenth century editions of their plays in England. *T. C. Rising, M.A. 1933 London, King's College*

Livy and Horace on the origins of the Roman drama. *R. A. Browne, Ph.D. 1931 Cambridge*

Popularity and decline of Roman drama. *R. McKernan, M.A. 1918 National University of Ireland*

The Roman attitude to drama before the death of Augustus. *M. Boys, M.A. 1947 Leeds*

The Roman theatre. *R. H. Tudor, M.Litt. 1936 Durham*

Theatre: Russia
The origin and early history of the theatre in Russia, 1672 to 1756. *B. Malnick, Ph.D. 1936 London, School of Slavonic and East European Studies*

A study of the academic drama in Russia and the Ukraine in the seventeenth and eighteenth centuries, with special reference to its Polish origins. *L. R. Lewitter, Ph.D. 1950 Cambridge*

Theatre: South Africa
Theatres and plays in Natal, 1846-1897. *N. S. Freeman, M.A. 1949 Birmingham*

Theatre: Spain
The character of Don Pedro in the chronicles, romancero, and Spanish theatre up to 1700. *N. E. Gardiner, M.Litt. 1939 Cambridge*

Culteranism in the Spanish theatre of the seventeenth century, with particular reference to the works of Calderón de la Barca. *E. M. Wilson, Ph.D. 1933 Cambridge*

The Spanish stage in the time of Shakespeare and Lope de Vega. *J. Garcia Lora, M.A. 1947 Birmingham*

A study in the dramatic relationships of France, Spain and England in the seventeenth century. *L. du G. Peach, Ph.D. 1921 Sheffield*

Theatre: Switzerland
Das Streben nach dem Drama in der deutschschweizerischen Literatur des neunzehnten und beginnenden zwanzigsten Jahrhunderts. *P. Lang, M.A. 1923 London*

Theatre Royal (Birmingham)
The Theatre Royal, Birmingham. *J. E. Cunningham, M.A. 1949 Birmingham*

Thebes
Methods of representing hair in the wall-paintings of Theban tombs. *E. J. H. Mackay, M.A. 1922 Bristol*

Theism
See also God; Transcendentalism; and Martineau, J.

Theism contd.
The aesthetic approach to theism. *T. W. Taylor, Ph.D. 1935 Cambridge*

The argument from design. *W. L. Northridge, M.A. 1920 Belfast*

Arguments for theism from design in nature with special reference to Hume, Paley, and Kant. *P. P. Elliott, B.Litt. 1926 Oxford*

The Bridgewater Treatises: their theological significance. *M. C. Thompson, Ph.D. 1949 Edinburgh*

A comparison between Christian theism and the religious beliefs of certain tribes in West Africa. *E. N. Jones, B.Litt. 1925 Oxford*

The idea of the supernatural and of the transcendent in primitive and modern theistic thought. *T. J. E. Hopkins, M.A. 1934 Liverpool*

The moral ideal and its bearing on theism. *G. Charlesworth, M.A. 1945 Liverpool*

The moral judgments and their theistic implications. *Y. L. Jackson, Ph.D. 1940 Edinburgh*

Plato's philosophical theism. *J. W. Griffiths, M.A. 1920 Wales*

Plato's philosophical theism. *J. W. Griffiths, M.A. 1919 London*

The psychological approach to theism. *N. A. Turner-Smith, B.Litt. 1923 Oxford*

The rational, the arational, and the irrational in the epistemology of theism: an essay in the philosophy of faith. *J. F. Butler, Ph.D. 1936 Manchester*

Restatements of the moral argument for God in recent British theism. *H. P. Van Dusen, Ph.D. 1932 Edinburgh*

The scholastic approach to theism. *H. S. Box, Ph.D. 1933 London, External Degree*

Some aspects of modern theism. *G. J. M. Pearce, M.A. 1946 Birmingham*

Some aspects of theism, particularly of its treatment by three modern theistic authors: A. S. Pringle-Pattison, F. R. Tennant, G. D. Hicks. *G. T. Eddy, M.A. 1940 Birmingham*

A study of the relation of Plato's philosophy to theism. *C. H. Rose, M.A. 1922 Birmingham*

Theism and ideas of value. *D. E. Williams, M.A. 1924 Wales*

Theism and the problem of evil. *J. R. Jones, M.A. 1929 Wales*

Theism, old and new. *J. Fahey, M.A. 1917 National University of Ireland*

The theistic philosophy of Hermann Lotze. *A. K. Rule, Ph.D. 1923 Edinburgh*

Themistocles
Cimon and Themistocles: a comparison and a contrast. *A. W. Barth, M.A. 1907 London*

Theobald, Lewis
The work of Theobald and his predecessors on the text of Shakespeare. *H. M. King, Ph.D. 1940 London, External Degree*

Theodore, of Tarsus, Saint, Archbishop
Theodore of Tarsus, Archbishop of Canterbury, A.D. 668-690. *R. H. Whitaker, Ph.D. 1948 Edinburgh*

Theodoret, Bishop of Cyros
Theodoret, bishop of Cyros and follower of the Antioch school in the Monophysite controversy, A.D. 441-457. *J. Malathouras, B.Litt. 1921 Oxford*

Theology
This heading includes general and Christian theology. See also under the names of individual religions and sects. See also Agnosticism; Angels; Apologetics; Atonement; Bible; Christian Union; Church, Doctrine of; Conscience; Creation and the Fall; Determinism; Epistemology; Eschatology; Ethics; Evil; Faith; Fate; Forgiveness; Free Will; God; Grace; Holy Spirit; Immanence; Jesus Christ; Justification; Kingdom of God; Logos; Metaphysics; Neoplatonism; Patristics; Prayer; Predestination; Prophecy; Providence; Punishment; Redemption; Religious Conversion; Repentance; Revelation; Sacraments; Sacrifice; Saints; Salvation; Sin; Soul; Supernatural; Theism; Transcendentalism; Trinity.

Aberdeen divines, being a history of the chair of divinity at King's College, Aberdeen, 1620-. *G. D. Henderson, D.Litt. 1931 Glasgow*

1. The Christology of Clement of Alexandria. 2. The theology of the Wisdom literature. *R. B. Tollinton, B.D. 1905 Oxford*

Theology contd.
A comparison between the metaphysics of St. Thomas Aquinas and the metaphysics of Aristotle to illustrate the relation of Scholasticism and Aristotelianism. *H. J. W. Carpenter, B.Litt. 1926 Oxford*

The controversy between Karl Barth and Emil Brunner concerning natural theology. *J. Henderson, Ph.D. 1940 Edinburgh*

A critical edition of the *Quattuor determinationes patris Willelmi Wydeforde de ordine fratrum minorum contre Wycliff et Wyclyvianos in materia de religion*. *M. D. Dobson, B.Litt. 1932 Oxford*

Doctrina poetarum: a survey of the doctrinal content of English poetry from Caedmon to Scott in the light of the *Summa theologica* of St. Thomas Aquinas. *S. J. C. Gaffney, Ph.D. 1938 National University of Ireland*

Existence and analogy. *E. L. Mascall, D.D. 1948 Oxford*

1. Illustrations of the doctrines of Christianity from natural religion. 2. The value of evidences in Christian theology. *H. R. Huckin, B.D. 1874 Oxford*

The influence of Hegel's philosophy upon theology in Wales from 1850 to the present day. *P. J. Jones, M.A. 1927 Wales*

Kant's view of the relation between theology and ethics. *W. M. Watt, B.Litt. 1933 Oxford*

Piers Plowman as a work of moral theology. *G. Hjort, Ph.D. 1932 Cambridge*

A re-examination of the so-called 'theology of Aristotle'. *G. L. Lewis, D.Phil. 1950 Oxford*

The relation of theology to epistemology, with special reference to Hume. *R. J. Tree, M.A. 1939 Wales*

The relations between theology and music viewed in the light of the works of theologians and the decisions of ecclesiastical authorities. *E. R. Routley, B.D. 1946 Oxford*

1. The re-union of the Christian Church, viewed under some of its present aspects. 2. Man in God's image as revealed in Scripture. *J. P. Way, B.D. & D.D. 1896 Oxford*

The rise and growth of the liberal theology in New England to 1825. *J. F. King, Ph.D. 1939 Edinburgh*

Robert of Orford and his place in the scholastic controversies at Oxford in the late thirteenth century, with an edition of his *Reprobationes* of Giles of Rome. *A. P. Vella, B.Litt. 1946 Oxford*

1. St. Paul's claim for dogmatic theology. 2. The resurrection of Jesus Christ: the keystone of the faith. *W. C. Eppstein, B.D. & D.D. 1905 Oxford*

1. The scope and method of rational theology. 2. The proof of the being of God. *H. J. Bidder, B.D. 1877 Oxford*

An sgáthán spioradálta (The spiritual mirror). *J. Faulkner, Ph.D. 1945 National University of Ireland*

1. Some aspects of theology of Methodius of Olympus. 2. Some features of the theological language of the *Dialects* of Adamantius. *C. Jenkins, B.D. & D.D. 1924 Oxford*

The structure of Caroline moral theology. *H. R. McAdoo, D.D. 1949 Dublin, Trinity College*

A study of some Oxford Schoolmen of the middle of the fourteenth century, with special reference to Worcester Cathedral ms. F.65. *S. L. Forte, B.Litt. 1947 Oxford*

A survey of the fundamental ideas in the mind of Christ as interpreted in the theological literature of Britain and America since *Ecce homo* (1865). *A. White, Ph.D. 1927 Edinburgh*

Tennyson's religious, social and political ideas in relation to his time. *L. J. Smethurst, M.A. 1948 London, King's College*

Theology in English poetry. *S. J. C. Gaffney, Ph.D. 1941 National University of Ireland*

Theology in the English poets of the Victorian era. *L. S. Peake, B.Litt. 1926 Oxford*

The thought of Léon Bloy: an interpretation of the life and character of Léon Bloy, with special reference to his theology. *M. H. Williams, M.A. 1950 Wales*

A translation of theological terms and ideas into the languages of evangelization, ancient and modern, particularly those of the Bantu family. *W. A. Norton, B.Litt. 1916 Oxford*

1. The witness of the Old Testament to the immanence of God in nature and in man. 2. The theology of the Pastoral Epistle. *W. H. Fremantle, B.D. & D.D. 1895 Oxford*

Theology: Study of
For references to theological studies and writers, see under Church History; Patristics; Philosophy; King's College, Aberdeen; and Abelard, P.; Andrewes, L.; Anselm, Saint; Arminius, J.; Arnauld, A.; Barth, K.; Bonaventura, Saint; Boston, T.; Browne, R.; Bunyan, J.; Bushnell, H.; Butler, J., Bishop; Calvin, J.; Campbell, J. M.; Carlyle, T.; Cartwright, T.; Chalmers, T.; Channing, W. E.; Clémanges, N. P. de; Coleridge, S. T.; Denck, H.; Duns Scotus, J.; Eckhart, J.; Edwards, J.; Erasmus, D.; Erskine, T.; Fairbairn, A. M.; Fraser, J.; Gerdil, G. S.; Gorham, G. C.; Hooker, R.; Hügel, F. von, Baron; Hugh, of Saint Victor; Hus, J.; John, of Salisbury; Knox, J.; Lamennais, F. R. de; Langton, S., Archbishop; Law, W.; Le Clerc, J.; Leighton, R., Archbishop; Luther, M.; Malebranche, N.; Maurice, F. D.; Molinos, M. de; Morison, J.; Mozley, J. B.; Newman, J. H.; Orford, R., Bishop; Otto, R.; Owen, J.; Paley, W.; Pascal, B.; Pecock, R., Bishop; Pennington, I.; Psichari, E.; Rashdall, H.; Richard, of Saint Victor; Ritschl, A.; Robertson, F. W.; Rolle, R.; Schleiermacher, F. D. E.; Smith, S.; South, R.; Suarez, F. de; Taylor, J.; Thomas Aquinas, Saint; Toplady, A. M.; Tschudi, G.; Tucker, J.; Tyrell, G.; Ullerston, R.; Warburton, W., Bishop; Watson, R., Bishop; Wesley, J.; Whitefield, G.; William, of Occam.

Théophile, de Viau
The debt of English poetry in the seventeenth century to Théophile and Saint-Amant. *J. Short, B.Litt. 1941 Oxford*

Theophrastus
Studies on the botanical researches and method of Theophrastos. *V. Sinnatamby, M.Sc. 1948 London, University College*

Theosophy
The early years of George Russell (AE) and his connection with the theosophical movement. *W. M. Gibbon, Ph.D. 1947-48 Dublin, Trinity College*

1. Some heads of a Christian answer to the neo-Buddhist theosophy. 2. Some considerations, scriptural and modern, concerning sin. *T. S. Lea, B.D. 1905 Oxford*

Thermometers
See also Heat.

The development of the thermometer from 300 B.C. to A.D. *H. Shaw, M.Sc. 1922 London*

Thessaly
The history of Thessaly. *R. Williams, M.A. 1903 Wales*

The history of Thessaly up to 323 B.C. *E. J. Lloyd, M.A. 1914 Wales*

Thessaly in the thirteenth century B.C. and the origin of the Centaur-Lapithai myth. *N. Bachtin, Ph.D. 1934 Cambridge*

Thevet, André
André Thevet: his work as a geographer. *R. E. Fowler, B.Litt. 1930 Oxford*

Thibaudet, Albert
A contribution to the study of Albert Thibaudet as a critic of the novel. *M. K. Leiper, Ph.D. 1939 London, University College*

Thibault, Jacques Anatole François
See France, Anatole.

Thinking
See also Logic; Philosophy; Psychology.

A logical examination of non-propositional forms of thought, with special reference to aesthetics. *C. M. Fremlin, B.Litt. 1938 Oxford*

The part played by kinaesthetic experience in perception and in thinking. *W. Strzalkowski, D.Phil. 1946 Oxford*

The part played by symbols in thinking, with special reference to belief, and cognate states. *J. L. Evans, D.Phil. 1945 Oxford*

Psychological researches into the nature of thinking. *H. F. Friedlander, M.A. 1946 Birmingham*

The relation of thought to reality. *H. A. Overstreet, B.Sc. 1901 Oxford*

A study of abstract thinking and linguistic development with reference to the education of a child of 'average' intelligence. *I. E. Campbell, Ph.D. 1943 Reading*

A study of the possibility of improving habits of thought in school children by a training in logic. *E. F. White, M.A. 1935 London, Institute of Education*

The subconscious factors of mental process considered in relation to thought. *A. M. Bodkin, M.A. 1902 Wales*

Thirty Years' War
The diplomatic relations between England and Germany during the Thirty Years' War, with an introductory chapter on their relations between 1603 and 1618. *E. A. Beller, D.Phil. 1923 Oxford*

Thomas à Becket, Saint, Archbishop
Contribution to the study of the life of Thomas Becket, with special reference to the mss. of the poem *De Sancto Thoma, archiepiscopo cantuariensi*. *H. H. Hodge, M.A. 1923 Oxford*

The tradition of Saint Thomas of Canterbury in literature, art and religion. *A. B. Cottle, M.A. 1947 Wales*

Thomas Aquinas, Saint
Causality in Al-Ghazali, Averroes, and Aquinas. *M. Fakhry, Ph.D. 1949 Edinburgh*

A comparison between the metaphysics of St. Thomas Aquinas and the metaphysics of Aristotle to illustrate the relation of Scholasticism and Aristotelianism. *H. J. W. Carpenter, B.Litt. 1926 Oxford*

The concept of creation in the metaphysics of St. Thomas. *J. F. Cummins, M.A. 1943 National University of Ireland*

The content of our natural knowledge of God in the philosophy of St. Thomas Aquinas. *E. Quinn, M.A. 1948 Leeds*

Doctrina poetarum. *H. M. Gaffney, M.A. 1939 National University of Ireland*

Doctrina poetarum: a survey of the doctrinal content of English poetry from Caedmon to Scott in the light of the *Summa theologica* of St. Thomas Aquinas. *S. J. C. Gaffney, Ph.D. 1938 National University of Ireland*

The ethics of S. Thomas Aquinas considered in regard to their relevance to present day problems. *H. S. Marshall, M.A. 1934 Bristol*

Evil according to St Thomas. *C. Lucey, M.A. 1930 National University of Ireland*

Exemplary causality in the philosophy of St. Thomas. *P. Creed, M.A. 1947 National University of Ireland*

God and creatures in the philosophy of St. Thomas Aquinas and A. N. Whitehead. *W. A. Whitehouse, B.Litt. 1940 Oxford*

The influence of the pseudo Dionysius the Areopagite on the philosophy of St. Thomas Aquinas. *S. J. Curtis, Ph.D. 1931 London, External Degree*

Knowledge of the particular in St. Thomas Aquinas, including a discussion of the principle of individuation. *W. G. Maclagan, Ph.D. 1928 Edinburgh*

The law of nature: the Patristic conception as contrasted with the Thomist. *J. Dalby, B.D. 1942 Oxford*

Man's knowledge of God as treated by St. Thomas Aquinas. *R. L. Patterson, Ph.D. 1933 London, University College*

The method of reflection in the philosophy of St. Thomas. *T. F. Fitzgerald, M.A. 1950 National University of Ireland*

The notion of *virtus moralis* in S. Thomas Aquinas and its sources. *B. B. Magrath, B.Litt. 1948 Oxford*

The philosophy of law of St. Thomas Aquinas. *F. H. Hunt, Ph.D. 1942 Cambridge*

St. Thomas and the problem of evil. *T. Connellan, M.A. 1944 National University of Ireland*

The scholasticism of Christianity and of Islam so far as they are represented by the *Summa contra gentiles* of St. Thomas Aquinas and the *Nihayatu-l-igdam fi ilmil-kalam* of Al Shahrastani. *A. Guillaume, B.D. & D.D. 1934 Oxford*

Some aspects of the Thomist theory of knowledge, in their metaphysical reference. *A. Mallouk, B.Litt. 1947 Oxford*

The teaching of Dante on the human intellect, with special reference to the doctrine of St. Thomas Aquinas. *F. S. Foster, Ph.D. 1947 Cambridge*

The theory and aim of education; some Thomistic principles. *P. O'C. Ryan, M.A. 1929 National University of Ireland*

The theory of active and passive intellect from Aristotle to Aquinas. *S. J. Curtis, M.A. 1922 London*

The theory of substance as developed by Aquinas, considered with reference to later philosophy. *C. P. Ryan, D.Phil. 1948 Oxford*

Thomistic concept of natural law in ethics. *M. B. Crowe, M.A. 1945 National University of Ireland*

Thomas Aquinas, Saint contd.
1. The Thomistic doctrine of the sacramental form or matter. 2. The reality of the Holy Spirit's indwelling in the souls of the sanctified. *W. K. Firminger, B.D. 1905 Oxford*

Thought and sense in the philosophy of St. Thomas Aquinas. *P. H. Williams, M.A. 1949 Wales*

The transcendent relation of reality to truth as the fundamental tenet of the philosophy of St. Thomas Aquinas. *L. L. Keyes, B.Litt. 1934 Oxford*

The transformation of an old ideal: Aristotle-Aquinas-modern idealism. *H. W. Perkins, M.A. 1928 Bristol*

Truth, unity, and goodness as aspects of being in the writings of St. Thomas Aquinas. *W. W. S. March, B.D. 1941 Oxford*

Thomas, David (Dafydd Ddu of Eryri)
Dafydd Ddu o Eryri a'i gysylltiadau llenyddol (Dafydd Ddu of Eryri and his literary connections). *G. T. Roberts, M.A. 1929 Wales*

Thomas of Erceldoune
Thomas of Erceldoune: edited with an introduction notes and a glossary. *I. M. Nixon, Ph.D. 1947 Edinburgh*

Thomas, of Woodstock, Duke of Gloucester
The career of Thomas, Duke of Gloucester. *H. G. Wright, M.A. 1931 London, Birkbeck College*

Thomas, Owen
A review and revision of the biography of John Jones, Talsarn, by Owen Thomas. *D. E. Jenkins, M.A. 1924 Liverpool*

Thomas Robert (Ap Fychan)
Ap Fychan; ei fywyd, a'i waith, a'i gysylltiadau llenyddol (Ap Fychan: life, work and literary connections). *W. Williams, M.A. 1931 Wales*

Thomas, Saint and Apostle
1. The Apostle Jude: is he to be identified with Jude the servant of Jesus Christ and brother of James? 2. SS. Philip, Bartholomew, Matthew, and Thomas: being an inquiry from New Testament records into the second group in the Apostolate. *A. C. Evans, B.D. 1901 Oxford*

Thomism
See Thomas Aquinas, Saint.

Thompson, Francis
Aspects of the nineteenth century quest for God as reflected in the works of Thomas Hardy, Robert Browning and Francis Thompson. *A. M. Granville, M.A. 1950 Wales*

Francis Thompson. *W. V. Russell, M.A. 1937 National University of Ireland*

Francis Thompson. *E. Sullivan, M.A. 1927 National University of Ireland*

Francis Thompson: a study of his relation to George Herbert, Henry Vaughan and Richard Crashaw. *C. Bergin, M.A. 1948 National University of Ireland*

The life and works of Francis Thompson. *J. G. Hodge, M.A. 1936 Wales*

The nature of the mystical in the poetry of Francis Thompson. *T. McClintock, M.A. 1947 Manchester*

The poetry and prose of Francis Thompson: a critical study. *H. A. Ladd, B.Litt. 1923 Oxford*

The poetry of Francis Thompson. *D. L. Jones, M.A. 1936 Wales*

Problem of evil in Francis Thompson's poetry. *F. X. Lobo, M.A. 1945 National University of Ireland*

Three modern mystics: Thompson, Patmore, Hopkins. *J. M. Ryan, M.A. 1937 National University of Ireland*

Thomson, James
Barthold Hennrich Brockes' translation of James Thomson's *Seasons* and the influence of the *Seasons* on descriptive native nature poetry in Germany, with special reference to the poetry of Brockes and Christian Ewald von Kleist's poem *Der Frühling. G. E. W. Booy, M.A. 1940 Bristol*

James Thomson: poet of nature and reason. *E. S. Taylor, Ph.D. 1943 Edinburgh*

James Thomson (B.V.): his connexion with contemporary fashions in thought and literature. *M. J. Wolfe, B.Litt. 1940 Oxford*

Thoresby, Ralph
Ralph Thoresby and his circle, with special reference to the state of English historical scholarship in his time. *J. J. Saunders, M.A. 1936 London, External Degree*

Thornton, Henry
Wage theories in the nineteenth century, with special reference to Thornton. *A. C. McCarthy, M.Econ.Sc. 1941 National University of Ireland*

Thought
See Thinking.

Thraco-Illyrian Language
The Thraco-Illyrian language. *B. F. C. Atkinson, Ph.D. 1926 Cambridge*

Thread Industry
The gold and silver thread monopolies granted by James I, 1611-1621. *M. A. Abrams, Ph.D. 1930 London, School of Economics and Political Science*

Thucydides
A comparison of the principles and methods of Herodotus and Thucydides as historians. *T. B. Davis, M.A. 1901 Wales*

A comparison of the treatment of historical subjects by Aristophanes and Thucydides. *W. J. Jones, M.A. 1911 Wales*

A comparison of Thucydides and Aristophanes. *W. Jones, M.A. 1902 Wales*

The composition of Thucydides' *History. J. F. Counihan, M.A. 1939 National University of Ireland*

Thurston, John Bates, Sir
The career of Sir John Thurston, Governor of Fiji, 1888-1897. *J. Millington, M.A. 1947 London, Birkbeck College*

Tiberias
The city of Tiberias in the third and fourth centuries. *S. Mestel, M.A. 1918 London*

Tibet
Contributions to the climatology and geomorphology of Sino-Tibet and central China. *J. B. Hanson-Lowe, Ph.D. 1949 London, External Degree*

Western Tibet: a record of a threatened civilization. *C. L. H. Geary, Ph.D. 1948 London, External Degree*

Tibullus
The love of nature and rustic life in Horace, Tibullus, and Propertius. *M. J. Wrigley, M.A. 1933 Manchester*

Tickell, Thomas
Thomas Tickell: a study of his life and works. *J. E. Butt, B.Litt. 1928 Oxford*

Tieck, Johann Ludwig
An analysis of the short stories by Ludwig Tieck and Friedrich Hebbel, with special reference to style and structure. *H. H. J. Jensen, M.A. 1947 London, Bedford College*

J. L. Tieck and the *Volksbücher. A. M. Capell, M.A. 1912 London*

Ludwig Tieck's Shakespearean criticism. *H. Moses, M.A. 1939 London, University College*

The place of Italy in the life and works of Ludwig Tieck. *E. C. V. Stopp, Ph.D. 1938 Cambridge*

The relation of music and poetry as reflected in the works of Tieck, Wackenroder and Brentano. *M. E. Atkinson, M.A. 1947 London, Bedford College*

Tieck and Runge: a study in the relationship of literature and the fine arts in the German Romantic period, with special reference to Franz Sternbald. *J. B. C. Grundy, Ph.D. 1929 London*

Tiercelin, Louis
Louis Tiercelin and the Breton renascence. *R. Delaney, Ph.D. 1936 Leeds*

Tierney, George
George Tierney. *H. K. Olphin, M.A. 1933 London, King's College*

Tikhon, of Voronezh, Saint
St. Tikhon of Voronezh. *N. Gorodetzky, D.Phil. 1944 Oxford*

Timber
See Forestry.

Time
A critical account of the problem of time in its philosophical aspects. *D. Crowther, Ph.D. 1925 Glasgow*

The effects of time interval on recall. *V. N. Hall, M.A. 1935 London, King's College*

Freewill and time: a consideration of the metaphysical implications in regard to the nature of time, of the ethical doctrine of freewill. *A. E. Teale, B.Litt. 1937 Oxford*

An historical review of the nature of time and its connexion with value, in so far as these bear on the problems of personal freedom and human purpose. *W. A. Merrylees, B.Litt. 1923 Oxford*

The ideas of time and history in the development of thought up to the end of the eighteenth century. *W. von Leyden, D.Phil. 1944 Oxford*

Time contd.
An inquiry into the perception and memory of time relations, and particularly into the development of the time concept among high school children. *J. N. W. Hanter, Ph.D. 1934 Edinburgh*

On the cause of anomalous determinations of time. *M. R. Madwar, Ph.D. 1926 Edinburgh*

The problem of time. *S. G. Panandikar, M.Litt. 1931 Cambridge*

The problem of time: a critical examination in the light of recent discussions. *L. E. Thomas, M.A. 1938 Wales*

The problem of time, with special reference to its importance for modern thought. *M. F. Cleugh, Ph.D. 1936 London, Bedford College*

1. The psychology of time. 2. Modern psychology and education. *M. Sturt, Ph.D. 1932 Birmingham*

The sense of time and its relation to the teaching of chronology. *M. Kaye, M.A. 1933 Leeds*

Some experimental investigations on the length of the seconds pendulum, 1735-1830. *A. T. L. Rimmer, M.Sc. 1939 London, University College*

A theological study of the relationship of time and eternity, with special reference to the modern philosophy of history. *J. Marsh, D.Phil. 1946 Oxford*

Tin Industry
The economics of tin control. *P. Ungphakorn, Ph.D. 1949 London, School of Economics and Political Science*

Tinplate Industry
See Iron and Steel Industry.

Tipperary
History of Abbey School, Tipperary. *T. Crowley, M.A. 1943 National University of Ireland*

Titus and Vespasian
See Romances.

Titus Livius
See Livy.

Tobacco Industry
Anglo-American relations in the tobacco trade to the end of the nineteenth and the beginning of the twentieth century. *H. Chasey, M.A. 1950 Bristol*

The history of the tobacco trade in England. *A. Rive, M.Litt. 1927 Cambridge*

Tockwith Priory
The Cartulary of Tockwith. *G. C. Ransome, M.A. 1930 Manchester*

Tocqueville, Alexis Charles Henri Clérel de
Rousseau and De Tocqueville. *V. Buranelli, M.A. 1948 National University of Ireland*

Toleration
See Religious Tolerance.

Toller, Ernst
Ernst Toller. *R. W. Buckley, M.A. 1928 Liverpool*

Tolstoi, Leo Nikolaievich, Count
The influence of the Russian novel on French thinkers and writers, with particular reference to Tolstoy and Dostoevsky. *F. W. J. Hemmings, D.Phil. 1949 Oxford*

Le roman russe en France à la fin du dix-neuvième siècle considéré au point de vue de l'influence exercée par Tolstoi sur Paul Margueritte et Romain Rolland. *L. Godinski, Ph.D. 1923 London*

The reception and influence of the works of Leo Tolstoy in England, 1870-1910. *S. M. Price, M.A. 1936 Manchester*

Tombs
See also Burials.

Funerary monuments of India. *G. S. Ghuryne, Ph.D. 1923 Cambridge*

Megalithic chambered tombs of North-West Clare. *R. de Valera, M.A. 1944 National University of Ireland*

Tongues, Gift of
See Gift of Tongues.

Tonson, Jacob
Jacob Tonson. *T. Prince, M.A. 1932 Wales*

The life and work of Jacob Tonson. *G. F. Papali, Ph.D. 1934 London, University College*

Tools (Archaeology)
See also Axes.

The tools of Neanderthal man. *C. B. M. McBurney, Ph.D. 1948 Cambridge*

Toplady, Augustus Montague
Augustus Montague Toplady, hymn-writer and theologian, with special reference to his controversy with John Wesley. *J. Maycock, Ph.D. 1946 Edinburgh*

217

Trade: Ireland contd.
The trade of Dublin. *D. K. Smee, Ph.D. 1929 London*

Trade relations between Ireland and France, 1660-1793. *L. Cullen, M.A. 1956 National University of Ireland*

Trade: Italy
Commercial relations between England and Venice in the thirteenth and fourteenth centuries. *G. F. Shaw, M.A. 1909 London*

A general sketch of the history of the Italian merchants in England, 1272-1399, especially in connection with the wool trade. *A. Neild, M.A. 1914 London*

Trade: Japan
The industry and trade of Japan in modern times. *S. Uyehara, M.Sc. 1926 London*

Trade: Latin America
Historical study of Anglo-South American trade, with special reference to the period, 1807-1825. *J. S. Jones, Ph.D. 1934 London, School of Economics and Political Science*

Trade: Netherlands
Anglo-Flemish trading relations in the later Middle Ages. *L. M. Seckler, Ph.D. 1932 London, University College*

Trade: Nigeria
Extra-territorial non-mining companies in Nigeria in peace and war. *H. Mars, B.Litt. 1945 Oxford*

Trade: North America
American trade restrictions and British commerce 1808-12. *M. G. Knox, B.Litt. 1938 Oxford*

Trade: Poland
Foreign trade of Poland between 1918 and 1939 with special reference to the trade with Britain. *S. Florecki, Ph.D. 1943 Edinburgh*

Trade: Portugal
The commercial relations of England and Portugal: 1487-1807. *A. B. W. Chapman, D.Sc. 1907 London*

The commercial relations of England and Portugal: the Middle Ages. *V. M. Shillington, D.Sc. 1907 London*

Trade: Rome
Commerce in the time of the Empire between Italy and other countries. *W. W. Griffiths, M.A. 1922 Wales*

A dissertation on trade routes of the province of Asia Minor within the first three centuries of the Christian era. *A. H. Watts, Ph.D. 1926 London*

Trade: Rumania
Foreign trade of Roumania. *P. R. Gheorghiu, Ph.D. 1932 London, School of Economics and Political Science*

Trade: Spain
Cultivation in Spain, with some reference to trade between Spain and Great Britain. *F. F. Laidler, M.Sc. 1930 Wales*

Spanish economic policy and its relation to trade with England, culminating in the Treaty of 1667. *J. C. Salyer, B.Litt. 1948 Oxford*

Trade: Turkey
British trade with Turkey and the decline of the Levant Company, 1790-1825. *I. S. Russell, M.A. 1932 Manchester*

Trade: United States
British policy in its relation to the commerce and navigation of the United States of America from 1794 to 1807. *W. H. Elkins, D.Phil. 1936 Oxford*

Commercial relations between Great Britain and the United States of America from 1783 to 1794. *W. H. Elkins, B.Litt. 1935 Oxford*

The House of Hancock, business in Boston, 1724 to 1775. *W. T. Baxter, Ph.D. 1946 Edinburgh*

Trade: U.S.S.R
The foreign trade of Soviet Russia. *L. Segal, Ph.D. 1936 London, School of Economics and Political Science*

Soviet trade and distribution, 1917-1937: the growth of planned consumption. *E. M. Chossudowsky, Ph.D. 1940 Edinburgh*

Trade Associations
The economic significance and organization of trade associations in the United Kingdom. *W. J. Deneen, M.Sc. 1933 London, School of Economics and Political Science*

Trade Cycles
A 100% reserve plan in relation to monetary theories of the trade cycle. *J. E. Weinrich, M.Sc. 1948 London, School of Economics and Political Science*

Trade Cycles contd.
An attempt to interpret, with the aid of recent trade cycle theory, the cyclical fluctuations in the U.S.A. since the war of 1914-18. *T. Wilson, Ph.D. 1940 London, School of Economics and Political Science*

British trade fluctuations, 1868-86: a chronicle and a commentary. *W. W. Rostow, B.Litt. 1938 Oxford*

Budgetary policy, with special reference to the trade cycle. *R. P. N. Poduval, Ph.D. 1940 London, University College*

Capital structure and depression. *L. M. Lachmann, M.Sc. 1935 London, School of Economics and Political Science*

Certain aspects of the international transmission of cyclical fluctuations, 1870-1913. *J. S. Pesmazoglu, Ph.D. 1950 Cambridge*

Commercial fluctuations and currency disturbances of the seventeenth century. *W. J. Hinton, M.A. 1915 Wales*

Cyclical fluctuations in British export trade, 1924-38. *H. Soong, Ph.D. 1950 Cambridge*

International aspects of the trade-cycle international transfer of inflationary and deflationary movements. *T. Scitovszky, M.Sc. 1938 London, School of Economics and Political Science*

International cycles and Canada's balance of payments of 1921-33. *V. W. Malach, Ph.D. 1948 London, School of Economics and Political Science*

Polish monetary policy and trade fluctuations, 1924-1939. *S. Smierzchalski, M.Sc. 1945 London, School of Economics and Political Science*

The process of recovery from trade depression, with special reference to Great Britain, 1931-6. *G. L. S. Shackle, D.Phil. 1940 Oxford*

Sequence of movements of indices of industrial fluctuations in Great Britain (1885-1914 and 1919-1930). *J. R. H. Shaul, M.Sc. 1934 London, School of Economics and Political Science*

Some social aspects of the business cycle. *D. S. Thomas, Ph.D. 1924 London*

The variations of real wages and profit margins in relation to the trade cycle. *S. C. Tsiang, Ph.D. 1945 London, School of Economics and Political Science*

Wage policy in relation to industrial fluctuations. *A. G. Pool, Ph.D. 1939 London, External Degree*

Trade, International
See also Commodities; Customs and Excise; Free Trade; Tariffs; Trade.

The application of certain Keynesian concepts to international trade, with special reference to the multiplier. *E. J. Mishan, M.Sc. 1948 London, School of Economics and Political Science*

Britain's colonies in world trade. *F. Meyer, Ph.D. 1945 London, School of Economics and Political Science*

Bulk purchase in international trade. *J. H. Davies, M.A. 1948 Wales*

Import quotas, as used by European countries since 1929, with special reference to France. *F. A. Haight, M.Sc. 1934 London, School of Economics and Political Science*

Inconvertible paper money in relation to the foreign exchanges and international trade. *W. H. Lyon, M.A. 1925 Liverpool*

The international trade position of Canada, 1913-1933: an examination of the causes and characteristics of the balance of payments and the balance of trade. *W. E. Duffett, M.Sc. 1935 London, School of Economics and Political Science*

New Zealand's policy in international trade and its relation to employment policy. *K. A. Blakey, M.Sc. 1947 London, School of Economics and Political Science*

The problems of international exchange in 1914-1920. *A. M. Lewis, M.A. 1921 Wales*

The regulation of tariffs by recent international agreements, as exemplified by the practice of Great Britain and the United States. *C. H. McKenna, B.Litt. 1938 Oxford*

Studies in economic development and international trade. *I. G. Patel, Ph.D. 1950 Cambridge*

Tariffs and stability in commercial relations in the post-war period, with special regard to Central Europe. *V. Jalea, Ph.D. 1931 Birmingham*

The theory and practice of credit insurance in international trade. *E. Shenkman, Ph.D. 1934 London, School of Economics and Political Science*

Trade Unions
See also Industrial Relations.

Trade Unions contd.
An account of trade unionism in South Africa. *E. Gitsham, M.A. 1926 Leeds*

The economic policy of trade unions in Great Britain in the post-war period, as illustrated by the proceedings of the Trade Union Congress. *D. E. Ackroyd, B.Litt. 1936 Oxford*

The Engineers' Union, Book 1. The millwrights and 'old mechanics'. *W. McLaine, Ph.D. 1939 London, External Degree*

The general strike during one hundred years. *A. Plummer, M.Sc. 1927 London*

The history of the trade unions in the Yorkshire woollen and worsted industries during the nineteenth and twentieth centuries. *J. F. Weatherhead, B.Litt. 1925 Oxford*

The history of trade unionism in the coal-mining industry of north Wales up to 1914. *E. Rogers, M.A. 1928 Wales*

The international administrative unions. *H. R. Turkel, B.Litt. 1930 Oxford*

International trade union organization. *H. Burgess, M.Sc. 1934 London, School of Economics and Political Science*

The law relating to combinations. *A. L. Haslam, D.Phil. 1929 Oxford*

An outline of the activities of some trade unions of south Wales, with reference to the question of compulsory membership. *P. S. Thomas, M.A. 1920 Wales*

The political thought and practice of American trade unionism, 1906-18. *I. M. Karson, Ph.D. 1949 London, School of Economics and Political Science*

The progress of labour organization in the pottery industry of Great Britain. *W. H. Warburton, B.Litt. 1928 Oxford*

The relation of the first international working men's association to the war of 1870 and the ensuing communard movements in Paris, Lyons, and Marseilles. *C. D. Edwards, B.Litt. 1924 Oxford*

Syndicalism and industrial unionism in England until 1918. *E. L. Burdick, D.Phil. 1950 Oxford*

The teachings of Karl Marx: their influence on English labour organizations, 1850-1900. *H. Morgans, M.A. 1936 Wales*

Trade disputes in Great Britain: a brief enquiry into causes of, and an examination of methods of dealing with these, and particularly the experience and possibilities of conciliation and arbitration, and with a reference to Indian labour. *B. V. Narayanaswamy, Ph.D. 1929 Edinburgh*

Trade union law in the United Kingdom, the United States, and the Republic of China. *C. C. Liu, M.Litt. 1949 Cambridge*

Trade unions and the state. *W. Milne-Bailey, Ph.D. 1934 London, School of Economics and Political Science*

Voluntary associations within the state, 1900-1934, with special reference to the place of trade unions in relation to the State in Great Britain. *C. B. Macpherson, M.Sc. 1935 London, School of Economics and Political Science*

Workers' Producers' Associations in Palestine. *H. Gabrieli, B.Litt. 1935 Oxford*

Traeth Mawr
The history of Traeth Mawr and the industrial results of the formation of the embankment. *W. M. Richards, M.A. 1925 Wales*

Tragedy
Tragedy as a literary form. See also Theatre. For individual writers, see under their names.

The colloquial element in the language of Attic tragedy. *P. T. Stevens, Ph.D. 1939 Aberdeen*

A comparison of the use of the *Sententia*, considered as a typical rhetorical ornament, in the tragedies of Seneca, and in those of Gascoigne, Kyd, Jonson, Marston, and Greville. *G. K. Hunter, D.Phil. 1950 Oxford*

The composition of the chorus in Greek tragedy. *M. K. Norris, M.A. 1928 London*

The development of the tragic consciousness in Elizabethan drama. *C. F. Obermeyer, Ph.D. 1928 London*

Divination in Greek tragedy. *F. A. Dunne, M.A. 1945 National University of Ireland*

Divination in Homer and the tragedians. *T. Fahy, M.A. 1914 National University of Ireland*

Tragedy contd.
The dramatic works of Roger Boyle, Earl of Orrery, with special reference to the rise of the heroic tragedy, including an annotated text of the unprinted *Zoroastres*. *F. W. Payne, M.A. 1923 London*

Elizabethan and Jacobean revenge tragedies in relation to their ethical and psychological background. *W. A. Armstrong, M.A. 1940 Sheffield*

Elizabethan tragedy contrasted with the classical drama of Corneille and Racine. *F. E. Jope, M.A. 1910 Birmingham*

English tragedies in the Greek form with studies of the principal plays. *M. R. Fenning, M.A. 1929 Birmingham*

English tragedy of the romantic period, 1790-1821, with special reference to German influences. *M. W. Cooke, M.A. 1910 London*

The evolution of French classical tragedy in the eighteenth century to the death of Voltaire. *I. H. Williams, Ph.D. 1930 Wales*

An examination of some recent theories on Greek tragedy in their bearing upon the interpretation of certain plays. *K. Andrews, M.A. 1929 London*

Female characterization in Jacobean tragedy, with special consideration of the tragedies of Heywood, Webster, Middleton, Beaumont and Fletcher. *A. E. Bufton, M.A. 1939 Wales*

Fifth century B.C. views on the purpose of Greek tragedy. *B. E. Stirrup, M.A. 1948 Manchester*

French tragedy from 1680 to 1778; a critical survey and a study in evolution. *L. G. Marcus, M.Litt. 1946 Cambridge*

Friedrich Hebbel's theory of tragedy. *C. A. M. Sym, Ph.D. 1936 Edinburgh*

Hercules in Greek and Roman tragedy (Euripides, Sophocles, Seneca). *L. Ball, M.A. 1937 Manchester*

The idea of tragedy in the Renaissance. *F. E. Budd, Ph.D. 1928 London*

Influence of Elizabethan drama on heroic tragedy. *J. D. Carey, M.A. 1929 London*

The influence of oracles on human conduct in Greek tragedy. *M. Smith, M.A. 1950 Manchester*

Le développement de la tragédie racinienne jusqu'à *Andromaque*. *H. T. Barnwell, M.A. 1949 Birmingham*

The philosophy of tragedy. *J. C. T. Downes, M.A. 1949 Liverpool*

The place of Jean de Schelandre in the development of the French tragedy. *H. Smitherman, M.A. 1912 London*

The place of nature in French classical tragedy. *E. E. MacCabe, M.A. 1920 National University of Ireland*

Revenge tragedy from Kyd to Webster: its basis in the society of the age. *E. B. De Chickera, B.Litt. 1950 Oxford*

A review and criticism of theories on the origin of Greek tragedy. *E. B. Hall, M.A. 1915 London*

The Roman conception of tragedy as exemplified especially in Seneca. *R. A. Browne, M.A. 1927 Wales*

Rotrou's conception of the tragic, with reference to *Hercule Mourant* and *Venceslas*. *F. K. Dawson, M.A. 1950 Manchester*

The significance of domestic drama in English literature, with special reference to four extant Elizabethan domestic tragedies, and with an excursus on their authorship. *H. M. Davies, M.A. 1911 Wales*

The sources and inspiration of Montchrestien's dramatic works and his place in French tragedy. *D. S. Moss, M.A. 1927 Wales*

Themes and conventions of Elizabethan tragedy. *M. C. Bradbrook, Ph.D. 1934 Cambridge*

Theory of tragedy in England, 1660-1702. *D. L. Harley, B.Litt. 1934 Oxford*

The theory of tragedy in the works of Paul Ernst, Wilhelm von Scholz, and Samuel Lublinski, with special reference to the influence of Hebbel. *J. W. McFarlane, B.Litt. 1948 Oxford*

Tragedy in France in the eighteenth century, 1700-1789: its literary and sociological value. *H. C. Ault, D.Litt. 1948 Birmingham*

The use of revenge as a tragic theme in Greek tragedy, Seneca, and Elizabethan revenge plays. *J. S. Middlemas, M.A. 1949 Manchester*

Tragedy contd.
Women in Elizabethan and Jacobean tragedy: a study of the principal conventions and influences governing the treatment of women characters in English tragedy. *J. M. Morrell, M.A. 1931 London, Royal Holloway College*

Traherne, Thomas
Platonism and mysticism in J. Donne, H. Vaughan and T. Traherne. *C. G. M. Roberts, M.A. 1913 Bristol*

Studies in the writings of Thomas Traherne. *J. W. Proud, M.A. 1914 London*

The study of T. Traherne. *F. M. Pither, M.A. 1915 Birmingham*

Thomas Traherne. *H. Q. Iredale, M.A. 1933 Birmingham*

Thomas Traherne: a study of his life and works. *E. L. Thomas, M.A. 1932 Wales*

Thomas Traherne and his circle: a literary and biographical study. *G. I. Wade, Ph.D. 1933 London, University College*

Trajan, Emperor
Roman society in the reign of Trajan as seen in the writings of Tacitus, Juvenal and Pliny the Younger. *M. M. Gough, M.A. 1908 Birmingham*

Trakl, Georg
Das Verfallsproblem bei Georg Trakl. *I. V. Morris, M.A. 1936 Belfast*

Transcendentalism
The idea of the supernatural and of the transcendent in primitive and modern theistic thought. *T. J. E. Hopkins, M.A. 1934 Liverpool*

Transfiguration, The
See Jesus Christ.

Transkei
The Transkeian territories: a study in acculturation. *D. D. Davies, M.A. 1948 Wales*

Translations
The changing values in the critical and literary outlook of the seventeenth century, as manifested in English verse translation from the Greek and Latin classics. *S. Musgrove, D.Phil. 1944 Oxford*

Cicero as a translator. *E. M. Montgomery, M.A. 1931 London, Bedford College*

Cicero's study of Greek literature, with special reference to Cicero as a translator. *M. D. J. Adams, M.A. 1932 Wales*

The methods of the medieval translators of Greek philosophical works into Latin. *L. Minio-Paluello, D.Phil. 1947 Oxford*

Pope's version of the *Iliad*, considered as illustrating his theory of translation and his conception of the heroic style. *W. H. Jowsey, B.Litt. 1949 Oxford*

A study of sixteenth century English translations of the *Aeneid*: Surrey, Phaer and Stanyhurst. *G. D. Willcock, M.A. 1913 London*

The theory of translation in France in the eighteenth century. *C. B. West, M.Litt. 1927 Cambridge*

Transmigration
See Soul.

Transport
See also Air Transport; Railways; Road Transport; Shipping.

The administration of the system of transportation of British convicts, 1763-1793. *W. Oldham, Ph.D. 1933 London, King's College*

Carriage by air and sea. *J. H. Heires, B.Litt. 1948 Oxford*

A century's extension of passenger transport facilities (1830-1930) within the present London Transport Board's area, and its relation to population spread. *M. L. Moore, Ph.D. 1948 London, Birkbeck College*

Co-ordination of inland transport in Great Britain. *J. L. Grumbridge, Ph.D. 1939 London, School of Economics and Political Science*

Costs and modes of transport in Ireland. *E. J. Coyne, M.A. 1921 National University of Ireland*

The costs of transport and the location of industry in Great Britain and Egypt. *A. A. A. Ismail, Ph.D. 1942 Birmingham*

The development of inland transport in Eire. *P. B. Brown, M.Econ.Sc. 1946 National University of Ireland*

The development of transport and its effect on industries in the Bristol district. *J. Sagar, M.A. 1936 Bristol*

The future of internal transport in Great Britain. *R. E. Freeman, B.Litt. 1921 Oxford*

Transport contd.
A geographical study of China, with special reference to the means of transport. *C. M. Bao, Ph.D. 1940 London, School of Economics and Political Science*

A history of inland transport in Ireland down to the period of railways. *P. O'Kelly, M.Sc. 1922 London*

The industrial development of the Llynfi, Ogmore and Garw valleys, with special reference to transport facilities in the are. *T. Bevan, M.A. 1928 Wales*

Influence of the cost of inland transport on the development of production, trade and traffic, with special reference to India. *F. P. Antia, Ph.D. 1930 London, School of Economics and Political Science*

Ireland's systems of internal transport, their development and the State in relation to them. *T. Morrin, M.Econ.Sc. 1947 National University of Ireland*

The law as to C.I.F. contracts. *H. Goitein, LL.D. 1926 London*

The Midland transportation question. Sketches, statistical and otherwise. *Kelly T. H, M.Com. 1928 Birmingham*

On the treatment of transport costs in pure theory. *B. Courtney, M.Com.Sc. 1944 Belfast*

The recent course of gross investment in inland transport in Great Britain and the influence of government action upon it. *K. F. Glover, M.Sc. 1949 London, School of Economics and Political Science*

Subsidization of inland transport: its extent and consequences. *B. S. Agarwala, Ph.D. 1933 London, School of Economics and Political Science*

Transport and communication in medieval Wales. *W. H. Waters, M.A. 1923 Wales*

Transport development in west Yorkshire from the Industrial Revolution to the present day to the present day. *J. L. Hanson, Ph.D. 1949 London, External Degree*

Transport in the West Midlands from 1660 to 1840. *D. W. Blundell, M.Com, 1933 Birmingham*

The turnpike trusts of Wales: a study in transport economics. *E. W. Barton, M.A. 1915 Wales*

Transportation
The transportation system in the seventeenth century, with special reference to the West Indies. *A. E. Smith, D.Phil. 1933 Oxford*

Transvaal
British relations with the Transvaal from 1874 to 1881. *W. G. Murray, D.Phil. 1937 Oxford*

Travancore
The development of political institutions in the State of Travancore, A.D. 1885-1924. *V. M. Ittyerah, B.Litt. 1930 Oxford*

Principles of reconstruction of a curriculum suited to the village conditions in India, with special reference to Travancore. *P. S. Abraham, M.Ed. 1944 Leeds*

Travel
See Voyages and Travels.

Treason
Offences against the State in Roman law and the courts which were competent to take cognizance of them. *P. M. Schisas, LL.D. 1924 London*

The treason legislation of the reign of Henry VIII. *I.D. Thornley, M.A. 1917 London*

Treaties, Law of
See also Capitulations; Law, International; Servitudes.

Law of ratification. *E. O. Walford, LL.D. 1932 London, External Degree*

The legal obligations arising out of treaty relations between China and other states. *M. T. Z. Tyau, LL.D. 1916 London*

Tree of Knowledge
See Creation and the Fall.

Tregaron
Tregaron: a sociological study of a Welsh rural community. *E. Jones, Ph.D. 1947 Wales*

Treitschke, Heinrich von
The idea of the German 'national mission' as expressed by Fichte, List and Treitschke. *S. G. Graber, M.Sc. 1949 London, School of Economics and Political Science*

Trent, Council of
See Church History: Reformation and Counter-Reformation.

Trent, River
The Middle Trent Valley: a study in the East Midland type of development. *R. P. Brady, M.A. 1933 Manchester*

Trevet, Nicolas
See Trivet, N.

Trevisa, John of
See John, of Trevisa.

Tri Truagha na Sgéalaidheachta
Tuairisgí Nádúra i *Tri Truagha na Sgéalaidheachta* (Accounts of nature in the *Three Sorrowful Stories*). *M. Ní Mhathghamhna, M.A. 1943 National University of Ireland*

Triconodon
Studies on the primates: (1) brains of Eocene primates interpreted from endocranial casts; (2) a new interpretation of Wadjak Man; (3) a restoration of the skull and brain of the Jurassic mammal, Triconodon. *G. D. Pinkley, Ph.D. 1935 London, University College*

Trinidad and Tobago
The effect of the slave emancipation in British Guiana and Trinidad. *J. R. Maclean, B.Litt. 1931 Oxford*

The legislative council of Trinidad and Tobago. *H. M. Craig, B.Litt. 1949 Oxford*

Trinity, The
Anti-Trinitarianism in England in the seventeenth century. *H. M. Nolan, B.Litt. 1910 Oxford*

Athrawiaeth y Drindod a pherson Crist yng Nghymru o 1860 (The doctrine of the Trinity and the Person of Christ in Wales from 1860). *C. Rogers, M.A. 1934 Wales*

1. The Christian idea of sin and original sin. 2. The doctrine of the Trinity in the early Fathers. *E. J. Bicknell, B.D. & D.D. 1923 Oxford*

A critical and philosophical examination of the doctrine of the Holy Trinity. *C. W. Lowry, D.Phil. 1933 Oxford*

1. The doctrine of the Blessed Trinity. 2. Scripture aspects of the Atonement. *B. W. Randolph, B.D. & D.D. 1901 Oxford*

The doctrine of the Godhead in St.Gregory Nazianzen, with special reference to its Trinitarian and Christological aspects. *D. Martynowski, B.Litt. 1939 Oxford*

1. The doctrine of the Holy Trinity. 2. Prophecy and the prophets of Israel. *N. Davies, B.D. 1924 Oxford*

1. The doctrine of the Holy Trinity in the New Testament. 2. The authorship of the second Epistle of St. Peter. *S. Addleshaw, B.D. 1909 Oxford*

1. The doctrine of the Holy Trinity. 2. The reality of the resurrection of Christ. *S. C. Morgan, B.D. & D.D. 1881 Oxford*

1. The doctrine of the Holy Trinity. 2. The doctrine of the atonement. *R. G. Fookes, B.D. 1903 Oxford*

1. The doctrine of the Holy Trinity. 2. The prophecy of Hosea. *W. Gardiner, B.D. 1881 Oxford*

1. The doctrine of the Trinity in St. Paul's Epistles. 2. The growth of Christian dogma and of Christian belief as evidenced by the apologists of the second century. *W. A. Spooner, B.D. & D.D. 1903 Oxford*

The evolution of the doctrine of the most Holy Trinity, considered mainly in its exposition by Greek Patristic authors, and studies in its true meaning. *G. L. Prestige, D.D. 1934 Oxford*

1. God and the world. 2. The cultus of the Sacred Heart in light of the hypostatic union. *W. Farrar, B.D. 1895 Oxford*

1. How Luke was written. 2. New light on the significance of the word 'hypostasis'. *E. W. Lummis, B.D. & D.D. 1924 Oxford*

1. Miracles in the light of modern science. 2. The Trinitarian formula in the writings of Novatian. *W. Y. Fausset, B.D. 1914 Oxford*

1. On the history of the doctrine of the Holy Trinity. 2. On miracles. *L. J. T. Darwall, B.D. 1886 Oxford*

1. On the Holy Trinity. 2. On the sacraments. *A. B. O. Wilberforce, B.D. & D.D. 1897 Oxford*

1. On the Septuagint. 2. On the doctrine of the Holy Trinity. *F. J. Bryant, B.D. & D.D. 1886 Oxford*

Trinity, The, College of, Arundel
The organisation of a college of secular priests as illustrated by the records of the College of Holy Trinity, Arundel, 1380-1544. *R. B. K. Petch, M.A. 1940 London, King's College*

Tristan
See Romances.

Trivet, Nicolas
The Anglo-Norman *Chronicle* of Nicolas Trivet. *A. Rutherford, Ph.D. 1932 London, Birkbeck College*

Nicholas Trevet: a study of his life and works, with special reference to his Anglo-Norman chronicle. *R. J. Dean, D.Phil. 1938 Oxford*

Troeltsch, Ernst
The concept of norms in the theology of Ernst Troeltsch. *L. S. Eby, Ph.D. 1932 Edinburgh*

A study of Troeltsch's treatment of Christianity as a doctrine of society. *K. T. Henderson, B.Litt. 1925 Oxford*

Troilus and Cressida
See Romances.

Trollope, Anthony
Anthony Trollope. *P. Burke, M.A. 1936 National University of Ireland*

Tropics
Climatic aspect of the permanent settlement of the white man in the tropics: an essay in acclimatization. *G. J. Cons, M.A. 1929 London*

Troubadours
See also Gontier, de Soignies; Peirol.

Etude littéraire des premiers trouvères (douzième siècle). *E. Kerr, M.A. 1947 Belfast*

Troy
(a) The origin and development of the heroic poem in England, with some account of its relationship to the heroic romance and the heroic play; (b) The Trojan legend in England. *A. E. Parsons, D.Litt. 1932 London, External Degree*

The chronological problem of the Trojan War. *V. R. d'A. Desborough, B.Litt. 1939 Oxford*

The Helen myth in Greek literature. *W. C. Reid, M.A. 1948 Belfast*

Sdair na Traoi do réir láimhscríbhinne A.11 (*The history of Troy* as in ms. A.11). *S. M. MacGiolla Mhártain, M.A. 1945 National University of Ireland*

The source and growth of the legend of the association of Troy with the foundation of Rome. *M. E. M. Hamilton, M.A. 1932 London, Bedford College*

Studies in the Troy story in Middle English. *B. D. Wright, Ph.D. 1924 London*

Tógáil Troi (*The taking of Troy*). *T. O'Sléibhin, M.A. 1949 National University of Ireland*

The Trojan as conceived by Greeks of the fifth century B.C.: a comparison between the literary and artistic records. *G. C. Cook, M.A. 1937 London, University College*

Trumpet of Heaven
Trompa na bhFlaitheas (*The trumpet of Heaven*). *A. MacLochlainn, M.A. 1948 National University of Ireland*

Trusts
Comparative study of the law affecting corporate trustees in the United States of America, New Zealand and England. *J. L. Robson, Ph.D. 1939 London, University College*

The law of trusts in the eighteenth century up to the death of Lord Hardwicke. *B. F. Brown, D.Phil. 1932 Oxford*

Trusts, Charitable
An examination of trust concept with reference to its compatibility with French law together with a few notes on the wakf. *F. T. Arsan, B.Litt. 1948 Oxford*

Law of educational trusts or educational endowments. *A. E. Ikin, LL.D. 1917 London*

Some aspects of charitable trusts. *M. Saunders, LL.M. 1950 Sheffield*

Truth
See also Philosophy; and Kant, Immanuel; Thomas Aquinas, Saint.

Aspects of the problem of knowledge and truth. *L. A. Reid, M.A. 1923 Wales*

Byron's artistic truth. *T. Keegan, M.A. 1941 National University of Ireland*

The coherence notion of truth as in Mr. Joachim, and the pragmatic theory of truth as in the writings of Professor James. *E. C. Childs, M.A. 1909 London*

A critical exposition of Mr. Bradley's view of truth. *V. B. Evans, M.A. 1922 Wales*

A critical study of Mr. Bradley's view of truth. *V. B. Evans, B.Litt. 1923 Oxford*

Truth contd.
Degrees of truth and reality. *S. E. Hooper, M.A. 1918 London*

An examination of the nature and significance of Plato's theory of degrees of sapheneia. *W. F. Hicken, D.Phil. 1949 Oxford*

Fluency and lying: an experiment designed to study the relations between a number of tests of fluency and temperamental and intellectual traits, and also their relationship to a behaviour problem, namely, lying. *G. M. Hammond, M.A. 1946 London, Birkbeck College*

The idealist theory of truth. *E. T. Evans, M.A. 1948 Wales*

The pragmatic theory of truth, with especial regard to the question whether it implies a distinction between reality as it is known and reality as it is in itself. *S. S. S. Browne, B.Litt. 1929 Oxford*

Professor Collingwood's conception of the relations between metaphysics and history, and its consequences for the theory of truth. *C. K. Grant, D.Phil. 1949 Oxford*

The relations between voluntarism and pragmatism as illustrated by the development of French voluntaristic philosophy from Maine de Biran to Professor Bergson: with especial reference to the Bergsonian notion of truth and its development in the 'new philosophy'. *L. S. Stebbing, M.A. 1912 London*

Some aspects of truth, static and developmental. *W. T. Tutton, M.A. 1921 Liverpool*

Truth and certitude according to the Louvain School. *R. J. Gleeson, M.A. 1920 National University of Ireland*

Truth, unity, and goodness as aspects of being in the writings of St. Thomas Aquinas. *W. W. S. March, B.D. 1941 Oxford*

Tschudi, Gilg
A treatise on purgatory by Tschudi. *I. A. Knowles, Ph.D. 1925 Glasgow*

Tuberculosis
Tuberculosis: an historical survey. *M. F. J. Moir, M.D. 1927 Aberdeen*

Tucker, Josiah
The life and works of Josiah Tucker. *H. G. Brown, M.A. 1925 Bristol*

Tudur Penllyn
The works of Tudur Penllyn and Ieuan Brydydd Hir Hynaf. *A. Jenkins, M.A. 1921 Wales*

Tudur, Sion
A collection of the poems of Sion Tudur. *W. U. Williams, M.A. 1906 Wales*

Tughluq, Muhammad bin
The rise and fall of Muhammad bin Tughluq (1325-51). *M. Husain, Ph.D. 1935 London, School of Oriental and African Studies*

Tulsidās
The religious and moral teaching of Tulsidās in his poem *Rāmcharitmanās. J. M. Macfie, Ph.D. 1929 Edinburgh*

Tungus
Notes on the Reindeer Tungus of Manchuria. *E. J. Lindgren, Ph.D. 1936 Cambridge*

Tunis
The establishment of the French Protectorate over Tunis: its diplomatic history from the Congress of Berlin to the formation of the Triple Alliance, July 1878 to May 1882. *T. Lewis, M.A. 1950 Wales*

The Great Powers and Tunis, 1878-1881. *M. M. Safwat, Ph.D. 1940 London, School of Economics and Political Science*

Tunis from 1855 to 1879: primarily based on the dispatches of Consul-General Richard Wood. *M. M. Safwat, M.A. 1937 Liverpool*

Tunstall, Cuthbert, Bishop
A calendar of the register of Cuthbert Tunstall, Bishop of Durham. *G. Hinde, Ph.D. 1933 London, External Degree*

Turberville, George
A study of the poems of George Turberville. *G. E. Ford, M.A. 1914 London*

Turgot, Anne Robert Jacques, Baron de l'Aulne
Turgot: intendent of Limoges, 1761 to 1774. *D. Dakin, Ph.D. 1936 London, Birkbeck College*

Turgot: social and economic reform. *E. A. Gearing, M.A. 1911 Liverpool*

Turkey
See also Bosphorus; Dardanelles; Smyrna.

Turkey contd.
British foreign policy in the Near East, 1903-1909, with special reference to projects for the internal reform of the Ottoman Empire. *W. E. Walters, M.A. 1937 Wales*

The commercial and diplomatic relations of England and Turkey, 1680-1699. *A. C. Wood, B.Litt. 1923 Oxford*

Cyprus under the Turks, 1571-1878. *H. C. Luke, B.Litt. 1919 Oxford*

Great Britain and Turkey, 1878-85. *R. A. Spencer, D.Phil. 1950 Oxford*

The international juridical condition, in respect of nationality, of the former inhabitants of the Ottoman Empire under the Treaty of Lausanne, in Egypt and in the mandated territories. *P. P. J. Ghali, B.Litt. 1931 Oxford*

The rise of the Turkish Empire in central Asia (A.D. 552-615). *Y.-F. Chu, B.Litt. 1937 Oxford*

Sir Henry Elliott, British Ambassador at Constantinople, 1867-77, with particular reference to the period 1867-74. *D. T. Rees, M.A. 1940 Wales*

A study in Turanian history based on Chinese original sources. *H. W. Thomasson, M.A. 1925 Manchester*

A study of cultural change with special reference to Turkey. *M. Turhan, Ph.D. 1949 Cambridge*

A study of the official and unofficial relations between Greece and Turkey from the armistice of Mudros to the present day. *E. L. B. Curtis, M.Sc. 1933 London, School of Economics and Political Science*

Turkey and state succession. *O. Eralp, Ph.D. 1939 London, External Degree*

Turkish and Egyptian rule in Arabia, 1810-1841. *A. H. M. El-Batrik, Ph.D. 1947 London, School of Oriental and African Studies*

Turner, Francis, Bishop
A study of Francis Turner, bishop of Ely, 1684-90, with special reference to his political activity. *C. Emmott, B.Litt. 1930 Oxford*

Turnpikes
See Roads.

Tuscany
Bishop Scipio dei Ricci and the Synod of Pistoia: a critical survey. *C. A. Bolton, B.Litt. 1937 Oxford*

Tuscany and the Italian Risorgimento, 1859-60. *F. J. Skinner, M.A. 1921 London*

Twm o'r Nant
Bywyd a gwaith Twm o'r Nant a'i le yn hanes yr Anterliwt (The life and work of Twm o'r Nant and his place in the history of the 'Interlude'). *G. M. Ashton, M.A. 1944 Wales*

A critical study of the writings of Thomas Edwards (Twm o'r Nant), 1737-1810. *E. Hughes, M.A. 1942 Liverpool*

Tyard, Pontus de
The Platonic conception of love in the work of Pontus de Tyard. *H. O. C. Phillips, M.A. 1949 Wales*

Tyndale, William
Heresies of William Tyndale: a thesis. *H. W. Callow, M.A. 1911 Liverpool*

Tyneside
The Reform movement in Tyneside and Wearside, 1812-1832. *M. B. G. Allan, M.A. 1919 Liverpool*

Typography
See Printing.

Tyrconnell
History of Tir Conaill in the 16th century. *J. O'Donnell, M.A. 1946 National University of Ireland*

Tyrconnell, Richard Talbot, 1st Earl of
The political significance of the career of the Earl of Tyrconnell in Irish history and its relation to the cause of James II. 1685 to 1691. *M. E. Brady, M.Litt. 1932 Cambridge*

Tyrell, George
The religious thought of George Tyrell, Roman Catholic modernist. *E. P. Turnbach, Ph.D. 1942 Edinburgh*

Tyrwhitt, Thomas
Thomas Tyrwhitt (1730-86) and his contribution to English scholarship. *T. J. A. Monaghan, D.Phil. 1947 Oxford*

Tyuchev, Fyodor Ivanovich
The life and poetry of Tyutchev. *M. P. Webb, Ph.D. 1927 London*

U Pok Ni
Konmara Pya Zat, by U Pok Ni, edited with introduction, translation and commentary. *H. Pe, Ph.D. 1944 London, School of Oriental and African Studies*

Udall, Nicholas
The life and work of Nicholas Udall, 1506-1556. *A. R. Moon, M.A. 1926 London*

Uganda
See also Bari, The; Kipsigi, The.

Native development in Buganda. *L. P. Mair, Ph.D. 1933 London, School of Economics and Political Science*

Ugarit
See Ras Shamra-Ugarit.

Ugaritic Language
The Ras Shamra texts: translated with introductions and commentaries. *T. H. C. Gaster, A. 1936 London, Institute of Archaeology*

Uhland, Johann Ludwig
The old German elements in the poems of Ludwig Uhland. *J. A. Walsh, M.A. 1918 National University of Ireland*

Ukraine
Polish-Ukrainian relations, 1919-39. *Z. Sliwowski, B.Phil. 1947 Oxford*

Some historical factors in the formation of the Ukrainian people. *J. Jagodzinski, M.A. 1942 Liverpool*

Ullerston, Richard
Richard Ullerston. *A. H. Wood, M.A. 1936 Manchester*

Ulster
See Northern Ireland.

Umundri, The
The divine Umundri Kings of Igboland. *M. D. W. Jeffreys, Ph.D. 1934 London, University College*

Unanimism
See also French Literature: Twentieth Century.

Emile Zola as a precursor of Jules Romains and *l'unanimisme*. *C. Z. Ruston, B.Litt. 1944 Oxford*

The theory and application of unanimism in the poetical works of Jules Romains. *P. M. Reese, M.A. 1934 Wales*

Unconscious
The concept of the 'unconscious' and its importance for psychology. *L. G. Tucker, M.A. 1924 Liverpool*

Modern theories of the unconscious. *W. L. Northridge, Ph.D. 1922 Belfast*

Plotinus's conception of the unconscious. *D. D. Stuurman, B.Litt. 1937 Oxford*

Unemployment
See Employment.

Unit Trusts
See also Investment; Stocks and Shares.

British unit trusts: their organization and investment policy. *R. C. Clements, B.Litt. 1938 Oxford*

Unit trusts. *C. H. Walker, Ph.D. 1938 London, School of Economics and Political Science*

Unitarianism
See also Channing, W. E.; Firmin, T.; Price, R.

English Presbyterian thought from 1662 to the foundation of the Unitarian Movement. *O. M. Griffiths, Ph.D. 1933 Bristol*

Thomas Firmin, F.R.S. (1632-1697). *H. W. Stephenson, D.Phil. 1949 Oxford*

United Brethren, The
The Renewed Church of the United Brethren, 1722 to 1930. *W. G. C. Addison, Ph.D. 1931 London, External Degree*

United Nations
See also International Court of Justice; International Labour Organization; League of Nations.

The British Commonwealth and the United Nations. *C. C. Aikman, Ph.D. 1948 London, School of Economics and Political Science*

The framing of the security chapters of the United Nations Charter, 1942-6. *E. W. Hughes, B.Phil. 1947 Oxford*

United Provinces
See Agra and Oudh, United Provinces of.

United States
See also Chicago; Georgia; Los Angeles; Louisiana; New York; Virginia; etc.

United States: Constitution
A comparative study of the offices of the Prime Minister of Great Britain and the President of the United States of America: a study in comparative political institutions. *T. F. Fan, M.Sc. 1933 London, School of Economics and Political Science*

A comparison of the constitutions of the United States and Australia. *B. Jones, M.A. 1924 Wales*

Criticism and defence of the Constitution of the Senate of the U.S.A. during the campaign for ratification, 1787-1789. *J. M. Shelat, M.A. 1933 London, King's College*

The influence of Montesquieu upon the American constitution. *R. W. Ferguson, M.A. 1912 London*

The presidency of the U.S.A. and the premiership of Great Britain: a comparative study of patronage. *E. G. Ashcroft, M.Sc. 1946 London, School of Economics and Political Science*

The reception of the American constitution in Britain, 1787-1848. *D. H. Pattinson, M.A. 1941 Birmingham*

Some elements of recent constitutional and administrative tendencies in France, Germany and United States of America: an introductory study. *H. Finer, M.Sc. 1922 London*

United States: Economics
The economic development of the American colonies, with special reference to the relations with the mother country. *C. A. Joseph, M.Com. 1928 Birmingham*

Elements of instability in the economic expansion of America, 1921-29. *M. M. Junaid, Ph.D. 1932 London, School of Economics and Political Science*

The integration of industry in the United States of America and Great Britain, with special reference to financial control and the capitalization of joint-stock companies. *H. A. Marquand, M.A. 1928 Wales*

The repudiation of state debts by States of the United States of America in the nineteenth century. *G. L. Ridgeway, B.Litt. 1928 Oxford*

United States: Foreign Affairs
American diplomatic policy in China, 1928-33. *J. W. Christopher, D.Phil. 1948 Oxford*

Anglo-American arbitration policies, 1890-1914. *O. Gollancz, Ph.D. 1940 Cambridge*

Anglo-American relations with regard to the Panama Canal project, 1897-1903. *S. P. Kramer, M.Litt. 1938 Cambridge*

Anglo-American rivalry in Mexico and South America. *E. J. Pratt, D.Phil. 1929 Oxford*

Aspects of Anglo-American relations, 1899-1906. *L. M. Gelber, B.Litt. 1933 Oxford*

British public opinion on Anglo-American relations, 1805-1812. *D. R. Currie, Ph.D. 1935 Saint Andrew's*

The government of the United States and Latin American independence. *J. J. Auchmuty, Ph.D. 1935 Dublin, Trinity College*

A history of the development of British public opinion of Anglo-American relations, 1783-1794. *D. S. Reid, Ph.D. 1934 Saint Andrew's*

The influence of the Barbary States in international relations, with special reference to the United States. *R. K. Irons, D.Phil. 1934 Oxford*

The mission to Spain of Pierre Soulé, 1853-5: a study in the Cuban diplomacy of the United States, with special reference to contemporary opinion. *A. A. Ettinger, D.Phil. 1930 Oxford*

The relations of Great Britain and the United States of America during the Spanish-American War of 1898. *H. Holroyde, M.A. 1947 Sheffield*

The relations of Great Britain and America, especially from 1861-1866. *E. E. Baker, M.A. 1920 Birmingham*

The slave trade and Anglo-American relations, 1807-1862. *A. T. Milne, M.A. 1930 London, University College*

The United States and the League of Nations, with special reference to co-operation. *H. L. Sainer, M.Sc. 1946 London, School of Economics and Political Science*

The work and policy of the United States in Panama. *C. B. Wallis, M.Litt. 1939 Cambridge*

United States: Geography
Economic geography of North America. *W. McComish, M.Sc. 1936 London, External Degree*

Geographical influences of the exploration of America west of the Mississippi, 1800-50. *E. W. Gilbert, B.Litt. 1928 Oxford*

United States: History
See also Calhoun, J. C.; Jefferson, T.; Smith, W.

Bristol voyages to the New World between 1576 and 1612. *E. R. Gath, M.A. 1914 Bristol*

The British attitude towards the American Civil War. *C. I. Payne, M.A. 1928 Birmingham*

The causes of the revolution in New York, 1691-1760: a study of taxation and of the effects of England's commercial restrictions, prefaced by a sketch of the colony's political history. *B. Miles, B.Litt. 1905 Oxford*

English opinion on the American War of Independence. *T. P. Brockway, B.Litt. 1925 Oxford*

French and Spanish opinion of the American Civil War, with some reference to English and other continental opinion. . *E. J. Pratt, B.Litt. 1925 Oxford*

The Howes and the American Revolution. *T. S. Anderson, D.Phil. 1930 Oxford*

Maryland and the American Revolution. *M. J. Broadbent, M.A. 1949 Sheffield*

The more immediate effects of the American revolution on Ireland (1775-1785). *T. M. O'Connor, M.A. 1938 Belfast*

The movement of opinion in England concerning America prior to the declaration of American independence. *D. G. Martin, M.A. 1911 Liverpool*

The West Indies in the American Revolution. *M. J. Hewitt, D.Phil. 1937 Oxford*

United States: Politics and Government
Administrative legislation and adjudication in Great Britain and the United States. *E. R. Baltzell, D.Phil. 1923 Oxford*

British administration of the American colonies, 1689-1783. *J. D. Doty, B.Litt. 1923 Oxford*

A comparison of the British system of colonial government in the American colonies during the half-century preceding the Revolution with that in British Canada before the rebellion of 1837. *W. J. Mulholland, B.Litt. 1920 Oxford*

The distribution of functions among central government departments in the United Kingdom, with some comparison of the United States of America and British dominions. *C. N. Yang, D.Phil. 1948 Oxford*

The redistribution of seats in American state legislatures. *J. W. Douglas, D.Phil. 1949 Oxford*

United States: Social History
The influence of American ideas at Frankfurt-am-Main, 1848-9. *J. A. Hawgood, M.A. 1928 London*

The influence of the relations between groups upon the inner life of groups, with special reference to black and white in the Southern States of the United States during the nineteenth century. *H. W. Roberts, M.A. 1934 London, School of Economics and Political Science*

A sociological analysis of some intellectual groups in American society from 1912-1930. *D. H. Schwartz, Ph.D. 1940 London, School of Economics and Political Science*

Universals
On the consciousness of the universal and the individual. *F. A. P. Aveling, D.Sc. 1912 London*

On the nature of universals. *N. Ertel, M.A. 1911 London*

Scientia intuitiva and the concrete universal. *J. R. Jones, M.A. 1935 Wales*

Some medieval and modern theories of the universal. *E. H. Knight, Ph.D. 1935 London, External Degree*

The theory of universals, with special reference to Locke, Berkeley and Hume. *O. R. Davies, M.A. 1937 Wales*

Unity of the universal. *C. Martin, M.A. 1941 National University of Ireland*

Universities
See Education, Higher; and under the names of individual universities.

University Extension
See Education, Adult.

Upanishads
See Sanskrit Literature.

Urbanization
See also Town and Country Planning.

Food and leisure among the African youth of Leopoldville (Belgian Congo): a study of the adaptation of African youth to urban life. *S. A. M. A. J. M. Comhaire-Sylvain, B.Litt. 1948 Oxford*

Urbanization contd.
Some problems of urbanization in India: based on a study of Madras City. *C. W. Ranson, B.Litt 1937 Oxford*

Urdu Language
A critical history of Urdu language and literature down to the year 1720. *S. G. M. Qadr, Ph.D. 1930 London, School of Oriental and African Studies*

The teaching of Urdu in India, with special reference to the Punjab. *K. Mohyeddin, M.Ed. 1927 Leeds*

Urdu as the medium of higher instruction. *S. B. Sayeed, M.Ed. 1935 Leeds*

Urdu Literature
A comparative study of the *Nau Tarz i Murassa*, and a history of Urdu prose from the earliest times down to 1775. *S. S. Husain, Ph.D. 1933 London, School of Oriental and African Studies*

A critical history of Urdu language and literature down to the year 1720. *S. G. M. Qadr, Ph.D. 1930 London, School of Oriental and African Studies*

Hāli as poet, critic and biographer, and his influence on Urdu literature. *M. T. Husain, Ph.D. 1935 London, School of Oriental and African Studies*

India's contribution to imaginative English literature. *R. Pitman, M.A. 1920 Birmingham*

The influence of English literature on Urdu literature. *S. A. Latif, Ph.D. 1924 London*

Urfi
Faizi, Urfi, and Naziri (poets of Akbar's Court). *A. W. Khan, Ph.D. 1932 London, School of Oriental and African Studies*

Ursins, Jean Juvenal des, Archbishop
See Juvenal des Ursins, J., Archbishop.

Uruguayan Literature
See Herrera y Reissig, J.

Ussher, James, Archbishop
The doctrine of the church as exemplified in the life and works of James Ussher, Archbishop of Armagh. *R. B. Knox, Ph.D. 1948 Belfast*

U.S.S.R
See also Russia.

The development of industry, agriculture and transport in the Soviet Arctic and sub-Arctic north of 60 degrees. *C. J. Webster, M.A. 1949 London, School of Slavonic and East European Studies*

Distribution of the national income in the U.S.S.R. *G. C. Huang, M.A. 1932 Liverpool*

The foreign policy of Soviet Russia in Europe, 1917-1939. *E. Bogomas, M.Sc. 1945 London, School of Economics and Political Science*

Planning and production control in Soviet State industries. *G. R. Barker, M,Com. 1950 Birmingham*

The political system in the U.S.S.R. *T. D. Hou, M.Sc. 1936 London, School of Economics and Political Science*

Soviet economic life and the general categories of economic analysis: comparative studies of the forms of value, distribution and production under Soviet and other systems of economic organization. *H. E. Ronimois, Ph.D. 1949 London, School of Economics and Political Science*

Studies in the development of the national economy of the U.S.S.R. *A. M. Baykov, Ph.D. 1942 Birmingham*

Usury
See also Interest.

Bargains with money-lenders. *H. H. L. Bellot, D.C.L. 1906 Oxford*

The Church of England and usury. *H. S. Swabey, B.D. 1949 Durham*

Comparative aspects of the law of unjust enrichment. *E. S. Busuttil, B.Litt. 1949 Oxford*

The English view of usury and the distribution of wealth in the later Middle Ages. *H. G. Richardson, M.A. 1912 London*

Usury and the principles of the Muhammadan law. *M. S. Ali Khan, D.Phil. 1928 Oxford*

Uthred, of Boldon
Uthred of Boldon: a study in fourteenth century political theory. *C. H. Thompson, Ph.D. 1936 Manchester*

Utilitarianism
The educational theory of the English Utilitarians. *A. H. Cheshire, M.A. 1923 Liverpool*

The English Utilitarians and education. *D. Gandy, M.A. 1921 Liverpool*

Utilitarianism contd.
A study of Utilitarian ethics. *M. Sopote, B.Sc. 1908 Oxford*

Utility (Economics)
The development of utility theory and welfare economics. *L. W. McKenzie, B.Litt. 1949 Oxford*

Utopias
Early and modern conceptions of Utopia. *W. A. Robbins, M.A. 1911 Birmingham*

English utopian fiction (up to 1870; with a glance forward). *K. F. Laurie, M.A. 1930 London, University College*

Utopia in nineteenth century English literature. *H. C. Sherwood, M.A. 1934 Birmingham*

Utopian literature. *H. M. Deacon, M.A. 1930 Birmingham*

Uvata
The *Rigveda Prātisākhya* with the commentary of Uvata, edited from the manuscripts with introduction, critical and additional notes, English translation, and several appendices. *M. D. Shastri, D.Phil. 1922 Oxford*

Vagrancy
Elizabethan rogues and vagabonds: their life, manners and representation in contemporary literature, especially in connexion with the so-called coney-catching pamphlets of Robert Greene. *F. Aydelotte, B.Litt. 1907 Oxford*

Pauperism and vagrancy in Cambridgeshire to 1834. *E. M. Hampson, Ph.D. 1931 Cambridge*

The treatment of vagrancy and the relief of the poor and destitute in the Tudor period, based upon the local records of London to 1552 and Hull to 1576. *K. Anderson, Ph.D. 1933 London, Royal Holloway College*

Vaishnavites
See Hinduism.

Valdés, Armando Palacio
Armando Palacio Valdés y su obra. *J. F. Buckley, M.A. 1942 National University of Ireland*

Valdés, Juan de
A critical edition of the British Museum manuscript of the *Dialogo de las Lenguas*, with a prefatory essay in three part. *J. H. Perry, M.A. 1920 London, School of Economics and Political Science*

Valencia, Spain
The social geography of the Huerta of Valencia. *J. M. Houston, D.Phil. 1950 Oxford*

Valerius Flaccus, Gaius
The influence of the *Aeneid* on the *Argonautica* of Valerius Flaccus. *A. N. Marlow, M.A. 1938 London, Queen Mary College*

A study of the *Argonautica* of Valerius Flaccus. *J. C. Wiseman, Ph.D. 1934 Aberdeen*

Valéry, Paul
Paul Valéry. *H. C. F. Johnston, Litt.D. 1937 Dublin, Trinity College*

Paul Valéry and the Mallarmean heritage: a literary and psychological study. *R. S. Jones, Ph.D. 1949 London, King's College*

The philosophy of Paul Valéry as expressed in his poetry. *R. S. Jones, M.A. 1942 Wales*

Valle Crucis Abbey, Denbighshire
The history of Valle Crucis Abbey, Denbighshire. *E. J. Fisher, M.A. 1929 Liverpool*

Valorization
Valorization under public auspices. *J. Kipps, B.Litt. 1929 Oxford*

Value (Economics)
Advertising, salesmanship, and the theory of value. *T. H. Silcock, D.Phil. 1936 Oxford*

The ethics of economic values. *P. Byrne, M.A. 1932 National University of Ireland*

Labour theory of value in classical economics. *E. L. Kennedy, M.A. 1946 National University of Ireland*

An luach sa chóus eacnomaidheachta fé stiúir (Value in a planned economy). *P. J. Lynch, Ph.D. 1939 National University of Ireland*

Soviet economic life and the general categories of economic analysis: comparative studies of the forms of value, distribution and production under Soviet and other systems of economic organization. *H. E. Ronimois, Ph.D. 1949 London, School of Economics and Political Science*

A study of economic concepts of income and capital valuation, with special reference to accountancy. *G. B. Sanderson, Ph.D. 1942 London, School of Economics and Political Science*

Value (Economics) contd.
The theory of value on the capital market. *H. Makower, Ph.D. 1937 London, School of Economics and Political Science*

Value (Philosophy)
The conception of value in psychological medicine. *C. P. Blacker, D.M. 1931 Oxford*

An essay towards a logical theory of value. *M. E. Clarke, Ph.D. 1926 London*

An historical review of the nature of time and its connexion with value, in so far as these bear on the problems of personal freedom and human purpose. *W. A. Merrylees, B.Litt. 1923 Oxford*

A metaphysic of value. *M. Cashell, M.A. 1949 National University of Ireland*

Principles of the adjudgment of value in literature from Sanskrit sources. *S. Dasgupta, Ph.D. 1948 Cambridge*

The problem of value in early modern philosophy: a study of Descartes, Geulincx and Spinoza. *D. J. McCracken, Ph.D. 1936 Belfast*

The problem of value in early modern philosophy, with special reference to Descartes. *D. J. McCracken, M.A. 1934 Belfast*

A psychological study of value, with special reference to the noegenetic theory. *J. H. Ball, M.A. 1931 London, University College*

Theism and ideas of value. *D. E. Williams, M.A. 1924 Wales*

The treatment of the idea of value in recent philosophical literature. *E. W. Hill, M.A. 1921 Liverpool*

Value. *S. G. Williamson, M.A. 1937 Birmingham*

Value and the philosophy of the absolute with special reference to the philosophy of Bosanquet. *J. G. F. Potter, B.Litt. 1935 Oxford*

Vane, Henry, Sir
The careers and opinions of Hugh Peters and Sir Henry Vane the Younger. *J. M. Patrick, B.Litt. 1936 Oxford*

A report on the sources available for an account of the life of Sir Henry Vane, junior, during the period 1649-62. *E. M. Emlyn, M.A. 1928 Liverpool*

Sir Henry Vane the Elder. *E. B. Wells, M.A. 1923 Manchester*

Varro, Marcus Terentius
A critical study of the life and works of Varro. *J. H. Jones, Ph.D. 1936 London, University College*

The indebtedness of Vergil to Varro in the composition of the *Georgics*: a study in parallelism. *N. P. Bentley, M.A. 1929 Manchester*

Vases
See Ceramics.

Vaughan, Henry
Francis Thompson: a study of his relation to George Herbert, Henry Vaughan and Richard Crashaw. *C. Bergin, M.A. 1948 National University of Ireland*

Henry Vaughan. *L. C. Martin, B.Litt. 1913 Oxford*

Henry Vaughan. *J. Caball, M.A. 1940 National University of Ireland*

Henry Vaughan: a study in the relation of poetry and mysticism. *M. M. Bruckshaw, M.A. 1950 Manchester*

Henry Vaughan: with a special study of his imagery. *E. Holmes, B.Litt. 1928 Oxford*

Henry Vaughan, Silurist: a study of his life and writings, his relation to his age and subsequent influence. *D. L. Graham, Ph.D. 1934 Birmingham*

Platonism and mysticism in J. Donne, H. Vaughan and T. Traherne. *C. G. M. Roberts, M.A. 1913 Bristol*

The religious element in the letters and poems of Donne, and in the works of Browne and Vaughan. *R. E. George, B.Litt. 1915 Oxford*

The sources and nature of the thought of Henry Vaughan. *R. H. Walters, M.A. 1946 Bristol*

Studies in the poetry of Henry Vaughan. *A. J. Chiappe, Ph.D. 1942 Cambridge*

A study of Henry Vaughan. *H. M. Catlow, M.A. 1916 Birmingham*

Vaughan, John
Hanes yr S.P.C.K. yn Sir Gaerfyrddin o 1700 hyd 1750, gyda chyfeiriad arbennig at John Vaughan, Cwrt Derllys, a'i waith (The history of the S.P.C.K. in Carmarthenshire from 1700 to 1750, with special reference to John Vaughan, Cwrt Derllys, and his work). *M. Clement, M.A. 1940 Wales*

Vaughan, Richard, 2nd Earl of Carbery
Richard Vaughan, 2nd Earl of Carbery (1606-1686). *T. S. Williams, M.A. 1936 Wales*

Vaughan, Robert
The lives and labours of John Jones and Robert Vaughan, scribes of the sixteenth and seventeenth centuries. *S. Jones, M.A. 1926 Wales*

Vauvenargues, Luc de Clapiers, Marquis de
Luc de Clapiers, Marquis de Vauvenargues (1715-1747). *M. G. Wallas, Ph.D. 1926 London*

Vedanta
See Philosophy: India.

Vedas
Early Buddhist ballads and their relations to the older Upanishadic literature. *S. R. M. R. Katre, Ph.D. 1932 London, School of Oriental and African Studies*

An index to Sāyana Bhasya on Rig Veda Mandal II. *G. R. Raddi, M.A. 1930 London, School of Oriental and African Studies*

The Nirukta and the Nighantu. *L. Sarup, Ph.D. 1920 Oxford*

On the interpretation of some doubtful words in the *Atharvaveda*. *T. Choudhury, Ph.D. 1930 London, School of Oriental and African Studies*

The origin and development of Indian religion as presented by Vedic literature to the end of the Sutra period. *P. S. Deshmukh, D.Phil. 1927 Oxford*

The position of women in early India, as it appears in the Vedic literature and the sacred law. *S. Rao, B.Litt. 1936 Oxford*

The position of women in the Vedic ritual. *J. Chaudhuri, Ph.D. 1934 London, School of Oriental and African Studies*

The *Rigveda Prātisākhya* with the commentary of Uvata, edited from the manuscripts with introduction, critical and additional notes, English translation, and several appendices. *M. D. Shastri, D.Phil. 1922 Oxford*

A Rigvedic index: being a complete collection of Sayana's interpretations of Rigvedic words, both when those interpretations are inconsistent with one another and when they differ from the interpretations of western scholars. *C. Kunhan Raja, Ph.D. 1924 Oxford*

Visnu in the *Rgveda* and after until the epic period. *M. S. Gladstone, Ph.D. 1928 Cambridge*

Vega Carpio, Lope Félix de
La Dragontea of Lope de Vega: a critical and annotated edition, together with a preliminary essay on Lope as an epic poet. *A. K. James, Ph.D. 1935 London, External Degree*

Quelques traces de L'influence espagnole au théâtre français du 17e siècle: Lope de Vega et J. Rotrou. *F. Astley, M.A. 1928 Birmingham*

The Spanish stage in the time of Shakespeare and Lope de Vega. *J. Garcia Lora, M.A. 1947 Birmingham*

Vega, Garcilaso de la
Garcilaso de la Vega. *E. A. Parker, B.Litt. 1922 Oxford*

Vega, Ventura de la
The original dramatic productions of Ventura de la Vega. *J. H. Mundy, M.A. 1939 Liverpool*

Vegetable Industry
The organization of wholesale distribution in Great Britain of fruit, flowers, and vegetables of domestic and foreign origin. *W. Drake, M.Com. 1941 London, External Degree*

The wholesale marketing of vegetables in Birmingham. *B. N. Knapp, M.Com. 1948 Birmingham*

Vendée
Jean-Baptiste Carrier and the Terror in the Vendée. *E. H. Carrier, M.A. 1915 Liverpool*

Venice
Commercial relations between England and Venice in the thirteenth and fourteenth centuries. *G. F. Shaw, M.A. 1909 London*

The theory of Roman and Renaissance vault construction, with special reference to the Pantheon, Rome, and Santa Maria della Salute, Venice. *A. G. S. Fidler, M.A. 1936 Liverpool*

The Venice legend in German literature since 1880. *D. M. Hall, Ph.D. 1936 London, Birkbeck College*

Ventadorn, Bernard de
The syntax of Bernard de Ventadorn. *A. Leach, M.A. 1932 Manchester*

Verhaeren, Emile
Emile Verhaeren and his place in the history of modern poetry. *P.M. Jones, B.Litt. 1923 Oxford*

Verhaeren, Emile contd.
The versification of Emile Verhaeren. *J. Barber, M.A. 1922 Manchester*

Whitman in France; Whitman and the origin of the *vers libre*: Whitman and Verhaeren; the origins of the *vers libre*. *P. M. Jones, M.A. 1916 Wales*

Verlaine, Paul
The versification of Paul Verlaine. *F. E. Lonsdale, M.A. 1933 Manchester*

Verne, Jules
Módh smaointe na Frainnce dá fhoillsiú 'sa Ghaedhilge: ó scríbhinní Fhenelon agus Iúles Bherne (French philosophy as illustrated in Irish, from the writings of Fénélon and Jules Verne). *T. O'Rathaille, M.A. 1933 National University of Ireland*

Verrall, Arthur Woollgar
A reconsideration of Verrall's criticism of Euripides. *A. C. Edwards, M.A. 1931 Birmingham*

Verri, Pietro
Pietro Verri's *Caffè* and periodical literature in Italy during the second half of the eighteenth century. *A. Del Re, M.A. 1921 London*

Vespasianus, Titus Flavius, Emperor
A commentary, mainly, but not exclusively, devoted to its historical aspects, on the *Vita Divi Vespasiani* of C. Suetonius Tranquillus. *A. W. Braithwaite, B.Litt. 1926 Oxford*

Study of the version of *Titus and Vespasian* contained in the ms. British Museum additional 10289. *M. E. D. Honey, M.A. 1907 London*

Vestfirðir
A topographical study of the sagas of the Vestfirðir and of their traditions. *I. L. Gordon, Ph.D. 1930 Leeds*

Vetālapañcavimśati
A critical study of Ksemendra's version of the *Vetālapañcavimśati*. *Y. D. Sharma, B.Litt. 1941 Oxford*

Veterinary Law
The law relating to medical, dental, and veterinary practice. *F. Bullock, LL.D. 1928 London*

Veuillot, Louis François
Louis Veuillot: critique littéraire. *R. Dawid, M.A. 1947 Liverpool*

Veuillot as a literary critic. *E. J. M. Gauthier, Ph.D. 1934 London, King's College*

Viaud, Louis Marie Julien
See Loti, Pierre.

Victoria, Australia
The economic development of the coastal regions of Victoria and New South Wales. *H. Swift, M.A. 1939 Liverpool*

Vielé-Griffin, Francis
Nature and symbol in the works of Francis Vielé-Griffin. *A. Crone, B.Litt. 1939 Oxford*

Viennet, Jean Pons Guillaume
J. P. G. Viennet, l'homme et l'écrivain d'après ses mémoires inédits, ses épitres, ses satires et ses fables. *A. Head, Ph.D. 1948 London, Birkbeck College*

Vignola, Giacomo Barozzi da
Giacomo Barozzi da Vignola, 1507-1573, architect. *E. Williams, M.A. 1932 Liverpool*

Vigny, Alfred de, Comte
Alfred de Vigny: le progrès de sa pensée à travers ses oeuvres. *M. S. Russell, M.A. 1933 Belfast*

Alfred de Vigny - poète et philosophe. *J. Scannell, M.A. 1915 National University of Ireland*

Alfred de Vigny's translation of Othello: its place in the history of French drama. *M. E. O'Dowd, M.A. 1917 National University of Ireland*

A contribution to the study of the sources of some of Alfred de Vigny's poems. *J. G. Tarbet, Ph.D. 1932 London, University College*

Ducis and De Vigny considered as interpreters of Shakespeare. *R. J. Evans, M.A. 1909 Wales*

La vérité historique des oeuvres de Vigny. *E. M. Greenwood, M.A. 1913 Leeds*

The *Othello* of Alfred de Vigny as compared with that of Shakespeare. *M. Whiteley, M.A. 1920 Manchester*

The philosophy of Alfred de Vigny as reflected in his published work. *J. Davies, M.A. 1905 Wales*

Vijayanagara Empire, The
Social and political life in the Vijayanagara Empire, A.D. 1346-1646. *B. A. Saletore, Ph.D. 1931 London, School of Oriental and African Studies*

Vikings
See Norsemen.

Villages
See also Settlements.

The derelict villages of Durham County. A. Temple, M.Litt. 1940 Durham

Kaihsienkung: economic life in a Chinese village. H. T. Fei, Ph.D. 1938 London, School of Economics and Political Science

The treatment of village life in the first four collections of Berthold Auerbach's Schwarzwälder Dorfgeschichten. P. S. Pargeter, M.A. 1947 Birmingham

Village-patterns and distributions in East Devon. H. M. Mortimer, M.A. 1940 London, External Degree

Villalobos, Lopez de
See Lopez de Villalobos, R.

Vincent de Paul, Saint
The assistance of the poor in Paris and in the northeastern French provinces, 1614 to 1660, with special reference to the letters of S. Vincent de Paul. E. Archer, Ph.D. 1936 London, School of Economics and Political Science

Vinci, Leonardo da
See Leonardo da Vinci.

Violin
Aptitude tests for performance on violinda (violin-type instrument). H. B. Priestley, M.A. 1949 London, Institute of Education

Virelay
See Poetry, French.

Virgil
The attitude of Virgil and other Augustan poets to the religion of Rome. A. J. McIver, B.Litt. 1932 Oxford

The characteristics of the Augustan age reflected in Virgil and Horace. G. Etheridge, M.A. 1911 Birmingham

The growth of the Aeneid. M. M. Crump, M.A. 1919 London

How far did Virgil, Horace and Tacitus supply the want of a middle voice in Latin by the use of the so-called passive?. M. Cartwright, M.A. 1906 Wales

Imtheachta Aenísa agus Aeneis Bhergil (The travels of Aeneas in Vergil's Aeneid). S. O'Mordha, M.A. 1939 National University of Ireland

The indebtedness of Vergil to Varro in the composition of the Georgics: a study in parallelism. N. P. Bentley, M.A. 1929 Manchester

The influence of Apollonius Rhodius on Vergil, with special reference to the romance of Aeneid IV. C. M. Worsley, M.A. 1925 Manchester

The influence of the Aeneid on the Argonautica of Valerius Flaccus. A. N. Marlow, M.A. 1938 London, Queen Mary College

The Italian element in Vergil's mythology. E. M. Palmer, M.A. 1929 Manchester

On the Culex, Ciris, Catalecta, Copa and Moretum attributed to Vergil, with special reference to style and grammar. E. John, M.A. 1909 London

On the preservation of ancient scholia on Virgil in Latin glossaries. H. J. Thomson, D. Litt. 1922 Saint Andrew's

The poems of Virgil considered in connection with the geography of Italy, including the natural features and animal and plant life. A. H. Birch, M.A. 1912 Wales

A study of Gawayne Douglas's translation of Vergil's Aeneid. I. M. Le Chavetois, M.A. 1909 London

A study of sixteenth century English translations of the Aeneid: Surrey, Phaer and Stanyhurst. G. D. Willcock, M.A. 1913 London

A study of Virgil's methods of adapting Homer, based on Macrobius's list of parallel passages. R. F. Morgan, M.A. 1936 Wales

Vergil and Homer: a study of the fifth book of Vergil's Aeneid. W. S. Booth, M.A. 1925 Manchester

Vergil's Roman campagna. B. Tilly, Ph.D. 1940 London, External Degree

Virgil and Roman learning as applied to the Aeneid. R. T. Moore, M.A. 1920 London

Virgil and Tennyson: a parallel study. L. S. Graham, M.A. 1917 Birmingham

Virgil as an observer of nature. A. I. Craig, M.A. 1909 Birmingham

Virgil glosses in Latin glossaries. A. F. G. Dall, Ph.D. 1922 Saint Andrew's

Virgil contd.
Virgil's treatment of Roman history. G. A. L. Heward, M.A. 1908 Wales

Virgil's use of Homer and Euripides in the third book of the Aeneid. N. E. Sutton, M.A. 1948 Manchester

Virgin Mary
See Mary, Virgin.

Virginia
1. Bristol and Virginia in the seventeenth century. 2. Bristol merchants, shipwrights, etc. from the Burgess Books, 1607-1700. N. C. P. Tyack, M.A. 1930 Bristol

Visconti, Giangaleazzo, Duke of Milan
Giangaleazzo Visconti, Duke of Milan, and the unity of Italy. D. M. Bueno de Mesquita, Ph.D. 1939 Cambridge

Vishnu
Visnu in the Rgveda and after until the epic period. M. S. Gladstone, Ph.D. 1928 Cambridge

Visual Perception
See Perception.

Visuddhimagga
See Buddhism.

Vitalism
A critical exposition of mechanism and vitalism, with special reference to their philosophical implications. H. Williams, M.A. 1932 Wales

Vitelli, Paolo
The problem of Paolo Vitelli, condottiere in the service of Florence. E. B. Darke, M.A. 1909 London

Vitta, Emile
La poésie d'Emile Vitta. H. Rench, M.A. 1933 Birmingham

Vivarium
The monastery of Vivarium and its historical importance. M. Stanley, B.Litt. 1939 Oxford

Vivekananda
A comparison of the pagan apologetic of Celsus against Christianity as contained in Origen's Contra Celsum, and the neo-Hindu attitude to Christianity as represented in the works of Vivekananda, and an estimate of the value of Origen's reply for Christian apologetics against neo-Hinduism. J. R. Chandran, B.Litt. 1949 Oxford

Vives, Juan Luis
Vives and aspects of renaissance education. K. O'Shea, M.A. 1926 National University of Ireland

Vocational Education
See Education, Vocational.

Vocational Guidance
See also Careers.

The contribution of a secondary school to vocational adjustment. R. M. Jones, M.Ed. 1944 Manchester

Education and employment: a study of the employments of juveniles with reference to vocational guidance and education. B. P. Jones, M.Ed. 1927 Manchester

The need for vocational guidance: a study of three comparable groups of ex-secondary schoolgirls. W. H. van O. Bruyn, M.A. 1940 London, Institute of Education

The predictive value of certain vocational tests, with special reference to personnel selection in the Army. M. S. Stevenson, M.Sc. 1944 London, University College

A scheme of vocational guidance for use in an educational area. A. Macdonald, Ph.D. 1939 Edinburgh

A study in vocational guidance, with special reference to the importance of interests. A. Crowther, Ph.D. 1937 Cambridge

A study of children's vocational interests and their relation to school interests. S. B. Ahmed, M.Ed. 1949 Leeds

Vocational and occupational guidance. K. H. R. Edwards, M.A. 1939 Liverpool

Vocational guidance and selection in Harrogate. A. Taylor, M.Ed. 1937 Leeds

Vocational guidance in secondary schools. H. A. T. Simmonds, M.A. 1931 London, Day Training College

A vocational investigation of some of the factors affecting the early industrial careers of elementary-school boys. A. W. Heim, Ph.D. 1940 Cambridge

Vocational Training
See Education, Vocational.

Vogelweide, Walther von der
The political poetry of Walther von der Vogelweide. A. J. P. Crick, M.A. 1936 London, King's College

Voiture, Vincent
Voiture and the Hôtel de Rambouillet: a study of the brilliant period of the esprit précieux. C. D. Webb, M.A. 1905 London

Volition
See Will.

Volney, Constantin François Chasseboeuf de, Comte
Volney et la littérature française à la fin du dix-huitième siècle. M. D. Moorhead, M.A. 1922 Belfast

Voltaire, François Marie Arouët de
Bolingbroke and Voltaire: a comparative study of their philosophical and religious ideas. A. S. Hurn, B.Litt. 1915 Oxford

The influence of the French revolutionary theorists (Voltaire, Rousseau, D'Holbach etc.) upon Shelley. G. C. Rosser, M.A. 1939 Wales

The influence of Voltaire upon Anatole France. H. E. Whittle, Ph.D. 1939 London, External Degree

Le pessimisme de Voltaire entre 1759 et 1769. K. Rockett, M.A. 1939 Manchester

Les parodies dramatiques des oeuvres de Voltaire. M. J. Laird, M.A. 1912 Leeds

A study of the chapters concerning the history of the Jews in Voltaire's Introduction à l'essai sur les moeurs et l'esprit des nations. E. Koutaissoff, B.Litt. 1939 Oxford

Swift et Voltaire. B. F. Rice, M.A. 1935 Birmingham

Voltaire's conception of the origin and function of morality. J. M. Jeffreys, M.A. 1947 London, University College

Voluntary Associations
See also Philanthropic Societies.

The place of charity and voluntary social service in the life of the community. C. Braithwaite, Ph.D. 1938 London, External Degree

The problem of liberty in relation to the development of voluntary associations. W. E. Styler, M.A. 1937 Birmingham

The relations between the State and voluntary associations in theory and practice during the last fifty years. C. B. Macintosh, Cert.Litt. 1920 Oxford

The relations of statutory and voluntary authorities in public administration in England and Wales. M. McKie, B.Litt. 1930 Oxford

The respective spheres of the State and of voluntary organizations in the prevention and relief of poverty in London at the present day. L. H. Bell, M.A. 1935 London, School of Economics and Political Science

Voluntary associations within the state, 1900-1934, with special reference to the place of trade unions in relation to the State in Great Britain. C. B. Macpherson, M.Sc. 1935 London, School of Economics and Political Science

Voyages and Travels
See also Drake, F., Sir; Hakluyt, R.

Barrès en voyage: le monde extérieur dans les oeuvres de Maurice Barrès. J. R. Taylor, M.A. 1930 Wales

A bibliography of travel books translated from English into French during the period 1750-1800. S. Roberts, M.A. 1949 Leeds

Bristol voyages to the New World between 1576 and 1612. E. R. Gath, M.A. 1914 Bristol

A description and classification of the mss. of the Navigatio Sancti Brendani. C. E. Low, D.Phil. 1934 Oxford

Expediciones por el norte de America del sur en siglo XVI. J. G. Healy, M.A. 1931 National University of Ireland

Fford y Brawt Odric, o'r Llanstephan ms. 2; ei gymharu âr gwreiddiol, gyda nodiadau gramadegol a geirfa (The journey of Brother Odoric, from the Llanstephan ms. 2; compared with the original and with grammatical notes and a vocabulary). S. J. Williams, M.A. 1925 Wales

French travellers in England from 1820 to 1830. E. Jones, M.A. 1925 Wales

The grand tour in Italy in the sixteenth, seventeenth and eighteenth centuries. E. M. Hutton, Ph.D. 1937 Cambridge

Voyages and Travels contd.
The history of St. Helena and the route to the Indies, 1659-1702. *W. C. Palmer, M.A. 1924 London*

The literature of travel from 1350-1750. *W. J. H. Watkins, M.A. 1919 Wales*

Medieval travel as illustrated by the wardrobe accounts of Henry, Earl of Derby, 1390-1393. *G. Stretton, M.A. 1924 London*

South African travel literature in English to the end of the seventeenth century. *N. H. MacKenzie, Ph.D. 1940 London, University College*

The Principal Navigations, Voyages, Traffiques, and Discoveries of the English Nation, by Richard Hakluyt. *F. West, M.A. 1927 Liverpool*

Travel descriptions in Middle High German Arthurian epics. *M. O'C. Walshe, M.A. 1935 London, University College*

Travel in Italy in the first century before Christ. *A. H. Watts, M.A. 1915 London*

Welsh seamen, navigators and colonizers, Elizabethan and Jacobean, together with some history of Welsh maritime and colonizing activity during the period. *E. R. Williams, M.A. 1915 Wales*

Vulgate
See Bible: Versions.

Wackenroder, Wilhelm Heinrich
The relation of music and poetry as reflected in the works of Tieck, Wackenroder and Brentano. *M. E. Atkinson, M.A. 1947 London, Bedford College*

Wade, Claude, Sir
The diplomatic career of Sir Claude Wade: a study of British relations with the Sikhs and Afghans, July 1823 to March 1840. *E. R. Kapadia, M.A. 1938 London, School of Oriental and African Studies*

Wade, Thomas
A study of Thomas Wade: poet and dramatist, 1805-1875. *S. I. Stevenson, M.A. 1929 London*

Wages and Salaries
See also Industrial Relations.

Alfred Marshall as an economist, with special reference to wages and working class. *P. Whelan, M.Econ.Sc. 1945 National University of Ireland*

An analysis of wage-rates in Britain in relation to employment levels since 1920. *W. H. Mason, M.Sc. 1949 London, External Degree*

British incomes and property. *J. C. Stamp, D.Sc. 1916 London*

Changes of wage rates in certain industries during the last 30-40 years, and in particular, the relations between changes in rates and changes in earnings, and their causes. *J. W. F. Rowe, M.Sc. 1923 London*

A consideration of the theory of womens' wages, and an attempt to test the truth of certain reasons which have been adduced by economic writers for the relatively lower wage-level of women in industry as compared with that of men. *P. B. Wylde-Brown, M.A. 1930 Birmingham*

A critical examination of methods of industrial remuneration, with special reference to the requirement of British industry. *N. C. Hunt, Ph.D. 1948 Edinburgh*

Economic analysis of wage regulation in Australia, 1920-1947. *J. E. Isaac, Ph.D. 1949 London, School of Economics and Political Science*

The impact of international economic fluctuations on employment and incomes in New Zealand, 1929-1939, and the nature and effects of public policy towards it, with some comparative study of Australia and Canada in the same period. *N. S. McIvor, Ph.D. 1949 London, School of Economics and Political Science*

An investigation into wage incentives and their effect on production, with comparisons between Great Britain and the United States. *S. K. Reed, Ph.D. 1950 Edinburgh*

National guilds as a wage system. *M. Healy, M.A. 1920 National University of Ireland*

Problems of wages and wage regulations. *W. D. Jones, M.Sc. 1936 London, External Degree*

The regulation of wages in England under the Statute of Artificers. *N. M. Hindmarsh, Ph.D. 1932 London, External Degree*

The relationship between wages theories and social organization. *J. R. Kirwan, B.Phil. 1948 Oxford*

The settlement of wages in government employment. *E. C. Shepherd, B.Litt. 1923 Oxford*

Wages and Salaries contd.
Some contributions to a study of work, wages and prices in Wales in the sixteenth century. *A. B. Jones, M.A. 1933 Wales*

Some problems in wages policy. *C. D. Finch, Ph.D. 1949 London, School of Economics and Political Science*

Some problems of wages and their regulation in Great Britain since 1918. *A. G. B. Fisher, Ph.D. 1924 London*

Studies in the theory of wage rates. *P. H. Asher, M.Sc. 1935 Cambridge*

A study of the methods of state regulation of wages, with special reference to their possible applications in India. . *S. B. L. Nigam, Ph.D. 1949 London, School of Economics and Political Science*

A study on the minimum wage. *J. H. Richardson, Ph.D. 1927 London*

Systems of remuneration of labour in agriculture in relation to efficiency and performance. *W. Mackenzie, B.Litt. 1948 Oxford*

The variations of real wages and profit margins in relation to the trade cycle. *S. C. Tsiang, Ph.D. 1945 London, School of Economics and Political Science*

Wage policy in relation to industrial fluctuations. *A. G. Pool, Ph.D. 1939 London, External Degree*

Wage theories in the nineteenth century, with special reference to Thornton. *A. C. McCarthy, M.Econ.Sc. 1941 National University of Ireland*

Wage-rates: 1750-1800. *G. H. A. Stephens, B.Litt. 1931 Oxford*

Wages and capitalist production. *V. G. Edelberg, Ph.D. 1935 London, School of Economics and Political Science*

Wages and the State. *E. M. Burns, Ph.D. 1926 London*

Wages policy and the price level. *K. S. Isles, M.Sc. 1934 Cambridge*

Wakefield
The city of Wakefield: a study of the growth and functions of an urban settlement. *R. Bentham, M.A. 1939 London, University College*

A history of popular education in Wakefield, 1780-1902. *C. Brown, M.Ed. 1937 Leeds*

The social history of Wakefield and neighbourhood in the seventeenth century. *S. Waters, M.A. 1932 Leeds*

Wakefield and district as a traditional area in the Yorkshire, Derbyshire and Nottinghamshire coalfield. *E. H. Varley, M.Sc. 1935 London, Birkbeck College*

Wakf
See Trusts, Charitable.

Wales: Economics
Certain aspects of the Industrial Revolution in South Wales, 1760-1850. *A. H. John, Ph.D. 1940 Cambridge*

The economic, industrial and social history of Ebbw Vale during the period 1775-1927, being a study in the origin and development of an industrial district of south Wales in all its aspects. *A. G. Jones, M.A. 1929 Wales*

The evolution of industries and settlements between Merthyr Tydfil and Abergavenny from 1740 to 1840. *C. Davies, M.A. 1949 Wales*

The industrial development of Merioneth, 1750-1820, being an investigation into the economic organization and history of certain distinctive industries in the county during this period. *M. J. Jones, M.A. 1937 Wales*

The industrial development of the Rhondda Valleys to 1910. *E. D. Lewis, M.A. 1940 Wales*

The industrial development of the Llynfi, Ogmore and Garw valleys, with special reference to transport facilities in the are. *T. Bevan, M.A. 1928 Wales*

The industrial history of the Rhymney Valley, with regard to the iron, steel and tinplate industries, coal mining, lead mining, smelting and quarrying. *J. Davies, M.Sc. 1926 Wales*

Some contributions to a study of work, wages and prices in Wales in the sixteenth century. *A. B. Jones, M.A. 1933 Wales*

Wales: Geography
The denudation chronology of northeast Wales. *A. N. Harris, Ph.D. 1947 London, Birkbeck College*

The geographical distribution of religious denominations in Wales in its relation to racial and social factors. *J. E. Daniel, M.A. 1928 Wales*

Wales: Geography contd.
The morphology of the Welsh border towns: a study in historical geography. *P. D. Wood, M.A. 1950 Wales*

North Wales and Merseyside. *D. Williams, M.A. 1932 Liverpool*

Wales: History
See also Black Death; Chartists; and Cornwall, Richard, Earl of; Giraldus, Cambrensis; Glyndwr, O.; Hywel, Dda; Morys, H. (Eos Ceiriog); Vaughan, R., 2nd Earl of Carbery; Wynn, C. W. W., Sir.

The boroughs of north Wales: their parliamentary history from the Act of Union to the first Reform Act (1535-1832). *G. Roberts, M.A. 1929 Wales*

The contribution of Wales to the British Empire in the sixteenth and seventeenth centuries. *W. A. Bebb, M.A. 1920 Wales*

A contribution to the study of early invasions of Wales. *H. Higgins, M.A. 1921 Liverpool*

The *cymwds* of Gwynedd prior to the Edwardian conquest of Wales. *G. L. Jones, M.A. 1919 Wales*

The Edwardian settlement of North Wales. *W. H. Waters, M.Litt. 1926 Cambridge*

The growth and development of the municipal element in the principality of north Wales up to the close of the fourteenth century. *E. A. Lewis, M.A. 1902 Wales*

The history of Wales during the reign of Edward II, 1307-1327. *J. C. Davies, M.A. 1914 Wales*

Nonconformist academies in Wales (1662-1862). *H. P. Roberts, M.A. 1922 Liverpool*

The Norman conquests in Wales up to 1100 A.D. *J. W. Wilkinson, M.A. 1901 Wales*

Norse relations with Wales. *B. G. Charles, M.A. 1932 Wales*

The policy of Powys in the twelfth and thirteenth centuries. *F. L. Rees, M.A. 1911 Wales*

The political history of Wales from 1350 to 1485, as reflected in the literature of the period. *C. H. Thomas, M.A. 1936 Wales*

The principality of Wales under Edward the Black Prince. *D. L. Evans, B.Litt. 1930 Oxford*

The Rebecca riots in Wales. *M. Williams, M.A. 1913 Wales*

Richard, Earl of Cornwall, King of the Romans (1257-1272). *F. R. Lewis, M.A. 1934 Wales*

Richard Vaughan, 2nd Earl of Carbery (1606-1686). *T. S. Williams, M.A. 1936 Wales*

The turnpike trusts of Wales: a study in transport economics. *E. W. Barton, M.A. 1915 Wales*

Wales and piracy: a study in Tudor administration, 1500-1640. *C. E. Hughes, M.A. 1937 Wales*

Wales and the border counties in relation to the Popish plot. *I. M. O'Leary, M.A. 1924 Wales*

Wales and the Marches in the reign of Edward II, with special reference to Glamorgan and the revolt of Llewelyn Bren. *T. A. Dyke, M.A. 1912 Wales*

Wales in the seventeenth century. *J. C. Morrice, B.Litt. 1920 Oxford*

Wales under the Propagation Act, 1650-3. *T. Richards, M.A. 1934 Wales*

The Welsh soldier in England's armies of the thirteenth and fourteenth centuries. *T. L. Williams, M.A. 1915 Wales*

Wales: Politics and Government
The influence of the French Revolution on the political and social life of Wales. *W. P. Williams, M.A. 1925 Wales*

Welsh politics from Mortimers Cross to Bosworth Field. *W. G. Jones, M.A. 1908 Liverpool*

Wales: Social History
The Caernarvonshire squires, 1558-1625. *E. G. Jones, M.A. 1936 Wales*

The history of the Honourable Society of Cymmrodorion. *H. M. Jones, M.A. 1939 Wales*

The influence of the French Revolution on the political and social life of Wales. *W. P. Williams, M.A. 1925 Wales*

The influence of the Methodist movement on social life in Wales. *E. C. Lloyd, B.Litt. 1921 Oxford*

Movements towards social reform in south Wales during the period 1832-1850. *L. Williams, M.A. 1933 Wales*

Wales: Social History contd.
The religious and social condition of Wales at the outbreak of the Glyndwr movement, with special reference to the attitude of the clergy, both regular and secular, to the movement. *J. R. Gabriel, M.A. 1906 Wales*

The social and religious history of Wales from 1350 to 1550 as reflected in the literature of the period. *C. H. Thomas, Ph.D. 1940 National University of Ireland*

Social conditions in Wales under the Tudors and Stuarts. *J. C. Morrice, Ph.D. 1924 Oxford*

The social determination of ideologies: being a study of a Welsh mining community. *G. H. Armbruster, Ph.D. 1940 London, School of Economics and Political Science*

Social life in Wales in the eighteenth century as illustrated in its popular literature of the period. *T. H. Jones, M.A. 1922 Wales*

A social survey of a rural parish in Wales. *H. Williams- Jones, M.A. 1929 Liverpool*

Wales and the Welsh in English literature from the beginning of the sixteenth to the beginning of the nineteenth century. *W. J. Hughes, M.A. 1919 Wales*

The wayside entertainer in Wales in the nineteenth century. *R. W. Jones, M.A. 1939 Liverpool*

The Welsh character and his development in English drama, 1590-1642. *B. Pierce-Jones, M.A. 1949 Manchester*

Waliullah, Shah
The practical theology and ethics of Shah Waliullah of Dihli. *A. J. Halepota, D.Phil. 1949 Oxford*

Wallasey
The growth of Wallasey and its future development. *W. B. Thorp, M.A. 1936 Liverpool*

Wallis, John
The development of mathematical notation from Wallis to John Bernoulli. *W. Howells, Ph.D. 1933 London, External Degree*

John Wallis, and his place in the history of science. *J. F. Scott, Ph.D. 1935 London, University College*

Translation and analysis of the *Arithmetica infinitorum* of J. Wallis (1656). *G. A. Dickinson, M.Sc. 1936 Liverpool*

Walls
Walls: material, social and individual: a study of the defences raised by man in his later evolutionary development. *J. S. Brooks, M.A. 1935 Bristol*

Walpole, Horace, 4th Earl of Orford
Criticism of Horace Walpole's treatment of William Pitt, Earl of Chatham, 1760-1768. *G. M. Dalrymple, M.A. 1909 Liverpool*

Horace Walpole as reflective of the literary tastes and tendencies of the eighteenth century. *R. Papperovitch, M.A. 1926 Liverpool*

Walpole, Hugh Seymour, Sir
The influence of *The Castle of Otranto* on the English novel, excluding the novels of Scott, up to 1820. *K. K. Mehrotra, B.Litt. 1933 Oxford*

Walsh, William
A critical edition of the poems of William Walsh (1662-1708) in Bodleian manuscript Malone 9. *E. Rhodes, M.A. 1949 London, Birkbeck College*

The life and works of William Walsh, with a special study of the letters and poems of 1692 and of ms. Malone 9. *P. C. Freeman, B.Litt. 1934 Oxford*

William Walsh, poet and critic. *B. E. McLauchlan, M.A. 1948 Birmingham*

Walsingham, Francis, Sir
Sir Francis Walsingham. *C. Read, B.Litt. 1909 Oxford*

Walter, Edmund
A study of the life and poetry of Edmund Walter. *M. C. Deas, Ph.D. 1931 Cambridge*

Walwyn, William
The life and works of William Walwyn the Leveller. *S. H. Knapton, M.A. 1949 London, Queen Mary College*

The part played by Walwyn and Overton in the Leveller Movement. *J. E. Speak, M.A. 1949 Leeds*

Wang an Shih
Wang an Shih, a rejected reformer. *H. R. Williamson, D.Litt. 1932 London, External Degree*

War and Peace
See also Armed Forces; Armour; Christianity and Political and Social Questions; League of Nations; United Nations; Weapons.

War and Peace contd.
The British attitude to the second Hague Conference: a study of newspaper opinion in England, 1906-7. *R. J. Parry, M.A. 1937 Wales*

Christian attitudes to war and peace: a study of the four main types, with a foreword by W. P. Paterson. *T. S. K. Scott-Craig, Ph.D. 1938 Edinburgh*

1. The Christian's duty to the State. 2. The lawfulness of war. *J. G. W. Tuckey, B.D. 1924 Oxford*

The development of the 'just war' conception, especially since Grotius. *G. D. Roos, B.Litt. 1936 Oxford*

Economic phenomena before and after war. *S. Secerov, M.Sc. 1918 London*

Effects of war on national economy. *C. Morris, M.A. 1945 National University of Ireland*

English poetry and war. *M. A. O'Shea, M.A. 1931 National University of Ireland*

The estimation of the effects of air attack. *H. W. G. Deeks, M.Sc. 1948 London, External Degree*

1. The function of the prophets in Christian Church, as it may be gathered from the New Testament. 2. The Christian view of war. *J. G. Tetley, B.D. & D.D. 1901 Oxford*

Functions of banks in finance of peace and war. *J. Busteed, M.Comm. 1926 National University of Ireland*

International legal and military control of cables and wireless in time of war, with special reference to the present war. *G. I. Phillips, B.Litt. 1918 Oxford*

Labour and war: the theory of labour action to prevent war. *B. F. Braatoy, Ph.D. 1934 London, School of Economics and Political Science*

The law of contraband of war. *H. R. Pyke, LL.D. 1916 London*

The League of Nations and the problem of a universal peace organization. *G. Schwarzenberger, Ph.D. 1936 London, School of Economics and Political Science*

The organization of peace through collective security, 1934-1938. *E. Strickler, M.Sc. 1949 London, School of Economics and Political Science*

The policy of Switzerland in the construction of the collective peace system. *J. B. Knapp, B.Litt. 1936 Oxford*

The problem of war to the religious thinker of the sixteenth century. *R. F. Wright, Ph.D. 1937 London, King's College*

The psychological and ethical basis of the problem of peace. *H. V. Hall, M.A. 1932 Wales*

Psychological aspects of advertising in war. *N. M. Hindmarsh, M.Sc. 1943 London, King's College*

The psychological roots of war. *A. C. Osburn, B.Litt. 1938 Oxford*

Public opinion and the movement for disarmament, 1888-98. *M. Tate, B.Litt. 1935 Oxford*

The pursuit of disarmament, Geneva, 1920-33: a study in international procedure. *S. Woo, M.Sc. 1938 London, School of Economics and Political Science*

A study of the attitude towards war of a group of secondary school-children, aged 14-15. *S. Dutt, M.A. 1949 London, Institute of Education*

A study of the reactions of older children to air-raid conditions in 1940-41. *M. H. Ouseley, M.A. 1948 London, Institute of Education*

War and peace in English poetry, 1780-1830. *R. A. Jones, M.A. 1948 Wales*

Warburton, Bartholomew Elliott George
A study of Warburton's *The Crescent and the Cross* in relation to the literary interest in the Near East shown by English romantic writers in the eighteenth and the earlier nineteenth centuries. *M. S. Abdel-Hamid, M.A. 1948 Bristol*

Warburton, William, Bishop
The literary life and writings of William Warburton. *B. S. Kesavan, M.A. 1936 London, Birkbeck College*

Warburton and the Warburtonians. *A. W. Evans, Litt.D. 1932 Dublin, Trinity College*

Ward, Edward
Ned Ward. *L. W. Herron, Ph.D. 1941 London, University College*

Ward, James
Empiricism in the philosophy of James Ward. *A. H. Murray, B.Litt. 1928 Oxford*

The idea of God in the philosophy of William James and James Ward. *S. J. Theodore, B.Litt. 1925 Oxford*

Wardlaw, Ralph
Ralph Wardlaw, 1779-1853, with particular reference to his theory of the atonement and the rise of Congregationalism in Scotland. *R. D. Hyslop, Ph.D. 1947 Edinburgh*

Wardship
See Child Welfare.

Warham, William
William Warham as statesman, scholar, and patron. *K. E. Hardy, B.Litt. 1943 Oxford*

Warton, Joseph
Joseph Warton. *P. Parker, B.Litt. 1929 Oxford*

Joseph Warton as a literary critic. *R. M. Baine, B.Litt. 1939 Oxford*

Warton, Thomas
The correspondence of Bishop Percy and Thomas Warton. *M. G. Robinson, B.Litt. 1935 Oxford*

Literary history in England in the eighteenth century, before Warton's *History of English poetry*. *T. A. H. Scott, B.Litt. 1939 Oxford*

Warwick, County
Population migration to and from Warwickshire and Staffordshire, 1841-1901. *R. Lawton, M.A. 1950 Liverpool*

Water and Water Supply
See also Oases.

The contribution of water power development to the progress of the cotton-spinning industry, with particular reference to the Bolton district (period 1770-1845). *E. J. Foulkes, M.A. 1943 Wales*

The domestic water supply in the Wealden District in its geographical aspect. *S. G. Davis, M.Sc. 1939 London, Birkbeck College*

Geographical and historical aspects of the public water supply of London, 1852-1902. *R. W. Morris, Ph.D. 1941 London, Birkbeck College*

A geographical study of water resources of England and Wales and their use in large-scale supplies of piped water to cities. *A. Biggs, M.Sc. 1949 London, School of Economics and Political Science*

On the common law of England with respect to waters, with special references to the possibility of applying it to varying natural circumstances. *W. A. B. Musgrave, D.C.L. 1890 Oxford*

Right to support of land and buildings by underground water and semi-solids. *F. B. Brook, LL.M. 1932 Cambridge*

The ritual significance of water. *P. L. Collignon, Ph.D. 1929 London*

Watercourses in the parish of St. Margaret's, Westminster, in the seventeenth century: a problem of local administration. *A. C. Wood, B.Litt. 1938 Oxford*

Waterford
A history of Waterford: its life and government from 1150-1800. *F. C. Morris, M.A. 1915 Wales*

Waterhouse Charity, The
A history of the Waterhouse Charity, Halifax. *J. Clayton, M.A. 1943 Leeds*

Waterways
See Canals; Rivers.

Watson, Richard, Bishop
Richard Watson, bishop of Llandaff, 1737-1816. *P. R. Smythe, B.D. 1937 Oxford*

Watson, William, Sir
A study of the chemistries of Lemery, Freind, Baume, and Watson, and of the development of chemical thought from 1675 to 1787. *S. D. M. Waters, M.Sc. 1931 London*

Watts, Isaac
Isaac Watts' work in hymnology, with special regard to its derivative and original features. *H. Escott, Ph.D. 1950 Edinburgh*

Waya, The
The Wayas of Nyasaland. *H. S. Stannus, Ph.D. 1926 London*

Wealth
Distribution of wealth in an Indian province. *H. C. Seth, Ph.D. 1926 London*

The English view of usury and the distribution of wealth in the later Middle Ages. *H. G. Richardson, M.A. 1912 London*

The relation of wealth to welfare. *W. A. Robson, Ph.D. 1925 London*

Wealth contd.
The use of wealth by the Romans from 150 to 50 B.C. *E. Thomas, M.A. 1947 London, Birkbeck College*

Work and wealth in Southampton: an essay in civic economy. *P. Ford, Ph.D. 1933 London, External Degree*

Weapons
See also Armour; Ballistics.

The halberd in bronze-age Europe: a study in pre-historic origins, evolution, distribution and chronology. *J. P. Reardon, Ph.D. 1936 National University of Ireland*

Weapons and conduct of Hebrew warfare as illustrated in the Old Testament. *W. Davies, M.A. 1929 Wales*

Wearside
The Reform movement in Tyneside and Wearside, 1812-1832. *M. B. G. Allan, M.A. 1919 Liverpool*

Weathering
See Erosion.

Weavers' Company
The history of the London Weavers' Company. *F. Consitt, B.Litt. 1929 Oxford*

Weaving Industry
The hand loom weavers in the Stockport area, 1784-94. *G. Taylor, M.A. 1922 Manchester*

Webster, John
The art of Webster. *B. Doody, M.A. 1934 National University of Ireland*

A critical edition of the *Famous Historie of Sir Thomas Wyat*, by Thomas Dekker and John Webster. *E. M. F. Martin, M.A. 1930 London, University College*

Female characterization in Jacobean tragedy, with special consideration of the tragedies of Heywood, Webster, Middleton, Beaumont and Fletcher. *A. E. Bufton, M.A. 1939 Wales*

John Webster. *F. Allen, M.A. 1914 Birmingham*

John Webster, a study. *D. M. Farr, Ph.D. 1947 Leeds*

John Webster and the early seventeenth century background. *L. Whitworth, M.A. 1947 Liverpool*

The literary reputation of John Webster to 1830. *T. L. Wang, B.Litt. 1949 Oxford*

Some aspects of the style of John Webster: a study of *The Duchess of Malfi* and *The White Devil. N. V. L. Hilt, Ph.D. 1949 Birmingham*

The use and purpose of imagery in the tragedy of Webster, Tourneur and Middleton. *J. R. Jones, M.A. 1941 Wales*

Webster's imagery and what it tells us. *J. A. Storey, Ph.D. 1944 Dublin, Trinity College*

Wedderburn, Alexander, 1st Earl of Rosslyn
Some political aspects of the career of Alexander Wedderburn, Lord Loughborough and Earl of Rosslyn. *H. C. Sheridan, M.A. 1919 Liverpool*

Weelkes, Thomas
Thomas Weelkes and the English tradition. *D. M. Arnold, M.A. 1950 Sheffield*

Weights and Measures
See Measurement.

Welfare Economics
See also Social Services; Child Welfare.

The development of utility theory and welfare economics. *L. W. McKenzie, B.Litt. 1949 Oxford*

Postulates of welfare economics. *H. Myint, Ph.D. 1943 London, School of Economics and Political Science*

The provision for the welfare of women and young workers in the cotton industry. *R. K. K. Lee, M.A. 1949 Liverpool*

The relation of wealth to welfare. *W. A. Robson, Ph.D. 1925 London*

The theory of welfare and control. *W. J. Baumol, Ph.D. 1949 London, School of Economics and Political Science*

The theory of welfare economics. *I. M. D. Little, D.Phil. 1949 Oxford*

Welfare work. *E. D. Proud, D.Sc. 1916 London*

Wellesley, Arthur, 1st Duke of Wellington
The influence of Wellington on the internal politics of France, 1815-18. *A. I. Jones, B.Litt. 1935 Oxford*

Wellesley, Richard Colley, 1st Marquis
The constitutional relations of the Marquess Wellesley with the home authorities. *B. L. Frazer, M.A. 1917 Liverpool*

Wellington, Arthur Wellesley, First Duke of
The foreign policy of Wellington, 1828-30. *A. C. F. Beales, M.A. 1927 London*

Wellington, Duke of
See Wellesley, Arthur, 1st Duke of Wellington.

Wells, Herbert George
A study of H. G. Wells's contributions to education. *T. G. Evans, M.A. 1931 Wales*

Welsh Language
Astudiaeth fanwl o gystrawen, testunau rhyddiath Cymraeg canol a gyhoeddwyd yn y *Bulletin of the Board of Celtic Studies* (An exact study of the syntax of the medieval Welsh prose texts published in the *Bulletin of the Board of Celtic Studies*). *D. S. Evans, M.A. 1948 Wales*

A comparison of the phonetic systems of English and Welsh, and the application of such comparative study in the practical teaching of English in Welsh schools. *M. Davies, M.A. 1923 Wales*

Cystrawen arddodiaid ym Mhedair Cainc y Mabinogi (The syntax of prepositions in the Four Branches of the Mabinogi). *M. Rees, M.A. 1935 Wales*

Cystrawen y ferf mewn Cymraeg canol (The syntax of the verb in medieval Welsh). *T. J. Morgan, M.A. 1930 Wales*

Cystrawen y frawddeg yn y Pedair Cainc yn Llyfr Gwyn Rhydderch (The syntax of the sentence in the Four Branches in the White Book of Rhydderch). *G. M. Richards, M.A. 1933 Wales*

Ffyrfiau berfol rhai o destunau cymraeg yr unfed ganrif ar bymtheg, y testunau a gyhoeddwyd ym Mulletin Bwrdd y Gwybodau Celtaidd a chylchgronau eraill (Verbal forms in some sixteenth century Welsh texts as published in the *Bulletin of the Board of Celtic Studies* and other periodicals). *R. J. Davies, M.A. 1933 Wales*

Fragments of Gospels and pseudo-Gospels in medieval Welsh. *J. Jenkins, B.Litt. 1919 Oxford*

The history of Welsh orthography up to 1620. *O. R. Hughes, M.A. 1905 Wales*

Iaith a ieithwedd y cerddi rhydd cynnar (The language and style of the early free poems). *H. M. Evans, M.A. 1937 Wales*

Initial mutations in medieval Welsh. *J. D. Brown, M.A. 1900 Wales*

Inter-relations of Ireland and Wales as evidenced by the tradition, languages and literatures of both countries. *C. O'Rahilly, M.A. 1919 Wales*

The language and style of William Salesbury. *D. Mark, M.A. 1903 Wales*

The language of Williams, Pantycelyn, with special reference to vocabulary and grammatical forms. *C. J. Davies, M.A. 1923 Wales*

Orgraff y Gymraeg o gyfnod y Dr. William Owen Pughe hyd ddiwygiad yr orgraff (The orthography of the Welsh language from the period of Dr. William Owen Pugh to the reform). *W. I. Jones, M.A. 1924 Wales*

A study of the development of the science of grammar in its earliest stages in Wales, with particular reference to the grammatical works of Einion Offeiriad, Dafydd Ddu Hiraddug and Simwnt Fychan. *J. T. Jones, M.A. 1925 Wales*

The verbal forms in the *Mabinogion* and *Bruts. G. J. Williams, M.A. 1918 Wales*

The verbal forms of the *Mabinogion* and *Bruts. W. Griffith, M.A. 1904 Wales*

The Welsh version of the *Historia regum Britanniae* in Peniarth ms.44 collated with the *Red book* version, together with notes on the influence of the original on the style and construction of the Welsh, and a glossary of Welsh words whose use is illustrated by the Latin. *B. Jones, M.A. 1915 Wales*

Yr iaith Gymraeg, ei horgraff a'i chystrawen (The Welsh language, its orthography and syntax). *D. T. Evans, M.A. 1927 Wales*

Welsh Language: Dialects
Astudiaeth o Gymraeg llafar ardai Ceinwydd (A study of the spoken Welsh of the district of New Quay). *J. J. G. Davies, Ph.D. 1934 Wales*

The Dyfi: its people, antiquities, dialects, folklore and placenames studied in correlation to one another, with a special aim of ascertaining what degree of correlation there may be between physical anthropology, archaeology and dialect distribution. *I. C. Peate, M.A. 1924 Wales*

An enquiry into the dialect of Gower. *R. R. Griffiths, M.A. 1923 Wales*

Gramadeg tafodiaith dyffryn Aman (The grammar of the dialect of the Amman Valley). *R. O. Rees, M.A. 1936 Wales*

Welsh Language: Dialects contd.
The spoken dialect of Anglesey. *A. M. Jones, M.A. 1926 Wales*

The spoken dialect of the Ogwr Basin, Glamorgan. *T. I. Phillips, M.A. 1933 Wales*

Tafodiaith Cwmtawe (The dialect of the Tawe Valley). *D. G. Evans, M.A. 1930 Wales*

Tafodiaith hen blwyf Llangatwg (Castellnedd) (The dialect of the old parish of Llangatwg (Neath)). *C. B. H. Lewis, M.A. 1932 Wales*

The vicissitudes of the Welsh language in the Marches of Wales, with special reference to its territorial distribution in modern times. *W. H. Rees, Ph.D. 1947 Wales*

Welsh Language: Etymology
Aspects of Welsh lexicography in the nineteenth century, with special reference to the contribution of Daniel Silvan Evans. *R. E. Hughes, M.A. 1941 Liverpool*

The English element in Welsh. *T. H. Williams, M.A. 1911 Wales*

English loan words in literary Welsh. *R. W. Jones, M.A. 1907 Wales*

Latin loan words in Welsh and words that are cognate in Welsh and Latin. *J. Lloyd-Jones, B.Litt. 1908 Oxford*

Loan words in Welsh. *T. H. Parry-Williams, B.Litt. 1911 Oxford*

Some points of contact between Welsh and Breton. *R. W. Parry, M.A. 1912 Wales*

Welsh Language: Study and Teaching
Bilingual education in Wales, with special reference to the teaching of Welsh. *E. Evans, M.A. 1924 Wales*

The development of the study of the national language, literature and history in the educational system of Wales. *J. Hughes, M.A. 1922 Wales*

A survey of bilingualism in Wales and the Marches. *W. H. Rees, M.A. 1941 Liverpool*

Welsh Literature: General
Bardism and romance; a study of the Welsh literary tradition. *T. G. Jones, M.A. 1915 Wales*

Cyfriniaeth yn llenyddiaeth Gymreig (Mysticism in Welsh literature). *J. I. Williams, M.A. 1926 Wales*

Dychanau ac ymrysonau'r beirdd Cymreig hyd ddiwdd yr eilfed ganrif ar bymtheg (The satires and contentions of the Welsh bards to the end of the seventeenth century). *O. Thomas, M.A. 1928 Wales*

Hanes a llenyddiaeth cychwyniad a datblygiad mudiad y wladfa Gymreig ym Mhatagonia (The history and literature of the origin and development of the Welsh colony in Patagonia). *N. H. Cadfan, M.A. 1942 Wales*

Inter-relations of Ireland and Wales as evidenced by the tradition, languages and literatures of both countries. *C. O'Rahilly, M.A. 1919 Wales*

Llenyddiaeth Gymraeg y Wladfa (The Welsh literature of the Colony (in Patagonia)). *R. B. Williams, M.A. 1931 Wales*

The social nexus of Welsh literature. *J. Thomas, M.A. 1923 Liverpool*

Traddodiad llenyddol Deau Ceredigion, 1600-1850 (The literary tradition of southern Cardiganshire, 1600-1850). *G. Bowen, M.A. 1943 Wales*

Welsh Literature: Early and Medieval
See also Amlyn ac Amic; Aneirin; Brut y Brenhinoedd; Cynddelw Brydydd Mawr; Dafydd Llwyd ap Llywelyn ap Gruffudd; Fynglwyd, Iorwerth; Geoffrey, of Monmouth; Giraldus, Cambrensis; Guto'r Glyn; Gwidw; Hywel Davi; Ieuan Brydydd Hir Hynaf; Lewis Glyn Cothi; Llawdden; Mabinogion; Red Book of Hergest; Rhys Nanmor; Romances; Tudur Penllyn; Vision de Saint Paul.

Astudiaeth fanwl o gystrawen, testunau rhyddiath Cymraeg canol a gyhoeddwyd yn y *Bulletin of the Board of Celtic Studies* (An exact study of the syntax of the medieval Welsh prose texts published in the *Bulletin of the Board of Celtic Studies*). *D. S. Evans, M.A. 1948 Wales*

Cerddi'r Saint a'u cymharu â'r buchedau cyfatebol (The poems of the Saints and their comparison with the corresponding lives). *D. J. Jones, M.A. 1929 Wales*

Chwedl Myrddin yn y canu cynnar (The legend of Myrddin in early poetry). *A. O. H. Jarman, M.A. 1936 Wales*

A comparison between *Owein a Luned* and *Yvain, or Le Chevalier au Lion. M. Morgan, M.A. 1910 Wales*

Welsh Literature: Early and Medieval contd.
Early vaticinatory material in Welsh, with a study of some English parallels known to Welsh writers. *M. E. Griffiths, M.A. 1927 Wales*

The political history of Wales from 1350 to 1485, as reflected in the literature of the period. *C. H. Thomas, M.A. 1936 Wales*

The social and religious history of Wales from 1350 to 1550 as reflected in the literature of the period. *C. H. Thomas, Ph.D. 1940 National University of Ireland*

Tri thestun ffug-hanesyddol Cymraeg (Peniarth ms. 20, td. 1-64, British Museum addl. ms. 12, 193, Peniarth ms. 215, td. 374-402 - a'u cyd-destunau) a'u cysylltiad â'r testunau Lladin gwreiddiol (Three Welsh pseudo-historical texts (Peniarth ms. 20, pp. 1-64, British Museum Addl. ms. 12, 193, Peniarth ms. 215, pp. 374-402 -and their contexts) and their connections with the original latin texts). *T. Jones, M.A. 1935 Wales*

Ystorya Addaf a Val a cauas Elen y Grog: tarddiad, cynnwys ac arddull y testunau Cymraeg a'u lledaeniad (*The history of Adam* and *How Helen found the Cross*; Source, content, and style of the Welsh texts, and their diffusion). *T. G. Jones, M.A. 1936 Wales*

Welsh Literature: Sixteenth Century
See also Arwystl, Huw; Dafydd, Meurig; Dafydd Trefor; Gruffudd ab Ieuan ap Llywelyn Fychan; Gruffydd Hiraethog; Jones, Llywelyn; Lleyn, William; Llywelyn ap Rhisiart; Morus Dwyfech; Nanmor, Dafydd; Phylip, Siôn; Prys, Edmwnd; Salesbury, William; Tudur, Sion.

Gweithian barddonol Huw Arwystl (The poetical works of Huw Arwystl). *J. A. Jones, M. A. 1926 Wales*

Welsh Literature: Seventeenth Century
See also Davies, James (Iaco ap Dewi); Davies, John; Humphreys, H.; Bishop; Jones, John (Gellilyfdy); Morris, E.; Morys, H. (Eos Ceiriog); Prys, T.; Vaughan, H.; Vaughan, R.

Y dylanwadau llenyddol, crefyddol ac athronyddol ar Forgan Llwyd (Literary, religious and philosophical influences on Morgan Llwyd). *E. L. Evans, M.A. 1926 Wales*

Welsh Literature: Eighteenth Century
See also Evans, E.; Evans, T.; Jones, R.; Rowland, D.; Samuel, E.; Twm o'r Nant; Wynn, W.

Bywyd a gwaith Twm o'r Nant a'i le yn hanes yr Anterliwt (The life and work of Twm o'r Nant and his place in the history of the 'Interlude'). *G. M. Ashton, M.A. 1944 Wales*

Cysylltiad y diwygiadau crefyddol o 1730 hyd 1850 â llenyddiaeth y cyfnod (The connection of religious revivals from 1730 to 1850 with the literature of the period). *L. E. Evans, M.A. 1934 Wales*

Evan Evans (Ieuan Fardd), 1731-1788. Hanes ei fywyd a'i gysylltiadau llenyddol (Evan Evans (Ieuan Fardd), 1731-1788. The history of his life and his literary connections). *A. Lewis, M.A. 1950 Wales*

The literary movement in west Wales in the first half of the eighteenth century and its religious associations. *T. O. Williams, M.A. 1923 Wales*

Social life in Wales in the eighteenth century as illustrated in its popular literature of the period. *T. H. Jones, M.A. 1922 Wales*

Yr anterliwd Gymraeg (The Welsh interlude). *G. G. Evans, M.A. 1938 Wales*

Yr anterliwt Gymraeg: ei ffynonellau, ei chrefftwaithm a'i gwerth fel arwddocâd o ddiwylliant y bobl (The Welsh 'interlude'; its sources, craftsmanship, and value as an indication of the culture of the people). *T. J. R. Jones, M.A. 1939 Wales*

Welsh Literature: Nineteenth Century
See also Ambrose, W. (Emrys); Ap Rhys, G.; Davies, W. (Gwalter Mechain); Edwards, R.; Evans, J. (I. D. Ffraid); Jones, E. (Ieuan Gwynedd); Jones, John (Glanygors); Jones, John Morris, Sir; Pryse, J. R. (Golyddan); Rees, W. (Gwilym Hiraethog); Stephens, T.; Thomas, D. (Dafydd Ddu of Eryri); Thomas, O.; Williams, J.; Williams, P. B.; Williams, W.

Cyfraniad Methodistiaeth Galfinaidd i lenyddiaeth Gymraeg o 1811 hyd 1864 (The contribution of Calvinistic Methodism to the literature of Wales from 1811 ro 1864). *J. P. Williams, M.A. 1928 Wales*

Cysylltiad y diwygiadau crefyddol o 1730 hyd 1850 â llenyddiaeth y cyfnod (The connection of religious revivals from 1730 to 1850 with the literature of the period). *L. E. Evans, M.A. 1934 Wales*

Welsh Literature: Nineteenth Century contd.
Dylanwad y chwyldro Ffrengig ar lenyddiaeth Cymru (The influence of the French Revolution on the literature of Wales). *J. J. Evans, M.A. 1926 Wales*

Dylanwadau Ffrengig ar lenyddiaeth Gymreig y bedwaredd ganrif ar bymtheg (French influences on nineteenth century Welsh literature). *E. M. Evans, M.A. 1926 Wales*

Lle John Morris Jones yn yr adfywiad llenyddol o 1886 (The place of John Morris Jones in the literary revival from 1886). *G. J. Evans, M.A. 1945 Wales*

Merched llên Cymru o 1850 i 1914 (The women of the literature of Wales from 1850 to 1914). *I. M. Jones, M.A. 1935 Wales*

Political elements in Welsh literature, 1788-1840. *J. J. Williams, M.A. 1923 Liverpool*

Welshpool
The castle and town of Welshpool during the twelfth and thirteenth centuries. *A. G. Jones, M.A. 1911 Wales*

Wenlock
A historical and archaeological account of Wenlock Priory and its dependent churches from the earliest times to 1307. *E. A. Gee, M.A. 1937 Birmingham*

Wentworth, John, Sir
Sir John Wentworth and his times. *K. E. Stokes, Ph.D. 1938 London, King's College*

Werner, Abraham Gottlob
The life and work of A. G. Werner, 1749-1817, and his influence on his contemporaries. *M. M. Mathews, M.Sc. 1935 London, University College*

Wernher, der Gartenäre
See Meier Helmbrecht.

Wesley, Charles
The catholic element in the hymns of Charles Wesley. *A. S. Denyer, B.D. 1943 Leeds*

Charles Wesley and his poetry. *Y. D. Tseng, B.Litt. 1936 Oxford*

Wesley, John
Augustus Montague Toplady, hymn-writer and theologian, with special reference to his controversy with John Wesley. *J. Maycock, Ph.D. 1946 Edinburgh*

The doctrine of assurance in the experience and thought of the eighteenth century, with special reference to John Wesley. *A. S. Yates, Ph.D. 1949 Leeds*

Early Methodism in Bristol, with special reference to J. Wesley's visits to the city, 1739-90, and their impression on the people. *W. A. Goss, M.A. 1932 Bristol*

An examination of the views of John Wesley in relation to the Protestant Reformation. *R. G. Ashman, Ph.D. 1949 Wales*

The Holy Spirit from Arminius to Wesley. *H. Watkin-Jones, D.D. 1929 Cambridge*

The influence of Arminius upon the theology of John Wesley. *A. H. S. Pask, Ph.D. 1940 Edinburgh*

John Wesley and education. *A. H. Body, M.Ed. 1935 Manchester*

John Wesley's religious teaching and his social and economic views. *E. D. Bebb, B.Litt. 1944 Oxford*

Methodism from the death of Wesley, 1791, to the Wesleyan centenary, 1839. *R. F. Wearmouth, M.A. 1928 Birmingham*

The path to perfection, an examination and restatement of John Wesley's doctrine of Christian perfection. *W. E. Sangster, Ph.D. 1942 London, Richmond College*

The political ideas and influence of John Wesley. *M. L. Edwards, M.A. 1927 Wales*

The relation of William Law to John Wesley and the beginnings of Methodism. *E. W. Baker, Ph.D. 1941 Edinburgh*

The soteriology of John Wesley. *P. W. Hoon, Ph.D. 1936 Edinburgh*

Wesleyan Methodism's contribution to national education (1739-1902). *H. Cloke, M.A. 1936 London, King's College*

Wesleyanism
See Methodism.

Wessex
See also Edward, the Elder, King of Wessex; Egberht, King of Wessex.

A comparison of the local administration and law courts of the Carolingian Empire with those of the West Saxon kings. *H. M. Cam, M.A. 1909 London*

Wessex contd.
Contributions to the knowledge of the drainage, morphology and structure of the Wessex region of southern England. *D. L. Linton, M.Sc. 1930 London, King's College*

Edward the Elder and the Danes. *F. T. Wainwright, Ph.D. 1944 Reading*

An historical and political geography of Wessex. *K. I. James, M.A. 1950 Wales*

The life and times of Egberht, King of Wessex, 802 to 839. *A. J. Thorogood, M.A. 1931 Reading*

West Harling, Norfolk
The Gawdys of West Harling, Norfolk: a study of education and social life in the seventeenth century. *C. D. Price, M.A. 1950 Wales*

West Indies
See also Antilles; Barbados; British Guiana; Jamaica; Trinidad and Tobago.

British commercial policy in the West Indies from 1783 to 1793. *H. M. Allen, Ph.D. 1928 London*

British relations with the Spanish colonies in the Caribbean 1713-1739. *L. F. Horsfall, M.A. 1935 London, King's College*

The Caribbean in international politics, 1670-1707. *W. G. Bassett, Ph.D. 1934 London, King's College*

The colonial agents of the British West India Islands from the first appointment to the close of the eighteenth century. *L. M. Penson, Ph.D. 1921 London*

The English and the West Indies under the early Stuarts. *C. A. Taylor, M.A. 1938 National University of Ireland*

The free port system in the British West Indies, 1766-1815. *L. F. Horsfall, Ph.D. 1939 London, King's College*

The government of the British colonies in the West Indies. *H. H. Wrong, B.Litt. 1922 Oxford*

The problem of federation in the British West Indies during the nineteenth century. *L. M. Young, Ph.D. 1947 Cambridge*

The transportation system in the seventeenth century, with special reference to the West Indies. *A. E. Smith, D.Phil. 1933 Oxford*

The West Indies in the American Revolution. *M. J. Hewitt, D.Phil. 1937 Oxford*

Westminster
Watercourses in the parish of St. Margaret's, Westminster, in the seventeenth century: a problem of local administration. *A. C. Wood, B.Litt. 1938 Oxford*

Westminster Conference
See Presbyterianism.

Wey, Francis
Francis Wey: his life and works. *E. M. Prickett, M.A. 1933 London, East London College*

Wey, River
The Wey River Basin: a study of human settlement and economic development in the valley, with particular reference to present day conditions. *G. A. T. F. Hooper, M.A. 1935 London, Birkbeck College*

Wheat Trade
The agriculture of the semi-arid regions of the Middle West of the U.S.A. considered in relation to wheat cultivation. *J. R. Sanctuary, M.A. 1940 London, External Degree*

The developments of the grain trade in the twentieth century, and their influence on the world wheat situation. *G. S. Cartwright, B.Litt. 1932 Oxford*

The economics of the distribution of wheat. *P. T. Barry, M.Econ.Sc. 1936 National University of Ireland*

A geographical study of wheat and the wheat trade in Europe. *A. Booker, B.Litt. 1929 Oxford*

The marketing of the world's wheat crop. *M. H. Alsop, M.Sc. 1938 London, School of Economics and Political Science*

Production and international exchange of wheat, with reference to the economic geography of India, and a further reference to world wheat position. *S. K. Bedekar, M.Sc. 1936 Wales*

Whetstone, George
The non-dramatic works of George Whetstone. *D. M. Mead, M.A. 1919 London*

Whewell, William
The methodology of William Whewell. *E. E. Perrin, M.Sc. 1927 London*

Whigs
See also Liberalism.

The place of Lord Brougham in the history of the Whig Party. *A. Aspinall, Ph.D. 1924 Manchester*

White Earth Reservation
The structure and development of the brush-prairie of the White Earth Indian Reservation. *J. Ewing, D.Sc. 1916 Aberdeen*

White Horse, Hills and Vale of
See Wiltshire.

White, William Hale
The life and thought of William Hale White. *H. A. Smith, Ph.D. 1939 Birmingham*

William Hale White (Mark Rutherford). *A. J. Smith, M.A. 1933 Liverpool*

Whitefield, George
The theology of George Whitefield, 1714-1770. *C. B. Sherriff, Ph.D. 1950 Edinburgh*

Whitehead, Alfred North
Creativity, process and entity in the philosophy of A. N. Whitehead. *M. Haldar, Ph.D. 1949 London, King's College*

An enquiry into the foundations of Whitehead's metaphysic of experience. *I. Leclerc, Ph.D. 1949 London, King's College*

God and creatures in the philosophy of St. Thomas Aquinas and A. N. Whitehead. *W. A. Whitehouse, B.Litt. 1940 Oxford*

The philosophy of Whitehead. *W. Mays, Ph.D. 1945 Cambridge*

The treatment of the idea of the individual in the philosophies of Bernard Bosanquet, J. M. E. McTaggart and A. N. Whitehead. *B. E. Jones, M.A. 1942 Manchester*

Whitgift, John, Archbishop
John Whitgift: his character and work. *E. J. Balley, M.A. 1927 Belfast*

The life and work of John Whitgift, 1532-1604. *P. M. Dawley, Ph.D. 1938 Cambridge*

The rise and decline of Calvinism in England during the archiepiscopate of Whitgift. *B. M. H. Thompson, B.Litt. 1932 Oxford*

Whitman, Walt
The mystical element in Walt Whitman. *J. H. Bodgener, M.A. 1932 Liverpool*

Whitman in France; Whitman and the origin of the *vers libre*: Whitman and Verhaeren; the origins of the *vers libre*. *P. M. Jones, M.A. 1916 Wales*

Whytt, Robert
The life and work of Robert Whytt, M.D., F.R.C.P., F.R.S., Professor of Medicine in the University of Edinburgh. *R. M. Barclay, M.D. 1922 Edinburgh*

Wicksell, Knut
Wicksell's theory of interest and influence. *S. Adler, M.Sc. 1932 London, School of Economics and Political Science*

Widmann, Leonhard
Sprachliche, literarische und kulturelle Untersuchung der *Regensburger Chronik* des Leonhard Widmann. *F. Gossman, M.A. 1940 London, King's College*

Wilbrandt, Adolf
Adolf Wilbrandt as a dramatist. *E. H. Jones, M.A. 1936 Wales*

Wilde, George
An edition of the play *Love's Hospital* (1636), with some account of the author, George Wilde. *K. M. Tancock, M.A. 1933 London, University College*

Wilde, Oscar
The development and significance of Oscar Wilde's theory of art and its influence upon his works. *W. M. Cubbon, M.A. 1948 Manchester*

Wilde, Robert
Robert Wilde: his life and works. *J. M. Stokes, B.Litt. 1930 Oxford*

Wilkes, John
The political ideas of the English Radicals, particularly in Nonconformist circles, from John Lilburne to John Wilkes. *B. H. Lewis, M.A. 1926 Wales*

Wilkins, William
William Wilkins, R. A. *G. Walkley, M.Litt. 1939 Cambridge*

Will
See also Determinism; Free Will.

The bondage of the will in the light of post-Reformation theology. *J. I. Jones, M.A. 1946 Wales*

Will contd.
The doctrine of the freedom of the will according to English empiricism and transcendental idealism. *J. L. Williams, B.Sc. 1904 Oxford*

The effects of volition and affective states upon muscular work. *R. P. R. Westgate, Ph.D. 1934 London, King's College*

An experimental study of the frustration of will-acts and conation. *K. L. Philp, Ph.D. 1933 London, King's College*

Freedom of the will according to Kant and the English Idealists. *J. L. Williams, M.A. 1902 Wales*

A further study of volitional frustration in respect of uncompleted tasks. *T. Walsh, Ph.D. 1942 London, King's College*

1. Genesis i, ii.1-7, iii.17-19; Psalm xix.1-3, xcv.3-7: evolution and providence. 2. St. Mark ix.48; St. John iii.36: eternal justice. 3. Genesis iii.1-10; Romans vii.18,19: will in Christian ethics. *A. J. Nilson, D.D. 1885 Oxford*

The influence of conation upon mental and manual operations. *J. Caughey, Ph.D. 1929 London*

The influence of volition upon the perception (cognition) of visual items, relations and correlates. *E. O. Mercer, Ph.D. 1935 London, King's College*

Influences of volition in mental testing, or influences of conation on cognition. *E. H. Wild, Ph.D. 1926 London*

Intellect and will, and their relation. *T. A. Conroy, M.A. 1911 National University of Ireland*

Modern theories of the will. *R. F. A. Hoernle, B.Sc. 1907 Oxford*

The nature and extent of conative control of some contents of consciousness. *W. J. Messer, M.Sc. 1927 London*

On the measurement of conation: an enquiry into volitional processes. *R. C. McCarthy, Ph.D. 1925 London*

On the memory of completed and uncompleted tasks: a study of volitional frustration. *T. Walsh, M.A. 1940 London, King's College*

The phenomenology of acts of choice: an analysis of volitional consciousness. *H. M. Wells, Ph.D. 1925 London*

Plato's psychology in its bearing on the development of will. *M. H. Wood, M.A. 1905 London*

The problem of the will considered with special reference to the English school of idealists and the relation of their conclusions briefly to the doctrine of grace. *C. R. Batten, M.A. 1927 London*

The relation of feeling and conation, with special reference to the hedonic and hormic theories. *Y. Pan, Ph.D. 1930 London, University College*

The relations between voluntarism and pragmatism as illustrated by the development of French voluntaristic philosophy from Maine de Biran to Professor Bergson: with especial reference to the Bergsonian notion of truth and its development in the 'new philosophy'. *L. S. Stebbing, M.A. 1912 London*

The voluntarism of Duns Scotus. *T. F. McDonagh, M.A. 1923 National University of Ireland*

William, of Nassyngton
William of Nassyngton's *Mirror of Life*, or *Speculum Vitae*: a Middle English poem. *D. I. Price, M.A. 1914 Wales*

William, of Occam
The theories of Cardinal Pierre d'Ailly concerning forms of government in Church and State with special reference to his interest in suggestions made by William of Occam. *A. E. Roberts, M.A. 1931 London, Bedford College*

William of Ockham's attitude to political authority and its relation to the history of his time. *J. B. Morrall, B.Litt. 1949 Oxford*

William, of Waddington
Contribution à l'étude du *Manuel des Péchés*. *E. J. F. Arnould, Ph.D. 1936 London, External Degree*

A new edition of *Handlyng synne* and *Medytacyuns*. *G. H. Naish, Ph.D. 1936 London, External Degree*

William, of Wydford
A critical edition of the *Quattuor determinationes patris Willelmi Wydeforde de ordine fratrum minorum contre Wycliff et Wyclyvianos in materia de religion*. *M. D. Dobson, B.Litt. 1932 Oxford*

Williams, John
Bywydd a gwaith John Williams, Rhos: awdur yr oraclau bywiol (The life and work of John Williams, Rhos, author of the living oracles). *W. Phillips, M.A. 1947 Wales*

Williams, John, Archbishop
The political and ecclesiastical activities of Bishop Williams in relation to the history of his times. *M. E. Hudson, M.A. 1926 London*

Williams, Peter Bailey
Bywyd a gwaith Peter Bailey Williams (The life and work of Peter Bailey Williams). *G. T. Roberts, M.A. 1935 Wales*

Williams, William
The influence of the Methodist revival on Welsh hymnology, with particular reference to the hymns of William Williams of Pantycelyn. *L. Jones, B.Litt. 1922 Oxford*

The language of Williams, Pantycelyn, with special reference to vocabulary and grammatical forms. *C. J. Davies, M.A. 1923 Wales*

A study of the hymnology of the Methodist revival in Wales, with particular reference to the hymns of Williams, Pantycelyn. *L. Jones, M.A. 1921 Wales*

Williamson, Alexander William
The work of Williamson and its relation to the type theory of Wurtz. *J. Harris, M.Sc. 1926 London*

Wills
See Succession.

Wilmot, John, Earl of Rochester
The literary significance of John Wilmot, Earl of Rochester. *H. Judge, M.A. 1934 Birmingham*

Wilson, John
An edition of John Wilson's *The cheats*. *M. C. Nahm, B.Litt. 1929 Oxford*

The life of Christopher North. *E. Swann, Ph.D. 1932 Leeds*

Wilson, John Cook
Cook Wilson's view of the relation between knowing and the activities of thinking which are not knowing. *J. Coutts, B.Litt. 1940 Oxford*

The province of logic and its relation to grammar, metaphysics, and psychology with special reference to the view of Cook Wilson. *R. G. F. Robinson, B.Litt. 1927 Oxford*

The theory of judgment in the philosophies of F. H. Bradley and John Cook Wilson. *M. Ahmed, Ph.D. 1937 London, University College*

Wilson, Robert, the Elder
The life and works of Robert Wilson, the Elder. *F. Nevey, M.A. 1916 London*

Wilson, Robert Thomas, Sir
The career of Sir Robert Wilson (1777-1849) with special reference to his diplomatic and military activities during the years 1806-15. *G. M. D. G. Costigan, B.Litt. 1930 Oxford*

Wilson, Thomas Woodrow, President
The principle of self-determination, with special reference to President Wilson. *T. H. Kuo, B.Litt. 1935 Oxford*

Wiltshire
A comparison between the geographical bases of the rural economic life of the Vale of White Horse and that of the White Horse Hills. *M. E. Webb, B.Litt. 1936 Oxford*

A regional geography of North Wiltshire. *W. Wakefield, M.Sc. 1944 Bristol*

The scarplands of the Wiltshire-Gloucestershire-Somerset borders: a regional study, with particular reference to urban and rural settlement. *I. G. Youldon, M.A. 1945 London, King's College*

Wiltshire: a geographical and social study. *H. E. Bracey, Ph.D. 1948 London, Birkbeck College*

Winchcombe Abbey
The history of Winchcombe Abbey. *G. T. Haigh, M.Litt. 1944 Durham*

Winchcombe, Gloucestershire
A critical study of the sources of the Annals of Winchcombe, Faustina B.i.ff.21-29b, 1182-1232. *E. John, M.A. 1950 Manchester*

Winchelsey, Robert de, Archbishop
Archbishop Winchelsey: a sketch of a critical period in the relations between Church and State. *F. Barton, M.A. 1912 London*

Winchester
City of Winchester, the first book of Ordinances, 1552-1609, transcribed and annotated. *T. Atkinson, M.A. 1940 Bristol*

The importance of Winchester as capital of England from the tenth to the twelfth century. *P. Meadows, M.A. 1911 London*

Windsor
The central and local financial organisation and administrative machinery of the royal free chapel of St. George within the castle of Windsor from its foundation (1348) to the treasurership of William Gillot (1415-16). *A. K. B. Roberts, Ph.D. 1943 London, Royal Holloway College*

Wine Trade
The Gascon wine trade of Southampton during the reigns of Henry VI and Edward IV. *M. K. James, B.Litt. 1948 Oxford*

History of trade relations between Bordeaux and Britain in the eighteenth century, with special reference to the wine and spirit trade. *A. E. Roberts, M.A. 1926 Wales*

Wisbech
The function of Wisbech in relation to its geographical setting. *R. W. L. Melbourne, M.A. 1939 London, Birkbeck College*

Wisdom
The concept of wisdom in Greek and Hebrew literature. *J. P. Dempsey, M.A. 1946 National University of Ireland*

Wisdom Literature
See Bible: Old Testament.

Wise, Thomas, Sir
Sir Thomas Wise and the Central Society of Education. *I. D. Harry, M.A. 1932 Wales*

Wishart, George
Life of George Wishart. *O. H. Walker, Ph.D. 1924 Edinburgh*

Witchcraft
Demonology, magic, and witchcraft in the English drama, 1580-1642. *F. M. N. Trefethen, M.Litt. 1950 Cambridge*

The witch in the English drama. *M. M. C. Pollard, Cert.Litt. 1917 Oxford*

Witchcraft and the Church of Scotland subsequent to the Reformation. *J. Gilmore, Ph.D. 1948 Glasgow*

Witherspoon, John
John Witherspoon: his Scottish ministry. *W. O. Brackett, Ph.D. 1935 Edinburgh*

Wolf, John
John Wolf, printer and publisher, 1579-1601; a bibliographical survey. *H. R. Hoppe, M.A. 1933 London, King's College*

Wollaston, William Hyde
The life and work of W. H. Wollaston. *A. W. Kent, M.Sc. 1931 London*

Wolsey, Thomas, Cardinal
Wolsey's colleges at Oxford and Ipswich. *F. Bate, M.A. 1905 Liverpool*

Wolverhampton
Wolverhampton and the Great Civil War, 1642-1645. *T. J. Larkin, M.A. 1928 Birmingham*

Women
The changing ideal of womanhood in the novel and its relation to the feminist movement, 1837 to 1873. *M. P. Nicolson Thomson, Ph.D. 1947 Cambridge*

The development of the feminist idea in England (1789-1833). *R. J. T. Saywell, M.A. 1936 London, King's College*

Le féminisme de Madame de Staël. *E. M. Standring, M.A. 1941 Manchester*

Representative Victorian women. *M. A. Bald, Ph.D. 1921 Edinburgh*

A study of Chaucer's diction and terms for womanly beauty. *S. Ganguly, Ph.D. 1940 London, University College*

Women: Education
See also Co-education; Girls: Education.
An account of the education of women and girls in England in the time of the Tudors. *D. M. Meads, Ph.D. 1929 London*

Discovering the Bluestockings, a neglected constellation of clever women. *M. L. Robbie, Ph.D. 1947 Edinburgh*

The early history of female education in India. *R. B. Mathur, Ph.D. 1947 London, School of Oriental and African Studies*

The education of English women in the seventeenth century. *P. W. Smith, M.A. 1921 London*

The education of women in Bengal, with special reference to that of the nineteenth and twentieth centuries. *R. Bannerjea, M.Ed. 1938 Leeds*

The education of women in England, 1603-1715. *E. S. Bier, B.Litt. 1928 Oxford*

Women: Education contd.
The education of women in France from 1700 to 1789 as shown in the literature of the period. *R. F. C. Davies, Ph.D. 1934 London, Birkbeck College*

Education of women in the early nineteenth century: some French points of view. *L. Gavan Duffy, M.A. 1916 National University of Ireland*

The education of women under the Roman Empire. *E. Symes, M.A. 1909 London*

Female education in Bengal. *V. I. Alphonso, M.A. 1931 London, King's College*

The higher education and employment of women in the twentieth century. *E. Y. Angus, M.A. 1931 London, School of Economics and Political Science*

History of women's higher education during the nineteenth century. *H. Donovan, M.A. 1919 National University of Ireland*

The progress and development of the education of women in India. *M. I. Tahur, M.Ed. 1928 Leeds*

Report of a tour to the west coast of Africa to study the education of women, 1928-29. Some notes on the Bachama tribe, Nigeria, 1928. *E. S. Fegan, Dip. Anthropology 1929 Cambridge*

Some aspects of feminine education in England during the seventeenth century. *F. Cameron, M.A. 1949 Liverpool*

Women's education in India. *I. Khan, M.A. 1947 London, Institute of Education*

Women: Psychology
Emotional fluctuations in women. *M. Kerr, Ph.D. 1938 London, Bedford College*

Some theories of feminine attitudes and so-called character traits: a study in ideologies. *V. Klein, Ph.D. 1944 London, School of Economics and Political Science*

Women Authors
See Women in Literature.

Women in Industry
A consideration of the theory of womens' wages, and an attempt to test the truth of certain reasons which have been adduced by economic writers for the relatively lower wage-level of women in industry as compared with that of men. *P. B. Wylde-Brown, M.A. 1930 Birmingham*

Domestic workers in hospitals: a field of women's employment. *M. S. Eaton, Ph.D. 1948 London, School of Economics and Political Science*

The higher education and employment of women in the twentieth century. *E. Y. Angus, M.A. 1931 London, School of Economics and Political Science*

Woman and child industrial labour in the Bombay Presidency. *Z. A. Ahmad, Ph.D. 1935 London, School of Economics and Political Science*

Women at work. *J. O'Leary, M.A. 1945 National University of Ireland*

Women in the textile industries and trade of fifteenth century England. *M. K. Dale, M.A. 1928 London*

Women workers and the Industrial Revolution, 1750-1850. *I. Pinchbeck, Ph.D. 1930 London, School of Economics and Political Science*

The work of women in agriculture in the late eighteenth and early nineteenth centuries, and the influence of the agrarian revolution thereon. *I. Pinchbeck, M.A. 1927 London*

Women in Literature
The changing ideal of womanhood in the novel and its relation to the feminist movement, 1837 to 1873. *M. P. Nicolson Thomson, Ph.D. 1947 Cambridge*

The characterization of women in the English novel from Richardson to the Brontës. *E. Evans, M.A. 1931 Wales*

The characterization of women in Plautus and Terence and the fragments of Menander. *M. Watts, M.A. 1919 London*

An examination of the methods of Dickens and Thackeray in the characterization of women. *E. C. McGahan, M.A. 1946 Wales*

Female characterization in Jacobean tragedy, with special consideration of the tragedies of Heywood, Webster, Middleton, Beaumont and Fletcher. *A. E. Bufton, M.A. 1939 Wales*

The female characters in Grillparzer's drama, as contrasted with those in Goethe's and Schiller's. *A. V. Burgess, M.A. 1907 Wales*

Feminist writers of the seventeenth century, with special reference to François Poulain de la Barre. *S. A. Richards, M.A. 1912 London*

Women in Literature contd.
The greater women novelists of the Victorian age. *E. M. Dolan, M.A. 1945 National University of Ireland*

The heritage of Cordelia; the early influences which have moulded the later poets' conception of woman. *M. A. Murphy, M.A. 1932 National University of Ireland*

Irish women writers 1800-35. *S. J. C. Harrison, Ph.D. 1947 Dublin, Trinity College*

Les femmes selon Dumas: une étude. *M. T. Gibson, M.A. 1915 Birmingham*

Merched llên Cymru o 1850 i 1914 (The women of the literature of Wales from 1850 to 1914). *I. M. Jones, M.A. 1935 Wales*

The position of woman in the seventeenth century and her influence on the literature. *M. M. Burrows, M.A. 1912 Birmingham*

The position of women as reflected in medieval German didactic literature. *E. D. Barber, M.A. 1940 Manchester*

Richardson's influence on the women novelists of the eighteenth century. *U. Todd-Naylor, Ph.D. 1935 London, University College*

Some pioneer women novelists and their contribution to the eighteenth century novel, 1688-1740. *F. Smith, Ph.D. 1926 London*

Woman in the early romantic school of German literature. *M. G. Maddison, M.A. 1910 Birmingham*

The women characters of W. S. Landor. *D. G. Cope, M.A. 1917 Birmingham*

Women in ancient comedy. *A. Page, M.A. 1947 Manchester*

Women in Elizabethan and Jacobean tragedy: a study of the principal conventions and influences governing the treatment of women characters in English tragedy. *J. M. Morrell, M.A. 1931 London, Royal Holloway College*

The women in Shakespeare's plays: a critical study from the dramatic and psychological points of view, and in relation to the development of Shakespeare's art. *A. M. Mackenzie, D.Litt. 1924 Aberdeen*

Women novelists before Jane Austen. *B. E. Hughes, M.A. 1915 Wales*

The women of George Meredith. *E. Conroy, M.A. 1912 Wales*

The women of Sophocles. *K. N. Toy, M.A. 1911 Birmingham*

The women of Sophocles and Aeschylus. *A. Hill, M.A. 1910 London*

Women writers in Germany in the beginning of the nineteenth century, with special reference to Annette von Droste-Hülshoff. *E. Matthews, M.A. 1925 Wales*

Women's share in the development of the English novel, 1621-1818. *B. G. MacCarthy, Ph.D. 1939 National University of Ireland*

Women, Status of
Changes in the status of women during the nineteenth century as reflected in Bengali literature. *J. Sen, Ph.D. 1924 London*

A comparative study of the economic position of women in Great Britain and Poland in the inter-war period. *I. Florecka, Ph.D. 1945 Edinburgh*

Evolution of the proprietary status of woman under the common law of the Hindus with special reference to the quantum of interest in immovable property acquired by way of inheritance and partition. *B. M. Patnaik, LL.M. 1948 London, School of Economics and Political Science*

In multis iuris nostri articulis deterior est condicio feminarum quam masculorum - Dig. i.5.9. *P. F. Aldred, D.C.L. 1881 Oxford*

The life and social conditions of women in the primitive Islamic community as depicted in the eighth volume of Ibn Sa'd's *Tabaqat al Kubra* and the sixth volume of Ibn Hanbal's *Musnad. G. H. Stern, Ph.D. 1937 London, School of Oriental and African Studies*

The position of woman in the seventeenth century and her influence on the literature. *M. M. Burrows, M.A. 1912 Birmingham*

The position of women among the Romans. *A. M. Holmes, M.A. 1932 London, University College*

The position of women as reflected in medieval German didactic literature. *E. D. Barber, M.A. 1940 Manchester*

Women, Status of contd.
The position of women in ancient Egypt. *M. S. Palmer, M.A. 1929 Manchester*

The position of women in ancient India according to the *Dharmásaestras. S. N. Ajgaonkar, B.Litt. 1925 Oxford*

The position of women in Australian aboriginal society. *P. M. Kaberry, Ph.D. 1938 London, School of Economics and Political Science*

The position of women in contemporary France. *F. I. Clark, M.Sc. 1935 London, School of Economics and Political Science*

The position of women in early India, as it appears in the Vedic literature and the sacred law. *S. Rao, B.Litt. 1936 Oxford*

The position of women in Icelandic life and social economy as shown in the Icelandic sagas. *R. G. Thomas, M.A. 1939 Wales*

The position of women in Norway in Viking times. *E. S. Eames, M.Litt. 1950 Cambridge*

The position of women in the Vedic ritual. *J. Chaudhuri, Ph.D. 1934 London, School of Oriental and African Studies*

The rights and duties of Englishwomen: an investigation of present day law and opinion. *E. Reiss, Ph.D. 1924 Manchester*

The social and legal position of women in ancient India as represented by a critical study of the epics: the *Mahabharata* and the *Ramayana. S. N. Ajgaonkar, D.Phil. 1927 Oxford*

The status of woman in Islam. *L. B. Jones, M.A. 1941 Wales*

The status of women among the southern Bantu. *P. J. Bradney, B.Sc. 1950 Oxford*

Vicissitudes of the Greek - chiefly of the Athenian - woman. *L. T. Davies, M.A. 1906 London*

Woman's rights and feminism in the contemporary French theatre. *C. R. Bagley, B.Litt. 1922 Oxford*

Wonders of the East
The Wonders of the East; the Anglo-Saxon prose translation from Cotton ms. Vitellius A.XV, collated with the text of Cotton ms. Tiberius B.V., Vol.1. *B. L. Garrad, Ph.D. 1925 London*

Wood, Charles, Sir
The origin and development in Bengal of the principles involved in Sir Charles Wood's despatch on education of 19th July, 1854. *D. P. Sinha, M.A. 1939 London, School of Oriental and African Studies*

Wood, Richard, Sir
Tunis from 1855 to 1879: primarily based on the dispatches of Consul-General Richard Wood. *M. M. Safwat, M.A. 1937 Liverpool*

Wood, Robert
The life and work of 'Palmyra' Wood: a biographical study. *J. Moncur, Ph.D. 1929 Saint Andrew's*

Woodard, Nathaniel
The life and work of Nathaniel Woodard, with special reference to the influence of the Oxford movement on English education in the nineteenth century. *R. Perry, M.A. 1932 Bristol*

Woodlands
See Forestry.

Woodwork
The nomenclature of chips and shavings in France: a study in linguistic geography. *M. R. Roberts, M.A. 1933 Manchester*

'Technique' and 'content' in woodwork courses. *H. Lamb, M.Ed. 1941 Leeds*

Woollen Industry
See also Staple.

The rise and decline of the serge industry in the southwest of England, with special reference to the eighteenth century. *W. G. Hoskins, M.Sc. 1929 London*

The theory of futures trading with special reference to the marketing of wool. *G. J. Blau, Ph.D. 1942 London, School of Economics and Political Science*

World consumption of clothing wools. *F. J. C. Cronjé, Ph.D. 1939 Cambridge*

Woollen Industry: Great Britain
The characteristics of wool production and woollen manufacture in Wales in relation to the geographical features of the principality. *A. M. Jones, M.Sc. 1925 Wales*

A comparative study of the economics of the woollen industry of Scotland and the Panjab. *J. M. Sirajuddin, Ph.D. 1927 Edinburgh*

Woollen Industry: Great Britain contd.
The development of the West of England woollen industry from 1550 to 1640. *K. E. Barford, M.A. 1923 London*

Edward III's war finance, 1337-41: transactions in wool and credit operations. *E. B. Fryde, D.Phil. 1947 Oxford*

The employment of juveniles and young persons (14-18) in the West Riding wool textile industry, with some reference to the effect of the raising of the school-leaving age and release for part-time further education. *J. W. Scarf, B.Phil. 1947 Oxford*

The English wool trade during the thirteenth century. *F. Miller, B.Litt. 1921 Oxford*

A general sketch of the history of the Italian merchants in England, 1272-1399, especially in connection with the wool trade. *A. Neild, M.A. 1914 London*

The Gloucestershire woollen industry in the eighteenth and nineteenth centuries. *R. Perry, Ph.D. 1946 London, External Degree*

The historical geography of the Norfolk and Suffolk woollen industry. *J. S. Bishop, M.A. 1929 London*

A historical geography of the Cotswold woollen industry in the nineteenth and early twentieth centuries. *I. Ellis, M.A. 1946 Wales*

A history of Clare, Suffolk, with special reference to its development as a borough during the Middle Ages, and to its importance as a centre of the woollen industry in the fifteenth to seventeenth centuries. *G. A. Thornton, Ph.D. 1927 London*

A history of the Shrewsbury Drapers' Company during the seventeenth century, with particular reference to the Welsh woollen trade. *D. J. Evans, M.A. 1950 Wales*

The history of the trade unions in the Yorkshire woollen and worsted industries during the nineteenth and twentieth centuries. *J. F. Weatherhead, B.Litt. 1925 Oxford*

The history of the Yorkshire woollen and worsted industries from the earliest times up to the Industrial Revolution. *H. Heaton, M.Com. 1914 Birmingham*

1. The monastic wool trade of the thirteenth century. 2. The Italian bankers and the English Crown. *R. J. Whitwell, B.Litt. 1903 Oxford*

The pastoral custom and local wool trade of medieval Sussex, 1085-1485. *A. M. M. Melville, M.A. 1931 London, King's College*

Post-war raw material price variations in the woollen and worsted industries. *F. H. Eastwood, M.Comm. 1935 Leeds*

The relation between technical and economic factors in the development of the wool textile industry. *G. W. Glover, M.A. 1936 Leeds*

Shrewsbury, Oswestry, and the Welsh wool trade in the seventeenth century, especially in connexion with the crisis and Parliament of 1621. *T. C. Mendenhall, B.Litt. 1936 Oxford*

The Welsh woollen industry: recent history and present position. *G. Evans, M.A. 1948 Wales*

The West of England woollen industry, 1750-1840. *J. H. Morris, M.Sc. 1934 London, School of Economics and Political Science*

The Wiltshire woollen industry, chiefly in the sixteenth and early seventeenth centuries. *G. D. Ramsay, D.Phil. 1939 Oxford*

Woollen trade and industry in the rural areas of Gloucestershire. *F. C. Raggatt, M.A. 1933 Bristol*

Woollen Industry: Other Countries
A comparative study of the economics of the woollen industry of Scotland and the Panjab. *J. M. Sirajuddin, Ph.D. 1927 Edinburgh*

The Low Country cloth towns at the end of the thirteenth century. *O. D. Rudkin, M.A. 1916 Liverpool*

The woollen industry of Ireland. *J. G. Muldowney, M.A. 1928 National University of Ireland*

Worcester, John Tiptoft, Earl of
John Tiptoft, Earl of Worcester. *R. J. Mitchell, B.Litt. 1929 Oxford*

Worcestershire
A study of the changes in the distribution and density of population in Worcestershire during the period 1841-1931, and of the geographical factors involved. *E. R. G. Wood, M.A. 1950 Birmingham*

Wordsworth, Dorothy
Dorothy Wordsworth: her mind and art. *F. Thompson, M.A. 1926 Birmingham*

Wordsworth, William
The affinity between the aesthetic and social philosophy of Ruskin and the teaching of Wordsworth. *M. E. Needham, M.A. 1931 Birmingham*

The attitude of Wordsworth and Byron towards Napoleon. *R. Griffith, M.A. 1949 Wales*

The development of the political ideas of Wordsworth and Shelley, with special reference to their conception of freedom. *G. O. Roberts, M.A. 1938 Wales*

The educational ideas of Wordsworth. *H. E. Winn, M.A. 1925 London*

An examination of Wordsworth's poetry, particularly his lesser known and later poetry, considered as experimental work, whether in technique or content. *B. G. Brooks, Ph.D. 1937 London, External Degree*

The influence on educational thought of (1) Ruskin (2) Wordsworth. *W. O. Delaney, M.A. 1924 Liverpool*

The literary relations of Wordsworth and M. Arnold. *M. E. Green, M.A. 1927 Birmingham*

The mutual influence of William Wordsworth and Samuel Taylor Coleridge. *J. Bradshaw, M.A. 1914 Liverpool*

Mysticism in the poetry of Wordsworth, Shelley and Tagore. *B. Sengupta, B.Litt. 1947 Dublin, Trinity College*

Mysticism in Wordsworth. *J. Adams, M.A. 1927 Wales*

Pantheism in English poetry, with special reference to Wordsworth and Shelley. *J. I. Wensley, M.A. 1917 Wales*

A psychological study of the poetical imagination of Wordsworth and Shelley. *E. M. E. Haydon, M.A. 1914 London*

Stoicism and Wordsworth. *I. Watson, M.A. 1911 Birmingham*

A study of the chief elements of mystical thought in English writers up to the time of Blake and Wordsworth. *M. Richards, M.A. 1921 Birmingham*

A textual and critical study of Wordsworth's *An evening walk* and *Descriptive sketches. P. B. Bartlett, B.Litt. 1928 Oxford*

Wordsworth and education. *P. Sandbach, M.A. 1926 Liverpool*

Wordsworth and his influence upon English poetry. *C. H. Hipkins, M.A. 1916 Birmingham*

Wordsworth, Coleridge, Byron, Shelley and the French Revolution. *P. R. Griffin, M.A. 1925 National University of Ireland*

Wordsworth's political development. *F. M. Todd, Ph.D. 1948 London, University College*

Work
Correlation between increase in amplitude and decrement in work curves. *D. F. Ward, M.Sc. 1939 London, University College*

Incentives to work and their relation to health and efficiency with particular reference to workers in the building industry. *N. M. Davis, Ph.D. 1948 London, School of Hygiene and Tropical Medicine*

Individual differences in fluctuation in output of mental work. *A. Z. Saleh, Ph.D. 1948 London, University College*

The movements for shorter hours, 1840-75. *J. S. Hodgson, D.Phil. 1940 Oxford*

1. The place of education in the life of the ancient Hebrews. 2. St. Paul's ideal of labour. *F. T. Ingle, B.D. 1923 Oxford*

The relationship between intelligence and speed of working. *C. G. Adams, M.A. 1925 Bristol*

Some aspects of mental work. *W. H. Entwistle, Ph.D. 1932 London, Day Training College*

Work and wealth in Southampton: an essay in civic economy. *P. Ford, Ph.D. 1933 London, External Degree*

Workhouses
See Poor Law.

Working Class
See Labour.

World War I, 1914-1918
A comparison of the war taxation of Great Britain and the United States of America from 1914. *D. M. Sandral, B.Litt. 1922 Oxford*

Economic effects of the Great War 1914-18 on Ireland. *F. McDermott, M.A. 1940 National University of Ireland*

The economics of reparations. *E. M. Sage, M.A. 1930 Wales*

Yoruba, The contd.
The religion of the Yorubas, especially in relation to the religion of ancient Egypt. *J. O. Lucas, D.D. 1942 Durham*

The sociology of the Yoruba. *N. A. Fadipe, Ph.D. 1940 London, School of Economics and Political Science*

Yoruba paganism, or the religious beliefs of the West African negroes, particularly of the Yoruba tribes of southern Nigeria. *S. S. Farrow, Ph.D. 1924 Edinburgh*

Young, Edward
Edward Young: a study of his life and works. *W. A. Jones, M.A. 1949 Wales*

Young Irelanders
  See Ireland: History.

Young, Thomas
The acoustical and optical work of Thomas Young in relation to his contemporaries. *J. F. Robertson, M.Sc. 1938 London, University College*

Youth Organizations
The background of youth work in a rural area. *K. Mann, M.A. 1945 London, King's College*

The educational value of self-government in a youth club. *V. S. Pate, M.A. 1948 Birmingham*

The influence of the Youth Movement on German education. *G. Thomson, Ph.D. 1935 Glasgow*

The influence of the Youth Movement on German literature. *L. S. Booth, M.A. 1930 Leeds*

Youth activities in west Wiltshire: a survey of youth organizations existing in this area, together with an investigation into some of the problems arising therefrom. *R. J. Butchers, M.A. 1944 London, Institute of Education*

A youth movement for this country. *A. J. Drewett, M.A. 1943 Sheffield*

Ypres
Introduction à l'étude de la ville d'Ypres. *F. Justice, M.A. 1940 National University of Ireland*

Yucatán
British activities in Yucatan and on the Moskito shore in the eighteenth century. *J. McLeish, M.A. 1926 London*

Yugoslavia
The geographical background of political problems associated with the Italo-Jugoslav frontier. *A. E. F. Moodie, Ph.D. 1942 London, Birkbeck College*

Yvain
  See Romances.

Zanzibar
History of British relations with Zanzibar, 1800-1886. *O. T. Lewis, M.A. 1936 Wales*

Zeromski, Stefan
Stefan Zeromski, 1864-1925; his life and work. *I. E. Favell, M.A. 1949 Birmingham*

Zola, Emile
Dutch criticism of Zola between 1876-1902. *E. L. Janssen, M.A. 1921 London*

Emile Zola: a critical account of his ideas. *W. Fear, Ph.D. 1949 Leeds*

Emile Zola as a precursor of Jules Romains and l'unanimisme. *C. Z. Ruston, B.Litt. 1944 Oxford*

The influence of Emile Zola on English literature. *D. G. Lewis, M.A. 1943 Wales*

Les soirées de Médan as a manifesto of naturalism. *J. J. Starck, Ph.D. 1948 London, King's College*

The popular element in the vocabulary and syntax of *L'Assommoir* of E. Zola, 1877. *H. Bottomley, M.A. 1931 Manchester*

The socialistic tendencies of Emile Zola as expressed in his literary works. *F. S. McCutcheon, M.A. 1929 Wales*

Zoroastrianism
The Pahlavi *Rivayat* preceding the *Dadistan i Denij*, transcription and translation of the hitherto untranslated portions, with philological notes. *H. P. Mirza, Ph.D. 1940 London, School of Oriental and African Studies*

Zorrilla, Francisco de Rojas
  See Rojas Zorrilla, F. de.

Zuckmayer, Carl
Individualism in the *Deutsche Dramen* of Carl Zuckmayer. *M. Graham, M.A. 1950 Belfast*

Zulu, The
  See Bantu, The.

Author Index

Aaron, R. I.
The history and value of the distinction between intellect and intuition. *D.Phil. 1926 Oxford*

Aaron, R. I.
The relations of history and science. *M.A. 1923 Wales*

Abbayambal, U.
State policy and economic development in Mysore State since 1881. *Ph.D. 1931 London, School of Economics and Political Science*

Abbott, C. B.
Christopher Smart. *B.Litt. 1927 Oxford*

Abbott, C. C.
The life and work of George Darley. *Ph.D. 1926 Cambridge*

Abbott, I. D. A.
The English yeomanry in the seventeenth century. *B.Litt. 1928 Oxford*

Abbott, K.
The influence of the German hexameter on the English in the eighteenth and nineteenth centuries. *M.A. 1931 London, King's College*

Abbott, R.
The contribution of J. B. J. D. Boussingault (1802-1887) to the knowledge of plant nutrition. *M.Sc. 1939 London, University College*

Abbott, R.
A geographical study of California. *M.A. 1949 London, External Degree*

Abbott, W. C.
The Pensionary or Long Parliament of Charles II. *B.Litt. 1897 Oxford*

Abdel-Hamid, A. N.   *see* Hamid, A. N. A.

Abdel-Hamid, M. S.
A study of Warburton's *The Crescent and the Cross* in relation to the literary interest in the Near East shown by English romantic writers in the eighteenth and the earlier nineteenth centuries. *M.A. 1948 Bristol*

Abdel-Kader, A. H.
Al-Junayd: a study of a third/ninth century mystic with an edition and annotated translation of his writings. *Ph.D. 1948 London, School of Oriental and African Studies*

Abelson, A.
A comparative study of the mental ability of normal and subnormal children. *D.Sc. 1920 London*

Abelson, J.
The immanence of God in Rabbinical literature. *M.A. 1909 London*

Abelson, J.
Maimonides on the Jewish creed. *M.A. 1909 London*

Aberbach, M.
Palestine under Roman administration 6-66 A.D. *M.A. 1947 Leeds*

Abercrombie, N. J.
The life and work of Pierre Nicole. *D.Phil. 1933 Oxford*

Aberdein, J. W.
The life and work of John Galt. *Ph.D. 1934 Aberdeen*

Abernethy, D. A. N.
Charles Lever: Irish novelist. *B.Litt. 1937 Dublin, Trinity College*

Abraham, J. E.
Some ethical implications of the new psychology. *M.A. 1926 Belfast*

Abraham, J. H.
The idea of substance in Locke's philosophy. *M.A. 1930 London, University College*

Abraham, P. S.
Principles of reconstruction of a curriculum suited to the village conditions in India, with special reference to Travancore. *M.Ed. 1944 Leeds*

Abrahams, E. B.
Greek dress. *M.A. 1907 London*

Abram, A.
The effects produced by economic changes upon social life in England in the fifteenth century. *D.Sc. 1909 London*

Abrams, M. A.
The gold and silver thread monopolies granted by James I, 1611-1621. *Ph.D. 1930 London, School of Economics and Political Science*

Abrioux, O.
A study in French of Georges Duhamel. *Ph.D. 1949 Aberdeen*

Abson, P.
Anglo-Norman didactic literature of the thirteenth century, and An Anglo-Norman life of St. Edward the Confessor. *Ph.D. 1921 Sheffield*

Abulleef, H. K. S.
The financial question and the reorganization of the Egyptian administration, 1865-1885. *M.A. 1948 Bristol*

Acheson, E. C.
Monetary and financial experiments in the U. S. A., 1933-35. *Ph.D. 1939 London, School of Economics and Political Science*

Ackermann, R.
The origins of Byronism in English literature. *M.A. 1924 Birmingham*

Ackerson, L.
The development and application of statistical methods in the prediction of ability. *B.Sc. 1925 Oxford*

Ackroyd, D. E.
The economic policy of trade unions in Great Britain in the post-war period, as illustrated by the proceedings of the Trade Union Congress. *B.Litt. 1936 Oxford*

Ackroyd, P. R.
The problem of Maccabean psalms, with special reference to the psalms of Solomon. *Ph.D. 1945 Cambridge*

Acon, H. B.
Modern idealistic logic and the problem of relations. *D.Phil. 1935 Oxford*

Acum, T. E. A.
A study of the place-names of the pre-Conquest Kentish charters. *M.A. 1923 London*

Acworth, A. W.
Financial reconstruction in England, 1815-1822. *B.Litt. 1925 Oxford*

Adair, P. M.
The debt of the eighteenth century novel to the drama. *M.A. 1942 Belfast*

Adam, J. I.
Gustave Flaubert as a literary critic. *M.A. 1927 Manchester*

Adamiyat, F.
The diplomatic relations of Persia with Britain, Russia and Turkey, 1815-1830. *Ph.D. 1949 London, School of Economics and Political Science*

Adams, A. E.
A study of conditions related to the delinquency of a group of boys in an approved school. *M.A. 1944 London, Institute of Education*

Adams, A. W.
The Latin text of the Johannine epistles, with special reference to the Spanish family. *B.D. 1950 Oxford*

Adams, C. E.
Contributions to the study of the vocabulary of sport in contemporary German. *M.A. 1935 Liverpool*

Adams, C. F.
The influence of Mohammedanism on Western civilization. *M.A. 1910 London*

Adams, C. G.
The relationship between intelligence and speed of working. *M.A. 1925 Bristol*

Adams, E. M.
The history of Sardinia under the Roman Republic. *M.A. 1917 London*

Adams, G.   .
The Carthaginians as depicted in Livy, Polybius, and other ancient writers. *M.A. 1922 London*

Adams, H.
A survey of local government in Hertfordshire, 1700 to 1832. *Ph.D. 1931 London, External Degree*

Adams, I. D.
Coleridge's contributions to periodical literature. *M.A. 1935 London, Bedford College*

Adams, J.
Mysticism in Wordsworth. *M.A. 1927 Wales*

Adams, M.
The British attitude to German colonial development, 1880-1885. *M.A. 1935 London, Bedford College*

Adams, M. D. J.
Cicero's study of Greek literature, with special reference to Cicero as a translator. *M.A. 1932 Wales*

Adams, R.
'Divine personality', studied in the light of recent tendencies in philosophy and theology. *Ph.D. 1946 Dublin, Trinity College*

Adams, R. H.
An investigation into backwardness in arithmetic in the junior school. *M.A. 1940 London, Institute of Education*

Adams, T. H.
Contemporary English opinion of Goethe as a dramatic poet. *M.A. 1908 Birmingham*

Adams, W. S.
The organization of retail trade in the borough of Llanelly, with special reference to the retailing of foodstuffs. *M.A. 1940 Wales*

Adcock, C. J.
A factorial analysis of temperament factors. *Ph.D. 1947 London, Birkbeck College*

Addison, M.
The Lough Neagh shore area: its physical evolution and human utilization. *M.Sc. 1945 Belfast*

Addison, W.
The life and writings of Thomas Boston of Ettrick. *Ph.D. 1936 Edinburgh*

Addison, W. G. C.
The Renewed Church of the United Brethren, 1722 to 1930. *Ph.D. 1931 London, External Degree*

Addleshaw, G. W. O.
The contribution of Pope Benedict XIV to Church government, with special reference to the episcopate. *B.D. 1935 Oxford*

Addleshaw, S.
1. The doctrine of the Holy Trinity in the New Testament. 2. The authorship of the second Epistle of St. Peter. *B.D. 1909 Oxford*

Addy, A. H.
La langue de Paul Arène (1843-1896). *M.A. 1936 Leeds*

Aden, J.
1. The communion of saints. 2. The resurrection of the dead. *B.D. & D.D. 1876 Oxford*

Adige, V. R.
A history of self-government in India from ancient times to 1914. *B.Litt. 1924 Oxford*

Adikaram, K. K. D. E. W. B.
State of Buddhism in Ceylon as revealed by the Pali commentaries of the fifth century, A.D. *Ph.D. 1933 London, School of Oriental and African Studies*

Adinarayansih, S. P.
The psychology of colour prejudice. *M.A. 1939 London, University College*

Adiseshiah, M. S.
Seasonal variations in the demand for money. *Ph.D. 1938 London, School of Economics and Political Science*

Adler, S.
Wicksell's theory of interest and influence. *M.Sc. 1932 London, School of Economics and Political Science*

Adrian, A. W. H.
1. On the kingdom of God as depicted in the New Testament. 2. On miracles. *B.D. 1892 Oxford*

Adshead, F.
The direction and control of foreign trade by the State under the Stuarts, 1603-1688. *M.A. 1908 London*

Afifii, A. E.
The mystical philosophy of Muhyid-Dín Ibnul-'Arabí. *Ph.D. 1930 Cambridge*

Agard, W. R.
The metopes of the treasury of the Athenians at Delphi. *B.Litt. 1923 Oxford*

Agarwala, B. S.
Subsidization of inland transport: its extent and consequences. *Ph.D. 1933 London, School of Economics and Political Science*

Agnew, I. M.
A comparative study of the figures of speech in early Provençal and Italian lyrical poetry, down to and including Dante's *Vita nuova* and *Rime. Ph.D. 1926 Edinburgh*

Agnew, R. A.
Molinos and the implications of the spirit of quietism. *Ph.D. 1935 Edinburgh*

Agrawala, J.
Principles and practice of health insurance as applied to India. *Ph.D. 1948 Wales*

Aguilar de Leon, J. L.
The responsibility of states and the Calvo and Drago doctrines. *D.Phil. 1947 Oxford*

Ahearne, A. M.
Victor Hugo et le mélodrame. *M.A. 1942 National University of Ireland*

Ahern, H.
El romanticismo en España. *M.A. 1929 National University of Ireland*

Ahmad, E.
Settlements in the United Provinces of Agra and Oudh. *Ph.D. 1949 London, School of Economics and Political Science*

Ahmad, G.
An investigation into the problems of forgetting of different kinds of material by school children. *M.Ed. 1937 Leeds*

Ahmad, K. S.
The agricultural geography of the Punjab. *Ph.D. 1939 London, University College*

Ahmad, M. B.
An outline of the system of the administration of justice under the Muslims in India, based mainly upon cases decided by Muslim courts between 1206 and 1750. *M.Litt. 1939 Cambridge*

Ahmad, M. G. I.
Contribution of India to Arabic literature. *Ph.D. 1929 London*

Ahmad, Q.
The Taluqdari law of Oudh, with special reference to the alienation of property *inter vivos*, and its devolution on death testate and intestate. *LL.D. 1928 London*

Ahmad, R.
Mental and moral culture in India in the Middle Ages. *Ph.D. 1932 London, King's College*

Ahmad, R.
Persian poets in India and their works. *M.A. 1926 London*

Ahmad, S. M.
Geographical materials in the writings of al-Mas'udi. *B.Litt. 1947 Oxford*

Ahmad, S. S. B.
A critical estimate of Insha Allah Khan Insha as poet and grammarian. *Ph.D. 1949 London, School of Oriental and African Studies*

Ahmad Shah, E.
The problem of evil with special reference to Hindu philosophy. *B.Litt. 1922 Oxford*

Ahmad, Z. A.
Woman and child industrial labour in the Bombay Presidency. *Ph.D. 1935 London, School of Economics and Political Science*

Ahmed, A. M.
Cotton production, with special reference to Egypt. *M.Sc. 1946 London, External Degree*

Ahmed, M.
The theory of judgment in the philosophies of F. H. Bradley and John Cook Wilson. *Ph.D. 1937 London, University College*

Ahmed, M. K.
Moral reasoning of the child and its relation to mental age. *M.A. 1936 London, University College*

Ahmed, N. L.
The reign of the Emperor Shah Jehan. *B.Litt. 1927 Oxford*

Ahmed, S. B.
A study of children's vocational interests and their relation to school interests. *M.Ed. 1949 Leeds*

Ahmedali, S. A.
Ibn as-Sikkit's *Islāh al-Mantiq* according to the recensions of Al-Qālī and At-Tibrīzī. *D.Phil. 1936 Oxford*

Aiken, W. A.
The administration of Daniel Finch, second Earl of Nottingham, as Secretary of State under Queen Anne, 1702-4. *M.Litt. 1933 Cambridge*

Aikin-Sneath, B.
Comedy and the theory of comedy in Germany from 1700-1750, with special reference to foreign influences. *Ph.D. 1935 London, University College*

Aikman, C. C.
The British Commonwealth and the United Nations. *Ph.D. 1948 London, School of Economics and Political Science*

Ailes, E. H.
Substance and procedure in the conflict of laws. *D.Phil. 1929 Oxford*

Ainslie, J. L.
The doctrine of orders in the Reformed Churches in the sixteenth and seventeenth centuries. *Ph.D. 1935 Edinburgh*

Airey, J. C.
Proceedings in Parliament with regard to the government of India, 1763-1773. *M.A. 1911 Liverpool*

Airston, W.
Goethe and Hauptmann: comparative study. *M.A. 1914 Birmingham*

Aitken, D. F.
A study of the English romance of *Sir Tristrem* in relation to its source. *B.Litt. 1927 Oxford*

Aitken, J. M.
Rhetoric in Euripides and Menander. *B.Litt. 1936 Oxford*

Aitken, J. M.
The trial of George Buchanan before the Lisbon Inquisition. *Ph.D. 1938 Edinburgh*

Aitken, M. Y. H.
Etude sur *le Miroir, ou les Evangiles des données* de Robert de Gretham. *Ph.D. 1921 Saint Andrew's*

Aiyangar, K. R. Ramaswami *see* Ramaswami Aiyangar, K. F.

Aiyappan, A.
Culture change in south-western India. *Ph.D. 1937 London, School of Economics and Political Science*

Aiyar, A. S. S.
Literary groups of the first half of the eighteenth century. *Ph.D. 1935 London, King's College*

Ajgaonkar, S. N.
The position of women in ancient India according to the *Dharmásaestras. B.Litt. 1925 Oxford*

Ajgaonkar, S. N.
The social and legal position of women in ancient India as represented by a critical study of the epics: the *Mahabharata* and the *Ramayana. D.Phil. 1927 Oxford*

Ajgaonkar, V. A.
The problem of the higher education of girls in the Bombay Presidency. *M.Ed. 1940 Leeds*

Akhtar, S. M.
The growth and development of the Indian tea industry and trade. *Ph.D. 1932 London, School of Economics and Political Science*

Akhunji, A. R.
A critical enquiry into the training of defective children in England. *M.Ed. 1932 Leeds*

Akil, F. H.
Curves of output produced by one individual. *Ph.D. 1949 London, University College*

Alagiyawanna, K. L. V.
A comparative study of some forms of adult education in England, the United States, Denmark and Sweden, with special reference to rural areas, together with a scheme of adult education in Ceylon. *M.A. 1948 London, Institute of Education*

Alan, M. E.
Ronsard's natural history. *B.Litt. 1943 Dublin, Trinity College*

Alcock, R.
La famosa toledana of Juan de Quiro. *M.A. 1916 Liverpool*

Aldred, P. F.
In multis iuris nostri articulis deterior est condicio feminarum quam masculorum - *Dig.* i.5.9. *D.C.L. 1881 Oxford*

Alexander, A. F. O'D.
The war with France in 1377. *Ph.D. 1934 London, External Degree*

Alexander, D. J.
The analysis of teachers' estimates and pupils' performance at the stage of entry to secondary education. *M.A. 1947 London, Institute of Education*

Alexander, E. A.
L'influence de Guillaume de Lorris sur quelques poètes français du quatorzième siècle. *M.A. 1948 Belfast*

Alexander, I. P.
Arthur Hugh Clough and his poetry. *M.A. 1939 Birmingham*

Alexander, J. M. G.
The Scots vernacular revival. *M.A. 1913 London*

Alexander, J. M. G.
The ancient Egyptian canals between the Mediterranean and the Red Sea: their problems for the sciences of geology, geography, engineering and history. *D.Sc. 1919 Glasgow*

Alexander, W. P.
Intelligence, concrete and abstract: a study in differential traits. *Ph.D. 1936 Glasgow*

Al-Hashimi, M.
Tabir al-Ruya (interpretation of dreams): sources, philosophy, influence, etc. *Ph.D. 1948 London, School of Oriental and African Studies*

Al-Hilli, A. H.
Elementary education in Irak in the times of the 'Abbāsids. *Ph.D. 1949 Manchester*

Ali, A.
Mirza 'Abdu'r-Rahim Khan-i-Khanan: soldier, statesman and patron of letters. *Ph.D. 1932 Cambridge*

Ali, H.
Deviations from the Anglo-Muhammadan law with reference to the Maplahs of Malabar. *LL.D. 1931 London, University College*

Ali Khan, M. S.
Usury and the principles of the Muhammadan law. *D.Phil. 1928 Oxford*

Ali, M. A.
State and private enterprise in education in British India. *M.Ed. 1928 Leeds*

Ali, S. A. el   *see* El Ali, S. A.

Ali, S. M.
A geographical study of the Ghaggar Plain. *Ph.D. 1939 London, Birkbeck College*

Ali, Z.
Diwan of Ibn Hani. *D.Phil. 1925 Oxford*

Ali, Z.
Ibn Hani and his times. *B.Litt. 1924 Oxford*

Allam, M. M.
An edition of: Al-Qártajanní's *Maqsúrah. Ph.D. 1945 Manchester*

Allan, J. B.
The Book of the Covenant (Ex.xx.22-xxiii.33): a new appreciation. *Ph.D. 1926 Edinburgh*

Allan, J. R. F.
An examination of the purpose of the municipal high school for girls, in the light of changes in the social structure of Britain since the war. *M.A. 1939 Liverpool*

Allan, K.
The recreations and amusements of the industrial working class in the second quarter of the nineteenth century, with special reference to Lancashire. *M.A. 1947 Manchester*

Allan, M. B. G.
The Reform movement in Tyneside and Wearside, 1812-1832. *M.A. 1919 Liverpool*

Allan, W.
1. Verifications of Scripture from Egypt and the Holy Land. 2. The perpetual obligation of the Sabbath. *B.D. & D.D. 1892 Oxford*

Allard, E. M. A. A. J.
Animistic beliefs in Malaya. *D.Phil. 1941 Oxford*

Allardice, J. T.
Syntax of Terence. *D.Litt. 1926 Saint Andrew's*

Allardyce, A.
Reality and spirit. *M.A. 1924 Bristol*

Allaway, A. J.
The coal industry in the seventeenth century. *B.A. 1931 Sheffield*

Allen, A. M.
Modern experiments in American banking reorganization. *Ph.D. 1938 London, School of Economics and Political Science*

Allen, B.
The alliterative diction of early Middle English poetry. *M.A. 1921 London*

Allen, B.
A study of the controversy concerning the application of Roman canon law in England during the Middle Ages. *B.Litt. 1923 Oxford*

Allen, B. F.
The genealogy of the C. text manuscripts of *Piers Plowman. M.A. 1923 London*

Allen, C. F.
Theodor Storm's prose style: a study in the evolution of the literary style and construction of novellen based on the original mss. *Ph.D. 1926 Edinburgh*

Allen, D. K.
Jesus' conception of man in the Synoptic Gospels. *Ph.D. 1928 Edinburgh*

Allen, E. A.
Temperamental tests: an experimental investigation into some points of character and temperament. *Ph.D. 1926 London*

Allen, E. L.
The problem of Mark: the sources, composition and historical value of St. Mark's Gospel. *Ph.D. 1923 London*

Allen, F.
John Webster. *M.A. 1914 Birmingham*

Allen, F. H.
A study in divine immanence in man. *B.D. 1944 Oxford*

Allen, G. B.
A commentary on: St. John xix.35-37; xx.30-31; xxi.24-25. *D.D. 1923 Oxford*

Allen, G. B.
1. The nature, origin, and early history of Arianism. 2. The later history and development of Arianism. *B.D. 1919 Oxford*

Allen, G. C.
The history of an eighteenth century combination in the copper-mining industry. *M.Com. 1922 Birmingham*

Allen, G. C.
The industrial development of Birmingham and the Black Country, 1860-1914. *Ph.D. 1928 Birmingham*

Allen, H. M.
British commercial policy in the West Indies from 1783 to 1793. *Ph.D. 1928 London*

Allen, J.
The *Defence of Guenevere* and other poems by W. Morris. *M.A. 1913 Bristol*

Allen, J. D.
The purpose of the elementary school. *M.A. 1928 Liverpool*

Allen, L.
The function of poetry and primitive psychology in the work of Jules Supervielle. *M.A. 1949 Manchester*

Allen, P. S.
Opus epistolarum Desiderii Erasmi Roterodami. *D.Litt. 1925 Oxford*

Allen, R.
François Coppée: a critical study of his works. *M.A. 1923 Wales*

Allen, R.
The principle of nonsubscription to creeds and confessions of faith as exemplified in Irish Presbyterian history. *Ph.D. 1944 Belfast*

Allen, R.
Scottish ecclesiastical influence upon Irish Presbyterianism from the non-subscription controversy to the union of the synods. *M.A. 1940 Belfast*

Allen, W. F.
La muse française et l'école romantique. *M.A. 1909 Wales*

Allen, W. S.
Linguistic problems and their treatment in antiquity. *Ph.D. 1948 Cambridge*

Allenby, A. I.
A psychological study of the origins of monotheism. *D.Phil. 1949 Oxford*

Allin, W. E.
Poor law adminstration in Glamorganshire before the Poor Law Amendment Act of 1834. *M.A. 1936 Wales*

Allison, J. E.
The geographical development of Birkenhead. *M.A. 1939 Liverpool*

Allison, L. H.
Perseveration. *M.A. 1937 Reading*

Allott, K. C. B.
An edition of the poetical works of William Habington with a critical introduction. *B.Litt. 1938 Oxford*

Allott, M.   *see* Farris, M.

Allott, R. M.
An examination of the basis of the distinction between primary and secondary characterisation in conflict of laws. *LL.M. 1948 Sheffield*

Allott, S.
Children in Greek literature from the heroic to the golden age. *B.Litt. 1943 Dublin, Trinity College*

Allsebrook, W. B. J.
The Court of Requests in the reign of Elizabeth. *M.A. 1936 London, University College*

Allt, W. G.
The organ and its music from medieval times to Johann Sebastian Bach. *Mus. Doc. 1930 Edinburgh*

Alphonso, V. I.
Female education in Bengal. *M.A. 1931 London, King's College*

Alsop, H.
The influence of France on M. Arnold. *M.A. 1914 Birmingham*

Alsop, M. H.
The marketing of the world's wheat crop. *M.Sc. 1938 London, School of Economics and Political Science*

Alter, S. N.
Studies in Bahaism. *Ph.D. 1923 Edinburgh*

Alton, E. S.
An experimental contribution to the function of imagery. *Ph.D. 1932 London, University College*

Alty, W.
An examination of the charges brought against the friars by Matthew Paris. *M.A. 1911 Wales*

Alwis, E. H. de   *see* De Alwis, E. H.

Ambedkar, B. R.
The problem of the rupee. *D.Sc. 1923 London*

Ambedkar, B. R.
Provincial decentralization of imperial finance in British India. *M.Sc. 1921 London*

Ambrose, G.
George Gascoigne, his life and works. *B.Litt. 1926 Oxford*

Ambrose, G. P.
The Levant Company after 1640. *B.Litt. 1933 Oxford*

Amburger, H. S. M.
Die Familiengeschichte der Köler. *Ph.D. 1928 London*

Ames, J. G.
The growth of the English periodical in the eighteenth century. *B.Litt. 1899 Oxford*

Amma, C. P. K.
The effect of nursery training on the responses of children in the Merrill-Terman tests. *M.Ed. 1920 Leeds*

Ammär, A. M.
The people of Sharqiya: their racial history, serology, physical characters, demography and conditions of life. *Ph.D. 1940 Manchester*

Ammar, H. M.
An enquiry into inequalities of educational opportunities in Egypt. *M.A. 1949 London, Institute of Education*

Amos, H. D.
The value of intelligence tests in the selection of candidates for entrance to secondary schools. *M.A. 1930 Wales*

Anagnostopoulos, B.
A study of the life and writings of St. John of Damascus. *B.Litt. 1950 Oxford*

Anand, M. R.
The treatment of relations by Locke and Hume. *Ph.D. 1929 London*

Ananthan, K. R. K.
The development of education in Mysore and present day needs. *M.Ed. 1937 Leeds*

Andalib-i-Shadani, W. H.
The Muslim historians of India, from 1205-1259. *Ph.D. 1934 London, School of Oriental and African Studies*

Anderson, A.
The knowledge of Greek in England in Anglo-Saxon times. *B.Litt. 1922 Oxford*

Anderson, A. C.
A commentary on the Book of Joshua, with a translation on the basis of Massoretic text and the Septuagint Version. *Ph.D. 1943 Dublin, Trinity College*

Anderson, A. H.
The Burgh of the Canongate and its court. *Ph.D. 1949 Edinburgh*

Anderson, A. L.
Conrad Ferdinand Meyer in his relationship to the theory of the Novelle. *Ph.D. 1924 Edinburgh*

Anderson, D.
A study of the influence of the Bible on the life and literature of Scotland in the seventeenth century. *Ph.D. 1932 Glasgow*

Anderson, E. T.
The intonation of American English. *M.A. 1939 London, University College*

Anderson, H.
The conception of the Resurrection, in the Apocrypha and Pseudepigrapha. *Ph.D. 1950 Glasgow*

Anderson, J.
The influence of neo-Platonism on the life and thought of St. Augustine. *Ph.D. 1927 Glasgow*

Anderson, J. D.
The greater English monasteries and their knights, 1066-1215. *B.Litt. 1948 Oxford*

Anderson, J. O.
Classical etymology as revealed in Greek and Latin literature. *M.A. 1930 London, Bedford College*

Anderson, K.
The treatment of vagrancy and the relief of the poor and destitute in the Tudor period, based upon the local records of London to 1552 and Hull to 1576. *Ph.D. 1933 London, Royal Holloway College*

Anderson, M. A.
The character of British relations with France, 1859-1865. *M.A. 1949 London, Bedford College*

Arnold, I. D. O.
Linguistic study of an unedited manuscript of the *Apparition maistre Jehan de Meun* by Honoré Bonet (1398), with particular reference to the elimination of hiatus. *M.A. 1927 Wales*

Arnold, J. B.
The sea fisheries of Northern Ireland. *M.Com.Sc. 1942 Belfast*

Arnott, J. F.
The *Hellenics* of Walter Savage Landor: an introductory study. *B.Litt. 1938 Oxford*

Arnould, E. J. F.
Contribution à l'étude du *Manuel des Péchés*. *Ph.D. 1936 London, External Degree*

Arora, H. S.
Agricultural education in the Punjab. *Ph.D. 1934 London, School of Economics and Political Science*

Arrowsmith, F. A.
The Pacific ports of Canada. *M.A. 1936 London, School of Economics and Political Science*

Arsan, F. T.
An examination of trust concept with reference to its compatibility with French law together with a few notes on the wakf. *B.Litt. 1948 Oxford*

Arschavir, A.
The development of the British railway station. *M.A. 1948 Manchester*

Arscott, C. M.
The relation of parents to schools: an enquiry into the advisability and the practicability of organizing co-operation between the home and the school. *M.Ed. 1922 Manchester*

Arscott, C. M.
A study of some of the influences traceable in the poetry of William Morris. *M.A. 1917 London*

Arscott, C. M.
A study of *The Life and death of Jason, The earthly Paradise*, and *Sigurd the Volsung*, with special reference to Morris's treatment of his sources. *Ph.D. 1928 London*

Arsitch, V. T.
Durkheim's conception of religion. *B.Litt. 1922 Oxford*

Arthurs, J. B.
The verbal system in bardic poetry. *M.A. 1942 Belfast*

Arulnandy, S.
Relations and complex qualities. *M.Sc. 1931 London, University College*

Asfour, S. Z. A.
Departmental legislation and the problem of safeguards in England and Egypt. *Ph.D. 1949 Manchester*

Ashcroft, E. G.
The presidency of the U.S.A. and the premiership of Great Britain: a comparative study of patronage. *M.Sc. 1946 London, School of Economics and Political Science*

Ashdown, E.
A study of the work of Henry James, George Gissing, Samuel Butler, and George Moore, more particularly in its relation to the development of the theory of the novel in the later nineteenth century. *Ph.D. 1927 London*

Asher, P. H.
Studies in the theory of wage rates. *M.Sc. 1935 Cambridge*

Ashford, F.
An estimate of Caravaggio and his influence on the succeeding generation in Italy. *M.A. 1936 London, University College*

Ashley, A.
The social policy of Bismarck. *M.A. 1912 Birmingham*

Ashley, M. P.
Financial and commercial policy under the Protectorate. *D.Phil. 1933 Oxford*

Ashley, W. S.
The early development of Shelley. *M.A. 1908 Birmingham*

Ashman, R. G.
An examination of the views of John Wesley in relation to the Protestant Reformation. *Ph.D. 1949 Wales*

Ashmole, B.
Greek sculpture of the period between Pheidias and Praxiteles. *B.Litt. 1924 Oxford*

Ashraf, K. M.
Life and conditions of the people of Hindustan (1200-1550 A.D.). *Ph.D. 1932 London, School of Oriental and African Studies*

Ashthana, G. D.
Old English and Hindu ballads. *Ph.D. 1928 London*

Ashton, A.
1. The meaning of the word κύριοσ in the Septuagint and in the New Testament. 2. The prophet of Israel in his relation to God. *B.D. 1909 Oxford*

Ashton, F.
The theory of the novel from 1850 to 1900. *M.A. 1931 Manchester*

Ashton, G. M.
Bywyd a gwaith Twm o'r Nant a'i le yn hanes yr Anterliwt(The life and work of Twm o'r Nant and his place in the history of the 'Interlude'). *M.A. 1944 Wales*

Ashton, M. M.
The history of Rivington Grammar School. *M.Ed. 1929 Manchester*

Ashton, S. D.
A survey of educational development in the borough of Ashton-under-Lyne, with special reference to Albion Schools and to the period 1840-1938. *M.Ed. 1938 Manchester*

Ashur, M. S.
The Nationalist movement in Egypt, 1879-1882. *M.A. 1925 Birmingham*

Ashwell, K. E.
Otway: his indebtedness in tragedy to French drama and to the *Nouvelles de Saint-Réal*. *M.A. 1908 London*

Ashworth, A. H.
La comparaison des idées de Rousseau et de Fénelon sur l'education. *M.A. 1911 Liverpool*

Ashworth, H. I.
The design and development of the commercial hotel. *M.A. 1930 Manchester*

Ashworth, M. M.
The evolution of the Tory party, 1783-1815. *M.A. 1925 Manchester*

Asirvatham, J. E.
Herbert Spencer's theory of social justice. *Ph.D. 1925 Edinburgh*

Askar, R. M.
Animism in the child's conception of the world: an experimental criticism and verification of Professor Piaget's enquiries into child animism. *M.A. 1932 Birmingham*

Asnodkar, M. N.
The organization of the Indian money market. *M.Sc. 1923 London*

Aspinall, A.
The administrative and judicial reforms of Lord Cornwallis in Bengal, 1786-1793, excluding the permanent settlement. *M.A. 1922 Manchester*

Aspinall, A.
The place of Lord Brougham in the history of the Whig Party. *Ph.D. 1924 Manchester*

Astington, E.
A basic minimum French vocabulary. *M.Ed. 1950 Manchester*

Astington, E.
The social and intellectual background of the 'déclassé' members of the Paris Commune of 1871. *M.A. 1939 Manchester*

Astley, F.
Quelques traces de L'influence espagnole au théâtre français du 17e siècle: Lope de Vega et J. Rotrou. *M.A. 1928 Birmingham*

Aston, S. C.
The poems of the Provençal troubadour Peirol. *Ph.D. 1940 Cambridge*

Ata, M.
Persian history from 820-1056 A.D. *Ph.D. 1932 Dublin, Trinity College*

Atherton, W.
The modern approach in science teaching, having particular reference to courses for secondary school pupils of 11-16 years of age. *M.Ed. 1939 Manchester*

Atik, A. A.
The poetry of Abu Firas al-Hamdani. *D.Phil. 1948 Oxford*

Atiya, A. S.
Nicopolis: a study based on eastern and western sources, and an examination of the battlefield and its approaches. *Ph.D. 1933 London, School of Oriental and African Studies*

Atkins, E. M.
The Tory attitude towards parliamentary reform (1815-1832). *M.A. 1931 London, King's College*

Atkins, S. H.
A study of Thomas Campion as critic and poet. *M.A. 1931 London, King's College*

Atkins, S. H.
A study of verse-satire and epigram, 1595-1603. *Ph.D. 1937 London, External Degree*

Atkinson, B. F. C.
The Thraco-Illyrian language. *Ph.D. 1926 Cambridge*

Atkinson, C. C.
1. The evolution of the revelation of God traced through the crises in the history of Israel during the period from Moses to Elijah. 2. The evolution of the revelation of God traced through the crises in the history of Israel during the eighth century B.C. *B.D. & D.D. 1898 Oxford*

Atkinson, C. W.
A comparative investigation of the influence of geography and practical biology on the understanding of the forms of reasoning involved in civics. *M.Ed. 1949 Leeds*

Atkinson, D. M.
A re-examination of the problem of radical-changing verbs in the Hispanic languages with a critical account of the theories so far brought forward to explain them. *M.A. 1948 Sheffield*

Atkinson, J.
Johannine interpretation: the episodes in the fourth Gospel as symbolic of various types of spiritual characters and attitude. *M.Litt. 1950 Durham*

Atkinson, M. E.
The relation of music and poetry as reflected in the works of Tieck, Wackenroder and Brentano. *M.A. 1947 London, Bedford College*

Atkinson, N. F.
Political life of Lord Melbourne. *M.A. 1919 Liverpool*

Atkinson, R. A.
Denmark and Britain. *M.Com.Sc. 1933 Belfast*

Atkinson, R. M. M.
Stammering in children and a method of treatment. *M.Ed. 1922 Manchester*

Atkinson, T.
City of Winchester, the first book of Ordinances, 1552-1609, transcribed and annotated. *M.A. 1940 Bristol*

Atkinson, W. C.
El maestro Fernan Pérez de Oliva. *M.A. 1925 Belfast*

Attlee, B. H. B.
1. The biblical conception of the kingdom of heaven. 2. 'Tu es Petrus'. *B.D. 1910 Oxford*

Attlee, B. H. B.
Dissertations on St. Luke xxiii.43; St. Matthew xxvii.27,28; St. Matthew xix.3-11. *D.D. 1924 Oxford*

Atto, C. H.
The Society for the Encouragement of Learning and its place in the history of publishing. *Ph.D. 1938 London, King's College*

Aubry, P. J. A.
Ozanam, historien et critique littéraire. *Ph.D. 1932 London, Birkbeck College*

Auchmuty, J. J.
The government of the United States and Latin American independence. *Ph.D. 1935 Dublin, Trinity College*

Aughterson, W. V.
The influence of radical doctrine in the French Revolution on English drama in the time of Thomas Holcroft, 1776 to 1806. *Ph.D. 1936 London, King's College*

Auld, D. M.
Quelques aspects de l'étude de Pierre Loti. *M.A. 1929 Birmingham*

·Auld, M.
The agrarian programme of the democratic party, 78-59 B.C. *M.A. 1905 Liverpool*

Ault, H. C.
England and her writers in the works of Anatole France (1844-1924). *M.A. 1928 Birmingham*

Ault, H. C.
Tragedy in France in the eighteenth century, 1700-1789: its literary and sociological value. *D.Litt. 1948 Birmingham*

Ault, H. K.
An investigation into the causes of backwardness in geography among secondary school children. *M.A. 1940 London, Institute of Education*

Ault, O. E.
The relation of certain problems to the training of teachers in the United States, Ontario, France, Scotland and Germany. *Ph.D. 1935 Edinburgh*

Aung, M. H.
The Burmese drama - with reference to the Elizabethan drama. *Ph.D. 1933 Dublin, Trinity College*

Aung, M. H.
The position of ecclesiastics in Burmese Buddhist law. *B.Litt. 1939 Dublin, Trinity College*

Austen, W. G.
Jacopone dei Benedetti da Todi: a religious poet of the thirteenth century. *B.Litt. 1925 Oxford*

Austen-Leigh, A. H.
1. The sacrament of the Lord's Supper. 2. The obligation of the decalogue upon Christians. *B.D. 1872 Oxford*

Austin, F. E.
1. The eschatology of the Gospels. 2. The authorship and destination of the Epistle to the Hebrews. *B.D. 1907 Oxford*

Austin, F. E.
Expositions of I Corinthians xv.29; St. Mark xiii.26; Hebrews v.6. *D.D. 1911 Oxford*

Austin, G. H.
English local finance. *Ph.D. 1921 Sheffield*

Austin, R. P.
The origin, significance, and history of the Stoichedon style in Greek inscriptions. *B.Litt. 1935 Oxford*

Auty, P.
The Cistercian Movement in the north of England, with special reference to the early history of Byland Abbey. *B.Litt. 1934 Oxford*

Aveling, F. A. P.
On the consciousness of the universal and the individual. *D.Sc. 1912 London*

Awad, L. H. K.
The theory and practice of 'poetic diction' in English, with reference to the same in Arabic and French. *M.Litt. 1941 Cambridge*

Awad, M.
The conflict of nationalism and imperialism with particular reference to the Near and Middle East. *Ph.D. 1926 London*

Awad, M.
The geographical aspects of the Mosul Question. *M.A. 1926 Liverpool*

Aydelotte, F.
Elizabethan rogues and vagabonds: their life, manners and representation in contemporary literature, especially in connexion with the so-called coney-catching pamphlets of Robert Greene. *B.Litt. 1907 Oxford*

Aydelotte, W. O.
Bismarck and British colonial policy: the problem in South-West Africa, 1883-1885. *Ph.D. 1935 Cambridge*

Aykroyd, P.
Louis de Cardonnel. *Ph.D. 1927 Dublin, Trinity College*

Ayoub, A. R. M. A.
The verbal piece in Egyptian Arabic: a morphological study. *M.A. 1949 London, School of Oriental and African Studies*

Ayouty, M. Y. el- *see* El-Ayouty, M. Y.

Ayre, J. L.
The Christology of the earliest gospel. *Ph.D. 1922 Edinburgh*

Ayres, G. L. A.
Fluctuation in new capital issues on the London money market, 1899-1913. *M.Sc. 1934 London, School of Economics and Political Science*

Ayscough, H. H.
An account of the progress of penal reform in England from 1810-1930, together with some conclusions. *Ph.D. 1933 London, School of Economics and Political Science*

Azeemullah, S.
The ethical and social doctrines of Bishop Berkeley. *M.A. 1924 London*

Azmy, I.
George Eliot as an analyst of the social life of England in the nineteenth century. *M.A. 1949 Sheffield*

Babbage, S. B.
The Church of England and Puritanism during the primacy of Bancroft, 1604-1610. *Ph.D. 1940 London, King's College*

Baber, F. T.
The historical geography of the Forest of Dean. *M.A. 1949 Wales*

Bach, R.
Feuerbach's reconstruction of philosophy as the study of man. *M.A. 1948 London, Birkbeck College*

Bachtin, N.
Thessaly in the thirteenth century B.C. and the origin of the Centaur-Lapithai myth. *Ph.D. 1934 Cambridge*

Backhouse, W. H.
The religious and moral training of the adolescent. *M.Ed. 1940 Leeds*

Bacon, J. C.
Identity, individuality, personality. *Ph.D. 1924 Bristol*

Bacon, J. C.
Recent psychological theories of self-consciousness. *M.A. 1923 Wales*

Badcock, A. J.
Aspects of the idea of God in western thought. *M.A. 1949 Liverpool*

Badcock, F. J.
1. The Council of Constantinople and the Nicene Creed. 2. The early Roman baptismal creed. *B.D. & D.D. 1922 Oxford*

Bader, R. V. G.
The origins of the Young England Movement. *B.Phil. 1950 Saint Andrew's*

Badger, A. B.
On the pronouns in seventeenth and eighteenth century English. *M.A. 1930 London, University College*

Bagchi, R.
Banks and industrial finance in India. *Ph.D. 1937 London, University College*

Baggally, J. W.
The light thrown by the klephtic ballads on the history of Greece in the period (1715 to 1821) before the war of Independence. *B.Litt. 1935 Oxford*

Baggs, T. A.
The rise and progress of Euphuism in English literature. *M.A. 1912 Birmingham*

Bagley, C. R.
Woman's rights and feminism in the contemporary French theatre. *B.Litt. 1922 Oxford*

Bagley, D.
Critical analysis of objective studies in the teaching of English. *M.A. 1935 London, Institute of Education*

Bagot, J. H.
Significant factors in the growth of juvenile delinquency. *M.A. 1939 Liverpool*

Bahadoorsingh, I. J.
Communal representation and Indian self-government. *B.Litt. 1944 Oxford*

Baikie, J. E. M.
The Caesarean text *inter pares*. *M.Litt. 1935 Cambridge*

Bailes, J. L.
A study in the living Durham dialect: a contribution to an English linguistic atlas. *M.A. 1948 Leeds*

Bailey, B. L.
Trade routes between mainland Greece and the West, from the Geometric Age until the end of the sixth century B.C. *M.A. 1935 London, Westfield College*

Bailey, C. H.
A survey of the theories of the conduction of electricity through solutions from 1800-1876 (Carlisle and Nicholson to Kohlrausch). *M.Sc. 1938 London, External Degree*

Bailey, D. S.
The English Reformation as reflected in the life and works of Thomas Becon, 1512 to 1567. *Ph.D. 1947 Edinburgh*

Bailey, E.
The production and marketing of cocoa in the western provinces of Nigeria, with some consideration of government control of marketing and prices from 1939 to 1946. *M.A. 1947 Sheffield*

Bailey, E. E.
General principles of liability for tort. *D.Phil. 1932 Oxford*

Bailey, H. W.
The Iranian recension of the Pahlavi *Bundahesh*: a philological and critical treatment of the text, with translation. *D.Phil. 1933 Oxford*

Bailey, J. H. S.
1. The historical and religious value of Genesis and its claim to be regarded as an inspired book. 2. Recent theories concerning the origin of life, and their probable effect upon religious thought and belief. *B.D. 1913 Oxford*

Bailey, J. H. Shackleton *see* Shackleton Bailey, J. H.

Bailey, M. F.
A short study in the early history of photography. *M.Sc. 1946 London, University College*

Bailey, M. N.
The prose works of John Donne. *M.A. 1913 Birmingham*

Bailey, R. R.
The hedonism of Jeremy Bentham. *Ph.D. 1938 London, University College*

Bailey, S. J.
Assignments of debts in England from the twelfth to the twentieth centuries. *LL.M. 1930 Cambridge*

Bailey, T. R.
Eighteenth century poetical miscellanies. *Ph.D. 1933 London, External Degree*

Bailey, W. Milne- *see* Milne-Bailey, W.

Baillie, A. W.
Examination and criticism of Hoeffding's contribution to the psychology of religious conviction. *M.A. 1924 Manchester*

Baily, R. C. J.
The parliamentary history of Reading between 1750 and 1850. *M.A. 1944 Reading*

Baine, R. M.
Joseph Warton as a literary critic. *B.Litt. 1939 Oxford*

Bains, I.
British policy in relation to Portuguese claims in West Africa, 1876 to 1884. *M.A. 1940 London, Bedford College*

Bainton, E.
The modern democratic movement as reflected in the English poets. *M.A. 1911 Birmingham*

Bairactaris, A.
The contemplation of supersensible being in Plato's writings, compared with the apprehension of God through Christ in the writings of St. Paul. *B.Litt. 1944 Oxford*

Baird, M.
The collaboration of Dekker and Middleton. *B.Litt. 1928 Oxford*

Baird-Smith, W. F. *see* Smith, W. F. Baird-

Bajwa, K. S.
A study of the development of agriculture in the Punjab and its economic effects. *Ph.D. 1928 Leeds*

Baker, A. M.
Figure paintings on rood screens in the churches of Norfolk and south Devonshire. *Ph.D. 1938 London, Courtauld Institute of Art*

Baker, C. H. C.
Exegeses of: St.Luke xxiv.21; Acts ii.3,4; St.John iii.5. *D.D. 1886 Oxford*

Baker, C. H. C.
1. The Resurrection of Christ. 2. The Ascension of Christ. *B.D. 1882 Oxford*

Baker, E. E.
The relations of Great Britain and America, especially from 1861-1866. *M.A. 1920 Birmingham*

Baker, E. W.
The relation of William Law to John Wesley and the beginnings of Methodism. *Ph.D. 1941 Edinburgh*

Baker, J.
Criminality in youth: a medico-legal study. *M.D. 1901 Aberdeen*

Baker, J.
The longer commentary of R. David Kimchi on the Psalms (chap. 120-150). *Ph.D. 1931 Dublin, Trinity College*

Baker, J. N. L.
The effects of irrigation on movements of population, and on the food supply of the world, with special reference to America. *B.Litt. 1924 Oxford*

Baker, L. A.
An account of the 'direct method' in modern language teaching, its origin and development. *M.Ed. 1924 Manchester*

Baker, M.
George Ellis, Esquire: a study. *M.A. 1923 London*

Baker, M.
The influence of orthography upon pronunciation in sixteenth and seventeenth century French. *M.A. 1934 Manchester*

Baker, R. J.
The sociological function of intellectuals in modern society: a study of some social movements in post-war Germany. *Ph.D. 1936 London, School of Economics and Political Science*

Baker, R. L.
Palmerston's attitude towards Mehemet Ali, 1834-8, with an introduction on the development of the Near Eastern question, 1788-1834. *B.Litt. 1928 Oxford*

Baker, R. P.
The *Iphigenia in Aulis* of Euripides. *M.A. 1926 Birmingham*

Baker, R. W.
The hearsay rule. *B.Litt. 1947 Oxford*

Baker, S.
1. The doctrine of baptism. 2. The intermediate state. *B.D. 1901 Oxford*

Baker, S.
Expositions of: Acts ii.42: the Christian fellowship; Acts xv.6: the ministry in the Apostolic age; St. John xvii.22: the prayer of the Lord that his Church might be one. *D.D. 1905 Oxford*

Baker, S. J. K.
East African studies. *M.A. 1931 Liverpool*

Baker, T. H. L.
The doctrine of the knowledge of God. *B.D. 1950 Cambridge*

Baker, W.
Exegeses of: John xix.25-27; I Thessalonians ii.1-12; I Peter iii.18-20. *D.D. 1874 Oxford*

Baker, W.
1. The state of the departed. 2. The communion of Saints. *B.D. 1871 Oxford*

Baker, W. S.
The religious thought and influence of Thomas Arnold of Rugby. *Ph.D. 1950 Edinburgh*

Bakir, A. M.
Egyptian epistolography from the eighteenth to the twenty-first dynasties. *B.Litt. 1941 Oxford*

Bakir, A. M.
Slavery in Pharaonic Egypt. *D.Phil. 1946 Oxford*

Balaguer, M.
Law as the basis of morality in the philosophy of Hobbes, Cumberland and Locke. *Ph.D. 1937 London, University College*

Balakrishna, R.
Industrial development of Mysore. *Ph.D. 1939 London, School of Economics and Political Science*

Bald, M. A.
English influences on the written form of the language and on the literature of Scotland, 1500-1625. *B.Litt. 1925 Oxford*

Bald, M. A.
Representative Victorian women. *Ph.D. 1921 Edinburgh*

Bald, R. C.
Thomas Middleton. *Ph.D. 1929 Cambridge*

Baldwin, G.
Staging in England from the earliest times to 1576, with special reference to the stage directions. *M.A. 1931 Manchester*

Baldwin, J. R.
Aberdeen and Anglo-French diplomatic relations, 1841-6. *B.Litt. 1936 Oxford*

Baliga, B. S.
The influence of the home government on land revenue and judicial administration in the presidency of Fort William in Bengal from 1807-1822. *Ph.D. 1934 London, School of Oriental and African Studies*

Balin, S.
The life and poetry of Jean Richepin. *M.A. 1937 Sheffield*

Balint, M.
Individual differences of behaviour in early infancy, and an objective method for recording them. *M.Sc. 1945 Manchester*

Ball, A. H. R.
John Ruskin as a critic of literature. *M.A. 1921 Birmingham*

Ball, A. H. R.
John Ruskin as a writer of prose. *M.A. 1924 Liverpool*

Ball, J. H.
A psychological study of value, with special reference to the noegenetic theory. *M.A. 1931 London, University College*

Ball, L.
Hercules in Greek and Roman tragedy (Euripides, Sophocles, Seneca). *M.A. 1937 Manchester*

Ball, L. P.
The critical writings of W. P. Ker. *M.A. 1940 Liverpool*

Ballantine, J.
Lopez de Villalobos: a critical study. *M.A. 1932 Belfast*

Ballantyne, J. C.
On the significance of inter-communication in the philosophy of religion. *M.A. 1930 Liverpool*

Balley, E. J.
John Whitgift: his character and work. *M.A. 1927 Belfast*

Ballin, H. H.
The organization of electricity supply in Great Britain. *Ph.D. 1942 London, School of Economics and Political Science*

Baltzell, E. R.
Administrative legislation and adjudication in Great Britain and the United States. *D.Phil. 1923 Oxford*

Bambridge, A. H.
The philosophic and psychological implications of Christian Science. *B.Litt. 1930 Oxford*

Bamforth, W.
British interests in the Tigris-Euphrates Valley, 1856-88. *M.A. 1948 London, Bedford College*

Bandyopadhyay, N.
Kant's view of our knowledge of the self. *Ph.D. 1932 London, University College*

Banerjea, P.
1. Public administration in ancient India. 2. A study of Indian economics. *D.Sc. 1916 London*

Banerjee, B.
Realism in contemporary Bengali poetry as compared and considered with reference to realism in English poetry from the last decade of the nineteenth century. *Ph.D. 1937 London, King's College*

Banerjee, B. B.
An edition of the dramatic works of John Sheffield, Duke of Buckinghamshire. *B.Litt. 1937 Oxford*

Banerjee, S. K.
Evolution and character of the Elizabethan lyric. *Ph.D. 1931 Edinburgh*

Banerji, A. N.
Financing of local authorities in British India. *Ph.D. 1941 London, School of Economics and Political Science*

Banerji, H. K.
Fielding as an observer of life and a reformer of contemporary manners. *B.Litt. 1923 Oxford*

Banerji, P.
Instincts and education: an enquiry concerning the instincts in education. *M.Ed. 1927 Leeds*

Banerji, S.
The history of Humayun from 1530-1540 A.D. *Ph.D. 1925 London*

Banerji Sastri, A.
Origin and development of Māgadhī. *D.Phil. 1922 Oxford*

Banks, E. G.
1. Prayer. 2. The intermediate state. *B.D. & D.D. 1890 Oxford*

Banks, E. K. C.
Factor-analysis applied to current problems in psychology, with special reference to data obtained from H. M. forces. *Ph.D. 1945 London, University College*

Banks, R.
A study of the seventeenth century masque. *M.A. 1912 Birmingham*

Bannell, J. G.
Mental development with special reference to school conditions and health. *M.A. 1916 Liverpool*

Bannerjea, R.
The education of women in Bengal, with special reference to that of the nineteenth and twentieth centuries. *M.Ed. 1938 Leeds*

Bannerjee, G. C.
A critical edition of Jasper Mayne's *The citie match* and *The amorous warre*, with a biographical and critical introduction. *B.Litt. 1936 Oxford*

Bao, C. M.
A geographical study of China, with special reference to the means of transport. *Ph.D. 1940 London, School of Economics and Political Science*

Barakat, G. E.
The status of aliens in Egypt since 1937, with a sketch of the historical development of their position and a comparison of the present law in Egypt with the British law as to aliens. *B.Litt. 1950 Oxford*

Barbeau, F. C. J. M.
Some aspects of the totemism of north-west America. *B.Sc. 1910 Oxford*

Barber, A. V.
A study of sound and unsound currency in Massachusetts from 1690 to 1763. *B. Litt. 1929 Oxford*

Barber, E. D.
The position of women as reflected in medieval German didactic literature. *M.A. 1940 Manchester*

Barber, G. C.
The concept of sin in the great religions of the East. *Ph.D. 1938 London, Richmond College*

Barber, J.
The versification of Emile Verhaeren. *M.A. 1922 Manchester*

Barber, P.
The League of Nations and national minorities. *M.A. 1924 Wales*

Barber, W. H.
The penetration of the philosophy of Leibniz in France. *D.Phil. 1950 Oxford*

Barbour, C. E.
The new psychology and the Christian doctrine of sin. *Ph.D. 1927 Edinburgh*

Barbour, G. F.
On philosophical aspects of Christian ethics. *Ph.D. 1910 Edinburgh*

Barbour, W. T.
The history of contract in early English equity. *B.Litt. 1912 Oxford*

Barclay, A.
Calvin's doctrine of the Lord's Supper in its relation to other sacramental types. *Ph.D. 1926 Edinburgh*

Barclay, R. M.
The life and work of Robert Whytt, M.D., F.R.C.P., F.R.S., Professor of Medicine in the University of Edinburgh. *M.D. 1922 Edinburgh*

Bardon, D. T.
Aspects of prognosis in psychiatry. *M.D. 1943 Dublin, Trinity College*

Bardsley, C. B.
Education in relation to employment in a rural area and in an industrial area. *M.A. 1939 Liverpool*

Barfield, A. O.
Poetic diction. *B.Litt. 1927 Oxford*

Barford, K. E.
The development of the West of England woollen industry from 1550 to 1640. *M.A. 1923 London*

Barger, H.
Monetary policy and dynamic change. *Ph.D. 1937 London, School of Economics and Political Science*

Bargery, G. P.
Hausa-English dictionary and English-Hausa vocabulary. *D.Litt. 1937 London, School of Oriental and African Studies*

Barkakoty, A. K.
The growth of local self-government in Assam, 1874-1919. *Ph.D. 1949 London, School of Oriental and African Studies*

Barker, A. E.
Studies in the background of Milton's prose. *Ph.D. 1937 London, University College*

Barker, F. E.
Richard Crashaw, poet and mystic: a critical biography. *M.A. 1922 London*

Barker, G. M.
Etude de l'enfant chez quelques romanciers du 19e siècle. *M.A. 1916 Birmingham*

Barker, G. R.
Planning and production control in Soviet State industries. *M.Com. 1950 Birmingham*

Barker, H. J.
Nodier, conteur. *M.A. 1923 Liverpool*

Barker, J.
1. The doctrine of God the Holy Spirit. 2. The Old Testament revelation: a divine preparation for the Incarnation. *B.D. 1902 Oxford*

Barker, J.
Expositions of Genesis i,ii; Isaiah lii.15-liii; St. John i.1-18. *D.D. 1906 Oxford*

Barker, J.
Jules Romains: sa vie, sa poésie, sa pensée. *M.A. 1941 Birmingham*

Barker, J. W.
El Libro de buen amor of Juan Ruiz. *Ph.D. 1924 Cambridge*

Barker, L. F.
Les idées de Madame de Maintenon sur l'éducation des filles, comparées à celles qui ont cours à notre époque. *M.A. 1912 Liverpool*

Barker, L. G. E.
The life and writings of John Byrom. *M.A. 1933 London, University College*

Barker, M. A.
The humanitarian novel in England and France, 1830-1870. *Ph.D. 1938 London, External Degree*

Barker, M. L.
A historical and critical survey of the study of speech-melody, 1775 to 1923. *Ph.D. 1925 Edinburgh*

Barker, W. M.
Quelques conteurs français du 19e siècle. *M.A. 1918 Birmingham*

Barkley, J. M.
The Eucharistic rite in the liturgy of the Church of Scotland. *D.D. 1949 Dublin, Trinity College*

Barkley, J. M.
The heart of the Christian life or Christian worship in its history and teaching. *Ph.D. 1946 Dublin, Trinity College*

Barling, T. J.
L'enseignement supérieur et la Révolution française. *M.A. 1948 Birmingham*

Barlingay, D. S.
Philosophical atomism: a comparative study of the theories of Hume and Bertrand Russell. *M.A. 1927 London*

Barlingay, W. S.
A critical discussion of the status of sense-data. *Ph.D. 1930 London, University College*

Barlow, F.
A critical edition of the letters of Arnulf of Lisieux. *D.Phil. 1937 Oxford*

Barlow, F.
A study of certain letter books in the possession of the Dean and Chapter of Durham as illustrations of the life of the Church in England in the later thirteenth century. *B.Litt. 1934 Oxford*

Barlow, J. E.
The mystery religions and the Christian sacraments. *B.D. 1942 Leeds*

Barlow, W.
The dialect of Radcliffe: a contribution to a survey of the regional dialects of Lancashire. *M.A. 1934 Liverpool*

Barna, T.
Redistribution of incomes through public finance in 1937. *Ph.D. 1943 London, School of Economics and Political Science*

Barnard, E. G.
The education system of French Protestant Switzerland (Cantons of Geneva, Vaud and Neuchâtel). *M.A. 1931 London, King's College*

Barnard, H. C.
Madame de Maintenon and Saint Cyr. *M.A. 1928 London*

Barnard, H. Clive- *see* Clive-Barnard, H.

Barnard, T. T.
Regulation of marriage in the New Hebrides. *Ph.D. 1924 Cambridge*

Barnard, W. S.
Charles Le Goffic: his poetry and poetic criticism. *M.A. 1937 London, Bedford College*

Barnes, A. G.
The history of the Flavian period, and in particular of the reign of Domitian, especially as reflected in the works of the poets Juvenal, Martial, and Statius. *M.A. 1936 Manchester*

Barnes, A. M.
Leclerc et la république des lettres. *D.Phil. 1935 Oxford*

Barnes, B.
Goethe's knowledge of French literature. *B.Litt. 1926 Oxford*

Barnes, E. M. A.
The reflection of contemporary religious thought in the essays of the eighteenth century. *M.A. 1913 Birmingham*

Barnes, G. P.
The evolution of the Merlin story in twelfth and thirteenth century French literature. *M.A. 1950 Manchester*

Barnes, J.
Social sympathy and the scientific impulse in the naturalistic work of Gerhart Hauptmann. *M.A. 1937 Manchester*

Barnes, M. W.
The firm of Lintot. *M.A. 1942 London, Bedford College*

Barnes, S. E.
The development of organized leisure-time activities for young persons in England, with particular reference to London. *M.A. 1947 London, Institute of Education*

Barnett, A. J.
The Four Hundred and the Thirty. *M.A. 1901 Birmingham*

Barnett, K. M.
The influence of Romanticism on Renan's historical treatment of religious beliefs. *M.A. 1931 London, Bedford College*

Barnett, M.
The gift of the spirit in the New Testament, with special reference to Glossolalia. *M.A. 1946 Manchester*

Barnett, R. W.
British foreign policy in relation to the Russo-Japanese war. *B.Litt. 1937 Oxford*

Barnett, T. R.
Queen Margaret and the influence she exerted on the Celtic Church in Scotland. *Ph.D. 1925 Edinburgh*

Barns, J. W. B.
The character and use of anthologies among the Greek literary papyri, together with an edition of some unpublished papyri. *D.Phil. 1946 Oxford*

Barnwell, H. T.
Le développement de la tragédie racinienne jusqu'à *Andromaque*. *M.A. 1949 Birmingham*

Baron, D. K.
The development of the spa in England and Wales. *M.A. 1938 Manchester*

Baron, G.
A critical survey of the auxiliary means of selection employed in examinations in public elementary schools for free special places in secondary schools. *M.Ed. 1937 Leeds*

Baron, J.
Exegeses of: Judges v.24; St. Luke i.15; Romans xvi.5. *B.D. & D.D. 1878 Oxford*

Baron, W. P.
Certain aspects of coast erosion in the English Channel with special reference to the coast-defence problems of the town of Sidmouth, Devon. *M.A. 1931 London, External Degree*

Baron, W. P.
The economic geography of the county of Devon: a study of the factors controlling the geographical distribution of the chief occupations. *Ph.D. 1938 London, External Degree*

Barou, N. I.
International co-operative banking (co-operative banking and co-operative banks of the world). *Ph.D. 1933 London, School of Economics and Political Science*

Barpujari, H.
British administration in Assam (1825-45), with special reference to the hill-tribes on the frontier. *Ph.D. 1949 London, School of Oriental and African Studies*

Barr, G. B. T.
Certain related topics in highway law. *LL.M. 1936 Cambridge*

Barra, T. de la
Some aspects of industrial organization. *Ph.D. 1924 Glasgow*

Barras, W. D.
Objective tests of the fluency factor, with special reference to its relation to ability in school subjects. *M.A. 1938 London, Institute of Education*

Barratt, D. M.
The condition of the English parish clergy from the Reformation to 1660, with special reference to the dioceses of Oxford, Gloucester, and Worcester. *D.Phil. 1949 Oxford*

Barrett, A. J.
Yeats and Celtic mythology. *M.A. 1948 National University of Ireland*

Barrett, B. C.
Santa Teresa y sus obras. *M.A. 1948 National University of Ireland*

Barrett, C. K.
The Holy Spirit and the Gospel tradition. *B.D. 1948 Cambridge*

Barrett, F.
Uí Fidgente, a kingdom of the Eoganachta. *M.A. 1942 National University of Ireland*

Barrett, G. B.
Louis Aragon, a survey of his work from 1919 to 1936. *M.A. 1936 Birmingham*

Barrett, I.
On aspect in Germanic. *M.A. 1936 Liverpool*

Barrett, K. I.
Studies in the life and writings of George Herbert. *M.A. 1934 London, King's College*

Barrett, W. P.
Matthew Prior and his literary relations with France. *Ph.D. 1932 Cambridge*

Barrington, E. C.
The human geography of the Island of Guernsey. *M.A. 1934 London, Birkbeck College*

Barrington-Ward, M. J.
1. The sinlessness of Christ. 2. The Resurrection as the main evidence for Christianity. *B.D. & D.D. 1919 Oxford*

Barron, B.
A study of the effect of the following factors: nature of the work, lack of social intercourse, limitation of educational possibilities, migration of population and low social status upon the mental life of the modern English agricultural labourers, with special reference to Oxfordshire. *B.Litt. 1923 Oxford*

Barrow, G. W. S.
Scottish royal ecclesiastical policy, 1107-1214, with special reference to foreign influence in the spread of the monastic orders and the personnel of the episcopate in Scotland. *B.Litt. 1950 Oxford*

Barrow, R. H.
Slavery in the first two centuries of the Roman Empire. *B.Litt. 1926 Oxford*

Barrow, W. M.
Studies in the history of Liverpool, 1756-1783. *M.A. 1925 Liverpool*

Barruadh, S.
Aithbheochaint na Gaedhilge(The Irish language revival). *M.A. 1928 National University of Ireland*

Barry, A. Milner- *see* Milner-Barry, A.

Barry, F. V.
A study of children's books from 1700-1825. *B.Litt. 1921 Oxford*

Barry, J. G.
Survivals of Irish monastic church organisation in late medieval and early modern times. *M.A. 1949 National University of Ireland*

Barry, M. H.
The application in Roman-Dutch law of the principle *mobilia non habent sequelam* with special reference to the law of South Africa. *B.Litt. 1925 Oxford*

Barry, P.
The hylomorphic concept in psychology. *M.A. 1942 National University of Ireland*

Barry, P. T.
The economics of the distribution of wheat. *M.Econ.Sc. 1936 National University of Ireland*

Barry, R. G.
A review of savings and savings institutions. *M.Comm. 1948 National University of Ireland*

Barry, V. A. A.
A critical examination of Bossuet's attitude on the question of the Gallican Church. *B.Litt. 1920 Oxford*

Barry, W.
The literary aspect of Burke. *M.A. 1949 National University of Ireland*

Bartels, F. L.
The provision and administration of education in the Gold Coast from 1765 to 1865. *M.A. 1949 London, Institute of Education*

Barter, A.
The teaching of history. *M.A. 1926 Liverpool*

Barth, A. W.
Cimon and Themistocles: a comparison and a contrast. *M.A. 1907 London*

Bartholomew, K.
A population study of Aust Agder fylke (county), Norway. *M.Sc. 1949 London, University College*

Bartleet, E. B.
Expositions of Philippians ii.5-13; St. Luke iv.1-14; St. John viii.36-47. *D.D. 1915 Oxford*

Bartleet, E. B.
1. Growth of the doctrine of Jesus Christ in the Pauline Epistles. 2. The doctrine of the future life. *B.D. 1902 Oxford*

Bartlett, D.B.
An investigation into the attitudes of boys and girls towards the content of, and the methods of, teaching geography in grammar schools. *M.A. 1948 London, Institute of Education*

Bartlett, E. M.
The analysis of some types of aesthetic judgment. *Ph.D. 1934 London, Bedford College*

Bartlett, M. G.
The land utilisation and agriculture of Somerset. *M.Sc. 1945 Bristol*

Bartlett, P. B.
A textual and critical study of Wordsworth's *An evening walk* and *Descriptive sketches. B.Litt. 1928 Oxford*

Bartlett, R. J.
The history of a list of nonsense syllables committed to memory in 1912, being a preliminary enquiry into the process of forgetting. *M.Sc. 1921 London*

Barton, E. V.
An essay on the method of Henry James. *M.A. 1950 Reading*

Barton, E. W.
The turnpike trusts of Wales: a study in transport economics. *M.A. 1915 Wales*

Barton, F.
Archbishop Winchelsey: a sketch of a critical period in the relations between Church and State. *M.A. 1912 London*

Barton, F. T.
Shakespeare criticism in France in the nineteenth century. *B.Litt. 1919 Oxford*

Bartrum, E.
1. The use and authority of the Apocrypha. 2. The occasion and purpose of the Epistle to the Romans. *B.D. & D.D. 1885 Oxford*

Barua, A.
The editing of the *Petakopadesa*, with critical apparatus and commentary. *Ph.D. 1933 London, School of Oriental and African Studies*

Barua, B.
A cultural history of Assam of the early period, *c.*400 A.D.-1200 A.D. *Ph.D. 1947 London, School of Oriental and African Studies*

Barún, R. de *see* De Barún, R.

Barwise, W.
The syntax of *Le Charroi de Nîmes. M.A. 1936 Manchester*

Basdekas, H.
The teaching of the Eastern Church with regard to the Holy Eucharist in the sixteenth and seventeenth centuries. *B.Litt. 1914 Oxford*

Baskomb, C. G. H.
1. The atonement. 2. The spiritual body. *B.D. 1905 Oxford*

Baslow, W. H.
1. Infant baptism. 2. The commission given to those receiving the order of Priesthood in the Church of England. *B.D. & D.D. 1895 Oxford*

Bassett, G. W.
An experimental study of mental processes involved in the comprehension of historical narrative. *Ph.D. 1940 London, Institute of Education*

Bassett, H. C.
Golyddan; ei fywyd a'i weithiau, gyda chyfeiriad arbennig at yr arwrgerdd Gymraeg(Golyddan; his life and his works, with special reference to the Welsh epic). *M.A. 1935 Wales*

Bassett, J. G. Tilney- *see* Tilney-Bassett, J. G.

Bassett, T. M.
A study of local government in Wales under the Commonwealth with special reference to its relations with the central authority. *M.A. 1941 Wales*

Bassett, W. G.
The Caribbean in international politics, 1670-1707. *Ph.D. 1934 London, King's College*

Bastable, J. D.
An analysis of belief. *Ph.D. 1945 National University of Ireland*

Bastable, J. D.
Problem of belief. *M.A. 1938 National University of Ireland*

Bastable, P. K.
Does man aspire naturally to the vision of God?. *Ph.D. 1945 National University of Ireland*

Bastable, P. K.
Relation. *M.A. 1939 National University of Ireland*

Baster, A. S. J.
Financial integration within the British Empire. *M.Comm. 1930 London, School of Economics and Political Science*

Baster, A. S. J.
The history and present position of English banks operating in foreign countries. *Ph.D. 1934 London, External Degree*

Bastin, A. G.
The place of educational visits in the teaching of science in primary (junior) and secondary schools, and the facilities for such visits in London and other English cities. *M.A. 1948 Bristol*

Bastow, A.
A metrical examination of the Middle High German poem *Meier Helmbrecht. M.A. 1935 Leeds*

Basu, A.
A survey and critical study of some experiments in 'national' education in India. *M.A. 1932 London, King's College*

Basu, J.
Culture-contact among the Plains Gars of eastern Bengal. *Ph.D. 1947 London, University College*

Basu, L.
Indian writers of English verse. *B.Litt. 1926 Oxford*

Basu, P.
The relations between Oudh and the East India Company from 1785 to 1801. *Ph.D. 1938 London, School of Oriental and African Studies*

Basu, R. *see* Bannerjea, R.

Basu, T.
Economic and political relations of India with Iran and Afghanistan since 1900. *M.Litt. 1942 Cambridge*

Batcheler, L. E. M.
The South Sea Company and the Assiento. *M.A. 1924 London*

Batchelor, F. S.
The influence of Roman law on the development of the consensual contracts in the law of Scotland. *Ph.D. 1938 Glasgow*

Batchelor, G. E.
The acting tradition in England between 1800 and 1830, with special reference to Shakespeare's plays. *Ph.D. 1939 London, King's College*

Batchelor, G. E.
A study of the manuscripts of theatrical and dramatic interest preserved in the British Museum, 1660-1720. *M.A. 1929 London*

Bate, E.
Les neólogismes de *Notre Dame* de Victor Hugo. *M.A. 1924 Leeds*

Bate, F.
The Declaration of Indulgence of 1672, including an introduction tracing the development of the question of toleration from 1660 to 1672. *B.Litt. 1907 Oxford*

Bate, F.
Wolsey's colleges at Oxford and Ipswich. *M.A. 1905 Liverpool*

Bateman, J. V.
The nature and function of the categories in the philosophy of Immanuel Kant, James Ward, S. Alexander. *Ph.D. 1933 Edinburgh*

Bates, E. P.
Some aspects of the work of the Anglo-Latin twelfth century satirists: the loan words in Gothic, with some account of the pronunciation of that language. *M.A. 1910 London*

Bateson, F. H.
Dissertation sur *La chanson de Floovant. M.A. 1932 Leeds*

Bateson, F. H.
La chanson de Floovant: étude critique et édition. *D. Litt. 1938 Leeds*

Bateson, F. N. W.
Post-Restoration comedy, 1700-25. *B.Litt. 1926 Oxford*

Batho, E. C.
James Hogg: the Ettrick Shepherd. *M.A. 1920 London*

Bathurst, G. C.
An examination of the learning process, with special reference to the Gestalt psychology. *Ph.D. 1939 London, Institute of Education*

Bathurst, M. E.
Indefeasibility of registered titles: a comparative study. *Ph.D. 1949 Cambridge*

Batrawi, A. M. el *see* El Batrawi, A. M.

Batrik, A. H. M. El- *see* El-Batrik, A. H. M.

Batt, F. R.
Interference with contract and unfair competition. *M.A. 1933 Wales*

Batten, C. R.
The problem of the will considered with special reference to the English school of idealists and the relation of their conclusions briefly to the doctrine of grace. *M.A. 1927 London*

Batten, T. C.
The teaching of elementary mathematics in secondary schools. *M.A. 1934 Liverpool*

Batterberry, R. P. J.
Mixed education in Ireland 1824-1884. *Ph.D. 1939 National University of Ireland*

Battersby, W. J.
St. John Baptist de la Salle: the work of the Brothers of the Christian Schools, and its significance in the history of English education. *Ph.D. 1947 London, Birkbeck College*

Baty, T.
The law of contraband with reference to transit to neutral ports. *D.C.L. 1901 Oxford*

Baudewyns, J. J. J.
The determinants of the level of employment. *B.Phil. 1947 Oxford*

Bauer, M. A.
An analysis of the influence of social conditions on different causes of infant deaths and on stillbirths and neonatal deaths in county boroughs of England and Wales during the years 1928-1938. *M.Sc. 1944 Birmingham*

Baumol, W. J.
The theory of welfare and control. *Ph.D. 1949 London, School of Economics and Political Science*

Baxter, F. C.
Criticism and appreciation of Elizabethan drama: Dryden to Swinburne. *Ph.D. 1933 Cambridge*

Baxter, J.
The organization of the brewing industry. *Ph.D. 1945 London, External Degree*

Baxter, W. T.
The House of Hancock, business in Boston, 1724 to 1775. *Ph.D. 1946 Edinburgh*

Baykov, A. M.
Studies in the development of the national economy of the U.S.S.R. *Ph.D. 1942 Birmingham*

Bayley, C. C.
Judicial investigations under the Dictum of Kenilworth, Cambridgeshire. *M.A. 1929 Manchester*

Baylis, G.
The factory system and the factory acts, 1802-1850. *M.A. 1930 Birmingham*

Bazbur Rehman, M.
Jahiz: his life and work. *Ph.D. 1923 Cambridge*

Bazeley, M. L.
The Forest of Dean in its relations with the Crown during the twelfth and thirteenth centuries. *M.A. 1911 London*

Bazire, J.
An edition of the metrical life of St. Robert of Knaresborough. *M.A. 1949 Leeds*

Beach, D. M.
The phonetics of Pekingese. *Ph.D. 1923 London*

Beach, D. M.
The phonetics of the Hottentot language. *D.Litt. 1932 London, University College*

Beacham, A.
The development of organized marketing in the British coal industry. *M.A. 1937 Liverpool*

Beacham, A.
The problem of industrial restriction: a comparative study of industrial reorganization in the British basic industries, 1929-39. *Ph.D. 1942 Belfast*

Beaglehole, C. H.
Revival of Anglicanism during the Restoration period, with special reference to the diocese of Durham. *M.Litt. 1947 Durham*

Beaglehole, E.
Rights in property: a psychological study. *Ph.D. 1931 London, School of Economics and Political Science*

Beaglehole, J. C.
The Royal instructions to colonial governors, 1783-1854: a study in British colonial policy. *Ph.D. 1929 London*

Beale, W. J.
The religious conception of intermediary beings in relation to the idea of causation. *Ph.D. 1935 Sheffield*

Beales, A. C. F.
The foreign policy of Wellington, 1828-30. *M.A. 1927 London*

Beard, D. L.
Origin and early development of Presbyterianism in Virginia. *Ph.D. 1932 Edinburgh*

Beard, R.
The East India Co. crisis (1770-1773). *M.A. 1928 Birmingham*

Beard, R. M.
An investigation into the interests and personal attitudes of adolescents educated in schools organized according to the Dalton Plan. *M.A. 1949 London, Institute of Education*

Beardwood, A.
The legal and economic relations between alien merchants and the central government in England, 1350-77. *D.Phil. 1929 Oxford*

Beardwood, A.
The position of foreign merchants in England during the reign of Edward III, mainly from the legal standpoint. *B.Litt. 1924 Oxford*

Beasley, B. R.
The place of the congregation in liturgical worship. *M.A. 1945 Leeds*

Beasley, I. M.
The dramatic art of Ostrovsky. *Ph.D. 1931 London, External Degree*

Beaumont, E.
The Catholic revival in French literature from Huysmans to Péguy. *M.A. 1940 London, King's College*

Beaumont, E.
Léon Bloy. *Ph.D. 1943 London, External Degree*

Beaumont, H.
Great Civil War in Shrewsbury. *M.A. 1934 Sheffield*

Beaven, R. H.
The psychology of conscience, with special reference to its relation to the Christian doctrine of man. *M.Litt. 1939 Cambridge*

Beaver, S. H.
The geography of the iron industry of Northamptonshire, Rutland and South Lincolnshire. *M.A. 1931 London, University College*

Bebb, E. D.
John Wesley's religious teaching and his social and economic views. *B.Litt. 1944 Oxford*

Bebb, E. D.
Protestant nonconformity and some social and economic questions, 1660-1800. *Ph.D. 1934 Sheffield*

Bebb, L. J. M.
1. The ministry of John the Baptist. 2. The sources, purpose, and arrangement of St. Luke's Gospel. *B.D. 1899 Oxford*

Bebb, W. A.
The contribution of Wales to the British Empire in the sixteenth and seventeenth centuries. *M.A. 1920 Wales*

Bebbington, P. S.
Samuel Garbett, 1717-1803, a Birmingham pioneer. *M.Com. 1938 Birmingham*

Beck, L. J.
The elements of representation: a critical study of the philosophy of O. Hamelin. *D.Phil. 1936 Oxford*

Beck, R.
The sources of Grillparzer's *Ein Bruderzwist in Habsburg* (1849). *M.A. 1926 London*

Beck, R.
Studies in the development of the Berlin salons during 1800-1820. *Ph.D. 1928 London*

Beckerlegge, O. A.
Le secré de secrez of Pierre d'Abernun; a critical edition. *Ph.D. 1938 Sheffield*

Becket, E. M.
The development of education in Nottingham during the nineteenth and the early twentieth century with special reference to the history of University College. *M.A. 1922 London*

Becket, E. M.
The history of education and educational institutions in Nottinghamshire, excluding the City of Nottingham, from 1800 to 193. *Ph.D. 1936 London, External Degree*

Beckett, J. C.
The relations between the Irish Presbyterians and the government from the Declaration of Indulgence (1687) to the repeal of the Test Act (1780). *M.A. 1942 Belfast*

Beckh, G. F.
Goethe as a political thinker. *M.A. 1918 Bristol*

Beckinsale, R. P.
A geographical survey of the textile industries of the West of England. *D.Phil. 1949 Oxford*

Beckwith, F.
Peter Desmaizeaux (1673?-1745): life and works. *M.A. 1936 Leeds*

Beddis, L. G.
Education in some ideal commonwealths. *M.Ed. 1932 Manchester*

Beddow, J. F. H.
The history of the fourth Parliament of William III. *B.Litt. 1913 Oxford*

Beddy, J. P.
Profits. *D.Econ.Sc. 1941 National University of Ireland*

Bedekar, S. K.
Production and international exchange of wheat, with reference to the economic geography of India, and a further reference to world wheat position. *M.Sc. 1936 Wales*

Bedell, B. J.
An investigation into the mental abilities of the children of Trinidad. *Ph.D. 1950 Edinburgh*

Bedell, G. W.
Residence of an individual for purposes of income tax. *LL.M. 1932 Cambridge*

Bedson, C. M.
Jean-Christophe et la musique. *M.A. 1942 Birmingham*

Bedwell, F.
1. That the doctrine of a future state did form part of the revelation to man in the times preceding our Lord's birth. 2. That the so-called doctrine of final perseverance can be established by sufficient evidence from Holy Scripture, and is held by the Church of England in her seventeenth Article. *B.D. 1874 Oxford*

Bee, H. H. C.
The origin and development of prayer and its place in the life of primitive peoples. *M.A. 1942 Leeds*

Beebe, H. T.
1. Genesis iv.2; Hebrews xi.4; xii.24: Abel's sacrifice. 2. St. Matthew xxvii.5-7; Romans vi.9: the Resurrection of Jesus and its effect on believers. 3. Romans viii.1-4, 14-17, 29-39: the work of the Holy Spirit. *D.D. 1893 Oxford*

Beebe, H. T.
1. On justification by faith. 2. On Hades. *B.D. 1889 Oxford*

Beebee, E. M.
John Pym. *M.A. 1915 Birmingham*

Beeby, C. E.
1. The future life in light of the theory of evolution. 2. The doctrine of salvation. *B.D. 1888 Oxford*

Beeby, C. E.
The relation between the simultaneous constituents in an act of skill. *Ph.D. 1927 Manchester*

Beech, E.
The social, economic and administrative development of Chadderton, 1847-1914. *M.A. 1949 Manchester*

Beech, E. A.
Economics and organization of the glass improvement industry in England. *M.Sc. 1940 London, External Degree*

Beecher, L. J.
Language teaching in Kikuyu schools. *M.A. 1937 London, Institute of Education*

Beeching, H. C.
1. On the doctrine of the atonement in the Old Testament. 2. On the doctrine of the atonement in the New Testament. *B.D. & D.D. 1911 Oxford*

Beemer, H.
Rank among the Swazi of the protectorate. *Ph.D. 1943 London, School of Economics and Political Science*

Beer, E. S. de see de Beer, E. S.

Beer, P.
The sermons of Henry King. *B.Litt. 1944 Oxford*

Beers, W. A.
The principles of individual right. *LL.D. 1944 Dublin, Trinity College*

Beese, F. K.
The slave in ancient comedy. *M.A. 1939 Wales*

Beese, M. A.
A critical edition of the poems printed by John Donne the Younger in 1660 as written by William Herbert, Earl of Pembroke, and Sir Benjamin Ruddier. *B.Litt. 1935 Oxford*

Beeston, A. F. L.
The preparation of a handbook of south Arabian epigraphy. *D.Phil. 1937 Oxford*

Beeston, G. R.
The development of the historical novel from 1830 to 1880. *M.A. 1929 Wales*

Behrens, E. B.
The International Labour Office (League of Nations): certain aspects of international administration raised in connection with the early development of the International Labour Organization. *Ph.D. 1924 London*

Beilby, O. J.
The productivity of labour and standards of living in British agriculture, and a comparison with selected countries abroad. *B.Litt. 1935 Oxford*

Belasco, P. S.
Authority in Church and State, with special reference to the seventeenth century. *Ph.D. 1928 London*

Belasco, P. S.
The political ideas of the Quakers of the seventeenth century. *M.Sc. 1926 London*

Belgrave, M. D.
A sketch of the progress of English Shakespearian study, with special reference to the nineteenth century. *M.A. 1908 London*

Bell, A. E.
The physical and astronomical work of Christian Huygens considered in relation to that of his contemporaries. *Ph.D. 1942 London, University College*

Bell, A. E.
A study of simple harmonic motion, 1450-1850. *M.Sc. 1938 London, University College*

Bell, C. C.
An investigation of the attitude of training college students towards the importance of good speech. *M.A. 1934 London, Institute of Education*

Bell, C. G.
A text of Edward Fairfax's *Eclogues*, with an introductory essay on Fairfax's place in the history of English poetry. *B.Litt. 1939 Oxford*

Bell, G. E.
Martin Luther as an educator. *M.Ed. 1949 Durham*

Bell, H. G.
The law of domicile in relation to death duties. *LL.D. 1914 London*

Bell, I. C.
The overseas trade of the United Kingdom, with special reference to trade with the dominions and trade policies since 1919. *M.A. 1941 Wales*

Bell, J. G.
The technique of the Odyssey. *M.A. 1938 Manchester*

Bell, L. H.
The respective spheres of the State and of voluntary organizations in the prevention and relief of poverty in London at the present day. *M.A. 1935 London, School of Economics and Political Science*

Bell, M. H.
The life and writings of Nicolas de Clémanges: a study in repercussions of the Schism and Conciliar Movement. *M.A. 1948 London, Bedford College*

Bellamy, D. S.
Religious teaching in secondary schools. *M.Ed. 1932 Leeds*

Bellamy, J.
Exegeses of: John xxi.20, etc.; John v.6; Matthew vi.11. *D.D. 1872 Oxford*

Beller, E. A.
The diplomatic relations between England and Germany during the Thirty Years' War, with an introductory chapter on their relations between 1603 and 1618. *D.Phil. 1923 Oxford*

Bellot, H. H. L.
Bargains with money-lenders. *D.C.L. 1906 Oxford*

Belmore, H. W.
Rilke's craftsmanship: an analysis of his poetic style. *M.A. 1947 London, External Degree*

Beloff, M.
Public order and popular disturbances in England, 1689-1714. *B.Litt. 1937 Oxford*

244

Belshaw, C. S.
Economic aspects of culture contact in eastern Melanesia, with special reference to the influence of a monetary economy. *Ph.D. 1948 London, School of Economics and Political Science*

Belshaw, H.
Agricultural fluctuations. *Ph.D. 1926 Cambridge*

Belshaw, J. P.
Depression, recovery and reconstruction in New Zealand, 1929-1937: the effects of economic depression, of economic nationalism and of changes in world economic trends upon a pastoral-producing country. *Ph.D. 1937 Manchester*

Belton, L. J.
An examination of the meaning and use of the term intuition. *M.A. 1946 Sheffield*

Belton, L. J.
The psychology of religious belief. *M.A. 1927 Birmingham*

Beneragama, D. C. P.
A critical edition of the *Batavataya*, with an essay on its position in the Pali grammatical literature. *M.A. 1949 London, School of Oriental and African Studies*

Benham, F. C.
The prosperity of Australia: an economic analysis. *Ph.D. 1928 London*

Benjamin, E. R.
The interpretation of Plato's *Timaeus*. *Ph.D. 1928 Edinburgh*

Benjamin, V. D.
Some representative versions of the Faust-theme in English literature. *M.A. 1936 Manchester*

Benn, M. B.
The romantic element in the prose-works of Hermann Hesse. *M.A. 1948 London, University College*

Benn, T. V.
Bibliographie critique des ouvrages de Louis Sébastien Mercier. *Ph.D. 1925 Leeds*

Bennett, E.
An edition of the prologues to Gavin Douglas's *Eneados*. *B.Litt. 1938 Oxford*

Bennett, E.
The supernatural in German drama of the early nineteenth century. *M.A. 1919 Birmingham*

Bennett, H. J. R.
Social aspects of the Chartist movement. *M.A. 1927 Birmingham*

Bennett, H. R.
Literary parody and burlesque of the seventeenth and eighteenth centuries. *M.A. 1914 London*

Bennett, J.
Empedocles, the poet; his style and metre. *Ph.D. 1940 Dublin, Trinity College*

Bennett, J. A. W.
The history of Old English and Old Norse studies in England from the time of Francis Junius till the end of the eighteenth century. *D.Phil. 1938 Oxford*

Bennett, J. P.
A geographical study of the port of Antwerp. *M.A. 1933 Liverpool*

Bennett, L. C.
A study of the influence of politics on poetry during the years 1640 to 1660. *M.A. 1924 London*

Bennett, L. G.
The development and present structure of the horticultural industry of Middlesex and the London region. *Ph.D. 1950 Reading*

Bennett, T. F.
Shaw's contribution to the theory and practice of modern English drama. *M.A. 1929 Wales*

Bennett, W.
An investigation into mathematical abilities most closely related to logical and critical thinking. *M.A. 1948 London, Institute of Education*

Bennison, J.
Medieval fairs in England. *M.A. 1911 London*

Bennison, W.
The law of the foreshore and the right of access thereto. *LL.D. 1914 London*

Benoy, J.
1. The sacrificial worship of the Hebrews. 2. The miraculous element in the Gospels. *B.D. 1891 Oxford*

Benson, E.
A history of education in York, 1780-1902. *Ph.D. 1933 London, External Degree*

Bentham, M. A.
French contributions to the science of heat in the first half of the nineteenth century. *M.Sc. 1928 London*

Bentham, R.
The city of Wakefield: a study of the growth and functions of an urban settlement. *M.A. 1939 London, University College*

Bentley, E. R.
The contribution of modern psychology to literary criticism. *B.Litt. 1939 Oxford*

Bentley, G. E.
Studies in the theatrical companies and actors of Elizabethan times, with special reference to the period 1616-1642. *Ph.D. 1930 London, East London College*

Bentley, N. P.
The indebtedness of Vergil to Varro in the composition of the *Georgics*: a study in parallelism. *M.A. 1929 Manchester*

Benton, J. K.
Recent psychological theories of the origin of religion. *Ph.D. 1934 Edinburgh*

Benton, S.
The barony of Odysseus. *B.Litt. 1933 Oxford*

Berbiers, J. D.
Les idées de Montesquieu sur la religion. *M.A. 1929 Liverpool*

Beresford, J. R.
The theory of conscience or moral sense, as found in some eighteenth century writers. *M.A. 1914 Liverpool*

Bergerhoff, S.
Historical studies in the syntax and phraseology of present-day English. *Ph.D. 1945 Leeds*

Bergin, C.
Francis Thompson: a study of his relation to George Herbert, Henry Vaughan and Richard Crashaw. *M.A. 1948 National University of Ireland*

Berkowitz, S.
An edition, with introduction, critical notes, and translation, of the commentary of Rabbi David Kimhi on Amos. *Ph.D. 1939 Cambridge*

Berlas, A. B.
An enquiry into the development of training of teachers. *M.A. 1949 London, Institute of Education*

Bermingham, R.
The rise of individualism, with special reference to Locke. *M.A. 1937 National University of Ireland*

Bernard, G. V.
Primary education in the Central Provinces and Berar. *M.Ed. 1939 Leeds*

Bernard, M. I. D. J. A. A.
Juan del Encina and the origin of the Spanish drama. *M.A. 1931 London, King's College*

Bernardin, J. B.
The doctrine of the Holy Spirit in St. Luke and Acts. *B.Litt. 1925 Oxford*

Berneaud, J. M.
A portrayal of childhood in German fiction from Keller to Carcesa. *Ph.D. 1950 Saint Andrew's*

Bernhard, R. C.
The control of money. *M.Sc. 1936 London, School of Economics and Political Science*

Bernstein, E.
Quickness and intelligence: an enquiry concerning the existence of a general speed factor. *Ph.D. 1922 London*

Berridge, A. R.
A factorial analysis of ability in school physics. *M.A. 1947 London, Institute of Education*

Berrigan, A. M.
Contribution in theory and practice to the English novel, 1859-1914. *Ph.D. 1931 Dublin, Trinity College*

Berry, C. A. F.
The villas of Roman Britain, and their place in the life of the province. *Ph.D. 1949 London, External Degree*

Berry, J. B.
The temptations of Jesus, with special reference to the history of their interpretation. *Ph.D. 1930 Edinburgh*

Berryman, M.
Lyons as a market of ideas from B.C. 43-1307 A.D. *M.A. 1910 London*

Berthen, E. A. J.
The theory of personality in modern philosophy from Kant to Lotze. *M.A. 1911 London*

Bertram, I. D.
The cult of Isis in Italy under the Empire. *M.A. 1934 London, Bedford College*

Best, A. E.
Berkeley's argument against Newtonian mathematics and its metaphysical implications. *Ph.D. 1948 London, King's College*

Best, A. E.
The doctrine of knowledge of John Locke and contemporary English Platonism. *M.A. 1940 Manchester*

Best, A. M.
The financing and organization of the household of the Queens of England during the first part of the fourteenth century. *M.A. 1916 London*

Best, E.
One body in Christ: a study in the relationship of the Church to Christ in the teaching of the Apostle Paul. *Ph.D. 1948 Belfast*

Best, I.
A study of the archetypes in children's fantasies. *M.A. 1949 Leeds*

Best, S. E. J.
The East Riding of Yorkshire: a study in agricultural geography. *Ph.D. 1927 Leeds*

Best, S. H.
The poetry of John Davidson, 1857-1909. *M.A. 1931 Birmingham*

Beston, T.
The psychosis and the psychoneuroses. *M.D. 1920 London*

Bethall, S. L.
The winter's tale: a study. *M.A. 1950 Wales*

Betteridge, H. T.
Macpherson's *Ossian* in the works of Johann Gottfried v. Herder. *M.A. 1933 Birmingham*

Betts, E. A.
The Johannine doctrine of the Holy Spirit. *Ph.D. 1932 Edinburgh*

Beukes, P.
State and culture, with special reference to Fichte and von Humboldt. *B.Litt. 1936 Oxford*

Bevan, T.
The industrial development of the Llynfi, Ogmore and Garw valleys, with special reference to transport facilities in the are. *M.A. 1928 Wales*

Bevan, T. H.
The use of poetry by Thomas Hardy. *M.A. 1936 Wales*

Bévenot, N. M.
Notes sur un choix d'oeuvres dramatiques au dix-neuvième siècle. *M.A. 1913 Liverpool*

Beveridge, I. M.
A study of the literary works of the Comte de Gobineau. *M.A. 1923 London*

Beveridge, W. H.
Unemployment in Britain, with special reference to the period from 1909 to the present time. *D.Sc. 1930 London, School of Economics and Political Science*

Bevers, C.
The treatment of some scientific activities in the senior school. *M.Ed. 1935 Leeds*

Beverstock, A. G.
An analysis of the abilities, interests and qualities of personality of a representative group of engineering apprentices. *M.A. 1946 London, Institute of Education*

Bevington, S. M.
Factors in occupational maladjustment: a comparative study of the careers of employed and unemployed lads in a typical London district. *Ph.D. 1933 London, External Degree*

Bewkes, E. G.
John McLeod Campbell, theologian: his theological development and trial and a new interpretation of his theory of the atonement. *Ph.D. 1924 Edinburgh*

Bey, A. M. K. el *see* El Bey, A. M. K.

Beyleveld, G. P.
The British fruit market: with special reference to South Africa. *M.Sc. 1940 London, School of Economics and Political Science*

Beynon, B. L.
The conflict between rationalism and romanticism in the works of Ernest Renan. *M.Litt. 1936 Cambridge*

Beynon, O.
The lead mining industry of Cardiganshire, 1700-1830. *M.A. 1938 Wales*

Beyon, K. M.
The oracle at Dodona. *M.A. 1928 Bristol*

Bhai, H. S.
An historical survey of the financial policy (with its economic and general results) of the Government of India, from 1857 to 1900. *Ph.D. 1934 Leeds*

Bhai, H. S.
The project method, illustrated from the history of India during the British period. *M.Ed. 1935 Leeds*

Bhaldraithe, T. MacD. de *see* De Bhaldraithe, T. MacD.

Bhalla, S.
The psychological needs of children: a critical survey with a discussion of confirmatory evidence. *M.A. 1949 London, Institute of Education*

Bhan, J. N.
The problem of federation in India, with special reference to economic relations. *Ph.D. 1949 London, School of Economics and Political Science*

Bhan, R. K.
Recent economic depression in India, with reference to agriculture and rural life. *Ph.D. 1940 London, School of Economics and Political Science*

Bhan, S.
A study of modern principles of mental hygiene, with special reference to Indian education. *M.A. 1937 London, Institute of Education*

Bhanot, V. H.
An investigation into the possibility of measuring attitude towards mathematics by means of a test based on values and situations. *M.A. 1949 London, Institute of Education*

Bharucha, K. B.
The history of the cotton-mill industry in western India. *Ph.D. 1927 London*

Bhat, V. G.
Studies in the Sanskrit drama. *Ph.D. 1933 Cambridge*

Bhatt, G. U.
The system of education in Germany since the war. *M.Ed. 1931 Leeds*

Bhatt, J. M.
The function of scepticism in the development of knowledge. *Ph.D. 1934 London, University College*

Bhatt, R. S.
Some social aspects of the minority problem in India. *M.A. 1936 London, School of Economics and Political Science*

Bhatt, V. M.
Exchange control and clearing agreements in 1931-37. *M.Sc. 1939 London, School of Economics and Political Science*

Bhattacharya, B. C.
Development of social and political ideas in Bengal, 1858-84. *Ph.D. 1934 London, School of Oriental and African Studies*

Bhattacharya, S.
Some philosophical problems in the *Bhagavata Purāna*. *Ph.D. 1947 London, School of Oriental and African Studies*

Bhuyan, S. K.
East India Company's relations with Assam, 1771 to 1826. *Ph.D. 1938 London, School of Oriental and African Studies*

Bibby, E.
The puritan classical movement of Elizabeth's reign. *M.A. 1929 Manchester*

Bibby, S. D.
The causal situation with regard to personal behaviour. *M.A. 1948 Birmingham*

Bick, Y. A.
The chemical studies of Michael Lomonossov, 1711-1765. *M.Sc. 1949 London, University College*

Bickersteth, F. M. E.
An attempt to trace the course of the development of some mental capacities by the application of mental tests to children from five to fifteen years of age. *Cert.Sc. 1916 Oxford*

Bickersteth, M. E.
Psychochromaesthesia: an investigation of the nature and development of coloured thinking in childhood. *Ph.D. 1923 Edinburgh*

Bickersteth, S.
1. The resurrection. 2. Christianity necessary to a true view of personality. *B.D. & D.D. 1905 Oxford*

Bicknell, E. J.
1. The Christian idea of sin and original sin. 2. The doctrine of the Trinity in the early Fathers. *B.D. & D.D. 1923 Oxford*

Bidder, H. J.
1. The scope and method of rational theology. 2. The proof of the being of God. *B.D. 1877 Oxford*

Bier, E. S.
The education of women in England, 1603-1715. *B.Litt. 1928 Oxford*

Biesheuvel, S.
The nature of temperament: a study of some fundamental factors. *Ph.D. 1933 Edinburgh*

Bigby, D. A.
The relations between England and France during the Great Rebellion: the Civil War. *M.A. 1912 London*

Bigg, C.
1. Grace and free will in reference to the language of Scripture and to some later theories. 2. The Epistle to the Galatians. *B.D. & D.D. 1876 Oxford*

Biggar, H. P.
The constitutional history of Canada in its earlier days; and the early trading companies of New France. *B.Litt. 1899 Oxford*

Biggs, A.
A geographical study of water resources of England and Wales and their use in large-scale supplies of piped water to cities. *M.Sc. 1949 London, School of Economics and Political Science*

Biggs, C. R. D.
Expositions of: Philippians i.3-26; Philippians i.27-ii.11; Philippians iii.1-21. *D.D. 1900 Oxford*

Biggs, C. R. W.
1. The doctrinal significance of the Lord's Supper. 2. The Gospel according to St. Luke in its literary relations to the Gospels according to the other Synoptists and to St. John. *B.D. 1896 Oxford*

Bilbrough, H.
Galsworthy's conception of comedy. *M.A. 1948 Manchester*

Bilgerig, N. G.
Hilaire Belloc; a literary study. *M.A. 1949 National University of Ireland*

Billen, A. V.
An examination of the Munich and Wurtzburg fragments of the old Latin Pentateuch. *Ph.D. 1923 London*

Billig, L.
Clausulae and Platonic chronology. *M.A. 1920 London*

Billing, G. C.
Some aspects of protection and its relation to economic development in New Zealand. *Ph.D. 1934 London, School of Economics and Political Science*

Billingham, P. H.
The Civil War in Warwickshire, 1642-6, with an introduction on the representation of Warwickshire in the Long Parliament. *B.Litt. 1927 Oxford*

Billington, W. C. R.
The Prussian aristocracy in the social novels of Theodor Fontane. *M.A. 1946 Birmingham*

Binas, A. M.
Glossaire des vieux mots qu'on trouve dans *Le dit de Poissy*, poème écrit en avril 1400 par Christine de Pisan. *M.A. 1926 Leeds*

Binchy, W. F.
Study of early English charters. *M.A. 1929 National University of Ireland*

Bindley, T. H.
1. The Chalcedonian definition of the faith, and the inter-relation of the four great heresies on the Incarnation. 2. The historic value of the episcopate in the early Church as a witness and a guarantee. *B.D. 1893 Oxford*

Bindoff, S. T.
Great Britain and the Scheldt, 1814-1839. *M.A. 1933 London, University College*

Bingham, C. R.
Lessing's *Laokoon* and its English predecessors. *M.A. 1938 London, University College*

Birch, A. H.
A comparison of the styles of Gaudentius of Brescia, the *De Sacramentis* (ascribed to St. Ambrose) and the *Disdascalia Apostolorum* or *Fragmenta Veronensia*. *Ph.D. 1924 London*

Birch, A. H.
The poems of Virgil considered in connection with the geography of Italy, including the natural features and animal and plant life. *M.A. 1912 Wales*

Birch, B. G.
A contribution to the study of Grimmelshausen. *M.A. 1932 Bristol*

Birch, R. S.
Psychological meaning with special reference to logical meaning. *Ph.D. 1927 Edinburgh*

Birch, T. W.
The development of industry and trade in the Middle Severn Valley. *M.Sc. 1933 London, External Degree*

Birchall, H.
Some economic aspects of the organisation and operation of commercial air transport. *Ph.D. 1936 London, External Degree*

Bird, C. H. Golding- *see* Golding-Bird, C. H.

Bird, D. M. G.
A review of fifteenth century church music in England, with special reference to the Pepys ms. 1236. *M.Litt. 1941 Cambridge*

Bird, G. Golding- *see* Golding-Bird, G.

Bird, R.
Civic factions in London and their relation to political parties, 1376-99. *M.A. 1922 London*

Birmingham, J.
The prose style of George Meredith. *M.A. 1927 Liverpool*

Birnie, M. B.
Jesus' teaching on man and modern psychological theories. *M.A. 1947 Bristol*

Biro, S. S.
The German policy of the pre-Fructidorian Directory. *D.Phil. 1929 Oxford*

Birrell, J. H.
British post-war trade with the British Commonwealth nations, expecially in its geographical aspects. *Ph.D. 1927 Edinburgh*

Birtwell, M. H.
Les idées politiques de George Sand. *M.A. 1926 Manchester*

Birtwhistle, T. M.
The development of abolitionism, 1807-23. *M.A. 1948 London, Birkbeck College*

Birtwistle, J. A.
A comparative study of the results of homogeneous and heterogeneous work in mental arithmetic. *M.A. 1936 London, Institute of Education*

Bishop, C. R.
A study of Pope's satire. *Ph.D. 1937 London, King's College*

Bishop, E. W.
Education in France during the Revolutionary and Napoleonic era (1789-1815). *M.A. 1927 London*

Bishop, E. W.
Education in the Commonwealth, 1642-60. *Ph.D. 1942 London, King's College*

Bishop, J.
The forms and psychology of worship in the Free Church tradition, with special reference to Methodism. *M.A. 1947 Bristol*

Bishop, J. S.
The historical geography of the Norfolk and Suffolk woollen industry. *M.A. 1929 London*

Bishop, N. R.
The problems and development of cartelization in the British tar industry. *Ph.D. 1944 London, External Degree*

Bishop, W. A. C.
Secondary school selection. *M.Sc. 1940 Wales*

Bisson, S. W.
Claude Fauchet's knowledge of Old French literature. *B.Litt. 1929 Oxford*

Black, A. M.
The educational work of Robert Owen. *Ph.D. 1949 Saint Andrew's*

Black, D.
The incidence of income taxes. *Ph.D. 1937 Glasgow*

Black, G. A.
Novalis, Friedrich von Hardenberg, in English translation. *Ph.D. 1936 London, University College*

Black, M.
An Aramaic approach to the Gospels and Acts. *D.Litt. 1944 Glasgow*

Black, M.
The theories of logical positivism. *Ph.D. 1939 London, University College*

Black, M. M.
The influence of the 'free place' scholarship on twentieth century education in England. *M.Ed. 1939 Manchester*

Black, R. D. C.
Study of the economic writings of S. Mountifort Longfield. *Ph.D. 1943 Dublin, Trinity College*

Black, W. S.
Education and the creation of a common culture. *M.Ed. 1937 Manchester*

Blackbird, E. W.
The poetry of Dante Gabriel Rossetti, with special reference to style. *M.A. 1934 Liverpool*

Blackburn, J. M.
An analysis of learning curves and of factors in economical learning. *Ph.D. 1934 Cambridge*

Blacker, C. P.
The conception of value in psychological medicine. *D.M. 1931 Oxford*

Blackett, J. F.
Fifty years of public health and social welfare in Bath, 1896-1945. *M.A. 1949 Bristol*

Blackman, E. C.
Marcion and his influence. *B.D. 1947 Cambridge*

Blackshaw, W.
The value and limitations of biological principles in social science. *B.Sc. 1914 Oxford*

Blackstone, B.
George Herbert and Nicholas Ferrar: a study of thought and imagery in Jacobean devotional literature. *Ph.D. 1936 Cambridge*

Blackwell, A. M.
An analysis of the factors entering into mathematical ability, with special reference to children of 11 and 12. *M.A. 1938 London, Institute of Education*

Blackwell, E.
The life, times and work of Erasmus Darwin. *M.A. 1949 London, Royal Holloway College*

Blacow, J.
The psychology of the unconscious, with special reference to mental disorder, its cause and cure. *M.A. 1936 Liverpool*

Blaghd, E. P. de   see De Blaghd, E. P.

Blair, A. F.
The economic, social, and administrative problem of the congested districts of Ireland. *M.Comm. 1930 National University of Ireland*

Blair, H. A.
Belief in beings superhuman and subhuman: an examination of the part played by this belief in the Patristic theology up to the Council of Nicaea. *B.D. 1945 Oxford*

Blair, W.
Risk, interest rates, and security prices. *B.Litt. 1938 Oxford*

Blake, A. H.
The history syllabus of the senior school, being a consideration of the principles of selection. *M.A. 1934 London, Institute of Education*

Blake, J. W.
International rivalry in West Africa (1454-1559). *M.A. 1935 London, King's College*

Blake, T. W. Jex-   see Jex-Blake, T. W.

Blake, W. J.
On the causes and course of the rebellion of 1549 in Devon and Cornwall. *M.A. 1909 London*

Blakeley, L.
Introduction and notes to the *Reves tale. M.A. 1946 Birmingham*

Blakeley, L.
Studies in the language of the Lindisfarne Gospels. *Ph.D. 1949 Birmingham*

Blakeway, C. E.
1. The consideration of our Lord's Messianic consciousness in the light of his use of the Old Testament. 2. A critical study of the pericope in St. John vii.53-viii.11. *B.D. & D.D. 1910 Oxford*

Blakey, D.
A study of the publications of the Minerva Press: 1790-1820. *Ph.D. 1933 London, King's College*

Blakey, K. A.
New Zealand's policy in international trade and its relation to employment policy. *M.Sc. 1947 London, School of Economics and Political Science*

Blakiston, H. E. D.
Expositions: Exodus xxiv.9-11; St.Luke xxii.17-20; Romans v.19. *D.D. 1907 Oxford*

Blakiston, H. E. D.
1. On the origin and affinities of the Lord's Supper and the Passover. 2. On the traces of Gentilism in Christianity. *B.D. 1901 Oxford*

Blanch, I. V.   see Harriss, I. V.

Blanshard, P. V.
Some metaphysical implications of the judgment. *B.Sc. 1920 Oxford*

Blatcher, M.
The working of the Court of King's Bench in the fifteenth century. *Ph.D. 1936 London, University College*

Blau, G. J.
The theory of futures trading with special reference to the marketing of wool. *Ph.D. 1942 London, School of Economics and Political Science*

Blaxter, K. L.
The maintenance of the winter milk supply during war-time. *Ph.D. 1944 Reading*

Bleby, M. L.
The rise and development of the pastoral, with special reference to the English pastoral. *M.A. 1906 Birmingham*

Blenkinsop, E. S.
Bürger's originality. *B.Litt. 1935 Oxford*

Blevin, W. P.
The ethical theory of Bishop Butler. *M.A. 1908 London*

Bligh, D. L.
Shakespeare's prose. *M.A. 1921 National University of Ireland*

Bliss, A. J.
Sir Orfeo: introduction, text, commentary, and glossary. *B.Litt. 1948 Oxford*

Bloch, M.
A critical translation of the *Ikkarim* of Joseph Albo, with a consideration of his philosophic system and a general survey of the teaching and disputations of Jewish theologians in regard to the question of what constitutes the articles of fundamentals of the Jewish faith. *M.A. 1930 Wales*

Blomfield, J. E.
The origins of Old English orthography, with special reference to the representation of the spirants and w. *B.Litt. 1935 Oxford*

Bloomer, D.
An investigation into the influence of written corrections of the work in arithmetic and English in a senior girls' school. *M.A. 1944 Liverpool*

Bloor, C.
The psychological doctrine of temperament. *M.A. 1925 London*

Blore, G. J.
Exegeses of: II Corinthians iii.4-11; 12-18; Ephesians i.3-14. *D.D. 1874 Oxford*

Blore, G. J.
1. The use of the word θυσιαστήριον and its Latin equivalent in primitive times. 2. The use of the word τράπεα and its Latin equivalent in primitive times. *B.D. 1874 Oxford*

Blore, R. P. H.
The principle of balance in the curriculum. *M.A. 1921 London*

Bluck, R. S. H.
The *Greater Alcibiades* attributed to Plato: an introduction and commentary, together with an appendix on the language and the style. *Ph.D. 1949 Edinburgh*

Blumberg, N. B.
The German Communist movement, 1918-1923. *D.Phil. 1950 Oxford*

Blundell, D. W.
Transport in the West Midlands from 1660 to 1840. *M.Com, 1933 Birmingham*

Blundell, H. J. Weld-   see Weld-Blundell, H. J.

Blundell, J. E.
The horticultural industries of Worcestershire. *M.Com. 1929 Birmingham*

Blunt, A. F.
The history of theories of painting in Italy and France, 1400-1700, with special reference to Poussin. *Ph.D. 1935 Cambridge*

Blunt, A. W. F.
1. The theology of Justin Martyr. 2. Justin Martyr and the New Testament canon. *B.D. 1918 Oxford*

Blyth, T. A.
1.The subjects and efficacy of holy baptism. 2. Theories opposed to the fact of the Resurrection of our Lord. *B.D. 1888 Oxford*

Blyth, T. A.
Exegeses of: I Samuel xiii.7-25 (The witch of Endor); Psalm xviii.7-17 (David's song of deliverance); Zechariah i.8,9,10; St. Matthew xvii.10, etc. (The guardianship of angels). *D.D. 1892 Oxford*

Blythe, K.
The tragedies of Thomas Goff. *M.A. 1940 Sheffield*

Blyton, M. H.
Paul the Deacon, and the *Historia Langobardorum. M.A. 1935 London, Birkbeck College*

Boase, A. M.
The fortunes of Montaigne. *Ph.D. 1930 Cambridge*

Boast, W. J.
Relations of Pope Gregory the Great with the churches in the Roman Empire of the East. *M.A. 1931 Birmingham*

Boaz, G. D.
The psychological role of the mother in the origin of the religious sentiment: a psychological study of mother-goddess cults, with special reference to India. *D.Phil. 1942 Oxford*

Boden, C. E.
The borough organization of Southampton in the sixteenth century. *M.A. 1920 London*

Boden, I.
History and development of company law in Great Britain and Ireland. *M.A. 1947 National University of Ireland*

Bodenham, R. J. W.
The growth and development of regional literature in the West Midlands. *M.A. 1932 Birmingham*

Bodgener, J. H.
The mystical element in Walt Whitman. *M.A. 1932 Liverpool*

Bodkin, A. M.
The subconscious factors of mental process considered in relation to thought. *M.A. 1902 Wales*

Bodkin, M. McD.
Shakespeare's history. *M.A. 1922 National University of Ireland*

Bodonheli, J.
John Knox's superintendents. *Ph.D. 1936 Aberdeen*

Body, A. H.
John Wesley and education. *M.Ed. 1935 Manchester*

Bogie, D. J.
An investigation into the preparation of consolidated statements for holding companies. *Ph.D. 1948 Edinburgh*

Bogomas, E.
The foreign policy of Soviet Russia in Europe, 1917-1939. *M.Sc. 1945 London, School of Economics and Political Science*

Bohannan, P. J.
A study of the symbolism of political authority in Africa. *B.Sc. 1949 Oxford*

Bolas, W.
An examination of the postulate that there is no improvement over the session in English language in the pre-senior part-time day courses at a technical school, involving the formulation of two equivalent tests in English. *M.A. 1948 Birmingham*

Bolgar, R. R.
The development of Hellenism during the fifteenth and sixteenth centuries. *Ph.D. 1940 Cambridge*

Bolshakoff, S.
The doctrine of the unity of the Church, with special reference to the works of Khomaikov and Moehler. *D.Phil. 1943 Oxford*

Bolsover, G. H.
Great Britain, Russia and the Eastern Question (1832-1841). *Ph.D. 1933 London, King's College*

Bolte, C. G.
The Soviet Question in British politics. *B.Litt. 1949 Oxford*

Boltiansky, S. R.
The application of the test from imagery to certain plays in the Beaumont-Fletcher canon with a view to ascertaining the shares therein of J. Fletcher and P. Massinger. *Ph.D. 1938 Manchester*

Bolton, C. A.
Bishop Scipio dei Ricci and the Synod of Pistoia: a critical survey. *B.Litt. 1937 Oxford*

Bolton, C. A.
Electrical engineering economics. *M.Sc. 1928 London*

Bolton, W. T. H.
The domestic policy of Robert Harley and the Tory Ministry from 1710-1714. *M.A. 1930 London, Bedford College*

Bond, B. H.
A psychological approach to the teaching of geometry. *M.A. 1935 Birmingham*

Bond, G.
The geology, climates and cultures of the Pleistocene period in Matabeleland, southern Rhodesia. *Ph.D. 1949 London, External Degree*

Bonifazi, C.
The attack on Christendom made by Kierkegaard and Nietzsche. *M.A. 1950 Bristol*

Bonnar, J. A. K.
On the incidence, causation, and treatment of juvenile delinquency. *M.Sc. 1948 Cambridge*

Bonnerjee, A.
A critical review of contemporary criticism of Burke's *Reflections on the Revolution in France*. *M.Sc. 1938 London, School of Economics and Political Science*

Bonsall, B. S.
Speeches of the states (The Kuo Yü): a translation with introduction and notes. *D.Litt. 1932 London, External Degree*

Bonser, A. H.
The inter-relation of the doctrine of the work of Christ and the person of Christ during the first five centuries of the Church. *B.D. 1948 Leeds*

Bonser, W.
A comparative study of magical practices among the Anglo-Saxons. *Ph.D. 1927 London*

Bonsey, A. W.
The sociology of religion, with special reference to the works of Professor Durkheim and other writers to *L'Année Sociologique*. *B.Litt. 1930 Oxford*

Booker, A.
A geographical study of wheat and the wheat trade in Europe. *B.Litt. 1929 Oxford*

Booker, H. S.
Certain aspects of food consumption, with special reference to milk. *M.Sc. 1938 London, School of Economics and Political Science*

Boon, E. P.
The land utilisation of Cheshire. *M.Sc. 1941 London, King's College*

Boone, G.
The Poor Law of 1601, with some consideration of modern developments of the poor law problem. *M.A. 1917 Birmingham*

Boorman, S. C.
The reputation of Tennyson from the date of his earliest work up to the present time. *M.A. 1935 London, Queen Mary College*

Booth, H.
A study of Robert Bridges and the influence of his thought and technique on modern poetry. *B.Litt. 1938 Oxford*

Booth, L. S.
The influence of the Youth Movement on German literature. *M.A. 1930 Leeds*

Booth, M.
The diplomatic relations between England and France during the years 1558-1564. *M.A. 1934 London, University College*

Booth, N. H.
Hours of work in the coal-mining industry of Great Britain since the early part of the nineteenth century, with special reference to Northumberland and Durham, and with an account of certain movements connected therewith. *B.Litt. 1930 Oxford*

Booth, R. L.
The German worker-poets. *M.A. 1943 Leeds*

Booth, W. S.
Vergil and Homer: a study of the fifth book of Vergil's *Aeneid*. *M.A. 1925 Manchester*

Booy, G. E. W.
Barthold Hennrich Brockes' translation of James Thomson's *Seasons* and the influence of the *Seasons* on descriptive native nature poetry in Germany, with special reference to the poetry of Brockes and Christian Ewald von Kleist's poem *Der Frühling*. *M.A. 1940 Bristol*

Borrah, M. I.
The life and works of Amire Hasan Dihlavi. *Ph.D. 1931 London, School of Oriental and African Studies*

Borthwick, T.
A contribution to the demography (including some remarks on the climate, hygienic, and other conditions) of South Australia. *M.D. 1891 Edinburgh*

Bose, A.
A study of English poetry from 1830 to 1850. *D.Phil. 1947 Oxford*

Bose, A. C.
Mysticism in poetry; a study of AE, W. B. Yeats and Rabindranath Tagore. *Ph.D. 1937 Dublin, Trinity College*

Bose, M.
An analysis of some case records from a London child guidance clinic. *M.A. 1947 London, Institute of Education*

Bose, R.
The Vedānta doctrine according to Nimbārka, with a translation of his *Bhāsya*, together with the supercommentary of Srīnivāsa. *D.Phil. 1937 Oxford*

Bosher, R. S.
The Laudian Party, 1649-1662, and its influence on the Church settlement of the Restoration. *Ph.D. 1949 Cambridge*

Bostock, E. B.
The spiritual outlook of Ralph Waldo Emerson. *Ph.D. 1948 Edinburgh*

Bostock, J. K.
A critical edition of *Meister Albertus Lere* with introduction and notes. *Ph.D. 1922 London*

Bostock, J. K.
Die Mittelhochdeutschen Uebersetzungen der Traktate des Albertanus Brixiensis. *B.Litt. 1924 Oxford*

Boswell, E.
The court stage, 1660-1702. *Ph.D. 1930 London, University College*

Boswell, K. C.
Southampton: a factor in the economic development of the Hampshire Basin. *M.Sc. 1936 London, External Degree*

Botting, J. G. G.
Some special aspects of British income tax. *M.Sc. 1945 London, External Degree*

Bottomley, H.
The popular element in the vocabulary and syntax of *L'Assommoir* of E. Zola, 1877. *M.A. 1931 Manchester*

Bottomore, T. B.
An examination of some recent theories of social progress. *M.Sc. 1949 London, School of Economics and Political Science*

Boughton, C. H. K.
1. On the nature of authority. 2. On the essential elements of ordination. *B.D. 1915 Oxford*

Boulton, M.
A study of William Richardson, with special reference to his Shakespearian criticism. *B.Litt. 1948 Oxford*

Bourbel, A. C. de. *see* de Bourbel, A. C.

Bourde, A. J. M. A.
The influence of England on the French 'Agronomes', 1750-1789. *Ph.D. 1949 Cambridge*

Bourke, J. V.
Banking and currency in Ireland. *M.Comm. 1933 National University of Ireland*

Bourne, D.
Robertson's position in drama. *M.A. 1931 London, University College*

Bourne, J. A.
The life and works of Gonzalo de Céspedes y Meneses, with bibliographical notes on the Spanish novel of the seventeenth century. *Ph.D. 1937 Cambridge*

Bourne, P. W. N.
Exegeses of: Acts xxvi.19-70; i.8; St.John xv.5. *D.D. 1887 Oxford*

Bouropoulos, N.
The judicial function in the modern state. *Ph.D. 1949 London, School of Economics and Political Science*

Boustead, H. W.
1. The dramatic structure of the Apocalypse. 2. The mystical interpretation of the Apocalypse. *B.D. & D.D. 1905 Oxford*

Bowden, L. D.
The theory of logical types. *B.Litt. 1950 Oxford*

Bowen, B. M.
Emily Brontë. *M.A. 1947 Birmingham*

Bowen, E.
Southwest Wales: a study of physical anthropological characters in correlation with various distributions. *M.A. 1926 Wales*

Bowen, E. M.
Aspects of taxation and expenditure in the United Kingdom, 1890-1914, with special reference to the growth of the social services. *M.A. 1934 Wales*

Bowen, J.
A study of *pays* as units of regional treatment: a comparison of France and England. *M.A. 1935 Liverpool*

Bowen, G.
Traddodiad llenyddol Deau Ceredigion, 1600-1850(The literary tradition of southern Cardiganshire, 1600-1850). *M.A. 1943 Wales*

Bower, I. M.
The place-names of Lindsey (north Lincolnshire). *Ph.D. 1940 Leeds*

Bower, P. A.
The balance of external payments of Nigeria during 1936. *B.Litt. 1946 Oxford*

Bower, W. G.
Early Greek thought on the life of the soul after death. *M.A. 1905 London*

Bowers, J. L.
The cosmology of Plato and the background of early Greek philosophy. *B.Litt. 1950 Dublin, Trinity College*

Bowes, I.
Cleveland and Teesside: a geographical study of population and occupational changes since 1800. *M.A. 1948 London, Bedford College*

Bowie, D.
Ce que Molière doit aux auteurs latins. *M.A. 1912 Liverpool*

Bowley, A. H.
A study of the factors influencing the general development of the child during the pre-school years by means of record forms. *Ph.D. 1940 London, External Degree*

Bowley, M. E.
The place of Nassau William Senior (1790 to 1864) in the development of economic thought. *Ph.D. 1936 London, External Degree*

Bowley, V. E. A.
Victor Hugo and the English stage. *M.A. 1927 London*

Bowley, V. E. A.
Victor Hugo in the light of English criticism and opinion during the nineteenth century. *Ph.D. 1944 London, Queen Mary College*

Bowman, F. L.
An historical enquiry into the teaching of history in the elementary training college and public elementary school, with some consideration of both the development of the study of history and of pedagogic theory in relation to the problem of teaching history in the training college. *M.Ed. 1919 Manchester*

Bowman, J.
Intellectual and moral claims in education:an historico-philosophical argument. *M.A. 1929 National University of Ireland*

Bowman, J.
The Pharisees: a critical investigation. *D.Phil. 1945 Oxford*

Bowman, M. J.
Ancient musical instruments of Ireland. *B.Mus. 1933 National University of Ireland*

Bowman, M. J.
Place names and antiquities of the Barony of Duhallow. *M.A. 1934 National University of Ireland*

Bowmer, J. C.
The sacrament of the Lord's Supper in early Methodism. *M.A. 1949 Leeds*

Box, H. S.
The scholastic approach to theism. *Ph.D. 1933 London, External Degree*

Box, K.
Keats' literary theories, as expressed in his letters and as exemplified in his poems. *M.A. 1947 Manchester*

Boyce, T.
The imagination of the school-child and its relation to his proficiency in the different subjects of the elementary school curriculum. *M.A. 1917 Liverpool*

Boyd, H.
Exegeses of: Romans vii.14-25; vii.28-30; ix.5. *B.D. & D.D. 1879 Oxford*

Boyd, H. A.
The cathedral system in the Church of Ireland since the disestablishment. *B.Litt. 1950 Dublin, Trinity College*

Boyd, J.
A critical study of the writings of Forrest Reid. *B.Litt. 1945 Dublin, Trinity College*

Boyd, J.
Experiment in form and characterization in the twentieth century novel. *M.A. 1938 Belfast*

Boyd, J.
Goethe's knowledge of English literature. *B.Litt. 1923 Oxford*

Boyd, M. R.
Three fifteenth century manuscripts of *Renaud de Montauban* (British Museum, Royal 16 G. ii, Royal 15 E. vi and Sloane 960). *M.A. 1905 London*

Boyd, W.
Jean Jacques Rousseau. *D.Phil. 1911 Glasgow*

Boydell, N. Y.
An interpretation of the distribution of the population within the United Provinces of Agra and Oudh. *M.Sc. 1938 Leeds*

Boyer de la Giroday, F.
The international sugar problem. *B.Phil. 1947 Oxford*

Boyle, J.
Les traductions françaises de l'*Utopie* et l'influence de Thomas Morus en France au seizième siècle. *M.A. 1949 Liverpool*

Boyle, J. A.
Studies on the *Ta'rikh-i-Jahān-Gushā* of Juvayni. *Ph.D. 1947 London, School of Oriental and African Studies*

Boyle, J. W.
Jour de cendres and *Seinte confessioun*; an ed. of two Anglo-Norman poems from the ms. 312 in T.C.D. *B.Litt. 1942 Dublin, Trinity College*

Boys, D. G.
Matthew Arnold's theory and practice of poetry. *M.A. 1923 London*

Boys, J. L. Verney-　*see* Verney-Boys, J. L.

Boys, M.
The Roman attitude to drama before the death of Augustus. *M.A. 1947 Leeds*

Braatoy, B. F.
Labour and war: the theory of labour action to prevent war. *Ph.D. 1934 London, School of Economics and Political Science*

Bracewell, C. C.
The Residency in Oudh during the administration of Warren Hastings, 1772-85. *M.A. 1922 Manchester*

Bracey, H. E.
Wiltshire: a geographical and social study. *Ph.D. 1948 London, Birkbeck College*

Bracken, J. R.
British relations with France from the establishment of the Directory to the coup d'état of Fructidor. *B.Litt. 1939 Oxford*

Brackett, W. O.
John Witherspoon: his Scottish ministry. *Ph.D. 1935 Edinburgh*

Brackwell, C.
The Church of England and society, 1830-1850. *M.A. 1949 Birmingham*

Bradbrook, M. C.
Themes and conventions of Elizabethan tragedy. *Ph.D. 1934 Cambridge*

Bradbury, J. B.
The religious development of the adolescent. *M.Ed. 1947 Manchester*

Bradbury, L. J.
A survey of the wrapping paper industry. *M.Com. 1922 Birmingham*

Bradbury, M. A. H.
The poetry of Clément Marot. *M.A. 1915 Belfast*

Braddock, A. P.
The activities of Catholics in the matter of education in England. *M.A. 1917 London*

Bradford, E. E.
The epistle to the Romans. *D.D. 1912 Oxford*

Bradford, E. E.
1. Predestination and free will. 2. The resurrection of the holy. *B.D. 1904 Oxford*

Bradford, E. J. G.
Ability, variability and improvability. *M.Sc. 1920 London*

Bradley, E. M.
The teaching of geography in England from 1886 to 1916. *M.Ed. 1917 Manchester*

Bradley, J. T.
The psychology of error. *Ph.D. 1930 London, External Degree*

Bradley, M. S.
The Christian principle of redemption in its application to penal reform. *B.Litt. 1929 Oxford*

Bradley, P.
International administrative legislation under the Covenant of the League of Nations (with special reference to municipal application). *Ph.D. 1936 London, School of Economics and Political Science*

Bradley, P. B.
Naval expeditions to Ireland at the time of the French Revolution. *M.A. 1923 National University of Ireland*

Bradley, W. J.
Sir William Wyse, Irish pioneer in educational reform. *Ph.D. 1945 Dublin, Trinity College*

Bradley, W. L.
The theology of P. T. Forsyth, 1848 to 1921. *Ph.D. 1949 Edinburgh*

Bradney, P. J.
The status of women among the southern Bantu. *B.Sc. 1950 Oxford*

Bradshaw, F.
Self-government in Canada and how it was achieved: the story of Lord Durham's Report. *D.Sc. 1904 London*

Bradshaw, J.
The mutual influence of William Wordsworth and Samuel Taylor Coleridge. *M.A. 1914 Liverpool*

Bradshaw, J.
A psychological study of the development of religious beliefs among children and young persons. *M.Sc. 1949 London, University College*

Brady, H.
The personnel of Parliament, 1571. *M.A. 1927 Manchester*

Brady, M. E.
The political significance of the career of the Earl of Tyrconnell in Irish history and its relation to the cause of James II. 1685 to 1691. *M.Litt. 1932 Cambridge*

Brady, P.
Satire in Elizabethan drama. *Ph.D. 1942 National University of Ireland*

Brady, P.
Spenser as a satirist. *M.A. 1936 National University of Ireland*

Brady, R. P.
The Middle Trent Valley: a study in the East Midland type of development. *M.A. 1933 Manchester*

Brady, T.
John of Salisbury and 12th century humanism. *M.A. 1931 National University of Ireland*

Bradyll-Johnson, L.
Exegeses of: St. John xvii.1-5; 6-19; 19-26. *D.D. 1922 Oxford*

Bradyll-Johnson, L.
1. The intermediate state. 2. The resurrection of the body. *B.D. 1918 Oxford*

Braham, E. G.
The concept of self from Descartes to Kant, with some reference to immortality. *Ph.D. 1935 London, King's College*

Braham, E. G.
Personality and immortality in modern philosophy. *M.A. 1927 Bristol*

Braham, E. G.
The problem of self and immortality. *B.A. 1925 Bristol*

Braham, E. G.
Some aspects of personality in British and American idealism from the time of T. H. Green, with some reference to immortality. *M.A. 1930 Liverpool*

Brahmachari, S.
Moral attitudes in relation to upbringing, personal adjustment and social opinion. *Ph.D. 1938 London, University College*

Braithwaite, A. W.
A commentary, mainly, but not exclusively, devoted to its historical aspects, on the *Vita Divi Vespasiani* of C. Suetonius Tranquillus. *B.Litt. 1926 Oxford*

Braithwaite, C.
The place of charity and voluntary social service in the life of the community. *Ph.D. 1938 London, External Degree*

Braley, E. F.
The state and education in the 18th century. *LL.D. 1932 Dublin, Trinity College*

Bramall, E. J. N.
The life and poetical works of Richard Barnfield. *B.Litt. 1930 Oxford*

Brameld, N. M.
Local government under the Tudors. *M.A. 1916 London*

Bramley, T.
1. Ecclesiastes. 2. The doctrine of the Resurrection. *B.D. & D.D. 1890 Oxford*

Brampton, C. K.
The *Defensor minor* of Marsilius de Mainardini of Padua. *B.Litt. 1922 Oxford*

Bramstedt, E. Kohn-　*see* Kohn-Bramstedt, E.

Bramston, J.
1. Holy baptism. 2. Holy communion. *B.D. 1872 Oxford*

Bramwell, B.
Changes in the economic structure of the British shipping industry since the Great War. *M.A. 1939 Liverpool*

Brand, H. W.
West Ham, its educational problems and its educational facilities. *M.A. 1935 London, King's College*

Brandon, S. G. F.
The effect of the fall of Jerusalem in A.D. 70 on the Christian Church. *B.D. 1939 Leeds*

Brandon, S. G. F.
1. The political consciousness of the Marcan gospel. 2. The origins of Alexandrian Christianity. 3. The historical element in some ancient religions. *D.D. 1943 Leeds*

Brandt, J. A.
The influence of Emilio Castelar on the formation and fortunes of the Spanish Republic of 1873. *B.Litt. 1925 Oxford*

Branfoot, A. I. S.
A critical survey of the Narodnik movement, 1861-1881. *Ph.D. 1926 London*

Branigan, J. J.
The teaching of geography in postwar secondary education. *M.A. 1945 Leeds*

Bransby, E. R.
An investigation into the consumer-demand for milk in the city of Leeds. *Ph.D. 1938 London, External Degree*

Bransby, E. R.
A problem in agricultural marketing: an investigation in Yorkshire and Sussex into the consumer-demand for milk. *M.Sc. 1935 London, South Eastern Agricultural College*

Branthwaite, T. A.
Expositions of Genesis i.1-2; Romans viii.14-16; Romans viii.22. *D.D. 1907 Oxford*

Branthwaite, T. A.
1. The Pauline authorship of the Epistle to the Ephesians. 2. The date and authorship of the Athanasian Creed. *B.D. 1903 Oxford*

Branton, N.
Some effects of state interference in the British coal industry, with special reference to the period 1930-39. *Ph.D. 1944 London, External Degree*

Branton, N.
A study of business organization in the printing trade. *M.Com. 1937 London, External Degree*

Brash, W. B.
The English mystics of the fourteenth century. *B.Litt. 1919 Oxford*

Brasington, B. G.
A study in regional division as applied to the northern part of Tanganyika Territory. *Ph.D. 1935 London, Birkbeck College*

Braun, M.
Legendary and historical figures in Hellenistic-Oriental popular literature. *Ph.D. 1937 Cambridge*

Bray, J. F. L.
A statistical study of the economic forces affecting the rate of interest with special reference to recent developments. *Ph.D. 1935 London, School of Economics and Political Science*

Brayshaw, C. M.
The economics of Yorkshire farming: a study based on the accounts of thirty-two Yorkshire farms for the period 1928-34. *M.Sc. 1937 Leeds*

Bready, J. W.
The influence of Christianity on social progress as illustrated by the career of Lord Shaftesbury. *Ph.D. 1927 London*

Breathnac, M.
Matthew Arnold's classical ideal. *M.A. 1939 National University of Ireland*

Breathnach, L.
Aistriúcháin ar scéal beathadh Mhaitiais Talbóid ó Bhéarla an Athar Séamus Ó Casaide (A translation from the English of a biography of Matthew Talbot by Fr. Séamas Ó Casaide). *M.A. 1936 National University of Ireland*

Breathnach, R.
Dréachtaí filíochta a cumadh do sna Grásaigh, i gCo. Cille Coinnigh, idir 1704 agus 1742(Poetry composed for the Grace family in Co. Kilkenny between 1704 and 1742). *M.A. 1938 National University of Ireland*

Breathnach, S.
An t-aighneas idir chill agus tuaith 'sa tsean-scéaluidheacht Ghaedhilge(The conflict between church and state in Old Irish storytelling). *M.A. 1940 National University of Ireland*

Brebner, J. B.
The history of Nova Scotia prior to 1763. *B.Litt. 1925 Oxford*

Bredahl-Petersen, M. A. F. *see* Petersen, M. A. F. Bredahl

Bree, W.
1. On original sin. 2. On justification. *B.D. & D.D. 1893 Oxford*

Breen, H. A.
The Pre-Raphaelite group of poets. *M.A. 1948 National University of Ireland*

Breen, M.
James Shirley, dramatist. *M.A. 1936 National University of Ireland*

Breen, T. W.
Caedmon: the first English poet. *M.A. 1951 National University of Ireland*

Brehaut, L.
Is the general standpoint of the *Theodicée* inconsistent with the philosophical views expressed in Leibnitz' other works?. *B.Sc. 1913 Oxford*

Brenan, M. A.
1. Catholic education in Ireland, 1774-1824: illustrated from the diocesan records of Kildare and Leighlin. 2. The Confraternity of Christian Doctrine in Ireland, 1775-1835. *Ph.D. 1934 National University of Ireland*

Brennan, H.
Baironizm v poezii Lermontova(Byronism in the poetry of Lermontov). *M.A. 1915 London*

Brennan, J. D.
The regionalism of Thomas Hardy. *M.A. 1948 National University of Ireland*

Brennan, M. P.
Bohemond I of Antioch. *M.A. 1943 Belfast*

Brennan, P.
Post-audit examination of government accounts. *M.A. 1945 National University of Ireland*

Brereton, C. A.
1. The Christology of St. John of Damascus. 2. The Eucharistic doctrine of St. John of Damascus. *B.D. 1910 Oxford*

Brereton, G. E.
A critical edition of *De Graunz Jaianz*. *B.Litt. 1930 Oxford*

Breslin, J. P.
Gawain Douglas. *M.A. 1942 National University of Ireland*

Bretherton, J.
The ethical basis of the State's authority. *M.A. 1937 Liverpool*

Brett, R. L.
Shaftesbury (the author of *The Characteristics*) as a literary critic. *B.Litt. 1940 Oxford*

Brettle, L.
The geographical basis, character and organization of the import trade of London from the East Indies, with special reference to the twentieth century. *B.Litt. 1930 Oxford*

Brettle, R. E.
English masques, 1604-1640, with special reference to Ben Jonson. *M.A. 1922 London*

Brettle, R. E.
John Marston. *D.Phil. 1927 Oxford*

Brewer, J. R.
The third Earl of Shaftesbury and the background of English romanticism. *M.A. 1947 London, University College*

Brewer, W. D. D.
Wilhelm Roscher, his life and works. *M.Com. 1924 Birmingham*

Brewin, J. L.
Biological research in the early days of the Royal Society. *M.Sc. 1937 London, University College*

Brewin, K. A.
Agrarian conditions in east Berkshire, 1560-1660. *M.A. 1918 London*

Briault, E. W. H.
The historical geography of a part of east Sussex from 1780, with special reference to agriculture. *Ph.D. 1939 London, Birkbeck College*

Brice, J. I.
The influence of Hume in British theology. *Ph.D. 1948 London, Richmond College*

Bridges, H. P.
The liberty of the subject in England during the period 1803-1832. *LL.D. 1926 London*

Bridges, H. P.
The psychology of shape. *M.A. 1931 London, King's College*

Bridges, J. S.
Evolution in the law and practice of blockade. *LL.D. 1919 London*

Bridges, S. F.
Thomas Chaundler. *B.Litt. 1949 Oxford*

Bridgewater, J. M.
A study of psychodrama as a classroom technique. *M.A. 1949 London, Institute of Education*

Bridson, T. H.
Open-air schools. *M.Ed. 1942 Manchester*

Bridston, K. R.
Law and gospel and their relationship in the theology of Luther. *Ph.D. 1949 Edinburgh*

Brien, C.
The Cistercian movement. *M.A. 1926 Birmingham*

Brier, A.
A critical inquiry into the practical value of mental tests in secondary schools. *M.Ed. 1924 Leeds*

Briers, P. M.
The medieval borough of Henley: 1. its history; 2. its constitution. *B.Litt. 1935 Oxford*

Briggs, E. R.
The political academies of France in the early eighteenth century, with special reference to the Club de l'Entresol, and to its founder the Abbé Pierre-Joseph Alary. *Ph.D. 1932 Cambridge*

Briggs, F.
Expositions of St. Matthew xxviii.1-15: I Corinthians xv.35-50; St. Luke xxiv.36-49. *D.D. 1919 Oxford*

Briggs, F.
1. The priesthood of Christ in the Epistle to the Hebrews. 2. The redemption. *B.D. 1910 Oxford*

Bright, J. F.
1. General characteristics of the Epistles of the New Testament, with special illustration from the Epistle of St.James. 2.General characteristics of the Epistles of St.Paul, with special illustration from the Epistle to the Galatians. *B.D. & D.D. 1884 Oxford*

Brimson, B. E.
The Church in the reign of Edward I, with special reference to the register of Archbishop Peckham. *M.A. 1909 Wales*

Brind, M.
Life of Charles K. Bushe, Lord Chief Justice. *M.A. 1919 National University of Ireland*

Brinker, R.
The influence of sanctuaries on the legislation and history of early Israel. *M.A. 1944 Manchester*

Brinker, R.
Studies in the language and style of the book Jeremiah. *M.A. 1942 Liverpool*

Brinkmann, C.
The relations between England and Germany from 1660 to 1688. *B.Litt. 1907 Oxford*

Brinkworth, E. R. C.
A study of the visitation books of the archdeaconry of Buckingham, 1633-6. *B.Litt. 1948 Oxford*

Brinn, M. H.
English verse-drama from Yeats to Auden. *M.A. 1950 Wales*

Brinton, C. C.
The political thought of the English Romanticists. *D.Phil. 1923 Oxford*

Brinton, P. R.
1. A comparison of the idea of divine sonship in Pauline and Johannine theology. The origin of the title Κύριοσ as applied to our Lord in the New Testament. *B.D. & D.D. 1922 Oxford*

Bristow, E.
Christianity in Asia, and evidences of the Church's power and influence in the province to A.D.325, in the light of Christian epigraphy. *M.A. 1926 Manchester*

Brittain, D.
Prosper Mérimée and England. *M.A. 1926 Manchester*

Britten, A. G. R.
Le caractère d'Aimeri de Narbonne d'après les chansons *Girart de Vienne, Aimeri de Narbonne, Les Enfances Guillaume, Les Narbonnais, Le Siège de Basbastre, La Prise de Cordres et de Sebille* et *La Mort Aimeri*. *M.A. 1936 London, Birkbeck College*

Britton, G. C.
The affiliations of Germanic. *M.A. 1949 Birmingham*

Britton, R. F.
La philosophie du retour à la nature chez Jean-Jacques Rousseau, et applications practiques de son système. *M.A. 1949 Liverpool*

Broad, E. G.
The Christian churches and the formation and maintenance of a system of state-aided elementary education in England and Wale. *M.A. 1938 Bristol*

Broadbent, C. F. B.
The attitude of the Greek dramatic poets to the religious cults of their day. *M.A. 1920 London*

Broadbent, M. J.
Maryland and the American Revolution. *M.A. 1949 Sheffield*

Broadhurst, B. M.
Some aspects of the relation of primitive medicine to magic. *B.Sc. 1928 Oxford*

Brock, F. H. C.
The influence of the aesthetic point of view upon the ethics of Aristotle. *M.A. 1904 London*

Brock, P. M. L.
The development of mathematical geography among the Greeks. *M.A. 1935 London, King's College*

Brock, W. R.
Lord Liverpool and Liberal Toryism, 1820 to 1827. *Ph.D. 1943 Cambridge*

Brockbank, J. L.
The history of the municipality of the city of York from 1638-1663 as illustrated mainly from house books (vols. 36 and 37) containing the minutes of the proceedings of the corporation. *M.A. 1910 London*

Brockhurst, B. J.
The life and works of Stephen Batman, 15?-1584. *M.A. 1947 London, Westfield College*

Brockington, A. A.
A study of Robert Browning's influence and reputation in the twentieth century. *Ph.D. 1931 London, External Degree*

Brocklebank, R. S. G.
An inquiry into the changing distribution of population in the Chilterns since 1821. *Ph.D. 1937 London, University College*

Brockway, T. P.
English opinion on the American War of Independence. *B.Litt. 1925 Oxford*

Brodie, D. M.
Life and works of Edmund Dudley. *Ph.D. 1935 Cambridge*

Brodie, I.
An inquiry into the sources of the Book of Anan, the founder of Karaism. *B.Litt. 1921 Oxford*

Brodie, J.
Equity and the lapse of time. *LL.M. 1936 Leeds*

Brodie, P. H.
The development of the militant spirit among primitive peoples. *B.Sc. 1917 Oxford*

Brodie, R. R.
Some aspects of a fall in the rate of mortality as affecting the financial position of friendly societies and sickness funds. *Ph.D. 1932 London, External Degree*

Brodszky, P.
The novels of Henry Mackenzie. *M.A. 1941 Birmingham*

Brogden, M. I.
The fantastic element in the characters of E. T. A. Hoffmann. *B.Litt. 1947 Oxford*

Bromage, B. W.
Henry James: with special reference to his longer novels. *M.A. 1924 Birmingham*

Bromiley, G. W.
Herder's contribution to the Romantic philosophy of history, with special reference to the theological implications. *Ph.D. 1943 Edinburgh*

Bromiley, W. P.
The development of the white community in Natal, 1845-72. *Ph.D. 1937 London, King's College*

Bromley, J. *see* Robertson, J.

Brook, A.
1. The creed of the Christian Church. 2. St. Paul's Epistles considered as a whole, with special reference to his teaching on justification. *B.D. 1893 Oxford*

Brook, D.
The influence of Christianity on the family and domestic relations in Roman law. *D.C.L. 1896 Oxford*

Brook, D. E.
Nature in English poetry from 1610 to 1660. *M.A. 1936 Liverpool*

Brook, F. B.
Right to support of land and buildings by underground water and semi-solids. *LL.M. 1932 Cambridge*

Brook, G. L.
A new edition of the Middle British lyrics of ms. Harley 2253 in the British Museum. *Ph.D. 1934 Leeds*

Brook, S.
A study of allegorical representation in *Piers Plowman*. *M.A. 1947 Manchester*

Brooke, T. H.
An edition of the memoirs of Sir Hugh Cholmley, with a contribution on his life and on the Civil War in Yorkshire. *B.Litt. 1937 Oxford*

Brooke, W. E.
The sermons of Donne and Taylor. *M.A. 1935 Birmingham*

Brooker, R. W.
Cirencester and its region: a study in Cotteswold geography. *M.A. 1937 Reading*

Brookfield, G. P.
Contributions to the development of English medieval architecture based largely on a first-hand study of various monuments in Oxford. *B.Litt. 1925 Oxford*

Brookfield, S. H.
The historical background of the English land law from 1535. *M.A. 1935 Liverpool*

Brooks, B. G.
An examination of Wordsworth's poetry, particularly his lesser known and later poetry, considered as experimental work, whether in technique or content. *Ph.D. 1937 London, External Degree*

Brooks, C.
Antonio Panizzi, scholar and patriot. *Ph.D. 1929 Manchester*

Brooks, C.
An edition of the correspondence between Thomas Percy and Dr. Richard Farmer (B.M. Add. ms. 28222). *B.Litt. 1932 Oxford*

Brooks, E. K.
Manners and morals in the English novel between Richardson and Jane Austen. *M.A. 1942 Leeds*

Brooks, H. F.
The complete works of John Oldham (1653-83): edited with an introduction, biographical and critical textual apparatus, and explanatory notes: with an appendix, containing an analysed transcript of the autograph drafts of Oldham's poems in ms. Rawlinson Poet. 123. *D.Phil. 1939 Oxford*

Brooks, H. F.
John Oldham (1653-83), *Satyrs on the Jesuits*: a critical text with introduction and notes. *B.Litt. 1934 Oxford*

Brooks, H. L.
The Polish Upper Silesian coal industry since the War. *M.Sc. 1939 London, School of Economics and Political Science*

Brooks, J. S.
Walls: material, social and individual: a study of the defences raised by man in his later evolutionary development. *M.A. 1935 Bristol*

Brooks, K. G.
André Gide. *M.A. 1931 Birmingham*

Brooks, K. R.
Edition of the Old English poem *Andreas*. *D.Phil. 1941 Oxford*

Brooks, L.
The London compulsory day continuation schools: January, 1921-July, 1922. *M.A. 1923 London*

Brooks, M. M.
The character sketch: its growth and development in English literature. *M.A. 1914 London*

Brooks, W. E. St.J.
Register of the hospital of S. John the Baptist without the New Gate. *Litt.D. 1935 Dublin, Trinity College*

Brooksbank, K.
The day continuation school in England. *M.Ed. 1939 Manchester*

Broome, D. M.
The exchequer in the reign of Edward III, 1327-1377: a preliminary investigation. *Ph.D. 1923 Manchester*

Broome, J. H.
An agent in Anglo-French relationships: Pierre Desmaizeaux. *Ph.D. 1949 London, University College*

Brotherton, F. F.
The life and work of Louis-Benoit Picard. *M.A. 1943 Manchester*

Brough, J.
The concept. *M.A. 1911 Wales*

Broughton, D.
Alexander Pope as a satirist in prose. *M.A. 1943 London, Birkbeck College*

Broughton, D.
An edition of the complete works of William Diaper. *Ph.D. 1947 Leeds*

Broughton, E. S.
Orientalism in English poetry. *M.A. 1919 London*

Broughton, G. M.
Sense-perception according to Kant. *M.A. 1909 London*

Broughton, G. M.
The social and economic consequences of the development of the factory system in India as compared with England. *D.Sc. 1924 London*

Brown, A.
An edition of the play *Wyt and science* by John Redford, from British Museum additional manuscript 15233. *M.A. 1949 London, University College*

Brown, A.
The place of redemptive mediation in the history of religion. *M.A. 1938 Leeds*

Brown, A. J.
Liquidity-preference: a study of investment. *D.Phil. 1939 Oxford*

Brown, A. W.
The effect of the Bankruptcy and Deeds of Arrangement Act of 1913 on the law relating to bankruptcy. *LL.M. 1916 Liverpool*

Brown, B. F.
The law of trusts in the eighteenth century up to the death of Lord Hardwicke. *D.Phil. 1932 Oxford*

Brown, B. F.
The teaching of physics to junior pupils, ages $11^1/_2$ to $14^1/_2$ years, with particular regard to the period 12 $^1/_2$ to $13^1/_2$ years. *M.A. 1938 Liverpool*

Brown, C.
A history of popular education in Wakefield, 1780-1902. *M.Ed. 1937 Leeds*

Brown, C. K. F.
The Church of England's contribution to popular education in England after 1833. *B.Litt. 1941 Oxford*

Brown, C. K. F.
The history of the English clergy, 1800-1900. *D.Phil. 1949 Oxford*

Brown, C. K. F.
Treasures of the Surrey churches in the diocese of Guildford. *M.A. 1942 Leeds*

Brown, C. M. P.
Social reform in New Zealand. *M.Sc. 1938 Cambridge*

Brown, E. M.
The counter-reformation in Ireland under the Tudor sovereigns. *M.A. 1922 National University of Ireland*

Brown, E. M. L.
The history of stereochemistry up to 1890. *M.Sc. 1949 London, University College*

Brown, F. E.
Social questions in Balzac's novels. *Ph.D. 1934 London, King's College*

Brown, F. K.
A life of William Godwin. *D.Phil. 1925 Oxford*

Brown, F. W.
The history of the introduction of infinitesimals. *M.Sc. 1930 London*

Brown, G. A.
Moral and psychological factors in repentance. *Ph.D. 1939 Edinburgh*

Brown, G. H.
The place of Sir Arthur Hesilrige in English politics, 1659-60. *B.Litt. 1948 Oxford*

Brown, G. K.
The effect of the religious reformation on Italy between 1520 and 1550. *Ph.D. 1931 Edinburgh*

Brown, G. W.
The economic history of Liberia. *Ph.D. 1938 London, School of Economics and Political Science*

Brown, H.
Dramatic creation as exemplified in Shakespeare's plays. *D.Litt. 1927 Glasgow*

Brown, H.
Varieties of pronunciation in sixteenth century standard English (the vowels of stressed syllables). *B.Litt. 1926 Oxford*

Brown, H. G.
The life and works of Josiah Tucker. *M.A. 1925 Bristol*

Brown, H. M.
Methodism and the Church of England in Cornwall, 1738-1838: a historical survey of Cornish Methodism, its rise, growth, and relation to the Church of England. *Ph.D. 1947 London, External Degree*

Brown, H. R.
An enquiry into the financial implications of the educational reforms proposed by the Federal Council of Teachers in Northern Ireland. *M.Com.Sc. 1944 Belfast*

Brown, I. V.
Educational practice in relation to industry and commerce. *M.A. 1919 London*

Brown, J. C.
The origin and early history of the office of notary, with a foreword by the Right Honourable the Viscount Dunedin. *Ph.D. 1935 Edinburgh*

Brown, J. D.
Initial mutations in medieval Welsh. *M.A. 1900 Wales*

Brown, J. H. L.
The problem of John the Baptist. *Ph.D. 1940 Glasgow*

Brown, M.
L'appréciation de Shakespeare en France: avec mention particuliere des traductions et des représentations de Macbeth, 1700 à 1900. *M.A. 1948 Birmingham*

Brown, M.
A study of the works of William Baldwin, with special reference to his connection with *The Mirror for Magistrates*. *M.A. 1912 London*

Brown, P. B.
The development of inland transport in Eire. *M.Econ.Sc. 1946 National University of Ireland*

Brown, P. B. Wylde-   *see* Wylde-Brown, P. B.

Brown, P. C.
Shakespeare's debt to Latin poetry. *M.A. 1912 Birmingham*

Brown, R.
John Oldham, poet and satirist. *B.Litt. 1927 Oxford*

Brown, R. F.
A critical analysis of sixty-five periodicals published in Madrid between 1823-1854. *M.A. 1934 Liverpool*

Brown, R. F.
The development of the novel in Spain between 1700 and 1849 and its relation to public taste in narrative prose. *Ph.D. 1939 Liverpool*

Brown, S. E.
The protection of a purchaser under the old law and the new. *LL.M. 1927 Leeds*

Brown, S. L.
1. A critical introduction to the study of Hosea. 2. A critical translation of Hosea. *B.D. & D.D. 1924 Oxford*

Brown, S. M.
The effect of the religious movement on the origin and early growth of the Milanese commune during the eleventh century. *B.Litt. 1929 Oxford*

Brown, S. W.
The distribution of rural population with particular reference to the Vale of Evesham. *B.Litt. 1925 Oxford*

Brown, T.
Cost analysis in the gas industry. *M.Com. 1946 Birmingham*

Brown, U. M.
An edition of the *Saga of Porgils and Haflioi* (from Sturlunga Saga). *B.Litt. 1949 Oxford*

Brown, V. M.
An experimental study of a new method of grammar teaching and its bearing on composition. *M.A. 1936 London, Institute of Education*

Brown, W.
Etude sur le vocabulaire de Prosper Mérimée au point de vue du néologisme. *M.A. 1925 Leeds*

Brown, W. E.
Heinrich Luden and the origins of the Luden Nationalist movement. *M.A. 1929 Birmingham*

Brown, W. J.
The place of the junior technical school in the national system of education, with special reference to Bury. *M.Ed. 1933 Manchester*

Browne, A. H.
1. The Antichrist. 2. The prophet of the New Testament. *B.D. & D.D. 1905 Oxford*

Browne, C. G.
1. The Incarnation in relation to our daily life. 2. The priesthood of the laity in the Church of Christ. *B.D. & D.D. 1908 Oxford*

Browne, G. W. G.
Factors affecting the total flow of cheque-payments in the non-financial circulation through the clearing banks, 1919-37. *B.Litt. 1939 Oxford*

Browne, M. F.
Positivism with special reference to Auguste Comte and the Viennese circle of philosophy. *M.A. 1944 National University of Ireland*

Browne, O'D. T. D.
The Rotunda Hospital - 1745-1945. *Litt. D. 1947 Dublin, Trinity College*

Browne, R. A.
Livy and Horace on the origins of the Roman drama. *Ph.D. 1931 Cambridge*

Browne, R. A.
The Roman conception of tragedy as exemplified especially in Seneca. *M.A. 1927 Wales*

Browne, R. C.
An experimental study of some of the psychological problems which arise in pilots who use the beam approach method of landing aircraft. *D.M. 1946 Oxford*

Browne, S. S. S.
The pragmatic theory of truth, with especial regard to the question whether it implies a distinction between reality as it is known and reality as it is in itself. *B.Litt. 1929 Oxford*

Browne, W. L.
William Blake and his critics. *M.A. 1944 National University of Ireland*

Browning, D. C.
Ms. Balliol 354: Richard Hill's *Commonplace Book. B.Litt. 1935 Oxford*

Browning, W. R. F.
The relevance of the ethical teaching of Jesus to the conditions of this world order: an examination of the Sermon on the Mount. *B.D. 1948 Oxford*

Brownless, V. T.
An investigation into the possibility of the development of spatial perception in children in their first year of secondary education, in preparation for their introduction to formal geometry. *M.A. 1949 London, King's College*

Brownlie, W. M.
The establishment of state intermediate education in France. *Ph.D. 1934 Glasgow*

Brownlow, G. S.
Retail goodwill valuation. *M.Sc. 1940 London, External Degree*

Broxap, M.
Peter de Rivaux. *M.A. 1925 Manchester*

Bruce, F. R. C.
Expositions of St. Matthew iv.1-11: Christ's temptation; St. Luke xxii.39-44: the agony in Gethsemane; II Thessalonians ii.3-10: the second coming of Christ. *D.D. 1908 Oxford*

Bruce, F. R. C.
1. The neo-Platonic tribute to the faith. 2. A study of the two records of our Lord's genealogy. *B.D. 1904 Oxford*

Bruce, J. P.
A translation with critical notes of a ms. in the British Museum written by the Chinese Emperor Ch'ien Hung, and entitled *A treatise on the recognition of faults. M.A. 1907 London*

Bruckshaw, B.
George Chapman: a critical assessment of his poetry, dramatic and non-dramatic, with particular reference to his philosophical development insofar as it influences his medium. *M.A. 1950 Manchester*

Bruckshaw, M. M.
Henry Vaughan: a study in the relation of poetry and mysticism. *M.A. 1950 Manchester*

Bruen, K. E.
The agricultural geography of the Irrawaddy delta, with special reference to rice. *M.A. 1939 London, University College*

Brunicardi, M. H. J.
The ruined parish churches of the diocese of Cork. *M.A. 1913 National University of Ireland*

Brunner, C. T.
A study of the growth of motor traffic, with special reference to the relation between the increased cost of highways maintenance and the growth of motor traffic and to the proper distribution of that cost. *M.A. 1924 Manchester*

Bruyn, W. H. van O.
The need for vocational guidance: a study of three comparable groups of ex-secondary schoolgirls. *M.A. 1940 London, Institute of Education*

Bryan, P. W.
An enquiry into the major geographical factors conditioning the production and distribution of coal and iron in the United States of America. *Ph.D. 1924 London*

Bryant, A. D.
Neo-Hellenism in French literature from 1850-1900. *Ph.D. 1931 London, East London College*

Bryant, F. J.
1. On the Septuagint. 2. On the doctrine of the Holy Trinity. *B.D. & D.D. 1886 Oxford*

Bryant, R. W. G.
The English canal system in its geographical and industrial relations. *M.Sc. 1939 London, School of Economics and Political Science*

Bryant, S.
Organized character. *D.Sc. 1884 London*

Bryant, W. H.
The Rolliad and *The Anti-Jacobin* as literary satire. *M.A. 1934 Wales*

Bryce, J.
Stendhal: ce qu'il a écrit et ce qu'il a lu en anglais. *M.A. 1911 Birmingham*

Brydon, R. S.
The finances of James VI, 1567-1603. *Ph.D. 1925 Edinburgh*

Bryer, M. L.
The constructional methods of ancient Hellenic architecture. *B.litt. 1940 Oxford*

Bryett, H.
The primary school in England: survey and a forecast. *M.A. 1929 Liverpool*

Bryn Thomas, W.
Church of England finances. *Ph.D. 1942 London, School of Economics and Political Science*

Buch, M. A.
Rise and growth of Indian liberalism. *Ph.D. 1937 London, School of Economics and Political Science*

Buchan, H. A.
A critical edition, with introduction and explanatory notes, of ms. Malone 14. *B.Litt. 1934 Oxford*

Buchanan, J. R.
Muhammad's idea of the last judgment and its sources. *Ph.D. 1927 Edinburgh*

Buchanan, N.
Efficiency in production control. *Ph.D. 1937 Belfast*

Buchanan, R. O.
The pastoral industries of New Zealand: a study in economic geography. *Ph.D. 1932 London, University College*

Buchan-Sydserff, M.
Liverpool during the Seven Years War. *M.A. 1934 Liverpool*

Bucher, J. R.
The relation to the Old Testament of the synoptic teaching of Jesus, with some comparison of the attitude shown in the Epistles of Paul and in the Epistle to the Hebrews. *Ph.D. 1940 Edinburgh*

Buchinger, H.
Englische Ubersetzungen von Martin Luthers geistlichen Liedern bis zum Jahre 1800. *M.A. 1939 Bristol*

Buckby, C. W.
A comparative study of the various systems of economic development in East Africa. *Ph.D. 1932 London, School of Economics and Political Science*

Buckerfield, M. J.
A regional study of south Cambridgeshire, with reference to relevant contiguous areas. *M.A. 1946 London, Birkbeck College*

Buckland, C. S. B.
Metternich and the English Government from the Peace of Schönbrünn. *B.Litt. 1930 Oxford*

Buckle, E. M.
French fairy tales in the eighteenth century. *Ph.D. 1927 London*

Buckler, G. G.
The intellectual and moral standards of Anna Comnena. *D.Phil. 1927 Oxford*

Buckley, A.
The judicial proceedings under the Dictum of Kenilworth in Sussex and Kent. *M.A. 1927 Manchester*

Buckley, C. J.
The use of schools as instruments of democracy. *M.Sc. 1948 London, School of Economics and Political Science*

Buckley, C. T. R.
William Shippen as an opposition leader (1714-43). *B.Litt. 1930 Oxford*

Buckley, J. F.
Armando Palacio Valdés y su obra. *M.A. 1942 National University of Ireland*

Buckley, J. K.
Joseph Parkes of Birmingham and the part which he played in radical reform movements from 1825 to 1845. *M.A. 1924 London*

Buckley, R. W.
Ernst Toller. *M.A. 1928 Liverpool*

Buckpitt, G. E.
The maintenance of efficiency in road passenger transport undertakings under conditions of monopoly. *M.Sc. 1948 London, External Degree*

Budd, F. E.
The idea of tragedy in the Renaissance. *Ph.D. 1928 London*

Budden, E. S.
A study of memory and its importance for the theory of knowledge. *D.Phil. 1935 Oxford*

Budge, A. J. B.
A geographical study of the distribution of the engineering industry in England and Wales. *M.A. 1933 Liverpool*

Bueno de Mesquita, D. M.
Giangaleazzo Visconti, Duke of Milan, and the unity of Italy. *Ph.D. 1939 Cambridge*

Buer, M. C.
Health, wealth, and population in the early days of the Industrial Revolution. *D.Sc. 1927 London*

Bufton, A. E.
Female characterization in Jacobean tragedy, with special consideration of the tragedies of Heywood, Webster, Middleton, Beaumont and Fletcher. *M.A. 1939 Wales*

Buhler, C. F.
The *Dicts and Sayings of the philosophers. Litt.D. 1947 Dublin, Trinity College*

Bühler, C. F.
The sources of the *Court of Sapience*; a Middle English religious and didactic poem. *Ph.D. 1930 Dublin, Trinity College*

Bülbring, M.
The literary relations between Germany and the Netherlands in the sixteenth century. *M.A. 1939 London, University College*

Bulcock, H.
Intuition and discursive understanding. *M.A. 1919 Liverpool*

Bull, G.
Political individualism of John Locke. *M.Litt. 1933 Cambridge*

Bull, S. L.
An historical and critical analysis of British health insurance. *M.Sc. 1938 London, School of Economics and Political Science*

Bull, W. M.
Elementary education among the Greeks during the sixth, fifth and fourth centuries B.C., dealing with both educational practice, theory and criticism. *M.A. 1932 London, King's College*

Bullen, F. T.
The influence of Guy de Maupassant on the English short story, 1800-1900. *M.A. 1928 Liverpool*

Bullett, S.
The British Museum manuscript Arundel 230, with particular reference to the Psalms, and the *Livre des créatures. M.A. 1910 London*

Bullock, C.
Sir Orfeo, edited with introduction, notes, translation and glossary. *Ph.D. 1926 London*

Bullock, F.
The law relating to medical, dental, and veterinary practice. *LL.D. 1928 London*

Bullock, F. W. B.
Religious conversion in Great Britain (1700-1850): a psychological and historical enquiry. *M.Litt. 1934 Cambridge*

Bullock, F. W. B.
Religious societies (*ecclesiolae in ecclesia*) from 1500 to 1800, excluding those of the Church of Rome. *Ph.D. 1938 Cambridge*

Bulsara, J. F.
A comparative study of some aspects of ritual in the simpler and more developed communities. *Ph.D. 1930 London, School of Economics and Political Science*

Bunker, S. K.
The attitude of the Church to the race problem in central South Africa during the nineteenth century, viewed in the light of New Testament principles. *B.Litt. 1933 Oxford*

Buntine, M. A.
Adult education: a survey from the beginning of the nineteenth century. *Ph.D. 1925 Edinburgh*

Buranelli, V.
Rousseau and De Tocqueville. *M.A. 1948 National University of Ireland*

Burca, S. de *see* Burke, J.

Burchardt, C. J. B.
English accounts and views of Norwegian life and literature, especially in the nineteenth century. *B.Litt. 1918 Oxford*

Burdick, E. L.
Syndicalism and industrial unionism in England until 1918. *D.Phil. 1950 Oxford*

Burgess, A. V.
The female characters in Grillparzer's drama, as contrasted with those in Goethe's and Schiller's. *M.A. 1907 Wales*

Burgess, C.
A study of some influences in the development of the British beet-sugar industry. *Ph.D. 1932 Cambridge*

Burgess, H.
International trade union organization. *M.Sc. 1934 London, School of Economics and Political Science*

Burgess, H. J.
The educational history of the National Society, 1811-1833. *M.A. 1949 London, Institute of Education*

Burgin, E. L.
Administration of foreign estates. *LL.D. 1913 London*

Burgis, H.
German influence on Scott. *M.A. 1916 London*

Burke, J.
Canamhaint oirthuaiscirt Mhuigheo(The dialects of south-east Mayo). *M.A. 1941 National University of Ireland*

Burke, J. F.
The metaphysics of the spiritual life; the philosophy of Rudolf Eucken. *M.A. 1945 National University of Ireland*

Burke, J. F.
The reform of Irish land tenures. *D.Sc. 1917 London*

Burke, J. T.
An edition of Hogarth's *Analysis of Beauty*, with an appendix of excerpts from the original manuscript drafts and a study of Hogarth's place in the aesthetic criticism of the eighteenth century. *M.A. 1935 London, King's College*

Burke, P.
Anthony Trollope. *M.A. 1936 National University of Ireland*

Burke, T. A.
Irish Catholics and Legislative Union, 1800. *M.A. 1943 National University of Ireland*

Burkhardt, F. H.
The influence of Spinozism on the religious philosophy of German Idealism. *B.Litt. 1935 Oxford*

Burkill, T. A.
Cause, value and God. *Ph.D. 1941 Manchester*

Burkill, T. A.
A criticism of the Kantian dualism. *M.A. 1940 Manchester*

Burkill, T. A.
An examination of the central themes of St. Mark's Gospel in relation to the beliefs of the Apostolic Church. *D.Phil. 1947 Oxford*

Burleigh, E. C.
Monotheistic ideas in Hebrew Wisdom literature and their influence on early Christianity. *M.A. 1950 Bristol*

Burleigh, J. H. S.
The teaching of John Hus concerning the Church. *B.Litt. 1922 Oxford*

Burley, G. H. C.
The French ascendancy in Scotland, 1554-1560. *M.A. 1929 Birmingham*

Burmester, O. H. E.
Bohairic pericopae of Wisdom and Sirach and Coptic Church Offices. *Ph.D. 1933 Cambridge*

Burne, P.
The moral theory of Jeremy Bentham and William Paley. *M.A. 1948 London, Bedford College*

Burnell, N. H.
Glossaire aux branches II et Va du *Roman du Renart*. *M.A. 1926 Leeds*

Burnet, G. B.
The rise, progress, and decline of the Quaker movement in Scotland. *Ph.D. 1937 Glasgow*

Burnett, E.
Romans de caserne à tendances naturalistes, 1887-1899. *Ph.D. 1937 Leeds*

Burnett-Hurst, A. R.
Labour and housing in an Indian city: a study in the economic conditions of the wage-earning classes in Bombay. *M.Sc. 1923 London*

Burnicle, D.
Dunbar's debt to Chaucer. *M.A. 1934 Birmingham*

Burningham, G. W.
The Christian doctrine of immortality, in the light of anthropological evidence and philosophic principles. *M.A. 1935 Leeds*

Burns, A. R.
Money and monetary policy in early times. *Ph.D. 1926 London*

Burns, D. G.
A study of the suitability of certain courses used in the teaching of French to first year grammar school pupils. *M.A. 1949 Birmingham*

Burns, D. K.
The Epistle to the Hebrews: an enquiry into its relation to primitive tradition. *Ph.D. 1933 Edinburgh*

Burns, E. M.
Wages and the State. *Ph.D. 1926 London*

Burns, H. R.
Rainer Maria Rilke's *Mir zur Feier* and *Die frühen Gedichte*: a study in the development of his style. *Ph.D. 1926 Edinburgh*

Burns, R. E.
An historical and comparative study of patentability. *B.Litt. 1935 Oxford*

Burr, E. G.
1. The nature and being of God. 2. The doctrine of the sacraments as 'effective signs of grace'. *B.D. & D.D. 1909 Oxford*

Burr, J.
A view of Anglo-French relations, 1389-1399. *M.A. 1936 Liverpool*

Burrage, C.
The rise and development of English separatist and separatistic congregations during the years 1553-1640. *B.Litt. 1909 Oxford*

Burroughs, E. A.
1. The conception of personality in relation to the present outlook and to the Christian doctrine of God. 2. Intercommunion and Christian reunion. *B.D. & D.D. 1921 Oxford*

Burroughs, G. E. R.
Selection of students for training as teachers. *Ph.D. 1950 Birmingham*

Burrow, A. I.
Three centuries of Birmingham educational development. *M.A. 1931 Birmingham*

Burrow, T.
The language of the Kharosthi documents from Chinese Turkestan. *Ph.D. 1936 Cambridge*

Burrows, H. R.
Studies in social science: 1. The housing problem in Bristol. 2. Some social and economic effects of alcohol consumption. *M.Com. 1932 Leeds*

Burrows, L. R.
Charles Dickens and the eighteenth century tradition of the novel. *M.A. 1948 Sheffield*

Burrows, M. F.
R. S. Hawker, poet and mystic: a study of his life, character and writings. *M.A. 1925 London*

Burrows, M. M.
The position of woman in the seventeenth century and her influence on the literature. *M.A. 1912 Birmingham*

Burrows, R. M. le F.
Rabindranath Tagore - poet, mystic and teacher. *B.Litt. 1947 Dublin, Trinity College*

Burstein, S. R.
The relation between corn-gods and other world deities. *M.A. 1924 Wales*

Burston, W. H.
History and education for citizenship in grammar schools. *M.A. 1947 Bristol*

Burton, B. E.
Sir John Harington's translation of *Orlando Furioso*. *B.Litt. 1939 Oxford*

Burton, E. J.
Collaboration between playwrights in the Elizabethan drama. *M.A. 1930 London, University College*

Burton, F.
Minor English verse narrative, 1600-1651. *M.A. 1936 Sheffield*

Burton, J. W.
Restrictive intervention. *Ph.D. 1942 London, School of Economics and Political Science*

Burton, K. G.
The early newspaper press in Berkshire (1723 to 1855). *M.A. 1950 Reading*

Burtt, L. M.
Persecution and toleration in the period 1660 to 1690. *M.A. 1922 Birmingham*

Bury, J. H.
The development of co-education in English secondary schools. *M.A. 1941 Reading*

Busby, O. M.
Studies in the development of the fool in the Elizabethan drama. *M.A. 1916 London*

Buse, S. I.
The syntax of New Testament Greek in the light of recent papyrological discoveries. *M.A. 1945 Wales*

Bushe-Fox, P. L.
Cases in English courts concerning unrecognized states or governments. *LL.M. 1935 Cambridge*

Busher, T. S.
Exegeses of: Mark ix.1-8; 9-13; 14-29. *B.D. & D.D. 1924 Oxford*

Bushnell, G. H. S.
Archaeology of the Santa Elena Peninsula in southwest Ecuador. *Ph.D. 1947 Cambridge*

Bushrod, W. T.
The development of the great affiliated friendly societies from their humble and often obscure origins in the eighteenth century. *M.A. 1924 Manchester*

Busia, K. A.
The position of the chief in the modern political systems of Ashanti: a study of the influence of contemporary social changes on Ashanti political institutions. *D.Phil. 1947 Oxford*

Bussby, F.
the Semitic background of the Synoptics. *B.D. 1947 Durham*

Busschau, W. J.
The theory of gold supply with special reference to the problems of the Witwatersrand. *D.Phil. 1936 Oxford*

Bussell, F. W.
1. Doctrine of the work and office of Christ, with special reference to the atonement, during the first three centuries. 2. The relations of faith and reason in the Christian system, especially during the Apostolic and sub-Apostolic period. *B.D. 1892 Oxford*

Bussell, F. W.
Exegeses of: Genesis xii.4; xv.12; Romans iv.16,17. *D.D. 1897 Oxford*

Bussey, O.
The religious awakening of 1858-60 in Great Britain and Ireland. *Ph.D. 1947 Edinburgh*

Busteed, J.
Functions of banks in finance of peace and war. *M.Comm. 1926 National University of Ireland*

Busuttil, E. S.
Comparative aspects of the law of unjust enrichment. *B.Litt. 1949 Oxford*

Butcher, E. E.
Bristol Corporation of the Poor, 1696-1834. *M.A. 1930 Bristol*

Butcher, H. L. M.
The Ika-Ibo people, Benin Province, S. Nigeria. *Dip. Anthropology. 1931 Cambridge*

Butcher, N. F. H.
A comparative study of the effects of continuous and intermittent auditory distraction on the mental output of children. *M.A. 1938 London, Institute of Education*

Butchers, R. J.
Youth activities in west Wiltshire: a survey of youth organizations existing in this area, together with an investigation into some of the problems arising therefrom. *M.A. 1944 London, Institute of Education*

Butler, C. D.
The assessment of social attitudes of school children. *M.A. 1949 London, Institute of Education*

Butler, D. C.
Some social and religious aspects of ancestor worship in China. *Ph.D. 1929 Edinburgh*

Butler, F.
Experimental methods in terrestrial magnetism in the late eighteenth and early nineteenth centuries. *M.Sc. 1934 London, University College*

Butler, F. H. C.
Early contributions to our knowledge of respiration. *M.Sc. 1928 London*

Butler, H. J.
The Abbey Theatre and the principal writers connected therewith. *M.A. 1925 National University of Ireland*

Butler, J. B.
The farm worker's standard of living: a study of conditions in Shropshire in 1939. *M.Sc. 1946 London, External Degree*

Butler, J. B.
A survey of egg supplies and consumption in a Midland market town. *M.Com. 1939 Birmingham*

Butler, J. F.
The rational, the arational, and the irrational in the epistemology of theism: an essay in the philosophy of faith. *Ph.D. 1936 Manchester*

Butler, M. E.
A survey of the geographical factors that have controlled the history of Lonsdale. *M.A. 1921 Liverpool*

Butt, J. E.
Thomas Tickell: a study of his life and works. *B.Litt. 1928 Oxford*

Butterworth, E. M.
Sacred verse and the Oxford Movement. *M.A. 1923 Liverpool*

Buttler, E. A.
The Christian element in Shelley's religious thought. *M.A. 1919 Birmingham*

Button, C. N.
Scottish mysticism in the seventeenth century, with special reference to Samuel Rutherford. *Ph.D. 1927 Edinburgh*

Buxton, C. R.
Hoffmann and Nerval. *M.A. 1950 Manchester*

Bygott, J.
Lincolnshire: some aspects of its geography, with special reference to the Wolds. *B.Sc. 1914 Oxford*

Byl, F. V. van der
La renaissance de l'éducation en France, 1764-1833. *Ph.D. 1934 Dublin, Trinity College*

Byles, A. T. P.
Critical edition of Caxton's *Fayttes of armes and of chivalrye. Ph.D. 1933 London, External Degree*

Byles, A. T. P.
Introduction and glossary to the *Book of the Ordre of Chyvalry*, translated and printed by William Caxton from a French version of the Catalan tract by Ramon Lull, entitled *Le Libre del Orde de Cavayleria*; and to Adam Loutfut's Scottish transcription, made in 1494 and contained in Harleian ms. 6149 at the British Museum. *M.A. 1925 London*

Byles, P. G.
Educational needs and opportunities in English villages, 1870-1902. *B.Litt. 1925 Oxford*

Byrne, B. M.
Extension of governmental activity in the economic sphere in the Irish Free State from 1922-1935. *M.A. 1935 National University of Ireland*

Byrne, E. M.
An attempt to ascertain the conditions and final import of a rational experience. *M.A. 1940 National University of Ireland*

Byrne, J.
Representative documents of 'aesthetic' criticism, 1866-1923, in England. *M.A. 1935 Manchester*

Byrne, J. J.
British war finance for 12 months, April 1, 1940-April, 1941. *M.A. 1941 National University of Ireland*

Byrne, J. J.
Right to educate. *M.A. 1942 National University of Ireland*

Byrne, J. J.
A study of British war finance in 1914 to 1919 and 1939 to 1943. *M.Sc. 1943 Cambridge*

Byrne, M. J.
Irish maritime development. *M.Econ.Sc. 1946 National University of Ireland*

Byrne, P.
The ethics of economic values. *M.A. 1932 National University of Ireland*

Byrne, P. C.
Social service in the Irish Free State. *M.A. 1937 National University of Ireland*

Byrne, T. W.
Judicial proceedings under the Dictum de Kenilworth, Northamptonshire. *M.A. 1932 Manchester*

Byrom, H. J.
An investigation of Nicholas Grimald's association with Tottel's *Miscellany. M.A. 1927 London*

Caball, J.
Henry Vaughan. *M.A. 1940 National University of Ireland*

Cabot, J. M.
The Rumanian claims in Hungary before the peace conference. *B.Litt. 1924 Oxford*

Cadfan, N. H.
Hanes a llenyddiaeth cychwyniad a datblygiad mudiad y wladfa Gymreig ym Mhatagonia(The history and literature of the origin and development of the Welsh colony in Patagonia). *M.A. 1942 Wales*

Cadman, W. H.
The meaning of the title 'Son of Man' in the Gospels. *B.Litt. 1920 Oxford*

Cadoux, C. J.
A history of Smurna from the earliest times to 180 A.D. *M.A. 1911 London*

Cadvan-Jones, E.
The idea of mediation as applied to Jesus Christ in the New Testament. *M.Litt. 1927 Cambridge*

Cady, F. W.
An investigation into the sources and language of the Townley mysteries with a view to determining the possible diversity of authorship. *B.Litt. 1908 Oxford*

Caff, W. R. M.
The history of the development of the steam engine to the year 1850, with special reference to the work of West-country engineers. *M.Sc. 1937 London, External Degree*

Caffyn, E. R. E.
An investigation into the development of musical ability of children in a selective general school, with special reference to the effects of age, intelligence and training, together with a plan for a one-year course of work in rudiments of music and musical appreciation. *M.A. 1946 Reading*

Cahill, T. M.
1. Early Irish journalism 2. The early newsheets. *M.A. 1937 National University of Ireland*

Caine, C. L.
The use of graphs and charts in the mining industry. *M.A. 1948 Sheffield*

Caird, C. B.
The New Testament conception of δόξα. *D.Phil. 1944 Oxford*

Cairncross, A. K.
Home and foreign investment in Great Britain, 1870-1913. *Ph.D. 1936 Cambridge*

Cairncross, A. S.
Matthew Arnold: a study of his youth and ideas. *D.Litt. 1932 Glasgow*

Cairns, A.
God's love in the teaching of Jesus according to the synoptic Gospels. *Ph.D. 1937 Belfast*

Cairns, M. B.
Judicial control exercised over local authorities compared with that exercised over Government departments. *M.A. 1947 Bristol*

Caldicott, J. W.
1. Christ descended into hell. 2. After we have received the Holy Ghost, we may depart from grace given, and fall into sin, and by the grace of God we may arise again, and amend our lives. *B.D. & D.D. 1874 Oxford*

Caldwell, F. H.
Group psychology in its bearing on homiletics. *Ph.D. 1934 Edinburgh*

Caldwell, T.
The Christ-mysticism of St. Paul. *Ph.D. 1927 Saint Andrew's*

Callaghan, J.
Ethics of Plato. *M.A. 1915 National University of Ireland*

Callaghan, T.
Saint Augustine's philosophy of liberal education. *Ph.D. 1942 National University of Ireland*

Callan, C. E.
Alice Meynell. *M.A. 1926 Birmingham*

Callan, P.
The siege of Galway, 1651-1652. *M.A. 1931 National University of Ireland*

Callender, M. H.
Roman amphorae. *Ph.D. 1950 Durham*

Callow, H. W.
Heresies of William Tyndale: a thesis. *M.A. 1911 Liverpool*

Callus, D. A. P.
The problem of the plurality of forms at the University of Oxford in the thirteenth century. *D.Phil. 1938 Oxford*

Calvert, M. E.
The construction and validation of a test of mental ability. *M.A. 1946 London, Institute of Education*

Calvert, R. C.
The natural basis of sculptural forms. *M.A. 1936 Belfast*

Cam, H. M.
A comparison of the local administration and law courts of the Carolingian Empire with those of the West Saxon kings. *M.A. 1909 London*

Cambitoglou, A.
Selected south Italian vases of the Manchester Museum. *M.A. 1948 Manchester*

Cambridge, A. M.
The study of Icelandic in England in the eighteenth century. *M.A. 1931 London, University College*

Cameron, A. E.
A comparative study of the mathematical abilities of girls and boys in secondary schools. *M.A. 1923 London*

Cameron, A. I.
James Kennedy, Bishop of St. Andrews. *Ph.D. 1924 Edinburgh*

Cameron, D.
The ecclesiastical politics of Archibald Johnston, Lord Wariston, 1611-1663. *Ph.D. 1930 Edinburgh*

Cameron, F.
Some aspects of feminine education in England during the seventeenth century. *M.A. 1949 Liverpool*

Cameron, H. M.
The educational theory involved in the philosophy of Hegel. *M.A. 1918 London*

Cameron, J.
Celtic law: with special reference to the *Senchus Mór* and the *Book of Aicill*, and a critical examination of the traces of an early Gaelic system of law in Scotland. *Ph.D. 1935 Glasgow*

Cameron, K. N.
A critical study of Cyril Tourneur. *B.Litt. 1934 Oxford*

Camfield, F. W.
The social condition of England during the seventeenth century as illustrated by the Southampton documents. *M.A. 1907 London*

Campbell, A.
Certain dangers to health which result from the present system of public elementary education in Scotland. *M.D. 1883 Glasgow*

Campbell, A.
The production of dipthongs by 'breaking' in Old English from 700 to 900. *B.Litt. 1931 Oxford*

Campbell, A.
A review of the criticisms of Keats and Shelley in *The Edinburgh, The Quarterly* and *Blackwood's. M.A. 1929 Liverpool*

Campbell, D.
The influence of the western Caliphate on the medical system of Europe. *B.Sc. 1923 Oxford*

Campbell, D. J.
Pliny: *Natural History*, book 2, vol. 1 (2). *Ph.D. 1935 Aberdeen*

Campbell, E. M. J.
The history of cartographical symbols. *M.A. 1946 London, Birkbeck College*

Campbell, I. E.
A study of abstract thinking and linguistic development with reference to the education of a child of 'average' intelligence. *Ph.D. 1943 Reading*

Campbell, J.
The life and works of Barnaby Rich. *B.Litt. 1921 Oxford*

Campbell, J. J.
Life in Vandal Africa (A.D.429-533). *M.A. 1934 Belfast*

Campbell, J. K.
Joseph Hall (1574-1656), satirist, character writer and controversialist. *M.A. 1937 London, Birkbeck College*

Campbell, K. W.
The life and works of John Dyer. *Cert.Litt. 1918 Oxford*

Campbell, P. C.
Chinese coolie emigration to countries within the British Empire. *M.Sc. 1922 London*

Campbell, R. J.
1. Some non-Jewish sources of the Christian religion. 2. The Maccabean period as an element in the preparation for Christianity. *B.D. & D.D. 1919 Oxford*

Campbell, R. M.
John Wilson Croker's contributions to the *Quarterly review*, with and estimate of his work in them as a literary critic. *B.Litt. 1937 Oxford*

Campbell, R. M.
Preferential tariffs in the British Empire. *Ph.D. 1929 London*

Campbell, W. McM.
Samuel Rutherford, propagandist and exponent of Scottish Presbyterianism: an exposition of his position and influence in the doctrine and politics of the Scottish church. *Ph.D. 1937 Edinburgh*

Campion, W. J.
The Renaissance humanists and education. *Ph.D. 1940 National University of Ireland*

Candioglou, J. E.
Public international law as relating to international rivers. *LL.D. 1919 London*

Cane, W. A.
The relations between England and Scotland during the minority of Alexander III and during the Barons' War. *M.A. 1923 Manchester*

Canfield, F. W.
Revelation and the Holy Spirit. *D.D. 1933 London, External Degree*

Canham, D.
Style in composition. *M.A. 1923 National University of Ireland*

Cannon, D. J.
Kantian and scholastic theory of knowledge. *M.A. 1945 National University of Ireland*

Cantle, A.
Quo warranto proceedings for the county of Lancaster. *M.A. 1935 London, King's College*

Caomhánach, S. *see* Kavanagh, J.

Capell, A.
The linguistic position of south-eastern Papua. *Ph.D. 1938 London, School of Oriental and African Studies*

Capell, A. M.
J. L. Tieck and the *Volksbücher*. *M.A. 1912 London*

Capon, A. J. E.
Pierre Jurieu: his political ideas and activities. *Ph.D. 1939 London, External Degree*

Carberry, H. P.
The Clare election, 1828. *M.A. 1934 Liverpool*

Cardwell, H. B.
Personal relationships in the work of D. H. Lawrence. *M.A. 1947 Leeds*

Carey, J. D.
Influence of Elizabethan drama on heroic tragedy. *M.A. 1929 London*

Carey, N.
Factors in the mental processes of school children. 1. Visual and autditory imagery. 2. On the nature of the specific mental factors. 3. Factors concerned in the school subjects. *D.Sc. 1916 London*

Carleton, A. P.
A study of the life and writings of St. Ignatius of Antioch, and St. Irenaeus, with special reference to their personal religion and its influence on their work and teaching. *D.D. 1934 Oxford*

Carlisle, H. *see* Ludlam, H.

Carmichael, M.
La description de la nature dans les oeuvres d'Alphonse Daudet. *M.A. 1916 Liverpool*

Carmichael, O. C.
Instinct: its nature and place in human life. *B.Sc. 1917 Oxford*

Carnegie, F. A. R.
Problems connected with the three texts of *Piers the Plowman. M.A. 1923 London*

Carnell, F. G.
The history of English agricultural imports and exports, 1660-1713. *B.Litt. 1945 Oxford*

Carney, P.
The place of mental arithmetic. *M.A. 1934 National University of Ireland*

Carpenter, B.
The light thrown by Plautus on Roman social life of his time. *M.A. 1917 London*

Carpenter, E. F.
The life and times of Thomas Tenison, 1636-1715. *Ph.D. 1943 London, King's College*

Carpenter, E. F.
Thomas Sherlock, Bishop of Bangor, Salisbury and London, 1728-61: his work for Church and State. *M.A. 1934 London, King's College*

Carpenter, H. J. W.
A comparison between the metaphysics of St. Thomas Aquinas and the metaphysics of Aristotle to illustrate the relation of Scholasticism and Aristotelianism. *B.Litt. 1926 Oxford*

Carpenter, J. C.
A pioneer in the work of propagating a knowledge of England and English literature in France, being an investigation into the Abbé Prévost's relations with England and English literature, with special reference to his *Le pour et contre, Cleveland, Mémoires d'un homme de qualité* and *Lettres de Mentor à un jeune seigneur. M.A. 1915 Wales*

Carpenter, J. R.
Population fluctuation studies in biotic communities. *B.Sc. 1938 Oxford*

Carpenter, J. S.
The law relating to legal remedies against debtors, treated historically and comparatively. *LL.D. 1918 London*

Carr, A.
The nature of sleep: a critical survey of the principal theories. *B.Litt. 1949 Oxford*

Carr, B. M. H.
A history of the Kentish dialect, with special reference to agricultural terms. *M.A. 1947 London, King's College*

Carr, C. T.
Die altsaechsischen Nominalkomposita: ihrer Bildung und Bedeutung nach Untersucht. *M.A. 1926 Manchester*

Carr, H. J.
A critical exposition of the social and economic ideas of John Francis Bray; and an estimate of his influence upon Karl Marx. *Ph.D. 1943 London, External Degree*

Carr, M. E. J.
The development of mathematical theories of electricity prior to Maxwell, with special reference to the concept potential. *M.Sc. 1949 London, University College*

Carrick, E.
The life and works of Fulk Greville: a study of his poetry and of the political and religious ideas revealed in it (1554-1628). *M.A. 1936 London, Bedford College*

Carrier, E. H.
Jean-Baptiste Carrier and the Terror in the Vendée. *M.A. 1915 Liverpool*

Carrington, H. E.
The development of technical education in England, with special reference to Leeds. *M.Ed. 1945 Leeds*

Carrington, J. F.
A comparative study of some Central African gong-languages. *Ph.D. 1946 London, External Degree*

Carrington, N. T.
John Bunyan as a literary artist. *M.A. 1926 Birmingham*

Carrington, R. C.
The development of social and economic life at Pompeii. *D.Phil. 1933 Oxford*

Carroll, B. G.
Constitutions of Archbishop Chichele. *M.A. 1932 Manchester*

Carroll, H. F.
Spiritualism of Plato and Aristotle. *M.A. 1913 National University of Ireland*

Carroll, M.
Othello in Shakespeare criticism. *M.A. 1946 National University of Ireland*

Carrothers, W. A.
Emigration from the British Isles, 1815-1921. *Ph.D. 1921 Edinburgh*

Carruthers, S. W.
The *Westminster Confession of Faith*: being an account of the printing and preparation of its seven leading editions to which is appended a critical text with notes thereon. *Ph.D. 1929 Edinburgh*

Carslaw, R. McG.
Farm management research technique. *Ph.D. 1931 Cambridge*

Carson, J. G.
Some aspects of R. Browning's philosophy of love. *M.A. 1920 Birmingham*

Carsten, F. L.
The development of the 'manorial' system (*Grundherrschaft* and *Gutsherrschaft*) in north-eastern Germany until the end of the sixteenth century. *D.Phil. 1942 Oxford*

Carter, A. E. C.
The work of Arnold Bennett as a novelist. *M.A. 1927 Birmingham*

Carter, A. T.
The defence of compulsive necessity in the civil law. *D.C.L. 1893 Oxford*

Carter, E. B.
The development of satire in prose, 1640-1660. *M.A. 1948 Manchester*

Carter, G. R.
The modern tendency towards industrial combination in some spheres of British industry: its forms and developments, their causes and determinant circumstances. *M.A. 1911 Wales*

Carter, J.
A functional classification of settlement in Breckland. *B.Litt. 1950 Oxford*

Carter, L. J.
The image of God in man: an enquiry into the doctrine of human nature. *D.D. 1943 Durham*

Carter, T. Le M.
Canada in the International Labour Organisation. *M.Sc. 1939 London, School of Economics and Political Science*

Cartman, J.
The history and present state of Hinduism in Ceylon. *M.A. 1950 Manchester*

Cartwright, G. S.
The developments of the grain trade in the twentieth century, and their influence on the world wheat situation. *B.Litt. 1932 Oxford*

Cartwright, M.
How far did Virgil, Horace and Tacitus supply the want of a middle voice in Latin by the use of the so-called passive?. *M.A. 1906 Wales*

Carus-Wilson, E. M. *see* Wilson, E. M. Carus-

Carver, P. L.
Palsgrave's translation of *Acolastus* (by Gulielmus Fullonius). *Ph.D. 1934 Leeds*

Casady, E. R.
Henry Howard, Earl of Surrey. *B.Litt. 1931 Oxford*

Case, F. W. E.
A comparison of the mental patterns of English children with those of a comparable age in British Guiana. *M.A. 1947 London, Institute of Education*

Casey, G.
La doctrine de l'a priori chez Aristote. *M.A. 1934 National University of Ireland*

Casey, P. J.
Ferguson and Anglo-Irish literature. *M.A. 1946 National University of Ireland*

Casey, P. J.
Sir Samuel Ferguson: his life and work. *Ph.D. 1948 National University of Ireland*

Casey, R. P.
Studies in Clement of Alexandria. *Ph.D. 1924 Cambridge*

Casey, T. J.
Der offene Weg: Rainer Maria Rilke. *M.A. 1949 National University of Ireland*

Cash, E. F.
L'archaisme et les procédés littéraires chez P. L. Courier. *M.A. 1914 Birmingham*

Cash, I.
Nature and scope of private nuisance. *B.Litt. 1939 Oxford*

Cashell, M.
A metaphysic of value. *M.A. 1949 National University of Ireland*

Casher, C. J.
1. The deity of Christ and of the Holy Spirit as revealed in the New Testament. 2. The Scriptural evidence for the Resurrection of Christ. *B.D. 1899 Oxford*

Casher, C. J.
Expositions of: St. Matthew iv.3, 4: St. Luke iv.3,4: the first temptation; St. Matthew iv.5; St. Luke iv.9: the second temptation; St. Matthew iv.8-11; St. Luke iv.5-8: the third temptation. *D.D. 1903 Oxford*

Caspari, F. W. E. C.
The influence of the Renaissance on the English conception of the State. *B.Litt. 1936 Oxford*

Casper, E. R.
The refugee and international law. *LL.M. 1948 London, University College*

Cass, F. V.
Essai sur *Eugénie Grandet* et *Un coeur simple. M.A. 1920 Birmingham*

Cassidy, F. S.
An experimental research on the problem of teaching geography to backward boys in present day senior schools. *M.Ed. 1937 Leeds*

Cassidy, J. F.
Preparation of accounts from incomplete records. *M.Comm. 1947 National University of Ireland*

Cassirer, H. W.
Commentary on Kant's *Critique of Judgment. Ph.D. 1938 Glasgow*

Cassirer, R.
The Irish influence on the Liberal movement in England, 1789-1832, with special reference to the period 1815-32. *Ph.D. 1940 London, School of Economics and Political Science*

Casson, L. F.
The diction of alliterative poetry in English in the fourteenth and fifteenth centuries. *B.Litt. 1937 Oxford*

Casson, L. F.
The romance of Sir Degrevant: edited from the mss, at Lincoln and Cambridge, with introduction, notes and glossary. . *Ph.D. 1942 Edinburgh*

Casson, T. E.
The relation of form and subject in the romantic movement of English Literature. *B.Litt. 1911 Oxford*

Cast, B. M. D.
An investigation on methods of marking composition. *M.A. 1939 London, University College*

Castello, D.
Ictus lengthening in Homer. *M.A. 1912 London*

Cater, J. J.
The sentiment of nationality. *Ph.D. 1924 Edinburgh*

Catling, G. M.
The history of the knowledge of the spectrum. *M.Sc. 1926 London*

Catlow, H. M.
A study of Henry Vaughan. *M.A. 1916 Birmingham*

Cattell, R. B.
Perseveration tests of temperament. *M.A. 1932 London, Day Training College*

Cattell, R. B.
The subjective character of cognition and the presensational development of perception. *Ph.D. 1929 London*

Caughey, J.
The influence of conation upon mental and manual operations. *Ph.D. 1929 London*

Cavalier, H. R.
1. Christianity and pantheism. 2. The heavenly priesthood of our Lord. *B.D. 1906 Oxford*

Cave, M. C.
Antonio Conti e il suo posto nella letteratura del settecento. *M.A. 1922 London*

Cavenagh, F. A.
The ethical end of Plato's theory of ideas. *M.A. 1909 London*

Cavers, D. L.
The Surrey dialect in Middle English in relation to the dialects of the adjacent counties. *B.Litt. 1929 Oxford*

Cawley, A. C.
A study of the language of the various texts of Trevisa's translation of Higden's *Polychronicon. M.A. 1938 London, University College*

Cawley, F.
The transcendence of Jesus Christ: a study of the unique features of his person and work, with special reference to the fourth Gospel. *Ph.D. 1934 Edinburgh*

Caws, A. G.
The perception of tachistoscopically exposed letters. *Ph.D. 1933 London, King's College*

Cawte, L. H.
Great Britain and the suppression of the Cuban slave trade, 1817-1865. *M.A. 1934 London, King's College*

Cazalet, W. G.
The doctrine of Calvin: parts I and II. *B.D. & D.D. 1924 Oxford*

Cazenove, J. G.
1. Although the eternal power and divinity of the Creator may be learnt by reason, yet man in his present condition needs the aid of revelation to enlighten him respecting the duties of religion. 2. St. Paul is the author of the two Epistles to the Thessalonians. *B.D. & D.D. 1874 Oxford*

Cedervall, E. W.
The influence of Italian literature on Spenser and Sidney. *M.A. 1920 Wales*

Cerný, L.
The day of Jahweh and some relevant problems. *B.Litt. 1944 Oxford*

Chadburn, J. H. P.
A critical and literary study of Baudelaire's *Fleurs du Mal. B.Litt. 1929 Oxford*

Chadwick, A.
The perception of musical relationships by school children: an anlysis of experimental data and a discussion of practical and theoretical issues. *M.Ed. 1949 Leeds*

Chadwick, C.
Du Bartas et la bible. *M.A. 1949 Liverpool*

Chadwick, D. E.
An index verborum to the Lindisfarne Gospels. *M.A. 1934 Leeds*

Chadwick, D. L.
The criticisms of Walter Pater. *M.A. 1928 Birmingham*

Chadwick, G. F.
The character of open spaces in the modern town plan. *M.A. 1950 Manchester*

Chadwick, J. H.
Schelling to Feuerbach. *M.A. 1910 London*

Chafy-Chafy, W. K. W.
1. On Antichrist. 2. On infant baptism. *B.D. & D.D. 1891 Oxford*

Chakravarti, P. C.
The art of war in Ancient India. *Ph.D. 1938 London, School of Oriental and African Studies*

Chakravarty, A. C.
Postwar English poetry. *D.Phil. 1937 Oxford*

Chakravarty, N. P.
Translation of some Kharosthi documents. *Ph.D. 1924 Cambridge*

Chaldecott, J. A.
The scientific works of Léon Foucault. *M.Sc. 1949 London, University College*

Chalk, E. S.
1. The Sermon on the Mount in light of today. 2. The Christian argument from the study of ethnology. *B.D. 1921 Oxford*

Chalmers, W. N.
Personality and its relation to the school as an ideal society. *M.A. 1924 Liverpool*

Chaloner, N. I.
The literary criticism of C. Lamb. *M.A. 1916 Birmingham*

Chaloner, W. H.
The social and economic development of Crewe, 1800-1923. *Ph.D. 1939 Manchester*

Chaloner, W. H.
The social and economic development of Crewe, 1830-1880. *M.A. 1937 Manchester*

Chamberlain, M. G.
A study of agnosticism and intellectual doubt in the age of Shakespeare as expressed in the literature of the period, with special reference to Marston and the Inns of Court circle. *M.A. 1934 London, King's College*

Chamberlain, V. C.
An enquiry into the nature of the difficulties experienced by university students in choosing a career. *M.A. 1950 Manchester*

Chambers, J. D.
Nottinghamshire in the eighteenth century: a study of the movements leading to the industrial revolutions of the nineteenth century. *Ph.D. 1927 London*

Chambers, S. P.
The equilibrium analysis of a monetary economy. *M.Sc. 1934 London, School of Economics and Political Science*

Champ, J. M.
A study of the attitude of women (students, teachers and former teachers) towards teaching as a career. *M.A. 1948 London, Institute of Education*

Champenois, J. J.
The rise of the critical review in the eighteenth century. *B.Litt. 1913 Oxford*

Champernowne, H. I.
The psychological interview (a survey of methods and practical results in cases of educational and occupational difficulty). *Ph.D. 1940 London, School of Hygiene and Tropical Medicine*

Champion, H. J.
The establishment of British government in Isle St. John (Prince Edward Island) 1758-1784. *M.A. 1934 London, King's College*

Champion, S. A.
Abbreviation by initials: a tendency in modern language studies, with special reference to the French press, 1919-1945. *M.A. 1949 London, University College*

Champness, R.
Early history of the English law relating to letters patent tor inventions. *LL.M. 1930 Cambridge*

Champneys, W.
The accommodation for the sick provided at certain public schools for boys in England. *D.M. 1929 Oxford*

Chance, J.
The school group - its leaders and leadership. *M.A. 1933 Birmingham*

Chance, M. E. Clayton- see Clayton-Chance, M. E.

Chance, R. J. F.
City State and Nation State: a study of the political theory of Plato and Aristotle in relation to the modern State. *Ph.D. 1927 London*

Chance, T. W.
The date, structure and authorship of the Book of Deuteronomy. *M.A. 1900 Wales*

Chand, B.
Discretionary powers in the Indian Government, with special reference to district administration. *Ph.D. 1938 London, School of Economics and Political Science*

Chand, T.
The influence of Islam on Indian culture. *D.Phil. 1922 Oxford*

Chandler, F. W.
A catalogue of names of persons in the German court epics: an examination of the literary sources and dissemination together with notes on the etymologies of the more important names. *M.A. 1936 London, Birkbeck College*

Chandler, M.
The confusion between moral and aesthetic ideas in Greek literary criticism and philosophy. *M.A. 1933 London, Royal Holloway College*

Chandler, S. L.
The Anglican Church and political parties, 1701-1737. *M.A. 1930 Birmingham*

Chandra, A. K.
Protection of minorities of shareholders by the law. *LL.D. 1944 Dublin, Trinity College*

Chandra, L.
The political and cultural history of the Panjab, including the North West Frontier Province in its earliest period. *Ph.D. 1940 London, School of Oriental and African Studies*

Chandra, M.
Studies in Indian dancing as depicted in painting and sculpture and the representations of the musical ragas in painting. *Ph.D. 1934 London, School of Oriental and African Studies*

Chandra, P.
The relations between the Board of Commissioners for the Affairs of India and the Court of Directors, 1784-1816. *Ph.D. 1933 London, School of Economics and Political Science*

Chandran, J. R.
A comparison of the pagan apologetic of Celsus against Christianity as contained in Origen's *Contra Celsum*, and the neo-Hindu attitude to Christianity as represented in the works of Vivekananda, and an estimate of the value of Origen's reply for Christian apologetics against neo-Hinduism. *B.Litt. 1949 Oxford*

Chang, C.
The English police system and its applicability to rural China. *Ph.D. 1937 London, School of Economics and Political Science*

Chang, H. C.
Early Elizabethan dramatic style with particular regard to the works of George Reele. *Ph.D. 1949 Edinburgh*

Chang, K.
Budget control: a study of fiscal policy as an instrument for regulating economic fluctuations. *M.A. 1947 Leeds*

Chang, K. C.
The philosophy of Moh Tih. *M.A. 1926 Liverpool*

Chang, T. C.
Cyclical movements in the balance of payments. *Ph.D. 1948 Cambridge*

Chang, T. T.
The finance of co-operative organizations with special reference to methods of financing agricultural co-operatives, including state assistance. *M.Sc. 1938 Wales*

Chang, W. S.
The development, significance, and some limitations of Hegel's ethical teaching. *D.Phil. 1923 Oxford*

Chang, Y. N.
The method of teaching English in Chinese middle schools. *M.Ed. 1937 Leeds*

Chang, Y. T.
The economic development and prospects of Inner Mongolia (Chahar, Suiyuan, and Niugria). *M.A. 1929 Liverpool*

Channing, H. A.
The influence of other philosophies on later Stoicism. *M.A. 1948 London, Royal Holloway College*

Chapelhow, J.
1. The canon of Scripture. 2. The Church. *B.D. 1876 Oxford*

Chapelhow, J.
1. I Corinthians xv.29: baptism for the dead. 2. II Corinthians xii.7: St. Paul's thorn in the flesh. 3. I Peter iii.18-20: the spirits in prison. *D.D. 1893 Oxford*

Chapin, L. T.
The British background of the American theory of judicial review. *Ph.D. 1938 Edinburgh*

Chaplin, W. N.
The control of the press in England before the granting of the charter to the Stationers' Company. *M.A. 1935 London*

Chapman, A. B. W.
The commercial relations of England and Portugal: 1487-1807. *D.Sc. 1907 London*

Chapman, C. T.
A study in soteriology with special reference to the ransom theory in its origin, historical setting and significance. *Ph.D. 1946 London, King's College*

Chapman, D.
The application of the social survey to problems of housing and town and country planning. *Ph.D. 1948 London, External Degree*

Chapman, E. F.
The development of critical theories in England, 1660-1771. *Ph.D. 1935 London, King's College*

Chapman, P. F.
Biographical study of T. Norton. *M.A. 1931 Bristol*

Chapman, R.
Fortune in Elizabethan drama: an attempt to discover, chiefly from plays written between 1570 and 1620, the conception of that period concerning the person and activities of the goddess Fortuna. *M.A. 1947 London, King's College*

Chapman, R. B.
British relations with Mexico, 1859-62. *B.Litt. 1936 Oxford*

Chapman, T.
The working of the principle of co-option, with special reference to education committees. *M.A. 1938 Manchester*

Chapman, T. A.
A commentary on Philippians ii.5-11; Colossians i.13-19; Hebrews i.1-3. *D.D. 1924 Oxford*

Chapman, T. A.
1. The doctrine of the being and nature of God. 2. The Incarnation of our Lord. *B.D. 1907 Oxford*

Chapman, W. C.
The distribution of traditional types of buildings on the Welsh borderland. *M.A. 1936 Manchester*

Chapman, W. D.
Town and country planning in Cheshire, with special reference to the policy of decentralisation and the maintenance of the agricultural industry. *M.A. 1946 Manchester*

Chappell, M. G.
The Select Committee of 1861 on colonial military expenditure and its antecedents. *M.A. 1934 London, Westfield College*

Chapple, G. F.
The correspondence of the City of London. *Ph.D. 1938 London, Birkbeck College*

Charles, B. G.
Non-Celtic placenames in Wales and Monmouthshire. *Ph.D. 1935 London, University College*

Charles, B. G.
Norse relations with Wales. *M.A. 1932 Wales*

Charles, H. R.
An edition of Book I of Hooker's *Ecclesiastical polity* with an introductory essay dealing with the subject matter of the book and with the author's position in the history of political thought. *M.A. 1928 Wales*

Charles, M.
A study of the teaching of Jesus in its application to modern economic problems. *B.Litt. 1935 Oxford*

Charles, P. A.
The press articles of Charles Nodier. *M.A. 1931 Wales*

Charlesworth, G.
The moral ideal and its bearing on theism. *M.A. 1945 Liverpool*

Charlesworth, J.
Liability for dangerous things. *LL.D. 1922 London*

Charlesworth, R.
The history of education in Warrington. *M.Ed. 1936 Manchester*

Charlesworth, S.
The problem of the North in the early years of Queen Elizabeth's reign. *Ph.D. 1931 Sheffield*

Charlton, J. M. T.
Middle Attic black-figure painting, with special reference to vases in the Manchester district. *M.A. 1940 Manchester*

Charmoy, F. d'E. de *see* de Charmoy, F. d'E.

Chart, D. A.
An economic history of Ireland. *Litt.D. 1922 Dublin, Trinity College*

Chart, M. M. C.
A comparison of the function of imagination in the fine arts and in philosophy. *M.A. 1939 Reading*

Chary, K. V.
A statistical analysis of the performance of boys and girls in science (physics and chemistry). *M.A. 1948 London, Institute of Education*

Chasey, H.
Anglo-American relations in the tobacco trade to the end of the nineteenth and the beginning of the twentieth century. *M.A. 1950 Bristol*

Chatterjee, P. H.
Studies of labour wastage and sickness absence. *Ph.D. 1941 London, University College*

Chatterji, B. R.
Indian political and cultural influence in Cambodia (Kambuja) from the sixth to the fourteenth centuries. *Ph.D. 1926 London*

Chatterji, S. C.
The introduction of a vocational bias into schools in North India. *M.A. 1939 Leeds*

Chatterji, S. C.
A system of physical education for schoolboys in India. *M.Ed. 1928 Leeds*

Chatterji, S. C.
The training of teachers in India. *Ph.D. 1942 Dublin, Trinity College*

Chatterji, S. P.
A comparative study in the methods employed in England and France for the grouping of children and young persons in different types of schools. *Ph.D. 1936 London, King's College*

Chaturvedi, H. R.
The future of agricultural co-operation in the United Provinces: an examination of co-operative experience in parts of Europe, America and India with special reference to the problems of agricultural co-operation in the United Provinces. *Ph.D. 1940 Wales*

Chaturvedi, H. S. D.
Tagore at Shantinekatan, or Sir Rabindranath Tagore's educational experiment at Shantinekatan. *M.Ed. 1929 Leeds*

Chaturvedi, S. N.
The history and development of rural education in the United Provinces of Agra and Oudh, from 1840 to 1926. *M.A. 1931 London, King's College*

Chaudhuri, J.
The position of women in the Vedic ritual. *Ph.D. 1934 London, School of Oriental and African Studies*

Chaundy, L. W.
The contribution of certain nineteenth century scientists to the development of educational values. *M.A. 1950 Reading*

Chaundy, L. W.
Some studies in animal heat. *M.Sc. 1938 London, King's College*

Chavasse, C. L.
The bride of Christ; an enquiry into the nuptial element in early Christianity. *B.Litt. 1940 Dublin, Trinity College*

Chavetois, G. A. le *see* Le Chavetois, G. A.

Chavetois, I. M. le *see* Le Chavetois, I. M.

Checkland, S. G.
The political economists and the politicians from Waterloo to the Reform Bill. *M. Com. 1947 Birmingham*

Cheema, M. S.
The rise to power of Ranjit Singh. *B.Litt. 1925 Oxford*

Cheeseman, E. A.
Epidemics in schools: a statistical analysis of data of the sickness experience in eighteen public schools, collected during the years 1935 to 1939. *Ph.D. 1947 London, School of Hygiene and Tropical Medicine*

Cheetham, G. B.
The development of the iron and steel industry of North Lancashire and South Cumberland in relation to geographical factors. *M.Sc. 1937 Leeds*

Cheetham, J. O.
The history, condition and prospects of the South Wales coalfield, considered mainly from the point of view of markets and industrial organisation. *M.A. 1921 Wales*

Cheever, M. D. F.
The origin of scientific excavation in Egypt and its development during the nineteenth century. *M.A. 1938 London, University College*

Chegwidden, C.
Some aspects of the social position of the professional teacher at various periods in the history of education. *M.A. 1933 Wales*

Chelliah, D. D.
A history of educational policy of the Straits Settlements from 1800 to 1925 (*circa*). *Ph.D. 1940 London, External Degree*

Chen, L.
Oscillation at the threshold and in mental work. *Ph.D. 1934 London, University College*

Chen, M.
The improvement of vocational education in China. *M.A. 1938 Leeds*

Chen, M. S.
The monetary and banking policy of Great Britain during and since the great depression. *M.Sc. 1939 London, School of Economics and Political Science*

Chen, T. C.
China's frontier's problems. *Ph.D. 1937 London, School of Economics and Political Science*

Chen, T. C.
Recognition in international law. *D.Phil. 1948 Oxford*

Ch'en, Y.
The International Settlement at Shanghai. *Ph.D. 1940 London, School of Economics and Political Science*

Cheng, C. C.
The transition from individualist to socialist political thinking in England. *B.Phil. 1948 Oxford*

Cheng, F. T.
The rules of private international law determining capacity to contract. *LL.D. 1916 London*

Cheng, H. T.
The problem of marketing foreign goods in China. *M.Sc. 1938 Cambridge*

Cheng, J. C.
Some aspects of the Taiping rebellion in China, 1850-64. *Ph.D. 1950 Cambridge*

Cheng, K. C.
The presentation of the Manchurian Question in the English press 1931-1933. *Ph.D. 1938 London, School of Economics and Political Science*

Cheng, S. G.
Modern China: a political study. *D.Sc. 1921 London*

Cheng, S. M.
Babouvism and the theory of proletarian dictatorship. *Ph.D. 1934 London, School of Economics and Political Science*

Cheng, T. C.
The education of overseas Chinese: a comparative study of Hong Kong, Singapore and the East Indies. *M.A. 1949 London, Institute of Education*

Cheng, T. T.
The problems of monetary reform in China. *M.Sc. 1937 London, School of Economics and Political Science*

Cherian, K. V.
A dissertation upon Benjamin Disraeli as a man of letters. *M.A. 1932 Liverpool*

Cherrick, B.
The arguments for the unity of God in medieval Jewish philosophy. *M.A. 1937 Manchester*

Cherry, A. C.
A life of Charles Knight (1791 to 1873) with special reference to his political and educational activities. *M.A. 1942 London, King's College*

Cheshire, A. H.
The educational theory of the English Utilitarians. *M.A. 1923 Liverpool*

Cheshire, G. C.
The modern law of real property. *D.C.L. 1927 Oxford*

Chesney, E.
The sequestration of estates 1643-1660. *Ph.D. 1928 Sheffield*

Chesshire, R. S. P.
1. The *Quicumque Vult*. 2. The discipline of the early Church. *B.D. & D.D. 1910 Oxford*

Chesters, E. M.
Sir Thomas More and education. *M.A. 1923 Liverpool*

Chettle, E. G.
Contribution à étude de Flore et Blanceflor. *M.A. 1920 Birmingham*

Chevenix Trench, S. M.
Relations between English monasteries and their patrons in the thirteenth century. *B.Litt. 1950 Oxford*

Chew, H. M.
English ecclesiastical baronies and knight service, especially in the thirteenth and fourteenth centuries. *Ph.D. 1926 London*

Chew, H. M.
Scutages and aids in England, particularly in the fourteenth century. *M.A. 1921 London*

Chi, C. H.
Personnel administration in public utility enterprises, with special reference to railways and to Chinese conditions. *M.Sc. 1938 London, School of Economics and Political Science*

Chiappe, A. J.
Studies in the poetry of Henry Vaughan. *Ph.D. 1942 Cambridge*

Chick, E.
A preliminary investigation of the pedigree of the B-text mss. of *Piers Plowman*. *M.A. 1914 London*

Chickera, E. B. de *see* De Chickera, E. B.

Chien, C. L.
The place of judiciary in the modern state with special reference to the English judiciary. *Ph.D. 1936 London*

Ch'ien, C. S.
China in the English literature of the eighteenth century. *B.Litt. 1937 Oxford*

Chilcott, C. M.
The influence of Plato on the philosophy of the Empire 53-180 A.D. *M.A. 1922 London*

Child, C. J.
Johann Gottlieb Fichte and the genesis of the Nationalist movement in Germany. *M.A. 1934 Birmingham*

Child, R. L.
The doctrine of grace as illustrated by the experience and teaching of St. Paul, Augustine, and Luther. *B.Litt. 1925 Oxford*

Childe, V. G.
Indo-European influences in Hellenic civilization down to the end of the Bronze Age. *B.Litt. 1916 Oxford*

Childs, E. C.
The coherence notion of truth as in Mr. Joachim, and the pragmatic theory of truth as in the writings of Professor James. *M.A. 1909 London*

Childs, S.
The lords' ordainers and their work: a sketch of baronial government. *M.A. 1910 London*

Childs, T. J.
An edition of *Nosce teipsum* by Sir John Davies, with a prefatory study of his poetry. *B.Litt. 1939 Oxford*

Chilton, A.
The colloquial movement in English prose from 1660 to 1704. *M.A. 1948 London, Queen Mary College*

Chilton, A.
1. The relation of confirmation to baptism. 2. The meaning and use of the Messianic titles: 'Christ', 'Son of David', 'Son of God', 'Son of Man'. *B.D. & D.D. 1906 Oxford*

Chilver, G. E. F.
The social and economic history of Cisalpine Gaul under the early Empire to the death of Trajan. *D.Phil. 1936 Oxford*

Chinn, W. L.
A juvenile court survey. *M.A. 1933 Birmingham*

Chirgwin, A. M.
The evolution of the idea of God. *M.A. 1921 Bristol*

Chisholm, A.
1. Labour's Magna Carta. 2. The international labour organizations of the League of Nations. *D.Litt. 1922 Glasgow*

Chishti, K. A.
The British conquest of Sind. *M.A. 1938 London, School of Oriental and African Studies*

Chiu, V. Y.
The Chinese constitution. *Ph.D. 1921 London*

Chi-wu Chu, C.
The relation between international law and municipal law. *D.Phil. 1949 Oxford*

Cho, T. L.
Joint stock banking in China. *M.Sc. 1937 London, School of Economics and Political Science*

Choilleadh, B. M. *see* MacGiolla Choilleadh, B.

Chopra, V. K.
A study of methods of national income measurements, with special reference to the problems of India. *Ph.D. 1949 London, School of Economics and Political Science*

Chossudowsky, E. M.
Soviet trade and distribution, 1917-1937: the growth of planned consumption. *Ph.D. 1940 Edinburgh*

Chothia, F. S.
A comparative study of the curriculum (with special reference to science) of the secondary schools of England and the U.S.A.; and implications for the curriculum of Bombay secondary schools. *M.A. 1948 London, Institute of Education*

Choudhury, K. P.
A study of interests in relation to the needs of children. *M.A. 1948 London, Institute of Education*

Choudhury, T.
On the interpretation of some doubtful words in the *Atharvaveda*. *Ph.D. 1930 London, School of Oriental and African Studies*

Chow, P. G.
A hundred years of economic relations between China and Great Britain, 1834-1934. *Ph.D. 1938 Edinburgh*

Chow, T. K.
Economic background of the modern diplomacy of the Great Powers in the Far East since the World War. *M.Sc. 1934 London, School of Economics and Political Science*

Chowdary, V. V.
Criminal responsibilities in India. *LL.D. 1928 London*

Chrétien, G. L.
A comparative study of the problem of consent in the formation of contract in French and English law. *D.Phil. 1949 Oxford*

Chrimes, S. B.
John, first Duke of Bedford: his work and policy in England, 1389-1435. *M.A. 1929 London*

Chrimes, S. B.
Studies in constitutional ideas in England during the fifteenth century. *Ph.D. 1933 Cambridge*

Christelow, A.
The part of Castile in the Hundred Years' War. *B.Litt. 1934 Oxford*

Christian, C. J.
The relation of the Methodist movement to political thought in England, 1800-1850, with special reference to Methodist records. *M.A. 1936 Manchester*

Christie, A. H.
Harappa in Asia. *M.A. 1950 Manchester*

Christie, I. M.
Studies in the thought of Thomas Carlyle. *M.A. 1947 Belfast*

Christie, T.
Certain mental disorders in relation to gross antisocial conduct. *M.D. 1936 Saint Andrew's*

Christie, W. A.
The history and development of the Sunday school in England. *M.A. 1937 Liverpool*

Christopher, J. W.
American diplomatic policy in China, 1928-33. *D.Phil. 1948 Oxford*

Christophersen, P. H.
The early history of ballad literature, with special reference to English and Scandinavian ballads. *Ph.D. 1943 Cambridge*

Chu, C. Chi-wu *see* Chi-wu Chu, C.

Chu, K. C.
The reorganisation of company capital. *M.Com. 1939 Birmingham*

Chu, Y.-F.
The rise of the Turkish Empire in central Asia (A.D. 552-615). *B.Litt. 1937 Oxford*

Chubb, B. H.
The application of the Local Government Act, 1929, to London. *M.Sc. 1940 London, School of Economics and Political Science*

Chubb, F. B.
The powers of inquisition into and control over public finance exercised by the House of Commons, more especially by its committees. *D.Phil. 1950 Oxford*

Chubb, J. N.
Error and illusion. *D.Phil. 1937 Oxford*

Chubb, N. F.
A critical examination of Sigmund Freud's theory of personality. *M.A. 1937 London, University College*

Chung, T. Y.
The historical novels of six Victorian writers: Thackeray, Dickens, Charles Kingsley, George Eliot, Meredith and Walter Pater. *Ph.D. 1936 Edinburgh*

Chung-Sieu, C.
British loans to China from 1860 to 1913, with special reference to the period 1894-1913. *Ph.D. 1940 London, School of Economics and Political Science*

Church, A. F.
La syntaxe des propositions adverbiales dans *Huon de Bordeaux*. *M.A. 1934 London, Birkbeck College*

Church, L. F.
Oglethorpe and social and religious movements in England and Georgia. *Ph.D. 1928 London*

Church, R. J.
The railways of West Africa: a geographical and historical analysis. *Ph.D. 1943 London, External Degree*

Church, R. W.
A critical exposition of the theory of knowledge in Malebranche. *D.Phil. 1930 Oxford*

Churchard, M. B. A.
An analysis of the industrial and agricultural life of south-east England. *Ph.D. 1933 London, Bedford College*

Ciniphéic, A. M. De.
La sensibilité d'Eugénie de Guérin. *M.A. 1947 National University of Ireland*

Citron, B.
The evangelical doctrine of conversion, Lutheran and Reformed. *Ph.D. 1946 Edinburgh*

Clancy, T. J.
Social security and Ireland. *M.Econ.Sc. 1951 National University of Ireland*

Clapham, J. H.
The ability to arrange concepts in order and the relation of this ability to reasoning. *M.A. 1935 London, Institute of Education*

Clapham, M.
School societies: their organization as part of the curriculum. *M.Ed. 1939 Leeds*

Clark, A. J.
The evolution of radical theory after the Reformation. *M.A. 1910 London*

Clark, E. M.
Konko-kyo: a sect of modern Shintoism. *Ph.D. 1924 Edinburgh*

Clark, F. I.
The position of women in contemporary France. *M.Sc. 1935 London, School of Economics and Political Science*

Clark, F. S.
The nature and effect of floating securities. *LL.D. 1922 London*

Clark, G.
Co-education: an analysis of the work and principles of the mixed schools. *M.A. 1937 Liverpool*

Clark, H. V.
The scope and value of psychological testing, with special reference to the examination of scholarship candidates for further education. *M.A. 1936 Liverpool*

Clark, H. W.
Personnel in retail distribution, with special reference to the training of juvenile employees. *M.Com. 1937 Birmingham*

Clark, I. M.
The history of Church discipline in Scotland. *Ph.D. 1926 Aberdeen*

Clark, J. M.
Zur Geschichte der umschreibenden Konjugation im Deutschen. *M.A. 1913 London*

Clark, J. N. C.
The annotations of Ekkehart IV in the Orosius ms. St. Gall 621: a contribution to the question of the nature of ancient glosses. *Ph.D. 1931 Edinburgh*

Clark, M. E.
British diplomacy and the recognition of Louis Napoleon. *M.A. 1922 London, King's College*

Clark, M. J. *see* McCormick, M. J.

Clark, N.
An edition of *The royall slave* by William Cartwright, with a consideration of the manuscript newly acquired by the British Museum together with a short life of Cartwright and a general survey of his dramatic works. *M.A. 1932 London, University College*

Clark, R. B.
Brother Elias and the government of the Franciscan Order, 1217-39. *Ph.D. 1950 Cambridge*

Clark, R. H.
Pierre Claude François Daunou (1761-1840); a literary and biographical essay. *Ph.D. 1939 London, Queen Mary College*

Clark, R. H.
Un critique littéraire de l'époque romantique: Gustave Planche. *M.A. 1934 London, Queen Mary College*

Clark, W. H.
The conception of the mission of the Church in early reformed theology, with special reference to Calvin's theology and practice in Geneva. *Ph.D. 1928 Edinburgh*

Clarke, A. J.
John Ford. *M.A. 1916 National University of Ireland*

Clarke, B. F.
Aspects of inhibition. *B.Litt. 1948 Oxford*

Clarke, C. P. R.
Gibraltar as a British possession to 1783. *B.Litt. 1934 Oxford*

Clarke, E. B.
Economic changes in the manor of Cranborne (Dorset) in the sixteenth and seventeenth centuries. *B.Litt. 1939 Oxford*

Clarke, E. L.
An enquiry into the present state of educational opportunity in England and Wales. *M.Ed. 1935 Durham*

Clarke, E. R.
The interpretation of age frequency data. *M.Ed. 1933 Manchester*

Clarke, G.
The range and nature of the factors in perceptual tests. *Ph.D. 1937 London, University College*

Clarke, G. R.
The political and social teachings of the Young Irelanders, 1842-1848. *M.A. 1936 Belfast*

Clarke, H.
Charles Dickens' contribution to the social novel, 1836-1850. *M.A. 1947 Birmingham*

Clarke, J. J.
The economics of housing. *M.A. 1919 Liverpool*

Clarke, J. L.
The language and literature of Dublin - a survey 1172-1942. *M.A. 1938 National University of Ireland*

Clarke, M. E.
The conception of creation considered in its bearing upon the relation of the finite individual to God. *M.A. 1920 London*

Clarke, M. E.
An essay towards a logical theory of value. *Ph.D. 1926 London*

Clarke, O. F.
Introduction to Berdyaev. *B.D. 1950 Oxford*

Clarke, R. D.
Some secular activities of the English Dominicans during the reigns of Edward I, Edward II, and Edward III (1272-1377). *M.A. 1930 London, University College*

Classe, A.
The rhythm of English prose. *D.Litt. 1940 Glasgow*

Claxton, M. E.
An experimental investigation of the benefit derived from the employment of specially designed equipment for instruction in fundamental electrical and radio theory. *M.Ed. 1950 Durham*

Claye, A. N.
1. The doctrine of the person of Christ in the Fathers of the first two centuries. 2. The doctrine of the Holy Eucharist in the same period. *B.D. & D.D. 1907 Oxford*

Clayton, A.
Le monde politique dans Balzac. *M.A. 1930 Manchester*

Clayton, C. P.
The sociological novel in the nineteenth century. *M.A. 1912 Wales*

Clayton, J.
A history of the Waterhouse Charity, Halifax. *M.A. 1943 Leeds*

Clayton, M.
The tale of the Argonauts. *M.A. 1926 London*

Clayton, N.
Naval administration 1603-1628. *Ph.D. 1935 Leeds*

Clayton-Chance, M. E.
Chateaubriand and Flaubert. *M.A. 1921 Birmingham*

Cleak, D. S.
A geographical study of the Ndola District, northern Rhodesia, with special reference to the copper mining industry. *M.Sc. 1938 Bristol*

Cleak, K. C.
Anglo-Persian relations, 1856-1907. *M.A. 1938 Bristol*

Cleary, J. P.
Death duties on entailed estates. *LL.D. 1927 London*

Cleaver, F. H.
An anthropometric study of Welsh and English populations. *M.A. 1936 Wales*

Cledwyn, N. E.
La langue et le style de Maurice Barrès. *M.A. 1933 Wales*

Clegg, A. B.
External examinations in the schools and their probable development: a critical survey. *M.A. 1935 London, King's College*

Clegg, R.
Economic geography of medieval Yorkshire. *M.A. 1923 Liverpool*

Clegg, R. S.
Histoire générale de la ville de Chauny (Aisne) de sa fondation au commencement de la Troisième République. *M.A. 1939 Leeds*

Clement, E. H.
The meaning and the development of the cult of Mars at Rome. *B.Litt. 1939 Oxford*

Clement, J.
The development of the catechism and of the catechetical instruction of children in the church consequent upon the religious changes in Germany during the sixteenth century. *M.A. 1945 National University of Ireland*

Clement, M.
Hanes yr S.P.C.K. yn Sir Gaerfyrddin o 1700 hyd 1750, gyda chyfeiriad arbennig at John Vaughan, Cwrt Derllys, a'i waith(The history of the S.P.C.K. in Carmarthenshire from 1700 to 1750, with special reference to John Vaughan, Cwrt Derllys, and his work). *M.A. 1940 Wales*

Clements, R. C.
British unit trusts: their organization and investment policy. *B.Litt. 1938 Oxford*

Clements, R. S.
Cardinal Newman's doctrine of authority in religion. *Ph.D. 1931 Edinburgh*

Cleobury, F. H.
Finite and absolute experience: a study in contrasts. *Ph.D. 1941 London, External Degree*

Clerk, M. E. M.
The French sonnet. *Ph.D. 1922 Edinburgh*

Cleugh, M. F.
The problem of time, with special reference to its importance for modern thought. *Ph.D. 1936 London, Bedford College*

Cleveland-Stevens, L.
English railways, their development and their relation to the state. *D.Sc. 1915 London*

Cliff, M. E.
The scope and value of the open-air school. *M.D. 1934 Manchester*

Clifford, E. A. H.
Milton and civil liberty. *M.A. 1941 Reading*

Clift, A. L.
Railway statistics: their history and economic significance. *M.Com. 1925 Birmingham*

Clinton, D. K.
The London Missionary Society in South Africa during the years 1798-1836. *B.Litt. 1935 Oxford*

Clitheroe, E. L.
The Mormon doctrine of salvation and the nineteenth century background. *Ph.D. 1936 Edinburgh*

Clitheroe, T.
The life of Samuel Roberts, a Sheffield philanthropist 1763-1848. *M.A. 1940 Leeds*

Clive-Barnard, M.
The little schools of Port Royal. *B.Litt. 1911 Oxford*

Cloke, H.
Wesleyan Methodism's contribution to national education (1739-1902). *M.A. 1936 London, King's College*

Clough, M.
The coal resources of Russia. *M.Sc. 1931 London, School of Economics and Political Science*

Clulow, F. M.
The York, Chester and Towneley cycles: a comparison of their contents and their outstanding characteristics of treatment. *M.A. 1933 Birmingham*

Clune, G.
Canamhainti an Chláir(Dialects of Co. Clare). *Ph.D. 1936 National University of Ireland*

Clyde, W. M.
The struggle for the freedom of the press from Caxton to Cromwell. *Ph.D. 1929 Saint Andrew's*

Coakley, D. J.
Tariffs for farmers. *M.Comm. 1928 National University of Ireland*

Coates, H. J.
The musical style of Palestrina: its relation to plain chant and its use of the leading motif system. *Ph.D. 1938 London, Trinity College*

Coates, W. D.
English Benedictines in the century preceding the dissolution, with special reference to their connexion with the universities and with learning. *B.Litt. 1931 Oxford*

Coates, W. H.
The incidence of income tax. *Ph.D. 1928 London*

Cobb, M. B. B.
The breakdown of the Anglo-Austrian Alliance, 1748-1756. *M.A. 1935 London, University College*

Cobban, A. B. C.
The political thought of Edmund Burke. *Ph.D. 1926 Cambridge*

Cobbett, W. P.
An examination of the law of partnership in Roman law, with special reference to points of analogy and contrast in English law. *D.C.L. 1887 Oxford*

Cobham, G. W.
A survey of the principal economic activities of the Chesterfield district, realistically and historically treated. *M.Sc. 1942 London, External Degree*

Coburn, K. H.
A critical edition of Coleridge's marginalia to Tennemann's *Geschichte der Philosophie* (1798-1817), with introduction and notes. *B.Litt. 1932 Oxford*

Cochrane, A. C.
The relation of Karl Barth to the historic creeds and standards of the Church. *Ph.D. 1937 Edinburgh*

Cochrane, D.
A study in demand analysis. *Ph.D. 1949 Cambridge*

Cockburn, D.
A statistical study of the judgments of a group of teachers as shown by their preferences among their pupils. *M.Ed. 1949 Durham*

Cocking, J. M.
The esthetics of Stephane Mallarmé: a study in development. *M.A. 1939 London, King's College*

Cockroft, E.
A study of the life and dramatic works of Arthur Murphy. *Ph.D. 1931 London, External Degree*

Cocks, H. F. L.
By faith alone: an inquiry into the nature of saving faith. *D.D. 1942 London, New College*

Coffey, D. J.
René Bazin. *M.A. 1933 National University of Ireland*

Coffin, R. P.
The prose works of John Donne. *B.Litt. 1921 Oxford*

Cogan, N.
Carlyle and Emerson. *M.A. 1915 National University of Ireland*

Coghlan, J. J.
The poetry of Thomas Moore. *M.A. 1920 National University of Ireland*

Cohen, A.
The Jewish economic, religious and social life in medieval Europe, as illustrated by the *Responsa* of Rabbi Meir ben Baruch of Rothenburg (1215-1293). *Ph.D. 1941 Wales*

Cohen, A.
1. The Rabbinic literature as an aid to the lexicography of the Hebrew bible. 2. Arabisms in Rabbinic literature. *Ph.D. 1923 London*

Cohen, H. M.
An investigation concerning the inter-relations of social and economic status, Stanford-Binet and performance I.Q., estimates of probable vocational success, the Otis Primary A Group intelligence test in a group of mentally defective children, and the free association test as a measure of intelligence. *M.D. 1936 Liverpool*

Cohen, I.
An analytic and experimental study of relation and correlate finding. *M.A. 1936 London, University College*

Cohen, I.
A statistical study of physical and mental types. *Ph.D. 1940 London, University College*

Cohen, M. M.
Arthur Schnitzler. *M.A. 1935 Birmingham*

Cohen, S.
Judicial proceedings under the Dictum of Kenilworth, Cambridgeshire. *M.A. 1929 Manchester*

Cohn, E.
Comparative jurisprudence and legal reform. *Ph.D. 1946 London, University College*

Coker, G. B. A.
Jurisdiction of English courts in relation to foreign immovables. *LL.M. 1947 London, University College*

Colbeck, E. C.
The cooperative marketing of eggs. *M.Com. 1933 Leeds*

Colbeck, E. C.
The development of commercial education on Merseyside since 1900. *M.A. 1945 Liverpool*

Colbert, M.
Sheridan Le Fanu. *M.A. 1946 National University of Ireland*

Colborn, A. F.
A critical text of *Hali Meidhad*, together with a grammar and glossarial notes. *B.Litt. 1934 Oxford*

Coldicott, H. R. S.
Peter Pindar: satirist. *B.Litt. 1913 Oxford*

Coldwell, M.
The use of poetry as a dramatic medium in the twentieth century. *M.A. 1940 Wales*

Cole, A. R.
1. Second Epistle of St. John. 2. Third Epistle of St. John. *B.D. 1874 Oxford*

Cole, D. H.
Imperial military geography. *Litt.D. 1935 Dublin, Trinity College*

Cole, H.
Humphrey Stafford, first Duke of Buckingham: an estimate of the significance of his political activities. *M.A. 1945 London, King's College*

Cole, K. C.
A comparison between the English and American principles of civil liability for tort. *B.Litt. 1924 Oxford*

Cole, M. M.
An analysis of the major geographic factors affecting the production and utilization of building material in certain areas. *Ph. D. 1947 London, Bedford College*

Cole, P. D. P. H. de E.
Bacon's knowledge and use of the Bible. *D.Phil. 1950 Oxford*

Cole, R.
The statistical significance of certain psychoanalytical types in children. *M.A. 1947 London, University College*

Cole, R. A.
Adjectives of light and colour in Greek lyric poetry. *Ph.D. 1948 Dublin, Trinity College*

Cole, R. A.
An edition of: a manuscript of the seventeenth century containing unpublished Hebrew poems by Sa'adia Longo from the *Cairo Genizah*. *M.A. 1948 Manchester*

Coleby, L. J. M.
The chemical studies of P. J. Maquer (1718-1784). *M.Sc. 1935 London, University College*

Coleby, L. J. M.
Studies in the chemical work of Stahl. *Ph.D. 1938 London, University College*

Coleiro, E.
St. Jerome's *Letters* and *Lives of the Hermits*, with reference to (i) art and style; (ii) social and historical significance. *Ph.D. 1949 London, King's College*

Coleman, M.
Celtic settlement and agriculture in central Sussex. *M.A. 1944 London, External Degree*

Coles, J.
The origins and course of Coleridge's reaction against Locke and Kant. *M.A. 1949 Wales*

Coles, R.
Historical geography of southeast Essex. *Ph.D. 1934 London, King's College*

Coles, R.
The organization of the egg industry, with special reference to England and Wales. *M.Sc. 1938 London, School of Economics and Political Science*

Colfer, J. M.
The development of industries in Eire since 1924, with special reference to (a) employment, and (b) the national income and its distribution. *M.Econ.Sc. 1944 National University of Ireland*

Colgrave, B.
Tennyson's religious beliefs. *M.A. 1910 Birmingham*

Collar, D. J.
A statistical survey in a London school of arithmetical ability, with its relation to other subjects of the school curriculum. *M.A. 1919 London*

Collas, J. P.
A critical examination of the *Atlas linguistique de la France* in so far as it concerns the island of Guernsey. *B.Litt. 1934 Oxford*

Colledge, J. E.
Studies in the language of manners in England from the eleventh to the eighteenth centuries. *M.A. 1935 Liverpool*

Collender, B.
Irish maritime development. *M.Econ.Sc. 1946 National University of Ireland*

Collie, E. R.
On the upper limit of the growth of intelligence as determined by mental testing. *Ph.D. 1925 Edinburgh*

Collie, F. A.
The history and nature of the dowry among the ancient Greeks. *M.A. 1905 Wales*

Collier, F.
The family economy of the workers in the cotton industry during the period of the Industrial Revolution, 1784-1833. *M.A. 1921 Manchester*

Collier, L. B.
A detailed survey of the history and development of the south Wales coal industry, *c.*1750 to *c.*1850. *Ph.D. 1941 London, External Degree*

Collieu, E. G.
The Radical attitude towards the Monarchy and the House of Lords, 1868-85. *B. Litt. 1936 Oxford*

Collignon, P. L.
The ritual significance of water. *Ph.D. 1929 London*

Collins, A. H.
The life and writings of John Dyer (1701-1757). *M.A. 1930 London, King's College*

Collins, A. S.
The profession of letters, 1780-1832: a study of the relation of author to patron, publisher, and public. *Ph.D. 1927 London*

Collins, A. S.
The relation between author, patron, publisher, and public: 1726-1780. *M.A. 1923 London*

Collins, B. A.
Jewish education in Talmud and contemporary sources. *M.A, 1946 National University of Ireland*

Collins, B. E.
Etude du pessimisme de Guy de Maupassant. *M.A. 1933 Birmingham*

Collins, D. C.
The collection and dissemination of news during the time of Shakespeare, with particular reference to the news pamphlets, 1590-1610. *Ph.D. 1938 London, External Degree*

Collins, D. S.
Shakespeare's use of astrological terms, with an introduction on astrology and popular astrological knowledge of the period. *M.A. 1932 London, King's College*

Collins, E.
The relation between intelligence and various forms of practical ability. *M.A. 1935 Birmingham*

Collins, H. E.
A study of Balzac's literary criticism. *Ph.D. 1937 London, Birkbeck College*

Collins, H. F.
The sea novel in French literature, 1830-1870. *M.A. 1924 London*

Collins, K. E.
Le pessimisme sous l'occupation allemande, 1940-1944: un aspect de la littérature contemporaine. *M.A. 1947 Birmingham*

Collins, M.
An enquiry into the relation of language to emotion, with special reference to its influence on thought and behaviour. *M.A. 1921 Liverpool*

Collins, M. H. A.
The life and works of Frederic Reynolds, dramatist, 1764-1841. *M.A. 1929 London*

Collinson, M. M.
The history of free trade in France during the eighteenth and nineteenth century, with special reference to the individual thinkers. *M.Com. 1944 Birmingham*

Collinson, W. E.
Die niederdeutsche gereimte Katharinenlegende der Brüsseler Hs.No.II.143, und ihr Verhältnis zu dem mitteldeutschen Wolfenbüttler Fragmenten: Text und Untersuchung. *M.A. 1912 London*

Colman, B. *see* Thompson, B.

Colombo, C. J.
Prize law during the Great War. *LL.D. 1925 London*

Colonna, I. M. L.
The major declamations of Pseudo-Quintilian. *M.A. 1939 London, University College*

Colquhoun, E.
Report on the study of Julio Herrera y Reissig. *M.A. 1944 Liverpool*

Colquhoun, G.
La littérature et la langue françaises dans l'oeuvre et dans la vie de R. L. Stevenson. *M.A. 1933 Liverpool*

Colson, A. M.
The revolt of the Hampshire agricultural labourers and its causes, 1812-1831. *M.A. 1937 London, King's College*

Coltman, C. M.
The belief in immortality as a religious sanction for progress. *B.Litt. 1922 Oxford*

Coltman, C. M.
The development of the concept of justice in English modern philosophy. *M.A. 1912 London*

Coltman, I. C.
Religious separation and moral authority: some aspects of religious intolerance in England, 1603-1660. *M.A. 1949 London, School of Economics and Political Science*

Colvile, K. N.
Scottish culture in the seventeenth century (1603-1660). *Ph.D. 1930 Edinburgh*

Colyer, M. M.
Records of tax assessments, 1642-1651. *M.A. 1922 London, King's College*

Combaux, P. G. A.
Present British Government policy with regard to the control of, and the assistance to, the private sector of industry. *M.Sc. 1948 London, School of Economics and Political Science*

Comber, L. C.
The scientific interests of children in relation to the teaching of science. *M.A. 1938 London, Institute of Education*

Comerford, F.
Philosophical survey of Roman religion. *M.A. 1946 National University of Ireland*

Comhaire, J. L. L.
Urban native administration in tropical Africa, British and Belgian. *D.Phil. 1948 Oxford*

Comhaire-Sylvain, S. A. M. A. J. M.
Food and leisure among the African youth of Leopoldville (Belgian Congo): a study of the adaptation of African youth to urban life. *B.Litt. 1948 Oxford*

Common, S.
The economics of the settlement of the Prairie Provinces of Canada, 1900-1931. *Ph.D. 1933 London, School of Economics and Political Science*

Conan, A. R.
Recent monetary problems of some primary producing countries. *M.Sc. 1938 London, School of Economics and Political Science*

Concannon, T.
Burke: a revaluation. *M.A. 1940 National University of Ireland*

Conditt, M. U.
Schleiermacher's idea of God. *Ph.D. 1923 Edinburgh*

Conkling, W. E.
An examination of the literary and historical evidence of the Resurrection of Jesus Christ, together with an estimate of its value from the standpoint of modern thought. *B.Litt. 1922 Oxford*

Conlin, A. C.
L'action dans la tragédie de Racine. *M.A. 1949 National University of Ireland*

Conlon, J. P.
Rude stone monuments of the northern portion of Co. Cork. *M.A. 1913 National University of Ireland*

Conlon, M. E.
Economic problems of Germany. *M.Econ.Sc. 1932 National University of Ireland*

Conlon, M. J.
Cardinal Gerdil and ontologism. *M.A. 1924 National University of Ireland*

Conlon, M. V.
Local Government in Ireland. *M.A. 1931 National University of Ireland*

Conn, J. C.
The contribution of Thomas Erskine of Linlathen and his writings to Scottish theology. *Ph.D. 1935 Saint Andrew's*

Conneely, M. A.
Study as an aim in primary teaching. *M.A. 1935 National University of Ireland*

Connell, D.
The vision of God in St. Augustine and Malebranche: a comparison. *M.A. 1947 National University of Ireland*

Connell, K. H.
The population of Ireland from 1750 to 1846, and the social and economic factors associated with its increase. *Ph.D. 1948 London, External Degree*

Connell, R. C.
A comparison of settlements of registered land in England and Australasia. *Ph.D. 1948 London, King's College*

Connell, W. F.
The educational philosophy and influence of Matthew Arnold. *Ph.D. 1948 London, Institute of Education*

Connellan, T.
St. Thomas and the problem of evil. *M.A. 1944 National University of Ireland*

Conning, G. R.
The place of prophetic intercession in Old Testament religion. *Ph.D. 1934 Edinburgh*

Connolly, M. J.
The towns of Roman Britain. *M.A. 1943 National University of Ireland*

Connolly, P. P.
Roger Ascham. *M.A. 1949 National University of Ireland*

Connolly, S.
The Platonism of Augustine's ascent to God. *M.A. 1950 National University of Ireland*

Connolly, T. J.
A contrast between private enterprise and nationalisation of industry. *M.A. 1927 National University of Ireland*

Connor, L. R.
Fertility of marriage and population growth. *M.Sc. 1926 London*

Connor, M. M.
The operations of underwriting and issuing houses, with particular reference to the Irish Free State. *M.Comm. 1937 National University of Ireland*

Conrad, H. R.
Chanson de geste and prose romance in French literature of the fifteenth and early sixteenth centuries. *Ph.D. 1937 Cambridge*

Conroy, E.
The women of George Meredith. *M.A. 1912 Wales*

Conroy, T. A.
Intellect and will, and their relation. *M.A. 1911 National University of Ireland*

Cons, G. J.
Climatic aspect of the permanent settlement of the white man in the tropics: an essay in acclimatization. *M.A. 1929 London*

Consitt, F.
The history of the London Weavers' Company. *B.Litt. 1929 Oxford*

Consitt, F.
The value of films in the teaching of history. *Ph.D. 1931 Leeds*

Constable, K. M.
A variorum text of the sonnets of Michael Drayton and a critical study of the different versions. *B.Litt. 1929 Oxford*

Conway, A. A.
New Orleans as a port of immigration. *M.A. 1949 London, University College*

Conway, A. E.
The relations of Henry VII with Scotland and Ireland (1485-1497) illustrated from episodes in the life of Sir Henry Wyatt (c. 1460-1537). *M.A. 1926 London*

Conway, E. S.
A study of factors that influenced action in regard to the education of the unemployed boy during the inter-war years. *M.A. 1941 Liverpool*

Conway, S.
Geographical factors conditioning the eastward spread of Islam in Asia. *M.A. 1926 Liverpool*

Conzen, G.
The historical geography of Chester. *M.A. 1942 Manchester*

Coogan, M. F.
Some aspects of the chantry system in Lancashire. *M.A. 1944 Manchester*

Cook, D.
The representative history of the county, town and university of Cambridge, 1689-1832. *Ph.D. 1935 London, University College*

Cook, E.
A portion of west Sussex: a study of agriculture and population. *M.A. 1939 Liverpool*

Cook, E. J.
A critical examination of the theory that the fourth gospel was written to supplement and interpret the current synoptic record. *B.Litt. 1929 Oxford*

Cook, F. S.
The value of the new-type examination for assessing attainment in biology. *M.A. 1936 London, Institute of Education*

Cook, G. C.
The Trojan as conceived by Greeks of the fifth century B.C.: a comparison between the literary and artistic records. *M.A. 1937 London, University College*

Cook, H. J.
The Greek versions of Esther. *M.A. 1948 Birmingham*

Cook, J.
The vernacular English literature, 871-1066, as illustrative of the social history of that period. *M.A. 1931 Wales*

Cook, M. S. M.
An edition of the Brogyntyn manuscript of John Fletcher's *Demetrius and Enanthe*, with an examination of its relationship to the text as printed in the first folio of 1647. *B.Litt. 1950 Oxford*

Cook, W. G. H.
The civil responsibility of lunatics. *LL.D. 1920 London*

Cook, W. G. H.
The evolution of the franchise in England, with special reference to the Reform Act of 1869, and to the political influence of organized Christianity. *M.Sc. 1922 London*

Cooke, A. R.
The relations between Great Britain and Russia from 1848 to 1856. *M.A. 1920 Birmingham*

Cooke, G. A.
1. Isaiah lii.13-liii.12: the servant of the Lord. 2. Genesis xv; xvii; Exodus xx and other connected passages in Deuteronomy and Jeremiah: the covenant in Israel. 3. Ezekiel xxxiii-xxxix: the new age: Israel restored. *D.D. 1909 Oxford*

Cooke, G. K.
English grammarians, 1450-1650: a critical survey, a study in the development of a logical system of grammar for English. *M.A. 1938 London, Queen Mary College*

Cooke, K. S.
An investigation of some of the factors involved in arithmetical ability in school children. *Ph.D. 1933 London, External Degree*

Cooke, M. M.   *see* Shea, M. M.

Cooke, M. W.
English tragedy of the romantic period, 1790-1821, with special reference to German influences. *M.A. 1910 London*

Cooke, R. G.
The foundations of the law of bankruptcy. *LL.M. 1924 Manchester*

Cooke, S. E.
Le développement du sentiment de la nature chez les poètes français depuis le Moyen Age jusqu'après le Romantisme. *M.A. 1909 Birmingham*

Cooksey, H. C.
Jules Renard, 1864-1910. *M.A. 1924 London*

Coolidge, A. C.
Henry Fielding, critic of his times. *Ph.D. 1937 Dublin, Trinity College*

Coolidge, A. C.
The reaction against the prose romance of the seventeenth century, with special reference to *The adventures of Covent Garden*. *B.Litt. 1929 Oxford*

Coombes, A. H.
1. A neglected factor in the criticism of the fourth Gospel. 2. The perplexities of St. John. *B.D. & D.D. 1924 Oxford*

Coombes, D. M.
An enquiry into the careers of these pupils who enter the secondary school after their second attempt in the admission examination. *M.A. 1935 Birmingham*

Coombs, H. C.
Dominion exchanges and central bank problems arising therefrom. *Ph.D. 1934 London, School of Economics and Political Science*

Coomer, D.
The aims and practices of the English Dissenters from the end of Anne's reign to the rise of the Wesleyan Movement. *M.A. 1944 Liverpool*

Coope, G.
Shelley and Plato: a study in literary relationship. *M.A. 1931 Birmingham*

Cooper, A.
Stoicism in Latin poetry (to the end of the Augustan period). *M.A. 1918 Birmingham*

Cooper, D. J.
Emily Brontë, with special reference to her poems. *M.A. 1946 Leeds*

Cooper, D. M.
The theology of Novatian. *Ph.D. 1944 London, King's College*

Cooper, F. R.
The theme of honour as present in the English drama, 1485-1642, with special reference to the dramatic use of the duel. *M.A. 1946 London, King's College*

Cooper, M. M.
The nature of demand for dairy produce in the United Kingdom, with particular reference to New Zealand supplies. *B.Litt. 1937 Oxford*

Cooper, M. M.
The social background of Shaw's early plays. *M.A. 1947 Sheffield*

Cooper, W. M.
Roger Bacon. *M.A. 1910 London*

Coopland, G. W.
The Abbey of St. Bertin and its neighbourhood, 900-1350. *D.Litt. 1914 Liverpool*

Cope, D. G.
The women characters of W. S. Landor. *M.A. 1917 Birmingham*

Cope, S. R.
The history of Boyd, Benfield and Co: a study in the merchant banking in the last decade of the eighteenth century. *Ph.D. 1947 London, School of Economics and Political Science*

Copeland, J. L.
The relations between the Mendicant Friars and the secular clergy in England during the century after the issue of the bull *Super Cathedram* (1300). *M.A. 1937 London, Royal Holloway College*

Copley, G. J.
A study of the *Parker Chronicle* (449-597 A.D.) in the light of more recent archaeological, place name and topographical evidence. *Ph.D. 1947 London, King's College*

Copley, J.
English songs and carols of the fifteenth century: text and transcriptions of the music. *M.A. 1940 Leeds*

Corbett, E. W.
The development of education in the Isle of Man. *M.Ed. 1931 Manchester*

Corbett, J. A.
Matthew Arnold and Germany. *Ph.D. 1937 London, University College*

Corbett, M.
The influence of the metaphysical poets on postwar poetry. *M.A. 1938 National University of Ireland*

Corbett, P. B.
A century of epigrams: the influence of Latin epigram upon English epigram in the Elizabethan age, with special reference to Martial. *M.A. 1938 Sheffield*

Corboy, J.
Jesuit Mission to Ireland. *M.A. 1941 National University of Ireland*

Cordery, M. A.
Keats' theory and practice of poetry. *M.A. 1939 Reading*

Cordingley, H.
Handwork and science: their contribution to cultural education. *M.Ed. 1938 Leeds*

Corea, J. C. A.
Fluctuations in meaning (in binocular rivalry). *M.A. 1939 London, University College*

Corkery, D.
The method of metaphysics according to Bergson. *M.A. 1937 National University of Ireland*

Corkery, D.
Rinn an bheatha: gur féidir áirdeagnuíocht a bheith ann, á thagairt go speisialta do M. Bergson(The apex of life). *Ph.D. 1944 National University of Ireland*

Corkery, D.
Synge and Anglo-Irish literature. *M.A. 1929 National University of Ireland*

Corkery, J. J.
Gaelic catechisms in Ireland. *M.A. 1944 National University of Ireland*

Corlett, J.
A survey of the financial aspect of elementary education. *Ph.D. 1928 London*

Corlette, J. C.
1. The relation of the Old to the New Testament 2. The Kingdom of God. *B.D. & D.D. 1879 Oxford*

Cormack, W. S.
An economic history of shipbuilding and marine engineering. *Ph.D. 1930 Glasgow*

Cornea, V.
The rationalization of agricultural production and marketing, with special reference to recent developments in central Europe. *B.Litt. 1933 Oxford*

Cornelius, B. E.
A critical study of Dewey's theory of moral values. *Ph.D. 1924 Edinburgh*

Corner, H. G.
Expositions of: St. Matthew xii.31,32: the blasphemy against the Holy Ghost; Romans viii.19-23: the groaning creation; Galatians iii.20. *D.D. 1905 Oxford*

Corner, H. G.
1. On the doctrine of God the Son. 2. On the doctrine of God the Holy Ghost. *B.D. 1901 Oxford*

Cornforth, G. A. E.
William Cowper: his attitude to nature and religion. *M.A. 1929 Birmingham*

Cornish, R. T.
The Stockholm region: a geographical study. *M.Sc. 1949 London, King's College*

Cornwell, J.
The construction, standardization and validation of an orally presented group test of intelligence for children between the ages of 8 and 11. *M.A. 1950 Birmingham*

Corrigan, H. S. W.
British policy and opinion and the second Hague conference. *M.A. 1934 London, King's College*

Corson, J. C.
The English Revolution and the doctrines of resistance and non-resistance, 1688 to 1714: a study in sovereignty. *Ph.D. 1934 Edinburgh*

Corston, J. B.
The conception of redemption in the gnostic theologies of the first and second centuries. *Ph.D. 1938 Edinburgh*

Corvesor, D.
Shakespeare adaptations from Dryden to Garrick. *Ph.D. 1926 London*

Cosens, W. R.
A commentary on Romans vi.1-4; Mark ix.44,46,48. *B.D. & D.D. 1872 Oxford*

Cosgrove, I. K.
Three homilies against the Jews by Jacob of Serug, edited with introduction, translation and notes. *Ph.D. 1931 London, External Degree*

Costa, H. L. da *see* Da Costa, H. L.

Costa, P. de *see* De Costa, P.

Costello, E.
Thomas Nashe and English fiction. *M.A. 1932 National University of Ireland*

Costello, E. M.
The problem of the backward child.. *M.A. 1938 National University of Ireland*

Costello, S.
The life of Ramón de Perellós, Viscount of Roda and Perellós. *M.A. 1930 Belfast*

Coster, F. G. H.
The Vale of Somerset: study of economic development and types of settlement in relation to physical character. *Cert.Litt. 1919 Oxford*

Costigan, G. M. D. G.
The career of Sir Robert Wilson (1777-1849) with special reference to his diplomatic and military activities during the years 1806-15. *B.Litt. 1930 Oxford*

Costigan, H. A.
Education and the apprentice. *M.A. 1938 Liverpool*

Costley-White, H.
1. The Christian view of the natural world. 2. The unjust steward. *B.D. & D.D. 1924 Oxford*

Cott, J.
1. On the origin of the daily service. 2. The aim and structure of the daily service. *B.D. & D.D. 1874 Oxford*

Cotterill, M. K.
Social life in Athens as depicted in Aristophanes. *M.A. 1907 London*

Cottle, A. B.
The tradition of Saint Thomas of Canterbury in literature, art and religion. *M.A. 1947 Wales*

Cotton, E. E.
British wartime finance. *M.Com.Sc. 1943 Belfast*

Cotton, J. M. S.
Politian's vernacular poems and their relation to his theory of poetry. *B.Litt. 1934 Oxford*

Cotton, M. K. R.
The condition of the clergy at the time of the Reformation in England. *M.A. 1916 London*

Cotton, O. J. K.
An enquiry into the correlation of certain mental tests with ability in different types of English composition. *M.A. 1932 Birmingham*

Cotton, R. P.
The recent history and the present state of the marketing of milk and dairy produce in Northern Ireland. *M.Com.Sc. 1942 Belfast*

Cottrell, E. M. B.
The Catholics in England, 1649-60, with special reference to their political significance. *B.Litt. 1932 Oxford*

Cottrell, N. G.
Education in the ideal states of the seventeenth century. *M.A. 1935 Birmingham*

Cottrell, T. E.
The philosophy of Cicero. *M.A. 1914 Birmingham*

Cottrill, F.
A study of Anglo-Saxon stone sculpture in central and southern England. *M.A. 1931 London, University College*

Couch, L.
Klopstock in England: a chapter in Anglo-German literary relations. *Ph.D. 1928 London*

Coulborn, A. P. R.
The economic and political preliminaries of the Crusade of Henry Despenser, Bishop of Norwich in 1383. *Ph.D. 1931 London, University College*

Coulson, D. H.
The supply of education in England and the growth of public provision, 1833-1921. *M.Ed. 1939 Leeds*

Coulson, H. J.
Anglican Eucharistic theology from 1700 to 1845. *B.Litt. 1939 Oxford*

Counihan, J. F.
The composition of Thucydides' *History*. *M.A. 1939 National University of Ireland*

Couper, J. M.
The historical background of the raider ballads of Liddesdale. *Ph.D. 1948 Aberdeen*

Couper, M. M.
The evolution of the Spanish *comedia* from the close of the seventeenth century to the present day, with special reference to the period 1835-1898. *Ph.D. 1936 Edinburgh*

Courie, J. A.
The effect of civilization on the Maori race, with special reference to health and disease. *M.D. 1913 Glasgow*

Course, J. R.
The significance of 'mana' in primitive life and thought. *M.A. 1940 Leeds*

Courtney, B.
On the treatment of transport costs in pure theory. *M.Com.Sc. 1944 Belfast*

Courtney, S.
Les jeunes filles dans le théâtre d'Alfred de Musset. *M.A. 1950 National University of Ireland*

Cousins, W. M.
The emancipation of the slaves in Jamaica and its results. *Ph.D. 1928 London*

Coutts, A.
The Reformation and the religion of the spirit: a critical study of the life and teaching of Hans Denck. *Ph.D. 1921 Edinburgh*

Coutts, D. V.
Studies in the mental imagery experienced by young adolescents during the silent reading of descriptive passages. *Ph.D. 1947 London, Institute of Education*

Coutts, J.
Cook Wilson's view of the relation between knowing and the activities of thinking which are not knowing. *B.Litt. 1940 Oxford*

Couturier, L. M. J.
La dette anglaise de Victor Hugo. *M.A. 1912 London*

Couzens, F. C.
Density, distribution and housing of population in the middle Derwent basin. *M.A. 1937 London, Birkbeck College*

Couzens, F. C.
The growth of the borough and the distribution and density of population in the Chesterfield region since the Industrial Revolution. *Ph.D. 1941 London, External Degree*

Coveney, D. K.
A descriptive catalogue of the mss. in the library at University College, London, with an appendix of unpublished medieval German documents. *Ph.D. 1930 London, University College*

Coventry, F.
Sentiment and sensibility in English literature of the eighteenth century. *Ph.D. 1942 Cambridge*

Coverdale, R.
The present status of the theory of association in the psychology of thought. *B.Litt. 1949 Oxford*

Cowan, G.
Bede's use of cases and prepositions in his historical works. *M.Litt. 1936 Cambridge*

Cowan, R. M. W.
The newspaper in Scotland. *D.Litt. 1946 Glasgow*

Cowan, R. W. T.
Some problems in the working of the Australian federation, 1927-37. *B.Litt. 1939 Oxford*

Cowcher, W. B.
The incidence of local rates and of taxes upon the unearned increment of land. *B.Litt. 1914 Oxford*

Cowell, F. R.
State publishing: its methods and problems. *Ph.D. 1938 London, External Degree*

Cowell, P. M.
The attitude of the British Government to the Portuguese revolution of 1826-1834. *M.A. 1927 London*

Cowie, L. W.
The conflict of social, political and religious ideals in English education, 1660-1714. *M.A. 1947 London, King's College*

Cowley, L. D.
The religious ideas of Edmund Burke. *Ph.D. 1947 London, External Degree*

Cowper, C. L. H.
An historical study of the provision made for the social (as distinct from the scholastic) welfare of children and young persons in England since 1800. *M.A. 1930 London, King's College*

Cox, A.
Philip Massinger. *M.A. 1913 National University of Ireland*

Cox, E. M.
Shelley's outlook on life as revealed in his poetry. *M.A. 1916 National University of Ireland*

Cox, J. E.
1. The Scriptures: the rule of faith. 2. The Church. *B.D. & D.D. 1870 Oxford*

Cox, J. W.
Mechanical aptitude, its existence, nature and measurement. *D.Sc. 1928 London*

Cox, J. W.
Some factors in visual perception. *M.Sc. 1919 London*

Cox, M. A.
Rousseau and English poetry, 1785-1824. *M.A. 1911 Birmingham*

Cox, M. D.
Mercantile interests in the House of Commons, 1710-13. *M.A. 1949 Manchester*

Cox, R. G.
Nineteenth century periodical criticism, 1800-1860. *Ph.D. 1940 Cambridge*

Cox, R. M.
The administration of the Twelfth Dynasty: a phase in the development of government in ancient Egypt. *M.A. 1935 London, University College*

Coxhill, W. T.
Brasenose College in the time of Principal Ralph Cawley (1770-7). *B.Litt. 1946 Oxford*

Coxon, W. V. T.
Matthew Arnold as a dramatic poet. *M.A. 1935 Liverpool*

Coyle, E.
Poetry of Alfred Noyes. *M.A. 1933 National University of Ireland*

Coyne, E. J.
Costs and modes of transport in Ireland. *M.A. 1921 National University of Ireland*

Coyne, T. J.
Agricultural credit in Ireland. *M.A. 1922 National University of Ireland*

Crabtree, A. I.
Marriage and family life among educated Africans in urban areas of the Gold Coast. *M.Sc. 1949 London, School of Economics and Political Science*

Cracknell, S. H.
An experimental investigation into some aspects of character. *Ph.D. 1939 London, King's College*

Cracknell, S. H.
Suggestibility in children. *M.Sc. 1922 London*

Craddock, E. A.
The French critics of Shakespeare, with a bibliography of works dealing with the history of Shakespearean study, criticism, and representation in France. *M.A. 1914 London*

Cragg, A. K.
Islam in the twentieth century: the relevance of Christian theology and the relation of the Christian mission to its problems. *D.Phil. 1950 Oxford*

Craggs, C. M.
A critical enquiry into the growth and development of junior instruction centres. *M.Ed. 1936 Leeds*

Craig, A. I.
Virgil as an observer of nature. *M.A. 1909 Birmingham*

Craig, G. A.
The Luxemburg crisis of 1867, with special reference to British policy. *B.Litt. 1938 Oxford*

Craig, H. M.
The legislative council of Trinidad and Tobago. *B.Litt. 1949 Oxford*

Craig, H. T.
Exegeses of: St.Matthew iv.1-4; iv.5-11; St. John xvii.11-21. *D.D. 1886 Oxford*

Craig, H. T.
1. The tradition, chronology, and prophecy of the Old Testament coincident with the history of the world. 2. The infinite Creator of immortal man. *B.D. 1886 Oxford*

Craig, J.
The artificial or 'precious' element in French literature during the period 1627-1730, from d'Urfé to Marivaux. *M.A. 1910 London*

Craig, J. D.
Ancient editions of Terence. *D.Litt. 1929 Saint Andrew's*

Craig, M. J. W.
Walter Savage Landor. *Ph.D. 1944 Dublin, Trinity College*

Craig, R.
The theoretical basis of William Temple's social teaching. *Ph.D. 1950 Saint Andrew's*

Craig, T. S. K. Scott- *see* Scott-Craig, T. S. K.

Craigie, J.
Thomas Hudson's *Histoire of Judith*, edited with an introduction, notes, appendices, and glossary. *Ph.D. 1940 Edinburgh*

Cramp, H. J.
Experimental methods on electricity during the first quarter of the nineteenth century, with special reference to the development of Voltaic apparatus. *M.Sc. 1937 London, King's College*

Crandall, W. W.
A catalogue of the drawings of James Gibbs in the Ashmolean Museum and their connexion with his life and work. *B.Litt. 1933 Oxford*

Crane, S. M.
An experimental investigation of aesthetic judgment. *M.A. 1946 London, University College*

Cratchley, W. J.
Edward Copleston, bishop of Llandaff. *B.Litt. 1938 Oxford*

Cratchley, W. J.
Influence of the theory of evolution on the Christian doctrine of the atonement. *M.A. 1933 Bristol*

Cratchley, W. J.
The theology of John Newman. *Ph.D. 1936 Bristol*

Crawford, E. A.
Towards Christian education; a psychological approach. *Ph.D. 1946 Dublin, Trinity College*

Crawford, S. J.
A critical edition of the *Handboc* or *Enchiridion* of Byrhtferth. *D.Phil. 1930 Oxford*

Crawford, S. J.
A new edition of the Old English translation of the *Hexameron* of Basil (usually ascribed to Aelfric), with a collation of all the existing mss., and an introduction on the sources, authorship, and language of the translation. *B.Litt. 1912 Oxford*

Crean, P. J.
A study of the life and times of Kitty Clive. *Ph.D. 1933 London, External Degree*

Creaven, J. A.
The philosophy of personalism, a study in the philosophy of the human person. *M.A. 1941 National University of Ireland*

Creed, J. M.
The Gospel according to St. Luke. *D.D. 1930 Cambridge*

Creed, P.
Exemplary causality in the philosophy of St. Thomas. *M.A. 1947 National University of Ireland*

Creighton, J. A. McC.
The Μόροι of Xenophon, with an introduction and commentary. *M.A. 1938 Belfast*

Cremin, C. C.
Phases of Corcyraean history. *M.A. 1931 National University of Ireland*

Cresswell, J.
English agriculture, 1760-1830. *M.Sc. 1935 London, External Degree*

Cretney, J. H.
The 'country' in Restoration comedy. *M.A. 1950 Nottingham*

Crews, C. C.
The last period of the great farm of the English customs (1660-1671). *M.A. 1935 London, King's College*

Crick, A. J. P.
The political poetry of Walther von der Vogelweide. *M.A. 1936 London, King's College*

Criddle, C. G.
The life of Christopher Love and his relation to contemporary movements. *M.A. 1933 Wales*

Cripps, R. S.
1. The contribution of the prophets of Israel. 2. The atonement in history and life. *B.D. 1929 Cambridge*

Crisham, M. T.
Value of present-day infant school training methods. *M.A. 1935 National University of Ireland*

Cristureanu, T.
International co-operation: a study of its causes and forms. *Ph.D. 1932 London, School of Economics and Political Science*

Crocket, H. E.
An investigation of social attitudes in school children. *Ph.D. 1940 London, University College*

Crockett, P. D.
An inquiry into the nature and methods of the assistance rendered by banking to commercial enterprise in the United States of America, as compared with England and Germany particularly. *B.Litt. 1923 Oxford*

Crofts, J. E. V.
The metaphysical style: its use and development. *B.Litt. 1914 Oxford*

Crofts, R. A.
Some recent continental commercial banking developments, with special reference to Belgium, France, Germany, Norway and Switzerland. *M.Sc. 1938 London, External Degree*

Croker, W. G.
St. Christopher in Old and Middle English literature and in the contemporary iconography. *M.A. 1931 Wales*

Crompton, J.
Lollard doctrine, with special reference to the controversy over image-worship and pilgrimages. *B.Litt. 1950 Oxford*

Crone, A.
Nature and symbol in the works of Francis Vielé-Griffin. *B.Litt. 1939 Oxford*

Cronin, M. F.
Problems of the two-teacher school. *M.A. 1935 National University of Ireland*

Cronjé, F. J. C.
World consumption of clothing wools. *Ph.D. 1939 Cambridge*

Cronkhite, L. W.
The aims and method of ethics. *B.Sc. 1908 Oxford*

Cronkshaw, P.
A history of the boot, shoe and slipper industries in Rossendale. *M.A. 1945 Manchester*

Crook, R. A.
An edition of the *Prose life of St. Margaret (Seinte Marherete)*, based on ms. Bodley 34 and ms. Reg. 17.A.XXVII, with a grammar and a glossary which will consider parallels in other texts of the same group. *Ph.D. 1929 Oxford*

Cropper, R. C. F.
Freight transport by road: economic competition and economic regulation. *M.Sc. 1949 London, School of Economics and Political Science*

Crosby, A. Essex- *see* Essex-Crosby, A.

Crosby, E. A.
Madame Riccoboni: her life and works; her place in the literary history of the eighteenth century. *M.A. 1919 London*

265

Darvall, F. O.
The Luddite disturbances and the machinery of order. *Ph.D. 1933 London, External Degree*

Darwall, L. J. T.
1. On the history of the doctrine of the Holy Trinity. 2. On miracles. *B.D. 1886 Oxford*

Das, B.
A study of L. H. Myers as a philosophical novelist. *B.Litt. 1950 Oxford*

Das Gupta, C. C.
The development of the Kharosthi script. *Ph.D. 1947 Cambridge*

Das Gupta, J. C.
The new psychology and education. *Ph.D. 1941 Dublin, Trinity College*

Das, H.
Sir William Norris, Bart., and his embassy to Aurangzeb (1657-1702). *B.Litt. 1923 Oxford*

Das, K. K.
Bills of rights and federal constitutions. *Ph.D. 1947 Cambridge*

Das, N.
Industrial finance and management in India. *Ph.D. 1937 London, School of Economics and Political Science*

Das, P. C.
Eighteenth century ideas of taste as reflected chiefly in the poetry of the period. *Ph.D. 1936 Edinburgh*

Das, S.
An edition of the Old English poem *Crist* A and B, lines 1 to 866. *Ph.D. 1936 London, University College*

Das, S.
An examination of Bradley's philosophy. *Ph.D. 1929 London*

Das, S.
The history and literature of the Gauīyad Vaisnavas and their relation to other medieval Vaisnavas schools. *Ph.D. 1935 London, School of Oriental and African Studies*

Das, S.
Problems of primary education in Assam. *M.Ed. 1940 Leeds*

Das, S. K.
Divine power: being a historical study based on Sanskrit texts. *Ph.D. 1925 London*

Dasgupta, A.
The conception of surplus in theoretical economics. *Ph.D. 1936 London, School of Economics and Political Science*

Dasgupta, A.
Relations of the Governor General and Council with the Governor and Council of Madras under the Regulation Act, 1773. *Ph.D. 1930 London, School of Oriental and African Studies*

Dasgupta, J.
Psychological theories of play and their influence upon education theory and practice. *M.A. 1949 London, Institute of Education*

Dasgupta, J. K.
A critical study of the life and novels of Bankimcandra. *Ph.D. 1933 London, School of Oriental and African Studies*

Dasgupta, L.
A comparative study of the mathematical ability of boys and girls in a secondary school from 12 to 14 years of age. *M.A. 1948 London, Institute of Education*

Dasgupta, S.
Contemporary idealists and their critics. *Ph.D. 1922 Cambridge*

Dasgupta, S.
The Paramara dynasty of Malwa. *M.A. 1922 London*

Dasgupta, S.
Principles of the adjudgment of value in literature from Sanskrit sources. *Ph.D. 1948 Cambridge*

Dastur, C. J.
The Retrospective Review: its origin, aims, and contributors. *B.Litt. 1939 Oxford*

Dasvarma, S. L.
Education for world-citizenship: the modern doctrines of instinct, heredity, social science, and aesthetics, and their bearing on educational aim, method, organization and administration. *M.A. 1922 London, University College*

Datta Guptar, S. K.
Monograph on the modern law relating to criminal appeals to the King in Council. *LL.M. 1931 Cambridge*

Datta, N.
Some aspects of Mahayana and its relation with Hinayana. *D.Litt. 1930 London, School of Oriental and African Studies*

Datta, N. K.
The Vedanta: its place as a system of metaphysics. *Ph.D. 1921 London*

Datta, P.
The origin and early history of public debt in India. *Ph.D. 1931 London, School of Economics and Political Science*

Datta, S.
A critical exposition of Indian constitutional reforms with special reference to 'dyarchy'. *Ph.D. 1923 London*

Datta, S.
The downfall of Tipu Sultan, 1793-99. *Ph.D. 1924 London*

Daube, D.
Formalism and progress in the early Roman law of delict. *Ph.D. 1936 Cambridge*

Daudpota, U. M. K.
The influence of Arabic poetry on the development of Persian poetry. *Ph.D. 1927 Cambridge*

Daula, A. M.
The speech and customs of the Cūhrās of the Panjab. *Ph.D. 1935 London, School of Oriental and African Studies*

Daunton-Fear, R.
Anglicanism during the Civil War and the Commonwealth. *M.A. 1943 Bristol*

Daval, H.
The development of the *Bodhisattva* doctrine in Buddhist Sanskrit literature. *Ph.D. 1930 London, School of Oriental and African Studies*

Dave, K. J.
Effect of practice in intelligence tests. *M.A. 1938 London, University College*

Dave, T. N.
A study of the Gujarati language in the sixteenth century, with special reference to the ms. Balavabodha to Upadisamata. *Ph.D. 1931 London, School of Oriental and African Studies*

Davenport, A.
Studies in the prose works of Walter Savage Landor. *M.A. 1936 Liverpool*

Davenport, G. M.
James Joyce's use of symbolism. *B.Litt. 1950 Oxford*

Davenport, M.
The relation between Herodotus and Sophocles. *M.A. 1936 Manchester*

Davey, C. M.
A comparison of verbal (oral) and pictorial tests of intelligence. *Ph.D. 1924 London*

Davey, C. M.
The personnel of Parliament, 1597. *M.A. 1927 Manchester*

Davey, P. C.
A conspectus of the scientific work of Sir Humphrey Davy, Bart. *M.Sc. 1949 London, University College*

Davey, R. C. W.
The disposal of woodland produce. *M.Sc. 1938 London*

David, A. A.
1. Passages from the Gospels of St. Matthew and St. Mark in which Jesus enjoins 'silence'. 2. Examination of passages in which is recorded the impression made by Jesus on various classes of those who first listened to him. *B.D. & D.D. 1910 Oxford*

David, E.
Nature as revealed in the work of Auguste Brizeux. *M.A. 1934 Wales*

David, E.
The teaching of geography in primary schools: an investigation as to the psychological approach in the teaching of different aspects of geography to children of primary school age. *M.A. 1944 Birmingham*

David, F. D.
Contribution à l'étude de la pensée de Pierre Leroux. *M.A. 1916 London*

David, I.
The movement towards imperial preference in Great Britain and the self-governing dominions in recent years, with special reference to some aspects of empire marketing. *M.A. 1930 Wales*

David, R. J. A.
Mistake in the English law of contract. *Ph.D. 1935 Cambridge*

Davidson, D.
The influence of England on the Scottish Reformation. *Ph.D. 1926 Edinburgh*

Davidson, D.
The religious relations of England and Scotland in the early reformation period. *B.Litt. 1923 Oxford*

Davidson, J. G.
An investigation into the theoretical and practical aspects of office mechanization. *Ph.D. 1939 Edinburgh*

Davidson, J. W.
European penetration of the South Pacific, 1779 to 1842. *Ph.D. 1943 Cambridge*

Davidson, M.
The theories of an ice age. *M.Sc. 1914 Belfast*

Davidson, T.
An examination of the grants of land made to the Scottish Church in the twelfth and thirteenth centuries, with special reference to secular services. *Ph.D. 1930 Edinburgh*

Davie, T. M.
Jung's theory of psychological types: a critical estimate. *Ph.D. 1931 Edinburgh*

Davies, A.
The attitude of Wales towards the Reformation. *M.A. 1911 Wales*

Davies, A.
A re-survey of the morphology of the nose of the different races of mankind in relation to environment. *M.Sc. 1931 Wales*

Davies, A.
The rural Third Estate in France in 1789: a study in opinion. *M.A. 1939 Wales*

Davies, A. B. O.
The Council of the League of Nations: a constitutional study, with special reference to its composition. *M.A. 1930 Wales*

Davies, A. E.
The relation of thought to existence in Anselm's statement of the ontological argument. *M.A. 1918 London*

Davies, B. L.
Changes in land utilization in the Towy Valley, Carmarthenshire, since the end of the eighteenth century. *M.A. 1938 Wales*

Davies, C.
The evolution of industries and settlements between Merthyr Tydfil and Abergavenny from 1740 to 1840. *M.A. 1949 Wales*

Davies, C. C.
The north west frontier of India, 1890-1908. *Ph.D. 1926 Cambridge*

Davies, C. G.
A case of visual aphasia. *M.A. 1941 London, King's College*

Davies, C. H.
The physical anthropology of the Gower Peninsula, studied in correlation with its settlements, archaeology, folklore and placenames. *M.A. 1927 Wales*

Davies, C. J.
The language of Williams, Pantycelyn, with special reference to vocabulary and grammatical forms. *M.A. 1923 Wales*

Davies, C. M.
English literature of the Picturesque School (c. 1680 to 1780) in relation to the art of printing. *M.A. 1931 London, Westfield College*

Davies, C. S.
Agricultural change in east Cheshire, 1780-1830. *M.A. 1949 Manchester*

Davies, D.
Christian ethics in Victorian philosophy. *B.Litt. 1932 Oxford*

Davies, D.
A critical examination of Kant's treatment of the self. *M.A. 1920 Wales*

Davies, D.
Problems raised by Kant's treatment of the self. *Ph.D. 1923 Glasgow*

Davies, D.
Recent industrial changes in the Afan district (Glamorganshire), with special reference to the development of Port Talbot. *M.A. 1915 Wales*

Davies, D. C.
Dante Gabriel Rossetti and his influence on English poetry until the end of the nineteenth century: a study of the poetic tendencies of the period, 1870-1900. *M.A. 1924 Wales*

Davies, D. C.
The relations of Egypt and Syria-Palestine, with special reference to Old Testament history. *M.A. 1923 Liverpool*

Davies, D. D.
The Transkeian territories: a study in acculturation. *M.A. 1948 Wales*

Davies, D. E.
A general survey of the School Board Movement as it affected Monmouthshire, with special reference to the town of Newport. *M.A. 1927 Wales*

Davies, D. H. M.
The worship of the English Puritans during the sixteenth, seventeenth and early eighteenth centuries. *D.Phil. 1943 Oxford*

Davies, D. J.
The condition of England during the revolutionary and Napoleonic periods, as illustrated by the history of Birmingham between the years 1789-1815. *M.A. 1924 Wales*

Davies, D. J.
The conditions of the rural population of England and Wales, 1870-1928, in relation to migration and its effects in age and sex selection; income and standards of living; changes in social organization. *Ph.D. 1931 Wales*

Davies, D. J.
The Greek mysteries as presented in the early Christian Fathers. *M.A. 1915 Wales*

Davies, D. J.
The south Wales anthracite industry, with special reference to changes in business organization since government decontrol in 1921, and their social effects. *M.A. 1930 Wales*

Davies, D. T.
The critical system of Ferdinand Brunetière. *M.A. 1928 Wales*

Davies, D. T.
The influence of asceticism on ideas of Christian morality from Clement and Tertullian to Siricius. *M.A. 1914 Wales*

Davies, D. W.
A history of social and economic theory in Palestine down to the monarchy. *M.A. 1938 Wales*

Davies, E.
The British iron and steel trades since 1920. *M.A. 1937 Wales*

Davies, E.
The characteristics of the early Christian Church in Wales, considered especially in relation to the Churches in Ireland and in Gaul. *B.Litt. 1934 Oxford*

Davies, E.
The Duke of Bedford and his friends. *M.A. 1908 Liverpool*

Davies, E.
A study of the small landowner and of the tenantry during the years 1780-1832 on the basis of the land tax assessments. *D.Phil. 1926 Oxford*

Davies, E. G.
The social ideas of Eugène Brieux as expressed in his dramatic works. *M.A. 1938 Wales*

Davies, E. I.
The hand-made nail trade of Birmingham and district. *M.Com. 1933 Birmingham*

Davies, E. M.
Thomas Hudson (1701-1779), his life and work. *M.A. 1938 London, Courtauld Institute of Art*

Davies, E. M.
The work and influence of the friars in England for the first 50 years. *M.A. 1915 Birmingham*

Davies, E. M. E.
Port developments and commerce of Newport, 1835-1935. *M.A. 1938 Wales*

Davies, E. O.
A critical edition of *Pasquin* and *The historical register* by Henry Fielding. *B.Litt. 1948 Oxford*

Davies, E. T.
The influence of Locke on Rousseau. *M.A. 1914 Wales*

Davies, E. T.
The political ideas of Algernon Sidney. *M.A. 1940 Wales*

Davies, G.
Victor Hugo comme critique de Shakespeare, avec une étude spéciale de son oeuvre intitulée *William Shakespeare. M.A. 1915 Wales*

Davies, G. D.
The historical fiction of the eighteenth century and the first fourteen years of the nineteenth. *M.A. 1916 Wales*

Davies, G. D. M.
The study of rhetoric in England as represented in the educational writings of the sixteenth century, and a classified catalogue of educational writings published in England and of English educational works published abroad before 1640. *M.A. 1934 London, King's College*

Davies, G. H.
The Covenant in the life of Israel. *B.Litt. 1933 Oxford*

Davies, G. H.
An investigation into the origin and growth of the conception of theocracy in Israel. *M.A. 1929 Wales*

Davies, G. J.
Leopoldo Alas (Clarín), his work and his contemporaries. *Ph.D. 1938 Leeds*

Davies, G. L.
The democratic spirit in English poetry up to the time of the French Revolution. *M.A. 1929 Wales*

Davies, G. N. M.
N. F. S. Grundtvig and the Danish Folk High School Movement. *Ph.D. 1928 Wales*

Davies, G. R. C.
The administrative staff of the Roman emperors at Rome from Augustus to Alexander Severus. *D.Phil. 1947 Oxford*

Davies, G. V. M.
The correlation of industries in southeast Lancashire, with special reference to the potentialities of other European and eastern textile countries in world trade. *M.Sc. 1930 Wales*

Davies, H.
A study of Gottfried Keller's three last *Novellen* cycles, with special reference to his *Weltanschauung. M.A. 1937 Wales*

Davies, H. E.
The rules of international private law relating to the transfer of movable, immovables, and choses in action. *LL.D. 1928 London*

Davies, H. E.
Social reform in the novels of Charles Dickens. *M.A. 1935 Wales*

Davies, H. I.
A study of certain doctrines found in Bosanquet's logic. *Ph.D. 1936 Cambridge*

Davies, H. J.
An investigation in the use of informal objective tests in physics in the lower forms of a secondary school. *M.Sc. 1942 Wales*

Davies, H. M.
The financial control of British joint stock companies. *M.Com. 1940 Birmingham*

Davies, H. M.
The place of the Royal Institution of South Wales in the history of scientific and general education in the nineteenth century. *M.A. 1940 Wales*   ·

Davies, H. M.
The significance of domestic drama in English literature, with special reference to four extant Elizabethan domestic tragedies, and with an excursus on their authorship. *M.A. 1911 Wales*

Davies, H. S.
Some principles of health education in their historical relationships. *M.D. 1946 London, School of Hygiene and Tropical Medicine and London, King's College*

Davies, J.
The Hebrews and the Babylonian captivity. *M.A. 1934 Liverpool*

Davies, J.
The industrial history of the Rhymney Valley, with regard to the iron, steel and tinplate industries, coal mining, lead mining, smelting and quarrying. *M.Sc. 1926 Wales*

Davies, J.
A philosophical analysis of the claim of religion to be a guide to human conduct, individual and social. *M.A. 1940 Wales*

Davies, J.
The philosophy of Alfred de Vigny as reflected in his published work. *M.A. 1905 Wales*

Davies, J. A.
A study of Berkeley's exposition of his new principle, from the *Commonplace book* to the second edition of the *Principles of human knowledge* (1734). *B. Litt. 1938 Oxford*

Davies, J. B.
The syntax of Marie de France as studied in her *Lais. M.A. 1938 Wales*

Davies, J. C.
The history of Wales during the reign of Edward II, 1307-1327. *M.A. 1914 Wales*

Davies, J. D.
The reputation of Alexander Pope during the early years of the nineteenth century, 1800-30. *M.A. 1940 London, Queen Mary College*

Davies, J. E.
A re-examination of the apparent antithesis between the theological doctrine of grace and the ethical doctrine of the categorical imperative. *B.Litt. 1944 Oxford*

Davies, J. H.
Bulk purchase in international trade. *M.A. 1948 Wales*

Davies, J. I.
A study of Swinburne's relations with France. *M.A. 1932 Wales*

Davies, J. J. G.
Astudiaeth o Gymraeg llafar ardai Ceinwydd(A study of the spoken Welsh of the district of New Quay). *Ph.D. 1934 Wales*

Davies, J. L.
An economic survey of a grazing district in the Welland Valley. *M.Sc. 1927 Wales*

Davies, J. M.
The growth of settlement in the Swansea Valley. *M.A. 1942 Wales*

Davies, J. P.
The relations between ethics and metaphysics, with special reference to the works of Spinoza, Kant and T. H. Green. *M.A. 1922 Wales*

Davies, J. S.
The attitude of Euripides towards the popular religious thought of the day. *M.A. 1907 Wales*

Davies, J. T.
A critical examination of the theory of sublimation, together with a consideration of its relevance for religion. *Ph.D. 1944 London, Richmond College*

Davies, J. T.
The Welsh Church and Welsh politics in the war of Owen Glyndwr. *M.A. 1920 Liverpool*

Davies, J. V.
The diocese of St. David's during the first half of the eighteenth century, including a study of the relevant data in the *Ottley Papers. M.A. 1936 Wales*

Davies, L.
The origin of Hebrew prophecy. 2. The development of prophecy in Israel after the time of Samuel. *B.D. & D.D. 1919 Oxford*

Davies, L. N. A.
The history of the Barry Dock and Railways Company in relation to the development of the south Wales coalfield. *M.A. 1938 Wales*

Davies, L. T.
Vicissitudes of the Greek - chiefly of the Athenian - woman. *M.A. 1906 London*

Davies, M.
A comparison of the phonetic systems of English and Welsh, and the application of such comparative study in the practical teaching of English in Welsh schools. *M.A. 1923 Wales*

Davies, M.
History of our knowledge of fermentation. *M.Sc. 1928 London*

Davies, M.
Lotze's conception of divine personality. *M.A. 1910 London*

Davies, M.
The megalithic monuments of the coastlands of the Irish Sea and North Channel. *Ph.D. 1942 Manchester*

Davies, M.
Study of the prosody and diction of Hardy's lyric poetry. *M.A. 1943 Wales*

Davies, M. A.
The idea of God in Descartes, Spinoza and Leibniz. *M.A. 1935 Wales*

Davies, M.
The German Aufklärung as reflected in the works and character of Friedrich von Hagedorn. *M.A. 1938 Wales*

Davies, M. H.
Monumentum Ancyranum compared with other authorities for the life of Augustus. *M.A. 1912 Wales*

Davies, M. M.
A critical examination of the interpretation of man in the early writings of Karl Marx. *M.A. 1948 Wales*

Davies, M. M.
A statistical study of individual preferences with olfactory stimuli. *M.A. 1938 London, University College*

Davies, M. R. R.
Constitutional principles re-examined in the light of modern administrative law. *Ph.D. 1948 Cambridge*

Davies, M. R. R.
Rating reform. *M.LL. 1943 Leeds*

Davies, N.
1. The doctrine of the Holy Trinity. 2. Prophecy and the prophets of Israel. *B.D. 1924 Oxford*

Davies, N. D.
The philosophical implications of the doctrine of the person of Christ in the definition of Chalcedon. *B.D. 1927 Oxford*

Davies, O.
Roman mines in Europe. *Litt.D. 1947 Dublin, Trinity College*

Davies, O. G.
Le portrait dans la littérature en prose au dix-septième siècle. *M.A. 1938 Bristol*

Davies, O. R.
The theory of universals, with special reference to Locke, Berkeley and Hume. *M.A. 1937 Wales*

Davies, P. E.
An examination of the views of Edward Irving concerning the person and work of Jesus Christ. *Ph.D. 1928 Edinburgh*

Davies, R. C.
A study of John Marston as a satirist, considered generally and with special reference to contemporary writers. *M.A. 1922 London*

Davies, R. E.
Problem of authority in the continental reformers. *B.D. 1946 Cambridge*

Davies, R. E.
Thomas Hood: a critical study. *Ph.D. 1937 London, University College*

Davies, R. F. C.
The child and childhood in the poetry of the French Romantic period, studied particularly in the works of Lamartine, Vigny, Victor Hugo, Sainte Beuve and De Musset. *M.A. 1929 Wales*

Davies, R. F. C.
The education of women in France from 1700 to 1789 as shown in the literature of the period. *Ph.D. 1934 London, Birkbeck College*

Davies, R. J.
Ffyrfiau berfol rhai o destunau cymraeg yr unfed ganrif ar bymtheg, y testunau a gyhoeddwyd ym Mulletin Bwrdd y Gwybodau Celtaidd a chylchgronau eraill(Verbal forms in some sixteenth century Welsh texts as published in the *Bulletin of the Board of Celtic Studies* and other periodicals). *M.A. 1933 Wales*

Davies, R. O.
1. On repentance. 2. On faith. *B.D. 1889 Oxford*

Davies, R. O.
1. Romans vii.12: internal evidence of the divine origin of the law of Moses. *D.D. 1893 Oxford*

Davies, R. T.
Social problems and social theories during the sixteenth century (1520-70), with special reference to the writings of More, Starkey, Crowley, Ascham, Latimer and Elyott. *M.A. 1921 Wales*

Davies, S. H.
The novel technique of John Galsworthy. *M.A. 1932 Wales*

Davies, S. H.
Technical theory and practice in George Meredith's novels. *Ph.D. 1935 London, King's College*

Davies, T. E.
The character of Cicero as exhibited in his letters. *M.A. 1916 Wales*

Davies, T. E.
Cyfraniad Dr. William Rees (Gwilym Hiraethog) i fywyda llên ei gyfnod(The contribution of Dr. William Rees to contemporary life and literature). *M.A. 1931 Wales*

Davies, T. G.
La vision de Saint Paul: a comparative study in the French, Latin and Welsh literatures of the Middle Ages. *M.A. 1934 Wales*

Davies, T. H.
1. The approximate date of the Acts of the Apostles. 2. The descent into Hades. *B.D. 1905 Oxford*

Davies, T. H.
1. St. Luke xxii.14-20: the institution of the Eucharist. 2. I Corinthians xv.3-8: the witness of St. Paul to the resurrection. 3. I Corinthians xv.29: baptizing for the dead. *D.D. 1910 Oxford*

Davies, T. M.
Retailers' buying associations. *M.A. 1936 Wales*

Davies, T. O.
An examination of Mozley's treatment of the Augustinian doctrines of grace and pre-destination. *B.Litt. 1925 Oxford*

Davies, T. R.
The Globe and the Romantic tendency. *M.A. 1904 Wales*

Davies, T. W. L.
The bardic order in the fifteenth century. *M.A. 1910 Wales*

Davies, W.
British diplomatic relations with China, 1854-1869. *M.A. 1938 Wales*

Davies, W.
A contribution to the study of the *Chanson de Geste de Simon de Pouille*. *M.A. 1921 London*

Davies, W.
Phylipiaid Ardudwy, with the poems of Sion Phylip in the Cardiff Free Library collection. *M.A. 1912 Wales*

Davies, W.
Weapons and conduct of Hebrew warfare as illustrated in the Old Testament. *M.A. 1929 Wales*

Davies, W. B.
Chwedi *Troelus a Chresyd* yn Gymraeg fel y ceir hi yn llawysgrif Peniarth 106(The legend of *Troilus and Cressida* in Welsh as it is found in ms. Peniarth 106). *M.A. 1932 Wales*

Davies, W. D.
Paul and Rabbinic Judaism. *D.D. 1948 Wales*

Davies, W. E.
Experimental work in educational guidance in a mixed selective central school. *M.Ed. 1943 Manchester*

Davies, W. H.
The influence of recent changes in the social environment on the outlook and habits of individuals, with special reference to mining communities in south Wales. *M.A. 1933 Wales*

Davies, W. H.
The life and times of Hiero II, King of Syracuse. *M.A. 1935 Wales*

Davies, W. J.
A description of the trade and shipping of Hull during the seventeenth century, and the trade organizations and kindred societies within the port. *M.A. 1937 Wales*

Davies, W. J.
Dissertation on the relations of morality and religion. *M.A. 1946 Liverpool*

Davies, W. J. F.
The sea in Old English poetry. *M.A. 1948 Wales*

Davies, W. L.
Prudentius and the problems of his age: an exposition and appreciation of the *Apotheosis* and *Hamartigenia* of Aurelius Prudentius Clemens. *M.A. 1939 Wales*

Davies, W. M. R.
The three Welsh versions of the New Testament 1567, 1588, and 1620, critically compared, with special reference to the Greek original, the Latin Vulgate and the English version. *M.A. 1910 Wales*

Davies, W. N. G.
The Amandebele tribes of southern Rhodesia: the problems of Western influence on native life and modifications of geographical and cultural values. *M.Sc. 1934 Wales*

Davies, W. P.
The history and significance of the early Elizabethan drama. *M.A. 1910 Wales*

Davies, W. R.
The evidence of Salvian for the causes of the fall of the Roman Empire in the West. *M.A. 1941 Wales*

Davies, W. R.
The influence of the boy actor on Shakespeare's dramatic technique. *B.Litt. 1938 Oxford*

Davies, W. S.
Giraldus Cambrensis: *De Invectionibus*, transcribed from the Vatican manuscript and edited with an historical introduction. *M.A. 1921 Wales*

Davies, W. T.
A critical study of the dramatic work of John Bale and its relation to the English dramatic tradition and contemporary developments. *B.Litt. 1936 Oxford*

Davies, Y.
The ethical idea of love and its central position in Christian ethics down to St. Cyprian. *B.Litt. 1918 Oxford*

Davis, A. G.
The law relating to commercial letters of credit. The relationship between banker and seller under a confirmed credit promised to perform an existing duty. *Ph.D. 1939 London, School of Economics and Political Science*

Davis, A. K.
The political thought of Victorian poets. *B.Litt. 1923 Oxford*

Davis, B. E. C.
A study of Spenser's *Complaints*. *M.A. 1915 London*

Davis, D. G.
The Evangelical revival in eighteenth century England as reflected in the life and work of William Romaine, 1714-1795. *Ph.D. 1949 Edinburgh*

Davis, D. M.
1. The resurrection of Jesus Christ in its relation to the Christian faith. 2. The person and work of the Holy Spirit. *B.D. & D.D. 1909 Oxford*

Davis, E. J.
Lollardry in London on the eve of the Reformation. *M.A. 1913 London*

Davis, F.
Le tornoiement antecrist by Huon de Méry. *Ph.D. 1935 London, External Degree*

Davis, F. N.
The introduction of Christianity into the British Islands, illustrated by the lives of the saints. *B.Litt. 1905 Oxford*

Davis, G. A.
Bernard Shaw in Germany: the first phase. *M.A. 1930 London, King's College*

Davis, H. C.
A comparative study of children in English and French literature 1900 to 1914. *M.A. 1934 London, East London College*

Davis, H. H.
Hannah More as a blue stocking. *B.Litt. 1927 Oxford*

Davis, H. M.
Irish trade in the time of Strafford. *M.A. 1911 London*

Davis, J. A. M.
A study of confidence in a group of secondary school children. *M.A. 1944 London, Institute of Education*

Davis, J. C. W.
John Owen, D.D., Puritan preacher and ecclesiastical statesman, with particular reference to his proposals for a settlement of religion and his views on toleration. *M.A. 1949 Liverpool*

Davis, J. G.
The theology of William Blake. *B.D. 1946 Oxford*

Davis, M.
A review of the radical and type theories in organic chemistry from the time of Berzelius to that of Kekulé, including the development of the theory of valency. *M.Sc. 1927 London*

Davis, N. M.
Incentives to work and their relation to health and efficiency with particular reference to workers in the building industry. *Ph.D. 1948 London, School of Hygiene and Tropical Medicine*

Davis, R. S.
A study of certain aspects of word order in the prose works of Julius Caesar. *M.A. 1938 Wales*

Davis, S. G.
The domestic water supply in the Wealden District in its geographical aspect. *M.Sc. 1939 London, Birkbeck College*

Davis, S. G.
The geographical growth and development of Hong Kong, 1841-1941. *Ph.D. 1946 London, External Degree*

Davis, T. B.
A comparison of the principles and methods of Herodotus and Thucydides as historians. *M.A. 1901 Wales*

Davis, W. B. S.
A study of missionary policy and methods in Bengal from 1793 to 1905. *Ph.D. 1942 Edinburgh*

Davison, D.
Andrew Marvell and the culture of his time: a study in the relationship of his poetry to some aspects of seventeenth century society. *M.A. 1949 Sheffield*

Davson, H. F. P.
1. The evidence for the resurrection of Jesus Christ. 2. The divinity of Christ argued from his claim to sinlessness. *B.D. 1908 Oxford*

Davy, J. J.
Stock Exchange and state control. *M.A. 1924 National University of Ireland*

Daw, M. E.
The rôle of the parson in the literature of the eighteenth century in England and Germany. *M.A. 1937 London, King's College*

Dawe, C. V.
An economic interpretation of the agricultural statistics relating to the Bristol Advisory Province. *Ph.D. 1935 Bristol*

Dawe, C. V.
An economic interpretation of the agricultural returns of the Bristol advisory province. *Ph.D. 1932 Leeds*

Dawe, C. V.
A study of juvenile unemployment in West Ham. *M.Comm. 1933 Leeds*

Dawid, R.
Louis Veuillot: critique littéraire. *M.A. 1947 Liverpool*

Dawley, P. M.
The life and work of John Whitgift, 1532-1604. *Ph.D. 1938 Cambridge*

Dawn, A. F.
The history of freedom of speech and of the press in England since 1900. *M.Sc. 1933 London, School of Economics and Political Science*

Dawod, T. H. O. M.
The phonetics of the dialect of Il Karnak (upper Egypt). *M.A. 1949 London, School of Oriental and African Studies*

Dawson, A. A.
The economic organization of small farms in the Northeast of Scotland. *Ph.D. 1930 Aberdeen*

Dawson, D. J.
The political activity and influence of the House of Lords, 1603-1629. *B.Litt. 1950 Oxford*

Dawson, F. K.
Rotrou's conception of the tragic, with reference to *Hercule Mourant* and *Venceslas*. *M.A. 1950 Manchester*

Dawson, G. G.
Healing. *D.D. 1936 Cambridge*

Dawson, G. G.
Healing, pagan and Christian. *Ph.D. 1935 London, Richmond College*

Dawson, J. M.
The juvenile employment service. *M.A. 1948 London, Bedford College*

Dawson, M.
The Orange Free State: a study in the inter-relation of geography and history. *M.A. 1926 London*

Dawson, M.
The poetry of Mr. Walter de la Mare. *M.A. 1931 Liverpool*

Dawson, N.
Hugh Kelly (1739-77). *B.Litt. 1931 Oxford*

Dawson, R. M.
The history of the Canadian civil service. *M.Sc. 1920 London*

Dawson, R. M.
The principle of official independence. *D.Sc. 1922 London*

Dawson, R. V.
Prognostic tests of aptitude in modern foreign languages, with special reference to French. *M.Ed. 1947 Leeds*

Dawson, T. H.
The influence of German aesthetic thought on the conception of romanticism in England, 1790-1830. *Ph.D. 1925 London*

Day, A. A.
The origins of Latin love-elegy. *Ph.D. 1937 London, University College*

Day, A. E. B.
1. The Old Testament in the light of the Egyptian monuments. 2. Natural science as it affects scriptural truth. *B.D. 1908 Oxford*

Day, A. E. B.
Three expositions of Holy Scripture on the earliest conception of the nature of the Christian ministry. *D.D. 1913 Oxford*

Day, E. H.
Expositions of: St. Matthew i. and St. Luke ii; St. Luke xxiv.13-36; I Corinthians xv.29. *D.D. 1905 Oxford*

Day, E. Hermitage- *see* Hermitage-Day, E.

Day, J. T.
The Norse settlements in northwest Yorkshire. *M.A. 1939 Liverpool*

Day, M. E.
The quarrel between poetry and philosophy. *M.A. 1911 Birmingham*

Day, P. W.
The first settlement of the maritime nations in the Spanish Antilles. *M.A. 1916 London*

Dayal, P.
The agricultural geography of Bihar. *Ph.D. 1947 London, School of Economics and Political Science*

Daysh, G. H. J.
A geographical study of the port of Southampton. *B.Litt. 1925 Oxford*

De Alwis, E. H.
The effect of change of meaning on periodicity in the perception of ambiguous figures. *M.A. 1940 London, University College*

De Barún, C.
Torugheacht Shaidhbhe inghne Eoghain Oig(The pursuit of Sadhbh, daughter of Eoghan Og). *M.A. 1932 National University of Ireland*

de Beer, E. S.
The development of parties during the ministry of Danby. *M.A. 1923 London*

De Bhaldraithe, T. MacD.
Canamhain chois fhairrge(Dialects of the sea side). *Ph.D. 1942 National University of Ireland*

De Blaghd, E. P.
Dánta polaitíochta san Ghaoluinn, 1782-1848(Political poems in the Gaoluinn, 1782-1848). *M.A. 1946 National University of Ireland*

de Bourbel, A. C.
1. The meaning, necessity, and morality of the Christian atonement. 2. The sacrament of the Lord's Supper considered as satisfying certain needs of human nature. *B.D. 1896 Oxford*

De Burca, S. *see* Burke, J.

de Charmoy, F. d'E.
Obligation contract in French and English law. *LL.M. 1936 Cambridge*

De Chickera, E. B.
Revenge tragedy from Kyd to Webster: its basis in the society of the age. *B.Litt. 1950 Oxford*

De Ciniphéic, A. M. *see* Ciniphéic, A. M. De.

De Costa, P.
Imagery of Kalidasa and the theory of poetics. *Ph.D. 1949 London, School of Oriental and African Studies*

De, D.
A historical survey of Pancaratra religion. *Ph.D. 1931 London, School of Oriental and African Studies*

De Graft-Johnson, J. C.
Co-operation in agriculture and banking in British West Africa. *Ph.D. 1946 Edinburgh*

De Hora, L. E. D. H. *see* Horanszky de Hora, L. E. D.

De, J. C.
The dynasties of the Gupta period. *M.A. 1922 London*

de Kalb, E. W.
An elucidation of the death of Christopher Marlowe, through an examination of the lives and interests of certain of his associates. *Ph.D. 1929 Cambridge*

de Kiewiet, C. W. *see* Kiewiet, C. W. de

de Kretser, B.
The Buddhist conception of man in relation to the Christian conception. *Ph.D. 1948 Edinburgh*

de la Barra, T. *see* Barra, T. de la

de la Giroday, F. Boyer *see* Boyer de la Giroday, F.

De La Mare, K.
The place of the olive in the economy of the Mediterranean region. *B.Litt. 1930 Oxford*

De la Perrelle, L. P.
Humanism in German secondary education: an attempt to trace its influence in the XIXth and XXth centuries. *Ph.D. 1940 London, King's College*

De Leon, J. L. Aguilar *see* Aguilar de Leon, J. L.

de Lingen, J. R. K. *see* Lingen, J. R. K. de

De Mel, B. W.
The relation between the psychological and religious interpretations of man. *B.Litt. 1947 Oxford*

De Menasce, J. A. M.
An examination of Kant's early writings in their relation to the critical works, with special reference to the method, the transcendental logic, and the theory of truth and error. *B.Litt. 1925 Oxford*

de Montgomery, A. H. V.
Pierre Allix, life and writings. *Ph.D. 1935 London, Birkbeck College*

De Montgomery, B. G.
British and Continental labour policy: the political labour movement and labour legislation in Great Britain, France, and the Scandinavian countries, 1900-1922. *D.Phil. 1923 Oxford*

de Mourgues, O. M. H. L.
Metaphysical, baroque, and précieux poetry during the late Renaissance in France: a study in parallelism. *Ph. D. 1950 Cambridge*

De St. Mathurin, S. C.
Les idées biologiques de Diderot et leur influence sur son oeuvre romanesque. *B.Litt. 1932 Oxford*

de Silva, C. R.
Ceylon under the British occupation: its political and economic development, 1795-1833. *Ph.D. 1932 London, King's College*

De Silva, H. R.
An analysis of the visual perception of movement. *Ph.D. 1928 Cambridge*

de Valera, R.
Megalithic chambered tombs of North-West Clare. *M.A. 1944 National University of Ireland*

De Villiers, D. I.
An investigation into the relationship between attainment in school arithmetic and interest in the practical and theoretical aspects of the subject. *Ph.D. 1949 London, Institute of Education*

de Voil, W. H. *see* Voil, W. H. de

De Wolf, C.
The recurrence of the death theme in Spanish poetry from minstrel to 20th century. *Ph.D. 1938 Dublin, Trinity College*

De Zoysa, A. P.
Observances, beliefs and customs in Sinhalese villages. *Ph.D. 1928 London*

Deacon, H. M.
Utopian literature. *M.A. 1930 Birmingham*

Deakin, B. Y.
The effect of George Eliot the thinker on George Eliot the novelist. *M.A. 1947 Manchester*

Dean, F. H.
A comparative study of the law of partnership in England and France. *LL.M. 1932 Manchester*

Dean, K. W.
Bury St. Edmund's as a literary centre, with particular reference to the activities of Miles Blomefield, b.1525, and Cox Macro, 1683-1767. *M.A. 1925 London*

Dean, R. J.
Nicholas Trevet: a study of his life and works, with special reference to his Anglo-Norman chronicle. *D.Phil. 1938 Oxford*

Dean, S.
Acquisition of easements in English law. *LL.M. 1926 Liverpool*

Deane, C. V.
Dramatic theory and the rhymed heroic play. *Ph.D. 1929 Cambridge*

Dearle, N. B.
Industrial training, with special reference to the conditions prevailing in London. *D.Sc. 1915 London*

Dearmer, P.
1. Body and soul. 2. Christianity and art. *B.D. & D.D. 1911 Oxford*

Deary, J. C.
The first folio. *M.A. 1916 National University of Ireland*

Deas, M. C.
A study of the life and poetry of Edmund Walter. *Ph.D. 1931 Cambridge*

Decreus, J. C. van L.
Influences dans le drame de Paul Claudel. *M.A. 1945 Leeds*

Deeks, H. W. G.
The estimation of the effects of air attack. *M.Sc. 1948 London, External Degree*

Deeley, A. P.
The light thrown by the papal registers on papal provisions, and some ecclesiastical abuses in the English Church during the time of Pope John XXII. *M.A. 1927 Manchester*

Deeming, H.
The relations of English poets and patrons between 1780-1830. *M.A. 1922 London*

Dehkan, A. A.
Question of international law in Anglo-Iranian diplomatic relations. *Ph.D. 1938 London, School of Economics and Political Science*

Deighton, H. S.
Clerical taxation and consent in the reign of Edward I. *B.Litt. 1935 Oxford*

Del Re, A.
Pietro Verri's *Caffè* and periodical literature in Italy during the second half of the eighteenth century. *M.A. 1921 London*

Delaney, R.
Louis Tiercelin and the Breton renascence. *Ph.D. 1936 Leeds*

Delaney, W. O.
The influence on educational thought of (1) Ruskin (2) Wordsworth. *M.A. 1924 Liverpool*

Delany, K. F.
Robert Kilwardby's *Tractatus de ortu scientiarum*. *B.Litt. 1925 Oxford*

Delap, P.
Men under stress. *M.D. 1945 Dublin, Trinity College*

Delgado, L.
The economic development of the Argentine, with special reference to Anglo-Argentinian relations. *Ph.D. 1939 London, School of Economics and Political Science*

Deller, E.
The liberty of the subject. *LL.D. 1916 London*

Delo-Dosumu, A. O. *see* Dosumu, A. O. Delo-

Demant, V. A.
The influence of anthropomorphic art on religious belief and practice. *B.Litt. 1924 Oxford*

Dempsey, J. P.
The concept of wisdom in Greek and Hebrew literature. *M.A. 1946 National University of Ireland*

Dempsey, M.
A contribution to the study of the sources of the *Génie du Christianisme*. *Ph.D. 1927 London*

Dempsey, M.
The political career of Lord Randolph Churchill. *M.A. 1949 Liverpool*

Dempsey, T.
The Delphic oracle: its early history influence and fall. *M.A. 1916 National University of Ireland*

Dempsey, V. P.
Pope and Boileau. *M.A. 1921 National University of Ireland*

Dempster, J. J. B.
An investigation into the use of estimated factor scores in describing and comparing a group of secondary and senior school boys of 11+. *M.A. 1944 London, Institute of Education*

Denard, W. V.
Cicero's ideas on deity and universe. *B.Litt. 1948 Dublin, Trinity College*

Deneen, W. J.
The economic significance and organization of trade associations in the United Kingdom. *M.Sc. 1933 London, School of Economics and Political Science*

Denholm-Young, N.
The lands of Isabella de Fortibus, Countess of Aumale: a study in thirteenth century administration. *B.Litt. 1929 Oxford*

Denman, D. R.
The practical application of wartime agricultural policy, with special reference to Highland regions. *Ph.D. 1945 London, External Degree*

Denman, D. R.
Tenant-right valuations. *M.Sc. 1940 London, External Degree*

Denmark, F. L.
The development of language expression and language appreciation in the congenitally deaf child. *M.A. 1930 Liverpool*

Denne, E.
The aims of physics teaching in secondary schools. *M.Sc. 1946 London, External Degree*

Dennes, W. R.
The method and presuppositions of group psychology. *D.Phil. 1923 Oxford*

Dennis, C. P. L.
The complete poems of Alekséy Vasil'evich Kol'tsóv, translated from the Russian with introduction and commentary. *Ph.D. 1922 London*

Dennis, L.
The Nottinghamshire coalfield: a geographical interpretation. *M.A. 1936 London, External Degree*

Dent, K. S.
The British navy and the Anglo-American war of 1812-1815. *M.A. 1949 Leeds*

Denton, E. J. Willing- *see* Willing-Denton, E. J.

Denton, E. R.
Individual differences in fluctuation of attention. *M.A. 1943 London, University College*

Denton, E. R.
Measuring fluctuation in mental work. *Ph.D. 1949 London, University College*

d'Entrèves, A. P.
Richard Hooker. *D.Phil. 1933 Oxford*

Denyer, A. S.
The catholic element in the hymns of Charles Wesley. *B.D. 1943 Leeds*

Deoras, V. R.
The political history of Maharashtra from the earliest times to circa 1000 A.D. *Ph.D. 1940 London, School of Oriental and African Studies*

Dermer, E. C.
1. The Resurrection of our Lord. 2. Justification. *B.D. 1874 Oxford*

Derrett, J. D. M.
The dynastic history of the Hoysala kings. *Ph.D. 1949 London, School of Oriental and African Studies*

Derry, T. K.
The enforcement of a seven years' apprenticeship under the statute of artificers. *D.Phil. 1931 Oxford*

Desai, K. D.
The teaching of English in the middle and high schools in the Presidency of Bombay. *M.Ed. 1938 Leeds*

Desai, M. M.
A study of surprise. *Ph.D. 1937 London, University College*

Desai, M. R.
A history of education in ancient India, from the earliest times to the beginning of the Christian era: from the *Rig-Veda* to the Smritis. *M.Ed. 1935 Leeds*

Desai, R. C.
Consumer expenditure in India, 1931-32 to 1940-41. *Ph.D. 1948 Cambridge*

Desai, S. P.
Studies in natural philosophy of India. *M.Sc. 1934 London, University College*

Desai, Y. T.
Agricultural co-operation in the Bombay Presidency. *M.Sc. 1930 London, School of Economics and Political Science*

Desborough, V. R. d'A.
The chronological problem of the Trojan War. *B.Litt. 1939 Oxford*

Deshmukh, C. D.
The problem of individuality and its implications for modern idealism. *Ph.D. 1933 London, University College*

Deshmukh, P. S.
The origin and development of Indian religion as presented by Vedic literature to the end of the Sutra period. *D.Phil. 1927 Oxford*

Deshmukh, R. V.
Court life in ancient India, A.D. 300-700. *B.Litt. 1929 Oxford*

Deshpande, S.
The development of the cotton industry in India from the early nineteenth century. *B.Litt. 1924 Oxford*

Desmond, R. W.
The press and foreign affairs. *Ph.D. 1936 London, School of Economics and Political Science*

Develin, J. C.
The development of education in Spain since 1900. *D.Phil. 1935 Oxford*

Develin, J. C.
Local government in France since 1918, with special reference to the financial and administrative relations of central and local authorities. *B.Litt. 1934 Oxford*

Devilly, P. B.
The spirit of 18th century Ireland as reflected in its literature (in the English language). *M.A. 1937 National University of Ireland*

Devilly, P. B.
The treatment of nature in Elizabethan literature. *M.A. 1936 National University of Ireland*

Devine, M.
1. The place of the Wisdom literature in the Old Testament. 2. Leading thoughts in the Book of Job. *B.D. & D.D. 1923 Oxford*

Devitt, T. C.
Irish agriculture, 1929-1936. *M.A. 1937 National University of Ireland*

Devlin, F. T.
Ernest Psichari: l'homme et son oeuvre. *M.A. 1938 National University of Ireland*

Devonshire, M. G.
1. The English novel in France (1830-1835). 2. Index alphabétique des auteurs de romans anglais publiés en France de 1830 à 1835. *M.A. 1915 London*

Devonshire, M. G.
The English novel in France, 1848-1870. *Ph.D. 1931 London, External Degree*

Dew, E. N.
1. The intermediate state. 2. The nature of Christ's risen body. *B.D. 1890 Oxford*

Dewar, A. C.
The first Dutch war. *B.Litt. 1917 Oxford*

Dewar, H. R. Maund *see* Maund Dewar, H. R.

Dewick, E. C.
The Christian attitude to other religions. *D.D. 1950 Cambridge*

Dewick, E. C.
The indwelling God. *B.D. 1938 Cambridge*

Dexter, T. F. G.
The excavation of the Old Parish Church of Perranzabaloe. *Ph.D. 1922 Saint Andrew's*

Dey, H. L.
Indian tariffs in relation to industry and taxation. *D.Sc. 1933 London, School of Economics and Political Science*

Dezsar, V. M. F. M. A. Rudnyánsky de *see* Rudnyánszky de Dezsar, V. M. F. M. A.

Dezsö, L.
A study of the person of Jesus Christ in the Synoptic Gospels. *Ph.D. 1930 Aberdeen*

Dhamoon, S. S.
The source of morality in human nature. *M.A. 1932 London, King's College*

Dhar, B.
Factorial analysis and its bearing on selection and placement of workers in the Tata iron and steel factory, Jamshedpur, India: first survey. *Ph.D. 1947 Edinburgh*

Dhar, L.
A critical edition and translation of the *Padumavati* of Malik Muhammad Jayasi: a study of the Hindi (Avadhi) language in the sixteenth century. *Ph.D. 1940 London, School of Oriental and African Studies*

Dharkar, C. D.
Lord Macaulay and the Indian Legislative Council (1834-1838). *M.A. 1931 London, School of Oriental and African Studies*

Dhavale, V. N.
The critical theories of Dr. I. A. Richards. *D.Phil. 1949 Oxford*

Dhumé, S. M.
The problem of banking in India: its present situation, development, and reform. *Ph.D. 1922 London*

Dias, M. M.
Life and works of Charles Johnson (1679-1748). *M.A. 1941 London, Birkbeck College*

Dibden, H.
Mathematics teaching in senior schools based on the suggestions of the Board of Education pamphlet no. 101. *M.A. 1937 Bristol*

Dicker, J. A.
An examination of benefits to be derived from school educational visits. *M.A. 1940 London, Institute of Education*

Dicker, M. E.
Local peculiarities of handwriting in documentary papyri of the Roman period. *M.A. 1929 London*

Dickie, W. M.
The scientific method and achievement of Aristotle and Bacon. *Ph.D. 1925 Aberdeen*

Dickinson, E. B.
A study of the numerous causes chiefly psychological, of stammering in school children. *M.D. 1939 Glasgow*

Dickinson, E. G.
A genetic study of the third dimension in child art, with special reference to certain aspects of phenomenal regression. *Ph.D. 1940 London, Institute of Education*

Dickinson, G. A.
Translation and analysis of the *Arithmetica infinitorum* of J. Wallis (1656). *M.Sc. 1936 Liverpool*

Dickinson, J. C.
The history of the Augustinian canons in England before 1215, with special reference to the spread of their foundations and their relations with the secular clergy. *B.Litt. 1937 Oxford*

Dickinson, M. W.
Andreas Capellanus' *De amore*: a re-interpretation. *M.A. 1950 Birmingham*

Dickinson, R. E.
The distribution and functions of urban settlements in East Anglia. *Ph.D. 1934 London, University College*

Dickinson, W. C.
Sheriffs and sheriff courts in Scotland prior to the union of the Crowns in 1603, with special reference to the Fife records at the sixteenth century. *Ph.D. 1924 Saint Andrew's*

Dickson, C. H.
The life and works of Ulric Guttinguer: being a contribution to the history of the Romantic movement in France. *Ph.D. 1940 London, University College*

Dickson, D.
Marcus Junius Brutus: his life, times, and writings. *Ph.D. 1937 Edinburgh*

Dickson, M. E.
The life and works of Samuel and William Rowley, with a special examination of the evidence for the authorship of the more important doubtful plays and of plays written in collaboration. *M.A. 1931 London, East London College*

Dickson, R. J.
An investigation into the causes, extent and character of emigration from the northern parts of Ireland to colonial America, with particular reference to the activities in Ireland of promoters of American lands. *Ph.D. 1949 Belfast*

Dickson, T. E.
Psychological studies of art, with special reference to pictorial art. *Ph.D. 1937 Edinburgh*

Diggle, M.
The treatment in literature of the ideal of chivalry in the nineteenth century with reference to medieval documents. . *M.Litt. 1928 Cambridge*

Dighton, W.
An edition of the poems of Sidney Godolphin. *B.Litt. 1927 Oxford*

Dijk, S. J. P. van *see* Van Dijk, S. J. P.

Dike, E. B.
The obsolescence of words: a study, based chiefly on the *New English Dictionary*, of changes in our vocabulary since circa 1650. *Ph.D. 1933 Edinburgh*

Dillistone, F. W.
A comparison of ideas of salvation in Hinduism and Christianity, with special reference to the Bhakti religions. *B.D. 1933 Oxford*

Dillon, B.
Major novels of Henry James. *M.A. 1947 National University of Ireland*

Dimitrieff, V.
The implications of perfection as capable of realization in the finite self, being a consideration of the ethical conditions of personality. *M.A. 1919 London*

Dimont, C. T.
Exegeses of Proverbs xxi.3; Jeremiah xxxi.33,34; Wisdom vii.15. *D.D. 1923 Oxford*

Dimont, C. T.
1. Varying treatment of the Pharisees in the Synoptic Gospels. 2. The theory of Christian almsgiving from the sub-Apostolic age to the Reformation. *B.D. 1911 Oxford*

Dimsey, S. E.
Guarini and the English pastoral. *B.Litt. 1927 Oxford*

Din, A. H. M. Nizámu'd- *see* Nizámu'd-Din, A. H. M.

Din, S.
Fitzgerald and the Persian poets, with an edition of *Salaman and Absal*; also a literal translation in English of the original poem by the Persian poet, Jami. *B.Litt. 1933 Oxford*

Dineen, P. N.
Sgotha cainte na Gaedhilge(Irish idioms). *M.A. 1942 National University of Ireland*

Dingwall, E. J.
Notes on artificial cranial deformation: a contribution to the study of ethnic mutilations. *Ph.D. 1929 London*

Dinsmore, E. R.
Science and observation. *M.A. 1935 London, Institute of Education*

Dinwoodie, M. J. C.
The settlement of the Hebrews in Canaan. *Ph.D. 1936 Edinburgh*

Dior, M.
La religion et les hommes. *M.A. 1943 National University of Ireland*

Distance, D.
L'Angleterre dans l'oeuvre de Mme. de Staël. *M.A. 1935 Belfast*

Ditcher, G. B.
A discourse on the law relating to the doctrine of remoteness of damage. *LL.M. 1949 Sheffield*

Ditchfield, L.
Etude préliminaire à une biographie de Gustave Flaubert. *M.A. 1932 Birmingham*

Diverrès, A. H.
Paul Féval: le romantique, le Breton, le chrétien. *M.A. 1938 Wales*

Diverres, P. R. Y. M.
Contribution à l'étude de la botanologie celtique: les noms de plantes des *Four Ancient Books of Wales*. *M.A. 1915 Liverpool*

Divine, T. F.
The theory of interest and the concept of social justice. *Ph.D. 1938 London, School of Economics and Political Science*

Dix, G. E. A.
1. The *Treatise on the Apostolic tradition* of St. Hippolytus. 2. The theology of confirmation in relation to baptism. 3. The shape of the liturgy. *B.D. & D.D. 1949 Oxford*

Dix, G. H.
The old wives' tale by G. Peele: a study of the literary and folklore aspects of the play. *M.A. 1910 London*

Dixon, G. W.
The colonial administrations of Sir Thomas Maitland. *B.Litt. 1938 Oxford*

Dixon, H. T.
Expositions of St. John i.1-18: the prologue; St. John xviii.33-38: within the praetorium; Ephesians i.1-14: the doctrine of grace. *D.D. 1908 Oxford*

Dixon, H. T.
1. The prophets of the Old Testament and their influence. 2. St. Paul's conception of Christ. *B.D. 1904 Oxford*

Dixon, M. I.
Hawking literature in Anglo-Norman. *M.Litt. 1929 Cambridge*

Dixon, N.
The placenames of Midlothian. *Ph.D. 1947 Edinburgh*

Djamour, J.
Fanaticism: a psychological analysis. *M.A. 1947 London, School of Economics and Political Science*

Djang, T. K.
Factory inspection in Great Britain. *Ph.D. 1940 London, School of Economics and Political Science*

Dobb, M. H.
Capitalist enterprise and social progress. *Ph.D. 1925 London*

Dobbins, D. J.
The mystical theology of St. Bonaventura. *B.Litt. 1925 Oxford*

Dobby, E. H. G.
The political geography of Malaya. *Ph.D. 1945 London, Birkbeck College*

Doble, E.
History of the Eastern Counties Railway in relation to contemporary economic development. *Ph.D. 1939 London, School of Economics and Political Science*

Dobson, D. P.
1. The teaching of pre-history in schools. 2. The archaeology of Somerset. *Litt.D. 1932 Dublin, Trinity College*

Dobson, E. B.
A survey of the land utilization of Banffshire and Angus. *M.A. 1947 London, King's College*

Dobson, J.
A study of anatomical eponymous nomenclature. *M.Sc. 1944 Manchester*

Dobson, M. D.
A critical edition of the *Quattuor determinationes patris Willelmi Wydeforde de ordine fratrum minorum contre Wycliff et Wyclyvianos in materia de religion*. *B.Litt. 1932 Oxford*

Docking, D. L.
The Spasmodic School of poetry. *M.A. 1924 Liverpool*

Docking, S. J.
Illustrations supplementing a thesis on the development of Protestant church architecture in Manhattan Island, New York City. *M.A. 1932 Liverpool*

Dodd, A. D.
Regeneration and the new psychology, with special reference to character changes. *Ph.D. 1935 Edinburgh*

Dodd, E. E.
The philosophy of Heraclitus as contained in his fragments. *M.A. 1920 Wales*

Dodd, J. A.
The campaign of Xerxes from the Persian side. *M.A. 1913 London*

Dodds, W. M. T.
Prolegomena to a study of Robert South: a bibliography of his miscellaneous works (1654-1717) with appendices. *M.A. 1946 London, University College*

Dodwell, B.
The Sokemen of the southern Danelaw in the eleventh century. *M.A. 1936 London, Bedford College*

Doherty, F. M.
Governor William Franklin. *B.Litt. 1931 Oxford*

Doherty, J. P.
Athenian agora. *M.A. 1949 National University of Ireland*

Doherty, M. A.
L'évolution de la pensée de Charles Péguy. *M.A. 1936 Birmingham*

Doise, M. A.
La pensée religieuse de Sully-Prudhomme d'après son oeuvre poétique. *M.A. 1935 London, King's College*

Dolan, E. M.
The greater women novelists of the Victorian age. *M.A. 1945 National University of Ireland*

Dolley, A. H. F.
The British income tax since 1900. *B.Litt. 1929 Oxford*

Dolley, R. C. F.
Titus Oates and the Popish plot. *M.A. 1911 London*

Dollond, I. I.
The law of contraband. *B.Litt. 1941 Dublin, Trinity College*

Don, A. V. R.
A critical survey of the advances made in surgery and anatomy in the *Corpus Hippocraticum* and the *De Medicina* of Celsus, with a short history of surgery and anatomy from the earliest times down to the beginning of the Christian era. *Ch.M. 1922 Aberdeen*

Donald, M. P. N. *see* Nicolson Thomson, M. P.

Donaldson, G.
The relations between the English and Scottish Presbyterian movements to 1604. *Ph.D. 1938 London, University College*

Donaldson, J. M.
Das Werden und Vergehen von Sitte und Brauch in Hessen und Wales. *Ph.D. 1939 Edinburgh*

Donaldson, M.
Abilities and disabilities of minors in the law of South Africa and Ceylon and allied systems. *B.Litt. 1949 Oxford*

Donegan, M.
Chaucer and Langland as painters of English life. *M.A. 1948 National University of Ireland*

Donges, T. E.
The liability for safe carriage of goods in Roman-Dutch law. *LL.D. 1925 London*

Doniach, A. S.
A study of the *Tibb-el-Nufus* (medicine of the soul) of Rabbi Joseph-bar-Jehuda (Aqnin), from the Bodleian ms. Huntingdon 518, together with a short life of the author. *B.Litt. 1921 Oxford*

Donington, R.
English instrumental music from the Reformation to the Restoration, with particular reference to the first half of the seventeenth century. *B.Litt. 1946 Oxford*

Donlon, W. C.
La comédie en France entre Molière et Marivaux. *M.A. 1937 London, King's College*

Donnan, E. A.
A comparison of Shakespeare's use of Holinshed and Plutarch in his English and Greek-Roman history plays. *Ph.D. 1950 Manchester*

Donnellan, C.
Pre-Johnson developments in English lexicography. *M.A. 1932 National University of Ireland*

Donnelly, E.
Roches, Lords of Fermoy. *M.A. 1929 National University of Ireland*

Donnelly, E.
Social services in Eire. *Ph.D. 1943 Dublin, Trinity College*

Donnelly, F.
Robert Southwell. *M.A. 1929 National University of Ireland*

Donnelly, T. F.
Cults of Rhodes. *M.A. 1938 National University of Ireland*

Donner, H. W.
Thomas Lovell Beddoes: the making of a poet. *D.Phil. 1934 Oxford*

Donner, H. W.
Thomas Lovell Beddoes and the dramatists of the Elizabethan Age. *B.Litt. 1932 Oxford*

Donovan, H.
History of women's higher education during the nineteenth century. *M.A. 1919 National University of Ireland*

Donovan, J.
Instinctive aspects of education. *M.A. 1935 National University of Ireland*

Donovan, M. F.
Les romans historiques de Paul Adams (1789-1830). *M.A. 1946 London, Birkbeck College*

Donovan, M. J. D. *see* O'Sullivan, M. J. D.

Donovan, P. F.
King Lear, a study. *M.A. 1928 National University of Ireland*

Donovan, T.
Free will and determinism. *M.A. 1914 National University of Ireland*

Dons, A. L. F.
The Muhammadan *jizyah* or capitation tax. *B.Litt. 1922 Oxford*

Dony, J. G.
The history of the straw hat and straw plaiting industries of Great Britain to 1914, with special reference to the social conditions of the workers engaged in them. *Ph.D. 1941 London, School of Economics and Political Science*

Doody, B.
The art of Webster. *M.A. 1934 National University of Ireland*

Doolan, D. C.
The development of industries in Eire since 1924, with special reference to (a) employment, and (b) The national income and its distribution. *M.Econ.Sc. 1944 National University of Ireland*

Doolan, M. F.
Some aspects of the cult of medievalism in nineteenth century poetry. *M.A. 1936 Belfast*

Doorly, V. E. L.
The influence of English diplomacy on Italy. *M.A. 1912 London*

Doraiswamy, R.
The effect of the breakdown of the international gold standard on India. *M.Sc. 1937 London, School of Economics and Political Science*

Doran, D. J.
Self-sufficiency in the Irish Free State. *M.A. 1936 National University of Ireland*

Dosumu, A. O. Delo-
The real and the apparent in mature sense-perception. *M.A. 1923 London*

Doty, J. D.
British administration of the American colonies, 1689-1783. *B.Litt. 1923 Oxford*

Dougary, E. A. M.
The materials for biography, the handling of the materials, and the techniques employed to reveal character and personality, with special reference to the work of Lockhart, Froude and Lytton Strachey, in the light of recent psychological investigation. *Ph.D. 1942 Edinburgh*

Doughty, O.
English lyric in the eighteenth century. *B.Litt. 1923 Oxford*

Douglas, G. W.
A survey of the resources of tanning materials and the leather industry of Bhopal State, India. *M.Sc. 1935 Leeds*

Douglas, J. W.
The redistribution of seats in American state legislatures. *D.Phil. 1949 Oxford*

Douglas, M. B.
The rise of 'metaphysical' poetry in England. *M.A. 1913 Birmingham*

Douglass, H. K.
Standards of Catholicism during the period of the Councils and at the Reformation. *B.Litt. 1921 Oxford*

Douie, D. L.
The nature and extent of the heresy of the Fraticelli. *Ph.D. 1930 Manchester*

Doveton, D. M.
The human geography of Swaziland. *B.Litt. 1937 Oxford*

Dowdall, L. J. G. D.
1.The doctrine of the atonement. 2. Inspiration. *B.D. 1881 Oxford*

Dowdell, E. G.
The economic administration of Middlesex from the accession of Charles II to the death of George II: studies in the records of Quarter-sessions. *D.Phil. 1929 Oxford*

Dowling, H. M.
The life of George Peele, dramatist, with the text, canon and interpretation of his works. *M.A. 1934 Wales*

Dowling, P. J.
The Popular Catholic School in Ireland. *Ph.D. 1929 London*

Dowling, T. A. G.
The sea in Shelley. *M.A. 1946 National University of Ireland*

Down, W. C.
The occupation of the Falkland Islands. *Ph.D. 1927 Cambridge*

Downer, A. C.
1. The nature and purpose of the Pentecostal gift. 2. The Holy Spirit in the Church. *B.D. & D.D. 1908 Oxford*

Downes, J. C. T.
The philosophy of tragedy. *M.A. 1949 Liverpool*

Downes, W. J.
Experience in relation to the real. *M.A. 1923 London*

Downey, D.
Problems in teaching of history in Irish primary schools. *M.A. 1934 National University of Ireland*

Downing, A. B.
A study of the conception of conscience in the philosophy of Martin Heidegger and Karl Jaspers. *M.A. 1947 Manchester*

Downing, E. T.
The works of Coventry Patmore. *B.Litt. 1930 Oxford*

Downs, E. V.
English literature: the rudiments of its art and craft. *M.A. 1921 Wales*

Downs, F. J.
The preparatory department as it exists in some public, grammar, and secondary schools, and its curriculum. *M.Ed. 1944 Leeds*

Dowson, D.
The poetry of Charles Guérin, with special reference to his versification. *M.A. 1922 Manchester*

Dowson, E. R.
L'inspiration satirique d'Auguste Barbier. *M.A. 1921 Leeds*

Dowson, F. C. W.
La psychologie et les idées dans le théâtre de François de Curel. *M.A. 1929 Birmingham*

Doxford, W. B. D.
Liu Hsiang and the Hsin Hsü. *Ph.D. 1937 London, School of Oriental and African Studies*

Doyle, B. J.
Sir Walter Scott. *M.A. 1938 National University of Ireland*

Doyle, J. E.
Don Luis de Góngora. *M.A. 1929 National University of Ireland*

Doyle, P.
The relation of Church and State with special reference to the growth of the idea of religious toleration in England under James I, 1603-1616. *M.A. 1928 London*

Doyle, S.
The significance of British policy towards Spain, 1859-68. *M.A. 1949 London, Bedford College*

Drake, E. F.
The policy of the German *Reichsbank* from stabilization to the Hoover moratorium (1924-1932). *B.Litt. 1935 Oxford*

Drake, J.
Pleasure as a criterion of worth. *M.A. 1917 London*

Drake, R. M.
Tests of musical talent. *Ph.D. 1931 London, University College*

Drake, W.
The organization of wholesale distribution in Great Britain of fruit, flowers, and vegetables of domestic and foreign origin. *M.Com. 1941 London, External Degree*

Draper, F. W. M.
The early plays of Louis-Charles Caiquiez, melodramatist (1762-1842): his literary ascendants and descendants. *Ph.D. 1927 London*

Drever, J.
Instinct in man: a contribution to the psychology of education. *Ph.D. 1916 Edinburgh*

Drew, C. E. S.
Politics and parties in the county of Buckinghamshire, 1678-1715. *B.Litt. 1931 Oxford*

Drew, G. C.
The role of incentives in animal learning. *M.A. 1948 Bristol*

Drew, L. L. J.
An experimental enquiry into the methods of selection for technical education, based on multiple factor analysis. *M.Ed. 1944 Leeds*

Drewett, A. J.
A youth movement for this country. *M.A. 1943 Sheffield*

Driver, C. H.
Political and social ideas in England, 1820-37. *M.A. 1926 London*

Dron, I. M.
The dialogue in Italian in the sixteenth century. *Ph.D. 1940 Edinburgh*

Druce, J. G. F.
The rôle of men of science in the Czech National Revival Movement, 1790-1848. *M.A. 1942 London, School of Slavonic and East European Studies*

Druller, I. D.
The personal element in the essays of Elia. *M.A. 1919 Birmingham*

Drummond, A. L.
Edward Irving and the gift of tongues: an historical and psychological study. *Ph.D. 1930 Edinburgh*

Drummond, G. A.
The attitude of backward adolescents towards their school life and work. *M.A. 1947 London, Institute of Education*

Drummond, G. F.
Government control of food prices. *M.Sc. 1923 London*

Drummond, J. G.
The working of the Bengal Legislative Council under the Government of India Act, 1919. . *Ph.D. 1939 Cambridge*

Drury, C. M.
Christian missions and foreign relations in China: an historical study. *Ph.D. 1932 Edinburgh*

D'Souza, L. P.
An examination of Indian education since the year 1813, in the light of modern educational principles. *M.A. 1935 London, Institute of Education*

Du Feu, V. M.
The use of verbal prefixes in Russian. *M.A. 1949 London, School of Slavonic and East European Studies*

Dube, D. L.
War and post-war public debt of India. *Ph.D. 1930 London, School of Economics and Political Science*

Duckworth, F.
The primitive in the psychology of the modern child. *M.A. 1940 Leeds*

Duckworth, G.
The Jesuits and the Council of Trent. *B. Litt. 1939 Oxford*

Dudden, F. H.
1. St. Mark xiv.21 and viii.38: 'Son of Man' in the Synoptic Gospels. 2. St. Mark i.11; St. Luke iii.22: 'Son of God' in the Synoptic Gospels. 3. St. Matthew xi.18-19: Our Lord's attitude towards asceticism. *D.D. 1907 Oxford*

Dudden, F. H.
1. The theology of Gregory the Great. 2. Gregory's doctrine of man and the means of grace. *B.D. 1903 Oxford*

Dudeja, J. N.
The teaching of humanities in India. *M.A. 1934 Leeds*

Dudley, D.
The interaction of England and India during the early years of George III. *M.A. 1909 Liverpool*

Dudlyke, E. R.
The economic geography of the milk supply of London. *M.A. 1937 London, School of Economics and Political Science*

Duff, A. M.
Freedmen in the early Roman Empire. *B.Litt. 1926 Oxford*

Duff, J.
The letters of St. Jerome as illustrating the condition of society in the fourth century. *B.Litt. 1925 Oxford*

Duff, R. A.
Spinoza's political and ethical philosophy. *Ph.D. 1904 Glasgow*

Duffett, W. E.
The international trade position of Canada, 1913-1933: an examination of the causes and characteristics of the balance of payments and the balance of trade. *M.Sc. 1935 London, School of Economics and Political Science*

Duffin, P. B.
The ancient *Lives* of Agesilaus. *M.A. 1946 Belfast*

Duffy, C. Gavan-
The Senate in the Irish constitution. *M.A. 1947 National University of Ireland*

Duffy, E. M. T.
Mythomystes and *The tale of Narcissus* by Henry Reynolds: edited with introduction and notes. *M.A. 1948 Liverpool*

Duffy, J.
Educational theories of the French Revolution. *M.A. 1949 National University of Ireland*

Duffy, L. Gavan
Education of women in the early nineteenth century: some French points of view. *M.A. 1916 National University of Ireland*

Duffy, M. J.
Charles Lever, novelist. *M.A. 1949 National University of Ireland*

Dugan, A. B.
Walter Pope: a study of his life and works. *B.Litt. 1935 Oxford*

Duggan, L.
The problem of Lord Essex in Ireland. *M.A. 1926 National University of Ireland*

Duggan, L.
The role of memory in education. *Ph.D. 1948 National University of Ireland*

Duggan, M.
Rome, Greece and Macedon to 196 B.C. *M.A. 1934 National University of Ireland*

Duggan, T. F.
Irish rural economics. *M.A. 1921 National University of Ireland*

Dugmore, C. W.
The non-Eucharistic services of the early Church. *B.D. 1940 Oxford*

Duke, W. K.
Foreign lending. *M.Sc. 1939 London, School of Economics and Political Science*

Duminy, J. P.
Continuity and infinity in modern mathematics and philosophy. *B.Sc. 1923 Oxford*

Dunbar, K.
Kant's philosophy of religion: Professor Laird's notes and extract from Professor Taylor's report. *M.A. 1915 Belfast*

Dunbar, N. C. H.
The development of the conception of the proper law of a contract in English private international law. *Ll.M. 1940 Sheffield*

Duncan, C. P.
The influence of the stage and its appurtenances on drama. *M.A. 1949 National University of Ireland*

Duncan, J. L.
The end and aim of law. *Ph.D. 1931 Edinburgh*

Duncan, L. C.
A study of the course of forward exchange rates during the last few years. *M.Sc. 1934 London, School of Economics and Political Science*

Duncan, V. G. Kirk- *see* Kirk-Duncan, V. G.

Duncan, W. G. K.
Liberalism in England 1880-1914. *Ph.D. 1931 London, School of Economics and Political Science*

Duncan-Jones, A. E.
1. Ethical language. 2. Meaning and generality (and three other papers). *Ph.D. 1937 Birmingham*

Duncanson, J. D.
The *Mémoires* of Guillaume and Martin Du Bellay: a contribution to the history of French historiography in the sixteenth century. *M.A. 1938 London, King's College*

Duncum, B. M.
The development of inhalation anaesthesia, with special reference to the years 1846-1900. *D.Phil. 1945 Oxford*

Dunham, A.
Political unrest in upper Canada, 1815-1836. *Ph.D. 1924 London*

Dunham, A. G.
The history of Miletus down to the anabasis of Alexander. *M.A. 1913 London*

Dunkley, B.
Greek fountain buildings before 300 B.C. *M.A. 1936 London, University College*

Dunkley, E. H.
Paul Eliasen and the Danish Reformation. *B.D. 1942 Oxford*

Dunkley, E. H.
The Reformation in Denmark. *D.D. 1945 Oxford*

Dunkurley, R.
The origin and value of the Agrapha. *Ph.D. 1927 London*

Dunlap, S. R.
An edition of the poetical works of Thomas Carew, with introduction and notes. *D.Phil. 1939 Oxford*

Dunlap, S. R.
The vernacular writings of King James VI and I. *B.Litt. 1937 Oxford*

Dunlop, J.
English apprenticeship and child labour: a history. *D.Sc. 1912 London*

Dunlop, J. E.
The poems attributed to Bion and Moschus. English commentary, with a new translation, introductory essays, and a complete index verborum. *Ph.D. 1944 London, External Degree*

Dunlop, J. K.
The development of the British Army, 1899 to 1914. *Ph.D. 1936 London, Queen Mary College*

Dunn, E. C.
Contemporary life, literature and society as reflected in Ben Jonson's works. *Ph.D. 1922 London*

Dunn, M. F.
The use of song in the Elizabethan drama. *M.A. 1929 Liverpool*

Dunn, P. J.
The political and ecclesiastical activities of William Nicolson, Bishop of Carlisle (1702-1718). *M.A. 1931 London, King's College*

Dunn, P. N.
A critical study of the novels of D. Alonso de Castillo Solorzano. *M.A. 1949 London, King's College*

Dunn, R.
Etude lexicographique sur les *Mémoires secrets* (1762) par Louis Petit de Bachaumont. *M.A. 1934 Leeds*

Dunne, F. A.
Divination in Greek tragedy. *M.A. 1945 National University of Ireland*

Dunne, P. M.
Social services in Ireland. *M.Econ.Sc. 1948 National University of Ireland*

Dunning, T. G.
God the absolute. *Ph.D. 1926 Glasgow*

Dunning, T. P.
Interpretation of text of *Piers Plowman*. *M.A. 1936 National University of Ireland*

Dunning, T. P.
Piers Plowman: an interpretation of A-Text. *Ph.D. 1938 National University of Ireland*

Dunsby, C.
Plato's idea of God and the soul in their mutual relations. *M.A. 1912 Birmingham*

Dunsdon, M. I.
The problem of illusions of reversible perspective and the effect of conation upon them. *M.A. 1931 Reading*

Dunstan, G. R.
Parish clergy in the diocese of Exeter in the century after the Black Death. *M.A. 1939 Leeds*

Dunstan, W. R.
Height and weight of school children in East Sussex. *M.Sc. 1923 London*

Durant, H. W.
The problem of leisure. *Ph.D. 1940 London, External Degree*

Duri, A. A. A. K.
Studies on the economic life of Mesopotamia in the tenth century. *Ph.D. 1942 London, School of Oriental and African Studies*

Durrani, M. A. K.
A general geographical account of the N. W. F. Province of India. *M.A. 1939 London, School of Economics and Political Science*

Dury, G. H.
Guernsey. *M.A. 1944 London, External Degree*

Dusen, H. P. van *see* Van Dusen, H. P.

Dustan, W. G.
Sir Walter Scott and the drama with some account of the theatre in Edinburgh. *Ph.D. 1933 Edinburgh*

Duthie, G. I.
Elizabethan pirated dramas, with special reference to the 'bad' quartos of *Hamlet, Henry V, Romeo and Juliet*: with an appendix on the problem of *The Taming of the Shrew*. *Ph.D. 1939 Edinburgh*

Dutt, B.
A comparison of English and Scottish education, 1870-1948. *M.Ed. 1950 Leeds*

Dutt, N. K. *see* Datta, N. K.

Dutt, P. K.
Power resources and utilization in the United Provinces. *M.A. 1947 London, School of Economics and Political Science*

Dutt, S.
A study of the attitude towards war of a group of secondary school-children, aged 14-15. *M.A. 1949 London, Institute of Education*

Dutton, R. W.
A study of the prognostic value of examinations set as a test for admission into Middlesex secondary schools. *M.A. 1934 London, Institute of Education*

Duval, S. P.
1. Comparison of the teaching of St. Paul and St. James as to faith and works. 2. The consideration of St. Paul's expectation as to the conversion of the Jews in Romans ix, x, xi. *B.D. and D.D. 1912 Oxford*

Duynstee, A. E. M.
Over-saving, or Keynes doctrine. *M.Econ.Sc. 1947 National University of Ireland*

Dyer, E. F.
New aspects of dramatic work in secondary schools, with especial reference to the value of a model stage. *M.Ed. 1935 Durham*

Dyer, L. J.
A report on the recent development and present position of education for industry in Belgium. *M.A. 1939 London, King's College*

Dyer, S. G.
The citrus fruit growing industry: its geographical distribution and conditions. *Ph.D. 1930 London, Birkbeck College*

Dyer, W. J.
The Gold Coast, a geographical study. *M.A. 1934 Bristol*

Dyke, T. A.
Wales and the Marches in the reign of Edward II, with special reference to Glamorgan and the revolt of Llewelyn Bren. *M.A. 1912 Wales*

Dykes, K. C.
The doctrine of original sin in the light of some recent psychological and anthropological theories. *M.A. 1943 Manchester*

Dyment, S. A.
The propagation of sound in air, in solids, and in liquids: the development of the subject during the period c.1615-c.1830. *M.Sc. 1930 London*

Dymes, D. M. E.
The original language of the *Ancren Riwle*. *M.A. 1922 London*

Dymond, D.
The elements of Hildebrand's conception of the Church. *M.A. 1915 London*

Dyson, H. V. D.
John Ford. *B.Litt. 1924 Oxford*

Eaglestone, A. A.
Major John Cartwright: his place in contemporary radical movements. *B.Litt. 1930 Oxford*

Eames, E. S.
The position of women in Norway in Viking times. *M.Litt. 1950 Cambridge*

Eames, H.
Pride, love, and reason in the characters of the *nueva Comedia. M.Litt. 1933 Cambridge*

Earl, A.
Judges. *B.D. 1932 Cambridge*

Eason, H. J.
Prehistoric man in the Medway Valley. *B.Sc. 1928 Oxford*

Easson, D. E.
Scottish monasticism: its relations with the Crown and the Church to the year 1378. *Ph.D. 1928 Saint Andrew's*

East, E. D.
Theories of light to Fresnel. *M.Sc. 1926 London*

East, J.
The form and function of settlements in relation to types of farming in England and Wales, with an analysis of specific examples chosen from the west Midlands and elsewhere. *Ph.D. 1947 London, University College and London, External Degree*

Easterling, R. C.
The friars in Wales. *M.A. 1912 Wales*

Eastham, M.
Education among some preliterate peoples. *M.A. 1940 Leeds*

Eastlake, A. E.
The influence of English literature on the German novel and drama in the period 1880-1900. *Ph.D. 1937 London, Birkbeck College*

Eastwood, D. M.
The revival of Pascal in France, 1880-1923. *D.Phil. 1933 Oxford*

Eastwood, F. H.
Post-war raw material price variations in the woollen and worsted industries. *M.Comm. 1935 Leeds*

Eastwood, W.
Smollett as critic of social conditions in eighteenth century England. *M.A. 1949 Sheffield*

Eaton, G. H.
A survey of the manor in seventeenth century Gower. *M.A. 1936 Wales*

Eaton, M. S.
Domestic workers in hospitals: a field of women's employment. *Ph.D. 1948 London, School of Economics and Political Science*

Eaton, R. S.
Die Verwertung der Quellen und Motive in Scheffels *Ekkehard* und *Hugideo. M.A. 1930 Manchester*

Eattell, E. A.
The Terman-Merrill intelligence scale in testing institutionalized epileptics. *M.Sc. 1945 London, Birkbeck College*

Eby, L. S.
The concept of norms in the theology of Ernst Troeltsch. *Ph.D. 1932 Edinburgh*

Eccleshall, M. M.
Price control in Great Britain, 1939-1946, with special reference to non-food consumers' goods. *B.Litt. 1950 Oxford*

Eck, H. V. S.
1. The Incarnation. 2. The Christian doctrine of sin. *B.D. & D.D. 1924 Oxford*

Eckel, M. W.
A study of the idea of conscience, with particular reference to the thought of Jeremy Taylor. *B.Litt. 1950 Oxford*

Eddy, G. T.
Some aspects of theism, particularly of its treatment by three modern theistic authors: A. S. Pringle-Pattison, F. R. Tennant, G. D. Hicks. *M.A. 1940 Birmingham*

Edees, E. S.
The influence of the *Metamorphoses* of Ovid on Lucan. *M.A. 1931 Manchester*

Edelberg, V. G.
Wages and capitalist production. *Ph.D. 1935 London, School of Economics and Political Science*

Edelstein, C. S.
Le Juif au théâtre en France. *M.A. 1922 Leeds*

Edgar, R.
Organization of junior technical education from 1913 to the Education Act of 1944. *M.A. 1946 Manchester*

Edgar, W.
Ideas of life and religion in pre-historic Scotland, with special reference to Mediterranean influences. *Ph.D. 1934 Glasgow*

Edge, B. M. A.
Lady Luxborough and her circle. *M.A. 1930 Birmingham*

Edge, S. W.
The stoicism of Seneca. *M.A. 1927 Liverpool*

Edgell, B.
Lotze's logic and its relations to current logical doctrine in England. *M.A. 1899 Wales*

Edgell, B.
Theories of memory. Studies in the theory of memory. *D.Litt. 1924 Wales*

Edgell, T. C. P.
English trade and policy in Borneo and the adjacent islands, 1667-1786. *M.A. 1935 London, King's College*

Edkins, E.
Sir Thomas More and the divorce. *M.A. 1916 Liverpool*

Edmonds, E. J.
Tri tonna dibhfheirge Dé agus *Beatha Chaitriona*(*The three surges of God's wrath* and *The life of Catherine*). *M.A. 1930 National University of Ireland*

Edmondson, B. L.
Contemporary theories of French prosody as exemplified in the works of Jean Moréas. *M.A. 1922 Manchester*

Edmonds-Smith, E.
The eschatology of the third Gospel. *B.D. 1929 Oxford*

Edward, K.
Schleiermacher's theory of the nature of religious experience. *Ph.D. 1915 Edinburgh*

Edward, W. A.
The *Suasoriae* of Seneca the Elder. *D.Litt. 1924 Glasgow*

Edwards, A. C.
The development of armour and costume from the fourteenth century to the seventeenth century as illustrated in the memorial brasses of Essex. *M.A. 1937 Bristol*

Edwards, A. C.
A reconsideration of Verrall's criticism of Euripides. *M.A. 1931 Birmingham*

Edwards, A. T. G.
The life and work of Henry James, with special reference to the development of his attitude to the craft of letters, and to the 'international situation'. *M.A. 1931 Wales*

Edwards, C. D.
The relation of the first international working men's association to the war of 1870 and the ensuing communard movements in Paris, Lyons, and Marseilles. *B.Litt. 1924 Oxford*

Edwards, D. A.
The Virgin Birth in history and faith. *B.D. 1943 Oxford*

Edwards, D. M.
The organization of the Athenian pottery industry. *M.A. 1940 Manchester*

Edwards, D. M.
The philosophy of religion. *Ph.D. 1925 London*

Edwards, E. D.
Prose literature of the T'ang period as contained in the T'ang collection of reprints. *D.Litt. 1931 London, External Degree*

Edwards, E. W.
British policy in relation to Morocco, 1902-6. *M.A. 1939 Wales*

Edwards, F. B.
Naturalization as a sub-division of private international law. *B.Litt. 1913 Oxford*

Edwards, G.
A comparative investigation of the influence of mechanical and linguistic training on the understanding of the forms of reasoning involved in civics. *M.Ed. 1949 Leeds*

Edwards, G.
A study of the Daucleddau coalfield, Pembrokeshire. *M.A. 1950 Birmingham*

Edwards, H.
Personal immortality as a moral postulate. *D.Phil. 1922 Liverpool*

Edwards, H. A.
The western shores of the Indian Ocean before Vasco da Gama. *M.A. 1930 London, Birkbeck College*

Edwards, H. B.
A study of the technique of German drama from Goethe to Hebbel. *M.A. 1936 Wales*

Edwards, H. L. R.
The humanism of John Skelton, with special reference to his translation of Diodorus Siculus. *Ph.D. 1938 Cambridge*

Edwards, H. L. R.
The life and works of John Skelton. *M.A. 1934 Wales*

Edwards, I. ap O.
Local government in the principality of Wales during the sixteenth and seventeenth centuries, as illustrated mainly by the extant data relating to the county of Merioneth. *M.A. 1924 Wales*

Edwards, I. E.
Colonial policy and slavery in South Africa, 1806-26. *B.Litt. 1937 Oxford*

Edwards, I. E.
The colonial policy of the Liverpool administration, with special reference to British settlement in South Africa. *M.A. 1931 Wales*

Edwards, J.
Edward Samuel: ei oes a'i waith(Edward Samuel; his age and his work). *M.A. 1924 Wales*

Edwards, J. O.
The psychological basis of memory. *Ph.D. 1928 London*

Edwards, K.
The clergy of the English secular cathedrals in the fourteenth century, with special reference to the church of Salisbury. *Ph.D. 1940 Manchester*

Edwards, K.
The personnel and political activities of the English Episcopate during the reign of Edward II. *M.A. 1937 London, Royal Holloway College*

Edwards, K. C.
The Grand Duchy of Luxembourg: its human and economic geography. *Ph.D. 1948 London, External Degree*

Edwards, K. C.
The human and economic development of Nottingham and the associated district. *M.A. 1931 London, External Degree*

Edwards, K. H.
An experimental study of perseveration. *M.Sc. 1934 Cambridge*

Edwards, K. H.
Some aspects of employment psychology. *M.Ed. 1932 Durham*

Edwards, K. H. R.
Vocational and occupational guidance. *M.A. 1939 Liverpool*

Edwards, M. L.
The political ideas and influence of John Wesley. *M.A. 1927 Wales*

Edwards, M. L.
The social and political influence of Methodism in the Napoleonic period. *Ph.D. 1934 London, King's College*

Edwards, N. M.
Contemporary lyrical poetry. *M.A. 1925 Wales*

Edwards, O. M. L.
Developments in the evaluation of Baudelaire's poetry, with some reference to English critics (1857-1917). *M.A. 1946 Wales*

Edwards, P. W.
Sir Kenelm Digby: a study of his life and works, chiefly between the years 1633-1644. *M.A. 1946 Birmingham*

Edwards, R.
The application of factor analysis to the study of the individual items of a non-verbal test. *M.Ed. 1950 Manchester*

Edwards, R. D.
History of the laws against the nonconforming churches in Ireland in the 17th and 18th centuries. *M.A. 1931 National University of Ireland*

Edwards, R. N.
Ezekiel and the law of holiness in Leviticus. *M.A. 1921 Wales*

Edwards, R. W.
The history of penal laws against Irish Catholics from 1534 to 1691 (Treaty of Limerick). *Ph.D. 1934 London, King's College*

Edwards, T. D. O.
A critical survey of recent British work on the Church and ministry. *M.A. 1940 Bristol*

Edwards, T. J.
The disposal of the monastic property in the diocese of Llandaff at the time of the Reformation. *M.A. 1928 Wales*

Edwards, W.
The Eleusinian mysteries, with special reference to their influence upon Plato. *M.A. 1914 Wales*

Edwards, W. E.
The attitudes of France to the South American colonies, 1822-6. *Ph.D. 1933 Cambridge*

Edwardson, J.
The conditions and needs of the cottage homes child (poor law), together with a short history of the rise and development of the cottage homes system. *M.A. 1923 Liverpool*

Eeles, G. N.
Guizot as a historian of England. *B.Litt. 1926 Oxford*

Egan, J.
Forus feasa ar ghraiméir lobháin(An outline of the Louvain grammar). *M.A. 1938 National University of Ireland*

Egan, J. P.
Graimeir Ghaedhilge na mBráthair(The Brothers' Irish grammar). *Ph.D. 1945 National University of Ireland*

Egerton, R.
Legal aid. *LL.M. 1946 Cambridge*

Egger, M.
A comparative study of the English, Scottish, and Hungarian popular ballad. *Ph.D. 1928 London*

Egger, V. T. C. E. F.
Nationalist currents in nineteenth-century socialist doctrines. *Ph.D. 1949 London, School of Economics and Political Science*

Egger-Booth, L. S. *see* Booth, L. S.

Ehrhardt, A. A. T.
City-state and Church. *Ph.D. 1944 Cambridge*

Ehrlich, L.
The origins of the petition of right. *B.Litt. 1916 Oxford*

Eichholz, D. E.
The pseudo-platonic dialogue *Eryxias*. *M.Litt. 1934 Cambridge*

Eichner, H.
Thomas Mann's relation to Goethe and its significance for his own development. *Ph.D. 1949 London, University College*

Eid, N. M.
An investigation into the out-of-school activities of a group of adolescents. *M.A. 1948 London, Institute of Education*

Eisel, H. W. C.
A brief history of education in Durham County in the eighteenth century, with a special reference to elementary education. *M.Ed. 1941 Durham*

Eker, J.
The syntax of the past participle in the Middle French period, c. 1320-c. 1500. *M.A. 1930 Manchester*

Ekere, C. A.
Education in Nigeria: a critical study of policy and practice in the light of modern principles of education. *M.A. 1945 London, Institute of Education*

El Ali, S. A.
The early history of Basra: a study of the organization of an Islamic Misr. *D.Phil. 1949 Oxford*

El Batrawi, A. M.
The racial history of Egypt and Nubia from predynastic to present times. *Ph.D. 1940 London, University College*

El Bey, A. M. K.
The public finances of modern Egypt, with special reference to the period 1876-1942. *Ph.D. 1946 London, School of Economics and Political Science*

el Dabbagh, A. H.
A geographical analysis of the date-palm industry of Iraq. *M.A. 1948 Birmingham*

el Kaissouni, A. M.
Monetary policy in agricultural raw material producing countries, with special reference to Egypt. *Ph.D. 1942 London, School of Economics and Political Science*

El Koussy, A. A. H.
An investigation of the factors in tests involving the visual perception of space. *Ph.D. 1934 London, University College*

El Labban, I. A. E. M.
An analysis of mental patterns and their function in the process of education. *M.A. 1938 London, Institute of Education*

el Saaty, H. *see* Saaty, H. el

El-Ayouty, M. Y.
Studies in the development of the English novel in the late nineteenth and early twentieth centuries, with special reference to tragic themes and treatment. *Ph.D. 1950 Belfast*

El-Batrik, A. H. M.
Turkish and Egyptian rule in Arabia, 1810-1841. *Ph.D. 1947 London, School of Oriental and African Studies*

Elcock, W. D.
Vocabulaire ethnographique d'une région des Pyrénées centrales. *M.A. 1933 Manchester*

El-Ghareib, R. M. *see* Ghareib, R. M. El-

El-Gritley, A. A. I.
The structure of modern industry in Egypt. *Ph.D. 1947 London, School of Economics and Political Science*

Elias, T. O.
Nigerian land law and custom. *Ph.D. 1949 London, University College*

Eliash, M.
The *Risalah* of Shafi'ı. *B.Litt. 1919 Oxford*

Eliot, K. M.
The beginnings of English trade with Guinea and the East Indies, 1550-1599. *M.A. 1915 London*

Eliot, P. F.
1. The ethical and spiritual ideas of the Psalms. 2. The doctrine of the Messiah in the Psalms. *B.D. & D.D. 1891 Oxford*

Elkin, A. P.
Ritual and mythology in Australia: an historic study. *Ph.D. 1927 London*

Elkin, P. K.
The attitude to allegory in poetry (1660-1715) as expressed in critical writings and as exemplified in selected allegorical poems. *B.Litt. 1949 Oxford*

Elkins, W. H.
British policy in its relation to the commerce and navigation of the United States of America from 1794 to 1807. *D.Phil. 1936 Oxford*

Elkins, W. H.
Commercial relations between Great Britain and the United States of America from 1783 to 1794. *B.Litt. 1935 Oxford*

El-Koussy, A. A. H. *see* Koussy, A. A. H. el-

Elliot, W. M.
The holiness of God in John Calvin and Rudolph Otto. *Ph.D. 1938 Edinburgh*

Elliott, P. P.
Arguments for theism from design in nature with special reference to Hume, Paley, and Kant. *B.Litt. 1926 Oxford*

Elliott, W. Y.
The pragmatic revolt in politics. *D.Phil. 1923 Oxford*

Ellis, A. G.
The relations between abilities in grammar school subjects and their bearing upon school organization. *M.Ed. 1948 Durham*

Ellis, C.
Hubert de Burgh. *M.A. 1912 Wales*

Ellis, D. K.
The philosophy of Joseph Conrad. *M.A. 1949 Wales*

Ellis, D. M.
Astudiaeth o enwau lleoedd (plwyfi, trefydd, pentrefydd, tref-ddegymau, mynddoedd, afonydd, cymeodd, llynnoedd) sir Drefaldwyn(A study of place names (parishes, towns and villages, townships, mountains, rivers, valleys, lakes) of Montgomeryshire). *M.A. 1935 Wales*

Ellis, E. L.
The Whig Party, 1702-1708. *M.A. 1949 Wales*

Ellis, F. P.
The effect of environment on the health and efficiency of men in warships. *M.D. 1947 Manchester*

Ellis, G.
A history of the slate quarryman in Caernarvonshire in the nineteenth century. *M.A. 1931 Wales*

Ellis, H. L.
The marketing of non-ferrous metals. *M.Com. 1926 Birmingham*

Ellis, H. R.
Eschatology and manticism in Old Norse literature. *Ph.D. 1940 Cambridge*

Ellis, I.
A historical geography of the Cotswold woollen industry in the nineteenth and early twentieth centuries. *M.A. 1946 Wales*

Ellis, J. O.
The structure of neologisms in Russian and Czech. *Ph.D. 1948 London, School of Slavonic and East European Studies*

Ellis, O. C. de C.
Cleopatra on the English stage. *M.A. 1946 Sheffield*

Ellis, T. I.
The history of education in Wales from 1870, with special reference to secondary education to 1920. *M.A. 1930 Wales*

Ellis, W. P.
Alain Chartier and the political conditions of France in the year 1422. *M.A. 1934 Liverpool*

Ellis-Fermor, U. M.
An account of the English stage in the last years before Garrick. *B.Litt. 1922 Oxford*

Ellison, A. J.
Evidence of a prisoner's character. *LL.M. 1928 Cambridge*

Ellmann, R. D.
W. B. Yeats: the fountain years. *B.Litt. 1947 Dublin, Trinity College*

Ellowitz, J.
The history of the theories of chemical affinity from Boyle to Berzelius. *M.Sc. 1927 London*

Elman, P.
Jewish finance in England, 1216-1290, with special reference to royal revenue. *M.A. 1935 London, School of Economics and Political Science*

Elmes, T. I.
Alice Meynell. *M.A. 1949 National University of Ireland*

Elmslie, W. A. L.
How came our faith. *D.D. 1947 Cambridge*

el-Nowaihi, N. M. M.
Animals in ancient Arabic poetry. *Ph.D. 1942 London, School of Oriental and African Studies*

el-Sharani, Z. *see* Sharani, Z. el-

Elsley, R. C.
Juno in Arcadia: an edition of the anonymous masque in the British Museum ms. Egerton 1994, with introduction and notes. *M.A. 1950 Birmingham*

Elston, C. S.
A study, critical, historical and linguistic, of the earliest relations between Celts and Germans. *Ph.D. 1933 London, Birkbeck College*

Elston, C. S. *see* Edelstein, C. S.

Eltoft, H. C. R.
The exegesis of Rashi, with reference to his commentary on the Pentateuch. *M.A. 1927 Manchester*

Elton, G. R.
Thomas Cromwell: aspects of his administrative work. *Ph.D. 1949 London, University College*

Elvey, G. R.
Systems of limitation of currency. *B.Litt. 1926 Oxford*

Elwell, E. S.
1. Exegesis of St. John iii.5 in connexion with Galatians iii.27. 2. St. Matthew xxvi.26-28 in connexion with St. Mark xiv.22-24; St. Luke xxii.19,20; I Corinthians xi.23-26, 3. Exegesis of Titus i.5. *D.D. 1882 Oxford*

Elwell, E. S.
1. On eternal punishment. 2. On Anglican orders. *B.D. 1878 Oxford*

El-Zayat, M. H.
Persian influence on Arabic court literature in the first three centuries of the Hijra. *D.Phil. 1947 Oxford*

Emanuel, H. D.
The Latin life of St. Cadoc: a textual and lexicographical study. *M.A. 1950 Wales*

Embling, J. F.
Count Beust: a study in lost causes. *M.A. 1934 Bristol*

Emerson, N. D.
The political career of the Right Hon. John Foster, last speaker of the Irish House of Commons. *Ph.D. 1930 Dublin, Trinity College*

Emerson, R.
The theory of sovereignty in Germany from 1811 to 1921. *Ph.D. 1927 London*

Emerton, W. P.
De conjecturis ultimarum voluntatum. *D.C.L. 1883 Oxford*

Emlyn, E. M.
A report on the sources available for an account of the life of Sir Henry Vane, junior, during the period 1649-62. *M.A. 1928 Liverpool*

Emmet, C. W.
1. The Acts and the Pauline Epistles. 2. The Epistle to the Romans. *B.D. 1917 Oxford*

Emmott, C.
A study of Francis Turner, bishop of Ely, 1684-90, with special reference to his political activity. *B.Litt. 1930 Oxford*

Empson, I. M.
The influence of the ballad on nineteenth century poetry, with special reference to Rossetti, Morris and Swinburne. *M.A. 1933 Reading*

Empson, J. D.
Livestock improvement in the dairy industry of England and Wales: a study of economic factors involved. *B.Litt. 1950 Oxford*

Emre, A. S.
Location of industrial establishments. *M.Sc. 1946 London, School of Economics and Political Science*

Emrich, C. L.
The history and place of public policy in English private law. *D.Phil. 1938 Oxford*

Encinas, J. A.
Totemism among the ancient Peruvians. *M.Sc. 1928 Cambridge*

Endacott, G. B.
The progress of enclosures in the county of Dorset since 1700. *B.Litt. 1938 Oxford*

Endicott, N. J.
Specimen of an edition of Nathan Field's *A Woman is a Weathercocke* (1612) and *Amends for Ladies* (1618, 1639). *B.Litt. 1929 Oxford*

Enever, F. A.
History of the law of distress for rent and damage feasant. *LL.D. 1929 London*

Engel, R. van
Les idées de Balzac sur la littérature. *M.A. 1929 Liverpool*

England, E. I.
The plain of Hereford: a geographical study of the evolution of local life. *M.A. 1935 Liverpool*

England, F. E.
Kant's conception of God in its metaphysical development, together with a translation of the *Nova Dilucidatio*. *Ph.D. 1928 London*

England, F. E.
Kant's distinction between constitutive and regulative principles of knowledge. *M.A. 1922 London*

England, S. L.
Social and political comedy in France from 1815 to 1848, and its origins. *Ph.D. 1932 London, East London College*

Ensor, M. H.
The influence of the Italian *Risorgimento* in English literature. *M.A. 1917 Wales*

Entrèves, A. P. d' *see* d'Entrèves, A. P.

Entwistle, R.
The eighteenth century rhetoricians. *Ph.D. 1930 London, Birkbeck College*

Entwistle, W. H.
Some aspects of mental work. *Ph.D. 1932 London, Day Training College*

Ephgrave, M.
Grammar and vocabulary of the works of Gonzalo de Berceo. *Ph.D. 1935 Leeds*

Eppstein, W. C.
1. St. Paul's claim for dogmatic theology. 2. The resurrection of Jesus Christ: the keystone of the faith. *B.D. & D.D. 1905 Oxford*

Epstein, I.
The *Responsa* of Rabbi Solomon ben Adreth of Barcelona, 1235-1310, as a source of the history of Spain. Studies in the communal life of the Jews in Spain as reflected in the *Responsa*. *Ph.D. 1923 London*

Eralp, O.
Turkey and state succession. *Ph.D. 1939 London, External Degree*

Erasmus, R. P. B.
The communal idea in Bantu law. *B.Sc. 1944 Oxford*

Erin, H.
The attitude of the Talmud towards trade and commerce. *M.A. 1937 Manchester*

Errandonea, I.
Sophoclei chori persona tragica. *B.Litt. 1922 Oxford*

Erskine, C.
1. The growth ot belief in a future state. 2. The organization and worship of the early Christian Churches as exhibited in the New Testament. *B.D. 1901 Oxford*

Ertel, N.
On the nature of universals. *M.A. 1911 London*

Escott, H.
Isaac Watts' work in hymnology, with special regard to its derivative and original features. *Ph.D. 1950 Edinburgh*

Esdaile, J. E. K.
The Oxford school of sculptors from 1550-1800. *B.Litt. 1935 Oxford*

Espey, J. J.
English criticism of American literature during the period 1800 to 1850 as reflected in the periodicals. *B.Litt. 1938 Oxford*

Essex-Crosby, A.
Joint stock companies in Great Britain, 1890-1930. *M.Com. 1937 London, School of Economics and Political Science*

Esskildsen, E. Y.
On the liturgy of the Swedish Church: a) mass offices prepared by individuals between 1535 and 1576; b) mass offices prepared by committees between 1599 and 1716. *B.D. 1917 Oxford*

Ethelburga, Sister *see* Hogan, M.

Etheridge, G.
The characteristics of the Augustan age reflected in Virgil and Horace. *M.A. 1911 Birmingham*

Etherington, J. R. M.
The life of Archbishop Juxon. *B.Litt. 1940 Oxford*

Etscheit, E. C. V. *see* Stopp, E. C. V.

Ettinger, A. A.
The mission to Spain of Pierre Soulé, 1853-5: a study in the Cuban diplomacy of the United States, with special reference to contemporary opinion. *D.Phil. 1930 Oxford*

Evans, A. A.
William Blake and the romantic fallacy. *M.A. 1937 Bristol*

Evans, A. C.
1. The Apostle Jude: is he to be identified with Jude the servant of Jesus Christ and brother of James? 2. SS. Philip, Bartholomew, Matthew, and Thomas: being an inquiry from New Testament records into the second group in the Apostolate. *B.D. 1901 Oxford*

Evans, A. J.
A history of education in Bradford during the period of the Bradford School Board (1870-1904). *M.A. 1947 Leeds*

Evans, A. W.
Warburton and the Warburtonians. *Litt.D. 1932 Dublin, Trinity College*

Evans, B.
A history of the trade disputes and the formation and operation of the several sliding scale agreements in the South Wales coal trade, 1870 to 1903, with special reference to the work of Sir William Thomas Lewis, 1st Baron Merthyr of Senghenydd. *M.A. 1944 Wales*

Evans, B. B.
The sources of Dr. Johnson's *Lives of the Poets*. *B.Litt. 1930 Oxford*

Evans, B. I.
Studies in the language and syntax of Ben Jonson. *M.A. 1922 London*

Evans, B. M.
The Welsh coal trade during the Stuart period, 1603-1709. *M.A. 1928 Wales*

Evans, B. P.
The family of Mortimer. *Ph.D. 1934 Wales*

Evans, C.
The rise and progress of the periodical press in Wales up to 1860. *M.A. 1926 Wales*

Evans, C. M.
The medieval borough of Beaumaris and the commote of Dindaethwy, 1200-1600. *M.A. 1949 Wales*

Evans, C. W. L.
Exposition of passages from the twelfth chapter of the Epistle to the Romans: the ethical scheme of St. Paul. *D.D. 1914 Oxford*

Evans, C. W. L.
1. Progressive revelation as illustrated in the history of Israel. 2. Asceticism and Christianity. *B.D. 1909 Oxford*

Evans, D.
The classic, romantic and specific Spanish elements in the dramas of Grillparzer and Halm. *M.A. 1912 Wales*

Evans, D. B.
Andreas Gryphius and the Elizabethan drama. *M.A. 1950 Wales*

Evans, D. E.
The British income tax in the twentieth century, with special reference to public enquiries and to the legislation relating to the subject. *M.A. 1925 Wales*

Evans, D. E.
A grammatical and lexical study of the Greek inscriptions of Phrygia in Asia Minor. *B.Litt. 1917 Oxford*

Evans, D. E.
A study of the Laconian dialect. *M.A. 1913 Wales*

Evans, D. G.
Tafodiaith Cwmtawe(The dialect of the Tawe Valley). *M.A. 1930 Wales*

Evans, D. H.
The development of farm mechanization in England and Wales. *M.Sc. 1949 Nottingham*

Evans, D. J.
A history of the Shrewsbury Drapers' Company during the seventeenth century, with particular reference to the Welsh woollen trade. *M.A. 1950 Wales*

Evans, D. L.
The principality of Wales under Edward the Black Prince. *B.Litt. 1930 Oxford*

Evans, D. O.
The French romantic drama on modern subjects. *D.Phil. 1923 Oxford*

Evans, D. S.
Astudiaeth fanwl o gystrawen, testunau rhyddiath Cymraeg canol a gyhoeddwyd yn y *Bulletin of the Board of Celtic Studies*(An exact study of the syntax of the medieval Welsh prose texts published in the *Bulletin of the Board of Celtic Studies*). *M.A. 1948 Wales*

Evans, D. T.
Yr iaith Gymraeg, ei horgraff a'i chystrawen(The Welsh language, its orthography and syntax). *M.A. 1927 Wales*

Evans, E.
Arwystli and Cyfeilog in the sixteenth and seventeenth centuries: an agrarian and social study. *M.A. 1939 Wales*

Evans, E.
Bilingual education in Wales, with special reference to the teaching of Welsh. *M.A. 1924 Wales*

Evans, E.
The characterization of women in the English novel from Richardson to the Brontës. *M.A. 1931 Wales*

Evans, E.
The ecclesiastical and philosophical background of Origen's thought, with special reference to the work *De principiis*. *B.D. 1925 Oxford*

Evans, E.
The manor of Headington. *B.Litt. 1928 Oxford*

Evans, E.
Scarron and the Realistic Movement of the seventeenth century. *M.A. 1937 Wales*

Evans, E. D.
Euripides and his relation to the religion of his time. *M.A. 1909 Wales*

Evans, E. E.
Contributions to prehistoric archaeology, with special reference to Northern Ireland. *D.Sc. 1939 Wales*

Evans, E. E.
A study of the origins and distributions of some late Bronze Age industries in Western Europe. *M.A. 1931 Wales*

Evans, E. L.
Y dylanwadau llenyddol, crefyddol ac athronyddol ar Forgan Llwyd(Literary, religious and philosophical influences on Morgan Llwyd). *M.A. 1926 Wales*

Evans, E. M.
Dylanwadau Ffrengig ar lenyddiaeth Gymreig y bedwaredd ganrif ar bymtheg(French influences on nineteenth century Welsh literature). *M.A. 1926 Wales*

Evans, E. R.
Philosophic thought in the works of Romain Rolland. *M.A. 1932 Wales*

Evans, E. T.
The idealist theory of truth. *M.A. 1948 Wales*

Evans, F. M. G. *see* Higham, F. M. G.

Evans, G.
Charles Watkin Williams Wynn, 1775-1850. *M.A. 1935 Wales*

Evans, G.
The concept of monotheism in its historical manifestations. *M.A. 1924 Bristol*

Evans, G.
The Welsh woollen industry: recent history and present position. *M.A. 1948 Wales*

Evans, G. G.
Yr anterliwd Gymraeg(The Welsh interlude). *M.A. 1938 Wales*

Evans, G. J.
Lle John Morris Jones yn yr adfywiad llenyddol o 1886(The place of John Morris Jones in the literary revival from 1886). *M.A. 1945 Wales*

Evans, G. M.
1. Holy baptism. 2. Redemption and the salvation consequent upon it. *B.D. 1908 Oxford*

Evans, H. A.
Report of an investigation into the secondary school careers of children who were not selected by the head teachers of elementary schools as likely to benefit by a secondary education. *M.A. 1938 Birmingham*

Evans, H. B.
A bibliography of eighteenth century English translations of certain French philosophic writers of the Age of Reason. *M.A. 1938 Birmingham*

Evans, H. G. J.
Louis Lambert and the philosophy of Balzac. *Ph.D. 1949 London, King's College*

Evans, H. K.
A study of the junior instruction centre based on material from the Wrexham district. *M.A. 1937 Liverpool*

Evans, H. M.
Iaith a ieithwedd y cerddi rhydd cynnar(The language and style of the early free poems). *M.A. 1937 Wales*

Evans, H. W.
Defects in local government arising from the distribution of areas, with special reference to north Wales. *LL.M. 1938 Wales*

Evans, I.
Christian socialism: its rise and development, its economic and social results, and its relation to other working class movements. *M.A. 1912 Wales*

Evans, J.
Magical jewels of the Middle Ages and Renaissance, particularly in England. *Cert.Litt. 1920 Oxford*

Evans, J.
1. On the intermediate state. 2. On demoniacal possession. *B.D. & D.D. 1906 Oxford*

Evans, J.
A study of ornament in western Europe from 1180 to the middle of the seventeenth century. *D.Litt. 1930 London, University College*

Evans, J. A.
Expositions of I Timothy ii.8; I Peter i.10-12; II Peter i.20-21. *D.D. 1915 Oxford*

Evans, J. A.
1. The problem of pain as treated in the Book of Job. 2. The place of the resurrection ot our Lord in the plan of salvation. *B.D. 1907 Oxford*

Evans, J. D.
The internationalism in the work and thought of William Ewart Gladstone, with reference to present-day theory and practice of internationalism. *M.A. 1938 Wales*

Evans, J. F.
The attitude of Chaucer towards chivalry, the Church and the people, compared with that of Langland, Wycliffe and Gower. *M.A. 1911 Wales*

Evans, J. J.
Dylanwad y chwyldro Ffrengig ar lenyddiaeth Cymru(The influence of the French Revolution on the literature of Wales). *M.A. 1926 Wales*

Evans, J. K.
The influence of English writers on Gérard de Nerval. *M.A. 1939 Manchester*

Evans, J. L.
The part played by symbols in thinking, with special reference to belief, and cognate states. *D.Phil. 1945 Oxford*

Evans, J. M.
A monograph on the native education among the North American Indians, and its effect upon adult behaviour. *M.Ed. 1923 Manchester*

Evans, J. T.
The two main parts of the Book of Isaiah compared and contrasted with a more detailed investigation of the several parts of Deutero-Isaiah in regard to matter, style and authorship. *M.A. 1905 Wales*

Evans, K. M.
A study of attitude towards teaching as a career. *M.A. 1946 London, King's College*

Evans, L. E.
Cysylltiad y diwygiadau crefyddol o 1730 hyd 1850 â llenyddiaeth y cyfnod(The connection of religious revivals from 1730 to 1850 with the literature of the period). *M.A. 1934 Wales*

Evans, L. G.
A syntactical study of the verb in modern French, with special reference to Pierre Hamp. *M.A. 1928 Manchester*

Evans, L. M.
The relation of Chaucer to chivalry. *M.A. 1911 Wales*

Evans, L. W.
The regional development of the metallurgical industries of south-east Carmarthenshire. *M.A. 1937 Wales*

Evans, M.
The history of the Modern Movement in Welsh poetry. *M.A. 1921 Wales*

Evans, M.
The language of the Elizabethan drama. *Ph.D. 1940 Cambridge*

Evans, M. H.
The attitude of the Roman Government to Christianity from Nero to Marcus Aurelius. *M.A. 1909 Wales*

Evans, M. P.
The conception of the self in Locke, Berkeley and Hume. *M.A. 1934 Wales*

Evans, O. E.
The Junior Instruction Centre. *M.A. 1939 Liverpool*

Evans, O. T.
The origins and milieux of the Parnasse. *M.A. 1932 Wales*

Evans, P. C. C.
Sir John Perrot. *M.A. 1940 Wales*

Evans, P. L.
The Englishman as a character in the French fiction of the eighteenth century. *M.A. 1923 Manchester*

Evans, R. J.
Ducis and De Vigny considered as interpreters of Shakespeare. *M.A. 1909 Wales*

Evans, R. L.
Diderot et la musique. *M.A. 1932 Birmingham*

Evans, R. R.
English ballads: their origin and literature. *M.A. 1911 Wales*

Evans, R. W.
Y daroganau Cymraeg hyd at amser y Tuduriaid, gan roi sylw arbennig i'r cywyddau brud(The Welsh prophecies up to the time of the Tudors, with special reference to the prophetic cywyddau). *M.A. 1935 Wales*

Evans, S.
Dream literature in the English Romantic period (1780-1830), with a consideration of some writers of the later nineteenth century. *M.A. 1938 Wales*

Evans, S.
An examination of Sir Humphrey Machworth's industrial activities, with special reference to the Governor and Company of the Mine Adventurers of England. *M.A. 1950 Wales*

Evans, S. G.
Thomas Smith, merchant adventurer. *M.A. 1949 Leeds*

Evans, S. H.
The divine sympathy: an essay on kenotic Christology. *B.D. 1944 Durham*

Evans, T.
The conception of teleology in modern philosophy from Descartes to Kant. *M.A. 1927 Wales*

Evans, T.
Political thought in Wales, 1789-1846. *M.A. 1924 Wales*

Evans, T.
The syntax of the New Testament compared with Attic Greek. *M.A. 1903 Wales*

Evans, T. G.
A study of H. G. Wells's contributions to education. *M.A. 1931 Wales*

Evans, T. L.
Bywyd a gwaith Dr. Lewis Edwards(The life and work of Dr. Lewis Edwards). *M.A. 1948 Wales*

Evans, T. P.
The methods employed by the Council of the League of Nations to settle international disputes in pursuance of the terms of the Covenant. *Ph.D. 1930 London, School of Economics and Political Science*

Evans, V. B.
A critical exposition of Mr. Bradley's view of truth. *M.A. 1922 Wales*

Evans, V. B.
A critical study of Mr. Bradley's view of truth. *B.Litt. 1923 Oxford*

Evans, W. A.
Gower: a regional study, with special reference to agricultural geography. *M.A. 1948 Wales*

Evans, W. A.
A statistical study of the development of Nonconformity in north Wales in the nineteenth century, with special reference to the period 1850-1901. *M.A. 1928 Liverpool*

Evans, W. G.
Aristotle's treatment of social problems in its bearing upon modern life. *M.A. 1918 Wales*

Evans, W. S.
Conceptions of property in England from Harrington to Marx. *Ph.D. 1942 Sheffield*

Evans-Pritchard, E. E. *see* Pritchard, E. E. Evans-

Everett, D.
A study of the Middle English prose Psalter of Richard Rolle of Hampole. *M.A. 1920 London*

Evers, W. K.
Disputes about episcopal elections in England in the reign of Henry III, with special reference to some unpublished Durham documents. *B.Litt. 1936 Oxford*

Ewan, G.
The philosophy of J. F. Fries. *Ph.D. 1921 Edinburgh*

Ewart, H. J.
Transformation of the Highlands of Scotland. *Ph.D. 1935 Aberdeen*

Ewbank, W. W.
The poems of Cicero. *Ph.D. 1932 London, External Degree*

Ewen, A. H.
Plato and Pythagoreanism. *M.A. 1923 London*

Ewens, E. G.
Maria Edgeworth and the novel. *Ph.D. 1946 Dublin, Trinity College*

Ewing, A. C.
Kant's treatment of causality. *D.Phil. 1923 Oxford*

Ewing, J.
The structure and development of the brush-prairie of the White Earth Indian Reservation. *D.Sc. 1916 Aberdeen*

Exelby, H. R.
The Industrial Revolution in the textile industries of Wiltshire. *M.A. 1928 Bristol*

Exley, C. F.
A survey of the learning process with special reference to perception, with experimental work on three forms of perception. *M.Ed. 1927 Leeds*

Exley, M.
Naval construction in the reign of James I. *M.A. 1949 Leeds*

Eybers, G. von W.
Constitutional development at the Cape of Good Hope, 1795-1854. *M.A. 1916 London*

Eyre, P. D.
1. The Logos as the interpreter of God the Father. 2. The Book of Job critically considered with special reference to the faith and needs of the present day. *B.D. & D.D. 1900 Oxford*

Eysenck, H. J.
Experimental and statistical investigation of some factors influencing aesthetic judgments. *Ph.D. 1940 London, University College*

Fadipe, N. A.
The sociology of the Yoruba. *Ph.D. 1940 London, School of Economics and Political Science*

Fadner, F. L.
Development of pan-Slavist thought in Russia from Karazin to Danilevski, 1800-1870. *Ph.D. 1949 London, School of Slavonic and East European Studies*

Fagan, E. H. de L.
Some aspects of the King's household in the reign of Henry V, 1413-1422. *M.A. 1935 London, University College*

Fage, J. D.
The achievement of self-government in Southern Rhodesia, 1898-1923. *Ph.D. 1950 Cambridge*

Fahey, J.
Theism, old and new. *M.A. 1917 National University of Ireland*

Fahmy, A. H.
The educational ideas of the Muslims in the middle ages. *M.A. 1937 Birmingham*

Fahmy, A. M.
Muslim sea power in the eastern Mediterranean from the seventh to the tenth century: studies in naval organization. *Ph.D. 1948 London, School of Oriental and African Studies*

Fahmy, M.
Spasmophemia. *Ph.D. 1949 Cambridge*

Fahmy, M. H.
The legal principles governing the situational status of Egypt. *LL.D. 1928 London*

Fahy, T.
Divination in Homer and the tragedians. *M.A. 1914 National University of Ireland*

Faint, R. W.
An examination of the critical periodical literature of the Romantic revival. *M.A. 1925 London*

Fair, P. E. C.
Structure and function of judgement. *M.A. 1915 National University of Ireland*

Fairbank, J. K.
British policy in relation to the origin of the Chinese Imperial Maritime Customs Service, 1850-4 inclusive. *B.Litt. 1931 Oxford*

Fairbank, J. K.
The origin of the Chinese maritime customs. *D.Phil. 1936 Oxford*

Fairgrieve, A.
The economic possibilities of the northern and eastern savannas. *M.A. 1924 Liverpool*

Fairhurst, H.
Historical geography of the Makerfield district in south Lancashire. *M.A. 1922 Liverpool*

Fairhurst, H.
Iron age settlements in Kintyre: Kildonan Bay. *Ph.D. 1940 Glasgow*

Fairhurst, H.
Some aspects of the early historical geography of Scotland. *M.A. 1933 Liverpool*

Fairlie, A. A. B.
L'élément barbare chez Leconte de Lisle. *D.Phil. 1943 Oxford*

Fairs, G. H.
Criminal transportation, its theory and practice, with special reference to Australia. *M.A. 1932 Bristol*

Faithfull, C. E.
The relation between the individual good and the social good, in Plato. *M.A. 1915 London*

Fakhry, M.
Causality in Al-Ghazali, Averroes, and Aquinas. *Ph.D. 1949 Edinburgh*

Falconer, A. F.
The correspondence of Bishop Percy with Sir David Dalrymple, Lord Hailes, and George Paton of Edinburgh, with introduction and notes. *B.Litt. 1934 Oxford*

Falconer, W.
An enquiry into the social and political state of Scotland as reflected in the *Basilicon Doron* of James I. *Ph.D. 1925 Edinburgh*

Falk, E. H.
Etude sur la conception intuitive de l'action dramatique dans le théâtre français de 1885 à 1904. *Ph.D. 1942 Manchester*

Fan, T. F.
A comparative study of the offices of the Prime Minister of Great Britain and the President of the United States of America: a study in comparative political institutions. *M.Sc. 1933 London, School of Economics and Political Science*

Fargher, R.
La *Décade philosophique* et la fin de la philosophie en France au début du dix-neuvième siècle. *D.Phil. 1941 Oxford*

Fargher, R.
Mably and Montesquieu. *B.Litt. 1938 Oxford*

Farid, I. A.
The introduction of perennial irrigation in Egypt and its effects on the rural economy and population problems of the country. *Ph.D. 1937 London, University College*

Faris, J. A.
A consideration of certain connected problems about belief and cognate states of mind. *B.Litt. 1938 Oxford*

Farkas, P. L.
The fourth noble truth: a study in Buddhist ethics. *Ph.D. 1931 Aberdeen*

Farley, F. A.
A psychological enquiry into the function and importance of habit in human life. *M.A. 1934 Leeds*

Farmer, H. G.
A musical history of the Arabs: from the days of idolatry to the time of the Buwaihids. *Ph.D. 1926 Glasgow*

Farmer, I. M.
The young child's idea of its personal environment as seen in drawings. *M.A. 1949 Birmingham*

Farnsworth, A.
The residence and domicil of corporations. *Ph.D. 1938 London, External Degree*

Farr, D. M.
John Webster, a study. *Ph.D. 1947 Leeds*

Farr, G.
Commentary on the Book of Hosea by Dionysius Bar Salibi. *M.A. 1945 Manchester*

Farran, C. E.
1. The theory of sacraments and the varying use of the term in theology. 2. Confirmation or laying on of hands as recorded and taught in the New Testament. *B.D. & D.D. 1910 Oxford*

Farrar, D. H.
Images and literary imagery. *Ph.D. 1931 London, Bedford College*

Farrar, M. F.
The load factor as a factor in fixing rates and charges for public utility undertakings. *M.A. 1930 Leeds*

Farrar, W.
1. God and the world. 2. The cultus of the Sacred Heart in light of the hypostatic union. *B.D. 1895 Oxford*

Farrell, A. B.
The making of the ratio-studiorum, 1548-1599 A.D. *Ph.D. 1932 National University of Ireland*

Farrell, B. A.
The possibility of mathematics in the philosophy of Kant. *B.Litt. 1939 Oxford*

Farren, S.
Some aspects of the proper law. *LL.M. 1947 London, University College*

Farrington, B.
Shelley's translations from Greek. *M.A. 1917 National University of Ireland*

Farrington, E. M.
Calvin as a literary artist. *M.A. 1945 Belfast*

Farris, M.
Action, theme and symbol in the novels of E. M. Forster. *M.A. 1946 Liverpool*

Farris, M.
The element of symbolism in the later novels and stories of Henry James. *Ph.D. 1949 Liverpool*

Farrow, S. S.
Yoruba paganism, or the religious beliefs of the West African negroes, particularly of the Yoruba tribes of southern Nigeria. *Ph.D. 1924 Edinburgh*

Faulkner, A.
Parrthas an Anma le Antóin Gearnon(*The Paradise of the soul* by Antóin Gearnon). *M.A. 1938 National University of Ireland*

Faulkner, J.
An sgáthán spioradálta(The spiritual mirror). *Ph.D. 1945 National University of Ireland*

Faulks, W. T.
Recherches sur la syntaxe de Jacques de Longuyon dans *les voeux du paon*, manuscript w. *M.A. 1932 Birmingham*

Fausset, W. Y.
1. Miracles in the light of modern science. 2. The Trinitarian formula in the writings of Novatian. *B.D. 1914 Oxford*

Favell, I. E.
Stefan Zeromski, 1864-1925; his life and work. *M.A. 1949 Birmingham*

Fawcett, C. B.
The Fiord peoples. *B.Litt. 1913 Oxford*

Fawcett, W. A.
St. Helen's, 1845 and afterwards: an illustration of educational developments. *M.A. 1936 Liverpool*

Fay, C. R.
Co-operation at home and abroad: a description and analysis. *D.Sc. 1909 London*

Feachem, R. W. de F.
The material culture of the Bay Islands. *M.Sc. 1948 Cambridge*

Fear, R. Daunton- *see* Daunton-Fear, R.

Fear, W.
Émile Zola: a critical account of his ideas. *Ph.D. 1949 Leeds*

Feavearyear, A. E.
Currency history and the currency problem, 1914-1923. *M.Sc. 1923 London*

Feaver, E. K.
The controversy concerning miracles in England during the seventeenth and eighteenth centuries, with special reference to the period 1700-1750. *Ph.D. 1937 Edinburgh*

Febvre, L.
Geoffrey Chaucer and Guillaume de Machaut. *M.A. 1948 National University of Ireland*

Feeley, J.
Philosophy and science. *M.A. 1948 National University of Ireland*

Fegan, E. S.
Report of a tour to the west coast of Africa to study the education of women, 1928-29. Some notes on the Bachama tribe, Nigeria, 1928. *Dip. Anthropology 1929 Cambridge*

Fei, C. C.
The literary reputation of John Keats in England from 1817 to 1888. *M.A. 1937 Liverpool*

Fei, H. T.
Kaihsienkung: economic life in a Chinese village. *Ph.D. 1938 London, School of Economics and Political Science*

Feibusch, E. M.
The Old French metrical versions of the prophecies of Merlin. *B.Litt. 1928 Oxford*

Feldman, A.
The parables and similes of the Rabbis: agricultural and pastoral. *Ph.D. 1925 London*

Feldman, R. V.
An enquiry into the philosophical significance and justification of self-respect. *Ph.D. 1937 London, University College*

Feldmann, M.
An exposition of the contents of an unpublished treatise in manuscript by Gersonides, concerning *Hokhmath Hatekhuna*, astronomy. *M.A. 1941 Manchester*

Fellheimer, J.
The Englishman's conception of the Italian in the age of Shakespeare. *M.A. 1935 London, King's College*

Fenelon, K. G.
The economics of road transport. *Ph.D. 1926 Edinburgh*

Feng, S. C.
Foreign banking in China. *M.Sc. 1938 London, School of Economics and Political Science*

Fenn, M.
The conditions of moral responsibility. *M.A. 1948 Wales*

Fenning, M. R.
English tragedies in the Greek form with studies of the principal plays. *M.A. 1929 Birmingham*

Fenton, A. W. E.
Ancient Greek astronomy, with special reference to navigation and nautical astronomy. *Ph.D. 1937 London, Birkbeck College*

Fenwick, L.
The phonology and accidence of the Cotton ms. of the *Cursor mundi* considered with especial reference to the Northumbrian dialect of Old English. *M.A. 1947 Manchester*

Fenwick, M. E.
The enquiry into complaints against the ministers of Eleanor of Castile (1291-1292), its administrative and legal significanc. *M.A. 1931 London, Royal Holloway College*

Ferguson, A. E.
Etude lexicographique des mots intéressants dans l'oeuvre de Gustave Aimard, étudiés dans ses romans écrits pendant les cinq années 1858-1862. *M.A. 1936 Leeds*

Ferguson, G. A.
The reliability of mental tests. *Ph.D. 1940 Edinburgh*

Ferguson, R. W.
The influence of Montesquieu upon the American constitution. *M.A. 1912 London*

Ferguson, T.
A clinical survey of the applicability of intelligence tests to the study of mental deficiency in children. *M.D. 1924 Edinburgh*

Fermor, U. M. Ellis- *see* Ellis-Fermor, U. M.

Fernando, C. N. V.
A study of the history of Christianity in Ceylon in the British period from 1796 to 1903, with special reference to the Protestant missions. *B.Litt. 1942 Oxford*

Ferns, F. E. B.
Principles of justice observed by courts of justice in England. *LL.M. 1956 Manchester*

Ferrario, M. T.
The relation between court and literature in the seventeenth century (1579-1700). *M.A. 1917 Birmingham*

Ferriday, A.
The place of chemistry in a rural secondary school. *M.Sc. 1930 Liverpool*

Fertleman, B.
The last days of Aaron according to the Midrash *Petirat-Aharon. M.A. 1937 Manchester*

Ffoulkes, J. F.
The armourer and his craft. *B.Litt. 1912 Oxford*

Fidler, A. G. S.
The theory of Roman and Renaissance vault construction, with special reference to the Pantheon, Rome, and Santa Maria della Salute, Venice. *M.A. 1936 Liverpool*

Fidler, M.
The revolutionary novel, 1780-1820. *M.A. 1928 Manchester*

Field, A. G.
The expedition to Mauritius in 1810 and the establishment of British control. *M.A. 1932 London, Birkbeck College*

Field, A. M.
The development of government in Newfoundland, 1638-1713. *M.A. 1924 London*

Field, E. E.
Rural settlements and the distribution of rural population in Northamptonshire. *M.Sc. 1931 London, External Degree*

Field, G. C.
Modern developments of realism. *B.Sc. 1912 Oxford*

Field, H. E.
Re-building character of delinquent youth: a study of the English Borstal system and of the responses of individuals to its methods of treatment. *Ph.D. 1933 London, Institute of Education*

Field, M. J.
Religion and medicine among the Ga people of the Gold Coast. *Ph.D. 1936 London, University College*

Field, R.
An enquiry into the relative achievements of boys and girls at a first School Certificate examination, in the six commoner subjects of the curriculum. *M.A. 1935 Birmingham*

Field, T.
1. Baptism and the forgiveness of sins. 2. Absolution and the forgiveness of sins. *B.D. & D.D. 1897 Oxford*

Fielden, O. *see* Lamont, O.

Fieldhouse, A. E.
A study of backwardness in singing among school children. *Ph.D. 1937 London, Institute of Education*

Fielding, D. D.
The Roman province of Judaea before 70 A.D. *M.A. 1933 Manchester*

Fielding, I. J.
The geographical background of white settlement in the Kenya highlands. *M.Sc. 1947 London, School of Economics and Political Science*

Fielding, J. T.
The place of the evening institute in further education in the East Midlands. *M.Ed. 1950 Nottingham*

Fielding, W. R.
The teaching of science in the junior school. *M.Ed. 1932 Manchester*

Fikry, A. R.
Economic development of Egypt since 1876. *M.Sc. 1918 London*

Filby, F. A.
The development of analytical method in chemistry from 1790 to 1830. *M.Sc. 1929 London*

Filby, F. A.
A history of food adulteration and analysis from the earliest times, to the work of Frederick Accum (1820). *Ph.D. 1933 London, University College*

Fildes, L. G.
Word deafness: a psychological contribution to the study of mental defect. *Ph.D. 1929 London*

Filmer, H. A.
Gay Lussac's law of gaseous volumes and the influence on chemical theory up to 1860. *M.Sc. 1928 London*

Finch, C. D.
Some problems in wages policy. *Ph.D. 1949 London, School of Economics and Political Science*

Finch, R. G.
1. The history of the canon of the Old Testament, together with the Mishna and Tosephta tractate *Yadaim*. 2. The Tosephta tractate *Aboda Zara. Ph.D. 1931 London, External Degree*

Finch, T. F.
Agricultural limits in the Dublin mountains. *M.Sc. 1948 Dublin, Trinity College*

Finch, W. H.
Hermann Stehr: sein Leben und sein Werk. *M.A. 1940 Liverpool*

Findlay, D. F.
The fabric rolls of Exeter cathedral, 1374-1514. *Ph.D. 1939 Leeds*

Findlay, E. J.
An enquiry into the physical conditions and social circumstances of mentally subnormal children attending elementary schools in the city of Lincoln. *M.D. 1934 Glasgow*

Finer, H.
Representative government and a parliament of industry: a study of the German Federal Economic Council. *D.Sc. 1923 London*

Finer, H.
Some elements of recent constitutional and administrative tendencies in France, Germany and United States of America: an introductory study. *M.Sc. 1922 London*

Finkelstein, T.
The contribution of the English courts to the development of international law. *B.Litt. 1939 Oxford*

Finlay, A. M.
The influence of equitable ideas concerning property in the development of the law of contract as illustrated by (1) the passing of property under invalid contracts, and (2) contracts for the benefit of third persons. *Ph.D. 1938 London, School of Economics and Political Science*

Finlay, E.
Trends in the men's tailoring industry of Great Britain. *Ph.D. 1947 London, External Degree*

Finn, D. J.
Greek sculpture and painting. *M.A. 1910 National University of Ireland*

Finney, K. E.
Eichendorff's ideas of romanticism. *M.A. 1913 Birmingham*

Finney, R. R.
The importance and place of physical sciences in a liberal education, with special reference to the study of physical chemistry in a secondary school curriculum. *M.A. 1928 Liverpool*

Firminger, W. K.
Exegeses of Acts xx.28; xvii.22-31; Ephesians iii.28. *D.D. 1919 Oxford*

Firminger, W. K.
The history of the occupation and rural administration of Bengal by the English Company from the time of Clive to the permanent settlement under Cornwallis. *B.Litt. 1913 Oxford*

Firminger, W. K.
1. The Thomistic doctrine of the sacramental form or matter. 2. The reality of the Holy Spirit's indwelling in the souls of the sanctified. *B.D. 1905 Oxford*

Firth, C. B.
Some aspects of the religious history of Norfolk in the fifteenth century. *M.A. 1910 London*

Firth, N. M.
La vie et les poésies de Jean Moréas. *M.A. 1923 Leeds*

Firth, R. W.
Economic organization of Polynesian societies. *Ph.D. 1927 London*

Fisch, H.
A critical study of the prose-works of Bishop Joseph Hall, 1574-1656. *B.Litt. 1948 Oxford*

Fisch, S.
An edition of: Midrash *Haggadol* to the first five chapters of Numbers. *M.A. 1933 Manchester*

Fisch, S.
The Midrash *Haggadol*, its authorship, its sources and its importance in Rabbinic literature. *Ph.D. 1936 Manchester*

Fischel, H.A.
The Rabbinic conception of prophecy. *Ph.D. 1945 Edinburgh*

Fish, M. E.
The relation of Catullus and the Augustan elegiac Latin poets to Alexandrian literature. *M.A. 1918 London*

Fish, T.
The tablets from Drehem. *Ph.D. 1928 Cambridge*

Fisher, A.
The critics of the eighteenth century, before Wordsworth and Coleridge. *M.A. 1911 London*

Fisher, A. G. B.
Some problems of wages and their regulation in Great Britain since 1918. *Ph.D. 1924 London*

Fisher, C.
The economic geography of southern Rhodesia, with special reference to communications. *M.A. 1924 Liverpool*

Fisher, E.
W. S. Landor as a critic. *M.A. 1914 Birmingham*

Fisher, E. J.
The history of Valle Crucis Abbey, Denbighshire. *M.A. 1929 Liverpool*

Fisher, F. J.
The influence and development of the industrial guilds in the larger provincial towns under James I and Charles I, with special reference to the formation of new corporations for the control of industry. *M.A. 1931 London, School of Economics and Political Science*

Fisher, J.
The elegy in the eighteenth century. *B.Litt. 1929 Oxford*

Fisher, J. M.
Some aspects of primitive medicine. *Ph.D. 1949 Cambridge*

Fisher, J. W.
The development of Rhodesia under the British South Africa Company (1890-1914), with some indication of subsequent developments. *M.A. 1924 Wales*

Fisher, K. A.
The growth of humanitarian feeling towards animals as shown in English poetry. *M.A. 1929 Wales*

Fisher, M.
The struggles of the European powers for possession in Guiana, 1667-1713. *M.A. 1926 London*

Fisher, M. J.
The eastern element in Lamartine. *Ph.D. 1942 London, King's College*

Fisher, M. J.
Les romans de Lamartine. *M.A. 1937 London, King's College*

Fisher, M. L. E.
An edition of Middleton's *Women beware women* and *A chaste maid in Cheapside*, with an introduction and notes. *B.Litt. 1937 Oxford*

Fisher, N. H.
The contribution of Robert Barnes to the English Reformation. *M.A. 1950 Birmingham*

Fishman, I.
The history of Jewish education in Central Europe from the beginning of the seventeenth century to 1782 (the Edict of Toleration issued by Joseph II of Austria). *Ph.D. 1941 London, External Degree*

Fisk, A. G.
The fundamental ideas of the Holiness Code in relation to the prophetic teaching. *Ph.D. 1930 Edinburgh*

Fison, J. E.
The blessing of the Holy Spirit. *B.D. 1950 Oxford*

Fitch, M. G.
The history of the training of teachers for secondary schools in England (approx. 1846 to 1930). *M.A. 1931 London, King's College*

Fitch, T.
Caroline puritanism as exemplified in the life and work of William Prynne. *Ph.D. 1949 Edinburgh*

Fitch, W.
The theology of Christian conversion in the light of New Testament teaching, and with special reference to the works of Søren Kierkegaard. *Ph.D. 1946 Glasgow*

Fitter, L. E.
Macpherson's *Ossian. M.A. 1908 Birmingham*

Fitzgerald, M. P.
Ballads: English, Scotch and Irish. *M.A. 1924 National University of Ireland*

Fitzgerald, T. F.
The method of reflection in the philosophy of St. Thomas. *M.A. 1950 National University of Ireland*

Fitzgerald, W.
Early Ireland: an essay in historical geography. *M.A. 1925 Liverpool*

Fitzgibbon, J.
The Leveller Movement. *M.A. 1939 National University of Ireland*

Fitzhardinge, L. F.
The development of the Roman fleets under the Empire. *B.Litt. 1933 Oxford*

Fitzhardinge, U. C.
The policy of the Roman Government towards non-Roman religions from Augustus to Trajan, with special reference to the treatment of such religions in Rome and Italy. *B.Litt. 1940 Oxford*

Fitzpatrick, B.
Breaks with tradition: an inquiry, with special reference to the gradual development of the industrial element in education. *M.A. 1938 National University of Ireland*

Fitzpatrick, J. I.
Dairying in the Irish agricultural economy. *Ph.D. 1946 Dublin, Trinity College*

Fitzpatrick, M. S.
Mind and the universal frame. *M.A. 1934 National University of Ireland*

Fitzpatrick, T.
History of independent Corinth. *M.A. 1915 National University of Ireland*

Fitzsimons, J.
Catholic popular education in Ireland (1750-1870). *Ph.D. 1941 National University of Ireland*

Flack, W. S.
Mental tests as a means of classifying secondary school pupils in mathematics. *M.Sc. 1924 Birmingham*

Flack, W. S.
The relative significance of various types of mental tests for education prognosis. *Ph.D. 1929 London*

Flajszer, J. L.
The doctrine of poverty in its religious, social and political aspects, as illustrated by some XII-XIII century movements. *Ph.D. 1943 London, School of Economics and Political Science*

Flanagan, J. G.
Church reform in Ireland before 1550. *M.A. 1946 National University of Ireland*

Flanagan, L.
Studies in the development of the parish of Bradford, 1800-1847. *M.A. 1931 Liverpool*

Flatley, M.
Canamhaintí Gaedhilge(Irish dialects). *M.A. 1933 National University of Ireland*

Flatley, M.
Lebor Gabala(*The book of invasions*). *M.A. 1934 National University of Ireland*

Flavell, J. S.
Arithmetic in the junior school. *M.A. 1942 Birmingham*

Fleck, J. McP.
Irenaeus and the fourth gospel: the value of his testimony. *Ph.D. 1925 Edinburgh*

Fleet, W. F.
The underworld and its deities in the Ras Shamra texts. *M.A. 1938 Manchester*

Fleischmann, A. G.
The neumes and Irish liturgical mss. *M.A. 1932 National University of Ireland*

Fleming, C. E.
Democratic planning in Australia, 1919-1939. *B.Litt. 1949 Oxford*

Fleming, C. M.
A survey of reading ability. *Ph.D. 1931 Glasgow*

Fleming, E. see Pléamonn, B.

Fleming, J. G.
Matrimonial causes in the conflict of laws: a comparative study. *D.Phil. 1948 Oxford*

Fleming, W. K.
1. A study of the first Epistle of St. Peter in its relation to the Apostle's character and history. 2. The action of divine grace through distinctive channels of human personality. *B.D. 1909 Oxford*

Flemington, W. F.
The New Testament doctrine of baptism. *B.D. 1948 Cambridge*

Flemming, W.
The place and value of mathematics in secondary schools. *M.A. 1949 Liverpool*

Flenley, R.
The English civic chronicles during the fifteenth and sixteenth centuries. *B.Litt. 1910 Oxford*

Fletcher, B. A.
Education as a factor in colonial development, with special reference to Java. *M.A. 1934 Bristol*

Fletcher, E. G. M.
The carrier's liability. *LL.D. 1932 London, External Degree*

Fletcher, F. T. H.
Etude sur la langue de Jacques de Longuyon. *M.A. 1923 Birmingham*

Fletcher, F. T. H.
Montesquieu and English thought. *D.Litt. 1935 Birmingham*

Fletcher, G. M.
The status of French and English in the Neutral Islands, 1635-1763. *M.A. 1930 London, King's College*

Fletcher, J.
A critical appreciation and survey of the works of Nicholas Rowe. *B.Litt. 1939 Oxford*

Fletcher, J.
Jonathan Swift: an Augustan poet. *M.A. 1950 Manchester*

Fletcher, M. A.
A study of the Knights of the Shire returned to Parliament by Bedfordshire during the Middle Ages. *M.A. 1933 London, University College*

Flew, R. N.
How far is it true that the Christianity of the end of the second century is a departure from the teaching and ideals of the New Testament?. *B.D. 1925 Oxford*

Fligg, H.
A history of elementary education in Leeds prior to 1870. *M.Ed. 1938 Leeds*

Flight, A. T.
Legislation relating to mining, XIX century, 1840-1887. *Ph.D. 1937 London, School of Economics and Political Science*

Flitcroft, J.
The constitutions for the promotion of University graduates in England, 1417-1438. *M.A. 1937 Manchester*

Flockhart, M. C.
Guillaume Thomas Francis Raynal: his life, writings, political views, and his influence on the French Revolution. *B.Litt. 1923 Oxford*

Flood, W. E.
Some problems in the presentation of popular science. *Ph.D. 1949 Birmingham*

Florance, A. W.
Poetry and the rustic in the eighteenth century. *M.A. 1935 Bristol*

Florecka, I.
A comparative study of the economic position of women in Great Britain and Poland in the inter-war period. *Ph.D. 1945 Edinburgh*

Florecki, S.
Foreign trade of Poland between 1918 and 1939 with special reference to the trade with Britain. *Ph.D. 1943 Edinburgh*

Flower, J. C.
Recent developments of psychological study upon religion. *Ph.D. 1925 Cambridge*

Floyer, J. K.
1. The life of St. Dunstan. 2. The work of St. Dunstan at Glastonbury. *B.D. & D.D. 1922 Oxford*

Flynn, M.
Thomas Fuller, D. D. *M.A. 1936 National University of Ireland*

Flynn, M. J.
The French theatre in the 18th century. *M.A. 1943 National University of Ireland*

Foakes, R. A.
The revenger's tragedy and *The atheist's tragedy*: some notes on their style and on the authorship problem. *M.A. 1949 Birmingham*

Fodrio, C.
A study of the French banking system, with special reference to the financing of industry and to the French investment policy during the period 1815-1914. *Ph.D. 1941 London, School of Economics and Political Science*

Fogarty, J.
Asinius Pollio and his part in the Roman Revolution. *M.A. 1943 National University of Ireland*

Fogg, W.
The influence of physical conditions upon human life in the Sebou Basin. *M.A. 1928 Manchester*

Foley, C. M.
Eugène Le Roy. *M.A. 1929 Birmingham*

Foley, J.
The pilgrim's progress of John Bunyan: sources of the allegory. *M.A. 1949 National University of Ireland*

Folland, M. D. B.
Extra curricular activity: its place and scope in the two senior forms of a secondary (grammar) school. *M.A. 1946 Birmingham*

Follows, J. W.
Antecedents of the International Labour Organization. *B.Litt. 1932 Oxford*

Fong, S.
A comparative study of the aesthetic judgments of English and Chinese children in picture appreciation. *M.A. 1938 Birmingham*

Fontaine, B. L. S.
Human problems of organisation in industry. *M.Sc. 1939 London, University College*

Fookes, R. G.
1. The doctrine of the Holy Trinity. 2. The doctrine of the atonement. *B.D. 1903 Oxford*

Foot, M. R. D.
The policies of Stanley, Granville, and Gladstone towards Luxemburg, Belgium, and Alsace-Lorraine, 1867-1871. *B.Litt. 1950 Oxford*

Forbes, J. D.
Strategy and tactics in medieval Scotland. *Ph.D. 1927 Edinburgh*

Forbes, J. K.
The linen industry of Northern Ireland. *M.Sc. 1939 London, External Degree*

Forbes, J. M.
A study of emotion by means of free association in conjunction with the psycho-galvanic reflex. *Ph.D. 1935 London, University College*

Forbes, J. R. M.
Rise and earliest development of Christian monasticism with a study of its origin. *Ph.D. 1928 Edinburgh*

Ford, G. E.
A study of the poems of George Turberville. *M.A. 1914 London*

Ford, J. A.
The theory of the kenosis as based upon the New Testament. *Ph.D. 1928 Edinburgh*

Ford, K.
Milton, as he reveals himself in his prose. *M.A. 1919 National University of Ireland*

Ford, P.
Work and wealth in Southampton: an essay in civic economy. *Ph.D. 1933 London, External Degree*

Forde, D.
The prehistoric geography of Brittany: a study of the megalithic civilization. *Ph.D. 1928 London*

Formby, C. W.
1. The unveiling of the Fall. 2. Re-creation: a new aspect of evolution. *B.D. & D.D. 1924 Oxford*

Forrest, J.
The Elizabethan Ovid: a study of the Ovidian spirit in Elizabethan poetry, 1589 to 1616. *Ph.D. 1945 Edinburgh*

Forrester, E. G.
Northamptonshire county elections and electioneering (1695-1832), based mainly on the Isham and Cartwright muniments. *B.Litt. 1939 Oxford*

Forrester, I. E. V.
The Middlesex magistrate, 1760 to 1820: social and economic aspects of the work of J.P.'s. *M.A. 1934 London, School of Economics and Political Science*

Forrester, J. F.
A study of the attitudes of adolescents to their own intellectual, social and spiritual development. *Ph.D. 1946 London, Institute of Education*

Forsey, G. F.
The Palatine manuscript of Sophocles. *M.A. 1912 London*

Forster, J. M.
Swinburne and the Italian Risorgimento. *M.A. 1934 Birmingham*

Forsyth, T. M.
The development and significance of English philosophic method. *D. Phil. 1908 Edinburgh*

Forsyth, W. D.
Migration to Australia and New Zealand: post-war experience, present position, and future possibilities. *B.Litt. 1939 Oxford*

Forsythe, E. E. B.
Early traditions concerning King Arthur's family: a study in comparative chronology. *M.A. 1938 Belfast*

Forte, S. L.
A study of some Oxford Schoolmen of the middle of the fourteenth century, with special reference to Worcester Cathedral ms. F.65. *B.Litt. 1947 Oxford*

Fortes, M.
A new application of the theory of neogenesis to the problem of mental testing. *Ph.D. 1930 London, University College*

Fortune, R. F.
On initiative magic. *Dip. Anthropology. 1912 Cambridge*

Foster, C.
The influence of science teaching on the development of secondary education, with particular reference to the City of Birmingham. *M.A. 1940 London, King's College*

Foster, C.
An investigation into certain factors concerning the admission of pupils to secondary schools in Somerset. *M.A. 1934 Bristol*

Foster, F. S.
The teaching of Dante on the human intellect, with special reference to the doctrine of St. Thomas Aquinas. *Ph.D. 1947 Cambridge*

Foster, I. L.
Astudiaeth o chwedl *Culhwch ac Olwen*(A study of the legend of Culhwch and Olwen). *M.A. 1935 Wales*

Foster, J.
The Christian Church of the T'ang Dynasty. *M.A. 1938 Birmingham*

Foster, J. M.
The influence of Spenser on Milton. *M.A. 1945 London, King's College*

Foster, K.
A contribution to the study of nineteenth century slang. *M.A. 1929 London*

Foster, S. E.
The shipmoney levies under Charles I, and their influence upon local feeling. *M.A. 1914 London*

Foster, W. T.
The natural man and the noble savage in English literature in the seventeenth and eighteenth centuries. *B.Litt. 1916 Oxford*

Fothergill, F. S.
Latin in the secondary school. *M.Ed. 1937 Durham*

Fothergill, I. M.
Napoléon et sa légende à travers le roman, le conte et la nouvelle jusqu'à la fin du Second Empire. *M.A. 1928 Wales*

Foulds, G. A.
The psychological functions involved in the child's use of fantasy and fiction; and, the child's response to fictional characters and its relationship to personality traits. *M.A. 1943 Liverpool*

Foulger, T. R.
The psychological approach to religious education. *M.A. 1930 London, Day Training College*

Foulkes, E. J.
The contribution of water power development to the progress of the cotton-spinning industry, with particular reference to the Bolton district (period 1770-1845). *M.A. 1943 Wales*

Fountain, A. M. *see* Griffiths, A. M.

Fowler, F. J.
A geographical analysis of the development of the Canal Colonies region of the Punjab. *Ph.D. 1938 Leeds*

Fowler, G.
Les Oberlé de R. Bazin: le fond géographique et politique. *M.A. 1928 Birmingham*

Fowler, H. L.
The development of concepts. *Ph.D. 1928 London*

Fowler, R. E.
André Thevet: his work as a geographer. *B.Litt. 1930 Oxford*

Fowler, W. J.
The Crown and municipal corporations, 1679 to 1688: an aspect of the English revolution. *M.A. 1935 Reading*

Fox, C.
Archaeology of the Cambridge region. *Ph.D. 1922 Cambridge*

Fox, H. G.
Napoleon III and the panic of 1859. *M.A. 1930 Birmingham*

Fox, L.
The historical novel until the time of Scott. *M.A. 1943 Leeds*

Fox, L.
The honor of Leicester: a study in descent and administration, with special reference to the Leicestershire fees of the honor. *M.A. 1938 Manchester*

Fox, P. D.
Mgr. Dupanloup as an educator. *M.A. 1949 National University of Ireland*

Fox, P. L. Bushe- *see* Bushe-Fox, P. L.

Foxell, W. J.
The expressiveness of music. *Ph.D. 1927 London*

Foxwell, A. K.
Sir Thomas Wyatt and his poems. *M.A. 1910 London*

Fozzard, I.
The political importance of the newspaper press in the French Restoration period, 1814-30. *B.Litt. 1949 Oxford*

Fradin, J. M. B.
Ralph Neville, Bishop of Chichester and Chancellor. *B.Litt. 1942 Oxford*

Francis, C. A.
Character and importance of the religious settlement in Tudor England. *M.A. 1936 National University of Ireland*

Francis, C. M.
Thomas Campion (1567-1620): a study of his English works, with particular reference to the influence of music and classical studies on his theory and practice as a metrist. *B.Litt. 1938 Oxford*

Francis, E. A.
The Anglo-Norman versions of the life of St. Margaret. *M.A. 1922 London*

Francis, E. M.
Some relationships between power and economic development, with special reference to California. *Ph.D. 1939 Cambridge*

Francis, F. G.
The attitude of Aristophanes towards the traditional conception of religion and religious observances in Athens. *M.A. 1921 London*

Francis, G. M.
Literary criticism of Plautus, ancient and modern. *M.A. 1948 Wales*

Francis, J. H.
Thomas Hardy: His views on life and nature. *M.A. 1913 Wales*

Francis, K. H.
The decline of chivalry as shown in the French literature of the fifteenth century, with special reference to poetry and drama. *Ph.D. 1948 London, External Degree*

Francoudi, T.
The capitulations and the mixed tribunals generally. *LL.D. 1915 London*

Frangopulo, N. J.
A history of Queen Elizabeth's Grammar School, Ashbourne, Derbyshire. *M.Ed. 1937 Leeds*

Frankel, I.
Peshat (plain exegesis) in Talmudic and Midrashic literature. *Ph.D. 1949 Dublin, Trinity College*

Frankel, S. H.
South African railway policy, with special reference to rates and the development of the primary industries. *Ph.D. 1928 London*

Frankfort, H.
Studies in early pottery of the Near East. *M.A. 1923 London*

Franklin, H. L.
A study of the passion narratives, with special reference to the Last Supper. *B.Litt. 1935 Oxford*

Franklin, R. E.
Medical education and the rise of the general practitioner, 1760-1860. *Ph.D. 1950 Birmingham*

Franks, R. S.
The theories of the atonement of Anselm and Grotius. *B.Litt. 1899 Oxford*

Fraser, J.
James Fraser of Brea, 1639 to 1699: his life and writings, with special reference to his theory of universal redemption and its influence on religious thought in Scotland. *Ph.D. 1944 Edinburgh*

Fraser, D. E.
The development of the road system in Glamorgan up to 1844, with special reference to turnpike roads. *M.A. 1940 Wales*

Fraser, F.
Robert Owen and Christian Socialism. *Ph.D. 1927 Edinburgh*

Fraser, G.
A study of moral education. *B.Sc. 1923 Oxford*

Fraser, H. M.
An historical account of beekeeping in Greece and Rome during the classical period. *Ph.D. 1930 London, External Degree*

Frayn, J. M.
The Roman Apollo and kindred deities. *Ph.D. 1945 Edinburgh*

Frayn, R. S.
Revelation and the unconscious. *Ph.D. 1940 London, Richmond College*

Frazer, B. L.
The constitutional relations of the Marquess Wellesley with the home authorities. *M.A. 1917 Liverpool*

Frazer, H. A.
History and law of Irish local taxation. *M.Sc. 1936 London, External Degree*

Frazer, J. E.
Lyman Beecher, theologian and social reformer. *Ph.D. 1937 Edinburgh*

Frazer, N. L.
The English in the South of France from the accession of Henry III to the death of the Black Prince. *M.A. 1906 London*

Frazer-Hurst, H. D.
Coleridge as a religious thinker. *Ph.D. 1939 Dublin, Trinity College*

Frebault, C.
La vie coloniale dans le roman anglais et français: étude sur Rudyard Kipling et Pierre Loti. *M.A. 1926 Birmingham*

Fréchet, A. L. G.
Ernest Renan: moraliste. *Ph.D. 1943 Belfast*

Frechtling, L. E.
British policy in the Middle East, 1874-80. *D.Phil. 1939 Oxford*

Freedman, H.
The life of the Jews in Spain in the times of R. Asher B. Jechiel, as furnished by his *Responsa*. *Ph.D. 1930 London, External Degree*

Freedman, M.
The sociology of race relations in southeast Asia with special reference to British Malaya. *M.A. 1948 London, School of Economics and Political Science*

Freeling, D.
The earlier history of the Home Rule movement. *M.A. 1927 Birmingham*

Freeman, A. J.
An investigation into the causes that render large numbers of boys unable to obtain employment on reaching early manhood, with special reference to the conditions of boy life and labour in Birmingham. *B.Litt. 1914 Oxford*

Freeman, E. F.
Education et morale dans les écoles en France. *M.A. 1934 Birmingham*

Freeman, G. S. P.
Phrygia and Montanism. *B.Litt. 1940 Oxford*

Freeman, I. C. H.
The works of Aldous Huxley, with special reference to his philosophy. *M.A. 1939 Wales*

Freeman, K.
The work and life of Solon. *M.A. 1922 Wales*

Freeman, M. E.
The horse in Greek Art, from earliest times until the death of Alexander the Great. *M.A. 1937 London, University College*

Freeman, N. S.
Theatres and plays in Natal, 1846-1897. *M.A. 1949 Birmingham*

Freeman, P. C.
The life and works of William Walsh, with a special study of the letters and poems of 1692 and of ms. Malone 9. *B.Litt. 1934 Oxford*

Freeman, R.
The English emblem books. *Ph.D. 1941 Cambridge*

Freeman, R. E.
The future of internal transport in Great Britain. *B.Litt. 1921 Oxford*

Freeman, W. A.
An enquiry into the attitudes of secondary school boys and girls towards arithmetic. *M.A. 1948 Birmingham*

Fremantle, W. H.
1. The witness of the Old Testament to the immanence of God in nature and in man. 2. The theology of the Pastoral Epistle. *B.D. & D.D. 1895 Oxford*

Fremantle, W. R.
Exegeses of: St. John xvi.8; xvi.10; Exodus xxxiv.7. *B.D. & D.D. 1876 Oxford*

Fremlin, C. M.
A logical examination of non-propositional forms of thought, with special reference to aesthetics. *B.Litt. 1938 Oxford*

French, D. M.
The relations of the state to electricity undertakings in Great Britain and Germany. *B.Litt. 1934 Oxford*

French, P. W.
Indian logic in the light of Western thought. *M.A. 1919 London*

French, P. W.
The international right of aerial navigation. *LL.D. 1915 London*

Frend, W. H. C.
The social and economic background of Christianity in North Africa down to 430, with special reference to the Donatist schism. *D.Phil. 1940 Oxford*

Freston, P. M.
Children's conception of adult life. *M.A. 1945 London, Birkbeck College and London, King's College*

Fretter, A.
The influence of Platonic philosophy on Elizabethan poetry. *M.A. 1911 Birmingham*

Freybyia, J. St.
The European recovery programme. *M.Econ.Sc. 1950 National University of Ireland*

Freyer, G. D.
Machiavelli. *Ph.D. 1940 Dublin, Trinity College*

Friedlander, H. F.
Psychological researches into the nature of thinking. *M.A. 1946 Birmingham*

Friedlander, M.
An edition of: the *Sha'ar ha-Razin* of Todros Abulafia. *M.A. 1930 Manchester*

Friedlander, M.
The historical continuity of Hebrew, with special reference to its medieval and modern phases. *Ph.D. 1933 Manchester*

Friedman, M.
The local law applicable to contracts with a foreign element. *LL.M. 1940 Leeds*

Friedmann, O.
Propaganda in National Socialist Germany. *M.Sc. 1947 London, School of Economics and Political Science*

Friend, A. C.
Life and works of Odo of Cheriton. *D.Phil. 1936 Oxford*

Friend, P. E.
The outlaw in French literature. *M.A. 1922 London, University College*

Fries, F. T.
Anglo-Italian relations, 1884-5, and the Italian occupation of Massawah. *Ph.D. 1940 Cambridge*

Frisby, C. B.
Field research in flying training. *Ph.D. 1947 London, King's College and London, Birkbeck College*

Frith, H. I.
'New realism' contrasted with 'critical realism'. *M.A. 1924 Manchester*

Frizelle, J. D.
Marian poetry in Irish, a comparative study. *M.A. 1949 National University of Ireland*

Frodd, A. McK.
A geographical study of Saudi Arabia. *M.A. 1937 Liverpool*

Frost, E.
Christian healing; a consideration of the place of spiritual healing in the Church of today in the light of examination of the doctrine and practice of the Ante-Nicene Church. *Ph.D. 1940 London, King's College*

Frost, K. T.
Studies in Greek athletic art. *B.Litt. 1907 Oxford*

Frost, M. M.
Treatment of the rustic and the citizen in Elizabethan drama. *M.A. 1916 London*

Fry, A. H.
The land utilisation in Wiltshire, with special reference to Salisbury Plain. *M.A. 1939 London, Birkbeck College*

Fry, D. B.
Articulation tests: an application of experimental phonetic methods to measuring the efficiency of communication systems. *Ph.D. 1947 London, University College*

Fryde, E. B.
Edward III's war finance, 1337-41: transactions in wool and credit operations. *D.Phil. 1947 Oxford*

Fryer, D. W.
The land utilisation of Huntingdonshire. *M.Sc. 1942 London, School of Economics and Political Science*

Fryer, W. R.
The Comte de Mirabeau in England. *B.Litt. 1940 Oxford*

Fu, T.
A criticism of pragmatism. *M.A. 1917 Birmingham*

Fuchs, L. G.
Contributions to an industrial psychology of the blind. *M.A. 1949 London, Birkbeck College*

Fudge, M. K.
English leather glove trade. *M.A. 1930 Bristol*

Fulford, J. L. L.
1. The eschatological beliefs of Jesus. 2. Extract teaching *in re* synoptic Gospels. *B.D. & D.D. 1913 Oxford*

Fulford, R. J.
The teaching of geometry: historically and psychologically treated, with an experimental investigation in reference to the correlation of imagery and geometrical ability. *M.Sc. 1923 Birmingham*

Fullam, P.
Mystical poetry of William Blake. *M.A. 1931 National University of Ireland*

Fuller, A. R. B.
The minor corporations of the secular cathedrals of the province of Canterbury (excluding the Welsh sees) between the thirteenth century and 1536, with special reference to the minor canons of St. Paul's Cathedral from their origin in the twelfth century to the visitations of Bishop Gilson in 1724. *M.A. 1947 London, Birkbeck College*

Fuller, B. A. G.
A history of the rise and development of the problem of evil in ancient European philosophy up to the end of the second century A.D. *B.Sc. 1905 Oxford*

Fuller, G. J.
Shrewsbury, historical geography and present survey. *M.A. 1940 London, External Degree*

Fulton, A. A.
And the word became flesh. *Ph.D. 1947 Dublin, Trinity College*

Fundaminsky, S.
Tosefta *Pesachim*, translated and annotated, with a comparative study of Mishnah and Tosefta *Pesachim*. *Ph.D. 1949 London, External Degree*

Furby, G. E. P.
The English novel in France from 1836-1848. *M.A. 1920 London*

Fussell, E. M.
The history of the Cluniacs in England and Wales. *M.A. 1917 Wales*

Fussell, J. H.
Music in primary and secondary schools with special regard to its aesthetic and disciplinary values. *M.A. 1936 Bristol*

Fynne, R. J.
Montessori and her inspirers. *M.A. 1921 London*

Gabriel, J. R.
The religious and social condition of Wales at the outbreak of the Glyndwr movement, with special reference to the attitude of the clergy, both regular and secular, to the movement. *M.A. 1906 Wales*

Gabrieli, H.
Workers' Producers' Associations in Palestine. *B.Litt. 1935 Oxford*

Gadd, M. L.
English monumental brasses of the fifteenth and early sixteenth centuries with special reference (a) to the conditions of their manufacture, (b) to their characteristic forms and distribution. *M.A. 1936 Manchester*

Gadsby, E. J.
Clara Reeve. *M.A. 1926 London*

Gadson, M. E.
The nature of change in Aristotle's *Metaphysics*. *M.A. 1912 London*

Gaffney, H. M.
Doctrina poetarum. *M.A. 1939 National University of Ireland*

Gaffney, J. P.
Heathenism and its echo in Anglo-Saxon poetry. *M.A. 1935 National University of Ireland*

Gaffney, S. J. C.
Doctrina poetarum: a survey of the doctrinal content of English poetry from Caedmon to Scott in the light of the *Summa theologica* of St. Thomas Aquinas. *Ph.D. 1938 National University of Ireland*

Gaffney, S. J. C.
Theology in English poetry. *Ph.D. 1941 National University of Ireland*

Gain, F. A.
The doctrine of the Church in Anglican theology, 1833-52, with particular reference to the conception of doctrinal authority. *B.Litt. 1950 Oxford*

Gairola, C. K.
Cultural history of the Satavahana Dynasty. *Ph.D. 1949 London, School of Oriental and African Studies*

Gale, A. H.
The incidence and causes of minor degrees of deafness in elementary school children. *D.M. 1933 Oxford*

Galin, S.
The evolution of the physical units. *Ph.D. 1934 London, University College*

Galin, S.
The method of Descartes. *M.Sc. 1927 London*

Galletley, M. H.
Contributions à l'étude de la poésie d'Auguste Angellier. *M.A. 1928 Birmingham*

Galleymore, J. F.
Francis Jammes. *M.A. 1942 Birmingham*

Gallie, W. B.
The part played by the use of symbols in the attainment of knowledge. *B.Litt. 1937 Oxford*

Gallon, R.
A survey of junior instruction centres, with special reference to Durham County. *M.Ed. 1940 Manchester*

Galloway, A. D.
The cosmic significance of Christian redemption. *Ph.D. 1950 Cambridge*

Galloway, G.
Studies in the philosophy of religion. *D.Phil. 1905 Saint Andrew's*

Galloway, J.
Reactions in literature of the relations between Scotland and England in the seventeenth and eighteenth centuries: an attempt at tracing England's literary discovery of Scotland. *Ph.D. 1930 Edinburgh*

Galpin, A. J.
1. The word σωμα in the New Testament. 2. The teaching of St. Paul's prayers. *B.D. & D.D. 1910 Oxford*

Galpin, H. F.
The antiquity and development of the office of coroner: a study in English legal history. *D.C.L. 1896 Oxford*

Galway, M.
Some aspects of modern criticism. *M.A. 1929 Belfast*

Gamble, G. G.
The early history of Hunslet. *M.A. 1948 Leeds*

Gamble, G. G.
The evolution of the English elementary day school up to 1902, containing a history of the Hunslet national schools. *M.Ed. 1945 Leeds*

Gamble, H. R.
1. The origin and religious significance of the Jewish Sabbath. 2. The history and meaning of the Christian Sunday. *B.D. & D.D. 1919 Oxford*

Gandy, D.
The English Utilitarians and education. *M.A. 1921 Liverpool*

Ganguli, D.
The history of the Paramara Dynasty in Malwa, Arthuna and Chandravati (A.D. 808-1310). *Ph.D. 1931 London, School of Oriental and African Studies*

Ganguly, J. N. C.
Hindu political authority. *M.A. 1924 Birmingham*

Ganguly, S.
A study of Chaucer's diction and terms for womanly beauty. *Ph.D. 1940 London, University College*

Gannon, J.
Irish land and its problems. *M.A. 1939 National University of Ireland*

Gaon, S. I.
The influence of Alfonso Tostado on the Pentateuch commentary of Abravanel. *Ph.D. 1943 London, Jews' College*

Garantch, D.
The International Labour Organization as an international legislator. *Ph.D. 1940 London, School of Economics and Political Science*

Garcia Lora, J.
The Spanish stage in the time of Shakespeare and Lope de Vega. *M.A. 1947 Birmingham*

Garden, D. J.
Business control by budget. *Ph.D. 1936 Manchester*

Gardiner, H. C.
The last days of the medieval religious stage, particularly in England. *Ph.D. 1941 Cambridge*

Gardiner, M. A.
Social life in Roman Africa. *M.A. 1931 Belfast*

Gardiner, N. E.
The character of Don Pedro in the chronicles, romancero, and Spanish theatre up to 1700. *M.Litt. 1939 Cambridge*

Gardiner, P. L.
The nature of historical explanation. *B.Litt. 1950 Oxford*

Gardiner, W.
1. The doctrine of the Holy Trinity. 2. The prophecy of Hosea. *B.D. 1881 Oxford*

Gardner, C. J.
Some aspects of Canadian legislation with regard to trade practices and business policy. *M.Sc. 1940 London, School of Economics and Political Science*

Gardner, D. E. M.
An experimental investigation into some effects upon children of infant school methods based on spontaneous activity as compared with more formal methods. *M.A. 1940 Leeds*

Gardner, J. C.
The origin and nature of the legal rights of spouses and children in the Scottish law of succession. *Ph.D. 1927 Edinburgh*

Gardner, L.
Le clergé dans l'oeuvre de Balzac. *M.A. 1925 Manchester*

Gardner, R.
Stephen: a study of his religious outlook and of its affinities in pre-Christian Jewish thought and in the New Testament. *Ph.D. 1934 Saint Andrew's*

Gardner, R. V.
Joseph Bouchardy and French melodrama. *M.A. 1947 London, External Degree*

Gardner, R. W.
An economic study of the ownership and tenure of agricultural land in Oxfordshire. *Ph.D. 1950 Reading*

Gardner, T. C.
Administrative aspects of the government's evacuation scheme, with special reference to Oxford and Oxfordshire. *B.Litt. 1940 Oxford*

Gardner, W. H.
Gerard Manley Hopkins: a study of poetic idiosyncrasy in relation to poetic tradition. *Ph.D. 1942 London, External Degree*

Garland, H. B.
Aspects of the development of the Viennese theatre between 1866 and 1914. *Ph.D. 1935 Cambridge*

Garland, W. R.
Continuation schools, with special reference to the continuative clauses of the Education Act, 1918. *M.Sc. 1925 London*

Garner, W.
A supplementary school course in geometry, designed for more advanced students. *M.Ed. 1930 Manchester*

Garnett, A.
Insolation and relief: their bearing on the human geography of Alpine regions. *Ph.D. 1938 London, External Degree*

Garnett, C. B.
Kants' view of space about 1769. *Ph.D. 1932 Edinburgh*

Garrad, B. L.
The practice of blood-letting among the English from the earliest times. *B.Litt. 1921 Oxford*

Garrad, B. L.
The Wonders of the East; the Anglo-Saxon prose translation from Cotton ms. Vitellius A.XV, collated with the text of Cotton ms. Tiberius B.V., Vol.1. *Ph.D. 1925 London*

Garrard, L. A.
The elements in early Christianity, down to the end of the fourth century, which helped to prepare the way for later Christian intolerance, and the relation of these elements to the early Christian conception of God as love. *B.D. 1935 Oxford*

Garrett, A. J.
Historical geography of the upper Brent. *M.A. 1935 London, King's College*

Garrett, H. E.
Desirable objectives for the milk-producing industry in Great Britain: some problems involved and their prospect of solution. *B.Litt. 1950 Oxford*

Garrett, J.
The ancient stone monuments of the eastern entries into Ireland from the sea, and their British connections. *M.A. 1939 Manchester*

Garrett, K. I.
Lord Ellenborough's ideas on Indian policy. *M.A. 1935 London, Birkbeck College*

Garrod, D. A. E.
The upper palaeolithic age in the British Isles. *B.Sc. 1925 Oxford*

Garry, B.
Tóruidheacht ar Lorg Chriosta(Following the footsteps of Christ). *M.A. 1945 National University of Ireland*

Garry, N.
The education of the crippled child in England. *M.A. 1933 Leeds*

Garside, B.
History of Hampton-upon-Thames in the sixteenth and seventeenth centuries, with special reference to educational foundations. *M.A. 1930 London, University College*

Garst, J.
A geographical study of the Los Angeles region of southern California. *Ph.D. 1931 Edinburgh*

Garstang, J.
El Arabah: explorations and excavations at Abydos, 1899-1900, including observations on modes of burial from the end of the old kingdom to the nineteenth dynasty; on the morphology of ceramic and other types; and on the dates of Egyptian employment of materials. *B.Litt. 1902 Oxford*

Gary, A. T.
The political and economic relations of English and American Quakers, 1750-85. *D.Phil. 1935 Oxford*

Gary, F.
The plays of Cyril Tourneur. *B.Litt. 1930 Oxford*

Gash, N.
The unrest in rural England in 1830, with special reference to Berkshire. *B.Litt. 1934 Oxford*

Gaskell, A.
The colonization and settlement of Manchuria. *M.A. 1932 Liverpool*

Gaskill, P. A.
Some aspect of the prose style of Edward Gibbon. *M.A. 1934 Liverpool*

Gaster, T. H. C.
The Ras Shamra texts: translated with introductions and commentaries. *A. 1936 London, Institute of Archaeology*

Gately, J.
Marlowe's influence on Shakespeare and *Richard III* . *M.A. 1912 National University of Ireland*

Gates, S. M.
History of Numidia under the Roman Republic. *M.A. 1917 London*

Gateson, M. A.
An edition of *The Shadow of Night*, by George Chapman. *B.Litt. 1938 Oxford*

Gath, E. R.
Bristol voyages to the New World between 1576 and 1612. *M.A. 1914 Bristol*

Gatley, G. H.
The relationship between classic sculpture and architecture. *M.A. 1925 Manchester*

Gattegno, C.
The mathematical definition of education. *M.A. 1948 London, Institute of Education*

Gaught, A. S.
Geographical factors in the development of the Maritime Provinces. *M.A. 1932 London, King's College*

Gaught, A. S.
Some geographical aspects of the agriculture of Durham. *Ph.D. 1939 London, External Degree*

Gauld, W. A.
The Eastern Question and European diplomacy in the period 1876-1878, with special reference to British policy. *M.A. 1923 Liverpool*

Gaunt, A.
The Christianity of Tertullian, studied in its growth and historical relations. *B.Litt. 1912 Oxford*

Gauntlett, F. E.
Sir Walter Scott in Germany. *M.A. 1920 London*

Gauthier, E. J. M.
Veuillot as a literary critic. *Ph.D. 1934 London, King's College*

Gautier, J. M. H.
An edition of: Châteaubriand, Lettre à M. de Fontanes sur la campagne romaine. *M.A. 1950 Manchester*

Gavan-Duffy, C. see Duffy, C. Gavan-

Gavan-Duffy, L. see Duffy, L. Gavan

Gavin, C. I.
Louis Philippe. *Ph.D. 1931 Aberdeen*

Gawel, S. F.
The problem of economic development of backward countries (with special reference to Poland). *B.Litt. 1947 Oxford*

Gayer, A. D.
Unemployment in British industries, 1815-1850. *D.Phil. 1931 Oxford*

Gaynor, J.
Dionysius the second: tyrant of Syracuse. *M.A. 1947 National University of Ireland*

Gear, F. B.
The contribution of William James to the philosophy and psychology of religion. *Ph.D. 1939 Edinburgh*

Gearhart, H. A.
Conversion: a comparison of the results formulated by recent American psychology of religion with the teaching and experience of the New Testament. *Ph.D. 1924 Edinburgh*

Gearing, E. A.
Turgot: social and economic reform. *M.A. 1911 Liverpool*

Geary, A.
A history of the introduction and development of projective methods in geometry. *M.Sc. 1928 London*

Geary, B. H. N. G.
A study of fifteenth century English lyric verse from manuscripts and printed editions, with special attention to metrical form. *B.Litt. 1934 Oxford*

Geary, C. L. H.
A discussion of the geographical factors affecting the distribution of population in Ceylon. *M.A. 1929 London*

Geary, C. L. H.
Western Tibet: a record of a threatened civilization. *Ph.D. 1948 London, External Degree*

Gebhardt, E. R.
An edition of William Cartwright's *The ordinary*. *B.Litt. 1933 Oxford*

Geddes, A.
Human geography of Bengal. *Ph.D. 1935 Edinburgh*

Geddes, W.
The use of fictions in English law. *M.A. 1931 Liverpool*

Geddes, W. R.
An analysis of cultural change in Fiji. *Ph.D. 1948 London, School of Economics and Political Science*

Gee, E. A.
A historical and archaeological account of Wenlock Priory and its dependent churches from the earliest times to 1307. *M.A. 1937 Birmingham*

Gee, H.
1. The conception of the Church in Holy Scripture and the early Christian writers. 2. The conception of the Church in the writings of the Reformers. *B.D. & D.D. 1898 Oxford*

Gee, O. R.
Charles Jenkinson as Secretary at War, with special reference to the period from the general election of September 1780 to the fall of North's administration in March 1782. *B.Litt. 1949 Oxford*

Gee, S. S.
General Boulanger. *M.A. 1938 Bristol*

Geffen, Z. N.
Serial publication and the development of the art of
the major novelists, c. 1845-1870. *M.Litt. 1949
Cambridge*

Gelber, L. M.
Aspects of Anglo-American relations, 1899-1906.
B.Litt. 1933 Oxford

Gelly, M.
Early Methodist associations and societies in
Wales. *M.A. 1919 Wales*

George, C. O.
Indirect taxation in the United Kingdom, 1913-14
to 1924-25. *Ph.D. 1934 London, External Degree*

George, H. V.
La philosophie de La Mettrie. *M.A. 1946 Birmingham*

George, K. R. N. St. J. Wykeham- *see* Wykeham-George, K. R. N. St. J.

George, M. J.
The concordats between the Holy See and England
in the fourteenth and fifteenth centuries. *M.A.
1915 Liverpool*

George, P.
The money and foreign exchange problems, with
special reference to the monetary experience of
Great Britain and the course of the dollar-sterling
exchange in 1919-1925. *M.Sc. 1928 Wales*

George, R. E.
The religious element in the letters and poems of
Donne, and in the works of Browne and Vaughan.
B.Litt. 1915 Oxford

George, S. E. I.
The poetical works of Syr Dafydd Trefor. *M.A.
1929 Wales*

Georgević, I.
Religious controversies in the sixteenth century,
and their influence in France and England. *B.Litt.
1919 Oxford*

Gerhardi, W. A.
Anton Chehov: a critical study. *B.Litt. 1923 Oxford*

Gérin-Lajoie, P.
Process of constitutional amendment in Canada.
D.Phil. 1948 Oxford

Gerould, G. H.
The north English homily collection, with a study of
the tales contained therein. *B.Litt. 1901 Oxford*

Gerschewitsch, I.
A grammar of Manichean Sogdian. *Ph.D. 1943
London, School of Oriental and African Studies*

Gething, H. M.
La Bretagne, peinte par deux écrivains contempor-
ains, A. le Braz et C. le Goffic. *M.A. 1921
Birmingham*

Gey van Pittins, E. F. W.
Nationality within the British Commonwealth of
Nations. *Ph.D. 1928 London*

Ghali, P. P. J.
The international juridical condition, in respect of
nationality, of the former inhabitants of the Otto-
man Empire under the Treaty of Lausanne, in
Egypt and in the mandated territories. *B.Litt. 1931
Oxford*

Ghareib, R. M. El-
Factorial analysis of practical ability and its relation
to other intellectual abilities and personality traits.
Ph.D. 1950 Edinburgh

Ghate, B. G.
The problem of rural indebtedness in Indian economic life. *Ph.D. 1937 London, School of Economics and Political Science*

Ghatge, M. B.
A study of methods of investigation and research in
marketing, and an assessment of their contributions
to the solution of problems of producers and to the
general economic efficiency of the organizations
lying between producers and consumers. *Ph.D.
1936 Wales*

Gheorghiu, P. R.
Foreign trade of Roumania. *Ph.D. 1932 London,
School of Economics and Political Science*

Ghey, F. L.
The relation of θεωρία to πράξισ in Plato's
Republic and Aristotle's *Ethics*. *M.A. 1907 London*

Ghorbal, S.
The beginnings of the Egyptian Question and the
rise of Mehemet Ali, 1800-1812. *M.A. 1924 London*

Ghosal, A. K.
An administrative study of the development of civil
service in India during the Company's régime.
*Ph.D. 1940 London, School of Economics and
Political Science*

Ghose, D. C.
International monetary policy since 1919, with special reference to India. *M.Sc. 1948 London, School
of Economics and Political Science*

Ghose, N. N.
Evolution of Bengal: an outline of its historical
geography from the earliest times to the end of the
Moslem period. . *M.A. 1933 Liverpool*

Ghosh, A. K.
An analysis of the Indian price structure from
1861. *Ph.D. 1949 London, School of Economics
and Political Science*

Ghosh, B.
Comparative survey of education in Burma and a
few countries with a rural background, e.g., Turkey
and Scandinavia. *M.A. 1947 London, Institute of
Education*

Ghosh, B.
The Indian salt industry, trade and taxation,
1756-1932. *Ph.D. 1933 London, School of Economics and Political Science*

Ghosh, B.
The *Khandakhā-dyaka* of Brahmagupta, with the
commentaries of Prthūdaka for the first part, and
Varuna for the second part, critically edited and
translated. *D.Phil. 1940 Oxford*

Ghosh, J. C.
An edition of the works of Thomas Otway, with
biography and commentary. *D.Phil. 1929 Oxford*

Ghosh, J. C.
The life and works of Thomas Otway. *B.Litt. 1923
Oxford*

Ghosh, R.
An experimental study of humour. *Ph.D. 1938
London, University College*

Ghosh, S.
The temporal arrangement of errors or failures in
perceptual work. *Ph.D. 1949 London, University
College*

Ghuryne, G. S.
Funerary monuments of India. *Ph.D. 1923 Cambridge*

Gibb, H. A. R.
The Arabic conquest of Transoxania. *M.A. 1922
London*

Gibb, W. J.
Light thrown by the works of Lucian on contemporary life. *Ph.D. 1929 London*

Gibbins, H. J.
1. The problem of the second Epistle of St. John. 2.
The references to the Holy Spirit in the Epistle of
Clement of Rome to the Corinthians. *B.D. 1904
Oxford*

Gibbon, J. G.
Unemployment insurance: a study of schemes of
assisted insurance. *D.Sc. 1911 London*

Gibbon, W. M.
The early years of George Russell (AE) and his
connection with the theosophical movement. *Ph.D.
1947-48 Dublin, Trinity College*

Gibbons, F.
The prose works of W. Morris. *M.A. 1915
Birmingham*

Gibbs, F. W.
The life and work of Herman Boerhaave, with
particular reference to his influence in chemistry.
Ph.D. 1949 London, University College

Gibbs, F. W.
Some studies in the history of soap manufacture.
M.Sc. 1937 London, University College

Gibbs, J.
The visions and locutions of St. Theresa. *B.Litt.
1940 Oxford*

Gibbs, J. M.
A contribution to the standardization of the
Terman-Merrill intelligence test. *M.A. 1939 Lon-
don, University College*

Gibbs, M. E.
The episcopate in the reign of Henry III. *B.Litt.
1932 Oxford*

Gibbs, M. E.
Lord John Russell and the development of relations between Parliament, Cabinet and parties,
1832-1852. *M.A. 1928 Manchester*

Gibbs, N. H.
The history of Reading in the later Middle Ages,
considered with special reference to the importance
of the gild merchant in medieval seignorial
boroughs. *D.Phil. 1935 Oxford*

Gibson, E. C. S.
1. On the interpretation of the Apocalypse. 2. On
the structure of the Eucharistic office. *B.D. & D.D.
1895 Oxford*

Gibson, F. M.
Dickens et Daudet. *M.A. 1913 Birmingham*

Gibson, G. H.
The nature and significance of Christian sociology.
M.A. 1936 Bristol

Gibson, G. H.
The structure of community: a study in personal
relationships. *Ph.D. 1945 London, University College*

Gibson, J. A.
British opinion on the federation of Canada. *B.Litt.
1934 Oxford*

Gibson, J. A.
The life of Sir Edmund Walker Head, Bart. *D.Phil.
1938 Oxford*

Gibson, J. A.
The lyrical poems of the Harleian ms. 2253, British
Museum. *M.A. 1914 London*

Gibson, M. B.
Les romans champêtres de George Sand. *M.A.
1940 Belfast*

Gibson, M. T.
Les femmes selon Dumas: une étude. *M.A. 1915
Birmingham*

Gibson, R. J. Harvey-
Outlines of the history of botany. *D.Sc. 1920 Aberdeen*

Gibson, W. E.
Elkanah Settle: his life and works. *M.A. 1938
Wales*

Gilbert, D.
Ideals of education in Isocrates and Plato. *M.A.
1937 London, Westfield College*

Gilbert, E. W.
Geographical influences of the exploration of
America west of the Mississippi, 1800-50. *B.Litt.
1928 Oxford*

Gilbert, T. W.
1. Eternal life in St. John's Gospel. 2. The leading
ideas of the Acts of the Apostles. *B.D. 1912 Oxford*

Gilbert, T. W.
Exegeses of St. John xx.30,31; I John v.13; Acts
vi.13,14. *D.D. 1923 Oxford*

Gilbertson, J. C.
The Rhenish school of German philology. *M.A.
1938 Manchester*

Gilcriest, G. H.
Lord George Germain. *M.A. 1914 Liverpool*

Giles, E. L. G.
The growth of realism in Elizabethan fiction, with
special reference to Greene, Nashe and Deloney.
M.A. 1937 Wales

Giles, E. L. G.
The growth of realism in the fiction of the sixteenth
and seventeenth centuries, with special reference to
the development of the picaresque novel. *Ph.D.
1943 London, Birkbeck College*

Giles, P. M.
The economic and social development of Stockport, 1815-1836. *M.A. 1950 Manchester*

Giles, R. A.
The constitutional history of the Church in
Australia. *B.Litt. 1929 Oxford*

Gilham, E. L.
Roman society of the Republic as revealed in the
comic poets. *M.A. 1920 London*

Gill, A.
Le pédant dans la comédie italienne du cinquecento, et sa descendance directe dans la
comédie française jusqu'à Molière. *M.A. 1934
Manchester*

Gill, C. J.
Education and industrialism: a study of the way in
which changes in industrial organizations have led
to changes in the use of child labour, and to the
growth in England of a system of education based
on compulsory school attendance. *M.A. 1938
Liverpool*

Gill, D. M.
The evolution of the administration of the Treasury
in England during the years 1660-1714. *M.A. 1919
London*

Gill, F. C.
Methodism and the English Romantic Movement. *M.A. 1936 Liverpool*

Gill, J.
The manuscript tradition of the *Practica* of the Council of Florence. *Ph.D. 1949 London, King's College*

Gill, M. H.
Paul Scarron et la littérature espagnole: les emprunts et l'influence espagnole dans son oeuvre. *M.A. 1932 Leeds*

Gill, R.
The poetry of Alexander Blok. *Ph.D. 1938 London, External Degree*

Gill, W. C.
Dissertation on the Peace of Amiens and its rupture. *M.A. 1908 Leeds*

Gillam, S. G.
The correspondence of Arthur Charlett (Master of University College, 1692-1722) in its antiquarian and historical aspects. *B.Litt. 1948 Oxford*

Gillan, I. T.
The Christian inscriptions of North Africa: a study in the popular religion of the early (Western) Church. *Ph.D. 1943 Edinburgh*

Gillespie, R. A.
The early career, accession and domestic policy of the Emperor Domitian. *M.A. 1937 London, Birkbeck College*

Gillies, E. L.
The indigenous tribes of British Columbia and European influence upon them. *Ph.D. 1923 Edinburgh*

Gillies, M. M.
A dissertation on *Medea. Ph.D. 1924 Edinburgh*

Gillis, D. H.
The determinants of Canadian federalism. *Ph.D. 1948 London, School of Economics and Political Science*

Gillon, R. M.
John Davidson of Prestonpans, (1549?-1604). *Ph.D. 1935 Edinburgh*

Gilmore, J.
Witchcraft and the Church of Scotland subsequent to the Reformation. *Ph.D. 1948 Glasgow*

Gim, S.
The phonetics of the Korean language. *M.A. 1937 London, University College*

Ginigé, A.
The distribution of population and the development of settlements in Ceylon. *M.A. 1930 London, School of Economics and Political Science*

Ginsberg, H. L.
Studies on the Hebrew verb. *Ph.D. 1930 London, External Degree*

Ginsberg, M.
The metaphysic of Malebranche. *M.A. 1915 London*

Ginsberg, M.
Sifra (voluntary offerings). *Ph.D. 1934 London, King's College*

Ginsberg, M.
Translation of *Sifre*, chapters 1-3, with introduction and notes. *M.A. 1930 London, King's College*

Ginsburg, H. H.
The development of the Dutch political party system, 1848-1901. *B.Litt. 1948 Oxford*

Ginsburg, L.
The attitude of Judaism towards the sacrificial system. *B.Litt. 1936 Oxford*

Giovannini, M.
A study of the dramatic works of John Banks, including a critical edition of *Vertue betray'd or, Anna Bullen: a tragedy. B.Litt. 1938 Oxford*

Giroday, F. Boyer de la *see* Boyer de la Giroday, F.

Gitsham, E.
An account of trade unionism in South Africa. *M.A. 1926 Leeds*

Gittins, C. E.
Condorcet as an educationalist. *M.A. 1935 Wales*

Gittins, J. S.
The relation of intelligence to performance in school. *M.A. 1936 London, Institute of Education*

Gladden, E. N.
The attainment of efficiency in the state service. *Ph.D. 1936 London, External Degree*

Gladish, D. M.
The Tudor Privy Council. *M.A. 1915 London*

Gladstone, M. S.
Visnu in the *Rgveda* and after until the epic period. *Ph.D. 1928 Cambridge*

Glaister, J.
Necessity for legislative reform in Scotland in regard to uncertified deaths. *M.D. 1885 Glasgow*

Glanville, G. C.
The Old Testament morality. *B.Litt. 1937 Oxford*

Glason, J. A.
Scientific method in the teaching of geography with special reference to the teaching of geography in 'modern schools'. *M.A. 1932 Reading*

Glass, D. V.
Recent changes in fertility in certain European countries, with particular reference to the provision of social incentives to parenthood. *Ph.D. 1940 London, External Degree*

Glassey, W.
The attitude of grammar school pupils and their parents to education, religion and sport. *M.Ed. 1943 Manchester*

Glasson, T. F.
The second advent: the origin of the New Testament doctrine. *D.D. 1945 London, Richmond College*

Glazebrook, M. G.
1. The poetical structure of Isaiah xl-lv. 2. The genuineness of the second Epistle to the Thessalonians. *B.D. & D.D. 1903 Oxford*

Gleason, J. H.
British conceptions of Russia and Russian policy, 1837-41. *B.Litt. 1932 Oxford*

Gleave, H. C.
A critical edition of the Ethiopic text of Canticles. *B.Litt. 1948 Oxford*

Gleave, J. T.
Education development in the county of Aachen after the war, with specific reference to teachers. *M.Ed. 1947 Durham*

Gleeson, R. J.
Truth and certitude according to the Louvain School. *M.A. 1920 National University of Ireland*

Glen, C.
A contribution to the psychology of common sexual perversions. *M.D. 1939 Glasgow*

Glendenning, F. J.
The Hasmonean dynasty in Jewish literature before A.D. 70. *M.A. 1949 Sheffield*

Glendon, E. T.
Europe and Morocco, particularly from 1900-1911. *M.A. 1923 Birmingham*

Glenister, D. A.
An investigation of the scientific interests of girls aged 12-13 years. *M.A. 1932 London, Day Training College*

Glickman, L.
The use of musical instruments in Jewish and Assyro-Babylonian religious ceremonial compared. *M.A. 1942 Manchester*

Glover, E. A.
1. The doctrine of the Lord's Supper. 2. The doctrine of the atonement. *B.D. 1902 Oxford*

Glover, E. A.
Expositions of: Romans i.17; viii.2; xi.34. *D.D. 1906 Oxford*

Glover, G. W.
The relation between technical and economic factors in the development of the wool textile industry. *M.A. 1936 Leeds*

Glover, K. F.
The recent course of gross investment in inland transport in Great Britain and the influence of government action upon it. *M.Sc. 1949 London, School of Economics and Political Science*

Gluckmann, H. M.
The realm of the supernatural among the southeastern Bantu. *D.Phil. 1936 Oxford*

Glucksohn, N.
A contribution towards the standardization of the new revised Stanford Binet test of intelligence (Terman and Merrill) for use with English children aged four to six years. *M.A. 1939 London, University College*

Glun, H. H.
History of the Vulgate in England from Alcuin to Roger Bacon. *Ph.D. 1932 Cambridge*

Glynn, J. K.
The private member of Parliament, 1833-1868. *Ph.D. 1949 London, School of Economics and Political Science*

Gobat, J. D.
Error and variability of judgment in routine work: their relation to assessments of character. *Ph.D. 1938 London, External Degree*

Godakumbura, C. E.
An historical examination of Sinhalese case-syntax from the beginning of the tenth century to the end of the thirteenth century A.D. *Ph.D. 1945 London, External Degree*

Goddard, C. E.
The origin of the Semitic alphabet. *Ph.D. 1927 Edinburgh*

Goddard, F. G.
1. The mediatorship of Christ as viewed from the standpoint of personality. 2. An examination of faith, with special reference to its definition in Hebrews xi. *B.D. 1907 Oxford*

Goddard, Z. W.
The lower classes in the novel from Lesage to 1789. *M.A. 1932 London, King's College*

Goddard, Z. W.
Rétif de la Brétonne. *Ph.D. 1935 London, King's College*

Godfrey, C.
A study of Keats's *Endymion. M.A. 1949 Liverpool*

Godfrey, D. R.
The novels of Aldous Huxley as an expression of a philosophy of life. *Ph.D. 1949 Dublin, Trinity College*

Godfrey, J. T.
Size of holdings, with particular reference to Irish conditions. *M.Econ.Sc. 1942 National University of Ireland*

Godin, H. J. G.
Jules Janin, l'homme et le critique dramatique. *M.A. 1938 Belfast*

Godin, H. J. G.
Jules Janin, romancier et conteur. *Ph.D. 1940 Belfast*

Godinski, L.
Le roman russe en France à la fin du dix-neuvième siècle considéré au point de vue de l'influence exercée par Tolstoi sur Paul Margueritte et Romain Rolland. *Ph.D. 1923 London*

Godwin, E. T. H.
Atonement in the light of the development of the idea of sacrifice. *B.D. 1940 Leeds*

Goffin, C. W.
Conditions of agricultural and pastoral work in British East Africa. *M.A. 1930 London, Birkbeck College*

Goffin, K. M.
The development and value of the conception of individuality. *M.A. 1910 London*

Goffin, R. C.
The life and poems of William Cartwright. *M.A. 1914 London*

Goggin, S. E.
A general view of the influence of the French drama on that of England between 1660 and 1714. *M.A. 1908 London*

Gohain, B.
Human sacrifice and head-hunting in Assam. *M.A. 1937 London, University College*

Gohar, H. M.
The effect of geographical factors on the spread of Islam with special reference to Africa. *M.A. 1930 Bristol*

Goitein, E. S.
Buckingham's influence on England's policy with regard to France (from October, 1623). *M.A. 1926 London*

Goitein, H.
The law as to C.I.F. contracts. *LL.D. 1926 London*

Golden, K.
Prós na Gaeilge(Irish prose). *Ph.D. 1947 National University of Ireland*

Golding, C. E.
The principle of arbitration in English law treated historically. *LL.D. 1927 London*

Golding, S. R.
A critical study of *The Fair maid of the exchange* and its attribution to Thomas Heywood, and the relation of the play to Markham and Machin's *Dumb knight* and the works of John Day and Thomas Dekker. *M.A. 1922 London*

Golding, S. R.
Studies in John Day. *Ph.D. 1930 London, King's College*

Golding-Bird, C. H.
1. Internal evidences of revelation in Holy Scripture. 2. The immutability of God. *B.D. 1908 Oxford*

Golding-Bird, G.
1. Inspiration. 2. Apostolic succession of the Christian ministry. *B.D. & D.D. 1912 Oxford*

Goldman, S.
The development of historical writing among the Moslems in Spain. *D.Phil. 1936 Oxford*

Goldman, S.
English capital theory in the light of recent developments (with special reference to Ricardo and Jevons). *M.Sc. 1933 London, School of Economics and Political Science*

Goldner, E. M.
The theory of ideas in Antoine Arnauld. *B.Litt. 1938 Oxford*

Goldschmidt, L.
Four centuries of school education in the Pottery Towns and Newcastle-under-Lyme, 1548-1948. *M.A. 1948 Birmingham*

Goldstraw, H.
An examination of certain portions of the French element in Chaucer's vocabulary. *M.A. 1931 Manchester*

Goldstraw, H.
The rise and development of education in the Staffordshire Potteries. *M.Ed. 1935 Manchester*

Goldstücker, E.
Humour, irony, and satire as employed by the young German writers. *B.Litt. 1942 Oxford*

Goldthorp, L. M.
The Franciscans and Dominicans in Yorkshire. *M.A. 1932 Leeds*

Gollancz, M. E. H. J.
The system of gaol delivery as illustrated in the extant gaol delivery rolls of the fifteenth century. *M.A. 1936 London, King's College*

Gollancz, O.
Anglo-American arbitration policies, 1890-1914. *Ph.D. 1940 Cambridge*

Golomb, L.
The relation of morality to self-consciousness in the philosophy of T. H. Green. *M.A. 1946 Sheffield*

Gomersall, E. E.
A new statement of the facts regarding the movements of peoples in China, with respect to the natural features. *M.Sc. 1921 Wales*

Gomez, O. A.
Taxation and capital formation. *M.Sc. 1942 London, School of Economics and Political Science*

Gomez Orbaneja, A.
The control of agricultural prices by the State and other bodies, with special reference to British experience and the possibility of its application to post-war European agriculture. *B.Litt. 1946 Oxford*

Gompertz, M.
Short history of ancient agriculture. *Ph.D. 1926 London*

Gomulicki, B. R.
The development and present status of the trace theory of memory. *B.Litt. 1950 Oxford*

Gooch, R. K.
The committees (commissions) in the chambers of the French Parliament (1875 to present time) and their influence on ministerial responsibility. *Ph.D. 1924 Oxford*

Good, C. W.
The influence of the form of a question upon children. *M.A. 1937 London, University College*

Good, D.
Economic and political origins of the Labour party from 1884 to 1906. *Ph.D. 1936 London, School of Economics and Political Science*

Goodacre, N. W.
The place of architecture in a liberal education. *M.A. 1933 Liverpool*

Goodall, G. W.
Some temperament traits in relation to industrial efficiency: a study of a group of workers by interviews, tests, assessments and records. *Ph.D. 1938 London, School of Hygiene and Tropical Medicine*

Goodall, N.
Principles and characteristics of missionary policy during the last fifty years, as illustrated by the history of the London Missionary Society. *D.Phil. 1950 Oxford*

Goodbody, M. L.
Some aspects of Goethe's *Pandora*. *M.A. 1938 Bristol*

Goode, J.
The architectonics of *Paradise lost*. *M.A. 1921 Birmingham*

Goode, J.
John Milton: the making of an epic poet. *D.Litt. 1929 Birmingham*

Goodenough, E. R.
The theology of Justin Martyr. *D.Phil. 1923 Oxford*

Gooder, A.
The parliamentary representation of the county of York from the earliest Parliaments to 1601. *Ph.D. 1933 Leeds*

Gooderson, C. O.
Vénus et sa chambre dans *Les voeux du paon* de Jacques de Longuyon. *M.A. 1942 Birmingham*

Goodfellow, D. M.
Culture contact between Bantu and European in South-East Africa as illustrated by the life of Sir Theophilus Shepstone. *Ph.D. 1932 London, School of Economics and Political Science*

Gooding, H. B.
1. Christian baptism. 2. St. Paul's belief in the divinity of Our Lord. *B.D. 192[Oxford*

Goodison, R. R.
England and the Orangist Party from 1665 to 1672. *M.A. 1934 London, University College*

Goodman, A. I.
Residual capacity to hear of pupils in schools for the deaf. *M.D. 1947 Manchester*

Goodman, G. N.
The historical novel in Scott and his imitators. *M.A. 1914 Birmingham*

Goodman, I.
Al t'he kaboteca (Be not like your fathers): a polemical work by Ephodi (Prophiat Duran), critically edited on the basis of manuscripts and provided with a translation. *Ph.D. 1935 Glasgow*

Goodman, P. H.
The political career of William, third Lord Howard of Escrick (1626?-94). *B.Litt. 1948 Oxford*

Goodman, T.
An approach to a contemporary aesthetic through the 20th century visual arts. *Ph.D. 1945 Dublin, Trinity College*

Goodson, D. C.
Palestine as a type region of the Mohammedan world. *M.A. 1935 Reading*

Goodson, J. B.
The appraisal of agricultural productivity. *M.A. 1939 London, Birkbeck College*

Goodwin, D. R. T.
A study of the change in meaning of French criminal law terms, with special reference to colloquial and literary usage. *M.A. 1936 Manchester*

Goodwin, R. M.
An analysis of the stock and flow of money in England and Wales since 1925. *B.Litt. 1937 Oxford*

Goom, W.
The mathematical education of the adolescent, with particular reference to the work in central and senior schools. *M.Ed. 1937 Manchester*

Gooneratne, D. D. M.
The Sinhalese in Ceylon: a study in historical and social geography. *M.A. 1930 Liverpool*

Gopal, M.
The literary criticism of Walter Pater. *B.Litt. 1933 Oxford*

Gopal, M. H.
Financial history of Mysore, 1799-1831. *Ph.D. 1930 London, School of Economics and Political Science*

Gopalaswami, M. V.
Economy in motor learning. *Ph.D. 1923 London*

Gopsill, G. H.
The relation between the State and the development of a system of popular education in England and Wales. *M.A. 1938 Birmingham*

Gordon, A. L.
The public corporation in Great Britain. *D.Phil. 1936 Oxford*

Gordon, D. B.
The conception of the covenant in the thought of Israel prior to the exile. *Ph.D. 1938 Edinburgh*

Gordon, D. C. B.
The political and educational ideas and ideals of John Knox. *Ph.D. 1926 Edinburgh*

Gordon, D. J.
The *commedia erudita* and Elizabethan Comedy. *Ph.D. 1941 Cambridge*

Gordon, F. A.
The economic aspect of coal-mining in South Yorkshire. *M.Com. 1926 Birmingham*

Gordon, H.
The early development of the university extension movement under the influence of James Stuart. *M.A. 1941 Sheffield*

Gordon, I. A.
John Skelton and the early Renaissance: a biographical and critical study. *Ph.D. 1936 Edinburgh*

Gordon, I. L.
A topographical study of the sagas of the Vestfirðirand of their traditions. *Ph.D. 1930 Leeds*

Gordon, J.
The *Liturgia sacra* and *Professio fidei catholicae* of Valerandus. *Ph.D. 1928 Edinburgh*

Gordon, M.
The social ideas of Dumas fils. *M.A. 1924 Liverpool*

Gordon, M. J.
A study of the provision for vocational training in the advanced courses of girls' secondary schools, with special reference to electricity. *M.A. 1941 London, King's College*

Gordon, M. L.
The place of oligarchy in the development of Greece. *Cert.Litt. 1917 Oxford*

Gordon, T. C.
The prophecies of Jeremiah: a new translation, from a revised Hebrew text, with brief expositions. *Ph.D. 1934 Glasgow*

Gordon Walker, P. C.
Sir Stafford Northcote's sinking fund and the redemption of debt between 1874 and 1914. *B.Litt. 1930 Oxford*

Gorner, J. V.
Two Spanish Romantics: Antonio García Gutiérrez and Juan Eugenio Hartzenbusch. *M.A. 1929 Liverpool*

Gorner, V. J.
Hull and the North Sea coastlands. *M.Sc. 1948 London, External Degree*

Gorodetzky, N.
The humiliated Christ in modern Russian thought. *B.Litt. 1938 Oxford*

Gorodetzky, N.
St. Tikhon of Voronezh. *D.Phil. 1944 Oxford*

Gorski, T. A.
Ptolemaic temple architecture in Egypt: an analysis of the Greek and Egyptian elements. *M.A. 1948 London, University College*

Goskar, K. L.
The form of the plateau in south Wales. *M.Sc. 1935 Wales*

Gosling, D. K.
The parish registers of the Churches of SS. Philip and Jacob and of St. Thomas in Bristol in 1812. *M.A. 1934 Bristol*

Gosling, S. B.
The development of the port of Montreal: a study of the modification of geographical values. *M.A. 1932 Reading*

Goss, M. G.
The development of university participation in the training of teachers in England and Wales. *M.A. 1949 London, King's College*

Goss, W. A.
Early Methodism in Bristol, with special reference to J. Wesley's visits to the city, 1739-90, and their impression on the people. *M.A. 1932 Bristol*

Gossman, F.
Sprachliche, literarische und kulturelle Untersuchung der *Regensburger Chronik* des Leonhard Widmann. *M.A. 1940 London, King's College*

Goudge, H. L.
1. The relation of the Church to the kingdom of God. 2. The meaning of the words of institution in I Corinthians xi.24, 25. *B.D. & D.D. 1910 Oxford*

Gough, E. J.
1. The grace of confirmation. 2. The Christian observance of the Lord's day. *B.D. & D.D. 1900 Oxford*

Gough, M. M.
Roman society in the reign of Trajan as seen in the writings of Tacitus, Juvenal and Pliny the Younger. *M.A. 1908 Birmingham*

Gould, H. E.
The minor Latin didactic poets. *M.A. 1931 London, Birkbeck College*

Gould, S. C.
Critical and historical edition of B. L. de Muralt's *Letters describing the character and customs of the English and French nations*, 1726, with an introduction and notes. *B.Litt. 1931 Oxford*

Gould, S. C.
Literary and social dandyism in England and France between 1780 and 1850. *D.Phil. 1950 Oxford*

Gouldson, K.
A critical survey of the drama of Rojas Zorilla. *M.A. 1939 Liverpool*

Gourvitch, I.
An examination of the third book of *Britannia's Pastorals* and its attribution to William Browne of Tavistock, with a study of English fairy poetry from the time of Spenser, indicating Browne's position in its development. *M.A. 1923 London*

Gourvitch, I.
The life and work of Drayton with particular reference to the *Polyolbion* and its sources. *Ph.D. 1930 London, King's College*

Gowda, A. C. D.
Some mental determinants of scholastic achievement. *M.Ed. 1932 Leeds*

Gowde, T. V. Thimme *see* Thimme Gowda, T. V.

Gower, P. W.
Problems of religious psychology in the works of the French naturalistic and psychological novelists. *M.A. 1932 London, King's College*

Gowrie, S.
Education in Madras. *M.A. 1948 Bristol*

Goyne, K.
The life of Colley Cibber. *M.A. 1937 London, Courtauld Institute of Art*

Graber, S. G.
The idea of the German 'national mission' as expressed by Fichte, List and Treitschke. *M.Sc. 1949 London, School of Economics and Political Science*

Grace, H. M.
The great roll of the pipe for the ninth year of the reign of King Richard the first, Michaelmas 1197 (pipe roll 43) now first typed from the original in the custody of the Master of the Rolls. *M.A. 1929 Reading*

Grace, J.
Henri de Boulainvilliers: historian and philosopher. *Ph.D. 1932 Cambridge*

Grace, S. W.
A primer of French pronunciation. *M.A. 1920 London*

Grace, W. F. F.
The Congress policy of Napoleon III. *M.A. 1925 Liverpool*

Grace, W. F. F.
Great Britain and the Polish Question, 1863. *Ph.D. 1925 Cambridge*

Gradon, P. O. E.
A critical edition of Cynewulf's *Elene*. *Ph.D. 1948 London, King's College*

Grafe, I.
Epilegomena to Bacchylides. *B.Litt. 1940 Oxford*

Graft-Johnson, J. C. De *see* De Graft-Johnson, J. C.

Graham, D. L.
Henry Vaughan, Silurist: a study of his life and writings, his relation to his age and subsequent influence. *Ph.D. 1934 Birmingham*

Graham, E. H.
Judicial investigations under the Dictum of Kenilworth, Northamptonshire. *M.A. 1930 Manchester*

Graham, E. S. *see* Eames, E. S.

Graham, G. S.
British policy and Canada, 1774-91: a study in eighteenth century mercantilism. *Ph.D. 1929 Cambridge*

Graham, J. E. L.
Canadian monetary and fiscal developments since 1929. *B.Litt. 1939 Oxford*

Graham, J. K.
An historical study of the career of Hugh O'Neill, second earl of Tyrone, 1550c.-1616. *M.A. 1938 Belfast*

Graham, L. S.
Virgil and Tennyson: a parallel study. *M.A. 1917 Birmingham*

Graham, M.
Individualism in the *Deutsche Dramen* of Carl Zuckmayer. *M.A. 1950 Belfast*

Graham, M.
The works of Alice Meynell. *M.A. 1942 Birmingham*

Graham, O.
The jute industry of Dundee, 1830-1855. *M.A. 1928 Manchester*

Graham, P. M. M.
An investigation into the psychological factors of linguistic ability. *M.A. 1942 London, Institute of Education*

Grahy, M.
Sources of wit and humour in Plautus. *M.A. 1930 National University of Ireland*

Grain, M. C.
Recent trends in the delinquency of girls: a study of cases recorded by the City of Oxford Education Authority, Nov. 1933-Dec. 1946. *B.Litt. 1949 Oxford*

Graneek, J. J.
Anti-semitism in the Greco-Roman Diaspora (323 B.C.-325 A.D.). *M.A. 1938 Birmingham*

Grant, A.
Continuity and change in education: the origins of elementary education in England at the beginning of the nineteenth century, and recent proposals for development and change. *M.A. 1930 Liverpool*

Grant, A.
Inspiration in the ancient world: examination of the beliefs current among the Ancient Greeks and Romans in regard to inspiration whether experienced in a state of ectasy or in full consciousness. *M.A. 1939 London, King's College*

Grant, A. R. H.
Exegeses of: John xx.17; Hebrews x.12-13; Romans viii.34. *D.D. 1924 Oxford*

Grant, A. R. H.
1. Holy baptism. 2. The Resurrection and the modern mind. *B.D. 1920 Oxford*

Grant, B. C.
The teaching of Latin by the Jesuits, with special reference to the *ratio studiorum*. *M.A. 1920 Wales*

Grant, C. K.
Professor Collingwood's conception of the relations between metaphysics and history, and its consequences for the theory of truth. *D.Phil. 1949 Oxford*

Grant, J. K.
Some changes brought about by wartime evacuation in the conduct of public elementary schools and in the attainments of their pupils. *M.A. 1943 Liverpool*

Grant, J. W.
The dissenting Reformed Churches of England with respect to the doctrine of the Church from 1870 to 1940, with special reference to the Congregational Churches. *D.Phil. 1948 Oxford*

Grant, R. K. J.
The administration of the royal forests of England during the thirteenth century. *Ph.D. 1938 Wales*

Grant, V. B.
Jamaican land law. *LL.M. 1948 London, External Degree*

Grant, W. M.
An interpretation of the apocalyptic teaching of Jesus. *Ph.D. 1928 Aberdeen*

Granville, A. M.
Aspects of the nineteenth century quest for God as reflected in the works of Thomas Hardy, Robert Browning and Francis Thompson. *M.A. 1950 Wales*

Gratz, E. L. R.
Henri de Bornier: les sources de son inspiration et les influences qu'il a subies. *M.A. 1912 London*

Grave, W. W.
The poetical works of Pero Guillén de Sevilla. *Ph.D. 1928 Cambridge*

Gravenall, B.
A contribution to the study of Catulle Mendès as critic. *Ph.D. 1939 London, University College*

Graves, J. T. R.
A critical survey of Board of Education policy in relation to resulting reforms in post-primary and secondary education since 1904. *B.Litt. 1939 Oxford*

Graves, R. C.
The part played by the intention of the parties in determining the system of law applicable. *LL.D. 1925 London*

Graves, R. R.
The illogical element in poetry, with a study of its application by romantic and limitation by classical poets. *B.Litt. 1925 Oxford*

Graveson, R. H.
Status in the common law. *Ph.D. 1941 London, King's College*

Graw, F. J.
Non-linguistic tests of mental ability. *Ph.D. 1926 London*

Gray, G. D. B.
South Yorkshire: a regional study. *M.A. 1946 London, King's College*

Gray, H. B.
1. The parabolic teaching of our Saviour. 2. The temptation of our Saviour. *B.D. & D.D. 1892 Oxford*

Gray, H. D.
The antecedents and meaning of the modern evangelical conception of grace. *Ph.D. 1935 Edinburgh*

Gray, J.
The ethical implications of modern psychology. *M.A. 1928 Birmingham*

Gray, J.
Historical conditions in patriarchal Palestine in the light of recent archaeological research. *Ph.D. 1949 Edinburgh*

Gray, J. C.
Local government, finance and functions in Wales, as affected by post-war changes. *M.A. 1941 Wales*

Gray, J. W.
A survey of the German university system during the Weimar Republic. *M.A. 1936 London, King's College*

Gray, K.
Some contributions to the early history of Nonconformity in Rossendale. *M.A. 1942 Wales*

Gray, M. H.
L'esthétique de Francis Jammes. *M.A. 1949 Liverpool*

Gray, R. D.
Alchemical symbolism in Goethe's scientific and literary works. *Ph.D. 1949 Cambridge*

Gray, W. B.
The administration of Scotland during the reigns of Charles II and James VII. *B.Litt. 1920 Oxford*

Gray, W. B.
The military forces and the public revenue of Scotland, 1660-1688. *Ph.D. 1921 Edinburgh*

Greatbatch, W. A.
The notion of matter in the later philosophy of Plato. *M.A. 1922 London*

Greaves, H. M.
Keats as literary critic. *M.A. 1918 Birmingham*

Greaves, I. C.
The organization of labour in tropical agriculture. *Ph.D. 1934 London, School of Economics and Political Science*

Greaves, M.
The life and work of Robert Bage. *B.Litt. 1938 Oxford*

Greaves, R. W.
The activities of the corporation of the borough of Leicester from 1688 to 1835. *D.Phil. 1936 Oxford*

Grebenik, E.
Some aspects of population in Bristol. *M.Sc. 1941 London, School of Economics and Political Science*

Green, C. A. H.
Expositions of St. Mark x; xii.1-37; xii.37-44; and xiii. *D.D. 1911 Oxford*

Green, C. A. H.
1. The witness to the divinity of our Lord. 2. Operations of the Holy Spirit in the individual soul. *B.D. 1907 Oxford*

Green, E. M.
The rival claims of Sparta and Macedon to the leadership of Greece in the late third century B.C. *M.A. 1924 London*

Green, E. R. R.
The economic history of the Lagan Valley, 1800-50. *B.Litt. 1945 Dublin, Trinity College*

Green, F. H. W.
The geography of the Moray Firth lowlands, with special reference to distribution of settlements, and with special attention to the tract between the rivers Ness and Spey; Inverness and Cullen. *M.Sc. 1935 London, School of Economics and Political Science*

Green, F. W.
The Gospel according to St. Matthew: *The Clarendon Bible*, Clarendon press, 1936. *B.D. 1944 Oxford*

Green, G. H.
The day dream and the terror dream. *M.A. 1926 Wales*

Green, G. H.
The daydreams of children: their importance for education. *B.Litt. 1921 Oxford*

Green, G. H.
The daydreams of children from infancy to adolescence considered as evidence of the nature of psychological development. *Ph.D. 1925 London*

Green, H. A. C.
The medieval conception of heaven and hell as shown by English religious and didactic literature from 1150. *M.A. 1923 London*

Green, J. T.
Matthew Arnold's imagery: a study in poetic method. *Ph.D. 1948 Leeds*

Green, M. E.
The literary relations of Wordsworth and M. Arnold. *M.A. 1927 Birmingham*

Green, M. M.
The Minnesingers in relation to contemporary politics. *M.A. 1909 Birmingham*

Green, R. G. L.
Andrew Lang as a writer of fairy tales and romances. *B.Litt. 1944 Oxford*

Green, R. W.
Recent progress in the application of theories of taxation. *B.Litt. 1920 Oxford*

Green, S. M. B.
The development of the road (motor) haulage industry in Great Britain, with special reference to the years 1918-46. *B.Phil. 1948 Oxford*

Green, T. F.
Some problems of secondary education in the light of group psychology. *M.A. 1927 Sheffield*

Green, T. L.
A survey of the teaching and learning of biology. *M.A. 1943 Bristol*

Green, V.
The Franciscans in medieval English life (1224-1348). *B.Litt. 1936 Oxford*

Green, V. H. H.
Bishop Reginald Pecock. *B.D. 1945 Cambridge*

Greenberg, M. M.
British trade and the opening of China, 1800-1842. *Ph.D. 1949 Cambridge*

Greene, T. M.
Kant's religious theory and its relation to English deism. *Ph.D. 1924 Edinburgh*

Greening, E. P.
Some psychological concepts of Alfred Adler. *M.A. 1940 Manchester*

Greening, M. C.
A study of Snorri Sturlason's *Saga of Olaf Tryggvasn. M.A. 1931 London, Westfield College*

Greenleaves, H.
An analysis of the opposition to the major-generals, with special reference to Yorkshire and the North. *B.Litt. 1927 Oxford*

Greenwood, E. M.
La vérité historique des oeuvres de Vigny. *M.A. 1913 Leeds*

Greenwood, F. W. T.
Expositions of St. John x.10; xiv.6; xviii.37. *B.D. & D.D. 1908 Oxford*

Greenwood, G.
The status of the federal system under the Australian constitution. *Ph.D. 1939 London, School of Economics and Political Science*

Greenwood, H. D.
The origins and early history of independency in Suffolk to 1688. *B.Litt. 1949 Oxford*

Greenwood, J. S. E. T.
The nature of geometrical axioms, being an essay on the theory of geometrical knowledge. *M.A. 1922 London*

Greenwood, N.
A vocational study of chemistry with its applications to education. *M.Ed. 1924 Leeds*

Gregg, P. E.
John Lilburne and his relation to the first phase of the Leveller Movement, 1638-1649. *Ph.D. 1939 London, School of Economics and Political Science*

Gregory, A. L.
Judicial proceedings under the Dictum of Kenilworth, East Berkshire. *M.A. 1927 Manchester*

Gregory, A. L.
The *Questiones* of Stephen Langton. *Ph.D. 1929 Manchester*

Gregory, J. B.
A bibliographical and reference guide to the life and works of Dante Gabriel Rossetti, with a study of the Pre-Raphaelite Movement. *Ph.D. 1931 London, King's College*

Gregory, J. E.
The pragmatic reaction to absolute idealism in English philosphy. *M.A. 1949 Sheffield*

Gregory, J. W.
The idea of the soul in primitive religion. *M.A. 1939 Leeds*

Gregory, M.
An attempted synthesis of Christian spiritual healing and psychotherapy. *D.Phil. 1938 Oxford*

Gregory, M.
Cymdeithes Cymreigyddion y Fenni a'i chynhyrchion pwsicaf gyda sylw manylach i waith Thomas Stephens, Merthyr(The Cymreigyddion y Fenni Society and its most important productions, with special reference to the work of Thomas Stephens of Merthyr). *M.A. 1948 Wales*

Gregory, M.
A new translation of the Book of Psalms from Hebrew into Amharic. *B.Litt. 1936 Oxford*

Gregory, M. V.
The place of social and economic history in education. *M.Ed. 1929 Manchester*

Gregory, T. E. G.
Tariffs: a study in method. *D.Sc. 1922 London*

Gregson, A. L.
A rational justification of the main principles of Advaita-Vedanta philosophy. *Ph.D. 1947 London, Birkbeck College*

Grensted, L. W.
1. The later Roman view of the Christian doctrine of the atonement. 2. The development of the penal theory of the atonement. *B.D. 1922 Oxford*

Gretton, M. S.
The works of George Meredith. *B.Litt. 1926 Oxford*

Greville, S. E.
Briton and Maori: a comparative study of the relations between the races, 1840-1848. *M.A. 1910 London*

Grewal, D. K.
Fluctuations of attention during short periods of work. *Ph.D. 1933 London, University College*

Grewe, F. H.
Aspects of the religious thought of S.T. Coleridge. *M.A. 1947 Sheffield*

Grey, J. H.
The religious thought of Phillips Brooks and its significance. *Ph.D. 1938 Edinburgh*

Gribble, C. W.
Realistic tendencies in French prose fiction of the seventeenth century, with special reference to the realistic novel in the nineteenth century. *M.A. 1923 Wales*

Grice, J. W.
National and local finance: a review of the relations between the central and local authorities in England, France, Belgium, and Prussia during the nineteenth century. *D.Sc. 1911 London*

Grierson, D. M.
A study of joy based on the theory found in Shand's *Foundations of character. M.A. 1917 London*

Grierson, G. K.
The political relations of the Chatham party. *M.A. 1907 Liverpool*

Grieser, N. J.
The British investor and his sources of information. *M.Sc. 1940 London, School of Economics and Political Science*

Griffin, A. H.
French in a Midland grammar school. *M.A. 1936 Birmingham*

Griffin, G. J.
Robert Hall, 1764-1831: a study of his thought and work. *Ph.D. 1948 Edinburgh*

Griffin, P. R.
Wordsworth, Coleridge, Byron, Shelley and the French Revolution. *M.A. 1925 National University of Ireland*

Griffin, S. G.
People v. prince: some political doctrines of Mariana and the early Jesuits. *M.A. 1931 National University of Ireland*

Griffith, D. M.
A comparative study of the Sunday School Movement in England and Wales. *M.A. 1923 Wales*

Griffith, E. S.
The development of city government in the United States and the United Kingdom, with special reference to the period since 1870. *D.Phil. 1925 Oxford*

Griffith, H. D.
Evolution. *Ph.D. 1946 Dublin, Trinity College*

Griffith, J. A. G.
The constitutional significance of delegated legislation. *LL.M. 1948 London, School of Economics and Political Science*

Griffith, M. C.
The council in Ireland, 1399-1452. *B.Litt. 1935 Oxford*

Griffith, R.
The attitude of Wordsworth and Byron towards Napoleon. *M.A. 1949 Wales*

Griffith, W.
The verbal forms of the *Mabinogion* and *Bruts. M.A. 1904 Wales*

Griffiths, A. M.
The microscope in school: a consideration of the problems involved in the use of the microscope for the study of the flowering plant. *M.Ed. 1931 Leeds*

Griffiths, B. R.
Syntaxe du *Roman de Reinbert. M.A. 1947 London, University College*

Griffiths, E. L.
The psychological grounds of preference of shapes by school children. *M.A. 1927 Wales*

Griffiths, E. M.
Relations between England and France, 1589-1603. *M.A. 1921 Birmingham*

Griffiths, E. R.
The reaction of English Pembrokeshire to the social and intellectual movement of modern Wales since 1689. *M.A. 1927 Wales*

Griffiths, E. T.
A study of some texts belonging to the Map-cycle in Italy, and especially of the *Chantari di Lancilotto*, with a short introduction on the history of the Arthurian tradition in Italy. *M.A. 1914 Wales*

Griffiths, G. C.
The dramatic work of Stephen Phillips. *M.A. 1934 Wales*

Griffiths, G. M.
Enwau lleoedd yng nghymydau Caerwedros a Mabwynion, Ceredigion(The placenames in the commotes of Cardiganshire and Mabwynion). *M.A. 1948 Wales*

Griffiths, G. S.
The debt of Chaucer to Boccaccio. *B.Litt. 1925 Oxford*

Griffiths, J. E. S.
Girls' initiation ceremony among the Amapondo. *Dip. Anthropology 1931 Cambridge*

Griffiths, J. G.
The influence of ancient Egypt on Greek and Mycenaean religious cults before the Hellenistic age. *M.A. 1936 Liverpool*

Griffiths, J. G.
The quarrel of Horus and Seth, from Egyptian and classical sources. *D.Phil. 1950 Oxford*

Griffiths, J. W.
Plato's philosophical theism. *M.A. 1920 Wales*

Griffiths, J. W.
Plato's philosophical theism. *M.A. 1919 London*

Griffiths, M. E.
Early vaticinatory material in Welsh, with a study of some English parallels known to Welsh writers. *M.A. 1927 Wales*

Griffiths, O. M.
English Presbyterian thought from 1662 to the foundation of the Unitarian Movement. *Ph.D. 1933 Bristol*

Griffiths, P. J. B.
The sea and seafaring as described in the *Islendinga Sögur. M.A. 1935 Wales*

Griffiths, R.
The *à priori* elements in religious experience: an epistemological study. *Ph.D. 1930 Edinburgh*

Griffiths, R. F.
A study of imagination in children of five years. *M.Sc. 1931 London, University College*

Griffiths, R. J.
Quintilian's theory of education. *M.A. 1914 Wales*

Griffiths, R. R.
An enquiry into the dialect of Gower. *M.A. 1923 Wales*

Griffiths, T. H.
The development of south Wales anthracite coal area, with special reference to its industrial and labour organizations. *M.A. 1922 Wales*

Griffiths, T. J.
The connection between France and England in the reign of Louis XI. *M.A. 1917 Wales*

Griffiths, W. E.
The Roman occupation of north Wales and Chester. *M.A. 1947 Wales*

Griffiths, W. J.
Victorian theories of literary art. *M.A. 1931 Wales*

Griffiths, W. W.
Commerce in the time of the Empire between Italy and other countries. *M.A. 1922 Wales*

Griggs, E. L.
A biography of Hartley Coleridge. *Ph.D. 1927 London*

Grime, A.
John Corbet, 1619-1680. *Ph.D. 1932 Edinburgh*

Grimes, W. F.
Castle Lyons, the works-depot of the twentieth Legion at Holt, Denbighshire: a description and history of the site, with a catalogue of the pottery and other objects found, its place in the history of the Roman occupation of north Wales, together with a study of an aspect of the Romano-British pottery industry. *M.A. 1930 Wales*

Grimsditch, H. B.
William Beckford of Fonthill: a critical study. *M.A. 1925 Liverpool*

Grimshaw, H. A.
The problems of English elementary education since 1870: the evolution of opinion and the development of the system. . *M.Sc. 1918 London*

Grimshaw, I. G.
Religious revivals in the light of modern psychological theory. *Ph.D. 1933 Edinburgh*

Grimshaw, M. I.
The Great Powers and the Far East, from the seizure of Kiao-chau to the Boxer Settlement, 1897-1901. *M.A. 1929 Birmingham*

Grimsley, R.
Jean d'Alembert: his activity and his thought. *D.Phil. 1948 Oxford*

Grindley, D.
Recent developments in the mathematical theory of mapping. *M.A. 1929 Wales*

Gripaios, H.
The co-ordination of market forces in ocean tramp shipping, with special reference to the period 1920-1939. *M.Sc. 1949 London, School of Economics and Political Science*

Grisdale, D. M.
Middle English sermons from the Worcester chapter: ms. F 10, edited. *M.A. 1936 Leeds*

Gritley, A. A. I. el- *see* El-Gritley, A. A. I.

Grobel, M. C.
The Society for the Diffusion of Useful Knowledge, 1826-48. *M.A. 1933 London, University College*

Grocock, T. A.
Religious instruction in secondary schools: an enquiry and some suggestions. *M.A. 1940 Birmingham*

Groom, B.
On ornamental words (a preliminary essay): a contribution to the study of poetic diction in English literature. *M.A. 1915 London*

Grose, N. P.
Studies in the life and English works of Richard Stonyhurst (1547-1618). *M.A. 1948 London, Westfield College*

Gross, E. R.
The weak man as 'hero' in the works of Gerhart Hauptmann. *M.A. 1947 Belfast*

Grosse, J. M.
Public policy in English law. *LL.M. 1948 Sheffield*

Grossu, M.
A survey of the problems of reorganization of the cotton industry of Great Britain. *Ph.D. 1941 Manchester*

Grove, R. B.
An investigation into public opinion and the passing of the Education Act of 1870. *M.A. 1949 London, Institute of Education*

Grove, R. B.
School journeys and visits: their place in modern education. *M.A. 1940 Leeds*

Grubb, I.
Social conditions in Ireland in the seventeeth and eighteenth centuries, as illustrated by early Quaker records. *M.A. 1916 London*

Grumbridge, J. L.
Co-ordination of inland transport in Great Britain. *Ph.D. 1939 London, School of Economics and Political Science*

Grundy, J.
Giles Fletcher the Younger: a bibliographical and critical study. *M.A. 1947 London, Bedford College*

Grundy, J. B. C.
Tieck and Runge: a study in the relationship of literature and the fine arts in the German Romantic period, with special reference to Franz Sternbald. *Ph.D. 1929 London*

Grünwald, E.
Louis Philippe's France as seen by English women. *Ph.D. 1948 London, University College*

Gryziecka, M.
Divergence between the marginal private and marginal social net product in foreign investments. *M.Sc. 1949 London, School of Economics and Political Science*

Guder, G.
A comparison of Friedrich Hölderlin and John Keats in their respective backgrounds. *Ph.D. 1942 Edinburgh*

Guenena, M. S.
A comparative study of the rules of private international law relating to partnerships and to corporations, with special reference to the laws of France and of Egypt. *LL.D. 1924 London*

Guerreiro, A. D.
Problems in the measurement of national income and wealth. *B.Litt. 1945 Oxford*

Guershoon, A. I.
Certain aspects of Russian proverbs. *Ph.D. 1938 London, School of Slavonic and East European Studies*

Guest, A. W.
A geographical description of the basin of the River Sinu, in the State of Colombia, South America, with special reference to the geographical conditions of selected areas. *B.Sc. 1930 Oxford*

Guest, N. E. L.
Daniel O'Connell and Catholic emancipation. *M.A. 1931 Birmingham*

Guha, N. S.
The economic development of Assam. *M.Comm. 1937 Leeds*

Guhathakurta, J.
Indian coal trade. *M.Sc. 1937 London, School of Economics and Political Science*

Guhathakurta, P.
The Bengali drama: its origin and development. *Ph.D. 1926 London*

Guiles, A. P.
Mental therapy and the forgiveness of sins: a clinical view of the results of sin, with psychological studies of religious leaders as approaches to the application of the work of Christ in the experience of forgiveness. *Ph.D. 1934 Edinburgh*

Guillaume, A.
The scholasticism of Christianity and of Islam so far as they are represented by the *Summa contra gentiles* of St. Thomas Aquinas and the *Nihayatu-l-igdam fi ilmil-kalam* of Al Shahrastani. *B.D. & D.D. 1934 Oxford*

Guirdham, A.
The differential diagnosis of depressive states, with an inquiry into the suicidal impulse: an investigation conducted by a method of experimental psychology. *B.Sc. 1935 Oxford*

Gulland, J. A.
Criminal law reform during Peel's tenure of office as Home Secretary, 1822-27. *M.A. 1930 London, University College*

Gullick, C. F. W. R.
The geographical development of West Cornwall. *B.Litt. 1934 Oxford*

Gummer, E. N.
The reception of the works of Charles Dickens in Germany. *B.Litt. 1938 Oxford*

Gunawardena, D. C.
Studies in the biological work of John Ray. *M.Sc. 1934 London, University College*

Gunn, H. D.
Some anthropological aspects of Mexican immigrant settlement in Dallas, Texas. *M.A. 1949 London, School of Economics and Political Science*

Gunn, J. A.
A study in the development of French thought in the second half of the nineteenth century. *Ph.D. 1921 Liverpool*

Gupta, A. K. D.
A study of the song-books and poetical miscellanies of the seventeenth century. *Ph.D. 1931 Edinburgh*

Gupta, C. C. Das *see* Das Gupta, C. C.

Gupta, K.
British monetary policy and practice, 1927-33. *M.Sc. 1938 London, University College*

Gupta, K. B. S.
An enquiry into some perseverative tendencies in school children. *M.Ed. 1928 Leeds*

Gupta, K. M.
The land-system in South India between c.800 A.D. and 1200 A.D. *Ph.D. 1926 London*

Gupta, P.
Baji Rao II. *Ph.D. 1936 London, School of Oriental and African Studies*

Gupta, S.
British policy on the northeast Frontier of India (1826-86). *D.Phil. 1948 Oxford*

Gupta, S.
Shakspeare in India: a general survey of Shakespeare's vogue in India. *Ph.D. 1924 London*

Gupta, S. B.
The reasoning of children aged 7 years. *M.Ed. 1932 Leeds*

Gupta, S. K.
The works of Kalidasa. *B.Litt. 1913 Oxford*

Guptar, S. K. Datta *see* Datta Guptar, S. K.

Gurbaxani, H. M.
Mysticism in the early nineteenth century poetry in England. *Ph.D. 1928 London*

Gurney, D. St.J. C.
An experimental enquiry into the value of silent reading in the teaching of modern languages in schools. *M.Ed. 1931 Leeds*

Gurney, O. R.
Hittite prayers of Mursili II. *D.Phil. 1939 Oxford*

Gurrey, P.
The noun and pronoun of address in the seventeenth and eighteenth centuries. *Ph.D. 1926 London*

Guthkelch, A. C. L.
1. The ancient and modern learning of England. 2. The *Battle of the Books*. *M.A. 1907 London*

Guthrie, M.
The tonal structure of Bemba. *Ph.D. 1945 London, School of Oriental and African Studies*

Gutteridge, H. C.
The law of bankers' commercial credits. *LL.D. 1928 London*

Gwilliam, G. H.
1. The language in which our Lord taught. 2. Supposed quotations from the Apostolic liturgy in the New Testament. *B.D. 1890 Oxford*

Gwynn, A. ap
A comparison of the Welsh version of *Amyln ac Amic* with the French and Latin versions, with study of the grammatical forms and syntax of the Welsh version. *M.A. 1926 Wales*

Gwynn, A. O.
Roman education under the Empire. *M.A. 1915 National University of Ireland*

Gwynn, A. O.
Roman education under the Empire. *B.Litt. 1919 Oxford*

Gwynne, G. E.
Madame de Staël et les idéologues. *M.A. 1949 Wales*

Gyani, S. S.
Philosophy of Sikhism. *Ph.D. 1938 London, School of Oriental and African Studies*

Haarhoff, T. J.
Schools in Gaul from the defeat of the Franks by Julian to their rise under Chlodowig. *B.Litt. 1918 Oxford*

Haas, V.
Sensation and experience: an enquiry into the data of psychology. *M.A. 1944 Wales*

Habakkuk, E. G.
The physique of elementary school children, with special reference to their mentality: a statistical study bearing on social economics. *M.Sc. 1924 Wales*

Habel, S. T.
John Foster, 1770-1843, and his contribution to religious thought. *Ph.D. 1945 Edinburgh*

Haber, L. F.
The growth and development of the chemical industry. *Ph.D. 1949 London, External Degree*

Habibullah, A. B. M.
The sultanate of Delhi, 1206 to 1290 A.D. *Ph.D. 1936 London, School of Oriental and African Studies*

Hack, R. K.
The temple of Zeus at Olympia. *B.Litt. 1908 Oxford*

Hackett, J.
The Pauline notion of baptismal re-birth and the mystery religions. *M.A. 1942 National University of Ireland*

Hackett, J. W.
Saladin's campaign of 1188 in northern Syria, with particular reference to the northern defences of the principality of Antioch. *B.Litt. 1937 Oxford*

Hackett, K. P.
Phases of education in Galway city during the 18th and early part of the 19th century. *M.A. 1935 National University of Ireland*

Hackett, W. M.
Critical edition of a portion of the epic poem (of Girart de Roussillon), with study of the language of the poet and of the existing manuscripts. *M.A. 1937 Manchester*

Hackett, W. M.
A critical edition of the epic poem Girart de Roussillon, with notes, complete glossary, and linguistic introduction. *D.Phil. 1950 Oxford*

Haddakin, L. F.
Stoicism and political theory in the tragedies of George Chapman. *M.A. 1948 London, University College*

Hadden, M. A.
The problem of the European child in Shanghai (China). *M.D. 1933 Dublin, Trinity College*

Haddick, J. E. K.
The effect of modern criticism upon the cultural and religious values of the Old Testament. *Ph.D. 1946 Dublin, Trinity College*

Haddon, E. B.
Notes on ethnography of the Bari, Uganda. *Dip. Anthropology. 1912 Cambridge*

Hadfield, P.
Iranian influence on Jewish and Christian eschatology. *B.D. 1944 Leeds*

Hadjiantoniou, G. A.
Cyril Lucaris, his life and works. *Ph.D. 1948 Edinburgh*

Hadkins, V. R.
A comparative study of the economic development of the mandated territories in Africa. *M.Sc. 1940 Sheffield*

Hadley, W.
The *Life of Alexander* in English prose (Thornton ms.). *M.A. 1922 London*

Hafez, M. A. R.
The Alexandria cotton market. *M.A. 1938 Manchester*

Hague, D. C.
The cost problems and price policies of industrial enterprises: a study into the relationships between economic theory and practical business policies. *M.Com. 1949 Birmingham*

Haider, S.
The land problems of Iraq. *Ph.D. 1942 London, School of Economics and Political Science*

Haigh, G. T.
The history of Winchcombe Abbey. *M.Litt. 1944 Durham*

Haight, F. A.
Import quotas, as used by European countries since 1929, with special reference to France. *M.Sc. 1934 London, School of Economics and Political Science*

Haikal, Y.
The role of the Prime Minister in France. *Ph.D. 1936 London, School of Economics and Political Science*

Haikel, A. A. F.
The financial problems of Great Britain during the war 1939-1945, with special reference to Anglo-Egyptian financial relations. *M.Comm. 1948 Leeds*

Haines, T. J. H.
The life and works of Wilkie Collins. *M.A. 1936 Wales*

Hainsworth, G.
L'influence de l'Angleterre dans la littérature française dans la première moitié du dix-septième siècle: esquisse de cette question. *M.A. 1929 Leeds*

Hainsworth, P.
An edition of *Sir Percyvell of Gales*. *M.A. 1930 Leeds*

Halcrow, E. M.
The administration and agrarian policy of the manors of Durham Cathedral Priory. *B.Litt. 1949 Oxford*

Haldar, M.
Creativity, process and entity in the philosophy of A. N. Whitehead. *Ph.D. 1949 London, King's College*

Hale, C. A.
The grammar schools of Cheshire. *M.A. 1935 Bristol*

Hale, E. M.
Essay on the Byzantine revival, 717-1071. *M.A. 1913 Birmingham*

Hale, F.
The influence of Latin drama on Elizabethan drama. *M.A. 1920 Birmingham*

Halepota, A. J.
The practical theology and ethics of Shah Waliullah of Dihli. *D.Phil. 1949 Oxford*

Hales, R.
Balzac; *De amicitia*. *M.A. 1950 National University of Ireland*

Haley, K. H. D.
The ministerial career of the first Earl of Shaftesbury, 1660-73. *B.Litt. 1949 Oxford*

Halford, F. B.
The versification of Joachim du Bellay. *M.A. 1918 London*

Halket, E. C.
Sources and dialect of a French didactic poem on geography. *M.A. 1919 London*

Hall, A. R.
Ballistics in the seventeenth century. *Ph.D. 1950 Cambridge*

Hall, B.
Italian financiers of the fifteenth and sixteenth centuries with special reference to Pallavicino and Spinola and their share in Elizabethan finance. *M.Sc. 1928 London*

Hall, B.
The trade of Newcastle-upon-Tyne and the northeast coast, 1600-1640. *Ph.D. 1933 London, School of Economics and Political Science*

Hall, D. E. C.
Albert Samain. *M.A. 1936 London, Bedford College*

Hall, D. G. E.
1. Early English intercourse with Burma, 1587-1743. 2. The Dalhousie-Phayre correspondence, 1852-1856. *D.Litt. 1931 London, King's College*

Hall, D. G. E.
The mercantile aspect of English foreign policy during the reign of Charles II. *M.A. 1917 London*

Hall, D. M.
The Venice legend in German literature since 1880. *Ph.D. 1936 London, Birkbeck College*

Hall, E.
Medievalism in the works of Rossetti and William Morris. *M.A. 1912 London*

Hall, E. B.
A review and criticism of theories on the origin of Greek tragedy. *M.A. 1915 London*

Hall, E. M.
Childhood in English poetry. *M.A. 1921 Wales*

Hall, E. M.
A study of children's activity with plastic material and some interpretations of play in infancy. *M.A. 1938 Birmingham*

Hall, F. G.
The bank of Ireland 1783-1846. *Litt.D. 1949 Dublin, Trinity College*

Hall, F. G.
The trend of banking in Ireland since 1800. *Ph.D. 1944 Dublin, Trinity College*

Hall, G. M.
Prostitution and sex promiscuity in several countries at the present time. *M.A. 1932 Liverpool*

Hall, H.
Local government and central control. *D.C.L. 1906 Oxford*

Hall, H. B.
The dramas of Joaquín Dicenta. *M.A. 1950 Liverpool*

Hall, H. D.
The development of ideas as to the relations which should exist between the United Kingdom and the Dominions since the grant of responsible self-government. *B.Litt. 1920 Oxford*

Hall, H. L.
Australia and England: a study in imperial relations. *Ph.D. 1934 London, School of Economics and Political Science*

Hall, H. V.
The psychological and ethical basis of the problem of peace. *M.A. 1932 Wales*

Hall, I. V.
The sugar trade of Bristol. *M.A. 1925 Bristol*

Hall, J. A.
An historical survey of science instruction in Liverpool. *M.A. 1930 Liverpool*

Hall, K. R. L.
Experimental study of some verbal factors in perceiving and remembering. *D.Phil. 1949 Oxford*

Hall, L. E.
Possessory liens in English law. *LL.D. 1916 London*

Hall, M. G.
Roger, Bishop of Worcester (1164-79). *B.Litt. 1940 Oxford*

Hall, M. L.
Roman ideas of immortality. *M.A. 1919 Bristol*

Hall, T. W.
Some considerations on the teaching of mathematics. *M.A. 1936 National University of Ireland*

Hall, V. N.
The effects of time interval on recall. *M.A. 1935 London, King's College*

Hall, W.
The teaching of science in England during the latter half of the nineteenth century, and Huxley's influence on its development. *M.A. 1931 Sheffield*

Hall, W. L.
Athanasius' theory of redemption in the light of modern expositors. *Ph.D. 1934 Edinburgh*

Hallam, A. D.
Hebraic studies in seventeenth century England. *M.A. 1949 Leeds*

Hallesy, H. F.
The development of scientific and philosophical prose in the seventeenth century. *M.A. 1949 Wales*

Hallett, E.
Cotton finance and its relation to the currency and credit system of Egypt. *Ph.D. 1946 London, External Degree*

Halliday, G.
Visual training in the Royal Navy during the war years: an historical and critical study. *M.Ed. 1950 Manchester*

Halliday, W. R.
The waters of divination. *B.Litt. 1910 Oxford*

Halligan, P. J.
The problem of error. *M.A. 1946 National University of Ireland*

Hallis, F.
An examination of some modern theories of the relation of state to law, with special reference to their application to the juristic doctrine of corporate personality. *D.Phil. 1927 Oxford*

Halliwell, A.
Standard speech and dialects in sixteenth century France. *M.A. 1933 Manchester*

Halliwell, T.
The literary influences of the Oxford Movement from 1833-1850. *M.A. 1944 Manchester*

Halloran, J. H.
La question de l'adultérie dans le théâtre français, 1750-1850. *M.A. 1928 Leeds*

Halls, H. A. W.
Canada's balance of indebtedness, 1919-1933. *M.Sc. 1937 London, School of Economics and Political Science*

Halper, B.
The participial formations of the germinate verbs. *M.A. 1909 London*

Halsey, F.
The usage and influence of the Psalter in Middle and Early Modern English with special reference to the Penitential Psalms. *M.A. 1933 London, King's College*

Halstead, D.
The Luddite disturbances throughout the cotton manufacturing area in 1812. *M.A. 1917 Liverpool*

Ham, E. B.
Some of the continuations of the medieval French romance of *Alexander. D.Phil. 1927 Oxford*

Hambly, W. D.
Tattooing and other forms of body-marking among primitive peoples. *B.Sc. 1918 Oxford*

Hambrook, A.
The commercial relations between England and France from 1660 to 1714. *M.Sc. 1928 London*

Hamdani, A. H. F.
Doctrines and history of the Ismā'ili Da'wat in Yemen. *Ph.D. 1931 London, School of Oriental and African Studies*

Hamdani, V. A.
A critical study of the sources for the history of the Saljūqs of Persia and Syria. *D.Phil. 1938 Oxford*

Hamdi, M. M.
A statistical survey of the development of capital investment in Egypt since 1880. *Ph.D. 1943 London, School of Economics and Political Science*

Hamdi, S. A.
The civil war between Amin and Ma'mūn. *M.A. 1948 London, School of Oriental and African Studies*

Hamer, D.
France in the writings of Henry James; a bibliography of the writings of Henry James. *M.A. 1924 Liverpool*

Hamid, A. N. A.
Ricardo's contributions to financial theory examined in the light of modern theory. *Ph.D. 1936 Leeds*

Hamid, M. S. Abdel- *see* Abdel-Hamid, M. S.

Hamid, S. A.
The most economical unit of memorizing with recitation. *Ph.D. 1926 London*

Hamid, S. A.
Some factors of effectiveness in mental ('intelligence') tests. *M.A. 1923 London*

Hamilton, A. D. B.
Barbados and the Confederation Question, 1871-1885. *Ph.D. 1947 London, External Degree*

Hamilton, H.
History of the brass and copper industries of England from Elizabethan times to the Industrial Revolution. *D.Litt. 1925 Glasgow*

Hamilton, H. C.
Castlereagh and the Holy Alliance. *M.A. 1926 Birmingham*

Hamilton, J. A.
A history of Byzantine architecture with special reference to problems of origin and evolution of plan. *Ph.D. 1925 Edinburgh*

Hamilton Jenkin, A. K.
Richard Carew. *B.Litt. 1924 Oxford*

Hamilton, K. M.
The relationship of the arts in English critical theory of the eighteenth century, with special reference to the years 1750-1780, excluding periodical essays. *M.A. 1940 London, University College*

Hamilton, M. C.
The Irish Labour Court. *M.Econ.Sc. 1949 National University of Ireland*

Hamilton, M. E. M.
The source and growth of the legend of the association of Troy with the foundation of Rome. *M.A. 1932 London, Bedford College*

Hamilton, P. M.
A comparative study of the recent ethical theories of idealism, pragmatism, and realism. *B.Litt. 1922 Oxford*

Hamilton, R.
A study of the aims and technique of William Painter, as shown in his selection and treatment of the sources of *A Palace of pleasure. M.A. 1949 Wales*

Hamilton, R. W.
Emotional factors in juvenile delinquency. *B.Sc. 1941 Oxford*

Hamilton, S. B.
History of ideas on the behaviour of materials under stress (from 1650 to 1850). *M.Sc. 1934 London, University College*

Hamlyn, H. M.
The circulating libraries of the eighteenth century. *M.A. 1948 London, Birkbeck College*

Hammad, S. I.
French and British influences in Egyptian education. *M.A. 1949 London, Institute of Education*

Hammelmann, H. A. A. P. O.
A comparative study of the law of evidence in the Continental and common law systems. *D.Phil. 1947 Oxford*

Hammerton, H. J.
The place of seasonal ritual in the medieval English drama. *M.A. 1944 Leeds*

Hammond, G. M.
Fluency and lying: an experiment designed to study the relations between a number of tests of fluency and temperamental and intellectual traits, and also their relationship to a behaviour problem, namely, lying. *M.A. 1946 London, Birkbeck College*

Hammond, H.
The sermon as persuasion in late seventeenth century France and England: a study of Bossuet, Bourdaloue, Barrow, and South. *Ph.D. 1950 Cambridge*

Hammond, M.
The constitution of the Roman principate under Augustus in theory and practice, with a special consideration of the edicts from Cyrene and the value of the speech of Maecenas in Dio lii as evidence for the Augustan age. *B.Litt. 1928 Oxford*

Hammond, M.
Music as a didactic element in Renascence literature. *M.A. 1912 London*

Hammond, R. J.
The social and economic circumstances of Ket's rebellion, 1549. *M.A. 1934 London, School of Economics and Political Science*

Hamnett, J. H.
The part played by the French Oratory in the secondary education of France during the years 1614-1792. *M.A. 1947 Birmingham*

Hampson, E. M.
Cambridgeshire and its lunatic paupers and criminals. *M.A. 1926 Liverpool*

Hampson, E. M.
Pauperism and vagrancy in Cambridgeshire to 1834. *Ph.D. 1931 Cambridge*

Hampton, H. W.
The effects of the French Revolution on English literature, with special reference to Burke. *M.A. 1910 Birmingham*

Hampton, R. G.
International regulation in the meat trade. *Ph.D. 1938 London, School of Economics and Political Science*

Hamson, C. J.
Patent rights for scientific discoveries. *LL.M. 1935 Cambridge*

Han, S. T.
The problem of the relationship between mind and body. *M.A. 1912 Liverpool*

Hancock, S. T. R.
Education and the army. *M.Ed. 1949 Manchester*

Hancox, M. K.
A study of Diderot's novel *La religieuse. M.A. 1944 Birmingham*

Handasyde, F. E.
A critical study of George Granville, Lord Lansdowne. *B.Litt. 1931 Oxford*

Handcock, W. D.
Recent critiques of the doctrine of the sovereignty with special reference to the writings of Professor Leon Duguit. *B.Litt. 1930 Oxford*

Handcock, W. D.
The theory of sovereignty in history. *M.A. 1926 Bristol*

Handler, A. B.
Henri Linguet: his political and social theory. *M.Sc. 1934 London, School of Economics and Political Science*

Handley, J. E.
The Irish in Scotland, 1798-1845. *M.A. 1941 National University of Ireland*

Handley, J. E.
Scottish farming in the eighteenth century. *Ph.D. 1933 London, External Degree*

Handley, M.
The child in poetry. *M.A. 1906 Birmingham*

Hands, L.
1. Utrum Christus venisset si Adam non peccasset. 2. The New Testament doctrine of the Christian character and its development. *B.D. 1907 Oxford*

Hanks, H.
The educational welfare of the industrial adolescent, with special reference to day continuation schools. *M.A. 1940 London, King's College*

Hanlon, M.
Analytic and synthetic propositions. *M.A. 1945 National University of Ireland*

Hanly, M.
Malone as Shakespearean commentator. *M.A. 1913 National University of Ireland*

Hann, A. E. J.
A commentary on Pliny's *Natural History*, book VII. *Ph.D. 1949 London, Birkbeck College*

Hann, A. F. J.
A Vatican manuscript of Aristophanes' *Clouds* (codex Palatinus 116). *M.A. 1936 London, University College*

Hanna, A. J.
The history of Nyasaland and northeastern Rhodesia, 1875-95. *Ph.D. 1948 London, King's College*

Hanna, J. M.
The development of road transport in conjunction with railways for the conveyance of merchandise in England and Wales. *M.Sc. 1936 London, School of Economics and Political Science*

Hannah, J. J.
1. The purpose of the Epistle to St. James. 2. The Church and Scripture. *B.D. & D.D. 1909 Oxford*

Hannay-Thompson, J. H.
The administration of ports. *Ph.D. 1938 Edinburgh*

Hannen, R. B.
An historical examination into baptismal usage in the reformed churches of Scotland. *Ph.D. 1948 Glasgow*

Hanrahan, J. G.
Evil and world order in Shakespeare's tragedies. *M.A. 1947 National University of Ireland*

Hans, N.
History of Russian educational policy, 1801-1917. *Ph.D. 1926 London*

Hansford, F. S.
An outline of the development of ideas on magnetism from 1600-1820. *M.Sc. 1931 London*

Hansford, S. H.
The evolution of technique in Chinese jade carving. *M.A. 1946 London, Courtauld Institute of Art*

Hanson, C.
Some elements of sentimentalism in the literature of the eighteenth century. *M.A. 1948 Sheffield*

Hanson, J. B.
Henri de Régnier: le poète. *D.Phil. 1945 Oxford*

Hanson, J. L.
A history of education in Halifax during the nineteenth century. *M.Ed. 1940 Leeds*

Hanson, J. L.
Transport development in west Yorkshire from the Industrial Revolution to the present day to the present day. *Ph.D. 1949 London, External Degree*

Hanson, L. W.
The Tory Party in the reign of George I. *B.Litt. 1930 Oxford*

Hanson, R. P. C.
Origen's doctrine of tradition. *D.D. 1950 Dublin, Trinity College*

Hanson-Lowe, J. B.
Contributions to the climatology and geomorphology of Sino-Tibet and central China. *Ph.D. 1949 London, External Degree*

Hansson, C. T.
Contributions to the study of the influence of German loanwords in Swedish vocabulary. *M.A. 1949 Liverpool*

Hanter, J. N. W.
An inquiry into the perception and memory of time relations, and particularly into the development of the time concept among high school children. *Ph.D. 1934 Edinburgh*

Haq, A.
Abu Tammam and his times. *B.Litt. 1922 Oxford*

Haq, A.
Abu Tammam and his times. *D.Phil. 1925 Oxford*

Haq, M. A.
Dīwān Ibn Sanā' al Mulk, with commentary and indexes. *D.Phil. 1938 Oxford*

Haque, S.
Ibn Taimiya and his projects of reform. *Ph.D. 1937 London, School of Oriental and African Studies*

Haque, S. A.
The education of the depressed classes in India. *M.Ed. 1938 Leeds*

Harbison, J.
Modern Irish literature in the English language. *M.A. 1928 Belfast*

Harbord, S. M. *see* Vos, S. M.

Harcourt-Smith, G. M. H.
The treatment of the supernatural in English literature from Shakespeare to Coleridge together with some consideration of the subject in its relation to the metaphysical and mystical side of literature. *M.A. 1907 London*

Hardie, F. M.
Parliamentary reform in Great Britain: a critical analysis of existing proposals, with constructive comments. *D.Phil. 1937 Oxford*

Hardie, J. B.
Arabic musical instruments, from a ms. in the Farmer collection. *Ph.D. 1946 Glasgow*

Harding, F. J. W.
Matthew Arnold (the critic) as an interpreter of France. *B.Litt. 1948 Oxford*

Harding, J. N.
A study of Matthew Arnold and Ernest Renan as representative of the spirit of frustration in England and France in the nineteenth century. *M.A. 1947 Wales*

Harding, J. N.
A study of the development of the critical thought of Paul Elmer More. *Ph.D. 1949 Birmingham*

Harding, L. N.
Some business aspects of association football and county cricket in England: a study of certain aspects of the organization of games dependent upon gate receipts. *M.Sc. 1941 London, School of Economics and Political Science*

Harding, O. J.
The Cleveland district of Yorkshire: an essay in local geography. *M.Sc. 1929 Leeds*

Harding, R.
Education for industry on the northeast coast. *M.Ed. 1934 Durham*

Harding, R. E. M.
The pianoforte: its history traced to the Great Industrial Exhibition of 1851. *Ph.D. 1931 Cambridge*

Harding, W. E.
The psychological and philosophical implications of the kenotic Christology. *M.A. 1932 Manchester*

Hardman, E.
A geographical study of the Vale of Evesham. *M.A. 1930 Manchester*

Hardwick, J. C.
The mechanical view of nature since Descartes. *B.Sc. 1923 Oxford*

Hardy, B. G.
Coleridge's theory of communication. *M.A. 1949 London, University College*

Hardy, K. E.
William Warham as statesman, scholar, and patron. *B.Litt. 1943 Oxford*

Hardy, P. R.
Victor Cousin and the Romantic Movement. *M.A. 1932 London, King's College*

Hardy, S. H.
An account of the needle industry up to the beginning of the factory system. *M.Com. 1940 Birmingham*

Hardy, S. M.
William Huskisson (1770-1834), imperial statesman and economist. *Ph.D. 1943 London, Birkbeck College*

Hare, A. E. C.
Labour migration: a study of the mobility of labour. *Ph.D. 1933 London, School of Economics and Political Science*

Harford, J. B.
Studies in the book of Ezekiel. *D.D. 1935 Cambridge*

Hargrave, J.
Social and economic conditions in the industrial towns of the West Riding of Yorkshire in the hungry forties. *M.A. 1940 Leeds*

Hargreaves, E. L.
Some reversions to former standards of money. *Ph.D. 1924 London*

Hargreaves, J. D.
Anglo-French relations, 1904-1906. *M.A. 1948 Manchester*

Hargreaves, J. J.
Labour conditions in the road motor transport industry. *B.Litt. 1938 Oxford*

Harichandan, J.
The history of education in Orissa. *M.Ed. 1947 Leeds*

Haring, C. H.
The buccaneers in Jamaica. *B.Litt. 1909 Oxford*

Harland, S. F. H.
The structure of the short story. *M.A. 1949 Leeds*

Harley, D. L.
Theory of tragedy in England, 1660-1702. *B.Litt. 1934 Oxford*

Harley, J. L.
Report of an enquiry into the occupations, further education and leisure interests of a number of girl wage-earners from elementary and central schools in the Manchester district, with special reference to the influence of school training on their use of leisure. *M.Ed. 1937 Manchester*

Harlow, V. T.
Constitutional and economic development in Barbados, 1640-1685. *B.Litt. 1923 Oxford*

Harman, C. J.
The significance of the effects of changes in data, and in particular in the supply of money, upon the structure of industrial production in a modern capitalist economy. *M.Sc. 1935 London, External Degree*

Harman, R. C.
Factors determining the size of gas undertakings. *M.Sc. 1938 London, School of Economics and Political Science*

Harmer, L. C.
The life and works of Lancelot de Carle. *Ph.D. 1937 Cambridge*

Harmshaw, R. O.
Samuel Butler as a satirist. *M.A. 1928 Birmingham*

Harney, J. A.
An inquiry into the procedure of the Supreme Court of New South Wales. *B.Litt. 1939 Oxford*

Harney, K. J.
Influence of Spenser on succeeding poets. *M.A. 1919 National University of Ireland*

Harold, H. G.
John Wyclif and his interpretation of the sacraments. *Ph.D. 1940 Edinburgh*

Harper, H. D.
Exegeses of: St. Matthew xiii.55; St. Matthew i.1; I Timothy ii.5. *B.D. & D.D. 1878 Oxford*

Harper, I. M.
A history of the real Old Timers of Fort Edmonton (Canada) and its hinterland. *M.Litt. 1932 Cambridge*

Harper, K.
The foundations of the doctrine of the Logos in the prologue to the fourth gospel. *M.Litt. 1947 Durham*

Harper, R.
Psychological and psychophysical studies of craftsmanship in dairying. *Ph.D. 1949 Reading*

Harper, T.
The Hellenistic background of New Testament thought. *Ph.D. 1929 Glasgow*

Harper, W.
The leisure activities of adolescents: an investigation of the psychological functions of the various leisure activities of adolescents in a particular town, with some special references to the cinema and reading. *M.A. 1942 Manchester*

Harper, W. P.
Public borrowing, 1649-1660, with special reference to government borrowing in the City of London between 1640 and 1650. *M.Sc. 1927 London*

Harries, J. M.
Departmental stores. *M.A. 1950 Sheffield*

Harries, L.
Barddoniaeth Huw Cae Llwyd, Ieuan ap Huw Cae Llwyd, Ieuan Dyfi a Gwerful Mechain. *M.A. 1933 Wales*

Harrington, C. S.
Influence of Malthus on economic thought. *M.A. 1915 National University of Ireland*

Harris, A. N.
The denudation chronology of northeast Wales. *Ph.D. 1947 London, Birkbeck College*

Harris, A. N.
The ports of Western India: a study in the physical, economic and historical factors controlling port development. *M.A. 1932 Reading*

Harris, A. N. V.
Psychological and social differences between A, B and C groups in senior schools, and their relation to the differential birth rate. *M.A. 1942 Birmingham*

Harris, C.
1. The condition of our Lord's body between his Resurrection and Ascension. 2. The narratives of the Ascension, critically compared and harmonized. *B.D. 1898 Oxford*

Harris, C.
Expositions of: I Corinthians xv.1-11; 12-23; 35-58. *D.D. 1905 Oxford*

Harris, C. R. S.
The philosophy of John Duns Scotus. *Ph.D. 1924 Oxford*

Harris, D. G. T.
Musical education in Tudor times, 1485-1603. *M.A. 1938 Liverpool*

Harris, E.
1. The doctrine of the Incarnation as expounded by Wyclif. 2. Coincidences between the Epistle to St.James and the Sermon on the Mount. *B.D. & D.D. 1888 Oxford*

Harris, E. E.
The bearing of the conception of evolution upon the problem of the inclusion of individual minds within reality as a whole. *B.Litt. 1933 Oxford*

Harris, E. E.
The followers of Goya. *Ph.D. 1934 London, University College*

Harris, E. F.
Le parler de Bar-le-Duc au moyen âge de'après des documents d'archives. *M.A. 1924 Birmingham*

Harris, E. H.
The influence of the Faust legend on English poetry. *M.A. 1912 Belfast*

Harris, G. B.
The economic aspects of Fascism. *M.Com.Sc. 1932 Belfast*

Harris, H.
The Greek, the barbarian and the slave. *M.Litt. 1929 Cambridge*

Harris, H. M.
A study of the development of the meaning of the word 'romance' (romantic) as used in literary criticism. *M.A. 1911 London*

Harris, J.
The work of Williamson and its relation to the type theory of Wurtz. *M.Sc. 1926 London*

Harris, J. G.
Sacrifice in the period of the Hebrew monarchy: its theory and practice. *M.A. 1950 Wales*

Harris, J. R.
Economic and social development in St. Helens in the latter half of the eighteenth century. *M.A. 1950 Manchester*

Harris, M.
British migration to western Australia, 1829-1850. *Ph.D. 1934 London, School of Economics and Political Science*

Harris, M. E. A.
Studies in the lyric poetry of Wilhelm Müller, with special reference to his relations to the Romanticists. *Ph.D. 1922 London*

Harris, M. L.
Etude sur la correspondence de François-René de Châteaubriand, des années 1789-1823. *M.A. 1914 Birmingham*

Harris, N. T.
The Pope-Bowles controversy. *M.A. 1925 London*

Harris, N. T.
Pope's relations with his contemporaries. *Ph.D. 1933 London, University College*

Harris, R. W.
The social, economic and political problems of the Stuart settlement of Jamaica. *M.A. 1943 Bristol*

Harris, S.
Types of agricultural villages and related systems of land utilization and division in western France and its islands. *M.Sc. 1930 Wales*

Harris, S. B.
The historical geography (ancient) of Northamptonshire and the southeast Midlands. *M.Sc. 1945 London, External Degree*

Harris, W. H.
Hywel Dda, together with an outline of the origins, affinities, and history of the laws called after his name. *B.Litt. 1913 Oxford*

Harris, W. J. A.
Japanese foreign policy since 1915, with special reference to the events in 1931 and 1932. *M.Sc. 1940 London, School of Economics and Political Science*

Harrison, A.
English factory legislation considered with regard to its economic effects and methods of administration. *D.Sc. 1903 London*

Harrison, A. C.
R. Southey and his poetry. *M.A. 1920 Birmingham*

Harrison, A. V.
A survey of my present situation in technical education, including its relation with industry. *M.A. 1938 Bristol*

Harrison, C.
Addison's literary criticism. *Ph.D. 1946 Leeds*

Harrison, D.
Conspiracy as a tort and as a crime in English law, treated historically. *LL.D. 1923 London*

Harrison, F. M.
Some aspects of music in England in the seventeenth century. *Ph.D. 1935 London, Royal College of Music*

Harrison, G. B.
A study of the Stationers' Register for the years 1591-1594, in relation to the social life and literature of the period. *Ph.D. 1928 London*

Harrison, H. D.
The main economic results of industrial psychology. *M.Com. 1923 Birmingham*

Harrison, J.
An economic study of dairy herd depreciation. *M.Sc. 1939 Reading*

Harrison, K.
Aurelius Prudentius Clemens *Contra Symmachum*, Books I-II, including introduction, translation, commentary, bibliography, together with translation of Symmachus' third *Relatio* and St. Ambrose's reply. *Ph.D. 1935 Dublin, Trinity College*

Harrison, M.
The Education Act, 1944, and its development from earlier legislation. *M.A. 1945 Leeds*

Harrison, M.
Some aspects of needed educational reform. *M.Ed. 1942 Leeds*

Harrison, R. M.
The work of Charles Péguy. *Ph.D. 1933 London, Westfield College*

Harrison, S. J. C.
Irish women writers 1800-35. *Ph.D. 1947 Dublin, Trinity College*

Harrison, W. E. C.
Maritime activity under Henry VII. *M.A. 1931 London, King's College*

Harriss, I. V.
The effects of the Reformation on the social conditions of England, 1535-1570. *M.A. 1915 Birmingham*

Harrop, A. J.
England and New Zealand. *Ph.D. 1926 Cambridge*

Harry, E. L.
An economic and social survey of the parish of Badsey, Worcestershire, in which the population is engaged in an intensive form of agriculture. *M.Sc. 1931 Wales*

Harry, I. D.
Sir Thomas Wise and the Central Society of Education. *M.A. 1932 Wales*

Harry, R. T.
Psychological laws and economic activity. *M.A. 1924 Wales*

Hart, A. T.
Life and times of John Sharp. *B.D. 1944 Cambridge*

Hart, B.
The psychology of insanity. *M.D. 1912 London*

Hart, D. I.
Disraeli. *M.A. 1921 Birmingham*

Hart, E. F.
The relationship between English poetry and music in the seventeenth century. *M.A. 1949 London, King's College*

Hart, G. E.
Anglicanism: its progress until 1626. *M.A. 1922 Bristol*

Hart, I. I. B.
The mechanical investigations of Leonardo da Vinci, with special reference to his researches on flight. *Ph.D. 1924 London*

Hart, M. C.
The Upper House during the Protectorates of Oliver and Richard Cromwell. *M.A. 1929 London*

Hart, N. Y. *see* Boydell, N. Y.

Hart, T. A.
The Hesychast controversy, with special reference to the *Byzantina historia* of Nicephorus Gregoras and the *Historia* of John Cantacuzenus. *M.A. 1949 London, Bedford College*

Harte, A. H. W.
A functional conception of the training of post-primary school teachers, with special reference to New Zealand. *Ph.D. 1948 London, Institute of Education*

Harte, R. H.
The Eleusinian mysteries. *M.A. 1927 Belfast*

Hartford, R. R.
The system of Erigena, a study in Christian thought. *D.D. 1948 Dublin, Trinity College*

Hartill, P.
The rational necessity of Christ's atonement. *B.D. 1927 Oxford*

Hartland, R. W.
Influences anglaises sur le roman historique français. *M.A. 1913 Birmingham*

Hartland, R. W.
Walter Scott et le roman frénétique. *D.Litt. 1927 Birmingham*

Hartland-Swann, J. J.
The influence of religious dogma on metaphysical speculation in the philosophy of Descartes, with special reference to the psychological aspect. *Ph.D. 1946 London, External Degree*

Hartland-Swann, J. J.
Philosophy and poetry: a study of their combination and an evaluation of its success. *B.Litt. 1949 Oxford*

Hartley, G. W.
The function of English studies in educational reconstruction. *M.A. 1945 Leeds*

Hartley, G. W.
Training in style through literary appreciation, with special reference to pupils aged ten to fifteen. *M.Ed. 1927 Leeds*

Hartley, J. C.
Maurice Maeterlinck: a study of the development of his drama and philosophy. *M.A. 1950 Sheffield*

Hartman, D. A.
The press and the modern state. *Ph.D. 1930 London, School of Economics and Political Science*

Hartmann, C. A. H.
Spanish sea power in the Mediterranean during the reign of Philip II. *B.Litt. 1922 Oxford*

Hartnett, P.
Antiquities of E. Muskerry. *M.A. 1939 National University of Ireland*

Hartog, W. G.
A contribution to the study of the melodrama of Guilbert de Pixerécourt, with special reference to his treatment of his sources. *M.A. 1908 London*

Hartridge, R. A. R.
The Vicarage system in Western Europe in the later middle ages, c.1200-1500. *Ph.D. 1929 London*

Harvey, G. E.
The history of Burma up to 1824. *B.Litt. 1923 Oxford*

Harvey, H.
The poetical works of John Skelton, Laureate, 1460-1529. *M.A. 1912 London*

Harvey, H. S.
Gerard Langbaine the Younger. *B.Litt. 1937 Oxford*

Harvey, J.
John Sturm. *Ph.D. 1926 Glasgow*

Harvey, P. G.
The council under Henry IV. *B.Litt. 1932 Oxford*

Harvey, R. J.
Observations on the extraneous influences and culture-contacts in the Tanganyika Territory in their bearing on problems of native education. *B.Sc. 1937 Oxford*

Harvey, W. N. W.
The psychology of S. Paul. *B.Litt. 1941 Dublin, Trinity College*

Harvey, W. N. W.
The two Oxford movements. *D.D. 1947 Dublin, Trinity College*

Harvey-Gibson, R. J. *see* Gibson, R. J. Harvey-

Harwin, S. A.
A study and comparison of French and Welsh texts of the story of Gwidw. *M.A. 1929 Wales*

Harwood, M. K. B.
An analysis of factors in certain tests of sensory recognition. *M.A. 1935 London, Institute of Education*

Harwood, M. K. B.
The curve of output during a continued series of tasks varying in nature. *M.Sc. 1937 London, University College*

Harwood, M. K. B.
An illustrative study of examination marks by the methods of factor analysis and the analysis of variance. *Ph.D. 1943 London, Bedford College*

Hasan, A. N. M. A.
Western influences in the Arabic literature of Egypt and Syria between 1820 and 1879. *Ph.D. 1931 London, School of Oriental and African Studies*

Hasan, H.
Falakī-i-Shirwānī: his times, life and works. *Ph.D. 1929 London*

Hasan, I.
The political structure of the Mughal Empire in northern India and its practical working up to the year 1657. *Ph.D. 1932 London, School of Oriental and African Studies*

Hasan, M.
The life and works of Nathaniel Lee. *D.Phil. 1937 Oxford*

Hasan, S.
The early history of the Buwaihid Dynasty beginning with 320 to 356 A.H. *Ph.D. 1928 London*

Hasan, S. N.
The Chisti and Suhrawardi movements in India to the middle of the sixteenth century. *D.Phil. 1948 Oxford*

Hasan, S. Z.
Realism: an attempt to trace its origin and its development. *D.Phil. 1925 Oxford*

Hasegawa, K.
Theories of pleasure-unpleasure and its relation to action. *Ph.D. 1926 Edinburgh*

Hashim, A.
A study of the attitudes of secondary school pupils towards certain school subjects. *M.A. 1948 London, Institute of Education*

Hashimi, M. Al- *see* Al-Hashimi, M.

Hashmi, B. A.
Development of Muslim education in India under the British rule. *M.A. 1927 Leeds*

Hashmi, S. Y.
Persian poetry of the kings of India. *Ph.D. 1933 London, School of Oriental and African Studies*

Haslam, A. L.
The law relating to combinations. *D.Phil. 1929 Oxford*

Haslam, E. P.
Control schemes in raw materials and foodstuffs in relation to the problems of the dairy industry in New Zealand. *B.Litt. 1938 Oxford*

Haslam, M. M.
History of the discovery of the gases of the air and of their physical and chemical properties. *M.Sc. 1929 London*

Hasler, W. J.
Canada in boom and depression, 1924 to 1935. *M.Sc. 1936 London, School of Economics and Political Science*

Hasluck, E. L.
The teaching of history. *M.A. 1919 London*

Hass, J. G.
Jules Levallois. *M.A. 1929 Birmingham*

Hassall, W. O.
A study of the nunnery of St. Mary Clerkenwell and its property with an edition of its cartulary. *D.Phil. 1941 Oxford*

Hassan, H. I.
Some aspects of Shī'īte propaganda under the Fātimids in Egypt. *Ph.D. 1927 London*

Hassan, M. S.
The rebirth of a nation: the kingdom of Irak. *M.A. 1928 London*

Hassanein, H.
Infantile mortality in Egypt, with some reference to the experience of Great Britain. *Ph.D. 1945 London, School of Economics and Political Science*

Hastings, G. W.
The place of Cowper in eighteenth century literature. *M.A. 1908 Wales*

Hastings, J. M.
St. Stephen's Chapel and the architecture of the fourteenth century in London. *Ph.D. 1947 Cambridge*

Hastings, J. W.
The original doctrines of the Disciples of Christ: a critical evaluation. *Ph.D. 1929 Edinburgh*

Hastings, W. F.
The education of English Catholics, 1559-1800. *M.A. 1923 London*

Hatch, H. G.
A Christological study, being a critical investigation of Christological data supplied from an examination of Gospel sources on the lines of an acceptance of the four-document hypothesis. *Ph.D. 1928 London*

Hatch, J. E.
1. The prophets of Israel up to the fall of Samaria. 2. The function of prophecy illustrated by the prophets of Judah. *B.D. & D.D. 1915 Oxford*

Hateley, D. M.
The authentic philosophy of W. Pater. *M.A. 1921 Birmingham*

Hatfield, E. J.
Theories of heredity in the nineteenth century. *M.Sc. 1928 London*

Hatfield, H. A.
Etude sur les procédés littéraires de B. de St. Pierre. *M.A. 1913 Birmingham*

Hatto, A. T.
A Middle German Apocalypse edited from the manuscript British Museum, add. 15243. *M.A. 1934 London, King's College*

Hatton, J. D.
Race and racism in the Union of South Africa. *M.A. 1948 National University of Ireland*

Hatton, R. M. R. H.
Diplomatic relations between Great Britain and the Dutch Republic, 1714-1721. *Ph.D. 1947 London, University College*

Hauger, E. G.
The achievement of Thomas Hood as a serious poet. *M.A. 1948 Leeds*

Haunch, T. O.
The planning, design and equipment of residential colleges for the training of teachers. *M.A. 1950 Sheffield*

Havens, P. S.
John Hall: a study of his non-political works. *B.Litt. 1928 Oxford*

Havergal, F. T.
1. The abodes of the departed. 2. The holy angels. *B.D. & D.D. 1888 Oxford*

Havill, E. E.
The Parliamentary representation of Monmouthshire and the Monmouth boroughs, 1536-1832. *M.A. 1949 Wales*

Haward, W. I.
The transactions between the merchants of the Staple and the Lancastrian government, 1449-1461. *Ph.D. 1932 London, Bedford College*

Hawdon, F. E.
A survey of English Shakespearean criticism, 1907-1939. *M.A. 1948 London, External Degree*

Hawes, A. J. G.
The Christology of St. Hilary of Poitiers. *Ph.D. 1928 London*

Hawes, G. K.
The right of private judgment in matters of conduct: its growth and value. *M.A. 1931 Manchester*

Hawgood, J. A.
The influence of American ideas at Frankfurt-am-Main, 1848-9. *M.A. 1928 London*

Hawk, G. E.
England's literary debt to Spain, 1603-1642. *B.Litt. 1928 Oxford*

Hawkes, A. J.
A contribution to the study of Hans Friedrich Blunck: a study of the trilogy *Gewalt über das Feuer, Kampf der Gestirne, Streit mit den Göttern*. *M.A. 1933 Liverpool*

Hawkes, L. R.
A regional study of the agricultural landscape of the north Exe basin. *M.A. 1938 London, Birkbeck College*

Hawkins, A. D.
Some investigations concerning the work of a central school in relation to the future occupations of its pupils. *M.Sc. 1933 Birmingham*

Hawkins, E. B.
Sir Harry Smith in South Africa. *B.Litt. 1923 Oxford*

Hawkins, L. M.
The political faith of the English nonjurors. *Ph.D. 1927 London*

Hawkins, R. M.
An enquiry into the relationship between the synoptic record of the teaching of Jesus and the Book of Isaiah, with reference to the Septuagint version. *Ph.D. 1927 Edinburgh*

Hawkins, T. H.
The history of education in the British army up to 1939. *M.Ed. 1945 Leeds*

Hawkridge, P. B.
The kingdom at the threshold: a study of the apocalyptic element in English puritanism in the sixteenth and seventeenth centuries. *Ph.D. 1943 London, Richmond College*

Hawksworth, J. M.
Delegation in local government law. *LL.M. 1950 Sheffield*

Hawksworth, L.
La vie et l'oeuvre de Jean Lahor. *M.A. 1939 Liverpool*

Hawley, F.
On the relationship of the Japanese language. Sketch of a history of Japanese literary studies made by Europeans. . *M.A. 1933-34 Liverpool*

Haworth, H. R.
The Resurrection in the New Testament. *B.D. 1939 Leeds*

Haworth, P.
An edition of British Museum ms. Harley 2257. *B.Litt. 1928 Oxford*

Haworth, T. O.
The religious use of symbol in Crashaw and his predecessors. *M.A. 1950 Manchester*

Hawthorne, J. E.
An endeavour to compile a test to ascertain whether a subject possesses particular capacity for science. *M.Ed. 1924 Leeds*

Hay, R. L.
The technical education of the mine worker with special reference to the effect of the industry on the receptivity of the student. *M.Ed. 1935 Durham*

Hay, R. Milton *see* Milton Hay, R.

Haycocks, N.
La vie au foyer: usages et coutumes au moyen âge d'après la littérature populaire de l'époque, et particulièrement les fabliaux. Essai historique et linguistique. *M.A. 1929 Manchester*

Hayden, M. J.
Localisation of industrial production in Eire. *M.Econ.Sc. 1938 National University of Ireland*

Haydock, G. H.
Empiricism: a critical examination of the empirical theory of knowledge as this is expounded in certain of the works of Locke and Berkeley. *Ph.D. 1946 Glasgow*

Haydock, G. H.
The significance of the religious consciousness with special reference to Bosanquet and Ritschl. *B.Litt. 1920 Oxford*

Haydon, E. M. E.
A psychological study of the poetical imagination of Wordsworth and Shelley. *M.A. 1914 London*

Hayens, K.
Theodor Fontane. *D.Litt. 1921 Glasgow*

Hayes, A.
Federal Reserve gold policy, 1921-32, and the working of the gold standard. *B.Litt. 1933 Oxford*

Hayes, A. E.
A study of employment in coalmining and agriculture in the Wrexham area. *M.A. 1948 Liverpool*

Hayes, C. J.
The romance of *Eracle* by Gautier d'Arras: its sources, composition, and place in contemporary literature. *B.Litt. 1935 Oxford*

Hayes, J. M.
Fr. Gerard Manley Hopkins. *M.A. 1941 National University of Ireland*

Hayes, N.
Essai sur la poésie symboliste en France. *M.A. 1920 National University of Ireland*

Hayes, R. M.
Music in education. *M.A. 1947 National University of Ireland*

Hayes-McCoy, G. A.
Service of Scottish mercenary forces in Ireland. *M.A. 1932 National University of Ireland*

Hayes-McCoy, G. A.
The service of the Scottish mercenary forces in Ireland, from 1565 to 1603, with an account of the mercenary system in Ireland and of its effect on Scottish history. *Ph.D. 1934 Edinburgh*

Hayes-Robinson, T.
1. St. Athanasius' exposition of the divinity and Incarnation of our Lord in the anti-Arian orations. 2. St. Augustine's exposition of grace, free-will, and predestination in his anti-Pelagian treatises. *B.D. 1906 Oxford*

Haynes, E. J.
Exposition of the Book of Revelation: introduction, chapter i; ii.1-17; ii.18; iii. *D.D. 1905 Oxford*

Haynes, E. J.
1. The witness of the New Testament to the inspiration of the Old Testament. 2. The theology of the Epistle to the Hebrews compared with that of St. John's Gospel. *B.D. 1900 Oxford*

Haynes, E. J. M.
The human geography of the English pottery industry. *B.Litt. 1925 Oxford*

Haynes, J.
A study in Chaucer: the English poet's nature lore. *M.A. 1917 National University of Ireland*

Hazlett, H.
A history of the English forces employed in Ireland, 1641-1649. *M.A. 1935 Belfast*

Hazlett, H.
A history of the military forces operating in Ireland, 1641-1649. *Ph.D. 1938 Belfast*

Hazlitt, V. H.
The acquisition of motor habits. *M.A. 1917 London*

Hazzard, L. B.
The mysticism of the fourth Gospel. *Ph.D. 1927 Edinburgh*

Head, A.
J. P. G. Viennet, l'homme et l'écrivain d'après ses mémoires inédits, ses épitres, ses satires et ses fables. *Ph.D. 1948 London, Birkbeck College*

Head, G. W.
Six great Anglicans. *B.D. 1929 Cambridge*

Headlam, A. C.
1. Acts vii.38; St. Luke vii.3; St. Matthew xvi.21: the pre-Christian doctrine of the Εκκλησία, and non-political organizations. 2. St. Matthew xvi.18: Gospel teaching direct or indirect, as to the Εκκλησία. 3. Acts ii.42: the earliest Christian community. *D.D. 1903 Oxford*

Headlam, A. C.
1. The integrity of the Epistle to the Romans. 2. The argument and theology of Romans ix-xi. *B.D. 1895 Oxford*

Headley, M. G.
Barddoniaeth Llawdden a Rhys Nanmor(The poetry of Llawdden and Rhys Nanmor). *M.A. 1938 Wales*

Healey, E.
The plateau: a study of periods of arrested progress in motor learning. *M.Ed. 1934 Leeds*

Healey, E. W.
Poetry of the Great War. *M.A. 1939 National University of Ireland*

Healey, F. G.
Rousseau et Napoléon. *M.A. 1949 Birmingham*

Healey, W.
The school report and record as a factor in the junior scholarship examination. *M.Ed. 1939 Leeds*

Healy, B.
Moral and national aspects of platonic and modern play. *M.A. 1940 National University of Ireland*

Healy, J. G.
Expediciones por el norte de America del sur en siglo XVI. *M.A. 1931 National University of Ireland*

Healy, J. G.
Los Alemanes en la conquista de América. *Ph.D. 1936 National University of Ireland*

Healy, M.
National guilds as a wage system. *M.A. 1920 National University of Ireland*

Heap, E. B.
The rights and duties of third parties. *LL.M. 1938 Leeds*

Hearnshaw, F. J. C.
The court leet of Southampton and leet jurisdiction in general. *M.A. 1908 London*

Heaslip, K. W.
Irish Gaelic literature (verse) in translation. *B.Litt. 1950 Dublin, Trinity College*

Heath, F. L.
A contribution to the study of the plays of Alfred Capus. *Ph.D. 1930 London, University College*

Heath, H. G.
The origin, development and structure of the short story in English. *M.A. 1922 London*

Heath, H. T.
The letters of Samuel Pepys and his immediate family circle. *B.Litt. 1938 Oxford*

Heathcote, A. W.
Prolegomena to the study of the relationship between science and religion. *Ph.D. 1949 London, External Degree*

Heathcote, J. P.
Excavations at Bronze Age burial mounds on Stanton Moor. *M.A. 1930 Sheffield*

Heathcote, N. H. de V.
Studies in the history of the physical sciences. *Ph.D. 1947 London, External Degree*

Heather, P. J.
Custom and belief connected with precious stones, as shown in the Middle English verse of the fourteenth century. *Ph.D. 1931 London, External Degree*

Heaton, H.
The history of the Yorkshire woollen and worsted industries from the earliest times up to the Industrial Revolution. *M.Com. 1914 Birmingham*

Heaton, W. J.
The influence of Plotinus upon the religious philosphy of St. Augustine, with special reference to the points of difference between neoplatonism and Christianity. *M.A. 1930 Reading*

Heavy, M. M.
The Galatians. *M.A. 1928 National University of Ireland*

Heavyside, M. J.
The analysis and testing of civics in a school civics experiment. *M.Ed. 1949 Leeds*

Hebb, H. E.
A study of the language of Chateaubriand's 'American' books, viz., *Atala, René, Les Natchez* and the *Voyage en Amérique*, with additional notes on the language of *Le dernier Abencérage*. *M.A. 1926 Leeds*

Hechinger, E. J.
Les idées de Maurice Barrès. *M.A. 1946 Birmingham*

Hecker, W. R.
A study of the choice of occupation among secondary school pupils. *M.A. 1937 London, Institute of Education*

Hedley, E. N. V.
Paul Heyse's dramatic use of language in his *Novellen*. *M.A. 1949 Belfast*

Hedley, R. M.
The administration of the navy in the reign of Edward III. *M.A. 1922 Manchester*

Hegarty, E.
Filidheacht na Ruarcach(The poetry of O'Rourke). *M.A. 1939 National University of Ireland*

Hegarty, E. J.
The social function of interest. *M.A. 1949 National University of Ireland*

Hegazy, A. E. M.
New developments in costing techniques as an aid to managerial control. *Ph.D. 1950 Birmingham*

Hehir, D. N.
Philosophy of the early Christian apologists. *M.A. 1931 National University of Ireland*

Heim, A. W.
A vocational investigation of some of the factors affecting the early industrial careers of elementary-school boys. *Ph.D. 1940 Cambridge*

Heinemann, H. J.
The status of the labourer in Jewish law and society in the Tannaitic period. *M.A. 1949 Manchester*

Heinrich, T. A.
Payne Knight, Price, and the picturesque. *M.Litt. 1936 Cambridge*

Heires, J. H.
Carriage by air and sea. *B.Litt. 1948 Oxford*

Heithaus, C. H.
The temples of Syria of the Roman period: their dates and developments, according to the evidence of structure, decoration and inscriptions. *Ph.D. 1940 London, University College*

Heller, E.
Thomas Mann: a study of his work in relation to the main currents of thought in nineteenth-century Germany. *Ph.D. 1948 Cambridge*

Hellman, O. L. M.
L'amitié masculine dans les romans courtois. *M.A. 1945 London, Birkbeck College*

Helmer, E.
The mandates system in the B and C territories. *Ph.D. 1928 London*

Helmer-Hirschberg, O.
Logical types from the axiomatic point of view. *Ph.D. 1936 London, Bedford College*

Hemingway, R.
The sea in the poetry of Victor Hugo. *M.A. 1917 Liverpool*

Hemmant, M.
The Exchequer Chamber, being the assembly of all the judges of England for matters of law. *Ph.D. 1929 London*

Hemmings, F. W. J.
The influence of the Russian novel on French thinkers and writers, with particular reference to Tolstoy and Dostoevsky. *D.Phil. 1949 Oxford*

Hempstock, T. A.
A comparative study of the training of full-time teachers of commercial subjects in England and France 1946 to 1949. *M.A. 1950 Sheffield*

Henchy, J. A.
Fosterage in early and medieval Ireland. *Ph.D. 1942 National University of Ireland*

Hencken, H. O'N.
The bronze and iron ages in Devon and Cornwall. *Ph.D. 1930 Cambridge*

Hendershot, H. B.
Albrecht Ritschl and the problem of value. *Ph.D. 1933 Edinburgh*

Henderson, B. L. K.
The town charters granted under the Protectorate. *M.A. 1909 London*

Henderson, G.
Gaelic dialects. *B.Litt. 1899 Oxford*

Henderson, G. B.
The European Concert, June 1854-July 1855. *Ph.D. 1934 Cambridge*

Henderson, G. D.
Aberdeen divines, being a history of the chair of divinity at King's College, Aberdeen, 1620-. *D.Litt. 1931 Glasgow*

Henderson, H. C. K.
The agricultural geography of the Adur Basin in its regional setting. *Ph.D. 1935 London, Birkbeck College*

Henderson, J.
The controversy between Karl Barth and Emil Brunner concerning natural theology. *Ph.D. 1940 Edinburgh*

Henderson, K. T.
A study of Troeltsch's treatment of Christianity as a doctrine of society. *B.Litt. 1925 Oxford*

Henderson, M. B.
Etude sur la poésie de Victor Hugo et de Tennyson. *M.A. 1915 Birmingham*

Henderson, N. K.
A study of sociability with special reference to backward children in a secondary modern school. *Ph.D. 1949 London, Institute of Education*

Henderson, P. A. Wright- *see* Wright-Henderson, P. A.

Henderson, R. F.
The new issue market and the finance of industry. *Ph.D. 1950 Cambridge*

Henderson, T. C.
The ecclesiastical policy of Cardinal Ximénex. *Ph.D. 1939 Edinburgh*

Henderson, W. O.
Lancashire cotton famine. *Ph.D. 1932 London, School of Economics and Political Science*

Heneman, H. J.
The German Presidency. *Ph.D. 1934 London, School of Economics and Political Science*

Henley, P.
Spenser in Ireland. *M.A. 1926 National University of Ireland*

Henn, K.
The hand-made nail trade of Dudley and district. *M.Com. 1927 Birmingham*

Henning, D. V.
The geography of Michelstown, its demesne and surrounding country, in the Barony of Condons and Clangibbon about the year 1841. *M.Sc. 1948 Dublin, Trinity College*

Hennings, M. A.
The local administration of the sheriff in the thirteenth century. *M.A. 1916 London*

Henriques, L. F.
The social structure of Jamaica, with special reference to racial distinctions. *D.Phil. 1948 Oxford*

Henriques, U. R. Q.
Grievances of the English clergy in the late thirteenth and early fourteenth centuries, with special reference to the *gravamina* of 1309. *B.Litt. 1940 Oxford*

Henry, C. J.
Ernest Psichari. *M.A. 1949 National University of Ireland*

Henry, P.
Economic theories of the nineteenth century which were based on a critical study of the conception of nationality. *M.Econ.Sc. 1941 National University of Ireland*

Henry, T. W.
Moral and religious education at Athens in the fifth century B.C. *M.A. 1915 Liverpool*

Henshaw, T.
Milton as a politician and a political thinker. *M.A. 1926 Wales*

Henson, H. H.
1. The influence of critical theory on the interpretation and authority of Holy Scripture. 2. Apostolic discipline as illustrated by St. Paul's epistles to the Corinthians. *B.D. 1897 Oxford*

Henstock, E. C.
The history of mechanics up to and including the work of Newton. *Ph.D. 1938 London, External Degree*

Henstock, E. C.
The rise of mechanics. *M.Sc. 1934 London, University College*

Henthorne, T. K.
The teaching of physics in secondary schools up to the standard of the school certificate examination. *M.A. 1933 Liverpool*

Hentschel, E. C.
The Byronic superman in England and Germany. *M.A. 1936 London, University College*

Hentze, M.
Pre-Fascist Italy: the rise and fall of the parliamentary régime. *Ph.D. 1938 London, School of Economics and Political Science*

Henwood, F. C.
The West Riding rhubarb industry. *M.Com. 1934 Birmingham*

Herbert, J. W.
Constitutional struggles in Jamaica, 1748-1776. *M.A. 1927 London*

Herbert, S.
1. Nationality and its problems. 2. The fall of feudalism in France. *M.A. 1923 Wales*

Herbert, W. F.
The operation of the Education Act of 1936 in a county area. *M.Ed. 1943 Manchester*

Herbruck, R. W.
The restraint of trade in relation to commercial combinations. *B.Litt. 1927 Oxford*

Herbstmann, J.
A historical study of the Jewish medieval exegesis on the Book of Amos. *M.A. 1943 Manchester*

Herdson, A. C. M.
The development of education in Sunderland during the nineteenth century. *M.Ed. 1931 Durham*

Herlihy, M. F.
Poetry and prose of James Stephens. *M.A. 1945 National University of Ireland*

Herman, J.
English drama from Robertson. *Ph.D. 1921 Cambridge*

Herman, N. D.
The rise and decline of the German Social Democratic Party. *M.A. 1949 Sheffield*

Hermitage-Day, E.
1. Considerations on eternal punishment. 2. The baptism of infants. *B.D. 1901 Oxford*

Hermus, C. L. T.
A middle Dutch version of the *Speculum humanae salvationis*. *Ph.D. 1937 London, External Degree*

Hernaman, M. O.
The development of communications in northwest Wales. *M.A. 1945 London, Birkbeck College*

Herne, E. M.
Archbishop Parker and the Anglican Settlement, 1558-1563. *M.A. 1928 Birmingham*

Heron, A.
Cultural and psychological problems in education for parenthood. *M.Sc. 1949 Manchester*

Heron, D.
A second study of extreme alcoholism in adults, with special reference to the Home Office inebriate reformatory data. *D.Sc. 1912 London*

Heron, W.
Literary appreciation in the elementary school. *M.Ed. 1923 Leeds*

Herrick, H. M.
Cardinal Newman. *M.A. 1932 Liverpool*

Herrington, E. I.
British measures for the suppression of the slave trade from the west coast of Africa, 1807-1833. *M.A. 1923 London*

Herrmann, W.
The visual impressions in the poems of Leconte de Lisle. *M.A. 1950 Bristol*

Herron, L. W.
Ned Ward. *Ph.D. 1941 London, University College*

Herzmark, P. M.
Studien zur Entstehungsgeschichte von Chamissos *Peter Schlemihl. M.A. 1926 London*

Herzog, J.
Semikha or the laying on of the hands of the sacrifice. *M.A. 1912 London*

Hesketh-Williams, P. K.
The earlier literary criticism of Samuel Johnson. *B.Litt. 1940 Oxford*

Hettiaratchi, D. E.
A critical study of the *Vesaturu-da-Sanne. Ph.D. 1948 London, External Degree*

Hettinger, J.
The ultra-perceptive faculty. *Ph.D. 1939 London, King's College*

Heuser, H. K. M.
Exchange control. *Ph.D. 1938 London, School of Economics and Political Science*

Heward, G. A. L.
Virgil's treatment of Roman history. *M.A. 1908 Wales*

Hewat, E. G. K.
A comparison of Hebrew and Chinese wisdom, as exemplified in the Book of Proverbs and the Analects of Confucius. *Ph.D. 1934 Edinburgh*

Hewetson, E. M.
Ruskin as a literary critic. *M.A. 1938 London, King's College*

Hewitt, F. S.
A study of certain aspects of the psychology of the pre-adolescent child. *M.A. 1945 Liverpool*

Hewitt, H. J.
The economic and social history of Cheshire in the reign of the three Edwards. *Ph.D. 1926 London*

Hewitt, H. J.
Monasticism in Cheshire. *M.A. 1917 Liverpool*

Hewitt, M. J.
The West Indies in the American Revolution. *D.Phil. 1937 Oxford*

Hewitt, R.
The development of the Tees-side industrial area. *M.Sc. 1940 London, University College*

Hewlett, A. D.
Beyond the Dalton plan: a new practical attempt to find a more satisfactory basis for individual work and responsibility in an English secondary school. *M.A. 1929 London*

Hewlett, A. D.
The University of Oxford and the Church of England in the time of William Laud. *B.Litt. 1934 Oxford*

Hewlett, E. L.
The work of the British and Foreign School Society in the training of teachers. *M.Ed. 1932 Manchester*

Hewlett, R. D.
Agricultural co-operation in Sweden and its relations with the state 1929 to 1947. *Ph.D. 1950 Reading*

Hewson, J. T.
The relations between schoolmaster and administrator: from the point of view of the secondary school, with special reference to: the legislation and developments during recent years; a comparison of the systems of England and those of Germany and France; the relations existing between the internal (the schoolmaster) and the external (the governors and director) authority of the school. *M.Ed. 1931 Durham*

Heyes, M. T.
Cicero and the supernatural. *M.A. 1922 Liverpool*

Heyes, M. T.
Sannazaro: a study of his Latin works. *Ph.D. 1933 London, External Degree*

Heywood, C. L.
The evolution of the river system of Northern Britain. *M.Sc. 1946 London, King's College and London, Birkbeck College*

Heywood, C. L.
An investigation of the factors involved in the geographical work of boys and girls. *M.A. 1938 London, Institute of Education*

Heyworth, H.
A study of the life, thought and works of Hermann Löns. *M.A. 1939 Leeds*

Hicken, W. F.
An examination of the nature and significance of Plato's theory of degrees of sapheneia. *D.Phil. 1949 Oxford*

Hickmore, M. A. S.
The shipbuilding industry on the east and south coasts of England in the fifteenth century. *M.A. 1937 London, School of Economics and Political Science*

Hicks, F. C. N.
1. The meaning and history of Jewish sacrifice and sacrificial ideas. 2. The attitude to sacrifice of the critics of the Old Testament. *B.D. & D.D. 1924 Oxford*

Hicks, F. W. P.
The medieval history of St. James' Bristol. *M.A. 1932 Bristol*

Hicks, J. F.
A translation, with a commentary, of the sermons of Father John Healy of Dunleer. *M.A. 1947 Belfast*

Hicks, J. R.
The positions of the skilled and less skilled workman in the engineering and building trades (1914-25). *B.Litt. 1927 Oxford*

Higginbotham, M.
The career of A. J. Mundella, with special reference to his Sheffield connections. *M.A. 1941 Sheffield*

Higginbotham, P. J.
An investigation into the use of leaderless group discussions on topics of importance to the self and in the community with a group of adolescents. *M.A. 1949 London, Institute of Education*

Higgins, A. J. B.
Studies in the vocabulary and syntax of the *Expositio Evangelii secundum Lucam* of Saint Ambrose. *M.A. 1937 Wales*

Higgins, A. J. B.
Tatian's *Diatessaron*: introductory studies, with a portion of the Arabic version. *Ph.D. 1945 Manchester*

Higgins, B. H.
The psychological factor in economic theory. *M.Sc. 1935 London, School of Economics and Political Science*

Higgins, D.
England and the Bourbon restoration. *M.A. 1922 Liverpool*

Higgins, H.
A contribution to the study of early invasions of Wales. *M.A. 1921 Liverpool*

Higgins, L. S.
Changes in the sand dune coasts of south Wales, with special reference to an investigation in the Newton-Merthyr Mawr area. *M.A. 1932 Wales*

Higgins, S. E.
Théophile Gautier: critique d'art. *M.A. 1947 Belfast*

Higginson, J. H.
The dame schools of Great Britain. *M.A. 1939 Leeds*

Higginson, J. H.
An experimental investigation of the musical response of school-children. *M.Ed. 1935 Leeds*

Higham, F. M. G.
The principal secretaries of state under the earlier Stuarts. *Ph.D. 1921 Manchester*

Highet, J.
Moral authority: an examination of external and internal authority in morals. *D.Phil. 1947 Oxford*

Highfield, H.
Some psychological characteristics of educationally retarded children. *M.A. 1935 London, University College*

Highfield, M. E.
The diagnostic significance of the Terman-Merrill scale. *M.A. 1945 London, University College and London, Institute of Education*

Highmore, G.
A factorial analysis of athletic ability preparatory to the formation of a series of prognostic tests. *Ph.D. 1949 London, Institute of Education*

Hight, G. A.
A biographical study of the western Icelandic sagas, giving a full account of the lives of the principal characters, with genealogical tables showing their descent from the first settlers. *B.Litt. 1918 Oxford*

Higson, C. W. J.
La Passiun de Seint Edmund (Gonville and Caius College ms. 435). *Ph.D. 1937 Cambridge*

Hildburgh, W. L.
Medieval Spanish enamels. *Ph.D. 1937 London, University College*

Hildebrandt, F.
Gospel and humanitarianism. *Ph.D. 1941 Cambridge*

Hildyard, M. O.
A study of the literary criticism of John Gibson Lockhart, with a bibliography of his critical writings. *Ph.D. 1928 London*

Hiley, R. W.
1. The atonement. 2. The inspiration of the Scriptures. *B.D. & D.D. 1885 Oxford*

Hill, A.
La vie de saint Jean l'aumônier. *M.A. 1936 Sheffield*

Hill, A.
The women of Sophocles and Aeschylus. *M.A. 1910 London*

Hill, A. B.
A physiological and economic study of the diets of workers in rural areas as compared with those of workers resident in urban districts. *Ph.D. 1926 London*

Hill, A. H.
The influence of Roman satire on English literature. *M.A. 1910 Birmingham*

Hill, A. S. H.
The moderate Royalists and Puritans, and the conception of sovereignty in England prior to the Civil War. *Ph.D. 1933 London, School of Economics and Political Science*

Hill, B.
An index significationum to the Anglo-Saxon gloss to the Lindisfarne Gospels. *M.A. 1949 Birmingham*

Hill, B. M.
The growth of the Russian psychological novel. *Ph.D. 1931 London, King's College*

Hill, D. A.
A geographical interpretation of the land utilization of the Belfast region. *M.A. 1948 London, External Degree*

Hill, D. J.
The religion of Apuleius. *M.A. 1940 Leeds*

Hill, E. W.
The treatment of the idea of value in recent philosophical literature. *M.A. 1921 Liverpool*

Hill, G. B.
Selection for commercial courses in junior technical schools. *M.Ed. 1950 Manchester*

Hill, H. S. McC.
The growth and development of international law in Africa. *D.C.L. 1900 Oxford*

Hill, J.
A critical study of Quintilian's system of language teaching. *M.A. 1930 Sheffield*

Hill, L. G.
A study of the attitude of children to the house system with particular reference to its incentive value in the secondary modern school. *M.Ed. 1950 Nottingham*

Hill, M. C.
A study, mainly from royal Wardrobe accounts, of the nature and organization of the King's messenger service from the reign of John to that of Edward III inclusive. *M.A. 1939 London, Royal Holloway College*

Hill, N. V. L.
The social and literary environment of Byron's *Don Juan. M.A. 1946 Birmingham*

Hill, N. V. L.
Some aspects of the style of John Webster: a study of *The Duchess of Malfi* and *The White Devil. Ph.D. 1949 Birmingham*

Hill, P.
Government aid to the cultivator in Egypt. *M.Com.* *1933 Birmingham*

Hill, R. L.
The attitude of the Tory Party to labour questions, 1832-46. *B.Litt. 1928 Oxford*

Hill, R. M. T.
Ecclesiastical letter-books of the thirteenth century. *B.Litt. 1936 Oxford*

Hill, T.
The phonetics of a Nyanja speaker, with particular reference to the phonological structure of the word. *M.A. 1948 London, School of Oriental and African Studies*

Hill, T. E.
Karl Heim's conception of the approach to knowledge of God. *Ph.D. 1937 Edinburgh*

Hillard, A. E.
1. Certain Jewish modes of thought and teaching: their influence on the form in which truth is presented in the Gospels. 2. How far and in what sense is it possible to maintain such a distinction as that implied in the phase 'essential doctrine'?. *B.D. & D.D. 1907 Oxford*

Hillary, H. C.
The development of education in Barnsley in the nineteenth century, prior to direct state intervention. *M.A. 1941 Sheffield*

Hillī, A. H. al- *see* Al-Hillī, A. H.

Hilliard, F. H.
The nature of man in the living religions. *Ph.D. 1944 London, King's College*

Hilliard, H. D.
Greek and Judaistic individualism in the Hellenistic age, in their similarity and contrast, and their relation to the concept of the Messiah. *M.A. 1932 Bristol*

Hillman, H. V.
The application of scientific method to the teaching of chemistry. *M.A. 1947 London, Institute of Education*

Hills, A. C.
Some early Tudor dialogues, referred to by Sir Thomas More in his controversial works; with an account of Bishop Barlow. *M.A. 1938 London, King's College*

Hilton, R. H.
Aspects of the economic development of some Leicestershire estates in the fourteenth and fifteenth centuries. *D.Phil. 1940 Oxford*

Hilton, R. J.
Word order in Old Provençal, with special reference to Flamenca and the poems of Bertran de Born. *B.Litt. 1938 Oxford*

Hilton, W. G.
The ethical ideas of John Locke and their antecedents. *M.A. 1929 Manchester*

Hilton-Simpson, M. W.
Medicine among the Berbers of the Aurés. *B.Sc. 1921 Oxford*

Himmelweit, H. T.
The study of temperament of neurotic persons by means of aspiration tests. *Ph.D. 1945 London, Maudsley Hospital*

Hinchley, A.
The influence of environment on the fen children of Holland, Lincs. *M.Ed. 1939 Durham*

Hinchliffe, A.
The development of Marlowe's attitude towards aspiration. *M.A. 1948 Manchester*

Hinde, G.
A calendar of the register of Cuthbert Tunstall, Bishop of Durham. *Ph.D. 1933 London, External Degree*

Hinde, R. S. E.
Humanitarian and religious elements in early English prison reform, 1773-1835. *B.Phil. 1948 Oxford*

Hinden, R.
Palestine: an experiment in colonization. *Ph.D. 1939 London, External Degree*

Hindia, M. E. A. A.
Cotton production in the Nile basin outside Egypt. *M.A. 1943 London, School of Economics and Political Science*

Hindmarsh, N. M.
Psychological aspects of advertising in war. *M.Sc. 1943 London, King's College*

Hindmarsh, N. M.
The regulation of wages in England under the Statute of Artificers. *Ph.D. 1932 London, External Degree*

Hinds, H. E. G.
The religious philosophy of Samuel Taylor Coleridge. *Ph.D. 1935 Edinburgh*

Hindshaw, W.
The attitude of society towards the young since the Industrial Revolution. *M.Ed. 1920 Manchester*

Hines, H. J.
Oscillation of attention: an enquiry into the effect of the degree of oscillation of ambiguous figures of varying degrees of meaning. *M.Sc. 1935 London, University College*

Hingley, G. C.
Shakespeare's debt to classical antiquity. *M.A. 1912 Birmingham*

Hinnebusch, W. A.
Studies in thirteenth century English Dominican history. *D.Phil. 1939 Oxford*

Hinton, E. M.
A biography of Barnabe Riche. *B.Litt. 1928 Oxford*

Hinton, J.
Jean-Alexandre Buchon and his relations with England. *M.A. 1928 London*

Hinton, W. J.
Commercial fluctuations and currency disturbances of the seventeenth century. *M.A. 1915 Wales*

Hipkin, G. M.
The social and economic condition of the Holland division of Lincolnshire from 1642 to 1660. *B.Litt. 1930 Oxford*

Hipkins, C. H.
Wordsworth and his influence upon English poetry. *M.A. 1916 Birmingham*

Hipkins, J. C.
The historical play in the age of Elizabeth. *M.A. 1910 Birmingham*

Hird, J. H.
Examen de vocabulaire des *Travailleurs de la mer*. *M.A. 1925 Leeds*

Hirsch, D. von
British opinion in regard to Austria (1844 to 1867). *Ph.D. 1946 Cambridge*

Hirsch, W.
Rabbinic ideas of the soul. *Ph.D. 1946 London, External Degree*

Hirschberg, O. Helmer- *see* Helmer-Hirschberg, O.

Hirschwald, H.
Karl Barth's conception of grace and its place in his theology. *D.Phil. 1945 Oxford*

Hirst, A. J. C.
The law of negligence, with particular reference to children. *LL.M. 1929 Leeds*

Hirst, E. W.
The doctrine of conscience in British philosophy. *B.Sc. 1908 Oxford*

Hirst, E. W.
The doctrine of conscience in British philosophy. *M.A. 1908 London*

Hirst, M.
The position of the soul and its relation to the ideas in Plato's metaphysic. *M.A. 1912 London*

Hirst, M. E.
The recent controversy over the ideal theory of Plato. *M.A. 1911 Birmingham*

Hiscock, P. R.
Some problems connected with the influence of the freedmen upon the civil service under Claudius. *M.A. 1947 Reading*

Hitch, T. K.
The question of personnel in a socialized industry. *Ph.D. 1937 London, School of Economics and Political Science*

Hitchcock, E. V.
The *Donet* by Reginald Pecock, collated with the *Poore mennis myrrour*. *Ph.D. 1924 London*

Hitchcock, F. R. M.
Irenaeus of Lugdunum. *Litt.D. 1949 Dublin, Trinity College*

Hitchcock, R. W.
A history of Charity School education and a statistical survey of some measures of educational growth. *Ph.D. 1938 London, King's College*

Hitchcock, R. W.
A statistical study of the growth of charity schools. *M.A. 1933 London, Institute of Education*

Hitchens, A. C.
The persistence of the romantic spirit in modern French poetry. *M.A. 1938 London, King's College*

Hitchens, A. C.
The romantic element in Rostand, with special reference to *Cyrano de Bergerac* and *Chantecler*. *M.A. 1927 Manchester*

Hjort, G.
Piers Plowman as a work of moral theology. *Ph.D. 1932 Cambridge*

Hla, B.
The automatization of voluntary movements. *Ph.D. 1934 London, King's College*

Ho, T. I.
Ancient and modern educational theory in China. *Ph.D. 1936 London, Institute of Education*

Hoare, A. D. M.
The works of Morris and of Yeats in relation to early saga literature. *Ph.D. 1930 Cambridge*

Hoare, A. D. M.
The works of William Morris in relation to the Norse sagas. *M.Litt. 1927 Cambridge*

Hoare, A. M.
Nicholas Ferrar, with special reference to the *Story books of Little Gidding*. *M.A. 1924 London*

Hoballah, M. F.
Spinoza's conception of human individuality. *Ph.D. 1943 London, University College*

Hobby, B. F.
The testing of aptitude for foreign languages. *M.A. 1942 Birmingham*

Hobhouse, W.
1. Eternal life in relation to the Incarnation. 2. The idea of the Church in the Gospels. *B.D. & D.D. 1918 Oxford*

Hobson, C. K.
The export of capital. *D.Sc. 1914 London*

Hockey, S. L.
The economic geography of Gloucestershire. *M.A. 1935 Bristol*

Hodcroft, F. W.
The language of the *Cronica de Morea*. *M.A. 1950 Manchester*

Hodge, A. J.
Prayer and its psychology. *Ph.D. 1930 London, External Degree*

Hodge, C. E.
The Abbey of St. Albans under John of Whethamstede. *Ph.D. 1933 Manchester*

Hodge, H. H.
Contribution to the study of the life of Thomas Becket, with special reference to the mss. of the poem *De Sancto Thoma, archiepiscopo cantuariensi*. *M.A. 1923 London*

Hodge, J. G.
The life and works of Francis Thompson. *M.A. 1936 Wales*

Hodge, S. E. J.
An analysis of dramatic speech in English literature before 1550. *M.A. 1947 London, Birkbeck College*

Hodges, H. A.
A critical examination of Dilthey's theory of the historical and social studies only. *D.Phil. 1932 Oxford*

Hodges, T. M.
History of Port of Cardiff in relation to its hinterland with special reference to the years 1830-1914. *M.Sc. 1946 London, External Degree*

Hodgett, G. A. F.
The dissolution of the monasteries in Lincolnshire. *M.A. 1947 London, External Degree*

Hodgetts, C. W.
The old English gild system. *M.A. 1941 Leeds*

Hodgkins, W.
Some consideration of the causes of defects in the rhythm of speech. *M.A. 1938 Manchester*

Hodgkinson, L. A.
The administration of the Earl of Leicester in the United Provinces. *M.A. 1925 Liverpool*

Hodgkiss, F. D.
Robert Hallum. *M.A. 1931 Manchester*

Hodgson, E.
An edition of three tragedies by Nathaniel Lee: *Sophonisba, The Rival Queeens, Theodosius*; with bibliographical and critical introduction and notes. *M.A. 1947 Leeds*

Hodgson, F. W.
The reorganization of an independent school. *M.A. 1950 Birmingham*

Hodgson, H. B.
The growth, development and modern functions of the county borough of Bradford. *M.A. 1939 Leeds*

Hodgson, H. B.
The use and value of folklore in the teaching of geography. *M.Ed. 1935 Leeds*

Hodgson, J. S.
The movements for shorter hours, 1840-75. *D.Phil. 1940 Oxford*

Hodgson, L. M.
The distribution of woodland, present and past, in the Nant Ffrancon Valley, and other parts of Caernarvonshire. *M.Sc. 1933 Wales*

Hodgson, P.
An edition, from the manuscripts, of some of the prose pieces which have been attributed to the author of the *Cloud of unknowing* with an introduction and notes. *B.Litt. 1934 Oxford*

Hodgson, P.
An edition from the manuscripts of the *Cloud of Unknowing*, with an introduction, notes, and glossary. *D.Phil. 1936 Oxford*

Hodgson, S. E.
The suppression of chantries in England. *M.A. 1931 Leeds*

Hodnett, D. K.
Suggestions concerning the date and authorship of the *Modus Tenendi Parliamentum*. *M.A. 1918 Bristol*

Hoernle, R. F. A.
Modern theories of the will. *B.Sc. 1907 Oxford*

Hogan, A. J.
The liturgical origin and the didactic purpose of the medieval drama. *Ph.D. 1928 Cambridge*

Hogan, C. A.
Some modern theories of perception. *B.Litt. 1931 Oxford*

Hogan, E. A. *see* Devlin, F. T.

Hogan, J. J.
An investigation into the history of the use of English in Ireland in medieval times, with special reference to the nature of the dialects and the influence of standard English. *B.Litt. 1926 Oxford*

Hogan, J. J.
Romantic poets and language. *M.A. 1923 National University of Ireland*

Hogan, M.
A historical sketch of the curricula of secondary schools. *M.A. 1944 National University of Ireland*

Hogan, W. C.
The housing movement in Ireland. *M.Econ.Sc. 1942 National University of Ireland*

Hogan, W. J.
Prose works of James Stephens. *M.A. 1949 National University of Ireland*

Hogarth, A. H.
The present position of the housing problem in and around London. *D.M. 1908 Oxford*

Hogarth, O. J.
Exegeses of: Ephesians i.1; iv.4; iv.25. *D.D. 1922 Oxford*

Hogbin, H. I. P.
The maintenance of order in Oceania. *M.Sc. 1931 London, School of Economics and Political Science*

Hogg, H. W.
Problems suggested by the names and traditions of the Iraelitish tribes. *B.Litt. 1904 Oxford*

Hogg, P. L.
Currency and banking developments in the French overseas Empire, 1939-1945. *Ph.D. 1947 London, School of Economics and Political Science*

Hogg, P. L.
The problems of the Bank of England and the Federal Reserve System since 1927. *M.Sc. 1935 London, School of Economics and Political Science*

Hogg, W. H.
The Rainfall régimes of the Western United States of America. *M.Sc. 1938 London, University College*

Hoggart, H. R.
The impact of politics on literature in the reign of Queen Anne. *M.A. 1940 Leeds*

Hoggarth, N. R.
The relative values of certain individual and group methods used in practice periods in the teaching of elementary mathematics. *M.A. 1938 London, Institute of Education*

Holbrooke, S. W. B.
Argument for the resurrection. 2. Infant baptism. *B.D. 1907 Oxford*

Holbrooke, S. W. B.
Expositions of St. John i.1-13; vi.70-71; ix.15-17. *D.D. 1913 Oxford*

Holden, C. G.
Imperial subventions towards services administered by local authorities in England and Wales. *M.Com. 1925 Birmingham*

Holden, G. H.
Edmond Rostand et son oeuvre dramatique. *M.A. 1922 Birmingham*

Holden, G. R.
Loans and financial reconstruction in Austria. *B.Litt. 1934 Oxford*

Holden, K. H.
Judicial proceedings in Cambridgeshire under the Dictum of Kenilworth. *M.A. 1929 Manchester*

Holder, E.
Les interprétations critiques de la littérature anglaise en France pendant le Second Empire. *M.A. 1928 Leeds*

Holding, G. E.
The structure and scenic arrangements of the Greek theatre. *M.A. 1907 Wales*

Holdsworth, H.
A social and economic history of the Higlands of Scotland from the Revolution of 1689 to the Forty-five. *M.A. 1936 Leeds*

Holdsworth, L.
Remedial reading for dull senior boys. *M.Ed. 1939 Leeds*

Holgate, G.
A short history of the growth of Redcliffe. *M.A. 1934 Bristol*

Holgate, H. C. F.
Bank accounting: an examination and comparison of the accounting systems of the commercial banks in Great Britain and certain other European countries, with brief reference to the history of the matter in England. *Ph.D. 1938 London, External Degree*

Holland, J. J.
Combined agricultural and literary education in Ireland, 1765-1865. *Ph.D. 1926 National University of Ireland*

Holland, J. M.
Shore dwellers of ancient Ireland. *M.A. 1912 National University of Ireland*

Holland, T. R.
Education in British Somaliland. *M.A. 1949 Reading*

Hollas, H.
A study of climatic correlations, with special reference to the Indian monsoon, based upon a review of conditions in abnormal seasons. *M.A. 1933 Manchester*

Holleman, W. J.
A study of the rules of private international law relating to the transfer and acquisition of rights in movable property, *inter vivos*, with the exception of bankruptcy. *B.Litt. 1924 Oxford*

Holliday, L. A.
Merioneth, part 33 of the *Land of Britain*: the final report of the land utilization survey. *Ph.D. 1948 London, King's College*

Hollings, J. E.
Matthew Arnold: a study of his influence on secondary school curricula. *M.A. 1931 Birmingham*

Hollingworth, G. E.
The influence of the morality play upon the regular Elizabethan drama. *M.A. 1915 London*

Hollingworth, K. M.
Experimental investigations in the study of heat in the eighteenth century. *M.Sc. 1948 London, University College*

Hollis, A. M.
The relations between the Roman Government and Christianity down to the end of the second century. *B.D. 1931 Oxford*

Hollis, A. W.
The personal relationship in teaching. *M.A. 1935 Birmingham*

Hollis, F. J.
The archaeology of Herod's Temple: incorporating a commentary on the tractate *Middoth*. *D.D. 1931 London, King's College*

Holloway, C. J.
Language and intelligence. *D.Phil. 1947 Oxford*

Holloway, H.
The Byzantine liturgies. *M.A. 1918 Belfast*

Holloway, H.
The Norwegian rite: a study of the Byzantine liturgy. *D.D. 1934 Belfast*

Holloway, J. L.
The prelude to the Great Trek. *D.Sc. 1917 London*

Holloway, O. E.
Matthew Arnold's debt to Sainte-Beuve and Renan. *B.Litt. 1930 Oxford*

Hollowood, A. B.
Industrial geography of north Staffordshire. *M.Sc. 1940 London, External Degree*

Holly, C. C.
Plato and fine art. *M.A. 1942 National University of Ireland*

Holman, E. W.
A thesis on the function of the municipal secondary school, and schools of similar type, in the scheme of educational development and reform. *M.Ed. 1920 Manchester*

Holmes, A. M.
The position of women among the Romans. *M.A. 1932 London, University College*

Holmes, A. R.
Some effects of the slum clearance schemes of the London County Council. *M.Sc. 1947 London, School of Economics and Political Science*

Holmes, D. A.
Marketing research. *M.A. 1946 National University of Ireland*

Holmes, E.
Henry Vaughan: with a special study of his imagery. *B.Litt. 1928 Oxford*

Holmes, E.
Studies in the language of Milton: parts 1-2. *M.A. 1923 Liverpool*

Holmes, J.
British public opinion regarding Indian policy at the time of the mutiny. *M.A. 1936 London, Birkbeck College*

Holmes, J. M.
Contributions to Australian geography. *Ph.D. 1934 Glasgow*

Holmstrom, J. E.
The comparative economics of railways and roads for pioneer development abroad. *Ph.D. 1932 London, School of Economics and Political Science*

Holmyard, E. J.
Rise and development of chemistry in medieval Islam. *M.Sc. 1925 Bristol*

Holmyard, E. J.
1. Work on the history of chemistry in medieval Islam. 2. Work on the teaching of chemistry in this country. *D.Litt. 1928 Bristol*

Holroyd, G. H.
Education for leisure in the elementary school. *M.A. 1941 Leeds*

Holroyde, H.
The relations of Great Britain and the United States of America during the Spanish-American War of 1898. *M.A. 1947 Sheffield*

Holt, B. *see* Smith, B.

Holt, J. F.
Some aspects of the social philosophy of Karl Marx. *B.Litt 1943 Dublin, Trinity College*

Holt, M. M.
The origins in Greece of some physical and astral theories of the early Stoics. *M.Litt. 1938 Cambridge*

Holt, R. V.
The life of Viscount Castlereagh, second Marquess of Londonderry. *B.Litt. 1910 Oxford*

Honey, M. E. D.
Study of the version of *Titus and Vespasian* contained in the ms. British Museum additional 10289. *M.A. 1907 London*

Honeybourne, M. B.
The extent and value of the lands in London and Southwark occupied by the religious houses (including the prebends of St. Paul's and St. Martin's le Grand), the parish churches and churchyards, and the inns of the abbots and bishops, before the dissolution of the monasteries. *M.A. 1930 London, Bedford College*

Honeyman, P. A. W.
State regulation of labour and industry in New South Wales. *M.A. 1922 Manchester*

Honniball, V. F.
Some aspects of Shakespeare's philosophy of life. *M.A. 1911 Birmingham*

Hood, J. C. F.
Icelandic church saga. *D.D. 1943 Durham*

Hood, L. J. S.
Belize, a tropical port and its hinterland. *M.A. 1935 London, Birkbeck College*

Hook, R.
Richard Graves (1715-1804). *M.A. 1935 London, King's College*

Hooke, B. G. E.
A third study of the English skull, with special reference to the Faringdon Street crania (with a subsidiary paper). *M.Sc. 1927 London*

Hooker, E. M.
The Greek altar: its origins and its forms and functions down to 146 B.C. (the literary and archaeological evidence). *M.A. 1947 London, University College and London, Birkbeck College*

Hooker, G. T. W.
Public festivals in Athenian life: the place of Attic public festivals in the lives of the people of Athens from the sixth to the fourth century B.C. *M.A. 1947 London, University College and London, Birkbeck College*

Hooker, S. M.
Literary criticism in the plays of Aristophanes. *M.A. 1913 London*

Hoon, B. E.
The organisation of the English customs system, 1696 to 1786. *Ph.D. 1934 London, King's College*

Hoon, P. W.
The soteriology of John Wesley. *Ph.D. 1936 Edinburgh*

Hooper, A. D.
The activities of the League of Nations in relation to the traffic of opium and other dangerous drugs, in particular, emphasizing the illicit traffic as a significant factor in the situation. *M.A. 1936 Wales*

Hooper, A. G.
An edition of *Hrómundar saga Greipssonar*. *M.A. 1930 Leeds*

Hooper, A. G.
An edition of the *Bragða Olvis* saga and rimur. *Ph.D. 1932 Leeds*

Hooper, C. W. J.
Music in elementary education. *M.A. 1942 Leeds*

Hooper, G. A. T. F.
The Wey River Basin: a study of human settlement and economic development in the valley, with particular reference to present day conditions. *M.A. 1935 London, Birkbeck College*

Hooper, H. M.
The development and a criticism of the theory and practice of education as found in imaginative literature of the nineteenth century and after. *M.A. 1920 London*

Hooper, J. P.
Poetical works of Samuel Daniel. *M.A. 1938 National University of Ireland*

Hooper, S. E.
Degrees of truth and reality. *M.A. 1918 London*

Hooper, W.
The law of illegitimacy. *LL.D. 1911 London*

Hooper, W.
1. On creation. 2. On the person of Christ. *B.D. & D.D. 1887 Oxford*

Hooson, J.
The political and social organization of Gaul under the Roman Empire. *M.A. 1912 Wales*

Hooton, E. A.
The pre-Hellenistic stage in the evolution of the literary art at Rome. *B.Litt. 1913 Oxford*

Hooton, F. G.
The economics of guaranteed trade. *D.Phil. 1949 Oxford*

Hope, H.
The development of education in Bury to 1870. *M.Ed. 1933 Manchester*

Hope, L. P.
The significance of Canossa. *Ph.D. 1931 Edinburgh*

Hope, N. V.
Ministerial stipends in the Church of Scotland from 1560 to 1633. *Ph.D. 1944 Edinburgh*

Hope, R. B.
Dr. Thomas Percival, a medical pioneer and social reformer, 1740-1804. *M.A. 1947 Manchester*

Hope, R. S.
Profits in British industry from 1924 to 1935: an investigation into the profits made by certain public companies in Great Britain in the years from 1924 to 1935. *D.Phil. 1949 Oxford*

Hopf, C. L. R. A.
Martin Bucer and the English Reformation. *D.Phil. 1943 Oxford*

Hopferwieser, R. A.
Leisure as a planning problem, with special reference to the Birmingham conurbation. *M.Com. 1950 Birmingham*

Hopkins, A. W.
Anglo-Russian relations and the formation of the Anglo-Russian Agreement, 1903-1907. *M.A. 1937 Wales*

Hopkins, E. A.
The stoicism of Lucius Annaeus Seneca, with special reference to ethics. *M.A. 1943 London, Bedford College*

Hopkins, J.
Charles Reade: his methods, characterizations, and place in English literature. *M.A. 1929 Wales*

Hopkins, K. D.
Punishment in schools. *M.A. 1938 Birmingham*

Hopkins, P. C.
Unacknowledged motivations in some social movements. *Ph.D. 1927 London*

Hopkins, T. J. E.
The idea of the supernatural and of the transcendent in primitive and modern theistic thought. *M.A. 1934 Liverpool*

Hopkinson, J. H.
1. The relation of the Psalms to Christ. 2. The resurrection of Jesus Christ. *B.D. & D.D. 1909 Oxford*

Hopkirk, D. S.
Archbishop Leighton: his characteristic position as theologian and ecclesiastic. *B.Litt. 1926 Oxford*

Hopkirk, D. S.
A study of the accommodation movements between Presbytery and Episcopacy in the seventeenth century in Scotland, England and Ireland. *Ph.D. 1946 Edinburgh*

Hopp, M.
Exposé des données actuelles de la question des idées religieuses de Montaigne. *M.A. 1926 London*

Hoppe, H. R.
John Wolf, printer and publisher, 1579-1601; a bibliographical survey. *M.A. 1933 London, King's College*

Hopper, R. J.
Athenian foreign trade in the fifth and fourth centuries B.C. *Ph.D. 1936 Cambridge*

Hopps, L. R.
The animal story in German literature from the *Ecbasis Captivi* to Goethe's *Reineke Fuchs*. *B.Litt. 1940 Oxford*

Hopwood, P. G. S.
The religious experience of the Church of the Apostolic Age. *B.Litt. 1925 Oxford*

Hopwood, P. S. S.
The religious experience of the primitive Church. *Ph.D. 1935 Glasgow*

Hora, F. R. H.
The treatment of problems of heredity before the twentieth century. *M.Sc. 1926 London*

Hora, L. E. D. H. de *see* Horanszky de Hora, L. E. D.

Horanszky de Hora, L. E. D.
Researches in the history of the rights of the subject in England. *Ph.D. 1927 Aberdeen*

Horden, J. R. B.
The story of *Argalus and Parthenia*. *B.Litt. 1946 Oxford*

Horgan, J.
Comedy in the Irish theatre; its genius. *M.A. 1936 National University of Ireland*

Horgan, J.
Metaphysical analogy. *Ph.D. 1938 National University of Ireland*

Horgan, J. D.
The psychological study of reasoning. *M.A. 1923 National University of Ireland*

Hornby-Priddin, D. M.
The art of the dance in French literature from Theophile Gautier to Paul Valéry. *Ph.D. 1948 London, Bedford College*

Horne, C. J.
Life and works of Dr. Wm. King of Christ Church (1663-1712). *B.Litt. 1940 Oxford*

Horne, D. H. T.
A comparison of the free topic method with the experiment demonstration method of teaching science in a senior school. *M.A. 1942 London, Institute of Education*

Horne, R. E.
A study of the ideas of Paul Claudel, as expressed in his plays and poems. *M.A. 1939 Wales*

Horner, F. B.
Export demand: an attempt to measure the price and income elasticities of demand for Australian exports in 1938. *Ph.D. 1948 London, School of Economics and Political Science*

Hornik, M. P.
Policy of Baron von Holstein. *D.Phil. 1942 Oxford*

Hornik, T. M.
The child's environment and its influence on the development of character and the origin of the neuroses. *B.Sc. 1943 Oxford*

Hornsby, H. M.
A commentary on the subject matter of the *Noctes Atticae* of Aulus Gellius, Bk. I. *Ph.D. 1931 Dublin, Trinity College*

Hornsby, J. T.
John Glas: a study of the origins, development and influence of the Glasite Movement. *Ph.D. 1936 Edinburgh*

Horrocks, A. J.
Thomas Hardy's analysis of human nature: a psychological study of the Wessex novels. *Ph.D. 1931 London, External Degree*

Horrocks, J. L.
Livian usage with respect to sequence of tenses in *oratio obliqua*. *M.A. 1937 Liverpool*

Horrwitz, W. B. P.
Legal problems of limited companies in English and German law, with references to American law. *D.Phil. 1946 Oxford*

Horsefield, J. K.
The evolution and significance of the principles of the Bank Charter Act of 1844. *B.A. 1937 Bristol*

Horsefield, J. K.
Some aspects of Bank of England policy, 1780-1850. *M.A. 1949 Bristol*

Horsfall, L. F.
British relations with the Spanish colonies in the Caribbean 1713-1739. *M.A. 1935 London, King's College*

Horsfall, L. F.
The free port system in the British West Indies, 1766-1815. *Ph.D. 1939 London, King's College*

Horsfall, T. E. P.
A study of Milton's reputation at home and abroad between the years 1660-1714. *B.Litt. 1929 Oxford*

Horsfield, A. E.
Henry VII's relations with Scotland and Ireland, 1485-98. *Litt.D. 1932 Dublin, Trinity College*

Horsfield, K. A.
The influence of the French novelists on Theodor Fontane, with reference to the German novel of the latter part of the nineteenth century. *M.A. 1933 Manchester*

Horst, S. T. van der. *see* Van der Horst, S. T.

Horton, H.
North Lancashire: its economic condition in the thirteenth and fourteenth centuries. *M.A. 1949 Manchester*

Horton, J. W.
The relations of Sir Robert Peel with the Crown, 1837-46. *B.Litt. 1950 Oxford*

Horwill, G.
Price determination under monopoly and competition: a theory of structural integration. *M.Com. 1948 Birmingham*

Hoskins, I. H.
An approach to the study of education in the light of an evolutionary psychology. *M.A. 1948 London, Institute of Education*

Hoskins, V. H.
Vocational guidance and selection, with special reference to the industries and occupations of Sheffield. *Ph.D. 1926 Sheffield*

Hoskins, W. G.
The ownership and occupation of the land in Devonshire, 1650-1800. *Ph.D. 1938 London, External Degree*

Hoskins, W. G.
The rise and decline of the serge industry in the southwest of England, with special reference to the eighteenth century. *M.Sc. 1929 London*

Hotblack, K.
Chatham's colonial policy. *D.Sc. 1917 London*

Hou, J. C.
An historical geography of Peiping. *Ph.D. 1949 Liverpool*

Hou, S. T.
The currency and banking problems of China. *Ph.D. 1935 Liverpool*

Hou, T. D.
The political system in the U.S.S.R. *M.Sc. 1936 London, School of Economics and Political Science*

Houblon, T. H. A.
1. The unity of the Church. 2. The person and work of God the Holy Ghost. *B.D. & D.D. 1903 Oxford*

Houghton, A. M.
The use of plant-motives in marginalia of English illuminated manuscripts of the fourteenth and fifteenth centuries. *M.A. 1942 Manchester*

Houghton, C.
Household economics: its place in the scheme of national education. *M.Ed. 1918 Manchester*

Houghton, C.
The plays of Sean O'Casey. *M.A. 1942 Birmingham*

Houghton, E. J. W.
Expositions of St. Matthew v.17-48; I Corinthians xv.1-11; I Peter i.11-ii.17. *D.D. & B.D. 1909 Oxford*

Houghton, S. M.
The civil administration of Ireland, 1801-1846. *M.A. 1924 Manchester*

Houlihan, C.
William Cowper and the eighteenth century. *M.A. 1949 National University of Ireland*

Hourd, M. J.
The literary criticism of Richard Hurd (1719-1808). *B.Litt. 1932 Oxford*

Hourihane, M.
History of Irish fisheries. *M.A. 1927 National University of Ireland*

House, W. J.
1. Christus condemnator. 2. The Johannine idea of life. *B.D. and D.D. 1924 Oxford*

Houseman, J. W.
The government and growth of the parish of Halifax, 1760-1848. *M.A. 1928 Liverpool*

Houseman, R. E.
David Stow, his life and work, 1793-1864. *M.Ed. 1938 Manchester*

Houseman, R. E.
The evolution of British public opinion with regard to Germany as reflected in the press and journals of opinion between 1895 and 1903. *M.A. 1934 London, Birkbeck College*

Housley, H.
The development of the felt hat manufacturing industry of Lancashire and Cheshire. *M.A. 1929 Manchester*

Houston, G. A. C.
The evolution of the historical drama in Germany during the first half of the nineteenth century. *M.A. 1919 London*

Houston, J. M.
Distribution of settlements in the Solway Firth Plain. *B.Sc. 1946 Oxford*

Houston, J. M.
The social geography of the Huerta of Valencia. *D.Phil. 1950 Oxford*

Hovell, E. M. W.
Arthur Golding's translation of Ovid's *Metamorphoses. M.A. 1909 London*

Howard, B. S.
A study of aptitude for engineering drawing at the age of 13, with reference to the selection of entrants to technical schools. *M.A. 1945 London, Institute of Education*

Howard, C. C.
Speed and accuracy as related to intelligence and perseverance. *Ph.D. 1932 London, University College*

Howard, D.
The English activities on the north coast of Australia in the first half of the nineteenth century. *M.A. 1924 London*

Howard, H. E.
The genesis of the Crimean War. *M.A. 1932 London, King's College*

Howard, J.
The nature and methods of parliamentary control over foreign policy in France since the signature of the Treaty of Versailles, 28 June 1919. *B.Litt. 1938 Oxford*

Howard, J. H.
Phases of poor law policy and administration, 1760-1834. *M.A. 1921 Liverpool*

Howard, T. E.
Toryism from 1745 to 1761. *M.A. 1939 Liverpool*

Howard, W. N.
An investigation into the relative value of methods of teaching science in selective central schools. *M.Sc. 1930 Sheffield*

Howard-Robinson, M. F.
Thomas Rotherham, Archbishop of York and Chancellor of England: his life and times. *M.A. 1940 Sheffield*

Howarth, A. T.
Charles Rennie Mackintosh and the secessionist movement in architecture. *Ph.D. 1949 Glasgow*

Howarth, B. L.
A critical study of the spellings of the two oldest French Psalters: 1. The Oxford, or Montebourg Psalter, 2. The Cambridge, or Canterbury Psalter. *M.A. 1936 Manchester*

Howarth, R. G.
An edition of the poems of James Shirley as contained in the 1646 *Poems*, Bodl. ms. Rawl. Poet. 88 and B.M. Add. ms. 33998. *B.Litt. 1931 Oxford*

Howarth, W.
The German elements in the aesthetic of the age of Wordsworth; being studies in Coleridge's aesthetic and literary theory, and its relation to contemporary German thought. *Litt.D. 1928 Manchester*

Howarth, W.
Some aesthetic and psychological factors in the appreciation of poetry. *M.Ed. 1920 Manchester*

Howe, G. M.
The application of air photography to a study of the agricultural geography of northwest Cardiganshire. *M.Sc. 1949 Wales*

Howe, J. W. A.
The immutability of God. *B.D. 1948 Durham*

Howells, E. J.
Movements of mining population in the anthracite area of south Wales. *M.Sc. 1938 Wales*

Howells, G.
The place of the *Bhagavadgītā* in Indian thought. *B.Litt. 1906 Oxford*

Howells, W.
The development of algebraic notation up to the middle of the seventeenth century. *M.Sc. 1930 London*

Howells, W.
The development of mathematical notation from Wallis to John Bernoulli. *Ph.D. 1933 London, External Degree*

Howes, H. W.
The cult and pilgrimage of St. James of Compostela, Spain, and their effects on the life and thought of the people in the northwestern corner of Spain. *M.A. 1938 Wales*

Howes, H. W.
Santiago de Compostela, Galicia, Spain: an attempt to prove that it was a prehistoric settlement. *M.Sc. 1924 Wales*

Howes, W. H.
The functional aspects of the legend of St. James of Compostela. *Ph.D. 1934 London, School of Economics and Political Science*

Howie, D.
Aspects of personality: a study in the inter-correlation of certain estimates of personal qualities. *Ph.D. 1936 London, Institute of Education*

Howland, R. D.
Fabian thought and social change in England from 1884-1914. *Ph.D. 1942 London, School of Economics and Political Science*

Howlett, M. N.
The social life of 'the town' as represented by some of the Elizabethan dramatists. *M.A. 1912 London*

Howrie, M. D.
1. The use of *exempla* in Middle High German Literature. 2. The legend of the Virgin as knight. *Ph.D. 1922 London*

Howse, E. M. F.
The Clapham Sect. *Ph.D. 1934 Edinburgh*

Hoy, J. D.
Adult education in England. *M.A. 1931 Birmingham*

Hoyle, M. L.
Judicial proceedings under the Dictum de Kenilworth, Buckingham. *M.A. 1928 Manchester*

Hoyle, M. L.
Judicial proceedings under the Dictum de Kenilworth. *Ph.D. 1934 Manchester*

Hoyle, S. H. S.
Labiche's technique of comedy. *M.A. 1935 Manchester*

Hozayyen, S. A. S.
The Arabian East and the Far East: their commercial and cultural relations during the Graeco-Roman and the Perso-Arabian periods. *M.A. 1933 Liverpool*

Hsia, C. L.
Treaty relations between China and Great Britain: a study of international law and diplomacy. *Ph.D. 1922 Edinburgh*

Hsiang, J. K.
Civil service discipline in modern democracies: an essay on the code of official conduct in England, U.S.A. and France. *M.Sc. 1938 London, School of Economics and Political Science*

Hsieh, J. T.
The state in relation to agriculture since 1929, with special reference to the agricultural policies of Great Britain and the United States of America. *B.Litt. 1938 Oxford*

Hsu, C. P.
Biography in the nineteenth century as illustrated by seven biographies of English men of letters. *B.Litt. 1947 Oxford*

Hsu, L. K.
The functioning of a north China family. *Ph.D. 1940 London, School of Economics and Political Science*

Hsü, T.-S.
Buddhist ideas in China on the origin of man and a translation of the *Yuen Fen Lun. B.Litt. 1925 Oxford*

Hsu, Y. N.
The British cotton industry in depression. *Ph.D. 1941 Cambridge*

Hu, P.
A study of the intelligence of Anglo-Chinese children. *M.Sc. 1936 London, University College*

Huang, G. C.
Distribution of the national income in the U.S.S.R. *M.A. 1932 Liverpool*

Huang, J.
A short history of Shakespearean production. *M.Litt. 1937 Cambridge*

Huang, T.
The legal status of the Chinese abroad. *Ph.D. 1936 London, School of Economics and Political Science*

Huband, D. I. E.
The early and late Morris. *M.A. 1924 Birmingham*

Hubbard, C. E. B.
A survey of religious life in Birmingham, 1790-1830. *M.A. 1935 Birmingham*

Hubbard, D. G. B.
Early Quaker education. *M.A. 1939 London, King's College*

Hubbuck, A. R.
John Byrom, F.R.S., 1691-1763: his religious thought and its relation to the movements of his time. *Ph.D. 1947 Edinburgh*

Huckin, H. R.
Exegeses of: Isaiah xxxii.8; St. Matthew v.48; St. Luke xv.7. *D.D. 1874 Oxford*

Huckin, H. R.
1. Illustrations of the doctrines of Christianity from natural religion. 2. The value of evidences in Christian theology. *B.D. 1874 Oxford*

Huddleston, J.
Industrial relations in the distributive trades, with special reference to the Co-operative Movement. *M.A. 1938 Leeds*

Hudson, H. L.
Adult education in the county of Cornwall: its development and present position. *M.A. 1946 London, King's College*

Hudson, J.
Political theory and educational practice. *M.A. 1941 Liverpool*

Hudson, M. E.
The political and ecclesiastical activities of Bishop Williams in relation to the history of his times. *M.A. 1926 London*

Hudson-Williams, A.
The syntax and language of Dracontius. *M.Litt. 1934 Cambridge*

Huehns, G.
Antinomianism in the period of English history, 1640-1660. *Ph.D. 1947 London, School of Economics and Political Science*

Hugessen, N. R. Knatchbull- *see* Knatchbull-Hugessen, N. R.

Huggins, K. H.
Studies in British urban geography. *Ph.D. 1940 Glasgow*

Hugh, E.
A comparison of the use of the subjunctive in Gautier d'Arras and Chrétien de Troyes. *M.A. 1919 Wales*

Hugh, R. L.
Annibyniaeth yng Ngorllewin Morgannwg, 1646-1816(Congregationalism in West Glamorgan, 1646-1816). *M.A. 1945 Wales*

Hughes, A. G.
An investigation into the comparative intelligence and attainments of Jewish and non-Jewish school-children. *Ph.D. 1928 London*

Hughes, A. G.
The practice value of games in arithmetic operations. *M.Ed. 1922 Leeds*

Hughes, A. W.
A study of the Abbe de Fénelon's treatise *De l'éducation des filles*, considered in relation to the educational ideas of his contemporaries. *M.A. 1944 Wales*

Hughes, B. E.
Women novelists before Jane Austen. *M.A. 1915 Wales*

Hughes, C. E.
Tendencies of seventeenth century thought as exhibited in the writings of Lord Halifax. *M.A. 1932 London, Bedford College*

Hughes, C. E.
Wales and piracy: a study in Tudor administration, 1500-1640. *M.A. 1937 Wales*

Hughes, C. F.
The development of the poor laws in Caernarvonshire and Anglesey, 1815-1914. *M.A. 1945 Wales*

Hughes, D.
A study of social and constitutional tendencies in the early years of Edward III, as illustrated more especially by the events connected with the ministerial enquiries of 1340, and the following years. *M.A. 1913 London*

Hughes, D. T.
Simon de Montfort and his times. *M.A. 1910 Wales*

Hughes, E.
The changes in the numbers of agricultural labourers and in their wages and efficiency during the past fifty years, and the causes of these changes, with special reference to Wales. *M.A. 1909 Wales*

Hughes, E.
A critical study of the writings of Thomas Edwards (Twm o'r Nant), 1737-1810. *M.A. 1942 Liverpool*

Hughes, E. B.
Châteaubriand's earliest critics in England, 1797-1822. *Ph.D. 1939 London, Queen Mary College*

Hughes, E. B.
Cromwell in French literature of the Restoration period, 1815-1830. *M.A. 1931 London, East London College*

Hughes, E. G.
Seneca's philosophy. *M.A. 1908 Birmingham*

Hughes, E. H.
Emotional development in young children. *Ph.D. 1934 London, Bedford College*

Hughes, E. R.
Walter Savage Landor as a satirist and controversialist in the spheres of law and religion. *M.A. 1949 Wales*

Hughes, E. W.
An analysis of the records of some 750 male probationers in the city of Coventry. *M.A. 1942 Birmingham*

Hughes, E. W.
The framing of the security chapters of the United Nations Charter, 1942-6. *B.Phil. 1947 Oxford*

Hughes, G.
The plays of W. Somerset Maugham. *M.A. 1939 Wales*

Hughes, G. H.
Bywyd a gwaith Iaco ab Dewi(The life and work of Iaco ab Dewi). *M.A. 1939 Wales*

Hughes, G. W.
The life and work of Alexander Knox, 1757-1831. *Ph.D. 1937 Edinburgh*

Hughes, G. W.
The social and economic status of the elementary school teacher in England, 1833-1870. *M.Ed. 1936 Manchester*

Hughes, H. C.
An essay introductory to the *De pauperie Salvatoris* of Richard Fitzralph, books v-vii. *Ph.D. 1928 Manchester*

Hughes, H. O.
Vocational aspects of education - elementary, secondary and technical. *M.A. 1933 Birmingham*

Hughes, I. A.
Prognostic tests for the selection of students for advanced courses in needlework. *M.A. 1935 London, Institute of Education*

Hughes, I. T.
A large scale survey of groups of pre-historic earthworks in central Wales and along the Welsh Border. *M.A. 1927 Wales*

Hughes, J.
The development of the study of the national language, literature and history in the educational system of Wales. *M.A. 1922 Wales*

Hughes, J. B. W.
Life and writings of Richard Taverner. *M.A. 1932 London, King's College*

Hughes, J. C.
Hebrew and Jewish sources of the *Qûran*. *M.A. 1909 Wales*

Hughes, J. R.
How far does Roman comedy represent Roman life and sentiment?. *M.A. 1907 Wales*

Hughes, J. V.
Les comédies-ballets de Molière. *M.A. 1947 Liverpool*

Hughes, L.
St. Jerome's Epistles. *B.D. & D.D. 1923, Oxford*

Hughes, M.
Society in French comedy from the death of Molière to 1715. *M.A. 1925 Wales*

Hughes, M. C.
Richard Baxter, man of letters. *M.A. 1935 Liverpool*

Hughes, M. D. A.
The history of religion in Wales from 1600 to 1640. *B.Litt. 1930 Oxford*

Hughes, O. R.
The history of Welsh orthography up to 1620. *M.A. 1905 Wales*

Hughes, R.
The effects of the Boer War on British diplomatic relations (1899-April, 1904). *M.A. 1941 Wales*

Hughes, R. E.
Aspects of Welsh lexicography in the nineteenth century, with special reference to the contribution of Daniel Silvan Evans. *M.A. 1941 Liverpool*

Hughes, R. E.
Bywyd a gwaith William Wynn, Llangynhafal(The life and work of William Wynn, Llangynhafal). *M.A. 1940 Wales*

Hughes, R. O.
The religious institutions of the Hebrews and Jews referred to in the Hexateuch, studied in themselves and as they represent the development of religious conceptions. *M.A. 1914 Wales*

Hughes, R. W.
Charles Baudelaire. *D.Litt. 1932 London, King's College*

Hughes, S. T.
Rationalisation in relation to the economic situation of the British motor industry. *M.Com. 1950 Birmingham*

Hughes, T. J.
A social study of the parish of Aberdaron in the Llŷn peninsula. *M.A. 1950 Wales*

Hughes, T. R.
A contribution to the history of elementary education in north Wales up to 1870, with special reference to national schools. *M.A. 1935 Liverpool*

Hughes, T. R.
A contribution to the history of elementary education in Manchester, up to 1870, with special reference to national schools. *M.Ed. 1937 Manchester*

Hughes, T. R.
The melancholy element in English poetry from Widsith to Chaucer. *M.A. 1928 Wales*

Hughes, T. R.
The London Magazine (1820-9). *B.Litt. 1931 Oxford*

Hughes, U. W.
A biographical sketch of Robert Burnell, with materials for his life. *B.Litt. 1936 Oxford*

Hughes, V. L.
Social survey of East Kent coalfield. *Ph.D. 1934 London, School of Economics and Political Science*

Hughes, W. D. F.
The doctrines of the Church and the ministry held by the principal Anglican and Continental reformers. *B.Litt. 1923 Oxford*

Hughes, W. E.
The treatment of Odysseus in Homeric and post-Homeric Greek poetry. *M.A. 1913 Wales*

Hughes, W. J.
Wales and the Welsh in English literature from the beginning of the sixteenth to the beginning of the nineteenth century. *M.A. 1919 Wales*

Hughes-Roberts, H.   *see* Roberts, H. Hughes-

Huie, W. P.
The theology of Thomas Chalmers. *Ph.D. 1949 Edinburgh*

Hulbert, N. F.
Historical survey of the Somerset and Bristol fairs. *M.A. 1935 Bristol*

Hull, A.
The financial basis of the established Church of England. *M.A. 1938 Leeds*

Hulme, C.
The text of the Fillingham *Otuel* with a thesis upon it (ms. additional 37492, British Museum). *M.A. 1922 London*

Hulme, H. M.
Dialect in Tudor drama. *M.A. 1937 London, Courtauld Institute of Art*

Hulme, H. M.
Studies in language mainly in relation to Derbyshire, Staffordshire and Shropshire from 1500 to 1700, from Church accounts. *Ph.D. 1947 London, External Degree*

Hulyalkar, S. G.
Aristotle's theory of perception. *M.A. 1939 London, University College*

Humber, R. L.
The political ideas of John C. Calhoun. *B.Litt. 1923 Oxford*

Humbert, H. F.
Hampton Court Conference. *Ph.D. 1940 Edinburgh*

Hume, E. G.
A study of backwardness in reading among London elementary school children. *M.A. 1926 London*

Humphreys, D.
Types of social life illustrated by the writings of Gerald of Wales. *B.Litt. 1936 Oxford*

Humphreys, D. W.
The genesis of the American system of vocational education. *M.A. 1936 London, King's College*

Humphreys, E. H.
The origin, ideal and early history of monachism. *M.A. 1925 Bristol*

Humphreys, E. O.
A summary of recent research bearing on the relation of social factors to the incidence of rheumatic diseases in childhood, with an analysis of new data bearing on the subject. *M.A. 1930 Liverpool*

Humphreys, G. S.
A biographical and literary study of Stephen Hawes, with special reference to the minor poems. *M.A. 1928 London*

Humphreys, K. A. C.
Operational methods in mathematics from Leibniz to Fourier. *M.Sc. 1949 London, External Degree*

Humphreys, K. W.
The provision of books in the centrally-organized religious orders before 1400. *B.Litt. 1949 Oxford*

Humphreys, R. A.
Lord Shelburne and British imperialism, 1763-83. *Ph.D. 1933 Cambridge*

Hunt, E. A.
The idea of the Deity in primitive thought. *M.A. 1939 Leeds*

Hunt, E. M. C.
The fall of paganism. *M.A. 1913 Birmingham*

Hunt, E. W.
The Pauline interpretation of history: an examination of Romans xi-xii. *B.D. 1946 Birmingham*

Hunt, F. H.
The philosophy of law of St. Thomas Aquinas. *Ph.D. 1942 Cambridge*

Hunt, H. J.
Socialism and romanticism in France, 1830-1848. *D.Phil. 1931 Oxford*

Hunt, J.
Medieval armour in Ireland, as exemplified on existing effigial monuments. *M.A. 1945 National University of Ireland*

Imper, A. D.
The economics of farm management in a section of Aberdeenshire. *Ph.D. 1928 Aberdeen*

Imrie, D. S. M.
Edinburgh Magazine: 1739-1826. *Ph.D. 1936 Saint Andrew's*

Inayatullah, S.
The influence of physical environment upon Arabian life and institutions. *Ph.D. 1932 London, School of Oriental and African Studies*

Ince, M. J.
Eighteenth century literary criticism up to Dr. Johnson, with particular reference to the criticism of Shakespeare, Milton and the metaphysical poets. *M.A. 1948 Manchester*

Indiramma, B.
A critical enquiry into adult education with some suggestions for its application to India. *M.Ed. 1930 Leeds*

Ineson, D. G.
The development of legislation relating to the powers of railway companies to charge for the carriage of merchandise traffic. *LL.D. 1923 Leeds*

Ing, C. M.
Metrical theory and practice in the Elizabethan lyric. *D.Phil. 1949 Oxford*

Inge, W. R.
Faith. *D.D. 1909 Cambridge*

Ingham, E.
1603-1685: Presbyterians and Independents, their relations to the government and its effect on their relations with one anothe. *M.A. 1935 Manchester*

Ingham, J. G.
An investigation into the relationship between memory and intelligence. *Ph.D. 1949 London, Institute of Psychiatry*

Ingham, J. K. B.
A geographical survey of the basin of the Warwickshire Stour. *M.Sc. 1938 Leeds*

Ingham, K.
The achievements of Christian missionaries in India, 1794-1833. *D.Phil. 1949 Oxford*

Ingle, F. T.
1. The place of education in the life of the ancient Hebrews. 2. St. Paul's ideal of labour. *B.D. 1923 Oxford*

Inglis, A.
James Gregory: a survey of his work in mathematical analysis. *Ph.D. 1933 Saint Andrew's*

Inglis, B.
Freedom of the press in Ireland 1784-1842. *Ph.D. 1950 Dublin, Trinity College*

Inglis, W. B.
The rise of the Scottish Chaucerians. *Ph.D. 1930 Glasgow*

Ingold, K. M.
Prométhée dans la littérature allemande. *M.A. 1924 Belfast*

Ingram, E. G.
A literary analysis of the *Grettissaga* showing the composite nature of the Old Norse historical saga. *M.A. 1908 London*

Ingroville, P. C.
1. The Book of Revelation. 2. The doctrine of the Church of England on the Lord's Supper compared with Scripture and the teaching of the primitive Church, and also with the teaching of the Church of Rome. *B.D. 1909 Oxford*

Inman, D. M.
A study of the general knowledge of London school children in relation to intelligence. *Ph.D. 1936 London, Institute of Education*

Insh, G. P.
Scottish colonial schemes prior to the Union. *D.Litt. 1922 Glasgow*

Instein, H.
Edward I as a foreign statesman. *B.Litt. 1933 Oxford*

Ion, R. H.
The theology of the early Friends with special reference to that of Isaac Pennington. *B.D. 1947 Oxford*

Iovetz-Tereshchenko, N. M.
Some problems of the *Tale of the expedition of Igor*, a Russian poem of the twelfth century. *B.Litt. 1928 Oxford*

Iovetz-Tereshchenko, N. M.
A study on friendship-love in adolescence. *Ph.D. 1933 London, King's College*

Iqbal, A. A.
The conception of self-consciousness in pre-Kantian and Kantian philosophy. *M.A. 1924 London*

Iredale, H. Q.
Thomas Traherne. *M.A. 1933 Birmingham*

Ireland, J. E. de C.
The sea in education. *Ph.D. 1950 Dublin, Trinity College*

Ireland, P. W.
Government and administration of Iraq: a study in political development. *Ph.D. 1936 London, School of Economics and Political Science*

Ireson, J. C.
The cult of obscurity in French symbolist poetry. *M.A. 1949 London, External Degree*

Irons, R. K.
The influence of the Barbary States in international relations, with special reference to the United States. *D.Phil. 1934 Oxford*

Irvine, A. J.
The development of musical ability with special reference to aural technique and sight reading. *Ph.D. 1940 Glasgow*

Irvine, J. S. W.
The doctrine of sin in the theology of John Bunyan. *Ph.D. 1930 Edinburgh*

Irvine, M. H.
The old and new elements in Spenser's poetry. *M.Litt. 1932 Cambridge*

Irwin, P. J.
A study of the English dialects of Ireland, 1172-1800. *Ph.D. 1935 London, Birkbeck College*

Irwin, P. J.
A study of the vocabulary of the English settlers in Ireland before 1600. *M.A. 1931 London, Birkbeck College*

Irwin, W. H.
Marvell and poetry. *M.A. 1935 National University of Ireland*

Isaac, J.
Economics of migration. *Ph.D. 1942 London, School of Economics and Political Science*

Isaac, J. E.
Economic analysis of wage regulation in Australia, 1920-1947. *Ph.D. 1949 London, School of Economics and Political Science*

Isaacs, H. M.
The ecclesiastical and religious position in the diocese of Llandaff in the reign of Queen Elizabeth. *M.A. 1928 Wales*

Isaacs, Z. M.
Three plays of Thomas Randolph: *Aristippus, The Conceited pedler, The Muses looking-glasse*: with introduction, collations and notes. *Ph.D. 1926 Sheffield*

Ishaque, M.
Poets and poetry of modern Iran. *Ph.D. 1940 London, School of Oriental and African Studies*

Ish-Shalom, M.
Jehuda Halevi and Chaim Nachman Bialik. *Ph.D. 1938 London, School of Oriental and African Studies*

Islam, F.
An experimental investigation into the comparative validity of some non-verbal tests of intelligence. *M.A. 1934 Leeds*

Islam, H.
An experimental study of some tests of perseveration. *M.Ed. 1940 Leeds*

Isles, K. S.
Wages policy and the price level. *M.Sc. 1934 Cambridge*

Ismail, A. A. A.
The costs of transport and the location of industry in Great Britain and Egypt. *Ph.D. 1942 Birmingham*

Ismail, D. A.
The law as to the transfer of title in sale of goods. *LL.M. 1934 Leeds*

Ispir, V. G.
The nature and development of the idea of God as held by the primitive peoples of central Africa. *B.Sc. 1914 Oxford*

Isserlin, B. S. J.
The settlement of Palestine in the Bronze age and its connexion with geographical and human factors. *B.Litt. 1948 Oxford*

Ittyerah, V. M.
The development of political institutions in the State of Travancore, A.D. 1885-1924. *B.Litt. 1930 Oxford*

Ivatt, E. C.
Studies in the diction of Spenser. *M.A. 1911 London*

Ives, D. V.
The seven deadly sins in English literature. *M.A. 1931 London, Westfield College*

Ives, R. B.
Disraeli as a writer of political novels. *M.A. 1924 Birmingham*

Ivor, D.
The principles of federal public finance. *Ph.D. 1947 London, School of Economics and Political Science*

Iyengar, S.
Keats and Spenser. *M.A. 1936 London, University College*

Jack, F. M. S.
Joseph Conrad. *M.A. 1941 Birmingham*

Jacka, A. J.
The influence of present day linguistic theory on the teaching of modern languages in schools. *M.A. 1934 London, Institute of Education*

Jacka, H. T.
The dissolution of the English nunneries. *M.A. 1917 London*

Jackson, A.
The life and work of Nicholas Rowe, 1674-1718. *M.A. 1929 London*

Jackson, A.
London theatres, 1700 to 1714, as reflected in the periodical press of the time. *Ph.D. 1936 London, External Degree*

Jackson, C.
A collected edition of the hitherto uncollected and unpublished poems of Matthiás Jochumsson. *M.A. 1931 Leeds*

Jackson, C.
Matthias Jochumsson: a biographical and critical study. *Ph.D. 1934 Manchester*

Jackson, C. H.
The development of the individual. *Ph.D. 1941 Dublin, Trinity College*

Jackson, F.
The Hundred of Leyland after the Conquest. *M.A. 1913 Liverpool*

Jackson, G. B.
The teaching of geometry in secondary schools. *M.Ed. 1924 Manchester*

Jackson, G. S.
The conflict of musical opinion in the early eighteenth century: based on a study of certain critical writings of the period. *B.Litt. 1949 Oxford*

Jackson, J. J.
Byron and Shelley considered as types of the revolutionary spirit. *M.A. 1912 London*

Jackson, L.
Analysis of aggression among problem children: a study of its incidence and immediate nature. *B.Sc. 1942 Oxford*

Jackson, L.
Investigation into factors influencing the direction of aggressive impulses into (a) delinquency, (b) neurosis, (c) positive achievement. *D.Phil. 1949 Oxford*

Jackson, M. L.
Some aspects of expression in the poetry of the early nineteenth century. *M.A. 1940 Belfast*

Jackson, M. V.
International relations on the south east coast of Africa, 1796-1856. *Ph.D. 1938 London, King's College*

Jackson, R.
An examination of the deductive logic of J. S. Mill. *D.Litt. 1938 Saint Andrew's*

Jackson, R. W.
An historical survey of the law of inevitable accident. *LL.D. 1936 Dublin, Trinity College*

Jackson, R. W.
Jonathan Swift: dean and pastor. *Litt. D. 1939 Dublin, Trinity College*

Jackson, T. E. A. K.
Industrial relations in road transport. *Ph.D. 1946 Manchester*

Jackson, T. H.
The teaching of mathematics: an enquiry into the aims and methods in schools of various types, with a view to securing a greater degree of coordination between (a) school and school, (b) school and after-school activities. *M.Ed. 1937 Manchester*

Jackson, W. E.
Les confidences de Samain dans le *Jardin de l'Infante. M.A. 1926 Birmingham*

Jackson, W. G.
An historical study of the provision for play and recreation in Manchester. *M.Ed. 1940 Manchester*

Jackson, Y. L.
The moral judgments and their theistic implications. *Ph.D. 1940 Edinburgh*

Jacob, E. F.
Baronial reform and rebellion, 1259-1267. *Ph.D. 1924 Oxford*

Jacob, K. K.
Art judgement in school children: being an experimental study of the appreciation of pictures by secondary school boys. *M.A. 1931 Leeds*

Jacobs, O.
The literary theory of Jules Laforgue. *B.Litt. 1950 Oxford*

Jacobson, D.
Blood relationships of the Old Testament. *Ph.D. 1936 Cambridge*

Jacombs, M. E.
The Jewish community in Rome, from its foundation until A.D. 313. *M.A. 1915 Birmingham*

Jafri, S. A. H.
An index of the traditionists quoted in *Kitāb al Kharāj* of Abū Yūsuf, together with a biography of the author. *Ph.D. 1932 London, School of Oriental and African Studies*

Jager, M.
The development of the idea of the animal as a symbol of harmony in English literature. *Ph.D. 1932 Cambridge*

Jagger, J. H.
The sound images in Spenser's poetry. *M.A. 1909 London*

Jagodzinski, J.
Some historical factors in the formation of the Ukrainian people. *M.A. 1942 Liverpool*

Jagtiani, H. M.
The role of the state in the development of railways. *M.Sc. 1923 London*

Jahagirdar, R. V.
Kanarese influence in Old Marathi (Jñānesvari). *M.A. 1928 London*

Jahangir Khan, M.
The northwest frontier policy of the Mughals, 1556-1658. *Ph.D. 1937 Cambridge*

Jahans, G. A.
An enquiry into the abilities of adolescent boys in elementary schools in Bristol. *M.A. 1934 Bristol*

Jahoda, G.
Aspects of the sociology of J. M. Robertson. *M.Sc. 1947 London, School of Economics and Political Science*

Jain, B. D.
Phonology of Panjābī as spoken about Ludhiana. *Ph.D. 1926 London*

Jain, L. C.
Indigenous banking in India. *Ph.D. 1928 London*

Jalea, V.
Tariffs and stability in commercial relations in the post-war period, with special regard to Central Europe. *Ph.D. 1931 Birmingham*

Jalland, T. F.
This, our sacrifice. *B.D. 1934 Oxford*

James, A.
The selection of children for secondary education. *M.Sc. 1925 Birmingham*

James, A. J.
Aspects of the economic geography of Sumatra. *M.A. 1949 Wales*

James, A. K.
La Dragontea of Lope de Vega: a critical and annotated edition, together with a preliminary essay on Lope as an epic poet. *Ph.D. 1935 London, External Degree*

James, A. W.
Kant's view of object and objectivity. *M.A. 1908 London*

James, C. M.
The treatment of Old Norse literature in the works of William Morris, with particular reference to *Sigurd the Volsung. M.A. 1932 Wales*

James, D. G.
The status of secondary qualities in the light of contemporary research. *M.A. 1928 Wales*

James, D. W.
James Joyce and the evolution of the creative artist: a study of his life and works in relation to the age and his environment. *M.A. 1936 Wales*

James, E. F.
Swinburne, *The Queen Mother* and the *Mary Stuart* trilogy: an investigation into Swinburne's sources of inspiration and into the use made of historical documents. *M.A. 1932 Bristol*

James, E. M.
A concise history of the beginning of the ionic theory, its development from the end of the eighteenth century to the conclusion of Faraday's work. *M.Sc. 1926 London*

James, E. O.
The cult of the dead in North America. *Ph.D. 1925 London*

James, E. O.
The relation of ritual to belief in primitive cult, with special reference to the magico-religious customs of the Australian Aborigines. *B.Litt. 1916 Oxford*

James, E. O.
The unpublished poems of Lewis Glyn Cothi as found in the Peniarth manuscripts. *M.A. 1911 Wales*

James, G. F.
The Lords Commissioners of the Admiralty, 1689-1714. *M.A. 1937 Birmingham*

James, H. A.
1. Idolatry. 2. The place of unity in the ideal of a Church. *B.D. 1874 Oxford*

James, H. I.
The development of the doctrine of the atonement in English theology during the nineteenth century. *B.Litt. 1930 Oxford*

James, H. J.
Talhaiarn. *M.A. 1919 Wales*

James, H. L.
1. St. Paul and the mystery religions. 2. The Incarnation and the Eucharist. *B.D. & D.D. 1924 Oxford*

James, J.
The problem of suffering in the Old Testament. *M.A. 1941 Wales*

James, J. C.
An attempt to trace the rise of English literary criticism. *M.A. 1914 Wales*

James, J. W.
A history of the origins and development of the Celtic church in Wales, between the years 450 A.D. and 630 A.D. *D.D. 1931 Durham*

James, J. W.
The significance of rhythm in musical education. *M.A. 1938 Liverpool*

James, K. I.
An historical and political geography of Wessex. *M.A. 1950 Wales*

James, L.
The Indian problem in eastern and southern Africa. *M.A. 1940 Liverpool*

James, M.
Social and economic policy and projects during the interregnum, 1640-1660. *Ph.D. 1927 London*

James, M. K.
The Gascon wine trade of Southampton during the reigns of Henry VI and Edward IV. *B.Litt. 1948 Oxford*

James, N. G. B.
Peter Collinson, F.R.S., F.S.A., and his circle of friends. *B.Litt. 1923 Oxford*

James, P. G.
British policy in relation to the Gold Coast, 1815-1850. *M.A. 1935 London, King's College*

James, P. J.
1. The redemption. 2. The Church in the Epistle to the Ephesians. *B.D. 1910 Oxford*

James, R. D.
The population and settlement in Northern Ireland. *M.A. 1948 Wales*

James, R. L.
The philosophic and aristocratic opposition to the Flavian emperors. *Ph.D. 1938 London, University College*

James, R. L. Langford- *see* Langford-James, R. L.

James, T. J.
The early history of Newcastle Emlyn, to include a study of the data relating to the castle, town and lordship down to the Act of Union, 1536. *M.A. 1913 Wales*

James, T. J.
The educational ideas of the Encyclopaedists. *Ph.D. 1946 London, External Degree*

James, W.
The ideas of François de Curel as expressed in his dramatic works. *M.A. 1931 Wales*

James, W. S.
The development of the gas laws from Boyle to Van der Waals. *M.Sc. 1928 London*

Jameson, A. J.
Strathmore in the eighteenth century. A study in historical geography. *M.Sc. 1938 Manchester*

Jamieson, A. B.
Burns and religion. *M.A. 1928 Birmingham*

Jamieson, J.
The influence of the Rev. Henry Cooke on the political life of Ulster. *M.A. 1950 Belfast*

Jamison, W. N.
The idea of the unity of the Church: a study of its development in the first three centuries. *Ph.D. 1948 Edinburgh*

Janssen, E. L.
Dutch criticism of Zola between 1876-1902. *M.A. 1921 London*

Jardine, E. E.
Principles of science, with application to certain problems in the teaching of physics and chemistry. *M.A. 1916 Liverpool*

Jarman, A. O. H.
Chwedl Myrddin yn y canu cynnar(The legend of Myrddin in early poetry). *M.A. 1936 Wales*

Jarman, T. L.
The history of the Society for the Diffusion of Useful Knowledge. *B.Litt. 1933 Oxford*

Jarrett, H. R.
The Gambia. *M.Sc. 1947 London, External Degree*

Jarvis, J. B.
Changes in land utilization in the southeast of Denbighshire, 1840-1938. *M.A. 1940 Wales*

Jasper, R. C. D.
The parliamentary representation of Grampound. *M.A. 1940 Leeds*

Jauncey, E.
The doctrine of grace: historically and dogmatically considered. *D.D. 1940 Durham*

Jaworczykowski, J. B.
Legal philosophy of Edmund Burke. *D.Phil. 1949 Oxford*

Jay, A.
Nivelle de la Chaussée et *La comédie larmoyante. M.A. 1913 Liverpool*

Jay, L. J.
Geographical factors in the growth of Brisbane, Australia. *M.A. 1949 Birmingham*

Jayasuriya, J. E.
A factor analysis of tests of functional thinking in mathematics. *M.A. 1949 London, Institute of Education*

Jayasuriya, T. D.
The bilingual problem in Ceylon. *M.A. 1931 London, Day Training College*

Jayawickrame, N. A.
A critical analysis of the Pali Sutta Nipata illustrating its gradual growth. *Ph.D. 1947 London, School of Oriental and African Studies*

Jeaffreson, J. W.
The mensuration of French verse-rhythm based upon experimental investigation of the properties of stress-accent. *M.A. 1924 London*

Jeffares, A. N.
The sources and symbolism of the later poems of William Butler Yeats. *Ph.D. 1945 Dublin, Trinity College*

Jeffares, A. N.
W. B. Yeats: man and poet. *D.Phil. 1947 Oxford*

Jeffares, G. P. F.
André Gide and the individual. *Ph.D. 1950 Dublin, Trinity College*

Jefferson, D. W.
An edition of Burke's *Sublime and Beautiful*, with notes, and an introduction dealing with the place of Burke in English aesthetics in the eighteenth century. *B.Litt. 1937 Oxford*

Jefferson, H.
Henri Duclos. *Ph.D. 1942 Dublin, Trinity College*

Jefferson, W. H.
The metaphysical problems involved in the nature and range of the concept of freedom and its relation to the concept of mechanism. *M.A. 1922 Liverpool*

Jeffery, A.
The foreign vocabulary of the *Qurân*. *Ph.D. 1929 Edinburgh*

Jeffery, A. J. W.
The effect of a recruitment film on the attitude of school leavers to nursing as a career. *M.Ed. 1950 Manchester*

Jeffery, J. S.
Experimental studies in aesthetic appreciation. *B.Sc. 1940 Oxford*

Jeffery, M. R.
Introduction and glossary to the Old English version of Bede's *Ecclesiastical history of the English people*. *M.A. 1935 Leeds*

Jeffery, V. M.
Italian and English pastoral drama of the Renaissance: a comparative study. *M.A. 1922 London*

Jeffreys, J. B.
Trends in business organisation in Great Britain since 1856, with special reference to the financial structure of companies, the mechanism of investment and the relations between the shareholder and the company. *Ph.D. 1938 London, School of Economics and Political Science*

Jeffreys, J. M.
Voltaire's conception of the origin and function of morality. *M.A. 1947 London, University College*

Jeffreys, M. D. W.
The divine Umundri Kings of Igboland. *Ph.D. 1934 London, University College*

Jelf, C. E.
1. 'One baptism for the remission of sins'. 2. 'The communion of saints'. *B.D. & D.D. 1907 Oxford*

Jellicoe, S.
The eschatology of the Psalter: a study in the religious development of Israel as reflected in the Psalms, with special reference to the destinies of the individual and the nation. *B.D. 1944 Durham*

Jenkin, A. K. Hamilton *see* Hamilton Jenkin, A. K.

Jenkin, A. M.
Imagery and learning. *M.A. 1930 London, Bedford College*

Jenkin, A. M.
Imagery and learning: a further study. *Ph.D. 1933 London, Bedford College*

Jenkin, G. B.
Production in the consumers' co-operative movement. *M.Com. 1934 Birmingham*

Jenkins, A.
The works of Tudur Penllyn and Ieuan Brydydd Hir Hynaf. *M.A. 1921 Wales*

Jenkins, A. E. R.
The English Moor, or The Mock-marriage, by Richard Brome, edited from the manuscript in the library of Lichfield Cathedral. *B.Litt. 1941 Oxford*

Jenkins, B.
The aims and work of Richard Price, 1723-1791. *M.A. 1927 Wales*

Jenkins, C.
1. Some aspects of theology of Methodius of Olympus. 2. Some features of the theological language of the *Dialects* of Adamantius. *B.D. & D.D. 1924 Oxford*

Jenkins, D.
The attitude of the German Government towards membership of the League of Nations. *M.A. 1939 Wales*

Jenkins, D.
Bywyd a gwaith Huw Morys (Pont y Meibon) (1622-1709). *M.A. 1948 Wales*

Jenkins, D.
The laws of Hywel Dda. *LL.M. 1949 Cambridge*

Jenkins, D. E.
A review and revision of the biography of John Jones, Talsarn, by Owen Thomas. *M.A. 1924 Liverpool*

Jenkins, D. H.
Barddoniaeth arwrol yn y Gymraeg(Heroic poetry in Welsh). *M.A. 1924 Wales*

Jenkins, D. J.
A brief sketch of the Hebrew conception of man in the Old Testament. *M.A. 1937 Wales*

Jenkins, D. L.
Accented verse: a study of the development of free metre poetry in Welsh literature until the beginning of the seventeenth century. *M.A. 1921 Wales*

Jenkins, D. M.
Some aspects of the French element in the Middle English lyric. *M.A. 1912 London*

Jenkins, E.
The satirical element in Petronius. *M.A. 1932 Wales*

Jenkins, E. M.
Madame Louise Ackermann. *M.A. 1928 Leeds*

Jenkins, H.
The life and work of Henry Chettle (c. 1560-1607). *M.A. 1933 London, University College*

Jenkins, I.
A comparative study of the French, Welsh and Latin versions of the *Purgatoire de Saint Patrice (Purdan Padrif)*. *M.A. 1929 Wales*

Jenkins, J.
Fragments of Gospels and pseudo-Gospels in medieval Welsh. *B.Litt. 1919 Oxford*

Jenkins, J. E. C.
Population in Central Wales: changes in number and distribution, 1801-1931. *M.A. 1939 London, King's College*

Jenkins, J. W.
An analysis of the factors entering into results of tests based upon the logical principles of mathematics. *Ph.D. 1939 London, Institute of Education*

Jenkins, M.
Boileau: his influence and reputation in English literature. *M.A. 1932 Birmingham*

Jenkins, R. J. H.
Dedalus: a study of Dorian plastic art in the seventh century B.C. *Ph.D. 1936 Cambridge*

Jenkins, S. P.
A study of Lord Berners' translation, *Arthur of Little Britain*, with a prefatory life of the author. *B.Litt. 1946 Oxford*

Jenkins, T. H.
The Portuguese in India and the East Indies 1497-1548. *M.A. 1924 Birmingham*

Jenkins, T. W.
The influence of German thought in English literature of the first half of the nineteenth century. *M.A. 1926 Wales*

Jenkins, W. J.
The early history of the iron industry in the Dudley area, with special reference to the claims of Dudley. *M.A. 1929 Wales*

Jenkins, W. J.
A history of the proprietary chapels of Bath. *M.A. 1947 Bristol*

Jenkins, W. O.
1. The gradual development of the doctrine of a future life in Holy Scripture, with special reference to the teaching of St. Paul on the resurrection-body in I Corinthians xv. 2. The Logos-Christology deduced from the writings of St. Paul. *B.D. & D.D. 1907 Oxford*

Jenks, J. E. F.
The evolution of modern land-settlement policy in Australasia. *B.Litt. 1930 Oxford*

Jennings, E. H.
Le Romantisme. *M.A. 1909 Birmingham*

Jennings, J. W.
German historiography and the evolution of German political ideas in the nineteenth century. *Ph.D. 1949 London, School of Economics and Political Science*

Jennings, R. H.
The social implications of the teaching of St. Paul. *Ph.D. 1938 Edinburgh*

Jennings, V. B.
Coláistí na Bainríoghna, a mbunú 's a mbliadhanta tosaigh 1845-1856(Queen's Colleges, their foundation and early years, 1845-1856). *M.A. 1947 National University of Ireland*

Jensen, A. E.
The revival of early literature in England and Scotland from Percy to Scott, 1765-1802. *Ph.D. 1933 Edinburgh*

Jensen, H. H. J.
An analysis of the short stories by Ludwig Tieck and Friedrich Hebbel, with special reference to style and structure. *M.A. 1947 London, Bedford College*

Jephcott, A. P.
Studies of employed adolescent girls in relation to their development and social background. *M.A. 1949 Wales*

Jeremy, G. A.
The social and economic effects of the development of multiple shops in the United Kingdom and the United States of America. *M.A. 1927 Wales*

Jerman, H. N.
The archaeology of east central Wales. *M.A. 1934 Wales*

Jervis, H. V.
L'influence littéraire de Jean Jacques Rousseau en Angleterre. *M.A. 1913 Liverpool*

Jessop, H.
Settlement types and their distribution in northeast Yorkshire. *M.Sc. 1938 Leeds*

Jessop, J. C.
An historical survey of education in Angus to the year 1872 from original and contemporary sources, embracing early education and the beginning of systematic education; the parish school system; burgh schools, schools of industry and the origin and establishment of infant schools. *Ph.D. 1930 Saint Andrew's*

Jessop, T. E.
Twentieth century realism in England and America. *B.Litt. 1924 Oxford*

Jessopp, A.
1. That a brief summary of credenda was drawn up at a very early date in Apostolic times and probably by the Apostolic College, the reception of which was a condition of baptism; and that this preliminary summary was subsequently amplified and expanded by a more full statement with which the baptized were furnished for their edification and advancement in Christian knowledge. 2. A consideration of such passages in the Apostolic writings as apparently contain quotations from this primitive creed. *B.D. & D.D. 1870 Oxford*

Jewett Williams, H. L.
To what extent do the discourses ascribed to Christ in the fourth Gospel preserve His own words?. *B.Litt. 1912 Oxford*

Jewitt, E. P.
The relation of grammar and composition to the training of appreciation. *M.A. 1923 London*

Jex-Blake, T. W.
1. The authorship of the Epistle to the Hebrews. 2. Galatians iii. 20. *B.D. & D.D. 1873 Oxford*

Jha, L.
Mithila and Magadha, 700 A.D.-1100 A.D. *Ph.D. 1948 London, School of Oriental and African Studies*

Jha, S.
An edition of the unpublished Maithili ms., the *Padavali* of Govindadasa, with an analysis of its grammar and phonology. *Ph.D. 1934 London, School of Oriental and African Studies*

Jha, V. S.
A comparison of the philosophic systems of Malebranche and Berkeley. *Ph.D. 1927 London*

Joannidis, B.
The doctrine of predestination in St. Paul and Stoicism. *B.Litt. 1932 Oxford*

Job, E. H.
The stoic element in Horace. *M.A. 1933 Manchester*

Job, T.
Satire in English nineteenth century verse. *M.A. 1925 Wales*

Jocz, J.
A study in the relationship between the Jewish people and Jesus Christ. *Ph.D. 1945 Edinburgh*

Joels, E. A.
Contributions to a commentary on Cicero's speech *Pro Rabirio Postumo*. *M.A. 1924 London*

Johanns, P.
The philosophic system of Sankara. *B.Litt. 1921 Oxford*

Johanson, E. J.
The psychological approach to the problem of sin. *B.Litt. 1929 Oxford*

Johari, G. P.
The intellectual life of A. H. Clough, with particular reference to his poetry. *B.Litt. 1949 Oxford*

John, A. H.
Certain aspects of the Industrial Revolution in South Wales, 1760-1850. *Ph.D. 1940 Cambridge*

John, D. G.
An economic and historical survey of the development of the anthracite industry with special reference to the Swansea Valley. *M.A. 1923 Wales*

John, E.
A critical study of the sources of the Annals of Winchcombe, Faustina B.i.ff.21-29b, 1182-1232. *M.A. 1950 Manchester*

John, E.
On the *Culex, Ciris, Catalecta, Copa* and *Moretum* attributed to Vergil, with special reference to style and grammar. *M.A. 1909 London*

John, E. L.
The social and economic ideas of William Morris and their relation to those of his times. *M.A. 1944 Wales*

John, G.
The romance of the *Seven Sages of Rome* in the French, Latin and Welsh literatures of the Middle Ages. *M.A. 1926 Wales*

John, I. J.
German policy in Central Europe, 1933-37. *M.Sc. 1939 London, School of Economics and Political Science*

John, J. E.
Mycenaean religion. *M.A. 1915 Wales*

John, L. B.
The parliamentary representation of Glamorgan, 1536-1832. *M.A. 1934 Wales*

John, M.
The development of English socialism from 1848 to 1884. *M.A. 1934 London, Bedford College*

John, M. B.
An analysis of the cartographical material in John Speed's *Theatre of the Empire of Great Britaine*. *M.Sc. 1945 Wales*

John, T. G.
The political novels of Disraeli. *M.A. 1918 Wales*

John, V. K.
Law of landlord and tenant in Malabar. *LL.D. 1926 London*

John, W.
A critical appreciation of the modern short story, with particular reference to Mr. A. E. Coppard. *M.A. 1936 Wales*

John, W. H.
The inter-relations of nature and supernature in Von Hügel's *Philosophy of Religion*. *M.A. 1941 Wales*

John, W. R.
The history of the growth and organization of the copper industry of Swansea and district. *M.A. 1912 Wales*

John, W. T.
The Dreyfus affairs in the life and works of Charles Péguy. *Ph.D. 1948 London, King's College*

Johnes, E. G.
Sir R. J. Wilmot Horton, Bart., politician and pamphleteer. *M.A. 1936 Bristol*

Johnes, M. H.
La genèse de la doctrine littéraire de Pierre Leroux. *M.A. 1949 Wales*

Johns, D. S.
The doctrinaire novel, 1760-1830, with special reference to J. J. Rousseau. *M.A. 1926 Manchester*

Johns, E. M.
Report upon an enquiry into a child's vocabulary: how far it is indicative of intelligence and influence by social status. *M.A. 1949 Reading*

Johnson, A. R.
An investigation of the problem of Greek influence upon the religious thought of Judaism in the Hellenistic age. *Ph.D. 1931 Wales*

Johnson, B. L. C.
The charcoal iron trade in the Midlands, 1690-1720. *M.A. 1950 Birmingham*

Johnson, D. C.
Public opinion and Parliament since 1832. *B.Litt. 1922 Oxford*

Johnson, D. W. J.
Sir James Graham as politician and Home Secretary, 1818-46. *B.Litt. 1948 Oxford*

Johnson, F.
Evening education in England, with special reference to London. *Ph.D. 1937 London, King's College*

Johnson, F.
The London Polytechnic movement, with special reference to Quintin Hogg. *M.A. 1929 London*

Johnson, G.
The idea of the Church in the New Testament and its development in the first two centuries. *Ph.D. 1941 Cambridge*

Johnson, G. A.
Algunas ideas religiosas y morales de Cervantes. *M.A. 1942 National University of Ireland*

Johnson, G. C.
The military and naval terms in the Norman and Anglo-Saxon chronicles of the twelfth century. *Ph.D. 1949 Leeds*

Johnson, G. F.
Education for the engineering industry with special reference to Wakefield and the West Riding. *M.Ed. 1940 Leeds*

Johnson, G. R.
The moral dynamic of the Christian experience according to St. Paul. *Ph.D. 1922 Edinburgh*

Johnson, H.
A commentary on Acts xv.1-6; 6-12; 13-21. *D.D. 1924 Oxford*

Johnson, H.
1. Israel and society: the Jewish religion's contribution towards social integration. 2. Christianity and society: our Lord's work considered sociologically. *B.D. 1917 Oxford*

Johnson, J. C. De Graft- *see* De Graft-Johnson, J. C.

Johnson, J. I. B.
Education and the social novel. *M.A. 1947 Bristol*

Johnson, L. Bradyll- *see* Bradyll-Johnson, L.

Johnson, R. V.
Marlowe's presentation of human destiny. *M.A. 1949 Manchester*

Johnson, S.
The history and development of the conveyance on sale of land. *LL.D. 1916 London*

Johnson, S. C.
A history of emigration from the United Kingdom to North America, 1763-1912. *D.Sc. 1913 London*

Johnson, W.
The setting and characters in the novels of Pereda. *M.A. 1936 Birmingham*

Johnson, W. H.
Roger Bacon. *M.A. 1913 Birmingham*

Johnston, A. S.
Leconte de Lisle: animalier. *M.A. 1936 Belfast*

Johnston, C. E.
A comparison of the currency and banking systems of Canada and the United States, with some reference to that of Great Britain. *B.Litt. 1920 Oxford*

Johnston, E. D.
A study of the New Testament sources for the life of Jesus. *Ph.D. 1950 Manchester*

Johnston, F. R.
The cult of St. Bridget of Sweden in fifteenth century England. *M.A. 1947 Manchester*

Johnston, H. C. F.
Paul Valéry. *Litt.D. 1937 Dublin, Trinity College*

Johnston, J.
Gerhart Hauptmann. *M.A. 1914 National University of Ireland*

Johnston, J. O.
1. The doctrine involved in Article XIII. 2. The historical account of the doctrine. *B.D. & D.D. 1914 Oxford*

Johnston, S. H. F.
Hubert de Burgh. *B.Litt. 1933 Oxford*

Johnston, T. A.
Christianity in Africa, A.D. 180-258. *M.A. 1924 National University of Ireland*

Johnstone, A.
Theories of light to the time of Fresnel. *M.Sc. 1926 London*

Johnstone, A. H.
Das deutsche Bild vom heutigen England nach Uebersetzungen und Schulbüchern, 1918-1932. *Ph.D. 1934 Edinburgh*

Johnstone, J.
Grillparzer and England. *M.A. 1931 Birmingham*

Johnstone, S. M.
Samuel Marsden: a pioneer of civilization in the South Seas. *M.A. 1928 Belfast*

Johri, S. R.
The effect of coaching and practice on intelligence tests. *M.Ed. 1937 Leeds*

Jolles, C. A. B. E.
Theodor Fontane and England; a critical study in Anglo-German literary relations in the nineteenth century. *M.A. 1947 London, Birkbeck College*

Jolles, O. J. M.
The cultural, commercial and political relations between the State of Hamburg and Great Britain from 1890 to 1914. *M.A. 1938 Wales*

Jolley, F.
The paradox of evil. *M.A. 1949 Liverpool*

Jolley, L. J.
The heroic couplet in the eighteenth century: a study of critical theory and poetic practice, with special emphasis on the development of style and content. *M.A. 1938 London, University College*

Jolliffe, M. F.
The financial reconstruction of Austria by the League of Nations, with reference to its economic consequences. *M.A. 1930 Wales*

Jolly, A. L.
An analysis of the variation in costs of milk production. *Ph.D. 1940 London, South Eastern Agricultural College*

Jolly, A. R.
Sensational elements in Dickens and Collins. *M.A. 1943 Manchester*

Jones, A.
The Christology of the Apocalypse. *M.A. 1937 Wales*

Jones, A. A.
The king in Israel. *M.A. 1947 Birmingham*

Jones, A. B.
Some contributions to a study of work, wages and prices in Wales in the sixteenth century. *M.A. 1933 Wales*

Jones, A. D.
Distribution of population in New Brunswick and Prince Edward Island. *M.A. 1933 Liverpool*

Jones, A. E.
The relations between Great Britain and Russia, 1870-1899. *M.A. 1917 Birmingham*

Jones, A. E. Duncan- *see* Duncan-Jones, A. E.

Jones, A. G.
The castle and town of Welshpool during the twelfth and thirteenth centuries. *M.A. 1911 Wales*

Jones, A. G.
The economic, industrial and social history of Ebbw Vale during the period 1775-1927, being a study in the origin and development of an industrial district of south Wales in all its aspects. *M.A. 1929 Wales*

Jones, A. G.
The study of Elizabethan literature at the end of the eighteenth and the beginning of the nineteenth centuries. *B.Litt. 1923 Oxford*

Jones, A. I.
The influence of Wellington on the internal politics of France, 1815-18. *B.Litt. 1935 Oxford*

Jones, A. M.
The characteristics of wool production and woollen manufacture in Wales in relation to the geographical features of the principality. *M.Sc. 1925 Wales*

Jones, A. M.
The spoken dialect of Anglesey. *M.A. 1926 Wales*

Jones, A. Watkin *see* Watkin Jones, A.

Jones, B.
A comparison of the constitutions of the United States and Australia. *M.A. 1924 Wales*

Jones, B.
The non-military aspects of the Roman occupation of Wales. *M.A. 1935 Wales*

Jones, B.
The Welsh version of the *Historia regum Britanniae* in Peniarth ms.44 collated with the *Red book* version, together with notes on the influence of the original on the style and construction of the Welsh, and a glossary of Welsh words whose use is illustrated by the Latin. *M.A. 1915 Wales*

Jones, B. E.
The treatment of the idea of the individual in the philosophies of Bernard Bosanquet, J. M. E. McTaggart and A. N. Whitehead. *M.A. 1942 Manchester*

Jones, B. L.
The evolutionary hypothesis and its implications: a critical exposition and discussion with special reference to the theories of naturalistic, creative and emergent evolution. *M.A. 1934 Liverpool*

Jones, B. M.
Henry Fielding and his attitude towards the law and towards legal reform. *M.A. 1932 Wales*

Jones, B. P.
Education and employment: a study of the employments of juveniles with reference to vocational guidance and education. *M.Ed. 1927 Manchester*

Jones, B. Pierce- *see* Pierce-Jones, B.

Jones, C.
The idea of *Wandlung* in German literature. *M.A. 1935 London, Birkbeck College*

Jones, C. E.
1. The life and works of Thomas Love Peacock. 2. A bibliography of Thomas Love Peacock. *Ph.D. 1927 London*

Jones, C. E.
The teaching of history of boys of eleven to fifteen. *M.Ed. 1926 Leeds*

Jones, C. F.
The French sources of Sterne. *Ph.D. 1931 London, Birkbeck College*

Jones, C. G.
A critical study of John Locke's examination of Père Malebranche's opinion of seeing all things in God. *M.A. 1949 Wales*

Jones, C. M.
Une édition critique de la traduction Anglo-Normande de *La chronique de Turpin*, de Guillaume de Briane, avec introduction, notes et glossaire. *M.A. 1927 Wales*

Jones, D.
The metaphysical basis of ethics. *M.A. 1904 Wales*

Jones, D. A.
A critical examination of recent theories of the date of Deuteronomy. *M.A. 1943 Wales*

Jones, D. B.
The teaching of Latin by the Jesuits, with special reference to the *ratio studiorum*. *M.A. 1922 Wales*

Jones, D. C.
A critical examination of the philosophic principles basic to Karl Marx's *Capital*. *M.A. 1946 Wales*

Jones, D. C.
Tennyson's diction. *M.A. 1925 Liverpool*

Jones, D. C. Sealy- *see* Sealy-Jones, D. C.

Jones, D. H.
The origins of the English Independents. *M.A. 1929 Birmingham*

Jones, D. J.
Bugeilgerddi a rhieingerddi Cymraeg y 18fed a'r 19eg ganrif(Welsh pastoral and love poems of the eighteenth and nineteenth centuries). *M.A. 1930 Wales*

Jones, D. J.
Cerddi'r Saint a'u cymharu â'r bucheddau cyfatebol(The poems of the Saints and their comparison with the corresponding lives). *M.A. 1929 Wales*

Jones, D. J.
The Elizabethan lyric and its relations with contemporary music. *M.A. 1939 Wales*

Jones, D. J.
The social aspects of the rise and decay of literary culture in Mold and Holywell, 1820-1900. *M.A. 1929 Liverpool*

Jones, D. J.
Some recent theories with regard to the metaphysical foundations of ethics. *M.A. 1912 Wales*

Jones, D. J. O.
Hanes a llafur llenyddol Daniel Rowland(The life and literary work of Daniel Rowland). *M.A. 1937 Wales*

Jones, D. L.
The poetry of Francis Thompson. *M.A. 1936 Wales*

Jones, D. M.
The conception of teleology, with special reference to the views of Spinoza, Leibniz, and Kant. *M.A. 1911 Wales*

Jones, D. O.
The eschatology of the ancient Celts. *M.A. 1927 Wales*

Jones, D. P.
The primacy of the practical reason. *M.A. 1920 Liverpool*

Jones, D. R.
The history of Welsh domestic art from the sixteenth century as exhibited in the native furniture, with a study of its relation to the furniture of other parts of the British Isles and the continent of Europe. *M.A. 1925 Wales*

Jones, D. R.
The poems of Iorwerth Fynglwyd. *M.A. 1909 Wales*

Jones, D. T.
Interest as a factor in the transfer of training from the inculcation of mathematical principles to problems in reasoning. *M.A. 1937 London, Institute of Education*

Jones, E.
Anglo-Russian relations from 1878-1885, with special reference to central Asia. *M.A. 1934 Wales*

Jones, E.
The development and organization of the artificial silk industry in Great Britain. *M.A. 1940 Wales*

Jones, E.
The doctrine of the parousia in Paul and the Synoptic Gospels. *B.Litt. 1924 Oxford*

Jones, E.
The evolution of settlement in the Teify Valley. *M.Sc. 1945 Wales*

Jones, E.
French travellers in England from 1820 to 1830. *M.A. 1925 Wales*

Jones, E.
La lutte romantique à l'Académie Française. *M.A. 1922 Birmingham*

Jones, E.
Nicholas Love's fifteenth century translation of the *Meditationes vitae Christi*: a study, with special reference to the Passion section. *M.A. 1949 London, Bedford College*

Jones, E.
Suffering as a religious problem, with special reference to the Book of Job and the Psalter. *M.A. 1944 Wales*

Jones, E.
Tregaron: a sociological study of a Welsh rural community. *Ph.D. 1947 Wales*

Jones, E.
The word of God in some Accadian psalms. *M.A. 1949 Manchester*

Jones, E. Cadvan- *see* Cadvan-Jones, E.

Jones, E. E.
John Bale, Protestant. *M.A. 1910 Wales*

Jones, E. G.
The Caernarvonshire squires, 1558-1625. *M.A. 1936 Wales*

Jones, E. G.
Great Britain and the economic development of the Argentine Republic. *M.A. 1929 Wales*

Jones, E. H.
Adolf Wilbrandt as a dramatist. *M.A. 1936 Wales*

Jones, E. H.
A study of industrial relations in the British tinplate industry, 1874-1939. *M.A. 1940 Wales*

Jones, E. I.
The development in religious and ethical thought as discerned in the *Iliad* and the *Odyssey*. *M.A. 1915 Wales*

Jones, E. J.
The enclosure movement in Anglesey, 1788-1866. *M.A. 1924 Wales*

Jones, E. M.
The inspiration and sources of Marguerite de Navarre. *M.A. 1929 Wales*

Jones, E. M.
Theories of consumption, with reference to demand for and supply of foodstuffs in Great Britain. *M.A. 1939 Wales*

Jones, E. N.
A comparison between Christian theism and the religious beliefs of certain tribes in West Africa. *B.Litt. 1925 Oxford*

Jones, E. P.
The history of the town and castle of Pembroke to 1603. *M.A. 1905 Wales*

Jones, E. R.
Anglesey placenames: a contribution to Welsh history and ethnography. *M.A. 1911 Wales*

Jones, E. R.
Political theories in England during the seventeenth century, with special reference to the social contract. *M.A. 1903 Wales*

Jones, E. W.
Psychological problems in the teaching of geography. *M.A. 1931 London, Day Training College*

Jones, F. C.
System of extra-territoriality in Japan, 1855-99. *M.A. 1930 Bristol*

Jones, F. J.
The poems in prose of Charles Baudelaire. *B.Litt. 1949 Oxford*

Jones, F. L.
The structure of the novel in Jane Austen, and its relationship to the work of her predecessors. *M.A. 1935 London, Queen Mary College*

Jones, F. M.
C. Blount, 8th Lord Mountjoy. *M.A. 1946 National University of Ireland*

Jones, F. W.
The legend of Gawain: its Celtic origins and its treatment in English literature. *M.A. 1911 Wales*

Jones, G.
Bywyd a gwaith Edward Morris, Perthi Llwydion(The life and work of Edward Morris, Perthi Llwydion). *M.A. 1941 Wales*

Jones, G.
Legal procedure and the conduct of the feud in the Icelandic sagas. *M.A. 1929 Wales*

Jones, G. H.
The development of Jacobite ideas and policy, 1689-1746. *D.Phil. 1950 Oxford*

Jones, G. H.
1. The Hebrew doctrine of immortality in the light of other religions. 2. The Hebrew doctrine of sacrifice in the light of other religions. *B.D. & D.D. 1907 Oxford*

Jones, G. H.
Music and education. *M.A. 1932 Birmingham*

Jones, G. L.
The art of George Moore: his theory and practice. *M.A. 1936 Liverpool*

Jones, G. L.
The *cymwds* of Gwynedd prior to the Edwardian conquest of Wales. *M.A. 1919 Wales*

Jones, G. L.
The position of the Jewish community in Palestine in the first two centuries after the Exile. *M.A. 1930 Wales*

Jones, G. M.
Anglesey placenames. *M.A. 1926 Wales*

Jones, G. N.
The Norman lordship of Glamorgan: its settlement and early organization to the death of Gilbert de Clare, 1314. *M.A. 1921 Wales*

Jones, G. P.
Exegeses of I Corinthians ii.6-16; xii.7-11; II Corinthians xii.16. *D.D. 1923 Oxford*

Jones, G. P.
The founding of the Congo Free State, with special reference to the work of Sir Henry Morton Stanley. *M.A. 1935 Wales*

Jones, G. P.
1. The teaching of St. Paul on the Church in the Epistle to the Ephesians. 2. The teaching of St. Paul on the Holy Spirit. *B.D. 1908 Oxford*

Jones, G. R.
The transition in Welsh poetry between 1450 and 1600. *M.A. 1925 Wales*

Jones, G. R. J.
The military geography of Gwynedd in the thirteenth century. *M.A. 1949 Wales*

Jones, G. T.
Bywyd a gwaith Roger Edwards o'r Wyddgrug(The life and work of Roger Edwards of Mold). *M.A. 1933 Wales*

Jones, G. T.
A study of certain industries in relation to increasing and diminishing returns. *Ph.D. 1929 Cambridge*

Jones, G. T. Salusbury *see* Salusbury-Jones, G. T.

Jones, G. V.
The sources, growth, and value of English modernism. *B.Litt. 1931 Oxford*

Jones, H.
1. The development of Hebrew monotheism. 2. The prophecies of Amos. *B.D. 1924 Oxford*

Jones, H.
The theory of sovereignty in the philosophy of Thomas Hobbes. *M.A. 1936 Liverpool*

Jones, H. A.
The structure and conditions of authorship of the Old English poem on St. Guthlac. *M.A. 1938 Manchester*

Jones, H. Cunliffe- *see* Cunliffe-Jones, H.

Jones, H. G.
A critical account of certain experiments in the realist approach to the teaching of mathematics in post-primary schools. *M.A. 1941 Liverpool*

Jones, H. G.
John Kelsall: a study in religious and economic history. *M.A. 1938 Wales*

Jones, H. L.
The development of commercial education in England, from medieval times. *M.Ed. 1927 Manchester*

Jones, H. L.
The development of leasehold tenure in South Lancashire, with special reference to the seventeenth century. *M.A. 1924 Manchester*

Jones, H. M.
The history of the Church in the reign of Edward III. *M.A. 1914 Wales*

Jones, H. M.
The history of the Honourable Society of Cymmrodorion. *M.A. 1939 Wales*

Jones, H. Morris- *see* Morris-Jones, H.

Jones, H. Stanley- *see* Stanley-Jones, H.

Jones, H. T.
The psychology of aesthetic experience: instinctive reaction in aesthetic experience. *B.Sc. 1924 Oxford*

Jones, H. V. M.
A comparison of the teachings of Spinoza and McTaggart on immortality. *M.A. 1936 Wales*

Jones, H. W.
The history of the Royal Society (1667) by Thomas Sprat, bishop of Rochester, edited from the original copies and mss, together with the comments of Henry Stubbe and others; remarks on the life of the author; a list of his works; notes, appendices and bibliography. *Ph.D. 1948 Leeds*

Jones, H. Watkin- *see* Watkin-Jones, H.

Jones, H. Williams-
A social survey of a rural parish in Wales. *M.A. 1929 Liverpool*

Jones, I.
Changes in the theory and public opinion concerning the status and interests of a wage-earning class in Great Britain during the period 1600-1800. *M.A. 1928 Wales*

Jones, I.
Matthew Arnold's place in English criticism. *M.A. 1924 Wales*

Jones, I. A.
Greek loan words in Latin literature down to the time of Cicero. *M.A. 1915 Wales*

Jones, I. B.
Popular medical knowledge in fourteenth century English literature. *M.A. 1934 Liverpool*

Jones, I. G.
The international regulation of sugar bounties. *M.A. 1940 Wales*

Jones, I. M.
Merched llên Cymru o 1850 i 1914(The women of the literature of Wales from 1850 to 1914). *M.A. 1935 Wales*

Jones, I. M.
The origins and development to 1892 of the Indian National Congress. *M.A. 1946 London, School of Oriental and African Studies*

Jones, I. W.
A comparative study of two methods of approach in the teaching of Latin. *M.A. 1949 London, Institute of Education*

Jones, J.
An account of the treatment of the fundamental operations of arithmetic, as applied to whole numbers, fractions and decimals, in the printed English Arithmetics, up to and including Cocker's *Arithmetic* (1678). *M.Sc. 1931 Wales*

Jones, J.
The influence of Greek life and Greek culture on the writings and teachings of St. Paul. *M.A. 1919 Wales*

Jones, J. A.
Gweithian barddonol Huw Arwystl(The poetical works of Huw Arwystl). *M. A. 1926 Wales*

Jones, J. D.
Sir Gawain and the magic sword. *M.A. 1925 Wales*

Jones, J. G.
The religious philosophy of Newman. *Ph.D. 1934 Edinburgh*

Jones, J. H.
A critical study of the life and works of Varro. *Ph.D. 1936 London, University College*

Jones, J. H.
The effects of tariffs on industries, with especial reference to the tinplate industry. *M.A. 1904 Wales*

Jones, J. H.
The influence of Greece on Roman *satura*. *M.A. 1933 Wales*

Jones, J. I.
The bondage of the will in the light of post-Reformation theology. *M.A. 1946 Wales*

Jones, J. I.
The relationship between iconography of the Middle Ages and medieval English drama. *M.A. 1939 Wales*

Jones, J. J.
The native Italian element in early Roman religion as illustrated by Latin literature up to the end of the first century B.C. *M.A. 1919 Wales*

Jones, J. L.
The affinities of Italic and Celtic. *M.A. 1909 Wales*

Jones, J. L. Morgan- *see* Morgan-Jones, J. L.

Jones, J. Lloyd- *see* Lloyd-Jones, J.

Jones, J. M.
An economic survey of some aspects of farming in Wales. *M.A. 1926 Wales*

Jones, J. R.
The popular element in the language of Plautus. *M.A. 1911 Wales*

Jones, J. R.
A re-examination of some questions at issue between idealists and realists with regard to the subject-object relation and the nature of mind. *D.Phil. 1946 Oxford*

Jones, J. R.
Scientia intuitiva and the concrete universal. *M.A. 1935 Wales*

Jones, J. R.
Theism and the problem of evil. *M.A. 1929 Wales*

Jones, J. R.
The use and purpose of imagery in the tragedy of Webster, Tourneur and Middleton. *M.A. 1941 Wales*

Jones, J. S.
English foreign trade in the first half of the nineteenth century, together with some observations on the war period of 1793-1814. *M.Sc. 1928 London*

Jones, J. S.
Historical study of Anglo-South American trade, with special reference to the period, 1807-1825. *Ph.D. 1934 London, School of Economics and Political Science*

Jones, J. T.
Rhetoric in Welsh oratory and poetry, 1789-1840. *M.A. 1924 Liverpool*

Jones, J. T.
A study of the development of the science of grammar in its earliest stages in Wales, with particular reference to the grammatical works of Einion Offeiriad, Dafydd Ddu Hiraddug and Simwnt Fychan. *M.A. 1925 Wales*

Jones, J. W.
The reciprocal influence of Roman law and Christianity. *Ph.D. 1925 London*

Jones, J. Westbury- *see* Westbury-Jones, J.

Jones, K.
Nestroys Parodien: ihre Technik und Methode. *M.A. 1927 London*

Jones, K. M.
The *Revue britannique*: its origins in 1825 and its early history to 1840. *M.A. 1938 Wales*

Jones, L.
The influence of the Methodist revival on Welsh hymnology, with particular reference to the hymns of William Williams of Pantycelyn. *B.Litt. 1922 Oxford*

Jones, L.
Lead and silver industry in Wales, 1558-1750. *B.Litt. 1924 Oxford*

Jones, L.
The lead industry in Cardiganshire. *M.A. 1915 Wales*

Jones, L.
A study of the hymnology of the Methodist revival in Wales, with particular reference to the hymns of Williams, Pantycelyn. *M.A. 1921 Wales*

Jones, L. B.
The status of woman in Islam. *M.A. 1941 Wales*

Jones, L. G. E.
The training of teachers in England and Wales: a critical survey. *Ph.D. 1926 London*

Jones, L. M.
The conception of bliss in the Old Testament. *M.A. 1941 Wales*

Jones, L. M.
Hanes llenyddol y *Gwyliedydd* (1822-1837), gyda mynegai i'w gynnwys(The literary history of the *Gwyliedydd* (1822-1837), with an index to its contents). *M.A. 1936 Wales*

Jones, L. R.
A geographical study of the localization and migration of iron and steel manufacture in the North East of England (Northumberland, Durham, and the North Riding). *Ph.D. 1925 London*

Jones, L. S.
Church and chapel as sources and centres of education in Wales during the second half of the nineteenth century. *M.A. 1940 Liverpool*

Jones, L. W.
Theory and practice of psychology, and other papers. *D.Sc. 1939 Wales*

Jones, M.
A collection of the acta of John, Lord of Ireland and Count of Mortain, with a study of his household. *M.A. 1949 Manchester*

Jones, M.
Expositions of Acts xx.15-38: St. Paul's address to the elders at Miletus; Matthew iv.23: the Christ of eschatology; Hebrews i.1: The Epistle to Hebrews. *D.D. 1914 Oxford*

Jones, M.
The history of the lordship and castle of Chirk, 1282-1660. *M.A. 1920 Wales*

Jones, M.
Some organizations of industrial employers in England in the early nineteenth century. *M.A. 1933 Manchester*

Jones, M.
William de Braose. *M.A. 1901 Wales*

Jones, M. A.
The Book of Job. *M.A. 1927 Birmingham*

Jones, M. D.
The Arthurian legend in English literature down to and including Malory. *M.A. 1908 Wales*

Jones, M. H.
Anglo-French relations (1871-1904), with special reference to the problem of the Franco-German rivalry. *M.A. 1938 Wales*

Jones, M. H.
The life and letters of Christopher Love, 1618-1651. *M.A. 1932 Wales*

Jones, M. H.
The origin and growth of the Methodist Movement in Wales in the eighteenth century, in the light of the unpublished mss. correspondence of Howell Harris at Trevecka. *Ph.D. 1929 Wales*

Jones, M. J.
The industrial development of Merioneth, 1750-1820, being an investigation into the economic organization and history of certain distinctive industries in the county during this period. *M.A. 1937 Wales*

Jones, M. K.
The slave trade at Mauritius, 1811-29. *B.Litt. 1936 Oxford*

Jones, M. P.
The influence of French literary theory and practice on the work of George Gissing and George Moore. *M.A. 1936 Wales*

Jones, M. S. S.
The abnormal subject and responsibility for crime. *M.D. 1926 Liverpool*

Jones, M. S. S.
Observations of the evolution of public health law and administration with special reference to its bearing on mother and child. *M.D. 1925 Liverpool*

Jones, M. W. E.
Social history and domestic manners as reflected in the works of Gustav Freytag and Wilhelm Raabe. *M.A. 1932 Wales*

Jones, N.
A critical edition of the *Vigilles des mors* of Pierre de Nesson, based on the two manuscripts in the British Museum. *M.A. 1942 Wales*

Jones, N.
An investigation into the curriculum of girls' secondary schools. *M.A. 1927 London*

Jones, O. A.
A comparison of the texts of the *Brut y Brenhinoedd* as found in the *Red book of Hergest* and in the Peniarth ms. 44, concluded in Llanstephan ms. 1. *M.A. 1914 Wales*

Jones, O. L.
Hellas and its background. *M.A. 1937 Birmingham*

Jones, P. H.
The Church under the Lancastrians. *M.A. 1910 Wales*

Jones, P. J.
The influence of Hegel's philosophy upon theology in Wales from 1850 to the present day. *M.A. 1927 Wales*

Jones, P. J.
The Malatesta of Rimini. *D.Phil. 1950 Oxford*

Jones, P. M.
Whitman in France; Whitman and the origin of the *vers libre*: Whitman and Verhaeren; the origins of the *vers libre*. *M.A. 1916 Wales*

Jones, P.M.
Emile Verhaeren and his place in the history of modern poetry. *B.Litt. 1923 Oxford*

Jones, R.
Gabriele d'Annunzio, with special reference to his sojourn to France from 1911-1915. *M.A. 1943 Wales*

Jones, R.
The nature and first principle of taxation. *D.Sc. 1915 London*

Jones, R.
Rural depopulation in Wales, 1881-1901. *M.A. 1911 Belfast*

Jones, R.
St. Paul's conception of the Spirit. *D.D. 1928 Belfast*

Jones, R. A.
Knowledge Chartism: a study of the influence of Chartism on nineteenth century educational development in Great Britain. *M.A. 1938 Birmingham*

Jones, R. A.
Mme. de Staël and England: a study of Mme. de Staël's English acquaintances, and of her reputation and influence in England. *M.A. 1928 London*

Jones, R. A.
Theodore Hook: his life and works. *M.A. 1932 Wales*

Jones, R. A.
War and peace in English poetry, 1780-1830. *M.A. 1948 Wales*

Jones, R. B.
Nationalism in the works of Maurice Barrès. *M.A. 1934 Wales*

Jones, R. E. A.
Marie Antoinette and the French Revolution. *M.A. 1946 Wales*

Jones, R. G.
The law of diplomatic immunity. *Ph.D. 1949 Cambridge*

Jones, R. M.
The contribution of a secondary school to vocational adjustment. *M.Ed. 1944 Manchester*

Jones, R. M.
The Welsh novel. *M.A. 1923 Wales*

Jones, R. O.
Some Spanish biographies of Sir Thomas More. *M.A. 1949 London, King's College*

Jones, R. S.
Paul Valéry and the Mallarmean heritage: a literary and psychological study. *Ph.D. 1949 London, King's College*

Jones, R. S.
The philosophy of Paul Valéry as expressed in his poetry. *M.A. 1942 Wales*

Jones, R. T.
The life, work and thought of Vavasor Powell (1617-70). *D.Phil. 1947 Oxford*

Jones, R. W.
English loan words in literary Welsh. *M.A. 1907 Wales*

Jones, R. W.
The wayside entertainer in Wales in the nineteenth century. *M.A. 1939 Liverpool*

Jones, R. W. Lloyd- *see* Lloyd-Jones, R. W.

Jones, S.
Disintegration of the personality in the work of Marcel Proust. *M.A. 1940 Wales*

Jones, S.
The lives and labours of John Jones and Robert Vaughan, scribes of the sixteenth and seventeenth centuries. *M.A. 1926 Wales*

Jones, S.
The metaphysical basis of the work of Marcel Proust. *Ph.D. 1949 Cambridge*

Jones, S. B.
Quality, quantity and relation with special reference to the philosophy of Hegel. *M.A. 1923 Wales*

Jones, S. J.
The domestic horse and perforated stone axes in antiquity as studied by archaeological and folklore evidence, with some suggestions as to their connections with movements of peoples. *M.A. 1928 Wales*

Jones, S. J.
Ieuan Gwynedd: ei fywyd a'i waith(Ieuan Gwynedd; his life and his work). *M.A. 1931 Wales*

Jones, S. S.
The position of small States in the League of Nations. *D.Phil. 1936 Oxford*

Jones, T.
The ethical doctrine of Alexandre Dumas fils, as expressed in his plays. *M.A. 1941 Wales*

Jones, T.
Tri thestun ffug-hanesyddol Cymraeg (Peniarth ms. 20, td. 1-64, British Museum addl. ms. 12, 193, Peniarth ms. 215, td. 374-402 - a'u cyd-destunau) a'u cysylltiad â'r testunau Lladin gwreiddiol(Three Welsh pseudo-historical texts (Peniarth ms. 20, pp. 1-64, British Museum Addl. ms. 12, 193, Peniarth ms. 215, pp. 374-402 -and their contexts) and their connections with the original latin texts). *M.A. 1935 Wales*

Jones, T. B.
The life of St. David by Giraldus Cambrensis. *M.A. 1934 Wales*

Jones, T. C.
The history of the Counter-Reformation in Wales. *B.Litt. 1924 Oxford*

Jones, T. E.
Ffwleriaeth yng Nghumru(Fullerism in Wales). *M.A. 1934 Wales*

Jones, T. E.
The history of the Industrial Revolution in Monmouthshire. *M.A. 1929 Wales*

Jones, T. G.
Bardism and romance; a study of the Welsh literary tradition. *M.A. 1915 Wales*

Jones, T. G.
Ystorya Addaf a *Val a cauas Elen y Grog*: tarddiad, cynnwys ac arddull y testunau Cymraeg a'u lledaeniad(*The history of Adam* and *How Helen found the Cross*; Source, content, and style of the Welsh texts, and their diffusion). *M.A. 1936 Wales*

Jones, T. H.
The imagery of the metaphysical poets of the seventeenth century. *M.A. 1949 Wales*

Jones, T. H.
Social life in Wales in the eighteenth century as illustrated in its popular literature of the period. *M.A. 1922 Wales*

Jones, T. H.
The value of sentiment to the characterization in the novels of Samuel Richardson. *M.A. 1946 Wales*

Jones, T. I. J.
The Enclosure Movement in south Wales during the Tudor and early Stuart periods. *M.A. 1936 Wales*

Jones, T. J. R.
Yr anterliwt Gymraeg: ei ffynonellau, ei chrefftwaithm a'i gwerth fel arwddocâd o ddiwylliant y bobl(The Welsh 'interlude'; its sources, craftsmanship, and value as an indication of the culture of the people). *M.A. 1939 Wales*

Jones, T. R.
Walter Bagehot: writer and critic. *M.A. 1932 Wales*

Jones, T. T.
The significance for metaphysics of the presuppositions of morality. *M.A. 1929 Wales*

Jones, V. T.
Modern British drama in relation to the plays of Ibsen. *M.A. 1928 Liverpool*

Jones, W.
A comparison of Thucydides and Aristophanes. *M.A. 1902 Wales*

Jones, W. A.
Edward Young: a study of his life and works. *M.A. 1949 Wales*

Jones, W. A. Pritchard- *see* Pritchard-Jones, W. A.

Jones, W. D.
Problems of wages and wage regulations. *M.Sc. 1936 London, External Degree*

Jones, W. G.
The life and works of Henry Rowlands. *M.A. 1936 Wales*

Jones, W. G.
Welsh politics from Mortimers Cross to Bosworth Field. *M.A. 1908 Liverpool*

Jones, W. H.
Methods in farm management analysis: an economic investigation with some illustrations and results. *M.Sc. 1933 Wales*

Jones, W. I.
The Aden dialect of Arabic: a study of its grammatical peculiarities as compared with the classical language. *M.A. 1940 Wales*

Jones, W. I.
Orgraff y Gymraeg o gyfnod y Dr. William Owen Pughe hyd ddiwygiad yr orgraff(The orthography of the Welsh language from the period of Dr. William Owen Pugh to the reform). *M.A. 1924 Wales*

Jones, W. J.
A comparison of the treatment of historical subjects by Aristophanes and Thucydides. *M.A. 1911 Wales*

Jones, W. L.
Immanence. *M.A. 1930 Wales*

Jones, W. L.
A psychological study of religious conversion. *M.A. 1935 Reading*

Jones, W. L.
The social and psychological conditions of the rise and development of Methodism. *Ph.D. 1939 Liverpool*

Jones, W. P.
The syntax of New Testament compared with Attic Greek. *M.A. 1902 Wales*

Jones, W. R.
A comparative study of the nature poetry of Ieuen Glan Geirionydd, Alun, Islwyn and Ceiriog. *M.A. 1923 Wales*

Jones, W. R.
The history of the port of Hull to the end of the fourteenth century. *M.A. 1943 Wales*

Jones, W. R.
Tests for the examination of the effect of bilingualism on intelligence. *M.A. 1933 Wales*

Jones, W. T.
Royce's theory of the individual. *B.Litt. 1933 Oxford*

Jones-Roberts, E. *see* Roberts, E. Jones-

Jope, F. E.
Elizabethan tragedy contrasted with the classical drama of Corneille and Racine. *M.A. 1910 Birmingham*

Jopson, C. M.
Investigations into the Judaeo-Spanish of the Balkan Peninsula, with particular reference to Roumania and Yugoslavia. *Ph.D. 1930 London, King's College*

Jordan, D.
An analysis of the attitude of children towards certain school subjects, and the measure of correlation between attitude and attainment. *M.A. 1937 London, Institute of Education*

Jordan, P.
Montesquieu: his political and economic ideas. *Ph.D. 1930 London, External Degree*

Jordan, P.
Montesquieu: his political and economic ideas. *Ph.D. 1930 London, School of Economics and Political Science*

Jordan, W. M.
The problems of French security, 1918-1920, with special reference to the military terms and the western frontier of Germany. *Ph.D. 1940 London, School of Economics and Political Science*

Jordon, W. M.
The silk industry in London, 1760-1830, with special reference to the condition of the wage-earners and the policy of the Spitalfields Acts. *M.A. 1931 London, University College*

Jory, J. J.
History of coal during the Industrial Revolution. *Ph.D. 1931 London, External Degree*

Jory, J. J.
The letter-writers of the eighteenth century. *M.A. 1912 Wales*

Joscelyne, A. E.
1. The Epistle to the Galatians. 2. The mission of John the Baptist. *B.D. 1894 Oxford*

Joscelyne, A. E.
Expositions of: II Kings xxii: reforms of Josiah; Acts vii: the defence of Stephen; The Epistle to Philemon: St. Paul's treatment of slavery. *D.D. 1898 Oxford*

Joselin, A. G.
The analysis of a pictorial test of intelligence. *M.A. 1947 London, Institute of Education*

Joseph, B.
Nationality: its meaning, developments and problems. *Ph.D. 1928 London*

Joseph, B.
The *Responsa* of R. Benjamin (Ze'eb) ben Matisyahu: a contribution to the history of Jews in southern Europe at the end of the fifteenth and the beginning of the sixteenth centuries. *Ph.D. 1942 London, University College*

Joseph, B. L.
Monologue, soliloquy and aside in the pre-Restoration drama. *D.Phil. 1946 Oxford*

Joseph, C. A.
The economic development of the American colonies, with special reference to the relations with the mother country. *M.Com. 1928 Birmingham*

Joseph, G. I.
The law of mistake in contract. *B.Litt. 1936 Oxford*

Joseph, M. K.
The life and works of William Falconer (1732-70). *B.Litt. 1939 Oxford*

Joseph, P.
China's political fin-de-siècle, 1900: a study in the diplomatic relations of the powers with China. *Ph.D. 1926 London*

Joshi, K. L.
The *London Journal*, 1719-1738. *M.A. 1937 London, Courtauld Institute of Art*

Joshi, L. D.
The Khasa family law in the Himalayan districts of the United Provinces, India. *LL.D. 1927 London*

Joshi, P. M.
The kingdom of Bijāpur. *Ph.D. 1935 London, School of Oriental and African Studies*

Joshua, A.
The history of the development of studies in the marketing of agricultural produce and theories of marketing reforms, with some reference to the development of marketing studies in India. *M.Sc. 1936 Wales*

Jowett, G. T.
1. The intermediate state. 2. The date and authorship of the Apocalypse. *B.D. & D.D. 1909 Oxford*

Jowsey, W. H.
Pope's version of the *Iliad*, considered as illustrating his theory of translation and his conception of the heroic style. *B.Litt. 1949 Oxford*

Joy, F. W.
1. The Lord's Prayer: its origin, comprehensiveness, and suitability, both as a form and a model. 2. The genuineness of the pastoral epistles. *B.D. & D.D. 1895 Oxford*

Joyce, A. H.
Italian art in the works of Robert Browning. *M.A. 1904 Birmingham*

Joyce, G. C.
1. Deuteronomy xviii.9-22: inspiration and prophecy. 2. Isaiah vi and xxi.1-10: the prophetic call, audition, and vision. I Corinthians xii-xiv: the psychology of Christian prophecy, introductory to tongues and prophecy in the Corinthian Church. *D.D. 1909 Oxford*

Joyce, G. C.
1. The doctrine of the fall in relation to evolution. 2. The fall and the Incarnation. *B.D. 1904 Oxford*

Joyce, L. S.
Individual experimental work in physics in the junior forms of grammar schools. *M.Ed. 1949 Durham*

Joyce, M. P.
Transcription of Harcourt Papers. *M.A. 1947 National University of Ireland*

Joynson, R. B.
The perception of size and its connexion with the perception of space. *B.Litt. 1949 Oxford*

Jucker, N. S.
The political papers of Charles Jenkinson, 1760-1765. *M.A. 1936 Manchester*

Judd, J. M.
The history and significance of the early Elizabethan drama. *M.A. 1914 Wales*

Judek, S.
The development of the electricity supply industry in Great Britain. *Ph.D. 1947 Edinburgh*

Judge, H.
The literary significance of John Wilmot, Earl of Rochester. *M.A. 1934 Birmingham*

Judson, K. I.
Early history of the manor and parish of Bradford (W. Riding, Yorks). *M.A. 1933 London, Birkbeck College*

Jukes, C. D.
Etude sur l'authenticité du 5e livre de Rabelais. *M.A. 1924 Birmingham*

Jump, J. D.
A full critical edition of *Rollo, Duke of Normandy; or, the bloody brother. M.A. 1936 Liverpool*

Junaid, M. M.
Elements of instability in the economic expansion of America, 1921-29. *Ph.D. 1932 London, School of Economics and Political Science*

Junankar, N. S.
The conceptions of time, space, and motion in early Indian philosophy. *D.Phil. 1937 Oxford*

Junankar, N. S.
The criticisms of the Sāmkhya philosophy in the texts of other Indian systems. *B.Litt. 1935 Oxford*

Jung, L.
Fallen angels in Jewish, Christian, and Mohammedan literature. *Ph.D. 1922 London*

Jung, M. U. I. S.
Muslim law of marriage. *LL.D. 1926 Dublin, Trinity College*

Jupp, T. H.
Economic development of Morocco under French protection. *M.A. 1935 Bristol*

Justice, F.
Introduction à l'étude de la ville d'Ypres. *M.A. 1940 National University of Ireland*

Justice, F. E. J.
The abuse of rights. *Ph.D. 1943 National University of Ireland*

Kaberry, P. M.
The position of women in Australian aboriginal society. *Ph.D. 1938 London, School of Economics and Political Science*

Kader, A. H. Abdel- *see* Abdel-Kader, A. H.

Kafafi, M. A. S.
The *Bayān al-Adyān* by Abu'l Maīl Muhammad ibn Ubayd Allāh: translation, introduction and notes. *Ph.D. 1949 London, School of Oriental and African Studies*

Kaftal, G.
The iconography of local saints in Tuscan painting from the thirteenth to the end of the fifteenth century. *D.Phil. 1946 Oxford*

Kagan, K.
Ususfructus and *dominium. M.Litt. 1945 Cambridge*

Kahn, L. W.
Types of social ideals in German literature (from Sturm-und-Drang to Romanticism). *M.A. 1936 London, University College*

Kaissouni, A. M. el *see* el Kaissouni, A. M.

Kalisch, S.
A critical study of Abravanel's *Commentary on Kings. M.A. 1943 Manchester*

Kallukaren, P. P.
Industrial banking in India. *Ph.D. 1923 London*

Kalota, R. S.
A history of the education of the Shudra untouchables before and under the British rule in India, c. 2000 B.C. to 1947. *M. Ed. 1950 Durham*

Kamat, V. V.
Measuring intelligence of Indian children. *Ph.D. 1939 Edinburgh*

Kamel, N.
The national characteristics of the modern Egyptians. *M.A. 1942 London, School of Economics and Political Science*

Kamen, A.
Christina Rossetti: as a lyrical poet. *M.A. 1927 Wales*

Kanani, A. H. K. M. Z.
The development of *El-Ghazal* in Arabic poetry. *Ph.D. 1948 London, School of Oriental and African Studies*

Kanapathippillai, K.
The study of the language of the Tamil inscriptions of the seventh and eighth centuries A.D. *Ph.D. 1936 London, School of Oriental and African Studies*

Kane, G. J.
The B-text of *Piers Plowman*, passus XVIII-XX. *Ph.D. 1946 London, University College*

Kankan, T. B.
Interests of boys in relation to mental ability and environment. *M.Ed. 1936 Leeds*

Kanta, S.
A critical edition of the *Atharvaprātiśākhya* with a comparative study of the *Caturādhyāyikā*, with translation and notes. *D.Phil. 1937 Oxford*

Kapadia, E. R.
The diplomatic career of Sir Claude Wade: a study of British relations with the Sikhs and Afghans, July 1823 to March 1840. *M.A. 1938 London, School of Oriental and African Studies*

Kapur, I. M.
Post-war developments in monetary theory. *M.Sc. 1934 London, School of Economics and Political Science*

Kapur, R. K.
A study of the burlesque drama from D'Avenant to Fielding. *B.Litt. 1934 Oxford*

Kar, B. C.
Psychological theories of instinct and their influence on educational theory and practice. *M.A. 1949 London, Institute of Education*

Karim, F. A.
The Persian *Ghazal*: its origin, development and characteristics. *B.Litt. 1932 Oxford*

Karmel, P. H.
The measurement of reproductivity in relation to the conflict between male and female measures. *Ph.D. 1949 Cambridge*

Karson, I. M.
The political thought and practice of American trade unionism, 1906-18. *Ph.D. 1949 London, School of Economics and Political Science*

Karvé, B. D.
An experimental investigation of 'fluency' (of imagination and association), in school children. *M.Ed. 1929 Leeds*

Kassim, M.
The history of the Suez Canal Concession, 1854-1866. *M.A. 1924 London*

Kastner, L. E.
Histoire du rondeau en France et de ses dérivés des origines à la Pléiade. *M.A. 1933 Manchester*

Kato, B.
A translation into English of part of the *Miao fa lien hua ching. B.Litt. 1925 Oxford*

Katre, S. R. M. R.
Early Buddhist ballads and their relations to the older Upanishadic literature. *Ph.D. 1932 London, School of Oriental and African Studies*

Katz, W. P. M.
The text of the Septuagint: its corruptions and their emendation. *Ph.D. 1945 Cambridge*

Kaul, B. N.
Some aspects of the population problem in Burma. *Ph.D. 1930 London, School of Economics and Political Science*

Kaul, R. N.
The theory of judgment in Bradley and Bosanquet. *B.Litt. 1928 Oxford*

Kavanagh, J.
The letter R (Hessen's Irish lexicon). *Ph.D. 1940 National University of Ireland*

Kavanagh, K.
English elegy. *M.A. 1933 National University of Ireland*

Kavanagh, P.
The history of Anglo-Irish drama from the earliest period up to 1750. *Ph.D. 1944 Dublin, Trinity College*

Kavanagh, T.
Drámaidheacht na Gaedhilge(The dramatisation of Irish). *M.A. 1929 National University of Ireland*

Kay, B. L. V.
La théorie de l'éducation chez Molière. *M.A. 1912 Liverpool*

Kay, L. H.
Lessing's knowledge and criticism of English literature. *M.A. 1912 Birmingham*

Kay, L. J.
Physical science in the non-selective modern school. *M.A. 1929 London*

Kay, S. J.
Some aspects of the problem of the educable mentally defective child and its place in society. *M.A. 1935 Liverpool*

Kaye, M.
Problems of democratic education. *Ph.D. 1928 London*

Kaye, M.
The sense of time and its relation to the teaching of chronology. *M.A. 1933 Leeds*

Kaye, R. A.
Néologismes dans *la Comédie humaine* de H. de Balzac, 1829-1832. *M.A. 1923 Leeds*

Kean, A. W. G.
The history of *mens rea* in the law of homicide. *M.Litt. 1939 Cambridge*

Keane, C. E.
Lebar lapiderachta Fionnguine Meic Maeltuile: a medieval Irish lapidary. *M.A. 1941 National University of Ireland*

Keane, D.
The function and influence of privy councillors in Parliament in the early seventeenth century. *M.A. 1930 London, University College*

Keane, F. J.
Spenser's debt to Ariosto and Tasso. *M.A. 1920 National University of Ireland*

Keane, M. J. C.
History of the free trade movement and its effects on Irish trade and commerce. *M.A. 1922 National University of Ireland*

Keane, W. F.
The Physiocrats and Adam Smith. *M.A. 1915 National University of Ireland*

Kear, M.
Richard Jefferies: the interpreter of nature. *M.A. 1925 Liverpool*

Kearns, A. J.
Latin influence on Tudor comedy. *M.A. 1935 National University of Ireland*

Keates, H. A.
1. The origin of the expectation of the early Advent of our Blessed Lord. 2. The relation of the Epistle to the Hebrews to St. Paul's Epistles. *B.D. 1904 Oxford*

Keating, H. M.
The factors which have influenced settlement and the movements of population within the plain of Nottingham. *Ph.D. 1933 London, External Degree*

Keating, H. M.
The historical geography of the Newark area as illustrating changes in the importance of geographical factors. *M.A. 1929 London*

Keating, M. G.
Meditations on the Supper of Our Lord. *M.A. 1919 Bristol*

Keay, F. E.
Ancient Indian education: an enquiry into its origin, development, and ideals. *M.A. 1917 London*

Keays-Young, J. M.
England and the English in the Icelandic sagas. *B.Litt. 1928 Oxford*

Keeble, T. W.
The burlesque of mythology in seventeenth century Spanish poetry. *Ph.D. 1948 London, King's College*

Keegan, E.
The early poetry of W. B. Yeats. *M.A. 1941 National University of Ireland*

Keegan, K. M.
Sir Francis Drake: explorer. *M.A. 1924 Birmingham*

Keegan, T.
Byron's artistic truth. *M.A. 1941 National University of Ireland*

Keeley, K. M.
The detection and trial of Lollards from 1414-1428. *M.A. 1936 Manchester*

Keeling, S. V.
Antoine Arnauld and the Cartesian theory of representative ideas. *M.A. 1926 London*

Keene, A. C.
1. The doctrine of sacrifice. 2. The doctrine of atonement. *B.D. 1906 Oxford*

Keene, A. C.
Expositions of St. John iii.46-54; St. John ix.1-38; St. John v.1-14. *D.D. 1910 Oxford*

Keeney, G. S.
The occupation of the counties Northumberland, Durham, Cumberland, and Westmorland from the fourth to the eighth centuries, as revealed by the archaeological and historical evidence. *B. Litt. 1935 Oxford*

Keep, E. T.
The account of individuation in Plato's early dialogues. *M.A. 1947 Wales*

Keet, C. C.
Some liturgical and ceremonial aspects of Jewish worship exhibited in the Psalter. *Ph.D. 1927 London*

Kefalas, A.
The place of instinct in the evolution of the mind in man and the lower animals from the biological and psychological points of view. *M.A. 1926 Liverpool*

Kehoe, B. P.
Hegel and Germany. *Ph.D. 1932 National University of Ireland*

Keir, W. A. S.
E. M. Forster: a critical and historical estimate. *B.Litt. 1949 Oxford*

Keith, A. B.
The theory of State succession, with special reference to English and Colonial law. *D.C.L. 1907 Oxford*

Kelchner, G. D.
Dreams in Old Norse literature and their affinities in folklore. *Ph.D. 1934 Cambridge*

Kelleher, H. F.
Scoto-Irish intercourse in the latter part of the sixteenth century. *M.A. 1931 National University of Ireland*

Kelleher, J.
Robert Burns as the culmination of a literary tradition. *M.A. 1938 National University of Ireland*

Kelleher, M.
Logic and mathematics, with special reference to Bertrand Russell. *M.A. 1942 National University of Ireland*

Kelleher, P.
Some modern theories of intelligence: exposition and criticism. *M.A. 1934 National University of Ireland*

Kellems, J. R.
The theology of Alexander Campbell in relation to the origin of the Disciples. *Ph.D. 1926 Edinburgh*

Kellems, V. E.
The biography of Barton Warren Stone, with particular reference to the origin of the Christian Church in the west, and its influence on the Disciples of Christ. *Ph.D. 1928 Edinburgh*

Keller, R. E.
An enquiry into the use of adjectives denoting beauty in Middle High German. *M.A. 1949 Manchester*

Kelley, L. W.
The early years of Richard, Earl of Cornwall. *M.A. 1912 Liverpool*

Kelly, J.
Dramatic aspect of Browning's poetry. *M.A. 1930 National University of Ireland*

Kelly, J. F.
The psychology of the emotions. *M.A. 1945 National University of Ireland*

Kelly, J. J.
George Shiels as the exponent of modern Irish comedy. *M.A. 1951 National University of Ireland*

Kelly, T.
A study of the Civil Service of Northern Ireland. *M.A. 1936 Belfast*

Kelly, T. F.
The administration of Thomas Drummond in Ireland (1835-40). *M.A. 1941 National University of Ireland*

Kelly T. H.
The Midland transportation question. Sketches, statistical and otherwise. *M.Com. 1928 Birmingham*

Kelly, T. H.
Wages and labour organization in the brass trades of Birmingham and district. *Ph.D. 1930 Birmingham*

Kelsall, M.
A study in the teaching of English composition in a girls' modern secondary school: an investigation into the relative merits of two different methods. *M.A. 1947 Liverpool*

Kelso, A. P.
Schleiermacher's ethics. *B.Sc. 1913 Oxford*

Kemp, E. W.
Ecclesiastical authority and the canonizations of saints in the western Church. *B.D. 1944 Oxford*

Kemp, J. N.
Greek poetry and the sea. *M.A. 1938 London, University College*

Kenadjian, E. B.
Bunyan's use of allegory in relation to the earlier English tradition. *M.A. 1929 Manchester*

Kendall, O. P. F.
A historical and cultural survey of the Roman limes of Germania Superior and Raetia. *M.A. 1931 London, University College*

Kendall, W. L.
The political theory of J. S. Mill. *M.Sc. 1926 London*

Kendra, E.
Palestine in the seventh and sixth centuries B.C. in the light of archaeology. *M.A. 1948 Leeds*

Kendrick, T. D.
The megalithic remains of the Channel Islands. *B.Sc. 1924 Oxford*

Kennedy, B. A.
The struggle for tenant-right in Ulster, 1829 to 1850. *M.A. 1943 Belfast*

Kennedy, C. A.
Survey of the history of education in Corca Laighdne (Diocese of Ross) from earliest times to 1825. *M.A. 1942 National University of Ireland*

Kennedy, E. L.
Labour theory of value in classical economics. *M.A. 1946 National University of Ireland*

Kennedy, E. M.
La psychologie de Molière. *M.A. 1916 National University of Ireland*

Kennedy, J.
The doctrine of reward and retribution in the *Book of Proverbs*. *Ph.D. 1934 Glasgow*

Kennedy, M. A.
Some comparisons between Welsh and Irish love poetry. *M.A. 1943 National University of Ireland*

Kennedy, S. G.
The plantation of Ulster. *M.A. 1925 National University of Ireland*

Kennedy, W.
English taxation, 1640-1799. *D.Sc. 1913 London*

Kennelly, M.
Some aspects of Jesuit education before the suppression. *M.A. 1948 National University of Ireland*

Kennett, B.
Notes on some tribes of Kabba province. *Dip. Anthropology. 1931 Cambridge*

Kenny, E. J. A.
Quaestiones hydraulicae. *M.Litt. 1936 Cambridge*

Kenny, J. J.
Law reform in England since 1921. *M.A. 1949 National University of Ireland*

Kenny. K. A.
A consideration of geographical factors influencing the distribution of population in British Columbia. *M.A. 1934 London, Bedford College*

Kent, A. R.
An English translation of *Liber regularum* by Tyconius Afer. *M.A. 1943 Sheffield*

Kent, A. W.
The life and work of W. H. Wollaston. *M.Sc. 1931 London*

Kent, J.
Encumbered Estates Act. *M.A. 1931 National University of Ireland*

Kenworthy, F.
The industrial development of Ashton-under-Lyne, 1780-1850. *M.A. 1929 Manchester*

Kenworthy, P. F.
Rural settlement in East Cheshire: a study in historical geography. *M.A. 1949 Manchester*

Kenwrick, G. J.
The relation of social and educational theory at the opening of the nineteenth century. *M.A. 1927 London*

Kenyon, E. M.
William Morris as an interpreter of northern legend. *M.A. 1928 Manchester*

Keogh, W.
The pantheism of Spinoza. *M.A. 1930 National University of Ireland*

Keppel, D. H. E.
1. On the Gospel of St. John. 2. On St. Augustine's treatise *De civitate dei*. *B.D. 1906 Oxford*

Kepple, S.
A survey of taxation and government expenditure in the Irish Free State, 1922-1936. *M.A. 1938 National University of Ireland*

Ker, N. R.
A study of the additions and alterations in mss. Bodley 340 and 342. *B.Litt. 1933 Oxford*

Ker, R. E.
Simonides of Ceos. *M.A. 1930 Belfast*

Kerby, W. M.
The life and literary activities of Baculard d'Arnaud, with special reference to his novels. *Ph.D. 1921 London*

Kerley, H. W.
The relation of St. Paul's ethics to his doctrine of salvation. *Ph.D. 1949 Edinburgh*

Kermode, J. F.
Some aspects of seventeenth century learning as exhibited in the *Davideis* of Abraham Cowley. *M.A. 1947 Liverpool*

Kerr, B. M.
Irish immigration into Great Britain, 1798-1838. *B.Litt. 1939 Oxford*

Kerr, D. G. G.
The work of Sir Edmund Head in British North America 1848-61. *Ph.D. 1937 London, King's College*

Kerr, E.
Etude littéraire des premiers trouvères (douzième siècle). *M.A. 1947 Belfast*

Kerr, H. T.
The relation between the person of Christ and the principle of redemption, especially as propounded by D. F. Strauss, A. E. Biedermann and E. P. W. Troeltsch. *Ph.D. 1936 Edinburgh*

Kerr, M.
Emotional fluctuations in women. *Ph.D. 1938 London, Bedford College*

Kerr, M.
An experimental investigation of auditory imagery. *M.A. 1931 Manchester*

Kerr, M. P.
The organization and administration of the Tres Galliae, 49 B.C.-283 A.D. *M.A. 1924 Manchester*

Kerr, S. A.
Hume's doctrine of imagination. *B.Litt. 1930 Oxford*

Kerrigo, J. H.
The novels of T. L. Peacock. *M.A. 1921 Birmingham*

Kerrison, S. E.
Coventry and the Municipal Corporations Act, 1835: an investigation of the workings of Coventry Corporation mainly between 1750 and 1835, and a critical examination of the Commissioners' Report of 1833. *M.A. 1939 Birmingham*

Kershaw, E. see Brooks, E. K.

Kershaw, J. D.
The municipal borough as a health unit. *M.D. 1939 London, University College*

Kershaw, R. N.
The composition, organization, and character of the House of Commons, 1640-1653. *B.Litt. 1923 Oxford*

Kersley, R. H.
Quasi-contract. *LL.M. 1932 Cambridge*

Kesavan, B. S.
The literary life and writings of William Warburton. *M.A. 1936 London, Birkbeck College*

Kesterton, B.
The social and emotional effects of the recreational film on adolescents of 13 and 14 years of age in the West Bromwich area. *Ph.D. 1948 Birmingham*

Ketelbey, D. M.
A comparative study of federation in the United States, in Switzerland, and in Germany, with reference to federation in the British Empire. *M.A. 1917 Birmingham*

Kettle, A. C.
The relation of political and social ideas to the novel of the English romantic revival. *Ph.D. 1942 Cambridge*

Kettler, H. K.
Baroque survivals in literary theory and practice of the early German enlightenment, 1700-1750. *Ph.D. 1938 Cambridge*

Kevin, C.
Matthew Arnold as a critic of literature. *M.A. 1930 National University of Ireland*

Keyes, H. M.
Keats and Hazlitt in their personal and literary relations. *B.Litt. 1937 Oxford*

Keyes, L. L.
The transcendent relation of reality to truth as the fundamental tenet of the philosophy of St. Thomas Aquinas. *B.Litt. 1934 Oxford*

Khan, A.
International production and exchange of rice, with special reference to production, market demand and consumption of rice in India and Burma. *Ph.D. 1939 Wales*

Khan, A. A.
The production, marketing and consumption of the chief oil seeds in India and the supply and use of oil seeds in the United Kingdom. *Ph.D. 1940 Wales*

Khan, A. F. M. A.
Muhammadan education in Bengal, with special reference to primary education. *M.Ed. 1940 Leeds*

Khan, A. M.
An experiment in the measurement and modification of attitude towards mathematics. *M.A. 1948 London, Institute of Education*

Khan, A. R.
The organization and control of education in Bengal. *M.Ed. 1940 Leeds*

Khan, A. W.
Faizi, Urfi, and Naziri (poets of Akbar's Court). *Ph.D. 1932 London, School of Oriental and African Studies*

Khan, G. H. D. see Dārāb Khan, G. H.

Khan, G. M.
Relation of intuition and intellect. *M.A. 1933 London, King's College*

Khan, I.
Women's education in India. *M.A. 1947 London, Institute of Education*

Khan, I. M.
A critical edition of the Persian correspondence of Col. Sir John Murray. *M.A. 1925 London*

Khan, I. M.
The industrial competitive strength of the United Kingdom compared with that of some other industrial countries, with special reference to the post-war period. *Ph.D. 1932 Leeds*

Khan, K.
Principles of educational reconstruction, with special reference to conditions in the North West Frontier Province. *M.Ed. 1938 Leeds*

Khan, K. A.
Fīhi ma īhi, or the table-talk of Jalālu'ddīn Rūmī. *Ph.D. 1942 Cambridge*

Khan, M. A.
Symbolism in English metaphysical poetry, with special reference to Donne, Herbert and Vaughan. *Ph.D. 1948 London, Queen Mary College*

Khan, M. A. M.
A critical edition, with notes and indices, of the *Kitāb al Tashbīhāt* of Ibn Abī 'Aun. *Ph.D. 1939 Cambridge*

Khan, M. A. W.
The financial problems of Indian states under federation. *Ph.D. 1935 London, School of Economics and Political Science*

Khan, M. F.
A study of the methods for the validation of test items. *M.A. 1948 London, Institute of Education*

Khan, M. H.
The influence of Western education in India. *Ph.D. 1942 Dublin, Trinity College*

Khan, M. I. R.
Some geographical factors in the history of the Punjab from 712 A.D. to 1605 A.D. with special reference to river control of settlement. *Ph.D. 1930 London, University College*

Khan, M. Jahangir see Jahangir Khan, M.

Khan, M. M.
Problems of public finance arising in federal constitutions. *M.Sc. 1936 London*

Khan, M. Q. H.
A critical survey of the growth of primary education in the Punjab since the annexation, 1847-1947, British period. *M.A. 1949 London, King's College*

Khan, M. S. Ali see Ali Khan, M. S.

Khanna, K. C.
Anglo-Sikh relations (1839-49). *Ph.D. 1932 London, School of Oriental and African Studies*

Khanolkar, V. P.
Secondary education in the Bombay Presidency (excluding Sind): its past, present and future; being a study in the evolution and the present state of the system. *M.A. 1933 London, King's College*

Kher, N. Y.
The organization and methods of agricultural co-operation in the British Isles and the possibility of their application in the Central Provinces of India. *Ph.D. 1949 Wales*

Khergamvala, J. S.
Assignment of contracts and choses in action. *LL.D. 1915 London*

Khosla, J. N.
The French Senate. *Ph.D. 1933 London, School of Economics and Political Science*

Khulousy, S. A. D. A. A.
Shiism and its influence on Arabic literature. *Ph.D. 1947 London, External Degree*

Kidd, B. J.
Expositions of: St. Luke xii.42,43: the ministry, a stewardship; I Corinthians xii: the spiritual gifts of the Church; Romans ix.4: the Covenant or Church principle. *D.D. 1904 Oxford*

Kidd, B. J.
1. On the later medieval doctrine of the Eucharistic sacrifice. 2. On the relation of confirmation to baptism according to the New Testament. *B.D. 1898 Oxford*

Kidd, C. B.
Phenomenology and the theory of moral values. *Ph.D. 1935 Saint Andrew's*

Kidd, R. H.
Wit and humour in early Greek literature. *B.Litt. 1941 Dublin, Trinity College*

Kidd, R. H.
Wit and humour in early Greek literature. *M.A. 1941 National University of Ireland*

Kiernan, T. J.
The financial administration of Ireland to 1817. *Ph.D. 1930 London, School of Economics and Political Science*

Kiewiet, C. W. de
The policy of the British Government towards the South African Dutch republics, 1848-1872. *Ph.D. 1927 London*

Kilburn, K.
The use of imagery in the odes of Pindar. *M.A. 1950 Liverpool*

Kilduff, M.
A comparative study of the supernatural element in Elizabethan drama and in modern drama. *M.A. 1937 Liverpool*

Kilgour, A.
The records of the *Fratres Arvales*. *Ph.D. 1939 Saint Andrew's*

Kilpatrick, G. D.
The origins of the Gospel according to St. Matthew. *B.D. 1944 Oxford*

Kilpatrick, J. W.
Protestant missions in Jamaica, being a critical survey of mission policy from 1754 to the present day. *Ph.D. 1944 Edinburgh*

Kimball, E. G.
Frank almoign: a study of ecclesiastical tenure in England chiefly in the fourteenth and fifteenth centuries. *B.Litt. 1927 Oxford*

Kimball, P. C.
The monetary reform of 1821. *B.Litt. 1930 Oxford*

Kimble, G. H.
The mapping of West Africa in the fourteenth and fifteenth centuries, as illustrative of the development of geographical ideas. *M.A. 1931 London, King's College*

Kimpton, E. C.
Shakespeare and Molière, with special reference to comedy. *M.A. 1908 London*

King, A.
The relations of the British Government with the émigrés and royalists of western France, 1793-1795. *Ph.D. 1931 London, University College*

King, A. H.
The influence of French literature upon German prose and dramatic literature from 1880 to 1900. *Ph.D. 1934 London, Birkbeck College*

King, A. W.
Malaya, with special reference to the influence of soil and climate conditions on agriculture. *M.A. 1936 Bristol*

King, C. A. M.
The movement of sand on beaches by waves and other action. *Ph.D. 1950 Cambridge*

King, C. R.
Origin of belief in one God in the Greek world. *M.A. 1932 London, Birkbeck College*

King, D. J. C.
The assignability of choses in action at common law. *LL.M. 1939 Bristol*

King, E. J.
The moral and religious ideas of Aeschylus and Pindar. *M.A. 1937 Manchester*

King, E. M.
The relation of Shakespeare to Lyly. *M.A. 1908 London*

King, G.
The principles of Christian hermeneutics studied in its chief varieties. *Ph.D. 1928 London*

King, H.
The influence of Keats during the late nineteenth century. *M.A. 1923 Birmingham*

King, H.
A report on an investigation of land-utilization in east Yorkshire before the enclosures. *M.A. 1933 Liverpool*

King, H. M.
The work of Theobald and his predecessors on the text of Shakespeare. *Ph.D. 1940 London, External Degree*

King, J. F.
The rise and growth of the liberal theology in New England to 1825. *Ph.D. 1939 Edinburgh*

King, J. M.
The social and intellectual background of the Reign of Queen Anne as reflected in the *Tatler* and *Spectator. M.A. 1938 London, King's College*

King, J. S.
Cost accounting as applied to agriculture as an aid to more productive farming. *Ph.D. 1928 London*

King, K. C.
The Hürnen Seyfrid: a study in origins. *Ph.D. 1938 London, University College*

King, R. H.
Religion as an integrative principle in human personality. *M.Litt. 1938 Cambridge*

King, R. W.
Henry Francis Cary, 1772-1844, translator of Dante: a study. *M.A. 1919 London*

King, S. G.
The personnel organization of the British civil service: a study of structure as related to function. *M.Sc. 1945 London, External Degree*

King, S. H.
Contributions towards the study of the historical geography of Norfolk, with special reference to West Norfolk. *M.A. 1937 London, King's College*

King, S. H.
Contributions towards the study of the historical geography of Lincolnshire. *Ph.D. 1945 London, King's College*

King, S. M.
L'appel du Rhin dans les oeuvres de Maurice Barrès avant la publication des *Bastions de l'Est*: l'influence allemande et l'évolution de sa pensée relative au problème du Rhin. *M.A. 1932 Leeds*

King, S. T.
James Silk Buckingham (1786-1855), social and political reformer. *M.A. 1933 London, King's College*

King, T. H.
A geographical study of electricity generation and distribution in the northwest region. *M.A. 1949 Liverpool*

King, T. M.
Nature in the poetry of Robert Burns. *B.Litt. 1943 Dublin, Trinity College*

King, W.
An economic and social analysis of the effects of state-aid for industrial training and professional education, with special reference to the Swansea and Aberystwyth districts. *M.A. 1921 Wales*

King, W.
A statistical study of the rural population of Wales in the nineteenth and twentieth centuries. *Ph.D. 1929 Wales*

King, W. H.
A comparative study of the factors entering into the boys' and girls' results in a special place examination. *M.A. 1945 London, Institute of Education*

King, W. H.
A critical analysis of the results of a school certificate examination. *Ph.D. 1949 London, Institute of Education*

King, W. J.
Rainfall variability: world and continental distribution. *M.Sc. 1938 London, Queen Mary College*

King, W. T. C.
History of the London discount market. *Ph.D. 1936 London, School of Economics and Political Science*

Kinghorn, J.
A study of certain aspects of nineteenth century periodical criticism (1798-1842) especially in its influence on and attitude to new literary movements. *Ph.D. 1939 Edinburgh*

Kings, A. T.
An introduction to the economic development of the mechanical engineering industry, 1750-1900. *M.Sc. 1923 London*

Kingsford, M. R.
The life, work and influence of W. H. G. Kingston. *B.Litt. 1946 Oxford*

Kingston, H. P.
The influence of William Godwin on Shelley. *M.A. 1932 Birmingham*

Kingston, P. W.
Ideas and revelation. *B.D. 1928 Cambridge*

Kinnear, F. G.
Gottfried Keller's *Züricher Novellen. Ph.D. 1922 Edinburgh*

Kinnes, J. R.
A study of Ste. Beuve's criticisms of English and German literatures. *Ph.D. 1928 Edinburgh*

Kinsella, C.
Padraig Colum. *M.A. 1949 National University of Ireland*

Kinsey, E. A. W.
The work of Sir Robert Peel as Secretary of State for the Home Department, 1822-1830. *M.A. 1927 Manchester*

Kinsey, W. W.
Some aspects of Lancashire radicalism, 1816-21. *M.A. 1927 Manchester*

Kipps, J.
Valorization under public auspices. *B.Litt. 1929 Oxford*

Kiralfy, A. K.
The action on the case: the development of the action as reflected on the plea rolls of the sixteenth and seventeenth centuries. *Ph.D. 1949 London, King's College*

Kirby, E. S.
The economic organization of Manchoukuo, with particular reference to specific features exemplifying the special characteristics of the modern economic system in the Far East. *Ph.D. 1938 London, External Degree*

Kirby, J. L.
The Hungerford family in the later middle ages. *M.A. 1939 London, King's College*

Kirby, K. H. B.
Britain and Britons in the eyes of the eighteenth-century Germans. *Ph.D. 1934 London, King's College*

Kirby, K. H. B.
Heine in England in the nineteenth century. *M.A. 1927 London*

Kirk, K. E.
1. Conscience and moral law. 2. Cases of conscience. *B.D. 1922 Oxford*

Kirk, M.
Parliamentary enclosure in Bulmer Wapontake. *M.A. 1948 Leeds*

Kirkaldy, A. W.
The Northmen in France. *B.Litt. 1902 Oxford*

Kirk-Duncan, V. G.
Some Hellenic elements in the works of Abelard. *B.Litt. 1941 Oxford*

Kirk-Duncan, V. G.
A study of certain aspects of *prima facie* extra-sensory cognition. *D.Phil. 1944 Oxford*

Kirkland, D.
Alain Chartier's *Quadrilogue invectif. M.A. 1935 Liverpool*

Kirkland, D.
Remonstrances au Roy pour la réformation du royaume, by Jean Juvenal des Ursins, with introduction and notes. *Ph.D. 1938 Liverpool*

Kirkman, E.
The epithet and Colette. *M.A. 1942 Leeds*

Kirkus, A. M.
The great roll of the pipe for the ninth year of the reign of King John, Michaelmas, 1207 (pipe roll 53). *M.A. 1942 Reading*

Kiroff, N. Y.
Industrial fuel problems under wartime conditions. *M.Sc. 1943 Leeds*

Kirsch, C. E.
The theology of James Morison, with special reference to his theories of the atonement. *Ph.D. 1939 Edinburgh*

Kirstein, J.
Das Rilke-Problem der Mehrdeutigkeit. *M.A. 1946 National University of Ireland*

Kirwan, J. R.
The relationship between wages theories and social organization. *B.Phil. 1948 Oxford*

Kirwan, L. P.
Lower Nubia in the early Byzantine period. *B.Litt. 1935 Oxford*

Kirzner, W.
The Oath of the Lord, being a critical and analytical exposition of the Halakhah of the judicial imposition of the Biblical oath of the Bailees in conjunction with a discussion of the general laws relevant to it. *M.A. 1930 London, King's College*

Kirzner, W.
Some ancient asseverations and affirmations in the light of cultural anthropology. *M.Sc. 1934 London, School of Economics and Political Science*

Kishen, B. R.
Some consequences of M'Alister Donoghue (pauper) v. Stevenson, 1932, A.C. 562. *LL.M. 1943 Leeds*

Kissin, I.
Co-operation and credit in forestry. *D.Phil. 1944 Oxford*

Kitchen, L. E.
Selection for secondary education. *M.A. 1945 Bristol*

Kitchin, A. W. Menzies- *see* Menzies-Kitchin, A. W.

Kitchin, G.
Sir Roger L'Estrange: pamphleteer, essayist, and man of letters; with an estimation of his influence on the development of English prose. *B.Litt. 1910 Oxford*

Kite, J. C.
British foreign policy, 1850-1871. *M.A. 1916 Birmingham*

Klat, P. J.
Land tenure in Syria and Lebanon and its economic effects, with some suggestions for reform. *B.Phil. 1948 Oxford*

Klein, A.
The logical theory of the term: a critical examination of the traditional doctrine. *M.A. 1910 London*

Klein, J. W. G.
Romain Rolland's dramatic works and theories. *Ph.D. 1935 London, King's College*

Klein, V.
Some theories of feminine attitudes and so-called character traits: a study in ideologies. *Ph.D. 1944 London, School of Economics and Political Science*

Klingender, F. D.
The black-coated worker in London. *Ph.D. 1934 London, School of Economics and Political Science*

Knapp, B. N.
The wholesale marketing of vegetables in Birmingham. *M.Com. 1948 Birmingham*

Knapp, C.
1. The doctrine of the Paraclete as found in St. John xiv-xvi. 2. The preface to St. Luke's Gospel. 3. The authorship and date of Psalm cxix. *D.D. 1906 Oxford*

Knapp, C.
1. The kingdom of God. 2. The biblical and Augustinian use of the term 'grace'. *B.D. 1902 Oxford*

Knapp, J. B.
The policy of Switzerland in the construction of the collective peace system. *B.Litt. 1936 Oxford*

Knapton, S. H.
The life and works of William Walwyn the Leveller. *M.A. 1949 London, Queen Mary College*

Knatchbull-Hugessen, N. R.
Can a neutral monist theory of knowledge give an adequate account of memory. *B.Litt. 1938 Oxford*

Knesebeck, G.-L. von dem *see* Von dem Knesebeck, G.-L.

Knetes, C.
The sacred ministry and its relation to marriage in the Holy Eastern Orthodox Church. *B.Litt. 1909 Oxford*

Knight, C. M.
The importance of the Veronese palimpsest in the first decade of Livy. *M.A. 1910 London*

Knight, D.
J. J. Bodmer's contribution to the knowledge and appreciation of Middle High German Literature. *M.A. 1949 London, Bedford College*

Knight, E. A.
Eratosthenes as a representative of Hellenistic culture. *M.A. 1930 London, King's College*

Knight, E. H.
Some medieval and modern theories of the universal. *Ph.D. 1935 London, External Degree*

Knight, H.
D'Aubigné as a poet. *D.Phil. 1939 Oxford*

Knight, H.
The language and style of Mathurin Régnier. *B.Litt. 1935 Oxford*

Knight, J. G.
The chemical studies of Hermann Boerhaave, 1668-1738. *M.Sc. 1934 London, University College*

Knight, L. S.
Welsh schools of the fifteenth and sixteenth centuries. *M.A. 1914 Wales*

Knight, W. H. J.
A study of the Middlesex junior technical school entrance examination: being an investigation into the methods adopted and their value for the selection of junior technical school pupils. *M.A. 1949 London, Institute of Education*

Knight, W. S. M.
Public policy in English law. *B.Litt. 1923 Oxford*

Knights, L. C.
Aspects of the economic and social background of comedy in the early seventeenth century. *Ph.D. 1936 Cambridge*

Knobloch, E.
Controversies about the gold standard, 1921-1932: a critical survey of the international literature. *M.Sc. 1935 London, School of Economics and Political Science*

Knopf, I. C.
The English background to the works of Hans Grimm. *M.A. 1939 London, University College*

Knowles, D.
La renaissance de l'idéalisme et sa réaction sur le théâtre en France, 1890-1900. *M.A. 1931 Leeds*

Knowles, I. A.
A treatise on purgatory by Tschudi. *Ph.D. 1925 Glasgow*

Knowles, K. D.
1. The divine fatherhood. 2. The Apostles' Creed. *B.D. & D.D. 1924 Oxford*

Knowles, V.
Studies in the late plays of Euripides. *M.A. 1938 Manchester*

Knowling, R. J.
1. The Catholic Epistles in relation to the Gospels. 2. Some thoughts on Christian evidences and recent criticism. *B.D. & D.D. 1896 Oxford*

Knowlson, G. A.
Jean V, Duke of Brittany (1399-1442) in relation to England. *M.A. 1934 Liverpool*

Knox, E.
The political influence of William Cobbett, 1794-1815. *M.A. 1907 Liverpool*

Knox, H. M.
The educational writings of Simon Somerville Laurie, M.A., LL.D., F.E.I.S., F.R.S.E., 1829-1909, first Bell Professor of the theory, history and art of education in the University of Edinburgh, 1876-1903. *Ph.D. 1949 Edinburgh*

Knox, M. G.
American trade restrictions and British commerce 1808-12. *B.Litt. 1938 Oxford*

Knox, R. B.
The decline of the native Irish monasticism from the ninth to the twelfth centuries. *M.A. 1944 Belfast*

Knox, R. B.
The doctrine of the church as exemplified in the life and works of James Ussher, Archbishop of Armagh. *Ph.D. 1948 Belfast*

Knox, S.
The use of music in the Elizabethan theatre: an enquiry into the dramatic value of the musical element in the drama of the Elizabethan period. *M.Litt. 1939 Durham*

Koenigsgarten, H. F.
The German drama under the influence of the Great War and the revolution. *D.Phil. 1944 Oxford*

Koeppler, H.
Study of the antecedents of the *De Claris jurisconsultis* of Diplovatatius. *D.Phil. 1936 Oxford*

Koerner, M.
Quellen-Studien zu Theodor Körners *Leier und Schwert. M.A. 1912 London*

Kohn-Bramstedt, E.
Class distinctions as reflected in the German novel of the nineteenth century: aristocracy: middle classes: intellectuals, 1830 to 1900. *Ph.D. 1936 London, School of Economics and Political Science*

Königsberger, H. G.
The government of Sicily under Philip II of Spain: a study in the practice of empire. . *Ph.D. 1949 Cambridge*

Konovaloff, S.
Monetary reconstruction in Czechoslovakia. *B.Litt. 1927 Oxford*

Kopanitsas, D.
Four essays in economic inertia. *M.Sc. 1950 Cambridge*

Koren, W.
A study of the relationship between the diplomatic and commercial policies of France, Germany, Italy, Russia, and Austria-Hungary, 1871-1914. *B.Litt. 1934 Oxford*

Körner, S.
Propositions asserting entailment relations. *Ph.D. 1944 Cambridge*

Korninger, S.
Lord Byron and Nikolaus Lenau: a comparative study. *M.A. 1950 Sheffield*

Kostanecki, J.
The influence of inflation and deflation on banking, based on a comparison of conditions in eastern and western Europe. *Ph.D. 1927 London*

Kothare, A. N.
The history of the law of conservation of matter. *M.Sc. 1937 London, University College*

Kotwal, G. R.
The person of quality in Restoration comedy. *B.Litt. 1938 Oxford*

Koussy, A. A. H. el-
A study of mechanical ability, with special reference to sex differences. *M.Sc. 1932 Birmingham*

Koussy, A. A. H. el *see* El Koussy, A. A. H.

Koutaissoff, E.
A study of the chapters concerning the history of the Jews in Voltaire's *Introduction à l'essai sur les moeurs et l'esprit des nations. B.Litt. 1939 Oxford*

Kramer, S. P.
Anglo-American relations with regard to the Panama Canal project, 1897-1903. *M.Litt. 1938 Cambridge*

Kramm, H. H. W.
The conception of Church order and ministry under Luther and the early Lutheran Church considered in the light of non-Roman Christianity in Scandinavia, Germany, and the British Isles to-day. *D.Phil. 1940 Oxford*

Krass, L.
The phonetics of Estonian (including some notice of intonation). *M.A. 1943 London, University College*

Kretser, B. de *see* de Kretser, B.

Krishna, B.
Commercial relations between India and England, 1600-1757. *Ph.D. 1922 London*

Krishna, L. Rama *see* Rama Krishna, L.

Krishnaswami, A.
Capital development of India, 1860-1913. *Ph.D. 1941 London, School of Economics and Political Science*

Krizewsky, M.
The limits of obligation. *M.A. 1923 London*

Kronheimer, E. F. C.
Problems of personality development in the light of graphological analysis. *B.Sc. 1942 Oxford*

Kryński, S. L. Przegonia- *see* Przegonia-Kryński, S. L.

Kuhar, A. L.
The conversion of the Slovenes. *Ph.D. 1950 Cambridge*

Kularatnam, K.
The physiographic evolution of Ceylon. *M.A. 1944 London, External Degree*

Kumarappa, B.
Ramanuja's conception of the Deity. *Ph.D. 1930 London, School of Oriental and African Studies*

Kunhan Raja, C.
A Rigvedic index: being a complete collection of Sayana's interpretations of Rigvedic words, both when those interpretations are inconsistent with one another and when they differ from the interpretations of western scholars. *Ph.D. 1924 Oxford*

Kuo, T. H.
The principle of self-determination, with special reference to President Wilson. *B.Litt. 1935 Oxford*

Kurhade, S. K.
A study of modern developments in agricultural co-operation in parts of Europe and North America, with reference to the problem of co-operation in India. *M.Sc. 1936 Wales*

Kuriyan, G.
Regional geography of Kerala. *Ph.D. 1946 London, External Degree*

Kurvinen, A.
An edition of *Syre Gawene and the Carle of Carelyle. B.Litt. 1949 Oxford*

Kyd, G. O.
The Scottish answer to Hume. *B.Litt. 1932 Oxford*

Kydd, R. M.
An analysis of Hume's views on the influence of reason on conduct. *B.Litt. 1944 Oxford*

Kynaston, A. M.
The life and writings of Charlotte Lennox, 1720-1804. *M.A. 1936 London, Birkbeck College*

Kyrle, H. J. R. Money- *see* Money-Kyrle, H. J. R.

Kyrle, R. E. Money-
The meaning of sacrifice. *Ph.D. 1929 London*

La Mare, K. de *see* De La Mare, K.

Labban, I. A. E. M. el *see* El Labban, I. A. E. M.

Laborde, E. D.
The Battle of Maldon. *Ph.D. 1931 London, External Degree*

Lacey, T. W.
Study of the Hebrew prophets. *M.A. 1931 Bristol*

Lachmann, L. M.
Capital structure and depression. *M.Sc. 1935 London, School of Economics and Political Science*

Lack, M. E.
The position and duties of the King's almoner, 1255-1327. *M.A. 1949 London, Royal Holloway College*

Ladborough, R. W.
Maucroix. *Ph.D. 1935 Cambridge*

Ladd, H. A.
The poetry and prose of Francis Thompson: a critical study. *B.Litt. 1923 Oxford*

Lagarde, P. H. J.
The scientific method of Pascal. *B.Litt. 1933 Oxford*

Lahey, G.
A critical study of Newman's *Apologia pro vita sua. B.Litt. 1949 Oxford*

Lahiri, P.
Studies in the word-order of Sanskrit prose. *Ph.D. 1933 London, School of Oriental and African Studies*

Lai, R. C.
Reorganisation of the Punjab Government, 1847-57. *Ph.D. 1937 London, School of Oriental and African Studies*

Laidler, F. F.
Cultivation in Spain, with some reference to trade between Spain and Great Britain. *M.Sc. 1930 Wales*

Laidlow, W. A.
The history of Delos. *Litt.D. 1933 Dublin, Trinity College*

Lailavoix, L.
La captivité de Charles d'Orléans d'après les manuscrits anglais. *M.A. 1911 London*

Lainée, H. G.
1. The teaching of Holy Scripture with regard to the nature and ministry of angels. 2. The teaching of the Gospel according to St. John on the person and work of the Holy Spirit. *B.D. 1906 Oxford*

Laing, W. A. G.
Preliminary medical education. *M.D. 1886 Glasgow*

Laird, M. J.
Les parodies dramatiques des oeuvres de Voltaire. *M.A. 1912 Leeds*

Lajoie, P. Gérin- *see* Gérin-Lajoie, P.

Lake, D. E.
Individual psychology - its nature, assumptions and limitations. *M.A. 1939 Bristol*

Lakhani, G. T.
Study of the causal factors and subsequent development of excessive shyness, lack of self-confidence and allied conditions among children. *Ph.D. 1934 Edinburgh*

Lal, D. I.
The history and present status of adult education in the Punjab (India). *M.A. 1948 London, Institute of Education*

Lal, H.
International gold movements. *Ph.D. 1949 London, School of Economics and Political Science*

Lall, G.
The Panjab as a sovereign state, 1799-1839. *Ph.D. 1923 London*

Lall, S.
An intelligence and educational survey of the eleven-year-olds in the government high schools of the United Provinces of Agra and Oudh, India. *Ph.D. 1945 Edinburgh*

Lamb, A. C.
An anthropological survey of the Mende people of Sierra Leone, with special reference to their social structure and material culture and their relation to the geographical environment. *Ph.D. 1946 Leeds*

Lamb, A. C.
The place of fear as a determinant of religious thought and practice. *M.A. 1942 Sheffield*

Lamb, H.
'Technique' and 'content' in woodwork courses. *M.Ed. 1941 Leeds*

Lamb, J. A.
A study of the use of the Psalms in Christian worship, as reflected in the pre-Reformation liturgies and service-books. *Ph.D. 1946 Edinburgh*

Lamb, M.
Roman life and manners as depicted in Martial and Juvenal. *M.A. 1920 London*

Lamb, N. J.
Ramón Pérez de Ayala. *M.A. 1940 Liverpool*

Lamb, V. M.
Migration in Great Britain since 1927, with special reference to the industrial population. *B.Litt. 1939 Oxford*

Lamb, W. K.
British labour and Parliament, 1867-1893. *Ph.D. 1934 London, School of Economics and Political Science*

Lambert, C. M.
A study of interest in school subjects among secondary school pupils at different ages (a contribution to educational guidance). *M.A. 1944 London, Institute of Education*

Lambert, E. W.
The contributions of Priestley, Ingenhausz, Senebier and N. T. de Saussure to our knowledge of photosynthesis and respiration. *M.Sc. 1937 London, External Degree*

Lambert, F. J.
The history of the doctrine of scripture up to the Reformation. *Ph.D. 1943 London, External Degree*

Lambert, M.
The Saar territory as a factor in international relations, 1920-1932. *Ph.D. 1936 London, School of Economics and Political Science*

Lambert, S.
The influence of Parliament upon the foreign policy of the Gladstone Government, 1868-74. *M.A. 1949 London, Bedford College*

Lambton, A. K. S.
Contributions to the study of Seljūq institutions. *Ph.D. 1939 London, School of Oriental and African Studies*

Lamnin, T. P.
The Scottish Chaucerians. *M.A. 1941 National University of Ireland*

Lamont, D.
Richard Crashaw. *M.A. 1941 National University of Ireland*

Lamont, J. H. P.
The critical system of Hippolyte Taine. *M.A. 1926 Wales*

Lamont, O.
The De Burgh earls of Ulster. *M.A. 1947 Belfast*

Lampert, C.
The philosophical implications of the sacramental principle. *D.Phil. 1943 Oxford*

Lancaster, J. T.
Mrs Gaskell, with special reference to the social reform novel, 1830-1850. *M.Litt. 1927 Cambridge*

Lancaster, M.
The treatment of national character in the novels of Charles Lever. *M.A. 1935 Liverpool*

Land, C. E. L.
The novels of William Godwin. *M.A. 1938 Birmingham*

Land, W. L.
A study of the influence of the Victorian home on the religious development of the child in the last three decades of the nineteenth century. *B.Litt. 1948 Oxford*

Landau, J.
Parliamentary institutions and political parties in Egypt, 1866-1924. *Ph.D. 1949 London, School of Oriental and African Studies*

Landaw, L.
Hebrew-German romances and tales and their relation to the romantic literature of the Middle Ages. *M.A. 1911 London*

Lander, J. R.
The administration of the Yorkist kings. *M.Litt. 1950 Cambridge*

Lander, T. J.
The idea of the fear of God in the Old and New Testaments. *M.A. 1938 Bristol*

Landers, W. M.
La vie et l'oeuvre de Jacques de Cambry (1749-1807). *Ph.D. 1946 London, External Degree*

Lane, E.
1. The fourfold account of the resurrection of Jesus Christ in the light of the fourfold purpose of the four Gospel writers. 2. The authorship of the Epistle to the Hebrews. *B.D. & D.D. 1905 Oxford*

Lane, E. V.
The historical geography of the Sheffield iron and steel industries. *M.A. 1923 Liverpool*

Lane, H. T.
The life and writings of John Cary. *M.A. 1932 Bristol*

Lane, M.
The position of England towards the Baltic powers, i.e. Denmark and Sweden including the Hanse towns, from 1689-1697. *M.A. 1911 London*

Lang, D. M.
Alexander Nikolaevich and his contacts with French and German thinkers. *Ph.D. 1950 Cambridge*

Lang, E.
1. The justice of the atonement. 2. The omnipresence of God and eschatology. *B.D. & D.D. 1908 Oxford*

Lang, E. M.
The enforcement of the Lateran decrees in England in the reign of Henry III. *B.Litt. 1931 Oxford*

Lang, P.
Das Streben nach dem Drama in der deutschschweizerischen Literatur des neunzehnten und beginnenden zwanzigsten Jahrhunderts. *M.A. 1923 London*

Langan, I. W.
Contributions to the psychology of the blind: a non-verbal group test of general ability. *Ph.D. 1949 Reading*

Langdon, J. N.
An experimental study of certain forms of manual dexterity. *Ph.D. 1933 London, External Degree*

Langford-James, R. L.
1. The doctrine of justification as set forth by St. Paul and St. James in their writings. 2. The evidence from the New Testament for the divinity of our Lord. *B.D. 1904 Oxford*

Langford-James, R. L.
Expositions of Jeremiah vii.23; Exekiel xviii.4; St. John xvii.3. *D.D. 1910 Oxford*

Langley, G. H.
The ontological proof of the existence of God in modern philosophy from Descartes to Kant. *M.A. 1909 London*

Langley, S. J.
The history and development of the iron and steel welded tube trade, with particular reference to the rise and eventual decline of the trade in the town of Wednesbury, Staffordshire. *M.Com. 1948 Birmingham*

Langnas, A. I.
The relations between Great Britain and the Spanish colonies, 1808-12. *Ph.D. 1938 London, School of Economics and Political Science*

Langrick, A. E.
The dialect of Bubwith in the East Riding of Yorkshire. *M.A. 1949 Leeds*

Langstadt, E.
The conception of the *Civitas Christiana* in the thought of the early Church. *Ph.D. 1938 Cambridge*

Langstaff, J. B.
The order for the administration of the Lord's Supper or Holy Communion as set forth in the prayer books of the Church of England, of the Church of Scotland, and of the Episcopal Church in the United States of America. *B.Litt. 1916 Oxford*

Langton, E.
The Jewish and Christian doctrine of good and evil spirits: its origin and development. *D.D. 1942 London, External Degree*

Lannin, T. P.
The effects of bilingualism on mental development. *Ph.D. 1946 National University of Ireland*

Lansdale, M.
Sir William d'Avenant as a transition dramatist. *M.A. 1929 Manchester*

Laracy, E. D.
Louise Labé. *M.A. 1940 National University of Ireland*

Larcombe, H. J.
The development of subscription charity schools in England and Wales, from the close of the seventeenth to the close of the eighteenth century, with special reference to London and district. *Ph.D. 1928 London*

Larcombe, H. J.
The progress of education in Bristol. *M.A. 1924 Bristol*

Large, E. J. C.
Shakespeare and the comic spirit. *M.A. 1923 Birmingham*

Larkin, T. J.
Wolverhampton and the Great Civil War, 1642-1645. *M.A. 1928 Birmingham*

Larkin, W.
Karl Marx and his system. *M.A. 1916 National University of Ireland*

Larkin, W.
The theory of property in the eighteenth century: its historical antecedents with special reference to England and Locke. *Ph.D. 1928 London*

Larmor, W. J.
Effects of the war on Irish linen industry. *M.Com.Sc. 1921 Belfast*

Larmour, R. V.
Antoine Arnauld's critique of Malebranche's philosophy as it is contained in *Des vraies et des fausses idées*. *M.A. 1945 Belfast*

Larsen, H. W.
Some theoretical aspects of industrialization of advanced agricultural countries, illustrated from New Zealand experience. *Ph.D. 1948 London, University College*

Lascelles, M. M.
Alexander and the earthly paradise in medieval English literature. *B.Litt. 1927 Oxford*

Latham, A. M. C.
The poems of Sir Walter Ralegh. *B.Litt. 1927 Oxford*

Latham, L. C.
The decay of the manorial system during the first half of the fifteenth century, with special reference to manorial jurisdiction and the decline of villeinage, as exemplified in the records of twenty-six manors in the counties of Berkshire, Hampshire, and Wiltshire. *M.A. 1928 London*

Latif, S. A.
The influence of English literature on Urdu literature. *Ph.D. 1924 London*

Latimer, E. C.
Stevenson's method as writer and critic. *M.A. 1917 Liverpool*

Laughlin, T. A.
The history of the Hull Grammar School. *M.Ed. 1945 Leeds*

Laurie, K. F.
English utopian fiction (up to 1870; with a glance forward). *M.A. 1930 London, University College*

Laurier, L. N.
Marivaux' debt to his predecessors in the drama. *Ph.D. 1941 London, King's College*

Lauterpacht, H.
Private law analogies in international law, with special reference to international arbitration. *LL.D. 1925 London*

Lavault, J. L. A.
Food price policy in the United Kingdom during the war, 1939-45. *B.Phil. 1947 Oxford*

Lavelle, A. B.
The problem of evil in the philosophy of Leibniz. *Ph.D. 1935 Sheffield*

Lavelle, M.
The origin and growth of the German ballad. *M.A. 1918 National University of Ireland*

Laver, R.
John Newton and the early Methodists. *B.Litt. 1923 Oxford*

Lavin, M. J.
The construction of the novel and Jane Austen. *M.A. 1936 National University of Ireland*

Law, M. M.
The growth of British influence in Abyssinia and on the African coast of the Red Sea from 1840 to 1885. *M.A. 1931 London, King's College*

Law, S.
The first two years of general science work in a secondary school. *M.Ed. 1937 Manchester*

Law, W.
Exegeses of: John xiv, xv, and xvi. *D.D. 1924 Oxford*

Law, W. S.
1. The interpretation of Psalm cx. 2. The authenticity of the Epistle of St. James. *B.D. 1898 Oxford*

Lawlor, N. D.
Contemporary poetic drama. *M.A. 1944 National University of Ireland*

Lawlor, W. S.
Agricultural education in Ireland; a history. *M.A. 1927 National University of Ireland*

Lawrence, A. W.
The dating of early Hellenistic statues. *B.Litt. 1925 Oxford*

Lawrence, E. M.
An investigation into the relation between intelligence and inheritance. *Ph.D. 1930 London, School of Economics and Political Science*

Lawrence, H. T.
Les lectures de Madame de Sévigné. *M.A. 1934 Leeds*

Lawrence, I. H. W.
Suggestion in relation to the moral value of ideas. *M.A. 1911 London*

Lawrence, J. F.
Somerset 1800-1830: an inquiry into social and economic conditions. *M.Litt. 1941 Durham*

Lawrence, L.
The rise of neo-classic architecture in England. *M.A. 1937 London, Courtauld Institute of Art*

Lawrenson, T. E.
Le théâtre de Jean Giraudoux. *M.A. 1941 Manchester*

Lawson, A. C.
1. Early Christian prophecy. 2. St. Hippolytus and the Church. *B.D. 1924 Oxford*

Lawson, A. C.
The sources of the *De ecclesiasticis officiis* of St. Isidore of Seville. *D.D. 1937 Oxford*

Lawson, J.
The biblical theology of St. Irenaeus. *B.D. 1949 Cambridge*

Lawson, J.
Gardens and gardening in the Roman world. *M.A. 1945 Manchester*

Lawson, J.
A study of the parliamentary burgesses during the first half of the fifteenth century, based on the returns of London, York, Norwich, Bristol and Southampton between 1413 and 1437. *M.A. 1936 Manchester*

Lawson, M. S.
An account of the dialect of Staithes in the North Riding of Yorkshire. *M.A. 1949 Leeds*

Lawson, T. S.
Scottish poetics and literary criticism from James VI to Francis Jeffrey. *Ph.D. 1930 Edinburgh*

Lawton, C. L.
The theory of bank rate. *M.Sc. 1934 London, School of Economics and Political Science*

Lawton, H. W.
Roman civilization in the three Gauls during the first three centuries of Roman rule. *M.A. 1923 Wales*

Lawton, J. A.
A survey of science teaching in the senior school. *M.A. 1941 Leeds*

Lawton, J. S.
British and American Christology from 1889-1914. *B.D. 1944 Oxford*

Lawton, J. S.
The place of miracle in Christian apologetics in Great Britain from 1688 to the present day. *D.Phil. 1950 Oxford*

Lawton, R.
Population migration to and from Warwickshire and Staffordshire, 1841-1901. *M.A. 1950 Liverpool*

Laycock, E. K.
Some studies in the moral climate of the mid-eighteenth century in England, as expressed in a representative selection of the prose literature of the period 1740-1786. *M.Litt. 1946 Cambridge*

Laycock, S. R.
An experimental investigation into adaptability to new situations. *Ph.D. 1927 London*

Lazarus, H. M.
Schools and methods of Jewish education in Palestine and Babylon up to the close of the Talmud. *M.A. 1913 London*

Lazarus, S. C.
Personality in recent philosophy. *Ph.D. 1924 Oxford*

Lazenby, W. C.
The social and economic history of Styal, 1750-1850. *M.A. 1949 Manchester*

Le Chavetois, G. A.
The legislation of Caius Gracchus considered especially in relation to the Order of the Equites. *M.A. 1912 London*

Le Chavetois, I. M.
A study of Gawayne Douglas's translation of Vergil's *Aeneid. M.A. 1909 London*

Le Lièvre, A.
Linguistic activity at the court of Henry VIII. *Ph.D. 1950 Cambridge*

Le May, R. S.
Buddhist art in Siam. *Ph.D. 1937 Cambridge*

Le Mesurier, A. M. C.
The Anglo-French struggle for the control of Dutch foreign policy, 1755 to 1763. *M.A. 1934 London, University College*

Le Patourel, J. H.
A study of the administration of the Channel Islands in the thirteenth and early fourteenth centuries, based mainly upon the assize rolls and other unprinted documents. *D.Phil. 1934 Oxford*

Lea, E. M.
Classical mythology and classical subjects in the work of some of the nineteenth century poets. *M.A. 1921 Birmingham*

Lea, T. S.
Expositions of Acts i: the pre-Pentecostal Church; Acts ii-v.16: Pentecost and the first or Sadducee persecution; Acts v.17-vi. *D.D. 1910 Oxford*

Lea, T. S.
1. Some heads of a Christian answer to the neo-Buddhist theosophy. 2. Some considerations, scriptural and modern, concerning sin. *B.D. 1905 Oxford*

Leach, A.
The syntax of Bernard de Ventadorn. *M.A. 1932 Manchester*

Leach, E. R.
Cultural change, with special reference to the hill tribes of Burma and Assam. *Ph.D. 1947 London, School of Economics and Political Science*

Leadbeater, D. T. V.
The influence of Spanish picaresque fiction on English novelists to the end of the eighteenth century. *M.A. 1942 Wales*

Leahy, D. J.
English as spoken in Cork City. *M.A. 1915 National University of Ireland*

Leahy, J. A.
The State and industry in Ireland. *M.Econ.Sc. 1948 National University of Ireland*

Leahy, M.
The poetry of Joseph Mary Plunkett. *M.A. 1949 National University of Ireland*

Leahy, P. J.
Adalbert Stifter. *M.A. 1945 National University of Ireland*

Leakey, L. S. B.
The Stone Age archeology of Kenya Colony. *Ph.D. 1931 Cambridge*

Leaper, W. A.
Growth of sabbatarianism in England from 1558 to 1658. *M.A. 1919 National University of Ireland*

Learoyd, W. H. A.
The personification of supreme evil in Christian thought: a study of origins. *D.D. 1940 Durham*

Leary, G. A.
The fables of Phaedrus: a commentary critical and exegetical, with an introduction on the poet, his style, language and prosody, the mss, and the development of the fable in classical literature. *M.A. 1947 Manchester*

Leatherbarrow, J. S.
Lancashire Elizabethan recusants. *M.A. 1940 Manchester*

Leatherland, H. F.
Christian sociology, 1920-1940: a review and critical estimate of the main trends of the period. *Ph.D. 1947 Edinburgh*

Leathley, S. A.
1. The history of marriage and divorce. 2. The development of monogamy among the Jews in the Old Testament. *B.D. & D.D. 1916 Oxford*

Leaver, H. G.
Cicero's recall from exile. *M.A. 1924 Manchester*

Leavis, F. R.
Relationship of journalism to literature. *Ph.D. 1924 Cambridge*

Leavis, Q. D.
Fiction and the reading public. *Ph.D. 1932 Cambridge*

Lebon, J. H. G.
Contributions to the economic geography of Ayrshire. *Ph.D. 1946 London, External Degree*

Lebus, M.
Contingency. *M.A. 1919 London*

Leclerc, I.
An enquiry into the foundations of Whitehead's metaphysic of experience. *Ph.D. 1949 London, King's College*

Leddy, J. F.
Seneca the philosopher as a source for Roman private life. *B.Litt. 1934 Oxford*

Leddy, J. F.
The social legislation of the Roman Empire from Augustus to Constantine, and the policy of its authors. *D.Phil. 1938 Oxford*

Lee, A.
French literature and the adolescent: an inquiry into the interests of adolescents as a basis of the selection of French literature for sixth forms. *M.A. 1937 London, Institute of Education*

Lee, B.
Mary Tudor's Irish policy and the Counter-Reformation. *M.A. 1930 National University of Ireland*

Lee, C.
The system of Chinese public finance: a comparative study. *Ph.D. 1935 London, School of Economics and Political Science*

Lee, E. K.
The religious thought of St. John. *M.Litt. 1945 Durham*

Lee, F. M.
George Eliot. *M.A. 1941 Birmingham*

Lee, G. A.
The powers of government in the constitution of Ireland. *M.A. 1941 National University of Ireland*

Lee, G. E.
The theory of punishment, with special reference to education. *M.A. 1917 London*

Lee, G. S. T.
Horace as a literary critic. *M.A. 1908 London*

Lee, H. I.
Malta as a British colony, 1824-1851. *M.A. 1949 London, Bedford College*

Lee, H.-S.
Central control and the employment of Exchequer grants in British local government. *Ph.D. 1950 Glasgow*

Lee, M. P.
The Geneva treatment of the Manchurian and Abyssinian crises. *Ph.D. 1946 London, School of Economics and Political Science*

Lee, P.
Earl Grey's native policy in South Africa, with special reference to Natal. *M.A. 1930 Sheffield*

Lee, P. J.
Seneca the younger as a critic of his age. *M.A. 1934 Manchester*

Lee, R. K. K.
The provision for the welfare of women and young workers in the cotton industry. *M.A. 1949 Liverpool*

Lee, R. S.
The interpretation of some aspects of Christian doctrine and practice in the light of Sigmund Freud's conceptions of the development and structure of the mind. *D.Phil. 1947 Oxford*

Lee, R. S.
Religion as a factor in personal synthesis. *B.Litt. 1927 Oxford*

Lee, S. T.
North Kiangsu: a study in regional geography. *M.Sc. 1939 Cambridge*

Lee, T.
Aos ealadhan agus oifige in Eirinn(Art students and their function in Ireland). *M.A. 1927 National University of Ireland*

Lee, W.
Studien über die älteren Minnesänger mit Ubersetzungsversuchen. *M.A. 1903 Birmingham*

Leech, A. J.
The place of children's books in English education during the first half of the nineteenth century, with special reference to the Hofland Collection. *M.Ed. 1941 Leeds*

Leech, C. E. J.
Life and Works of Thomas Southerne. *M.A. 1932 London, East London College*

Leech, C. E. J.
Private performances and amateur theatricals (excluding the academic stage) from 1580 to 1660, with an edition of one or more of the plays presented before the Earl of Westmorland, 1640-1650. *Ph.D. 1935 London, Queen Mary College*

Leech, H. C. L.
A political and economic history of the development of internal civil aviation in Great Britain, 1919-1939. *M.A. 1950 Manchester*

Leek, D. M.
Otto Ludwig's character portrayal. *B.Litt. 1948 Oxford*

Leeman, W.
1. The authorship of the Pastoral Epistles. 2. The controversies dealt with in the Pastoral Epistles. *B.D. & D.D. 1915 Oxford*

Leese, F. E.
A calendar and analysis, with introduction, of two Elizabethan port books (E190/5/1 and E190/5/6). *B.Litt. 1950 Oxford*

Leese, J.
The history and character of educational inspection in England. *Ph.D. 1934 London, King's College*

Leese, J.
The history of Calais under the deputyship of Arthur Plantagenet, Lord Lisle, 1533-1540. *M.A. 1929 Manchester*

Leese, J.
The history of elementary school inspection, 1839-1902. *M.Ed. 1931 Manchester*

Lees-Smith, H. B.
Second chambers in theory and practice. *D.Sc. 1927 London*

Lee-Woolf, J. P.
Pauline ethics, with special reference to eschatology. *B.D. 1942 Oxford*

Leff, B.
Some aspects of the measurement of technical aptitude in boys aged 12 years, with special reference to Alexander's performance scale. *M.A. 1949 London, Institute of Education*

Legge, M. D.
A description of the manuscripts of *La Lumiere as Lais*, by Pierre de Peckham, an Anglo-Norman poem of the thirteenth century, and a comparison of the poem with its Latin source. *B.Litt. 1928 Oxford*

Legh, K. L. Wood- *see* Wood-Legh, K. L.

Lehane, A. P.
Hopkins and Milton. *M.A. 1949 National University of Ireland*

Leheta, M. F.
Economic federation with special references from the individual conditions of Egypt, past and present. *Ph.D. 1926 Leeds*

Leheta, M. F.
Labour question in Egypt. *M.Com. 1923 Birmingham*

Lehmann, A. G.
The aesthetic doctrines of French Symbolism. *D.Phil. 1948 Oxford*

Lehmann, O. H. M.
The Hebrew conception of nature, especially as illustrated by the prophets. *B.Litt. 1947 Oxford*

Lehrman, S. M.
A commentary on the Book of Joel, by Jefeth Ibn Ali the Karaite. *Ph.D. 1927 London*

Leigh, A. H. Austen- *see* Austen-Leigh, A. H.

Leighton, W. H.
A comparison of the influence of Wycliffe and Luther upon the Reformation in England. *M.A. 1927 Birmingham*

Leighton, W. H.
Wyclif and Lollardry in England. *M.A. 1925 Birmingham*

Leiper, M. K.
A contribution to the study of Albert Thibaudet as a critic of the novel. *Ph.D. 1939 London, University College*

Leishmann, J. B.
The three *Parnassus Plays*. *B.Litt. 1928 Oxford*

Leitch, A. H.
The relevancy of Calvin to modern issues within Protestantism. *Ph.D. 1941 Cambridge*

Leith-Ross, S. M.
The origin and development of the Old French virelay. *B.Litt. 1938 Oxford*

Lejeune, C. A. J.
Le théâtre de Jean Giraudoux: sa conception, sa réalization. *M.A. 1950 Liverpool*

Lemarchand, E. W.
The development of the concept of natural regions, and its value in the furtherance of geographical thought. *M.A. 1929 London*

Lemarchant, A.
The evolution of religion in Greece from the earliest times to the time of Hesiod. *M.A. 1920 Belfast*

Lemmey, T.
A commentary on St. John xvi.7; 8-11; I Corinthians xii.8-11. *D.D. 1924 Oxford*

Lemmey, T.
1. Justification by faith, as set forth in the writings of St. Paul. 2. Some New Testament evidences for the divinity of our Lord. *B.D. 1907 Oxford*

Lemon, H. W.
The theory of education in Plato's *Laws*. *M.Ed. 1920 Manchester*

Lemon, T. W.
1. The proper mode of holy baptism. 2. The proper subjects of holy baptism. *B.D. & D.D. 1889 Oxford*

Lencz, S. G.
The authorship and authenticity of the Johannine Epistles. *Ph.D. 1933 Aberdeen*

Lenfant, J. H. A. M.
British capital export, 1900-1913. *Ph.D. 1949 London, School of Economics and Political Science*

Lennon, A.
The teaching of botany in the history of secondary education. *M.Ed. 1921 Manchester*

Lennon, F. K.
A defence of abstraction. *M.A. 1943 National University of Ireland*

Lennon, F. W.
Bacon's English style. *M.A. 1936 National University of Ireland*

Lennon, T. W.
Some aspects of the sufferings of Catholics under the penal laws in the reign of James I. *M.A. 1939 Liverpool*

Leon, J. L. Aguilar de. *see* Aguilar de Leon, J. L.

Leonard, G. S.
Classification of children in the elementary school. *M.A. 1927 Birmingham*

Leonard, P. F.
Irish bankruptcy law. *M.A. 1943 National University of Ireland*

Leonard, T.
Individual differences and moral training. *M.A. 1938 National University of Ireland*

Leopold, K. B.
Aesthetic appreciation: a comparison of two methods of training appreciation in poetry. *M.A. 1930 London, King's College*

Lerner, A.
The economics of control: a theory of authoritarian pricing and production. *Ph.D. 1942 London, School of Economics and Political Science*

Leser, C. E. V.
Family budget data and price elasticities of demand. *M.Sc. 1941 London, School of Economics and Political Science*

Leslie, B. M.
The comedy of humours and the comedy of manners. *M.A. 1923 Belfast*

Leslie, M. I.
Felicia Hemans: the basis of a biography by Temple Lane (pseud.). *Ph.D. 1943 Dublin, Trinity College*

Lester, J. R.
The isolation of France. *M.A. 1937 Birmingham*

Lester, P. H.
1. The New Testament teaching on the Second Advent considered in the light of subsequent history. 2. The relation of natural science to theology. *B.D. 1908 Oxford*

Lester, R.
An examination of the *Epigrammata* of Sir Thomas More and of their importance in his life and writings. *M.A. 1937 London, King's College*

Letcher, H. P.
The writ of habeas corpus. *LL.D. 1934 London, External Degree*

Levene, A.
The early Syrian Fathers on Genesis from a Syrian manuscript on the Pentateuch in the Mingana collections. *Ph.D. 1936 London, External Degree*

Leventhal, A. J.
Postwar tendencies in French literature. *Ph.D. 1933 Dublin, Trinity College*

Lever, J. W.
The evolution of the Elizabethan sonnet. *M.A. 1945 Manchester*

Leverton, H.
A critical examination of the educational theory of Quintilian. *M.Ed. 1939 Leeds*

Levey, M. F.
The acquisition of sovereignty over unappropriated territory. *LL.D. 1914 London*

Levine, I.
Reason and morals: an enquiry into the first principles of ethics. *D.Litt. 1924 Glasgow*

Levine, I. H.
The Life and works of Rabbi Eliezer bar Nathan of Mainz. *Ph.D. 1939 London, Jews' College*

Levy, A. B.
Mistake in contract. *LL.M. 1942 Bristol*

Levy, P.
Lessing's study and knowledge of English language and literature. *M.A. 1935 London, University College*

Levy, R. H.
The blessings of Moses in post-Biblical Jewish literature: Targum versions considered and compared with the Talmud, Midrash and medieval commentators down to Abrabanel, as well as with those of Moses Mendelsohhn and Malbim. *M.A. 1945 Manchester*

Lew, M. S.
The works of Rabbi Moses Isserls as a source of the history of the Jews in Poland in the sixteenth century. *Ph.D. 1941 London, Jews' College*

Lewis, A.
The English activities of Cardinal Ottobuono, Legate of the Holy See. *M.A. 1937 Manchester*

Lewis, A.
Evan Evans (Ieuan Fardd), 1731-1788. Hanes ei fywyd a'i gysylltiadau llenyddol(Evan Evans (Ieuan Fardd), 1731-1788. The history of his life and his literary connections). *M.A. 1950 Wales*

Lewis, A.
The literary and philanthropic societies of the eighteenth century: their services to and influence upon Welsh literature. *M.A. 1921 Wales*

Lewis, A.
The next step in education: raising the school-leaving age to fifteen years. *M.Ed. 1931 Manchester*

Lewis, A. B.
Descriptions of the Devil and his works in early English literature and the development of these ideas in relation to doctrine. *Ph.D. 1939 London, University College*

Lewis, A. M.
The problems of international exchange in 1914-1920. *M.A. 1921 Wales*

Lewis, A. M.
The theory and practice of film observation: and experimental investigation into the child's attitudes to educational and entertainment films. *M.A. 1938 London, Institute of Education*

Lewis, B.
Studies on the history of the Qarmati and Ismaili movements from the eighth to the eleventh centuries. *Ph.D. 1939 London, External Degree*

Lewis, B. A.
A critical analysis of didactic methods in chemistry and their effect upon the educational development of the child. *M.A. 1930 Liverpool*

Lewis, B. A.
The political system of the Murle. *B.Sc. 1950 Oxford*

Lewis, B. B.
An examination of the architectural aspects of railway development in Great Britain. *M.A. 1944 Liverpool*

Lewis, B. H.
The political ideas of the English Radicals, particularly in Nonconformist circles, from John Lilburne to John Wilkes. *M.A. 1926 Wales*

Lewis, B. J. I.
Twentieth-century criticism of the sociological theories of Karl Marx, and especially of his economic or materialistic interpretation of history. *M.A. 1932 Wales*

Lewis, C. B. H.
Tafodiaith hen blwyf Llangatwg (Castellnedd)(The dialect of the old parish of Llangatwg (Neath)). *M.A. 1932 Wales*

Lewis, C. N.
The growth of the doctrine of the conservation of energy, up to and including the work of Joule. *M.Sc. 1937 London, External Degree*

Lewis, D. G.
The influence of Emile Zola on English literature. *M.A. 1943 Wales*

Lewis, D. G.
Sir Thomas Morgan, Bart., 1604-1679, 'soldier of fortune'. *M.A. 1930 Wales*

Lewis, D. J.
The influence of Ossian on the chief French writers of the Romantic period. *M.A. 1909 Wales*

Lewis, E. A.
The growth and development of the municipal element in the principality of north Wales up to the close of the fourteenth century. *M.A. 1902 Wales*

Lewis, E. A.
The medieval boroughs of Snowdonia. *M.A. 1912 Wales*

Lewis, E. D.
The industrial development of the Rhondda Valleys to 1910. *M.A. 1940 Wales*

Lewis, E. G.
The relationship of form and content in the work of Donne. *M.A. 1932 Wales*

Lewis, E. L.
An inquiry into the prospects that the children of the unskilled have of becoming skilled. *Ph.D. 1923 Glasgow*

Lewis, E. L.
The slate industry in north Wales, with special reference to Merioneth. *M.A. 1917 Wales*

Lewis, E. M.
An edition of 4 Charles I. Rot. Pat. 4 Car.I. 33A-33C: The Ditchfield Grant of September 25. *M.A. 1930 Leeds*

Lewis, E. P.
Expositions of I Corinthians xv.20-58: the Resurrection; St. John iii.3-5; Genesis i: the Creation. *D.D. 1904 Oxford*

Lewis, E. P.
1. The Incarnation. 2. Apostolic succession. *B.D. 1896 Oxford*

Lewis, E. R.
The Franco-Italian rapprochement, 1898-1902. *M.A. 1937 Wales*

Lewis, F. R.
Richard, Earl of Cornwall, King of the Romans (1257-1272). *M.A. 1934 Wales*

Lewis, F. R.
Studies in the history and administration of the German Church from 1225 to 1275, with special reference to the Province of Cologne. *D.Phil. 1936 Oxford*

Lewis, G. A.
Different views of the nature of mental activity, more especially in connection with educational theory. *M.A. 1908 Wales*

Lewis, G. E. D.
A comparative study of the intelligence and educability of Malays and Chinese in Malaya and its significance in relation to educational policy. *Ph.D. 1949 London, Institute of Education*

Lewis, G. I.
An investigation of changes in population density and distribution, together with changes in agricultural practice, in Pembrokeshire during the period 1831-1931. *M.A. 1937 Birmingham*

Lewis, G. L.
A re-examination of the so-called 'theology of Aristotle'. *D.Phil. 1950 Oxford*

Lewis, H.
An examination of Welsh versions of the *Historia regum Britanniae*, with reference to the original. *M.A. 1913 Wales*

Lewis, H. D.
The moral philosophy of T. H. Green. *B.Litt. 1935 Oxford*

Lewis, H. D.
The problem of moral freedom with reference to its discussion in recent philosophy and in particular in the *Ethics* of Nicolai Hartmann. *M.A. 1934 Wales*

Lewis, H. M.
The relative distribution of landscape and figure art in Western Europe with some inquiry as to the causes. *Ph.D. 1937 London, Courtauld Institute of Art*

Lewis, H. V. W.
The political influence of Pope Gregory the Great in Italy. *M.A. 1913 Wales*

Lewis, J.
Charles Churchill. *M.A. 1945 Bristol*

Lewis, J.
The relations between central and local government in England and Wales in the period 1923-1933, treated with reference both to the policy and to the public discussions. *M.A. 1936 Wales*

Lewis, J.
Some aspects of the history and development of dairying in Carmarthenshire. *M.Sc. 1948 Wales*

Lewis, J. H.
The history of the borough of Kenfig to 1485. *M.A. 1922 Wales*

Lewis, L. F.
The seasonal distribution (of temperature) over the British Isles. *M.Sc. 1947 Bristol*

Lewis, L. I.
The main aspects of the post-war drama. *M.A. 1933 Wales*

Lewis, M.
The part the press played: the influence of the Press upon international relationships during the years 1896-1914. *M.A. 1930 Birmingham*

Lewis, M. M.
The development of language in children. *Ph.D. 1935 London, External Degree*

Lewis, M. M.
Outlines of the history of the study of English in theory and practice (1550-1800). *M.A. 1922 London*

Lewis, N. A.
The selection of entrants to the junior technical school. *M.Ed. 1944 Manchester*

Lewis, N. B.
Persons and politics in the early years of Richard II, 1377-1388. *M.A. 1928 Manchester*

Lewis, N. B.
The relations of France and England in the reign of Richard II. *M.A. 1922 Manchester*

Lewis, O. T.
History of British relations with Zanzibar, 1800-1886. *M.A. 1936 Wales*

Lewis, P. A.
The Norman element in the novels of Jules Barbey d'Aurevilly. *M.A. 1921 Wales*

Lewis, R. A.
Edwin Chadwick and the public health movement, 1832-1854. *Ph.D. 1949 Birmingham*

Lewis, R. A.
Two partnerships of the Knights: a study of the Midland iron industry in the eighteenth century. *M.A. 1949 Birmingham*

Lewis, R. P. W.
A critical study of the idea of dimensions. *M.Sc. 1949 Wales*

Lewis, S. E.
The diplomatic relations between England and Germany, 1898-1902. *M.A. 1930 London, School of Economics and Political Science*

Lewis, T.
The establishment of the French Protectorate over Tunis: its diplomatic history from the Congress of Berlin to the formation of the Triple Alliance, July 1878 to May 1882. *M.A. 1950 Wales*

Lewis, T.
The planning and conditions of settlement in Wales during the Dark Ages and medieval period, from first-hand knowledge obtained by means of archaeological investigations. *M.Sc. 1927 Wales*

Lewis, T. A.
St. Paul's doctrine of Christ, especially its development as revealed in his extant writings. *B.D. 1951 Oxford*

Lewis, T. E.
The doctrine of judicial precedent: its history and importance as a source of law. *Ph.D. 1928 Cambridge*

Lewis, T. H.
Carmarthenshire under the Tudors. *M.A. 1919 Wales*

Lewis, T. H.
Local government in Wales, sixteenth to eighteenth centuries, as exemplified by the work of the Quarter Sessions in the County. *Ph.D. 1941 London, External Degree*

Lewis, W.
The pedagogics of school handiwork. *M.A. 1913 Wales*

Lewis, W. A.
The economics of loyalty contracts. *Ph.D. 1940 London, School of Economics and Political Science*

Lewis, W. B.
Some tendencies and characteristics of the contemporary novel. *M.A. 1927 Wales*

Lewis, W. H.
Robert Greene's later prose works. *M.A. 1927 Bristol*

Lewis, W. J.
The economic geography of the tinplate industry in south Wales. *M.Sc. 1943 London, External Degree*

Lewis, W. L.
The determinism of Jonathan Edwards. *M.A. 1949 Bristol*

Lewis, W. M.
The Puritans and music, with special reference to the Commonwealth period. *M.A. 1917 Wales*

Lewitter, L. R.
A study of the academic drama in Russia and the Ukraine in the seventeenth and eighteenth centuries, with special reference to its Polish origins. *Ph.D. 1950 Cambridge*

Lewy, C.
Some philosophical considerations about the survival of death. *Ph.D. 1943 Cambridge*

Leybourne, G. G.
Recent and prospective population trends in Great Britain and certain other countries. *M.A. 1935 Liverpool*

Leyden, W. von *see* von Leyden, W.

Li, C.
A comparison of Shelley and Li Po as poets of nature. *B.Litt. 1936 Oxford*

Li, M. H.
The great recoinage of 1696-99 (a particular study of the question on currency devaluation). *Ph.D. 1937 London, School of Economics and Political Science*

Liang, Y. H.
Cash-shop banks and their relationship to the banking system of China. *M.A. 1936 Liverpool*

Liberty, S.
The imperial policy of Claudius as reflected in the New Testament. *B.D. & D.D. 1939 Oxford*

Lichtenstädter, I.
An introduction to the *Kitâb al-Muhabbar* of Muhammad ibn Habîb, together with an edition of its first twenty folios, with indices and explanatory notes. *D.Phil. 1937 Oxford*

Liddall, M. E.
Experiments in the maintenance of industrial peace. *B.A. 1923 Bristol*

Liddell, J. R.
The first century of the library of Corpus Christi College, Oxford (1517-1617). *B.Litt. 1933 Oxford*

Liddell, M. F.
German sea poetry. *D.Phil. 1925 Birmingham*

Lidden, H. W.
The growth of self-government in the Borough of Southampton as illustrated by its charters and letters patent. *Ph.D. 1923 London*

Liddicoat, J. H. W.
The part played by Great Britain in the separation of Brazil from Portugal, 1821-1825. *M.A. 1927 London*

Liddle, M. G.
The bourgeois in French literature of the fourteenth century. *Ph.D. 1925 London*

Liebschuetz, H.
Early medieval humanism, as exemplified in the life and writings of John of Salisbury. *M.A. 1947 London, External Degree*

Liepmann, K. K.
The daily ebb and flow of labour between home and workplace in English industrial areas. *Ph.D. 1942 London, School of Economics and Political Science*

Lièvre, A. Le *see* Le Lièvre, A.

Lightbound, T.
A biographical sketch of Sir George Savile, 1726-1784, with an appendix of his letters. *M.A. 1916 Liverpool*

Lightbown, J.
The dialect of the *Pricke of Conscience*, together with a collation of mss. Galba E IX and Harley 4196. *M.A. 1935 Leeds*

Lightley, J. W.
The movement towards 'scribism' in the history of Israel. *M.A. 1912 Belfast*

Lilly, G.
The prose style of John Donne in his *Sermons*. *M.A. 1947 Liverpool*

Lim, K. T.
A study of English vital statistics, with special emphasis on marriage statistics and social or occupational class differences. *Ph.D. 1938 Liverpool*

Limentani, U.
The significance of Mazzini's literary work. *Ph.D. 1947 London, Birkbeck College*

Limrick, M. F. R.
The significance of rhythm in the Platonic system of education. *M.A. 1915 Liverpool*

Lincoln, J. S.
The dream in primitive cultures. *Ph.D. 1935 London, School of Economics and Political Science*

Lindgren, E. J.
Notes on the Reindeer Tungus of Manchuria. *Ph.D. 1936 Cambridge*

Lindley, J. R.
The history of education in Lichfield, as illustrating the development of education in England. *M.A. 1942 Birmingham*

Lindley, M.
Queen Caroline and literature. *M.A. 1927 Liverpool*

Lindop, D. E.
The diocese of Coventry and Lichfield during the Reformation, with special reference to parochial life. *B.Litt. 1937 Oxford*

Lindores, E. A.
The Oriental tale in English prose fiction from 1740 to 1839. *M.A. 1924 Manchester*

Lindsay, J. H.
Accessory elements in Chinese Buddhist sculpture to the end of the sixth century. *M.A. 1938 London, Courtauld Institute of Art*

Lindsay, J. M.
Recurrent themes in the works of Thomas Mann. *Ph.D. 1950 Aberdeen*

Lindsay, R. J. M.
The *carmen famosum* of the neoteric school. *M.A. 1950 Belfast*

Lindsay, R. R.
The Celtic monastics on the Continent. *Ph.D. 1927 Glasgow*

Lindsay, W. J.
A study of the *Analects* of Confucius. *M.A. 1925 Belfast*

Lindsay-Macdougall, K. F.
A study of the University letter book (FF) 1509-1535. *B.Litt. 1950 Oxford*

Lindsey, D.
Reactions to colour and form. *M.A. 1947 Manchester*

Line, W.
The growth of visual perception in children. *Ph.D. 1929 London*

Lineham, A. W.
Etude sur l'éloquence de la chaire française du 17e siècle. *M.A. 1905 Birmingham*

Lineham, J.
The concept of activity. *Ph.D. 1922 Bristol*

Lines, G. W. R.
Divisional executives under the Education Act, 1944. *M.Ed. 1948 Leeds*

Ling, B.
Parliaments and the Peace Treaty: a comparative study of the reactions of the British and French Parliaments to the Treaty of Peace of 1919. *Ph.D. 1938 London, School of Economics and Political Science*

Lingen, J. R. K. de
Concordance to the *Bhagavad Gita*; supplement: annotated translation of the *Bhagavad Gita*. *Ph.D. 1948 Edinburgh*

Linton, D. L.
Contributions to the knowledge of the drainage, morphology and structure of the Wessex region of southern England. *M.Sc. 1930 London, King's College*

Lintott, J. N. T.
The history of chemical methods of detecting arsenic up to the year 1860. *M.Sc. 1935 London, University College*

Lion, A. A.
A conception of religion deduced from the works of Giovanni Gentile. *B.Litt. 1927 Oxford*

Lion, A. A.
The problem of error in the contribution of Kant to modern idealistic logic. *D.Phil. 1930 Oxford*

Lipman, V. D.
Problems of areas in English local government. *D.Phil. 1947 Oxford*

Lippincott, B. E.
Critics of democracy: Carlyle, Arnold, Stephen (Fitzjames), Maine, Lecky. *Ph.D. 1931 London, School of Economics and Political Science*

Lipstein, K.
Critical studies upon the texts and the theory of the *beneficium cedendarum actionum* and *venditio nominis*. *Ph.D. 1937 Cambridge*

Liptrot, E. M.
Use of the Greek myth in English literature from 1800 to 1850. *M.A. 1929 Manchester*

Lissau, R.
Wilhelm Meister's Wanderjahre; a critical re-examination and re-valuation. *M.A. 1941 London, University College*

Lister, H.
Allan Ramsay and the Scottish vernacular revival (circa seventeenth and eighteenth centuries). *M.A. 1934 London, Birkbeck College*

Lister, J. M.
1. St. Paul's thorn in the flesh. 2. A critical examination of the use of φιλεῖν and ἀγαπᾶν in the New Testament, with special reference to the exegesis of St. John xxi.15-17. *B.D. & D.D. 1899 Oxford*

Lister, W.
An edition of the Middle English romance *Ywaine and Gawain*. *M.A. 1939 Manchester*

Lister, W.
Secular instruction and incidental information in English vernacular sermon literature of the later Middle Ages, 1150-1450. *M.Ed. 1945 Manchester*

Liston, R. T. L.
John Calvin's doctrine of the sovereignty of God. *Ph.D. 1930 Edinburgh*

Liston, T. K.
Economic aspects of company law. *M.A. 1925 National University of Ireland*

Listowel, W. F., Earl of
A critical history of the main currents of modern aesthetics. *Ph.D. 1932 London, King's College*

Little, A.
Plato and the subconscious. *M.A. 1923 National University of Ireland*

Little, I. M. D.
The theory of welfare economics. *D.Phil. 1949 Oxford*

Little, K. L.
The anthropology of some coloured communities in Great Britain with comparative material on colour prejudice. *Ph.D. 1945 London, School of Economics and Political Science*

Little, V. A. S.
The Christology of Clement of Alexandria. *D.Phil. 1938 Oxford*

Little, V. A. S.
The Christology of the second century apologists, with special reference to the philosophical influences. *B.Litt. 1920 Oxford*

Littlejohns, W. N.
Studies in the history and influence of the education of boys at Port Royal and in the older Oratorian colleges of France. *M.A. 1948 London, King's College*

Littleton, T. A.
A history of the development of the Eucharist to 150 A.D. *B.D. 1948 Leeds*

Liu, C. C.
Trade union law in the United Kingdom, the United States, and the Republic of China. *M.Litt. 1949 Cambridge*

Liu, C. H.
The ethnology of China proper. *B.Sc. 1932 Oxford*

Liu, E.-L.
A study of the rainfall fluctuations in China: their causes and effects. *D.Phil. 1940 Oxford*

Liu, N.
Reform of Chinese city government based on European experience. *Ph.D. 1931 London, School of Economics and Political Science*

Liu, S. Y.
A comparative study of the English and American money markets. *Ph.D. 1927 London*

Liu, T. C. S.
The Chinese banking with special reference to modern banks. *M.Com. 1931 Leeds*

Liversidge, J. E. A.
Roman villas in Britain. *M.Litt. 1949 Cambridge*

Liversidge, P. H.
The use of plastics in modern building. *M.A. 1950 Sheffield*

Livingstone, A. D.
Irenaeus and Gnosticism. *Ph.D. 1934 Edinburgh*

Living-Taylor, M.
Les dieux ont soif (de Anatole France): étude sur la documentation et la genèse du roman. *M.A. 1942 Manchester*

Llewellyn, E. C.
The influence of Middle Dutch and Middle Low German on English speech. *B. Litt. 1930 Oxford*

Lloyd, A.
The years between: an enquiry into the bases of co-education for adolescents, and some account of its practice. *M.A. 1936 Birmingham*

Lloyd, A. H.
The place of coinage in Greek foreign trade down to the end of the fifth century B.C. *Ph.D. 1929 Cambridge*

Lloyd, A. M.
Balzac et ses contemporains. Balzac journaliste. *M.A. 1935 London, King's College*

Lloyd, D. M.
Astudiaeth feirniadol o farddoniaeth Cynddelw Brydydd Mawr, o ran iaith a gwerth llenyddol(A critical study of the poetry of Cynddelw Brydydd Mawr, with special reference to language and literary value). *M.A. 1932 Wales*

Lloyd, D. W.
The coal export trade of the United Kingdom, 1910-1920, with special reference to south Wales. *M.A. 1922 Wales*

Lloyd, E.
Robert Owen and social legislation. *M.A. 1932 Wales*

Lloyd, E. A.
The Co-operative Movement in Italy, with special reference to agriculture, labour and production. *M.A. 1925 Wales*

Lloyd, E. C.
The influence of the Methodist movement on social life in Wales. *B.Litt. 1921 Oxford*

Lloyd, E. J.
Astudiaeth feirniadol o'r Didache a llenyddiaeth Gristionogol arall o gynnyrch y ddwy ganrif gyntaf, a ysgrifennwyd yn yr iaith Roeg, ynghyda chyfeiriad arbennig at ddatblygiad y Weinidogaeth a'r Gwasanaethau Eglwysig(A critical study of the Didache and other Christian literature in Greek of the first and second centuries, with special reference to the development of the ministry and the church services). *Ph.D. 1946 Wales*

Lloyd, E. J.
The history of the Eisteddfod. *M.A. 1913 Wales*

Lloyd, E. J.
The history of Thessaly up to 323 B.C. *M.A. 1914 Wales*

Lloyd, E. R.
L'oeuvre française de Carlo Goldoni. *M.A. 1938 Manchester*

Lloyd, E. W.
A contribution to the study of life, personality and works of Pedro Lopez de Ayala, 1332-1407. *Ph.D. 1930 London, King's College*

Lloyd, G. G.
The treatment of the Mosaic Law in the Epistle to the Hebrews with some comparison of the Pauline attitude. *Ph.D. 1946 Edinburgh*

Lloyd, G. R. M.
A study of the prophecies of Zechariah. *B.Litt. 1935 Oxford*

Lloyd, G. T.
Samuel Daniel. *M.A. 1931 Birmingham*

Lloyd, H. A.
Theories of punishment. *M.A. 1937 Wales*

Lloyd, I. M.
The influence of the Bible in English literature of the nineteenth century. *M.A. 1920 Wales*

Lloyd, J.
Gweithiau Gruffudd ab Ieuan ap Llywelyn Fychan(The works of Gruffudd ab Ieuan ap Llywelyn Fychan). *M.A. 1911 Wales*

Lloyd, M. D. I.
Some phases of the historical German drama since Schiller's death: the patriotic, the antique Roman and the revolutionary. *M.A. 1912 Wales*

Lloyd, R. G.
The life and work of the Rev. John Owen D.D., the Puritan divine, with special reference to the Socinian controversies of the seventeenth century. *Ph.D. 1942 Edinburgh*

Lloyd, R. L. H.
The work of the 'deputation of reform' during the early stages of the Council of Basel. *B.Litt. 1936 Oxford*

Lloyd, T.
The geography and administration of northern Canada. *D.Sc. 1949 Bristol*

Lloyd Thomas, M. G.
The life of John Philips. *B.Litt. 1925 Oxford*

Lloyd, W. A.
The discipline of the Society of Friends as a regular national body, with particular reference to church government based on a study of the epistles of the yearly meetings, 1669 to 1738. *Ph.D. 1947 Cambridge*

Lloyd, W. E.
The prose tales of William Morris. *M.A. 1930 Liverpool*

Lloyd-Jones, J.
Latin loan words in Welsh and words that are cognate in Welsh and Latin. *B.Litt. 1908 Oxford*

Lloyd-Jones, R. W.
A survey of the history of Bosley. *M.A. 1943 Liverpool*

Lo, C. S.
A study of the moral philosophy of Hsün-tze with special reference to the relation between knowledge and morality. *B.Litt. 1939 Oxford*

Lobb, K. M.
The terror novel and Sir Walter Scott: a study in literary influence. *Ph.D. 1939 London, External Degree*

Lobo, F. X.
Problem of evil in Francis Thompson's poetry. *M.A. 1945 National University of Ireland*

Lock, W.
1. The Old Testament an essential part of the revelation of God. 2. On the Epistle to the Ephesians. *B.D. & D.D. 1896 Oxford*

Locke, H. W.
Democracy as a practical ideal. *M.A. 1922 Birmingham*

Lockhart, L.
Nādir Shāh. *Ph.D. 1935 London, School of Oriental and African Studies*

Lockhart, W. C.
The evangelical revival as reflected in the life and works of John William de la Fléchère, 1729-1785. *Ph.D. 1936 Edinburgh*

Lockitt, C. H.
The social relations of England and France, 1763-1793, in connection with their effect on the Revolutionary era. *M.A. 1911 London*

Lockwood, F. W.
Faith healing under the Roman Empire: a translation of the sacred orations of Aristides Aelius, together with an introduction. *M.A. 1935 London, Birkbeck College*

Lockwood, J. F.
The place of Dionysius of Halicarnassus in the development of prose-criticism. *Ph.D. 1936 London, University College*

Lockwood, W. B.
The Old Saxon vocabulary and its relationship to the other Germanic dialects. *M.A. 1946 Bristol*

Lodge, L.
Les idées littéraires de Fénelon. *M.A. 1929 London*

Lodge, M. S.
Some medieval elements in early Tudor poetry. *M.A. 1948 Sheffield*

Loewenheim, M.
An experimental investigation into cognitive development in infants of one to two years of age. *Ph.D. 1945 London, University College*

Lofthouse, A.
Le *Tristan* d'Eilhart d'Oberg. *M.A. 1939 Manchester*

Lofthouse, M.
Le *pèlerinage de la vie humaine* de Guillaume de Deguileville d'après le texte du manuscrit French 2 de la John Rylands Library, Manchester. *M.A. 1929 Manchester*

Loftus, P. J.
National income of Palestine. *Ph.D. 1948 London, External Degree*

Logan, D. W.
Donatio mortis causa in Roman, English, and American law. *D.Phil. 1939 Oxford*

Lokanathan, P. S.
Industrial organization in India, with special reference to industrial finance and labour. *D.Sc. 1934 London, School of Economics and Political Science*

London, E. H.
Charles Dickens as a regional novelist. *M.A. 1949 Wales*

Long, A. J.
The evolutionary theory of sin. *B.D. 1948 Oxford*

Long, E. P. E.
Le groupe Delécluze et son rôle dans le mouvement romantique. *M.A. 1938 Liverpool*

Long, I. L. M.
An investigation into the relationship between interest in and knowledge of school geography, by means of a series of attitude tests. *M.A. 1949 London, Institute of Education*

Long, J. R.
Location theory and the clothing industry: a study of the factors of industrial location, with particular reference to their influence on the clothing industry. *Ph.D. 1949 Leeds*

Long, S. R. C.
Le Père Rapin, critique littéraire. *Ph.D. 1936 London, Birkbeck College*

Long, T. H. D.
Expositions of: Genesis iii: the doctrine of the Fall; Ephesians iv.1-16: the unity of the Church and the functions of its ministers; I Corinthians xi.18-34. *D.D. 1909 Oxford*

Long, T. H. D.
1. The hypostatic union. 2. The nature of our Lord's resurrection body. *B.D. 1904 Oxford*

Long, V. J.
The anti-social child within the school. *M.A. 1939 Bristol*

Longfield, K.
Anglo-Irish trade in the sixteenth century. *M.A. 1926 London*

Longford, W. W.
Expositions of I Corinthians viii.4,5,6; Romans viii.7-10; Romans iii.21-25. *D.D. 1915 Oxford*

Longford, W. W.
1. Logos Christology: its validity and value. 2. The nature of the Gospel and its place in sacramental theory. *B.D. 1911 Oxford*

Longmore, K. M.
The tourist industry of Great Britain; its present problems and future prospects. *M.Com. 1950 Birmingham*

Longstaff, G. B.
Studies in statistics: social, political, and medical. *M.D. 1891 Oxford*

Lonsdale, F. E.
The versification of Paul Verlaine. *M.A. 1933 Manchester*

Lonsdale, H.
Victor Hugo et la peine de mort. *M.A. 1922 Leeds*

Loo, G. H. van *see* Van Loo, G. H.

Loomis, R. S.
Illustrations of the romances in medieval English art. *B.Litt. 1913 Oxford*

Looney, M.
The development of the modern infant school. *M.A. 1928 National University of Ireland*

Loos, A. W.
The theology of A. M. Fairbairn. *Ph.D. 1939 Edinburgh*

Lord, M. B.
Italian immigration into the Argentine Republic. *M.A. 1939 Manchester*

Lord, P.
History of education in Oldham. *M.Ed. 1938 Manchester*

Lorimer, K. J.
Eugene O'Neill and modern dramatic technique. *M.A. 1947 London, Bedford College*

Lorrain-Smith, E.
The migration of farmers in relation to the economic development of agriculture in Great Britain since 1880. *B.Litt. 1931 Oxford*

Loseby, H. V.
A comparison of the educational system of Athens (400-300 B.C.) with that of England at the present day. *M.Ed. 1934 Leeds*

Lough, J.
Some aspects of the life and thought of Baron d'Holbach. *Ph.D. 1938 Cambridge*

Loughran, P.
The mid-Victorian novel-in-verse. *M.A. 1944 Sheffield*

Lovell, G. F.
1. The relation of the Church to the Gospels. 2. The external evidences for the Gospels in the second century. *B.D. 1876 Oxford*

Low, C. E.
A description and classification of the mss. of the *Navigatio Sancti Brendani*. *D.Phil. 1934 Oxford*

Low, T.
The influence of the Crusades on the contemporary religious life in Scotland. *Ph.D. 1933 Glasgow*

Lowe, F. G.
The Didache and early Christianity. *M.A. 1932 Bristol*

Lowe, F. G.
Early doctrine of the Kingdom of God. *B.A. 1929 Bristol*

Lowe, F. G.
1. The life and teaching of Irenaeus. 2. Irenaean fragments. *Ph.D. 1938 Bristol*

Lowe, H. N.
A study of the educational system of Holland. *M.A. 1927 Liverpool*

Lowe, J.
The Biblical use of the word μάρτυσ and the idea of martyrdom. *M.A. 1939 Manchester*

Lowe, J. B. Hanson- *see* Hanson-Lowe, J. B.

Lowe, J. C.
Saint Evremond in England. *M.A. 1932 Birmingham*

Lowe, J. E.
Magic in Greek and Latin literature. *M.A. 1922 London*

Lowe, L. L. S.
Mr. Customer Smythe, customer of the Port of London, 1570-89. *B.Litt. 1950 Oxford*

Löwenstein, A.
The sources of Hebbel's *Agnes Bernauer*. *M.A. 1908 London*

Lowery, H.
An experimental study of musical ability in schoolchildren. *M.Ed. 1927 Leeds*

Lowman, G. S.
The phonetics of the Lettish language. *Ph.D. 1931 London, University College*

Lowndes, G. A. N.
The growth of the public system of education in England and Wales, 1895-1935. *B.Litt. 1937 Oxford*

Lowry, C. W.
A critical and philosophical examination of the doctrine of the Holy Trinity. *D.Phil. 1933 Oxford*

Lowry, E. C.
The administration of the estates of Merton College in the fourteenth century. *D.Phil. 1933 Oxford*

Lowther, H.
Misfits in a secondary grammar school: a study of academic failures, 1935-1944. *M.Ed. 1948 Manchester*

Loyn, H. H.
Kingship and nobility in Anglo-Saxon England to the time of Alfred the Great. *M.A. 1949 Wales*

Lucas, A. G.
The problems arising out of Shakespeare's *Troilus and Cressida*. *M.A. 1913 Wales*

Lucas, C. V. M.
The composition and functions of the local councils of the cities of the province of Africa under the early Roman Empire up to Constantine. *Ph.D. 1937 London, Westfield College*

Lucas, J. O.
The religion of the Yorubas, especially in relation to the religion of ancient Egypt. *D.D. 1942 Durham*

Lucas, M. B.
Samuel Clarke and his contemporaries: a revaluation of Clarke's philosophical position based upon an examination of his relations with his contemporaries. *Ph.D. 1940 London, King's College*

Lucas, W. I.
English comedians in Germany in the sixteenth and seventeenth centuries. *M.A. 1930 Bristol*

Luce, A. A.
Berkeley and Malebranche. *Litt.D. 1943 Dublin, Trinity College*

Luce, A. F.
Feudalism in Jersey. *M.A. 1924 London*

Lucey, C.
Evil according to St Thomas. *M.A. 1930 National University of Ireland*

Luckman, W. F.
Shakespeare's philosophy of love. *M.A. 1929 Birmingham*

Lucy, M.
Vocabulary to lives of St. Carthage. *M.A. 1915 National University of Ireland*

Ludford, L.
Industrial unrest. *M.Com. 1918 Birmingham*

Ludlam, H.
The recitative of Lully. *M.A. 1948 Sheffield*

Ludowyk, E. F. C.
English and English education in Ceylon. *Ph.D. 1936 Cambridge*

Ludwig, W. P.
The relation of Jewish-Alexandrian theology, especially in Philo, to the Pauline Epistles. *Ph.D. 1937 Edinburgh*

Luery, A. E.
Rural education. *M.Ed. 1921 Leeds*

Luke, F. D.
The poetry of Arthur Rimbaud. *D.Phil. 1947 Oxford*

Luke, H. C.
Cyprus under the Turks, 1571-1878. *B.Litt. 1919 Oxford*

Luke, W. R.
Changes in the distribution of the population since 1800. *M.A. 1939 London, External Degree*

Lumby, J. H.
A calendar of the de Hoghton deeds and papers. *M.A. 1936 Liverpool*

Lummis, E. W.
1. How Luke was written. 2. New light on the significance of the word 'hypostasis'. *B.D. & D.D. 1924 Oxford*

Lumsden, A.
Pedro Espinosa and his work. *M.A. 1943 Liverpool*

Lund, H. M. L.
The problem of history and drama in German dramatic theory and practice in the nineteenth century. *M.A. 1943 London, Bedford College*

Lund, S. M.
The comedy of manner, 1700-1780. *Ph.D. 1933 London, East London College*

Lund, S. M.
The life and works of George Colman the Elder. *M.A. 1928 London*

Lunn, J.
The Black Death, 1348-49, with special reference to cathedral registers for the mortality of the clergy. *Ph.D. 1931 Cambridge*

Lusher, P. G.
Studies in the guild drama in London, from 1515 to 1550, in the records of the Drapers' Company. *Ph.D. 1940 London, University College*

Lutov, P. T.
The historical and religious background of Isaiah xl-lxvi. *B.Litt. 1934 Oxford*

Lutsky, G. S. N.
Aldous Huxley's quest for truth; a study of the ideas as developed in his novels and other writings. *M.A. 1943 Birmingham*

Lutzki, M.
The history and principles of the Hebrew professional scribes. *B.Litt. 1935 Oxford*

Luzzetti, C. A.
The construction of the London underground railways: a study of the creation of an important public utility by private enterprise. *B.Litt. 1939 Oxford*

Lyell, J. P. R.
A commentary on certain aspects of the Spanish Armada drawn from contemporary sources. *B.Litt. 1932 Oxford*

Lyke, G. M.
A study of the character of the main changes in the production and distribution of agricultural produce in Cardiganshire in medieval and modern times. *M.A. 1917 Wales*

Lynam, M. E.
Chatterton, Thomas. *M.A. 1946 National University of Ireland*

Lynch, B. J.
Industrial administration. *Ph.D. 1934 Belfast*

Lynch, D. J.
Gerard Manley Hopkins: poetic imagery. *M.A. 1950 National University of Ireland*

Lynch, G. J. J.
The revival of Roman Catholicism in South Wales in the late eighteenth and early nineteenth centuries. *M.A. 1941 Wales*

Lynch, I. K.
Evolution and history of local government law in Ireland. *M.A. 1948 National University of Ireland*

Lynch, M. C.
John Mitchel. *M.A. 1943 National University of Ireland*

Lynch, N.
Earlier and later seventeenth century prose. *M.A. 1930 National University of Ireland*

Lynch, P. J.
Labour in the Third Reich. *M.Econ.Sc. 1936 National University of Ireland*

Lynch, P. J.
An luach sa chóus eacnomaidheachta fé stiúir(Value in a planned economy). *Ph.D. 1939 National University of Ireland*

Lynch, P. J.
The reading approach in modern language teaching, with some reference to Australian needs and conditions. *M.A. 1938 National University of Ireland*

Lynch, S. *see* O'Connell, S.

Lyne, H. F.
The Aristotelian and scholastic doctrine of opposition. *M.A. 1945 National University of Ireland*

Lyon, E. W.
Napoleon Bonaparte and the sale of Louisiana to the United States. *B.Litt. 1928 Oxford*

Lyon, W. H.
Inconvertible paper money in relation to the foreign exchanges and international trade. *M.A. 1925 Liverpool*

Lyons, F. S. L.
Irish parliamentary representation 1891-1910. *Ph.D. 1947 Dublin, Trinity College*

Lyons, H. T.
Evacuation problems: a study of difficult children in hostels. *M.A. 1943 London, Institute of Education*

Lyons, J. G.
Registration of title to land in Eire. *M.A. 1946 National University of Ireland*

Lyons, W. H.
Two old French religious poems from a ms. in the library of Trinity College, Dublin. *Ph.D. 1937 Dublin, Trinity College*

Lysaght, D. J.
Chemistry at the early meetings of the Royal Society of London. *M.Sc. 1934 London, University College*

Lysaght, D. J.
Chemistry at the Royal Society, 1687-1727. *Ph.D. 1937 London, University College*

Lythgoe, N. L.
A historical survey of the teaching of Latin from medieval times. *M.Ed. 1918 Manchester*

Ma, Y. C.
The technique of government borrowing: a study of the methods employed by the British Treasury in its borrowing operations, 1914-39. *Ph.D. 1942 London, School of Economics and Political Science*

Mabbott, J. D.
The development of the platonic theory of forms. *B.Litt. 1923 Oxford*

Maber, G. L.
Nicholas Ferrar and George Herbert: their work and times. *M.A. 1947 Manchester*

Mac A'ghoill, T.
Múineadh litridheachta na Gaedhilge 'sa nGaedhealtacht(The teaching of Irish literature in the Irish-speaking area). *M.A. 1934 National University of Ireland*

Mac an Fhailghigh, E.
A contribution to Celtic philology. *M.A. 1939 National University of Ireland*

Mac Aodhagáin, P. *see* Egan, J.

Mac Confhaola, M. G.
Uí Chonchubhair Chonnacht sa bhfilídheacht(The O'Connors of Connaught in poetry). *M.A. 1942 National University of Ireland*

Mac Craith, C. *see* McGrath, J. A.

Mac Cuinn, S.
Léightheoireacht agus caitheamh-aimsire bhua-chaillí an bhaile mhór(The reading and pastimes of boys in big towns). *M.A. 1942 National University of Ireland*

Mac Dhubhain, A.
Filídheacht mhuintir Chobhtaigh(The poetry of the Coffey family). *M.A. 1940 National University of Ireland*

Mac Donagh, M.
Eachtra Choinn Láidir Mic Bacaigh binne Gul-ban(The adventures of Conn Láidir son of Bacach binne Gulban). *M.A. 1939 National University of Ireland*

Mc Donagh, M. J.
An edition of the first section of the text (Book of Ballymote, fasc. 119b-127a) with indexes and variae lectiones. *M.A. 1940 National University of Ireland*

Mc Donagh, P.
Ainmneacha aiteann i gCondae Mhuigheo(The names of furze in Co. Mayo). *M.A. 1948 National University of Ireland*

Mac Donnell, D. N.
Language and nature study. *M.A. 1934 National University of Ireland*

Mac Eamuinn, E. *see* Edmonds, E. J.

Mac Eoinín, U. *see* Jennings, V. B.

Mac Philbin, T. *see* Plover, T.

Macadam, M. F. L.
Middle Egyptian stelae in the British Museum to the end of the Middle Kingdom. *D.Phil. 1935 Oxford*

McAdoo, H. R.
Seventeenth century satire in Irish, with special reference to the Párliment Cholinne Tomáis. *Ph.D. 1940 Dublin, Trinity College*

McAdoo, H. R.
The structure of Caroline moral theology. *D.D. 1949 Dublin, Trinity College*

McAdoo, T. E.
The part played by Kinsale in history from Elizabeth to Cromwell. *M.A. 1914 National University of Ireland*

MacAlister, V.
The Donne world picture. *M.A. 1944 National University of Ireland*

McAlpine, J. W.
The validity of mystical knowledge. *Ph.D. 1931 Edinburgh*

McAlpine, R. J.
The reform movement in England previous to the French Revolution. *M.A. 1907 Liverpool*

McAndrew, A.
Law and equity. *M.A. 1936 National University of Ireland*

Macandrǿw, R. M.
Naturalism in Spanish poetry from the origins to 1900. *D.Litt. 1929 Aberdeen*

McAra, M. J. A.
Bradley's treatment of 'appearance'. *M.A. 1926 London*

McArthur, J. S.
An examination of the Chalcedonian Christology. *B.D. 1929 Oxford*

McArthur, W.
French song in the seventeenth century: poets and musicians. *M.A. 1925 London*

McArthur, W.
An inquiry into the extent and nature of Ben Jonson's familiar knowledge of classical Latin authors, and the reflection and influence of that knowledge on his work and character. *Ph.D. 1940 Glasgow*

Macassey, E. L.
1. The mission of the Twelve. 2. The teaching of the Christ on the kingdom. *B.D. 1924 Oxford*

Macaulay, J. S. A.
The history of the staple at Westminster in the reign of Richard II. *B.Litt. 1934 Oxford*

Macauliffe, M. M.
The poetry of the Catholic revival. *M.A. 1938 National University of Ireland*

Macbeth, M. E.
A study of special measures designed to improve the nutriture of certain population groups in the United Kingdom which are particularly susceptible to malnutrition. *B.Litt. 1947 Oxford*

McBriar, A. M.
Fabian doctrine and its influence in English politics. *D.Phil. 1949 Oxford*

MacBride, D.
Henri de Régnier: poète symboliste. *M.A. 1937 Belfast*

McBride, M. A. J.
The plays of Robert Browning in their dramatic and in their spiritual aspects. *M.A. 1919 London*

McBryan, I. M. J.
German Romanticism. *M.A. 1916 National University of Ireland*

MacBryde, D. D.
The righteousness of God in the conception of St. Paul, with special reference to the Epistle to the Romans. *Ph.D. 1943 Edinburgh*

McBurney, C. B. M.
The tools of Neanderthal man. *Ph.D. 1948 Cambridge*

MacCabe, E. E.
The place of nature in French classical tragedy. *M.A. 1920 National University of Ireland*

McCabe, I. M. J. *see* McBryan, I. M. J.

McCabe, J. O.
Great Britain and the evolution of the western part of the international boundary of Canada. *Ph.D. 1941 Glasgow*

McCabe, W. H.
An introduction to the Jesuit theatre. *Ph.D. 1929 Cambridge*

McCaffrey, J. O. M.
The influence of Celtic literature on that of England. *M.A. 1938 National University of Ireland*

McCain, C. R.
Preaching in eighteenth century Scotland: a comparative study of the extant sermons of Ralph Erskine, 1685-1752; John Erskine, 1721-1803; and Hugh Blair, 1718-1800. *Ph.D. 1949 Edinburgh*

McCall, P.
The distinctive features of the Christian doctrine of atonement as brought out by by the comparative study of religion. *M.A. 1947 Leeds*

McCallister, W. J.
Freedom in education: a critical interpretation of some historical views. *Ph.D. 1930 London, External Degree*

McCallum, M. M. C.
The dramatic art of Mira de Amescua. *M.A. 1936 Liverpool*

McCann, D.
English monarchy fifteenth to seventeenth century. *M.A. 1939 National University of Ireland*

McCann, E. K.
L'influence de la philosophie de Bergson sur l'oeuvre littéraire de Marcel Proust. *M.A. 1933 Liverpool*

McCann, F.
Research on the saga-lists called *A* & *B* contained in, respectively, *The Book of Leinster* and ms.H.3.17 (T.C.D.) and mss.23.N.10 (R.I.A.), Rawl. B512 and Harleian 5280, together with research on the tales included therein, with special emphasis upon those which are now lost. *M.A. 1950 Belfast*

McCann, J.
Asceticism; an historical study. *Ph.D. 1944 Dublin, Trinity College*

McCann, R. E.
The metaphysic of St. Bonaventure. *M.A. 1936 National University of Ireland*

MacCarthaigh, D.
Stair agus seanchas Iár-Mhúscraighe, agus filíocht le S. Máistir O'Conaill agus le Tadhg O'Síothcháin, agus giotaí le fillibh(The history and lore of West Muskerry, and poetry by S. Máistir O'Conaill, Tadhg O'Síothcháin and others). *M.A. 1937 National University of Ireland*

MacCarthaigh, L.
Filíocht ó láimscríbhinn ó co. an Chláir. Filíocht Stainndis Aodha Uí Ghráda, Bhriain Uí Luanna agus Shéamais Mhic Chruitinn(Poetry from a manuscript from Co. Clare, including the poetry of Stainndis Aodh O'Gráda, Briain O'Luanna and Séamas Mac Cruitinn). *M.A. 1937 National University of Ireland*

McCarthy, A. C.
Wage theories in the nineteenth century, with special reference to Thornton. *M.Econ.Sc. 1941 National University of Ireland*

McCarthy, B.
Hiero II. king of Syracuse (B.C. 269-215). *M.A. 1950 National University of Ireland*

MacCarthy, B. G.
Browning's psychology of genius as shown in *Pauline; Paracelsus; Andrea del Sarto; Cleon*. *M.A. 1927 National University of Ireland*

MacCarthy, B. G.
Women's share in the development of the English novel, 1621-1818. *Ph.D. 1939 National University of Ireland*

MacCarthy, C. J. F.
The economics of inheritance in Ireland. *M.Comm. 1949 National University of Ireland*

MacCarthy, C. P.
Income tax in Ireland. *M.Comm. 1918 National University of Ireland*

McCarthy, C. P.
War taxation. *M.Comm. 1918 National University of Ireland*

McCarthy, D.
Causality. *M.A. 1940 National University of Ireland*

McCarthy, E. E.
A history of the social credit movement. *M.A. 1947 Leeds*

MacCarthy, E. M.
Maria Edgeworth; a study in Anglo-Irish literature. *M.A. 1934 National University of Ireland*

McCarthy, L. P.
St. Just: his place in the French Revolution. *B.Litt. 1927 Oxford*

McCarthy, M.
Some aspects of the Geraldine rebellion. *M.A. 1926 National University of Ireland*

McCarthy, P. J.
An economic history of the Port of Cork from 1813 to 1900. *M.Econ.Sc. 1949 National University of Ireland*

McCarthy, R. C.
On the measurement of conation: an enquiry into volitional processes. *Ph.D. 1925 London*

McCaul, S. M. P.
Economic survey of pharmaceutical retailing. *M.Econ.Sc. 1949 National University of Ireland*

MacCauley, J. A.
John Philpot Curran. *M.A. 1939 National University of Ireland*

MacCauley, L.
Gates of the Euxine. *M.A. 1919 National University of Ireland*

McClatchey, D.
The parish clergy of rural Oxfordshire from the institution of Bishop John Butler (1777) to the translation of Bishop Samuel Wilberforce (1869), with particular reference to their non-ecclesiastical activities. *D.Phil. 1949 Oxford*

McClean, R. J.
Sankt Stephans Leben. *M.A. 1930 London, School of Economics and Political Science*

McClintock, T.
The nature of the mystical in the poetry of Francis Thompson. *M.A. 1947 Manchester*

McCloy, S. T.
A comparative study of the old and new types of revivalism, with special relation to the influence of contemporary religious thought and practice. *B.Litt. 1922 Oxford*

Maccoby, S.
English radicalism, 1832-1852. *Ph.D. 1934 London, School of Economics and Political Science*

McCombe, B. *see* Bramwell, B.

McComish, W.
Economic geography of North America. *M.Sc. 1936 London, External Degree*

MacConformhaoile, M. C.
Sgoláirí Ceiltise(Celtic scholars). *M.A. 1936 National University of Ireland*

MacConroi, M.
Nua fhilidheacht na Gaedilge(Modern Irish poetry). *M.A. 1926 National University of Ireland*

McConville, M. A.
The Anglo-Norman element in Irish poetry from 1200 A.D. to 1600 A.D. *M.A. 1946 Belfast*

MacCormac, M. J.
Aspects of Irish industrialisation. *M.A. 1948 National University of Ireland*

McCormick, E. H.
Literature in New Zealand. *M.Litt. 1936 Cambridge*

McCormick, M. J.
Choiseul's foreign policy relative to England. *M.A. 1911 Liverpool*

McCornish, W.
Trade of Northern Ireland, 1922-1939: a study in economic geography. *Ph.D. 1949 London, External Degree*

McCourt, D.
Rundale and its social concomitants. *M.A. 1947 Belfast*

McCourt, D.
The Rundale system in Ireland: a study of its geographical distribution and social relations. *Ph.D. 1950 Belfast*

McCourt, I.
Gottfried Keller's Weltanschauung. *Ph.D. 1932 Edinburgh*

McCown, D. B.
Municipal tribunals and international law: The development of international law by English and French courts in the nineteenth century. *Ph.D. 1938 London, School of Economics and Political Science*

McCoy, G. A. Hayes- *see* Hayes-McCoy, G. A.

McCoy, S. M. M.
Education in Ireland in the sixteenth century. *Ph.D. 1936 National University of Ireland*

McCracken, D. J.
The problem of value in early modern philosophy, with special reference to Descartes. *M.A. 1934 Belfast*

McCracken, D. J.
The problem of value in early modern philosophy: a study of Descartes, Geulincx and Spinoza. *Ph.D. 1936 Belfast*

McCracken, E. M.
The composition and distribution of woods in Northern Ireland from the sixteenth century down to the establishment of the first Ordnance Survey. *M.Sc. 1944 Belfast*

McCracken, J. L.
Central and local administration in Ireland under George II. *Ph.D. 1948 Belfast*

McCracken, J. L.
The undertakers in Ireland and their relations with the Lords Lieutenant, 1724-1771. *M.A. 1942 Belfast*

McCrae, A. J.
A contribution to the study of *Le chemin de vaillance*, a fifteenth-century allegorical poem by Jean de Courcy. *Ph.D. 1934 London, University College*

McCrea, A.
The new psychology, its origins, and development. *M.A. 1924 Belfast*

McCririck, V. N. R.
Costumbrismo in the novels of Pérez Galdós. *M.A. 1949 Birmingham*

McCulloh, G. O.
The theism of James Martineau. *Ph.D. 1938 Edinburgh*

MacCunn, F. J.
The contemporary English view of Napoleon. *B.Litt. 1913 Oxford*

MacCurtain, S.
Bunadas na h-economuíocta(The basis of economics). *M.A. 1928 National University of Ireland*

McCusker, H. C.
John Bale, antiquary and biographer. *M.A. 1934 London, University College*

McCutcheon, F. S.
The socialistic tendencies of Emile Zola as expressed in his literary works. *M.A. 1929 Wales*

McCutcheon, K. L.
Yorkshire fairs and markets to the end of the eighteenth century. *M.Litt. 1935 Durham*

McDermott, F.
Economic effects of the Great War 1914-18 on Ireland. *M.A. 1940 National University of Ireland*

McDermott, J.
The history of the agricultural geography of Great Britain since 1800. *M.Sc. 1943 London, External Degree*

MacDermott, L.
Constitutional law. *M.A. 1934 National University of Ireland*

MacDermott, M.
Francis Ledwidge. *M.A. 1946 National University of Ireland*

MacDermott, M.
The verbal system of the *Book of Leinster* version of the *Táin bó Cúalnge*. *M.A. 1939 National University of Ireland*

Macdermott, M. M.
Vowel sounds in poetry, their music and tone colour. *Ph.D. 1941 Glasgow*

Macdiarmid, A. A. J.
The hospital-school and the residential special school, with particular reference to teaching in orthopaedic hospital wards. *Ph.D. 1946 Glasgow*

McDiarmid, M. P.
Robert Fergusson and his relation to Scottish vernacular poetry. *B.Litt. 1938 Oxford*

MacDomhnaill, S.
Dánta agus amhráin an fhile Séan O' Gadhra. *M.A. 1936 National University of Ireland*

MacDonagh, D.
T. S. Eliot as poet. *M.A. 1939 National University of Ireland*

McDonagh, T. F.
The voluntarism of Duns Scotus. *M.A. 1923 National University of Ireland*

Macdonald, A.
The place names of the county of West Lothian. *Ph.D. 1937 Edinburgh*

Macdonald, A.
A scheme of vocational guidance for use in an educational area. *Ph.D. 1939 Edinburgh*

Macdonald, A. B.
The worship of the early Christian Church as reflected in the New Testament literature, and its influence on the development of doctrine. *Ph.D. 1932 Edinburgh*

McDonald, A. H.
The sources and compositions of Livy, books XXXI-XLV. *Ph.D. 1938 Cambridge*

MacDonald, C.
Fielding's plays. *B.Litt. 1924 Oxford*

Macdonald, D. F.
Population movements in Scotland, 1770-1850. *D.Phil. 1933 Oxford*

MacDonald, E. M.
The prose works of Thomas Deloney. *M.A. 1931 Birmingham*

McDonald, G.
The plays of Fielding, and their influence on the technique of the novels. *M.A. 1939 Liverpool*

Macdonald, H. L.
A palaeographical study of the manuscript of Cicero's *De Oratore* (Harl. 2736) in the British Museum. *M.A. 1924 London*

Macdonald, I. I.
The interpretation of the Song of Solomon in the Spanish mystics. *Ph.D. 1930 Cambridge*

Macdonald, J. H.
An introduction to an edition of the poems of Robert Southwell. *B.Litt. 1930 Oxford*

MacDonald, K. R.
The Isle of Sheppey and the Swale. *M.A. 1949 London, King's College*

MacDonald, M.
The logical characteristics of expression. *Ph.D. 1934 London, University College*

MacDonald, M.
A study of the main causes for the failure of the attempt to introduce a democratic form of government in Austria after the war, with special reference to the constitution of 1920. *B.Litt. 1939 Oxford*

MacDonald, M.
Three religious poets of the seventeenth century. *M.A. 1933 National University of Ireland*

Macdonald, N.
The imperial land regulations as applied to Canada, 1763-1841. *Ph.D. 1932 Edinburgh*

McDonald, O. H.
Music and the theory of signs. *M.Litt. 1949 Cambridge*

MacDonald, R.
The ethical value of education as provided and presented by public authorities during the past thirty years (1890-1920). *M.A. 1925 Liverpool*

MacDonald, R.
The methodology of John Herschel and some of its subsequent developments. *M.Sc. 1927 London*

Macdonald, S. E. F.
The adaptations of Shakespeare by Jean-François Ducis; with special reference to the influence of the classical tradition on French tragedy. *Ph.D. 1929 Edinburgh*

McDonnel, J.
Pérez de Ayala, novelist. *B.Litt. 1947 Oxford*

McDonnell, E. M.
An analysis of 'p' (perseveration) tests, with special reference to schizophrenic conditions. *M.A. 1934 London, University College*

MacDonogh, J. A. M.
The religion of Jean Racine. *B.Litt. 1939 Dublin, Trinity College*

McDougall, D.
Primitive beliefs about the dead as a preparation for the Christian doctrine of immortality. *Ph.D. 1937 Edinburgh*

MacDougall, K. F. Lindsay- see Lindsay-Macdougall, K. F.

MacDougall, W.
The French conquest and administration of the Milanese, 1499-1572. *D.Litt. 1924 Glasgow*

McDowall, C.
Exegeses of: Romans iii.21-26; iv.13-25; v. 1-11. *D.D. & B.D. 1882 Oxford*

McDowell, F.
Expositions of: Romans viii.18-24; I Corinthians xv.29; Hebrews vi.4-6. *D.D. 1897 Oxford*

McDowell, F.
1. On the credibility of miracles. 2. The efficacy of the sacraments. *B.D. 1890 Oxford*

McDowell, R. B.
Social and political ideas in Ireland in the 18th century. *Ph.D. 1938 Dublin, Trinity College*

Mace, D. R.
Origins of the Christian sex ethic. *Ph.D. 1942 Manchester*

Mace, F. A.
The trade and industry of Devonshire in the later Middle Ages. *M.A. 1925 London*

McEachran, F.
Herder's Humanitätsideal. *B.Litt. 1930 Oxford*

McEldowney, M. M.
The fairy tales and fantasies of George Macdonald. *B.Litt. 1934 Oxford*

McElligott, M.
Gerald Griffin. *M.A. 1936 National University of Ireland*

McElligott, M.
Gerald Griffin; a study in Anglo-Irish literature. *M.A. 1936 National University of Ireland*

McElligott, T. J. F.
The creative work of Canon Sheehan. *M.A. 1942 National University of Ireland*

McElroy, K. L.
Life and work of William Laud, 1628-39, with special reference to his social and political activities. *D.Phil. 1943 Oxford*

McElroy, K. L.
The place of the parish in local government, 1600-1650. *B.Litt. 1925 Oxford*

McElroy, R. G.
Impossiblity of performance of contract. *Ph.D. 1934 Cambridge*

McElwain, D. W.
A psychological study of ownership in children. *Ph.D. 1937 London, University College*

McEwan, J. W.
The historical setting of the Scottish covenants of the reign of Charles I. *Ph.D. 1930 Glasgow*

McFadden, W.
Ferdinando Texeda: a complete analysis of his work together with a study of his stay in England (1621? to 1631?), being a contribution to the solution of the problems connected with him. *M.A. 1933 Belfast*

MacFarlane, D. L.
The introduction and development of Wesleyanism in Scotland. *Ph.D. 1931 Edinburgh*

McFarlane, J. W.
The theory of tragedy in the works of Paul Ernst, Wilhelm von Scholz, and Samuel Lublinski, with special reference to the influence of Hebbel. *B.Litt. 1948 Oxford*

McFarlane, K.
The legal incidence of the death duties. *LL.D. 1933 London, External Degree*

McFarlane, M.
A study in practical ability. *Ph.D. 1924 London*

Macfie, J. M.
The religious and moral teaching of Tulsidās in his poem *Rāmcharitmanās*. *Ph.D. 1929 Edinburgh*

McGahan, E. C.
An examination of the methods of Dickens and Thackeray in the characterization of women. *M.A. 1946 Wales*

McGann, M. J.
From inspiration to erudition: studies in the development of the notion 'poeta doctus'. *M.A. 1950 Belfast*

McGartoll, J.
Great Southern Railways Company. *M.A. 1939 National University of Ireland*

McGearty, L.
Stoff, Stimmungen und Form der Lyrik Hugo von Hofmannsthals. *M.A. 1947 National University of Ireland*

McGeogh, A.
Labour in the merchant service 1850-1920. *M.Com. 1921 Birmingham*

MacGibney, L. E.
Some aspects of the development of seventeenth century comedy. *M.A. 1942 Belfast*

MacGillivray, A. M.
Myopia and the education of the myopic scholar in Scotland. *M.D. 1930 Saint Andrew's*

MacGinley, J. J.
The judiciary in relation to legislation and constitutional development during the reigns of Henry VII and Henry VIII. *M.A. 1915 London*

MacGiolla Choilleadh, B.
Taighde ar dheilbh-eolas na meán-Gaeilge(An investigation of the morphology of Middle Irish). *M.A. 1943 National University of Ireland*

MacGiolla Mhártain, S. M.
Sdair na Traoi do réir láimhscríbhinne A.11(*The history of Troy* as in ms. A.11). *M.A. 1945 National University of Ireland*

MacGiollacuda, M.
An gearr-scéal sa nua-Ghaedhilg(The short story in modern Irish). *M.A. 1946 National University of Ireland*

McGoris, M.
Sheridan. *M.A. 1941 National University of Ireland*

McGovern, W. M.
Buddhist cosmology. *D.Phil. 1922 Oxford*

McGrath, J. A.
Duanaire bhrathar mbocht d'Ord S. Froinsias(Poems of the Franciscan Brothers). *Ph.D. 1945 National University of Ireland*

McGrath, J. A.
Pádraig Dubh O'Cuirnín tiugh-fhile na nGael(Pádraig Dubh O'Cuirnín, popular poet of the Irish). *Ph.D. 1945 National University of Ireland*

McGrath, J. S. F.
Newman's work for university education in Ireland. *D.Phil. 1948 Oxford*

Mcgrath, M. P.
The melancholy humour - a study of one aspect of English literature, circa 1590-1640. *M.A. 1943 Bristol*

McGrath, P. V.
The marketing of food, fodder and livestock in the London area in the seventeenth century, with some reference to the sources of supply. *M.A. 1947 London, Queen Mary College*

McGrath, T. J.
Philosophy of certitude. *M.A. 1915 National University of Ireland*

MacGregor, A. J.
Historical landmarks in the treatment of insanity. *M.D. 1892 Edinburgh*

McGregor, A. M.
The crowd: collective and individual aspects in Elizabethan drama, 1580-1610. *M.A. 1927 London*

Macgregor, G. H. C.
The Gospel of John. *B.D. 1929 Cambridge*

MacGregor, J.
The history of adult and technical education in Skipton-in-Craven, during the nineteenth century. *M.Ed. 1949 Leeds*

MacGregor, J. G.
An analysis of the function of aesthetic experience in religion. *D.Phil. 1945 Oxford*

MacGregor, J. G.
An inquiry into the origins of the Presbyterian Church polity in Scotland, as devised by the reformers of the sixteenth century. *Ph.D. 1923 Edinburgh*

Macgregor, J. J.
The history of land-ownership since 1870, with special reference to conditions in Cambridgeshire. *B.Litt. 1938 Oxford*

MacGregor, M. B.
Ecclesiastical polity and religious life in Scotland during the Commonwealth and Protectorate. *Ph.D. 1929 Glasgow*

Macgregor, M. E.
The life and works of Mrs. Amelia Opie. *Ph.D. 1932 London, King's College*

Macgregor, M. L.
The Roman Collegia. *M.A. 1931 London, Birkbeck College*

McGregor, R.
Native segregation in Southern Rhodesia: a study of social policy. *Ph.D. 1940 London, External Degree*

McGuane, M. D.
The economic effect of some aspects of our current taxation system. *M.A. 1949 National University of Ireland*

McGuffie, T. H.
Life in the British Army in relation to social conditions. *M.A. 1940 London, King's College*

McGuinness, T. W.
Changes of population in west Cornwall with the rise and decline of mining. *M.Sc. 1938 London, Birkbeck College*

McGuinness, T. W.
Population changes in Cornwall in relation to economic resources. *Ph.D. 1944 London, King's College*

McGuire, J. B.
Realism in Irish drama. *Ph.D. 1941 Dublin, Trinity College*

McGwynn, J. F. J. *see* Mac Cuinn, S.

McHale, J. P.
Present system of direct taxation in Eire. *M.Comm. 1947 National University of Ireland*

McHardy, R. S.
Hebrew prophecy as illustrated by the vision and message of second Isaiah. *B.Litt. 1923 Oxford*

McHardy, W. D.
A preparation for an edition of a critical text of selected chapters of the Syriac version of Ecclesiasticus. *D.Phil. 1943 Oxford*

Machin, F.
Labour organization of miners of South Yorkshire from 1858-1914. *B.Litt. 1930 Oxford*

Machin, I. W. J.
Popular religious works of the eighteenth century: their vogue and influence. *Ph.D. 1939 London, External Degree*

Machin, M. I.
Dualism in Greek and Roman mythology. *Ph.D. 1933 London, University College*

McHugh, G. P.
The evolution of local administration in English elementary education during the period 1833-1930 with special consideration of the problems of finance, administrative areas and inspection. *M.Ed. 1932 Durham*

McHugh, J. H.
Education in Ireland in the penal times. *M.A. 1941 National University of Ireland*

McHugh, M. M.
La chanson de Roland : its origin and its language. *M.A. 1920 National University of Ireland*

McHugh, R. J.
Newman, his work in Ireland, and his educational theory and practice. *Ph.D. 1947 National University of Ireland*

McIlvenna, E. G. C.
The satire of the Philistine and philistinism in German literature from Sturm und Drang to Heine. *Ph.D. 1936 Edinburgh*

McIlwraith, A. K.
The life and writings of Philip Massinger. *D.Phil. 1931 Oxford*

MacInerney, J. F.
The medieval English lyric. *M.A. 1932 National University of Ireland*

Macinnes, A. M. F.
The kingdom of God in the apostolic writings. *Ph.D. 1922 Edinburgh*

MacInnes, J.
The rise and development of the evangelical movement in the Highlands of Scotland from 1688 to 1800. *Ph.D. 1941 Edinburgh*

McInnes, J. H.
Training for commerce in post-primary schools. *M.Ed. 1934 Durham*

McInnes, M.
The human geography of Sheffield and the surrounding district. *B.Litt. 1923 Oxford*

McIntosh, A. J.
The British ports in relation to the export trade of Birmingham. *Ph.D. 1935 London, External Degree*

Macintosh, C. B.
The relations between the State and voluntary associations in theory and practice during the last fifty years. *Cert.Litt. 1920 Oxford*

McIntosh, D. M.
An investigation of methods of examination at the 'qualifying stage'. *Ph.D. 1939 Saint Andrew's*

McIntosh, N. R.
The attitude of W. S. Landor towards the political situations of his day. *M.A. 1914 Birmingham*

McIntyre, J.
The language of the Pauline epistles considered in its bearing on the possible Pauline authorship of the pastoral epistles. *M.Litt. 1946 Durham*

McIntyre, S. S.
The social and cultural basis of prejudice. *Ph.D. 1950 Edinburgh*

McIver, A. J.
The attitude of Virgil and other Augustan poets to the religion of Rome. *B.Litt. 1932 Oxford*

McIver, J. A.
The regional and economic geography of Dumfriesshire. *M.Sc. 1948 London, School of Economics and Political Science*

Maciver, R. M.
Community: a sociological study, being an attempt to set out the nature and fundamental laws of social life. *D.Phil. 1915 Edinburgh*

McIvor, N. S.
The impact of international economic fluctuations on employment and incomes in New Zealand, 1929-1939, and the nature and effects of public policy towards it, with some comparative study of Australia and Canada in the same period. *Ph.D. 1949 London, School of Economics and Political Science*

Mack, F. M.
An edition of *Seinte Marherta*. *Ph.D. 1934 London, King's College*

Mackarness, C. C.
1. On the principles of worship in the Book of Common Prayer. 2. On the separate services in the Book of Common Prayer. *B.D. & D.D. 1914 Oxford*

Mackay, A. L. G.
The Australian banking and credit system. *M.Litt. 1931 Cambridge*

Mackay, A. R. F.
New Zealand public finance. *Ph.D. 1936 London, School of Economics and Political Science*

Mackay, E. J. H.
A cemetery at Kish. A Sumerian palace. Jemdet Nasr. Bahrein and Hemamieh. Mohenjo-Daro. *D.Litt. 1933 Bristol*

Mackay, E. J. H.
Methods of representing hair in the wall-paintings of Theban tombs. *M.A. 1922 Bristol*

McKay, J.
Ben Jonson and the Latin comedy. *M.A. 1939 National University of Ireland*

Mackay, J. J.
The sentiment of place in English poetry from 1700-1780. *M.A. 1937 London, Bedford College*

MacKean, W. H.
1. The origin of Christian monasticism in Egypt. 2. The history of Christian monasticism in Egypt to the close of the fourth century. *B.D. & D.D. 1919 Oxford*

McKee, E. M. W.
George Lillo, 1693-1739. *B.Litt. 1939 Oxford*

McKellar, T. P. H.
A psychological study of human aggressiveness. *Ph.D. 1949 London, University College*

McKelvie, R. F. S.
Expositions of St. Matthew i.18-25; St. Luke i.26-38; St. John i.1-18. *D.D. 1919 Oxford*

McKenna, C. H.
The regulation of tariffs by recent international agreements, as exemplified by the practice of Great Britain and the United States. *B.Litt. 1938 Oxford*

McKennan, D. L.
The *Orthographia gallica*: Trinity College manuscript. *M.A. 1935 Belfast*

Mackenzie, A. M.
The women in Shakespeare's plays: a critical study from the dramatic and psychological points of view, and in relation to the development of Shakespeare's art. *D.Litt. 1924 Aberdeen*

Mackenzie, B. A.
Some phonological features of the dialect of London and of the surrounding areas in the fifteenth century. *B.Litt. 1926 Oxford*

Mackenzie, E. K. A.
The literary works of Bishop Percy, with special reference to the antiquarian studies of the eighteenth century. *Ph.D. 1943 London, Westfield College*

Mackenzie, E. M.
Jeremy Taylor: a study of his style. *M.Litt. 1938 Cambridge*

Mackenzie, G. A.
The romantic poetry of S. T. Coleridge. *M.A. 1926 Birmingham*

MacKenzie, H. M.
The petty Scots novel. *Ph.D. 1945 Edinburgh*

Mackenzie, H. S.
The influence of environment on the form of the gospel of Jesus. *Ph.D. 1925 Edinburgh*

McKenzie, J.
The Germanic numerals and numeral-systems. *Ph.D. 1938 Leeds*

McKenzie, L. W.
The development of utility theory and welfare economics. *B.Litt. 1949 Oxford*

Mackenzie, M.
Hegel's theory and practice of education, and problems of girls' education in elementary schools. *M.A. 1908 Wales*

Mackenzie, M. H.
The policy of Lord Palmerston in the Near Eastern Question from the date of his accession to office in November, 1830, to the date of his retirement in August, 1841. *B.Litt. 1928 Oxford*

MacKenzie, N. H.
South African travel literature in English to the end of the seventeenth century. *Ph.D. 1940 London, University College*

Mackenzie, W.
Systems of remuneration of labour in agriculture in relation to efficiency and performance. *B.Litt. 1948 Oxford*

McKeough, M. F.
The Blessed Virgin Mary in Middle English verse. *M.A, 1939 National University of Ireland*

McKeough, M. N.
Religious lyric verse in fifteenth century England. *Ph.D. 1941 National University of Ireland*

McKernan, O.
A study of the poetry of the Irish *Annals* up to the year 1,000 A.D. *M.A. 1938 Belfast*

McKernan, R.
Popularity and decline of Roman drama. *M.A. 1918 National University of Ireland*

Mackie, A. W.
A critical investigation into the philosophical, ecclesiastical and other influences on Ernest Renan's *Vie de Jésus*. *Ph.D. 1931 Glasgow*

Mackie, J. L.
British sugar taxation since the Napoleonic wars. *Ph.D. 1939 London, School of Economics and Political Science*

McKie, M.
The main tendencies in English political philosophy in the nineteenth century. *M.A. 1925 Wales*

McKie, M.
The relations of statutory and voluntary authorities in public administration in England and Wales. *B.Litt. 1930 Oxford*

Mackie, R. A.
Richard Mulcaster and his pedagogic doctrines: a study of the realistic movement in Elizabethan education. *Ph.D. 1933 Glasgow*

McKindlay, J. L.
Economic aspects of the production and distribution of branded food products. *M.A. 1939 Liverpool*

Mackinlay, C.
The relation of religion to morals in Christianity. *M.Litt. 1940 Durham*

Mackinlay, M. M. M.
Dekker and the artizan in the Elizabethan drama. *M.A. 1949 Manchester*

McKinlay, R.
Semitisms in the New Testament in the light of later popular Greek. *Ph.D. 1927 Glasgow*

MacKinnon, A.
The doctrine of the atonement in the light of Christ's teaching and ministry. *Ph.D. 1924 Glasgow*

McKinnon, A. T.
Kierkegaard's critique of rationalism. *Ph.D. 1950 Edinburgh*

Mackinnon, I. F.
Settlements and churches in Nova Scotia, 1749-1776: the origin of Protestant Churches in relation to settlement, from the founding of Halifax to the American Revolution. *Ph.D. 1930 Edinburgh*

Mackinnon, J. M.
The English Poor Law of 1834, with special reference to its working between 1834 and 1847: a study in social pathology. *M.A. 1930 London, University College*

Mackintosh, A. M.
A study in the use of advisory bodies by the Ministry of Agriculture and Fisheries, since 1919. *B.Litt. 1949 Oxford*

Mackintosh, H. S.
An investigation into the social and educational aspects of pupil migration in Scotland. *Ph.D. 1941 Aberdeen*

McKisack, M.
Parliament in the reign of Richard II. *B.Litt. 1924 Oxford*

Mackness, G.
Exegeses of Romans iii.21-26; Romans v.1-11; I Corinthians x.23-xi.1. *D.D. 1871 Oxford*

Mackness, G.
1. Holy Scripture, the sole rule of faith. 2. On the limits to be imposed upon the exercise of private judgment in the interpretation of the rule of faith. *B.D. 1871 Oxford*

Mackworth, N. H.
Researches in the measurement of human performance. *Ph.D. 1947 Cambridge*

McLachlan, H. J.
The curricula of the Dissenting Academies in the reign of George III. *M.A. 1930 Manchester*

McLachlan, H. J.
The rise and spread of Socinianism in England before 1689. *D.Phil. 1949 Oxford*

McLachlan, J. O.
Anglo-Spanish diplomatic and commercial relations, 1731-59. *Ph.D. 1937 Cambridge*

Maclagan, W. G.
Knowledge of the particular in St. Thomas Aquinas, including a discussion of the principle of individuation. *Ph.D. 1928 Edinburgh*

McLaine, W.
The Engineers' Union, Book 1. The millwrights and 'old mechanics'. *Ph.D. 1939 London, External Degree*

McLaren, V. M.
Retardation in children of high intelligence. *Ph.D. 1950 Glasgow*

McLauchlan, B. E.
William Walsh, poet and critic. *M.A. 1948 Birmingham*

MacLaughlin, E.
Art of Marlowe. *M.A. 1916 National University of Ireland*

Maclay, D. T.
Army psychiatry in and out of battle: its relationship to the soldier and to the service. *M.D. 1947 Glasgow*

Maclean, A. H.
The origins of the political opinions of John Locke. *Ph.D. 1948 Cambridge*

Maclean, J. A.
The sources for the history of the Highlands. *Ph.D. 1939 Aberdeen*

Maclean, J. R.
The effect of the slave emancipation in British Guiana and Trinidad. *B.Litt. 1931 Oxford*

MacLean, M. M.
La critique littéraire d'Etienne Pasquier dans les *Recherches de la France* et les *Lettres*. *M.A. 1941 Liverpool*

McLean, W. H.
The wider applications of the principles of town-planning. *Ph.D. 1929 Glasgow*

McLeish, J.
British activities in Yucatan and on the Moskito shore in the eighteenth century. *M.A. 1926 London*

McLeish, W. A.
A quantitative investigation of the effect of scientific lending on certain industries as viewed from the aspect of banking. *Ph.D. 1939 Edinburgh*

McLellan, N. J.
Chartism and the Churches, with special reference to Lancashire: an account of the Churches and social reform in the Chartist period. *Ph.D. 1947 Edinburgh*

McLellan, R. D.
Roman and imperial sentiment in the literature of the Empire: Augustus to Constantine. *Ph.D. 1934 London, University College*

MacLeod, A. N.
The social morality of Confucianism: a Christian appraisal. *Ph.D. 1938 Edinburgh*

MacLeod, C.
Wooden figure sculpture in Ireland until the 17th century. *M.A, 1944 National University of Ireland*

Macleod, J. W.
The British moralists. *B.Litt. 1933 Oxford*

MacLeod, M. K.
The Yezidis, or 'devil-worshippers' of Assyria: an investigation into their social and religious cult. *Ph.D. 1933 Edinburgh*

McLernan, M. C.
The works of Alice Meynell. *M.A. 1937 Liverpool*

McLernon, R. R.
La pensée dans la poésie de Lamartine. *Ph.D. 1940 Belfast*

McLintock, A. H.
The establishment of constitutional government in Newfoundland, 1783-1832. *Ph.D. 1938 London, King's College*

MacLochlainn, A.
Trompa na bhFlaitheas(The trumpet of Heaven). *M.A. 1948 National University of Ireland*

McLoughlin, J. E.
Christina Rossetti. *M.A. 1947 National University of Ireland*

MacLoughlin, J. M.
The reality of morals. *Ph.D. 1942 National University of Ireland*

McLuhan, M.
The place of Thomas Nashe in the learning of his time. *Ph.D. 1944 Cambridge*

Maclure, E. C.
1. The efficacy of prayer. 2. The efficacy of sacraments. *B.D. & D.D. 1890 Oxford*

MacLysaght, E.
Everyday life in Ireland in the second half of the seventeenth century. *M.A. 1937 National University of Ireland*

McMahon, J. F.
An edition of three unedited sermons by John Fisher (1459-1535), together with a bibliography of his printed works. *B.Litt. 1949 Oxford*

McMahon, J. T.
Methods of teaching religion. *Ph.D. 1928 National University of Ireland*

MacMathúna, C.
Staidéar ar roinnt seanamhrán Gaelige(A study of a selection of old Irish songs). *M.A. 1949 National University of Ireland*

Macmeeken, A. M.
The intelligence of a representative group of Scottish children. *Ph.D. 1939 Edinburgh*

McMillan, D.
A contribution to the study of the *Enfances Guillaume* in the versions contained in the mss. Royal 20D XI (British Museum, London) and français 24369 (Bibliothèque Nationale, Paris). *Ph.D. 1938 London, University College*

MacMillan, D. N.
The doctrine of the person and work of Christ in Horace Bushnell's theology. *Ph.D. 1935 Edinburgh*

Macmillan, E.
The relationship of Warren Hastings to the government of Oudh. *M.A. 1912 Liverpool*

Macmillan, M.
Introduction and notes to Pope's Homer's *Iliad*. *D.Litt. 1902 Birmingham*

Macmillan, M.
Matheran folk songs. *D.Litt. 1903 Birmingham*

Macmillan, M.
The tragedy of *Julius Caesar*. *D.Litt. 1902 Birmingham*

MacMillan, R. A. C.
The crowning phase in the critical philosophy. *Ph.D. 1912 Glasgow*

McMillan, W.
The worship of the Scottish Reformed Church, 1550-1638. *Ph.D. 1925 Edinburgh*

Macmullan, H. M.
A critical edition of *St. Patrick for Ireland* (1640) by James Shirley. *B.Litt. 1931 Oxford*

McMurray, C. W.
Stone and pillar cult among the Western Semites, with special reference to the Hebrews. *Ph.D. 1934 Edinburgh*

MacNab, T. M. A.
Scottish Lollardry and its contribution to the Reformation in Scotland, with special reference to the Lollards of the West. *Ph.D. 1933 Glasgow*

McNamara, P. M.
Inter-relation between geographical factors and population decline in Ireland since the famine of 1845-47. *Ph.D. 1932 London, School of Economics and Political Science*

McNaughton, A.
A study in the phenomena of prostration arising from a conviction of sin. *Ph.D. 1937 Edinburgh*

McNaulty, M.
Some aspects of the history of the administration of the Poor laws in Birmingham between 1730 and 1834. *M.A. 1942 Birmingham*

McNeil, B. E.
Studien zur Erklärung der Gedankenwelt R. M. Rilkes. *Ph.D. 1929 Edinburgh*

MacNeill, F. E.
An investigation into temperament: its relation to intelligence, and special abilities. *Ph.D. 1942 Edinburgh*

McNeur, R. W.
John Calvin's conception of the seat of authority in religion. *Ph. D. 1950 Edinburgh*

MacNulty, B. A.
Some characters of the Red Branch saga. *M.A. 1920 National University of Ireland*

MacNutt, W. S.
British rule in Nova Scotia, 1713-1784. *M.A. 1932 London, King's College*

Macodrum, M. M.
Survivals of the English and Scottish popular ballads in Canada: a study of the ways of tradition with verse. *Ph.D. 1927 Glasgow*

MacOireachtaigh, S.
Beatha Mhaolmhodaigh naomhtha(The life of St. Maolmodach). *M.A. 1934 National University of Ireland*

MacPhail, A.
Historical and other notes on the administration of the Anatomy Act. *M.D. 1923 Glasgow*

McPhee, W. A.
The economic revolution in British West Africa. *Ph.D. 1925 London*

McPherson, A.
Disputatio I. Eccii et M. Lutheri, Lipsiae, Labita 1519: translation with critical introduction and notes. *Ph.D. 1931 Edinburgh*

Macpherson, A. C.
The interpretation of the fourth Gospel. *Ph.D. 1940 Cambridge*

Macpherson, A. L.
André Rivoire. *M.A. 1949 London, University College*

Macpherson, C. B.
Voluntary associations within the state, 1900-1934, with special reference to the place of trade unions in relation to the State in Great Britain. *M.Sc. 1935 London, School of Economics and Political Science*

Macpherson, H. C.
The later convenanting movement, with special reference to religion and ethics. *Ph.D. 1923 Edinburgh*

Macpherson, J.
The Gaelic dialect of North Uist. *Ph.D. 1945 Edinburgh*

MacPhillips, M.
Cornelius O'Mulrian, Bishop of Killaloe (1576-1617) and the Counter-Reformation. *M.A. 1928 National University of Ireland*

McPolin, F.
The teacher's functions. *Ph.D. 1941 National University of Ireland*

MacPolin, F.
Technique of examining children, based on the *New Examiner* by Dr. P. B. Ballard (1923). *M.A. 1934 National University of Ireland*

McQuaid, J.
Musicians of the Scottish Reformation, with special reference to Crown policy c.1560-1650. *Ph.D. 1949 Edinburgh*

McQuaid, J. C.
A Roman of the early Empire: Lucius Annaeus Seneca. *M.A, 1918 National University of Ireland*

MacQueen, E. E.
The General Assembly of the Kirk as the rival of the Scottish Parliament, 1560-1618. *Ph.D. 1927 Saint Andrew's*

McQueen, E. N.
The distribution of attention. *D.Sc. 1917 London*

McQuitty, J. L.
Contributory negligence. *LL.D. 1940 Dublin, Trinity College*

Macrae, A.
History of the clan Macrae. *M.A. 1905 London*

Macrae, C.
Scotland and the Wars of the Roses, 1435-85. *D.Phil. 1939 Oxford*

McRae, C. R.
Some effects of social and educational opportunities upon mental tests. *Ph.D. 1925 London*

McRae, W. A.
The nature and scope of civil liability in nuisance. *B.Litt. 1936 Oxford*

MacRéamoinn, S.
Taighde ar feidhm na réimíreann mbriathardha(An investigation of the function of verbal prefixes). *M.A. 1943 National University of Ireland*

McRitchie, M. M.
A study of a hitherto unconsidered Yvain manuscript (National Library of Wales, add. ms.444W - Yvain Williams ms.530). *M.A. 1929 Wales*

McShane, P. J.
Spenser as philosopher. *M.A. 1935 Birmingham*

McSweeney, M.
Poverty and the wage-earning classes. *M.A. 1914 National University of Ireland*

McSweeney, P.
Turlough Luineach O'Neill. *M.A. 1927 National University of Ireland*

MacTaggart, M. M.
An investigation of the causes of backwardness at the qualifying stage, with particular reference to the percentage of children scholastically retarded owing to unsuitability of curriculum. Non-scholastic tests, mechanical aptitude tests, technical information tests, and a practical test for 'backward' children. *Ph.D. 1928 Edinburgh*

McVail, E. M.
An inquiry into the housing of seasonal workers in Scotland. *M.D. 1915 Glasgow*

Macvane, J. F.
The life and work of Fulke Greville, Lord Brooke. *B.Litt. 1935 Oxford*

MacWhite, E.
Some aspects of the Irish date bronze age, based on a study of the hoards of the period. *M.A. 1944 National University of Ireland*

MacWilliam, J.
The relation of the Christian revelation to history, with special reference to Ritschlian and Hegelian tendencies. *B.Litt. 1911 Oxford*

Macwillie, J.
Mathematics and natural science in English education. *M.A. 1933 Liverpool*

Madan, A. H.
The circumstances of the Treaty of Dover. *M.A. 1909 Birmingham*

Madden, A. F.
The attitude of the Evangelicals to the Empire and imperial problems (1820-1850). *D.Phil. 1950 Oxford*

Madden, A. F.
The influence of the evangelical spirit on a policy of trusteeship towards native races, as illustrated by the records of certain missionary societies dealing with New Zealand (1814-54). *B.Litt. 1939 Oxford*

Madden, M.
Nature observance in Anglo-Saxon poetry. *M.A. 1937 National University of Ireland*

Maddison, M. G.
Woman in the early romantic school of German literature. *M.A. 1910 Birmingham*

Maddocks, G. M.
The literature of the religious revival in eighteenth century England. *M.A. 1950 Wales*

Madge, S. J.
The Domesday of Crown Lands: a study of the Parliamentary confiscations, surveys and sales during the Commonwealth. *D.Sc. 1938 London, School of Economics and Political Science*

Madge, S. J.
Rural Middlesex under the Commonwealth: a study based principally upon the Parliamentary surveys of the royal estates. *M.Sc. 1922 London*

Madgen, W.
The doctrines of God and freedom in the philosophy of Spinoza. *M.A. 1928 Liverpool*

Madgwick, R. B.
The quality of immigration into eastern Australia before 1851. *D.Phil. 1935 Oxford*

Madwar, M. R.
On the cause of anomalous determinations of time. *Ph.D. 1926 Edinburgh*

Magee, F. J.
Natural science in Irish rural schools. *M.A. 1921 National University of Ireland*

Magee, J.
Dissolution of English monasteries: social and economic effects. *M.A. 1941 National University of Ireland*

Magill, C. P.
The development of the reading public in Germany during the period 1840-1848: a critical investigation. *Ph.D. 1938 London, University College*

Magrah, M. H.
Bankers and non-routine customers: an examination of their practical relationship. *M.Comm. 1931 London, School of Economics and Political Science*

Magrath, B. B.
The notion of *virtus moralis* in S. Thomas Aquinas and its sources. *B.Litt. 1948 Oxford*

Magson, E. H.
How we judge our fellows: an investigation into the value of an interview as a means of estimating general intelligence. *D.Sc. 1925 London*

MagUidhir, S. M.
Dáibhí O'Bruadair; a bheatha agus a shaothar(Daibhí O'Bruadair: his life and work). *M.A. 1937 National University of Ireland*

Maguire, C.
Relativity of human knowledge. *M.A. 1911 National University of Ireland*

Maguire, J. F.
Agricultural geography of southwest Lancashire. *M.A. 1939 Liverpool*

Maher, J.
Ireland and U.S. slavery. *M.A. 1929 National University of Ireland*

Mahmood, A. W.
The Governor-Generalship of Sir John Shore, 1793-8. *B.Litt. 1939 Oxford*

Mahmood, M. M.
Rural co-operation in India. *B.Litt. 1922 Oxford*

Mahmoud, Z. N.
Self-determination. *Ph.D. 1947 London, King's College*

Mahon, H. P.
Poetry of James Elroy Flecker. *M.A. 1942 National University of Ireland*

Mahoney, J. C.
Jean Mairet and his tragedies. *B.Litt. 1932 Oxford*

Mahony, T.
The place and value of human geography in Irish primary schools. *M.A. 1934 National University of Ireland*

Mahood, M. M.
The transition from Jacobean to Restoration comedy, with special reference to social and theatrical factors. *M.A. 1944 London, King's College*

Maini, P. L.
The Indian problem in Kenya. *M.Sc. 1944 London, School of Economics and Political Science*

Mainwaring, J.
The aesthetic judgment. *D.Litt. 1940 Birmingham*

Mainwaring, J.
Psychological factors in musical education and in the musical development of the child. *M.A. 1931 Birmingham*

Mair, L. P.
Native development in Buganda. *Ph.D. 1933 London, School of Economics and Political Science*

Majid, S. A.
Industrial geography of Bihar. *Ph.D. 1949 London, School of Economics and Political Science*

Majmudar, P. N.
A study of metres in the older *Upanisads*. *M.A. 1930 London, School of Oriental and African Studies*

Major, H. D. A.
Exegeses of: Mark i.1; iv.1; viii.27-30. *D.D. 1924 Oxford*

Major, H. D. A.
1. The tree of the knowledge of good and evil. 2. $A\iota\acute{\omega}\nu\iota o\sigma$: its meaning and use in the New Testament. *B.D. 1916 Oxford*

Major, K.
A study of the archiepiscopal household of Stephen Langton and a collection of his acta. *B.Litt. 1931 Oxford*

Majumbar, D. N.
A changing austric culture. *Ph.D. 1935 Cambridge*

Majumdar, J. K.
The ethical implications of a monadistic metaphysic. *Ph.D. 1923 London*

Makhdumi, M. A.
Secondary education in the Punjab. *M.Ed. 1939 Leeds*

Makhzangi, M. H.
A study of certain aspects of education in England and in Egypt. *M.A. 1933 Birmingham*

Makings, S. M.
The economics of poor land arable farming; based on surveys of difficult farming areas in the east Midlands. *Ph.D. 1943 London, External Degree*

Makiya, M. S.
Architecture and the Mediterranean climate. *Ph.D. 1946 Cambridge*

Makower, H.
The theory of value on the capital market. *Ph.D. 1937 London, School of Economics and Political Science*

Malach, V. W.
International cycles and Canada's balance of payments of 1921-33. *Ph.D. 1948 London, School of Economics and Political Science*

Malalasekera, G. P.
1. Dictionary of Pali Proper Names. 2. Vamsatthappakasini, or commentary on the *Mahaevamsa*. 3. The extended *Mahāvamsa*. *D. Lit. 1938 London, External Degree*

Malalasekera, G. P.
A history of the Pali literature of Ceylon. *Ph.D. 1925 London*

Malan, A.
1. The Christian's expectations of a palingenesis mundi finds valuable support from reason and science. 2. St.Luke xvi.9. *B.D. 1877 Oxford*

Malan, A. N.
1. The scientific aspect of biblical eschatology. 2. The parable of the unjust steward. *B.D. & D.D. 1898 Oxford*

Malan, G. H.
An absolute logical criterion. *D.Phil. 1916 Glasgow*

Malathouras, J.
Theodoret, bishop of Cyros and follower of the Antioch school in the Monophysite controversy, A.D. 441-457. *B.Litt. 1921 Oxford*

Malbon, G.
The relations between Crown and Baronage in England between 1216 and 1232, with especial reference to the administration of Hubert de Burgh. *M.A. 1940 London, External Degree*

Malcolm, C. A.
The office of sheriff in Scotland: its origin and early development. *Ph.D. 1922 Edinburgh*

Malcolm, L. W. G.
Medical museums: an historical and bibliographical study. *Ph.D. 1933 Cambridge*

Malcolm-Smith, E. F.
The international relations of Serbia 1848-1860. *Ph.D. 1926 Cambridge*

Malik, M. B.
The development of Hindustani in its early stages, especially as seen in translations and adaptations from Persian. *Ph.D. 1939 London, School of Oriental and African Studies*

Malinowski, B. G.
The family among the Australian aborigines: a sociological study. *D.Sc. 1916 London*

Malinowski, S. G.
The natives of Mailu: preliminary results of the Robert Mond research work in British New Guinea. *D.Sc. 1916 London*

Malits, M. H.
The origins of Yiddish in the German language. *M.A. 1942 Wales*

Mall, T.
A critical edition of Bhava-bhuti's drama *Mahae-vīra-caritam*. *B.Litt. 1914 Oxford*

Malley, E.
The financial administration of the Bridgewater Estate, 1780-1800. *M.A. 1929 Manchester*

Malley, W. J.
The organization of elementary education in Liverpool since the passing of the Education Act of 1918, with special reference to the provision of facilities for post-primary education. *M.A. 1936 Liverpool*

Mallik, B. K.
The problem of freedom. *B.Sc. 1924 Oxford*

Mallin, J. E.
Johann Christian Brandes: an examination of the plays of this dramatist contained in his *Sämtliche dramatische Schriften*, with notes on sources and translations of the plays and an account of the author's life, together with a list of his works. *M.A. 1908 London*

Mallinson, A.
The coinage of ancient Palestine from the second century B.C. to the fourth century of the Christian era. *B.Litt. 1924 Oxford*

Mallinson, J. W.
The Chaco dispute: a study of pacific methods of settling international disputes. *M.Sc. 1939 London, School of Economics and Political Science*

Mallinson, V.
Henri Barbusse, critique de notre temps. *M.A. 1936 Leeds*

Mallison, J. C.
The dramatic work of Sir Robert Howard. *M.A. 1923 Manchester*

Mallouk, A.
Some aspects of the Thomist theory of knowledge, in their metaphysical reference. *B.Litt. 1947 Oxford*

Malnick, B.
The origin and early history of the theatre in Russia, 1672 to 1756. *Ph.D. 1936 London, School of Slavonic and East European Studies*

Malone, M. I.
Bettina von Arnim. *M.A. 1924 National University of Ireland*

Malt, P. A.
Le rôle de la religion dans la *Comédie humaine* de Balzac. *M.A. 1937 London, King's College*

Manbre, S. T.
St. Peter Thomas, 1305-1366. *M.A. 1937 Liverpool*

Manders, C. R. S.
Education under changing government, with special reference to Alsace since the Great War. *M.A. 1939 London, Institute of Education*

Mangan, F. J.
Local registration of title in Saorstát Eireann. *M.A. 1932 National University of Ireland*

Mangan, J.
James Clarence Mangan. *M.A. 1932 National University of Ireland*

Manheim, E.
Security, authority and society; an ethnological introduction into sociology. *Ph.D. 1937 London, School of Economics and Political Science*

Manley, E. R.
On certain Greek particles. *M.A. 1921 London*

Mann, C. W.
Some influences of Greek philosophy on Jewish thought and teaching in Apocryphal literature and Philo Judaeus. *M.A. 1934 Liverpool*

Mann, D.
The Babylonian-Hebrew punctuation. *M.A. 1906 London*

Mann, F. A. A.
The legal aspect of money, with special reference to comparative and private international law. *LL.D. 1938 London, School of Economics and Political Science*

Mann, F. O.
The works of Thomas Deloney. *B.Litt. 1912 Oxford*

Mann, J.
The *Responsa* of the Babylonian Geonim as a source of Jewish history. *M.A. 1915 London*

Mann, J. G.
The evolution of defensive armour in England, France, and Italy in the first half of the fourteenth century. *B.Litt. 1923 Oxford*

Mann, K.
The background of youth work in a rural area. *M.A. 1945 London, King's College*

Mann, S.
The phonology of the Indo-European elements in Albanian. *M.A. 1940 Bristol*

Manning, F. E.
Sir Robert Peel the elder, and early factory legislation. *M.A. 1932 Bristol*

Manning, P. A.
The limits to the effectiveness of the system of payment by results as an incentive to production. *M.A. 1924 Manchester*

Manning, P. A.
The postwar relations of skilled and unskilled labour in the printing, building and engineering industries. *Ph.D. 1933 London, School of Economics and Political Science*

Mannion, T.
Internal trade; its function and importance in economic development. *M.A. 1925 National University of Ireland*

Manns, F. G. E.
Some aspects of English educational administration. *M.Sc. 1936 London, School of Economics and Political Science*

Mansergh, P. N. S.
The constitution and government of the Irish Free State. *B.Litt. 1933 Oxford*

Mansergh, P. N. S.
A study of devolution, with special reference to the government of Northern Ireland. *D.Phil. 1936 Oxford*

Manson, J.
Regionalism in Spanish fiction from 1654 to the present day, with especial reference to Pereda. *Ph.D. 1938 Edinburgh*

Mansoor, M.
Basis for a Samaritan grammar. *Ph.D. 1944 Dublin, Trinity College*

Manvell, A. R.
The study of W. B. Yeats' poetic career with special reference to his lyrical poems. *Ph.D. 1938 London, External Degree*

Manzalaoui, M. A.
Some English translations of Arabic imaginative literature (1704-1838): a study of their portrayal of the Arab world, with an estimate of their influence on nineteenth century English literature. *B.Litt. 1947 Oxford*

Mar, T. T. G.
Anglo-Chinese diplomacy, 1895-1911. *Ph.D. 1929 London*

Marais, J. S.
The colonization of New Zealand. *D.Phil. 1925 Oxford*

Marcantoni, J. D.
The minor poems of Petronius, with special reference to his literary and philosopical outlook. *M.A. 1938 London, Queen Mary College*

March, W. W. S.
Truth, unity, and goodness as aspects of being in the writings of St. Thomas Aquinas. *B.D. 1941 Oxford*

Marcon, D. V.
Matthew Arnold as a literary critic. *M.A. 1940 London, King's College*

Marcousé, R.
The decoration of Norman baptismal fonts in relation to English twelfth century sculpture. *Ph.D. 1940 London, Courtauld Institute of Art*

Marcus, L. G.
French tragedy from 1680 to 1778; a critical survey and a study in evolution. *M.Litt. 1946 Cambridge*

Mardiros, A. M.
An examination of some problems of Marxist philosophy. *M.Litt. 1943 Cambridge*

Mare, K. de la *see* De La Mare, K.

Margulies, S.
A critical comparison between *Pirke Aboth* and *Aboth de Rabbi Nathan*, with special reference to their relationship and a possible common source. *M.A. 1949 Manchester*

Marin, C. E. H.
La philosophie de l'expérience moral: Frédéric Rauh. *B.Litt. 1921 Oxford*

Maritch, D.
The Christology of St. Athanasius. *B.Litt. 1921 Oxford*

Mark, D.
The language and style of William Salesbury. *M.A. 1903 Wales*

Mark, J.
Poetics and poetry in seventeenth-century Germany: a study in traditionalism. *Ph.D. 1939 Cambridge*

Mark, J. M.
L'influence des évènements politiques jusqu'à la grande guerre (1914) sur l'oeuvre d'Anatole France. *M.A. 1939 Belfast*

Markey, J.
Anglo-Irish writers of comedies, 1690-1790. *M.A. 1929 National University of Ireland*

Markham, S. F.
British occupation of the Ionian Islands, 1815-64. *B.Litt. 1926 Oxford*

Marks, V. M. W.
Study of the lives of seven saints in the ms. Cotton Domitian XI, British Museum. *M.A. 1915 London*

Markus, R. I.
The origins of the Cartesian view of rational explanation and certain aspects of its influence on later philosophy. *Ph.D. 1950 Manchester*

Markus, R. I.
The relation between the theory of knowledge and metaphysics in the philosophical system of Samuel Alexander. *M.A. 1948 Manchester*

Marley, J. G.
A statistical and economic survey of certain aspects of the beef producing, dairying and cattle rearing industries in Great Britian between 1939 and 1945. *M.A. 1947 Manchester*

Marlow, A. N.
The influence of the *Aeneid* on the *Argonautica* of Valerius Flaccus. *M.A. 1938 London, Queen Mary College*

Marnane, M. M.
Correlation of religion in Catholic pedagogy. *M.A. 1948 National University of Ireland*

Marquand, H. A.
The integration of industry in the United States of America and Great Britain, with special reference to financial control and the capitalization of joint-stock companies. *M.A. 1928 Wales*

Marriott, G. L.
1. On anthropomorphism in Scripture and doctrine. 2. On seven new homilies of Macarias. *B.D. 1918 Oxford*

Marriott, H.
Exegeses of Matthew v.1-2; 3-12; 28-29. *D.D. 1920 Oxford*

Marriott, H.
1. On the persistence of Arcanism. 2. On the place of mysticism in Christianity. *B.D. 1915 Oxford*

Mars, H.
Efficiency of capital raising, investment and financial administration in consumers' co-operative production. *M.Com. 1937 Birmingham*

Mars, H.
Extra-territorial non-mining companies in Nigeria in peace and war. *B.Litt. 1945 Oxford*

Mars, J.
The balance of external payments of the Gold Coast for the fiscal years 1936-37 to 1938-39. *M.A. 1942 Bristol*

Marsden, I. F.
Emmanuel Signoret: l'homme et l'oeuvre. *M.A. 1927 Leeds*

Marsh, E.
La 'théorie du silence' au théâtre et l'oeuvre dramatique de Jean-Jacques Bernard. *M.A. 1933 Birmingham*

Marsh, E. A. J.
Obligations between man and man in Euripides. *M.A. 1906 London*

Marsh, J.
A theological study of the relationship of time and eternity, with special reference to the modern philosophy of history. *D.Phil. 1946 Oxford*

Marshall, A. D. B.
The marketing of Canadian bacon. *B.Litt. 1938 Oxford*

Marshall, A. H.
Local authorities: internal financial control. *Ph.D. 1937 London, External Degree*

Marshall, A. J.
The changes in visual acuity during the course of dark adaptation. *Ph.D. 1939 London, University College*

Marshall, D.
The English Poor Laws and social conditions. *Ph.D. 1926 Cambridge*

Marshall, D.
The moral teaching of Euripides. *M.A. 1913 Birmingham*

Marshall, D. W. H.
The organization of the English occupation in Scotland, 1296-1461. *B.Litt. 1925 Oxford*

Marshall, G. H.
Norman Lincolnshire. *M.A. 1948 Leeds*

Marshall, H. S.
The ethics of S. Thomas Aquinas considered in regard to their relevance to present day problems. *M.A. 1934 Bristol*

Marshall, L. B.
An anthology of seventeenth century verse by poets hitherto almost unknown, with accounts of their lives and a critical survey of their work. *Ph.D. 1932 London, University College*

Marshall, L. B.
The life and letters of Matthew Gregory Lewis (1775-1818). *M.A. 1929 London*

Marshall, L. H.
A systematic account of the ethical teaching of the New Testament. *Ph.D. 1948 London, External Degree*

Marshall, M. E. Sandbach- *see* Sandbach-Marshall, M. E.

Marshall, O. R.
A historical study of the law relating to the assignment of choses in action. *Ph.D. 1948 London, University College*

Marshall, S. F.
The validity and reliability of a secondary school entrance test: being the follow-up over a period of six years of the examination in a rural area. *M.A. 1940 London, Institute of Education*

Marshall, T. H.
The changing meaning of leisure and the problems created. *M.A. 1942 London, Institute of Education*

Marshall, W. A.
The scientific history of the steam engine. *M.Sc. 1930 London*

Marson, G. L.
Coventry: a study in urban geography. *M.A. 1949 Liverpool*

Marston, F. A.
The organization and procedure of the Paris Peace Conference of 1919. *Ph.D. 1943 London, School of Economics and Political Science*

Martell, J. S.
Origins of self-government in Nova Scotia, 1815-1836. *Ph.D. 1935 London, King's College*

Marten, N. A.
The style of the *Honourable history of Friar Bacon and Friar Bungay. M.A. 1948 Birmingham*

Martienssen, H. M.
An enquiry concerning the architectural theory and practice of Sir William Chambers, R.A. *Ph.D. 1949 London, Courtauld Institute of Art*

Martin, A. F.
The economic geography of Newfoundland. *B.Sc. 1938 Oxford*

Martin, A. P.
The writings of C. Velleius Paterculus: his style and grammar. *M.A. 1908 London*

Martin, A. W.
The rubber market. *M.Com. 1911 Birmingham*

Martin, C.
Unity of the universal. *M.A. 1941 National University of Ireland*

Martin, C. B.
Lord Selkirk's work in Canada. *B.Litt. 1912 Oxford*

Martin, C. J.
The commentaries on the *Politics* of Aristotle in the late thirteenth and early fourteenth centuries, with reference to the thought and political life of the time. *D.Phil. 1949 Oxford*

Martin, C. P.
Pre-historic man in Ireland. *Sc.D. 1935 Dublin, Trinity College*

Martin, D. G.
The movement of opinion in England concerning America prior to the declaration of American independence. *M.A. 1911 Liverpool*

Martin, E. C.
The British West African settlements 1751-1821: a study in local administration. *Ph.D. 1924 London*

Martin, E. C.
The English establishments on the Gold Coast in the second half of the eighteenth century. *M.A. 1921 London*

Martin, E. J.
1. On the policy of the Emperor Julian. 2. On the theology of the Emperor Julian. *B.D. 1914 Oxford*

Martin, E. M. F.
A critical edition of the *Famous Historie of Sir Thomas Wyat*, by Thomas Dekker and John Webster. *M.A. 1930 London, University College*

Martin, F. A.
Plato's ideal of justice. *M.A. 1944 National University of Ireland*

Martin, H. V.
The message of Karl Barth in relation to Hinduism. *M.A. 1937 Bristol*

Martin, H. V.
The wings of faith. *Ph.D. 1947 Bristol*

Martin, J. B.
The discount policy of the Federal Reserve system. *B.Litt. 1933 Oxford*

Martin, J. L., Sir
Juan de Herrera, 1530-97: his life, art, and influence on the architecture of the sixteenth and seventeenth centuries in Spain. *M.A. 1932 Manchester*

Martin, K. L. P.
British policy towards Canada, 1812-1837. *B.Litt. 1921 Oxford*

Martin, L. C.
Henry Vaughan. *B.Litt. 1913 Oxford*

Martin, M.
Thomas Parnell: his life and works. *B.Litt. 1930 Oxford*

Martin, M. H.
Law and the community, being aspects of political experiment and the theory in the sixth and fifth centuries in Hellas. *D.Phil. 1936 Oxford*

Martin, N. C.
A study of responses to poetry. *M.A. 1949 London, Institute of Education*

Martin, R.
1. On the existence of God. 2. On the sufficiency of Holy Scripture for salvation. *B.D. & D.D. 1886 Oxford*

Martin, R. J. E.
Vocabulary tests for French. *M.A. 1932 London, King's College*

Martin, Sir J. L.
The position of José de Churriguera in the development of Spanish Baroque architecture. *Ph.D. 1936 Manchester*

Martineau, E. I. J.
Quakerism and public service, chiefly between 1832 and 1867. *B.Litt. 1938 Oxford*

Martlew, G.
Education in Nigeria. *M.A. 1934 Liverpool*

Martyn, E. H.
Administrative and clerical staffs in the local government service of England and Wales. *M.Sc. 1922 London*

Martyn, G. W.
Experimental studies of mental fatigue. *D.Sc. 1913 London*

Martynowski, D.
The doctrine of the Godhead in St.Gregory Nazianzen, with special reference to its Trinitarian and Christological aspects. *B.Litt. 1939 Oxford*

Mary Dominic, Sister *see* Dickinson, M. W.

Mary St. John, Sister. *see* MacPhillips, M.

Mary St. Joseph, Mother *see* Callan, P.

Mascall, E. L.
Existence and analogy. *D.D. 1948 Oxford*

Mason, A. C.
The development of Kant's ethical philosophy, with especial reference to his English precursors. *M.A. 1913 London*

Mason, A. T.
The historical novel. *M.A. 1923 Birmingham*

Mason, E. S.
Dumping. *B.Litt. 1923 Oxford*

Mason, G. M.
Le sentiment poétique chez Flaubert. *M.A. 1945 Bristol*

Mason, J.
Scottish experiments in rural education from the eighteenth century to the present day, with special reference to rural arts and crafts. *Ph.D. 1931 Edinburgh*

Mason, J. E.
The dominie in English literature. *M.A. 1928 Birmingham*

Mason, J. E.
The relationship between imagery and the teaching of English. *M.Ed. 1928 Leeds*

Mason, W. H.
An analysis of wage-rates in Britain in relation to employment levels since 1920. *M.Sc. 1949 London, External Degree*

Masoroon, M. B.
Metaphysical poetry in the seventeenth century. *M.A. 1933 Bristol*

Massey, A. W.
The nature of the self: an historical survey from Descartes to James, with a constructive essay. *M.A. 1935 Liverpool*

Masterman, S. R.
International rivalry in Samoa, 1845-1884. *M.A. 1933 London, Bedford College*

Masterman, W.
The practical utility to English lawyers of the study of Roman law. *D.C.L. 1881 Oxford*

Masters, D. C. C.
The Reciprocity Treaty of 1854: its history, its relation to British colonial and foreign policy and to the development of Canadian fiscal autonomy. *D.Phil. 1935 Oxford*

Masterson, W. E.
Jurisdiction in marginal seas over foreign smuggling vessels and subjects. *LL.D. 1928 London*

Matchette, R. L.
The mind of God in creation: or a philosophic enquiry into the nature of creation. *M.A. 1920 Belfast*

Mateescu, D. G.
The economic organisation of the Rumanian oilfields, with special reference to the problems of international competition. *Ph.D. 1929 Birmingham*

Mather, F. C.
The machinery of public order in England during the Chartist period, 1837-1848. *M.A. 1948 Manchester*

Mathew, D. J.
A study of Spanish and Celtic influences on Elizabethan history. *Litt.D. 1933 Dublin, Trinity College*

Mathews, H. F.
The contribution of Methodism to popular education, 1800-1850. *M.A. 1946 Liverpool*

Mathews, M. M.
The life and work of A. G. Werner, 1749-1817, and his influence on his contemporaries. *M.Sc. 1935 London, University College*

Mathews, T.
The history and significance of the early Elizabethan drama. *M.A. 1908 Wales*

Mathias, J.
The intellectual and social phenomena which determined the triumph of Christianity in Italy. *M.A. 1925 Wales*

Mathias, R. G.
The economic policy of the Board of Trade, 1696-1714. *B.Litt. 1939 Oxford*

Mathias, S. Y.
Lord Liverpool as prime minister. *M.A. 1913 Liverpool*

Mathias, W. A.
Astudiaeth o weithgarwch llenyddol William Salesbury(A study of the literary activity of William Salesbury). *M.A. 1949 Wales*

Mathur, M. C.
The financial relationship between Great Britain and Northern Ireland 1931 to 1945. *M.Com.Sc. 1947 Belfast*

Mathur, R. B.
The early history of female education in India. *Ph.D. 1947 London, School of Oriental and African Studies*

Mathur, V. N. S.
Agricultural development of western United Provinces. *M.A. 1938 London, Birkbeck College*

Mattha, G.
Demotic ostraka from the collections at Oxford, Paris, Berlin, Vienna, and Cairo. *D.Phil. 1936 Oxford*

Mattha, G.
A descriptive report on publications dealing with Greek and demotic ostraca. *B.Litt. 1933 Oxford*

Matthai, J.
Agricultural co-operation in British India. *B.Litt. 1917 Oxford*

Matthai, J.
Village government in British India. *D.Sc. 1916 London*

Matthews, E.
Women writers in Germany in the beginning of the nineteenth century, with special reference to Annette von Droste-Hülshoff. *M.A. 1925 Wales*

Matthews, G.
The experience of salvation in the sub-Apostolic period. *B.Litt. 1910 Oxford*

Matthews, G. M.
The poet and the public, 1800-1850: an investigation into the relations between the writers of non-dramatic verse and their readers. *B.Litt. 1950 Oxford*

Matthews, H.
Personnel of the Parliament of 1584-85. *M.A. 1948 London, University College*

Matthews, H. A.
The climate and climatic regions of Chile. *Ph.D. 1931 London, University College*

Matthews, J. H.
The part played by the aristocracy in the later Carolingian Empire, with special reference to Germany. *Ph.D. 1949 Cambridge*

Matthews, J. L.
The early history of the logos doctrine - the idea in Greek philosophy, with an appendix showing its relation to Hellenism, Judaism and the New Testament. *Ph.D. 1936 London, New College*

Matthews, M. E.
The advantages and disadvantages of co-education. *M.A. 1925 Birmingham*

Matthews, P. T.
Reichsbank policy, 1923-1934. *M. Com. 1934 Birmingham*

Matthews, T. F. G.
The Scilly Islands during Tudor and Stuart times (approx. 1547-1700). *B.Litt. 1943 Oxford*

Matthews, W.
English pronunciation in the seventeenth and eighteenth centuries: and essays upon shorthand and literature. *Ph.D. 1934 London, Birkbeck College*

Matthews, W.
The influence of Byron on Russian poetry. *Ph.D. 1926 London*

Matthews, W.
A study of the pronunciation of English during the seventeenth and eighteenth centuries as shown by the contemporary writers of shorthand. *M.A. 1931 London, Birkbeck College*

Matthews, W. K.
English influences in Russian literature, from 1700 to 1830. *M.A. 1923 Manchester*

Matthews, W. R.
Moral evil in relation to modern cosmological theory. *M.A. 1912 London*

Matthiessen, F. O.
Oliver Goldsmith as essayist and critic. *B.Litt. 1925 Oxford*

Maule, H. G.
A study in the laundry industry of the general conditions of work and management which may influence the health and well-being of laundry operatives. *Ph.D. 1949 London, School of Hygiene and Tropical Medicine*

Maund, C. A. M.
A critical examination of Hume's epistemolgy with reference to its bearing on modern problems. *Ph.D. 1936 London, Bedford College*

Maund Dewar, H. R.
Tests of artistic appreciation. *Ph.D. 1937 London, University College*

Maung, K.
A survey of the history of education in Burma before the British conquest and after. *M.A. 1929 London*

Maung Thein
Customary law of Buddhist marriages in British Burma. *Ph.D. 1941 London, University College*

Maura, B.
The authenticity of the chronicler's account of the restoration of Israel in the light of Ezra and Nehemiah: a critical and historical study. *Ph.D. 1943 Edinburgh*

Maurice, F. C. F.
The size of the Persian army in the invasion of Greece 480 B.C. *D.Litt. 1930 London*

Maw, D. P.
The philosophy of Menander and its sources. *M.A. 1948 Manchester*

Maw, G. F.
An analysis of the factor patterns obtained from tests of history given to boys of different ages. *M.A. 1937 London, Institute of Education*

Mawson, E. G.
The Chatham Chest. *M.A. 1931 Liverpool*

Maxse, R. E. B.
The reception of the works of Jacob Boehme in England in the seventeenth and eighteenth centuries. *B.Litt. 1935 Oxford*

Maxton, G. S.
A special enquiry into agricultural developments during the mid-eighteenth century on the estate of the Earl of Marchmont in Berwickshire. *Ph.D. 1935 Edinburgh*

Maxwell, D. E. S.
The poetry of T. S. Eliot. *Ph.D. 1950 Dublin, Trinity College*

Maxwell, H. F.
The ascetical element in St. Paul. *B.Litt. 1934 Oxford*

Maxwell, I. R.
The influence of French farce on English sixteenth century drama. *B.Litt. 1935 Oxford*

Maxwell, J. J.
The early dialectic of Plato. *M.A. 1908 London*

Maxwell, R. M.
Deutschlands Einfluss auf die englisch-irische Literatur in der ersten Hälfte des 19. Jahrhunderts. *M.A. 1944 National University of Ireland*

Maxwell, W. D.
The first and second editions (English and Latin) of the service book used by the English congregation of Marian exiles in Geneva, 1556-1559; arranged in parallel columns, and edited with introduction and notes showing the origins and usages of the rite. *Ph.D. 1929 Edinburgh*

Maxwell, W. N.
Lessons of the war for psychological theory. *M.A. 1921 Belfast*

May, A.
The theme of Antony and Cleopatra in English drama. *B.Litt. 1937 Oxford*

May, E. I.
A study on the *De Jerusalem celeste* and the *De Babilonia infernale* of Giacomino da Verona. *Ph.D. 1928 London*

May, G.
The English criminal and criminal ecclesiastical law of sex morality and its effect upon the organization of the family. *LL.D. 1933 London, School of Economics and Political Science*

May, J. M. F.
The coinages of Illyria and Paeonia from the early fourth century B.C. until the establishment of Roman provinces in these countries. *B.Litt. 1937 Oxford*

May, R. S. le *see* Le May, R. S.

May, T. E.
Aspects of the style of the *Criticón* of Baltasar Gracián with reference to the theories of his *Agudeza y arte de ingenio*. *M.A. 1937 Manchester*

May, T. H.
1. The place and work of the prophets in the Catholic Church. 2. The laying on of hands. *B.D. & D.D. 1924 Oxford*

Mayall, H. S.
Nature in the poetry of Ronsard. *M.A. 1931 Manchester*

Maycock, J.
Augustus Montague Toplady, hymn-writer and theologian, with special reference to his controversy with John Wesley. *Ph.D. 1946 Edinburgh*

Maycock, J.
Evolution and freedom: does evolution preclude moral freedom?. *M.A. 1938 Liverpool*

Mayer, C. A.
Satire in French literature from 1525 to 1560, with particular reference to the sources and the technique. *Ph.D. 1949 London, University College*

Mayer, U. P.
The agrarian question in Iraq. *D.Phil. 1944 Oxford*

Mayers, B. M.
Political theory of Alexander Hamilton. *Ph.D. 1938 London, School of Economics and Political Science*

Maynard, W. A.
English song in the seventeenth century. *B.Litt. 1950 Oxford*

Maynard-Smith, H.
1. The authenticity of the Epistle of St. James. 2. Our Lord's brethren. *B.D. & D.D. 1923 Oxford*

Mayne, J.
The influence of the religious and ethical idealism of the prophets on the cultus of old Israel. *Ph.D. 1934 Edinburgh*

Mayo, H. B.
Newfoundland, the tenth province of Canada: the case for union examined. *D.Phil. 1948 Oxford*

Mayor, A. H.
Cervantes, with special reference to *Don Quixote*, in English literature until 1781. *B.Litt. 1926 Oxford*

May-Oung, M. S.
Sir Charles Crosthwaite and the consolidation of Burma. *B.Litt. 1930 Oxford*

Mays, W.
The philosophy of Whitehead. *Ph.D. 1945 Cambridge*

M'Caw, L. S.
The Black Mountains. A physical, agricultural and geographical survey, 1932-6. *M.A. 1936 Manchester*

Mead, D. M.
The non-dramatic works of George Whetstone. *M.A. 1919 London*

Mead, G. J. de C.
The financial relations between the Crown and the City of London in the reigns of Edward I to Henry VII (excluding Parliamentary taxation). *M.A. 1936 London, King's College*

Mead, W. R.
The geographical background to community of interests among the northern European peoples. *Ph.D. 1947 London, External Degree*

Mead, W. R.
A geographical consideration of the successive re-orientations in the foreign trade of Finland, with special emphasis on the post war period. *M.Sc. 1939 London, School of Economics and Political Science*

Meadows, P.
The importance of Winchester as capital of England from the tenth to the twelfth century. *M.A. 1911 London*

Meads, D. M.
An account of the education of women and girls in England in the time of the Tudors. *Ph.D. 1929 London*

Means, P. B.
The relation of the human soul to God in Hinduism and Christianity. *B.Litt. 1923 Oxford*

Meara, G.
The fortunes of rationalism in English political thought from the publication of Burke's *Reflections on the French Revolution* to the end of the nineteenth century. *M.A. 1933 Wales*

Meara, G.
Juvenile unemployment in the south Wales industrial region: an economic and statistical enquiry. *Ph.D. 1935 Wales*

Mears, J. C.
The nature of religious knowledge according to Pascal. *M.A. 1948 Wales*

Mears, R. A. F.
The history of Methodism in the eighteenth century. *B.Litt. 1925 Oxford*

Mechling, W. H.
Studies in the life and culture of the Malecites and Micmacs. *B.Litt. 1916 Oxford*

Mecklenburg, P.
Hans Carossa and the Goethean tradition. *Ph.D. 1944 National University of Ireland*

Medalie, H.
Ishmael and Hagar in the post-Biblical and Islamic literature. *M.A. 1941 Manchester*

Medalie, H. H.
Ha-Hinukh - attributed to R. Aharon Hal-Lewi, Barcelona (13th century) - a translation and critical study. *Ph.D. 1944 Dublin, Trinity College*

Medlicott, W. N.
British foreign policy in the Near East from the Congress of Berlin to the accession of Ferdinand of Coburg. *M.A. 1926 London*

Meecham, H. G.
The letters of Aristeas in relation to the Biblical and Apocryphal writings. *Ph.D. 1929 Manchester*

Meek, H. G.
Criminal law as applied to bankruptcy. *LL.M. 1929 Cambridge*

Meek, R. L.
The development of the concept of surplus in economic thought from Mun to Mill. *Ph.D. 1949 Cambridge*

Meenai, S. A.
Robert Torrens. *M.Sc. 1948 London, School of Economics and Political Science*

Megaw, M. I.
The ecclesiastical relations of the reign of Stephen, with special reference to St. Bernard and the Cistercian reforming party, 1135-1154. *M.A. 1939 Belfast*

Mehrotra, K. K.
The influence of *The Castle of Otranto* on the English novel, excluding the novels of Scott, up to 1820. *B.Litt. 1933 Oxford*

Mehta, C. A.
India's balance of international payments, 1910-11 to 1929-30. *Ph.D. 1934 London, School of Economics and Political Science*

Mehta, J. M.
A study in rural economy of Gujarat containing suggestions for reconstruction. *Ph.D. 1929 London*

Mehta, M. S.
The relations of the British Government in India with the Indian States, 1813-1823. *Ph.D. 1928 London*

Mehta, N. B.
Indian railways: rates and regulation. *Ph.D. 1925 London*

Meiklejohn, J.
The application of musical tests to the study of individual reactions to music. *Ph.D. 1940 Glasgow*

Meiklejohn, W.
Salient features of Scottish education. *M.A. 1931 National University of Ireland*

Meissner, J. L. G.
The Celtic church in England after the synod of Whitby. *M.A. 1927 Belfast*

Mekie, D. C. T.
Effects of government interference in modifying the influence of natural advantages. *Ph.D. 1925 Edinburgh*

Mel, B. W. de *see* De Mel, B. W.

Melbourne, A. C. V.
Constitutional development in New South Wales, 1788-1856. *Ph.D. 1931 London, King's College*

Melbourne, R. W. L.
The function of Wisbech in relation to its geographical setting. *M.A. 1939 London, Birkbeck College*

Meldrum, A. N.
Avogadro and Dalton: the standing in chemistry of their hypotheses. *D.Sc. 1904 Aberdeen*

Meldrum, M. S.
Croce and the *Einfühlung* theory on the relation of feeling to the work of art. *B.Litt. 1941 Oxford*

Meldrum, N.
The General Assembly of the Church of Scotland in the year 1638: a study from contemporary documents of its origin, proceedings and importance. *Ph.D. 1924 Edinburgh*

Melia, T. S.
Seanuiocla Chonnacht le minighthe's nótaí(Proverbs of Connaught, with the author's notes). *Ph.D. 1938 National University of Ireland*

Melinek, A.
Conception of reward and punishment in the Tannaitic Midrash (Mekiltah, Sifra and Sifre). *Ph.D. 1944 London, Jews' College*

Mellone, M. A.
A factorial study of picture tests for young children, with special reference to the appearance of a space factor among boys. *Ph.D. 1944 Edinburgh*

Mellor, G.
A linguistic study of the Franco-Italian epics. *M.A. 1950 Manchester*

Mellor, G. R.
British policy in relation to Sierra Leone, 1808-1852. *M.A. 1935 London, King's College*

Mellowes, C. L.
Geographical basis of natural silk industry of West Pennines. *M.A. 1933 London, External Degree*

Melville, A. M. M.
The pastoral custom and local wool trade of medieval Sussex, 1085-1485. *M.A. 1931 London, King's College*

Menary, G.
The life and letters of Duncan Forbes of Culloden, Lord President of the Court of Session, 1685-1747. *D.Litt. 1937 Glasgow*

Menasce, J. A. M. de *see* De Menasce, J. A. M.

Mendelsohn, L.
Some Rabbinical beliefs and customs connected with death and mourning. *M.A. 1910 London*

Mendenhall, T. C.
Shrewsbury, Oswestry, and the Welsh wool trade in the seventeenth century, especially in connexion with the crisis and Parliament of 1621. *B.Litt. 1936 Oxford*

Mendis, G. C.
A historical criticism of *Mahavamsa*. *Ph.D. 1931 London, School of Oriental and African Studies*

Mendoza, J. Pereira- *see* Pereira-Mendoza, J.

Meng, F. C.
The principles of political obligation of the modern state. *B.Litt. 1938 Oxford*

Menon, C. A.
Ezuttaccan and his age. *Ph.D. 1938 London, School of Oriental and African Studies*

Menon, C. P. S.
Early history of astronomy and cosmology in India. *M.Sc. 1930 London*

Menon, I. N.
The State and the moral life. *B.Litt. 1922 Oxford*

Menon, V. K. K.
The psychology of reasoning, being an experimental study of the mental processes involved in reasoning. *M.A. 1929 London*

Menon, V. K. N.
The development of the poetry of William Butler Yeats. *Ph.D. 1939 Edinburgh*

Menteath, T. A. Stuart- *see* Stuart-Menteath, T. A.

Menton, B. P.
The relations between the English and Irish banking systems with special reference to the adjustment of the balance of payments between the countries, 1929-1939. *Ph.D. 1947 London, External Degree*

Menzies-Kitchin, A. W.
The economic possibilities of land settlement. *Ph.D. 1939 Cambridge*

Mepham, W. A.
The history of the drama in Essex from the fifteenth century to the present time. *Ph.D. 1937 London, Queen Mary College*

Mercer, D. F.
Trends in modern criticism, 1800-1940. *B.Litt. 1949 Oxford*

Mercer, E. O.
The influence of volition upon the perception (cognition) of visual items, relations and correlates. *Ph.D. 1935 London, King's College*

Merchant, W. M.
Shakespeare illustration and design. *M.A. 1950 Wales*

Mercier, V. H. S.
Realism in Anglo-Irish fiction, 1916-1940. *Ph.D. 1945 Dublin, Trinity College*

Merdinger, C. J.
A history of civil engineering. *D.Phil. 1949 Oxford*

Meredith, G. P.
An investigation into some aspects of the problem of transfer of training. *M.Ed. 1926 Leeds*

Meredith, H. J.
Agricultural marketing in Breconshire, with special reference to different types of farming. *M.A. 1926 Wales*

Meredith, H. J.
A historical and economic study of the development and organization of the market gardening industry in the Vale of Evesham. *B.Litt. 1929 Oxford*

Merrall, A.
A glossary to the Middle English poem *Genesis and Exodus*, with explanatory notes on the text. *M.A. 1941 Manchester*

Merriman, R. B.
A biography of Thomas Cromwell. *B.Litt. 1899 Oxford*

Merritt, N.
The Romans and immortality. *M.A. 1933 Birmingham*

Merritt, W. B.
The Reformation and the English universities. *M.A. 1938 National University of Ireland*

Merry, W. J.
James Hogg. *D.Litt. 1922 Glasgow*

Merrylees, W. A.
An historical review of the nature of time and its connexion with value, in so far as these bear on the problems of personal freedom and human purpose. *B.Litt. 1923 Oxford*

Merryweather, H. H.
1. The atonement. 2. Sunday, or the Lord's day. *B.D. 1905 Oxford*

Mertner, E.
The structure of the story in Rudyard Kipling's work. *M.A. 1937 Wales*

Mesiha, W.
Marketing of perishable agricultural products. *M.Com. 1930 Birmingham*

Mesquita, D. M. Bueno de
See Bueno de Mesquita, D. M.

Mess, H. A.
Factory legislation and its administration, 1891-1924. *Ph.D. 1926 London*

Messer, W. J.
The nature and extent of conative control of some contents of consciousness. *M.Sc. 1927 London*

Messer, W. J.
The pedagogical conclusion of psychological study of attention. *M.A. 1930 Reading*

Mestel, S.
The city of Tiberias in the third and fourth centuries. *M.A. 1918 London*

Mesurier, A. M. C. le *see* Le Mesurier, A. M. C.

Metcalf, H.
Foreign exchange control. *M.Com. 1939 Leeds*

Metcalf, R.
A study of French word-order in the sixteenth century with special reference to inversion of the subject. *M.A. 1949 Leeds*

Metcalfe, O.
The influence of socio-economic factors on school progress and personality development. *M.A. 1950 Birmingham*

Metford, J. C. J.
Alberto Lista y Aragón: a report on investigations of his life and work. *M.A. 1940 Liverpool*

Metlitzky, D.
Prolegomena for a study of Arabic influences on the literature and thought of the English middle ages. *M.A. 1938 London, University College*

Mews, H.
Middle class conduct books in the seventeenth century. *M.A. 1934 London, King's College*

Mewse, E.
The relation between artistic ability and intelligence. *M.Ed. 1934 Durham*

Meyer, A. M.
Religious currents in modern German-Swiss literature. *M.A. 1923 Liverpool*

Meyer, F.
Britain's colonies in world trade. *Ph.D. 1945 London, School of Economics and Political Science*

Meyer, L. B.
Richard II's coup d'état of 1397. *M.A. 1908 London*

Meyer, S. B.
The industries of the south of Russia and the competition with England. *M.Com. 1910 Birmingham*

Mhac an tSaoi, M. C.
Faisnéis bhreise ar Phiaras Fhirtéar(Further information on Piaras Firtéar). *M.A. 1945 National University of Ireland*

Mhártain, S. M. M. *see* MacGiolla Mhártain, S. M.

Michael, D. P. M.
The life and works of Arthur Machen, with special reference to his novels and tales. *M.A. 1940 Wales*

Michael, J. H.
The Jews in the city of Rome during the first centuries B.C. and A.D., including a study of the references to them in Greek and Latin writers. *M.A. 1913 Wales*

Michaels, P. M.
International Labour Organization as an object lesson in international functional co-operation. *M.Sc. 1949 London, School of Economics and Political Science*

Michel, G. C. O.
The French element in the *Ancrene Riwle*. *M.A. 1950 Bristol*

Michell, G. A.
1. The history of the doctrine of satisfaction from Tertullian to St. Ambrose. 2. The history of the doctrine of satisfaction from St. Augustine to St. Anselm. *B.D. & D.D. 1924 Oxford*

Micklem, E. R.
The miracles of healing in the New Testament in the light of modern psychological and psychotherapeutical research. *B.Litt. 1921 Oxford*

Micklem, P. A.
1. The primitive Church and its organization. 2. The kingdom of heaven in the Gospel of St. Matthew. *B.D. & D.D. 1924 Oxford*

Middlemas, J. S.
The use of revenge as a tragic theme in Greek tragedy, Seneca, and Elizabethan revenge plays. *M.A. 1949 Manchester*

Middleton, G.
Studies in the orations of Libanius. *D.Litt. 1920 Aberdeen*

Middleton, J. F. M.
Systems of land tenure among the Bantu peoples of East Africa. *B.Sc. 1949 Oxford*

Middleton, T. M.
An enquiry into the use of leisure amongst the working classes of Liverpool. *M.A. 1931 Liverpool*

Midgley, C.
The geography of Roman Britain and its human relationships. *M.Sc. 1927 Sheffield*

Midgley, C. W.
The Arthurian legend and its revival in the nineteenth century. *M.A. 1920 Birmingham*

Midgley, E. G.
Pope's knowledge of English literature from Chaucer to Dryden. *B.Litt. 1950 Oxford*

Midgley, L. M.
Edmund, Earl of Cornwall, and his place in history. *M.A. 1930 Manchester*

Mihra, R. D.
The consideration of alternative methods of co-operative organization in agriculture and a comparison of the results achieved by certain selected countries, viz. Great Britain, Ireland and Denmark. *B.Litt. 1925 Oxford*

Mildon, W. H.
Puritanism in Hampshire and the Isle of Wight from the reign of Elizabeth to the Restoration. *Ph.D. 1934 London, External Degree*

Miles, B.
The causes of the revolution in New York, 1691-1760: a study of taxation and of the effects of England's commercial restrictions, prefaced by a sketch of the colony's political history. *B.Litt. 1905 Oxford*

Miles, F. N.
The limitations imposed upon Latin lyric poetry by the special nature of the Latin language, with special reference to Horace and Catullus. *M.A. 1933 Wales*

Miles, G. H.
Preference and affective influence as factors in recall. *D.Sc. 1916 London*

Miles, G. J.
The Chinese in southeastern Asia and the East Indies. *M.A. 1932 London, Birkbeck College*

Miles, G. P. L.
Primitive agriculture. *Ph.D. 1942 London, School of Economics and Political Science*

Miles, H.
The Coventry silk-ribbon industry from the introduction of the use of the Dutch engine loom (c.1770) to the Cobden Commercial Treaty (1860). *B.Litt. 1930 Oxford*

Miles, W. F.
Development of English literary criticism during the eighteenth century. *Ph.D. 1922 Cambridge*

Miletitch, D.
The substance and method of our Lord's teaching viewed in the light of modern educational and psychological thought. *B.Litt. 1922 Oxford*

Mill, A. J.
Records of early drama in Scotland. *Ph.D. 1925 Saint Andrew's*

Millar, D. H.
Lionel Johnson, 1867 to 1902: a biographical and critical study. *M.A. 1947 Belfast*

Millar, G. D.
The influence of the earlier romanticists on E. T. A. Hoffmann. *M.A. 1915 London*

Millar, L.
Christian education in the first four centuries. *Ph.D. 1944 Dublin, Trinity College*

Millard, H. I.
The fate of the Knight Templars in England, with special reference to their lands. *M.A. 1918 Wales*

Millen, E. L.
The doctrine of the Parousia in the New Testament, with special reference to the Epistles of St. Paul. *B.D. 1939 Oxford*

Miller, A. B.
Growth of the idea of religious toleration in England from 1689 to 1727. *Ph.D. 1939 Edinburgh*

Miller, A. J.
The religious teaching of Rufus M. Jones. *Ph.D. 1936 Edinburgh*

Miller, A. T.
The life of James Sharp, archbishop of St. Andrews. *Ph.D. 1940 Edinburgh*

Miller, D. E.
Concerning propositions and their truth. *M.A. 1931 London, Bedford College*

Miller, D. M.
The Greek novel. *M.A. 1912 London*

Miller, F.
The English wool trade during the thirteenth century. *B.Litt. 1921 Oxford*

Miller, F. M.
Some influences upon perception. *M.A. 1937 London, King's College*

Miller, G. M.
The positions and elementarie of Richard Mulcaster. *M.A. 1934 Leeds*

Miller, H.
The administration of the poor laws in Ireland till 30th November, 1921, and in Northern Ireland from the 1st December, 1921, till present date. *M.Com.Sc. 1942 Belfast*

Miller, H. C.
Adult education in North Staffordshire: its history and development. *M.Ed. 1928 Manchester*

Miller, M.
A phonology of the old Northumbrian texts. *Ph.D. 1930 Leeds*

Miller, M. S.
The economic development of Russia from 1905-1914: with special reference to trade, industry and finance. *Ph.D. 1925 London*

Miller, R.
A critical and experimental study in the development of moral ideas. *Ph.D. 1928 Edinburgh*

Miller, R. F.
The fear of God: a study of the fear of God in the Christian religion. *Ph.D. 1930 Edinburgh*

Miller, T. E.
An economic survey of the agriculture of Airedale and Calder Valley. *M.Sc. 1935 Leeds*

Millidge, A. P.
A contribution to the study of the development of the French novel in the pre-romantic period. *M.A. 1932 Reading*

Milligan, F. S.
Politics and industry in the state. *M.A. 1921 Birmingham*

Milligan, R. A. C.
A study of Saint Lambert, the man and the poet. *B.Phil. 1950 Saint Andrew's*

Millington, E. C.
History of the theories of colour vision from Young (1800) to the present time. *M.Sc. 1930 London*

Millington, E. C.
Studies in cohesion, 1650-1850. *Ph.D. 1943 London, External Degree*

Millington, J.
The career of Sir John Thurston, Governor of Fiji, 1888-1897. *M.A. 1947 London, Birkbeck College*

Millington, N. F.
Homework and leisure time activities. *M.A. 1938 Birmingham*

Millor, W. J.
A critical edition of the text of the latters of John of Salisbury. *Ph.D. 1939 London, University College*

Mills, C. C.
1. The resurrection of Jesus Christ. 2. The ministry of angels as revealed in Holy Scripture. *B.D. & D.D. 1909 Oxford*

Mills, L. A.
British Malaya, 1824-1867, with an introductory sketch of its history from 1786-1824. *Ph.D. 1924 Oxford*

Mills, M. A.
Histoire de la publication des *Confessions* (1775-1789): contribution aux études Rousseauistes. *M.A. 1940 Leeds*

Mills, M. H.
Constitutional and diplomatic aspects of the ordinances of 1311. *M.A. 1912 London*

Mills, R. C.
English colonization theories, 1830-1842, with special reference to the economic and political development of the Australian colonies. *D.Sc. 1915 London*

Mills, S. R.
Prognostic tests of ability in modern languages. *M.A. 1941 London, Courtauld Institute of Art*

Millward, A. S.
League sanctions: an account of the origins and interpretations of Article XVI of the Covenant, and an attempt to estimate its significance. *M.Sc. 1934 London, School of Economics and Political Science*

Milne, A. T.
The slave trade and Anglo-American relations, 1807-1862. *M.A. 1930 London, University College*

Milne, C. H.
Reconstruction of the Old-Latin text or texts of the Gospels used by Saint Augustine, with a study of their character. *D.Litt. 1926 Aberdeen*

Milne, C. H. M.
A critical edition of Bede on the seven Catholic Epistles (or the major part thereof), based on the two early Oxford manuscripts. *D.Phil. 1941 Oxford*

Milne, D. J.
The Rye House Plot: with special reference to its place in the Exclusion Contest and its consequences till 1685. *Ph.D. 1949 London, Bedford College*

Milne, E. W.
Studies in human geography in the highland regions of Norway. *D.Sc. 1934 Aberdeen*

Milne, J. J.
Quelques personnages comiques dans les mystères français de la Passion et autres du quinzième siècle. *D.Litt. 1926 Birmingham*

Milne, R. D.
The influence of Swiss theory and practice on the Weimar Constitution, 1919. *M.A. 1934 London, King's College*

Milne, W. S.
1. The typical significance of the history of the children of Israel. 2. The teaching of St. Paul with regard to the Holy Spirit. *B.D. 1889 Oxford*

Milne-Bailey, W.
Trade unions and the state. *Ph.D. 1934 London, School of Economics and Political Science*

Milner, J. L.
L'influence espagnole sur la comédie française du dix-septième siècle. *M.A. 1913 Liverpool*

Milner, J. R.
Théophile Gautier et le dandysme. *M.A. 1939 Leeds*

Milner-Barry, A.
Percy's *Reliques* and the ballads of Burger. *M.A. 1922 Birmingham*

Milnes, G. R.
Baudelairism in France and England. *M.A. 1911 London*

Milnes, H.
The educational value of chemistry with proposals for its treatment in the school curriculum. *M.A. 1928 Liverpool*

Milton Hay, R.
1. The influence of the Continental Reformation upon the Thirty-nine Articles. *B.D. 1924 Oxford*

Milum, J. P.
Evolution and the spirit of man. *Ph.D. 1926 London*

Milverton, F. J.
An experimental investigation into the effects of physical training on personality. *M.Ed. 1940 Leeds*

Milward, W. E.
An enquiry into the state of public opinion from the establishment of King Henry VIII's supremacy over the Church to the close of the Lincolnshire rebellion. *M.A. 1907 Liverpool*

Miner, H. B.
The doctrine of the "inner light": its European development immediately prior to the foundation of the Society of Friends, and in that Society from the time of George Fox to the present day. *Ph.D. 1936 Edinburgh*

Ming, Y.
The principles and policies of the Nine Power Treaty of 1922 in the light of subsequent developments. *D.Phil. 1941 Oxford*

Mingay, J. M.
The history of the οἰκείωσιϛ doctrine, with special reference to Cicero *De Finibus* v. *B.Litt. 1950 Oxford*

Minio-Paluello, L.
The methods of the medieval translators of Greek philosophical works into Latin. *D.Phil. 1947 Oxford*

Minty, L. M.
American banking methods. *Ph.D. 1924 London*

Mirchandani, G. T.
Rural education in the Bombay Presidency. *M.Ed. 1938 Leeds*

Mirz, N. K.
Co-education, with special reference to the adolescent. *M.A. 1931 Leeds*

Mirza, A.
Short historical sketches of Ayur-Vedic or Hindu system of medicine. *M.D. 1900 Edinburgh*

Mirza, H. P.
The Pahlavi *Rivayat* preceding the *Dadistan i Denij*, transcription and translation of the hitherto untranslated portions, with philological notes. *Ph.D. 1940 London, School of Oriental and African Studies*

Mirza, M. W.
The life and works of Amir Khusrau. *Ph.D. 1930 London, School of Oriental and African Studies*

Mishan, E. J.
The application of certain Keynesian concepts to international trade, with special reference to the multiplier. *M.Sc. 1948 London, School of Economics and Political Science*

Mishra, J. N.
Financial burden of the war, 1914-1918. *M.Sc. 1946 London, School of Economics and Political Science*

Misra, B. B.
The judicial administration of the East India Company in Bengal, 1765-1782. *Ph.D. 1947 London, School of Oriental and African Studies*

Misra, B. P.
Novels of George Moore. *Ph.D. 1947 Dublin, Trinity College*

Misra, B. R.
Indian provincial finance (1919-37), with special reference to the United Provinces. *Ph.D. 1939 London, School of Economics and Political Science*

Misra, L. N.
Indian commodity market speculation. *Ph.D. 1932 London, School of Economics and Political Science*

Misra, S.
Development of Indian public finance during the war, April 1939 to March 1946. *Ph.D. 1949 London, School of Economics and Political Science*

Mitchell, A.
A descriptive and critical bibliography of Leigh Hunt's prose writings. *Ph.D. 1924 Edinburgh*

Mitchell, A. B.
The economic function of organized speculation in commodities. *B.Litt. 1938 Oxford*

Mitchell, A. G.
A critical edition of Piers Plowman, context, prologue and passus i-iv. *Ph.D. 1939 London, University College*

Mitchell, C.
Matthias Grünewald. *B.Litt. 1938 Oxford*

Mitchell, D. N.
Thomas Mann: the development of his social philosophy and its relation to his art. *M.A. 1945 Leeds*

Mitchell, E. A. E.
English influences on French historians during the seventeenth century. *M.Litt. 1932 Cambridge*

Mitchell, E. G.
Sir George Beaumont, and his contacts with English Romanticism. *M.A. 1938 London, Queen Mary College*

Mitchell, F.
The influence of charity on education in England. *M.Ed. 1930 Manchester*

Mitchell, F. W.
The nature of mathematical thinking. *Ph.D. 1937 London, Institute of Education*

Mitchell, J. C.
Social organization of the Yao people of southern Nyasaland. *D.Phil. 1950 Oxford*

Mitchell, M. E. C.
The distribution of early bronze age types in Scotland. *Ph.D. 1933 Edinburgh*

Mitchell, R. D.
Archibald McLean, 1733-1812, Baptist pioneer in Scotland. *D. 1950 Edinburgh*

Mitchell, R. J.
John Tiptoft, Earl of Worcester. *B.Litt. 1929 Oxford*

Mitchell, W. F.
English pulpit oratory from Andrewes to Tillotson: a study of its literary aspects. *B.Litt. 1931 Oxford*

Mitchiner, W. M.
Anselm and his circle: a study of the historical importance of his letters. *M.A. 1945 London, Bedford College*

Mitra, B.
The influence of the home government on the development of the land revenue and judicial administration in the presidency of Fort William in Bengal from 1823 to 1840. *M.A. 1936 London, School of Oriental and African Studies*

Mitrany, D.
The land and the peasant in Roumania. *Ph.D. 1931 London, School of Economics and Political Science*

Mitrany, D.
The rural revolution in Rumania and in south eastern Europe. *Ph.D. 1929 London*

Mitton, C. L.
The problem of the authorship of the Epistle to the Ephesians. *Ph.D. 1949 London, External Degree*

Miyamoto, S.
Early Mahayana Buddhism with special reference to the doctrine of Nagarjuna. *D.Phil. 1927 Oxford*

Moar, A.
The teaching of the mother tongue in Great Britain and France and the educational and psychological principles underlying it. *Ph.D. 1940 London, Institute of Education*

Modak, M. S.
Vedanta and Spinoza: a comparative study. *Ph.D. 1928 London*

Moddy, J.
Le roman social d'Eugène Süe. *B.Litt. 1925 Oxford*

Moens, M.
A comparison of the treatment of romantic motives in Sir Philip Sidney's *Arcadia* and in typical earlier and later romances. *M.A. 1912 London*

Moffat, A. B.
Natural science as an element in a liberal education: its proper place and treatment in the curriculum of schools. *M.A. 1934 Liverpool*

Moffat, J. L.
Moral preoccupations in the life and work of Marcel Proust. *Ph.D. 1948 Bristol*

Moffat, M. M.
La controverse sur la moralité du théâtre après la lettre à d'Alembert de J. J. Rousseau. *M.A. 1930 Liverpool*

Moffat, P. S.
Some mental changes in the growth of children and their significance for education. *Ph.D. 1938 Edinburgh*

Moffatt, J.
An introduction to the literature of the New Testament. *D.Litt. 1911 Glasgow*

Moffit, L. W.
The economic and social condition of England on the eve of the Industrial Revolution, with special reference to Lancashire. *Ph.D. 1921 Edinburgh*

Mogey, J. McF.
Rural life in Northern Ireland and other papers. *D.Sc. 1948 Belfast*

Mohajer, A. R.
The project method applied to the teaching of elementary science in Indian schools. *M.Ed. 1937 Leeds*

Mohammed, A. G.
The recent development of the tax system in Egypt. *M.Com. 1940 Leeds*

Mohammed, A. Z.
Psychological enquiry as to the factors involved in the appreciation of pictures among adults and children. *M.Sc. 1933 Birmingham*

Mohanty, R. N.
A comparative study of Indian and English education. *M.A. 1940 Leeds*

Mohsin, S. M.
Factors affecting the reliability of self-estimates in answering personality questionnaires. *Ph.D. 1948 Edinburgh*

Mohyeddin, K.
The teaching of Urdu in India, with special reference to the Punjab. *M.Ed. 1927 Leeds*

Mohy-ud-Din, A. *see* Ud-Din, A. M.

Moir, I. A.
Codex Climaci rescriptus graecus. *Ph.D. 1943 Cambridge*

Moir, M. F. J.
Tuberculosis: an historical survey. *M.D. 1927 Aberdeen*

Moir, R.
The grounds of pessimism in Thomas Hardy's view of life. *M.A. 1947 Manchester*

Moir, T. L.
The Addled Parliament of 1614. *Ph.D. 1950 Dublin, Trinity College*

Mole, C. M.
The progress of French in Alsace-Lorraine since the war. *M.A. 1925 Birmingham*

Moller, A. W. R.
The history of English coal mining, 1500-1750. *D.Phil. 1933 Oxford*

Moller, A. W. R.
The history of English coal-mining in the seventeenth century. *B.Litt. 1923 Oxford*

Moller, L. F.
Public policy in private international law. *B.Litt. 1938 Oxford*

Mollett, J. A.
An economic study of the supply of agricultural labour in Buckinghamshire. *M.Sc. 1949 Reading*

Molloy, W. F.
Saint-Just and the French Revolution. *M.A. 1915 National University of Ireland*

Moloney, J. C. U.
The Irish fishing industry. *M.A. 1950 National University of Ireland*

Molony, J. T.
Mistake in the law of contract. *LL.M. 1933 Cambridge*

Molyneux, W. E.
The work of Vittorio Alfieri considered in relation to the author's attitude to religion. *M.A. 1947 Manchester*

Monaghan, J. J.
A social and economic history of Belfast, 1801-1825. *Ph.D. 1940 Belfast*

Monaghan, J. J.
A social and economic history of Belfast, 1790-1800. *M.A. 1936 Belfast*

Monaghan, T. J. A.
Thomas Tyrwhitt (1730-86) and his contribution to English scholarship. *D.Phil. 1947 Oxford*

Moncur, R.
The life and work of 'Palmyra' Wood: a biographical study. *Ph.D. 1929 Saint Andrew's*

Money-Kyrle, H. J. R.
Anglo-Saxon magic. *B.Sc. 1924 Oxford*

Money-Kyrle, R. E. *see* Kyrle, R. E. Money-

Monnaie, L. F.
Le Normand d'après Guy de Maupassant. *M.A. 1926 London*

Montague, F. R.
A critical and comparative survey of modern tendencies in commercial education at home and abroad. *M.Ed. 1936 Leeds*

Montgomery, A. V. H. de *see* de Montgomery, A. H. V.

Montgomery, B. G. de *see* De Montgomery, B. G.

Montgomery, E. M.
Cicero as a translator. *M.A. 1931 London, Bedford College*

Montgomery, M.
Friedrich Hölderlin's place in the German neo-Hellenic movement. *B. Litt. 1918 Oxford*

Moodie, A. E. F.
The geographical background of political problems associated with the Italo-Jugoslav frontier. *Ph.D. 1942 London, Birkbeck College*

Moody, T. W. D.
The Londonderry plantation, with special reference to the resulting relations between the Crown and the city, 1609-41. *Ph.D. 1934 London, University College*

Moon, A. R.
The life and work of Nicholas Udall, 1506-1556. *M.A. 1926 London*

Moon, R. W.
The measurement of profit and the incidence of taxation. *B.Phil. 1948 Oxford*

Moor, C.
1. The development of Judaism and its influence upon Christianity. 2. Christian life in the first days of the Church. *B.D. 1904 Oxford*

Moor, C.
Expositions of Romans x-xi; Acts xviii.15-34; I Timothy iii and v. *D.D. 1908 Oxford*

Moor, F.
1. The threefold ministry. 2. Infant baptism. *B.D. 1888 Oxford*

Moor, M. F.
The place of rhetoric in education in the first century A.D. and at the present day. *B.Litt. 1922 Oxford*

Moore, C. A. I.
The state of Roman agriculture in the time of the Gracchi. *M.A. 1914 London*

Moore, D. E.
Moore en France de 1757 à 1830. *M.A. 1934 Liverpool*

Moore, E.
Exegeses of: II Corinthians iv.6-7; St. John xxi.24-25; Romans vii.7-25. *D.D. 1878 Oxford*

Moore, E. F. B.
The study of apprehension of deity from the psychological and epistemological point of view. *Ph.D. 1944 Dublin, Trinity College*

Moore, F. C.
The influence of the French Revolution on the English Romantic poets. *M.A. 1918 London*

Moore, H. K.
1. The interpretation of the Acts, with especial reference to Professor Ramsay's South Galatian theory. 2. Our Lord's use of π÷στισ. *B.D. & D.D. 1898 Oxford*

Moore, H. M.
Dekker as a dramatist. *M.A. 1933 National University of Ireland*

Moore, M.
Economic nationalism. *M.Econ.Sc. 1943 National University of Ireland*

Moore, M.
The meaning of freedom. *M.A. 1922 Birmingham*

Moore, M. C.
The history of the agitation against the stamp duty on newspapers, 1830-1855. *M.A. 1935 London, King's College*

Moore, M. C.
The study of the primary emotions in young children with special reference to the emotion of fear. *M.A. 1914 Liverpool*

Moore, M. F.
Feudal aspect of Domesday survey of Somerset and Dorset in connexion with the Barony of Moiun (Dunster Castle) and analogous feudal estates, based upon contemporary public and local records. *Ph.D. 1930 London, King's College*

Moore, M. L.
A century's extension of passenger transport facilities (1830-1930) within the present London Transport Board's area, and its relation to population spread. *Ph.D. 1948 London, Birkbeck College*

Moore, M. S.
Unwritten laws of Greece. *M.A. 1947 National University of Ireland*

Moore, R.
The late eighteenth and early nineteenth century editions of the metaphysical poets, with notes on their editors and publishers: an enquiry into the revival of interest in metaphysical poetry and the influence of that revival. *M.A. 1932 London, King's College*

Moore, R. C.
The application of the Binet-Simon scale to normal English children. *M.Sc. 1919 Liverpool*

Moore, R. C.
The industrial training and education of apprentices. *M.A. 1921 Manchester*

Moore, R. C.
1. Tests of reasoning processes and their relation to general mental ability. 2. The mental differences between the sexes. *M.A. 1915 Liverpool*

Moore, R. L.
1. The biblical teaching as to the Resurrection. 2. The Patristic teaching as to the Resurrection. *B.D. 1924 Oxford*

Moore, R. T.
Virgil and Roman learning as applied to the *Aeneid*. *M.A. 1920 London*

Moore, W. D.
The life, works, and learning of Pedro Mejía, with a study of the sources of the *Silva de Varia Lección*. *M.A. 1934 Belfast*

Moore, W. I.
L'Université impériale. *M.A. 1920 London*

Moorhead, F. J.
The letters of Nicholas Poillevilain de Clémanges, 1363(4)-1437. *M.A. 1936 Liverpool*

Moorhead, M. D.
Volney et la littérature française à la fin du dix-huitième siècle. *M.A. 1922 Belfast*

Mootham, O. H.
The doctrine of continuous voyage, 1756-1815. *M.Sc. 1926 London*

Moran, J. R.
Romanization of the three Gauls. *M.A. 1919 National University of Ireland*

Morant, G. M.
1. A first study of the Tibetan skull. 2. A study of the Nepalese skull. *M.Sc. 1922 London*

Morant, G. M.
A study of Egyptian craniology from prehistoric to Roman times. *D.Sc. 1926 London*

Morant, V. E.
Historical geography of Maidstone. *M.A. 1948 London, Birkbeck College*

Morehouse, F. M. I.
Migration from the United Kingdom to North America, 1840-1850. *Ph.D. 1926 Manchester*

Moreno, E.
The religious and philosophical background of Mateo Alemán with reference to the *Guzmán de Alfarache*. *Ph.D. 1944 Cambridge*

Moreton, F. E.
Co-education: a statistical enquiry into the attitude of teachers towards co-education, and a comparative study of the emotional development of children trained in co-educational and other institutions. *Ph.D. 1939 London, Institute of Education*

Moreton, F. E.
A statistical enquiry into the religious ideas of children, and some application in religious education. *M.A. 1931 Birmingham*

Morey, G. E.
The administration of the counties of Norfolk and Suffolk in the reign of Henry IV. *M.A. 1941 London, University College*

Morgan, A.
Linguistic ability considered in relation to general intelligence in senior school children. *M.A. 1940 Wales*

Morgan, B. E.
The city of Mari, with special reference to the archaeological material. *M.A. 1950 Manchester*

Morgan, D. H.
The teaching of Christ on social questions. *M.A. 1944 Wales*

Morgan, D. R.
The Guianas. *M.Sc. 1938 London, External Degree*

Morgan, D. T.
Industrial and social conditions in the Wrexham coalfield (1800-1860). *M.A. 1927 Liverpool*

Morgan, H. L.
English poetry and the Second World War. *M.A. 1950 Wales*

Morgan, I.
The nonconformity of Richard Baxter. *Ph.D. 1944 London, Richmond College*

Morgan, I. J.
The origins and development of the university movement in Wales, with particular reference to the period 1800-1889. *M.A. 1929 Wales*

Morgan, J. H.
A study of the economic development of the commote of Carnwyllion from 1500. *M.A. 1933 Wales*

Morgan, J. H.
Traethawd beirniadol ar fywyd a gwaith John Jones, Glanygors(Critical essay on the life and work of John Jones, Glanygors). *M.A. 1929 Wales*

Morgan, J. L.
The economic administration of Coupar Angus Abbey, 1440-1560. *Ph.D. 1929 Glasgow*

Morgan, J. R.
The contributions of Robert Hooke to the physical sciences. *M.Sc. 1931 London, University College*

Morgan, J. R.
The development of a safety lamp. *M.Sc. 1927 London*

Morgan, K. E.
Aims and problems in the teaching of poetry at the secondary school stage. *M.A. 1948 Liverpool*

Morgan, L. G.
The teaching of science to the Chinese. *M.A. 1932 London, Day Training College*

Morgan, L. T.
Mental fatigue. *M.A. 1924 Bristol*

Morgan, M.
A comparison between *Owein a Luned* and *Yvain, or Le Chevalier au Lion*. *M.A. 1910 Wales*

Morgan, M.
Christ Church, Canterbury, and the *sede vacante* jurisdiction of Canterbury during the thirteenth century. *B.Litt. 1938 Oxford*

Morgan, M.
The English priories and manors of the Abbey of Bec-Hellouin. *D.Phil. 1942 Oxford*

Morgan, M. M.
Gweithiau llenyddol y Parch. William Ambrose, Porthmadog (Emrys)(Literary works of Rev. William Ambrose (Emrys) of Portmadoc). *M.A. 1933 Wales*

Morgan, M. M.
The *Meditations on the Passion* ascribed to Richard Rolle. *M.A. 1947 London, Bedford College*

Morgan, O. I.
A study of the training for leisure occupations offered in a senior girls' school in an industrial area, together with an industrial enquiry into the use made of this training by the girls after their entry into employment. *M.Ed. 1942 Manchester*

Morgan, R. F.
A study of Virgil's methods of adapting Homer, based on Macrobius's list of parallel passages. *M.A. 1936 Wales*

Morgan, R. M.
The boroughs of Radnor to the Act of Union and beyond. *M.A. 1911 Wales*

Morgan, S. C.
1. The doctrine of the Holy Trinity. 2. The reality of the resurrection of Christ. *B.D. & D.D. 1881 Oxford*

Morgan, T. J.
Cystrawen y ferf mewn Cymraeg canol(The syntax of the verb in medieval Welsh). *M.A. 1930 Wales*

Morgan, T. L.
The operation of the provisions of the Law of Property Act, 1925, regarding undivided shares in land. *LL.M. 1938 Wales*

Morgan, W.
The influence of Milton upon the poetry of the eighteenth century. *M.A. 1918 Wales*

Morgan, W. G.
The mobility of labour in the principal industries of Somersetshire, 1923-1933. *M.A. 1934 Wales*

Morgan, W. J. C.
The dramatic art of Pinero. *M.A. 1933 Wales*

Morgan, W. L.
A study of the *Grosstadtroman* in modern German literature. *M.A. 1936 Wales*

Morgan-Jones, J. L.
Education in Caernarvonshire, considered in relation to the social and cultural background. *B.Litt. 1938 Oxford*

Morgans, H.
The teachings of Karl Marx: their influence on English labour organizations, 1850-1900. *M.A. 1936 Wales*

Morison, E. F.
Expositions of three selected passages from the Book of Leviticus. *D.D. 1916 Oxford*

Morison, E. F.
1. The relation of priest and prophet in the history of Israel before the exile. 2. St. Basil the Great and the monastic life. *B.D 1912 Oxford*

Morison, I. A.
The Dutch barrier, 1709-1719. *Ph.D. 1929 London*

Morisset, G. M. M.
L'inspiration antique dans *La jeunesse du Nanny de Lyesse* par François Habert. *M.A. 1929 London*

Morisset, G. M. M.
Ovide en France durant la première partie du seizième siècle. *Ph.D. 1934 London, Birkbeck College*

Morland, M. A.
Anthony Earl of Shaftesbury (1671-1713) and the German classical writers of the eighteenth century. *Ph.D. 1946 London, External Degree*

Morley, A. H.
The new constitutions of Europe: a comparative study of post-war European constitutions, with special reference to Germany, Poland, Czechoslovakia, the Kingdom of the Serbs, Croats, and Slovenes, and the Baltic States. *B.Litt. 1925 Oxford*

Morley, F. S.
British opinion on the development of the commonwealth of nations, 1895-1914. *Ph.D. 1932 Edinburgh*

Morley, J. G.
Psychology of the language and style of préciosité. *B.Litt. 1939 Oxford*

Morling, N. A.
Price policy in the short period. *M.Com. 1931 Birmingham*

Morrall, J. B.
William of Ockham's attitude to political authority and its relation to the history of his time. *B.Litt. 1949 Oxford*

Morrell, J. M.
Women in Elizabethan and Jacobean tragedy: a study of the principal conventions and influences governing the treatment of women characters in English tragedy. *M.A. 1931 London, Royal Holloway College*

Morrell, W. P.
British colonial administration, 1841-52. *D.Phil. 1927 Oxford*

Morrice, J. C.
The poems of William Lleyn. *M.A. 1902 Wales*

Morrice, J. C.
Social conditions in Wales under the Tudors and Stuarts. *Ph.D. 1924 Oxford*

Morrice, J. C.
Wales in the seventeenth century. *B.Litt. 1920 Oxford*

Morrin, T.
Ireland's systems of internal transport, their development and the State in relation to them. *M.Econ.Sc. 1947 National University of Ireland*

Morris, A. G.
The educational theories of François Rabelais. *M.Ed. 1939 Manchester*

Morris, A. G.
The teaching of free composition in modern languages. *M.A. 1944 Liverpool*

Morris, A. K.
The attitude of Herodotus towards the gods and religion. *M.A. 1939 Wales*

Morris, B. H.
The effects of a stock market boom upon industry and commerce with special reference to American experience, 1924-30. *B.Litt. 1933 Oxford*

Morris, C.
Effects of war on national economy. *M.A. 1945 National University of Ireland*

Morris, C. J.
Outline of social life in Central Nepal. *Dip. Anthropology. 1931 Cambridge*

Morris, C. J.
Social life in Nepal. *M.Sc. 1935 Cambridge*

Morris, D. R. C.
Prayer and the four Gospels. *B.D. 1947 Oxford*

Morris, E. H.
An enquiry into the psychological, ethical and religious implications underlying the concept of forgiveness. *M.A. 1930 Wales*

Morris, E. M. D.
The education of girls in England from 1600 to 1800. *M.A. 1926 London*

Morris, F. C.
A history of Waterford: its life and government from 1150-1800. *M.A. 1915 Wales*

Morris, F. G.
Physical controls in the historical geography of the Sussex estuaries. *M.A. 1931 London, School of Economics and Political Science*

Morris, F. G.
The South Cotswolds. *M.A. 1933 Bristol*

Morris, G.
The English stage and the English scene (Elizabeth to Victoria). *M.A. 1950 National University of Ireland*

Morris, G. E.
The language of the Middle English lyric. *B.A. 1937 Sheffield*

Morris, G. E.
Soldiers' songs of the thirteenth and fourteenth centuries. *M.A. 1947 Sheffield*

Morris, G. R.
Geographical factors in the evolution of Portugal as a political unit. *M.A. 1936 Liverpool*

Morris, G. S.
Scott's use of fact in the novels: a study in the relation of fact and fiction. *M.A. 1938 Wales*

Morris, H.
The lyrics and songs of the Elizabethan drama. *M.A. 1912 Wales*

Morris, I. F.
The relation of the doctrine of the Word of God to the doctrine of the *imago Dei*: a study in the theology of Karl Barth. *Ph.D. 1941 Edinburgh*

Morris, I. V.
Das Verfallsproblem bei Georg Trakl. *M.A. 1936 Belfast*

Morris, J.
The position and teaching of science in co-educational schools. *M.A. 1929 Liverpool*

Morris, J. H.
The West of England woollen industry, 1750-1840. *M.Sc. 1934 London, School of Economics and Political Science*

Morris, J. V.
The political and social novels of Charles Kingsley. *M.A. 1921 Wales*

Morris, K.
The causes of Anti-Romanist fanaticism in Great Britain in the eighteenth century, with special reference to the Lord George Gordon Riots. *M.A. 1926 Wales*

Morris, M. M.
The implications of immortality in the moral consciousness. *M.A. 1925 Wales*

Morris, N.
Elementary education in the Babylonian Talmud. *M.A. 1932 London, King's College*

Morris, N. R.
The law and practice relating to habitual criminals. *Ph.D. 1949 London, School of Economics and Political Science*

Morris, P. P.
Charlotte Brontë. *M.A. 1945 National University of Ireland*

Morris, R. H.
1. The authorship of the Epistle to the Hebrews. 2. The authorship of the fourth Gospel as proved from internal evidence. *B.D. & D.D. 1884 Oxford*

Morris, R. I.
The application of the hormic theory in psychology to the theory of religious education. *Ph.D. 1945 Edinburgh*

Morris, R. W.
Geographical and historical aspects of the public water supply of London, 1852-1902. *Ph.D. 1941 London, Birkbeck College*

Morris, S. T.
A study of some economic aspects of the sheep industry of Devon, with special reference to changes in the practice of sheep farming on the red loams of mid-Devon. *M.Sc. 1936 Wales*

Morris, W. D.
The agricultural regions of the U.S.S.R. *M.Sc. 1946 London, King's College*

Morris-Jones, H.
The ethical theory of Nietzsche. *B.Litt. 1937 Oxford*

Morrison, A. A.
The doctrine of the Christ in St. Mark's Gospel. *Ph.D. 1948 Saint Andrew's*

Morrison, J. M.
The structure of the Gospel according to St. Mark approached from the standpoint of Formgeschichte, with a special consideration of (a) Mark ii.1.-iii.6 and (b) Mark xi.15-xii.40. *B.Litt. 1934 Oxford*

Morrison, M. G.
The influence of Catullus in the sixteenth century in France. *Ph.D. 1940 Cambridge*

Morrissey, S.
Forestry in Ireland. *M.A. 1938 National University of Ireland*

Morrissey, W.
The poetry of Gerard Manley Hopkins. *M.A. 1937 Liverpool*

Morrow, I. F. D.
The Black Sea question during the Crimean War. *Ph.D. 1927 Cambridge*

Morse, B. J.
The influence of German literature on English literature in the early nineteenth century, with special reference to Thomas Carlyle. *M.A. 1929 Wales*

Mortimer, H. M.
Village-patterns and distributions in East Devon. *M.A. 1940 London, External Degree*

Mortimer, N. B.
The position of Part III Authorities in the English education system. *Ph.D. 1946 London, External Degree*

Mortimer, R. C.
The origins of private penance. *B.D. 1938 Oxford*

Mortimer, R. S.
Bristol Quakerism. *M.A. 1946 Bristol*

Morton, A.
The singing guilds in the Old Testament. *Ph.D. 1944 Saint Andrew's*

Morton, A. M.
William Morris's treatment of his Icelandic sources. *B.Litt. 1935 Oxford*

Morton, A. W.
The contribution of the Evangelical revival to the philosophy and practice of education. *D.Phil. 1949 Oxford*

Morton, I. C.
Lessings ethische Ansichten. *M.A. 1925 Birmingham*

Morton, W. L.
Newfoundland in colonial policy, 1775-1793. *B.Litt. 1935 Oxford*

Mosby, F.
A history of the settlement of the western firths of Iceland. *M.A. 1931 Leeds*

Mosby, J. E. G.
The agricultural geography of Norfolk, with special reference to changes in land utilisation and human occupancy. *Ph.D. 1938 London, School of Economics and Political Science*

Moscherosch, G. P.
The nature and function of dogma in the symbolo-fidéisme of the Paris School. *Ph.D. 1950 Edinburgh*

Moscrop, S. F.
Craftsmanship in Conrad. *M.A. 1926 Liverpool*

Moser, W. L.
The evolution of the theory and doctrine of the Church of England, as exemplified by Ockham, Wyclif and Cranmer. *Ph.D. 1927 Edinburgh*

Moses, H.
Ludwig Tieck's Shakespearean criticism. *M.A. 1939 London, University College*

Moshinsky, P.
The relation between the distribution of intelligence and the social environment. *Ph.D. 1937 London, School of Economics and Political Science*

Mosley, F. M.
Du Bartas in his relation to English literature, with special reference to Milton. *M.A. 1916 London*

Mosley, J. K.
The impassibility of God. *D.D. 1926 Cambridge*

Moss, C. T.
The telescopes of Sir William Herschel. *M.Sc. 1949 London, University College*

Moss, D. S.
The sources and inspiration of Montchrestien's dramatic works and his place in French tragedy. *M.A. 1927 Wales*

Moss, F. W.
Le théâtre de Clara Gazul. *M.A. 1924 Leeds*

Moss, F. W.
Rabelais the educator. *M.Ed. 1928 Leeds*

Moss, P. G.
The teaching of geography in the secondary school, with special reference to maps and map-work. *M.A. 1931 Liverpool*

Moss, R.
The origins and influence of Methodism in the north Staffordshire Potteries before 1820. *M.A. 1949 London, Birkbeck College*

Murphy, N.
Le mouvement régionaliste dans la littérature française moderne et l'oeuvre de Henry Bordeaux. *M.A. 1926 National University of Ireland*

Murray, A. E.
A history of the commercial and financial relations between England and Ireland from the period of the Revolution. *D.Sc. 1903 London*

Murray, A. H.
Empiricism in the philosophy of James Ward. *B.Litt. 1928 Oxford*

Murray, A. H.
A study in the philosophy of Charles Bernard Renouvier, with special reference to his theory of knowledge. *D.Phil. 1931 Oxford*

Murray, A. R. M.
Realist theories of perception. *Ph.D. 1932 Cambridge*

Murray, A. V.
The relations between Abelard and St. Bernard. *B.Litt. 1930 Oxford*

Murray, C. H.
The history of Christian baptism. *B.Litt. 1927 Oxford*

Murray, F.
The state and compulsory education. *M.A. 1943 National University of Ireland*

Murray, H.
An investigation into the stability of personal relations among educationally sub-normal children living in an institution. *M.Sc. 1949 Sheffield*

Murray, J. P.
The nature and knowledge of God (or the Absolute) in the philosophy of Plotinus. *Ph.D. 1928 London*

Murray, J. P.
The theory of sense-perception in the writings of Plotinus. *M.A. 1924 London*

Murray, J. W.
The effect of the Education Act of 1918 on future local educational organization. *M.A. 1923 Liverpool*

Murray, K. A. H.
Factors affecting the prices of livestock in Great Britain. *B.Litt. 1931 Oxford*

Murray, K. M. E.
The growth of the organization of the Cinque Ports Confederation. *B.Litt. 1932 Oxford*

Murray, L. A.
The return to the Golden Age in Spanish Literature. *M.A. 1924 Liverpool*

Murray, L. J.
Realistic novel in the Elizabethan Age. *M.A. 1913 National University of Ireland*

Murray, M. A.
Excavations in Malta. *D.Litt. 1932 London, University College*

Murray, R.
Molière as a national dramatist of France. *M.A. 1916 National University of Ireland*

Murray, W. G.
British relations with the Transvaal from 1874 to 1881. *D.Phil. 1937 Oxford*

Murray, W. M.
Hilaire Belloc, essayist. *M.A. 1948 National University of Ireland*

Murray, R. N.
The education of Jamaica: its historical background and possible future developments. *M.A. 1947 London, Institute of Education*

Murrell, E. S.
A comparative study of Girart de Roussillon and the Tristan poems. *B.Litt. 1926 Oxford*

Musafar, K. C.
Romantic drama, 1780-1830, considered in the light of the theatrical history of the period. *Ph.D. 1924 London*

Musgrave, C.
The early inhabitants of the Oxford neighbourhood, with special reference to Cassington. *B.Sc. 1939 Oxford*

Musgrave, C. A.
Household administration in the fourteenth century, with special reference to the household of Elizabeth de Burgh, Lady of Clare. *M.A. 1923 London*

Musgrave, M.
Michael of Kildare: earliest traces of Anglo-Irish poetry. *M.A. 1912 National University of Ireland*

Musgrave, W. A. B.
On the common law of England with respect to waters, with special references to the possibility of applying it to varying natural circumstances. *D.C.L. 1890 Oxford*

Musgrove, S.
The changing values in the critical and literary outlook of the seventeenth century, as manifested in English verse translation from the Greek and Latin classics. *D.Phil. 1944 Oxford*

Musson, J. W.
William Dunbar and John Skelton. *M.A. 1939 Bristol*

Mutschmann, H.
The place names of Nottinghamshire. *M.A. 1912 Liverpool*

Mutton, A. F. A.
An analysis of some of the interactions of geography and history in the Arun and Adur valleys. *M.A. 1932 London, Bedford College*

Mutton, A. F. A.
Some aspects of the evolution and distribution of settlement and industries in the Black Forest region considered in relation to the geographical setting. *Ph.D. 1937 London, Bedford College*

Myers, C. V.
Tom Taylor: life and works. *M.Litt. 1933 Cambridge*

Myers, H. S.
A study of newspapers of the Civil War, Commonwealth and Protectorate, in certain of their literary aspects. *M.A. 1921 London*

Myers, J. F.
The common law in the sixteenth century. *M.A. 1950 Liverpool*

Myint, N.
Postulates of welfare economics. *Ph.D. 1943 London, School of Economics and Political Science*

Myres, J. P. H.
The foreign policy of Charles Albert (1848-9), with special reference to England. *B.Litt. 1932 Oxford*

Myres, M. W.
1. The place of the ark in the religious thought of the early Israelites. 2. The revelation of Yahweh in tradition and history. *B.D. & D.D. 1924 Oxford*

Nacnab, M.
Barnabe Googe. *M.A. 1918 London*

Nadel, S. F.
The political and religious structure of Nupe society (northern Nigeria). *Ph.D. 1935 London, School of Economics and Political Science*

Nadkarni, L. M.
Effects of the world economic depression on Far Eastern currencies. *M.Sc. 1937 London, School of Economics and Political Science*

Nagchaudhuri, U.
Poetic drama of the nineteenth century, from 1800 to 1830. *Ph.D. 1927 London*

Nagib, A. F.
Recent changes in the structure and training of labour in the British engineering industry, and their future trends. *Ph.D. 1945 Manchester*

Nagle, J.
Richard Cantillon; his position in the history of economic doctrines. *M.Sc. 1930 National University of Ireland*

Nagle, M. T.
Modern English lyrics (1850-1936). *M.A. 1937 National University of Ireland*

Nahapiet, K.
Reasoning in children from 7 to 11 years of age. *M.A. 1933 Birmingham*

Nahm, M. C.
An edition of John Wilson's *The cheats*. *B.Litt. 1929 Oxford*

Nainar, S. M. H.
The knowledge of India possessed by Arab geographers down to the fourteenth century A.D., with special reference to southern India. *Ph.D. 1938 London, School of Oriental and African Studies*

Naish, G. H.
A new edition of *Handlyng synne* and *Medytacyuns*. *Ph.D. 1936 London, External Degree*

Naish, J. P.
North Italian Christianity, A.D.350-461. *B.Litt. 1921 Oxford*

Nakar, S. E.
A factorial analysis of reasoning ability. *M.A. 1949 London, Institute of Education*

Nakavi, S. M. H.
A critical survey of the educational development and conditions in the state of Hyderabad (Deccan) with suggestions and recommendations for further improvement. *M.Ed. 1937 Leeds*

Namasivayam, S.
Constitutional developments in Ceylon during the period 1928-48. *B.Phil. 1948 Oxford*

Nanavutty, P.
Some Eastern influences on William Blake's *Prophetic Books*. *M.Litt. 1938 Cambridge*

Nance, J. T.
1. The doctrine of the resurrection in the Book of Job. 2. The connection between free-will and eternal punishment. *B.D. 1881 Oxford*

Nandimath, S. C.
Theology of the *Saivagamas*, being a survey of the doctrines of the Saiva Siddhanta and Virasaivism. *Ph.D. 1930 London, School of Oriental and African Studies*

Nankivell, J. W. H.
A survey of attempts at religious comprehension in the Church of England in the seventeenth century, with special reference to the period from the Restoration to the Revolution. *B.Litt. 1943 Oxford*

Napolitan, L.
Some aspects of the fruit growing industry in the County of Kent. *M.Sc. 1946 London, School of Economics and Political Science*

Narasimhia, A. N. P.
A grammar of the old Kanarese inscriptions, including a study of Sanskrit and Prakrit loanwords. *Ph.D. 1933 London, School of Oriental and African Studies*

Narayanaswamy, B. V.
Trade disputes in Great Britain: a brief enquiry into causes of, and an examination of methods of dealing with these, and particularly the experience and possibilities of conciliation and arbitration, and with a reference to Indian labour. *Ph.D. 1929 Edinburgh*

Narborough, F. D. V.
A commentary on the Epistle to the Hebrews. *B.D. 1931 Oxford*

Narsian, S. J.
Rural education in Sind. *M.Ed. 1938 Leeds*

Nash, A. S.
Problems of method in the social sciences. *M.Sc. 1938 London, School of Economics and Political Science*

Nash, E. N.
Poverty and some of its effects upon schoolchildren. *M.Ed. 1941 Durham*

Nash, J.
History of legal procedure in Ireland since 1600. *M.A. 1945 National University of Ireland*

Nasim, M.
The effect of legislative enactments and judicial pronouncements on the civil law of the Muhammadans in the United Provinces of Agra and Oudh on matters other than family relations, administration and arbitration. *LL.D. 1929 London*

Nasr, M. A.
Walter Bagehot: a study in Victorian ideas. *Ph.D. 1949 London, School of Economics and Political Science*

Nassour, A. J.
The political thought of Thomas Paine. *D.Phil. 1947 Oxford*

Nat, B. S.
Estimation of stature from long bones in U. P. Indians. *M.D. 1930 Saint Andrew's*

Nath, S.
An investigation into the significance of teachers' assessments of the personal attributes of their pupils for secondary school selection. *M.A. 1948 London, Institute of Education*

Natzio, K.
The penetration of English ideas into France (1680-1720), with special reference to Pierre Bayle. *B.Litt. 1929 Oxford*

Nayar, T. B.
Studies in South Indian pottery. *M.A. 1931 London, University College*

Naylor, U. Todd- *see* Todd-Naylor, U.

Nazim, M.
Sultán Mahmúd of Ghazna and his times. *Ph.D. 1928 Cambridge*

Neal, A. B.
The place of practical instruction in education. *M.A. 1923 Wales*

Niblett, W. R.
The function of the literary critic, with special reference to the work of Hazlitt. *B.Litt. 1930 Oxford*

Nic Concairrge, C.
Saoghal agus saothar triair sgríobhnóirí Gaedhilge : Pádraig Mac Piarais, Micheál Breathnach agus Pádraig O'Conaire(The lives and works of three Irish writers: Pádraig Mac Piarais, Micheál Breathnach and Pádraig O'Conaire). *M.A. 1941 National University of Ireland*

Nic Craith, S.
Págántacht san Ruadhraigheacht agus san Fhiannaigheacht(Paganism in the Red Branch Cycle and the Fenian Cycle). *M.A. 1939 National University of Ireland*

Nic Dhonnchadha, M. *see* Mc Donagh, M. J.

NicDhonnchadha, M. *see* Mac Donagh, M.

Nicholas, T. J.
The value of apprentice ability tests in Birmingham junior technical school entrance examination. *M.A. 1942 Birmingham*

Nicholls, A. W.
French refugees in England from the Restoration to the death of William III. *B.Litt. 1923 Oxford*

Nicholls, R. E.
Life, works and literary theories of Jacques-Joseph du Guet. *Ph.D. 1936 London, University College*

Nichols, I.
The education of children in hospital schools. *M.A. 1938 Liverpool*

Nichols, J. F.
Custodia essexae: a study of the conventual property held by the Priory of Christ Church, Canterbury, in the counties of Essex, Suffolk and Norfolk. *Ph.D. 1930 London, King's College*

Nicholson, J.
A contribution to the study of French as taught in England: thirteenth to fifteenth centuries. *Ph.D. 1936 London, University College*

Nicholson, J. E.
The educational needs of the senior school boy. *M.Ed. 1940 Manchester*

Nicholson, J. H.
Social contacts of education. *M.A. 1923 Bristol*

Nicholson, J. L.
Variations in working-class family expenditure. *M.Sc. 1949 London, School of Economics and Political Science*

Nickoloff, N.
The authority of oecumenical councils, in the Eastern Orthodox, the Roman Catholic, and the Anglican Churches. *B.Litt. 1925 Oxford*

Nicol, A. T.
The concept of continuity: its development in Greek thought before Aristotle. *Ph.D. 1938 Cambridge*

Nicolson, A.
The feeling aspect of the religious consciousness. *Ph.D. 1929 Edinburgh*

Nicolson Thomson, M. P.
The changing ideal of womanhood in the novel and its relation to the feminist movement, 1837 to 1873. *Ph.D. 1947 Cambridge*

Nigam, S. B. L.
A study of the methods of state regulation of wages, with special reference to their possible applications in India. . *Ph.D. 1949 London, School of Economics and Political Science*

Nightingale, J. L.
1659-1660: a study in the interaction of political and religious forces in the period between the fall of Richard Cromwell and the restoration of Charles II. *M.Litt. 1936 Durham*

Niklaus, N.
Contribution à l'étude de Jean Moréas. *Ph.D. 1934 London, University College*

Nilson, A. J.
1. Genesis i, ii.1-7, iii.17-19; Psalm xix.1-3, xcv.3-7: evolution and providence. 2. St. Mark ix.48; St. John iii.36: eternal justice. 3. Genesis iii.1-10; Romans vii.18,19: will in Christian ethics. *D.D. 1885 Oxford*

Nimmo, A. B.
L'influence d'André Chénier sur l'oeuvre de Victor Hugo jusqu'á 1840. *M.A. 1948 Liverpool*

Nisbet, E. Y.
An inquiry into the purchasing power of the drachma in ancient Greece for the purpose of determining, if possible, the material conditions which prevailed in Athens during her existence as an independent state. *Ph.D. 1948 Glasgow*

Nixon, A. J.
The principle of authority in the Free Churches. *Ph.D. 1930 London, External Degree*

Nixon, I. M.
Thomas of Erceldoune: edited with an introduction notes and a glossary. *Ph.D. 1947 Edinburgh*

Niyogi, J. P.
The evolution of the Indian income tax. *Ph.D. 1929 London*

Nizámu'd-Din, A. H. M.
Introduction to the *Jawámi'u'l-hikáyát wu lawámi'ur-riwáyát*. *Ph.D. 1924 Cambridge*

Noble, E.
The novels and short stories of the Conte de Gobineau. *Ph.D. 1931 Dublin, Trinity College*

Noble, E.
The study of Milton in the first half of the eighteenth century. *M.A. 1914 London*

Nock, A. E. M.
L'esthétique de Gustave Flaubert dans sa correspondence et dans ses oeuvres. *M.A. 1921 London*

Noël-Paton, M. O.
The Triple Alliance and the War of Devolution. *Ph.D. 1931 London, University College*

Nokes, G. D.
The history and scope of the offence of blasphemy cognizable by the courts Christian and the courts of common law in England. *LL.D. 1927 London*

Nolan, C. C. *see* Nolan, H.

Nolan, D. P.
Stair an oideachais i bhfairche Chluain-fearta, 1700-1885(The history of education in the diocese of Clonfert, 1700-1885). *M.A. 1941 National University of Ireland*

Nolan, H.
The social life and doctrine of St. Thomas More. *M.A. 1942 National University of Ireland*

Nolan, H. M.
Anti-Trinitarianism in England in the seventeenth century. *B.Litt. 1910 Oxford*

Nolan, N. G.
The Irish emigration: a study in demography. *Ph.D. 1936 National University of Ireland*

Nolloth, H. E.
1. St. Mark iv.26-29: the secret growth of the seed of the kingdom. 2. Revelation iv.4-11: the vision of the four-and-twenty elders, and the four living beings. 3. Revelation xx.1-8: the prophecy of the millennial reign. *D.D. 1894 Oxford*

Noonan, J. A.
A critical edition of the works of Guillaume de Ferrières, with a study of his life. *D.Phil. 1933 Oxford*

Norburn, R. G.
Disinterestedness and its conditions: a limited comparison between the ethics of Christianity and of scientific humanism as represented in particular by the *Ethics* of Professor Nicholai Hartmann. *M.A. 1940 Manchester*

Norden, P. Weil- *see* Weil-Norden, P.

Norenius, A. C.
Dramatic criticism in early nineteenth century periodicals (1800-1830), and its influence on the contemporary drama. *Ph.D. 1931 London, East London College*

Norman, A. H.
The philosophy of A. S. Pringle-Pattison. *B.Litt. 1936 Oxford*

Norman, E.
Observations on the speech of a child. *M.A. 1931 Reading*

Norman, F.
Marien Himmelfahrt: ein mittelhochdeutsches Gedicht kritisch. *M.A. 1925 London*

Norman, G. M.
Horace: his views on life. *M.A. 1919 Birmingham*

Normoyle, M. J. D.
Foras focal an Athar Peadar O'Laoghaire(The vocabulary of Father Peter O'Leary). *Ph.D. 1942 National University of Ireland*

Norris, B. A.
The religious thought of Richard Price, 1723-1791. *Ph.D. 1950 Edinburgh*

Norris, M. E.
Alcestis. *M.A. 1910 London*

Norris, M. K.
The composition of the chorus in Greek tragedy. *M.A. 1928 London*

Norrish, P. L.
The life of Robert Spencer, 2nd Earl of Sunderland, 1640-1702, with special reference to his work as secretary of state. *M.A. 1936 Liverpool*

North, R. J.
Catholicism in the work of François Mauriac. *M.A. 1947 London, King's College*

Northend, F. M.
Henry Arthur Jones and the dramatic renaissance in England. *M.A. 1940 London, Bedford College*

Northridge, W. L.
The argument from design. *M.A. 1920 Belfast*

Northridge, W. L.
Modern theories of the unconscious. *Ph.D. 1922 Belfast*

Norton, A. R.
An attempt to assess the importance of some of the usually accepted causes of mental abnormality: a clinical and statistical study of 500 psychiatric patients. *D.M. 1947 Oxford*

Norton, G. R.
The adaptation of native custom and belief to modern conditions of civilization in South Africa. *M.A. 1939 Leeds*

Norton, M.
Byron, the dramatist. *M.A. 1940 Birmingham*

Norton, P. R.
Dialogus Palladii de vita S. Ioannis Chrysostomi. *D.Phil. 1923 Oxford*

Norton, W. A.
A translation of theological terms and ideas into the languages of evangelization, ancient and modern, particularly those of the Bantu family. *B.Litt. 1916 Oxford*

Norwell, F. A.
Advanced instruction in the elementary school. *M.A. 1931 Liverpool*

Noshy, I.
The problem of Greek and Egyptian influences in Ptolemaic architecture and sculpture. *Ph.D. 1934 London, University College*

Noss, J. B.
Modern psychology and the Catholic doctrine of the person of Christ. *Ph.D. 1928 Edinburgh*

Notcutt, H. C.
An interpretation of Keats' *Endymion*. *Ph.D. 1921 London*

Nowaihi, N. M. M. el- *see* el-Nowaihi, N. M. M.

Noyes, H. H.
The novels of George Moore. *Ph.D. 1938 London, Birkbeck College*

Nremicarne, A. J. T.
The ban of the Bari. *M.Sc. 1914 London*

Nugent, W.
Church and state in early Christian Ireland. *M.A. 1949 National University of Ireland*

Nunn, E. R. H.
The subject matter of history in junior schools. *M.A. 1929 London*

Nunn, G.
Science in the senior school. *M.A. 1937 Liverpool*

Nunn, T. P.
The aim and achievement of scientific method: an epistemological essay. *D.Sc. 1907 London*

Nurse, A. J.
A survey of the history and development of the selective central school in England and of similar types of post primary schools in France: a comparison of educational theory and practice. *M.A. 1939 London, King's College*

Nurullah, S.
A study of rhythm and psychological methods of developing regularity of time and stress in movement. *M.Ed. 1927 Leeds*

Nusbaum, D.
Cold: its demands and suggestions: a study of the importance of environment in the development of Eskimo culture. *D.Phil. 1939 Oxford*

Nuttall, C.
Budgetary policy, rates of interest, and company profits during the recovery period, 1932-1937. *Ph.D. 1940 Birmingham*

Nuttall, E. R.
The economic objects and results of land legislation in Ireland in the Gladstonian era. *M.A. 1936 Wales*

Nuttall, G. F.
Faith and reason in the works of Bishop Pecock. *B.D. 1937 Oxford*

O'Cuiv, B.
Relative construction in Middle Irish; a study of some morphological and syntactical changes in the expression of the relative. *M.A. 1940 National University of Ireland*

O'Dea, M. E.
The policy of the Tudors in regard to the mines in Ireland. *M,A. 1931 National University of Ireland*

O'Dell, A. C.
Historical geography of the Shetland Islands. *M.Sc. 1933 London, King's College*

Odell, W. A.
Roman Philhellenism as a factor in the literary revival of Greek under Hadrian and Antonines. *M.A. 1920 Birmingham*

Odling, M. G.
The experimental basis of Robert Boyle's objections to the Aristotelian and alchemical doctrines. *M.Sc. 1928 London*

O'Doherty, E. F.
Ethics of right and good. *M.A. 1939 National University of Ireland*

O'Doherty, E. F.
The process of abstraction and concept formation. *Ph.D. 1946 Cambridge*

O'Doherty, J.
Researches in association: a psycho-physical essay. *M.A. 1915 National University of Ireland*

O'Doherty, M.
The Nibelungen saga in Celtic literature. *M.A. 1916 National University of Ireland*

O'Doherty, R.
Turf in Ireland. *M.A. 1942 National University of Ireland*

O'Domhnalláin, P.
Beatha san Phroinsias maille le brollach agus gluais(*The life of St. Francis*, with preface and commentary). *M.A. 1937 National University of Ireland*

O'Domnabháin, R.
An uimhir dhéide i saothar na n-úghdar seo leanas. 1. An t-ath. P. O'Laoghaire. 2. P. O'Conaire. 3. An Seabhac(The number two as used in the works of P. O'Laoghaire, P. O'Conaire, and An Seabhac). *M.A. 1942 National University of Ireland*

O'Donnchadha, P. see Mc Donagh, P.

O'Donnchadha, S. B.
An Leabhar Muimhneach(The Book of Munster). *M.A. 1937 National University of Ireland*

O'Donnell, J.
History of Tir Conaill in the 16th century. *M.A. 1946 National University of Ireland*

O'Donnell, J. P.
James Shirley. *M.A. 1939 National University of Ireland*

O'Donnell, P.
Nasalization in Irish. *M.A. 1915 National University of Ireland*

O'Donoghue, B. J.
The commercial utilization of Java citronella oil. *Ph.D. 1928 National University of Ireland*

O'Donoghue, D.
Filíocht Mháire Bhuidhe Ní Laeri(The poems of Máire Buidhe Ní Laeri). *M.A. 1929 National University of Ireland*

O'Donoghue, D.
Some metaphysical aspects of modern physical science. *M.A. 1945 National University of Ireland*

O'Donoghue, J. R.
The Dream of Rood and Ruthwell Cross. *M.A. 1929 National University of Ireland*

O'Donoghue, M. E.
Clár na láimhscríbhinní san leabharlainn, Coláiste no hOllscoile Corcaigh(Catalogue of manuscripts in the library of University College, Cork). *Ph.D. 1943 National University of Ireland*

O'Donovan, A.
Ancient mining in Spain. *M.Litt. 1934 Cambridge*

O'Donovan, J.
Cato Minor. *M.A. 1945 National University of Ireland*

O'Donovan, J.
An economic history of live stock in Ireland since the famine. *B.Litt. 1931 Oxford*

O'Donovan, M.
Les trois manières de Ronsard. *M.A. 1946 National University of Ireland*

O'Donovan, M. H.
Bourdaloue and the Bible. *M.A. 1926 London*

O'Dowd, M. E.
Alfred de Vigny's translation of Othello: its place in the history of French drama. *M.A. 1917 National University of Ireland*

O'Driscoll, E.
The poor in English literature. *M.A. 1917 National University of Ireland*

O'Driscoll, E. J.
Celtic ethnology and culture. *M.A. 1928 National University of Ireland*

O'Driscoll, F.
Early Corca Laidhe history. *M.A. 1943 National University of Ireland*

O'Droigheain, M.
Taighde i gcóir stair litridheachta na Nua Ghaedhilge ó 1882 anuas(Research on the history of modern Irish literature since 1882). *M.A. 1929 National University of Ireland*

O'Duinnin, P. see Dineen, P. N.

O'Dwyer, M.
Shakespeare's prose. *M.A. 1930 National University of Ireland*

Oeser, O. A.
Some experiments on the abstraction of form and colour. *Ph.D. 1932 Cambridge*

O'Fachtna, A. see Faulkner, J.

O'Faoláin, P.
Matamaitice 'sna bun-scoileannaibh(Mathematics in primary schools). *M.A. 1928 National University of Ireland*

O'Faoláin, T.
Cnuasacht béaloideasa ós na Déisibh(Folklore from the Deise). *M.A. 1942 National University of Ireland*

O'Farrell, B.
Le militaire vu par Balzac. *M.A. 1945 National University of Ireland*

O'Farrell, D. F.
The development of industries in Eire since 1924, with special reference to (a) employment, (b) the national income and its distribution. *M.Econ.Sc. 1944 National University of Ireland*

O'Fearchair, S.
An dírbheathaisńeis sa Ghaedhilg(Autobiography in Irish). *M.A. 1945 National University of Ireland*

O'Ferrall, J. L.
Music in general education. *M.A. 1927 National University of Ireland*

Offler, H. S.
The Emperor Lewis IV and the Curia from 1330 to 1347: canon law and international politics in the first half of the fourteenth century. *Ph.D. 1939 Cambridge*

Offor, R.
Letras Armas de la Provincia del Paraguay de los años de 1626 y 1627. *Ph.D. 1926 London*

Offord, M. Y.
An edition of *The parlement of the thre ages.* *B.Litt. 1948 Oxford*

O'Flaherty, K.
A. E. Housman. *M.A. 1939 National University of Ireland*

O'Flaherty, K. M.
Le mal de René. *Ph.D. 1943 National University of Ireland*

O'Flaherty, M.
Saothar filídheachta Thuileagna Uí Mhaolchonaire(The poetic works of Tuileagna O'Maolchonaire). *M.A. 1936 National University of Ireland*

O'Flaherty, M. A.
Aided Diarmata Meic Fergusso Cerrbeoil(The violent death of Diarmad son of Fergus Cerrbeoil). *M.A. 1948 National University of Ireland*

O'Flaithfhile, M. see Flatley, M.

O'Flynn, D. J.
Agricultural credit in Ireland. *M.Econ.Sc. 1942 National University of Ireland*

O'Flynn, L. G.
Problems in the teaching of English. *M.A. 1936 National University of Ireland*

O'Flynn, T.
Coleridge's dramatic criticism. *M.A. 1946 National University of Ireland*

Ogata, K.
The co-operative movement in Japan. *Ph.D. 1923 London*

Ogg, G.
The chronology of the public ministry of Jesus. *D.Litt. 1936 Saint Andrew's*

Ogilvie, A.
The physical geography of the Moray Firth from Golspie to Port Gordon. *B.Sc. 1915 Oxford*

O'Gioballáin, C.
Buaidh na Naomh-Chroiche; aistriú a rinne Bonaventura O'Conchubhair, O.F.M. ar *Triumphus Crucis* le Girolamo Savonarola(*The triumph of the Holy Cross*; a translation by Bonaventura O'Conchubhair, O.F.M. of *Triumphus Crucis* by Girolamo Savonarola). *M.A. 1938 National University of Ireland*

O'Góilidhe, C. see Golden, K.

O'Gorman, M.
Prose works of Chaucer. *M.A. 1937 National University of Ireland*

O'Grady, W. H. A.
Studies of Ireland under Strafford. *Litt.D. 1922 Dublin, Trinity College*

O'h-Allmháin, R.
Geinealaigh Earann(Irish genealogies). *M.A. 1942 National University of Ireland*

O'Halloran, R. J.
Family allowances. *M.Econ.Sc. 1940 National University of Ireland*

O'Hanlon, A.
Seamus O'Kelly. *M.A. 1946 National University of Ireland*

O'Hanrahan, R.
Irish local government. *M.A. 1927 National University of Ireland*

O'Hara, G.
Habitus and habit. *M.A. 1949 National University of Ireland*

O'hArgain, G.
An Bhoromha as *Leabhar mor Leacáin*, 295 ro a 24-310 ro a 12(The Boru tribute, from the *Book of Lecan*, 295r 24-310r 12). *M.A. 1950 National University of Ireland*

O'Hart, S.
Public works policy. *M.A. 1938 National University of Ireland*

O'hEalnighthe, D.
Stiúraitheoir an pheacaigh(The director of the sinner). *M.A. 1943 National University of Ireland*

O'hEidhin, P. see Hynes, P.

O'hInnse, S.
Fosterage in old Irish law. *M.A. 1940 National University of Ireland*

O'h-Innse, S. A. see Henchy, J. A.

Ohn, M.
A survey of the development of education in Burma. *M.Ed. 1940 Leeds*

O'hOisin, S.
Eachtra Muireadhaigh Mhic Diaindheirg(The adventures of Muireadach son of Diaindearg). *M.A. 1945 National University of Ireland*

O'hUallacháin, B.
Eagar ar shleachta as 24 p9(An edition of extracts from ms. 24 p9). *M.A. 1941 National University of Ireland*

O'hUallacháin, S.
Saothar Mháire(The work of Máire). *M.A. 1939 National University of Ireland*

O'hUigín, L.
Stair an Naoimhgréadhla; aistriúchán(A translation of *Stair an Naoimhghréadhla*). *M.A. 1939 National University of Ireland*

O'hUllacháin, P.
Amhráin ghrádha ó'n Mhumhain; cnuasacht a bailigheadh as láimhsgríbhinní Phádruig Fhéirtéir, Coláiste na h-Oillsgoile Baile Atha Cliath(Love songs from Munster; a collection from the manuscripts of Pádraig Feirtéar in University College Dublin). *M.A. 1939 National University of Ireland*

O'Kane, W. McK.
The study of law: an essential element in a modern liberal education. *LL.D. 1940 Belfast*

O'Keeffe, D.
Democracy in English fiction. *M.A. 1941 National University of Ireland*

O'Kelly, B. P.
Fundamental rights articles in the Irish constitution. *M.A. 1946 National University of Ireland*

O'Kelly, J. B. S.
Novels of Thomas Hardy. *M.A. 1948 National University of Ireland*

O'Kelly, M. J.
A survey of the antiquities in the Barony of Small County, Co. Limerick. *M.A. 1941 National University of Ireland*

O'Kelly, P.
Coim mheas na gcanamhan(A comparison of dialects). *M.A. 1944 National University of Ireland*

O'Kelly, P.
A history of inland transport in Ireland down to the period of railways. *M.Sc. 1922 London*

O'Kelly, R. T.
Shakespeare's final vision: the *Tempest. M.A. 1941 National University of Ireland*

O'Laochdha, T. P.
An chómhacht a bhí ag an Athair Peadar O'Laoghaire agus ag Pádraig O'Conaire(The extent of the influence of Father Peadar O'Laoghaire and Pádraig O'Conaire). *M.A. 1941 National University of Ireland*

O'Laoghaire, D.
Eachtra an Mhadraidh Mhaoil(The adventures of An Madradh Maol). *M.A. 1942 National University of Ireland*

O'Laoghaire, S.
Eachtraí buile Shuibhne ingaedhilg an lae indiu(The adventures of Buile Suibhne, in modern Irish). *M.A. 1929 National University of Ireland*

O'Laoighidh, P.
Sgoltacha agus sgoláirí Fairche na Gaillimhe, 1500-1731(Schools and scholars of the diocese of Galway, 1500-1731). *M.A. 1946 National University of Ireland*

O'Laoighidh, T. S.
An t-athair Tomás O'Ceallaigh agus a shaothar, maille le réamh-rádh, nótaí agus eile(Fr. Tomás O'Ceallaigh and his work, with preface, notes etc). *M.A. 1941 National University of Ireland*

Oldfield, J.
The problem of capital punishment. *D.C.L. 1901 Oxford*

Oldfield, M.
Parliament and Convocation, with special reference to the pontificate of Henry Chichele, 1413-1443. *M.A. 1938 Manchester*

Oldfield, W. J.
1. Sin: 'Η αμαρτί α εστιν η ανομία. 2. The atonement: 'Ο Θεόσ αγάπη εστίν. *B.D. & D.D. 1907 Oxford*

Oldham, A. L.
1. On the creed in the Acts. 2. On the appointment of rites and ceremonies in the Church. *B.D. & D.D. 1905 Oxford*

Oldham, H. W.
An experimental investigation of certain phenomena due to oscillation in mental efficiency. *M.A. 1931 Reading*

Oldham, H.W.
An investigation of school mathematics, mainly with the object of discovering by scientific method whether or not it is justifiable to include arithmetic, algebra and geometry as one group for school certificate and matriculation examination. *Ph.D. 1936 Reading*

Oldham, W.
The administration of the system of transportation of British convicts, 1763-1793. *Ph.D. 1933 London, King's College*

Oldroyd, A.
Education and employment. *M.A. 1915 Liverpool*

O'Leary, C.
The poetry of John Donne. *M.A. 1949 National University of Ireland*

O'Leary, F. L.
Irish Parliament of Queen Anne. *M.A. 1944 National University of Ireland*

O'Leary, I. M.
Wales and the border counties in relation to the Popish plot. *M.A. 1924 Wales*

O'Leary, J.
George Peele, (1558-1596?): poet and dramatist. *M.A. 1935 National University of Ireland*

O'Leary, J.
Women at work. *M.A. 1945 National University of Ireland*

O'Leary, M.
Edwin Muir and Scottish letters. *M.A. 1948 National University of Ireland*

O'Leary, M. A.
Monumenta vetera corcagiensia, being a survey of all antiquarian remains within and around the city of Cork. *M.A. 1931 National University of Ireland*

O'Leary, M. F. M.
Education with a tradition: an account of the educational work of the Society of the Sacred Heart, 1800-1935. *Ph.D. 1935 London, External Degree*

Oli, E. I.
The human geography of Nigeria in relation to physical aspects, with special reference to agriculture. *M.A. 1945 London, External Degree*

O'Lionnain, T. *see* Leonard, T.

Oliver, J. L.
An investigation into the efficacy of outdoor work in improving the attainment of training college students in, and their attitude towards, the subject of geography. *M.A. 1948 London, Institute of Education*

Oliver, R.
Psychological functions of leisure reading. *M.A. 1949 Manchester*

Oliver, R. A. C.
The application of psychological tests to certain problems of native education in East Africa. *Ph.D. 1933 Edinburgh*

Olphin, H. K.
George Tierney. *M.A. 1933 London, King's College*

Olsen, C. P. M.
The older settlements of north Northumberland: a study in geography and history. *M.A. 1947 London, University College*

Olson, H.
The new Hebrew Book of Enoch. *Ph.D. 1924 London*

Olszewska, E. S.
A history of the Scandinavian influence on the English language. *B.Litt. 1934 Oxford*

O'Luing, S.
Comparáid idir an *Pharsalia* agus an *Cath Cathardha*(*Pharsalia* and *Cath Cathardha* compared). *M.A. 1939 National University of Ireland*

O'Mahony, E.
The ideal of science. *M.A. 1919 National University of Ireland*

O'Mahony, J.
Gods and men; conceptions of a moral order in Aeschylus and Herodotus. *M.A. 1950 National University of Ireland*

O'Mahony, J. F.
The sea in English poetry. *M.A. 1942 National University of Ireland*

O'Mahony, M. A.
An outlook on agriculture and industry in post-war Eire. *M.Econ.Sc. 1945 National University of Ireland*

O'Mahony, M. M.
Poetry of the Victorian age as represented by Browning and Arnold. *M.A. 1942 National University of Ireland*

O'Mahony, T.
William Carleton, novelist; a study in Anglo-Irish literature. *M.A. 1934 National University of Ireland*

O'Maille, T. S. *see* Melia, T. S.

O'Maolchatha, P.
Sgéalta as *Leabhar Laighean*(Tales from the *Book of Leinster*). *M.A. 1936 National University of Ireland*

O'Maolchumaidh, M. U.
Critic liteardha ar saothar an Athar Peadar O'Laoghaire(A literary criticism of the work of Father Peadar O'Laoghaire). *M.A. 1931 National University of Ireland*

O'Maoldhomhnaigh, P. P.
Nua-litríocht na Gaedhilge agus cainnt na ndaoine(Modern Irish literature and popular expression). *M.A. 1943 National University of Ireland*

O'Maonaigh, C.
Smaointe beatha Chríost, i astriú gaedhilge a chuir Tomas Gruamdha O Bruacháin (fl. c.1450), ar an *Meditationes vitae Christi*(*Thoughts on the life of Christ*; an Irish translation by Tomás Gruamdha O Bruacháin (fl. c.1450) of *Meditaciones vitae Christi*). *M.A. 1941 National University of Ireland*

O'Mathghamhna, D.
Taighde ar na h-iolraidh atá le fagháil i saothar an Athar Pheadair(Research on the plural forms used in the work of Father Peadar). *M.A. 1944 National University of Ireland*

O'Mathghamhna, S.
Dánta as láimhscríbhinn i gColáiste Cholmáin, Mainistir Fhearmuighe(Poems from a manuscript in St. Colman's College, Fermoy). *M.A. 1939 National University of Ireland*

O'Meara, J. F. G.
A critical study of external examinations and of their influence on secondary education. *M.A. 1944 National University of Ireland*

O'Meara, J. J.
Prolegomena to the *Contra academicos* of St. Augustine. *D.Phil. 1945 Oxford*

O'Meara, P.
The rural bias and the rural primary school. *M.A. 1935 National University of Ireland*

O'Meara, T. J.
The correlation of history and geography in the primary schools. *M.A. 1936 National University of Ireland*

O'Morain, S. C.
Tráchtas ar Phádraig Mac Piarais(A thesis on Pádraig Mac Piarais). *M.A. 1931 National University of Ireland*

O'Mordha, M.
Meon agus tréithe na ndaoine sa nua-sgéalaidheacht(The mind and characteristics of the ordinary people in modern literature). *M.A. 1946 National University of Ireland*

O'Mordha, S.
Imtheachta Aenísa agus *Aeneis* Bhergil(The travels of Aeneas in Vergil's *Aeneid*). *M.A. 1939 National University of Ireland*

O'Murchadha, D. F.
Iarmbéarladha na Gaedhilge agus a dtionchur ar an ainm(Irish particles and their influence on the noun). *M.A. 1941 National University of Ireland*

O'Murchadha, T.
Micheál Og O'Longáin. *M.A. 1940 National University of Ireland*

O'Nealon, M. R.
Catholic continuity in English education. *M.A. 1933 National University of Ireland*

O'Neill, C. M.
Origins of Hellenistic king-worship. *M.A. 1927 National University of Ireland*

O'Neill, J.
A history of Corinth from the earliest times to the death of Alexander. *M.A. 1919 National University of Ireland*

O'Neill, J. P.
Employment trends in Saorstát Eireann. *M.A. 1937 National University of Ireland*

O'Neill, M. B.
The influence of Sir Byrom Bramwell on poliomyelitis. *M.D. 1949 Edinburgh*

O'Neill, T. P.
Organisation and administration of relief during the great famine. *M.A. 1946 National University of Ireland*

Ong, H. S.
Rice growing in British Malaya. *M.A. 1936 London, External Degree*

Onians, R. B.
Studies in primitive thought. *Ph.D. 1926 Cambridge*

O'Niatháin, P.
Log-Ainmneacha Barúntacht Uí Bhadhamhna agus an Bharraigh Ruaidh(The place names of the Baronies of Ibane and Barryroe). *M.A. 1942 National University of Ireland*

O'Nolan, M.
Alain-Fournier. *M.A. 1943 National University of Ireland*

O'Nuallain, D. *see* Nolan, D. P.

O'Nualláin, N. *see* Nolan, N. G.

Oppenheimer, H.
The constitution of the German Republic. *Ph.D. 1924 London*

Oppenheimer, H.
The criminal responsibility of lunatics: a study in comparative law. *LL.D. 1908 London*

Oppermann, C. J. A.
The Counter-Reformation in Sweden. *M.A. 1922 London*

Oppermann, C. J. A.
Sweden and the Papacy, 822-1248. *Ph.D. 1931 London, External Degree*

O'Raghallaigh, P. G.
Comhainmneacha, samhail-ainmneacha agus diúltadha Gaedhilge(Irish synonyms, homonyms and negatives). *M.A. 1947 National University of Ireland*

O'Raghallaigh, T. *see* Reilly, T.

O'Rahilly, C.
Inter-relations of Ireland and Wales as evidenced by the tradition, languages and literatures of both countries. *M.A. 1919 Wales*

Oram, H. C.
Industrial Revolution and the textile industries of Somerset. *M.A. 1930 Bristol*

Oras, H.
Milton's editors and commentators from Patrick Hume to Todd. *B.Litt. 1928 Oxford*

O'Rathaille, T.
Módh smaointe na Frainnce dá fhoillsiú 'sa Ghaedhilge: ó scríbhinní Fhenelon agus Iúles Bherne(French philosophy as illustrated in Irish, from the writings of Fénélon and Jules Verne). *M.A. 1933 National University of Ireland*

Orbaneja, A. Gomez *see* Gomez Orbaneja, A.

Orde, F.
The psychological conditions in two representative factories. *M.A. 1937 London, University College*

O'Reilly, J. L.
Educational principles in the practice of Don Bosco and his successors. *M.A. 1948 National University of Ireland*

Orgel, V. G.
André Spire. *Ph.D. 1942 Dublin, Trinity College*

O'Riáin, S.
Uimhreacha i saothar an ath. P. O'Laoghaire(Numbers as used in the work of Father Peadar O'Laoghaire). *M.A. 1939 National University of Ireland*

O'Riordáin, S. P. *see* Reardon, J. P.

O'Riordan, M.
Satirical poems of Thomas Moore. *M.A. 1946 National University of Ireland*

Orme, E. L.
Religious toleration in England in the years immediately following the Restoration. *M.A. 1918 Bristol*

Ormiston, M.
An enquiry into the bearing of general and special abilities upon scholastic success at the beginning and end of the secondary school career. *Ph.D. 1937 Leeds*

Ormsby, H. R.
The geography of France: regional and economic. *D.Sc. 1932 London, School of Economics and Political Science*

Orna, N. E.
The relation between theory and practice in Elizabethan and Jacobean comedy, 1570-1616. *M.A. 1948 London, University College*

O'Rónáin, C.
Drámaidheacht na scol(School dramatics). *M.A. 1938 National University of Ireland*

Orr, J.
The preparation of a critical edition of a thirteenth century French satirical poem *La Bible de Guiot de Provins*, with a linguistic and literary study and a glossary. *B.Litt. 1913 Oxford*

Orr, J. E.
A factual and analytical account of the religious awakening in the United Kingdom in the years 1855-65. *D.Phil. 1948 Oxford*

Orr, S. S.
Plato's theory of ethics as contained in the early dialogues. *M.A. 1942 Belfast*

Orrick, J. B.
Matthew Arnold as a critic. *B.Litt. 1927 Oxford*

Orrin, J. E. S.
A study of the changes in the geographical distribution of industry and population in England and Wales during the twentieth century. *M.A. 1932 Wales*

Orsman, M. E.
Some changes in the distribution of population in Brittany. *M.A. 1932 Wales*

Orton, H.
The living dialect of Byers Green. *B.Litt. 1924 Oxford*

Orton, W. A.
A survey of British industrial history, 1914-1921. *M.Sc. 1921 London*

O'Ruairc, A.
Psychological factors governing the education and culture of primitive peoples. *M.A. 1943 National University of Ireland*

Osborn, G. E.
The psychology of Christian public worship: a study in the more practical aspects of some of the typical liturgies and worships of Western Christianity. *Ph.D. 1935 Edinburgh*

Osborn, J. M.
Dryden: the biographies before 1900. *B.Litt. 1937 Oxford*

Osborn, R. R.
The political importance of English Protestant nonconformity, 1673-88. *B. Litt. 1937 Oxford*

Osborne, F. M.
The work of religious societies in English education, 1660-1870. *M.A. 1925 London*

Osburn, A. C.
The psychological roots of war. *B.Litt. 1938 Oxford*

O'Scannláin, R. A.
Eachtra Chonaill Ghulban(The adventures of Conall Gulban). *M.A. 1941 National University of Ireland*

Oschinsky, D.
English manorial accountancy in the thirteenth and early fourteenth centuries, with special reference to the didactic treatises on the subject. *M.A. 1942 London, School of Economics and Political Science*

O'Shea, A. B.
Andrew Marvell (1621-78); an interpretation. *M.A. 1950 National University of Ireland*

O'Shea, J.
Psychology of Plato. *M.A. 1915 National University of Ireland*

O'Shea, K.
Vives and aspects of renaissance education. *M.A. 1926 National University of Ireland*

O'Shea, M.
The homocentric attitude of Swift's writings. *M.A. 1935 National University of Ireland*

O'Shea, M. A.
English poetry and war. *M.A. 1931 National University of Ireland*

O'Sléibhín, T.
Tógáil Troí(The taking of Troy). *M.A. 1949 National University of Ireland*

Osley, A. S.
Plutarch's *Life of Crassus*: with historical commentary. *Ph.D. 1942 London, External Degree*

O'Spolláin, M. A.
Seanmóirí na Gaeilge(Irish sermons). *M.A. 1948 National University of Ireland*

Ostick, E.
The influence of Ibsen's theatre in both its range and quality on English drama. *M.A. 1928 Bristol*

O'Suilleabháin, P. *see* O'Sullivan, P.

O'Sullivan, D.
In defence of the farmer. *Ph.D. 1947 National University of Ireland*

O'Sullivan, H.
A commentary on Racine's *Andromaque*: a study of vocabulary, syntax, style. *M.A. 1945 Manchester*

O'Sullivan, M. J. D.
Old Galway: history of an English colony in Ireland. *D.Litt. 1943 National University of Ireland*

O'Sullivan, P.
Lucerna Fidelium le Froinsias O'Maolmhuaidh(*Lucerna Fidelium* by Froinsias O'Maolmhuaidh). *M.A. 1944 National University of Ireland*

O'Sullivan, T. M.
The financing of industry in Ireland, excluding the six counties of N.I. *M.Econ.Sci. 1947 National University of Ireland*

O'Sullivan, W.
An economic history of Cork City to 1800. *M.A. 1936 National University of Ireland*

Oswald Edwards, T. D. *see* Edwards, T. D. O.

Oswin, G. M.
A study of Randolph's *Amyntas* and its relation to contemporary pastoral drama. *B.Litt. 1941 Oxford*

O'Tatháin, M. R.
Amhráin is dánta Dhaibhí de Barra(Songs and poems of Daibhí de Barra). *M.A. 1932 National University of Ireland*

O'Tierney, F. J.
Teaching of modern languages (with special reference to Irish) in primary schools. *M.A. 1913 National University of Ireland*

O'Tierney, R.
Duanta Eoghain Uí Dhonnghaile agus duanta eile ó indé(The poems of Eoghan O'Donnghaile and other poems of yesterday). *M.A. 1937 National University of Ireland*

O'Tighearnaigh, R. *see* O'Tierney, R.

Ottaway, A. K. C.
An experimental study of the biological interests of school children. *M.A. 1935 London, Institute of Education*

Otter, M. E.
Types of land use in Caernarvonshire. *M.A. 1945 Liverpool*

Otter, R. J.
An analysis of the correlations between results of mathematical tests compiled according to the principles of Gestalt psychology and a teacher's estimate of mathematical ability in school children. *M.A. 1949 London, Institute of Education*

Otter, W. H.
Higher education: its organization, administration and finance, with special reference to the county borough of Bootle. *M.A. 1936 Liverpool*

Ottley, R.
The style and syntax of the *Historia ecclesiastica* of Bede. *M.A. 1935 London, Queen Mary College*

O'Tuama, S.
Dánta droch-shaoil (1800-1845)(Poems of the hard life, 1800-1845). *M.A. 1931 National University of Ireland*

Otway-Ruthven, A. J.
The King's Secretary and the Signet Office in the fifteenth century. *Ph.D. 1937 Cambridge*

Ough, C. J.
East Anglican church architecture of the fourteenth anf fifteenth centuries, with special reference to the churches of the Stour Valley. *M.A. 1939 London, King's College*

Oung, M. S. May- *see* May-Oung, M. S.

Ouseley, M. H.
A study of the reactions of older children to air-raid conditions in 1940-41. *M.A. 1948 London, Institute of Education*

Outram, A. E.
Some conventions of Elizabethan drama. *D.Phil. 1939 Oxford*

Overington, S.
An organization for the senior school and its influence upon curricula. *M.A. 1942 Sheffield*

Overstreet, H. A.
The relation of thought to reality. *B.Sc. 1901 Oxford*

Owen, A.
Attempts made before the sixteenth century to improve the speaking and writing of the French language in England. *M.A. 1921 Wales*

Owen, A. D. K.
Problems of juvenile employment. *M.Com. 1929 Leeds*

Owen, A. T.
Parthia and her relations with Rome from 27 B.C. to A.D. 228. *M.A. 1920 Wales*

Owen, C. A.
Thomas Killigrew: critical study. *B.Litt. 1939 Oxford*

Owen, D. E. T.
Composition as mental and aesthetic training. *M.Ed. 1919 Manchester*

Owen, D. L.
A comparison of *Piers Plowman* with some earlier and contemporary French allegories. *M.A. 1909 London*

Owen, D. M.
1. Holy Scripture: the rule of faith. 2. 'I believe in one God'. *B.D. 1877 Oxford*

Owen, E. H.
Bywyd a gwaith Dr. Owen Owen Roberts, 1793-1866(Life and work of Dr. Owen Owen Roberts, 1793-1866). *M.A. 1939 Wales*

Owen, G.
History of the town and castle of Cardigan. *M.A. 1907 Wales*

Owen, G. D.
Agrarian conditions and changes in west Wales during the sixteenth century, with special reference to monastic and chantry lands. *Ph.D. 1935 Wales*

Owen, H.
The law of Wales and the Marches as connected with the history of English law. *D.C.L. 1900 Oxford*

Owen, J.
The relations of science to philosophy, with special reference to the conceptions of substance and causation. *M.A. 1908 Wales*

Owen, J. T.
Gwallter Mechain: ei hanes, ei waith a'i safonau beirniadol(Gwallter Mechain; his life story, his work, and his standards of criticism). *M.A. 1928 Wales*

Owen, L.
Feudal law in the *chansons de geste. M.A. 1914 Wales*

Owen, L.
1. The history of Old Testament prophecy. 2. The study of the Psalms. *B.D. 1924 Oxford*

Owen, L.
The Russian peasant movement, 1906-1917. *Ph.D. 1933 London, King's College*

Owen, M. B.
Justin Martyr and his witness to the beliefs, practice and sufferings of the Christians of his day. *M.A. 1941 Wales*

Owen, M. G.
Studies in the language of Robert Smith Surtees (1805-1864). *M.A. 1939 Liverpool*

Owen, R. G.
Brwydr y 'Ddau Gyfansoddiad', 1877-1885(The conflict of the 'Two Constitutions', 1877-1885). *M.A. 1941 Wales*

Owen, R. H.
The public life of John, 4th Duke of Bedford (1710-1771). *M.A. 1923 Wales*

Owen, T. J.
The educational and literary work of Griffith Jones, Llanddowror. *M.A. 1923 Wales*

Owen, W.
The dualism of practical reason. *M.A. 1915 Wales*

Owen, W. J.
The present position of the discussion concerning formal training. *M.A. 1920 Wales*

Owen, W. T.
Expressionist drama in modern Germany. *M.A. 1931 Wales*

Owens, O.
Gweithiau barddonol Morus Dwyfech(The poetic works of Morus Dwyfech). *M.A. 1944 Wales*

Owst, G. R.
Medieval preaching in England as illustrated by the period c.1350 to 1450. *Ph.D. 1924 London*

Owthwaite, A. H.
A critical survey of commercial and technical education in England and Wales. *M.A. 1945 Sheffield*

Oxenham, F. N.
1. The Athanasian Creed consonant with the word of God. 2. The true doctrine of election involves no injustice. *B.D. & D.D. 1896 Oxford*

Oxley, J. E.
The dialect of Lindsey. *M.A. 1934 London, King's College*

Oxley, J. E.
English political satire, 1800-1830. *Ph.D. 1941 London, Birkbeck College*

Pacey, W. C. D.
A study of the reception of French realistic fiction in Victorian England and of its influence upon the English novel. *Ph.D. 1941 Cambridge*

Pachauri, A. R.
A study of the Gestalten problem concerning completed and uncompleted test-items. *Ph.D. 1934 London, University College*

Packer, P. W.
Guy de Maupassant's works in England. *Ph.D. 1946 London, Birkbeck College*

Padfield, W.
Les mots dialectaux dans la littérature française contemporaine. *M.A. 1921 Liverpool*

Padgett, W. W.
Étude sur le vocabulaire du *Voyage en Espagne* de Théophile Gautier. *M.A. 1924 Leeds*

Pafford, J. H. P.
Kynge Johan re-edited, with a study of the language of Bale in appendix. *M.A. 1929 London*

Page, A.
Women in ancient comedy. *M.A. 1947 Manchester*

Page, A. G. D.
Philarète Chasles and his connection with England. *M.A. 1931 London, East London College*

Page, A. H.
Ekkehard's *Waltharius. M.A. 1932 London, Bedford College*

Page, B. S.
The life and philosophy of Numenius. *M.A. 1926 Birmingham*

Page, F.
Lexique des premiers poètes romantiques, 1820-1830. *M.A. 1914 London*

Page, F. M.
The organization of the manor, with reference to the estates of Crowland Abbey. *Ph.D. 1930 Cambridge*

Page, H. H.
Movements for Anglo-Russian reconciliation and alliance from March 1890 to December 1903. *M.A. 1933 Birmingham*

Page, N. M. G.
A study of emigration from Great Britain, 1802 to 1860. *Ph.D. 1931 London, School of Economics and Political Science*

Painter, W. A.
Medieval philosophy and the approach to modern thought. *Ph.D. 1929 Bristol*

Pak, C. W.
A comparative study of the family law in the Chinese and English legal systems. *Ph.D. 1940 London, King's College*

Pakey, C.
The theory and practice of Chinese democracy. *Ph.D. 1939 London, School of Economics and Political Science*

Palca, J.
A regional analysis of English milk production. *M.Sc. 1944 London, School of Economics and Political Science*

Pallot, E. C.
The ideas of incarnation in the non-Christian religions, and the Christian doctrine of the incarnation. *Ph.D. 1938 London, Richmond College*

Palmer, A. E.
Aeschines as a statesman. *M.A. 1921 Birmingham*

Palmer, E. M.
The Italian element in Vergil's mythology. *M.A. 1929 Manchester*

Palmer, J. J. E.
Literary patronage in the time of Dryden. *B.Litt. 1940 Oxford*

Palmer, L. R.
The language of the non-literary papyri of the first four centuries. *Ph.D. 1933 Cambridge*

Palmer, M.
A comparative study of the war poetry of Siegfried Sassoon and Wilfred Owen. *M.A. 1950 Manchester*

Palmer, M. S.
The position of women in ancient Egypt. *M.A. 1929 Manchester*

Palmer, M. S.
A study of shabti-figures, with special reference to the Manchester collection. *Ph.D. 1945 Manchester*

Palmer, W. C.
The activities of the English East India Company in Persia and the Persian Gulf, 1616-57. *Ph.D. 1933 London, King's College*

Palmer, W. C.
The history of St. Helena and the route to the Indies, 1659-1702. *M.A. 1924 London*

Palser, E. M.
Henry Brooke, 1703-1783. *M.A. 1907 London*

Palsson, S. L.
The journal (Sept. 1st-Oct. 10th, 1807) of the Icelander, Magnus Stephensen: a newly-discovered manuscript, edited with translation, notes, glossary and appendices. *M.A. 1947 Leeds*

Paluello, L. Minio- *see* Minio-Paluello, L.

Pan, Y.
The relation of feeling and conation, with special reference to the hedonic and hormic theories. *Ph.D. 1930 London, University College*

Panandikar, S. G.
The problem of time. *M.Litt. 1931 Cambridge*

Panandikar, S. G.
1. Some aspects of the economic consequences of the war for India. 2. The wealth and welfare of the Bengal Delta. *Ph.D. 1921 London*

Panandikar, S. G.
The wealth and welfare of the Bengal delta. *D.Sc. 1926 London*

Pandalai, K. K.
Succession and partition in Marumakkatayam law. *LL.D. 1914 London*

Pandit, B. S.
An edition with translation, grammatical study, and glossary of a text *Nala-ki bata. Ph.D. 1933 London, School of Oriental and African Studies*

Pandit, P. B.
Selections from *Sadavasyaka vrtti* of Tarunaprabha, critically edited: a study of the Gujrati language in the fourteenth century A.D. *Ph.D. 1949 London, School of Oriental and African Studies*

Pannett, D. A.
A comparison of girls' junior technical schools in London and Paris. *M.A. 1939 London, King's College*

Panton, J. H.
The assessment of teaching ability with special reference to men students in training. *M.A. 1934 London, Institute of Education*

Pao, K. Y.
The public accounts and statistical returns of English railways. *M.Com. 1912 Birmingham*

Pao, P. Y.
Deconcentration and decentralisation in modern local government. *Ph.D. 1937 London, School of Economics and Political Science*

Papaioannou, J. G. Zighdis- *see* Zighdis-Papaioannou, J. G.

Papali, G. F.
The life and work of Jacob Tonson. *Ph.D. 1934 London, University College*

Papenfus, E. M.
Les théories dramatiques de Francisque Sarcey. *Ph.D. 1926 London*

Papperovitch, R.
Horace Walpole as reflective of the literary tastes and tendencies of the eighteenth century. *M.A. 1926 Liverpool*

Parasher, S. C.
The development of the Indian civil service. *M.Sc. 1947 London, School of Economics and Political Science*

Pardoe, D.
A survey of the early work on the diffraction of light. *M.Sc. 1946 London, External Degree*

Parfitt, H. G.
An examination of certain prose rhythms as used in the works of Lyly, Browne, Milton, Lamb and Shaw. *M.A. 1940 Wales*

Pargeter, H. J.
Woman versus man: a study of the relationships and differences between the sexes as a source of tragedy in the life and chief dramas of F. Hebbel. *M.A. 1950 Birmingham*

Pargeter, P. S.
The treatment of village life in the first four collections of Berthold Auerbach's *Schwarzwälder Dorfgeschichten. M.A. 1947 Birmingham*

Paris, H. J.
The Rev. William Gilpin and the cult of the picturesque. *B.Litt. 1938 Oxford*

Parish, E. L.
A critical text of the C-text of *Piers Plowman*, passus 9 and 10. *M.A. 1933 London, University College*

Park, J. T.
Charles Yorke, 1764-1770: an analysis of his private and political correspondence as contained in the Hardwicke mss. *M.A. 1949 Manchester*

Parke, H. W.
The second Spartan Empire, 405-379 B.C. *Litt.D. 1933 Dublin, Trinity College*

Parker, B. N.
Politics in the novels of Honoré de Balzac. *M.A. 1929 London*

Parker, D. O.
Political movements in the West Riding, 1815-32. *M.A. 1923 Manchester*

Parker, E.
A study of John Dyer, in the light of new manuscript material. *B.Litt. 1938 Oxford*

Parker, E. A.
Garcilaso de la Vega. *B.Litt. 1922 Oxford*

Parker, E. A.
The treatment of friendship by Schiller and Shakespeare. *M.A. 1911 Birmingham*

Parker, G.
Herder's relationship to German romanticism, with special reference to the theory of literary criticism. *D.Phil. 1939 Oxford*

Parker, H. H.
The hop industry. *Ph.D. 1933 London, External Degree*

Parker, L. A.
Enclosure in Leicestershire, 1485-1607. *M.A. 1948 London, External Degree*

Parker, M.
Social and political aspects of the development of municipal government in Kenya, with special reference to Nairobi. *Ph.D. 1949 London, School of Economics and Political Science*

Parker, M. V. H.
Shakespeare and the idea of justice. *B.Litt. 1950 Oxford*

Parker, P.
Joseph Warton. *B.Litt. 1929 Oxford*

Parker, W. A.
The Bishops and the poor law, 1782-1834. *M.A. 1939 Manchester*

Parker, W. G.
A psychological estimate of evangelical experience. *Ph.D. 1948 London, Richmond College*

Parker, W. H.
The influence of physical geography upon the history of settlement and distribution of population in Sussex. *B.Sc. 1939 Oxford*

Parker, W. R.
A critical study of Milton's *Samson Agonistes*. *B.Litt. 1934 Oxford*

Parkes, H. E.
Cost accounts in the metal industry. *M.Com. 1920 Birmingham*

Parkes, J. W.
The religious element in anti-Semitism up to the time of Charlemagne in the West and Leo the Isaurian in the East. *D.Phil. 1934 Oxford*

Parkes, M. M. *see* Holt, M. M.

Parkinson, C. N.
Trade and war in the eastern seas, 1803-1810. *Ph.D. 1935 London, King's College*

Parkinson, J. W.
The central school and its place in English education. *M.Ed. 1920 Manchester*

Parks, W. A.
An analytical survey of the influence of the development of chemical theory during the nineteenth century upon the evolution of chemical industry, with special reference to East London. *M.Sc. 1950 London, West Ham Municipal College*

Parrinder, E. G. S.
West African religion, illustrated from the beliefs and practices of the Yoruba, Ewe, Akan and kindred peoples. *Ph.D. 1946 London, External Degree*

Parrish, W. J.
A survey of the history of science teaching in English schools since 1870. *M.Sc. 1926 London*

Parry, A. W.
Education in England in the middle ages. *D.Sc. 1919 London*

Parry, A. W.
An investigation into the extent to which a social conception of education is to be found in the works of English writers of the eighteenth and nineteenth centuries. *M.A. 1911 Wales*

Parry, B. M.
The political importance of Dr. Price. *M.A. 1934 Liverpool*

Parry, D.
The development of the regional novel since Hardy, being an appreciation of its technique and a study of its exponents from Thomas Hardy to the present day, with especial reference to Arnold Bennett, Eden Phillpotts, Sheila Kaye-Smith and Mary Webb. *M.A. 1932 Wales*

Parry, E.
Chinese ethics. *M.A. 1943 Leeds*

Parry, E.
Chinese religion: an approach through the Hakka Chinese dictionary. *B.D. 1940 Leeds*

Parry, E. D.
Stephen Langton as a defender of English liberty. *M.A. 1923 Wales*

Parry, E. J.
British policy and the Spanish marriages, 1841-1846. *Ph.D. 1934 London, School of Economics and Political Science*

Parry, E. J.
The diplomatic relations between England and France from 1898 to June 1905: the policy of M. Delcassé and the making of the Anglo-French *Entente*. *M.A. 1932 Wales*

Parry, E. O.
Flint: the castle and town in the thirteenth and fourteenth centuries. *M.A. 1927 Wales*

Parry, H. J.
Athrawiaeth y 'kenosis' mewn diwinyddiarth Gymraeg (Phil. ii, 5-8)(The doctrine of the 'kenosis' in Welsh theology (Phil. ii, 5-8)). *M.A. 1938 Wales*

Parry, J. B.
The rôle of attention in aesthetic experience. *Ph.D. 1940 London, University College*

Parry, J. E.
A critical exegesis of the concept of freedom in the educational systems of Pestalozzi and Herbart. *B.Litt. 1928 Oxford*

Parry, J. E.
Plato's doctrine of personal immortality. *M.A. 1918 Wales*

Parry, J. H.
The audiencia of New Galicia in the sixteenth century: a study in Spanish colonial government. *Ph.D. 1939 Cambridge*

Parry, J. P.
William Blake and the religious background of his writings. *M.A. 1947 Liverpool*

Parry, N. O.
Quintilian's theory of education. *M.A. 1919 Wales*

Parry, O.
The parliamentary representation of Wales and Monmouthshire during the nineteenth century, but mainly until 1870. *M.A. 1924 Wales*

Parry, R. I.
The attitude of the Welsh Independents towards working class movements, including public education, from 1815 to 1870. *M.A. 1931 Wales*

Parry, R. J.
The British attitude to the second Hague Conference: a study of newspaper opinion in England, 1906-7. *M.A. 1937 Wales*

Parry, R. St. J. *see* St. John Parry, R.

Parry, R. W.
Some points of contact between Welsh and Breton. *M.A. 1912 Wales*

Parry, T.
Bywyd a gwaith y Dr. Siôn Dafydd Rhys(The life and work of Dr. John David Rhys). *M.A. 1929 Wales*

Parry, W. D.
Literary criticism in the age of Pope. *M.A. 1919 Wales*

Parry, W. H.
Mathematical education. *M.A. 1912 National University of Ireland*

Parry-Williams, T. H.
Loan words in Welsh. *B.Litt. 1911 Oxford*

Parshad, J. D.
Some aspects of Indian foreign trade, 1757-1893. *Ph.D. 1928 London*

Parsloe, C. G.
The minute book of the Bedford Corporation, 1647-1664. *M.A. 1949 London, University College*

Parslow, L. C.
The factors contributing to successful mathematical attainment in boys and girls of a secondary school. *M.A. 1942 London, Institute of Education*

Parsons, A. E.
(a) The origin and development of the heroic poem in England, with some account of its relationship to the heroic romance and the heroic play; (b) The Trojan legend in England. *D.Litt. 1932 London, External Degree*

Parsons, A. E.
Some aspects of the life and literary work of William Chamberlayne of Shaftesbury, 1619-1689. *Ph.D. 1924 London*

Parsons, D. M.
Christina Rossetti: the imagery in her English poetry. *M.A. 1948 London, King's College*

Parsons, E.
Religious and philosophical ideas reflected in the novel, 1870 to 1900. *Ph.D. 1936 London, External Degree*

Parsons, E.
The tragic aspect of life, as presented by T. Hardy. *M.A. 1932 Birmingham*

Parsons, E. J. S.
The proclamations issued by Charles I during the years 1642-6, both during his progress to Oxford and his residence there until the surrender of the city in 1646, relating especially to Oxford and neighbouring counties. *B.Litt. 1935 Oxford*

Parsons, H. R.
Anglo-Norman books of courtesy and nurture. *B.Litt. 1927 Oxford*

Parsons, L.
Studies in the life and works of Joshua Sylvester (1564-1618). *M.A. 1948 London, Westfield College*

Parsons, R. G.
1. The character and composition of the fourth Gospel. 2. The origin and authorship of the fourth Gospel. *B.D. & D.D. 1924 Oxford*

Partridge, E. H.
The evidence of contemporary French memoirs, letters and periodicals with regard to the influence of English literature. *B.Litt. 1924 Oxford*

Paruleker, R. V.
The problem of education in the Bombay Presidency, with special reference to higher education. *M.Ed. 1924 Leeds*

Parvathi, N. I.
The school curriculum in relation to life. *M.A. 1934 Leeds*

Pascoe, F. L.
A comparison of the aims, conditions and methods of teaching French to the child and the adult, with special reference to secondary schools and London senior commercial institutes. *M.A. 1929 London*

Pask, A. H. S.
The influence of Arminius upon the theology of John Wesley. *Ph.D. 1940 Edinburgh*

Pasricha, B. R.
A study of vocational wishes of a group of secondary school pupils in relation to their interests, scholastic attainments and attitudes. *M.A. 1949 London, Institute of Education*

Pasricha, H. L.
A study of agricultural co-operation in India based upon foreign experience. *Ph.D. 1931 London, School of Economics and Political Science*

Passé, H. A.
The English language in Ceylon. *Ph.D. 1948 London, External Degree*

Passey, W. E.
Houses of correction in England and Wales. *M.A. 1936 Liverpool*

Passey, W. E.
The principles of the treatment of ex-service men from the time of Elizabeth. *Dip.Soc.Sci. 1924 Liverpool*

Pastor, A. R.
The theology of Plotinus. *B.Litt. 1920 Oxford*

Pate, V. S.
The educational value of self-government in a youth club. *M.A. 1948 Birmingham*

Patel, A. M.
The industrial geography of the United Provinces of Agra and Oudh. *M.A. 1948 London, University College*

Patel, I. G.
Studies in economic development and international trade. *Ph.D. 1950 Cambridge*

Patel, M. A. M.
Provincial autonomy of Bombay. *M.Sc. 1947 London, School of Economics and Political Science*

Paterson, A. C.
Practical estimation of pupil's progress in secondary schools. *Ph.D. 1928 Glasgow*

Paterson, A. R.
Educational aspects of the Romantic Movement in Britain. *Ph.D. 1941 Glasgow*

Paterson, J.
History of Newfoundland, 1713-1763. *M.A. 1931 London, King's College*

Paterson, J.
Marriage law and ceremonial in the Code of Hammarapi. *Ph.D. 1929 Glasgow*

Patnaik, B. M.
Evolution of the proprietary status of woman under the common law of the Hindus with special reference to the quantum of interest in immovable property acquired by way of inheritance and partition. *LL.M. 1948 London, School of Economics and Political Science*

Paton, M. O. Noël- *see* Noël-Paton, M. O.

Paton, R.
Evolution and the Christian doctrine of human worth: a vindication of human values from the standpoint of biology, anthropology and psychology. *Ph.D. 1931 Edinburgh*

Paton, S. H.
A study of Alsace at the present time, with particular reference to its cultural history and conditions. *B.Litt. 1936 Oxford*

Patourel, J. H. le *see* Le Patourel, J. H.

Patrick, D. G. M.
Christianity on the offensive: a study in the task and method of Christian apologetics, with special reference to the work of Blaise Pascal and Søren Kierkegaard. *Ph.D. 1943 Edinburgh*

Patrick, J. M.
The careers and opinions of Hugh Peters and Sir Henry Vane the Younger. *B.Litt. 1936 Oxford*

Patrinacos, N.
The nature of sex: a study of the metaphysical and moral character of sex. *D.Phil. 1950 Oxford*

Patterson, G.
The earlier poetic method of T. S. Eliot and its background. *M.Litt. 1937 Dublin, Trinity College*

Patterson, R. F.
Ben Jonson's conversations with William Drummond of Hawthornden. *D.Litt. 1922 Glasgow*

Patterson, R. L.
Man's knowledge of God as treated by St. Thomas Aquinas. *Ph.D. 1933 London, University College*

Pattinson, D. H.
The reception of the American constitution in Britain, 1787-1848. *M.A. 1941 Birmingham*

Pattison, B.
Music and poetry in the sixteenth century. *Ph.D. 1934 Cambridge*

Pattison, J. S.
The economics of Henry Dunning MacLeod. *Ph.D. 1940 London, School of Economics and Political Science*

Patton, J. V.
Christianity and education in the first five centuries A.D. *B.Litt. 1916 Oxford*

Patton, M. W.
William Hazlitt. *M.A. 1937 National University of Ireland*

Patton, S.
De Quincey. *M.A. 1943 National University of Ireland*

Paul, B. C.
The development of marriage in ancient India. *Ph.D. 1949 London, School of Oriental and African Studies*

Paul, J. D. S.
Mining in the Lake counties in the sixteenth century. *Ph.D. 1926 London*

Paul, R. S.
Oliver Cromwell's view of his political mission in the light of his theological and ecclesiastical presuppositions. . *D.Phil. 1949 Oxford*

Paulden, M. O.
The Hebrew conquest of Canaan. *M.A. 1931 Liverpool*

Paulin, L. V.
John Rich and the eighteenth century stage. *M.A. 1936 London, University College*

Pavlovitch, V.
St. Basil's conception of Christian monasticism. *B.Litt. 1922 Oxford*

Pavlovsky, G. A.
The economics of Russian farming, with particular reference to the years 1900-1916. *Ph.D. 1929 London*

Pawley, G. C.
A factorial analysis of the abilities involved in the learning of school chemistry. *M.A. 1937 London, Institute of Education*

Payling, L. W. H.
The place-names of Holland, south-east Lincolnshire. *Ph.D. 1940 London, University College*

Payling, L. W. H.
The place-names of Kesteven. *M.A. 1936 Leeds*

Paylor, W. J.
An edition of the *Characters* of Sir Thomas Overbury. *B.Litt. 1933 Oxford*

Payne, C. H. W.
The administration of and succession to estates in the Straits Settlements. *LL.D. 1932 London, External Degree*

Payne, C. I.
The British attitude towards the American Civil War. *M.A. 1928 Birmingham*

Payne, E. A.
The Saktas of Bengal. *B.Litt. 1927 Oxford*

Payne, E. M.
The problem of listening to music. *M.A. 1933 Bristol*

Payne, E. O.
Property in land in south Bedforshire, with special reference to the land tax assessments, 1750-1832. *Ph.D. 1939 London, School of Economics and Political Science*

Payne, E. R.
The agricultural geography of the East Midlands-Market Harborough-Rugby area. *M.Sc. 1945 Wales*

Payne, F. W.
The dramatic works of Roger Boyle, Earl of Orrery, with special reference to the rise of the heroic tragedy, including an annotated text of the unprinted *Zoroastres*. *M.A. 1923 London*

Payne, F. W.
Staging in the Restoration: with special reference to stage directions in the plays of the time. *Ph.D. 1926 London*

Payne, R. C.
Agrarian conditions on the Wiltshire estates of the Duchy of Lancaster, the Lords Hungerford and the Bishopric of Winchester in the thirteenth, fourteenth and fifteenth centuries. *Ph.D. 1940 London, School of Economics and Political Science*

Paynter, A. M.
The origin and development of the English prose essay to the making of the *Tatler*. *M.A. 1910 London*

Pe, H.
Konmara Pya Zat, by U Pok Ni, edited with introduction, translation and commentary. *Ph.D. 1944 London, School of Oriental and African Studies*

Peace, F. G.
Robert Eyres Landor. *M.A. 1931 Leeds*

Peach, L. du G.
A study in the dramatic relationships of France, Spain and England in the seventeenth century. *Ph.D. 1921 Sheffield*

Peacock, R.
The Great War in German lyrical poetry, 1914-18. *M.A. 1930 Leeds*

Peake, L. S.
Theology in the English poets of the Victorian era. *B.Litt. 1926 Oxford*

Peake, M. I.
London and the Wars of the Roses, 1445-1461. *M.A. 1925 London*

Pearce, A.
Certain adverbial usages in Chaucer. *M.A. 1928 Manchester*

Pearce, G. J. M.
Some aspects of modern theism. *M.A. 1946 Birmingham*

Pearce, J.
An economic survey of the management and utilization of grassland in Great Britain. *Ph.D. 1950 Reading*

Pearmain, H. F.
Horsham and its functions, local and regional: past, present and future. *M.A. 1944 London, Birkbeck College*

Pearn, B. R.
The Ionian Islands under the administration of Sir Thomas Maitland, 1816-1824. *M.A. 1924 London*

Pearn, F. E.
A booke yntytuled *Of goode maneres*. *M.A. 1914 London*

Pearson, A.
An investigation of mental abilities by means of non-verbal auditory material. *M.Ed. 1944 Leeds*

Pearson, E.
The economic development of the Erewash Valley: a study in economic geography. *M.Sc. 1936 London, External Degree*

Pearson, F. J.
The influence of chemical theory upon chemical nomenclature and symbolism from the period of Lavoisier to that of Laurent. *M.Sc. 1929 London*

Pearson, H. D.
The clergyman, the schoolmaster and the governess in the novel of the eighteenth century. *M.A. 1920 London*

Pearson, L. S.
Continuation and technical education in the Irish Free State. *M.A. 1932 London, King's College*

Pearson, W. W.
The theory of evolution in science, ethics and religion, with special reference to its teleological nature, tracing the development of the theory in question from Lamarck to our own day. *B.Sc. 1907 Oxford*

Peaston, A. E.
The use of liturgical orders of service in the worship of the so-called Presbyterian Dissenters. *B.Litt. 1936 Oxford*

Peate, I. C.
The Dyfi: its people, antiquities, dialects, folklore and placenames studied in correlation to one another, with a special aim of ascertaining what degree of correlation there may be between physical anthropology, archaeology and dialect distribution. *M.A. 1924 Wales*

Peate, I. C.
The Welsh house: a study in folk culture, and other papers. *D.Sc. 1941 Wales*

Peaty, M. J.
Percy's *Reliques* and its influence. *M.A. 1914 Birmingham*

Peck, A. L.
Pseudo-Hippocrates philosophus. *Ph.D. 1929 Cambridge*

Peck, D. R.
Some studies in the history of ideas on the discontinuity of matter and energy. *M.Sc. 1946 London, External Degree*

Peck, L. D. F.
The course of public opinion and legal decision, including legislation, relating to economic combination and monopoly, mainly in Great Britain, in the period 1880-1914. *M.A. 1929 Wales*

Peck, W. E.
The life of Percy Bysshe Shelley, 1792-1818. *D.Phil. 1922 Oxford*

Pecker, G. F.
Parliament and the affairs of the East India Company, 1765-1784. *M.A. 1910 Liverpool*

Peddie, J. R.
The Scottish universities, 1826-1906. *D.Litt. 1927 Glasgow*

Pedley, R.
Brigantes: a study in the early history of the northern Pennines. *Ph.D. 1939 Durham*

Pedley, W. H.
Labour on the land since 1920. *B.Litt. 1940 Oxford*

Peel, A.
Puritanism and its Presbyterian development in the time of Elizabeth. *B.Litt. 1912 Oxford*

Peel, E. A.
An analysis of the factors underlying the process of observation. *M.A. 1938 London, Institute of Education*

Peel, E. A.
A statistical study of the preference of a group of children and adults as shown by certain tests of aesthetic appreciation. *Ph.D. 1945 London, Institute of Education*

Peers, E. A.
The beginnings of French prose fiction. *M.A. 1915 London*

Peers, H.
Syncope and apocope in Old English. *M.A. 1932 Leeds*

Peet, R. M.
Problems of land tenure in modern Africa. *M.Sc. 1948 London, School of Economics and Political Science*

Peggs, A. D.
A history of Bahamian education. *M.Ed. 1947 Durham*

Pei, H. C.
Anglo-Chinese diplomatic relations. *Ph.D. 1939 London, School of Economics and Political Science*

Pelan, M. M.
Floire et Blancheflor. *Ph.D. 1937 Belfast*

Pelham, R. A.
The economic geography of Sussex during the fourteenth century, with special reference to the county's relations with lands across the sea. *M.A. 1930 Wales*

Pellizzi, C.
Le lettere italiane del nostro secolo. *D.Litt. 1932 London, University College*

345

Pells, E. G.
The English elementary school considered as an agent of social transformation, 1870-1918. *B.Litt. 1928 Oxford*

Pendlebury, B. J.
Dryden's heroic plays. *M.A. 1921 Birmingham*

Pendleton, E. B.
Affinities and differences between Giovanni Pascoli and English and French poets: English and French inspiration in his poetry. *M.A. 1947 London, Bedford College and London, Birkbeck College*

Pendleton, J. W.
The prose works of John Hall of Durham. *B.Litt. 1934 Oxford*

Penn, C. D.
The navy under the early Stuarts and its influence on English history. *M.A. 1913 London*

Penn, L. P.
Ethical monotheism in Israel before Amos. *B.D. & D.D. 1924 Oxford*

Pennington, A.
A study of leisure-time interests. *M.Ed. 1950 Durham*

Penny, H. H.
An analysis of current views of the nature of intelligence. *Ph.D. 1935 London, Institute of Education*

Penny, J. M. F.
Domestic furniture and utensils of the Han period. *M.A. 1941 London, Courtauld Institute of Art*

Penrose, C.
Soviet agriculture. *M.Sc. 1946 London, School of Economics and Political Science and London, External Degree*

Penson, L. M.
The colonial agents of the British West India Islands from the first appointment to the close of the eighteenth century. *Ph.D. 1921 London*

Pentreath, A. G.
1. The communion of saints. 2. The Athanasian Creed. *B.D. 1897 Oxford*

Pentreath, A. G.
Expositions of: Isaiah liii; The Book of the Prophet Jonah; I Peter iii.18-20. *D.D. 1901 Oxford*

Pentreath, F. R.
1. The creeds: their origin and value. 2. The intermediate state. *B.D. 1874 Oxford*

Pentreath, F. R.
Exegeses of: St. John vii.17; II Peter i.21; Romans iii.21-26. *D.D. 1878 Oxford*

Percival, G.
Φιλία: an edition of Aristotle, *Nicomachean Ethics*, VIII and IX. *Ph.D. 1938 Cambridge*

Percival, S. W.
Charles Dickens and Charles Kingsley as social critics. *M.A. 1947 Manchester*

Percival, W.
The historians of the French Revolution prior to 1823. *M.A. 1929 Manchester*

Pereira-Mendoza, J.
Rashi as philologist. *M.A. 1939 Manchester*

Perera, D. J. N.
Education in Ceylon. *M.A. 1920 London*

Perera, H. S.
The qualitative analysis of intelligence tests. *M.A. 1922 London*

Perera, N. M.
Some aspects of comparative parliamentary procedure. *Ph.D. 1932 London, School of Economics and Political Science*

Peristiany, J.
The social institutions of the Kipsigi tribe. *D.Phil. 1938 Oxford*

Perkins, H. W.
The transformation of an old ideal: Aristotle-Aquinas-modern idealism. *M.A. 1928 Bristol*

Perks, M. T.
A critical edition with introduction and commentary of Spenser's *A view of the present state of Ireland*. *B.Litt. 1924 Oxford*

Perlmann, M.
Moslem polemics against Jews and Judaism. *Ph.D. 1941 London, School of Oriental and African Studies*

Perrelle, L. P. de la *see* De la Perrelle, L. P.

Perrett, E.
The strain of Protestantism in the works of André Gide. *M.A. 1928 Wales*

Perrin, E. E.
The methodology of William Whewell. *M.Sc. 1927 London*

Perrott, M. E.
The foundation and early history of the Irish Society, 1609-25. *M.A. 1920 London*

Perry, A. L. M.
An investigation of recent tendencies in secondary education in England and America, and their implications for the reorganization of secondary education in New Zealand. *Ph.D. 1938 London, Institute of Education*

Perry, C. R.
Expositions of: I Corinthians ix.19-22; St. Mark ix.38-40; St. Luke xx.21-26. *D.D. 1901 Oxford*

Perry, C. R.
1. The language used by Christ. 2. The organization of the early Christian Churches. *B.D. 1892 Oxford*

Perry, F. C.
A grammar of the dialect of Farmborough (North Somerset): historical and descriptive, with dialect specimens and an appendix on the Scandinavian element. *M.A. 1917 Leeds*

Perry, J.
John Spottiswoode, Archbishop and Chancellor, as churchman, historian and theologian. *Ph.D. 1950 Edinburgh*

Perry, J. H.
A critical edition of the British Museum manuscript of the *Dialogo de las Lenguas*, with a prefatory essay in three part. *M.A. 1920 London, School of Economics and Political Science*

Perry, R.
The Gloucestershire woollen industry in the eighteenth and nineteenth centuries. *Ph.D. 1946 London, External Degree*

Perry, R.
The life and work of Nathaniel Woodard, with special reference to the influence of the Oxford movement on English education in the nineteenth century. *M.A. 1932 Bristol*

Perry, R. M.
Jahweh, the God of love: a study in Old Testament theology. *Ph.D. 1937 Edinburgh*

Perry, W. J.
The children of the sun: a study in the early history of civilization. *D.Sc. 1929 London*

Perryn, G. A.
1. The visible Church of Christ is a congregation of faithful men, in which the pure word of God is preached, and the sacraments be duly ministered according to Christ's ordinance - Article XIX. 2. It is not lawful for the Church to ordain anything that is contrary to God's word - Article XX. *B.D. & D.D. 1871 Oxford*

Peshitch, D.
The theological teaching of Justin Martyr. *B.Litt. 1921 Oxford*

Pesmazoglu, J. S.
Certain aspects of the international transmission of cyclical fluctuations, 1870-1913. *Ph.D. 1950 Cambridge*

Petch, R. B. K.
The organisation of a college of secular priests as illustrated by the records of the College of Holy Trinity, Arundel, 1380-1544. *M.A. 1940 London, King's College*

Petegorsky, D. W.
The Digger Movement in the English Revolution. *Ph.D. 1940 London, School of Economics and Political Science*

Peter, D.
The organization of a climatological station in a secondary school, and the introduction of this work into the geography syllabus. *M.Ed. 1930 Manchester*

Peter, D.
A study of the port of Fleetwood, with special reference to its position in the west coast fishing industry. *M.A. 1932 Manchester*

Peter, I. S.
The Anglo-Saxon epic as exemplified by *Beowulf* considered in the light of the Indian epic *Rāmayana*. *Ph.D. 1930 London, King's College*

Peters, J. T.
The Dunkers: their origins, migrations, doctrines, and development. *Ph.D. 1942 Edinburgh*

Peters, R. S.
The nature of psychological enquiries. *M.A. 1949 London, Birkbeck College*

Petersen, M. A. F. Bredahl
Dr. Johannes Macchabaeus (John MacAlpin): Scotland's contribution to the Reformation in Denmark. *Ph.D. 1937 Edinburgh*

Peterson, J. L.
Adolescence: a study of elementary school leavers and public schoolboys of the same age. *M.A. 1939 London, University College*

Petherick, C.
Count Aehrenthal: a study in the foreign policy of Austria-Hungary, 1906-1912. *M.A. 1936 Bristol*

Petre, E. O. G. Turville- *see* Turville-Petre, E. O. G.

Pettet, E. C.
Shakespeare and the neo-romance. *B.Litt. 1944 Dublin, Trinity College*

Pettyfer, J. C.
L'histoire dans *Les hommes de bonne volonté* by J. Romains. *M.A. 1948 Birmingham*

Pflaum, K. B.
Belief. *B.Litt. 1945 Oxford*

Phelps, W. C.
Anatole France, critique de son milieu. *M.A. 1933 Birmingham*

Philip, C. T.
Standardization of intelligence and aptitude tests in their mother tongue for secondary school children. *M.A. 1944 London, Institute of Education*

Philippakis, B.
The Attic *stamnos*. *D.Phil. 1950 Oxford*

Philips, C. H.
The influence of the East India Company 'interest' on the English government, 1813-1833. *M.A. 1937 Liverpool*

Phillips, A. J.
Intelligence tests and their uses in the secondary school. *M.Ed. 1926 Manchester*

Phillips, C. H.
Foreign deities worshipped in Israel in the period of the monarchy: their character and origin. *M.A. 1938 Wales*

Phillips, D. D.
John Penry and the Marprelate controversy in the light of recent research. *M.A. 1914 Wales*

Phillips, E. M.
Sainte-Beuve's critical appreciation of English literature. *M.A. 1923 Wales*

Phillips, E. M. G. van Zwanenberg *see* van Zwanenberg Phillips, E. M. G.

Phillips, G.
The poets of the Oxford Movement. *M.A. 1926 Liverpool*

Phillips, G. E.
Mental fatigue. *D.Sc. 1920 London*

Phillips, G. I.
International legal and military control of cables and wireless in time of war, with special reference to the present war. *B.Litt. 1918 Oxford*

Phillips, H. E. I.
The Court of Star Chamber, 1603-41, with special reference to the period 1625-41. *M.A. 1939 London, University College*

Phillips, H. O. C.
The Platonic conception of love in the work of Pontus de Tyard. *M.A. 1949 Wales*

Phillips, J.
The doctrine of the Word in relation to the Holy Scriptures as presented in the theology of Karl Barth. *B.Litt. 1930 Oxford*

Phillips, J. E.
The educational value of the study of physics from the standpoint of method. *M.A. 1924 Wales*

Phillips, J. F.
The Agriculture Act, 1947. *LL.M. 1949 Cambridge*

Phillips, J. L.
1. The Church in the Epistle to the Ephesians. 2. The Christ of the fourth Gospel. *B.D. 1913 Oxford*

Phillips, J. L.
Exegeses of St. Mark xvi.6,11; I Corinthians xv.8. *D.D. 1920 Oxford*

Phillips, J. R. E.
Some aspects of the economics of consumption. *M.A. 1938 Wales*

Phillips, L. R.
Individual differences in dark adaptation. *Ph.D. 1939 London, University College*

Phillips, L. R.
A study of the effect upon learning of a training in certain principles of attention and memorization. *M.A. 1936 London, Institute of Education*

Phillips, M.
A colonial autocracy: New South Wales under Governor Macquarie, 1810-1821. *D.Sc. 1908 London*

Phillips, M.
The European Powers and the British occupation of Egypt, 1882-1885. *M.A. 1937 Wales*

Phillips, M.
Supernaturalism in English poetry, 1750-1850. *Ph.D. 1930 London, East London College*

Phillips, M. G.
Byron and the 'Postscript of the Augustans'. *M.A. 1916 London*

Phillips, P. E.
English literature in the critical work of Taine. *M.A. 1931 Wales*

Phillips, R. H. S.
The political economy of town planning. *Ph.D. 1941 London, School of Economics and Political Science*

Phillips, S.
1. The sufficiency of Holy Scripture. 2. The communion of saints. *B.D. & D.D. 1889 Oxford*

Phillips, T. I.
The spoken dialect of the Ogwr Basin, Glamorgan. *M.A. 1933 Wales*

Phillips, T. O.
Bywyd a gwaith Meurig Dafydd (Llanisien) a Llywelyn Siôn (Llangewydd)(The life and work of Meurig Dafydd (Llanisien) and Llywelyn Jones (Llangewydd)). *M.A. 1937 Wales*

Phillips, W.
Bywydd a gwaith John Williams, Rhos: awdur yr oraclau bywiol(The life and work of John Williams, Rhos, author of the living oracles). *M.A. 1947 Wales*

Phillips, W.
The influence of Roman law on the history and doctrine of the Christian church during the first three centuries. *Ph.D. 1931 Edinburgh*

Phillips, W. F.
The influence of anthropomorphism upon the Christian view of God, and the world. *B.Litt. 1911 Oxford*

Phillipson, H. M.
Some historical examples in the Roman moralists. *M.A. 1929 Manchester*

Phillipson, W. O.
The doctrine of the atonement and modern thought. *M.A. 1937 Bristol*

Philp, K. L.
An experimental study of the frustration of will-acts and conation. *Ph.D. 1933 London, King's College*

Philpot, A. E.
A study of the layout of school books in its relevant appreciation and comprehension. *M.A. 1948 London, Institute of Education*

Philpot, M. G.
A study of the dramatic monologue, with special consideration of its development in the Victorian age. *M.A. 1920 London*

Philpot, R. J.
Military unrest as described by Tacitus. *M.A. 1950 Wales*

Philpott, S. J. F.
Fluctuations in human output. *D.Sc. 1932 London, University College*

Philpott, W. E.
Origin and growth of the protectorate system, with special study of the system as developed in British colonial history 1800 to 1848. *M.A. 1934 London, King's College*

Phipps, C. B.
The antecedents and history of Irish Romanesque architecture. *B.Litt. 1940 Dublin, Trinity College*

Phipps, C. B.
The monastic round towers of Ireland. *Ph.D. 1935 Dublin, Trinity College*

Phipps, W. E.
An enquiry into the correlation of motor ability with 'g'. *M.A. 1939 Birmingham*

Pichler, E. T.
Le symbolisme de la pauvreté dans l'oeuvre de Léon Bloy. *M.A. 1945 Birmingham*

Pick, M.
The work of Lady Gregory: her contribution to the Irish dramatic and literary revival. *M.A. 1940 London, Bedford College*

Pickard, O. G.
Midland immigrations. *M.Com. 1940 Birmingham*

Pickering, J. R.
The development of the theory of substitution in the benzene nucleus, 1875-1923. *M.Sc. 1929 London*

Pickering, R. H.
L'évolution sémantique du mot 'raison' d'après les textes du XVIIe siècle. *M.A. 1946 Manchester*

Pickering, W. A.
The life and works of John Gay. *M.A. 1934 Birmingham*

Pickersgill, J. W.
Catholic opinion and the ecclesiastical policy of the government in France (1869-70). *B.Litt. 1933 Oxford*

Pickett, K.
The Gestalt theory of learning and some of its implications for educational theory and practice. *B.Litt. 1949 Oxford*

Pickford, C. E.
The story of Aléxandre l'Orfelin: a critical edition. *M.A. 1948 Manchester*

Pickford, R. W.
Psychological problems in the history of painting. *D.Litt. 1947 Glasgow*

Pickford, R. W.
A study of some mental processes involved in reading. *Ph.D. 1932 Cambridge*

Pickles, I. L. *see* Gordon, I. L.

Pickles, T. H.
The mathematical laboratory in secondary schools. *M.Ed. 1926 Leeds*

Pickles, W.
Pierre-Joseph Proudhon et Karl Marx. *M.A. 1927 Leeds*

Pickthall, J.
Revelation: an interpretation in the terms of modern conceptions of personality. *Ph.D. 1924 Edinburgh*

Pickup, E. M.
An edition of selected letters of John Aubrey. *B.Litt. 1935 Oxford*

Picton, J. G.
Bank advances to industry. *M.Com. 1933 Birmingham*

Piddington, R. O. R.
Culture and neurosis. *Ph.D. 1935 London, School of Economics and Political Science*

Pidgeon, A. L.
The development of Canadian naval bases. *B.Litt. 1948 Oxford*

Pienaar, W. J. B.
Justus van Effen and English influences in Dutch literature. *Ph.D. 1925 London*

Piennaar, W. J.
Perseveration and difficult children. *Ph.D. 1929 London*

Pierce, F. W.
La creación del mundo: a narrative poem on the cosmogony, by Alonso de Acevedo. *M.A. 1939 Belfast*

Pierce-Jones, B.
The Welsh character and his development in English drama, 1590-1642. *M.A. 1949 Manchester*

Pieris, H. E.
A comparative study of the interests of adolescent girls in certain urban and rural areas. *M.A. 1949 London, Institute of Education*

Pietrkiewicz, J. M.
A comparative study of English lyric poetry from a Polish point of view, illustrated by an anthology, a critical commentary, and verse translations into Polish. *Ph.D. 1947 London, King's College*

Piggott, H. E.
The moral development of the child. *M.A. 1903 Wales*

Piggott, S.
The life and work of Dr. William Stukeley (1687-1765). *B.Litt. 1946 Oxford*

Pilgrim, J. E.
The cloth industry in Essex and Suffolk. *M.A. 1938 London, School of Economics and Political Science*

Pilgrim, R. W.
Franco-Scottish relations from 1290 to 1390. *B.Litt. 1936 Oxford*

Pilkington, D. D.
English compound nouns of the type used in personal descriptions; a supplement to the chronology of the new English dictionary. *M.A. 1920 London*

Pilkington, E. M.
Regional survey and its application in schools. *M.Ed. 1921 Manchester*

Pilkington, R.
Liens accessory of securities. *LL.M. 1928 Leeds*

Pillai, P. P.
Industrial conditions in modern India. *Ph.D. 1923 London*

Pillai, R. P. B.
A study of the threshold in relation to subliminal impressions and allied phenomena. *Ph.D. 1938 London, University College*

Pillay, K. K.
Local self-government in the Madras Presidency, 1850-1919. *D.Phil. 1948 Oxford*

Pilsbury, W. A.
A consideration of some of the text books on modern history used in secondary schools since 1860 illustrating the development in the theory and practice of history teaching. *M.A. 1944 Reading*

Pimlott, J. A. R.
The evidence of English visitors on the social and economic conditions of France, 1763-89 (May). *B.Litt. 1934 Oxford*

Pimontel, A.
The land of Israel as an idea and ideal in Biblical literature. *M.A. 1937 Manchester*

Pinchbeck, D.
The sermons of Jofroi de Waterford, with a critical, historical and philological study of the text. *Ph.D. 1936 London, Birkbeck College*

Pinchbeck, I.
Women workers and the Industrial Revolution, 1750-1850. *Ph.D. 1930 London, School of Economics and Political Science*

Pinchbeck, I.
The work of women in agriculture in the late eighteenth and early nineteenth centuries, and the influence of the agrarian revolution thereon. *M.A. 1927 London*

Pinchin, H.
Expositions of: I Corinthians xv.29; I St. Peter iii.18-20; Genesis xlix.10. *D.D. 1899 Oxford*

Pinchin, H. T.
1. The Christian doctrine and some non-Christian theories of sin. 2. The nature and reaonableness of prayer. *B.D. 1895 Oxford*

Pink, M. A.
The influence of Shakespeare on the eighteenth century drama (1700-1780). *M.A. 1920 London*

Pinkley, G. D.
Studies on the primates: (1) brains of Eocene primates interpreted from endocranial casts; (2) a new interpretation of Wadjak Man; (3) a restoration of the skull and brain of the Jurassic mammal, Triconodon. *Ph.D. 1935 London, University College*

Pinsent, A.
Education as a pure science. *M.A. 1921 London*

Pinto, V. de S.
The life and works of Sir Charles Sedley. *D.Phil. 1927 Oxford*

Piplani, B. M.
Municipal enterprise in Germany : a study of German local utilities before and after the war. *Ph.D. 1939 London, School of Economics and Political Science*

Pires, E. A.
The growth and present status of Catholic secondary education in the province of Bombay. *M.A. 1942 London, Institute of Education*

Pither, F. M.
The study of T. Traherne. *M.A. 1915 Birmingham*

Pitman, M. C.
Studies in the work of Henry Peacham. *M.A. 1933 London, Royal Holloway College*

Pitman, R.
India's contribution to imaginative English literature. *M.A. 1920 Birmingham*

Pitt, P.
Early archaic red-figure vase painting during the period 530-510 B.C. *M.A. 1937 Birmingham*

Pittins, E. F. W. Gey van *see* Gey van Pittins, E. F. W.

Pitt-Rivers, G. L. F.
The clash of race and the clash of culture. *B.Sc. 1926 Oxford*

Pitts, H.
The Kingdom of God in English literature. *M.A. 1920 National University of Ireland*

Pitts, J.
The freewill problem in modern philosophy from Descartes to Kant. *Ph.D. 1933 London, External Degree*

Pitts, R. C.
Jean Nicolas Grou, 1731-1803, the man and his work. *Ph.D. 1947 Edinburgh*

Plant, G. S.
The idea of toleration under the later Stuarts. *Ph.D. 1936 London, School of Economics and Political Science*

Plant, M.
The economic aspects of book production and distribution between 1500 and 1650. *M.Sc. 1934 London, School of Economics and Political Science*

Plant, M.
The English book trade: an economic history of the making and sale of books. *D.Sc. 1939 London, School of Economics and Political Science*

Platnauer, M.
The Emperor Lucius Septimus Severus. *B.Litt. 1915 Oxford*

Platt, J.
English colloquial idiom in the eighteenth century. *Ph.D. 1925 London*

Platt, R.
Relations between aesthetic thought and painting in England in the eighteenth century. *M.A. 1948 Reading*

Platts, A.
Land administration in Iraq from the Muhammadan period to present times, based on original Arabic sources and official administration reports. *Ph.D. 1927 London*

Pléamonn, B.
An tAthair Peadar Ua Laoghaire agus Pádraig Mac Piarais, i gcomh-mheas agus i gcodarsna(Father Peadar Ua Laoghaire and Pádraig Mac Piarais, compared and contrasted). *M.A. 1943 National University of Ireland*

Pleass, C. J.
The Betes. *Dip. Anthropology. 1928 Cambridge*

Pléimeanne, C.
Tráchtas ar fhilídheacht na 17 aoise(A treatise on 17th century poetry). *M.A. 1933 National University of Ireland*

Pletcher, M. S.
Human personality as reflected in the psychology of the New Testament. *B.Litt. 1911 Oxford*

Plommer, W. H.
Plutarch's *Life of Pericles. D.Phil. 1948 Oxford*

Plover, T.
Pádraig Og O'Conaire agus Máire: saoghal agus saothar na mbeirte(Pádraig Og O'Conaire and Máire: their lives and works). *M.A. 1950 National University of Ireland*

Plucknett, T. F. T.
The Great Council in the fifteenth century. *M.A. 1917 London*

Plumb, J.
Early nonconformity in Lincolnshire. *M.A. 1940 Sheffield*

Plumb, J. H.
Elections to the House of Commons in the reign of William III. *Ph.D. 1936 Cambridge*

Plume, G. A.
The enclosure movement in Caernarvonshire, with special reference to the Porth-yr-aur papers. *M.A. 1935 Wales*

Plumley, J. M.
Burial customs of the Near East with special reference to the Old Testament. *M.Litt. 1939 Durham*

Plummer, A.
The general strike during one hundred years. *M.Sc. 1927 London*

Plummer, A.
The life of James Bronterre O'Brien. *B.Litt. 1928 Oxford*

Pocock, L. G.
Notes on Cicero: *In Vatinium. M.A. 1924 London*

Poduval, R. P. N.
Budgetary policy, with special reference to the trade cycle. *Ph.D. 1940 London, University College*

Poel, J. van der *see* Van der Poel, J.

Polderman, F.
L'oeuvre d'Iwan Gilkin. *M.A. 1917 Birmingham*

Pollard, A. H.
A study of mortality and fertility trends and of various indices related thereto. *Ph.D. 1948 London, External Degree*

Pollard, H. A.
The solution of concrete problems. *M.A. 1942 Birmingham*

Pollard, J. L.
An edition with translation of: Ibn Ja'far; chapter the eleventh of *Liqāh al-Khawātir wa-jilā'al-basā'ir. M.A. 1950 Manchester*

Pollard, J. R. T.
Some problems connected with birds in Greek religion. *B.Litt. 1947 Oxford*

Pollard, M. M. C.
The witch in the English drama. *Cert.Litt. 1917 Oxford*

Pollard, S. D.
The inter-relations of balances of payments and internal economic conditions, considered with special reference to selected countries in the period 1927-31. *B.Litt. 1935 Oxford*

Pollock, T.
Singing disability in school children. *M.Ed. 1950 Durham*

Polonsky, A.
The evolution of the law of torts in Palestine. *LL.M. 1940 Leeds*

Polsky, S.
The legal attitude toward mental abnormality: a comparative analysis of the historical and modern criminal law tests of responsibility, with respect to insanity, in England, Scotland and the United States of America. *Ph.D. 1950 Edinburgh*

Polychroniades, G.
Methods of research on farm management. *B.Litt. 1941 Oxford*

Polyvios, P. J.
Public policy in company law. *B.Litt. 1944 Oxford*

Pomfret, J.
Tirso de Molina and the *nueva comedia. M.A. 1935 Birmingham*

Pool, A. G.
Wage policy in relation to industrial fluctuations. *Ph.D. 1939 London, External Degree*

Pool, E. M.
Alfred de Musset et la littérature anglaise. *M.A. 1914 Liverpool*

Poole, E. P.
The lesser novels, 1740-1770. *M.A. 1930 London, East London College*

Poole, R. B.
1. St. Paul's claim to be a true Apostle and the spiritual father of the Galatians (Galatians i.1,2,11,12). 2. The inadequacy of the law and its proper function and position (Galatians iii.24). 3. The attitude and responsibilities of Christians under the new law of liberty (Galatians v.i;vi.7,8). *D.D. 1886 Oxford*

Poole, S. B. R.
Ecclesiastical opinion in England on the Eastern Question from the Treaty of Paris to the Treaty of Berlin. *M.A. 1934 London, King's College*

Poonen, E.
The theories of the origin of species critically viewed. *M.D. 1889 Aberdeen*

Pope, D. M.
The *roman comique* in England. *M.A. 1906 London*

Pope, E. A.
Natal education: its history and methods. *M.A. 1916 Liverpool*

Pope, R. W. M.
1. Demoniacal possession. 2. The intermediate state. *B.D. 1877 Oxford*

Pope, S. R.
Verbal imagery and figures of speech in Propertius: a study of some aspects of poetic technique. *M.A. 1942 Liverpool*

Popham, F. S.
Religious education. *Ph.D. 1933 Dublin, Trinity College*

Popham, K. M. A.
Octovien de Saint Gelais's translation of Ovid's *Heroides. B.Litt. 1937 Oxford*

Popovitch, M.
The conception of eternal life, with special reference to the Johannine writings. *B.Litt. 1922 Oxford*

Popovitch, V.
Shakespeare in Serbia. *Ph.D. 1925 London*

Popplewell, N.
The influences of Puritanism on English life and character. *Ph.D. 1931 Edinburgh*

Porcher, G. L.
1. The Hebrew sabbath. 2. The Christian Sunday. *B.D. 1923 Oxford*

Port, F. J.
The characteristics of administrative law. *LL.D. 1927 London*

Porter, C. B.
The legal conception of criminal responsibility in view of modern theories of criminology. *Ph.D. 1924 Edinburgh*

Porter, C. H.
The influence of Addison. *M.A. 1909 London*

Porter, I.
Aspects of the early English opera libretto. *Ph.D. 1938 Leeds*

Porter, W. E.
The establishment of the original text of Peter Langtoft's chronicle, part 2, as translated by Robert Mannyng of Brunne, by a collation of the two extant mss. - Petyt ms. 511, vol. 7, in the Inner Temple Library and Lambeth ms. 131, in the Lambeth Palace Library. *M.A. 1930 Leeds*

Porter, W. H.
The 'Ecole Unique' in France: an historical survey of the movement, an appreciation of its aims, with some reference to political and social implications, and an account of the objects hitherto achieved. *M.A. 1938 London, Courtauld Institute of Art*

Portus, G. V.
The various societies in the Church of England in the first half of the eighteenth century. *B.Litt. 1911 Oxford*

Posnette, G. M.
The Russia Company. *M.A. 1919 Birmingham*

Postan, M.
The financing of trade in the later Middle Ages, with special reference to the English trade in the fifteenth century. *M.Sc. 1926 London*

Pothan, A. M.
The teaching of English as a second language in India, with special reference to Hyderabad Deccan. *M.Ed. 1938 Leeds*

Potter, E. J.
Influence of Jonson on Restoration comedy (1660-1700). *M.A. 1939 London, King's College*

Potter, G. R.
Education in the fourteenth and fifteenth centuries, with special reference to the development of the universities of northern Europe. *Ph.D. 1927 Cambridge*

Potter, J. G. F.
Value and the philosophy of the absolute with special reference to the philosophy of Bosanquet. *B.Litt. 1935 Oxford*

Potter, J. O.
Le toponyme baki: étude philologique sur l'apport francique dans la Wallonie. *M.A. 1950 Birmingham*

Potter, S.
On grammatical mood in Ben Jonson's comedies. *M.A. 1924 London*

Potter, S.
The relationship of the Old English version of Bede to Werferth's Gregory on the one hand, and to Alfred's translations on the other. *B.Litt. 1923 Oxford*

Potts, E. W. M.
Prognostic tests of school geometry. *M.A. 1934 London, Institute of Education*

Pouliot, V.
The notion of substance in the *Metaphysics* of Aristotle. *B.Litt. 1933 Oxford*

Pound, A. G.
The importance of Halesowen Abbey in the life of the English people. *M.A. 1926 Birmingham*

Pounder, K.
Eugene O'Neill. *M.A. 1947 Birmingham*

Pounds, N. J. G.
The historical geography of Cornwall. *Ph.D. 1945 London, External Degree*

Povah, A.
Exegeses of St. Luke viii.9-10; Romans xiv and xv.3; Hebrews x.37. *D.D. 1890 Oxford*

Powar, A. G.
The reign of Shahu Chhatrapati, 1708-1749 A.D. *Ph.D. 1934 London, School of Oriental and African Studies*

Powdermaker, H.
A sociological study of leadership in primitive society. *Ph.D. 1928 London*

Powell, A. F.
Sainte-Beuve et l'Angleterre: le critique et le poète dans leurs rapports avec certains écrivains anglais. *M.A. 1920 London*

Powell, E.
The history and importance of the Latin versions of the Gospels in the light of modern criticism. *M.A. 1948 Leeds*

Powell, E. T.
The evolution of the money market (1835-1915). *D.Sc. 1915 London*

Powell, G. G.
The original acoustical work of Ernst Florens Friedrich Chladni and its influence on his immediate successors. *M.Sc. 1950 Wales*

Powell, G. L.
Tentatives toward European union: a survey of the progress made in the last half-century in the development of selected public international organizations which tend toward unifying Europe. *B.Litt. 1949 Oxford*

Powell, H. T.
The doctrine of the fall: a question of validity. *D.D. 1929 Durham*

Powell, I. G.
The adhesion of the Royal Navy to Parliament at the outbreak of the Civil War. *M.A. 1919 London*

Powell, J. H.
Determinism in Calvin. *Ph.D. 1928 Edinburgh*

Powell, J. W.
An investigation into the effects of National Socialism on secondary education in Germany and some problems involved in its reconstruction. *M.Ed. 1948 Durham*

Powell, M.
A geographical survey of the Mendip Hills showing their effect upon human activities in the region. *B.Sc. 1927 Oxford*

Powell, M. J.
1. Christ the representative man. 2. The Epistle of St. Paul the Apostle to the Ephesians. *B.D. & D.D. 1907 Oxford*

Powell, M. J.
An edition of the Pauline Epistles contained in ms. Parker 32, Corpus Christi College, Cambridge. *M.A. 1914 London*

Powell, N. S. B.
The conceptions of natural law and natural right, with special reference to Hobbes, Spinoza, Locke and Rousseau. *M.A. 1932 Wales*

Powell, P. H.
Christophorus Kormart's adaptations of Pierre Corneille's *Polyeucte* and *Héraclius* and their relation to the contemporary German drama of the seventeenth century. *M.A. 1936 Wales*

Powell, S.
A century of English prose satire. *M.A. 1914 National University of Ireland*

Powell, S. M.
The character of Percival in the Arthurian legend. *M.A. 1902 Wales*

Powell, W.
Difficulties in the conception of an infinite God. *M.A. 1910 Wales*

Powell, W. H.
1. The prophets: the characteristics of their teaching, and their influence on the religious and political life of Israel. 2. The resurrection of our Lord: its evidences and its hints as to a future life. *B.D. & D.D. 1909 Oxford*

Power, E.
Das bürgerliche Trauerspiel. *M.A. 1927 National University of Ireland*

Power, E. E.
Some chapters in the history of English nunneries in the later Middle Ages. *M.A. 1916 London*

Power, E. R. R.
The social structure of an English county town. *Ph.D. 1937 London, School of Economics and Political Science*

Powis, A. K.
The Whigs and their relations with William III from 1689-1698. *M.A. 1947 London, King's College*

Powis, G. J.
Sports centres; their planning and construction. *M.A. 1948 Sheffield*

Powles, L. V.
The mysticism of George Sand. *Ph.D. 1939 London, External Degree*

Powley, E. B.
The English Navy during the Revolution of 1688 and its condition at the commencement of the reign of William III and Mary. *B.Litt. 1925 Oxford*

Powley, E. B.
The family of de la Pomerai of Beri, 1066-1719, with appendix post 1720. *M.A. 1941 Liverpool*

Prager, T.
German banking in depression and recovery, 1930-1935. *Ph.D. 1943 London, School of Economics and Political Science*

Prais, S. J.
The building of econometric models, with special reference to the investment process. *M.Com 1950 Birmingham*

Prakasha, V.
The reliability of certain tests of practical ability. *M.A. 1949 London, Institute of Education*

Prankerd, A. A.
The Twelve Tables. *D.C.L. 1887 Oxford*

Prasad, B.
Theory of government in ancient India. *Ph.D. 1926 London*

Prasad, J.
Indian epistemology. *Ph.D. 1930 Cambridge*

Prasad, J.
Psychological factors in serial reproduction. *M.Sc. 1930 Cambridge*

Prasad, Y.
The life and career of Mir Qamaruddin Nizamul Mulk Asaf Jah I. *Ph.D. 1927 London*

Prased, B.
The state in ancient India (North): a study in the structure and practical working of political institutions in Northern India in ancient times. *D.Sc. 1928 London*

Prashad, G.
Influence of European political doctrines upon the evolution of the Indian Government institutions and practice (1858-1938). *Ph.D. 1942 London, School of Economics and Political Science*

Pratt, C. L. G.
The claim of physiology to be regarded as one of the humanities. *M.A. 1936 Liverpool*

Pratt, D. G.
The doctrine of baptismal regeneration in the Church of England, with special reference to the Prayer Books of 1549, 1552, and 1662. *B.D. 1951 Oxford*

Pratt, E. J.
Anglo-American rivalry in Mexico and South America. *D.Phil. 1929 Oxford*

Pratt, E. J.
French and Spanish opinion of the American Civil War, with some reference to English and other continental opinion. . *B.Litt. 1925 Oxford*

Pratt, J. H.
An examination of certain Chinese institutions, customs, aesthetic concepts, and achievements, with a view to determining how far they could be naturalized in the practice and teaching of the Christian Church in China. *B.Litt. 1935 Oxford*

Pratt, L. J. B.
Child training in Sierra Leone: a description of education in relation to society. *M.Ed. 1949 Durham*

Pratt, M. *see* Exley, M.

Pratt, S. A. J.
Methods of investigation and research in agricultural and rural economies, with special reference to economic and social studies in tropical Africa. *B.Litt. 1949 Oxford*

Preedy, G. L.
A study of the supernatural in Middle English verse romances. *M.A. 1918 Bristol*

Preedy, J. B. K.
The chariot group of the Mausoleum. *M.A. 1909 London*

Prendergast, E.
Prehistoric discoveries in Co. Dublin. *M.A. 1947 National University of Ireland*

Prendergast, J.
Galen's physiology, with special reference to the vascular system. *B.Litt. 1930 Oxford*

Prendergast, M. J.
Dissolution of monasteries in England: social and economic results. *M.A. 1937 National University of Ireland*

Prendergast, W. J.
A translation, with commentary, of the *Makāmas* of Badī-al-Zamān Hamadhānī. *B.Litt. 1914 Oxford*

Prendeville, P. L.
History of the Dublin Chamber of Commerce, 1760-1860. *M.Comm. 1930 National University of Ireland*

Presanis, A.
Banking and monetary problems of Greece from 1931-1939. *M.Sc. 1946 London, School of Economics and Political Science*

Prescot, H. K.
The economics and political theory of William Godwin and his debt to French thinkers. *D.Phil. 1931 Oxford*

Prescott, F.
History of our knowledge on fermentation. *Ph.D. 1930 London, University College*

Pressly, H. E.
Evangelicalism in England in the first half of the nineteenth century as exemplified in the life and works of William Jay, 1769-1853. *Ph.D. 1950 Edinburgh*

Presswood, R. E.
An experimental study of concepts in adolescence. *M.Ed. 1934 Leeds*

Presswood, W. L.
The influence of Auguste Comte and the rise of positivism in England up to the formation of the English Positivist Society in 1867. *Ph.D. 1935 Sheffield*

Prest, A. R.
War economics of primary producing countries. *Ph.D. 1949 Cambridge*

Prest, W.
The coal industry. *M.A. 1934 Leeds*

Prestige, G. L.
1. The documentary evidence for the Virgin Birth. 2. The doctrine of the Virgin Birth. *B.D. 1923 Oxford*

Prestige, G. L.
The evolution of the doctrine of the most Holy Trinity, considered mainly in its exposition by Greek Patristic authors, and studies in its true meaning. *D.D. 1934 Oxford*

Preston, R. A.
The life and career of William Blathwayt, 1649-1717. *M.A. 1932 Leeds*

Preus, H. A.
Luther's doctrine of the Church in his early writings. *Ph.D. 1928 Edinburgh*

Prevelakis, E.
British policy towards the change of dynasty in Greece in the years 1862-3. *B.Litt. 1949 Oxford*

Price, A. E.
Emotional development and the infant school: the play curriculum as an aid to emotional adjustment and growth. *M.A. 1940 Leeds*

Price, C. D.
The Gawdys of West Harling, Norfolk: a study of education and social life in the seventeenth century. *M.A. 1950 Wales*

Price, C. J. L.
Contributions to the history of the English theatre and drama in Wales, 1737-1843. *M.A. 1939 Wales*

Price, D. I.
William of Nassyngton's *Mirror of Life*, or *Speculum Vitae*: a Middle English poem. *M.A. 1914 Wales*

Price, D. J.
The economic development of the Swansea area. *M.A. 1932 London, School of Economics and Political Science*

Price, D. K.
A comparative study of the higher classes of administrative officials, in the British Civil Service on the one hand, and the American Federal system on the other. *B.Litt. 1935 Oxford*

Price, D. T.
The Church in the reign of Edward I. *M.A. 1907 Wales*

Price, E. J. J.
An experimental analysis of certain performance tests. *B.Sc. 1939 Oxford*

Price, E. M.
Ralph, Lord Cromwell, and his household: studies in relation to household accounts in the possession of Lord de l'Isle and Dudley. *M.A. 1949 London, King's College*

Price, E. S.
A dissertation comprising a critical commentary and analysis of the system of intuitional ethics expounded by R. Price. *M.A. 1930 Bristol*

Price, F. D.
The administration of the diocese of Gloucester, 1547-79. *B.Litt. 1940 Oxford*

Price, G. R.
Exegeses of: Deuteronomy xviii.15; Zechariah xiii.7; St.Matthew xix.17. *D.D. & B.D. 1880 Oxford*

Price, H.
The scope, curriculum and organization of the modern school. *M.A. 1935 Liverpool*

Price, H. H.
The object of perception. *B.Sc. 1923 Oxford*

Price, J. G. T.
The law of maritime liens. *LL.D. 1940 Wales*

Price, J. G. T.
The recent history of the law of maritime liens. *M.A. 1935 Wales*

Price, J. H.
Adolescent attitudes to authority: an investigation of the psychological factors underlying the opinions of objective authority held by young people in a particular town, and determining what they actually do when authority is exercised over them. *M.A. 1943 Manchester*

Price, J. M.
The laws against Roman Catholic recusants, illustrated from the history of the North Riding of Yorkshire. *M.A. 1922 Wales*

Price, O. T. W.
The economics of use and conservation of agricultural land, with particular reference to grasslands in England and Wales. *D.Phil. 1949 Oxford*

Price, S. J. M.
1. The doctrine of the mediation of Christ. 2. The testimony of the Church as to the doctrine of the descent of Christ into hell. *B.D. & D.D. 1905 Oxford*

Price, S. M.
The reception and influence of the works of Leo Tolstoy in England, 1870-1910. *M.A. 1936 Manchester*

Price, S. M.
Sex problems in boys' secondary schools. *M.Ed. 1940 Manchester*

Price, T. W.
The possessory remedies in Roman-Dutch law. *Ph.D. 1941 Cambridge*

Price, T. W.
Social legislation and theory in Great Britain from 1906 to 1914. *B.Litt. 1930 Oxford*

Price, W. J.
The historical, non-dramatic poetry of the period 1550-1642. *M.A. 1914 Liverpool*

Price, W. W.
A history of the attempts towards reunion between the Anglican and the Eastern-Orthodox churches (especially since the sixteenth century). *M.A. 1929 Birmingham*

Prichard, M. F.
The treatment of poverty in Norfolk, from 1700 to 1859. *Ph.D. 1950 Cambridge*

Prichard, N. G. M.
The psychology of evidence. *M.Sc. 1930 London, King's College*

Prichard, W. J.
Development councils: a study of state co-operation with private industry. *M.Com. 1949 Leeds*

Prickett, E. M.
Francis Wey: his life and works. *M.A. 1933 London, East London College*

Priddin, D. M. Hornby- *see* Hornby-Priddin, D. M.

Prideaux, S. P. T.
1. Enquiry into the nature of sacrifice. 2. Primitive sacrifice as perfected and completed by Christianity. *B.D. 1912 Oxford*

Prideaux, S. P. T.
Expositions on St. Matthew xxiv; St. Mark xiii; St. Luke xxi. *D.D. 1917 Oxford*

Priest, G. B.
Gottfried Keller and the German Künstlerroman. *M.A. 1945 Manchester*

Priestley, E.
Percussion playing and recorder playing in schools. *M.Ed. 1942 Leeds*

Priestley, H. B.
Aptitude tests for performance on violinda (violin-type instrument). *M.A. 1949 London, Institute of Education*

Priestley, H. E.
British policy in the Italian Question (1866-1871). *Ph.D. 1931 London, Birkbeck College*

Priestley, H. E.
The prehistoric age as a subject for school study, incorporating a proposed school text-book on prehistory for children of the ages of 11 and 12. *M.Ed. 1928 Leeds*

Priestley, L.
The word order of subject, verb, régimes and attributes in Commines. *M.A. 1948 Leeds*

Priestley, M. A.
The problem of Anglo-French commercial rivalry in the reign of Charles II. *B.Litt. 1949 Oxford*

Primmer, W. C.
Education in rural England. *M.Ed. 1945 Manchester*

Prince, A. E.
Military system of Edward III. *B.Litt. 1929 Oxford*

Prince, T.
Jacob Tonson. *M.A. 1932 Wales*

Pringle, A. D.
A contribution to the study of the Bantu race (Zulus) in Natal, with reference to (1) their mode of living, racial customs and social conditions and (2) their physical and mental diseases. *M.D. 1916 Aberdeen*

Pritchard, C.
1. On the anticipative or prophetic character of the several stages of the Creation. 2. The order of the hours of the day in the Gospel according to St. John is the same as that in the other Gospels. *B.D. & D.D. 1880 Oxford*

Pritchard, D. D.
The slate industry of north Wales: a study of the changes in economic organization from 1780 to the present day. *M.A. 1935 Wales*

Pritchard, E.
The influence of the coal trade on the merchant shipping and foreign trade of Great Britain during the second half of the nineteenth century. *B.Litt. 1925 Oxford*

Pritchard, E. E. Evans-
The social organization of the Azande of the Bahr-el-Ghazal province of the Anglo-Egyptian Sudan. *Ph.D. 1928 London*

Pritchard, E. H.
Anglo-Chinese relations and the Macartney embassy (1775-1800). *D.Phil. 1933 Oxford*

Pritchard, F. C.
The history and development of boys' preparatory schools in England. *M.A. 1938 London, King's College*

Pritchard, F. C.
The Methodist contribution to nineteenth century secondary education. *Ph.D. 1947 London, External Degree*

Pritchard, J.
The source and implication of the New Testament quotations in the *Apologies* of Justin Martyr. *M.A. 1905 Wales*

Pritchard, R. J.
The 'servant' idea in the Old Testament: its origin, its development and influence upon the Israelitish nation, with an enquiry into an alleged similar conception among other nations. *M.A. 1930 Wales*

Pritchard-Jones, W. A.
Biology in education. *M.Ed. 1935 Durham*

Proby, J. C. P.
Henry VIII and the Irish Church. *B.Litt. 1925 Oxford*

Procter, H.
Juvenile delinquency, with special reference to the Children and Young Persons Act, 1933: a survey of the work of the Lancashire Education Authority in carrying out the duties imposed upon it by the Children and Young Persons Act, 1933. *M.A. 1942 Liverpool*

Proctor, G. V. G.
Some characteristics of English poetry between the two world wars, 1919-1939. *B.Litt. 1949 Dublin, Trinity College*

Proctor, S. M.
The origins and early history of savings banks in Great Britain. *M.A. 1929 Liverpool*

Pronger, W. A.
The life and works of Thomas Gascoigne. *B.Litt. 1932 Oxford*

Proper, B.
The Anglo-Norman manuscripts of the chanson de geste, *Aspremont*. *M.A. 1913 London*

Propert, E. J.
An economic survey of the printing industry in Bristol. *M.A. 1934 Bristol*

Proserpio, L.
The fundamental problems of neo-scholastic epistemology. *M.A. 1913 Liverpool*

Prosser, D. S.
The geography of the drainage areas of the Cynon and Clydach Rivers on the eve of the Industrial Revolution. *M.Sc. 1945 Wales*

Prosser, R. A. E.
The political parties in Athens during the Peloponnesian War. *M.A. 1926 Bristol*

Prothero, R. M.
The cultural contacts existing between the Bristol Channel coastlands in prehistoric times. *M.A. 1947 Wales*

Proud, E. D.
Welfare work. *D.Sc. 1916 London*

Proud, J. W.
Studies in the writings of Thomas Traherne. *M.A. 1914 London*

Prouty, C. T.
An edition, with indtroduction, notes, and glossary, of George Gascoigne's *A hundreth sundrie flowres*. *Ph.D. 1939 Cambridge*

Pruden, E. H.
Calvin's doctrine of Holy Scripture. *Ph.D. 1931 Edinburgh*

Pryce, A. R. Rhys- *see* Rhys-Pryce, A. R.

Pryce, F. N.
The pottery of the Hellenistic period to the rise of the Aretine wares. *M.A. 1913 Wales*

Pryde, G. S.
Scots burgh finances prior to 1707. *Ph.D. 1926 Saint Andrew's*

Pryke, W. M.
1. Use of the Old Testament in the primitive Christian apologetic. 2. Examination of the speeches in the Acts of the Apostles with reference to this apologetic. *B.D. 1916 Oxford*

Pryor, M.
1. The incarnation. 2. The atonement. *B.D. & D.D. 1906 Oxford*

Prys, G. M.
A study of the development of Lamennais' thought. *M.A. 1923 Wales*

Przegonia-Kryński, S. L.
Patriotism in English poetry, 1702-1832. *B.Litt. 1947 Oxford*

Pugh, T. B.
The lands and servants of the Dukes of York to 1415. *B.Litt. 1948 Oxford*

Pugsley, A. J.
Contribution towards the study of the economic development of Bristol in the eighteenth and nineteenth centuries. *M.A. 1921 Bristol*

Pullan, J. M.
An examination of school text books in chemistry. *M.A. 1932 London, Day Training College*

Pullan, L.
1. The Christian conception of sin. 2. The idea of atonement in the Old Testament. *B.D. & D.D. 1921 Oxford*

Pulling, U. E.
The history of Oriental cults among the Greeks. *M.A. 1911 London*

Purcell, A. C.
The teaching of modern languages. *M.A. 1945 National University of Ireland*

Purcell, C. P.
The Catholic body in England from 1715 to 1829, with special reference to the Catholic laity. *B.Litt. 1927 Oxford*

Purcell, M.
A contribution to the study of Chateaubriand's *Vie de Pance*. *M.A. 1931 London, University College*

Purcell, M. B.
Une histoire du *Sillon*. *M.A. 1931 Birmingham*

Purcell, P.
Keats and criticism. *M.A. 1937 National University of Ireland*

Purcell, V. W. W. S.
Education in modern China, with special reference to the influence upon it of Western civilization. *Ph.D. 1936 Cambridge*

Purchase, H. G.
The law relating to documents of title to goods. *LL.D. 1931 London, King's College*

Purchon, I.
A comparative study of the *fora* of the Roman Empire. *M.A. 1933 Wales*

Purdie, E.
The literary ballad in England during the romantic period. *Cert.Litt. 1923 Oxford*

Purdie, E.
The story of Judith in German and English Literature. *M.A. 1916 London*

Puri, A. A.
Muslim rule in Sind in the eighth, ninth and tenth centuries. *Ph.D. 1936 London, School of Oriental and African Studies*

Purkis, G. S.
The *Decameron* of Boccaccio, translated into French by Laurent de Premierfait, 1414. *M.A. 1923 London*

Purkis, G. S.
Giovanni Pascoli: a contribution to the study of his Italian poems. *Ph.D. 1927 London*

Purushottam, T. A.
A study of individual differences in the fluctuations of attention. *Ph.D. 1932 London, University College*

Purvis, J. S.
A medieval act book. *B.D. 1943 Cambridge*

Purvis, J. S.
The records of the Ecclesiastical Commission at York, 1562-1585. *D.D. 1948 Cambridge*

Purvis, T. A.
1. The Incarnation. 2. The atonement. *B.D. & D.D. 1905 Oxford*

Puscariu, A.
The Danube: its history and its economic and political development. *Ph.D. 1928 Birmingham*

Putnam, G. E.
Theory and practice of the inheritance taxes in the American commonwealth. *B.Litt. 1910 Oxford*

Pye, G. A.
A study of the Middle English Breton lays, with reference to fairy lore, folk-lore and origins. *M.A. 1936 London, Birkbeck College*

Pye, M. W.
Henri de Latouche. *Ph.D. 1928 London*

Pye, P.
Keats as a critic. *M.A. 1917 National University of Ireland*

Pyke, C. E.
Lucretius as translator of Epicurus: a study in poetical mood. *M.A. 1939 Bristol*

Pyke, H. R.
The law of contraband of war. *LL.D. 1916 London*

Pyle, W. F.
English heroic line structure from Chaucer to Wyatt. *Ph.D. 1933 Dublin, Trinity College*

Pym, G. W.
Projects of crusade in the fifteenth century. *M.A. 1925 Liverpool*

Pyne, C. A.
Industrial revival in Eire. *M.Econ.Sc. 1938 National University of Ireland*

Qadr, S. G. M.
A critical history of Urdu language and literature down to the year 1720. *Ph.D. 1930 London, School of Oriental and African Studies*

Qaiyum, A.
Some economic aspects of printing. *M.Com. 1939 Leeds*

Qazi, S. A.
A short history of elementary education in the United Provinces of Agra and Oudh (India) 1813-1935. *M.Ed. 1937 Leeds*

Quan, S.
The ethical and literary appreciation: a critical analysis of Aristotle's *Poetics* in relation to current theories of aesthetics, with particular reference to the teaching of literary appreciation in schools. *M.A. 1945 London, King's College*

Quayle, T.
The influence of French on the development of the English vocabulary from 1600 onwards. *M.A. 1913 London*

Quayle, W. C.
The psychology of the use of a map. *M.A. 1916 Liverpool*

Queenan, J. J.
Pioneer movements in Catholic education, Cork City, 1750-1850. *M.A. 1928 National University of Ireland*

Quibell, C. L.
1. The purpose of the Incarnation. 2. The kingdom of Christ in the New Testament. *B.D. 1910 Oxford*

Quick, F. E.
Reason and the limits of reason. *M.A. 1933 Liverpool*

Quick, L. E. H.
The elements of Chaucer's narrative art. *M.A. 1917 Bristol*

Quigley, P.
Litríocht na Gaedhilge in san gceathru asis deag(Irish Literature in the fourteenth century). *M.A. 1951 National University of Ireland*

Quilter, F. W.
Exegeses of the fall: Genesis iii.1-6; the atonement: Hebrews ix.11-14; the inspiration of Holy Scripture: II Timothy iii. 15-17. *D.D. 1872 Oxford*

Quilter, F. W.
1. The limits of conscience. 2. The doctrine of eternal rewards and punishments. *B.D. 1872 Oxford*

Quine, E.
The development of scientific pedagogy. *B.Sc. 1914 Liverpool*

Quine, W. E.
The peerage under Pitt, 1784-1806. *M.A. 1931 Liverpool*

Quine, W. E.
The selection and training of pupils for commerce in the senior school. *M.Ed. 1945 Leeds*

Quinn, D. B.
Tudor rule in Ireland in the reigns of Henry VII and Henry VIII, with special reference to the Anglo-Irish financial administration. *Ph.D. 1934 London, King's College*

Quinn, E.
The content of our natural knowledge of God in the philosophy of St. Thomas Aquinas. *M.A. 1948 Leeds*

Quinn, K. M.
A comparison between the styles of Old English and Norse historical prose. *M.A. 1932 London, King's College*

Quinton, A.
L'idée de l'antiquité Gréco-Latin dans Jean-Jacques Rousseau. *M.A. 1924 Liverpool*

Quinton, G. E.
The development of the idea of personal immortality in pagan Rome, with special reference to the metrical epitaphs in Buecheler's collection. *M.A. 1934 Bristol*

Quirk, A.
The movement for Catholic emancipation, 1807-1829. *M.A. 1913 Liverpool*

Quirk, C. R.
The interpretation of diphthongal spellings in Old English, with special reference to the phonological problems presented by the fracture spellings in Cambridge University Library manuscript Ii.1.33. *M.A. 1949 London, University College*

Quraishi, M. A. H.
An inquiry into the boy and girl welfare movement in England. *M.Ed. 1930 Leeds*

Qureshi, D. M.
Agricultural resources of western Pakistan: a statistico-economical survey. *M.Sc. 1949 London, School of Economics and Political Science*

Qureshi, I. H.
The administration of the sultanate of Delhi. *Ph.D. 1939 Cambridge*

Qureshi, M. M. A. I.
Agricultural credit: being a study of recent developments in farm credit administration in the United States. *Ph.D. 1935 Dublin, Trinity College*

Raalte, L. F. R. van *see* Van Raalte, L. F. R.

Rabbinowitz, J.
A critical and exegetical commentary on Mishnah tractate *Megillah*. *Ph.D. 1930 Manchester*

Rabin, C.
The evolution of the syntax of post-biblical Hebrew. *D.Phil. 1943 Oxford*

Rabin, C.
Studies in early Arabic dialects. *Ph.D. 1939 London, School of Oriental and African Studies*

Rabinowicz, M. H.
Life and times of Rabbi Joseph Colon (Kolom), 1420-1480. *Ph.D. 1948 London, Jews' College*

Rabinowitz, L. I.
The social life of the Jews of N. France in the XII-XIV centuries, as reflected in the Rabbinical literature of the period. *Ph.D. 1937 London, External Degree*

Radcliffe, J. D.
Income tax and its evasion: a history of post-war practice. *M.Com.Sc. 1938 Belfast*

Radcliffe, N. C. W.
1. The doctrine of a future life in the Old and New Testaments 2. The authorship of the Pastoral Epistles. *B.D. & D.D. 1909 Oxford*

Radcliffe, W.
Servants and satellites: a consideration of some minor Italian social types of the eighteenth century attendant upon the giovin signore of Parini's satire *Il giorno. M.A. 1937 Manchester*

Raddi, G. R.
An index to Sāyana Bhasya on Rig Veda Mandal II. *M.A. 1930 London, School of Oriental and African Studies*

Radford, E.
Fifty years of Greek vase-painting: Euphronios and his contemporaries. *M.A. 1913 London*

Radice, A. E. *see* Murray, A. E.

Radice, E. A.
Factors governing the supply of savings in Great Britain since the war. *D.Phil. 1938 Oxford*

Rae, J.
Researches in medical history, being an investigation into the causes of death of the kings of England from William I to William IV. *M.D. 1911 Aberdeen*

Rae, N. F. C.
Julia Domna. *Ph.D. 1932 Saint Andrew's*

Rae, S. F.
The concept of public opinion and its measurement. *Ph.D. 1939 London, School of Economics and Political Science*

Raeburn, W. A. L.
Conflict of laws relating to the collection of assets in bankruptcy. *LL.M. 1949 London, School of Economics and Political Science*

Rafilovitch, D.
Views concerning the epistemology of morals held by some of the British moralists of the eighteenth century, with especial reference to the anti-empiricist views of Richard Price and Thomas Reid. *D.Phil. 1940 Oxford*

Ragg, L.
1. The atonement. 2. The witness of the Church. *B.D. 1905 Oxford*

Ragg, L.
1. The sources of St. Luke's Gospel. 2. St. Luke vi.20-49. 3. St. Luke xxi.1-xxii.20. *D.D. 1923 Oxford*

Raggatt, F. C.
Self-government in the secondary school. *M.Ed. 1949 Durham*

Raggatt, F. C.
Woollen trade and industry in the rural areas of Gloucestershire. *M.A. 1933 Bristol*

Raghaillaigh, M.
Recent aspects of the co-operative movement in Ireland. *M.A. 1929 National University of Ireland*

Raghaviah, W. B.
Indian foreign trade, 1900-1931 and its economic background. *Ph.D. 1937 Edinburgh*

Rahilly, I.
Francis Jammes. *M.A. 1940 National University of Ireland*

Rahim, A.
The Mogul diplomacy from Akbar to Aurangzeb. *Ph.D. 1932 London, School of Oriental and African Studies*

Rahman, A. F. M. K.
Rise and fall of the Rohilla power in Hindustan, 1707 to 1774. *Ph.D. 1936 London, School of Oriental and African Studies*

Rahman, B.
A critical study of the educational problem in Bengal, with special reference to secondary education. *M.Ed. 1927 Leeds*

Rahman, F.
Avicenna's psychology: a critical edition, English translation, and commentary of *Kitab al-Najot, ii.6. D.Phil. 1949 Oxford*

Rahman, H.
Some aspects of the examination problem. *M.A. 1936 Birmingham*

Rahman, M. F.
The Bengali Muslims and English education (1765-1835). *M.A. 1948 London, Institute of Education*

Railton, W. K.
Mrs. Gaskell: life and works. *M.A. 1940 Wales*

Rainbow, S. G.
English expeditions to the Dutch East Indies during the Revolutionary and Napoleonic Wars. *M.A. 1933 London, East London College*

Raine, S. G.
Perseveration, perseverance, character and intelligence. *Ph.D. 1935 London, King's College*

Raj, J. S.
The monetary theories of John Locke. *M.Sc. 1937 London, University College*

Raj, K. N.
The monetary policy of the Reserve Bank of India with special reference to the structural and institutional factors in the economy. *Ph.D. 1947 London, School of Economics and Political Science*

Raja, C. K. *see* Kunhan Raja, C.

Rajan, B.
Paradise lost and the seventeenth-century reader. *Ph.D. 1946 Cambridge*

Rajapakse, L. A.
The principles of the Roman-Dutch law of delict as illustrated in the law of Ceylon, with a special chapter on the liability of the Crown to be sued in tort in Ceylon. *LL.D. 1925 London*

Rajkhowa, S. C.
Education and language problems in Assam. *M.A. 1948 London, Institute of Education*

Raju, J. B.
Philosophical proofs of the existence of God. *B.Sc. 1914 Oxford*

Raleigh, T.
Some difficulties with the English law of suretyship. *D.C.L. 1896 Oxford*

Ralph, R. G.
Realism in English poetry, 1700-1783. *M.A. 1940 London, King's College*

Ralph, R. G.
Realism in English poetry, 1700-1832. *Ph.D. 1947 London, External Degree*

Ralphs, F. L.
An anthropometric survey of the male adolescents of the Sheffield district. *Ph.D. 1934 Sheffield*

Rama Krishna, L.
Panjabi Sufi poets. *Ph.D. 1934 London, School of Oriental and African Studies*

Rama Rao, K. G.
Comparative value of certain verbal and non-verbal (primarily perceptual) tests and their relation to tests of mechanical ability. *Ph.D. 1933 London, University College*

Ramaswami Aiyangar, K. F.
British Indian amdinistration: an historical study. *M.Sc. 1936 London, School of Economics and Political Science*

Ramaswamy, K. R.
Educational administration. *M.Ed. 1929 Leeds*

Ramkrishniah, M.
The development of education in H.E.H. the Nizam's dominions. *M.Ed. 1946 Leeds*

Ramm, A.
European alliances and ententes, 1879-85: a study of contemporary British information. *M.A. 1937 London, Bedford College*

Ramsay, A. A. W.
Idealism and foreign policy: a study on the relations of Great Britain with Germany and France, 1860-1890. *Ph.D. 1925 Edinburgh*

Ramsay, G. D.
Government and industry during the Protectorate (1653-8). *B.Litt. 1933 Oxford*

Ramsay, G. D.
The Wiltshire woollen industry, chiefly in the sixteenth and early seventeenth centuries. *D.Phil. 1939 Oxford*

Ramsay, J. C.
The Darien scheme and the Church of Scotland. *Ph.D. 1949 Edinburgh*

Ramsbotham, R. B.
An enquiry into the collections of the land revenue in Bengal, 1772-1774, from the appointment of the Committee of Circuit, May, 1772, until the introduction of the provisions of the Regulating Act, October, 1774. *B.Litt. 1924 Oxford*

Ramsden, D. M.
The psychology of the boy group with special reference to school scout troup. *M.Ed. 1934 Leeds*

Ramzi, M. J.
The development of political thought and practice in Islam, 1-232 A.H./622-847 A.D. *Ph.D. 1948 Glasgow*

Ramzy, I.
An experiment in assessing personality. *Ph.D. 1948 London, University College*

Randall, R. W.
1. The theological virtue of faith. 2. The teaching of the Apostles on the duty of receiving the faith revealed by God. *B.D. & D.D. 1892 Oxford*

Randall, T.
1. The communion of saints. 2. The authorship of the Pastoral Epistles. *B.D. 1889 Oxford*

Randle, H. N.
Indian logic of Nyaya system. *D.Phil. 1927 Oxford*

Randolph, B. W.
1. The doctrine of the Blessed Trinity. 2. Scripture aspects of the Atonement. *B.D. & D.D. 1901 Oxford*

Rangachar, C.
An experimental study of school children with regard to some racial mental differences. *M.Ed. 1930 Leeds*

Ranganathan, V. R.
Saiva Siddhānta: a religio-philosophical system of south India. *B.Litt. 1923 Oxford*

Ranganayakula, G.
The cotton industry in the Madras Presidency, with special reference to the domestic and factory systems. *B.Litt. 1926 Oxford*

Ranger, A. W. G.
The Roman and English law of mortgage. *D.C.L. 1884 Oxford*

Rankin, W.
Tertullian the jurist. *Ph.D. 1929 Aberdeen*

Ransome, G. C.
The Cartulary of Tockwith. *M.A. 1930 Manchester*

Ransome, M. E.
The general election of 1710. *M.A. 1938 London, Royal Holloway College*

Ranson, C. W.
Some problems of urbanization in India: based on a study of Madras City. *B.Litt 1937 Oxford*

Rao, A. V.
The life and works of George, Lord Lyttleton, 1709-1773. *Ph.D. 1929 London*

Rao, C. R.
The application of statistical methods to problems of biological classification. *Ph.D. 1948 Cambridge*

Rao, K. G. Rama *see* Rama Rao, K. G.

Rao, K. K.
Distribution of powers between the federal and state legislatures in the draft-constitution of India. *LL.M. 1949 London, University College and London, School of Oriental and African Studies*

Rao, M. H.
Vocational education in India, with special reference to the Central Provinces and Berar. *M.Ed. 1939 Leeds*

Rao, S.
The position of women in early India, as it appears in the Vedic literature and the sacred law. *B.Litt. 1936 Oxford*

Rao, T. N. K.
An experimental study into the backwardness of elementary schoolboys in arithmetic. *M.Ed. 1934 Leeds*

Rao, V. K. R. V.
The national income of British India, 1931-32. *Ph.D. 1937 Cambridge*

Rao, W. L.
Criminal responsibility in English law. *Ph.D. 1931 Sheffield*

Rapaport, I.
Slavery in ancient Mesopotamia and its bearing on the Old Testament. *M.A. 1939 London, King's College*

Rashad, I.
An Egyptian in Ireland. *Ph.D. 1922 National University of Ireland*

Rashed, Z. E.
The Peace of Paris, 1763. *Ph.D. 1949 Liverpool*

Rashidi, Z. R. G.
Land reclamation in the Nile Delta: its geographical background and significance. *M.A. 1940 Leeds*

Ratcliffe, J. F.
Unified field theories: the theories of Kaluza and Klein, Weyl, Eddington and Einstein. *M.Sc. 1934 Wales*

Rath, B. N.
Development of education in Orissa under the British (1803-1946). *M.A. 1948 London, Institute of Education*

Ratha, R.
The study of fluctuations in homogeneous mental tasks. *Ph.D. 1949 London, University College*

Rathbone, E.
The influence of bishops and of members of cathedral bodies in the intellectual life of England, 1066 to 1216. *Ph.D. 1936 London, King's College*

Ratledge, E. D.
The relation of the seventeenth century 'character' to the comedy of manners. *M.A. 1933 Manchester*

Ratnasuriya, M. D.
An examination of Sikhavalanda. *Ph.D. 1931 London, External Degree*

Rattray, R. S.
Customs of the Ashanti relating to birth, puberty, marriage, and death. *B.Sc. 1925 Oxford*

Raum, O. F.
The educational system of the Chaga, with special reference to 1. The light thrown by social anthropology on the origins of education. 2. The theories of the nature of education and of educational psychology. 3. The educational planning of the present day. *Ph.D. 1938 London, External Degree*

Ravden, M.
Some family factors in the development of children's behaviour patterns. *Ph.D. 1947 London, External Degree*

Raven, C. E.
Apollinarianism. *D.D. 1923 Cambridge*

Raven, J. C.
The performances of related individuals in tests mainly educative and mainly reproductive mental tests used in genetic studies. *M.Sc. 1936 London, King's College*

Ravi Varma, R. V.
Ancient Indian jewellery (from the earliest times to the medieval period). *M.A. 1933 London, University College*

Rawle, W. J.
The growth of free trade ideas, 1800-1830. *M.Com. 1939 Birmingham*

Rawlinson, A. E. J.
1. The resurrection of Jesus Christ considered as a historical and dogmatic problem. 2. The outlook of Jesus upon the future. *B.D. 1921 Oxford*

Rawlley, R. C.
Economic organization of the export trade of Kashmir and Indian silks, with special reference to their utilization in the British and the French markets. *M.Sc. 1918 London*

Rawlley, R. C.
Economics of the silk industry: a study in industrial organization. *D.Sc. 1919 London*

Rawnsley, W. A.
The place of natural history in English literature, 1789-1846. *M.A. 1938 London, King's College*

Rawson, C. P.
An investigation into the phenomena of aggressiveness. *M.Sc. 1934 London, School of Economics and Political Science*

Rawson, C. P.
Some aspects of evacuation. *Ph.D. 1943 Reading*

Ray, D.
The construction and validation of a group test of intelligence for English children of 13 years of age upwards. *M.A. 1948 London, Institute of Education*

Ray, H.
The dynastic history of northern India from *c.* 916 to 1196 A.D. *Ph.D. 1930 London, School of Oriental and African Studies*

Ray, S.
Anglo-Indian poetry. *Ph.D. 1929 London*

Ray, S.
The idea of liberty in relation to State and non-State organizations in England. *Ph.D. 1922 London*

Ray, S.
John Moore, 1729 to 1802. *Ph.D. 1936 London, University College*

Raybould, A. B.
Factors conditioning achievement in French among a group of adolescents. *M.A. 1946 Birmingham*

Rayburn, B.
A critical survey of theories relating to the origin of the Germanic and High German sound-shifts, with an introduction on the general problem of sound-change. *M.A. 1942 Manchester*

Raychaudhuri, B.
The fundamental principles of Sankara-Vedānta. *Ph.D. 1922 London*

Raychaudhuri, D.
The life and work of Sir Aston Cokain. *M.A. 1933 London, University College*

Raychaudhuri, G.
History of the Western Chalukyas (political and administrative). *Ph.D. 1948 London, School of Oriental and African Studies*

Rayner, B. A.
The historical geography of the Furness iron industry. *M.A. 1924 Liverpool*

Rayner, D.
Aspects of the history of the Commons in the fourteenth century. *Ph.D. 1934 Manchester*

Rayner, W. R.
The settlement of Indians on the margins of the Indian Ocean. *M.A. 1934 London, Birkbeck College*

Raynes, E. M.
A critical edition, with introduction, glossary and notes of the Old English poem *Phoenix. M.A. 1948 London, Bedford College*

Re, A. del *see* Del Re, A.

Read, A. W.
The place of Johnson's dictionary in the history of English lexicography. *B.Litt. 1933 Oxford*

Read, C.
Sir Francis Walsingham. *B.Litt. 1909 Oxford*

Read, K. E.
The relationship between food-production and social structure in simple societies. *Ph.D. 1948 London, School of Economics and Political Science*

Read, M. H.
Primitive economics with special reference to culture contact. *Ph.D. 1934 London, School of Economics and Political Science*

Reaney, M. J.
The pscyhology of the 'organized group game' with special reference to its place in the play system and its educational value. *D.Sc. 1916 London*

Reaney, P. H.
The place-names of Essex. *Ph.D. 1931 London, East London College*

Reardon, J. P.
The halberd in bronze-age Europe: a study in pre-historic origins, evolution, distribution and chronology. *Ph.D. 1936 National University of Ireland*

Reardon, J. P.
The place-names and antiquities of Kinalmeaky Barony, Co. Cork. *M.A. 1930 National University of Ireland*

Reason, H. A.
Historical survey of theories concerning the elementary nature of matter, with special reference to the four element theory and its overthrow by modern scientific work. *M.Sc. 1936 London, External Degree*

Reason, P. M.
Agricultural price records: an account of the methods of recording prices and a guide to the published wholesale price records of England and Wales. *M.Sc. 1934 Reading*

Rebbeck, D.
The history of iron shipbuilding on the Queen's Island up to July, 1874. *Ph.D. 1950 Belfast*

Rebbeck, D.
The shipyards of Britain - a geographical and historical analysis. *B.Litt. 1946 Dublin, Trinity College*

Reckert, F. S.
The Galician revival in the nineteenth and twentieth centuries, in both Castilian and Galician culture. *M.Litt. 1949 Cambridge*

Record, S. P.
The Tacitean use of prepositions, with a few remarks on the tendency of Latin to become an analytical language. *M.A. 1907 London*

Redbond, W. J.
Sea terms in early English literature. *M.A. 1934 London, King's College*

Reddi, O. V.
The burden of British public debt. *M.Sc. 1949 London, University College*

Redford, A.
Labour migration in England, 1800-1850. *Ph.D. 1922 Manchester*

Redmond, J.
Luis de León; vida y obras. *M.A. 1933 National University of Ireland*

Redmond, M. F.
The borough of Tewkesbury, 1575-1714. *M.A. 1950 Birmingham*

Redpath, R. T. H.
Four philosophical controversies engaged in by Leibniz and certain other philosophers of the later seventeenth and early eighteenth centuries. *Ph.D. 1940 Cambridge*

Reed, A. W.
Studies in the life of John Heywood and the Canon Heywood. *M.A. 1916 London*

Reed, C. G.
A metrical study of subject preferences in a boys' secondary school: an account of an experiment in the measurement of attitude. *M.Ed. 1939 Manchester*

Reed, F. O.
Public worship in sixteenth century Calvinism. *B.Litt. 1934 Oxford*

Reed, H.
Early life and works of Thomas Hardy, 1840-1878. *M.A. 1936 Birmingham*

Reed, J. C.
Humphrey Moseley, bookseller. *B.Litt. 1928 Oxford*

Reed, L.
The *Tiers Estat* in medieval French literature. *M.A. 1945 Wales*

Reed, R. C.
The Reform Bills of 1884 and 1885. *M.A. 1949 Wales*

Reed, S. K.
An investigation into wage incentives and their effect on production, with comparisons between Great Britain and the United States. *Ph.D. 1950 Edinburgh*

Reed, W. M. O.
The use of pictorial effect in the poetry of Aeschylus, Sophocles, and Euripides. *M.A. 1918 London*

Reedy, L. D.
Russian realism and the development of the English novel, 1880-1914 - a study in literary influence. *Ph.D. 1938 Dublin, Trinity College*

Reel, C. J.
Benedict Canfield (William Fitch), Capuchin: the man and his writings. *B.Litt. 1948 Oxford*

Rees, A. W.
The international organization of railway communications. *M.A. 1938 Wales*

Rees, B.
Rhai agweddau ar ganu rhydd cynnar Cymru, g yda sylw arbennig i'w gysylltiadau â chanu Saesneg(Some aspects of the free early poetry of Wales, with special reference to its connections with English poetry). *M.A. 1940 Wales*

Rees, C.
The influence exercised by the development of English prose and literary criticism upon the teaching of the vernacular tongue and study of literature in English schools. *M.A. 1909 Wales*

Rees, C. E.
MacCurdy's doctrine of patterns. *M.Sc. 1930 Bristol*

Rees, D.
Post-war biographies: their character and literary value. *M.A. 1934 Wales*

Rees, D. T.
Sir Henry Elliott, British Ambassador at Constantinople, 1867-77, with particular reference to the period 1867-74. *M.A. 1940 Wales*

Rees, D. W.
The influence of topographical conditions on the English campaigns in Wales in the twelfth and thirteenth centuries. *M.A. 1923 Wales*

Rees, E.
The increasing rigour in mathematical demonstration: a historical study. *M.A. 1926 Wales*

Rees, F. L.
The policy of Powys in the twelfth and thirteenth centuries. *M.A. 1911 Wales*

Rees, G.
The origin and development of Old Testament prophecy, with an examination of alleged similar phenomena among non-Israelitish people. *M.A. 1917 Wales*

Rees, G.
A study of Rémy de Gourmont as a literary critic, with special reference to his connection with the Symbolist Movement in French poetry from 1885-1900. *M.A. 1937 Wales*

Rees, G. B.
C. F. Hebbel's realism in theory and practice. *Ph.D. 1926 London*

Rees, G. O.
Etudes d'exotisme contemporain: les romanciers français et l'extrême-orient. *M.A. 1940 Wales*

Rees, H.
Efrydiau yn nharddiad a datblygiad geirfa ac arddull beirdd Cymraeg y cynfnod 1800-1842(Studies on the source and development of the vocabulary and style of Welsh poets of the period 1800-1842). *M.A. 1929 Wales*

Rees, H.
The northeastern expansion of London since 1770. *M.Sc. 1946 London, School of Economics and Political Science*

Rees, H.
Some poetic treatments of the Faust problem, illustrating its development before and after Goethe. *M.A. 1910 Wales*

Rees, J. M.
A comparative view of the cost of living, and standard of life and comfort, obtaining in a new and in an old country, as exemplified in the cases of South Africa and England. *M.A. 1911 Wales*

Rees, M.
Cystrawen arddodiaid ym Mhedair Cainc y Mabinogi(The syntax of prepositions in the Four Branches of the Mabinogi). *M.A. 1935 Wales*

Rees, P. T.
The Cibbers, father and son, as actors, dramatists and writers. *M.A. 1931 Wales*

Rees, R. O.
Gramadeg tafodiaith dyffryn Aman(The grammar of the dialect of the Amman Valley). *M.A. 1936 Wales*

Rees, S. G.
Galsworthy's contribution to modern drama. *M.A. 1937 Wales*

Rees, T.
The Holy Spirit in thought and experience. *Ph.D. 1922 London*

Rees, T. D. M.
Some aspects of the problem of sovereignty. *M.A. 1949 Wales*

Rees, T. H. J.
Datblygiad y gelfyddyd ysgrifennu caneuon yng Nghymru yn y XIX ganrif(The development of the art of song-writing in Wales in the XIX century). *M.A. 1930 Wales*

Rees, T. O.
The tale of mystery and terror. *M.A. 1937 Wales*

Rees, W.
An agrarian survey of South Wales and the March, 1282-1415. *D.Sc. 1920 London*

Rees, W.
The Cynic philosophers in the second century of the Christian era. *M.A. 1917 Wales*

Rees, W.
The Cynics from the first century to the fall of the Western Empire, with a special study of the problem of fate and free-will as treated by the Stoics and Cynics of the same period. *B.Litt. 1919 Oxford*

Rees, W.
An edition of *Hrafnkelssaga Freysgotha*, with introduction, normalized text, notes and glossary. *M.A. 1921 Wales*

Rees, W.
English literary criticism from Shaftesbury's *Characteristics* to Reynolds' *Discourses. Ph.D. 1926 London*

Rees, W.
The lordship of Brecon, 1066-1325. *M.A. 1914 Wales*

Rees, W.
Malthus and his relation to contemporary economic writers. *M.A. 1927 Wales*

Rees, W. H.
A survey of bilingualism in Wales and the Marches. *M.A. 1941 Liverpool*

Rees, W. H.
The vicissitudes of the Welsh language in the Marches of Wales, with special reference to its territorial distribution in modern times. *Ph.D. 1947 Wales*

Reese, A. D.
Ritual background of Celtic heroes and saints: a study of some of the survivals of pagan elements in early Celtic Christianity. *M.A. 1937 Wales*

Reese, H.
The castle and borough of Pembroke during the Middle Ages. *M.A. 1927 Wales*

Reese, P. M.
The theory and application of unanimism in the poetical works of Jules Romains. *M.A. 1934 Wales*

Reeve, E. G.
Some problems in the selection of service personnel. *M.Sc. 1948 London, University College*

Richards, T. T.
The interests of boys in the junior forms of a secondary school in relation to the teaching of science. *M.Sc. 1939 Wales*

Richards, W.
The works of Gruffydd Hiraethog. *M.A. 1925 Wales*

Richards, W. L.
Gwaith Dafydd Llwyd o Fathafarn(The work of Dafydd Llwyd of Mathafarn). *M.A. 1947 Wales*

Richards, W. M.
A general survey of the slate industry of Caernarvonshire and Merionethshire. *M.A. 1933 Liverpool*

Richards, W. M.
The history of Traeth Mawr and the industrial results of the formation of the embankment. *M.A. 1925 Wales*

Richardson, A.
Christian apologetics. *D.D. 1948 Oxford*

Richardson, A.
The concept of emergent evolution. *M.A. 1929 Liverpool*

Richardson, A.
An examination of the nature and function of miracle stories in the formation of the Gospel tradition. *B.D. 1940 Oxford*

Richardson, A. E.
1. The position of Jesus Christ in Mohammedanism. 2. Our risen Lord's appearances in Galilee. *B.D. 1902 Oxford*

Richardson, D.
The reality of extra-intellectual knowledge, with special reference to Bergson and pragmatism. *M.A. 1917 Wales*

Richardson, G. W.
The persecution under Diocletian. *M.A. 1924 London*

Richardson, H.
The use of Anglo-Norman in private and public documents of the fourteenth and fifteenth centuries. *B.Litt. 1939 Oxford*

Richardson, H. G.
The English view of usury and the distribution of wealth in the later Middle Ages. *M.A. 1912 London*

Richardson, J. A.
A factorial analysis of the reading ability in 10 year old primary school children. *M.A. 1949 Birmingham*

Richardson, J. E.
An experiment of group methods of teaching English composition with some consideration of their effects on attainment and attitude and a sociometric study of the groups involved. *M.A. 1948 London, Institute of Education*

Richardson, J. H.
A study on the minimum wage. *Ph.D. 1927 London*

Richardson, L. J. D.
Agma: a contribution to Greek alphabetology. *M.A. 1942 Wales*

Richardson, R. D.
The causes of the present conflict of ideals in the Church of England. *B.Litt. 1923 Oxford*

Richey, M. F.
Ein Beitrag zum Studium der geistlichen Lyrik des siebzehnten Jahrhunderts. *M.A. 1916 London*

Richmond, H. M.
A study of Henry Mackenzie. *Ph.D. 1923 London*

Richmond, M. W. Wakefield- *see* Wakefield-Richmond, M. V.

Rickaby, J.
The origin and extent of civil authority. *B.Sc. 1901 Oxford*

Rickman, S.
Paul Claudel. *M.A. 1936 Birmingham*

Ridd, P. M.
The Anglo-German Conventions of 1898 and their position in Anglo-German relations. *M.A. 1932 Bristol*

Riddell, D. M.
A critical analysis of recent investigations into the psychology of adolescence. *M.A. 1936 London, Institute of Education*

Riddell, H. G.
The English press and the Moroccan crisis of 1911. *M.A. 1949 Liverpool*

Riddell, J.
A study of the history and development of the School Medical Service in Liverpool from 1908 to 1939, and an attempt to assess its consequences on the health of the Liverpool school child. *M.A. 1946 Liverpool*

Riddell, R. G.
Imperial land policy, 1783-1848. *B.Litt. 1934 Oxford*

Riddick, S.
Charles Middleton, afterward Lord Barham, and naval administration, 1778-1805. *M.A. 1939 Liverpool*

Rideout, E. H.
The operation of the English Navigation Acts during the eighteenth century. *M.A. 1931 Liverpool*

Rider, B. C.
The Greek house. *M.A. 1906 London*

Rider, S. W.
Geographical considerations affecting, and arising from the location and development of the copper and allied industries of the Swansea district. *M.Sc. 1923 Wales*

Ridgeway, G. L.
The repudiation of state debts by States of the United States of America in the nineteenth century. *B.Litt. 1928 Oxford*

Ridgway, J.
Exegeses from the Epistle to the Hebrews. *D.D. 1870 Oxford*

Ridley, E. E. A.
Alcibiades. *M.A. 1909 London*

Ridley, K. B.
A definition of Keats' idea of poetry based on an examination of (1) his letters, (2) variants of his poems, (3) sources of his poems. *B.Litt. 1923 Oxford*

Ridout, E. S. F.
The commercial law of ancient Athens to 323 B.C. *Ph.D. 1935 London, University College*

Ridout, E. S. F.
The distribution of power between the federal government and the constituent states in Greek federations. *M.A. 1926 London*

Rifaat, M. A.
The monetary system of Egypt. *Ph.D. 1935 London, School of Economics and Political Science*

Rigby, F. F.
The Anglican 'via media', with special reference to the ecclesiastical conditions in Lancashire during the years 1660-1689. *M.A. 1943 Manchester*

Rigby, F. F.
The effect of the Reformation on the supply of schools in England during the sixteenth century. *M.Ed. 1941 Manchester*

Rigg, M. T.
The revival of Latin Literature in the eighth century A.D. *M.A. 1935 London, Birkbeck College*

Rigg, W. H.
1. The problem of St. John's Gospel. 2. Personal immortality. *B.D. & D.D. 1921 Oxford*

Righton, N. P.
Anglo-Belgian relations and their influence on British foreign policy in general, 1833-1839. *M.A. 1927 London*

Riker, T. W.
The political career of Henry Fox in the years 1753-1763. *B.Litt. 1908 Oxford*

Riley, W.
The finance of capital expenditure by English local authorities. *M.A. 1931 Manchester*

Riley, W. A.
St. Louis: a study of medieval kingship. *M.A. 1917 Liverpool*

Rimmer, A. T. L.
Some aspects of the development of English technical education. *M.A. 1946 Bristol*

Rimmer, A. T. L.
Some experimental investigations on the length of the seconds pendulum, 1735-1830. *M.Sc. 1939 London, University College*

Rintoul, D.
Robert Southey: a critical biography. *Ph.D. 1940 Edinburgh*

Riordan, U.
Les idées sociales de Charles Péguy. *M.A. 1931 National University of Ireland*

Rising, T. C.
An investigation of the development and character of the influence of Terence and Plautus on the earlier English drama, with some account of fifteenth and sixteenth century editions of their plays in England. *M.A. 1933 London, King's College*

Ritchie, A. C.
Types and antitypes of the Passion in English medieval art, twelfth and thirteenth centuries. *Ph.D. 1935 London, Courtauld Institute of Art*

Ritchie, J. M.
A historical sketch of organized effort on behalf of the blind in Great Britain. *Ph.D. 1927 Edinburgh*

Ritchie, O. M.
The forensic theory of the atonement in its psychological aspects. *Ph.D. 1933 Edinburgh*

Rive, A.
The history of the tobacco trade in England. *M.Litt. 1927 Cambridge*

Rivers, G. L. F. Pitt *see* Pitt-Rivers, G. L. F.

Rivett, C.
The nature and function of adolescent leisure pursuits. *M.A. 1947 Manchester*

Rix, M. E.
An economic analysis of existing English legislation concerning the limited liability company. *M.Sc. 1936 London, External Degree*

Rizvi, S. M. T.
An economic and regional geography of the United Provinces of Agra and Oudh. *Ph.D. 1937 London, External Degree*

Rizvi, S. M. Z.
Agricultural credit in India: a comparative study of arrangements for provision of agricultural credit in India and abroad. *B.Litt. 1949 Oxford*

Roach, A. W.
The food supply of Great Britain. *M.Sc. 1938 London, External Degree*

Roach, K. M.
The teaching of religious knowledge in secondary schools. *M.A. 1934 Birmingham*

Robb, B. K.
Fashions in gynecology during the last century, with remarks thereon. *M.D. 1884 Aberdeen*

Robb, N. A.
The literary and artistic manifestations of neo-Platonism in the Italian Renaissance. *D.Phil. 1933 Oxford*

Robbie, H. J. L.
A history of English religious poetry from 1500 to 1700. *Ph.D. 1928 Cambridge*

Robbie, M. L.
Discovering the Bluestockings, a neglected constellation of clever women. *Ph.D. 1947 Edinburgh*

Robbins, I. C.
A critical study of the political activities of Andrew Marvell. *Ph.D. 1926 London*

Robbins, R. F.
A critical examination of the first Epistle of St. Paul to the Corinthians, with special reference to the background of the Corinthian Church. *Ph.D. 1950 Edinburgh*

Robbins, R. H.
The medieval English religious lyric. *Ph.D. 1938 Cambridge*

Robbins, W. A.
Early and modern conceptions of Utopia. *M.A. 1911 Birmingham*

Robert, C. E.
Handwerk und Handwerker in der deutschen erzählenden Literatur vom Ausgang des achtzehnten Jahrhunderts bis zur Gegenwart. *M.A. 1939 Liverpool*

Roberts, A.
Changes in the marketing of coal brought about by the Coal Mines Act of 1930, with special reference to Lancashire. *Ph.D. 1939 Manchester*

Roberts, A.
A critical study of some mechanical aids in the teaching of botany. *M.A. 1933 London, Institute of Education*

Roberts, A. E.
History of trade relations between Bordeaux and Britain in the eighteenth century, with special reference to the wine and spirit trade. *M.A. 1926 Wales*

Roberts, A. E.
The theories of Cardinal Pierre d'Ailly concerning forms of government in Church and State with special reference to his interest in suggestions made by William of Occam. *M.A. 1931 London, Bedford College*

Roberts, A. K. B.
The central and local financial organisation and administrative machinery of the royal free chapel of St. George within the castle of Windsor from its foundation (1348) to the treasurership of William Gillot (1415-16). *Ph.D. 1943 London, Royal Holloway College*

Roberts, A. M.
Preliminary studies on the alliterative version of the *Gest hystoriale* as compared with the original Latin of Guido delle Colonne. *M.A. 1920 London*

Roberts, B. H.
An economic study of cattle and sheep production, with particular reference to Welsh farm stock enterprises. *M.Sc. 1949 Wales*

Roberts, B. J.
The agriculture and agricultural implements of the Hebrews. *M.A. 1936 Wales*

Roberts, C. G. M.
Platonism and mysticism in J. Donne, H. Vaughan and T. Traherne. *M.A. 1913 Bristol*

Roberts, D. C.
Some aspects of the history of the lordship of Oswestry to A.D. 1300. *M.A. 1939 Wales*

Roberts, D. E.
An analysis of the 'one-inch to the mile' ordnance survey map of Great Britain, with special reference to the methods of production and the persistence or change of conventional symbols throughout successive editions of the map. *M.Sc. 1946 Wales*

Roberts, D. E.
The religious philosophy of Hastings Rashdall. *Ph.D. 1936 Edinburgh*

Roberts, D. E.
The religious thought of Thomas Carlyle. *Ph.D. 1948 Edinburgh*

Roberts, D. E.
The theory of reality as perfect, with special reference to its bearing on ethics. *M.A. 1916 Wales*

Roberts, D. E. J.
The coal industry of the U.S.S.R. *M.Sc. 1948 London, School of Economics and Political Science*

Roberts, D. G.
Lucian as a critic and lover of art. *M.A. 1910 London*

Roberts, D. M.
The history of the town and castle of Carmarthen to 1603. *M.A. 1908 Wales*

Roberts, D. T.
The conflict between the logical and the historical standpoint in fundamental questions of grammar, with reference to Latin. *M.A. 1907 Wales*

Roberts, E.
The judicial proceedings under the Dictum of Kenilworth, West Berkshire. *M.A. 1927 Manchester*

Roberts, E.
The standard of life. *M.Sc. 1928 London*

Roberts, E. H.
A study of the growth of the provision of public facilities for leisure time occupations by local authorities of Merseyside. *M.A. 1933 Liverpool*

Roberts, E. Jones-
Richard Jones o'r Wern: his life and work. *M.A. 1947 Liverpool*

Roberts, E. K. R. R.
A contribution to the study of emigration from north Wales to the United States of America, 1800-1850. *M.A. 1931 Liverpool*

Roberts, E. M.
Characteristics of the grammar and style of Bion and Moschus. *M.A. 1908 London*

Roberts, E. P.
Gweirydd ap Rhys: ei fywyd a'i waith(Gweirydd ap Rhys: his life and his work). *M.A. 1941 Wales*

Roberts, E. S.
French works in contemporary British reviews (1800-1820). *M.A. 1928 Liverpool*

Roberts, E. S.
Llysieulyfr meddyginiaethol a briodolir i William Salesbury(A medicinal herbal attributed to William Salesbury). *M.A. 1917 Wales*

Roberts, F.
The psychology of C. G. Jung in relation to religious thought and experience. *M.A. 1946 Birmingham*

Roberts, G.
The boroughs of north Wales: their parliamentary history from the Act of Union to the first Reform Act (1535-1832). *M.A. 1929 Wales*

Roberts, G. D.
Discipline of Greek armies. *M.A. 1927 Wales*

Roberts, G. D.
The history of the study of the classics in Wales during the sixteenth century. *B.Litt. 1923 Oxford*

Roberts, G. J.
The conditions of labour in Israel as portrayed in the Old Testament and the Mishnah. *M.A. 1936 Wales*

Roberts, G. O.
The development of the political ideas of Wordsworth and Shelley, with special reference to their conception of freedom. *M.A. 1938 Wales*

Roberts, G. T.
Bywyd a gwaith Peter Bailey Williams(The life and work of Peter Bailey Williams). *M.A. 1935 Wales*

Roberts, G. T.
Dafydd Ddu o Eryri a'i gysylltiadau llenyddol(Dafydd Ddu of Eryri and his literary connections). *M.A. 1929 Wales*

Roberts, H.
A history of local government in the West Riding of Yorkshire since 1888. *M.Com. 1943 Leeds*

Roberts, H.
Judicial investigations under the Dictum of Kenilworth, Essex. *M.A. 1928 Manchester*

Roberts, H.
Proofs of the being of God. *M.A. 1921 Wales*

Roberts, H.
Religious experience and its objective reference. *Ph.D. 1927 Cambridge*

Roberts, H. Hughes-
Welsh hagiography with special reference to Saint Margaret. *M.A. 1949 Liverpool*

Roberts, H. L.
Political aspects of the agrarian problem in Roumania, 1918-45. *D.Phil. 1948 Oxford*

Roberts, H. P.
Nonconformist academies in Wales (1662-1862). *M.A. 1922 Liverpool*

Roberts, H. W.
The influence of the relations between groups upon the inner life of groups, with special reference to black and white in the Southern States of the United States during the nineteenth century. *M.A. 1934 London, School of Economics and Political Science*

Roberts, J. E.
The controversy regarding Richard Dugdale, the 'Surey demoniac'. *M.A. 1944 Manchester*

Roberts, J. R.
The nature, need and destiny of man in Jewish thought from the Exile to the Advent. *M.A. 1941 Wales*

Roberts, J. W.
Edmwnd Prys: hanes ei fywyd a chasgliad o'i weithiau(Edmwnd Prys; the history of his life and a collection of his works). *M.A. 1938 Wales*

Roberts, M.
The Whig Party, 1807-12. *D.Phil. 1935 Oxford*

Roberts, M. J.
The attempts at Presbyterian-Episcopal accommodation in Scotland and their influence on modern movements of unity. *Ph.D. 1949 Glasgow*

Roberts, M. J.
Goethe's influence on Byron and Scott. *M.A. 1915 Wales*

Roberts, M. R.
The nomenclature of chips and shavings in France: a study in linguistic geography. *M.A. 1933 Manchester*

Roberts, N.
The presentation of the liberal middle class in the novels and *Novellen* of Friedrich Spielhagen. *M.A. 1949 Birmingham*

Roberts, R.
Studies in the morphology and syntax of the Vespasian Psalter. *Ph.D. 1934 Leeds*

Roberts, R. E.
Prudentius' treatment of Roman religion. *M.A. 1938 Wales*

Roberts, R. F.
Bywyd a gwaith Dr. John Davies, Mallwyd(The life and work of Dr. John Davies, Mallwyd). *M.A. 1950 Wales*

Roberts, R. O.
The history of the public debts of the United Kingdom from 1815 to 1939, and the economic doctrine relating thereto. *M.A. 1942 Wales*

Roberts, R. S.
The Arthurian legend in English literature. *M.A. 1901 Wales*

Roberts, S.
A bibliography of travel books translated from English into French during the period 1750-1800. *M.A. 1949 Leeds*

Roberts, S. H.
History of French colonial policy, 1870-1925. *D.Sc. 1929 London*

Roberts, T.
The poetical works of Dafydd Nanmor. *M.A. 1910 Wales*

Roberts, T.
The poetical works of Gruffudd ab Ieuan ap Llywelyn Fychan. *M.A. 1910 Wales*

Roberts, W. B.
Butler's contribution to ethical science. *M.A. 1917 Liverpool*

Roberts, W. E.
The social and political satire in the novel of the eighteenth century (1740-1780), with special reference to Fielding and Smollett. *M.A. 1932 Wales*

Roberts, W. F. J.
A critical edition of *Hali Meidenhad*. *Ph.D. 1949 London, University College*

Roberts, W. F. J.
The ellipsis of the subject pronoun (and related phenomena) in English in the twelfth, thirteenth and fourteenth centuries. *M.A. 1933 London, University College*

Roberts, W. L.
Bywyd a gwaith John Evans (I. D. Ffraid)(Life and work of John Evans (I. D. Ffraid)). *M.A. 1950 Wales*

Robertson, A.
1. The atonement. 2. St. Paul's doctrine of Christian ethics in relation to the Holy Spirit. *B.D. & D.D. 1897 Oxford*

Robertson, A.
The biography of Sir Robert Moray, 1608-1673. *B.Litt. 1912 Oxford*

Robertson, A. J.
Anglo-Saxon charters. *Ph.D. 1934 Cambridge*

Robertson, A. J.
Report on hydrographical investigations in the Faroe-Shetland Channel and the northern part of the North Sea during the years 1904-1905. *D.Sc. 1906 Saint Andrew's*

Robertson, A. M.
Anthropological account of the Aborigines of western Australia together with the climate, the diseases, and the productions of the country. *M.D. 1883 Edinburgh*

Robertson, A. S.
The coin hoards of Roman Britain. *M.A. 1936 London, University College*

Robertson, C. E.
The psychology of musical appreciation: an analysis of the bases and nature of the experience of listening to music. *Ph.D. 1936 Durham*

Robertson, C. J.
The sugar trade: a study in economic geography. *Ph.D. 1930 London, School of Economics and Political Science*

Robertson, E. L.
Shelley's philosophic thought, with special reference to his view of immortality. *M.Litt. 1941 Cambridge*

Robertson, F. W.
The rise of a Scottish navy, 1460-1513. *Ph.D. 1934 Edinburgh*

Robertson, G.
On the nature of dipsomania, with reference to consciousness and volition. *M.D. 1894 Aberdeen*

Robertson, H. M.
The causes and progress of the growth of economic individualism in England in the sixteenth and at the beginning of the seventeenth century. *Ph.D. 1930 Cambridge*

Robertson, H. M.
The growth of economic individualism in England in modern times: Part I : introductory to the end of the Middle Ages. *M.A. 1926 Leeds*

Robertson, J.
1. The doctrine of the future life in the Old Testament. 2. The origin of Hebrew prophecy. *B.D. and D.D. 1897 Oxford*

Robertson, J.
Owen Felltham: a critical study. *M.A. 1937 Liverpool*

Robertson, J. F.
The acoustical and optical work of Thomas Young in relation to his contemporaries. *M.Sc. 1938 London, University College*

Robertson, L. A.
English foreign policy during the reign of William III: in particular the relations of England with the Swiss Protestants. *B.Litt. 1926 Oxford*

Roberts-Thomson, E.
The relation of Baptists to Disciples (Churches) of Christ. *M.A. 1949 Bristol*

Robins, M.
Investigation of the dependence of tests of attainment in school subjects on 'g', 'f' and 'p' factors. *M.A. 1939 London, King's College*

Robinson, A. R.
Fontane as a social novelist. *Ph.D. 1950 Edinburgh*

Robinson, E. F.
Diplomatic relations between England and Serbia from the return of Milos to the death of Michael, 1859-1867. *M.A. 1925 London*

Robinson, E. H.
Floire et Blancheflor: a critical edition of the popular version. *M.A. 1935 Manchester*

Robinson, E. M. B.
The administrative relations between England and Ireland, 1660-1670. *M.A. 1927 Manchester*

Robinson, E. M. M.
The issue between Bradley and his critics concerning the nature and reality of relations. *B.Litt. 1937 Oxford*

Robinson, E. W.
Persian miniature painting in the Bodleian. *B.Litt. 1938 Oxford*

Robinson, F.
The region of Ormskirk. *M.A. 1928 Liverpool*

Robinson, F. H.
The coal mining industry in Great Britain: yesterday, today and tomorrow. *M.Sc. 1927 London*

Robinson, F. W.
William Ellis and his work for education. *M.A. 1919 London*

Robinson, G. E.
Legal liability of public authorities and local administrative bodies. *LL.D. 1914 London*

Robinson, G. M. N.
La jeunesse de Corneille et la formation de son génie. *M.A. 1948 Birmingham*

Robinson, H.
The economic significance of weights and measures: a study in the progress towards uniformity. *M.A. 1948 Liverpool*

Robinson, H.
1. Sufficiency of Holy Scripture for salvation - Article VI. 2. The sacrament of the Lord's Supper - Article XXVIII. *B.D. & D.D. 1871 Oxford*

Robinson, H. M.
1. The divinity of the Son. 2. The personality of the Holy Ghost. *B.D. 1876 Oxford*

Robinson, H. M.
Exegeses of: I Corinthians vii-xi; xi-xiv; xv; xvi. *D.D. 1876 Oxford*

Robinson, H. S.
English Shakespearian criticism in the eighteenth century. *M.Litt. 1930 Cambridge*

Robinson, H. W.
Labour mobility: its measurement and causes. *D.Phil. 1939 Oxford*

Robinson, H. W.
A mathematical and statistical analysis of economic phenomena connected with the building industry. *Ph.D. 1937 London, School of Economics and Political Science*

Robinson, I. H.
The life and works of Hester Chapone. *B.Litt. 1936 Oxford*

Robinson, J. A. T.
Thou who art. *Ph.D. 1946 Cambridge*

Robinson, K.
Characterisation in the *Chanson de Geste* of *Girart de Vienne*, by Bertrand de Bar-sur-Aube. *M.A. 1937 London, Royal Holloway College*

Robinson, L.
Judaea under the procurators. *M.Litt. 1927 Cambridge*

Robinson, M. F. Howard- *see* Howard-Robinson, M. F.

Robinson, M. G.
The correspondence of Bishop Percy and Thomas Warton. *B.Litt. 1935 Oxford*

Robinson, N. H. G.
The claim of morality. *D.Litt. 1948 Glasgow*

Robinson, R. G. F.
The province of logic and its relation to grammar, metaphysics, and psychology with special reference to the view of Cook Wilson. *B.Litt. 1927 Oxford*

Robinson, T. H.
The antecedents and beginnings of the Amalgamated Society of Engineers. *B.Litt. 1928 Oxford*

Robinson, T. Hayes- *see* Hayes-Robinson, T.

Robson, A. H.
The education of children engaged in industry in England, 1833-76. *Ph.D. 1930 London, King's College*

Robson, C. A.
The French version of the sermons of Maurice de Sully. *B.Litt. 1939 Oxford*

Robson, E.
Some letters of Sir James Murray. *M.A. 1948 Manchester*

Robson, J. L.
Comparative study of the law affecting corporate trustees in the United States of America, New Zealand and England. *Ph.D. 1939 London, University College*

Robson, R. J.
The Oxfordshire election of 1754. *B.Litt. 1947 Oxford*

Robson, W. A.
The relation of wealth to welfare. *Ph.D. 1925 London*

Robson, W. F.
L'education des filles d'après les idées de Fénelon. *M.A. 1924 Liverpool*

Robson, W. N.
The principles of legal liability for trespass and injuries by animals. *LL.D. 1914 Leeds*

Roby, W.
The history of the Levant Company 1603-1681: a study in commercial history. *M.A. 1927 Manchester*

Roche, J. C.
The history, development and organisation of the Birmingham jewellery trade. *M.Com. 1926 Birmingham*

Roche, J. L.
De Alexandri Magni fortuna aut virtute apud Plutarchum. *M.A. 1937 National University of Ireland*

Roche, J. W.
Life and works of William Bell Scott. *M.A. 1930 London, University College*

Rochester, C. P.
The C child, with special reference to the C child in senior schools. *M.A. 1939 Birmingham*

Rochester, H.
The application of vocational selection and guidance methods in a technical college. *M.A. 1938 Birmingham*

Rockett, K.
Le pessimisme de Voltaire entre 1759 et 1769. *M.A. 1939 Manchester*

Rockey, O.
The political theory of Thomas Jefferson. *B.Litt. 1925 Oxford*

Rockow, L.
Contemporary political thought in England. *Ph.D. 1925 London*

Rocks, M.
The philosophy of G. K. Chesterton. *M.A. 1941 National University of Ireland*

Roderick, A. J.
Agrarian conditions in Herefordshire and the adjacent border during the later Middle Ages. *Ph.D. 1938 London, School of Economics and Political Science*

Roderick, A. J.
A study of Anglo-Welsh political relations, with special reference to constitutional matters, 1218-1282. *M.A. 1935 Wales*

Rodgers, A.
Mundart Peter Roseggers, mit einer Abhandlung über seine Leben und seine Waldheimat aus seinen längeren Romanen. *M.A. 1931 Leeds*

Rodgers, A.
Part- and full-time vocational schools in Germany. *M.Ed. 1939 Leeds*

Rodgers, D. D. E.
The industrial geography of Liverpool and district. *M.A. 1933 Liverpool*

Rodgers, H. B.
Preston: the interrelations of town and region. *M.A. 1950 Manchester*

Roe, F. C.
Les valets et les servantes dans la comédie de Molière. *M.A. 1920 Birmingham*

Roebuck, C. M.
Samuel Daniel: a biographical and critical study. *B.Litt. 1926 Oxford*

Roediger, C. F.
The State railways of Europe. *B.Litt. 1909 Oxford*

Rogers, C.
Athrawiaeth y Drindod a pherson Crist yng Nghymru o 1860(The doctrine of the Trinity and the Person of Christ in Wales from 1860). *M.A. 1934 Wales*

Rogers, D. J.
The syntax of Chaucer's *Troilus and Criseyde*. *M.A. 1925 Wales*

Rogers, D. J.
The syntax of *Cursor Mundi*. *B.Litt. 1932 Oxford*

Rogers, D. R.
The Eliu and Jahweh speeches in the Book of Job, investigated from the literary and linguistic points of view. *M.A. 1915 Wales*

Rogers, E.
The history of trade unionism in the coal-mining industry of north Wales up to 1914. *M.A. 1928 Wales*

Rogers, E. B.
The external affairs of Canada, 1926-1934. *M.Sc. 1935 London, School of Economics and Political Science*

Rogers, F. C.
The Evangelical revival and Congregationalism. *M.A. 1909 Liverpool*

Rogers, F. H.
The Bristol craft guilds during the sixteenth and seventeenth centuries. *M.A. 1949 Bristol*

Rogers, L. E.
An edition of British Museum ms. Harley 2372. *B.Litt. 1934 Oxford*

Rogers, M. S. Vercoe- *see* Vercoe-Rogers, M. S.

Rogers, N. M.
The settlement of labour disputes in Canada. *B.Litt. 1922 Oxford*

Rogers, R. S.
Athrawiaeth y diewedd(The doctrine of the end). *M.A. 1934 Wales*

Rogers, T. C.
The life, work and influence of George Lillo. *Ph.D. 1937 London, Queen Mary College*

Roggendorff, H.
Heian literature, with special reference to the Uta-Monogatari. *M.A. 1940 London, School of Oriental and African Studies*

Rolbant, S.
Inquiry into institutional safeguards on the freedom of the individual in the modern democratic state. *Ph.D. 1946 London, School of Economics and Political Science*

Roll, E.
Early industrial organisation: a history of the firm of Boulton and Watt. *Ph.D. 1930 Birmingham*

Rollinson, D.
Local finance (England and Wales). *M.Com. 1924 Birmingham*

Rollinson, W. W.
Sir Robert Peel and the Free Trade movement in the first half of the nineteenth century, especially during the years 1842-1847. *M.A. 1930 Birmingham*

Rollo, W.
The Basque dialect of Manquina. *D.Litt. 1929 Glasgow*

Rombo, G.
Contribuzione allo studio biografico e critico di Paolo Antonio Rolli, in base a nuove recerche e documenti inediti, con speciale rifermento alle sue attività letterarie in Inghilterra. *Ph.D. 1937 London, Bedford College*

Rona, F.
Currency and banking in central Europe, 1919-1938. *M.Sc. 1947 London, School of Economics and Political Science*

Ronan, S. J.
Irish death duty code. *M.A. 1947 National University of Ireland*

Ronimois, H. E.
Soviet economic life and the general categories of economic analysis: comparative studies of the forms of value, distribution and production under Soviet and other systems of economic organization. *Ph.D. 1949 London, School of Economics and Political Science*

Rooke, B. E.
An edition of the *Friend* by S. T. Coleridge. *Ph.D. 1949 London, University College*

Rooney, B. P.
Metal-workers in early Ireland. *M.A. 1946 National University of Ireland*

Roos, G. D.
The development of the 'just war' conception, especially since Grotius. *B.Litt. 1936 Oxford*

Rooum, J. M.
An experimental investigation into the processes of solving arithmetical problems by children in a modern school. *M.Ed. 1936 Leeds*

Roper, J. I.
The influence of geography upon the development, distribution, and organization of the leather industry of Great Britain. *B.Litt. 1924 Oxford*

Rose, A.
Many-valued logic. *M.Sc. 1950 Manchester*

Rose, A. N.
A historical study of the ethical atmosphere at the beginning of the Christian era. *M.A. 1912 Birmingham*

Rose, C. H.
A study of the relation of Plato's philosophy to theism. *M.A. 1922 Birmingham*

Rose, D.
The relation of the Christian doctrine and experience of forgiveness to psychological health. *M.A. 1948 Birmingham*

Rose, F. H. E. T.
The committee system in local government. *M.Sc. 1938 London, School of Economics and Political Science*

Rose, M. A.
Petitions in Parliament under the Lancastrians, from, or relating to, towns. *M.A. 1926 London*

Rose, S.
Ovid in English literature. *M.A. 1922 London*

Rose, W.
The development of *Weltschmerz* in German literature from *Werther* to the beginning of the Romantic movement. *Ph.D. 1923 London*

Rose, W.
Ethical and social features of the German people in the fifteenth and sixteenth centuries, as represented in the Volkslied of the period. *M.A. 1914 Birmingham*

Roseby, M.
A study of Oehlenschläger. *M.A. 1913 London*

Rosedale, H. G.
1. Church government. 2. The Apocrypha in relation to the Church. *B.D. 1897 Oxford*

Rosedale, H. G.
Expositions of: St. Matthew iv.1-10; Acts vii.2-53; I Corinthians xiv.34,35; I Timothy ii.11-12. *D.D. 1901 Oxford*

Rosedale, W. E.
1. The authorship of the Pastoral Epistles. 2. The discipline of the primitive Church in regard to errors in faith and morals, as it may be gathered from the New Testament. *B.D. & D.D. 1909 Oxford*

Rosen, K.
A study of the Musar movement. *M.A. 1943 Manchester*

Rosen, S. McK.
The individual in some recent British thought. *Ph.D. 1931 London, School of Economics and Political Science*

Rosenau, H.
The architectural development of the synagogue. *Ph.D. 1940 London, Courtauld Institute of Art*

Rosenfeld, S. M.
Prologues and epilogues of the Restoration period, 1660-1700, considered in relation to the audience, theatrical conditions, and the dramatic productivity of the age. *M.A. 1925 London*

Rosetti, R. V.
Observation of a method of teaching English in secondary schools. *M.A. 1949 London, Institute of Education*

Rosevere, A. M. B.
Charles Péguy as a literary critic. *Ph.D. 1938 London, King's College*

Rosevere, A. M. B.
The place of the aesthetic in education, as determined by changing social conditions, and its place in the curriculum. *M.A. 1940 Reading*

Roskell, J. S.
The personnel of the House of Commons in 1422. *D.Phil. 1941 Oxford*

Ross, A.
New Zealand aspirations in the Pacific in the nineteenth century. *Ph.D. 1950 Cambridge*

Ross, B. R.
Contribution to the study of the geomorphology and drainage development of the Lower Thames Basin. *Ph.D. 1932 London, External Degree*

Ross, C.
Studies in the chemical work of Claude Louis Berthollet (1748-1822). *M.Sc. 1934 London, University College*

Ross, C.
Studies in the history of dyeing. *Ph.D. 1946 London, University College*

Ross, C. D.
The Yorkshire baronage, 1399-1433. *D.Phil. 1950 Oxford*

Ross, D. J. A.
The place of Gaston Paris in romance studies. *M.A. 1936 London, University College*

Ross, D. J. A.
Some thirteenth century French versions of the *Chirurgia* of Roger of Salerno. *Ph.D. 1940 London, University College*

Ross, J. S.
The doctrine of recapitulation in its application to the teaching of mathematics. *M.A. 1923 London*

Ross, L. L.
The effect of the advance in scientific knowledge upon seventeenth century literature. . *M.A. 1912 Birmingham*

Ross, M.
The philosophical positions of Malebranche and Berkeley. *M.A. 1920 London*

Ross, P. I.
La vocation dans les romans de P. Loti. *M.A. 1927 Birmingham*

Ross, S. M. Leith- *see* Leith-Ross, S. M.

Ross, T. A.
Servitudes in the law of Scotland: principles, sources and influences which have affected the law. *Ph.D. 1932 Edinburgh*

Rosser, D. T.
A regional and economic survey of the anthracite area of Carmarthenshire. *M.A. 1948 Wales*

Rosser, G. C.
The influence of the French revolutionary theorists (Voltaire, Rousseau, D'Holbach etc.) upon Shelley. *M.A. 1939 Wales*

Rost, F. E. B.
Report on existing educational institutions in Denmark. *M.A. 1928 London*

Rosteutscher, J. H. W.
The history of the German controversy on the origin of language. *Ph.D. 1937 Cambridge*

Rostow, W. W.
British trade fluctuations, 1868-86: a chronicle and a commentary. *B.Litt. 1938 Oxford*

Rostowski, R.
A study of the economics of international migration, 1820-1914. *Ph.D. 1943 Edinburgh*

Roth, C.
The last Florentine Republic, 1527-1530. *D.Phil. 1925 Oxford*

Roth, C.
The last Florentine Republic, to the fall of Niccolo Capponi. *B.Litt. 1923 Oxford*

Roth, G. K.
Modern Fiji: changes in native custom. *M.Sc. 1937 Cambridge*

Roth, H. L.
A critical discussion of the sources of Spinoza, with special reference to Maimonides and Descartes. *D.Phil. 1922 Oxford*

Roth, N.
Environment and the theories of instinct. *M.A. 1936 London, King's College*

Roth, N.
Political thought and the population problem. *M.Sc. 1939 London, School of Economics and Political Science*

Rothenberg, W.
Attempt and participation in Roman penal law. *M.Litt. 1941 Cambridge*

Rothenstein, J. K. N.
The development of colour and design in nineteenth century painting, with special reference to the conflict between the academic revolutionary traditions. *Ph.D. 1932 London, University College*

Rothney, G. O.
British policy in the North American cod fisheries with special reference to foreign competition, 1776-1819. *Ph.D. 1939 London, King's College*

Rothney, G. O.
The history of Newfoundland and Labrador, 1754 to 1783. *M.A. 1934 London, King's College*

Rothwell, H.
A preliminary study of the chronicles and instruments for a constitutional history of the years 1296-1301 in England. *Ph.D. 1930 Cambridge*

Rothwell, M. M.
Judicial proceedings under the Dictum de Kenilworth, in Northamptonshire. *M.A. 1929 Manchester*

Round, F. E.
The early history of Roman Catholic emancipation, 1760-1793. *M.A. 1930 Birmingham*

Round, L. M.
The judicial proceedings under the Dictum of Kenilworth, Surrey. Revised text. *M.A. 1928 Manchester*

Round, M. G.
The living dialect of Broughton-in-Furness. *M.A. 1949 Leeds*

Rourke, S. T.
Bread making: evolution of the industry and the organisation of a modern bakery. *M.Comm. 1927 National University of Ireland*

Rout, D.
New education for the new India. *B.Litt. 1948 Dublin, Trinity College*

Routledge, F. J.
Bodleian mss. relating to the later Tudors, with special reference to the currency literature of the period. *B.Litt. 1920 Oxford*

Routley, E. R.
The relations between theology and music viewed in the light of the works of theologians and the decisions of ecclesiastical authorities. *B.D. 1946 Oxford*

Rowan, B. L.
The Leix-Offaly Plantation. *M.A. 1940 National University of Ireland*

Rowbottom, D.
Pneumatics in the seventeenth century. *M.Sc. 1943 London, External Degree*

Rowe, B. J. H.
John, Duke of Bedford, as regent of France, 1422-35: his policy and administration in the North. *B.Litt. 1927 Oxford*

Rowe, C. F.
The theoretical drawings of Inigo Jones: their sources and scope. *M.A. 1947 London, Warburg Institute*

Rowe, J. H.
Notes on the early history of the Hundred of Penwith in Cornwall, with a more detailed history of the parish of Phillack with its dependent chapelry of Gwithian. *M.A. 1931 Leeds*

Rowe, J. W. F.
Changes of wage rates in certain industries during the last 30-40 years, and in particular, the relations between changes in rates and changes in earnings, and their causes. *M.Sc. 1923 London*

Rowe, K. M.
A critical study of the life and works of Sir John Denham. *M.A. 1931 Reading*

Rowland, E. J.
The political and social organization of Gaul under the Roman Empire. *M.A. 1910 Wales*

Rowland, I.
A survey and criticism of the scope of natural science teaching in girls' secondary schools with proposals for increasing its practical value. *M.A. 1927 Liverpool*

Rowland, J.
Durkheim's social theory with special reference to the position of the individual in society. *M.A. 1948 London, Bedford College*

Rowland, S. C.
The education of an Athenian. *M.A. 1912 London*

Rowlands, E. R.
A critical study of the *Peshitta* text of Psalms, books III and IV (Psalms 73-106), in relation to the Massoretic text and the Septuagint version. *M.A. 1939 Wales*

Rowlands, W.
Barddoniaeth Tomos Prys o Blas Iolyn(The poetry of Thomas Prys of Plas Iolyn). *M.A. 1912 Wales*

Rowlandson, J.
Auguste Barbier: sa vie et son oeuvre. *Ph.D. 1942 Durham*

Rowley, H. H.
A comparison of the grammar and vocabulary of the Aramaic portions of the Old Testament with those of the Aramaic papyri and inscriptions. *B.Litt. 1928 Oxford*

Rowley, R. G.
The effects of notice on contracts for the sale of land with particular reference to the registration of land charges. *LL.D. 1948 Leeds*

Rowley, R. G.
Recent developments in the law of restrictive covenants affecting land. *LL.M. 1942 Leeds*

Roy, H. C.
The epic in Hindi literature. *Ph.D. 1949 London, School of Oriental and African Studies*

Roy, S.
An examination of the ultimate postulates of morality. *M.A. 1913 London*

Royds, A.
The relationship of juvenile delinquency and environment in an industrial town. *M.Ed. 1936 Manchester*

Royds, T. F.
1. The scientific objections to the utility of prayer. 2. The Book of Job and the problems arising out of it. *B.D. 1910 Oxford*

Royle, C. H.
A critical edition of the poems of Gontier de Soignies. *B.Litt. 1937 Oxford*

Royston, P.
An investigation into the relative efficacy of different methods of speech instruction, including some study of factors influencing speech. *M.A. 1945 London, Institute of Education*

Rozdon, P. N.
Individual differences in colour memory. *Ph.D. 1932 Edinburgh*

Rozelaar, L. A.
Le Romantisme du *Memorial de Sainte-Helene* et son influence sur Victor Hugo. *M.A. 1924 London*

Ruairc, M. Ní *see* Ní Ruairc, M.

Ruan, J. J.
Habits in moral training. *M.A. 1936 National University of Ireland*

Rubie, A. E.
1. The origin and characteristics of St. Mark's Gospel, and its relation to the other Synoptic Gospels. 2. The authorship, date, sources, and historical credibility of the Acts of the Apostles. *B.D. & D.D. 1904 Oxford*

Rubin, A.
Social criticism in the Hungarian novel (1620-1850). *Ph.D. 1945 London, External Degree*

Ruck, B. A.
John Galsworthy: some ideas in the plays and novels, in the essays and stories. *M.A. 1928 Birmingham*

Rudall, R. J.
The foundation of South Australia. *B.Litt. 1911 Oxford*

Ruddock, A. A.
The trade of Southampton with the Mediterranean. *Ph.D. 1940 London, School of Economics and Political Science*

Ruddock, J. W.
Economics of the Consumers' Co-Operative Movement. *M.Sc. 1939 London, School of Economics and Political Science*

Ruddock, N. H. C.
1. Justification. 2. The forgiveness of sins. *B.D. and D.D. 1898 Oxford*

Rude, B. S.
A study of the conception of life in the synoptic teaching of Jesus, and its development in the Pauline and Johannine writings. *Ph.D. 1938 Edinburgh*

Rudkin, E. H.
1. Studies in the Holy Eucharist. 2. Ecclesiastes. *B.D. 1924 Oxford*

Rudkin, O. D.
The Low Country cloth towns at the end of the thirteenth century. *M.A. 1916 Liverpool*

Rudkin, O. D.
Thomas Spence and his connections. *M.A. 1924 London*

Rudnyánszky de Dezsar, V. M. F. M. A.
Goldoni and Gozzi. *B.Litt. 1941 Dublin, Trinity College*

Rudra, A.
The position of the Viceroy and Governor of India. *Ph.D. 1938 London, School of Economics and Political Science*

Ruffell, J. V.
William Barnes: study of the man and poet and of his work in connection with Dorset and the Dorset dialect. *Ph.D. 1948 London, External Degree*

Ruini, C.
La politica agraria della Granbrettagna. *M.Com. 1940 Birmingham*

Rule, A. K.
The theistic philosophy of Hermann Lotze. *Ph.D. 1923 Edinburgh*

Rule, A. M. B.
John Bunyan: an original literary artist. *M.A. 1929 Birmingham*

Rumsey, G. R.
The contribution of science teaching to moral training. *M.A. 1926 London*

Rumyaneck, J.
The economic and social development of the Jews in England, 1730-1860. *Ph.D. 1933 London, School of Economics and Political Science*

Rundle, A. S. R.
The gradual breakdown of inflexion in the Indo-European languages. *Ph.D. 1949 London, External Degree*

Rupp, E. G.
Studies in the making of the English Protestant tradition. *B.D. 1946 Cambridge*

Ruscoe, R. G.
The place of mathematical history in school mathematics. *M.A. 1925 London*

Rushe, M. M. M.
Taighde ar dheilbheolus an 13-14 céad. Corus briathardha *Beatha Fheichin Thobhair*(A study of 13th and 14th century morphology. The verbal system of *Beatha Fheichin Thobhair*). *M.A. 1948 National University of Ireland*

Rushforth, M.
John Taylor, water poet and journalist. *M.A. 1934 London, University College*

Rushton, A.
The physical and agricultural geography of the Maltese Islands. *M.Sc. 1948 London, External Degree*

Rushton, J.
Birmingham: an analysis of geographical influences on the metal industries. *M.Sc. 1936 London, Bedford College*

Rushton, J. L.
The influence of Spenser on English literature of the early eighteenth century, 1700-1750. *Ph.D. 1934 Sheffield*

Rusk, W. M. R.
The relationship of instinctive and rational factors in the religous attitude: a psychological inquiry. *Ph.D. 1927 Edinburgh*

Russell, C. S.
Form and function. *D.Sc. 1921 Glasgow*

Russell, D. S.
The psychology of the Apocalyptists, 200 B.C.-A.D. 100. *B.Litt. 1945 Oxford*

Russell, F. R. J.
Ricarda Huch and E. G. Kolbenheyer as historical novelists: a contribution to the problem of the development of the historical novel in Germany. *M.A. 1937 London, University College*

Russell, F. T.
Social security in south Rhodesia. *Ph.D. 1947 London, External Degree*

Russell, I. S.
British trade with Turkey and the decline of the Levant Company, 1790-1825. *M.A. 1932 Manchester*

Russell, I. S.
The later history of the Levant Company, 1753-1825. *Ph.D. 1935 Manchester*

Russell, J. A.
The novel of the Netherlands: a comparative study. *Ph.D. 1928 Glasgow*

Russell, J. B.
An examination of the doctrine of the inner light in the apology of Rt. Barclay. *Ph.D. 1931 Edinburgh*

Russell, M. H.
Sterne: an autobiography extracted from his writings. *B.Litt. 1930 Oxford*

Russell, M. S.
Alfred de Vigny: le progrès de sa pensée à travers ses oeuvres. *M.A. 1933 Belfast*

Russell, O. R.
A study of the factors underlying the intercorrelations of verbal, mathematical, and form perception tests. *Ph.D. 1935 Edinburgh*

Russell, W. V.
Francis Thompson. *M.A. 1937 National University of Ireland*

Russell-Wood, J.
Chemistry in Great Britain from 1727 to 1774, with special reference to the life and scientific works of William Brownrigg, M.D., F.R.S. *Ph.D. 1948 London, External Degree*

Rust, E. C.
Eschatology and the Christian understanding of history, with special reference to the biblical and metaphysical background. *B.D. 1947 Oxford*

Ruston, C. Z.
Emile Zola as a precursor of Jules Romains and *l'unanimisme*. *B.Litt. 1944 Oxford*

Rutherford, A.
The Anglo-Norman *Chronicle* of Nicolas Trivet. *Ph.D. 1932 London, Birkbeck College*

Rutherford, E. J.
Biology and education. *M.A. 1927 Liverpool*

Ruthven, A. J. Otway- *see* Otway-Ruthven, A. J.

Rutland, E. H. C.
The decentralization of industry. *Ph.D. 1934 London, School of Economics and Political Science*

Rutland, W. R.
The early work of Thomas Hardy. *1935. 195. Oxford*

Rutland, W. R.
Thomas Hardy. *D.Phil. 1937 Oxford*

Rutter, D.
An enquiry into the predictive value of grammar school entrance examinations. *M.Ed. 1949 Durham*

Ryan, C. P.
The theory of substance as developed by Aquinas, considered with reference to later philosophy. *D.Phil. 1948 Oxford*

Ryan, E. F.
Development of the idea of Rome up to the fall of the Western Empire. *M.A. 1911 National University of Ireland*

Ryan, J. M.
Three modern mystics: Thompson, Patmore, Hopkins. *M.A. 1937 National University of Ireland*

Ryan, P. J.
The ancient classics: their place in modern education. *M.A. 1927 National University of Ireland*

Ryan, P. O'C.
The theory and aim of education; some Thomistic principles. *M.A. 1929 National University of Ireland*

Ryan, P. P.
Fundamental rights. *M.A. 1941 National University of Ireland*

Ryan, W. J. L.
The nature and effects of protective policy in Ireland from 1922-1939. *Ph.D. 1949 Dublin, Trinity College*

Ryder, J. P.
Density of population in Europe, including special treatment of two countries about 1801 and 1861. *M.A. 1935 Manchester*

Ryder, R.
The teaching of general science in a secondary modern school for boys. *M.A. 1948 Liverpool*

Rynd, R. F.
1. The attitude of Christ towards the civil society of his day. 2. The Gospel and asceticism. *B.D. 1910 Oxford*

Saad, L.
Geographical study of Minufiya province: the physical character and the human response. *Ph.D. 1950 Reading*

Saaty, H. el
Juvenile delinquency in Egypt. *Ph.D. 1946 London, School of Economics and Political Science*

Sachar, A. L.
The Victorian House of Lords. *Ph.D. 1923 Cambridge*

Sachse, F. M.
A study of the legal and administrative records of Dacca as illustrating the policy of Warren Hastings in East Bengal. *B.Litt. 1934 Oxford*

Sachse, W. L.
Critical edition of the Norwich Mayor's Court minute books (1630-3), with introduction describing functions of the court at that time. *B.Litt. 1937 Oxford*

Sadeque, A.
The problem of the standards of the Indian currency. *Ph.D. 1948 London, School of Economics and Political Science*

Sadeque, S. F.
Some unpublished Arabic texts relating to the reign of Baybars I. *Ph.D. 1948 London, School of Oriental and African Studies*

Saer, H. A.
English contributions to experiments in French drama in the eighteenth century. *Ph.D. 1934 London, Bedford College*

Safely, J.
The moral dynamic in the synoptic teaching of Jesus. *Ph.D. 1928 Edinburgh*

Saffell, C. R. T.
Pétrus Borel: a study of his life, work and importance in French literature. *Ph.D. 1941 London, External Degree*

Safwat, M. M.
The Great Powers and Tunis, 1878-1881. *Ph.D. 1940 London, School of Economics and Political Science*

Safwat, M. M.
Tunis from 1855 to 1879: primarily based on the dispatches of Consul-General Richard Wood. *M.A. 1937 Liverpool*

Sagar, J.
The development of transport and its effect on industries in the Bristol district. *M.A. 1936 Bristol*

Sage, E. M.
The economics of reparations. *M.A. 1930 Wales*

Sageman, P.
An examination into the present educational opportunities for Egyptian girls in Egypt. *M.A. 1937 London, King's College*

Sagmaster, J. W.
The influence of German aesthetic philosophy on Samuel Taylor Coleridge's theory of poetry. *B.Litt. 1928 Oxford*

Sahair, M.
Circular mentality and the pyknic body type. *Ph.D. 1930 London, University College*

Said, G. E. M. A.
Production policies and their impact on problems of marketing and international trade in modern Egypt. *Ph.D. 1949 Birmingham*

Said, M. M.
The specific nature of colour and form memories. *M.Sc. 1929 Birmingham*

Saigh, E. J. S.
Eastern influences in Chaucer with special reference to the Arabs. *Ph.D. 1946 London, King's College*

Saigh, E. J. S.
English travellers in Syria. *M.A. 1942 Leeds*

Sainer, H. L.
The United States and the League of Nations, with special reference to co-operation. *M.Sc. 1946 London, School of Economics and Political Science*

St. John Parry, R.
Romans. *D.D. 1913 Cambridge*

St. Mathurin, S. C. de *see* De St. Mathurin, S. C.

Saklani, B. P.
Development of secondary education in the United Provinces, India, under British rule: being a critical account of secondary education from the beginning to the present time. *M.Ed. 1948 Leeds*

Saksena, B. P.
History of Shahgahan of Dihli. *Ph.D. 1931 London, School of Oriental and African Studies*

Saksena, G. S.
Some factors detrimental to agriculture in the United Provinces. *Ph.D. 1931 London, School of Economics and Political Science*

Saksena, S. K.
The nature of consciousness in Hindu philosophy. *Ph.D. 1939 London, School of Oriental and African Studies*

Saleh, A. Z.
Individual differences in fluctuation in output of mental work. *Ph.D. 1948 London, University College*

Salem, M. S.
The cult of Isis in Italy: an account of its external history. *Ph.D. 1937 Liverpool*

Saletore, B. A.
Social and political life in the Vijayanagara Empire, A.D. 1346-1646. *Ph.D. 1931 London, School of Oriental and African Studies*

Salisbury, M.
The English law of wills treated historically and especially with suggestions for advisable reforms. *LL.D. 1911 London*

Salmon, D. M.
Marcel Schwob et les écrivains anglosaxons, précédé d'un aperçu sur Marcel Schwob et la littérature anglo-saxonne. *M.A. 1927 Leeds*

Salmon, E. T.
Studies in pre-Gracchan colonization. *Ph.D. 1933 Cambridge*

Salmon, M.
William the Marshal. *M.A. 1909 Wales*

Salmon, V. G.
A study of the language of the metrical chronicle of Robert of Gloucester. *M.A. 1949 London, University College*

Salmon, W.
Sources of theory of 'Lordship and grace'. *M.A. 1934 National University of Ireland*

Salmons, M.
The influence of Cervantes on English literature of the eighteenth century. *M.A. 1929 Manchester*

Salt, M. C. L.
English embassies to France in the reign of Edward I: their personnel, powers, equipment and objects. *M.A. 1927 London*

Salt, W. E.
Industrial combination and unemployment. *M.A. 1924 Sheffield*

Salter, D. M. R.
The dramatic art of John Marston. *M.A. 1920 Bristol*

Salu, M. B.
Grammar of the *Ancrene Wisse* (phonology and accidence). *B.Litt. 1949 Oxford*

Salusbury-Jones, G. T.
Some aspects of street life in medieval England. *B.Litt. 1938 Dublin, Trinity College*

Salyer, J. C.
Spanish economic policy and its relation to trade with England, culminating in the Treaty of 1667. *B.Litt. 1948 Oxford*

Salzberger, L. S.
Hölderlin's Anschauungen vom Beruf des Dichters in Zusammenhang mit dem Stil seiner Dichtung. *D.Phil. 1950 Oxford*

Samad, A.
A short thesis on the origin and development of science teaching in English schools. *M.A. 1930 Leeds*

Samaraweera, D. D.
Early history of Buddhist education in Ceylon (third century B.C. to sixteenth century A.D.). *M.A. 1949 London, Institute of Education*

Sambrook, G. A.
Criticism of Spenser in the eighteenth century. *M.A. 1929 Liverpool*

Samek, R. A.
Public policy in private international law. *M.Litt. 1948 Cambridge*

Sampson, B.
The British peasant, 1770-1820, as reflected in our literature. *M.A. 1921 London*

Samson, E. M. F.
Maria Edgeworth: her place in the history of the English novel. *B.Litt. 1925 Oxford*

Samuel, B.
The international adjustment of monetary and banking systems and the proposals made since the war for the solution of the problem. *M.A. 1928 Wales*

Samuel, J.
Problems of public finance in the federal states of Canada and Australia, with special reference to the scheme for India. *M.Com. 1937 Leeds*

Samuel, P.
The origin and evolution of the Assembly of the League of Nations. *M.A. 1935 Wales*

Samuel, R.
Heinrich von Kleist's participation in the political movements of the years 1805-9. *Ph.D. 1938 Cambridge*

Sanai, M.
An investigation of social and political attitudes. *Ph.D. 1949 London, University College*

Sanaullah
The decline of the Saljuqid Empire (1092-1117). *Ph.D. 1935 London, School of Oriental and African Studies*

Sanborn, F. R.
An introduction to English maritime and commercial law. *Ph.D. 1924 Oxford*

Sanctuary, J. R.
The agriculture of the semi-arid regions of the Middle West of the U.S.A. considered in relation to wheat cultivation. *M.A. 1940 London, External Degree*

Sandall, P. H.
Elementary schools and schoolbooks in England at the close of the eighteenth and beginning of the nineteenth centuries. *M.A. 1929 London*

Sandars, J. S.
The doctrine of culpa. *D.C.L. 1885 Oxford*

Sanday, W. I.
The poetry of Thomas Campbell. *B.Litt. 1943 Oxford*

Sandbach, P.
Wordsworth and education. *M.A. 1926 Liverpool*

Sandbach-Marshall, M. E.
The religious philosophy of Herder and Schleiermacher studied in relation to the influence upon them of Leibniz, Spinoza, and Kant. *M.A. 1928 London*

Sandeen, E. E.
The novels in *The Gentleman's Journal*. *B.Litt. 1933 Oxford*

Sandelius, W. E.
Parliamentary government as it exists in Sweden. *B.Litt. 1923 Oxford*

Sanders, C.
The psychological needs of children and their relation to behaviour. *Ph.D. 1938 London, Institute of Education*

Sanders, D. R.
Introduction to a study of the linguistic influence of France on Spain in the Middle Ages. *M.A. 1930 Manchester*

Sanders, H. G.
The direct and indirect influences of geographical conditions upon Hebrew religion. *M.A. 1937 Manchester*

Sanders, I. J.
Some contributions to thirteenth century feudal geography. *D.Phil. 1938 Oxford*

Sanders, T. H.
A study in Japanese economics. *M.Com. 1914 Birmingham*

Sanderson, G. B.
A study of economic concepts of income and capital valuation, with special reference to accountancy. *Ph.D. 1942 London, School of Economics and Political Science*

Sanderson, G. D.
Relations of the British Government and the Roman Catholic Church in Ireland 1508-1829. *Ph.D. 1930 Dublin, Trinity College*

Sanderson, J. E.
John Bright as a critic of foreign policy. *M.A. 1923 Birmingham*

Sanderson, R. E.
Exegesis of Luke xxii.19-20. *B.D. & D.D. 1874 Oxford*

Sandilands, D. N.
The history of the Midland glass industry, with special reference to the flint glass section. *M.Com. 1927 Birmingham*

Sandmann, M. M. G.
Subject and predicate: a contribution to the theory of grammatical analysis. *D.Litt. 1949 Glasgow*

Sandral, D. M.
A comparison of the war taxation of Great Britain and the United States of America from 1914. *B.Litt. 1922 Oxford*

Sandys-Wood, A.
Rome and Parthia, 70-29 B.C. *B.Litt. 1949 Oxford*

Sangster, P.
The path to perfection, an examination and restatement of John Wesley's doctrine of Christian perfection. *Ph.D. 1942 London, Richmond College*

Sankalia, H. D.
The archaeology of Gujarat (A.D. 400-1300). *Ph.D. 1937 London, University College*

Sankar, S.
The Vaikhânasa Dharma Praśna. *M.A. 1915 London*

Sanker, L. M.
The date and origin of Midrash psalms. *Ph.D. 1944 London, Jews' College*

Sankey, J.
La religion et l'église dans l'oeuvre de Stendhal. *M.A. 1935 Liverpool*

Sankey, W. H.
Naval developments under Henry VIII. *M.A. 1926 Manchester*

Sankey, W. H.
The teaching of history in the preparatory school. *M.Ed. 1923 Manchester*

Sanmarti, J.
A study of the theories of Thomas Attwood and contemporary advocates of paper money in England. *Ph.D. 1948 London, School of Economics and Political Science*

Santmyer, H. H.
Clara Reeve: her life and works. *B.Litt. 1927 Oxford*

Santvoord, G. van *see* Van Santvoord, G.

Sanyal, H. N.
The rural organization of an Indian province (Bengal) dealing with land tenures, etc. *Ph.D. 1928 London*

Sanyal, N.
Development of Indian railways, 1842-1928. *Ph.D. 1929 London*

Sanyal, S. P.
The cooperative organization in British India. *M.A. 1940 Leeds*

Saran, P.
The provincial government of the Mughals: 1556 to 1659 A.D. *Ph.D. 1936 London, School of Oriental and African Studies*

Saraswat, D. S.
Production and marketing of milk and milk products in United Kingdom and western Europe with special reference to co-operative methods and their application under Indian conditions. *Ph.D. 1949 Glasgow*

Sarathchandra, E. R.
A critical examination of some theories of the external world in Indian philosophy. *M.A. 1949 London, University College*

Sarathchandra, E. R. de S.
The psychology of perception in Pali Buddhism, with special reference to the theory of Bhavanga. *Ph.D. 1948 London, External Degree*

Sardesai, V. N.
Some problems in the nasalization of Marāthī. *M.A. 1929 London*

Sargeant, H. H.
The study of the pre-Shakespearian drama before Malone. *B.Litt. 1940 Oxford*

Sargeaunt, M. J.
John Ford. *B.Litt. 1931 Oxford*

Sargent, C. P.
A geographical study of the boot and shoe trade in England. *M.Sc. 1932 London, University College*

Sargent, W. E.
The psychology of unbelief. *Ph.D. 1941 Edinburgh*

Sarjeant, D.
The public library service under English local government. *Ph.D. 1935 London, School of Economics and Political Science*

Sarjent, B. K.
The teaching of the vernacular in French secondary schools: a study in methods. *M.A. 1940 Reading*

Sarkar, K. M.
The foreign policy of Lord Minto, 1807-13. *M.Litt. 1937 Cambridge*

Sarkar, M. P.
The teaching of economics in the secondary schools of India. *M.Ed. 1927 Leeds*

Sarkar, S. C.
Some aspects of the earliest social history of India, especially the pre-Buddhistic ages. *D.Phil. 1923 Oxford*

Sarker, R.
The socio-economic organization of northern India (c.200 A.D.-c.600 A.D.). *Ph.D. 1947 London, School of Oriental and African Studies*

Sarmiento, E.
A contribution to the study of the influence of Baltasar Gracián (1601 to 1658), with an index to the moral ideas of the *Criticón* and to the aesthetic ideas of the *Agudeza* with a complete bibliography of Gracianism. *Ph.D. 1931 London, King's College*

Sarofim, E.
England and the criminal legislation of Egypt, from 1882. *D.Phil. 1949 Oxford*

Sarson, G. M.
The geographical reasons for the growth of the population of south Staffordshire, east Warwickshire and Leicestershire from 1801-1931. *Ph.D. 1937 London, External Degree*

Sarup, L.
The Nirukta and the Nighantu. *Ph.D. 1920 Oxford*

Sastri, A. B. *see* Banerji Sastri, A.

Sastri, K. N. V.
The administration of Mysore under Sir Mark Cubbon (1834 to 1861). *Ph.D. 1931 London, University College*

Sastri, N. S.
Development of large scale industries in India and their localisation. *Ph.D. 1943 London, School of Economics and Political Science*

Saswadkar, N. G.
Accent in Gujarāti. *M.A. 1929 London*

Sathaye, S. G.
'Instrumentalism': a methodological exposition of the philosophy of John Dewey. *Ph.D. 1944 London, University College*

Sato, I. R.
A comparative study of some aspects of modern Japanese and English fiction. *M.Litt. 1939 Cambridge*

Sauerzweig, U.
Matthew Arnold and Germany. *M.A. 1938 National University of Ireland*

Saum, C. M.
England and the Great Schism of the West. *M.A. 1916 Liverpool*

Saunders, C. K.
Italian influence on the Elizabethan lyrics, more especially in connection with madrigals connection with madrigals. *M.A. 1909 London*

Saunders, D. A. P.
W. H. Ireland: his life and works. *M.A. 1936 Wales*

Saunders, D. B.
Dr. Johnson's knowledge of the English writers to the year 1600 (excluding Shakespeare). *B.Litt. 1935 Oxford*

Saunders, E. J.
Gweithiau Lewys Morganwg(The works of Lewys Morganwg). *M.A. 1922 Wales*

Saunders, H. W.
Finance accounts of Norwich Cathedral Priory, 1272-1377. *D. Litt. 1927 Glasgow*

Saunders, I. J.
Some political activities of the Franciscan friars in England in the thirteenth century. *M.A. 1935 Wales*

Saunders, J. B.
The Chalcedonian formula in the twentieth century: an examination of recent trends in Christology. *B.D. 1947 Oxford*

Saunders, J. J.
Ralph Thoresby and his circle, with special reference to the state of English historical scholarship in his time. *M.A. 1936 London, External Degree*

Saunders, J. W.
The poet and his audience: non-dramatic poetry of the sixteenth century. *B.Litt. 1949 Oxford*

Saunders, K. A.
The meaning of the term 'Son of God' in the Synoptic Gospels, and its antecedents. *B.Litt. 1922 Oxford*

Saunders, M.
Some aspects of charitable trusts. *LL.M. 1950 Sheffield*

Saunders, W. R.
A geographical study of the recent distribution of population and types of settlement in mid-Wales and along the central Welsh border, with special reference to Radnorshire. *B.Litt. 1925 Oxford*

Sauvain, A.
Co-operation between county education authorities and authorities for elementary education only, with special reference to the county council of the West Riding of Yorkshire and the Borough of Ossett. *M.Ed. 1943 Manchester*

Savage, C. I.
Economic problems of the road passenger transport industry with special reference to the history of the West Midlands. *M.Com. 1949 Birmingham*

Saverimuttu, P.
Some influences that changed the educational system of Ceylon between 1900 and 1945. *M.A. 1949 London, Institute of Education*

Savigny, W. B.
The genesis of Herder's literary theories. *M.A. 1939 Manchester*

Savill, L. E. M.
The development of military training in schools in the British Isles. *M.A. 1937 London, King's College*

Savory, H. J.
The historical geography of the River Plate region, 1810-1900. *M.A. 1937 Manchester*

Savory, H. N.
From what directions and at what times Britain was invaded by bearers of early Iron Age culture. *D.Phil. 1938 Oxford*

Saw, R. L.
An examination of the notion of cause in the light of recent contributions to the philosophy of nature. *Ph.D. 1927 London*

Sawdon, E. W.
An exercise book of the geography of China. *M.A. 1922 Birmingham*

Sawdon, E. W.
Should children learn poems as 'wholes' or in 'parts'. *M.A. 1926 Birmingham*

Sawyerr, H. A. E.
The Sierra Leone patois: a study of its growth and structure, with special reference to the teaching of English in Sierra Leone. *M.Ed. 1940 Durham*

Saxby, I. B.
Some conditions affecting the growth and permanence of desires. *D.Sc. 1918 London*

Saxon-Snell, B. O. *see* Snell, B. O. S.

Saxton, C. C.
Costing and prices in British industry. *D.Phil. 1941 Oxford*

Saxton, J. H.
Christian Morgenstern's relations to Nietzsche. *M.A. 1936 London, University College*

Saxton, M. C.
Geographical factors affecting the cotton industry in Lancashire as compared with India. *M.A. 1921 Liverpool*

Sayce, R. A.
The French biblical epic in the seventeenth century. *D.Phil. 1949 Oxford*

Sayce, R. U.
Hilltop camps, with special reference to those of north Cardiganshire. *M.A. 1920 Wales*

Sayeed, S. B.
Urdu as the medium of higher instruction. *M.Ed. 1935 Leeds*

Sayons, K. M.
Analysis of humour. *B.Litt. 1949 Oxford*

Saywell, R. J. T.
The development of the feminist idea in England (1789-1833). *M.A. 1936 London, King's College*

Scammell, E. H.
Position of a tenant for life under a trust for sale of land. *LL.M. 1948 London, King's College*

Scammell, W. McC.
The present and future organization of British ports and harbours. *M.Com.Sc. 1947 Belfast*

Scanlan, C. H.
Political philosophy of Suarez. *M.A. 1939 National University of Ireland*

Scannell, J.
Alfred de Vigny - poète et philosophe. *M.A. 1915 National University of Ireland*

Scarf, J. W.
The employment of juveniles and young persons (14-18) in the West Riding wool textile industry, with some reference to the effect of the raising of the school-leaving age and release for part-time further education. *B.Phil. 1947 Oxford*

Scarfe, F. H.
The French background in English poetry, 1850-1900. *M.Litt. 1939 Cambridge*

Scarfe, N. V.
The post-war tendencies in agriculture in the county of Essex. *M.A. 1933 London, University College*

Scargill, M. H.
The phonology and morphology of the Rushworth Gospels, known as Rushworth 1. *Ph.D. 1940 Leeds*

Scargill, R. E.
The reputation and influence of the English romantic poets in England from 1824 (the death of Byron) to 1850 (the death of Wordsworth). *M.A. 1933 London, King's College*

Scarre, A. M.
The Saxon element in early Irish history. *M.A. 1908 Liverpool*

Schaeffer, J. N.
The representation of locality in Greek art, and the ancient texts related thereto. *B.Litt. 1908 Oxford*

Schaik, J. J. van *see* Van Schaik, J. J.

Schapera, I.
The tribal system in South Africa: a study of the Bushmen and Hottentots. *Ph.D. 1929 London*

Schenck, F.
Foreign chivalry at the Court of Edward III. *B.Litt. 1912 Oxford*

Schenk, H. G. A. V.
The social and economic background of attempts at a Concert of Europe from 1804 to 1825. *D.Phil. 1943 Oxford*

Schisas, P. M.
Offences against the State in Roman law and the courts which were competent to take cognizance of them. *LL.D. 1924 London*

Schlatter, R. B.
The social and economic ideas in the writings of religious leaders, 1660-1688. *D.Phil. 1938 Oxford*

Schlatter, R. B.
The treatment of social and economic questions by Anglican divines during the reign of Charles II. *B.Litt. 1935 Oxford*

Schlepegrell, A. F. K.
German borrowings abroad, 1924-30. *B.Litt. 1934 Oxford*

Schlesinger, R. A. J.
Federalism in central and eastern Europe. *Ph.D. 1945 London, University College*

Schlumberger, B. J.
Studies on fatality in sentimental pre-Romantic French literature, 1725-62. *M.A. 1922 London*

Schmidt, C. H.
The relation between language and thought as illustrated by the experience of teaching through a foreign medium. *1922 B.Litt Oxford*

Schmidt, J. M.
The waiver of jurisdictional immunities. *Ph.D. 1941 Cambridge*

Schoberth, F. W.
Die Neuromantik in Drama Herbert Eulenbergs. *M.A. 1937 Wales*

Schofield, M. M.
The correspondence between King George III and John Robinson. *M.A. 1937 Manchester*

Schofield, T.
Etude lexicographique sur le vocabulaire des textes réunis sous la lettre 'G' du *Glossaire archéologique* vol. 1, de Victor Gay. *M.A. 1933 Leeds*

Scholefield, G. H.
The Pacific, its past and future and the policy of the great powers from the eighteenth century. *D.Sc. 1919 London*

Scholes, A. G.
Education for Empire settlement: a study of juvenile migration. *Ph.D. 1930 Edinburgh*

Schonell, F. E.
An experimental study of diagnostic tests in English. *M.A. 1940 London, University College*

Schonell, F. E.
An investigation into the educability of children suffering from cerebral palsy, spastic paralysis. *Ph.D. 1950 Birmingham*

Schonell, F. J.
An investigation into disability in spelling. *Ph.D. 1932 London, Day Training College*

Schper, A.
Christian Hebraists in sixteenth-century England. *Ph.D. 1944 London, Courtauld Institute of Art*

Schram, O. K.
The chief elements in Norfolk placenames: a contribution to the study of place nomenclature. *M.A. 1924 Wales*

Schram, O. K.
The place names of Norfolk. *Ph.D. 1927 Cambridge*

Schulz, G.
Some aspects of the British iron and steel industry from 1927-35, with special reference to the tinplate and steel sheet industry. *B.Litt. 1938 Oxford*

Schumacher, D. F.
Herder's treatment of his English sources in the Volkslieder. *M.A. 1936 London, University College*

Schwartz, B.
Law and the executive. *Ph.D. 1948 Cambridge*

Schwartz, D. H.
A sociological analysis of some intellectual groups in American society from 1912-1930. *Ph.D. 1940 London, School of Economics and Political Science*

Schwarz, H. F.
Anglo-Austrian relations during the reign of the Emperor Joseph II. *B.Litt. 1931 Oxford*

Schwarz, W.
The fables of Aesop in the German literature of the fifteenth century, with special reference to Steinhoewel's translation. *M.A. 1939 London, University College*

Schwarz, W.
Luther's translation of the Bible in the light of humanistic scholarship. *Ph.D. 1949 London, University College*

Schwarz, Z.
The social and political ideas of Maimonides. *M.Sc. 1926 London*

Schwarzchild, A.
Joy and sorrow and the like in the poetic language of Klopstock, Schiller and Goethe. *Ph.D. 1940 Edinburgh*

Schwarzenberger, G.
The League of Nations and the problem of a universal peace organization. *Ph.D. 1936 London, School of Economics and Political Science*

Scitovszky, T.
International aspects of the trade-cycle international transfer of inflationary and deflationary movements. *M.Sc. 1938 London, School of Economics and Political Science*

Sclare, M.
Social insurance, a study of the destitution caused by the early death of the wage earner. *M.A. 1923 Leeds*

Scobie, R. A.
The technology and economics of fishing in relation to Hawaiian culture. *M.A. 1949 London, School of Economics and Political Science*

Scola, P.
The Lothians. Reports of the Land Utilization Survey of Britain, parts 16-18. *M.Sc. 1944 London, School of Economics and Political Science*

Scotland, A.
The genesis of Shakespeare's *Hamlet. Ph.D. 1930 Glasgow*

Scotland, J.
Literary life in England and France betwen the years 1066 and 1400. *M.Litt. 1929 Cambridge*

Scotney, P. H.
An examination of the theory and practice of appointments in the reigns of Henry III and Edward I (1216-1307), and of their historical significance. *M.A. 1927 London*

Scott, A.
Childhood in English poetry. *M.A. 1935 Belfast*

Scott, A. A.
Frau Welt: ein Beitrag zur Sittengeschichte des deutschen Mittelalters. *M.A. 1918 London*

Scott, C. H.
The laying on of hands in the New Testament and in Christian usage. *B.D. 1924 Oxford*

Scott, D. R.
A study in the doctrine of forgiveness and atonement. *Ph.D. 1923 Saint Andrew's*

Scott, E. M.
Le parler de Toul et de ses environs d'après des documents d'archives. *M.A. 1923 London*

Scott, F. R.
The annexation of Savoy and Nice by Napoleon III, 1860. *B.Litt. 1924 Oxford*

Scott, H.
The medieval Irish Parliament. *M.A. 1914 London*

Scott, J.
The Baptists in Scotland. *Ph.D. 1927 Glasgow*

Scott, J. F.
John Wallis, and his place in the history of science. *Ph.D. 1935 London, University College*

Scott, J. P.
The phonology of the placenames of Shropshire. *M.A. 1924 Liverpool*

Scott, J. W.
Recent philosophy and recent social movements. *D. Phil. 1919 Glasgow*

Scott, J. W. W.
An analytic study of the sources of Spenser's diction in *Shepheardes Calender. Ph.D. 1928 Saint Andrew's*

Scott, K. B. *see* Ridley, K. B.

Scott, L.
Under-Secretaries of State, 1755-1775. *M.A. 1950 Manchester*

Scott, M. J.
Joseph Conrad. *M.A. 1926 Birmingham*

Scott, P.
The agricultural geography of Swaziland. *M.Sc. 1947 London, School of Economics and Political Science*

Scott, S. H.
The relation of the Eastern Churches to Rome before the schism of Photius. *D.Phil. 1927 Oxford*

Scott, S. H.
The theology of St. Cyril of Alexandria. *B.Litt. 1911 Oxford*

Scott, S. M.
The old French prose romance *L'estoire del Saint Graal* and its relation to Robert de Borron's poem *Le roman de l'estoire dou Graal. M.A. 1935 Manchester*

Scott, T.
The poetry and criticism of Matthew Arnold compared. *M.A. 1948 Manchester*

Scott, T. A. H.
Literary history in England in the eighteenth century, before Warton's *History of English poetry. B.Litt. 1939 Oxford*

Scott, W. A. G.
Smollett's reputation and influence in the eighteenth century, chiefly as novelist. *B.Litt. 1948 Oxford*

Scott, W. F.
The early life and services of Sir John Jervis, Lord St. Vincent, and their influence on his later career and character. *B.Litt. 1929 Oxford*

Scott, W. F.
The naval chaplain in Stuart times. *D.Phil. 1935 Oxford*

Scott, W. P.
Shelley in Italy, and his use of Italian literature. *B.Litt. 1925 Oxford*

Scott, W. R.
The philosophy of Francis Hutcheson and of James Arbuckle, showing the position of both in the Molesworth-Shaftesbury School and the relation of the former to the Enlightenment in Scotland. *D.Phil. 1900 Saint Andrew's*

Scott-Craig, T. S. K.
Christian attitudes to war and peace: a study of the four main types, with a foreword by W. P. Paterson. *Ph.D. 1938 Edinburgh*

Scotter, W. H.
International rivalry in the bights of Benin and Biafra, 1815-1885. *Ph.D. 1934 London, King's College*

Scouloudi, I.
Alien immigration into and alien communities in London, 1558 to 1640. *M.Sc. 1936 London, School of Economics and Political Science*

Screech, S. D.
Bossuet and mysticism. *Ph.D. 1934 London, Birkbeck College*

Scrimgeour, R. M.
The development of letter writing in the seventeenth century with a study of its bearing on the essay and the novel. *M.A. 1928 London*

Scrimiger, E. M.
The career of the Earl of Shelburne, 1760-1783. *M.A. 1909 Liverpool*

Scrivens, A. G.
An objective study of the factors underlying ability in verbal expression. *M.A. 1933 London, Institute of Education*

Scrivens, W.
The practice and functions of local government as illustrated in Lancashire towns in the century before the Municipal Corporations Act (1835) with a consideration of the more immediate effects of the reform. *M.A. 1934 Liverpool*

Scullard, H. H.
Some neglected aspects of Scipio Africanus. *Ph.D. 1930 London, University College*

Scully, F. M.
Dissent and democracy. *M.A. 1937 Bristol*

Scully, F. M.
Relations between Church and State in England between 1829 and 1839. *B.Litt. 1935 Oxford*

Seabourne, M. A. I.
George Meredith: his aims and achievements as a novelist. *M.A. 1936 Wales*

Seal, A. M.
Sir P. Sidney's *Astrophel and Stella*. *M.A. 1917 Birmingham*

Sealy-Jones, D. C.
The protection of persons acquiring interests in land from limited owners. *LL.M. 1947 London, External Degree*

Searle, D. E.
The foreign policy of the Gladstone administration of 1880-1885, with special reference to German policy in South-west Africa. *M.A. 1933 Wales*

Searle, J. C.
An inquiry into the nature, extent and implications of the socialism of the French Revolution, during the period of the revolutionary government. *Ph.D. 1935 London, School of Economics and Political Science*

Seary, E. R.
Ebenezer Elliott: a study, including an edition of his works. *Ph.D. 1932 Sheffield*

Seaton, M. E.
A study of the relations between England and the Scandinavian countries in the seventeenth century, based upon the evidence of acquaintance in English writers with Scandinavian languages, literatures, and myths. *M.A. 1920 London*

Seccombe, H. G.
The life and work of Sir Francis Kynaston. *B.Litt. 1933 Oxford*

Secerov, S.
Economic phenomena before and after war. *M.Sc. 1918 London*

Seckler, L. M.
Anglo-Flemish trading relations in the later Middle Ages. *Ph.D. 1932 London, University College*

Seckler, L. M.
The building of the Hanseatic League from its earliest days until 1370. *M.A. 1929 Birmingham*

Seddon, R.
A factorial analysis of skill in commercial subjects at the secondary school level. *Ph.D. 1949 London, Institute of Education*

Seddon, R. H.
Sculpture in Britain, with special reference to its nature as a community art between 500 B.C. and 1900 A.D., being an analysis of the progress of community psychological states in Britain and its relation to the development of British sculpture. *Ph.D. 1946 Reading*

Sedlo, J.
The influence of John Hus on Europe to the time of the Reformation, with special reference to central and eastern Europe. *Ph.D. 1943 Edinburgh*

Seed, G.
The social and administrative reforms of Lord William Bentinck. *Ph.D. 1949 Saint Andrew's*

Seeds, M. E. *see* Alan, M. E.

Segal, J. B.
History of the Passover. *D.Phil. 1939 Oxford*

Segal, L.
The foreign trade of Soviet Russia. *Ph.D. 1936 London, School of Economics and Political Science*

Segal, L.
The romantic movement in Russia. *M.A. 1919 Birmingham*

Segal, P.
The development of thought in the writings and work of William Morris. *M.A. 1939 London, University College*

Segal, S.
A critical synopsis of Malbim's *Meir Löb be Jehiel Michael*, commentary on the Book of Hosea in the light of earlier Jewish interpretation. *M.A. 1944 Manchester*

Segar, M. G. T.
The life and works of Ambrose Philips. *B.Litt. 1929 Oxford*

Seidmann, G.
Die Gestaltungsmittel der Komoedie bei Johann Nestroy. *M.A. 1945 Belfast*

Sekler, E. F.
The development of the British staircase. *Ph.D. 1948 London, Warburg Institute*

Sekyi, W. E. G.
The relation between the state and the individual considered in the light of its bearing on the conception of duty. *M.A. 1918 London*

Selim, H. K.
Post-war changes in the agricultural geography of Egypt. *M.A. 1939 Liverpool*

Sellers, H.
The life and works of Samuel Daniel. *B.Litt. 1916 Oxford*

Sellers, R. V.
Two ancient Christologies. *D.D. 1939 Cambridge*

Selley, W. T.
A critical examination of a deductive method of teaching history in secondary schools. *M.Ed. 1939 Manchester*

Selley, W. T.
The family and early life of Sixtus V. *M.A. 1934 Bristol*

Sells, D. M. D.
An enquiry into the operation of the British trade boards system. *Ph.D. 1923 London*

Selway, A. H.
The philosophical background of the Oxford Movement of the nineteenth century. *M.A. 1940 Manchester*

Selwood, E. H.
Classification of communities by means of occupations. *Ph.D. 1932 London, Birkbeck College*

Selwyn, P.
Causes of poverty among the rural populations of the Arab states. *B.Litt. 1947 Oxford*

Semper, E.
The curriculum of the technical high school with special reference to Bradford. *M.Ed. 1946 Leeds*

Semple, S. H.
Quaestiones exegeticae Sidonianae. *Ph.D. 1927 Cambridge*

Semple, W. H.
In Apollinaris Sidonii *Carmina quaestiones et notae exegeticae*. *M.A. 1929 Belfast*

Sen, A.
A study of the Rorschach test. *Ph.D. 1949 London, University College*

Sen, B.
Some historical aspects of the inscriptions of Bengal from the fifth to the twelfth century A.D. *Ph.D. 1933 London, School of Oriental and African Studies*

Sen, D. M.
A comparison of the philosophical system of Leibniz and Berkeley. *Ph.D. 1928 London*

Sen, J.
Changes in the status of women during the nineteenth century as reflected in Bengali literature. *Ph.D. 1924 London*

Sen, J. M.
The state in its relation to education in India. *M.Ed. 1922 Leeds*

Sen, K. T.
Group consciousness, with special reference to educational applications. *Ph.D. 1922 Edinburgh*

Sen, S.
Daniel De Foe, his mind and art. *M.Litt. 1947 Cambridge*

Sen, S.
The military system of the Mahrattas: its origin and development from the time of Shivaji to the fall of the Mahratta Empire. *B.Litt. 1927 Oxford*

Sen, S.
Sir James Steuart. *Ph.D. 1947 London, School of Economics and Political Science*

Sen, S. N.
The development of primary and post-primary education in England during the present century. *M.A. 1937 Leeds*

Sendall, H. W.
From initiation to conversion. *M.A. 1942 Leeds*

Sengupta, B.
Mysticism in the poetry of Wordsworth, Shelley and Tagore. *B.Litt. 1947 Dublin, Trinity College*

Sengupta, S. K.
The poetic development of W. B. Yeats, with a study of some texts. *Ph.D. 1936 Leeds*

Senior, G. F.
The theme of 'Bildung' in *Wilhelm Meister*, and the moral and religious teaching of the early Carlyle to 1843. *M.A. 1950 Manchester*

Senior, W. H.
An account of an investigation into the labour force employed on farms. *M.Sc. 1929 Reading*

Sephton, A. E. G.
De Quincey's prose style. *M.A. 1946 Liverpool*

Sepianu, F. C.
Milton's reputation in France in the seventeenth century. *B.Litt. 1941 Oxford*

Serjeant, R. B.
A history of Islamic textiles up to the Mongol conquest. *Ph.D. 1940 Cambridge*

Serjeantson, M. S.
The dialects of the West Midlands between 1150-1450. *D.Phil. 1926 Oxford*

Servais, Y.
The art of Katherine Mansfield. *M.A. 1937 National University of Ireland*

Seth, H. C.
Distribution of wealth in an Indian province. *Ph.D. 1926 London*

Sewell, M. E.
The construction of poetry with special reference to the *Illuminations* of Rimbaud, together with *Bateau ivre* and *Un coup de dés*. *Ph.D. 1949 Cambridge*

Sewell, W. A.
Milton's treatise *On Christian doctrine* and its relation to *Paradise lost*. *B.Litt. 1933 Oxford*

Sexton, E. H. L.
A descriptive and bibliographical list of Irish figure sculptures of the early Christian period, with a critical assessment of their significance. *B.Litt. 1940 Oxford*

Sexton, J.
Irish continuation school and the adolescent. *M.A. 1942 National University of Ireland*

Seymour, A. H.
The effects of different conditions of temperature and ventilation on the mental output and mental fatigues of school children. *Ph.D. 1936 London, University College*

Seymour, J. H. C.
A critical study of the novels of Robert Bage (1728-1801) and a consideration of their place in the history of the English novel. *M.A. 1936 London, King's College*

Seymour, M. A.
The organization, personnel and functions of the medieval hospital in the later Middle Ages. *M.A. 1946 London, King's College*

Seymour, O. C.
The religion of the Cherokee Indians. *Ph.D. 1934 Edinburgh*

Shackle, G. L. S.
Industrial fluctuations in a changing economy. *Ph.D. 1937 London, School of Economics and Political Science*

Shackle, G. L. S.
The process of recovery from trade depression, with special reference to Great Britain, 1931-6. *D.Phil. 1940 Oxford*

Shackleton Bailey, J. H.
A commentary on: Genesis i.1; ii.8; vi.17. *D.D. 1923 Oxford*

Shadani, W. H. Andalib-i- *see* Andalib-i-Shadani, W. H.

Shadman, S. F.
The relations of Britain and Persia, 1800-1815. *Ph.D. 1939 London, School of Economics and Political Science*

Shadwell, C. L.
The Universities and College Estates Acts, 1858-1880. *D.C.L. 1898 Oxford*

Shaffner, F. I.
History of the theory of international gold movements. *B.Litt. 1928 Oxford*

Shah, E. Ahmad *see* Ahmad Shah, E.

Shah, N. J.
History of Indian tariff. *Ph.D. 1923 London*

Shah, S. Y.
A history of elementary education in the Punjab. *M.A. 1937 Bristol*

Shah, Y.
The social life and institutions of Jhang and suggestions for their reorganization. *M.Ed. 1925 Leeds*

Shahla, G. D.
The Arab conception of the ideal teacher in Arabic pedagogical literature. *M.A. 1938 London, Institute of Education*

Shaikh, B. K.
Sind: its educational past and present. *M.Ed. 1938 Leeds*

Shakespeare, J. J.
A statistical enquiry into the relative popularity of school subjects in the elementary schools of Worcestershire. *M.A. 1934 Birmingham*

Shalom, M. Ish- *see* Ish-Shalom, M.

Shamin, M. I.
A critical survey of theories underlying experimental study of the effects of reward and punishment on school learning. *M.A. 1948 London, Institute of Education*

Shanahan, C. M.
The influence of Baudelaire, Laforgue and Corbière on the poetry of T. S. Eliot. *M.A. 1949 Manchester*

Shanahan, E. W.
The production and the consumption of animal foodstuffs, with special reference to the British Empire. *D.Sc. 1919 London*

Shankar, G.
An edition of the *Kapphinābhyudaya* of Sivasvāmin with a discussion of the Prākrit exemplified in it. *B. Litt. 1933 Oxford*

Shannon, E.
A study of the mythology and legend in the creative poetry of William Morris. *M.A. 1938 National University of Ireland*

Shannon, E. F.
Tennyson and the reviewers, 1827-51: a study of the growth of Tennyson's reputation and of the influence of the critics upon his poetry. *D.Phil. 1949 Oxford*

Shannon, R. A.
A study of parish government: illustrated by documents from the parish chest of Eye, Northants. *M.A. 1949 London, External Degree*

Shannon, T. L.
The religious thought of Robertson of Brighton. *Ph.D. 1946 Edinburgh*

Shapcott, G. M.
A study of the workings of Milton's imagination as revealed in the portrayal of the chief characters in *Paradise Lost, Paradise Regained* and *Samson Agonistes*. *M.A. 1930 London, Bedford College*

Shapira, I.
The relief of the Jewish disabilities in England (1829-58). *M.A. 1934 London, Queen Mary College*

Shapiro, I. A.
The early life and poetry of John Donne. *M.A. 1926 Birmingham*

Sharani, Z. el-
The curriculum in girls' secondary schools, with special reference to England and Egypt. *M.A. 1939 Bristol*

Sharkawy, M. A. el M. M.
Problems of the development of French West Africa, as illustrated by Senegal and the Ivory Coast. *M.A. 1931 Liverpool*

Sharma, Y. D.
A critical study of Ksemendra's version of the *Vetālapañcaviṁśati*. *B.Litt. 1941 Oxford*

Sharma, Y. D.
Indian civil law according to Kautilya. *D.Phil. 1945 Oxford*

Sharp, D. E.
The doctrine of matter and form in the early English Franciscans. *D.Phil. 1927 Oxford*

Sharp, G. R.
The physical work of C. A. de Coulomb. *M.Sc. 1936 London, University College*

Sharp, I. G.
A study of the practice and procedure of arbitration and conciliation as a voluntary principle in some British industries, with an account of state action in the field. *Ph.D. 1940 London, School of Economics and Political Science*

Sharp, L. W.
The expansion of the English language in Scotland. *Ph.D. 1927 Cambridge*

Sharp, M.
Contributions to the history of the earldom and county of Chester, 1237-1399, with a study of the household of Edward the Black Prince and its relations with Cheshire. *Ph.D. 1925 Manchester*

Sharpe, J. F.
A contribution to the early history of Flintshire, with special reference to the See of St. Asaph. *M.A. 1924 Liverpool*

Sharper, L. L.
1. Sacrifice. 2. Atonement. *B.D. 1874 Oxford*

Sharples, K. S.
Evolutionary aspects and critical analysis of the English criminal law in its relation to mental disorder, with particular reference to crimes against the person. *LL.M. 1950 Manchester*

Sharrock, R. I.
The methods and models of Bunyan's allegories. *B.Litt. 1947 Oxford*

Shastri, M. D.
The *Rigveda Praetisākhya* with the commentary of Uvata, edited from the manuscripts with introduction, critical and additional notes, English translation, and several appendices. *D.Phil. 1922 Oxford*

Shastri, P. D.
The doctrine of *Maya* in the system of the Vedanta. *B.Sc. 1911 Oxford*

Shastri, S. K.
Political and social ideas of Victor Considérant. *M.Sc. 1936 London, School of Economics and Political Science*

Shattock, E. A.
The relation between morality and religion in primitive society. *B.Litt. 1927 Oxford*

Shaul, J. R. H.
Sequence of movements of indices of industrial fluctuations in Great Britain (1885-1914 and 1919-1930). *M.Sc. 1934 London, School of Economics and Political Science*

Shave, D. W.
The Amazon Basin, with special reference to its economical development. *M.Sc. 1933 London, Birkbeck College*

Shave, L. H.
The development of natural philosophy as reflected by the English and French Encyclopaedias of the eighteenth century. *Ph.D. 1941 London, University College*

Shaw, F.
Aislinge Oenguso (The vision of Oengus). *M.A. 1931 National University of Ireland*

Shaw, F. B.
Le scepticisme de Prosper Mérimée. *M.A. 1923 Birmingham*

Shaw, G. F.
Commercial relations between England and Venice in the thirteenth and fourteenth centuries. *M.A. 1909 London*

Shaw, H.
The development of the thermometer from 300 B.C. to A.D. *M.Sc. 1922 London*

Shaw, J.
Seventeenth century pamphlets and the development of prose style. *M.A. 1949 Leeds*

Shaw, J. J. S.
A biography of Thomas Clifford, first Lord Clifford of Chudleigh. *Ph.D. 1935 Glasgow*

Shaw, L. M.
Colley Cibber, actor-manager, dramatist and historian of the theatre. *M.A. 1928 Liverpool*

Shaw, P. E. O.
The Catholic Apostolic church, sometimes called Irvingite: an historical study. *Ph.D. 1935 Edinburgh*

Shaw, P. E. O.
The early tractarians and the eastern Church. *B.Litt. 1924 Oxford*

Shawcross, K. M.
The Literary Gazette under the editorship of William Jerdan. *B.Litt. 1937 Oxford*

Shaxby, J. M.
The constitutional position of the Church in the Norman kingdom of Sicily, 1130-94, with special reference to the relations between papacy, monarchy, metropolitan and immediate sees. *B.Litt. 1933 Oxford*

Shea, M. M.
Zur Entwickelungsgeschichte der Kunstballade. *M.A. 1918 National University of Ireland*

Sheard, J. A.
The dialect of Lower Calderdale (Yorks). *Ph.D. 1940 London, King's College*

Sheard, W.
The construction of a test of scientific method. *M.Ed. 1950 Manchester*

Shearer, T.
The Percy Grainger materials preserved in the Anderson papers in the National Library of Scotland. *B.Litt. 1935 Oxford*

Shearman, H. F.
The economic results of the disestablishment of the Irish Church. *Ph.D. 1944 Dublin, Trinity College*

Sheehy, E. J.
Land and peasant in Anglo-Irish literature. *M.A. 1932 National University of Ireland*

Sheehy, M.
Outline of international economic disintegration and reconstruction. *M.Econ.Sc. 1944 National University of Ireland*

Sheehy, M. J.
J. E. Cairnes. *M.Econ.Sc. 1941 National University of Ireland*

Sheen, H. E.
The Oxford Movement in a Manchester parish: the Miles Platting case. *M.A. 1941 Manchester*

Sheen, K. J.
Development of ideas in the works of Paul Adam. *Ph.D. 1935 London, University College*

Shehata, S. A. A. M.
The organisation of education in Egypt, with special reference to the future of elementary (primary) education. *M.A. 1940 London, Institute of Education*

Sheikh, A. A.
Punjab industries. *M.A. 1945 London, University College*

Sheil, M.
Intuition in Bergson's philosophy. *M.A. 1931 National University of Ireland*

Shelat, J. M.
Criticism and defence of the Constitution of the Senate of the U.S.A. during the campaign for ratification, 1787-1789. *M.A. 1933 London, King's College*

Sheldrick, A. J.
Some tendencies and developments in recent poetry. *M.A. 1921 Wales*

Shelley, C. L.
A study of the German novel between 1850 and 1870 in its relations to French and English influences. *M.A. 1930 Wales*

Shembekar, V. S.
The place and problems of rural reconstruction in the development of Indian agriculture. *Ph.D. 1941 Wales*

Shendarkar, D. D.
An experimental investigation in teaching to solve problems in arithmetic and the light it throws on the doctrine of formal training. *Ph.D. 1930 London, Day Training College*

Shenfield, A.
A statistical study in the structure of industry. *M.Com. 1939 Birmingham*

Shenkman, E.
The theory and practice of credit insurance in international trade. *Ph.D. 1934 London, School of Economics and Political Science*

Shenoy, B. R.
Some aspects of a central bank for India. *M.Sc. 1933 London, School of Economics and Political Science*

Sheperd, K. M.
The presentation of King Arthur in medieval romance, with special reference to Middle English. *M.A. 1907 London*

Shepherd, A. P.
1. Man's solution of the problem of sin. 2. God's solution of the problem of sin. *B.D. 1924 Oxford*

Shepherd, C. Y.
Some economics aspects of the cacao industry of Trinidad. *Ph.D. 1937 London, External Degree*

Shepherd, D. P.
An edition of the poems of John Cunningham (1729-73). *B.Litt. 1941 Oxford*

Shepherd, E. C.
The settlement of wages in government employment. *B.Litt. 1923 Oxford*

Shepherd, G. T.
Aspects of the devotion to the Blessed Virgin Mary in thirteenth-century English lyric poetry. *M.A. 1948 London, King's College*

Shepherd, T. B.
Methodism and the literature of the eighteenth century. *Ph.D. 1938 London, Birkbeck College*

Shepherd, T. B.
A study of Charles Churchill. *M.A. 1934 London, Birkbeck College*

Shepherd, W. H.
A cultural comparison between Alsace and Lorraine, including an account of the regions round Strasbourg and Nancy. *M.A. 1944 Manchester*

Shepley, W. H.
A study of psycho-somatic correlations, with especial reference to the affective states. *M.D. 1943 Manchester*

Sheppard, E. A.
Studies in the language of Bellenden's *Boece*. *Ph.D. 1936 London, University College*

Sheppard, J. E.
1. The communion of saints. 2. The nature of the Resurrection body. *B.D. & D.D. 1900 Oxford*

Sheppard, N. J.
Arthur Hugh Clough and his age. *M.A. 1938 National University of Ireland*

Sheppard, T. V.
Iceland, in the light of modern geography. *M.Sc. 1935 London, King's College*

Sheppard, W. J. L.
1. The Lord's coming and the world's end. 2. The Revelation of St. John. *B.D. & D.D. 1922 Oxford*

Shere, S. A.
The Lodi dynasty A.D. 1451 to 1526. *M.A. 1934 London, School of Oriental and African Studies*

Sheridan, H. C.
Some political aspects of the career of Alexander Wedderburn, Lord Loughborough and Earl of Rosslyn. *M.A. 1919 Liverpool*

Sheridan, M.
W. B. Yeats. *M.A. 1945 National University of Ireland*

Sheridan, M. D. H.
The scholastic attainments of children with impaired hearing. *M.A. 1945 Liverpool*

Sheridan, N. J.
Sir Thomas Browne. *M.A. 1934 National University of Ireland*

Sherman, J.
De summi numinis existentia. *M.A. 1716 Glasgow*

Sherman, L. R.
Religious teaching in early English literature before the Conquest. *B.Litt. 1914 Oxford*

Sherriff, C. B.
The theology of George Whitefield, 1714-1770. *Ph.D. 1950 Edinburgh*

Sherwin-White, A. N.
The types of political relation established between Rome and other communities in Italy from the earliest recorded times to the close of the Republic, and their contribution to the conception of citizenship adopted by the Roman Empire during the first three centuries A.D. *D.Phil. 1937 Oxford*

Sherwood, H. C.
Utopia in nineteenth century English literature. *M.A. 1934 Birmingham*

Shiah, N.
Ancient Egyptian beads. *Ph.D. 1946 London, University College*

Shibeika, M. A.
The Sudan and the Mahdist Revolution of 1881-85. *Ph.D. 1949 London, Bedford College*

Shield, A. R. P.
Jonathan Swift, 1696-1717: early satires and politics. *M.A. 1939 Birmingham*

Shields, F. R.
The problem of humanism. *M.A. 1906 London*

Shields, R. W.
Metempsychosis in Western thought. *B.D. 1943 Leeds*

Shillington, V. M.
The commercial relations of England and Portugal: the Middle Ages. *D.Sc. 1907 London*

Shiman, R. G.
The United States and Old World diplomacy, 1898 to 1914, with special reference to China. *Ph.D. 1930 London, School of Economics and Political Science*

Shirley, F. J. J.
The politics of Hooker. *Ph.D. 1931 London, External Degree*

Shirname, T. G.
The scope and method of research in agricultural economics, with special reference to Indian agriculture. *Ph.D. 1932 Wales*

Shorney, A. B.
The agricultural geography of Devon. *M.Sc. 1943 London, External Degree*

Short, J.
The debt of English poetry in the seventeenth century to Théophile and Saint-Amant. *B.Litt. 1941 Oxford*

Short, J.
Thesis on the philosophic character of English fourteenth century mysticism. *Ph.D. 1929 Edinburgh*

Shortt, C.
A study of the mercantile system: an analysis of its influence on England, Ireland and the American colonies. *M.A. 1929 National University of Ireland*

Shrives, J.
Les différentes formes d'imagination chez Leconte de Lisle. *M.A. 1924 Birmingham*

Shrock, A. T.
R. Jonah b. Abraham of Gerona: his life and ethical works. *Ph.D. 1936 London, External Degree*

Shropshire, D. W. T.
Ancestor worship among the southern Bantu. *B.Litt. 1927 Oxford*

Shropshire, D. W. T.
The religious institutions and beliefs of the southern Bantu, and their bearing on the problems of the Christian missionary. *D.Phil. 1937 Oxford*

Shukla, M. M.
A study of friendship among adolescents. *M.A. 1948 London, Institute of Education*

Shukla, M. M.
A study of inductive reasoning in children of about 13 years of age. *M.A. 1948 London, Institute of Education*

Shukry, M. F.
The Khedive Ismail and slavery in the Sudan. *Ph.D. 1935 Liverpool*

Shukry, M. F.
The mission of General Gordon in the Sudan, 18 January, 1884-26 January 1885. *M.A. 1937 Liverpool*

Shutt, R. J. H.
A special study of the language and contents of Josephus' *Jewish Antiquities*, books 11-20. *Ph.D. 1936 Durham*

Shuttleworth, C. W.
Tests of mechanical aptitude. *M.A. 1941 London, Institute of Education*

Siddinqi, A. M. M. A. A.
History of the development of mercantile law in India, with special reference to the law of incorporated trading companies. *LL.D. 1928 London*

Siddiq, S. M.
A critical examination of the *Tarikh-i-Bayhaqi*. *Ph.D. 1930 London, School of Oriental and African Studies*

Siddiqi, A. H.
Caliphate and kingship in medieval Persia. *Ph.D. 1934 London, School of Oriental and African Studies*

Siddiqi, M. Z.
Origin and development of Arabian medicine. *Ph.D. 1925 Cambridge*

Sideropoulo, E.
Knowledge: pure and perceptual. *Ph.D. 1931 London, University College*

Sidersky, M.
Assyrian prayers and hymns. *B.Litt. 1922 Oxford*

Sidgwick, R.
'The mirror of fools': a study in church history chiefly of the twelfth century. *M.A. 1908 Birmingham*

Siebenberg, P. J.
French monetary policy 1930 to 1939. *M.Com. 1946 Birmingham*

Sieu, C. Chung- *see* Chung-Sieu, C.

Silcock, H.
A statistical examination of post-war developments of selected public social services on Merseyside. *M.A. 1941 Liverpool*

Silcock, T. H.
Advertising, salesmanship, and the theory of value. *D.Phil. 1936 Oxford*

Silk, W. A.
British foreign policy in relation to Japan, 1890 to 1902. *M.A. 1944 Wales*

Sillick, C. B. M.
The city port of Plymouth: an essay in geographical interpretation. *Ph.D. 1938 London, Bedford College*

Silman, E. I. H.
The development of rationalization in the Leeds men's tailoring industry, with particular reference to scientific management. *Ph.D. 1933 Leeds*

Silsby, E.
The origin of the sense of sin in man. *M.Sc. 1921 London*

Silva, C. R. de *see* de Silva, C. R.

Silva, H. R. de *see* De Silva, H. R.

Silva, R.
The religious dramas of Calderón. *M.A. 1939 Liverpool*

Simcock, V.
The literary programme of the early *Arcadia* with special reference to poetic diction. *M.A. 1950 Liverpool*

Simister, O. E.
A study of Matthew Arnold's literary criticism, with special reference to the influence of Sainte-Beuve on Arnold. *M.A. 1936 Birmingham*

Simkin, C. G. F.
An analysis of economic fluctuations in New Zealand. *D.Phil. 1949 Oxford*

Simkins, E.
The agricultural geography of the coast plains of South India. *M.A. 1927 Liverpool*

Simkins, M.
Essai et notes sur *Trois contes* de G. Flaubert. *M.A. 1925 Birmingham*

Simmonds, H. A. T.
Vocational guidance in secondary schools. *M.A. 1931 London, Day Training College*

Simmonds, L. F. R.
A comparative study of the scientific interests of adults and of boys of the same social class. *M.A. 1936 London, Institute of Education*

Simmonds, L. F. R.
The controversy between Proust and Berthollet on the invariability of chemical proportions. *M.Sc. 1931 London*

Simmons, B.
Some aspects of the treatment of the Psalms and of the song of Solomon in English eighteenth century literature. *M.A. 1937 London, King's College*

Simms, G. O.
The text of *Codex Cenannensis*. *Ph.D. 1950 Dublin, Trinity College*

Simms, V. H.
The organisation of the Whig Party during the exclusion crisis 1678 to 81. *M.A. 1934 London, University College*

Simons, H.
The development of Keats's idea of poetry. *M.A. 1927 Wales*

Simons, H. J.
A study of the criminal law and its administration in South Africa, Southern Rhodesia and Kenya. *Ph.D. 1936 London, School of Economics and Political Science*

Simons, J. B.
A critical study of the novels of Arnold Bennett. *M.A. 1932 Wales*

Simons, L. C.
The ecclesiastical history of Glamorgan during the Middle Ages up to 1188, with special reference to the period A.D. 1056-1188. *M.A. 1914 Wales*

Simpson, A.
The Convention Parliament, 1688-9. *D.Phil. 1939 Oxford*

Simpson, A. F.
Certainty through faith: an examination of the religious philosophy of Peter Taylor Forsyth. *Ph.D. 1949 London, External Degree*

Simpson, A. R.
Greek elementary education and its critics (down to Aristotle). *Ph.D. 1944 London, External Degree*

Simpson, C. A.
The early traditions of Israel. *B.D. & D.D. 1944 Oxford*

Simpson, C. A.
The regional geography of the Cotteswolds. *B.Sc. 1923 Oxford*

Simpson, D. C.
Exegeses of Zechariah ix.9; Tobit xiii.6; xiv.9. *D.D. 1923 Oxford*

Simpson, D. C.
1. The meaning of criticism, with special reference to the higher criticism of the Pentateuch. 2. The divine purpose in Hebrew religion. *B.D. 1919 Oxford*

Simpson, E. B.
A measurement of the effect of group discussion on the understanding and appreciation of films. *M.A. 1947 London, Institute of Education*

Simpson, E. M.
The prose works of John Donne. *D.Phil. 1923 Oxford*

Simpson, G. F.
English nature poetry of the eighteenth century. *B.Litt. 1925 Oxford*

Simpson, I. *see* Sinovitch, I.

Simpson, I. J.
Education in Aberdeenshire before 1872. *Ph.D. 1942 Aberdeen*

Simpson, J. G.
1. Christ, our righteousness. 2. The doctrine of the Holy Spirit. *B.D. & D.D. 1909 Oxford*

Simpson, M. M.
The conception of fate, and its development in the Latin literature of the later Republic and the early Empire. *M.A. 1919 Liverpool*

Simpson, M. W. Hilton- *see* Hilton-Simpson, M. W.

Simpson, W. D.
The Castle of Kildrummy: its place in Scottish history and architecture. *D.Litt. 1923 Aberdeen*

Sims, A.
Education for the Christian ministry. *M.A. 1945 Bristol*

Sims, B. H.
The servant of the Lord: the influence of the Old Testament conception on the literature of the New Testament (with special reference to Isaiah lii.13-liii.12). *B.Litt. 1943 Oxford*

Sims, G. F.
The aesthetic appreciation of music and its training. *M.A. 1938 Birmingham*

Sims, M. G.
A critical analysis of the presentation of ideas connected with the figure of the hero in the works of Stefan George and his circle. *M.A. 1947 London, Birkbeck College*

Simson, W. A.
An enquiry into curiosity as shown in the written questions of children and adolescents. *M.A. 1946 Birmingham*

Sinclair, A.
The problem of tenure of assistant masters in secondary schools. *M.Ed. 1940 Manchester*

Sinclair, C.
Scoto-Celtic architecture: its place among the styles. *Ph.D. 1932 Glasgow*

Sinclair, M. S.
William Smith, American loyalist, 1728-83. *B.Litt. 1928 Oxford*

Sinclair, O. W.
The influence of 1848 on education. *M.A. 1916 London*

Sinclair, W. M.
1. On the Epistle to the Hebrews. 2. On the proportional reward. *B.D. 1888 Oxford*

Sinclair, W. M.
St. John's Gospel vi.28-65, and the first Epistle of St. John, chapters i and iv. *D.D. 1892 Oxford*

Singer, A. F.
The survival of the Romano-Austrians. *B.Litt. 1948 Oxford*

Singer, H. W.
Materials for the study of urban ground rent. *Ph.D. 1937 Cambridge*

Singh, A.
Purposes and methods of recording and accounting as applied to agriculture, with special reference to provision and use of economic data relating to agriculture in India. *Ph.D. 1937 Wales*

Singh, G.
Elementary education in India and abroad. *M.Sc. 1918 London*

Singh, P.
Economics of agricultural marketing in India, with particular reference to oilseeds, the determination of prices, and proposals for future marketing policy. *B.Litt. 1949 Oxford*

Singh, T.
Co-operative credit in the Punjab. *Ph.D. 1927 London*

Singleton, R.
Earl of Tyrone's rebellion. *M.A. 1915 Liverpool*

Singleton, W. A.
The development of nursery and elementary schools in Great Britain. *M.A. 1945 Liverpool*

Singleton, W. A.
An investigation into the structural and decorative characteristics of traditional domestic architecture in selected areas within the counties of Lancashire, Cheshire and Derbyshire. *Ph.D. 1949 Manchester*

Sinha, B. P.
Decline of the kingdom of Magadha from *c.*455 A.D. to *c.*1000 A.D. *Ph.D. 1948 London, School of Oriental and African Studies*

Sinha, C. P.
Relation between intelligence quotient and curves of output (mental). *M.Sc. 1949 London, University College*

Sinha, C. S.
Distribution of population in the United Provinces of Agra and Oudh (India). *M.A. 1933 London, Birkbeck College*

Sinha, D. P.
The origin and development in Bengal of the principles involved in Sir Charles Wood's despatch on education of 19th July, 1854. *M.A. 1939 London, School of Oriental and African Studies*

Sinha, H.
Sovereignty in ancient Indian polity: a study in the evolution of the early Indian state. *Ph.D. 1935 London, School of Oriental and African Studies*

Sinha, K. D.
The role of interpolated experience in remembering. *M.Sc. 1949 Cambridge*

Sinha, R.
The press and crime. *M.Sc. 1949 London, School of Economics and Political Science*

Sinha, R. K.
The literary influences on D. H. Lawrence's poems and novels. *D.Phil. 1950 Oxford*

Sinha, S.
Post-war labour legislation in India: a comparison with Japan. *Ph.D. 1932 London, School of Economics and Political Science*

Sinnatamby, V.
Studies on the botanical researches and method of Theophrastos. *M.Sc. 1948 London, University College*

Sinovitch, I.
L'influence de l'école Saint-Simonienne sur la littérature française jusqu'en 1850. *M.A. 1922 Leeds*

Sirajuddin, J. M.
A comparative study of the economics of the woollen industry of Scotland and the Panjab. *Ph.D. 1927 Edinburgh*

Siriex, P. H.
The deviations of the parliamentary system of the United Kingdom since 1911. *B.Litt. 1934 Oxford*

Sisam, K.
An edition of the Salisbury Psalter (Salisbury ms. 150), with introduction and critical notes. *B.Litt. 1915 Oxford*

Sisson, R. A.
The work and significance of William Perkins. *M.Litt. 1949 Cambridge*

Sitaram, K. N.
Puranas: their composition and correlation. *Ph.D. 1922 London*

Sivaprakasam, K.
Oscillation of attention. *Ph.D. 1934 London, University College*

Sivaprakasam, K.
Quantitive and qualitative analysis of imagination. *M.Sc. 1931 London, University College*

Skeffington, O. L. S.
Jules Romains, the apostle of unanimism. *Ph.D. 1935 Dublin, Trinity College*

Skeffington, O. S.
Jules Romains, the apostle of unanimism: a critical review of his contribution to literature. *Ph.D. 1935 National University of Ireland*

Skelton, C.
An investigation into the reliability of various entrance examinations for pupils about to enter secondary and central selective schools. *M.A. 1938 Leeds*

Skelton, E.
The Court of Star Chamber in the reign of Queen Elizabeth. *M.A. 1931 London, University College*

Skemp, J. B.
Plato's later philosophy of motion. *Ph.D. 1937 Edinburgh*

Skenhouse, A. C.
A geographical enquiry into the modern settlement and economic development of Palestine. *M.Sc. 1949 London, External Degree*

Skentelbery, M. L.
The revival of the sonnet. *M.A. 1941 National University of Ireland*

Skillicorn, A. H.
The Education Act of 1870: an analysis of underlying ideas and opinions, and their influence on the English educational system. *M.Sc. 1927 London*

Skilling, H. G.
The German-Czech national conflict in Bohemia, 1879-1893. *Ph.D. 1940 London, School of Slavonic and East European Studies*

Skinner, F. J.
Tuscany and the Italian Risorgimento, 1859-60. *M.A. 1921 London*

Skinner, G. H.
The geography of Cornwall and its control over human activity. *M.A. 1934 Bristol*

Skinner, J. W.
Emile Montégut: critic of English literature. *Ph.D. 1926 London*

Skinner, W. A.
An investigation into assessment of teaching ability in teachers of technical subjects. *M.A. 1949 London, Institute of Education*

Skinner, W. A.
The investigation of factors useful in predicting teaching ability with special reference to the teaching of mathematics and science. *M.Ed. 1947 Manchester*

Skirrow, P. W.
The union of England and Scotland considered with regard to the action of English statesmen and the development of opinion in England. *B.Litt. 1927 Oxford*

Skone, G. W.
Manorial organization in medieval Pembrokeshire. *M.A. 1928 Wales*

Skrimshire, N. E.
The evolution of the Assembly of the League of Nations as a parliamentary body. *M.Sc. 1932 London, School of Economics and Political Science*

Skrine, J. H.
1. On the historic Christ. 2. On the sacraments. *B.D. & D.D. 1912 Oxford*

Skues, M. T.
The practice of Eastern cults at Rome and their influence to 200 A.D. *M.A. 1908 London*

Slade, E. H.
A history of the Londonderry shirt industry. *M.A. 1937 Belfast*

Slater, H.
The syllabus, teaching and value of geography in a rural fenland grammar school. *M.Ed. 1933 Manchester*

Slater, W.
1. The teaching of the New Testament as to the divinity of our Lord and Saviour Jesus Christ. 2. The internal evidence as to the Johannine authorship of the fourth Gospel. *B.D. 1889 Oxford*

Sleigh, R. S.
Sufficiency of Christianity. *Ph.D. 1923 Aberdeen*

Sleight, G. F.
The diagnosis and treatment of the dull and backward child. *Ph.D. 1933 London, Day Training College*

Sleight, W. G.
The problem of the relation between the ultimate ground and the individual members of the universe, as treated by Spinoza and Leibniz. *M.A. 1907 London*

Slevin, J. G.
The idea of God in the philosophy of Fichte. *M.A. 1939 National University of Ireland*

Sliwowski, Z.
Polish-Ukrainian relations, 1919-39. *B.Phil. 1947 Oxford*

Slocombe, C. S.
The construction of mental tests. *Ph.D. 1925 London*

Sloman, A. E.
The sources of Calderon's *Principe constante*. *D.Phil. 1948 Oxford*

Slosser, G. J.
An historical and critical study of the Christian unity movements since the Peace of Westphalia. *Ph.D. 1928 London*

Slotki, I. W.
The writing and recital of ancient Hebrew poetry. *D.Litt. 1932 Manchester*

Slotki, J. J.
Hebrew education from 1000 to 150 B.C. *M.A. 1929 Manchester*

Slotki, J. J.
The towns and districts of Mesopotamia in the second millenium B.C. according to the inscriptions of Tiglathpileser I. *Ph.D. 1946 Manchester*

Smail, R. C.
Military methods employed by the Latin states in Syria, 1097 to 1192. *Ph.D. 1948 Cambridge*

Smailes, A. E.
Population in the dales of North East England. *M.A. 1934 London, University College*

Small, F. G.
The history of science teaching in English schools since 1870. *M.Sc. 1926 London*

Small, G. W.
The use of case in Old English to express comparison. *B.Litt. 1927 Oxford*

Small, L. M.
Gunnlaugssaga Ormstungu: a critical edition. *Ph.D. 1925 Edinburgh*

Smalley, B.
Biblical commentators of the twelfth and thirteenth centuries, viewed as historical material, with special reference to the commentaries of Stephen Langton. *Ph.D. 1929 Manchester*

Smalley, F. A.
An investigation of the methods of presentation of Christianity to the Gentiles by the early Church, and an examination of China's religious heritage with a view to similarity of approach. *B.Litt. 1933 Oxford*

Smallpage, E.
The slave trade in European diplomacy, 1814-1818. *M.A. 1922 Liverpool*

Smallpage, P.
The life of the Reverend Robert Dall, 1745-1828. *M.A. 1929 Liverpool*

Smallwood, F. T.
Sir W. Scott and H. Heine: an enquiry into the relations between the two writers. *M.A. 1910 Birmingham*

Smart, A.
Sir Walter Scott: his influence on life and letters. *Ph.D. 1938 Aberdeen*

Smart, A. E.
The development of sacramental ideas in relation to the institution of marriage. *M.A. 1942 Leeds*

Smart, E. L.
Collation of a reprint of *Jack Jugggler* prepared in collaboration with Dr. W. W. Greg for the Malone Society, with an essay on the development of the Tudor interlude as a dramatic form. *M.A. 1934 London, University College*

Smart, H. E.
Kabir and the movements springing from his influence. *B.Litt. 1921 Oxford*

Smart, J. E.
Some aspects of educational administration, with special reference to its organization and problems in boroughs and county boroughs. *Ph.D. 1930 London, School of Economics and Political Science*

Smart, T. B.
The Stepmother by Sir Robert Stapylton. *M.A. 1938 Sheffield*

Smedley, L. S.
The Wytham scheme: an experiment in open-air education. *M.A. 1942 Sheffield*

Smee, D. K.
An analysis of the geographical conditions influencing the development of the stock industries in the Irish Free State. *M.A. 1927 London*

Smee, D. K.
The trade of Dublin. *Ph.D. 1929 London*

Smerdon, E. W.
Chinese medicine: a comparison with Renaissance and Stuart medicine. *M.D. 1913 Edinburgh*

Smethurst, L. J.
Tennyson's religious, social and political ideas in relation to his time. *M.A. 1948 London, King's College*

Smewing, E. M.
Scientific method in ancient and medieval times. *M.Sc. 1934 London, University College*

Smierzchaiski, S.
Polish monetary policy and trade fluctuations, 1924-1939. *M.Sc. 1945 London, School of Economics and Political Science*

Smit, L. van Z.
Nature in the works of Annette von Droste-Hülshoff. *Ph.D. 1932 London, University College*

Smith, A.
Ethical aspects of the family. *Ph.D. 1945 London, School of Economics and Political Science*

Smith, A. C.
Frederick Denison Maurice. *M.A. 1950 Sheffield*

Smith, A. C.
The language of J. K. Huysmans. *Ph.D. 1930 London, King's College*

Smith, A. D.
The development of rates of postage. *D.Sc. 1917 London*

Smith, A. E.
Offa of Mercia in history and tradition. *M.A. 1942 Leeds*

Smith, A. E.
The transportation system in the seventeenth century, with special reference to the West Indies. *D.Phil. 1933 Oxford*

Smith, A. H.
The place-names of the North Riding of Yorkshire. *Ph.D. 1926 Leeds*

Smith, A. J.
William Hale White (Mark Rutherford). *M.A. 1933 Liverpool*

Smith, A. J. M.
Studies in the metaphysical poets of the Anglican Church in the seventeenth century. *Ph.D. 1931 Edinburgh*

Smith, A. M.
Post-entry training in the civil service: a study of the positive state. *Ph.D. 1945 London, School of Economics and Political Science*

Smith, A. V.
A study of the prose works of R. Greene. *M.A. 1927 Birmingham*

Smith, B.
Two obedientiary rolls of Selby Abbey. *M.A. 1949 Leeds*

Smith, B. A.
Some existing anomalies in British income tax law affecting resident foreigners and non-resident British subjects. *LL.D. 1927 London*

Smith, B. H.
The origins of the tariff reform movement. *M.A. 1938 Birmingham*

Smith, B. T. D.
The Gospel according to St Matthew. *B.D. 1928 Cambridge*

Smith, B. T. D.
Parables of the synoptic Gospels. *D.D. 1937 Cambridge*

Smith, C.
The religious ideas of Renan. *Ph.D. 1949 London, King's College*

Smith, C.
Some aspects of the thought of Julien Benda. *M.A. 1937 Manchester*

Smith, C. A.
A reconsideration of some of the more important rules governing equitable apportionments between tenant for life and remainderman. *Ll.M. 1938 Sheffield*

Smith, C. G.
Joseph Hume, M.P.: political activities, 1818-1825. *M.A. 1921 Liverpool*

Smith, C. H. J.
A study of the factor pattern of the social conscience of intending teachers. *M.A. 1947 London, Institute of Education*

Smith, C. T.
The external relations of life assurance companies (ordinary branch): an historical view. *M.Sc. 1945 London, School of Economics and Political Science*

Smith, D. C.
A thesis on Robert Browne (1550?-1633) as churchman and theologian. *Ph.D. 1936 Edinburgh*

Smith, D. H.
The recent industrialization of the northern and western sectors of Greater London. *Ph.D. 1933 London, Birkbeck College*

Smith, D. M.
The development of literary criticism in England until 1800, as seen by the treatment of the works of Geoffrey Chaucer and Edmund Spenser. *M.A. 1923 Wales*

Smith, D. M.
Robert Garnier et quelques aspects de la poésie dramatique au seizième siècle. *M.A. 1940 Wales*

Smith, E.
Higher education in Lancashire in the nineteenth century. *B.Litt. 1922 Oxford*

Smith, E. E.
The friars in England. *M.A. 1908 Birmingham*

Smith, E. Edmonds- *see* Edmonds-Smith, E.

Smith, E. F. Malcolm- *see* Malcolm-Smith, E. F.

Smith, E. H.
The economic organization of the medieval borough with special reference to Leicester and its guild merchants. *M.A. 1912 Wales*

Smith, E. I.
Experiments in technique: a study of the plays of Harley Granville Barker. *M.A. 1948 Liverpool*

Smith, E. Lorrain- *see* Lorrain-Smith, E.

Smith, E. M.
Corporate religious worship as practised in a group of secondary modern schools, and its value to adolescents. *M.A. 1946 Birmingham*

Smith, F.
The life and work of Sir James Kay-Shuttleworth. *Ph.D. 1923 Wales*

Smith, F.
The peasantry, Orthodox clergy, dissenters, and Jews, as seen by Leskov. *M.A. 1948 London, School of Slavonic and East European Studies*

Smith, F.
Some pioneer women novelists and their contribution to the eighteenth century novel, 1688-1740. *Ph.D. 1926 London*

Smith, F. A.
Minor comedies in the eighteenth century. *M.A. 1929 Birmingham*

Smith, F. J.
English theories of moral obligation from Hobbes to Stephen. *B.Sc. 1900 Oxford*

Smith, F. T.
The land utilisation reports of Sutherlandshire: with a special account of the reclamation schemes and the deer forests. *M.Sc. 1938 London, King's College*

Smith, F. V.
Explanatory concepts in the theory of personality. *Ph.D. 1948 London, Birkbeck College*

Smith, G.
A psychological study of poetry-writing by children. *D.Phil. 1940 Oxford*

Smith, G. B.
Cicero's educational theory. *M.Ed. 1934 Manchester*

Smith, G. M. H. Harcourt- *see* Harcourt-Smith, G. M. H.

Smith, G. S.
Play centres in England. *M.Ed. 1921 Manchester*

Smith, H.
Retailing costs and technical progress. *B.Litt. 1934 Oxford*

Smith, H. A.
The life and thought of William Hale White. *Ph.D. 1939 Birmingham*

Smith, H. B.
An historical study of the agriculture of part of south-eastern Sussex from 1780. *M.A. 1940 London, Birkbeck College*

Smith, H. B. Lees- *see* Lees-Smith, H. B.

Smith, H. G.
The reform movement in Birmingham, 1830-1884. *Ph.D. 1930 London, External Degree*

Smith, H. J.
A study of the relation between the imaginative and rational aspects of religion. *B.Litt. 1936 Oxford*

Smith, H. K.
The relations between the Church of England and the state from 1838 to 1870. *M.A. 1946 Sheffield*

Smith, H. Maynard- *see* Maynard-Smith, H.

Smith, H. R. C.
1. The import and rendering of the word διαθήκη in Hebrews ix. 2. The personality and identity of St. Mary Magdalen. *B.D. & D.D. 1891 Oxford*

Smith, J.
The non-Babylonian oracles in the Book of the Prophet Ezechiel, (chapters i-xxxvii). *Ph.D. 1929 Edinburgh*

Smith, J.
Telecommunications: their significance as a factor in economic developments. *Ph.D. 1946 London, External Degree*

Smith, J. A.
1. The atonement. 2. The Holy Spirit. *B.D. & D.D. 1898 Oxford*

Smith, J. A.
The avowynge of King Arthur, Sir Gawan, Sir Kaye, and Sir Bawdewyn of Bretan: a Middle English romance from the Ireland ms. *M.A. 1938 Leeds*

Smith, J. C.
Principles of governing the exercise of the powers and duties of local authorities. *LL.M. 1948 Leeds*

Smith, J. H.
Economic studies of the poultry industry. *M.Sc. 1937 Wales*

Smith, J. M.
The French background of Middle Scots literature. *Ph.D. 1933 Edinburgh*

Smith, J. W. A.
The curriculum of the Dissenting Academies, with special reference to factors determining it, 1660-1800. *M.Ed. 1950 Durham*

Smith, K. M. G.
Histoire poétique de Guillaume au court nez: recherches sur les chansons de geste. *Ph.D. 1925 Leeds*

Smith, L. G.
An investigation into the teaching of science to non-science specialists at the post-certificate stage, with special reference to the needs of these pupils in later life. *M.A. 1934 London, Institute of Education*

Smith, L. M.
Some aspects of staff organization in the Postal Service with special reference to (a) the general history and development of the movement since 1895; (b) the struggle for official recognition; (c) the efforts to secure full civil rights; and (d) the working of Whitleyism. *B.Litt. 1931 Oxford*

Smith, L. P. F.
Analysis of the agricultural systems of the six and the twenty-six counties. *M.A. 1948 National University of Ireland*

Smith, M.
The influence of oracles on human conduct in Greek tragedy. *M.A. 1950 Manchester*

Smith, M.
The life and teachings of Rābia' al-'Adawiyya al-Qayriyya of Basra together with some account of the place of the women saints in Islam. *Ph.D. 1928 London*

Smith, M.
The nervous temperament: its definition and history: its expression in industry and importance from the point of view of health and efficiency. *D.Sc. 1930 London, School of Hygiene and Tropical Medicine*

Smith, M. D.
Periods of arrested progress in the acquisition of skill. *Ph.D. 1930 Cambridge*

Smith, M. J.
La place de Rousseau dans le mouvement pédagogique en France aux dix-septième et dix-huitième siècles. *Ph.D. 1935 Edinburgh*

Smith, M. L.
Illustrations of the form, grammar, and language of the Epistle of St. Paul to the Romans. *B.D. & D.D. 1913 Oxford*

Smith, M. M.
An investigation into the development of number concepts in young children. *M.A. 1943 Leeds*

Smith, M. N.
An edition of *Sir Amadace*. *M.A. 1934 Leeds*

Smith, M. S.
A contribution to the history of the educational tradition inherited from Madame de Maintenon. *Ph.D. 1927 London*

Smith, M. W.
Economic relations between England and Russia in the sixteenth century. *M.A. 1918 Wales*

Smith, M. Wretts- *see* Wretts-Smith, M.

Smith, N.
L'influence du culte de la forme sur la pensée de J. M. de Heredia. *M.A. 1918 Birmingham*

Smith, N.
Studies in the Cartesian philosophy. *D.Phil. 1903 Saint Andrew's*

Smith, N. A. Turner- *see* Turner-Smith, N. A.

Smith, N. E. V.
Austro-British relations 1863-1866, with special reference to the German question. *M.A. 1935 London, King's College*

Smith, N. M.
The value of Clarendon as a historian. *M.A. 1906 Wales*

Smith, O.
A new translation of the Icelandic *Saga of Hoensa-Dorir*. *M.A. 1945 Bristol*

Smith, P. F.
The mental and moral discipline of handicraft in schools. *M.A. 1931 Liverpool*

Smith, P. M.
The creative imagination of Henri de Régnier. *B.Litt. 1938 Oxford*

Smith, P. W.
The education of English women in the seventeenth century. *M.A. 1921 London*

Smith, R. A. L.
Canterbury Cathedral priory: a study in monastic administration. *Ph.D. 1941 Cambridge*

Smith, R. A. L.
The history of Pershore Abbey and its estates. *M.A. 1938 London, School of Economics and Political Science*

Smith, S.
The great roll of the pipe for the seventh year of the reign of King John, Michaelmas 1205. *Ph.D. 1937 Reading*

Smith, S. E.
The special character of Eckhart's mysticism studied with reference in particular to his German works. *B.Litt. 1946 Oxford*

Smith, S. R.
The Ibo people. *Ph.D. 1930 Cambridge*

Smith, S. S.
Social ideas in comedy, 1860-1920. *B.Litt. 1924 Oxford*

Smith, T. A.
The present condition of historical drama in England. *M.A. 1934 Bristol*

Smith, T. C.
The practice and doctrine of baptism in primitive Christianity. *Ph.D. 1949 Edinburgh*

Smith, V.
The dramatic work of Henry Bataille. *B.Litt. 1927 Oxford*

Smith, V. C.
Free banking. *Ph.D. 1935 London, School of Economics and Political Science*

Smith, W. E.
The ethical limitations of some modern psychology. *M.A. 1934 Leeds*

Smith, W. E.
Medieval English satire. *M.A. 1914 Birmingham*

Smith, W. E. L.
Episcopal appointments and patronage in the reign of Edward II: a study in the relations of Church and State. *Ph.D. 1931 Edinburgh*

Smith, W. F. Baird-
The philosophy of the conditioned. *M.A. 1922 Liverpool*

Smith, W. M.
The marketing of Australian and New Zealand primary products. *Ph.D. 1932 London, School of Economics and Political Science*

Smith-Dampier, J. L. D.
1. On the divinity of Christ, as shown by his possession of the incommunicable attributes of God. 2. Internal evidence of the Johannine authorship of the fourth Gospel. *B.D. 1905 Oxford*

Smitherman, H.
The place of Jean de Schelandre in the development of the French tragedy. *M.A. 1912 London*

Smithson, R. J.
The Anabaptist movement. *Ph.D. 1933 Glasgow*

Smyth, A. M.
An investigation into the interest of children in school geography, with special reference to the development of interest in girls between the ages of 11 and 16 years. *M.A. 1946 London, Institute of Education*

Smyth, K. P.
The book of Micheas. *Ph.D. 1947 National University of Ireland*

Smyth, K. P.
Development of ethical thought of Plato and Aristotle. *M.A. 1933 National University of Ireland*

Smyth, P. C.
Irish land purchase. *M.Comm. 1928 National University of Ireland*

Smyth, W. H.
The ethics of punishment. *M.A. 1920 Belfast*

Smythe, P. R.
Richard Watson, bishop of Llandaff, 1737-1816. *B.D. 1937 Oxford*

Sneath, B. Aikin- *see* Aikin-Sneath, B.

Snee, E. J.
The development of modern German prose fiction since 1880. *M.A. 1910 London*

Snelgrove, G. W.
The work and theories of Jonathan Richardson the Elder (1665 to 1745). *Ph.D. 1936 London, Courtauld Institute of Art*

Snell, B. O. S.
On the derivation and meaning of some ancient building terms. *M.A. 1924 London*

Snow, R. H.
Thomas Lovell Beddoes: his life and work. *B.Litt. 1925 Oxford*

Snow, W. G. S.
The times, life and thought of Patrick Forbes, Bishop of Aberdeen, 1618-1635. *Ph.D. 1940 Edinburgh*

Sodhi, H. S.
The idea of punishment in moral and political theory. *Ph.D. 1931 London, University College*

Sofer, C.
Some recent trends in the status history of the coloured people of South Africa. *M.Sc. 1949 London, School of Economics and Political Science*

Soga, W. A.
Ethnology of the Bomvanas. *M.D. 1894 Glasgow*

Sokkar, M. T.
The post-war industrial development of Egypt. *M.Com. 1940 Leeds*

Solaru, T. T.
Problems of teacher training in Nigeria considered in connection with educational developments in British tropical Africa. *M.A. 1948 London, Institute of Education*

Solberg, C. T.
The Independent Labour Party. *B.Litt. 1939 Oxford*

Solloway, J.
Expositions of: Hebrews xii.1-2; 3-17; 18-29. *D.D. 1905 Oxford*

Solloway, J.
1. The times and prophecy of Amos. 2. The chronology of the life of our Lord. *B.D. 1901 Oxford*

Solmsen, F. H. R.
Rome and Roman models in Cicero's philosophical and rhetorical writings. *Ph.D. 1936 Cambridge*

Solmsen, L.
The purpose and function of the speeches in Herodotus. *M.Litt. 1938 Cambridge*

Solo, C. S.
From research laboratory to production line: a study in the economics of technological change. *Ph.D. 1949 London, School of Economics and Political Science*

Somerville, D. H.
Shrewsbury, 1660-1718. *D.Litt. 1933 Glasgow*

Somerville, D. K.
English pulpit oratory in its relation to literary style and thought, 1680-1850. *Ph.D. 1943 Aberdeen*

Sommer, E.
Studies in the life and philosophy of Robert Kilwardby. *Ph.D. 1936 Cambridge*

Soni, H. R.
Basic Indian industries. *M.Sc. 1925 London*

Soni, H. R.
Indian industry and its problems (vol. 1: factors in industrial development). *D.Sc. 1933 London, School of Economics and Political Science*

Soong, H.
Cyclical fluctuations in British export trade, 1924-38. *Ph.D. 1950 Cambridge*

Soper, D. O.
Edmond Richer and the revival of Gallicanism, 1600-1630. *Ph.D. 1929 London*

Sopote, M.
A study of Utilitarian ethics. *B.Sc. 1908 Oxford*

Sorley, H. T.
Shah Abdul Latif of Bhit, his poetry, life and times: a study of literary, social and economic conditions in eighteenth century Sind. *D.Litt. 1938 Aberdeen*

Soutar, G.
Nature studies in Greek poetry. *D.Litt. 1898 Saint Andrew's*

Southall, D. M.
Editors of Shakespeare. *M.A. 1923 Birmingham*

Southall, I. M.
Christ in German epic and dramatic literature. *M.A. 1914 Birmingham*

Southeard, W. D.
The attitude of the prophets towards the cult, with special reference to Jeremiah and Deuteronomy. *Ph.D. 1949 London, King's College*

Southern, A. C.
Elizabethan recusant literature, 1559-1582. *Ph.D. 1946 London, University College*

Southerns, A. B.
Chaucer and mediaeval romantic literature. *M.A. 1913 National University of Ireland*

Southerns, C. H.
The transition from epic to romance. *M.A. 1913 National University of Ireland*

Southgate, B. A.
A survey of the estuary of the river Tees. *D.Sc. 1936 Aberdeen*

Southgate, D. G.
The transition from Whiggism to liberalism. *D.Phil. 1949 Oxford*

Southward, E. C.
The *Lai du Cor* and its importance in the development of the chief Arthurian characters. *Ph.D. 1939 London, External Degree*

Souttar, R.
The law relating to the sale of intoxicating liquors in England and other countries. *D.C.L. 1903 Oxford*

Souza, A. M. J. B.
Contribution á l'étude du théâtre en France pendant la révolution. *Ph.D. 1926 London*

Souza, L. P. d' *see* D'Souza, L. P.

Sove, B.
The eschatology of the Book of Job. *B.Litt. 1931 Oxford*

Soward, F. H.
The purpose and immediate operation of the Canada Act of 1791. *B.Litt. 1922 Oxford*

Soyer, N. F.
The history of the recapitulation theory. *M.Sc. 1929 London*

Spalt, K. H. G.
Adalbert Stifter's attitude towards the state. *M.A. 1938 Birmingham*

Spalt, K. H. G.
Social factors in German-Swiss literature since 1850. *Ph.D. 1940 Birmingham*

Sparks, B. W.
A contribution to the geomorphology of the South Downs. *M.A. 1949 London, University College*

Sparks, H. F. D.
John the Baptist and his disciples in Patristic theology: a short study in ancient Scriptural exegesis. *B.D. 1937 Oxford*

Sparks, H. J.
The development of Portsmouth as a naval base as illustrating the growth of British naval policy. *M.A. 1911 London*

Sparrow, W. J.
An enquiry into the variation of precision of movement with age during adolescence. *M.A. 1934 Birmingham*

Spate, O. H. K.
London, 1801-51: a geographical study. *Ph.D. 1938 Cambridge*

Spaulding, H. B.
A comparative and critical study of the income tax laws of Great Britain and the United States. *Ph.D. 1926 London*

Speak, G. M.
A critical estimate of Richard Doddridge Blackmore's novels. *M.A. 1949 Leeds*

Speak, J. E.
The part played by Walwyn and Overton in the Leveller Movement. *M.A. 1949 Leeds*

Speak, L.
Residential adult education in England. *M.A. 1949 Leeds*

Speake, J. G.
The medieval borough of Shrewsbury. *M.A. 1939 Wales*

Speakman, S. O.
The dramatic art of Rojas Zorrilla. *B.Litt. 1939 Oxford*

Spear, T. G. P.
English social life in India in the eighteenth century. *Ph.D. 1932 Cambridge*

Spearing, E. M.
The Elizabethan translations of Seneca's tragedies. *M.A. 1912 London*

Spedding, R. K.
Akhenaten and the growth and development of monotheism in Hebrew prophecy: a comparison and a survey. *M.A. 1932 Liverpool*

Speight, K.
Spirito e motivi dei poeti crepuscolari. *M.A. 1933 Manchester*

Speight, K.
Thomas James Mathias and his place in Anglo-Italian literary relations. *M.Litt. 1938 Cambridge*

Speller, N.
Subject and object: a study of some aspects of the new realism. *M.A. 1917 Birmingham*

Spence, M.
Charles Kingsley and education. *M.A. 1945 Bristol*

Spence, T. H.
The Southern Presbyterian Church and the doctrine of the spirituality of the Church. *Ph.D. 1929 Edinburgh*

Spencer, B.
Shakespeare dans la vie et l'oeuvre de Hector Berlioz. *M.A. 1936 Leeds*

Spencer, B. M.
William Dobson. *M.A. 1937 London, Courtauld Institute of Art*

Spencer, F. A. M.
1. The application of our Lord's moral teaching to modern needs. 2. The Lord's Prayer as a guide to public worship. *B.D. 1923 Oxford*

Spencer, F. H.
Municipal origins: an account of English private bill legislation relating to local government, 1740-1835; with a chapter on private bill procedure. *D.Sc. 1911 London*

Spencer, H.
The Church and the councils of the early fifth century. *M.A. 1915 Liverpool*

Spencer, H. B.
The comedies of Thomas May. *B.Litt. 1933 Oxford*

Spencer, P. H.
The social novel in France, 1848-1871. *Ph.D. 1949 Cambridge*

Spencer, R. A.
Great Britain and Turkey, 1878-85. *D.Phil. 1950 Oxford*

Sperber, S.
The place of the prophet in Talmud and Midrashic literature. *M.A. 1945 Manchester*

Spicer, E. E.
Aristotle's conception of the soul. *M.A. 1933 London, King's College*

Spicer, W. K.
A study of the life and work of Thomas James Mathias, 1754-1835. *M.A. 1946 London, Birkbeck College*

Spink, G. W.
Ferdinand Freiligraths Verbannungsjahre in London. *Ph.D. 1931 Edinburgh*

Spink, J. S.
Un manuscrit inédit de Jean-Jacques Rousseau: la première rédaction des lettres écrites de la montagne. *M.A. 1932 Leeds*

Spinks, A. G. S.
Archetypes and apocalypse: a study of apocalyptic literature from the standpoint of Jungian psychology. *Ph.D. 1946 London, King's College*

Spinks, A. G. S.
A psychological study of some aspects of the religious consciousness of seventeenth century England: considered with particular reference to the psychological factors involved in the development of English 'dissent'. *M.A. 1939 London, University College*

Spiro, R. H.
John Loudon McAdam, colossus of roads. *Ph.D. 1950 Edinburgh*

Spooner, R. T.
An examination of the Labour Party during its formative years, 1900-1920. *M.A. 1949 Birmingham*

Spooner, W. A.
1. The doctrine of the Trinity in St. Paul's Epistles. 2. The growth of Christian dogma and of Christian belief as evidenced by the apologists of the second century. *B.D. & D.D. 1903 Oxford*

Spratt, A. V.
The influence of paleontology on the theory of evolution. *M.Sc. 1927 London*

Spratt, J.
Agrarian conditions in Norfolk and Suffolk during the first half of the seventeenth century. *M.A. 1935 London, School of Economics and Political Science*

Spriggs, G. N.
Theories of light and electricity in the eighteenth century. *M.Sc. 1926 London*

Springall, L. M.
The Norfolk agricultural labourer, 1834-1884. *Ph.D. 1935 London, School of Economics and Political Science*

Springett, W. D.
Exegeses of: Numbers xxii; Daniel v; Acts vii. *D.D. 1888 Oxford*

Springett, W. D.
The priesthood of Christ, of Christians, and of the Christian ministry. 2. Public worship in the Christian Church, as described in or inferred from the New Testament. *B.D. 1880 Oxford*

Spruill, C. P.
The creation and liquidation of public debt in the United Kingdom during the eighteenth and nineteenth centuries, economically and financially regarded. *B.Litt. 1922 Oxford*

Spurdle, F. G.
The development of executive government in Barbados and the Leeward Islands, 1660 to 1783. *Ph.D. 1931 London, King's College*

Spyero, H. A.
1. The part taken by the Holy Spirit in the salvation of man. 2. The law of Moses: a preparation for the reception of Christianity. *B.D. 1873 Oxford*

Sreenivasachar, P.
The political history of the Telugu country, from *c.* A.D. 1000 to A.D. 1565. *Ph.D. 1933 London, School of Oriental and African Studies*

Srinivas, M. N.
The social function of religion in a South Indian community. *D.Phil. 1947 Oxford*

Srinivasan, M.
Marketing of Indian agricultural produce in the United Kingdom. *Ph.D. 1942 Wales*

Srivastava, R. S.
Some aspects of agricultural marketing in India, with reference to developments in Western marketing systems. *B.Litt. 1948 Oxford*

Stacey, M. W.
An enquiry into the stability of attitudes and interests of a group of adolescent girls. *M.A. 1948 London, Institute of Education*

Stacey, S. B.
A study of the attitude of adolescents towards school life and work. *M.A. 1949 London, Institute of Education*

Stadler, E. M. R.
The history of the literary criticism of Shakespeare in Germany. *B.Litt. 1912 Oxford*

Stafford, F. J.
Texts and text-books in the teaching of French and German. *M.Ed. 1918 Manchester*

Stamp, J. C.
British incomes and property. *D.Sc. 1916 London*

Stanbridge, J. W.
1. The divinity of the Holy Spirit. 2. Episcopal government in the early Church. *B.D. 1876 Oxford*

Stanbury, F. E.
The social ideas of Charles Dickens, and their influence upon his art as a novelist. *M.A. 1934 Wales*

Standring, E. M.
Le féminisme de Madame de Staël. *M.A. 1941 Manchester*

Stang, M. U.
The scientific materialism of Georg Büchner: a critical study. *M.A. 1942 London, External Degree*

Staniforth, A. B.
Shakespeare on the London stage in the days of Coleridge, Hazlitt, and Lamb. *B.Litt. 1933 Oxford*

Stanley, G. F. G.
Political unrest in the Canadian Northwest, with special reference to the first Riel Rebellion, 1869-70. *B.Litt. 1932 Oxford*

Stanley, G. F. G.
The second Riel Rebellion, 1870-86. *D.Phil. 1935 Oxford*

Stanley, M.
The monastery of Vivarium and its historical importance. *B.Litt. 1939 Oxford*

Stanley-Jones, H.
The short story from Scott to Stevenson. *B.Litt. 1925 Oxford*

Stanner, W. E. H.
Economic changes in north Australian tribes. *Ph.D. 1938 London, School of Economics and Political Science*

Stannus, H. S.
The Wayas of Nyasaland. *Ph.D. 1926 London*

Stansfield, A.
Das dritte Reich: a study of the idea of the 'third kingdom' in German literature, with special reference to the classical and romantic periods. *M.A. 1932 Manchester*

Stapledon, W. O.
Meaning. *Ph.D. 1925 Liverpool*

Staples, D. J.
Sensibilité auditive de Lamartine. *M.A. 1949 London, Birkbeck College*

Stapleton, A. B.
A critical study of Defoe's *Review*, and other journals of its day, with particular emphasis on the social life of the age. *Ph.D. 1924 London*

Star, L. P.
The psychology of religious expression and its relation to religious education. *Ph.D. 1942 Dublin, Trinity College*

Starck, J. J.
Les soirées de Médan as a manifesto of naturalism. *Ph.D. 1948 London, King's College*

Starke, D.
England and the English as presented in Michelet's *History of France. M.A. 1922 London*

Starr, A. J.
A study of the function of Ipswich as a centre in East Anglia, and its development as a port since 1805. *M.Sc. 1939 London, Birkbeck College*

Starrels, S. E.
Supernatural birth in historical religions. *Ph.D. 1936 London, King's College*

Statman, J.
The rise and development of the Ketubah. *M.A. 1910 London*

Staton, W.
The teaching of science in elementary schools. *M.A. 1935 Liverpool*

Stauffer, D. A.
English biography before 1700. *D.Phil. 1927 Oxford*

Staynor, E. V.
The psychology of reasoning with special reference to educational problems. *M.A. 1932 London, Day Training College*

Stead, H. G.
Statistics and psychology. *Ph.D. 1925 London*

Stead, L. M.
Fielding en France. *M.A. 1914 Leeds*

Stead, W. F.
Robert Southwell. *B.Litt. 1936 Oxford*

Stebbing, L. S.
A modern introduction to logic. *D.Litt. 1931 London, Bedford College*

Stebbing, L. S.
The relations between voluntarism and pragmatism as illustrated by the development of French voluntaristic philosophy from Maine de Biran to Professor Bergson: with especial reference to the Bergsonian notion of truth and its development in the 'new philosophy'. *M.A. 1912 London*

Stede, D. A. L.
The concrete expression of abstract ideas in Indian philosophy, with special reference to comparison as means of evidence. *Ph.D. 1938 London, School of Oriental and African Studies*

Stedman, A. R.
The history of Marlborough Grammar School, 1550-1944, with some account of the medieval Hospital of St. John Baptist, Marlborough. *M.A. 1945 London, King's College*

Stedman, R. E.
An examination of Bosanquet's doctrine of self-transcendence. *Ph.D. 1930 Edinburgh*

Steel, J. H.
Style in Spenser. *D. Litt. 1917 Glasgow*

Steel, R. W.
The human geography of Sierre Leone. *B.Sc. 1939 Oxford*

Steer, K. A.
The archaeology of Roman Durham. *Ph.D. 1938 Durham*

Stefanovici, J. O.
Comparative phonetics of English and Roumanian. *Ph.D. 1927 London*

Stein, R.
Scientific terminology and analogy in Coleridge's poetic theory and practice. *B.Litt. 1946 Oxford*

Steiner, F. B.
A comparative study of the forms of slavery. *D.Phil. 1949 Oxford*

Steiner, W. A. F. P.
Transfers of shares and debentures in private international law. *LL.M. 1948 London, School of Economics and Political Science*

Stephen, J. L.
Occupational interests in relation to intelligence. *M.A. 1938 London, University College*

Stephen, J. S.
The history of roads in the Highlands. *Ph.D. 1936 Aberdeen*

Stephen, R.
The poetical works of Bedo Aerddrem, Bedo Brwynllys and Bedo Phylip Bach. *M.A. 1907 Wales*

Stephen, R. A.
On the history and development of obstetrical forceps, with special reference to the application and use of Kielland forceps. *M.D. 1933 Aberdeen*

Stephens, A. E.
Plymouth Dock: a survey of the development of the Royal Dockyard in Hamoaze during the sailing ship era. *Ph.D. 1940 London, Birkbeck College*

Stephens, A. E.
Plymouth Haven. *M.Sc. 1936 London, Birkbeck College*

Stephens, G. H. A.
Wage-rates: 1750-1800. *B.Litt. 1931 Oxford*

Stephens, G. M.
A study of Chaucer's narrative methods in *The Book of Duchesse, The Parlement of foules, The Hous of fame, Troilus and Criseyde* and *The Canterbury tales. M.A. 1933 Wales*

Stephens, M. B.
La poésie de Léon Dierx. *M.A. 1929 Belfast*

Stephens, R. R.
Le théâtre classique en France et la tradition nationale. *M.Litt. 1935 Durham*

Stephens, W. E. D.
An examination of the sources of the *Thidrikssaga. M.A. 1937 London, University College*

Stephens, W. J.
Kant's conception of the freedom of the will. *M.A. 1905 Wales*

Stephens, W. R. W.
1. A critical study of St. Anselm's treatise *Cur deus homo*? 2. The internal evidence for the authenticity of the Gospel according to St. John. *B.D. 1895 Oxford*

Stephens, W. R. W.
Expositions of I St. Peter i.1-ii, 10; I St. Peter ii.11-iii.22; I St. Peter iv and v. *D.D. 1901 Oxford*

Stephenson, C. E.
A psychological approach to Amos and Hosea. *M.A. 1946 Birmingham*

Stephenson, E.
William Prynne's ideal State Church, and his views on the sectaries, Independents. *M.A. 1929 Manchester*

Stephenson, H. W.
Thomas Firmin, F.R.S. (1632-1697). *D.Phil. 1949 Oxford*

Stephenson, J.
The geography of Berkshire, with special reference to agriculture. *M.A. 1936 London, School of Economics and Political Science*

Stephenson, J.
Gerard Manley Hopkins and his poetry. *M.A. 1939 National University of Ireland*

Stephenson, J.
The manufacturers' agent. His economic and social significance. *D.Sc. 1922 London*

Stephenson, W.
Mental tests and their relation to the central factor. *Ph.D. 1930 London, University College*

Stern, G. H.
The life and social conditions of women in the primitive Islamic community as depicted in the eighth volume of Ibn Sa'd's *Tabaqat al Kubra* and the sixth volume of Ibn Hanbal's *Musnad. Ph.D. 1937 London, School of Oriental and African Studies*

Stern, H. H.
The social development of a child from birth to 18 months. *M.A. 1947 London, King's College*

Stern, J. P.
The problem of the aphorism in the writing of G. C. Lichtenberg. *Ph.D. 1950 Cambridge*

Steuart, E. M.
The origin and development of the Roman *satura. M.A. 1914 London*

Stevanovic, B.
The experimental study of the mental processes involved in judgment. *Ph.D. 1926 London*

Steven, I.
Capacity and pricing in the British iron and steel industry under the Federation. *B.Litt. 1940 Oxford*

Stevens, C. E.
Sidonius Apollinaris and his age. *B.Litt. 1930 Oxford*

Stevens, J. R.
An examination of the factors which link Bristol dock policy with the development of the tramp shipping of the port, 1840-1890. *M.A. 1940 Bristol*

Stevens, L. Cleveland- see Cleveland-Stevens, L.

Stevens, P. T.
The colloquial element in the language of Attic tragedy. *Ph.D. 1939 Aberdeen*

Stevens, T. M.
The doctrine of invention in its connexion with the law relating to letters patent for inventions. *D.C.L. 1897 Oxford*

Stevenson, A. H. L.
The life and works of Sydney Owenson, Lady Morgan. *B.Litt. 1935 Oxford*

Stevenson, G. S. C.
A study of Scottish vernacular poetry in the reign of James VI; with a new text of the poems of Alexander Montgomerie. *B.Litt. 1911 Oxford*

Stevenson, J. A. C.
The influence of Hobbes, Locke and Berkeley on the English and Scottish aestheticians of the eighteenth century. *Ph.D. 1949 Edinburgh*

Stevenson, J. C.
The influence of the Bible on English literature of the seventeenth century. *M.A. 1914 Birmingham*

Stevenson, M. S.
The predictive value of certain vocational tests, with special reference to personnel selection in the Army. *M.Sc. 1944 London, University College*

Stevenson, S. I.
A study of Thomas Wade: poet and dramatist, 1805-1875. *M.A. 1929 London*

Steward, R. G.
Government planning: changing opinions, 1931-1947. *M.Sc. 1949 London, School of Economics and Political Science*

Stewart, A. A.
The study of personality in English neo-classical literature. *Ph.D. 1933 London, King's College*

Stewart, B. J.
Administrative beginnings in British Burma, 1826-1843. *Ph.D. 1931 London, School of Oriental and African Studies*

Stewart, D. H. G.
Christianity and modern humanism. *Ph.D. 1939 Edinburgh*

Stewart, J.
The missionary activity of the ancient Nestorian Church. *Ph.D. 1925 Edinburgh*

Stewart, J. C.
The letters of Synesius of Cyrene, Metropolitan Bishop of Ptolemais in the Libyan Pentapolis, tr. into English with a commentary and an introductory essay. *Ph.D. 1923 Edinburgh*

Stewart, J. D.
A comprehensive survey of the mathematical education of engineers. *Ph.D. 1948 Aberdeen*

Stewart, J. McK.
The philosophy of Henri Bergson. *D.Phil. 1911 Edinburgh*

Stewart, K. R.
Magico-religious beliefs and practices in primitive society: a sociological interpretation of their therapeutic aspects. *Ph.D. 1948 London, School of Economics and Political Science*

Stewart, R. A.
The use of the Old Testament in the Epistle to the Hebrews. *M.Litt. 1947 Cambridge*

Stewart, W. A. C.
A critical estimate of the educational theory and practice of the Society of Friends as seen in their schools in England. *Ph.D. 1947 London, Institute of Education*

Stewart, W. D.
Some psychological aspects of employment in the coal-mining industry, with special reference to the Ayrshire coalfield in Scotland. *B.Litt. 1933 Oxford*

Stewart, W. F. S.
The book of Jonah. *B.Litt. 1945 Dublin, Trinity College*

Stigant, G. B.
A review of recent work on primitive Japanese Shinto. *M.Sc. 1936 London, School of Economics and Political Science*

Stilliard, N. H.
The rise and development of legitimate trade in palm oil with West Africa. *M.A. 1938 Birmingham*

Stirk, J. L.
The development in ancient Greece of the concept of number in arithmetic and geometry. *M.Sc. 1947 London, University College*

Stirrup, B. E.
Fifth century B.C. views on the purpose of Greek tragedy. *M.A. 1948 Manchester*

Stockdale, W. H.
The reliability of group tests as tests of intelligence. *M.Ed. 1924 Manchester*

Stocks, C. A.
Social anthropology of the Lapchas. *B.Sc. 1927 Oxford*

Stocks, J. E.
1. The Christian use of the Old Testament Apocrypha. 2. Some aspects of the value to the Church of St. Paul's first Epistle to the Corinthians. *B.D. & D.D. 1909 Oxford*

Stockwell, H. C. R.
The image in the works of Marcel Proust. *Ph.D. 1942 London, King's College*

Stockwin, R. F.
Amédée Prouvost: poète, 1877-1909. *M.A. 1936 Birmingham*

Stoddart, A. L.
The influence of Molière on Restoration comedy (1660-1720). *M.A. 1919 Birmingham*

Stoffregen, E. A.
Restriction of the supply of staple commodities. *Ph.D. 1931 London, School of Economics and Political Science*

Stojanovic, M. D.
Serbia in international politics from the insurrection of Herzegovina (1875) to the Congress of Berlin (1878). *Ph.D. 1930 London, King's College*

Stoker, J. T.
L'ambassade française à Londres, 1792-1793. *M.A. 1935 Leeds*

Stokes, E. M.
The formation and modification of mental attitudes towards mathematics. *M.Sc. 1946 Manchester*

Stokes, H. G.
Art in Roman life as shown in the works of Cicero. *B.Litt. 1934 Oxford*

Stokes, J. M.
Robert Wilde: his life and works. *B.Litt. 1930 Oxford*

Stokes, K. E.
Sir John Wentworth and his times. *Ph.D. 1938 London, King's College*

Stokoe, T. H.
Exegeses of St. Matthew xi.2-10; I Corinthians xii.31-xiii.13; Galatians iv.21-v.1. *D.D. 1871 Oxford*

Stokoe, T. H.
1. 'I believe in one God'. 2. 'I look for the resurrection of the dead'. *B.D. 1871 Oxford*

Stone, D.
1. The providential preparation for the Church of Christ. 2. The revelation of the Church in the Gospels. *B.D. & D.D. 1909 Oxford*

Stone, J.
The modifications made necessary in the doctrine of sovereignty in international law by the creation of the League of Nations. *LL.M. 1930 Leeds*

Stone, L.
Peacock and the novel of ideas. *M.A. 1949 National University of Ireland*

Stone, T. G.
The struggle for power on the Senegal and Gambia, 1660-1713. *M.A. 1921 London*

Stone, V. C.
A study of some social and industrial problems involved in modern, large-scale employment of labour in unskilled work, based on observation and investigation in a wartime filling factory. *M.A. 1945 Liverpool*

Stonehouse, G. G. V. J. H. T.
1. The literary problem of Habakkuk i.1-ii.4. 2. Israel's deliverance from exile in relation to the Gentile world: Isaiah xl-lv. *B.D. 1910 Oxford*

Stoneman, E. T.
Motivation of attempted suicide: an investigation of 87 cases of unsuccessful suicide, Edinburgh, 1932 to 1933. *Ph.D. 1933 Edinburgh*

Stopp, E. C. V.
The place of Italy in the life and works of Ludwig Tieck. *Ph.D. 1938 Cambridge*

Stopp, F. J.
The art of exposition in Lessing's prose works, with special reference to the polemical writings. *Ph.D. 1948 London, University College*

Storey, J. A.
Webster's imagery and what it tells us. *Ph.D. 1944 Dublin, Trinity College*

Storey, J. E.
Philosophical issues raised by mystical experience. *M.A. 1929 Liverpool*

Storey, T. H.
Humour in the novels of Paul Fechter. *M.A. 1940 Belfast*

Stott, F. C.
A study of the fundamental concepts of biology and their influence upon methods of teaching biology in schools. *M.A. 1945 London, Institute of Education*

Stott, J.
A history of the development of adult education in England. *M.A. 1930 Liverpool*

Stott, P. E.
On the French element in the English regional dialects. *M.A. 1934 Liverpool*

Stoudt, J. J.
The mysticism of Jacob Böhme, with special reference to his dialectic. *Ph.D. 1943 Edinburgh*

Stout, G. D.
Leigh Hunt, journalist, essayist, and critic. *B.Litt. 1923 Oxford*

Stowe, L.
Froebel's principles and their relationship to the theory and practice of infant education today. *M.A. 1940 Leeds*

Stoyanovic, J.
The religious philosophy in Russia in the nineteenth century. *Ph.D. 1926 London*

Stoyanović, J.
Vladimir Solovieff's religious philosophy. *B.Litt. 1919 Oxford*

Stoyanovitch, M.
The teaching of salvation in the orations of St. Gregory of Nazianzus. *B.Litt. 1922 Oxford*

Stoyanovsky, J.
The mandate for Palestine. *LL.D. 1927 London*

Straelen, H. J. J. M. van *see* van Straelen, H. J. J. M.

Strain, J.
Causality and freedom. *M.A. 1920 Belfast*

Stranks, C. J.
The life, times and writings of Jeremy Taylor. *M.Litt. 1937 Durham*

Stranz, W. J.
The political career of Henry Goulburn, 1784-1856. *M.Litt. 1950 Durham*

Strasheim, J. J.
Some aspects of the developing 'intelligence'. *Ph.D. 1925 London*

Stratford, E. C. W.
The history of English patriotism. *D.Sc. 1913 London*

Stratford, N.
Une introduction aux *Miracles de Nostre Dame par personnages*. *M.A. 1941 Sheffield*

Straw, S. D.
A critical survey of the Old French element in English surnames. *M.A. 1919 London*

Straw, W.
A study of the linguistic features of the first Prayer Book of Edward VI (1549). *M.A. 1924 London*

Streatfeild, F.
Constitutional history of the French Church, 1438-1682. *D.Phil. 1921 Oxford*

Streatfeild, F.
1. The influence of the Apocrypha upon the language of the New Testament. 2. Paulinisms in the Epistle to the Hebrews, and their relationship to the problem of its authorship. *B.D. 1916 Oxford*

Street, F.
The relations of the bishops and citizens of Salisbury (New Sarum) between 1225 and 1612. *M.A. 1915 London*

Streichenberger, J. A.
A comparison between the English limited company and the French société anonyme. *B.Litt. 1932 Oxford*

Stretton, G.
Medieval travel as illustrated by the wardrobe accounts of Henry, Earl of Derby, 1390-1393. *M.A. 1924 London*

Stribley, F. U.
John Ruskin as social reformer. *M.A. 1925 Birmingham*

Strickler, E.
The organization of peace through collective security, 1934-1938. *M.Sc. 1949 London, School of Economics and Political Science*

Strong, C. F.
Palmerston and the dawn of Italian independence, 1830-1851. *Ph.D. 1925 London*

Strong, C. F.
The policy of Great Britain with reference to the Continental revolutions of 1848-9. *M.A. 1921 London*

Strong, J.
The history of secondary education in Scotland. *M.A. 1908 London*

Strong, T. B.
1. The doctrine of the objective presence in the Eucharist. 2. The Church and the world. *B.D. 1899 Oxford*

Strong, T. B.
Expositions of: St. John xx.22-23: the power of absolution given to the Church; I John iii.19, 20: the Christian doctrine of conscience; Galatians ii.19-20: individual religion and the Church. *D.D. 1902 Oxford*

Stroud, D. A.
Mens rea or imputability under the law of England. *LL.D. 1913 London*

Stroud, L. J.
The history of Quaker education in England, 1647-1903. *M.Ed. 1945 Leeds*

Stroud, L. J.
John Ford (1801-1875): the life, work and influence of a Quaker schoolmaster. *Ph.D. 1947 London, External Degree*

Struge, C.
The life and times of John Dudley, Earl of Warwick and Duke of Northumberland, 1504(?)-1553. *Ph.D. 1927 London*

Struthers, J.
A study of the leisure activities of school children in a Middlesex secondary (mixed) school. *M.A. 1939 London, Institute of Education*

Strzalkowski, W.
The part played by kinaesthetic experience in perception and in thinking. *D.Phil. 1946 Oxford*

Stuart, A. G.
The significance in the philosophy of religion of the integration of personality through adaptation to reality. *B.Litt. 1932 Oxford*

Stuart, A. L.
Poetry and other arts in relation to life. *Ph.D. 1944 Dublin, Trinity College*

Stuart, D. D.
Southey, as seen in his epics. *B.Litt. 1939 Oxford*

Stuart, E. C. P.
Some aspects of the political and administrative history of Gascony from 1303-1307. *Ph.D. 1927 London*

Stuart, J. W. L.
The nature of mathematics. *M.Sc. 1946 London, External Degree*

Stuart, M.
The learning methods of mental defectives. *M.Ed. 1944 Manchester*

Stuart-Menteath, T. A.
Land utilization in Somerset. *B.Sc. 1937 Oxford*

Stubbings, F. H.
An investigation of Mycenaean pottery from the Levant and of some local variations of Mycenaean pottery. *Ph.D. 1948 Cambridge*

Stubbins, T. E.
The reliability of an entrance scholarship examination as a means of predicting school certificate results. *M.Ed. 1937 Leeds*

Stubbs, J. G.
Chemistry at the Académie Royale des Sciences from its foundation in 1666 to the middle of the eighteenth century. *Ph.D. 1939 London, Queen Mary College*

Stubbs, J. G.
The discovery of halogen. *M.Sc. 1931 London*

Sturgiss, B. E. S.
A study of the respective places and contributions of parent and teacher in child education, with special reference to the parent and parent-teacher organizations in France and England. *M.A. 1937 Bristol*

Sturman, R. H.
The internal organization of English secondary schools for boys during the middle decades of the nineteenth century. *M.A. 1932 London, King's College*

Sturman, W. M.
The history of the Nunnery of St. Mary and St. Michael outside Stamford. *M.A. 1944 London, Queen Mary College*

Sturt, M.
1. The psychology of time. 2. Modern psychology and education. *Ph.D. 1932 Birmingham*

Stuttard, J. C.
The historical geography of the Forest of Dean during the seventeenth century. *M.Sc. 1942 Cambridge*

Stuurman, D. D.
Plotinus's conception of the unconscious. *B.Litt. 1937 Oxford*

Style, C. M.
Exegeses of: St.John i.4: Romans x.2; I Corinthians xv.14. *D.D. 1880 Oxford*

Styler, W. E.
The problem of liberty in relation to the development of voluntary associations. *M.A. 1937 Birmingham*

Subhan, A.
An inquiry into the causes of the failure of the Mu'tazilite movement. *B.Litt. 1945 Oxford*

Subhan, A.
Secondary education for boys in Bengal. *M.A. 1938 Leeds*

Subley, G. V. W.
The philosophy of prayer, developed on a psychological basis. *M.A. 1927 London*

Subotić, D.
Serbian traditional folk-poetry in England, France, and Germany in the nineteenth century. *B.Litt. 1927 Oxford*

Subramania, I.
The *Bhaeratifyanaetyaśastra*, translated with introduction and notes. *M.A. 1919 London*

Sudbury, P. G.
The medieval boroughs of Pembrokeshire. *M.A. 1947 Wales*

Suffolk, J. C.
The novel of industrial town life from Mrs. Gaskell to Arnold Bennett. *M.A. 1939 Sheffield*

Sugathadasa, D. G.
A crtical review of researches in the United Kingdom on selection for secondary education, with suggestions for their application to Ceylon. *M.A. 1948 London, Institute of Education*

Suhrawardy, S. A. B.
A critical survey of the development of the Urdu novel and short story. *Ph.D. 1941 London, School of Oriental and African Studies*

Sukhatme, A. V.
1. Extension of statistical theory to certain problems arising in sampling inspection in industry. 2. A critical comparison of Neyman and Pearson's 'L1' test and certain alternative tests. *Ph.D. 1935 London, University College*

Sullivan, E.
Francis Thompson. *M.A. 1927 National University of Ireland*

Sullivan, G. D.
Irish parliamentary representation, 1800-1830. *B.Litt. 1950 Dublin, Trinity College*

Sullivan, J.
The measurement of mental ability and school achievement. *M.A. 1926 National University of Ireland*

Sullivan, J.
Memory; a psychological study. *M.A. 1915 National University of Ireland*

Sumangala, S.
The rules of discipline of Buddhist Sāmanera (novices). *B.Litt. 1920 Oxford*

Sumithra, D. G.
An experimental investigation into the distribution of intelligence in different schools by means of non-verbal tests. *M.Ed. 1933 Leeds*

Sun, K. T.
Education for citizenship in China. *M.A. 1936 Leeds*

Sundaram, L.
Revenue administration of the Sirkars under the E.I.C. down to 1802. *Ph.D. 1930 London, School of Oriental and African Studies*

Sundaram, M. S.
A critical edition of James Shirley's *The court secret*. *B.Litt. 1934 Oxford*

Sunday, W. F.
The development of Luther's conception of liberty as found in his early writings (until 1521). *Ph.D. 1924 Edinburgh*

Super, R. H.
The English poetry of Walter Savage Landor before 1812. *B.Litt. 1937 Oxford*

Sur, R. K.
An experimental investigation of memory of school children, with special reference to Bergson's theory. *M.Ed. 1929 Leeds*

Suratgar, M. L. K.
Traces of Persian influence upon English literature during the fifteenth and sixteenth centuries. *Ph.D. 1939 London, University College*

Surman, A. H.
The voluntary day continuation schools in London. *M.A. 1949 London, Institute of Education*

Surman, C. E.
Classical Presbyterianism in England, 1643-1660. *M.A. 1949 Manchester*

Suryanarayanan, S. S.
A comparative study of the *Advaita Vēdānta* and of D. H. Bradley. *B.Litt. 1917 Oxford*

Susman, A. S.
Selections from Solomon ben Reuben Bonfed, translated with introduction. *M.A. 1942 Manchester*

Sutcliffe, A.
Social satire and literary burlesque in *Punch*, 1841-1850. *M.A. 1937 Manchester*

Sutcliffe, F. G. *see* Peace, F. G.

Sutcliffe, W. D.
English book-reviewing in the last half of the eighteenth century. *D.Phil. 1943 Oxford*

Sutherland, A.
English alchemists before the sixteenth century. *M.Sc. 1930 London*

Sutherland, A. J. B.
The so-called Glasgow School of Painting. *M.A. 1938 London, Courtauld Institute of Art*

Sutherland, D.
Islay: a study in island geography. *Ph.D. 1929 Glasgow*

Sutherland, D. J. S.
The history of the teaching of science in Scottish schools. *Ph.D. 1939 Saint Andrew's*

Sutherland, H. E. G.
The correlation between intelligence and size of family. *Ph.D. 1930 Edinburgh*

Sutherland, I.
A statistical study of the incidence of still births in England and Wales and its possible relation to social influences. *D.Phil. 1948 Oxford*

Sutherland, I. L. G.
A critical examination of some current tendencies in the theory of human conduct. *Ph.D. 1924 Glasgow*

Sutherland, J. D.
The speed factor in intelligent reactions. *Ph.D. 1931 Edinburgh*

Sutherland, J. R.
Nicholas Rowe. *B.Litt. 1926 Oxford*

Suttle, E. F. A.
The life and musical works of Henry Aldrich. *B.Litt. 1938 Oxford*

Sutton, C. T.
Maritime settlements and disputes. *M.Com. 1936 London, School of Economics and Political Science*

Sutton, D. M.
The drawings by Raphael in the Ashmolean Museum, Oxford: an account of the formation of the collection and its acquisition by the University. *B.Litt. 1944 Oxford*

Sutton, I.
Observations on 'neurotic' casualties in the Middle East. *M.D. 1947 Manchester*

Sutton, N. E.
Virgil's use of Homer and Euripides in the third book of the *Aeneid*. *M.A. 1948 Manchester*

Swabey, H. S.
The Church of England and usury. *B.D. 1949 Durham*

Swaim, J. C.
The historical character of the fourth Gospel. *Ph.D. 1931 Edinburgh*

Swaine, D. R.
The indebtedness of Klopstock to English literature. *M.A. 1919 Wales*

Swainson, B. M.
The development of moral ideas in children and adolescents. *D.Phil. 1949 Oxford*

Swainson, B. M.
A study of rural settlement in Somerset. *M.A. 1932 London, External Degree*

Swale, W. R.
Schools and schoolmasters in Dickens. *M.A. 1933 Birmingham*

Swales, T. H.
Parliamentary enclosures in Lindsey, or the enclosures of the eighteenth and nineteenth centuries as they affected Lindsey. *M.A. 1936 Leeds*

Swallow, M. A.
History of the development of the means of communication in the County of Monmouth. *Ph.D. 1932 London, School of Economics and Political Science*

Swaminathan, V. S.
Distribution of population in the Tamil country. *M.Sc. 1931 London, University College*

Swann, E.
The life of Christopher North. *Ph.D. 1932 Leeds*

Swann, J. J. Hartland- *see* Hartland-Swann, J. J.

Swanson, Z.
A factorial analysis of mental tests. *Ph.D. 1950 Edinburgh*

Swarbrick, J. W.
Some conceptions of Sheol: a study in Old Testament eschatology. *M.A. 1922 Manchester*

Swartwout, R. E.
The services of monks to art. *M.Litt. 1932 Cambridge*

Swartz, R. T.
An edition of Robert Heath's *Clarastella* of 1650. *B. Litt. 1929 Oxford*

Swayne, W. S.
1. Our Lord's knowledge as man. 2. St. Paul and his Gospel. *B.D. 1918 Oxford*

Sweeney, M.
The concept of natural law in the history of economic thought. *M.A. 1947 National University of Ireland*

Sweeney, M. V.
English Catholic education from the Reformation to Catholic emancipation (1580-1829). *M.Ed. 1946 Leeds*

Sweet, J. M.
English preaching, 1221-1293. *B.Litt. 1950 Oxford*

Sweetapple, H. D. S.
1. Some general characteristics of St. Paul's Epistles, with special illustrations from the Epistle to the Galatians. 2. The intention and use of sacraments in the Christian Church. *B.D. & D.D. 1908 Oxford*

Sweetinburgh, F. E.
Edward I and the church. *M.A. 1917 Birmingham*

Sweeting, E. J.
Studies in early Tudor criticism, literary and linguistic, up to 1558. *M.A. 1938 London, Royal Holloway College*

Sweetman, E. J.
Blessed Robert Southwell, S.J. *M.A. 1936 National University of Ireland*

Swift, E.
The machinery of manorial administration, with special reference to the lands of the Bishopric of Winchester, 1208-1454. *M.A. 1930 London, King's College*

Swift, H.
The economic development of the coastal regions of Victoria and New South Wales. *M.A. 1939 Liverpool*

Swift, T. M.
The significance of the romantic hero in the work of W. B. Yeats. *M.A. 1950 Manchester*

Swinburn, L. M.
De Lanterne of Lig't, transcribed from the ms. Harleian 2324, with an introduction, notes and glossary. M.A. 1914 London

Sydserff, M. Buchan- see Buchan-Sydserff, M.

Syed, M. H.
Qasi Mahmud Bahri: a mystic poet of the twelfth century A.H.; his times, life and work. Ph.D. 1932 London, School of Oriental and African Studies

Syed, Z.
Development of the educational system in Hyderabad, Deccan. M.Ed. 1938 Leeds

Sykes, E. C.
The agricultural geography and related distribution of population in Northumberland. M.A. 1931 Liverpool

Sykes, J.
English local authority expenditure, 1913-32. Ph.D. 1935 Leeds

Sykes, J. M.
Ideals in school music. M.A. 1939 Bristol

Sykes, L. C.
Madame Cottin et le roman sentimental. D.Phil. 1940 Oxford

Sykes, M. H.
The New Testament idea of the Church: an historical study, with particular reference to its Hebrew and Jewish background. Ph.D. 1948 Manchester

Sykes, N.
Edmund Gibson, Bishop of London (1669-1748). D.Phil. 1923 Oxford

Sylvain, S. A. M. A. J. M. Comhaire- see Comhaire-Sylvain, S. A. M. A. J. M.

Sylvester, G. H.
Some implications of post-war educational reconstruction in the Bristol area. M.A. 1944 Bristol

Sym, C. A. M.
Friedrich Hebbel's theory of tragedy. Ph.D. 1936 Edinburgh

Symes, C.
A study of George Chapman's Shadow of night. M.A. 1948 Birmingham

Symes, E.
The education of women under the Roman Empire. M.A. 1909 London

Symes, J.
The vend of coal, 1700-1830. M.A. 1928 Leeds

Symonds, H. E.
The Council of Trent and Anglican formularies. B.D. 1932 Oxford

Symonds, J. S.
Local government areas and the replanning of the Black Country. M.Com. 1948 Birmingham

Symons, W. G.
Control and management in co-operative retail societies. M.Com. 1936 Birmingham

Szantyr, K. U.
Extradition of political offenders. M.Litt. 1949 Cambridge

Szladits, C.
Some aspects of the discharge of contracts in English and Continental law. LL.M. 1949 London, School of Economics and Political Science

Tachibana, S.
The ' Gift of the good doctrine', containing introduction, translation and notes. B.Litt. 1920 Oxford

Tachibana, S.
Ethics of Pāli Buddhism. D.Phil. 1922 Oxford

Taffa, W. A.
The borough franchise in the first half of the seventeenth century. M.A. 1926 London

Taffs, W. A.
Lord Odo Russell as British Ambassador in Berlin, 1872-1878. Ph.D. 1932 London, University College

Tahur, M. I.
The progress and development of the education of women in India. M.Ed. 1928 Leeds

Tai, H. L.
Feudal society in ancient China. Ph.D. 1939 London, School of Economics and Political Science

Taji, J. A. B.
State revenues in Palestine. M.A. 1937 Leeds

Talbot, G. B.
The method of teaching the English group of subjects in junior technical schools. M.A. 1939 Wales

Talbot, R. T.
1. The place of the prophet in the New Testament. 2. The doctrine of the New Testament as to the moral aspect of war. B.D. & D.D. 1906 Oxford

Talbot Rice, D.
To inquire into the physical characters of the ancient inhabitants of Kish, and to compare them with those of the modern inhabitants. B.Sc. 1927 Oxford

Talib, M. A.
The development of history teaching in schools and its application to the Indian high school. M.Ed. 1941 Leeds

Talookdar, B. K.
A survey of Anglo-Indian poetry. Ph.D. 1935 Dublin, Trinity College

Talukder, A. H.
Individual experience in the philosophy of Leibniz. M.A. 1935 London, University College

Tamblin, W. J.
Geographical factors influencing intensive agriculture in southwest England. M.Sc. 1945 London, King's College

Tamlyn, J. H.
Théophile Gautier. M.A. 1921 Wales

Tancock, C. C.
1. St. Paul and his relations to the Galatian Church. 2. Our Lord's teaching by hard sayings and parables. B.D. & D.D. 1899 Oxford

Tancock, K. M.
An edition of the play Love's Hospital (1636), with some account of the author, George Wilde. M.A. 1933 London, University College

Tancock, L. W.
A contribution to the study of the social and industrial novel in France between 1830 and 1900. Ph.D. 1931 London, University College

Tannan, M. L.
Banking law and practice in India. M.Com. 1927 Birmingham

Tanner, E. B.
Inspiration in science: a study of the genesis of scientific ideas. M.Sc. 1932 Liverpool

Tarbet, J. G.
A contribution to the study of the sources of some of Alfred de Vigny's poems. Ph.D. 1932 London, University College

Targett, A. B.
The earls and earldom of Chester to 1254. M.A. 1913 Wales

Tarnowski, S.
Some aspects of the administrative control of local government in England. Ph.D. 1936 London, School of Economics and Political Science

Tarrant, D.
The genesis of Plato's theory of ideas. M.A. 1909 London

Tarrant, D.
The Hippias major attributed to Plato, with introductory essay and commentary. Ph.D. 1931 London, External Degree

Tarshis, L.
The marginal productivity of capital, with special reference to the U.S.A. Ph.D. 1940 Cambridge

Taseer, M. D.
India and the Near East in English literature. Ph.D. 1936 Cambridge

Tata, M. A.
Agricultural problems and conditions in the Bombay Presidency, 1870-1914. M.Sc. 1922 London

Tate, A. C.
On purchasing. M.Com. 1934 Birmingham

Tate, M.
Public opinion and the movement for disarmament, 1888-98. B.Litt. 1935 Oxford

Tate, R. B.
The life, works and ideas of Cardinal Margarit. M.A. 1950 Belfast

Tate, W. E.
Parliamentary enclosure in Oxfordshire, 1696-1882. B.Litt. 1947 Oxford

Tatham, G.
Southwest Lancashire: a study of the recent changes in industry and population. M.A. 1932 Liverpool

Tatlock, R.
The philosophy of Peter Abelard. M.A. 1938 Leeds

Tattersall, R. W.
1. On the Incarnation. 2. On justification by faith. B.D. 1892 Oxford

Tave, S. M.
Comic theory and criticism from Steele to Hazlitt. D.Phil. 1950 Oxford

Taylor, A.
Vocational guidance and selection in Harrogate. M.Ed. 1937 Leeds

Taylor, A. A.
The career of Peter of Gavaston and his place in history. M.A. 1938 London, Royal Holloway College

Taylor, A. C. R.
English verse drama: its history and its place in the twentieth century. M.Litt. 1934 Cambridge

Taylor, A. J.
The astronomical method of Kepler. Ph.D. 1932 London, University College

Taylor, A. J.
Concentration and localization of the British cotton industry, 1825-1850. M.A. 1947 Manchester

Taylor, A. J.
The methodology of Descartes. M.Sc. 1927 London

Taylor, B.
Charles Nodier: romancier et conteur, 1780-1844. M.A. 1938 Birmingham

Taylor, C.
The coastal lands of southwest Lancashire and some of their problems. M.A. 1932 Liverpool

Taylor, C. A.
The English and the West Indies under the early Stuarts. M.A. 1938 National University of Ireland

Taylor, C. E. see Armstrong, C. E.

Taylor, D. C.
A life of William Congreve. B.Litt. 1925 Oxford

Taylor, E.
The poetry of Charles Cotton. M.A. 1937 Liverpool

Taylor, E. A.
An experimental approach to remedial reading for dull and backward junior pupils. M.Ed. 1942 Leeds

Taylor, E. G. R.
Studies in Tudor geography. D.Sc. 1930 London, External Degree

Taylor, E. S.
James Thomson: poet of nature and reason. Ph.D. 1943 Edinburgh

Taylor, F.
An edition of: Thome Elmham Gesta Henrici Quinti. Ph.D. 1938 Manchester

Taylor, F.
The religion of Pierre Loti. M.A. 1934 Manchester

Taylor, F. S.
A conspectus of Greek alchemy. Ph.D. 1932 London, University College

Taylor, F. S.
The theoretical basis and practical methods of transmutation of metals as practised by the early alchemists (before 800 A.D.). B.Sc. 1925 Oxford

Taylor, F. W.
The economics of advertising. M.Sc. 1932 London, School of Economics and Political Science

Taylor, G.
An edition of the Middle English romance of Athelston. M.A. 1934 Leeds

Taylor, G.
The hand loom weavers in the Stockport area, 1784-94. M.A. 1922 Manchester

Taylor, G. E.
The Privy Council under the Tudors. M.A. 1928 Birmingham

Taylor, H. A.
The concept of the reason and of its function in seventeenth and eighteenth century philosophy and literature. Ph.D. 1938 London, University College

Taylor, H. W.
The pastoral in the eighteenth century. M.A. 1914 Birmingham

Taylor, J.
Railway organization and administration. Ph.D. 1925 Edinburgh

Taylor, J. E.
The political and administrative system of Sulla. B.Litt. 1924 Oxford

Taylor, J. F.
The Dynasts by T. Hardy. M.A. 1925 Birmingham

Taylor, J. G.
Our Lady of Batersey: the story of Battersea Church and parish told from original sources. Ph.D. 1926 London

Taylor, J. R.
Barrès en voyage: le monde extérieur dans les oeuvres de Maurice Barrès. *M.A. 1930 Wales*

Taylor, L.
The chronicles of Pedro the Cruel - Pedro Lopez de Ayala. *Ph.D. 1931 Glasgow*

Taylor, L. B.
The Anglican tendencies in the Scottish Reformation and their bearing on the significance of the Concordat of Leith. *B.Litt. 1932 Oxford*

Taylor, M. E.
The influence of Platonism on certain French authors of the sixteenth century. *M.Litt. 1930 Cambridge*

Taylor, M. Living- *see* Living-Taylor, M.

Taylor, N.
Early development of views regarding acids, alkalies, and salts, until the time of Graham. *M.Sc. 1930 London*

Taylor, O. R.
The theory of the epic in France in the eighteenth century. *M.A. 1939 Wales*

Taylor, R. A.
Conditions in the elementary school system of today, which result in strain, physical and mental, upon the child. *M.A. 1929 Manchester*

Taylor, R. H.
An exposition of: Acts of the Apostles vii: Stephen's defence: Hebrews vii-ix: the heavenly priesthood of Christ: Romans viii, ix: St. Paul's doctrine of election. *D.D. 1900 Oxford*

Taylor, R. H.
1. The heavenly doctrine of St. Mark. 2. Our Lord's use of the Old Testament. *B.D. 1895 Oxford*

Taylor, R. R.
International private law in Scotland with special reference to the choice of law. *Ph.D. 1947 Glasgow*

Taylor, S. A.
The policy of industrial concentration during the war, with special reference to the hosiery industry. *Ph.D. 1949 London, School of Economics and Political Science*

Taylor, S. A.
The structure and organization of the British hosiery industry. *M.Sc. 1942 London, School of Economics and Political Science*

Taylor, T. S.
Henry Bullinger of Zurich: his place in the Reformation with special reference to England. *B.Litt. 1912 Oxford*

Taylor, T. W.
The aesthetic approach to theism. *Ph.D. 1935 Cambridge*

Taylor, V.
The historical evidence for the Virgin birth. *Ph.D. 1922 London*

Taylor, V. L.
The staging of Elizabethan plays. *M.A. 1911 Birmingham*

Taylor, W.
A list of Arabic words in the English vocabulary. *M.A. 1932 Leeds*

Taylor, W.
The Scottish Privy Council, 1603-1625: its composition and its work. *Ph.D. 1950 Edinburgh*

Taylor, W. M.
An historical investigation into the survival of Anglo-Saxon personal names into the English surname period. *M.A. 1914 London*

Taylor, Z.
Remarques sur la diction poétique de l'école romane. *M.A. 1928 Manchester*

Teale, A. E.
Freewill and time: a consideration of the metaphysical implications in regard to the nature of time, of the ethical doctrine of freewill. *B.Litt. 1937 Oxford*

Teasdale, H.
The prevalence of eidetic imagery among schoolchildren and its educational significance. *M.Ed. 1932 Leeds*

Tebbs, S. N.
1. The Sacraments. 2. Faith and works. *B.D. 1874 Oxford*

Tee, R. H. R.
The equitable doctrine of election. *LL.D. 1923 London*

Teggin, J. R.
The conservation and repair of medieval ecclesiastical buildings, with particular reference to certain selected examples. *M.A. 1938 Manchester*

Teidhirs, P.
Díoscán de dhánta gearra(A short selection of syllabic poems). *M.A. 1948 National University of Ireland*

Telfer, J. M.
A critical study of the episodic Tristan poems. *B.Litt. 1949 Oxford*

Telfer, W.
The treasure of São Roque: a sidelight on the Reformation. *B.D. 1932 Cambridge*

Telford, J. H.
Burmese animism or animism in Kengtung State, Burma. *Ph.D. 1933 Edinburgh*

Temkin, S. D.
The influence of public opinion on the development of English law from 1880-1914. *M.A. 1938 Liverpool*

Temple, A.
The derelict villages of Durham County. *M.Litt. 1940 Durham*

Temple, H.
1. The preaching of Christ and his Apostles. 2. In what sense and with what limitations is it true to say that correct theological belief is necessary to salvation?. *B.D. & D.D. 1899 Oxford*

Templeman, G.
The place of the secular clergy in the society of fifteenth century England. *M.A. 1936 London, School of Economics and Political Science*

Templeton, J. H.
The idea of creation in Christian thought. *B.Litt. 1943 Dublin, Trinity College*

Templeton, J. H.
The originality of Christianity. *Ph.D. 1946 Dublin, Trinity College*

Templeton, T.
The psychology of economics. *Ph.D. 1927 Glasgow*

Tenen, C.
Adolescent attitudes to authority at work. *M.A. 1945 Manchester*

Tenen, C.
Psychological aspects of the change from school to work. *Ph.D. 1948 Manchester*

Teniswood, W. V.
The policy of Great Britain regarding Australia, 1850-1900. *Ph.D. 1936 Edinburgh*

Tereshchenko, N. M. Iovetz- *see* Iovetz-Tereshchenko, N. M.

Terhune, A. M.
The life of Edward Fitzgerald. *Ph.D. 1940 Cambridge*

Terry, C. W.
The Civil War in Somerset, 1642-1646. *M.A. 1913 London*

Terry, F. H. K.
Religious education: revolution or renaissance?. *Ph.D. 1939 National University of Ireland*

Tetley, J. G.
1. The function of the prophets in Christian Church, as it may be gathered from the New Testament. 2. The Christian view of war. *B.D. & D.D. 1901 Oxford*

Tew, J. H. B.
Costs, prices, and investment in the British iron and steel industries 1924-37. *Ph.D. 1941 Cambridge*

Tew, M. M.
A comparative study of bride wealth in Africa, with special reference to kinship structure and tribal organization. *B.Sc. 1948 Oxford*

Thacher, J. S.
The paintings of Francisco de Herrera the Elder. *Ph.D. 1936 London, Courtauld Institute of Art*

Thakur, B.
The idealism of Collier and Berkeley. *Ph.D. 1937 London, University College*

Thaper, K. S.
Biography of Maharaja Dalip Singh. *B.Litt. 1934 Oxford*

Theilkuhl, W.
Mittelhochdeutsche Ritterdichtung in frühneuhochdeutscher Zeit. *M.A. 1929 London*

Theodore, S. J.
The idea of God in the philosophy of William James and James Ward. *B.Litt. 1925 Oxford*

Thimann, I. C.
A contribution to the study of the historical comedies of Scribe. *Ph.D. 1934 London, University College*

Thimme Gowda, T. V.
A study of the attitudes of teachers in England towards their course of training. *M.A. 1946 London, Institute of Education*

Thom, W. C.
Church order in Scotland. *Ph.D. 1924 Aberdeen*

Thomas, A. B.
Deimier. *M.A. 1907 Wales*

Thomas, A. L.
The syntax of archaic Latin, with special reference to the usage of Catullus and Lucretius. *M.A. 1913 Wales*

Thomas, A. M.
The poems of Leonidas of Tarentum. *M.A. 1937 Wales*

Thomas, B.
The life and character of Lorenzo de Medici, with special consideration of the conflicting views entertained by historians. *M.A. 1921 Wales*

Thomas, B.
The 'noblesse' in France in 1789: a study of opinion. *M.A. 1950 Wales*

Thomas, B.
The south Wales coal trade in its international and marketing aspects, 1921-1926. *M.A. 1928 Wales*

Thomas, B.
Studies in labour supply and labour costs. *Ph.D. 1932 London, School of Economics and Political Science*

Thomas, B. C.
A study of the educational values of physical tests and measurements for boys 11+ to 15+. *M.Ed. 1945 Manchester*

Thomas, B. E.
Growth of the naturalist drama in Germany, with special reference to Gerhart Hauptmann. *M.A. 1931 Wales*

Thomas, B. P.
Le romantisme et le théâtre de Victor Hugo. *M.A. 1916 Birmingham*

Thomas, B. S.
The geography and ethnography of unknown South Arabia. *Ph.D. 1935 Cambridge*

Thomas, C. H.
The political history of Wales from 1350 to 1485, as reflected in the literature of the period. *M.A. 1936 Wales*

Thomas, C. H.
The social and religious history of Wales from 1350 to 1550 as reflected in the literature of the period. *Ph.D. 1940 National University of Ireland*

Thomas, C. M. B.
The marketing of padi in Siam. *M.A. 1933 Bristol*

Thomas, D.
Ffynonellau, arddull a chymeriad gwaith llenyddol Theophilus Evans(Sources, style and character of the literary work of Theophilus Evans). *M.A. 1937 Wales*

Thomas, D.
A study of a rural and maritime community in the nineteenth century, with special reference to the relation between agriculture and shipping. *M.A. 1928 Liverpool*

Thomas, D. E.
English social life as displayed in the literature of the thirteenth and fourteenth centuries. *B.Litt. 1921 Oxford*

Thomas, D. H.
The development of technical education in England from 1851-1889, with special reference to economic factors. *Ph.D. 1940 London, School of Economics and Political Science*

Thomas, D. J.
Emynyddiaeth Cymru hyd 1740(The hymnology of Wales up to 1740). *M.A. 1922 Wales*

Thomas, D. L.
The individualism of André Gide: its character and origin. *M.A. 1945 Wales*

Thomas, D. S.
Some social aspects of the business cycle. *Ph.D. 1924 London*

Thomas, E.
The crisis of 1825. *M.Sc. 1938 London, School of Economics and Political Science*

Thomas, E.
A scheme of industrial and technical education with special reference to rural areas. *M.A. 1920 Wales*

Thomas, E.
A study of the social and economic influence of the small unit of cultivation. *B.Litt. 1926 Oxford*

Thomas, E.
The use of wealth by the Romans from 150 to 50 B.C. *M.A. 1947 London, Birkbeck College*

Thomas, E.
The Welsh church under Edward I. *M.A. 1912 Wales*

Thomas, E. E.
1. Lotze's theory of reality. 2. Lotze's relation to idealism. *D.Litt. 1922 Wales*

Thomas, E. E.
The relation between Leibniz and Lotze. *M.A. 1910 Wales*

Thomas, E. H.
Mysticism in nineteenth century English literature. *M.A. 1924 Wales*

Thomas, E. L.
Thomas Traherne: a study of his life and works. *M.A. 1932 Wales*

Thomas, E. M.
The slave's *peculium* in Rome and the protection afforded to it by Roman law before the year 180 A.D. *M.A. 1927 Wales*

Thomas, E. M.
The trade gilds of the Eastern provinces of the Roman Empire (exclusive of Egypt) during the first three centuries A.D. *B.Litt. 1934 Oxford*

Thomas, E. R.
The foundations of Welsh education: a study of the relationship of an educational system to its social environment. *M.A. 1943 Birmingham*

Thomas, E. R.
Marcus Lucanus as a representative stoic and rhetorician of the Neronian period. *M.A. 1920 Wales*

Thomas, F. C.
Ability and knowledge: the standpoint of the London School. *M.Sc. 1935 London, King's College*

Thomas, F. C.
On the standardization of group tests of intelligence, and the interpretation of their results. *M.A. 1930 London, Day Training College*

Thomas, F. C.
The recruitment of secondary school pupils. *Ph.D. 1939 London, External Degree*

Thomas, G.
The life and work of Anthony Bek, bishop of Durham. *M.A. 1915 Wales*

Thomas, G. H.
Changing values in Egyptian agriculture from 1800 to the present time. *M.A. 1939 London, Birkbeck College*

Thomas, G. I.
An enquiry into the development of a new method of class music teaching based on the principles of Gestalt psychology. *Ph.D. 1949 London, Institute of Education*

Thomas, G. I.
The industrial history of the parish of Aberdare from 1800-1900. *M.A. 1943 Wales*

Thomas, G. I.
A study of the development as a school subject of music from the beginning of the nineteenth century to the present time in England and Wales, with special reference to official reports. *M.A. 1943 Wales*

Thomas, G. W.
A study of the development towards the principles and practice of modern education as shown in the Dissenting Academies in England. *M.A. 1949 London, Institute of Education*

Thomas, H.
Catalogue raisonné of the subjunctive in Plautus. *D.Litt. 1909 Birmingham*

Thomas, H.
The geography of the chemical industry of western Europe. *M.A. 1923 Wales*

Thomas, H.
A historico-geographical survey of the alkali industry of Great Britain from 1789 to the present day. *Ph.D. 1935 London, Birkbeck College*

Thomas, H. D.
The works of Hywel Davi. *M.A. 1913 Wales*

Thomas, H. J.
The tinplate industry, 1914-23. *M.Com. 1923 Birmingham*

Thomas, H. L.
Some barbaric elements in Carolingian art: an evaluation of Keltic, Germanic and Steppe influences in the art of the West. *Ph.D. 1949 Edinburgh*

Thomas, H. P.
Music and drama have a common origin. *Ph.D. 1939 London, Trinity College*

Thomas, J.
The economic development of the North Staffordshire potteries since 1730, with special reference to the Industrial Revolution. *Ph.D. 1934 London, School of Economics and Political Science*

Thomas, J.
A history of education in the towns of Barry and Penarth together with the neighbouring parishes of Leckwith, Llandough juxta Penarth, Lavernock, Sully, St.Andrews, Wenvoe, Highlight, Perthkerry and Penmark during the period 1860-1930. *M.A. 1933 Wales*

Thomas, J.
The rise of education in England. *M.A. 1902 London*

Thomas, J.
The social nexus of Welsh literature. *M.A. 1923 Liverpool*

Thomas, J.
The south Wales coalfield during government control, 1914-1921. *M.A. 1925 Wales*

Thomas, J. A.
The English idea of the 'social contract' theory of government in English political theory, from the Reformation to the Revolution of 1688. *M.A. 1923 Wales*

Thomas, J. A.
An enquiry into the change in the character of the House of Commons 1832-1901. *Ph.D. 1926 London*

Thomas, J. E. H.
The relation of the concepts of immanence and personality. *M.A. 1920 Liverpool*

Thomas, J. G.
A geographical study of the Eire-Northern Ireland boundary. *M.A. 1949 Wales*

Thomas, J. G. T.
The kenotic theory in its bearing on the humanity of Our Lord. *B.D. 1947 Leeds*

Thomas, J. G. T.
The life and work of Griffith Jones, Llanddowror, 1683-1761. *M.A. 1940 Leeds*

Thomas, J. H.
The socialistic theory of Anatole France as expressed in his literary works. *M.A. 1928 Wales*

Thomas, J. H.
Town sanitation in the sixteenth century, based on the records of a group of provincial towns. *B.Litt. 1929 Oxford*

Thomas, J. K.
The bias of Hazlitt. *M.A. 1931 Liverpool*

Thomas, J. N.
Determinism in the theological system of Jonathan Edwards. *Ph.D. 1937 Edinburgh*

Thomas, L.
The Reformation in the diocese of Llandaff. *B.Litt. 1926 Oxford*

Thomas, L. E.
The problem of time: a critical examination in the light of recent discussions. *M.A. 1938 Wales*

Thomas, L. J.
The history of the counties of Glamorgan and Monmouth during the Great Civil War, 1642-1648. *M.A. 1914 Wales*

Thomas, L. M.
A study of the 'Familiar letters of James Howell. *M.A. 1931 Wales*

Thomas, M.
The ethical philosophy of Richard Price. *M.A. 1921 Wales*

Thomas, M. F.
The Banims; a study in Anglo-Irish literature. *M.A. 1935 National University of Ireland*

Thomas, M. G. Lloyd *see* Lloyd Thomas, M. G.

Thomas, M. I.
Grammatical characteristics of Lycurgus. *M.A. 1907 London*

Thomas, M. I.
Life in Spain during the fifth and sixth centuries A.D. (based chiefly on the works of contemporary Latin writers). *Ph.D. 1934 London, External Degree*

Thomas, M. W.
The development of factory legislation from 1833-47: a study of legislative and administrative evolution. *Ph.D. 1948 London, University College*

Thomas, M. W.
The organization of the English factories in the East Indies, 1600-1642. *M.A. 1920 London*

Thomas, O.
Dychanau ac ymrysonau'r beirdd Cymreig hyd ddiwdd yr eilfed ganrif ar bymtheg(The satires and contentions of the Welsh bards to the end of the seventeenth century). *M.A. 1928 Wales*

Thomas, P. G.
The literary correspondence (1757-1781) of Bishop Percy. *M.A. 1928 Wales*

Thomas, P. J.
Development of the Indian administrative and financial system, 1858-1905, with special reference to the relations between the central government and the provinces. *D.Phil. 1935 Oxford*

Thomas, P. J.
Manufactured Indian cotton goods in England and their influence on English economic history about 1680-1720. *B.Litt. 1922 Oxford*

Thomas, P. S.
An outline of the activities of some trade unions of south Wales, with reference to the question of compulsory membership. *M.A. 1920 Wales*

Thomas, P. V.
Eugène Brieux. *M.A. 1912 London*

Thomas, R.
The development of descriptive poems in the English poetry of the eighteenth century. *M.A. 1949 Wales*

Thomas, R.
The influence of Trajano Boccalini's *Ragguagli de Parnaso* upon the English literature of the seventeenth and early eighteenth centuries. *M.A. 1921 Wales*

Thomas, R.
The moral theory of Richard Price. *Ph.D. 1928 London*

Thomas, R.
A study of the psychology of the creative processes, with particular reference to literary production. *D.Sc. 1932 Wales*

Thomas, R. E.
Ribbon development in selected areas around Birmingham. *M.Com. 1949 Birmingham*

Thomas, R. G.
Aspects of the Sturlung age, with special reference to *Sturlunga Saga*: a study in the life and literature of Iceland during the twelfth and thirteenth centuries. *Ph.D. 1943 Wales*

Thomas, R. G.
The position of women in Icelandic life and social economy as shown in the Icelandic sagas. *M.A. 1939 Wales*

Thomas, R. J.
Astudiaeth o enwau lleoedd cwmwd Meisgyn, gyda sylw arbennig i blwyf Llantrisant(A study of the placenames of the commote of Meisgyn, with special reference to the parish of Llantrisant). *M.A. 1933 Wales*

Thomas, S. E.
The rise and growth of English joint stock banking. *Ph.D. 1934 London, External Degree*

Thomas, S. G.
Contribution to the study of the style in the earliest French prose romances. *Ph.D. 1948 London, University College*

Thomas, T. G.
The local cults of ancient Latium outside Rome, with the exception of Ostia. *M.A. 1930 Wales*

Thomas, T. J.
James Howell and his relation to France, the French language and literature. *M.A. 1926 Wales*

Thomas, T. T.
The diminutive in Roman *satura*. *M.A. 1946 Wales*

Thomas, W. Bryn *see* Bryn Thomas, W.

Thomas, W. H.
A historical survey and critique of the theories propounded concerning the Carolingian legends. *M.A. 1929 Wales*

Thomas, W. H. G.
1. The doctrine of the New Testament on the Supper of the Lord. 2. The doctrine of the Church of England on the Supper of the Lord. *B.D. 1901 Oxford*

Thomas, W. H. G.
Expositions of: St. John xx.30, 31: the purpose and plan of the fourth Gospel; Romans 1.17: the righteousness of God; Ephesians 1.22,23. *D.D. 1906 Oxford*

Thomas, W. J.
The economics of the store cattle industry, with special reference to Wales. *M.Sc. 1946 Wales*

Thomas, W. P.
Nonconformist academies in Wales in the eighteenth century. *M.A. 1928 Wales*

Thomason, M. B.
The crusades of St. Louis. *M.A. 1913 Birmingham*

Thomasson, H. W.
A study in Turanian history based on Chinese original sources. *M.A. 1925 Manchester*

Thompson, B.
An edition of the Old English poem of *Saint Guthlac*. *Ph.D. 1931 Leeds*

Thompson, B. M. H.
The rise and decline of Calvinism in England during the archiepiscopate of Whitgift. *B.Litt. 1932 Oxford*

Thompson, C. A.
Sir Thomas More as a satirist in his epigrams and *Utopia*. *B.Litt. 1947 Oxford*

Thompson, C. H.
The economic implications of conditions in the production and marketing of primary commodities since the Great War. *M.Com. 1939 Birmingham*

Thompson, C. H.
Uthred of Boldon: a study in fourteenth century political theory. *Ph.D. 1936 Manchester*

Thompson, C. J.
1. Reasonableness of the considerations which form the ground of Christian hope. 2. The moral value of the doctrine of final judgement. *B.D. & D.D. 1893 Oxford*

Thompson, C. M.
The function of reason in relation to the moral idea and the part played by experience. *M.A. 1922 London*

Thompson, E.
The history of the port of Lancaster, with special reference to the years 1750-1825. *M.A. 1935 Manchester*

Thompson, E.
The idea of sovereignty of the people, and the constitutional legislation of the French National Assembly, 1789-1791. *Ph.D. 1948 London, External Degree*

Thompson, E. A.
The Arcadian League, 371-338 B.C. *B.Litt. 1937 Dublin, Trinity College*

Thompson, E. J.
The poetry and dramas of Rabindranath Tagore. *Ph.D. 1924 London*

Thompson, E. M.
The doctrine of baptism. *B.D. 1927 Oxford*

Thompson, F.
Dorothy Wordsworth: her mind and art. *M.A. 1926 Birmingham*

Thompson, F. F.
The psychology of eucharistic worship. *Ph.D. 1938 Edinburgh*

Thompson, G. F.
The basis of Christian morals in the second and third centuries. *M.A. 1924 Sheffield*

Thompson, G. L. S.
The origins of Congregationalism in Scotland. *Ph.D. 1932 Edinburgh*

Thompson, J.
The life and times of Marcus Licinius Crassus, Triumvir. *Ph.D. 1941 Edinburgh*

Thompson, J.
Organic rhythm. *M.A. 1920 National University of Ireland*

Thompson, J.
The relations between James VI and I and Carlo Emanuele I, Duke of Savoy. *Ph.D. 1942 Saint Andrew's*

Thompson, J. H. Hannay *see* Hannay-Thompson, J. H.

Thompson, L. F.
Kotzebue: a reconsideration of his place in European drama. *M.A. 1926 London*

Thompson, M. C.
The Bridgewater Treatises: their theological significance. *Ph.D. 1949 Edinburgh*

Thompson, P. E.
L'évolution des thèmes poétiques dans l'oeuvre de Jean Moréas. *M.A. 1950 Manchester*

Thompson, R. S.
A study of elementary education in Malta and the problems affecting its development. *M.Ed. 1943 Durham*

Thompson, R. W.
The category of personality in relation to Kant's three postulates of the practical reason: freedom, immortality, God. *M.A. 1907 London*

Thompson, T. F.
St. Simon and Carlyle to 1835. *M.A. 1939 Birmingham*

Thomson, D.
The conception of political party in England in the period 1740-83. *Ph.D. 1938 Cambridge*

Thomson, E. E. B.
Scotland under Lauderdale. *Ph.D. 1928 Saint Andrew's*

Thomson, E. Roberts- *see* Roberts-Thomson, E.

Thomson, G.
The influence of the Youth Movement on German education. *Ph.D. 1935 Glasgow*

Thomson, H. J.
On the preservation of ancient scholia on Virgil in Latin glossaries. *D. Litt. 1922 Saint Andrew's*

Thomson, J. C.
The history and present position of Chinese surgery; surgical characteristics of the Chinese, and the prospects of western surgical practice in China. *M.D. 1892 Edinburgh*

Thomson, M. A.
The office of Secretary of State, 1681-1782. *D.Phil. 1931 Oxford*

Thomson, M. P. N. *see* Nicolson Thomson, M. P.

Thomson, P. W.
The influence of Chaucer, Gower, and Lydgate on the Scottish poets in the fifteenth and early sixteenth centuries. *B.Litt. 1915 Oxford*

Thomson, R. B.
The architectural design of streets. *M.A. 1947 Sheffield*

Thomson, S. H.
Sources of the theological doctrines of Wycliffe. *B.Litt. 1926 Oxford*

Thomson, W. S.
P. R. O. assize roll 505, edited with an introduction on the war-time administration of Lincolnshire, 1294-98. *Ph.D. 1939 Edinburgh*

Thoothi, N. A.
Discussion and determination of the most adequate method to be employed in the study of the inter-relation and interaction of the economic, ethical, and religious factors in the life of organized communities, as illustrated in the case of the Vaishnava communities of Gujerat. *D.Phil. 1925 Oxford*

Thorburn, T. J.
The Resurrection narratives. *D.D. 1911 Cambridge*

Thorn, G. A.
An examination of the historical basis of the *Roman d'Eustache le Moine*. *M.A. 1949 Leeds*

Thorne, E. H.
Vincenzo Martinelli and his circle in London, 1748-1774. *Ph.D. 1946 London, University College*

Thornley, I.D.
The treason legislation of the reign of Henry VIII. *M.A. 1917 London*

Thornley, P. E.
Folklore in Elizabethan prose literature. *M.A. 1929 Wales*

Thornton, A. *see* Schwarzchild, A.

Thornton, C. G.
Landnámabók: the book of the settlement of Iceland. *Ph.D. 1938 Cambridge*

Thornton, D.
Henry Dundas and the government of India, 1784-1800. *M.A. 1925 Liverpool*

Thornton, F. B.
The bases of Pope's *Essay on man*. *B.Litt. 1937 Oxford*

Thornton, G. A.
A history of Clare, Suffolk, with special reference to its development as a borough during the Middle Ages, and to its importance as a centre of the woollen industry in the fifteenth to seventeenth centuries. *Ph.D. 1927 London*

Thornton, M.
The work of the Catholic Church in British tropical Africa: a study in co-operation. *Ph.D. 1933 London, External Degree*

Thorogood, A. J.
The life and times of Egberht, King of Wessex, 802 to 839. *M.A. 1931 Reading*

Thorp, N. M.
The study and literary treatment of the *Nibelungen* legend and *Nibelungenlied* from 1752 to the present time. *D.Phil. 1938 Oxford*

Thorp, W. B.
The growth of Wallasey and its future development. *M.A. 1936 Liverpool*

Thorpe, H.
The geography of rural settlement in the Durham region. *M.Litt. 1937 Durham*

Thorpe, L. G. M.
A first contribution to the study of the linguistics of the unpublished thirteenth century prose-romance entitled *Le Roman de Laurin, fils de Marques le Seneschal*. *Ph.D. 1949 London, External Degree*

Thoviss, R. H.
Nature of religious experience. *Ph.D. 1923 Cambridge*

Thraves, L. H.
The Gordon riots, 1780. *M.A. 1910 Liverpool*

Thrift, I. E.
Manners and morals of the seventeenth and eighteenth centuries as revealed in books written for the young. *Ph.D. 1935 London, King's College*

Throssell, T.
Joseph Conrad: a study of his style. *M.A. 1947 Liverpool*

Thrupp, S. L.
A study of the merchant class of London in the fifteenth century, with special reference to the Company of Grocers. *Ph.D. 1931 London, University College*

Thwaites, M. R.
A study of *The ring and the book*. *B.Litt. 1947 Oxford*

Thyagaraju, A. F.
A study of the themes of weak verbs in Old English and the older stages of the other Germanic languages. *M.A. 1935 London, King's College*

Tibble, J. W.
John Clare: a life. *M.A. 1935 Leeds*

Tibbott, G.
Emynwyr gogledd Cymru hyd y flwyddyn 1800(The hymn-writers of North Wales to 1800). *M.A. 1926 Wales*

Tien, J. K.
Religious cults and social structure of the Shan States of the Yunnen-Burma frontier. *Ph.D. 1948 London, School of Economics and Political Science*

Tierney, J. J.
1. Early Spartan civilisation. 2. Influence of Dionysus cult on Roman religion. *M.A. 1932 National University of Ireland*

Tiffin, W. J.
Errors in French prose composition made by school children under examination conditions. *M.Ed. 1929 Leeds*

Tiffin, W. J.
Trois poèmes de Christine de Pisan: (a) *L'epistre au dieu d'amour*; (b) *Le dit de la rose*; (c) *Le débat de deux amants*. *M.A. 1929 Leeds*

Tigg, E. R.
Medieval themes in modern German drama since 1900. *Ph.D. 1937 London, External Degree*

Tiley, J. C. G.
Baron Friedrich von Hügel's place in the modernist movement. *B.Litt. 1940 Oxford*

Tillett, M. G.
Madame Campan and her work at Ecouen. *M.A. 1941 Reading*

Tillotson, A.
The correspondence between Edmond Malone and Thomas Percy (preserved in the Bodleian in mss. 26, 27, 37 and 39). *B.Litt. 1933 Oxford*

Tillotson, G.
The *Britannia's Pastorals* and *The Shepherd's Pipe* of William Browne. *B.Litt. 1930 Oxford*

Tilly, B.
An account of pedimental composition from the earliest monuments to the Parthenon. *M.A. 1932 London, Bedford College*

Tilly, B.
Vergil's Roman campagna. *Ph.D. 1940 London, External Degree*

Tilney-Bassett, J. G.
Robert Armin. *B.Litt. 1935 Oxford*

Timings, F. L.
The Birmingham steel pen trade. *M.Com. 1926 Birmingham*

Tin, P. M.
The Buddhist doctrine of insight, with special reference to the Pali text called *The path of purity*, ch. xx-xxii of *Visuddhimagga*. *B.Litt. 1922 Oxford*

Ting, S.
Studies of the Scottish shoreline. *Ph.D. 1937 Glasgow*

Tinsley, E. J.
The *Sermons* of Lancelot Andrewes in their relation to the growth of Anglican theology, and to the impact of doctrinal ideas upon literature in the Jacobean period. *B.D. 1944 Durham*

Tippett, L. H. C.
On the extreme individuals and the range of samples taken from a normal population. *M.Sc. 1926 London*

Tirol, M. M.
Les cabinets de lecture en France, 1800-1850. *Ph.D. 1926 London*

Tisdell, D. J.
The interests of some junior technical school boys. *M.A. 1942 Birmingham*

Titmuss, C. M.
D. G. Rossetti. *M.A. 1924 Birmingham*

Titterton, M.
The child in the German drama, from the time of Goethe and Schiller. *M.A. 1908 Birmingham*

Tizard, J.
Industrial relations in the British Co-operative Movement. *B.Litt. 1949 Oxford*

Tizard, L. J.
St. Paul's doctrine of justification: its origin, significance, and adequacy. *B.Litt. 1929 Oxford*

Tobias, A.
The development of the Rabbinate in central Europe during the years 1348-1648. *Ph.D. 1945 London, Jews' College*

Tobin, J.
Essay on economic planning. *M.Econ.Sc. 1938 National University of Ireland*

Todd, E. C. E.
The administrative and legal implications of tribunals concerned with town and country planning. *LL.M. 1951 Manchester*

Todd, F. M.
Wordsworth's political development. *Ph.D. 1948 London, University College*

Todd, G. F.
Joint stock company failures, 1862-1914. *B.Litt. 1932 Oxford*

Todd, H.
The technical high school, with special reference to girls. *M.Ed. 1941 Leeds*

Todd, M.
Civic government of Durham, 1780-1835. *M.A. 1924 Liverpool*

Todd-Naylor, U.
Charlotte Lennox. *B.Litt. 1931 Oxford*

Todd-Naylor, U.
Richardson's influence on the women novelists of the eighteenth century. *Ph.D. 1935 London, University College*

Toibin, S.
Bearlagair na saor(Masons' jargon). *M.A. 1931 National University of Ireland*

Tolley, I. H.
The mendicants and English education in the thirteenth century. *M.A. 1924 London*

Tollinton, R. B.
1. The Christology of Clement of Alexandria. 2. The theology of the Wisdom literature. *B.D. 1905 Oxford*

Tolson, J. E.
The *Summa* of Petrus Helias on Priscian, *Institutiones Grammaticae*, XVII and XVIII. *M.A. 1950 Liverpool*

Tomkinson, F.
The history of the Aramaeans down to the fall of Nineveh, 612 B.C. *M.A. 1932 Wales*

Tomkinson, F. E.
The education theory of Benedetto Croce. *M.A. 1929 Liverpool*

Tomkinson, W. S.
The novels of Daniel Defoe. *B.Litt. 1925 Oxford*

Tomlinson, F. W.
Burke and the French Revolution. *M.Sc. 1928 London*

Tomlinson, H. E.
The historical development of heraldic terms, with especial consideration of 'armes parlantes'. *M.A. 1942 Manchester*

Tomlinson, J. L.
Training for industry and commerce: present defects and future remedies. *M.Com. 1937 Leeds*

Tompkins, J. B.
The four quarter concept in aboriginal America. *Ph.D. 1934 London, University College*

Tompkins, J. M. S.
The work of Mrs. Radcliffe and its influence on later writers. *M.A. 1921 London*

Toms, E.
The Abbey of Chertsey and its manors under Abbot John de Rutherwyk, 1307-1347. *Ph.D. 1935 London, King's College*

Toms, E. W.
The Old Testament and the future life. *M.A. 1925 Wales*

Toner, F. J.
Newman and intellectual culture. *M.A. 1945 National University of Ireland*

Tonge, W.
The nature of moral obligation. *M.A. 1940 Manchester*

Tonkinson, E.
The Walsall and Midlands leather trades; a study in their history and organisation from the earliest times to the present day. *M.Com. 1948 Birmingham*

Tooley, M. J.
The *Defensor pacis* of Marsilio of Padua and John of Jandun: its relation to political theories developed in France during the reign of Philip IV. *M.A. 1921 London*

Toomay, J. B.
Critical examination of the religious position of Josiah Royce. *Ph.D. 1934 Edinburgh*

Toorn, K. van den *see* van den Toorn, K.

Topham, M.
An examination into some elements of Spenser's psychological vocabulary, with reference to that of Chaucer. *M.A. 1931 Manchester*

Topping, C. J. H.
A comparative study of the language of the Anglo-Norman Bills of Eyre and similar documents of the Channel Isles, Gloucestershire, London and a northern area (Lancashire). *Ph.D. 1934 London, Birkbeck College*

Topping, J. F.
A survey of industrial trends in employment in the West Riding of Yorkshire since 1921. *M.Com. 1946 Leeds*

Topping, R.
The metaphysical implications of freedom. *M.A. 1937 Belfast*

Torbarina, J.
Influence of Italian literature on Ragusan poetry in the sixteenth century. *Ph.D. 1930 London, King's College*

Torrance, W. G.
Rural education. *M.A. 1930 Birmingham*

Tough, D. L. W.
The last years of a frontier: a history of the borders during the reign of Elizabeth. *B.Litt. 1920 Oxford*

Toulmin, S. E.
The place of reason in ethics. *Ph.D. 1949 Cambridge*

Toussaint, M. M. A.
Printing in the Mascarene Islands (Ile de France and Bourbon) from 1767 to 1810. *Ph.D. 1947 London, External Degree*

Towers, J. E.
The origins of the Hebrew psalter. *M.A. 1934 Manchester*

Towne, M. M.
The Platonic conception of the soul and its relation to the ideas. *M.A. 1928 London*

Towneley-Worsthorne, S. P. E. C. W.
Venetian operatic stage, 1637-1700. *D.Phil. 1950 Oxford*

Townend, M.
The Volsung episode in the *Prose Edda* (*Edda Snorra Sturlasonar*): the Volsung episode in relation to its sources. *M.A. 1942 Leeds*

Townson, J. A.
The individual and his relation to the common good. *M.A. 1934 Liverpool*

Toy, H. S.
History of Helston, 1768-91. *M.A. 1931 Bristol*

Toy, K. N.
The women of Sophocles. *M.A. 1911 Birmingham*

Toy, R. H.
The influence of the university on the development of its region. *Ph.D. 1950 Dublin, Trinity College*

Toye, D. B.
The history of the Bosphorus and the Dardanelles, with special reference to treaty relations: a study in international law and diplomacy. *LL.D. 1925 London*

Toye, E. C.
Abolitionist societies (1787-1838). *M.A. 1936 London, King's College*

Trafford, E. E.
Personnel of the Parliament of 1593. *M.A. 1948 London, University College*

Trafford, W. P. C.
The economic and political problems of Japanese colonization. *M.A. 1919 Wales*

Traneker, K. G.
Les idées courtoises dans l'*Ipomeden* de Hue de Roteland. *M.A. 1927 Birmingham*

Tranmer, E.
Eugène Fromentin, his life and works. *M.A. 1921 Birmingham*

Tranter, A. V.
Evasion in taxation. *Ph.D. 1927 London*

Travers, B. H.
Macquarie, Governor of New South Wales, 1809-1821. *B.Litt. 1949 Oxford*

Traversi, D. A. U. Antona- *see* Antona-Traversi, D. A. U.

Travis, J. E.
The vocabulary of sport in present-day France. *M.A. 1933 Manchester*

Travis, M. A.
The reform of the dual system in England and Wales, 1941-44. *M.A. 1949 London, King's College*

Treadgold, D. W.
The growth and interrelations of political groups and parties in Russia, 1898-May 1906. *D.Phil. 1949 Oxford*

Treadgold, M.
George Chapman: life and works (exclusive of translations); the relationship of the poems to the tragedies, 1559-1634. *M.A. 1936 London, Bedford College*

Treanor, J.
P. H. Pearse as an educationalist. *M.A. 1942 National University of Ireland*

Tree, R. J.
An examination of Hume's treatment of the problems of divine existence and providence. *B.Litt. 1941 Oxford*

Tree, R. J.
The relation of theology to epistemology, with special reference to Hume. *M.A. 1939 Wales*

Trefethen, F. M. N.
Demonology, magic, and witchcraft in the English drama, 1580-1642. *M.Litt. 1950 Cambridge*

Tregear, T. R.
Wuhan: its local and wider environment. *Ph.D. 1934 London, External Degree*

Treharne, S. C. M.
Prudentius *Psychomachia* and French allegorical poetry of the Middle Ages. *M.A. 1929 Wales*

Treiman, I.
The history of the English law of bankruptcy, with special reference to the origins, continental sources, and early development of the principal features of the law. *D.Phil. 1927 Oxford*

Treloar, B. G.
The development of *préciosité* in the seventeenth century: a literary and social study. *D.Phil. 1948 Oxford*

Tremearne, A. J. N.
Bullfighting in Nigeria and Portugal: a humane sport. *M.Sc. 1914 London*

Trenaman, H. R.
The metaphysical status of religion. *Ph.D. 1935 London, King's College*

Trench, S. M. Chevenix *see* Chevenix Trench, S. M.

Treneer, A.
A critical examination of the prose and verse of C. M. Doughty. *B.Litt. 1931 Oxford*

Trenerry, C. J.
The origin and early history of insurance, including the contract of bottomry. *D.Sc. 1907 London*

Trenur, A.
George Meredith. *M.A. 1922 London*

Trevelyan, E. J.
The law relating to minors as applied by the British courts in India. *D.C.L. 1906 Oxford*

Treves, A. E. S.
De l'emploi des images, metaphores et comparaisons dans *Madame Bovary. B.Litt. 1929 Oxford*

Trevor, D.
Public opinion and the acquisition of Bechuanaland and Rhodesia, 1868-1896. *Ph.D. 1936 London, School of Economics and Political Science*

Trevor, J.
A study of the English skull in medieval times, with special reference to crania in the Department of Human Anatomy, Oxford, and at Rothwell Parish Church, near Kettering, Northamptonshire. *B.Sc. 1934 Oxford*

Tribble, H. W.
The doctrine of sanctification in the theology of Karl Barth. *Ph.D. 1937 Edinburgh*

Triebel, L. A.
The Nuremberg legend of the crocodile. *M.A. 1914 London*

Tripathi, R. S.
History of Kanauj to the Moslem conquest. *Ph.D. 1929 London*

Tristram, F. H.
The use of the subjunctive mood in the *Mémoires du Duc de Saint-Simon. M.A. 1913 Wales*

Tristram, H. T.
Synesius as a representative of Greek thought and culture during the period immediately preceding its eclipse. *B.Litt. 1925 Oxford*

Trivedi, P. K.
Studies of expression in children's free drawing and their response to aesthetic and other pictorial tests. *M.Ed. 1949 Durham*

Trivett, J. V.
Attitudes in the secondary (modern) school: an experimental investigation. *M.A. 1949 Bristol*

Trodden, L. E.
Banking systems of Ireland. *M.A. 1926 National University of Ireland*

Trood, S. M. E.
The political thought of Sir Robert Filmer and his royalist contemporaries. *M.A. 1922 London*

Trood, S. M. E.
Popular ideas concerning government during the latter half of the seventeenth century. *D.Litt. 1932 London, External Degree*

Trott, A. L.
The history of church schools in Swansea during the nineteenth century to 1870. *M.A. 1941 Wales*

Trott, C. D. J.
The historical geography of the Neath region up to the eve of the Industrial Revolution. *M.A. 1946 Wales*

Trotter, E.
The parish in the seventeenth century in the North Riding. *M.A. 1913 London*

Trotter, R. J. F.
The nature of personality. *M.A. 1947 Liverpool*

Troughton, N. A.
La réaction contre le naturalisme autour de 1890 dans le roman. *M.A. 1928 Belfast*

Trounce, A. M.
An edition of the Middle English romance of *Athelston* with literary and linguistic introduction, notes, and a glossary. *B.Litt. 1932 Oxford*

Troutman, O. T.
The textile industry of Australia. *M.Com. 1939 Birmingham*

Trouton, D. S.
A psychological and statistical study of certain psychoanalytical character types. *M.A. 1947 London, University College*

Troy, M. J.
A commentary on Aristotle's *Metaphysics*, Book 12. *M.A. 1942 National University of Ireland*

Truscott, M. J.
The influences of the improvements in agriculture during the reigns of George I and George II. *M.A. 1914 London*

Tsao, D. F.
A comparative study of drawing ability in English children by the Goodenough scale. *M.A. 1935 London, University College*

Tsao, J. C.
Time intervals in learning and memory. *Ph.D. 1949 Cambridge*

Tseng, C.-Y.
The evolution of inscriptions on bronzes during the Chou period. *M.A. 1937 London, Courtauld Institute of Art*

Tseng, Y. D.
Charles Wesley and his poetry. *B.Litt. 1936 Oxford*

Tsiang, S. C.
The variations of real wages and profit margins in relation to the trade cycle. *Ph.D. 1945 London, School of Economics and Political Science*

Tsou, P. C.
A regional study of Shantung and its significance in the life of north China. *M.A. 1939 Liverpool*

Tucker, A. K.
François de Curel, dramatist and philosopher. *Ph.D. 1931 London, University College*

Tucker, A. K.
George Sand as a political theorist. *M.A. 1922 London*

Tucker, A. N.
The comparative phonetics of the Suto-Chuana group of Bantu languages. *Ph.D. 1929 London*

Tucker, D. R.
The development of quarter sessions government in Devon in the nineteenth century and the transition to county council government. *M.A. 1949 London, External Degree*

Tucker, E. F. C.
An inquiry into the changes in the human cranium from palaeolithic times onwards, with special reference to the British Isles. *B.Sc. 1927 Oxford*

Tucker, G. N.
The economic history of the province of Canada, 1845-1851. *Ph.D. 1930 Cambridge*

Tucker, H. F. G.
The Press and the colonies. *M.A. 1936 Bristol*

Tucker, H. N.
The nature and scope of public policy in English law. *D.C.L. 1946 Oxford*

Tucker, L. G.
The concept of the 'unconscious' and its importance for psychology. *M.A. 1924 Liverpool*

Tucker, M. G.
The career of Prince Kaunitz, Austrian chancellor, 1753-1792. *M.A. 1937 Bristol*

Tuckey, J. G. W.
1. The Christian's duty to the State. 2. The lawfulness of war. *B.D. 1924 Oxford*

Tudor, R. H.
The Roman theatre. *M.Litt. 1936 Durham*

Tugwood, J. R.
The origins of dynamo-electric apparatus. *M.Sc. 1945 London, University College*

Tulloch, W. J.
The *De tribus processionibus* of Richard of Saint Victor: a critical text with introduction. *M.A. 1945 Liverpool*

Tumbleton, T.
An quis civis in duabus civitatibus esse possit?. *D.C.L. 1886 Oxford*

Tunnicliffe, A. C.
Plato's conception of beauty, and its bearing on the development of the theory of ideas. *M.A. 1911 London*

Tuomey, T.
Normality of Shakespeare. *M.A. 1931 National University of Ireland*

Tupholme, B. S.
1. On the holy Catholic Church. 2. On the sacraments. *B.D. & D.D. 1888 Oxford*

Tupholme, W. S.
Exegeses of I Timothy i.3; i.18; II Timothy i.13. *D.D. 1921 Oxford*

Tupholme, W. S.
1. The Incarnation of our Lord. 2. The three creeds. *B.D. 1903 Oxford*

Tupling, G. H.
Studies in the economic development of Rossendale. *Ph.D. 1925 London*

Turberville, A. S.
The House of Lords in the reign of William III, 1688-1702. *B.Litt. 1912 Oxford*

Turhan, M.
A study of cultural change with special reference to Turkey. *Ph.D. 1949 Cambridge*

Turkel, H. R.
The international administrative unions. *B.Litt. 1930 Oxford*

Turnbach, E. P.
The religious thought of George Tyrell, Roman Catholic modernist. *Ph.D. 1942 Edinburgh*

Turnbull, A. C.
The Jacobites in England and Wales, 1689-1723. *M.A. 1949 Liverpool*

Turnbull, G. H.
The educational ideas of Wolfgang Ratke. *M.A. 1913 Liverpool*

Turner, A. B.
Some comparisons between evening class attenders in the Black Country and non-attenders. *M.A. 1932 Bristol*

Turner, A. C.
The House of Commons and foreign policy between the first and second Reform Acts. *B.Litt. 1948 Oxford*

Turner, B. C.
The polite novel after Jane Austen. *B.Litt. 1944 Oxford*

Turner, D. M.
General ability and the relation between general and specific ability at different stages of school life. *M.A. 1922 London*

Turner, D. M.
History of science teaching in England. *Ph.D. 1928 London*

Turner, E. C.
The auditing of private limited company accounts in its relations to taxation. *M.Com. 1923 Birmingham*

Turner, E. M.
The life and work of Charles Cotton. *B.Litt. 1935 Oxford*

Turner, F. W.
Scientific method as exemplified in qualitative analysis. *M.A. 1928 London*

Turner, H. A.
The making of modern Liverpool, 1760-1820. *M.A. 1939 Birmingham*

Turner, H. E. W.
The Antiochene exegesis of Holy Scripture up to the Council of Chalcedon. *B.D. 1940 Oxford*

Turner, H. M. *see* MacKenzie, H. M.

Turner, J. A.
Plato and the poets. *M.A. 1932 National University of Ireland*

Turner, J. E.
The metaphysical basis of moral obligation. *M.A. 1921 Liverpool*

Turner, J. E.
A theory of direct realism and the relation of realism to idealism. *Ph.D. 1925 Liverpool*

Turner, J. E. S.
The chief Roman satirists and the historical value of their works, as a picture of their times. *M.A. 1918 Birmingham*

Turner, L. F.
The Elizabethan drama as the newspaper of the age; a study of the influence of external controlling factors on the drama of the early seventeenth century as a potential medium for reflecting popular opinion on political and social questions. *M.A. 1938 London, University College*

Turner, L. M.
The business world in France as revealed in the works of Balzac. *M.A. 1923 Manchester*

Turner, M. E.
Some aspects of the English Carmelites in the first half of the fifteenth century. *M.A. 1933 Manchester*

Turner, W. G.
British policy in reference to Mehemet Ali, 1839-41. *M.A. 1928 London*

Turner-Smith, N. A.
The psychological approach to theism. *B.Litt. 1923 Oxford*

Turpin, J. J.
1. The Old Testament: a progressive revelation of the divine character. 2. The miraculous element in the Gospels. *B.D. 1908 Oxford*

Turpin, K. C.
The political evolution of Robert Harley, 1702-12. *B.Litt. 1940 Oxford*

Turville-Petre, E. O. G.
An edition of *Viga Glúms Saga* from the manuscripts, with introduction and notes. *B.Litt. 1934 Oxford*

Tuting, W. C.
1. Apostolic teaching and the teaching of the creeds in relation to that of our Lord. 2. The doctrine of immortality, Jewish and Christian. *B.D. & D.D. 1911 Oxford*

Tutton, W. T.
Some aspects of truth, static and developmental. *M.A. 1921 Liverpool*

Twamley, W. H. B.
The importance of the religious bodies in the political development of England between the end of the eighteenth century and the beginning of the Oxford Movement. *Ph.D. 1925 Cambridge*

Tweddle, W. A.
A statistical examination of how industry adapts itself to changes in the volume of output and the effects of such changes on the amounts of fixed and working capital employed. *Ph.D. 1938 Cambridge*

Twomey, P. V.
Apprenticeship at home and abroad. *M.Comm. 1950 National University of Ireland*

Twyman, E. M.
William Morris. *M.A. 1924 Birmingham*

Tyabji, K.
Limited interests in Muhammadan law. *B.Litt. 1947 Oxford*

Tyack, N. C. P.
1. Bristol and Virginia in the seventeenth century. 2. Bristol merchants, shipwrights, etc. from the Burgess Books, 1607-1700. *M.A. 1930 Bristol*

Tyau, M. T. Z.
The legal obligations arising out of treaty relations between China and other states. *LL.D. 1916 London*

Tylecote, M.
The mechanics' institute movement in Lancashire and Yorkshire, 1824 to 1850, with special reference to the institutions at Manchester, Ashton-under-Lyne and Huddersfield. *Ph.D. 1930 Manchester*

Tyler, A. E.
The press of Robert Estienne, 1526-1550: a historical study. *D.Phil. 1949 Oxford*

Tyler, C. E.
England in the Icelandic sagas. *Ph.D. 1926 Sheffield*

Tyree, W. E.
The Christian interpretation of history as exemplified in the writings of Jacques Maritain and Reinhold Niebuhr. *Ph.D. 1949 Edinburgh*

Tyrer, F.
A record of ten years' work and experience in the teaching of biology in a senior elementary school. *M.A. 1940 Liverpool*

Tyrrell, B. D.
Some aspects of the geological work of Johan Jacob Scheuchzer including a translation of his *Herbarium Deluvianum* of 1709. *M.Sc. 1934 London, University College*

Tyrrell, G. A.
The work and importance of W. Caxton. *M.A. 1922 Birmingham*

Tyson, G.
Some apparent effects of co-education, suggested by a statistical investigation of examination results. *M.Ed. 1930 Manchester*

Tyson, M.
The early history of *Placita coram rege*. *Ph.D. 1927 Manchester*

Tyszynski, H.
International commodity agreements and world trade expansion. *Ph.D. 1949 London, School of Economics and Political Science*

Ua Buachalla, D. F.
Barúntacht Mhúscraighe(The barony of Muskerry). *M.A. 1942 National University of Ireland*

Ua Buachalla, D. P.
Review of agricultural legislation in Eire, 1922-42. *M.Econ.Sc. 1943 National University of Ireland*

Ua Danacair, C.
The Irish house. *M.A. 1945 National University of Ireland*

Ua Flaithbheartaigh, M. *see* O'Flaherty, M.

Ua Loinghsigh, E.
Tráchtas ar an seana-shaoghal(An account of life long ago). *M.A. 1936 National University of Ireland*

Ua Nualláin, B.
Tráchtas ar nádúir-fhilíocht na Gaedhilge(A treatise on Irish nature poetry). *M.A. 1934 National University of Ireland*

Ud-Din, A. M.
The rise of Persian independence 820-1056 A.D. *Ph.D. 1935 Dublin, Trinity College*

Udoma, E. U.
Law and British administration in South-eastern Nigeria. *Ph.D. 1944 Dublin, Trinity College*

Uí Chroitigh, M. B.
Séadna. *M.A. 1942 National University of Ireland*

Ullmann, S.
The principles of semantics. *D.Litt. 1948 Glasgow*

Ulug, H. T.
Commercial banking in Turkey, with reference to the experience of certain other countries. *M.Sc. 1946 London, School of Economics and Political Science*

Ulyatt, K. W.
The early history of chemical studies on mineral waters. *M.Sc. 1948 London, University College*

Uncles, W.
The evolution of English literary criticism. *M.A. 1928 Belfast*

Underdown, P. T.
The parliamentary history of the City of Bristol, 1750-1790. *M.A. 1948 Bristol*

Underhill, A. M.
The rise of journalism to Defoe. *M.A. 1929 Birmingham*

Underhill, M. M.
The religious observances ordained for every day of the Hindu year, with special reference to customs observed in the Maratha country, together with the origin of these observances, whether traceable to legends, astronomical causes, or other sources. *B.Litt. 1921 Oxford*

Underwood, A. C.
The biblical doctrine of conversion. *B.Litt. 1920 Oxford*

Underwood, J. J.
The English religious lyric in the Middle Ages. *M.A. 1937 National University of Ireland*

Underwood, V. P.
An Anglo-Norman metrical Brut of the fourteenth century. *Ph.D. 1937 London, University College*

Ungphakorn, P.
The economics of tin control. *Ph.D. 1949 London, School of Economics and Political Science*

Unmack, E. A.
1. Some aspects of modern criticism with reference to the Book of Jonah. 2. St. Paul's doctrine of the Church. *B.D. 1924 Oxford*

Unmack, E. R. W.
A comparative study of speech development and motor co-ordination in children of twenty-four to forty months by means of specially devised tests. *Ph.D. 1939 London, University College*

Unterman, B.
The schools of Shammai and Hillel with special reference to their influence upon the development of the Jewish *Halachah*. *M.A. 1937 Liverpool*

Unwin, J. D.
An enquiry into the relation between sexual opportunity and cultural condition among uncivilised peoples. *Ph.D. 1931 Cambridge*

Upcott, A. W.
1. The testimony of St. Paul with regard to the resurrection of our Lord compared with that of the four Evangelists. 2. A study of the sterner side of the character of our Lord as evidenced in the narratives of the Evangelists. *B.D. & D.D. 1906 Oxford*

Uprichard, E. M.
The relationship between interest, aptitude and achievement as shown by an enquiry into curricula in four secondary modern schools. *Ph.D. 1947 London, Institute of Education*

Upright, N.
The City of Coventry in the Restoration period, 1660-1688. *M.A. 1944 Manchester*

Ure, P.
Aspects of the mythology in W. B. Yeats' poetry. *M.A. 1944 Liverpool*

Uren, A. R.
A critical exposition of the methods and results of the American School of religious psychology: a study in the psychology of religion. *Ph.D. 1924 Edinburgh*

Urie, D. McK. L.
Sacrifice at Ugarit. *Ph.D. 1944 Saint Andrew's*

Urwin, E. C.
Christian ethics and social institutions in the fourth century, with special reference to Augustine. *M.A. 1920 London*

Urwin, G. G.
The standard of appreciation shown by the public during the conclusion of the Napoleonic War of the period of depression and insurgence, 1800-1830. *M.A. 1947 London, External Degree*

Utley, W.
The social and economic conditions of the members of the *Collegia* from Constantine to Theodosius II. *M.A. 1925 London*

Uyehara, S.
The industry and trade of Japan in modern times. *M.Sc. 1926 London*

Vaidya, R. N.
The silver market during and since the war. *M.Sc. 1923 London*

Vainstein, J.
Biblical land and property laws, with some account of their amplification in the Mishnah. *Ph.D. 1946 Glasgow*

Vajiranana, P.
Buddhist meditation according to the Pāli Canon of the Thera-Vāda School. *Ph.D. 1936 Cambridge*

Vakil, C. N.
Indian finance, 1860-1898: from the mutiny to the stabilization of exchange. *M.Sc. 1921 London*

Vakil, J. A.
An experimental investigation into the perseverative errors of school children in arithmetic. *M.Ed. 1936 Leeds*

Vakil, K. S.
Indian education and possible lines of its advancement. *M.Ed. 1923 Leeds*

Valentine, C. H.
Modern psychology and the validity of Christian experience. *Ph.D. 1926 London*

Valentine, L. E.
A critical examination of the two main versions of the Book of Job by Bishops Morgan and Parry, with special reference to the Hebraisms in these versions, together with a new translation of the book into idiomatic Welsh. *M.A. 1921 Wales*

Valentine, M. S.
A survey of the position and prospects of domestic industries in north China. *M.A. 1938 Liverpool*

Valera, R. de *see* de Valera, R.

Valerio, M. A.
John of Salisbury: a pre-Renaissance humanist. *M.A. 1946 National University of Ireland*

Vali, F. A.
International servitudes: rights in foreign territory. *Ph.D. 1932 London, School of Economics and Political Science*

Valiuddin, M.
The philosophy of Schopenhauer in relation to pragmatism, with some reference to the history of Bergson. *Ph.D. 1927 London*

Vaman Rao, V. C.
Education and the English industrial revolution. *Ph.D. 1939 Dublin, Trinity College*

van den Teorn, K.
The case for teaching economics in schools. *M.Ed. 1939 Leeds*

Van der Byl, F. V. *see* Byl, F. V. van der

Van der Horst, S. T.
The market for native labour in South Africa. *Ph.D. 1939 London, School of Economics and Political Science*

Van der Poel, J.
The railway and customs policy of the South African states and colonies. *Ph.D. 1929 London*

Van Dijk, S. J. P.
The origin of the breviary 'according to the use of the Roman Curia'. *D.Phil. 1950 Oxford*

Van Dusen, H. P.
Restatements of the moral argument for God in recent British theism. *Ph.D. 1932 Edinburgh*

van Engel, R. *see* Engel, R. van

Van Loo, G. H.
The economics of J. E. Cairnes. *M.Sc. 1938 London, University College*

Van Pittins, E. F. W. G. *see* Gey van Pittins, E. F. W.

Van Raalte, L. F. R.
The significance of Friedrich Hebbel for the German drama of the later nineteenth century. *M.A. 1922 London*

van Rensburg, J. P. J.
An introduction and commentary to Apuleius: *Metamorphosis* XI. *M.A. 1938 London, University College*

Van Santvoord, G.
The pamphlets of Greene. *B.Litt. 1917 Oxford*

Van Schaik, J. J.
Private international law of contracts on a comparative basis. *D.Phil. 1949 Oxford*

van Straelen, H. J. J. M.
Yoshida Shōin, forerunner of the Meiji restoration. *Ph.D. 1949 Cambridge*

van Zwanenberg Phillips, E. M. G.
English impressionist artists in the nineteenth century. *M.A. 1938 London, Courtauld Institute of Art*

Van Zÿl Smit, L. *see* Smit, L. van Z.

Vanshi, Y.
The cult of Rudra-Siva: an historical survey. *Ph.D. 1938 London, School of Oriental and African Studies*

Varley, B.
The history of Stockport Grammar School. *M.Ed. 1943 Manchester*

Varley, E. H.
Wakefield and district as a traditional area in the Yorkshire, Derbyshire and Nottinghamshire coalfield. *M.Sc. 1935 London, Birkbeck College*

Varley, W. J.
The origin of settlements in the Cheshire Plain: an essay in historical geography. *M.A. 1934 Wales*

Varma, G. C.
Local finance in India. *Ph.D. 1932 London, School of Economics and Political Science*

Varma, J. N.
History of the cotton industry of India. *M.Sc. 1922 London*

Varma, K. G.
Indo-Aryan loan-words in Malayalam, with a study of some Dravidian loans in Sanskrit. *Ph.D. 1934 London, School of Oriental and African Studies*

Varma, R. V. Ravi *see* Ravi Varma, R. V.

Varma, S. P.
True and false orientalism, with special reference to Hinduism and India, in the English poetry of the nineteenth century. *Ph.D. 1926 London*

Varughese, M.
A comparative study of the mental development of European and south Indian children. *M.A. 1937 London, Bedford College*

Vasiliu, V. G.
A comparative study of the Roumanian and British income tax. *Ph.D. 1932 London, School of Economics and Political Science*

Vasudevaiya, G.
The history of education in Madras, with special reference to elementary education. *M.Ed. 1939 Leeds*

Vasudevaiya, T.
The people's banks, with special reference to developments in Germany and Great Britain, together with a consideration of the value of its experience to India. *M.A. 1936 Leeds*

Vaughan, E. J.
A Vatican manuscript of the Greek fabulist Ignatius Diaconus. *M.A. 1928 London*

Vaughan, H. C.
The dramatic work of Allan Monkhouse. *M.A. 1949 Wales*

Vaughan, H. J.
The economics of production on grass and arable farms. *B.Sc. 1924 Oxford*

Vavkoukis, T. S.
The theory of adoption as found in Roman law, and its development in certain countries. *B.Litt. 1909 Oxford*

Veale, E. W.
Burgage tenure in medieval Bristol. *LL.D. 1931 London, University College*

Veinoglou, A.
Black figured skyphoi. *M.A. 1941 Reading*

Veitch, J.
The domestic relations of George Canning. *M.A. 1927 Liverpool*

Veitch, J.
George Canning and the Tory schism, 1809-1822. *Ph.D. 1932 Liverpool*

Vella, A. P.
Robert of Orford and his place in the scholastic controversies at Oxford in the late thirteenth century, with an edition of his *Reprobationes* of Giles of Rome. *B.Litt. 1946 Oxford*

Venables, E. M.
1. The experience of religion. 2. The religion of experience. *B.D. 1924 Oxford*

Vercoe-Rogers, M. S.
Climatic cycles and their influence upon human history. *M.A. 1928 London*

Verghese, P. T.
An experimental study of standardized tests for selecting secondary school pupils. *M.Ed. 1938 Leeds*

Verkinderen, A.
The position of agriculture in the Low Countries in relation to their economic union, to their wealth and welfare, and to international organization of agriculture. *B.Litt. 1948 Oxford*

Verney-Boys, J. L.
Normandy in the works of Gustave Flaubert. *M.A. 1947 London, King's College*

Vernon, P. E.
The psychology of music, with special reference to its appreciation, perception, and composition. *Ph.D. 1932 Cambridge*

Verroeulst, M. J. J.
Fuel policy in France and Great Britain. *B.Phil. 1947 Oxford*

Versfeld, M.
The cogito ergo sum: an analytic study in the metaphysics of René Descartes. *Ph.D. 1934 Glasgow*

Vesavevala, P. M.
A study of the problem of infant education. *M.Ed. 1931 Leeds*

Vévar, A. M.
Rustics and rural life in the novels of George Eliot, George Meredith and Thomas Hardy. *M.A. 1940 Wales*

Viani, M.
Antonio Fogazzaro: *Romanziere*. *M.A. 1941 National University of Ireland*

Vibart, H. H. R.
Family allowances and the compensation fund. *B.Litt. 1924 Oxford*

Vicary, T. C.
An investigation into the use of non-verbal tests of intelligence in India. *M.A. 1938 London, Institute of Education*

Vickery, K. O. A.
The place of health education in the advancement of public health. *M.D. 1947 London, St. Bartholomew's Hospital Medical College*

Vidyarthy, D. P.
Sentiment and sensibility in English prose fiction from Samuel Richardson to Ann Radcliffe, with special reference to character-delineation. *Ph.D. 1949 London, King's College*

Viljoen, S. P. du T.
Studies in economic methodology. *Ph.D. 1928 London*

Villiers, D. I. de *see* De Villiers, D. I.

Vinaver, E.
The romance of *Tristan and Iseult* in Malory's *Le Morte Darthur*: a study of the sources. *B.Litt. 1922 Oxford*

Vinay, J. P. A.
The comparative phonetics of French and the dialects of Caux and Bray. *M.A. 1937 London, University College*

Vince, S. W. E.
The utilization of Caithness, Ross and Cromarty, Perth, Argyll and the Hebrides. *M.Sc. 1947 London, School of Economics and Political Science*

Vincent, A.
Current British payments agreements. *M.Sc. 1947 London, School of Economics and Political Science*

Vincent, E. B.
A study of English natural theology in the seventeenth century, illustrating some results of the influence of the scientific spirit upon religious thought in England during the earlier years of the Royal Society. *B.Litt. 1927 Oxford*

Vincent, E. R. P.
Gabriele Rossetti in England. *D.Phil. 1933 Oxford*

Vincent, H. C.
Nature and conditions of memory progress. *M.A. 1919 Liverpool*

Vincent, H. M.
The influence of the Italian Question on Anglo-French relations, 1856-60, from the Treaty of Paris to the annexation of Savoy and Nice. *B.Litt. 1948 Oxford*

Vincent, L. M. E.
Landforms of the western slopes of the Pennines. *B.Sc. 1924 Oxford*

Vincent, W. A. L.
The State and school education, 1640-60, in England and Wales: a survey based on printed sources. *B.Litt. 1944 Oxford*

Vine, C. H.
Examination of the life and homilies of Aelfric. *B.A. 1913 Bristol*

Vine, W. E.
Literary and philosophical models and sources of the satirical writings of Horace. *M.A. 1905 London*

Vinnicombe, D. M.
The sea in French poetry from 1870 to the present day. *M.A. 1928 London*

Vinter, E.
Treatise on the law of fiduciary relationships. *LL.M. 1932 Cambridge*

Vira, R.
A critical edition of the *Kapisthala-Katha-Samhita*, first astaka. *Ph.D. 1930 London, School of Oriental and African Studies*

Vivian, D. W. F. St. C.
A study of the private and political life of General Paoli during his thirty years' exile in England. *M.Litt. 1948 Cambridge*

Vohra, D. N.
Some critical problems of Australian federalism. *M.Sc. 1934 London, School of Economics and Political Science*

Voil, W. H. de
The origin and history of the Old Catholic group of churches, their doctrinal and liturgical position; and the development of their relations with other non-papal communions. *Ph.D. 1937 Edinburgh*

Vollans, E. C.
The county borough of Derby in relation to the surrounding region. *B.Litt. 1949 Oxford*

Volpi, E.
Manzoni. *M.A. 1941 National University of Ireland*

Von dem Knesebeck, G.-L.
The progress of land settlement in England since 1892, with an historical introduction. *B.Litt. 1935 Oxford*

Von Hirsch, D. *see* Hirsch, D. von

von Leyden, W.
The ideas of time and history in the development of thought up to the end of the eighteenth century. *D.Phil. 1944 Oxford*

Vorontzoff, T.
The sources of book V of Malory's *Morte d'Arthur* and his treatment of them. *B.Litt. 1936 Oxford*

Vos, S. M.
Three religious moralists. *M.Litt. 1950 Cambridge*

Vosper, E. F.
The history of the study of Spanish in England from 1500 to 1808. *B.Litt. 1926 Oxford*

Vrooman, F. B.
The economic geography of north-west Canada with special reference to the agricultural possibilities. *B.Sc. 1910 Oxford*

Vyas, M. T.
Ancient Indian education. *M.A. 1926 London*

Wace, H.
1. On the import of the controversy respecting the historical character of the Gospels. 2. On the present state of the controversy. *B.D. 1882 Oxford*

Waddell, H. C.
The 'common' or Hellenistic Greek in the light of recent research. *M.A. 1921 Belfast*

Waddell, W. G.
The traditional estimate of Menander, as affected by the discovery of the new fragments. *M.A. 1914 London*

Waddy, C.
An introduction to the chronicle called *Muffaril al Kutub li Akhbar Bani Ayyub* by Jamal ad Din b. Wasi. *Ph.D. 1934 London, School of Oriental and African Studies*

Wade, G.
The contribution of Francis Bacon to religious and ethical thought. *M.A. 1944 Leeds*

Wade, G. I.
Thomas Traherne and his circle: a literary and biographical study. *Ph.D. 1933 London, University College*

Wade, G. W.
1. The leading methods of Old Testament prophecy. 2. The teaching of the prophets in regard to Jehovah's relation to Israel. *B.D. & D.D. 1901 Oxford*

Wade, M. M.
The personal disputes between Henry III and Simon and Eleanor de Montfort. *B.Litt. 1939 Oxford*

Wade, W. W.
Public opinion in international relations. *M.Sc. 1948 London, School of Economics and Political Science*

Wadman, D. C.
The Anglo-French and Anglo-Belgian military and naval conversations from the *Entente* to the Great War. *M.A. 1939 Wales*

Wadsworth, G. C.
The General Assembly of 1610: a critical investigation. *Ph.D. 1930 Edinburgh*

Waechter, J.
The Mesolithic age in the Middle East. *Ph.D. 1949 Cambridge*

Wagle, N. M.
Recent progress of central banking in the British Empire. *M.Sc. 1937 London, School of Economics and Political Science*

Wagner, G.
Psychological factors in saving and spending. *M.A. 1939 London, University College*

Wagner, M. J. M.
Quintus of Smyrna. *M.A. 1932 London, University College*

Wagstaff, E.
The political aspect of the South Sea bubble. *M.A. 1934 London, University College*

Waidson, H. M.
F. M. Klinger's attitude to religion. *M.A. 1938 Birmingham*

Wain, W. A.
A study in comparative literature, based on the works of S. Daniel, J. du Bellay. *M.A. 1921 Birmingham*

Wainwright, F. T.
Edward the Elder and the Danes. *Ph.D. 1944 Reading*

Wainwright, G. A.
The Keftiu-people of the Egyptian monuments. *B.Litt. 1914 Oxford*

Wainwright, G. A.
Meydum and Memphis: the formula in the light of mythology. *B.A. 1911 Bristol*

Waite, A.
Perceptual ability of defective children. *M.A. 1938 London, King's College*

Waite, H.
Association of fingerprints. *D.Sc. 1915 London*

Waites, J. A.
An enquiry into the attitudes of adults in a Lancashire urban area towards property. *M.A. 1944 Manchester*

Waites, J. A.
The place of property in English culture. *Ph.D. 1946 Manchester*

Wake, W. C.
Greek medicine in the fifth and fourth centuries B.C. *M.Sc. 1946 London, External Degree*

Wakefield, G. P.
The construction of Joseph Conrad's novels and stories. *M.A. 1950 Liverpool*

Wakefield, M. E.
Ownership in relation to character. *M.A. 1917 London*

Wakefield, W.
A regional geography of North Wiltshire. *M.Sc. 1944 Bristol*

Wakefield-Richmond, M. V.
The life and works of Mrs. Aphra Behn, with a special study of *Oroonoko. B.Litt. 1949 Oxford*

Wakelam, B. B.
The backward child in the elementary school. *M.A. 1942 Birmingham*

Walden, R. W. L.
An evaluation of the position of regional and other studies in geography in the curricula envisaged for the three main streams in secondary education in England and Wales. *M.A. 1949 Wales*

Wales, A. E.
The life and work of Smithson Tennant M.D., F.R.S., 1761-1815, with an account of some aspects of eighteenth and early nineteenth century science. *M.Sc. 1940 Leeds*

Wales, A.E.
The life and work of Sir Jonathan Hutchinson, 1828-1913, with an account of his family biography and of some aspects of nineteenth century life and thought, particularly in science and medicine. *Ph.D. 1948 Leeds*

Wales, F. H.
1. Prophecy in the Christian Church. 2. The evolution of the episcopate. *B.D. 1897 Oxford*

Wales, H. G. Q.
Siamese state ceremonies: their history and function. *Ph.D. 1932 London, School of Economics and Political Science*

Waley, D. P.
Medieval Orvieto: the political history of an Italian city state, 1157-1334. *Ph.D. 1950 Cambridge*

Walford, A. J.
Buenos Aires and the Argentine Confederation, 1852-1861. *M.A. 1934 London, Birkbeck College*

Walford, A. J.
The political career of Bartolome Mitre, 1852-1891. *Ph.D. 1940 London, University College*

Walford, E. O.
Law of ratification. *LL.D. 1932 London, External Degree*

Waligorski, A. O.
The language of suggestion, magic and propaganda. *Ph.D. 1938 London, School of Economics and Political Science*

Walker, A.
The history of the manufacture of sulphuric acid up to 1860. *M.Sc. 1934 London, University College*

Walker, A.
Studies in the works of Thomas Lodge. *Ph.D. 1926 London*

Walker, A. J.
J. J. Rousseau et son influence dans l'enseignement pratique, surtout en France et en Angleterre. *M.A. 1906 Birmingham*

Walker, A. S.
Napoleon III and Russia. *M.A. 1917 Birmingham*

Walker, B.
A study of Tacitus' motives and techniques in the writing of the *Annals. M.A. 1947 Manchester*

Walker, C. H.
Unit trusts. *Ph.D. 1938 London, School of Economics and Political Science*

Walker, C. T. H.
Manilius. *B.Litt. 1902 Oxford*

Walker, D.
1. The date of St. Luke's Gospel and the Acts of the Apostles. 2. St. Paul's visits to Jerusalem recorded in the Acts and in the Epistle to the Galatians. *B.D. 1901 Oxford*

Walker, D.
Expositions of: Acts ii.4: ἤρξαντο λαλεῖν ετέραισ γλώσσαισ; the gift of tongues; Romans iii.25: ὃν προέθετο ο θεὸσ ιλαστήριον διά τησ πίστεωσ εν τω αυτου αἵματι: the meaning of ιλαστήριον; Galatians iii.15: the legal terminology of the Epistle to the Galatians and its bearing on the question of the churches addressed by St. Paul. *D.D. 1904 Oxford*

Walker, D. A.
A theoretical and experimental study of the nature and extent of predetermination of score-scatter by the type of test-paper used. *Ph.D. 1937 Edinburgh*

Walker, D. P.
French verse in classical metres, and the music to which it was set, of the last quarter of the sixteenth century. *D.Phil. 1940 Oxford*

Walker, E.
The development of communications in Glamorgan, with special reference to the growth of industry between 1760 and 1840. *M.A. 1947 Wales*

Walker, E. C.
The history of enthusiasm as a factor in the religious and social problems of the eighteenth century. *Ph.D. 1930 London, King's College*

Walker, E. R.
Unemployment and depression in Australia, 1929-32. *Ph.D. 1933 Cambridge*

Walker, F.
The historical geography of southwest Lancashire prior to the Industrial Revolution. *M.A. 1937 Liverpool*

Walker, F. A.
Exegeses of: Revelation i.1-4; Romans iv.1-3; I Corinthians x.16. *D.D. 1883 Oxford*

Walker, F. A.
1. On holy baptism. 2. On episcopal government. *B.D. 1879 Oxford*

Walker, F. B.
Political opinion in the north of England, 1780-1837. *M.A. 1913 Belfast*

Walker, J.
The influence of geographical factors on the economic evolution of Scotland to the beginning of the eighteenth century, mainly as revealed in the development of overseas trade, especially that of the Clyde ports. *Ph.D. 1928 Edinburgh*

Walker, J.
The Republican Party in England from the Restoration to the Revolution, 1660-1688. *Ph.D. 1931 Manchester*

Walker, J. C.
The early history of the Presbyterian church in western Canada from the earliest times to the year 1881. *Ph.D. 1928 Edinburgh*

Walker, J. M.
1. The origin and development of the Apostles' Creed. 2. The real meaning of the Arian controversy. *B.D. & D.D. 1914 Oxford*

Walker, L. J.
Cognition: its psychological analysis, its metaphysical conditions, and its epistemological value. *M.A. 1909 London*

Walker, N. M. T.
The educational ideas of Herbert Spencer. *Ph.D. 1929 Glasgow*

Walker, O. H.
Life of George Wishart. *Ph.D. 1924 Edinburgh*

Walker, P. C. Gordon *see* Gordon Walker, P. C.

Walker, R. F.
Le vocabulaire d'Alphonse de Châteaubriant. *M.A. 1936 Leeds*

Walker, W. C.
1. The beginnings of the scientific career of Joseph Priestley. 2. The detection and estimation of electric charges in the eighteenth century. 3. Animal electricity before Galvani. *Ph.D. 1937 London, University College*

Walker, W. C.
The electro-chemical researches of Sir Humphrey Davy. *M.Sc. 1929 London*

Walker, W. H. T.
The Norfolk Rising under Robert Kett, 1549. *M.A. 1921 Wales*

Walkley, G.
William Wilkins, R. A. *M.Litt. 1939 Cambridge*

Wall, T.
Academic writings of Irish exiles in the seventeenth century. *Ph.D. 1943 National University of Ireland*

Wall, W. D.
The adolescent child, the newspaper reading of adolescents and adults during the War, and five other papers. *Ph.D. 1947 Birmingham*

Wallace, H. M.
Foreign influences on Scottish politics, 1578-1582. *M.A. 1932 London, Westfield College*

Wallace, J. P.
A history and survey of the road-transport operations of the British railways. *M.A. 1947 Wales*

Wallace, R. L.
The articles of the Church of Ireland of 1615. *Ph.D. 1949 Edinburgh*

Wallace, R. N. R.
Fluctuations of attention and the perception of meaning. *M.A. 1935 London, University College*

Wallas, M. G.
Luc de Clapiers, Marquis de Vauvenargues (1715-1747). *Ph.D. 1926 London*

Wallbank, A. M. M.
The origin of the Independents in the reign of Elizabeth. *M.A. 1927 Birmingham*

Wallenstein, A.
Some unpublished Hebrew poems of the fifteenth and sixteenth centuries forming part of the Montefiore collection of manuscripts, transcribed, translated and annotated. *M.A. 1941 Manchester*

Wallenstein, M.
Ancient Hebrew poetry as illustrated by a ms. of the seventeenth century from the *Cairo Genizah. Ph.D. 1938 Manchester*

Waller, C. H.
1. The true interpretation of Genesis i. and ii.1-4.
2. The meaning of 'the generations of the heavens and the earth' in Genesis ii.4. *B.D. & D.D. 1891 Oxford*

Wallis, C. B.
The work and policy of the United States in Panama. *M.Litt. 1939 Cambridge*

Wallis, E. W.
The Church in Shetland during the sixteenth and seventeenth centuries. *Ph.D. 1940 Edinburgh*

Wallis, W. D.
The conditions psychological and sociological of the development of individuality amongst peoples of rudimentary culture. *B.Sc. 1910 Oxford*

Walls, W. B.
The effect of six months' instruction in school subjects on some mental factors of adults. *M.Ed. 1945 Leeds*

Walmsley, D. M.
The development of dramatic opera in England. *Ph.D. 1928 London*

Walmsley, D. M.
A study of Thomas Shadwell. *M.A. 1924 London*

Walmsley, W. G.
A linguistic study of the Tournay charters acquired by the British Museum in 1914. *M.A. 1921 London*

Walpole, K. A.
Emigration to British North America under the early Passenger Acts, 1803-1842. *M.A. 1929 London*

Walpole, R. N.
La tradition manuscrite et la phonétique des principaux textes de la version Johannis de *La Chronique de Turpin*. *M.A. 1936 Wales*

Walsh, D.
Victorian drama as the reflection of the age. *M.A. 1942 National University of Ireland*

Walsh, H. E.
An outline of the history of education in Bradford before 1870. *M.Ed. 1936 Leeds*

Walsh, J. A.
The old German elements in the poems of Ludwig Uhland. *M.A. 1918 National University of Ireland*

Walsh, J. E.
Climatic variation in the Argentine, with special reference to problems of climatic classification. *M.Sc. 1934 London, Birkbeck College*

Walsh, J. J.
Employment and unemployment in the 26 counties. *M.Econ.Sc. 1941 National University of Ireland*

Walsh, M.
Philip Massinger. *M.A. 1931 National University of Ireland*

Walsh, P.
Ancient history of Dunlavin. *M.A. 1926 National University of Ireland*

Walsh, R.
Anglo-Norman literature in Leinster, 1170-1570. *Ph.D. 1941 National University of Ireland*

Walsh, R. B.
Irish maritime development. *M.Econ.Sc. 1946 National University of Ireland*

Walsh, T.
A further study of volitional frustration in respect of uncompleted tasks. *Ph.D. 1942 London, King's College*

Walsh, T.
On the memory of completed and uncompleted tasks: a study of volitional frustration. *M.A. 1940 London, King's College*

Walsh, T. F.
Character: an essay on natural ethics. *M.A. 1914 National University of Ireland*

Walsh, T. V.
Some principles involved in the teaching of handwork, with special reference to the junior school. *M.A. 1941 Leeds*

Walsh, W.
The idea of the state and its realisation. *M.A. 1936 National University of Ireland*

Walshaw, R. S.
Changes in the trend and distribution of our school population, and their effects on education. *M.Ed. 1940 Manchester*

Walshaw, R. S.
Population movements in the British Isles since 1921. *M.A. 1937 Liverpool*

Walshe, M. O'C.
Travel descriptions in Middle High German Arthurian epics. *M.A. 1935 London, University College*

Walshe, P. T.
Irish education since the union, a historical and critical study. *Ph.D. 1928 Dublin, Trinity College*

Walter, J. H.
An edition of the *Launching of the Mary*. *M.A. 1930 London, University College*

Walter, J. H.
The plays and poems of Henry Glapthorne, with a biography and critical apparatus. *Ph.D. 1935 London, University College*

Walters, A. C. D.
A study of English dramatic criticism during the period 1870-1900, with special reference to the work of Bernard Shaw, William Archer, A. B. Walkley, and H. A. Jones. *M.A. 1944 Wales*

Walters, D. E.
Vavasor Powell (1617-1670): an account of his life, with special reference to religious movements in Wales in his time. *M.A. 1933 Liverpool*

Walters, D. E.
The Wisdom literature of the Hebrews. *M.A. 1903 Wales*

Walters, E. H.
Retentivity in the special senses. *Ph.D. 1929 London*

Walters, G.
The doctrine of the Holy Spirit in John Calvin. *Ph.D. 1949 Edinburgh*

Walters, M.
Francis Bacon and the theory and practice of formal rhetoric. *D.Phil. 1940 Oxford*

Walters, M.
The literary and rhetorical background of Francis Bacon as an English man of letters. *M.A. 1938 London, Royal Holloway College*

Walters, R. H.
The sources and nature of the thought of Henry Vaughan. *M.A. 1946 Bristol*

Walters, W. E.
British foreign policy in the Near East, 1903-1909, with special reference to projects for the internal reform of the Ottoman Empire. *M.A. 1937 Wales*

Walters, W. J.
The reconstruction of the iron, steel and tinplate industries of south Wales since the war. *M.A. 1928 Wales*

Walton, E. M.
The gold standard in South Africa, a gold-producing country, 1920-34. *B.Litt. 1943 Oxford*

Walton, F. T.
An examination of the supernormal psychical phenomena recorded in Latin literature. *M.A. 1934 Birmingham*

Walton, G.
The English writings of Abraham Cowley. *M.Litt. 1939 Cambridge*

Walton, J. K.
E. M. Forster. *B.Litt. 1944 Dublin, Trinity College*

Walton, L. B.
Galdós as creator of the modern Spanish novel. *B.Litt. 1926 Oxford*

Walton, P. C.
A geography of the East Anglican herring fishery. *M.A. 1948 London, King's College*

Walwyn, A. F.
A study of the learning process. *M.A. 1921 London*

Wang, C. S.
The village school and rural reconstruction in China. *M.A. 1941 London, Institute of Education*

Wang, D.
The judicial system of Fascist Italy. *Ph.D. 1939 London, School of Economics and Political Science*

Wang, H. K.
The incorporate person. *Ph.D. 1941 London, University College*

Wang, P. H.
The struggle for supremacy in the Pacific. *M.Sc. 1937 London, School of Economics and Political Science*

Wang, S. T.
The Margary Affair and the Convention of Chefoo. *B.Litt. 1938 Oxford*

Wang, T. L.
The literary reputation of John Webster to 1830. *B.Litt. 1949 Oxford*

Wanklin, G. I.
Quelques aspects de Maurice Maeterlinck. *M.A. 1928 Birmingham*

Wanklyn, C. A.
The novels of D. H. Lawrence: a critical study. *M.A. 1950 Sheffield*

Wanning, A.
Some changes in the prose style of the seventeenth century. *Ph.D. 1938 Cambridge*

Warburton, F. W.
Influence of rest pauses on fluctuations of mental output. *Ph.D. 1945 London, University College*

Warburton, F. W.
Influence of short rest pauses on fluctuations in mental output. *M.A. 1938 London, University College*

Warburton, W. H.
The economic ideas of the urban industrial working class of England during the years 1800-1850. *M.Com. 1939 Birmingham*

Warburton, W. H.
The progress of labour organization in the pottery industry of Great Britain. *B.Litt. 1928 Oxford*

Ward, A. E. S.
1. Indirect proofs of the Resurrection. 2. The influence of dissent upon the Church of England. *B.D. & D.D. 1924 Oxford*

Ward, B. E.
The social organization of the Ewe-speaking people: an analytical and comparative study. *M.A. 1948 London, School of Economics and Political Science*

Ward, B. J.
An initial study of Quintilian's theory of education. *M.A. 1943 National University of Ireland*

Ward, D.
The medieval lordship of Montgomery. *M.A. 1924 Wales*

Ward, D. F.
Correlation between increase in amplitude and decrement in work curves. *M.Sc. 1939 London, University College*

Ward, E.
Vittorio Alfieri's influence and reputation in France and England. *M.A. 1932 Manchester*

Ward, F. E.
The artistic method of Thomas Hardy, novelist. *M.A. 1921 Birmingham*

Ward, F. M.
Richard Locke: a record of a strenuous life. *M.A. 1937 Bristol*

Ward, J. G. S.
The activities of Spain on the Pacific Coast of South America, and her war with the 'Confederation of the Andes' (Chile, Peru, Bolivia and Ecuador), 1860-1886. *Ph.D. 1939 London, Birkbeck College*

Ward, J. N.
Christian moral judgment: an enquiry into the character of Christian moral judgment as evidenced by a study of St. Paul's conception of the relation between law and gospel. *M.A. 1944 Manchester*

Ward, K. M.
Grace O'Malley: a 16th century heroine of the province of Connaught. *M.A. 1934 National University of Ireland*

Ward, L. E.
A geographical study of the expansion of Japan in relation to the Japanese population problem. *M.A. 1932 Liverpool*

Ward, M. J. Barrington- see Barrington-Ward, M. J.

Ward, P. J.
Madame de Genlis, educationist. *Ph.D. 1934 Cambridge*

Ward, R. A.
Aristotelian antecedents in the philosophical vocabulary of the New Testament. *M.A. 1946 London, Birkbeck College*

Ward, R. A.
Aristotelian usages in the philosophical vocabulary of the New Testament. *Ph.D. 1949 London, Birkbeck College*

Ward, R. M. C.
The headship of Jesus Christ as taught and vindicated by the Reformed Presbyterian Church in North America in relation to civil government. *Ph.D. 1939 Edinburgh*

Ward, S. M.
Ausdrucksverstärkung im Mittelhochdeutschen: mit besonderer Berücksichtigung der Zusammensetzungen. *M.A. 1949 Birmingham*

Ward, W. C. J.
The proper scope of quantitative work in science in secondary schools, with particular reference to chemistry. *M.A. 1927 London*

Ward, W. E. F.
The antecedents of the political and ecclesiastical ideas of Arnold of Brescia and his relation to the civic movement in Italy. *B.Litt. 1924 Oxford*

Ward, W. J.
1. On the disputed verses, I John v.7,8. 2. On the Incarnation. *B.D. 1904 Oxford*

Wardale, W. L.
Albrecht van Borgunnien's treatise on medicine and its sources. *M.A. 1927 Liverpool*

Wardle, F.
Matthew Arnold and Walter Pater: a study in critical attitudes. *M.A. 1940 Manchester*

Wardman, H. W.
Aesthetic of Renan. *Ph.D. 1949 London, University College*

Wardman, O.
Le théâtre naturaliste: origin and development. *Ph.D. 1930 London, External Degree*

Wardrop, C. W. I.
The doctrine of atonement in Coleridge and Maurice. *Ph.D. 1932 Edinburgh*

Ware, C. S.
A study of the sublime, with special reference to the theory of Edmund Burke. *M.A. 1949 Wales*

Wareham, K.
The early historical geography of Lindsey. *M.A. 1919 Liverpool*

Warhadpande, N. R.
A new approach to the problem of individual differences, abilities and types, and their bearing on educational methods and systems. *B.Litt. 1949 Oxford*

Warman, F. S. G.
1. Romans iii.21-26: the doctrine of the atonement in St. Paul. 2. Romans iii.24-25; I Timothy ii.6: propitiation, redemption, reconciliation, ransom, justification. 3. Luke xvi.1-13: parable of the unrighteous steward. *D.D. 1911 Oxford*

Warman, F. S. G.
1. The Virgin birth of the Lord Jesus Christ. 2. The person of our Lord and the kenotic theory. *B.D. 1907 Oxford*

Warner, F. M.
Shakespeare on the modern English stage. *Ph.D. 1928 London*

Warner, L. E.
Devolution in industry: an enquiry into the scale of production in the boot and shoe manufacturing industry. *M.Com. 1925 Birmingham*

Warner, T. E.
The influence of Jewish eschatology upon the New Testament. *B.Litt. 1939 Dublin, Trinity College*

Warner, W. J.
The humanitarian movement in England in the eighteenth century, with special reference to the relation between the revival in religious life and industrial change: a study in the sociology of religion. *Ph.D. 1929 London*

Warren, A. H.
Richard Hengist Horne: a literary biography. *B.Litt. 1939 Oxford*

Warren, F. E.
1. Pelagianism. 2. Recent attempts to establish undogmatic Christianity in India. *B.D. 1873 Oxford*

Warren, J. H.
Local public utilities in relation to local government. *M.A. 1936 Liverpool*

Warren, L. M.
The drainage of the Fens and its effects upon the parishes of the south divison of the Bedford level, 1600-1850. *M.A. 1927 London*

Warren, R. P.
A study of John Marston's satires, 1598-9. *B.Litt. 1930 Oxford*

Warriner, D.
Combination in German industries, 1924-1928. *Ph.D. 1930 London, School of Economics and Political Science*

Warrington, S.
A national employment service: Great Britain's experience. *M.Sc. 1947 London, External Degree*

Warting, W. K.
The effects of war conditions on elementary education in the Borough of Altrincham. *M.Ed. 1943 Manchester*

Washbrook, M. A.
The history and criticism of the theory of acquired characteristics. *M.Sc. 1929 London*

Washington, G. T.
The measure of damages in actions for breach of mercantile contract. *B.Litt. 1930 Oxford*

Washington, J. H.
Education in the Union of South Africa. *Ph.D. 1924 London*

Washington, J. H.
The unification of South Africa, 1806-1909. *M.Sc. 1921 London*

Wason, M. O.
A study of the conditions which led to the Athenian and Spartan tyrannies, and the effect of these tyrannies on the foreign policy of other states. *Ph.D. 1946 Glasgow*

Wastell, R. E. P.
British imperial policy in relation to Madagascar, 1810-1896. *Ph.D. 1944 London, King's College*

Wastell, R. E. P.
History of slave compensation, 1833-45. *M.A. 1933 London, King's College*

Waterfield, R.
1. The Resurrection of Christ. 2. The Virgin Birth of Christ. *B.D. & D.D. 1924 Oxford*

Waterman, F. E. *see* Schonell, F. E.

Waters, S.
The social history of Wakefield and neighbourhood in the seventeenth century. *M.A. 1932 Leeds*

Waters, S. D. M.
A study of the chemistries of Lemery, Freind, Baume, and Watson, and of the development of chemical thought from 1675 to 1787. *M.Sc. 1931 London*

Waters, W. H.
The Edwardian settlement of North Wales. *M.Litt. 1926 Cambridge*

Waters, W. H.
Transport and communication in medieval Wales. *M.A. 1923 Wales*

Waterson, A.
A study of the work and methods of Henry Briggs with special reference to the theory of interpolation. *Ph.D. 1941 Saint Andrew's*

Waterson, N. M.
Mary II of England and her life during the years 1689-1694: influence on politics, on the Anglican Church, and on society. *B.Litt. 1925 Oxford*

Waterson, N. M.
Some aspects of social and political life in England during the nineteenth century in relation to contemporary theory. *M.A. 1921 Birmingham*

Watkin, E. E.
The development of the south Wales tinplate industry, with special reference to 1919-1939. *M.A. 1949 Wales*

Watkin Jones, A.
Political ideas in Wales during the latter half of the eighteenth century as reflected in ballad literature. *B.Litt. 1926 Oxford*

Watkin, M.
Ystorya *Bown o Hamtwn*. *M.A. 1913 Wales*

Watkin, W. R.
Poems of Bedo Brwynllys. *M.A. 1909 Wales*

Watkin-Jones, H.
The Holy Spirit from Arminius to Wesley. *D.D. 1929 Cambridge*

Watkins, D. H.
The West Penwith Peninsula of Cornwall, considered from the point of view of archaeological evidences concerning development of settlements. *M.A. 1930 Wales*

Watkins, E. R. L.
The demarcation of industries. *M.Com. 1931 Birmingham*

Watkins, G. D.
A geographical study of Madras City. *M.Sc. 1929 London*

Watkins, I. M.
Welsh blood groups: a contribution to the anthropology of the Welsh people. *M.Sc. 1946 Wales*

Watkins, J. H.
Michault Taillevent: poet of fifteenth-century Burgundy. *M.A. 1948 Wales*

Watkins, S. H.
The rise of English literary criticism. *M.A. 1907 Wales*

Watkins, W. B. C.
Johnson's knowledge of English poetry before 1650. *B.Litt. 1931 Oxford*

Watkins, W. J. H.
The literature of travel from 1350-1750. *M.A. 1919 Wales*

Watson, A.
The early iconography of the Tree of Jesse. *Ph.D. 1935 London, External Degree*

Watson, C. S.
The rationale of the rules of evidence, being an enquiry into the basis and development of the principal rules of evidence in English law, with a few suggestions for reform. *LL.D. 1917 London*

Watson, D. W. H.
Lord Herbert of Cherbury: a study of his personality and writings. *M.A. 1950 Liverpool*

Watson, H. A.
The nature of man. *D.D. 1911 Cambridge*

Watson, I.
Stoicism and Wordsworth. *M.A. 1911 Birmingham*

Watson, J. A.
British extraterritorial jurisdiction. *LL.D. 1927 London*

Watson, J. E.
The educational activities of Baptists in England during the eighteenth and nineteenth centuries with particular reference to the Northwest. *M.A. 1947 Liverpool*

Watson, K.
Obstetrical difficulties of a recently qualified doctor, with some observations on the teaching of obstetrics to undergraduates. *M.D. 1941 Dublin, Trinity College*

Watson, L.
A comparison between the tragedies and histories of Shakespeare with special reference to the heroes. *M.A. 1910 Birmingham*

Watson, L.
Modern theories of the fall of man and original sin. *M.Litt. 1949 Durham*

Watson, M.
The theme of flying in German literature. *M.A. 1939 London, Birkbeck College*

Watson, T. J.
A history of deaf education in Scotland, 1760-1939. *Ph.D. 1949 Edinburgh*

Watson, W. C.
The place and teaching of English in early adolescence. *M.A. 1914 Liverpool*

Watt, W. M.
Free will and predestination in early Islam. *Ph.D. 1944 Edinburgh*

Watt, W. M.
Kant's view of the relation between theology and ethics. *B.Litt. 1933 Oxford*

Watters, A. C.
History of the British Churches of Christ. *Ph.D. 1940 Edinburgh*

Wattie, M.
The pronouns and pronominal adjectives in early Scots down to 1603. *B.Litt. 1927 Oxford*

Watts, A. F.
The contribution of abnormal psychology to the problems of normal education. *M.A. 1917 London*

Watts, A. H.
A dissertation on trade routes of the province of Asia Minor within the first three centuries of the Christian era. *Ph.D. 1926 London*

Watts, A. H.
Travel in Italy in the first century before Christ. *M.A. 1915 London*

Watts, C. E. N.
A comparative study of secondary education in two rural areas, considered in relation to the social and economic backgrounds, and the educational progress and subsequent careers of the pupils. *M.Sc. 1946 Wales*

Watts, M.
The characterization of women in Plautus and Terence and the fragments of Menander. *M.A. 1919 London*

Watts, W. T.
A comparative study of the effects of auditory and other distractions on the output and accuracy in simple addition. *M.A. 1938 London, Institute of Education*

Way, A. G.
The character and sources of the legends connected with the House of Atreus. *M.A. 1935 London, King's College*

Way, J. P.
1. The re-union of the Christian Church, viewed under some of its present aspects. 2. Man in God's image as revealed in Scripture. *B.D. & D.D. 1896 Oxford*

Wayper, C. L.
The relations between Great Britain and Austria-Hungary from the rising in Herzegovina to the Conference of Constantinople. *Ph.D. 1950 Cambridge*

Weale, M. M.
Chapman's method of translating Homer: being studies in books I, II, and XVIII of the *Iliad*, and book V of the *Odyssey*. *M.A. 1920 London*

Wearmouth, R. F.
Methodism and the working classes of England (1800-1850). *Ph.D. 1935 London, School of Economics and Political Science*

Wearmouth, R. F.
Methodism from the death of Wesley, 1791, to the Wesleyan centenary, 1839. *M.A. 1928 Birmingham*

Weatherhead, J. F.
The history of the trade unions in the Yorkshire woollen and worsted industries during the nineteenth and twentieth centuries. *B.Litt. 1925 Oxford*

Weatherhead, L. D.
The contribution of Victorian poets to the development of the idea of immortality. *M.A. 1926 Manchester*

Weaver, F. J.
The Constable de Bourbon. *M.A. 1906 London*

Webb, B.
De imperii civilis origine. *M.A. 1750 Glasgow*

Webb, C. D.
Voiture and the Hôtel de Rambouillet: a study of the brilliant period of the *esprit précieux*. *M.A. 1905 London*

Webb, E.
Character and intelligence: an attempt at an exact study of character. *D.Sc. 1914 London*

Webb, E. M.
L'analyse d'un échec; étude sur le journal intime d'Henri-Frédéric Amiel. *M.A. 1942 Birmingham*

Webb, E. W.
The relation of certain factors of imagery and immediate memory to geometrical ability. *M.A. 1949 London, Institute of Education*

Webb, H.
A consideration of certain aspects of teaching arithmetic. *M.A. 1945 Bristol*

Webb, J. H.
1. The use and importance of the Old Testament in the first two centuries. 2. The first Epistle of Clement critically and dogmatically examined, with special reference to the Old Testament. *B.D. & D.D. 1907 Oxford*

Webb, M. E.
A comparison between the geographical bases of the rural economic life of the Vale of White Horse and that of the White Horse Hills. *B.Litt. 1936 Oxford*

Webb, M. P.
The life and poetry of Tyutchev. *Ph.D. 1927 London*

Webb, S.
The training of women teachers in British India. *M.A. 1930 London, King's College*

Webber, K.
Heine's imagery, in its relation to his personality and thought. *D.Phil. 1943 Oxford*

Webster, A.
Thackeray's attitude towards the society of his time, as revealed in his writings of 1836-1847. *M.A. 1948 Manchester*

Webster, A. W.
Problems of English rural administration illustrated by the three parishes of St. Mary Cray, St. Paul's Cray and Orpington, Kent. *M.Sc. 1922 London*

Webster, C. J.
The development of industry, agriculture and transport in the Soviet Arctic and sub-Arctic north of 60 degrees. *M.A. 1949 London, School of Slavonic and East European Studies*

Webster, C. M.
Dr. Robert South. *B.D. 1951 Oxford*

Webster, D. A. R. H.
The reception of Thomas Mann in England and America, a critical study. *M.A. 1940 London, University College*

Webster, H. E.
John Hawkesworth: a biography and a critical study of his work in the periodicals. *M.A. 1949 London, Birkbeck College*

Webster, M. G. A.
Roman villas in Britain: their nature and distribution. *M.A. 1920 Liverpool*

Webster, W.
A thesis on re-organization in rural elementary education, based on independent observation and study, 1924-1928. *M.Ed. 1928 Leeds*

Wechsler, A.
Descartes' world, or Treatise on light. *M.Sc. 1931 London*

Wecter, D.
The family correspondence of David Garrick. *B.Litt. 1929 Oxford*

Wedeck, J.
Ability to estimate character. *Ph.D. 1933 London, University College*

Weeks, E. J.
Some tests of disposition. *M.A. 1927 London*

Weeks, E. P.
Methods of government control of agriculture in New Zealand, the United States of America, Italy, and Germany. *D.Phil. 1940 Oxford*

Weeks, E. P.
Quantitative restriction of imports to Great Britain in relation to imperial trade. *B. Litt. 1936 Oxford*

Wei, F. C.
A study of the Chinese moral traditions and its social values. *Ph.D. 1929 London*

Wei, Y. S.
British diplomacy and the Anglo-Congo Treaty of 1894. *Ph.D. 1949 Cambridge*

Weil, R.
The use of lyrics in German drama. *B.Litt. 1950 Oxford*

Weil, R. W. E.
Thoman Mann's writings on Goethe (with special reference to his novel *Lotte in Weimar*. *B.Litt. 1950 Dublin, Trinity College*

Weil-Norden, P.
Shakespeare's dramatic technique in the opening scenes of his tragedies. *M.A. 1950 Birmingham*

Weinberg, A.
The influence of Auguste Comte on the economics of John Stuart Mill. *Ph.D. 1949 London, External Degree*

Weiner, A.
England and the Teutonic *Hanse*. *M.A. 1904 Wales*

Weingreen, J.
A study in ancient Hebrew education. *Ph.D. 1931 Dublin, Trinity College*

Weinrich, J. E.
A 100% reserve plan in relation to monetary theories of the trade cycle. *M.Sc. 1948 London, School of Economics and Political Science*

Weinstock, M. B.
The position of London in national affairs, 1658-1661, having special regard to political and economic aspects. *M.A. 1934 London, School of Economics and Political Science*

Weinstock, O.
Revolt and Christian orthodoxy in the German lyric since 1890. *M.A. 1949 Leeds*

Weir, A. J.
British opinion and colonial policy, 1783-1839, in particular, the origin of the ideas of the colonial reformers. *Ph.D. 1924 Edinburgh*

Weir, C. J. M.
A critical lexicon of the Accadian prayers in the rituals of expiation, with an investigation of the principles which distinguish the various series of Babylonian expiation rituals. *D.Phil. 1930 Oxford*

Weir, E. A.
Pragmatism and education: the philosophy of John Dewey. *M.A. 1943 Manchester*

Weis, P. R.
Mishnah *Horayoth*, with critical and explanatory notes. *M.A. 1942 Manchester*

Weise, R. W.
The problem of international technical assistance to China. *M.Sc. 1940 London, School of Economics and Political Science*

Weiskrantz, L.
Interaction of figural after-effects. *B.Sc. 1950 Oxford*

Weiss, H.
Aristotle's conception of chance in nature and in human life. *M.Litt. 1945 Cambridge*

Weiss, R.
Humanism in England during the fifteenth century up to 1485. *D.Phil. 1938 Oxford*

Weiss, S. J.
The economics of air transport. *Ph.D. 1938 London, School of Economics and Political Science*

Weissbruth, A.
Some aspects of the relation between Neo-Platonism and Christianity in the later Roman Empire. *M.A. 1937 London, University College*

Weisz, D.
A critical investigation into the relationship of the hermeneutical rules of the Halakah to those of the Hagadah. *M.A. 1948 Manchester*

Weisz, S. J.
A comparison of the views of Aaron ben Joseph in his *Sefer Hamibhar* and his Halakic poems with the accepted views of the Karaites and Rabbanites concerning the Sabbath and other Jewish festivals. *M.A. 1942 Manchester*

Welch, J. W.
The Isoko clans of the Niger Delta. *Ph.D. 1937 Cambridge*

Welch, P. J.
The maritime powers and the evolution of war aims of the Grand Alliance, 1701-1704. *M.A. 1940 London, University College*

Weld-Blundell, H. J.
The religious history of the Abyssinian races. *B.Litt. 1911 Oxford*

Weldon, J. M.
The treatment of causality in the philosophy of Hume. *M.A. 1930 National University of Ireland*

Wellesz, E. F.
External influences on west European art in the twelfth century, with special reference to Spain and the neighbouring countries. *B.Litt. 1948 Oxford*

Wells, B.
Walter Pater as an exponent of aestheticism. *M.A. 1950 Manchester*

Wells, E. B.
Sir Henry Vane the Elder. *M.A. 1923 Manchester*

Wells, E. N.
Kenilworth castle and priory. *M.A. 1923 Birmingham*

Wells, F. A.
The British hosiery trade: its history and organization. *Ph.D. 1931 London, School of Economics and Political Science*

Wells, G. A.
A critical examination of Herder's thought, with special reference to its parallels in Coleridge. *M.A. 1949 London, University College*

Wells, H. M.
The phenomenology of acts of choice: an analysis of volitional consciousness. *Ph.D. 1925 London*

Wells, L. St. A.
The apocryphal Gospels. *B.D. 1928 Oxford*

Wells, O. S.
The value of agricultural output in different regions. *M.Sc. 1937 Cambridge*

Wells, P. F.
The philosophy of Guillaume Apollinaire as revealed in his poetry. *M.A. 1948 Wales*

Wells, T. A. G.
An economic geography of commercialized agriculture with special reference to North America. *Ph.D. 1947 London, External Degree*

Welt, F.
Comparison between the divorce law of the British Commonwealth, U.S.A., and certain continental systems of law, with particular regard to the execution of foreign judgments. *Ph.D. 1941 Edinburgh*

Welton, L. J. F.
Nicolai Clenardi epistolae. *Ph.D. 1935 Liverpool*

Wenger, E. L.
The part of experience in theological knowledge. *B.D. 1947 Oxford*

Wenham, L. P.
A history of Richmond School, Yorkshire. *M.Ed. 1947 Durham*

Wensley, A. J.
The measurement and causes of the localisation of industry, with special reference to the industries of Birmingham and distric. *M.Com. 1936 Birmingham*

Wensley, J. I.
Pantheism in English poetry, with special reference to Wordsworth and Shelley. *M.A. 1917 Wales*

Wentz, W. Y. E.
The psychological nature and origin of the belief in fairies in Celtic countries. *B.Sc. 1910 Oxford*

Werner, C. G.
The problem of evil in the thought of F. R. Tennant. *Ph.D. 1950 Edinburgh*

Werner, F. E. L. E. M.
George Borrow. *M.A. 1924 Birmingham*

West, C. B.
Courtoisie in Anglo-Norman literature. *Ph.D. 1936 London, Birkbeck College*

West, C. B.
The theory of translation in France in the eighteenth century. *M.Litt. 1927 Cambridge*

West, F.
The Principal Navigations, Voyages, Traffiques, and Discoveries of the English Nation, by Richard Hakluyt. *M.A. 1927 Liverpool*

West, G.
A study of the life and works of William Julius Mickle, translator of *The Lusiad* (1734-1788). *M.A. 1932 London, King's College*

West, G. H.
1. On the subservience of evil to the purposes of God. 2. On the office of the Holy Spirit as the perfector of the works of God the Father. *B.D. & D.D. 1889 Oxford*

West, H. W.
The social and religious thought of Charles Kingsley and his place in the English Christian Socialist Movement of 1848-54. *Ph.D. 1947 Edinburgh*

West, J. C.
The authorship of the Johannine literature. *B.D. 1926 Oxford*

West, J. H.
The primitive conception of worship. *M.A. 1945 Leeds*

West, J. R.
A critical edition of the twelfth century sections of Cott. ms. Galba E ii (register of the Abbey of St. Benet of Holme). *Ph.D. 1927 London*

West, M. P.
The position of English in a national system of education for Bengal. *D.Phil. 1927 Oxford*

Westall, E.
Sully: l'homme et son oeuvre d'aprés *Les économies royales*. *M.A. 1947 Liverpool*

Westburgh, E. M.
Personality analysis from the clinical point of view. *Ph.D. 1933 Edinburgh*

Westbury-Jones, J.
Fate, determinism and free will in religion and philosophy. *D.D. 1936 Oxford*

Westcott, I. M.
A study of the fictitious element in the seventeenth century pamphlet literature. *B.Litt. 1925 Oxford*

Western, W.
The administration of the city and county borough of Belfast. *M.A. 1944 Belfast*

Westgate, R. P. R.
The effects of volition and affective states upon muscular work. *Ph.D. 1934 London, King's College*

Westworth, O. A.
The Albion Steam Flour Mill: a chapter in the Boulton and Watt co-partnership. *M.Com. 1930 Birmingham*

Wetherill, A.
The significance of long-term persistence to successful attainment in the grammar school. *M.Ed. 1946 Leeds*

Whale, G. B. M.
The causes of the movement for radical parliamentary reform in England, between 1763 and 1789, with special reference to the influence of the so-called Rational Protestants. *B.Litt. 1930 Oxford*

Whale, P. B.
The German credit banks and the money market 1900-1914. *M.Com. 1924 Birmingham*

Whalley, W.
An historical account of Catholic education in England, with special reference to educational activities in the Salford diocese. *M.Ed. 1938 Manchester*

Whalley, W.
Slavery and its abolition, particularly with regard to England's efforts for its extinction to the year 1846, and with especial reference to the West Indies. *M.A. 1926 Manchester*

Wharam, M. E.
The economic effects of the taxation of business reserves, with particular reference to allowances for depreciation and obsolescence. *M.A. 1931 Birmingham*

Wharhirst, G. E.
The Reformation in the diocese of Lincoln as illustrated by the life and work of Bishop Longland (1521-47). *B. Litt. 1938 Oxford*

Wheble, C. L.
The London lighterage trade: its history, organisation and economics. *M.Sc. 1939 London, School of Economics and Political Science*

Wheeler, D. K.
Factors in mechanical ability in adults. *Ph.D. 1948 London, University College*

Wheeler, E. C.
An investigation into backwardness in arithmetic among London elementary school children. *M.A. 1927 London*

Wheeler, G. C. W. C.
Mono-Alu folklore. *D.Sc. 1927 London*

Wheeler, L. R.
The development of vitalistic theories in biology, especially from 1800 to 1933. *Ph.D. 1937 London, External Degree*

Wheeler, O. A.
Anthropomorphism and science: a study of the development of ejective cognition in the individual and the race. *D.Sc. 1916 London*

Wheeler, O. A.
The objective mode of cognition: its metaphysical ground, logical sphere and the modification in its use in the passage from primitive man to the positive scientist. *M.A. 1911 Wales*

Wheeler, R. E. M.
The origins of Byzantine art. *M.A. 1912 London*

Wheeler, T. B.
The seventeenth century character, with a brief sketch of its anticipations in English literature, and a bibliography of character books published in the seventeenth and eighteenth centuries. *M.A. 1911 Wales*

Wheeler, W. J.
The individual and the group in education. *M.A. 1936 Birmingham*

Whelan, J.
The 'prentice years of English poetry. *M.A. 1926 National University of Ireland*

Whelan, J. J.
Method of teaching the intermediate Latin course in secondary schools. *M.A. 1935 National University of Ireland*

Whelan, M. E.
A study of the Jesuit Mission of 1580 with particular reference to its effects on Catholicism in England. *M.A. 1927 Liverpool*

Whelan, P.
Alfred Marshall as an economist, with special reference to wages and working class. *M.Econ.Sc. 1945 National University of Ireland*

Whetwall, E. M. M.
Some essential conditions of symbolism. *Ph.D. 1927 London*

Whibley, M.
Anglo-Sardinian relations: January, 1859-March, 1860. *M.A. 1923 London*

Whileblood, S. M.
Anglo-Papal relations, 1213-1216. *M.A. 1948 Manchester*

Whisker, R. F.
John, Duke of Albany, 1481-1536, servant of Scotland and France. *M.A. 1939 Liverpool*

Whitaker, R. H.
Theodore of Tarsus, Archbishop of Canterbury, A.D. 668-690. *Ph.D. 1948 Edinburgh*

Whitaker, S. P.
A study of the life and works of Sir John Berkenhead. *M.A. 1915 London*

Whitaker, T. M.
A comparative review of rainfall régimes with a marked winter maximum in areas bordering the Eastern Mediterranean. . *M.A. 1941 Manchester*

Whitaker, W. B.
Sunday in the eighteenth century, 1677-1837. *Ph.D. 1937 London, King's College*

Whitaker, W. B.
Thomas Cartwright and Cambridge, 1547-71. *M.A. 1924 Bristol*

White, A.
A survey of the fundamental ideas in the mind of Christ as interpreted in the theological literature of Britain and America since *Ecce homo* (1865). *Ph.D. 1927 Edinburgh*

White, A. J.
Some problems in the teaching of science. *M.A. 1926 London*

White, A. M.
The influence of the Bible on the work of Paul Claudel. *Ph.D. 1932 London, Westfield College*

White, A. N. Sherwin- *see* Sherwin-White, A. N.

White, B. M. J.
The *Eclogues*, life and literary activities of Alexander Barclay. *M.A. 1926 London*

White, E.
The influence of Böhm-Bawerk on American theories of capital and interest. *M.Sc. 1935 London, School of Economics and Political Science*

White, E. A.
The hardware export trade. *M.Com. 1922 Birmingham*

White, E. E.
Work of Cuvier. *M.Sc. 1947 London, External Degree*

White, E. F.
The jurisdiction of the Privy Council under the Tudors. *M.A. 1918 London*

White, E. F.
A study of the possibility of improving habits of thought in school children by a training in logic. *M.A. 1935 London, Institute of Education*

White, H. Costley- *see* Costley-White, H.

White, H. D. J.
An application of mental tests to university students. *Ph.D. 1926 London*

White, H. J.
1. Doctrinal effect of the Vulgate text. 2. Original righteousness, as conceived by the Fathers, Schoolmen, and Reformers. *B.D. & D.D. 1918 Oxford*

White, H. S.
Nathaniel Hawthorne: a monograph. *B.Litt. 1922 Oxford*

White, J.
Studies in pre-Lockian psychology. *D.Sc. 1898 London*

White, J. E.
A contribution to the study of the ideas of Rémy de Gourmont. *Ph.D. 1934 London, University College*

White, J. H.
The contributions to the establishment of the atomic theory made by John Dalton and his contemporaries. *M.Sc. 1927 London*

White, J. H.
The history of the phlogiston theory. *Ph.D. 1932 London, University College*

White, J. M.
The fens of north Armagh. *Ph.D. 1932 Belfast*

White, J. W.
French provincial life in the novels of Edouard Estaunié, with some reference to contemporary writers. *M.A. 1949 London, King's College and London, Birkbeck College*

White, K.
Theory and practice of corporative economics. *B.Litt. 1937 Oxford*

White, L. F. W.
The administration of education, 1902-1914. *Ph.D. 1934 London, School of Economics and Political Science*

White, M.
Mérimée nouvelliste. *M.A. 1941 National University of Ireland*

White, M. K.
William Godwin: his life, work and influences. *M.A. 1921 Sheffield*

White, O.
Developments since 1870 in the teaching of religion in the public elementary schools of England, with special reference to senior schools. *B.Litt. 1939 Oxford*

White, P.
The prosodic and historical aspects of some poems by S. T. Coleridge. *M.A. 1925 Birmingham*

White, R. A.
A transcript and catalogue of Bodleian ms. Malone 16. *B.Litt. 1931 Oxford*

White, R. E. O.
Hume's theory of ethics: a study of the *Enquiry concerning the Principles of Morals. M.A. 1950 Liverpool*

Whitefoord, B.
An exposition of: St. Luke xxiv.13-35; Acts vii.1-53 (St. Stephen's apology); the Epistle to Philemon. *D.D. 1899 Oxford*

Whitefoord, B.
1. Presence of a creed in the New Testament. 2. The Resurrection, or the cardinal features of Apostolic teaching. *B.D. 1895 Oxford*

Whitehead, E.
A critical and historical study of the relations between the State and education from 1886 to 1926. *B.Litt. 1934 Oxford*

Whitehead, F.
The development of Latin *u* and Germanic *w* in the Romance languages. *D.Phil. 1933 Oxford*

Whitehead, G.
The relation of repression to cultural development. *Ph.D. 1939 Edinburgh*

Whitehead, W. Y.
The influence of apocalyptic on the mind of Jesus. *Ph.D. 1929 Glasgow*

Whitehill, W. M.
Spanish romanesque architecture of the eleventh century. *Ph.D. 1934 London, Courtauld Institute of Art*

Whitehouse, F.
The crusade of Shelley against tyranny. *M.A. 1922 Birmingham*

Whitehouse, M. D.
The political activity of Clodius, particularly in relation to the triumvirs. *M.A. 1916 London*

Whitehouse, S. P.
The idea of teleology in the light of modern philosophy. *B.Litt. 1938 Oxford*

Whitehouse, W. A.
God and creatures in the philosophy of St. Thomas Aquinas and A. N. Whitehead. *B.Litt. 1940 Oxford*

Whitehouse, W. E.
Early distribution and valleyward movement of population in south Britain; a relief model of Wales; climatology in correlation with geography; human geography in Britain. *M.A. 1916 Wales*

Whitehouse, W. J.
Some aspects of the history of the English friars in the thirteenth century. *M.A. 1923 Birmingham*

Whiteley, C. H.
Empiricism. *Ph.D. 1950 Birmingham*

Whiteley, J. L.
Palladas of Alexandria. *M.A. 1934 London, Birkbeck College*

Whiteley, J. L.
The Periplus of the Erythraean Sea. *Ph.D. 1940 London, Birkbeck College*

Whiteley, M.
The *Othello* of Alfred de Vigny as compared with that of Shakespeare. *M.A. 1920 Manchester*

Whiteley, W. M.
Survey of the effects of the 1939-45 war and of the immigration of former city-dwellers on a Midland township. *M.Com. 1948 Birmingham*

Whitfield, A. S.
Elizabeth Cleghorn Gaskell: a study of her writings. *B.Litt. 1926 Oxford*

Whitfield, E. A.
Gabriel Bonnot de Mably. *Ph.D. 1928 London*

Whitfield, G. J. N.
A survey of the books published in English between 1603 and 1608, with a view to determining the interests of the reading public during those years. *M.A. 1935 London, King's College*

Whiting, W. A.
Studies in the treatment of the child in English literature. *M.A. 1921 London*

Whitley, C. F.
The exilic age and contemporary thought. *Ph.D. 1949 Dublin, Trinity College*

Whitman, W. F.
The doctrine of the Church and the sacraments in Hugh of Saint Victor. *B.Litt. 1924 Oxford*

Whitmarsh, A. J.
The historical significance of science. *M.Sc. 1941 Birmingham*

Whitmarsh, W. F. H.
Les idées de Leconte de Lisle. *M.A. 1925 Birmingham*

Whitson, A. M.
The constitutional development of Jamaica, with special reference to the control of the revenue, 1660-1729. *M.A. 1928 Manchester*

Whitt, P. B.
Montaigne in England in the seventeenth century, with special reference to the *Essay. Ph.D. 1934 London, East London College*

Whittaker, E.
A study of profits, with special reference to the profits of farms in the East of Scotland. *Ph.D. 1932 Edinburgh*

Whittaker, M.
Fragments of Attic comedy. *M.Litt. 1934 Cambridge*

Whittaker, P. H.
On child life in medieval English literature. *M.A. 1932 Liverpool*

Whitter, J.
A survey of the economic and administrative life of Kingston-upon-Thames between 1660-1720. *M.Sc. 1933 London, School of Economics and Political Science*

Whittington, J. M.
Shakespeare's actors: their importance and possible influence upon Shakespeare as a playwright. *M.A. 1948 Manchester*

Whittle, H. E.
The influence of Voltaire upon Anatole France. *Ph.D. 1939 London, External Degree*

Whitty, R. G. H.
The Court of Taunton in the sixteenth and seventeenth centuries. *M.A. 1932 London, External Degree*

Whitty, R. G. H.
The history of Taunton under the Tudors and Stuarts. *Ph.D. 1938 London, External Degree*

Whitwell, R. J.
1. The monastic wool trade of the thirteenth century. 2. The Italian bankers and the English Crown. *B.Litt. 1903 Oxford*

Whitworth, E. C.
The parliamentary franchise in the English boroughs in the Stuart period. *M.A. 1926 London*

Whitworth, L.
John Webster and the early seventeenth century background. *M.A. 1947 Liverpool*

Whyatt, C. B.
The Baptists and political and social conditions in Lancashire during the Industrial Revolution, 1760-1832. *M.A. 1948 Manchester*

Whyatt, P.
A study of Thomas Otway. *B.Litt. 1915 Oxford*

Whyte, A. J. B.
The early life and letters of Cavour. *Litt.D. 1927 Dublin, Trinity College*

Whyte, R. M.
Land utilization survey of Breconshire. *M.A. 1943 Wales*

Wibberley, G. P.
Some aspects of livestock marketing in Great Britain and North America. *Ph.D. 1941 Wales*

Wickelgren, F. L.
La Mothe le Vayer: contribution à l'étude du libertinage au dix-septième siècle. *M.A. 1922 London*

Wickenden, H. J.
Emigration from Taunton to N. England 1625-1645. *M.A. 1929 Bristol*

Wicks, C. W.
The influence of French writers on Matthew Arnold. *M.A. 1922 Bristol*

Wicks, J.
An analysis of the nature, history and content of the doctrine of public policy in relation to the common law. *B.Litt. 1941 Oxford*

Wicks, M. C. W.
A history of the Italian exiles in London, 1816-1848. *Ph.D. 1930 Edinburgh*

Wickwar, W. H.
The struggle for the freedom of the press, 1819-1832. *M.A. 1926 London*

Widdows, E. J.
An idealist conception of history. *Ph.D. 1922 Bristol*

Widdows, E. J.
The subject of evil in Greek philosophy. *M.A. 1911 Bristol*

Wiener, F. I.
Hans Sachs's dramatic adaptation of *Dares and Dictys. M.A. 1945 Manchester*

Wiesenberg, E.
The Halakah in Pseudojonathan on the Pentateuch (Part 1: Festivals and marriage laws). *Ph.D. 1952 London, Jews' College*

Wiggs, K. I.
Unemployment in Germany (since the war). *Ph.D. 1932 London, School of Economics and Political Science*

Wigham, E. L.
W. B. Yeats as a symbolic poet. *M.A. 1925 Birmingham*

Wightman, E. M.
The 7th Earl of Shaftesbury as a social reformer. *M.A. 1923 Birmingham*

Wightman, W. P. D.
Science and monism: an historical and critical discussion of the monistic tendencies in the natural sciences. *Ph.D. 1933 London, External Degree*

Wigley, W. E.
The conception of Até from Homer to Aeschylus. *M.A. 1940 Birmingham*

Wigoder, G. B.
The religious philosophy of Abraham bar Hiyya, with a re-edition and translation into English of his *Hegyon Ha-nephesh. D.Phil. 1947 Oxford*

Wijeratne, B. P. F.
Phonology of the Sinhalese inscriptions up to the end of the tenth century A.D. *Ph.D. 1944 London, School of Oriental and African Studies*

Wijesekera, O. H. de A.
Syntax of the cases in the Pāli Nikāyas. *Ph.D. 1936 London, School of Oriental and African Studies*

Wilberforce, A. B. O.
1. On the Holy Trinity. 2. On the sacraments. *B.D. & D.D. 1897 Oxford*

Wilcher, L. C.
The working of federalism in Australia. *B.Litt. 1933 Oxford*

Wilcox, F. M.
The elementary school and national life. *M.A. 1930 Liverpool*

Wilcox, H. A.
The prehistoric woodlands and marshlands of England. *M.A. 1927 Liverpool*

Wild, E. H.
Influences of volition in mental testing, or influences of conation on cognition. *Ph.D. 1926 London*

Wild, K. W.
George Darley and the Elizabethan revival in the Romantic period. *M.A. 1914 Liverpool*

Wildblood, M. E.
Some aspects of the English post-war novel. *M.A. 1926 Wales*

Wilde, R. W.
The concept of sea in psycho-therapy. *Ph.D. 1945 Dublin, Trinity College*

Wilde, R. W.
The relations between Calvinism and social and political thought in the United Kingdom. *M.A. 1933 Manchester*

Wilder, W. B. C.
1. True and false conceptions of the Eucharist as a sacrifice. 2. The grounds of the observance of the Lord's day. *B.D. 1902 Oxford*

Wilkes, L.
Considerations on the teaching of mathematics, especially geometry - being mainly a comparison of the 'oral' method and the method of 'learning by experience'. *M.A. 1930 Birmingham*

Wilkie, H. I.
Realism in the Elizabethan drama, with special reference to citizen comedy. *Ph.D. 1923 Edinburgh*

Wilkie, J. S.
The biologist's approach to the mind-body problem. *Ph.D. 1949 London, University College*

Wilkins, H. J.
1. The Lord's day. 2. The intermediate state. *B.D. & D.D. 1906 Oxford*

Wilkins, M.
The treatment of love and marriage in classical Greek literature. *M.A. 1924 London*

Wilkins, P. M.
Historical geography of Surrey about the year 1800. *M.Sc. 1942 London, School of Economics and Political Science*

Wilkins, R. C. J.
The problem of evil in pre-Christian religions. *M.A. 1940 Leeds*

Wilkinson, A. M.
The verse satires of Daniel Defoe. *M.A. 1949 Manchester*

Wilkinson, E. H.
The historical geography of Herefordshire. *Ph.D. 1945 Bristol*

Wilkinson, E. M.
A critical study of Johann Elias Schlegel's aesthetic and dramatic theory. *Ph.D. 1943 London, Bedford College*

Wilkinson, H. G.
Adolescent education in county boroughs and industrial districts, and the place of physics in the reorganised schools. *M.Ed. 1932 Durham*

Wilkinson, H. R.
Ethnographic maps of Macedonia, 1730-1918. *M.A. 1948 Liverpool*

Wilkinson, J.
Matthew Arnold and the literary criticism of the early nineteenth century, with special reference to Jeffrey and Hazlitt: a comparison of methods and evaluations. *M.A. 1947 Manchester*

Wilkinson, J. T.
The Reverend Richard Baxter and Margaret Charlton: being an examination of *The Breviate of a Life of Margaret Charlton* by Richard Baxter (1681). *M.A. 1930 Birmingham*

Wilkinson, J. W.
The Norman conquests in Wales up to 1100 A.D. *M.A. 1901 Wales*

Wilkinson, M. K.
The development of Parliamentary opinion in respect to education, 1832-1870. *M.A. 1925 Wales*

Wilkinson, W.
The Alexander legend in medieval England. *M.A. 1933 Leeds*

Wilkinson, W. E.
Foreign marriages and divorces: the rules of private international law relating to marriage and divorce. *LL.D. 1918 London*

Wilks, J. A.
Bestrafte Untreue, eine allegorische mittelhochdeutsche Minnerede, herausgegeben. *M.A. 1920 London*

Willan, T. S.
The commonwealth surveys for the North Riding of Yorkshire. *B.Litt. 1932 Oxford*

Willan, T. S.
English coasting trade and inland navigation from 1600 to 1750. *D.Phil. 1934 Oxford*

Willatts, E. C.
The land utilisation of the London basin: a study of the existing conditions and historical changes, 1840-1935. *Ph.D. 1937 London, External Degree*

Willcock, G. D.
A study of sixteenth century English translations of the *Aeneid*: Surrey, Phaer and Stanyhurst. *M.A. 1913 London*

Willetts, M. H.
The lyrical poems of W. Blake. *M.A. 1921 Birmingham*

Willetts, R. F.
Three plays of Euripides in relation to the social background of his time. *M.A. 1938 Birmingham*

Willetts, W. Y.
Features distinctive of Buddhist sculpture in China. *M.A. 1946 London, Courtauld Institute of Art*

Williams, A. C.
Edmond Halley and his influence upon the progress of science in the seventeenth century. *Ph.D. 1940 London, University College*

Williams, A. C.
Edmond Halley and the problems of terrestrial magnetism. *M.Sc. 1937 London, University College*

Williams, A. D.
The theological and religious teaching of William Ellery Channing. *Ph.D. 1937 Edinburgh*

Williams, A. F. O'N.
1. Problems in the philosophy of religion raised and answered in the Book of Job. 2. St. Paul's teaching in the letters addressed to the Corinthian Church. *B.D. 1908 Oxford*

Williams, A. H.
The rise and growth of Welsh Wesleyan Methodism to 1858. *M.A. 1932 Wales*

Williams, A. H. N.
The Roman occupation of west Cumberland. *M.A. 1927 Wales*

Williams, A. Hudson- *see* Hudson-Williams, A.

Williams, A. J.
England a papal fief: repudiation. *M.A. 1925 Liverpool*

Williams, A. L.
A manual of Christian evidences. *D.D. 1911 Cambridge*

Williams, A. R.
Erotic and neurotic traits in post-Victorian English literature. *M.A. 1939 Wales*

Williams, B.
The last embassy of Sir Austin Henry Layard (March, 1877-August, 1878). *M.A. 1939 Wales*

Williams, B. H. G.
The historical evidence contained in Aristophanes and in the fragments of the Old Attic Comedy. *B.Litt. 1932 Oxford*

Williams, C. A. E.
La littérature française dans l'enseignement secondaire de garçons en France. *M.A. 1936 Birmingham*

Williams, C. E. E.
Exegeses of: St.John i.18; I Corinthians xv.29; St.Matthew xviii.19. *D.D. 1886 Oxford*

Williams, C. E. E.
1. Justification by faith. 2. Christianity as a civilizing agent. *B.D. 1882 Oxford*

Williams, C. G.
A study of the development of the poetry of William Blake, up to and including *The Marriage of Heaven and Hell*, with special reference to the growth of his mystical conceptions. *M.A. 1934 Wales*

Williams, C. R.
The industrialization of Flintshire in the nineteenth century, being an examination of the changes and development in the principal industries from 1815 to 1914. *M.A. 1950 Wales*

Williams, C. R. M.
Molière: his philosophy of religion. *M.A. 1922 Wales*

Williams, C. W.
Purposes and workings of the Federal Reserve System comparatively treated. *B.Litt. 1923 Oxford*

Williams, D.
Gray and romanticism. *M.A. 1907 Wales*

Williams, D.
The ideas of democracy in the eighteenth century as shown in the writings of Condorcet. *M.A. 1928 Wales*

Williams, D.
North Wales and Merseyside. *M.A. 1932 Liverpool*

Williams, D. E.
Theism and ideas of value. *M.A. 1924 Wales*

Williams, D. J.
Examinations: their origins, development and functions. *M.A. 1946 Liverpool*

Williams, D. J.
The philosophy of M. Bergson, with special reference to his theory of knowledge. *M.A. 1916 Wales*

Williams, D. J. E.
The indebtedness of Shakespeare and English writers to Montaigne and his *Essays*. *M.A. 1917 Wales*

Williams, D. T.
The importance of the Channel Islands in British relations with the Continent during the thirteenth and fourteenth centuries: a study in historical geography. *M.A. 1927 Wales*

Williams, E.
Giacomo Barozzi da Vignola, 1507-1573, architect. *M.A. 1932 Liverpool*

Williams, E. A.
The classical element in English poetry of the nineteenth century. *M.A. 1908 Wales*

Williams, E. D.
A standardized test of literary appreciation. *M.A. 1937 London, University College*

Williams, E. E.
The conomic aspect of the abolition of the West Indian slave trade and slavery. *D.Phil. 1938 Oxford*

Williams, E. M.
The geometrical concepts of children from five to eight years of age. *M.A. 1934 London, Institute of Education*

Williams, E. R.
Child portraiture in English prose. *M.A. 1912 Bristol*

Williams, E. R.
Welsh seamen, navigators and colonizers, Elizabethan and Jacobean, together with some history of Welsh maritime and colonizing activity during the period. *M.A. 1915 Wales*

Williams, E. V.
The phonology and accidence of the O.E. glosses in ms. Cotton Vespasian A1 (Vespasian Psalter). *B.Litt. 1935 Oxford*

Williams, F.
The educational aims of pioneers in elementary Welsh education, 1730-1870. *M.A. 1929 Wales*

Williams, F. E.
The social anthropology of a western Papuan tribe (Morehead River). *B.Sc. 1934 Oxford*

Williams, F. H. S.
The tea trade. *M.Sc. 1938 London, School of Economics and Political Science*

Williams, F. H. T.
A study of the dialect of the Old English homilies in the twelfth century ms. Vespasian D XIV. *M.A. 1945 London, King's College*

Williams, F. J.
The dramatic works of Antoine le Metel, Sieur d'Ouville. *Ph.D. 1936 London, Birkbeck College*

Williams, F. J.
Practical mathematics: the approach of the post-primary pupil to the study of mathematics. *M.Ed. 1928 Manchester*

Williams, F. M.
The older French element in the vocabulary of the English dialects. *B.Litt. 1947 Oxford*

Williams, F. R.
The biblical theology of the New Testament. *B.D. 1924 Oxford*

Williams, G.
The life and work of Bishop Richard Davies. *M.A. 1947 Wales*

Williams, G. A.
Handicraft in education: its rise and progress in English elementary and secondary schools. *M.A. 1936 Liverpool*

Williams, G. J.
The verbal forms in the *Mabinogion* and *Bruts*. *M.A. 1918 Wales*

Williams, G. L.
The history of tortious liability for animals. *Ph.D. 1936 Cambridge*

Williams, G. P.
Books of character of the seventeenth century. *M.A. 1906 Wales*

Williams, G. P.
Edition du *Biaus Descouneus* de Renaud de Beaujeu avec introduction et glossaire. *M.A. 1915 Wales*

Williams, G. R.
A study of the syntax and vocabulary of the *De excidio Britanniae* of Gildas. *M.A. 1935 Wales*

Williams, H.
The conception of justice in leading British moralists of the eighteenth and nineteenth centuries. *M.Litt. 1944 Cambridge*

Williams, H.
A critical exposition of mechanism and vitalism, with special reference to their philosophical implications. *M.A. 1932 Wales*

Williams, H. B.
The life and works of Sir Richard Fanshawe, 1608 to 1666. *M.A. 1934 London, East London College*

Williams, H. B.
A study of English local government from a legal standpoint, with particular reference to the early development of country administration, illustrated by a comparison of the application of certain principles of local government in medieval and in modern times. *LL.D. 1925 London*

Williams, H. E.
Life and works of Sir Henry Taylor. *M.A. 1948 London, Queen Mary College*

Williams, H. G.
Essex schools before 1600. *M.A. 1924 London*

Williams, H. H.
The religious thought of Thomas Erskine of Linlathen: its origin, nature and influence. *B.D. 1943 Leeds*

Williams, H. L.
A critical study of the drama of Paul Hervieu (1857-1915). *M.A. 1935 Wales*

Williams, H. L.
Safonau beirniadu barddoniaeth yng Nghymru yn y bedwaredd ganrif ar bymtheg(The standards of the criticism of poetry in Wales in the nineteenth century). *M.A. 1935 Wales*

Williams, H. L. Jewitt *see* Jewitt Williams, H. L.

Williams, H. S.
Some aspects of the measurement and maturation of mechanical aptitude in boys aged 12 to 14. *Ph.D. 1948 London, Institute of Education*

Williams, H. W.
The relationship of artist and armourer in Europe during the sixteenth century, with particular reference to etching and allied techniques. *Ph.D. 1935 London, Courtauld Institute of Art*

Williams, I.
The Book of Aneirin. M.A. 1907 Wales

Williams, I. H.
The evolution of French classical tragedy in the eighteenth century to the death of Voltaire. *Ph.D. 1930 Wales*

Williams, J.
Education in Egypt before British control. *M.Ed. 1934 Durham*

Williams, J.
The London coffee-houses, and their literary associations down to the death of Anne. *B.Litt. 1936 Oxford*

Williams, J.
Patriotism in Old French literature: eleventh to fifteenth century. *Ph.D. 1933 London, External Degree*

Williams, J.
The statute of frauds, paragraph 4, in the light of its judicial interpretation. *Ph.D. 1932 Cambridge*

Williams, J. E.
The life and work of František Palacky, with special reference to his political ideas of nationality and government. *M.A. 1925 Wales*

Williams, J. E. C.
Breuddwyd Pawl a Phurdan Padrig(The Dream of St. Paul and The Purgatory of St. Patrick). M.A. 1936 Wales

Williams, J. H.
A study of the contribution of the Church in Wales to the development of Welsh hymnology, with special reference to the period A.D. 1740 to A.D. 1900. *M.A. 1940 Liverpool*

Williams, J. I.
Cyfriniaeth yn llenyddiaeth Gymreig(Mysticism in Welsh literature). *M.A. 1926 Wales*

Williams, J. J.
History of the laws, usages and constitutions of the early English boroughs; the original constitution of municipal corporations; and the source of their powers of legislation and administration. *LL.D. 1928 Sheffield*

Williams, J. J.
Political elements in Welsh literature, 1788-1840. *M.A. 1923 Liverpool*

Williams, J. K.
Noun valency in French: a study of the determination of the noun and a contribution to the study of the word-group. *M.A. 1933 Wales*

Williams, J. L.
The doctrine of the freedom of the will according to English empiricism and transcendental idealism. *B.Sc. 1904 Oxford*

Williams, J. L.
Freedom of the will according to Kant and the English Idealists. *M.A. 1902 Wales*

Williams, J. L.
Gwaith Guto'r Glyn(The work of Guto'r Glyn). *M.A. 1927 Wales*

Williams, J. L.
Technical education in north Wales and its relation to industry, commerce and agriculture, 1938-1939. *M.A. 1944 Liverpool*

Williams, J. M.
An experimental and theoretical study of humour in children. *M.A. 1945 London, University College*

Williams, J. M.
The theme of the deserted heroine in classical literature. *M.A. 1935 Wales*

Williams, J. M.
The works of some fifteenth century Glamorgan bards: Ieuan Gethyn ap Ieuan ap Lleision, Rhys Brydydd, Rhisiart ap Rhys, Gwilym Tew, Llywelyn ap Hywel ap Gronwy, Lang Lewys, Llywelyn Goch y Dant, Gruffydd ap Dafydd Fychan, Ieuan Du'r Bilwg. *M.A. 1923 Wales*

Williams, J. P.
Cyfraniad Methodistiaeth Galfinaidd i lenyddiaeth Gymraeg o 1811 hyd 1864(The contribution of Calvinistic Methodism to the literature of Wales from 1811 ro 1864). *M.A. 1928 Wales*

Williams, J. S.
The aims and methods of the English humanist educators of the sixteenth century. *M.A. 1914 Liverpool*

Williams, J. V.
The work of W. H. Hudson. *M.A. 1950 Wales*

Williams, J. W.
1. Early Christian missions in some of their relations to heathen religion. 2. The importance and function of the Book of Esther in the canon. *B.D. 1896 Oxford*

Williams, J. W.
The foreign policy of England from the peace of Nimeguen to the death of King Charles II. *B.Litt. 1910 Oxford*

Williams, J. W.
Hanes athrawiaeth yr iawn yng Nghymru yn y bedwaredd ganrif ar bymtheg(The history of the doctrine of the atonement in Wales in the nineteenth century). *M.A. 1939 Wales*

Williams, L.
Movements towards social reform in south Wales during the period 1832-1850. *M.A. 1933 Wales*

Williams, L. F. R.
The history of the abbey of St. Alban's. *B.Litt. 1913 Oxford*

Williams, L. M.
International relations between Great Britain, Germany and the United States in the Samoan Islands. *M.A. 1938 Wales*

Williams, M.
The Chartist movement in Wales. *M.A. 1919 Wales*

Williams, M.
The effect on general reasoning ability of training in functional thinking in arithmetic. *M.A. 1938 London, Institute of Education*

Williams, M.
The extent to which Wolfram von Eschenbach is indebted for his poem *Parzival* to French and other foreign sources. *M.A. 1907 Wales*

Williams, M.
The history of the study of plant response to stimuli. *M.Sc. 1927 London*

Williams, M.
1. The letters of William Shenstone. 2. William Shenstone: a chapter in eighteenth century taste. *D.Litt. 1939 London, External Degree*

Williams, M.
The Rebecca riots in Wales. *M.A. 1913 Wales*

Williams, M.
William Shenstone: a chapter in eighteenth century taste. *Ph.D. 1928 London*

Williams, M. F.
The Society of Friends in Glamorgan, 1654-1900. *M.A. 1950 Wales*

Williams, M. H.
The thought of Léon Bloy: an interpretation of the life and character of Léon Bloy, with special reference to his theology. *M.A. 1950 Wales*

Williams, M. I.
A sociological and statistical study of the population of the Vale of Glamorgan during the first half of the nineteenth century. *M.A. 1939 Wales*

Williams, M. R.
William Godwin, philosopher and man of letters. *M.A. 1923 Bristol*

Williams, N.
The political career of Lord Brougham from 1805 to 1830. *M.A. 1913 Liverpool*

Williams, N.
Problems of population and education in the new housing estates, with special reference to Norris Green. *M.A. 1938 Liverpool*

Williams, N. P.
1. The Gospel narratives of the Resurrection. 2. The sources of St. Mark's Gospel. *B.D. 1921 Oxford*

Williams, N. V.
Some aspects of the cult of the Virgin Mary in medieval French literature. *M.A. 1927 Wales*

Williams, O. C.
The historical development of private bill procedure and standing orders in the House of Commons. *B.C.L. & D.C.L. 1946 Oxford*

Williams, O. T.
An investigation of the rimes and phonology of Barbour's *Bruce. M.A. 1908 Wales*

Williams, P. H.
Thought and sense in the philosophy of St. Thomas Aquinas. *M.A. 1949 Wales*

Williams, P. K. Hesketh- *see* Hesketh-Williams, P. K.

Williams, P. T.
The industrial history of Flintshire in the nineteenth century. *M.A. 1933 Liverpool*

Williams, R.
A critical study of the novels of Thomas Hardy. *M.A. 1914 Wales*

Williams, R.
The history of Thessaly. *M.A. 1903 Wales*

Williams, R.
The use of standardized tests in recording the mental progress of elementary school children, and the value of such records in selecting individuals for higher education. *M.A. 1935 Liverpool*

Williams, R. B.
Llenyddiaeth Gymraeg y Wladfa(The Welsh literature of the Colony (in Patagonia)). *M.A. 1931 Wales*

Williams, R. G.
Hanes Antinomiaeth yng Nghymru, 1650 hyd 1850(The history of Antinomianism in Wales, 1650-1850). *M.A. 1934 Wales*

Williams, R. M.
The teaching of Spanish to Welsh-speaking pupils. *M.A. 1939 Liverpool*

Williams, S. A.
Teaching pupils how to study, with special reference to the study of history. *M.A. 1918 London*

Williams, S. J.
Fford y Brawt Odric, o'r Llanstephan ms. 2; ei gymharu âr gwreiddiol, gyda nodiadau gramadegol a geirfa(*The journey of Brother Odoric*, from the Llanstephan ms. 2; compared with the original and with grammatical notes and a vocabulary). *M.A. 1925 Wales*

Williams, T.
Aspects of the agrarian problem in Wales in the sixteenth century. *M.A. 1928 Wales*

Williams, T. D. F.
Genesis of national socialism. *M.A. 1946 National University of Ireland*

Williams, T. G.
The relation of Chaucer to chivalry. *M.A. 1909 Wales*

Williams, T. H.
The English element in Welsh. *M.A. 1911 Wales*

Williams, T. H.
Spurley Hey's contribution to the origin and development of central schools. *M.A. 1938 Sheffield*

Williams, T. H.
A study of the placenames of Merioneth. *M.A. 1931 Wales*

Williams, T. H. Parry- *see* Parry-Williams, T. H.

Williams, T. L.
The Welsh soldier in England's armies of the thirteenth and fourteenth centuries. *M.A. 1915 Wales*

Williams, T. O.
The literary movement in west Wales in the first half of the eighteenth century and its religious associations. *M.A. 1923 Wales*

Williams, T. P.
Germany's relations to France in drama and criticism between 1870 and 1890. *M.A. 1936 Wales*

Williams, T. S.
The historical, economic and cultural importance of the Loess soil of Europe. *M.Sc. 1928 Wales*

Williams, T. S.
Richard Vaughan, 2nd Earl of Carbery (1606-1686). *M.A. 1936 Wales*

Williams, U. M.
The influence on concepts of the personality of recent advances in physiology. *B.Litt. 1949 Oxford*

Williams, V. E. N.
Caerwent and the Roman occupation of South Wales. *M.A. 1924 Wales*

Williams, W.
Ap Fychan; ei fywyd, a'i waith, a'i gysylltiadau llenyddol(Ap Fychan: life, work and literary connections). *M.A. 1931 Wales*

Williams, W.
The available data for the Black Death in Wales. *M.A. 1920 Wales*

Williams, W. D.
The influence of Nietzsche's French reading on his thought and writing. *D.Phil. 1950 Oxford*

Williams, W. G.
A critical study of the writings of Robert Jones, Rhoslan. *M.A. 1937 Liverpool*

Williams, W. G.
The slaves of Greek comedy compared with those of Plautus and Terence. *M.A. 1911 London*

Williams, W. J.
The influence of Milton on English poetry up to 1770. *M.A. 1907 Wales*

Williams, W. L.
A comparative study of four Old French versions of the life of Saint Catherine of Alexandria. *M.A. 1944 Wales*

Williams, W. P.
The influence of the French Revolution on the political and social life of Wales. *M.A. 1925 Wales*

Williams, W. S.
Religious ideas in the *Carmina Latina Epigraphica. M.A. 1939 Wales*

Williams, W. T.
The oecumenical creeds of the ancient church: problems of their origin and development. *M.A. 1943 Wales*

Williams, W. T.
The relations between Henry VII and Wales. *M.A. 1914 Wales*

Williams, W. U.
A collection of the poems of Sion Tudur. *M.A. 1906 Wales*

Williams-Jones, H. *see* Jones, H. Williams-

Williamson, D. M.
The legation of Cardinal Otto, 1237-41. *M.A. 1947 Manchester*

Williamson, E. H.
The New Testament doctrine of perfection. *Ph.D. 1935 Dublin, Trinity College*

Williamson, E. H.
New Testament eschatology in its bearing upon ethics. *B.Litt. 1939 Dublin, Trinity College*

Williamson, H. P.
An examination of some recent developments in testing personality, and an experimental investigation on the measurement of personality in senior school-children. *M.Sc. 1929 Birmingham*

Williamson, H. R.
All for China: an account of the life and labour of Mrs. E. H. Edwards of Taiynanfu, Shensi. *M.A. 1922 London*

Williamson, H. R.
Wang an Shih, a rejected reformer. *D.Litt. 1932 London, External Degree*

Williamson, J. A.
Cromwell and Mazarin, 1656-1658: an account of the Anglo-French alliance leading to the conquest of Dunkirk. *M.A. 1909 London*

Williamson, J. G.
Mistake in the formation of contracts. *B.Litt. 1938 Oxford*

Williamson, M. G.
The non-Celtic placenames of the Scottish border counties. *Ph.D. 1943 Edinburgh*

Williamson, M. T.
English personal letters and private diaries of 1640-1680: a study of the general mental attitude of the period as illustrated by individual types, together with a brief examination of the colloquial language of the time. *Ph.D. 1929 London*

Williamson, P. H.
Coleridge on Shakespeare: an essay in correlation. *M.A. 1948 Manchester*

Williamson, R. T.
The religious thought of James Montgomery. *Ph.D. 1950 Edinburgh*

Williamson, S. G.
Value. *M.A. 1937 Birmingham*

Willing, G. M.
The influence of the Spanish picaresque novel in the French literature of the seventeenth century, with special reference to Sorel's *Francion* (1623-33). *B.Litt. 1931 Oxford*

Willing-Denton, E. J.
Boswell in the newspapers from the death of Johnson to his own death. *B.Litt. 1935 Oxford*

Willis, D. M.
The imagery of Paul Claudel. *M.A. 1933 Manchester*

Willis, G. G.
An analysis, with commentary, of Saint Augustine of Hippo's treatises on marriage, the *De bono conjugali*, the *De adulterinis conjugiis* and the *De nuptiis et concupiscentia. M.A. 1939 Manchester*

Willis, L. M.
The interpretation of the pediments of the Parthenon. *M.A. 1910 London*

Willis, S. J.
The principle of individuality in education. *Ph.D. 1930 Dublin, Trinity College*

Willmott, F. C.
The provision of schemes of work in the English subjects for pupils of the new age group in senior modern schools. *M.A. 1940 Bristol*

Willoughby, J. M.
1. The doctrine of resurrection. 2. The rational basis of faith. *B.D. 1902 Oxford*

Willoughby, J. M.
Expositions of St. John xiv.16-17; xv.26; xvi.7-18. *D.D. 1906 Oxford*

Willoughby, L. A.
Zwei unbekannte Fassungen von Gedichten: über die *Fünfzehn Zeichen* und *Das jüngste Gericht*: Text und Untersuchungen. *M.A. 1903 London*

Willoughby, R. M. P.
The distinctions and anomalies arising out of the equitable doctrine of the legal estate. *LL.D. 1911 London*

Wills, J. H.
A discussion of the relative share of Apollonius, Hipparchus, and Ptolemy in the evolution of the theory of eccentrics and epicycles. *M.Sc. 1931 London*

Wilmer, R. H.
Issues dividing western Christendom on the doctrine of the Church in the sixteenth and seventeenth centuries. *D.Phil. 1948 Oxford*

Wilmott, A. E.
A study of Caxton's Ovid. *M.A. 1909 London*

Wilshere, P. N.
An attempt to consider a syllabus in world history suitable for a 'senior' school. *M.A. 1931 London, Day Training College*

Wilson, A. E.
An enquiry into the methods of teaching geography and sources of geography material. *M.Ed. 1934 Leeds*

Wilson, A. E.
The fall of paganism. *M.A. 1914 Birmingham*

Wilson, A. E.
The fall of paganism in the Western Roman Empire, 311-395 A.D. *D.Litt. 1927 Birmingham*

Wilson, A. J. N.
Immigration and settlement in the province of Dalmatia from the first Roman contacts to the death of Commodus. *D.Phil. 1949 Oxford*

Wilson, A. M.
The life and ministry of Chauvelin, with particular reference to French foreign policy between 1731 and 1737. *B.Litt. 1927 Oxford*

Wilson, B.
A study of the early writings of Tertullian with particular reference to the *Apologeticum. M.A. 1948 Liverpool*

Wilson, B. N.
The changes of the Reformation period in Durham and Northumberland. *Ph.D. 1939 Durham*

Wilson, C. E.
An edition of the *Masnavi*, by Jalalu'd-Dīn Rūmī, Vol. I - Translation; Vol. II - Commentary. *Ph.D. 1925 London*

Wilson, C. I.
A study of the mss. of the *Chanson d'Aspremont* in the Bibliothèque Nationale in Paris. *Ph.D. 1923 London*

Wilson, C. R.
History of the East India Company's settlement at Calcutta, 1711-1717, Vol. II. *B.Litt. 1901 Oxford*

Wilson, D.
An investigation, using the discussion group technique, of some of the social relationships of secondary modern school children. *M.A. 1949 Liverpool*

Wilson, D. F.
Psychology and religious education. *B.Litt. 1927 Oxford*

Wilson, D. K.
(1) Some of the textbooks used in the teaching of elementary mathematics in Scotland prior to the year 1800. (2) Development of the mathematical curriculum in the Scottish schools during the same period. *Ph.D. 1932 Glasgow*

Wilson, E.
Rhythm and its significance in musical education: a study of the fundamental principles of rhythm, their development in musical composition and their rôle in musical education. *M.A. 1941 Leeds*

Wilson, E.
Scottish university studies, 1800-1850. *M.Ed. 1948 Leeds*

Wilson, E. F.
Educational experience in the present war-time army and its bearing on national problems of education. *M.Ed. 1944 Leeds*

Wilson, E. G.
Resumption of cash payments: the problems as illustrated by the experience of various countries in the nineteenth century. *Ph.D. 1928 London*

Wilson, E. M.
Culteranism in the Spanish theatre of the seventeenth century, with particular reference to the works of Calderón de la Barca. *Ph.D. 1933 Cambridge*

Wilson, E. M. Carus-
The overseas trade of Bristol in the later Middle Ages: a study of English commerce, 1399-1485. *M.A. 1926 London*

Wilson, F. H.
The social and economic history of Ostia. *D.Phil. 1935 Oxford*

Wilson, F. P.
The plague pamphlets of T. Dekker, with an account of the plague in London from 1603 to 1630. *D.Litt. 1921 Birmingham*

Wilson, F. P.
The prose works of Dekker. *M.A. 1912 Birmingham*

Wilson, F. P.
The prose works of Thomas Dekker. *B.Litt. 1913 Oxford*

Wilson, G. B.
Alcohol and the nation. *Ph.D. 1939 London, External Degree*

Wilson, H. S.
The basis of musical artistry. *Ph.D. 1948 London, Trinity College*

Wilson, I. M.
An outline of the history of mycology up to about 1884. *M.Sc. 1931 London*

Wilson, J. C.
Muhammad's prophetic office as portrayed in the Qur'ān. *Ph.D. 1949 Edinburgh*

Wilson, J. H.
A critical evaluation of certain scales of intelligence, with special reference to the effects of coaching and practice. *Ph.D. 1929 London*

Wilson, J. H.
A survey, historical and critical, of intelligence tests. *M.Ed. 1923 Leeds*

Wilson, J. S.
The administrative work of the Lord Chancellor in the early seventeenth century. *Ph.D. 1927 London*

Wilson, K. M.
Music and English poetry. *Ph.D. 1925 Cambridge*

Wilson, M. A.
The composition and recruitment of the agricultural labour force and their bearing on future supply. *B.Litt. 1949 Oxford*

Wilson, M. E.
The ocean port of Chicago. *M.Sc. 1926 London*

Wilson, N.
Charles Lamb. *M.A. 1939 National University of Ireland*

Wilson, O. M.
André Chénier: poète du dix-huitième siècle. *M.A. 1933 Belfast*

Wilson, R.
The import of capital. *D.Phil. 1930 Oxford*

Wilson, R. A.
The pre-war biographies of Romain Rolland and their place in the ensemble of his work and of the period up to 1914. *Ph.D. 1937 Saint Andrew's*

Wilson, R. J.
1. Revelation and inspiration. 2. Christ incarnate, the reconciler and restorer of fallen man. *B.D. & D.D. 1894 Oxford*

Wilson, R. K.
Early settlement in the South Island of New Zealand, with special reference to the North and East. *M.A. 1947 London, University College*

Wilson, R. M.
An edition of the Middle English homily *Sawles Warde*, with notes, glossary and full critical and textual apparatus. *M.A. 1931 Leeds*

Wilson, R. McL.
Diaspora Judaism and syncretism, with special reference to the question of the origins of Gnosticism. *Ph.D. 1946 Cambridge*

Wilson, S. K.
American colonial colleges. *Ph.D. 1925 Cambridge*

Wilson, T.
An attempt to interpret, with the aid of recent trade cycle theory, the cyclical fluctuations in the U.S.A. since the war of 1914-18. *Ph.D. 1940 London, School of Economics and Political Science*

Wilson, T. J.
La Calprenède, romancier. *D.Phil. 1927 Oxford*

Wilson, W. G.
A critical investigation into the unity, date, and authorship of the 4th Gospel, and its relationship to the Johannine epistles. *Ph.D. 1949 Dublin, Trinity College*

Wiltshire, H. C.
The acting tradition in England during the period 1730-1760. *M.A. 1935 London, Queen Mary College*

Wimms, J. H.
The relative effects of fatigue and practice, including an experimental investigation, with reference to certain varieties of mental work. *M.A. 1906 Wales*

Winawer, H. M.
The Jewish Question in the district of Wilno in 1880-1914. *B.Phil. 1948 Oxford*

Windsor, R.
The *Parlement* of Paris under Charles VI and Charles VII. *M.A. 1940 Liverpool*

Wing, H. D.
Musical ability and appreciation: an investigation into its measurement, distribution and development: a contribution to the psychology of music using a new series of standardized tests. *Ph.D. 1941 London, University College*

Wing, H. D.
Tests of musical ability. *M.A. 1936 London, Institute of Education*

Wingate, S. D.
The medieval Latin versions of the Aristotelian scientific corpus, with special reference to the biological works. *Ph.D. 1931 London, University College*

Winn, H. E.
The educational ideas of Wordsworth. *M.A. 1925 London*

Winnicki, T. Z.
Labour's foreign policy, 1919-24. *M.Litt. 1950 Cambridge*

Winram, G.
Soil erosion in North America. *M.A. 1944 London, External Degree*

Winslow, E. A.
Budget studies and the measurement of living costs and standards. *Ph.D. 1923 London*

Winstanley, C. H.
Leaders of humanism in English education: Humphrey, Duke of Gloucester, William Grocyn, Thomas Linacre, Bishop Richard Foxe. *M.A. 1930 Liverpool*

Winstedt, E. O.
The manuscripts of Prudentius. *B.Litt. 1903 Oxford*

Winter, H. J.
The historical development of Ohm's law and the evolution of a standard of electrical resistance. *Ph.D. 1946 London, External Degree*

Winterbourn, R.
An investigation into the development of the attitudes of children towards authority. *Ph.D. 1941 London, Institute of Education*

Winters, R. L.
Francis Lambert of Avignon (1487-1530): a study in Reformation origins. *Ph.D. 1936 Edinburgh*

Wirszubski, C.
Libertas as a political idea at Rome during the late Republic and early Principate. *Ph.D. 1947 Cambridge*

Wisdom, J. O.
Hegel and modern philosophy. *Ph.D. 1933 Dublin, Trinity College*

Wise, A. R.
L'art de la prose chez Pierre Loti. *M.A. 1935 Birmingham*

Wise, C. G.
Education in Mauritius, with special reference to the Royal College. *M.Ed. 1932 Manchester*

Wiseman, J. C.
A study of the *Argonautica* of Valerius Flaccus. *Ph.D. 1934 Aberdeen*

Wiskemann, E. M.
Great Britain and the Roman question. *M.Litt. 1928 Cambridge*

Withers, R. F. J.
Morphological correspondence in modern biology. *M.Sc. 1948 London, University College*

Withrington, J. W.
An analysis of factors entering into geometrical ability. *M.A. 1936 London, Institute of Education*

Witt, R. E.
Albinus and the history of Middle Platonism. *Ph.D. 1934 Cambridge*

Witte, W.
Art and the artist in Schiller's poetry: a critical study. *M.A. 1943 London, External Degree*

Witte, W.
Recent German prose usage. *Ph.D. 1935 Aberdeen*

Wittgenstein, L.
Tractatus logicophilosophicus. M.Litt. 1929 Cambridge

Wohlgemuth, S. A.
On the after effect of seen movement. *D.Sc. 1911 London*

Wölcken, F. E.
The unity of thought in the early works of Stefan George. *Ph.D. 1937 Edinburgh*

Woledge, B.
La langue de *l'Atre perilleux*, poème de la Table Ronde. *M.A. 1928 Leeds*

Wolf, C. de see De Wolf, C.

Wolfe, C. W.
Hegelian epistemology. *B.Litt. 1938 Dublin, Trinity College*

Wolfe, M. J.
James Thomson (B.V.): his connexion with contemporary fashions in thought and literature. *B.Litt. 1940 Oxford*

Wolff, T. A.
The Russian Romantics and English literature. *M.A. 1947 London, Bedford College*

Wollman, D. C.
Public health in Leeds, 1836-1848. *M.A. 1949 Leeds*

Wolters, A. W. P.
The development of the theory of space from Descartes to Kant. *M.A. 1910 London*

Woo, C. S.
The British cotton trade with China. *M.Com. 1913 Birmingham*

Woo, S.
The pursuit of disarmament, Geneva, 1920-33: a study in international procedure. *M.Sc. 1938 London, School of Economics and Political Science*

Woo, T. D.
The recent extension of cotton growing. *M.Com. 1912 Birmingham*

Woo, T. L.
Dextrality and sinistrality of hand and eye. *Ph.D. 1928 London*

Wood, A.
Hamlet dans les oeuvres françaises depuis 1700 jusqu'à la *Préface du Cromwell. M.A. 1920 Liverpool*

Wood, A. C.
The commercial and diplomatic relations of England and Turkey, 1680-1699. *B.Litt. 1923 Oxford*

Wood, A. C.
Fulk-Fitz-Warin: text and a study of the language. *M.A. 1911 London*

Wood, A. C.
A history of the Levant Company. *D.Phil. 1934 Oxford*

Wood, A. C.
Watercourses in the parish of St. Margaret's, Westminster, in the seventeenth century: a problem of local administration. *B.Litt. 1938 Oxford*

Wood, A. H.
Richard Ullerston. *M.A. 1936 Manchester*

Wood, A. Sandys- see Sandys-Wood, A.

Wood, C. W.
Science in the secondary school: its adaptation to an appreciation of life. *M.Ed. 1933 Manchester*

Wood, E. R. G.
A study of the changes in the distribution and density of population in Worcestershire during the period 1841-1931, and of the geographical factors involved. *M.A. 1950 Birmingham*

Wood, F. T.
Henry Carey, poet, dramatist and satirist. *Ph.D. 1930 London, External Degree*

Wood, G. A.
The Anglo-Saxon riddles. *M.A. 1909 Wales*

Wood, G. M.
The history and development of nursery education in Manchester and Salford. *M.Ed. 1934 Manchester*

Wood, H. J.
An agricultural atlas of Scotland. *Ph.D. 1931 London, External Degree*

Wood, H. P.
New type achievement examinations in science. *M.Ed. 1941 Manchester*

Wood, H. W.
The terror novel in French literature: its influence on the French novel of 1820-45. *M.A. 1922 London*

Wood, J.
Vocalisation of the proper names in the Pentateuch according to a Syriac manuscript, Add. 12138, in the British Museum. *M.A. 1940 Manchester*

Wood, J. Russell- see Russell-Wood, J.

Wood, K.
Milton criticism from Addison to de Quincey. *M.A. 1950 Sheffield*

Wood, K. W.
English naval administration at the close of the seventeenth century. *M.A. 1935 Leeds*

Wood, L. R.
Agriculture in Jersey. *Ph.D. 1934 London, External Degree*

Wood, M. E.
Norman domestic architecture in England. *M.A. 1934 London, University College*

Wood, M. H.
Plato's psychology in its bearing on the development of will. *M.A. 1905 London*

Wood, N.
Religious uniformity and English education in the sixteenth century. *Ph.D. 1928 London*

Wood, P. D.
The morphology of the Welsh border towns: a study in historical geography. *M.A. 1950 Wales*

Wood, R. J.
The beacons of North England, with special reference to the geographical plan of those provided in Elizabethan times. *M.Sc. 1937 London, School of Economics and Political Science*

Wood, T.
The defence of the north-west border of England against the Scots in the first half of the fourteenth century. *M.A. 1937 Manchester*

Wood, T.
English casuistry of the seventeenth century and its relations with medieval and Jesuit casuistry. *M.A. 1947 Leeds*

Wood, T.
Jeremy Taylor and seventeenth century English casuistry, with special reference to the *Ductor dubitantium. B.D. 1945 Leeds*

Wood, V. C.
France in the life and works of Dickens. *M.A. 1949 Liverpool*

Woodall, M. W.
Gainsborough's landscape drawings and their place in the development of English landscape drawing and painting. *Ph.D. 1937 London, Courtauld Institute of Art*

Woodcock, A. C.
The problems of the European community in Kenya. *M.A. 1949 Leeds*

Woodcock, B. L.
Pre-Reformation Church courts in the diocese of Canterbury. *B.Litt. 1950 Oxford*

Woodcock, O. H.
War service in a tropical country: (1) the effect of temperament; (2) as a factor in the causation of mental breakdown. *M.D. 1918 Manchester*

Woodford, H. G.
The place of the individual in some sociological theories. *B.A. 1924 Bristol*

Wood-Legh, K. L.
County representatives in the Parliaments of Edward III. *B.Litt. 1929 Oxford*

Wood-Legh, K. L.
Some aspects of Church life in England during the reign of Edward III. *Ph.D. 1933 Cambridge*

Woodman, C.
Dramatic monologue of Browning. *M.A. 1948 National University of Ireland*

Woods, E. H.
The transition from the Synoptic to the Johannine version of the life and teaching of Jesus. *Ph.D. 1924 Edinburgh*

Woods, F.
Civic liberty in the 20th century. *M.A. 1935 National University of Ireland*

Woods, F. H.
1. On the atonement. 2. On infant baptism. *B.D. 1881 Oxford*

Woods, F. U.
The political activities of the 'Saints', 1800-1833. *M.A. 1924 Manchester*

Woods, S. R.
The problem of religious education in secondary schools. *M.A. 1943 Bristol*

Woodsworth, C. J.
Canada and the Far East. *Ph.D. 1940 London, School of Economics and Political Science*

Woodward, A.
The life and works of Katherine Philips. *Cert.Litt. 1920 Oxford*

Woodward, F. W. M.
Expositions of the Epistle of Jude 1-8; 9-16; 17-25. *D.D. 1910 Oxford*

Woodward, F. W. M.
1. The meaning of the Transfiguration. 2. The Gospel histories in the Koran dogmatically considered. *B.D. 1906 Oxford*

Wooldridge, S. D.
Anglo-Chinese relations, 1834-1860. *M.A. 1930 Birmingham*

Woolf, B. L.
The authority of Jesus and its foundation: an examination of the Gospels and the Book of Acts. *Ph.D. 1926 Edinburgh*

Woolf, J. P. Lee- *see* Lee-Woolf, J. P.

Woolf, M. S.
Goethe's knowledge of English literature. *M.A. 1907 Birmingham*

Woolf, R. E.
An edition of the Old English *Juliana*. *B.Litt. 1949 Oxford*

Woolley, S. F.
The comparative study of parliamentary representation in the new borough constituencies created in 1832. *M.A. 1937 London, External Degree*

Woosnam, L.
Geoffrey of Monmouth's *Chronicle* and its influence on English literature. *M.A. 1913 Wales*

Woosnam, L.
Inscriptions on old English coins up to 1154. *Ph.D. 1921 Cambridge*

Wootton, F.
The physical work of Descartes. *M.Sc. 1927 London*

Wootton, M. E. M.
A critical study of Kleist's tales, with special reference to their importance in the development of the German Novelle. *M.A. 1936 London, Bedford College*

Worboys, J. S. A.
Man's sense of moral obligation: the inevitable psychological aspect of a universal ethical process by which man in his freedom deals with the necessity of self-transcendence through some accepted principle of value. *Ph.D. 1936 London, External Degree*

Worcester, D. K.
East Sussex landownership: the structure of rural society in an area of old enclosure, 1733-87. *Ph.D. 1950 Cambridge*

Worden, C. N.
The teaching of Latin in England: a critical and historical survey. *Ph.D. 1938 London, King's College*

Wordsworth, E. C.
Some 'voluntary' taxes of the Roman Empire. *M.A. 1912 Birmingham*

Worgan, D. A.
Central and local government in Germany, with reference to the Weimar Constitution of 1919. *M.A. 1932 Wales*

Wormald, S.
A critical enquiry into the teaching of modern languages in France. *M.Ed. 1933 Leeds*

Wormald, S.
Une étude du vocabulaire des premières oeuvres en prose de Victor Hugo (1823-1834). *M.A. 1924 Leeds*

Worsley, C. M.
The influence of Apollonius Rhodius on Vergil, with special reference to the romance of *Aeneid* IV. *M.A. 1925 Manchester*

Worsthorne, S. P. E. C. W. Towneley- *see* Towneley-Worsthorne, S. P. E. C. W.

Worth, J. G.
Education and the French Revolution. *B.Litt. 1921 Oxford*

Worthington, E.
A comparison of free-place and fee-paying boys in a municipal secondary school (1916-1925), together with investigations concerning the reliability of the admission examination. *M.A. 1930 Birmingham*

Wortley, B. A.
The interpretation of company law in the light of equitable principles, with particular regard to the duties of directors and promoters. *LL.M. 1934 Leeds*

Wostenholm, C. D.
An examination of the manner in which prose passages are memorised by pupils between the ages of 10 and 13. *M.Sc. 1936 Sheffield*

Wozencroft, G.
The history of the town, lordship and castle of Builth from the eleventh to the sixteenth centuries. *M.A. 1919 Wales*

Wozencroft, G.
The relations between England and France during the Aberdeen-Guizot Ministries (1841-6). *Ph.D. 1932 London, King's College*

Wragg, E.
Henry V as conqueror in France, and the Lancastrian experiment in Normandy. *M.A. 1916 Birmingham*

Wragg, R. B.
Kitchens: a thesis on domestic and large kitchens, including those to hospitals, canteens, schools and hotels. *M.A. 1947 Sheffield*

Wragg, S. R.
An economic survey of small holdings in the Vale of Evesham. *M.A. 1937 Bristol*

Wray, M.
La bourgeoisie de province dans l'oeuvre de Balzac. *M.A. 1925 Manchester*

Wrenne, L. J.
Standish James O'Grady. *M.A. 1944 National University of Ireland*

Wretts-Smith, M.
The policy and activities of the Muscovy Company in the late sixteenth and early seventeenth centuries. *M.Sc. 1920 London*

Wright, A. F.
An inquiry into the socio-religious character of Chinese civilization, with special reference to those features conducive to the acceptance of Buddhism. *B.Litt. 1937 Oxford*

Wright, B. D.
Studies in the Troy story in Middle English. *Ph.D. 1924 London*

Wright, B. M.
A study of the influence of various types of incentives upon learning. *Ph.D. 1938 Edinburgh*

Wright, C. E.
The cultivation of saga during the Dark Ages. *Ph.D. 1936 Cambridge*

Wright, C. J.
Miracles in history and in modern thought. *Ph.D. 1931 London, External Degree*

Wright, D. G.
The theology of John Locke. *Ph.D. 1938 Edinburgh*

Wright, E.
Fulke Greville and his literary relations. *M.A. 1930 Manchester*

Wright, E. G.
Bishop Humphrey Humphreys (1648-1712): a study of the literary and antiquarian movements in Wales in the seventeenth and early eighteenth centuries. *M.A. 1948 Liverpool*

Wright, E. M.
Lamartine et Byron. *M.A. 1938 London, King's College*

Wright, F.
The economics of the gas industry. *M.A. 1925 Leeds*

Wright, F. C. Y. C.
The Secretariat General of the League of Nations: an experiment into international administration. *Ph.D. 1931 London, External Degree*

Wright, F. W.
The relations between Louis Napoleon and Great Britain from 1848 to the outbreak of the Crimean war. *M.A. 1925 Birmingham*

Wright, G.
An economic survey of St.Vincent. *M.Com. 1928 Leeds*

Wright, G. H. B.
1. The doctrine of immortality in the Old Testament. 2. Development of the doctrine of the fatherhood of God in the Old and New Testaments. *B.D. 1891 Oxford*

Wright, G. H. B.
Exegeses of: Job v; vi; and xix.25-29. *D.D. 1891 Oxford*

Wright, H. G.
The career of Thomas, Duke of Gloucester. *M.A. 1931 London, Birkbeck College*

Wright, H. N.
Early law and religion: a study in the relationship between the primitive rules of law and the early ideas of magic and religion. *LL.D. 1919 London*

Wright, H. R. C.
Free trade and protection in the Netherlands, 1819-1825. *Ph.D. 1949 Cambridge*

Wright, J.
De summo bono. *M.A. 1761 Glasgow*

Wright, L.
The auditorium. *M.A. 1934 Liverpool*

Wright, L. St. A.
Exegeses of: John iii.1-13; 14-21; I Corinthians xi.23-29. *D.D. 1924 Oxford*

Wright, L. St. A.
1. The Gallican liturgy. 2. Consecration and communion in the English rite. *B.D. 1916 Oxford*

Wright, M. M.
The influence of the romantic poem of Ariosto upon the critical thought of the Renaissance. *M.A. 1947 Manchester*

Wright, M. M.
Shakespeare and the Italian 'novellieri'. *Ph.D. 1950 Manchester*

Wright, M. R. E.
The economic history of Bermuda in the nineteenth century. *M.A. 1928 Bristol*

Wright, R.
La langue de Charles de Bernard. *M.A. 1927 Leeds*

Wright, R. F.
The origin of the sea codes. *LL.D. 1943 Dublin, Trinity College*

Wright, R. F.
The problem of war to the religious thinker of the sixteenth century. *Ph.D. 1937 London, King's College*

Wright, S.
Overstress in endurance tests. *M.Sc. 1934 Belfast*

Wright, T.
Grammar of the dialect of Tarbolton (Ayrshire). *Ph.D. 1929 Glasgow*

Wright, W. S.
The history of Homeric criticism among the Greeks. *M.A. 1927 London*

Wright-Henderson, P. A.
1. The value of the theory of accommodation as applied to moral difficulties in the Old Testament. 2. The place of miracles among the evidences for Christianity. *B.D. & D.D. 1903 Oxford*

Wrigley, M. J.
The love of nature and rustic life in Horace, Tibullus, and Propertius. *M.A. 1933 Manchester*

Wrong, H. H.
The government of the British colonies in the West Indies. *B.Litt. 1922 Oxford*

Wu, C. Y.
Richardson's conception of narrative art. *M.A. 1949 Liverpool*

Wu, C. Y.
The theory of international price relationships: an historical survey. *Ph.D. 1937 London, School of Economics and Political Science*

Wu, E. Y.
The evolution of Marx's social and political ideas, with special reference to the period 1840-1848. *Ph.D. 1939 London, School of Economics and Political Science*

Wu, G. D.
Prehistoric pottery in China. *Ph.D. 1937 London, Courtauld Institute of Art*

Wu, H. T.
The treatment of Europe in Chinese school textbooks. *M.A. 1949 London, Institute of Education*

Wu, J. C. C.
The rice economy of China. *Ph.D. 1948 Liverpool*

Wu, W. H.
The position of the peasant in modern China. *Ph.D. 1939 London, School of Economics and Political Science*

Wu, Y. L.
Capital formation and the economic order: an analytical study, with special reference to the case of a poor country. . *Ph.D. 1946 London, School of Economics and Political Science*

Wulff, W. P.
Rosa anglica. *Ph.D. 1931 National University of Ireland*

Wun, M.
The development of the Burmese language in the medieval period. *B.Litt. 1939 Oxford*

Wyatt, S.
An experimental investigation of children's vocabularies, with special reference to the effect of bilingualism on vocabulary. *M.Ed. 1918 Manchester*

Wyatt, T. S.
Some Cambridge contacts with France during Tudor and early Stuart times. *M.Litt. 1938 Cambridge*

Wykeham-George, K. R. N. St. J.
English canonists in the later Middle Ages: a historical biographical and literary study. *B.Litt. 1937 Oxford*

Wyld, H. C. K.
The relation of standard English to the modern dialects in their treatment of the gutturals. *B.Litt. 1899 Oxford*

Wylde-Brown, P. B.
A consideration of the theory of womens' wages, and an attempt to test the truth of certain reasons which have been adduced by economic writers for the relatively lower wage-level of women in industry as compared with that of men. *M.A. 1930 Birmingham*

Wylie, H. E.
The relation of the Wisdom literature to the fourth Gospel. *Ph.D. 1931 Edinburgh*

Wylie, R. C.
Catholic doctine and practice in the English Church during the period 1570-1625. *B.Litt. 1929 Oxford*

Wynne, W. H.
The development of land policy in Australia with special reference to New South Wales. *Ph.D. 1926 Cambridge*

Xavier, P. F.
The evolution of the economic geography of early Ceylon. *M.A. 1930 Liverpool*

Yabsley, D.
La plainte du Désiré by Jean Lemaire: critical edition with notes. *M.A. 1929 London*

Yajnik, R. K.
The influence of British drama on the Indian stage, with special reference to western India. *Ph.D. 1932 London, East London College*

Yang, C. N.
The distribution of functions among central government departments in the United Kingdom, with some comparison of the United States of America and British dominions. *D.Phil. 1948 Oxford*

Yang, J. P.
The political ideas of Saint-Just, with special reference to the work of the Committee of Public Safety. *B.Litt. 1937 Oxford*

Yanoshevitch, M.
The problem of the second marriage of priests in the Orthodox Church of the East. *B.Litt. 1921 Oxford*

Yare, H.
Contemporary English opinions of the French literature of 1820-1840. *M.A. 1927 Liverpool*

Yates, A. S.
The doctrine of assurance in the experience and thought of the eighteenth century, with special reference to John Wesley. *Ph.D. 1949 Leeds*

Yates, D.
Grillparzer and his early tragic heroines: Sappho, Medea, Hero. *M.A. 1925 Birmingham*

Yates, E.
Cowper, as revealed in his letters and poems. *M.A. 1917 Birmingham*

Yates, E.
The growth and progress of the electrical manufacturing industry in Great Britain. *M.A. 1937 Manchester*

Yates, J. E.
The Greek philosophical background of *pneuma*, in its relation to early Christian thought. *M.A. 1939 Manchester*

Yates, K. M.
The Elihu speeches: an investigation into the style, language, theology, meaning and authorship. *Ph.D. 1932 Edinburgh*

Yates, M. F.
The political career of Laurence Hyde, Earl of Rochester, in its illustration of government policy, and party groupings under Charles II and James II. *Ph.D. 1935 London, Royal Holloway College*

Yates, N.
English agriculture and the labourer, 1840-1885, with special reference to the depression of the 'seventies'. *M.A. 1930 Birmingham*

Yates, R. A.
Erosion levels of the river Avon drainage basin: a comparative account of the various methods of cartographic analysis. *M.Sc. 1950 Bristol*

Yates, T. J. A.
The principals and mechanisms of education among primitive peoples and the applications of these in European-controlled education of the natives in Africa. *Ph.D. 1933 London, School of Economics and Political Science*

Yealy, F. J.
Emerson and the romantic revival. *Ph.D. 1930 Cambridge*

Yeaxlee, B. A.
The psychology of primary and middle adolescence in relation to religious education. *B.Litt. 1936 Oxford*

Yeaxlee, B. A.
Spiritual values in adult education. *Ph.D. 1925 London*

Yeivin, S.
Private architecture in Fayyum villages of the Roman period. *M.A. 1928 London*

Yeldham, F. A.
A study of mathematical methods in England to the thirteenth century. *Ph.D. 1932 London, University College*

Yelissiye, A.
The history of the Church of Serbia from the foundation of its independence to the fall of the patriarchate (1219-1463 A.D.). *B.Litt. 1919 Oxford*

Yevtic, P.
The conception of *karma* and reincarnation in Hindu religion and philosophy. *Ph.D. 1927 London*

Yevtić, P.
History of the Serbian Church under Turkish rule. *B.Litt. 1919 Oxford*

Yockney, M. E.
A study of ballad collections edited in the eighteenth century. *B.Litt. 1949 Oxford*

Yodaiken, L. H.
Children's games. *B.Litt. 1942 Dublin, Trinity College*

You, P. S.
The techniques of sampling with special reference to demographic enquiries in undeveloped countries. *Ph.D. 1949 London, School of Economics and Political Science*

Youldon, I. G.
The scarplands of the Wiltshire-Gloucestershire-Somerset borders: a regional study, with particular reference to urban and rural settlement. *M.A. 1945 London, King's College*

Young, A. F.
The geography and administration of services in the county of Cumberland. *M.A. 1934 Liverpool*

Young, D. W.
History of the Birmingham gun trade. *M.Com. 1936 Birmingham*

Young, E. M.
The contribution of Henry James to the development of the modern novel. *M.A. 1931 Wales*

Young, J. A.
The physical and historical background of the Dee estuary. *M.A. 1926 Liverpool*

Young, J. I.
Relations, historical and literary, between Ireland and Scandinavia from the ninth century to the thirteenth. *Ph.D. 1930 Cambridge*

Young, J. M. Keays- *see* Keays-Young, J. M.

Young, L. G.
State intervention in education in England under the Early Stuarts. *M.A. 1938 London, King's College*

Young, L. M.
The problem of federation in the British West Indies during the nineteenth century. *Ph.D. 1947 Cambridge*

Young, N. Denholm- *see* Denholm-Young, N.

Young, P. C.
Jewish conceptions of the Messiah and the kingdom of God as reflected in certain specified texts between 150 B.C. and A.D. 100, with special reference to the political implications. *B.Litt. 1940 Oxford*

Young, R. G.
Henry Melvill, 1798 to 1871: a study of his theological thought and homiletical method. *Ph.D. 1949 Edinburgh*

Young, R. L.
Problems presented by easements to the purchaser of land. *B.Litt. 1935 Oxford*

Yovanovitch, S. Y.
Grace and freewill in St. Paul and St. Augustine. *B.Litt. 1920 Oxford*

Yu, S. P.
China as treated by English and French writers in the first half of the eighteenth century. *B.Litt. 1932 Oxford*

Yu, Y.
The English Cabinet. *Ph.D. 1937 London, School of Economics and Political Science*

Yule, E. P.
An investigation into the relation between association and intelligence. *Ph.D. 1934 Saint Andrew's*

Yule, H. W.
1. Whether the baptism of young children is in any wise to be retained in the Church. 2. Transubstantiation overthrows the nature of a sacrament. *B.D. 1877 Oxford*

Yusuf, N. J. M.
Hastings' experiment in the judicial system. *Ph.D. 1930 London, School of Economics and Political Science*

Yusufuddin, K. M.
Practical education. *M.A. 1930 Leeds*

Zafiriou, R.
The concept of capital in economic theory. *Ph.D. 1945 London, School of Economics and Political Science*

Zagday, M. I. H.
The administration of a deceased's estate in Muhammadan law: an historical and comparative study. *Ph.D. 1945 London, University College*

Zaina, L. A.
Le développement des idées littéraires en Bretagne sous la Restauration vu dans les pages du *Lycée Armoricain*, 1823-1831. *M.A. 1947 Liverpool*

Zakaria, M.
A comparative study of theories of factor analysis and their relations to analysis of variance, with special reference to psychology and education. *M.A. 1948 London, Institute of Education*

Zakaria, R. A.
Muslims in India: a political analysis (from 1885-1906). *Ph.D. 1948 London, School of Oriental and African Studies*

Zamick, M.
Dr. Edmund Castell, 1606-1685: studies of some aspects of eastern learning in seventeenth-century Britain. *Ph.D. 1934 Saint Andrew's*

Zaun, A. A.
A study of the idea of the verbal inspiration of the Scriptures with special reference to the reformers and post-reformation thinkers of the sixteenth and seventeenth centuries. *Ph.D. 1937 Edinburgh*

Zawadzki, K. K. F.
State control of investment. *M.Sc. 1949 London, School of Economics and Political Science*

Zayat, M. H. el- *see* El-Zayat, M. H.

Zema, D. B.
The influence of economic factors in the Gregorian reform of the eleventh century. *Ph.D. 1940 Cambridge*

Zentler, A. P.
Aspects of resale price control, with special reference to conditions in the U.K. *M.Sc. 1941 London, School of Economics and Political Science*

Zernick, R. H.
The imagery in the works of Fritz Reuter. *M.A. 1947 London, Birkbeck College*

Zernov, N.
The unity of the Church and the reunion of the Churches. *D.Phil. 1932 Oxford*

Ziada, M. M.
Foreign relations of Egypt in the fifteenth century (1422-1517). *Ph.D. 1930 Liverpool*

Ziegelmeyer, E. H.
The relation between empiricism and scepticism in Hume's theory of knowledge. *Ph.D. 1938 London, King's College*

Zighdis-Papaioannou, J. G.
Modern monetary theories in France. *Ph.D. 1939 London, School of Economics and Political Science*

Zok, T. C.
Fluctuation of attention at and near the threshold. *M.A. 1938 London, University College*

Zoond, V.
The housing legislation in England, 1851-67, with special reference to London. *M.A. 1932 London, King's College*

Zoysa, A. P. de *see* De Zoysa, A. P.

Zucker, E. M. M.
A history of the workhouse system to the end of the eighteenth century, with special reference to the period from 1722 to 1732, and the industrial aspect. *M.A. 1925 Manchester*

Zwanenberg Phillips, E. M. G. van *see* van Zwanenberg Phillips, E. M. G.